WITHDRAW

D1257374

COMMODITY PRICES

COMMODITY PRICES

CATHERINE FRIEDMAN, EDITOR

SECOND EDITION

A Source Book and Index Providing References to Wholesale, Retail, and Other Quotations for More Than 10,000 Agricultural, Commercial, Industrial, and Consumer Products

Gale Research Inc. • DETROIT • LONDON

Catherine Friedman, *Editor*

Monica M. Hubbard, *Coordinating Editor*

Special thanks to Dennis LaBeau

Mary Beth Trimper, *Production Manager*
Marilyn Jackman, *External Production Associate*

Arthur Chartow, *Art Director*
Cynthia D. Baldwin and Bernadette M. Gornie, *Graphic Designers*
C. J. Jonik, *Keyliner*

Laura Bryant, *Production Supervisor*
Louise Gagne, *Internal Production Associate*
Yolanda Y. Latham, *Internal Production Assistant*

835 Penobscot Bldg.
Detroit, MI 48226-4094

ISBN 0-8103-0499-6

Printed in the United States of America
Published simultaneously in the United Kingdom
by Gale Research International Limited
(An affiliated company of Gale Research Inc.)

Contents

Introduction

Commodities are the raw materials from which almost everything we use is manufactured. The prices of agricultural products, chemicals, energy, metals, and other commodities have a direct impact on the costs we face on a daily basis and are closely watched economic indicators. Economists, researchers, stock brokers, investors, and many business executives, therefore, rely on up-to-date information on commodity prices and trends. This data can sometimes be difficult to locate. *Commodity Prices* makes this search easier by indexing 198 publications that regularly report commodity prices; more than 14,000 commodity prices are recorded for over 10,400 commodities.

Sources for *Commodity Prices* range from domestic and international trade publications and newsletters to U.S. and foreign government documents. Types of prices indexed include cash, retail, spot, future, or whatever the original source specifies. Commodities include agricultural products (both food and non-food), chemicals, metals, minerals, and some manufactured products (such as wine). Foreign exchange rates are also identified if found in the original source.

Arrangement and Entry Coverage

Commodity Prices is arranged alphabetically by specific commodity name, with multiple sources cited alphabetically under the commodity name. Cross references are included to help the user access information. A complete entry will include:

- the commodity name
- commodity price source
- price frequency
- effective market(s)
- units of measure
- type of price
- time period covered

However, not every entry includes each of these items of information since the original sources may not cover them all.

Sample Entry

Each numbered item is explained below in the paragraph with the corresponding number.

1 **EGGS: GRADE AA LARGE**
2 **Source:** *California Farmer.* 3 **Price Frequency:** Semi-monthly.
4 **Effective Market(s):** Northern California, Los Angeles. 5 **Units of Measure:** Cents per dozen. 6 **Type of Price:** Price to chain stores.
7 **Time Period Covered:** Latest week, month ago, year ago.

1 Commodity Name: The names of commodities appear as published in the price source. They have not been changed or edited unless necessary to improve access.

2 Price Source: The complete name of the publication where the commodity price is found.

3 Price Frequency: This identifies the time intervals (daily, weekly, monthly, etc.) for which the commodity price is available. This may or may not correspond to the publication frequency of the price source. For example, a publication may be published quarterly, but the commodity price it contains may be presented on a monthly and quarterly basis. The frequency for this price then, will be monthly and quarterly.

4 Effective Market(s): Identifies the geographic area(s) for which price data is available. For less than six markets, the name of each market is included. For six markets or more, the entry specifies the number of markets but does not list each one separately. For lesser known markets, state postal codes or countries are used, e.g., Conway (KS).

5 Units of Measure: When the original source provides a quantitative measure for the price (dollars per lb. or Thai baht per metric ton) it has been included. The only abbreviation used under this heading is "lb." for "pound." If international currency is used, the country has been cited. If domestic currency is used, it is listed only as dollars or cents. Units of measure are presented as found in the price source publication.

6 Type of Price: This is the type of commodity price found in the price source, for example, spot, wholesale, retail, or price received by farmer.

7 Time Period Covered: Each entry specifies how much historical price data is presented in the price source. Many of the indexed publications present commodity price data for several years.

Publishers Index

A complete listing of the original sources used to compile *Commodity Prices* is provided in the Publishers Index. Information cited includes:

- publication name
- publisher
- address and telephone number
- frequency of publication
- subscription price
- single-issue price
- brief description of the commodity prices included in the publication

Acknowledgments

Compiling this book has been a challenge. Without the support, encouragement and, in some cases, editorial skills of friends, colleagues, and family, it would never have been completed. I would like to thank Herminio Reyes, the Arizona connection (including Linda DeFato and Shelley Grebles), my friends and colleagues in San Diego, especially Robert Carande, Carolyn Fields, Joan Freeman-Goodwin, Linda Muroi, Michael Perkins, Iliana Sonntag, Ginny Steel, Doug Stewart, Judy Thompson, Anne Turhollow, Phillip White, and Carole Wilson, and my family in Illinois and Ohio. I would also like thank everyone else who put up with me during the final stages of this book's production, especially my editors at Gale Research, Monica Hubbard and Ann Evory.

Suggestions

We welcome your comments and suggestions for *Commodity Prices* which can be addressed:

Commodity Prices
Gale Research Inc.
835 Penobscot Building
Detroit, MI 48226-4094

Commodity Prices

ABACA: G

Source: *FAO Quarterly Bulletin of Statistics.* **Price Frequency:** monthly, annually. **Effective Market(s):** European ports. **Units of Measure:** Dollars per 1000 kilograms, dollars per metric ton. **Time Period Covered:** latest 3 years.

ABACA: G, HAND CLEANED, BICOL

Source: *Fibre Market News.* **Price Frequency:** weekly. **Effective Market(s):** New York. **Units of Measure:** cents per lb. **Time Period Covered:** latest week.

ABACA: G, MACHINE CLEANED, CEBU/ LEYTE

Source: *Fibre Market News.* **Price Frequency:** weekly. **Effective Market(s):** New York. **Units of Measure:** cents per lb. **Time Period Covered:** latest week.

ABACA: I/S2, HAND CLEANED, BICOL

Source: *Fibre Market News.* **Price Frequency:** weekly. **Effective Market(s):** New York. **Units of Measure:** cents per lb. **Time Period Covered:** latest week.

ABACA: I/S2, MACHINE CLEANED, CEBU/ LEYTE

Source: *Fibre Market News.* **Price Frequency:** weekly. **Effective Market(s):** New York. **Units of Measure:** cents per lb. **Time Period Covered:** latest week.

ABACA: JK

Source: *FAO Quarterly Bulletin of Statistics.* **Price Frequency:** monthly, annually. **Effective Market(s):** European ports. **Units of Measure:** Dollars per 1000 kilograms, dollars per metric ton. **Time Period Covered:** latest 3 years.

ABACA: JK, MACHINE CLEANED, DAVAO

Source: *Fibre Market News.* **Price Frequency:** weekly. **Effective Market(s):** New York. **Units of Measure:** cents per lb. **Time Period Covered:** latest week.

ABACA: S-G, MACHINE CLEANED, DAVAO

Source: *Fibre Market News.* **Price Frequency:** weekly. **Effective Market(s):** New York. **Units of Measure:** cents per lb. **Time Period Covered:** latest week.

ABACA: S-I/S2, MACHINE CLEANED, DAVAO

Source: *Fibre Market News.* **Price Frequency:** weekly. **Effective Market(s):** New York. **Units of Measure:** cents per lb. **Time Period Covered:** latest week.

ABACA: S2

Source: *FAO Quarterly Bulletin of Statistics.* **Price Frequency:** monthly, annually. **Effective Market(s):** European ports. **Units of Measure:** Dollars per 1000 kilograms, dollars per metric ton. **Time Period Covered:** latest 3 years.

ABACA: S3, MACHINE CLEANED, CEBU/ LEYTE

Source: *Fibre Market News.* **Price Frequency:** weekly. **Effective Market(s):** New York. **Units of Measure:** cents per lb. **Time Period Covered:** latest week.

ABACA: S3, MACHINE CLEANED, DAVAO

Source: *Fibre Market News.* **Price Frequency:** weekly. **Effective Market(s):** New York. **Units of Measure:** cents per lb. **Time Period Covered:** latest week.

ABALONE: BLACK, WHOLE, FROZEN, DOMESTIC

Source: *Seafood Price-Current.* **Price Frequency:** semiweekly. **Effective Market(s):** West Coast. **Units of Measure:** Dollars per lb. **Type of Price:** first receiver. **Time Period Covered:** latest day.

ABALONE: LIVE, JAPANESE

Source: *Weekly Statistical Fishery Report.* **Price Frequency:** weekly. **Effective Market(s):** Tokyo. **Units of Measure:** Dollars per lb. **Type of Price:** wholesale. **Time Period Covered:** 2 weeks ago, month ago.

ABALONE: NO. 1, WHITE, FROZEN, DOMESTIC

Source: *Seafood Price-Current.* **Price Frequency:** semiweekly. **Effective Market(s):** West Coast. **Units of Measure:** Dollars per lb. **Type of Price:** first receiver. **Time Period Covered:** latest day.

ABALONE: NO. 2, WHITE, FROZEN, DOMESTIC

Source: *Seafood Price-Current.* **Price Frequency:** semiweekly. **Effective Market(s):** West Coast. **Units of Measure:** Dollars per lb. **Type of Price:** first receiver. **Time Period Covered:** latest day.

ABS: 10% GLASS

Source: *Plastics Technology.* **Price Frequency:** monthly. **Units of Measure:** cents per lb., cents per cubic inch. **Type of Price:** bulk list, market. **Time Period Covered:** latest month.

ABS: 30% GLASS

Source: *Plastics Technology.* **Price Frequency:** monthly. **Units of Measure:** cents per lb., cents per cubic inch. **Type of Price:** bulk list, market. **Time Period Covered:** latest month.

ABS: EXTRA HIGH IMPACT

Source: *Plastics Technology.* **Price Frequency:** monthly. **Units of Measure:** cents per lb., cents per cubic inch. **Type of Price:** bulk list, market. **Time Period Covered:** latest .

ABS: FITTINGS

Source: *Plastics Technology.* **Price Frequency:** monthly. **Units of Measure:** cents per lb., cents per cubic inch. **Type of Price:** bulk list, market. **Time Period Covered:** latest month.

ABS: FLAME RETARDANT

Source: *Plastics Technology.* **Price Frequency:** monthly. **Units of Measure:** cents per lb., cents per cubic inch. **Type of Price:** bulk list, market. **Time Period Covered:** latest month.

ABS: HIGH HEAT

Source: *Plastics Technology.* **Price Frequency:** monthly. **Units of Measure:** cents per lb., cents per cubic inch. **Type of Price:** bulk list, market. **Time Period Covered:** latest month.

ABS: HIGH IMPACT

Source: *Chemical Marketing Reporter.* **Price Frequency:** weekly. **Effective Market(s):** New York. **Units of Measure:** Dollars per lb. **Type of Price:** spot. **Time Period Covered:** latest week.

Source: *Journal of Commerce and Commercial.* **Price Frequency:** weekly in Tuesday issue. **Units of Measure:** Dollars per lb. **Type of Price:** spot. **Time Period Covered:** latest week.

Source: *Plastics Technology.* **Price Frequency:** monthly. **Units of Measure:** cents per lb., cents per cubib inch. **Type of Price:** bulk list, market. **Time Period Covered:** latest month.

ABS: INJECTION MOLDING GRADE, MEDIUM IMPACT

Source: *Purchasing.* **Price Frequency:** monthly. **Units of Measure:** cents per lb. **Type of Price:** transaction. **Time Period Covered:** latest day, month ago, 6 months ago, year ago.

ABS: LOW IMPACT

Source: *Chemical Marketing Reporter.* **Price Frequency:** weekly. **Effective Market(s):** New York. **Units of Measure:** Dollars per lb. **Type of Price:** spot. **Time Period Covered:** latest week.

ABS: MEDIUM IMPACT

Source: *Chemical Marketing Reporter.* **Price Frequency:** weekly. **Effective Market(s):** New York. **Units of Measure:** Dollars per lb. **Type of Price:** spot. **Time Period Covered:** latest week.

Source: *Plastics Technology.* **Price Frequency:** monthly. **Units of Measure:** cents per lb., cents per cubic inch. **Type of Price:** bulk list, market. **Time Period Covered:** latest month.

ABS: MOLDING GRADE, HIGH IMPACT, HIGH GLOSS

Source: *Modern Plastics.* **Price Frequency:** quarterly in January, April, July & October issues. **Units of Measure:** cents per lb. **Type of Price:** market. **Time Period Covered:** latest 3 years.

ABS: PIPE GRADE

Source: *Chemical Marketing Reporter.* **Price Frequency:** weekly. **Effective Market(s):** New York. **Units of Measure:** Dollars per lb. **Type of Price:** spot. **Time Period Covered:** latest week.

Source: *Journal of Commerce and Commercial.* **Price Frequency:** weekly in Tuesday issue. **Units of Measure:** Dollars per lb. **Type of Price:** spot. **Time Period Covered:** latest week.

ABS: TRANSPARENT

Source: *Plastics Technology.* **Price Frequency:** monthly. **Units of Measure:** cents per lb., cents per cubic inch. **Type of Price:** bulk list, market. **Time Period Covered:** latest month.

ABS PIPE

Source: *Plastics Technology.* **Price Frequency:** monthly. **Units of Measure:** cents per lb., cents per cubic inch. **Type of Price:** bulk list, market. **Time Period Covered:** latest month.

ABS PLATING

Source: *Journal of Commerce and Commercial.* **Price Frequency:** weekly in Tuesday issue. **Units of Measure:** Dollars per lb. **Type of Price:** spot. **Time Period Covered:** latest week.

Source: *Plastics Technology.* **Price Frequency:** monthly. **Units of Measure:** cents per lb., cents per cubic inch. **Type of Price:** bulk list, market. **Time Period Covered:** latest month.

ABS SHEET

Source: *Plastics Technology.* **Price Frequency:** monthly. **Units of Measure:** cents per lb., cents per cubic inch. **Type of Price:** bulk list, market. **Time Period Covered:** latest month.

ABS/NYLON ALLOY

Source: *Plastics Technology.* **Price Frequency:** monthly. **Units of Measure:** cents per lb., cents per cubic inch. **Type of Price:** bulk list, market. **Time Period Covered:** latest month.

ABS/POLYCARBONATE ALLOY

Source: *Plastics Technology.* **Price Frequency:** monthly. **Units of Measure:** cents per lb., cents per cubic inch. **Type of Price:** bulk list, market. **Time Period Covered:** latest month.

ABS/POLYVINYL CHLORIDE ALLOY

Source: *Plastics Technology.* **Price Frequency:** monthly. **Units of Measure:** cents per lb., cents per cubic inch. **Type of Price:** bulk list, market. **Time Period Covered:** latest month.

ACETAL COPOLYMER

Source: *Plastics Technology.* **Price Frequency:** monthly. **Units of Measure:** cents per lb. **Type of Price:** bulk list, market. **Time Period Covered:** latest month.

ACETAL COPOLYMER: 25% GLASS

Source: *Plastics Technology.* **Price Frequency:** monthly. **Units of Measure:** cents per lb., cents per cubic inch. **Type of Price:** bulk list, market. **Time Period Covered:** latest month.

ACETAL HOMOPOLYMER

Source: *Plastics Technology.* **Price Frequency:** monthly. **Units of Measure:** cents per lb., cents per cubic inch. **Type of Price:** bulk list, market. **Time Period Covered:** latest month.

ACETAL HOMOPOLYMER: 20% GLASS

Source: *Plastics Technology.* **Price Frequency:** monthly. **Units of Measure:** cents per lb., cents per cubic inch. **Type of Price:** bulk list, market. **Time Period Covered:** latest month.

ACETAL POLYMER: EXTRUSION

Source: *Journal of Commerce and Commercial.* **Price Frequency:** weekly in Tuesday issue. **Units of Measure:** Dollars per lb. **Type of Price:** spot. **Time Period Covered:** latest week.

ACETALDEHYDE

Source: *Chemical Marketing Reporter.* **Price Frequency:** weekly. **Effective Market(s):** New York, West. **Units of Measure:** Dollars per lb. **Type of Price:** spot. **Time Period Covered:** latest week.

ACETAMINOPHEN

see N-Acetyl-p-aminophenol.

ACETANILIDE: TECHNICAL, FLAKED

Source: *Chemical Marketing Reporter.* **Price Frequency:** weekly. **Effective Market(s):** New York. **Units of Measure:** Dollars per lb. **Type of Price:** spot. **Time Period Covered:** latest week.

ACETATE FILAMENT YARN

see Yarn: Acetate Filament.

ACETATE STAPLE

Source: *Journal of Commerce and Commercial.* **Price Frequency:** weekly in Tuesday issue. **Units of Measure:** Dollars per lb. **Type of Price:** spot. **Time Period Covered:** latest week.

ACETIC ACID

Source: *Purchasing.* **Price Frequency:** quarterly in January, April, July, and October issues. **Units of Measure:** cents per lb. **Type of Price:** transaction. **Time Period Covered:** latest 5 quarters.

ACETIC ACID: GLACIAL, USP

Source: *Journal of Commerce and Commercial.* **Price Frequency:** weekly in Friday issue. **Units of Measure:** Dollars per lb. **Type of Price:** spot. **Time Period Covered:** latest week.

ACETIC ACID: TECHNICAL GRADE

Source: *Chemical Marketing Reporter.* **Price Frequency:** weekly. **Effective Market(s):** New York. **Units of Measure:** Dollars per lb. **Type of Price:** spot. **Time Period Covered:** latest week.

Source: *Journal of Commerce and Commercial.* **Price Frequency:** weekly in Thursday issue. **Units of Measure:** Dollars per lb. **Type of Price:** spot. **Time Period Covered:** latest week.

ACETIC ANHYDRIDE

Source: *Chemical Marketing Reporter.* **Price Frequency:** weekly. **Effective Market(s):** East, West. **Units of Measure:** Dollars per lb. **Type of Price:** spot. **Time Period Covered:** latest week.

Source: *Journal of Commerce and Commercial.* **Price Frequency:** weekly in Thursday issue. **Units of Measure:** Dollars per lb. **Type of Price:** spot. **Time Period Covered:** latest week.

ACETOACET-O-ANISIDIDE

Source: *Chemical Marketing Reporter.* **Price Frequency:** weekly. **Effective Market(s):** New York. **Units of Measure:** Dollars per lb. **Type of Price:** spot. **Time Period Covered:** latest week.

ACETOACET-O-CHLOROANILIDE

Source: *Chemical Marketing Reporter.* **Price Frequency:** weekly. **Effective Market(s):** New York. **Units of Measure:** Dollars per lb. **Type of Price:** spot. **Time Period Covered:** latest week.

ACETOACET-O-TOLUIDIDE

Source: *Chemical Marketing Reporter.* **Price Frequency:** weekly. **Effective Market(s):** New York. **Units of Measure:** Dollars per lb. **Type of Price:** spot. **Time Period Covered:** latest week.

ACETOACET-M-XYLIDIDE

Source: *Chemical Marketing Reporter.* **Price Frequency:** weekly. **Effective Market(s):** New York. **Units of Measure:** Dollars per lb. **Type of Price:** spot. **Time Period Covered:** latest week.

ACETOACETANILIDE

Source: *Chemcial Marketing Reporter.* **Price Frequency:** weekly. **Effective Market(s):** New York. **Units of Measure:** Dollars per lb. **Type of Price:** spot. **Time Period Covered:** latest week.

ACETONE

Source: *Chemical Marketing Reporter.* **Price Frequency:** weekly. **Effective Market(s):** California, East, West of the Rockies excluding California. **Units of Measure:** Dollars per lb. **Type of Price:** spot. **Time Period Covered:** latest week.

Source: *Journal of Commerce and Commercial.* **Price Frequency:** weekly in Wednesday issue. **Effective Market(s):** Gulf. **Units of Measure:** Dollars per lb. **Type of Price:** spot. **Time Period Covered:** latest week.

Source: *Purchasing.* **Price Frequency:** quarterly in January, April, July, and October issues. **Units of Measure:** cents per lb. **Type of Price:** transaction. **Time Period Covered:** latest 5 quarters.

ACETONITRILE

Source: *Chemical Marketing Reporter.* **Price Frequency:** weekly. **Effective Market(s):** New York. **Units of Measure:** Dollars per lb. **Type of Price:** spot. **Time Period Covered:** latest week.

ACETOPHENETIDIN

see Phenacetin.

ACETOPHENONE: PERFUME GRADE

Source: *Chemical Marketing Reporter.* **Price Frequency:** weekly. **Effective Market(s):** New York. **Units of Measure:** Dollars per lb. **Type of Price:** spot. **Time Period Covered:** latest week.

ACETOPHENONE: TECHNICAL GRADE

Source: *Chemical Marketing Reporter.* **Price Frequency:** weekly. **Effective Market(s):** New York. **Units of Measure:** Dollars per lb. **Type of Price:** spot. **Time Period Covered:** latest week.

N-ACETYL-P-AMINOPHENOL

Source: *Chemical Marketing Reporter.* **Price Frequency:** weekly. **Effective Market(s):** New York. **Units of Measure:** Dollars per kilo. **Type of Price:** spot. **Time Period Covered:** latest week.

ACETYLENE: BLACK, 50% COMPRESSED, IMPORTED

Source: *Chemical Marketing Reporter.* **Price Frequency:** weekly. **Effective Market(s):** New York. **Units of Measure:** Dollars per lb. **Type of Price:** spot. **Time Period Covered:** latest week.

ACETYLENE: BLACK, 100% COMPRESSED, IMPORTED

Source: *Chemical Marketing Reporter.* **Price Frequency:** weekly. **Effective Market(s):** New York. **Units of Measure:** Dollars per lb. **Type of Price:** spot. **Time Period Covered:** latest week.

ACETYLENE TETRABROMIDE

Source: *Chemical Marketing Reporter.* **Price Frequency:** weekly. **Effective Market(s):** New York. **Units of Measure:** Dollars per lb. **Type of Price:** spot. **Time Period Covered:** latest week.

ACETYLSALICYLIC ACID: USP

see also Aspirin.

Source: *Journal of Commerce and Commercial.* **Price Frequency:** weekly in Friday issue. **Units of Measure:** Dollars per lb. **Type of Price:** spot. **Time Period Covered:** latest week.

ACETYLTRIBUTYL CITRATE

Source: *Chemical Marketing Reporter.* **Price Frequency:** weekly. **Effective Market(s):** New York. **Units of Measure:** Dollars per lb. **Type of Price:** spot. **Time Period Covered:** latest week.

ACIDS

Source: *Journal of Commerce and Commercial.* **Price Frequency:** weekly in Thursday issue. **Units of Measure:** Dollars per lb. **Type of Price:** spot. **Time Period Covered:** latest week.

ACIDSPAR: DRY

Source: *Industrial Minerals.* **Price Frequency:** monthly. **Effective Market(s):** Rotterdam. **Units of Measure:** Dollars per metric tonne. **Type of Price:** producer & dealer. **Time Period Covered:** latest month.

Source: *Industrial Minerals.* **Price Frequency:** monthly. **Effective Market(s):** main European port. **Units of Measure:** British pounds per metric tonne. **Type of Price:** producer & dealer. **Time Period Covered:** latest month.

ACIDSPAR: DRY, SOUTH AFRICAN

Source: *Industrial Minerals.* **Price Frequency:** monthly. **Effective Market(s):** Durban (South Africa). **Units of Measure:** Dollars per metric tonne. **Type of Price:** producer & dealer. **Time Period Covered:** latest month.

ACIDSPAR: FILTERCAKE, MEXICAN

Source: *Industrial Minerals.* **Price Frequency:** monthly. **Effective Market(s):** Tampico (Mexico). **Units of Measure:** Dollars per metric tonne. **Type of Price:** producer & dealer. **Time Period Covered:** latest month.

ACIDSPAR: UNITED STATES

Source: *Industrial Minerals.* **Price Frequency:** monthly. **Effective Market(s):** Illinois. **Units of Measure:** Dollars per short ton. **Type of Price:** producer & dealer. **Time Period Covered:** latest month.

ACRYLAMIDE: SOLID

Source: *Chemical Marketing Reporter.* **Price Frequency:** weekly. **Effective Market(s):** New York. **Units of Measure:** Dollars per lb. **Type of Price:** spot. **Time Period Covered:** latest week.

ACRYLAMIDE: SOLUTION

Source: *Chemical Marketing Reporter.* **Price Frequency:** weekly. **Effective Market(s):** New York. **Units of Measure:** Dollars per lb. **Type of Price:** spot. **Time Period Covered:** latest week.

ACRYLIC: GENERAL PURPOSE

Source: *Journal of Commerce and Commercial.* **Price Frequency:** weekly in Tuesday issue. **Units of Measure:** Dollars per lb. **Type of Price:** spot. **Time Period Covered:** latest week.

Source: *Plastics Technology.* **Price Frequency:** monthly. **Units of Measure:** cents per lb., cents per cubic inch. **Type of Price:** bulk list, market. **Time Period Covered:** latest month.

ACRYLIC: IMPACT

Source: *Journal of Commerce and Commercial.* **Price Frequency:** weekly in Tuesday issue. **Units of Measure:** Dollars per lb. **Type of Price:** spot. **Time Period Covered:** latest week.

Source: *Plastics Technology.* **Price Frequency:** monthly. **Units of Measure:** cents per lb., cents per cubic inch. **Type of Price:** bulk list, market. **Time Period Covered:** latest month.

ACRYLIC ACID: GLACIAL

Source: *Chemical Marketing Reporter.* **Price Frequency:** weekly. **Effective Market(s):** New York. **Units of Measure:** Dollars per lb. **Type of Price:** spot. **Time Period Covered:** latest week.

ACRYLIC ACID: TECHNICAL

Source: *Chemical Marketing Reporter.* **Price Frequency:** weekly. **Effective Market(s):** New York. **Units of Measure:** Dollars per lb. **Type of Price:** spot. **Time Period Covered:** latest week.

ACRYLIC FIBER: 3.0 DENIER

Source: *ATI, America's Textiles International.* **Price Frequency:** monthly. **Time Period Covered:** latest month, 6 months ago, year ago.

ACRYLIC STAPLE

Source: *JTN: The International Textile Magazine.* **Price Frequency:** monthly. **Effective Market(s):** Taiwan. **Units of Measure:** Dollars per lb. **Type of Price:** export. **Time Period Covered:** latest month.

ACRYLIC STAPLE: 1.2-1.5 DENIER

Source: *Journal of Commerce and Commercial.* **Price Frequency:** weekly in Tuesday issue. **Units of Measure:** Dollars per lb. **Type of Price:** spot. **Time Period Covered:** latest week.

ACRYLIC STAPLE: 2 DENIER

Source: *Journal of Commerce and Commercial.* **Price Frequency:** weekly in Tuesday issue. **Units of Measure:** Dollars per lb. **Type of Price:** spot. **Time Period Covered:** latest week.

ACRYLIC STAPLE: 3 DENIER

Source: *Journal of Commerce and Commercial.* **Price Frequency:** weekly in Tuesday issue. **Units of Measure:** Dollars per lb. **Type of Price:** spot. **Time Period Covered:** latest week.

ACRYLIC STAPLE: FOR WORSTED BLENDS

Source: *JTN: The International Textile Magazine.* **Price Frequency:** monthly. **Effective Market(s):** Japan. **Units of Measure:** Japanese yen per kilogram. **Type of Price:** spot. **Time Period Covered:** latest month.

ACRYLIC YARN
see Yarn: Acrylic.

ACRYLONITRILE

Source: *Chemical Marketing Reporter.* **Price Frequency:** weekly. **Effective Market(s):** New York. **Units of Measure:** Dollars per lb. **Type of Price:** spot. **Time Period Covered:** latest week.

Source: *Cotton and Wool Situation and Outlook Report.* **Price Frequency:** monthly. **Units of Measure:** cents per lb. **Type of Price:** spot. **Time Period Covered:** latest year.

Source: *Modern Plastics.* **Price Frequency:** quarterly in January, April, July & October issues. **Units of Measure:** cents per lb. **Type of Price:** market. **Time Period Covered:** latest 3 years.

ACRYLONITRILE BUTADIENE STYRENE
see ABS.

ACRYLONITRILE COPOLYMER: EXTRUSION

Source: *Plastics Technology*. **Price Frequency:** monthly. **Units of Measure:** cents per lb., cents per cubic inch. **Type of Price:** bulk list, market. **Time Period Covered:** latest month.

ACRYLONITRILE COPOLYMER: INJECTION

Source: *Plastics Technology.* **Price Frequency:** monthly. **Units of Measure:** cents per lb., cents per cubic inch. **Type of Price:** bulk list, market. **Time Period Covered:** latest month.

ACRYLONITRILE TANKS

Source: *Journal of Commerce and Commercial.* **Price Frequency:** weekly in Thursday issue. **Units of Measure:** Dollars per lb. **Type of Price:** spot. **Time Period Covered:** latest day.

ADIPIC ACID

Source: *Journal of Commerce and Commercial.* **Price Frequency:** weekly in Thursday issue. **Units of Measure:** Dollars per lb. **Type of Price:** spot. **Time Period Covered:** latest week.

ADIPIC ACID: RESIN GRADE

Source: *Chemical Marketing Reporter.* **Price Frequency:** weekly. **Effective Market(s):** New York. **Units of Measure:** Dollars per lb. **Type of Price:** spot. **Time Period Covered:** latest week.

AFRICAN VIOLETS: POTTED, LESS THAN 5″

Source: *Floriculture Crops.* **Price Frequency:** annually. **Effective Market(s):** 17 domestic markets, United States. **Units of Measure:** Dollars per unit. **Type of Price:** commercial wholesale. **Time Period Covered:** latest 2 years.

AFRICAN VIOLETS: POTTED, MORE THAN 5″

Source: *Floriculture Crops.* **Price Frequency:** annually. **Effective Market(s):** 11 domestic markets, United States. **Units of Measure:** Dollars per unit. **Type of Price:** commercial wholesale. **Time Period Covered:** latest 2 years.

AGAR: POWDERED, USP

Source: *Chemical Marketing Reporter.* **Price Frequency:** weekly. **Effective Market(s):** New York. **Units of Measure:** Dollars per lb. **Type of Price:** spot. **Time Period Covered:** latest week.

AGRICULTURAL RAW MATERIALS

Source: *Monthly Commodity Price Bulletin.* **Price Frequency:** monthly, annually. **Effective Market(s):** developing countries. **Units of Measure:** index. **Type of Price:** free market price index. **Time Period Covered:** latest 5 years.

Source: *Monthly Commodity Price Bulletin Supplement.* **Price Frequency:** monthly, quarterly, annually. **Units of Measure:** index. **Type of Price:** free market index. **Time Period Covered:** latest 20 years.

Source: *UNCTAD Commodity Yearbook.* **Price Frequency:** annually. **Units of Measure:** index. **Type of Price:** price index. **Time Period Covered:** latest 12 years.

AHI (FISH)
see Tuna: Yellowfin.

ALACHLOR: EMULSIFIABLE CONCENTRATE

Source: *Agricultural Prices Annual Summary.* **Price Frequency:** semiannually. **Effective Market(s):** United States. **Units of Measure:** Dollars per 5 gallons. **Type of Price:** average paid by farmer. **Time Period Covered:** latest 6 years.

ALCOHOL

Source: *Colorado Beverage Analyst.* **Price Frequency:** monthly. **Effective Market(s):** Colorado. **Units of Measure:** Dollars per case. **Type of Price:** wholesale by brand. **Time Period Covered:** latest month.

Source: *Illinois Beverage Journal.* **Price Frequency:** monthly. **Effective Market(s):** Illinois. **Units of Measure:** Dollars per case. **Type of Price:** wholesale by brand. **Time Period Covered:** latest month.

ALCOHOL: DENATURED

Source: *Standard & Poor's Statistical Service Current Statistics.* **Price Frequency:** monthly, annually. **Units of Measure:** cents per gallon. **Time Period Covered:** latest 4 years.

ALCOHOL: ETHYL

Source: *Commodity Year Book.* **Price Frequency:** monthly, annually. **Effective Market(s):** New York. **Units of Measure:** index. **Type of Price:** wholesale price index. **Time Period Covered:** latest 13 years.

ALCOHOL: GRAIN

Source: *Kentucky Beverage Journal.* **Price Frequency:** monthly. **Effective Market(s):** Kentucky. **Units of Measure:** Dollars per bottle, dollars per case. **Type of Price:** wholesale by brand. **Time Period Covered:** latest month.

ALCOHOL: SYNTHETIC, C8-C10

Source: *Chemical Marketing Reporter.* **Price Frequency:** weekly. **Effective Market(s):** New York. **Units of Measure:** Dollars per lb. **Type of Price:** spot. **Time Period Covered:** latest week.

ALCOHOL: SYNTHETIC, C12-C13

Source: *Chemical Marketing Reporter.* **Price Frequency:** weekly. **Effective Market(s):** New York. **Units of Measure:** Dollars per lb. **Type of Price:** spot. **Time Period Covered:** latest week.

ALCOHOL: SYNTHETIC, C14-C15

Source: *Chemical Marketing Reporter.* **Price Frequency:** weekly. **Effective Market(s):** New York. **Units of Measure:** Dollars per lb. **Type of Price:** spot. **Time Period Covered:** latest week.

ALCOHOL: SYNTHETIC, C16-C18

Source: *Chemical Marketing Reporter.* **Price Frequency:** weekly. **Effective Market(s):** New York. **Units of Measure:** Dollars per lb. **Type of Price:** spot. **Time Period Covered:** latest week.

ALDEHYDE: C10, CAPRIC

Source: *Chemical Marketing Reporter.* **Price Frequency:** weekly. **Effective Market(s):** New York. **Units of Measure:** Dollars per lb. **Type of Price:** spot. **Time Period Covered:** latest week.

ALDEHYDE: C11, SATURATED

Source: *Chemical Marketing Reporter.* **Price Frequency:** weekly. **Effective Market(s):** New York. **Units of Measure:** Dollars per lb. **Type of Price:** spot. **Time Period Covered:** latest week.

ALDEHYDE: C12, LAURIC

Source: *Chemical Marketing Reporter.* **Price Frequency:** weekly. **Effective Market(s):** New York. **Units of Measure:** Dollars per lb. **Type of Price:** spot. **Time Period Covered:** latest week.

ALE

Source: *Illinois Beverage Journal.* **Price Frequency:** monthly. **Effective Market(s):** Illinois. **Units of Measure:** Dollars per case. **Type of Price:** wholesale by brand. **Time Period Covered:** latest month.

Source: *Nevada Beverage Index.* **Price Frequency:** monthly. **Effective Market(s):** Nevada. **Units of Measure:** Dollars per unit. **Type of Price:** wholesale by brand. **Time Period Covered:** latest month.

ALFALFA

Source: *Farm and Dairy.* **Price Frequency:** weekly, seasonally. **Effective Market(s):** Ohio, Pennsylvania. **Units of Measure:** Dollars per load. **Type of Price:** auction high, auction low. **Time Period Covered:** latest week.

Source: *Lancaster Farming.* **Price Frequency:** weekly. **Effective Market(s):** Pennsylvania. **Units of Measure:** Dollars per ton. **Type of Price:** auction. **Time Period Covered:** latest week.

Source: *Washington Farmer-Stockman.* **Price Frequency:** monthly, seasonally. **Effective Market(s):** Washington. **Units of Measure:** Dollars per ton. **Type of Price:** received by farmer. **Time Period Covered:** latest month, month ago, year ago.

ALFALFA: 17% PROTEIN, DEHYDRATED

Source: *Milling & Baking News.* **Price Frequency:** weekly. **Units of Measure:** Dollars per ton. **Time Period Covered:** latest week.

ALFALFA: 17% PROTEIN, DEHYDRATED, REGROUND

Source: *Feedstuffs.* **Price Frequency:** weekly. **Effective Market(s):** 12 domestic markets. **Units of Measure:** Dollars per bulk ton. **Time Period Covered:** latest week.

ALFALFA HAY

Source: *Agricultural Prices.* **Price Frequency:** monthly. **Effective Market(s):** United States. **Units of Measure:** Dollars per ton. **Type of Price:** received by farmer. **Time Period Covered:** latest 2 months, year ago.

Source: *Agricultural Prices.* **Price Frequency:** monthly. **Effective Market(s):** 29 domestic markets, United States. **Units of Measure:** Dollars per ton. **Type of Price:** received by farmer. **Time Period Covered:** latest month.

Source: *California Farmer.* **Price Frequency:** semimonthly. **Effective Market(s):** 5 California markets. **Units of Measure:** Dollars per ton. **Time Period Covered:** latest week, month ago, year ago.

Source: *Commodity Year Book.* **Price Frequency:** annually. **Effective Market(s):** United States. **Units of Measure:** Dollars per 100 lbs. **Type of Price:** paid by farmer. **Time Period Covered:** latest 2 years.

Source: *Hay Market News.* **Price Frequency:** weekly, seasonally. **Effective Market(s):** 16 domestic markets. **Units of Measure:** Dollars per ton. **Type of Price:** cash. **Time Period Covered:** latest week, month ago, year ago.

Source: *Illinois Farm Report.* **Price Frequency:** monthly. **Effective Market(s):** Illinois. **Units of Measure:** Dollars per ton. **Type of Price:** average received by farmers. **Time Period Covered:** latest 2 months, year ago.

ALFALFA HAY: FAIR QUALITY

Source: *Oregon Farmer-Stockman.* **Price Frequency:** monthly, seasonally. **Effective Market(s):** Lower Columbia Basin (OR). **Time Period Covered:** latest month.

Source: *Washington Farmer-Stockman.* **Price Frequency:** monthly, seasonally. **Effective Market(s):** Columbia Basin (OR). **Units of Measure:** Dollars per ton. **Time Period Covered:** latest month, month ago.

ALFALFA HAY: GOOD QUALITY

Source: *Oregon Farmer-Stockman.* **Price Frequency:** monthly. **Effective Market(s):** Klamath Falls/Tulelake (OR), Lower Columbia Basin (OR). **Time Period Covered:** latest month.

Source: *Washington Farmer-Stockman.* **Price Frequency:** monthly, seasonally. **Effective Market(s):** Columbia Basin (OR). **Units of Measure:** Dollars per ton. **Time Period Covered:** latest month, month ago.

ALFALFA HAY: PREMIUM QUALITY

Source: *Oregon Farmer-Stockman.* **Price Frequency:** monthly. **Effective Market(s):** Klamath Falls/Tulelake (OR), Lower Columbia Basin (OR). **Time Period Covered:** latest month.

ALFALFA HAY CUBES

Source: *Drovers Journal.* **Price Frequency:** semiweekly, seasonally. **Effective Market(s):** 8 domestic markets. **Time Period Covered:** selected day.

Source: *Oregon Farmer-Stockman.* **Price Frequency:** monthly. **Effective Market(s):** Lower Columbia Basin (OR). **Time Period Covered:** latest month.

Source: *Washington Farmer-Stockman.* **Price Frequency:** monthly, seasonally. **Effective Market(s):** Columbia Basin (OR). **Units of Measure:** Dollars per ton. **Time Period Covered:** latest month, month ago.

ALFALFA MEAL: 17% PROTEIN, DEHYDRATED, REGROUND

Source: *Grain and Feed Market News.* **Price Frequency:** weekly, seasonally. **Effective Market(s):** 6 domestic markets. **Units of Measure:** Dollars per ton. **Type of Price:** wholesale. **Time Period Covered:** latest week, week ago, year ago.

ALFALFA MEAL: DEHYDRATED

Source: *Feed Situation and Outlook Report.* **Price Frequency:** monthly. **Effective Market(s):** Kansas City. **Units of Measure:** Dollars per ton. **Time Period Covered:** latest 8 months.

ALFALFA MEAL PELLETS: 15% PROTEIN, SUNCURED

Source: *Grain and Feed Market News.* **Price Frequency:** weekly, seasonally. **Effective Market(s):** Kansas City, Los Angeles, Portland, Toledo (OH). **Units of Measure:** Dollars per ton. **Type of Price:** wholesale. **Time Period Covered:** latest week, week ago, year ago.

ALFALFA MEAL PELLETS: DEHYDRATED, REGROUND

Source: *California Farmer.* **Price Frequency:** semimonthly. **Effective Market(s):** Southern California, Northern California. **Units of Measure:** Dollars per ton. **Time Period Covered:** latest week, month ago, year ago.

ALFALFA PELLETS: 13% PROTEIN, SUNCURED

Source: *Feedstuffs.* **Price Frequency:** weekly. **Effective Market(s):** 7 domestic markets. **Units of Measure:** Dollars per bulk ton. **Time Period Covered:** latest week.

ALFALFA PELLETS: 15% PROTEIN, SUNCURED

Source: *Feedstuffs.* **Price Frequency:** weekly. **Effective Market(s):** 7 domestic markets. **Units of Measure:** Dollars per bulk ton. **Time Period Covered:** latest week.

ALFALFA PELLETS: 17% PROTEIN, DEHYDRATED

Source: *Feedstuffs.* **Price Frequency:** weekly. **Effective Market(s):** 12 domestic markets. **Units of Measure:** Dollars per bulk ton. **Time Period Covered:** latest week.

Source: *Feedstuffs.* **Price Frequency:** weekly. **Effective Market(s):** Kansas City. **Units of Measure:** Dollars per ton. **Time Period Covered:** latest week, week ago, 6 months ago, year ago.

ALFALFA PELLETS: DEHYDRATED

Source: *Drovers Journal.* **Price Frequency:** semiweekly, seasonally. **Effective Market(s):** 8 domestic markets. **Time Period Covered:** selected day.

ALFALFA PELLETS: SUNCURED

Source: *Drovers Journal.* **Price Frequency:** semiweekly, seasonally. **Effective Market(s):** 8 domestic markets. **Time Period Covered:** selected day.

ALFALFA SEED: CERTIFIED

Source: *Agricultural Prices Annual Summary.* **Price Frequency:** semiannually. **Effective Market(s):** United States. **Units of Measure:** Dollars per 100 lbs. **Type of Price:** average paid by farmer. **Time Period Covered:** latest 6 years.

ALFALFA SEED: UNCERTIFIED

Source: *Agricultural Prices Annual Summary.* **Price Frequency:** semiannually. **Effective Market(s):** United States. **Units of Measure:** Dollars per 100 lbs. **Type of Price:** average paid by farmer. **Time Period Covered:** latest 6 years.

ALFALFA SPROUTS

Source: *New Zealand Farmer.* **Price Frequency:** weekly, seasonally. **Effective Market(s):** New Zealand. **Units of Measure:** New Zealand dollars per punnet. **Time Period Covered:** latest week.

ALGERIA DINAR

Source: *International Wheat Council Market Report.* **Price Frequency:** weekly. **Effective Market(s):** London. **Units of Measure:** Algerian dinar per United States dollar. **Type of Price:** foreign exchange. **Time Period Covered:** latest 5 weeks.

ALGIN

see Sodium Alginate.

ALKALI BLUE: DRY, FLUSHED

Source: *Chemical Marketing Reporter.* **Price Frequency:** weekly. **Effective Market(s):** New York, West of the Rockies. **Units of Measure:** Dollars per lb. **Type of Price:** spot. **Time Period Covered:** latest week.

ALKYD

Source: *Plastics Technology.* **Price Frequency:** monthly. **Units of Measure:** cents per lb., cents per cubic inch. **Type of Price:** bulk list, market. **Time Period Covered:** latest month.

ALKYDS: TYPE 1, LONG SOYBEAN OIL

Source: *Journal of Commerce and Commercial.* **Price Frequency:** weekly in Wednesday issue. **Units of Measure:** Dollars per lb. **Type of Price:** spot. **Time Period Covered:** latest week.

ALKYDS: TYPE 3, MEDIUM SOY, LINSEED OIL

Source: *Journal of Commerce and Commercial.* **Price Frequency:** weekly in Wednesday issue. **Units of Measure:** Dollars per lb. **Type of Price:** spot. **Time Period Covered:** latest week.

ALKYLATE

Source: *Oil Buyers' Guide.* **Price Frequency:** weekly. **Effective Market(s):** Venezuela. **Units of Measure:** Dollars per gallon. **Type of Price:** official. **Time Period Covered:** latest week.

ALLSPICE
see also Pimento.

ALLSPICE: GUATEMALAN/HONDURAN
Source: *Chemical Marketing Reporter.* **Price Frequency:** weekly. **Effective Market(s):** New York. **Units of Measure:** Dollars per lb. **Type of Price:** spot. **Time Period Covered:** latest week.

ALLSPICE: JAMAICAN
Source: *Chemical Marketing Reporter.* **Price Frequency:** weekly. **Effective Market(s):** New York. **Units of Measure:** Dollars per lb. **Type of Price:** spot. **Time Period Covered:** latest week.

ALLSPICE OIL
Source: *Journal of Commerce and Commercial.* **Price Frequency:** weekly in Tuesday issue. **Units of Measure:** Dollars per lb. **Type of Price:** spot. **Time Period Covered:** latest week.

ALLYL ALCOHOL
Source: *Chemical Marketing Reporter .* **Price Frequency:** weekly. **Effective Market(s):** Bayport (TX). **Units of Measure:** Dollars per lb. **Type of Price:** spot. **Time Period Covered:** latest week.

ALLYL BROMIDE
Source: *Chemical Marketing Reporter.* **Price Frequency:** weekly. **Effective Market(s):** New York. **Units of Measure:** Dollars per lb. **Type of Price:** spot. **Time Period Covered:** latest week.

ALLYL CAPROATE
Source: *Chemical Marketing Reporter.* **Price Frequency:** weekly. **Effective Market(s):** New York. **Units of Measure:** Dollars per lb. **Type of Price:** spot. **Time Period Covered:** latest week.

ALLYL CHLORIDE
Source: *Chemical Marketing Reporter.* **Price Frequency:** weekly. **Effective Market(s):** New York. **Units of Measure:** Dollars per lb. **Type of Price:** spot. **Time Period Covered:** latest week.

ALLYL ISOTHIOCYANATE
Source: *Chemical Marketing Reporter.* **Price Frequency:** weekly. **Effective Market(s):** New York. **Units of Measure:** Dollars per lb. **Type of Price:** spot. **Time Period Covered:** latest week.

ALMOND HULLS
Source: *Los Angeles Times.* **Price Frequency:** daily. **Effective Market(s):** Los Angeles. **Units of Measure:** Dollars per ton. **Type of Price:** cash. **Time Period Covered:** latest day.

ALMOND OIL: BITTER
Source: *U. S. Essential Oil Trade.* **Price Frequency:** annually. **Effective Market(s):** United States. **Units of Measure:** Dollars per kilogram. **Type of Price:** import value. **Time Period Covered:** latest 3 years.

ALMOND OIL: BITTER, ARTIFICIAL
see Benzaldehyde.

ALMOND OIL: BITTER, NATURAL
Source: *Chemical Marketing Reporter.* **Price Frequency:** weekly. **Effective Market(s):** New York. **Units of Measure:** Dollars per lb. **Type of Price:** spot. **Time Period Covered:** latest week.

ALMONDS
Source: *Agricultural Prices Annual Summary.* **Price Frequency:** annually. **Effective Market(s):** California, Hawaii. **Units of Measure:** Dollars per lb. **Type of Price:** average received by farmer. **Time Period Covered:** latest 6 years.

Source: *Fruit and Tree Nuts Situation and Outlook Yearbook.* **Price Frequency:** annually. **Effective Market(s):** California. **Units of Measure:** cents per lb. **Type of Price:** grower. **Time Period Covered:** latest 20 years.

ALOE: CAPE
Source: *Chemical Marketing Reporter.* **Price Frequency:** weekly. **Effective Market(s):** New York. **Units of Measure:** Dollars per lb. **Type of Price:** spot. **Time Period Covered:** latest week.

ALOE: CAPE, POWDERED
Source: *Chemical Marketing Reporter.* **Price Frequency:** weekly. **Effective Market(s):** New York. **Units of Measure:** Dollars per lb. **Type of Price:** spot. **Time Period Covered:** latest week.

ALOE: CURACAO
Source: *Chemical Marketing Reporter.* **Price Frequency:** weekly. **Effective Market(s):** New York. **Units of Measure:** Dollars per lb. **Type of Price:** spot. **Time Period Covered:** latest week.

ALOE: CURACAO, POWDERED
Source: *Chemical Marketing Reporter.* **Price Frequency:** weekly. **Effective Market(s):** New York. **Units of Measure:** Dollars per lb. **Type of Price:** spot. **Time Period Covered:** latest week.

ALOE GUMS: SOUTH AFRICAN/CURACAO
Source: *Journal of Commerce and Commercial.* **Price Frequency:** weekly in Monday issue. **Units of Measure:** Dollars per lb. **Type of Price:** spot. **Time Period Covered:** latest week.

ALOE VERA
Source: *Journal of Commerce and Commercial.* **Price Frequency:** weekly in Monday issue. **Units of Measure:** Dollars per lb. **Type of Price:** spot. **Time Period Covered:** latest week.

ALOIN: NF
Source: *Chemical Marketing Reporter.* **Price Frequency:** weekly. **Effective Market(s):** New York. **Units of Measure:** Dollars per lb. **Type of Price:** spot. **Time Period Covered:** latest week.

ALUM: AMMONIUM, FCC, POWDERED
Source: *Chemical Marketing Reporter.* **Price Frequency:** weekly. **Effective Market(s):** New York. **Units of Measure:** Dollars per 100 lbs. **Type of Price:** spot. **Time Period Covered:** latest week.

ALUM: AMMONIUM, TECHNICAL, GRANULAR

Source: *Chemical Marketing Reporter.* **Price Frequency:** weekly. **Effective Market(s):** New York. **Units of Measure:** Dollars per 100 lbs. **Type of Price:** spot. **Time Period Covered:** latest week.

ALUM: POTASSIUM, FCC, POWDERED

Source: *Chemical Marketing Reporter.* **Price Frequency:** weekly. **Effective Market(s):** New York. **Units of Measure:** Dollars per 100 lbs. **Type of Price:** spot. **Time Period Covered:** latest week.

ALUM: POTASSIUM, TECHNICAL, GRANULAR

Source: *Chemical Marketing Reporter.* **Price Frequency:** weekly. **Effective Market(s):** New York. **Units of Measure:** Dollars per 100 lbs. **Type of Price:** spot. **Time Period Covered:** latest week.

ALUMINA: ACTIVATED, GRANULAR

Source: *Chemical Marketing Reporter.* **Price Frequency:** weekly. **Effective Market(s):** New York. **Units of Measure:** Dollars per ton. **Type of Price:** spot. **Time Period Covered:** latest week.

ALUMINA: CALCINED

Source: *Chemical Marketing Reporter.* **Price Frequency:** weekly. **Effective Market(s):** New York. **Units of Measure:** Dollars per ton. **Type of Price:** spot. **Time Period Covered:** latest week.

Source: *Industrial Minerals.* **Price Frequency:** monthly. **Effective Market(s):** United Kingdom. **Units of Measure:** British pounds per metric tonne. **Type of Price:** dealer. **Time Period Covered:** latest month.

ALUMINA: CALCINED, MEDIUM SODA CONTENT

Source: *Industrial Minerals.* **Price Frequency:** monthly. **Effective Market(s):** main European port. **Units of Measure:** British pounds per metric tonne. **Type of Price:** producer & dealer. **Time Period Covered:** latest month.

ALUMINA: FUSED, BROWN

Source: *Industrial Minerals.* **Price Frequency:** monthly. **Effective Market(s):** main European port. **Units of Measure:** British pounds per metric tonne. **Type of Price:** producer & dealer. **Time Period Covered:** latest month.

ALUMINA: FUSED, WHITE

Source: *Industrial Minerals.* **Price Frequency:** monthly. **Effective Market(s):** main European port. **Units of Measure:** British pounds per metric tonne. **Type of Price:** producer & dealer. **Time Period Covered:** latest month.

ALUMINA TRIHYDRATE: WHITE

Source: *Chemical Marketing Reporter.* **Price Frequency:** weekly. **Effective Market(s):** New York. **Units of Measure:** Dollars per ton. **Type of Price:** spot. **Time Period Covered:** latest week.

ALUMINIUM

see Aluminum.

ALUMINUM

Source: *Business Week.* **Price Frequency:** weekly. **Units of Measure:** cents per lb. **Time Period Covered:** latest 2 weeks.

Source: *Economic and Energy Indicators.* **Price Frequency:** monthly, quarterly, annually. **Units of Measure:** cents per lb. **Time Period Covered:** latest 3 months, quarters, and years.

Source: *Far Eastern Economic Review.* **Price Frequency:** weekly. **Effective Market(s):** London. **Units of Measure:** Dollars per tonne. **Time Period Covered:** latest week, week ago, 3 months ago, year ago.

Source: *Financial Times.* **Price Frequency:** daily. **Effective Market(s):** London. **Units of Measure:** Dollars per tonne. **Type of Price:** free market. **Time Period Covered:** latest day.

Source: *Investor's Daily.* **Price Frequency:** daily. **Effective Market(s):** New York. **Units of Measure:** Dollars per lb. **Type of Price:** spot. **Time Period Covered:** latest 2 days.

Source: *Iron Age.* **Price Frequency:** monthly. **Effective Market(s):** London. **Units of Measure:** cents per lb. **Type of Price:** consumer. **Time Period Covered:** latest month.

Source: *Journal of Commerce and Commercial.* **Price Frequency:** daily. **Effective Market(s):** London. **Units of Measure:** Dollars per ton. **Type of Price:** spot . **Time Period Covered:** latest day.

Source: *Los Angeles Times.* **Price Frequency:** daily. **Effective Market(s):** London. **Units of Measure:** Dollars per pound. **Type of Price:** cash. **Time Period Covered:** latest day.

Source: *Minerals Today.* **Price Frequency:** bimonthly. **Units of Measure:** cents per lb. **Time Period Covered:** latest month, month ago.

Source: *New York Times.* **Price Frequency:** daily. **Effective Market(s):** New York. **Units of Measure:** Dollars per lb. **Type of Price:** cash. **Time Period Covered:** latest 2 days.

Source: *Northern Miner.* **Price Frequency:** daily. **Effective Market(s):** Midwest. **Units of Measure:** cents per lb. **Type of Price:** producer. **Time Period Covered:** selected day.

Source: *Northern Miner.* **Price Frequency:** daily. **Effective Market(s):** London. **Units of Measure:** Dollars per tonne. **Type of Price:** spot. **Time Period Covered:** week ago.

Source: *UNCTAD Commodity Yearbook.* **Price Frequency:** annually. **Effective Market(s):** London. **Units of Measure:** Dollars per metric ton. **Type of Price:** cash. **Time Period Covered:** latest 12 years.

ALUMINUM: 99.5% MINIMUM

Source: *Commodity Trade and Price Trends.* **Price Frequency:** annually. **Effective Market(s):** Europe. **Units of Measure:** Dollars per metric ton, 1980 constant dollars per metric ton. **Time Period Covered:** latest 29 years.

Source: *Commodity Trade and Price Trends.* **Price Frequency:** annually. **Effective Market(s):** London. **Units of Measure:** Dollars per metric ton, 1980 constant dollars per metric ton. **Type of Price:** bid/asked . **Time Period Covered:** latest 8 years.

ALUMINUM: 99.5% OR MORE

Source: *Chemical Marketing Reporter.* **Price Frequency:** weekly. **Effective Market(s):** New York. **Units of Measure:** Dollars per lb. **Type of Price:** spot. **Time Period Covered:** latest week.

ALUMINUM: 99.5% PURITY

Source: *E&MJ.* **Price Frequency:** monthly. **Effective Market(s):** London. **Units of Measure:** cents per lb. **Type of Price:** spot close. **Time Period Covered:** selected dates.

Source: *E&MJ.* **Price Frequency:** monthly. **Effective Market(s):** London. **Units of Measure:** cents per lb. **Type of Price:** spot close. **Time Period Covered:** latest month.

ALUMINUM: 99.7% PURITY

Source: *E&MJ.* **Price Frequency:** monthly. **Effective Market(s):** New York. **Units of Measure:** cents per lb. **Type of Price:** merchant. **Time Period Covered:** selected dates.

Source: *E&MJ.* **Price Frequency:** monthly. **Effective Market(s):** New York. **Units of Measure:** cents per lb. **Type of Price:** closing, merchant. **Time Period Covered:** latest month.

Source: *Financial Times.* **Price Frequency:** daily. **Effective Market(s):** London. **Units of Measure:** Dollars per tonne. **Type of Price:** cash. **Time Period Covered:** latest day, day ago.

Source: *Survey of Current Business.* **Price Frequency:** monthly, annually. **Effective Market(s):** United States. **Units of Measure:** Dollars per lb. **Type of Price:** average. **Time Period Covered:** latest year.

ALUMINUM: 99.7% PURITY, FUTURES

Source: *E&MJ.* **Price Frequency:** monthly. **Effective Market(s):** New York. **Units of Measure:** cents per lb. **Type of Price:** futures. **Time Period Covered:** selected dates.

ALUMINUM: CANADA

Source: *International Financial Statistics.* **Price Frequency:** monthly, quarterly, annually. **Effective Market(s):** United Kingdom. **Units of Measure:** cents per lb., index. **Type of Price:** market price, price index. **Time Period Covered:** latest 5 months, latest 5 quarters, latest 5 years.

Source: *International Financial Statistics Yearbook.* **Price Frequency:** annually. **Effective Market(s):** United Kingdom. **Units of Measure:** cents per lb. **Type of Price:** wholesale. **Time Period Covered:** latest 30 years.

ALUMINUM: COMMON ALLOY SHEET 3003

Source: *Purchasing.* **Price Frequency:** monthly. **Units of Measure:** cents per lb. **Type of Price:** transaction. **Time Period Covered:** latest day, month ago, 6 months ago, year ago.

ALUMINUM: COPPER MAXIMUM 0.6%

Source: *American Metal Market.* **Price Frequency:** daily. **Effective Market(s):** United States. **Units of Measure:** cents per lb. **Type of Price:** list. **Time Period Covered:** latest day.

ALUMINUM: FOUNDRY GRADE

Source: *American Metal Market.* **Price Frequency:** daily. **Effective Market(s):** United States. **Units of Measure:** cents per lb. **Type of Price:** list. **Time Period Covered:** latest day.

ALUMINUM: FUTURES

Source: *Barron's.* **Price Frequency:** weekly. **Effective Market(s):** New York. **Units of Measure:** cents per lb. **Type of Price:** futures. **Time Period Covered:** latest week.

Source: *Investor's Daily.* **Price Frequency:** daily. **Effective Market(s):** New York. **Units of Measure:** cents per lb. **Type of Price:** futures. **Time Period Covered:** latest day.

Source: *Wall Street Journal.* **Price Frequency:** daily. **Effective Market(s):** New York. **Units of Measure:** cents per lb. **Type of Price:** futures. **Time Period Covered:** next contract month.

ALUMINUM: FUTURES, DECEMBER

Source: *Commodity Year Book.* **Price Frequency:** monthly. **Effective Market(s):** New York. **Units of Measure:** cents per lb. **Type of Price:** futures. **Time Period Covered:** past 3 years.

ALUMINUM: HIGH GRADE

Source: *American Metal Market.* **Price Frequency:** daily. **Effective Market(s):** London. **Units of Measure:** Dollars per metric ton. **Type of Price:** cash. **Time Period Covered:** latest 2 days.

Source: *Asian Wall Street Journal.* **Price Frequency:** daily. **Effective Market(s):** London. **Units of Measure:** Dollars per metric ton. **Type of Price:** spot. **Time Period Covered:** latest day.

Source: *Journal of Commerce and Commercial.* **Price Frequency:** daily. **Effective Market(s):** London. **Units of Measure:** British pounds per metric ton. **Type of Price:** spot. **Time Period Covered:** latest day, day ago.

Source: *Monthly Commodity Price Bulletin.* **Price Frequency:** monthly, annually. **Effective Market(s):** London. **Units of Measure:** Dollars per metric ton. **Type of Price:** cash. **Time Period Covered:** latest 5 years.

Source: *Monthly Commodity Price Bulletin Supplement.* **Price Frequency:** monthly, quarterly, annually. **Effective Market(s):** London. **Units of Measure:** Dollars per tonne. **Time Period Covered:** latest 20 years.

Source: *New York Times.* **Price Frequency:** daily. **Effective Market(s):** London. **Units of Measure:** Dollars per metric ton. **Type of Price:** spot. **Time Period Covered:** latest day.

Source: *The Times.* **Price Frequency:** daily. **Effective Market(s):** London. **Units of Measure:** Dollars per tonne. **Type of Price:** cash. **Time Period Covered:** latest day.

Source: *Wall Street Journal.* **Price Frequency:** daily. **Effective Market(s):** London. **Units of Measure:** Dollars per metric ton. **Type of Price:** spot. **Time Period Covered:** latest day, 3 months ago.

ALUMINUM: SECONDARY 380, 3% ZINC

Source: *Purchasing.* **Price Frequency:** monthly. **Units of Measure:** cents per lb. **Type of Price:** transaction. **Time Period Covered:** latest day, month ago, 6 months ago, year ago.

ALUMINUM: STANDARD GRADE

Source: *Monthly Commodity Price Bulletin Supplement.* **Price Frequency:** monthly, quarterly, annually. **Effective Market(s):** London. **Units of Measure:** British ponds per tonne, dollars per tonne. **Type of Price:** cash. **Time Period Covered:** latest 20 years.

Source: *Monthly Commodity Price Bulletin.* **Price Frequency:** monthly, annually. **Effective Market(s):** London . **Units of Measure:** British pounds per metric ton, cents per lb. **Type of Price:** cash. **Time Period Covered:** latest 5 years.

ALUMINUM: STEEL DEOXIDIZING, GRADE 1

Source: *American Metal Market.* **Price Frequency:** daily. **Effective Market(s):** United States. **Units of Measure:** cents per lb. **Type of Price:** list. **Time Period Covered:** latest day.

ALUMINUM ACETATE

Source: *Chemical Marketing Reporter.* **Price Frequency:** weekly. **Effective Market(s):** New York. **Units of Measure:** Dollars per lb. **Type of Price:** spot. **Time Period Covered:** latest week.

ALUMINUM CANSTOCK

Source: *Purchasing.* **Price Frequency:** quarterly in January, April, July, and October issues. **Units of Measure:** cents per lb. **Type of Price:** transaction. **Time Period Covered:** latest 5 quarters.

ALUMINUM CHLORIDE

Source: *Chemical Marketing Reporter.* **Price Frequency:** weekly. **Effective Market(s):** New York. **Units of Measure:** Dollars per 100 lb. **Type of Price:** spot. **Time Period Covered:** latest week.

ALUMINUM EXTRUSIONS

Source: *Purchasing.* **Price Frequency:** quarterly in January, April, July, and October issues. **Units of Measure:** cents per lb. **Type of Price:** transaction. **Time Period Covered:** latest 5 quarters.

ALUMINUM FORMATE: DIBASIC

Source: *Chemical Marketing Reporter.* **Price Frequency:** weekly. **Effective Market(s):** New York. **Units of Measure:** Dollars per lb. **Type of Price:** spot. **Time Period Covered:** latest week.

ALUMINUM HYDROXIDE: DRIED, GEL, NF

Source: *Chemical Marketing Reporter.* **Price Frequency:** weekly. **Effective Market(s):** New York. **Units of Measure:** Dollars per lb. **Type of Price:** spot. **Time Period Covered:** latest week.

ALUMINUM INGOT

Source: *Asian Wall Street Journal.* **Price Frequency:** daily. **Effective Market(s):** Midwest. **Units of Measure:** Dollars per lb. **Type of Price:** cash. **Time Period Covered:** latest 2 days, year ago.

Source: *Wall Street Journal.* **Price Frequency:** daily. **Effective Market(s):** Midwest. **Units of Measure:** Dollars per lb. **Time Period Covered:** latest day, day ago, year ago.

ALUMINUM INGOT: 99.7% MINIMUM

Source: *Journal of Commerce and Commercial.* **Price Frequency:** daily. **Effective Market(s):** Europe. **Units of Measure:** Dollars per ton. **Type of Price:** spot. **Time Period Covered:** latest day.

ALUMINUM INGOT: 99.7% PURE

Source: *Japan Economic Journal.* **Price Frequency:** weekly. **Effective Market(s):** Tokyo. **Units of Measure:** Japanese yen per ton. **Type of Price:** trader. **Time Period Covered:** latest 2 weeks.

ALUMINUM INGOT: ALLOYED, DOMESTIC

Source: *American Metal Market.* **Price Frequency:** daily. **Effective Market(s):** United States. **Units of Measure:** cents per lb. **Type of Price:** producer. **Time Period Covered:** latest day.

ALUMINUM INGOT: SECONDARY

Source: *American Metal Market.* **Price Frequency:** daily. **Effective Market(s):** United States. **Units of Measure:** cents per lb. **Type of Price:** list. **Time Period Covered:** latest day.

ALUMINUM INGOT: UNALLOYED, 99.5%

Source: *Purchasing.* **Price Frequency:** monthly. **Units of Measure:** cents per lb. **Type of Price:** transaction. **Time Period Covered:** latest day, month ago, 6 months ago, year ago.

ALUMINUM INGOT: UNALLOYED, 99.7%

Source: *American Metal Market.* **Price Frequency:** daily. **Effective Market(s):** London. **Units of Measure:** Dollars per metric ton. **Type of Price:** spot. **Time Period Covered:** latest day.

Source: *American Metal Market.* **Price Frequency:** daily. **Effective Market(s):** New York. **Units of Measure:** cents per lb. **Type of Price:** merchant. **Time Period Covered:** latest day.

ALUMINUM INGOT: UNALLOYED, 99.7%, FUTURES

Source: *American Metal Market.* **Price Frequency:** daily. **Effective Market(s):** New York. **Units of Measure:** cents per lb. **Type of Price:** futures. **Time Period Covered:** latest day.

ALUMINUM OXIDE AMORPHOUS

see Alumina: Calcined.

ALUMINUM PASTE: LEAFING GRADE, LINING, STANDARD

Source: *Chemical Marketing Reporter.* **Price Frequency:** weekly. **Effective Market(s):** New York. **Units of Measure:** Dollars per lb. **Type of Price:** spot. **Time Period Covered:** latest week.

ALUMINUM PASTE: LEAFING GRADE, LINING, EXTRA FINE

Source: *Chemical Marketing Reporter.* **Price Frequency:** weekly. **Effective Market(s):** New York. **Units of Measure:** Dollars per lb. **Type of Price:** spot. **Time Period Covered:** latest week.

ALUMINUM PHENOLSULFONATE: PURIFIED

Source: *Chemical Marketing Reporter.* **Price Frequency:** weekly. **Effective Market(s):** New York. **Units of Measure:** Dollars per kilo. **Type of Price:** spot. **Time Period Covered:** latest week.

ALUMINUM POWDER: ATOMIZED

Source: *American Metal Market.* **Price Frequency:** daily. **Units of Measure:** Dollars per lb. **Type of Price:** wholesale. **Time Period Covered:** latest day.

ALUMINUM POWDER: FLAKE, EXTRA FINE

Source: *American Metal Market.* **Price Frequency:** daily. **Units of Measure:** Dollars per lb. **Type of Price:** wholesale. **Time Period Covered:** latest day.

ALUMINUM POWDER: LEAFING GRADE, LINING, STANDARD

Source: *Chemical Marketing Reporter.* **Price Frequency:** weekly. **Effective Market(s):** New York. **Units of Measure:** Dollars per lb. **Type of Price:** spot. **Time Period Covered:** latest week.

ALUMINUM POWDER: LEAFING GRADE, LINING, EXTRA FINE

Source: *Chemical Marketing Reporter.* **Price Frequency:** weekly. **Effective Market(s):** New York. **Units of Measure:** Dollars per lb. **Type of Price:** spot. **Time Period Covered:** latest week.

ALUMINUM POWDER PASTE: LINING, STANDARD

Source: *American Metal Market.* **Price Frequency:** daily. **Units of Measure:** Dollars per lb. **Type of Price:** wholesale. **Time Period Covered:** latest day.

ALUMINUM RICH ALLOY

Source: *American Metal Market.* **Price Frequency:** daily. **Effective Market(s):** United States. **Units of Measure:** cents per lb. **Type of Price:** producer. **Time Period Covered:** latest day.

ALUMINUM SCRAP: 1S

Source: *American Metal Market.* **Price Frequency:** daily. **Effective Market(s):** Toronto. **Units of Measure:** Canadian cents per lb. **Type of Price:** dealer buying. **Time Period Covered:** latest day.

ALUMINUM SCRAP: BORINGS AND TURNINGS

Source: *Iron Age.* **Price Frequency:** monthly. **Effective Market(s):** New York. **Units of Measure:** cents per lb. **Type of Price:** dealer. **Time Period Covered:** latest month.

ALUMINUM SCRAP: BORINGS AND TURNINGS, AS IS

Source: *American Metal Market.* **Price Frequency:** daily. **Effective Market(s):** Los Angeles, New York. **Units of Measure:** cents per lb. **Type of Price:** dealer buying. **Time Period Covered:** latest day.

ALUMINUM SCRAP: BORINGS AND TURNINGS, CLEAN AND DRY

Source: *American Metal Market.* **Price Frequency:** daily. **Effective Market(s):** 14 domestic markets, Montreal, Toronto. **Units of Measure:** cents per lb., Canadian cents per lb. **Type of Price:** dealer buying. **Time Period Covered:** latest day.

ALUMINUM SCRAP: BORINGS, CLEAN AND DRY

Source: *Iron Age.* **Price Frequency:** monthly. **Units of Measure:** cents per lb. **Type of Price:** refinery. **Time Period Covered:** latest month.

ALUMINUM SCRAP: CAN STOCK CLIPPINGS, CLEAN

Source: *American Metal Market.* **Price Frequency:** daily. **Units of Measure:** cents per lb. **Type of Price:** smelter buying. **Time Period Covered:** latest day.

ALUMINUM SCRAP: CAST, OLD

Source: *Iron Age.* **Price Frequency:** monthly. **Units of Measure:** cents per lb. **Type of Price:** refinery. **Time Period Covered:** latest month.

ALUMINUM SCRAP: CLIPPINGS

Source: *American Metal Market.* **Price Frequency:** daily. **Effective Market(s):** Los Angeles, New York. **Units of Measure:** cents per lb. **Type of Price:** dealer buying. **Time Period Covered:** latest day.

Source: *Commmodity Year Book.* **Price Frequency:** monthly, annually. **Effective Market(s):** New York. **Units of Measure:** cents per lb. **Time Period Covered:** latest 2 years.

ALUMINUM SCRAP: CLIPPINGS, MEDIUM

Source: *American Metal Market.* **Price Frequency:** daily. **Effective Market(s):** 14 domestic markets, Montreal, Toronto. **Number of Sources:** 3. **Units of Measure:** cents per lb., Canadian cents per lb. **Type of Price:** dealer buying. **Time Period Covered:** latest day.

ALUMINUM SCRAP: CLIPPINGS, MIXED

Source: *American Metal Market.* **Price Frequency:** daily. **Number of Sources:** 1. **Units of Measure:** cents per lb. **Type of Price:** smelter buying. **Time Period Covered:** latest day.

ALUMINUM SCRAP: CLIPPINGS, MIXED, HIGH COPPER ALLOY

Source: *American Metal Market.* **Price Frequency:** daily. **Number of Sources:** 4. **Units of Measure:** cents per lb. **Type of Price:** smelter buying. **Time Period Covered:** latest day.

ALUMINUM SCRAP: CLIPPINGS, MIXED, LOW COPPER ALLOY

Source: *American Metal Market.* **Price Frequency:** daily. **Effective Market(s):** 14 domestic markets, Montreal, Toronto. **Number of Sources:** 5. **Units of Measure:** cents per lb., Canadian cents per lb. **Type of Price:** dealer buying. **Time Period Covered:** latest day.

Source: *American Metal Market.* **Price Frequency:** daily. **Number of Sources:** 3. **Units of Measure:** cents per lb. **Type of Price:** smelter buying, specialty consumer buying. **Time Period Covered:** latest day.

Source: *Iron Age.* **Price Frequency:** monthly. **Effective Market(s):** New York. **Number of Sources:** 3. **Units of Measure:** cents per lb. **Type of Price:** dealer. **Time Period Covered:** latest month.

ALUMINUM SCRAP: CLIPPINGS, MIXED, NEW

Source: *Iron Age.* **Price Frequency:** monthly. **Number of Sources:** 2. **Units of Measure:** cents per lb. **Type of Price:** refinery. **Time Period Covered:** latest month.

ALUMINUM SCRAP: CLIPPINGS, SEGREGATED

Source: *Iron Age.* **Price Frequency:** monthly. **Effective Market(s):** New York. **Number of Sources:** 7. **Units of Measure:** cents per lb. **Type of Price:** dealer. **Time Period Covered:** latest month.

ALUMINUM SCRAP: CLIPPINGS, SEGREGATED, LOW COPPER ALLOY

Source: *American Metal Market.* **Price Frequency:** daily. **Effective Market(s):** 14 domestic markets, Montreal, Toronto. **Number of Sources:** 6. **Units of Measure:** cents per lb., Canadian cents per lb. **Type of Price:** dealer buying. **Time Period Covered:** latest day.

Source: *American Metal Market.* **Price Frequency:** daily. **Number of Sources:** 7. **Units of Measure:** cents per lb. **Type of Price:** specialty consumer buying. **Time Period Covered:** latest day.

ALUMINUM SCRAP: SHEET AND CAST, OLD

Source: *American Metal Market.* **Price Frequency:** daily. **Units of Measure:** cents per lb. **Type of Price:** smelter buying. **Time Period Covered:** latest day.

Source: *American Metal Market.* **Price Frequency:** daily. **Effective Market(s):** 14 domestic markets, Montreal, Toronto. **Units of Measure:** cents per lb., Canadian cents per lb. **Type of Price:** dealer buying. **Time Period Covered:** latest day.

Source: *Iron Age.* **Price Frequency:** monthly. **Effective Market(s):** New York. **Units of Measure:** cents per lb. **Type of Price:** dealer. **Time Period Covered:** latest month.

ALUMINUM SCRAP: SHEET, OLD

Source: *Iron Age.* **Price Frequency:** monthly. **Units of Measure:** cents per lb. **Type of Price:** refinery. **Time Period Covered:** latest month.

ALUMINUM SCRAP: SOLIDS

Source: *American Metal Market.* **Price Frequency:** daily. **Effective Market(s):** Detroit. **Units of Measure:** cents per lb. **Type of Price:** dealer buying. **Time Period Covered:** latest day.

ALUMINUM SCRAP: TURNINGS, CLEAN AND DRY

Source: *American Metal Market.* **Price Frequency:** daily. **Units of Measure:** cents per lb. **Type of Price:** smelter buying. **Time Period Covered:** latest day.

ALUMINUM SCRAP BEVERAGE CANS: USED

Source: *American Metal Market.* **Price Frequency:** daily. **Units of Measure:** cents per lb. **Type of Price:** producer. **Time Period Covered:** latest day.

ALUMINUM SCRAP CRANK CASES

Source: *Commodity Year Book.* **Price Frequency:** monthly, annually. **Effective Market(s):** New York. **Units of Measure:** cents per lb. **Type of Price:** dealers' buying prices. **Time Period Covered:** latest 5 years.

ALUMINUM SCRAP UTENSILS

Source: *American Metal Market.* **Price Frequency:** daily. **Effective Market(s):** Toronto. **Units of Measure:** Canadian cents per lb. **Type of Price:** dealer buying. **Time Period Covered:** latest day.

ALUMINUM SHEET: 3 X 8 FOOT

Source: *ENR.* **Price Frequency:** monthly in second issue of month. **Effective Market(s):** 10 domestic markets. **Units of Measure:** Dollars per 100 lbs. **Type of Price:** spot. **Time Period Covered:** latest month.

ALUMINUM SIDING: SCRAP

Source: *American Metal Market.* **Price Frequency:** daily. **Units of Measure:** cents per lb. **Type of Price:** smelter buying, specialty consumer buying. **Time Period Covered:** latest day.

ALUMINUM SIDING: SCRAP, PAINTED

Source: *American Metal Market.* **Price Frequency:** daily. **Effective Market(s):** Toronto. **Units of Measure:** Canadian cents per lb. **Type of Price:** dealer buying. **Time Period Covered:** latest day.

ALUMINUM STEARATE

Source: *Chemical Marketing Reporter.* **Price Frequency:** weekly. **Effective Market(s):** New York. **Units of Measure:** Dollars per lb. **Type of Price:** spot. **Time Period Covered:** latest week.

ALUMINUM SULFATE: DRY, COMMERCIAL

Source: *Journal of Commerce and Commercial.* **Price Frequency:** weekly in Thursday issue. **Effective Market(s):** East. **Units of Measure:** Dollars per ton. **Type of Price:** spot. **Time Period Covered:** latest day.

ALUMINUM SULFATE: DRY, IRON FREE

Source: *Chemical Marketing Reporter.* **Price Frequency:** weekly. **Effective Market(s):** Northeast. **Units of Measure:** Dollars per ton. **Type of Price:** spot. **Time Period Covered:** latest week.

ALUMINUM SULFATE: GRANULAR, USP

Source: *Chemical Marketing Reporter.* **Price Frequency:** weekly. **Effective Market(s):** New York. **Units of Measure:** Dollars per lb. **Type of Price:** spot. **Time Period Covered:** latest week.

ALUMINUM SULFATE: GROUND, COMMERCIAL

Source: *Chemical Marketing Reporter.* **Price Frequency:** weekly. **Effective Market(s):** East/Gulf Coasts, West Coast. **Units of Measure:** Dollars per ton. **Type of Price:** spot. **Time Period Covered:** latest week.

ALUMINUM SULFATE: LIQUID, COMMERCIAL

Source: *Chemical Marketing Reporter.* **Price Frequency:** weekly. **Effective Market(s):** New York. **Units of Measure:** Dollars per ton. **Type of Price:** spot. **Time Period Covered:** latest week.

Source: *Journal of Commerce and Commercial.* **Price Frequency:** weekly in Thursday issue. **Effective Market(s):** East. **Units of Measure:** Dollars per ton. **Type of Price:** spot. **Time Period Covered:** latest week.

ALUMINUM SULFATE: LIQUID, IRON FREE

Source: *Chemical Marketing Reporter.* **Price Frequency:** weekly. **Effective Market(s):** New York. **Units of Measure:** Dollars per lb. **Type of Price:** spot. **Time Period Covered:** latest week.

Source: *Journal of Commerce and Commercial.* **Price Frequency:** weekly in Thursday issue. **Effective Market(s):** East. **Units of Measure:** Dollars per lb. **Type of Price:** spot. **Time Period Covered:** latest week.

ALUMINUM TRIHYDRATE

see ATH.

AMBER JACK (FISH): FRESH

Source: *Seafood Price-Current.* **Price Frequency:** semiweekly. **Effective Market(s):** Gulf/Southeast. **Units of Measure:** Dollars per lb. **Type of Price:** sale by first receiver. **Time Period Covered:** latest day.

2-AMINO-4-CHLOROPHENOL: DRY AND GROUND

Source: *Chemical Marketing Reporter.* **Price Frequency:** weekly. **Effective Market(s):** New York. **Units of Measure:** Dollars per lb. **Type of Price:** spot. **Time Period Covered:** latest week.

2-AMINO-2-ETHYL-1,3-PROPANEDIOL

Source: *Chemical Marketing Reporter.* **Price Frequency:** weekly. **Effective Market(s):** New York. **Units of Measure:** Dollars per lb. **Type of Price:** spot. **Time Period Covered:** latest week.

AMINO FUNCTIONAL SILANE

see Silane: Amino Functional.

2-AMINO-2-METHYL-1-PROPANOL: 95%

Source: *Chemical Marketing Reporter.* **Price Frequency:** weekly. **Effective Market(s):** New York. **Units of Measure:** Dollars per lb. **Type of Price:** spot. **Time Period Covered:** latest week.

AMINOACETIC ACID: TECHNICAL GRADE

Source: *Chemical Marketing Reporter.* **Price Frequency:** weekly. **Effective Market(s):** New York. **Units of Measure:** Dollars per lb. **Type of Price:** spot. **Time Period Covered:** latest week.

AMINOACETIC ACID: USP

Source: *Chemical Marketing Reporter.* **Price Frequency:** weekly. **Effective Market(s):** New York. **Units of Measure:** Dollars per lb. **Type of Price:** spot. **Time Period Covered:** latest week.

P-AMINOBENZOIC ACID

Source: *Journal of Commerce and Commercial.* **Price Frequency:** weekly in Friday issue. **Units of Measure:** Dollars per kilo. **Type of Price:** spot. **Time Period Covered:** latest week.

P-AMINOBENZOIC ACID: USP

Source: *Chemical Marketing Reporter.* **Price Frequency:** weekly. **Effective Market(s):** New York. **Units of Measure:** Dollars per kilo. **Type of Price:** spot. **Time Period Covered:** latest week.

AMINOETHYL ETHANOLAMINE

Source: *Chemical Marketing Reporter.* **Price Frequency:** weekly. **Effective Market(s):** New York. **Units of Measure:** Dollars per lb. **Type of Price:** spot. **Time Period Covered:** latest week.

N-AMINOETHYL PIPERAZINE

Source: *Chemical Marketing Reporter.* **Price Frequency:** weekly. **Effective Market(s):** New York. **Units of Measure:** Dollars per lb. **Type of Price:** spot. **Time Period Covered:** latest week.

O-AMINOPHENOL

Source: *Chemical Marketing Reporter.* **Price Frequency:** weekly. **Effective Market(s):** Charlotte (NC). **Units of Measure:** Dollars per lb. **Type of Price:** spot. **Time Period Covered:** latest week.

P-AMINOPHENOL

Source: *Chemical Marketing Reporter.* **Price Frequency:** weekly. **Effective Market(s):** Raleigh (NC). **Units of Measure:** Dollars per kilo. **Type of Price:** spot. **Time Period Covered:** latest week.

P-AMINOSALICYLIC ACID: USP

Source: *Journal of Commerce and Commercial.* **Price Frequency:** weekly in Friday issue. **Units of Measure:** Dollars per lb. **Type of Price:** spot. **Time Period Covered:** latest week.

AMMONIA

Source: *Commodity Year Book.* **Price Frequency:** annually. **Effective Market(s):** Gulf Coast. **Units of Measure:** Dollars per short ton. **Time Period Covered:** latest 8 years.

AMMONIA: AGRICULTURAL

Source: *Energy Pricing News: Petrochemical Report.* **Price Frequency:** bimonthly. **Effective Market(s):** Eastern Canada, Western Canada. **Units of Measure:** Canadian dollars per tonne. **Type of Price:** contract. **Time Period Covered:** latest month.

AMMONIA: ANHYDROUS

Source: *Journal of Commerce and Commercial.* **Price Frequency:** weekly in Thursday issue. **Effective Market(s):** Louisiana. **Units of Measure:** Dollars per ton. **Type of Price:** spot. **Time Period Covered:** latest week.

AMMONIA: ANHYDROUS, FERTILIZER GRADE

Source: *Agricultural Prices.* **Price Frequency:** monthly. **Effective Market(s):** 9 domestic markets, United States. **Units of Measure:** Dollars per ton. **Type of Price:** paid by farmer. **Time Period Covered:** latest month.

Source: *Agricultural Prices Annual Summary.* **Price Frequency:** semiannually. **Effective Market(s):** 6 domestic markets, United States. **Units of Measure:** Dollars per ton. **Type of Price:** average paid by farmer. **Time Period Covered:** latest year, for US quarterly latest 6 years.

Source: *Chemical Marketing Reporter.* **Price Frequency:** weekly. **Effective Market(s):** Midwest, Gulf Coast. **Units of Measure:** Dollars per ton. **Type of Price:** spot. **Time Period Covered:** latest week.

AMMONIA: AQUA TANKS

Source: *Journal of Commerce and Commercial.* **Price Frequency:** weekly in Thursday issue. **Effective Market(s):** Southeast. **Units of Measure:** Dollars per ton. **Type of Price:** spot. **Time Period Covered:** latest week.

AMMONIA: AQUEOUS

Source: *Chemical Marketing Reporter.* **Price Frequency:** weekly. **Effective Market(s):** East of the Rockies. **Units of Measure:** Dollars per ton. **Type of Price:** spot. **Time Period Covered:** latest week.

AMMONIA: AQUEOUS, FERTILIZER GRADE

Source: *Agricultural Prices.* **Price Frequency:** monthly. **Effective Market(s):** 9 domestic markets, United States. **Units of Measure:** Dollars per ton. **Type of Price:** paid by farmer. **Time Period Covered:** latest month.

Source: *Agricultural Prices Annual Summary.* **Price Frequency:** semiannually. **Effective Market(s):** Northwest, Southwest, United States. **Units of Measure:** Dollars per ton. **Type of Price:** average paid by farmer. **Time Period Covered:** latest year, for US quarterly latest 6 years.

AMMONIAC SAL: GALVANIZING GRADE

Source: *Chemical Marketing Reporter.* **Price Frequency:** weekly. **Effective Market(s):** New York. **Units of Measure:** Dollars per 100 lbs. **Type of Price:** spot. **Time Period Covered:** latest week.

AMMONIACAL LIQUOR

see Ammonia: Aqueous.

AMMONIUM ACETATE: PURIFIED CRYSTAL

Source: *Journal of Commerce and Commercial.* **Price Frequency:** weekly in Friday issue. **Units of Measure:** Dollars per lb. **Type of Price:** spot. **Time Period Covered:** latest week.

AMMONIUM BIBORATE: GRANULAR

Source: *Chemical Marketing Reporter.* **Price Frequency:** weekly. **Effective Market(s):** New York. **Units of Measure:** Dollars per lb. **Type of Price:** spot. **Time Period Covered:** latest week.

AMMONIUM BIBORATE: POWDER

Source: *Chemical Marketing Reporter.* **Price Frequency:** weekly. **Effective Market(s):** New York. **Units of Measure:** Dollars per lb. **Type of Price:** spot. **Time Period Covered:** latest week.

AMMONIUM BICARBONATE

Source: *Chemical Marketing Reporter.* **Price Frequency:** weekly. **Effective Market(s):** New York. **Units of Measure:** Dollars per 100 lbs. **Type of Price:** spot. **Time Period Covered:** latest week.

AMMONIUM BICHROMATE: PHOTO-LITHO GRADE, GRANULAR

Source: *Chemical Marketing Reporter.* **Price Frequency:** weekly. **Effective Market(s):** New York. **Units of Measure:** Dollars per lb. **Type of Price:** spot. **Time Period Covered:** latest week.

AMMONIUM BIFLUORIDE

Source: *Chemical Marketing Reporter.* **Price Frequency:** weekly. **Effective Market(s):** New York. **Units of Measure:** Dollars per lb. **Type of Price:** spot. **Time Period Covered:** latest week.

AMMONIUM BROMIDE: 42% SOLUTION

Source: *Journal of Commerce and Commercial.* **Price Frequency:** weekly in Friday issue. **Units of Measure:** Dollars per lb. **Type of Price:** spot. **Time Period Covered:** latest week.

AMMONIUM BROMIDE: GRANULAR, NF, DOMESTIC

Source: *Chemical Marketing Reporter.* **Price Frequency:** weekly. **Effective Market(s):** New York. **Units of Measure:** Dollars per lb. **Type of Price:** spot. **Time Period Covered:** latest week.

AMMONIUM CHLORIDE

Source: *Journal of Commerce and Commercial.* **Price Frequency:** weekly in Thursday issue. **Units of Measure:** Dollars per 50 lbs. **Type of Price:** spot. **Time Period Covered:** latest week.

AMMONIUM CHLORIDE: GRANULAR, USP

Source: *Chemical Marketing Reporter.* **Price Frequency:** weekly. **Effective Market(s):** New York. **Units of Measure:** Dollars per lb. **Type of Price:** spot. **Time Period Covered:** latest week.

AMMONIUM CHLORIDE: WHITE, TECHNICAL GRADE, FINE, GRANULAR

Source: *Chemical Marketing Reporter.* **Price Frequency:** weekly. **Effective Market(s):** New York. **Units of Measure:** Dollars per 100 lb. **Type of Price:** spot. **Time Period Covered:** latest week.

AMMONIUM CITRATE: DIBASIC

Source: *Chemical Marketing Reporter.* **Price Frequency:** weekly. **Effective Market(s):** New York. **Units of Measure:** Dollars per lb. **Type of Price:** spot. **Time Period Covered:** latest week.

AMMONIUM DIMOLYBDATE

Source: *Chemical Marketing Reporter.* **Price Frequency:** weekly. **Effective Market(s):** New York. **Units of Measure:** Dollars per lb. **Type of Price:** spot. **Time Period Covered:** latest week.

AMMONIUM FLUOBORATE: TECHNICAL GRADE

Source: *Chemical Marketing Reporter.* **Price Frequency:** weekly. **Effective Market(s):** New York. **Units of Measure:** Dollars per lb. **Type of Price:** spot. **Time Period Covered:** latest week.

AMMONIUM HEPTAMOLYBDATE: CRYSTALLINE

Source: *Chemical Marketing Reporter.* **Price Frequency:** weekly. **Effective Market(s):** New York. **Units of Measure:** Dollars per lb. **Type of Price:** spot. **Time Period Covered:** latest week.

AMMONIUM LAURYL SULFATE

Source: *Chemical Marketing Reporter.* **Price Frequency:** weekly. **Effective Market(s):** New York. **Units of Measure:** Dollars per lb. **Type of Price:** spot. **Time Period Covered:** latest week.

AMMONIUM LIGNIN: SULFONATE, LIQUID

Source: *Chemical Marketing Reporter.* **Price Frequency:** weekly. **Effective Market(s):** West Coast. **Units of Measure:** Dollars per ton. **Type of Price:** spot. **Time Period Covered:** latest week.

AMMONIUM NITRATE

Source: *Commodity Year Book.* **Price Frequency:** annually. **Effective Market(s):** Corn Belt. **Units of Measure:** Dollars per short ton. **Time Period Covered:** latest 8 years.

Source: *Journal of Commerce and Commercial.* **Price Frequency:** weekly in Thursday issue. **Effective Market(s):** East. **Units of Measure:** Dollars per ton. **Type of Price:** spot. **Time Period Covered:** latest week.

AMMONIUM NITRATE: FERTILIZER GRADE

Source: *Agricultural Prices.* **Price Frequency:** monthly. **Effective Market(s):** 9 domestic markets, United States. **Units of Measure:** Dollars per ton. **Type of Price:** paid by farmer. **Time Period Covered:** latest month.

AMMONIUM NITRATE: FERTILIZER GRADE, DOMESTIC

Source: *Chemical Marketing Reporter.* **Price Frequency:** weekly. **Effective Market(s):** Southeast. **Units of Measure:** Dollars per ton. **Type of Price:** spot. **Time Period Covered:** latest week.

AMMONIUM NITRATE: FETILIZER GRADE, 33.5% NITROGEN

Source: *Agricultural Prices Annual Summary.* **Price Frequency:** semiannually. **Effective Market(s):** 8 domestic markets, United States. **Units of Measure:** Dollars per ton. **Type of Price:** average paid by farmer. **Time Period Covered:** latest year, for US quarterly latest 6 years.

AMMONIUM OXALATE: TECHNICAL GRADE, FINE, GRANULAR

Source: *Chemical Marketing Reporter.* **Price Frequency:** weekly. **Effective Market(s):** New York. **Units of Measure:** Dollars per lb. **Type of Price:** spot. **Time Period Covered:** latest week.

AMMONIUM PENTABORATE: GRANULAR

Source: *Chemical Marketing Reporter.* **Price Frequency:** weekly. **Effective Market(s):** New York . **Units of Measure:** Dollars per lb. **Type of Price:** spot. **Time Period Covered:** latest week.

AMMONIUM PENTABORATE: POWDER

Source: *Chemical Marketing Reporter.* **Price Frequency:** weekly. **Effective Market(s):** New York. **Units of Measure:** Dollars per lb. **Type of Price:** spot. **Time Period Covered:** latest week.

AMMONIUM PERSULFATE

Source: *Chemical Marketing Reporter.* **Price Frequency:** weekly. **Effective Market(s):** New York. **Units of Measure:** Dollars per lb. **Type of Price:** spot. **Time Period Covered:** latest week.

AMMONIUM PHOSPHATE

see Di- and Monoammonium Phosphates.

AMMONIUM SILICOFLUORIDE

Source: *Chemical Marketing Reporter.* **Price Frequency:** weekly. **Effective Market(s):** New York. **Units of Measure:** Dollars per lb. **Type of Price:** spot. **Time Period Covered:** latest week.

AMMONIUM SULFATE: LARGE GRANULAR

Source: *Chemical Marketing Reporter.* **Price Frequency:** weekly. **Effective Market(s):** New York. **Units of Measure:** Dollars per ton. **Type of Price:** spot. **Time Period Covered:** latest week.

Source: *Journal of Commerce and Commercial.* **Price Frequency:** weekly in Thursday issue. **Units of Measure:** Dollars per ton. **Type of Price:** spot. **Time Period Covered:** latest week.

AMMONIUM SULFATE: STANDARD, COMMERCIAL

Source: *Chemical Marketing Reporter.* **Price Frequency:** weekly. **Effective Market(s):** New York. **Units of Measure:** Dollars per ton. **Type of Price:** spot. **Time Period Covered:** latest week.

AMMONIUM SULFATE: TECHNICAL GRADE

Source: *Chemical Marketing Reporter.* **Price Frequency:** weekly. **Effective Market(s):** New York. **Units of Measure:** Dollars per ton. **Type of Price:** spot. **Time Period Covered:** latest week.

AMMONIUM SULFIDE: LIQUID

Source: *Chemical Marketing Reporter.* **Price Frequency:** weekly. **Effective Market(s):** New York. **Units of Measure:** Dollars per ton. **Type of Price:** spot. **Time Period Covered:** latest week.

AMMONIUM SULFOCYANIDE: TECHNICAL GRADE

see Ammonium Thiocyanate.

AMMONIUM THIOCYANATE: TECHNICAL GRADE, CRYSTALLINE

Source: *Chemical Marketing Reporter.* **Price Frequency:** weekly. **Effective Market(s):** New York. **Units of Measure:** Dollars per lb. **Type of Price:** spot. **Time Period Covered:** latest week.

AMMONIUM THIOCYANATE: TECHNICAL GRADE, SOLUTION

Source: *Chemical Marketing Reporter.* **Price Frequency:** weekly. **Effective Market(s):** New York. **Units of Measure:** Dollars per lb. **Type of Price:** spot. **Time Period Covered:** latest week.

AMMONIUM THIOSULFATE: PHOTOGRAPHIC

Source: *Chemical Marketing Reporter.* **Price Frequency:** weekly. **Effective Market(s):** New York. **Units of Measure:** Dollars per lb. **Type of Price:** spot. **Time Period Covered:** latest week.

AMMONIUM ZIRCONYL CARBONATE: SOLUTION

Source: *Chemical Marketing Reporter.* **Price Frequency:** weekly. **Effective Market(s):** New York. **Units of Measure:** Dollars per lb. **Type of Price:** spot. **Time Period Covered:** latest week.

AMYL ACETATE: PRIMARY MIXED ISOMERS

Source: *Chemical Marketing Reporter.* **Price Frequency:** weekly. **Effective Market(s):** New York . **Units of Measure:** Dollars per lb. **Type of Price:** spot. **Time Period Covered:** latest week.

AMYL ALCOHOL: PRIMARY MIXED ISOMERS

Source: *Chemcial Marketing Reporter.* **Price Frequency:** weekly. **Effective Market(s):** New York. **Units of Measure:** Dollars per lb. **Type of Price:** spot. **Time Period Covered:** latest week.

AMYL CINNAMIC ALDEHYDE

Source: *Chemical Marketing Reporter.* **Price Frequency:** weekly. **Effective Market(s):** New York. **Units of Measure:** Dollars per lb. **Type of Price:** spot. **Time Period Covered:** latest week.

Source: *Journal of Commerce and Commercial.* **Price Frequency:** weekly in Tuesday issue. **Units of Measure:** Dollars per lb. **Type of Price:** spot. **Time Period Covered:** latest week.

AMYL SALICYLATE

Source: *Journal of Commerce and Commercial.* **Price Frequency:** weekly in Tuesday issue. **Units of Measure:** Dollars per lb. **Type of Price:** spot. **Time Period Covered:** latest week.

P-TERT-AMYLPHENOL

Source: *Chemical Marketing Reporter.* **Price Frequency:** weekly. **Effective Market(s):** New York. **Units of Measure:** Dollars per lb. **Type of Price:** spot. **Time Period Covered:** latest week.

AMYRIS OIL

Source: *Chemical Marketing Reporter.* **Price Frequency:** weekly. **Effective Market(s):** New York. **Units of Measure:** Dollars per lb. **Type of Price:** spot. **Time Period Covered:** latest week.

Source: *Journal of Commerce and Commercial.* **Price Frequency:** weekly in Tuesday issue. **Units of Measure:** Dollars per lb. **Type of Price:** spot. **Time Period Covered:** latest week.

ANCHOVY MEAL

Source: *Feedstuffs.* **Price Frequency:** weekly. **Effective Market(s):** Los Angeles, San Francisco. **Units of Measure:** Dollars per bulk ton. **Time Period Covered:** latest week.

ANDALUSITE: TRANSVAAL

Source: *Industrial Minerals.* **Price Frequency:** monthly. **Effective Market(s):** main European port. **Units of Measure:** British pounds per metric tonne. **Type of Price:** producer & dealer. **Time Period Covered:** latest month.

ANETHOLE: TECHNICAL GRADE

Source: *Chemical Marketing Reporter.* **Price Frequency:** weekly. **Effective Market(s):** New York. **Units of Measure:** Dollars per kilo. **Type of Price:** spot. **Time Period Covered:** latest week.

ANETHOLE: USP

Source: *Chemical Marketing Reporter.* **Price Frequency:** weekly. **Effective Market(s):** New York. **Units of Measure:** Dollars per lb. **Type of Price:** spot. **Time Period Covered:** latest week.

Source: *Journal of Commerce and Commercial.* **Price Frequency:** weekly in Tuesday issue. **Units of Measure:** Dollars per lb. **Type of Price:** spot. **Time Period Covered:** latest week.

ANGELICA ROOT: WHOLE

Source: *Journal of Commerce and Commercial.* **Price Frequency:** weekly in Monday issue. **Units of Measure:** Dollars per lb. **Type of Price:** spot. **Time Period Covered:** latest week.

ANGELICA ROOT OIL

Source: *Chemical Marketing Reporter.* **Price Frequency:** weekly. **Effective Market(s):** New York. **Units of Measure:** Dollars per kilo. **Type of Price:** spot. **Time Period Covered:** latest week.

ANILINE

Source: *Chemical Marketing Reporter.* **Price Frequency:** weekly. **Effective Market(s):** New York. **Units of Measure:** Dollars per lb. **Type of Price:** spot. **Time Period Covered:** latest week.

Source: *Journal of Commerce and Commercial.* **Price Frequency:** weekly in Wednesday issue. **Units of Measure:** Dollars per lb. **Type of Price:** spot. **Time Period Covered:** latest week.

ANIMAL AND VEGETABLE FAT

Source: *Feedstuffs.* **Price Frequency:** weekly. **Effective Market(s):** 7 domestic markets. **Units of Measure:** Dollars per lb. **Time Period Covered:** latest week.

ANIMAL BYPRODUCTS

Source: *Feedstuffs.* **Price Frequency:** weekly. **Units of Measure:** Dollars per bulk ton. **Time Period Covered:** latest week.

ANIMAL FAT

Source: *Feed Situation and Outlook Report.* **Price Frequency:** monthly. **Effective Market(s):** Kansas City. **Units of Measure:** cents per lb. **Time Period Covered:** latest 8 months.

Source: *Feedstuffs.* **Price Frequency:** weekly. **Effective Market(s):** 10 domestic markets. **Units of Measure:** Dollars per bulk ton. **Time Period Covered:** latest week.

Source: *Grain and Feed Market News.* **Price Frequency:** weekly, seasonally. **Effective Market(s):** Kansas City, Minneapolis, San Francisco. **Units of Measure:** cents per lb. **Type of Price:** wholesale. **Time Period Covered:** latest week, week ago, year ago.

ANIMAL FEED: WHEY POWDER/MILK REPLACER

Source: *Dairy Foods.* **Price Frequency:** monthly. **Effective Market(s):** Central States, Eastern area. **Units of Measure:** Dollars per lb. **Time Period Covered:** latest month.

ANISE OIL

Source: *Chemical Marketing Reporter.* **Price Frequency:** weekly. **Effective Market(s):** New York. **Units of Measure:** Dollars per kilo. **Type of Price:** spot. **Time Period Covered:** latest week.

Source: *U. S. Essential Oil Trade.* **Price Frequency:** annually. **Effective Market(s):** United States. **Units of Measure:** Dollars per kilogram. **Type of Price:** import value. **Time Period Covered:** latest 3 years.

ANISE OIL: CHINESE

Source: *Prices of Selected Asia/Pacific Products.* **Price Frequency:** monthly. **Effective Market(s):** United Kingdom/North European ports. **Units of Measure:** British pounds per kilogram. **Type of Price:** wholesale high, wholesale low. **Time Period Covered:** latest month.

ANISE OIL: DRUM, CHINESE

Source: *Prices of Selected Asia/Pacific Products.* **Price Frequency:** monthly. **Effective Market(s):** Hong Kong. **Units of Measure:** Hong Kong dollars per kilogram. **Type of Price:** wholesale high, wholesale low. **Time Period Covered:** latest month.

ANISE OIL: STAR

Source: *Journal of Commerce and Commercial.* **Price Frequency:** weekly in Tuesday issue. **Units of Measure:** Dollars per lb. **Type of Price:** spot. **Time Period Covered:** latest week.

ANISE SEED: CHINESE

Source: *Chemical Marketing Reporter.* **Price Frequency:** weekly. **Effective Market(s):** New York. **Units of Measure:** Dollars per lb. **Type of Price:** spot. **Time Period Covered:** latest week.

Source: *Prices of Selected Asia/Pacific Products.* **Price Frequency:** monthly. **Effective Market(s):** New York. **Units of Measure:** Dollars per lb. **Type of Price:** spot high, spot low. **Time Period Covered:** latest month.

ANISE SEED: SPANISH

Source: *Chemical Marketing Reporter.* **Price Frequency:** weekly. **Effective Market(s):** New York. **Units of Measure:** Dollars per lb. **Type of Price:** spot. **Time Period Covered:** latest week.

Source: *U. S. Spice Trade.* **Price Frequency:** annually. **Effective Market(s):** New York. **Units of Measure:** cents per lb. **Type of Price:** spot. **Time Period Covered:** latest 3 years.

ANISE SEED: STAR, CHINESE

Source: *U. S. Spice Trade.* **Price Frequency:** annually. **Effective Market(s):** New York. **Units of Measure:** cents per lb. **Type of Price:** spot. **Time Period Covered:** latest 3 years.

ANISE SEED: TURKISH

Source: *Chemical Marketing Reporter.* **Price Frequency:** weekly. **Effective Market(s):** New York. **Units of Measure:** Dollars per lb. **Type of Price:** spot. **Time Period Covered:** latest week.

Source: *Prices of Selected Asia/Pacific Products.* **Price Frequency:** monthly. **Effective Market(s):** New York. **Units of Measure:** Dollars per lb. **Type of Price:** spot high, spot low. **Time Period Covered:** latest month.

Source: *U. S. Spice Trade.* **Price Frequency:** annually. **Effective Market(s):** New York. **Units of Measure:** cents per lb. **Type of Price:** spot. **Time Period Covered:** latest 3 years.

ANISIC ALDEHYDE

Source: *Chemical Marketing Reporter.* **Price Frequency:** weekly. **Effective Market(s):** New York. **Units of Measure:** Dollars per lb. **Type of Price:** spot. **Time Period Covered:** latest week.

O-ANISIDINE

Source: *Journal of Commerce and Commercial.* **Price Frequency:** weekly in Wednesday issue . **Units of Measure:** Dollars per lb. **Type of Price:** spot. **Time Period Covered:** latest week.

O-ANISIDINE: IMPORTED

Source: *Chemical Marketing Reporter.* **Price Frequency:** weekly. **Effective Market(s):** New York. **Units of Measure:** Dollars per lb. **Type of Price:** spot. **Time Period Covered:** latest week.

P-ANISIDINE: IMPORTED, CAST SOLID

Source: *Chemical Marketing Reporter.* **Price Frequency:** weekly. **Effective Market(s):** New York. **Units of Measure:** Dollars per lb. **Type of Price:** spot. **Time Period Covered:** latest week.

P-ANISIDINE: IMPORTED, FLAKES

Source: *Chemical Marketing Reporter.* **Price Frequency:** weekly. **Effective Market(s):** New York. **Units of Measure:** Dollars per lb. **Type of Price:** spot. **Time Period Covered:** latest week.

ANTARTIC QUEEN (FISH): SKINLESS, BONLESS, FROZEN, CHILEAN

Source: *Seafood Price-Current.* **Price Frequency:** semiweekly. **Effective Market(s):** Mid-Atlantic. **Units of Measure:** Dollars per lb. **Type of Price:** first receiver. **Time Period Covered:** latest day.

ANTHRANILIC ACID: PURIFIED

Source: *Chemical Marketing Reporter.* **Price Frequency:** weekly. **Effective Market(s):** New York. **Units of Measure:** Dollars per lb. **Type of Price:** spot. **Time Period Covered:** latest week.

ANTHRAQUINONE

Source: *Journal of Commerce and Commercial.* **Price Frequency:** weekly in Wednesday issue. **Units of Measure:** Dollars per lb. **Type of Price:** spot. **Time Period Covered:** latest week.

ANTHURIUMS: CUT, HAWAII

Source: *Floriculture Crops.* **Price Frequency:** annually. **Effective Market(s):** United States. **Units of Measure:** cents per unit. **Type of Price:** commercial wholesale. **Time Period Covered:** latest 2 years.

ANTIFREEZE: PERMANENT TYPE

Source: *Agricultural Prices.* **Price Frequency:** semiannually. **Effective Market(s):** United States. **Units of Measure:** Dollars per gallon. **Type of Price:** paid by farmer. **Time Period Covered:** latest year.

Source: *Agricultural Prices Annual Summary.* **Price Frequency:** semiannually. **Effective Market(s):** United States. **Units of Measure:** Dollars per gallon. **Type of Price:** average paid by farmer. **Time Period Covered:** latest 6 years.

ANTIMONY

Source: *American Metal Market.* **Price Frequency:** daily. **Units of Measure:** Dollars per lb. **Type of Price:** merchant. **Time Period Covered:** latest day.

Source: *Chemical Marketing Reporter.* **Price Frequency:** weekly. **Effective Market(s):** New York. **Units of Measure:** Dollars per lb. **Type of Price:** spot. **Time Period Covered:** latest week.

Source: *Commodity Year Book.* **Price Frequency:** annually. **Effective Market(s):** New York. **Units of Measure:** cents per lb. **Type of Price:** dealer price. **Time Period Covered:** latest 3 years.

Source: *E&MJ.* **Price Frequency:** monthly. **Units of Measure:** Dollars per lb. **Type of Price:** merchant. **Time Period Covered:** selected dates.

Source: *E&MJ.* **Price Frequency:** monthly. **Units of Measure:** Dollars per lb. **Type of Price:** merchant. **Time Period Covered:** latest month.

Source: *Northern Miner.* **Price Frequency:** daily. **Effective Market(s):** New York. **Units of Measure:** cents per lb. **Type of Price:** producer. **Time Period Covered:** selected day.

ANTIMONY: 99.5%

Source: *Investor's Daily.* **Price Frequency:** daily. **Effective Market(s):** New York. **Units of Measure:** Dollars per lb. **Type of Price:** spot. **Time Period Covered:** latest 2 days.

Source: *New York Times.* **Price Frequency:** daily. **Effective Market(s):** New York. **Units of Measure:** Dollars per lb. **Type of Price:** cash. **Time Period Covered:** latest 2 days.

ANTIMONY: 99.6% MINIMUN

Source: *Economic and Energy Indicators.* **Price Frequency:** monthly, quarterly, annually. **Units of Measure:** Dollars per metric ton. **Time Period Covered:** latest 3 months, quarters, and years.

ANTIMONY: 99.6% MINIMUM

Source: *Journal of Commerce and Commercial.* **Price Frequency:** daily. **Effective Market(s):** Europe. **Units of Measure:** Dollars per ton. **Type of Price:** spot. **Time Period Covered:** latest day.

ANTIMONY: DOMESTIC

Source: *Commodity Year Book.* **Price Frequency:** annually. **Effective Market(s):** United States. **Units of Measure:** cents per lb. **Time Period Covered:** latest 3 years.

Source: *Iron Age.* **Price Frequency:** monthly. **Effective Market(s):** Laredo (TX). **Units of Measure:** Dollars per lb. **Type of Price:** consumer. **Time Period Covered:** latest month.

ANTIMONY: FOREIGN

Source: *Commodity Year Book.* **Price Frequency:** annually. **Effective Market(s):** New York. **Units of Measure:** cents per lb. **Time Period Covered:** latest 3 years.

ANTIMONY: MAXIMUM

Source: *Modern Plastics.* **Price Frequency:** quarterly in February, May, August & November issues. **Units of Measure:** Dollars per lb. **Type of Price:** list. **Time Period Covered:** latest year.

ANTIMONY: MINIMUM

Source: *Modern Plastics.* **Price Frequency:** quarterly in February, May, August & November issues. **Units of Measure:** Dollars per lb. **Type of Price:** list. **Time Period Covered:** latest year.

ANTIMONY BATTERY ALLOY

Source: *American Metal Market.* **Price Frequency:** daily. **Effective Market(s):** Montreal/Toronto. **Units of Measure:** Canadian dollars per lb. **Time Period Covered:** latest day.

ANTIMONY FLUOBORATE: LIQUID CONCENTRATED

Source: *Chemical Marketing Reporter.* **Price Frequency:** weekly. **Effective Market(s):** New York. **Units of Measure:** Dollars per lb. **Type of Price:** spot. **Time Period Covered:** latest week.

ANTIMONY IN ALLOY: DOMESTIC

Source: *American Metal Market.* **Price Frequency:** daily. **Effective Market(s):** United States. **Units of Measure:** Dollars per lb. **Time Period Covered:** latest day.

ANTIMONY OXIDE

Source: *American Metal Market.* **Price Frequency:** daily. **Effective Market(s):** United States. **Units of Measure:** Dollars per lb. **Time Period Covered:** latest day.

Source: *E&MJ.* **Price Frequency:** monthly. **Units of Measure:** Dollars per lb. **Time Period Covered:** selected dates.

Source: *E&MJ.* **Price Frequency:** monthly. **Units of Measure:** Dollars per lb. **Time Period Covered:** latest month.

Source: *Industrial Minerals.* **Price Frequency:** monthly. **Effective Market(s):** Antwerp (Belguim). **Units of Measure:** British pounds per metric tonne. **Type of Price:** producer & deal. **Time Period Covered:** latest month.

Source: *Journal of Commerce and Commercial.* **Price Frequency:** weekly in Wednesday issue. **Units of Measure:** Dollars per lb. **Type of Price:** spot. **Time Period Covered:** latest week.

ANTIMONY OXIDE: HIGH TINT

Source: *Chemical Marketing Reporter.* **Price Frequency:** weekly. **Effective Market(s):** East of the Rockies. **Units of Measure:** Dollars per lb. **Type of Price:** spot. **Time Period Covered:** latest week.

ANTIMONY TRICHLORIDE: ANHYDROUS, SOLID

Source: *Chemical Marketing Reporter.* **Price Frequency:** weekly. **Effective Market(s):** New York. **Units of Measure:** Dollars per lb. **Type of Price:** spot. **Time Period Covered:** latest week.

ANTIMONY TRIOXIDE

Source: *Commodity Year Book.* **Price Frequency:** annually. **Effective Market(s):** United States. **Units of Measure:** cents per lb. **Time Period Covered:** latest 2 years.

APERITIFS

Source: *Colorado Beverage Analyst.* **Price Frequency:** monthly. **Effective Market(s):** Colorado. **Units of Measure:** Dollars per case. **Type of Price:** wholesale by brand. **Time Period Covered:** latest month.

Source: *Illinois Beverage Journal.* **Price Frequency:** monthly. **Effective Market(s):** Illinois. **Units of Measure:** Dollars per case. **Type of Price:** wholesale by brand. **Time Period Covered:** latest month.

APLITE: GLASS GRADE

Source: *Industrial Minerals.* **Price Frequency:** monthly. **Effective Market(s):** Montpelier (VA). **Units of Measure:** Dollars per metric tonne. **Type of Price:** producer & dealer. **Time Period Covered:** latest month.

APOMORPHINE HYDROCHLORIDE: NF

Source: *Chemical Marketing Reporter.* **Price Frequency:** weekly. **Effective Market(s):** New York. **Units of Measure:** Dollars per gram. **Type of Price:** spot. **Time Period Covered:** latest week.

APPLE PEARS: HOSUI, CALIFORNIAN

Source: *Lancaster Farming.* **Price Frequency:** weekly, seasonally. **Effective Market(s):** Pennsylvania. **Units of Measure:** Dollars per carton. **Type of Price:** market. **Time Period Covered:** latest week.

APPLE PEARS: SHINSEIKI, CALIFORNIAN

Source: *Lancaster Farming.* **Price Frequency:** weekly, seasonally. **Effective Market(s):** Pennsylvania. **Units of Measure:** Dollars per carton. **Type of Price:** market. **Time Period Covered:** latest week.

APPLES

Source: *Commodity Year Book.* **Price Frequency:** monthly, annually. **Effective Market(s):** United States. **Units of Measure:** cents per lb. **Type of Price:** price received by growers. **Time Period Covered:** latest 12 years.

Source: *Commodity Year Book.* **Price Frequency:** annually. **Units of Measure:** cents per lb. **Type of Price:** price received by growers. **Time Period Covered:** latest 12 years.

Source: *Commodity Year Book.* **Price Frequency:** annually. **Effective Market(s):** United States. **Units of Measure:** cents per lb. **Type of Price:** farm price. **Time Period Covered:** latest 12 years.

Source: *Fruit and Tree Nuts Situation and Outlook Yearbook.* **Price Frequency:** annually. **Effective Market(s):** United States. **Units of Measure:** cents per lb. **Type of Price:** grower. **Time Period Covered:** latest 20 years.

Source: *The Grower.* **Price Frequency:** monthly, seasonally. **Effective Market(s):** 6 domestic markets. **Units of Measure:** Dollars per bushel. **Time Period Covered:** latest year.

APPLES: CANNED

Source: *Marketing Appalachian District Apples.* **Price Frequency:** annually. **Effective Market(s):** 11 domestic markets. **Units of Measure:** Dollars per ton. **Time Period Covered:** latest 2 years.

APPLES: COMMERCIAL CROP

Source: *Marketing Appalachian District Apples.* **Price Frequency:** annually. **Effective Market(s):** 36 domestic markets. **Units of Measure:** Dollars per lb. **Time Period Covered:** latest 3 years.

APPLES: CORTLAND

Source: *Fresh Fruit and Vegetable Prices.* **Price Frequency:** monthly, seasonally. **Effective Market(s):** Hudson Valley (NY). **Units of Measure:** Dollars per unit. **Type of Price:** average price at shipping point. **Time Period Covered:** latest year.

APPLES: CORTLAND, HUDSON VALLEY (NY)

Source: *Fresh Fruit and Vegetable Prices.* **Price Frequency:** monthly, seasonally. **Effective Market(s):** New York City. **Units of Measure:** Dollars per carton. **Type of Price:** average wholesale price. **Time Period Covered:** latest year.

APPLES: DRIED

Source: *Marketing Appalachian District Apples.* **Price Frequency:** annually. **Effective Market(s):** California, all other states, United States. **Units of Measure:** Dollars per ton. **Time Period Covered:** latest 2 years.

APPLES: FOR VINEGAR, WINE, JAM, ETC

Source: *Marketing Appalachian District Apples.* **Price Frequency:** annually. **Effective Market(s):** 9 domestic markets. **Units of Measure:** Dollars per ton. **Time Period Covered:** latest 2 years.

APPLES: FRESH

Source: *Agricultural Outlook.* **Price Frequency:** monthly, annually. **Effective Market(s):** United States. **Units of Measure:** cents per lb. **Type of Price:** price received by farmer. **Time Period Covered:** monthly latest 6 months, annually latest 3 years.

Source: *Agricultural Prices.* **Price Frequency:** monthly. **Effective Market(s):** United States. **Units of Measure:** Dollars per lb. **Type of Price:** received by farmer. **Time Period Covered:** latest 2 months, year ago.

Source: *Agricultural Prices Annual Summary.* **Price Frequency:** annually. **Effective Market(s):** 27 domestic markets, United States. **Units of Measure:** Dollars per lb. **Type of Price:** average received by farmer. **Time Period Covered:** latest 2 years, for US latest 6 years.

Source: *Fruit and Tree Nuts Situation and Outlook Yearbook.* **Price Frequency:** annually. **Effective Market(s):** United States. **Units of Measure:** cents per lb. **Type of Price:** grower. **Time Period Covered:** latest 20 years.

Source: *Marketing Appalachian District Apples.* **Price Frequency:** annually. **Effective Market(s):** 30 domestic markets. **Units of Measure:** Dollars per lb. **Time Period Covered:** latest 3 years.

Source: *Washington Farmer-Stockman.* **Price Frequency:** monthly, seasonally. **Effective Market(s):** Washington. **Units of Measure:** Dollars per lb. **Type of Price:** received by farmer. **Time Period Covered:** latest month, month ago, year ago.

APPLES: FROZEN

Source: *Marketing Appalachian District Apples.* **Price Frequency:** annually. **Effective Market(s):** 8 domestic markets. **Units of Measure:** Dollars per ton. **Time Period Covered:** latest 2 years.

APPLES: GOLDEN DELICIOUS

Source: *California Farmer.* **Price Frequency:** semimonthly, seasonally. **Effective Market(s):** Sonoma County (CA). **Units of Measure:** Dollars per 38 lb. carton. **Time Period Covered:** latest week, year ago.

Source: *Fresh Fruit and Vegetable Prices.* **Price Frequency:** monthly, seasonally. **Effective Market(s):** 6 domestic markets. **Units of Measure:** Dollars per unit. **Type of Price:** average price at shipping point. **Time Period Covered:** latest year.

Source: *Marketing Appalachian District Apples.* **Price Frequency:** weekly, seasonally. **Effective Market(s):** Appalachian District. **Units of Measure:** Dollars per traypack carton, dollars per film bag. **Time Period Covered:** latest year.

Source: *Marketing Appalachian District Apples.* **Price Frequency:** weekly, seasonally. **Effective Market(s):** Atlanta, Baltimore, New York, Pittsburgh, Philadelphia. **Units of Measure:** Dollars per traypack carton, dollars per film bag. **Time Period Covered:** latest year.

Source: *Oregon Farmer-Stockman.* **Price Frequency:** monthly, seasonally. **Effective Market(s):** Yakima Valley (WA). **Units of Measure:** Dollars per traypack carton. **Time Period Covered:** latest month.

Source: *The Packer.* **Price Frequency:** weekly, seasonally. **Effective Market(s):** varies. **Units of Measure:** Dollars per traypack carton. **Type of Price:** price received by farmer. **Time Period Covered:** latest week.

APPLES: GOLDEN DELICIOUS, WASHINGTON

Source: *Lancaster Farming.* **Price Frequency:** weekly, seasonally. **Effective Market(s):** Pennsylvania. **Units of Measure:** Dollars per tray pack. **Type of Price:** market. **Time Period Covered:** latest week.

APPLES: GRANNY SMITH

Source: *California Farmer.* **Price Frequency:** semimonthly, seasonally. **Effective Market(s):** San Joaquin Valley. **Units of Measure:** Dollars per 40 lb. carton. **Time Period Covered:** latest week, month ago, year ago.

Source: *Fresh Fruit and Vegetable Prices.* **Price Frequency:** monthly, seasonally. **Effective Market(s):** Central/Southern San Joaquin Valley (CA), Yakima Valley/Wenatchee District (WA). **Units of Measure:** Dollars per unit. **Type of Price:** average price at shipping point. **Time Period Covered:** latest year.

Source: *Oregon Farmer-Stockman.* **Price Frequency:** monthly, seasonally. **Effective Market(s):** Yakima Valley (WA). **Units of Measure:** Dollars per traypack carton. **Time Period Covered:** latest month.

Source: *The Packer.* **Price Frequency:** weekly, seasonally. **Effective Market(s):** varies. **Units of Measure:** Dollars per traypack carton. **Type of Price:** price received by farmer. **Time Period Covered:** latest week.

APPLES: GRANNY SMITH, ARGENTINE

Source: *Lancaster Farming.* **Price Frequency:** weekly, seasonally. **Effective Market(s):** Pennsylvania. **Units of Measure:** Dollars per tray pack. **Type of Price:** market. **Time Period Covered:** latest week.

APPLES: GRANNY SMITH, AUSTRALIAN

Source: *Lancaster Farming.* **Price Frequency:** weekly, seasonally. **Effective Market(s):** Pennsylvania. **Units of Measure:** Dollars per tray pack. **Type of Price:** market. **Time Period Covered:** latest week.

APPLES: GRANNY SMITH, CHILEAN

Source: *Fresh Fruit and Vegetable Prices.* **Price Frequency:** monthly, seasonally. **Effective Market(s):** New York City/Philadelphia. **Units of Measure:** Dollars per unit. **Type of Price:** dock price. **Time Period Covered:** latest year.

APPLES: GRANNY SMITH, NEW ZEALAND

Source: *Lancaster Farming.* **Price Frequency:** weekly, seasonally. **Effective Market(s):** Pennsylvania. **Units of Measure:** Dollars per tray pack. **Type of Price:** market. **Time Period Covered:** latest week.

APPLES: GRAVENSTEIN

Source: *California Farmer.* **Price Frequency:** semi-monthly, seasonally. **Effective Market(s):** Sonoma County (CA). **Units of Measure:** Dollars per 38 lb. carton. **Time Period Covered:** latest week, month ago, year ago.

APPLES: JONATHAN

Source: *Fresh Fruit and Vegetable Prices.* **Price Frequency:** monthly, seasonally. **Effective Market(s):** Michigan. **Units of Measure:** Dollars per unit. **Type of Price:** average price at shipping point. **Time Period Covered:** latest year.

APPLES: JONATHAN, MICHIGAN

Source: *Fresh Fruit and Vegetable Prices.* **Price Frequency:** monthly, seasonally. **Effective Market(s):** Chicago. **Units of Measure:** Dollars per carton. **Type of Price:** average wholesale price. **Time Period Covered:** latest year.

APPLES: JUICE AND CIDER

Source: *Marketing Appalachian District Apples.* **Price Frequency:** annually. **Effective Market(s):** 17 domestic markets. **Units of Measure:** Dollars per ton. **Time Period Covered:** latest 2 years.

APPLES: MCINTOSH

Source: *Fresh Fruit and Vegetable Prices.* **Price Frequency:** monthly, seasonally. **Effective Market(s):** Michigan, Hudson Valley (NY), Lake Champlain/Mohawk Valley (NY), Western/Central New York. **Units of Measure:** Dollars per unit. **Type of Price:** average price at shipping point. **Time Period Covered:** latest year.

APPLES: MCINTOSH, HUDSON VALLEY (NY)

Source: *Fresh Fruit and Vegetable Prices.* **Price Frequency:** monthly, seasonally. **Effective Market(s):** New York City. **Units of Measure:** Dollars per carton. **Type of Price:** average wholesale price. **Time Period Covered:** latest year.

APPLES: MCINTOSH, LAKE CHAMPLAIN (NY)

Source: *Fresh Fruit and Vegetable Prices.* **Price Frequency:** monthly, seasonally. **Effective Market(s):** New York City. **Units of Measure:** Dollars per carton. **Type of Price:** average wholesale price. **Time Period Covered:** latest year.

APPLES: MCINTOSH, MICHIGAN

Source: *Fresh Fruit and Vegetable Prices.* **Price Frequency:** monthly, seasonally. **Effective Market(s):** Chicago. **Units of Measure:** Dollars per carton. **Type of Price:** average wholesale price. **Time Period Covered:** latest year.

APPLES: MCINTOSH, NEW ENGLAND

Source: *Fresh Fruit and Vegetable Price.* **Price Frequency:** monthly, seasonally. **Effective Market(s):** New York City. **Units of Measure:** Dollars per carton. **Type of Price:** average wholesale price. **Time Period Covered:** latest year.

APPLES: PIPPIN

Source: *California Farmer.* **Price Frequency:** semi-monthly, seasonally. **Effective Market(s):** Santa Cruz County (CA). **Units of Measure:** Dollars per 38 lb. carton. **Time Period Covered:** latest week, year ago.

APPLES: PROCESSED

Source: *Marketing Appalachian District Apples.* **Price Frequency:** annually. **Effective Market(s):** 29 domestic markets. **Units of Measure:** Dollars per ton. **Time Period Covered:** latest 3 years.

APPLES: PROCESSED, CANNED

Source: *Fruit and Tree Nuts Situation and Outlook Yearbook.* **Price Frequency:** annually. **Effective Market(s):** United States. **Units of Measure:** Dollars per ton. **Type of Price:** grower. **Time Period Covered:** latest 20 years.

APPLES: PROCESSED, DRIED

Source: *Fruit and Tree Nuts Situation and Outlook Yearbook.* **Price Frequency:** annually. **Effective Market(s):** United States. **Units of Measure:** Dollars per ton. **Type of Price:** grower. **Time Period Covered:** latest 20 years.

APPLES: PROCESSED, FROZEN

Source: *Fruit and Tree Nuts Situation and Outlook Yearbook.* **Price Frequency:** annually. **Effective Market(s):** United States. **Units of Measure:** Dollars per ton. **Type of Price:** grower. **Time Period Covered:** latest 20 years.

APPLES: PROCESSED, JUICE AND CIDER

Source: *Fruit and Tree Nuts Situation and Outlook Yearbook.* **Price Frequency:** annually. **Effective Market(s):** United States. **Units of Measure:** Dollars per ton. **Type of Price:** grower. **Time Period Covered:** latest 20 years.

APPLES: PROCESSED, OTHER TYPES

Source: *Fruit and Tree Nuts Situation and Outlook Yearbook.* **Price Frequency:** annually. **Effective Market(s):** United States. **Units of Measure:** Dollars per ton. **Type of Price:** grower. **Time Period Covered:** latest 20 years.

APPLES: RED DELICIOUS

Source: *Agricultural Outlook.* **Price Frequency:** monthly. **Effective Market(s):** Washington. **Units of Measure:** Dollars per carton tray pack. **Time Period Covered:** latest year.

Source: *California Farmer.* **Price Frequency:** semi-monthly, seasonally. **Effective Market(s):** Santa Cruz County (CA). **Units of Measure:** Dollars per 38 lb. carton. **Time Period Covered:** latest week, month ago, year ago.

Source: *Fresh Fruit and Vegetable Prices.* **Price Frequency:** monthly, seasonally. **Effective Market(s):** 8 domestic markets. **Units of Measure:** Dollars per unit. **Type of Price:** average price at shipping point. **Time Period Covered:** latest year.

Source: *Fruit and Tree Nuts Situation and Outlook Yearbook.* **Price Frequency:** annually. **Effective Market(s):** United States. **Units of Measure:** Dollars per lb. **Type of Price:** retail. **Time Period Covered:** latest 9 years.

Source: *Marketing Appalachian District Apples.* **Price Frequency:** weekly, seasonally. **Effective Market(s):** Appalachian District. **Units of Measure:** Dollars per traypack carton, dollars per film bag. **Time Period Covered:** latest year.

Source: *Marketing Appalachian District Apples.* **Price Frequency:** weekly, seasonally. **Effective Market(s):** Atlanta, Baltimore, New York, Pittsburgh, Philadelphia. **Units of Measure:** Dollars per film bag, dollars per traypack. **Type of Price:** wholesale. **Time Period Covered:** latest year.

Source: *The Packer.* **Price Frequency:** weekly, seasonally. **Effective Market(s):** varies. **Units of Measure:** Dollars per traypack carton. **Type of Price:** price received by farmer. **Time Period Covered:** latest week.

APPLES: RED DELICIOUS, CANADIAN

Source: *Lancaster Farming.* **Price Frequency:** weekly, seasonally. **Effective Market(s):** Pennsylvania. **Units of Measure:** Dollars per tray pack. **Type of Price:** market. **Time Period Covered:** latest week.

APPLES: RED DELICIOUS, HUDSON VALLEY (NY)

Source: *Fresh Fruit and Vegetable Prices.* **Price Frequency:** monthly, seasonally. **Effective Market(s):** New York City. **Units of Measure:** Dollars per carton. **Type of Price:** average wholesale price. **Time Period Covered:** latest year.

APPLES: RED DELICIOUS, MICHIGAN

Source: *Fresh Fruit and Vegetable Prices.* **Price Frequency:** monthly, seasonally. **Effective Market(s):** Chicago. **Units of Measure:** Dollars per carton. **Type of Price:** average wholesale price. **Time Period Covered:** latest year.

APPLES: RED DELICIOUS, WASHINGTON

Source: *Fresh Fruit and Vegetable Prices.* **Price Frequency:** monthly, seasonally. **Effective Market(s):** Chicago, New York City. **Units of Measure:** Dollars per carton. **Type of Price:** average wholesale price. **Time Period Covered:** latest year.

Source: *Lancaster Farming.* **Price Frequency:** weekly, seasonally. **Effective Market(s):** Pennsylvania. **Units of Measure:** Dollars per tray pack. **Type of Price:** market. **Time Period Covered:** latest week.

APPLES: RED DELICIOUS, WASHINGTON EXTRA FANCY

Source: *Oregon Farmer-Stockman.* **Price Frequency:** monthly, seasonally. **Effective Market(s):** Yakima Valley (WA). **Units of Measure:** Dollars per traypack carton. **Time Period Covered:** latest month.

APPLES: ROME

Source: *Marketing Appalachian District Apples.* **Price Frequency:** weekly, seasonally. **Effective Market(s):** Atlanta, Pittsburgh. **Units of Measure:** Dollars per film bag, dollars per traypack. **Type of Price:** wholesale. **Time Period Covered:** latest year.

APPLES: ROME, RED

Source: *Fresh Fruit and Vegetable Prices.* **Price Frequency:** monthly, seasonally. **Effective Market(s):** Appalachian District. **Units of Measure:** Dollars per unit. **Type of Price:** average price at shipping point. **Time Period Covered:** latest year.

Source: *Marketing Appalachian District Apples.* **Price Frequency:** weekly, seasonally. **Effective Market(s):** Appalachian District. **Units of Measure:** Dollars per traypack carton, dollars per film bag. **Time Period Covered:** latest year.

APPLES: ROYAL GALA

Source: *The Packer.* **Price Frequency:** weekly, seasonally. **Effective Market(s):** varies. **Units of Measure:** Dollars per traypack carton. **Type of Price:** price received by farmer. **Time Period Covered:** latest week.

APPLES: SLICED, FROZEN

Source: *HRI-Buyer's Guide.* **Price Frequency:** weekly. **Effective Market(s):** Northeastern area. **Units of Measure:** Dollars per case. **Type of Price:** price paid by dining places & institutions. **Time Period Covered:** latest week.

APPLES: STAYMAN

Source: *Marketing Appalachian District Apples.* **Price Frequency:** weekly, seasonally. **Effective Market(s):** Pittsburgh, Philadelphia. **Units of Measure:** Dollars per film bag, dollars per traypack. **Type of Price:** wholesale. **Time Period Covered:** latest year.

APPLES: STAYMAN, RED

Source: *Fresh Fruit and Vegetable Prices.* **Price Frequency:** monthly, seasonally. **Effective Market(s):** Appalachian District. **Units of Measure:** Dollars per unit. **Type of Price:** average price at shipping point. **Time Period Covered:** latest year.

Source: *Marketing Appalachian District Apples.* **Price Frequency:** weekly, seasonally. **Effective Market(s):** Appalachian District. **Units of Measure:** Dollars per traypack carton, dollars per film bag. **Time Period Covered:** latest year.

APPLES: YORK, RED

Source: *Marketing Appalachian District Apples.* **Price Frequency:** weekly, seasonally. **Effective Market(s):** Appalachian District. **Units of Measure:** Dollars per traypack carton, dollars per film bag. **Time Period Covered:** latest year.

APRICOT KERNEL OIL

Source: *Chemical Marketing Reporter.* **Price Frequency:** weekly. **Effective Market(s):** New York. **Units of Measure:** Dollars per lb. **Type of Price:** spot. **Time Period Covered:** latest week.

APRICOTS

Source: *Agricultural Prices Annual Summary.* **Price Frequency:** annually. **Effective Market(s):** California, Washington, Utah, United States. **Units of Measure:** Dollars per ton. **Type of Price:** average received by farmer. **Time Period Covered:** latest 3 years, for US latest 6 years.

Source: *Lancaster Farming.* **Price Frequency:** weekly, seasonally. **Effective Market(s):** Pennsylvania. **Units of Measure:** Dollars per unit. **Type of Price:** market. **Time Period Covered:** latest week.

APRICOTS: DERBY ROYAL AND ROYAL

Source: *Fresh Fruit and Vegetable Prices.* **Price Frequency:** monthly, seasonally. **Effective Market(s):** Winter/Brentwood/Western San Joaquin Valley (CA). **Units of Measure:** Dollars per lug. **Type of Price:** average price at shipping point. **Time Period Covered:** latest year.

APRICOTS: PERFECTION

Source: *Fresh Fruit and Vegetable Prices.* **Price Frequency:** monthly, seasonally. **Effective Market(s):** Yakima Valley/Wenatchee (WA). **Units of Measure:** Dollars per lug. **Type of Price:** average price at shipping point. **Time Period Covered:** latest year.

APRICOTS: PERFECTION AND RIVALS, 1-5/8″ MINIMUM

Source: *Oregon Farmer-Stockman.* **Price Frequency:** monthly, seasonally. **Effective Market(s):** Yakima Valley (WA). **Units of Measure:** Dollars per 24 lb. carton. **Time Period Covered:** latest month.

ARABIC GUM: CLEANED KORDOFAN TIERS, NF

Source: *Chemical Marketing Reporter.* **Price Frequency:** weekly. **Effective Market(s):** New York. **Units of Measure:** Dollars per lb. **Type of Price:** spot. **Time Period Covered:** latest week.

ARABIC GUM: POWDER

Source: *Chemical Marketing Reporter.* **Price Frequency:** weekly. **Effective Market(s):** New York. **Units of Measure:** Dollars per lb. **Type of Price:** spot. **Time Period Covered:** latest week.

Source: *Journal of Commerce and Commercial.* **Price Frequency:** weekly in Monday issue. **Units of Measure:** Dollars per lb. **Type of Price:** spot. **Time Period Covered:** latest week.

ARABIC GUM: SPRAY DRIED

Source: *Chemical Marketing Reporter.* **Price Frequency:** weekly. **Effective Market(s):** New York. **Units of Measure:** Dollars per lb. **Type of Price:** spot. **Time Period Covered:** latest week.

Source: *Journal of Commerce and Commercial.* **Price Frequency:** weekly in Monday issue. **Units of Measure:** Dollars per lb. **Type of Price:** spot. **Time Period Covered:** latest week.

ARAMID (TEXTILE)

Source: *Journal of Commerce and Commercial.* **Price Frequency:** weekly in Tuesday issue. **Units of Measure:** Dollars per lb. **Type of Price:** spot. **Time Period Covered:** latest week.

ARGENTINA AUSTRALS

Source: *Barron's.* **Price Frequency:** weekly. **Effective Market(s):** New York. **Units of Measure:** Argentine Australs per United States dollar. **Type of Price:** foreign exchange. **Time Period Covered:** latest 2 weeks.

Source: *International Wheat Council Market Report.* **Price Frequency:** weekly. **Effective Market(s):** London. **Units of Measure:** Argentine australs per United States dollar. **Type of Price:** foreign exchange. **Time Period Covered:** latest 5 weeks.

Source: *New York Times.* **Price Frequency:** daily. **Effective Market(s):** New York. **Units of Measure:** Argentine australs per United States dollar. **Type of Price:** financial foreign exchange rate. **Time Period Covered:** latest 2 days.

Source: *The Times.* **Price Frequency:** daily. **Effective Market(s):** London. **Units of Measure:** Argentine australs per British pound. **Type of Price:** foreign exchange. **Time Period Covered:** latest day.

ARMAGNAC

Source: *Colorado Beverage Analyst.* **Price Frequency:** monthly. **Effective Market(s):** Colorado. **Units of Measure:** Dollars per case. **Type of Price:** wholesale by brand. **Time Period Covered:** latest month.

Source: *Illinois Beverage Journal.* **Price Frequency:** monthly. **Effective Market(s):** Illinois. **Units of Measure:** Dollars per case. **Type of Price:** wholesale by brand. **Time Period Covered:** latest month.

Source: *Kentucky Beverage Journal.* **Price Frequency:** monthly. **Effective Market(s):** Kentucky. **Units of Measure:** Dollars per bottle, dollars per case. **Type of Price:** wholesale by brand. **Time Period Covered:** latest month.

ARROWROOT POWDER

Source: *Journal of Commerce and Commercial.* **Price Frequency:** weekly in Monday issue. **Units of Measure:** Dollars per lb. **Type of Price:** spot. **Time Period Covered:** latest week.

ARSENIC: BLACK LUMPY, 99%

Source: *Economic and Energy Indicators.* **Price Frequency:** monthly, quarterly, annually. **Units of Measure:** Dollars per metric ton. **Time Period Covered:** latest 3 months, quarters, and years.

ARSENIC: CRUDE

see Arsenious Trioxide.

ARSENIC: WHITE

See Arsenic Trioxide.

ARSENIC METAL: DOMESTIC

Source: *Commodity Year Book.* **Price Frequency:** annually. **Effective Market(s):** United States. **Units of Measure:** cents per lb. **Time Period Covered:** latest 11 years.

ARSENIC TRIOXIDE: DOMESTIC

Source: *Commodity Yearbook.* **Price Frequency:** annually. **Effective Market(s):** Tacoma (WA). **Units of Measure:** cents per lb. **Time Period Covered:** latest 11 years.

ARSENIC TRIOXIDE: MEXICAN

Source: *Commodity Year Book.* **Price Frequency:** annually. **Effective Market(s):** Laredo (TX). **Units of Measure:** cents per lb. **Time Period Covered:** latest 11 years.

ARSENIOUS TRIOXIDE

Source: *Chemical Marketing Reporter.* **Price Frequency:** weekly. **Effective Market(s):** New York. **Units of Measure:** Dollars per lb. **Type of Price:** spot. **Time Period Covered:** latest week.

ARTICHOKES

Source: *Fresh Fruit and Vegetable Prices.* **Price Frequency:** monthly, seasonally. **Effective Market(s):** Central California. **Units of Measure:** Dollars per carton. **Type of Price:** average price at shipping point. **Time Period Covered:** latest year.

Source: *Lancaster Farming.* **Price Frequency:** weekly, seasonally. **Effective Market(s):** Pennsylvania. **Units of Measure:** Dollars per carton. **Type of Price:** market. **Time Period Covered:** latest week.

Source: *The Packer.* **Price Frequency:** weekly, seasonally. **Effective Market(s):** varies. **Units of Measure:** Dollars per . **Type of Price:** price received by farmer. **Time Period Covered:** latest week.

ARTICHOKES: FRESH, CALIFORNIA

Source: *HRI-Buyer's Guide.* **Price Frequency:** weekly. **Effective Market(s):** Northeastern area. **Units of Measure:** Dollars per case. **Type of Price:** price paid by dining places & institutions. **Time Period Covered:** latest week.

ARTICHOKES: GLOBE TYPE, CALIFORNIA

Source: *Fresh Fruit and Vegetable Prices.* **Price Frequency:** monthly, seasonally. **Effective Market(s):** Chicago, New York City. **Units of Measure:** Dollars per carton. **Type of Price:** average wholesale price. **Time Period Covered:** latest year.

ASAFETIDA GUM

Source: *Journal of Commerce and Commercial.* **Price Frequency:** weekly in Monday issue. **Units of Measure:** Dollars per lb. **Type of Price:** spot. **Time Period Covered:** latest week.

ASBESTOS: CANADIAN CHRYSOTILE, GROUP NO. 3

Source: *Industrial Minerals.* **Price Frequency:** monthly. **Effective Market(s):** Quebec. **Units of Measure:** Canadian dollars per metric tonne. **Type of Price:** producer. **Time Period Covered:** latest month.

ASBESTOS: CANADIAN CHRYSOTILE, GROUP NO. 4

Source: *Industrial Minerals.* **Price Frequency:** monthly. **Effective Market(s):** Quebec. **Units of Measure:** Canadian dollars per metric tonne. **Type of Price:** producer. **Time Period Covered:** latest month.

ASBESTOS: CANADIAN CHRYSOTILE, GROUP NO. 5

Source: *Industrial Minerals.* **Price Frequency:** monthly. **Effective Market(s):** Quebec. **Units of Measure:** Canadian dollars per metric tonne. **Type of Price:** producer. **Time Period Covered:** latest month.

ASBESTOS: CANADIAN CHRYSOTILE, GROUP NO. 6

Source: *Industrial Minerals.* **Price Frequency:** monthly. **Effective Market(s):** Quebec. **Units of Measure:** Canadian dollars per metric tonne. **Type of Price:** producer. **Time Period Covered:** latest month.

ASBESTOS: CANADIAN CHRYSOTILE, GROUP NO. 7

Source: *Industrial Minerals.* **Price Frequency:** monthly. **Effective Market(s):** Quebec. **Units of Measure:** Canadian dollars per metric tonne. **Type of Price:** producer. **Time Period Covered:** latest month.

ASCORBIC ACID: USP

Source: *Chemical Marketing Reporter.* **Price Frequency:** weekly. **Effective Market(s):** New York. **Units of Measure:** Dollars per kilo. **Type of Price:** spot. **Time Period Covered:** latest week.

Source: *Journal of Commerce and Commerical.* **Price Frequency:** weekly in Friday issue. **Units of Measure:** Dollars per kilo. **Type of Price:** spot. **Time Period Covered:** latest week.

L-ASCORBIC ACID: USP

Source: *Journal of Commerce and Commercial.* **Price Frequency:** weekly in Friday issue. **Units of Measure:** Dollars per kilo. **Type of Price:** spot. **Time Period Covered:** latest week.

ASH

Source: *Volume and Value of Sawtimber Stumpage Sold from National Forests by Selected Species and Region.* **Price Frequency:** quarterly, annually. **Effective Market(s):** Eastern region. **Units of Measure:** Dollars per 1000 board feet. **Type of Price:** average. **Time Period Covered:** latest quarter, latest year.

ASH: WHITE

Source: *Timber Mart-South.* **Price Frequency:** quarterly. **Effective Market(s):** Arkansas. **Units of Measure:** Dollars per 1000 board feet . **Type of Price:** bid. **Time Period Covered:** latest quarter.

ASPARAGUS

Source: *Agricultural Prices Annual Summary.* **Price Frequency:** annually. **Effective Market(s):** 6 domestic markets. **Units of Measure:** Dollars per 100 lbs. **Type of Price:** average received by farmer. **Time Period Covered:** latest 6 years.

Source: *Agricultural Prices Annual Summary.* **Price Frequency:** monthly, seasonally. **Effective Market(s):** California, Michigan, Washington, United States. **Units of Measure:** Dollars per 100 lbs. **Type of Price:** average received by farmer. **Time Period Covered:** latest 3 years, for US latest 6 years.

Source: *California Farmer.* **Price Frequency:** semimonthly, seasonally. **Effective Market(s):** Stockton Delta (CA), Imperial/Coachella/Palo Verde Valley, Salinas (CA). **Units of Measure:** Dollars per 30 lb. crate. **Time Period Covered:** latest week, month ago, year ago.

Source: *Lancaster Farming.* **Price Frequency:** weekly, seasonally. **Effective Market(s):** Pennsylvania. **Units of Measure:** Dollars per carton/crate. **Type of Price:** market. **Time Period Covered:** latest week.

ASPARAGUS: CALIFORNIA

Source: *Fresh Fruit and Vegetable Prices.* **Price Frequency:** monthly, seasonally. **Effective Market(s):** Chicago, New York City. **Units of Measure:** Dollars per crate/carton. **Type of Price:** average wholesale price. **Time Period Covered:** latest year.

ASPARAGUS: CHILEAN

Source: *Fresh Fruit and Vegetable Prices.* **Price Frequency:** monthly, seasonally. **Effective Market(s):** New York City. **Units of Measure:** Dollars per carton. **Type of Price:** average price at shipping point. **Time Period Covered:** latest year.

ASPARAGUS: CUT AND TIPS, FROZEN

Source: *HRI-Buyer's Guide.* **Price Frequency:** weekly. **Effective Market(s):** Northeastern area. **Units of Measure:** Dollars per case. **Type of Price:** price paid by dining places & institutions. **Time Period Covered:** latest week.

ASPARAGUS: FIELD RUN

Source: *Fresh Fruit and Vegetable Prices.* **Price Frequency:** monthly, seasonally. **Effective Market(s):** Michigan, Swedesboro (NJ), Vineland (NJ), Yakima (WA). **Units of Measure:** Dollars per crate. **Type of Price:** average price at shipping point. **Time Period Covered:** latest year.

ASPARAGUS: FRESH

Source: *Agricultural Prices.* **Price Frequency:** monthly. **Effective Market(s):** United States. **Units of Measure:** Dollars per 100 lbs. **Type of Price:** received by farmer. **Time Period Covered:** latest 2 months, year ago.

ASPARAGUS: FRESH, LOOSE, LARGE, CALIFORNIA

Source: *HRI-Buyer's Guide.* **Price Frequency:** weekly. **Effective Market(s):** Northeastern area. **Units of Measure:** Dollars per case. **Type of Price:** price paid by dining places & institutions. **Time Period Covered:** latest week.

ASPARAGUS: GREEN, LOOSE

Source: *Fresh Fruit and Vegetable Prices.* **Price Frequency:** monthly, seasonally. **Effective Market(s):** Imperial/Coachella/Palo Verde Valley (CA)/Calexico (CA), Stockton/Delta District (CA), Salinas District (CA). **Units of Measure:** Dollars per crate. **Type of Price:** average price at shipping point. **Time Period Covered:** latest year.

ASPARAGUS: MEXICO

Source: *Fresh Fruit and Vegetable Prices.* **Price Frequency:** monthly, seasonally. **Effective Market(s):** Chicago, New York City. **Units of Measure:** Dollars per crate/carton. **Type of Price:** average wholesale price. **Time Period Covered:** latest year.

ASPARAGUS: WASHINGTON

Source: *Fresh Fruit and Vegetable Prices.* **Price Frequency:** monthly, seasonally. **Effective Market(s):** Chicago, New York City. **Units of Measure:** Dollars per crate/carton. **Type of Price:** average wholesale price. **Time Period Covered:** latest year.

ASPARAGUS SPEARS: MEDIUM, FROZEN

Source: *HRI-Buyer's Guide.* **Price Frequency:** weekly. **Effective Market(s):** Northeastern area. **Units of Measure:** Dollars per case. **Type of Price:** price paid by dining places & institutions. **Time Period Covered:** latest week.

ASPEN

Source: *Volume and Value of Sawtimber Stumpage Sold from National Forests by Selected Species and Region.* **Price Frequency:** quarterly, annually. **Effective Market(s):** Eastern region, Rocky Mountain region, Southwestern region, Intermountain region. **Units of Measure:** Dollars per 1000 board feet. **Type of Price:** average. **Time Period Covered:** latest quarter, latest year.

ASPHALT: CUTBACK

Source: *Oil Buyers' Guide.* **Price Frequency:** weekly. **Effective Market(s):** Venezuela. **Units of Measure:** Dollars per barrel. **Type of Price:** official. **Time Period Covered:** latest week.

ASPHALT: CUTBACK, MC800

Source: *ENR.* **Price Frequency:** monthly in first issue of month. **Effective Market(s):** 16 domestic markets, Montreal, Toronto. **Units of Measure:** Dollars per ton. **Type of Price:** spot. **Time Period Covered:** latest month.

ASPHALT: EMULSION, RAPID SET

Source: *ENR.* **Price Frequency:** monthly in first issue of month. **Effective Market(s):** 16 domestic markets, Montreal, Toronto. **Units of Measure:** Dollars per ton. **Type of Price:** spot. **Time Period Covered:** latest month.

ASPHALT: EMULSION, SLOW SET

Source: *ENR.* **Price Frequency:** monthly in first issue of month. **Effective Market(s):** 11 domestic markets, Montreal. **Units of Measure:** Dollars per ton. **Type of Price:** spot. **Time Period Covered:** latest month.

ASPHALT: INDUSTRIAL GRADE

Source: *Oil Buyers' Guide.* **Price Frequency:** weekly. **Effective Market(s):** Venezuela. **Units of Measure:** Dollars per barrel. **Type of Price:** official. **Time Period Covered:** latest week.

ASPHALT: PAVING, AC-20

Source: *ENR.* **Price Frequency:** monthly in first issue of month. **Effective Market(s):** 16 domestic markets, Montreal, Toronto. **Units of Measure:** Dollars per ton. **Type of Price:** spot. **Time Period Covered:** latest month.

ASPHALT: PENETRATION GRADE

Source: *Oil Buyers' Guide.* **Price Frequency:** weekly. **Effective Market(s):** Venezuela. **Units of Measure:** Dollars per barrel. **Type of Price:** official. **Time Period Covered:** latest week.

ASPHALT GILSONITE

see Gilsonite.

ASPHALT PETROLEUM CUTBACK

Source: *Chemical Marketing Reporter.* **Price Frequency:** weekly. **Effective Market(s):** East Coast. **Units of Measure:** Dollars per ton. **Type of Price:** spot. **Time Period Covered:** latest week.

ASPHALT PETROLEUM CUTBACK: EMULSION

Source: *Chemical Marketing Reporter.* **Price Frequency:** weekly. **Effective Market(s):** East Coast. **Units of Measure:** Dollars per ton. **Type of Price:** spot. **Time Period Covered:** latest week.

ASPHALT PETROLEUM CUTBACK: STEAM REFINED, 40-300 Penetration

Source: *Chemical Marketing Reporter.* **Price Frequency:** weekly. **Effective Market(s):** New York. **Units of Measure:** Dollars per ton. **Type of Price:** spot. **Time Period Covered:** latest week.

ASPHALT PETROLEUM CUTBACK: STEEP ROOFING GRADE

Source: *Chemical Marketing Reporter.* **Price Frequency:** weekly. **Effective Market(s):** New York. **Units of Measure:** Dollars per ton. **Type of Price:** spot. **Time Period Covered:** latest week.

ASPIRIN: 10% GRANULATION, WHITE

Source: *Chemical Marketing Reporter.* **Price Frequency:** weekly. **Effective Market(s):** New York. **Units of Measure:** Dollars per lb. **Type of Price:** spot. **Time Period Covered:** latest week.

ASPIRIN: 100% GRANULATION, WHITE

Source: *Chemical Marketing Reporter.* **Price Frequency:** weekly. **Effective Market(s):** New York. **Units of Measure:** Dollars per lb. **Type of Price:** spot. **Time Period Covered:** latest week.

ASPIRIN: CRYSTALLINE, POWDERED, USP

Source: *Chemical Marketing Reporter.* **Price Frequency:** weekly. **Effective Market(s):** New York. **Units of Measure:** Dollars per lb. **Type of Price:** spot. **Time Period Covered:** latest week.

ATH: EXTRA FINE, MAXIMUM

Source: *Modern Plastics.* **Price Frequency:** quarterly in February, May, August & November issues. **Units of Measure:** Dollars per lb. **Type of Price:** list. **Time Period Covered:** latest year.

ATH: EXTRA FINE, MINIMUM

Source: *Modern Plastics.* **Price Frequency:** quarterly in February, May, August & November issues. **Units of Measure:** Dollars per lb. **Type of Price:** list. **Time Period Covered:** latest year.

ATH: FINE, MAXIMUM

Source: *Modern Plastics.* **Price Frequency:** quarterly in February, May, August & November issues. **Units of Measure:** Dollars per lb. **Type of Price:** list. **Time Period Covered:** latest year.

ATH: FINE, MINIMUM

Source: *Modern Plastics.* **Price Frequency:** quarterly in February, May, August & November issues. **Units of Measure:** Dollars per lb. **Type of Price:** list. **Time Period Covered:** latest year.

ATH: MEDIUM, MAXIMUM

Source: *Modern Plastics.* **Price Frequency:** quarterly in February, May, August & November issues. **Units of Measure:** Dollars per lb. **Type of Price:** list. **Time Period Covered:** latest year.

ATH: MEDIUM, MINIMUM

Source: *Modern Plastics.* **Price Frequency:** quarterly in February, May, August & November issues. **Units of Measure:** Dollars per lb. **Type of Price:** list. **Time Period Covered:** latest year.

ATRAZINE: 80%, WETTABLE POWDER

Source: *Agricultural Prices Annual Summary.* **Price Frequency:** semiannually. **Effective Market(s):** United States. **Units of Measure:** Dollars per 5 lbs. **Type of Price:** average paid by farmer. **Time Period Covered:** latest 6 years.

ATROPINE SULFATE: USP

Source: *Chemical Marketing Reporter.* **Price Frequency:** weekly. **Effective Market(s):** New York. **Units of Measure:** Dollars per ounce. **Type of Price:** spot. **Time Period Covered:** latest week.

ATTAPULGITE

Source: *Industrial Minerals.* **Price Frequency:** monthly. **Effective Market(s):** United Kingdom. **Units of Measure:** British pounds per metric tonne. **Type of Price:** producer & dealer. **Time Period Covered:** latest month.

ATTAR OF ROSES

Source: *U. S. Essential Oil Trade.* **Price Frequency:** annually. **Effective Market(s):** United States. **Units of Measure:** Dollars per kilogram. **Type of Price:** import value. **Time Period Covered:** latest 3 years.

AUSTRALIA DOLLARS

Source: *American Metal Market.* **Price Frequency:** daily. **Effective Market(s):** New York. **Units of Measure:** Australian dollars per United States dollar. **Type of Price:** foreign exchange. **Time Period Covered:** latest day.

Source: *Asian Wall Street Journal.* **Price Frequency:** daily. **Effective Market(s):** United States. **Units of Measure:** Australian dollars per SDR. **Type of Price:** foreign exchange. **Time Period Covered:** latest 2 days.

Source: *Asian Wall Street Journal.* **Price Frequency:** daily. **Effective Market(s):** Asia. **Units of Measure:** United States dollars per Australian dollar. **Type of Price:** foreign exchange. **Time Period Covered:** latest 2 days.

Source: *Barron's.* **Price Frequency:** weekly. **Effective Market(s):** New York. **Units of Measure:** Australian dollars per United States dollar. **Type of Price:** foreign exchange. **Time Period Covered:** latest 2 weeks.

Source: *The Economist.* **Price Frequency:** weekly. **Effective Market(s):** London. **Units of Measure:** Australian dollars per United States dollar, per British pound, per SDR, per ECU. **Type of Price:** foreign exhange. **Time Period Covered:** latest week.

Source: *International Wheat Council Market Report.* **Price Frequency:** weekly. **Effective Market(s):** London. **Units of Measure:** Australian dollars per United States dollar. **Type of Price:** foreign exchange. **Time Period Covered:** latest 5 weeks.

Source: *New York Times.* **Price Frequency:** daily. **Effective Market(s):** New York. **Units of Measure:** Australian dollars per United States dollars. **Type of Price:** foreign exchange. **Time Period Covered:** latest 2 days.

Source: *The Times.* **Price Frequency:** daily. **Effective Market(s):** London. **Units of Measure:** Australian dollars per British pound. **Type of Price:** foreign exchange. **Time Period Covered:** latest day.

AUSTRALIA DOLLARS: FUTURES

Source: *Asian Wall Street Journal.* **Price Frequency:** daily. **Effective Market(s):** Chicago. **Units of Measure:** United States dollars per Australian dollar. **Type of Price:** foreign exchange futures. **Time Period Covered:** latest 2 days.

Source: *Barron's.* **Price Frequency:** weekly. **Effective Market(s):** New York. **Units of Measure:** United States dollars per Australian dollar. **Type of Price:** foreign exchange futures. **Time Period Covered:** latest week.

Source: *Los Angeles Times.* **Price Frequency:** daily. **Effective Market(s):** Chicago. **Units of Measure:** United States dollars per Australian dollar. **Type of Price:** foreign exchange futures. **Time Period Covered:** latest day.

Source: *Urner Barry's Price-Current.* **Price Frequency:** daily. **Units of Measure:** United States dollars per Australian dollars. **Type of Price:** foreign exchange futures. **Time Period Covered:** latest day.

AUSTRIA SCHILLINGS

Source: *Asian Wall Street Journal.* **Price Frequency:** daily. **Effective Market(s):** United States. **Units of Measure:** Austrian schillings per ECU, per SDR. **Type of Price:** foreign exchange. **Time Period Covered:** latest 2 days.

Source: *Barron's.* **Price Frequency:** weekly. **Effective Market(s):** New York. **Units of Measure:** Austrian Schillings per United States dollar. **Type of Price:** foreign exchange. **Time Period Covered:** latest 2 weeks.

Source: *New York Times.* **Price Frequency:** daily. **Effective Market(s):** New York. **Units of Measure:** Austrian schillings per United States dollars. **Type of Price:** foreign exchange. **Time Period Covered:** latest 2 days.

Source: *Timber Bulletin.* **Price Frequency:** monthly, annually. **Units of Measure:** Austrian schillings per United States dollar. **Type of Price:** foreign exchange. **Time Period Covered:** latest 2 years.

AUTOMOBILES: 4 DOOR SEDAN, COMPACT, NEW

Source: *Agricultural Prices Annual Summary.* **Price Frequency:** semiannually. **Effective Market(s):** United States. **Units of Measure:** Dollars per automobile. **Type of Price:** average paid by farmer. **Time Period Covered:** latest 6 years.

AUTOMOBILES: 4 DOOR SEDAN, INTERMEDIATE, NEW

Source: *Agricultural Prices Annual Summary.* **Price Frequency:** semiannually. **Effective Market(s):** United States. **Units of Measure:** Dollars per automobile. **Type of Price:** average paid by farmer. **Time Period Covered:** latest 6 years.

AUTOMOBILES: 4 DOOR SEDAN, STANDARD, NEW

Source: *Agricultural Prices Annual Summary.* **Price Frequency:** semiannually. **Effective Market(s):** United States. **Units of Measure:** Dollars per automobile. **Type of Price:** average paid by farmer. **Time Period Covered:** latest 6 years.

AVOCADO OIL

Source: *Chemical Marketing Reporter.* **Price Frequency:** weekly. **Effective Market(s):** New York. **Units of Measure:** Dollars per lb. **Type of Price:** spot. **Time Period Covered:** latest week.

AVOCADOS

Source: *Agricultural Prices Annual Summary.* **Price Frequency:** annually. **Effective Market(s):** California, Florida, United States. **Units of Measure:** Dollars per ton. **Type of Price:** average received by farmer. **Time Period Covered:** latest 3 years, for US latest 6 years.

Source: *Fruit and Tree Nuts Situation and Outlook Yearbook.* **Price Frequency:** annually. **Effective Market(s):** California, Florida, United States. **Units of Measure:** Dollars per ton. **Type of Price:** grower. **Time Period Covered:** latest 20 years.

Source: *The Grower.* **Price Frequency:** monthly, seasonally. **Units of Measure:** Dollars per carton. **Time Period Covered:** latest year.

Source: *New Zealand Farmer.* **Price Frequency:** weekly, seasonally. **Effective Market(s):** New Zealand. **Units of Measure:** New Zealand dollars per bushel. **Time Period Covered:** latest week.

AVOCADOS: BACON

Source: *California Farmer.* **Price Frequency:** semimonthly, seasonally. **Effective Market(s):** Southern California. **Units of Measure:** Dollars per 25 lb. carton/lug. **Time Period Covered:** latest week, month ago, year ago.

AVOCADOS: BERNECKER

Source: *The Packer.* **Price Frequency:** weekly, seasonally. **Effective Market(s):** varies. **Units of Measure:** Dollars per traypack carton. **Type of Price:** price received by farmer. **Time Period Covered:** latest week.

AVOCADOS: DUPUIS

Source: *The Packer.* **Price Frequency:** weekly, seasonally. **Effective Market(s):** varies. **Units of Measure:** Dollars per traypack carton. **Type of Price:** price received by farmer. **Time Period Covered:** latest week.

AVOCADOS: FRESH

Source: *HRI-Buyers Guide.* **Price Frequency:** weekly. **Effective Market(s):** Northeastern area. **Units of Measure:** Dollars per carton. **Type of Price:** price paid by dining places & institutions. **Time Period Covered:** latest week.

AVOCADOS: FUERTE

Source: *California Farmer.* **Price Frequency:** semimonthly, seasonally. **Effective Market(s):** Southern California. **Units of Measure:** Dollars per 25 lb. carton/lug. **Time Period Covered:** latest week, month ago, year ago.

Source: *New Zealand Farmer.* **Price Frequency:** weekly, seasonally. **Effective Market(s):** New Zealand. **Units of Measure:** New Zealand dollars per bushel/tray. **Time Period Covered:** latest week.

AVOCADOS: GREEN SKIN VARIETIES

Source: *Fresh Fruit and Vegetable Prices.* **Price Frequency:** monthly, seasonally. **Effective Market(s):** South Florida. **Units of Measure:** Dollars per carton. **Type of Price:** average price at shipping point. **Time Period Covered:** latest year.

AVOCADOS: GREEN SKIN VARIETIES, CALIFORNIA

Source: *Lancaster Farming.* **Price Frequency:** weekly, seasonally. **Effective Market(s):** Pennsylvania. **Units of Measure:** Dollars per carton. **Type of Price:** market. **Time Period Covered:** latest week.

AVOCADOS: GREEN SKIN VARIETIES, FLORIDA

Source: *Fresh Fruit and Vegetable Prices.* **Price Frequency:** monthly, seasonally. **Effective Market(s):** New York City. **Units of Measure:** Dollars per carton. **Type of Price:** average wholesale price. **Time Period Covered:** latest year.

AVOCADOS: HASS

Source: *California Farmer.* **Price Frequency:** semimonthly. **Effective Market(s):** Southern California. **Units of Measure:** Dollars per 25 lb. carton/lug. **Time Period Covered:** latest week, month ago, year ago.

Source: *Fresh Fruit and Vegetable Prices.* **Price Frequency:** monthly, seasonally. **Effective Market(s):** South/Central California. **Units of Measure:** Dollars per carton. **Type of Price:** average price at shipping point. **Time Period Covered:** latest year.

Source: *The Packer.* **Price Frequency:** weekly, seasonally. **Effective Market(s):** varies. **Units of Measure:** Dollars per traypack carton. **Type of Price:** price received by farmer. **Time Period Covered:** latest week.

AVOCADOS: HASS, CALIFORNIA

Source: *Fresh Fruit and Vegetable Prices.* **Price Frequency:** monthly, seasonally. **Effective Market(s):** Chicago, New York City. **Units of Measure:** Dollars per carton. **Type of Price:** average wholesale price. **Time Period Covered:** latest year.

Source: *Lancaster Farming.* **Price Frequency:** weekly, seasonally. **Effective Market(s):** Pennsylvania. **Units of Measure:** Dollars per carton. **Type of Price:** market. **Time Period Covered:** latest week.

AVOCADOS: NADIR

Source: *The Packer.* **Price Frequency:** weekly, seasonally. **Effective Market(s):** varies. **Units of Measure:** Dollars per traypack carton. **Type of Price:** price received by farmer. **Time Period Covered:** latest week.

AVOCADOS: REED

Source: *California Farmer.* **Price Frequency:** semimonthly, seasonally. **Effective Market(s):** Southern California. **Units of Measure:** Dollars per 25 lb. carton/lug. **Time Period Covered:** latest week, year ago.

AVOCADOS: SIMMONDS

Source: *The Packer.* **Price Frequency:** weekly, seasonally. **Effective Market(s):** varies. **Units of Measure:** Dollars per traypack carton. **Type of Price:** price received by farmer. **Time Period Covered:** latest week.

AVOCADOS: ZUTANO

Source: *California Farmer.* **Price Frequency:** semimonthly, seasonally. **Effective Market(s):** Southern California, San Joaquin Valley. **Units of Measure:** Dollars per 25 lb. carton/lug. **Time Period Covered:** latest week, month ago, year ago.

AZALEAS: POTTED, FINISHED, FLORIST, LESS THAN 5″

Source: *Floriculture Crops.* **Price Frequency:** annually. **Effective Market(s):** 19 domestic markets, United States. **Units of Measure:** Dollars per unit. **Type of Price:** commercial wholesale. **Time Period Covered:** latest 2 years.

AZALEAS: POTTED, FINISHED, FLORIST, MORE THAN 5″

Source: *Floriculture Crops.* **Price Frequency:** annually. **Effective Market(s):** 28 domestic markets, United States. **Units of Measure:** Dollars per unit. **Type of Price:** commercial wholesale. **Time Period Covered:** latest 2 years.

AZO: ORANGE

Source: *Chemical Marketing Reporter.* **Price Frequency:** weekly. **Effective Market(s):** New York. **Units of Measure:** Dollars per lb. **Type of Price:** spot. **Time Period Covered:** latest week.

AZO: YELLOW

Source: *Chemical Marketing Reporter.* **Price Frequency:** weekly. **Effective Market(s):** East of the Rockies. **Units of Measure:** Dollars per lb. **Type of Price:** spot. **Time Period Covered:** latest week.

AZO G: YELLOW PIGMENT

Source: *Chemical Marketing Reporter.* **Price Frequency:** weekly. **Effective Market(s):** New York. **Units of Measure:** Dollars per lb. **Type of Price:** spot. **Time Period Covered:** latest week.

AZODICARBONAMIDE

Source: *Modern Plastics.* **Price Frequency:** quarterly in February, May, August & November issues. **Units of Measure:** Dollars per lb. **Type of Price:** list. **Time Period Covered:** latest year.

BA-CD

see Barium-Cadmium.

BABBITT: SCRAP, MIXED

Source: *American Metal Market.* **Price Frequency:** daily. **Effective Market(s):** 6 domestic markets, Montreal, Toronto. **Units of Measure:** cents per lb., Canadian cents per lb. **Type of Price:** dealer buying. **Time Period Covered:** latest day.

BACITRACIN: NON-STERILE, USP

Source: *Chemical Marketing Reporter.* **Price Frequency:** weekly. **Effective Market(s):** New York. **Units of Measure:** Dollars per million units. **Type of Price:** spot. **Time Period Covered:** latest week.

BACON

Source: *Livestock and Poultry Update.* **Price Frequency:** monthly. **Units of Measure:** cents per lb. **Type of Price:** retail. **Time Period Covered:** latest 3 months, year ago.

Source: *Porkpro Newsletter.* **Price Frequency:** weekly. **Effective Market(s):** Chicago. **Units of Measure:** Dollars per lb. **Type of Price:** retail. **Time Period Covered:** latest day, week ago, year ago.

BACON: CANADIAN STYLE, CURED AND SMOKED, UNSLICED

Source: *Meat Price Report.* **Price Frequency:** weekly. **Units of Measure:** cents per lb. **Type of Price:** price paid to wholesaler. **Time Period Covered:** latest week.

BACON: CANADIAN STYLE, DOMESTIC

Source: *HRI-Buyer's Guide.* **Price Frequency:** weekly. **Effective Market(s):** Northeastern area. **Units of Measure:** Dollars per lb. **Type of Price:** price paid by dining places & institutions. **Time Period Covered:** latest week.

BACON: SLAB

Source: *HRI-Buyer's Guide.* **Price Frequency:** weekly. **Effective Market(s):** Northeastern area. **Units of Measure:** Dollars per lb. **Type of Price:** price paid by dining places & institutions. **Time Period Covered:** latest week.

BACON: SLICED

Source: *Livestock and Poultry Situation and Outlook Report.* **Price Frequency:** monthly. **Units of Measure:** Dollars per lb. **Type of Price:** retail. **Time Period Covered:** latest 3 years.

BACON: SLICED, CURED AND SMOKED, SKINLESS, IRREGULAR SLICES

Source: *Meat Price Report.* **Price Frequency:** weekly. **Units of Measure:** cents per lb. **Type of Price:** price paid to wholesaler. **Time Period Covered:** latest week.

BACON: SLICED, CURED AND SMOKED, SKINLESS, LAID FLAT, Separated

Source: *Meat Price Report.* **Price Frequency:** weekly. **Units of Measure:** cents per lb. **Type of Price:** price paid to wholesaler. **Time Period Covered:** latest week.

BACON: SLICED, CURED AND SMOKED, SKINLESS, SINGLE PACK

Source: *Meat Price Report.* **Price Frequency:** weekly. **Units of Measure:** cents per lb. **Type of Price:** price paid to wholesaler. **Time Period Covered:** latest week.

BACON: SLICED, LAYERS

Source: *HRI-Buyer's Guide.* **Price Frequency:** weekly. **Effective Market(s):** Northeastern area. **Units of Measure:** Dollars per lb. **Type of Price:** price paid by dining places & institutions. **Time Period Covered:** latest week.

BAGS

see also specific types of bags, e.g., Burlap Bag.

BAGS: COFFEE, SANTOS

Source: *Fibre Market News.* **Price Frequency:** weekly. **Units of Measure:** cents per bag. **Time Period Covered:** latest week.

BAGS: GRASS

Source: *Fibre Market News.* **Price Frequency:** weekly. **Units of Measure:** cents per bag. **Time Period Covered:** latest week.

BAGS: GROCERY, VARIETY

Source: *Pulp & Paper Week.* **Price Frequency:** monthly, irregularly. **Units of Measure:** index. **Type of Price:** price index. **Time Period Covered:** latest 3 months.

BAGS: GUNNIES, SHORT

Source: *Fibre Market News.* **Price Frequency:** weekly. **Units of Measure:** cents per bag. **Time Period Covered:** latest week.

BAGS: PEANUT, LARGE

Source: *Fibre Market News.* **Price Frequency:** weekly. **Units of Measure:** cents per bag. **Time Period Covered:** latest week.

BAGS: SPECIALTY, LINERS

Source: *Pulp & Paper Week.* **Price Frequency:** monthly, irregularly. **Units of Measure:** index. **Type of Price:** price index. **Time Period Covered:** latest 3 months.

BAGS AND SACKS: PAPER

Source: *Pulp & Paper Week.* **Price Frequency:** monthly, irregularly. **Units of Measure:** index. **Type of Price:** price index. **Time Period Covered:** latest 3 months.

BAHRAIN DINAR

Source: *The Times.* **Price Frequency:** daily. **Effective Market(s):** London. **Units of Measure:** Bahrain dinar per British pound. **Type of Price:** foreign exchange. **Time Period Covered:** latest day.

BALER: PICK-UP, AUTOMATIC TIE

Source: *Agricultural Prices.* **Price Frequency:** annually. **Effective Market(s):** United States. **Units of Measure:** Dollars each. **Type of Price:** paid by farmer. **Time Period Covered:** latest year.

Source: *Agricultural Prices Annual Summary.* **Price Frequency:** annually. **Effective Market(s):** United States. **Units of Measure:** Dollars each. **Type of Price:** average paid by farmer. **Time Period Covered:** latest 6 years.

BALER TWINE

Source: *Agricultural Prices.* **Price Frequency:** semiannually. **Effective Market(s):** United States. **Units of Measure:** Dollars per 40 lb. bale. **Type of Price:** paid by farmer. **Time Period Covered:** latest year.

Source: *Agricultural Prices Annual Summary.* **Price Frequency:** quarterly. **Effective Market(s):** United States. **Units of Measure:** Dollars per 40 lb. bale. **Type of Price:** average paid by farmer. **Time Period Covered:** latest 6 years.

BALL CLAY: AIR DRIED, SHREDDED

Source: *Industrial Minerals.* **Price Frequency:** monthly. **Effective Market(s):** main European port. **Units of Measure:** British pounds per metric tonne. **Type of Price:** producer & dealer. **Time Period Covered:** latest month.

BALL CLAY: AIR FLOATED, DOMESTIC

Source: *Chemical Marketing Reporter.* **Price Frequency:** weekly. **Effective Market(s):** Indiana. **Units of Measure:** Dollars per ton. **Type of Price:** spot. **Time Period Covered:** latest week.

BALL CLAY: AIR FLOATED, PULVERISED

Source: *Industrial Minerals.* **Price Frequency:** monthly. **Effective Market(s):** main European port. **Units of Measure:** British pounds per metric tonne. **Type of Price:** producer & dealer. **Time Period Covered:** latest month.

BALL CLAY: CRUSHED, MOISTURE REPELLENT, DOMESTIC

Source: *Chemical Marketing Reporter.* **Price Frequency:** weekly. **Effective Market(s):** Indiana. **Units of Measure:** Dollars per ton. **Type of Price:** spot. **Time Period Covered:** latest week.

BALL CLAY: REFINED, NOODLED

Source: *Industrial Minerals.* **Price Frequency:** monthly. **Effective Market(s):** main European port. **Units of Measure:** British pounds per metric tonne. **Type of Price:** producer & dealer. **Time Period Covered:** latest month.

BALSAM: COPAIBA

Source: *Journal of Commerce and Commercial.* **Price Frequency:** weekly in Monday issue. **Units of Measure:** Dollars per lb. **Type of Price:** spot. **Time Period Covered:** latest week.

BALSAM: PERU

Source: *Journal of Commerce and Commercial.* **Price Frequency:** weekly in Monday issue. **Units of Measure:** Dollars per lb. **Type of Price:** spot. **Time Period Covered:** latest week.

BALSAM: TOLU

Source: *Chemical Marketing Reporter.* **Price Frequency:** weekly. **Effective Market(s):** New York. **Units of Measure:** Dollars per lb. **Type of Price:** spot. **Time Period Covered:** latest week.

Source: *Journal of Commerce and Commercial.* **Price Frequency:** weekly in Monday issue. **Units of Measure:** Dollars per lb. **Type of Price:** spot. **Time Period Covered:** latest week.

BAMBOO SHOOTS: NO. 1 CAN, TAIWANESE

Source: *Prices of Selected Asia/ Pacific Products.* **Price Frequency:** monthly, seasonally. **Effective Market(s):** Tokyo. **Units of Measure:** Japanese yen per case. **Type of Price:** wholesale high, wholesale low. **Time Period Covered:** latest month.

BANANAS

Source: *Agricultural Prices Annual Summary.* **Price Frequency:** annually. **Effective Market(s):** California, Hawaii. **Units of Measure:** Dollars per lb. **Type of Price:** average received by farmer. **Time Period Covered:** latest 6 years.

Source: *Fruit and Tree Nuts Situation and Outlook Yearbook.* **Price Frequency:** annually. **Effective Market(s):** United States. **Units of Measure:** Dollars per lb. **Type of Price:** retail. **Time Period Covered:** latest 9 years.

Source: *Statistical Bulletin of the South Pacific: Retail Price Indexes.* **Price Frequency:** annually. **Effective Market(s):** 18 South Pacific markets. **Units of Measure:** Australian dollars per kilogram. **Type of Price:** retail. **Time Period Covered:** latest year.

Source: *Prices of Selected Asia/Pacific Products.* **Price Frequency:** monthly, seasonally. **Effective Market(s):** Sydney (Australia). **Units of Measure:** Australian dollars per case. **Type of Price:** wholesale high, wholesale low. **Time Period Covered:** latest month.

BANANAS: CAVENDISH/VALERY, CENTRAL AMERICA

Source: *Monthly Commodity Price Bulletin Supplement.* **Price Frequency:** monthly, quarterly, annually. **Effective Market(s):** Hamburg. **Units of Measure:** West German marks per tonne, dollars per tonne. **Time Period Covered:** latest 20 years.

BANANAS: CENTRAL AMERICA

Source: *FAO Quarterly Bulletin of Statistics.* **Price Frequency:** monthly, annually. **Effective Market(s):** Hamburg. **Units of Measure:** West German marks per 1000 kilograms, dollars per metric ton. **Type of Price:** importer to wholesaler. **Time Period Covered:** latest 3 years.

Source: *Monthly Commodity Price Bulletin.* **Price Frequency:** monthly, annually. **Effective Market(s):** North Sea ports. **Units of Measure:** Deutsche marks per metric ton, cents per lb. **Time Period Covered:** latest 5 years.

Source: *UNCTAD Commodity Yearbook.* **Price Frequency:** annually. **Effective Market(s):** North Sea ports. **Units of Measure:** Dollars per metric ton. **Type of Price:** free market. **Time Period Covered:** latest 12 years.

BANANAS: CENTRAL AMERICA/ECUADOR

Source: *Monthly Commodity Price Bulletin Supplement.* **Price Frequency:** monthly, quarterly, annually. **Effective Market(s):** Atlantic Gulf/Pacific ports. **Units of Measure:** cents per lb. **Time Period Covered:** latest 20 years.

Source: *Monthly Commodity Price Bulletin.* **Price Frequency:** monthly, annually. **Effective Market(s):** United States ports. **Units of Measure:** cents per lb. **Time Period Covered:** latest 5 months.

Source: *UNCTAD Commodity Yearbook.* **Price Frequency:** annually. **Effective Market(s):** United States ports. **Units of Measure:** Dollars per metric ton. **Type of Price:** free market. **Time Period Covered:** latest 12 years.

BANANAS: ECUADOR

Source: *Commodity Trade and Price Trends.* **Price Frequency:** annually. **Effective Market(s):** Hamburg. **Units of Measure:** cents per kilogram, 1980 constant cents per kilogram. **Time Period Covered:** latest 25 years.

BANANAS: FRESH

Source: *HRI-Buyers Guide.* **Price Frequency:** weekly. **Effective Market(s):** Northeastern area. **Units of Measure:** Dollars per carton. **Type of Price:** price paid by dining places & institutions. **Time Period Covered:** latest week.

BANANAS: FRESH, PHILIPPINES

Source: *Prices of Selected Asia/Pacific Products.* **Price Frequency:** monthly, seasonally. **Effective Market(s):** Tokyo. **Units of Measure:** Japanese yen per carton. **Type of Price:** trade high, trade low. **Time Period Covered:** latest month.

BANANAS: GREEN, FIRST CLASS, ANY ORIGIN

Source: *Commodity Trade and Price Trends.* **Price Frequency:** annually. **Units of Measure:** cents per kilogram, 1980 constant cents per kilogram. **Type of Price:** import. **Time Period Covered:** latest 37 years.

BANANAS: GREEN, FIRST CLASS, CENTRAL AMERICAN

Source: *FAO Quarterly Bulletin of Statistics.* **Price Frequency:** monthly, annually. **Effective Market(s):** New York. **Units of Measure:** Dollars per 40 lb. box, dollars per metric ton. **Time Period Covered:** latest 3 years.

BANANAS: IMPORTED

Source: *Fresh Fruit and Vegetable Prices.* **Price Frequency:** monthly, seasonally. **Effective Market(s):** Chicago, New York City. **Units of Measure:** Dollars per carton. **Type of Price:** average wholesale price. **Time Period Covered:** latest year.

Source: *Lancaster Farming.* **Price Frequency:** weekly, seasonally. **Effective Market(s):** Pennsylvania. **Units of Measure:** Dollars per carton. **Type of Price:** market. **Time Period Covered:** latest week.

BANANAS: LATIN AMERICA

Source: *International Financial Statistics.* **Price Frequency:** monthly, quarterly, annually. **Effective Market(s):** United States ports. **Units of Measure:** cents per lb., index. **Type of Price:** market price, price index. **Time Period Covered:** latest 5 months, latest 5 quarters, latest 5 years.

Source: *International Financial Statistics Yearbook.* **Price Frequency:** annually. **Effective Market(s):** United States ports. **Units of Measure:** cent per lb. **Type of Price:** wholesale. **Time Period Covered:** latest 30 years.

BANANAS: MARTINIQUE

Source: *FAO Quarterly Bulletin of Statistics.* **Price Frequency:** monthly, annually. **Effective Market(s):** French ports. **Units of Measure:** French francs per kilogram, dollars per metric ton. **Time Period Covered:** latest 3 years.

BANANAS: PETITE, IMPORTED

Source: *Lancaster Farming.* **Price Frequency:** weekly, seasonally. **Effective Market(s):** Pennsylvania. **Units of Measure:** Dollars per pack. **Type of Price:** market. **Time Period Covered:** latest week.

BANANAS: PHILIPPINES

Source: *FAO Quarterly Bulletin of Statistics.* **Price Frequency:** monthly, annually. **Effective Market(s):** Japan. **Units of Measure:** Japanese yen per kilogram, dollars per metric ton. **Time Period Covered:** latest 3 years.

Source: *Japan Economic Journal.* **Price Frequency:** weekly. **Effective Market(s):** Japan. **Units of Measure:** Japanese yen per 12 kilograms. **Type of Price:** wholesale. **Time Period Covered:** latest 2 weeks.

BANANAS: WINDWARD ISLANDS

Source: *Prices of Selected Asia/Pacific Products.* **Price Frequency:** monthly, seasonally. **Effective Market(s):** United Kingdom. **Units of Measure:** British pence per kilogram. **Type of Price:** wholesale high, wholesale low. **Time Period Covered:** latest month.

BARACUDA: FILLETS, FRESH, HAWAIIAN

Source: *Seafood Price-Current.* **Price Frequency:** semiweekly. **Effective Market(s):** Hawaii. **Units of Measure:** Dollars per lb. **Type of Price:** sale by first receiver. **Time Period Covered:** latest day.

BARACUDA: WHOLE, FRESH, HAWAIIAN

Source: *Seafood Price-Current.* **Price Frequency:** semiweekly. **Effective Market(s):** Hawaii. **Units of Measure:** Dollars per lb. **Type of Price:** sale by first receiver. **Time Period Covered:** latest day.

BARBERRY BARK: GROUND

Source: *Journal of Commerce and Commercial.* **Price Frequency:** weekly in Monday issue. **Units of Measure:** Dollars per lb. **Type of Price:** spot. **Time Period Covered:** latest week.

BARBITAL: NF

Source: *Chemical Marketing Reporter.* **Price Frequency:** weekly. **Effective Market(s):** New York. **Units of Measure:** Dollars per kilo. **Type of Price:** spot. **Time Period Covered:** latest week.

BARBITAL-SODIUM: NF

Source: *Chemical Marketing Reporter.* **Price Frequency:** weekly. **Effective Market(s):** New York. **Units of Measure:** Dollars per kilo. **Type of Price:** spot. **Time Period Covered:** latest week.

BARITE: DRY GROUND, SOUTHERN, OFF COLOR, COARSE

Source: *Chemical Marketing Reporter.* **Price Frequency:** weekly. **Effective Market(s):** New York. **Units of Measure:** Dollars per lb. **Type of Price:** spot. **Time Period Covered:** latest week.

BARITE: UNBLEACHED, EXTRA FINE, PIGMENT GRADE

Source: *Chemical Marketing Reporter.* **Price Frequency:** weekly. **Effective Market(s):** New York. **Units of Measure:** Dollars per ton. **Type of Price:** spot. **Time Period Covered:** latest week.

BARITE: WATER GROUND, WHITE

Source: *Chemical Marketing Reporter.* **Price Frequency:** weekly. **Effective Market(s):** New York. **Units of Measure:** Dollars per lb. **Type of Price:** spot. **Time Period Covered:** latest week.

BARIUM CARBONATE

Source: *Chemical Marketing Reporter.* **Price Frequency:** weekly. **Effective Market(s):** New York. **Units of Measure:** Dollars per ton. **Type of Price:** spot. **Time Period Covered:** latest week.

Source: *Journal of Commerce and Commercial.* **Price Frequency:** weekly in Thursday issue. **Units of Measure:** Dollars per lb. **Type of Price:** spot. **Time Period Covered:** latest week.

BARIUM CHLORATE

Source: *Chemical Marketing Reporter.* **Price Frequency:** weekly. **Effective Market(s):** New York. **Units of Measure:** Dollars per lb. **Type of Price:** spot. **Time Period Covered:** latest week.

BARIUM CHLORIDE: CRYSTAL

Source: *Journal of Commerce and Commercial.* **Price Frequency:** weekly in Thursday issue. **Units of Measure:** Dollars per lb. **Type of Price:** spot. **Time Period Covered:** latest week.

BARIUM CHLORIDE: PURIFIED, CRYSTALLINE

Source: *Chemical Marketing Reporter.* **Price Frequency:** weekly. **Effective Market(s):** New York. **Units of Measure:** Dollars per lb. **Type of Price:** spot. **Time Period Covered:** latest week.

BARIUM CHLORIDE: TECHNICAL GRADE, ANHYDROUS

Source: *Chemical Marketing Reporter.* **Price Frequency:** weekly. **Effective Market(s):** New York. **Units of Measure:** Dollars per 100 lbs. **Type of Price:** spot. **Time Period Covered:** latest week.

BARIUM CHLORIDE: TECHNICAL GRADE, CRYSTALLINE

Source: *Chemical Marketing Reporter.* **Price Frequency:** weekly. **Effective Market(s):** New York. **Units of Measure:** Dollars per 100 lbs. **Type of Price:** spot. **Time Period Covered:** latest week.

BARIUM MONOHYDRATE

Source: *Chemical Marketing Reporter.* **Price Frequency:** weekly. **Effective Market(s):** New York. **Units of Measure:** Dollars per 100 lbs. **Type of Price:** spot. **Time Period Covered:** latest week.

BARIUM NITRATE

Source: *Chemical Marketing Reporter.* **Price Frequency:** weekly. **Effective Market(s):** New York. **Units of Measure:** Dollars per 100 lbs. **Type of Price:** spot. **Time Period Covered:** latest week.

BARIUM OCTAHYDRATE: CRYSTALLINE

Source: *Chemical Marketing Reporter.* **Price Frequency:** weekly. **Effective Market(s):** New York. **Units of Measure:** Dollars per 100 lbs. **Type of Price:** spot. **Time Period Covered:** latest week.

BARIUM PEROXIDE

Source: *Chemical Marketing Reporter.* **Price Frequency:** weekly. **Effective Market(s):** New York. **Units of Measure:** Dollars per lb. **Type of Price:** spot. **Time Period Covered:** latest week.

BARIUM STEARATE

Source: *Chemical Marketing Reporter.* **Price Frequency:** weekly. **Effective Market(s):** New York. **Units of Measure:** Dollars per lb. **Type of Price:** spot. **Time Period Covered:** latest week.

BARIUM SULFATE: POWDERED, X-RAY DIAGNOSIS GRADE, USP

Source: *Chemical Marketing Reporter.* **Price Frequency:** weekly. **Effective Market(s):** New York. **Units of Measure:** Dollars per lb. **Type of Price:** spot. **Time Period Covered:** latest week.

BARIUM SULFATE: TECHNICAL GRADE

see Barite and Blanc Fixe.

BARIUM SULFIDE

Source: *Chemical Marketing Reporter.* **Price Frequency:** weekly. **Effective Market(s):** New York. **Units of Measure:** Dollars per ton. **Type of Price:** spot. **Time Period Covered:** latest week.

BARIUM-CADMIUM: MAXIMUM

Source: *Modern Plastics.* **Price Frequency:** quarterly in February, May, August & November issues. **Units of Measure:** Dollars per lb. **Type of Price:** list. **Time Period Covered:** latest year.

BARIUM-CADMIUM: MINIMUM

Source: *Modern Plastics.* **Price Frequency:** quarterly in February, May, August & November issues. **Units of Measure:** Dollars per lb. **Type of Price:** list. **Time Period Covered:** latest year.

BARLEY

Source: *Agra Europe.* **Price Frequency:** weekly. **Effective Market(s):** 9 European markets. **Units of Measure:** national currency per tonne. **Type of Price:** average. **Time Period Covered:** latest week.

Source: *Agricultural Outlook.* **Price Frequency:** annually. **Units of Measure:** Dollars per bushel. **Type of Price:** farm. **Time Period Covered:** latest 6 years.

Source: *Agricultural Prices.* **Price Frequency:** monthly, seasonally. **Effective Market(s):** 12 domestic markets, United States. **Units of Measure:** Dollars per bushel. **Type of Price:** received by farmer. **Time Period Covered:** latest 2 months.

Source: *Agricultural Prices Annual Summary.* **Price Frequency:** monthly, annually. **Effective Market(s):** 11 domestic markets, United States. **Units of Measure:** Dollars per bushel. **Type of Price:** average received by farmer. **Time Period Covered:** latest 2 years, for US latest 6 years.

Source: *Agricultural Prices Annual Summary.* **Price Frequency:** annually. **Effective Market(s):** 29 domestic markets, United States. **Units of Measure:** Dollars per bushel. **Type of Price:** average received by farmer. **Time Period Covered:** latest 2 years, for US latest 6 years.

Source: *Agricultural Trade Highlights.* **Price Frequency:** monthly. **Units of Measure:** Dollars per metric ton. **Time Period Covered:** latest week, month ago, year ago.

Source: *Commodity Year Book.* **Price Frequency:** annually. **Effective Market(s):** Duluth (MN). **Units of Measure:** Dollars per bushel. **Type of Price:** price received by farmers. **Time Period Covered:** latest 9 years.

Source: *Feed Situation and Outlook Report.* **Price Frequency:** annually. **Units of Measure:** Dollars per bushel. **Type of Price:** received by farmers. **Time Period Covered:** latest 5 years.

Source: *Feed Situation and Outlook Report.* **Price Frequency:** monthly, annually. **Effective Market(s):** United States. **Units of Measure:** Dollars per bushel. **Type of Price:** received by farmers. **Time Period Covered:** latest 6 years.

Source: *Feedstuffs.* **Price Frequency:** weekly. **Effective Market(s):** Atlanta, Kansas City, Los Angeles, San Francisco. **Units of Measure:** Dollars per 100 lbs. **Time Period Covered:** latest week.

Source: *Feedstuffs.* **Price Frequency:** weekly. **Effective Market(s):** Los Angeles. **Units of Measure:** Dollars per 100 lbs. **Time Period Covered:** latest week, week ago, 6 months ago, year ago.

Source: *Standard & Poor's Statistical Service Current Statistics.* **Price Frequency:** monthly, annually. **Effective Market(s):** Minneapolis. **Units of Measure:** cents per bushel. **Time Period Covered:** latest 4 years.

Source: *Washington Farmer-Stockman.* **Price Frequency:** monthly, seasonally. **Effective Market(s):** Washington. **Units of Measure:** Dollars per bushel. **Type of Price:** received by farmer. **Time Period Covered:** latest month, month ago, year ago.

BARLEY: ALL TYPES

Source: *Agricultural Prices.* **Price Frequency:** monthly. **Effective Market(s):** United States. **Units of Measure:** Dollars per bushel. **Type of Price:** received by farmer. **Time Period Covered:** latest 2 months, year ago.

BARLEY: EUROPEAN ECONOMIC COMMUNITY

Source: *International Wheat Council Market Report.* **Price Frequency:** weekly, seasonally. **Effective Market(s):** France, United Kingdom, Spain. **Units of Measure:** Dollars per metric ton. **Type of Price:** export. **Time Period Covered:** latest 5 weeks.

BARLEY: FEED

Source: *Agricultural Outlook.* **Price Frequency:** monthly, annually. **Effective Market(s):** Duluth (MN). **Units of Measure:** Dollars per bushel. **Type of Price:** wholesale. **Time Period Covered:** monthly latest 5 months, annually latest 4 years.

Source: *Agricultural Prices.* **Price Frequency:** monthly. **Effective Market(s):** United States. **Units of Measure:** Dollars per bushel. **Type of Price:** received by farmer. **Time Period Covered:** latest 2 months, year ago.

Source: *Agricultural Prices Annual Summary.* **Price Frequency:** annually. **Effective Market(s):** United States. **Units of Measure:** Dollars per bushel. **Type of Price:** average received by farmer. **Time Period Covered:** latest 6 years.

Source: *Agricultural Prices Annual Summary.* **Price Frequency:** monthly, annually. **Effective Market(s):** United States. **Units of Measure:** Dollars per bushel. **Type of Price:** average received by farmer. **Time Period Covered:** latest 6 years.

Source: *Farmers Weekly.* **Price Frequency:** weekly, seasonally. **Effective Market(s):** Great Britain. **Units of Measure:** British pounds per tonne. **Type of Price:** spot. **Time Period Covered:** latest week, week ago, year ago.

Source: *Farmers Weekly.* **Price Frequency:** weekly, seasonally. **Effective Market(s):** 13 British markets. **Units of Measure:** British pounds per tonne. **Type of Price:** spot. **Time Period Covered:** latest week.

Source: *Farmers Weekly.* **Price Frequency:** weekly, seasonally. **Effective Market(s):** 50 British markets. **Units of Measure:** British pounds per tonne. **Type of Price:** farm. **Time Period Covered:** latest week.

Source: *Feed Situation and Outlook Report.* **Price Frequency:** monthly, annually. **Effective Market(s):** United States. **Units of Measure:** Dollars per bushel. **Type of Price:** received by farmers. **Time Period Covered:** latest 6 years.

Source: *Minneapolis Grain Exchange Statistical Annual.* **Price Frequency:** daily, seasonally. **Effective Market(s):** Minneapolis, Duluth (MN). **Units of Measure:** cents per bushel. **Type of Price:** cash. **Time Period Covered:** latest year.

Source: *Montana Farmer-Stockman.* **Price Frequency:** monthly, seasonally. **Effective Market(s):** 9 Montana markets. **Type of Price:** elevator bid. **Time Period Covered:** latest month.

Source: *Scottish Farmer.* **Price Frequency:** monthly. **Effective Market(s):** 6 Scottish markets, Great Britain. **Units of Measure:** British pounds per tonne. **Type of Price:** average spot. **Time Period Covered:** latest month.

BARLEY: FEED, AUSTRALIAN

Source: *International Wheat Council Market Report.* **Price Frequency:** weekly, seasonally. **Effective Market(s):** East Coast. **Units of Measure:** Dollars per metric ton. **Type of Price:** export. **Time Period Covered:** latest 5 weeks.

BARLEY: FEED, GREAT BRITAIN

Source: *Financial Times.* **Price Frequency:** daily. **Effective Market(s):** London. **Units of Measure:** British pounds per tonne. **Type of Price:** spot. **Time Period Covered:** latest day.

BARLEY: FEED, NO. 2

Source: *Doane's Agricultural Report.* **Price Frequency:** weekly. **Effective Market(s):** Duluth (MN). **Units of Measure:** Dollars per bushel. **Time Period Covered:** latest week, week ago, year ago.

Source: *Journal of Commerce and Commercial.* **Price Frequency:** daily. **Effective Market(s):** Duluth (MN). **Units of Measure:** Dollars per bushel. **Type of Price:** spot supplier. **Time Period Covered:** latest day.

BARLEY: FEED, NO. 2, CANADIAN

Source: *International Wheat Council Market Report.* **Price Frequency:** weekly, seasonally. **Effective Market(s):** Rotterdam. **Units of Measure:** Dollars per metric ton. **Type of Price:** import. **Time Period Covered:** latest 5 weeks.

BARLEY: FEED, NO. 2 OR BETTER

Source: *Commodity Year Book.* **Price Frequency:** annually. **Effective Market(s):** Duluth (MN). **Units of Measure:** Dollars per bushel. **Time Period Covered:** latest 9 years.

Source: *Commodity Year Book.* **Price Frequency:** monthly, annually. **Effective Market(s):** Duluth (MN). **Units of Measure:** cents per bushel. **Time Period Covered:** latest 7 years.

Source: *Feed Situation and Outlook Report.* **Price Frequency:** monthly, annually. **Effective Market(s):** Duluth (MN). **Units of Measure:** Dollars per bushel. **Type of Price:** average, cash. **Time Period Covered:** latest 6 years.

BARLEY: FEED, NO. 3

Source: *International Wheat Council Market Report.* **Price Frequency:** weekly, seasonally. **Effective Market(s):** Duluth (MN). **Units of Measure:** Dollars per metric ton. **Type of Price:** export. **Time Period Covered:** latest 5 weeks.

BARLEY: FUTURES

Source: *Asian Wall Street Journal.* **Price Frequency:** daily. **Effective Market(s):** Winnepeg. **Units of Measure:** Canadian dollars per ton. **Type of Price:** futures. **Time Period Covered:** latest day.

Source: *Farmers Weekly.* **Price Frequency:** weekly. **Effective Market(s):** Baltic Exchange. **Units of Measure:** British pounds per tonne. **Type of Price:** futures. **Time Period Covered:** next 6 contract months.

Source: *Financial Times.* **Price Frequency:** daily. **Effective Market(s):** London. **Units of Measure:** British pounds per tonne. **Type of Price:** futures. **Time Period Covered:** latest week for next 2 contract months.

Source: *Investor's Daily.* **Price Frequency:** daily. **Effective Market(s):** Winnepeg. **Units of Measure:** Canadian dollars per ton. **Type of Price:** futures. **Time Period Covered:** latest day.

Source: *The Times.* **Price Frequency:** daily. **Effective Market(s):** London. **Units of Measure:** British pounds per tonne. **Type of Price:** futures. **Time Period Covered:** latest day for next 2 contract months.

Source: *Wall Street Journal.* **Price Frequency:** daily. **Effective Market(s):** Winnipeg. **Units of Measure:** Canadian dollars per ton. **Type of Price:** futures. **Time Period Covered:** next 6 contract months.

BARLEY: FUTURES, MAY

Source: *Commodity Year Book.* **Price Frequency:** monthly. **Effective Market(s):** Winnipeg. **Units of Measure:** Canadian dollars per tonne. **Type of Price:** futures. **Time Period Covered:** latest 6 years.

BARLEY: MALTING

Source: *Agricultural Outlook.* **Price Frequency:** monthly, annually. **Effective Market(s):** Minneapolis. **Units of Measure:** Dollars per bushel. **Type of Price:** wholesale. **Time Period Covered:** monthly latest 5 months, annually latest 4 years.

Source: *Agricultural Prices.* **Price Frequency:** monthly. **Effective Market(s):** United States. **Units of Measure:** Dollars per bushel. **Type of Price:** received by farmer. **Time Period Covered:** latest 2 months, year ago.

Source: *Agricultural Prices Annual Summary.* **Price Frequency:** annually. **Effective Market(s):** United States. **Units of Measure:** Dollars per bushel. **Type of Price:** average received by farmer. **Time Period Covered:** latest 6 years.

Source: *Agricultural Prices Annual Summary.* **Price Frequency:** monthly, annually. **Effective Market(s):** United States. **Units of Measure:** Dollars per bushel. **Type of Price:** average received by farmer. **Time Period Covered:** latest 6 years.

Source: *Farmers Weekly.* **Price Frequency:** weekly, seasonally. **Effective Market(s):** 13 British markets. **Units of Measure:** British pounds per tonne. **Type of Price:** spot. **Time Period Covered:** latest week.

Source: *Feed Situation and Outlook Report.* **Price Frequency:** monthly, annually. **Effective Market(s):** United States. **Units of Measure:** Dollars per bushel. **Type of Price:** received by farmers. **Time Period Covered:** latest 6 years.

Source: *Montana Farmer-Stockman.* **Price Frequency:** monthly, seasonally. **Effective Market(s):** 9 Montana markets. **Type of Price:** elevator bid. **Time Period Covered:** latest month.

Source: *Montana Farmer-Stockman.* **Price Frequency:** monthly, seasonally. **Effective Market(s):** Minneapolis. **Units of Measure:** Dollars per 100 lbs. **Type of Price:** cash. **Time Period Covered:** latest month.

BARLEY: MALTING, NO. 3, 65% PLUMP

Source: *Grain and Feed Market News.* **Price Frequency:** daily, seasonally. **Effective Market(s):** Minneapolis. **Units of Measure:** Dollars per bushel. **Type of Price:** cash bid. **Time Period Covered:** latest week, year ago.

BARLEY: MALTING, NO. 3 OR BETTER

Source: *Commodity Year Book.* **Price Frequency:** annually. **Effective Market(s):** Duluth (MN). **Units of Measure:** Dollars per bushel. **Time Period Covered:** latest 9 years.

Source: *Feed Situation and Outlook Report.* **Price Frequency:** annually. **Effective Market(s):** Minneapolis. **Units of Measure:** Dollars per bushel. **Type of Price:** average. **Time Period Covered:** latest 5 years.

BARLEY: MALTING, NO. 3 OR BETTER, 65% OR BETTER PLUMP

Source: *Feed Situation and Outlook Report.* **Price Frequency:** monthly, annually. **Effective Market(s):** Minneapolis. **Units of Measure:** Dollars per bushel. **Type of Price:** cash. **Time Period Covered:** latest 6 years.

BARLEY: MALTING, PREMIUM

Source: *Scottish Farmer.* **Price Frequency:** monthly. **Effective Market(s):** 7 Scottish markets, Great Britain. **Units of Measure:** British pounds per tonne. **Type of Price:** average spot. **Time Period Covered:** latest 2 months.

BARLEY: MINNEAPOLIS SPECIALTY

Source: *Minneapolis Grain Exchange Statistical Annual.* **Price Frequency:** daily, seasonally. **Effective Market(s):** Minneapolis. **Units of Measure:** cents per bushel. **Type of Price:** cash. **Time Period Covered:** latest year.

BARLEY: NO. 1, CANADIAN

Source: *FAO Quarterly Bulletin of Statistics.* **Price Frequency:** monthly, annually. **Effective Market(s):** Thunder Bay (Canada). **Units of Measure:** Canadian dollars per 1000 kilograms, dollars per metric ton. **Time Period Covered:** latest 3 years.

BARLEY: NO. 2

Source: *California Farmer.* **Price Frequency:** semimonthly. **Effective Market(s):** Los Angeles, Stockton (CA). **Units of Measure:** Dollars per 100 lbs. **Time Period Covered:** latest week, month ago, year ago.

Source: *Feed Situation and Outlook Report.* **Price Frequency:** annually. **Effective Market(s):** Portland (OR). **Units of Measure:** Dollars per bushel. **Type of Price:** average. **Time Period Covered:** latest 5 years.

Source: *Grain and Feed Market News.* **Price Frequency:** daily, seasonally. **Effective Market(s):** Duluth (MN), Portland, Stockton (CA), Los Angeles. **Units of Measure:** Dollars per bushel. **Type of Price:** cash bid. **Time Period Covered:** latest week, year ago.

Source: *Grain and Feed Market News.* **Price Frequency:** daily, seasonally. **Effective Market(s):** Duluth (MN), East Coast, Pacific Northwest. **Units of Measure:** Dollars per bushel. **Type of Price:** export bid. **Time Period Covered:** latest week, year ago.

Source: *Grain and Feed Market News.* **Price Frequency:** weekly, seasonally. **Effective Market(s):** Los Angeles, Portland, Duluth (MN). **Units of Measure:** Dollars per ton. **Type of Price:** wholesale. **Time Period Covered:** latest week, week ago, year ago.

Source: *Idaho Farmer-Stockman.* **Price Frequency:** monthly. **Effective Market(s):** Portland (OR). **Units of Measure:** Dollars per 100 lbs. **Time Period Covered:** latest month, month ago.

Source: *Idaho Farmer-Stockman.* **Price Frequency:** monthly. **Effective Market(s):** Denver, Omaha (NE), Portland (OR), Stockton (CA). **Units of Measure:** Dollars per 100 lbs. **Time Period Covered:** latest month.

Source: *Los Angeles Times.* **Price Frequency:** daily. **Effective Market(s):** Los Angeles. **Units of Measure:** Dollars per 100 lbs. **Type of Price:** cash. **Time Period Covered:** latest day.

Source: *Montana Farmer-Stockman.* **Price Frequency:** monthly, seasonally. **Effective Market(s):** Portland (OR). **Units of Measure:** Dollars per 100 lbs. **Type of Price:** cash. **Time Period Covered:** latest month, month ago.

Source: *Montana Farmer-Stockman.* **Price Frequency:** monthly. **Effective Market(s):** Portland (OR). **Type of Price:** cash. **Time Period Covered:** latest month, month ago.

Source: *Oregon Farmer-Stockman.* **Price Frequency:** monthly. **Effective Market(s):** Portland (OR). **Units of Measure:** Dollars per 100 lbs. **Type of Price:** cash. **Time Period Covered:** latest month, month ago.

Source: *Utah Farmer-Stockman.* **Price Frequency:** monthly. **Effective Market(s):** Ogden (UT), Denver, Omaha, Portland, Stockton (CA). **Units of Measure:** Dollars per 100 lbs. **Type of Price:** cash. **Time Period Covered:** latest month, month ago.

Source: *Washington Farmer-Stockman.* **Price Frequency:** monthly, seasonally. **Effective Market(s):** Portland (OR). **Units of Measure:** Dollars per 100 lbs. **Type of Price:** cash. **Time Period Covered:** latest month, month ago.

BARLEY: NO. 2, CANADIAN

Source: *International Wheat Council Market Report.* **Price Frequency:** weekly, seasonally. **Effective Market(s):** St. Lawrence (Canada). **Units of Measure:** Dollars per metric ton. **Type of Price:** export. **Time Period Covered:** latest 5 weeks.

BARLEY: NO. 2, UNITED STATES

Source: *International Wheat Council Market Report.* **Price Frequency:** weekly, seasonally. **Effective Market(s):** Rotterdam. **Units of Measure:** Dollars per metric ton. **Type of Price:** import. **Time Period Covered:** latest 5 weeks.

BARLEY: NO. 2, WESTERN, PORTLAND

Source: *Commodity Year Book.* **Price Frequency:** annually. **Effective Market(s):** Duluth (MN). **Units of Measure:** Dollars per bushel. **Time Period Covered:** latest 9 years.

BARLEY: NO. 3

Source: *Lancaster Farming.* **Price Frequency:** weekly. **Effective Market(s):** Pennsylvania. **Units of Measure:** Dollars per bushel. **Type of Price:** auction. **Time Period Covered:** latest week.

BARLEY: OVER 65% PLUMP, AZURE

Source: *Minneapolis Grain Exchange Statistical Annual.* **Price Frequency:** daily, seasonally. **Effective Market(s):** Minneapolis. **Units of Measure:** cents per bushel. **Type of Price:** cash. **Time Period Covered:** latest year.

BARLEY: OVER 65% PLUMP, MOREX

Source: *Minneapolis Grain Exchange Statistical Annual.* **Price Frequency:** daily, seasonally. **Effective Market(s):** Minneapolis. **Units of Measure:** cents per bushel. **Type of Price:** cash. **Time Period Covered:** latest year.

BARLEY: SCANDINAVIAN

Source: *International Wheat Council Market Report.* **Price Frequency:** weekly, seasonally. **Effective Market(s):** Rotterdam. **Units of Measure:** Dollars per metric ton. **Type of Price:** import. **Time Period Covered:** latest 5 weeks.

BARLEY: TOP QUALITY

Source: *Asian Wall Street Journal.* **Price Frequency:** daily. **Effective Market(s):** Minneapolis. **Units of Measure:** Dollars per bushel. **Type of Price:** cash. **Time Period Covered:** latest 2 days, year ago.

Source: *Farm and Dairy.* **Price Frequency:** weekly, seasonally. **Effective Market(s):** Minneapolis. **Units of Measure:** Dollars per bushel. **Time Period Covered:** latest week, year ago.

Source: *Wall Street Journal.* **Price Frequency:** daily. **Effective Market(s):** Minneapolis. **Units of Measure:** dollars per bushel. **Time Period Covered:** latest day, day ago, year ago.

BARLEY FEED

Source: *Feedstuffs.* **Price Frequency:** weekly. **Effective Market(s):** Buffalo, Kansas City. **Units of Measure:** Dollars per bulk ton. **Time Period Covered:** latest week.

BARLEY FOR SEED

see Seed Barley.

BARLEY STRAW

Source: *Scottish Farmer.* **Price Frequency:** weekly. **Effective Market(s):** Scotland. **Units of Measure:** British pounds per tonne. **Type of Price:** average farmer's buying-in. **Time Period Covered:** latest week.

BARLEY STRAW: 2ND CLASS

Source: *Farmers Weekly.* **Price Frequency:** weekly, seasonally. **Effective Market(s):** 10 British markets. **Units of Measure:** British pounds per tonne. **Type of Price:** merchant's buying. **Time Period Covered:** latest week.

BARLEY STRAW: 2ND QUALITY

Source: *Scottish Farmer.* **Price Frequency:** weekly. **Effective Market(s):** Scotland. **Units of Measure:** British pounds per tonne. **Type of Price:** average farmer's buying-in. **Time Period Covered:** latest week.

BARLEY STRAW: BEST QUALITY

Source: *Scottish Farmer.* **Price Frequency:** weekly. **Effective Market(s):** Scotland. **Units of Measure:** British pounds per tonne. **Type of Price:** average farmer's buying-in. **Time Period Covered:** latest week.

BARLEY STRAW: FEED

Source: *Farmers Weekly.* **Price Frequency:** weekly, seasonally. **Effective Market(s):** 10 British markets. **Units of Measure:** British pounds per tonne. **Type of Price:** merchant's buying. **Time Period Covered:** latest week.

BARROWS AND GILTS

Source: *Agricultural Prices.* **Price Frequency:** monthly. **Effective Market(s):** United States. **Units of Measure:** Dollars per 100 lbs. **Type of Price:** received by farmer. **Time Period Covered:** latest 2 months, year ago.

Source: *Agricultural Prices.* **Price Frequency:** monthly. **Effective Market(s):** 20 domestic markets, United States. **Units of Measure:** Dollars per 100 lbs. **Type of Price:** received by farmer. **Time Period Covered:** latest 2 months.

Source: *Doane's Agricultural Report.* **Price Frequency:** weekly. **Effective Market(s):** Omaha (NE). **Units of Measure:** Dollars per 100 lbs. **Time Period Covered:** latest week, week ago, year ago.

Source: *Livestock and Poultry Situation and Outlook Report.* **Price Frequency:** quarterly, annually. **Effective Market(s):** 7-market average. **Units of Measure:** Dollars per 100 lbs. **Time Period Covered:** latest 2 years.

Source: *Livestock and Poultry Update.* **Price Frequency:** monthly. **Effective Market(s):** 7-market average. **Units of Measure:** Dollars per 100 lbs. **Time Period Covered:** latest 3 months, year ago.

BARROWS AND GILTS: SLAUGHTER

Source: *Livestock and Poultry Situation and Outlook Report.* **Price Frequency:** monthly. **Effective Market(s):** Soiux City (IA), 7-market average. **Units of Measure:** Dollars per 100 lbs. **Time Period Covered:** latest year.

BARROWS AND GILTS: SLAUGHTER, NO. 1 AND 2

Source: *Livestock and Poultry Situation and Outlook Report.* **Price Frequency:** monthly. **Effective Market(s):** Omaha (NE). **Units of Measure:** Dollars per 100 lbs. **Time Period Covered:** latest year.

BARYTES: GROUND, API

Source: *Industrial Minerals.* **Price Frequency:** monthly. **Effective Market(s):** Gulf Coast. **Units of Measure:** Dollars per metric tonne. **Type of Price:** wholesale, retail. **Time Period Covered:** latest month.

BARYTES: GROUND, OCMA

Source: *Industrial Minerals.* **Price Frequency:** monthly. **Effective Market(s):** Aberdeen (Scotland), Greater Yarmouth (England). **Units of Measure:** British pounds per metric tonne. **Type of Price:** producer & dealer. **Time Period Covered:** latest month.

BARYTES: GROUND, WHITE, PAINT GRADE

Source: *Industrial Minerals.* **Price Frequency:** monthly. **Effective Market(s):** United Kingdom. **Units of Measure:** British pounds per metric tonne. **Type of Price:** producer & dealer. **Time Period Covered:** latest month.

BARYTES: MICRONISED

Source: *Industrial Minerals.* **Price Frequency:** monthly. **Effective Market(s):** United Kingdom. **Units of Measure:** British pounds per metric tonne. **Type of Price:** produceer & dealer. **Time Period Covered:** latest month.

BARYTES: UNGROUND, OCMA

Source: *Industrial Minerals.* **Price Frequency:** monthly. **Effective Market(s):** Morocco. **Units of Measure:** Dollars per metric tonne. **Type of Price:** producer & dealer. **Time Period Covered:** latest month.

BARYTES: WATER GROUND

Source: *Journal of Commerce and Commercial.* **Price Frequency:** weekly in Wednesday issue. **Units of Measure:** Dollars per ton. **Type of Price:** spot. **Time Period Covered:** latest week.

BASIL: DOMESTIC

Source: *U. S. Spice Trade.* **Price Frequency:** annually. **Effective Market(s):** New York. **Units of Measure:** cents per lb. **Type of Price:** spot. **Time Period Covered:** latest 3 years.

BASIL: EGYPTIAN

Source: *Chemical Marketing Reporter.* **Price Frequency:** weekly. **Effective Market(s):** New York. **Units of Measure:** Dollars per lb. **Type of Price:** spot. **Time Period Covered:** latest week.

Source: *U. S. Spice Trade.* **Price Frequency:** annually. **Effective Market(s):** New York. **Units of Measure:** cents per lb. **Type of Price:** spot. **Time Period Covered:** latest 3 years.

BASIL: FRENCH

Source: *Chemical Marketing Reporter.* **Price Frequency:** weekly. **Effective Market(s):** New York. **Units of Measure:** Dollars per lb. **Type of Price:** spot. **Time Period Covered:** latest week.

Source: *U. S. Spice Trade.* **Price Frequency:** annually. **Effective Market(s):** New York. **Units of Measure:** cents per lb. **Type of Price:** spot. **Time Period Covered:** latest 3 years.

BASIL OIL: COMORES

Source: *Chemical Marketing Reporter.* **Price Frequency:** weekly. **Effective Market(s):** New York. **Units of Measure:** Dollars per kilo. **Type of Price:** spot. **Time Period Covered:** latest week.

BASIL OIL: EGYPTIAN

Source: *Chemical Marketing Reporter.* **Price Frequency:** weekly. **Effective Market(s):** New York. **Units of Measure:** Dollars per lb. **Type of Price:** spot. **Time Period Covered:** latest week.

BASIL OIL: SWEET

Source: *Journal of Commerce and Commercial.* **Price Frequency:** weekly in Tuesday issue. **Units of Measure:** Dollars per lb. **Type of Price:** spot. **Time Period Covered:** latest week.

BASS: SEA, FILLETS, FRESH

Source: *Seafood Price-Current.* **Price Frequency:** semiweekly. **Effective Market(s):** West Coast. **Units of Measure:** Dollars per lb. **Type of Price:** sale by first receiver. **Time Period Covered:** latest day.

BASS: SEA, WHITE, DRESSED, WHOLE, FRESH

Source: *Seafood Price-Current.* **Price Frequency:** semiweekly. **Effective Market(s):** West Coast. **Units of Measure:** Dollars per lb. **Type of Price:** sale by first receiver. **Time Period Covered:** latest day.

BASS: SEA, WHOLE, FRESH

Source: *Seafood Price-Current.* **Price Frequency:** semiweekly. **Effective Market(s):** Mid-Atlantic, Boston, New Bedford (MA), Portland (ME). **Units of Measure:** Dollars per lb. **Type of Price:** sale by first receiver, auction price. **Time Period Covered:** latest day.

BASS: SEA, WHOLE, FRESH, MEXICAN

Source: *Seafood Price-Current.* **Price Frequency:** semiweekly. **Effective Market(s):** West Coast. **Units of Measure:** Dollars per lb. **Type of Price:** sale by first receiver. **Time Period Covered:** latest day.

BASSWOOD

Source: *Volume and Value of Sawtimber Stumpage Sold from National Forests by Selected Species and Region.* **Price Frequency:** quarterly, annually. **Effective Market(s):** Eastern region. **Units of Measure:** Dollars per 1000 board feet. **Type of Price:** average. **Time Period Covered:** latest quarter, latest year.

BASSWOOD, CUCUMBER, AND YELLOW POPLAR SAWTIMBER

Source: *Volume and Value of Sawtimber Stumpage Sold from National Forests by Selected Species and Region.* **Price Frequency:** quarterly, annually. **Effective Market(s):** Southern region. **Units of Measure:** Dollars per 1000 board feet. **Type of Price:** average. **Time Period Covered:** latest quarter, latest year.

BASTNAESITE CONCENTRATES: LEACHED

Source: *Industrial Minerals.* **Price Frequency:** monthly. **Effective Market(s):** main European port. **Units of Measure:** Dollars per lb. rare earth oxide. **Type of Price:** producer & dealer. **Time Period Covered:** latest month.

BATISTE FABRIC

Source: *DNR: Daily News Record.* **Price Frequency:** quarterly. **Units of Measure:** Dollars per yard. **Time Period Covered:** latest 3 quarters.

Source: *JTN: The International Textile Magazine.* **Price Frequency:** monthly. **Effective Market(s):** Japan. **Units of Measure:** Japanese yen per yard. **Type of Price:** spot. **Time Period Covered:** latest month.

BATTERIES: SCRAP, WHOLE

Source: *American Metal Market.* **Price Frequency:** daily. **Units of Measure:** Dollars per 100 lbs. **Time Period Covered:** latest day.

Source: *Iron Age.* **Price Frequency:** monthly. **Effective Market(s):** New York. **Units of Measure:** cents per lb. **Type of Price:** dealer. **Time Period Covered:** latest month.

BATTERIES: SCRAP, WHOLE, DRAINED, OLD

Source: *American Metal Market.* **Price Frequency:** daily. **Effective Market(s):** 14 domestic markets, Montreal, Toronto. **Units of Measure:** cents per lb., Canadian cents per lb. **Type of Price:** dealer buying. **Time Period Covered:** latest day.

BATTERY: STORAGE, 12 VOLT

Source: *Agricultural Prices.* **Price Frequency:** semiannually. **Effective Market(s):** United States. **Units of Measure:** Dollars each. **Type of Price:** paid by farmer. **Time Period Covered:** latest year.

Source: *Agricultural Prices Annual Summary.* **Price Frequency:** quarterly. **Effective Market(s):** United States. **Units of Measure:** Dollars each. **Type of Price:** average paid by farmer. **Time Period Covered:** latest 6 years.

BATTERY ACID

Source: *Chemical Marketing Reporter.* **Price Frequency:** weekly. **Effective Market(s):** New York. **Units of Measure:** Dollars per ton. **Type of Price:** spot. **Time Period Covered:** latest week.

BATTERY PLATES: SCRAP, CLEAN

Source: *American Metal Market.* **Price Frequency:** daily. **Effective Market(s):** 14 domestic markets, Montreal, Toronto. **Units of Measure:** cents per lb., Canadian cents per lb. **Type of Price:** dealer buying. **Time Period Covered:** latest day.

BATTERY PLATES: SCRAP, WITH SEPARATORS

Source: *American Metal Market.* **Price Frequency:** daily. **Effective Market(s):** Boston, Philadelphia, San Francisco. **Units of Measure:** cents per lb. **Type of Price:** dealer buying. **Time Period Covered:** latest day.

BAUXITE

Source: *Commodity Year Book.* **Price Frequency:** annually. **Effective Market(s):** United States. **Units of Measure:** Dollars per ton. **Time Period Covered:** latest 10 years.

BAUXITE: ABRASIVE GRADE

Source: *Industrial Minerals.* **Price Frequency:** monthly. **Effective Market(s):** main European port. **Units of Measure:** Dollars per metric tonne. **Type of Price:** producer & dealer. **Time Period Covered:** latest month.

BAUXITE: GRADE I, CHINESE

Source: *Industrial Minerals.* **Price Frequency:** monthly. **Effective Market(s):** main European port. **Units of Measure:** British pounds per metric tonne. **Type of Price:** producer & dealer. **Time Period Covered:** latest month.

BAUXITE: GRADE II, CHINESE

Source: *Industrial Minerals.* **Price Frequency:** monthly. **Effective Market(s):** main European port. **Units of Measure:** British pounds per metric tonne. **Type of Price:** producer & dealer. **Time Period Covered:** latest month.

BAUXITE: GUYANA

Source: *International Financial Statistics.* **Price Frequency:** quarterly, annually. **Effective Market(s):** Baltimore (MD). **Units of Measure:** Dollars per metric ton, index. **Type of Price:** market price, price index. **Time Period Covered:** latest quarter, latest 4 years.

Source: *International Financial Statistics Yearbook.* **Price Frequency:** annually. **Effective Market(s):** Baltimore (MD). **Units of Measure:** Dollars per metric ton. **Type of Price:** wholesale. **Time Period Covered:** latest 30 years.

BAUXITE: JAMAICAN

Source: *Commodity Trade and Price Trends.* **Price Frequency:** annually. **Effective Market(s):** United States. **Units of Measure:** Dollars per metric ton, 1980 constant dollars per metric ton. **Type of Price:** import. **Time Period Covered:** latest 37 years.

BAUXITE: REFACTORY GRADE

Source: *Industrial Minerals.* **Price Frequency:** monthly. **Effective Market(s):** main European port. **Units of Measure:** Dollars per metric tonne. **Type of Price:** producer & dealer. **Time Period Covered:** latest month.

BAUXITE: REFRACTORY GRADE, CALCINED

Source: *Chemical Marketing Reporter.* **Price Frequency:** weekly. **Effective Market(s):** Baltimore (MD)/Mobile (AL). **Units of Measure:** Dollars per metric ton. **Type of Price:** spot. **Time Period Covered:** latest week.

BAUXITE: REFRACTORY GRADE, GUYANA

Source: *Industrial Minerals.* **Price Frequency:** monthly. **Effective Market(s):** Baltimore (MD), Gulf Coast. **Units of Measure:** Dollars per metric tonne. **Type of Price:** producer & dealer. **Time Period Covered:** latest month.

BAY OIL: NF

Source: *Chemical Marketing Reporter.* **Price Frequency:** weekly. **Effective Market(s):** New York. **Units of Measure:** Dollars per lb. **Type of Price:** spot. **Time Period Covered:** latest week.

Source: *Journal of Commerce and Commercial.* **Price Frequency:** weekly in Tuesday issue. **Units of Measure:** Dollars per lb. **Type of Price:** spot. **Time Period Covered:** latest week.

BAYBERRY WAX

Source: *Chemical Marketing Reporter.* **Price Frequency:** weekly. **Effective Market(s):** New York. **Units of Measure:** Dollars per lb. **Type of Price:** spot. **Time Period Covered:** latest week.

BEAN SPROUTS

Source: *New Zealand Farmer.* **Price Frequency:** weekly, seasonally. **Effective Market(s):** New Zealand. **Units of Measure:** New Zealand dollars per tray. **Time Period Covered:** latest week.

BEANS

Source: *Farmers Weekly.* **Price Frequency:** monthly, seasonally. **Effective Market(s):** Essex (England), Lincolnshire (England). **Units of Measure:** British pounds per tonne. **Type of Price:** spot. **Time Period Covered:** latest month.

Source: *Washington Farmer-Stockman.* **Price Frequency:** monthly, seasonally. **Effective Market(s):** Washington. **Units of Measure:** Dollars per 100 lbs. **Type of Price:** received by farmer. **Time Period Covered:** latest month, month ago, year ago.

BEANS: BABY LIMA

Source: *Bean Market News.* **Price Frequency:** weekly. **Effective Market(s):** California. **Units of Measure:** Dollars per 100 lbs. **Type of Price:** dealer. **Time Period Covered:** latest week, week ago, year ago.

Source: *Bean Market Summary.* **Price Frequency:** monthly, annually. **Effective Market(s):** California. **Units of Measure:** Dollars per 100 lbs. **Type of Price:** dealer. **Time Period Covered:** latest 5 years.

Source: *Vegetable and Specialties Situation and Outlook Report.* **Price Frequency:** annually. **Units of Measure:** Dollars per 100 lbs. **Type of Price:** dealer. **Time Period Covered:** latest 7 years.

BEANS: BABY LIMA, DRY

Source: *California Farmer.* **Price Frequency:** semimonthly. **Effective Market(s):** California. **Units of Measure:** Dollars per 100 lbs. **Time Period Covered:** latest week, month ago, year ago.

BEANS: BLACK MATPE, GRADE A, THAI

Source: *Prices of Selected Asia/Pacific Products.* **Price Frequency:** monthly, seasonally. **Effective Market(s):** Bangkok. **Units of Measure:** Thai baht per 100 kilograms. **Type of Price:** wholesale high, wholesale low. **Time Period Covered:** latest month.

BEANS: BLACKEYE

Source: *Bean Market News.* **Price Frequency:** weekly. **Effective Market(s):** California. **Units of Measure:** Dollars per 100 lbs. **Type of Price:** dealer. **Time Period Covered:** latest week, week ago, year ago.

Source: *Bean Market Summary.* **Price Frequency:** monthly, annually. **Effective Market(s):** California. **Units of Measure:** Dollars per 100 lbs. **Type of Price:** dealer. **Time Period Covered:** latest 5 years.

Source: *Vegetable and Specialties Situation and Outlook Report.* **Price Frequency:** annually. **Units of Measure:** Dollars per 100 lbs. **Type of Price:** dealer. **Time Period Covered:** latest 7 years.

BEANS: BLACKEYE, DRY

Source: *California Farmer.* **Price Frequency:** semimonthly. **Effective Market(s):** California. **Units of Measure:** Dollars per 100 lbs. **Time Period Covered:** latest week, month ago, year ago.

BEANS: CRANBERRY TYPE, FRESH

Source: *HRI-Buyers Guide.* **Price Frequency:** weekly. **Effective Market(s):** Northeastern area. **Units of Measure:** Dollars per crate. **Type of Price:** price paid by dining places & institutions. **Time Period Covered:** latest week.

BEANS: DARK RED KIDNEY

Source: *FAO Quarterly Bulletin of Statistics.* **Price Frequency:** monthly, annually. **Effective Market(s):** United Kingdom. **Units of Measure:** British pounds per 1000 kilograms, dollars per metric ton. **Time Period Covered:** latest 3 years.

BEANS: DRY, EDIBLE

Source: *Agricultural Outlook.* **Price Frequency:** monthly, annually. **Effective Market(s):** United States. **Units of Measure:** Dollars per 100 lbs. **Type of Price:** price received by farmer. **Time Period Covered:** monthly latest 6 months, annually latest 3 years.

Source: *Agricultural Prices.* **Price Frequency:** monthly. **Effective Market(s):** United States. **Units of Measure:** Dollars per 100 lbs. **Type of Price:** received by farmer. **Time Period Covered:** latest 2 months, year ago.

Source: *Agricultural Prices.* **Price Frequency:** monthly, seasonally. **Effective Market(s):** 9 domestic markets, United States. **Units of Measure:** Dollars per 100 lbs. **Type of Price:** received by farmer. **Time Period Covered:** latest 2 months.

Source: *Agricultural Prices Annual Summary.* **Price Frequency:** annually. **Effective Market(s):** 13 domestic markets, United States. **Units of Measure:** Dollars per 100 lbs. **Type of Price:** average received by farmer. **Time Period Covered:** latest 2 years, for US latest 6 years.

Source: *Vegetable and Specialties Situation and Outlook Report.* **Price Frequency:** monthly, annually. **Effective Market(s):** United States. **Units of Measure:** Dollars per 100 lbs. **Type of Price:** grower. **Time Period Covered:** latest 4 years.

BEANS: DRY, NAVY BEAN-PINTO

Source: *FAo Quarterly Bulletin of Statistics.* **Price Frequency:** monthly, annually. **Effective Market(s):** Washington. **Units of Measure:** Dollars per 100 lbs., dollars per metric ton. **Type of Price:** dealer. **Time Period Covered:** latest 3 years.

BEANS: FEED

Source: *Farmers Weekly.* **Price Frequency:** weekly, seasonally. **Effective Market(s):** Great Britain. **Units of Measure:** British pounds per tonne. **Type of Price:** spot. **Time Period Covered:** latest week, week ago, year ago.

BEANS: FRENCH CUT, FROZEN

Source: *HRI-Buyer's Guide.* **Price Frequency:** weekly. **Effective Market(s):** Northeastern area. **Units of Measure:** Dollars per case. **Type of Price:** price paid by dining places & institutions. **Time Period Covered:** latest week.

BEANS: GARBANZO

Source: *Bean Market News.* **Price Frequency:** weekly. **Effective Market(s):** California. **Units of Measure:** Dollars per 100 lbs. **Type of Price:** dealer. **Time Period Covered:** latest week, week ago, year ago.

Source: *Bean Market Summary.* **Price Frequency:** monthly, annually. **Effective Market(s):** California. **Units of Measure:** Dollars per 100 lbs. **Type of Price:** dealer. **Time Period Covered:** latest 5 years.

Source: *Vegetable and Specialties Situation and Outlook Report.* **Price Frequency:** annually. **Units of Measure:** Dollars per 100 lbs. **Type of Price:** dealer. **Time Period Covered:** latest 7 years.

BEANS: GREAT NORTHERN

Source: *Bean Market News.* **Price Frequency:** weekly. **Effective Market(s):** Western Nebraska/Eastern Wyoming, Idaho. **Units of Measure:** Dollars per 100 lbs. **Type of Price:** dealer. **Time Period Covered:** latest week, last week, year ago.

Source: *Bean Market News.* **Price Frequency:** weekly. **Effective Market(s):** Western Nebraska/Eastern Wyoming. **Units of Measure:** Dollars per 100 lbs. **Type of Price:** grower. **Time Period Covered:** latest week, week ago.

Source: *Bean Market Summary.* **Price Frequency:** monthly, annually. **Effective Market(s):** Western Nebraska/Eastern Wyoming. **Units of Measure:** Dollars per 100 lbs. **Type of Price:** dealer, price paid to grower. **Time Period Covered:** latest 5 years.

Source: *Idaho Farmer-Stockman.* **Price Frequency:** monthly. **Effective Market(s):** Denver. **Type of Price:** price to grower. **Time Period Covered:** latest month, month ago.

Source: *Vegetable and Specialties Situation and Outlook Report.* **Price Frequency:** annually. **Units of Measure:** Dollars per 100 lbs. **Type of Price:** dealer. **Time Period Covered:** latest 7 years.

Source: *Washington Farmer-Stockman.* **Price Frequency:** monthly, seasonally. **Effective Market(s):** Denver. **Units of Measure:** Dollars per 100 lbs. **Type of Price:** price to grower. **Time Period Covered:** latest month, month ago.

BEANS: GREEN TYPE

Source: *Lancaster Farming.* **Price Frequency:** weekly, seasonally. **Effective Market(s):** Pennsylvania. **Units of Measure:** Dollars per bushel. **Type of Price:** market. **Time Period Covered:** latest week.

BEANS: GREEN TYPE, FLAT

Source: *Fresh Fruit and Vegetable Prices.* **Price Frequency:** monthly, seasonally. **Effective Market(s):** Nogales (AZ). **Units of Measure:** Dollars per lb. **Type of Price:** average price at shipping point. **Time Period Covered:** latest year.

BEANS: GREEN TYPE, GEORGIA

Source: *Fresh Fruit and Vegetable Prices.* **Price Frequency:** monthly, seasonally. **Effective Market(s):** Chicago. **Units of Measure:** Dollars per bushel container. **Type of Price:** average wholesale price. **Time Period Covered:** latest year.

BEANS: GREEN TYPE, GRADE A, THAI

Source: *Prices of Selected Asia/Pacific Products.* **Price Frequency:** monthly, seasonally. **Effective Market(s):** Bangkok. **Units of Measure:** Thai baht per 100 kilograms. **Type of Price:** wholesale high, wholesale low. **Time Period Covered:** latest month.

BEANS: GREEN TYPE, ROUND

Source: *Fresh Fruit and Vegetable Prices.* **Price Frequency:** monthly, seasonally. **Effective Market(s):** Florida, Vineland (NJ), South Georgia, Western North Carolina. **Units of Measure:** Dollars per carton. **Type of Price:** average price at shipping point. **Time Period Covered:** latest year.

Source: *Lancaster Farming.* **Price Frequency:** weekly, seasonally. **Effective Market(s):** Pennsylvania. **Units of Measure:** Dollars per bushel. **Type of Price:** market. **Time Period Covered:** latest week.

Source: *The Packer.* **Price Frequency:** weekly, seasonally. **Effective Market(s):** varies. **Units of Measure:** Dollars per crate. **Type of Price:** price received by farmer. **Time Period Covered:** latest week.

BEANS: GREEN TYPE, ROUND, FLORIDA

Source: *Fresh Fruit and Vegetable Prices.* **Price Frequency:** monthly, seasonally. **Effective Market(s):** Chicago, New York City. **Units of Measure:** Dollars per bushel container. **Type of Price:** average wholesale price. **Time Period Covered:** latest year.

BEANS: GREEN TYPE, ROUND, ILLINOIS

Source: *Fresh Fruit and Vegetable Prices.* **Price Frequency:** monthly, seasonally. **Effective Market(s):** Chicago. **Units of Measure:** Dollars per bushel container. **Type of Price:** average wholesale price. **Time Period Covered:** latest year.

BEANS: GREEN TYPE, ROUND, LONG ISLAND (NY)

Source: *Fresh Fruit and Vegetable Prices.* **Price Frequency:** monthly, seasonally. **Effective Market(s):** New York City. **Units of Measure:** Dollars per bushel container. **Type of Price:** average wholesale price. **Time Period Covered:** latest year.

BEANS: GREEN TYPE, ROUND, NEW JERSEY

Source: *Fresh Fruit and Vegetable Prices.* **Price Frequency:** monthly, seasonally. **Effective Market(s):** New York City. **Units of Measure:** Dollars per bushel container. **Type of Price:** average wholesale price. **Time Period Covered:** latest year.

BEANS: GREEN TYPE, SMALL, NEW STOCK, THAI

Source: *Prices of Selected Asia/Pacific Products.* **Price Frequency:** monthly, seasonally. **Effective Market(s):** Hong Kong. **Units of Measure:** Hong Kong dollars per picul. **Type of Price:** wholesale high, wholesale low. **Time Period Covered:** latest month.

BEANS: LARGE LIMA

Source: *Bean Market News.* **Price Frequency:** weekly. **Effective Market(s):** California. **Units of Measure:** Dollars per 100 lbs. **Type of Price:** dealer. **Time Period Covered:** latest week, week ago, year ago.

Source: *Bean Market Summary.* **Price Frequency:** monthly, annually. **Effective Market(s):** California. **Units of Measure:** Dollars per 100 lbs. **Type of Price:** dealer. **Time Period Covered:** latest 5 years.

Source: *Vegetable and Specialties Situation and Outlook Report.* **Price Frequency:** annually. **Units of Measure:** Dollars per 100 lbs. **Type of Price:** dealer. **Time Period Covered:** latest 7 years.

BEANS: LARGE LIMA, DRY

Source: *California Farmer.* **Price Frequency:** semimonthly. **Effective Market(s):** California. **Units of Measure:** Dollars per 100 lbs. **Time Period Covered:** latest week, month ago, year ago.

BEANS: LIGHT RED KIDNEY

Source: *Bean Market News.* **Price Frequency:** weekly. **Effective Market(s):** California. **Units of Measure:** Dollars per 100 lbs. **Type of Price:** dealer. **Time Period Covered:** latest week, week ago, year ago.

Source: *Bean Market Summary.* **Price Frequency:** monthly, annually. **Effective Market(s):** California. **Units of Measure:** Dollars per 100 lbs. **Type of Price:** dealer. **Time Period Covered:** latest 5 years.

Source: *Vegetable and Specialties Situation and Outlook Report.* **Price Frequency:** annually. **Units of Measure:** Dollars per 100 lbs. **Type of Price:** dealer. **Time Period Covered:** latest 7 years.

BEANS: LIGHT RED KIDNEY, DRY

Source: *California Farmer.* **Price Frequency:** semimonthly. **Effective Market(s):** California. **Units of Measure:** Dollars per 100 lbs. **Time Period Covered:** latest week, month ago, year ago.

BEANS: LIMA

Source: *Lancaster Farming.* **Price Frequency:** weekly, seasonally. **Effective Market(s):** Pennsylvania. **Units of Measure:** Dollars per bushel. **Type of Price:** market. **Time Period Covered:** latest week.

BEANS: LIMA, FORDHOOK, FROZEN

Source: *HRI-Buyer's Guide.* **Price Frequency:** weekly. **Effective Market(s):** Northeastern area. **Units of Measure:** Dollars per case. **Type of Price:** price paid by dining places & institutions. **Time Period Covered:** latest week.

BEANS: NAVY

Source: *Vegetable and Specialties Situation and Outlook Report.* **Price Frequency:** annually. **Units of Measure:** Dollars per 100 lbs. **Type of Price:** dealer. **Time Period Covered:** latest 7 years.

BEANS: PINK

Source: *Bean Market News.* **Price Frequency:** weekly. **Effective Market(s):** Idaho, Washington. **Units of Measure:** Dollars per 100 lbs. **Type of Price:** dealer. **Time Period Covered:** latest week, week ago, year ago.

Source: *Bean Market News.* **Price Frequency:** weekly. **Effective Market(s):** Idaho, Washington. **Units of Measure:** Dollars per 100 lbs. **Type of Price:** grower. **Time Period Covered:** latest week, week ago.

Source: *Bean Market News.* **Price Frequency:** weekly. **Effective Market(s):** California. **Units of Measure:** Dollars per 100 lbs. **Type of Price:** dealer. **Time Period Covered:** latest week, week ago, year ago.

Source: *Bean Market Summary.* **Price Frequency:** monthly, annually. **Effective Market(s):** California, Southern Idaho. **Units of Measure:** Dollars per 100 lbs. **Type of Price:** dealer. **Time Period Covered:** latest 5 years.

Source: *Bean Market Summary.* **Price Frequency:** monthly, annually. **Effective Market(s):** Southern Idaho. **Units of Measure:** Dollars per 100 lbs. **Type of Price:** price paid to grower. **Time Period Covered:** latest 5 years.

Source: *Idaho Farmer-Stockman.* **Price Frequency:** monthly. **Effective Market(s):** Denver. **Type of Price:** price to grower. **Time Period Covered:** latest month, month ago.

Source: *Vegetable and Specialties Situation and Outlook Report.* **Price Frequency:** annually. **Units of Measure:** Dollars per 100 lbs. **Type of Price:** dealer. **Time Period Covered:** latest 7 years.

Source: *Washington Farmer-Stockman.* **Price Frequency:** monthly, seasonally. **Effective Market(s):** Denver. **Units of Measure:** Dollars per 100 lbs. **Type of Price:** price to grower. **Time Period Covered:** latest month, month ago.

BEANS: PINTO

Source: *Bean Market News.* **Price Frequency:** weekly. **Effective Market(s):** 8 domestic markets. **Units of Measure:** Dollars per 100 lbs. **Type of Price:** dealer. **Time Period Covered:** latest week, week ago, year ago.

Source: *Bean Market News.* **Price Frequency:** weekly. **Effective Market(s):** 8 domestic markets. **Units of Measure:** Dollars per 100 lbs. **Type of Price:** grower. **Time Period Covered:** latest week, week ago.

Source: *Bean Market Summary.* **Price Frequency:** monthly, annually. **Effective Market(s):** Northern Colorado. **Units of Measure:** Dollars per 100 lbs. **Type of Price:** dealer, price paid to grower. **Time Period Covered:** latest 5 years.

Source: *Idaho Farmer-Stockman.* **Price Frequency:** monthly. **Effective Market(s):** Denver. **Type of Price:** price to grower. **Time Period Covered:** latest month, month ago.

Source: *Vegetable and Specialties Situation and Outlook Report.* **Price Frequency:** annually. **Units of Measure:** Dollars per 100 lbs. **Type of Price:** dealer. **Time Period Covered:** latest 7 years.

Source: *Washington Farmer-Stockman.* **Price Frequency:** monthly, seasonally. **Effective Market(s):** Denver. **Units of Measure:** Dollars per 100 lbs. **Type of Price:** price to grower. **Time Period Covered:** latest month, month ago.

BEANS: POLE

Source: *The Packer.* **Price Frequency:** weekly, seasonally. **Effective Market(s):** varies. **Units of Measure:** Dollars per carton. **Type of Price:** price received by farmer. **Time Period Covered:** latest week.

BEANS: RED, CHINESE

Source: *Prices of Selected Asia/Pacific Products.* **Price Frequency:** monthly, seasonally. **Effective Market(s):** Tokyo. **Units of Measure:** 1000 Japanese yen per 60 kilograms. **Type of Price:** high, low. **Time Period Covered:** latest month.

BEANS: ROUND, FRESH

Source: *HRI-Buyers Guide.* **Price Frequency:** weekly. **Effective Market(s):** Northeastern area. **Units of Measure:** Dollars per crate. **Type of Price:** price paid by dining places & institutions. **Time Period Covered:** latest week.

BEANS: SMALL RED

Source: *Bean Market News.* **Price Frequency:** weekly. **Effective Market(s):** Idaho, Washington. **Units of Measure:** Dollars per 100 lbs. **Type of Price:** dealer. **Time Period Covered:** latest week, last week, year ago.

Source: *Bean Market News.* **Price Frequency:** weekly. **Effective Market(s):** Idaho, Washington. **Units of Measure:** Dollars per 100 lbs. **Type of Price:** grower. **Time Period Covered:** latest week, week ago.

Source: *Bean Market Summary.* **Price Frequency:** monthly, annually. **Effective Market(s):** Southern Idaho. **Units of Measure:** Dollars per 100 lbs. **Type of Price:** dealer, price paid to grower. **Time Period Covered:** latest 5 years.

Source: *Idaho Farmer-Stockman.* **Price Frequency:** monthly. **Effective Market(s):** Denver. **Type of Price:** price to grower. **Time Period Covered:** latest month, month ago.

Source: *Vegetable and Specialties Situation and Outlook Report.* **Price Frequency:** annually. **Units of Measure:** Dollars per 100 lbs. **Type of Price:** dealer. **Time Period Covered:** latest 7 years.

Source: *Washington Farmer-Stockman.* **Price Frequency:** monthly, seasonally. **Effective Market(s):** Denver. **Units of Measure:** Dollars per 100 lbs. **Type of Price:** price to grower. **Time Period Covered:** latest month, month ago.

BEANS: SMALL RED, THAI

Source: *Prices of Selected Asia/Pacific Products.* **Price Frequency:** monthly, seasonally. **Effective Market(s):** Hong Kong. **Units of Measure:** Hong Kong dollars per picul. **Type of Price:** wholesale high, wholesale low. **Time Period Covered:** latest month.

BEANS: SMALL WHITE

Source: *Bean Market Summary.* **Price Frequency:** monthly, annually. **Effective Market(s):** California. **Units of Measure:** Dollars per 100 lbs. **Type of Price:** dealer. **Time Period Covered:** latest 5 years.

Source: *Vegetable and Specialties Situation and Outlook Report.* **Price Frequency:** annually. **Units of Measure:** Dollars per 100 lbs. **Type of Price:** dealer. **Time Period Covered:** latest 7 years.

BEANS: SNAP, CANNED

Source: *Vegetable and Specialties Situation and Outlook Report.* **Price Frequency:** monthly. **Units of Measure:** Dollars per case. **Type of Price:** wholesale. **Time Period Covered:** latest month, year ago.

BEANS: SNAP, FROZEN

Source: *Vegetable and Specialties Situation and Outlook Report.* **Price Frequency:** monthly. **Units of Measure:** Dollars per case. **Type of Price:** food service, retail. **Time Period Covered:** latest month, year ago.

BEANS: STRING, FROZEN

Source: *HRI-Buyer's Guide.* **Price Frequency:** weekly. **Effective Market(s):** Northeastern area. **Units of Measure:** Dollars per case. **Type of Price:** price paid by dining places & institutions. **Time Period Covered:** latest week.

BEANS: WAX, FRESH

Source: *HRI-Buyers Guide.* **Price Frequency:** weekly. **Effective Market(s):** Northeastern area. **Units of Measure:** Dollars per crate. **Type of Price:** price paid by dining places & institutions. **Time Period Covered:** latest week.

BEANS: WAX, YELLOW

Source: *Lancaster Farming.* **Price Frequency:** weekly, seasonally. **Effective Market(s):** Pennsylvania. **Units of Measure:** Dollars per bushel. **Type of Price:** market. **Time Period Covered:** latest week.

BEDDING PLANTS: FLOWERING AND FOLIAR TYPES, FLATS

Source: *Floriculture Crops.* **Price Frequency:** annually. **Effective Market(s):** 29 domestic markets, United States. **Units of Measure:** Dollars per unit. **Type of Price:** commercial wholesale. **Time Period Covered:** latest 2 years.

BEDDING PLANTS: FLOWERING AND FOLIAR TYPES, POTTED, LESS Than 5″

Source: *Floriculture Crops.* **Price Frequency:** annually. **Effective Market(s):** 29 domestic markets, United States. **Units of Measure:** Dollars per unit. **Type of Price:** commercial wholesale. **Time Period Covered:** latest 2 years.

BEDDING PLANTS: FLOWERING AND FOLIAR TYPES, POTTED, MORE Than 5″

Source: *Floriculture Crops.* **Price Frequency:** annually. **Effective Market(s):** 29 domestic markets, United States. **Units of Measure:** Dollars per unit. **Type of Price:** commercial wholesale. **Time Period Covered:** latest 2 years.

BEDDING PLANTS: VEGETABLE TYPES, FLATS

Source: *Floriculture Crops.* **Price Frequency:** annually. **Effective Market(s):** 29 domestic markets, United States. **Units of Measure:** Dollars per unit. **Type of Price:** commercial wholesale. **Time Period Covered:** latest 2 years.

BEDDING PLANTS: VEGETABLE TYPES, POTTED, LESS THAN 5″

Source: *Floriculture Crops.* **Price Frequency:** annually. **Effective Market(s):** 26 domestic markets, United States. **Units of Measure:** Dollars per unit. **Type of Price:** commercial wholesale. **Time Period Covered:** latest 2 years.

BEDDING PLANTS: VEGETABLE TYPES, POTTED, MORE THAN 5″

Source: *Floriculture Crops.* **Price Frequency:** annually. **Effective Market(s):** 26 domestic markets, United States. **Units of Measure:** Dollars per unit. **Type of Price:** commercial wholesale. **Time Period Covered:** latest 2 years.

BEECH BOARDS: SLAVONIAN

Source: *Timber Bulletin.* **Price Frequency:** monthly, annually. **Effective Market(s):** Italy. **Units of Measure:** 1000 Italian lire per cubic meter. **Time Period Covered:** monthly latest 2 years, annually latest 6 years.

BEEF

Source: *Agricultural Outlook.* **Price Frequency:** annually. **Effective Market(s):** United States. **Units of Measure:** Dollars per 100 lbs. **Type of Price:** primary market. **Time Period Covered:** latest 2 years.

Source: *Agricultural Outlook.* **Price Frequency:** monthly, annually. **Effective Market(s):** Chicago. **Units of Measure:** Dollars per 100 lbs. **Type of Price:** retail. **Time Period Covered:** monthly latest 6 months, annually latest 3 years.

Source: *Commodity Year Book.* **Price Frequency:** annually. **Units of Measure:** cents per lb. **Type of Price:** retail. **Time Period Covered:** latest 7 years.

Source: *New Zealand Farmer.* **Price Frequency:** weekly, seasonally. **Effective Market(s):** 8 New Zealand markets. **Units of Measure:** New Zealand cents per kilogram. **Type of Price:** export. **Time Period Covered:** latest week.

BEEF: 600-900 LBS

Source: *Asian Wall Street Journal.* **Price Frequency:** daily. **Effective Market(s):** Mid-United States. **Units of Measure:** Dollars per lb. **Type of Price:** cash. **Time Period Covered:** latest 2 days, year ago.

Source: *Investor's Daily.* **Price Frequency:** daily. **Effective Market(s):** Midwest. **Units of Measure:** Dollars per 100 lbs. **Type of Price:** spot. **Time Period Covered:** latest 2 days.

Source: *New York Times.* **Price Frequency:** daily. **Effective Market(s):** Midwest. **Units of Measure:** Dollars per 100 lbs. **Type of Price:** cash. **Time Period Covered:** latest 2 days.

BEEF: 700-900 LBS

Source: *Farm and Dairy.* **Price Frequency:** weekly, seasonally. **Effective Market(s):** Mid-United States. **Units of Measure:** Dollars per lb. **Time Period Covered:** latest week, year ago.

Source: *Wall Street Journal.* **Price Frequency:** daily. **Effective Market(s):** Mid-United States. **Units of Measure:** Dollars per lb. **Time Period Covered:** latest day, day ago, year ago.

BEEF: ALL ORIGINS

Source: *International Financial Statistics.* **Price Frequency:** monthly, quarterly, annually. **Effective Market(s):** United States ports. **Units of Measure:** cents per lb., index. **Type of Price:** market price, price index. **Time Period Covered:** latest 5 months, latest 5 quarters, latest 5 years.

Source: *International Financial Statistics Yearbook.* **Price Frequency:** annually. **Effective Market(s):** United States ports. **Units of Measure:** cents per lb. **Type of Price:** wholesale. **Time Period Covered:** latest 30 years.

BEEF: ALL ORIGINS, MAINLY AUSTRALIA

Source: *Monthly Commodity Price Bulletin.* **Price Frequency:** monthly, annually. **Effective Market(s):** United States ports. **Units of Measure:** cents per lb. **Type of Price:** average import. **Time Period Covered:** latest 5 years.

Source: *UNCTAD Commodity Yearbook.* **Price Frequency:** annually. **Effective Market(s):** United States ports. **Units of Measure:** Dollars per metric ton. **Type of Price:** free market. **Time Period Covered:** latest 12 years.

BEEF: ALL TYPES, FRESH

Source: *Livestock and Poultry Situation and Outlook Report.* **Price Frequency:** monthly. **Effective Market(s):** Central United States. **Units of Measure:** cents per lb. **Type of Price:** wholesale. **Time Period Covered:** latest year.

BEEF: ARGENTINE

Source: *FAO Quarterly Bulletin of Statistics.* **Price Frequency:** monthly, annually. **Effective Market(s):** Argentina. **Units of Measure:** Dollars per 1000 kilograms, dollars per metric ton. **Type of Price:** export. **Time Period Covered:** latest 3 years.

BEEF: BONELESS, 85% LEAN, FROZEN

Source: *Commodity Trade and Price Trends.* **Price Frequency:** annually. **Units of Measure:** cents per kilogram, 1980 cents per kilogram. **Type of Price:** import. **Time Period Covered:** latest 37 years.

BEEF: BONELESS, 90% LEAN, FRESH

Source: *Livestock and Poultry Update.* **Price Frequency:** monthly. **Effective Market(s):** Central United States. **Units of Measure:** Dollars per 100 lbs. **Type of Price:** wholesale. **Time Period Covered:** latest 3 months, year ago.

BEEF: BONELESS, 90% LEAN, FROZEN, IMPORTED, MAINLY Australian

Source: *Monthly Commodity Price Bulletin Supplement.* **Price Frequency:** monthly, quarterly, annually. **Units of Measure:** cents per lb. **Type of Price:** import. **Time Period Covered:** latest 20 years.

BEEF: BONELESS, AUSTRALIAN

Source: *FAO Quarterly Bulletin of Statistics.* **Price Frequency:** monthly, annually. **Effective Market(s):** United States. **Units of Measure:** Dollars per 100 kilograms. **Time Period Covered:** latest 3 years.

BEEF: BONELESS, FROZEN, ARGENTINE

Source: *Commodity Trade and Price Trends.* **Price Frequency:** annually. **Effective Market(s):** European Economic Community. **Units of Measure:** cents per kilogram, 1980 constant cents per kilogram. **Type of Price:** export. **Time Period Covered:** latest 33 years.

BEEF: CANNER AND CUTTER

Source: *Commodity Year Book.* **Price Frequency:** annually. **Effective Market(s):** Midwest. **Units of Measure:** cents per lb. **Time Period Covered:** latest 4 years.

BEEF: CHOICE

Source: *Livestock and Poultry Situation and Outlook Report.* **Price Frequency:** monthly. **Effective Market(s):** Central United States. **Units of Measure:** cents per lb. **Type of Price:** retail. **Time Period Covered:** latest year.

BEEF: CHOICE 3, BONELESS

Source: *Livestock, Meat, Wool Market News.* **Price Frequency:** weekly, seasonally. **Effective Market(s):** East Coast, Central United States, California. **Units of Measure:** Dollars per 100 lbs. **Type of Price:** wholesale. **Time Period Covered:** latest week, year ago.

BEEF: CHOICE, BONE IN

Source: *Meat Price Report.* **Price Frequency:** weekly. **Units of Measure:** cents per lb. **Type of Price:** price paid to wholesaler. **Time Period Covered:** latest week.

BEEF: CHOICE, DICED

Source: *Meat Price Report.* **Price Frequency:** weekly. **Units of Measure:** cents per lb. **Type of Price:** price paid to wholesaler. **Time Period Covered:** latest week.

BEEF: CHOICE, GROUND

Source: *Livestock and Poultry Situation and Outlook Report.* **Price Frequency:** monthly. **Units of Measure:** Dollars per lb. **Type of Price:** retail. **Time Period Covered:** latest 3 years.

BEEF: CHOICE, GROUND, COARSE

Source: *National Provisioner.* **Price Frequency:** daily. **Units of Measure:** cents per lb. **Time Period Covered:** latest week.

BEEF: CHOICE, GROUND, REGULAR 75% LEAN

Source: *Meat Price Report.* **Price Frequency:** weekly. **Units of Measure:** cents per lb. **Type of Price:** price paid to wholesaler. **Time Period Covered:** latest week.

BEEF: CHOICE, GROUND, REGULAR, TVP ADDED

Source: *Meat Price Report.* **Price Frequency:** weekly. **Units of Measure:** cents per lb. **Type of Price:** price paid to wholesaler. **Time Period Covered:** latest week.

BEEF: CHOICE, GROUND, SPECIAL 80% LEAN

Source: *Meat Price Report.* **Price Frequency:** weekly. **Units of Measure:** cents per lb. **Type of Price:** price paid to wholesaler. **Time Period Covered:** latest week.

BEEF: CHOICE, YIELD GRADE 3

Source: *Livestock and Poultry Situation and Outlook Report.* **Price Frequency:** monthly, quarterly, annually. **Units of Measure:** cents per lb. **Type of Price:** retail. **Time Period Covered:** monthly latest year, quarterly latest 2 years, annually latest 5 years.

BEEF: CORNED, ARGENTINE

Source: *International Financial Statistics.* **Price Frequency:** quarterly, annually. **Effective Market(s):** Argentina. **Units of Measure:** cents per lb., index. **Type of Price:** market price, price index. **Time Period Covered:** latest quarter, latest 4 years.

Source: *International Financial Statistics Yearbook.* **Price Frequency:** annually. **Effective Market(s):** Argentina. **Units of Measure:** cents per lb. **Type of Price:** wholesale. **Time Period Covered:** latest 30 years.

BEEF: CORNED, CANNED

Source: *Statistical Bulletin of the South Pacific: Retail Price Indexes.* **Price Frequency:** annually. **Effective Market(s):** 18 South Pacific markets. **Units of Measure:** Australian dollars per 340 grams. **Type of Price:** retail. **Time Period Covered:** latest year.

BEEF: CUTOUT

Source: *Livestock and Poultry Situation and Outlook Report.* **Price Frequency:** monthly. **Effective Market(s):** Central United States. **Units of Measure:** Dollars per 100 lbs. **Type of Price:** wholesale. **Time Period Covered:** latest year.

Source: *Livestock and Poultry Update.* **Price Frequency:** monthly. **Effective Market(s):** Central United States. **Units of Measure:** Dollars per 100 lbs. **Type of Price:** wholesale. **Time Period Covered:** latest 3 months, year ago.

BEEF: FRESH, BONELESS, 50% LEAN TRIMMINGS

Source: *National Provisioner.* **Price Frequency:** daily. **Effective Market(s):** Midwest River area. **Units of Measure:** cents per lb. **Time Period Covered:** latest week.

BEEF: FRESH, BONELESS, 75% LEAN TRIMMINGS

Source: *National Provisioner.* **Price Frequency:** daily. **Effective Market(s):** Midwest River area. **Units of Measure:** cents per lb. **Time Period Covered:** latest week.

BEEF: FRESH, BONELESS, 85% LEAN TRIMMINGS

Source: *National Provisioner.* **Price Frequency:** daily. **Effective Market(s):** Midwest River area. **Units of Measure:** cents per lb. **Time Period Covered:** latest week.

BEEF: FRESH, BONELESS, 90% LEAN TRIMMINGS

Source: *National Proivisioner.* **Price Frequency:** daily. **Effective Market(s):** Midwest River area. **Units of Measure:** cents per lb. **Time Period Covered:** latest week.

BEEF: FROZEN, ARGENTINE

Source: *International Financial Statistics.* **Price Frequency:** quarterly, annually. **Effective Market(s):** Argentina. **Units of Measure:** cents per lb., index. **Type of Price:** market price, price index. **Time Period Covered:** latest quarter, latest 4 years.

Source: *International Financial Statistics Yearbook.* **Price Frequency:** annually. **Effective Market(s):** Argentina. **Units of Measure:** cents per lb. **Type of Price:** wholesale. **Time Period Covered:** latest 30 years.

BEEF: GROUND

Source: *Livestock and Poultry Update.* **Price Frequency:** monthly. **Units of Measure:** cents per lb. **Type of Price:** retail. **Time Period Covered:** latest 3 months, year ago.

BEEF: GROUND, 80% LEAN

Source: *Porkpro Newsletter.* **Price Frequency:** weekly. **Effective Market(s):** Chicago. **Units of Measure:** Dollars per lb. **Type of Price:** retail. **Time Period Covered:** latest day, week ago, year ago.

BEEF: IRELAND

Source: *International Financial Statistics.* **Price Frequency:** quarterly, annually. **Effective Market(s):** London. **Units of Measure:** cents per lb., index. **Type of Price:** market price, price index. **Time Period Covered:** latest quarter, latest 4 years.

Source: *International Financial Statistics Yearbook.* **Price Frequency:** annually. **Effective Market(s):** London. **Units of Measure:** cents per lb. **Type of Price:** wholesale. **Time Period Covered:** latest 30 years.

BEEF: REGULAR, GROUND, BULK

Source: *HRI-Buyer's Guide.* **Price Frequency:** weekly. **Effective Market(s):** Northeastern area. **Units of Measure:** Dollars per lb. **Type of Price:** price paid by dining places & institutions. **Time Period Covered:** latest week.

BEEF: SLICED, PROCESS DRIED

Source: *Meat Price Report.* **Price Frequency:** weekly. **Units of Measure:** cents per lb. **Type of Price:** price paid to wholesaler. **Time Period Covered:** latest week.

BEEF: SPECIAL, GROUND, 80% LEAN, BULK

Source: *HRI-Buyer's Guide.* **Price Frequency:** weekly. **Effective Market(s):** Northeastern area. **Units of Measure:** Dollars per lb. **Type of Price:** price paid by dining places & institutions. **Time Period Covered:** latest week.

BEEF: STEER, CHOICE

Source: *California Farmer.* **Price Frequency:** semimonthly. **Effective Market(s):** California. **Units of Measure:** Dollars per 100 lbs. **Time Period Covered:** latest week, month ago, year ago.

BEEF: UNITED STATES

Source: *International Financial Statistics.* **Price Frequency:** monthly, quarterly, annually. **Effective Market(s):** New York. **Units of Measure:** cents per lb., index. **Type of Price:** market price, price index. **Time Period Covered:** latest 4 months, latest 5 quarters, latest 5 years.

Source: *International Financial Statistics Yearbook.* **Price Frequency:** annually. **Effective Market(s):** New York. **Units of Measure:** cents per lb. **Type of Price:** wholesale. **Time Period Covered:** latest 30 years.

BEEF ARM CHUCK: CHOICE

Source: *National Provisioner.* **Price Frequency:** daily. **Units of Measure:** cents per lb. **Time Period Covered:** latest week.

BEEF ARM CHUCK: CHOICE 2-3

Source: *Livestock, Meat, Wool Market News.* **Price Frequency:** weekly, seasonally. **Effective Market(s):** East Coast, Central United States, California. **Units of Measure:** Dollars per 100 lbs. **Type of Price:** wholesale. **Time Period Covered:** latest week, year ago.

BEEF ARMBONE CHUCK: CHOICE 2-3

Source: *Livestock, Meat, Wool Market News.* **Price Frequency:** weekly, seasonally. **Effective Market(s):** Central United States, California. **Units of Measure:** Dollars per 100 lbs. **Type of Price:** average. **Time Period Covered:** latest week, year ago.

BEEF BOTTOM GOOSENECK ROUND: CHOICE

Source: *HRI-Buyer's Guide.* **Price Frequency:** weekly. **Effective Market(s):** Northeastern area. **Units of Measure:** Dollars per lb. **Type of Price:** price paid by dining places & institutions. **Time Period Covered:** latest week.

Source: *Meat Price Report.* **Price Frequency:** weekly. **Units of Measure:** cents per lb. **Type of Price:** price paid to wholesaler. **Time Period Covered:** latest week.

BEEF BOTTOM GOOSENECK ROUND: CHOICE, HEEL OUT, TRIMMED

Source: *Meat Price Report.* **Price Frequency:** weekly. **Units of Measure:** cents per lb. **Type of Price:** price paid to wholesaler. **Time Period Covered:** latest week.

BEEF BOTTOM GOOSENECK ROUND: SELECT

Source: *HRI-Buyer's Guide.* **Price Frequency:** weekly. **Effective Market(s):** Northeastern area. **Units of Measure:** Dollars per lb. **Type of Price:** price paid by dining places & institutions. **Time Period Covered:** latest week.

BEEF BOTTOM ROUND: CHOICE 2-3

Source: *Livestock, Meat, Wool Market News.* **Price Frequency:** weekly, seasonally. **Effective Market(s):** Central United States, California. **Units of Measure:** Dollars per 100 lbs. **Type of Price:** average. **Time Period Covered:** latest week, year ago.

BEEF BOTTOM SIRLOIN: FLAP, CHOICE 2-3

Source: *Livestock, Meat, Wool Market News.* **Price Frequency:** weekly, seasonally. **Effective Market(s):** Central United States, California. **Units of Measure:** Dollars per 100 lbs. **Type of Price:** average. **Time Period Covered:** latest week, year ago.

BEEF BOTTOM SIRLOIN BALL TIP: CHOICE

Source: *Meat Price Report.* **Price Frequency:** weekly. **Units of Measure:** cents per lb. **Type of Price:** price paid to wholesaler. **Time Period Covered:** latest week.

BEEF BOTTOM SIRLOIN BALL TIP: CHOICE 2-3

Source: *Livestock, Meat, Wool Market News.* **Price Frequency:** weekly, seasonally. **Effective Market(s):** Central United States, California. **Units of Measure:** Dollars per 100 lbs. **Type of Price:** average. **Time Period Covered:** latest week, year ago.

BEEF BOTTOM SIRLOIN BUTT: CHOICE

Source: *Meat Price Report.* **Price Frequency:** weekly. **Units of Measure:** cents per lb. **Type of Price:** price paid to wholesaler. **Time Period Covered:** latest week.

BEEF BOTTOM SIRLOIN TRIANGLE: CHOICE

Source: *Meat Price Report.* **Price Frequency:** weekly. **Units of Measure:** cents per lb. **Type of Price:** price paid to wholesaler. **Time Period Covered:** latest week.

BEEF BRAISING STEAK: CHOICE, SPECIAL

Source: *Meat Price Report.* **Price Frequency:** weekly. **Units of Measure:** cents per lb. **Type of Price:** price paid to wholesaler. **Time Period Covered:** latest week.

BEEF BRISKET: CHOICE

Source: *National Provisioner.* **Price Frequency:** daily. **Units of Measure:** cents per lb. **Time Period Covered:** latest week.

BEEF BRISKET: CHOICE 2-3

Source: *Livestock, Meat, Wool Market News.* **Price Frequency:** weekly, seasonally. **Effective Market(s):** Central United States, California. **Units of Measure:** Dollars per 100 lbs. **Type of Price:** average. **Time Period Covered:** latest week, year ago.

BEEF BRISKET: CHOICE 3

Source: *Livestock, Meat, Wool Market News.* **Price Frequency:** weekly, seasonally. **Effective Market(s):** East Coast, Central United States, California. **Units of Measure:** Dollars per 100 lbs. **Type of Price:** wholesale. **Time Period Covered:** latest week, year ago.

BEEF BRISKET: CHOICE, BONELESS, DECKLE OFF

Source: *Meat Price Report.* **Price Frequency:** weekly. **Units of Measure:** cents per lb. **Type of Price:** price paid to wholesaler. **Time Period Covered:** latest week.

BEEF BRISKET: CHOICE, BONELESS, FRESH, DECKLE OFF

Source: *HRI-Buyer's Guide.* **Price Frequency:** weekly. **Effective Market(s):** Northeastern area. **Units of Measure:** Dollars per lb. **Type of Price:** price paid by dining places & institutions. **Time Period Covered:** latest week.

BEEF BRISKET: CORNED, BONELESS, DECKLE OFF

Source: *Meat Price Report.* **Price Frequency:** weekly. **Units of Measure:** cents per lb. **Type of Price:** price paid to wholesaler. **Time Period Covered:** latest week.

BEEF BRISKET: CORNED, COOKED

Source: *Meat Price Report.* **Price Frequency:** weekly. **Units of Measure:** cents per lb. **Type of Price:** price paid to wholesaler. **Time Period Covered:** latest week.

BEEF BRISKET: CORNED, TRIMMED

Source: *HRI-Buyer's Guide.* **Price Frequency:** weekly. **Effective Market(s):** Northeastern area. **Units of Measure:** Dollars per lb. **Type of Price:** price paid by dining places & institutions. **Time Period Covered:** latest week.

BEEF BULL CARCASS: DRESSED, GRADE 1-2

Source: *Livestock, Meat, Wool Market News.* **Price Frequency:** weekly, seasonally. **Effective Market(s):** East Coast, Central United States, California. **Units of Measure:** Dollars per 100 lbs. **Type of Price:** wholesale. **Time Period Covered:** latest week, year ago.

BEEF BULL MEAT: BONELESS, IMPORTED

Source: *National Provisioner.* **Price Frequency:** daily. **Effective Market(s):** Midwest River area. **Units of Measure:** cents per lb. **Time Period Covered:** latest week.

BEEF BULL MEAT: CHOICE 3, BONELESS, FRESH

Source: *Livestock, Meat, Wool Market News.* **Price Frequency:** weekly, seasonally. **Effective Market(s):** East Coast, Central United States, California. **Units of Measure:** Dollars per 100 lbs. **Type of Price:** wholesale. **Time Period Covered:** latest week, year ago.

BEEF BULL MEAT: FRESH, BONELESS

Source: *National Provisioner.* **Price Frequency:** daily. **Effective Market(s):** Midwest River area. **Units of Measure:** cents per lb. **Time Period Covered:** latest week.

BEEF BUTT TENDERLOIN: CHOICE

Source: *Meat Price Report.* **Price Frequency:** weekly. **Units of Measure:** cents per lb. **Type of Price:** price paid to wholesaler . **Time Period Covered:** latest week.

BEEF BUTT TENDERLOIN: UTILITY

Source: *Meat Price Report.* **Price Frequency:** weekly. **Units of Measure:** cents per lb. **Type of Price:** price paid to wholesaler. **Time Period Covered:** latest week.

BEEF CARCASS: 700-900 LBS., MIDWEST

Source: *The Brock Report.* **Price Frequency:** weekly. **Units of Measure:** Dollars per 100 lbs. **Time Period Covered:** latest week, 2 weeks ago, year ago.

BEEF CARCASS: HEIFER, DRESSED, CHOICE 2

Source: *Livestock, Meat, Wool Market News.* **Price Frequency:** weekly, seasonally. **Effective Market(s):** East Coast, Central United States, California. **Units of Measure:** Dollars per 100 lbs. **Type of Price:** wholesale. **Time Period Covered:** latest week, year ago.

BEEF CARCASS: HEIFER, DRESSED, CHOICE 3

Source: *Livestock, Meat, Wool Market News.* **Price Frequency:** weekly, seasonally. **Effective Market(s):** California, Central United States, East Coast. **Units of Measure:** Dollars per 100 lbs. **Type of Price:** wholesale. **Time Period Covered:** latest week, year ago.

BEEF CARCASS: HEIFER, DRESSED, CHOICE 4

Source: *Livestock, Meat, Wool Market News.* **Price Frequency:** weekly, seasonally. **Effective Market(s):** California, Central United States, East Coast. **Units of Measure:** Dollars per 100 lbs. **Type of Price:** wholesale. **Time Period Covered:** latest week, year ago.

BEEF CARCASS: HEIFER, DRESSED, SELECT 1-3

Source: *Livestock, Meat, Wool Market News.* **Price Frequency:** weekly, seasonally. **Effective Market(s):** East Coast, Central United States, California. **Units of Measure:** Dollars per 100 lbs. **Type of Price:** wholesale. **Time Period Covered:** latest week, year ago.

BEEF CARCASS: STEER, CHOICE, FRESH

Source: *Commodity Year Book.* **Price Frequency:** annually. **Effective Market(s):** East Coast. **Units of Measure:** cents per lb. **Time Period Covered:** latest 7 years.

Source: *Survey of Current Business.* **Price Frequency:** monthly, annually. **Effective Market(s):** Central United States. **Units of Measure:** Dollars per lb. **Type of Price:** wholesale. **Time Period Covered:** latest year.

BEEF CARCASS: STEER, DRESSED, CHOICE 2

Source: *Livestock, Meat, Wool Market News.* **Price Frequency:** weekly, seasonally. **Effective Market(s):** East Coast, Central United States, California. **Units of Measure:** Dollars per 100 lbs. **Type of Price:** wholesale. **Time Period Covered:** latest week, year ago.

BEEF CARCASS: STEER, DRESSED, CHOICE 3

Source: *Livestock, Meat, Wool Market News.* **Price Frequency:** weekly, seasonally. **Effective Market(s):** East Coast, Central United States, California. **Units of Measure:** Dollars per 100 lbs. **Type of Price:** wholesale. **Time Period Covered:** latest week, year ago.

BEEF CARCASS: STEER, DRESSED, CHOICE 4

Source: *Livestock, Meat, Wool Market News.* **Price Frequency:** weekly, seasonally. **Effective Market(s):** East Coast, Central United States, California. **Units of Measure:** Dollars per 100 lbs. **Type of Price:** wholesale. **Time Period Covered:** latest week, year ago.

BEEF CARCASS: STEER, DRESSED, SELECT 1-3

Source: *Livestock, Meat, Wool Market News.* **Price Frequency:** weekly, seasonally. **Effective Market(s):** East Coast, Central United States, California. **Units of Measure:** Dollars per 100 lbs. **Type of Price:** wholesale. **Time Period Covered:** latest week, year ago.

BEEF CATTLE

Source: *Agricultural Outlook.* **Price Frequency:** monthly, annually. **Effective Market(s):** United States. **Units of Measure:** Dollars per 100 lbs. **Type of Price:** price received by farmer. **Time Period Covered:** monthly latest 6 months, annually latest 3 years.

Source: *Agricultural Prices.* **Price Frequency:** monthly. **Effective Market(s):** United States. **Units of Measure:** Dollars per 100 lbs. **Type of Price:** received by farmer. **Time Period Covered:** latest 2 months, year ago.

Source: *Agricultural Prices.* **Price Frequency:** monthly. **Effective Market(s):** United States. **Units of Measure:** Dollars per 100 lbs. **Type of Price:** received by farmer. **Time Period Covered:** latest 2 years.

Source: *Agricultural Prices.* **Price Frequency:** monthly. **Effective Market(s):** 35 domestic markets, United States. **Units of Measure:** Dollars per 100 lbs. **Type of Price:** received by farmer. **Time Period Covered:** latest 2 months.

Source: *Agricultural Prices Annual Summary.* **Price Frequency:** monthly, annually. **Effective Market(s):** 35 domestic markets, United States. **Units of Measure:** Dollars per 100 lbs. **Type of Price:** average received by farmer. **Time Period Covered:** latest year, for US latest 6 years.

Source: *Commodity Year Book.* **Price Frequency:** monthly, annually. **Units of Measure:** Dollars per 100 lbs. **Type of Price:** price received by farmers. **Time Period Covered:** latest 6 years.

Source: *Illinois Farm Report.* **Price Frequency:** monthly. **Effective Market(s):** Illinois. **Units of Measure:** Dollars per 100 lbs. **Type of Price:** average received by farmers. **Time Period Covered:** latest 2 months, year ago.

Source: *Kansas Business Review.* **Price Frequency:** monthly. **Effective Market(s):** Kansas. **Units of Measure:** Dollars per 100 lbs. **Time Period Covered:** latest month, month ago, year ago.

Source: *Livestock and Poultry Situation and Outlook Report.* **Price Frequency:** monthly. **Units of Measure:** Dollars per 100 lbs. **Type of Price:** farm. **Time Period Covered:** latest year.

Source: *Washington Farmer-Stockman.* **Price Frequency:** monthly, seasonally. **Effective Market(s):** Washington. **Units of Measure:** Dollars per 100 lbs. **Type of Price:** received by farmer. **Time Period Covered:** latest month, month ago, year ago.

BEEF CATTLE: FUTURES, JUNE

Source: *Commodity Year Book.* **Price Frequency:** monthly. **Effective Market(s):** Chicago. **Units of Measure:** cents per lb. **Type of Price:** futures. **Time Period Covered:** latest 6 years.

BEEF CATTLE: STORES

Source: *Scottish Farmer.* **Price Frequency:** weekly. **Effective Market(s):** Scotland. **Units of Measure:** British pence per kilogram. **Type of Price:** average. **Time Period Covered:** latest week.

BEEF CATTLE CONCENTRATE

Source: *Agricultural Prices.* **Price Frequency:** quarterly. **Effective Market(s):** United States. **Units of Measure:** Dollars per 100 lbs. **Type of Price:** paid by farmer. **Time Period Covered:** latest 2 quarters, year ago.

Source: *Agricultural Prices.* **Price Frequency:** monthly. **Effective Market(s):** 10 domestic markets, United States. **Units of Measure:** Dollars per 100 lbs. **Type of Price:** paid by farmer. **Time Period Covered:** latest month.

BEEF CATTLE CONCENTRATE: 32-36% PROTEIN

Source: *Agricultural Prices Annual Summary.* **Price Frequency:** quarterly. **Effective Market(s):** 10 domestic markets, United States. **Units of Measure:** Dollars per ton. **Type of Price:** average received by farmer. **Time Period Covered:** latest year, for US monthly latest 6 years.

Source: *Feed Situation and Outlook Report.* **Price Frequency:** quarterly, annually. **Effective Market(s):** United States. **Units of Measure:** Dollars per ton. **Type of Price:** paid by farmer. **Time Period Covered:** latest year.

BEEF CHEEK MEAT

Source: *National Provisioner.* **Price Frequency:** daily. **Effective Market(s):** Midwest River area. **Units of Measure:** cents per lb. **Time Period Covered:** latest week.

BEEF CHEEK MEAT: FROZEN

Source: *Livestock, Meat, Wool Market News.* **Price Frequency:** weekly, seasonally. **Effective Market(s):** Central United States. **Units of Measure:** Dollars per 100 lbs. **Time Period Covered:** latest week.

BEEF CHUCK: 2 PIECE, CHOICE 2-3, BONELESS

Source: *Livestock, Meat, Wool Market News.* **Price Frequency:** weekly, seasonally. **Effective Market(s):** Central United States, California. **Units of Measure:** Dollars per 100 lbs. **Type of Price:** average. **Time Period Covered:** latest week, year ago.

BEEF CHUCK: 2 PIECE SQUARE CUT, CHOICE 2-3

Source: *Livestock, Meat, Wool Market News.* **Price Frequency:** weekly, seasonally. **Effective Market(s):** Central United States, California. **Units of Measure:** Dollars per 100 lbs. **Type of Price:** average. **Time Period Covered:** latest week, year ago.

BEEF CHUCK: CHOICE

Source: *National Provisioner.* **Price Frequency:** daily. **Units of Measure:** cents per lb. **Time Period Covered:** latest week.

BEEF CHUCK: CHOICE, GROUND

Source: *Livestock and Poultry Situation and Outlook Report.* **Price Frequency:** monthly. **Units of Measure:** Dollars per lb. **Type of Price:** retail. **Time Period Covered:** latest 3 years.

BEEF CHUCK: FRESH, BONELESS

Source: *National Provisioner.* **Price Frequency:** daily. **Effective Market(s):** Midwest River area. **Units of Measure:** cents per lb. **Time Period Covered:** latest week.

BEEF CHUCK ROAST

Source: *Porkpro Newsletter.* **Price Frequency:** weekly. **Effective Market(s):** Chicago. **Units of Measure:** Dollars per lb. **Type of Price:** retail. **Time Period Covered:** latest day, week ago, year ago.

BEEF CHUCK ROAST: CHOICE, BONE IN

Source: *Livestock and Poultry Situation and Outlook Report.* **Price Frequency:** monthly. **Units of Measure:** Dollars per lb. **Type of Price:** retail. **Time Period Covered:** latest 3 years.

BEEF CHUCK ROLL: CHOICE

Source: *Meat Price Report.* **Price Frequency:** weekly. **Units of Measure:** cents per lb. **Type of Price:** price paid to wholesaler. **Time Period Covered:** latest week.

Source: *National Provisioner.* **Price Frequency:** daily. **Units of Measure:** cents per lb. **Time Period Covered:** latest week.

BEEF CHUCK ROLL: UTILITY

Source: *Meat Price Report.* **Price Frequency:** weekly. **Units of Measure:** cents per lb. **Type of Price:** price paid to wholesaler. **Time Period Covered:** latest week.

BEEF CHUCK STEAK: CHOICE, BONE IN

Source: *Livestock and Poultry Situation and Outlook Report.* **Price Frequency:** monthly. **Units of Measure:** Dollars per lb. **Type of Price:** retail. **Time Period Covered:** latest 3 years.

BEEF COW CARCASS: DRESSED, BONING

Source: *Livestock, Meat, Wool Market News.* **Price Frequency:** weekly, seasonally. **Effective Market(s):** East Coast, Central United States, California. **Units of Measure:** Dollars per 100 lbs. **Type of Price:** wholesale. **Time Period Covered:** latest week, year ago.

BEEF COW CARCASS: DRESSED, CANNER AND CUTTER

Source: *Livestock, Meat, Wool Market News.* **Price Frequency:** weekly, seasonally. **Effective Market(s):** East Coast, Central United States, California. **Units of Measure:** Dollars per 100 lbs. **Type of Price:** wholesale. **Time Period Covered:** latest week, year ago.

BEEF COW CARCASS: DRESSED, UTILITY AND BREAKING

Source: *Livestock, Meat, Wool Market News.* **Price Frequency:** weekly, seasonally. **Effective Market(s):** East Coast, Central United States, California. **Units of Measure:** Dollars per 100 lbs. **Type of Price:** wholesale. **Time Period Covered:** latest week, year ago.

BEEF CUBED STEAKS: CHOICE

Source: *Meat Price Report.* **Price Frequency:** weekly. **Units of Measure:** cents per lb. **Type of Price:** price paid to wholesaler. **Time Period Covered:** latest week.

BEEF CUBED STEAKS: CHOICE, SPECIAL

Source: *Meat Price Report.* **Price Frequency:** weekly. **Units of Measure:** cents per lb. **Type of Price:** price paid to wholesaler. **Time Period Covered:** latest week.

BEEF DIAMOND LOIN: CHOICE

Source: *National Provisioner.* **Price Frequency:** daily. **Units of Measure:** cents per lb. **Time Period Covered:** latest week.

BEEF DIAMOND LOIN: CHOICE 2-3

Source: *Livestock, Meat, Wool Market News.* **Price Frequency:** weekly, seasonally. **Effective Market(s):** Central United States, California. **Units of Measure:** Dollars per 100 lbs. **Type of Price:** average. **Time Period Covered:** latest week, year ago.

BEEF FEET: FROZEN

Source: *Livestock, Meat, Wool Market News.* **Price Frequency:** weekly, seasonally. **Effective Market(s):** Central United States. **Units of Measure:** Dollars per 100 lbs. **Time Period Covered:** latest week.

BEEF FLANK: CHOICE 3

Source: *Livestock, Meat, Wool Market News.* **Price Frequency:** weekly, seasonally. **Effective Market(s):** East Coast, Central United States, California. **Units of Measure:** Dollars per 100 lbs. **Type of Price:** wholesale. **Time Period Covered:** latest week, year ago.

BEEF FLANK STEAK: CHOICE

Source: *National Provisioner.* **Price Frequency:** daily. **Units of Measure:** cents per lb. **Time Period Covered:** latest week.

BEEF FLANK STEAK: CHOICE 2-3

Source: *Livestock, Meat, Wool Market News.* **Price Frequency:** weekly, seasonally. **Effective Market(s):** Central United States, California. **Units of Measure:** Dollars per 100 lbs. **Type of Price:** average. **Time Period Covered:** latest week, year ago.

BEEF FLANK STEAK: CHOICE, SKINNED

Source: *Meat Price Report.* **Price Frequency:** weekly. **Units of Measure:** cents per lb. **Type of Price:** price paid to wholesaler. **Time Period Covered:** latest week.

BEEF FLANK STEAK: CHOICE, SQUARED, SKINNED, PEELED

Source: *HRI-Buyer's Guide.* **Price Frequency:** weekly. **Effective Market(s):** Northeastern area. **Units of Measure:** Dollars per lb. **Type of Price:** price paid by dining places & institutions. **Time Period Covered:** latest week.

BEEF FLANK STEAK: PRIME, SKINNED

Source: *Meat Price Report.* **Price Frequency:** weekly. **Units of Measure:** cents per lb. **Type of Price:** price paid to wholesaler . **Time Period Covered:** latest week.

BEEF FLANK STEAK: SELECT, SQUARED, SKINNED, PEELED

Source: *HRI-Buyer's Guide.* **Price Frequency:** weekly. **Effective Market(s):** Northeastern area. **Units of Measure:** Dollars per lb. **Type of Price:** price paid by dining places & institutions. **Time Period Covered:** latest week.

BEEF FOR STEWING: CHOICE

Source: *HRI-Buyer's Guide.* **Price Frequency:** weekly. **Effective Market(s):** Northeastern area. **Units of Measure:** Dollars per lb. **Type of Price:** price paid by dining places & institutions. **Time Period Covered:** latest week.

BEEF FOR STEWING: CHOICE, LEAN

Source: *Meat Price Report.* **Price Frequency:** weekly. **Units of Measure:** cents per lb. **Type of Price:** price paid to wholesaler. **Time Period Covered:** latest week.

BEEF FOR STEWING: SELECT

Source: *HRI-Buyer's Guide.* **Price Frequency:** weekly. **Effective Market(s):** Northeastern area. **Units of Measure:** Dollars per lb. **Type of Price:** price paid by dining places & institutions. **Time Period Covered:** latest week.

BEEF FORE: STEER, CHOICE, YIELD 3

Source: *National Provisioner.* **Price Frequency:** daily. **Effective Market(s):** Midwest River area. **Units of Measure:** cents per lb. **Time Period Covered:** latest week.

BEEF FOREQUARTER: CHOICE 3

Source: *Livestock, Meat, Wool Market News.* **Price Frequency:** weekly, seasonally. **Effective Market(s):** East Coast, Central United States, California. **Units of Measure:** Dollars per 100 lbs. **Type of Price:** wholesale. **Time Period Covered:** latest week, year ago.

BEEF FORES: ENGLISH

Source: *Farmers Weekly.* **Price Frequency:** weekly. **Effective Market(s):** Great Britain. **Units of Measure:** British pence per lb. **Time Period Covered:** latest week.

BEEF FULL LOIN: CHOICE, TRIMMED

Source: *Meat Price Report.* **Price Frequency:** weekly. **Units of Measure:** cents per lb. **Type of Price:** price paid to wholesaler. **Time Period Covered:** latest week.

BEEF FULL LOIN: PRIME, TRIMMED

Source: *Meat Price Report.* **Price Frequency:** weekly. **Units of Measure:** cents per lb. **Type of Price:** price paid to wholesaler . **Time Period Covered:** latest week.

BEEF FULL PLATES: NO. 1

Source: *National Provisioner.* **Price Frequency:** daily. **Effective Market(s):** Midwest River area. **Units of Measure:** cents per lb. **Time Period Covered:** latest week.

BEEF FULL TENDERLOIN: CHOICE 2-3

Source: *Livestock, Meat, Wool Market News.* **Price Frequency:** weekly, seasonally. **Effective Market(s):** Central United States, California. **Units of Measure:** Dollars per 100 lbs. **Type of Price:** average. **Time Period Covered:** latest week, year ago.

BEEF FULL TENDERLOIN: CHOICE, 7/DOWN

Source: *Meat Price Report.* **Price Frequency:** weekly. **Units of Measure:** cents per lb. **Type of Price:** price paid to wholesaler. **Time Period Covered:** latest week.

BEEF FULL TENDERLOIN: CHOICE, 7/UP

Source: *Meat Price Report.* **Price Frequency:** weekly. **Units of Measure:** cents per lb. **Type of Price:** price paid to wholesaler. **Time Period Covered:** latest week.

BEEF FULL TENDERLOIN: CHOICE, DEFATTED, SIDE MUSCLE ON

Source: *Meat Price Report.* **Price Frequency:** weekly. **Units of Measure:** cents per lb. **Type of Price:** price paid to wholesaler. **Time Period Covered:** latest week.

BEEF FULL TENDERLOIN: CHOICE, SKINNED

Source: *Meat Price Report.* **Price Frequency:** weekly. **Units of Measure:** cents per lb. **Type of Price:** price paid to wholesaler. **Time Period Covered:** latest week.

BEEF FULL TENDERLOIN: CHOICE, SPECIAL, SIDE MUSCLE OFF

Source: *Meat Price Report.* **Price Frequency:** weekly. **Units of Measure:** cents per lb. **Type of Price:** price paid to wholesaler. **Time Period Covered:** latest week.

BEEF FULL TENDERLOIN: PRIME, 7/DOWN

Source: *Meat Price Report.* **Price Frequency:** weekly. **Units of Measure:** cents per lb. **Type of Price:** price paid to wholesaler. **Time Period Covered:** latest week.

BEEF FULL TENDERLOIN: PRIME, 7/UP

Source: *Meat Price Report.* **Price Frequency:** weekly. **Units of Measure:** cents per lb. **Type of Price:** price paid to wholesaler. **Time Period Covered:** latest week.

BEEF FULL TENDERLOIN: PRIME, DEFATTED, SIDE MUSCLE ON

Source: *Meat Price Report.* **Price Frequency:** weekly. **Units of Measure:** cents per lb. **Type of Price:** price paid to wholesaler. **Time Period Covered:** latest week.

BEEF FULL TENDERLOIN: UTILITY, 7/DOWN

Source: *Meat Price Report.* **Price Frequency:** weekly. **Units of Measure:** cents per lb. **Type of Price:** price paid to wholesaler. **Time Period Covered:** latest week.

BEEF FULL TENDERLOIN: UTILITY, 7/UP

Source: *Meat Price Report.* **Price Frequency:** weekly. **Units of Measure:** cents per lb. **Type of Price:** price paid to wholesaler. **Time Period Covered:** latest week.

BEEF FULL TENDERLOIN: UTILITY, DEFATTED, SIDE MUSCLE ON

Source: *Meat Price Report.* **Price Frequency:** weekly. **Units of Measure:** cents per lb. **Type of Price:** price paid to wholesaler. **Time Period Covered:** latest week.

BEEF FULL TENDERLOIN: UTILITY, SKINNED

Source: *Meat Price Report.* **Price Frequency:** weekly. **Units of Measure:** cents per lb. **Type of Price:** price paid to wholesaler. **Time Period Covered:** latest week.

BEEF FULL TENDERLOIN: UTILITY, SPECIAL, SIDE MUSCLE OFF

Source: *Meat Price Report.* **Price Frequency:** weekly. **Units of Measure:** cents per lb. **Type of Price:** price paid to wholesaler. **Time Period Covered:** latest week.

BEEF GOOSENECK: CHOICE

Source: *National Provisioner.* **Price Frequency:** daily. **Units of Measure:** cents per lb. **Time Period Covered:** latest week.

BEEF HEAD MEAT: FROZEN

Source: *Livestock, Meat, Wool Market News.* **Price Frequency:** weekly, seasonally. **Effective Market(s):** Central United States. **Units of Measure:** Dollars per 100 lbs. **Time Period Covered:** latest week.

BEEF HEARTS: BONE OUT

Source: *National Provisioner.* **Price Frequency:** daily. **Effective Market(s):** Midwest River area. **Units of Measure:** cents per lb. **Time Period Covered:** latest week.

BEEF HEARTS: REGULAR, BONE OUT, FROZEN

Source: *Livestock, Meat, Wool Market News.* **Price Frequency:** weekly, seasonally. **Effective Market(s):** Central United States. **Units of Measure:** Dollars per 100 lbs. **Time Period Covered:** latest week.

BEEF HIDE AND OFFAL

Source: *Livestock and Poultry Update.* **Price Frequency:** monthly. **Effective Market(s):** Central United States. **Units of Measure:** Dollars per 100 lbs. **Type of Price:** wholesale. **Time Period Covered:** latest 3 months, year ago.

BEEF HIND: HEIFER, CHOICE 3

Source: *Livestock, Meat, Wool Market News.* **Price Frequency:** weekly, seasonally. **Effective Market(s):** East Coast, Central United States, California. **Units of Measure:** Dollars per 100 lbs. **Type of Price:** wholesale. **Time Period Covered:** latest week, year ago.

BEEF HIND: STEER, CHOICE 3

Source: *Livestock, Meat, Wool Market News.* **Price Frequency:** weekly, seasonally. **Effective Market(s):** East Coast, Central United States, California. **Units of Measure:** Dollars per 100 lbs. **Type of Price:** wholesale. **Time Period Covered:** latest week, year ago.

BEEF HIND: STEER, CHOICE, YIELD 3

Source: *National Provisioner.* **Price Frequency:** daily. **Effective Market(s):** Midwest River area. **Units of Measure:** cents per lb. **Time Period Covered:** latest week.

BEEF HINDS: ENGLISH

Source: *Farmers Weekly.* **Price Frequency:** weekly. **Effective Market(s):** Great Britain. **Units of Measure:** British pence per lb. **Time Period Covered:** latest week.

BEEF HINDS: IRISH REPUBLIC

Source: *Meat and Dairy Products.* **Price Frequency:** monthly. **Effective Market(s):** London. **Units of Measure:** British pence per lb. **Type of Price:** average. **Time Period Covered:** latest 4 years.

BEEF INSIDE ROUND: COOKED

Source: *Meat Price Report.* **Price Frequency:** weekly. **Units of Measure:** cents per lb. **Type of Price:** price paid to wholesaler. **Time Period Covered:** latest week.

BEEF INSIDE ROUND: CORNED

Source: *Meat Price Report.* **Price Frequency:** weekly. **Units of Measure:** cents per lb. **Type of Price:** price paid to wholesaler. **Time Period Covered:** latest week.

BEEF KIDNEYS

Source: *National Provisioner.* **Price Frequency:** daily. **Effective Market(s):** Midwest River area. **Units of Measure:** cents per lb. **Time Period Covered:** latest week.

BEEF KIDNEYS: FROZEN

Source: *Livestock, Meat, Wool Market News.* **Price Frequency:** weekly, seasonally. **Effective Market(s):** Central United States. **Units of Measure:** Dollars per 100 lbs. **Time Period Covered:** latest week.

BEEF KIDNEYS FOR PET FOOD: INEDIBLE

Source: *Livestock, Meat, Wool Market News.* **Price Frequency:** weekly, seasonally. **Effective Market(s):** Central United States. **Units of Measure:** Dollars per 100 lbs. **Time Period Covered:** latest week.

BEEF KNUCKLE: CHOICE

Source: *Meat Price Report.* **Price Frequency:** weekly. **Units of Measure:** cents per lb. **Type of Price:** price paid to wholesaler. **Time Period Covered:** latest week.

Source: *National Provisioner.* **Price Frequency:** daily. **Units of Measure:** cents per lb. **Time Period Covered:** latest week.

BEEF KNUCKLE: CHOICE 2-3

Source: *Livestock, Meat, Wool Market News.* **Price Frequency:** weekly, seasonally. **Effective Market(s):** Central United States, California. **Units of Measure:** Dollars per 100 lbs. **Type of Price:** average. **Time Period Covered:** latest week, year ago.

BEEF KNUCKLE: CHOICE, SPECIAL

Source: *Meat Price Report.* **Price Frequency:** weekly. **Units of Measure:** cents per lb. **Type of Price:** price paid to wholesaler. **Time Period Covered:** latest week.

BEEF KNUCKLES SIRLOIN STRIP: SELECT, BONELESS

Source: *HRI-Buyer's Guide.* **Price Frequency:** weekly. **Effective Market(s):** Northeastern area. **Units of Measure:** Dollars per lb. **Type of Price:** price paid by dining places & institutions. **Time Period Covered:** latest week.

BEEF KNUCKLES SIRLOIN TIP: CHOICE, BONELESS

Source: *HRI-Buyer's Guide.* **Price Frequency:** weekly. **Effective Market(s):** Northeastern area. **Units of Measure:** Dollars per lb. **Type of Price:** price paid by dining places & institutions. **Time Period Covered:** latest week.

BEEF LIPS: UNSCALDED, FROZEN

Source: *Livestock, Meat, Wool Market News.* **Price Frequency:** weekly, seasonally. **Effective Market(s):** Central United States. **Units of Measure:** Dollars per 100 lbs. **Time Period Covered:** latest week.

BEEF LIVERS

Source: *Meat Price Report.* **Price Frequency:** weekly. **Units of Measure:** cents per lb. **Type of Price:** price paid to wholesaler. **Time Period Covered:** latest week.

BEEF LIVERS: PORTION CUT, FROZEN

Source: *Meat Price Report.* **Price Frequency:** weekly. **Units of Measure:** cents per lb. **Type of Price:** price paid to wholesaler. **Time Period Covered:** latest week.

BEEF LIVERS: REGULAR

Source: *National Provisioner.* **Price Frequency:** daily. **Effective Market(s):** Midwest River area. **Units of Measure:** cents per lb. **Time Period Covered:** latest week.

BEEF LIVERS: REGULAR, FROZEN

Source: *Livestock, Meat, Wool Market News.* **Price Frequency:** weekly, seasonally. **Effective Market(s):** Central United States. **Units of Measure:** Dollars per 100 lbs. **Time Period Covered:** latest week.

BEEF LIVERS: SELECTED, FROZEN

Source: *Livestock, Meat, Wool Market News.* **Price Frequency:** weekly, seasonally. **Effective Market(s):** Central United States. **Units of Measure:** Dollars per 100 lbs. **Time Period Covered:** latest week.

BEEF LIVERS: SLICED, FROZEN

Source: *Meat Price Report.* **Price Frequency:** weekly. **Units of Measure:** cents per lb. **Type of Price:** price paid to wholesaler. **Time Period Covered:** latest week.

BEEF LIVERS: STEER, WHOLE

Source: *HRI-Buyer's Guide.* **Price Frequency:** weekly. **Effective Market(s):** Northeastern area. **Units of Measure:** Dollars per lb. **Type of Price:** price paid by dining places & institutions. **Time Period Covered:** latest week.

BEEF LIVERS FOR PET FOOD: INEDIBLE

Source: *Livestock, Meat, Wool Market News.* **Price Frequency:** weekly, seasonally. **Effective Market(s):** Central United States. **Units of Measure:** Dollars per 100 lbs. **Time Period Covered:** latest week.

BEEF LOIN: CHOICE 3

Source: *Livestock, Meat, Wool Market News.* **Price Frequency:** weekly, seasonally. **Effective Market(s):** East Coast, Central United States, California. **Units of Measure:** Dollars per 100 lbs. **Type of Price:** wholesale. **Time Period Covered:** latest week, year ago.

BEEF LOIN: UNITED STATES

Source: *Japan Economic Journal.* **Price Frequency:** weekly. **Effective Market(s):** Japan. **Units of Measure:** Japanese yen per kilogram. **Type of Price:** wholesale. **Time Period Covered:** latest 2 weeks.

BEEF LUNGS FOR PET FOOD: INEDIBLE

Source: *Livestock, Meat, Wool Market News.* **Price Frequency:** weekly, seasonally. **Effective Market(s):** Central United States. **Units of Measure:** Dollars per 100 lbs. **Time Period Covered:** latest week.

BEEF MELTS FOR PET FOOD

Source: *Livestock, Meat, Wool Market News.* **Price Frequency:** weekly, seasonally. **Effective Market(s):** Central United States. **Units of Measure:** Dollars per 100 lbs. **Time Period Covered:** latest week.

BEEF OUTSIDE ROUND: CHOICE

Source: *Meat Price Report.* **Price Frequency:** weekly. **Units of Measure:** cents per lb. **Type of Price:** price paid to wholesaler. **Time Period Covered:** latest week.

BEEF OUTSIDE ROUND: COOKED

Source: *Meat Price Report.* **Price Frequency:** weekly. **Units of Measure:** cents per lb. **Type of Price:** price paid to wholesaler. **Time Period Covered:** latest week.

BEEF OUTSIDE ROUND: CORNED

Source: *Meat Price Report.* **Price Frequency:** weekly. **Units of Measure:** cents per lb. **Type of Price:** price paid to wholesaler. **Time Period Covered:** latest week.

BEEF OUTSIDE ROUND: UTILITY

Source: *Meat Price Report.* **Price Frequency:** weekly. **Units of Measure:** cents per lb. **Type of Price:** price paid to wholesaler. **Time Period Covered:** latest week.

BEEF PATTIES: CHOICE, GROUND, REGULAR, 75% LEAN

Source: *Meat Price Report.* **Price Frequency:** weekly. **Units of Measure:** cents per lb. **Type of Price:** price paid to wholesaler. **Time Period Covered:** latest week.

BEEF PATTIES: CHOICE, GROUND, REGULAR, TVP ADDED

Source: *Meat Price Report.* **Price Frequency:** weekly. **Units of Measure:** cents per lb. **Type of Price:** price paid to wholesaler. **Time Period Covered:** latest week.

BEEF PATTIES: CHOICE, GROUND, SPECIAL, 80% LEAN

Source: *Meat Price Report.* **Price Frequency:** weekly. **Units of Measure:** cents per lb. **Type of Price:** price paid to wholesaler. **Time Period Covered:** latest week.

BEEF PATTIES: GROUND, REGULAR

Source: *HRI-Buyer's Guide.* **Price Frequency:** weekly . **Effective Market(s):** Northeastern area. **Units of Measure:** Dollars per lb. **Type of Price:** price paid by dining places & institutions. **Time Period Covered:** latest week.

BEEF PATTIES: GROUND, SPECIAL, 80% LEAN

Source: *HRI-Buyer's Ghide.* **Price Frequency:** weekly. **Effective Market(s):** Northeastern area. **Units of Measure:** Dollars per lb. **Type of Price:** price paid by dining places & institutions. **Time Period Covered:** latest week.

BEEF PORTERHOUSE STEAK: CHOICE

Source: *Meat Price Report.* **Price Frequency:** weekly. **Units of Measure:** cents per lb. **Type of Price:** price paid to wholesaler. **Time Period Covered:** latest week.

BEEF PORTERHOUSE STEAK: CHOICE, BONE IN

Source: *Livestock and Poultry Situation and Outlook Report.* **Price Frequency:** monthly. **Units of Measure:** Dollars per lb. **Type of Price:** retail. **Time Period Covered:** latest 3 years.

BEEF PORTERHOUSE STEAK: PRIME

Source: *Meat Price Report.* **Price Frequency:** weekly. **Units of Measure:** cents per lb. **Type of Price:** price paid to wholesaler. **Time Period Covered:** latest week.

BEEF RIB: CHOICE

Source: *National Provisioner.* **Price Frequency:** daily. **Units of Measure:** cents per lb. **Time Period Covered:** latest week.

BEEF RIB: CHOICE 2-3

Source: *Livestock, Meat, Wool Market News.* **Price Frequency:** weekly, seasonally. **Effective Market(s):** Central United States, California. **Units of Measure:** Dollars per 100 lbs. **Type of Price:** average. **Time Period Covered:** latest week, year ago.

BEEF RIB: CHOICE 2-3, ROAST READY

Source: *Livestock, Meat, Wool Market News.* **Price Frequency:** weekly, seasonally. **Effective Market(s):** Central United States, California. **Units of Measure:** Dollars per 100 lbs. **Type of Price:** average. **Time Period Covered:** latest week, year ago.

BEEF RIB: CHOICE 3

Source: *Livestock, Meat, Wool Market News.* **Price Frequency:** weekly, seasonally. **Effective Market(s):** East Coast, Central United States, California. **Units of Measure:** Dollars per 100 lbs. **Type of Price:** wholesale. **Time Period Covered:** latest week, year ago.

BEEF RIB: CHOICE, 25/30

Source: *National Provisioner.* **Price Frequency:** daily. **Effective Market(s):** Midwest River area. **Units of Measure:** cents per lb. **Time Period Covered:** latest week.

BEEF RIB: CHOICE, 30/35

Source: *National Provisioner.* **Price Frequency:** daily. **Effective Market(s):** Midwest River area. **Units of Measure:** cents per lb. **Time Period Covered:** latest week.

BEEF RIB: CHOICE, OVEN PREPARED

Source: *HRI-Buyer's Guide.* **Price Frequency:** weekly. **Effective Market(s):** Northeastern area. **Units of Measure:** Dollars per lb. **Type of Price:** price paid by dining places & institutions. **Time Period Covered:** latest week.

Source: *Meat Price Report.* **Price Frequency:** weekly. **Units of Measure:** cents per lb. **Type of Price:** price paid to wholesaler. **Time Period Covered:** latest week.

BEEF RIB: CHOICE, PRIMAL

Source: *Meat Price Report.* **Price Frequency:** weekly. **Units of Measure:** cents per lb. **Type of Price:** price paid to wholesaler. **Time Period Covered:** latest week.

BEEF RIB: CHOICE, ROAST READY

Source: *HRI-Buyer's Guide.* **Price Frequency:** weekly. **Effective Market(s):** Northeastern area. **Units of Measure:** Dollars per lb. **Type of Price:** price paid by dining places & institutions. **Time Period Covered:** latest week.

BEEF RIB: CHOICE, ROAST READY, 18/DOWN

Source: *Meat Price Report.* **Price Frequency:** weekly. **Units of Measure:** cents per lb. **Type of Price:** price paid to wholesaler. **Time Period Covered:** latest week.

BEEF RIB: CHOICE, ROAST READY, 18/UP

Source: *Meat Price Report.* **Price Frequency:** weekly. **Units of Measure:** cents per lb. **Type of Price:** price paid to wholesaler. **Time Period Covered:** latest week.

BEEF RIB: PRIME, OVEN PREPARED

Source: *HRI-Buyer's Guide.* **Price Frequency:** weekly. **Effective Market(s):** Northeastern area. **Units of Measure:** Dollars per lb. **Type of Price:** price paid by dining places & institutions. **Time Period Covered:** latest week.

Source: *Meat Price Report.* **Price Frequency:** weekly. **Units of Measure:** cents per lb. **Type of Price:** price paid to wholesaler. **Time Period Covered:** latest week.

BEEF RIB: PRIME, PRIMAL

Source: *Meat Price Report.* **Price Frequency:** weekly. **Units of Measure:** cents per lb. **Type of Price:** price paid to wholesaler. **Time Period Covered:** latest week.

BEEF RIB: PRIME, ROAST READY

Source: *HRI-Buyer's Guide.* **Price Frequency:** weekly. **Effective Market(s):** Northeastern area. **Units of Measure:** Dollars per lb. **Type of Price:** price paid by dining places & institutions. **Time Period Covered:** latest week.

BEEF RIB: PRIME, ROAST READY, 18/DOWN

Source: *Meat Price Report.* **Price Frequency:** weekly. **Units of Measure:** cents per lb. **Type of Price:** price paid to wholesaler. **Time Period Covered:** latest week.

BEEF RIB: PRIME, ROAST READY, 18/UP

Source: *Meat Price Report.* **Price Frequency:** weekly. **Units of Measure:** cents per lb. **Type of Price:** price paid to wholesaler. **Time Period Covered:** latest week.

BEEF RIB: SELECT, OVEN PREPARED

Source: *HRI-Buyer's Guide.* **Price Frequency:** weekly. **Effective Market(s):** Northeastern area. **Units of Measure:** Dollars per lb. **Type of Price:** price paid by dining places & institutions. **Time Period Covered:** latest week.

BEEF RIB: SELECT, ROAST READY

Source: *HRI-Buyer's Guide.* **Price Frequency:** weekly. **Effective Market(s):** Northeastern area. **Units of Measure:** Dollars per lb. **Type of Price:** price paid by dining places & institutions. **Time Period Covered:** latest week.

BEEF RIB: UTILITY, PRIMAL

Source: *Meat Price Report.* **Price Frequency:** weekly. **Units of Measure:** cents per lb. **Type of Price:** pirce paid to wholesaler. **Time Period Covered:** latest week.

BEEF RIB ROAST

Source: *Livestock and Poultry Update.* **Price Frequency:** monthly. **Units of Measure:** cents per lb. **Type of Price:** retail. **Time Period Covered:** latest 3 months, year ago.

BEEF RIB ROAST: CHOICE

Source: *National Provisioner.* **Price Frequency:** daily. **Units of Measure:** cents per lb. **Time Period Covered:** latest week.

BEEF RIB ROAST: CHOICE, BONE IN

Source: *Livestock and Poultry Situation and Outlook Report.* **Price Frequency:** monthly. **Units of Measure:** Dollars per lb. **Type of Price:** retail. **Time Period Covered:** latest 3 years.

BEEF RIB ROLL: CHOICE 2-3

Source: *Livestock, Meat, Wool Market News.* **Price Frequency:** weekly, seasonally. **Effective Market(s):** Central United States, California. **Units of Measure:** Dollars per 100 lbs. **Type of Price:** average. **Time Period Covered:** latest week, year ago.

BEEF RIB STEAK: CHOICE, BONELESS

Source: *Meat Price Report.* **Price Frequency:** weekly. **Units of Measure:** cents per lb. **Type of Price:** price paid to wholesaler. **Time Period Covered:** latest week.

BEEF RIBEYE: CHOICE

Source: *National Provisioner.* **Price Frequency:** daily. **Units of Measure:** cents per lb. **Time Period Covered:** latest week.

BEEF RIBEYE ROLL: CHOICE, BONELESS, LIP ON

Source: *HRI-Buyer's Guide.* **Price Frequency:** weekly. **Effective Market(s):** Northeastern area. **Units of Measure:** Dollars per lb. **Type of Price:** price paid by dining places & institutions. **Time Period Covered:** latest week.

BEEF RIBEYE ROLL: CHOICE, LIP OFF

Source: *Meat Price Report.* **Price Frequency:** weekly. **Units of Measure:** cents per lb. **Type of Price:** price paid to wholesaler. **Time Period Covered:** latest week.

BEEF RIBEYE ROLL: CHOICE, LIP ON

Source: *Meat Price Report.* **Price Frequency:** weekly. **Units of Measure:** cents per lb. **Type of Price:** price paid to wholesaler. **Time Period Covered:** latest week.

BEEF RIBEYE ROLL: PRIME, BONELESS, LIP ON

Source: *HRI-Buyer's Guide.* **Price Frequency:** weekly. **Effective Market(s):** Northeastern area. **Units of Measure:** Dollars per lb. **Type of Price:** price paid by dining places & institutions. **Time Period Covered:** latest week.

BEEF RIBEYE ROLL: PRIME, LIP OFF

Source: *Meat Price Report.* **Price Frequency:** weekly. **Units of Measure:** cents per lb. **Type of Price:** price paid to wholesaler. **Time Period Covered:** latest week.

BEEF RIBEYE ROLL: PRIME, LIP ON

Source: *Meat Price Report.* **Price Frequency:** weekly. **Units of Measure:** cents per lb. **Type of Price:** price paid to wholesaler. **Time Period Covered:** latest week.

BEEF RIBEYE ROLL: PRIME, LIP ON STEAKS

Source: *Meat Price Report.* **Price Frequency:** weekly. **Units of Measure:** cents per lb. **Type of Price:** price paid to wholesaler. **Time Period Covered:** latest week.

BEEF RIBEYE ROLL: SELECT, BONELESS, LIP ON

Source: *HRI-Buyer's Guide.* **Price Frequency:** weekly. **Effective Market(s):** Northeastern area. **Units of Measure:** Dollars per lb. **Type of Price:** price paid by dining places & institutions. **Time Period Covered:** latest week.

BEEF RIBEYE ROLL: UTILITY, LIP OFF

Source: *Meat Price Report.* **Price Frequency:** weekly. **Units of Measure:** cents per lb. **Type of Price:** price paid to wholesaler. **Time Period Covered:** latest week.

BEEF RIBEYE ROLL STEAK: CHOICE

Source: *Meat Price Report.* **Price Frequency:** weekly. **Units of Measure:** cents per lb. **Type of Price:** price paid to wholesaler. **Time Period Covered:** latest week.

BEEF RIBEYE ROLL STEAK: CHOICE, LIP ON

Source: *Meat Price Report.* **Price Frequency:** weekly. **Units of Measure:** cents per lb. **Type of Price:** price paid to wholesaler. **Time Period Covered:** latest week.

BEEF RIBEYE ROLL STEAK: PRIME

Source: *Meat Price Report.* **Price Frequency:** weekly. **Units of Measure:** cents per lb. **Type of Price:** price paid to wholesaler. **Time Period Covered:** latest week.

BEEF RIBEYE ROLL STEAK: UTILITY

Source: *Meat Price Report.* **Price Frequency:** weekly. **Units of Measure:** cents per lb. **Type of Price:** price paid to wholesaler. **Time Period Covered:** latest week.

BEEF ROUGH FLANKS: NO. 1

Source: *National Provisioner.* **Price Frequency:** daily. **Effective Market(s):** Midwest River area. **Units of Measure:** cents per lb. **Time Period Covered:** latest week.

BEEF ROUND: CHOICE

Source: *National Provisioner.* **Price Frequency:** daily. **Units of Measure:** cents per lb. **Time Period Covered:** latest week.

BEEF ROUND: CHOICE 2-3

Source: *Livestock, Meat, Wool Market News.* **Price Frequency:** weekly, seasonally. **Effective Market(s):** Central United States, California. **Units of Measure:** Dollars per 100 lbs. **Type of Price:** average. **Time Period Covered:** latest week, year ago.

BEEF ROUND: CHOICE, PRIMAL

Source: *HRI-Buyer's Guide.* **Price Frequency:** weekly. **Effective Market(s):** Northeastern area. **Units of Measure:** Dollars per lb. **Type of Price:** price paid by dining places & institutions. **Time Period Covered:** latest week.

Source: *Meat Price Report.* **Price Frequency:** weekly. **Units of Measure:** cents per lb. **Type of Price:** price paid to wholesaler. **Time Period Covered:** latest week.

BEEF ROUND: CHOICE, RUMP AND SHANK OFF

Source: *Meat Price Report.* **Price Frequency:** weekly. **Units of Measure:** cents per lb. **Type of Price:** price paid to wholesaler. **Time Period Covered:** latest week.

BEEF ROUND: CHOICE, RUMP AND SHANK OFF, BONELESS

Source: *Meat Price Report.* **Price Frequency:** weekly. **Units of Measure:** cents per lb. **Type of Price:** price paid to wholesaler. **Time Period Covered:** latest week.

BEEF ROUND: HEIFER, CHOICE 3

Source: *Livestock, Meat, Wool Market News.* **Price Frequency:** weekly, seasonally. **Effective Market(s):** East Coast, Central United States, California. **Units of Measure:** Dollars per 100 lbs. **Type of Price:** wholesale. **Time Period Covered:** latest week, year ago.

BEEF ROUND: PRIME, PRIMAL

Source: *HRI-Buyer's Guide.* **Price Frequency:** weekly. **Effective Market(s):** Northeastern area. **Units of Measure:** Dollars per lb. **Type of Price:** price paid by dining places & institutions. **Time Period Covered:** latest week.

Source: *Meat Price Report.* **Price Frequency:** weekly. **Units of Measure:** cents per lb. **Type of Price:** price paid to wholesaler. **Time Period Covered:** latest week.

BEEF ROUND: PRIME, RUMP AND SHANK OFF

Source: *Meat Price Report.* **Price Frequency:** weekly. **Units of Measure:** cents per lb. **Type of Price:** price paid to wholesaler. **Time Period Covered:** latest week.

BEEF ROUND: PRIME, RUMP AND SHANK OFF, BONELESS

Source: *Meat Price Report.* **Price Frequency:** weekly. **Units of Measure:** cents per lb. **Type of Price:** price paid to wholesaler. **Time Period Covered:** latest week.

BEEF ROUND: SELECT, PRIMAL

Source: *HRI-Buyer's Guide.* **Price Frequency:** weekly. **Effective Market(s):** Northeastern area. **Units of Measure:** Dollars per lb. **Type of Price:** price paid by dining places & institutions. **Time Period Covered:** latest week.

BEEF ROUND: STEER, CHOICE 3

Source: *Livestock, Meat, Wool Market News.* **Price Frequency:** weekly, seasonally. **Effective Market(s):** East Coast, Central United States, California. **Units of Measure:** Dollars per 100 lbs. **Type of Price:** wholesale. **Time Period Covered:** latest week, year ago.

BEEF ROUND: UTILITY, PRIMAL

Source: *Meat Price Report.* **Price Frequency:** weekly. **Units of Measure:** cents per lb. **Type of Price:** price paid to wholesaler. **Time Period Covered:** latest week.

BEEF ROUND: UTILITY, RUMP AND SHANK OFF, BONELESS

Source: *Meat Price Report.* **Price Frequency:** weekly. **Units of Measure:** cents per lb. **Type of Price:** price paid to wholesaler. **Time Period Covered:** latest week.

BEEF ROUND ROAST: CHOICE, BONELESS

Source: *Livestock and Poultry Situation and Outlook Report.* **Price Frequency:** monthly. **Units of Measure:** Dollars per lb. **Type of Price:** retail. **Time Period Covered:** latest 3 years.

BEEF ROUND STEAK: CHOICE, BONELESS

Source: *Livestock and Poultry Situation and Outlook Report.* **Price Frequency:** monthly. **Units of Measure:** Dollars per lb. **Type of Price:** retail. **Time Period Covered:** latest 3 years.

BEEF SHORT LOIN: CHOICE

Source: *Meat Price Report.* **Price Frequency:** weekly. **Units of Measure:** cents per lb. **Type of Price:** price paid to wholesaler. **Time Period Covered:** latest week.

Source: *National Provisioner.* **Price Frequency:** daily. **Units of Measure:** cents per lb. **Time Period Covered:** latest week.

BEEF SHORT LOIN: CHOICE, TRIMMED

Source: *HRI-Buyer's Guide.* **Price Frequency:** weekly. **Effective Market(s):** Northeastern area. **Units of Measure:** Dollars per lb. **Type of Price:** price paid by dining places & institutions. **Time Period Covered:** latest week.

BEEF SHORT LOIN: PRIME

Source: *HRI-Buyer's Guide.* **Price Frequency:** weekly. **Effective Market(s):** Northeastern area. **Units of Measure:** Dollars per lb. **Type of Price:** price paid by dining places & institutions. **Time Period Covered:** latest week.

Source: *Meat Price Report.* **Price Frequency:** weekly. **Units of Measure:** cents per lb. **Type of Price:** price paid to wholesaler. **Time Period Covered:** latest week.

BEEF SHORT LOIN: SELECT

Source: *HRI-Buyer's Guide.* **Price Frequency:** weekly. **Effective Market(s):** Northeastern area. **Units of Measure:** Dollars per lb. **Type of Price:** price paid by dining places & institutions. **Time Period Covered:** latest week.

BEEF SHORT LOIN: UTILITY

Source: *Meat Price Report.* **Price Frequency:** weekly. **Units of Measure:** cents per lb. **Type of Price:** price paid to wholesaler. **Time Period Covered:** latest week.

BEEF SHORT PLATES: CHOICE 3

Source: *Livestock, Meat, Wool Market News.* **Price Frequency:** weekly, seasonally. **Effective Market(s):** East Coast, Central United States, California. **Units of Measure:** Dollars per 100 lbs. **Type of Price:** wholesale. **Time Period Covered:** latest week, year ago.

BEEF SHORT RIBS: CHOICE

Source: *HRI-Buyer's Guide.* **Price Frequency:** weekly. **Effective Market(s):** Northeastern area. **Units of Measure:** Dollars per lb. **Type of Price:** price paid by dining places & institutions. **Time Period Covered:** latest week.

BEEF SHORT RIBS: CHOICE, REGULAR

Source: *Meat Price Report.* **Price Frequency:** weekly. **Units of Measure:** cents per lb. **Type of Price:** price paid to wholesaler. **Time Period Covered:** latest week.

BEEF SHORT RIBS: CHOICE, SHORT PLATE

Source: *Meat Price Report.* **Price Frequency:** weekly. **Units of Measure:** cents per lb. **Type of Price:** price paid to wholesaler. **Time Period Covered:** latest week.

BEEF SHORT RIBS: CHOICE, TRIMMED

Source: *HRI-Buyer's Guide.* **Price Frequency:** weekly. **Effective Market(s):** Northeastern area. **Units of Measure:** Dollars per lb. **Type of Price:** price paid by dining places & institutions. **Time Period Covered:** latest week.

BEEF SHORT RIBS: SELECT

Source: *HRI-Buyer's Guide.* **Price Frequency:** weekly. **Effective Market(s):** Northeastern area. **Units of Measure:** Dollars per lb. **Type of Price:** price paid by dining places & institutions. **Time Period Covered:** latest week.

BEEF SHORT RIBS: SELECT, TRIMMED

Source: *HRI-Buyer's Guide.* **Price Frequency:** weekly. **Effective Market(s):** Northeastern area. **Units of Measure:** Dollars per lb. **Type of Price:** price paid by dining places & institutions. **Time Period Covered:** latest week.

BEEF SHOULDER CLOD: CHOICE

Source: *Meat Price Report.* **Price Frequency:** weekly. **Units of Measure:** cents per lb. **Type of Price:** price paid to wholesaler. **Time Period Covered:** latest week.

Source: *National Provisioner.* **Price Frequency:** daily. **Units of Measure:** cents per lb. **Time Period Covered:** latest week.

BEEF SHOULDER CLOD: CHOICE 2-3

Source: *Livestock, Meat, Wool Market News.* **Price Frequency:** weekly, seasonally. **Effective Market(s):** Central United States, California. **Units of Measure:** Dollars per 100 lbs. **Type of Price:** average. **Time Period Covered:** latest week, year ago.

BEEF SHOULDER CLOD: CHOICE, BONELESS

Source: *HRI-Buyer's Guide.* **Price Frequency:** weekly. **Effective Market(s):** Northeastern area. **Units of Measure:** Dollars per lb. **Type of Price:** price paid by dining places & institutions. **Time Period Covered:** latest week.

BEEF SHOULDER CLOD: FRESH, BONELESS

Source: *National Provisioner.* **Price Frequency:** daily. **Effective Market(s):** Midwest River area. **Units of Measure:** cents per lb. **Time Period Covered:** latest week.

BEEF SHOULDER CLOD: SELECT, BONELESS

Source: *HRI-Buyer's Guide.* **Price Frequency:** weekly. **Effective Market(s):** Northeastern area. **Units of Measure:** Dollars per lb. **Type of Price:** price paid by dining places & institutions. **Time Period Covered:** latest week.

BEEF SHOULDER CLOD: UTILITY

Source: *Meat Price Report.* **Price Frequency:** weekly. **Units of Measure:** cents per lb. . **Type of Price:** price paid to wholesaler. **Time Period Covered:** latest week.

BEEF SIDES: SCOTCH

Source: *Meat and Dairy Products.* **Price Frequency:** monthly. **Effective Market(s):** London. **Units of Measure:** British pence per lb. **Type of Price:** average. **Time Period Covered:** latest 4 years.

BEEF SIDES: SCOTCH KILLED

Source: *Farmers Weekly.* **Price Frequency:** weekly. **Effective Market(s):** Great Britain. **Units of Measure:** British pence per lb. **Time Period Covered:** latest week.

BEEF SIRLOIN BUTT: CHOICE, BONELESS, TRIMMED

Source: *HRI-Buyer's Guide.* **Price Frequency:** weekly. **Effective Market(s):** Northeastern area. **Units of Measure:** Dollars per lb. **Type of Price:** price paid by dining places & institutions. **Time Period Covered:** latest week.

Source: *Meat Price Report.* **Price Frequency:** weekly. **Units of Measure:** cents per lb. **Type of Price:** price paid to wholesaler. **Time Period Covered:** latest week.

BEEF SIRLOIN BUTT: PRIME, BONELESS, TRIMMED

Source: *HRI-Buyer's Guide.* **Price Frequency:** weekly. **Effective Market(s):** Northeastern area. **Units of Measure:** Dollars per lb. **Type of Price:** price paid by dining places & institutions. **Time Period Covered:** latest week.

Source: *Meat Price Report.* **Price Frequency:** weekly. **Units of Measure:** cents per lb. **Type of Price:** price paid to wholesaler. **Time Period Covered:** latest week.

BEEF SIRLOIN BUTT: SELECT, BONELESS, TRIMMED

Source: *HRI-Buyer's Guide.* **Price Frequency:** weekly. **Effective Market(s):** Northeastern area. **Units of Measure:** Dollars per lb. **Type of Price:** price paid by dining places & institutions. **Time Period Covered:** latest week.

BEEF SIRLOIN BUTT: UTILITY, BONELESS, TRIMMED

Source: *Meat Price Report.* **Price Frequency:** weekly. **Units of Measure:** cents per lb. **Type of Price:** price paid to wholesaler. **Time Period Covered:** latest week.

BEEF SIRLOIN FLAP: CHOICE

Source: *National Provisioner.* **Price Frequency:** daily. **Units of Measure:** cents per lb. **Time Period Covered:** latest week.

BEEF SIRLOIN LOIN END: CHOICE

Source: *Meat Price Report.* **Price Frequency:** weekly. **Units of Measure:** cents per lb. **Type of Price:** price paid to wholesaler. **Time Period Covered:** latest week.

BEEF SIRLOIN LOIN END: PRIME

Source: *Meat Price Report.* **Price Frequency:** weekly. **Units of Measure:** cents per lb. **Type of Price:** price paid to wholesaler. **Time Period Covered:** latest week.

BEEF SIRLOIN STEAK: CHOICE, BONE IN

Source: *Livestock and Poultry Situation and Outlook Report.* **Price Frequency:** monthly. **Units of Measure:** Dollars per lb. **Type of Price:** retail. **Time Period Covered:** latest 3 years.

BEEF SKIRT STEAK: CHOICE

Source: *HRI-Buyer's Guide.* **Price Frequency:** weekly. **Effective Market(s):** Northeastern area. **Units of Measure:** Dollars per lb. **Type of Price:** price paid by dining places & institutions. **Time Period Covered:** latest week.

BEEF SKIRT STEAK: SELECT

Source: *HRI-Buyer's Guide.* **Price Frequency:** weekly. **Effective Market(s):** Northeastern area. **Units of Measure:** Dollars per lb. **Type of Price:** price paid by dining places & institutions. **Time Period Covered:** latest week.

BEEF SKIRTS: INSIDE, CHOICE

Source: *Meat Price Report.* **Price Frequency:** weekly. **Units of Measure:** cents per lb. **Type of Price:** price paid to wholesaler. **Time Period Covered:** latest week.

BEEF SKIRTS: OUTSIDE, CHOICE

Source: *Meat Price Report.* **Price Frequency:** weekly. **Units of Measure:** cents per lb. **Type of Price:** price paid to wholesaler. **Time Period Covered:** latest week.

BEEF SKIRTS: OUTSIDE, CHOICE, PEELED

Source: *Meat Price Report.* **Price Frequency:** weekly. **Units of Measure:** cents per lb. **Type of Price:** price paid to wholesaler. **Time Period Covered:** latest week.

BEEF SQUARE CUT CHUCK: CHOICE

Source: *Meat Price Report.* **Price Frequency:** weekly. **Units of Measure:** cents per lb. **Type of Price:** price paid to wholesaler. **Time Period Covered:** latest week.

BEEF SQUARE CUT CHUCK: CHOICE, BONELESS

Source: *HRI-Buyer's Guide.* **Price Frequency:** weekly. **Effective Market(s):** Northeastern area. **Units of Measure:** Dollars per lb. **Type of Price:** price paid by dining places & institutions. **Time Period Covered:** latest week.

Source: *Meat Price Report.* **Price Frequency:** weekly. **Units of Measure:** cents per lb. **Type of Price:** price paid to wholesaler. **Time Period Covered:** latest week.

BEEF SQUARE CUT CHUCK: SELECT, BONELESS

Source: *HRI-Buyer's Guide.* **Price Frequency:** weekly. **Effective Market(s):** Northeastern area. **Units of Measure:** Dollars per lb. **Type of Price:** price paid by dining places & institutions. **Time Period Covered:** latest week.

BEEF SQUARE CUT CHUCK: UTILITY

Source: *Meat Price Report.* **Price Frequency:** weekly. **Units of Measure:** cents per lb. **Type of Price:** price paid to wholesaler. **Time Period Covered:** latest week.

BEEF SQUARE CUT CHUCK: UTILITY, BONELESS

Source: *Meat Price Report.* **Price Frequency:** weekly. **Units of Measure:** cents per lb. **Type of Price:** price paid to wholesaler. **Time Period Covered:** latest week.

BEEF STEER CARCASS: CHOICE

Source: *Commodity Year Book.* **Price Frequency:** monthly, annually. **Effective Market(s):** Midwest. **Units of Measure:** cents per lb. **Type of Price:** wholesale. **Time Period Covered:** latest 9 years.

Source: *Commodity Year Book.* **Price Frequency:** annually. **Effective Market(s):** Central United States. **Units of Measure:** cents per lb. **Time Period Covered:** latest 7 years.

BEEF STRIP LOIN: CHOICE

Source: *National Provisioner.* **Price Frequency:** daily. **Units of Measure:** cents per lb. **Time Period Covered:** latest week.

BEEF STRIP LOIN: CHOICE 2-3

Source: *Livestock, Meat, Wool Market News.* **Price Frequency:** weekly, seasonally. **Effective Market(s):** Central United States, California. **Units of Measure:** Dollars per 100 lbs. **Type of Price:** average. **Time Period Covered:** latest week, year ago.

BEEF STRIP LOIN: CHOICE, 10″ CUT, BONE IN, REGULAR

Source: *Meat Price Report.* **Price Frequency:** weekly. **Units of Measure:** cents per lb. **Type of Price:** price paid to wholesaler. **Time Period Covered:** latest week.

BEEF STRIP LOIN: CHOICE, BONE IN

Source: *HRI-Buyer's Guide.* **Price Frequency:** weekly. **Effective Market(s):** Northeastern area. **Units of Measure:** Dollars per lb. **Type of Price:** price paid by dining places & institutions. **Time Period Covered:** latest week.

BEEF STRIP LOIN: CHOICE, BONELESS

Source: *HRI-Buyer's Guide.* **Price Frequency:** weekly. **Effective Market(s):** Northeastern area. **Units of Measure:** Dollars per lb. **Type of Price:** price paid by dining places & institutions. **Time Period Covered:** latest week.

BEEF STRIP LOIN: CHOICE, SHORT CUT, BONELESS, 12/DOWN

Source: *Meat Price Report.* **Price Frequency:** weekly. **Units of Measure:** cents per lb. **Type of Price:** price paid to wholesaler. **Time Period Covered:** latest week.

BEEF STRIP LOIN: CHOICE, SHORT CUT, BONELESS, 12/UP

Source: *Meat Price Report.* **Price Frequency:** weekly. **Units of Measure:** cents per lb. **Type of Price:** price paid to wholesaler. **Time Period Covered:** latest week.

BEEF STRIP LOIN: PRIME, 10″ CUT, BONE IN, REGULAR

Source: *Meat Price Report.* **Price Frequency:** weekly. **Units of Measure:** cents per lb. **Type of Price:** price paid to wholesaler. **Time Period Covered:** latest week.

BEEF STRIP LOIN: PRIME, BONE IN

Source: *HRI-Buyer's Guide.* **Price Frequency:** weekly. **Effective Market(s):** Northeastern area. **Units of Measure:** Dollars per lb. **Type of Price:** price paid by dining places & institutions. **Time Period Covered:** latest week.

BEEF STRIP LOIN: PRIME, BONELESS

Source: *HRI-Buyer's Guide.* **Price Frequency:** weekly. **Effective Market(s):** Northeastern area. **Units of Measure:** Dollars per lb. **Type of Price:** price paid by dining places & institutions. **Time Period Covered:** latest week.

BEEF STRIP LOIN: PRIME, SHORT CUT, BONELESS, 12/DOWN

Source: *Meat Price Report.* **Price Frequency:** weekly. **Units of Measure:** cents per lb. **Type of Price:** price paid to wholesaler. **Time Period Covered:** latest week.

BEEF STRIP LOIN: PRIME, SHORT CUT, BONELESS, 12/UP

Source: *Meat Price Report.* **Price Frequency:** weekly. **Units of Measure:** cents per lb.

Type of Price: price paid to wholesaler. **Time Period Covered:** latest week.

BEEF STRIP LOIN: SELECT, BONE IN

Source: *HRI-Buyer's Guide.* **Price Frequency:** weekly. **Effective Market(s):** Northeastern area. **Units of Measure:** Dollars per lb. **Type of Price:** price paid by dining places & institutions. **Time Period Covered:** latest week.

BEEF STRIP LOIN: SELECT, BONELESS

Source: *HRI-Buyer's Guide.* **Price Frequency:** weekly. **Effective Market(s):** Northeastern area. **Units of Measure:** Dollars per lb. **Type of Price:** price paid by dining places & institutions. **Time Period Covered:** latest week.

BEEF STRIP LOIN: UTILITY, 10″ CUT, BONE IN, REGULAR

Source: *Meat Price Report.* **Price Frequency:** weekly. **Units of Measure:** cents per lb. **Type of Price:** price paid to wholesaler. **Time Period Covered:** latest week.

BEEF STRIP LOIN: UTILITY, SHORT CUT, BONELESS, 12/DOWN

Source: *Meat Price Report.* **Price Frequency:** weekly. **Units of Measure:** cents per lb. **Type of Price:** price paid to wholesaler. **Time Period Covered:** latest week.

BEEF STRIP LOIN STEAKS: CHOICE, SHORT CUT, BONE IN

Source: *Meat Price Report.* **Price Frequency:** weekly. **Units of Measure:** cents per lb. **Type of Price:** price paid to wholesaler. **Time Period Covered:** latest week.

BEEF STRIP LOIN STEAKS: CHOICE, SHORT CUT, BONELESS, CENTER Cut

Source: *Meat Price Report.* **Price Frequency:** weekly. **Units of Measure:** cents per lb. **Type of Price:** price paid to wholesaler . **Time Period Covered:** latest week.

BEEF STRIP LOIN STEAKS: CHOICE, SHORT CUT, BONELESS, Regular

Source: *Meat Price Report.* **Price Frequency:** weekly. **Units of Measure:** cents per lb. **Type of Price:** price paid to wholesaler. **Time Period Covered:** latest week.

BEEF STRIP LOIN STEAKS: PRIME, SHORT CUT, BONE IN

Source: *Meat Price Report.* **Price Frequency:** weekly. **Units of Measure:** cents per lb. **Type of Price:** price paid to wholesaler. **Time Period Covered:** latest week.

BEEF STRIP LOIN STEAKS: PRIME, SHORT CUT, BONELESS, CENTER Cut

Source: *Meat Price Report.* **Price Frequency:** weekly. **Units of Measure:** cents per lb. **Type of Price:** price paid to wholesaler. **Time Period Covered:** latest week.

BEEF STRIP LOIN STEAKS: PRIME, SHORT CUT, BONELESS, REGULAR

Source: *Meat Price Report.* **Price Frequency:** weekly. **Units of Measure:** cents per lb. **Type of Price:** price paid to wholesaler. **Time Period Covered:** latest week.

BEEF STROGANOFF STRIPS: CHOICE

Source: *Meat Price Report.* **Price Frequency:** weekly. **Units of Measure:** cents per lb. **Type of Price:** price paid to wholesaler. **Time Period Covered:** latest week.

BEEF SWEET BREADS: FROZEN

Source: *Livestock, Meat, Wool Market News.* **Price Frequency:** weekly, seasonally. **Effective Market(s):** Central United States. **Units of Measure:** Dollars per 100 lbs. **Time Period Covered:** latest week.

BEEF T-BONE STEAK

Source: *Livestock and Poultry Update.* **Price Frequency:** monthly. **Units of Measure:** cents per lb. **Type of Price:** retail. **Time Period Covered:** latest 3 months, year ago.

Source: *Porkpro Newsletter.* **Price Frequency:** weekly. **Effective Market(s):** Chicago. **Units of Measure:** Dollars per lb. **Type of Price:** retail. **Time Period Covered:** latest day, week ago, year ago.

BEEF T-BONE STEAK: CHOICE

Source: *Meat Price Report.* **Price Frequency:** weekly. **Units of Measure:** cents per lb. **Type of Price:** price paid to wholesaler. **Time Period Covered:** latest week.

BEEF T-BONE STEAK: CHOICE, BONE IN

Source: *Livestock and Poultry Situation and Outlook Report.* **Price Frequency:** monthly. **Units of Measure:** Dollars per lb. **Type of Price:** retail. **Time Period Covered:** latest 3 years.

BEEF T-BONE STEAK: PRIME

Source: *Meat Price Report.* **Price Frequency:** weekly. **Units of Measure:** cents per lb. **Type of Price:** price paid to wholesaler. **Time Period Covered:** latest week.

BEEF TENDERLOIN: CHOICE

Source: *National Provisioner.* **Price Frequency:** daily. **Units of Measure:** cents per lb. **Time Period Covered:** latest week.

BEEF TENDERLOIN: CHOICE, WHOLE, SPECIAL TRIM

Source: *HRI-Buyer's Guide.* **Price Frequency:** weekly. **Effective Market(s):** Northeastern area. **Units of Measure:** Dollars per lb. **Type of Price:** price paid by dining places & institutions. **Time Period Covered:** latest week.

BEEF TENDERLOIN: CHOICE, WHOLE, TRIMMED

Source: *HRI-Buyer's Guide.* **Price Frequency:** weekly. **Effective Market(s):** Northeastern area. **Units of Measure:** Dollars per lb. **Type of Price:** price paid by dining places & institutions. **Time Period Covered:** latest week.

BEEF TENDERLOIN: SELECT, WHOLE, SPECIAL TRIM

Source: *HRI-Buyer's Guide.* **Price Frequency:** weekly. **Effective Market(s):** Northeastern area. **Units of Measure:** Dollars per lb. **Type of Price:** price paid by dining places & institutions. **Time Period Covered:** latest week.

BEEF TENDERLOIN: SELECT, WHOLE, TRIMMED

Source: *HRI-Buyer's Guide.* **Price Frequency:** weekly. **Effective Market(s):** Northeastern area. **Units of Measure:** Dollars per lb. **Type of Price:** price paid by dining places & institutions. **Time Period Covered:** latest week.

BEEF TENDERLOIN STEAK: CHOICE, COMPLETELY SKINNED

Source: *Meat Price Report.* **Price Frequency:** weekly. **Units of Measure:** cents per lb. **Type of Price:** price paid to wholesaler. **Time Period Covered:** latest week.

BEEF TENDERLOIN STEAK: CHOICE, DEFATTED, SIDE MUSCLE ON

Source: *Meat Price Report.* **Price Frequency:** weekly. **Units of Measure:** cents per lb. **Type of Price:** price paid to wholesaler. **Time Period Covered:** latest week.

BEEF TENDERLOIN STEAK: CHOICE, SIDE MUSCLE ON

Source: *Meat Price Report.* **Price Frequency:** weekly. **Units of Measure:** cents per lb. **Type of Price:** price paid to wholesaler. **Time Period Covered:** latest week.

BEEF TENDERLOIN STEAK: CHOICE, SPECIAL, SIDE MUSCLE OFF, Skin On

Source: *Meat Price Report.* **Price Frequency:** weekly. **Units of Measure:** cents per lb. **Type of Price:** price paid to wholesaler. **Time Period Covered:** latest week.

BEEF TENDERLOIN STEAK: PRIME, COMPLETELY SKINNED

Source: *Meat Price Report.* **Price Frequency:** weekly. **Units of Measure:** cents per lb. **Type of Price:** price paid to wholesaler. **Time Period Covered:** latest week.

BEEF TENDERLOIN STEAK: PRIME, DEFATTED, SIDE MUSCLE ON

Source: *Meat Price Report.* **Price Frequency:** weekly. **Units of Measure:** cents per lb. **Type of Price:** price paid to wholesaler. **Time Period Covered:** latest week.

BEEF TENDERLOIN STEAK: PRIME, SIDE MUSCLE ON

Source: *Meat Price Report.* **Price Frequency:** weekly. **Units of Measure:** cents per lb. **Type of Price:** price paid to wholesaler. **Time Period Covered:** latest week.

BEEF TENDERLOIN STEAK: PRIME, SPECIAL, SIDE MUSCLE OFF, Skin On

Source: *Meat Price Report.* **Price Frequency:** weekly. **Units of Measure:** cents per lb. **Type of Price:** price paid to wholesaler. **Time Period Covered:** latest week.

BEEF TENDERLOIN STEAK: UTILITY, COMPLETELY SKINNED

Source: *Meat Price Report.* **Price Frequency:** weekly. **Units of Measure:** cents per lb. **Type of Price:** price paid to wholesaler. **Time Period Covered:** latest week.

BEEF THREE PIECE LOIN: CHOICE

Source: *National Provisioner.* **Price Frequency:** daily. **Units of Measure:** cents per lb. **Time Period Covered:** latest week.

BEEF TONGUE: CURED

Source: *Meat Price Report.* **Price Frequency:** weekly. **Units of Measure:** cents per lb. **Type of Price:** price paid to wholesaler. **Time Period Covered:** latest week.

BEEF TONGUE: FRESH

Source: *Meat Price Report.* **Price Frequency:** weekly. **Units of Measure:** cents per Lb. **Type of Price:** price paid to wholesaler. **Time Period Covered:** latest week.

BEEF TONGUE: FROZEN

Source: *Livestock, Meat, Wool Market News.* **Price Frequency:** weekly, seasonally. **Effective Market(s):** Central United States. **Units of Measure:** Dollars per 100 lbs. **Time Period Covered:** latest week.

BEEF TONGUE: NO. 1

Source: *National Provisioner.* **Price Frequency:** daily. **Effective Market(s):** Midwest River area. **Units of Measure:** cents per lb. **Time Period Covered:** latest week.

BEEF TONGUE: NO. 2

Source: *National Provisioner.* **Price Frequency:** daily. **Effective Market(s):** Midwest River area. **Units of Measure:** cents per lb. **Time Period Covered:** latest week.

BEEF TONGUE: SMOKED

Source: *HRI-Buyer's Guide.* **Price Frequency:** weekly. **Effective Market(s):** Northeastern area. **Units of Measure:** Dollars per lb. **Type of Price:** price paid by dining places & institutions. **Time Period Covered:** latest week.

Source: *Meat Price Report.* **Price Frequency:** weekly. **Units of Measure:** cents per lb. **Type of Price:** price paid to wholesaler. **Time Period Covered:** latest week.

BEEF TOP INSIDE ROUND: CHOICE

Source: *Meat Price Report.* **Price Frequency:** weekly. **Units of Measure:** cents per lb. **Type of Price:** price paid to wholesaler. **Time Period Covered:** latest week.

BEEF TOP INSIDE ROUND: CHOICE, BONELESS

Source: *HRI-Buyer's Guide.* **Price Frequency:** weekly. **Effective Market(s):** Northeastern area. **Units of Measure:** Dollars per lb. **Type of Price:** price paid by dining places & institutions. **Time Period Covered:** latest week.

BEEF TOP INSIDE ROUND: PRIME

Source: *Meat Price Report.* **Price Frequency:** weekly. **Units of Measure:** cents per lb. **Type of Price:** price paid to wholesaler. **Time Period Covered:** latest week.

BEEF TOP INSIDE ROUND: SELECT, BONELESS

Source: *HRI-Buyer's Guide.* **Price Frequency:** weekly. **Effective Market(s):** Northeastern area. **Units of Measure:** Dollars per lb. **Type of Price:** price paid by dining places & institutions. **Time Period Covered:** latest week.

BEEF TOP INSIDE ROUND: UTILITY

Source: *Meat Price Report.* **Price Frequency:** weekly. **Units of Measure:** cents per lb. **Type of Price:** price paid to wholesaler. **Time Period Covered:** latest week.

BEEF TOP ROUND: CHOICE 2-3

Source: *Livestock, Meat, Wool Market News.* **Price Frequency:** weekly, seasonally. **Effective Market(s):** Central United States, California. **Units of Measure:** Dollars per 100 lbs. **Type of Price:** average. **Time Period Covered:** latest week, year ago.

BEEF TOP SIRLOIN BUTT: CHOICE

Source: *National Provisioner.* **Price Frequency:** daily. **Units of Measure:** cents per lb. **Time Period Covered:** latest week.

BEEF TOP SIRLOIN BUTT: CHOICE 2-3

Source: *Livestock, Meat, Wool Market News.* **Price Frequency:** weekly, seasonally. **Effective Market(s):** Central United States, California. **Units of Measure:** Dollars per 100 lbs. **Type of Price:** average. **Time Period Covered:** latest week, year ago.

BEEF TOP SIRLOIN BUTT: CHOICE, BONELESS

Source: *HRI-Buyer's Guide.* **Price Frequency:** weekly. **Effective Market(s):** Northeastern area. **Units of Measure:** Dollars per lb. **Type of Price:** price paid by dining places & institutions. **Time Period Covered:** latest week.

BEEF TOP SIRLOIN BUTT: CHOICE, 10/DOWN

Source: *Meat Price Report.* **Price Frequency:** weekly. **Units of Measure:** cents per lb. **Type of Price:** price paid to wholesaler. **Time Period Covered:** latest week.

BEEF TOP SIRLOIN BUTT: CHOICE, 10/UP

Source: *Meat Price Report.* **Price Frequency:** weekly. **Units of Measure:** cents per lb. **Type of Price:** price paid to wholesaler. **Time Period Covered:** latest week.

BEEF TOP SIRLOIN BUTT: PRIME, BONELESS

Source: *HRI-Buyer's Guide.* **Price Frequency:** weekly. **Effective Market(s):** Northeastern area. **Units of Measure:** Dollars per lb. **Type of Price:** price paid by dining places & institutions. **Time Period Covered:** latest week.

BEEF TOP SIRLOIN BUTT: PRIME, 10/DOWN

Source: *Meat Price Report.* **Price Frequency:** weekly. **Units of Measure:** cents per lb. **Type of Price:** price paid to wholesaler. **Time Period Covered:** latest week.

BEEF TOP SIRLOIN BUTT: PRIME, 10/UP

Source: *Meat Price Report.* **Price Frequency:** weekly. **Units of Measure:** cents per lb. **Type of Price:** price paid to wholesaler. **Time Period Covered:** latest week.

BEEF TOP SIRLOIN BUTT: SELECT, BONELESS

Source: *HRI-Buyer's Guide.* **Price Frequency:** weekly. **Effective Market(s):** Northeastern area. **Units of Measure:** Dollars per lb. **Type of Price:** price paid by dining places & institutions. **Time Period Covered:** latest week.

BEEF TOP SIRLOIN BUTT: UTILITY, 10/UP

Source: *Meat Price Report.* **Price Frequency:** weekly. **Units of Measure:** cents per lb. **Type of Price:** price paid to wholesaler. **Time Period Covered:** latest week.

BEEF TOP SIRLOIN BUTT STEAK: CHOICE

Source: *Meat Price Report.* **Price Frequency:** weekly. **Units of Measure:** cents per lb. **Type of Price:** price paid to wholesaler. **Time Period Covered:** latest week.

BEEF TOP SIRLOIN BUTT STEAK: CHOICE, CENTER CUT

Source: *Meat Price Report.* **Price Frequency:** weekly. **Units of Measure:** cents per lb. **Type of Price:** price paid to wholesaler. **Time Period Covered:** latest week.

BEEF TOP SIRLOIN BUTT STEAK: CHOICE, SEMI-CENTER CUT

Source: *Meat Price Report.* **Price Frequency:** weekly. **Units of Measure:** cents per lb. **Type of Price:** price paid to wholesaler. **Time Period Covered:** latest week.

BEEF TOP SIRLOIN BUTT STEAK: PRIME

Source: *Meat Price Report.* **Price Frequency:** weekly. **Units of Measure:** cents per lb. **Type of Price:** price paid to wholesaler. **Time Period Covered:** latest week.

BEEF TOP SIRLOIN BUTT STEAK: PRIME, CENTER CUT

Source: *Meat Price Report.* **Price Frequency:** weekly. **Units of Measure:** cents per lb. **Type of Price:** price paid to wholesaler. **Time Period Covered:** latest week.

BEEF TOP SIRLOIN BUTT STEAK: PRIME, SEMI-CENTER CUT

Source: *Meat Price Report.* **Price Frequency:** weekly. **Units of Measure:** cents per lb. **Type of Price:** price paid to wholesaler. **Time Period Covered:** latest week.

BEEF TREPAS: FROZEN

Source: *Livestock, Meat, Wool Market News.* **Price Frequency:** weekly, seasonally. **Effective Market(s):** Central United States. **Units of Measure:** Dollars per 100 lbs. **Time Period Covered:** latest week.

BEEF TRIPE

Source: *National Provisioner.* **Price Frequency:** daily. **Effective Market(s):** Midwest River area. **Units of Measure:** cents per lb. **Time Period Covered:** latest week.

BEEF TRIPE: SCALDED, EDIBLE, FROZEN

Source: *Livestock, Meat, Wool Market News.* **Price Frequency:** weekly, seasonally. **Effective Market(s):** Central United States. **Units of Measure:** Dollars per 100 lbs. **Time Period Covered:** latest week.

BEER

Source: *Illinois Beverage Journal.* **Price Frequency:** monthly. **Effective Market(s):** Illinois. **Units of Measure:** Dollars per case. **Type of Price:** wholesale by brand. **Time Period Covered:** latest month.

Source: *Kentucky Beverage Journal.* **Price Frequency:** monthly. **Effective Market(s):** Kentucky. **Units of Measure:** Dollars per case. **Type of Price:** wholesale by brand. **Time Period Covered:** latest month.

Source: *Nevada Beverage Index.* **Price Frequency:** monthly. **Effective Market(s):** Nevada. **Units of Measure:** Dollars per unit. **Type of Price:** wholesale by brand. **Time Period Covered:** latest month.

Source: *Statistical Bulletin of the South Pacific: Retail Price Indexes.* **Price Frequency:** annually. **Effective Market(s):** 18 South Pacific markets. **Units of Measure:** Australian dollars per 370 milliliters. **Type of Price:** retail. **Time Period Covered:** latest year.

BEER: DOMESTIC

Source: *Colorado Beverage Analyst.* **Price Frequency:** monthly. **Effective Market(s):** Colorado. **Units of Measure:** Dollars per case. **Type of Price:** wholesale by brand. **Time Period Covered:** latest month.

BEER: IMPORTED

Source: *Colorado Beverage Analyst.* **Price Frequency:** monthly. **Effective Market(s):** Colorado. **Units of Measure:** Dollars per case. **Type of Price:** wholesale by brand. **Time Period Covered:** latest month.

BEESWAX

Source: *National Honey Market News.* **Price Frequency:** monthly, seasonally. **Effective Market(s):** Florida. **Units of Measure:** cents per lb. **Type of Price:** paid to beekeepers. **Time Period Covered:** latest month.

BEESWAX: AUSTRALIAN

Source: *Prices of Selected Asia/Pacific Products.* **Price Frequency:** monthly. **Effective Market(s):** United Kingdom. **Units of Measure:** Dollars per metric ton. **Type of Price:** high, low. **Time Period Covered:** latest month.

BEESWAX: DARK

Source: *Gleanings in Bee Culture.* **Price Frequency:** monthly. **Effective Market(s):** 10 domestic markets. **Units of Measure:** Dollars per lb. **Type of Price:** retail. **Time Period Covered:** latest month.

BEESWAX: LIGHT

Source: *Gleanings in Bee Culture.* **Price Frequency:** monthly. **Effective Market(s):** 10 domestic markets. **Units of Measure:** Dollars per lb. **Type of Price:** retail. **Time Period Covered:** latest month.

Source: *National Honey Market News.* **Price Frequency:** monthly, seasonally. **Effective Market(s):** Florida. **Units of Measure:** cents per lb. **Type of Price:** paid to beekeepers. **Time Period Covered:** latest month.

BEESWAX: REFINED, WHITE, BLEACHED

Source: *Chemical Marketing Reporter.* **Price Frequency:** weekly. **Effective Market(s):** New York. **Units of Measure:** Dollars per lb. **Type of Price:** spot. **Time Period Covered:** latest week.

BEESWAX: REFINED, WHITE, BLEACHED, BRICKS

Source: *Prices of Selected Asia/Pacific Products.* **Price Frequency:** monthly. **Effective Market(s):** New York. **Units of Measure:** Dollars per lb. **Type of Price:** spot high, spot low. **Time Period Covered:** latest month.

BEESWAX: REFINED, YELLOW

Source: *Chemical Marketing Reporter.* **Price Frequency:** weekly. **Effective Market(s):** New York. **Units of Measure:** Dollars per lb. **Type of Price:** spot. **Time Period Covered:** latest week.

Source: *Journal of Commerce and Commercial.* **Price Frequency:** weekly in Monday issue. **Units of Measure:** Dollars per lb. **Type of Price:** spot. **Time Period Covered:** latest week.

BEESWAX: REFINED, YELLOW, BRICKS

Source: *Prices of Selected Asia/Pacific Products.* **Price Frequency:** monthly. **Effective Market(s):** New York. **Units of Measure:** Dollars per lb. **Type of Price:** spot high, spot low. **Time Period Covered:** latest month.

BEESWAX: REFINED, YELLOW, SLABS

Source: *Prices of Selected Asia/Pacific Products.* **Price Frequency:** monthly. **Effective Market(s):** New York. **Units of Measure:** Dollars per lb. **Type of Price:** spot high, spot low. **Time Period Covered:** latest month.

BEESWAX: WHITE

Source: *Journal of Commerce and Commercial.* **Price Frequency:** weekly in Monday issue. **Units of Measure:** Dollars per lb. **Type of Price:** spot. **Time Period Covered:** latest week.

BEESWAX: WHITE, SLABS

Source: *Prices of Selected Asia/Pacific Products.* **Price Frequency:** monthly. **Effective Market(s):** New York. **Units of Measure:** Dollars per lb. **Type of Price:** spot high, spot low. **Time Period Covered:** latest month.

BEET PULP

Source: *Feedstuffs.* **Price Frequency:** weekly. **Effective Market(s):** 7 domestic markets. **Units of Measure:** Dollars per bulk ton. **Time Period Covered:** latest week.

BEET PULP: DRIED

Source: *Feedstuffs.* **Price Frequency:** weekly. **Effective Market(s):** 8 domestic markets. **Units of Measure:** Dollars per ton. **Time Period Covered:** latest week.

BEET PULP: SHREDDED

Source: *Los Angeles Times.* **Price Frequency:** daily. **Effective Market(s):** Los Angeles. **Units of Measure:** Dollars per ton. **Type of Price:** cash. **Time Period Covered:** latest day.

BEET PULP WITH MOLASSES: SHREDDED

Source: *California Farmer.* **Price Frequency:** semimonthly. **Effective Market(s):** California. **Units of Measure:** Dollars per ton. **Time Period Covered:** latest week, month ago, year ago.

BEET SUGAR

see Sugar: Beet.

BEET SUGAR: REFINED

Source: *Sugar and Sweetner Situation and Outlook Report.* **Price Frequency:** monthly, quarterly, annually. **Effective Market(s):** Midwest. **Units of Measure:** cents per lb. **Type of Price:** wholesale. **Time Period Covered:** latest 10 years.

BEETROOT

Source: *New Zealand Farmer.* **Price Frequency:** weekly, seasonally. **Effective Market(s):** New Zealand. **Units of Measure:** New Zealand dollars per case. **Time Period Covered:** latest week.

BEETS

Source: *Lancaster Farming.* **Price Frequency:** weekly, seasonally. **Effective Market(s):** Pennsylvania. **Units of Measure:** Dollars per crate. **Type of Price:** market. **Time Period Covered:** latest week.

BEETS: FRESH

Source: *HRI-Buyers Guide.* **Price Frequency:** weekly. **Effective Market(s):** Northeastern area. **Units of Measure:** Dollars per bunch. **Type of Price:** price paid by dining places & institutions. **Time Period Covered:** latest week.

BEETS: ILLINOIS

Source: *Fresh Fruit and Vegetable Prices.* **Price Frequency:** monthly, seasonally. **Effective Market(s):** Chicago. **Units of Measure:** Dollars per unit. **Type of Price:** average wholesale price. **Time Period Covered:** latest year.

BEETS: NEW JERSEY

Source: *Fresh Fruit and Vegetable Prices.* **Price Frequency:** monthly, seasonally. **Effective Market(s):** New York City. **Units of Measure:** Dollars per unit. **Type of Price:** average wholesale price. **Time Period Covered:** latest year.

BEETS: RED

Source: *Lancaster Farming.* **Price Frequency:** weekly, seasonally. **Effective Market(s):** Pennsylvania. **Units of Measure:** Dollars per bushel. **Type of Price:** market. **Time Period Covered:** latest week.

BEETS: TEXAS

Source: *Fresh Fruit and Vegetable Prices.* **Price Frequency:** monthly, seasonally. **Effective Market(s):** Chicago, New York City. **Units of Measure:** Dollars per unit. **Type of Price:** average wholesale price. **Time Period Covered:** latest year.

BELGIUM FRANCS

Source: *Asian Wall Street Journal.* **Price Frequency:** daily. **Effective Market(s):** United States. **Units of Measure:** Belgian francs per ECU, per SDR. **Type of Price:** foreign exchange. **Time Period Covered:** latest 2 days.

Source: *Barron's.* **Price Frequency:** weekly. **Effective Market(s):** New York. **Units of Measure:** Belgian francs per United States dollar. **Type of Price:** commercial foreign exchange rate, financial foreign exchange rate. **Time Period Covered:** latest 2 weeks.

Source: *The Economist.* **Price Frequency:** weekly. **Effective Market(s):** London. **Units of Measure:** Belgian francs per British pounds, per ECU, per SDR, per United States dollar. **Type of Price:** foreign exchange. **Time Period Covered:** latest week.

BELGUIM FRANCS

Source: *New York Times.* **Price Frequency:** daily. **Effective Market(s):** New York. **Units of Measure:** Belgian francs per United States dollars. **Type of Price:** commercial foreign exchange rate. **Time Period Covered:** latest 2 days.

Source: *Timber Bulletin.* **Price Frequency:** monthly, annually. **Units of Measure:** Belgian francs per United States dollar. **Type of Price:** foreign exchange. **Time Period Covered:** latest 2 years.

BELLADONNA: SOLID POWDER EXTRACT

Source: *Journal of Commerce and Commercial.* **Price Frequency:** weekly in Monday issue. **Units of Measure:** Dollars per lb. **Type of Price:** spot. **Time Period Covered:** latest week.

BENTONITE: API, WYOMING

Source: *Industrial Minerals.* **Price Frequency:** monthly. **Effective Market(s):** Wyoming. **Units of Measure:** Dollars per metric tonne. **Type of Price:** producer & dealer. **Time Period Covered:** latest month.

BENTONITE: CIVIL ENGINEERING GRADE

Source: *Industrial Minerals.* **Price Frequency:** monthly. **Effective Market(s):** main European port. **Units of Measure:** British pounds per metric tonne. **Type of Price:** producer & dealer. **Time Period Covered:** latest month.

BENTONITE: DOMESTIC

Source: *Chemical Marketing Reporter.* **Price Frequency:** weekly. **Effective Market(s):** New York. **Units of Measure:** Dollars per ton. **Type of Price:** spot. **Time Period Covered:** latest week.

BENTONITE: FOUNDRY GRADE, FULLER'S EARTH, SODA ASH TREATED

Source: *Industrial Minerals.* **Price Frequency:** monthly. **Effective Market(s):** United Kingdom. **Units of Measure:** British pounds per metric tonne. **Type of Price:** producer & dealer. **Time Period Covered:** latest month.

BENTONITE: FOUNDRY GRADE, WYOMING

Source: *Industrial Minerals.* **Price Frequency:** monthly. **Effective Market(s):** United Kingdom. **Units of Measure:** British pounds per metric tonne. **Type of Price:** producer & dealer. **Time Period Covered:** latest month.

BENTONITE: OCMA

Source: *Industrial Minerals.* **Price Frequency:** monthly. **Effective Market(s):** United Kingdom. **Units of Measure:** British pounds per metric tonne. **Type of Price:** producer & dealer. **Time Period Covered:** latest month.

BENTONITE: WYOMING

Source: *Industrial Minerals.* **Price Frequency:** monthly. **Effective Market(s):** Wyoming. **Units of Measure:** Dollars per metric tonne. **Type of Price:** producer & dealer. **Time Period Covered:** latest month.

BENZALDEHYDE: NF

Source: *Journal of Commerce and Commercial.* **Price Frequency:** weekly in Tuesday issue. **Units of Measure:** Dollars per lb. **Type of Price:** spot. **Time Period Covered:** latest week.

BENZALDEHYDE: TECHNICAL GRADE

Source: *Journal of Commerce and Commercial.* **Price Frequency:** weekly in Tuesday issue. **Units of Measure:** Dollars per lb. **Type of Price:** spot. **Time Period Covered:** latest week.

Source: *Journal of Commerce and Commercial.* **Price Frequency:** weekly in Wednesday issue. **Units of Measure:** Dollars per lb. **Type of Price:** spot. **Time Period Covered:** latest week.

BENZALDEHYDE: TECHNICAL GRADE, NF

Source: *Chemical Marketing Reporter.* **Price Frequency:** weekly. **Effective Market(s):** New York, West of the Rockies. **Units of Measure:** Dollars per lb. **Type of Price:** spot. **Time Period Covered:** latest week.

BENZENE

Source: *Cotton and Wool Situation and Outlook Report.* **Price Frequency:** monthly. **Units of Measure:** Dollars per gallon. **Type of Price:** spot. **Time Period Covered:** latest year.

Source: *Energy Pricing News: Petrochemical Report.* **Price Frequency:** bimonthly. **Units of Measure:** Canadian dollars per tonne. **Type of Price:** contract. **Time Period Covered:** latest month.

Source: *Journal of Commerce and Commercial.* **Price Frequency:** daily. **Units of Measure:** Dollars per lb. **Type of Price:** spot supplier. **Time Period Covered:** latest day.

Source: *Modern Plastics.* **Price Frequency:** quarterly in January, April, July & October issues. **Units of Measure:** cents per lb. **Type of Price:** market. **Time Period Covered:** latest 3 years.

Source: *Purchasing.* **Price Frequency:** monthly. **Effective Market(s):** United States. **Units of Measure:** cents per lb. **Type of Price:** transaction. **Time Period Covered:** latest day, month ago, 6 months ago, year ago.

BENZENE: INDUSTRIAL BARGES

Source: *Journal of Commerce and Commercial* . **Price Frequency:** weekly in Wednesday issue. **Effective Market(s):** Gulf. **Units of Measure:** Dollars per gallon. **Type of Price:** spot. **Time Period Covered:** latest week.

BENZENE: INDUSTRIAL OR NITRATION

Source: *Chemical Marketing Reporter.* **Price Frequency:** weekly. **Effective Market(s):** New York. **Units of Measure:** Dollars per gallon. **Type of Price:** spot. **Time Period Covered:** latest week.

BENZENE: PURE

Source: *Japan Economic Journal.* **Price Frequency:** weekly. **Effective Market(s):** Tokyo. **Units of Measure:** Japanese yen per kilogram. **Time Period Covered:** latest 2 weeks.

BENZIDINE: ORANGE, LIQUID

Source: *Chemical Marketing Reporter.* **Price Frequency:** weekly. **Effective Market(s):** New York. **Units of Measure:** Dollars per lb. **Type of Price:** spot. **Time Period Covered:** latest week.

BENZIDINE: ORANGE, POWDERED

Source: *Chemical Marketing Reporter.* **Price Frequency:** weekly. **Effective Market(s):** New York. **Units of Measure:** Dollars per lb. **Type of Price:** spot. **Time Period Covered:** latest week.

BENZIDINE: YELLOW, AAA

Source: *Chemical Marketing Reporter.* **Price Frequency:** weekly. **Effective Market(s):** New York. **Units of Measure:** Dollars per lb. **Type of Price:** spot. **Time Period Covered:** latest week.

BENZIDINE: YELLOW, AAOA

Source: *Chemical Marketing Reporter.* **Price Frequency:** weekly. **Effective Market(s):** New York. **Units of Measure:** Dollars per lb. **Type of Price:** spot. **Time Period Covered:** latest week.

BENZIDINE: YELLOW, AAOT

Source: *Chemical Marketing Reporter.* **Price Frequency:** weekly. **Effective Market(s):** New York. **Units of Measure:** Dollars per lb. **Type of Price:** spot. **Time Period Covered:** latest week.

BENZOCAINE: USP

Source: *Chemical Marketing Reporter.* **Price Frequency:** weekly. **Effective Market(s):** New York. **Units of Measure:** Dollars per kilogram. **Type of Price:** spot. **Time Period Covered:** latest week.

BENZODIHYDROPYRONE

Source: *Chemical Marketing Reporter.* **Price Frequency:** weekly. **Effective Market(s):** New York. **Units of Measure:** Dollars per lb. **Type of Price:** spot. **Time Period Covered:** latest week.

BENZOIC ACID: TECHNICAL GRADE

Source: *Chemical Marketing Reporter.* **Price Frequency:** weekly. **Effective Market(s):** New York. **Units of Measure:** Dollars per lb. **Type of Price:** spot. **Time Period Covered:** latest week.

BENZOIC ACID: USP

Source: *Journal of Commerce and Commercial.* **Price Frequency:** weekly in Friday issue. **Units of Measure:** Dollars per lb. **Type of Price:** spot. **Time Period Covered:** latest week.

BENZOIN GUM: SUMATRA

Source: *Chemical Marketing Reporter.* **Price Frequency:** weekly. **Effective Market(s):** New York. **Units of Measure:** Dollars per lb. **Type of Price:** spot. **Time Period Covered:** latest week.

Source: *Journal of Commerce and Commercial.* **Price Frequency:** weekly in Monday issue. **Units of Measure:** Dollars per lb. **Type of Price:** spot. **Time Period Covered:** latest week.

BENZOPHENONE

Source: *Modern Plastics.* **Price Frequency:** quarterly in February, May, August & November issues. **Units of Measure:** Dollars per lb. **Type of Price:** list. **Time Period Covered:** latest year.

BENZOPHENONE: CRYSTALS, NF

Source: *Chemical Marketing Reporter.* **Price Frequency:** weekly. **Effective Market(s):** New York. **Units of Measure:** Dollars per lb. **Type of Price:** spot. **Time Period Covered:** latest week.

BENZOPHENONE: FLAKES, NF

Source: *Chemical Marketing Reporter.* **Price Frequency:** weekly. **Effective Market(s):** New York. **Units of Measure:** Dollars per lb. **Type of Price:** spot. **Time Period Covered:** latest week.

BENZOPHENONE: TECHNICAL GRADE, FLAKES

Source: *Chemical Marketing Reporter.* **Price Frequency:** weekly. **Effective Market(s):** New York. **Units of Measure:** Dollars per lb. **Type of Price:** spot. **Time Period Covered:** latest week.

2,2-BENZOTHIAZYL DISULFIDE

see Mercaptobenzothiazyl Disulfide.

BENZOTRIAZOLE: FLAKE

Source: *Chemical Marketing Reporter.* **Price Frequency:** weekly. **Effective Market(s):** New York. **Units of Measure:** Dollars per lb. **Type of Price:** spot. **Time Period Covered:** latest week.

BENZOTRIAZOLE: PHOTO-GRADE

Source: *Chemical Marketing Reporter.* **Price Frequency:** weekly. **Effective Market(s):** New York. **Units of Measure:** Dollars per lb. **Type of Price:** spot. **Time Period Covered:** latest week.

BENZOTRIAZOLE: POWDERED

Source: *Chemical Marketing Reporter.* **Price Frequency:** weekly. **Effective Market(s):** New York. **Units of Measure:** Dollars per lb. **Type of Price:** spot. **Time Period Covered:** latest week.

BENZOYL CHLORIDE

Source: *Chemical Marketing Reporter.* **Price Frequency:** weekly. **Effective Market(s):** New York. **Units of Measure:** Dollars per lb. **Type of Price:** spot. **Time Period Covered:** latest week.

BENZOYL PEROXIDE: PASTE, 50% AND 55% FORMULATIONS

Source: *Chemical Marketing Reporter.* **Price Frequency:** weekly. **Effective Market(s):** New York. **Units of Measure:** Dollars per lb. **Type of Price:** spot. **Time Period Covered:** latest week.

BENZOYL PEROXIDE: REGULAR GRANULAR, 70-78%

Source: *Chemical Marketing Reporter.* **Price Frequency:** weekly. **Effective Market(s):** New York. **Units of Measure:** Dollars per lb. **Type of Price:** spot. **Time Period Covered:** latest week.

BENZYL ACETATE

Source: *Chemical Marketing Reporter.* **Price Frequency:** weekly. **Effective Market(s):** New York. **Units of Measure:** Dollars per lb. **Type of Price:** spot. **Time Period Covered:** latest week.

Source: *Journal of Commerce and Commercial.* **Price Frequency:** weekly in Tuesday issue. **Units of Measure:** Dollars per lb. **Type of Price:** spot. **Time Period Covered:** latest week.

BENZYL ALCOHOL: NF

Source: *Chemical Marketing Reporter.* **Price Frequency:** weekly. **Effective Market(s):** New York. **Units of Measure:** Dollars per lb. **Type of Price:** spot. **Time Period Covered:** latest week.

BENZYL ALCOHOL: TECHNICAL GRADE

Source: *Chemical Marketing Reporter.* **Price Frequency:** weekly. **Effective Market(s):** New York. **Units of Measure:** Dollars per lb. **Type of Price:** spot. **Time Period Covered:** latest week.

BENZYL BENZOATE

Source: *Chemical Marketing Reporter.* **Price Frequency:** weekly. **Effective Market(s):** New York. **Units of Measure:** Dollars per lb. **Type of Price:** spot. **Time Period Covered:** latest week.

Source: *Journal of Commerce and Commercial.* **Price Frequency:** weekly in Tuesday issue. **Units of Measure:** Dollars per lb. **Type of Price:** spot. **Time Period Covered:** latest week.

BENZYL CHLORIDE

Source: *Journal of Commerce and Commercial.* **Price Frequency:** weekly in Wednesday issue. **Units of Measure:** Dollars per lb. **Type of Price:** spot. **Time Period Covered:** latest week.

BENZYL CHLORIDE: TECHNICAL GRADE

Source: *Chemical Marketing Reporter.* **Price Frequency:** weekly. **Effective Market(s):** New York. **Units of Measure:** Dollars per lb. **Type of Price:** spot. **Time Period Covered:** latest week.

BENZYL CINNAMATE

Source: *Chemical Marketing Reporter.* **Price Frequency:** weekly. **Effective Market(s):** New York. **Units of Measure:** Dollars per lb. **Type of Price:** spot. **Time Period Covered:** latest week.

N-BENZYL-N,N-DIMETHYLAMINE

Source: *Chemical Marketing Reporter.* **Price Frequency:** weekly. **Effective Market(s):** New York. **Units of Measure:** Dollars per lb. **Type of Price:** spot. **Time Period Covered:** latest week.

BENZYL FORMATE

Source: *Chemical Marketing Reporter.* **Price Frequency:** weekly. **Effective Market(s):** New York. **Units of Measure:** Dollars per lb. **Type of Price:** spot. **Time Period Covered:** latest week.

BENZYL ISOEUGENOL

Source: *Chemical Marketing Reporter.* **Price Frequency:** weekly. **Effective Market(s):** New York. **Units of Measure:** Dollars per lb. **Type of Price:** spot. **Time Period Covered:** latest week.

BENZYL PROPIONATE

Source: *Chemical Marketing Reporter.* **Price Frequency:** weekly. **Effective Market(s):** New York. **Units of Measure:** Dollars per lb. **Type of Price:** spot. **Time Period Covered:** latest week.

BENZYL SALICYLATE

Source: *Chemical Marketing Reporter.* **Price Frequency:** weekly. **Effective Market(s):** New York. **Units of Measure:** Dollars per lb. **Type of Price:** spot. **Time Period Covered:** latest week.

BENZYLIDINE ACETONE

Source: *Chemical Marketing Reporter.* **Price Frequency:** weekly. **Effective Market(s):** New York. **Units of Measure:** Dollars per lb. **Type of Price:** spot. **Time Period Covered:** latest week.

BENZYLISOEUGENOL

Source: *Journal of Commerce and Commercial.* **Price Frequency:** weekly in Tuesday issue. **Units of Measure:** Dollars per lb. **Type of Price:** spot. **Time Period Covered:** latest week.

BERGAMOT OIL

Source: *U. S. Essential Oil Trade.* **Price Frequency:** annually. **Effective Market(s):** United States. **Units of Measure:** Dollars per kilogram. **Type of Price:** import value. **Time Period Covered:** latest 3 years.

BERGAMOT OIL: ITALIAN

Source: *Chemical Marketing Reporter.* **Price Frequency:** weekly. **Effective Market(s):** New York. **Units of Measure:** Dollars per kilo. **Type of Price:** spot. **Time Period Covered:** latest week.

Source: *Journal of Commerce and Commercial.* **Price Frequency:** weekly in Tuesday issue. **Units of Measure:** Dollars per lb. **Type of Price:** spot. **Time Period Covered:** latest week.

BERYLLIUM: 98.5%, POWDER BLEND

Source: *American Metal Market.* **Price Frequency:** weekly. **Effective Market(s):** Elmore (OH). **Units of Measure:** Dollars per lb. base copper. **Time Period Covered:** latest week.

BERYLLIUM ALUMINUM

Source: *American Metal Market.* **Price Frequency:** weekly. **Effective Market(s):** Detroit/Elmore (OH)/Reading (PA). **Units of Measure:** Dollars per lb. base copper. **Time Period Covered:** latest week.

BERYLLIUM CASTING ALLOY

Source: *American Metal Market.* **Price Frequency:** weekly. **Units of Measure:** Dollars per lb. base copper. **Time Period Covered:** latest week.

BERYLLIUM COPPER: ROD, BAR AND WIRE

Source: *American Metal Market.* **Price Frequency:** weekly. **Units of Measure:** Dollars per lb. base copper. **Time Period Covered:** latest week.

BERYLLIUM COPPER: ROD, BAR AND WIRE, NO. 25

Source: *E&MJ.* **Price Frequency:** monthly. **Units of Measure:** Dollars per lb. **Time Period Covered:** selected dates.

Source: *E&MJ.* **Price Frequency:** monthly. **Units of Measure:** Dollars per lb. **Time Period Covered:** latest month.

BERYLLIUM COPPER: STRIP

Source: *American Metal Market.* **Price Frequency:** weekly. **Units of Measure:** Dollars per lb. base copper. **Time Period Covered:** latest week.

BERYLLIUM COPPER: STRIP, NO. 25

Source: *E&MJ.* **Price Frequency:** monthly. **Units of Measure:** Dollars per lb. **Time Period Covered:** selected dates.

Source: *E&MJ.* **Price Frequency:** monthly. **Units of Measure:** Dollars per lb. **Time Period Covered:** latest month.

BERYLLIUM COPPER: STRIP NO. 25

Source: *Iron Age.* **Price Frequency:** monthly. **Units of Measure:** Dollars per lb. Be. **Type of Price:** consumer. **Time Period Covered:** latest month.

BERYLLIUM COPPER MASTER ALLOY INGOT

Source: *American Metal Market.* **Price Frequency:** weekly. **Effective Market(s):** Detroit/Elmore (OH)/ Reading (PA). **Units of Measure:** Dollars per lb. contained beryllium. **Time Period Covered:** latest week.

BERYLLIUM INGOTS: VACUUM CAST

Source: *American Metal Market.* **Price Frequency:** weekly. **Effective Market(s):** Elmore (OH). **Units of Measure:** Dollars per lb. base copper. **Time Period Covered:** latest week.

BERYLLIUM OXIDE POWDER

Source: *American Metal Market.* **Price Frequency:** weekly. **Units of Measure:** Dollars per lb. base copper. **Time Period Covered:** latest week.

BERYLLIUM POWDER

Source: *American Metal Market.* **Price Frequency:** daily. **Units of Measure:** Dollars per lb. **Type of Price:** wholesale. **Time Period Covered:** latest day.

BERYLLIUM POWDER: SP200F

Source: *Iron Age.* **Price Frequency:** monthly. **Units of Measure:** Dollars per lb. **Type of Price:** consumer. **Time Period Covered:** latest month.

BERYLLIUM-ALUMINUM: 5% BERYLLIUM

Source: *Iron Age.* **Price Frequency:** monthly. **Units of Measure:** Dollars per lb. contained Be. **Type of Price:** consumer. **Time Period Covered:** latest month.

BETAHYDROXYNAPHTHOIC ACID

see b-Oxynaphthoic Acid.

BEVERAGES: NON-SPIRITUOUS

Source: *Colorado Beverage Analyst.* **Price Frequency:** monthly. **Effective Market(s):** Colorado. **Units of Measure:** Dollars per unit. **Type of Price:** wholesale by brand. **Time Period Covered:** latest month.

BEVERAGES: TROPICAL

Source: *Monthly Commodity Price Bulletin.* **Price Frequency:** monthly, annually. **Effective Market(s):** developing countries. **Units of Measure:** index. **Type of Price:** free market price index. **Time Period Covered:** latest 5 years.

Source: *Monthly Commodity Price Bulletin Supplement.* **Price Frequency:** monthly, quarterly, annually. **Units of Measure:** index. **Type of Price:** free market index. **Time Period Covered:** latest 20 years.

BEVERAGES PRICE INDEX

Source: *UNCTAD Commodity Yearbook.* **Price Frequency:** annually. **Units of Measure:** index. **Type of Price:** price index. **Time Period Covered:** latest 12 years.

BEZENE HEXACHLORIDE: 99% GAMMA ISOMER

see Lindane.

BHT

see Butylated Hydroxytoluene.

BIOTIN: CRYSTALLINE

Source: *Chemical Marketing Reporter.* **Price Frequency:** weekly. **Effective Market(s):** New York. **Units of Measure:** Dollars per gram. **Type of Price:** spot. **Time Period Covered:** latest week.

BIPHENYL

see Diphenyl.

BIRCH: PAPER

Source: *Volume and Value of Sawtimber Stumpage Sold from National Forests by Selected Species and Region.* **Price Frequency:** quarterly, annually. **Effective Market(s):** Eastern region. **Units of Measure:** Dollars per 1000 board feet. **Type of Price:** average. **Time Period Covered:** latest quarter, latest year.

BIRCH: YELLOW

Source: *Volume and Value of Sawtimber Stumpage Sold from National Forests by Selected Species and Region.* **Price Frequency:** quarterly, annually. **Effective Market(s):** Eastern region. **Units of Measure:** Dollars per 1000 board feet. **Type of Price:** average. **Time Period Covered:** latest quarter, latest year.

BIRCH TAR OIL: RECTIFIED

Source: *Journal of Commerce and Commmercial.* **Price Frequency:** weekly in Tuesday issue. **Units of Measure:** Dollars per lb. **Type of Price:** spot. **Time Period Covered:** latest week.

BIRDS OF PARADISE: CUT, HAWAII

Source: *Floriculture Crops.* **Price Frequency:** annually. **Effective Market(s):** United States. **Units of Measure:** cents per unit. **Type of Price:** commercial wholesale. **Time Period Covered:** latest 2 years.

BISILICATE: GROUND

Source: *Journal of Commerce and Commercial.* **Price Frequency:** weekly in Wednesday issue. **Units of Measure:** Dollars per lb. **Type of Price:** spot. **Time Period Covered:** latest week.

BISMUTH

Source: *Commodity Year Book.* **Price Frequency:** annually. **Effective Market(s):** New York. **Units of Measure:** Dollars per lb. **Type of Price:** foreign producer price. **Time Period Covered:** latest 11 years.

Source: *E&MJ.* **Price Frequency:** monthly. **Units of Measure:** Dollars per lb. **Type of Price:** merchant. **Time Period Covered:** selected dates.

Source: *E&MJ.* **Price Frequency:** monthly. **Units of Measure:** Dollars per lb. **Type of Price:** merchant. **Time Period Covered:** latest month.

Source: *Northern Miner.* **Price Frequency:** daily. **Effective Market(s):** New York. **Units of Measure:** Dollars per lb. **Type of Price:** producer. **Time Period Covered:** selected day.

BISMUTH: 99.99% MINIMUM

Source: *Journal of Commerce and Commercial.* **Price Frequency:** daily. **Effective Market(s):** Europe. **Units of Measure:** Dollars per lb. **Type of Price:** spot. **Time Period Covered:** latest day.

BISMUTH NITRATE: PURIFIED, CRYSTALLINE

Source: *Chemical Marketing Reporter.* **Price Frequency:** weekly. **Effective Market(s):** New York. **Units of Measure:** Dollars per lb. **Type of Price:** spot. **Time Period Covered:** latest week.

BISMUTH OXYCHLORIDE

Source: *Chemical Marketing Reporter.* **Price Frequency:** weekly. **Effective Market(s):** New York. **Units of Measure:** Dollars per lb. **Type of Price:** spot. **Time Period Covered:** latest week.

BISMUTH SUBCARBONATE

Source: *Journal of Commerce and Commercial.* **Price Frequency:** weekly in Friday issue. **Units of Measure:** Dollars per lb. **Type of Price:** spot. **Time Period Covered:** latest week.

BISMUTH SUBCARBONATE: MEDIUM POWDER, USP

Source: *Chemical Marketing Reporter.* **Price Frequency:** weekly. **Effective Market(s):** New York. **Units of Measure:** Dollars per lb. **Type of Price:** spot. **Time Period Covered:** latest week.

BISMUTH SUBGALLATE

Source: *Journal of Commerce and Commercial.* **Price Frequency:** weekly in Friday issue. **Units of Measure:** Dollars per lb. **Type of Price:** spot. **Time Period Covered:** latest week.

BISMUTH SUBGALLATE: PURIFIED

Source: *Chemical Marketing Reporter.* **Price Frequency:** weekly. **Effective Market(s):** New York. **Units of Measure:** Dollars per lb. **Type of Price:** spot. **Time Period Covered:** latest week.

BISMUTH SUBNITRATE

Source: *Journal of Commerce and Commercial.* **Price Frequency:** weekly in Friday issue. **Units of Measure:** Dollars per lb. **Type of Price:** spot. **Time Period Covered:** weekly.

BISMUTH SUBNITRATE: POWDERED, NF

Source: *Chemical Marketing Reporter.* **Price Frequency:** weekly. **Effective Market(s):** New York. **Units of Measure:** Dollars per lb. **Type of Price:** spot. **Time Period Covered:** latest week.

BISMUTH SUBSALICYLATE

Source: *Journal of Commerce and Commercial.* **Price Frequency:** weekly in Friday issue. **Units of Measure:** Dollars per lb. **Type of Price:** spot. **Time Period Covered:** latest week.

BISMUTH SUBSALICYLATE: PURIFIED, POWDERED

Source: *Chemical Marketing Reporter.* **Price Frequency:** weekly. **Effective Market(s):** New York. **Units of Measure:** Dollars per lb. **Type of Price:** spot. **Time Period Covered:** latest week.

BISMUTH TRIOXIDE

Source: *Journal of Commerce and Commercial.* **Price Frequency:** weekly in Friday issue. **Units of Measure:** Dollars per lb. **Type of Price:** spot. **Time Period Covered:** latest week.

BISMUTH TRIOXIDE: REAGENT POWDERED

Source: *Chemical Marketing Reporter.* **Price Frequency:** weekly. **Effective Market(s):** New York. **Units of Measure:** Dollars per lb. **Type of Price:** spot. **Time Period Covered:** latest week.

BISPHENOL-A: EPOXY GRADE

Source: *Chemical Marketing Reporter.* **Price Frequency:** weekly. **Effective Market(s):** New York. **Units of Measure:** Dollars per lb. **Type of Price:** spot. **Time Period Covered:** latest week.

BISPHENOL-A: POLYCARBONATE GRADE

Source: *Chemical Marketing Reporter.* **Price Frequency:** weekly. **Effective Market(s):** New York. **Units of Measure:** Dollars per lb. **Type of Price:** spot. **Time Period Covered:** latest week.

BITTERS

Source: *Beverage Media.* **Price Frequency:** monthly. **Effective Market(s):** New York. **Units of Measure:** Dollars per unit. **Type of Price:** wholesale by brand. **Time Period Covered:** latest month.

Source: *Illinois Beverage Journal.* **Price Frequency:** monthly. **Effective Market(s):** Illinois. **Units of Measure:** Dollars per case. **Type of Price:** wholesale by brand. **Time Period Covered:** latest month.

BLACKBERRIES

Source: *Lancaster Farming.* **Price Frequency:** weekly, seasonally. **Effective Market(s):** Pennsylvania. **Units of Measure:** Dollars per unit. **Type of Price:** market. **Time Period Covered:** latest week.

BLANC FIXE: SYNTHETIC, IMPORTED

Source: *Chemical Marketing Reporter.* **Price Frequency:** weekly. **Effective Market(s):** New York. **Units of Measure:** Dollars per lb. **Type of Price:** spot. **Time Period Covered:** latest week.

BLENDED WHISKEY

Source: *Colorado Beverage Analyst.* **Price Frequency:** monthly. **Effective Market(s):** Colorado. **Units of Measure:** Dollars per case. **Type of Price:** wholesale by brand. **Time Period Covered:** latest month.

Source: *Kentucky Beverage Journal.* **Price Frequency:** monthly. **Effective Market(s):** Kentucky. **Units of Measure:** Dollars per bottle, dollars per case. **Type of Price:** wholesale by brand. **Time Period Covered:** latest month.

BLOCKS: CEMENT

Source: *Agricultural Prices.* **Price Frequency:** quarterly. **Effective Market(s):** United States. **Units of Measure:** Dollars per 100. **Type of Price:** paid by farmer. **Time Period Covered:** latest 2 quarters, year ago.

BLOOD

Source: *National Provisioner.* **Price Frequency:** weekly. **Effective Market(s):** Midwest. **Units of Measure:** Dollars per ton. **Time Period Covered:** latest week.

BLOOD MEAL: 80%

Source: *National Provisioner.* **Price Frequency:** weekly. **Effective Market(s):** Chicago. **Units of Measure:** Dollars per ton. **Time Period Covered:** latest week.

BLOOD MEAL: 85%

Source: *Livestock, Meat, Wool Market News.* **Price Frequency:** weekly, seasonally. **Effective Market(s):** Central United States, Panhandle area, California. **Units of Measure:** Dollars per bulk ton. **Time Period Covered:** latest week.

BLOOD MEAL: FLASH DRIED

Source: *Feedstuffs.* **Price Frequency:** weekly. **Effective Market(s):** Atlanta, Memphis, Minneapolis/St. Paul. **Units of Measure:** Dollars per bulk ton. **Time Period Covered:** latest week.

BLOOD ROOT

Source: *Journal of Commerce and Commercial.* **Price Frequency:** weekly in Monday issue. **Units of Measure:** Dollars per lb. **Type of Price:** spot. **Time Period Covered:** latest week.

BLUEBERRIES

Source: *Fresh Fruit and Vegetable Prices.* **Price Frequency:** monthly, seasonally. **Effective Market(s):** West/Central Michigan, South/Central New Jersey, North Carolina. **Units of Measure:** Dollars per flat. **Type of Price:** average price at shipping point. **Time Period Covered:** latest year.

BLUEBERRIES: BLUECROP

Source: *The Packer.* **Price Frequency:** weekly, seasonally. **Effective Market(s):** varies. **Units of Measure:** Dollars per tray. **Type of Price:** price received by farmer. **Time Period Covered:** latest week.

BLUEBERRIES: CULTIVATED, FROZEN

Source: *HRI-Buyer's Guide.* **Price Frequency:** weekly. **Effective Market(s):** Northeastern area. **Units of Measure:** Dollars per case. **Type of Price:** price paid by dining places & institutions. **Time Period Covered:** latest week.

BLUEBERRIES: ELLIOT

Source: *The Packer.* **Price Frequency:** weekly, seasonally. **Effective Market(s):** varies. **Units of Measure:** Dollars per tray. **Type of Price:** price received by farmer. **Time Period Covered:** latest week.

BLUEBERRIES: GEORGIA

Source: *Fresh Fruit and Vegetable Prices.* **Price Frequency:** monthly, seasonally. **Effective Market(s):** Chicago. **Units of Measure:** Dollars per pint. **Type of Price:** average wholesale price. **Time Period Covered:** latest year.

BLUEBERRIES: MICHIGAN

Source: *Fresh Fruit and Vegetable Prices.* **Price Frequency:** monthly, seasonally. **Effective Market(s):** Chicago, New York City. **Units of Measure:** Dollars per pint. **Type of Price:** average wholesale price. **Time Period Covered:** latest year.

BLUEBERRIES: NEW JERSEY

Source: *Fresh Fruit and Vegetable Prices.* **Price Frequency:** monthly, seasonally. **Effective Market(s):** New York City. **Units of Measure:** Dollars per pint. **Type of Price:** average wholesale price. **Time Period Covered:** latest year.

Source: *Lancaster Farming.* **Price Frequency:** weekly, seasonally. **Effective Market(s):** Pennsylvania. **Units of Measure:** Dollars per flat. **Type of Price:** market. **Time Period Covered:** latest week.

Source: *The Packer.* **Price Frequency:** weekly, seasonally. **Effective Market(s):** varies. **Units of Measure:** Dollars per tray. **Type of Price:** price received by farmer. **Time Period Covered:** latest week.

BLUEBERRIES: NORTH CAROLINA

Source: *Fresh Fruit and Vegetable Prices.* **Price Frequency:** monthly, seasonally. **Effective Market(s):** Chicago, New York City. **Units of Measure:** Dollars per pint. **Type of Price:** average wholesale price. **Time Period Covered:** latest year.

BLUEFISH: FILLETS, FRESH

Source: *Seafood Price-Current.* **Price Frequency:** semiweekly. **Effective Market(s):** Mid-Atlantic, New England. **Units of Measure:** Dollars per lb. **Type of Price:** sale by first receiver. **Time Period Covered:** latest day.

BLUEFISH: WHOLE, FRESH

Source: *HRI-Buyers Guide.* **Price Frequency:** weekly. **Effective Market(s):** New York. **Units of Measure:** Dollars per lb. **Type of Price:** price paid by dining places & institutions. **Time Period Covered:** latest week.

Source: *Seafood Price-Current.* **Price Frequency:** semiweekly. **Effective Market(s):** Mid-Atlantic, Boston, New Bedford (MA), Portland (ME). **Units of Measure:** Dollars per lb. **Type of Price:** sale by first receiver, auction price. **Time Period Covered:** latest day.

BLUEGRASS SEED: PROPRIETARY

Source: *Agricultural Prices Annual Summary.* **Price Frequency:** semiannually. **Effective Market(s):** United States. **Units of Measure:** Dollars per lb. **Type of Price:** average paid by farmer. **Time Period Covered:** latest 6 years.

BLUEGRASS SEED: PUBLIC AND COMMON

Source: *Agricultural Prices Annual Summary.* **Price Frequency:** semiannually. **Effective Market(s):** United States. **Units of Measure:** Dollars per lb. **Type of Price:** average paid by farmer. **Time Period Covered:** latest 6 years.

BOAR

Source: *Farm and Dairy.* **Price Frequency:** weekly, seasonally. **Effective Market(s):** Ohio, Pennsylvania. **Units of Measure:** Dollars per head. **Type of Price:** auction high, auction low. **Time Period Covered:** latest week.

BOAR HAMS

Source: *HRI-Buyer's Guide.* **Price Frequency:** weekly. **Effective Market(s):** Northeastern area. **Units of Measure:** Dollars per lb. **Type of Price:** wholesale. **Time Period Covered:** latest week.

Source: *Urner Barry's Price-Current.* **Price Frequency:** daily. **Units of Measure:** Dollars per lb. **Type of Price:** wholesale. **Time Period Covered:** latest day.

Source: *Urner Barry's Price-Current, West Coast Edition.* **Price Frequency:** semiweekly. **Effective Market(s):** West Coast. **Units of Measure:** Dollars per lb. **Type of Price:** wholesale. **Time Period Covered:** latest day.

BOAR SADDLES

Source: *HRI-Buyer's Guide.* **Price Frequency:** weekly. **Effective Market(s):** Northeastern area. **Units of Measure:** Dollars per lb. **Type of Price:** wholesale. **Time Period Covered:** latest week.

Source: *Urner Barry's Price-Current.* **Price Frequency:** daily. **Units of Measure:** Dollars per lb. **Type of Price:** wholesale. **Time Period Covered:** latest day.

Source: *Urner Barry's Price-Current, West Coast Edition.* **Price Frequency:** semiweekly. **Effective Market(s):** West Coast. **Units of Measure:** Dollars per lb. **Type of Price:** wholesale. **Time Period Covered:** latest day.

BOIS DE ROSE OIL

Source: *Journal of Commerce and Commercial.* **Price Frequency:** weekly in Tuesday issue. **Units of Measure:** Dollars per lb. **Type of Price:** spot. **Time Period Covered:** latest week.

Source: *U. S. Essential Oil Trade.* **Price Frequency:** annually. **Effective Market(s):** United States. **Units of Measure:** Dollars per kilogram. **Type of Price:** import value. **Time Period Covered:** latest 3 years.

BOIS DE ROSE OIL: BRAZILIAN

Source: *Chemical Marketing Reporter.* **Price Frequency:** weekly. **Effective Market(s):** New York. **Units of Measure:** Dollars per lb. **Type of Price:** spot. **Time Period Covered:** latest week.

BOLOGNA

Source: *Livestock and Poultry Situation and Outlook Report.* **Price Frequency:** monthly. **Units of Measure:** Dollars per lb. **Type of Price:** retail. **Time Period Covered:** latest 3 years.

Source: *Meat Price Report.* **Price Frequency:** weekly. **Units of Measure:** cents per lb. **Type of Price:** price paid to wholesaler. **Time Period Covered:** latest week.

BON TONER: RED 48

Source: *Chemical Marketing Reporter.* **Price Frequency:** weekly. **Effective Market(s):** New York. **Units of Measure:** Dollars per lb. **Type of Price:** spot. **Time Period Covered:** latest week.

BON TONER: RED 52

Source: *Chemical Marketing Reporter.* **Price Frequency:** weekly. **Effective Market(s):** New York. **Units of Measure:** Dollars per lb. **Type of Price:** spot. **Time Period Covered:** latest week.

BONDED WHISKEY

Source: *Colorado Beverage Analyst.* **Price Frequency:** monthly. **Effective Market(s):** Colorado. **Units of Measure:** Dollars per case. **Type of Price:** wholesale by brand. **Time Period Covered:** latest month.

Source: *Kentucky Beverage Journal.* **Price Frequency:** monthly. **Effective Market(s):** Kentucky. **Units of Measure:** Dollars per bottle, dollars per case. **Type of Price:** wholesale by brand. **Time Period Covered:** latest month.

BONE AND MEAT MEAL

Source: *Feedstuffs.* **Price Frequency:** weekly. **Effective Market(s):** 10 domestic markets. **Units of Measure:** Dollars per bulk ton. **Time Period Covered:** latest week.

BONE MEAL: 50% PROTEIN

Source: *Wall Street Journal.* **Price Frequency:** daily. **Effective Market(s):** Illinois. **Units of Measure:** Dollars per ton. **Time Period Covered:** latest day, day ago, year ago.

BONE MEAL: STEAMED

Source: *Chemical Marketing Reporter.* **Price Frequency:** weekly. **Effective Market(s):** Midwest plants. **Units of Measure:** Dollars per ton. **Type of Price:** spot. **Time Period Covered:** latest week.

Source: *Journal of Commerce and Commercial.* **Price Frequency:** weekly in Thursday issue. **Units of Measure:** Dollars per ton. **Type of Price:** spot. **Time Period Covered:** latest week.

Source: *Prices of Selected Asia/Pacific Products.* **Price Frequency:** monthly. **Effective Market(s):** New York. **Units of Measure:** Dollars per metric ton. **Type of Price:** spot high, spot low. **Time Period Covered:** latest month.

BONE MEAL: STEAMED, IMPORTED

Source: *Prices of Selected Asia/Pacific Products.* **Price Frequency:** monthly. **Effective Market(s):** Tokyo. **Units of Measure:** 1000 Japanese yen per metric ton. **Type of Price:** primary wholesale high, primary wholesale low. **Time Period Covered:** latest month.

BONE PHOSPHATE: DEFLUORINATED OF LIME

see Defluorinated Phosphate.

BONE PHOSPHATE: PRECIPITATED

see Calcium Phosphate Tribasic.

BORAX: ANHYDROUS

Source: *Industrial Minerals.* **Price Frequency:** monthly. **Effective Market(s):** United Kingdom. **Units of Measure:** British pounds per metric tonne. **Type of Price:** producer & dealer. **Time Period Covered:** latest month.

Source: *Journal of Commerce and Commercial.* **Price Frequency:** weekly in Thursday issue. **Units of Measure:** Dollars per ton. **Type of Price:** spot. **Time Period Covered:** latest week.

BORAX: DECAHYDRATE, REFINED, BRITISH

Source: *Industrial Minerals.* **Price Frequency:** monthly. **Effective Market(s):** main European port. **Units of Measure:** British pounds per metric tonne. **Type of Price:** producer & dealer . **Time Period Covered:** latest month.

BORAX: NF

see Sodium Borate.

BORAX: PENTAHYDRATE, REFINED, BRITISH

Source: *Industrial Minerals.* **Price Frequency:** monthly. **Effective Market(s):** main European port. **Units of Measure:** British pounds per metric tonne. **Type of Price:** producer & dealer. **Time Period Covered:** latest month.

BORAX: TECHNICAL GRADE, ANHYDROUS, 99%

Source: *Chemical Marketing Reporter.* **Price Frequency:** weekly. **Effective Market(s):** New York. **Units of Measure:** Dollars per ton. **Type of Price:** spot. **Time Period Covered:** latest week.

BORAX: TECHNICAL GRADE, DECAHYDRATE, GRANULAR, 99-1/2%

Source: *Chemical Marketing Reporter.* **Price Frequency:** weekly. **Effective Market(s):** New York. **Units of Measure:** Dollars per ton. **Type of Price:** spot. **Time Period Covered:** latest week.

BORAX: TECHNICAL GRADE, PENTAHYDRATE, GRANULAR, 99-1/2%

Source: *Chemical Marketing Reporter.* **Price Frequency:** weekly. **Effective Market(s):** New York. **Units of Measure:** Dollars per ton. **Type of Price:** spot. **Time Period Covered:** latest week.

BORIC ACID: REFINED, GRANULAR, BRITISH

Source: *Industrial Minerals.* **Price Frequency:** monthly. **Effective Market(s):** main European port. **Units of Measure:** British pounds per metric tonne. **Type of Price:** producer & dealer. **Time Period Covered:** latest month.

BORIC ACID: TECHNICAL GRADE

Source: *Journal of Commerce and Commercial.* **Price Frequency:** weekly in Thursday issue. **Units of Measure:** Dollars per lb. **Type of Price:** spot. **Time Period Covered:** latest week.

BORIC ACID: TECHNICAL GRADE, GRANULAR, 99.9%

Source: *Chemical Marketing Reporter.* **Price Frequency:** weekly. **Effective Market(s):** New York. **Units of Measure:** Dollars per ton. **Type of Price:** spot. **Time Period Covered:** latest week.

BORON TRICHLORIDE: CP

Source: *Chemical Marketing Reporter.* **Price Frequency:** weekly. **Effective Market(s):** New York. **Units of Measure:** Dollars per lb. **Type of Price:** spot. **Time Period Covered:** latest week.

BORON TRIFLUORIDE

Source: *Chemical Marketing Reporter.* **Price Frequency:** weekly. **Effective Market(s):** New York. **Units of Measure:** Dollars per lb. **Type of Price:** spot. **Time Period Covered:** latest week.

BORON TRIFLUORIDE: ETHERATE

Source: *Chemical Marketing Reporter.* **Price Frequency:** weekly. **Effective Market(s):** New York. **Units of Measure:** Dollars per lb. **Type of Price:** spot. **Time Period Covered:** latest week.

BORON TRIFLUORIDE: PHENOLATE

Source: *Chemical Marketing Reporter.* **Price Frequency:** weekly. **Effective Market(s):** New York. **Units of Measure:** Dollars per lb. **Type of Price:** spot. **Time Period Covered:** latest week.

BOURBON WHISKEY

Source: *Kentucky Beverage Journal.* **Price Frequency:** monthly. **Effective Market(s):** Kentucky. **Units of Measure:** Dollars per bottle, dollars per case. **Type of Price:** wholesale by brand. **Time Period Covered:** latest month.

BOVINE SKIN: DRIED, THAI

Source: *Prices of Selected Asia/Pacific Products.* **Price Frequency:** monthly, seasonally. **Effective Market(s):** Bangkok. **Units of Measure:** Thai baht per kilogram. **Type of Price:** wholesale high, wholesale low. **Time Period Covered:** latest month.

BOVINE SKIN: LARGE SALTED SHEET, THAI

Source: *Prices of Selected Asia/Pacific Products.* **Price Frequency:** monthly, seasonally. **Effective Market(s):** Bangkok. **Units of Measure:** Thai baht per kilogram. **Type of Price:** wholesale high, wholesale low. **Time Period Covered:** latest month.

BOXBOARD: 20-PT, CLAY COATED, RECYCLED, 80 BRIGHT

Source: *Purchasing.* **Price Frequency:** monthly. **Units of Measure:** Dollars per ton. **Type of Price:** transaction. **Time Period Covered:** latest day, month ago, 6 months ago, year ago.

BOXBOARD: RECYCLED FOLDING, 20-PT CHIPBOARD, BENDING

Source: *Pulp & Paper Week.* **Price Frequency:** monthly, usually in last issue of month. **Effective Market(s):** Eastern United States. **Units of Measure:** Dollars per short ton. **Type of Price:** estimated transaction. **Time Period Covered:** latest 3 months, year ago.

BOXBOARD: RECYCLED FOLDING, 20-PT CLAY COATED, 80 BRIGHT

Source: *Pulp & Paper Week.* **Price Frequency:** monthly, usually in last issue of month. **Effective Market(s):** Eastern United States. **Units of Measure:** Dollars per short ton. **Type of Price:** estimated transaction. **Time Period Covered:** latest 3 months, year ago.

BOXES: CORRUGATED, OLD

Source: *Journal of Commerce and Commercial.* **Price Frequency:** daily. **Effective Market(s):** 5-market average. **Units of Measure:** Dollars per ton. **Type of Price:** spot supplier. **Time Period Covered:** latest day.

BOXES: PAPER, SETUP

Source: *Pulp & Paper Week.* **Price Frequency:** monthly, irregularly. **Units of Measure:** index. **Type of Price:** price index. **Time Period Covered:** latest 3 months.

BOXES AND CONTAINERS: PAPER

Source: *Pulp & Paper Week.* **Price Frequency:** monthly, irregularly. **Units of Measure:** index. **Type of Price:** price index. **Time Period Covered:** latest 3 months.

BRAKE REALIGNMENT: MATERIALS AND LABOR

Source: *Agricultural Prices Annual Summary.* **Price Frequency:** semiannually. **Effective Market(s):** United States. **Units of Measure:** Dollars each time. **Type of Price:** average paid by farmer. **Time Period Covered:** latest 6 years.

BRAN

Source: *Agricultural Prices.* **Price Frequency:** quarterly. **Effective Market(s):** United States. **Units of Measure:** Dollars per 100 lbs. **Type of Price:** paid by farmer. **Time Period Covered:** latest 2 quarters, year ago.

Source: *Agricultural Prices.* **Price Frequency:** monthly. **Effective Market(s):** 10 domestic markets, United States. **Units of Measure:** Dollars per 100 lbs. **Type of Price:** paid by farmer. **Time Period Covered:** latest month.

Source: *Agricultural Prices Annual Summary.* **Price Frequency:** quarterly. **Effective Market(s):** 10 domestic markets, United States. **Units of Measure:** Dollars per 100 lbs. **Type of Price:** average received by farmer. **Time Period Covered:** latest year, for US monthly latest 6 years.

BRAN MILLFEEDS

Source: *Feedstuffs.* **Price Frequency:** weekly. **Effective Market(s):** 9 domestic markets. **Units of Measure:** Dollars per bulk ton. **Time Period Covered:** latest week.

Source: *Feedstuffs.* **Price Frequency:** weekly. **Effective Market(s):** 9 domestic markets. **Units of Measure:** Dollars per ton. **Time Period Covered:** latest week.

BRANDY

Source: *Beverage Media.* **Price Frequency:** monthly. **Effective Market(s):** New York. **Units of Measure:** Dollars per unit. **Type of Price:** wholesale by brand. **Time Period Covered:** latest month.

Source: *Colorado Beverage Analyst.* **Price Frequency:** monthly. **Effective Market(s):** Colorado. **Units of Measure:** Dollars per case. **Type of Price:** wholesale by brand. **Time Period Covered:** latest month.

Source: *Illinois Beverage Journal.* **Price Frequency:** monthly. **Effective Market(s):** Illinois. **Units of Measure:** Dollars per case. **Type of Price:** wholesale by brand. **Time Period Covered:** latest month.

Source: *Indiana Beverage Journal.* **Price Frequency:** monthly. **Effective Market(s):** Indiana. **Units of Measure:** Dollars per case, dollars per bottle. **Type of Price:** wholesale by brand. **Time Period Covered:** latest month.

Source: *Kentucky Beverage Journal.* **Price Frequency:** monthly. **Effective Market(s):** Kentucky. **Units of Measure:** Dollars per bottle, dollars per case. **Type of Price:** wholesale by brand. **Time Period Covered:** latest month.

Source: *Nevada Beverage Index.* **Price Frequency:** monthly. **Effective Market(s):** Nevada. **Units of Measure:** Dollars per unit. **Type of Price:** wholesale by brand. **Time Period Covered:** latest month.

Source: *Rhode Island Beverage Journal.* **Price Frequency:** monthly. **Effective Market(s):** Rhode Island. **Units of Measure:** Dollars per unit. **Type of Price:** wholesale by brand. **Time Period Covered:** latest month.

BRASS PIPE

Source: *Iron Age.* **Price Frequency:** monthly. **Effective Market(s):** New York. **Units of Measure:** cents per lb. **Type of Price:** dealer. **Time Period Covered:** latest month.

BRASS POWDER

Source: *American Metal Market.* **Price Frequency:** daily. **Units of Measure:** Dollars per lb. **Type of Price:** wholesale. **Time Period Covered:** latest day.

BRASS SCRAP: CLIPPINGS, NEW, SOFT

Source: *Iron Age.* **Price Frequency:** monthly. **Effective Market(s):** New York. **Units of Measure:** cents per lb. **Type of Price:** dealer. **Time Period Covered:** latest month.

BRASS SCRAP: CLIPPINGS, YELLOW, NEW

Source: *American Metal Market.* **Price Frequency:** daily. **Effective Market(s):** 14 domestic markets, Montreal, Toronto. **Units of Measure:** cents per lb., Canadian cents per lb. **Type of Price:** dealer buying. **Time Period Covered:** latest day.

BRASS SCRAP: LIGHT YELLOW

Source: *American Metal Market.* **Price Frequency:** daily. **Effective Market(s):** 14 domestic markets, Montreal, Toronto. **Units of Measure:** cents per lb., Canadian cents per lb. **Type of Price:** dealer buying. **Time Period Covered:** latest day.

BRASS SCRAP: PIPE

Source: *American Metal Market.* **Price Frequency:** daily. **Effective Market(s):** 14 domestic markets, Montreal, Toronto. **Units of Measure:** cents per lb., Canadian cents per lb. **Type of Price:** dealer buying. **Time Period Covered:** latest day.

BRASS SCRAP: RED

Source: *Iron Age.* **Price Frequency:** monthly. **Units of Measure:** cents per lb. **Type of Price:** mill. **Time Period Covered:** latest month.

BRASS SCRAP: REFINERY

Source: *American Metal Market.* **Price Frequency:** daily. **Units of Measure:** cents per lb. **Type of Price:** refinery. **Time Period Covered:** latest day.

BRASS SCRAP: ROD ENDS, FREE CUTTING

Source: *Iron Age.* **Price Frequency:** monthly. **Units of Measure:** cents per lb. **Type of Price:** mill. **Time Period Covered:** latest month.

BRASS SCRAP: ROD ENDS, YELLOW

Source: *American Metal Market.* **Price Frequency:** daily. **Effective Market(s):** 14 domestic markets, Montreal, Toronto. **Units of Measure:** cents per lb., Canadian cents per lb. **Type of Price:** dealer buying. **Time Period Covered:** latest day.

BRASS SCRAP: ROD TURNINGS, YELLOW

Source: *American Metal Market.* **Price Frequency:** daily. **Effective Market(s):** 14 domestic markets, Montreal, Toronto. **Units of Measure:** cents per lb., Canadian cents per lb. **Type of Price:** dealer buying. **Time Period Covered:** latest day.

BRASS SCRAP: SOLIDS, RED

Source: *American Metal Market.* **Price Frequency:** daily. **Effective Market(s):** 14 domestic markets, Montreal, Toronto. **Units of Measure:** cents per lb., Canadian cents per lb. **Type of Price:** dealer buying. **Time Period Covered:** latest day.

BRASS SCRAP: SOLIDS, YELLOW

Source: *American Metal Market.* **Price Frequency:** daily. **Effective Market(s):** East, Midwest. **Units of Measure:** cents per lb. **Time Period Covered:** latest day.

BRASS SCRAP: SOLIDS, YELLOW, HEAVY

Source: *Iron Age.* **Price Frequency:** monthly. **Units of Measure:** cents per lb. **Type of Price:** refinery. **Time Period Covered:** latest month.

BRASS SCRAP: TURNINGS

Source: *American Metal Market.* **Price Frequency:** daily. **Effective Market(s):** East, Midwest. **Units of Measure:** cents per lb. **Time Period Covered:** latest day.

BRASS SCRAP: TURNINGS AND BORINGS, MIXED, YELLOW

Source: *American Metal Market.* **Price Frequency:** daily. **Effective Market(s):** 14 domestic markets, Montreal, Toronto. **Units of Measure:** cents per lb., Canadian cents per lb. **Type of Price:** dealer buying. **Time Period Covered:** latest day.

BRASS SCRAP: TURNINGS AND BORINGS, RED

Source: *American Metal Market.* **Price Frequency:** daily. **Effective Market(s):** 14 domestic markets, Montreal, Toronto. **Units of Measure:** cents per lb., Canadian cents per lb. **Type of Price:** dealer buying. **Time Period Covered:** latest day.

BRASS SCRAP: TURNINGS, YELLOW, HEAVY

Source: *Iron Age.* **Price Frequency:** monthly. **Units of Measure:** cents per lb. **Type of Price:** refinery. **Time Period Covered:** latest month.

BRASS SCRAP: YELLOW

Source: *Iron Age.* **Price Frequency:** monthly. **Units of Measure:** cents per lb. **Type of Price:** mill. **Time Period Covered:** latest month.

BRASS SHEET

Source: *Purchasing.* **Price Frequency:** quarterly in January, April, July, and October issues. **Units of Measure:** cents per lb. **Type of Price:** transaction. **Time Period Covered:** latest 5 quarters.

BRAZIL CRUZADOS

Source: *Barron's.* **Price Frequency:** weekly. **Effective Market(s):** New York. **Units of Measure:** Brazilian cruzados per United States dollar. **Type of Price:** foreign exchange. **Time Period Covered:** latest 2 weeks.

Source: *International Wheat Council Market Report.* **Price Frequency:** weekly. **Effective Market(s):** London. **Units of Measure:** Brazilian cruzados per United States dollar. **Type of Price:** foreign exchange. **Time Period Covered:** latest 5 weeks.

Source: *New York Times.* **Price Frequency:** daily. **Effective Market(s):** New York. **Units of Measure:** Brazilian Cruzados per United States dollars. **Type of Price:** foreign exchange. **Time Period Covered:** latest 2 days.

Source: *The Times.* **Price Frequency:** daily. **Effective Market(s):** London. **Units of Measure:** Brazilian cruzado per British pound. **Type of Price:** foreign exchange. **Time Period Covered:** latest day.

BREWERS' DRIED GRAINS

Source: *Feed Situation and Outlook Report.* **Price Frequency:** monthly. **Effective Market(s):** Milwaukee. **Units of Measure:** Dollars per ton. **Time Period Covered:** latest 8 months.

Source: *Feedstuffs.* **Price Frequency:** weekly. **Effective Market(s):** Chicago. **Units of Measure:** Dollars per ton. **Time Period Covered:** latest week, week ago, 6 months ago, year ago.

Source: *Feedstuffs.* **Price Frequency:** weekly. **Effective Market(s):** 8 domestic markets. **Units of Measure:** Dollars per ton. **Time Period Covered:** latest week.

Source: *Grain and Feed Market News.* **Price Frequency:** weekly, seasonally. **Effective Market(s):** Milwaukee, St. Louis. **Units of Measure:** Dollars per ton. **Type of Price:** wholesale. **Time Period Covered:** latest week, week ago, year ago.

BREWERS' PRODUCTS: GRAINS, DRIED

Source: *Feedstuffs.* **Price Frequency:** weekly. **Effective Market(s):** 8 domestic markets. **Units of Measure:** Dollars per bulk ton. **Time Period Covered:** latest week.

BREWERS' PRODUCTS: YEAST, DRIED

Source: *Feedstuffs.* **Price Frequency:** weekly. **Effective Market(s):** 8 domestic markets. **Units of Measure:** Dollars per lb. **Time Period Covered:** latest week.

BREWERS' RICE

Source: *Rice Market News.* **Price Frequency:** weekly, seasonally. **Effective Market(s):** Arkansas, Texas, Louisiana, California. **Units of Measure:** Dollars per 100 lbs. **Type of Price:** bulk. **Time Period Covered:** latest week, year ago.

BRICKS: COMMON BUILDING

Source: *Standard & Poor's Statistical Service Current Statistics.* **Price Frequency:** monthly, annually. **Units of Measure:** Dollars per 1000. **Time Period Covered:** latest 3 years.

BRICKS: STANDARD MODULAR

Source: *ENR.* **Price Frequency:** monthly in first issue of month. **Effective Market(s):** 16 domestic markets, Montreal, Toronto. **Units of Measure:** Dollars per thousand. **Type of Price:** spot. **Time Period Covered:** latest month.

BRISKET

see Beef Brisket.

BRITISH POUNDS

see Great Britain Pounds Sterling.

BROADCLOTH

Source: *DNR: Daily News Record.* **Price Frequency:** quarterly. **Units of Measure:** Dollars per yard. **Time Period Covered:** latest 3 quarters.

Source: *JTN: The International Textile Magazine.* **Price Frequency:** monthly. **Effective Market(s):** Japan. **Units of Measure:** Japanese yen per yard. **Type of Price:** spot. **Time Period Covered:** latest month.

BROADWOVENS: GRAY, SYNTHETIC

Source: *Commodity Year Book.* **Price Frequency:** monthly, annually. **Units of Measure:** index. **Type of Price:** price index. **Time Period Covered:** latest 5 years.

BROCCOLI

Source: *Agricultural Prices Annual Summary.* **Price Frequency:** annually. **Effective Market(s):** Arizona, California, average of other states, United States. **Units of Measure:** Dollars per 100 lbs. **Type of Price:** average received by farmer. **Time Period Covered:** latest 6 years.

Source: *Agricultural Prices Annual Summary.* **Price Frequency:** monthly, seasonally. **Effective Market(s):** California, United States. **Units of Measure:** Dollars per 100 lbs. **Type of Price:** average received by farmer. **Time Period Covered:** latest 3 years, for US latest 6 years.

Source: *California Farmer.* **Price Frequency:** semimonthly. **Effective Market(s):** Salinas/Watsonville (CA), Santa Maria/Guadalupe/Oceano/Lompoc (CA), Central San Joaquin Valley, Imperial/Coachella/Palo Verde Valleys (CA). **Units of Measure:** Dollars per 23 lb. carton. **Time Period Covered:** latest week, month ago, year ago.

Source: *Fresh Fruit and Vegetable Prices.* **Price Frequency:** monthly, seasonally. **Effective Market(s):** 6 domestic markets. **Units of Measure:** Dollars per carton. **Type of Price:** average price at shipping point. **Time Period Covered:** latest year.

Source: *The Grower.* **Price Frequency:** monthly, seasonally. **Effective Market(s):** Salinas (CA). **Units of Measure:** Dollars per carton. **Time Period Covered:** latest year, year ago, 2 years ago.

Source: *Lancaster Farming.* **Price Frequency:** weekly, seasonally. **Effective Market(s):** Pennsylvania. **Units of Measure:** Dollars per carton. **Type of Price:** market. **Time Period Covered:** latest week.

Source: *New Zealand Farmer.* **Price Frequency:** weekly, seasonally. **Effective Market(s):** New Zealand. **Units of Measure:** New Zealand dollars per case. **Time Period Covered:** latest week.

Source: *The Packer.* **Price Frequency:** weekly, seasonally. **Effective Market(s):** varies. **Units of Measure:** Dollars per carton. **Type of Price:** price received by farmer. **Time Period Covered:** latest week.

BROCCOLI: CALIFORNIA

Source: *Fresh Fruit and Vegetable Prices.* **Price Frequency:** monthly, seasonally. **Effective Market(s):** Chicago, New York City. **Units of Measure:** Dollars per carton. **Type of Price:** average wholesale price. **Time Period Covered:** latest year.

BROCCOLI: CHOPPED, FROZEN

Source: *HRI-Buyer's Guide.* **Price Frequency:** weekly. **Effective Market(s):** Northeastern area. **Units of Measure:** Dollars per case. **Type of Price:** price paid by dining places & institutions. **Time Period Covered:** latest week.

BROCCOLI: FRESH

Source: *Agricultural Prices.* **Price Frequency:** monthly. **Effective Market(s):** United States. **Units of Measure:** Dollars per 100 lbs. **Type of Price:** received by farmer. **Time Period Covered:** latest 2 months, year ago.

Source: *HRI-Buyers Guide.* **Price Frequency:** weekly. **Effective Market(s):** Northeastern area. **Units of Measure:** Dollars per carton. **Type of Price:** price paid by dining places & institutions. **Time Period Covered:** latest week.

Source: *Vegetable and Specialties Situation and Outlook Report.* **Price Frequency:** monthly, annually. **Effective Market(s):** United States. **Units of Measure:** Dollars per 100 lbs. **Type of Price:** received by grower. **Time Period Covered:** latest 4 years.

BROCCOLI: ILLINOIS

Source: *Fresh Fruit and Vegetable Prices.* **Price Frequency:** monthly, seasonally. **Effective Market(s):** Chicago. **Units of Measure:** Dollars per carton. **Type of Price:** average wholesale price. **Time Period Covered:** latest year.

BROCCOLI SPEARS: FROZEN

Source: *HRI-Buyer's Guide.* **Price Frequency:** weekly. **Effective Market(s):** Northeastern area. **Units of Measure:** Dollars per case. **Type of Price:** price paid by dining places & institutions. **Time Period Covered:** latest week.

Source: *Vegetable and Specialties Situation and Outlook Report.* **Price Frequency:** monthly. **Units of Measure:** Dollars per case. **Type of Price:** food service, retail. **Time Period Covered:** latest month, year ago.

BROILER BACKS AND NECKS: READY-TO-COOK

Source: *Poultry Market Statistics.* **Price Frequency:** monthly, annually. **Effective Market(s):** Chicago, Detroit, Northeast. **Units of Measure:** Dollars per lb. **Type of Price:** average to first receiver. **Time Period Covered:** latest year.

BROILER BREASTS: LINE RUN, READY-TO-COOK

Source: *Poultry Market Statistics.* **Price Frequency:** monthly, annually. **Effective Market(s):** Chicago, Detroit, Northeast. **Units of Measure:** Dollars per lb. **Type of Price:** average to first receiver. **Time Period Covered:** latest year.

BROILER BREASTS: RIBS ON, READY-TO-COOK

Source: *Poultry Market Statistics.* **Price Frequency:** monthly, annually. **Effective Market(s):** Chicago, Detroit, Northeast. **Units of Measure:** Dollars per lb. **Type of Price:** average to first receiver. **Time Period Covered:** latest year.

BROILER BREASTS: SKINNED, BONELESS, READY-TO-COOK

Source: *Poultry Market Statistics.* **Price Frequency:** monthly, annually. **Effective Market(s):** Chicago, Detroit, Northeast. **Units of Measure:** Dollars per lb. **Type of Price:** average to first receiver. **Time Period Covered:** latest year.

BROILER GIZZARDS: READY-TO-COOK

Source: *Poultry Market Statistics.* **Price Frequency:** monthly, annually. **Effective Market(s):** Chicago, Detroit, Northeast. **Units of Measure:** Dollars per lb. **Type of Price:** average to first receiver. **Time Period Covered:** latest year.

BROILER GROWER FEED

Source: *Agricultural Outlook.* **Price Frequency:** monthly, annually. **Units of Measure:** Dollars per ton. **Type of Price:** wholesale. **Time Period Covered:** monthly latest 6 months, annually latest 3 years.

Source: *Agricultural Prices.* **Price Frequency:** quarterly. **Effective Market(s):** United States. **Units of Measure:** Dollars per ton. **Type of Price:** paid by farmer. **Time Period Covered:** latest 2 quarters, year ago.

Source: *Agricultural Prices.* **Price Frequency:** monthly. **Effective Market(s):** 10 domestic markets, United States. **Units of Measure:** Dollars per ton. **Type of Price:** paid by farmer. **Time Period Covered:** latest month.

Source: *Agricultural Prices Annual Summary.* **Price Frequency:** quarterly. **Effective Market(s):** 10 domestic markets, United States. **Units of Measure:** Dollars per ton. **Type of Price:** average received by farmer. **Time Period Covered:** latest year, for US monthly latest 6 years.

Source: *Feed Situation and Outlook Report.* **Price Frequency:** quarterly, annually. **Effective Market(s):** United States. **Units of Measure:** Dollars per ton. **Type of Price:** paid by farmer. **Time Period Covered:** latest year.

BROILER LEG QUARTERS: READY-TO-COOK

Source: *Poultry Market Statistics.* **Price Frequency:** monthly, annually. **Effective Market(s):** Chicago, Detroit, Northeast. **Units of Measure:** Dollars per lb. **Type of Price:** average to first receiver. **Time Period Covered:** latest year.

BROILER LEGS: READY-TO-COOK

Source: *Poultry Market Statistics.* **Price Frequency:** monthly, annually. **Effective Market(s):** Chicago, Detroit, Northeast. **Units of Measure:** Dollars per lb. **Type of Price:** average to first receiver. **Time Period Covered:** latest year.

BROILER LIVERS: READY-TO-COOK

Source: *Poultry Market Statistics.* **Price Frequency:** monthly, annually. **Effective Market(s):** Chicago, Detroit, Northeast. **Units of Measure:** Dollars per lb. **Type of Price:** average to first receiver. **Time Period Covered:** latest year.

BROILER WINGS: READY-TO-COOK

Source: *Poultry Market Statistics.* **Price Frequency:** monthly, annually. **Effective Market(s):** Chicago, Detroit, Northeast. **Units of Measure:** Dollars per lb. **Type of Price:** average to first receiver. **Time Period Covered:** latest year.

BROILER-FRYER BREASTS: RIB ON

Source: *Poultry Market Statistics.* **Price Frequency:** weekly. **Effective Market(s):** Arkansas. **Units of Measure:** Dollars per lb. **Type of Price:** weighted average. **Time Period Covered:** latest year.

BROILER-FRYER BREASTS: SKINNED, BONELESS

Source: *Poultry Market Statistics.* **Price Frequency:** weekly. **Effective Market(s):** Arkansas. **Units of Measure:** Dollars per lb. **Type of Price:** weighted average. **Time Period Covered:** latest year.

BROILER-FRYER LEG QUARTERS

Source: *Poultry Market Statistics.* **Price Frequency:** weekly. **Effective Market(s):** Arkansas. **Units of Measure:** Dollars per lb. **Type of Price:** weighted average. **Time Period Covered:** latest year.

BROILER-FRYER LEGS

Source: *Poultry Market Statistics.* **Price Frequency:** weekly. **Effective Market(s):** Arkansas. **Units of Measure:** Dollars per lb. **Type of Price:** weighted average. **Time Period Covered:** latest year.

BROILER-FRYER WINGS

Source: *Poultry Market Statistics.* **Price Frequency:** weekly. **Effective Market(s):** Arkansas. **Units of Measure:** Dollars per lb. **Type of Price:** weighted average. **Time Period Covered:** latest year.

BROILER-FRYERS

Source: *Poultry Market Statistics.* **Price Frequency:** monthly, annually. **Effective Market(s):** Florida, Los Angeles, San Francisco. **Units of Measure:** cents per lb. **Type of Price:** delivered to retailer. **Time Period Covered:** latest year.

BROILER-FRYERS: GRADE A, READY-TO-COOK

Source: *Poultry Market Statistics.* **Price Frequency:** weekly. **Effective Market(s):** 13 Domestic markets. **Units of Measure:** cents per lb. **Type of Price:** weighted average. **Time Period Covered:** latest year.

BROILER-FRYERS: READY-TO-COOK

Source: *Poultry Market Statistics.* **Price Frequency:** weekly. **Effective Market(s):** 12-city average. **Units of Measure:** cents per lb. **Type of Price:** weighted average. **Time Period Covered:** latest 4 years.

BROILER-FRYERS: WITHOUT GIBLETS, READY-TO-COOK

Source: *Poultry Market Statistics.* **Price Frequency:** weekly. **Effective Market(s):** Central, East, West. **Units of Measure:** cents per lb. **Type of Price:** first receiver. **Time Period Covered:** latest year.

BROILERS

see also Broiler-Fryers, Chickens, Fryers, Hens, Roasters.

Source: *Agra Europe.* **Price Frequency:** weekly. **Effective Market(s):** 9 European markets. **Units of Measure:** national currency per live kilogram. **Type of Price:** average. **Time Period Covered:** latest week.

Source: *Agricultural Outlook.* **Price Frequency:** quarterly, annually. **Effective Market(s):** 12-city average. **Units of Measure:** cents per lb. **Type of Price:** past averages. **Time Period Covered:** latest year.

Source: *Agricultural Outlook.* **Price Frequency:** monthly, annually. **Effective Market(s):** United States. **Units of Measure:** cents per lb. **Type of Price:** price received by farmer. **Time Period Covered:** monthly latest 6 months, annually latest 3 years.

Source: *Agricultural Outlook.* **Price Frequency:** monthly, annually. **Effective Market(s):** 12-city average. **Units of Measure:** cents per lb. **Type of Price:** wholesale. **Time Period Covered:** monthly latest 6 months, annually latest 3 years.

Source: *Agricultural Prices.* **Price Frequency:** monthly. **Effective Market(s):** United States. **Units of Measure:** Dollars per lb. **Type of Price:** received by farmer. **Time Period Covered:** latest 2 months, year ago.

Source: *Agricultural Prices.* **Price Frequency:** monthly. **Effective Market(s):** 11 domestic markets, United States. **Units of Measure:** Dollars per lb. **Type of Price:** received by farmer. **Time Period Covered:** latest month.

Source: *Agricultural Trade Highlights.* **Price Frequency:** monthly. **Units of Measure:** Dollars per metric ton. **Type of Price:** first receiver. **Time Period Covered:** latest week, month ago, year ago.

Source: *Commodity Year Book.* **Price Frequency:** quarterly, annually. **Effective Market(s):** United States. **Units of Measure:** cents per lb. **Type of Price:** farm, city. **Time Period Covered:** latest 5 years.

Source: *Commodity Year Book.* **Price Frequency:** monthly, annually. **Effective Market(s):** United States. **Units of Measure:** cents per lb. **Type of Price:** wholesale. **Time Period Covered:** latest 5 years.

Source: *Commodity Year Book.* **Price Frequency:** annually. **Effective Market(s):** 4-region area. **Units of Measure:** cents per lb. **Type of Price:** retail. **Time Period Covered:** latest 5 years.

Source: *Commodity Year Book.* **Price Frequency:** annually. **Effective Market(s):** Georgia. **Units of Measure:** cents per lb. **Time Period Covered:** latest 7 years.

Source: *Doane's Agricultural Report.* **Price Frequency:** weekly. **Effective Market(s):** 12-city weighted average. **Units of Measure:** cents per lb. **Time Period Covered:** latest week, week ago, year ago.

Source: *FAO Quarterly Bulletin of Statistics.* **Price Frequency:** monthly, annually. **Effective Market(s):** United States. **Units of Measure:** Dollars per 100 lbs., dollars per metric ton. **Type of Price:** farm. **Time Period Covered:** latest 3 years.

Source: *Feedstuffs.* **Price Frequency:** weekly. **Effective Market(s):** 12-city average. **Units of Measure:** cents per lb. **Time Period Covered:** latest week, week ago, 6 months ago, year ago.

Source: *Livestock and Poultry Situation and Outlook Report.* **Price Frequency:** quarterly, annually. **Effective Market(s):** 12-market average. **Units of Measure:** cents per lb. **Type of Price:** wholesale. **Time Period Covered:** latest 2 years.

Source: *Livestock and Poultry Update.* **Price Frequency:** monthly. **Effective Market(s):** Georgia, 12-city average. **Units of Measure:** cents per lb. **Type of Price:** wholesale. **Time Period Covered:** latest 3 months, year ago.

Source: *Poultry Times.* **Price Frequency:** biweekly. **Effective Market(s):** 9 domestic markets, 12-city average. **Units of Measure:** cents per lb. **Time Period Covered:** week ago, 3 weeks ago.

Source: *Washington Farmer-Stockman.* **Price Frequency:** monthly, seasonally. **Effective Market(s):** Washington. **Units of Measure:** Dollars per lb. **Type of Price:** received by farmer. **Time Period Covered:** latest month, month ago, year ago.

BROILERS: DRESSED

Source: *Investor's Daily.* **Price Frequency:** daily. **Units of Measure:** Dollars per lb. **Type of Price:** spot. **Time Period Covered:** latest 2 days.

Source: *New York Times.* **Price Frequency:** daily. **Units of Measure:** Dollars per lb. **Type of Price:** cash. **Time Period Covered:** latest 2 days.

BROILERS: FRESH, SPLIT OR QUARTERED

Source: *Meat Price Report.* **Price Frequency:** weekly. **Units of Measure:** cents per lb. **Type of Price:** price paid to wholesaler. **Time Period Covered:** latest week.

BROILERS: GRADE A, DRESSED

Source: *Asian Wall Street Journal.* **Price Frequency:** daily. **Effective Market(s):** New York. **Units of Measure:** Dollars per lb. **Type of Price:** cash. **Time Period Covered:** latest 2 days, year ago.

Source: *Wall Street Journal.* **Price Frequency:** daily. **Effective Market(s):** New York. **Units of Measure:** Dollars per lb. **Time Period Covered:** latest day, day ago, year ago.

BROILERS: GRADE A, READY-TO-COOK, ICED

Source: *Feedstuffs.* **Price Frequency:** weekly. **Effective Market(s):** Chicago. **Units of Measure:** cents per lb. **Time Period Covered:** latest week, week ago, 6 months ago, year ago.

BROILERS: GRADE A, WHOLE, FRESH, PLUG OUT

Source: *Meat Price Report.* **Price Frequency:** weekly. **Units of Measure:** cents per lb. **Type of Price:** price paid to wholesaler. **Time Period Covered:** latest week.

BROILERS: LIVE

Source: *Standard & Poor's Statistical Service Current Statistics.* **Price Frequency:** monthly, annually. **Effective Market(s):** Georgia. **Units of Measure:** Dollars per lb. **Time Period Covered:** latest 5 years.

Source: *Survey of Current Business.* **Price Frequency:** monthly, annually. **Effective Market(s):** Georgia. **Units of Measure:** Dollars per lb. **Type of Price:** average. **Time Period Covered:** latest year.

BROILERS: WEST GERMAN

Source: *FAO Quarterly Bulletin of Statistics.* **Price Frequency:** monthly, annually. **Effective Market(s):** West Germany. **Units of Measure:** West German marks per kilogram, dollars per metric ton. **Type of Price:** farm. **Time Period Covered:** latest 3 years.

BROILERS-FRYERS

see also Broilers, Chickens, Fryers, Hens, Roasters.

BROMINE

Source: *Chemical Marketing Reporter.* **Price Frequency:** weekly. **Effective Market(s):** New York. **Units of Measure:** Dollars per lb. **Type of Price:** spot. **Time Period Covered:** latest week.

Source: *Journal of Commerce and Commercial.* **Price Frequency:** weekly in Friday issue. **Units of Measure:** Dollars per lb. **Type of Price:** spot. **Time Period Covered:** latest week.

BROMINE: PURIFIED

Source: *Industrial Minerals.* **Price Frequency:** monthly. **Effective Market(s):** main European port. **Units of Measure:** Dollars per lb. **Type of Price:** producer & dealer. **Time Period Covered:** latest month.

BROMOCHLOROMETHANE

Source: *Chemical Marketing Reporter.* **Price Frequency:** weekly. **Effective Market(s):** Midland. **Units of Measure:** Dollars per lb. **Type of Price:** spot. **Time Period Covered:** latest week.

BRONZE: SCRAP, COMMERCIAL

Source: *Iron Age.* **Price Frequency:** monthly. **Units of Measure:** cents per lb. **Type of Price:** mill. **Time Period Covered:** latest month.

BRONZE: SCRAP, HIGH GRADE, LOW LEAD

Source: *American Metal Market.* **Price Frequency:** daily. **Effective Market(s):** San Francisco. **Units of Measure:** cents per lb. **Type of Price:** dealer buying. **Time Period Covered:** latest day.

BRUSSEL SPROUTS

Source: *Lancaster Farming.* **Price Frequency:** weekly, seasonally. **Effective Market(s):** Pennsylvania. **Units of Measure:** Dollars per unit. **Type of Price:** market. **Time Period Covered:** latest week.

BRUSSEL SPROUTS: CALIFORNIA

Source: *Fresh Fruit and Vegetable Prices.* **Price Frequency:** monthly, seasonally. **Effective Market(s):** Chicago, New York City. **Units of Measure:** Dollars per carton. **Type of Price:** average wholesale price. **Time Period Covered:** latest year.

BRUSSEL SPROUTS: FRESH

Source: *HRI-Buyers Guide.* **Price Frequency:** weekly. **Effective Market(s):** Northeastern area. **Units of Measure:** Dollars per tray. **Type of Price:** price paid by dining places & institutions. **Time Period Covered:** latest week.

BRUSSEL SPROUTS: OHAKUNE

Source: *New Zealand Farmer.* **Price Frequency:** weekly, seasonally. **Effective Market(s):** New Zealand. **Units of Measure:** New Zealand dollars per bag/crate. **Time Period Covered:** latest week.

BUCKTHORN BARK

Source: *Journal of Commerce and Commercial.* **Price Frequency:** weekly in Monday issue. **Units of Measure:** Dollars per lb. **Type of Price:** spot. **Time Period Covered:** latest week.

BUFFALO BURGER: GROUND

Source: *HRI-Buer's Guide.* **Price Frequency:** weekly. **Effective Market(s):** Northeastern area. **Units of Measure:** Dollars per lb. **Type of Price:** wholesale. **Time Period Covered:** latest week.

BUFFALO CHUCK ROAST: BONELESS

Source: *HRI-Buyer's Guide.* **Price Frequency:** weekly. **Effective Market(s):** Northeastern area. **Units of Measure:** Dollars per lb. **Type of Price:** wholesale. **Time Period Covered:** latest week.

BUFFALO RIBEYES: BONELESS

Source: *HRI-Buyer's Guide.* **Price Frequency:** weekly. **Effective Market(s):** Northeastern area. **Units of Measure:** Dollars per lb. **Type of Price:** wholesale. **Time Period Covered:** latest week.

BUFFALO SKIN: DRIED, GRADE A, THAI

Source: *Prices of Selected Asia/Pacific Products.* **Price Frequency:** monthly, seasonally. **Effective Market(s):** Bangkok. **Units of Measure:** Thai baht per kilogram. **Type of Price:** wholesale high, wholesale low. **Time Period Covered:** latest month.

BUFFALO SKIN: SALTED, GRADE A, THAI

Source: *Prices of Selected Asia/Pacific Products.* **Price Frequency:** monthly, seasonally. **Effective Market(s):** Bangkok. **Units of Measure:** Thai baht per kilogram. **Type of Price:** wholesale high, wholesale low. **Time Period Covered:** latest month.

BULL CALVES: CHAROLAIS

Source: *Farmers Weekly.* **Price Frequency:** weekly. **Effective Market(s):** Great Britain. **Units of Measure:** British pounds per head. **Time Period Covered:** latest week, week ago, year ago.

BULL CALVES: HEREFORD

Source: *Farmers Weekly.* **Price Frequency:** weekly. **Effective Market(s):** Great Britain. **Units of Measure:** British pounds per head. **Time Period Covered:** latest week, week ago, year ago.

BULLS

Source: *New Zealand Farmer.* **Price Frequency:** weekly, seasonally. **Effective Market(s):** 8 New Zealand markets. **Units of Measure:** New Zealand cents per kilogram. **Type of Price:** export. **Time Period Covered:** latest week.

BULLS: ADULT, STORE

Source: *New Zealand Farmer.* **Price Frequency:** weekly, seasonally. **Effective Market(s):** 7 New Zealand markets. **Units of Measure:** New Zealand dollars per head. **Time Period Covered:** latest 2 weeks.

BULLS: FEEDER, MEDIUM AND LARGE FRAME 1

Source: *Montana Farmer-Stockman.* **Price Frequency:** monthly, seasonally. **Effective Market(s):** Billings (MT). **Units of Measure:** Dollars per 100 lbs. **Type of Price:** cash auction. **Time Period Covered:** latest month.

BULLS: GRADE 1-2

Source: *Livestock, Meat, Wool Market News.* **Price Frequency:** weekly. **Effective Market(s):** Omaha, Sioux City, South St. Paul, Lancaster County (PA). **Units of Measure:** Dollars per 100 lbs. **Type of Price:** average. **Time Period Covered:** latest week, year ago.

BULLS: SLAUGHTER

Source: *Montana Farmer-Stockman.* **Price Frequency:** monthly, seasonally. **Effective Market(s):** Billings (MT), Riverton (WY). **Units of Measure:** Dollars per 100 lbs. **Type of Price:** cash auction. **Time Period Covered:** latest month.

BULLS: SLAUGHTER, YIELD GRADE 1

Source: *Utah Farmer-Stockman.* **Price Frequency:** monthly. **Effective Market(s):** Spanish Fork (UT), Salina (UT). **Units of Measure:** Dollars per 100 lbs. **Type of Price:** auction. **Time Period Covered:** latest month.

BULLS: SLAUGHTER, YIELD GRADE 1-2

Source: *Oregon Farmer-Stockman.* **Price Frequency:** monthly. **Effective Market(s):** Oregon/Washington. **Time Period Covered:** latest month.

Source: *Washington Farmer-Stockman.* **Price Frequency:** monthly, seasonally. **Effective Market(s):** Washington/Oregon. **Units of Measure:** Dollars per 100 lbs. **Time Period Covered:** latest month.

BULLS: SLAUGHTER, YIELD GRADE 2 AND BULLS FOR FURTHER Breeding

Source: *Utah Farmer-Stockman.* **Price Frequency:** monthly. **Effective Market(s):** Spanish Fork (UT), Salina (UT). **Units of Measure:** Dollars per 100 lbs. **Type of Price:** auction. **Time Period Covered:** latest month.

BULLS: SLAUGHTER, YOUNG

Source: *Drovers Journal.* **Price Frequency:** semiweekly. **Effective Market(s):** 8 domestic markets. **Units of Measure:** Dollars per 100 lbs. **Time Period Covered:** latest week.

BULLS: YEARLING, STORE

Source: *New Zealand Farmer.* **Price Frequency:** weekly, seasonally. **Effective Market(s):** 7 New Zealand markets. **Units of Measure:** New Zealand dollars per head. **Time Period Covered:** latest 2 weeks.

BULLS: YOUNG

Source: *Scottish Farmer.* **Price Frequency:** weekly. **Effective Market(s):** Ayr (Scotland), Carlisle (Scotland), Edinburgh (Scotland), Paisley (Scotland), Stirling (Scotland), Scotland. **Units of Measure:** British pence per kilogram. **Type of Price:** average. **Time Period Covered:** latest week.

BULLS: YOUNG, ARGENTINE

Source: *FAO Quarterly Bulletin of Statistics.* **Price Frequency:** monthly, annually. **Effective Market(s):** Buenos Aires. **Units of Measure:** Argentine pesos per kilogram, dollars per metric ton. **Type of Price:** wholesale. **Time Period Covered:** latest 3 years.

BULLS: YOUNG, DEADWEIGHT

Source: *Farmers Weekly.* **Price Frequency:** weekly, seasonally. **Effective Market(s):** Great Britain. **Units of Measure:** British pence per kilogram. **Time Period Covered:** latest week.

Source: *Scottish Farmer.* **Price Frequency:** weekly. **Effective Market(s):** Scotland. **Units of Measure:** British pence per kilogram. **Type of Price:** average. **Time Period Covered:** latest week.

BUNNIES

Source: *Lacanster Farming.* **Price Frequency:** weekly. **Effective Market(s):** Pennsylvania. **Units of Measure:** Dollars each. **Type of Price:** auction. **Time Period Covered:** latest week.

BURLAP

Source: *Commodity Year book.* **Price Frequency:** monthly, annually. **Effective Market(s):** New York. **Units of Measure:** cents per yard. **Type of Price:** wholesale. **Time Period Covered:** latest 7 years.

BURLAP: 7 OUNCES, 36″

Source: *Fibre Market News.* **Price Frequency:** weekly. **Effective Market(s):** Bangladesh, Calcutta. **Units of Measure:** cents per yard. **Time Period Covered:** latest month.

BURLAP: 7.5 OUNCES, 36″

Source: *Fibre Market News.* **Price Frequency:** weekly. **Effective Market(s):** Bangladesh, Calcutta. **Units of Measure:** cents per yard. **Time Period Covered:** latest month.

BURLAP: 7.5 OUNCES, 40″

Source: *Fibre Market News.* **Price Frequency:** weekly. **Effective Market(s):** Bangladesh, Calcutta. **Units of Measure:** cents per yard. **Time Period Covered:** latest month.

BURLAP: 8.9 OUNCES, 40″

Source: *Fibre Market News.* **Price Frequency:** weekly. **Effective Market(s):** Bangladesh, Calcutta. **Units of Measure:** cents per yard. **Time Period Covered:** latest month.

BURLAP: 10 OUNCES, 36″

Source: *Fibre Market News.* **Price Frequency:** weekly. **Effective Market(s):** Bangladesh, Calcutta. **Units of Measure:** cents per yard. **Time Period Covered:** latest month.

BURLAP: 10 OUNCES, 40″

Source: *Asian Wall Street Journal.* **Price Frequency:** daily. **Effective Market(s):** New York. **Units of Measure:** Dollars per yard. **Type of Price:** cash. **Time Period Covered:** latest 2 days, year ago.

Source: *Commodity Trade and Price Trends.* **Price Frequency:** annually. **Effective Market(s):** New York. **Units of Measure:** cents per meter, 1980 constant cents per meter. **Type of Price:** spot. **Time Period Covered:** latest 37 years.

Source: *CRB Commodity Index Report.* **Price Frequency:** weekly. **Effective Market(s):** New York. **Units of Measure:** Dollars per yard. **Type of Price:** spot. **Time Period Covered:** latest week.

Source: *Fibre Market News.* **Price Frequency:** weekly. **Effective Market(s):** Bangladesh, Calcutta. **Units of Measure:** cents per yard. **Time Period Covered:** latest month.

Source: *Journal of Commerce and Commercial.* **Price Frequency:** daily. **Effective Market(s):** New York. **Type of Price:** spot supplier. **Time Period Covered:** latest day.

Source: *Wall Street Journal.* **Price Frequency:** daily. **Effective Market(s):** New York. **Units of Measure:** Dollars per yard. **Time Period Covered:** latest day, day ago, year ago.

BURLAP: 10.4 OUNCES, 36″

Source: *Fibre Market News.* **Price Frequency:** weekly. **Effective Market(s):** Bangladesh, Calcutta. **Units of Measure:** cents per yard. **Time Period Covered:** latest month.

BURLAP BAGS: POTATO, 50 LB

Source: *Fibre Market News.* **Price Frequency:** weekly. **Units of Measure:** cents per bag. **Time Period Covered:** latest week.

BURLAP BAGS: POTATO, 100 LB

Source: *Fibre Market News.* **Price Frequency:** weekly. **Units of Measure:** cents per bag. **Time Period Covered:** latest week.

BUTADIENE

Source: *Chemical Marketing Reporter.* **Price Frequency:** weekly. **Effective Market(s):** New York. **Units of Measure:** Dollars per lb. **Type of Price:** spot. **Time Period Covered:** latest week.

Source: *Journal of Commerce and Commercial.* **Price Frequency:** weekly in Thursday issue. **Units of Measure:** Dollars per lb. **Type of Price:** spot. **Time Period Covered:** latest week.

Source: *Modern Plastics.* **Price Frequency:** quarterly in January, April, July & October issues. **Units of Measure:** cents per lb. **Type of Price:** market. **Time Period Covered:** latest 3 years.

Source: *Purchasing.* **Price Frequency:** quarterly in January, April, July, and October issues. **Units of Measure:** cents per lb. **Type of Price:** transaction. **Time Period Covered:** latest 5 quarters.

BUTANE

Source: *International Butane/Propane Newsletter.* **Price Frequency:** semimonthly. **Effective Market(s):** East Coast (US), Japan, Mediterranean, Rotterdam, South Korea. **Units of Measure:** Dollars per metric ton. **Time Period Covered:** latest week.

Source: *Oil Buyers' Guide.* **Price Frequency:** weekly. **Effective Market(s):** Venezuela. **Units of Measure:** Dollars per metric ton. **Type of Price:** official. **Time Period Covered:** latest week.

Source: *Oil Buyers' Guide.* **Price Frequency:** weekly. **Effective Market(s):** 14 international markets. **Units of Measure:** Dollars per metric ton. **Type of Price:** spot. **Time Period Covered:** latest week.

Source: *Oil Buyers' Guide International.* **Price Frequency:** daily, weekly. **Effective Market(s):** 7 international markets. **Type of Price:** spot. **Time Period Covered:** latest week.

Source: *Oil Buyers' Guide International.* **Price Frequency:** weekly. **Effective Market(s):** Venezuela. **Units of Measure:** Dollars per barrel. **Type of Price:** official. **Time Period Covered:** latest week.

Source: *Petroleum Economist.* **Price Frequency:** monthly. **Effective Market(s):** Middle East, Northwest Europe, United States. **Units of Measure:** Dollars per metric ton/cents per gallon. **Time Period Covered:** latest month.

Source: *Petroleum Economist.* **Price Frequency:** monthly. **Effective Market(s):** Mediterranean, North Europe, United States. **Units of Measure:** Dollars per metric ton/cents per gallon. **Type of Price:** spot. **Time Period Covered:** latest month.

BUTANE: ABU DHABI

Source: *International Butane/Propane Newsletter.* **Price Frequency:** semimonthly. **Effective Market(s):** Abu Dhabi. **Units of Measure:** Dollars per metric ton. **Type of Price:** producer. **Time Period Covered:** latest week.

BUTANE: ALGERIA

Source: *International Butane/Propane Newsletter.* **Price Frequency:** semimonthly. **Effective Market(s):** Algeria. **Units of Measure:** Dollars per metric ton. **Type of Price:** producer. **Time Period Covered:** latest week.

BUTANE: ISO-BUTANE, VENEZUELA

Source: *International Butane/Propane Newsletter.* **Price Frequency:** semimonthly. **Effective Market(s):** Venezuela. **Units of Measure:** Dollars per metric ton. **Type of Price:** producer. **Time Period Covered:** latest week.

BUTANE: KUWAIT

Source: *International Butane/Propane Newsletter.* **Price Frequency:** semimonthly. **Effective Market(s):** Kuwait. **Units of Measure:** Dollars per metric ton. **Type of Price:** producer. **Time Period Covered:** latest week.

BUTANE: MIX

Source: *Oil Buyers' Guide.* **Price Frequency:** daily, weekly. **Effective Market(s):** Los Angeles. **Units of Measure:** cents per gallon. **Type of Price:** spot. **Time Period Covered:** latest week.

BUTANE: MONT BELVIEU

Source: *International Butane/Propane Newsletter.* **Price Frequency:** semimonthly. **Effective Market(s):** Mont Belvieu (TX). **Units of Measure:** cents per gallon. **Type of Price:** producer. **Time Period Covered:** latest week.

BUTANE: NORMAL

Source: *Asian Wall Street Journal.* **Price Frequency:** daily. **Effective Market(s):** Mont Belvieu (TX). **Units of Measure:** Dollars per gallon. **Type of Price:** spot. **Time Period Covered:** latest 2 days, year ago.

Source: *Energy Pricing News: Petrochemical Report.* **Price Frequency:** bimonthly. **Effective Market(s):** Edmonton (Canada), Sarnia (Canada). **Units of Measure:** Canadian dollars per cubic meter. **Type of Price:** contract. **Time Period Covered:** latest month.

Source: *Oil & Gas Journal.* **Price Frequency:** monthly in third issue of month. **Effective Market(s):** Conway (KS), Mont Belvieu (TX). **Units of Measure:** cents per gallon. **Type of Price:** spot. **Time Period Covered:** latest 2 months.

Source: *Oil Buyers' Guide.* **Price Frequency:** daily, weekly. **Effective Market(s):** Los Angeles, Mont Belvieu (TX), Conway (KS), Sarnia (Canada). **Units of Measure:** cents per gallon. **Type of Price:** spot. **Time Period Covered:** latest week.

BUTANE: NORMAL, VENEZUELA

Source: *International Butane/Propane Newsletter.* **Price Frequency:** semimonthly. **Effective Market(s):** Venezuela. **Units of Measure:** Dollars per metric ton. **Type of Price:** producer. **Time Period Covered:** latest week.

BUTANE: NORTH SEA

Source: *International Butane/Propane Newsletter.* **Price Frequency:** semimonthly. **Effective Market(s):** North Sea. **Units of Measure:** Dollars per metric ton. **Type of Price:** producer. **Time Period Covered:** latest week.

BUTANE: QATAR

Source: *International Butane/Propane Newsletter.* **Price Frequency:** semimonthly. **Effective Market(s):** Qatar. **Units of Measure:** Dollars per metric ton. **Type of Price:** producer. **Time Period Covered:** latest week.

BUTANE: SAUDI ARABIA

Source: *International Butane/Propane Newsletter.* **Price Frequency:** semimonthly. **Effective Market(s):** Saudi Arabia. **Units of Measure:** Dollars per metric ton. **Type of Price:** producer. **Time Period Covered:** latest week.

1,4-BUTANEDIOL

Source: *Chemical Marketing Reporter.* **Price Frequency:** weekly. **Effective Market(s):** New York . **Units of Measure:** Dollars per lb. **Type of Price:** spot. **Time Period Covered:** latest week.

1-BUTENE

Source: *Chemical Marketing Reporter.* **Price Frequency:** weekly. **Effective Market(s):** New York. **Units of Measure:** Dollars per lb. **Type of Price:** spot. **Time Period Covered:** latest week.

BUTTER

Source: *Statistical Bulletin of the South Pacific: Retail Price Indexes.* **Price Frequency:** annually. **Effective Market(s):** 18 South Pacific markets. **Units of Measure:** Australian dollars per 250 grams. **Type of Price:** retail. **Time Period Covered:** latest year.

Source: *World Dairy Situation.* **Price Frequency:** semiannually. **Effective Market(s):** North Europe/World ports. **Units of Measure:** Dollars per metric ton. **Time Period Covered:** latest 7 years.

BUTTER: 90 SCORE

Source: *Monthly Price Review.* **Price Frequency:** daily. **Effective Market(s):** East, Midwest. **Units of Measure:** Dollars per lb. **Type of Price:** spot. **Time Period Covered:** latest month.

Source: *Weekly Insiders Dairy & Egg Letter.* **Price Frequency:** weekly, annually. **Units of Measure:** Dollars per lb. **Type of Price:** wholesale 5 day average. **Time Period Covered:** latest week, week ago, year ago, 2 years ago.

BUTTER: 92 SCORE

Source: *Monthly Price Review.* **Price Frequency:** daily. **Effective Market(s):** East, Midwest. **Units of Measure:** Dollars per lb. **Type of Price:** spot. **Time Period Covered:** latest month.

Source: *Weekly Insiders Dairy & Egg Letter.* **Price Frequency:** weekly, annually. **Units of Measure:** Dollars per lb. **Type of Price:** wholesale 5 day average. **Time Period Covered:** latest week, week ago, year ago, 2 years ago.

BUTTER: 92 SCORE, FRESH

Source: *Weekly Insiders Dairy & Egg Letter.* **Price Frequency:** monthly. **Units of Measure:** Dollars per lb. **Type of Price:** wholesale. **Time Period Covered:** latest month, month ago.

BUTTER: 93 SCORE

Source: *Monthly Price Review.* **Price Frequency:** daily. **Effective Market(s):** East, Midwest. **Units of Measure:** Dollars per lb. **Type of Price:** spot. **Time Period Covered:** latest month.

Source: *Weekly Insiders Dairy & Egg Letter.* **Price Frequency:** weekly, annually. **Units of Measure:** Dollars per lb. **Type of Price:** wholesale 5 day average. **Time Period Covered:** latest week, week ago, year ago, 2 years ago.

BUTTER: 93 SCORE, CANADA

Source: *Meat and Dairy Products.* **Price Frequency:** monthly. **Effective Market(s):** Canada. **Units of Measure:** Canadian dollars per kilogram. **Type of Price:** average. **Time Period Covered:** latest 3 years.

BUTTER: ADVERTISED BRANDS

Source: *Weekly Insiders Dairy & Egg Letter.* **Price Frequency:** weekly, annually. **Effective Market(s):** New York. **Units of Measure:** Dollars per lb. **Type of Price:** retail. **Time Period Covered:** latest week, week ago, year ago, 2 years ago.

BUTTER: CHIPS/PATTIES

Source: *Dairy Market Statistics.* **Price Frequency:** monthly, annually. **Effective Market(s):** Central States, California cities, East Coast cities. **Units of Measure:** Dollars per lb. **Type of Price:** wholesale. **Time Period Covered:** latest year.

BUTTER: CHOICEST, NETHERLANDS

Source: *Meat and Dairy Products.* **Price Frequency:** monthly. **Effective Market(s):** Netherlands. **Units of Measure:** Dutch guilders per kilogram. **Type of Price:** average. **Time Period Covered:** latest 3 years.

BUTTER: CONTINENTALS

Source: *Dairy Market Statistics.* **Price Frequency:** monthly, annually. **Effective Market(s):** Central States, East Coast cities. **Units of Measure:** Dollars per lb. **Type of Price:** wholesale. **Time Period Covered:** latest year.

BUTTER: DANISH

Source: *FAO Quarterly Bulletin of Statistics.* **Price Frequency:** monthly, annually. **Effective Market(s):** London. **Units of Measure:** British pounds per 1000 kilograms, dollars per metric ton. **Type of Price:** wholesale. **Time Period Covered:** latest 3 years.

BUTTER: DUTCH

Source: *FAO Quarterly Bulletin of Statistics.* **Price Frequency:** monthly, annually. **Effective Market(s):** Netherlands. **Units of Measure:** Dutch guilders per 100 kilograms, dollars per metric ton. **Type of Price:** factory. **Time Period Covered:** latest 3 years.

BUTTER: ENGLISH

Source: *Meat and Dairy Products.* **Price Frequency:** monthly. **Effective Market(s):** United Kingdom. **Units of Measure:** British pounds per tonne. **Type of Price:** average. **Time Period Covered:** latest 3 years.

BUTTER: FIRST QUALITY, FRANCE

Source: *Meat and Dairy Products.* **Price Frequency:** monthly. **Effective Market(s):** France. **Units of Measure:** French francs per kilogram. **Type of Price:** average. **Time Period Covered:** latest 3 years.

BUTTER: GRADE A

Source: *Agricultural Outlook.* **Price Frequency:** monthly, annually. **Effective Market(s):** Chicago. **Units of Measure:** cents per lb. **Type of Price:** wholesale. **Time Period Covered:** monthly latest 6 months, annually latest 3 years.

Source: *Commodity Year Book.* **Price Frequency:** monthly, annually. **Effective Market(s):** Chicago. **Units of Measure:** cents per lb. **Type of Price:** wholesale. **Time Period Covered:** latest 7 years.

Source: *Dairy Foods.* **Price Frequency:** weekly. **Effective Market(s):** Chicago. **Units of Measure:** Dollars per lb. **Time Period Covered:** latest 4 weeks.

Source: *Dairy Market Statistics.* **Price Frequency:** weekly, monthly. **Effective Market(s):** Chicago. **Units of Measure:** Dollars per lb. **Type of Price:** spot. **Time Period Covered:** latest year.

Source: *Dairy Market Statistics.* **Price Frequency:** monthly, annually. **Effective Market(s):** Chicago. **Units of Measure:** Dollars per lb. **Type of Price:** wholesale. **Time Period Covered:** latest year.

Source: *Dairy Situation and Outlook Report.* **Price Frequency:** monthly, annually. **Effective Market(s):** Chicago. **Units of Measure:** cents per lb. **Type of Price:** wholesale. **Time Period Covered:** latest year.

Source: *FAO Quarterly Bulletin of Statistics.* **Price Frequency:** monthly, annually. **Effective Market(s):** Chicago. **Units of Measure:** Dollars per 100 lbs., dollars per metric ton. **Type of Price:** wholesale. **Time Period Covered:** latest 3 years.

Source: *Federal Milk Order Market Statistics Annual Summary.* **Price Frequency:** monthly, annually. **Effective Market(s):** Chicago. **Units of Measure:** Dollars per lb. **Time Period Covered:** latest 2 years.

Source: *Federal Milk Order Market Statistics.* **Price Frequency:** monthly, annually. **Effective Market(s):** Chicago. **Units of Measure:** Dollars per lb. **Type of Price:** wholesale. **Time Period Covered:** latest 2 years.

BUTTER: GRADE A, 92 SCORE

Source: *Journal of Commerce and Commercial.* **Price Frequency:** daily. **Effective Market(s):** Chicago. **Units of Measure:** Dollars per lb. **Type of Price:** spot supplier. **Time Period Covered:** latest day.

BUTTER: GRADE AA

Source: *Asian Wall Street Journal.* **Price Frequency:** daily. **Effective Market(s):** Chicago. **Units of Measure:** Dollars per lb. **Type of Price:** cash. **Time Period Covered:** latest 2 days, year ago.

Source: *California Farmer.* **Price Frequency:** semimonthly. **Effective Market(s):** California. **Units of Measure:** Dollars per lb. **Type of Price:** prices to retailers. **Time Period Covered:** latest week, month ago, year ago.

Source: *Commodity Year Book.* **Price Frequency:** annually. **Effective Market(s):** California, Chicago. **Units of Measure:** Dollars per lb. **Type of Price:** wholesale. **Time Period Covered:** latest 8 years.

Source: *Dairy Foods.* **Price Frequency:** weekly. **Effective Market(s):** Chicago. **Units of Measure:** Dollars per lb. **Time Period Covered:** latest 4 weeks.

Source: *Dairy Market Statistics.* **Price Frequency:** weekly, monthly. **Effective Market(s):** Chicago. **Units of Measure:** Dollars per lb. **Type of Price:** spot. **Time Period Covered:** latest year.

Source: *Dairy Market Statistics.* **Price Frequency:** monthly, annually. **Effective Market(s):** Chicago. **Units of Measure:** Dollars per lb. **Type of Price:** wholesale. **Time Period Covered:** latest year.

Source: *Dairy Market Statistics.* **Price Frequency:** monthly, annually. **Effective Market(s):** California plants. **Units of Measure:** Dollars per lb. **Type of Price:** average. **Time Period Covered:** latest year.

Source: *Farm and Dairy.* **Price Frequency:** weekly, seasonally. **Effective Market(s):** Chicago. **Units of Measure:** Dollars per lb. **Time Period Covered:** latest week, year ago.

Source: *Investor's Daily.* **Price Frequency:** daily. **Effective Market(s):** Chicago. **Units of Measure:** Dollars per lb. **Type of Price:** spot. **Time Period Covered:** latest 2 days.

Source: *New York Times.* **Price Frequency:** daily. **Effective Market(s):** Chicago. **Units of Measure:** Dollars per lb. **Type of Price:** cash. **Time Period Covered:** latest 2 days.

Source: *Wall Street Journal.* **Price Frequency:** daily. **Effective Market(s):** Chicago. **Units of Measure:** Dollars per lb. **Time Period Covered:** latest day, day ago, year ago.

Source: *Weekly Insiders Dairy & Egg Letter.* **Price Frequency:** weekly, annually. **Effective Market(s):** New York. **Units of Measure:** Dollars per lb. **Type of Price:** retail. **Time Period Covered:** latest week, week ago, year ago, 2 years ago.

BUTTER: GRADE AA, 1/4 LB. PRINTS

Source: *Dairy Market Statistics.* **Price Frequency:** monthly, annually. **Effective Market(s):** Central States, California cities, East Coast cities. **Units of Measure:** Dollars per lb. **Type of Price:** wholesale. **Time Period Covered:** latest year.

BUTTER: GRADE AA, 1 LB. PRINTS

Source: *Dairy Market Statistics.* **Price Frequency:** monthly, annually. **Effective Market(s):** Central States, California cities, East Coast cities. **Units of Measure:** Dollars per lb. **Type of Price:** wholesale. **Time Period Covered:** latest year.

BUTTER: GRADE AA, 93 SCORE

Source: *CRB Commodity Index Report.* **Price Frequency:** weekly. **Effective Market(s):** Chicago. **Units of Measure:** Dollars per lb. **Type of Price:** spot. **Time Period Covered:** latest week.

Source: *Meat and Dairy Products.* **Price Frequency:** monthly. **Effective Market(s):** United States. **Units of Measure:** cents per lb. **Type of Price:** average. **Time Period Covered:** latest 3 years.

BUTTER: GRADE B

Source: *Dairy Foods.* **Price Frequency:** weekly. **Effective Market(s):** Chicago. **Units of Measure:** Dollars per lb. **Time Period Covered:** latest 4 weeks.

Source: *Dairy Market Statistics.* **Price Frequency:** weekly, monthly. **Effective Market(s):** Chicago. **Units of Measure:** Dollars per lb. **Type of Price:** spot. **Time Period Covered:** latest year.

BUTTER: HOUSE BRANDS

Source: *Weekly Insiders Dairy & Egg Letter.* **Price Frequency:** weekly, annually. **Effective Market(s):** New York. **Units of Measure:** Dollars per lb. **Type of Price:** retail. **Time Period Covered:** latest week, week ago, year ago, 2 years ago.

BUTTER: NEW ZEALAND

Source: *International Financial Statistics.* **Price Frequency:** monthly, quarterly, annually. **Effective Market(s):** London, New Zealand. **Units of Measure:** cents per lb., index. **Type of Price:** market price, price index. **Time Period Covered:** latest month, latest 4 quarters, latest 5 years.

Source: *International Financial Statistics Yearbook.* **Price Frequency:** annually. **Effective Market(s):** London, New Zealand. **Units of Measure:** cents per lb. **Type of Price:** wholesale. **Time Period Covered:** latest 30 years.

BUTTER: REDDIES

Source: *Dairy Market Statistics.* **Price Frequency:** monthly, annually. **Effective Market(s):** Central States, California cities, East Coast cities. **Units of Measure:** Dollars per lb. **Type of Price:** wholesale. **Time Period Covered:** latest year.

BUTTER: SALTED, GRADE A, 92 SCORE, 1 POUND QUARTERS

Source: *Urner Barry's Price-Current.* **Price Frequency:** daily. **Units of Measure:** Dollars per lb. **Type of Price:** price from warehouse. **Time Period Covered:** latest day.

BUTTER: SALTED, GRADE A, 92 SCORE, 1 POUND SOLIDS

Source: *Urner Barry's Price-Current.* **Price Frequency:** daily. **Units of Measure:** Dollars per lb. **Type of Price:** price from warehouse. **Time Period Covered:** latest day.

BUTTER: SALTED, GRADE A, 92 SCORE, BULK

Source: *Urner Barry's Price-Current.* **Price Frequency:** daily. **Effective Market(s):** East, Midwest. **Units of Measure:** Dollars per lb. **Type of Price:** spot. **Time Period Covered:** latest day.

BUTTER: SALTED, GRADE AA

Source: *Dairy Market Statistics.* **Price Frequency:** monthly, annually. **Effective Market(s):** Northeast, North Central, South, West, United States. **Units of Measure:** Dollars per lb. **Type of Price:** retail. **Time Period Covered:** latest year.

Source: *Federal Milk Order Market Statistics.* **Price Frequency:** monthly. **Effective Market(s):** Northeast, North Central, South, West, United States. **Units of Measure:** Dollars per lb. **Type of Price:** retail. **Time Period Covered:** latest year to date.

BUTTER: SALTED, GRADE AA, 93 SCORE, 1 POUND QUARTERS

Source: *Urner Barry's Price-Current.* **Price Frequency:** daily. **Units of Measure:** Dollars per lb. **Type of Price:** price from warehouse. **Time Period Covered:** latest day.

BUTTER: SALTED, GRADE AA, 93 SCORE, 1 POUND SOLIDS

Source: *Urner Barry's Price-Current.* **Price Frequency:** daily. **Units of Measure:** Dollars per lb. **Type of Price:** price from warehouse. **Time Period Covered:** latest day.

BUTTER: SALTED, GRADE AA, 93 SCORE, BULK

Source: *Urner Barry's Price-Current.* **Price Frequency:** daily. **Effective Market(s):** East, Midwest. **Units of Measure:** Dollars per lb. **Type of Price:** spot. **Time Period Covered:** latest day.

BUTTER: SALTED, GRADE B, 90 SCORE, 1 POUND QUARTERS

Source: *Urner Barry's Price-Current.* **Price Frequency:** daily. **Units of Measure:** Dollars per lb. **Type of Price:** price from warehouse. **Time Period Covered:** latest day.

BUTTER: SALTED, GRADE B, 90 SCORE, 1 POUND SOLIDS

Source: *Urner Barry's Price-Current.* **Price Frequency:** daily. **Units of Measure:** Dollars per lb. **Type of Price:** price from warehouse. **Time Period Covered:** latest day.

BUTTER: SALTED, GRADE B, 90 SCORE, BULK

Source: *Urner Barry's Price-Current.* **Price Frequency:** daily. **Effective Market(s):** East, Midwest. **Units of Measure:** Dollars per lb. **Type of Price:** spot. **Time Period Covered:** latest day.

BUTTER: WEST GERMANY

Source: *Meat and Dairy Products.* **Price Frequency:** monthly. **Effective Market(s):** West Germany. **Units of Measure:** West German marks per kilogram. **Type of Price:** average. **Time Period Covered:** latest 3 years.

BUTTER POWDER SNUBBER

Source: *Federal Milk Order Market Statistics Annual Summary.* **Price Frequency:** monthly, annually. **Units of Measure:** Dollars per 100 lbs. **Time Period Covered:** latest 2 years.

Source: *Federal Milk Order Market Statistics.* **Price Frequency:** monthly, annually. **Effective Market(s):** Chicago. **Units of Measure:** Dollars per 100 lbs. **Time Period Covered:** latest 2 years.

BUTTERCUPS (VEGETABLE)

see Pumpkin: Buttercup.

BUTTERFAT: CREAM, FLUID

Source: *Monthly Price Review.* **Price Frequency:** daily. **Units of Measure:** Dollars per lb. **Type of Price:** spot. **Time Period Covered:** latest month.

BUTTERFISH: ROUND, FROZEN

Source: *Weekly Statistical Fishery Report.* **Price Frequency:** weekly. **Effective Market(s):** Tokyo. **Units of Measure:** Dollars per lb. **Type of Price:** wholesale. **Time Period Covered:** 2 weeks ago, month ago.

BUTTERFISH: WHOLE, FRESH

Source: *Seafood Price-Current.* **Price Frequency:** semiweekly. **Effective Market(s):** Mid-Atlantic, Boston, Bedford (MA), Portland (ME). **Units of Measure:** Dollars per lb. **Type of Price:** sale by first receiver, auction price. **Time Period Covered:** latest day.

BUTTERMILK: DRY, HUMAN

Source: *Dairy Foods.* **Price Frequency:** monthly. **Effective Market(s):** New York, Philadelphia, South. **Units of Measure:** Dollars per lb. **Time Period Covered:** latest month.

BUTTERMILK: DRY, SACKED

Source: *Feedstuffs.* **Price Frequency:** weekly. **Effective Market(s):** Ft. Worth, Minneapolis/St. Paul. **Units of Measure:** Dollars per 100 lbs. **Time Period Covered:** latest week.

BUTTERMILK: DRY, SWEET CREAM, SPRAY, BAGS, KNOWN BRANDS

Source: *Urner Barry's Price-Current.* **Price Frequency:** daily. **Units of Measure:** Dollars per lb. **Time Period Covered:** latest day.

BUTTERMILK: DRY, SWEET CREAM, SPRAY, BAGS, UNKNOWN BRANDS

Source: *Urner Barry's Price-Current.* **Price Frequency:** daily. **Units of Measure:** Dollars per lb. **Time Period Covered:** latest day.

BUTTERMILK: SWEET CREAM

Source: *Dairy Market Statistics.* **Price Frequency:** monthly, annually. **Effective Market(s):** Central States. **Units of Measure:** Dollars per lb. **Type of Price:** . **Time Period Covered:** latest year.

BUTTERMILK POWDER

Source: *Dairy Market Statistics.* **Price Frequency:** monthly, annually. **Effective Market(s):** Eastern area, Western area. **Units of Measure:** Dollars per lb. **Time Period Covered:** latest year.

Source: *Dairy Market Statistics.* **Price Frequency:** monthly, annually. **Effective Market(s):** Southern area. **Units of Measure:** Dollars per lb. **Type of Price:** wholesale . **Time Period Covered:** latest year.

BUTTERMILK POWDER: SWEET CREAM

Source: *Milling & Baking News.* **Price Frequency:** weekly. **Units of Measure:** cents per lb. **Time Period Covered:** latest week.

BUTTERMILK PRODUCT

Source: *Dairy Market Statistics.* **Price Frequency:** monthly, annually. **Effective Market(s):** Central States. **Units of Measure:** Dollars per lb. **Type of Price:** . **Time Period Covered:** latest year.

Source: *Milling & Baking News.* **Price Frequency:** weekly . **Units of Measure:** cents per lb. **Time Period Covered:** latest week.

BUTTERNUT (VEGETABLE)

see Pumpkin: Butternut.

BUTTEROLL

Source: *World Dairy Situation.* **Price Frequency:** semi-annually. **Effective Market(s):** North Europe/World ports. **Units of Measure:** Dollars per metric ton. **Time Period Covered:** latest 7 years.

BUTYL ACETATE

Source: *Journal of Commerce and Commercial.* **Price Frequency:** weekly in Wednesday issue. **Units of Measure:** Dollars per lb. **Type of Price:** spot. **Time Period Covered:** latest week.

N-BUTYL ACETATE: SYNTHETIC

Source: *Chemical Marketing Reporter.* **Price Frequency:** weekly. **Effective Market(s):** New York. **Units of Measure:** Dollars per lb. **Type of Price:** spot. **Time Period Covered:** latest week.

N-BUTYL ACRYLATE

Source: *Chemical Marketing Reporter.* **Price Frequency:** weekly. **Effective Market(s):** East. **Units of Measure:** Dollars per lb. **Type of Price:** spot. **Time Period Covered:** latest week.

BUTYL ALCOHOL: SYNTHETIC

Source: *Journal of Commerce and Commercial.* **Price Frequency:** weekly in Friday issue. **Units of Measure:** Dollars per lb. **Type of Price:** spot. **Time Period Covered:** latest week.

N-BUTYL ALCOHOL: SYNTHETIC

Source: *Chemical Marketing Reporter.* **Price Frequency:** weekly. **Effective Market(s):** New York. **Units of Measure:** Dollars per lb. **Type of Price:** spot. **Time Period Covered:** latest week.

SEC-BUTYL ALCOHOL: SYNTHETIC

Source: *Chemical Marketing Reporter.* **Price Frequency:** weekly. **Effective Market(s):** New York. **Units of Measure:** Dollars per lb. **Type of Price:** spot. **Time Period Covered:** latest week.

TERT-BUTYL ALCOHOL: SYNTHETIC

Source: *Chemical Marketing Reporter.* **Price Frequency:** weekly. **Effective Market(s):** East. **Units of Measure:** Dollars per lb. **Type of Price:** spot. **Time Period Covered:** latest week.

BUTYL ALDEHYDE

see Butyraldehyde.

BUTYL BENZYL PHTHALATE

Source: *Chemical Marketing Reporter.* **Price Frequency:** weekly. **Effective Market(s):** New York. **Units of Measure:** Dollars per lb. **Type of Price:** spot. **Time Period Covered:** latest week.

N-BUTYL CHLORIDE

Source: *Chemical Marketing Reporter.* **Price Frequency:** weekly. **Effective Market(s):** New York. **Units of Measure:** Dollars per lb. **Type of Price:** spot. **Time Period Covered:** latest week.

6-TERT-BUTYL-M-CRESOL

see Mono-tert-butyl-m-cresol.

BUTYL CYCLOHEXYL PHTHALATE

Source: *Chemical Marketing Reporter.* **Price Frequency:** weekly. **Effective Market(s):** New York. **Units of Measure:** Dollars per lb. **Type of Price:** spot. **Time Period Covered:** latest week.

N-BUTYL ETHER

Source: *Chemical Marketing Reporter.* **Price Frequency:** weekly. **Effective Market(s):** New York. **Units of Measure:** Dollars per lb. **Type of Price:** spot. **Time Period Covered:** latest week.

BUTYL ISODECYL PHTHALATE

Source: *Chemical Marketing Reporter.* **Price Frequency:** weekly. **Effective Market(s):** New York. **Units of Measure:** Dollars per lb. **Type of Price:** spot. **Time Period Covered:** latest week.

N-BUTYL LACTATE

Source: *Chemical Marketing Reporter.* **Price Frequency:** weekly. **Effective Market(s):** New York. **Units of Measure:** Dollars per lb. **Type of Price:** spot. **Time Period Covered:** latest week.

BUTYL METHACRYLATE

Source: *Chemical Marketing Reporter.* **Price Frequency:** weekly. **Effective Market(s):** New York. **Units of Measure:** Dollars per lb. **Type of Price:** spot. **Time Period Covered:** latest week.

BUTYL OCTYL PHTHALATE

Source: *Chemical Marketing Reporter.* **Price Frequency:** weekly. **Effective Market(s):** East. **Units of Measure:** Dollars per lb. **Type of Price:** spot. **Time Period Covered:** latest week.

BUTYL OLEATE: DISTILLED

Source: *Chemical Marketing Reporter.* **Price Frequency:** weekly. **Effective Market(s):** New York. **Units of Measure:** Dollars per lb. **Type of Price:** spot. **Time Period Covered:** latest week.

BUTYL PHTHALATE

see Dibutyl Phthalate.

BUTYL STEARATE: COSMETIC

Source: *Chemical Marketing Reporter.* **Price Frequency:** weekly. **Effective Market(s):** New York. **Units of Measure:** Dollars per lb. **Type of Price:** spot. **Time Period Covered:** latest week.

BUTYL STEARATE: TECHNICAL GRADE

Source: *Chemical Marketing Reporter.* **Price Frequency:** weekly. **Effective Market(s):** New York. **Units of Measure:** Dollars per lb. **Type of Price:** spot. **Time Period Covered:** latest week.

BUTYLAMINE

see Mono-, Di, and Tributylamine.

TERT-BUTYLAMINE

Source: *Chemical Marketing Reporter.* **Price Frequency:** weekly. **Effective Market(s):** New York. **Units of Measure:** Dollars per lb. **Type of Price:** spot. **Time Period Covered:** latest week.

BUTYLATE: EMULSIFIABLE CONCENTRATE

Source: *Agricultural Prices Annual Summary.* **Price Frequency:** semiannually. **Effective Market(s):** United States. **Units of Measure:** Dollars per 5 gallons. **Type of Price:** average paid by farmer. **Time Period Covered:** latest 6 years.

BUTYLATED HYDROXYANISOLE: FOOD GRADE

Source: *Chemical Marketing Reporter.* **Price Frequency:** weekly. **Effective Market(s):** New York. **Units of Measure:** Dollars per lb. **Type of Price:** spot. **Time Period Covered:** latest week.

BUTYLATED HYDROXYTOLUENE: FOOD AND FEED GRADES

Source: *Chemical Marketing Reporter.* **Price Frequency:** weekly. **Effective Market(s):** New York. **Units of Measure:** Dollars per lb. **Type of Price:** spot. **Time Period Covered:** latest week.

BUTYLATED HYDROXYTOLUENE: TECHNICAL GRADE

Source: *Chemical Marketing Reporter.* **Price Frequency:** weekly. **Effective Market(s):** New York. **Units of Measure:** Dollars per lb. **Type of Price:** spot. **Time Period Covered:** latest week.

1,3-BUTYLENE GLYCOL

Source: *Chemical Marketing Reporter.* **Price Frequency:** weekly. **Effective Market(s):** New York. **Units of Measure:** Dollars per lb. **Type of Price:** spot. **Time Period Covered:** latest week.

N-BUTYLLITHIUM: 15% HEXANE SOLUTION

Source: *Chemical Marketing Reporter.* **Price Frequency:** weekly. **Effective Market(s):** New York. **Units of Measure:** Dollars per lb. **Type of Price:** spot. **Time Period Covered:** latest week.

P-TERT-BUTYLPHENOL

Source: *Chemical Marketing Reporter.* **Price Frequency:** weekly. **Effective Market(s):** New York. **Units of Measure:** Dollars per lb. **Type of Price:** spot. **Time Period Covered:** latest week.

BUTYLTIN: MAXIMUM

Source: *Modern Plastics.* **Price Frequency:** quarterly in February, May, August & November issues. **Units of Measure:** Dollars per lb. **Type of Price:** list. **Time Period Covered:** latest year.

BUTYLTIN: MINIMUM

Source: *Modern Plastics.* **Price Frequency:** quarterly in February, May, August & November issues. **Units of Measure:** Dollars per lb. **Type of Price:** list. **Time Period Covered:** latest year.

BUTYRALDEHYDE

Source: *Chemical Marketing Reporter.* **Price Frequency:** weekly. **Effective Market(s):** New York. **Units of Measure:** Dollars per lb. **Type of Price:** spot. **Time Period Covered:** latest week.

BUTYRIC ACID

Source: *Chemical Marketing Reporter.* **Price Frequency:** weekly. **Effective Market(s):** New York. **Units of Measure:** Dollars per lb. **Type of Price:** spot. **Time Period Covered:** latest week.

BUTYRIC ETHER

see Ethyl Butyrate.

BUTYROLACTONE

Source: *Chemical Marketing Reporter.* **Price Frequency:** weekly. **Effective Market(s):** New York. **Units of Measure:** Dollars per lb. **Type of Price:** spot. **Time Period Covered:** latest week.

N-BUTYRONITRILE

Source: *Chemical Marketing Reporter.* **Price Frequency:** weekly. **Effective Market(s):** New York. **Units of Measure:** Dollars per lb. **Type of Price:** spot. **Time Period Covered:** latest week.

CAB

see Cellulose Acetate Butyrate.

CABBAGE

Source: *California Farmer.* **Price Frequency:** semimonthly, seasonally. **Effective Market(s):** Imperial/Coachella/Palo Verde Valleys. **Units of Measure:** Dollars per 50 lb. carton. **Time Period Covered:** latest week, month ago, year ago.

Source: *Statistical Bulletin of the South Pacific: Retail Price Indexes.* **Price Frequency:** annually. **Effective Market(s):** 18 South Pacific markets. **Units of Measure:** Australian dollars per kilogram. **Type of Price:** retail. **Time Period Covered:** latest year.

CABBAGE: BOK CHOY

Source: *Lancaster Farming.* **Price Frequency:** weekly, seasonally. **Effective Market(s):** Pennsylvania. **Units of Measure:** Dollars per carton. **Type of Price:** market. **Time Period Covered:** latest week.

CABBAGE: CHINESE

Source: *Lancaster Farming.* **Price Frequency:** weekly, seasonally. **Effective Market(s):** Pennsylvania. **Units of Measure:** Dollars per carton. **Type of Price:** market. **Time Period Covered:** latest week.

Source: *New Zealand Farmer.* **Price Frequency:** weekly, seasonally. **Effective Market(s):** New Zealand. **Units of Measure:** New Zealand dollars per case. **Time Period Covered:** latest week.

CABBAGE: CHINESE, NAPPA

Source: *Lancaster Farming.* **Price Frequency:** weekly, seasonally. **Effective Market(s):** Pennsylvania. **Units of Measure:** Dollars per carton. **Type of Price:** market. **Time Period Covered:** latest week.

CABBAGE: DANISH

Source: *Fresh Fruit and Vegetable Prices.* **Price Frequency:** monthly, seasonally. **Effective Market(s):** West/Central New York. **Units of Measure:** Dollars per bag. **Type of Price:** average price at shipping point. **Time Period Covered:** latest year.

CABBAGE: DRUMHEAD

Source: *New Zealand Farmer.* **Price Frequency:** weekly, seasonally. **Effective Market(s):** New Zealand. **Units of Measure:** New Zealand dollars per crate. **Time Period Covered:** latest week.

CABBAGE: FRESH

Source: *HRI-Buyers Guide.* **Price Frequency:** weekly. **Effective Market(s):** Northeastern area. **Units of Measure:** Dollars per crate. **Type of Price:** price paid by dining places & institutions. **Time Period Covered:** latest week.

CABBAGE: GREEN

Source: *Lancaster Farming.* **Price Frequency:** weekly, seasonally. **Effective Market(s):** Pennsylvania. **Units of Measure:** Dollars per unit. **Type of Price:** market. **Time Period Covered:** latest week.

CABBAGE: GREEN, FLORIDA

Source: *Fresh Fruit and Vegetable Prices.* **Price Frequency:** monthly, seasonally. **Effective Market(s):** New York City. **Units of Measure:** Dollars per crate/carton. **Type of Price:** average wholesale price. **Time Period Covered:** latest year.

CABBAGE: GREEN, GEORGIA

Source: *Fresh Fruit and Vegetable Prices.* **Price Frequency:** monthly, seasonally. **Effective Market(s):** Chicago. **Units of Measure:** Dollars per crate/carton. **Type of Price:** average wholesale price. **Time Period Covered:** latest year.

CABBAGE: GREEN, ILLINOIS

Source: *Fresh Fruit and Vegetable Prices.* **Price Frequency:** monthly, seasonally. **Effective Market(s):** Chicago. **Units of Measure:** Dollars per crate/carton. **Type of Price:** average wholesale price. **Time Period Covered:** latest year.

CABBAGE: GREEN, INDIANA

Source: *Fresh Fruit and Vegetable Prices.* **Price Frequency:** monthly, seasonally. **Effective Market(s):** Chicago. **Units of Measure:** Dollars per crate/carton. **Type of Price:** average wholesale price. **Time Period Covered:** latest year.

CABBAGE: GREEN, NEW JERSEY

Source: *Fresh Fruit and Vegetable Prices.* **Price Frequency:** monthly, seasonally. **Effective Market(s):** New York City. **Units of Measure:** Dollars per crate/carton. **Type of Price:** average wholesale price. **Time Period Covered:** latest year.

CABBAGE: GREEN, NEW YORK

Source: *Fresh Fruit and Vegetable Prices.* **Price Frequency:** monthly, seasonally. **Effective Market(s):** New York City. **Units of Measure:** Dollars per crate/carton. **Type of Price:** average wholesale price. **Time Period Covered:** latest year.

CABBAGE: GREEN, ROUND

Source: *Fresh Fruit and Vegetable Prices.* **Price Frequency:** monthly, seasonally. **Effective Market(s):** 12 domestic markets. **Units of Measure:** Dollars per carton/crate. **Type of Price:** average price at shipping point. **Time Period Covered:** latest year.

CABBAGE: GREEN, TEXAS

Source: *Fresh Fruit and Vegetable Prices.* **Price Frequency:** monthly, seasonally. **Effective Market(s):** Chicago. **Units of Measure:** Dollars per crate/carton. **Type of Price:** average wholesale price. **Time Period Covered:** latest year.

CABBAGE: RED

Source: *Lancaster Farming.* **Price Frequency:** weekly, seasonally. **Effective Market(s):** Pennsylvania. **Units of Measure:** Dollars per unit. **Type of Price:** market. **Time Period Covered:** latest week.

Source: *New Zealand Farmer.* **Price Frequency:** weekly, seasonally. **Effective Market(s):** New Zealand. **Units of Measure:** New Zealand dollars per crate. **Time Period Covered:** latest week.

CABBAGE: RED, FRESH

Source: *HRI-Buyers Guide.* **Price Frequency:** weekly. **Effective Market(s):** Northeastern area. **Units of Measure:** Dollars per crate. **Type of Price:** price paid by dining places & institutions. **Time Period Covered:** latest week.

CABBAGE: ROUND GREEN

Source: *The Packer.* **Price Frequency:** weekly, seasonally. **Effective Market(s):** varies. **Units of Measure:** Dollars per carton. **Type of Price:** price received by farmer. **Time Period Covered:** latest week.

CABBAGE: SAVOY

Source: *Lancaster Farming.* **Price Frequency:** weekly, seasonally. **Effective Market(s):** Pennsylvania. **Units of Measure:** Dollars per unit. **Type of Price:** market. **Time Period Covered:** latest week.

Source: *New Zealand Farmer.* **Price Frequency:** weekly, seasonally. **Effective Market(s):** New Zealand. **Units of Measure:** New Zealand dollars per crate. **Time Period Covered:** latest week.

CABBAGE: SAVOY, FRESH

Source: *HRI-Buyers Guide.* **Price Frequency:** weekly. **Effective Market(s):** Northeastern area. **Units of Measure:** Dollars per crate. **Type of Price:** price paid by dining places & institutions. **Time Period Covered:** latest week.

CABLE: ELECTRIC, INDOOR

Source: *Agricultural Prices.* **Price Frequency:** annually. **Effective Market(s):** United States. **Units of Measure:** Dollars per 100 feet. **Type of Price:** paid by farmer. **Time Period Covered:** latest year.

Source: *Agricultural Prices Annual Summary.* **Price Frequency:** semiannually. **Effective Market(s):** United States. **Units of Measure:** Dollars per 100 feet. **Type of Price:** average price paid by farmer. **Time Period Covered:** latest 6 years.

CACO3

see Calcium Carbonate.

CADMIUM

Source: *Chemical Marketing Reporter.* **Price Frequency:** weekly. **Effective Market(s):** New York. **Units of Measure:** Dollars per lb. **Type of Price:** spot. **Time Period Covered:** latest week.

Source: *E&MJ.* **Price Frequency:** monthly. **Units of Measure:** Dollars per lb. **Type of Price:** producer. **Time Period Covered:** selected dates.

Source: *Iron Age.* **Price Frequency:** monthly. **Units of Measure:** Dollars per lb. **Type of Price:** consumer. **Time Period Covered:** latest month.

Source: *Northern Miner.* **Price Frequency:** daily. **Effective Market(s):** New York. **Units of Measure:** Dollars per lb. **Type of Price:** producer. **Time Period Covered:** selected day.

CADMIUM: RED, DARK SHADE

Source: *Journal of Commerce and Commercial.* **Price Frequency:** weekly in Wednesday issue. **Units of Measure:** Dollars per lb. **Type of Price:** spot. **Time Period Covered:** latest week.

CADMIUM: RED, DARK SHADE, CHEMICALLY PURE

Source: *Chemical Marketing Reporter.* **Price Frequency:** weekly. **Effective Market(s):** East of the Rockies. **Units of Measure:** Dollars per lb. **Type of Price:** spot. **Time Period Covered:** latest week.

CADMIUM: RED, LIGHT SHADE, CHEMICALLY PURE

Source: *Chemical Marketing Reporter.* **Price Frequency:** weekly. **Effective Market(s):** East of the Rockies. **Units of Measure:** Dollars per lb. **Type of Price:** spot. **Time Period Covered:** latest week.

CADMIUM: RED, MEDIUM LIGHT SHADE, CHEMICALLY PURE

Source: *Chemical Marketing Reporter.* **Price Frequency:** weekly. **Effective Market(s):** East of the Rockies. **Units of Measure:** Dollars per lb. **Type of Price:** spot. **Time Period Covered:** latest week.

CADMIUM: RED, MEDIUM SHADE

Source: *Journal of Commerce and Commercial.* **Price Frequency:** weekly in Wednesday issue. **Units of Measure:** Dollars per lb. **Type of Price:** spot. **Time Period Covered:** latest week.

CADMIUM: RED, MEDIUM SHADE, CHEMICALLY PURE

Source: *Chemical Marketing Reporter.* **Price Frequency:** weekly. **Effective Market(s):** East of the Rockies. **Units of Measure:** Dollars per lb. **Type of Price:** spot. **Time Period Covered:** latest week.

CADMIUM: YELLOW, ALL SHADES, CHEMICALLY PURE

Source: *Chemical Marketing Reporter.* **Price Frequency:** weekly. **Effective Market(s):** east of the Rockies. **Units of Measure:** Dollars per lb. **Type of Price:** spot. **Time Period Covered:** latest week.

CADMIUM CHLORIDE: 20% SOLUTION

Source: *Chemical Marketing Reporter.* **Price Frequency:** weekly. **Effective Market(s):** New York. **Units of Measure:** Dollars per gallon. **Type of Price:** spot. **Time Period Covered:** latest week.

CADMIUM FLUOBORATE: LIQUID CONCENTRATE

Source: *Chemical Marketing Reporter.* **Price Frequency:** weekly. **Effective Market(s):** New York. **Units of Measure:** Dollars per lb. **Type of Price:** spot. **Time Period Covered:** latest week.

CADMIUM INGOTS/STICKS: 99.95% MINIMUM

Source: *Journal of Commerce and Commercial.* **Price Frequency:** daily. **Effective Market(s):** Europe. **Units of Measure:** Dollars per lb. **Type of Price:** spot. **Time Period Covered:** latest day.

CADMIUM LITHOPONE: YELLOW

Source: *Journal of Commerce and Commercial.* **Price Frequency:** weekly in Wednesday issue. **Units of Measure:** Dollars per lb. **Type of Price:** spot. **Time Period Covered:** latest week.

CADMIUM MERCURY LITHOPONE: MAROON SHADE

Source: *Chemical Marketing Reporter.* **Price Frequency:** weekly. **Effective Market(s):** East of the Rockies. **Units of Measure:** Dollars per lb. **Type of Price:** spot. **Time Period Covered:** latest week.

CADMIUM NITRATE: PURIFIED, FLAKE

Source: *Chemical Marketing Reporter.* **Price Frequency:** weekly. **Effective Market(s):** New York. **Units of Measure:** Dollars per lb. **Type of Price:** spot. **Time Period Covered:** latest week.

CADMIUM POWDER

Source: *American Metal Market.* **Price Frequency:** daily. **Units of Measure:** Dollars per lb. **Time Period Covered:** latest day.

CADMIUM SELENIDE: ORANGE, LIGHT SHADE

Source: *Journal of Commerce and Commercial.* **Price Frequency:** weekly in Wednesday issue. **Units of Measure:** Dollars per lb. **Type of Price:** spot. **Time Period Covered:** latest week.

CADMIUM SELENIDE LITHOPONE: ORANGE, DEEP SHADE

Source: *Chemical Marketing Reporter.* **Price Frequency:** weekly. **Effective Market(s):** East of the Rockies. **Units of Measure:** Dollars per lb. **Type of Price:** spot. **Time Period Covered:** latest week.

CADMIUM SELENIDE LITHOPONE: ORANGE, LIGHT SHADE

Source: *Chemical Marketing Reporter.* **Price Frequency:** weekly. **Effective Market(s):** East of the Rockies. **Units of Measure:** Dollars per lb. **Type of Price:** spot. **Time Period Covered:** latest week.

CADMIUM SELENIDE LITHOPONE: RED, DARK SHADE

Source: *Chemical Marketing Reporter.* **Price Frequency:** weekly. **Effective Market(s):** East of the Rockies. **Units of Measure:** Dollars per lb. **Type of Price:** spot. **Time Period Covered:** latest week.

CADMIUM SELENIDE LITHOPONE: RED, LIGHT SHADE

Source: *Chemical Marketing Reporter.* **Price Frequency:** weekly. **Effective Market(s):** East of the Rockies. **Units of Measure:** Dollars per lb. **Type of Price:** spot. **Time Period Covered:** latest week.

Source: *Journal of Commerce and Commercial.* **Price Frequency:** weekly in Wednesday issue. **Units of Measure:** Dollars per lb. **Type of Price:** spot. **Time Period Covered:** latest week.

CADMIUM SELENIDE LITHOPONE: RED, MAROON SHADE

Source: *Chemical Marketing Reporter.* **Price Frequency:** weekly. **Effective Market(s):** East of the Rockies. **Units of Measure:** Dollars per lb. **Type of Price:** spot. **Time Period Covered:** latest week.

CADMIUM SELENIDE LITHOPONE: RED, MEDIUM LIGHT SHADE

Source: *Chemical Marketing Reporter.* **Price Frequency:** weekly. **Effective Market(s):** East of the Rockies. **Units of Measure:** Dollars per lb. **Type of Price:** spot. **Time Period Covered:** latest week.

CADMIUM SELENIDE LITHOPONE: RED, MEDIUM SHADE

Source: *Chemical Marketing Reporter.* **Price Frequency:** weekly. **Effective Market(s):** East of the Rockies. **Units of Measure:** Dollars per lb. **Type of Price:** spot. **Time Period Covered:** latest week.

CADMIUM SELENIDE LITHOPONE: YELLOW, ALL SHADES

Source: *Chemical Marketing Reporter.* **Price Frequency:** weekly. **Effective Market(s):** East of the Rockies. **Units of Measure:** Dollars per lb. **Type of Price:** spot. **Time Period Covered:** latest week.

CADMIUM STICKS AND BALLS

Source: *Commodity Year Book.* **Price Frequency:** annually. **Effective Market(s):** United States. **Units of Measure:** Dollars per lb. **Time Period Covered:** latest 11 years.

CADMIUM SULFATE: 20% SOLUTION

Source: *Chemical Marketing Reporter.* **Price Frequency:** weekly. **Effective Market(s):** New York. **Units of Measure:** Dollars per gallon. **Type of Price:** spot. **Time Period Covered:** latest week.

CAFFEINE: NATURAL, ANHYDROUS

Source: *Journal of Commerce and Commercial.* **Price Frequency:** weekly in Friday issue. **Units of Measure:** Dollars per lb. **Type of Price:** spot. **Time Period Covered:** latest week.

CAFFEINE: NATURAL, ANHYDROUS, POWDERED, CRYSTALLINE, IMPORTED

Source: *Chemical Marketing Reporter.* **Price Frequency:** weekly. **Effective Market(s):** New York. **Units of Measure:** Dollars per lb. **Type of Price:** spot. **Time Period Covered:** latest week.

CAFFEINE: SYNTHETIC

Source: *Journal of Commerce and Commercial.* **Price Frequency:** weekly in Friday issue. **Units of Measure:** Dollars per lb. **Type of Price:** spot. **Time Period Covered:** latest week.

CAFFEINE: SYNTHETIC, ANHYDROUS, POWDERED, CRYSTALLINE, USP, DOMESTIC

Source: *Chemical Marketing Reporter.* **Price Frequency:** weekly. **Effective Market(s):** New York. **Units of Measure:** Dollars per lb. **Type of Price:** spot. **Time Period Covered:** latest week.

CALAMINE: USP

Source: *Chemical Marketing Reporter.* **Price Frequency:** weekly. **Effective Market(s):** New York. **Units of Measure:** Dollars per lb. **Type of Price:** spot. **Time Period Covered:** latest week.

CALAMUS OIL

Source: *Chemical Marketing Reporter.* **Price Frequency:** weekly. **Effective Market(s):** New York. **Units of Measure:** Dollars per lb. **Type of Price:** spot. **Time Period Covered:** latest week.

CALCIUM: CROWN

Source: *Iron Age.* **Price Frequency:** monthly. **Number of Sources:** Dollars per lb. **Type of Price:** consumer. **Time Period Covered:** latest month.

CALCIUM ACETATE: PURIFIED, POWDERED

Source: *Chemical Marketing Reporter.* **Price Frequency:** weekly. **Effective Market(s):** New York. **Units of Measure:** Dollars per lb. **Type of Price:** spot. **Time Period Covered:** latest week.

CALCIUM BROMIDE: 54% SOLUTION

Source: *Journal of Commerce and Commercial.* **Price Frequency:** weekly in Friday issue. **Units of Measure:** Dollars per lb. **Type of Price:** spot. **Time Period Covered:** latest week.

CALCIUM CARBIDE: GENERATING GRADE

Source: *Journal of Commerce and Commercial.* **Price Frequency:** weekly in Thursday issue. **Units of Measure:** Dollars per ton. **Type of Price:** spot. **Time Period Covered:** latest week.

CALCIUM CARBIDE: STANDARD, GENERATOR SIZE

Source: *Chemical Marketing Reporter.* **Price Frequency:** weekly. **Effective Market(s):** New York. **Units of Measure:** Dollars per ton. **Type of Price:** spot. **Time Period Covered:** latest week.

CALCIUM CARBONATE: 3 MICRON

Source: *Modern Plastics.* **Price Frequency:** quarterly in February, May, August & November issues. **Units of Measure:** Dollars per lb. **Type of Price:** list. **Time Period Covered:** latest year.

CALCIUM CARBONATE: 5 MICRON

Source: *Modern Plastics.* **Price Frequency:** quarterly in February, May, August & November issues. **Units of Measure:** Dollars per lb. **Type of Price:** list. **Time Period Covered:** latest year.

CALCIUM CARBONATE: COATED

Source: *Industrial Minerals.* **Price Frequency:** monthly. **Effective Market(s):** United Kingdom. **Units of Measure:** British pounds per metric tonne. **Type of Price:** producer & dealer. **Time Period Covered:** latest month.

CALCIUM CARBONATE: COATED, FINE

Source: *Chemical Marketing Reporter.* **Price Frequency:** weekly. **Effective Market(s):** New York. **Units of Measure:** Dollars per ton. **Type of Price:** spot. **Time Period Covered:** latest week.

CALCIUM CARBONATE: COATED, ULTRAFINE

Source: *Chemical Marketing Reporter.* **Price Frequency:** weekly. **Effective Market(s):** New York. **Units of Measure:** Dollars per ton. **Type of Price:** spot. **Time Period Covered:** latest week.

CALCIUM CARBONATE: DRY

Source: *Journal of Commerce and Commercial.* **Price Frequency:** weekly in Friday issue. **Units of Measure:** Dollars per bulk ton. **Type of Price:** spot. **Time Period Covered:** latest week.

CALCIUM CARBONATE: DRY, COARSE

Source: *Chemical Marketing Reporter.* **Price Frequency:** weekly. **Effective Market(s):** New York. **Units of Measure:** Dollars per ton. **Type of Price:** spot. **Time Period Covered:** latest week.

CALCIUM CARBONATE: DRY, FINE

Source: *Chemical Marketing Reporter.* **Price Frequency:** weekly. **Effective Market(s):** New York. **Units of Measure:** Dollars per ton. **Type of Price:** spot. **Time Period Covered:** latest week.

CALCIUM CARBONATE: DRY, MEDIUM

Source: *Chemical Marketing Reporter.* **Price Frequency:** weekly. **Effective Market(s):** New York. **Units of Measure:** Dollars per ton. **Type of Price:** spot. **Time Period Covered:** latest week.

CALCIUM CARBONATE: EXTRA LIGHT, USP

Source: *Chemical Marketing Reporter.* **Price Frequency:** weekly. **Effective Market(s):** New York. **Units of Measure:** Dollars per ton. **Type of Price:** spot. **Time Period Covered:** latest week.

CALCIUM CARBONATE: HEAVY, USP

Source: *Chemical Marketing Reporter.* **Price Frequency:** weekly. **Effective Market(s):** New York. **Units of Measure:** Dollars per ton. **Type of Price:** spot. **Time Period Covered:** latest week.

CALCIUM CARBONATE: LIGHT TO MEDIUM, USP

Source: *Chemical Marketing Reporter.* **Price Frequency:** weekly. **Effective Market(s):** New York. **Units of Measure:** Dollars per ton. **Type of Price:** spot. **Time Period Covered:** latest week.

CALCIUM CARBONATE: PRECIPITATE, TECHNICAL GRADE

Source: *Chemical Marketing Reporter.* **Price Frequency:** weekly. **Effective Market(s):** New York. **Units of Measure:** Dollars per ton. **Type of Price:** spot. **Time Period Covered:** latest week.

CALCIUM CARBONATE: PRECIPITATE, ULTRAFINE

Source: *Chemical Marketing Reporter.* **Price Frequency:** weekly. **Effective Market(s):** New York. **Units of Measure:** Dollars per ton. **Type of Price:** spot. **Time Period Covered:** latest week.

CALCIUM CARBONATE: SLURRY, FINE

Source: *Chemical Marketing Reporter.* **Price Frequency:** weekly. **Effective Market(s):** New York. **Units of Measure:** Dollars per ton. **Type of Price:** spot. **Time Period Covered:** latest week.

CALCIUM CARBONATE: SLURRY, ULTRAFINE

Source: *Chemical Marketing Reporter.* **Price Frequency:** weekly. **Effective Market(s):** New York. **Units of Measure:** Dollars per ton. **Type of Price:** spot. **Time Period Covered:** latest week.

CALCIUM CARBONATE: UNCOATED

Source: *Industrial Minerals.* **Price Frequency:** monthly. **Effective Market(s):** United Kingdom. **Units of Measure:** British pounds per metric tonne. **Type of Price:** producer & dealer. **Time Period Covered:** latest month.

CALCIUM CARBONATE: VERY FINE, HIGH PURITY, USP

Source: *Chemical Marketing Reporter.* **Price Frequency:** weekly. **Effective Market(s):** New York. **Units of Measure:** Dollars per ton. **Type of Price:** spot. **Time Period Covered:** latest week.

CALCIUM CHLORIDE: 77-80%, FLAKE

Source: *Journal of Commerce and Commercial.* **Price Frequency:** weekly in Thursday issue. **Units of Measure:** Dollars per ton. **Type of Price:** spot. **Time Period Covered:** latest week.

CALCIUM CHLORIDE: 90%, PELLET

Source: *Journal of Commerce and Commercial.* **Price Frequency:** weekly in Thursday issue. **Units of Measure:** Dollars per ton. **Type of Price:** spot. **Time Period Covered:** latest week.

CALCIUM CHLORIDE: 94-97%, PELLET

Source: *Journal of Commerce and Commercial.* **Price Frequency:** weekly in Thursday issue. **Units of Measure:** Dollars per ton. **Type of Price:** spot. **Time Period Covered:** latest week.

CALCIUM CHLORIDE: ANHYDROUS, 94-97%, FLAKE OR PELLET

Source: *Chemical Marketing Reporter.* **Price Frequency:** weekly. **Effective Market(s):** New York. **Units of Measure:** Dollars per ton. **Type of Price:** spot. **Time Period Covered:** latest week.

CALCIUM CHLORIDE: BRINING GRADE

Source: *Chemical Marketing Reporter.* **Price Frequency:** weekly. **Effective Market(s):** New York. **Units of Measure:** Dollars per ton. **Type of Price:** spot. **Time Period Covered:** latest week.

CALCIUM CHLORIDE: CONCENTRATED, REGULAR GRADE, 77-80%, FLAKE

Source: *Chemical Marketing Reporter.* **Price Frequency:** weekly. **Effective Market(s):** New York. **Units of Measure:** Dollars per ton. **Type of Price:** spot. **Time Period Covered:** latest week.

CALCIUM CHLORIDE: GRANULAR, USP

Source: *Chemical Marketing Reporter.* **Price Frequency:** weekly. **Effective Market(s):** New York. **Units of Measure:** Dollars per lb. **Type of Price:** spot. **Time Period Covered:** latest week.

CALCIUM CHLORIDE: LIQUID, 45%

Source: *Chemical Marketing Reporter.* **Price Frequency:** weekly. **Effective Market(s):** New York. **Units of Measure:** Dollars per ton. **Type of Price:** spot. **Time Period Covered:** latest week.

CALCIUM CHLORIDE: LIQUID, 100%

Source: *Chemical Marketing Reporter.* **Price Frequency:** weekly. **Effective Market(s):** New York. **Units of Measure:** Dollars per ton. **Type of Price:** spot. **Time Period Covered:** latest week.

CALCIUM CITRATE

Source: *Journal of Commerce and Commercial.* **Price Frequency:** weekly in Friday issue. **Units of Measure:** Dollars per lb. **Type of Price:** spot. **Time Period Covered:** latest week.

CALCIUM CITRATE: PURIFIED

Source: *Chemical Marketing Reporter.* **Price Frequency:** weekly. **Effective Market(s):** New York. **Units of Measure:** Dollars per lb. **Type of Price:** spot. **Time Period Covered:** latest week.

CALCIUM CYANAMIDE: INDUSTRIAL GRADE, ANHYDROUS

Source: *Chemical Marketing Reporter.* **Price Frequency:** weekly. **Effective Market(s):** New York. **Units of Measure:** Dollars per ton. **Type of Price:** spot. **Time Period Covered:** latest week.

CALCIUM GLUCONATE: POWDERED, USP

Source: *Chemical Marketing Reporter.* **Price Frequency:** weekly. **Effective Market(s):** New York. **Units of Measure:** Dollars per lb. **Type of Price:** spot. **Time Period Covered:** latest week.

CALCIUM GLUCONATE: USP

Source: *Journal of Commerce and Commercial.* **Price Frequency:** weekly in Friday issue. **Units of Measure:** Dollars per lb. **Type of Price:** spot. **Time Period Covered:** latest week.

CALCIUM GLYCEROPHASPHATE

Source: *Journal of Commerce and Commercial.* **Price Frequency:** weekly in Friday issue. **Units of Measure:** Dollars per lb. **Type of Price:** spot. **Time Period Covered:** latest week.

CALCIUM HYDRIDE: LUMP

Source: *Chemical Marketing Reporter.* **Price Frequency:** weekly. **Effective Market(s):** New York. **Units of Measure:** Dollars per lb. **Type of Price:** spot. **Time Period Covered:** latest week.

CALCIUM HYPOCHLORITE

Source: *Chemical Marketing Reporter.* **Price Frequency:** weekly. **Effective Market(s):** New York. **Units of Measure:** Dollars per 100 lbs. **Type of Price:** spot. **Time Period Covered:** latest week.

CALCIUM HYPOPHOSPHITE

Source: *Chemical Marketing Reporter.* **Price Frequency:** weekly. **Effective Market(s):** New York. **Units of Measure:** Dollars per kilo. **Type of Price:** spot. **Time Period Covered:** latest week.

CALCIUM IODATE: FCC

Source: *Chemical Marketing Reporter.* **Price Frequency:** weekly. **Effective Market(s):** New York. **Units of Measure:** Dollars per lb. **Type of Price:** spot. **Time Period Covered:** latest week.

CALCIUM IODIDE

Source: *Chemical Marketing Reporter.* **Price Frequency:** weekly. **Effective Market(s):** New York. **Units of Measure:** Dollars per kilo. **Type of Price:** spot. **Time Period Covered:** latest week.

CALCIUM LACTATE: PENTAHYDRATE, POWDERED, NF

Source: *Chemical Marketing Reporter.* **Price Frequency:** weekly. **Effective Market(s):** New York. **Units of Measure:** Dollars per lb. **Type of Price:** spot. **Time Period Covered:** latest week.

CALCIUM LACTATE: SPECIAL GRANULAR, DRIED GRADE

Source: *Chemical Marketing Reporter.* **Price Frequency:** weekly. **Effective Market(s):** New York. **Units of Measure:** Dollars per lb. **Type of Price:** spot. **Time Period Covered:** latest week.

CALCIUM LACTATE: TRIHYDRATE, POWDERED, NF

Source: *Chemical Marketing Reporter.* **Price Frequency:** weekly. **Effective Market(s):** New York. **Units of Measure:** Dollars per lb. **Type of Price:** spot. **Time Period Covered:** latest week.

CALCIUM LIGNIN SULFONATE: LIQUID, 50%

Source: *Chemical Marketing Reporter.* **Price Frequency:** weekly. **Effective Market(s):** West Coast. **Units of Measure:** Dollars per ton. **Type of Price:** spot. **Time Period Covered:** latest week.

CALCIUM NAPHTHENATE: LIQUID, 4% CALCIUM

Source: *Chemical Marketing Reporter.* **Price Frequency:** weekly. **Effective Market(s):** East of the Rockies. **Units of Measure:** Dollars per lb. **Type of Price:** spot. **Time Period Covered:** latest week.

CALCIUM PANTOTHENATE: USP

Source: *Journal of Commerce and Commercial.* **Price Frequency:** weekly in Friday issue. **Units of Measure:** Dollars per kilo. **Type of Price:** spot. **Time Period Covered:** latest week.

DL-CALCIUM PANTOTHENATE: CALCIUM CHLORIDE COMPLEX, FEED GRADE

Source: *Chemical Marketing Reporter.* **Price Frequency:** weekly. **Effective Market(s):** New York. **Units of Measure:** Dollars per lb. **Type of Price:** spot. **Time Period Covered:** latest week.

DL-CALCIUM PANTOTHENATE: FEED GRADE

Source: *Chemical Marketing Reporter.* **Price Frequency:** weekly. **Effective Market(s):** New York. **Units of Measure:** Dollars per kilo. **Type of Price:** spot. **Time Period Covered:** latest week.

D-CALCIUM PANTOTHENATE: USP

Source: *Chemical Marketing Reporter.* **Price Frequency:** weekly. **Effective Market(s):** New York. **Units of Measure:** Dollars per kilo. **Type of Price:** spot. **Time Period Covered:** latest week.

CALCIUM PHOSPHATE: DIBASIC, ANHYDROUS, USP

Source: *Chemical Marketing Reporter.* **Price Frequency:** weekly. **Effective Market(s):** New York. **Units of Measure:** Dollars per 100 lbs. **Type of Price:** spot. **Time Period Covered:** latest week.

CALCIUM PHOSPHATE: DIBASIC, DENTIFICE GRADE

Source: *Chemical Marketing Reporter.* **Price Frequency:** weekly. **Effective Market(s):** New York. **Units of Measure:** Dollars per 60 lbs. **Type of Price:** spot. **Time Period Covered:** latest week.

CALCIUM PHOSPHATE: DIBASIC, DIHYDRATE, USP

Source: *Chemical Marketing Reporter.* **Price Frequency:** weekly. **Effective Market(s):** New York. **Units of Measure:** Dollars per 100 lbs. **Type of Price:** spot. **Time Period Covered:** latest week.

CALCIUM PHOSPHATE: DIBASIC, FEED GRADE, 18-1/2% PHOSPHATE

Source: *Chemical Marketing Reporter.* **Price Frequency:** weekly. **Effective Market(s):** New York. **Units of Measure:** Dollars per ton. **Type of Price:** spot. **Time Period Covered:** latest week.

CALCIUM PHOSPHATE: MONOBASIC, ANHYDROUS, FOOD GRADE

Source: *Chemical Marketing Reporter.* **Price Frequency:** weekly. **Effective Market(s):** New York. **Units of Measure:** Dollars per 100 lbs. **Type of Price:** spot. **Time Period Covered:** latest week.

CALCIUM PHOSPHATE: MONOBASIC, MONOHYDRATE, FOOD GRADE

Source: *Chemical Marketing Reporter.* **Price Frequency:** weekly. **Effective Market(s):** New York. **Units of Measure:** Dollars per 100 lbs. **Type of Price:** spot. **Time Period Covered:** latest week.

CALCIUM PHOSPHATE: TRIBASIC, PRECIPITATED, NF

Source: *Chemical Marketing Reporter.* **Price Frequency:** weekly. **Effective Market(s):** New York. **Units of Measure:** Dollars per 100 lbs. **Type of Price:** spot. **Time Period Covered:** latest week.

CALCIUM PROPIONATE

Source: *Chemical Marketing Reporter.* **Price Frequency:** weekly. **Effective Market(s):** New York. **Units of Measure:** Dollars per lb. **Type of Price:** spot. **Time Period Covered:** latest week.

CALCIUM SILICATE: HYDRATED

Source: *Chemical Marketing Reporter.* **Price Frequency:** weekly. **Effective Market(s):** New York. **Units of Measure:** Dollars per lb. **Type of Price:** spot. **Time Period Covered:** latest week.

CALCIUM SILICATE: PAINT GRADE

see Wollastonite.

CALCIUM STEARATE: MAXIMUM

Source: *Modern Plastics.* **Price Frequency:** quarterly in February, May, August & November issues. **Units of Measure:** Dollars per lb. **Type of Price:** list. **Time Period Covered:** latest year.

CALCIUM STEARATE: MINIMUM

Source: *Modern Plastics.* **Price Frequency:** quarterly in February, May, August & November issues. **Units of Measure:** Dollars per lb. **Type of Price:** list. **Time Period Covered:** latest year.

CALOMEL POWDER

Source: *Journal of Commerce and Commercial.* **Price Frequency:** weekly in Friday issue. **Units of Measure:** Dollars per lb. **Type of Price:** spot. **Time Period Covered:** latest week.

CALOMEL POWDER: MILD, NF

Source: *Chemical Marketing Reporter.* **Price Frequency:** weekly. **Effective Market(s):** New York. **Units of Measure:** Dollars per lb. **Type of Price:** spot. **Time Period Covered:** latest week.

CALVES

Source: *Agricultural Outlook.* **Price Frequency:** monthly, annually. **Effective Market(s):** United States. **Units of Measure:** Dollars per 100 lbs. **Type of Price:** price received by farmer. **Time Period Covered:** monthly latest 6 months, annually latest 3 years.

Source: *Agricultural Prices.* **Price Frequency:** monthly. **Effective Market(s):** United States. **Units of Measure:** Dollars per 100 lbs. **Type of Price:** received by farmer. **Time Period Covered:** latest 2 months, year ago.

Source: *Agricultural Prices.* **Price Frequency:** monthly. **Effective Market(s):** 35 domestic markets, United States. **Units of Measure:** Dollars per 100 lbs. **Type of Price:** received by farmer. **Time Period Covered:** latest 2 months.

Source: *Commodity Year Book.* **Price Frequency:** monthly, annually. **Effective Market(s):** United States. **Units of Measure:** Dollars per 100 lbs. **Type of Price:** price received by farmers. **Time Period Covered:** latest 6 years.

Source: *Illinois Farm Report.* **Price Frequency:** monthly. **Effective Market(s):** Illinois. **Units of Measure:** Dollars per 100 lbs. **Type of Price:** average received by farmers. **Time Period Covered:** latest 2 months, year ago.

Source: *Kansas Business Review.* **Price Frequency:** monthly. **Effective Market(s):** Kansas. **Units of Measure:** Dollars per 100 lbs. **Type of Price:** received by farmer. **Time Period Covered:** latest month, month ago, year ago.

Source: *Lancaster Farming.* **Price Frequency:** weekly. **Effective Market(s):** Pennsylvania, Virginia. **Units of Measure:** Dollars per head. **Type of Price:** auction. **Time Period Covered:** latest week.

Source: *Livestock and Poultry Situation and Outlook Report.* **Price Frequency:** monthly. **Units of Measure:** Dollars per 100 lbs. **Type of Price:** farm. **Time Period Covered:** latest year.

Source: *Washington Farmer-Stockman.* **Price Frequency:** monthly, seasonally. **Effective Market(s):** Washington. **Units of Measure:** Dollars per 100 lbs. **Type of Price:** prices received by farmers. **Time Period Covered:** latest month, month ago, year ago.

CALVES: ALL VARIETIES

Source: *Farmers Weekly.* **Price Frequency:** weekly. **Effective Market(s):** Great Britain. **Units of Measure:** British pounds per head. **Type of Price:** average. **Time Period Covered:** latest week, week ago, two weeks ago.

CALVES: BEEF

Source: *Agricultural Prices Annual Summary.* **Price Frequency:** annually. **Effective Market(s):** 50 domestic markets, United States. **Units of Measure:** Dollars per 100 lbs. **Type of Price:** average price received by farmer. **Time Period Covered:** latest 2 years, for US latest 6 years.

Source: *Agricultural Prices Annual Summary.* **Price Frequency:** monthly. **Effective Market(s):** 35 domestic markets, United States. **Units of Measure:** Dollars per 100 lbs. **Type of Price:** average price received by farmer. **Time Period Covered:** latest year, for US latest 6 years.

CALVES: BEEF, KEEPING

Source: *Scottish Farmer.* **Price Frequency:** weekly. **Effective Market(s):** Ayr (Scotland), Lanark (Scotland), Paisley (Scotland), Stirling (Scotland). **Units of Measure:** British pounds per head. **Type of Price:** top, average. **Time Period Covered:** latest week.

CALVES: BELGIAN BLUE X

Source: *Farmers Weekly.* **Price Frequency:** weekly. **Effective Market(s):** 14 British markets. **Units of Measure:** British pounds per head. **Type of Price:** average. **Time Period Covered:** latest week.

CALVES: BULL

Source: *Farm and Dairy.* **Price Frequency:** weekly, seasonally. **Effective Market(s):** Ohio, Pennsylvania. **Units of Measure:** Dollars per head. **Type of Price:** auction high, auction low. **Time Period Covered:** latest week, year ago.

CALVES: CHAROLAIS X

Source: *Farmers Weekly.* **Price Frequency:** weekly. **Effective Market(s):** 14 British markets. **Units of Measure:** British pounds per head. **Type of Price:** average. **Time Period Covered:** latest week.

CALVES: CHOICE

Source: *Farm and Dairy.* **Price Frequency:** weekly, seasonally. **Effective Market(s):** Ohio, Pennsylvania. **Units of Measure:** Dollars per head. **Type of Price:** auction high, auction low. **Time Period Covered:** latest week, year ago.

CALVES: COMMON

Source: *Farm and Dairy.* **Price Frequency:** weekly, seasonally. **Effective Market(s):** Ohio, Pennsylvania. **Units of Measure:** Dollars per head. **Type of Price:** auction high, auction low. **Time Period Covered:** latest week, year ago.

CALVES: CROSSBRED

Source: *Farm and Dairy.* **Price Frequency:** weekly, seasonally. **Effective Market(s):** Ohio, Pennsylvania. **Units of Measure:** Dollars per head. **Type of Price:** auction high, auction low. **Time Period Covered:** latest week, year ago.

CALVES: DAIRY, KEEPING

Source: *Scottish Farmer.* **Price Frequency:** weekly. **Effective Market(s):** Ayr (Scotland), Lanark (Scotland), Paisley (Scotland), Stirling (Scotland). **Units of Measure:** British pounds per head. **Type of Price:** top, average. **Time Period Covered:** latest week.

CALVES: FRIESIAN

Source: *Farmers Weekly.* **Price Frequency:** weekly. **Effective Market(s):** 14 British markets. **Units of Measure:** British pounds per head. **Type of Price:** average. **Time Period Covered:** latest week.

CALVES: GOOD

Source: *Farm and Dairy.* **Price Frequency:** weekly, seasonally. **Effective Market(s):** Ohio, Pennsylvania. **Units of Measure:** Dollars per head. **Type of Price:** auction high, auction low. **Time Period Covered:** latest week, year ago.

CALVES: HEIFER

Source: *Farm and Dairy.* **Price Frequency:** weekly, seasonally. **Effective Market(s):** Ohio, Pennsylvania. **Units of Measure:** Dollars per head. **Type of Price:** auction high, auction low. **Time Period Covered:** latest week, year ago.

CALVES: HEREFORD CROSS

Source: *Farmers Weekly.* **Price Frequency:** weekly. **Effective Market(s):** 14 British markets. **Units of Measure:** British pounds per head. **Type of Price:** average. **Time Period Covered:** latest week.

CALVES: KILLING

Source: *Scottish Farmer.* **Price Frequency:** weekly. **Effective Market(s):** Ayr (Scotland), Lanark (Scotland), Paisley (Scotland), Stirling (Scotland). **Units of Measure:** British pounds per head. **Type of Price:** top, average. **Time Period Covered:** latest week.

CALVES: LIGHT AND THIN

Source: *Farm and Dairy.* **Price Frequency:** weekly, seasonally. **Effective Market(s):** Ohio, Pennsylvania. **Units of Measure:** Dollars per head. **Type of Price:** auction high, auction low. **Time Period Covered:** latest week, year ago.

CALVES: LIMOUSIN X

Source: *Farmers Weekly.* **Price Frequency:** weekly. **Effective Market(s):** 14 British markets. **Units of Measure:** British pounds per head. **Type of Price:** average. **Time Period Covered:** latest week.

CALVES: MEDIUM

Source: *Farm and Dairy.* **Price Frequency:** weekly, seasonally. **Effective Market(s):** Ohio, Pennsylvania. **Units of Measure:** Dollars per head. **Type of Price:** auction high, auction low. **Time Period Covered:** latest week, year ago.

CALVES: SIMMENTAL X

Source: *Farmers Weekly.* **Price Frequency:** weekly. **Effective Market(s):** 14 British markets. **Units of Measure:** British pounds per head. **Type of Price:** average. **Time Period Covered:** latest week.

CALVES: SLAUGHTER

Source: *Livestock, Meat, Wool Market News.* **Price Frequency:** weekly, seasonally. **Effective Market(s):** Georgia, Louisville, New York, South St. Paul. **Units of Measure:** Dollars per 100 lbs. **Type of Price:** average. **Time Period Covered:** latest week, year ago.

CALVES: SLAUGHTER, CHOICE

Source: *Livestock, Meat, Wool Market News.* **Price Frequency:** weekly, seasonally. **Effective Market(s):** Georgia, Louisville, New York, South St. Paul. **Units of Measure:** Dollars per 100 lbs. **Type of Price:** average. **Time Period Covered:** latest week, year ago.

CALVES: SLAUGHTER, GOOD

Source: *Livestock, Meat, Wool Market News.* **Price Frequency:** weekly, seasonally. **Effective Market(s):** Georgia, Louisville, New York, South St. Paul. **Units of Measure:** Dollars per 100 lbs. **Type of Price:** average. **Time Period Covered:** latest week, year ago.

CALVES: STEER

Source: *Agriculture.* **Price Frequency:** weekly. **Effective Market(s):** 8 domestic markets, 8-market average. **Units of Measure:** Dollars per 100 lbs. **Time Period Covered:** latest week, week ago, year ago.

CALVES: VEAL

see Veal Calves, Vealers.

CALVES LIVER

Source: *Meat Price Report.* **Price Frequency:** weekly. **Units of Measure:** cents per lb. **Type of Price:** price paid to wholesaler. **Time Period Covered:** latest week.

CALVES SKINS

Source: *National Provisioner.* **Price Frequency:** weekly. **Effective Market(s):** Chicago. **Time Period Covered:** latest week, year ago.

CAMBRIC FABRIC

Source: *JTN: The International Textile Magazine.* **Price Frequency:** monthly. **Effective Market(s):** Japan. **Units of Measure:** Japanese yen per yard. **Type of Price:** spot. **Time Period Covered:** latest month.

CAMPHOR: MONOBROMATED

Source: *Chemical Marketing Reporter.* **Price Frequency:** weekly. **Effective Market(s):** New York. **Units of Measure:** Dollars per lb. **Type of Price:** spot. **Time Period Covered:** latest week.

CAMPHOR: NATURAL

Source: *Journal of Commerce and Commercial.* **Price Frequency:** weekly in Friday issue. **Units of Measure:** Dollars per lb. **Type of Price:** spot. **Time Period Covered:** latest week.

CAMPHOR: POWDERED, USP

Source: *Chemical Marketing Reporter.* **Price Frequency:** weekly. **Effective Market(s):** New York. **Units of Measure:** Dollars per kilo. **Type of Price:** spot. **Time Period Covered:** latest week.

CAMPHOR: SYNTHETIC, REFINED

Source: *Chemical Marketing Reporter.* **Price Frequency:** weekly. **Effective Market(s):** New York. **Units of Measure:** Dollars per lb. **Type of Price:** spot. **Time Period Covered:** latest week.

CAMPHOR: SYNTHETIC, TECHNICAL GRADE

Source: *Chemical Marketing Reporter.* **Price Frequency:** weekly. **Effective Market(s):** New York. **Units of Measure:** Dollars per lb. **Type of Price:** spot. **Time Period Covered:** latest week.

Source: *Journal of Commerce and Commercial.* **Price Frequency:** weekly in Friday issue. **Units of Measure:** Dollars per lb. **Type of Price:** spot. **Time Period Covered:** latest week.

CAMPHOR: SYNTHETIC, USP

Source: *Journal of Commerce and Commercial.* **Price Frequency:** weekly in Friday issue. **Units of Measure:** Dollars per lb. **Type of Price:** spot. **Time Period Covered:** latest week.

CAMPHOR OIL

Source: *U. S. Essential Oil Trade.* **Price Frequency:** annually. **Effective Market(s):** United States. **Units of Measure:** Dollars per kilogram. **Type of Price:** import value. **Time Period Covered:** latest 3 years.

CAMPHOR OIL: SPECIFIC GRAVITY 1.070

Source: *Chemical Marketing Reporter.* **Price Frequency:** weekly. **Effective Market(s):** New York. **Units of Measure:** Dollars per lb. **Type of Price:** spot. **Time Period Covered:** latest week.

CAMPHOR OIL: WHITE, FORMOSAN

Source: *Chemical Marketing Reporter.* **Price Frequency:** weekly. **Effective Market(s):** New York. **Units of Measure:** Dollars per lb. **Type of Price:** spot. **Time Period Covered:** latest week.

CAMPHOR OIL: YELLOW

Source: *Chemical Marketing Reporter.* **Price Frequency:** weekly. **Effective Market(s):** New York. **Units of Measure:** Dollars per lb. **Type of Price:** spot. **Time Period Covered:** latest week.

CANADA DOLLARS

Source: *American Metal Market.* **Price Frequency:** daily. **Units of Measure:** Canadian dollars per United States dollar. **Type of Price:** foreign exchange. **Time Period Covered:** latest day.

Source: *Asian Wall Street Journal.* **Price Frequency:** daily. **Effective Market(s):** United States. **Units of Measure:** Canadian dollars per ECU, per SDR. **Type of Price:** foreign exchange. **Time Period Covered:** latest 2 days.

Source: *Barron's.* **Price Frequency:** weekly. **Effective Market(s):** New York. **Units of Measure:** Canadian dollars per United States dollar. **Type of Price:** foreign exchange. **Time Period Covered:** latest 2 weeks.

Source: *Commodity Year Book.* **Price Frequency:** monthly, annually. **Units of Measure:** Canadian dollars per United States dollars. **Type of Price:** foreign exchange. **Time Period Covered:** latest 5 years.

Source: *The Economist.* **Price Frequency:** weekly. **Effective Market(s):** London. **Units of Measure:** Canadian dollars per United States dollar, per British pound, per ECU, per SDR. **Type of Price:** foreign exchange. **Time Period Covered:** latest week.

Source: *International Wheat Council Market Report.* **Price Frequency:** weekly. **Effective Market(s):** London. **Units of Measure:** Canadian dollars per United States dollars. **Type of Price:** foreign exchange. **Time Period Covered:** latest 5 weeks.

Source: *New York Times.* **Price Frequency:** daily. **Effective Market(s):** New York. **Units of Measure:** Canadian dollars per United States dollars. **Type of Price:** foreign exchange. **Time Period Covered:** latest 2 days.

Source: *Timber Bulletin.* **Price Frequency:** monthly, annually. **Units of Measure:** Canadian dollars per United States dollar. **Type of Price:** foreign exchange. **Time Period Covered:** latest 2 years.

CANADA DOLLARS: FUTURES

Source: *Asian Wall Street Journal.* **Price Frequency:** daily. **Effective Market(s):** Chicago. **Units of Measure:** United States Dollars per Canadian dollars. **Type of Price:** foreign exchange futures. **Time Period Covered:** latest day.

Source: *Barron's.* **Price Frequency:** weekly. **Units of Measure:** United States dollars per Canadian dollar. **Type of Price:** foreign exchange futures. **Time Period Covered:** latest week.

Source: *Los Angeles Times.* **Price Frequency:** daily. **Effective Market(s):** Chicago. **Units of Measure:** United States dollars per Canadian dollar. **Type of Price:** foreign exchange futures. **Time Period Covered:** latest day.

Source: *New York Times.* **Price Frequency:** daily. **Effective Market(s):** Chicago. **Units of Measure:** United States dollars per Canadian dollar. **Type of Price:** foreign exchange futures. **Time Period Covered:** latest day.

Source: *Urner Barry's Price-Current.* **Price Frequency:** daily. **Units of Measure:** United States dollars per Canadian dollars. **Type of Price:** foreign exchange futures. **Time Period Covered:** latest day.

CANADIAN BACON
see Bacon: Canadian.

CANADIAN WHISKEY
Source: *Colorado Beverage Analyst.* **Price Frequency:** monthly. **Effective Market(s):** Colorado. **Units of Measure:** Dollars per case. **Type of Price:** wholesale by brand. **Time Period Covered:** latest month.

Source: *Illinois Beverage Journal.* **Price Frequency:** monthly. **Effective Market(s):** Illinois. **Units of Measure:** Dollars per case. **Type of Price:** wholesale by brand. **Time Period Covered:** latest month.

Source: *Kentucky Beverage Journal.* **Price Frequency:** monthly. **Effective Market(s):** Kentucky. **Units of Measure:** Dollars per bottle, dollars per case. **Type of Price:** wholesale by brand. **Time Period Covered:** latest month.

CANANGA OIL
Source: *Journal of Commerce and Commercial.* **Price Frequency:** weekly in Tuesday issue. **Units of Measure:** Dollars per lb. **Type of Price:** spot. **Time Period Covered:** latest week.

Source: *U. S. Essential Oil Trade.* **Price Frequency:** annually. **Effective Market(s):** United States. **Units of Measure:** Dollars per kilogram. **Type of Price:** import value. **Time Period Covered:** latest 3 years.

CANANGA OIL: INDONESIAN
Source: *Chemical Marketing Reporter.* **Price Frequency:** weekly. **Effective Market(s):** New York. **Units of Measure:** Dollars per kilo. **Type of Price:** spot. **Time Period Covered:** latest week.

Source: *Prices of Selected Asia/Pacific Products.* **Price Frequency:** monthly. **Effective Market(s):** New York. **Units of Measure:** Dollars per kilogram. **Type of Price:** spot high, spot low. **Time Period Covered:** latest month.

CANANGA OIL: JAVANESE
Source: *Prices of Selected Asia/Pacific Products.* **Price Frequency:** monthly. **Effective Market(s):** North European ports/United Kingdom. **Units of Measure:** British pounds per kilogram. **Time Period Covered:** latest month.

CANDELILLA WAX
see Wax: Candelilla.

CANDELILLA WAX: CRUDE
Source: *Chemical Marketing Reporter.* **Price Frequency:** weekly. **Effective Market(s):** New York. **Units of Measure:** Dollars per lb. **Type of Price:** spot. **Time Period Covered:** latest week.

CANDELILLA WAX: REFINED
Source: *Chemical Marketing Reporter.* **Price Frequency:** weekly. **Effective Market(s):** New York. **Units of Measure:** Dollars per lb. **Type of Price:** spot. **Time Period Covered:** latest week.

CANE SUGAR
see Sugar: Cane.

CANOLA: FUTURES
Source: *Asian Wall Street Journal.* **Price Frequency:** daily. **Effective Market(s):** Winnepeg. **Units of Measure:** Canadian dollars per ton. **Type of Price:** futures. **Time Period Covered:** latest day.

CANOLA MEAL: 36% PROTEIN
Source: *Feedstuffs.* **Price Frequency:** weekly. **Effective Market(s):** Buffalo (NY), Minneapolis/St. Paul, Montreal, Toronto. **Units of Measure:** Dollars per bulk ton. **Time Period Covered:** latest week.

CANOLA OIL
Source: *Milling & Baking News.* **Price Frequency:** weekly. **Effective Market(s):** Midwest. **Units of Measure:** cents per lb. **Type of Price:** spot bulk. **Time Period Covered:** latest week.

CANTALOUPS
Source: *California Farmer.* **Price Frequency:** semimonthly, seasonally. **Effective Market(s):** Westside District (CA). **Units of Measure:** Dollars per 1/2 carton. **Time Period Covered:** latest week, month ago, year ago.

Source: *Fresh Fruit and Vegetable Prices.* **Price Frequency:** monthly, seasonally. **Effective Market(s):** Arizona/Palo Verde Valley (CA), Arkansas Valley (CA), Lower Rio Grande Valley (TX), Westside District (CA). **Units of Measure:** Dollars per carton. **Type of Price:** average price at shipping point. **Time Period Covered:** latest year.

Source: *Lancaster Farming.* **Price Frequency:** weekly, seasonally. **Effective Market(s):** Pennsylvania. **Units of Measure:** Dollars per carton. **Type of Price:** market. **Time Period Covered:** latest week.

Source: *The Packer.* **Price Frequency:** weekly, seasonally. **Effective Market(s):** varies. **Units of Measure:** Dollars per unit. **Type of Price:** price received by farmer. **Time Period Covered:** latest week.

CANTALOUPS: CALIFORNIA
Source: *Fresh Fruit and Vegetable Prices.* **Price Frequency:** monthly, seasonally. **Effective Market(s):** Chicago, New York City. **Units of Measure:** Dollars per carton/crate. **Type of Price:** average wholesale price. **Time Period Covered:** latest year.

CANTALOUPS: CARIBBEAN IMPORTS
Source: *Fresh Fruit and Vegetable Prices.* **Price Frequency:** monthly, seasonally. **Effective Market(s):** South Florida. **Units of Measure:** Dollars per crate. **Type of Price:** price paid at point of entry. **Time Period Covered:** latest year.

CANTALOUPS: CHILEAN
Source: *Fresh Fruit and Vegetable Prices.* **Price Frequency:** monthly, seasonally. **Effective Market(s):** New York City/Philadelphia. **Units of Measure:** Dollars per carton. **Type of Price:** price paid at point of entry. **Time Period Covered:** latest year.

CANTALOUPS: FRESH
Source: *HRI-Buyers Guide.* **Price Frequency:** weekly. **Effective Market(s):** Northeastern area. **Units of Measure:** Dollars per carton. **Type of Price:** price paid by dining places & institutions. **Time Period Covered:** latest week.

CANTALOUPS: MEXICAN

Source: *Fresh Fruit and Vegetable Prices.* **Price Frequency:** monthly, seasonally. **Effective Market(s):** Nogales (AZ), South Texas. **Units of Measure:** Dollars per crate. **Type of Price:** price paid at point of entry. **Time Period Covered:** latest year.

Source: *Fresh Fruit and Vegetable Prices.* **Price Frequency:** monthly, seasonally. **Effective Market(s):** Chicago, New York City. **Units of Measure:** Dollars per carton/crate. **Type of Price:** average wholesale price. **Time Period Covered:** latest year.

CANTALOUPS: TEXAS

Source: *Fresh Fruit and Vegetable Prices.* **Price Frequency:** monthly, seasonally. **Effective Market(s):** Chicago, New York City. **Units of Measure:** Dollars per carton/crate. **Type of Price:** average wholesale price. **Time Period Covered:** latest year.

CAP

see Cellulose Acetate Propionate.

CAPACITORS: CERAMIC MONOLITHIC, 0.1 MICROFARAD AXIAL

Source: *Purchasing.* **Price Frequency:** monthly. **Units of Measure:** cents each. **Type of Price:** transaction. **Time Period Covered:** latest day, month ago, 6 months ago, year ago.

CAPACITORS: TANTALUM, 1.0 MICROFARAD AXIAL

Source: *Purchasing.* **Price Frequency:** monthly. **Units of Measure:** Dollars each. **Type of Price:** transaction. **Time Period Covered:** latest day, month ago, 6 months ago, year ago.

CAPONS

Source: *Meat Price Report.* **Price Frequency:** weekly. **Units of Measure:** cents per lb. **Type of Price:** price paid to wholesaler. **Time Period Covered:** latest week.

Source: *Weekly Insiders Turkey Letter.* **Price Frequency:** weekly. **Effective Market(s):** New York. **Units of Measure:** cents per lb. **Type of Price:** retail. **Time Period Covered:** latest week, week ago, year ago.

CAPONS: GRADE A, READY-TO-COOK, FROZEN

Source: *Urner Barry's Price Current.* **Price Frequency:** daily. **Units of Measure:** Dollars per lb. **Type of Price:** price to first receivers. **Time Period Covered:** latest day.

CAPONS: PLANT GRADE B, SEWN, FROZEN

Source: *Urner Barry's Price-Current.* **Price Frequency:** daily. **Units of Measure:** Dollars per lb. **Type of Price:** price to first receivers. **Time Period Covered:** latest day.

CAPONS: PLANT GRADE B, UNSEWN, FROZEN

Source: *Urner Barry's Price-Current.* **Price Frequency:** daily. **Units of Measure:** Dollars per lb. **Type of Price:** price to first receivers. **Time Period Covered:** latest day.

CAPONS: READY-TO-COOK, ICED

Source: *Urner Barry's Price-Current.* **Price Frequency:** daily. **Units of Measure:** Dollars per lb. **Type of Price:** price to first receivers. **Time Period Covered:** latest day.

CAPONS: WHOLE, FROZEN

Source: *HRI-Buyer's Guide.* **Price Frequency:** weekly. **Effective Market(s):** Northeastern area. **Units of Measure:** Dollars per lb. **Type of Price:** price paid by dining places & institutions. **Time Period Covered:** latest week.

CAPRIC ACID: COMMERCIAL, PURE

Source: *Chemical Marketing Reporter.* **Price Frequency:** weekly. **Effective Market(s):** New York. **Units of Measure:** Dollars per lb. **Type of Price:** spot. **Time Period Covered:** latest week.

CAPROLACTAM

Source: *Cotton and Wool Situation and Outlook Report.* **Price Frequency:** monthly. **Units of Measure:** cents per lb. **Type of Price:** spot. **Time Period Covered:** latest year.

CAPROLACTAM: FLAKE

Source: *Chemical Marketing Reporter.* **Price Frequency:** weekly. **Effective Market(s):** New York. **Units of Measure:** Dollars per lb. **Type of Price:** spot. **Time Period Covered:** latest week.

Source: *Journal of Commerce and Commercial.* **Price Frequency:** weekly in Thursday issue. **Units of Measure:** Dollars per lb. **Type of Price:** spot. **Time Period Covered:** latest week.

CAPROLACTAM: MOLTEN

Source: *Chemical Marketing Reporter.* **Price Frequency:** weekly. **Effective Market(s):** New York. **Units of Measure:** Dollars per lb. **Type of Price:** spot. **Time Period Covered:** latest week.

Source: *Journal of Commerce and Commercial.* **Price Frequency:** weekly in Thursday issue. **Units of Measure:** Dollars per lb. **Type of Price:** spot. **Time Period Covered:** latest week.

CAPRYL ALCOHOL: SECONDARY, 98%

Source: *Chemical Marketing Reporter.* **Price Frequency:** weekly. **Effective Market(s):** New York. **Units of Measure:** Dollars per lb. **Type of Price:** spot. **Time Period Covered:** latest week.

CAPRYLIC ACID: COMMERCIAL, PURE

Source: *Chemical Marketing Reporter.* **Price Frequency:** weekly. **Effective Market(s):** New York. **Units of Measure:** Dollars per lb. **Type of Price:** spot. **Time Period Covered:** latest week.

CAPSICUM PEPPERS: CHINESE

Source: *U. S. Spice Trade.* **Price Frequency:** annually. **Effective Market(s):** New York. **Units of Measure:** cents per lb. **Type of Price:** spot. **Time Period Covered:** latest 3 years.

CAPSICUM PEPPERS: INDIAN

Source: *U. S. Spice Trade.* **Price Frequency:** annually. **Effective Market(s):** New York. **Units of Measure:** cents per lb. **Type of Price:** spot. **Time Period Covered:** latest 3 years.

CAPSICUM PEPPERS: PAKISTAN

Source: *U. S. Spice Trade.* **Price Frequency:** annually. **Effective Market(s):** New York. **Units of Measure:** cents per lb. **Type of Price:** spot. **Time Period Covered:** latest 3 years.

CAPSICUMS

see also Peppers.

Source: *New Zealand Farmer.* **Price Frequency:** weekly, seasonally. **Effective Market(s):** New Zealand. **Units of Measure:** New Zealand dollars per case. **Time Period Covered:** latest week.

CAPSICUMS: GREEN

Source: *New Zealand Farmer.* **Price Frequency:** weekly, seasonally. **Effective Market(s):** New Zealand. **Units of Measure:** New Zealand dollars per kilogram. **Time Period Covered:** latest week.

CAPSICUMS: RED

Source: *New Zealand Farmer.* **Price Frequency:** weekly, seasonally. **Effective Market(s):** New Zealand. **Units of Measure:** New Zealand dollars per kilogram. **Time Period Covered:** latest week.

CAPSICUMS: YELLOW

Source: *New Zealand Farmer.* **Price Frequency:** weekly, seasonally. **Effective Market(s):** New Zealand. **Units of Measure:** New Zealand dollars per kilogram. **Time Period Covered:** latest week.

CAPTAN: 50%, WETTABLE POWDER

Source: *Agricultural Prices Annual Summary.* **Price Frequency:** semiannually. **Effective Market(s):** United States. **Units of Measure:** Dollars per lb. **Type of Price:** average price paid by farmer. **Time Period Covered:** latest 6 years.

CARAWAY OIL

Source: *Journal of Commerce and Commercial.* **Price Frequency:** weekly in Tuesday issue. **Units of Measure:** Dollars per lb. **Type of Price:** spot. **Time Period Covered:** latest week.

Source: *U. S. Essential Oil Trade.* **Price Frequency:** annually. **Effective Market(s):** United States. **Units of Measure:** Dollars per kilogram. **Type of Price:** import value. **Time Period Covered:** latest 3 years.

CARAWAY OIL: POLISH

Source: *Chemical Marketing Reporter.* **Price Frequency:** weekly. **Effective Market(s):** New York. **Units of Measure:** Dollars per lb. **Type of Price:** spot. **Time Period Covered:** latest week.

CARAWAY SEED: DUTCH

Source: *Chemical Marketing Reporter.* **Price Frequency:** weekly. **Effective Market(s):** New York. **Units of Measure:** Dollars per lb. **Type of Price:** spot. **Time Period Covered:** latest week.

Source: *U. S. Spice Trade.* **Price Frequency:** annually. **Effective Market(s):** New York. **Units of Measure:** cents per lb. **Type of Price:** spot. **Time Period Covered:** latest 3 years.

CARAWAY SEED: EGYPTIAN

Source: *Chemical Marketing Reporter.* **Price Frequency:** weekly. **Effective Market(s):** New York. **Units of Measure:** Dollars per lb. **Type of Price:** spot. **Time Period Covered:** latest week.

Source: *U. S. Spice Trade.* **Price Frequency:** annually. **Effective Market(s):** New York. **Units of Measure:** cents per lb. **Type of Price:** spot. **Time Period Covered:** latest 3 years.

CARAWAY SEED: POLISH

Source: *U. S. Spice Trade.* **Price Frequency:** annually. **Effective Market(s):** New York. **Units of Measure:** cents per lb. **Type of Price:** spot. **Time Period Covered:** latest 3 years.

CARBARYL: 80%, WETTABLE POWDER

Source: *Agricultural Prices Annual Summary.* **Price Frequency:** semiannually. **Effective Market(s):** United States. **Units of Measure:** Dollars per 10 lbs. **Type of Price:** average price paid by farmer. **Time Period Covered:** latest 6 years.

CARBOFURAN: GRANULAR

Source: *Agricultural Prices Annual Summary.* **Price Frequency:** semiannually. **Effective Market(s):** United States. **Units of Measure:** Dollars per 50 lbs. **Type of Price:** average price paid by farmer. **Time Period Covered:** latest 6 years.

CARBON

Source: *Journal of Commerce and Commercial.* **Price Frequency:** weekly in Thursday issue. **Units of Measure:** Dollars per ton. **Type of Price:** spot. **Time Period Covered:** latest week.

CARBON BLACK: FAST EXTRUDING

Source: *Chemical Marketing Reporter.* **Price Frequency:** weekly. **Effective Market(s):** New York. **Units of Measure:** Dollars per lb. **Type of Price:** spot. **Time Period Covered:** latest week.

CARBON BLACK: GENERAL PURPOSE

Source: *Chemical Marketing Reporter.* **Price Frequency:** weekly. **Effective Market(s):** New York. **Units of Measure:** Dollars per lb. **Type of Price:** spot. **Time Period Covered:** latest week.

Source: *Journal of Commerce and Commercial.* **Price Frequency:** weekly in Wednesday issue. **Units of Measure:** Dollars per lb. **Type of Price:** spot. **Time Period Covered:** latest week.

CARBON BLACK: HIGH ABRASION

Source: *Chemical Marketing Reporter.* **Price Frequency:** weekly. **Effective Market(s):** New York. **Units of Measure:** Dollars per lb. **Type of Price:** spot. **Time Period Covered:** latest week.

Source: *Journal of Commerce and Commercial.* **Price Frequency:** weekly in Wednesday issue. **Units of Measure:** Dollars per lb. **Type of Price:** spot. **Time Period Covered:** latest week.

CARBON BLACK: INTERMEDIATE SUPER ABRASION

Source: *Chemical Marketing Reporter.* **Price Frequency:** weekly. **Effective Market(s):** New York. **Units of Measure:** Dollars per lb. **Type of Price:** spot. **Time Period Covered:** latest week.

CARBON BLACK: SEMI-REINFORCING

Source: *Chemical Marketing Reporter.* **Price Frequency:** weekly. **Effective Market(s):** New York. **Units of Measure:** Dollars per lb. **Type of Price:** spot. **Time Period Covered:** latest week.

CARBON BLACK: SUPER ABRASION

Source: *Chemical Marketing Reporter.* **Price Frequency:** weekly. **Effective Market(s):** New York. **Units of Measure:** Dollars per lb. **Type of Price:** spot. **Time Period Covered:** latest week.

CARBON BLACK: THERMAL, MEDIUM

Source: *Chemical Marketing Reporter.* **Price Frequency:** weekly. **Effective Market(s):** New York. **Units of Measure:** Dollars per lb. **Type of Price:** spot. **Time Period Covered:** latest week.

CARBON BLACK OIL

Source: *Chemical Marketing Reporter.* **Price Frequency:** weekly. **Effective Market(s):** Gulf refineries, West Coast refineries. **Units of Measure:** Dollars per barrel. **Type of Price:** spot. **Time Period Covered:** latest week.

CARBON DISULFIDE

Source: *Chemical Marketing Reporter.* **Price Frequency:** weekly. **Effective Market(s):** New York. **Units of Measure:** Dollars per ton. **Type of Price:** spot. **Time Period Covered:** latest week.

Source: *Journal of Commerce and Commercial.* **Price Frequency:** weekly in Thursday issue. **Units of Measure:** Dollars per ton. **Type of Price:** spot. **Time Period Covered:** latest week.

CARBON STEEL

see Steel.

CARBON TETRACHLORIDE

Source: *Journal of Commerce and Commercial.* **Price Frequency:** weekly in Thursday issue. **Units of Measure:** Dollars per lb. **Type of Price:** spot. **Time Period Covered:** latest week.

CARBON TETRACHLORIDE: CHEMICALLY PURE, CONSUMERS

Source: *Chemical Marketing Reporter.* **Price Frequency:** weekly. **Effective Market(s):** New York. **Units of Measure:** Dollars per lb. **Type of Price:** spot. **Time Period Covered:** latest week.

CARBON TETRACHLORIDE: TECHNICAL GRADE

Source: *Chemical Marketing Reporter.* **Price Frequency:** weekly. **Effective Market(s):** New York. **Units of Measure:** Dollars per lb. **Type of Price:** spot. **Time Period Covered:** latest week.

Source: *Journal of Commerce and Commercial.* **Price Frequency:** weekly in Thursday issue. **Units of Measure:** Dollars per lb. **Type of Price:** spot. **Time Period Covered:** latest week.

CARBOXYMETHYL CELLULOSE

see CMC.

CARDAMOM

Source: *Prices of Selected Asia/Pacific Products.* **Price Frequency:** monthly, seasonally. **Effective Market(s):** Tokyo. **Units of Measure:** Japanese yen per kilogram. **Type of Price:** trade high, trade low. **Time Period Covered:** latest month.

CARDAMOM: BLEACHED "AA"

Source: *U. S. Spice Trade.* **Price Frequency:** monthly, annually. **Effective Market(s):** New York. **Units of Measure:** Dollars per lb. **Type of Price:** spot. **Time Period Covered:** latest 8 years.

CARDAMOM: BOLD MIXED, GUATEMALAN

Source: *Prices of Selected Asia/Pacific Products.* **Price Frequency:** monthly, seasonally. **Effective Market(s):** United Kingdom. **Units of Measure:** Bristish pounds per kilogram. **Type of Price:** spot high, spot low. **Time Period Covered:** latest month.

CARDAMOM: DECORTICATED

Source: *U. S. Spice Trade.* **Price Frequency:** monthly, annually. **Effective Market(s):** New York. **Units of Measure:** Dollars per lb. **Type of Price:** spot. **Time Period Covered:** latest 8 years.

CARDAMOM: GREENS, BOLD MIXED, GUATEMALAN

Source: *Fruit and Tropical Products.* **Price Frequency:** monthly, seasonally. **Effective Market(s):** London. **Units of Measure:** British pounds per tonne. **Type of Price:** month end. **Time Period Covered:** latest 2 years.

CARDAMOM: GREENS, EXTRA FANCY

Source: *U. S. Spice Trade.* **Price Frequency:** monthly, annually. **Effective Market(s):** New York. **Units of Measure:** Dollars per lb. **Type of Price:** spot. **Time Period Covered:** latest 8 years.

CARDAMOM: GREENS, GUATEMALAN

Source: *Prices of Selected Asia/Pacific Products.* **Price Frequency:** monthly, seasonally. **Effective Market(s):** North European ports/United Kingdom. **Units of Measure:** Dollars per kilogram. **Type of Price:** high, low. **Time Period Covered:** latest month.

CARDAMOM: GREENS, MIXED, GUATEMALAN

Source: *Prices of Selected Asia/Pacific Products.* **Price Frequency:** monthly, seasonally. **Effective Market(s):** United States. **Units of Measure:** Dollars per metric ton. **Type of Price:** spot high, spot low. **Time Period Covered:** latest month.

Source: *U. S. Spice Trade.* **Price Frequency:** monthly, annually. **Effective Market(s):** New York. **Units of Measure:** Dollars per lb. **Type of Price:** spot. **Time Period Covered:** latest 8 years.

CARDAMOM: GUATEMALAN

Source: *Chemical Marketing Reporter.* **Price Frequency:** weekly. **Effective Market(s):** New York. **Units of Measure:** Dollars per lb. **Type of Price:** spot. **Time Period Covered:** latest week.

Source: *Prices of Selected Asia/Pacific Products.* **Price Frequency:** monthly. **Effective Market(s):** United Kingdom/North European ports. **Units of Measure:** Dollars per kilogram. **Type of Price:** high, low. **Time Period Covered:** latest month.

CARDAMOM: LG, SRI LANKAN

Source: *Prices of Selected Asia/Pacific Products.* **Price Frequency:** monthly, seasonally. **Effective Market(s):** Colombo (Sri Lanka). **Units of Measure:** Sri Lankan rupees per kilogram. **Type of Price:** auction high, auction low. **Time Period Covered:** latest month.

CARDAMOM: LLG1, SRI LANKAN

Source: *Prices of Selected Asia/Pacific Products.* **Price Frequency:** monthly, seasonally. **Effective Market(s):** Colombo (Sri Lanka). **Units of Measure:** Sri Lankan rupees per kilogram. **Type of Price:** auction high, auction low. **Time Period Covered:** latest month.

CARDAMOM: LLG2, SRI LANKAN

Source: *Prices of Selected Asia/Pacific Products.* **Price Frequency:** monthly, seasonally. **Effective Market(s):** Colombo (Sri Lanka). **Units of Measure:** Sri Lankan rupees per kilogram. **Type of Price:** auction high, auction low. **Time Period Covered:** latest month.

CARDAMOM: SUN DRIED, GUATEMALAN

Source: *U. S. Spice Trade.* **Price Frequency:** monthly, annually. **Effective Market(s):** New York. **Units of Measure:** Dollars per lb. **Type of Price:** spot. **Time Period Covered:** latest 8 years.

CARDAMOM HUSKS

Source: *U. S. Spice Trade.* **Price Frequency:** monthly, annually. **Effective Market(s):** New York. **Units of Measure:** Dollars per lb. **Type of Price:** spot. **Time Period Covered:** latest 8 years.

CARDAMOM OIL

Source: *Journal of Commerce and Commercial.* **Price Frequency:** weekly in Tuesday issue. **Units of Measure:** Dollars per lb. **Type of Price:** spot. **Time Period Covered:** latest week.

CARDAMOM OIL: NF

Source: *Chemical Marketing Reporter.* **Price Frequency:** weekly. **Effective Market(s):** New York. **Units of Measure:** Dollars per lb. **Type of Price:** spot. **Time Period Covered:** latest week.

CARMINE: NO. 40, NF

Source: *Chemical Marketing Reporter.* **Price Frequency:** weekly. **Effective Market(s):** New York. **Units of Measure:** Dollars per lb. **Type of Price:** spot. **Time Period Covered:** latest week.

CARMINE: NO. 40, RED

Source: *Journal of Commerce and Commercial.* **Price Frequency:** weekly in Wednesday issue. **Units of Measure:** Dollars per lb. **Type of Price:** spot. **Time Period Covered:** latest week.

CARNATION SPRAYS

Source: *New Zealand Farmer.* **Price Frequency:** weekly, seasonally. **Effective Market(s):** New Zealand. **Units of Measure:** New Zealand dollars per bunch. **Time Period Covered:** latest week.

CARNATIONS

Source: *New Zealand Farmer.* **Price Frequency:** weekly, seasonally. **Effective Market(s):** New Zealand. **Units of Measure:** New Zealand dollars per bunch. **Time Period Covered:** latest week.

CARNATIONS: MINIATURE

Source: *Floriculture Crops.* **Price Frequency:** annually. **Effective Market(s):** 7 domestic markets, United States. **Units of Measure:** Dollars per unit. **Type of Price:** commercial wholesale. **Time Period Covered:** latest 2 years.

CARNATIONS: STANDARD

Source: *Floriculture Crops.* **Price Frequency:** annually. **Effective Market(s):** 6 domestic markets, United States. **Units of Measure:** cents per unit. **Type of Price:** commercial wholesale. **Time Period Covered:** latest 2 years.

CARNAUBA WAX

see Wax: Carnauba.

B-CAROTENE: 1%

Source: *Chemical Marketing Reporter.* **Price Frequency:** weekly. **Effective Market(s):** New York. **Units of Measure:** Dollars per lb. **Type of Price:** spot. **Time Period Covered:** latest week.

B-CAROTENE: 22%

Source: *Chemical Marketing Reporter.* **Price Frequency:** weekly. **Effective Market(s):** New York. **Units of Measure:** Dollars per lb. **Type of Price:** spot. **Time Period Covered:** latest week.

B-CAROTENE: 30%, IN VEGETABLE OIL

Source: *Chemical Marketing Reporter.* **Price Frequency:** weekly. **Effective Market(s):** New York. **Units of Measure:** Dollars per lb. **Type of Price:** spot. **Time Period Covered:** latest week.

B-CAROTENE POWDER: 10%

Source: *Chemical Marketing Reporter.* **Price Frequency:** weekly. **Effective Market(s):** New York. **Units of Measure:** Dollars per kilo. **Type of Price:** spot. **Time Period Covered:** latest week.

CARP

Source: *Seafood Price-Current.* **Price Frequency:** semiweekly. **Effective Market(s):** Mid-Atlantic, New England. **Units of Measure:** Dollars per lb. **Type of Price:** sale by first receiver. **Time Period Covered:** latest day.

CARP: BUFFALO

Source: *Seafood Price-Current.* **Price Frequency:** semiweekly. **Effective Market(s):** Mid-Atlantic, New England. **Units of Measure:** Dollars per lb. **Type of Price:** sale by first receiver. **Time Period Covered:** latest day.

CARP: JUMBO

Source: *Seafood Price-Current.* **Price Frequency:** semiweekly. **Effective Market(s):** Mid-Atlantic, New England. **Units of Measure:** Dollars per lb. **Type of Price:** sale by first receiver. **Time Period Covered:** latest day.

CARPETS

Source: *Textile World.* **Price Frequency:** monthly. **Units of Measure:** index. **Type of Price:** producer price index. **Time Period Covered:** latest 2 months, year ago.

CARRAGEENAN

Source: *Journal of Commerce and Commercial.* **Price Frequency:** weekly in Monday issue. **Units of Measure:** Dollars per lb. **Type of Price:** spot. **Time Period Covered:** latest week.

CARROTS

Source: *Agricultural Prices Annual Summary.* **Price Frequency:** annually. **Effective Market(s):** 12 domestic markets. **Units of Measure:** Dollars per 100 lbs. **Type of Price:** average price received by farmer. **Time Period Covered:** latest 6 years.

Source: *Agricultural Prices Annual Summary.* **Price Frequency:** monthly, seasonally. **Effective Market(s):** 6 domestic markets, United States. **Units of Measure:** Dollars per 100 lbs. **Type of Price:** average price received by farmer. **Time Period Covered:** latest 3 years, for US latest 6 years.

Source: *California Farmer.* **Price Frequency:** semimonthly. **Effective Market(s):** Kern (CA), Imperial/Coachella Valleys, Salinas/Gonzales (CA). **Units of Measure:** Dollars per 48 lb. bag. **Time Period Covered:** latest week, month ago, year ago.

Source: *Fresh Fruit and Vegetable Prices.* **Price Frequency:** monthly, seasonally. **Effective Market(s):** 8 domestic markets. **Units of Measure:** Dollars per sack. **Type of Price:** average price at shipping point. **Time Period Covered:** latest year.

Source: *The Grower.* **Price Frequency:** monthly, seasonally. **Effective Market(s):** Kern District (CA). **Units of Measure:** Dollars per 48 1-lb. bags. **Time Period Covered:** latest year, year ago, 2 years ago.

Source: *Lancaster Farming.* **Price Frequency:** weekly, seasonally. **Effective Market(s):** Pennsylvania. **Units of Measure:** Dollars per sack. **Type of Price:** market. **Time Period Covered:** latest week.

Source: *New Zealand Farmer.* **Price Frequency:** weekly, seasonally. **Effective Market(s):** New Zealand. **Units of Measure:** New Zealand dollars per bag. **Time Period Covered:** latest week.

Source: *The Packer.* **Price Frequency:** weekly, seasonally. **Effective Market(s):** varies. **Units of Measure:** Dollars per sack. **Type of Price:** price received by farmer. **Time Period Covered:** latest week.

CARROTS: CALIFORNIA

Source: *Fresh Fruit and Vegetable Prices.* **Price Frequency:** monthly, seasonally. **Effective Market(s):** Chicago, New York City. **Units of Measure:** Dollars per sack. **Type of Price:** average wholesale price. **Time Period Covered:** latest year.

Source: *Vegetable and Specialties Situation and Outlook Report.* **Price Frequency:** monthly. **Effective Market(s):** North Central, Northeast. **Units of Measure:** cents per lb. **Type of Price:** retail. **Time Period Covered:** latest month, year ago.

CARROTS: CANADIAN

Source: *Fresh Fruit and Vegetable Prices.* **Price Frequency:** monthly, seasonally. **Effective Market(s):** Chicago, New York City. **Units of Measure:** Dollars per sack. **Type of Price:** average wholesale price. **Time Period Covered:** latest year.

CARROTS: CLASS 1

Source: *Farmers Weekly.* **Price Frequency:** weekly. **Effective Market(s):** Birmingham (England), Bristol (England), Covent Garden (England), Glasgow (Scotland), Manchester (England). **Units of Measure:** British pence per unit. **Type of Price:** auction. **Time Period Covered:** latest week.

CARROTS: DICED, FROZEN

Source: *HRI-Buyer's Guide.* **Price Frequency:** weekly. **Effective Market(s):** Northeastern area. **Units of Measure:** Dollars per case. **Type of Price:** price paid by dining places & institutions. **Time Period Covered:** latest week.

CARROTS: FRESH

Source: *Agricultural Prices.* **Price Frequency:** monthly. **Effective Market(s):** United States. **Units of Measure:** Dollars per 100 lbs. **Type of Price:** received by farmer. **Time Period Covered:** latest 2 months, year ago.

Source: *HRI-Buyers Guide.* **Price Frequency:** weekly. **Effective Market(s):** Northeastern area. **Units of Measure:** Dollars per bag. **Type of Price:** price paid by dining places & institutions. **Time Period Covered:** latest week.

Source: *Vegetable and Specialties Situation and Outlook Report.* **Price Frequency:** monthly, annually. **Effective Market(s):** United States. **Units of Measure:** Dollars per 100 lbs. **Type of Price:** received by grower. **Time Period Covered:** latest 4 years.

CARROTS: MICHIGAN

Source: *Fresh Fruit and Vegetable Prices.* **Price Frequency:** monthly, seasonally. **Effective Market(s):** Chicago. **Units of Measure:** Dollars per sack. **Type of Price:** average wholesale price. **Time Period Covered:** latest year.

CARROTS: MINIATURE

Source: *Lancaster Farming.* **Price Frequency:** weekly, seasonally. **Effective Market(s):** Pennsylvania. **Units of Measure:** Dollars per carton. **Type of Price:** market. **Time Period Covered:** latest week.

CARROTS: OHAKUNE

Source: *New Zealand Farmer.* **Price Frequency:** weekly, seasonally. **Effective Market(s):** New Zealand. **Units of Measure:** New Zealand dollars per bag. **Time Period Covered:** latest week.

CARROTS: SLICED, FROZEN

Source: *HRI-Buyer's Guide.* **Price Frequency:** weekly. **Effective Market(s):** Northeastern area. **Units of Measure:** Dollars per case. **Type of Price:** price paid by dining places & institutions. **Time Period Covered:** latest week.

CARROTS: SPRING

Source: *New Zealand Farmer.* **Price Frequency:** weekly, seasonally. **Effective Market(s):** New Zealand. **Units of Measure:** New Zealand dollars per bag. **Time Period Covered:** latest week.

CARS: USED

Source: *Standard & Poor's Statistical Service Current Statistics.* **Price Frequency:** monthly. **Units of Measure:** Dollars each. **Type of Price:** average. **Time Period Covered:** latest 4 years.

L-CARVONE

Source: *Chemical Marketing Reporter.* **Price Frequency:** weekly. **Effective Market(s):** New York. **Units of Measure:** Dollars per lb. **Type of Price:** spot. **Time Period Covered:** latest week.

CASCARA BARK: BROKEN

Source: *Journal of Commerce and Commercial.* **Price Frequency:** weekly in Monday issue. **Units of Measure:** Dollars per lb. **Type of Price:** spot. **Time Period Covered:** latest week.

CASEIN

Source: *Milling & Baking News.* **Price Frequency:** weekly. **Effective Market(s):** United States ports. **Units of Measure:** Dollars per lb. **Time Period Covered:** latest week.

CASEIN: EDIBLE

Source: *Dairy Market Statistics.* **Price Frequency:** monthly, annually. **Units of Measure:** Dollars per lb. **Type of Price:** wholesale. **Time Period Covered:** latest year.

CASEIN: EDIBLE, ACID PRECIPITATED, GROUND, AUSTRALIAN, IMPORTED

Source: *Chemical Marketing Reporter.* **Price Frequency:** weekly. **Effective Market(s):** New York. **Units of Measure:** Dollars per lb. **Type of Price:** spot. **Time Period Covered:** latest week.

CASHEW KERNELS

Source: *Prices of Selected Asia/Pacific Products.* **Price Frequency:** monthly, seasonally. **Effective Market(s):** Tokyo. **Units of Measure:** Japanese yen per 453 grams. **Type of Price:** wholesale high, wholesale low. **Time Period Covered:** latest month.

CASHEW KERNELS: WHOLE, 320S, INDIAN

Source: *Prices of Selected Asia/Pacific Products.* **Price Frequency:** monthly, seasonally. **Effective Market(s):** United Kingdom, United Kingdom/North European ports. **Units of Measure:** Dollars per lb. **Type of Price:** spot high, spot low. **Time Period Covered:** latest month.

CASHEW KERNELS: WHOLE, 450S, INDIAN

Source: *Prices of Selected Asia/Pacific Products.* **Price Frequency:** monthly, seasonally. **Effective Market(s):** United Kingdom, United Kingdom/North European ports. **Units of Measure:** Dollars per lb. **Type of Price:** spot high, spot low. **Time Period Covered:** latest month.

CASSAVA PELLETS

Source: *FAO Quarterly Bulletin of Statistics.* **Price Frequency:** monthly, annually. **Effective Market(s):** Bangkok. **Units of Measure:** Thailand bahts per 100 kilograms, dollars per metric ton. **Type of Price:** wholesale. **Time Period Covered:** latest 3 years.

Source: *FAO Quarterly Bulletin of Statistics.* **Price Frequency:** monthly, annually. **Effective Market(s):** Rotterdam. **Units of Measure:** West German marks per 1000 kilograms, dollars per metric ton. **Time Period Covered:** latest 3 years.

CASSELLA ACID

Source: *Chemical Marketing Reporter.* **Price Frequency:** weekly. **Effective Market(s):** New York. **Units of Measure:** Dollars per lb. **Type of Price:** spot. **Time Period Covered:** latest week.

CASSIA

see also Cinnamon.

CASSIA: KORINTJI "A"

Source: *Chemical Marketing Reporter.* **Price Frequency:** weekly. **Effective Market(s):** New York. **Units of Measure:** Dollars per lb. **Type of Price:** spot. **Time Period Covered:** latest week.

CASSIA: KORINTJI "A", INDONESIAN

Source: *U. S. Spice Trade.* **Price Frequency:** annually. **Effective Market(s):** New York. **Units of Measure:** cents per lb. **Type of Price:** spot. **Time Period Covered:** latest 3 years.

CASSIA: KORINTJI "B"

Source: *Chemical Marketing Reporter.* **Price Frequency:** weekly. **Effective Market(s):** New York. **Units of Measure:** Dollars per lb. **Type of Price:** spot. **Time Period Covered:** latest week.

CASSIA: MADAGASCAR

Source: *U. S. Spice Trade.* **Price Frequency:** annually. **Effective Market(s):** New York. **Units of Measure:** cents per lb. **Type of Price:** spot. **Time Period Covered:** latest 3 years.

CASSIA: TAIWANESE

Source: *U. S. Spice Trade.* **Price Frequency:** annually. **Effective Market(s):** New York. **Units of Measure:** cents per lb. **Type of Price:** spot. **Time Period Covered:** latest 3 years.

CASSIA: VERA "AA", INDONESIAN

Source: *U. S. Spice Trade.* **Price Frequency:** annually. **Effective Market(s):** New York. **Units of Measure:** cents per lb. **Type of Price:** spot. **Time Period Covered:** latest 3 years.

CASSIA: WHOLE, CHINESE

Source: *Fruit and Tropical Products.* **Price Frequency:** monthly, seasonally. **Effective Market(s):** London. **Units of Measure:** British pounds per tonne. **Type of Price:** month end. **Time Period Covered:** latest 2 years.

CASSIA LIGNEA: VERA "AA", INDONESIAN

Source: *Prices of Selected Asia/Pacific Products.* **Price Frequency:** monthly, seasonally. **Effective Market(s):** United States, Netherlands. **Units of Measure:** Dollars per metric ton. **Type of Price:** high, low. **Time Period Covered:** latest month.

CASSIA LIGNEA: VERA AND KORINTJI, INDONESIAN

Source: *Prices of Selected Asia/Pacific Products.* **Price Frequency:** monthly, seasonally. **Effective Market(s):** Japan, Netherlands, Singapore, United States. **Units of Measure:** Dollars per metric ton. **Type of Price:** high, low. **Time Period Covered:** latest month.

CASSIA LIGNEA: WEST RIVER, CHINESE

Source: *Prices of Selected Asia/Pacific Products.* **Price Frequency:** monthly, seasonally. **Effective Market(s):** Hong Kong. **Units of Measure:** Hong Kong dollars per ton. **Type of Price:** wholesale high, wholesale low. **Time Period Covered:** latest month.

CASSIA LIGNEA: WHOLE, CHINESE

Source: *Prices of Selected Asia/Pacific Products.* **Price Frequency:** monthly, seasonally. **Effective Market(s):** United Kingdom/North European ports. **Units of Measure:** Dollars per metric ton. **Type of Price:** high, low. **Time Period Covered:** latest month.

CASSIA OIL

Source: *Journal of Commerce and Commercial.* **Price Frequency:** weekly in Tuesday issue. **Units of Measure:** Dollars per lb. **Type of Price:** spot. **Time Period Covered:** latest week.

Source: *U. S. Essential Oil Trade.* **Price Frequency:** annually. **Effective Market(s):** United States. **Units of Measure:** Dollars per kilogram. **Type of Price:** import value. **Time Period Covered:** latest 3 years.

CASSIA OIL: 85%, CHINESE

Source: *Prices of Selected Asia/Pacific Products.* **Price Frequency:** monthly. **Effective Market(s):** Hong Kong. **Units of Measure:** Hong Kong dollars per kilogram. **Type of Price:** wholesale high, wholesale low. **Time Period Covered:** latest month.

CASSIA OIL: CHINESE

Source: *Chemical Marketing Reporter.* **Price Frequency:** weekly. **Effective Market(s):** New York. **Units of Measure:** Dollars per lb. **Type of Price:** spot. **Time Period Covered:** latest week.

Source: *Prices of Selected Asia/Pacific Products.* **Price Frequency:** monthly. **Effective Market(s):** United Kingdom/North European ports. **Units of Measure:** British pounds per kilogram. **Type of Price:** high, low. **Time Period Covered:** latest month.

CASTOR OIL

Source: *Fruit and Tropical Products.* **Price Frequency:** monthly, annually. **Effective Market(s):** Rotterdam. **Units of Measure:** Dollars per tonne. **Type of Price:** average. **Time Period Covered:** monthly latest year, annually latest 2 years.

Source: *Oil World.* **Price Frequency:** weekly, monthly, annually. **Effective Market(s):** Rotterdam. **Units of Measure:** Dollars per tonne. **Type of Price:** lowest representative asking. **Time Period Covered:** weekly latest 3 weeks, monthly latest 2 months, annually latest 2 years.

Source: *Prices of Selected Asia/Pacific Products.* **Price Frequency:** monthly, seasonally. **Effective Market(s):** Tokyo. **Units of Measure:** Japanese yen per metric ton. **Type of Price:** high, low. **Time Period Covered:** latest month.

CASTOR OIL: ACIDS DEHYDRATED

Source: *Chemical Marketing Reporter.* **Price Frequency:** weekly. **Effective Market(s):** New York. **Units of Measure:** Dollars per lb. **Type of Price:** spot. **Time Period Covered:** latest week.

CASTOR OIL: BLOWN

Source: *Chemical Marketing Reporter.* **Price Frequency:** weekly. **Effective Market(s):** New York. **Units of Measure:** Dollars per lb. **Type of Price:** spot. **Time Period Covered:** latest week.

CASTOR OIL: CRUDE

Source: *Prices of Selected Asia/Pacific Products.* **Price Frequency:** monthly, seasonally. **Effective Market(s):** Rotterdam. **Units of Measure:** Dollars per metric ton. **Type of Price:** high, low. **Time Period Covered:** latest month.

CASTOR OIL: DEHYDRATED, BODIED

Source: *Chemical Marketing Reporter.* **Price Frequency:** weekly. **Effective Market(s):** New York. **Units of Measure:** Dollars per lb. **Type of Price:** spot. **Time Period Covered:** latest week.

CASTOR OIL: DEHYDRATED, UNBODIED

Source: *Chemical Marketing Reporter.* **Price Frequency:** weekly. **Effective Market(s):** New York. **Units of Measure:** Dollars per lb. **Type of Price:** spot. **Time Period Covered:** latest week.

CASTOR OIL: NO. 1, BRAZILIAN

Source: *Commodity Year Book.* **Price Frequency:** monthly, annually. **Effective Market(s):** New York. **Units of Measure:** cents per lb. **Type of Price:** wholesale. **Time Period Covered:** latest 5 years.

CASTOR OIL: NO. 1, BRAZILIAN, IMPORTED

Source: *Oil Crops Situation and Outlook.* **Price Frequency:** monthly. **Effective Market(s):** New York. **Units of Measure:** cents per lb. **Type of Price:** wholesale. **Time Period Covered:** latest 5 months.

CASTOR OIL: RAW, NO. 1, BRAZILIAN

Source: *Chemical Marketing Reporter.* **Price Frequency:** weekly. **Effective Market(s):** New York. **Units of Measure:** Dollars per lb. **Type of Price:** spot. **Time Period Covered:** latest week.

CASTOR OIL: REFINED

Source: *Chemical Marketing Reporter.* **Price Frequency:** weekly. **Effective Market(s):** New York. **Units of Measure:** Dollars per lb. **Type of Price:** spot. **Time Period Covered:** latest week.

CASTOR OIL: RICINOLEIC ACID

Source: *Chemical Marketing Reporter.* **Price Frequency:** weekly. **Effective Market(s):** New York. **Units of Measure:** Dollars per lb. **Type of Price:** spot. **Time Period Covered:** latest week.

CASTOR OIL: USP

Source: *Chemical Marketing Reporter.* **Price Frequency:** weekly. **Effective Market(s):** New York. **Units of Measure:** Dollars per lb. **Type of Price:** spot. **Time Period Covered:** latest week.

CATECHOL

Source: *Chemical Marketing Reporter.* **Price Frequency:** weekly. **Effective Market(s):** New York. **Units of Measure:** Dollars per lb. **Type of Price:** spot. **Time Period Covered:** latest week.

CATFISH

Source: *Aquaculture Situation and Outlook Report.* **Price Frequency:** monthly, annually. **Units of Measure:** cents per lb. **Type of Price:** received by processor. **Time Period Covered:** latest 20 years.

Source: *Catfish Production.* **Price Frequency:** monthly, annually. **Effective Market(s):** United States. **Units of Measure:** cents per lb. **Type of Price:** paid to producers. **Time Period Covered:** latest 15 years.

Source: *Seafood Price-Current.* **Price Frequency:** semiweekly. **Effective Market(s):** Mid-Atlantic, New England. **Units of Measure:** Dollars per lb. **Type of Price:** sale by first receiver. **Time Period Covered:** latest day.

CATFISH: FARM RAISED

Source: *Aquaculture Situation and Outlook Report.* **Price Frequency:** monthly, annually. **Units of Measure:** cents per lb. **Type of Price:** paid to processor. **Time Period Covered:** latest 20 years.

Source: *Catfish.* **Price Frequency:** monthly. **Effective Market(s):** United States. **Units of Measure:** Dollars per lb. **Type of Price:** paid to producers. **Time Period Covered:** latest 2 years.

CATFISH: FILLETS, FRESH

Source: *Aquaculture Situation and Outlook Report.* **Price Frequency:** monthly, annually. **Units of Measure:** cents per lb. **Time Period Covered:** latest 4 years.

Source: *Catfish.* **Price Frequency:** monthly. **Effective Market(s):** United States. **Units of Measure:** Dollars per lb. **Type of Price:** processor. **Time Period Covered:** latest month, year ago.

CATFISH: FILLETS, FROZEN

Source: *Aquaculture Situation and Outlook Report.* **Price Frequency:** monthly, annually. **Units of Measure:** cents per lb. **Time Period Covered:** latest 4 years.

Source: *Catfish.* **Price Frequency:** monthly. **Effective Market(s):** United States. **Units of Measure:** Dollars per lb. **Type of Price:** processor. **Time Period Covered:** latest month, year ago.

CATFISH: FRESH

Source: *Catfish.* **Price Frequency:** monthly. **Effective Market(s):** United States. **Units of Measure:** Dollars per lb. **Type of Price:** processor. **Time Period Covered:** latest month, year ago.

CATFISH: FRESH FARM RAISED, FILLETS, BREADED, FRESH

Source: *Seafood Price-Current.* **Price Frequency:** semiweekly. **Effective Market(s):** South. **Units of Measure:** Dollars per lb. **Type of Price:** first receiver. **Time Period Covered:** latest day.

CATFISH: FRESH FARM RAISED, FILLETS, BREADED, FROZEN

Source: *Seafood Price-Current.* **Price Frequency:** semiweekly. **Effective Market(s):** South. **Units of Measure:** Dollars per lb. **Type of Price:** first receiver. **Time Period Covered:** latest day.

CATFISH: FRESH FARM RAISED, NUGGETS, FRESH

Source: *Seafood Price-Current.* **Price Frequency:** semiweekly. **Effective Market(s):** South. **Units of Measure:** Dollars per lb. **Type of Price:** first receiver. **Time Period Covered:** latest day.

CATFISH: FRESH FARM RAISED, NUGGETS, FROZEN

Source: *Seafood Price-Current.* **Price Frequency:** semiweekly. **Effective Market(s):** South. **Units of Measure:** Dollars per lb. **Type of Price:** first receiver. **Time Period Covered:** latest day.

CATFISH: FRESH FARM RAISED, SHANK FILLETS, SKINLESS, BONELESS, FRESH

Source: *Seafood Price-Current.* **Price Frequency:** semiweekly. **Effective Market(s):** South. **Units of Measure:** Dollars per lb. **Type of Price:** first receiver. **Time Period Covered:** latest day.

CATFISH: FRESH FARM RAISED, SHANK FILLETS, SKINLESS, BONELESS, FROZEN

Source: *Seafood Price-Current.* **Price Frequency:** semiweekly. **Effective Market(s):** South. **Units of Measure:** Dollars per lb. **Type of Price:** first receiver. **Time Period Covered:** latest day.

CATFISH: FRESH FARM RAISED, STEAKS, FRESH

Source: *Seafood Price-Current.* **Price Frequency:** semiweekly. **Effective Market(s):** South. **Units of Measure:** Dollars per lb. **Type of Price:** first receiver. **Time Period Covered:** latest day.

CATFISH: FRESH FARM RAISED, STEAKS, FROZEN

Source: *Seafood Price-Current.* **Price Frequency:** semiweekly. **Effective Market(s):** South. **Units of Measure:** Dollars per lb. **Type of Price:** first receiver.

CATFISH: FRESH FARM RAISED, STRIPS OR FINGERS, BREADED, FRESH

Source: *Seafood Price-Current.* **Price Frequency:** semiweekly. **Effective Market(s):** South. **Units of Measure:** Dollars per lb. **Type of Price:** first receiver. **Time Period Covered:** latest day.

CATFISH: FRESH FARM RAISED, STRIPS OR FINGERS, BREADED, FROZEN

Source: *Seafood Price-Current.* **Price Frequency:** semiweekly. **Effective Market(s):** South. **Units of Measure:** Dollars per lb. **Type of Price:** first receiver. **Time Period Covered:** latest day.

Time Period Covered: latest day.

CATFISH: FRESH FARM RAISED, WHOLE, DRESSED, FRESH

Source: *Seafood Price-Current.* **Price Frequency:** semiweekly. **Effective Market(s):** South. **Units of Measure:** Dollars per lb. **Type of Price:** first receiver. **Time Period Covered:** latest day.

CATFISH: FRESH FARM RAISED, WHOLE, DRESSED, FROZEN

Source: *Seafood Price-Current.* **Price Frequency:** semiweekly. **Effective Market(s):** South. **Units of Measure:** Dollars per lb. **Type of Price:** first receiver. **Time Period Covered:** latest day.

CATFISH: FROZEN

Source: *Catfish.* **Price Frequency:** monthly. **Effective Market(s):** United States. **Units of Measure:** Dollars per lb. **Type of Price:** processor. **Time Period Covered:** latest month, year ago.

CATFISH: OCEAN

see also Wolffish.

CATFISH: OCEAN, FILLETS, FRESH

Source: *Seafood Price-Current.* **Price Frequency:** semiweekly. **Effective Market(s):** Mid-Atlantic, New England. **Units of Measure:** Dollars per lb. **Type of Price:** sale by first receiver. **Time Period Covered:** latest day.

CATFISH: OCEAN, FILLETS, PIN BONE IN, FROZEN, CANADIAN

Source: *Seafood Price-Current.* **Price Frequency:** semiweekly. **Effective Market(s):** Mid-Atlantic. **Units of Measure:** Dollars per lb. **Type of Price:** first receiver. **Time Period Covered:** latest day.

CATFISH: OCEAN, FILLETS, SKINLESS, BONELESS, FROZEN, CANADIAN

Source: *Seafood Price-Current.* **Price Frequency:** semiweekly. **Effective Market(s):** Mid-Atlantic. **Units of Measure:** Dollars per lb. **Type of Price:** first receiver. **Time Period Covered:** latest day.

CATFISH: PROCESSED, FRESH

Source: *Aquaculture Situation and Outlook Report.* **Price Frequency:** monthly, annually. **Units of Measure:** cents per lb. **Time Period Covered:** latest 4 years.

Source: *Catfish.* **Price Frequency:** monthly. **Effective Market(s):** United States. **Units of Measure:** Dollars per lb. **Type of Price:** processor. **Time Period Covered:** latest month, year ago.

CATFISH: PROCESSED, FROZEN

Source: *Aquaculture Situation and Outlook Report.* **Price Frequency:** monthly, annually. **Units of Measure:** cents per lb. **Time Period Covered:** latest 4 years.

Source: *Catfish.* **Price Frequency:** monthly. **Effective Market(s):** United States. **Units of Measure:** Dollars per lb. **Type of Price:** processor. **Time Period Covered:** latest month, year ago.

CATFISH: WHOLE, FRESH

Source: *Aquaculture Situation and Outlook Report.* **Price Frequency:** monthly, annually. **Units of Measure:** cents per lb. **Time Period Covered:** latest 4 years.

Source: *Catfish.* **Price Frequency:** monthly. **Effective Market(s):** United States. **Units of Measure:** Dollars per lb. **Type of Price:** processor. **Time Period Covered:** latest month, year ago.

CATFISH: WHOLE, FROZEN

Source: *Aquaculture Situation and Outlook Report.* **Price Frequency:** monthly, annually. **Units of Measure:** cents per lb. **Time Period Covered:** latest 4 years.

Source: *Catfish.* **Price Frequency:** monthly. **Effective Market(s):** United States. **Units of Measure:** Dollars per lb. **Type of Price:** processor. **Time Period Covered:** latest month, year ago.

CATNIP LEAVES

Source: *Journal of Commerce and Commercial.* **Price Frequency:** weekly in Monday issue. **Units of Measure:** Dollars per lb. **Type of Price:** spot. **Time Period Covered:** latest week.

CATTLE

see also Bulls, Calves, Cows, Heifers, Steers.

Source: *Agra Europe.* **Price Frequency:** weekly. **Effective Market(s):** 9 European markets. **Units of Measure:** national currency per kilogram. **Type of Price:** average. **Time Period Covered:** latest week.

Source: *The Brock Report.* **Price Frequency:** quarterly. **Effective Market(s):** Omaha (NE). **Units of Measure:** Dollars per 100 lbs. **Time Period Covered:** latest 4 years.

Source: *Farmers Weekly.* **Price Frequency:** weekly. **Effective Market(s):** over 170 British markets. **Units of Measure:** British pence per kilogram. **Type of Price:** auction. **Time Period Covered:** latest week.

Source: *Lancaster Farming.* **Price Frequency:** weekly. **Effective Market(s):** Pennsylvania, Virginia. **Units of Measure:** Dollars per head. **Type of Price:** auction. **Time Period Covered:** latest week.

Source: *New Zealand Farmer.* **Price Frequency:** weekly, seasonally. **Effective Market(s):** 7 New Zealand markets. **Units of Measure:** New Zealand cents per kilogram carcase weight. **Time Period Covered:** latest 2 weeks.

Source: *Standard & Poor's Statistical Service Current Statistics.* **Price Frequency:** monthly, annually. **Units of Measure:** Dollars per 100 lbs. **Time Period Covered:** latest 5 years.

Source: *The Times.* **Price Frequency:** daily. **Effective Market(s):** England/Wales, Great Britain, Scotland. **Units of Measure:** British pence per kilogram. **Type of Price:** average. **Time Period Covered:** latest day.

CATTLE: ADULT

Source: *FAO Quarterly Bulletin of Statistics.* **Price Frequency:** monthly, annually. **Effective Market(s):** European Economic Community. **Units of Measure:** ECU per 100 kilograms, dollars per metric ton. **Type of Price:** wholesale. **Time Period Covered:** latest 3 years.

CATTLE: BEEF

Source: *Agricultural Prices Annual Summary.* **Price Frequency:** annually. **Effective Market(s):** 50 domestic markets, United States. **Units of Measure:** Dollars per 100 lbs. **Type of Price:** average price received by farmer. **Time Period Covered:** latest 2 years, for US latest 6 years.

Source: *Illinois Farm Report.* **Price Frequency:** monthly. **Effective Market(s):** Illinois. **Units of Measure:** Dollars per 100 lbs. **Type of Price:** average received by farmers. **Time Period Covered:** latest 2 months, year ago.

CATTLE: BEEF, STORE

Source: *Scottish Farmer.* **Price Frequency:** weekly. **Effective Market(s):** 9 Scottish markets average. **Units of Measure:** British pounds per head. **Type of Price:** average. **Time Period Covered:** latest 2 weeks.

CATTLE: BONING, CANNER AND CUTTER

Source: *National Provisioner.* **Price Frequency:** daily. **Effective Market(s):** Midwest River. **Units of Measure:** cents per lb. **Time Period Covered:** latest week.

CATTLE: DAIRY, STORE

Source: *Scottish Farmer.* **Price Frequency:** weekly. **Effective Market(s):** 9 Scottish markets average. **Units of Measure:** British pounds per head. **Type of Price:** average. **Time Period Covered:** latest 2 weeks.

CATTLE: FAT

Source: *Agra Europe.* **Price Frequency:** weekly. **Effective Market(s):** 9 European markets. **Units of Measure:** national currency per kilogram. **Type of Price:** average. **Time Period Covered:** latest week.

Source: *Meat and Dairy Products.* **Price Frequency:** monthly. **Effective Market(s):** 9 international markets. **Units of Measure:** national currency per kilogram/lb. **Type of Price:** average. **Time Period Covered:** latest 3 years.

CATTLE: FED

Source: *The Brock Report.* **Price Frequency:** weekly. **Effective Market(s):** 5 domestic markets. **Units of Measure:** dollars per 100 lbs. **Type of Price:** top price. **Time Period Covered:** latest week, week ago.

CATTLE: FEEDER

Source: *The Brock Report.* **Price Frequency:** weekly. **Effective Market(s):** Amarillo (TX), Dodge City (KS), Oklahoma City, Sioux City (IA). **Units of Measure:** Dollars per 100 lbs. **Type of Price:** top price. **Time Period Covered:** latest week, week ago.

Source: *Farm and Dairy.* **Price Frequency:** weekly, seasonally. **Effective Market(s):** Ohio, Pennsylvania. **Units of Measure:** Dollars per head. **Type of Price:** auction high, auction low. **Time Period Covered:** latest week, year ago.

Source: *Investor's Daily.* **Price Frequency:** daily. **Effective Market(s):** Oklahoma. **Units of Measure:** Dollars per 100 lbs. **Type of Price:** spot. **Time Period Covered:** latest 2 days.

Source: *Livestock, Meat, Wool Market News.* **Price Frequency:** weekly, seasonally. **Effective Market(s):** 10 domestic markets. **Units of Measure:** Dollars per 100 lbs. **Type of Price:** average. **Time Period Covered:** latest week, year ago.

Source: *New York Times.* **Price Frequency:** daily. **Effective Market(s):** Oklahoma. **Units of Measure:** Dollars per 100 lbs. **Type of Price:** cash. **Time Period Covered:** latest 2 days.

CATTLE: FEEDER, CHOICE

Source: *Agricultural Outlook.* **Price Frequency:** monthly, annually. **Effective Market(s):** Kansas City. **Units of Measure:** Dollars per 100 lbs. **Type of Price:** market. **Time Period Covered:** monthly latest 6 months, annually latest 3 years.

CATTLE: FEEDER, FUTURES

Source: *Agriculture.* **Price Frequency:** weekly. **Effective Market(s):** Chicago. **Units of Measure:** cents per lb. **Type of Price:** futures. **Time Period Covered:** latest week, week ago.

Source: *Asian Wall Street Journal.* **Price Frequency:** daily. **Effective Market(s):** Chicago. **Units of Measure:** cents per lb. **Type of Price:** futures. **Time Period Covered:** latest day.

Source: *Barron's.* **Price Frequency:** weekly. **Effective Market(s):** Chicago. **Units of Measure:** cents per lb. **Type of Price:** futures. **Time Period Covered:** latest week.

Source: *Drovers Journal.* **Price Frequency:** weekly. **Effective Market(s):** Chicago. **Units of Measure:** Dollars per 100 lbs. **Type of Price:** futures. **Time Period Covered:** latest 6 weeks.

Source: *Feedstuffs.* **Price Frequency:** weekly. **Effective Market(s):** Chicago. **Units of Measure:** cents per lb. **Type of Price:** futures. **Time Period Covered:** latest week, week ago, latest season.

Source: *Investor's Daily.* **Price Frequency:** daily. **Effective Market(s):** Chicago. **Units of Measure:** cents per lb. **Type of Price:** futures. **Time Period Covered:** latest day.

Source: *Los Angeles Times.* **Price Frequency:** daily. **Effective Market(s):** Chicago. **Units of Measure:** cents per lb. **Type of Price:** futures. **Time Period Covered:** latest day.

Source: *New York Times.* **Price Frequency:** daily. **Effective Market(s):** Chicago. **Units of Measure:** cents per lb. **Type of Price:** futures. **Time Period Covered:** latest day.

Source: *Urner Barry's Price-Current.* **Price Frequency:** daily. **Effective Market(s):** Chicago. **Units of Measure:** cents per lb. **Type of Price:** futures. **Time Period Covered:** latest day.

Source: *Wall Street Journal.* **Price Frequency:** daily. **Effective Market(s):** Chicago. **Units of Measure:** cents per lb. **Type of Price:** futures. **Time Period Covered:** latest day.

CATTLE: FEEDER, MEDIUM AND LARGE NO. 1

Source: *Utah Farmer-Stockman.* **Price Frequency:** monthly, seasonally. **Effective Market(s):** Utah. **Units of Measure:** Dollars per bushel. **Type of Price:** range. **Time Period Covered:** latest month.

CATTLE: FUTURES

Source: *Barron's.* **Price Frequency:** weekly. **Effective Market(s):** Chicago. **Units of Measure:** cents per lb. **Type of Price:** futures. **Time Period Covered:** latest week.

Source: *Feedstuffs.* **Price Frequency:** weekly. **Effective Market(s):** Chicago. **Units of Measure:** cents per lb. **Type of Price:** futures. **Time Period Covered:** latest week, week ago, latest season.

Source: *Investor's Daily.* **Price Frequency:** daily. **Effective Market(s):** Chicago. **Units of Measure:** cents per lb. **Type of Price:** futures. **Time Period Covered:** latest day.

Source: *Lancaster Farming.* **Price Frequency:** daily. **Effective Market(s):** Chicago. **Type of Price:** futures. **Time Period Covered:** latest week.

Source: *Los Angeles Times.* **Price Frequency:** daily. **Effective Market(s):** Chicago. **Units of Measure:** cents per lb. **Type of Price:** futures. **Time Period Covered:** latest day.

Source: *The Times.* **Price Frequency:** daily. **Effective Market(s):** London. **Units of Measure:** British pence per kilogram. **Type of Price:** futures. **Time Period Covered:** latest day.

CATTLE: LIVE, FUTURES

Source: *Agriculture.* **Price Frequency:** weekly. **Effective Market(s):** Chicago. **Units of Measure:** cents per lb. **Type of Price:** futures. **Time Period Covered:** latest week, week ago.

Source: *Asian Wall Street Journal.* **Price Frequency:** daily. **Effective Market(s):** Chicago. **Units of Measure:** cents per lb. **Type of Price:** futures. **Time Period Covered:** latest day.

Source: *Financial Times.* **Price Frequency:** daily. **Effective Market(s):** Chicago. **Units of Measure:** cents per lb. **Type of Price:** futures. **Time Period Covered:** latest day.

Source: *National Provisioner.* **Price Frequency:** daily. **Effective Market(s):** Chicago. **Units of Measure:** cents per lb. **Type of Price:** futures. **Time Period Covered:** latest week.

Source: *New York Times.* **Price Frequency:** daily. **Effective Market(s):** Chicago. **Units of Measure:** cents per lb. **Type of Price:** futures. **Time Period Covered:** latest day.

Source: *Urner Barry's Price-Current.* **Price Frequency:** daily. **Effective Market(s):** Chicago. **Units of Measure:** cents per lb. **Type of Price:** futures. **Time Period Covered:** latest day.

Source: *Wall Street Journal.* **Price Frequency:** daily. **Effective Market(s):** Chicago. **Units of Measure:** cents per lb. **Type of Price:** futures. **Time Period Covered:** latest day.

CATTLE: LIVEWEIGHT

Source: *Financial Times.* **Price Frequency:** daily. **Effective Market(s):** London. **Units of Measure:** British pence per kilogram. **Type of Price:** spot. **Time Period Covered:** latest day.

CATTLE: OXEN

Source: *FAO Quarterly Bulletin of Statistics.* **Price Frequency:** monthly, annually. **Effective Market(s):** Australia. **Units of Measure:** Australian dollars per 100 kilograms, dollars per metric ton. **Type of Price:** wholesale. **Time Period Covered:** latest 3 years.

CATTLE: SLAUGHTER

Source: *Agricultural Outlook.* **Price Frequency:** monthly, annually. **Effective Market(s):** Omaha (NE). **Units of Measure:** Dollars per 100 lbs. **Type of Price:** market. **Time Period Covered:** monthly latest 6 months, annually latest 3 years.

Source: *Livestock, Meat, Wool Market News.* **Price Frequency:** weekly, seasonally. **Effective Market(s):** Lancaster County (PA), Omaha (NE), Sioux City (IA), South St. Paul. **Units of Measure:** Dollars per 100 lbs. **Type of Price:** average. **Time Period Covered:** latest week, year ago.

Source: *Oregon Farmer-Stockman.* **Price Frequency:** monthly, seasonally. **Effective Market(s):** Arizona/California, Central Plains, Midwest. **Units of Measure:** Dollars per 100 lbs. **Time Period Covered:** latest month.

CATTLE: SLAUGHTER, FUTURES

Source: *Drovers Journal.* **Price Frequency:** weekly. **Effective Market(s):** Chicago. **Units of Measure:** Dollars per 100 lbs. **Type of Price:** futures. **Time Period Covered:** latest 6 weeks.

CATTLE AND CALVES: FEEDER AND STOCKERS

Source: *Agricultural Prices.* **Price Frequency:** quarterly. **Effective Market(s):** United States. **Units of Measure:** Dollars per 100 lbs. **Type of Price:** paid by farmer. **Time Period Covered:** latest 2 quarters, year ago.

Source: *Agricultural Prices Annual Summary.* **Price Frequency:** quarterly. **Effective Market(s):** United States. **Units of Measure:** Dollars per 100 lbs. **Type of Price:** average price paid by farmer. **Time Period Covered:** latest 6 years.

CAULIFLOWER

Source: *Agricultural Prices.* **Price Frequency:** monthly. **Effective Market(s):** United States. **Units of Measure:** Dollars per 100 lbs. **Type of Price:** received by farmer. **Time Period Covered:** latest 2 months, year ago.

Source: *Agricultural Prices Annual Summary.* **Price Frequency:** annually. **Effective Market(s):** Arizona, California, average of other states, United States. **Units of Measure:** Dollars per 100 lbs. **Type of Price:** average price received by farmer. **Time Period Covered:** latest 6 years.

Source: *Agricultural Prices Annual Summary.* **Price Frequency:** monthly, seasonally. **Effective Market(s):** California, New York, United States. **Units of Measure:** Dollars per 100 lbs. **Type of Price:** average price received by farmer. **Time Period Covered:** latest 3 years, for US latest 6 years.

Source: *California Farmer.* **Price Frequency:** semimonthly. **Effective Market(s):** Imperial/Coachella/Palo Verde Valleys, Salinas/Watsonville (CA), Santa Maria/Guadalupe/Oceano/Lompoc (CA). **Units of Measure:** Dollars per 25 lb. carton. **Time Period Covered:** latest week, month ago, year ago.

Source: *Fresh Fruit and Vegetable Prices.* **Price Frequency:** monthly, seasonally. **Effective Market(s):** Oceano/Santa Maria District (CA), Salinas/Watsonville District (CA), Southern California/Western Arizona. **Units of Measure:** Dollars per carton. **Type of Price:** average price at shipping point. **Time Period Covered:** latest year.

Source: *Lancaster Farming.* **Price Frequency:** weekly, seasonally. **Effective Market(s):** Pennsylvania. **Units of Measure:** Dollars per carton. **Type of Price:** market. **Time Period Covered:** latest week.

Source: *New Zealand Farmer.* **Price Frequency:** weekly, seasonally. **Effective Market(s):** New Zealand. **Units of Measure:** New Zealand dollars per crate. **Time Period Covered:** latest week.

Source: *The Packer.* **Price Frequency:** weekly, seasonally. **Effective Market(s):** varies. **Units of Measure:** Dollars per carton. **Type of Price:** price received by farmer. **Time Period Covered:** latest week.

CAULIFLOWER: CALIFORNIA

Source: *Fresh Fruit and Vegetable Prices.* **Price Frequency:** monthly, seasonally. **Effective Market(s):** Chicago, New York City. **Units of Measure:** Dollars per carton. **Type of Price:** average wholesale price. **Time Period Covered:** latest year.

CAULIFLOWER: FRESH

Source: *HRI-Buyers Guide.* **Price Frequency:** weekly. **Effective Market(s):** Northeastern area. **Units of Measure:** Dollars per unit. **Type of Price:** price paid by dining places & institutions. **Time Period Covered:** latest week.

Source: *Vegetable and Specialties Situation and Outlook Report.* **Price Frequency:** monthly, annually. **Effective Market(s):** United States. **Units of Measure:** Dollars per 100 lbs. **Type of Price:** received by grower. **Time Period Covered:** latest 4 years.

CAULIFLOWER: FROZEN

Source: *HRI-Buyer's Guide.* **Price Frequency:** weekly. **Effective Market(s):** Northeastern area. **Units of Measure:** Dollars per case. **Type of Price:** price paid by dining places & institutions. **Time Period Covered:** latest week.

CAUSTIC POTASH

see also Potash: Caustic.

CAUSTIC SODA

see Soda: Caustic.

CEDAR: WESTERN RED

Source: *Random Lengths.* **Price Frequency:** weekly. **Effective Market(s):** coast mills, inland mills. **Units of Measure:** Dollars per 1000 board feet. **Type of Price:** price to wholesaler. **Time Period Covered:** latest week.

CEDAR SAWTIMBER: ALASKAN

Source: *Volume and Value of Sawtimber Stumpage Sold From National Forests by Selected Species and Region.* **Price Frequency:** quarterly, annually. **Effective Market(s):** Alaska, Pacific Northwest. **Units of Measure:** Dollars per 1000 board feet. **Type of Price:** average. **Time Period Covered:** latest quarter, latest year.

CEDAR SAWTIMBER: INCENSE

Source: *Volume and Value of Sawtimber Stumpage Sold From National Forests by Selected Species and Region.* **Price Frequency:** quarterly, annually. **Effective Market(s):** Pacific Northwest, Pacific Southwest. **Units of Measure:** Dollars per 1000 board feet. **Type of Price:** average. **Time Period Covered:** latest quarter, latest year.

CEDAR SAWTIMBER: PORT-ORFORD

Source: *Volume and Value of Sawtimber Stumpage Sold From National Forests by Selected Species and Region.* **Price Frequency:** quarterly, annually. **Effective Market(s):** Pacific Northwest, Pacific Southwest. **Units of Measure:** Dollars per 1000 board feet. **Type of Price:** average. **Time Period Covered:** latest quarter, latest year.

CEDAR SAWTIMBER: WESTERN RED

Source: *Volume and Value of Sawtimber Stumpage Sold From National Forests by Selected Species and Region.* **Price Frequency:** quarterly, annually. **Effective Market(s):** Alaska, Northern region, Pacific Northwest. **Units of Measure:** Dollars per 1000 board feet. **Type of Price:** average. **Time Period Covered:** latest quarter, latest year.

CEDAR SHAKES: WESTERN RED

Source: *Random Lengths.* **Price Frequency:** weekly. **Units of Measure:** Dollars per 1000 board feet. **Type of Price:** price to wholesaler. **Time Period Covered:** latest week.

CEDAR SHINGLES: WESTERN RED

Source: *Random Lengths.* **Price Frequency:** weekly. **Units of Measure:** Dollars per 1000 board feet. **Type of Price:** price to wholesaler. **Time Period Covered:** latest week.

CEDAR SIDING: WESTERN RED

Source: *Random Lengths.* **Price Frequency:** weekly. **Units of Measure:** Dollars per 1000 board feet. **Type of Price:** price to wholesaler. **Time Period Covered:** latest week.

CEDAR TIMBERS: WESTERN RED

Source: *Random Lengths.* **Price Frequency:** weekly. **Units of Measure:** Dollars per 1000 board feet. **Type of Price:** price to wholesaler. **Time Period Covered:** latest week.

CEDARLEAF OIL

Source: *Chemical Marketing Reporter.* **Price Frequency:** weekly. **Effective Market(s):** New York. **Units of Measure:** Dollars per lb. **Type of Price:** spot. **Time Period Covered:** latest week.

Source: *U. S. Essential Oil Trade.* **Price Frequency:** annually. **Effective Market(s):** United States. **Units of Measure:** Dollars per kilogram. **Type of Price:** import value. **Time Period Covered:** latest 3 years.

CEDARWOOD OIL

Source: *Journal of Commerce and Commercial.* **Price Frequency:** weekly in Tuesday issue. **Units of Measure:** Dollars per lb. **Type of Price:** spot. **Time Period Covered:** latest week.

Source: *U. S. Essential Oil Trade.* **Price Frequency:** annually. **Effective Market(s):** United States. **Units of Measure:** Dollars per kilogram. **Type of Price:** import value. **Time Period Covered:** latest 3 years.

CEDARWOOD OIL: CHINESE

Source: *Chemical Marketing Reporter.* **Price Frequency:** weekly. **Effective Market(s):** New York. **Units of Measure:** Dollars per lb. **Type of Price:** spot. **Time Period Covered:** latest week.

CEDARWOOD OIL: TEXAS

Source: *Chemical Marketing Reporter.* **Price Frequency:** weekly. **Effective Market(s):** New York. **Units of Measure:** Dollars per lb. **Type of Price:** spot. **Time Period Covered:** latest week.

CEDARWOOD OIL: VIRGINIA

Source: *Chemical Marketing Reporter.* **Price Frequency:** weekly. **Effective Market(s):** New York. **Units of Measure:** Dollars per lb. **Type of Price:** spot. **Time Period Covered:** latest week.

CEDROL: PRIME

Source: *Chemical Marketing Reporter.* **Price Frequency:** weekly. **Effective Market(s):** New York. **Units of Measure:** Dollars per lb. **Type of Price:** spot. **Time Period Covered:** latest week.

CEDRYL ACETATE: DISTILLED

Source: *Chemical Marketing Reporter.* **Price Frequency:** weekly. **Effective Market(s):** New York. **Units of Measure:** Dollars per lb. **Type of Price:** spot. **Time Period Covered:** latest week.

CELERY

Source: *Agricultural Prices Annual Summary.* **Price Frequency:** annually. **Effective Market(s):** 7 domestic markets. **Units of Measure:** Dollars per 100 lbs. **Type of Price:** average price received by farmer. **Time Period Covered:** latest 6 years.

Source: *Agricultural Prices Annual Summary.* **Price Frequency:** monthly, seasonally. **Effective Market(s):** California, Florida, Michigan, New York, United States. **Units of Measure:** Dollars per 100 lbs. **Type of Price:** average price received by farmer. **Time Period Covered:** latest 3 years, for US latest 6 years.

Source: *California Farmer.* **Price Frequency:** semimonthly. **Effective Market(s):** Salinas/Watsonville (CA), Santa Maria/Guadalupe/Oceano/Lompoc (CA), Southern California. **Units of Measure:** Dollars per 60 lb. crate. **Time Period Covered:** latest week, month ago, year ago.

Source: *Fresh Fruit and Vegetable Prices.* **Price Frequency:** monthly, seasonally. **Effective Market(s):** 6 domestic markets. **Units of Measure:** Dollars per crate. **Type of Price:** average price at shipping point. **Time Period Covered:** latest year.

Source: *The Grower.* **Price Frequency:** monthly, seasonally. **Effective Market(s):** Michigan. **Units of Measure:** Dollars per crate. **Time Period Covered:** latest year, year ago, 2 years ago.

Source: *Lancaster Farming.* **Price Frequency:** weekly, seasonally. **Effective Market(s):** Pennsylvania. **Units of Measure:** Dollars per carton. **Type of Price:** market. **Time Period Covered:** latest week.

Source: *New Zealand Farmer.* **Price Frequency:** weekly, seasonally. **Effective Market(s):** New Zealand. **Units of Measure:** New Zealand dollars per case/crate. **Time Period Covered:** latest week.

Source: *The Packer.* **Price Frequency:** weekly, seasonally. **Effective Market(s):** varies. **Units of Measure:** Dollars per crate/carton. **Type of Price:** price received by farmer. **Time Period Covered:** latest week.

CELERY: CALIFORNIA

Source: *Fresh Fruit and Vegetable Prices.* **Price Frequency:** monthly, seasonally. **Effective Market(s):** Chicago, New York City. **Units of Measure:** Dollars per crate/carton. **Type of Price:** average wholesale price. **Time Period Covered:** latest year.

Source: *Vegetable and Specialties Situation and Outlook Report.* **Price Frequency:** monthly. **Effective Market(s):** North Central, Northeast. **Units of Measure:** cents per lb. **Type of Price:** retail. **Time Period Covered:** latest month, year ago.

CELERY: FLORIDA

Source: *Fresh Fruit and Vegetable Prices.* **Price Frequency:** monthly, seasonally. **Effective Market(s):** Chicago, New York City. **Units of Measure:** Dollars per crate/carton. **Type of Price:** average wholesale price. **Time Period Covered:** latest year.

CELERY: FRESH

Source: *Agricultural Prices.* **Price Frequency:** monthly. **Effective Market(s):** United States. **Units of Measure:** Dollars per 100 lbs. **Type of Price:** received by farmer. **Time Period Covered:** latest 2 months, year ago.

Source: *Vegetable and Specialties Situation and Outlook Report.* **Price Frequency:** monthly, annually. **Effective Market(s):** United States. **Units of Measure:** Dollars per 100 lbs. **Type of Price:** received by grower. **Time Period Covered:** latest 4 years.

CELERY: MICHIGAN

Source: *Fresh Fruit and Vegetable Prices.* **Price Frequency:** monthly, seasonally. **Effective Market(s):** Chicago. **Units of Measure:** Dollars per crate/carton. **Type of Price:** average wholesale price. **Time Period Covered:** latest year.

CELERY: PASCAL, FRESH

Source: *HRI-Buyers Guide.* **Price Frequency:** weekly. **Effective Market(s):** Northeastern area. **Units of Measure:** Dollars per crate. **Type of Price:** price paid by dining places & institutions. **Time Period Covered:** latest week.

CELERY SEED

Source: *U. S. Spice Trade.* **Price Frequency:** monthly, annually. **Effective Market(s):** New York. **Units of Measure:** Dollars per lb. **Type of Price:** spot. **Time Period Covered:** latest 10 years.

CELERY SEED: INDIAN

Source: *Chemical Marketing Reporter.* **Price Frequency:** weekly. **Effective Market(s):** New York. **Units of Measure:** Dollars per lb. **Type of Price:** spot. **Time Period Covered:** latest week.

CELERY SEED OIL

Source: *Chemical Marketing Reporter.* **Price Frequency:** weekly. **Effective Market(s):** New York. **Units of Measure:** Dollars per lb. **Type of Price:** spot. **Time Period Covered:** latest week.

CELLULOSE ACETATE

Source: *Journal of Commerce and Commercial.* **Price Frequency:** weekly in Tuesday issue. **Units of Measure:** Dollars per lb. **Type of Price:** spot. **Time Period Covered:** latest week.

Source: *Plastics Technology.* **Price Frequency:** monthly. **Units of Measure:** cents per lb., cents per cubic inch. **Type of Price:** bulk list, market. **Time Period Covered:** latest month.

CELLULOSE ACETATE: POWDERED

Source: *Chemical Marketing Reporter.* **Price Frequency:** weekly. **Effective Market(s):** East. **Units of Measure:** Dollars per lb. **Type of Price:** spot. **Time Period Covered:** latest week.

CELLULOSE ACETATE BUTYRATE

Source: *Journal of Commerce and Commercial.* **Price Frequency:** weekly in Tuesday issue. **Units of Measure:** Dollars per lb. **Type of Price:** spot. **Time Period Covered:** latest week.

Source: *Plastics Technology.* **Price Frequency:** monthly. **Units of Measure:** cents per lb., cents per cubic inch. **Type of Price:** bulk list, market. **Time Period Covered:** latest month.

CELLULOSE ACETATE BUTYRATE: 38% BUTRYL CONTENT

Source: *Chemical Marketing Reporter.* **Price Frequency:** weekly. **Effective Market(s):** East. **Units of Measure:** Dollars per lb. **Type of Price:** spot. **Time Period Covered:** latest week.

CELLULOSE ACETATE BUTYRATE: 50% BUTRYL CONTENT

Source: *Chemical Marketing Reporter.* **Price Frequency:** weekly. **Effective Market(s):** East. **Units of Measure:** Dollars per lb. **Type of Price:** spot. **Time Period Covered:** latest week.

CELLULOSE ACETATE BUTYRATE: 55% BUTRYL CONTENT

Source: *Chemical Marketing Reporter.* **Price Frequency:** weekly. **Effective Market(s):** East. **Units of Measure:** Dollars per lb. **Type of Price:** spot. **Time Period Covered:** latest week.

CELLULOSE ACETATE BUTYRATE: POWDERED

Source: *Chemical Marketing Reporter.* **Price Frequency:** weekly. **Effective Market(s):** New York. **Units of Measure:** Dollars per lb. **Type of Price:** spot. **Time Period Covered:** latest week.

CELLULOSE ACETATE PROPIONATE

Source: *Plastics Technology.* **Price Frequency:** monthly. **Units of Measure:** cents per lb., cents per cubic inch. **Type of Price:** bulk list, market. **Time Period Covered:** latest month.

CELLULOSE GUM: PURE, HIGH VISCOSITY

Source: *Chemical Marketing Reporter.* **Price Frequency:** weekly. **Effective Market(s):** Hopewell (VA). **Units of Measure:** Dollars per lb. **Type of Price:** spot. **Time Period Covered:** latest week.

CELLULOSE GUM: STANDARD, LOW OR MEDIUM VISCOSITY

Source: *Chemical Marketing Reporter.* **Price Frequency:** weekly. **Effective Market(s):** Hopewell (VA). **Units of Measure:** Dollars per lb. **Type of Price:** spot. **Time Period Covered:** latest week.

CELLULOSE PROPIONATE

Source: *Journal of Commerce and Commercial.* **Price Frequency:** weekly in Tuesday issue. **Units of Measure:** Dollars per lb. **Type of Price:** spot. **Time Period Covered:** latest week.

CEMENT

Source: *ENR.* **Price Frequency:** monthly in first issue of month. **Effective Market(s):** 20-city average. **Units of Measure:** Dollars per ton. **Time Period Covered:** latest month.

Source: *Minerals Today.* **Price Frequency:** bimonthly. **Units of Measure:** Dollars per short ton. **Time Period Covered:** latest month, month ago.

CEMENT: 5 RAMS BRAND, CHINESE

Source: *Prices of Selected Asia/Pacific Products.* **Price Frequency:** monthly. **Effective Market(s):** Hong Kong. **Units of Measure:** Hong Kong dollars per metric ton. **Type of Price:** spot high. spot low. **Time Period Covered:** latest month.

CEMENT: HONG KONG

Source: *Prices of Selected Asia/Pacific Products.* **Price Frequency:** monthly. **Effective Market(s):** Hong Kong. **Units of Measure:** Hong Kong dollars per metric ton. **Type of Price:** spot high. spot low. **Time Period Covered:** latest month.

CEMENT: JAPANESE

Source: *Prices of Selected Asia/Pacific Products.* **Price Frequency:** monthly. **Effective Market(s):** Hong Kong. **Units of Measure:** Hong Kong dollars per metric ton. **Type of Price:** spot high. spot low. **Time Period Covered:** latest month.

CEMENT: MASONRY

Source: *ENR.* **Price Frequency:** monthly in first issue of month. **Effective Market(s):** 20 domestic markets, Montreal, Toronto. **Units of Measure:** Dollars per 70 lb. bag. **Type of Price:** spot. **Time Period Covered:** latest month.

CEMENT: PORTLAND

Source: *Agricultural Prices.* **Price Frequency:** quarterly. **Effective Market(s):** United States. **Units of Measure:** Dollars per 94 lbs. **Type of Price:** paid by farmer. **Time Period Covered:** latest 2 quarters, year ago.

Source: *Agricultural Prices Annual Summary.* **Price Frequency:** bimonthly. **Effective Market(s):** United States. **Units of Measure:** Dollars per bag. **Type of Price:** average price paid by farmer. **Time Period Covered:** latest 6 years.

Source: *Commodity Year Book.* **Price Frequency:** monthly, annually. **Units of Measure:** index. **Type of Price:** wholesale price index. **Time Period Covered:** latest 4 years.

CEMENT: PORTLAND, NORMAL, JAPANESE

Source: *Prices of Selected Asia/Pacific Products.* **Price Frequency:** monthly. **Effective Market(s):** Tokyo. **Units of Measure:** 1000 Japanese yen per metric ton. **Type of Price:** high, low. **Time Period Covered:** latest month.

CEMENT: PORTLAND, NORMAL, KOREAN

Source: *Prices of Selected Asia/Pacific Products.* **Price Frequency:** monthly. **Effective Market(s):** Tokyo. **Units of Measure:** 1000 Japanese yen per metric ton. **Type of Price:** high, low. **Time Period Covered:** latest month.

CEMENT: PORTLAND, NORMAL, TAIWANESE

Source: *Prices of Selected Asia/Pacific Products.* **Price Frequency:** monthly. **Effective Market(s):** Tokyo. **Units of Measure:** 1000 Japanese yen per metric ton. **Type of Price:** high, low. **Time Period Covered:** latest month.

CEMENT: PORTLAND, TYPE-1

Source: *ENR.* **Price Frequency:** monthly in first issue of month. **Effective Market(s):** 20 domestic markets, Montreal, Toronto. **Units of Measure:** Dollars per ton. **Type of Price:** spot. **Time Period Covered:** latest month.

CERAMIC DECANTERS

Source: *Colorado Beverage Analyst.* **Price Frequency:** monthly. **Effective Market(s):** Colorado. **Units of Measure:** Dollars per unit. **Type of Price:** wholesale by brand. **Time Period Covered:** latest month.

Source: *Illinois Beverage Journal.* **Price Frequency:** monthly. **Effective Market(s):** Illinois. **Units of Measure:** Dollars per unit. **Type of Price:** wholesale by brand. **Time Period Covered:** latest month.

CERIUM CONCENTRATE

Source: *Chemical Marketing Reporter.* **Price Frequency:** weekly. **Effective Market(s):** New York. **Units of Measure:** Dollars per lb. **Type of Price:** spot. **Time Period Covered:** latest week.

CERIUM HYDROXIDE

Source: *Chemical Marketing Reporter.* **Price Frequency:** weekly. **Effective Market(s):** New York. **Units of Measure:** Dollars per lb. **Type of Price:** spot. **Time Period Covered:** latest week.

CERIUM OXIDE: OPTICAL GRADE

Source: *Chemical Marketing Reporter.* **Price Frequency:** weekly. **Effective Market(s):** New York. **Units of Measure:** Dollars per lb. **Type of Price:** spot. **Time Period Covered:** latest week.

CETYL ALCOHOL: NF

Source: *Chemical Marketing Reporter.* **Price Frequency:** weekly. **Effective Market(s):** East. **Units of Measure:** Dollars per lb. **Type of Price:** spot. **Time Period Covered:** latest week.

CHAIN SAW: GASOLINE

Source: *Agricultural Prices.* **Price Frequency:** semiannually. **Effective Market(s):** United States. **Units of Measure:** Dollars each. **Type of Price:** paid by farmer. **Time Period Covered:** latest year.

Source: *Agricultural Prices Annual Summary.* **Price Frequency:** quarterly. **Effective Market(s):** United States. **Units of Measure:** Dollars each. **Type of Price:** average price paid by farmer. **Time Period Covered:** latest 6 years.

CHALK

see Calcium Carbonate.

CHAMOMILE FLOWERS: EGYPTIAN

Source: *Journal of Commerce and Commercial.* **Price Frequency:** weekly in Monday issue. **Units of Measure:** Dollars per lb. **Type of Price:** spot. **Time Period Covered:** latest week.

CHAMOMILE FLOWERS: HUNGARIAN

Source: *Chemical Marketing Reporter.* **Price Frequency:** weekly. **Effective Market(s):** New York. **Units of Measure:** Dollars per lb. **Type of Price:** spot. **Time Period Covered:** latest week.

Source: *Journal of Commerce and Commercial.* **Price Frequency:** weekly in Monday issue. **Units of Measure:** Dollars per lb. **Type of Price:** spot. **Time Period Covered:** latest week.

CHAMOMILE FLOWERS: ROMAN

Source: *Chemical Marketing Reporter.* **Price Frequency:** weekly. **Effective Market(s):** New York. **Units of Measure:** Dollars per lb. **Type of Price:** spot. **Time Period Covered:** latest week.

CHAMOMILE FLOWERS: WHOLE, EGYPTIAN

Source: *Chemical Marketing Reporter.* **Price Frequency:** weekly. **Effective Market(s):** New York. **Units of Measure:** Dollars per lb. **Type of Price:** spot. **Time Period Covered:** latest week.

CHAMOMILE OIL: BLUE, EGYPTIAN

Source: *Chemical Marketing Reporter.* **Price Frequency:** weekly. **Effective Market(s):** New York. **Units of Measure:** Dollars per lb. **Type of Price:** spot. **Time Period Covered:** latest week.

CHAMOMILE OIL: BLUE, HUNGARIAN

Source: *Chemical Marketing Reporter.* **Price Frequency:** weekly. **Effective Market(s):** New York. **Units of Measure:** Dollars per lb. **Type of Price:** spot. **Time Period Covered:** latest week.

CHAMPAGNE

see also Wines: Sparkling.

Source: *Beverage Media.* **Price Frequency:** monthly. **Effective Market(s):** New York. **Units of Measure:** Dollars per unit. **Type of Price:** wholesale by brand. **Time Period Covered:** latest month.

Source: *Indiana Beverage Journal.* **Price Frequency:** monthly. **Effective Market(s):** Indiana. **Units of Measure:** Dollars per case, dollars per bottle. **Type of Price:** wholesale by brand. **Time Period Covered:** latest month.

CHAMPAGNE: AMERICAN

Source: *Rhode Island Beverage Journal.* **Price Frequency:** monthly. **Effective Market(s):** Rhode Island. **Units of Measure:** Dollars per unit. **Type of Price:** wholesale by brand. **Time Period Covered:** latest month.

CHAMPAGNE: DOMESTIC

Source: *Colorado Beverage Analyst.* **Price Frequency:** monthly. **Effective Market(s):** Colorado. **Units of Measure:** Dollars per case. **Type of Price:** wholesale by brand. **Time Period Covered:** latest month.

CHAMPAGNE: IMPORTED

Source: *Colorado Beverage Analyst.* **Price Frequency:** monthly. **Effective Market(s):** Colorado. **Units of Measure:** Dollars per case. **Type of Price:** wholesale by brand. **Time Period Covered:** latest month.

Source: *Rhode Island Beverage Journal.* **Price Frequency:** monthly. **Effective Market(s):** Rhode Island. **Units of Measure:** Dollars per unit. **Type of Price:** wholesale by brand. **Time Period Covered:** latest month.

CHANNEL BEAMS

Source: *ENR.* **Price Frequency:** monthly in second issue of month. **Effective Market(s):** 17 domestic markets, Montreal, Toronto. **Units of Measure:** Dollars per 100 lbs. **Type of Price:** spot. **Time Period Covered:** latest month.

CHEESE

Source: *Agra Europe.* **Price Frequency:** weekly. **Effective Market(s):** 9 European markets. **Units of Measure:** national currency per tonne. **Type of Price:** average. **Time Period Covered:** latest week.

Source: *Commodity Year Book.* **Price Frequency:** monthly, annually. **Effective Market(s):** Wisconsin. **Units of Measure:** cents per lb. **Type of Price:** wholesale. **Time Period Covered:** latest 9 years.

Source: *Dairy Market Statistics.* **Price Frequency:** monthly. **Effective Market(s):** United States. **Units of Measure:** index. **Type of Price:** consumer price index. **Time Period Covered:** latest year.

Source: *Meat and Dairy Products.* **Price Frequency:** monthly. **Effective Market(s):** Wisconsin. **Units of Measure:** cents per lb. **Type of Price:** average. **Time Period Covered:** latest 3 years.

Source: *Monthly Price Review.* **Price Frequency:** daily. **Effective Market(s):** Northeast. **Units of Measure:** Dollars per lb. **Type of Price:** spot. **Time Period Covered:** latest month.

Source: *World Dairy Situation.* **Price Frequency:** semi-annually. **Effective Market(s):** North Europe/World ports. **Units of Measure:** Dollars per metric ton. **Type of Price:** average. **Time Period Covered:** latest 7 years.

CHEESE: AMERICAN PROCESS

Source: *Agricultural Outlook.* **Price Frequency:** monthly, annually. **Effective Market(s):** Wisconsin. **Units of Measure:** cents per lb. **Type of Price:** wholesale. **Time Period Covered:** monthly latest 6 months, annually latest 3 years.

Source: *Dairy Market Statistics.* **Price Frequency:** monthly, annually. **Effective Market(s):** North Central, Northeast, South, United States. **Units of Measure:** Dollars per lb. **Type of Price:** retail. **Time Period Covered:** latest year.

Source: *Dairy Market Statistics.* **Price Frequency:** monthly, annually. **Effective Market(s):** Eastern area, West Coast cities, Wisconsin. **Units of Measure:** Dollars per lb. **Type of Price:** wholesale. **Time Period Covered:** latest year.

Source: *Federal Milk Order Market Statistics.* **Price Frequency:** monthly. **Effective Market(s):** North Central, Northeast, South, United States. **Units of Measure:** Dollars per lb. **Type of Price:** retail. **Time Period Covered:** latest year to date.

Source: *HRI-Buyers Guide.* **Price Frequency:** weekly. **Effective Market(s):** Northeastern area. **Units of Measure:** Dollars per lb. **Type of Price:** price paid by dining places & institutions. **Time Period Covered:** latest week.

CHEESE: BARREL

Source: *Dairy Foods.* **Price Frequency:** monthly. **Effective Market(s):** Wisconsin. **Units of Measure:** Dollars per lb. **Time Period Covered:** latest month.

CHEESE: BELVILLE WHITE, CANADIAN

Source: *Meat and Dairy Products.* **Price Frequency:** monthly. **Effective Market(s):** Canada. **Units of Measure:** Canadian dollars per kilogram. **Type of Price:** wholesale. **Time Period Covered:** latest 3 years.

CHEESE: BLOCK

Source: *Dairy Foods.* **Price Frequency:** monthly. **Effective Market(s):** Wisconsin. **Units of Measure:** Dollars per lb. **Time Period Covered:** latest month.

CHEESE: BLUE, DANISH

Source: *HRI-Buyers Guide.* **Price Frequency:** weekly. **Effective Market(s):** Northeastern area. **Units of Measure:** Dollars per lb. **Type of Price:** price paid by dining places & institutions. **Time Period Covered:** latest week.

CHEESE: BLUE, DANISH, IMPORTED

Source: *Urner Barry's Price-Current.* **Price Frequency:** daily. **Units of Measure:** Dollars per lb. **Time Period Covered:** latest day.

CHEESE: BLUE, DOMESTIC

Source: *Dairy Foods.* **Price Frequency:** monthly. **Units of Measure:** Dollars per lb. **Time Period Covered:** latest month.

Source: *Dairy Market Statistics.* **Price Frequency:** monthly. **Effective Market(s):** New York, Wisconsin. **Units of Measure:** Dollars per lb. **Type of Price:** wholesale. **Time Period Covered:** latest year.

Source: *HRI-Buyers Guide.* **Price Frequency:** weekly. **Effective Market(s):** Northeastern area. **Units of Measure:** Dollars per lb. **Type of Price:** price paid by dining places & institutions. **Time Period Covered:** latest week.

Source: *Urner Barry's Price-Current.* **Price Frequency:** daily. **Units of Measure:** Dollars per lb. **Time Period Covered:** latest day.

CHEESE: BLUE, IMPORTED

Source: *Dairy Foods.* **Price Frequency:** monthly. **Units of Measure:** Dollars per lb. **Time Period Covered:** latest month.

Source: *Dairy Market Statistics.* **Price Frequency:** monthly. **Effective Market(s):** New York. **Units of Measure:** Dollars per lb. **Type of Price:** wholesale. **Time Period Covered:** latest year.

CHEESE: BRICK AND MUENSTER

Source: *Dairy Market Statistics.* **Price Frequency:** monthly, annually. **Effective Market(s):** Wisconsin. **Units of Measure:** Dollars per lb. **Type of Price:** wholesale. **Time Period Covered:** latest year.

CHEESE: CHEDDAR

Source: *California Farmer.* **Price Frequency:** semi-monthly. **Effective Market(s):** California. **Units of Measure:** Dollars per lb. **Type of Price:** wholesale. **Time Period Covered:** latest week, month ago, year ago.

Source: *Dairy Market Statistics.* **Price Frequency:** monthly, annually. **Effective Market(s):** Wisconsin. **Units of Measure:** Dollars per lb. **Type of Price:** wholesale. **Time Period Covered:** latest year.

Source: *Dairy Market Statistics.* **Price Frequency:** monthly, annually. **Effective Market(s):** Eastern area, West Coast cities. **Units of Measure:** Dollars per lb. **Type of Price:** wholesale. **Time Period Covered:** latest year.

Source: *Dairy Situation and Outlook Report.* **Price Frequency:** monthly, annually. **Effective Market(s):** Wisconsin. **Units of Measure:** cents per lb. **Type of Price:** wholesale. **Time Period Covered:** latest year.

Source: *Federal Milk Order Market Statistics.* **Price Frequency:** monthly. **Effective Market(s):** Wisconsin. **Units of Measure:** Dollars per lb. **Type of Price:** wholesale. **Time Period Covered:** latest 2 years.

Source: *HRI-Buyers Guide.* **Price Frequency:** weekly. **Effective Market(s):** Northeastern area. **Units of Measure:** Dollars per lb. **Type of Price:** price paid by dining places & institutions. **Time Period Covered:** latest week.

CHEESE: CHEDDAR, BARRELS

Source: *Dairy Market Statistics.* **Price Frequency:** weekly, monthly. **Units of Measure:** Dollars per lb. **Type of Price:** spot. **Time Period Covered:** latest year.

CHEESE: CHEDDAR, BLOCKS

Source: *Dairy Market Statistics.* **Price Frequency:** weekly, monthly. **Units of Measure:** Dollars per lb. **Type of Price:** spot. **Time Period Covered:** latest year.

Source: *Urner Barry's Price-Current.* **Price Frequency:** daily. **Units of Measure:** Dollars per lb. **Time Period Covered:** latest day.

CHEESE: CHEDDAR, DAISY

Source: *Urner Barry's Price-Current.* **Price Frequency:** daily. **Units of Measure:** Dollars per lb. **Time Period Covered:** lates day.

CHEESE: CHEDDAR, ENGLISH WHITE, RINDLESS

Source: *Meat and Dairy Products.* **Price Frequency:** monthly. **Effective Market(s):** United Kingdom. **Units of Measure:** British pounds per tonne. **Type of Price:** average. **Time Period Covered:** latest 3 years.

CHEESE: CHEDDAR, NATURAL

Source: *Dairy Market Statistics.* **Price Frequency:** monthly, annually. **Effective Market(s):** Northeast, South, West, United States. **Units of Measure:** Dollars per lb. **Type of Price:** retail. **Time Period Covered:** latest year.

Source: *Federal Milk Order Market Statistics.* **Price Frequency:** monthly. **Effective Market(s):** Northeast, South, West, United States. **Units of Measure:** Dollars per lb. **Type of Price:** retail. **Time Period Covered:** latest year to date.

CHEESE: CHEDDAR, PROCESSED, LOAF

Source: *Urner Barry's Price-Current.* **Price Frequency:** daily. **Units of Measure:** Dollars per lb. **Time Period Covered:** latest day.

CHEESE: CHEDDAR, PROCESSED, SLICED

Source: *Urner Barry's Price-Current.* **Price Frequency:** daily. **Units of Measure:** Dollars per lb. **Time Period Covered:** latest day.

CHEESE: CHEDDAR, SINGLE DAISY

Source: *Journal of Commerce and Commercial.* **Price Frequency:** daily. **Effective Market(s):** New York. **Units of Measure:** Dollars per lb. **Type of Price:** spot supplier. **Time Period Covered:** latest day.

Source: *Survey of Current Business.* **Price Frequency:** monthly, annually. **Effective Market(s):** Chicago. **Units of Measure:** Dollars per lb. **Type of Price:** wholesale. **Time Period Covered:** latest year.

CHEESE: CHEDDAR, WISCONSIN

Source: *FAO Quarterly Bulletin of Statistics.* **Price Frequency:** monthly, annually. **Effective Market(s):** United States. **Units of Measure:** Dollars per 100 lbs., dollars per metric ton. **Type of Price:** wholesale. **Time Period Covered:** latest 3 years.

CHEESE: CURRENT, CHEDDAR

Source: *Dairy Market Statistics.* **Price Frequency:** monthly, annually. **Effective Market(s):** Wisconsin. **Units of Measure:** Dollars per lb. **Type of Price:** average. **Time Period Covered:** latest year.

CHEESE: EDAM, DOMESTIC

Source: *Dairy Foods.* **Price Frequency:** monthly. **Units of Measure:** Dollars per lb. **Time Period Covered:** latest month.

Source: *Urner Barry's Price-Current.* **Price Frequency:** daily. **Units of Measure:** Dollars per lb. **Time Period Covered:** latest day.

CHEESE: EDAM, DUTCH, IMPORTED

Source: *Urner Barry's Price-Current.* **Price Frequency:** daily. **Units of Measure:** Dollars per lb. **Time Period Covered:** latest day.

CHEESE: EDAM, IMPORTED

Source: *Dairy Foods.* **Price Frequency:** monthly. **Units of Measure:** Dollars per lb. **Time Period Covered:** latest month.

Source: *Dairy Market Statistics.* **Price Frequency:** monthly. **Effective Market(s):** New York. **Units of Measure:** Dollars per lb. **Type of Price:** wholesale. **Time Period Covered:** latest year.

CHEESE: EMMENTHAL, 45% KEMPTON, WEST GERMAN

Source: *Meat and Dairy Products.* **Price Frequency:** monthly. **Effective Market(s):** West Germany. **Units of Measure:** West German marks per kilogram. **Type of Price:** average. **Time Period Covered:** latest 3 years.

CHEESE: GORGONZOLA, DOMESTIC

Source: *Dairy Foods.* **Price Frequency:** monthly. **Units of Measure:** Dollars per lb. **Time Period Covered:** latest month.

Source: *Dairy Market Statistics.* **Price Frequency:** monthly. **Effective Market(s):** New York. **Units of Measure:** Dollars per lb. **Type of Price:** wholesale. **Time Period Covered:** latest year.

Source: *Urner Barry's Price-Current.* **Price Frequency:** daily. **Units of Measure:** Dollars per lb. **Time Period Covered:** latest day.

CHEESE: GORGONZOLA, IMPORTED

Source: *Dairy Foods.* **Price Frequency:** monthly. **Units of Measure:** Dollars per lb. **Time Period Covered:** latest month.

Source: *Dairy Market Statistics.* **Price Frequency:** monthly. **Effective Market(s):** New York. **Units of Measure:** Dollars per lb. **Type of Price:** wholesale. **Time Period Covered:** latest year.

CHEESE: GORGANZOLA, ITALIAN, IMPORTED

Source: *Urner Barry's Price-Current.* **Price Frequency:** daily. **Units of Measure:** Dollars per lb. **Time Period Covered:** latest day.

CHEESE: GOUDA, BABY, IMPORTED

Source: *Dairy Market Statistics.* **Price Frequency:** monthly. **Effective Market(s):** New York. **Units of Measure:** Dollars per lb. **Type of Price:** wholesale. **Time Period Covered:** latest year.

CHEESE: GOUDA, DUTCH

Source: *FAO Quarterly Bulletin of Statistics.* **Price Frequency:** monthly, annually. **Effective Market(s):** Netherlands. **Units of Measure:** Dutch guilders per 100 kilograms, dollars per metric ton. **Type of Price:** national average. **Time Period Covered:** latest 3 years.

CHEESE: GOUDA, DUTCH, IMPORTED

Source: *Urner Barry's Price-Current.* **Price Frequency:** daily. **Units of Measure:** Dollars per lb. **Time Period Covered:** latest day.

CHEESE: GOUDA, FULL CREAM, NETHERLANDS

Source: *Meat and Dairy Products.* **Price Frequency:** monthly. **Effective Market(s):** Leeuwarden (Netherlands). **Units of Measure:** Dutch guilders per kilogram. **Type of Price:** average. **Time Period Covered:** latest 3 years.

CHEESE: GOUDA, LARGE, IMPORTED

Source: *Dairy Market Statistics.* **Price Frequency:** monthly. **Effective Market(s):** New York. **Units of Measure:** Dollars per lb. **Type of Price:** wholesale. **Time Period Covered:** latest year.

CHEESE: JARLSBERG BRAND, IMPORTED

Source: *Dairy Market Statistics.* **Price Frequency:** monthly. **Effective Market(s):** New York. **Units of Measure:** Dollars per lb. **Type of Price:** wholesale. **Time Period Covered:** latest year.

CHEESE: MONTEREY JACK

Source: *California Farmer.* **Price Frequency:** semimonthly. **Effective Market(s):** California. **Units of Measure:** Dollars per lb. **Type of Price:** wholesale. **Time Period Covered:** latest week, month ago, year ago.

Source: *Dairy Market Statistics.* **Price Frequency:** monthly, annually. **Effective Market(s):** West Coast cities, Wisconsin. **Units of Measure:** Dollars per lb. **Type of Price:** wholesale. **Time Period Covered:** latest year.

CHEESE: MOZZARELLA

Source: *HRI-Buyers Guide.* **Price Frequency:** weekly. **Effective Market(s):** Northeastern area. **Units of Measure:** Dollars per lb. **Type of Price:** price paid by dining places & institutions. **Time Period Covered:** latest week.

CHEESE: MOZZARELLA, DOMESTIC

Source: *Dairy Market Statistics.* **Price Frequency:** monthly. **Effective Market(s):** Wisconsin. **Units of Measure:** Dollars per lb. **Type of Price:** wholesale. **Time Period Covered:** latest year.

CHEESE: MOZZARELLA, LOAF, DOMESTIC

Source: *Urner Barry's Price-Current.* **Price Frequency:** daily. **Units of Measure:** Dollars per lb. **Time Period Covered:** latest day.

CHEESE: MOZZARELLA, PART SKIM, DOMESTIC

Source: *Urner Barry's Price-Current.* **Price Frequency:** daily. **Units of Measure:** Dollars per lb. **Time Period Covered:** latest day.

CHEESE: MUENSTER

Source: *Dairy Market Statistics.* **Price Frequency:** monthly, annually. **Effective Market(s):** Eastern area. **Units of Measure:** Dollars per lb. **Type of Price:** wholesale. **Time Period Covered:** latest year.

Source: *HRI-Buyers Guide.* **Price Frequency:** weekly. **Effective Market(s):** Northeastern area. **Units of Measure:** Dollars per lb. **Type of Price:** price paid by dining places & institutions. **Time Period Covered:** latest week.

Source: *Urner Barry's Price-Current.* **Price Frequency:** daily. **Units of Measure:** Dollars per lb. **Time Period Covered:** latest day.

CHEESE: PARMESAN, DOMESTIC

Source: *Dairy Foods.* **Price Frequency:** monthly. **Units of Measure:** Dollars per lb. **Time Period Covered:** latest month.

Source: *Urner Barry's Price-Current.* **Price Frequency:** daily. **Units of Measure:** Dollars per lb. **Time Period Covered:** latest week.

CHEESE: PARMESAN, IMPORTED

Source: *Dairy Foods.* **Price Frequency:** monthly. **Units of Measure:** Dollars per lb. **Time Period Covered:** latest month.

Source: *Dairy Market Statistics.* **Price Frequency:** monthly. **Effective Market(s):** New York. **Units of Measure:** Dollars per lb. **Type of Price:** wholesale. **Time Period Covered:** latest year.

CHEESE: PARMESAN, ITALIAN, IMPORTED

Source: *Urner Barry's Price Current.* **Price Frequency:** daily. **Units of Measure:** Dollars per lb. **Time Period Covered:** latest day.

CHEESE: PECORINO

Source: *HRI-Buyers Guide.* **Price Frequency:** weekly. **Effective Market(s):** Northeastern area. **Units of Measure:** Dollars per lb. **Type of Price:** price paid by dining places & institutions. **Time Period Covered:** latest week.

CHEESE: PECORINO ROMANO, GENUINE, DOMESTIC

Source: *Dairy Foods.* **Price Frequency:** monthly. **Units of Measure:** Dollars per lb. **Time Period Covered:** latest month.

CHEESE: PECORINO ROMANO, GENUINE, IMPORTED

Source: *Dairy Foods.* **Price Frequency:** monthly. **Units of Measure:** Dollars per lb. **Time Period Covered:** latest month.

Source: *Dairy Market Statistics.* **Price Frequency:** monthly. **Effective Market(s):** New York. **Units of Measure:** Dollars per lb. **Type of Price:** wholesale. **Time Period Covered:** latest year.

CHEESE: PECORINO ROMANO, GENUINE, ITALIAN, IMPORTED

Source: *Urner Barry's Price-Current.* **Price Frequency:** daily. **Units of Measure:** Dollars per lb. **Time Period Covered:** latest day.

CHEESE: PECORINO ROMANO SARDO, ITALIAN, IMPORTED

Source: *Urner Barry's Price-Current.* **Price Frequency:** daily. **Units of Measure:** Dollars per lb. **Time Period Covered:** latest day.

CHEESE: PECORINO SARDO, DOMESTIC

Source: *Dairy Foods.* **Price Frequency:** monthly. **Units of Measure:** Dollars per lb. **Time Period Covered:** latest month.

CHEESE: PECORINO SARDO, IMPORTED

Source: *Dairy Foods.* **Price Frequency:** monthly. **Units of Measure:** Dollars per lb. **Time Period Covered:** latest month.

Source: *Dairy Market Statistics.* **Price Frequency:** monthly. **Effective Market(s):** New York. **Units of Measure:** Dollars per lb. **Type of Price:** wholesale. **Time Period Covered:** latest year.

CHEESE: PROVOLONE, AGED, DOMESTIC

Source: *Urner Barry's Price-Current.* **Price Frequency:** daily. **Units of Measure:** Dollars per lb. **Time Period Covered:** latest day.

CHEESE: PROVOLONE, DOMESTIC

Source: *Dairy Foods.* **Price Frequency:** monthly. **Units of Measure:** Dollars per lb. **Time Period Covered:** latest month.

Source: *Dairy Market Statistics.* **Price Frequency:** monthly. **Effective Market(s):** New York, Wisconsin. **Units of Measure:** Dollars per lb. **Type of Price:** wholesale. **Time Period Covered:** latest year.

Source: *HRI-Buyers Guide.* **Price Frequency:** weekly. **Effective Market(s):** Northeastern area. **Units of Measure:** Dollars per lb. **Type of Price:** price paid by dining places & institutions. **Time Period Covered:** latest week.

CHEESE: PROVOLONE, FRESH, DOMESTIC

Source: *Urner Barry's Price-Current.* **Price Frequency:** daily. **Units of Measure:** Dollars per lb. **Time Period Covered:** latest day.

CHEESE: PROVOLONE, GIGANTI, IMPORTED

Source: *Dairy Market Statistics.* **Price Frequency:** monthly. **Effective Market(s):** New York. **Units of Measure:** Dollars per lb. **Type of Price:** wholesale. **Time Period Covered:** latest year.

CHEESE: PROVOLONE, IMPORTED

Source: *Dairy Foods.* **Price Frequency:** monthly. **Units of Measure:** Dollars per lb. **Time Period Covered:** latest month.

Source: *HRI-Buyers Guide.* **Price Frequency:** weekly. **Effective Market(s):** Northeastern area. **Units of Measure:** Dollars per lb. **Type of Price:** price paid by dining places & institutions. **Time Period Covered:** latest week.

CHEESE: PROVOLONE, ITALIAN, IMPORTED

Source: *Urner Barry's Price-Current.* **Price Frequency:** daily. **Units of Measure:** Dollars per lb. **Time Period Covered:** latest day.

CHEESE: REGGIANITO, ARGENTINE, IMPORTED

Source: *Dairy Market Statistics.* **Price Frequency:** monthly. **Effective Market(s):** New York. **Units of Measure:** Dollars per lb. **Type of Price:** wholesale. **Time Period Covered:** latest year.

Source: *Urner Barry's Price-Current.* **Price Frequency:** daily. **Units of Measure:** Dollars per lb. **Time Period Covered:** latest day.

CHEESE: ROMANO, ARGENTINE, IMPORTED

Source: *Urner Barry's Price-Current.* **Price Frequency:** daily. **Units of Measure:** Dollars per lb. **Time Period Covered:** latest day.

CHEESE: ROMANO, DOMESTIC

Source: *Dairy Foods.* **Price Frequency:** monthly. **Units of Measure:** Dollars per lb. **Time Period Covered:** latest month.

Source: *Dairy Market Statistics.* **Price Frequency:** monthly. **Effective Market(s):** New York. **Units of Measure:** Dollars per lb. **Type of Price:** wholesale. **Time Period Covered:** latest year.

CHEESE: ROMANO, IMPORTED

Source: *Dairy Foods.* **Price Frequency:** monthly. **Units of Measure:** Dollars per lb. **Time Period Covered:** latest month.

CHEESE: ROMANO SARDO, ARGENTINE, IMPORTED

Source: *Dairy Market Statistics.* **Price Frequency:** monthly. **Effective Market(s):** New York. **Units of Measure:** Dollars per lb. **Type of Price:** wholesale. **Time Period Covered:** latest year.

CHEESE: ROQUEFORT, DOMESTIC

Source: *Dairy Foods.* **Price Frequency:** monthly. **Units of Measure:** Dollars per lb. **Time Period Covered:** latest month.

CHEESE: ROQUEFORT, FRENCH, IMPORTED

Source: *Urner Barry's Price-Current.* **Price Frequency:** daily. **Units of Measure:** Dollars per lb. **Time Period Covered:** latest day.

CHEESE: ROQUEFORT, IMPORTED

Source: *Dairy Foods.* **Price Frequency:** monthly. **Units of Measure:** Dollars per lb. **Time Period Covered:** latest month.

Source: *Dairy Market Statistics.* **Price Frequency:** monthly. **Effective Market(s):** New York. **Units of Measure:** Dollars per lb. **Type of Price:** wholesale. **Time Period Covered:** latest year.

CHEESE: SWISS, AUSTRIAN

Source: *HRI-Buyers Guide.* **Price Frequency:** weekly. **Effective Market(s):** Northeastern area. **Units of Measure:** Dollars per lb. **Type of Price:** price paid by dining places & institutions. **Time Period Covered:** latest week.

CHEESE: SWISS, AUSTRIAN, IMPORTED

Source: *Dairy Market Statistics.* **Price Frequency:** monthly. **Effective Market(s):** New York. **Units of Measure:** Dollars per lb. **Type of Price:** wholesale. **Time Period Covered:** latest year.

Source: *Urner Barry's Price-Current.* **Price Frequency:** daily. **Units of Measure:** Dollars per lb. **Time Period Covered:** latest day.

CHEESE: SWISS, DANISH

Source: *HRI-Buyers Guide.* **Price Frequency:** weekly. **Effective Market(s):** Northeastern area. **Units of Measure:** Dollars per lb. **Type of Price:** price paid by dining places & institutions. **Time Period Covered:** latest week.

CHEESE: SWISS, DANISH, IMPORTED

Source: *Urner Barry's Price-Current.* **Price Frequency:** daily. **Units of Measure:** Dollars per lb. **Time Period Covered:** latest day.

CHEESE: SWISS, DOMESTIC

Source: *Dairy Foods.* **Price Frequency:** monthly. **Units of Measure:** Dollars per lb. **Time Period Covered:** latest month.

Source: *HRI-Buyers Guide.* **Price Frequency:** weekly. **Effective Market(s):** Northeastern area. **Units of Measure:** Dollars per lb. **Type of Price:** price paid by dining places & institutions. **Time Period Covered:** latest week.

CHEESE: SWISS, FINNISH

Source: *HRI-Buyers Guide.* **Price Frequency:** weekly. **Effective Market(s):** Northeastern area. **Units of Measure:** Dollars per lb. **Type of Price:** price paid by dining places & institutions. **Time Period Covered:** latest week.

CHEESE: SWISS, FINNISH, IMPORTED

Source: *Dairy Market Statistics.* **Price Frequency:** monthly. **Effective Market(s):** New York. **Units of Measure:** Dollars per lb. **Type of Price:** wholesale. **Time Period Covered:** latest year.

Source: *Urner Barry's Price-Current.* **Price Frequency:** daily. **Units of Measure:** Dollars per lb. **Time Period Covered:** latest day.

CHEESE: SWISS, GRADE A, DOMESTIC

Source: *Dairy Foods.* **Price Frequency:** monthly. **Effective Market(s):** Wisconsin. **Units of Measure:** Dollars per lb. **Time Period Covered:** latest month.

Source: *Dairy Market Statistics.* **Price Frequency:** monthly. **Effective Market(s):** New York, Western areas, Wisconsin. **Units of Measure:** Dollars per lb. **Type of Price:** wholesale. **Time Period Covered:** latest year.

Source: *Urner Barry's Price-Current.* **Price Frequency:** daily. **Units of Measure:** Dollars per lb. **Time Period Covered:** latest day.

CHEESE: SWISS, GRADE B, DOMESTIC

Source: *Urner Barry's Price-Current.* **Price Frequency:** daily. **Units of Measure:** Dollars per lb. **Time Period Covered:** latest day.

CHEESE: SWISS, IMPORTED

Source: *Dairy Foods.* **Price Frequency:** monthly. **Units of Measure:** Dollars per lb. **Time Period Covered:** latest month.

CHEESE: SWISS, SWITZERLAND

Source: *HRI-Buyers Guide.* **Price Frequency:** weekly. **Effective Market(s):** Northeastern area. **Units of Measure:** Dollars per lb. **Type of Price:** price paid by dining places & institutions. **Time Period Covered:** latest week.

CHEESE: SWISS, SWITZERLAND, IMPORTED

Source: *Dairy Market Statistics.* **Price Frequency:** monthly. **Effective Market(s):** New York. **Units of Measure:** Dollars per lb. **Type of Price:** wholesale. **Time Period Covered:** latest year.

Source: *Urner Barry's Price-Current.* **Price Frequency:** daily. **Units of Measure:** Dollars per lb. **Time Period Covered:** latest day.

CHEESE: SWISS WHEELS, IMPORTED

Source: *Dairy Market Statistics.* **Price Frequency:** monthly. **Effective Market(s):** New York. **Units of Measure:** Dollars per lb. **Type of Price:** wholesale. **Time Period Covered:** latest year.

CHEMICALS: HEAVY VOLUME

Source: *Journal of Commerce and Commerce.* **Price Frequency:** weekly in Thursday issue. **Units of Measure:** Dollars per lb., dollars per ton. **Type of Price:** spot. **Time Period Covered:** latest week.

CHENOPODIUM OIL: NF

Source: *Chemical Marketing Reporter.* **Price Frequency:** weekly. **Effective Market(s):** New York. **Units of Measure:** Dollars per lb. **Type of Price:** spot. **Time Period Covered:** latest week.

CHERRIES

Source: *Lancaster Farming.* **Price Frequency:** weekly, seasonally. **Effective Market(s):** Pennsylvania. **Units of Measure:** Dollars per unit. **Type of Price:** market. **Time Period Covered:** latest week.

CHERRIES: BING

Source: *California Farmer.* **Price Frequency:** semimonthly, seasonally. **Effective Market(s):** Stockton/Lodi/Linden (CA). **Units of Measure:** Dollars per 18 lb. lug. **Time Period Covered:** latest week, year ago.

Source: *Fresh Fruit and Vegetable Prices.* **Price Frequency:** monthly, seasonally. **Effective Market(s):** Stockton/Linden/Lodi (CA), Yakima Valley/Wenatchee (WA). **Units of Measure:** Dollars per lug. **Type of Price:** average price at shipping point. **Time Period Covered:** latest year.

Source: *Oregon Farmer-Stockman.* **Price Frequency:** monthly, seasonally. **Effective Market(s):** Yakima Valley (WA). **Units of Measure:** Dollars per 20 lb. carton. **Time Period Covered:** latest month.

CHERRIES: BING, CHILEAN

Source: *Fresh Fruit and Vegetable Prices.* **Price Frequency:** monthly, seasonally. **Effective Market(s):** New York City/Philadelphia. **Units of Measure:** Dollars per lug. **Type of Price:** dock price. **Time Period Covered:** latest year.

CHERRIES: CALIFORNIA

Source: *Fresh Fruit and Vegetable Prices.* **Price Frequency:** monthly, seasonally. **Effective Market(s):** Chicago, New York City. **Units of Measure:** Dollars per lug. **Type of Price:** average wholesale price. **Time Period Covered:** latest year.

CHERRIES: LAMBERT

Source: *Oregon Farmer-Stockman.* **Price Frequency:** monthly, seasonally. **Effective Market(s):** Yakima Valley (WA). **Units of Measure:** Dollars per 20 lb. carton. **Time Period Covered:** latest month.

CHERRIES: LARIAN

Source: *California Farmer.* **Price Frequency:** semimonthly, seasonally. **Effective Market(s):** Stockton/Linden (CA). **Units of Measure:** Dollars per 18 lb. lug. **Time Period Covered:** latest week, year ago.

CHERRIES: NORTHWEST

Source: *Fresh Fruit and Vegetable Prices.* **Price Frequency:** monthly, seasonally. **Effective Market(s):** Chicago, New York City. **Units of Measure:** Dollars per lug. **Type of Price:** average wholesale price. **Time Period Covered:** latest year.

CHERRIES: RED, SOUR, FROZEN

Source: *HRI-Buyer's Guide.* **Price Frequency:** weekly. **Effective Market(s):** Northeastern area. **Units of Measure:** Dollars per case. **Type of Price:** price paid by dining places & institutions. **Time Period Covered:** latest week.

CHERRIES: SWEET

Source: *Agricultural Prices Annual Summary.* **Price Frequency:** annually. **Effective Market(s):** 9 domestic markets, United States. **Units of Measure:** Dollars per ton. **Type of Price:** average price received by farmer. **Time Period Covered:** latest 3 years, for US latest 6 years.

CHERRIES: SWEET, FRESH

Source: *Fruit and Tree Nuts Situation and Outlook Yearbook.* **Price Frequency:** annually. **Effective Market(s):** United States. **Units of Measure:** Dollars per ton. **Type of Price:** grower. **Time Period Covered:** latest 20 years.

CHERRIES: SWEET, PROCESSING

Source: *Fruit and Tree Nuts Situation and Outlook Yearbook.* **Price Frequency:** annually. **Effective Market(s):** United States. **Units of Measure:** Dollars per ton. **Type of Price:** grower. **Time Period Covered:** latest 20 years.

CHERRIES: TART

Source: *Agricultural Prices Annual Summary.* **Price Frequency:** annually. **Effective Market(s):** 7 domestic markets, United States. **Units of Measure:** Dollars per ton. **Type of Price:** average price received by farmer. **Time Period Covered:** latest 3 years, for US latest 6 years.

CHERRIES: TART, FRESH

Source: *Fruit and Tree Nuts Situation and Outlook Yearbook.* **Price Frequency:** annually. **Effective Market(s):** United States. **Units of Measure:** Dollars per ton. **Type of Price:** grower. **Time Period Covered:** latest 20 years.

CHERRIES: TART, PROCESSING

Source: *Fruit and Tree Nuts Situation and Outlook Yearbook.* **Price Frequency:** annually. **Effective Market(s):** United States. **Units of Measure:** Dollars per ton. **Type of Price:** grower. **Time Period Covered:** latest 20 years.

CHERRY SAWTIMBER: BLACK

Source: *Volume and Value of Sawtimber Stumpage Sold From National Forests by Selected Species and Region.* **Price Frequency:** quarterly, annually. **Effective Market(s):** Eastern region. **Units of Measure:** Dollars per 1000 board feet. **Type of Price:** average. **Time Period Covered:** latest quarter, latest year.

CHICAGO ACID: DRY

Source: *Chemical Marketing Reporter.* **Price Frequency:** weekly. **Effective Market(s):** New York. **Units of Measure:** Dollars per lb. **Type of Price:** spot. **Time Period Covered:** latest week.

CHICK STARTER FEED

Source: *Agricultural Prices.* **Price Frequency:** quarterly. **Effective Market(s):** United States. **Units of Measure:** Dollars per ton. **Type of Price:** paid by farmer. **Time Period Covered:** latest 2 quarters, year ago.

Source: *Agricultural Prices.* **Price Frequency:** monthly. **Effective Market(s):** 10 domestic markets, United States. **Units of Measure:** Dollars per ton. **Type of Price:** paid by farmer. **Time Period Covered:** latest month.

Source: *Agricultural Prices Annual Summary.* **Price Frequency:** quarterly. **Effective Market(s):** 10 domestic markets, United States. **Units of Measure:** Dollars per ton. **Type of Price:** average price paid by farmer. **Time Period Covered:** latest year, for US latest 6 years.

Source: *Feed Situation and Outlook Report.* **Price Frequency:** quarterly. **Effective Market(s):** United States. **Units of Measure:** Dollars per ton. **Type of Price:** paid by farmer. **Time Period Covered:** latest 3 quarters.

CHICKEN: CAPONS

see Capons.

CHICKEN: COMMINUTED

Source: *Monthly Price Review.* **Price Frequency:** daily. **Effective Market(s):** Northeast. **Units of Measure:** Dollars per lb. **Type of Price:** spot. **Time Period Covered:** latest month.

CHICKEN: COMMINUTED, FRESH

Source: *Poultry Market Statistics.* **Price Frequency:** monthly, annually. **Effective Market(s):** Atlantic states coastal region. **Units of Measure:** cents per lb. **Type of Price:** average. **Time Period Covered:** latest year.

CHICKEN: COMMINUTED, FROZEN

Source: *Poultry Market Statistics.* **Price Frequency:** monthly, annually. **Effective Market(s):** Atlantic States coastal region. **Units of Measure:** cents per lb. **Type of Price:** average. **Time Period Covered:** latest year.

CHICKEN: COMMINUTED, NO KIDNEYS OR SEX GLANDS

Source: *Urner Barry's Price-Current.* **Price Frequency:** daily. **Effective Market(s):** Eastern area. **Units of Measure:** Dollars per lb. **Time Period Covered:** latest day.

CHICKEN: COMMINUTED, NO SKIN, FRESH

Source: *Urner Barry's Price-Current, West Coast Edition.* **Price Frequency:** semiweekly. **Effective Market(s):** West Coast. **Units of Measure:** Dollars per lb. **Time Period Covered:** latest day.

CHICKEN: COMMINUTED, NO SKIN, FROZEN

Source: *Monthly Price Review.* **Price Frequency:** daily. **Effective Market(s):** Northeast. **Units of Measure:** Dollars per lb. **Type of Price:** spot. **Time Period Covered:** latest month.

Source: *Urner Barry's Price-Current, West Coast Edition.* **Price Frequency:** semiweekly. **Effective Market(s):** West Coast. **Units of Measure:** Dollars per lb. **Time Period Covered:** latest day.

CHICKEN: COMMINUTED, WITH SKIN, FRESH

Source: *Urner Barry's Price-Current.* **Price Frequency:** daily. **Effective Market(s):** Eastern area. **Units of Measure:** Dollars per lb. **Time Period Covered:** latest day.

Source: *Urner Barry's Price-Current, West Coast Edition.* **Price Frequency:** semiweekly. **Effective Market(s):** West Coast. **Units of Measure:** Dollars per lb. **Time Period Covered:** latest day.

CHICKEN: COMMINUTED, WITH SKIN, FROZEN

Source: *Monthly Price Review.* **Price Frequency:** daily. **Effective Market(s):** Northeast. **Units of Measure:** Dollars per lb. **Type of Price:** spot. **Time Period Covered:** latest month.

Source: *Urner Barry's Price-Current.* **Price Frequency:** daily. **Effective Market(s):** Eastern area. **Units of Measure:** Dollars per lb. **Time Period Covered:** latest day.

Source: *Urner Barry's Price-Current, West Coast Edition.* **Price Frequency:** semiweekly. **Effective Market(s):** West Coast. **Units of Measure:** Dollars per lb. **Time Period Covered:** latest day.

CHICKEN BACKS AND NECKS

Source: *Lancaster Farming.* **Price Frequency:** weekly. **Effective Market(s):** Northeast. **Units of Measure:** cents per lb. **Type of Price:** negotiated. **Time Period Covered:** latest week.

Source: *Meat Price Report.* **Price Frequency:** weekly. **Units of Measure:** cents per lb. **Type of Price:** price paid to wholesaler. **Time Period Covered:** latest week.

Source: *Urner Barry's Price-Current.* **Price Frequency:** daily. **Units of Measure:** Dollars per lb. **Type of Price:** resale by first receivers. **Time Period Covered:** latest day.

CHICKEN BACKS AND NECKS: PRE-PACKAGED

Source: *Urner Barry's Price-Current.* **Price Frequency:** daily. **Effective Market(s):** New York. **Units of Measure:** Dollars per lb. **Type of Price:** price delivered warehouse. **Time Period Covered:** latest day.

CHICKEN BACKS AND NECKS: YELLOW

Source: *Urner Barry's Price-Current.* **Price Frequency:** daily. **Effective Market(s):** Northeast. **Units of Measure:** Dollars per lb. **Time Period Covered:** latest day.

CHICKEN BREAST PORTION: QUARTERED

Source: *Weekly Insiders Poultry Report.* **Price Frequency:** weekly. **Effective Market(s):** New York. **Units of Measure:** cents per lb. **Type of Price:** retail. **Time Period Covered:** latest week, week ago, year ago.

CHICKEN BREAST QUARTERS: PRE-PACKAGED

Source: *Urner Barry's Price-Current.* **Price Frequency:** daily. **Effective Market(s):** New York. **Units of Measure:** Dollars per lb. **Type of Price:** price delivered warehouse. **Time Period Covered:** latest day.

CHICKEN BREAST TENDERS: FRESH LINE RUN

Source: *Urner Barry's Price-Current.* **Price Frequency:** daily. **Effective Market(s):** Midwestern area, Northeastern area. **Units of Measure:** Dollars per lb. **Type of Price:** price delivered warehouse. **Time Period Covered:** latest day.

Source: *Urner Barry's Price-Current, West Coast Edition.* **Price Frequency:** semiweekly. **Effective Market(s):** Midwestern area, Northeastern area, Western area. **Units of Measure:** Dollars per lb. **Type of Price:** trucklot. **Time Period Covered:** latest day.

CHICKEN BREASTS

Source: *Livestock and Poultry Update.* **Price Frequency:** monthly. **Units of Measure:** cents per lb. **Type of Price:** retail. **Time Period Covered:** latest 3 months, year ago.

Source: *Urner Barry's Price-Current.* **Price Frequency:** daily. **Effective Market(s):** Midwestern area, Northeastern area. **Units of Measure:** Dollars per lb. **Type of Price:** price delivered warehouse. **Time Period Covered:** latest day.

Source: *Urner Barry's Price-Current.* **Price Frequency:** daily. **Units of Measure:** Dollars per lb. **Type of Price:** resale by first receivers. **Time Period Covered:** latest day.

Source: *Urner Barry's Price-Current, West Coast Edition.* **Price Frequency:** semiweekly. **Effective Market(s):** Midwestern area, Northeastern area, Western area. **Units of Measure:** Dollars per lb. **Type of Price:** trucklot. **Time Period Covered:** latest day.

Source: *Weekly Insiders Poultry Report.* **Price Frequency:** weekly. **Effective Market(s):** New York. **Units of Measure:** cents per lb. **Type of Price:** retail. **Time Period Covered:** latest week, week ago, year ago.

CHICKEN BREASTS: BONELESS

Source: *HRI-Buyers Guide.* **Price Frequency:** weekly. **Effective Market(s):** Northeastern area. **Units of Measure:** Dollars per lb. **Type of Price:** price paid by dining places & institutions. **Time Period Covered:** latest week.

Source: *Livestock and Poultry Update.* **Price Frequency:** monthly. **Effective Market(s):** Northeast. **Units of Measure:** cents per lb. **Type of Price:** wholesale. **Time Period Covered:** latest 3 months, year ago.

CHICKEN BREASTS: BONELESS, FRESH, TRIM MEAT

Source: *Urner Barry's Price-Current.* **Price Frequency:** daily. **Effective Market(s):** Midwestern area, Northeastern area. **Units of Measure:** Dollars per lb. **Type of Price:** price delivered warehouse. **Time Period Covered:** latest day.

Source: *Urner Barry's Price-Current, West Coast Edition.* **Price Frequency:** semiweekly. **Effective Market(s):** Midwestern area, Northeastern area, Western area. **Units of Measure:** Dollars per lb. **Type of Price:** trucklot. **Time Period Covered:** latest day.

CHICKEN BREASTS: BONELESS, PRE-PACKAGED

Source: *Urner Barry's Price-Current.* **Price Frequency:** daily. **Effective Market(s):** New York. **Units of Measure:** Dollars per lb. **Type of Price:** price delivered warehouse. **Time Period Covered:** latest day.

CHICKEN BREASTS: FRESH

Source: *HRI-Buyers Guide.* **Price Frequency:** weekly. **Effective Market(s):** Northeastern area. **Units of Measure:** Dollars per lb. **Type of Price:** price paid by dining places & institutions. **Time Period Covered:** latest week.

CHICKEN BREASTS: FRESH LINE RUN

Source: *Urner Barry's Price-Current, West Coast Edition.* **Price Frequency:** semiweekly. **Effective Market(s):** Midwestern area, Northeastern area, Western area. **Units of Measure:** Dollars per lb. **Type of Price:** trucklot. **Time Period Covered:** latest day.

CHICKEN BREASTS: FRONT HALF

Source: *Monthly Price Review.* **Price Frequency:** daily. **Effective Market(s):** Northeast. **Units of Measure:** Dollars per lb. **Type of Price:** spot. **Time Period Covered:** latest month.

Source: *Urner Barry's Price-Current.* **Price Frequency:** daily. **Effective Market(s):** Midwestern area, Northeastern area. **Units of Measure:** Dollars per lb. **Type of Price:** price delivered warehouse. **Time Period Covered:** latest day.

Source: *Urner Barry's Price-Current, West Coast Edition.* **Price Frequency:** semiweekly. **Effective Market(s):** Midwestern area, Northeastern area, Western area. **Units of Measure:** Dollars per lb. **Type of Price:** trucklot. **Time Period Covered:** latest day.

CHICKEN BREASTS: LINE RUN

Source: *Monthly Price Review.* **Price Frequency:** daily. **Effective Market(s):** Northeast. **Units of Measure:** Dollars per lb. **Type of Price:** spot. **Time Period Covered:** latest month.

Source: *Urner Barry's Price-Current.* **Price Frequency:** daily. **Effective Market(s):** Midwestern area, Northeastern area. **Units of Measure:** Dollars per lb. **Type of Price:** price delivered warehouse. **Time Period Covered:** latest day.

CHICKEN BREASTS: LINE RUN, YELLOW

Source: *Urner Barry's Price-Current.* **Price Frequency:** daily. **Effective Market(s):** Northeast. **Units of Measure:** Dollars per lb. **Time Period Covered:** latest day.

CHICKEN BREASTS: PRE-PACKAGED

Source: *Urner Barry's Price-Current.* **Price Frequency:** daily. **Effective Market(s):** New York. **Units of Measure:** Dollars per lb. **Type of Price:** price delivered warehouse. **Time Period Covered:** latest day.

CHICKEN BREASTS: RIBS ON

Source: *Livestock and Poultry Update.* **Price Frequency:** monthly. **Effective Market(s):** Northeast. **Units of Measure:** cents per lb. **Type of Price:** wholesale. **Time Period Covered:** latest 3 months, year ago.

CHICKEN BREASTS: SKIN ON, BONE IN, FRESH

Source: *Meat Price Report.* **Price Frequency:** weekly. **Units of Measure:** cents per lb. **Type of Price:** price paid to wholesaler. **Time Period Covered:** latest week.

CHICKEN BREASTS: SKIN ON, BONELESS

Source: *Urner Barry's Price-Current.* **Price Frequency:** daily. **Units of Measure:** Dollars per lb. **Type of Price:** resale by first receivers. **Time Period Covered:** latest day.

CHICKEN BREASTS: SKIN ON, BONELESS, FRESH

Source: *Meat Price Report.* **Price Frequency:** weekly. **Units of Measure:** cents per lb. **Type of Price:** price paid to wholesaler. **Time Period Covered:** latest week.

CHICKEN BREASTS: SKINLESS, BONELESS

Source: *Lancaster Farming.* **Price Frequency:** weekly. **Effective Market(s):** Northeast. **Units of Measure:** cents per lb. **Type of Price:** negotiated. **Time Period Covered:** latest week.

Source: *Monthly Price Review.* **Price Frequency:** daily. **Effective Market(s):** Northeast. **Units of Measure:** Dollars per lb. **Type of Price:** spot. **Time Period Covered:** latest month.

Source: *Urner Barry's Price-Current.* **Price Frequency:** daily. **Units of Measure:** Dollars per lb. **Type of Price:** resale by first receivers. **Time Period Covered:** latest day.

Source: *Weekly Statistical Fishery Report.* **Price Frequency:** weekly. **Effective Market(s):** New York. **Units of Measure:** Dollars per lb. **Time Period Covered:** latest day.

CHICKEN BREASTS: SKINLESS, BONELESS, FRESH

Source: *Meat Price Report.* **Price Frequency:** weekly. **Units of Measure:** cents per lb. **Type of Price:** price paid to wholesaler. **Time Period Covered:** latest week.

Source: *Urner Barry's Price-Current.* **Price Frequency:** daily. **Effective Market(s):** Midwestern area, Northeastern area. **Units of Measure:** Dollars per lb. **Type of Price:** price delivered warehouse. **Time Period Covered:** latest day.

Source: *Urner Barry's Price-Current, West Coast Edition.* **Price Frequency:** semiweekly. **Effective Market(s):** Midwestern area, Northeastern area, Western area. **Units of Measure:** Dollars per lb. **Type of Price:** trucklot. **Time Period Covered:** latest day.

CHICKEN BREASTS: SKINLESS, BONELESS, YELLOW

Source: *Urner Barry's Price-Current.* **Price Frequency:** daily. **Effective Market(s):** Northeast. **Units of Measure:** Dollars per lb. **Time Period Covered:** latest day.

CHICKEN BREASTS: SKINNLESS, RIBS ON

Source: *Lancaster Farming.* **Price Frequency:** weekly. **Effective Market(s):** Northeast. **Units of Measure:** cents per lb. **Type of Price:** negotiated. **Time Period Covered:** latest week.

CHICKEN BREASTS: YELLOW

Source: *Monthly Price Review.* **Price Frequency:** daily. **Effective Market(s):** Northeast. **Units of Measure:** Dollars per lb. **Type of Price:** spot. **Time Period Covered:** latest month.

Source: *Urner Barry's Price-Current.* **Price Frequency:** daily. **Effective Market(s):** Northeast. **Units of Measure:** Dollars per lb. **Time Period Covered:** latest day.

CHICKEN BREASTS: YELLOW, SKINLESS, BONELESS

Source: *Monthly Price Review.* **Price Frequency:** daily. **Effective Market(s):** Northeast. **Units of Measure:** Dollars per lb. **Type of Price:** spot. **Time Period Covered:** latest month.

CHICKEN CUTLETS

Source: *Weekly Insiders Poultry Report.* **Price Frequency:** weekly. **Effective Market(s):** New York. **Units of Measure:** cents per lb. **Type of Price:** retail. **Time Period Covered:** latest week, week ago, year ago.

CHICKEN DRUMS

Source: *Weekly Insiders Poultry Report.* **Price Frequency:** weekly. **Effective Market(s):** New York. **Units of Measure:** cents per lb. **Type of Price:** retail. **Time Period Covered:** latest week, week ago, year ago.

CHICKEN DRUMSTICKS

Source: *Urner Barry's Price-Current.* **Price Frequency:** daily. **Effective Market(s):** Midwestern area, Northeastern area. **Units of Measure:** Dollars per lb. **Type of Price:** price delivered warehouse. **Time Period Covered:** latest day.

Source: *Urner Barry's Price-Current.* **Price Frequency:** daily. **Units of Measure:** Dollars per lb. **Type of Price:** resale by first receivers. **Time Period Covered:** latest day.

Source: *Urner Barry's Price-Current, West Coast Edition.* **Price Frequency:** semiweekly. **Effective Market(s):** Midwestern area, Northeastern area, Western Area. **Units of Measure:** Dollars per lb. **Type of Price:** trucklot. **Time Period Covered:** latest day.

CHICKEN DRUMSTICKS: PRE-PACKAGED

Source: *Urner Barry's Price-Current.* **Price Frequency:** daily. **Effective Market(s):** New York. **Units of Measure:** Dollars per lb. **Type of Price:** price delivered warehouse. **Time Period Covered:** latest day.

CHICKEN DRUMSTICKS: YELLOW

Source: *Urner Barry's Price-Current.* **Price Frequency:** daily. **Effective Market(s):** Northeast. **Units of Measure:** Dollars per lb. **Time Period Covered:** latest day.

CHICKEN GIZZARDS

Source: *Lancaster Farming.* **Price Frequency:** weekly. **Effective Market(s):** Northeast. **Units of Measure:** cents per lb. **Type of Price:** negotiated. **Time Period Covered:** latest week.

Source: *Urner Barry's Price-Current.* **Price Frequency:** daily. **Units of Measure:** Dollars per lb. **Type of Price:** resale by first receivers. **Time Period Covered:** latest day.

CHICKEN GIZZARDS AND HEARTS: YELLOW

Source: *Urner Barry's Price-Current.* **Price Frequency:** daily. **Effective Market(s):** Northeast. **Units of Measure:** Dollars per lb. **Time Period Covered:** latest day.

CHICKEN GIZZARDS AND HEARTS: PRE-PACKAGED

Source: *Urner Barry's Price-Current.* **Price Frequency:** daily. **Effective Market(s):** New York. **Units of Measure:** Dollars per lb. **Type of Price:** price delivered warehouse. **Time Period Covered:** latest day.

CHICKEN HEARTS

Source: *Urner Barry's Price-Current.* **Price Frequency:** daily. **Units of Measure:** Dollars per lb. **Type of Price:** resale by first receivers. **Time Period Covered:** latest day.

CHICKEN KIEVS

Source: *Meat Price Report.* **Price Frequency:** weekly. **Units of Measure:** cents paid for each. **Type of Price:** price paid to wholesaler. **Time Period Covered:** weekly.

CHICKEN LEG PORTION: QUARTERED

Source: *Weekly Insiders Poultry Report.* **Price Frequency:** weekly. **Effective Market(s):** New York. **Units of Measure:** cents per lb. **Type of Price:** retail. **Time Period Covered:** latest week, week ago, year ago.

CHICKEN LEG QUARTERS

Source: *Lancaster Farming.* **Price Frequency:** weekly. **Effective Market(s):** Northeast. **Units of Measure:** cents per lb. **Type of Price:** negotiated. **Time Period Covered:** latest week.

Source: *Livestock and Poultry Update.* **Price Frequency:** monthly. **Effective Market(s):** Northeast. **Units of Measure:** cents per lb. **Type of Price:** wholesale. **Time Period Covered:** latest 3 months, year ago.

Source: *Monthly Price Review.* **Price Frequency:** daily. **Effective Market(s):** Northeast. **Units of Measure:** Dollars per lb. **Type of Price:** spot. **Time Period Covered:** latest month.

Source: *Urner Barry's Price-Current.* **Price Frequency:** daily. **Units of Measure:** Dollars per lb. **Type of Price:** resale by first receivers. **Time Period Covered:** latest day.

Source: *Urner Barry's Price-Current.* **Price Frequency:** daily. **Effective Market(s):** Midwestern area, Northeastern area. **Units of Measure:** Dollars per lb. **Type of Price:** price delivered warehouse. **Time Period Covered:** latest day.

Source: *Urner Barry's Price-Current, West Coast Edition.* **Price Frequency:** semiweekly. **Effective Market(s):** Midwestern area, Northeastern area, Western area. **Units of Measure:** Dollars per lb. **Type of Price:** trucklot. **Time Period Covered:** latest day.

CHICKEN LEG QUARTERS: PRE-PACKAGED

Source: *Urner Barry's Price-Current.* **Price Frequency:** daily. **Effective Market(s):** New York. **Units of Measure:** Dollars per lb. **Type of Price:** price delivered warehouse. **Time Period Covered:** latest day.

CHICKEN LEG QUARTERS: YELLOW

Source: *Monthly Price Review.* **Price Frequency:** daily. **Effective Market(s):** Northeast. **Units of Measure:** Dollars per lb. **Type of Price:** spot. **Time Period Covered:** latest month.

Source: *Urner Barry's Price-Current.* **Price Frequency:** daily. **Effective Market(s):** Northeast. **Units of Measure:** Dollars per lb. **Time Period Covered:** latest day.

CHICKEN LEGS

Source: *HRI-Buyers Guide.* **Price Frequency:** weekly. **Effective Market(s):** Northeastern area. **Units of Measure:** Dollars per lb. **Type of Price:** price paid by dining places & institutions. **Time Period Covered:** latest week.

Source: *Lancaster Farming.* **Price Frequency:** weekly. **Effective Market(s):** Northeast. **Units of Measure:** cents per lb. **Type of Price:** negotiated. **Time Period Covered:** latest week.

Source: *Livestock and Poultry Update.* **Price Frequency:** monthly. **Effective Market(s):** Northeast. **Units of Measure:** cents per lb. **Type of Price:** wholesale. **Time Period Covered:** latest 3 months, year ago.

Source: *Meat Price Report.* **Price Frequency:** weekly. **Units of Measure:** cents per lb. **Type of Price:** price paid to wholesaler. **Time Period Covered:** latest week.

Source: *Urner Barry's Price-Current.* **Price Frequency:** daily. **Effective Market(s):** Midwestern area, Northeastern area. **Units of Measure:** Dollars per lb. **Type of Price:** price delivered warehouse. **Time Period Covered:** latest day.

Source: *Urner Barry's Price-Current.* **Price Frequency:** daily. **Units of Measure:** Dollars per lb. **Type of Price:** resale by first receivers. **Time Period Covered:** latest day.

Source: *Urner Barry's Price-Current, West Coast Edition.* **Price Frequency:** semiweekly. **Effective Market(s):** Midwestern area, Northeastern area, Western area. **Units of Measure:** Dollars per lb. **Type of Price:** truckload. **Time Period Covered:** latest day.

Source: *Weekly Insiders Poultry Report.* **Price Frequency:** weekly. **Effective Market(s):** New York. **Units of Measure:** cents per lb. **Type of Price:** retail. **Time Period Covered:** latest week, week ago, year ago.

CHICKEN LEGS: PRE-PACKAGED

Source: *Urner Barry's Price-Current.* **Price Frequency:** daily. **Effective Market(s):** New York. **Units of Measure:** Dollars per lb. **Type of Price:** price delivered warehouse. **Time Period Covered:** latest day.

CHICKEN LEGS: WHOLE

Source: *Monthly Price Review.* **Price Frequency:** daily. **Effective Market(s):** Northeast. **Units of Measure:** Dollars per lb. **Type of Price:** spot. **Time Period Covered:** latest month.

CHICKEN LEGS: YELLOW

Source: *Monthly Price Review.* **Price Frequency:** daily. **Effective Market(s):** Northeast. **Units of Measure:** Dollars per lb. **Type of Price:** spot. **Time Period Covered:** latest month.

Source: *Urner Barry's Price-Current.* **Price Frequency:** daily. **Effective Market(s):** Northeast. **Units of Measure:** Dollars per lb. **Time Period Covered:** latest day.

CHICKEN LIVERS

Source: *HRI-Buyers Guide.* **Price Frequency:** weekly. **Effective Market(s):** Northeastern area. **Units of Measure:** Dollars per lb. **Type of Price:** price paid by dining places & institutions. **Time Period Covered:** latest week.

Source: *Lancaster Farming.* **Price Frequency:** weekly. **Effective Market(s):** Northeast. **Units of Measure:** cents per lb. **Type of Price:** negotiated. **Time Period Covered:** latest week.

Source: *Meat Price Report.* **Price Frequency:** weekly. **Units of Measure:** cents per lb. **Type of Price:** price paid to wholesaler. **Time Period Covered:** latest week.

Source: *Urner Barry's Price-Current.* **Price Frequency:** daily. **Units of Measure:** Dollars per lb. **Type of Price:** resale by first receivers. **Time Period Covered:** latest day.

CHICKEN LIVERS: PRE-PACKAGED

Source: *Urner Barry's Price-Current.* **Price Frequency:** daily. **Effective Market(s):** New York. **Units of Measure:** Dollars per lb. **Type of Price:** price delivered warehouse. **Time Period Covered:** latest day.

CHICKEN LIVERS: YELLOW

Source: *Urner Barry's Price-Current.* **Price Frequency:** daily. **Effective Market(s):** Northeast. **Units of Measure:** Dollars per lb. **Time Period Covered:** latest day.

CHICKEN MEAT: COMMINUTED, FRESH

Source: *Urner Barry's Price-Current, West Coast Edition.* **Price Frequency:** semiweekly. **Effective Market(s):** West Coast. **Units of Measure:** Dollars per lb. **Time Period Covered:** latest day.

CHICKEN MEAT: COMMINUTED, FROZEN

Source: *Urner Barry's Price-Current, West Coast Edition.* **Price Frequency:** semiweekly. **Effective Market(s):** West Coast. **Units of Measure:** Dollars per lb. **Time Period Covered:** latest day.

CHICKEN MEAT: COOKED AND FROZEN

Source: *HRI-Buyers Guide.* **Price Frequency:** weekly. **Effective Market(s):** Northeastern area. **Units of Measure:** Dollars per lb. **Type of Price:** price paid by dining places & institutions. **Time Period Covered:** latest week.

CHICKEN MEAT: NATURAL PROPORTION

Source: *HRI-Buyers Guide.* **Price Frequency:** weekly. **Effective Market(s):** Northeastern area. **Units of Measure:** Dollars per lb. **Type of Price:** price paid by dining places & institutions. **Time Period Covered:** latest week.

CHICKEN MEAT: WHITE

Source: *HRI-Buyers Guide.* **Price Frequency:** weekly. **Effective Market(s):** Northeastern area. **Units of Measure:** Dollars per lb. **Type of Price:** price paid by dining places & institutions. **Time Period Covered:** latest week.

CHICKEN MEAT: WHITE AND DARK, PULLED, COOKED

Source: *Meat Price Report.* **Price Frequency:** weekly. **Units of Measure:** cents per lb. **Type of Price:** price paid to wholesaler. **Time Period Covered:** latest week.

CHICKEN PARTS

Source: *Lancaster Farming.* **Price Frequency:** weekly. **Effective Market(s):** Northeast. **Units of Measure:** cents per lb. **Type of Price:** negotiated. **Time Period Covered:** latest week.

CHICKEN THIGHS

Source: *Urner Barry's Price-Current.* **Price Frequency:** daily. **Effective Market(s):** Midwestern area, Northeastern area. **Units of Measure:** Dollars per lb. **Type of Price:** price delivered warehouse. **Time Period Covered:** latest day.

Source: *Urner Barry's Price-Current.* **Price Frequency:** daily. **Units of Measure:** Dollars per lb. **Type of Price:** resale by first receivers. **Time Period Covered:** latest day.

Source: *Urner Barry's Price-Current, West Coast Edition.* **Price Frequency:** semiweekly. **Effective Market(s):** Midwestern area, Northeastern area, Western area. **Units of Measure:** Dollars per lb. **Type of Price:** trucklot. **Time Period Covered:** latest day.

Source: *Weekly Insiders Poultry Report.* **Price Frequency:** weekly. **Effective Market(s):** New York. **Units of Measure:** cents per lb. **Type of Price:** retail. **Time Period Covered:** latest week, week ago, year ago.

CHICKEN THIGHS: BRAZILIAN

Source: *Prices of Selected Asia/Pacific Products.* **Price Frequency:** monthly. **Effective Market(s):** Tokyo. **Units of Measure:** Japanese yen per kilogram. **Type of Price:** wholesale high, wholesale low. **Time Period Covered:** latest month.

CHICKEN THIGHS: PRE-PACKAGED

Source: *Urner Barry's Price-Current.* **Price Frequency:** daily. **Effective Market(s):** New York. **Units of Measure:** Dollars per lb. **Type of Price:** price delivered warehouse. **Time Period Covered:** latest day.

CHICKEN THIGHS: SKINLESS, BONELESS

Source: *Urner Barry's Price-Current.* **Price Frequency:** daily. **Units of Measure:** Dollars per lb. **Type of Price:** resale by first recievers. **Time Period Covered:** latest day.

CHICKEN THIGHS: SKINLESS, BONELESS, FRESH, SPECIAL TRIM

Source: *Urner Barry's Price-Current.* **Price Frequency:** daily. **Effective Market(s):** Midwestern area, Northeastern area. **Units of Measure:** Dollars per lb. **Type of Price:** price delivered warehouse. **Time Period Covered:** latest day.

CHICKEN THIGHS: SKINLESS, BONELESS, SPECIAL TRIM

Source: *Urner Barry's Price-Current, West Coast Edition.* **Price Frequency:** semiweekly. **Effective Market(s):** Midwestern area, Northeastern area, Western area. **Units of Measure:** Dollars per lb. **Type of Price:** trucklot. **Time Period Covered:** latest day.

CHICKEN THIGHS: THAI

Source: *Prices of Selected Asia/Pacific Products.* **Price Frequency:** monthly. **Effective Market(s):** Tokyo. **Units of Measure:** Japanese yen per kilogram. **Type of Price:** wholesale high, wholesale low. **Time Period Covered:** latest month.

CHICKEN THIGHS: UNITED STATES

Source: *Prices of Selected Asia/Pacific Products.* **Price Frequency:** monthly. **Effective Market(s):** Tokyo. **Units of Measure:** Japanese yen per kilogram. **Type of Price:** wholesale high, wholesale low. **Time Period Covered:** latest month.

CHICKEN THIGHS: YELLOW

Source: *Urner Barry's Price-Current.* **Price Frequency:** daily. **Effective Market(s):** Northeast. **Units of Measure:** Dollars per lb. **Time Period Covered:** latest day.

CHICKEN WINGS

Source: *HRI-Buyers Guide.* **Price Frequency:** weekly. **Effective Market(s):** Northeastern area. **Units of Measure:** Dollars per lb. **Type of Price:** price paid by dining places & institutions. **Time Period Covered:** latest week.

Source: *Lancaster Farming.* **Price Frequency:** weekly. **Effective Market(s):** Northeast. **Units of Measure:** cents per lb. **Type of Price:** negotiated. **Time Period Covered:** latest week.

Source: *Meat Price Report.* **Price Frequency:** weekly. **Units of Measure:** cents per lb. **Type of Price:** price paid to wholesaler. **Time Period Covered:** latest week.

Source: *Monthly Price Review.* **Price Frequency:** daily. **Effective Market(s):** Northeast. **Units of Measure:** Dollars per lb. **Type of Price:** spot. **Time Period Covered:** latest month.

Source: *Urner Barry's Price-Current.* **Price Frequency:** daily. **Effective Market(s):** Midwestern area, Northeastern area. **Units of Measure:** Dollars per lb. **Type of Price:** price delivered warehouse. **Time Period Covered:** latest day.

Source: *Urner Barry's Price-Current.* **Price Frequency:** daily. **Units of Measure:** Dollars per lb. **Type of Price:** resale by first receivers. **Time Period Covered:** latest day.

Source: *Urner Barry's Price-Current, West Coast Edition.* **Price Frequency:** semiweekly. **Effective Market(s):** Midwestern area, Northeastern area, Western area. **Units of Measure:** Dollars per lb. **Type of Price:** trucklot. **Time Period Covered:** latest day.

Source: *Weekly Insiders Poultry Report.* **Price Frequency:** weekly. **Effective Market(s):** New York. **Units of Measure:** cents per lb. **Type of Price:** retail. **Time Period Covered:** latest week, week ago, year ago.

CHICKEN WINGS: PRE-PACKAGED

Source: *Urner Barry's Price-Current.* **Price Frequency:** daily. **Effective Market(s):** New York. **Units of Measure:** Dollars per lb. **Type of Price:** price delivered warehouse. **Time Period Covered:** latest day.

CHICKEN WINGS: YELLOW

Source: *Monthly Price Review.* **Price Frequency:** daily. **Effective Market(s):** Northeast. **Units of Measure:** Dollars per lb. **Type of Price:** spot. **Time Period Covered:** latest month.

Source: *Urner Barry's Price-Current.* **Price Frequency:** daily. **Effective Market(s):** Northeast. **Units of Measure:** Dollars per lb. **Time Period Covered:** latest day.

CHICKENS

see also Broiler-Fryers, Broilers, Chicks, Fowl, Fryers, Hens, Roasters.

Source: *Agricultural Prices Annual Summary.* **Price Frequency:** annually. **Effective Market(s):** 50 domestic markets, United States. **Units of Measure:** Dollars per lb. **Type of Price:** average price received by farmer. **Time Period Covered:** latest 2 years, for US latest 6 years.

Source: *HRI-Buyers Guide.* **Price Frequency:** weekly. **Effective Market(s):** Northeastern area. **Units of Measure:** Dollars per lb. **Type of Price:** price paid by dining places & institutions. **Time Period Covered:** latest week.

Source: *Livestock and Poultry Situation and Outlook Report.* **Price Frequency:** monthly, annually. **Units of Measure:** cents per lb. **Type of Price:** farm, retail, wholesale average. **Time Period Covered:** latest 3 years.

Source: *Weekly Insiders Poultry Report.* **Price Frequency:** weekly. **Effective Market(s):** New York. **Units of Measure:** cents per lb. **Time Period Covered:** latest 3 years.

CHICKENS: CALIFORNIA GROWN, ICED

Source: *Urner Barry's Price-Current, West Coast Edition.* **Price Frequency:** semiweekly. **Effective Market(s):** Southern California. **Units of Measure:** Dollars per lb. **Type of Price:** trucklot. **Time Period Covered:** latest day.

CHICKENS: CANNER PACK, TRIM OR BETTER

Source: *Urner Barry's Price-Current.* **Price Frequency:** daily. **Effective Market(s):** Midwestern area, Northeastern area. **Units of Measure:** Dollars per lb. **Type of Price:** price delivered warehouse. **Time Period Covered:** latest day, latest 5 day average.

CHICKENS: CUT-UP, EIGHT PIECE CUT

Source: *Urner Barry's Price-Current.* **Price Frequency:** daily. **Units of Measure:** Dollars per lb. **Time Period Covered:** latest day.

CHICKENS: CUT-UP, NINE PIECE CUT

Source: *Urner Barry's Price-Current.* **Price Frequency:** daily. **Units of Measure:** Dollars per lb. **Time Period Covered:** latest day.

CHICKENS: CUT-UP, PRE-PACKAGED

Source: *Urner Barry's Price-Current.* **Price Frequency:** daily. **Effective Market(s):** New York. **Units of Measure:** Dollars per lb. **Type of Price:** price delivered warehouse. **Time Period Covered:** latest day.

CHICKENS: FROZEN

Source: *Statistical Bulletin of the South Pacific: Retail Price Indexes.* **Price Frequency:** annually. **Effective Market(s):** 18 South Pacific markets. **Units of Measure:** Australian dollars per kilogram. **Type of Price:** retail. **Time Period Covered:** latest year.

CHICKENS: GRADE A

Source: *Monthly Price Review.* **Price Frequency:** daily. **Effective Market(s):** Midwest, Northeast, West Coast. **Units of Measure:** Dollars per lb. **Type of Price:** spot. **Time Period Covered:** latest month.

Source: *Urner Barry's Price-Current.* **Price Frequency:** daily. **Effective Market(s):** Midwestern area, Northeastern area. **Units of Measure:** Dollars per lb. **Type of Price:** price delivered warehouse. **Time Period Covered:** latest day, latest 5 day average.

Source: *Urner Barry's Price-Current.* **Price Frequency:** daily. **Units of Measure:** Dollars per lb. **Type of Price:** resale by first receivers. **Time Period Covered:** latest day.

CHICKENS: GRADE A, FRESH, EVISERATED

Source: *Farmers Weekly.* **Price Frequency:** weekly. **Effective Market(s):** Smithfield (Great Britain). **Units of Measure:** British pence per lb. **Type of Price:** wholesale top, wholesale bottom. **Time Period Covered:** latest week.

CHICKENS: GRADE A, FRESH, UNEVISERATED

Source: *Farmers Weekly.* **Price Frequency:** weekly. **Effective Market(s):** Smithfield (Great Britain). **Units of Measure:** British pence per lb. **Type of Price:** wholesale top, wholesale bottom. **Time Period Covered:** latest week.

CHICKENS: GRADE A, ICED

Source: *Urner Barry's Price-Current, West Coast Edition.* **Price Frequency:** semiweekly. **Effective Market(s):** Southern California. **Units of Measure:** Dollars per lb. **Type of Price:** trucklot. **Time Period Covered:** latest day.

CHICKENS: GRADE A, ICED, SOUTHERN

Source: *Weekly Insiders Poultry Report.* **Price Frequency:** annually. **Effective Market(s):** New York. **Units of Measure:** cents per lb. **Time Period Covered:** latest 4 years.

CHICKENS: GRADE A, WHOLE

Source: *Weekly Statistical Fishery Report.* **Price Frequency:** weekly. **Effective Market(s):** New York. **Units of Measure:** Dollars per lb. **Time Period Covered:** latest day.

CHICKENS: GRADE A, YELLOW

Source: *Urner Barry's Price-Current.* **Price Frequency:** daily. **Effective Market(s):** Northeast. **Units of Measure:** Dollars per lb. **Type of Price:** prices delivered warehouse. **Time Period Covered:** latest day, latest 5 day average.

CHICKENS: GRADE A, YOUNG

Source: *Weekly Insiders Poultry Report.* **Price Frequency:** monthly, annually. **Effective Market(s):** Northeast. **Units of Measure:** cents per lb. **Type of Price:** average. **Time Period Covered:** latest 3 years.

CHICKENS: ICED

Source: *Weekly Insiders Poultry Report.* **Price Frequency:** annually. **Units of Measure:** cents per lb. **Type of Price:** wholesale. **Time Period Covered:** latest 3 years.

CHICKENS: MATURE

Source: *Agricultural Outlook.* **Price Frequency:** annually. **Effective Market(s):** United States. **Units of Measure:** cents per lb. **Type of Price:** primary market. **Time Period Covered:** latest 2 years.

CHICKENS: PLANT A

Source: *Urner Barry's Price-Current.* **Price Frequency:** daily. **Units of Measure:** Dollars per lb. **Type of Price:** resale by first receivers. **Time Period Covered:** latest day.

CHICKENS: PLANT A, ICED, SOUTHERN

Source: *Weekly Insiders Poultry Report.* **Price Frequency:** annually. **Effective Market(s):** New York. **Units of Measure:** cents per lb. **Time Period Covered:** latest 4 years.

CHICKENS: PLANT GRADE

Source: *Urner Barry's Price-Current.* **Price Frequency:** daily. **Effective Market(s):** Midwestern area, Northeastern area. **Units of Measure:** Dollars per lb. **Type of Price:** price delivered warehouse. **Time Period Covered:** latest day, latest 5 day average.

CHICKENS: PROCESSED, FRESH

Source: *Poultry Market Statistics.* **Price Frequency:** monthly, annually. **Effective Market(s):** Atlantic states coastal region. **Units of Measure:** cents per lb. **Type of Price:** average. **Time Period Covered:** latest year.

CHICKENS: PROCESSED, FROZEN

Source: *Poultry Market Statistics.* **Price Frequency:** monthly, annually. **Effective Market(s):** Atlantic states coastal region. **Units of Measure:** cents per lb. **Type of Price:** average. **Time Period Covered:** latest year.

CHICKENS: WHOLE

Source: *Porkpro Newsletter.* **Price Frequency:** weekly. **Effective Market(s):** Chicago. **Units of Measure:** Dollars per lb. **Type of Price:** retail. **Time Period Covered:** latest day, week ago, year ago.

Source: *Weekly Insiders Poultry Report.* **Price Frequency:** weekly. **Effective Market(s):** New York. **Units of Measure:** cents per lb. **Type of Price:** retail. **Time Period Covered:** latest week, week ago, year ago.

CHICKENS: WHOLE, FRESH

Source: *Livestock and Poultry Update.* **Price Frequency:** monthly. **Units of Measure:** cents per lb. **Type of Price:** retail. **Time Period Covered:** latest 3 months, year ago.

CHICKENS: WHOLE, PRE-PACKAGED, BAGGED

Source: *Urner Barry's Price-Current.* **Price Frequency:** daily. **Effective Market(s):** New York. **Units of Measure:** Dollars per lb. **Type of Price:** price delivered warehouse. **Time Period Covered:** latest day.

CHICKENS: WOGS

Source: *Urner Barry's Price-Current.* **Price Frequency:** daily. **Units of Measure:** Dollars per lb. **Time Period Covered:** latest day.

CHICKENS: YELLOW

Source: *Monthly Price Review.* **Price Frequency:** daily. **Effective Market(s):** Northeast. **Units of Measure:** Dollars per lb. **Type of Price:** spot. **Time Period Covered:** latest month.

CHICKENS: YOUNG, YELLOW

Source: *Weekly Insiders Poultry Report.* **Price Frequency:** monthly, annually. **Effective Market(s):** Northeast. **Units of Measure:** cents per lb. **Type of Price:** average. **Time Period Covered:** latest 3 years.

CHICKS: BROILER

Source: *Agricultural Prices.* **Price Frequency:** quarterly. **Effective Market(s):** United States. **Units of Measure:** Dollars per 100. **Type of Price:** paid by farmer. **Time Period Covered:** latest 2 quarters, year ago.

Source: *Agricultural Prices Annual Summary.* **Price Frequency:** quarterly. **Effective Market(s):** United States. **Units of Measure:** Dollars per 100. **Type of Price:** average price paid by farmer. **Time Period Covered:** latest 6 years.

CHICKS: EGG-TYPE

Source: *Agricultural Prices.* **Price Frequency:** quarterly. **Effective Market(s):** United States. **Units of Measure:** Dollars per 100. **Type of Price:** paid by farmer. **Time Period Covered:** latest 2 quarters, year ago.

Source: *Agricultural Prices Annual Summary.* **Price Frequency:** quarterly. **Effective Market(s):** United States. **Units of Measure:** Dollars per 100. **Type of Price:** average price paid by farmer. **Time Period Covered:** latest 6 years.

CHICORY ROOT: NATURAL

Source: *Journal of Commerce and Commercial.* **Price Frequency:** weekly in Monday issue. **Units of Measure:** Dollars per lb. **Type of Price:** spot. **Time Period Covered:** latest week.

CHILE PESOS

Source: *Barron's.* **Price Frequency:** weekly. **Effective Market(s):** New York. **Units of Measure:** Chilean pesos per United States dollar. **Type of Price:** official foreign exchange rate. **Time Period Covered:** latest 2 weeks.

Source: *New York Times.* **Price Frequency:** daily. **Effective Market(s):** New York. **Units of Measure:** Chilean pesos per United States dollars. **Type of Price:** official foreign exchange rate. **Time Period Covered:** latest 2 days.

CHILI PEPPER

see Pepper: Red.

CHILLIES: GREEN, THAI

Source: *Prices of Selected Asia/Pacific Products.* **Price Frequency:** monthly, seasonally. **Effective Market(s):** Netherlands. **Units of Measure:** Dutch guilders per kilogram. **Type of Price:** wholesale high, wholesale low. **Time Period Covered:** latest month.

CHILLIES: KENYAN

Source: *Prices of Selected Asia/Pacific Products.* **Price Frequency:** monthly, seasonally. **Effective Market(s):** United Kingdom, West Germany. **Units of Measure:** British pounds per kilogram, West German marks per kilogram. **Type of Price:** wholesale high, wholesale low. **Time Period Covered:** latest month.

CHILLIES: RED, THAI

Source: *Prices of Selected Asia/Pacific Products.* **Price Frequency:** monthly, seasonally. **Effective Market(s):** Netherlands. **Units of Measure:** Dutch guilders per kilogram. **Type of Price:** wholesale high, wholesale low. **Time Period Covered:** latest month.

CHILLIES: SMALL, CHINESE

Source: *Prices of Selected Asia/Pacific Products.* **Price Frequency:** monthly, seasonally. **Effective Market(s):** United Kingdom. **Units of Measure:** British pounds per metric ton. **Type of Price:** spot high, spot low. **Time Period Covered:** latest month.

CHILLIES: SMALL, TIENSIN

Source: *Fruit and Tropical Products.* **Price Frequency:** monthly, seasonally. **Effective Market(s):** London. **Units of Measure:** British pounds per tonne. **Type of Price:** month end. **Time Period Covered:** latest 2 years.

CHINA CLAY

see Kaolin.

CHINA YUAN

Source: *Asian Wall Street Journal.* **Price Frequency:** daily. **Effective Market(s):** China. **Units of Measure:** Chinese yuan per 8 national currencies. **Type of Price:** foreign exchange. **Time Period Covered:** latest day.

Source: *Barron's.* **Price Frequency:** weekly. **Effective Market(s):** New York. **Units of Measure:** Chinese yuan per United States dollar. **Type of Price:** foreign exchange. **Time Period Covered:** latest 2 weeks.

CHINESE WHISKEY

Source: *Colorado Beverage Analyst.* **Price Frequency:** monthly. **Effective Market(s):** Colorado. **Units of Measure:** Dollars per case. **Type of Price:** wholesale by brand. **Time Period Covered:** latest month.

CHINESE WINES

Source: *Colorado Beverage Analyst.* **Price Frequency:** monthly. **Effective Market(s):** Colorado. **Units of Measure:** Dollars per case. **Type of Price:** wholesale by brand. **Time Period Covered:** latest month.

CHISEL PLOW: DEEP TILLAGE

Source: *Agricultural Prices.* **Price Frequency:** semiannually. **Effective Market(s):** United States. **Units of Measure:** Dollars each. **Type of Price:** paid by farmer. **Time Period Covered:** latest year.

Source: *Agricultural Prices Annual Summary.* **Price Frequency:** semiannually. **Effective Market(s):** United States. **Units of Measure:** Dollars each. **Type of Price:** average price paid by farmer. **Time Period Covered:** latest 6 years.

CHITTERLINGS: FROZEN

Source: *National Provisioner.* **Price Frequency:** daily. **Effective Market(s):** Midwest River. **Units of Measure:** cents per lb. **Time Period Covered:** latest week.

CHLORAL HYDRATE: TECHNICAL

Source: *Journal of Commerce and Commercial.* **Price Frequency:** weekly in Friday issue. **Units of Measure:** Dollars per lb. **Type of Price:** spot. **Time Period Covered:** latest week.

CHLORATE: CRYSTAL

Source: *Journal of Commerce and Commercial.* **Price Frequency:** weekly in Thursday issue. **Units of Measure:** Dollars per ton. **Type of Price:** spot. **Time Period Covered:** latest week.

CHLORDONE: TECHNICAL GRADE

Source: *Journal of Commerce and Commercial.* **Price Frequency:** weekly in Thursday issue. **Units of Measure:** Dollars per lb. **Type of Price:** spot. **Time Period Covered:** latest week.

CHLORENDIC ANHYDRIDE: TECHNICAL GRADE

Source: *Chemical Marketing Reporter.* **Price Frequency:** weekly. **Effective Market(s):** New York. **Units of Measure:** Dollars per lb. **Type of Price:** spot. **Time Period Covered:** latest week.

CHLORINATED PARAFFIN: 40% CHLORINE

Source: *Chemical Marketing Reporter.* **Price Frequency:** weekly. **Effective Market(s):** New York. **Units of Measure:** Dollars per lb. **Type of Price:** spot. **Time Period Covered:** latest week.

CHLORINATED PARAFFIN: 50% CHLORINE

Source: *Chemical Marketing Reporter.* **Price Frequency:** weekly. **Effective Market(s):** New York. **Units of Measure:** Dollars per lb. **Type of Price:** spot. **Time Period Covered:** latest week.

CHLORINATED PARAFFIN: 60% CHLORINE

Source: *Chemical Marketing Reporter.* **Price Frequency:** weekly. **Effective Market(s):** New York. **Units of Measure:** Dollars per lb. **Type of Price:** spot. **Time Period Covered:** latest week.

CHLORINATED PARAFFIN: 70% CHLORINE, RESINOUS

Source: *Chemical Marketing Reporter.* **Price Frequency:** weekly. **Effective Market(s):** New York. **Units of Measure:** Dollars per lb. **Type of Price:** spot. **Time Period Covered:** latest week.

CHLORINATED RUBBER: 5, 10, 20 CENTIPOISES

Source: *Chemical Marketing Reporter.* **Price Frequency:** weekly. **Effective Market(s):** New York. **Units of Measure:** Dollars per lb. **Type of Price:** spot. **Time Period Covered:** latest week.

CHLORINATED RUBBER: 40 CENTIPOISES

Source: *Chemical Marketing Reporter.* **Price Frequency:** weekly. **Effective Market(s):** New York. **Units of Measure:** Dollars per lb. **Type of Price:** spot. **Time Period Covered:** latest week.

CHLORINATED RUBBER: 125 CENTIPOISES

Source: *Chemical Marketing Reporter.* **Price Frequency:** weekly. **Effective Market(s):** New York. **Units of Measure:** Dollars per lb. **Type of Price:** spot. **Time Period Covered:** latest week.

CHLORINATED RUBBER: 300 CENTIPOISES

Source: *Chemical Marketing Reporter.* **Price Frequency:** weekly. **Effective Market(s):** New York. **Units of Measure:** Dollars per lb. **Type of Price:** spot. **Time Period Covered:** latest week.

CHLORINE

Source: *Chemical Marketing Reporter.* **Price Frequency:** weekly. **Effective Market(s):** New York. **Units of Measure:** Dollars per ton. **Type of Price:** spot. **Time Period Covered:** latest week.

Source: *Journal of Commerce and Commercial.* **Price Frequency:** weekly in Thursday issue. **Units of Measure:** Dollars per 100 lbs. **Type of Price:** spot. **Time Period Covered:** latest week.

Source: *Purchasing.* **Price Frequency:** monthly. **Effective Market(s):** United States. **Units of Measure:** Dollars per ton. **Type of Price:** transaction. **Time Period Covered:** latest day, month ago, 6 months ago, year ago.

2-CHLORO-4-AMINOTOLUENE: TECHNICAL GRADE, LIQUID

Source: *Chemical Marketing Reporter.* **Price Frequency:** weekly. **Effective Market(s):** New York. **Units of Measure:** Dollars per lb. **Type of Price:** spot. **Time Period Covered:** latest week.

2-CHLORO-4-NITROANILINE: PASTE

Source: *Chemical Marketing Reporter.* **Price Frequency:** weekly. **Effective Market(s):** New York. **Units of Measure:** Dollars per lb. **Type of Price:** spot. **Time Period Covered:** latest week.

2-CHLORO-4-NITORANILINE: POWDERED

Source: *Chemical Marketing Reporter.* **Price Frequency:** weekly. **Effective Market(s):** New York. **Units of Measure:** Dollars per lb. **Type of Price:** spot. **Time Period Covered:** latest week.

4-CHLORO-2-NITROANILINE: PASTE

Source: *Chemical Marketing Reporter.* **Price Frequency:** weekly. **Effective Market(s):** New York. **Units of Measure:** Dollars per lb. **Type of Price:** spot. **Time Period Covered:** latest week.

4-CHLORO-2-NITROANILINE: POWDERED

Source: *Chemical Marketing Reporter.* **Price Frequency:** weekly. **Effective Market(s):** New York. **Units of Measure:** Dollars per lb. **Type of Price:** spot. **Time Period Covered:** latest week.

CHLOROACETIC ACID: MONO, HIGH PURITY, FLAKE

Source: *Chemical Marketing Reporter.* **Price Frequency:** weekly. **Effective Market(s):** New York. **Units of Measure:** Dollars per lb. **Type of Price:** spot. **Time Period Covered:** latest week.

O-CHLOROANILINE

Source: *Journal of Commerce and Commercial.* **Price Frequency:** weekly in Wednesday issue. **Units of Measure:** Dollars per lb. **Type of Price:** spot. **Time Period Covered:** latest week.

P-CHLOROANILINE

Source: *Journal of Commerce and Commercial.* **Price Frequency:** weekly in Wednesday issue. **Units of Measure:** Dollars per lb. **Type of Price:** spot. **Time Period Covered:** latest week.

P-CHLOROANILINE: FLAKE

Source: *Chemical Marketing Reporter.* **Price Frequency:** weekly. **Effective Market(s):** New York. **Units of Measure:** Dollars per lb. **Type of Price:** spot. **Time Period Covered:** latest week.

M-CHLOROANILINE: LIQUID

Source: *Journal of Commerce and Commercial.* **Price Frequency:** weekly in Wednesday issue. **Units of Measure:** Dollars per lb. **Type of Price:** spot. **Time Period Covered:** latest week.

O-CHLOROANILINE: LIQUID

Source: *Chemical Marketing Reporter.* **Price Frequency:** weekly. **Effective Market(s):** New York. **Units of Measure:** Dollars per lb. **Type of Price:** spot. **Time Period Covered:** latest week.

P-CHLOROANILINE: SOLID

Source: *Chemical Marketing Reporter.* **Price Frequency:** weekly. **Effective Market(s):** New York. **Units of Measure:** Dollars per lb. **Type of Price:** spot. **Time Period Covered:** latest week.

O-CHLOROBENZALDEHYDE

Source: *Chemical Marketing Reporter.* **Price Frequency:** weekly. **Effective Market(s):** New York. **Units of Measure:** Dollars per lb. **Type of Price:** spot. **Time Period Covered:** latest week.

P-CHLOROBENZALDEHYDE

Source: *Chemical Marketing Reporter.* **Price Frequency:** weekly. **Effective Market(s):** New York. **Units of Measure:** Dollars per lb. **Type of Price:** spot. **Time Period Covered:** latest week.

O-CHLOROBENZOIC ACID

Source: *Chemical Marketing Reporter.* **Price Frequency:** weekly. **Effective Market(s):** New York. **Units of Measure:** Dollars per lb. **Type of Price:** spot. **Time Period Covered:** latest week.

P-CHLOROBENZOIC ACID

Source: *Chemical Marketing Reporter.* **Price Frequency:** weekly. **Effective Market(s):** New York. **Units of Measure:** Dollars per lb. **Type of Price:** spot. **Time Period Covered:** latest week.

CHLOROFORM: NF

Source: *Chemical Marketing Reporter.* **Price Frequency:** weekly. **Effective Market(s):** New York. **Units of Measure:** Dollars per lb. **Type of Price:** spot. **Time Period Covered:** latest week.

CHLOROFORM: TECHNICAL GRADE

Source: *Chemical Marketing Reporter.* **Price Frequency:** weekly. **Effective Market(s):** New York. **Units of Measure:** Dollars per lb. **Type of Price:** spot. **Time Period Covered:** latest week.

O-CHLOROPHENOL

Source: *Chemical Marketing Reporter.* **Price Frequency:** weekly. **Effective Market(s):** New York. **Units of Measure:** Dollars per lb. **Type of Price:** spot. **Time Period Covered:** latest week.

P-CHLOROPHENOL

Source: *Chemical Marketing Reporter.* **Price Frequency:** weekly. **Effective Market(s):** New York. **Units of Measure:** Dollars per lb. **Type of Price:** spot. **Time Period Covered:** latest week.

CHLOROPHYLL: CONCENTRATE, WATER SOLUBLE, COPPERED, KK

Source: *Journal of Commerce and Commercial.* **Price Frequency:** weekly in Friday issue. **Units of Measure:** Dollars per kilo. **Type of Price:** spot. **Time Period Covered:** latest week.

CHLOROPICRIN: COMMERCIAL GRADE

Source: *Chemical Marketing Reporter.* **Price Frequency:** weekly. **Effective Market(s):** New York. **Units of Measure:** Dollars per lb. **Type of Price:** spot. **Time Period Covered:** latest week.

CHLOROSULFONIC ACID

Source: *Chemical Marketing Reporter.* **Price Frequency:** weekly. **Effective Market(s):** New York. **Units of Measure:** Dollars per ton. **Type of Price:** spot. **Time Period Covered:** latest week.

Source: *Journal of Commerce and Commercial.* **Price Frequency:** weekly in Thursday issue. **Units of Measure:** Dollars per lb. **Type of Price:** spot. **Time Period Covered:** latest week.

P-CHLOROTOLUENE: TECHNICAL GRADE

Source: *Chemical Marketing Reporter.* **Price Frequency:** weekly. **Effective Market(s):** New York. **Units of Measure:** Dollars per lb. **Type of Price:** spot. **Time Period Covered:** latest week.

CHLORPYRIFOS: EMULSIFIABLE CONCENTRATE

Source: *Agricultural Prices Annual Summary.* **Price Frequency:** semiannually. **Effective Market(s):** United States. **Units of Measure:** Dollars per 5 gallons. **Type of Price:** average price paid by farmer. **Time Period Covered:** latest 6 years.

CHOCOLATE LIQUOR

Source: *Commodity Year Book.* **Price Frequency:** annually. **Effective Market(s):** United States. **Units of Measure:** Dollars per metric ton. **Type of Price:** spot. **Time Period Covered:** latest 8 years.

CHOCOLATE LIQUOR: BRAZIL

Source: *World Cocoa Situation.* **Price Frequency:** monthly, annually. **Effective Market(s):** United States. **Units of Measure:** Dollars per metric ton. **Type of Price:** spot. **Time Period Covered:** latest 4 years.

CHOCOLATE LIQUOR: ECUADOR

Source: *World Cocoa Situation.* **Price Frequency:** monthly, annually. **Effective Market(s):** United States. **Units of Measure:** Dollars per metric ton. **Type of Price:** spot. **Time Period Covered:** latest 4 years.

CHOLECALCIFEROL: DRY

Source: *Chemical Marketing Reporter.* **Price Frequency:** weekly. **Effective Market(s):** New York. **Units of Measure:** Dollars per gram. **Type of Price:** spot. **Time Period Covered:** latest week.

CHOLINE BITARTRATE: CRYSTALLINE, 98% MINIMUM

Source: *Chemical Marketing Reporter.* **Price Frequency:** weekly. **Effective Market(s):** Springfield (MO). **Units of Measure:** Dollars per kilo. **Type of Price:** spot. **Time Period Covered:** latest week.

CHOLINE CHLORIDE: 60% DRY SUPPLEMENT

Source: *Chemical Marketing Reporter.* **Price Frequency:** weekly. **Effective Market(s):** New York. **Units of Measure:** Dollars per lb. **Type of Price:** spot. **Time Period Covered:** latest week.

CHOLINE CHLORIDE: FEED GRADE, 70% AQUEOUS

Source: *Chemical Marketing Reporter.* **Price Frequency:** weekly. **Effective Market(s):** East of the Rockies. **Units of Measure:** Dollars per lb. **Type of Price:** spot. **Time Period Covered:** latest week.

CHOLINE CHLORIDE: PHARMACEUTICAL

Source: *Chemical Marketing Reporter.* **Price Frequency:** weekly. **Effective Market(s):** Springfield (MO). **Units of Measure:** Dollars per kilo. **Type of Price:** spot. **Time Period Covered:** latest week.

CHOLINE DIHYDROGEN CITRATE: 98% MINIMUM

Source: *Chemical Marketing Reporter.* **Price Frequency:** weekly. **Effective Market(s):** Springfield (MO). **Units of Measure:** Dollars per kilo. **Type of Price:** spot. **Time Period Covered:** latest week.

CHROMATE

Source: *Journal of Commerce and Commercial.* **Price Frequency:** weekly in Thursday issue. **Units of Measure:** Dollars per lb. **Type of Price:** spot. **Time Period Covered:** latest week.

CHROME GREEN

Source: *Journal of Commerce and Commercial.* **Price Frequency:** weekly in Wednesday issue. **Units of Measure:** Dollars per lb. **Type of Price:** spot. **Time Period Covered:** latest week.

CHROME GREEN: EXTRA DEEP, CHEMICALLY PURE

Source: *Chemical Marketing Reporter.* **Price Frequency:** weekly. **Effective Market(s):** East of the Rockies. **Units of Measure:** Dollars per lb. **Type of Price:** spot. **Time Period Covered:** latest week.

CHROME GREEN: EXTRA LIGHT, CHEMICALLY PURE

Source: *Chemical Marketing Reporter.* **Price Frequency:** weekly. **Effective Market(s):** East of the Rockies. **Units of Measure:** Dollars per lb. **Type of Price:** spot. **Time Period Covered:** latest week.

CHROME GREEN: LIGHT

Source: *Chemical Marketing Reporter.* **Price Frequency:** weekly. **Effective Market(s):** East of the Rockies. **Units of Measure:** Dollars per lb. **Type of Price:** spot. **Time Period Covered:** latest week.

CHROME GREEN: MEDIUM

Source: *Chemical Marketing Reporter.* **Price Frequency:** weekly. **Effective Market(s):** East of the Rockies. **Units of Measure:** Dollars per lb. **Type of Price:** spot. **Time Period Covered:** latest week.

CHROME METAL: 99.0% MINIMUM

Source: *Journal of Commerce and Commercial.* **Price Frequency:** daily. **Effective Market(s):** Europe. **Units of Measure:** Dollars per lb. **Type of Price:** spot. **Time Period Covered:** latest day.

CHROME ORANGE: CHEMICALLY PURE

Source: *Chemical Marketing Reporter.* **Price Frequency:** weekly. **Effective Market(s):** East of the Rockies. **Units of Measure:** Dollars per lb. **Type of Price:** spot. **Time Period Covered:** latest week.

Source: *Journal of Commerce and Commercial.* **Price Frequency:** weekly in Wednesday issue. **Units of Measure:** Dollars per lb. **Type of Price:** spot. **Time Period Covered:** latest week.

CHROME ORE

Source: *Economic and Energy Indicators.* **Price Frequency:** monthly, quarterly, annually. **Time Period Covered:** latest 3 months, quarters, and years.

CHROME YELLOW: CHEMICALLY PURE

Source: *Chemical Marketing Reporter.* **Price Frequency:** weekly. **Effective Market(s):** East of the Rockies. **Units of Measure:** Dollars per lb. **Type of Price:** spot. **Time Period Covered:** latest week.

CHROME YELLOW: MEDIUM-DARK, CHEMICALLY PURE

Source: *Journal of Commerce and Commercial.* **Price Frequency:** weekly in Wednesday issue. **Units of Measure:** Dollars per lb. **Type of Price:** spot. **Time Period Covered:** latest week.

CHROMIC ACID: 99-3/4%

Source: *Chemical Marketing Reporter.* **Price Frequency:** weekly. **Effective Market(s):** New York. **Units of Measure:** Dollars per lb. **Type of Price:** spot. **Time Period Covered:** latest week.

Source: *Journal of Commerce and Commercial.* **Price Frequency:** weekly in Thursday issue. **Units of Measure:** Dollars per lb. **Type of Price:** spot. **Time Period Covered:** latest week.

CHROMITE: CHEMICAL GRADE, TRANSVAAL

Source: *Industrial Minerals.* **Price Frequency:** monthly. **Effective Market(s):** main European port. **Units of Measure:** Dollars per metric tonne. **Type of Price:** producer & dealer. **Time Period Covered:** latest month.

CHROMITE: FOUNDRY GRADE, TRANSVAAL

Source: *Industrial Minerals.* **Price Frequency:** monthly. **Effective Market(s):** main European port. **Units of Measure:** Dollars per metric tonne. **Type of Price:** producer & dealer. **Time Period Covered:** latest month.

CHROMITE: REFRACTORY GRADE, CONCENTRATES, PHILIPPINES

Source: *Industrial Minerals.* **Price Frequency:** monthly. **Effective Market(s):** main European port. **Units of Measure:** Dollars per metric tonne. **Type of Price:** producer & dealer. **Time Period Covered:** latest month.

CHROMITE: REFRACTORY GRADE, TRANSVAAL

Source: *Industrial Minerals.* **Price Frequency:** monthly. **Effective Market(s):** main European port. **Units of Measure:** Dollars per metric tonne. **Type of Price:** producer & dealer. **Time Period Covered:** latest month.

CHROMITE: SOUTH AFRICAN

Source: *Commodity Year Book.* **Price Frequency:** annually. **Effective Market(s):** United States. **Units of Measure:** Dollars per metric ton. **Time Period Covered:** latest 8 years.

CHROMITE: TURKISH

Source: *Commodity Year Book.* **Price Frequency:** annually. **Effective Market(s):** United States. **Units of Measure:** Dollars per metric ton. **Time Period Covered:** latest 8 years.

CHROMITE SAND: MOLDING GRADE

Source: *Industrial Minerals.* **Price Frequency:** monthly. **Effective Market(s):** United Kingdom. **Units of Measure:** British pounds per metric tonne. **Type of Price:** producer & dealer. **Time Period Covered:** latest month.

CHROMIUM: ALUMINOTHERMIC

Source: *American Metal Market.* **Price Frequency:** weekly. **Units of Measure:** Dollars per lb. **Type of Price:** producer. **Time Period Covered:** latest week.

CHROMIUM: ELECTROLYTIC

Source: *American Metal Market.* **Price Frequency:** weekly. **Units of Measure:** Dollars per lb. **Type of Price:** producer. **Time Period Covered:** latest week.

CHROMIUM: ELECTROLYTIC, 99.5%

Source: *Iron Age.* **Price Frequency:** monthly. **Number of Sources:** Dollars per lb. **Type of Price:** consumer. **Time Period Covered:** latest month.

CHROMIUM: ELECTROLYTIC, STANDARD

Source: *E&MJ.* **Price Frequency:** monthly. **Units of Measure:** Dollars per lb. **Time Period Covered:** latest month, selected dates.

CHROMIUM ACEATE: 7-1/2% SOLUTION

Source: *Chemical Marketing Reporter.* **Price Frequency:** weekly. **Effective Market(s):** New York. **Units of Measure:** Dollars per lb. **Type of Price:** spot. **Time Period Covered:** latest week.

CHROMIUM FLUORIDE

Source: *Chemical Marketing Reporter.* **Price Frequency:** weekly. **Effective Market(s):** New York. **Units of Measure:** Dollars per lb. **Type of Price:** spot. **Time Period Covered:** latest week.

CHROMIUM NITRATE

Source: *Chemical Marketing Reporter.* **Price Frequency:** weekly. **Effective Market(s):** New York. **Units of Measure:** Dollars per lb. **Type of Price:** spot. **Time Period Covered:** latest week.

CHROMIUM NITRATE: 10% METAL SOLUTION

Source: *Chemical Marketing Reporter.* **Price Frequency:** weekly. **Effective Market(s):** New York. **Units of Measure:** Dollars per lb. **Type of Price:** spot. **Time Period Covered:** latest week.

CHROMIUM OXIDE: EXTRA LIGHT, GREEN

Source: *Journal of Commerce and Commercial.* **Price Frequency:** weekly in Wednesday issue. **Units of Measure:** Dollars per lb. **Type of Price:** spot. **Time Period Covered:** latest week.

CHROMIUM OXIDE: HYDRATED

Source: *Chemical Marketing Reporter.* **Price Frequency:** weekly. **Effective Market(s):** New York. **Units of Measure:** Dollars per lb. **Type of Price:** spot. **Time Period Covered:** latest week.

CHROMIUM OXIDE: PURE

Source: *Chemical Marketing Reporter.* **Price Frequency:** weekly. **Effective Market(s):** New York. **Units of Measure:** Dollars per lb. **Type of Price:** spot. **Time Period Covered:** latest week.

CHROMIUM OXIDE: PURE, GREEN

Source: *Journal of Commerce and Commercial.* **Price Frequency:** weekly in Wednesday issue. **Units of Measure:** Dollars per lb. **Type of Price:** spot. **Time Period Covered:** latest week.

CHRYSANTHEMUM SPRAYS

Source: *New Zealand Farmer.* **Price Frequency:** weekly, seasonally. **Effective Market(s):** New Zealand. **Units of Measure:** New Zealand dollars per bunch. **Time Period Covered:** latest week.

CHRYSANTHEMUMS

Source: *New Zealand Farmer.* **Price Frequency:** weekly, seasonally. **Effective Market(s):** New Zealand. **Units of Measure:** New Zealand dollars per bunch. **Time Period Covered:** latest week.

CHRYSANTHEMUMS: POMPON

Source: *Floriculture Crops.* **Price Frequency:** annually. **Effective Market(s):** 14 domestic markets, United States. **Units of Measure:** Dollars per unit. **Type of Price:** commercial wholesale. **Time Period Covered:** latest 2 years.

CHRYSANTHEMUMS: POTTED HARDY/ GARDEN, LESS THAN 5″

Source: *Floriculture Crops.* **Price Frequency:** annually. **Effective Market(s):** 27 domestic markets, United States. **Units of Measure:** cents per unit. **Type of Price:** commercial wholesale. **Time Period Covered:** latest 2 years.

CHRYSANTHEMUMS: POTTED HARDY/ GARDEN, MORE THAN 5″

Source: *Floriculture Crops.* **Price Frequency:** annually. **Effective Market(s):** 27 domestic markets, United States. **Units of Measure:** cents per unit. **Type of Price:** commercial wholesale. **Time Period Covered:** latest 2 years.

CHRYSANTHEMUMS: POTTED, LESS THAN 5″

Source: *Floriculture Crops.* **Price Frequency:** annually. **Effective Market(s):** 24 domestic markets, United States. **Units of Measure:** Dollars per unit. **Type of Price:** commercial wholesale. **Time Period Covered:** latest 2 years.

CHRYSANTHEMUMS: POTTED, MORE THAN 5″

Source: *Floriculture Crops.* **Price Frequency:** annually. **Effective Market(s):** 27 domestic markets, United States. **Units of Measure:** Dollars per unit. **Type of Price:** commercial wholesale. **Time Period Covered:** latest 2 years.

CHRYSANTHEMUMS: STANDARD

Source: *Floriculture Crops.* **Price Frequency:** annually. **Effective Market(s):** 15 domestic markets, United States. **Units of Measure:** cents per unit. **Type of Price:** commercial wholesale. **Time Period Covered:** latest 2 years.

CIDER

Source: *Beverage Media.* **Price Frequency:** monthly. **Effective Market(s):** New York. **Units of Measure:** Dollars per unit. **Type of Price:** wholesale by brand. **Time Period Covered:** latest month.

Source: *Illinois Beverage Journal.* **Price Frequency:** monthly. **Effective Market(s):** Illinois. **Units of Measure:** Dollars per case. **Type of Price:** wholesale by brand. **Time Period Covered:** latest month.

Source: *Rhode Island Beverage Journal.* **Price Frequency:** monthly. **Effective Market(s):** Rhode Island. **Units of Measure:** Dollars per unit. **Type of Price:** wholesale by brand. **Time Period Covered:** latest month.

CIDER: SPARKLING

Source: *Illinois Beverage Journal.* **Price Frequency:** monthly. **Effective Market(s):** Illinois. **Units of Measure:** Dollars per case. **Type of Price:** wholesale by brand. **Time Period Covered:** latest month.

CIGARETTES

Source: *Statistical Bulletin of the South Pacific: Retail Price Indexes.* **Price Frequency:** annually. **Effective Market(s):** 18 South Pacific markets. **Units of Measure:** Australian dollars per 20. **Type of Price:** retail. **Time Period Covered:** latest year.

CIGARETTES: 100 MILLIMETER

Source: *Tobacco Situation and Outlook Report.* **Price Frequency:** semiannually. **Effective Market(s):** United States. **Units of Measure:** Dollars per 1000. **Type of Price:** wholesale. **Time Period Covered:** latest 10 years.

CIGARETTES: FILTERTIP

Source: *Tobacco Situation and Outlook Report.* **Price Frequency:** semiannually. **Effective Market(s):** United States. **Units of Measure:** Dollars per 1000. **Type of Price:** wholesale. **Time Period Covered:** latest 10 years.

CIGARETTES: KING SIZE

Source: *Tobacco Situation and Outlook Report.* **Price Frequency:** semiannually. **Effective Market(s):** United States. **Units of Measure:** Dollars per 1000. **Type of Price:** wholesale. **Time Period Covered:** latest 10 years.

CIGARETTES: STANDARD

Source: *Tobacco Situation and Outlook Report.* **Price Frequency:** semiannually. **Effective Market(s):** United States. **Units of Measure:** Dollars per 1000. **Type of Price:** wholesale. **Time Period Covered:** latest 10 years.

CINCHONA BARK: RED, BROKEN

Source: *Journal of Commerce and Commercial.* **Price Frequency:** weekly in Monday issue. **Units of Measure:** Dollars per lb. **Type of Price:** spot. **Time Period Covered:** latest week.

CINNAMIC ALCOHOL

Source: *Chemical Marketing Reporter.* **Price Frequency:** weekly. **Effective Market(s):** New York. **Units of Measure:** Dollars per lb. **Type of Price:** spot. **Time Period Covered:** latest week.

CINNAMIC ALDEHYDE

Source: *Chemical Marketing Reporter.* **Price Frequency:** weekly. **Effective Market(s):** New York. **Units of Measure:** Dollars per lb. **Type of Price:** spot. **Time Period Covered:** latest week.

CINNAMON

see also Cassia.

Source: *Chemical Marketing Reporter.* **Price Frequency:** weekly. **Effective Market(s):** New York. **Units of Measure:** Dollars per lb. **Type of Price:** spot. **Time Period Covered:** latest week.

Source: *Prices of Selected Asia/Pacific Products.* **Price Frequency:** monthly, seasonally. **Effective Market(s):** Tokyo. **Units of Measure:** Japanese yen per kilogram. **Type of Price:** trade high, trade low. **Time Period Covered:** latest month.

CINNAMON: H-2, CEYLON

Source: *U. S. Spice Trade.* **Price Frequency:** annually. **Effective Market(s):** New York. **Units of Measure:** cents per lb. **Type of Price:** spot. **Time Period Covered:** latest 3 years.

CINNAMON BARK: SEYCHELLES

Source: *Fruit and Tropical Products.* **Price Frequency:** monthly, seasonally. **Effective Market(s):** London. **Units of Measure:** British pounds per tonne. **Type of Price:** month end. **Time Period Covered:** latest 2 years.

Source: *Prices of Selected Asia/Pacific Products.* **Price Frequency:** monthly, seasonally. **Effective Market(s):** United Kigdom/North European ports. **Units of Measure:** Dollars per metric ton. **Type of Price:** high, low. **Time Period Covered:** latest month.

CINNAMON BARK OIL

Source: *Chemical Marketing Reporter.* **Price Frequency:** weekly. **Effective Market(s):** New York. **Units of Measure:** Dollars per lb. **Type of Price:** spot. **Time Period Covered:** latest week.

CINNAMON CORTEX: CHINESE

Source: *Prices of Selected Asia/Pacific Products.* **Price Frequency:** monthly, seasonally. **Effective Market(s):** Osaka. **Units of Measure:** Japanese yen per kilogram. **Type of Price:** trade high, trade low. **Time Period Covered:** latest month.

CINNAMON LEAF OIL

Source: *Chemical Marketing Reporter.* **Price Frequency:** weekly. **Effective Market(s):** New York. **Units of Measure:** Dollars per lb. **Type of Price:** spot. **Time Period Covered:** latest week.

Source: *Journal of Commerce and Commercial.* **Price Frequency:** weekly in Tuesday issue. **Units of Measure:** Dollars per lb. **Type of Price:** spot. **Time Period Covered:** latest week.

Source: *Prices of Selected Asia/Pacific Products.* **Price Frequency:** monthly. **Effective Market(s):** United Kingdom/North European ports. **Units of Measure:** British pounds per kilogram. **Type of Price:** high, low. **Time Period Covered:** latest month.

Source: *Prices of Selected Asia/Pacific Products.* **Price Frequency:** monthly. **Effective Market(s):** New York. **Units of Measure:** Dollars per lb. **Type of Price:** spot high, spot low. **Time Period Covered:** latest month.

CINNAMON LEAF OIL: SRI LANKAN

Source: *Prices of Selected Asia/Pacific Products.* **Price Frequency:** monthly. **Effective Market(s):** United Kingdom. **Units of Measure:** British pounds per kilogram. **Type of Price:** spot high, spot low. **Time Period Covered:** latest month.

CINNAMON OIL

Source: *U. S. Essential Oil Trade.* **Price Frequency:** annually. **Effective Market(s):** United States. **Units of Measure:** Dollars per kilogram. **Type of Price:** import value. **Time Period Covered:** latest 3 years.

CINNAMON OIL: ARTIFICIAL

Source: *Journal of Commerce and Commercial.* **Price Frequency:** weekly in Tuesday issue. **Units of Measure:** Dollars per lb. **Type of Price:** spot. **Time Period Covered:** latest week.

CITRAL: FCC

Source: *Journal of Commerce and Commercial.* **Price Frequency:** weekly in Tuesday issue. **Units of Measure:** Dollars per lb. **Type of Price:** spot. **Time Period Covered:** latest week.

CITRAL: NATURAL

Source: *Chemical Marketing Reporter.* **Price Frequency:** weekly. **Effective Market(s):** New York. **Units of Measure:** Dollars per lb. **Type of Price:** spot. **Time Period Covered:** latest week.

CITRAL: SYNTHETIC, FCC

Source: *Chemical Marketing Reporter.* **Price Frequency:** weekly. **Effective Market(s):** New York. **Units of Measure:** Dollars per lb. **Type of Price:** spot. **Time Period Covered:** latest week.

CITRIC ACID: ANHYDROUS, GRANULAR

Source: *Journal of Commerce and Commercial.* **Price Frequency:** weekly in Friday issue. **Units of Measure:** Dollars per lb. **Type of Price:** spot. **Time Period Covered:** latest week.

CITRIC ACID: ANHYDROUS, GRANULAR, USP

Source: *Chemical Marketing Reporter.* **Price Frequency:** weekly. **Effective Market(s):** east. **Units of Measure:** Dollars per lb. **Type of Price:** spot. **Time Period Covered:** latest week.

CITRIC ACID: HYDROUS, GRANULAR, USP

Source: *Chemical Marketing Reporter.* **Price Frequency:** weekly. **Effective Market(s):** New York. **Units of Measure:** Dollars per lb. **Type of Price:** spot. **Time Period Covered:** latest week.

CITRIC ACID CRYSTAL

Source: *Journal of Commerce and Commercial.* **Price Frequency:** weekly in Friday issue. **Units of Measure:** Dollars per lb. **Type of Price:** spot. **Time Period Covered:** latest week.

CITRIC ACID POWDER: ANHYDROUS

Source: *Chemical Marketing Reporter.* **Price Frequency:** weekly. **Effective Market(s):** east. **Units of Measure:** Dollars per lb. **Type of Price:** spot. **Time Period Covered:** latest week.

CITRIC ACID POWDER: USP

Source: *Journal of Commerce and Commercial.* **Price Frequency:** weekly in Friday issue. **Units of Measure:** Dollars per lb. **Type of Price:** spot. **Time Period Covered:** latest week.

CITRONELLA OIL

Source: *U. S. Essential Oil Trade.* **Price Frequency:** annually. **Effective Market(s):** United States. **Units of Measure:** Dollars per kilogram. **Type of Price:** import value. **Time Period Covered:** latest 3 years.

CITRONELLA OIL: CHINESE

Source: *Chemical Marketing Reporter.* **Price Frequency:** weekly. **Effective Market(s):** New York. **Units of Measure:** Dollars per lb. **Type of Price:** spot. **Time Period Covered:** latest week.

Source: *Journal of Commerce and Commercial.* **Price Frequency:** weekly in Tuesday issue. **Units of Measure:** Dollars per lb. **Type of Price:** spot. **Time Period Covered:** latest week.

Source: *Prices of Selected Asia/Pacific Products.* **Price Frequency:** monthly. **Effective Market(s):** Hong Kong. **Units of Measure:** Hong Kong dollars per kilogram. **Type of Price:** wholesale high, wholesale low. **Time Period Covered:** latest month.

Source: *Prices of Selected Asia/Pacific Products.* **Price Frequency:** monthly. **Effective Market(s):** New York, United Kingdom, United Kingdom/North European ports. **Units of Measure:** Dollars per lb., British pounds per kilogram. **Type of Price:** spot high, spot low. **Time Period Covered:** latest month.

CITRONELLA OIL: JAVANESE

Source: *Chemical Marketing Reporter.* **Price Frequency:** weekly. **Effective Market(s):** New York. **Units of Measure:** Dollars per lb. **Type of Price:** spot. **Time Period Covered:** latest week.

Source: *Prices of Selected Asia/Pacific Products.* **Price Frequency:** monthly. **Effective Market(s):** United Kingdom, United Kingdom/North European ports. **Units of Measure:** British pounds per kilogram. **Type of Price:** spot high, spot low. **Time Period Covered:** latest month.

CITRONELLA OIL: ORDINARY, SRI LANKAN

Source: *Prices of Selected Asia/Pacific Products.* **Price Frequency:** monthly. **Effective Market(s):** United Kingdom/North European ports. **Units of Measure:** British pounds per kilogram. **Type of Price:** high, low. **Time Period Covered:** latest month.

CITRONELLA OIL: REFINED

Source: *Prices of Selected Asia/Pacific Products.* **Price Frequency:** monthly. **Effective Market(s):** Tokyo. **Units of Measure:** Japanese yen per kilogram. **Type of Price:** high, low. **Time Period Covered:** latest month.

CITRONELLA OIL: SRI LANKAN

Source: *Prices of Selected Asia/Pacific Products.* **Price Frequency:** monthly. **Effective Market(s):** United Kingdom. **Units of Measure:** British pounds per kilogram. **Type of Price:** spot high, spot low. **Time Period Covered:** latest month.

CITRONELLAL

Source: *Chemical Marketing Reporter.* **Price Frequency:** weekly. **Effective Market(s):** New York. **Units of Measure:** Dollars per lb. **Type of Price:** spot. **Time Period Covered:** latest week.

CITRONELLOL

Source: *Chemical Marketing Reporter.* **Price Frequency:** weekly. **Effective Market(s):** New York. **Units of Measure:** Dollars per lb. **Type of Price:** spot. **Time Period Covered:** latest week.

Source: *Journal of Commerce and Commercial.* **Price Frequency:** weekly in Tuesday issue. **Units of Measure:** Dollars per lb. **Type of Price:** spot. **Time Period Covered:** latest week.

CITRONELLYL ACETATE

Source: *Chemical Marketing Reporter.* **Price Frequency:** weekly. **Effective Market(s):** New York. **Units of Measure:** Dollars per lb. **Type of Price:** spot. **Time Period Covered:** latest week.

CITRONELLYL FORMATE

Source: *Chemical Marketing Reporter.* **Price Frequency:** weekly. **Effective Market(s):** New York. **Units of Measure:** Dollars per lb. **Type of Price:** spot. **Time Period Covered:** latest week.

CITRUS OILS

Source: *U. S. Essential Oil Trade.* **Price Frequency:** annually. **Effective Market(s):** United States. **Units of Measure:** Dollars per kilogram. **Type of Price:** import value. **Time Period Covered:** latest 3 years.

CITRUS PULP

Source: *Agra Europe.* **Price Frequency:** weekly, irregularly. **Effective Market(s):** Rotterdam. **Units of Measure:** Dollars per tonne. **Type of Price:** average. **Time Period Covered:** latest week.

Source: *Farmers Weekly.* **Price Frequency:** weekly. **Effective Market(s):** Great Britain. **Units of Measure:** British pounds per tonne. **Type of Price:** spot. **Time Period Covered:** latest week.

CITRUS PULP: DRIED

Source: *Feedstuffs.* **Price Frequency:** weekly. **Effective Market(s):** Atlanta. **Units of Measure:** Dollars per ton. **Time Period Covered:** latest week, week ago, 6 months ago, year ago.

Source: *Feedstuffs.* **Price Frequency:** weekly. **Effective Market(s):** 8 domestic markets. **Units of Measure:** Dollars per ton. **Time Period Covered:** latest week.

CIVET: ARTIFICIAL

Source: *Chemical Marketing Reporter.* **Price Frequency:** weekly. **Effective Market(s):** New York. **Units of Measure:** Dollars per ounce. **Type of Price:** spot. **Time Period Covered:** latest week.

CIVET: NATURAL

Source: *Chemical Marketing Reporter.* **Price Frequency:** weekly. **Effective Market(s):** New York. **Units of Measure:** Dollars per ounce. **Type of Price:** spot. **Time Period Covered:** latest week.

CLAMS: CHERRYSTONE

Source: *HRI-Buyers Guide.* **Price Frequency:** weekly. **Effective Market(s):** New York. **Units of Measure:** Dollars per bushel. **Type of Price:** price paid by dining places & institutions. **Time Period Covered:** latest week.

CLAMS: CHERRYSTONE, IN SHELL, FRESH

Source: *Seafood Price-Current.* **Price Frequency:** semiweekly. **Effective Market(s):** New York. **Units of Measure:** Dollars per bushel. **Type of Price:** sale by first receiver. **Time Period Covered:** latest day.

CLAMS: CHOWDER

Source: *HRI-Buyers Guide.* **Price Frequency:** weekly. **Effective Market(s):** New York. **Units of Measure:** Dollars per bushel. **Type of Price:** price paid by dining places & institutions. **Time Period Covered:** latest week.

CLAMS: CHOWDER, FRESH

Source: *Seafood Price-Current.* **Price Frequency:** semiweekly. **Effective Market(s):** New York. **Units of Measure:** Dollars per bushel. **Type of Price:** sale by first receiver. **Time Period Covered:** latest day.

CLAMS: FRESH, MANILA

Source: *Seafood Price-Current.* **Price Frequency:** semiweekly. **Effective Market(s):** West Coast. **Units of Measure:** Dollars per lb. **Type of Price:** sale by first receiver. **Time Period Covered:** latest day.

CLAMS: LITTLENECK

Source: *HRI-Buyers Guide.* **Price Frequency:** weekly. **Effective Market(s):** New York. **Units of Measure:** Dollars per bushel. **Type of Price:** price paid by dining places & institutions. **Time Period Covered:** latest week.

CLAMS: LITTLENECK, IN SHELL, FRESH, LONG ISLAND

Source: *Seafood Price-Current.* **Price Frequency:** semiweekly. **Effective Market(s):** New York. **Units of Measure:** Dollars per bushel. **Type of Price:** sale by first receiver. **Time Period Covered:** latest day.

CLAMS: MINCED FOR CHOWDER

Source: *HRI-Buyers Guide.* **Price Frequency:** weekly. **Effective Market(s):** New York. **Units of Measure:** Dollars per case. **Type of Price:** price paid by dining places & institutions. **Time Period Covered:** latest week.

CLAMS: STEAMERS, IN SHELL, FRESH

Source: *Seafood Price-Current.* **Price Frequency:** semiweekly. **Effective Market(s):** New York. **Units of Measure:** Dollars per bushel. **Type of Price:** sale by first receiver. **Time Period Covered:** latest day.

CLAMS: TOPNECK

Source: *HRI-Buyers Guide.* **Price Frequency:** weekly. **Effective Market(s):** New York. **Units of Measure:** Dollars per bushel. **Type of Price:** price paid by dining places & institutions. **Time Period Covered:** latest week.

CLAMS: TOPNECK, IN SHELL, FRESH

Source: *Seafood Price-Current.* **Price Frequency:** semiweekly. **Effective Market(s):** New York. **Units of Measure:** Dollars per bushel. **Type of Price:** sale by first receiver. **Time Period Covered:** latest day.

CLAY
see specific kinds of clay, eg. Ball Clay.

CLAY: CHINA
see Kaolin.

CLAY PIPE

Source: *ENR.* **Price Frequency:** monthly in second issue of month. **Effective Market(s):** 14 domestic markets, Toronto. **Units of Measure:** Dollars per foot. **Type of Price:** spot. **Time Period Covered:** latest month.

CLEMENTINES: MOROCCAN

Source: *FAO Quarterly Bulletin of Statistics.* **Price Frequency:** monthly, annually, seasonally. **Effective Market(s):** France. **Units of Measure:** French francs per kilograms, dollars per metric ton. **Type of Price:** average. **Time Period Covered:** latest 3 years.

CLEMENTINES: SPANISH

Source: *FAO Quarterly Bulletin of Statistics.* **Price Frequency:** monthly, annually, seasonally. **Effective Market(s):** West Germany. **Units of Measure:** West German marks per 100 kilograms, dollars per metric ton. **Type of Price:** wholesale. **Time Period Covered:** latest 3 years.

CLOTH
see also Fabric.

CLOTH: BATISTE

Source: *DNR: Daily News Record.* **Price Frequency:** quarterly. **Units of Measure:** Dollars per yard. **Type of Price:** spot. **Time Period Covered:** latest 3 quarters.

CLOTH: BLENDS, 65/35

Source: *DNR: Daily News Record.* **Price Frequency:** quarterly. **Units of Measure:** Dollars per yard. **Type of Price:** spot. **Time Period Covered:** latest 3 quarters.

CLOTH: BROADCLOTH

Source: *DNR: Daily News Record.* **Price Frequency:** quarterly. **Units of Measure:** Dollars per yard. **Type of Price:** spot. **Time Period Covered:** latest 3 quarters.

CLOTH: DRILLS

Source: *DNR: Daily News Record.* **Price Frequency:** quarterly. **Units of Measure:** Dollars per yard. **Type of Price:** spot. **Time Period Covered:** latest 3 quarters.

CLOTH: HESSIAN

Source: *Prices of Selected Asia/Pacific Products.* **Price Frequency:** monthly. **Effective Market(s):** Hong Kong. **Units of Measure:** Hong Kong dollars per yard. **Type of Price:** high, low. **Time Period Covered:** latest month.

CLOTH: OSNABURGS

Source: *DNR: Daily News Record.* **Price Frequency:** quarterly. **Units of Measure:** Dollars per yard. **Type of Price:** spot. **Time Period Covered:** latest 3 quarters.

CLOTH: PRINT, 48″

Source: *CRB Commodity Index Report.* **Price Frequency:** weekly. **Effective Market(s):** New York. **Units of Measure:** Dollars per yard. **Type of Price:** spot. **Time Period Covered:** latest week.

Source: *Journal of Commerce and Commercial.* **Price Frequency:** daily. **Effective Market(s):** New York. **Units of Measure:** Dollars per lb. **Type of Price:** spot supplier. **Time Period Covered:** latest day.

CLOTH: PRINT, ALL COTTON

Source: *DNR: Daily News Record.* **Price Frequency:** quarterly. **Units of Measure:** Dollars per yard. **Type of Price:** spot. **Time Period Covered:** latest 3 quarters.

CLOTH: PRINT, POLYESTER/COTTON

Source: *DNR: Daily News Record.* **Price Frequency:** quarterly. **Units of Measure:** Dollars per yard. **Type of Price:** spot. **Time Period Covered:** latest 3 quarters.

Source: *Investor's Daily.* **Price Frequency:** daily. **Effective Market(s):** New York. **Units of Measure:** Dollars per yard. **Type of Price:** spot. **Time Period Covered:** latest 2 days.

CLOTH: PRINT, POLYESTER/COTTON, 48″

Source: *New York Times.* **Price Frequency:** daily. **Effective Market(s):** New York. **Units of Measure:** Dollars per yard. **Type of Price:** cash. **Time Period Covered:** latest 2 days.

Source: *Wall Street Journal.* **Price Frequency:** daily. **Effective Market(s):** New York. **Units of Measure:** Dollars per yard. **Time Period Covered:** latest day, day ago, year ago.

CLOTH: PRINT, POLYESTER/RAYON

Source: *DNR: Daily News Record.* **Price Frequency:** quarterly. **Units of Measure:** Dollars per yard. **Type of Price:** spot. **Time Period Covered:** latest 3 quarters.

CLOTH: PRINT, TEXTURED FILL

Source: *DNR: Daily News Record.* **Price Frequency:** quarterly. **Units of Measure:** Dollars per yard. **Type of Price:** spot. **Time Period Covered:** latest 3 quarters.

CLOTH: S. F. APPAREL DUCK

Source: *DNR: Daily News Record.* **Price Frequency:** quarterly. **Units of Measure:** Dollars per yard. **Type of Price:** spot. **Time Period Covered:** latest 3 quarters.

CLOTH: SHEETINGS

Source: *DNR: Daily News Record.* **Price Frequency:** quarterly. **Units of Measure:** Dollars per yard. **Type of Price:** spot. **Time Period Covered:** latest 3 quarters.

CLOTH: VOILE

Source: *DNR: Daily News Record.* **Price Frequency:** quarterly. **Units of Measure:** Dollars per yard. **Type of Price:** spot. **Time Period Covered:** latest 3 quarters.

CLOVE BUD OIL: MADAGASCAR

Source: *Chemical Marketing Reporter.* **Price Frequency:** weekly. **Effective Market(s):** New York. **Units of Measure:** Dollars per kilo. **Type of Price:** spot. **Time Period Covered:** latest week.

CLOVE LEAF OIL

Source: *Journal of Commerce and Commercial.* **Price Frequency:** weekly in Tuesday issue. **Units of Measure:** Dollars per lb. **Type of Price:** spot. **Time Period Covered:** latest week.

CLOVE LEAF OIL: INDONESIAN, REGULAR

Source: *Chemical Marketing Reporter.* **Price Frequency:** weekly. **Effective Market(s):** New York. **Units of Measure:** Dollars per kilo. **Type of Price:** spot. **Time Period Covered:** latest week.

CLOVE LEAF OIL: MADAGASCAR, REGULAR

Source: *Chemical Marketing Reporter.* **Price Frequency:** weekly. **Effective Market(s):** New York. **Units of Measure:** Dollars per kilo. **Type of Price:** spot. **Time Period Covered:** latest week.

CLOVE OIL

Source: *U. S. Essential Oil Trade.* **Price Frequency:** annually. **Effective Market(s):** United States. **Units of Measure:** Dollars per kilogram. **Type of Price:** import value. **Time Period Covered:** latest 3 years.

CLOVER SEED: LADINO

Source: *Agricultural Prices Annual Summary.* **Price Frequency:** semiannually. **Effective Market(s):** United States. **Units of Measure:** Dollars per lb. **Type of Price:** average price paid by farmer. **Time Period Covered:** latest 6 years.

CLOVER SEED: RED

Source: *Agricultural Prices Annual Summary.* **Price Frequency:** semiannually. **Effective Market(s):** United States. **Units of Measure:** Dollars per lb. **Type of Price:** average price paid by farmer. **Time Period Covered:** latest 6 years.

CLOVES

Source: *Prices of Selected Asia/Pacific Products.* **Price Frequency:** monthly, seasonally. **Effective Market(s):** Tokyo. **Units of Measure:** Japanese yen per kilogram. **Type of Price:** trade high, trade low. **Time Period Covered:** latest month.

CLOVES: BRAZILIAN

Source: *Chemical Marketing Reporter.* **Price Frequency:** weekly. **Effective Market(s):** New York. **Units of Measure:** Dollars per lb. **Type of Price:** spot. **Time Period Covered:** latest week.

Source: *U. S. Spice Trade.* **Price Frequency:** monthly, annually. **Effective Market(s):** New York. **Units of Measure:** Dollars per lb. **Type of Price:** spot. **Time Period Covered:** latest 10 years.

CLOVES: BRAZILIAN/CEYLONESE

Source: *U. S. Spice Trade.* **Price Frequency:** monthly, annually. **Effective Market(s):** New York. **Units of Measure:** Dollars per lb. **Type of Price:** spot. **Time Period Covered:** latest 10 years.

CLOVES: COMOROS

Source: *Fruit and Tropical Products.* **Price Frequency:** monthly, seasonally. **Effective Market(s):** London. **Units of Measure:** British pounds per tonne. **Type of Price:** month end. **Time Period Covered:** latest 2 years.

CLOVES: GRADE 1, SRI LANKAN

Source: *Prices of Selected Asia/Pacific Products.* **Price Frequency:** monthly, seasonally. **Effective Market(s):** Colombo (Sri Lanka). **Units of Measure:** Sri Lankan rupees per kilogram. **Type of Price:** auction high, auction low. **Time Period Covered:** latest month.

CLOVES: MADAGASCAR

Source: *Chemical Marketing Reporter.* **Price Frequency:** weekly. **Effective Market(s):** New York. **Units of Measure:** Dollars per lb. **Type of Price:** spot. **Time Period Covered:** latest week.

Source: *Fruit and Tropical Products.* **Price Frequency:** monthly, seasonally. **Effective Market(s):** London. **Units of Measure:** British pounds per tonne. **Type of Price:** month end. **Time Period Covered:** latest 2 years.

Source: *Prices of Selected Asia/Pacific Products.* **Price Frequency:** monthly, seasonally. **Effective Market(s):** Singapore, United States. **Units of Measure:** Dollars per metric ton. **Type of Price:** spot high, spot low. **Time Period Covered:** latest month.

Source: *Prices of Selected Asia/Pacific Products.* **Price Frequency:** monthly, seasonally. **Effective Market(s):** Japan, Netherlands. **Units of Measure:** Dollars per metric ton. **Type of Price:** high, low. **Time Period Covered:** latest month.

CLOVES: MADAGASCAR/ZANZIBAR

Source: *U. S. Spice Trade.* **Price Frequency:** monthly, annually. **Effective Market(s):** New York. **Units of Measure:** Dollars per lb. **Type of Price:** spot. **Time Period Covered:** latest 10 years.

CLOVES: TANZANIAN

Source: *Prices of Selected Asia/Pacific Products.* **Price Frequency:** monthly, seasonally. **Effective Market(s):** Japan, Netherlands, Singapore. **Units of Measure:** Dollars per metric ton. **Type of Price:** high, low. **Time Period Covered:** latest month.

CLOVES: ZANZIBAR

Source: *Chemical Marketing Reporter.* **Price Frequency:** weekly. **Effective Market(s):** New York. **Units of Measure:** Dollars per lb. **Type of Price:** spot. **Time Period Covered:** latest week.

CMC: DETERGENT MAKERS

Source: *Chemical Marketing Reporter.* **Price Frequency:** weekly. **Effective Market(s):** Somerset (PA). **Units of Measure:** Dollars per lb. **Type of Price:** spot. **Time Period Covered:** latest week.

CMC: PURIFIED, HIGH VISCOSITY

see Cellulose Gum.

CMC: TECHNICAL GRADE, 96% MINIMUM, LOW OR MEDIUM VISCOSITY

Source: *Chemical Marketing Reporter.* **Price Frequency:** weekly. **Effective Market(s):** Hopewell (VA). **Units of Measure:** Dollars per lb. **Type of Price:** spot. **Time Period Covered:** latest week.

COAL

Source: *Energy Statistics.* **Price Frequency:** monthly, annually. **Effective Market(s):** United States. **Units of Measure:** Dollars per ton, index. **Type of Price:** average mine, average import, average export, producer price index. **Time Period Covered:** monthly latest year, annually latest 8 years.

COAL: ANTHRACITE

Source: *Energy Statistics.* **Price Frequency:** monthly, annually. **Effective Market(s):** United States. **Units of Measure:** Dollars per ton, index. **Type of Price:** average mine, average import, average export, producer price index. **Time Period Covered:** monthly latest year, annually latest 8 years.

COAL: ANTHRACITE, CHESTNUT

Source: *Commodity Year Book.* **Price Frequency:** monthly, annually. **Units of Measure:** index. **Type of Price:** wholesale price index. **Time Period Covered:** latest 5 years.

COAL: AUSTRALIAN

Source: *International Financial Statistics.* **Price Frequency:** monthly, quarterly, annually. **Effective Market(s):** Australia. **Units of Measure:** Dollars per metric ton, index. **Type of Price:** market price, price index. **Time Period Covered:** latest 2 months, latest 4 quarters, latest 5 years.

Source: *International Financial Statistics Yearbook.* **Price Frequency:** annually. **Effective Market(s):** Australia. **Units of Measure:** Dollars per metric ton. **Type of Price:** wholesale. **Time Period Covered:** latest 30 years.

COAL: BITUMINOUS

Source: *Commodity Trade and Price Trends.* **Price Frequency:** annually. **Effective Market(s):** United States ports. **Units of Measure:** Dollars per metric ton, 1980 constant dollars per metric ton. **Type of Price:** export. **Time Period Covered:** latest 37 years.

Source: *Energy Statistics.* **Price Frequency:** monthly, annually. **Effective Market(s):** United States. **Units of Measure:** Dollars per ton, index. **Type of Price:** average mine, average import, average export, producer price index. **Time Period Covered:** monthly latest year, annually latest 8 years.

COAL: BITUMINOUS, SCREENINGS, FOR INDUSTRIAL USE

Source: *Commodity Year Book.* **Price Frequency:** monthly, annually. **Units of Measure:** index. **Type of Price:** wholesale price index. **Time Period Covered:** latest 3 years.

COAL: COKING

Source: *Energy Prices and Taxes.* **Price Frequency:** quarterly. **Effective Market(s):** Europe, International Energy Agency, Japan. **Units of Measure:** Dollars per metric ton. **Type of Price:** import. **Time Period Covered:** latest 2 years.

Source: *Energy Prices and Taxes.* **Price Frequency:** quarterly, annually. **Effective Market(s):** 10 international markets. **Units of Measure:** Dollars per metric ton, index. **Type of Price:** import, price index. **Time Period Covered:** quarterly latest 2 years, annually latest 9 years.

Source: *Energy Prices and Taxes.* **Price Frequency:** quarterly, annually. **Effective Market(s):** Australia, United States. **Units of Measure:** Dollars per metric ton, price index. **Type of Price:** export, index. **Time Period Covered:** quarterly latest 5 quarters, annually latest 9 years.

Source: *Energy Prices and Taxes.* **Price Frequency:** quarterly, annually. **Effective Market(s):** 28 international markets. **Units of Measure:** national currency per metric ton, national currency per ton of oil equivalent. **Time Period Covered:** quarterly latest year, annually latest 12 years.

COAL: COKING, AUSTRALIAN

Source: *Energy Prices and Taxes.* **Price Frequency:** quarterly, annually. **Effective Market(s):** European Community, Japan. **Units of Measure:** Dollars per metric ton. **Type of Price:** import. **Time Period Covered:** quarterly latest 5 quarters, annually latest 9 years.

COAL: COKING, CANADIAN

Source: *Energy Prices and Taxes.* **Price Frequency:** quarterly, annually. **Effective Market(s):** European Community, Japan. **Units of Measure:** Dollars per metric ton. **Type of Price:** import. **Time Period Covered:** quarterly latest 5 quarters, annually latest 9 years.

COAL: COKING, CHINESE

Source: *Energy Prices and Taxes.* **Price Frequency:** quarterly, annually. **Effective Market(s):** Japan. **Units of Measure:** Dollars per metric ton. **Type of Price:** import. **Time Period Covered:** quarterly latest 5 quarters, annually latest 9 years.

COAL: COKING, FOR INDUSTRIAL USE

Source: *Energy Prices and Taxes.* **Price Frequency:** annually. **Effective Market(s):** 10 international markets. **Units of Measure:** Dollars per metric ton, dollars per ton of oil equivalent. **Time Period Covered:** latest 8 years.

COAL: COKING, POLISH

Source: *Energy Prices and Taxes.* **Price Frequency:** quarterly, annually. **Effective Market(s):** European Community. **Units of Measure:** Dollars per metric ton. **Type of Price:** import. **Time Period Covered:** quarterly latest 5 quarters, annually latest 9 years.

COAL: COKING, SOUTH AFRICAN

Source: *Energy Prices and Taxes.* **Price Frequency:** quarterly, annually. **Effective Market(s):** European Community, Japan. **Units of Measure:** Dollars per metric ton. **Type of Price:** import. **Time Period Covered:** quarterly latest 5 quarters, annually latest 9 years.

COAL: COKING, U.S.S.R

Source: *Energy Prices and Taxes.* **Price Frequency:** quarterly, annually. **Effective Market(s):** European Community, Japan. **Units of Measure:** Dollars per metric ton. **Type of Price:** import. **Time Period Covered:** quarterly latest 5 quarters, annually latest 9 years.

COAL: COKING, UNITED STATES

Source: *Energy Prices and Taxes.* **Price Frequency:** quarterly, annually. **Effective Market(s):** European Community, Japan. **Units of Measure:** Dollars per metric ton. **Type of Price:** import. **Time Period Covered:** quarterly latest 5 quarters, annually latest 9 years.

COAL: STEAM

Source: *Energy Prices and Taxes.* **Price Frequency:** quarterly. **Effective Market(s):** Europe, International Energy Agency, Japan, United States. **Units of Measure:** Dollars per metric ton. **Type of Price:** import. **Time Period Covered:** latest 2 years.

Source: *Energy Prices and Taxes.* **Price Frequency:** quarterly, annually. **Effective Market(s):** 13 international markets. **Units of Measure:** Dollars per metric ton, index. **Type of Price:** import, price index. **Time Period Covered:** quarterly latest 2 years, annually latest 9 years.

Source: *Energy Prices and Taxes.* **Price Frequency:** quarterly, annually. **Effective Market(s):** Australia, United States. **Units of Measure:** Dollars per metric ton, price index. **Type of Price:** export, index. **Time Period Covered:** quarterly latest 5 quarters, annually latest 9 years.

COAL: STEAM, AUSTRALIAN

Source: *Energy Prices and Taxes.* **Price Frequency:** quarterly, annually. **Effective Market(s):** European Community, Japan. **Units of Measure:** Dollars per metric ton. **Type of Price:** import. **Time Period Covered:** quarterly latest 5 quarters, annually latest 9 years.

COAL: STEAM, CHINESE

Source: *Energy Prices and Taxes.* **Price Frequency:** quarterly, annually. **Effective Market(s):** European Community, Japan. **Units of Measure:** Dollars per metric ton. **Type of Price:** import. **Time Period Covered:** quarterly latest 5 quarters, annually latest 9 years.

COAL: STEAM, COLOMBIAN

Source: *Energy Prices and Taxes.* **Price Frequency:** quarterly, annually. **Effective Market(s):** European Community. **Units of Measure:** Dollars per metric ton. **Type of Price:** import. **Time Period Covered:** quarterly latest 5 quarters, annually latest 9 years.

COAL: STEAM, FOR ELECTRICITY GENERATION

Source: *Energy Prices and Taxes.* **Price Frequency:** quarterly, annually. **Effective Market(s):** 28 international markets. **Units of Measure:** national currency per metric ton, national currency per ton of oil equivalent. **Time Period Covered:** quarterly latest year, annually latest 12 years.

Source: *Energy Prices and Taxes.* **Price Frequency:** quarterly, annually. **Effective Market(s):** 13 international markets. **Units of Measure:** Dollars per metric ton, dollars per ton of oil equivalent. **Time Period Covered:** latest 8 years.

COAL: STEAM, FOR HOUSEHOLD USE

Source: *Energy Prices and Taxes.* **Price Frequency:** quarterly, annually. **Effective Market(s):** 28 international markets. **Units of Measure:** national currency per metric ton, national currency per ton of oil equivalent. **Time Period Covered:** quarterly latest year, annually latest 12 years.

COAL: STEAM, FOR INDUSTRIAL USE

Source: *Energy Prices and Taxes.* **Price Frequency:** quarterly, annually. **Effective Market(s):** 28 international markets. **Units of Measure:** national currency per metric ton, national currency per ton of oil equivalent. **Time Period Covered:** quarterly latest year, annually latest 12 years.

Source: *Energy Prices and Taxes.* **Price Frequency:** annually. **Effective Market(s):** 15 international markets. **Units of Measure:** Dollars per metric ton, dollars per ton of oil equivalent. **Time Period Covered:** latest 8 years.

COAL: STEAM, POLISH

Source: *Energy Prices and Taxes.* **Price Frequency:** quarterly, annually. **Effective Market(s):** European Community. **Units of Measure:** Dollars per metric ton. **Type of Price:** import. **Time Period Covered:** quarterly latest 5 quarters, annually latest 9 years.

COAL: STEAM, SOUTH AFRICAN

Source: *Energy Prices and Taxes.* **Price Frequency:** quarterly, annually. **Effective Market(s):** European Community, Japan. **Units of Measure:** Dollars per metric ton. **Type of Price:** import. **Time Period Covered:** quarterly latest 5 quarters, annually latest 9 years.

COAL: STEAM, U.S.S.R

Source: *Energy Prices and Taxes.* **Price Frequency:** quarterly, annually. **Effective Market(s):** European Community, Japan. **Units of Measure:** Dollars per metric ton. **Type of Price:** import. **Time Period Covered:** quarterly latest 5 quarters, annually latest 9 years.

COAL: STEAM, UNITED STATES

Source: *Energy Prices and Taxes.* **Price Frequency:** quarterly, annually. **Effective Market(s):** European Community, Japan. **Units of Measure:** Dollars per metric ton. **Type of Price:** import. **Time Period Covered:** quarterly latest 5 quarters, annually latest 9 years.

COALTAR PITCH: CRUDE

Source: *Journal of Commerce and Commercial.* **Price Frequency:** weekly in Wednesday issue. **Units of Measure:** Dollars per gallon. **Type of Price:** spot. **Time Period Covered:** latest week.

COALTAR PITCH: INDUSTRIAL GRADE, LIQUID

Source: *Chemical Marketing Reporter.* **Price Frequency:** weekly. **Effective Market(s):** New York. **Units of Measure:** Dollars per ton. **Type of Price:** spot. **Time Period Covered:** latest week.

COALTAR PITCH: ROOFING GRADE

Source: *Chemical Marketing Reporter.* **Price Frequency:** weekly. **Effective Market(s):** New York. **Units of Measure:** Dollars per ton. **Type of Price:** spot. **Time Period Covered:** latest week.

COBALT: 99%, CATHODES

Source: *Iron Age.* **Price Frequency:** monthly. **Number of Sources:** Dollars per lb. **Type of Price:** consumer. **Time Period Covered:** latest month.

COBALT: 99%, CATHODES, ETC

Source: *E&MJ.* **Price Frequency:** monthly. **Effective Market(s):** New York. **Units of Measure:** Dollars per lb. **Time Period Covered:** latest month, selected dates.

COBALT: 99%, EXTRA FINE

Source: *E&MJ.* **Price Frequency:** monthly. **Effective Market(s):** New York. **Units of Measure:** Dollars per lb. **Time Period Covered:** latest month, selected dates.

COBALT: 99%, POWDER

Source: *E&MJ.* **Price Frequency:** monthly. **Effective Market(s):** New York. **Units of Measure:** Dollars per lb. **Time Period Covered:** latest month, selected dates.

COBALT: 99%, "S" POWDER

Source: *E&MJ.* **Price Frequency:** monthly. **Units of Measure:** Dollars per lb. **Time Period Covered:** latest month, selected dates.

COBALT: 99.7%, CATHODES

Source: *Journal of Commerce and Commercial.* **Price Frequency:** daily. **Effective Market(s):** Europe. **Units of Measure:** Dollars per lb. **Type of Price:** spot. **Time Period Covered:** latest day.

COBALT: CATHODES

Source: *Commodity Year Book.* **Price Frequency:** annually. **Effective Market(s):** United States. **Units of Measure:** Dollars per lb. **Type of Price:** spot. **Time Period Covered:** latest 7 years.

Source: *Northern Miner.* **Price Frequency:** daily. **Effective Market(s):** United States. **Units of Measure:** Dollars per lb. **Type of Price:** producer. **Time Period Covered:** selected day.

COBALT ACETATE

Source: *Chemical Marketing Reporter.* **Price Frequency:** weekly. **Effective Market(s):** New York. **Units of Measure:** Dollars per lb. **Type of Price:** spot. **Time Period Covered:** latest week.

COBALT CARBONATE: POWDERED

Source: *Chemical Marketing Reporter.* **Price Frequency:** weekly. **Effective Market(s):** New York. **Units of Measure:** Dollars per lb. **Type of Price:** spot. **Time Period Covered:** latest week.

COBALT CHLORIDE

Source: *Chemical Marketing Reporter.* **Price Frequency:** weekly. **Effective Market(s):** New York. **Units of Measure:** Dollars per lb. **Type of Price:** spot. **Time Period Covered:** latest week.

COBALT HYDRATE

Source: *Chemical Marketing Reporter.* **Price Frequency:** weekly. **Effective Market(s):** New York. **Units of Measure:** Dollars per lb. **Type of Price:** spot. **Time Period Covered:** latest week.

COBALT METAL : 99.5-99.9%

Source: *Chemical Marketing Reporter.* **Price Frequency:** weekly. **Effective Market(s):** Chicago, New York. **Units of Measure:** Dollars per lb. **Type of Price:** spot. **Time Period Covered:** latest week.

COBALT NAPHTHENATE: LIQUID

Source: *Chemical Marketing Reporter.* **Price Frequency:** weekly. **Effective Market(s):** New York. **Units of Measure:** Dollars per lb. **Type of Price:** spot. **Time Period Covered:** latest week.

COBALT NITRATE

Source: *Chemical Marketing Reporter.* **Price Frequency:** weekly. **Effective Market(s):** New York. **Units of Measure:** Dollars per lb. **Type of Price:** spot. **Time Period Covered:** latest week.

COBALT OXIDE: 70-71% COBALT, IMPORTED

Source: *Chemical Marketing Reporter.* **Price Frequency:** weekly. **Effective Market(s):** New York. **Units of Measure:** Dollars per lb. **Type of Price:** spot. **Time Period Covered:** latest week.

COBALT OXIDE: BLACK, 72-73% COBALT, IMPORTED

Source: *Chemical Marketing Reporter.* **Price Frequency:** weekly. **Effective Market(s):** New York. **Units of Measure:** Dollars per lb. **Type of Price:** spot. **Time Period Covered:** latest week.

COBALT PHOSPHATE: POWDERED, 32.1% COBALT

Source: *Chemical Marketing Reporter.* **Price Frequency:** weekly. **Effective Market(s):** New York. **Units of Measure:** Dollars per lb. **Type of Price:** spot. **Time Period Covered:** latest week.

COBALT SULFATE: CRYSTALLINE

Source: *Chemical Marketing Reporter.* **Price Frequency:** weekly. **Effective Market(s):** East. **Units of Measure:** Dollars per lb. **Type of Price:** spot. **Time Period Covered:** latest week.

COBALT SULFATE: MONOHYDRATE

Source: *Chemical Marketing Reporter.* **Price Frequency:** weekly. **Effective Market(s):** New York. **Units of Measure:** Dollars per lb. **Type of Price:** spot. **Time Period Covered:** latest week.

COBALT TALLATE: 6% COBALT

Source: *Chemical Marketing Reporter.* **Price Frequency:** weekly. **Effective Market(s):** New York. **Units of Measure:** Dollars per lb. **Type of Price:** spot. **Time Period Covered:** latest week.

COBIA (FISH): FRESH

Source: *Seafood Price-Current.* **Price Frequency:** semiweekly. **Effective Market(s):** Gulf/Southeast. **Units of Measure:** Dollars per lb. **Type of Price:** sale by first receiver. **Time Period Covered:** latest day.

COCKS AND FAUCETS: BRASS

Source: *American Metal Market.* **Price Frequency:** daily. **Effective Market(s):** 14 domestic markets, Montreal, Toronto. **Units of Measure:** cents per lb., Canadian cents per lb. **Time Period Covered:** latest day.

Source: *Iron Age.* **Price Frequency:** monthly. **Number of Sources:** cents per lb. **Type of Price:** dealer, refinery, smelters. **Time Period Covered:** latest month.

COCKTAIL MIXES

Source: *Illinois Beverage Journal.* **Price Frequency:** monthly. **Effective Market(s):** Illinois. **Units of Measure:** Dollars per case. **Type of Price:** wholesale by brand. **Time Period Covered:** latest month.

COCKTAILS

Source: *Colorado Beverage Analyst.* **Price Frequency:** monthly. **Effective Market(s):** Colorado. **Units of Measure:** Dollars per case. **Type of Price:** wholesale by brand. **Time Period Covered:** latest month.

Source: *Kentucky Beverage Journal.* **Price Frequency:** monthly. **Effective Market(s):** Kentucky. **Units of Measure:** Dollars per bottle, dollars per case. **Type of Price:** wholesale by brand. **Time Period Covered:** latest month.

Source: *Rhode Island Beverage Journal.* **Price Frequency:** monthly. **Effective Market(s):** Rhode Island. **Units of Measure:** Dollars per unit. **Type of Price:** wholesale by brand. **Time Period Covered:** latest month.

COCKTAILS: PREPARED

Source: *Beverage Media.* **Price Frequency:** monthly. **Effective Market(s):** New York. **Units of Measure:** Dollars per unit. **Type of Price:** wholesale by brand. **Time Period Covered:** latest month.

Source: *Illinois Beverage Journal.* **Price Frequency:** monthly. **Effective Market(s):** Illinois. **Units of Measure:** Dollars per case. **Type of Price:** wholesale by brand. **Time Period Covered:** latest month.

Source: *Indiana Beverage Journal.* **Price Frequency:** monthly. **Effective Market(s):** Indiana. **Units of Measure:** Dollars per case, dollars per bottle. **Type of Price:** wholesale by brand. **Time Period Covered:** latest month.

Source: *Nevada Beverage Index.* **Price Frequency:** monthly. **Effective Market(s):** Nevada. **Units of Measure:** Dollars per unit. **Type of Price:** wholesale by brand. **Time Period Covered:** latest month.

COCOA

Source: *Commodity Trade and Price Trends.* **Price Frequency:** annually. **Effective Market(s):** New York/London. **Units of Measure:** cents per kilogram, 1980 constant cents per kilogram. **Type of Price:** average daily. **Time Period Covered:** latest 37 years.

Source: *Economic and Energy Indicators.* **Price Frequency:** monthly, quarterly, annually. **Units of Measure:** cents per lb. **Time Period Covered:** latest 3 months, quarters, and years.

Source: *Far Eastern Economic Review.* **Price Frequency:** weekly. **Effective Market(s):** New York. **Units of Measure:** Dollars per tonne. **Time Period Covered:** latest week, week ago, 3 months ago, year ago.

Source: *UNCTAD Commodity Yearbook.* **Price Frequency:** annually. **Effective Market(s):** New York/London. **Units of Measure:** Dollars per metric ton. **Type of Price:** average of daily prices. **Time Period Covered:** latest 12 years.

COCOA: FUTURES

Source: *Asian Wall Street Journal.* **Price Frequency:** daily. **Effective Market(s):** New York. **Units of Measure:** Dollars per ton. **Type of Price:** futures. **Time Period Covered:** latest day.

Source: *Barron's.* **Price Frequency:** weekly. **Effective Market(s):** New York. **Units of Measure:** Dollars per ton. **Type of Price:** futures. **Time Period Covered:** latest week.

Source: *Far Eastern Economic Review.* **Price Frequency:** weekly. **Effective Market(s):** New York. **Units of Measure:** Dollars per tonne. **Type of Price:** futures. **Time Period Covered:** latest week.

Source: *Financial Times.* **Price Frequency:** daily. **Effective Market(s):** New York. **Units of Measure:** Dollars per tonne. **Type of Price:** futures. **Time Period Covered:** latest day.

Source: *Fruit and Tropical Products.* **Price Frequency:** monthly, annually. **Effective Market(s):** London/New York. **Units of Measure:** SDR's per tonne. **Type of Price:** futures. **Time Period Covered:** latest 3 years.

Source: *Investor's Daily.* **Price Frequency:** daily. **Effective Market(s):** New York. **Units of Measure:** Dollars per ton. **Type of Price:** futures. **Time Period Covered:** latest day.

Source: *Los Angeles Times.* **Price Frequency:** daily. **Effective Market(s):** New York. **Units of Measure:** Dollars per ton. **Type of Price:** futures. **Time Period Covered:** latest day.

Source: *Monthly Commodity Price Bulletin Supplement.* **Price Frequency:** monthly, quarterly, annually. **Effective Market(s):** London. **Units of Measure:** cents per lb., SDRs per tonne. **Type of Price:** futures. **Time Period Covered:** latest 20 years.

Source: *New York Times.* **Price Frequency:** daily. **Effective Market(s):** New York. **Units of Measure:** Dollars per ton. **Type of Price:** futures. **Time Period Covered:** latest day.

Source: *The Times.* **Price Frequency:** daily. **Effective Market(s):** London. **Units of Measure:** British pounds per tonne. **Type of Price:** futures. **Time Period Covered:** latest day.

Source: *Wall Street Journal.* **Price Frequency:** daily. **Effective Market(s):** New York. **Units of Measure:** Dollars per ton. **Type of Price:** futures. **Time Period Covered:** latest day.

COCOA: FUTURES, 3 MONTHS

Source: *Monthly Commodity Price Bulletin.* **Price Frequency:** monthly, annually. **Effective Market(s):** New York/London. **Units of Measure:** cents per lb., SDRs per tonne. **Type of Price:** futures. **Time Period Covered:** latest 5 years.

COCOA: FUTURES, MARCH

Source: *Commodity Year Book.* **Price Frequency:** monthly. **Effective Market(s):** New York. **Units of Measure:** Dollars per tonne. **Type of Price:** futures. **Time Period Covered:** latest 5 years.

COCOA: GHANA

Source: *Commodity Trade and Price Trends.* **Price Frequency:** annually. **Effective Market(s):** New York. **Units of Measure:** cents per kilogram, 1980 constant cents per kilogram. **Type of Price:** spot. **Time Period Covered:** latest 37 years.

Source: *Fruit and Tropical Products.* **Price Frequency:** monthly, annually. **Effective Market(s):** London. **Units of Measure:** British pounds per tonne. **Type of Price:** spot. **Time Period Covered:** latest 3 years.

COCOA: IVORY COAST

Source: *Asian Wall Street Journal.* **Price Frequency:** daily. **Effective Market(s):** Eastern seaboard. **Units of Measure:** Dollars per metric ton. **Type of Price:** cash. **Time Period Covered:** latest 2 days, year ago.

Source: *Journal of Commerce and Commercial.* **Price Frequency:** daily. **Effective Market(s):** New York. **Units of Measure:** Dollars per tonne. **Type of Price:** spot supplier. **Time Period Covered:** latest day.

Source: *Wall Street Journal.* **Price Frequency:** daily. **Effective Market(s):** Eastern Seaboard. **Units of Measure:** Dollars per metric ton. **Time Period Covered:** latest day, day ago, year ago.

COCOA BEANS

Source: *Agricultural Outlook.* **Price Frequency:** monthly, annually. **Effective Market(s):** New York. **Units of Measure:** Dollars per lb. **Type of Price:** spot import. **Time Period Covered:** monthly latest 6 months, annually latest 3 years.

Source: *Commodity Year Book.* **Price Frequency:** annually. **Effective Market(s):** United States. **Units of Measure:** Dollars per metric ton. **Type of Price:** spot. **Time Period Covered:** latest 8 years.

Source: *FAO Quarterly Bulletin of Statistics.* **Price Frequency:** monthly, annually. **Effective Market(s):** New York/London. **Units of Measure:** Dollars per 100 lbs., dollars per metric ton. **Type of Price:** daily average. **Time Period Covered:** latest 3 years.

Source: *World Cocoa Situation.* **Price Frequency:** monthly, annually. **Effective Market(s):** New York. **Units of Measure:** cents per lb. **Time Period Covered:** latest 40 years.

COCOA BEANS: BRAZILIAN

Source: *International Financial Statistics.* **Price Frequency:** quarterly, annually. **Effective Market(s):** Brazil. **Units of Measure:** cents per lb., index. **Type of Price:** market price, price index. **Time Period Covered:** latest 3 quarters, latest 4 years.

Source: *International Financial Statistics Yearbook.* **Price Frequency:** annually. **Effective Market(s):** Brazil. **Units of Measure:** cents per lb. **Type of Price:** wholesale. **Time Period Covered:** latest 30 years.

Source: *World Cocoa Situation.* **Price Frequency:** monthly, annually. **Effective Market(s):** United States. **Units of Measure:** Dollars per metric ton. **Type of Price:** spot. **Time Period Covered:** latest 4 years.

COCOA BEANS: DOMINICAN REPUBLIC

Source: *World Cocoa Situation.* **Price Frequency:** monthly, annually. **Effective Market(s):** United States. **Units of Measure:** Dollars per metric ton. **Type of Price:** spot. **Time Period Covered:** latest 4 years.

COCOA BEANS: ECUADOR

Source: *World Cocoa Situation.* **Price Frequency:** monthly, annually. **Effective Market(s):** United States. **Units of Measure:** Dollars per metric ton. **Type of Price:** spot. **Time Period Covered:** latest 4 years.

COCOA BEANS: FUTURES

Source: *Commodity Year Book.* **Price Frequency:** monthly. **Effective Market(s):** New York. **Units of Measure:** cents per lb. **Type of Price:** futures. **Time Period Covered:** latest 9 years.

Source: *World Cocoa Situation.* **Price Frequency:** monthly, annually. **Effective Market(s):** New York. **Units of Measure:** Dollars per metric ton. **Type of Price:** futures. **Time Period Covered:** latest 25 years.

COCOA BEANS: GHANA

Source: *FAO Quarterly Bulletin of Statistics.* **Price Frequency:** monthly, annually. **Effective Market(s):** London. **Units of Measure:** British pounds per 1000 kilograms, dollars per metric ton. **Type of Price:** spot. **Time Period Covered:** latest 3 years.

Source: *International Financial Statistics.* **Price Frequency:** quarterly, annually. **Effective Market(s):** London. **Units of Measure:** cents per lb., index. **Type of Price:** market price, price index. **Time Period Covered:** latest 2 quarters, latest 4 years.

Source: *International Financial Statistics Yearbook.* **Price Frequency:** annually. **Effective Market(s):** London. **Units of Measure:** cents per lb. **Type of Price:** wholesale. **Time Period Covered:** latest 30 years.

COCOA BEANS: IVORY COAST

Source: *CRB Commodity Index Report.* **Price Frequency:** weekly. **Effective Market(s):** New York. **Units of Measure:** Dollars per tonne. **Type of Price:** spot. **Time Period Covered:** latest week.

Source: *Investor's Daily.* **Price Frequency:** daily. **Units of Measure:** Dollars per metric ton. **Type of Price:** spot. **Time Period Covered:** latest 2 days.

Source: *New York Times.* **Price Frequency:** daily. **Units of Measure:** Dollars per metric ton. **Type of Price:** cash. **Time Period Covered:** latest 2 days.

Source: *World Cocoa Situation.* **Price Frequency:** monthly, annually. **Effective Market(s):** United States. **Units of Measure:** Dollars per metric ton. **Type of Price:** spot. **Time Period Covered:** latest 4 years.

COCOA BEANS: MALAYSIAN

Source: *World Cocoa Situation.* **Price Frequency:** monthly, annually. **Effective Market(s):** United States. **Units of Measure:** Dollars per metric ton. **Type of Price:** spot. **Time Period Covered:** latest 4 years.

COCOA BEANS: NEW YORK/LONDON

Source: *International Financial Statistics.* **Price Frequency:** monthly, quarterly, annually. **Effective Market(s):** New York/London. **Units of Measure:** cents per lb., index. **Type of Price:** market price, price index. **Time Period Covered:** latest 5 months, latest 5 quarters, latest 5 years.

Source: *International Financial Statistics Yearbook.* **Price Frequency:** annually. **Effective Market(s):** New York/London. **Units of Measure:** cents per lb. **Type of Price:** wholesale. **Time Period Covered:** latest 30 years.

COCOA BUTTER

Source: *Chemical Marketing Reporter.* **Price Frequency:** weekly. **Effective Market(s):** New York. **Units of Measure:** Dollars per lb. **Type of Price:** spot. **Time Period Covered:** latest week.

Source: *Commodity Year Book.* **Price Frequency:** annually. **Effective Market(s):** United States. **Units of Measure:** Dollars per metric ton. **Type of Price:** spot. **Time Period Covered:** latest 8 years.

COCOA BUTTER: AFRICAN

Source: *World Cocoa Situation.* **Price Frequency:** monthly, annually. **Effective Market(s):** United States. **Units of Measure:** Dollars per metric ton. **Type of Price:** spot. **Time Period Covered:** latest 4 years.

COCOA BUTTER: AFRICAN STYLE

Source: *Investor's Daily.* **Price Frequency:** daily. **Units of Measure:** Dollars per metric ton. **Type of Price:** spot. **Time Period Covered:** latest 2 days.

Source: *New York Times.* **Price Frequency:** daily. **Units of Measure:** Dollars per metric ton. **Type of Price:** cash. **Time Period Covered:** latest 2 days.

COCOA BUTTER: NON-AFRICAN

Source: *World Cocoa Situation.* **Price Frequency:** monthly, annually. **Effective Market(s):** United States. **Units of Measure:** Dollars per metric ton. **Type of Price:** spot. **Time Period Covered:** latest 4 years.

COCOA BUTTERFAT RATIO

Source: *Milling & Baking News.* **Price Frequency:** weekly. **Effective Market(s):** East Coast, South America. **Units of Measure:** Dollars per lb. **Time Period Covered:** latest week.

COCOA CAKE

Source: *Commodity Year Book.* **Price Frequency:** annually. **Effective Market(s):** United States. **Units of Measure:** Dollars per metric ton. **Type of Price:** spot. **Time Period Covered:** latest 8 years.

Source: *World Cocoa Situation.* **Price Frequency:** monthly, annually. **Effective Market(s):** United States. **Units of Measure:** Dollars per metric ton. **Type of Price:** spot. **Time Period Covered:** latest 4 years.

COCOA CAKE RATIO

Source: *Milling & Baking News.* **Price Frequency:** weekly. **Effective Market(s):** Mew York. **Units of Measure:** cents per lb. **Time Period Covered:** latest week.

COCOA POWDER

Source: *Bakery Newsletter.* **Price Frequency:** weekly. **Effective Market(s):** New York. **Type of Price:** cash. **Time Period Covered:** last week.

Source: *Dairy Foods.* **Price Frequency:** monthly. **Effective Market(s):** New York. **Units of Measure:** Dollars per lb. **Time Period Covered:** latest 2 weeks.

COCOA POWDER: ALKALIZED, 10-12%

Source: *Milling & Baking News.* **Price Frequency:** weekly. **Effective Market(s):** East Coast. **Units of Measure:** cents per lb. **Time Period Covered:** latest week.

COCOA POWDER: BLACK ALKALIZED, 10-12%

Source: *Milling & Baking News.* **Price Frequency:** weekly. **Effective Market(s):** East Coast. **Units of Measure:** cents per lb. **Time Period Covered:** latest week.

COCOA POWDER: NATURAL BUTTERFAT, 16-18%

Source: *Milling & Baking News.* **Price Frequency:** weekly. **Effective Market(s):** East Coast. **Units of Measure:** cents per lb. **Time Period Covered:** latest week.

COCOA POWDER: NATURAL BUTTERFAT, 22-24%

Source: *Milling & Baking News.* **Price Frequency:** weekly. **Effective Market(s):** East Coast. **Units of Measure:** cents per lb. **Time Period Covered:** latest week.

COCOA POWDER: NATURAL BUTTERFAT, 10-12%

Source: *Milling & Baking News.* **Price Frequency:** weekly. **Effective Market(s):** East Coast. **Units of Measure:** cents per lb. **Time Period Covered:** latest week.

COCOA POWDER: RED ALKALIZED, 10-12%

Source: *Milling & Baking News.* **Price Frequency:** weekly. **Effective Market(s):** East Coast. **Units of Measure:** cents per lb. **Time Period Covered:** latest week.

COCOA POWDER: RED ALKALIZED, 16-18%

Source: *Milling & Baking News.* **Price Frequency:** weekly. **Effective Market(s):** East Coast. **Units of Measure:** cents per lb. **Time Period Covered:** latest week.

COCOA POWDER: RED ALKALIZED, 22-24%

Source: *Milling & Baking News.* **Price Frequency:** weekly. **Effective Market(s):** East Coast. **Units of Measure:** cents per lb. **Time Period Covered:** latest week.

COCOA POWDER RATIO

Source: *Milling & Baking News.* **Price Frequency:** weekly. **Effective Market(s):** New York. **Units of Measure:** cents per lb. **Time Period Covered:** latest week.

COCONUT: DESICCATED

Source: *Prices of Selected Asia/Pacific Products.* **Price Frequency:** monthly. **Effective Market(s):** United States. **Units of Measure:** Dollars per lb. **Type of Price:** high, low. **Time Period Covered:** latest month.

COCONUT: DESICCATED, FINE, PHILIPPINES

Source: *Prices of Selected Asia/Pacific Products.* **Price Frequency:** monthly. **Effective Market(s):** United Kingdom. **Units of Measure:** British pounds per metric ton. **Type of Price:** spot high, spot low. **Time Period Covered:** latest month.

COCONUT: DESICCATED, FINE, SRI LANKAN

Source: *Prices of Selected Asia/Pacific Products.* **Price Frequency:** monthly. **Effective Market(s):** United Kingdom. **Units of Measure:** British pounds per metric ton. **Type of Price:** spot high, spot low. **Time Period Covered:** latest month.

COCONUT: DESICCATED, MEDIUM, PHILIPPINES

Source: *Prices of Selected Asia/Pacific Products.* **Price Frequency:** monthly. **Effective Market(s):** United Kingdom. **Units of Measure:** British pounds per metric ton. **Type of Price:** spot high, spot low. **Time Period Covered:** latest month.

COCONUT: DESICCATED, MEDIUM, SRI LANKAN

Source: *Prices of Selected Asia/Pacific Products.* **Price Frequency:** monthly. **Effective Market(s):** United Kingdom. **Units of Measure:** British pounds per metric ton. **Type of Price:** spot high, spot low. **Time Period Covered:** latest month.

COCONUT EXPELLERS

Source: *Agra Europe.* **Price Frequency:** weekly, irregularly. **Effective Market(s):** Rotterdam. **Units of Measure:** Dollars per tonne. **Type of Price:** average. **Time Period Covered:** latest week.

COCONUT FIBRES: FEHRER MACHINE TWISTOMAT

Source: *Prices of Selected Asia/Pacific Products.* **Price Frequency:** monthly. **Effective Market(s):** main continental ports. **Units of Measure:** Dollars per metric ton. **Type of Price:** high, low. **Time Period Covered:** latest month.

COCONUT FIBRES: HACKLED, UNCUT, TWO TIES HB, SRI LANKAN

Source: *Prices of Selected Asia/Pacific Products.* **Price Frequency:** monthly. **Effective Market(s):** main continental ports. **Units of Measure:** Dollars per metric ton. **Type of Price:** high, low. **Time Period Covered:** latest month.

COCONUT OIL

Source: *Dairy Foods.* **Price Frequency:** monthly. **Effective Market(s):** Pacific coast. **Units of Measure:** Dollars per lb. **Time Period Covered:** latest 2 weeks.

Source: *Investor's Daily.* **Price Frequency:** daily. **Effective Market(s):** New Orleans. **Units of Measure:** Dollars per lb. **Type of Price:** spot. **Time Period Covered:** latest 2 days.

Source: *Milling & Baking News.* **Price Frequency:** weekly. **Effective Market(s):** ports. **Units of Measure:** cents per lb. **Type of Price:** spot bulk. **Time Period Covered:** latest week.

Source: *National Provisioner.* **Price Frequency:** daily. **Effective Market(s):** Pacific coast. **Units of Measure:** cents per lb. **Time Period Covered:** selected day.

Source: *New York Times.* **Price Frequency:** daily. **Effective Market(s):** New Orleans. **Units of Measure:** Dollars per lb. **Type of Price:** cash. **Time Period Covered:** latest 2 days.

Source: *World Oilseed Situation and Market Highlights.* **Price Frequency:** monthly, annually. **Effective Market(s):** Rotterdam, United States. **Units of Measure:** Dollars per metric ton. **Time Period Covered:** monthly latest 2 months, annually latest 2 years.

COCONUT OIL: CRUDE

Source: *Asian Wall Street Journal.* **Price Frequency:** daily. **Effective Market(s):** New Orleans. **Units of Measure:** Dollars per lb. **Type of Price:** cash. **Time Period Covered:** latest 2 days, year ago.

Source: *Chemical Marketing Reporter.* **Price Frequency:** weekly. **Effective Market(s):** New York, Pacific. **Units of Measure:** cents per lb. **Type of Price:** spot. **Time Period Covered:** latest week.

Source: *Commodity Year Book.* **Price Frequency:** monthly, annually. **Effective Market(s):** New York. **Units of Measure:** cents per lb. **Time Period Covered:** latest 8 years.

Source: *Oil Crops Situation and Outlook.* **Price Frequency:** monthly. **Effective Market(s):** New York. **Units of Measure:** cents per lb. **Type of Price:** wholesale. **Time Period Covered:** latest 5 months.

Source: *Prices of Selected Asia/Pacific Products.* **Price Frequency:** monthly, seasonally. **Effective Market(s):** Tokyo. **Units of Measure:** Japanese yen per kilogram. **Type of Price:** high, low. **Time Period Covered:** latest month.

Source: *Prices of Selected Asia/Pacific Products.* **Price Frequency:** monthly, seasonally. **Effective Market(s):** Liverpool. **Units of Measure:** British pounds per metric ton. **Type of Price:** high, low. **Time Period Covered:** latest month.

Source: *Prices of Selected Asia/Pacific Products.* **Price Frequency:** monthly, seasonally. **Effective Market(s):** New York. **Units of Measure:** Dollars per lb. **Type of Price:** spot high, spot low. **Time Period Covered:** latest month.

Source: *Wall Street Journal.* **Price Frequency:** daily. **Effective Market(s):** New Orleans. **Units of Measure:** Dollars per lb. **Time Period Covered:** latest day, day ago, year ago.

COCONUT OIL: CRUDE, PACIFIC

Source: *Journal of Commerce and Commercial.* **Price Frequency:** daily. **Units of Measure:** Dollars per lb. **Type of Price:** spot supplier. **Time Period Covered:** latest day.

COCONUT OIL: CRUDE, PHILIPPINES/ INDONESIAN

Source: *Prices of Selected Asia/Pacific Products.* **Price Frequency:** monthly, seasonally. **Effective Market(s):** Rotterdam. **Units of Measure:** Dollars per metric ton. **Type of Price:** high, low. **Time Period Covered:** latest month.

COCONUT OIL: PHILIPPINES

Source: *FAO Quarterly Bulletin of Statistics.* **Price Frequency:** monthly, annually. **Effective Market(s):** North Sea ports. **Units of Measure:** Dollars per 1000 kilograms, dollars per metric ton. **Time Period Covered:** latest 3 years.

Source: *Financial Times.* **Price Frequency:** daily. **Effective Market(s):** Rotterdam. **Units of Measure:** Dollars per tonne. **Type of Price:** spot. **Time Period Covered:** latest day.

Source: *International Financial Statistics.* **Price Frequency:** monthly, quarterly, annually. **Effective Market(s):** New York. **Units of Measure:** cents per lb., index. **Type of Price:** market price, price index. **Time Period Covered:** latest 5 months, latest 5 quarters, latest 5 years.

Source: *International Financial Statistics Yearbook.* **Price Frequency:** annually. **Effective Market(s):** New York, Philippines. **Units of Measure:** cents per lb. **Type of Price:** wholesale. **Time Period Covered:** latest 30 years.

Source: *International Financial Statistics.* **Price Frequency:** quarterly, annually. **Effective Market(s):** Philippines. **Units of Measure:** cents per lb. index. **Type of Price:** market price, price index. **Time Period Covered:** latest 3 quarters, latest 4 years.

Source: *Prices of Selected Asia/Pacific Products.* **Price Frequency:** monthly, seasonally. **Effective Market(s):** Hong Kong. **Units of Measure:** Hong Kong dollars per picul. **Type of Price:** wholesale high, wholesale low. **Time Period Covered:** latest month.

COCONUT OIL: PHILIPPINES/INDONESIAN

Source: *Commodity Trade and Price Trends.* **Price Frequency:** annually. **Effective Market(s):** Rotterdam. **Units of Measure:** Dollars per metric ton, 1980 constant dollars per metric ton. **Time Period Covered:** latest 37 years.

Source: *Fruit and Tropical Products.* **Price Frequency:** monthly, annually. **Effective Market(s):** Rotterdam. **Units of Measure:** Dollars per tonne. **Type of Price:** average. **Time Period Covered:** monthly latest year, annually latest 2 years.

Source: *Monthly Commodity Price Bulletin.* **Price Frequency:** monthly, annually. **Effective Market(s):** Rotterdam. **Units of Measure:** Dollars per metric ton. **Time Period Covered:** latest 5 years.

Source: *Monthly Commodity Price Bulletin Supplement.* **Price Frequency:** monthly, quarterly, annually. **Effective Market(s):** Rotterdam. **Units of Measure:** Dollars per tonne. **Time Period Covered:** latest 20 years.

Source: *Oil World.* **Price Frequency:** weekly, monthly, annually. **Effective Market(s):** Rotterdam. **Units of Measure:** Dollars per tonne. **Type of Price:** lowest representative asking. **Time Period Covered:** weekly latest 3 weeks, monthly latest 2 months, annually latest 2 years.

Source: *UNCTAD Commodity Yearbook.* **Price Frequency:** annually. **Effective Market(s):** Rotterdam. **Units of Measure:** Dollars per metric ton. **Type of Price:** free market. **Time Period Covered:** latest 12 years.

Source: *World Oilseed Situation and Market Highlights.* **Price Frequency:** monthly, annually. **Effective Market(s):** Rotterdam. **Units of Measure:** Dollars per metric ton. **Time Period Covered:** monthly latest year, annually latest 9 years.

COCONUT OIL: REFINED

Source: *Chemical Marketing Reporter.* **Price Frequency:** weekly. **Effective Market(s):** New York. **Units of Measure:** Dollars per lb. **Type of Price:** spot. **Time Period Covered:** latest week.

Source: *Prices of Selected Asia/Pacific Products.* **Price Frequency:** monthly, seasonally. **Effective Market(s):** Tokyo. **Units of Measure:** Japanese yen per kilogram. **Type of Price:** high, low. **Time Period Covered:** latest month.

COCONUT OIL: REFINED, SINGAPORE

Source: *Prices of Selected Asia/Pacific Products.* **Price Frequency:** monthly, seasonally. **Effective Market(s):** Hong Kong. **Units of Measure:** Hong Kong dollars per picul. **Type of Price:** high, low. **Time Period Covered:** latest month.

COCONUT OIL: SINGAPORE

Source: *Prices of Selected Asia/Pacific Products.* **Price Frequency:** monthly, seasonally. **Effective Market(s):** Hong Kong. **Units of Measure:** Hong Kong dollars per picul. **Type of Price:** wholesale high, wholesale low. **Time Period Covered:** latest month.

COCONUT OIL: THAI

Source: *Prices of Selected Asia/Pacific Products.* **Price Frequency:** monthly, seasonally. **Effective Market(s):** Bangkok. **Units of Measure:** Thai baht per 12.9 kilograms. **Type of Price:** wholesale high, wholesale low. **Time Period Covered:** latest month.

COCONUT OIL ACIDS: DISTILLED

Source: *Chemical Marketing Reporter.* **Price Frequency:** weekly. **Effective Market(s):** New York. **Units of Measure:** Dollars per lb. **Type of Price:** spot. **Time Period Covered:** latest week.

COCONUT OIL ACIDS: DOUBLE DISTILLED

Source: *Chemical Marketing Reporter.* **Price Frequency:** weekly. **Effective Market(s):** New York. **Units of Measure:** Dollars per lb. **Type of Price:** spot. **Time Period Covered:** latest week.

COCONUTS: 16'S, COTE D'IVOIRE

Source: *Prices of Selected Asia/Pacific Products.* **Price Frequency:** monthly, seasonally. **Effective Market(s):** West Germany. **Units of Measure:** West German marks per kilogram. **Type of Price:** wholesale high, wholesale low. **Time Period Covered:** latest month.

COCONUTS: 18'S, DOMINICAN REPUBLIC

Source: *Prices of Selected Asia/Pacific Products.* **Price Frequency:** monthly, seasonally. **Effective Market(s):** France. **Units of Measure:** French francs per kilogram. **Type of Price:** wholesale high, wholesale low. **Time Period Covered:** latest month.

COCONUTS: 20'S, DOMINICAN REPUBLIC

Source: *Prices of Selected Asia/Pacific Products.* **Price Frequency:** monthly, seasonally. **Effective Market(s):** Netherlands. **Units of Measure:** Dutch guilders per kilogram. **Type of Price:** wholesale high, wholesale low. **Time Period Covered:** latest month.

COCONUTS: 25'S, DOMINICAN REPUBLIC

Source: *Prices of Selected Asia/Pacific Products.* **Price Frequency:** monthly, seasonally. **Effective Market(s):** United Kingdom. **Units of Measure:** British pounds per kilogram. **Type of Price:** wholesale high, wholesale low. **Time Period Covered:** latest month.

COCONUTS: 25'S, SRI LANKAN

Source: *Prices of Selected Asia/Pacific Products.* **Price Frequency:** monthly, seasonally. **Effective Market(s):** United Kingdom. **Units of Measure:** British pounds per kilogram. **Type of Price:** wholesale high, wholesale low. **Time Period Covered:** latest month.

COCONUTS: 50'S, COTE D'IVOIRE

Source: *Prices of Selected Asia/Pacific Products.* **Price Frequency:** monthly, seasonally. **Effective Market(s):** Netherlands. **Units of Measure:** Dutch guilders per kilogram. **Type of Price:** wholesale high, wholesale low. **Time Period Covered:** latest month.

COCONUTS: DOMINICAN REPUBLIC

Source: *Lancaster Farming.* **Price Frequency:** weekly, seasonally. **Effective Market(s):** Pennsylvania. **Units of Measure:** Dollars per sack. **Type of Price:** market. **Time Period Covered:** latest week.

COCONUTS: TUPSAKAE, LARGE SIZE, THAI

Source: *Prices of Selected Asia/Pacific Products.* **Price Frequency:** monthly, seasonally. **Effective Market(s):** Bangkok. **Units of Measure:** Thai baht per 100 nuts. **Type of Price:** wholesale high, wholesale low. **Time Period Covered:** latest month.

COD: ALASKAN, FROZEN AT SEA

Source: *Seafood Price-Current.* **Price Frequency:** semiweekly. **Effective Market(s):** West Coast. **Units of Measure:** Dollars per lb. **Type of Price:** first receiver. **Time Period Covered:** latest day.

COD: BLACK

see also Sablefish.

COD: BLACK, FILLETS, FRESH

Source: *Seafoood Price-Current.* **Price Frequency:** semiweekly. **Effective Market(s):** West Coast. **Units of Measure:** Dollars per lb. **Type of Price:** sale by first receiver. **Time Period Covered:** latest day.

COD: BLACK, WHOLE, DRESSED, DOMESTIC

Source: *Seafood Price-Current.* **Price Frequency:** semiweekly. **Effective Market(s):** West Coast. **Units of Measure:** Dollars per lb. **Type of Price:** sale by first receiver. **Time Period Covered:** latest day.

COD: BLOCKS, IMPORTED

Source: *NMFS Green Sheet Supplement.* **Price Frequency:** weekly. **Effective Market(s):** New England. **Units of Measure:** Dollars per lb. **Type of Price:** processor. **Time Period Covered:** lastest week.

COD: BROWN ROCK, FILLETS, FRESH

Source: *Seafood Price-Current.* **Price Frequency:** semi-weekly. **Effective Market(s):** West Coast. **Units of Measure:** Dollars per lb. **Type of Price:** sale by first receiver. **Time Period Covered:** latest day.

COD: FILLETS, BONELESS, CANADIAN

Source: *NMFS Green Sheet Supplement.* **Price Frequency:** weekly. **Effective Market(s):** New England. **Units of Measure:** Dollars per lb. **Type of Price:** to primary wholesaler. **Time Period Covered:** lastest week.

COD: FILLETS, BONELESS, DANISH

Source: *NMFS Green Sheet Supplement.* **Price Frequency:** weekly. **Effective Market(s):** New England. **Units of Measure:** Dollars per lb. **Type of Price:** to primary wholesaler. **Time Period Covered:** lastest week.

COD: FILLETS, BONELESS, ICELANDIC

Source: *NMFS Green Sheet Supplement.* **Price Frequency:** weekly. **Effective Market(s):** New England. **Units of Measure:** Dollars per lb. **Type of Price:** to primary wholesaler. **Time Period Covered:** lastest week.

COD: FILLETS, BONELESS, NORWEGIAN

Source: *NMFS Green Sheet Supplement.* **Price Frequency:** weekly. **Effective Market(s):** New England. **Units of Measure:** Dollars per lb. **Type of Price:** to primary wholesaler. **Time Period Covered:** lastest week.

COD: FILLETS, BREADED, FROZEN

Source: *HRI-Buyers Guide.* **Price Frequency:** weekly. **Effective Market(s):** New York. **Units of Measure:** Dollars per case. **Type of Price:** price paid by dining places & institutions. **Time Period Covered:** latest week.

COD: FILLETS, CANADIAN

Source: *NMFS Green Sheet Supplement.* **Price Frequency:** weekly. **Effective Market(s):** New England. **Units of Measure:** Dollars per lb. **Type of Price:** to primary wholesaler. **Time Period Covered:** lastest week.

COD: FILLETS, DOMESTIC

Source: *NMFS Green Sheet Supplement.* **Price Frequency:** weekly. **Effective Market(s):** New England. **Units of Measure:** Dollars per lb. **Type of Price:** to primary wholesaler. **Time Period Covered:** lastest week.

COD: FILLETS, FRESH

Source: *HRI-Buyers Guide.* **Price Frequency:** weekly. **Effective Market(s):** New York. **Units of Measure:** Dollars per lb. **Type of Price:** price paid by dining places & institutions. **Time Period Covered:** latest week.

COD: FILLETS, FROZEN

Source: *HRI-Buyers Guide.* **Price Frequency:** weekly. **Effective Market(s):** New York. **Units of Measure:** Dollars per case. **Type of Price:** price paid by dining places & institutions. **Time Period Covered:** latest week.

COD: FILLETS, FROZEN, CANADIAN

Source: *Seafood Price-Current.* **Price Frequency:** semi-weekly. **Effective Market(s):** Mid-Atlantic. **Units of Measure:** Dollars per lb. **Type of Price:** first receiver. **Time Period Covered:** latest day.

COD: FILLETS, ICELANDIC

Source: *NMFS Green Sheet Supplement.* **Price Frequency:** weekly. **Effective Market(s):** New England. **Units of Measure:** Dollars per lb. **Type of Price:** to primary wholesaler. **Time Period Covered:** lastest week.

COD: FILLETS, SKINLESS, BONELESS, FROZEN, CANADIAN

Source: *Seafood Price-Current.* **Price Frequency:** semi-weekly. **Effective Market(s):** Mid-Atlantic. **Units of Measure:** Dollars per lb. **Type of Price:** first receiver. **Time Period Covered:** latest day.

COD: FILLETS, SKINLESS, BONELESS, FROZEN, ICELANDIC

Source: *Seafood Price-Current.* **Price Frequency:** semi-weekly. **Effective Market(s):** Mid-Atlantic. **Units of Measure:** Dollars per lb. **Type of Price:** first receiver. **Time Period Covered:** latest day.

COD: FILLETS, SKINLESS, FROZEN, CANADIAN

Source: *Seafood Price-Current.* **Price Frequency:** semi-weekly. **Effective Market(s):** Mid-Atlantic. **Units of Measure:** Dollars per lb. **Type of Price:** first receiver. **Time Period Covered:** latest day.

COD: FISH PORTIONS, BATTERED, COOKED

Source: *NMFS Green Sheet Supplement.* **Price Frequency:** weekly. **Effective Market(s):** New England. **Units of Measure:** Dollars per lb. **Type of Price:** to primary wholesalers. **Time Period Covered:** lastest week.

COD: FISH PORTIONS, BATTERED, RAW

Source: *NMFS Green Sheet Supplement.* **Price Frequency:** weekly. **Effective Market(s):** New England. **Units of Measure:** Dollars per lb. **Type of Price:** to primary wholesalers. **Time Period Covered:** lastest week.

COD: FISH PORTIONS, BREADED, COOKED

Source: *NMFS Green Sheet Supplement.* **Price Frequency:** weekly. **Effective Market(s):** New England. **Units of Measure:** Dollars per lb. **Type of Price:** to primary wholesalers. **Time Period Covered:** lastest week.

COD: FISH PORTIONS, BREADED, RAW

Source: *NMFS Green Sheet Supplement.* **Price Frequency:** weekly. **Effective Market(s):** New England. **Units of Measure:** Dollars per lb. **Type of Price:** to primary wholesalers. **Time Period Covered:** lastest week.

COD: FISH STICKS, BATTERED, COOKED

Source: *NMFS Green Sheet Supplement.* **Price Frequency:** weekly. **Effective Market(s):** New England. **Units of Measure:** Dollars per lb. **Type of Price:** to primary wholesalers. **Time Period Covered:** lastest week.

COD: FISH STICKS, BATTERED, RAW

Source: *NMFS Green Sheet Supplement.* **Price Frequency:** weekly. **Effective Market(s):** New England. **Units of Measure:** Dollars per lb. **Type of Price:** to primary wholesalers. **Time Period Covered:** lastest week.

COD: FISH STICKS, BREADED, COOKED

Source: *NMFS Green Sheet Supplement.* **Price Frequency:** weekly. **Effective Market(s):** New England. **Units of Measure:** Dollars per lb. **Type of Price:** to primary wholesalers. **Time Period Covered:** lastest week.

COD: FISH STICKS, BREADED, RAW

Source: *NMFS Green Sheet Supplement.* **Price Frequency:** weekly. **Effective Market(s):** New England. **Units of Measure:** Dollars per lb. **Type of Price:** to primary wholesalers. **Time Period Covered:** lastest week.

COD: LING, FILLETS, FRESH

Source: *Seafood Price-Current.* **Price Frequency:** semiweekly. **Effective Market(s):** West Coast. **Units of Measure:** Dollars per lb. **Type of Price:** sale by first receiver. **Time Period Covered:** latest day.

COD: LING, WHOLE, DRESSED

Source: *Seafood Price-Current.* **Price Frequency:** semiweekly. **Effective Market(s):** West Coast. **Units of Measure:** Dollars per lb. **Type of Price:** sale by first receiver. **Time Period Covered:** latest day.

COD: MARKET, FILLETS, BONELESS, FRESH

Source: *Seafood Price-Current.* **Price Frequency:** semiweekly. **Effective Market(s):** Mid-Atlantic, New England. **Units of Measure:** Dollars per lb. **Type of Price:** sale by first receiver. **Time Period Covered:** latest day.

COD: MARKET, WHOLE, HEAD OFF, FRESH

Source: *Seafood Price-Current.* **Price Frequency:** semiweekly. **Effective Market(s):** Boston, Mid-Atlantic, New Bedford (MA), Portland (ME). **Units of Measure:** Dollars per lb. **Type of Price:** sale by first receiver, auction price. **Time Period Covered:** latest day.

COD: MINCED, CANADIAN

Source: *Seafood Price-Current.* **Price Frequency:** semiweekly. **Effective Market(s):** New England. **Units of Measure:** Dollars per lb. **Time Period Covered:** latest day.

COD: MINCED, IMPORTED

Source: *NMFS Green Sheet Supplement.* **Price Frequency:** weekly. **Effective Market(s):** New England. **Units of Measure:** Dollars per lb. **Type of Price:** processor. **Time Period Covered:** lastest week.

COD: PROCESSORS FISH BLOCKS, CANADIAN/JAPANESE/ICELANDIC/NORWEGIAN

Source: *Seafood Price-Current.* **Price Frequency:** semiweekly. **Effective Market(s):** New England. **Units of Measure:** Dollars per lb. **Time Period Covered:** latest day.

COD: PROCESSORS FISH BLOCKS, KOREAN

Source: *Seafood Price-Current.* **Price Frequency:** semiweekly. **Effective Market(s):** New England. **Units of Measure:** Dollars per lb. **Time Period Covered:** latest day.

COD: RED ROCK, FILLETS, FRESH

Source: *Seafood Price-Current.* **Price Frequency:** semiweekly. **Effective Market(s):** West Coast. **Units of Measure:** Dollars per lb. **Type of Price:** sale by first receiver. **Time Period Covered:** latest day.

COD: SCROD, FILLETS, BONELESS, FRESH

Source: *Seafood Price-Current.* **Price Frequency:** semiweekly. **Effective Market(s):** Mid-Atlantic, New England. **Units of Measure:** Dollars per lb. **Type of Price:** sale by first receiver. **Time Period Covered:** latest day.

COD: SCROD, WHOLE, HEAD OFF, FRESH

Source: *Seafood Price-Current.* **Price Frequency:** semiweekly. **Effective Market(s):** Boston, Mid-Atlantic, New Bedford (MA), Portland (ME). **Units of Measure:** Dollars per lb. **Type of Price:** sale by first receiver, auction price. **Time Period Covered:** latest day.

COD: TRUE, FILLETS, FRESH

Source: *Seafood Price-Current.* **Price Frequency:** semiweekly. **Effective Market(s):** West Coast. **Units of Measure:** Dollars per lb. **Type of Price:** sale by first receiver. **Time Period Covered:** latest day.

COD: WHOLE, FRESH

Source: *HRI-Buyers Guide.* **Price Frequency:** weekly. **Effective Market(s):** New York. **Units of Measure:** Dollars per lb. **Type of Price:** price paid by dining places & institutions. **Time Period Covered:** latest week.

COD NAPE: CANADIAN

Source: *Seafood Price-Current.* **Price Frequency:** semiweekly. **Effective Market(s):** New England. **Units of Measure:** Dollars per lb. **Time Period Covered:** latest day.

COD OIL: REFINED

Source: *Chemical Marketing Reporter.* **Price Frequency:** weekly. **Effective Market(s):** Gloucester (MA). **Units of Measure:** Dollars per lb. **Type of Price:** spot. **Time Period Covered:** latest week.

COD TAILS: FROZEN, CANADIAN

Source: *Seafood Price-Current.* **Price Frequency:** semiweekly. **Effective Market(s):** Mid-Atlantic. **Units of Measure:** Dollars per lb. **Type of Price:** first receiver. **Time Period Covered:** latest day.

CODEINE ALKALOID: NF

Source: *Chemical Marketing Reporter.* **Price Frequency:** weekly. **Effective Market(s):** New York. **Units of Measure:** Dollars per kilo. **Type of Price:** spot. **Time Period Covered:** latest week.

CODEINE PHOSPHATE

Source: *Journal of Commerce and Commercial.* **Price Frequency:** weekly in Friday issue. **Units of Measure:** Dollars per kilo. **Type of Price:** spot. **Time Period Covered:** latest week.

CODEINE PHOSPHATE: USP

Source: *Chemical Marketing Reporter.* **Price Frequency:** weekly. **Effective Market(s):** New York. **Units of Measure:** Dollars per kilo. **Type of Price:** spot. **Time Period Covered:** latest week.

CODEINE SULFATE

Source: *Journal of Commerce and Commercial.* **Price Frequency:** weekly in Friday issue. **Units of Measure:** Dollars per kilo. **Type of Price:** spot. **Time Period Covered:** latest week.

CODEINE SULFATE: NF

Source: *Chemical Marketing Reporter.* **Price Frequency:** weekly. **Effective Market(s):** New York. **Units of Measure:** Dollars per kilo. **Type of Price:** spot. **Time Period Covered:** latest week.

CODLIVER OIL

Source: *Journal of Commerce and Commercial.* **Price Frequency:** weekly in Friday issue. **Units of Measure:** Dollars per gallon. **Type of Price:** spot. **Time Period Covered:** latest week.

CODLIVER OIL: NF

Source: *Chemical Marketing Reporter.* **Price Frequency:** weekly. **Effective Market(s):** New York. **Units of Measure:** Dollars per gallon. **Type of Price:** spot. **Time Period Covered:** latest week.

COFFEE

Source: *Agricultural Outlook.* **Price Frequency:** monthly, annually. **Effective Market(s):** New York. **Units of Measure:** Dollars per lb. **Type of Price:** spot import. **Time Period Covered:** monthly latest 6 months, annually latest 3 years.

Source: *Agricultural Prices Annual Summary.* **Price Frequency:** annually. **Effective Market(s):** California, Hawaii. **Units of Measure:** Dollars per lb. **Type of Price:** average price received by farmer. **Time Period Covered:** latest 6 years.

Source: *Economic and Energy Indicators.* **Price Frequency:** monthly, quarterly annually. **Units of Measure:** cents per lb. **Time Period Covered:** latest 3 months, quarters, and years.

Source: *Far Eastern Economic Review.* **Price Frequency:** weekly. **Effective Market(s):** New York. **Units of Measure:** cents per lb. **Time Period Covered:** latest week, week ago, 3 months ago, year ago.

Source: *International Financial Statistics.* **Price Frequency:** monthly, quarterly, annually. **Effective Market(s):** New York. **Units of Measure:** cents per lb., index. **Type of Price:** market price, price index. **Time Period Covered:** latest 5 months, latest 5 quarters, latest 5 years.

Source: *International Financial Statistics Yearbook.* **Price Frequency:** annually. **Effective Market(s):** New York. **Units of Measure:** cents per lb. **Type of Price:** wholesale. **Time Period Covered:** latest 30 years.

Source: *Monthly Commodity Price Bulletin.* **Price Frequency:** monthly, annually. **Units of Measure:** cents per lb. **Type of Price:** composite indicator price 1976. **Time Period Covered:** latest 5 years.

Source: *Monthly Commodity Price Bulletin.* **Price Frequency:** monthly, annually. **Units of Measure:** cents per lb. **Type of Price:** composite indicator price 1979. **Time Period Covered:** latest 5 years.

Source: *Monthly Commodity Price Bulletin Supplement.* **Price Frequency:** monthly, quarterly, annually. **Effective Market(s):** New York. **Units of Measure:** cents per lb. **Type of Price:** composite indicator price 1976. **Time Period Covered:** latest 20 years.

Source: *Monthly Commodity Price Bulletin Supplement.* **Price Frequency:** monthly, quarterly, annually. **Effective Market(s):** New York. **Units of Measure:** cents per lb. **Type of Price:** composite indicator price 1979. **Time Period Covered:** latest 10 years.

Source: *UNCTAD Commodity Yearbook.* **Price Frequency:** annually. **Units of Measure:** Dollars per metric ton. **Type of Price:** free market. **Time Period Covered:** latest 12 years.

COFFEE: "C", FUTURES

Source: *Financial Times.* **Price Frequency:** daily. **Effective Market(s):** New York. **Units of Measure:** cents per lb. **Type of Price:** futures. **Time Period Covered:** latest day.

Source: *Investor's Daily.* **Price Frequency:** daily. **Effective Market(s):** New York. **Units of Measure:** cents per lb. **Type of Price:** futures. **Time Period Covered:** latest day.

COFFEE: ALL GRADES, KENYAN

Source: *Fruit and Tropical Products.* **Price Frequency:** monthly. **Effective Market(s):** Kenya. **Units of Measure:** Kenya schillings per 50 kilos. **Type of Price:** auction. **Time Period Covered:** latest 5 years.

COFFEE: ANGOLAN

Source: *Commodity Trade and Price Trends.* **Price Frequency:** annually. **Effective Market(s):** New York. **Units of Measure:** cents per kilogram, 1980 constant cents per kilogram. **Type of Price:** spot. **Time Period Covered:** latest 37 years.

COFFEE: BRAZILIAN

Source: *Asian Wall Street Journal.* **Price Frequency:** daily. **Effective Market(s):** New York. **Units of Measure:** Dollars per lb. **Type of Price:** cash. **Time Period Covered:** latest 2 days, year ago.

Source: *Commodity Trade and Price Trends.* **Price Frequency:** annually. **Effective Market(s):** New York. **Units of Measure:** cents per kilogram, 1980 constant cents per kilogram. **Type of Price:** spot. **Time Period Covered:** latest 37 years.

Source: *Commodity Year Book.* **Price Frequency:** monthly, annually. **Effective Market(s):** New York. **Units of Measure:** cents per lb. **Type of Price:** spot. **Time Period Covered:** latest 8 years.

Source: *International Financial Statistics.* **Price Frequency:** monthly, quarterly, annually. **Effective Market(s):** New York. **Units of Measure:** cents per lb., index. **Type of Price:** market price, price index. **Time Period Covered:** latest 5 months, latest 5 quarters, latest 5 years.

Source: *International Financial Statistics.* **Price Frequency:** quarterly, annually. **Effective Market(s):** Brazil. **Units of Measure:** cents per lb. index. **Type of Price:** market price, price index. **Time Period Covered:** latest 3 quarters, latest 4 years.

Source: *International Financial Statistics Yearbook.* **Price Frequency:** annually. **Effective Market(s):** New York, Brazil. **Units of Measure:** cents per lb. **Type of Price:** wholesale. **Time Period Covered:** latest 30 years.

Source: *Wall Street Journal.* **Price Frequency:** daily. **Effective Market(s):** New York. **Units of Measure:** Dollars per lb. **Time Period Covered:** latest day, day ago, year ago.

COFFEE: BRAZILIAN AND OTHER ARABICAS

Source: *Monthly Commodity Price Bulletin.* **Price Frequency:** monthly, annually. **Effective Market(s):** New York. **Units of Measure:** cents per lb. **Time Period Covered:** latest 5 years.

Source: *Monthly Commodity Price Bulletin Supplement.* **Price Frequency:** monthly, quarterly, annually. **Effective Market(s):** New York. **Units of Measure:** cents per lb. **Time Period Covered:** latest 20 years.

Source: *UNCTAD Commodity Yearbook.* **Price Frequency:** annually. **Effective Market(s):** New York. **Units of Measure:** Dollars per metric ton. **Type of Price:** free market. **Time Period Covered:** latest 12 years.

COFFEE: COLOMBIAN

Source: *Asian Wall Street Journal.* **Price Frequency:** daily. **Effective Market(s):** New York. **Units of Measure:** Dollars per lb. **Type of Price:** cash. **Time Period Covered:** latest 2 days, year ago.

Source: *International Financial Statistics.* **Price Frequency:** monthly, quarterly, annually. **Effective Market(s):** Colombia, New York. **Units of Measure:** cents per lb., index. **Type of Price:** market price, price index. **Time Period Covered:** latest 2 months, latest 4 quarters, latest 5 years.

Source: *International Financial Statistics Yearbook.* **Price Frequency:** annually. **Effective Market(s):** Colombia, New York. **Units of Measure:** cents per lb. **Type of Price:** wholesale. **Time Period Covered:** latest 30 years.

Source: *Journal of Commerce and Commercial.* **Price Frequency:** daily. **Effective Market(s):** New York. **Units of Measure:** Dollars per ton. **Type of Price:** spot supplier. **Time Period Covered:** latest day.

COFFEE: COLOMBIAN MILD ARABICAS

Source: *Commodity Trade and Price Trends.* **Price Frequency:** annually. **Effective Market(s):** New York. **Units of Measure:** cents per kilogram, 1980 constant cents per kilogram. **Type of Price:** spot. **Time Period Covered:** latest 37 years.

Source: *Fruit and Tropical Products.* **Price Frequency:** monthly, annually. **Effective Market(s):** International Coffee Organization. **Units of Measure:** cents per lb. **Type of Price:** indicator. **Time Period Covered:** latest 4 years.

Source: *Monthly Commodity Price Bulletin.* **Price Frequency:** monthly, annually. **Effective Market(s):** New York. **Units of Measure:** cents per lb. **Time Period Covered:** latest 5 years.

Source: *Monthly Commodity Price Bulletin Supplement.* **Price Frequency:** monthly, quarterly, annually. **Effective Market(s):** New York. **Units of Measure:** cents per lb. **Type of Price:** average. **Time Period Covered:** latest 20 years.

COFFEE: COMPOSITE

Source: *Fruit and Tropical Products.* **Price Frequency:** monthly, annually. **Effective Market(s):** International Coffee Organization. **Units of Measure:** cents per lb. **Type of Price:** indicator. **Time Period Covered:** latest 4 years.

COFFEE: FUTURES

Source: *Asian Wall Street Journal.* **Price Frequency:** daily. **Effective Market(s):** London, New York. **Units of Measure:** British pounds per long ton, cents per lb. **Type of Price:** futures. **Time Period Covered:** latest day.

Source: *Barron's.* **Price Frequency:** weekly. **Effective Market(s):** New York. **Units of Measure:** cents per lb. **Type of Price:** futures. **Time Period Covered:** latest week.

Source: *Far Eastern Economic Review.* **Price Frequency:** weekly. **Effective Market(s):** New York. **Units of Measure:** cents per lb. **Type of Price:** futures. **Time Period Covered:** latest week.

Source: *Financial Times.* **Price Frequency:** daily. **Effective Market(s):** London. **Units of Measure:** British pounds per tonne. **Type of Price:** futures. **Time Period Covered:** latest day.

Source: *Los Angeles Times.* **Price Frequency:** daily. **Effective Market(s):** New York. **Units of Measure:** cents per lb. **Type of Price:** futures. **Time Period Covered:** latest day.

Source: *New York Times.* **Price Frequency:** daily. **Effective Market(s):** New York. **Units of Measure:** cents per lb. **Type of Price:** futures. **Time Period Covered:** latest day.

Source: *The Times.* **Price Frequency:** daily. **Effective Market(s):** London. **Units of Measure:** British pounds per tonne. **Type of Price:** futures. **Time Period Covered:** latest day.

Source: *Wall Street Journal.* **Price Frequency:** daily. **Effective Market(s):** New York. **Units of Measure:** cents per lb. **Type of Price:** futures. **Time Period Covered:** latest day.

COFFEE: FUTURES, MAY

Source: *Commodity Year Book.* **Price Frequency:** monthly. **Effective Market(s):** New York. **Units of Measure:** cents per lb. **Type of Price:** futures. **Time Period Covered:** latest 7 years.

COFFEE: GRADE AA, KENYAN

Source: *Fruit and Tropical Products.* **Price Frequency:** monthly. **Effective Market(s):** Kenya. **Units of Measure:** Kenya schillings per 50 kilos. **Type of Price:** auction. **Time Period Covered:** latest 5 years.

COFFEE: GRADE AB, KENYAN

Source: *Fruit and Tropical Products.* **Price Frequency:** monthly. **Effective Market(s):** Kenya. **Units of Measure:** Kenya schillings per 50 kilos. **Type of Price:** auction. **Time Period Covered:** latest 5 years.

COFFEE: GRADE C, KENYAN

Source: *Fruit and Tropical Products.* **Price Frequency:** monthly. **Effective Market(s):** Kenya. **Units of Measure:** Kenya schillings per 50 kilos. **Type of Price:** auction. **Time Period Covered:** latest 5 years.

COFFEE: GRADE TT, KENYAN

Source: *Fruit and Tropical Products.* **Price Frequency:** monthly. **Effective Market(s):** Kenya. **Units of Measure:** Kenya schillings per 50 kilos. **Type of Price:** auction. **Time Period Covered:** latest 5 years.

COFFEE: GREEN

Source: *Agricultural Outlook.* **Price Frequency:** monthly, annually. **Effective Market(s):** New York. **Units of Measure:** cents per lb. **Type of Price:** composite. **Time Period Covered:** monthly latest 5 months, annually latest 4 years.

Source: *FAO Quarterly Bulletin of Statistics.* **Price Frequency:** monthly, annually. **Units of Measure:** Dollars per 100 lbs., dollars per metric ton. **Type of Price:** international coffee agreement composite price. **Time Period Covered:** latest 3 years.

COFFEE: GREEN, COLOMBIAN MILD ARABICAS

Source: *FAO Quarterly Bulletin of Statistics.* **Price Frequency:** monthly, annually, seasonally. **Effective Market(s):** New York. **Units of Measure:** Dollars per 100 lbs., dollars per metric ton. **Time Period Covered:** latest 3 years.

COFFEE: GREEN, OTHER MILD ARABICAS

Source: *FAO Quarterly Bulletin of Statistics.* **Price Frequency:** monthly, annually. **Effective Market(s):** New York. **Units of Measure:** Dollars per 100 lbs., dollars per metric ton. **Time Period Covered:** latest 3 years.

COFFEE: GREEN, ROBUSTAS

Source: *FAO Quarterly Bulletin of Statistics.* **Price Frequency:** monthly, annually. **Effective Market(s):** New York. **Units of Measure:** Dollars per 100 lbs., dollars per metric ton. **Time Period Covered:** latest 3 years.

COFFEE: GREEN, UNWASHED ARABICAS, SANTOS NO. 4, BRAZILIAN

Source: *FAO Quarterly Bulletin of Statistics.* **Price Frequency:** monthly, annually. **Effective Market(s):** New York. **Units of Measure:** Dollars per 100 lbs., dollars per metric ton. **Time Period Covered:** latest 3 years.

COFFEE: GROUND ROAST, ALL PACKS

Source: *Commodity Year Book.* **Price Frequency:** monthly, annually. **Effective Market(s):** United States. **Units of Measure:** cents per lb. **Type of Price:** wholesale. **Time Period Covered:** latest 2 years.

COFFEE: INSTANT

Source: *Statistical Bulletin of the South Pacific: Retail Price Indexes.* **Price Frequency:** annually. **Effective Market(s):** 18 South Pacific markets. **Units of Measure:** Australian dollars per 100 grams. **Type of Price:** retail. **Time Period Covered:** latest year.

COFFEE: MEDLIN

Source: *Investor's Daily.* **Price Frequency:** daily. **Effective Market(s):** New York. **Units of Measure:** Dollars per lb. **Type of Price:** spot. **Time Period Covered:** latest 2 days.

Source: *New York Times.* **Price Frequency:** daily. **Effective Market(s):** New York. **Units of Measure:** Dollars per lb. **Type of Price:** cash. **Time Period Covered:** latest 2 days.

COFFEE: MILD

Source: *International Financial Statistics.* **Price Frequency:** monthly, quarterly, annually. **Effective Market(s):** New York. **Units of Measure:** cents per lb., index. **Type of Price:** market price, price index. **Time Period Covered:** latest 5 months, latest 5 quarters, latest 5 years.

Source: *International Financial Statistics Yearbook.* **Price Frequency:** annually. **Effective Market(s):** New York. **Units of Measure:** cents per lb. **Type of Price:** wholesale. **Time Period Covered:** latest 30 years.

COFFEE: MISCELLANEOUS, KENYAN

Source: *Fruit and Tropical Products.* **Price Frequency:** monthly. **Effective Market(s):** Kenya. **Units of Measure:** Kenya schillings per 50 kilos. **Type of Price:** auction. **Time Period Covered:** latest 5 years.

COFFEE: OTHER MILD ARABICAS

Source: *Commodity Trade and Price Trends.* **Price Frequency:** annually. **Effective Market(s):** New York. **Units of Measure:** cents per kilogram, 1980 constant cents per kilogram. **Type of Price:** spot. **Time Period Covered:** latest 37 years.

Source: *Fruit and Tropical Products.* **Price Frequency:** monthly, annually. **Effective Market(s):** Bremen/Hamburg. **Units of Measure:** cents per lb. **Type of Price:** average. **Time Period Covered:** latest 4 years.

Source: *Fruit and Tropical Products.* **Price Frequency:** monthly, annually. **Effective Market(s):** International Coffee Organization. **Units of Measure:** cents per lb. **Type of Price:** indicator. **Time Period Covered:** latest 4 years.

Source: *Monthly Commodity Price Bulletin.* **Price Frequency:** monthly, annually. **Effective Market(s):** New York, New York/Bremen/Hamburg. **Units of Measure:** cents per lb. **Time Period Covered:** latest 5 years.

Source: *Monthly Commodity Price Bulletin Supplement.* **Price Frequency:** monthly, quarterly, annually. **Effective Market(s):** Bremen/Hamburg, New York. **Units of Measure:** cents per lb. **Time Period Covered:** latest 20 years.

Source: *UNCTAD Commodity Yearbook.* **Price Frequency:** annually. **Effective Market(s):** New York. **Units of Measure:** Dollars per metric ton. **Type of Price:** free market. **Time Period Covered:** latest 12 years.

COFFEE: OTHER MILD ARABICAS, PRIME WASHED, MEXICAN

Source: *Fruit and Tropical Products.* **Price Frequency:** monthly, annually. **Effective Market(s):** New York. **Units of Measure:** cents per lb. **Type of Price:** average. **Time Period Covered:** latest 4 years.

COFFEE: OTHER MILD ARABICAS, PRIME WASHED, GUATEMALAN

Source: *Fruit and Tropical Products.* **Price Frequency:** monthly, annually. **Effective Market(s):** New York. **Units of Measure:** cents per lb. **Type of Price:** average. **Time Period Covered:** latest 4 years.

COFFEE: OTHER MILD ARABICAS, FUTURES

Source: *Fruit and Tropical Products.* **Price Frequency:** monthly, annually. **Effective Market(s):** New York. **Units of Measure:** cents per lb. **Type of Price:** futures. **Time Period Covered:** latest 4 years.

COFFEE: PARANA

Source: *Investor's Daily.* **Price Frequency:** daily. **Effective Market(s):** New York. **Units of Measure:** Dollars per lb. **Type of Price:** spot. **Time Period Covered:** latest 2 days.

Source: *New York Times.* **Price Frequency:** daily. **Effective Market(s):** New York. **Units of Measure:** Dollars per lb. **Type of Price:** cash. **Time Period Covered:** latest 2 days.

COFFEE: PHILIPPINES, FUTURES

Source: *Asian Wall Street Journal.* **Price Frequency:** daily. **Effective Market(s):** Manila. **Units of Measure:** Philippine pesos per kilo. **Type of Price:** futures. **Time Period Covered:** latest day.

COFFEE: ROASTED

Source: *Fruit and Tropical Products.* **Price Frequency:** quarterly, annually. **Effective Market(s):** 8 international markets. **Units of Measure:** national currency per kilogram/lb. **Type of Price:** retail. **Time Period Covered:** latest 2 years.

COFFEE: ROBUSTAS

Source: *Fruit and Tropical Products.* **Price Frequency:** monthly, annually. **Effective Market(s):** International Coffee Organization. **Units of Measure:** cents per lb. **Type of Price:** indicator. **Time Period Covered:** latest 4 years.

Source: *Monthly Commodity Price Bulletin.* **Price Frequency:** monthly, annually. **Effective Market(s):** Le Havre/Marseille/New York, New York. **Units of Measure:** cents per lb. **Time Period Covered:** latest 5 years.

Source: *Monthly Commodity Price Bulletin Supplement.* **Price Frequency:** monthly, quarterly, annually. **Effective Market(s):** Le Havre/Marseille, New York. **Units of Measure:** cents per lb. **Time Period Covered:** latest 20 years.

Source: *UNCTAD Commodity Yearbook.* **Price Frequency:** annually. **Effective Market(s):** New York. **Units of Measure:** Dollars per metric ton. **Type of Price:** free market. **Time Period Covered:** latest 12 years.

COFFEE: ROBUSTAS, FUTURES

Source: *Fruit and Tropical Products.* **Price Frequency:** monthly, annually. **Effective Market(s):** London. **Units of Measure:** British pounds per tonne. **Type of Price:** futures. **Time Period Covered:** latest 4 years.

COFFEE: ROBUSTAS, GRADE II, COTE D'IVOIRE

Source: *Fruit and Tropical Products.* **Price Frequency:** monthly, annually. **Effective Market(s):** New York. **Units of Measure:** cents per lb. **Type of Price:** average. **Time Period Covered:** latest 4 years.

COFFEE: ROBUSTAS, STANDARD, UGANDAN

Source: *Fruit and Tropical Products.* **Price Frequency:** monthly, annually. **Effective Market(s):** New York. **Units of Measure:** cents per lb. **Type of Price:** average. **Time Period Covered:** latest 4 years.

COFFEE: SANTOS NO. 4, BRAZILIAN

Source: *Fruit and Tropical Products.* **Price Frequency:** monthly, annually. **Effective Market(s):** International Coffee Organization. **Units of Measure:** cents per lb. **Type of Price:** indicator. **Time Period Covered:** latest 4 years.

Source: *Journal of Commerce and Commercial.* **Price Frequency:** daily. **Effective Market(s):** New York. **Units of Measure:** Dollars per ton. **Type of Price:** spot supplier. **Time Period Covered:** latest day.

COFFEE: SOLUBLE PER 16 OUNCES

Source: *Commodity Year Book.* **Price Frequency:** monthly, annually. **Effective Market(s):** United States. **Units of Measure:** cents per lb. **Type of Price:** wholesale. **Time Period Covered:** latest 2 years.

COFFEE: UGANDAN

Source: *International Financial Statistics.* **Price Frequency:** monthly, quarterly, annually. **Effective Market(s):** New York. **Units of Measure:** cents per lb., index. **Type of Price:** market price, price index. **Time Period Covered:** latest 5 months, latest 5 quarters, latest 5 years.

Source: *International Financial Statistics Yearbook.* **Price Frequency:** annually. **Effective Market(s):** New York. **Units of Measure:** cents per lb. **Type of Price:** wholesale. **Time Period Covered:** latest 30 years.

COGNAC

Source: *Beverage Media.* **Price Frequency:** monthly. **Effective Market(s):** New York. **Units of Measure:** Dollars per unit. **Type of Price:** wholesale by brand. **Time Period Covered:** latest month.

Source: *Colorado Beverage Analyst.* **Price Frequency:** monthly. **Effective Market(s):** Colorado. **Units of Measure:** Dollars per case. **Type of Price:** wholesale by brand. **Time Period Covered:** latest month.

Source: *Illinois Beverage Journal.* **Price Frequency:** monthly. **Effective Market(s):** Illinois. **Units of Measure:** Dollars per case. **Type of Price:** wholesale by brand. **Time Period Covered:** latest month.

Source: *Indiana Beverage Journal.* **Price Frequency:** monthly. **Effective Market(s):** Indiana. **Units of Measure:** Dollars per case, dollars per bottle. **Type of Price:** wholesale by brand. **Time Period Covered:** latest month.

Source: *Kentucky Beverage Journal.* **Price Frequency:** monthly. **Effective Market(s):** Kentucky. **Units of Measure:** Dollars per bottle, dollars per case. **Type of Price:** wholesale by brand. **Time Period Covered:** latest month.

Source: *Nevada Beverage Index.* **Price Frequency:** monthly. **Effective Market(s):** Nevada. **Units of Measure:** Dollars per unit. **Type of Price:** wholesale by brand. **Time Period Covered:** latest month.

Source: *Rhode Island Beverage Journal.* **Price Frequency:** monthly. **Effective Market(s):** Rhode Island. **Units of Measure:** Dollars per unit. **Type of Price:** wholesale by brand. **Time Period Covered:** latest month.

COINS: GOLD

Source: *Barron's.* **Price Frequency:** weekly. **Units of Measure:** Dollars per coin. **Time Period Covered:** latest week.

Source: *New York Times.* **Price Frequency:** daily. **Units of Measure:** Dollars per troy ounce. **Time Period Covered:** latest day.

COINS: GOLD, AMERICAN EAGLE

Source: *Asian Wall Street Journal.* **Price Frequency:** daily. **Units of Measure:** Dollars per troy ounce. **Type of Price:** cash. **Time Period Covered:** latest 2 days.

Source: *Barron's.* **Price Frequency:** weekly. **Units of Measure:** Dollars per coin. **Time Period Covered:** latest week.

Source: *Financial Times.* **Price Frequency:** daily. **Effective Market(s):** London. **Units of Measure:** Dollars per coin, British pounds per coin. **Time Period Covered:** latest day.

Source: *Investor's Daily.* **Price Frequency:** daily. **Effective Market(s):** New York. **Units of Measure:** Dollars per 1 troy ounce. **Type of Price:** spot. **Time Period Covered:** latest 2 days.

Source: *New York Times.* **Price Frequency:** daily. **Units of Measure:** Dollars per troy ounce. **Time Period Covered:** latest day.

Source: *The Times.* **Price Frequency:** daily. **Effective Market(s):** London. **Units of Measure:** Dollars per coin, British pounds per coin. **Time Period Covered:** latest day.

Source: *Wall Street Journal.* **Price Frequency:** daily. **Units of Measure:** Dollars per troy ounce. **Time Period Covered:** latest day, day ago, year ago.

COINS: GOLD, ANGEL

Source: *Financial Times.* **Price Frequency:** daily. **Effective Market(s):** London. **Units of Measure:** Dollars per coin, British pounds per coin. **Time Period Covered:** latest day.

COINS: GOLD, AUSTRALIAN KOALA

Source: *Barron's.* **Price Frequency:** weekly. **Units of Measure:** Dollars per coin. **Time Period Covered:** latest week.

COINS: GOLD, AUSTRIAN 100 CROWN

Source: *Investor's Daily.* **Price Frequency:** daily. **Effective Market(s):** New York. **Units of Measure:** Dollars per .9801 troy ounce. **Type of Price:** spot. **Time Period Covered:** latest 2 days.

Source: *New York Times.* **Price Frequency:** daily. **Units of Measure:** Dollars per troy ounce. **Time Period Covered:** latest day.

COINS: GOLD, AUSTRIAN CROWN

Source: *Barron's.* **Price Frequency:** weekly. **Units of Measure:** Dollars per coin. **Time Period Covered:** latest week.

COINS: GOLD, BRITANNIA

Source: *Financial Times.* **Price Frequency:** daily. **Effective Market(s):** London. **Units of Measure:** Dollars per coin, British pounds per coin. **Time Period Covered:** latest day.

Source: *The Times.* **Price Frequency:** daily. **Effective Market(s):** London. **Units of Measure:** Dollars per coin, British pounds per coin. **Time Period Covered:** latest day.

COINS: GOLD, CHINA PANDA

Source: *Investor's Daily.* **Price Frequency:** daily. **Effective Market(s):** New York. **Units of Measure:** Dollars per 1 troy ounce. **Type of Price:** spot. **Time Period Covered:** latest 2 days.

Source: *New York Times.* **Price Frequency:** daily. **Units of Measure:** Dollars per troy ounce. **Time Period Covered:** latest day.

COINS: GOLD, ISLE OF MAN NOBLE

Source: *Barron's.* **Price Frequency:** weekly. **Units of Measure:** Dollars per coin. **Time Period Covered:** latest week.

COINS: GOLD, KRUGERRAND

Source: *Asian Wall Street Journal.* **Price Frequency:** daily. **Units of Measure:** Dollars per troy ounce. **Type of Price:** cash. **Time Period Covered:** latest 2 days.

Source: *Barron's.* **Price Frequency:** weekly. **Units of Measure:** Dollars per coin. **Time Period Covered:** latest week.

Source: *Financial Times.* **Price Frequency:** daily. **Effective Market(s):** London. **Units of Measure:** Dollars per coin, British pounds per coin. **Time Period Covered:** latest day.

Source: *Investor's Daily.* **Price Frequency:** daily. **Effective Market(s):** New York. **Units of Measure:** Dollars per 1 troy ounce. **Type of Price:** spot. **Time Period Covered:** latest 2 days.

Source: *New York Times.* **Price Frequency:** daily. **Units of Measure:** Dollars per troy ounce. **Time Period Covered:** latest day.

Source: *The Times.* **Price Frequency:** daily. **Effective Market(s):** London. **Units of Measure:** Dollars per coin, British pounds per coin. **Time Period Covered:** latest day.

COINS: GOLD, KRUGERRAND, WHOLE

Source: *Wall Street Journal.* **Price Frequency:** daily. **Units of Measure:** Dollars per troy ounce. **Time Period Covered:** latest day, day ago, year ago.

COINS: GOLD, MAPLE LEAF

Source: *Asian Wall Street Journal.* **Price Frequency:** daily. **Units of Measure:** Dollars per troy ounce. **Type of Price:** cash. **Time Period Covered:** latest 2 days.

Source: *Barron's.* **Price Frequency:** weekly. **Units of Measure:** Dollars per coin. **Time Period Covered:** latest week.

Source: *Financial Times.* **Price Frequency:** daily. **Effective Market(s):** London. **Units of Measure:** Dollars per coin, British pounds per coin. **Time Period Covered:** latest day.

Source: *Investor's Daily.* **Price Frequency:** daily. **Effective Market(s):** New York. **Units of Measure:** Dollars per troy ounce. **Type of Price:** spot. **Time Period Covered:** latest 2 days.

Source: *New York Times.* **Price Frequency:** daily. **Units of Measure:** Dollars per troy ounce. **Time Period Covered:** latest day.

Source: *The Times.* **Price Frequency:** daily. **Effective Market(s):** London. **Units of Measure:** Dollars per coin, British pounds per coin. **Time Period Covered:** latest day.

Source: *Wall Street Journal.* **Price Frequency:** daily. **Units of Measure:** Dollars per troy ounce. **Time Period Covered:** latest day, day ago, year ago.

COINS: GOLD, MEXICAN 50 PESO

Source: *Investor's Daily.* **Price Frequency:** daily. **Effective Market(s):** New York. **Units of Measure:** Dollars per 1.2 troy ounce. **Type of Price:** spot. **Time Period Covered:** latest 2 days.

Source: *New York Times.* **Price Frequency:** daily. **Units of Measure:** Dollars per troy ounce. **Time Period Covered:** latest day.

COINS: GOLD, MEXICAN PESO

Source: *Barron's.* **Price Frequency:** weekly. **Units of Measure:** Dollars per coin. **Time Period Covered:** latest week.

COINS: GOLD, NEW SOVEREIGN

Source: *Financial Times.* **Price Frequency:** daily. **Effective Market(s):** London. **Units of Measure:** Dollars per coin, British pounds per coin. **Time Period Covered:** latest day.

Source: *The Times.* **Price Frequency:** daily. **Effective Market(s):** London. **Units of Measure:** Dollars per coin, British pounds per coin. **Time Period Covered:** latest day.

COINS: GOLD, NOBLE PLAT

Source: *Financial Times.* **Price Frequency:** daily. **Effective Market(s):** London. **Units of Measure:** Dollars per coin, British pounds per coin. **Time Period Covered:** latest day.

COINS: GOLD, OLD SOVEREIGN

Source: *Financial Times.* **Price Frequency:** daily. **Effective Market(s):** London. **Units of Measure:** Dollars per coin, British pounds per coin. **Time Period Covered:** latest day.

Source: *The Times.* **Price Frequency:** daily. **Effective Market(s):** London. **Units of Measure:** Dollars per coin, British pounds per coin. **Time Period Covered:** latest day.

COINS: PLATINUM

Source: *Barron's.* **Price Frequency:** weekly. **Units of Measure:** Dollars per coin. **Time Period Covered:** latest week.

COINS: SILVER, WHOLE

Source: *Wall Street Journal.* **Price Frequency:** daily. **Units of Measure:** Dollars per $1,000 face value. **Time Period Covered:** latest day, day ago, year ago.

COIR YARN

see Yarn: Coir.

COKE: OVEN FOUNDRY

Source: *Commodity Year Book.* **Price Frequency:** monthly, annually. **Effective Market(s):** Birmingham (AL). **Units of Measure:** index. **Type of Price:** wholesale price index. **Time Period Covered:** latest 7 years.

COLCHICUM ROOT

Source: *Journal of Commerce and Commercial.* **Price Frequency:** weekly in Monday issue. **Units of Measure:** Dollars per lb. **Type of Price:** spot. **Time Period Covered:** latest week.

COLCHICUM SEED

Source: *Journal of Commerce and Commercial.* **Price Frequency:** weekly in Monday issue. **Units of Measure:** Dollars per lb. **Type of Price:** spot. **Time Period Covered:** latest week.

COLD DUCK

Source: *Colorado Beverage Analyst.* **Price Frequency:** monthly. **Effective Market(s):** Colorado. **Units of Measure:** Dollars per case. **Type of Price:** wholesale by brand. **Time Period Covered:** latest month.

COLEMANITE: TURKISH

Source: *Industrial Minterals.* **Price Frequency:** monthly. **Effective Market(s):** main European port. **Units of Measure:** British pounds per metric tonne. **Type of Price:** producer & dealer. **Time Period Covered:** latest month.

COLLARD GREENS: FROZEN

Source: *HRI-Buyer's Guide.* **Price Frequency:** weekly. **Effective Market(s):** Northeastern area. **Units of Measure:** Dollars per case. **Type of Price:** price paid by dining places & institutions. **Time Period Covered:** latest week.

COLOMBIA PESOS

Source: *Barron's.* **Price Frequency:** weekly. **Effective Market(s):** New York. **Units of Measure:** Colombian pesos per United States dollar. **Type of Price:** foreign exchange. **Time Period Covered:** latest 2 weeks.

Source: *New York Times.* **Price Frequency:** daily. **Effective Market(s):** New York. **Units of Measure:** Colombian pesos per United States dollars. **Type of Price:** foreign exchange. **Time Period Covered:** latest 2 days.

COLORS: DRY

Source: *Journal of Commerce and Commercial.* **Price Frequency:** weekly in Wednesday issue. **Units of Measure:** Dollars per lb. **Type of Price:** spot. **Time Period Covered:** latest week.

COLTS

Source: *Lancaster Farming.* **Price Frequency:** weekly. **Effective Market(s):** Pennsylvania. **Units of Measure:** Dollars per head. **Type of Price:** auction. **Time Period Covered:** latest week.

COMBINE: SELF PROPELLED WITH GRAIN HEAD

Source: *Agricultural Prices.* **Price Frequency:** annually. **Effective Market(s):** United States. **Units of Measure:** Dollars each. **Type of Price:** paid by farmer. **Time Period Covered:** latest year.

Source: *Agricultural Prices Annual Summary.* **Price Frequency:** semiannually. **Effective Market(s):** United States. **Units of Measure:** Dollars each. **Type of Price:** average price paid by farmer. **Time Period Covered:** latest 6 years.

CONCH MEAT: FULLY CLEANED, COLOMBIA

Source: *NMFS Green Sheet Supplement.* **Price Frequency:** weekly. **Effective Market(s):** New York. **Units of Measure:** Dollars per lb. **Type of Price:** warehouse. **Time Period Covered:** lastest week.

CONCH MEAT: GRADE A, FROZEN, CARIBBEAN

Source: *Seafood Price-Current.* **Price Frequency:** semiweekly. **Effective Market(s):** Mid-Atlantic. **Units of Measure:** Dollars per lb. **Type of Price:** first receiver. **Time Period Covered:** latest day.

CONCH MEAT: NO. 1, FROZEN, CARIBBEAN

Source: *Seafood Price-Current.* **Price Frequency:** semiweekly. **Effective Market(s):** Mid-Atlantic. **Units of Measure:** Dollars per lb. **Type of Price:** first receiver. **Time Period Covered:** latest day.

CONCRETE BLOCK: HEAVYWEIGHT

Source: *ENR.* **Price Frequency:** monthly in first issue of month. **Effective Market(s):** 17 domestic markets, Montreal, Toronto. **Units of Measure:** Dollars per hundred. **Type of Price:** spot. **Time Period Covered:** latest month.

CONCRETE BLOCK: LIGHTWEIGHT

Source: *ENR.* **Price Frequency:** monthly in first issue of month. **Effective Market(s):** 18 domestic markets, Montreal, Toronto. **Units of Measure:** Dollars per hundred. **Type of Price:** spot. **Time Period Covered:** latest month.

CONCRETE BLOCK: SAND/GRAVEL

Source: *ENR.* **Price Frequency:** monthly in first issue of month. **Effective Market(s):** 20-city average. **Units of Measure:** Dollars per hundred. **Time Period Covered:** latest month.

CONCRETE BLOCKS

Source: *Agricultural Prices Annual Summary.* **Price Frequency:** bimonthly. **Effective Market(s):** United States. **Units of Measure:** Dollars per 100. **Type of Price:** average price paid by farmer. **Time Period Covered:** latest 6 years.

CONCRETE PIPE: REINFORCED

Source: *ENR.* **Price Frequency:** monthly in second issue of month. **Effective Market(s):** 18 domestic markets, Montreal, Toronto. **Units of Measure:** Dollars per foot. **Type of Price:** spot. **Time Period Covered:** latest month.

CONCRETE READY MIX: 3,000 PSI

Source: *ENR.* **Price Frequency:** monthly in first issue of month. **Effective Market(s):** 20 domestic markets, Montreal, Toronto. **Units of Measure:** Dollars per cubic yard. **Type of Price:** spot. **Time Period Covered:** latest month.

CONCRETE READY MIX: 4,000 PSI

Source: *ENR.* **Price Frequency:** monthly in first issue of month. **Effective Market(s):** 19 domestic markets, Montreal, Toronto. **Units of Measure:** Dollars per cubic yard. **Type of Price:** spot. **Time Period Covered:** latest month.

CONCRETE READY MIX: 5,000 PSI

Source: *ENR.* **Price Frequency:** monthly in first issue of month. **Effective Market(s):** 20 domestic markets, Montreal, Toronto. **Units of Measure:** Dollars per cubic yard. **Type of Price:** spot. **Time Period Covered:** latest month.

COOLERS: WINE

Source: *Colorado Beverage Analyst.* **Price Frequency:** monthly. **Effective Market(s):** Colorado. **Units of Measure:** Dollars per case. **Type of Price:** wholesale by brand. **Time Period Covered:** latest month.

Source: *Illinois Beverage Journal.* **Price Frequency:** monthly. **Effective Market(s):** Illinois. **Units of Measure:** Dollars per case. **Type of Price:** wholesale by brand. **Time Period Covered:** latest month.

Source: *Kentucky Beverage Journal.* **Price Frequency:** monthly. **Effective Market(s):** Kentucky. **Units of Measure:** Dollars per bottle, dollars per case. **Type of Price:** wholesale by brand. **Time Period Covered:** latest month.

COPAIBA BALSAM

Source: *Chemical Marketing Reporter.* **Price Frequency:** weekly. **Effective Market(s):** New York. **Units of Measure:** Dollars per lb. **Type of Price:** spot. **Time Period Covered:** latest week.

COPPER

Source: *American Metal Market.* **Price Frequency:** daily. **Effective Market(s):** London. **Units of Measure:** Dollars per metric ton. **Type of Price:** spot fix. **Time Period Covered:** latest day.

Source: *Business Week.* **Price Frequency:** weekly. **Units of Measure:** cents per lb. **Time Period Covered:** latest 2 weeks.

Source: *Far Eastern Economic Review.* **Price Frequency:** weekly. **Effective Market(s):** New York. **Units of Measure:** cents per lb. **Time Period Covered:** latest week, week ago, 3 months ago, year ago.

Source: *Financial Times.* **Price Frequency:** daily. **Effective Market(s):** London. **Units of Measure:** British pounds per tonne. **Type of Price:** spot. **Time Period Covered:** latest day.

Source: *Los Angeles Times.* **Price Frequency:** daily. **Effective Market(s):** United States. **Units of Measure:** Dollars per lb. **Type of Price:** cash. **Time Period Covered:** latest day.

Source: *Minerals Today.* **Price Frequency:** bimonthly. **Units of Measure:** cents per lb. **Time Period Covered:** latest month, month ago.

Source: *Northern Miner.* **Price Frequency:** daily. **Effective Market(s):** London. **Units of Measure:** British pounds per tonne. **Type of Price:** spot. **Time Period Covered:** week ago.

COPPER: CANADIAN

Source: *International Financial Statistics.* **Price Frequency:** quarterly, annually. **Effective Market(s):** Canada. **Units of Measure:** cents per lb., index. **Type of Price:** market price, price index. **Time Period Covered:** latest 2 quarters, latest 4 years.

Source: *International Financial Statistics Yearbook.* **Price Frequency:** annually. **Effective Market(s):** Canada. **Units of Measure:** cents per lb. **Type of Price:** wholesale. **Time Period Covered:** latest 30 years.

COPPER: CONTINUOUS CAST ROD PREMIUM

Source: *American Metal Market.* **Price Frequency:** daily. **Effective Market(s):** United States. **Units of Measure:** cents per lb. **Type of Price:** producer. **Time Period Covered:** latest day.

COPPER: ELECTROLYTIC

Source: *Investor's Daily.* **Price Frequency:** daily. **Units of Measure:** Dollars per lb. **Type of Price:** spot. **Time Period Covered:** latest 2 days.

Source: *New York Times.* **Price Frequency:** daily. **Units of Measure:** Dollars per lb. **Type of Price:** cash. **Time Period Covered:** latest 2 days.

COPPER: FUTURES

Source: *Barron's.* **Price Frequency:** weekly. **Effective Market(s):** New York. **Units of Measure:** cents per lb. **Type of Price:** futures. **Time Period Covered:** latest week.

Source: *Far Eastern Economic Review.* **Price Frequency:** weekly. **Effective Market(s):** New York. **Units of Measure:** cents per lb. **Type of Price:** futures. **Time Period Covered:** latest week.

Source: *Northern Miner.* **Price Frequency:** daily. **Effective Market(s):** New York. **Units of Measure:** cents per lb. **Type of Price:** futures. **Time Period Covered:** selected day.

COPPER: FUTURES, MAY

Source: *Commodity Year Book.* **Price Frequency:** monthly. **Effective Market(s):** New York. **Units of Measure:** cents per lb. **Type of Price:** futures. **Time Period Covered:** latest 6 years.

COPPER: GRADE 2

Source: *E&MJ.* **Price Frequency:** monthly. **Effective Market(s):** New York. **Units of Measure:** cents per lb. **Type of Price:** closing. **Time Period Covered:** latest month.

COPPER: GRADE A

Source: *American Metal Market.* **Price Frequency:** daily. **Effective Market(s):** London. **Units of Measure:** British pounds per metric ton. **Type of Price:** cash. **Time Period Covered:** latest day.

Source: *E&MJ.* **Price Frequency:** monthly. **Effective Market(s):** London. **Units of Measure:** cents per lb. **Type of Price:** closing cash bid. **Time Period Covered:** latest month, 3 months ago.

Source: *Financial Times.* **Price Frequency:** daily. **Effective Market(s):** London. **Units of Measure:** British pounds per tonne. **Type of Price:** cash. **Time Period Covered:** latest day.

Source: *Journal of Commerce and Commercial.* **Price Frequency:** daily. **Effective Market(s):** London. **Units of Measure:** British pounds per metric ton. **Type of Price:** spot. **Time Period Covered:** latest day, day ago.

Source: *Monthly Commodity Price Bulletin.* **Price Frequency:** monthly, annually. **Effective Market(s):** London. **Units of Measure:** British pounds per metric ton, cents per lb. **Type of Price:** cash. **Time Period Covered:** latest 5 years.

Source: *The Times.* **Price Frequency:** daily. **Effective Market(s):** London. **Units of Measure:** British pounds per tonne. **Type of Price:** cash. **Time Period Covered:** latest day.

COPPER: HIGH GRADE

Source: *UNCTAD Commodity Yearbook.* **Price Frequency:** annually. **Effective Market(s):** London. **Units of Measure:** Dollars per metric ton. **Type of Price:** cash. **Time Period Covered:** latest 12 years.

COPPER: HIGH GRADE, FUTURES

Source: *Asian Wall Street Journal.* **Price Frequency:** daily. **Effective Market(s):** New York. **Units of Measure:** cents per lb. **Type of Price:** futures. **Time Period Covered:** latest day.

Source: *Financial Times.* **Price Frequency:** daily. **Effective Market(s):** New York. **Units of Measure:** cents per lb. **Type of Price:** futures. **Time Period Covered:** latest day.

Source: *Investor's Daily.* **Price Frequency:** daily. **Effective Market(s):** New York. **Units of Measure:** cents per lb. **Type of Price:** futures. **Time Period Covered:** latest day.

Source: *New York Times.* **Price Frequency:** daily. **Effective Market(s):** New York. **Units of Measure:** cents per lb. **Type of Price:** futures. **Time Period Covered:** latest day.

COPPER: LIGHT

Source: *American Metal Market.* **Price Frequency:** daily. **Effective Market(s):** 14 domestic markets, Montreal, Toronto. **Units of Measure:** cents per lb., Canadian cents per lb. **Time Period Covered:** latest day.

COPPER: NO. 1, HEAVY

Source: *American Metal Market.* **Price Frequency:** daily. **Effective Market(s):** 14 domestic markets, Montreal, Toronto. **Units of Measure:** cents per lb., Canadian cents per lb. **Time Period Covered:** latest day.

COPPER: NO. 1, SCRAP

Source: *American Metal Market.* **Price Frequency:** daily. **Units of Measure:** Dollars per lb. **Time Period Covered:** latest day.

COPPER: NO. 2, HEAVY AND WIRE

Source: *American Metal Market.* **Price Frequency:** daily. **Effective Market(s):** 14 domestic markets, Montreal, Toronto. **Units of Measure:** cents per lb., Canadian cents per lb. **Time Period Covered:** latest day.

COPPER: NO. 2, HEAVY, SCRAP

Source: *Commodity Year Book.* **Price Frequency:** monthly, annually. **Effective Market(s):** New York. **Units of Measure:** cents per lb. **Type of Price:** dealer buying price. **Time Period Covered:** latest 9 years.

COPPER: NO. 2, SCRAP

Source: *American Metal Market.* **Price Frequency:** daily. **Units of Measure:** Dollars per lb. **Time Period Covered:** latest day.

Source: *American Metal Market.* **Price Frequency:** daily. **Units of Measure:** cents per lb. **Time Period Covered:** latest 3 days.

Source: *CRB Commodity Index Report.* **Price Frequency:** weekly. **Effective Market(s):** New York. **Units of Measure:** Dollars per lb. **Type of Price:** spot. **Time Period Covered:** latest week.

Source: *Journal of Commerce and Commercial.* **Price Frequency:** daily. **Effective Market(s):** New York. **Units of Measure:** cents per lb. **Type of Price:** spot supplier. **Time Period Covered:** latest day.

COPPER: OFHC BRAND PREMIUM

Source: *American Metal Market.* **Price Frequency:** daily. **Effective Market(s):** United States. **Units of Measure:** cents per lb. **Type of Price:** producer. **Time Period Covered:** latest day.

COPPER: SCRAP, LIGHT

Source: *American Metal Market.* **Price Frequency:** daily. **Units of Measure:** Dollars per lb. **Time Period Covered:** latest day.

Source: *Iron Age.* **Price Frequency:** monthly. **Number of Sources:** cents per lb. **Type of Price:** dealer, refinery, smelters. **Time Period Covered:** latest month.

COPPER: STANDARD, FUTURES

Source: *Wall Street Journal.* **Price Frequency:** daily. **Effective Market(s):** New York. **Units of Measure:** cents per lb. **Type of Price:** futures. **Time Period Covered:** latest day.

COPPER: UNITED KINGDOM

Source: *International Financial Statistics.* **Price Frequency:** monthly, quarterly, annually. **Effective Market(s):** London. **Units of Measure:** cents per lb., index. **Type of Price:** market price, price index. **Time Period Covered:** latest 5 months, latest 5 quarters, latest 5 years.

Source: *International Financial Statistics Yearbook.* **Price Frequency:** annually. **Effective Market(s):** London. **Units of Measure:** cents per lb. **Type of Price:** wholesale. **Time Period Covered:** latest 30 years.

COPPER: UNITED STATES

Source: *International Financial Statistics.* **Price Frequency:** annually. **Effective Market(s):** United States. **Units of Measure:** cents per lb., index. **Type of Price:** refinery, price index. **Time Period Covered:** latest 3 years.

Source: *International Financial Statistics Yearbook.* **Price Frequency:** annually. **Effective Market(s):** United States. **Units of Measure:** cents per lb. **Type of Price:** refinery. **Time Period Covered:** latest 30 years.

COPPER ACETATE: MONOHYDRATE, CRYSTALLINE, TECHNICAL GRADE

Source: *Chemical Marketing Reporter.* **Price Frequency:** weekly. **Effective Market(s):** New York. **Units of Measure:** Dollars per lb. **Type of Price:** spot. **Time Period Covered:** latest week.

COPPER BAR

Source: *Economic and Energy Indicators.* **Price Frequency:** monthly, quarterly, annually. **Units of Measure:** cents per lb. **Time Period Covered:** latest 3 months, quarters, and years.

COPPER BROMIDE

Source: *Chemical Marketing Reporter.* **Price Frequency:** weekly. **Effective Market(s):** New York. **Units of Measure:** Dollars per lb. **Type of Price:** spot. **Time Period Covered:** latest week.

COPPER CARBONATE: 55% COPPER

Source: *Journal of Commerce and Commercial.* **Price Frequency:** weekly in Thursday issue. **Units of Measure:** Dollars per lb. **Type of Price:** spot. **Time Period Covered:** latest week.

COPPER CARBONATE: 55% COPPER, DARK, DENSE

Source: *Chemical Marketing Reporter.* **Price Frequency:** weekly. **Effective Market(s):** New York. **Units of Measure:** Dollars per lb. **Type of Price:** spot. **Time Period Covered:** latest week.

COPPER CARBONATE: 55% COPPER, LIGHT, FLUFFY

Source: *Chemical Marketing Reporter.* **Price Frequency:** weekly. **Effective Market(s):** New York. **Units of Measure:** Dollars per lb. **Type of Price:** spot. **Time Period Covered:** latest week.

COPPER CATHODE INGOTS

Source: *Japan Economic Journal.* **Price Frequency:** weekly. **Effective Market(s):** Tokyo. **Units of Measure:** Japanese yen per ton. **Type of Price:** trader. **Time Period Covered:** latest 2 weeks.

COPPER CATHODES

Source: *American Metal Market.* **Price Frequency:** daily. **Units of Measure:** cents per lb. **Time Period Covered:** latest 3 days.

Source: *Asian Wall Street Journal.* **Price Frequency:** daily. **Units of Measure:** Dollars per lb. **Type of Price:** cash. **Time Period Covered:** latest 2 days, year ago.

Source: *E&MJ.* **Price Frequency:** monthly. **Effective Market(s):** New York. **Units of Measure:** cents per lb. **Type of Price:** merchant. **Time Period Covered:** latest month.

Source: *Iron Age.* **Price Frequency:** monthly. **Effective Market(s):** London. **Units of Measure:** cents per lb. **Type of Price:** consumer. **Time Period Covered:** latest month.

Source: *Northern Miner.* **Price Frequency:** daily. **Effective Market(s):** Canada, United States. **Units of Measure:** Canadian dollars per lb., dollars per lb. **Type of Price:** producer. **Time Period Covered:** selected day.

Source: *Purchasing.* **Price Frequency:** monthly. **Units of Measure:** cents per lb. **Type of Price:** transaction. **Time Period Covered:** latest day, month ago, 6 months ago, year ago.

Source: *Survey of Current Business.* **Price Frequency:** monthly, annually. **Effective Market(s):** United States. **Units of Measure:** Dollars per lb. **Type of Price:** producer. **Time Period Covered:** latest year.

Source: *Wall Street Journal.* **Price Frequency:** daily. **Units of Measure:** Dollars per lb. **Type of Price:** producer price. **Time Period Covered:** latest day, day ago, year ago.

COPPER CATHODES: FULL PLATE

Source: *American Metal Market.* **Price Frequency:** daily. **Effective Market(s):** United States. **Units of Measure:** cents per lb. **Type of Price:** producer. **Time Period Covered:** latest day.

Source: *E&MJ.* **Price Frequency:** monthly. **Effective Market(s):** United States. **Units of Measure:** cents per lb. **Type of Price:** producer. **Time Period Covered:** latest month.

COPPER CATHODES: HIGH GRADE

Source: *Asian Wall Street Journal.* **Price Frequency:** daily. **Effective Market(s):** London. **Units of Measure:** British pounds per metric ton. **Type of Price:** spot. **Time Period Covered:** latest 2 days, year ago.

Source: *New York Times.* **Price Frequency:** daily. **Effective Market(s):** London. **Units of Measure:** British pounds per metric ton. **Type of Price:** spot. **Time Period Covered:** latest day.

Source: *Wall Street Journal.* **Price Frequency:** daily. **Effective Market(s):** London. **Units of Measure:** British pounds per metric ton. **Type of Price:** spot. **Time Period Covered:** latest day, 3 months ago.

COPPER CHLORIDE: ANHYDROUS

Source: *Chemical Marketing Reporter.* **Price Frequency:** weekly. **Effective Market(s):** New York. **Units of Measure:** Dollars per lb. **Type of Price:** spot. **Time Period Covered:** latest week.

COPPER CHLORIDE: CUPRIC

Source: *Journal of Commerce and Commercial.* **Price Frequency:** weekly in Thursday issue. **Units of Measure:** Dollars per lb. **Type of Price:** spot. **Time Period Covered:** latest week.

COPPER CYANIDE: TECHNICAL GRADE

Source: *Chemical Marketing Reporter.* **Price Frequency:** weekly. **Effective Market(s):** New York. **Units of Measure:** Dollars per lb. **Type of Price:** spot. **Time Period Covered:** latest week.

COPPER FLUOBORATE: LIQUID, CONCENTRATED

Source: *Chemical Marketing Reporter.* **Price Frequency:** weekly. **Effective Market(s):** New York. **Units of Measure:** Dollars per lb. **Type of Price:** spot. **Time Period Covered:** latest week.

COPPER GLUCONATE: FCC

Source: *Chemical Marketing Reporter.* **Price Frequency:** weekly. **Effective Market(s):** New York. **Units of Measure:** Dollars per lb. **Type of Price:** spot. **Time Period Covered:** latest week.

COPPER NAPHTHENATE: LIQUID, 8% COPPER

Source: *Chemical Marketing Reporter.* **Price Frequency:** weekly. **Effective Market(s):** New York. **Units of Measure:** Dollars per lb. **Type of Price:** spot. **Time Period Covered:** latest week.

COPPER NITRATE: CRYSTALLINE

Source: *Chemical Marketing Reporter.* **Price Frequency:** weekly. **Effective Market(s):** New York. **Units of Measure:** Dollars per lb. **Type of Price:** spot. **Time Period Covered:** latest week.

COPPER OLEATE: SOLID, 6% COPPER

Source: *Chemical Marketing Reporte.* **Price Frequency:** weekly. **Effective Market(s):** New York. **Units of Measure:** Dollars per lb. **Type of Price:** spot. **Time Period Covered:** latest week.

COPPER OXIDE: CUPRIC, BLACK

Source: *Chemical Marketing Reporter.* **Price Frequency:** weekly. **Effective Market(s):** New York. **Units of Measure:** Dollars per lb. **Type of Price:** spot. **Time Period Covered:** latest week.

COPPER OXIDE: CUPROUS, 97%, USN

Source: *Chemical Marketing Reporter.* **Price Frequency:** weekly. **Effective Market(s):** New York. **Units of Measure:** Dollars per lb. **Type of Price:** spot. **Time Period Covered:** latest week.

COPPER POWDER: COMMERCIAL

Source: *American Metal Market.* **Price Frequency:** daily. **Units of Measure:** Dollars per lb. **Time Period Covered:** latest day.

COPPER POWDER: SPHERICAL

Source: *American Metal Market.* **Price Frequency:** daily. **Units of Measure:** Dollars per lb. **Time Period Covered:** latest day.

COPPER-8-QUINOLINOLATE: 10%, LIQUID EMULSION

Source: *Chemical Marketing Reporter.* **Price Frequency:** weekly. **Effective Market(s):** New York. **Units of Measure:** Dollars per lb. **Type of Price:** spot. **Time Period Covered:** latest week.

COPPER SHEET

Source: *Purchasing.* **Price Frequency:** quarterly in January, April, July and October issues. **Units of Measure:** cents per lb. **Type of Price:** average. **Time Period Covered:** latest 5 quarters.

COPPER SOLIDS: SCRAP

Source: *Iron Age.* **Price Frequency:** monthly. **Number of Sources:** cents per lb. **Type of Price:** consumer. **Time Period Covered:** latest month.

COPPER SULFATE: BASIC

Source: *Chemical Marketing Reporter.* **Price Frequency:** weekly. **Effective Market(s):** New York. **Units of Measure:** Dollars per lb. **Type of Price:** spot. **Time Period Covered:** latest week.

COPPER SULFATE: MONOHYDRATED, 35% COPPER

Source: *Chemical Marketing Reporter.* **Price Frequency:** weekly. **Effective Market(s):** New York. **Units of Measure:** Dollars per lb. **Type of Price:** spot. **Time Period Covered:** latest week.

COPPER SULFATE: PENTAHYDRATE, 99%, CRYSTALLINE

Source: *Chemical Marketing Reporter.* **Price Frequency:** weekly. **Effective Market(s):** New York. **Units of Measure:** Dollars per 100 lbs. **Type of Price:** spot. **Time Period Covered:** latest week.

COPPER TURNINGS: SCRAP

Source: *Iron Age.* **Price Frequency:** monthly. **Number of Sources:** cents per lb. **Type of Price:** consumer. **Time Period Covered:** latest month.

COPPER WIRE: NO. 1, SCRAP

Source: *Iron Age.* **Price Frequency:** monthly. **Number of Sources:** cents per lb. **Type of Price:** dealer, refinery, smelters. **Time Period Covered:** latest month.

COPPER WIRE: NO. 2, SCRAP

Source: *Asian Wall Street Journal.* **Price Frequency:** daily. **Effective Market(s):** New York. **Units of Measure:** Dollars per lb. **Type of Price:** cash. **Time Period Covered:** latest 2 days, year ago.

Source: *Iron Age.* **Price Frequency:** monthly. **Number of Sources:** cents per lb. **Type of Price:** dealer, refinery, smelters. **Time Period Covered:** latest month.

Source: *Wall Street Journal.* **Price Frequency:** daily. **Effective Market(s):** New York. **Units of Measure:** Dollars per lb. **Type of Price:** dealers selling price. **Time Period Covered:** latest day, day ago, year ago.

COPPER WIRE BAR

Source: *American Metal Market.* **Price Frequency:** daily. **Units of Measure:** cents per lb. **Time Period Covered:** latest 3 days.

Source: *E&MJ.* **Price Frequency:** monthly. **Effective Market(s):** United States. **Units of Measure:** cents per lb. **Type of Price:** producers. **Time Period Covered:** latest month.

Source: *Monthly Commodity Price Bulletin.* **Price Frequency:** monthly, annually. **Effective Market(s):** United States. **Units of Measure:** cents per lb. **Type of Price:** refinery. **Time Period Covered:** latest 5 years.

Source: *Monthly Commodity Price Bulletin Supplement.* **Price Frequency:** monthly, quarterly, annually. **Effective Market(s):** United States. **Units of Measure:** cents per lb. **Time Period Covered:** latest 20 years.

Source: *Purchasing.* **Price Frequency:** monthly. **Effective Market(s):** New York. **Units of Measure:** cents per lb. **Type of Price:** transaction. **Time Period Covered:** latest day, month ago, 6 months ago, year ago.

Source: *UNCTAD Commodity Yearbook.* **Price Frequency:** annually. **Effective Market(s):** United States. **Units of Measure:** Dollars per metric ton. **Type of Price:** refinery. **Time Period Covered:** latest 12 years.

COPPER WIRE BAR: ELECTROLYTIC

Source: *American Metal Market.* **Price Frequency:** daily. **Effective Market(s):** United States. **Units of Measure:** cents per lb. **Type of Price:** producer. **Time Period Covered:** latest day.

Source: *Commodity Trade and Price Trends.* **Price Frequency:** annually. **Effective Market(s):** London, New York. **Units of Measure:** Dollars per metric ton, 1980 constant dollars per metric ton. **Type of Price:** settlement, producer. **Time Period Covered:** latest 37 years.

Source: *Commodity Year Book.* **Price Frequency:** monthly, annually. **Effective Market(s):** United States. **Units of Measure:** cents per lb. **Type of Price:** producer price. **Time Period Covered:** latest 10 years.

Source: *Journal of Commerce and Commercial.* **Price Frequency:** daily. **Effective Market(s):** New York. **Units of Measure:** Dollars per lb. **Type of Price:** spot supplier. **Time Period Covered:** latest day.

Source: *Monthly Commodity Price Bulletin.* **Price Frequency:** monthly, annually. **Effective Market(s):** London. **Units of Measure:** British pounds per metric ton, cents per lb. **Type of Price:** cash. **Time Period Covered:** latest 5 years.

COPPER WIRE BAR: ELECTROLYTIC, DOMESTIC

Source: *Chemical Marketing Reporter.* **Price Frequency:** weekly. **Effective Market(s):** New York. **Units of Measure:** Dollars per lb. **Type of Price:** spot. **Time Period Covered:** latest week.

COPPER WIRE BAR: GRADE A, ELECTROLYTIC

Source: *Monthly Commodity Price Bulletin Supplement.* **Price Frequency:** monthly, quarterly, annually. **Units of Measure:** British pounds per tonne, dollars per tonne. **Type of Price:** cash. **Time Period Covered:** latest 20 years.

COPRA: PHILIPPINES

Source: *Commodity Trade and Price Trends.* **Price Frequency:** annually. **Effective Market(s):** European ports. **Units of Measure:** Dollars per metric ton, 1980 constant dollars per metric ton. **Time Period Covered:** latest 37 years.

Source: *Financial Times.* **Price Frequency:** daily. **Effective Market(s):** Rotterdam. **Units of Measure:** Dollars per tonne. **Type of Price:** spot. **Time Period Covered:** latest day.

Source: *International Financial Statistics.* **Price Frequency:** monthly, quarterly, annually. **Effective Market(s):** European ports. **Units of Measure:** Dollars per metric ton, index. **Type of Price:** market price, price index. **Time Period Covered:** latest 5 months, latest 5 quarters, latest 5 years.

Source: *International Financial Statistics Yearbook.* **Price Frequency:** annually. **Effective Market(s):** European ports, Philippines. **Units of Measure:** Dollars per metric ton. **Type of Price:** wholesale. **Time Period Covered:** latest 30 years.

COPRA: PHILIPPINES, FUTURES

Source: *Asian Wall Street Journal.* **Price Frequency:** daily. **Effective Market(s):** Manila. **Units of Measure:** Philippine centavos per kilo. **Type of Price:** futures. **Time Period Covered:** latest day.

COPRA: PHILIPPINES/INDONESIA

Source: *Fruit and Tropical Products.* **Price Frequency:** monthly, annually. **Effective Market(s):** European ports. **Units of Measure:** Dollars per tonne. **Type of Price:** average. **Time Period Covered:** monthly latest year, annually latest 2 years.

Source: *Monthly Commodity Price Bulletin.* **Price Frequency:** monthly, annually. **Effective Market(s):** European ports. **Units of Measure:** Dollars per metric ton. **Time Period Covered:** latest 5 years.

Source: *Monthly Commodity Price Bulletin Supplement.* **Price Frequency:** monthly, quarterly, annually. **Effective Market(s):** European ports. **Units of Measure:** Dollars per tonne. **Time Period Covered:** latest 20 years.

Source: *Oil World.* **Price Frequency:** weekly, monthly, annually. **Effective Market(s):** Northwest Europe. **Units of Measure:** Dollars per tonne. **Type of Price:** lowest representative asking. **Time Period Covered:** weekly latest 3 weeks, monthly latest 2 months, annually latest 2 years.

Source: *Prices of Selected Asia/Pacific Products.* **Price Frequency:** monthly. **Effective Market(s):** North West European ports. **Units of Measure:** Dollars per metric ton. **Type of Price:** high, low. **Time Period Covered:** latest month.

Source: *UNCTAD Commodity Yearbook.* **Price Frequency:** annually. **Effective Market(s):** European ports. **Units of Measure:** Dollars per metric ton. **Type of Price:** free market. **Time Period Covered:** latest 12 years.

Source: *World Oilseed Situation and Market Highlights.* **Price Frequency:** monthly, annually. **Effective Market(s):** Rotterdam. **Units of Measure:** Dollars per metric ton. **Time Period Covered:** latest 9 years.

COPRA EXPELLER PELLETS: 26% PROTEIN, PHILIPPINES

Source: *Oil World.* **Price Frequency:** weekly, monthly, annually. **Effective Market(s):** Hamburg. **Units of Measure:** Dollars per tonne. **Type of Price:** lowest representative asking export. **Time Period Covered:** weekly latest 3 weeks, monthly latest 2 months, annually latest 2 years.

Source: *World Oilseed Situation and Market Highlights.* **Price Frequency:** monthly, annually. **Effective Market(s):** Hamburg. **Units of Measure:** Dollars per metric ton. **Time Period Covered:** latest 9 years.

CORDIALS

Source: *Beverage Media.* **Price Frequency:** monthly. **Effective Market(s):** New York. **Units of Measure:** Dollars per unit. **Type of Price:** wholesale by brand. **Time Period Covered:** latest month.

Source: *Colorado Beverage Analyst.* **Price Frequency:** monthly. **Effective Market(s):** Colorado. **Units of Measure:** Dollars per case. **Type of Price:** wholesale by brand. **Time Period Covered:** latest month.

Source: *Illinois Beverage Journal.* **Price Frequency:** monthly. **Effective Market(s):** Illinois. **Units of Measure:** Dollars per case. **Type of Price:** wholesale by brand. **Time Period Covered:** latest month.

Source: *Indiana Beverage Journal.* **Price Frequency:** monthly. **Effective Market(s):** Indiana. **Units of Measure:** Dollars per case, dollars per bottle. **Type of Price:** wholesale by brand. **Time Period Covered:** latest month.

Source: *Kentucky Beverage Journal.* **Price Frequency:** monthly. **Effective Market(s):** Kentucky. **Units of Measure:** Dollars per bottle, dollars per case. **Type of Price:** wholesale by brand. **Time Period Covered:** latest month.

Source: *Nevada Beverage Index.* **Price Frequency:** monthly. **Effective Market(s):** Nevada. **Units of Measure:** Dollars per unit. **Type of Price:** wholesale by brand. **Time Period Covered:** latest month.

Source: *Rhode Island Beverage Journal.* **Price Frequency:** monthly. **Effective Market(s):** Rhode Island. **Units of Measure:** Dollars per unit. **Type of Price:** wholesale by brand. **Time Period Covered:** latest month.

CORDUROY: FEATHER WALE

Source: *JTN: The International Textile Magazine.* **Price Frequency:** monthly. **Effective Market(s):** Japan. **Units of Measure:** Japanese yen per yard. **Type of Price:** spot. **Time Period Covered:** latest month.

CORDUROY: MIDDLE WALE

Source: *JTN: The International Textile Magazine.* **Price Frequency:** monthly. **Effective Market(s):** Japan. **Units of Measure:** Japanese yen per yard. **Type of Price:** spot. **Time Period Covered:** latest month.

CORIANDER OIL

Source: *Journal of Commerce and Commercial.* **Price Frequency:** weekly in Tuesday issue. **Units of Measure:** Dollars per lb. **Type of Price:** spot. **Time Period Covered:** latest week.

CORIANDER OIL: USP

Source: *Chemical Marketing Reporter.* **Price Frequency:** weekly. **Effective Market(s):** New York. **Units of Measure:** Dollars per lb. **Type of Price:** spot. **Time Period Covered:** latest week.

CORIANDER SEED

Source: *Prices of Selected Asia/Pacific Products.* **Price Frequency:** monthly. **Effective Market(s):** United Kingdom/North European ports. **Units of Measure:** British pounds per metric ton. **Type of Price:** high, low. **Time Period Covered:** latest month.

CORIANDER SEED: EGYPTIAN

Source: *U. S. Spice Trade.* **Price Frequency:** annually. **Effective Market(s):** New York. **Units of Measure:** cents per lb. **Type of Price:** spot. **Time Period Covered:** latest 3 years.

CORIANDER SEED: MOROCCAN

Source: *Chemical Marketing Reporter.* **Price Frequency:** weekly. **Effective Market(s):** New York. **Units of Measure:** Dollars per lb. **Type of Price:** spot. **Time Period Covered:** latest week.

Source: *Fruit and Tropical Products.* **Price Frequency:** monthly, seasonally. **Effective Market(s):** London. **Units of Measure:** British pounds per tonne. **Type of Price:** month end. **Time Period Covered:** latest 2 years.

Source: *Prices of Selected Asia/Pacific Products.* **Price Frequency:** monthly. **Effective Market(s):** United Kingdom. **Units of Measure:** British pounds per metric ton. **Type of Price:** spot high, spot low. **Time Period Covered:** latest month.

Source: *U. S. Spice Trade.* **Price Frequency:** annually. **Effective Market(s):** New York. **Units of Measure:** cents per lb. **Type of Price:** spot. **Time Period Covered:** latest 3 years.

CORIANDER SEED: ROMANIAN

Source: *Chemical Marketing Reporter.* **Price Frequency:** weekly. **Effective Market(s):** New York. **Units of Measure:** Dollars per lb. **Type of Price:** spot. **Time Period Covered:** latest week.

Source: *U. S. Spice Trade.* **Price Frequency:** annually. **Effective Market(s):** New York. **Units of Measure:** cents per lb. **Type of Price:** spot. **Time Period Covered:** latest 3 years.

CORN

Source: *Agricultural Outlook.* **Price Frequency:** quarterly, annually. **Effective Market(s):** Chicago. **Units of Measure:** Dollars per bushel. **Type of Price:** average. **Time Period Covered:** latest year.

Source: *Agricultural Outlook.* **Price Frequency:** monthly, annually. **Effective Market(s):** United States. **Units of Measure:** Dollars per bushel. **Type of Price:** price received by farmer. **Time Period Covered:** monthly latest 6 months, annually latest 3 years.

Source: *Agricultural Outlook.* **Price Frequency:** annually. **Effective Market(s):** United States. **Units of Measure:** Dollars per bushel. **Type of Price:** farm. **Time Period Covered:** latest 6 years.

Source: *Agricultural Outlook.* **Price Frequency:** monthly, annually. **Effective Market(s):** Gulf ports. **Units of Measure:** Dollars per bushel. **Type of Price:** export. **Time Period Covered:** monthly latest 6 months, annually latest 3 years.

Source: *Agricultural Prices.* **Price Frequency:** monthly. **Effective Market(s):** United States. **Units of Measure:** Dollars per bushel. **Type of Price:** received by farmer. **Time Period Covered:** latest 2 months, year ago.

Source: *Agricultural Prices.* **Price Frequency:** monthly. **Effective Market(s):** United States. **Units of Measure:** Dollars per bushel. **Type of Price:** received by farmer. **Time Period Covered:** latest 2 years.

Source: *Agricultural Prices.* **Price Frequency:** monthly, seasonally. **Effective Market(s):** 17 domestic markets, United States. **Units of Measure:** Dollars per bushel. **Type of Price:** received by farmer. **Time Period Covered:** latest 2 months.

Source: *Agricultural Prices Annual Summary.* **Price Frequency:** annually. **Effective Market(s):** 48 domestic markets, United States. **Units of Measure:** Dollars per bushel. **Type of Price:** average price received by farmer. **Time Period Covered:** latest 2 years, for US latest 6 years.

Source: *Agricultural Prices Annual Summary.* **Price Frequency:** monthly, annually. **Effective Market(s):** 17 domestic markets. **Units of Measure:** Dollars per bushel. **Type of Price:** average price received by farmer. **Time Period Covered:** latest 2 years, for US latest 6 years.

Source: *Agricultural Trade Highlights.* **Price Frequency:** weekly. **Effective Market(s):** United States. **Units of Measure:** Dollars per metric ton. **Type of Price:** farm. **Time Period Covered:** latest week, month ago, year ago.

Source: *Agriculture.* **Price Frequency:** weekly. **Effective Market(s):** 7 domestic markets. **Units of Measure:** Dollars per bushel. **Time Period Covered:** latest week, wee ago.

Source: *The Brock Report.* **Price Frequency:** weekly. **Effective Market(s):** 10 domestic markets, Chatham (Canada). **Units of Measure:** Dollars per bushel. **Time Period Covered:** latest week, week ago.

Source: *Commodity Year Book.* **Price Frequency:** annually. **Effective Market(s):** United States. **Units of Measure:** Dollars per bushel. **Type of Price:** farm price. **Time Period Covered:** latest 9 years.

Source: *Feed Situation and Outlook Report.* **Price Frequency:** annually. **Units of Measure:** Dollars per bushel. **Type of Price:** average received by farmer. **Time Period Covered:** latest 5 years.

Source: *Feed Situation and Outlook Report.* **Price Frequency:** monthly, annually. **Effective Market(s):** United States. **Units of Measure:** Dollars per bushel. **Type of Price:** average received by farmer. **Time Period Covered:** latest 6 years.

Source: *Feedstuffs.* **Price Frequency:** weekly. **Effective Market(s):** 12 domestic markets. **Units of Measure:** Dollars per bushel. **Time Period Covered:** latest week.

Source: *Illinois Farm Report.* **Price Frequency:** monthly. **Effective Market(s):** Illinois. **Units of Measure:** Dollars per bushel. **Type of Price:** average received by farmers. **Time Period Covered:** latest 2 months, year ago.

Source: *Kansas Business Review.* **Price Frequency:** monthly. **Effective Market(s):** Kansas. **Units of Measure:** Dollars per bushel. **Type of Price:** received by farmer. **Time Period Covered:** latest month, month ago, year ago.

Source: *World Oilseed Situation and Market Highlights.* **Price Frequency:** monthly, annually. **Effective Market(s):** Rotterdam. **Units of Measure:** Dollars per metric ton, ECU per metric ton. **Time Period Covered:** monthly latest 2 months, annually latest 2 years.

CORN: ARGENTINE

Source: *World Agriculture Situation and Outlook.* **Price Frequency:** monthly, annually. **Effective Market(s):** Buenos Aires. **Units of Measure:** Dollars per metric ton. **Time Period Covered:** monthly latest year, annually latest 9 years.

Source: *World Grain Situation and Outlook.* **Price Frequency:** weekly, monthly, annually. **Effective Market(s):** Argentina. **Units of Measure:** Dollars per metric ton. **Type of Price:** export. **Time Period Covered:** weekly latest 3 months, monthly latest 3 years, annually latest 7 years.

CORN: DISTILLERS'

Source: *Farmers Weekly.* **Price Frequency:** weekly. **Effective Market(s):** Great Britain. **Units of Measure:** British pounds per tonne. **Type of Price:** spot. **Time Period Covered:** latest week.

CORN: EAR

Source: *Farm and Dairy.* **Price Frequency:** weekly, seasonally. **Effective Market(s):** Ohio, Pennsylvania. **Units of Measure:** Dollars per ton. **Type of Price:** auction high, auction low. **Time Period Covered:** latest week, year ago.

Source: *Lancaster Farming.* **Price Frequency:** weekly. **Effective Market(s):** Pennsylvania. **Units of Measure:** Dollars per ton. **Time Period Covered:** latest week.

CORN: FUTURES

Source: *Agriculture.* **Price Frequency:** weekly. **Effective Market(s):** Chicago. **Units of Measure:** cents per bushel. **Type of Price:** futures. **Time Period Covered:** latest week, week ago.

Source: *Asian Wall Street Journal.* **Price Frequency:** daily. **Effective Market(s):** Chicago. **Units of Measure:** cents per lb. **Type of Price:** futures. **Time Period Covered:** latest day.

Source: *Barron's.* **Price Frequency:** weekly. **Effective Market(s):** Chicago. **Units of Measure:** Dollars per bushel. **Type of Price:** futures. **Time Period Covered:** latest week.

Source: *Drovers Journal.* **Price Frequency:** weekly. **Effective Market(s):** Chicago. **Units of Measure:** cents per bushel. **Type of Price:** futures. **Time Period Covered:** latest 6 weeks.

Source: *Feedstuffs.* **Price Frequency:** weekly. **Effective Market(s):** Chicago. **Units of Measure:** cents per bushel. **Type of Price:** futures. **Time Period Covered:** latest week, week ago, latest season.

Source: *Grain and Feed Market News.* **Price Frequency:** weekly. **Effective Market(s):** Chicago. **Units of Measure:** Dollars per bushel. **Type of Price:** futures. **Time Period Covered:** latest week.

Source: *Investor's Daily.* **Price Frequency:** daily. **Effective Market(s):** Chicago. **Units of Measure:** Dollars per bushel. **Type of Price:** futures. **Time Period Covered:** latest day.

Source: *Lancaster Farming.* **Price Frequency:** daily. **Type of Price:** futures. **Time Period Covered:** latest week.

Source: *Los Angeles Times.* **Price Frequency:** daily. **Effective Market(s):** Chicago. **Units of Measure:** Dollars per bushel. **Type of Price:** futures. **Time Period Covered:** latest day.

Source: *Milling & Baking News.* **Price Frequency:** weekly. **Effective Market(s):** Chicago. **Units of Measure:** cents per bushel. **Type of Price:** futures. **Time Period Covered:** latest week, year ago, latest season.

Source: *New York Times.* **Price Frequency:** daily. **Effective Market(s):** Chicago. **Units of Measure:** Dollars per bushel. **Type of Price:** futures. **Time Period Covered:** latest day.

Source: *Urner Barry's Price-Current.* **Price Frequency:** daily. **Effective Market(s):** Chicago. **Units of Measure:** Dollars per bushel. **Type of Price:** futures. **Time Period Covered:** latest day.

Source: *Wall Street Journal.* **Price Frequency:** daily. **Effective Market(s):** Chicago. **Units of Measure:** cents per bushel. **Type of Price:** futures. **Time Period Covered:** latest day.

CORN: FUTURES, MAY

Source: *Commodity Year Book.* **Price Frequency:** monthly. **Effective Market(s):** Chicago. **Units of Measure:** cents per bushel. **Type of Price:** futures. **Time Period Covered:** latest 4 years.

CORN: HIGH FRUCTOSE

Source: *Feed Situation and Outlook Report.* **Price Frequency:** monthly. **Effective Market(s):** Midwest. **Units of Measure:** cents per lb. **Type of Price:** wholesale. **Time Period Covered:** latest 8 months.

CORN: NO. 2

Source: *Feedstuffs.* **Price Frequency:** weekly. **Effective Market(s):** Chicago. **Units of Measure:** Dollars per bushel. **Type of Price:** processor bid, terminal bid. **Time Period Covered:** latest week, week ago, 6 months ago, year ago.

Source: *Grain and Feed Market News.* **Price Frequency:** daily, seasonally. **Effective Market(s):** Memphis (TN). **Units of Measure:** Dollars per bushel. **Type of Price:** cash bid. **Time Period Covered:** latest week, year ago.

Source: *Idaho Farmer-Stockman.* **Price Frequency:** monthly. **Effective Market(s):** Portland (OR). **Units of Measure:** Dollars per 100 lbs. **Time Period Covered:** latest month, month ago.

Source: *Idaho Farmer-Stockman.* **Price Frequency:** monthly. **Effective Market(s):** Denver, Omaha (NE), Portland (OR), Stockton (CA). **Units of Measure:** Dollars per 100 lbs. **Time Period Covered:** latest month.

Source: *Investor's Daily.* **Price Frequency:** daily. **Effective Market(s):** Chicago. **Units of Measure:** Dollars per bushel. **Type of Price:** processor bid. **Time Period Covered:** latest 2 days.

Source: *Lancaster Farming.* **Price Frequency:** weekly. **Effective Market(s):** Pennsylvania. **Units of Measure:** Dollars per bushel. **Time Period Covered:** latest week.

Source: *Montana Farmer-Stockman.* **Price Frequency:** monthly, seasonally. **Effective Market(s):** Minneapolis, Portland (OR). **Units of Measure:** Dollars per bushel. **Type of Price:** cash. **Time Period Covered:** latest 2 months.

Source: *Montana Farmer-Stockman.* **Price Frequency:** monthly, seasonally. **Effective Market(s):** Gallatin Valley (MT), Southeast Montana. **Units of Measure:** Dollars per bushel. **Type of Price:** elevator bid. **Time Period Covered:** latest month.

Source: *Oregon Farmer-Stockman.* **Price Frequency:** monthly. **Effective Market(s):** Portland (OR). **Units of Measure:** Dollars per 100 lbs. **Type of Price:** cash. **Time Period Covered:** latest month, month ago.

Source: *Washington Farmer-Stockman.* **Price Frequency:** monthly, seasonally. **Effective Market(s):** Portland (OR). **Units of Measure:** Dollars per 100 lbs. **Type of Price:** cash. **Time Period Covered:** latest 2 months.

CORN: NO. 2, WHITE

Source: *Commodity Year Book.* **Price Frequency:** annually. **Effective Market(s):** Kansas City. **Units of Measure:** Dollars per bushel. **Time Period Covered:** latest 7 years.

Source: *Feed Situation and Outlook Report.* **Price Frequency:** monthly. **Effective Market(s):** Kansas City. **Units of Measure:** Dollars per bushel. **Type of Price:** wholesale. **Time Period Covered:** latest 8 months.

Source: *Grain and Feed Market News.* **Price Frequency:** daily, seasonally. **Effective Market(s):** Kansas City. **Units of Measure:** Dollars per bushel. **Type of Price:** cash bid. **Time Period Covered:** latest week, year ago.

CORN: NO. 2, YELLOW

Source: *Agricultural Outlook.* **Price Frequency:** monthly, annually. **Effective Market(s):** Chicago. **Units of Measure:** Dollars per bushel. **Type of Price:** wholesale. **Time Period Covered:** monthly latest 5 months, annually latest 4 years.

Source: *Asian Wall Street Journal.* **Price Frequency:** daily. **Effective Market(s):** Central Illinois. **Units of Measure:** Dollars per bushel. **Type of Price:** cash. **Time Period Covered:** latest 2 days, year ago.

Source: *California Farmer.* **Price Frequency:** semimonthly. **Effective Market(s):** Los Angeles, Stockton (CA). **Units of Measure:** Dollars per 100 lbs. **Time Period Covered:** latest week, month ago, year ago.

Source: *Commodity Year Book.* **Price Frequency:** annually. **Effective Market(s):** Gulf Ports (export), Los Angeles, St. Louis. **Units of Measure:** Dollars per bushel. **Time Period Covered:** latest 7 years.

Source: *Commodity Year Book.* **Price Frequency:** monthly, annually. **Effective Market(s):** Chicago. **Units of Measure:** cents per bushel. **Time Period Covered:** latest 8 years.

Source: *Commodity Year Book.* **Price Frequency:** monthly, annually. **Effective Market(s):** Omaha (NE). **Units of Measure:** Dollars per bushel. **Time Period Covered:** latest 8 years.

Source: *CRB Commodity Index Report.* **Price Frequency:** weekly. **Effective Market(s):** Chicago. **Units of Measure:** Dollars per bushel. **Type of Price:** spot. **Time Period Covered:** latest week.

Source: *Doane's Agricultural Report.* **Price Frequency:** weekly. **Effective Market(s):** Central Illinois. **Units of Measure:** Dollars per bushel. **Time Period Covered:** latest week, week ago, year ago.

Source: *Farm and Dairy.* **Price Frequency:** weekly, seasonally. **Effective Market(s):** Central Illinois. **Units of Measure:** Dollars per bushel. **Time Period Covered:** latest week, year ago.

Source: *Fedgazette.* **Price Frequency:** monthly. **Effective Market(s):** Minneapolis. **Units of Measure:** Dollars per bushel. **Time Period Covered:** latest 24 months.

Source: *Feed Situation and Outlook Report.* **Price Frequency:** annually. **Effective Market(s):** Gulf ports, Omaha (NE), St. Louis. **Units of Measure:** Dollars per bushel. **Type of Price:** average. **Time Period Covered:** latest 5 years.

Source: *Feed Situation and Outlook Report.* **Price Frequency:** monthly, annually. **Effective Market(s):** Central Illinois, Gulf, Omaha (NE), St. Louis. **Units of Measure:** Dollars per bushel. **Type of Price:** cash. **Time Period Covered:** latest 6 years.

Source: *Grain and Feed Market News.* **Price Frequency:** daily, seasonally. **Effective Market(s):** 6 domestic markets. **Units of Measure:** Dollars per bushel. **Type of Price:** cash bid. **Time Period Covered:** latest week, year ago.

Source: *Grain and Feed Market News.* **Price Frequency:** weekly, seasonally. **Effective Market(s):** 44 domestic markets. **Units of Measure:** Dollars per bushel. **Type of Price:** cash bid. **Time Period Covered:** latest week.

Source: *Grain and Feed Market News.* **Price Frequency:** daily, seasonally. **Effective Market(s):** East Coast, Gulf. **Units of Measure:** Dollars per bushel. **Type of Price:** export bid. **Time Period Covered:** latest week, year ago.

Source: *Grain and Feed Market News.* **Price Frequency:** weekly, seasonally. **Effective Market(s):** Illinois points, Kansas City, Omaha. **Units of Measure:** Dollars per ton. **Type of Price:** wholesale. **Time Period Covered:** latest week, week ago, year ago.

Source: *Idaho Farmer-Stockman.* **Price Frequency:** monthly. **Effective Market(s):** Ogden (UT). **Units of Measure:** Dollars per 100 lbs. **Time Period Covered:** latest month, month ago.

Source: *Livestock and Poultry Update.* **Price Frequency:** monthly. **Effective Market(s):** Central Illinois. **Units of Measure:** Dollars per bushel. **Time Period Covered:** latest 3 months, year ago.

Source: *Minneapolis Grain Exchange Statistical Annual.* **Price Frequency:** daily. **Effective Market(s):** Minneapolis. **Units of Measure:** cents per bushel. **Type of Price:** cash. **Time Period Covered:** latest year.

Source: *Minneapolis Grain Exchange Statistical Annual.* **Price Frequency:** monthly, annually. **Effective Market(s):** Minneapolis. **Units of Measure:** cents per bushel. **Type of Price:** cash. **Time Period Covered:** latest 10 years.

Source: *New York Times.* **Price Frequency:** daily. **Effective Market(s):** Chicago. **Units of Measure:** Dollars per bushel. **Type of Price:** cash. **Time Period Covered:** latest 2 days.

Source: *Standard & Poor's Statistical Service Current Statistics.* **Price Frequency:** monthly, annually. **Effective Market(s):** Chicago. **Units of Measure:** index. **Type of Price:** price index. **Time Period Covered:** latest 4 years.

Source: *Utah Farmer-Stockman.* **Price Frequency:** monthly, seasonally. **Effective Market(s):** Denver, Ogden (UT), Omaha, Portland, Stockton (CA). **Units of Measure:** Dollars per bushel. **Type of Price:** cash. **Time Period Covered:** latest 2 months.

Source: *Wall Street Journal.* **Price Frequency:** daily. **Effective Market(s):** Central Illinois. **Units of Measure:** Dollars per bushel. **Time Period Covered:** latest day, day ago, year ago.

CORN: NO. 2, YELLOW, 15.5% MOISTURE

Source: *Los Angeles Times.* **Price Frequency:** daily. **Effective Market(s):** Los Angeles. **Units of Measure:** Dollars per 100 lbs. **Type of Price:** cash. **Time Period Covered:** latest day.

CORN: NO. 3

Source: *Grain and Feed Market News.* **Price Frequency:** daily, seasonally. **Effective Market(s):** Pacific Northwest. **Units of Measure:** Dollars per bushel. **Type of Price:** export bid. **Time Period Covered:** latest week, year ago.

CORN: NO. 3, YELLOW

Source: *Economic and Energy Indicators.* **Price Frequency:** monthly, quarterly, annually. **Units of Measure:** Dollars per metric ton. **Time Period Covered:** latest 3 months, quarters, and years.

Source: *Journal of Commerce and Commercial.* **Price Frequency:** daily. **Effective Market(s):** Chicago. **Units of Measure:** Dollars per bushel. **Type of Price:** spot supplier. **Time Period Covered:** latest day.

Source: *World Agriculture Situation and Outlook.* **Price Frequency:** monthly, annually. **Effective Market(s):** Gulf ports. **Units of Measure:** Dollars per metric ton. **Time Period Covered:** monthly latest year, annually latest 9 years.

Source: *World Grain Situation and Outlook.* **Price Frequency:** weekly, monthly, annually. **Effective Market(s):** Gulf. **Units of Measure:** Dollars per metric ton. **Type of Price:** export. **Time Period Covered:** weekly latest 3 months, monthly latest 3 years, annually latest 7 years.

CORN: NO. 3, YELLOW, UNITED STATES

Source: *Agricultural Trade Highlights.* **Price Frequency:** weekly. **Effective Market(s):** Rotterdam. **Units of Measure:** Dollars per metric ton. **Type of Price:** asking. **Time Period Covered:** latest week, month ago, year ago.

Source: *Oil World.* **Price Frequency:** weekly, monthly, annually. **Effective Market(s):** Rotterdam. **Units of Measure:** Dollars per tonne. **Type of Price:** lowest representative asking. **Time Period Covered:** weekly latest 3 weeks, monthly latest 2 months, annually latest 2 years.

Source: *World Grain Situation and Outlook.* **Price Frequency:** weekly, monthly, annually. **Effective Market(s):** Rotterdam. **Units of Measure:** Dollars per metric ton. **Type of Price:** asking. **Time Period Covered:** weekly latest 7 months, monthly latest 2 years, annually latest 17 years.

CORN: SWEET

Source: *Agricultural Prices Annual Summary.* **Price Frequency:** monthly, seasonally. **Effective Market(s):** 11 domestic markets, United States. **Units of Measure:** Dollars per 100 lbs. **Type of Price:** average price received by farmer. **Time Period Covered:** latest 3 years, for US latest 6 years.

Source: *California Farmer.* **Price Frequency:** semimonthly, seasonally. **Effective Market(s):** Central San Joaquin Valley. **Units of Measure:** Dollars per 5 dozen carton. **Time Period Covered:** latest week, month ago, year ago.

Source: *The Grower.* **Price Frequency:** monthly, seasonally. **Effective Market(s):** East Coast. **Units of Measure:** Dollars per crate. **Time Period Covered:** latest year.

CORN: SWEET, BICOLOR

Source: *The Packer.* **Price Frequency:** weekly, seasonally. **Effective Market(s):** varies. **Units of Measure:** Dollars per crate. **Type of Price:** price received by farmer. **Time Period Covered:** latest week.

CORN: SWEET, CANNED

Source: *Vegetable and Specialties Situation and Outlook Report.* **Price Frequency:** monthly. **Units of Measure:** Dollars per case. **Type of Price:** wholesale. **Time Period Covered:** latest month, year ago.

CORN: SWEET, COB, FROZEN

Source: *Vegetable and Specialties Situation and Outlook Report.* **Price Frequency:** monthly. **Units of Measure:** Dollars per case. **Type of Price:** food service, retail. **Time Period Covered:** latest month, year ago.

CORN: SWEET, CUT, FROZEN

Source: *Vegetable and Specialties Situation and Outlook Report.* **Price Frequency:** monthly. **Units of Measure:** Dollars per case. **Type of Price:** food service, retail. **Time Period Covered:** latest month, year ago.

CORN: SWEET, FRESH

Source: *Agricultural Prices.* **Price Frequency:** monthly. **Effective Market(s):** United States. **Units of Measure:** Dollars per 100 lbs. **Type of Price:** received by farmer. **Time Period Covered:** latest 2 months, year ago.

Source: *Vegetable and Specialties Situation and Outlook Report.* **Price Frequency:** monthly, annually. **Effective Market(s):** United States. **Units of Measure:** Dollars per 100 lbs. **Type of Price:** received by grower. **Time Period Covered:** latest 4 years.

CORN: SWEET, WHITE

Source: *Lancaster Farming.* **Price Frequency:** weekly, seasonally. **Effective Market(s):** Pennsylvania. **Units of Measure:** Dollars per dozen. **Type of Price:** market. **Time Period Covered:** latest week.

Source: *The Packer.* **Price Frequency:** weekly, seasonally. **Effective Market(s):** varies. **Units of Measure:** Dollars per crate. **Type of Price:** price received by farmer. **Time Period Covered:** latest week.

CORN: SWEET, YELLOW

Source: *Fresh Fruit and Vegetable Prices.* **Price Frequency:** monthly, seasonally. **Effective Market(s):** 7 domestic markets. **Units of Measure:** Dollars per carton/crate. **Type of Price:** average price at shipping point. **Time Period Covered:** latest year.

Source: *The Packer.* **Price Frequency:** weekly, seasonally. **Effective Market(s):** varies. **Units of Measure:** Dollars per crate. **Type of Price:** price received by farmer. **Time Period Covered:** latest week.

CORN: SWEET, YELLOW, FLORIDA

Source: *Fresh Fruit and Vegetable Prices.* **Price Frequency:** monthly, seasonally. **Effective Market(s):** Chicago, New York City. **Units of Measure:** Dollars per crate. **Type of Price:** average wholesale price. **Time Period Covered:** latest year.

CORN: SWEET, YELLOW, ILLINOIS

Source: *Fresh Fruit and Vegetable Prices.* **Price Frequency:** monthly, seasonally. **Effective Market(s):** Chicago. **Units of Measure:** Dollars per crate. **Type of Price:** average wholesale price. **Time Period Covered:** latest year.

CORN: SWEET, YELLOW, NEW JERSEY

Source: *Fresh Fruit and Vegetable Prices.* **Price Frequency:** monthly, seasonally. **Effective Market(s):** New York City. **Units of Measure:** Dollars per crate. **Type of Price:** average wholesale price. **Time Period Covered:** latest year.

CORN: SWEET, YELLOW, NEW YORK

Source: *Fresh Fruit and Vegetable Prices.* **Price Frequency:** monthly, seasonally. **Effective Market(s):** New York City. **Units of Measure:** Dollars per crate. **Type of Price:** average wholesale price. **Time Period Covered:** latest year.

CORN: WHITE

Source: *Lancaster Farming.* **Price Frequency:** weekly, seasonally. **Effective Market(s):** Pennsylvania. **Units of Measure:** Dollars per crate. **Type of Price:** market. **Time Period Covered:** latest week.

CORN: WHOLE KERNEL, FROZEN

Source: *HRI-Buyer's Guide.* **Price Frequency:** weekly. **Effective Market(s):** Northeastern area. **Units of Measure:** Dollars per case. **Type of Price:** price paid by dining places & institutions. **Time Period Covered:** latest week.

CORN: YELLOW

Source: *Lancaster Farming.* **Price Frequency:** weekly, seasonally. **Effective Market(s):** Pennsylvania. **Units of Measure:** Dollars per dozen. **Type of Price:** market. **Time Period Covered:** latest week.

CORN: YELLOW, FRESH

Source: *HRI-Buyers Guide.* **Price Frequency:** weekly. **Effective Market(s):** Northeastern area. **Units of Measure:** Dollars per crate. **Type of Price:** price paid by dining places & institutions. **Time Period Covered:** latest week.

CORN EXTRACTIVES: CONDENSED, FERMENTED

Source: *Feedstuffs.* **Price Frequency:** weekly. **Effective Market(s):** Chicago, Kansas City. **Units of Measure:** Dollars per bulk ton. **Time Period Covered:** latest week.

CORN FOR SEED

see Seed Corn.

CORN GERM MEAL

Source: *Feedstuffs.* **Price Frequency:** weekly. **Effective Market(s):** Baltimore, Chicago, Kansas City. **Units of Measure:** Dollars per bulk ton. **Time Period Covered:** latest week.

CORN GLUTEN FEED

Source: *Asian Wall Street Journal.* **Price Frequency:** daily. **Effective Market(s):** Midwest. **Units of Measure:** Dollars per ton. **Type of Price:** cash. **Time Period Covered:** latest 2 days, year ago.

Source: *Feed Situation and Outlook Report.* **Price Frequency:** monthly. **Effective Market(s):** Illinois. **Units of Measure:** Dollars per ton. **Type of Price:** wholesale. **Time Period Covered:** latest 8 months.

Source: *Feedstuffs.* **Price Frequency:** weekly. **Effective Market(s):** Baltimore, Chicago, Kansas City. **Units of Measure:** Dollars per bulk ton. **Time Period Covered:** latest week.

Source: *Grain and Feed Market News.* **Price Frequency:** weekly, seasonally. **Effective Market(s):** Illinois points, Kansas City. **Units of Measure:** Dollars per ton. **Type of Price:** wholesale. **Time Period Covered:** latest week, week ago, year ago.

Source: *Wall Street Journal.* **Price Frequency:** daily. **Effective Market(s):** Midwest. **Units of Measure:** Dollars per ton. **Time Period Covered:** latest day, day ago, year ago.

CORN GLUTEN FEED: 21% PROTEIN

Source: *Milling & Baking News.* **Price Frequency:** weekly. **Effective Market(s):** Chicago, Southwest. **Units of Measure:** Dollars per ton. **Time Period Covered:** latest week.

CORN GLUTEN FEED: 60% PROTEIN

Source: *Grain and Feed Market News.* **Price Frequency:** weekly, seasonally. **Effective Market(s):** Illinois points, Kansas City. **Units of Measure:** Dollars per ton. **Type of Price:** wholesale. **Time Period Covered:** latest week, week ago, year ago.

CORN GLUTEN MEAL: 60% PROTEIN

Source: *Feed Situation and Outlook Report.* **Price Frequency:** monthly. **Effective Market(s):** Illinois. **Units of Measure:** Dollars per ton. **Type of Price:** wholesale. **Time Period Covered:** latest 8 months.

Source: *Feedstuffs.* **Price Frequency:** weekly. **Effective Market(s):** Baltimore, Chicago, Kansas City. **Units of Measure:** Dollars per bulk ton. **Time Period Covered:** latest week.

Source: *Feedstuffs.* **Price Frequency:** weekly. **Effective Market(s):** Chicago. **Units of Measure:** Dollars per ton. **Time Period Covered:** latest week, week ago, 6 months ago, year ago.

Source: *Milling & Baking News.* **Price Frequency:** weekly. **Effective Market(s):** Southwest. **Units of Measure:** Dollars per ton. **Time Period Covered:** latest week.

CORN GLUTEN PELLETS

Source: *Agra Europe.* **Price Frequency:** weekly, irregularly. **Effective Market(s):** Rotterdam. **Units of Measure:** Dollars per tonne. **Type of Price:** average. **Time Period Covered:** latest week.

CORN GLUTEN PELLETS: 23-24% PROTEIN

Source: *Oil World.* **Price Frequency:** weekly, monthly, annually. **Effective Market(s):** Rotterdam. **Units of Measure:** Dollars per tonne. **Type of Price:** lowest representative asking. **Time Period Covered:** weekly latest 3 weeks, monthly latest 2 months, annually latest 2 years.

Source: *World Oilseed Situation and Market Highlights.* **Price Frequency:** monthly, annually. **Effective Market(s):** Rotterdam. **Units of Measure:** Dollars per metric ton. **Time Period Covered:** latest 9 years.

CORN GRITS: BREWERS'

Source: *Feed Situation and Outlook Report.* **Price Frequency:** monthly. **Effective Market(s):** Chicago. **Units of Measure:** Dollars per 100 lbs. **Type of Price:** wholesale. **Time Period Covered:** latest 8 months.

Source: *Rice Situation and Outlook Report.* **Price Frequency:** monthly, annually. **Effective Market(s):** New York. **Units of Measure:** Dollars per 100 lbs. **Type of Price:** average. **Time Period Covered:** latest 9 years.

CORN HEAD FOR COMBINE

Source: *Agricultural Prices.* **Price Frequency:** annually. **Effective Market(s):** United States. **Units of Measure:** Dollars each. **Type of Price:** paid by farmer. **Time Period Covered:** latest year.

Source: *Agricultural Prices Annual Summary.* **Price Frequency:** annually. **Effective Market(s):** United States. **Units of Measure:** Dollars each. **Type of Price:** average price paid by farmer. **Time Period Covered:** latest 6 years.

CORN HOMINY: YELLOW

Source: *Los Angeles Times.* **Price Frequency:** daily. **Effective Market(s):** Los Angeles. **Units of Measure:** Dollars per ton. **Type of Price:** cash. **Time Period Covered:** latest day.

CORN MEAL

Source: *Agricultural Prices.* **Price Frequency:** quarterly. **Effective Market(s):** United States. **Units of Measure:** Dollars per 100 lbs. **Type of Price:** paid by farmer. **Time Period Covered:** latest 2 quarters, year ago.

Source: *Agricultural Prices.* **Price Frequency:** monthly. **Effective Market(s):** 10 domestic markets, United States. **Units of Measure:** Dollars per 100 lbs. **Type of Price:** paid by farmer. **Time Period Covered:** latest month.

Source: *Agricultural Prices Annual Summary.* **Price Frequency:** quarterly. **Effective Market(s):** 10 domestic markets, United States. **Units of Measure:** Dollars per 100 lbs. **Type of Price:** average price paid by farmer. **Time Period Covered:** latest year, for US latest 6 years.

Source: *Milling & Baking News.* **Price Frequency:** weekly. **Effective Market(s):** Chicago, New York. **Units of Measure:** Dollars per 100 lbs. **Time Period Covered:** latest week.

CORN MEAL: HOMINY FEED

see Hominy Feed.

CORN MEAL: YELLOW

Source: *Feed Situation and Outlook Report.* **Price Frequency:** monthly. **Effective Market(s):** New York. **Units of Measure:** Dollars per 100 lbs. **Type of Price:** wholesale. **Time Period Covered:** latest 8 months.

CORN OIL

Source: *Bakery Newsletter.* **Price Frequency:** weekly. **Effective Market(s):** Chicago. **Type of Price:** cash. **Time Period Covered:** last week.

Source: *Dairy Foods.* **Price Frequency:** monthly. **Effective Market(s):** Chicago. **Units of Measure:** Dollars per lb. **Time Period Covered:** latest 2 weeks.

Source: *Milling & Baking News.* **Price Frequency:** weekly. **Effective Market(s):** Decatur (IL). **Units of Measure:** cents per lb. **Type of Price:** spot bulk. **Time Period Covered:** latest week.

Source: *National Provisioner.* **Price Frequency:** daily. **Effective Market(s):** Midwest River. **Units of Measure:** cents per lb. **Time Period Covered:** selected day.

Source: *Oil World.* **Price Frequency:** weekly, monthly, annually. **Effective Market(s):** Midwest. **Units of Measure:** Dollars per tonne. **Type of Price:** lowest representative asking. **Time Period Covered:** weekly latest 3 weeks, monthly latest 2 months, annually latest 2 years.

CORN OIL: CRUDE

Source: *Chemical Marketing Reporter.* **Price Frequency:** weekly. **Effective Market(s):** Midwest. **Units of Measure:** cents per lb. **Type of Price:** spot. **Time Period Covered:** latest week.

Source: *World Oilseed Situation and Market Highlights.* **Price Frequency:** monthly, annually. **Effective Market(s):** Decatur (IL). **Units of Measure:** Dollars per metric ton. **Time Period Covered:** monthly latest year, annually latest 9 years.

CORN OIL: CRUDE, DRY MILL

Source: *Asian Wall Street Journal.* **Price Frequency:** daily. **Effective Market(s):** Chicago. **Units of Measure:** Dollars per lb. **Type of Price:** cash. **Time Period Covered:** latest 2 days, year ago.

Source: *Investor's Daily.* **Price Frequency:** daily. **Effective Market(s):** Chicago. **Units of Measure:** Dollars per lb. **Type of Price:** spot. **Time Period Covered:** latest 2 days.

Source: *New York Times.* **Price Frequency:** daily. **Effective Market(s):** Chicago. **Units of Measure:** Dollars per lb. **Type of Price:** cash. **Time Period Covered:** latest 2 days.

Source: *Wall Street Journal.* **Price Frequency:** daily. **Effective Market(s):** Chicago. **Units of Measure:** Dollars per lb. **Time Period Covered:** latest day, day ago, year ago.

CORN OIL: CRUDE, FOOTS (SOAPSTOCK), 95% ACID

Source: *Chemical Marketing Reporter.* **Price Frequency:** weekly. **Effective Market(s):** New York. **Units of Measure:** Dollars per lb. **Type of Price:** spot. **Time Period Covered:** latest week.

CORN OIL: CRUDE, WET MILL

Source: *Asian Wall Street Journal.* **Price Frequency:** daily. **Effective Market(s):** Chicago. **Units of Measure:** Dollars per lb. **Type of Price:** cash. **Time Period Covered:** latest 2 days, year ago.

Source: *Commodity Year Book.* **Price Frequency:** monthly, annually. **Effective Market(s):** Chicago. **Units of Measure:** cents per lb. **Type of Price:** spot. **Time Period Covered:** latest 10 years.

Source: *Wall Street Journal.* **Price Frequency:** daily. **Effective Market(s):** Chicago. **Units of Measure:** Dollars per lb. **Time Period Covered:** latest day, day ago, year ago.

CORN OIL: REFINED

Source: *Chemical Marketing Reporter.* **Price Frequency:** weekly. **Units of Measure:** Dollars per lb. **Type of Price:** spot. **Time Period Covered:** latest week.

CORN OIL: WET MILL

Source: *Oil Crops Situation and Outlook.* **Price Frequency:** monthly. **Effective Market(s):** Chicago. **Units of Measure:** cents per lb. **Type of Price:** wholesale. **Time Period Covered:** latest 5 months.

CORN OIL ACID

Source: *Chemical Marketing Reporter.* **Price Frequency:** weekly. **Effective Market(s):** New York. **Units of Measure:** Dollars per lb. **Type of Price:** spot. **Time Period Covered:** latest week.

CORN PICKER HUSKER

Source: *Agricultural Prices.* **Price Frequency:** annually. **Effective Market(s):** United States. **Units of Measure:** Dollars each. **Type of Price:** paid by farmer. **Time Period Covered:** latest year.

Source: *Agricultural Prices Annual Summary.* **Price Frequency:** annually. **Effective Market(s):** United States. **Units of Measure:** Dollars each. **Type of Price:** average price paid by farmer. **Time Period Covered:** latest 6 years.

CORN PLANTER: PLAIN

Source: *Agricultural Prices.* **Price Frequency:** annually. **Effective Market(s):** United States. **Units of Measure:** Dollars each. **Type of Price:** paid by farmer. **Time Period Covered:** latest year.

Source: *Agricultural Prices Annual Summary.* **Price Frequency:** annually. **Effective Market(s):** United States. **Units of Measure:** Dollars per machine. **Type of Price:** average price paid by farmer. **Time Period Covered:** latest 6 years.

CORN PLANTER: WITH FERTILIZER ATTACHMENT

Source: *Agricultural Prices.* **Price Frequency:** annually. **Effective Market(s):** United States. **Units of Measure:** Dollars each. **Type of Price:** paid by farmer. **Time Period Covered:** latest year.

Source: *Agricultural Prices Annual Summary.* **Price Frequency:** annually. **Effective Market(s):** United States. **Units of Measure:** Dollars each. **Type of Price:** average price paid by farmer. **Time Period Covered:** latest 6 years.

CORN SCREENINGS

Source: *Milling & Baking News.* **Price Frequency:** weekly. **Effective Market(s):** Kansas City. **Units of Measure:** Dollars per ton. **Time Period Covered:** latest week.

CORN STARCH

Source: *Feed Situation and Outlook Report.* **Price Frequency:** monthly. **Effective Market(s):** Midwest. **Units of Measure:** Dollars per 100 lbs. **Type of Price:** wholesale. **Time Period Covered:** latest 8 months.

CORN SUGAR

Source: *Feed Situation and Outlook Report.* **Price Frequency:** monthly. **Effective Market(s):** Midwest. **Units of Measure:** cents per lb. **Type of Price:** wholesale. **Time Period Covered:** latest 8 months.

CORN SWEETNER: HIGH FRUCTOSE

Source: *Dairy Foods.* **Price Frequency:** monthly. **Effective Market(s):** Chicago. **Units of Measure:** Dollars per 100 lbs. **Time Period Covered:** latest 2 weeks.

CORN SYRUP

Source: *Dairy Foods.* **Price Frequency:** monthly. **Effective Market(s):** Chicago. **Units of Measure:** Dollars per 100 lbs. **Time Period Covered:** latest 2 weeks.

Source: *Feed Situation and Outlook Report.* **Price Frequency:** monthly. **Effective Market(s):** Midwest/West. **Units of Measure:** cents per lb. **Type of Price:** wholesale. **Time Period Covered:** latest 8 months.

Source: *Milling & Baking News.* **Price Frequency:** weekly. **Effective Market(s):** 11 domestic markets. **Units of Measure:** cents per lb. **Time Period Covered:** latest week.

CORN SYRUP: 43 BAUME

Source: *Chemical Marketing Reporter.* **Price Frequency:** weekly. **Effective Market(s):** New York. **Units of Measure:** Dollars per 100 lbs. **Type of Price:** spot. **Time Period Covered:** latest week.

CORN SYRUP: 55%, WET/DRY

Source: *Milling & Baking News.* **Price Frequency:** weekly. **Effective Market(s):** 14 domestic markets. **Units of Measure:** cents per lb. **Time Period Covered:** latest week.

CORN SYRUP: HIGH FRUCTOSE, 42%, WET

Source: *Milling & Baking News.* **Price Frequency:** weekly. **Effective Market(s):** 14 domestic markets. **Units of Measure:** cents per lb. **Time Period Covered:** latest week.

CORN SYRUP: HIGH FRUCTOSE, 55%

Source: *Journal of Commerce and Commercial.* **Price Frequency:** daily. **Effective Market(s):** Midwest. **Units of Measure:** Dollars per 100 lbs. **Type of Price:** spot supplier. **Time Period Covered:** latest day.

CORN SYRUP: HIGH FRUCTOSE, FUTURES

Source: *Minneapolis Grain Exchange Statistical Annual.* **Price Frequency:** daily. **Effective Market(s):** Minneapolis. **Units of Measure:** Dollars per 100 lbs. **Type of Price:** futures. **Time Period Covered:** latest year.

CORN WHISKEY

Source: *Colorado Beverage Analyst.* **Price Frequency:** monthly. **Effective Market(s):** Colorado. **Units of Measure:** Dollars per case. **Type of Price:** wholesale by brand. **Time Period Covered:** latest month.

Source: *Kentucky Beverage Journal.* **Price Frequency:** monthly. **Effective Market(s):** Kentucky. **Units of Measure:** Dollars per bottle, dollars per case. **Type of Price:** wholesale by brand. **Time Period Covered:** latest month.

CORNED BEEF

see Beef: Corned.

CORNISH HENS

Source: *Meat Price Report.* **Price Frequency:** weekly. **Units of Measure:** cents paid per each. **Type of Price:** price paid to wholesaler. **Time Period Covered:** latest week.

CORNMINT OIL

Source: *U. S. Essential Oil Trade.* **Price Frequency:** annually. **Effective Market(s):** United States. **Units of Measure:** Dollars per kilogram. **Type of Price:** import value. **Time Period Covered:** latest 3 years.

CORTISONE ACETATE: USP

Source: *Chemical Marketing Reporter.* **Price Frequency:** weekly. **Effective Market(s):** New York. **Units of Measure:** Dollars per gram. **Type of Price:** spot. **Time Period Covered:** latest week.

COTTON

Source: *Agricultural Outlook.* **Price Frequency:** quarterly, annually. **Units of Measure:** cents per lb. **Type of Price:** spot average. **Time Period Covered:** latest year.

Source: *Agricultural Outlook.* **Price Frequency:** monthly, annually. **Effective Market(s):** Northern Europe. **Units of Measure:** cents per lb. **Type of Price:** average. **Time Period Covered:** monthly latest 5 months, annually latest 4 years.

Source: *Agricultural Outlook.* **Price Frequency:** monthly, annually. **Effective Market(s):** 8-market average. **Units of Measure:** cents per lb. **Type of Price:** export. **Time Period Covered:** monthly latest 6 months, annually latest 3 years.

Source: *Agriculture.* **Price Frequency:** weekly. **Effective Market(s):** San Joaquin Valley, South Delta, West Texas, 3-market average. **Units of Measure:** Dollars per 100 lbs. **Time Period Covered:** latest week.

Source: *The Brock Report.* **Price Frequency:** weekly. **Effective Market(s):** 5 domestic markets. **Units of Measure:** Dollars per bushel. **Time Period Covered:** latest week, week ago.

Source: *Economic and Energy Indicators.* **Price Frequency:** monthly, quarterly, annually. **Units of Measure:** cents per lb. **Time Period Covered:** latest 3 months, quarters, and years.

Source: *Far Eastern Economic Review.* **Price Frequency:** weekly. **Effective Market(s):** New York. **Units of Measure:** Dollars per lb. **Time Period Covered:** latest week, week ago, 3 months ago, year ago.

Source: *Standard & Poor's Statistical Service Current Statistics.* **Price Frequency:** monthly, annually. **Effective Market(s):** leading market average. **Units of Measure:** cents per lb. **Type of Price:** average. **Time Period Covered:** latest 4 years.

COTTON: 1-1/16″

Source: *CRB Commodity Index Report.* **Price Frequency:** weekly. **Effective Market(s):** 7-market average. **Units of Measure:** Dollars per lb. **Type of Price:** spot. **Time Period Covered:** latest week.

COTTON: 329, CHINESE

Source: *Cotton: World Statistics.* **Price Frequency:** monthly, annually. **Effective Market(s):** North Europe. **Units of Measure:** cents per lb. **Type of Price:** average. **Time Period Covered:** monthly latest 2 years, annually latest 3 years.

COTTON: A TYPE, AFRICAN

Source: *Cotton and Wool Situation and Outlook Report.* **Price Frequency:** weekly. **Effective Market(s):** Northern Europe. **Units of Measure:** cents per lb. **Time Period Covered:** latest 6 months.

COTTON: A TYPE, AUSTRALIAN

Source: *Cotton and Wool Situation and Outlook Report.* **Price Frequency:** weekly. **Effective Market(s):** Northern Europe. **Units of Measure:** cents per lb. **Time Period Covered:** latest 6 months.

COTTON: A TYPE, CALIFORNIA/ARIZONA

Source: *Cotton and Wool Situation and Outlook Report.* **Price Frequency:** weekly. **Effective Market(s):** Northern Europe. **Units of Measure:** cents per lb. **Time Period Covered:** latest 6 months.

COTTON: A TYPE, CENTRAL AMERICAN

Source: *Cotton and Wool Situation and Outlook Report.* **Price Frequency:** weekly. **Effective Market(s):** Northern Europe. **Units of Measure:** cents per lb. **Time Period Covered:** latest 6 months.

COTTON: A TYPE, CHINESE

Source: *Cotton and Wool Situation and Outlook Report.* **Price Frequency:** weekly. **Effective Market(s):** Northern Europe. **Units of Measure:** cents per lb. **Time Period Covered:** latest 6 months.

COTTON: A TYPE, MEMPHIS TERRITORY

Source: *Cotton and Wool Situation and Outlook Report.* **Price Frequency:** weekly. **Effective Market(s):** Northern Europe. **Units of Measure:** cents per lb. **Time Period Covered:** latest 6 months.

COTTON: A TYPE, MEXICAN

Source: *Cotton and Wool Situation and Outlook Report.* **Price Frequency:** weekly. **Effective Market(s):** Northern Europe. **Units of Measure:** cents per lb. **Time Period Covered:** latest 6 months.

COTTON: A TYPE, PAKISTAN

Source: *Cotton and Wool Situation and Outlook Report.* **Price Frequency:** weekly. **Effective Market(s):** Northern Europe. **Units of Measure:** cents per lb. **Time Period Covered:** latest 6 months.

COTTON: A TYPE, PARAGUAY

Source: *Cotton and Wool Situation and Outlook Report.* **Price Frequency:** weekly. **Effective Market(s):** Northern Europe. **Units of Measure:** cents per lb. **Time Period Covered:** latest 6 months.

COTTON: A TYPE, TURKEY

Source: *Cotton and Wool Situation and Outlook Report.* **Price Frequency:** weekly. **Effective Market(s):** Northern Europe. **Units of Measure:** cents per lb. **Time Period Covered:** latest 6 months.

COTTON: A TYPE, U.S.S.R

Source: *Cotton and Wool Situation and Outlook Report.* **Price Frequency:** weekly. **Effective Market(s):** Northern Europe. **Units of Measure:** cents per lb. **Time Period Covered:** latest 6 months.

COTTON: AFZAL 1-3/32", PAKISTAN

Source: *Cotton: World Statistics.* **Price Frequency:** monthly, annually. **Effective Market(s):** North Europe. **Units of Measure:** cents per lb. **Type of Price:** average. **Time Period Covered:** monthly latest 2 years, annually latest 22 years.

COTTON: AMERICAN PIMA

Source: *Agricultural Prices.* **Price Frequency:** annually. **Effective Market(s):** Arizona, California, New Mexico, Texas, United States. **Units of Measure:** Dollars per lb. **Type of Price:** received by farmer. **Time Period Covered:** latest 2 years.

Source: *Agricultural Prices Annual Summary.* **Price Frequency:** annually. **Effective Market(s):** Arizona, California, New Mexico, Texas, United States. **Units of Measure:** Dollars per lb. **Type of Price:** average price received by farmer. **Time Period Covered:** latest 2 years, for US latest 6 years.

Source: *Long Staple Cotton Review.* **Price Frequency:** annually. **Units of Measure:** cents per lb. **Type of Price:** farm, target. **Time Period Covered:** latest 8 years.

COTTON: AMERICAN PIMA, GRADE 1, STAPLE 44

Source: *Long Staple Cotton Review.* **Price Frequency:** monthly. **Units of Measure:** cents per lb. **Type of Price:** average. **Time Period Covered:** latest month, year ago.

COTTON: AMERICAN PIMA, GRADE 1, STAPLE 46

Source: *Long Staple Cotton Review.* **Price Frequency:** monthly. **Units of Measure:** cents per lb. **Type of Price:** average. **Time Period Covered:** latest month, year ago.

COTTON: AMERICAN PIMA, GRADE 2, STAPLE 44

Source: *Long Staple Cotton Review.* **Price Frequency:** monthly. **Units of Measure:** cents per lb. **Type of Price:** average. **Time Period Covered:** latest month, year ago.

COTTON: AMERICAN PIMA, GRADE 2, STAPLE 46

Source: *Long Staple Cotton Review.* **Price Frequency:** monthly. **Units of Measure:** cents per lb. **Type of Price:** average. **Time Period Covered:** latest month, year ago.

COTTON: AMERICAN PIMA, GRADE 3, 1-7/16"

Source: *Cotton: World Statistics.* **Price Frequency:** monthly, annually. **Effective Market(s):** North Europe. **Units of Measure:** cents per lb. **Type of Price:** average. **Time Period Covered:** monthly latest 2 years, annually latest 4 years.

COTTON: AMERICAN PIMA, GRADE 3, STAPLE 44

Source: *Long Staple Cotton Review.* **Price Frequency:** monthly. **Units of Measure:** cents per lb. **Type of Price:** average. **Time Period Covered:** latest month, year ago.

COTTON: AMERICAN PIMA, GRADE 3, STAPLE 46

Source: *Long Staple Cotton Review.* **Price Frequency:** monthly, annually. **Units of Measure:** cents per lb. **Type of Price:** average. **Time Period Covered:** monthly latest month, year ago, annually latest 8 years.

COTTON: AMERICAN PIMA, GRADE 4, STAPLE 44

Source: *Long Staple Cotton Review.* **Price Frequency:** monthly. **Units of Measure:** cents per lb. **Type of Price:** average. **Time Period Covered:** latest month, year ago.

COTTON: AMERICAN PIMA, GRADE 4, STAPLE 46

Source: *Long Staple Cotton Review.* **Price Frequency:** monthly. **Units of Measure:** cents per lb. **Type of Price:** average. **Time Period Covered:** latest month, year ago.

COTTON: AMERICAN PIMA, GRADE 5, STAPLE 44

Source: *Long Staple Cotton Review.* **Price Frequency:** monthly. **Units of Measure:** cents per lb. **Type of Price:** average. **Time Period Covered:** latest month, year ago.

COTTON: AMERICAN PIMA, GRADE 5, STAPLE 46

Source: *Long Staple Cotton Review.* **Price Frequency:** monthly. **Units of Measure:** cents per lb. **Type of Price:** average. **Time Period Covered:** latest month, year ago.

COTTON: AMERICAN PIMA, GRADE 6, STAPLE 44

Source: *Long Staple Cotton Review.* **Price Frequency:** monthly. **Units of Measure:** cents per lb. **Type of Price:** average. **Time Period Covered:** latest month, year ago.

COTTON: AMERICAN PIMA, GRADE 6, STAPLE 46

Source: *Long Staple Cotton Review.* **Price Frequency:** monthly. **Units of Measure:** cents per lb. **Type of Price:** average. **Time Period Covered:** latest month, year ago.

COTTON: AMERICAN UPLAND

Source: *Agricultural Prices.* **Price Frequency:** monthly. **Effective Market(s):** 10 domestic markets, United States. **Units of Measure:** Dollars per lb. **Type of Price:** received by farmer. **Time Period Covered:** latest 2 months.

COTTON: AMWZ, RAW, NEW CROP, TANZANIAN

Source: *Prices of Selected Asia/Pacific Products.* **Price Frequency:** monthly. **Effective Market(s):** Hong Kong. **Units of Measure:** Dollars per lb. **Type of Price:** high, low. **Time Period Covered:** latest month.

COTTON: B-557 SAWGIN

Source: *Asian Wall Street Journal.* **Price Frequency:** daily. **Effective Market(s):** Karachi. **Units of Measure:** Pakistani rupees per maund. **Type of Price:** closing. **Time Period Covered:** latest 2 days.

COTTON: BARAKAT, LONG STAPLE, SUDANESE

Source: *Monthly Commodity Price Bulletin Supplement.* **Price Frequency:** monthly, quarterly, annually. **Effective Market(s):** North Europe. **Units of Measure:** cents per lb. **Time Period Covered:** latest 20 years.

Source: *Monthly Commodity Price Bulletin.* **Price Frequency:** monthly, annually. **Effective Market(s):** North Europe. **Units of Measure:** cents per lb. **Time Period Covered:** latest 5 years.

COTTON: BS-1 GRADE, RAW, NEW CROP, PAKISTAN

Source: *Prices of Selected Asia/Pacific Products.* **Price Frequency:** monthly. **Effective Market(s):** Hong Kong. **Units of Measure:** Dollars per lb. **Type of Price:** high, low. **Time Period Covered:** latest month.

COTTON: C-1/2, 1-1/16″, ARGENTINE

Source: *Cotton: World Statistics.* **Price Frequency:** monthly, annually. **Effective Market(s):** North Europe. **Units of Measure:** cents per lb. **Type of Price:** average. **Time Period Covered:** monthly latest 2 years, annually latest 8 years.

COTTON: COARSE COUNT, ARGENTINE

Source: *Cotton and Wool Situation and Outlook Report.* **Price Frequency:** weekly. **Effective Market(s):** Northern Europe. **Units of Measure:** cents per lb. **Time Period Covered:** latest 6 months.

COTTON: COARSE COUNT, CHINESE

Source: *Cotton and Wool Situation and Outlook Report.* **Price Frequency:** weekly. **Effective Market(s):** Northern Europe. **Units of Measure:** cents per lb. **Time Period Covered:** latest 6 months.

COTTON: COARSE COUNT, NEW ORLEANS/ TEXAS

Source: *Cotton and Wool Situation and Outlook Report.* **Price Frequency:** weekly. **Effective Market(s):** Northern Europe. **Units of Measure:** cents per lb. **Time Period Covered:** latest 6 months.

COTTON: COARSE COUNT, PAKISTAN

Source: *Cotton and Wool Situation and Outlook Report.* **Price Frequency:** weekly. **Effective Market(s):** Northern Europe. **Units of Measure:** cents per lb. **Time Period Covered:** latest 6 months.

COTTON: COARSE COUNT, RUSSIAN

Source: *Cotton and Wool Situation and Outlook Report.* **Price Frequency:** weekly. **Effective Market(s):** Northern Europe. **Units of Measure:** cents per lb. **Time Period Covered:** latest 6 months.

COTTON: COARSE COUNT, SOUTHERN BRAZIL

Source: *Cotton and Wool Situation and Outlook Report.* **Price Frequency:** weekly. **Effective Market(s):** Northern Europe. **Units of Measure:** cents per lb. **Time Period Covered:** latest 6 months.

COTTON: COARSE COUNT, TURKISH

Source: *Cotton and Wool Situation and Outlook Report.* **Price Frequency:** weekly. **Effective Market(s):** Northern Europe. **Units of Measure:** cents per lb. **Time Period Covered:** latest 6 months.

COTTON: COTTON OUTLOOK INDEX A

Source: *Cotton: Review of the World Situation.* **Price Frequency:** annually. **Effective Market(s):** World. **Units of Measure:** cents per lb. **Type of Price:** average. **Time Period Covered:** latest 4 years.

Source: *Cotton: World Statistics.* **Price Frequency:** monthly, annually. **Effective Market(s):** North Europe. **Units of Measure:** cents per lb. **Type of Price:** average. **Time Period Covered:** monthly latest 2 years, annually latest 22 years.

Source: *Cotton and Wool Situation and Outlook Report.* **Price Frequency:** weekly, monthly, annually. **Effective Market(s):** Northern Europe. **Units of Measure:** cents per lb. **Time Period Covered:** weekly latest 6 months, monthly and annually latest 6 years.

Source: *Financial Times.* **Price Frequency:** daily. **Effective Market(s):** London. **Units of Measure:** cents per lb. **Type of Price:** spot. **Time Period Covered:** latest day.

COTTON: COTTON OUTLOOK INDEX A, MIDDLING 1-3/32"

Source: *Commodity Trade and Price Trends.* **Price Frequency:** annually. **Effective Market(s):** North Europe. **Units of Measure:** cents per kilogram, 1980 constant cents per kilogram. **Time Period Covered:** latest 37 years.

Source: *Monthly Commodity Price Bulletin.* **Price Frequency:** monthly, annually. **Effective Market(s):** Liverpool (England). **Units of Measure:** cents per lb. **Time Period Covered:** latest 5 years.

Source: *Monthly Commodity Price Bulletin Supplement.* **Price Frequency:** monthly, quarterly, annually. **Effective Market(s):** North Europe. **Units of Measure:** cents per lb. **Time Period Covered:** latest 20 years.

Source: *UNCTAD Commodity Yearbook.* **Price Frequency:** annually. **Effective Market(s):** North Europe. **Units of Measure:** Dollars per metric ton. **Type of Price:** free market. **Time Period Covered:** latest 12 years.

COTTON: COTTON OUTLOOK INDEX B

Source: *Cotton and Wool Situation and Outlook Report.* **Price Frequency:** monthly, annually. **Effective Market(s):** Northern Europe. **Units of Measure:** cents per lb. **Time Period Covered:** latest 6 years.

COTTON: COTTON OUTLOOK INDEX B, COARSE COUNT

Source: *Cotton and Wool Situation and Outlook Report.* **Price Frequency:** weekly. **Effective Market(s):** Northern Europe. **Units of Measure:** cents per lb. **Time Period Covered:** latest 6 months.

Source: *Cotton: World Statistics.* **Price Frequency:** monthly, annually. **Effective Market(s):** North Europe. **Units of Measure:** cents per lb. **Type of Price:** average. **Time Period Covered:** monthly latest 2 years, annually latest 20 years.

Source: *Monthly Commodity Price Bulletin.* **Price Frequency:** monthly, annually. **Effective Market(s):** Liverpool (England). **Units of Measure:** cents per lb. **Time Period Covered:** latest 5 years.

Source: *Monthly Commodity Price Bulletin Supplement.* **Price Frequency:** monthly, quarterly, annually. **Effective Market(s):** North Europe. **Units of Measure:** cents per lb. **Time Period Covered:** latest 20 years.

COTTON: EGYPTIAN

Source: *International Financial Statistics.* **Price Frequency:** monthly, quarterly, annually. **Effective Market(s):** Liverpool (England). **Units of Measure:** cents per lb., index. **Type of Price:** market price, price index. **Time Period Covered:** latest 5 months, latest 5 quartesr, latest 5 years.

Source: *International Financial Statistics Yearbook.* **Price Frequency:** annually. **Effective Market(s):** Liverpool (England). **Units of Measure:** cents per lb. **Type of Price:** wholesale . **Time Period Covered:** latest 30 years.

COTTON: FUTURES

Source: *Agriculture.* **Price Frequency:** weekly. **Effective Market(s):** New York. **Units of Measure:** cents per lb. **Type of Price:** futures. **Time Period Covered:** latest week, week ago.

Source: *Asian Wall Street Journal.* **Price Frequency:** daily. **Effective Market(s):** New York. **Units of Measure:** cents per lb. **Type of Price:** futures. **Time Period Covered:** latest day.

Source: *Barron's.* **Price Frequency:** weekly. **Effective Market(s):** New York. **Units of Measure:** cents per lb. **Type of Price:** futures. **Time Period Covered:** latest week.

Source: *Cotton: World Statistics.* **Price Frequency:** monthly. **Effective Market(s):** New York. **Units of Measure:** cents per lb. **Type of Price:** futures. **Time Period Covered:** latest 4 years.

Source: *DNR: Daily News Record.* **Price Frequency:** daily. **Units of Measure:** cents per lb. **Type of Price:** futures. **Time Period Covered:** latest day, day ago.

Source: *Far Eastern Economic Review.* **Price Frequency:** weekly. **Effective Market(s):** New York. **Units of Measure:** Dollars per lb. **Type of Price:** futures. **Time Period Covered:** latest week.

Source: *Financial Times.* **Price Frequency:** daily. **Effective Market(s):** New York. **Units of Measure:** cents per lb. **Type of Price:** futures. **Time Period Covered:** latest day.

Source: *Investor's Daily.* **Price Frequency:** daily. **Effective Market(s):** New York. **Units of Measure:** cents per lb. . **Type of Price:** futures. **Time Period Covered:** latest day.

Source: *Los Angeles Times.* **Price Frequency:** daily. **Effective Market(s):** New York. **Units of Measure:** cents per lb. **Type of Price:** futures. **Time Period Covered:** latest day.

Source: *New York Times.* **Price Frequency:** daily. **Effective Market(s):** New York. **Units of Measure:** cents per lb. **Type of Price:** futures. **Time Period Covered:** latest day.

Source: *Wall Street Journal.* **Price Frequency:** daily. **Effective Market(s):** New York. **Units of Measure:** cents per lb. **Type of Price:** futures. **Time Period Covered:** latest day.

COTTON: FUTURES, MAY

Source: *Commodity Year Book.* **Price Frequency:** monthly. **Effective Market(s):** New York. **Units of Measure:** cents per lb. **Type of Price:** futures. **Time Period Covered:** latest 8 years.

COTTON: GIZA 45, EGYPTIAN

Source: *UNCTAD Commodity Yearbook.* **Price Frequency:** annually. **Effective Market(s):** North Europe. **Units of Measure:** Dollars per metric ton. **Type of Price:** free market. **Time Period Covered:** latest 12 years.

COTTON: GIZA 45, EXTRA LONG STAPLE, EGYPTIAN

Source: *Monthly Commodity Price Bulletin.* **Price Frequency:** monthly, annually. **Effective Market(s):** North Europe. **Units of Measure:** cents per lb. **Time Period Covered:** latest 5 years.

Source: *Monthly Commodity Price Bulletin Supplement.* **Price Frequency:** monthly, quarterly, annually. **Effective Market(s):** North Europe. **Units of Measure:** cents per lb. **Time Period Covered:** latest 20 years.

COTTON: GIZA 69/75/81, EGYPTIAN

Source: *Cotton: World Statistics.* **Price Frequency:** monthly, annually. **Effective Market(s):** North Europe. **Units of Measure:** cents per lb. **Type of Price:** average. **Time Period Covered:** monthly latest 2 years, annually latest 22 years.

COTTON: GIZA 70, EGYPTIAN

Source: *Cotton: World Statistics.* **Price Frequency:** monthly, annually. **Effective Market(s):** North Europe. **Units of Measure:** cents per lb. **Type of Price:** average. **Time Period Covered:** monthly latest 2 years, annually latest 22 years.

Source: *FAO Quarterly Bulletin of Statistics.* **Price Frequency:** monthly, annually. **Effective Market(s):** Liverpool (England). **Units of Measure:** Dollars per 100 lbs., dollars per metric ton. **Time Period Covered:** latest 3 years.

COTTON: GRADE 31, STAPLE 34

Source: *Cotton Price Statistics.* **Price Frequency:** monthly, annually. **Effective Market(s):** United States. **Units of Measure:** cents per lb. **Type of Price:** average landed quotation, spot. **Time Period Covered:** latest 5 years.

Source: *Cotton Price Statistics Annual.* **Price Frequency:** monthly, annually. **Effective Market(s):** 8 domestic markets, United States. **Units of Measure:** cents per lb. **Type of Price:** spot. **Time Period Covered:** latest year, for US latest 6 years.

Source: *Cotton Price Statistics Annual.* **Price Frequency:** monthly, annually. **Effective Market(s):** Southeast, Memphis, California. **Units of Measure:** cents per lb. **Type of Price:** average landed mill price. **Time Period Covered:** latest 6 years.

COTTON: GRADE 41, STAPLE 34

Source: *Cotton Price Statistics.* **Price Frequency:** daily. **Effective Market(s):** 8 domestic markets. **Units of Measure:** cents per lb. **Type of Price:** spot. **Time Period Covered:** latest month.

Source: *Cotton Price Statistics.* **Price Frequency:** monthly, annually. **Effective Market(s):** United States. **Units of Measure:** cents per lb. **Type of Price:** average landed quotation, spot. **Time Period Covered:** latest 5 years.

Source: *Cotton Price Statistics Annual.* **Price Frequency:** annually. **Effective Market(s):** 10 domestic markets. **Units of Measure:** cents per lb. **Type of Price:** season average. **Time Period Covered:** latest 12 years.

Source: *Cotton Price Statistics Annual.* **Price Frequency:** daily, monthly. **Units of Measure:** cents per lb. **Type of Price:** spot. **Time Period Covered:** latest year.

Source: *Cotton Price Statistics Annual.* **Price Frequency:** monthly, annually. **Effective Market(s):** 8 domestic markets, United States. **Units of Measure:** cents per lb. **Type of Price:** spot. **Time Period Covered:** latest year, for US latest 40 years.

Source: *Cotton Price Statistics Annual.* **Price Frequency:** monthly, annually. **Effective Market(s):** California, Memphis, Oklahoma/Texas, Southeast. **Units of Measure:** cents per lb. **Type of Price:** average landed mill price. **Time Period Covered:** latest 6 years.

COTTON: GRADE 41, STAPLE 34, FUTURES

Source: *Cotton Price Statistics.* **Price Frequency:** daily, monthly. **Effective Market(s):** New York. **Units of Measure:** cents per lb. **Type of Price:** futures. **Time Period Covered:** latest month.

Source: *Cotton Price Statistics Annual.* **Price Frequency:** daily. **Effective Market(s):** New York. **Units of Measure:** cents per lb. **Type of Price:** futures. **Time Period Covered:** latest year.

COTTON: IZMIR/ANTALYA ST 1 WHITE, 1-3/32″ RG, TURKISH

Source: *Cotton: World Statistics.* **Price Frequency:** monthly, annually. **Effective Market(s):** North Europe. **Units of Measure:** cents per lb. **Type of Price:** average. **Time Period Covered:** monthly latest 2 years, annually latest 22 years.

COTTON: K-68 SAWGIN

Source: *Asian Wall Street Journal.* **Price Frequency:** daily. **Effective Market(s):** Karachi. **Units of Measure:** Pakistani rupees per maund. **Type of Price:** closing. **Time Period Covered:** latest 2 days.

COTTON: LONG MEDIUM STAPLE, EGYPTIAN

Source: *International Financial Statistics.* **Price Frequency:** quarterly, annually. **Effective Market(s):** Egypt. **Units of Measure:** cents per lb., index. **Type of Price:** market price, price index. **Time Period Covered:** latest 3 quarters, latest 4 years.

Source: *International Financial Statistics Yearbook.* **Price Frequency:** annually. **Effective Market(s):** Egypt. **Units of Measure:** cents per lb. **Type of Price:** wholesale . **Time Period Covered:** latest 30 years.

COTTON: LONG STAPLE, EGYPTIAN

Source: *International Financial Statistics.* **Price Frequency:** quarterly, annually. **Effective Market(s):** Egypt. **Units of Measure:** cents per lb., index. **Type of Price:** market price, price index. **Time Period Covered:** latest 3 quarters, latest 4 years.

Source: *International Financial Statistics Yearbook.* **Price Frequency:** annually. **Effective Market(s):** Egypt. **Units of Measure:** cents per lb. **Type of Price:** wholesale. **Time Period Covered:** latest 30 years.

COTTON: MEDIUM STAPLE, MIDDLING 1-3/32″, CENTRAL AMERICAN

Source: *Monthly Commodity Price Bulletin.* **Price Frequency:** monthly, annually. **Effective Market(s):** North Europe. **Units of Measure:** cents per lb. **Time Period Covered:** latest 5 years.

Source: *Monthly Commodity Price Bulletin Supplement.* **Price Frequency:** monthly, quarterly, annually. **Effective Market(s):** North Europe. **Units of Measure:** cents per lb. **Time Period Covered:** latest 20 years.

COTTON: MEDIUM STAPLE, MIDDLING 1-3/32″, MEMPHIS TERRITORY

Source: *Monthly Commodity Price Bulletin.* **Price Frequency:** monthly, annually. **Effective Market(s):** North Europe. **Units of Measure:** cents per lb. **Time Period Covered:** latest 5 years.

Source: *Monthly Commodity Price Bulletin Supplement.* **Price Frequency:** monthly, quarterly, annually. **Effective Market(s):** North Europe. **Units of Measure:** cents per lb. **Time Period Covered:** latest 20 years.

COTTON: MEDIUM STAPLE, MIDDLING 1-3/32″, MEXICAN

Source: *Monthly Commodity Price Bulletin.* **Price Frequency:** monthly, annually. **Effective Market(s):** North Europe. **Units of Measure:** cents per lb. **Time Period Covered:** latest 5 years.

Source: *Monthly Commodity Price Bulletin Supplement.* **Price Frequency:** monthly, quarterly, annually. **Effective Market(s):** North Europe. **Units of Measure:** cents per lb. **Time Period Covered:** latest 20 years.

COTTON: MENOUFI, FULLY GOOD, EGYPTIAN

Source: *Commodity Trade and Price Trends.* **Price Frequency:** annually. **Effective Market(s):** Liverpool. **Units of Measure:** cents per kilogram, 1980 constant cents per kilogram. **Time Period Covered:** latest 37 years.

COTTON: MEXICAN

Source: *International Financial Statistics Yearbook.* **Price Frequency:** annually. **Effective Market(s):** Mexico. **Units of Measure:** cents per lb. **Type of Price:** wholesale . **Time Period Covered:** latest 30 years.

COTTON: MIDDLING

Source: *California Farmer.* **Price Frequency:** semimonthly. **Effective Market(s):** Fresno (CA). **Units of Measure:** cents per lb. **Time Period Covered:** latest week, month ago, year ago.

COTTON: MIDDLING 1″

Source: *Commodity Trade and Price Trends.* **Price Frequency:** annually. **Effective Market(s):** Northern Europe. **Units of Measure:** cents per kilogram, 1980 constant cents per kilogram. **Time Period Covered:** latest 37 years.

COTTON: MIDDLING 1″, NEW ORLEANS/TEXAS

Source: *UNCTAD Commodity Yearbook.* **Price Frequency:** annually. **Effective Market(s):** North Europe. **Units of Measure:** Dollars per metric ton. **Type of Price:** free market. **Time Period Covered:** latest 12 years.

COTTON: MIDDLING 1-1/32″ TO 1-1/16″, RAW, UNITED STATES

Source: *Prices of Selected Asia/Pacific Products.* **Price Frequency:** monthly. **Effective Market(s):** Hong Kong. **Units of Measure:** Dollars per lb. **Type of Price:** high, low. **Time Period Covered:** latest month.

COTTON: MIDDLING 1-1/16″, NEW ORLEANS/TEXAS

Source: *Cotton: World Statistics.* **Price Frequency:** monthly, annually. **Effective Market(s):** North Europe. **Units of Measure:** cents per lb. **Type of Price:** average. **Time Period Covered:** monthly latest 2 years, annually latest 22 years.

COTTON: MIDDLING 1-3/32″

Source: *Agricultural Outlook.* **Price Frequency:** monthly, annually. **Effective Market(s):** United States. **Units of Measure:** cents per lb. **Type of Price:** average. **Time Period Covered:** monthly latest 5 months, annually latest 4 years.

COTTON: MIDDLING 1-3/32″, CALIFORNIA/ARIZONA

Source: *Cotton and Wool Situation and Outlook Report.* **Price Frequency:** monthly, annually. **Effective Market(s):** Northern Europe. **Units of Measure:** cents per lb. **Time Period Covered:** latest 6 years.

COTTON: MIDDLING 1-3/32″, CENTRAL AMERICAN

Source: *Cotton: World Statistics.* **Price Frequency:** monthly, annually. **Effective Market(s):** North Europe. **Units of Measure:** cents per lb. **Type of Price:** average. **Time Period Covered:** monthly latest 2 years, annually latest 22 years.

COTTON: MIDDLING 1-3/32″, MEMPHIS TERRITORY

Source: *Cotton and Wool Situation and Outlook Report.* **Price Frequency:** monthly, annually. **Effective Market(s):** Northern Europe. **Units of Measure:** cents per lb. **Time Period Covered:** latest 6 years.

Source: *Cotton: World Statistics.* **Price Frequency:** monthly, annually. **Effective Market(s):** North Europe. **Units of Measure:** cents per lb. **Type of Price:** average. **Time Period Covered:** monthly latest 2 years, annually latest 22 years.

COTTON: MIDDLING 1-3/32″, MEXICAN

Source: *Cotton: World Statistics.* **Price Frequency:** monthly, annually. **Effective Market(s):** North Europe. **Units of Measure:** cents per lb. **Type of Price:** average. **Time Period Covered:** monthly latest 2 years, annually latest 22 years.

Source: *UNCTAD Commodity Yearbook.* **Price Frequency:** annually. **Effective Market(s):** North Europe. **Units of Measure:** Dollars per metric ton. **Type of Price:** free market. **Time Period Covered:** latest 12 years.

COTTON: MIDDLING 1-3/32″, PARAGUAY

Source: *Cotton: World Statistics.* **Price Frequency:** monthly, annually. **Effective Market(s):** North Europe. **Units of Measure:** cents per lb. **Type of Price:** average. **Time Period Covered:** monthly latest 2 years, annually latest 4 years.

COTTON: MIDDLING 1-3/32″, U.S.S.R

Source: *Cotton: World Statistics.* **Price Frequency:** monthly, annually. **Effective Market(s):** North Europe. **Units of Measure:** cents per lb. **Type of Price:** average. **Time Period Covered:** monthly latest 2 years, annually latest 22 years.

COTTON: MIDDLING, AFRICAN FRANC ZONE

Source: *Cotton: World Statistics.* **Price Frequency:** monthly, annually. **Effective Market(s):** North Europe. **Units of Measure:** cents per lb. **Type of Price:** average. **Time Period Covered:** monthly latest 2 years, annually latest 4 years.

COTTON: MIDDLING, AUSTRALIAN

Source: *Cotton: World Statistics.* **Price Frequency:** monthly, annually. **Effective Market(s):** North Europe. **Units of Measure:** cents per lb. **Type of Price:** average. **Time Period Covered:** monthly latest 2 years, annually latest 5 years.

COTTON: MNH-93 SAWGIN

Source: *Asian Wall Street Journal.* **Price Frequency:** daily. **Effective Market(s):** Karachi. **Units of Measure:** Pakistani rupees per maund. **Type of Price:** closing. **Time Period Covered:** latest 2 days.

COTTON: MWANZA NO. 3, TANZANIAN

Source: *Cotton: World Statistics.* **Price Frequency:** monthly, annually. **Effective Market(s):** North Europe. **Units of Measure:** cents per lb. **Type of Price:** average. **Time Period Covered:** monthly latest 2 years, annually latest 16 years.

COTTON: NIAB-78 SAWGIN

Source: *Asian Wall Street Journal.* **Price Frequency:** daily. **Effective Market(s):** Karachi. **Units of Measure:** Pakistani rupees per maund. **Type of Price:** closing. **Time Period Covered:** latest 2 days.

COTTON: PIMA, GRADE 1, 1-9/16″, PERUVIAN

Source: *Cotton: World Statistics.* **Price Frequency:** monthly, annually. **Effective Market(s):** North Europe. **Units of Measure:** cents per lb. **Type of Price:** average. **Time Period Covered:** monthly latest 2 years, annually latest 22 years.

COTTON: PUNJAB 1505, PAKISTAN

Source: *Cotton: World Statistics.* **Price Frequency:** monthly, annually. **Effective Market(s):** North Europe. **Units of Measure:** cents per lb. **Type of Price:** average. **Time Period Covered:** monthly latest 2 years, annually latest 2 years.

COTTON: S.J.V. 1-1/8″, RAW, UNITED STATES

Source: *Prices of Selected Asia/Pacific Products.* **Price Frequency:** monthly. **Effective Market(s):** Hong Kong. **Units of Measure:** Dollars per lb. **Type of Price:** high, low. **Time Period Covered:** latest month.

COTTON: SHAMBAT B, SUDANESE

Source: *Cotton: World Statistics.* **Price Frequency:** monthly, annually. **Effective Market(s):** North Europe. **Units of Measure:** cents per lb. **Type of Price:** average. **Time Period Covered:** monthly latest 2 years, annually latest 22 years.

COTTON: SHORT STAPLE, MIDDLING 1″, NEW ORLEANS/TEXAS

Source: *Monthly Commodity Price Bulletin.* **Price Frequency:** monthly, annually. **Effective Market(s):** North Europe. **Units of Measure:** cents per lb. **Time Period Covered:** latest 5 years.

Source: *Monthly Commodity Price Bulletin Supplement.* **Price Frequency:** monthly, quarterly, annually. **Effective Market(s):** North Europe. **Units of Measure:** cents per lb. **Time Period Covered:** latest 20 years.

COTTON: STRICT LOW MIDDLING 15/16″

Source: *Cotton and Wool Situation and Outlook Report.* **Price Frequency:** monthly, annually. **Effective Market(s):** United States. **Units of Measure:** cents per lb. **Type of Price:** spot. **Time Period Covered:** monthly latest 2 years, annually latest 5 years.

COTTON: STRICT LOW MIDDLING 1″

Source: *Commodity Year Book.* **Price Frequency:** annually. **Effective Market(s):** United States. **Units of Measure:** cents per lb. **Time Period Covered:** latest 9 years.

Source: *Cotton and Wool Situation and Outlook Report.* **Price Frequency:** monthly, annually. **Effective Market(s):** United States. **Units of Measure:** cents per lb. **Type of Price:** spot. **Time Period Covered:** monthly latest 2 years, annually latest 5 years.

COTTON: STRICT LOW MIDDLING 1″, NEW ORLEANS/TEXAS

Source: *Cotton and Wool Situation and Outlook Report.* **Price Frequency:** monthly, annually. **Effective Market(s):** Northern Europe. **Units of Measure:** cents per lb. **Time Period Covered:** latest 6 years.

COTTON: STRICT LOW MIDDLING 1-1/32″

Source: *Commodity Year Book.* **Price Frequency:** annually. **Effective Market(s):** United States. **Units of Measure:** cents per lb. **Time Period Covered:** latest 9 years.

Source: *Cotton and Wool Situation and Outlook Report.* **Price Frequency:** monthly, annually. **Effective Market(s):** United States. **Units of Measure:** cents per lb. **Type of Price:** spot. **Time Period Covered:** monthly latest 2 years, annually latest 5 years.

COTTON: STRICT LOW MIDDLING 1-1/16″

Source: *Agricultural Outlook.* **Price Frequency:** monthly, annually. **Effective Market(s):** United States. **Units of Measure:** cents per lb. **Type of Price:** average. **Time Period Covered:** monthly latest 5 months, annually latest 4 years.

Source: *Asian Wall Street Journal.* **Price Frequency:** daily. **Effective Market(s):** Memphis. **Units of Measure:** Dollars per lb. **Type of Price:** cash. **Time Period Covered:** latest 2 days, year ago.

Source: *Business Week.* **Price Frequency:** weekly. **Units of Measure:** cents per lb. **Time Period Covered:** latest 2 weeks.

Source: *Commodity Year Book.* **Price Frequency:** monthly, annually. **Effective Market(s):** United States. **Units of Measure:** cents per lb. **Time Period Covered:** latest 9 years.

Source: *Commodity Year Book.* **Price Frequency:** annually. **Effective Market(s):** 8 domestic markets, United States. **Units of Measure:** Cents per lb. **Type of Price:** spot. **Time Period Covered:** Latest 9 years.

Source: *Cotton and Wool Situation and Outlook Report.* **Price Frequency:** monthly, annually. **Effective Market(s):** United States. **Units of Measure:** cents per lb. **Type of Price:** spot. **Time Period Covered:** monthly latest 2 years, annually latest 5 years.

Source: *Cotton and Wool Situation and Outlook Report.* **Price Frequency:** weekly. **Effective Market(s):** Northern Europe/World. **Units of Measure:** cents per lb. **Time Period Covered:** latest 7 months.

Source: *Cotton and Wool Situation and Outlook Report.* **Price Frequency:** monthly, annually. **Effective Market(s):** United States. **Units of Measure:** cents per lb. **Type of Price:** actual, raw fiber euivalent. **Time Period Covered:** monthly latest 2 years, annually latest 6 years.

Source: *Cotton and Wool Situation and Outlook Report.* **Price Frequency:** weekly. **Effective Market(s):** United States. **Units of Measure:** cents per lb. **Type of Price:** spot. **Time Period Covered:** latest 7 months.

Source: *Doane's Agricultural Report.* **Price Frequency:** weekly. **Effective Market(s):** 7 market average, adjusted world price. **Units of Measure:** cents per lb. **Time Period Covered:** latest week, week ago, year ago.

Source: *Investor's Daily.* **Price Frequency:** daily. **Units of Measure:** cents per lb. **Type of Price:** spot. **Time Period Covered:** latest 2 days.

Source: *Journal of Commerce and Commercial.* **Price Frequency:** daily. **Effective Market(s):** 8 market average. **Units of Measure:** Dollars per lb. **Type of Price:** spot supplier. **Time Period Covered:** latest day.

Source: *New York Times.* **Price Frequency:** daily. **Units of Measure:** cents per lb. **Type of Price:** cash. **Time Period Covered:** latest 2 days.

Source: *Wall Street Journal.* **Price Frequency:** daily. **Effective Market(s):** Memphis (TN). **Units of Measure:** Dollars per lb. **Time Period Covered:** latest day, day ago, year ago.

COTTON: STRICT LOW MIDDLING 1-3/32"

Source: *Commodity Year Book.* **Price Frequency:** monthly, annually. **Effective Market(s):** United States. **Units of Measure:** cents per lb. **Type of Price:** spot. **Time Period Covered:** latest 9 years.

Source: *Cotton and Wool Situation and Outlook Report.* **Price Frequency:** monthly, annually. **Effective Market(s):** United States. **Units of Measure:** cents per lb. **Type of Price:** spot. **Time Period Covered:** monthly latest 2 years, annually latest 5 years.

COTTON: STRICT LOW MIDDLING 1-1/16", FUTURES

Source: *Cotton and Wool Situation and Outlook Report.* **Price Frequency:** weekly. **Effective Market(s):** United States. **Units of Measure:** cents per lb. **Type of Price:** futures. **Time Period Covered:** latest 7 months.

COTTON: STRICT LOW MIDDLING 1-1/16", RAW

Source: *Prices of Selected Asia/Pacific Products.* **Price Frequency:** monthly. **Effective Market(s):** New York. **Units of Measure:** Dollars per lb. **Type of Price:** spot high, spot low. **Time Period Covered:** latest month.

COTTON: STRICT LOW MIDDLING 1-1/8"

Source: *Cotton and Wool Situation and Outlook Report.* **Price Frequency:** monthly, annually. **Effective Market(s):** United States. **Units of Measure:** cents per lb. **Type of Price:** spot. **Time Period Covered:** monthly latest 2 years, annually latest 5 years.

COTTON: STRICT MIDDLING 1-1/8", CALIFORNIA/ACALA

Source: *Cotton: World Statistics.* **Price Frequency:** monthly, annually. **Effective Market(s):** North Europe. **Units of Measure:** cents per lb. **Type of Price:** average. **Time Period Covered:** monthly latest 2 years, annually latest 21 years.

COTTON: STRICT MIDDLING 1-1/16", MEMPHIS TERRITORY

Source: *FAO Quarterly Bulletin of Statistics.* **Price Frequency:** monthly, annually. **Effective Market(s):** Liverpool. **Units of Measure:** Dollars per 100 lbs., dollars per metric ton. **Time Period Covered:** latest 3 years.

COTTON: SUDANESE

Source: *International Financial Statistics.* **Price Frequency:** quarterly, annually. **Effective Market(s):** Sudan. **Units of Measure:** cents per lb., index. **Type of Price:** market price, price index. **Time Period Covered:** latest 2 quarters, latest 3 years.

Source: *International Financial Statistics Yearbook.* **Price Frequency:** annually. **Effective Market(s):** Sudan. **Units of Measure:** cents per lb. **Type of Price:** wholesale. **Time Period Covered:** latest 30 years.

COTTON: TANGUIS GRADE 3, PERUVIAN

Source: *Cotton: World Statistics.* **Price Frequency:** monthly, annually. **Effective Market(s):** North Europe. **Units of Measure:** cents per lb. **Type of Price:** average. **Time Period Covered:** monthly latest 2 years, annually latest 22 years.

COTTON: TRETII, RUSSIAN

Source: *Cotton: World Statistics.* **Price Frequency:** monthly, annually. **Effective Market(s):** North Europe. **Units of Measure:** cents per lb. **Type of Price:** average. **Time Period Covered:** monthly latest 2 years, annually latest 3 years.

COTTON: TYPE 5/6, 1-1/16", BRAZILIAN

Source: *Cotton: World Statistics.* **Price Frequency:** monthly, annually. **Effective Market(s):** North Europe. **Units of Measure:** cents per lb. **Type of Price:** average. **Time Period Covered:** monthly latest 2 years, annually latest 3 years.

COTTON: UNITED STATES

Source: *International Financial Statistics.* **Price Frequency:** monthly, quarterly, annually. **Effective Market(s):** 10 market average. **Units of Measure:** cents per lb., index. **Type of Price:** market price, price index. **Time Period Covered:** latest 4 months, latest 5 quarters, latest 5 years.

Source: *International Financial Statistics Yearbook.* **Price Frequency:** annually. **Effective Market(s):** 10 market average. **Units of Measure:** cents per lb. **Type of Price:** wholesale. **Time Period Covered:** latest 30 years.

COTTON: UPLAND

Source: *Agricultural Outlook.* **Price Frequency:** monthly, annually. **Effective Market(s):** United States. **Units of Measure:** cents per lb. **Type of Price:** price received by farmer. **Time Period Covered:** monthly latest 6 months, annually latest 3 years.

Source: *Agricultural Prices.* **Price Frequency:** annually. **Effective Market(s):** 17 domestic markets, United States. **Units of Measure:** Dollars per lb. **Type of Price:** received by farmer. **Time Period Covered:** latest 2 years.

Source: *Agricultural Prices.* **Price Frequency:** monthly, seasonally. **Effective Market(s):** 10 domestic markets, United States. **Units of Measure:** Dollars per lb. **Type of Price:** received by farmer. **Time Period Covered:** latest 2 years.

Source: *Agricultural Prices Annual Summary.* **Price Frequency:** annually. **Effective Market(s):** 17 domestic markets, United States. **Units of Measure:** Dollars per lb. **Type of Price:** average price received by farmer. **Time Period Covered:** latest 2 years, for US latest 6 years.

Source: *Commodity Year Book.* **Price Frequency:** monthly, annually. **Effective Market(s):** United States. **Units of Measure:** cents per lb. **Type of Price:** price received by farmers. **Time Period Covered:** latest 9 years.

Source: *Cotton and Wool Situation and Outlook Report.* **Price Frequency:** monthly, annually. **Effective Market(s):** United States. **Units of Measure:** cents per lb. **Type of Price:** received by farmer. **Time Period Covered:** monthly latest 2 years, annually latest 5 years.

Source: *Cotton Price Statistics.* **Price Frequency:** monthly, annually. **Effective Market(s):** United States. **Units of Measure:** cents per lb. **Type of Price:** price received by farmers. **Time Period Covered:** latest 5 years.

Source: *Cotton Price Statistics Annual.* **Price Frequency:** monthly, annually. **Effective Market(s):** United States. **Units of Measure:** cents per lb. **Type of Price:** prices received by farmers. **Time Period Covered:** latest 6 years.

COTTON: UPLAND, EXTRA LONG STAPLE

Source: *Agricultural Outlook.* **Price Frequency:** annually. **Effective Market(s):** United States. **Units of Measure:** cents per lb. **Type of Price:** farm. **Time Period Covered:** latest 6 years.

COTTON EXPELLERS

Source: *Farmers Weekly.* **Price Frequency:** weekly. **Effective Market(s):** Great Britain. **Units of Measure:** British pounds per tonne. **Type of Price:** spot. **Time Period Covered:** latest week.

COTTON EXPELLERS: 43%, CHINESE

Source: *Oil World.* **Price Frequency:** weekly, monthly, annually. **Effective Market(s):** Denmark/United Kingdom. **Units of Measure:** Dollars per tonne. **Type of Price:** lowest representative asking. **Time Period Covered:** weekly latest 3 weeks, monthly latest 2 months, annually latest 2 years.

COTTON LINTERS FIRST CUT

Source: *Monthly Cotton Linters Review.* **Price Frequency:** monthly. **Effective Market(s):** South Central, Southeast, Southwest, West. **Units of Measure:** cents per lb. **Type of Price:** price received by oil mills. **Time Period Covered:** latest 2 months.

COTTON LINTERS SECOND CUT: 73% CELLULOSE BASIS

Source: *Monthly Cotton Linters Review.* **Price Frequency:** monthly. **Effective Market(s):** South Central, Southeast, Southwest, West. **Units of Measure:** cents per lb. **Type of Price:** price received by oil mills. **Time Period Covered:** latest 2 months.

COTTON PICKER

Source: *Agricultural Prices.* **Price Frequency:** annually. **Effective Market(s):** United States. **Units of Measure:** Dollars each. **Type of Price:** paid by farmer. **Time Period Covered:** latest year.

Source: *Agricultural Prices Annual Summary.* **Price Frequency:** annually. **Effective Market(s):** United States. **Units of Measure:** Dollars each. **Type of Price:** average price paid by farmer. **Time Period Covered:** latest 6 years.

COTTON YARN

see Yarn: Cotton.

COTTONSEED

Source: *Agricultural Prices.* **Price Frequency:** monthly. **Effective Market(s):** United States. **Units of Measure:** Dollars per ton. **Type of Price:** received by farmer. **Time Period Covered:** latest 2 months, year ago.

Source: *Agricultural Prices.* **Price Frequency:** monthly. **Effective Market(s):** 10 domestic markets, United States. **Units of Measure:** Dollars per lb. **Type of Price:** received by farmer. **Time Period Covered:** latest month.

Source: *Agricultural Prices Annual Summary.* **Price Frequency:** annually. **Effective Market(s):** 17 domestic markets, United States. **Units of Measure:** Dollars per ton. **Type of Price:** average price received by farmer. **Time Period Covered:** latest 2 years, for US latest 6 years.

Source: *Commodity Year Book.* **Price Frequency:** annually. **Effective Market(s):** United States. **Units of Measure:** Dollars per ton. **Type of Price:** farm price. **Time Period Covered:** latest 8 years.

Source: *Cottonseed Review.* **Price Frequency:** weekly during season. **Effective Market(s):** markets vary. **Units of Measure:** Dollars per ton. **Type of Price:** price paid to grower. **Time Period Covered:** latest week.

Source: *Feedstuffs.* **Price Frequency:** weekly. **Effective Market(s):** Ft. Worth, Los Angeles, Memphis, San Francisco. **Units of Measure:** Dollars per bulk ton. **Time Period Covered:** latest week.

Source: *Los Angeles Times.* **Price Frequency:** daily. **Effective Market(s):** Los Angeles. **Units of Measure:** Dollars per ton. **Type of Price:** cash. **Time Period Covered:** latest day.

Source: *Oil Crops Situation and Outlook.* **Price Frequency:** monthly, annually. **Effective Market(s):** United States. **Units of Measure:** Dollars per ton. **Type of Price:** average received by farmer. **Time Period Covered:** monthly latest year, annually latest 10 years.

Source: *Oil Crops Situation and Outlook.* **Price Frequency:** monthly. **Effective Market(s):** United States. **Units of Measure:** Dollars per ton. **Type of Price:** received by farmer. **Time Period Covered:** latest 5 months.

COTTONSEED FOR PLANTING

Source: *Agricultural Prices Annual Summary.* **Price Frequency:** annually. **Effective Market(s):** United States. **Units of Measure:** Dollars per 100 lbs. **Type of Price:** average price paid by farmer. **Time Period Covered:** latest 6 years.

COTTONSEED HULLS

Source: *Los Angeles Times.* **Price Frequency:** daily. **Effective Market(s):** Los Angeles. **Units of Measure:** Dollars per ton. **Type of Price:** cash. **Time Period Covered:** latest day.

COTTONSEED MEAL

Source: *Asian Wall Street Journal.* **Price Frequency:** daily. **Effective Market(s):** Clarksdale (MS). **Units of Measure:** Dollars per ton. **Type of Price:** cash. **Time Period Covered:** latest 2 days, year ago.

Source: *California Farmer.* **Price Frequency:** semimonthly. **Effective Market(s):** San Joaquin Valley. **Units of Measure:** Dollars per ton. **Time Period Covered:** latest week, month ago, year ago.

Source: *Commodity Year Book.* **Price Frequency:** monthly, annually. **Effective Market(s):** Memphis (TN). **Units of Measure:** Dollars per short ton. **Type of Price:** wholesale. **Time Period Covered:** latest 5 years.

Source: *Feedstuffs.* **Price Frequency:** weekly. **Effective Market(s):** Memphis (TN). **Units of Measure:** Dollars per ton. **Time Period Covered:** latest week, week ago, 6 months ago, year ago.

Source: *Feedstuffs.* **Price Frequency:** weekly. **Effective Market(s):** 8 domestic markets. **Units of Measure:** Dollars per ton. **Time Period Covered:** latest week.

Source: *Oil Crops Situation and Outlook.* **Price Frequency:** monthly, annually. **Effective Market(s):** Memphis (TN). **Units of Measure:** Dollars per ton. **Type of Price:** average received by farmer. **Time Period Covered:** monthly latest year, annually latest 10 years.

Source: *Wall Street Journal.* **Price Frequency:** daily. **Effective Market(s):** Clarksdale (MS). **Units of Measure:** Dollars per ton. **Time Period Covered:** latest day, day ago, year ago.

COTTONSEED MEAL: 41% PROTEIN

Source: *Agricultural Prices.* **Price Frequency:** quarterly. **Effective Market(s):** United States. **Units of Measure:** Dollars per 100 lbs. **Type of Price:** paid by farmer. **Time Period Covered:** latest 2 quarters, year ago.

Source: *Agricultural Prices.* **Price Frequency:** monthly. **Effective Market(s):** 10 domestic markets, United States. **Units of Measure:** Dollars per 100 lbs. **Type of Price:** paid by farmer. **Time Period Covered:** latest month.

Source: *Agricultural Prices Annual Summary.* **Price Frequency:** quarterly. **Effective Market(s):** 10 domestic markets, United States. **Units of Measure:** Dollars per 100 lbs. **Type of Price:** average price paid by farmer. **Time Period Covered:** latest year, for US latest 6 years.

Source: *Chemical Marketing Reporter.* **Price Frequency:** weekly. **Effective Market(s):** Memphis (TN). **Units of Measure:** Dollars per ton. **Type of Price:** spot. **Time Period Covered:** latest week.

Source: *Feed Situation and Outlook Report.* **Price Frequency:** quarterly. **Effective Market(s):** United States. **Units of Measure:** Dollars per 100 lbs. **Type of Price:** paid by farmer. **Time Period Covered:** latest 3 quarters.

Source: *Feed Situation and Outlook Report.* **Price Frequency:** monthly. **Effective Market(s):** Memphis (TN). **Units of Measure:** Dollars per ton. **Type of Price:** wholesale. **Time Period Covered:** latest 8 months.

Source: *Grain and Feed Market News.* **Price Frequency:** weekly, seasonally. **Effective Market(s):** California Hills, Kansas City, Memphis (TN), Portland (OR). **Units of Measure:** Dollars per ton. **Type of Price:** wholesale. **Time Period Covered:** latest week, week ago, year ago.

Source: *Los Angeles Times.* **Price Frequency:** daily. **Effective Market(s):** Los Angeles. **Units of Measure:** Dollars per ton. **Type of Price:** cash. **Time Period Covered:** latest day.

Source: *Milling & Baking News.* **Price Frequency:** weekly. **Effective Market(s):** Memphis (TN). **Units of Measure:** Dollars per ton. **Time Period Covered:** latest week.

Source: *Oil Crops Situation and Outlook.* **Price Frequency:** monthly. **Effective Market(s):** Memphis (TN). **Units of Measure:** Dollars per ton. **Time Period Covered:** latest 5 months.

Source: *World Oilseed Situation and Market Highlights.* **Price Frequency:** monthly, annually. **Effective Market(s):** Memphis (TN). **Units of Measure:** Dollars per metric ton. **Time Period Covered:** latest 9 years.

COTTONSEED MEAL PELLETS: 38% PROTEIN

Source: *World Oilseed Situation and Market Highlights.* **Price Frequency:** monthly, annually. **Effective Market(s):** Denmark. **Units of Measure:** Dollars per metric ton. **Time Period Covered:** latest 9 years.

COTTONSEED OIL

Source: *Bakery Newsletter.* **Price Frequency:** weekly. **Effective Market(s):** Mississippi Valley. **Type of Price:** cash. **Time Period Covered:** last week.

Source: *Journal of Commerce and Commercial.* **Price Frequency:** daily. **Effective Market(s):** Mississippi Valley. **Units of Measure:** Dollars per lb. **Type of Price:** spot supplier. **Time Period Covered:** latest day.

Source: *Milling & Baking News.* **Price Frequency:** weekly. **Effective Market(s):** Mississippi Valley. **Units of Measure:** cents per lb. **Type of Price:** spot bulk. **Time Period Covered:** latest week.

Source: *Oil Crops Situation and Outlook.* **Price Frequency:** monthly, annually. **Effective Market(s):** United States. **Units of Measure:** cent sper lb. **Type of Price:** average received by farmer. **Time Period Covered:** monthly latest year, annually latest 10 years.

COTTONSEED OIL: ACIDULATED (SOAPSTOCK)

Source: *Chemical Marketing Reporter.* **Price Frequency:** weekly. **Effective Market(s):** New York. **Units of Measure:** Dollars per lb. **Type of Price:** spot. **Time Period Covered:** latest week.

COTTONSEED OIL: CRUDE

Source: *Asian Wall Street Journal.* **Price Frequency:** daily. **Effective Market(s):** Mississippi Valley. **Units of Measure:** Dollars per lb. **Type of Price:** cash. **Time Period Covered:** latest 2 days, year ago.

Source: *Chemical Marketing Reporter.* **Price Frequency:** weekly. **Effective Market(s):** Mississippi Valley. **Units of Measure:** cents per lb. **Type of Price:** spot. **Time Period Covered:** latest week.

Source: *Commodity Year Book.* **Price Frequency:** monthly, annually. **Effective Market(s):** Southeastern Mills. **Units of Measure:** cents per lb. **Time Period Covered:** latest 7 years.

Source: *Investor's Daily.* **Price Frequency:** daily. **Effective Market(s):** Mississippi Valley. **Units of Measure:** Dollars per lb. **Type of Price:** spot. **Time Period Covered:** latest 2 days.

Source: *National Provisioner.* **Price Frequency:** daily. **Effective Market(s):** Midwest River Valley. **Units of Measure:** cents per lb. **Time Period Covered:** selected day.

Source: *New York Times.* **Price Frequency:** daily. **Effective Market(s):** Mississippi Valley. **Units of Measure:** Dollars per lb. **Type of Price:** cash. **Time Period Covered:** latest 2 days.

Source: *Oil Crops Situation and Outlook.* **Price Frequency:** monthly. **Effective Market(s):** United States. **Units of Measure:** cents per lb. **Type of Price:** wholesale. **Time Period Covered:** latest 5 months.

Source: *Wall Street Journal.* **Price Frequency:** daily. **Effective Market(s):** Mississippi Valley. **Units of Measure:** Dollars per lb. **Time Period Covered:** latest day, day ago, year ago.

Source: *World Oilseed Situation and Market Highlights.* **Price Frequency:** monthly, annually. **Effective Market(s):** Rotterdam, United States. **Units of Measure:** Dollars per metric ton. **Time Period Covered:** monthly latest year, annually latest 9 years.

COTTONSEED OIL: REFINED

Source: *Chemical Marketing Reporter.* **Price Frequency:** weekly. **Effective Market(s):** New York. **Units of Measure:** Dollars per lb. **Type of Price:** spot. **Time Period Covered:** latest week.

COTTONSEED OIL: UNITED STATES

Source: *Oil World.* **Price Frequency:** weekly, monthly, annually. **Effective Market(s):** Rotterdam. **Units of Measure:** Dollars per tonne. **Type of Price:** lowest representative asking. **Time Period Covered:** weekly latest 3 weeks, monthly latest 2 months, annually latest 2 years.

COTTONSEED OIL ACIDS: DISTILLED

Source: *Chemical Marketing Reporter.* **Price Frequency:** weekly. **Effective Market(s):** New York. **Units of Measure:** Dollars per lb. **Type of Price:** spot. **Time Period Covered:** latest week.

COUMARIN

Source: *Journal of Commerce and Commercial.* **Price Frequency:** weekly in Tuesday issue. **Units of Measure:** Dollars per lb. **Type of Price:** spot. **Time Period Covered:** latest week.

COUMARIN: CRYSTALLINE, NF

Source: *Chemical Marketing Reporter.* **Price Frequency:** weekly. **Effective Market(s):** New York. **Units of Measure:** Dollars per lb. **Type of Price:** spot. **Time Period Covered:** latest week.

COURGETTES

see also Zucchini.

Source: *New Zealand Farmer.* **Price Frequency:** weekly, seasonally. **Effective Market(s):** New Zealand. **Units of Measure:** New Zealand dollars per case. **Time Period Covered:** latest week.

COW-CALF PAIRS

Source: *Drovers Journal.* **Price Frequency:** semimonthly. **Effective Market(s):** 8 domestic markets. **Units of Measure:** Dollars per pair. **Time Period Covered:** selected day.

COWS

Source: *Farm and Dairy.* **Price Frequency:** weekly, seasonally. **Effective Market(s):** Ohio, Pennsylvania. **Units of Measure:** Dollars per head. **Type of Price:** auction high, auction low. **Time Period Covered:** latest week, year ago.

Source: *Scottish Farmer.* **Price Frequency:** weekly. **Effective Market(s):** Scotland. **Units of Measure:** British pence per kilogram. **Type of Price:** average. **Time Period Covered:** latest week.

COWS: AGED

Source: *Drovers Journal.* **Price Frequency:** semimonthly. **Effective Market(s):** 8 domestic markets. **Units of Measure:** Dollars per 100 lbs., dollars per head. **Time Period Covered:** selected day.

COWS: BEEF

Source: *Agricultural Prices.* **Price Frequency:** monthly. **Effective Market(s):** United States. **Units of Measure:** Dollars per 100 lbs. **Type of Price:** received by farmer. **Time Period Covered:** latest 2 month, year ago.

Source: *Agricultural Prices Annual Summary.* **Price Frequency:** annually. **Effective Market(s):** 50 domestic markets, United States. **Units of Measure:** Dollars per 100 lbs. **Type of Price:** average price received by farmer. **Time Period Covered:** latest 2 years, for US latest 6 years.

Source: *Agricultural Prices Annual Summary.* **Price Frequency:** monthly. **Effective Market(s):** 35 domestic markets, United States. **Units of Measure:** Dollars per 100 lbs. **Type of Price:** average price received by farmer. **Time Period Covered:** latest year, for US latest 6 years.

Source: *Farm and Dairy.* **Price Frequency:** weekly, seasonally. **Effective Market(s):** Ohio, Pennsylvania. **Units of Measure:** Dollars per head. **Type of Price:** auction high, auction low. **Time Period Covered:** latest week, year ago.

COWS: BEEF, CANNER AND CUTTER

Source: *Agricultural Outlook.* **Price Frequency:** monthly, annually. **Effective Market(s):** Chicago. **Units of Measure:** Dollars per 100 lbs. **Type of Price:** wholesale. **Time Period Covered:** monthly latest 6 months, annually latest 3 years.

Source: *Livestock and Poultry Situation and Outlook Report.* **Price Frequency:** monthly. **Effective Market(s):** Central United States. **Units of Measure:** Dollars per 100 lbs. **Type of Price:** wholesale. **Time Period Covered:** latest year.

Source: *Livestock and Poultry Update.* **Price Frequency:** monthly. **Effective Market(s):** Central United States. **Units of Measure:** Dollars per 100 lbs. **Type of Price:** wholesale. **Time Period Covered:** latest 3 months, year ago.

Source: *Meat and Dairy Products.* **Price Frequency:** monthly. **Effective Market(s):** Central United States. **Units of Measure:** Dollars per 100 lbs. **Type of Price:** wholesale. **Time Period Covered:** latest 4 years.

COWS: BONING AND BREAKING UTILITY

Source: *Dairy Situation and Outlook Report.* **Price Frequency:** monthly, annually. **Effective Market(s):** Omaha (NE). **Units of Measure:** Dollars per 100 lbs. **Time Period Covered:** latest 3 years.

COWS: BONING UTILITY

Source: *Livestock and Poultry Situation and Outlook Report.* **Price Frequency:** monthly. **Effective Market(s):** Omaha (NE). **Units of Measure:** Dollars per 100 lbs. **Time Period Covered:** latest year.

Source: *Livestock and Poultry Update.* **Price Frequency:** monthly. **Effective Market(s):** Omaha (NE). **Units of Measure:** Dollars per 100 lbs. **Time Period Covered:** latest 3 months, year ago.

Source: *National Provisioner.* **Price Frequency:** daily. **Effective Market(s):** Midwest River. **Units of Measure:** cents per lb. **Time Period Covered:** latest week.

COWS: BONING UTILITY AND CUTTER

Source: *Lancaster Farming.* **Price Frequency:** weekly. **Effective Market(s):** Pennsylvania, Virginia. **Units of Measure:** Dollars per head. **Type of Price:** auction. **Time Period Covered:** latest week.

COWS: BREAKING UTILITY

Source: *Livestock and Poultry Situation and Outlook Report.* **Price Frequency:** monthly. **Effective Market(s):** Omaha (NE). **Units of Measure:** Dollars per 100 lbs. **Time Period Covered:** latest year.

COWS: BREAKING UTILITY AND COMMERCIAL

Source: *Lancaster Farming.* **Price Frequency:** weekly. **Effective Market(s):** Pennsylvania, Virginia. **Units of Measure:** Dollars per head. **Type of Price:** auction. **Time Period Covered:** latest week.

COWS: BRED

Source: *Montana Farmer-Stockman.* **Price Frequency:** monthly, seasonally. **Effective Market(s):** Riverton (WY). **Units of Measure:** Dollars per head. **Type of Price:** cash auction. **Time Period Covered:** latest month.

COWS: CANNER

Source: *Livestock and Poultry Situation and Outlook Report.* **Price Frequency:** monthly. **Effective Market(s):** Omaha (NE). **Units of Measure:** Dollars per 100 lbs. **Time Period Covered:** latest year.

COWS: CANNER AND CUTTER

Source: *Commodity Year Book.* **Price Frequency:** annually. **Units of Measure:** Dollars per 100 lbs. **Type of Price:** wholesale. **Time Period Covered:** latest 4 years.

Source: *Drovers Journal.* **Price Frequency:** semimonthly. **Effective Market(s):** 8 domestic markets. **Units of Measure:** Dollars per 100 lbs. **Time Period Covered:** selected day.

Source: *Farm and Dairy.* **Price Frequency:** weekly, seasonally. **Effective Market(s):** Ohio, Pennsylvania. **Units of Measure:** Dollars per head. **Type of Price:** auction high, auction low. **Time Period Covered:** latest week, year ago.

COWS: CANNER AND LOW CUTTER

Source: *Lancaster Farming.* **Price Frequency:** weekly. **Effective Market(s):** Pennsylvania, Virginia. **Units of Measure:** Dollars per head. **Type of Price:** auction. **Time Period Covered:** latest week.

COWS: CAST

Source: *Scottish Farmer.* **Price Frequency:** weekly. **Effective Market(s):** 19 Scottish markets. **Units of Measure:** British pence per kilogram. **Type of Price:** liveweight. **Time Period Covered:** latest week.

COWS: COMMERCIAL

Source: *Commodity Year Book.* **Price Frequency:** annually. **Effective Market(s):** Omaha (NE). **Units of Measure:** Dollars per 100 lbs. **Type of Price:** wholesale. **Time Period Covered:** latest 5 years.

Source: *Livestock and Poultry Situation and Outlook Report.* **Price Frequency:** monthly. **Effective Market(s):** Omaha (NE). **Units of Measure:** Dollars per 100 lbs. **Time Period Covered:** latest year.

Source: *Livestock and Poultry Update.* **Price Frequency:** monthly. **Effective Market(s):** Omaha (NE). **Units of Measure:** Dollars per 100 lbs. **Time Period Covered:** latest 3 months, year ago.

COWS: CULL

Source: *Dairy Market Statistics.* **Price Frequency:** monthly, annually. **Effective Market(s):** 11 domestic markets. **Units of Measure:** Dollars per 100 lbs. **Time Period Covered:** latest year.

Source: *Farmers Weekly.* **Price Frequency:** weekly. **Effective Market(s):** 30 British markets. **Units of Measure:** British pence per kilogram. **Type of Price:** average. **Time Period Covered:** latest week.

Source: *Farmers Weekly.* **Price Frequency:** weekly. **Effective Market(s):** 7 British markets. **Units of Measure:** British pounds per head. **Time Period Covered:** latest week.

COWS: CULL, GRADE 1

Source: *Farmers Weekly.* **Price Frequency:** weekly. **Effective Market(s):** 30 British markets. **Units of Measure:** British pence per kilogram. **Time Period Covered:** latest week.

COWS: CULL, GRADE 2

Source: *Farmers Weekly.* **Price Frequency:** weekly. **Effective Market(s):** 30 British markets. **Units of Measure:** British pence per kilogram. **Time Period Covered:** latest week.

COWS: CULL, GRADE 3

Source: *Farmers Weekly.* **Price Frequency:** weekly. **Effective Market(s):** 30 British markets. **Units of Measure:** British pence per kilogram. **Time Period Covered:** latest week.

COWS: CULL, GRADE 4

Source: *Farmers Weekly.* **Price Frequency:** weekly. **Effective Market(s):** 30 British markets. **Units of Measure:** British pence per kilogram. **Time Period Covered:** latest week.

COWS: CUTTER

Source: *Livestock and Poultry Situation and Outlook Report.* **Price Frequency:** monthly. **Effective Market(s):** Omaha (NE). **Units of Measure:** Dollars per 100 lbs. **Time Period Covered:** latest year.

COWS: DAIRY

Source: *Scottish Farmer.* **Price Frequency:** weekly. **Effective Market(s):** Ayr (Scotland), Carlisle (Scotland), Lanark (Scotland), Paisley (Scotland), Stirling (Scotland). **Units of Measure:** British pounds per head. **Type of Price:** top, average. **Time Period Covered:** latest week.

COWS: DAIRY, FIRST CALVERS, FIRST QUALITY

Source: *Farmers Weekly.* **Price Frequency:** weekly. **Effective Market(s):** 16 British markets. **Units of Measure:** British pounds per head. **Type of Price:** average. **Time Period Covered:** latest week.

COWS: DAIRY, FIRST CALVERS, SECOND QUALITY

Source: *Farmers Weekly.* **Price Frequency:** weekly. **Effective Market(s):** 16 British markets. **Units of Measure:** British pounds per head. **Type of Price:** average. **Time Period Covered:** latest week.

COWS: DAIRY, FIRST QUALITY

Source: *Farmers Weekly.* **Price Frequency:** weekly. **Effective Market(s):** 16 British markets. **Units of Measure:** British pounds per head. **Type of Price:** average. **Time Period Covered:** latest week.

COWS: DAIRY, SECOND QUALITY

Source: *Farmers Weekly.* **Price Frequency:** weekly. **Effective Market(s):** 16 British markets. **Units of Measure:** British pounds per head. **Type of Price:** average. **Time Period Covered:** latest week.

COWS: DAIRY, TOP

Source: *Farm and Dairy.* **Price Frequency:** weekly, seasonally. **Effective Market(s):** Ohio, Pennsylvania. **Units of Measure:** Dollars per head. **Type of Price:** auction high, auction low. **Time Period Covered:** latest week, year ago.

COWS: FAT

Source: *Farm and Dairy.* **Price Frequency:** weekly, seasonally. **Effective Market(s):** Ohio, Pennsylvania. **Units of Measure:** Dollars per head. **Type of Price:** auction high, auction low. **Time Period Covered:** latest week, year ago.

COWS: FEEDER

Source: *Montana Farmer-Stockman.* **Price Frequency:** monthly, seasonally. **Effective Market(s):** Riverton (WY), Torrington (WY). **Units of Measure:** Dollars per head. **Type of Price:** cash auction. **Time Period Covered:** latest month.

COWS: GOOD

Source: *Farm and Dairy.* **Price Frequency:** weekly, seasonally. **Effective Market(s):** Ohio, Pennsylvania. **Units of Measure:** Dollars per head. **Type of Price:** auction high, auction low. **Time Period Covered:** latest week, year ago.

COWS: HEAVY, PRIME

Source: *New Zealand Farmer.* **Price Frequency:** weekly, seasonally. **Effective Market(s):** 7 New Zealand markets. **Units of Measure:** New Zealand dollars per head. **Time Period Covered:** latest 2 weeks.

COWS: LIGHT, PRIME

Source: *New Zealand Farmer.* **Price Frequency:** weekly, seasonally. **Effective Market(s):** 7 New Zealand markets. **Units of Measure:** New Zealand dollars per head. **Time Period Covered:** latest 2 weeks.

COWS: M

Source: *New Zealand Farmer.* **Price Frequency:** weekly, seasonally. **Effective Market(s):** 8 New Zealand markets. **Units of Measure:** New Zealand cents per kilogram. **Type of Price:** export. **Time Period Covered:** latest week.

COWS: MEDIUM, PRIME

Source: *New Zealand Farmer.* **Price Frequency:** weekly, seasonally. **Effective Market(s):** 7 New Zealand markets. **Units of Measure:** New Zealand dollars per head. **Time Period Covered:** latest 2 weeks.

COWS: MEDIUM TO GOOD

Source: *Farm and Dairy.* **Price Frequency:** weekly, seasonally. **Effective Market(s):** Ohio, Pennsylvania. **Units of Measure:** Dollars per head. **Type of Price:** auction high, auction low. **Time Period Covered:** latest week, year ago.

COWS: MILK

Source: *Agricultural Prices.* **Price Frequency:** monthly. **Effective Market(s):** United States. **Units of Measure:** Dollars per 100 lbs. **Type of Price:** received by farmer. **Time Period Covered:** latest 2 months, year ago.

Source: *Agricultural Prices.* **Price Frequency:** monthly. **Effective Market(s):** 33 domestic markets, United States. **Units of Measure:** Dollars per head. **Type of Price:** received by farmer. **Time Period Covered:** latest month.

Source: *Agricultural Prices Annual Summary.* **Price Frequency:** annually. **Effective Market(s):** 50 domestic markets, United States. **Units of Measure:** Dollars per head. **Type of Price:** average price received by farmer. **Time Period Covered:** latest 2 years, for US latest 6 years.

Source: *Agricultural Prices Annual Summary.* **Price Frequency:** quarterly. **Effective Market(s):** 35 domestic markets, United States. **Units of Measure:** Dollars per 100 lbs. **Type of Price:** average price received by farmer. **Time Period Covered:** latest year, for US latest 6 years.

Source: *Dairy Market Statistics.* **Price Frequency:** quarterly, annually. **Effective Market(s):** 11 domestic markets. **Units of Measure:** Dollars per head. **Time Period Covered:** latest year.

Source: *Farmers Weekly.* **Price Frequency:** weekly. **Effective Market(s):** Great Britain. **Units of Measure:** British pounds per head. **Time Period Covered:** latest week, week ago, year ago.

Source: *Fedgazette.* **Price Frequency:** monthly. **Effective Market(s):** Omaha (NE). **Units of Measure:** Dollars per head. **Time Period Covered:** latest 24 months.

Source: *Illinois Farm Report.* **Price Frequency:** monthly. **Effective Market(s):** Illinois. **Units of Measure:** Dollars per head. **Type of Price:** average received by farmers. **Time Period Covered:** latest 2 months, year ago.

Source: *Washington Farmer-Stockman.* **Price Frequency:** monthly, seasonally. **Effective Market(s):** Washington. **Units of Measure:** Dollars per head. **Type of Price:** prices received by farmers. **Time Period Covered:** latest month, month ago, year ago.

COWS: REPLACEMENT

Source: *Oregon Farmer-Stockman.* **Price Frequency:** monthly, seasonally. **Effective Market(s):** Klamath Falls (OR). **Units of Measure:** Dollars per 100 lbs. **Type of Price:** auction. **Time Period Covered:** latest month.

COWS: SLAUGHTER

Source: *Agricultural Prices.* **Price Frequency:** monthly. **Effective Market(s):** 35 domestic markets, United States. **Units of Measure:** Dollars per 100 lbs. **Type of Price:** received by farmer. **Time Period Covered:** latest 2 months.

Source: *Oregon Farmer-Stockman.* **Price Frequency:** monthly, seasonally. **Effective Market(s):** Klamath Falls (OR). **Units of Measure:** Dollars per 100 lbs. **Type of Price:** auction. **Time Period Covered:** latest month.

COWS: SLAUGHTER, BONING UTILITY

Source: *Montana Farmer-Stockman.* **Price Frequency:** monthly, seasonally. **Effective Market(s):** Billings (MT), Riverton (WY). **Units of Measure:** Dollars per 100 lbs. **Type of Price:** cash auction. **Time Period Covered:** latest month.

COWS: SLAUGHTER, BONING UTILITY 1-2

Source: *Livestock, Meat, Wool Market News.* **Price Frequency:** weekly, seasonally. **Effective Market(s):** Lancaster County (PA), Omaha, Sioux City (IA), South St. Paul. **Units of Measure:** Dollars per 100 lbs. **Type of Price:** average. **Time Period Covered:** latest week, year ago.

COWS: SLAUGHTER, BONING UTILITY AND HIGH CUTTER 1-3

Source: *Utah Farmer-Stockman.* **Price Frequency:** monthly, seasonally. **Effective Market(s):** Salina (UT), Spanish Fork (UT). **Units of Measure:** Dollars per 100 lbs. **Type of Price:** auction. **Time Period Covered:** latest month.

COWS: SLAUGHTER, BREAKING UTILITY

Source: *California Farmer.* **Price Frequency:** semimonthly. **Effective Market(s):** Stockton (CA). **Units of Measure:** Dollars per 100 lbs. **Time Period Covered:** latest week, month ago, year ago.

COWS: SLAUGHTER, BREAKING UTILITY 1-3

Source: *Livestock, Meat, Wool Market News.* **Price Frequency:** weekly, seasonally. **Effective Market(s):** Lancaster County (PA), Omaha, Sioux City (IA), South St. Paul. **Units of Measure:** Dollars per 100 lbs. **Type of Price:** average. **Time Period Covered:** latest week, year ago.

COWS: SLAUGHTER, BREAKING UTILITY AND COMMERCIAL

Source: *Montana Farmer-Stockman.* **Price Frequency:** monthly, seasonally. **Effective Market(s):** Billings (MT), Riverton (WY). **Units of Measure:** Dollars per 100 lbs. **Type of Price:** cash auction. **Time Period Covered:** latest month.

COWS: SLAUGHTER, BREAKING UTILITY AND COMMERCIAL 2-4

Source: *Utah Farmer-Stockman.* **Price Frequency:** monthly, seasonally. **Effective Market(s):** Salina (UT), Spanish Fork (UT). **Units of Measure:** Dollars per 100 lbs. **Type of Price:** auction. **Time Period Covered:** latest month.

COWS: SLAUGHTER, CANNER

Source: *Farm and Dairy.* **Price Frequency:** weekly, seasonally. **Effective Market(s):** Ohio, Pennsylvania. **Units of Measure:** Dollars per head. **Type of Price:** auction high, auction low. **Time Period Covered:** latest week, year ago.

COWS: SLAUGHTER, CANNER AND LOW CUTTER

Source: *Montana Farmer-Stockman.* **Price Frequency:** monthly, seasonally. **Effective Market(s):** Billings (MT), Riverton (WY). **Units of Measure:** Dollars per 100 lbs. **Type of Price:** cash auction. **Time Period Covered:** latest month.

COWS: SLAUGHTER, COMMERCIAL 2-4

Source: *Livestock, Meat, Wool Market News.* **Price Frequency:** weekly, seasonally. **Effective Market(s):** Lancaster County (PA), Omaha, Sioux City (IA), South St. Paul. **Units of Measure:** Dollars per 100 lbs. **Type of Price:** average. **Time Period Covered:** latest week, year ago.

COWS: SLAUGHTER, COMMERCIAL TO GOOD

Source: *Farm and Dairy.* **Price Frequency:** weekly, seasonally. **Effective Market(s):** Ohio, Pennsylvania. **Units of Measure:** Dollars per head. **Type of Price:** auction high, auction low. **Time Period Covered:** latest week, year ago.

COWS: SLAUGHTER, CULL

Source: *Farm and Dairy.* **Price Frequency:** weekly, seasonally. **Effective Market(s):** Ohio, Pennsylvania. **Units of Measure:** Dollars per head. **Type of Price:** auction high, auction low. **Time Period Covered:** latest week, year ago.

COWS: SLAUGHTER, CUTTER

Source: *Montana Farmer-Stockman.* **Price Frequency:** monthly, seasonally. **Effective Market(s):** Billings (MT). **Units of Measure:** Dollars per 100 lbs. **Type of Price:** cash auction. **Time Period Covered:** latest month.

COWS: SLAUGHTER, CUTTER 1-2

Source: *Livestock, Meat, Wool Market News.* **Price Frequency:** weekly, seasonally. **Effective Market(s):** Lancaster County (PA), Omaha, Sioux City (IA), South St. Paul. **Units of Measure:** Dollars per 100 lbs. **Type of Price:** average. **Time Period Covered:** latest week, year ago.

COWS: SLAUGHTER, CUTTER AND LOW DRESSING UTILITY

Source: *Utah Farmer-Stockman.* **Price Frequency:** monthly, seasonally. **Effective Market(s):** Spanish Fork (UT). **Units of Measure:** Dollars per 100 lbs. **Type of Price:** auction. **Time Period Covered:** latest month.

COWS: SLAUGHTER, UTILITY

Source: *Farm and Dairy.* **Price Frequency:** weekly, seasonally. **Effective Market(s):** Ohio, Pennsylvania. **Units of Measure:** Dollars per head. **Type of Price:** auction high, auction low. **Time Period Covered:** latest week, year ago.

COWS: SLAUGHTER, UTILITY 1-3

Source: *Livestock, Meat, Wool Market News.* **Price Frequency:** weekly. **Effective Market(s):** South St. Paul. **Units of Measure:** Dollars per 100 lbs. **Type of Price:** average. **Time Period Covered:** latest week, year ago.

COWS: SLAUGHTER, UTILITY 2-3

Source: *Oregon Farmer-Stockman.* **Price Frequency:** monthly. **Effective Market(s):** Oregon/Washington. **Time Period Covered:** latest month.

Source: *Washington Farmer-Stockman.* **Price Frequency:** monthly, seasonally. **Effective Market(s):** Oregon/Washington. **Units of Measure:** Dollars per 100 lbs. **Time Period Covered:** latest month.

COWS: STOCK, EARLY CALVERS

Source: *Montana Farmer-Stockman.* **Price Frequency:** monthly, seasonally. **Effective Market(s):** Billings (MT). **Units of Measure:** Dollars per head. **Type of Price:** cash auction. **Time Period Covered:** latest month.

COWS: UTILITY

Source: *Agricultural Outlook.* **Price Frequency:** monthly, annually. **Effective Market(s):** Kansas City. **Units of Measure:** Dollars per 100 lbs. **Type of Price:** market. **Time Period Covered:** monthly latest 6 months, annually latest 3 years.

Source: *Commodity Year Book.* **Price Frequency:** annually. **Effective Market(s):** Omaha (NE). **Units of Measure:** Dollars per 100 lbs. **Type of Price:** wholesale. **Time Period Covered:** latest 5 years.

Source: *Doane's Agricultural Report.* **Price Frequency:** weekly. **Effective Market(s):** Omaha (NE). **Units of Measure:** Dollars per 100 lbs. **Time Period Covered:** latest week, week ago, year ago.

Source: *Farm and Dairy.* **Price Frequency:** weekly, seasonally. **Effective Market(s):** Ohio, Pennsylvania. **Units of Measure:** Dollars per head. **Type of Price:** auction high, auction low. **Time Period Covered:** latest week, year ago.

COWS: UTILITY AND COMMON

Source: *Drovers Journal.* **Price Frequency:** semimonthly. **Effective Market(s):** 8 domestic markets. **Units of Measure:** Dollars per 100 lbs. **Time Period Covered:** selected day.

COWS: YELLOW, THIN

Source: *Farm and Dairy.* **Price Frequency:** weekly, seasonally. **Effective Market(s):** Ohio, Pennsylvania. **Units of Measure:** Dollars per head. **Type of Price:** auction high, auction low. **Time Period Covered:** latest week, year ago.

COWS: YOUNG AND MIDDLE-AGED

Source: *Drovers Journal.* **Price Frequency:** semimonthly. **Effective Market(s):** 8 domestic markets. **Units of Measure:** Dollars per 100 lbs., dollars per head. **Time Period Covered:** selected day.

CRAB CLAWS: STONE, JUMBO, FRESH

Source: *Seafood Price-Current.* **Price Frequency:** semiweekly. **Effective Market(s):** Gulf/Southeast. **Units of Measure:** Dollars per lb. **Type of Price:** sale by first receiver. **Time Period Covered:** latest day.

CRAB CLAWS: STONE, LARGE, FRESH

Source: *Seafood Price-Current.* **Price Frequency:** semiweekly. **Effective Market(s):** Gulf/Southeast. **Units of Measure:** Dollars per lb. **Type of Price:** sale by first receiver. **Time Period Covered:** latest day.

CRAB CLAWS: STONE, MEDIUM, FRESH

Source: *Seafood Price-Current.* **Price Frequency:** semiweekly. **Effective Market(s):** Gulf/Southeast. **Units of Measure:** Dollars per lb. **Type of Price:** slae by first receiver. **Time Period Covered:** latest day.

CRAB MEAT: BACKFIN, STEAMED, FRESH, LOUISIANA

Source: *Seafood Price-Current.* **Price Frequency:** semiweekly. **Effective Market(s):** Gulf/Southeast. **Units of Measure:** Dollars per lb. **Type of Price:** sale by first receiver. **Time Period Covered:** latest day.

CRAB MEAT: BLUE, BACKFIN, FRESH

Source: *Seafood Price-Current.* **Price Frequency:** semiweekly. **Effective Market(s):** Mid-Atlantic. **Units of Measure:** Dollars per lb. can. **Type of Price:** sale to first receiver. **Time Period Covered:** latest day.

CRAB MEAT: BLUE, BACKFIN, PASTEURIZED

Source: *Seafood Price-Current.* **Price Frequency:** semiweekly. **Effective Market(s):** Mid-Atlantic. **Units of Measure:** Dollars per lb. can. **Type of Price:** sale by first receiver. **Time Period Covered:** latest day.

CRAB MEAT: BLUE, CLAW, FRESH

Source: *Seafood Price-Current.* **Price Frequency:** semiweekly. **Effective Market(s):** Mid-Atlantic. **Units of Measure:** Dollars per lb. can. **Type of Price:** sale to first receiver. **Time Period Covered:** latest day.

CRAB MEAT: BLUE, CLAW, PASTEURIZED

Source: *Seafood Price-Current.* **Price Frequency:** semiweekly. **Effective Market(s):** Mid-Atlantic. **Units of Measure:** Dollars per lb. can. **Type of Price:** sale by first receiver. **Time Period Covered:** latest day.

CRAB MEAT: BLUE, FINGERS, FRESH

Source: *Seafood Price-Current.* **Price Frequency:** semiweekly. **Effective Market(s):** Mid-Atlantic. **Units of Measure:** Dollars per 12 ounce can. **Type of Price:** sale to first receiver. **Time Period Covered:** latest day.

CRAB MEAT: BLUE, FINGERS, PASTEURIZED

Source: *Seafood Price-Current.* **Price Frequency:** semiweekly. **Effective Market(s):** Mid-Atlantic. **Units of Measure:** Dollars per 12 ounce can. **Type of Price:** sale by first receiver. **Time Period Covered:** latest day.

CRAB MEAT: BLUE, JUMBO LUMP, FRESH

Source: *Seafood Price-Current.* **Price Frequency:** semiweekly. **Effective Market(s):** Mid-Atlantic. **Units of Measure:** Dollars per lb. can. **Type of Price:** sale by first receiver. **Time Period Covered:** latest day.

CRAB MEAT: BLUE, JUMBO LUMP, PASTEURIZED

Source: *Seafood Price-Current.* **Price Frequency:** semiweekly. **Effective Market(s):** Mid-Atlantic. **Units of Measure:** Dollars per lb. can. **Type of Price:** sale by first receiver. **Time Period Covered:** latest day.

CRAB MEAT: BLUE, SPECIAL, FRESH

Source: *Seafood Price-Current.* **Price Frequency:** semiweekly. **Effective Market(s):** Mid-Atlantic. **Units of Measure:** Dollars per lb. can. **Type of Price:** sale to first receiver. **Time Period Covered:** latest day.

CRAB MEAT: BLUE, SPECIAL, PASTEURIZED

Source: *Seafood Price-Current.* **Price Frequency:** semiweekly. **Effective Market(s):** Mid-Atlantic. **Units of Measure:** Dollars per lb. can. **Type of Price:** sale by first receiver. **Time Period Covered:** latest day.

CRAB MEAT: CLAW, STEAMED, FRESH, LOUISIANA

Source: *Seafood Price-Current.* **Price Frequency:** semiweekly. **Effective Market(s):** Gulf/Southeast. **Units of Measure:** Dollars per lb. **Type of Price:** sale by first receiver. **Time Period Covered:** latest day.

CRAB MEAT: DUNGENESS, FRESH

Source: *Seafood Price-Current.* **Price Frequency:** semiweekly. **Effective Market(s):** West Coast. **Units of Measure:** Dollars per lb. **Type of Price:** sale by first receiver. **Time Period Covered:** latest day.

CRAB MEAT: DUNGENESS, FROZEN

Source: *Seafood Price-Current.* **Price Frequency:** semiweekly. **Effective Market(s):** West Coast. **Units of Measure:** Dollars per lb. **Type of Price:** first receiver. **Time Period Covered:** latest day.

CRAB MEAT: FINGERS, STEAMED, FRESH, LOUISIANA

Source: *Seafood Price-Current.* **Price Frequency:** semiweekly. **Effective Market(s):** Gulf/Southeast. **Units of Measure:** Dollars per lb. **Type of Price:** sale by first receiver. **Time Period Covered:** latest day.

CRAB MEAT: JUMBO LUMP, STEAMED, FRESH, LOUISIANA

Source: *Seafood Price-Current.* **Price Frequency:** semiweekly. **Effective Market(s):** Gulf/Southeast. **Units of Measure:** Dollars per lb. **Type of Price:** sale by first receiver. **Time Period Covered:** latest day.

CRAB MEAT: KING, FROZEN, CHILEAN

Source: *Seafood Price-Current.* **Price Frequency:** semiweekly. **Effective Market(s):** West Coast. **Units of Measure:** Dollars per lb. **Type of Price:** first receiver. **Time Period Covered:** latest day.

CRAB MEAT: KING, FROZEN, DOMESTIC

Source: *Seafood Price-Current.* **Price Frequency:** semiweekly. **Effective Market(s):** West Coast. **Units of Measure:** Dollars per lb. **Type of Price:** first receiver. **Time Period Covered:** latest day.

CRAB MEAT: KING, MERUS, FROZEN, DOMESTIC

Source: *Seafood Price-Current.* **Price Frequency:** semiweekly. **Effective Market(s):** West Coast. **Units of Measure:** Dollars per lb. **Type of Price:** first receiver. **Time Period Covered:** latest day.

CRAB MEAT: KING, SALAD, FROZEN, DOMESTIC

Source: *Seafood Price-Current.* **Price Frequency:** semi-weekly. **Effective Market(s):** West Coast. **Units of Measure:** Dollars per lb. **Type of Price:** first receiver. **Time Period Covered:** latest day.

CRAB MEAT: RED, DOMESTIC

Source: *NMFS Green Sheet Supplement.* **Price Frequency:** weekly. **Effective Market(s):** New England. **Units of Measure:** Dollars per lb. **Type of Price:** to primary wholesalers. **Time Period Covered:** lastest week.

CRAB MEAT: SNOW, CANADIAN

Source: *NMFS Green Sheet Supplement.* **Price Frequency:** weekly. **Effective Market(s):** New England. **Units of Measure:** Dollars per lb. **Type of Price:** to primary wholesalers, warehouse. **Time Period Covered:** lastest week.

CRAB MEAT: SNOW, CLUSTERS, DOMESTIC

Source: *NMFS Green Sheet Supplement.* **Price Frequency:** weekly. **Effective Market(s):** New England. **Units of Measure:** Dollars per lb. **Type of Price:** to primary wholesalers. **Time Period Covered:** lastest week.

CRAB MEAT: SNOW, FROZEN, CANADIAN

Source: *Seafood Price-Current.* **Price Frequency:** semi-weekly. **Effective Market(s):** Mid-Atlantic. **Units of Measure:** Dollars per lb. **Type of Price:** first receiver. **Time Period Covered:** latest day.

CRAB MEAT: SNOW, FROZEN, CHILEAN

Source: *Seafood Price-Current.* **Price Frequency:** semi-weekly. **Effective Market(s):** Mid-Atlantic. **Units of Measure:** Dollars per lb. **Type of Price:** first receiver. **Time Period Covered:** latest day.

CRAB MEAT: SNOW, FROZEN, KOREAN

Source: *Seafood Price-Current.* **Price Frequency:** semi-weekly. **Effective Market(s):** Mid-Atlantic. **Units of Measure:** Dollars per lb. **Type of Price:** first receiver. **Time Period Covered:** latest day.

CRAB MEAT: SNOW, KOREAN

Source: *NMFS Green Sheet Supplement.* **Price Frequency:** weekly. **Effective Market(s):** New York. **Units of Measure:** Dollars per lb. **Type of Price:** warehouse. **Time Period Covered:** lastest week.

CRAB MEAT: SNOW, MERUS, FROZEN, KOREAN

Source: *Seafood Price-Current.* **Price Frequency:** semi-weekly. **Effective Market(s):** Mid-Atlantic. **Units of Measure:** Dollars per lb. **Type of Price:** first receiver. **Time Period Covered:** latest day.

CRAB MEAT: SNOW, SALAD, FROZEN, CANADIAN

Source: *Seafood Price-Current.* **Price Frequency:** semi-weekly. **Effective Market(s):** Mid-Atlantic. **Units of Measure:** Dollars per lb. **Type of Price:** first receiver. **Time Period Covered:** latest day.

CRAB MEAT: SPECIAL, STEAMED, FRESH, LOUISIANA

Source: *Seafood Price-Current.* **Price Frequency:** semi-weekly. **Effective Market(s):** Gulf/Southeast. **Units of Measure:** Dollars per lb. **Type of Price:** sale by first receiver. **Time Period Covered:** latest day.

CRABMEAT: BLUE

Source: *HRI-Buyers Guide.* **Price Frequency:** weekly. **Effective Market(s):** New York. **Units of Measure:** Dollars per lb. **Type of Price:** price paid by dining places & institutions. **Time Period Covered:** latest week.

CRABMEAT: KING

Source: *HRI-Buyers Guide.* **Price Frequency:** weekly. **Effective Market(s):** New York. **Units of Measure:** Dollars per case. **Type of Price:** price paid by dining places & institutions. **Time Period Covered:** latest week.

CRABMEAT: SNOW

Source: *HRI-Buyers Guide.* **Price Frequency:** weekly. **Effective Market(s):** New York. **Units of Measure:** Dollars per case. **Type of Price:** price paid by dining places & institutions. **Time Period Covered:** latest week.

CRABS: BLUE SOFT SHELL

Source: *HRI-Buyers Guide.* **Price Frequency:** weekly. **Effective Market(s):** New York. **Units of Measure:** Dollars per lb. **Type of Price:** price paid by dining places & institutions. **Time Period Covered:** latest week.

CRABS: BLUE, HOTEL, FROZEN, DOMESTIC

Source: *Seafood Price-Current.* **Price Frequency:** semi-weekly. **Effective Market(s):** Mid-Atlantic. **Units of Measure:** Dollars per lb. **Type of Price:** first receiver. **Time Period Covered:** latest day.

CRABS: BLUE, JUMBO, FROZEN, DOMESTIC

Source: *Seafood Price-Current.* **Price Frequency:** semi-weekly. **Effective Market(s):** Mid-Atlantic. **Units of Measure:** Dollars per lb. **Type of Price:** first receiver. **Time Period Covered:** latest day.

CRABS: BLUE, MEDIUM, FROZEN, DOMESTIC

Source: *Seafood Price-Current.* **Price Frequency:** semi-weekly. **Effective Market(s):** Mid-Atlantic. **Units of Measure:** Dollars per lb. **Type of Price:** first receiver. **Time Period Covered:** latest day.

CRABS: BLUE, PRIME, FROZEN, DOMESTIC

Source: *Seafood Price-Current.* **Price Frequency:** semi-weekly. **Effective Market(s):** Mid-Atlantic. **Units of Measure:** Dollars per lb. **Type of Price:** first receiver. **Time Period Covered:** latest day.

CRABS: BLUE, WHALE, FROZEN, DOMESTIC

Source: *Seafood Price-Current.* **Price Frequency:** semi-weekly. **Effective Market(s):** Mid-Atlantic. **Units of Measure:** Dollars per lb. **Type of Price:** first receiver. **Time Period Covered:** latest day.

CRABS: BROWN KING, LEG AND CLAW, FROZEN

Source: *Seafood Price-Current.* **Price Frequency:** semi-weekly. **Effective Market(s):** West Coast. **Units of Measure:** Dollars per lb. **Type of Price:** first receiver. **Time Period Covered:** latest day.

CRABS: DUNGENESS, WHOLE, COOKED, FRESH

Source: *Seafood Price-Current.* **Price Frequency:** semi-weekly. **Effective Market(s):** West Coast. **Units of Measure:** Dollars per lb. **Type of Price:** sale by first receiver. **Time Period Covered:** latest day.

CRABS: DUNGENESS, WHOLE, COOKED, FROZEN

Source: *Seafood Price-Current.* **Price Frequency:** semi-weekly. **Effective Market(s):** West Coast. **Units of Measure:** Dollars per lb. **Type of Price:** first receiver. **Time Period Covered:** latest day.

CRABS: DUNGENESS, WHOLE, LIVE

Source: *Seafood Price-Current.* **Price Frequency:** semi-weekly. **Effective Market(s):** West Coast. **Units of Measure:** Dollars per lb. **Type of Price:** sale by first receiver. **Time Period Covered:** latest day.

CRABS: HARD, NO. 1, JIMMIES, FRESH

Source: *Seafood Price-Current.* **Price Frequency:** semi-weekly. **Effective Market(s):** Mid-Atlantic. **Units of Measure:** Dollars per bushel. **Type of Price:** sale by first receiver. **Time Period Covered:** latest day.

CRABS: HARD, NO. 1, SOOK, FRESH

Source: *Seafood Price-Current.* **Price Frequency:** semi-weekly. **Effective Market(s):** Mid-Atlantic. **Units of Measure:** Dollars per bushel. **Type of Price:** sale by first receiver. **Time Period Covered:** latest day.

CRABS: HARD, NO. 2, JIMMIES, FRESH

Source: *Seafood Price-Current.* **Price Frequency:** semi-weekly. **Effective Market(s):** Mid-Atlantic. **Units of Measure:** Dollars per bushel. **Type of Price:** sale by first receiver. **Time Period Covered:** latest day.

CRABS: KING

Source: *HRI-Buyers Guide.* **Price Frequency:** weekly. **Effective Market(s):** New York. **Units of Measure:** Dollars per case. **Type of Price:** price paid by dining places & institutions. **Time Period Covered:** latest week.

CRABS: RED KING, LEG AND CLAW, FROZEN

Source: *Seafood Price-Current.* **Price Frequency:** semi-weekly. **Effective Market(s):** West Coast. **Units of Measure:** Dollars per lb. **Type of Price:** first receiver. **Time Period Covered:** latest day.

CRABS: SNOW, CLUSTER, FROZEN, CANADIAN

Source: *Seafood Price-Current.* **Price Frequency:** semi-weekly. **Effective Market(s):** Mid-Atlantic. **Units of Measure:** Dollars per lb. **Type of Price:** first receiver. **Time Period Covered:** latest day.

CRABS: SNOW, CLUSTER, FROZEN, DOMESTIC

Source: *Seafood Price-Current.* **Price Frequency:** semi-weekly. **Effective Market(s):** West Coast. **Units of Measure:** Dollars per lb. **Type of Price:** first receiver. **Time Period Covered:** latest day.

CRABS: SNOW, COCKTAIL CLAW, FROZEN, CANADIAN

Source: *Seafood Price-Current.* **Price Frequency:** semi-weekly. **Effective Market(s):** Mid-Atlantic. **Units of Measure:** Dollars per lb. **Type of Price:** first receiver. **Time Period Covered:** latest day.

CRABS: SNOW, COCKTAIL CLAW, FROZEN, DOMESTIC

Source: *Seafood Price-Current.* **Price Frequency:** semi-weekly. **Effective Market(s):** West Coast. **Units of Measure:** Dollars per lb. **Type of Price:** first receiver. **Time Period Covered:** latest day.

CRABS: SNOW, FROZEN, ALASKAN

Source: *Weekly Statistical Fishery Report.* **Price Frequency:** weekly. **Effective Market(s):** Tokyo. **Units of Measure:** Dollars per lb. **Type of Price:** wholesale. **Time Period Covered:** 2 weeks ago, month ago.

CRABS: SNOW, LEG AND CLAW, FROZEN, DOMESTIC

Source: *Seafood Price-Current.* **Price Frequency:** semi-weekly. **Effective Market(s):** West Coast. **Units of Measure:** Dollars per lb. **Type of Price:** first receiver. **Time Period Covered:** latest day.

CRABS: SOFT, HOTEL, FRESH

Source: *Seafood Price-Current.* **Price Frequency:** semi-weekly. **Effective Market(s):** Mid-Atlantic. **Units of Measure:** Dollars per dozen. **Type of Price:** sale to first receiver. **Time Period Covered:** latest day.

CRABS: SOFT, JUMBO, FRESH

Source: *Seafood Price-Current.* **Price Frequency:** semi-weekly. **Effective Market(s):** Mid-Atlantic. **Units of Measure:** Dollars per dozen. **Type of Price:** sale by first receiver. **Time Period Covered:** latest day.

CRABS: SOFT, MEDIUM, FRESH

Source: *Seafood Price-Current.* **Price Frequency:** semi-weekly. **Effective Market(s):** Mid-Atlantic. **Units of Measure:** Dollars per dozen. **Type of Price:** sale by first receiver. **Time Period Covered:** latest day.

CRABS: SOFT, PRIME, FRESH

Source: *Seafood Price-Current.* **Price Frequency:** semi-weekly. **Effective Market(s):** Mid-Atlantic. **Units of Measure:** Dollars per dozen. **Type of Price:** sale by first receiver. **Time Period Covered:** latest day.

CRABS: SOFT, WHALES, FRESH

Source: *Seafood Price-Current.* **Price Frequency:** semi-weekly. **Effective Market(s):** Mid-Atlantic. **Units of Measure:** Dollars per dozen. **Type of Price:** sale by first receiver. **Time Period Covered:** latest day.

CRANBERRIES

Source: *Agricultural Prices Annual Summary.* **Price Frequency:** annually. **Effective Market(s):** Massachusetts, New Jersey, Oregon, Washington, Wisconsin, United States. **Units of Measure:** Dollars per barrel. **Type of Price:** average price received by farmer. **Time Period Covered:** latest 3 years, for US latest 6 years.

Source: *Fruit and Tree Nuts Situation and Outlook Yearbook.* **Price Frequency:** annually. **Effective Market(s):** United States. **Units of Measure:** Dollars per barrel. **Type of Price:** grower. **Time Period Covered:** latest 20 years.

CRANBERRIES: EARLY BLACKS AND LATE HOWES, MASSACHUSETTS

Source: *Fresh Fruit and Vegetable Prices.* **Price Frequency:** monthly, seasonally. **Effective Market(s):** Chicago, New York City. **Units of Measure:** Dollars per carton. **Type of Price:** average wholesale price. **Time Period Covered:** latest year.

CRANBERRIES: WISCONSIN

Source: *Fresh Fruit and Vegetable Prices.* **Price Frequency:** monthly, seasonally. **Effective Market(s):** Chicago. **Units of Measure:** Dollars per carton. **Type of Price:** average wholesale price. **Time Period Covered:** latest year.

CREAM: CLASS II

Source: *Dairy Market Statistics.* **Price Frequency:** monthly, annually. **Effective Market(s):** Baltimore/Washington/Philadelphia, Boston, New York, Southern area. **Units of Measure:** Dollars per lb. butterfat. **Type of Price:** spot. **Time Period Covered:** latest year.

CREAM: FLUID

Source: *Urner Barry's Price-Current.* **Price Frequency:** daily. **Effective Market(s):** Northeast. **Units of Measure:** Dollars per lb. **Type of Price:** spot. **Time Period Covered:** latest day.

CREAM: SWEET, BUTTERMILK POWDER

Source: *Milling & Baking News.* **Price Frequency:** weekly. **Units of Measure:** cents per lb. **Time Period Covered:** latest week.

CREAM: SWEET, DRY

Source: *Monthly Price Review.* **Price Frequency:** daily. **Effective Market(s):** Northeast. **Units of Measure:** Dollars per lb. **Type of Price:** spot. **Time Period Covered:** latest month.

CREAM OF TARTAR

see also Potassium Bitartrate.

CREAM OF TARTAR: GRANULAR, NF

Source: *Journal of Commerce and Commercial.* **Price Frequency:** weekly in Friday issue. **Units of Measure:** Dollars per lb. **Type of Price:** spot. **Time Period Covered:** latest week.

CRENSHAW MELONS

Source: *Lancaster Farmer.* **Price Frequency:** weekly, seasonally. **Effective Market(s):** Pennsylvania. **Units of Measure:** Dollars per carton. **Type of Price:** market. **Time Period Covered:** latest week.

CREOSOTE: GRADE 1

Source: *Chemical Marketing Reporter.* **Price Frequency:** weekly. **Effective Market(s):** New York. **Units of Measure:** Dollars per gallon. **Type of Price:** spot. **Time Period Covered:** latest week.

Source: *Journal of Commerce and Commercial.* **Price Frequency:** weekly in Wednesday issue. **Effective Market(s):** East. **Units of Measure:** Dollars per gallon. **Type of Price:** spot. **Time Period Covered:** latest week.

CREOSOTE: SOLUTION 60/40

Source: *Chemical Marketing Reporter.* **Price Frequency:** weekly. **Effective Market(s):** New York. **Units of Measure:** Dollars per gallon. **Type of Price:** spot. **Time Period Covered:** latest week.

CREOSOTE: SOLUTION 80/20

Source: *Journal of Commerce and Commercial.* **Price Frequency:** weekly in Wednesday issue. **Units of Measure:** Dollars per lb. **Type of Price:** spot. **Time Period Covered:** latest week.

P-CRESIDINE: FUSED

Source: *Chemical Marketing Reporter.* **Price Frequency:** weekly. **Effective Market(s):** New York. **Units of Measure:** Dollars per lb. **Type of Price:** spot. **Time Period Covered:** latest week.

CRESOL

Source: *Journal of Commerce and Commercial.* **Price Frequency:** weekly in Wednesday issue. **Units of Measure:** Dollars per lb. **Type of Price:** spot. **Time Period Covered:** latest week.

M-CRESOL

Source: *Journal of Commerce and Commercial.* **Price Frequency:** weekly in Wednesday issue. **Units of Measure:** Dollars per lb. **Type of Price:** spot. **Time Period Covered:** latest week.

O-CRESOL

Source: *Journal of Commerce and Commercial.* **Price Frequency:** weekly in Wednesday issue. **Units of Measure:** Dollars per lb. **Type of Price:** spot. **Time Period Covered:** latest week.

P-CRESOL

Source: *Journal of Commerce and Commercial.* **Price Frequency:** weekly in Wednesday issue. **Units of Measure:** Dollars per lb. **Type of Price:** spot. **Time Period Covered:** latest week.

M-CRESOL: 95-98% PURE

Source: *Chemical Marketing Reporter.* **Price Frequency:** weekly. **Effective Market(s):** New York. **Units of Measure:** Dollars per lb. **Type of Price:** spot. **Time Period Covered:** latest week.

P-CRESOL: 98% PURE

Source: *Chemical Marketing Reporter.* **Price Frequency:** weekly. **Effective Market(s):** New York. **Units of Measure:** Dollars per lb. **Type of Price:** spot. **Time Period Covered:** latest week.

M,P-CRESOL: 99% PURE

Source: *Chemical Marketing Reporter.* **Price Frequency:** weekly. **Effective Market(s):** New York. **Units of Measure:** Dollars per lb. **Type of Price:** spot. **Time Period Covered:** latest week.

O-CRESOL: 99% PURE

Source: *Chemical Marketing Reporter.* **Price Frequency:** weekly. **Effective Market(s):** New York. **Units of Measure:** Dollars per lb. **Type of Price:** spot. **Time Period Covered:** latest week.

CRESYLIC ACID: COALTAR, DOMESTIC

Source: *Chemical Marketing Reporter.* **Price Frequency:** weekly. **Effective Market(s):** New York. **Units of Measure:** Dollars per lb. **Type of Price:** spot. **Time Period Covered:** latest week.

CRESYLIC ACID: DOMESTIC

Source: *Chemical Marketing Reporter.* **Price Frequency:** weekly. **Effective Market(s):** New York. **Units of Measure:** Dollars per lb. **Type of Price:** spot. **Time Period Covered:** latest week.

CREVALLE JACK (FISH): FILLETS, FRESH, HAWAIIAN

Source: *Seafood Price-Current.* **Price Frequency:** semi-weekly. **Effective Market(s):** Hawaii. **Units of Measure:** Dollars per lb. **Type of Price:** sale by first receiver. **Time Period Covered:** latest day.

CREVALLE JACK (FISH): WHOLE, FRESH, HAWAIIAN

Source: *Seafood Price-Current.* **Price Frequency:** semi-weekly. **Effective Market(s):** Hawaii. **Units of Measure:** Dollars per lb. **Type of Price:** sale by first receiver. **Time Period Covered:** latest day.

CROAKER (FISH): WHOLE, FRESH

Source: *Seafood Price-Current.* **Price Frequency:** semi-weekly. **Effective Market(s):** Boston, Mid-Atlantic, New Bedford (MA), Portland (ME). **Units of Measure:** Dollars per lb. **Type of Price:** sale by first receiver, auction price. **Time Period Covered:** latest day.

CROPS: ALL

Source: *Illinois Farm Report.* **Price Frequency:** monthly. **Effective Market(s):** Illinois. **Units of Measure:** index . **Type of Price:** index of prices received by farmers. **Time Period Covered:** latest 2 months, year ago.

CROTONIC ACID

Source: *Chemical Marketing Reporter.* **Price Frequency:** weekly. **Effective Market(s):** New York. **Units of Measure:** Dollars per lb. **Type of Price:** spot. **Time Period Covered:** latest week.

CRYOLITE: SYNTHETIC

Source: *Chemical Marketing Reporter.* **Price Frequency:** weekly. **Effective Market(s):** New York. **Units of Measure:** Dollars per ton. **Type of Price:** spot. **Time Period Covered:** latest week.

CUBE ROOT POWDER: 5% ROTENONE

Source: *Chemical Marketing Reporter.* **Price Frequency:** weekly. **Effective Market(s):** New York. **Units of Measure:** Dollars per lb. **Type of Price:** spot. **Time Period Covered:** latest week.

Source: *Journal of Commerce and Commercial.* **Price Frequency:** weekly in Thursday issue. **Units of Measure:** Dollars per lb. **Type of Price:** spot. **Time Period Covered:** latest week.

CUCUMBER, YELLOW POPLAR AND BASSWOOD SAWTIMBER

Source: *Volume and Value of Sawtimber Stumpage Sold From National Forests by Selected Species and Region.* **Price Frequency:** quarterly, annually. **Effective Market(s):** Southern region. **Units of Measure:** Dollars per 1000 board feet. **Type of Price:** average. **Time Period Covered:** latest quarter, latest year.

CUCUMBERS

Source: *Fresh Fruit and Vegetable Prices.* **Price Frequency:** monthly, seasonally. **Effective Market(s):** 11 domestic markets. **Units of Measure:** Dollars per carton/crate. **Type of Price:** average price at shipping point. **Time Period Covered:** latest year.

Source: *Lancaster Farming.* **Price Frequency:** weekly, seasonally. **Effective Market(s):** Pennsylvania . **Units of Measure:** Dollars per unit. **Type of Price:** market. **Time Period Covered:** latest week .

Source: *The Packer.* **Price Frequency:** weekly, seasonally. **Effective Market(s):** varies. **Units of Measure:** Dollars per carton. **Type of Price:** price received by farmer. **Time Period Covered:** latest week.

CUCUMBERS: CARIBBEAN IMPORTS

Source: *Fresh Fruit and Vegetable Prices.* **Price Frequency:** monthly, seasonally. **Effective Market(s):** South Florida. **Units of Measure:** Dollars per carton/crate. **Type of Price:** price paid at point of entry. **Time Period Covered:** latest year.

CUCUMBERS: FLORIDA

Source: *Vegetable and Specialties Situation and Outlook Report.* **Price Frequency:** monthly. **Effective Market(s):** North Central, Northeast. **Units of Measure:** cents per lb. **Type of Price:** retail. **Time Period Covered:** latest month, year ago.

CUCUMBERS: FRESH

Source: *HRI-Buyers Guide.* **Price Frequency:** weekly. **Effective Market(s):** Northeastern area. **Units of Measure:** Dollars per carton. **Type of Price:** price paid by dining places & institutions. **Time Period Covered:** latest week.

CUCUMBERS: KIRBY, FRESH

Source: *HRI-Buyers Guide.* **Price Frequency:** weekly. **Effective Market(s):** Northeastern area. **Units of Measure:** Dollars per basket. **Type of Price:** price paid by dining places & institutions. **Time Period Covered:** latest week.

CUCUMBERS: MEXICAN

Source: *Fresh Fruit and Vegetable Prices.* **Price Frequency:** monthly, seasonally. **Effective Market(s):** Nogales (AZ). **Units of Measure:** Dollars per carton/crate. **Type of Price:** price paid at point of entry. **Time Period Covered:** latest year.

CUCUMBERS: TELEGRAPH

Source: *New Zealand Farmer.* **Price Frequency:** weekly, seasonally. **Effective Market(s):** New Zealand. **Units of Measure:** New Zealand dollars each/per carton. **Time Period Covered:** latest week.

CUCUMBERS: WAXED, FLORIDA

Source: *Fresh Fruit and Vegetable Prices.* **Price Frequency:** monthly, seasonally. **Effective Market(s):** Chicago, New York City. **Units of Measure:** Dollars per crate/carton. **Type of Price:** average wholesale price. **Time Period Covered:** latest year.

CUCUMBERS: WAXED, ILLINOIS

Source: *Fresh Fruit and Vegetable Prices.* **Price Frequency:** monthly, seasonally. **Effective Market(s):** Chicago. **Units of Measure:** Dollars per crate/carton. **Type of Price:** average wholesale price. **Time Period Covered:** latest year.

CUCUMBERS: WAXED, MEXICAN

Source: *Fresh Fruit and Vegetable Prices.* **Price Frequency:** monthly, seasonally. **Effective Market(s):** Chicago, New York City. **Units of Measure:** Dollars per crate/carton. **Type of Price:** average wholesale price. **Time Period Covered:** latest year.

CUCUMBERS: WAXED, MICHIGAN

Source: *Fresh Fruit and Vegetable Prices.* **Price Frequency:** monthly, seasonally. **Effective Market(s):** Chicago. **Units of Measure:** Dollars per crate/carton. **Type of Price:** average wholesale price. **Time Period Covered:** latest year.

CUCUMBERS: WAXED, NEW JERSEY

Source: *Fresh Fruit and Vegetable Prices.* **Price Frequency:** monthly, seasonally. **Effective Market(s):** New York City. **Units of Measure:** Dollars per crate/carton. **Type of Price:** average wholesale price. **Time Period Covered:** latest year.

CUCUMBERS: WAXED, NEW YORK

Source: *Fresh Fruit and Vegetable Prices.* **Price Frequency:** monthly, seasonally. **Effective Market(s):** New York City. **Units of Measure:** Dollars per crate/carton. **Type of Price:** average wholesale price. **Time Period Covered:** latest year.

CUCUMBERS: WAXED, NORTH CAROLINA

Source: *Fresh Fruit and Vegetable Prices.* **Price Frequency:** monthly, seasonally. **Effective Market(s):** New York City. **Units of Measure:** Dollars per crate/carton. **Type of Price:** average wholesale price. **Time Period Covered:** latest year.

CUCUMBERS: WAXED, TEXAS

Source: *Fresh Fruit and Vegetable Prices.* **Price Frequency:** monthly, seasonally. **Effective Market(s):** Chicago. **Units of Measure:** Dollars per crate/carton. **Type of Price:** average wholesale price. **Time Period Covered:** latest year.

CULTIVATOR: ROW CROP

Source: *Agricultural Prices.* **Price Frequency:** annually. **Effective Market(s):** United States. **Units of Measure:** Dollars each. **Type of Price:** paid by farmer. **Time Period Covered:** latest year.

Source: *Agricultural Prices Annual Summary.* **Price Frequency:** annually. **Effective Market(s):** United States. **Units of Measure:** Dollars each. **Type of Price:** average price paid by farmer. **Time Period Covered:** latest 6 years.

CUMENE

Source: *Chemical Marketing Reporter.* **Price Frequency:** weekly. **Effective Market(s):** New York. **Units of Measure:** Dollars per lb. **Type of Price:** spot. **Time Period Covered:** latest week.

Source: *Journal of Commerce and Commercial.* **Price Frequency:** weekly in Thursday issue. **Units of Measure:** Dollars per lb. **Type of Price:** spot. **Time Period Covered:** latest week.

CUMIN SEED: CHINESE

Source: *U. S. Spice Trade.* **Price Frequency:** annually. **Effective Market(s):** New York. **Units of Measure:** cents per lb. **Type of Price:** spot. **Time Period Covered:** latest 3 years.

CUMIN SEED: INDIAN

Source: *Chemical Marketing Reporter.* **Price Frequency:** weekly. **Effective Market(s):** New York. **Units of Measure:** Dollars per lb. **Type of Price:** spot. **Time Period Covered:** latest week.

Source: *Fruit and Tropical Products.* **Price Frequency:** monthly, seasonally. **Effective Market(s):** London. **Units of Measure:** British pounds per tonne. **Type of Price:** month end. **Time Period Covered:** latest 2 years.

Source: *Prices of Selected Asia/Pacific Products.* **Price Frequency:** monthly. **Effective Market(s):** New York, United Kingdom/North European ports. **Units of Measure:** Dollars per lb., dollars per metric ton. **Type of Price:** spot high, spot low. **Time Period Covered:** latest month.

Source: *U. S. Spice Trade.* **Price Frequency:** annually. **Effective Market(s):** New York. **Units of Measure:** cents per lb. **Type of Price:** spot. **Time Period Covered:** latest 3 years.

CUMIN SEED: IRANIAN

Source: *Chemical Marketing Reporter.* **Price Frequency:** weekly. **Effective Market(s):** New York. **Units of Measure:** Dollars per lb. **Type of Price:** spot. **Time Period Covered:** latest week.

CUMIN SEED: PAKISTAN

Source: *U. S. Spice Trade.* **Price Frequency:** annually. **Effective Market(s):** New York. **Units of Measure:** cents per lb. **Type of Price:** spot. **Time Period Covered:** latest 3 years.

CUMIN SEED: TURKISH

Source: *Fruit and Tropical Products.* **Price Frequency:** monthly, seasonally. **Effective Market(s):** London. **Units of Measure:** British pounds per tonne. **Type of Price:** month end. **Time Period Covered:** latest 2 years.

Source: *U. S. Spice Trade.* **Price Frequency:** annually. **Effective Market(s):** New York. **Units of Measure:** cents per lb. **Type of Price:** spot. **Time Period Covered:** latest 3 years.

CUPRIC OXIDE: RED, TYPE 1

Source: *Journal of Commerce and Commercial.* **Price Frequency:** weekly in Wednesday issue. **Units of Measure:** Dollars per lb. **Type of Price:** spot. **Time Period Covered:** latest week.

CUPRIC OXIDE: RED, TYPE 2

Source: *Journal of Commerce and Commercial.* **Price Frequency:** weekly in Wednesday issue. **Units of Measure:** Dollars per lb. **Type of Price:** spot. **Time Period Covered:** latest week.

CUSK (FISH): FILLETS, FRESH

Source: *Seafood Price-Current.* **Price Frequency:** semiweekly. **Effective Market(s):** Mid-Atlantic, New England. **Units of Measure:** Dollars per lb. **Type of Price:** sale by first receiver. **Time Period Covered:** latest day.

CUSK (FISH): WHOLE, FRESH

Source: *Seafood Price-Current.* **Price Frequency:** semiweekly. **Effective Market(s):** Boston, Mid-Atlantic, New Bedford (MA), Portland (ME). **Units of Measure:** Dollars per lb. **Type of Price:** sale by first receiver, auction price. **Time Period Covered:** latest day.

CUTTLE FISH: DRIED, BELOW AVERAGE, HONG KONG

Source: *Prices of Selected Asia/Pacific Products.* **Price Frequency:** monthly. **Effective Market(s):** Hong Kong. **Units of Measure:** Hong Kong dollars per picul. **Type of Price:** wholesale high, wholesale low. **Time Period Covered:** latest month.

CUTTLE FISH: DRIED, MEDIUM, HONG KONG

Source: *Prices of Selected Asia/Pacific Products.* **Price Frequency:** monthly. **Effective Market(s):** Hong Kong. **Units of Measure:** Hong Kong dollars per picul. **Type of Price:** wholesale high, wholesale low. **Time Period Covered:** latest month.

CYANAZINE: LIQUID

Source: *Agricultural Prices Annual Summary.* **Price Frequency:** semiannually. **Effective Market(s):** United States. **Units of Measure:** Dollars per gallon. **Type of Price:** average price paid by farmer. **Time Period Covered:** latest 6 years.

CYANIDE

Source: *Journal of Commerce and Commercial.* **Price Frequency:** weekly in Thursday issue. **Units of Measure:** Dollars per lb. **Type of Price:** spot. **Time Period Covered:** latest week.

CYANIDE: 99% GRANULAR

Source: *Journal of Commerce and Commercial.* **Price Frequency:** weekly in Thursday issue. **Units of Measure:** Dollars per lb. **Type of Price:** spot. **Time Period Covered:** latest week.

CYANIDE FLUOBORATE

Source: *Journal of Commerce and Commercial.* **Price Frequency:** weekly in Thursday issue. **Units of Measure:** Dollars per lb. **Type of Price:** spot. **Time Period Covered:** latest week.

CYANIDE SULFATE: CRYSTAL

Source: *Journal of Commerce and Commercial.* **Price Frequency:** weekly in Thursday issue. **Units of Measure:** Dollars per 100 lbs. **Type of Price:** spot. **Time Period Covered:** latest week.

CYANURIC ACID

Source: *Chemical Marketing Reporter.* **Price Frequency:** weekly. **Effective Market(s):** New York. **Units of Measure:** Dollars per lb. **Type of Price:** spot. **Time Period Covered:** latest week.

CYCLAMEN ALDEHYDE: 50% MINIMUM ALDEHYDE CONTENT

Source: *Chemical Marketing Reporter.* **Price Frequency:** weekly. **Effective Market(s):** New York. **Units of Measure:** Dollars per lb. **Type of Price:** spot. **Time Period Covered:** latest week.

CYCLAMEN ALDEHYDE: 90-92% ALDEHYDE CONTENT

Source: *Chemical Marketing Reporter.* **Price Frequency:** weekly. **Effective Market(s):** New York. **Units of Measure:** Dollars per lb. **Type of Price:** spot. **Time Period Covered:** latest week.

CYCLAMEN ALDEHYDE: 96.5% ALDEHYDE CONTENT

Source: *Chemical Marketing Reporter.* **Price Frequency:** weekly. **Effective Market(s):** New York. **Units of Measure:** Dollars per lb. **Type of Price:** spot. **Time Period Covered:** latest week.

CYCLOHEXANE

Source: *Chemical Marketing Reporter.* **Price Frequency:** weekly. **Effective Market(s):** New York. **Units of Measure:** Dollars per gallon. **Type of Price:** spot. **Time Period Covered:** latest week.

Source: *Cotton and Wool Situation and Outlook Report.* **Price Frequency:** monthly. **Units of Measure:** Dollars per gallon. **Type of Price:** spot. **Time Period Covered:** latest year.

Source: *Journal of Commerce and Commercial.* **Price Frequency:** weekly in Wednesday issue. **Units of Measure:** Dollars per gallon. **Type of Price:** spot. **Time Period Covered:** latest week.

CYCLOHEXANOL: TECHNICAL GRADE

Source: *Chemical Marketing Reporter.* **Price Frequency:** weekly. **Effective Market(s):** New York. **Units of Measure:** Dollars per lb. **Type of Price:** spot. **Time Period Covered:** latest week.

CYCLOHEXANONE: TECHNICAL GRADE

Source: *Chemical Marketing Reporter.* **Price Frequency:** weekly. **Effective Market(s):** New York. **Units of Measure:** Dollars per lb. **Type of Price:** spot. **Time Period Covered:** latest week.

CYCLOHEXYLAMINE: TECHNICAL GRADE

Source: *Chemical Marketing Reporter.* **Price Frequency:** weekly. **Effective Market(s):** New York. **Units of Measure:** Dollars per lb. **Type of Price:** spot. **Time Period Covered:** latest week.

CYPRUS POUND

Source: *The Times.* **Price Frequency:** daily. **Effective Market(s):** London. **Units of Measure:** Cyprus pounds per British pound. **Type of Price:** foreign exchange. **Time Period Covered:** latest day.

2,4-D ACID: TECHNICAL GRADE

Source: *Chemical Marketing Reporter.* **Price Frequency:** weekly. **Effective Market(s):** New York. **Units of Measure:** Dollars per lb. **Type of Price:** spot. **Time Period Covered:** latest week.

2,4-D BUTYL ESTER: TECHNICAL GRADE

Source: *Chemical Marketing Reporter.* **Price Frequency:** weekly. **Effective Market(s):** New York. **Units of Measure:** Dollars per lb. **Type of Price:** spot. **Time Period Covered:** latest week.

2,4-D DIMETHYLAMINE SALT

Source: *Chemical Marketing Reporter.* **Price Frequency:** weekly. **Effective Market(s):** New York. **Units of Measure:** Dollars per gallon. **Type of Price:** spot. **Time Period Covered:** latest week.

2,4-D HERBICIDE: EMULSIFIABLE CONCENTRATE

Source: *Agricultural Prices Annual Summary.* **Price Frequency:** semiannually. **Effective Market(s):** United States. **Units of Measure:** Dollars per 5 gallons. **Type of Price:** paid by farmer. **Time Period Covered:** latest 6 years.

DABS: SEA, FILLETS, FRESH

Source: *HRI-Buyer's Guide.* **Price Frequency:** weekly. **Effective Market(s):** New York. **Units of Measure:** Dollars per lb. **Type of Price:** dealer. **Time Period Covered:** latest week.

DABS: SEA, FILLETS, FRESH, CANADIAN

Source: *Seafood Price-Current.* **Price Frequency:** semiweekly. **Effective Market(s):** Mid-Atlantic, New England. **Units of Measure:** Dollars per lb. **Type of Price:** sale by first receiver. **Time Period Covered:** latest day.

DABS: SEA, FILLETS, FRESH, DOMESTIC

Source: *Seafood Price-Current.* **Price Frequency:** semi-weekly. **Effective Market(s):** Mid-Atlantic, New England. **Units of Measure:** Dollars per lb. **Type of Price:** sale by first receiver. **Time Period Covered:** latest day.

DABS: SEA, WHOLE, FRESH

Source: *Seafood Price-Current.* **Price Frequency:** semi-weekly. **Effective Market(s):** Boston, Mid-Atlantic, New Bedford (MA), Portland (ME). **Units of Measure:** Dollars per lb. **Type of Price:** sale by first receiver, auction price. **Time Period Covered:** latest day.

DABS: WHOLE, SKINNED, TRIMMED, FRESH

Source: *Seafood Price-Current.* **Price Frequency:** semi-weekly. **Effective Market(s):** West Coast. **Units of Measure:** Dollars per lb. **Type of Price:** sale by first receiver. **Time Period Covered:** latest day.

DAFFODILS

Source: *New Zealand Farmer.* **Price Frequency:** weekly, seasonally. **Effective Market(s):** New Zealand. **Units of Measure:** New Zealand dollars per bunch. **Time Period Covered:** latest week.

DAIKON

Source: *Lancaster Farming.* **Price Frequency:** weekly, seasonally. **Effective Market(s):** Pennsylvania. **Units of Measure:** Dollars per crate. **Type of Price:** market. **Time Period Covered:** latest week.

DAIRY CONCENTRATE: 32% PROTEIN

Source: *Agricultural Prices Annual Summary.* **Price Frequency:** quarterly. **Effective Market(s):** 10 domestic markets, United States. **Units of Measure:** Dollars per ton. **Type of Price:** average paid by farmer. **Time Period Covered:** latest year, for US monthly for latest 6 years.

DAIRY FEED

Source: *Agricultural Prices.* **Price Frequency:** quarterly. **Effective Market(s):** United States. **Units of Measure:** Dollars per ton. **Type of Price:** paid by farmer. **Time Period Covered:** latest 2 quarters, year ago.

Source: *Agricultural Prices.* **Price Frequency:** monthly. **Effective Market(s):** 10 domestic markets, United States. **Units of Measure:** Dollars per ton. **Type of Price:** paid by farmer. **Time Period Covered:** latest month.

DAIRY FEED: 14% PROTEIN

Source: *Agricultural Prices Annual Summary.* **Price Frequency:** quarterly. **Effective Market(s):** 10 domestic markets, United States. **Units of Measure:** Dollars per ton. **Type of Price:** average paid by farmer. **Time Period Covered:** latest year, for US monthly for latest 6 years.

DAIRY FEED: 16% PROTEIN

Source: *Agricultural Prices Annual Summary.* **Price Frequency:** quarterly. **Effective Market(s):** 10 domestic markets, United States. **Units of Measure:** Dollars per ton. **Type of Price:** average paid by farmer. **Time Period Covered:** latest year, for US monthly for latest 6 years.

Source: *Feed Situation and Outlook Report.* **Price Frequency:** quarterly, annually. **Effective Market(s):** United States. **Units of Measure:** Dollars per ton. **Type of Price:** paid by farmer. **Time Period Covered:** latest 3 quarters, latest year.

DAIRY FEED: 18% PROTEIN

Source: *Agricultural Prices Annual Summary.* **Price Frequency:** quarterly. **Effective Market(s):** 10 domestic markets, United States. **Units of Measure:** Dollars per ton. **Type of Price:** average paid by farmer. **Time Period Covered:** latest year, for US monthly for latest 6 years.

DAIRY FEED: 20% PROTEIN

Source: *Agricultural Prices Annual Summary.* **Price Frequency:** quarterly. **Effective Market(s):** 10 domestic markets, United States. **Units of Measure:** Dollars per ton. **Type of Price:** average paid by farmer. **Time Period Covered:** latest year, for US monthly for latest 6 years.

DAIRY PRODUCTS

Source: *Illinois Farm Report.* **Price Frequency:** monthly. **Effective Market(s):** Illinois. **Units of Measure:** index. **Type of Price:** index of prices received by farmers. **Time Period Covered:** latest 2 months, year ago.

DAP: GENERAL PURPOSE

Source: *Plastics Technology.* **Price Frequency:** monthly. **Units of Measure:** cents per lb., cents per cubic inch. **Type of Price:** bulk list, market. **Time Period Covered:** latest month.

DATES

Source: *Agricultural Prices Annual Summary.* **Price Frequency:** annually. **Effective Market(s):** California, Hawaii. **Units of Measure:** Dollars per ton. **Type of Price:** average price received by farmer. **Time Period Covered:** latest 6 years.

DDVP

see Dimethyl Dichlorovinyl Phosphate.

DECANTERS: CERAMIC

Source: *Colorado Beverage Analyst.* **Price Frequency:** monthly. **Effective Market(s):** Colorado. **Units of Measure:** Dollars per case. **Type of Price:** wholesale by brand. **Time Period Covered:** latest month.

Source: *Illinois Beverage Journal.* **Price Frequency:** monthly. **Effective Market(s):** Illinois. **Units of Measure:** Dollars per case. **Type of Price:** wholesale by brand. **Time Period Covered:** latest month.

DECYL ALCOHOL: MIXED ISOMERS

Source: *Chemical Marketing Reporter.* **Price Frequency:** weekly. **Effective Market(s):** New York. **Units of Measure:** Dollars per lb. **Type of Price:** spot. **Time Period Covered:** latest week.

DECYL ALCOHOL: PERFUME GRADE

Source: *Chemical Marketing Reporter.* **Price Frequency:** weekly. **Effective Market(s):** New York. **Units of Measure:** Dollars per ton. **Type of Price:** spot. **Time Period Covered:** latest week.

DEHP

see Di-2-ethylhexyl Phthalate.

DENATURED ALCOHOL

see also Alcohol: Denatured.

DENATURED ALCOHOL: ETHYL, SD2B

Source: *Chemical Marketing Reporter.* **Price Frequency:** weekly. **Effective Market(s):** East. **Units of Measure:** Dollars per gallon. **Type of Price:** spot. **Time Period Covered:** latest week.

DENATURED ALCOHOL: ETHYL, SD3A

Source: *Chemical Marketing Reporter.* **Price Frequency:** weekly. **Effective Market(s):** East. **Units of Measure:** Dollars per gallon. **Type of Price:** spot. **Time Period Covered:** latest week.

DENATURED ALCOHOL: ETHYL, SD23A

Source: *Chemical Marketing Reporter.* **Price Frequency:** weekly. **Effective Market(s):** East. **Units of Measure:** Dollars per gallon. **Type of Price:** spot. **Time Period Covered:** latest week.

DENATURED ALCOHOL: ETHYL, SD23H

Source: *Chemical Marketing Reporter.* **Price Frequency:** weekly. **Effective Market(s):** East. **Units of Measure:** Dollars per gallon. **Type of Price:** spot. **Time Period Covered:** latest week.

DENATURED ALCOHOL: ETHYL, SD29

Source: *Chemical Marketing Reporter.* **Price Frequency:** weekly. **Effective Market(s):** East. **Units of Measure:** Dollars per gallon. **Type of Price:** spot. **Time Period Covered:** latest week.

DENATURED ALCOHOL: ETHYL, SD30

Source: *Chemical Marketing Reporter.* **Price Frequency:** weekly. **Effective Market(s):** East. **Units of Measure:** Dollars per gallon. **Type of Price:** spot. **Time Period Covered:** latest week.

DENATURED ALCOHOL: ETHYL, SD35A

Source: *Chemical Marketing Reporter.* **Price Frequency:** weekly. **Effective Market(s):** East. **Units of Measure:** Dollars per gallon. **Type of Price:** spot. **Time Period Covered:** latest week.

DENATURED ALCOHOL: ETHYL, SD40, BRUCINE FORMULA

Source: *Chemical Marketing Reporter.* **Price Frequency:** weekly. **Effective Market(s):** East. **Units of Measure:** Dollars per gallon. **Type of Price:** spot. **Time Period Covered:** latest week.

DENATURED ALCOHOL: ETHYL, SD40B, OPTIONAL FORMULA

Source: *Chemical Marketing Reporter.* **Price Frequency:** weekly. **Effective Market(s):** East. **Units of Measure:** Dollars per gallon. **Type of Price:** spot. **Time Period Covered:** latest week.

DENIM FABRIC: INDIGO

Source: *JTN: The International Textile Magazine.* **Price Frequency:** monthly. **Effective Market(s):** Japan. **Units of Measure:** Japanese yen per yard. **Type of Price:** spot. **Time Period Covered:** latest month.

DENMARK KRONERS

Source: *Asian Wall Street Journal.* **Price Frequency:** daily. **Effective Market(s):** United States. **Units of Measure:** Danish krone per ECU. **Type of Price:** foreign exchange. **Time Period Covered:** latest 2 days.

Source: *Barron's.* **Price Frequency:** weekly. **Effective Market(s):** New York. **Units of Measure:** Danish kroner per United States dollar. **Type of Price:** foreign exchange. **Time Period Covered:** latest 2 weeks.

Source: *New York Times.* **Price Frequency:** daily. **Effective Market(s):** New York. **Units of Measure:** Danish krone per United States dollar. **Type of Price:** foreign exchange. **Time Period Covered:** latest 2 days.

Source: *Timber Bulletin.* **Price Frequency:** monthly, annually. **Units of Measure:** Danish kroner per United States dollar. **Type of Price:** foreign exchange. **Time Period Covered:** latest 2 years.

DESOXYEPHEDRINE HYDROCHLORIDE

see Methamphetamine Hydrochloride.

DETERGENT ALKYLATE: STRAIGHT CHAIN DODECYLBENZENE

Source: *Chemical Marketing Reporter.* **Price Frequency:** weekly. **Effective Market(s):** New York. **Units of Measure:** Dollars per lb. **Type of Price:** spot. **Time Period Covered:** latest week.

DEUTSCHE MARKS

see West Germany Marks.

DEXTRINE: CANARY

Source: *Journal of Commerce and Commercial.* **Price Frequency:** weekly in Thursday issue. **Units of Measure:** Dollars per 100 lbs. **Type of Price:** spot. **Time Period Covered:** latest week.

DEXTRINE: CORN, CANARY DARK

Source: *Chemical Marketing Reporter.* **Price Frequency:** weekly. **Effective Market(s):** New York. **Units of Measure:** Dollars per 100 lbs. **Type of Price:** spot. **Time Period Covered:** latest week.

DEXTRINE: CORN, WHITE

Source: *Chemical Marketing Reporter.* **Price Frequency:** weekly. **Effective Market(s):** New York. **Units of Measure:** Dollars per 100 lbs. **Type of Price:** spot. **Time Period Covered:** latest week.

DEXTRINE: TUMERIC ALLEPPY

Source: *Journal of Commerce and Commercial.* **Price Frequency:** weekly in Thursday issue. **Units of Measure:** Dollars per 100 lbs. **Type of Price:** spot. **Time Period Covered:** latest week.

DEXTRINE: WHITE

Source: *Journal of Commerce and Commercial.* **Price Frequency:** weekly in Thursday issue. **Units of Measure:** Dollars per lb. **Type of Price:** spot. **Time Period Covered:** latest week.

DEXTROSE

Source: *Milling & Baking News.* **Price Frequency:** weekly. **Effective Market(s):** East, Midwest, West. **Units of Measure:** Dollars per lb. **Time Period Covered:** latest week.

DEXTROSE: ANHYDROUS, COMMERCIAL

Source: *Chemical Marketing Reporter.* **Price Frequency:** weekly. **Effective Market(s):** New York. **Units of Measure:** Dollars per 100 lbs. **Type of Price:** spot. **Time Period Covered:** latest week.

DEXTROSE: HYDRATED, COMMERCIAL

Source: *Chemical Marketing Reporter.* **Price Frequency:** weekly. **Effective Market(s):** New York, Western Zone. **Units of Measure:** Dollars per 100 lbs. **Type of Price:** spot. **Time Period Covered:** latest week.

DEXTROSE: SPECIAL, USP

Source: *Chemical Marketing Reporter.* **Price Frequency:** weekly. **Effective Market(s):** New York. **Units of Measure:** Dollars per 100 lbs. **Type of Price:** spot. **Time Period Covered:** latest week.

2,4-DI-TERT-AMYLPHENOL: MINIMUM 95.5%

Source: *Chemical Marketing Reporter.* **Price Frequency:** weekly. **Effective Market(s):** New York. **Units of Measure:** Dollars per lb. **Type of Price:** spot. **Time Period Covered:** latest week.

2,6-DI-TERT-BUTYL-P-CRESOL

see Butylated Hydroxytoluene.

DI-2-ETHYLHEXYL ADIPATE

see Dioctyl Adipate.

DI-2-ETHYLHEXYL AZELATE

see Dioctyl Azelate.

DI-2-ETHYLHEXYL PHTHALATE

see also Dioctyl Phthalate.

Source: *Modern Plastics.* **Price Frequency:** quarterly in February, May, August, November issues. **Units of Measure:** Dollars per lb. **Type of Price:** list. **Time Period Covered:** latest 4 quarters.

DI-ISO-OCTYL AZELATE

Source: *Chemical Marketing Reporter.* **Price Frequency:** weekly. **Effective Market(s):** East. **Units of Measure:** Dollars per lb. **Type of Price:** spot. **Time Period Covered:** latest week.

DI-ISO-OCTYL PHTHALATE

Source: *Chemical Marketing Reporter.* **Price Frequency:** weekly. **Effective Market(s):** New York. **Units of Measure:** Dollars per lb. **Type of Price:** spot. **Time Period Covered:** latest week.

DI-ISOBUTYL KETONE

Source: *Chemical Marketing Reporter.* **Price Frequency:** weekly. **Effective Market(s):** New York. **Units of Measure:** Dollars per lb. **Type of Price:** spot. **Time Period Covered:** latest week.

DI-ISOBUTYL PHTHALATE

Source: *Chemical Marketing Reporter.* **Price Frequency:** weekly. **Effective Market(s):** East. **Units of Measure:** Dollars per lb. **Type of Price:** spot. **Time Period Covered:** latest week.

DI-ISOBUTYLENE

Source: *Chemical Marketing Reporter.* **Price Frequency:** weekly. **Effective Market(s):** Houston. **Units of Measure:** Dollars per lb. **Type of Price:** spot. **Time Period Covered:** latest week.

DI-ISODECYL PHTHALATE

Source: *Chemical Marketing Reporter.* **Price Frequency:** weekly. **Effective Market(s):** New York. **Units of Measure:** Dollars per lb. **Type of Price:** spot. **Time Period Covered:** latest week.

DI-ISONONYL PHTHALATE

Source: *Chemical Marketing Reporter.* **Price Frequency:** weekly. **Effective Market(s):** New York. **Units of Measure:** Dollars per lb. **Type of Price:** spot. **Time Period Covered:** latest week.

DI-ISOPROPANOLAMINE

Source: *Chemical Marketing Reporter.* **Price Frequency:** weekly. **Effective Market(s):** New York. **Units of Measure:** Dollars per lb. **Type of Price:** spot. **Time Period Covered:** latest week.

DI-ISOPROPYLAMINE

Source: *Chemical Marketing Reporter.* **Price Frequency:** weekly. **Effective Market(s):** New York. **Units of Measure:** Dollars per lb. **Type of Price:** spot. **Time Period Covered:** latest week.

DI-O-TOLYLGUANIDINE: POWDERED

Source: *Chemical Marketing Reporter.* **Price Frequency:** weekly. **Effective Market(s):** New York. **Units of Measure:** Dollars per lb. **Type of Price:** spot. **Time Period Covered:** latest week.

DI-O-TOLYLTHIOUREA: TECHNICAL GRADE

Source: *Chemical Marketing Reporter.* **Price Frequency:** weekly. **Effective Market(s):** New York. **Units of Measure:** Dollars per lb. **Type of Price:** spot. **Time Period Covered:** latest week.

DIACETONE ALCOHOL: ACETONE FREE

Source: *Chemical Marketing Reporter.* **Price Frequency:** weekly. **Effective Market(s):** New York. **Units of Measure:** Dollars per lb. **Type of Price:** spot. **Time Period Covered:** latest week.

DIACETYL: FLAVOR GRADE

Source: *Chemical Marketing Reporter.* **Price Frequency:** weekly. **Effective Market(s):** New York. **Units of Measure:** Dollars per lb. **Type of Price:** spot. **Time Period Covered:** latest week.

DIAMMONIUM PHOSPHATE

Source: *Commodity Trade and Price Trends.* **Price Frequency:** annually. **Effective Market(s):** Gulf ports. **Units of Measure:** Dollars per metric ton, 1980 constant dollars per metric ton. **Time Period Covered:** latest 20 years.

DIAMMONIUM PHOSPHATE: FEED GRADE, 18% NITROGEN AND 20% PHOSPHATE

Source: *Chemical Marketing Reporter.* **Price Frequency:** weekly. **Effective Market(s):** Florida. **Units of Measure:** Dollars per ton. **Type of Price:** spot. **Time Period Covered:** latest week.

DIAMMONIUM PHOSPHATE: FERTILIZER GRADE

Source: *Journal of Commerce and Commercial.* **Price Frequency:** weekly in Thursday issue. **Effective Market(s):** Florida. **Units of Measure:** Dollars per ton. **Type of Price:** spot. **Time Period Covered:** latest week.

DIAMMONIUM PHOSPHATE: FERTILIZER GRADE, MINIMUM 18% NITROGEN AND 46% PHOSPHATE

Source: *Chemical Marketing Reporter.* **Price Frequency:** weekly. **Effective Market(s):** Florida. **Units of Measure:** Dollars per ton. **Type of Price:** spot. **Time Period Covered:** latest week.

DIAMMONIUM PHOSPHATE: FOOD GRADE

Source: *Chemical Marketing Reporter.* **Price Frequency:** weekly. **Effective Market(s):** New York. **Units of Measure:** Dollars per 100 lbs. **Type of Price:** spot. **Time Period Covered:** latest week.

DIAMMONIUM PHOSPHATE: TECHNICAL GRADE

Source: *Chemical Marketing Reporter.* **Price Frequency:** weekly. **Effective Market(s):** New York. **Units of Measure:** Dollars per 100 lbs. **Type of Price:** spot. **Time Period Covered:** latest week.

O-DIANISIDINE DIHYDROCHLORIDE: 100% MW 244

Source: *Chemical Marketing Reporter.* **Price Frequency:** weekly. **Effective Market(s):** New York. **Units of Measure:** Dollars per lb. **Type of Price:** spot. **Time Period Covered:** latest week.

DIARYLIDE YELLOW: OT, YELLOW 14

Source: *Chemical Marketing Reporter.* **Price Frequency:** weekly. **Effective Market(s):** New York. **Units of Measure:** Dollars per lb. **Type of Price:** spot. **Time Period Covered:** latest week.

DIATOMITE: CALCINED FILTER AIDS, UNITED STATES

Source: *Industrial Minerals.* **Price Frequency:** monthly. **Effective Market(s):** United Kingdom. **Units of Measure:** British pounds per mteric tonne. **Type of Price:** producer & dealer. **Time Period Covered:** latest month.

DIATOMITE: FLUX-CALCINED FILTER AIDS, UNITED STATES

Source: *Industrial Minerals.* **Price Frequency:** monthly. **Effective Market(s):** United Kingdom. **Units of Measure:** Birtish pounds per metric tonne. **Type of Price:** producer & dealer. **Time Period Covered:** latest month.

DIBUTYL MALEATE

Source: *Chemical Marketing Reporter.* **Price Frequency:** weekly. **Effective Market(s):** New York. **Units of Measure:** Dollars per lb. **Type of Price:** spot. **Time Period Covered:** latest week.

DIBUTYL PHTHALATE

Source: *Chemical Marketing Reporter.* **Price Frequency:** weekly. **Effective Market(s):** New York. **Units of Measure:** Dollars per lb. **Type of Price:** spot. **Time Period Covered:** latest week.

DIBUTYL SEBACATE

Source: *Chemical Marketing Reporter.* **Price Frequency:** weekly. **Effective Market(s):** New York. **Units of Measure:** Dollars per lb. **Type of Price:** spot. **Time Period Covered:** latest week.

DIBUTYLAMINE

Source: *Chemical Marketing Reporter.* **Price Frequency:** weekly. **Effective Market(s):** New York. **Units of Measure:** Dollars per lb. **Type of Price:** spot. **Time Period Covered:** latest week.

2,6-DICHLORO-4-NITROANILINE

Source: *Chemical Marketing Reporter.* **Price Frequency:** weekly. **Effective Market(s):** New York. **Units of Measure:** Dollars per lb. **Type of Price:** spot. **Time Period Covered:** latest week.

2,5-DICHLOROANILINE: FLAKE

Source: *Chemical Marketing Reporter.* **Price Frequency:** weekly. **Effective Market(s):** New York. **Units of Measure:** Dollars per lb. **Type of Price:** spot. **Time Period Covered:** latest week.

2,5-DICHLOROANILINE: FUSED

Source: *Chemical Marketing Reporter.* **Price Frequency:** weekly. **Effective Market(s):** New York. **Units of Measure:** Dollars per lb. **Type of Price:** spot. **Time Period Covered:** latest week.

3,4-DICHLOROANILINE: TECHNICAL GRADE, 88%, SOLID

Source: *Chemical Marketing Reporter.* **Price Frequency:** weekly. **Effective Market(s):** New York. **Units of Measure:** Dollars per lb. **Type of Price:** spot. **Time Period Covered:** latest week.

O-DICHLOROBENZENE: 80%

Source: *Journal of Commerce and Commercial.* **Price Frequency:** weekly in Wednesday issue. **Units of Measure:** Dollars per lb. **Type of Price:** spot. **Time Period Covered:** latest week.

O-DICHLOROBENZENE: REFINED, 98%

Source: *Chemical Marketing Reporter.* **Price Frequency:** weekly. **Effective Market(s):** New York. **Units of Measure:** Dollars per lb. **Type of Price:** spot. **Time Period Covered:** latest week.

O-DICHLOROBENZENE: TECHNICAL GRADE, 80%, SOLID

Source: *Chemical Marketing Reporter.* **Price Frequency:** weekly. **Effective Market(s):** New York. **Units of Measure:** Dollars per lb. **Type of Price:** spot. **Time Period Covered:** latest week.

P-DICHLOROBENZENE: DRY

Source: *Journal of Commerce and Commercial.* **Price Frequency:** weekly in Wednesday issue. **Units of Measure:** Dollars per lb. **Type of Price:** spot. **Time Period Covered:** latest week.

P-DICHLOROBENZENE: GRADED

Source: *Chemical Marketing Reporter.* **Price Frequency:** weekly. **Effective Market(s):** New York. **Units of Measure:** Dollars per lb. **Type of Price:** spot. **Time Period Covered:** latest week.

P-DICHLOROBENZENE: MOLTEN LIQUID

Source: *Journal of Commerce and Commercial.* **Price Frequency:** weekly in Wednesday issue. **Units of Measure:** Dollars per lb. **Type of Price:** spot. **Time Period Covered:** latest week.

DICHLOROPHENOXYACETIC ACID

see 2,4-D Acid.

DICYCLOHEXYL PHTHALATE

Source: *Chemical Marketing Reporter.* **Price Frequency:** weekly. **Effective Market(s):** New York. **Units of Measure:** Dollars per lb. **Type of Price:** spot. **Time Period Covered:** latest week.

DICYCLOHEXYLAMINE

Source: *Chemical Marketing Reporter.* **Price Frequency:** weekly. **Effective Market(s):** New York. **Units of Measure:** Dollars per lb. **Type of Price:** spot. **Time Period Covered:** latest week.

DICYCLOPENTADIENE: HIGH PURITY, 97-98%

Source: *Chemical Marketing Reporter.* **Price Frequency:** weekly. **Effective Market(s):** New York. **Units of Measure:** Dollars per lb. **Type of Price:** spot. **Time Period Covered:** latest week.

DIESEL FUEL

see also Fuel Oil, Gasoline, Oil, Petroleum.

Source: *Agricultural Prices Annual Summary.* **Price Frequency:** quarterly. **Effective Market(s):** 10 domestic markets, United States. **Units of Measure:** Dollars per gallon. **Type of Price:** average paid by farmer. **Time Period Covered:** latest year, for US monthly for latest 6 years.

Source: *Energy Pricing News Refined Fuel Report.* **Price Frequency:** semimonthly. **Effective Market(s):** 10 Canadian markets. **Units of Measure:** Canadian cents per liter. **Type of Price:** contract, delivered, rack, retail. **Time Period Covered:** latest week.

Source: *Oil Buyers' Guide.* **Price Frequency:** weekly. **Effective Market(s):** 6 Canadian markets. **Units of Measure:** Canadian cents per liter. **Type of Price:** rack. **Time Period Covered:** latest week.

Source: *Oil Buyers' Guide.* **Price Frequency:** weekly. **Effective Market(s):** 16 Canadian markets. **Units of Measure:** Canadian cents per liter. **Type of Price:** delivery for industrial accounts, rack. **Time Period Covered:** latest week.

Source: *Oil Buyers' Guide.* **Price Frequency:** daily. **Effective Market(s):** Los Angeles, San Francisco, Seattle/Portland. **Units of Measure:** cents per gallon. **Type of Price:** spot. **Time Period Covered:** latest week.

DIESEL FUEL: AUTOMOTIVE

Source: *Energy Prices and Taxes.* **Price Frequency:** quarterly, annually. **Effective Market(s):** 28 international markets. **Units of Measure:** national currency per litre, national currency per ton oil equivalent. **Time Period Covered:** varies.

Source: *Energy Prices and Taxes.* **Price Frequency:** annually. **Effective Market(s):** 25 international markets. **Units of Measure:** Dollars per litre, dollars per ton oil equivalent. **Time Period Covered:** latest 8 years.

DIETHANOLAMINE

Source: *Chemical Marketing Reporter.* **Price Frequency:** weekly. **Effective Market(s):** New York. **Units of Measure:** Dollars per lb. **Type of Price:** spot. **Time Period Covered:** latest week.

DIETHANOLAMINE LAURYL SULFATE

Source: *Chemical Marketing Reporter.* **Price Frequency:** weekly. **Effective Market(s):** New York. **Units of Measure:** Dollars per lb. **Type of Price:** spot. **Time Period Covered:** latest week.

DIETHYL BARBITURIC ACID

see Barbital.

DIETHYL CARBONATE

Source: *Chemical Marketing Reporter.* **Price Frequency:** weekly. **Effective Market(s):** New York. **Units of Measure:** Dollars per lb. **Type of Price:** spot. **Time Period Covered:** latest week.

DIETHYL ETHANOLAMINE: CHEMICALLY PURE

Source: *Chemical Marketing Reporter.* **Price Frequency:** weekly. **Effective Market(s):** New York. **Units of Measure:** Dollars per lb. **Type of Price:** spot. **Time Period Covered:** latest week.

DIETHYL ETHANOLAMINE: TECHNICAL GRADE

Source: *Chemical Marketing Reporter.* **Price Frequency:** weekly. **Effective Market(s):** New York. **Units of Measure:** Dollars per lb. **Type of Price:** spot. **Time Period Covered:** latest week.

DIETHYL OXALATE

Source: *Chemical Marketing Reporter.* **Price Frequency:** weekly. **Effective Market(s):** New York. **Units of Measure:** Dollars per lb. **Type of Price:** spot. **Time Period Covered:** latest week.

DIETHYL PHTHALATE

Source: *Chemical Marketing Reporter.* **Price Frequency:** weekly. **Effective Market(s):** New York. **Units of Measure:** Dollars per lb. **Type of Price:** spot. **Time Period Covered:** latest week.

DIETHYL PHTHALATE: ODORLESS COSMETIC GRADES

Source: *Chemical Marketing Reporter.* **Price Frequency:** weekly. **Effective Market(s):** New York. **Units of Measure:** Dollars per lb. **Type of Price:** spot. **Time Period Covered:** latest week.

DIETHYL SULFATE

Source: *Chemical Marketing Reporter.* **Price Frequency:** weekly. **Effective Market(s):** East. **Units of Measure:** Dollars per lb. **Type of Price:** spot. **Time Period Covered:** latest week.

DIETHYL THIOUREA

Source: *Chemical Marketing Reporter.* **Price Frequency:** weekly. **Effective Market(s):** New York. **Units of Measure:** Dollars per lb. **Type of Price:** spot. **Time Period Covered:** latest week.

DIETHYL TOLUAMIDE: META ISOMER

Source: *Chemical Marketing Reporter.* **Price Frequency:** weekly. **Effective Market(s):** New York. **Units of Measure:** Dollars per lb. **Type of Price:** spot. **Time Period Covered:** latest week.

N-N-DIETHYL-M-TOLUIDINE: TECHNICAL GRADE, LIQUID

Source: *Chemical Marketing Reporter.* **Price Frequency:** weekly. **Effective Market(s):** New York. **Units of Measure:** Dollars per lb. **Type of Price:** spot. **Time Period Covered:** latest week.

DIETHYLAMINE

Source: *Chemical Marketing Reporter.* **Price Frequency:** weekly. **Effective Market(s):** New York. **Units of Measure:** Dollars per lb. **Type of Price:** spot. **Time Period Covered:** latest week.

N,N-DIETHYLANILINE

Source: *Chemical Marketing Reporter.* **Price Frequency:** weekly. **Effective Market(s):** New York. **Units of Measure:** Dollars per lb. **Type of Price:** spot. **Time Period Covered:** latest week.

DIETHYLANILINE

Source: *Journal of Commerce and Commercial.* **Price Frequency:** weekly in Wednesday issue. **Units of Measure:** Dollars per lb. **Type of Price:** spot. **Time Period Covered:** latest week.

DIETHYLBENZENE

Source: *Chemical Marketing Reporter.* **Price Frequency:** weekly. **Effective Market(s):** New York. **Units of Measure:** Dollars per lb. **Type of Price:** spot. **Time Period Covered:** latest week.

DIETHYLENE GLYCOL

Source: *Chemical Marketing Reporter.* **Price Frequency:** weekly. **Effective Market(s):** East. **Units of Measure:** Dollars per lb. **Type of Price:** spot. **Time Period Covered:** latest week.

DIETHYLENE GLYCOL MONOBUTYL ETHER

Source: *Chemical Marketing Reporter.* **Price Frequency:** weekly. **Effective Market(s):** East. **Units of Measure:** Dollars per lb. **Type of Price:** spot. **Time Period Covered:** latest week.

DIETHYLENE GLYCOL MONOBUTYL ETHER ACETATE

Source: *Chemical Marketing Reporter.* **Price Frequency:** weekly. **Effective Market(s):** East. **Units of Measure:** Dollars per lb. **Type of Price:** spot. **Time Period Covered:** latest week.

DIETHYLENE GLYCOL MONOETHYL ETHER

Source: *Chemical Marketing Reporter.* **Price Frequency:** weekly. **Effective Market(s):** East. **Units of Measure:** Dollars per lb. **Type of Price:** spot. **Time Period Covered:** latest week.

DIETHYLENE GLYCOL MONOETHYL ETHER ACETATE

Source: *Chemical Marketing Reporter.* **Price Frequency:** weekly. **Effective Market(s):** East. **Units of Measure:** Dollars per lb. **Type of Price:** spot. **Time Period Covered:** latest week.

DIETHYLENE GLYCOL MONOMETHYL ETHER

Source: *Chemical Marketing Reporter.* **Price Frequency:** weekly. **Effective Market(s):** New York. **Units of Measure:** Dollars per lb. **Type of Price:** spot. **Time Period Covered:** latest week.

DIETHYLENETRIAMINE

Source: *Chemical Marketing Reporter.* **Price Frequency:** weekly. **Effective Market(s):** New York. **Units of Measure:** Dollars per lb. **Type of Price:** spot. **Time Period Covered:** latest week.

DIETHYLENETRIAMINE PENTAACETIC ACID: PENTASODIUM SALT SOLUTION

Source: *Chemical Marketing Reporter.* **Price Frequency:** weekly. **Effective Market(s):** New York. **Units of Measure:** Dollars per lb. **Type of Price:** spot. **Time Period Covered:** latest week.

DIGITOXIN: USP, IMPORTED

Source: *Chemical Marketing Reporter.* **Price Frequency:** weekly. **Effective Market(s):** New York. **Units of Measure:** Dollars per gram. **Type of Price:** spot. **Time Period Covered:** latest week.

DIGLYCOL LAURATE

Source: *Chemical Marketing Reporter.* **Price Frequency:** weekly. **Effective Market(s):** New York. **Units of Measure:** Dollars per lb. **Type of Price:** spot. **Time Period Covered:** latest week.

DIGLYCOL STEARATE

Source: *Chemical Marketing Reporter.* **Price Frequency:** weekly. **Effective Market(s):** New York. **Units of Measure:** Dollars per lb. **Type of Price:** spot. **Time Period Covered:** latest week.

DIHYDRAZINE SULFATE

Source: *Chemical Marketing Reporter.* **Price Frequency:** weekly. **Effective Market(s):** New York. **Units of Measure:** Dollars per lb. **Type of Price:** spot. **Time Period Covered:** latest week.

DIHYDROXYACETONE

Source: *Chemical Marketing Reporter.* **Price Frequency:** weekly. **Effective Market(s):** New York. **Units of Measure:** Dollars per kilo. **Type of Price:** spot. **Time Period Covered:** latest week.

DILAURYL 3,3-THIODIPROPIONATE

Source: *Chemical Marketing Reporter.* **Price Frequency:** weekly. **Effective Market(s):** New York. **Units of Measure:** Dollars per lb. **Type of Price:** spot. **Time Period Covered:** latest week.

DILL OIL: USP

Source: *Chemical Marketing Reporter.* **Price Frequency:** weekly. **Effective Market(s):** New York. **Units of Measure:** Dollars per lb. **Type of Price:** spot. **Time Period Covered:** latest week.

DILL SEED: DOMESTIC

Source: *U. S. Spice Trade.* **Price Frequency:** annually. **Effective Market(s):** New York. **Units of Measure:** cents per lb. **Type of Price:** spot. **Time Period Covered:** latest 3 years.

DILL SEED: INDIAN DEWHISKERED

Source: *U. S. Spice Trade.* **Price Frequency:** annually. **Effective Market(s):** New York. **Units of Measure:** cents per lb. **Type of Price:** spot. **Time Period Covered:** latest 3 years.

DIMETHYL ANTHRANILATE

Source: *Chemical Marketing Reporter.* **Price Frequency:** weekly. **Effective Market(s):** New York. **Units of Measure:** Dollars per lb. **Type of Price:** spot. **Time Period Covered:** latest week.

DIMETHYL BENZYL CARBINYL ACETATE

Source: *Chemical Marketing Reporter.* **Price Frequency:** weekly. **Effective Market(s):** New York. **Units of Measure:** Dollars per lb. **Type of Price:** spot. **Time Period Covered:** latest week.

DIMETHYL CARBONATE

Source: *Chemical Marketing Reporter.* **Price Frequency:** weekly. **Effective Market(s):** New York. **Units of Measure:** Dollars per lb. **Type of Price:** spot. **Time Period Covered:** latest week.

DIMETHYL DICHLOROVINYL PHOSPHATE

Source: *Chemical Marketing Reporter.* **Price Frequency:** weekly. **Effective Market(s):** New York. **Units of Measure:** Dollars per lb. **Type of Price:** spot. **Time Period Covered:** latest week.

DIMETHYL ETHANOLAMINE

Source: *Chemical Marketing Reporter.* **Price Frequency:** weekly. **Effective Market(s):** East. **Units of Measure:** Dollars per lb. **Type of Price:** spot. **Time Period Covered:** latest week.

DIMETHYL ETHER: AEROSOL GRADE

Source: *Chemical Marketing Reporter.* **Price Frequency:** weekly. **Effective Market(s):** New York. **Units of Measure:** Dollars per lb. **Type of Price:** spot. **Time Period Covered:** latest week.

DIMETHYL PHTHALATE

Source: *Chemical Marketing Reporter.* **Price Frequency:** weekly. **Effective Market(s):** New York. **Units of Measure:** Dollars per lb. **Type of Price:** spot. **Time Period Covered:** latest week.

DIMETHYL SEBACATE

Source: *Chemical Marketing Reporter.* **Price Frequency:** weekly. **Effective Market(s):** New York. **Units of Measure:** Dollars per lb. **Type of Price:** spot. **Time Period Covered:** latest week.

DIMETHYL SULFATE

Source: *Chemical Marketing Reporter.* **Price Frequency:** weekly. **Effective Market(s):** New York. **Units of Measure:** Dollars per lb. **Type of Price:** spot. **Time Period Covered:** latest week.

DIMETHYL SULFIDE

Source: *Chemical Marketing Reporter.* **Price Frequency:** weekly. **Effective Market(s):** New York. **Units of Measure:** Dollars per lb. **Type of Price:** spot. **Time Period Covered:** latest week.

DIMETHYL SULFOXIDE

Source: *Chemical Marketing Reporter.* **Price Frequency:** weekly. **Effective Market(s):** New York. **Units of Measure:** Dollars per lb. **Type of Price:** spot. **Time Period Covered:** latest week.

DIMETHYLACETAMIDE

Source: *Chemical Marketing Reporter.* **Price Frequency:** weekly. **Effective Market(s):** New York. **Units of Measure:** Dollars per lb. **Type of Price:** spot. **Time Period Covered:** latest week.

DIMETHYLAMINE: 25% SOLUTION

Source: *Chemical Marketing Reporter.* **Price Frequency:** weekly. **Effective Market(s):** New York. **Units of Measure:** Dollars per lb. **Type of Price:** spot. **Time Period Covered:** latest week.

DIMETHYLAMINE: 40% SOLUTION

Source: *Chemical Marketing Reporter.* **Price Frequency:** weekly. **Effective Market(s):** New York. **Units of Measure:** Dollars per lb. **Type of Price:** spot. **Time Period Covered:** latest week.

DIMETHYLAMINE: ANHYDROUS

Source: *Chemical Marketing Reporter.* **Price Frequency:** weekly. **Effective Market(s):** New York. **Units of Measure:** Dollars per lb. **Type of Price:** spot. **Time Period Covered:** latest week.

N,N-DIMETHYLANILINE

Source: *Chemical Marketing Reporter.* **Price Frequency:** weekly. **Effective Market(s):** New York. **Units of Measure:** Dollars per lb. **Type of Price:** spot. **Time Period Covered:** latest week.

N,N-DIMETHYLFORMAMIDE

Source: *Chemical Marketing Reporter.* **Price Frequency:** weekly. **Effective Market(s):** New York. **Units of Measure:** Dollars per lb. **Type of Price:** spot. **Time Period Covered:** latest week.

DIMETHYLPHTHALATE

Source: *Journal of Commerce and Commercial.* **Price Frequency:** weekly in Wednesday issue. **Units of Measure:** Dollars per lb. **Type of Price:** spot. **Time Period Covered:** latest week.

2,4-DINITROANILINE

Source: *Chemical Marketing Reporter.* **Price Frequency:** weekly. **Effective Market(s):** New York. **Units of Measure:** Dollars per lb. **Type of Price:** spot. **Time Period Covered:** latest week.

DINITROANILINE: ORANGE TONER, CHEMICALLY PURE

Source: *Chemical Marketing Reporter.* **Price Frequency:** weekly. **Effective Market(s):** East of the Rockies. **Units of Measure:** Dollars per lb. **Type of Price:** spot. **Time Period Covered:** latest week.

2,4-DINITROCHLOROBENZENE

Source: *Chemical Marketing Reporter.* **Price Frequency:** weekly. **Effective Market(s):** Charlotte (NC). **Units of Measure:** Dollars per lb. **Type of Price:** spot. **Time Period Covered:** latest week.

DINITROPHENOL

Source: *Journal of Commerce and Commercial.* **Price Frequency:** weekly in Wednesday issue. **Units of Measure:** Dollars per lb. **Type of Price:** spot. **Time Period Covered:** latest week.

2,4-DINITROPHENOL

Source: *Chemical Marketing Reporter.* **Price Frequency:** weekly. **Effective Market(s):** Charlotte (NC). **Units of Measure:** Dollars per lb. **Type of Price:** spot. **Time Period Covered:** latest week.

2,4-DINITROTOLUENE

Source: *Chemical Marketing Reporter.* **Price Frequency:** weekly. **Effective Market(s):** New York. **Units of Measure:** Dollars per lb. **Type of Price:** spot. **Time Period Covered:** latest week.

DINITROTOLUENE

Source: *Chemical Marketing Reporter.* **Price Frequency:** weekly. **Effective Market(s):** New York. **Units of Measure:** Dollars per lb. **Type of Price:** spot. **Time Period Covered:** latest week.

DIOCTYL ADIPATE

Source: *Chemical Marketing Reporter.* **Price Frequency:** weekly. **Effective Market(s):** East. **Units of Measure:** Dollars per lb. **Type of Price:** spot. **Time Period Covered:** latest week.

DIOCTYL AZELATE

Source: *Chemical Marketing Reporter.* **Price Frequency:** weekly. **Effective Market(s):** East. **Units of Measure:** Dollars per lb. **Type of Price:** spot. **Time Period Covered:** latest week.

DIOCTYL PHTHALATE

Source: *Chemical Marketing Reporter.* **Price Frequency:** weekly. **Effective Market(s):** New York. **Units of Measure:** Dollars per lb. **Type of Price:** spot. **Time Period Covered:** latest week.

Source: *Journal of Commerce and Commercial.* **Price Frequency:** weekly in Wednesday issue. **Units of Measure:** Dollars per lb. **Type of Price:** spot. **Time Period Covered:** latest week.

DIOCTYL SEBACATE: 99%

Source: *Chemical Marketing Reporter.* **Price Frequency:** weekly. **Effective Market(s):** New York. **Units of Measure:** Dollars per lb. **Type of Price:** spot. **Time Period Covered:** latest week.

1,4-DIOXANE

Source: *Chemical Marketing Reporter.* **Price Frequency:** weekly. **Effective Market(s):** East. **Units of Measure:** Dollars per lb. **Type of Price:** spot. **Time Period Covered:** latest week.

DIP OIL

see Tar Acid Oil.

DIPENTAERYTHRITOL

Source: *Chemical Marketing Reporter.* **Price Frequency:** weekly. **Effective Market(s):** East. **Units of Measure:** Dollars per lb. **Type of Price:** spot. **Time Period Covered:** latest week.

DIPENTENE: STEAM DISTILLED

Source: *Chemical Marketing Reporter.* **Price Frequency:** weekly. **Effective Market(s):** Florida. **Units of Measure:** Dollars per lb. **Type of Price:** spot. **Time Period Covered:** latest week.

DIPENTENE: SULFATE TURPENTINE DERIVED

Source: *Chemical Marketing Reporter.* **Price Frequency:** weekly. **Effective Market(s):** New York. **Units of Measure:** Dollars per lb. **Type of Price:** spot. **Time Period Covered:** latest week.

DIPHENHYDRAMINE HYDROCHLORIDE: USP, DOMESTIC

Source: *Chemical Marketing Reporter.* **Price Frequency:** weekly. **Effective Market(s):** New York. **Units of Measure:** Dollars per kilo. **Type of Price:** spot. **Time Period Covered:** latest week.

DIPHENYL

Source: *Journal of Commerce and Commercial.* **Price Frequency:** weekly in Wednesday issue. **Units of Measure:** Dollars per lb. **Type of Price:** spot. **Time Period Covered:** latest week.

DIPHENYL: 99.9%

Source: *Chemical Marketing Reporter.* **Price Frequency:** weekly. **Effective Market(s):** New York. **Units of Measure:** Dollars per lb. **Type of Price:** spot. **Time Period Covered:** latest week.

DIPHENYL GANIDINE

Source: *Journal of Commerce and Commercial.* **Price Frequency:** weekly in Thursday issue. **Units of Measure:** Dollars per lb. **Type of Price:** spot. **Time Period Covered:** latest week.

DIPHENYL OXIDE: TECHNICAL GRADE

Source: *Chemical Marketing Reporter.* **Price Frequency:** weekly. **Effective Market(s):** New York. **Units of Measure:** Dollars per lb. **Type of Price:** spot. **Time Period Covered:** latest week.

DIPHENYLAMINE: FLAKE

Source: *Journal of Commerce and Commercial.* **Price Frequency:** weekly in Wednesday issue. **Units of Measure:** Dollars per lb. **Type of Price:** spot. **Time Period Covered:** latest week.

DIPHENYLAMINE: G SALT

Source: *Journal of Commerce and Commercial.* **Price Frequency:** weekly in Wednesday issue. **Units of Measure:** Dollars per lb. **Type of Price:** spot. **Time Period Covered:** latest week.

DIPHENYLAMINE: MOLTEN

Source: *Chemical Marketing Reporter.* **Price Frequency:** weekly. **Effective Market(s):** New York. **Units of Measure:** Dollars per lb. **Type of Price:** spot. **Time Period Covered:** latest week.

Source: *Journal of Commerce and Commercial.* **Price Frequency:** weekly in Wednesday issue. **Units of Measure:** Dollars per lb. **Type of Price:** spot. **Time Period Covered:** latest week.

DIPHENYLAMINE: OCTYLATED, FLAKE

Source: *Chemical Marketing Reporter.* **Price Frequency:** weekly. **Effective Market(s):** New York. **Units of Measure:** Dollars per lb. **Type of Price:** spot. **Time Period Covered:** latest week.

DIPHENYLAMINE: REFINED, FLAKE

Source: *Chemical Marketing Reporter.* **Price Frequency:** weekly. **Effective Market(s):** New York. **Units of Measure:** Dollars per lb. **Type of Price:** spot. **Time Period Covered:** latest week.

DIPHENYLGUANIDINE

Source: *Chemical Marketing Reporter.* **Price Frequency:** weekly. **Effective Market(s):** New York. **Units of Measure:** Dollars per lb. **Type of Price:** spot. **Time Period Covered:** latest week.

DIPHENYLHYDANTOIN-SODIUM: USP

Source: *Chemical Marketing Reporter.* **Price Frequency:** weekly. **Effective Market(s):** New York. **Units of Measure:** Dollars per lb. **Type of Price:** spot. **Time Period Covered:** latest week.

DIPHENYLMETHANE

Source: *Journal of Commerce and Commercial.* **Price Frequency:** weekly in Wednesday issue. **Units of Measure:** Dollars per lb. **Type of Price:** spot. **Time Period Covered:** latest week.

DIPHENYLMETHANE 4,4-DI-ISOCYANATE: POLYMERIC

Source: *Chemical Marketing Reporter.* **Price Frequency:** weekly. **Effective Market(s):** New York. **Units of Measure:** Dollars per lb. **Type of Price:** spot. **Time Period Covered:** latest week.

DIPROPYLENE GLYCOL

Source: *Chemical Marketing Reporter.* **Price Frequency:** weekly. **Effective Market(s):** New York. **Units of Measure:** Dollars per lb. **Type of Price:** spot. **Time Period Covered:** latest week.

DIPROPYLENE GLYCOL MONOMETHYL ETHER

Source: *Chemical Marketing Reporter.* **Price Frequency:** weekly. **Effective Market(s):** New York. **Units of Measure:** Dollars per lb. **Type of Price:** spot. **Time Period Covered:** latest week.

DISK HARROW: TANDEM

Source: *Agricultural Prices.* **Price Frequency:** semiannually. **Effective Market(s):** United States. **Units of Measure:** Dollars each. **Type of Price:** paid by farmer. **Time Period Covered:** latest year.

Source: *Agricultural Prices Annual Summary.* **Price Frequency:** semiannually. **Effective Market(s):** United States. **Units of Measure:** Dollars each. **Type of Price:** average paid by farmer. **Time Period Covered:** latest 6 years.

DISTILLERS' DRIED GRAINS

Source: *Feed Situation and Outlook Report.* **Price Frequency:** monthly. **Effective Market(s):** Lawrenceburg (KY). **Units of Measure:** Dollars per ton. **Type of Price:** wholesale. **Time Period Covered:** latest 8 months.

Source: *Feedstuffs.* **Price Frequency:** weekly. **Effective Market(s):** 5 domestic markets. **Units of Measure:** Dollars per bulk ton. **Time Period Covered:** latest week.

DITRIDECYL PHTHALATE

Source: *Chemical Marketing Reporter.* **Price Frequency:** weekly. **Effective Market(s):** New York. **Units of Measure:** Dollars per lb. **Type of Price:** spot. **Time Period Covered:** latest week.

DIUNDECYL PHTHALATE

Source: *Chemical Marketing Reporter.* **Price Frequency:** weekly. **Effective Market(s):** New York. **Units of Measure:** Dollars per lb. **Type of Price:** spot. **Time Period Covered:** latest week.

DIVINYLBENZENE

Source: *Chemical Marketing Reporter.* **Price Frequency:** weekly. **Effective Market(s):** New York. **Units of Measure:** Dollars per lb. **Type of Price:** spot. **Time Period Covered:** latest week.

L-DODECANOL: SYNTHETIC

Source: *Chemical Marketing Reporter.* **Price Frequency:** weekly. **Effective Market(s):** New York. **Units of Measure:** Dollars per lb. **Type of Price:** spot. **Time Period Covered:** latest week.

DODECENYL SUCCINIC ANHYDRIDE

Source: *Chemical Marketing Reporter.* **Price Frequency:** weekly. **Effective Market(s):** New York. **Units of Measure:** Dollars per lb. **Type of Price:** spot. **Time Period Covered:** latest week.

DODECYLBENZENE

see Detergent Alkylate.

DODECYLPHENOL

Source: *Chemical Marketing Reporter.* **Price Frequency:** weekly. **Effective Market(s):** East. **Units of Measure:** Dollars per lb. **Type of Price:** spot. **Time Period Covered:** latest week.

DOLPHIN (FISH): FILLETS, FRESH, HAWAIIAN

Source: *Seafood Price-Current.* **Price Frequency:** semiweekly. **Effective Market(s):** Hawaii. **Units of Measure:** Dollars per lb. **Type of Price:** sale by first receiver. **Time Period Covered:** latest day.

DOLPHIN (FISH): FILLETS, FROZEN, TAIWAN AND JAPAN

Source: *Seafood Price-Current.* **Price Frequency:** semiweekly. **Effective Market(s):** West Coast. **Units of Measure:** Dollars per lb. **Type of Price:** first receiver. **Time Period Covered:** latest day.

DOLPHIN (FISH): FRESH

Source: *Seafood Price-Current.* **Price Frequency:** semiweekly. **Effective Market(s):** Gulf/Southeast. **Units of Measure:** Dollars per lb. **Type of Price:** sale by first receiver. **Time Period Covered:** latest day.

DOLPHIN (FISH): WHOLE, FRESH

Source: *Seafood Price-Current.* **Price Frequency:** semiweekly. **Effective Market(s):** Boston, Mid-Atlantic, New Bedford (MA), Portland (ME). **Units of Measure:** Dollars per lb. **Type of Price:** sale by first receiver, auction price. **Time Period Covered:** latest day.

DOLPHIN (FISH): WHOLE, FRESH, HAWAIIAN

Source: *Seafood Price-Current.* **Price Frequency:** semiweekly. **Effective Market(s):** Hawaii. **Units of Measure:** Dollars per lb. **Type of Price:** sale by first receiver. **Time Period Covered:** latest day.

DOLPHIN (FISH): WHOLE, FRESH, IMPORTS, CENTRAL AND SOUTH AMERICA

Source: *Seafood Price-Current.* **Price Frequency:** semiweekly. **Effective Market(s):** Miami. **Units of Measure:** Dollars per lb. **Type of Price:** sale by first receiver. **Time Period Covered:** latest day.

DOUGLAS FIR

Source: *Random Lengths.* **Price Frequency:** weekly. **Effective Market(s):** 8 domestic markets. **Units of Measure:** Dollars per 1000 board feet. **Type of Price:** delivered to wholesaler. **Time Period Covered:** latest week.

Source: *Volume and Value of Sawtimber Stumpage Sold From National Forests by Selected Species and Region.* **Price Frequency:** quarterly, annually. **Effective Market(s):** 8 domestic markets. **Units of Measure:** Dollars per 1000 board feet. **Type of Price:** average. **Time Period Covered:** latest quarter, latest year.

DOUGLAS FIR: GREEN, NO. 2 AND BETTER

Source: *Random Lengths.* **Price Frequency:** weekly. **Effective Market(s):** Portland. **Units of Measure:** Dollars per 1000 board feet. **Type of Price:** mill price to wholesaler. **Time Period Covered:** latest week.

DOUGLAS FIR: GREEN, SELECT AND COMMONS, PORTLAND

Source: *Random Lengths.* **Price Frequency:** weekly. **Effective Market(s):** California. **Units of Measure:** Dollars per 1000 board feet. **Type of Price:** mill price to wholesaler. **Time Period Covered:** latest week.

DOUGLAS FIR: GREEN, SELECT AND COMMONS, EUREKA

Source: *Random Lengths.* **Price Frequency:** weekly. **Effective Market(s):** California. **Units of Measure:** Dollars per 1000 board feet. **Type of Price:** mill price to wholesaler. **Time Period Covered:** latest week.

DOUGLAS FIR: GREEN, STANDARD AND BETTER

Source: *Random Lengths.* **Price Frequency:** weekly. **Effective Market(s):** Portland. **Units of Measure:** Dollars per 1000 board feet. **Type of Price:** mill price to wholesaler. **Time Period Covered:** latest week.

DOVES

Source: *Lancaster Farming.* **Price Frequency:** weekly. **Effective Market(s):** Pennsylvania. **Units of Measure:** Dollars each. **Type of Price:** auction. **Time Period Covered:** latest week.

DRILL: ELECTRIC, VARIABLE SPEED, REVERSIBLE

Source: *Agricultural Prices.* **Price Frequency:** annually. **Effective Market(s):** United States. **Units of Measure:** Dollars each. **Type of Price:** paid by farmer. **Time Period Covered:** latest year.

Source: *Agricultural Prices Annual Summary.* **Price Frequency:** semiannually. **Effective Market(s):** United States. **Units of Measure:** Dollars each. **Type of Price:** average paid by farmer. **Time Period Covered:** latest 6 years.

DRILLS CLOTH

Source: *DNR: Daily News Record.* **Price Frequency:** quarterly. **Units of Measure:** Dollars per yard. **Time Period Covered:** latest 3 quarters.

DRUGS: CRUDE

Source: *Journal of Commerce and Commercial.* **Price Frequency:** weekly in Monday issue. **Units of Measure:** Dollars per lb. **Type of Price:** spot. **Time Period Covered:** latest week.

DUCK BREASTS: BONELESS

Source: *Meat Price Report.* **Price Frequency:** weekly. **Units of Measure:** cents per lb. **Type of Price:** price paid to wholesaler. **Time Period Covered:** latest week.

DUCKLINGS

Source: *HRI-Buyers Guide.* **Price Frequency:** weekly. **Effective Market(s):** Northeastern area. **Units of Measure:** cents per lb. **Type of Price:** wholesale. **Time Period Covered:** latest week.

DUCKLINGS: GRADE A, FRESH, EVISERATED

Source: *Farmers Weekly.* **Price Frequency:** weekly. **Effective Market(s):** Smithfield (England). **Units of Measure:** British pence per lb. **Type of Price:** wholesale bottom, wholesale top. **Time Period Covered:** latest week.

DUCKLINGS: GRADE A, FRESH, UNEVISERATED

Source: *Farmers Weekly.* **Price Frequency:** weekly. **Effective Market(s):** Smithfield (England). **Units of Measure:** British pence per lb. **Type of Price:** wholesale bottom, wholesale top. **Time Period Covered:** latest week.

DUCKLINGS: GRADE A, READY-TO-COOK, FRESH

Source: *Poultry Market Statistics.* **Price Frequency:** monthly, annually. **Effective Market(s):** Chicago, New York. **Units of Measure:** Dollars per lb. **Type of Price:** average delivered to first receiver. **Time Period Covered:** latest year.

DUCKLINGS: GRADE A, READY-TO-COOK, FROZEN

Source: *Poultry Market Statistics.* **Price Frequency:** monthly, annually. **Effective Market(s):** Los Angeles, San Francisco. **Units of Measure:** Dollars per lb. **Type of Price:** average delivered to retailer. **Time Period Covered:** latest year.

Source: *Poultry Market Statistics.* **Price Frequency:** monthly, annually. **Effective Market(s):** Chicago, New York. **Units of Measure:** Dollars per lb. **Type of Price:** average delivered to first receiver. **Time Period Covered:** latest year.

DUCKS

Source: *Weekly Insiders Poultry Report.* **Price Frequency:** weekly. **Effective Market(s):** New York. **Units of Measure:** cents per lb. **Type of Price:** retail. **Time Period Covered:** latest week, week ago, year ago.

DUCKS: FRESH

Source: *Urner Barry's Price-Current.* **Price Frequency:** daily. **Effective Market(s):** Long Island, Midwest, Southeast. **Units of Measure:** Dollars per lb. **Type of Price:** delivered first receivers. **Time Period Covered:** latest day.

DUCKS: FROZEN

Source: *Urner Barry's Price-Current.* **Price Frequency:** daily. **Effective Market(s):** Long Island, Midwest, Midwest. **Units of Measure:** Dollars per lb. **Type of Price:** delivered first receivers. **Time Period Covered:** latest day.

DUCKS: LONG ISLAND

Source: *Weekly Insiders Poultry Report.* **Price Frequency:** annually. **Units of Measure:** cents per lb. **Type of Price:** wholesale. **Time Period Covered:** latest 3 years.

DUCKS: MALLARD

Source: *HRI-Buyers Guide.* **Price Frequency:** weekly. **Effective Market(s):** Northeastern area. **Units of Measure:** Dollars per lb. **Type of Price:** wholesale. **Time Period Covered:** latest week.

Source: *Urner Barry's Price-Current.* **Price Frequency:** daily. **Units of Measure:** Dollars per lb. **Type of Price:** wholesale. **Time Period Covered:** latest day.

Source: *Urner Barry's Price-Current, West Coast Edition.* **Price Frequency:** semiweekly. **Effective Market(s):** West Coast. **Units of Measure:** Dollars per lb. **Type of Price:** wholesale. **Time Period Covered:** latest week.

DUCKS: MUSCOVY

Source: *HRI-Buyers Guide.* **Price Frequency:** weekly. **Effective Market(s):** Northeastern area. **Units of Measure:** Dollars per lb. **Type of Price:** wholesale. **Time Period Covered:** latest week.

Source: *Lancaster Farming.* **Price Frequency:** weekly. **Effective Market(s):** Pennsylvania. **Units of Measure:** Dollars per lb. **Type of Price:** auction. **Time Period Covered:** latest week.

Source: *Urner Barry's Price-Current, West Coast Edition.* **Price Frequency:** semiweekly. **Effective Market(s):** West Coast. **Units of Measure:** Dollars per lb. **Type of Price:** wholesale. **Time Period Covered:** latest week.

DUCKS: MUSCOVY, DRAKES

Source: *Urner Barry's Price-Current.* **Price Frequency:** daily. **Units of Measure:** Dollars per lb. **Type of Price:** wholesale. **Time Period Covered:** latest day.

DUCKS: MUSCOVY, HENS

Source: *Urner Barry's Price-Current.* **Price Frequency:** daily. **Units of Measure:** Dollars per lb. **Type of Price:** wholesale. **Time Period Covered:** latest day.

DUCKS: PEKIN

Source: *Lancaster Farming.* **Price Frequency:** weekly. **Effective Market(s):** Pennsylvania. **Units of Measure:** Dollars per lb. **Type of Price:** auction. **Time Period Covered:** latest week.

DUCKS: WHOLE

Source: *Meat Price Report.* **Price Frequency:** weekly. **Units of Measure:** cents per lb. **Type of Price:** price paid to wholesaler. **Time Period Covered:** latest week.

DURALUMINUM: BORINGS AND TURNINGS

Source: *American Metal Market.* **Price Frequency:** daily. **Effective Market(s):** Buffalo. **Units of Measure:** cents per lb. **Type of Price:** dealer buying. **Time Period Covered:** latest day.

DURALUMINUM: CLIPPINGS

Source: *American Metal Market.* **Price Frequency:** daily. **Effective Market(s):** New York. **Units of Measure:** cents per lb. **Type of Price:** dealer buying. **Time Period Covered:** latest day.

Source: *Iron Age.* **Price Frequency:** monthly. **Units of Measure:** cents per lb. **Type of Price:** dealer. **Time Period Covered:** latest month.

DUTCH GUILDERS

see Netherlands Guilders.

DYE: A BL 9 BLUE 2G

Source: *Chemical Marketing Reporter.* **Price Frequency:** weekly. **Effective Market(s):** New York. **Units of Measure:** Dollars per lb. **Type of Price:** spot. **Time Period Covered:** latest week.

DYE: A BL 45 ALIZARINE BLUE SAP, CONCENTRATED

Source: *Chemical Marketing Reporter.* **Price Frequency:** weekly. **Effective Market(s):** New York. **Units of Measure:** Dollars per lb. **Type of Price:** spot. **Time Period Covered:** latest week.

DYE: A BL 90

Source: *Chemical Marketing Reporter.* **Price Frequency:** weekly. **Effective Market(s):** New York. **Units of Measure:** Dollars per lb. **Type of Price:** spot. **Time Period Covered:** latest week.

DYE: A BL 113 NAVY

Source: *Chemical Marketing Reporter.* **Price Frequency:** weekly. **Effective Market(s):** New York. **Units of Measure:** Dollars per lb. **Type of Price:** spot. **Time Period Covered:** latest week.

DYE: A BLK 1 126%

Source: *Chemical Marketing Reporter.* **Price Frequency:** weekly. **Effective Market(s):** New York. **Units of Measure:** Dollars per lb. **Type of Price:** spot. **Time Period Covered:** latest week.

DYE: A GR 16 333%

Source: *Chemical Marketing Reporter.* **Price Frequency:** weekly. **Effective Market(s):** New York. **Units of Measure:** Dollars per lb. **Type of Price:** spot. **Time Period Covered:** latest week.

DYE: A OR 7 11

Source: *Chemical Marketing Reporte.* **Price Frequency:** weekly. **Effective Market(s):** New York. **Units of Measure:** Dollars per lb. **Type of Price:** spot. **Time Period Covered:** latest week.

DYE: A OR 8 RO, EXTRA CONCENTRATED

Source: *Chemical Marketing Reporter.* **Price Frequency:** weekly. **Effective Market(s):** New York. **Units of Measure:** Dollars per lb. **Type of Price:** spot. **Time Period Covered:** latest week.

DYE: A OR 10 FAST OR G

Source: *Chemical Marketing Reporter.* **Price Frequency:** weekly. **Effective Market(s):** New York. **Units of Measure:** Dollars per lb.a. **Type of Price:** spot. **Time Period Covered:** latest week.

DYE: A OR 74 G 250%

Source: *Chemical Marketing Reporter.* **Price Frequency:** weekly. **Effective Market(s):** New York. **Units of Measure:** Dollars per lb. **Type of Price:** spot. **Time Period Covered:** latest week.

DYE: A R 1 2G

Source: *Chemical Marketing Reporter.* **Price Frequency:** weekly. **Effective Market(s):** New York. **Units of Measure:** Dollars per lb. **Type of Price:** spot. **Time Period Covered:** latest week.

DYE: A R 14 AZO RUBINE 133%

Source: *Chemical Marketing Reporter.* **Price Frequency:** weekly. **Effective Market(s):** New York. **Units of Measure:** Dollars per lb. **Type of Price:** spot. **Time Period Covered:** latest week.

DYE: A R 18 SCARLET 4R 150%

Source: *Chemical Marketing Reporter.* **Price Frequency:** weekly. **Effective Market(s):** New York. **Units of Measure:** Dollars per lb. **Type of Price:** spot. **Time Period Covered:** latest week.

DYE: A R 88 FAST RED A, CONCENTRATED

Source: *Chemical Marketing Reporter.* **Price Frequency:** weekly. **Effective Market(s):** New York. **Units of Measure:** Dollars per lb. **Type of Price:** spot. **Time Period Covered:** latest week.

DYE: A R 151 SILK RED 3B, CONCENTRATED

Source: *Chemical Marketing Reporter.* **Price Frequency:** weekly. **Effective Market(s):** New York. **Units of Measure:** Dollars per lb. **Type of Price:** spot. **Time Period Covered:** latest week.

DYE: A V 17 5BNS, CONCENTRATED

Source: *Chemical Marketing Reporter.* **Price Frequency:** weekly. **Effective Market(s):** New York. **Units of Measure:** Dollars per lb. **Type of Price:** spot. **Time Period Covered:** latest week.

DYE: A V 49 4BNS, CONCENTRATED

Source: *Chemical Marketing Reporter.* **Price Frequency:** weekly. **Effective Market(s):** New York. **Units of Measure:** Dollars per lb. **Type of Price:** spot. **Time Period Covered:** latest week.

DYE: A Y 17 FAST LIGHT YELLOW 2G

Source: *Chemical Marketing Reporter.* **Price Frequency:** weekly. **Effective Market(s):** New York. **Units of Measure:** Dollars per lb. **Type of Price:** spot. **Time Period Covered:** latest week.

DYE: A Y 23 TARTRAZINE, EXTRA CONCENTRATED

Source: *Chemical Marketing Reporter.* **Price Frequency:** weekly. **Effective Market(s):** New York. **Units of Measure:** Dollars per lb. **Type of Price:** spot. **Time Period Covered:** latest week.

DYE: B BL 9 2BN, LIQUID

Source: *Chemical Marketing Reporter.* **Price Frequency:** weekly. **Effective Market(s):** New York. **Units of Measure:** Dollars per lb. **Type of Price:** spot. **Time Period Covered:** latest week.

DYE: B BR 4 R, POWDER

Source: *Chemical Marketing Reporter.* **Price Frequency:** weekly. **Effective Market(s):** New York. **Units of Measure:** Dollars per lb. **Type of Price:** spot. **Time Period Covered:** latest week.

DYE: B G 1 JADE, CRYSTALS

Source: *Chemical Marketing Reporter.* **Price Frequency:** weekly. **Effective Market(s):** New York. **Units of Measure:** Dollars per lb. **Type of Price:** spot. **Time Period Covered:** latest week.

DYE: B GR 4 MALACHITE GREEN, CRYSTALS

Source: *Chemical Marketing Reporter.* **Price Frequency:** weekly. **Effective Market(s):** New York. **Units of Measure:** Dollars per lb. **Type of Price:** spot. **Time Period Covered:** latest week.

DYE: B V 1 METHYL VIOLET, CRYSTALS

Source: *Chemical Marketing Reporter.* **Price Frequency:** weekly. **Effective Market(s):** New York. **Units of Measure:** Dollars per lb. **Type of Price:** spot. **Time Period Covered:** latest week.

DYE: B V 10 RHODAMINE 540%

Source: *Chemical Marketing Reporter.* **Price Frequency:** weekly. **Effective Market(s):** New York. **Units of Measure:** Dollars per lb. **Type of Price:** spot. **Time Period Covered:** latest week.

DYE: B Y 2

Source: *Chemical Marketing Reporter.* **Price Frequency:** weekly. **Effective Market(s):** New York. **Units of Measure:** Dollars per lb. **Type of Price:** spot. **Time Period Covered:** latest week.

DYE: COALTAR, BLUE, FD AND C NO. 1

Source: *Chemical Marketing Reporter.* **Price Frequency:** weekly. **Effective Market(s):** New York. **Units of Measure:** Dollars per lb. **Type of Price:** spot. **Time Period Covered:** latest week.

DYE: COALTAR, BLUE, FD AND C NO. 2

Source: *Chemical Marketing Reporter.* **Price Frequency:** weekly. **Effective Market(s):** New York. **Units of Measure:** Dollars per lb. **Type of Price:** spot. **Time Period Covered:** latest week.

DYE: COALTAR, GREEN, D AND C NO. 5

Source: *Chemical Marketing Reporter.* **Price Frequency:** weekly. **Effective Market(s):** New York. **Units of Measure:** Dollars per lb. **Type of Price:** spot. **Time Period Covered:** latest week.

DYE: COALTAR, GREEN, D AND C NO. 6

Source: *Chemical Marketing Reporter.* **Price Frequency:** weekly. **Effective Market(s):** New York. **Units of Measure:** Dollars per lb. **Type of Price:** spot. **Time Period Covered:** latest week.

DYE: COALTAR, GREEN, FD AND C NO. 3

Source: *Chemical Marketing Reporter.* **Price Frequency:** weekly. **Effective Market(s):** New York. **Units of Measure:** Dollars per lb. **Type of Price:** spot. **Time Period Covered:** latest week.

DYE: COALTAR, RED, D AND C NO. 17

Source: *Chemical Marketing Reporter.* **Price Frequency:** weekly. **Effective Market(s):** New York. **Units of Measure:** Dollars per lb. **Type of Price:** spot. **Time Period Covered:** latest week.

DYE: COALTAR, RED, D AND C NO. 22

Source: *Chemical Marketing Reporter.* **Price Frequency:** weekly. **Effective Market(s):** New York. **Units of Measure:** Dollars per lb. **Type of Price:** spot. **Time Period Covered:** latest week.

DYE: COALTAR, RED, D AND C NO. 28

Source: *Chemical Marketing Reporter.* **Price Frequency:** weekly. **Effective Market(s):** New York. **Units of Measure:** Dollars per lb. **Type of Price:** spot. **Time Period Covered:** latest week.

DYE: COALTAR, RED, D AND C NO. 33

Source: *Chemical Marketing Reporter.* **Price Frequency:** weekly. **Effective Market(s):** New York. **Units of Measure:** Dollars per lb. **Type of Price:** spot. **Time Period Covered:** latest week.

DYE: COALTAR, RED, FD AND C NO. 3

Source: *Chemical Marketing Reporter.* **Price Frequency:** weekly. **Effective Market(s):** New York. **Units of Measure:** Dollars per lb. **Type of Price:** spot. **Time Period Covered:** latest week.

DYE: COALTAR, YELLOW, D AND C NO. 7

Source: *Chemical Marketing Reporter.* **Price Frequency:** weekly. **Effective Market(s):** New York. **Units of Measure:** Dollars per lb. **Type of Price:** spot. **Time Period Covered:** latest week.

DYE: COALTAR, YELLOW, D AND C NO. 8

Source: *Chemical Marketing Reporter.* **Price Frequency:** weekly. **Effective Market(s):** New York. **Units of Measure:** Dollars per lb. **Type of Price:** spot. **Time Period Covered:** latest week.

DYE: COALTAR, YELLOW, D AND C NO. 10

Source: *Chemical Marketing Reporter.* **Price Frequency:** weekly. **Effective Market(s):** New York. **Units of Measure:** Dollars per lb. **Type of Price:** spot. **Time Period Covered:** latest week.

DYE: COALTAR, YELLOW, FD AND C NO. 5

Source: *Chemical Marketing Reporter.* **Price Frequency:** weekly. **Effective Market(s):** New York. **Units of Measure:** Dollars per lb. **Type of Price:** spot. **Time Period Covered:** latest week.

DYE: COALTAR, YELLOW, FD AND C NO. 6

Source: *Chemical Marketing Reporter.* **Price Frequency:** weekly. **Effective Market(s):** New York. **Units of Measure:** Dollars per lb. **Type of Price:** spot. **Time Period Covered:** latest week.

DYE: COALTAR, YELLOW, NO. 11

Source: *Chemical Marketing Reporter.* **Price Frequency:** weekly. **Effective Market(s):** New York. **Units of Measure:** Dollars per lb. **Type of Price:** spot. **Time Period Covered:** latest week.

DYE: D BL 1 SKY BLUE 200%

Source: *Chemical Marketing Reporter.* **Price Frequency:** weekly. **Effective Market(s):** New York. **Units of Measure:** Dollars per lb. **Type of Price:** spot. **Time Period Covered:** latest week.

DYE: D BL 8 150%

Source: *Chemical Marketing Reporter.* **Price Frequency:** weekly. **Effective Market(s):** New York. **Units of Measure:** Dollars per lb. **Type of Price:** spot. **Time Period Covered:** latest week.

DYE: D BLK 22 FAST BLACK GR 150%

Source: *Chemical Marketing Reporter.* **Price Frequency:** weekly. **Effective Market(s):** New York. **Units of Measure:** Dollars per lb. **Type of Price:** spot. **Time Period Covered:** latest week.

DYE: D BR 230 FAST BROWN BRNB 200%

Source: *Chemical Marketing Reporter.* **Price Frequency:** weekly. **Effective Market(s):** New York. **Units of Measure:** Dollars per lb. **Type of Price:** spot. **Time Period Covered:** latest week.

DYE: D GR 26 BL 155%

Source: *Chemical Marketing Reporter.* **Price Frequency:** weekly. **Effective Market(s):** New York. **Units of Measure:** Dollars per lb. **Type of Price:** spot. **Time Period Covered:** latest week.

DYE: D OR 102 FAST ORANGE WS, CONCENTRATED 150%

Source: *Chemical Marketing Reporter.* **Price Frequency:** weekly. **Effective Market(s):** New York. **Units of Measure:** Dollars per lb. **Type of Price:** spot. **Time Period Covered:** latest week.

DYE: D OR 102 FAST ORANGE WSP, LIQUID

Source: *Chemical Marketing Reporter.* **Price Frequency:** weekly. **Effective Market(s):** New York. **Units of Measure:** $ per lb. **Type of Price:** spot. **Time Period Covered:** latest week.

DYE: D R 2 4B, EXTRA CONCENTRATED

Source: *Chemical Marketing Reporter.* **Price Frequency:** weekly. **Effective Market(s):** New York. **Units of Measure:** Dollars per lb. **Type of Price:** spot. **Time Period Covered:** latest week.

DYE: D R 31 BRILLIANT RED 12B 200%

Source: *Chemical Marketing Reporter.* **Price Frequency:** weekly. **Effective Market(s):** New York. **Units of Measure:** Dollars per lb. **Type of Price:** spot. **Time Period Covered:** latest week.

DYE: D R 80 FAST RED 8BLN

Source: *Chemical Marketing Reporter.* **Price Frequency:** weekly. **Effective Market(s):** New York. **Units of Measure:** Dollars per lb. **Type of Price:** spot. **Time Period Covered:** latest week.

DYE: D R 81 PAPER RED 8BL

Source: *Chemical Marketing Reporter.* **Price Frequency:** weekly. **Effective Market(s):** New York. **Units of Measure:** Dollars per lb. **Type of Price:** spot. **Time Period Covered:** latest week.

DYE: D Y 4 PAPER YELLOW 3GX 125%

Source: *Chemical Marketing Reporter.* **Price Frequency:** weekly. **Effective Market(s):** New York. **Units of Measure:** Dollars per lb. **Type of Price:** spot. **Time Period Covered:** latest week.

DYE: D Y 4 PAPER YELLOW 3GX, LIQUID

Source: *Chemical Marketing Reporter.* **Price Frequency:** weekly. **Effective Market(s):** New York. **Units of Measure:** Dollars per lb. **Type of Price:** spot. **Time Period Covered:** latest week.

DYE: D Y 11 STILBENE YELLOW GA, EXTRA CONCENTRATED

Source: *Chemical Marketing Reporter.* **Price Frequency:** weekly. **Effective Market(s):** New York. **Units of Measure:** Dollars per lb. **Type of Price:** spot. **Time Period Covered:** latest week.

DYE: D Y 27

Source: *Chemical Marketing Reporter.* **Price Frequency:** weekly. **Effective Market(s):** New York. **Units of Measure:** Dollars per lb. **Type of Price:** spot. **Time Period Covered:** latest week.

DYE: DIS BL 27 GG FS

Source: *Chemical Marketing Reporter.* **Price Frequency:** weekly. **Effective Market(s):** New York. **Units of Measure:** Dollars per lb. **Type of Price:** spot. **Time Period Covered:** latest week.

DYE: DIS OR 3 ORANGE GRA

Source: *Chemical Marketing Reporter.* **Price Frequency:** weekly. **Effective Market(s):** New York. **Units of Measure:** Dollars per lb. **Type of Price:** spot. **Time Period Covered:** latest week.

DYE: DIS OR 37 ORANGE OB

Source: *Chemical Marketing Reporter.* **Price Frequency:** weekly. **Effective Market(s):** New York. **Units of Measure:** Dollars per lb. **Type of Price:** spot. **Time Period Covered:** latest week.

DYE: DIS R 1 SCARLET BA

Source: *Chemical Marketing Reporter.* **Price Frequency:** weekly. **Effective Market(s):** New York. **Units of Measure:** Dollars per lb. **Type of Price:** spot. **Time Period Covered:** latest week.

DYE: DIS R 91 PINK FRL

Source: *Chemical Marketing Reporter.* **Price Frequency:** weekly. **Effective Market(s):** New York. **Units of Measure:** Dollars per lb. **Type of Price:** spot. **Time Period Covered:** latest week.

DYE: DIS V 1 3R

Source: *Chemical Marketing Reporter.* **Price Frequency:** weekly. **Effective Market(s):** New York. **Units of Measure:** Dollars per lb. **Type of Price:** spot. **Time Period Covered:** latest week.

DYE: DIS V 26 FRL

Source: *Chemical Marketing Reporter.* **Price Frequency:** weekly. **Effective Market(s):** New York. **Units of Measure:** Dollars per lb. **Type of Price:** spot. **Time Period Covered:** latest week.

DYE: DIS Y 3 YELLOW G

Source: *Chemical Marketing Reporter.* **Price Frequency:** weekly. **Effective Market(s):** New York. **Units of Measure:** Dollars per lb. **Type of Price:** spot. **Time Period Covered:** latest week.

DYE: DIS Y 54 YELLOW 3G

Source: *Chemical Marketing Reporter.* **Price Frequency:** weekly. **Effective Market(s):** New York. **Units of Measure:** Dollars per lb. **Type of Price:** spot. **Time Period Covered:** latest week.

DYE: V BLK 25 OLIVE TA, PASTE

Source: *Chemical Marketing Reporter.* **Price Frequency:** weekly. **Effective Market(s):** New York. **Units of Measure:** Dollars per lb. **Type of Price:** spot. **Time Period Covered:** latest week.

DYE: V G 1 JADE GREEN, DOUBLE PASTE

Source: *Chemical Marketing Reporter.* **Price Frequency:** weekly. **Effective Market(s):** New York. **Units of Measure:** Dollars per lb. **Type of Price:** spot. **Time Period Covered:** latest week.

DYE TANNING MATERIALS

Source: *Journal of Commerce and Commercial.* **Price Frequency:** weekly in Thursday issue. **Units of Measure:** Dollars per 100 lbs. **Type of Price:** spot. **Time Period Covered:** latest week.

E-GLASS GUN ROVING

Source: *Modern Plastics.* **Price Frequency:** quarterly in February, May, August, November issues. **Units of Measure:** Dollars per lb. **Type of Price:** list. **Time Period Covered:** latest 4 quarters.

EASTER LILIES: POTTED, LESS THAN 5″

Source: *Floriculture Crops.* **Price Frequency:** annually. **Effective Market(s):** 8 domestic markets, United States. **Units of Measure:** Dollars per unit. **Type of Price:** commercial wholesale. **Time Period Covered:** latest 2 years.

EASTER LILIES: POTTED, MORE THAN 5″

Source: *Floriculture Crops.* **Price Frequency:** annually. **Effective Market(s):** 27 domestic markets, United States. **Units of Measure:** Dollars per unit. **Type of Price:** commercial wholesale. **Time Period Covered:** latest 2 years.

ECHINACEA: PURPUREA

Source: *Journal of Commerce and Commercial.* **Price Frequency:** weekly in Monday issue. **Units of Measure:** Dollars per lb. **Type of Price:** spot. **Time Period Covered:** latest week.

ECHINACEA ROOT: POWDER

Source: *Journal of Commerce and Commercial.* **Price Frequency:** weekly in Monday issue. **Units of Measure:** Dollars per lb. **Type of Price:** spot. **Time Period Covered:** latest week.

ECUADOR SUCRES

Source: *Barron's.* **Price Frequency:** weekly. **Effective Market(s):** New York. **Units of Measure:** Ecuadorian sucre per United States dollar. **Type of Price:** floating foreign exchange rate. **Time Period Covered:** latest 2 weeks.

Source: *New York Times.* **Price Frequency:** daily. **Effective Market(s):** New York. **Units of Measure:** Ecuadorian sucre per United States dollar. **Type of Price:** floating foreign exchange rate. **Time Period Covered:** latest 2 days.

EGG BLENDS: WHOLE, WITH SWEETNERS

Source: *Milling & Baking News.* **Price Frequency:** weekly. **Units of Measure:** Dollars per lb. **Time Period Covered:** latest week.

EGG LIQUIDS

Source: *HRI-Buyers Guide.* **Price Frequency:** weekly. **Effective Market(s):** Northeastern area. **Units of Measure:** Dollars per lb. **Time Period Covered:** latest week.

EGG LIQUIDS: WHITES

Source: *Weekly Insiders Dairy & Egg Letter.* **Price Frequency:** weekly. **Units of Measure:** Dollars per lb. **Time Period Covered:** latest week.

EGG LIQUIDS: WHOLE

Source: *Weekly Insiders Dairy & Egg Letter.* **Price Frequency:** weekly. **Units of Measure:** Dollars per lb. **Time Period Covered:** latest week.

EGG LIQUIDS: YOLKS

Source: *Weekly Insiders Dairy & Egg Letter.* **Price Frequency:** weekly. **Units of Measure:** Dollars per lb. **Time Period Covered:** latest week.

EGG PRODUCTS: BLENDS

Source: *Urner Barry's Price-Current, West Coast Edition.* **Price Frequency:** semiweekly. **Effective Market(s):** West Coast. **Units of Measure:** Dollars per lb. **Time Period Covered:** latest week.

EGG PRODUCTS: BLENDS, FROZEN

Source: *Weekly Insiders Dairy & Egg Letter.* **Price Frequency:** weekly. **Units of Measure:** Dollars per lb. **Time Period Covered:** latest week.

EGG PRODUCTS: WHITES

Source: *Urner Barry's Price-Current, West Coast Edition.* **Price Frequency:** semiweekly. **Effective Market(s):** West Coast. **Units of Measure:** Dollars per lb. **Time Period Covered:** latest week.

EGG PRODUCTS: WHITES, FROZEN

Source: *Weekly Insiders Dairy & Egg Letter.* **Price Frequency:** weekly. **Units of Measure:** Dollars per lb. **Time Period Covered:** latest week.

EGG PRODUCTS: WHOLE

Source: *Urner Barry's Price-Current, West Coast Edition.* **Price Frequency:** semiweekly. **Effective Market(s):** West Coast. **Units of Measure:** Dollars per lb. **Time Period Covered:** latest week.

EGG PRODUCTS: WHOLE, FROZEN

Source: *Weekly Insiders Dairy & Egg Letter.* **Price Frequency:** weekly. **Units of Measure:** Dollars per lb. **Time Period Covered:** latest week.

EGG PRODUCTS: YOLKS

Source: *Urner Barry's Price-Current, West Coast Edition.* **Price Frequency:** semiweekly. **Effective Market(s):** West Coast. **Units of Measure:** Dollars per lb. **Time Period Covered:** latest week.

EGG PRODUCTS: YOLKS, FROZEN

Source: *Weekly Insiders Dairy & Egg Letter.* **Price Frequency:** weekly. **Units of Measure:** Dollars per lb. **Time Period Covered:** latest week.

EGG SOLIDS: ALBUMEN, SPRAY

Source: *Urner Barry's Price-Current.* **Price Frequency:** daily. **Units of Measure:** Dollars per lb. **Time Period Covered:** latest day.

Source: *Weekly Insiders Dairy & Egg Letter.* **Price Frequency:** weekly. **Units of Measure:** Dollars per lb. **Time Period Covered:** latest week.

EGG SOLIDS: BLENDS

Source: *Urner Barry's Price-Current.* **Price Frequency:** daily. **Units of Measure:** Dollars per lb. **Time Period Covered:** latest day.

Source: *Weekly Insiders Dairy & Egg Letter.* **Price Frequency:** weekly. **Units of Measure:** Dollars per lb. **Time Period Covered:** latest week.

EGG SOLIDS: WHITES

Source: *Milling & Baking News.* **Price Frequency:** weekly. **Units of Measure:** Dollars per lb. **Time Period Covered:** latest week.

EGG SOLIDS: WHOLE

Source: *Milling & Baking News.* **Price Frequency:** weekly. **Units of Measure:** Dollars per lb. **Time Period Covered:** latest week.

EGG SOLIDS: WHOLE, PLAIN

Source: *Urner Barry's Price-Current.* **Price Frequency:** daily. **Units of Measure:** Dollars per lb. **Time Period Covered:** latest day.

Source: *Weekly Insiders Dairy & Egg Letter.* **Price Frequency:** weekly. **Units of Measure:** Dollars per lb. **Time Period Covered:** latest week.

EGG SOLIDS: YOLKS

Source: *Milling & Baking News.* **Price Frequency:** weekly. **Units of Measure:** Dollars per lb. **Time Period Covered:** latest week.

Source: *Urner Barry's Price-Current.* **Price Frequency:** daily. **Units of Measure:** Dollars per lb. **Time Period Covered:** latest day.

Source: *Weekly Insiders Dairy & Egg Letter.* **Price Frequency:** weekly. **Units of Measure:** Dollars per lb. **Time Period Covered:** latest week.

EGGPLANT

Source: *Fresh Fruit and Vegetable Prices.* **Price Frequency:** monthly, seasonally. **Effective Market(s):** Pompano Beach (FL), South/Central Florida, North Carolina. **Units of Measure:** Dollars per carton/crate. **Type of Price:** average price at shipping point. **Time Period Covered:** latest year.

Source: *Lancaster Farming.* **Price Frequency:** weekly, seasonally. **Effective Market(s):** Pennsylvania. **Units of Measure:** Dollars per carton. **Type of Price:** market. **Time Period Covered:** latest week.

Source: *New Zealand Farmer.* **Price Frequency:** weekly, seasonally. **Effective Market(s):** New Zealand. **Units of Measure:** New Zealand dollars per kilogram. **Time Period Covered:** latest week.

EGGPLANT: FLORIDA

Source: *Fresh Fruit and Vegetable Prices.* **Price Frequency:** monthly, seasonally. **Effective Market(s):** Chicago, New York City. **Units of Measure:** Dollars per crate/carton. **Type of Price:** average wholesale price. **Time Period Covered:** latest year.

EGGPLANT: FRESH

Source: *HRI-Buyers Guide.* **Price Frequency:** weekly. **Effective Market(s):** Northeastern area. **Units of Measure:** Dollars per case. **Time Period Covered:** latest week.

EGGPLANT: ILLINOIS

Source: *Fresh Fruit and Vegetable Prices.* **Price Frequency:** monthly, seasonally. **Effective Market(s):** Chicago. **Units of Measure:** Dollars per crate/carton. **Type of Price:** average wholesale price. **Time Period Covered:** latest year.

EGGPLANT: ITALIAN TYPE, FRESH

Source: *HRI-Buyers Guide.* **Price Frequency:** weekly. **Effective Market(s):** Northeastern area. **Units of Measure:** Dollars per case. **Time Period Covered:** latest week.

EGGPLANT: MEXICO

Source: *Fresh Fruit and Vegetable Prices.* **Price Frequency:** monthly, seasonally. **Effective Market(s):** Nogales (AZ). **Units of Measure:** Dollars per carton/crate. **Type of Price:** price paid at point of entry. **Time Period Covered:** latest year.

Source: *Fresh Fruit and Vegetable Prices.* **Price Frequency:** monthly, seasonally. **Effective Market(s):** Chicago, New York City. **Units of Measure:** Dollars per crate/carton. **Type of Price:** average wholesale price. **Time Period Covered:** latest year.

EGGPLANT: NEW JERSEY

Source: *Fresh Fruit and Vegetable Prices.* **Price Frequency:** monthly, seasonally. **Effective Market(s):** New York City. **Units of Measure:** Dollars per crate/carton. **Type of Price:** average wholesale price. **Time Period Covered:** latest year.

EGGS

Source: *Agra Europe.* **Price Frequency:** weekly. **Effective Market(s):** 9 European markets. **Units of Measure:** national currency per dozen. **Type of Price:** average. **Time Period Covered:** latest week.

Source: *Agricultural Outlook.* **Price Frequency:** monthly, annually. **Effective Market(s):** United States. **Units of Measure:** cents per dozen. **Type of Price:** price received by farmers. **Time Period Covered:** monthly latest 6 months, annually latest 3 years.

Source: *Agricultural Prices Annual Summary.* **Price Frequency:** monthly, seasonally. **Effective Market(s):** United States. **Units of Measure:** cents per dozen. **Type of Price:** average received by farmer. **Time Period Covered:** monthly latest year, for US latest 6 years.

Source: *FAO Quarterly Bulletin of Statistics.* **Price Frequency:** monthly, annually. **Effective Market(s):** United States. **Units of Measure:** Dollars per 1200, dollars per metric ton. **Type of Price:** producer. **Time Period Covered:** latest 3 years.

Source: *Illinois Farm Report.* **Price Frequency:** quarterly. **Effective Market(s):** Illinois. **Units of Measure:** Dollars per dozen. **Type of Price:** average received by farmers. **Time Period Covered:** latest 2 months, year ago.

Source: *Livestock and Poultry Situation and Outlook Report.* **Price Frequency:** monthly, annually. **Units of Measure:** cents per dozen. **Type of Price:** farm. **Time Period Covered:** latest 3 years.

Source: *Standard & Poor's Statistical Service Current Statistics.* **Price Frequency:** monthly, annually. **Units of Measure:** cents per dozen. **Time Period Covered:** latest 5 years.

Source: *Statistical Bulletin of the South Pacific: Retail Price Indexes.* **Price Frequency:** annually. **Effective Market(s):** 18 South Pacific markets. **Units of Measure:** Australian dollars per . **Type of Price:** retail. **Time Period Covered:** latest year.

EGGS: ALL TYPES

Source: *Agricultural Prices.* **Price Frequency:** monthly. **Effective Market(s):** United States. **Units of Measure:** Dollars per dozen. **Type of Price:** received by farmer. **Time Period Covered:** latest 2 months, year ago.

Source: *Agricultural Prices Annual Summary.* **Price Frequency:** annually. **Effective Market(s):** 50 domestic markets, United States. **Units of Measure:** Dollars per dozen. **Type of Price:** average received by farmer. **Time Period Covered:** latest 2 years.

EGGS: BREAKING STOCK, NEST RUN

Source: *Urner Barry's Price-Current.* **Price Frequency:** daily. **Effective Market(s):** Midwest, Northeast, Southeast, South Central. **Units of Measure:** cents per dozen. **Type of Price:** general trading. **Time Period Covered:** latest day.

EGGS: BREAKING STOCK, UNDERGRADE AND CHECKS

Source: *Urner Barry's Price-Current.* **Price Frequency:** daily. **Effective Market(s):** Midwest, Northeast, Southeast, South Central. **Units of Measure:** cents per dozen. **Type of Price:** general trading. **Time Period Covered:** latest day.

EGGS: BROWN

Source: *Farm and Dairy.* **Price Frequency:** weekly, seasonally. **Effective Market(s):** Ohio, Pennsylvania. **Units of Measure:** Dollars per dozen. **Type of Price:** auction high, auction low. **Time Period Covered:** latest week.

EGGS: BROWN, EXTRA LARGE

Source: *Lancaster Farming.* **Price Frequency:** weekly. **Effective Market(s):** Northeast. **Units of Measure:** Dollars per dozen. **Type of Price:** auction. **Time Period Covered:** latest week.

Source: *Monthly Price Review.* **Price Frequency:** daily. **Effective Market(s):** Boston. **Units of Measure:** Dollars per dozen. **Type of Price:** spot. **Time Period Covered:** latest month.

EGGS: BROWN, GRADE A, EXTRA LARGE

Source: *Poultry Market Statistics.* **Price Frequency:** monthly, annually. **Effective Market(s):** New England area. **Units of Measure:** cents per dozen. **Type of Price:** farm. **Time Period Covered:** latest year.

EGGS: BROWN, GRADE A, JUMBO

Source: *Poultry Market Statistics.* **Price Frequency:** monthly, annually. **Effective Market(s):** New England area. **Units of Measure:** cents per dozen. **Type of Price:** farm. **Time Period Covered:** latest year.

EGGS: BROWN, GRADE A, LARGE

Source: *Poultry Market Statistics.* **Price Frequency:** monthly, annually. **Effective Market(s):** New England area. **Units of Measure:** cents per dozen. **Type of Price:** farm. **Time Period Covered:** latest year.

EGGS: BROWN, GRADE A, MEDIUM

Source: *Poultry Market Statistics.* **Price Frequency:** monthly, annually. **Effective Market(s):** New England area. **Units of Measure:** cents per dozen. **Type of Price:** farm. **Time Period Covered:** latest year.

EGGS: BROWN, GRADE A, SMALL

Source: *Poultry Market Statistics.* **Price Frequency:** monthly, annually. **Effective Market(s):** New England area. **Units of Measure:** cents per dozen. **Type of Price:** farm. **Time Period Covered:** latest year.

EGGS: BROWN, LARGE

Source: *Lancaster Farming.* **Price Frequency:** weekly. **Effective Market(s):** Northeast. **Units of Measure:** Dollars per dozen. **Type of Price:** auction. **Time Period Covered:** latest week.

Source: *Monthly Price Review.* **Price Frequency:** daily. **Effective Market(s):** Boston, Midwest, Northeast, Southeast, South Central. **Units of Measure:** Dollars per dozen. **Type of Price:** spot. **Time Period Covered:** latest month.

Source: *Weekly Insiders Dairy & Egg Letter.* **Price Frequency:** annually. **Effective Market(s):** Northeast. **Units of Measure:** cents per dozen. **Type of Price:** wholesale. **Time Period Covered:** latest 5 years.

Source: *Weekly Insiders Dairy & Egg Letter.* **Price Frequency:** weekly. **Effective Market(s):** Northeast, Midwest, Southeast, South Central. **Units of Measure:** cents per dozen. **Type of Price:** wholesale. **Time Period Covered:** latest week.

Source: *Weekly Insiders Dairy & Egg Letter.* **Price Frequency:** weekly. **Effective Market(s):** New York. **Units of Measure:** cents per dozen. **Type of Price:** retail. **Time Period Covered:** latest week, week ago, year ago, 2 years ago.

EGGS: BROWN, MEDIUM

Source: *Lancaster Farming.* **Price Frequency:** weekly. **Effective Market(s):** Northeast. **Units of Measure:** Dollars per dozen. **Type of Price:** auction. **Time Period Covered:** latest week.

Source: *Monthly Price Review.* **Price Frequency:** daily. **Effective Market(s):** Boston. **Units of Measure:** Dollars per dozen. **Type of Price:** spot. **Time Period Covered:** latest month.

EGGS: BROWN, SIZE 1, SCOTTISH

Source: *Scottish Farmer.* **Price Frequency:** weekly. **Effective Market(s):** Central Scotland. **Units of Measure:** British pence per dozen. **Type of Price:** producer to retailer. **Time Period Covered:** latest week.

EGGS: BROWN, SIZE 2, SCOTTISH

Source: *Scottish Farmer.* **Price Frequency:** weekly. **Effective Market(s):** Central Scotland. **Units of Measure:** British pence per dozen. **Type of Price:** producer to retailer. **Time Period Covered:** latest week.

EGGS: BROWN, SIZE 3, SCOTTISH

Source: *Scottish Farmer.* **Price Frequency:** weekly. **Effective Market(s):** Central Scotland. **Units of Measure:** British pence per dozen. **Type of Price:** producer to retailer. **Time Period Covered:** latest week.

EGGS: BROWN, SIZE 4, SCOTTISH

Source: *Scottish Farmer.* **Price Frequency:** weekly. **Effective Market(s):** Central Scotland. **Units of Measure:** British pence per dozen. **Type of Price:** producer to retailer. **Time Period Covered:** latest week.

EGGS: BROWN, SIZE 5, SCOTTISH

Source: *Scottish Farmer.* **Price Frequency:** weekly. **Effective Market(s):** Central Scotland. **Units of Measure:** British pence per dozen. **Type of Price:** producer to retailer. **Time Period Covered:** latest week.

EGGS: BROWN, SIZE 6, SCOTTISH

Source: *Scottish Farmer.* **Price Frequency:** weekly. **Effective Market(s):** Central Scotland. **Units of Measure:** British pence per dozen. **Type of Price:** producer to retailer. **Time Period Covered:** latest week.

EGGS: BROWN, SMALL

Source: *Lancaster Farming.* **Price Frequency:** weekly. **Effective Market(s):** Northeast. **Units of Measure:** Dollars per dozen. **Type of Price:** auction. **Time Period Covered:** latest week.

EGGS: BROWN, TABLE GRADE, EXTRA LARGE

Source: *Urner Barry's Price-Current.* **Price Frequency:** daily. **Effective Market(s):** Midwest, Northeast, Southeast, South Central. **Units of Measure:** cents per dozen. **Type of Price:** spot. **Time Period Covered:** latest day, 5 day average.

EGGS: BROWN, TABLE GRADE, LARGE

Source: *Urner Barry's Price-Current.* **Price Frequency:** daily. **Effective Market(s):** Northeast, Midwest, Southeast, South Central. **Units of Measure:** cents per dozen. **Type of Price:** spot. **Time Period Covered:** latest day, 5 day average.

EGGS: BROWN, TABLE GRADE, MEDIUM

Source: *Urner Barry's Price-Current.* **Price Frequency:** daily. **Effective Market(s):** Northeast, Midwest, Southeast, South Central. **Units of Measure:** cents per dozen. **Type of Price:** spot. **Time Period Covered:** latest day, 5 day average.

EGGS: BROWN, UNGRADED, SECONDS

Source: *Farmers Weekly.* **Price Frequency:** weekly. **Effective Market(s):** Great Britain. **Units of Measure:** British pence per dozen. **Type of Price:** farm. **Time Period Covered:** latest week.

EGGS: BROWN, UNGRADED, SIZE 1

Source: *Farmers Weekly.* **Price Frequency:** weekly. **Effective Market(s):** Great Britain. **Units of Measure:** British pence per dozen. **Type of Price:** farm. **Time Period Covered:** latest week.

EGGS: BROWN, UNGRADED, SIZE 2

Source: *Farmers Weekly.* **Price Frequency:** weekly. **Effective Market(s):** Great Britain. **Units of Measure:** British pence per dozen. **Type of Price:** farm. **Time Period Covered:** latest week.

EGGS: BROWN, UNGRADED, SIZE 3

Source: *Farmers Weekly.* **Price Frequency:** weekly. **Effective Market(s):** Great Britain. **Units of Measure:** British pence per dozen. **Type of Price:** farm. **Time Period Covered:** latest week.

EGGS: BROWN, UNGRADED, SIZE 4

Source: *Farmers Weekly.* **Price Frequency:** weekly. **Effective Market(s):** Great Britain. **Units of Measure:** British pence per dozen. **Type of Price:** farm. **Time Period Covered:** latest week.

EGGS: BROWN, UNGRADED, SIZE 5

Source: *Farmers Weekly.* **Price Frequency:** weekly. **Effective Market(s):** Great Britain. **Units of Measure:** British pence per dozen. **Type of Price:** farm. **Time Period Covered:** latest week.

EGGS: BROWN, UNGRADED, SIZE 6

Source: *Farmers Weekly.* **Price Frequency:** weekly. **Effective Market(s):** Great Britain. **Units of Measure:** British pence per dozen. **Type of Price:** farm. **Time Period Covered:** latest week.

EGGS: BROWN, UNGRADED, SIZE 7

Source: *Farmers Weekly.* **Price Frequency:** weekly. **Effective Market(s):** Great Britain. **Units of Measure:** British pence per dozen. **Type of Price:** farm. **Time Period Covered:** latest week.

EGGS: CHECK

Source: *Milling & Baking News.* **Price Frequency:** weekly. **Units of Measure:** Dollars per case. **Time Period Covered:** latest week.

EGGS: DRIED, ALBUMEN, SPRAY

Source: *Monthly Price Review.* **Price Frequency:** daily. **Units of Measure:** Dollars per lb. **Type of Price:** spot. **Time Period Covered:** latest month.

EGGS: DRIED, ALBUMENS

Source: *Poultry Market Statistics.* **Price Frequency:** monthly, annually. **Effective Market(s):** New York. **Units of Measure:** Dollars per lb. **Type of Price:** wholesale. **Time Period Covered:** latest year.

EGGS: DRIED, BLENDS

Source: *Poultry Market Statistics.* **Price Frequency:** monthly, annually. **Effective Market(s):** New York. **Units of Measure:** Dollars per lb. **Type of Price:** wholesale. **Time Period Covered:** latest year.

EGGS: DRIED, WHITES

Source: *Bakery Newsletter.* **Price Frequency:** weekly. **Effective Market(s):** Midwest, New York. **Units of Measure:** Dollars per lb. **Type of Price:** cash. **Time Period Covered:** latest week.

EGGS: DRIED, WHOLE

Source: *Bakery Newsletter.* **Price Frequency:** weekly. **Effective Market(s):** Midwest, New York. **Units of Measure:** Dollars per lb. **Type of Price:** cash. **Time Period Covered:** latest week.

Source: *Monthly Price Review.* **Price Frequency:** daily. **Units of Measure:** Dollars per lb. **Type of Price:** spot. **Time Period Covered:** latest month.

Source: *Poultry Market Statistics.* **Price Frequency:** monthly, annually. **Effective Market(s):** New York. **Units of Measure:** Dollars per lb. **Type of Price:** wholesale. **Time Period Covered:** latest year.

EGGS: DRIED, YOLKS

Source: *Bakery Newsletter.* **Price Frequency:** weekly. **Effective Market(s):** Midwest, New York. **Units of Measure:** Dollars per lb. **Type of Price:** cash. **Time Period Covered:** latest week.

Source: *Monthly Price Review.* **Price Frequency:** daily. **Units of Measure:** Dollars per lb. **Type of Price:** spot. **Time Period Covered:** latest month.

Source: *Poultry Market Statistics.* **Price Frequency:** monthly, annually. **Effective Market(s):** New York. **Units of Measure:** Dollars per lb. **Type of Price:** wholesale. **Time Period Covered:** latest year.

EGGS: EXTRA LARGE

Source: *Poultry Times.* **Price Frequency:** biweekly. **Effective Market(s):** New York. **Units of Measure:** cents per carton. **Type of Price:** delivered to store. **Time Period Covered:** week ago, 3 weeks ago.

Source: *Poultry Times.* **Price Frequency:** biweekly. **Effective Market(s):** Atlanta. **Units of Measure:** cents per carton. **Type of Price:** deliver to warehouse. **Time Period Covered:** 2 weeks ago, month ago.

EGGS: FANCY, LARGE

Source: *HRI-Buyers Guide.* **Price Frequency:** weekly. **Effective Market(s):** Northeastern area. **Units of Measure:** Dollars per loose dozen. **Time Period Covered:** latest week.

EGGS: FANCY, MEDIUM

Source: *HRI-Buyers Guide.* **Price Frequency:** weekly. **Effective Market(s):** Northeastern area. **Units of Measure:** Dollars per loose dozen. **Time Period Covered:** latest week.

EGGS: FANCY, PULLETS

Source: *HRI-Buyers Guide.* **Price Frequency:** weekly. **Effective Market(s):** Northeastern area. **Units of Measure:** Dollars per loose dozen. **Time Period Covered:** latest week.

EGGS: FROZEN

Source: *Lancaster Farming.* **Price Frequency:** weekly. **Effective Market(s):** Northeast. **Units of Measure:** cents per lb. in 30 lb. containers. **Type of Price:** wholesale. **Time Period Covered:** latest week.

EGGS: FROZEN, BLENDS

Source: *Monthly Price Review.* **Price Frequency:** daily. **Units of Measure:** Dollars per lb. **Type of Price:** spot. **Time Period Covered:** latest month.

Source: *Poultry Market Statistics.* **Price Frequency:** monthly, annually. **Effective Market(s):** New York/ Philadelphia. **Units of Measure:** cents per lb. **Time Period Covered:** latest year.

EGGS: FROZEN, BLENDS, 27-29% EGG SOLIDS

Source: *Urner Barry's Price-Current.* **Price Frequency:** daily. **Units of Measure:** cents per lb. **Time Period Covered:** latest day.

EGGS: FROZEN, BLENDS, 30-32% EGG SOLIDS

Source: *Urner Barry's Price-Current.* **Price Frequency:** daily. **Units of Measure:** cents per lb. **Time Period Covered:** latest day.

EGGS: FROZEN, BLENDS, 30-32% EGG SOLIDS, INSTITUTIONAL PACKS

Source: *Urner Barry's Price-Current.* **Price Frequency:** daily. **Units of Measure:** cents per lb. **Time Period Covered:** latest day.

EGGS: FROZEN, WHITES

Source: *Monthly Price Review.* **Price Frequency:** daily. **Units of Measure:** Dollars per lb. **Type of Price:** spot. **Time Period Covered:** latest month.

Source: *Poultry Market Statistics.* **Price Frequency:** monthly, annually. **Effective Market(s):** Chicago, New York/Philadelphia, San Francisco. **Units of Measure:** cents per lb. **Type of Price:** wholesale. **Time Period Covered:** latest year.

Source: *Urner Barry's Price-Current.* **Price Frequency:** daily. **Units of Measure:** cents per lb. **Time Period Covered:** latest day.

EGGS: FROZEN, WHITES, INSTITUTIONAL PACKS

Source: *Urner Barry's Price-Current.* **Price Frequency:** daily. **Units of Measure:** cents per lb. **Time Period Covered:** latest day.

EGGS: FROZEN, WHOLE

Source: *Monthly Price Review.* **Price Frequency:** daily. **Units of Measure:** Dollars per lb. **Type of Price:** spot. **Time Period Covered:** latest month.

Source: *Poultry Market Statistics.* **Price Frequency:** monthly, annually. **Effective Market(s):** New York/ Philadelphia, San Francisco. **Units of Measure:** cents per lb. **Time Period Covered:** latest year.

EGGS: FROZEN, WHOLE, ACTUAL 2

Source: *Urner Barry's Price-Current.* **Price Frequency:** daily. **Units of Measure:** cents per lb. **Time Period Covered:** latest day.

EGGS: FROZEN, WHOLE, ACTUAL 3

Source: *Urner Barry's Price-Current.* **Price Frequency:** daily. **Units of Measure:** cents per lb. **Time Period Covered:** latest day.

EGGS: FROZEN, WHOLE, INSTITUTIONAL PACKS

Source: *Urner Barry's Price-Current.* **Price Frequency:** daily. **Units of Measure:** cents per lb. **Time Period Covered:** latest day.

EGGS: FROZEN, WHOLE, LIGHT COLORED

Source: *Poultry Market Statistics.* **Price Frequency:** monthly, annually. **Effective Market(s):** Chicago, New York/Philadelphia. **Units of Measure:** cents per lb. **Type of Price:** wholesale. **Time Period Covered:** latest year.

EGGS: FROZEN, WHOLE, NO COLOR

Source: *Urner Barry's Price-Current.* **Price Frequency:** daily. **Units of Measure:** cents per lb. **Time Period Covered:** latest day.

EGGS: FROZEN, YOLKS

Source: *Monthly Price Review.* **Price Frequency:** daily. **Units of Measure:** Dollars per lb. **Type of Price:** spot. **Time Period Covered:** latest month.

EGGS: FROZEN, YOLKS, 43% SOLIDS, SALTED, NO COLOR

Source: *Urner Barry's Price-Current.* **Price Frequency:** daily. **Units of Measure:** cents per lb. **Time Period Covered:** latest day.

EGGS: FROZEN, YOLKS, 43% SOLIDS, SUGARED, NO COLOR

Source: *Urner Barry's Price-Current.* **Price Frequency:** daily. **Units of Measure:** cents per lb. **Time Period Covered:** latest day.

EGGS: FROZEN, YOLKS, 45% SOLIDS, ACTUAL 3

Source: *Urner Barry's Price-Current.* **Price Frequency:** daily. **Units of Measure:** cents per lb. **Time Period Covered:** latest day.

EGGS: FROZEN, YOLKS, 45% SOLIDS, ACTUAL 4

Source: *Urner Barry's Price-Current.* **Price Frequency:** daily. **Units of Measure:** cents per lb. **Time Period Covered:** latest day.

EGGS: FROZEN, YOLKS, 45% SOLIDS, NEPA 3

Source: *Urner Barry's Price-Current.* **Price Frequency:** daily. **Units of Measure:** cents per lb. **Time Period Covered:** latest day.

EGGS: FROZEN, YOLKS, 45% SOLIDS, UNDER NEPA 3

Source: *Urner Barry's Price-Current.* **Price Frequency:** daily. **Units of Measure:** cents per lb. **Time Period Covered:** latest day.

EGGS: FROZEN, YOLKS, SALTED

Source: *Poultry Market Statistics.* **Price Frequency:** monthly, annually. **Effective Market(s):** Chicago, New York/Philadelphia, San Francisco. **Units of Measure:** cents per lb. **Type of Price:** wholesale. **Time Period Covered:** latest year.

EGGS: FROZEN, YOLKS, SUGARED

Source: *Poultry Market Statistics.* **Price Frequency:** monthly, annually. **Effective Market(s):** Chicago, New York/Philadelphia, San Francisco. **Units of Measure:** cents per lb. **Type of Price:** wholesale. **Time Period Covered:** latest year.

EGGS: FROZEN, YOLKS, SUGARED, INSTITUTIONAL PACKS

Source: *Urner BArry's Price-Current.* **Price Frequency:** daily. **Units of Measure:** cents per lb. **Time Period Covered:** latest day.

EGGS: GRADE A OR BETTER, LARGE

Source: *Poultry Market Statistics.* **Price Frequency:** monthly, annually. **Effective Market(s):** Iowa, Missouri. **Units of Measure:** cents per dozen. **Type of Price:** farm. **Time Period Covered:** latest year.

EGGS: GRADE A OR BETTER, MEDIUM

Source: *Poultry Market Statistics.* **Price Frequency:** monthly, annually. **Effective Market(s):** Iowa, Missouri. **Units of Measure:** cents per dozen. **Type of Price:** farm. **Time Period Covered:** latest year.

EGGS: GRADE A OR BETTER, SMALL

Source: *Poultry Market Statistics.* **Price Frequency:** monthly, annually. **Effective Market(s):** Iowa, Missouri. **Units of Measure:** cents per dozen. **Type of Price:** farm. **Time Period Covered:** latest year.

EGGS: GRADE A, LARGE

Source: *Agricultural Outlook.* **Price Frequency:** quarterly, annually. **Effective Market(s):** New York. **Units of Measure:** cents per dozen. **Type of Price:** average. **Time Period Covered:** latest year.

Source: *Agricultural Outlook.* **Price Frequency:** annually. **Effective Market(s):** United States. **Units of Measure:** cents per dozen. **Type of Price:** wholesale. **Time Period Covered:** latest 4 years.

Source: *Agricultural Outlook.* **Price Frequency:** monthly, annually. **Effective Market(s):** New York. **Units of Measure:** cents per dozen. **Type of Price:** wholesale. **Time Period Covered:** monthly latest 6 months, annually latest 3 years.

Source: *Livestock and Poultry Situation and Outlook Report.* **Price Frequency:** quarterly, annually. **Effective Market(s):** New York. **Units of Measure:** cents per dozen. **Type of Price:** volume buyer. **Time Period Covered:** latest 2 years.

Source: *Livestock and Poultry Situation and Outlook Report.* **Price Frequency:** monthly, annually. **Effective Market(s):** 4-region average. **Units of Measure:** cents per dozen. **Type of Price:** retail. **Time Period Covered:** latest 3 years.

Source: *Livestock and Poultry Situation and Outlook Report.* **Price Frequency:** monthly, annually. **Effective Market(s):** New York. **Units of Measure:** cents per dozen. **Type of Price:** volume buyer. **Time Period Covered:** latest 3 years.

Source: *Livestock and Poultry Update.* **Price Frequency:** monthly. **Units of Measure:** cents per lb. **Type of Price:** retail. **Time Period Covered:** latest 3 months, year ago.

Source: *Livestock and Poultry Update.* **Price Frequency:** monthly. **Effective Market(s):** New York, 12-market average. **Units of Measure:** cents per dozen. **Type of Price:** wholesale. **Time Period Covered:** latest 3 months, year ago.

EGGS: GRADE AA, LARGE

Source: *California Farmer.* **Price Frequency:** semimonthly. **Effective Market(s):** Northern California, Los Angeles. **Units of Measure:** cents per dozen. **Type of Price:** price to chain stores. **Time Period Covered:** latest week, month ago, year ago.

EGGS: GRADEABLE NEST RUN, CLASS 1

Source: *Urner Barry's Price-Current.* **Price Frequency:** daily. **Effective Market(s):** Northeast, Midwest, Southeast, South Central. **Units of Measure:** cents per dozen. **Type of Price:** delivered. **Time Period Covered:** latest day.

EGGS: GRADEABLE NEST RUN, CLASS 2

Source: *Urner Barry's Price-Current.* **Price Frequency:** daily. **Effective Market(s):** Northeast, Midwest, Southeast, South Central. **Units of Measure:** cents per dozen. **Type of Price:** delivered. **Time Period Covered:** latest day.

EGGS: GRADEABLE NEST RUN, CLASS 3

Source: *Urner Barry's Price-Current.* **Price Frequency:** daily. **Effective Market(s):** Northeast, Midwest, Southeast, South Centra;. **Units of Measure:** cents per dozen. **Type of Price:** delivered. **Time Period Covered:** latest day.

EGGS: GRADEABLE NEST RUN, CLASS 4

Source: *Urner Barry's Price-Current.* **Price Frequency:** daily. **Effective Market(s):** Northeast, Midwest, Southeast, South Central. **Units of Measure:** cents per dozen. **Type of Price:** delivered. **Time Period Covered:** latest day.

EGGS: LARGE

Source: *Commodity Year Book.* **Price Frequency:** monthly, annually. **Effective Market(s):** Chicago. **Units of Measure:** cents per dozen. **Type of Price:** wholesale. **Time Period Covered:** latest 7 years.

Source: *Poultry Times.* **Price Frequency:** biweekly. **Effective Market(s):** New York. **Units of Measure:** cents per carton. **Type of Price:** delivered to store. **Time Period Covered:** week ago, 3 weeks ago.

Source: *Poultry Times.* **Price Frequency:** biweekly. **Effective Market(s):** Atlanta. **Units of Measure:** cents per carton. **Type of Price:** delivered to warehouse. **Time Period Covered:** 2 weeks ago, month ago.

Source: *Survey of Current Business.* **Price Frequency:** monthly, annually. **Effective Market(s):** Chicago. **Units of Measure:** Dollars per dozen. **Type of Price:** wholesale. **Time Period Covered:** latest 2 years.

Source: *Weekly Statistical Fishery Report.* **Price Frequency:** weekly. **Effective Market(s):** Northeast. **Units of Measure:** cents per dozen. **Type of Price:** spot. **Time Period Covered:** latest week.

EGGS: LIQUID

Source: *Urner Barry's Price-Current, West Coast Edition.* **Price Frequency:** semiweekly. **Effective Market(s):** West Coast. **Units of Measure:** Dollars per lb. **Time Period Covered:** latest week.

EGGS: LIQUID, UNPASTEURIZED

Source: *Poultry Market Statistics.* **Price Frequency:** weekly. **Effective Market(s):** Central States. **Units of Measure:** cents per lb. **Type of Price:** average. **Time Period Covered:** latest year.

EGGS: LIQUID, WHITES

Source: *Monthly Price Review.* **Price Frequency:** daily. **Units of Measure:** Dollars per lb. **Type of Price:** spot. **Time Period Covered:** latest month.

EGGS: LIQUID, WHITES, PASTEURIZED, CUSTOM PACK

Source: *Urner Barry's Price-Current.* **Price Frequency:** daily. **Units of Measure:** cents per lb. **Time Period Covered:** latest week.

EGGS: LIQUID, WHITES, UNPASTEURIZED

Source: *Poultry Market Statistics.* **Price Frequency:** monthly, annually. **Effective Market(s):** Southeast. **Units of Measure:** cents per lb. **Type of Price:** processor. **Time Period Covered:** latest year.

Source: *Urner Barry's Price-Current.* **Price Frequency:** daily. **Units of Measure:** cents per lb. **Time Period Covered:** latest week.

EGGS: LIQUID, WHOLE

Source: *Monthly Price Review.* **Price Frequency:** daily. **Units of Measure:** Dollars per lb. **Type of Price:** spot. **Time Period Covered:** latest month.

EGGS: LIQUID, WHOLE, PASTEURIZED, CUSTOM PACK

Source: *Urner Barry's Price-Current.* **Price Frequency:** daily. **Units of Measure:** cents per lb. **Time Period Covered:** latest day.

EGGS: LIQUID, WHOLE, UNPASTEURIZED

Source: *Urner Barry's Price Current.* **Price Frequency:** daily. **Units of Measure:** cents per lb. **Time Period Covered:** latest day.

EGGS: LIQUID, YOLKS

Source: *Monthly Price Review.* **Price Frequency:** daily. **Units of Measure:** Dollars per lb. **Type of Price:** spot. **Time Period Covered:** latest month.

EGGS: LIQUID, YOLKS, 43% SOLIDS, PASTEURIZED, CUSTOM PACK

Source: *Urner Barry's Price-Current.* **Price Frequency:** daily. **Units of Measure:** cents per lb. **Time Period Covered:** latest week.

EGGS: LIQUID, YOLKS, 43% SOLIDS, UNPASTEURIZED

Source: *Urner Barry's Price-Current.* **Price Frequency:** daily. **Units of Measure:** cents per lb. **Time Period Covered:** latest day.

EGGS: LIQUID, YOLKS, SALTED, 43% SOLIDS, 10% SALT

Source: *Urner Barry's Price-Current.* **Price Frequency:** daily. **Units of Measure:** cents per lb. **Time Period Covered:** latest day.

EGGS: MARKET

Source: *Agricultural Prices.* **Price Frequency:** monthly. **Effective Market(s):** United States. **Units of Measure:** Dollars per dozen. **Type of Price:** received by farmer. **Time Period Covered:** latest 2 months, year ago.

Source: *Agricultural Prices.* **Price Frequency:** monthly. **Effective Market(s):** 20 domestic markets, United States. **Units of Measure:** Dollars per dozen. **Type of Price:** received by farmer. **Time Period Covered:** latest month.

Source: *Agricultural Prices Annual Summary.* **Price Frequency:** monthly, seasonally. **Effective Market(s):** 20 domestic markets, United States. **Units of Measure:** cents per dozen. **Type of Price:** average received by farmer. **Time Period Covered:** monthly latest year, for US latest 6 years.

Source: *Agricultural Prices Annual Summary.* **Price Frequency:** annually. **Effective Market(s):** 50 domestic markets, United States. **Units of Measure:** Dollars per dozen. **Type of Price:** average received by farmer. **Time Period Covered:** latest 2 years.

EGGS: MEDIUM

Source: *Poultry Times.* **Price Frequency:** biweekly. **Effective Market(s):** New York. **Units of Measure:** cents per carton. **Type of Price:** delivered to store. **Time Period Covered:** week ago, 3 weeks ago.

Source: *Poultry Times.* **Price Frequency:** biweekly. **Effective Market(s):** Atlanta. **Units of Measure:** cents per carton. **Type of Price:** delivered to warehouse. **Time Period Covered:** 2 weeks ago, month ago.

EGGS: NEST RUNS

Source: *Milling & Baking News.* **Price Frequency:** weekly. **Units of Measure:** Dollars per case. **Time Period Covered:** latest week.

EGGS: NESTING RUN BREAKING STOCK

Source: *Poultry Market Statistics.* **Price Frequency:** monthly. **Effective Market(s):** 4-region average, Midwest, Northeast, South/Central, Southeast. **Units of Measure:** cents per dozen. **Type of Price:** weighted average. **Time Period Covered:** latest year.

EGGS: OFF GRADE, UNDERGRADES AND CHECKS

Source: *Lancaster Farming.* **Price Frequency:** weekly. **Effective Market(s):** Northeast. **Units of Measure:** Dollars per dozen. **Type of Price:** auction. **Time Period Covered:** latest week.

EGGS: PRESERVED, SHANGHAI

Source: *Prices of Selected Asia/Pacific Products.* **Price Frequency:** monthly. **Effective Market(s):** Hong Kong. **Units of Measure:** Hong Kong dollars per 1000 pieces. **Type of Price:** wholesale high, wholesale low. **Time Period Covered:** latest month.

EGGS: SIZE 1, SCOTTISH

Source: *Scottish Farmer.* **Price Frequency:** weekly. **Effective Market(s):** Scotland. **Units of Measure:** British pence per dozen. **Type of Price:** retailer to packer, consumer to packer. **Time Period Covered:** latest week.

EGGS: SIZE 2, SCOTTISH

Source: *Scottish Farmer.* **Price Frequency:** weekly. **Effective Market(s):** Scotland. **Units of Measure:** British pence per dozen. **Type of Price:** packer to producer, retailer to packer, consumer to packer. **Time Period Covered:** latest week.

EGGS: SIZE 3, SCOTTISH

Source: *Scottish Farmer.* **Price Frequency:** weekly. **Effective Market(s):** Scotland. **Units of Measure:** British pence per dozen. **Type of Price:** packer to producer, retailer to packer, consumer to packer. **Time Period Covered:** latest week.

EGGS: SIZE 4, SCOTTISH

Source: *Scottish Farmer.* **Price Frequency:** weekly. **Effective Market(s):** Scotland. **Units of Measure:** British pence per dozen. **Type of Price:** packer to producer, retailer to packer, consumer to packer. **Time Period Covered:** latest week.

EGGS: SIZE 5, SCOTTISH

Source: *Scottish Farmer.* **Price Frequency:** weekly. **Effective Market(s):** Scotland. **Units of Measure:** British pence per dozen. **Type of Price:** packer to producer, retailer to packer, consumer to packer. **Time Period Covered:** latest week.

EGGS: TABLE

Source: *Washington Farmer-Stockman.* **Price Frequency:** monthly. **Effective Market(s):** Washington. **Units of Measure:** Dollars per dozen. **Type of Price:** average received by farmer. **Time Period Covered:** latest month, month ago, year ago.

EGGS: TOP GRADE, EXTRA LARGE

Source: *Urner Barry's Price-Current, West Coast Edition.* **Price Frequency:** semiweekly. **Effective Market(s):** Southern California. **Units of Measure:** cents per dozen. **Time Period Covered:** latest week.

EGGS: TOP GRADE, JUMBO

Source: *Urner Barry's Price-Current, West Coast Edition.* **Price Frequency:** semiweekly. **Effective Market(s):** Southern California. **Units of Measure:** cents per dozen. **Time Period Covered:** latest week.

EGGS: TOP GRADE, LARGE

Source: *Urner Barry's Price-Current, West Coast Edition.* **Price Frequency:** semiweekly. **Effective Market(s):** Southern California. **Units of Measure:** cents per dozen. **Time Period Covered:** latest week.

EGGS: TOP GRADE, MEDIUM

Source: *Urner Barry's Price-Current, West Coast Edition.* **Price Frequency:** semiweekly. **Effective Market(s):** Southern California. **Units of Measure:** cents per dozen. **Time Period Covered:** latest week.

EGGS: TOP GRADE, SMALL

Source: *Urner Barry's Price-Current, West Coast Edition.* **Price Frequency:** semiweekly. **Effective Market(s):** Southern California. **Units of Measure:** cents per dozen. **Time Period Covered:** latest week.

EGGS: WEST GERMAN

Source: *FAO Quarterly Bulletin of Statistics.* **Price Frequency:** monthly, annually. **Effective Market(s):** West Germany. **Units of Measure:** West German marks per 100. **Type of Price:** producer . **Time Period Covered:** latest 3 years.

EGGS: WHITE

Source: *Farm and Dairy.* **Price Frequency:** weekly, seasonally. **Effective Market(s):** Ohio, Pennsylvania. **Units of Measure:** Dollars per dozen. **Type of Price:** auction high, auction low. **Time Period Covered:** latest week.

EGGS: WHITE, EXTRA LARGE

Source: *Lancaster Farming.* **Price Frequency:** weekly. **Effective Market(s):** Northeast. **Units of Measure:** Dollars per dozen. **Type of Price:** auction. **Time Period Covered:** latest week.

Source: *Monthly Price Review.* **Price Frequency:** daily. **Effective Market(s):** Northeast, Midwest, Southeast, South Central, Boston. **Units of Measure:** Dollars per dozen. **Type of Price:** spot. **Time Period Covered:** latest month.

Source: *Weekly Insiders Dairy & Egg Letter.* **Price Frequency:** weekly. **Effective Market(s):** New York. **Units of Measure:** cents per dozen. **Type of Price:** retail. **Time Period Covered:** latest week, week ago, year ago, 2 years ago.

EGGS: WHITE, FANCY, LARGE

Source: *Journal of Commerce and Commercial.* **Price Frequency:** daily. **Units of Measure:** cents per dozen. **Type of Price:** spot supplier. **Time Period Covered:** latest day.

EGGS: WHITE, GRADE A, EXTRA LARGE

Source: *Poultry Market Statistics.* **Price Frequency:** monthly. **Effective Market(s):** Florida, North Carolina. **Units of Measure:** cents per dozen. **Type of Price:** average delivered to retailer. **Time Period Covered:** latest year.

Source: *Poultry Market Statistics.* **Price Frequency:** weekly. **Effective Market(s):** 16 domestic markets. **Units of Measure:** cents per dozen. **Type of Price:** average to volume buyers. **Time Period Covered:** latest year.

Source: *Poultry Market Statistics.* **Price Frequency:** monthly, annually. **Effective Market(s):** Detroit. **Units of Measure:** cents per dozen. **Type of Price:** average. **Time Period Covered:** latest year.

Source: *Poultry Market Statistics.* **Price Frequency:** monthly, annually. **Effective Market(s):** 13 domestic markets. **Units of Measure:** cents per dozen. **Type of Price:** average to volume buyers. **Time Period Covered:** latest year.

EGGS: WHITE, GRADE A, JUMBO

Source: *Poultry Market Statistics.* **Price Frequency:** monthly, annually. **Effective Market(s):** Detroit. **Units of Measure:** cents per dozen. **Type of Price:** average. **Time Period Covered:** latest year.

EGGS: WHITE, GRADE A, LARGE

Source: *Feedstuffs.* **Price Frequency:** weekly. **Effective Market(s):** Chicago. **Units of Measure:** cents per dozen. **Time Period Covered:** latest week, week ago, 6 months ago, year ago.

Source: *Poultry Market Statistics.* **Price Frequency:** monthly. **Effective Market(s):** Florida, North Carolina. **Units of Measure:** cents per dozen. **Type of Price:** average delivered to retailer. **Time Period Covered:** latest year.

Source: *Poultry Market Statistics.* **Price Frequency:** weekly. **Effective Market(s):** 16 domestic markets. **Units of Measure:** cents per dozen. **Type of Price:** average to volume buyers. **Time Period Covered:** latest year.

Source: *Poultry Market Statistics.* **Price Frequency:** monthly, annually. **Effective Market(s):** Denver, Detroit. **Units of Measure:** cents per dozen. **Type of Price:** average. **Time Period Covered:** latest year.

Source: *Poultry Market Statistics.* **Price Frequency:** monthly, annually. **Effective Market(s):** 13 domesstic markets. **Units of Measure:** cents per dozen. **Type of Price:** average to volume buyers. **Time Period Covered:** latest year.

EGGS: WHITE, GRADE A, MEDIUM

Source: *Poultry Market Statistics.* **Price Frequency:** monthly. **Effective Market(s):** Florida, North Carolina. **Units of Measure:** cents per dozen. **Type of Price:** average delivered to retailer. **Time Period Covered:** latest year.

Source: *Poultry Market Statistics.* **Price Frequency:** weekly. **Effective Market(s):** 16 domestic markets. **Units of Measure:** cents per dozen. **Type of Price:** average to volume buyers. **Time Period Covered:** latest year.

Source: *Poultry Market Statistics.* **Price Frequency:** monthly, annually. **Effective Market(s):** Denver, Detroit. **Units of Measure:** cents per dozen. **Type of Price:** average. **Time Period Covered:** latest year.

Source: *Poultry Market Statistics.* **Price Frequency:** monthly, annually. **Effective Market(s):** 13 domesstic markets. **Units of Measure:** cents per dozen. **Type of Price:** average to volume buyers. **Time Period Covered:** latest year.

EGGS: WHITE, GRADE A, SMALL

Source: *Poultry Market Statistics.* **Price Frequency:** monthly, annually. **Effective Market(s):** Detroit. **Units of Measure:** cents per dozen. **Type of Price:** average. **Time Period Covered:** latest year.

Source: *Poultry Market Statistics.* **Price Frequency:** monthly. **Effective Market(s):** Florida, North Carolina. **Units of Measure:** cents per dozen. **Type of Price:** average delivered to retailer. **Time Period Covered:** latest year.

EGGS: WHITE, GRADE AA, EXTRA LARGE

Source: *Poultry Market Statistics.* **Price Frequency:** monthly, annually. **Effective Market(s):** Los Angeles. **Units of Measure:** Dollars per dozen. **Type of Price:** retail. **Time Period Covered:** latest year.

EGGS: WHITE, GRADE AA, LARGE

Source: *Poultry Market Statistics.* **Price Frequency:** monthly, annually. **Effective Market(s):** Denver. **Units of Measure:** cents per dozen. **Type of Price:** average. **Time Period Covered:** latest year.

Source: *Poultry Market Statistics.* **Price Frequency:** monthly, annually. **Effective Market(s):** Los Angeles. **Units of Measure:** Dollars per dozen. **Type of Price:** retail. **Time Period Covered:** latest year.

EGGS: WHITE, GRADE AA, MEDIUM

Source: *Poultry Market Statistics.* **Price Frequency:** monthly, annually. **Effective Market(s):** Denver. **Units of Measure:** cents per dozen. **Type of Price:** average. **Time Period Covered:** latest year.

Source: *Poultry Market Statistics.* **Price Frequency:** monthly, annually. **Effective Market(s):** Los Angeles. **Units of Measure:** Dollars per dozen. **Type of Price:** retail. **Time Period Covered:** latest year.

EGGS: WHITE, GRADE AA, SMALL

Source: *Poultry Market Statistics.* **Price Frequency:** monthly, annually. **Effective Market(s):** Denver. **Units of Measure:** cents per dozen. **Type of Price:** average. **Time Period Covered:** latest year.

EGGS: WHITE, GRADE B, LARGE

Source: *Poultry Market Statistics.* **Price Frequency:** monthly, annually. **Effective Market(s):** Denver. **Units of Measure:** cents per dozen. **Type of Price:** average. **Time Period Covered:** latest year.

EGGS: WHITE, GRADEABLE NEST RUN, CLASS 1

Source: *Poultry Market Statistics.* **Price Frequency:** monthly. **Effective Market(s):** 4-region average, Midwest, Northeast, South/Central, Southeast. **Units of Measure:** cents per dozen. **Type of Price:** weighted average. **Time Period Covered:** latest year.

EGGS: WHITE, GRADEABLE NEST RUN, CLASS 2

Source: *Poultry Market Statistics.* **Price Frequency:** monthly. **Effective Market(s):** 4-region average, Midwest, Northeast, South/Central, Southeast. **Units of Measure:** cents per dozen. **Type of Price:** weighted average. **Time Period Covered:** latest year.

EGGS: WHITE, GRADEABLE NEST RUN, CLASS 3

Source: *Poultry Market Statistics.* **Price Frequency:** monthly. **Effective Market(s):** 4-region average, Midwest, Northeast, South/Central, Southeast. **Units of Measure:** cents per dozen. **Type of Price:** weighted average. **Time Period Covered:** latest year.

EGGS: WHITE, GRADEABLE NEST RUN, CLASS 4

Source: *Poultry Market Statistics.* **Price Frequency:** monthly. **Effective Market(s):** 4-region average, Midwest, Northeast, South/Central, Southeast. **Units of Measure:** cents per dozen. **Type of Price:** weighted average. **Time Period Covered:** latest year.

EGGS: WHITE, JUMBO

Source: *Lancaster Farming.* **Price Frequency:** weekly. **Effective Market(s):** Northeast. **Units of Measure:** Dollars per dozen. **Type of Price:** auction. **Time Period Covered:** latest week.

Source: *Monthly Price Review.* **Price Frequency:** daily. **Effective Market(s):** Northeast, Midwest, Southeast, South Central. **Units of Measure:** Dollars per dozen. **Type of Price:** spot. **Time Period Covered:** latest month.

Source: *Weekly Insiders Dairy & Egg Letter.* **Price Frequency:** weekly. **Effective Market(s):** New York. **Units of Measure:** cents per dozen. **Type of Price:** retail. **Time Period Covered:** latest week, week ago, year ago, 2 years ago.

EGGS: WHITE, LARGE

Source: *Asian Wall Street Journal.* **Price Frequency:** daily. **Effective Market(s):** Chicago. **Units of Measure:** Dollars per dozen. **Type of Price:** cash. **Time Period Covered:** latest 2 days, year ago.

Source: *Farm and Dairy.* **Price Frequency:** weekly, seasonally. **Effective Market(s):** Chicago. **Units of Measure:** Dollars per dozen. **Time Period Covered:** latest week, year ago.

Source: *Investor's Daily.* **Price Frequency:** daily. **Effective Market(s):** New York. **Units of Measure:** cents per dozen. **Type of Price:** spot. **Time Period Covered:** latest 2 days.

Source: *Lancaster Farming.* **Price Frequency:** weekly. **Effective Market(s):** Northeast. **Units of Measure:** Dollars per dozen. **Type of Price:** auction. **Time Period Covered:** latest week.

Source: *Monthly Price Review.* **Price Frequency:** daily. **Effective Market(s):** Northeast, Midwest, Southeast, South Central, Boston. **Units of Measure:** Dollars per dozen. **Type of Price:** spot. **Time Period Covered:** latest month.

Source: *New York Times.* **Price Frequency:** daily. **Effective Market(s):** New York. **Units of Measure:** Dollars per dozen. **Type of Price:** cash. **Time Period Covered:** latest 2 days.

Source: *Poultry Market Statistics.* **Price Frequency:** monthly. **Effective Market(s):** 4-region average, Midwest, Northeast, South/Central, Southeast. **Units of Measure:** cents per dozen. **Type of Price:** weighted average. **Time Period Covered:** latest year.

Source: *Wall Street Journal.* **Price Frequency:** daily. **Effective Market(s):** Chicago. **Units of Measure:** Dollars per dozen. **Time Period Covered:** latest day, day ago, year ago.

Source: *Weekly Insiders Dairy & Egg Letter.* **Price Frequency:** annually. **Effective Market(s):** Northeast. **Units of Measure:** cents per dozen. **Type of Price:** wholesale. **Time Period Covered:** latest 5 years.

Source: *Weekly Insiders Dairy & Egg Letter.* **Price Frequency:** weekly. **Effective Market(s):** Northeast, Midwest, Southeast, South Central. **Units of Measure:** cents per dozen. **Type of Price:** wholesale. **Time Period Covered:** latest week.

Source: *Weekly Insiders Dairy & Egg Letter.* **Price Frequency:** weekly. **Effective Market(s):** New York. **Units of Measure:** cents per dozen. **Type of Price:** retail. **Time Period Covered:** latest week, week ago, year ago, 2 years ago.

EGGS: WHITE, MEDIUM

Source: *Lancaster Farming.* **Price Frequency:** weekly. **Effective Market(s):** Northeast. **Units of Measure:** Dollars per dozen. **Type of Price:** auction. **Time Period Covered:** latest week.

Source: *Monthly Price Review.* **Price Frequency:** daily. **Effective Market(s):** Northeast, Midwest, Southeast, South Central, Boston. **Units of Measure:** Dollars per dozen. **Type of Price:** spot. **Time Period Covered:** latest month.

Source: *Poultry Market Statistics.* **Price Frequency:** monthly. **Effective Market(s):** 4-region average, Midwest, Northeast, South/Central, Southeast. **Units of Measure:** cents per dozen. **Type of Price:** weighted average. **Time Period Covered:** latest year.

Source: *Weekly Insiders Dairy & Egg Letter.* **Price Frequency:** annually. **Effective Market(s):** Northeast. **Units of Measure:** cents per dozen. **Type of Price:** wholesale. **Time Period Covered:** latest 5 years.

Source: *Weekly Insiders Dairy & Egg Letter.* **Price Frequency:** weekly. **Effective Market(s):** Northeast, Midwest, Southeast, South Central. **Units of Measure:** cents per dozen. **Type of Price:** wholesale. **Time Period Covered:** latest week.

Source: *Weekly Insiders Dairy & Egg Letter.* **Price Frequency:** weekly. **Effective Market(s):** New York. **Units of Measure:** cents per dozen. **Type of Price:** retail. **Time Period Covered:** latest week, week ago, year ago, 2 years ago.

EGGS: WHITE, OFF GRADE

Source: *Lancaster Farming.* **Price Frequency:** weekly. **Effective Market(s):** Northeast. **Units of Measure:** Dollars per dozen. **Type of Price:** auction. **Time Period Covered:** latest week.

EGGS: WHITE, PULLETS

Source: *Lancaster Farming.* **Price Frequency:** weekly. **Effective Market(s):** Northeast. **Units of Measure:** Dollars per dozen. **Type of Price:** auction. **Time Period Covered:** latest week.

EGGS: WHITE, SMALL

Source: *Monthly Price Review.* **Price Frequency:** daily. **Effective Market(s):** Northeast, Midwest, Southeast, South Central. **Units of Measure:** Dollars per dozen. **Type of Price:** spot. **Time Period Covered:** latest month.

Source: *Poultry Market Statistics.* **Price Frequency:** monthly. **Effective Market(s):** 4-region average, Midwest, Northeast, South/Central, Southeast. **Units of Measure:** cents per dozen. **Type of Price:** weighted average. **Time Period Covered:** latest year.

Source: *Weekly Insiders Dairy & Egg Letter.* **Price Frequency:** annually. **Effective Market(s):** Northeast. **Units of Measure:** cents per dozen. **Type of Price:** wholesale. **Time Period Covered:** latest 5 years.

Source: *Weekly Insiders Dairy & Egg Letter.* **Price Frequency:** weekly. **Effective Market(s):** Northeast, Midwest, Southeast, South Central. **Units of Measure:** cents per dozen. **Type of Price:** wholesale. **Time Period Covered:** latest week.

EGGS: WHITE, TABLE GRADE, EXTRA LARGE

Source: *Urner Barry's Price-Current.* **Price Frequency:** daily. **Effective Market(s):** Northeast, Midwest, Southeast, South Central. **Units of Measure:** cents per dozen. **Type of Price:** spot. **Time Period Covered:** latest day, 5 day average.

EGGS: WHITE, TABLE GRADE, JUMBO

Source: *Urner Barry's Price-Current.* **Price Frequency:** daily. **Effective Market(s):** Northeast, Midwest, Southeast, South Central. **Units of Measure:** cents per dozen. **Type of Price:** spot . **Time Period Covered:** latest day, 5 day average.

EGGS: WHITE, TABLE GRADE, LARGE

Source: *Urner Barry's Price-Current.* **Price Frequency:** daily. **Effective Market(s):** Northeast, Midwest, Southeast, South Central. **Units of Measure:** cents per dozen. **Type of Price:** spot. **Time Period Covered:** latest day, 5 day average.

EGGS: WHITE, TABLE GRADE, MEDIUM

Source: *Urner Barry's Price-Current.* **Price Frequency:** daily. **Effective Market(s):** Northeast, Midwest, Southeast, South Central. **Units of Measure:** cents per dozen. **Type of Price:** spot. **Time Period Covered:** latest day, 5 day average.

EGGS: WHITE, TABLE GRADE, SMALL

Source: *Urner Barry's Price-Current.* **Price Frequency:** daily. **Effective Market(s):** Northeast, Midwest, Southeast, South Central. **Units of Measure:** cents per dozen. **Type of Price:** spot. **Time Period Covered:** latest day, 5 day average.

EGGS AND POULTRY

Source: *Illinois Farm Report.* **Price Frequency:** monthly. **Effective Market(s):** Illinois. **Units of Measure:** index . **Type of Price:** index of prices received by farmers. **Time Period Covered:** latest 2 months, year ago.

EGYPT POUNDS

Source: *International Wheat Council Market Report.* **Price Frequency:** weekly. **Effective Market(s):** London. **Units of Measure:** Egyptian pounds per United States dollar. **Type of Price:** foreign exchange. **Time Period Covered:** latest 5 weeks.

Source: *New York Times.* **Price Frequency:** daily. **Effective Market(s):** New York. **Units of Measure:** Egyptian pounds per United States dollar. **Type of Price:** foreign exchange. **Time Period Covered:** latest 2 days.

ELECTRICITY

Source: *Energy Statistics.* **Price Frequency:** monthly. **Effective Market(s):** 33 domestic markets. **Units of Measure:** Dollars per 500 kilowatt hours. **Type of Price:** residential. **Time Period Covered:** latest 16 months.

Source: *Energy Statistics.* **Price Frequency:** monthly, annually. **Effective Market(s):** United States. **Units of Measure:** Dollars per kilowatt hour, dollars per Btu. **Type of Price:** retail. **Time Period Covered:** monthly latest year, annually latest 15 years.

Source: *Gas Stats: Monthly Gas Utility Statistical Report.* **Price Frequency:** monthly. **Units of Measure:** index. **Type of Price:** price index. **Time Period Covered:** latest month, year ago.

Source: *Purchasing.* **Price Frequency:** quarterly in January, April, July, October issues. **Units of Measure:** cents per kilowatt hour. **Type of Price:** transaction. **Time Period Covered:** latest 5 quarters.

ELECTRICITY: FOR HOUSEHOLD USE

Source: *Energy Prices and Taxes.* **Price Frequency:** quarterly, annually. **Effective Market(s):** 28 international markets. **Units of Measure:** national currency per ton oil equivalent. **Time Period Covered:** varies.

Source: *Energy Prices and Taxes.* **Price Frequency:** annually. **Effective Market(s):** 25 international markets. **Units of Measure:** Dollars per kilowatt hour, dollars per ton oil equivalent. **Time Period Covered:** latest 8 years.

ELECTRICITY: FOR INDUSTRIAL USE

Source: *Energy Prices and Taxes.* **Price Frequency:** quarterly, annually. **Effective Market(s):** 28 international markets. **Units of Measure:** national currency per kilowatt hour, national currency per ton oil equivalent. **Time Period Covered:** varies.

Source: *Energy Prices and Taxes.* **Price Frequency:** annually. **Effective Market(s):** 25 international markets. **Units of Measure:** Dollars per kilowatt hour, dollars per ton oil equivalent. **Time Period Covered:** latest 8 years.

ELEMI GUM

Source: *Journal of Commerce and Commercial.* **Price Frequency:** weekly in Monday issue. **Units of Measure:** Dollars per lb. **Type of Price:** spot. **Time Period Covered:** latest week.

ELEVATOR: PORTABLE, WITHOUT POWER UNIT

Source: *Agricultural Prices.* **Price Frequency:** annually. **Effective Market(s):** United States. **Units of Measure:** Dollars each. **Type of Price:** paid by farmer. **Time Period Covered:** latest year.

Source: *Agricultural Prices Annual Summary.* **Price Frequency:** annually. **Effective Market(s):** United States. **Units of Measure:** Dollars each. **Type of Price:** average paid by farmer. **Time Period Covered:** latest 6 years.

ELM BARK

Source: *Journal of Commerce and Commercial.* **Price Frequency:** weekly in Monday issue. **Units of Measure:** Dollars per lb. **Type of Price:** spot. **Time Period Covered:** latest week.

EMERY: COARSE GRAIN

Source: *Industrial Minerals.* **Price Frequency:** monthly. **Effective Market(s):** main European port. **Units of Measure:** British pounds per metric tonne. **Type of Price:** producer & dealer. **Time Period Covered:** latest month.

EMERY: MEDIUM AND FINE GRAIN

Source: *Industrial Minerals.* **Price Frequency:** monthly. **Effective Market(s):** main European port. **Units of Measure:** British pounds per metric tonne. **Type of Price:** producer & dealer. **Time Period Covered:** latest month.

ENDIVE

Source: *Lancaster Farming.* **Price Frequency:** weekly, seasonally. **Effective Market(s):** Pennsylvania. **Units of Measure:** Dollars per crate. **Type of Price:** market. **Time Period Covered:** latest week.

ENDIVE: CALIFORNIA

Source: *Fresh Fruit and Vegetable Prices.* **Price Frequency:** monthly, seasonally. **Effective Market(s):** Chicago. **Units of Measure:** Dollars per carton. **Type of Price:** average wholesale price. **Time Period Covered:** latest year.

ENDIVE: FLORIDA

Source: *Fresh Fruit and Vegetable Prices.* **Price Frequency:** monthly, seasonally. **Effective Market(s):** Chicago, New York City. **Units of Measure:** Dollars per carton. **Type of Price:** average wholesale price . **Time Period Covered:** latest year.

ENDIVE: FRESH

Source: *HRI-Buyers Guide.* **Price Frequency:** weekly. **Effective Market(s):** Northeastern area. **Units of Measure:** Dollars per case. **Time Period Covered:** latest week.

ENDIVE: NEW JERSEY

Source: *Fresh Fruit and Vegetable Prices.* **Price Frequency:** monthly, seasonally. **Effective Market(s):** New York City. **Units of Measure:** Dollars per crate. **Type of Price:** average wholesale price. **Time Period Covered:** latest year.

ENDIVE AND ESCAROLE

Source: *Fresh Fruit and Vegetable Prices.* **Price Frequency:** monthly, seasonally. **Effective Market(s):** South/Central Florida. **Units of Measure:** Dollars per crate. **Type of Price:** average price at shipping point. **Time Period Covered:** latest year.

ENDRIN: TECHNICAL GRADE, 95-99%

Source: *Chemical Marketing Reporter.* **Price Frequency:** weekly. **Effective Market(s):** New York. **Units of Measure:** Dollars per lb. **Type of Price:** spot. **Time Period Covered:** latest week.

ENVELOPES

Source: *Pulp & Paper Week.* **Price Frequency:** monthly, irregularly. **Units of Measure:** index. **Type of Price:** price index. **Time Period Covered:** latest 3 months.

EPHEDRINE: SYNTHETIC, ANHYDROUS, USP

Source: *Chemical Marketing Reporter.* **Price Frequency:** weekly. **Effective Market(s):** New York. **Units of Measure:** Dollars per ounce. **Type of Price:** spot. **Time Period Covered:** latest week.

EPHEDRINE HYDROCHLORIDE: CRYSTALLINE, NF

Source: *Chemical Marketing Reporter.* **Price Frequency:** weekly. **Effective Market(s):** New York. **Units of Measure:** Dollars per kilo. **Type of Price:** spot. **Time Period Covered:** latest week.

EPHEDRINE HYDORCHLORIDE: NF

Source: *Journal of Commerce and Commercial.* **Price Frequency:** weekly in Friday issue. **Units of Measure:** Dollars per kilo. **Type of Price:** spot. **Time Period Covered:** latest week.

EPHEDRINE SULFATE

Source: *Journal of Commerce and Commercial.* **Price Frequency:** weekly in Friday issue. **Units of Measure:** Dollars per kilo. **Type of Price:** spot. **Time Period Covered:** latest week.

EPHEDRINE SULFATE: CRYSTALLINE, USP

Source: *Chemical Marketing Reporter.* **Price Frequency:** weekly. **Effective Market(s):** New York. **Units of Measure:** Dollars per kilo. **Type of Price:** spot. **Time Period Covered:** latest week.

EPICHLOROHYDRIN

Source: *Chemical Marketing Reporter.* **Price Frequency:** weekly. **Effective Market(s):** New York. **Units of Measure:** Dollars per lb. **Type of Price:** spot. **Time Period Covered:** latest week.

EPINEPHRINE BASE: SYNTHETIC, USP

Source: *Chemical Marketing Reporter.* **Price Frequency:** weekly. **Effective Market(s):** New York. **Units of Measure:** Dollars per gram. **Type of Price:** spot. **Time Period Covered:** latest week.

EPOXY: GENERAL PURPOSE RESIN

Source: *Plastics Technology.* **Price Frequency:** monthly. **Units of Measure:** cents per lb. **Type of Price:** bulk list, market. **Time Period Covered:** latest month.

EPOXY COMPOUNDS: NOVOLAC AND ANHYDRIDE GRADES FOR COILS, BUSHINGS, Transformers

Source: *Plastics Technology.* **Price Frequency:** monthly. **Units of Measure:** cents per lb., cents per cubic inch. **Type of Price:** bulk list, market. **Time Period Covered:** latest monthly.

EPOXY COMPOUNDS: NOVOLAC AND ANHYDRIDE GRADES FOR RESISTORS, CAPACITORS, Diodes

Source: *Plastics Technology.* **Price Frequency:** monthly. **Units of Measure:** cents per lb., cents per cubic inch. **Type of Price:** bulk list, market. **Time Period Covered:** latest month.

EPOXY COMPOUNDS: SEMICONDUCTOR, ANHYDRIDE GRADE

Source: *Plastics Technology.* **Price Frequency:** monthly. **Units of Measure:** cents per lb., cents per cubic inch. **Type of Price:** bulk list, market. **Time Period Covered:** latest month.

EPOXY COMPOUNDS: SEMICONDUCTOR, NOVOLAC GRADE

Source: *Plastics Technology.* **Price Frequency:** monthly. **Units of Measure:** cents per lb., cents per cubic inch. **Type of Price:** bulk list, market. **Time Period Covered:** latest month.

EPOXY FUNCTIONAL SILANE

see Silane: Epoxy Functional.

EPOXY RESIN: LIQUID

Source: *Chemical Marketing Reporter.* **Price Frequency:** weekly. **Effective Market(s):** New York. **Units of Measure:** Dollars per lb. **Type of Price:** spot. **Time Period Covered:** latest week.

EPOXY RESIN: SOLID

Source: *Chemical Marketing Reporter.* **Price Frequency:** weekly. **Effective Market(s):** New York. **Units of Measure:** Dollars per lb. **Type of Price:** spot. **Time Period Covered:** latest week.

EPS

see Polystyrene: Expandable.

EPSOM SALT

see also Magnesium Sulfate.

EPSOM SALT: TECHNICAL GRADE, 10%

Source: *Journal of Commerce and Commercial.* **Price Frequency:** weekly in Thursday issue. **Units of Measure:** Dollars per 100 lbs. **Type of Price:** spot. **Time Period Covered:** latest week.

ERGOT

Source: *Journal of Commerce and Commercial.* **Price Frequency:** weekly in Monday issue. **Units of Measure:** Dollars per lb. **Type of Price:** spot. **Time Period Covered:** latest week.

ERLICHEER

Source: *New Zealand Farmer.* **Price Frequency:** weekly, seasonally. **Effective Market(s):** New Zealand. **Units of Measure:** New Zealand dollars per bunch. **Time Period Covered:** latest week.

ERYTHORBIC ACID

Source: *Journal of Commerce and Commercial.* **Price Frequency:** weekly in Friday issue. **Units of Measure:** Dollars per lb. **Type of Price:** spot. **Time Period Covered:** latest week.

ERYTHORBIC ACID: POWDERED, GRANULAR

Source: *Chemical Marketing Reporter.* **Price Frequency:** weekly. **Effective Market(s):** New York. **Units of Measure:** Dollars per lb. **Type of Price:** spot. **Time Period Covered:** latest week.

ESCAROLE

Source: *Lancaster Farming.* **Price Frequency:** weekly, seasonally. **Effective Market(s):** Pennyslvania. **Units of Measure:** Dollars per crate. **Type of Price:** market. **Time Period Covered:** latest week.

ESCAROLE: CALIFORNIA

Source: *Fresh Fruit and Vegetable Prices.* **Price Frequency:** monthly, seasonally. **Effective Market(s):** Chicago. **Units of Measure:** Dollars per carton. **Type of Price:** average wholesale price. **Time Period Covered:** latest year.

ESCAROLE: FLORIDA

Source: *Fresh Fruit and Vegetable Prices.* **Price Frequency:** monthly, seasonally. **Effective Market(s):** Chicago, New York City. **Units of Measure:** Dollars per carton. **Type of Price:** average wholesale price. **Time Period Covered:** latest year.

ESCAROLE: FRESH

Source: *HRI-Buyers Guide.* **Price Frequency:** weekly. **Effective Market(s):** Northeastern area. **Units of Measure:** Dollars per case. **Time Period Covered:** latest week.

ESCAROLE: NEW JERSEY

Source: *Fresh Fruit and Vegetable Prices.* **Price Frequency:** monthly, seasonally. **Effective Market(s):** New York City. **Units of Measure:** Dollars per crate. **Type of Price:** average wholesale price. **Time Period Covered:** latest year.

ESTER GUM: GUM ROSIN TYPE

Source: *Chemical Marketing Reporter.* **Price Frequency:** weekly. **Effective Market(s):** 11 domestic markets. **Units of Measure:** Dollars per lb. **Type of Price:** spot. **Time Period Covered:** latest week.

ESTER GUM: WOOD ROSIN TYPE

Source: *Chemical Marketing Reporter.* **Price Frequency:** weekly. **Effective Market(s):** New York. **Units of Measure:** Dollars per lb. **Type of Price:** spot. **Time Period Covered:** latest week.

ETHANE

Source: *Energy Pricing News: Petrochemical Report.* **Price Frequency:** bimonthly. **Effective Market(s):** Edmonton (Canada). **Units of Measure:** Canadian dollars per cubic meter. **Type of Price:** contract. **Time Period Covered:** latest month.

Source: *Oil & Gas Journal.* **Price Frequency:** monthly in third issue of month. **Effective Market(s):** Mont Belvieu (TX), Conway (KS). **Units of Measure:** cents per gallon. **Type of Price:** spot. **Time Period Covered:** latest 2 months.

ETHANE GAS

Source: *Oil Buyers' Guide.* **Price Frequency:** daily, weekly. **Effective Market(s):** Conway (KS). **Units of Measure:** cents per gallon. **Type of Price:** spot. **Time Period Covered:** latest week.

ETHANE GAS: MIX

Source: *Oil Buyers' Guide.* **Price Frequency:** daily, weekly. **Effective Market(s):** Mont Belvieu (TX). **Units of Measure:** cents per gallon. **Type of Price:** spot. **Time Period Covered:** latest week.

ETHANE GAS: PURITY

Source: *Oil Buyers' Guide.* **Price Frequency:** daily, weekly. **Effective Market(s):** Mont Belvieu (TX). **Units of Measure:** cents per gallon. **Type of Price:** spot. **Time Period Covered:** latest week.

ETHANOL: 200 PROOF, SYNTHETIC

Source: *Purchasing.* **Price Frequency:** monthly. **Effective Market(s):** United States. **Units of Measure:** cents per gallon. **Type of Price:** transaction. **Time Period Covered:** latest day, month ago, 6 months ago, year ago.

ETHYL ACETATE: SYNTHETIC, 85-88%

Source: *Chemical Marketing Reporter.* **Price Frequency:** weekly. **Effective Market(s):** New York. **Units of Measure:** Dollars per lb. **Type of Price:** spot. **Time Period Covered:** latest week.

Source: *Journal of Commerce and Commercial.* **Price Frequency:** weekly in Friday issue. **Units of Measure:** Dollars per lb. **Type of Price:** spot. **Time Period Covered:** latest week.

ETHYL ACETATE: SYNTHETIC, 95-98%

Source: *Journal of Commerce and Commercial.* **Price Frequency:** weekly in Friday issue. **Units of Measure:** Dollars per lb. **Type of Price:** spot. **Time Period Covered:** latest week.

ETHYL ACETATE: SYNTHETIC, 99%

Source: *Chemical Marketing Reporter.* **Price Frequency:** weekly. **Effective Market(s):** New York. **Units of Measure:** Dollars per lb. **Type of Price:** spot. **Time Period Covered:** latest week.

ETHYL ACETOACETATE

Source: *Chemical Marketing Reporter.* **Price Frequency:** weekly. **Effective Market(s):** New York. **Units of Measure:** Dollars per lb. **Type of Price:** spot. **Time Period Covered:** latest week.

ETHYL ACRYLATE

Source: *Chemical Marketing Reporter.* **Price Frequency:** weekly. **Effective Market(s):** New York. **Units of Measure:** Dollars per lb. **Type of Price:** spot. **Time Period Covered:** latest week.

ETHYL ALCOHOL: 190 PROOF

Source: *Journal of Commerce and Commercial.* **Price Frequency:** weekly in Friday issue. **Effective Market(s):** East. **Units of Measure:** Dollars per gallon. **Type of Price:** spot. **Time Period Covered:** latest week.

ETHYL ALCOHOL: 190 PROOF, SYNTHETIC, USP

Source: *Chemical Marketing Reporter.* **Price Frequency:** weekly. **Effective Market(s):** East. **Units of Measure:** Dollars per gallon. **Type of Price:** spot. **Time Period Covered:** latest week.

ETHYL ALCOHOL: 200 PROOF

Source: *Journal of Commerce and Commercial.* **Price Frequency:** weekly in Friday issue. **Effective Market(s):** East. **Units of Measure:** Dollars per gallon. **Type of Price:** spot. **Time Period Covered:** latest week.

ETHYL ALCOHOL: 200 PROOF, ABSOLUTE

Source: *Chemical Marketing Reporter.* **Price Frequency:** weekly. **Effective Market(s):** New York. **Units of Measure:** Dollars per gallon. **Type of Price:** spot. **Time Period Covered:** latest week.

ETHYL ALCOHOL: DENATURED

see also Denatured Alcohol: Ethyl.

ETHYL ALCOHOL: FERMENTATION

Source: *Chemical Marketing Reporter.* **Price Frequency:** weekly. **Effective Market(s):** New York. **Units of Measure:** Dollars per gallon. **Type of Price:** spot. **Time Period Covered:** latest week.

ETHYL P-AMINOBENZOATE: NF

see Benzocaine.

ETHYL BENZOATE

Source: *Chemical Marketing Reporter.* **Price Frequency:** weekly. **Effective Market(s):** New York. **Units of Measure:** Dollars per lb. **Type of Price:** spot. **Time Period Covered:** latest week.

ETHYL BROMIDE: TECHNICAL GRADE, 98%

Source: *Chemical Marketing Reporter.* **Price Frequency:** weekly. **Effective Market(s):** New York. **Units of Measure:** Dollars per lb. **Type of Price:** spot. **Time Period Covered:** latest week.

ETHYL BUTYRATE

Source: *Chemical Marketing Reporter.* **Price Frequency:** weekly. **Effective Market(s):** New York. **Units of Measure:** Dollars per lb. **Type of Price:** spot. **Time Period Covered:** latest week.

ETHYL CELLULOSE: MEDIUM VISCOSITY

Source: *Chemical Marketing Reporter.* **Price Frequency:** weekly. **Effective Market(s):** New York. **Units of Measure:** Dollars per lb. **Type of Price:** spot. **Time Period Covered:** latest week.

ETHYL CELLULOSE: STANDARD VISCOSITY

Source: *Chemical Marketing Reporter.* **Price Frequency:** weekly. **Effective Market(s):** East. **Units of Measure:** Dollars per lb. **Type of Price:** spot. **Time Period Covered:** latest week.

ETHYL CELLULOSE: USP

Source: *Chemical Marketing Reporter.* **Price Frequency:** weekly. **Effective Market(s):** New York. **Units of Measure:** Dollars per lb. **Type of Price:** spot. **Time Period Covered:** latest week.

ETHYL CHLORIDE: TECHNICAL GRADE

Source: *Chemical Marketing Reporter.* **Price Frequency:** weekly. **Effective Market(s):** New York. **Units of Measure:** Dollars per lb. **Type of Price:** spot. **Time Period Covered:** latest week.

ETHYL ETHANOLAMINES

Source: *Chemical Marketing Reporter.* **Price Frequency:** weekly. **Effective Market(s):** East. **Units of Measure:** Dollars per lb. **Type of Price:** spot. **Time Period Covered:** latest week.

ETHYL ETHER: REFINED

Source: *Chemical Marketing Reporter.* **Price Frequency:** weekly. **Effective Market(s):** New York. **Units of Measure:** Dollars per lb. **Type of Price:** spot. **Time Period Covered:** latest week.

ETHYL HEXANOATE

Source: *Chemical Marketing Reporter.* **Price Frequency:** weekly. **Effective Market(s):** New York. **Units of Measure:** Dollars per lb. **Type of Price:** spot. **Time Period Covered:** latest week.

ETHYL IODIDE

Source: *Chemical Marketing Reporter.* **Price Frequency:** weekly. **Effective Market(s):** New York. **Units of Measure:** Dollars per lb. **Type of Price:** spot. **Time Period Covered:** latest week.

ETHYL METHACRYLATE

Source: *Chemical Marketing Reporter.* **Price Frequency:** weekly. **Effective Market(s):** New York. **Units of Measure:** Dollars per lb. **Type of Price:** spot. **Time Period Covered:** latest week.

N-ETHYL MORPHOLINE

Source: *Chemical Marketing Reporter.* **Price Frequency:** weekly. **Effective Market(s):** New York. **Units of Measure:** Dollars per lb. **Type of Price:** spot. **Time Period Covered:** latest week.

N-ETHYL-A-NAPHTHYLAMINE

Source: *Chemical Marketing Reporter.* **Price Frequency:** weekly. **Effective Market(s):** New York. **Units of Measure:** Dollars per lb. **Type of Price:** spot. **Time Period Covered:** latest week.

ETHYL OXALATE

see Diethyl Oxalate.

ETHYL PARATHION

see Parathion: Ethyl.

ETHYL SILICATE

Source: *Chemical Marketing Reporter.* **Price Frequency:** weekly. **Effective Market(s):** New York. **Units of Measure:** Dollars per lb. **Type of Price:** spot. **Time Period Covered:** latest week.

ETHYL SILICATE: DISTILLED

see Tetraethyl Orthosilicate.

N-ETHYL-O-TOLUIDINE

Source: *Chemical Marketing Reporter.* **Price Frequency:** weekly. **Effective Market(s):** New York. **Units of Measure:** Dollars per lb. **Type of Price:** spot. **Time Period Covered:** latest week.

N-ETHYL-M-TOLUIDINE: TECHNICAL GRADE, LIQUID

Source: *Chemical Marketing Reporter.* **Price Frequency:** weekly. **Effective Market(s):** New York. **Units of Measure:** Dollars per lb. **Type of Price:** spot. **Time Period Covered:** latest week.

ETHYL VANILLIN

Source: *Chemical Marketing Reporter.* **Price Frequency:** weekly. **Effective Market(s):** New York. **Units of Measure:** Dollars per lb. **Type of Price:** spot. **Time Period Covered:** latest week.

Source: *Journal of Commerce and Commercial.* **Price Frequency:** weekly in Tuesday issue. **Units of Measure:** Dollars per lb. **Type of Price:** spot. **Time Period Covered:** latest week.

ETHYLAMINE

see Mono-, Di- and Tri-Ethylamine.

N-ETHYLANILINE

Source: *Chemical Marketing Reporter.* **Price Frequency:** weekly. **Effective Market(s):** New York. **Units of Measure:** Dollars per lb. **Type of Price:** spot. **Time Period Covered:** latest week.

ETHYLBENZENE

Source: *Chemical Marketing Reporter.* **Price Frequency:** weekly. **Effective Market(s):** Houston. **Units of Measure:** Dollars per lb. **Type of Price:** spot. **Time Period Covered:** latest week.

ETHYLBENZENE: INDUSTRIAL BARGES

Source: *Journal of Commerce and Commercial.* **Price Frequency:** weekly in Wednesday issue. **Effective Market(s):** Gulf. **Units of Measure:** Dollars per lb. **Type of Price:** spot. **Time Period Covered:** latest week.

ETHYLENE

Source: *Chemical Marketing Reporter.* **Price Frequency:** weekly. **Effective Market(s):** New York. **Units of Measure:** Dollars per lb. **Type of Price:** spot. **Time Period Covered:** latest week.

Source: *Energy Pricing News: Petrochemical Report.* **Price Frequency:** bimonthly. **Effective Market(s):** Eastern Canada. **Units of Measure:** Canadian dollars per tonne. **Type of Price:** contract. **Time Period Covered:** latest month.

Source: *Japan Economic Journal.* **Price Frequency:** weekly. **Effective Market(s):** Tokyo. **Units of Measure:** Japanese yen per kilogram. **Type of Price:** market. **Time Period Covered:** latest 2 weeks.

Source: *Journal of Commerce and Commercial.* **Price Frequency:** weekly in Thursday issue. **Units of Measure:** Dollars per lb. **Type of Price:** spot. **Time Period Covered:** latest week.

Source: *Modern Plastics.* **Price Frequency:** quarterly in January, April, July, October issues. **Units of Measure:** cents per lb. **Type of Price:** market. **Time Period Covered:** latest 3 years.

Source: *Oil & Gas Journal.* **Price Frequency:** monthly in first issue of month. **Units of Measure:** cents per lb. **Time Period Covered:** latest month.

ETHYLENE: CRYOGENIC LIQUID

Source: *Purchasing.* **Price Frequency:** monthly. **Effective Market(s):** Gulf Coast. **Units of Measure:** cents per lb. **Type of Price:** transaction. **Time Period Covered:** latest day, month ago, 6 months ago, year ago.

ETHYLENE BRASSYLATE

Source: *Chemical Marketing Reporter.* **Price Frequency:** weekly. **Effective Market(s):** New York. **Units of Measure:** Dollars per lb. **Type of Price:** spot. **Time Period Covered:** latest week.

ETHYLENE DIBROMIDE

Source: *Chemical Marketing Reporter.* **Price Frequency:** weekly. **Effective Market(s):** New York. **Units of Measure:** Dollars per lb. **Type of Price:** spot. **Time Period Covered:** latest week.

ETHYLENE DICHLORIDE

Source: *Chemical Marketing Reporter.* **Price Frequency:** weekly. **Effective Market(s):** New York. **Units of Measure:** Dollars per lb. **Type of Price:** spot. **Time Period Covered:** latest week.

Source: *Journal of Commerce and Commercial.* **Price Frequency:** weekly in Thursday issue. **Units of Measure:** Dollars per lb. **Type of Price:** spot. **Time Period Covered:** latest week.

ETHYLENE GLYCOL

Source: *Cotton and Wool Situation and Outlook Report.* **Price Frequency:** monthly. **Units of Measure:** cents per lb. **Type of Price:** spot. **Time Period Covered:** latest year.

Source: *Japan Economic Journal.* **Price Frequency:** weekly. **Effective Market(s):** Tokyo. **Units of Measure:** Japanese yen per kilogram. **Type of Price:** market. **Time Period Covered:** latest 2 weeks.

ETHYLENE GLYCOL: ANTIFREEZE

Source: *Journal of Commerce and Commercial.* **Price Frequency:** weekly in Thursday issue. **Effective Market(s):** Gulf. **Units of Measure:** Dollars per lb. **Type of Price:** spot. **Time Period Covered:** latest week.

ETHYLENE GLYCOL: FIBER GRADE

Source: *Journal of Commerce and Commercial.* **Price Frequency:** weekly in Thursday issue. **Effective Market(s):** Gulf. **Units of Measure:** Dollars per lb. **Type of Price:** spot. **Time Period Covered:** latest week.

ETHYLENE GLYCOL: INDUSTRIAL GRADE

Source: *Chemical Marketing Reporter.* **Price Frequency:** weekly. **Effective Market(s):** New York. **Units of Measure:** Dollars per lb. **Type of Price:** spot. **Time Period Covered:** latest week.

ETHYLENE GLYCOL MONOBUTYL ETHER

Source: *Chemical Marketing Reporter.* **Price Frequency:** weekly. **Effective Market(s):** East. **Units of Measure:** Dollars per lb. **Type of Price:** spot. **Time Period Covered:** latest week.

ETHYLENE GLYCOL MONOBUTYL ETHER ACETATE

Source: *Chemical Marketing Reporter.* **Price Frequency:** weekly. **Effective Market(s):** East. **Units of Measure:** Dollars per lb. **Type of Price:** spot. **Time Period Covered:** latest week.

ETHYLENE GLYCOL MONOETHYL ETHER

Source: *Chemical Marketing Reporter.* **Price Frequency:** weekly. **Effective Market(s):** East. **Units of Measure:** Dollars per lb. **Type of Price:** spot. **Time Period Covered:** latest week.

ETHYLENE GLYCOL MONOETHYL ETHER ACETATE

Source: *Chemical Marketing Reporter.* **Price Frequency:** weekly. **Effective Market(s):** East. **Units of Measure:** Dollars per lb. **Type of Price:** spot. **Time Period Covered:** latest week.

ETHYLENE GLYCOL MONOMETHYL ETHER

Source: *Chemical Marketing Reporter.* **Price Frequency:** weekly. **Effective Market(s):** East. **Units of Measure:** Dollars per lb. **Type of Price:** spot. **Time Period Covered:** latest week.

ETHYLENE GLYCOL MONOMETHYL ETHER ACETATE

Source: *Chemical Marketing Reporter.* **Price Frequency:** weekly. **Effective Market(s):** East. **Units of Measure:** Dollars per lb. **Type of Price:** spot. **Time Period Covered:** latest week.

ETHYLENE GYLCOL: INDUSTRIAL GRADE

Source: *Journal of Commerce and Commercial.* **Price Frequency:** weekly in Thursday issue. **Effective Market(s):** Gulf. **Units of Measure:** Dollars per lb. **Type of Price:** spot. **Time Period Covered:** latest week.

ETHYLENE OXIDE

Source: *Chemical Marketing Reporter.* **Price Frequency:** weekly. **Effective Market(s):** New York. **Units of Measure:** Dollars per lb. **Type of Price:** spot. **Time Period Covered:** latest week.

Source: *Journal of Commerce and Commercial.* **Price Frequency:** weekly in Thursday issue. **Units of Measure:** Dollars per lb. **Type of Price:** spot. **Time Period Covered:** latest week.

ETHYLENE TRICHLORIDE

see Trichloroethylene.

ETHYLENE VINYL ACETATE

see EVA.

ETHYLENE-VINYL ALCOHOL COPOLYMER

see EVOH.

ETHYLENEDIAMINE: 99%

Source: *Chemical Marketing Reporter.* **Price Frequency:** weekly. **Effective Market(s):** New York. **Units of Measure:** Dollars per lb. **Type of Price:** spot. **Time Period Covered:** latest week.

ETHYLENEDIAMINE DIHYDRIODIDE

Source: *Chemical Marketing Reporter.* **Price Frequency:** weekly. **Effective Market(s):** New York. **Units of Measure:** Dollars per lb. **Type of Price:** spot. **Time Period Covered:** latest week.

ETHYLENEDIAMINE TETRAACETIC ACID: TETRASODIUM SALT, SOLUTION

Source: *Chemical Marketing Reporter.* **Price Frequency:** weekly. **Effective Market(s):** New York. **Units of Measure:** Dollars per lb. **Type of Price:** spot. **Time Period Covered:** latest week.

2-ETHYLHEXOIC ACID

Source: *Chemical Marketing Reporter.* **Price Frequency:** weekly. **Effective Market(s):** East. **Units of Measure:** Dollars per lb. **Type of Price:** spot. **Time Period Covered:** latest week.

2-ETHYLHEXYL ACRYLATE: STRAIGHT OR MIXED

Source: *Chemical Marketing Reporter.* **Price Frequency:** weekly. **Effective Market(s):** East. **Units of Measure:** Dollars per lb. **Type of Price:** spot. **Time Period Covered:** latest week.

2-ETHYLHEXYL ALCOHOL

Source: *Chemical Marketing Reporter.* **Price Frequency:** weekly. **Effective Market(s):** New York. **Units of Measure:** Dollars per lb. **Type of Price:** spot. **Time Period Covered:** latest week.

EUCALYPTOL

Source: *Journal of Commerce and Commercial.* **Price Frequency:** weekly in Tuesday issue. **Units of Measure:** Dollars per lb. **Type of Price:** spot. **Time Period Covered:** latest week.

EUCALYPTOL: NF, PORTUGUESE

Source: *Chemical Marketing Reporter.* **Price Frequency:** weekly. **Effective Market(s):** New York. **Units of Measure:** Dollars per kilo. **Type of Price:** spot. **Time Period Covered:** latest week.

EUCALYPTUS CITRIADORA: CHINESE

Source: *Chemical Marketing Reporter.* **Price Frequency:** weekly. **Effective Market(s):** New York. **Units of Measure:** Dollars per kilo. **Type of Price:** spot. **Time Period Covered:** latest week.

EUCALYPTUS OIL

Source: *U. S. Essential Oil Trade.* **Price Frequency:** annually. **Effective Market(s):** United States. **Units of Measure:** Dollars per kilogram. **Type of Price:** import value. **Time Period Covered:** latest 3 years.

EUCALYPTUS OIL: 70-75%

Source: *Journal of Commerce and Commercial.* **Price Frequency:** weekly in Tuesday issue. **Units of Measure:** Dollars per lb. **Type of Price:** spot. **Time Period Covered:** latest week.

EUCALYPTUS OIL: CHINESE, 80%

Source: *Chemical Marketing Reporter.* **Price Frequency:** weekly. **Effective Market(s):** New York. **Units of Measure:** Dollars per kilo. **Type of Price:** spot. **Time Period Covered:** latest week.

EUGENOL

Source: *Journal of Commerce and Commercial.* **Price Frequency:** weekly in Tuesday issue. **Units of Measure:** Dollars per lb. **Type of Price:** spot. **Time Period Covered:** latest week.

EUGENOL: USP

Source: *Chemical Marketing Reporter.* **Price Frequency:** weekly. **Effective Market(s):** New York. **Units of Measure:** Dollars per kilo. **Type of Price:** spot. **Time Period Covered:** latest week.

EUROPEAN CURRENCY UNITS

Source: *American Metal Market.* **Price Frequency:** daily. **Effective Market(s):** New York. **Units of Measure:** ECU per United States dollar. **Type of Price:** foreign exchange. **Time Period Covered:** latest day.

Source: *International Wheat Council Market Report.* **Price Frequency:** weekly. **Effective Market(s):** London. **Units of Measure:** ECU per United States dollar. **Type of Price:** foreign exchange. **Time Period Covered:** latest 5 weeks.

Source: *New York Times.* **Price Frequency:** daily. **Effective Market(s):** New York. **Units of Measure:** ECU per United States dollar. **Type of Price:** foreign exchange. **Time Period Covered:** latest 2 days.

EVA: EXTRUSION COAT

Source: *Plastics Technology.* **Price Frequency:** monthly. **Units of Measure:** cents per lb., cents per cubic inch. **Type of Price:** bulk list, market. **Time Period Covered:** latest month.

EVA: FILM EXTRUSION

Source: *Plastics Technology.* **Price Frequency:** monthly. **Units of Measure:** cents per lb., cents per cubic inch. **Type of Price:** bulk list, market. **Time Period Covered:** latest month.

EVA: INJECTION

Source: *Plastics Technology.* **Price Frequency:** monthly. **Units of Measure:** cents per lb., cents per cubic inch. **Type of Price:** bulk list, market. **Time Period Covered:** latest month.

EVOH

Source: *Plastics Technology.* **Price Frequency:** monthly. **Units of Measure:** cents per lb., cents per cubic inch. **Type of Price:** bulk list, market. **Time Period Covered:** latest monthly.

EWES

Source: *Farm and Dairy.* **Price Frequency:** weekly, seasonally. **Effective Market(s):** Ohio, Pennsylvania. **Units of Measure:** Dollars per head. **Type of Price:** auction high, auction low. **Time Period Covered:** latest week.

Source: *Scottish Farmer.* **Price Frequency:** weekly. **Effective Market(s):** Scotland. **Units of Measure:** British pence per kilogram. **Type of Price:** average. **Time Period Covered:** latest week.

Source: *Scottish Farmer.* **Price Frequency:** weekly. **Effective Market(s):** 33 Scottish markets. **Units of Measure:** British pence per kilogram. **Time Period Covered:** latest week.

EWES: BLACKFACE, STORE

Source: *Scottish Farmer.* **Price Frequency:** weekly. **Effective Market(s):** 9 Scottish markets average. **Units of Measure:** British pounds per head. **Type of Price:** average. **Time Period Covered:** latest 2 weeks.

EWES: CHEVIOT, STORE

Source: *Scottish Farmer.* **Price Frequency:** weekly. **Effective Market(s):** 9 Scottish markets average. **Units of Measure:** British pounds per head. **Type of Price:** average. **Time Period Covered:** latest 2 weeks.

EWES: CULL

Source: *Farmers Weekly.* **Price Frequency:** weekly. **Effective Market(s):** 17 British markets. **Units of Measure:** British pounds per head. **Time Period Covered:** latest week.

EWES: CULL, SHORN

Source: *Livestock, Meat, Wool Market News.* **Price Frequency:** weekly, seasonally. **Effective Market(s):** San Angelo (TX), West Fargo (ND), South St. Paul, Sioux Falls, Billings(MT). **Units of Measure:** Dollars per 100 lbs. **Type of Price:** average. **Time Period Covered:** latest week, year ago.

EWES: GOOD

Source: *Livestock and Poultry Situation and Outlook Report.* **Price Frequency:** monthly. **Effective Market(s):** San Angelo (TX), South St. Paul. **Units of Measure:** Dollars per 100 lbs. **Time Period Covered:** latest year.

Source: *Livestock and Poultry Update.* **Price Frequency:** monthly. **Effective Market(s):** San Angelo (TX). **Units of Measure:** Dollars per 100 lbs. **Time Period Covered:** latest 3 months, year ago.

EWES: GOOD, SHORN

Source: *Livestock, Meat, Wool Market News.* **Price Frequency:** weekly, seasonally. **Effective Market(s):** San Angelo (TX), West Fargo (ND), South St. Paul, Sioux Falls, Billings(MT). **Units of Measure:** Dollars per 100 lbs. **Type of Price:** average. **Time Period Covered:** latest week, year ago.

EWES: GOOD, STORE

Source: *New Zealand Farmer.* **Price Frequency:** weekly, seasonally. **Effective Market(s):** 7 New Zealand markets. **Units of Measure:** New Zealand dollars per head. **Time Period Covered:** latest 2 weeks.

EWES: GREYFACE, STORE

Source: *Scottish Farmer.* **Price Frequency:** weekly. **Effective Market(s):** 9 Scottish markets average. **Units of Measure:** British pounds per head. **Type of Price:** average. **Time Period Covered:** latest 2 weeks.

EWES: HALF BRED, STORE

Source: *Scottish Farmer.* **Price Frequency:** weekly. **Effective Market(s):** 9 Scottish markets average. **Units of Measure:** British pounds per head. **Type of Price:** average. **Time Period Covered:** latest 2 weeks.

EWES: HEAVY, PRIME

Source: *New Zealand Farmer.* **Price Frequency:** weekly, seasonally. **Effective Market(s):** 7 New Zealand markets. **Units of Measure:** New Zealand dollars per head. **Time Period Covered:** latest 2 weeks.

EWES: LIGHT, PRIME

Source: *New Zealand Farmer.* **Price Frequency:** weekly, seasonally. **Effective Market(s):** 7 New Zealand markets. **Units of Measure:** New Zealand dollars per head. **Time Period Covered:** latest 2 weeks.

EWES: LIGHT, STORE

Source: *New Zealand Farmer.* **Price Frequency:** weekly, seasonally. **Effective Market(s):** 7 New Zealand markets. **Units of Measure:** New Zealand dollars per head. **Time Period Covered:** latest 2 weeks.

EWES: MEDIUM, PRIME

Source: *New Zealand Farmer.* **Price Frequency:** weekly, seasonally. **Effective Market(s):** 7 New Zealand markets. **Units of Measure:** New Zealand dollars per head. **Time Period Covered:** latest 2 weeks.

EWES: SLAUGHTER

Source: *Lancaster Farming.* **Price Frequency:** weekly. **Effective Market(s):** Pennsylvania, Virginia. **Units of Measure:** Dollars per head. **Type of Price:** auction. **Time Period Covered:** latest week.

Source: *National Wool Market Review.* **Price Frequency:** weekly, seasonally. **Effective Market(s):** varies. **Units of Measure:** Dollars per head. **Time Period Covered:** latest weekly.

EWES: SLAUGHTER, CULL

Source: *Oregon Farmer-Stockman.* **Price Frequency:** monthly, seasonally. **Effective Market(s):** Midwest, Oklahoma City, Ft. Collins (CO). **Units of Measure:** Dollars per 100 lbs. **Time Period Covered:** latest month.

EWES: SLAUGHTER, CULL AND UTILITY

Source: *Montana Farmer-Stockman.* **Price Frequency:** monthly. **Effective Market(s):** Billings (MT). **Units of Measure:** Dollars per 100 lbs. **Type of Price:** cash auction. **Time Period Covered:** latest month.

EWES: SLAUGHTER, GOOD

Source: *Agricultural Outlook.* **Price Frequency:** monthly, annually. **Effective Market(s):** San Angelo (TX). **Units of Measure:** Dollars per 100 lbs. **Type of Price:** market. **Time Period Covered:** monthly latest 6 months, annually latest 3 years.

EWES: SLAUGHTER, MOSTLY GOOD

Source: *Montana Farmer-Stockman.* **Price Frequency:** monthly. **Effective Market(s):** Billings (MT). **Units of Measure:** Dollars per 100 lbs. **Type of Price:** cash auction. **Time Period Covered:** latest month.

EWES: SLAUGHTER, UTILITY

Source: *Montana Farmer-Stockman.* **Price Frequency:** monthly. **Effective Market(s):** Billings (MT). **Units of Measure:** Dollars per 100 lbs. **Type of Price:** cash auction. **Time Period Covered:** latest month.

Source: *Oregon Farmer-Stockman.* **Price Frequency:** monthly, seasonally. **Effective Market(s):** Ft. Collins (CO). **Units of Measure:** Dollars per 100 lbs. **Time Period Covered:** latest month.

EWES: SLAUGHTER, UTILITY AND GOOD

Source: *Idaho Farmer-Stockman.* **Price Frequency:** monthly. **Units of Measure:** Dollars per 100 lbs. **Time Period Covered:** latest month.

Source: *Oregon Farmer-Stockman.* **Price Frequency:** monthly, seasonally. **Effective Market(s):** Midwest, Oklahoma City. **Units of Measure:** Dollars per 100 lbs. **Time Period Covered:** latest month.

Source: *Utah Stockman-Farmer.* **Price Frequency:** monthly. **Units of Measure:** Dollars per 100 lbs. **Time Period Covered:** latest month.

EWES: STOCK

Source: *National Wool Market Review.* **Price Frequency:** weekly, seasonally. **Effective Market(s):** varies. **Units of Measure:** Dollars per head. **Time Period Covered:** latest weekly.

EWES: STOCK, MOSTLY MEDIUM

Source: *Montana Farmer-Stockman.* **Price Frequency:** monthly. **Effective Market(s):** Billings (MT). **Units of Measure:** Dollars per head. **Type of Price:** cash auction. **Time Period Covered:** latest month.

EWES: UTILITY, SHORN

Source: *Livestock, Meat, Wool Market News.* **Price Frequency:** weekly, seasonally. **Effective Market(s):** San Angelo (TX), West Fargo (ND), South St. Paul, Sioux Falls, Billings(MT). **Units of Measure:** Dollars per 100 lbs. **Type of Price:** average. **Time Period Covered:** latest week, year ago.

FABRIC

see also Cloth, and specific types of fabric, e.g., Pongee Fabric.

FABRIC: ACETATE LININGS

Source: *DNR: Daily News Record.* **Price Frequency:** quarterly. **Units of Measure:** dollars per yard. **Type of Price:** spot. **Time Period Covered:** latest 3 quarters.

FABRIC: ACETATE TAFFETA

Source: *DNR: Daily News Record.* **Price Frequency:** quarterly. **Units of Measure:** dollars per yard. **Type of Price:** spot. **Time Period Covered:** latest 3 quarters.

FABRIC: COTTON

Source: *JTN: The International Textile Magazine.* **Price Frequency:** monthly. **Effective Market(s):** Japan. **Units of Measure:** Japanese yen per yard. **Type of Price:** spot. **Time Period Covered:** latest month.

FABRIC: GRAY

Source: *JTN: The International Textile Magazine.* **Price Frequency:** monthly. **Effective Market(s):** Japan. **Units of Measure:** Japanese yen per yard. **Type of Price:** spot. **Time Period Covered:** latest month.

FABRIC: NYLON TAFFETA

Source: *DNR: Daily News Record.* **Price Frequency:** quarterly. **Units of Measure:** dollars per yard. **Type of Price:** spot. **Time Period Covered:** latest 3 quarters.

FABRIC: POLYESTER 65/COTTON 35

Source: *JTN: The International Textile Magazine.* **Price Frequency:** monthly. **Effective Market(s):** Japan. **Units of Measure:** Japanese yen per yard. **Type of Price:** spot. **Time Period Covered:** latest month.

FABRIC: POLYESTER FILAMENT

Source: *JTN: The International Textile Magazine.* **Price Frequency:** monthly. **Effective Market(s):** Japan. **Units of Measure:** Japanese yen per yard. **Type of Price:** spot. **Time Period Covered:** latest month.

FABRIC: POLYESTER/COTTON, GRAY

Source: *JTN: The International Textile Magazine.* **Price Frequency:** monthly. **Effective Market(s):** Taiwan. **Units of Measure:** Dollars per yard. **Type of Price:** export. **Time Period Covered:** latest month.

FABRIC: RAYON FILAMENT

Source: *JTN: The International Textile Magazine.* **Price Frequency:** monthly. **Effective Market(s):** Japan. **Units of Measure:** Japanese yen per yard. **Type of Price:** spot. **Time Period Covered:** latest month.

FABRIC: RAYON LININGS

Source: *DNR: Daily News Record.* **Price Frequency:** quarterly. **Units of Measure:** dollars per yard. **Type of Price:** spot. **Time Period Covered:** latest 3 quarters.

FABRICS: FINISHED

Source: *Textile World.* **Price Frequency:** monthly. **Units of Measure:** index. **Type of Price:** producer price index. **Time Period Covered:** latest 2 months, year ago.

FABRICS: GREIGE

Source: *Textile World.* **Price Frequency:** monthly. **Units of Measure:** index. **Type of Price:** producer price index. **Time Period Covered:** latest two months, year ago.

FARM PRODUCTS

Source: *Illinois Farm Report.* **Price Frequency:** monthly. **Effective Market(s):** Illinois. **Units of Measure:** index . **Type of Price:** index of prices received by farmers. **Time Period Covered:** latest 2 months, year ago.

FAT PRODUCTS

see specific types of fat, e.g., Animal Fat, see also Tallow, Grease.

FEATHER MEAL

Source: *Feed Situation and Outlook Report.* **Price Frequency:** monthly. **Effective Market(s):** Arkansas points. **Units of Measure:** Dollars per ton. **Type of Price:** wholesale. **Time Period Covered:** latest 8 months.

Source: *Grain and Feed Market News.* **Price Frequency:** weekly, seasonally. **Effective Market(s):** Arkansas points, Minneapolis. **Units of Measure:** Dollars per ton. **Type of Price:** wholesale. **Time Period Covered:** latest week, week ago, year ago.

Source: *Milling & Baking News.* **Price Frequency:** weekly. **Effective Market(s):** Kansas City. **Units of Measure:** Dollars per ton. **Time Period Covered:** latest week, week ago, year ago.

FEATHER MEAL: HYDROLYZED

Source: *Feedstuffs.* **Price Frequency:** weekly. **Effective Market(s):** 7 domestic markets. **Units of Measure:** Dollars per bulk ton. **Time Period Covered:** latest week.

Source: *National Provisioner.* **Price Frequency:** weekly. **Effective Market(s):** South. **Units of Measure:** Dollars per 100 lbs. **Time Period Covered:** latest week.

FEED GRAINS AND HAY

Source: *Illinois Farm Report.* **Price Frequency:** monthly. **Effective Market(s):** Illinois. **Units of Measure:** index . **Type of Price:** index of prices received by farmers. **Time Period Covered:** latest 2 months, year ago.

FEED GRINDER-MIXER

Source: *Agricultural Prices.* **Price Frequency:** semiannually. **Effective Market(s):** United States. **Units of Measure:** Dollars each. **Type of Price:** paid by farmer. **Time Period Covered:** latest year.

Source: *Agricultural Prices Annual Summary.* **Price Frequency:** annually. **Effective Market(s):** United States. **Units of Measure:** Dollars each. **Type of Price:** average paid by farmer. **Time Period Covered:** latest 6 years.

FEEDER CATTLE

see Cattle: Feeder.

FEEDER HEIFERS

see Heifers: Feeder.

FEEDER PIGS

see Pigs: Feeder.

FEEDER STEERS

see Steers: Feeder.

FELDSPAR: CERAMIC GRADE

Source: *Industrial Minerals.* **Price Frequency:** monthly . **Effective Market(s):** Spruce Pine (NC), Middleton (CT). **Units of Measure:** Dollars per short ton. **Type of Price:** producer & dealer. **Time Period Covered:** latest month.

FELDSPAR: CERAMIC GRADE, HIGH POTASH

Source: *Industrial Minerals.* **Price Frequency:** monthly. **Effective Market(s):** Monticello (GA). **Units of Measure:** Dollars per short ton. **Type of Price:** producer & dealer. **Time Period Covered:** latest month.

FELDSPAR: GLASS GRADE

Source: *Industrial Minerals.* **Price Frequency:** monthly. **Effective Market(s):** Spruce Pine (NC), Middleton (CT). **Units of Measure:** Dollars per short ton. **Type of Price:** producer & dealer. **Time Period Covered:** latest month.

FELDSPAR: GLASS GRADE, HIGH POTASH

Source: *Industrial Minerals.* **Price Frequency:** monthly. **Effective Market(s):** Monticello (GA). **Units of Measure:** Dollars per short ton. **Type of Price:** producer & dealer. **Time Period Covered:** latest month.

FELDSPAR POWDER: CERAMIC GRADE

Source: *Industrial Minerals.* **Price Frequency:** monthly. **Effective Market(s):** United Kingdom. **Units of Measure:** British pounds per metric tonne. **Type of Price:** producer & dealer. **Time Period Covered:** latest month.

FELDSPAR SAND: GLASS GRADE

Source: *Industrial Minerals.* **Price Frequency:** monthly. **Effective Market(s):** United Kingdom. **Units of Measure:** British pounds per metric tonne. **Type of Price:** producer & dealer. **Time Period Covered:** latest month.

FENCE: FIELD AND STOCK

Source: *Agricultural Prices.* **Price Frequency:** semiannually. **Effective Market(s):** United States. **Units of Measure:** Dollars per 20 rod roll. **Type of Price:** paid by farmer. **Time Period Covered:** latest year.

Source: *Agricultural Prices Annual Summary.* **Price Frequency:** quarterly. **Effective Market(s):** United States. **Units of Measure:** Dollars per 20 rod spool. **Type of Price:** average paid by farmer. **Time Period Covered:** latest 6 years.

FENCE CHARGER: SOLID STATE, ELECTRONIC

Source: *Agricultural Prices.* **Price Frequency:** annually. **Effective Market(s):** United States. **Units of Measure:** Dollars each. **Type of Price:** paid by farmer. **Time Period Covered:** latest year.

Source: *Agricultural Prices Annual Summary.* **Price Frequency:** semiannually. **Effective Market(s):** United States. **Units of Measure:** Dollars each. **Type of Price:** average paid by farmer. **Time Period Covered:** latest 6 years.

FENCE POST: STEEL

Source: *Agricultural Prices Annual Summary.* **Price Frequency:** quarterly. **Effective Market(s):** United States. **Units of Measure:** Dollars each. **Type of Price:** average paid by farmer. **Time Period Covered:** latest 6 years.

FENCE POST: STEEL, LINE

Source: *Agricultural Prices.* **Price Frequency:** semiannually. **Effective Market(s):** United States. **Units of Measure:** Dollars each. **Type of Price:** paid by farmer. **Time Period Covered:** latest year.

FENCE POST: WOOD, FARM LINE

Source: *Agricultural Prices.* **Price Frequency:** quarterly. **Effective Market(s):** United States. **Units of Measure:** Dollars each. **Type of Price:** paid by farmer. **Time Period Covered:** latest 2 quarters, year ago.

FENCE POST: WOOD, TREATED

Source: *Agricultural Prices Annual Summary.* **Price Frequency:** bimonthly. **Effective Market(s):** United States. **Units of Measure:** Dollars each. **Type of Price:** average paid by farmer. **Time Period Covered:** latest 6 years.

FENNEL OIL: SWEET, USP

Source: *Chemical Marketing Reporter.* **Price Frequency:** weekly. **Effective Market(s):** New York. **Units of Measure:** Dollars per lb. **Type of Price:** spot. **Time Period Covered:** latest week.

FENNEL SEED: CHINESE

Source: *Prices of Selected Asia/Pacific Products.* **Price Frequency:** monthly. **Effective Market(s):** United Kingdom. **Units of Measure:** British pounds per metric ton. **Type of Price:** spot high, spot low. **Time Period Covered:** latest month.

Source: *Prices of Selected Asia/Pacific Products.* **Price Frequency:** monthly. **Effective Market(s):** United Kingdom/North European ports. **Units of Measure:** Dollars per metric ton. **Type of Price:** high, low. **Time Period Covered:** latest month.

FENNEL SEED: EGYPTIAN

Source: *Chemical Marketing Reporter.* **Price Frequency:** weekly. **Effective Market(s):** New York. **Units of Measure:** Dollars per lb. **Type of Price:** spot. **Time Period Covered:** latest week.

Source: *U. S. Spice Trade.* **Price Frequency:** annually. **Effective Market(s):** New York. **Units of Measure:** cents per lb. **Type of Price:** spot. **Time Period Covered:** latest 3 years.

FENNEL SEED: INDIAN

Source: *Chemical Marketing Reporter.* **Price Frequency:** weekly. **Effective Market(s):** New York. **Units of Measure:** Dollars per lb. **Type of Price:** spot. **Time Period Covered:** latest week.

Source: *Prices of Selected Asia/Pacific Products.* **Price Frequency:** monthly. **Effective Market(s):** United Kingdom/North European ports. **Units of Measure:** Dollars per metric ton. **Type of Price:** high, low. **Time Period Covered:** latest month.

Source: *Prices of Selected Asia/Pacific Products.* **Price Frequency:** monthly. **Effective Market(s):** New York. **Units of Measure:** Dollars per lb. **Type of Price:** spot high, spot low. **Time Period Covered:** latest month.

Source: *U. S. Spice Trade.* **Price Frequency:** annually. **Effective Market(s):** New York. **Units of Measure:** cents per lb. **Type of Price:** spot. **Time Period Covered:** latest 3 years.

FENUGREEK SEED

Source: *Chemical Marketing Reporter.* **Price Frequency:** weekly. **Effective Market(s):** New York. **Units of Measure:** Dollars per lb. **Type of Price:** spot. **Time Period Covered:** latest week.

FENUGREEK SEED: AUSTRALIAN

Source: *U. S. Spice Trade.* **Price Frequency:** annually. **Effective Market(s):** New York. **Units of Measure:** cents per lb. **Type of Price:** spot. **Time Period Covered:** latest 3 years.

FENUGREEK SEED: INDIAN

Source: *U. S. Spice Trade.* **Price Frequency:** annually. **Effective Market(s):** New York. **Units of Measure:** cents per lb. **Type of Price:** spot. **Time Period Covered:** latest 3 years.

FENUGREEK SEED: MOROCCAN

Source: *Fruit and Tropical Products.* **Price Frequency:** monthly, seasonally. **Effective Market(s):** London. **Units of Measure:** British pounds per tonne. **Type of Price:** month end. **Time Period Covered:** latest 2 years.

Source: *U. S. Spice Trade.* **Price Frequency:** annually. **Effective Market(s):** New York. **Units of Measure:** cents per lb. **Type of Price:** spot. **Time Period Covered:** latest 3 years.

FERNS: LEATHERLEAF

Source: *Floriculture Crops.* **Price Frequency:** annually. **Effective Market(s):** Florida, Hawaii, Other States, United States. **Units of Measure:** Dollars per unit. **Type of Price:** commercial wholesale. **Time Period Covered:** latest 2 years.

FERRIC AMMONIUM CITRATE: BROWN, GREEN GRANULAR, NF

Source: *Chemical Marketing Reporter.* **Price Frequency:** weekly. **Effective Market(s):** New York. **Units of Measure:** Dollars per lb. **Type of Price:** spot. **Time Period Covered:** latest week.

FERRIC AMMONIUM OXALATE: FINE GRANULAR

Source: *Chemical Marketing Reporter.* **Price Frequency:** weekly. **Effective Market(s):** East. **Units of Measure:** Dollars per lb. **Type of Price:** spot. **Time Period Covered:** latest week.

FERRIC CHLORIDE: 42 BAUME, PHOTO GRADE

Source: *Chemical Marketing Reporter.* **Price Frequency:** weekly. **Effective Market(s):** New York. **Units of Measure:** Dollars per 100 lbs. **Type of Price:** spot. **Time Period Covered:** latest week.

FERRIC CHLORIDE: ANHYDROUS, TECHNICAL GRADE

Source: *Chemical Marketing Reporter.* **Price Frequency:** weekly. **Effective Market(s):** New York. **Units of Measure:** Dollars per lb. **Type of Price:** spot. **Time Period Covered:** latest week.

FERRIC CHLORIDE: SEWAGE GRADE

Source: *Chemical Marketing Reporter.* **Price Frequency:** weekly. **Effective Market(s):** New York. **Units of Measure:** Dollars per ton. **Type of Price:** spot. **Time Period Covered:** latest week.

FERRIC HYDROXYETHYLENE DIAMINETRIACETIC ACID: AGRICULTURAL GRADE, SODIUM Salt Solution, 5% Fe

Source: *Chemical Marketing Reporter.* **Price Frequency:** weekly. **Effective Market(s):** New York. **Units of Measure:** Dollars per lb. **Type of Price:** spot. **Time Period Covered:** latest week.

FERRIC HYDROXYETHYLENE DIAMINETRIACETIC ACID: INDUSTRIAL GRADE, SODIUM Salt Solution, 4.5% Fe

Source: *Chemical Marketing Reporter.* **Price Frequency:** weekly. **Effective Market(s):** New York, West. **Units of Measure:** Dollars per lb. **Type of Price:** spot. **Time Period Covered:** latest week.

FERRIC NITRATE: CRYSTALLINE

Source: *Chemical Marketing Reporter.* **Price Frequency:** weekly. **Effective Market(s):** New York. **Units of Measure:** Dollars per lb. **Type of Price:** spot. **Time Period Covered:** latest week.

FERRIC OXIDES

see Iron Oxides.

FERRIC PHOSPHATE: FCCG INSOLUBLE POWDER

Source: *Chemical Marketing Reporter.* **Price Frequency:** weekly. **Effective Market(s):** New York. **Units of Measure:** Dollars per lb. **Type of Price:** spot. **Time Period Covered:** latest week.

FERRIC PYROPHOSPHATE: SOLUBLE, PURIFIED

Source: *Chemical Marketing Reporter.* **Price Frequency:** weekly. **Effective Market(s):** New York. **Units of Measure:** Dollars per lb. **Type of Price:** spot. **Time Period Covered:** latest week.

FERRIC SULFATE: PARTLY HYDRATED

Source: *Chemical Marketing Reporter.* **Price Frequency:** weekly. **Effective Market(s):** New York. **Units of Measure:** Dollars per ton. **Type of Price:** spot. **Time Period Covered:** latest week.

FERROCHROME: 60-65%

Source: *E&MJ.* **Price Frequency:** monthly. **Units of Measure:** cents per lb. chromium. **Time Period Covered:** latest month.

FERROCHROME: HIGH CARBON

Source: *American Metal Market.* **Price Frequency:** weekly. **Units of Measure:** cents per lb. chromium. **Type of Price:** producer. **Time Period Covered:** latest week.

FERROCHROME-SILICON: LOW CARBON GRADE

Source: *American Metal Market.* **Price Frequency:** weekly. **Effective Market(s):** Pittsburgh. **Units of Measure:** cents per lb. chromium. **Type of Price:** producer. **Time Period Covered:** latest week.

FERROCOLUMBIUM

Source: *American Metal Market.* **Price Frequency:** weekly. **Units of Measure:** cents per lb. contained columbium. **Type of Price:** producer. **Time Period Covered:** latest week.

FERROMANGANESE: 78% MANGANESE

Source: *Commodity Year Book.* **Price Frequency:** monthly, annually. **Units of Measure:** Dollars per gross ton. **Time Period Covered:** latest 9 years.

FERROMANGANESE: HIGH CARBON

Source: *American Metal Market.* **Price Frequency:** weekly. **Units of Measure:** Dollars per gross ton. **Type of Price:** producer. **Time Period Covered:** latest week.

FERROMANGANESE: MEDIUM CARBON

Source: *E&MJ.* **Price Frequency:** monthly. **Units of Measure:** cents per lb. of manganese. **Time Period Covered:** latest month.

FERROMOLYBDENUM

Source: *Journal of Commerce and Commercial.* **Price Frequency:** daily. **Effective Market(s):** Europe. **Units of Measure:** Dollars per kilogram. **Type of Price:** spot. **Time Period Covered:** latest day.

FERROMOLYBDENUM: LUMP

Source: *American Metal Market.* **Price Frequency:** weekly. **Units of Measure:** cents per lb. of molybdenum. **Type of Price:** producer. **Time Period Covered:** latest week.

FERRONICKEL

Source: *American Metal Market.* **Price Frequency:** daily. **Units of Measure:** Dollars per lb. of nickel. **Type of Price:** market. **Time Period Covered:** latest day.

FERROSILICON: 50%, REGULAR

Source: *American Metal Market.* **Price Frequency:** weekly. **Units of Measure:** cents per lb. **Type of Price:** producer. **Time Period Covered:** latest week.

FERROSILICON: 75% MINIMUM

Source: *Journal of Commerce and Commercial.* **Price Frequency:** daily. **Effective Market(s):** Europe. **Units of Measure:** Dollars per ton. **Type of Price:** spot. **Time Period Covered:** latest day.

FERROSILICON: 75%, REGULAR

Source: *American Metal Market.* **Price Frequency:** weekly. **Units of Measure:** cents per lb. **Type of Price:** producer. **Time Period Covered:** latest week.

FERROSILICON: FOUNDRY ALLOY

Source: *American Metal Market.* **Price Frequency:** weekly. **Units of Measure:** cents per lb. **Type of Price:** producer. **Time Period Covered:** latest week.

FERROTITANIUM: LOS CARBON GRADE

Source: *American Metal Market.* **Price Frequency:** weekly. **Units of Measure:** cents per lb. contained titanium. **Type of Price:** producer. **Time Period Covered:** latest week.

FERROTUNGSTEN: HIGH PURITY 80%

Source: *American Metal Market.* **Price Frequency:** weekly. **Units of Measure:** cents per lb. **Type of Price:** producer. **Time Period Covered:** latest week.

FERROUS FLUOBORATE: LIQUID CONCENTRATED

Source: *Chemical Marketing Reporter.* **Price Frequency:** weekly. **Effective Market(s):** New York. **Units of Measure:** Dollars per lb. **Type of Price:** spot. **Time Period Covered:** latest week.

FERROUS GLUCONATE: NF

Source: *Chemical Marketing Reporter.* **Price Frequency:** weekly. **Effective Market(s):** East. **Units of Measure:** Dollars per lb. **Type of Price:** spot. **Time Period Covered:** latest week.

FERROUS GLUCONATE: USP

Source: *Journal of Commerce and Commercial.* **Price Frequency:** weekly in Friday issue. **Units of Measure:** Dollars per lb. **Type of Price:** spot. **Time Period Covered:** latest week.

FERROUS NAPHTHENATE: LIQUID, 6% IRON

Source: *Chemical Marketing Reporter.* **Price Frequency:** weekly. **Effective Market(s):** New York. **Units of Measure:** Dollars per lb. **Type of Price:** spot. **Time Period Covered:** latest week.

FERROUS SULFATE: CRYSTALLINE

Source: *Chemical Marketing Reporter.* **Price Frequency:** weekly. **Effective Market(s):** New York. **Units of Measure:** Dollars per lb. **Type of Price:** spot. **Time Period Covered:** latest week.

FERROUS SULFATE: HEPTAHYDRATE, GRANULAR

Source: *Chemical Marketing Reporter.* **Price Frequency:** weekly. **Effective Market(s):** New York. **Units of Measure:** Dollars per ton. **Type of Price:** spot. **Time Period Covered:** latest week.

FERROUS SULFATE: MOIST

Source: *Chemical Marketing Reporter.* **Price Frequency:** weekly. **Effective Market(s):** New York. **Units of Measure:** Dollars per ton. **Type of Price:** spot. **Time Period Covered:** latest week.

FERROUS SULFATE: MONOHYDRATE, GRANULAR

Source: *Chemical Marketing Reporter.* **Price Frequency:** weekly. **Effective Market(s):** New York. **Units of Measure:** Dollars per ton. **Type of Price:** spot. **Time Period Covered:** latest week.

FERROUS SULFATE: POWDERED, USP

Source: *Chemical Marketing Reporter.* **Price Frequency:** weekly. **Effective Market(s):** New York. **Units of Measure:** Dollars per lb. **Type of Price:** spot. **Time Period Covered:** latest week.

FERROVANADIUM

Source: *American Metal Market.* **Price Frequency:** weekly. **Units of Measure:** cents per lb. of vanadium. **Type of Price:** producer. **Time Period Covered:** latest week.

FERTILIZER

see also specific types of fertilizer, e.g., Muriate of Potash.

Source: *Agricultural Prices.* **Price Frequency:** monthly. **Effective Market(s):** 9 domestic markets, United States. **Units of Measure:** Dollars per ton. **Type of Price:** paid by farmer. **Time Period Covered:** latest month.

Source: *Agricultural Prices Annual Summary.* **Price Frequency:** semiannually. **Effective Market(s):** varies, United States. **Units of Measure:** Dollars per ton. **Type of Price:** average paid by farmer. **Time Period Covered:** latest year, for US quarterly for latest 6 years.

Source: *Journal of Commerce and Commercial.* **Price Frequency:** weekly in Thursday issue. **Units of Measure:** Dollars per ton. **Type of Price:** spot. **Time Period Covered:** latest week.

FERTILIZER: NITROGEN SOLUTION, 28%

Source: *Agricultural Prices Annual Summary.* **Price Frequency:** semiannually. **Effective Market(s):** North Central region, Northern Plains region, South Central region, United States. **Units of Measure:** Dollars per ton. **Type of Price:** average paid by farmer. **Time Period Covered:** latest year, for US quarterly for latest 6 years.

FERTILIZER: NITROGEN SOLUTION, 30%

Source: *Agricultural Prices Annual Summary.* **Price Frequency:** semiannually. **Effective Market(s):** Southeast region, United States. **Units of Measure:** Dollars per ton. **Type of Price:** average paid by farmer. **Time Period Covered:** latest year, for US quarterly for latest 6 years.

FERTILIZER: NITROGEN SOLUTION, 32%

Source: *Agricultural Prices Annual Summary.* **Price Frequency:** semiannually. **Effective Market(s):** North Central region, Northwest region, Southeast region, Southwest region, United States. **Units of Measure:** Dollars per ton. **Type of Price:** average paid by farmer. **Time Period Covered:** latest year, for US quarterly for latest 6 years.

FESCUE SEED: TALL, ALTA AND KENTUCKY

Source: *Agricultural Prices Annual Summary.* **Price Frequency:** semiannually. **Effective Market(s):** United States. **Units of Measure:** Dollars per 100 lbs. **Type of Price:** average paid by farmer. **Time Period Covered:** latest 6 years.

FIBERS

see also Yarn.

FIBERS: CELLULOSIC, ACETATE, 55 DENIER

Source: *DNR: Daily News Record.* **Price Frequency:** daily. **Units of Measure:** dollars per yard. **Time Period Covered:** latest day.

FIBERS: CELLULOSIC, ACETATE, 150 DENIER

Source: *DNR: Daily News Record.* **Price Frequency:** daily. **Units of Measure:** dollars per yard. **Time Period Covered:** latest day.

FIBERS: CELLULOSIC, HIGH MODULUS STAPLE

Source: *DNR: Daily News Record.* **Price Frequency:** daily. **Units of Measure:** dollars per yard. **Time Period Covered:** latest day.

FIBERS: CELLULOSIC, RAYON STAPLE

Source: *DNR: Daily News Record.* **Price Frequency:** daily. **Units of Measure:** dollars per yard. **Time Period Covered:** latest day.

FIBERS: MAN MADE

Source: *ATI, America's Textiles International.* **Price Frequency:** monthly. **Time Period Covered:** latest month, 6 months ago, year ago.

Source: *Textile World.* **Price Frequency:** monthly. **Units of Measure:** index. **Type of Price:** producer price index. **Time Period Covered:** latest 2 months, year ago.

FIBERS: NON-CELLULOSIC, ACRYLIC STAPLE BRANDED, 3 DENIER

Source: *DNR: Daily News Record.* **Price Frequency:** daily. **Units of Measure:** dollars per yard. **Time Period Covered:** latest day.

FIBERS: NON-CELLULOSIC, NYLON DULL/PRINS, 40 DENIER

Source: *DNR: Daily News Record.* **Price Frequency:** daily. **Units of Measure:** dollars per yard. **Time Period Covered:** latest day.

FIBERS: NON-CELLULOSIC, POLYESTER BLEND STAPLE BRANDED

Source: *DNR: Daily News Record.* **Price Frequency:** daily. **Units of Measure:** dollars per yard. **Time Period Covered:** latest day.

FIBERS: NON-CELLULOSIC, POLYESTER FEED, 150 DENIER

Source: *DNR: Daily News Record.* **Price Frequency:** daily. **Units of Measure:** dollars per yard. **Time Period Covered:** latest day.

FIBERS AND FILAMENTS

Source: *ATI, America's Textiles International.* **Price Frequency:** monthly. **Time Period Covered:** latest month, 6 months ago, year ago.

FIBREBOARD

Source: *Timber Bulletin.* **Price Frequency:** monthly, annually. **Effective Market(s):** Finland, Norway. **Units of Measure:** national currency per metric ton. **Type of Price:** export value. **Time Period Covered:** monthly latest 2 years, annually latest 6 years.

FIELD CULTIVATOR

Source: *Agricultural Prices.* **Price Frequency:** annually. **Effective Market(s):** United States. **Units of Measure:** Dollars each. **Type of Price:** paid by farmer. **Time Period Covered:** latest year.

Source: *Agricultural Prices Annual Summary.* **Price Frequency:** annually. **Effective Market(s):** United States. **Units of Measure:** Dollars each. **Type of Price:** average paid by farmer. **Time Period Covered:** latest 6 years.

FIGS

Source: *Agricultural Prices Annual Summary.* **Price Frequency:** annually. **Effective Market(s):** California, Hawaii. **Units of Measure:** Dollars per ton. **Type of Price:** average price received by farmer. **Time Period Covered:** latest 6 years.

Source: *Lancaster Farming.* **Price Frequency:** weekly, seasonally. **Effective Market(s):** Pennyslvania. **Units of Measure:** Dollars per unit. **Type of Price:** market. **Time Period Covered:** latest week.

FILBERTS

Source: *Agricultural Prices Annual Summary.* **Price Frequency:** annually. **Effective Market(s):** Oregon, Washington, United States. **Units of Measure:** Dollars per ton. **Type of Price:** average price received by farmer. **Time Period Covered:** latest 3 years, for US latest 6 years.

Source: *Fruit and Tree Nuts Situation and Outlook Yearbook.* **Price Frequency:** annually. **Effective Market(s):** Oregon, Washington, Oregon/Washington. **Units of Measure:** Dollars per ton. **Type of Price:** grower. **Time Period Covered:** latest 20 years.

FILE FOLDERS

Source: *Pulp & Paper Week.* **Price Frequency:** monthly, irregularly. **Units of Measure:** index. **Type of Price:** price index. **Time Period Covered:** latest 3 months.

FILLERS

Source: *Modern Plastics.* **Price Frequency:** quarterly in February, May, August, November issues. **Units of Measure:** Dollars per lb. **Type of Price:** list. **Time Period Covered:** latest 4 quarters.

FINISHED FABRICS

see Fabrics: Finished.

FINLAND MARKKA

Source: *Asian Wall Street Journal.* **Price Frequency:** daily. **Effective Market(s):** United States. **Units of Measure:** Finnish markkaa per ECU. **Type of Price:** foreign exchange. **Time Period Covered:** latest 2 days.

Source: *Barron's.* **Price Frequency:** weekly. **Effective Market(s):** New York. **Units of Measure:** Finnish markka per United States dollar. **Type of Price:** foreign exchange. **Time Period Covered:** latest 2 weeks.

Source: *New York Times.* **Price Frequency:** daily. **Effective Market(s):** New York. **Units of Measure:** Finnish Markka per United States dollar. **Type of Price:** foreign exchange. **Time Period Covered:** latest 2 days.

Source: *Timber Bulletin.* **Price Frequency:** monthly, annually. **Units of Measure:** Finnish markka per United States dollar. **Type of Price:** foreign exchange. **Time Period Covered:** latest 2 years.

Source: *The Times.* **Price Frequency:** daily. **Effective Market(s):** London. **Units of Measure:** Finland marka per British pound. **Type of Price:** foreign exchange. **Time Period Covered:** latest day.

FIR

Source: *Volume and Value of Sawtimber Stumpage Sold From National Forests by Selected Species and Region.* **Price Frequency:** quarterly, annually. **Effective Market(s):** 6 domestic markets. **Units of Measure:** Dollars per 1000 board feet. **Type of Price:** average. **Time Period Covered:** latest quarter, latest year.

FIR: GRAND

Source: *Volume and Value of Sawtimber Stumpage Sold From National Forests by Selected Species and Region.* **Price Frequency:** quarterly, annually. **Effective Market(s):** Northern region, Intermountain region, Pacific Northwest. **Units of Measure:** Dollars per 1000 board feet. **Type of Price:** average. **Time Period Covered:** latest quarter, latest year.

FIR: NOBLE

Source: *Volume and Value of Sawtimber Stumpage Sold From National Forests by Selected Species and Region.* **Price Frequency:** quarterly, annually. **Effective Market(s):** Pacific Northwest. **Units of Measure:** Dollars per 1000 board feet. **Type of Price:** average. **Time Period Covered:** latest quarter, latest year.

FIR: SHASTA RED

Source: *Volume and Value of Sawtimber Stumpage Sold From National Forests by Selected Species and Region.* **Price Frequency:** quarterly, annually. **Effective Market(s):** Pacific Northwest. **Units of Measure:** Dollars per 1000 board feet. **Type of Price:** average. **Time Period Covered:** latest quarter, latest year.

FIR: SUBALPINE

Source: *Volume and Value of Sawtimber Stumpage Sold From National Forests by Selected Species and Region.* **Price Frequency:** quarterly, annually. **Effective Market(s):** Northern region, Rocky Mountain region, Intermountain region, Pacific Northwest. **Units of Measure:** Dollars per 1000 board feet. **Type of Price:** average. **Time Period Covered:** latest quarter, latest year.

FIR: WHITE

Source: *Volume and Value of Sawtimber Stumpage Sold From National Forests by Selected Species and Region.* **Price Frequency:** quarterly, annually. **Effective Market(s):** Intermountain region, Pacific Northwest. **Units of Measure:** Dollars per 1000 board feet. **Type of Price:** average. **Time Period Covered:** latest quarter, latest year.

FIR AND LARCH: KILN DRIED, SELECT AND COMMONS

Source: *Random Lengths.* **Price Frequency:** weekly. **Units of Measure:** Dollars per 1000 board feet. **Type of Price:** mill price to wholesaler. **Time Period Covered:** latest week.

FIR LUMBER: 2X4

Source: *ENR.* **Price Frequency:** monthly in first issue of month. **Effective Market(s):** 20-city average. **Units of Measure:** Dollars per 1000 board feet. **Time Period Covered:** latest month.

FIR LUMBER: S4S

Source: *ENR.* **Price Frequency:** monthly in third issue of month. **Effective Market(s):** 18 domestic markets, Montreal. **Units of Measure:** Dollars per 1000 board feet. **Type of Price:** spot. **Time Period Covered:** latest month.

FIR OIL: CANADA

Source: *Chemical Marketing Reporter.* **Price Frequency:** weekly. **Effective Market(s):** New York. **Units of Measure:** Dollars per lb. **Type of Price:** spot. **Time Period Covered:** latest week.

FIR OIL: SIBERIA

Source: *Chemical Marketing Reporter.* **Price Frequency:** weekly. **Effective Market(s):** New York. **Units of Measure:** Dollars per lb. **Type of Price:** spot. **Time Period Covered:** latest week.

FISH: MACKEREL, CANNED

Source: *Statistical Bulletin of the South Pacific: Retail Price Indexes.* **Price Frequency:** annually. **Effective Market(s):** 18 South Pacific markets. **Units of Measure:** Australian dollars per . **Type of Price:** retail. **Time Period Covered:** latest year.

FISH MEAL

Source: *California Farmer.* **Price Frequency:** semimonthly. **Effective Market(s):** California. **Units of Measure:** Dollars per ton. **Time Period Covered:** latest week, month ago, year ago.

Source: *International Financial Statistics.* **Price Frequency:** monthly, quarterly, annually. **Effective Market(s):** Hamburg. **Units of Measure:** Dollars per metric ton, index. **Type of Price:** market price, price index. **Time Period Covered:** latest 5 months, latest 5 quarters, latest 5 years.

Source: *International Financial Statistics Yearbook.* **Price Frequency:** annually. **Effective Market(s):** Hamburg. **Units of Measure:** Dollars per metric ton. **Type of Price:** wholesale. **Time Period Covered:** latest 30 years.

Source: *Japan Economic Journal.* **Price Frequency:** weekly. **Effective Market(s):** Japan. **Units of Measure:** Japanese yen per kilogram. **Type of Price:** wholesale. **Time Period Covered:** latest 2 weeks.

FISH MEAL: 64% PROTEIN, CHILEAN

Source: *Milling & Baking News.* **Price Frequency:** weekly. **Effective Market(s):** Gulf. **Units of Measure:** Dollars per ton. **Time Period Covered:** latest week, week, ago, year ago.

FISH MEAL: 64-65% PROTEIN

Source: *Monthly Commodity Price Bulletin Supplement.* **Price Frequency:** monthly, quarterly, annually. **Effective Market(s):** Hamburg. **Units of Measure:** Dollars per tonne. **Time Period Covered:** latest 20 years.

Source: *Oil World.* **Price Frequency:** weekly, monthly, annually. **Effective Market(s):** Hamburg. **Units of Measure:** Dollars per tonne. **Type of Price:** lowest representative asking. **Time Period Covered:** weekly latest 3 weeks, monthly latest 2 months, annually latest 2 years.

Source: *UNCTAD Commodity Yearbook.* **Price Frequency:** annually. **Effective Market(s):** Hamburg. **Units of Measure:** Dollars per metric ton. **Type of Price:** free market. **Time Period Covered:** latest 12 years.

Source: *World Oilseed Situation and Market Highlights.* **Price Frequency:** monthly, annually. **Effective Market(s):** Hamburg. **Units of Measure:** Dollars per metric ton. **Time Period Covered:** monthly latest year, annually latest 9 years.

FISH MEAL: 64-65% PROTEIN, ANY ORIGIN

Source: *FAO Quarterly Bulletin of Statistics.* **Price Frequency:** monthly, annually. **Effective Market(s):** Hamburg. **Units of Measure:** Dollars per 1000 kilograms, dollars per metric ton. **Time Period Covered:** latest 3 years.

Source: *Monthly Commodity Price Bulletin.* **Price Frequency:** monthly, annually. **Effective Market(s):** Hamburg. **Units of Measure:** Dollars per metric ton. **Time Period Covered:** latest 5 years.

FISH MEAL: 65% PROTEIN

Source: *Feed Situation and Outlook Report.* **Price Frequency:** monthly. **Effective Market(s):** East Coast. **Units of Measure:** Dollars per ton. **Type of Price:** wholesale. **Time Period Covered:** latest 8 months.

FISH MEAL: 65% PROTEIN MINIMUM, IMPORTED, CHILEAN

Source: *Chemical Marketing Reporter.* **Price Frequency:** weekly. **Effective Market(s):** Atlantic/Gulf Ports. **Units of Measure:** Dollars per ton. **Type of Price:** spot. **Time Period Covered:** latest week.

FISH MEAL: 67% PROTEIN, DOMESTIC

Source: *Grain and Feed Market News.* **Price Frequency:** weekly, seasonally. **Effective Market(s):** East Coast, Gulf Coast, West Coast. **Units of Measure:** Dollars per ton. **Type of Price:** wholesale. **Time Period Covered:** latest week, week ago, year ago.

FISH MEAL: ICELAND

Source: *International Financial Statistics.* **Price Frequency:** monthly, quarterly, annually. **Effective Market(s):** Iceland. **Units of Measure:** Dollars per metric ton, index. **Type of Price:** market price, price index. **Time Period Covered:** latest month, latest quarter, latest 4 years.

Source: *International Financial Statistics Yearbook.* **Price Frequency:** annually. **Effective Market(s):** Iceland. **Units of Measure:** Dollars per metric ton. **Type of Price:** wholesale. **Time Period Covered:** latest 30 years.

FISH MEAL: MENHADEN

Source: *Feedstuffs.* **Price Frequency:** weekly. **Units of Measure:** Dollars per bulk ton. **Time Period Covered:** latest week.

Source: *Feedstuffs.* **Price Frequency:** weekly. **Effective Market(s):** Atlanta. **Units of Measure:** Dollars per ton. **Time Period Covered:** latest week, week ago, 6 months ago, year ago.

FISH MEAL: MENHADEN, 60% PROTEIN, GROUND, DOMESTIC

Source: *Chemical Marketing Reporter.* **Price Frequency:** weekly. **Effective Market(s):** Atlantic Port, Gulf Port. **Units of Measure:** Dollars per ton. **Type of Price:** spot. **Time Period Covered:** latest week.

FISH MEAL: PERUVIAN

Source: *Commodity Trade and Price Trends.* **Price Frequency:** annually. **Effective Market(s):** Hamburg. **Units of Measure:** Dollars per metric ton, 1980 constant dollars per metric ton. **Time Period Covered:** latest 28 years.

FISH MEAL: WHITE

Source: *Farmers Weekly.* **Price Frequency:** weekly, seasonally. **Effective Market(s):** Great Britain. **Units of Measure:** British pounds per tonne. **Type of Price:** spot. **Time Period Covered:** latest week.

FISH OIL

Source: *Oil World.* **Price Frequency:** weekly, monthly, annually. **Effective Market(s):** Northwest Europe. **Units of Measure:** Dollars per tonne. **Type of Price:** lowest representative asking. **Time Period Covered:** weekly latest 3 weeks, monthly latest 2 months, annually latest 2 years.

FISH OIL: CRUDE

Source: *Prices of Selected Asia/Pacific Products.* **Price Frequency:** monthly. **Effective Market(s):** North West European ports. **Units of Measure:** Dollars per metric ton. **Type of Price:** high, low. **Time Period Covered:** latest month.

Source: *Prices of Selected Asia/Pacific Products.* **Price Frequency:** monthly. **Effective Market(s):** Liverpool. **Units of Measure:** British pounds per metric ton. **Type of Price:** high, low. **Time Period Covered:** latest month.

FISH OIL: DENMARK

Source: *Prices of Selected Asia/Pacific Products.* **Price Frequency:** monthly. **Effective Market(s):** United Kingdom. **Units of Measure:** Dollars per metric ton. **Type of Price:** high, low. **Time Period Covered:** latest month.

FISH OIL: JAPANESE

Source: *Prices of Selected Asia/Pacific Products.* **Price Frequency:** monthly. **Effective Market(s):** Rotterdam. **Units of Measure:** Dollars per metric ton. **Type of Price:** high, low. **Time Period Covered:** latest month.

FISH OIL: MENHADEN, UNITED STATES

Source: *Prices of Selected Asia/Pacific Products.* **Price Frequency:** monthly. **Effective Market(s):** Rotterdam. **Units of Measure:** Dollars per metric ton. **Type of Price:** high, low. **Time Period Covered:** latest month.

FISH SOLUBLES

Source: *Feedstuffs.* **Price Frequency:** weekly. **Effective Market(s):** Atlanta, Chicago, Los Angeles, San Francisco. **Units of Measure:** Dollars per lb. **Time Period Covered:** latest week.

FLAME RETARDANTS

Source: *Modern Plastics.* **Price Frequency:** quarterly in February, May, August, November issues. **Units of Measure:** Dollars per lb. **Type of Price:** list. **Time Period Covered:** latest 4 quarters.

FLAX FOR SEED

see Seed Flax.

FLAXSEED

Source: *Agricultural Prices.* **Price Frequency:** monthly. **Effective Market(s):** United States. **Units of Measure:** Dollars per bushel. **Type of Price:** received by farmer. **Time Period Covered:** latest 2 months, year ago.

Source: *Agricultural Prices.* **Price Frequency:** monthly, seasonally. **Effective Market(s):** Minnesota, North Dakota, South Dakota, United States. **Units of Measure:** Dollars per bushel. **Type of Price:** received by farmer. **Time Period Covered:** latest 2 months.

Source: *Agricultural Prices Annual Summary.* **Price Frequency:** annually. **Effective Market(s):** Minnesota, North Dakota, South Dakota, United States. **Units of Measure:** Dollars per bushel. **Type of Price:** average price received by farmer. **Time Period Covered:** latest 2 years, for US latest 6 years.

Source: *Commodity Year Book.* **Price Frequency:** monthly, annually. **Effective Market(s):** United States. **Units of Measure:** cents per bushel. **Type of Price:** price received by farmers. **Time Period Covered:** latest 7 years.

Source: *Oil Crops Situation and Outlook.* **Price Frequency:** monthly. **Effective Market(s):** United States. **Units of Measure:** Dollars per bushel. **Type of Price:** received by farmer. **Time Period Covered:** latest 5 months.

FLAXSEED: FUTURES

Source: *Asian Wall Street Journal.* **Price Frequency:** daily. **Effective Market(s):** Winnepeg. **Units of Measure:** Canadian dollars per ton. **Type of Price:** futures. **Time Period Covered:** latest day.

Source: *Investor's Daily.* **Price Frequency:** daily. **Effective Market(s):** Winnepeg. **Units of Measure:** Canadian dollars per ton. **Type of Price:** futures. **Time Period Covered:** latest day.

Source: *Wall Street Journal.* **Price Frequency:** daily. **Effective Market(s):** Winnipeg. **Units of Measure:** Canadian dollars per ton. **Type of Price:** futures. **Time Period Covered:** latest day.

FLAXSEED: FUTURES, MAY

Source: *Commodity Year Book.* **Price Frequency:** monthly. **Effective Market(s):** Winnipeg . **Units of Measure:** Canadian dollars per tonne. **Type of Price:** futures. **Time Period Covered:** latest 3 years.

FLAXSEED: NO. 1

Source: *Grain and Feed Market News.* **Price Frequency:** daily, seasonally. **Effective Market(s):** Minneapolis. **Units of Measure:** Dollars per bushel. **Type of Price:** cash bid. **Time Period Covered:** latest week, year ago.

Source: *Minneapolis Grain Exchange Statistical Annual.* **Price Frequency:** monthly, annually. **Effective Market(s):** Minneapolis. **Units of Measure:** cents per bushel. **Type of Price:** cash. **Time Period Covered:** latest 10 years.

FLINT CLAY: CALCINED

Source: *Industrial Minerals.* **Price Frequency:** monthly. **Effective Market(s):** main European port. **Units of Measure:** British pounds per metric tonne. **Type of Price:** producer & dealer. **Time Period Covered:** latest month.

FLOORING: RED OAK, HARDWOOD LUMBER, SELECT

Source: *Journal of Commerce and Commercial.* **Price Frequency:** daily. **Type of Price:** spot supplier . **Time Period Covered:** latest day.

FLOORING: SOFTWOOD, YELLOW SOUTHERN PINE, C AND BETTER

Source: *Commodity Year Book.* **Price Frequency:** monthly, annually. **Units of Measure:** index. **Type of Price:** price index. **Time Period Covered:** latest 8 years.

FLOUNDER: BLOCKS, ATLANTIC

Source: *NMFS Green Sheet Supplement.* **Price Frequency:** weekly. **Effective Market(s):** New England. **Units of Measure:** Dollars per lb. **Type of Price:** processor. **Time Period Covered:** latest week.

FLOUNDER: BLOCKS, PACIFIC

Source: *NMFS Green Sheet Supplement.* **Price Frequency:** weekly. **Effective Market(s):** New England. **Units of Measure:** Dollars per lb. **Type of Price:** processor. **Time Period Covered:** latest week.

FLOUNDER: FILLETS, BREADED, FROZEN

Source: *HRI-Buyers Guide.* **Price Frequency:** weekly. **Effective Market(s):** New York. **Units of Measure:** Dollars per case. **Type of Price:** prices paid by dining places & institutions. **Time Period Covered:** latest week.

FLOUNDER: FILLETS, CANADIAN

Source: *NMFS Green Sheet Supplement.* **Price Frequency:** weekly. **Effective Market(s):** New England. **Units of Measure:** Dollars per lb. **Type of Price:** to primary wholesaler. **Time Period Covered:** latest week.

FLOUNDER: FILLETS, FRESH

Source: *Seafood Price-Current.* **Price Frequency:** semiweekly. **Effective Market(s):** West Coast. **Units of Measure:** Dollars per lb. **Type of Price:** sale by first receiver. **Time Period Covered:** latest day.

FLOUNDER: FILLETS, FROZEN

Source: *HRI-Buyers Guide.* **Price Frequency:** weekly. **Effective Market(s):** New York. **Units of Measure:** Dollars per case. **Type of Price:** prices paid by dining places & institutions. **Time Period Covered:** latest week.

FLOUNDER: FILLETS, HOLLAND

Source: *NMFS Green Sheet Supplement.* **Price Frequency:** weekly. **Effective Market(s):** New England. **Units of Measure:** Dollars per lb. **Type of Price:** to primary wholesaler. **Time Period Covered:** latest week.

FLOUNDER AND SOLE: ARROWTOOTH, SKINLESS, FROZEN, JAPANESE

Source: *Seafood Price-Current.* **Price Frequency:** semiweekly. **Effective Market(s):** Mid-Atlantic. **Units of Measure:** Dollars per lb. **Type of Price:** first receiver. **Time Period Covered:** latest day.

FLOUNDER AND SOLE: FILLETS, REGULAR, FROZEN, CANADIAN

Source: *Seafood Price-Current.* **Price Frequency:** semiweekly. **Effective Market(s):** Mid-Atlantic. **Units of Measure:** Dollars per lb. **Type of Price:** first receiver. **Time Period Covered:** latest day.

FLOUNDER AND SOLE: FROZEN, CANADIAN

Source: *Seafood Price-Current.* **Price Frequency:** semi-weekly. **Effective Market(s):** Mid-Atlantic. **Units of Measure:** Dollars per lb. **Type of Price:** first receiver. **Time Period Covered:** latest day.

FLOUNDER AND SOLE: KINGKLIP, GOLDEN, FROZEN, CHILEAN

Source: *Seafood Price-Current.* **Price Frequency:** semi-weekly. **Effective Market(s):** Mid-Atlantic. **Units of Measure:** Dollars per lb. **Type of Price:** first receiver. **Time Period Covered:** latest day.

FLOUNDER AND SOLE: SKINLESS, FROZEN, CANADIAN

Source: *Seafood Price-Current.* **Price Frequency:** semi-weekly. **Effective Market(s):** Mid-Atlantic. **Units of Measure:** Dollars per lb. **Type of Price:** first receiver. **Time Period Covered:** latest day.

FLOUNDER AND SOLE: SKINLESS, FROZEN, DANISH

Source: *Seafood Price-Current.* **Price Frequency:** semi-weekly. **Effective Market(s):** Mid-Atlantic. **Units of Measure:** Dollars per lb. **Type of Price:** first receiver. **Time Period Covered:** latest day.

FLOUNDER AND SOLE: SKINLESS, FROZEN, DUTCH

Source: *Seafood Price-Current.* **Price Frequency:** semi-weekly. **Effective Market(s):** Mid-Atlantic. **Units of Measure:** Dollars per lb. **Type of Price:** first receiver. **Time Period Covered:** latest day.

FLOUR: BAKERS' SHORT PATENT

Source: *Milling & Baking News.* **Price Frequency:** weekly. **Effective Market(s):** Kansas City. **Units of Measure:** Dollars per 100 lbs. **Type of Price:** bulk carlot. **Time Period Covered:** latest week, year ago.

FLOUR: BAKERS' STANDARD PATENT

Source: *Milling & Baking News.* **Price Frequency:** weekly. **Effective Market(s):** Kansas City. **Units of Measure:** Dollars per 100 lbs. **Type of Price:** bulk carlot. **Time Period Covered:** latest week, year ago.

FLOUR: CAKE, FANCY

Source: *Milling & Baking News.* **Price Frequency:** weekly. **Effective Market(s):** Chicago, New York. **Units of Measure:** Dollars per 100 lbs. **Type of Price:** bulk carlot. **Time Period Covered:** latest week, year ago.

FLOUR: CRACKER

Source: *Milling & Baking News.* **Price Frequency:** weekly. **Effective Market(s):** Chicago. **Units of Measure:** Dollars per 100 lbs. **Type of Price:** bulk carlot. **Time Period Covered:** latest week, year ago.

FLOUR: HARD WINTER

Source: *Asian Wall Street Journal.* **Price Frequency:** daily. **Effective Market(s):** Kansas City. **Units of Measure:** Dollars per 100 lbs. **Type of Price:** cash. **Time Period Covered:** latest 2 days, year ago.

Source: *Wall Street Journal.* **Price Frequency:** daily. **Effective Market(s):** Kansas City. **Units of Measure:** Dollars per 100 lbs. **Time Period Covered:** latest day, day ago, year ago.

FLOUR: HIGH GLUTEN

Source: *Milling & Baking News.* **Price Frequency:** weekly. **Effective Market(s):** Minneapolis, New York. **Units of Measure:** Dollars per 100 lbs. **Type of Price:** bulk carlot. **Time Period Covered:** latest week, year ago.

FLOUR: PASTRY

Source: *Milling & Baking News.* **Price Frequency:** weekly. **Effective Market(s):** Los Angeles. **Units of Measure:** Dollars per 100 lbs. **Type of Price:** bulk carlot. **Time Period Covered:** latest week, year ago.

FLOUR: PLAIN

Source: *Statistical Bulletin of the South Pacific: Retail Price Indexes.* **Price Frequency:** annually. **Effective Market(s):** 18 South Pacific markets. **Units of Measure:** Australian dollars per . **Type of Price:** retail. **Time Period Covered:** latest year.

FLOUR: RYE, WHITE

Source: *Milling & Baking News.* **Price Frequency:** weekly. **Effective Market(s):** Minneapolis, New York. **Units of Measure:** Dollars per 100 lbs. **Type of Price:** bulk carlot. **Time Period Covered:** latest week, year ago.

FLOUR: SECOND CLEAR

Source: *Milling & Baking News.* **Price Frequency:** weekly. **Effective Market(s):** Kansas City. **Units of Measure:** Dollars per 100 lbs. **Type of Price:** bulk carlot. **Time Period Covered:** latest week, year ago.

FLOUR: SEMOLINA

Source: *Milling & Baking News.* **Price Frequency:** weekly. **Effective Market(s):** Minneapolis, New York. **Units of Measure:** Dollars per 100 lbs. **Type of Price:** bulk carlot. **Time Period Covered:** latest week, year ago.

FLOUR: SOFT WINTER, STRAIGHT

Source: *Bakery Newsletter.* **Price Frequency:** weekly. **Effective Market(s):** Chicago. **Units of Measure:** Dollars per 100 lbs. **Type of Price:** bulk. **Time Period Covered:** latest week, year ago.

FLOUR: SOY, DEFATTED

Source: *Milling & Baking News.* **Price Frequency:** weekly. **Effective Market(s):** Midwest. **Units of Measure:** Dollars per 100 lbs. **Time Period Covered:** latest week.

FLOUR: SOY, SACKED

Source: *Milling & Baking News.* **Price Frequency:** weekly . **Effective Market(s):** Midwest. **Units of Measure:** Dollars per 100 lbs. **Time Period Covered:** latest week.

FLOUR: SPRING CLEAR, FANCY

Source: *Milling & Baking News.* **Price Frequency:** weekly. **Effective Market(s):** Minneapolis. **Units of Measure:** Dollars per 100 lbs. **Type of Price:** bulk carlot. **Time Period Covered:** latest week, year ago.

FLOUR: SPRING CLEAR, FIRST

Source: *Milling & Baking News.* **Price Frequency:** weekly. **Effective Market(s):** Minneapolis. **Units of Measure:** Dollars per 100 lbs. **Type of Price:** bulk carlot. **Time Period Covered:** latest week, year ago.

FLOUR: SPRING SHORT PATENT

Source: *Milling & Baking News.* **Price Frequency:** weekly. **Effective Market(s):** Minneapolis. **Units of Measure:** Dollars per 100 lbs. **Type of Price:** bulk carlot. **Time Period Covered:** latest week, year ago.

FLOUR: SPRING STANDARD

Source: *Bakery Newsletter.* **Price Frequency:** weekly. **Effective Market(s):** Minneapolis. **Units of Measure:** Dollars per 100 lbs. **Type of Price:** bulk. **Time Period Covered:** latest week, year ago.

Source: *New York Times.* **Price Frequency:** daily. **Effective Market(s):** Minneapolis. **Units of Measure:** Dollars per 100 lbs. **Type of Price:** cash. **Time Period Covered:** latest 2 days.

FLOUR: SPRING STANDARD PATENT

Source: *Investor's Daily.* **Price Frequency:** daily. **Effective Market(s):** Minneapolis. **Units of Measure:** Dollars per 100 lbs. **Type of Price:** spot. **Time Period Covered:** latest 2 days.

Source: *Milling & Baking News.* **Price Frequency:** weekly. **Effective Market(s):** Minneapolis, New York. **Units of Measure:** Dollars per 100 lbs. **Type of Price:** bulk carlot. **Time Period Covered:** latest week, year ago.

FLOUR: SPRING WHEAT

Source: *Commodity Year Book.* **Price Frequency:** monthly, annually. **Units of Measure:** index. **Type of Price:** wholesale price index. **Time Period Covered:** latest 4 years.

FLOUR: THIRD CLEAR

Source: *Milling & Baking News.* **Price Frequency:** weekly. **Effective Market(s):** Kansas City. **Units of Measure:** Dollars per 100 lbs. **Type of Price:** bulk carlot. **Time Period Covered:** latest week, year ago.

FLOUR: WHEAT, BAKERY

Source: *Commodity Year Book.* **Price Frequency:** annually. **Effective Market(s):** Kansas City, Minneapolis. **Units of Measure:** Dollars per 100 lbs. **Type of Price:** wholesale. **Time Period Covered:** latest 8 years.

Source: *Commodity Year Book.* **Price Frequency:** quarterly. **Effective Market(s):** Kansas City, Minneapolis. **Units of Measure:** Dollars per 100 lbs. **Type of Price:** wholesale. **Time Period Covered:** latest year.

FLOUR: WHOLE WHEAT

Source: *Millin & Baking News.* **Price Frequency:** weekly . **Effective Market(s):** Minneapolis. **Units of Measure:** Dollars per 100 lbs. **Type of Price:** bulk carlot. **Time Period Covered:** latest week, year ago.

FLOUR: WHOLE WHEAT, SPECIALTY

Source: *Milling & Baking News.* **Price Frequency:** weekly. **Effective Market(s):** Minneapolis. **Units of Measure:** Dollars per 100 lbs. **Type of Price:** bulk carlot. **Time Period Covered:** latest week, year ago.

FLOUR: WINTER STANDARD

Source: *Bakery Newsletter.* **Price Frequency:** weekly. **Effective Market(s):** Kansas City. **Units of Measure:** Dollars per 100 lbs. **Type of Price:** bulk. **Time Period Covered:** latest week, year ago.

FLOUR: WINTER/SPRING BLEND

Source: *Milling & Baking News.* **Price Frequency:** weekly. **Effective Market(s):** Los Angeles, New York. **Units of Measure:** Dollars per 100 lbs. **Type of Price:** bulk carlot. **Time Period Covered:** latest week, year ago.

FLOUR BY PRODUCTS OBTAINED

Source: *Commodity Year Book.* **Price Frequency:** quarterly, annually. **Effective Market(s):** Kansas City, Minneapolis. **Units of Measure:** Dollars per 100 lbs. **Type of Price:** wholesale. **Time Period Covered:** quarterly latest year, annually latest 8 years.

FLOWERING PLANTS: POTTED, LESS THAN 5″

Source: *Floriculture Crops.* **Price Frequency:** annually. **Effective Market(s):** 21 domestic markets, United States. **Units of Measure:** Dollars per unit. **Type of Price:** commercial wholesale. **Time Period Covered:** latest 2 years.

FLOWERING PLANTS: POTTED, MORE THAN 5″

Source: *Floriculture Crops.* **Price Frequency:** annually. **Effective Market(s):** 21 domestic markets, United States. **Units of Measure:** Dollars per unit. **Type of Price:** commercial wholesale. **Time Period Covered:** latest 2 years.

FLUKE (FISH): FILLETS, FRESH

Source: *Seafood Price-Current.* **Price Frequency:** semiweekly. **Effective Market(s):** Mid-Atlantic, New England. **Units of Measure:** Dollars per lb. **Type of Price:** sale by first receiver. **Time Period Covered:** latest day.

FLUKE (FISH): WHOLE, FRESH

Source: *Seafood Price-Current.* **Price Frequency:** semiweekly. **Effective Market(s):** Mid-Atlantic, Boston, New Bedford (MA), Portland (ME). **Units of Measure:** Dollars per lb. **Type of Price:** sale by first receiver, auction price. **Time Period Covered:** latest day.

FLUOBORIC ACID

Source: *Chemical Marketing Reporter.* **Price Frequency:** weekly. **Effective Market(s):** New York. **Units of Measure:** Dollars per lb. **Type of Price:** spot. **Time Period Covered:** latest week.

Source: *Journal of Commerce and Commercial.* **Price Frequency:** weekly in Thursday issue. **Units of Measure:** Dollars per lb. **Type of Price:** spot. **Time Period Covered:** latest week.

FLUORIDE: WHITE

Source: *Journal of Commerce and Commercial.* **Price Frequency:** weekly in Thursday issue. **Units of Measure:** Dollars per lb. **Type of Price:** spot. **Time Period Covered:** latest week.

FLUOROCARBON: NO. 11

Source: *Chemical Marketing Reporter.* **Price Frequency:** weekly. **Effective Market(s):** New York. **Units of Measure:** Dollars per lb. **Type of Price:** spot. **Time Period Covered:** latest week.

FLUOROCARBON: NO. 12

Source: *Chemical Marketing Reporter.* **Price Frequency:** weekly. **Effective Market(s):** New York. **Units of Measure:** Dollars per lb. **Type of Price:** spot. **Time Period Covered:** latest week.

FLUOROCARBON: NO. 22

Source: *Chemical Marketing Reporter.* **Price Frequency:** weekly. **Effective Market(s):** New York. **Units of Measure:** Dollars per lb. **Type of Price:** spot. **Time Period Covered:** latest week.

FLUOROCARBON: NO. 113

Source: *Chemical Marketing Reporter.* **Price Frequency:** weekly. **Effective Market(s):** New York. **Units of Measure:** Dollars per lb. **Type of Price:** spot. **Time Period Covered:** latest week.

FLUOROCARBON: NO. 114

Source: *Chemical Marketing Reporter.* **Price Frequency:** weekly. **Effective Market(s):** New York. **Units of Measure:** Dollars per lb. **Type of Price:** spot. **Time Period Covered:** latest week.

FLUOROPLASTICS

see Fluoropolymers.

FLUOROPOLYMER: CTFE

Source: *Journal of Commerce and Commercial.* **Price Frequency:** weekly in Tuesday issue. **Units of Measure:** Dollars per lb. **Type of Price:** spot. **Time Period Covered:** latest week.

Source: *Plastics Technology.* **Price Frequency:** monthly. **Units of Measure:** cents per lb., cents per cubic inch. **Type of Price:** bulk list, market. **Time Period Covered:** latest month.

FLUOROPOLYMER: ECTFE

Source: *Plastics Technology.* **Price Frequency:** monthly. **Units of Measure:** cents per lb., cents per cubic inch. **Type of Price:** bulk list, market. **Time Period Covered:** latest month.

FLUOROPOLYMER: ETFE

Source: *Plastics Technology.* **Price Frequency:** monthly. **Units of Measure:** cents per lb., cents per cubic inch. **Type of Price:** bulk list, market. **Time Period Covered:** latest month.

FLUOROPOLYMER: FEP

Source: *Journal of Commerce and Commercial.* **Price Frequency:** weekly in Tuesday issue. **Units of Measure:** Dollars per lb. **Type of Price:** spot. **Time Period Covered:** latest week.

Source: *Plastics Technology.* **Price Frequency:** monthly. **Units of Measure:** cents per lb., cents per cubic inch. **Type of Price:** bulk list, market. **Time Period Covered:** latest month.

FLUOROPOLYMER: PFA

Source: *Plastics Technology.* **Price Frequency:** monthly. **Units of Measure:** cents per lb., cents per cubic inch. **Type of Price:** bulk list, market. **Time Period Covered:** latest month.

FLUOROPOLYMER: PTFE

Source: *Journal of Commerce and Commercial.* **Price Frequency:** weekly in Tuesday issue. **Units of Measure:** Dollars per lb. **Type of Price:** spot. **Time Period Covered:** latest week.

Source: *Plastics Technology.* **Price Frequency:** monthly. **Units of Measure:** cents per lb., cents per cubic inch. **Type of Price:** bulk list, market. **Time Period Covered:** latest month.

FLUOROPOLYMER: PVDF

Source: *Plastics Technology.* **Price Frequency:** monthly. **Units of Measure:** cents per lb., cents per cubic inch. **Type of Price:** bulk list, market. **Time Period Covered:** latest month.

FLUORSPAR: ACIDSPAR

see Acidspar.

FLUORSPAR: METALLURGICAL

Source: *Industrial Minerals.* **Price Frequency:** monthly. **Effective Market(s):** United Kingdom. **Units of Measure:** British pounds per metric tonne. **Type of Price:** producer & dealer. **Time Period Covered:** latest month.

FLUORSPAR: METALLURGICAL, MEXICAN

Source: *Industrial Minerals.* **Price Frequency:** monthly. **Effective Market(s):** Tampico (Mexico). **Units of Measure:** Dollars per metric tonne. **Type of Price:** producer & dealer. **Time Period Covered:** latest month.

FLUOSILICIC ACID

see Hydrofluosilicic Acid.

FODDER

Source: *Scottish Farmer.* **Price Frequency:** weekly. **Effective Market(s):** Scotland. **Units of Measure:** British pound per tonne. **Type of Price:** average farmer buying-in. **Time Period Covered:** latest week.

FOLIC ACID: USP

Source: *Journal of Commerce and Commercial.* **Price Frequency:** weekly in Friday issue. **Units of Measure:** Dollars per kilo. **Type of Price:** spot. **Time Period Covered:** latest week.

FONOFOS: 20%, GRANULAR

Source: *Agricultural Prices Annual Summary.* **Price Frequency:** semiannually. **Effective Market(s):** United States. **Units of Measure:** Dollars per 50 lbs. **Type of Price:** average paid by farmer. **Time Period Covered:** latest 6 years.

FOOD

Source: *Dairy Market Statistics.* **Price Frequency:** monthly. **Effective Market(s):** United States. **Units of Measure:** index. **Type of Price:** consumer price index. **Time Period Covered:** latest year.

Source: *Monthly Commodity Price Bulletin.* **Price Frequency:** monthly, annually. **Effective Market(s):** developing countries. **Units of Measure:** index. **Type of Price:** free market price index. **Time Period Covered:** latest 5 years.

Source: *Monthly Commodity Price Bulletin Supplement.* **Price Frequency:** monthly, quarterly, annually. **Units of Measure:** index. **Type of Price:** free market index. **Time Period Covered:** latest 20 years.

Source: *UNCTAD Commodity Yearbook.* **Price Frequency:** annually. **Units of Measure:** index. **Type of Price:** price index. **Time Period Covered:** latest 12 years.

FOOD AND BEVERAGES PRICE INDEX

Source: *UNCTAD Commodity Yearbook.* **Price Frequency:** annually. **Units of Measure:** index. **Type of Price:** price index. **Time Period Covered:** latest 12 years.

FOOD AND TROPICAL BEVERAGES

Source: *Monthly Commodity Price Bulletin.* **Price Frequency:** monthly, annually. **Effective Market(s):** developing countries. **Units of Measure:** index. **Type of Price:** free market price index. **Time Period Covered:** latest 5 years.

Source: *Monthly Commodity Price Bulletin Supplement.* **Price Frequency:** monthly, quarterly, annually. **Units of Measure:** index. **Type of Price:** free market index. **Time Period Covered:** latest 20 years.

FOOD GRAINS

Source: *Illinois Farm Report.* **Price Frequency:** monthly. **Effective Market(s):** Illinois. **Units of Measure:** index . **Type of Price:** index of prices received by farmers. **Time Period Covered:** latest 2 months, year ago.

FOODSTUFFS

Source: *Business Week.* **Price Frequency:** weekly. **Units of Measure:** index. **Type of Price:** price index. **Time Period Covered:** latest 2 weeks.

FOOTWEAR

Source: *Commodity Year Book.* **Price Frequency:** monthly, annually. **Effective Market(s):** United States. **Units of Measure:** Dollars per pair. **Type of Price:** factory price. **Time Period Covered:** latest 9 years.

FORAGE HARVESTER

Source: *Agricultural Prices.* **Price Frequency:** annually. **Effective Market(s):** United States. **Units of Measure:** Dollars each. **Type of Price:** paid by farmer. **Time Period Covered:** latest year.

Source: *Agricultural Prices Annual Summary.* **Price Frequency:** annually. **Effective Market(s):** United States. **Units of Measure:** Dollars each. **Type of Price:** average paid by farmer. **Time Period Covered:** latest 6 years.

FOREIGN EXCHANGE

see individual nations' currencies, e.g., Austria Schillings.

FORMALDEHYDE: 37%, INHIBITED, 7% METHANOL

Source: *Chemical Marketing Reporter.* **Price Frequency:** weekly. **Effective Market(s):** Gulf. **Units of Measure:** Dollars per lb. **Type of Price:** spot. **Time Period Covered:** latest week.

FORMALDEHYDE: 37%, INHIBITED, 11-15% METHANOL

Source: *Chemical Marketing Reporter.* **Price Frequency:** weekly. **Effective Market(s):** Gulf. **Units of Measure:** Dollars per lb. **Type of Price:** spot. **Time Period Covered:** latest week.

FORMALDEHYDE: 37%, METHANOL FREE

Source: *Journal of Commerce and Commercial.* **Price Frequency:** weekly in Thursday issue. **Units of Measure:** Dollars per lb. **Type of Price:** spot. **Time Period Covered:** latest week.

FORMALDEHYDE: 37%, UNINHIBITED, METHANOL FREE

Source: *Chemical Marketing Reporter.* **Price Frequency:** weekly. **Effective Market(s):** Gulf. **Units of Measure:** Dollars per lb. **Type of Price:** spot. **Time Period Covered:** latest week.

FORMAMIDE

Source: *Chemical Marketing Reporter.* **Price Frequency:** weekly. **Effective Market(s):** New York. **Units of Measure:** Dollars per lb. **Type of Price:** spot. **Time Period Covered:** latest week.

FORMIC ACID: 90%

Source: *Chemical Marketing Reporter.* **Price Frequency:** weekly. **Effective Market(s):** New York. **Units of Measure:** Dollars per lb. **Type of Price:** spot. **Time Period Covered:** latest week.

Source: *Journal of Commerce and Commercial.* **Price Frequency:** weekly in Thursday issue. **Units of Measure:** Dollars per lb. **Type of Price:** spot. **Time Period Covered:** latest week.

FORMIC ACID: 95%

Source: *Chemical Marketing Reporter.* **Price Frequency:** weekly. **Effective Market(s):** New York. **Units of Measure:** Dollars per lb. **Type of Price:** spot. **Time Period Covered:** latest week.

FOWL

see also Broilers, Broiler-Fryers, Chickens, Hens, and specific types of fowl, e.g., Squab.

Source: *HRI-Buyers Guide.* **Price Frequency:** weekly. **Effective Market(s):** Northeastern area. **Units of Measure:** Dollars per lb. **Type of Price:** price paid by dining places & institutions. **Time Period Covered:** latest week.

Source: *Weekly Insiders Poultry Report.* **Price Frequency:** weekly. **Effective Market(s):** New York. **Units of Measure:** cents per lb. **Type of Price:** retail. **Time Period Covered:** latest week, week ago, year ago.

FOWL: CROSSBRED

Source: *Lancaster Farming.* **Price Frequency:** weekly. **Effective Market(s):** Pennsylvania. **Units of Measure:** Dollars per lb. **Type of Price:** auction. **Time Period Covered:** latest week.

FOWL: FRESH

Source: *Monthly Price Review.* **Price Frequency:** daily. **Effective Market(s):** Northeast. **Units of Measure:** Dollars per lb. **Type of Price:** spot. **Time Period Covered:** latest month.

FOWL: FRESH, ICED

Source: *Weekly Insiders Poultry Report.* **Price Frequency:** monthly. **Effective Market(s):** Northeast. **Units of Measure:** cents per lb. **Time Period Covered:** latest year.

FOWL: GRADE A, BOILING, FRESH, UNEVISERATED

Source: *Farmers Weekly.* **Price Frequency:** weekly. **Effective Market(s):** Smithfield (England). **Units of Measure:** British pence per lb. **Type of Price:** wholesale bottom, wholesale top. **Time Period Covered:** latest week.

FOWL: GRADE A, FROZEN

Source: *Weekly Insiders Poultry Report.* **Price Frequency:** annually. **Units of Measure:** cents per lb. **Type of Price:** wholesale. **Time Period Covered:** latest 3 years.

FOWL: GRADE B, FROZEN

Source: *Weekly Insiders Poultry Report.* **Price Frequency:** annually. **Units of Measure:** cents per lb. **Type of Price:** wholesale. **Time Period Covered:** latest 3 years.

FOWL: HEAVY TYPE, CANNER PACK

Source: *Poultry Market Statistics.* **Price Frequency:** monthly, annually. **Effective Market(s):** Southeast. **Units of Measure:** cents per lb. **Type of Price:** primary processor. **Time Period Covered:** latest year.

FOWL: HEAVY TYPE, FRESH, NECK OFF, CANNER PACK

Source: *Urner Barry's Price-Current.* **Price Frequency:** daily. **Units of Measure:** cents per lb. **Time Period Covered:** latest day.

FOWL: ICED

Source: *Weekly Insiders Poultry Report.* **Price Frequency:** annually. **Units of Measure:** cents per lb. **Type of Price:** wholesale. **Time Period Covered:** latest 3 years.

FOWL: LEGHORN, FRESH, NECK OFF, CANNER PACK

Source: *Urner Barry's Price-Current.* **Price Frequency:** daily. **Units of Measure:** cents per lb. **Time Period Covered:** latest day.

FOWL: LIGHT TYPE, CANNER PACK

Source: *Poultry Market Statistics.* **Price Frequency:** monthly, annually. **Effective Market(s):** Southeast. **Units of Measure:** cents per lb. **Type of Price:** primary processor. **Time Period Covered:** latest year.

FOWL: RED

Source: *Lancaster Farming.* **Price Frequency:** weekly. **Effective Market(s):** Pennsylvania. **Units of Measure:** Dollars per lb. **Type of Price:** auction. **Time Period Covered:** latest week.

FOWL: SEX LINK, FRESH, NECK OFF, CANNER PACK

Source: *Urner Barry's Price-Current.* **Price Frequency:** daily. **Units of Measure:** cents per lb. **Time Period Covered:** latest day.

FOWL: WHOLE, FRESH, CRYOVAC

Source: *Urner Barry's Price-Current.* **Price Frequency:** daily. **Effective Market(s):** Northeast, Southeast. **Units of Measure:** cents per lb. **Time Period Covered:** latest day.

FOWL: WHOLE, FRESH, ICED

Source: *Urner Barry's Price-Current.* **Price Frequency:** daily. **Effective Market(s):** Northeast, Southeast. **Units of Measure:** cents per lb. **Time Period Covered:** latest day.

FOWL: WHOLE, GRADE A, READY-TO-COOK, FROZEN

Source: *Urner Barry's Price-Current.* **Price Frequency:** daily. **Units of Measure:** cents per lb. **Time Period Covered:** latest day.

FOWL: WHOLE, GRADE B, READY-TO-COOK, FROZEN

Source: *Urner Barry's Price-Current.* **Price Frequency:** daily. **Units of Measure:** cents per lb. **Time Period Covered:** latest day.

FOWL MEAT: 46% WHITE AND 54% DARK, NATURAL PROPORTION

Source: *Urner Barry's Price-Current.* **Price Frequency:** daily. **Units of Measure:** Dollars per lb. **Time Period Covered:** latest day.

FOWL MEAT: 46% WHITE AND 54% DARK, NATURAL PROPORTION, SKIN ON

Source: *Urner Barry's Price-Current.* **Price Frequency:** daily. **Units of Measure:** Dollars per lb. **Time Period Covered:** latest day.

FOWL MEAT: DARK, BONELESS AND SKINLESS, FROZEN

Source: *Urner Barry's Price-Current.* **Price Frequency:** daily. **Units of Measure:** Dollars per lb. **Time Period Covered:** latest day.

FOWL MEAT: NATURAL PROPORTION, PULLED/DICED, COOKED AND FROZEN

Source: *Urner Barry's Price-Current.* **Price Frequency:** daily. **Units of Measure:** Dollars per lb. **Time Period Covered:** latest day.

FOWL MEAT: WHITE, BONELESS AND SKINLESS, FROZEN

Source: *Urner Barry's Price-Current.* **Price Frequency:** daily. **Units of Measure:** Dollars per lb. **Time Period Covered:** latest day.

FOWL MEAT: WHITE, PULLED/DICED, COOKED AND FROZEN

Source: *Urner Barry's Price-Current.* **Price Frequency:** daily. **Units of Measure:** Dollars per lb. **Time Period Covered:** latest day.

FOWL MEAT BROTH

Source: *Urner Barry's Price-Current.* **Price Frequency:** daily. **Units of Measure:** cents per lb. **Time Period Covered:** latest day.

FOWL MEAT FAT: RENDERED

Source: *Urner Barry's Price-Current.* **Price Frequency:** daily. **Units of Measure:** cents per lb. **Time Period Covered:** latest day.

FRAMING LUMBER

see Lumber: Framing.

FRANCE FRANCS

Source: *American Metal Market.* **Price Frequency:** daily. **Effective Market(s):** New York. **Units of Measure:** French francs per United States dollar. **Type of Price:** foreign exchange. **Time Period Covered:** latest day.

Source: *Asian Wall Street Journal.* **Price Frequency:** daily. **Effective Market(s):** United States. **Units of Measure:** French francs per ECU, per SDR. **Type of Price:** foreign exchange. **Time Period Covered:** latest 2 days.

Source: *Barron's.* **Price Frequency:** weekly. **Effective Market(s):** New York. **Units of Measure:** French francs per United States dollar. **Type of Price:** foreign exchange. **Time Period Covered:** latest 2 weeks.

Source: *The Economist.* **Price Frequency:** weekly. **Effective Market(s):** London. **Units of Measure:** French francs per United States dollar, per British pound, per SDR, per ECU. **Type of Price:** foreign exchange. **Time Period Covered:** latest week.

Source: *New York Times.* **Price Frequency:** daily. **Effective Market(s):** New York. **Units of Measure:** French francs per United States dollar. **Type of Price:** foreign exchange. **Time Period Covered:** latest 2 days.

Source: *Timber Bulletin.* **Price Frequency:** monthly, annually. **Units of Measure:** French francs per United States dollar. **Type of Price:** foreign exchange. **Time Period Covered:** latest 2 years.

FRANCE FRANCS: FUTURES

Source: *Barron's.* **Price Frequency:** weekly. **Effective Market(s):** Chicago. **Units of Measure:** United States dollars per French franc. **Type of Price:** foreign exchange futures. **Time Period Covered:** latest week.

FRANCS

see specific country name, e.g., France Francs.

FRANKFURTERS

Source: *Meat Price Report.* **Price Frequency:** weekly. **Units of Measure:** cents per lb. **Type of Price:** price paid to wholesaler. **Time Period Covered:** latest week.

FRANKFURTERS: ALL MEAT

Source: *Livestock and Poultry Situation and Outlook Report.* **Price Frequency:** monthly. **Units of Measure:** Dollars per lb. **Type of Price:** retail. **Time Period Covered:** latest 3 years.

FREESIAS

Source: *New Zealand Farmer.* **Price Frequency:** weekly, seasonally. **Effective Market(s):** New Zealand. **Units of Measure:** New Zealand dollars per bunch. **Time Period Covered:** latest week.

FROG LEGS: BANGLADESH AND INDIA, FROZEN

Source: *Seafood Price-Current.* **Price Frequency:** semiweekly. **Effective Market(s):** Mid-Atlantic. **Units of Measure:** Dollars per lb. **Type of Price:** first receiver. **Time Period Covered:** latest day.

FROG LEGS: SKINNED, BANGLADESH

Source: *NMFS Green Sheet Supplement.* **Price Frequency:** weekly. **Effective Market(s):** New York. **Units of Measure:** Dollars per lb. **Type of Price:** warehouse. **Time Period Covered:** latest week.

FRUCTOSE: CRYSTALLINE

Source: *Chemical Marketing Reporter.* **Price Frequency:** weekly. **Effective Market(s):** New York. **Units of Measure:** Dollars per lb. **Type of Price:** spot. **Time Period Covered:** latest week.

FRYERS

Source: *California Farmer.* **Price Frequency:** semimonthly. **Effective Market(s):** Los Angeles. **Units of Measure:** cents per lb. **Time Period Covered:** latest week, week ago, year ago.

FUEL OIL

see also Gasoil, Gasoline, Oil, Petroleum.

Source: *Gas Stats: Monthly Gas Utility Statistical Report.* **Price Frequency:** monthly. **Units of Measure:** index. **Type of Price:** price index. **Time Period Covered:** latest month, year ago.

Source: *Oil Buyers' Guide.* **Price Frequency:** weekly. **Effective Market(s):** Venezuela. **Units of Measure:** Dollars per barrel. **Type of Price:** official residential. **Time Period Covered:** latest week.

FUEL OIL: 0.3% SULFUR, LP

Source: *OPEC Bulletin.* **Price Frequency:** monthly. **Effective Market(s):** New York. **Units of Measure:** Dollars per barrel. **Time Period Covered:** latest 2 years.

FUEL OIL: 1.0% SULFUR

Source: *OPEC Bulletin.* **Price Frequency:** monthly. **Effective Market(s):** Italy, Rotterdam. **Units of Measure:** Dollars per barrel. **Time Period Covered:** latest 2 years.

FUEL OIL: 1.0% SULFUR, LP

Source: *OPEC Bulletin.* **Price Frequency:** monthly. **Effective Market(s):** New York. **Units of Measure:** Dollars per barrel. **Time Period Covered:** latest 2 years.

FUEL OIL: 2.0% SULFUR

Source: *OPEC Bulletin.* **Price Frequency:** monthly. **Effective Market(s):** Caribbean. **Units of Measure:** Dollars per barrel. **Time Period Covered:** latest 2 years.

FUEL OIL: 2.2% SULFUR

Source: *OPEC Bulletin.* **Price Frequency:** monthly. **Effective Market(s):** New York. **Units of Measure:** Dollars per barrel. **Time Period Covered:** latest 2 years.

FUEL OIL: 2.8% SULFUR

Source: *OPEC Bulletin.* **Price Frequency:** monthly. **Effective Market(s):** Carribean. **Units of Measure:** Dollars per barrel. **Time Period Covered:** latest 2 years.

FUEL OIL: 3.0% SULFUR

Source: *Japan Economic Journal.* **Price Frequency:** weekly. **Effective Market(s):** Tokyo. **Units of Measure:** Japanese yen per kiloliter. **Type of Price:** spot. **Time Period Covered:** latest 2 weeks.

FUEL OIL: 3.5% SULFUR

Source: *Japan Economic Journal.* **Price Frequency:** weekly. **Effective Market(s):** London, Singapore. **Units of Measure:** Dollars per ton. **Type of Price:** spot. **Time Period Covered:** latest 2 weeks.

Source: *OPEC Bulletin.* **Price Frequency:** monthly. **Effective Market(s):** Italy, Rotterdam. **Units of Measure:** Dollars per barrel. **Time Period Covered:** latest 2 years.

Source: *The Times.* **Price Frequency:** daily. **Effective Market(s):** Northwest Europe. **Units of Measure:** Dollars per metric ton. **Type of Price:** spot. **Time Period Covered:** latest day.

FUEL OIL: 180 C

Source: *OPEC Bulletin.* **Price Frequency:** monthly. **Effective Market(s):** Middle East Gulf, Singapore. **Units of Measure:** Dollars per barrel. **Time Period Covered:** latest 2 years.

FUEL OIL: 380 C

Source: *OPEC Bulletin.* **Price Frequency:** monthly. **Effective Market(s):** Singapore. **Units of Measure:** Dollars per barrel. **Time Period Covered:** latest 2 years.

FUEL OIL: BUNKER "C"

Source: *Oil Buyers' Guide International.* **Price Frequency:** weekly. **Effective Market(s):** Japan, Singapore. **Units of Measure:** Dollars per metric ton. **Type of Price:** spot. **Time Period Covered:** latest week.

Source: *Petroleum Economist.* **Price Frequency:** monthly. **Effective Market(s):** Bahamas, Bahrain, Curacao, Pulau Buxom (Singapore), Quoin Island. **Units of Measure:** Dollars per barrel. **Time Period Covered:** latest month.

FUEL OIL: FOR ELECTRICITY GENERATION

Source: *Commodity Year Book.* **Price Frequency:** annually. **Effective Market(s):** United States. **Units of Measure:** cents per kilowatt hour. **Time Period Covered:** latest 13 years.

FUEL OIL: HEAVY

Source: *Financial Times.* **Price Frequency:** daily. **Effective Market(s):** London. **Units of Measure:** Dollars per tonnne. **Type of Price:** spot. **Time Period Covered:** latest day.

FUEL OIL: HEAVY, 1.0% SULFUR, HIGH POUR

Source: *Petroleum Economist.* **Price Frequency:** monthly. **Effective Market(s):** Caribbean, Mediterranean, New York, Northwest Europe, Rotterdam. **Units of Measure:** Dollars per metric ton. **Type of Price:** spot. **Time Period Covered:** latest month.

FUEL OIL: HEAVY, 2.8% SULFUR

Source: *Petroleum Economist.* **Price Frequency:** monthly. **Effective Market(s):** Caribbean, Mediterranean, New York, Northwest Europe, Rotterdam. **Units of Measure:** Dollars per metric ton. **Type of Price:** spot. **Time Period Covered:** latest month.

FUEL OIL: HEAVY, 3.0% SULFUR

Source: *Energy Prices & Taxes.* **Price Frequency:** annually. **Effective Market(s):** Rotterdam. **Units of Measure:** Dollars per metric ton. **Type of Price:** spot. **Time Period Covered:** latest 15 years.

FUEL OIL: HEAVY, 3.5% SULFUR

Source: *Commodity Trade and Price Trends.* **Price Frequency:** annually. **Effective Market(s):** Europe. **Units of Measure:** Dollars per metric ton, 1980 constant dollars per metric ton. **Time Period Covered:** latest 17 years.

Source: *Oil Buyers' Guide International.* **Price Frequency:** weekly. **Effective Market(s):** Japan, Singapore. **Units of Measure:** Dollars per metric ton. **Type of Price:** spot. **Time Period Covered:** latest week.

Source: *Petroleum Economist.* **Price Frequency:** monthly. **Effective Market(s):** Caribbean, Mediterranean, New York, Northwest Europe, Rotterdam. **Units of Measure:** Dollars per metric ton. **Type of Price:** spot. **Time Period Covered:** latest month.

FUEL OIL: HEAVY, 180 CST

Source: *Oil Buyers' Guide.* **Price Frequency:** daily. **Effective Market(s):** Los Angeles, San Francisco, Seattle. **Units of Measure:** Dollars per metric ton. **Type of Price:** spot. **Time Period Covered:** latest week.

FUEL OIL: HEAVY, 380 CST

Source: *Oil Buyers' Guide.* **Price Frequency:** daily. **Effective Market(s):** Los Angeles, San Francisco, Seattle. **Units of Measure:** Dollars per metric ton. **Type of Price:** spot. **Time Period Covered:** latest week.

FUEL OIL: HEAVY, BUNKER "C"

Source: *Oil Buyers' Guide.* **Price Frequency:** daily. **Effective Market(s):** Los Angeles, San Francisco. **Units of Measure:** Dollars per metric ton. **Type of Price:** spot. **Time Period Covered:** latest week.

FUEL OIL: HEAVY, FOR ELECTRICITY GENERATION

Source: *Energy Prices and Taxes.* **Price Frequency:** quarterly, annually. **Effective Market(s):** 28 international markets. **Units of Measure:** national currency per metric ton, national currency per ton oil equivalent. **Time Period Covered:** varies.

Source: *Energy Prices and Taxes.* **Price Frequency:** annually. **Effective Market(s):** 17 international markets. **Units of Measure:** Dollars per metric ton, dollars per ton oil equivalent. **Time Period Covered:** latest 8 years.

FUEL OIL: HEAVY, FOR INDUSTRIAL USE

Source: *Energy Prices and Taxes.* **Price Frequency:** quarterly, annually. **Effective Market(s):** 28 international markets. **Units of Measure:** national currency per metric ton, national currency per ton oil equivalent. **Time Period Covered:** varies.

Source: *Energy Prices and Taxes.* **Price Frequency:** annually. **Effective Market(s):** 24 international markets. **Units of Measure:** Dollars per metric ton, dollars per ton oil equivalent. **Time Period Covered:** latest 8 years.

FUEL OIL: HEAVY, MARINE DIESEL

Source: *Oil Buyers' Guide.* **Price Frequency:** daily. **Effective Market(s):** Los Angeles, San Francisco, Seattle. **Units of Measure:** Dollars per metric ton. **Type of Price:** spot. **Time Period Covered:** latest week.

FUEL OIL: JET

Source: *Oil Buyers' Guide.* **Price Frequency:** daily. **Effective Market(s):** Los Angeles, San Francisco, Seattle. **Units of Measure:** cents per gallon. **Type of Price:** spot. **Time Period Covered:** latest week.

FUEL OIL: LIGHT

Source: *Petroleum Economist.* **Price Frequency:** monthly. **Effective Market(s):** Bahamas, Bahrain, Curacao, Pulau Buxom (Singapore), Quoin Island. **Units of Measure:** Dollars per barrel. **Time Period Covered:** latest month.

FUEL OIL: LIGHT, FOR HOUSEHOLD USE

Source: *Energy Prices and Taxes.* **Price Frequency:** quarterly, annually. **Effective Market(s):** 28 international markets. **Units of Measure:** national currency per 1000 litres, national currency per ton oil equivalent. **Time Period Covered:** varies.

Source: *Energy Prices and Taxes.* **Price Frequency:** annually. **Effective Market(s):** 24 international markets. **Units of Measure:** Dollars per 1000 litres, dollars per ton oil equivalent. **Time Period Covered:** latest 8 years.

FUEL OIL: LIGHT, FOR INDUSTRIAL USE

Source: *Energy Prices and Taxes.* **Price Frequency:** annually. **Effective Market(s):** 23 international markets. **Units of Measure:** Dollars per 1000 litres, dollars per ton oil equivalent. **Time Period Covered:** latest 8 years.

Source: *Energy Prices and Taxes.* **Price Frequency:** quarterly, annually. **Effective Market(s):** 28 international markets. **Units of Measure:** national currency per 1000 litres, national currency per ton oil equivalent. **Time Period Covered:** varies.

FUEL OIL: LOW

Source: *OPEC Bulletin.* **Price Frequency:** monthly. **Effective Market(s):** Singapore. **Units of Measure:** Dollars per barrel. **Time Period Covered:** latest 2 years.

FUEL OIL: MEDIUM

Source: *Petroleum Economist.* **Price Frequency:** monthly. **Effective Market(s):** Bahamas, Bahrain, Curacao, Pulau Buxom (Singapore), Quoin Island. **Units of Measure:** Dollars per barrel. **Time Period Covered:** latest month.

FUEL OIL: NO. 2

Source: *Asian Wall Street Journal.* **Price Frequency:** daily. **Effective Market(s):** New York. **Units of Measure:** Dollars per gallon. **Time Period Covered:** latest 2 days, year ago.

Source: *Energy Pricing News Refined Fuel Report.* **Price Frequency:** semimonthly. **Effective Market(s):** 10 Canadian markets. **Units of Measure:** Canadian cents per liter. **Type of Price:** contract, delivered, rack. **Time Period Covered:** latest week.

Source: *Investor's Daily.* **Price Frequency:** daily. **Effective Market(s):** New York. **Units of Measure:** Dollars per gallon. **Type of Price:** barge spot. **Time Period Covered:** latest 2 days.

Source: *New York Times.* **Price Frequency:** daily. **Effective Market(s):** New York. **Units of Measure:** Dollars per gallon. **Type of Price:** cash. **Time Period Covered:** latest 2 days.

Source: *Oil Buyers' Guide.* **Price Frequency:** weekly. **Effective Market(s):** Gulf Coast. **Units of Measure:** cents per gallon. **Type of Price:**. **Time Period Covered:** latest week.

Source: *Oil Buyers' Guide.* **Price Frequency:** daily. **Effective Market(s):** New York, Gulf Coast. **Units of Measure:** cents per gallon. **Type of Price:** spot. **Time Period Covered:** latest week.

Source: *Oil Buyers' Guide International.* **Price Frequency:** weekly. **Effective Market(s):** Gulf Coast. **Units of Measure:** cents per gallon. **Type of Price:** pipeline. **Time Period Covered:** latest week.

Source: *Purchasing.* **Price Frequency:** monthly. **Effective Market(s):** New York, United States. **Units of Measure:** cents per gallon. **Type of Price:** transaction. **Time Period Covered:** latest day, month ago, 6 months ago, year ago.

Source: *Wall Street Journal.* **Price Frequency:** daily. **Effective Market(s):** New York. **Units of Measure:** Dollars per gallon. **Time Period Covered:** latest day, day ago, year ago.

FUEL OIL: NO. 2, 0.2% SULFUR

Source: *Oil Buyers' Guide.* **Price Frequency:** weekly. **Effective Market(s):** East Coast. **Units of Measure:** cents per gallon. **Type of Price:** spot cargo, spot barge. **Time Period Covered:** latest week.

Source: *Oil Buyers' Guide International.* **Price Frequency:** weekly. **Effective Market(s):** Caribbean. **Units of Measure:** cents per gallon. **Type of Price:** spot. **Time Period Covered:** latest week.

Source: *Oil Buyers' Guide International.* **Price Frequency:** weekly. **Effective Market(s):** New York. **Units of Measure:** cents per gallon. **Type of Price:** spot barge. **Time Period Covered:** latest week.

Source: *Petroleum Economist.* **Price Frequency:** monthly. **Effective Market(s):** Caribbean, Mediterranean, New York, Northwest Europe, Rotterdam. **Units of Measure:** Dollars per metric ton. **Type of Price:** spot. **Time Period Covered:** latest month.

FUEL OIL: NO. 2, 0.2% SULFUR, CARIBBEAN

Source: *Oil Buyers' Guide.* **Price Frequency:** weekly. **Effective Market(s):** East Coast. **Units of Measure:** cents per gallon. **Type of Price:** spot. **Time Period Covered:** latest week.

FUEL OIL: NO. 2, 0.5% SULFUR

Source: *Oil Buyers' Guide International.* **Price Frequency:** weekly. **Effective Market(s):** Caribbean. **Units of Measure:** cents per gallon. **Type of Price:** spot. **Time Period Covered:** latest week.

Source: *Petroleum Economist.* **Price Frequency:** monthly. **Effective Market(s):** Caribbean, Mediterranean, New York, Northwest Europe, Rotterdam. **Units of Measure:** Dollars per metric ton. **Type of Price:** spot. **Time Period Covered:** latest month.

FUEL OIL: NO. 2, 0.5% SULFUR, CARIBBEAN

Source: *Oil Buyers' Guide.* **Price Frequency:** weekly. **Effective Market(s):** East Coast. **Units of Measure:** cents per gallon. **Type of Price:** spot . **Time Period Covered:** latest week.

FUEL OIL: NO. 2, 0.5% SULFUR, MEDITERRANEAN

Source: *Oil Buyers' Guide.* **Price Frequency:** weekly. **Effective Market(s):** East Coast. **Units of Measure:** cents per gallon. **Type of Price:** spot . **Time Period Covered:** latest week.

FUEL OIL: NO. 2, DISTILLATE

Source: *Commodity Year Book.* **Price Frequency:** monthly, annually. **Units of Measure:** index. **Type of Price:** price index. **Time Period Covered:** latest 14 years.

FUEL OIL: NO. 2, FUTURES

Source: *Oil Buyers' Guide.* **Price Frequency:** weekly. **Effective Market(s):** New York. **Units of Measure:** cents per gallon. **Type of Price:** futures. **Time Period Covered:** latest week.

Source: *Oil Buyers' Guide International.* **Price Frequency:** weekly. **Effective Market(s):** New York. **Units of Measure:** cents per gallon. **Type of Price:** futures. **Time Period Covered:** latest week.

FUEL OIL: NO. 4

Source: *Oil Buyers' Guide.* **Price Frequency:** weekly. **Effective Market(s):** 12 domestic markets. **Units of Measure:** Dollars per barrel. **Type of Price:** supplier's rack. **Time Period Covered:** latest week.

FUEL OIL: NO. 5

Source: *Oil Buyers' Guide.* **Price Frequency:** weekly. **Effective Market(s):** 12 domestic markets. **Units of Measure:** Dollars per barrel. **Type of Price:** supplier's rack. **Time Period Covered:** latest week.

FUEL OIL: NO. 6

Source: *Energy Pricing News Refined Fuel Report.* **Price Frequency:** semimonthly. **Effective Market(s):** 10 Canadian markets. **Units of Measure:** Canadian cents per liter. **Type of Price:** contract. **Time Period Covered:** latest week.

Source: *Oil Buyers' Guide.* **Price Frequency:** weekly. **Effective Market(s):** 12 domestic markets. **Units of Measure:** Dollars per barrel. **Type of Price:** supplier's rack. **Time Period Covered:** latest week.

Source: *Purchasing.* **Price Frequency:** monthly. **Effective Market(s):** United States. **Units of Measure:** Dollars per barrel. **Type of Price:** transaction. **Time Period Covered:** latest day, month ago, 6 months ago, year ago.

Source: *Standard & Poor's Statistical Service Current Statistics.* **Price Frequency:** monthly, annually. **Effective Market(s):** New York. **Units of Measure:** cents per gallon. **Time Period Covered:** latest 3 years.

FUEL OIL: NO. 6, 0.3% SULFUR

Source: *Oil Buyers' Guide.* **Price Frequency:** weekly. **Effective Market(s):** East Coast. **Units of Measure:** Dollars per barrel. **Type of Price:** spot cargo, spot barge. **Time Period Covered:** latest week.

Source: *Oil Buyers' Guide International.* **Price Frequency:** weekly. **Effective Market(s):** Atlantic Coast. **Units of Measure:** Dollars per barrel. **Type of Price:** spot. **Time Period Covered:** latest week.

FUEL OIL: NO. 6, 0.5% SULFUR

Source: *Oil Buyers' Guide.* **Price Frequency:** weekly. **Effective Market(s):** East Coast. **Units of Measure:** Dollars per barrel. **Type of Price:** spot cargo, spot barge. **Time Period Covered:** latest week.

Source: *Oil Buyers' Guide International.* **Price Frequency:** weekly. **Effective Market(s):** Atlantic Coast. **Units of Measure:** Dollars per barrel. **Type of Price:** spot. **Time Period Covered:** latest week.

FUEL OIL: NO. 6, 0.7% SULFUR

Source: *Oil Buyers' Guide.* **Price Frequency:** weekly. **Effective Market(s):** East Coast. **Units of Measure:** Dollars per barrel. **Type of Price:** spot cargo, spot barge. **Time Period Covered:** latest week.

Source: *Oil Buyers' Guide.* **Price Frequency:** weekly. **Effective Market(s):** Gulf Coast. **Units of Measure:** Dollars per barrel. **Type of Price:** . **Time Period Covered:** latest week.

Source: *Oil Buyers' Guide International.* **Price Frequency:** weekly. **Effective Market(s):** Gulf Coast. **Units of Measure:** Dollars per barrel. **Type of Price:** deepwater. **Time Period Covered:** latest week.

FUEL OIL: NO. 6, 1.0% SULFUR

Source: *Oil Buyers' Guide.* **Price Frequency:** weekly. **Effective Market(s):** Mediterranean, Northwest Europe. **Units of Measure:** Dollars per metric ton. **Type of Price:** cargo, barge. **Time Period Covered:** latest week.

Source: *Oil Buyers' Guide.* **Price Frequency:** weekly. **Effective Market(s):** East Coast. **Units of Measure:** Dollars per barrel. **Type of Price:** spot cargo, spot barge. **Time Period Covered:** latest week.

Source: *Oil Buyers' Guide.* **Price Frequency:** weekly. **Effective Market(s):** Gulf Coast. **Units of Measure:** Dollars per barrel. **Type of Price:** . **Time Period Covered:** latest week.

Source: *Oil Buyers' Guide International.* **Price Frequency:** weekly. **Effective Market(s):** Mediterranean, Northwest Europe. **Units of Measure:** Dollars per metric ton. **Type of Price:** cargo. **Time Period Covered:** latest week.

Source: *Oil Buyers' Guide International.* **Price Frequency:** weekly. **Effective Market(s):** Atlantic Coast. **Units of Measure:** Dollars per barrel. **Type of Price:** spot. **Time Period Covered:** latest week.

Source: *Oil Buyers' Guide International.* **Price Frequency:** weekly. **Effective Market(s):** Gulf Coast. **Units of Measure:** Dollars per barrel. **Type of Price:** deepwater. **Time Period Covered:** latest week.

FUEL OIL: NO. 6, 1.0% SULFUR, RESIDUAL

Source: *Oil & Gas Journal.* **Price Frequency:** weekly except second issue of month. **Effective Market(s):** New York, Rotterdam. **Units of Measure:** Dollars per barrel. **Type of Price:** spot. **Time Period Covered:** latest 3 weeks, year ago.

FUEL OIL: NO. 6, 1.5% SULFUR

Source: *Oil Buyers' Guide.* **Price Frequency:** weekly. **Effective Market(s):** 6 Canadian markets. **Units of Measure:** Canadian dollars per barrel. **Type of Price:** rack. **Time Period Covered:** latest week.

FUEL OIL: NO. 6, 2.2% SULFUR

Source: *Oil Buyers' Guide.* **Price Frequency:** weekly. **Effective Market(s):** East Coast. **Units of Measure:** Dollars per barrel. **Type of Price:** spot cargo, spot barge. **Time Period Covered:** latest week.

Source: *Oil Buyers' Guide International.* **Price Frequency:** weekly. **Effective Market(s):** Atlantic Coast. **Units of Measure:** Dollars per barrel. **Type of Price:** spot. **Time Period Covered:** latest week.

Source: *Oil Buyers' Guide International.* **Price Frequency:** weekly. **Effective Market(s):** Caribbean. **Units of Measure:** cents per gallon. **Type of Price:** spot. **Time Period Covered:** latest week.

FUEL OIL: NO. 6, 2.2% SULFUR, CARIBBEAN

Source: *Oil Buyers' Guide.* **Price Frequency:** weekly. **Effective Market(s):** East Coast. **Units of Measure:** Dollars per barrel. **Type of Price:** spot. **Time Period Covered:** latest week.

FUEL OIL: NO. 6, 2.5% SULFUR

Source: *Oil Buyers' Guide.* **Price Frequency:** weekly. **Effective Market(s):** 6 Canadian markets. **Units of Measure:** Canadian cents per barrel. **Type of Price:** rack. **Time Period Covered:** latest week.

FUEL OIL: NO. 6, 2.8% SULFUR

Source: *Oil Buyers' Guide.* **Price Frequency:** weekly. **Effective Market(s):** East Coast. **Units of Measure:** Dollars per barrel. **Type of Price:** spot cargo, spot barge. **Time Period Covered:** latest week.

Source: *Oil Buyers' Guide International.* **Price Frequency:** weekly. **Effective Market(s):** Atlantic Coast. **Units of Measure:** Dollars per barrel. **Type of Price:** spot. **Time Period Covered:** latest week.

Source: *Oil Buyers' Guide International.* **Price Frequency:** weekly. **Effective Market(s):** Caribbean. **Units of Measure:** cents per gallon. **Type of Price:** spot. **Time Period Covered:** latest week.

FUEL OIL: NO. 6, 2.8% SULFUR, CARIBBEAN

Source: *Oil Buyers' Guide.* **Price Frequency:** weekly. **Effective Market(s):** East Coast. **Units of Measure:** Dollars per barrel. **Type of Price:** spot . **Time Period Covered:** latest week.

FUEL OIL: NO. 6, 3.5% SULFUR

Source: *Oil Buyers' Guide.* **Price Frequency:** weekly. **Effective Market(s):** Mediterranean, Northwest Europe. **Units of Measure:** Dollars per metric ton. **Type of Price:** cargo, barge. **Time Period Covered:** latest week.

Source: *Oil Buyers' Guide International.* **Price Frequency:** weekly. **Effective Market(s):** Mediterranean, Northwest Europe. **Units of Measure:** Dollars per metric ton. **Type of Price:** cargo. **Time Period Covered:** latest week.

FUEL OIL: NO. 6, ORDINARY

Source: *Oil Buyers' Guide.* **Price Frequency:** weekly. **Effective Market(s):** Gulf Coast. **Units of Measure:** Dollars per barrel. **Type of Price:** . **Time Period Covered:** latest week.

Source: *Oil Buyers' Guide International.* **Price Frequency:** weekly. **Effective Market(s):** Gulf Coast. **Units of Measure:** Dollars per barrel. **Type of Price:** deepwater. **Time Period Covered:** latest week.

FUJIETTE FABRIC

Source: *JTN: The International Textile Magazine.* **Price Frequency:** monthly. **Effective Market(s):** Japan. **Units of Measure:** Japanese yen per yard. **Type of Price:** spot. **Time Period Covered:** latest month.

FUMARIC ACID: FOOD GRADE

Source: *Chemical Marketing Reporter.* **Price Frequency:** weekly. **Effective Market(s):** East. **Units of Measure:** Dollars per lb. **Type of Price:** spot. **Time Period Covered:** latest week.

FUMARIC ACID: TECHNICAL GRADE

Source: *Chemical Marketing Reporter.* **Price Frequency:** weekly. **Effective Market(s):** New York. **Units of Measure:** Dollars per lb. **Type of Price:** spot. **Time Period Covered:** latest week.

FUMARIC ACID: USP

Source: *Journal of Commerce and Commercial.* **Price Frequency:** weekly in Friday issue. **Units of Measure:** Dollars per lb. **Type of Price:** spot. **Time Period Covered:** latest week.

FURFURAL

Source: *Chemical Marketing Reporter.* **Price Frequency:** weekly. **Effective Market(s):** Cedar Rapids (IA)/ Belle Glade (FL). **Units of Measure:** Dollars per lb. **Type of Price:** spot. **Time Period Covered:** latest week.

FURFURYL ALCOHOL

Source: *Chemical Marketing Reporter.* **Price Frequency:** weekly. **Effective Market(s):** Memphis (TN)/Omaha (NE). **Units of Measure:** Dollars per lb. **Type of Price:** spot. **Time Period Covered:** latest week.

FURNACE BLACK

Source: *Journal of Commerce and Commercial.* **Price Frequency:** weekly in Wednesday issue. **Units of Measure:** Dollars per lb. **Type of Price:** spot. **Time Period Covered:** latest week.

FUTURES

see individual commodity names, e.g., Wheat: Futures.

G SALT

Source: *Chemical Marketing Reporter.* **Price Frequency:** weekly. **Effective Market(s):** New York. **Units of Measure:** Dollars per lb. **Type of Price:** spot. **Time Period Covered:** latest week.

GALBANUM GUM

Source: *Journal of Commerce and Commercial.* **Price Frequency:** weekly in Monday issue. **Units of Measure:** Dollars per lb. **Type of Price:** spot. **Time Period Covered:** latest week.

GALLIC ACID

Source: *Chemical Marketing Reporter.* **Price Frequency:** weekly. **Effective Market(s):** New York. **Units of Measure:** Dollars per kilo. **Type of Price:** spot. **Time Period Covered:** latest week.

Source: *Journal of Commerce and Commercial.* **Price Frequency:** weekly in Friday issue. **Units of Measure:** Dollars per kilo. **Type of Price:** spot. **Time Period Covered:** latest week.

GALLIUM: 99.99%

Source: *E&MJ.* **Price Frequency:** monthly. **Units of Measure:** Dollars per kilogram. **Time Period Covered:** latest month.

GALLIUM: 99.9999%, IMPORTED

Source: *E&MJ.* **Price Frequency:** monthly. **Units of Measure:** Dollars per kilogram. **Time Period Covered:** latest month.

GALLIUM: 99.99999%

Source: *E&MJ.* **Price Frequency:** monthly. **Units of Measure:** Dollars per kilogram. **Time Period Covered:** latest month.

GALLIUM INGOT: 99.9% MINIMUM

Source: *Journal of Commerce and Commercial.* **Price Frequency:** daily. **Effective Market(s):** Europe. **Units of Measure:** Dollars per kilogram. **Type of Price:** spot. **Time Period Covered:** latest day.

GAMBOGE GUM: PIPE

Source: *Journal of Commerce and Commercial.* **Price Frequency:** weekly in Monday issue. **Units of Measure:** Dollars per lb. **Type of Price:** spot. **Time Period Covered:** latest week.

GAMBOGE GUM: POWDER

Source: *Journal of Commerce and Commercial.* **Price Frequency:** weekly in Monday issue. **Units of Measure:** Dollars per lb. **Type of Price:** spot. **Time Period Covered:** latest week.

GAME BIRDS

Source: *Urner Barry's Price-Current, West Coast Edition.* **Price Frequency:** semiweekly. **Effective Market(s):** West Coast. **Units of Measure:** Dollars per lb. **Type of Price:** wholesale. **Time Period Covered:** latest week.

GARLIC

Source: *New Zealand Farmer.* **Price Frequency:** weekly, seasonally. **Effective Market(s):** New Zealand. **Units of Measure:** New Zealand dollars per kilogram. **Time Period Covered:** latest week.

GARLIC: FLAKE, CHINESE

Source: *Prices of Selected Asia/Pacific Products.* **Price Frequency:** monthly. **Effective Market(s):** Tokyo. **Units of Measure:** Japanese yen per kilogram. **Type of Price:** trade high, trade low. **Time Period Covered:** latest month.

GARLIC: FRESH

Source: *HRI-Buyers Guide.* **Price Frequency:** weekly. **Effective Market(s):** Northeastern area. **Units of Measure:** Dollars per case. **Time Period Covered:** latest week.

GARLIC: LARGE, NEW CROP, THAI

Source: *Prices of Selected Asia/Pacific Products.* **Price Frequency:** monthly. **Effective Market(s):** Bangkok. **Units of Measure:** Thai baht per kilogram. **Type of Price:** wholesale high, wholesale low. **Time Period Covered:** latest month.

GARLIC: SMALL, NEW CROP, THAI

Source: *Prices of Selected Asia/Pacific Products.* **Price Frequency:** monthly. **Effective Market(s):** Bangkok. **Units of Measure:** Thai baht per kilogram. **Type of Price:** wholesale high, wholesale low. **Time Period Covered:** latest month.

GARLIC: WHITE

Source: *Lancaster Farming.* **Price Frequency:** weekly, seasonally. **Effective Market(s):** Pennsylvania. **Units of Measure:** Dollars per lb. **Type of Price:** market. **Time Period Covered:** latest week.

GARLIC OIL: EGYPTIAN

Source: *Chemical Marketing Reporter.* **Price Frequency:** weekly. **Effective Market(s):** New York. **Units of Measure:** Dollars per kilo. **Type of Price:** spot. **Time Period Covered:** latest week.

GARNET: IDAHO

Source: *Industrial Minerals.* **Price Frequency:** monthly. **Effective Market(s):** Idaho. **Units of Measure:** Dollars per metric tonne. **Type of Price:** producer & dealer. **Time Period Covered:** latest month.

GAS

Source: *Gas Stats: Monthly Gas Utility Statistical Report.* **Price Frequency:** monthly. **Effective Market(s):** 6 domestic markets. **Units of Measure:** Dollars per MMBtu. **Type of Price:** spot to gas distribution companies. **Time Period Covered:** latest month.

GAS: ALL KINDS

Source: *Gas Stats: Monthly Gas Utility Statistical Report.* **Price Frequency:** monthly, annually. **Units of Measure:** Dollars per MMBtu. **Type of Price:** average. **Time Period Covered:** latest 24 months, latest 10 years.

GAS: COMMERCIAL

Source: *Gas Stats: Monthly Gas Utility Statistical Report.* **Price Frequency:** monthly, annually. **Units of Measure:** Dollars per MMBtu. **Type of Price:** average. **Time Period Covered:** latest 24 months, latest 10 years.

Source: *Gas Stats: Quarterly Report of Gas Industry Operations.* **Price Frequency:** quarterly. **Effective Market(s):** 10 domestic markets. **Units of Measure:** Dollars per MMBtu. **Type of Price:** average. **Time Period Covered:** latest quarter, latest year.

GAS: COMMERCIAL UTILITY

Source: *Gas Stats: Monthly Gas Utility Statistical Report.* **Price Frequency:** monthly. **Units of Measure:** Dollars per MMBtu. **Time Period Covered:** latest month, year ago.

GAS: ELECTRICITY GENERATION

Source: *Gas Stats: Monthly Gas Utility Statistical Report.* **Price Frequency:** monthly, annually. **Units of Measure:** Dollars per MMBtu. **Type of Price:** average. **Time Period Covered:** latest 12 months, latest 10 years.

Source: *Gas Stats: Quarterly Report of Gas Industry Operations.* **Price Frequency:** quarterly. **Effective Market(s):** 10 domestic markets. **Units of Measure:** Dollars per MMBtu. **Type of Price:** average. **Time Period Covered:** latest quarter, latest year.

GAS: ELECTRICITY GENERATION UTILITY

Source: *Gas Stats: Monthly Gas Utility Statistical Report.* **Price Frequency:** monthly. **Units of Measure:** Dollars per MMBtu. **Time Period Covered:** latest month, year ago.

GAS: INDUSTRIAL

Source: *Gas Stats: Monthly Gas Utility Statistical Report.* **Price Frequency:** monthly, annually. **Units of Measure:** Dollars per MMBtu. **Type of Price:** average. **Time Period Covered:** latest 24 months, latest 10 years.

Source: *Gas Stats: Quarterly Report of Gas Industry Operations.* **Price Frequency:** quarterly. **Effective Market(s):** 10 domestic markets. **Units of Measure:** Dollars per MMBtu. **Type of Price:** average. **Time Period Covered:** latest quarter, latest year.

GAS: INDUSTRIAL AND ELECTRIC GENERATION

Source: *Gas Stats: Monthly Gas Utility Statistical Report.* **Price Frequency:** monthly. **Units of Measure:** Dollars per MMBtu. **Type of Price:** average. **Time Period Covered:** latest 24 months.

GAS: INDUSTRIAL UTILITY

Source: *Gas Stats: Monthly Gas Utility Statistical Report.* **Price Frequency:** monthly. **Units of Measure:** Dollars per MMBtu. **Time Period Covered:** latest month, year ago.

GAS: LIQUIFIED PETROLEUM

Source: *Agricultural Prices.* **Price Frequency:** monthly. **Effective Market(s):** 10 domestic markets, United States. **Units of Measure:** Dollars per gallon. **Type of Price:** paid by farmer. **Time Period Covered:** latest month, for US quarterly for latest year.

Source: *Agricultural Prices Annual Summary.* **Price Frequency:** quarterly. **Effective Market(s):** 10 domestic markets, United States. **Units of Measure:** Dollars per gallon. **Type of Price:** average paid by farmer. **Time Period Covered:** latest year, for US monthly for latest 6 years.

GAS: LOUISIANA

Source: *World Oil.* **Price Frequency:** monthly. **Effective Market(s):** Northern Louisiana, Southern Louisiana. **Units of Measure:** Dollars per 1000 cubic feet. **Type of Price:** contract. **Time Period Covered:** latest month.

GAS: NATURAL

Source: *Energy Prices and Taxes.* **Price Frequency:** quarterly, annually. **Effective Market(s):** 6 international markets. **Units of Measure:** Dollars per ton oil equivalent. **Type of Price:** imports by pipeline. **Time Period Covered:** quarterly latest 5 quarters, annually latest 9 years.

Source: *Energy Prices and Taxes.* **Price Frequency:** quarterly, annually. **Effective Market(s):** Netherlands, Norway. **Units of Measure:** Dollars per ton oil equivalent. **Type of Price:** exports by pipeline. **Time Period Covered:** quarterly latest 5 quarters, annually latest 9 years.

Source: *Energy Pricing News Natural Gas Report.* **Price Frequency:** semimonthly. **Effective Market(s):** British Columbia, Alberta. **Units of Measure:** Canadian dollars per 1000 cubic feet. **Type of Price:** spot, direct sale. **Time Period Covered:** latest week.

Source: *Energy Statistics.* **Price Frequency:** monthly, annually. **Effective Market(s):** United States. **Units of Measure:** Dollars per 100 cubic feet, dollars per 1000 cubic feet. **Type of Price:** wellhead, import, export, interstate. **Time Period Covered:** monthly latest 2 years, annually latest 12 years.

Source: *Energy Statistics.* **Price Frequency:** annually. **Effective Market(s):** United States. **Units of Measure:** Dollars per 1000 cubic feet. **Type of Price:** average from producers, gatherers, &/or processing plant operators, average from interstate/intrastate pipelines or distributors, average of sales for resale. **Time Period Covered:** latest 6 years.

Source: *Energy Statistics.* **Price Frequency:** monthly, annually. **Effective Market(s):** United States. **Units of Measure:** Dollars per 1000 cubic feet. **Type of Price:** delivered to consumers. **Time Period Covered:** monthly latest year, annually latest 13 years.

Source: *Energy Statistics.* **Price Frequency:** monthly. **Effective Market(s):** 34 domestic markets. **Units of Measure:** Dollars per 40 therms, dollars per 100 therms. **Type of Price:** residential. **Time Period Covered:** latest 16 months.

Source: *Energy Statistics.* **Price Frequency:** monthly, annually. **Effective Market(s):** 51 domestic markets. **Units of Measure:** Dollars per 1000 cubic feet. **Type of Price:** average delivered to consumers. **Time Period Covered:** monthly latest year, annually latest 4 years.

Source: *Purchasing.* **Price Frequency:** monthly. **Effective Market(s):** United States. **Units of Measure:** Dollars per 1000 cubic feet. **Type of Price:** transaction. **Time Period Covered:** latest day, month ago, 6 months ago, year ago.

GAS: NATURAL, FOR ELECTRICITY GENERATION

Source: *Energy Prices and Taxes.* **Price Frequency:** quarterly, annually. **Effective Market(s):** 28 international markets. **Units of Measure:** national currency per unit value, national currency per ton oil equivalent. **Time Period Covered:** varies.

Source: *Energy Prices and Taxes.* **Price Frequency:** annually. **Effective Market(s):** 12 international markets. **Units of Measure:** Dollars per unit value, dollars per ton oil equivalent. **Time Period Covered:** latest 8 years.

GAS: NATURAL, FOR HOUSEHOLD USE

Source: *Energy Prices and Taxes.* **Price Frequency:** quarterly, annually. **Effective Market(s):** 28 international markets. **Units of Measure:** national currency per unit value, national currency per ton oil equivalent. **Time Period Covered:** varies.

Source: *Energy Prices and Taxes.* **Price Frequency:** annually. **Effective Market(s):** 12 international markets. **Units of Measure:** Dollars per unit value, dollars per ton oil equivalent. **Time Period Covered:** latest 8 years.

GAS: NATURAL, FOR INDUSTRIAL USE

Source: *Energy Prices and Taxes.* **Price Frequency:** quarterly, annually. **Effective Market(s):** 28 international markets. **Units of Measure:** national currency per unit value, national currency per ton oil equivalent. **Time Period Covered:** varies.

Source: *Energy Prices and Taxes.* **Price Frequency:** annually. **Effective Market(s):** 19 international markets. **Units of Measure:** Dollars per unit value, dollars per ton oil equivalent. **Time Period Covered:** latest 8 years.

GAS: NATURAL, FUTURES

Source: *Asian Wall Street Journal.* **Price Frequency:** daily. **Effective Market(s):** New York. **Units of Measure:** Dollars per million BTU's. **Type of Price:** futures. **Time Period Covered:** latest day.

GAS: NATURAL, LIQUIDS

Source: *Oil & Gas Journal.* **Price Frequency:** monthly in third issue of month. **Effective Market(s):** Mont Belvieu (TX), Conway (KS). **Units of Measure:** cents per gallon. **Type of Price:** spot. **Time Period Covered:** latest 2 months.

GAS: NATURAL, LIQUIFIED

Source: *Energy Prices and Taxes.* **Price Frequency:** quarterly, annually. **Effective Market(s):** France, Japan. **Units of Measure:** Dollars per ton oil equivalent. **Type of Price:** import. **Time Period Covered:** quarterly latest 5 quarters, annually latest 9 years.

GAS: NATURAL, PIPELINE

Source: *Oil & Gas Journal.* **Price Frequency:** monthly in second issue of month. **Effective Market(s):** 18 domestic markets. **Units of Measure:** Dollars per MMBTU. **Type of Price:** spot. **Time Period Covered:** latest month.

GAS: OKLAHOMA

Source: *World Oil.* **Price Frequency:** monthly. **Effective Market(s):** Northeastern OK, Northwestern OK, Southwestern OK, Southeastern OK. **Units of Measure:** Dollars per 1000 cubic feet. **Type of Price:** contract. **Time Period Covered:** latest month.

GAS: OTHER KINDS

Source: *Gas Stats: Monthly Gas Utility Statistical Report.* **Price Frequency:** annually. **Units of Measure:** Dollars per MMBtu. **Type of Price:** average. **Time Period Covered:** latest 10 years.

GAS: RESIDENTIAL

Source: *Gas Stats: Monthly Gas Utility Statistical Report.* **Price Frequency:** monthly, annually. **Units of Measure:** Dollars per MMBtu. **Type of Price:** average. **Time Period Covered:** latest 24 months, latest 10 years.

Source: *Gas Stats: Quarterly Report of Gas Industry Operations.* **Price Frequency:** Quarterly. **Effective Market(s):** 10 domestic markets. **Units of Measure:** Dollars per MMBtu. **Type of Price:** average. **Time Period Covered:** latest quarter, latest year.

GAS: RESIDENTIAL UTILITY

Source: *Gas Stats: Monthly Gas Utility Statistical Report.* **Price Frequency:** monthly. **Units of Measure:** Dollars per MMBtu. **Time Period Covered:** latest month, year ago.

GAS: TEXAS

Source: *World Oil.* **Price Frequency:** monthly. **Effective Market(s):** 12 Texan markets. **Units of Measure:** Dollars per 1000 cubic feet. **Type of Price:** contract. **Time Period Covered:** latest month.

GAS: UTILITY PIPE

Source: *Gas Stats: Monthly Gas Utility Statistical Report.* **Price Frequency:** monthly. **Units of Measure:** index. **Type of Price:** price index. **Time Period Covered:** latest month, year ago.

GAS OIL

see Gasoil.

GASOIL

Source: *Financial Times.* **Price Frequency:** daily. **Effective Market(s):** London. **Units of Measure:** Dollars per tonne. **Type of Price:** spot. **Time Period Covered:** latest day.

Source: *Japan Economic Journal.* **Price Frequency:** weekly. **Effective Market(s):** Tokyo. **Units of Measure:** Japanese yen per kiloliter. **Type of Price:** spot. **Time Period Covered:** latest 2 weeks.

Source: *Japan Economic Journal.* **Price Frequency:** weekly. **Effective Market(s):** Singapore. **Units of Measure:** Dollars per barrel. **Type of Price:** spot. **Time Period Covered:** latest 2 weeks.

Source: *Oil Buyers' Guide International.* **Price Frequency:** weekly. **Effective Market(s):** Japan, Singapore. **Units of Measure:** Dollars per metric ton. **Type of Price:** spot. **Time Period Covered:** latest week.

Source: *OPEC Bulletin.* **Price Frequency:** monthly. **Effective Market(s):** Caribbean, Italy, Middle East Gulf, New York, Rotterdam, Singapore. **Units of Measure:** Dollars per barrel. **Time Period Covered:** latest 2 years.

GASOIL: 0.2% SULFUR

Source: *Oil Buyers' Guide.* **Price Frequency:** weekly. **Effective Market(s):** Venezuela. **Units of Measure:** cents per gallon. **Type of Price:** official. **Time Period Covered:** latest week.

Source: *Oil Buyers' Guide International.* **Price Frequency:** weekly. **Effective Market(s):** Venezuela. **Units of Measure:** cents per gallon. **Type of Price:** official. **Time Period Covered:** latest week.

GASOIL: 0.3% SULFUR

Source: *Oil Buyers' Guide.* **Price Frequency:** weekly. **Effective Market(s):** Mediterranean, Northwest Europe. **Units of Measure:** Dollars per metric ton. **Type of Price:** cargo, barge. **Time Period Covered:** latest week.

Source: *Oil Buyers' Guide.* **Price Frequency:** weekly. **Effective Market(s):** Venezuela. **Units of Measure:** cents per gallon. **Type of Price:** official. **Time Period Covered:** latest week.

Source: *Oil Buyers' Guide International.* **Price Frequency:** weekly. **Effective Market(s):** Venezuela. **Units of Measure:** cents per gallon. **Type of Price:** official. **Time Period Covered:** latest week.

Source: *Oil Buyers' Guide International.* **Price Frequency:** weekly. **Effective Market(s):** Mediterranean, Northwest Europe. **Units of Measure:** Dollars per metric ton. **Type of Price:** cargo. **Time Period Covered:** latest week.

GASOIL: 0.5% SULFUR

Source: *Oil Buyers' Guide.* **Price Frequency:** weekly. **Effective Market(s):** Venezuela. **Units of Measure:** cents per gallon. **Type of Price:** official. **Time Period Covered:** latest week.

Source: *Oil Buyers' Guide International.* **Price Frequency:** weekly. **Effective Market(s):** Venezuela. **Units of Measure:** cents per gallon. **Type of Price:** official. **Time Period Covered:** latest week.

GASOIL: DIESEL, MINIMUM 53

Source: *Commodity Trade and Price Trends.* **Price Frequency:** annually. **Effective Market(s):** Europe. **Units of Measure:** Dollars per metric ton, 1980 constant dollars per metric ton. **Time Period Covered:** latest 20 years.

GASOIL: EUROPEAN COMMUNITY

Source: *The Times.* **Price Frequency:** daily. **Effective Market(s):** Northwest Europe. **Units of Measure:** Dollars per metric ton. **Type of Price:** spot. **Time Period Covered:** latest day.

GASOIL: EUROPEAN COMMUNITY QUALIFIED

Source: *Japan Economic Journal.* **Price Frequency:** weekly. **Effective Market(s):** London. **Units of Measure:** Dollars per ton. **Type of Price:** spot. **Time Period Covered:** latest 2 weeks.

GASOIL: FUTURES

Source: *Asian Wall Street Journal.* **Price Frequency:** daily. **Effective Market(s):** London. **Units of Measure:** Dollars per ton. **Type of Price:** futures. **Time Period Covered:** latest day.

Source: *Financial Times.* **Price Frequency:** daily. **Effective Market(s):** London. **Units of Measure:** Dollars per tonne. **Type of Price:** futures. **Time Period Covered:** latest day.

Source: *Oil Buyers' Guide International.* **Price Frequency:** weekly. **Effective Market(s):** London. **Units of Measure:** Dollars per metric ton. **Type of Price:** futures. **Time Period Covered:** latest 2 weeks.

Source: *The Times.* **Price Frequency:** daily. **Units of Measure:** Dollars per metric ton. **Type of Price:** futures. **Time Period Covered:** latest day.

Source: *Wall Street Journal.* **Price Frequency:** daily. **Effective Market(s):** London. **Units of Measure:** Dollars per ton. **Type of Price:** futures. **Time Period Covered:** latest day.

GASOIL: LIGHT

Source: *Energy Prices & Taxes.* **Price Frequency:** annually. **Effective Market(s):** Rotterdam. **Units of Measure:** Dollars per metric ton. **Type of Price:** spot. **Time Period Covered:** latest 15 years.

GASOLINE

Source: *Energy Prices and Taxes.* **Price Frequency:** quarterly, annually. **Effective Market(s):** 28 international markets. **Units of Measure:** national currency per litre, national currency per ton oil equivalent. **Time Period Covered:** varies.

Source: *Energy Prices and Taxes.* **Price Frequency:** annually. **Effective Market(s):** 25 international markets. **Units of Measure:** Dollars per litre, dollars per ton oil equivalent. **Time Period Covered:** latest 8 years.

Source: *Japan Economic Journal.* **Price Frequency:** weekly. **Effective Market(s):** Tokyo. **Units of Measure:** Japanese yen per kiloliter. **Type of Price:** spot. **Time Period Covered:** latest 2 weeks.

Source: *Petroleum Economist.* **Price Frequency:** monthly. **Effective Market(s):** Bahamas, Bahrain, Curacao, Pulau Buxom (Singapore), Quoin Island. **Units of Measure:** cents per gallon. **Time Period Covered:** latest month.

Source: *Standard & Poor's Statistical Service Current Statistics.* **Price Frequency:** monthly, annually. **Effective Market(s):** 55-market average. **Units of Measure:** cents per gallon. **Type of Price:** retail. **Time Period Covered:** latest 3 years.

GASOLINE: 87 OCTANE

Source: *Oil & Gas Journal.* **Price Frequency:** weekly except second issue of month. **Effective Market(s):** New York. **Units of Measure:** Dollars per barrel. **Type of Price:** spot. **Time Period Covered:** latest 3 weeks, year ago.

GASOLINE: 87 OCTANE, COLONIAL 48+ GRADE MEDITERRANEAN

Source: *Oil Buyers' Guide.* **Price Frequency:** weekly. **Effective Market(s):** East Coast. **Units of Measure:** cents per gallon. **Type of Price:** spot. **Time Period Covered:** latest week.

GASOLINE: 98 OCTANE

Source: *Oil & Gas Journal.* **Price Frequency:** weekly except second issue of month. **Effective Market(s):** Rotterdam. **Units of Measure:** Dollars per barrel. **Type of Price:** spot. **Time Period Covered:** latest 3 weeks, year ago.

GASOLINE: ALL TYPES

Source: *National Petroleum News.* **Price Frequency:** monthly. **Effective Market(s):** Northeast, North Central, South, West, United States. **Units of Measure:** Dollars per gallon. **Type of Price:** average. **Time Period Covered:** latest month.

GASOLINE: AVIATION

Source: *Petroleum Economist.* **Price Frequency:** monthly. **Effective Market(s):** Bahamas, Bahrain, Curacao, Pulau Buxom (Singapore), Quoin Island. **Units of Measure:** cents per gallon. **Time Period Covered:** latest month.

GASOLINE: DIESEL

Source: *Agricultural Prices.* **Price Frequency:** monthly. **Effective Market(s):** 10 domestic markets, United States. **Units of Measure:** Dollars per gallon. **Type of Price:** paid by farmer. **Time Period Covered:** latest month, for US quarterly for latest year.

GASOLINE: FURNACE

Source: *Oil Buyers' Guide.* **Price Frequency:** weekly. **Effective Market(s):** 16 Canadian markets. **Units of Measure:** Canadian cents per liter. **Type of Price:** delivery for industrial accounts, rack. **Time Period Covered:** latest week.

GASOLINE: LEADED

Source: *Survey of Current Business.* **Price Frequency:** monthly, annually. **Effective Market(s):** United States. **Units of Measure:** Dollars per gallon. **Type of Price:** retail. **Time Period Covered:** latest 2 years.

GASOLINE: NO. 2, FURNACE

Source: *Oil Buyers' Guide.* **Price Frequency:** weekly. **Effective Market(s):** 6 Canadian markets. **Units of Measure:** Canadian cents per liter. **Type of Price:** rack. **Time Period Covered:** latest week.

GASOLINE: NORMAL

Source: *Oil Buyers' Guide.* **Price Frequency:** daily, weekly. **Effective Market(s):** Los Angeles, Mont Belvieu (TX), Conway (KS). **Units of Measure:** cents per gallon. **Type of Price:** spot. **Time Period Covered:** latest week.

GASOLINE: PREMIUM

Source: *Energy Prices & Taxes.* **Price Frequency:** annually. **Effective Market(s):** Rotterdam. **Units of Measure:** Dollars per metric ton. **Type of Price:** spot. **Time Period Covered:** latest 15 years.

Source: *Energy Pricing News Refined Fuel Report.* **Price Frequency:** semimonthly. **Effective Market(s):** 10 Canadian markets. **Units of Measure:** Canadian cents per liter. **Type of Price:** rack, delivered, retail. **Time Period Covered:** latest week.

Source: *Financial Times.* **Price Frequency:** daily. **Effective Market(s):** London. **Units of Measure:** Dollars per tonnne. **Type of Price:** spot. **Time Period Covered:** latest day.

Source: *Investor's Daily.* **Price Frequency:** daily. **Effective Market(s):** New York. **Units of Measure:** Dollars per gallon. **Type of Price:** barge spot. **Time Period Covered:** latest 2 days.

Source: *OPEC Bulletin.* **Price Frequency:** monthly. **Effective Market(s):** Italy, Rotterdam, Singapore. **Units of Measure:** Dollars per barrel. **Time Period Covered:** latest 2 years.

Source: *Petroleum Economist.* **Price Frequency:** monthly. **Effective Market(s):** Caribbean, Mediterranean, New York, Northwest Europe, Rotterdam. **Units of Measure:** Dollars per metric ton. **Type of Price:** spot. **Time Period Covered:** latest month.

Source: *The Times.* **Price Frequency:** daily. **Effective Market(s):** Northwest Europe. **Units of Measure:** Dollars per metric ton. **Type of Price:** spot. **Time Period Covered:** latest day.

GASOLINE: PREMIUM, 92 OCTANE

Source: *Oil Buyers' Guide.* **Price Frequency:** weekly. **Effective Market(s):** Gulf Coast. **Units of Measure:** cents per gallon. **Type of Price:**. **Time Period Covered:** latest week.

Source: *Oil Buyers' Guide International.* **Price Frequency:** weekly. **Effective Market(s):** Gulf Coast. **Units of Measure:** cents per gallon. **Type of Price:** pipeline. **Time Period Covered:** latest week.

Source: *Oil Buyers' Guide International.* **Price Frequency:** weekly. **Effective Market(s):** New York. **Units of Measure:** cents per gallon. **Type of Price:** spot barge. **Time Period Covered:** latest week.

GASOLINE: PREMIUM, UNLEADED

Source: *Asian Wall Street Journal.* **Price Frequency:** daily. **Effective Market(s):** New York. **Units of Measure:** Dollars per gallon. **Time Period Covered:** latest 2 days, year ago.

Source: *National Petroleum News.* **Price Frequency:** monthly. **Effective Market(s):** Northeast, North Central, South, West, United States. **Units of Measure:** Dollars per gallon. **Type of Price:** average. **Time Period Covered:** latest month.

Source: *Oil Buyers' Guide.* **Price Frequency:** weekly. **Effective Market(s):** 6 Canadian markets. **Units of Measure:** Canadian cents per liter. **Type of Price:** rack. **Time Period Covered:** latest week.

Source: *Oil Buyers' Guide.* **Price Frequency:** weekly. **Effective Market(s):** 16 Canadian markets. **Units of Measure:** Canadian cents per liter. **Type of Price:** delivery for industrial accounts, rack. **Time Period Covered:** latest week.

Source: *Oil Buyers' Guide.* **Price Frequency:** daily. **Effective Market(s):** Los Angeles, San Francisco, Seattle/Portland. **Units of Measure:** cents per gallon. **Type of Price:** spot. **Time Period Covered:** latest week.

Source: *OPEC Bulletin.* **Price Frequency:** monthly. **Effective Market(s):** New York. **Units of Measure:** Dollars per barrel. **Time Period Covered:** latest 2 years.

GASOLINE: PREMIUM, UNLEADED, RVP

Source: *New York Times.* **Price Frequency:** daily. **Effective Market(s):** New York. **Units of Measure:** Dollars per gallon. **Type of Price:** cash. **Time Period Covered:** latest 2 days.

GASOLINE: PREMIUM, UNLEADED, FULL SERVICE

Source: *Super Automotive Service.* **Price Frequency:** monthly. **Effective Market(s):** 21 domestic markets. **Units of Measure:** Dollars per gallon. **Type of Price:** retail. **Time Period Covered:** latest month.

GASOLINE: PREMIUM, UNLEADED, SELF SERVICE

Source: *Super Automotive Service.* **Price Frequency:** monthly. **Effective Market(s):** 21 domestic markets. **Units of Measure:** Dollars per gallon. **Type of Price:** retail. **Time Period Covered:** latest month.

GASOLINE: REGULAR

Source: *Oil Buyers' Guide.* **Price Frequency:** weekly. **Effective Market(s):** Venezuela. **Units of Measure:** cents per gallon. **Type of Price:** official. **Time Period Covered:** latest week.

Source: *Oil Buyers' Guide International.* **Price Frequency:** weekly. **Effective Market(s):** Venezuela. **Units of Measure:** cents per gallon. **Type of Price:** official. **Time Period Covered:** latest week.

Source: *OPEC Bulletin.* **Price Frequency:** monthly. **Effective Market(s):** Italy. **Units of Measure:** Dollars per barrel. **Time Period Covered:** latest 2 years.

Source: *Petroleum Economist.* **Price Frequency:** monthly. **Effective Market(s):** Caribbean, Mediterranean, New York, Northwest Europe, Rotterdam. **Units of Measure:** Dollars per metric ton. **Type of Price:** spot. **Time Period Covered:** latest month.

GASOLINE: REGULAR, 89 OCTANE

Source: *Oil Buyers' Guide.* **Price Frequency:** weekly. **Effective Market(s):** Gulf Coast. **Units of Measure:** cents per gallon. **Type of Price:**. **Time Period Covered:** latest week.

Source: *Oil Buyers' Guide International.* **Price Frequency:** weekly. **Effective Market(s):** Gulf Coast. **Units of Measure:** cents per gallon. **Type of Price:** pipeline. **Time Period Covered:** latest week.

Source: *Oil Buyers' Guide International.* **Price Frequency:** weekly. **Effective Market(s):** New York. **Units of Measure:** cents per gallon. **Type of Price:** spot barge. **Time Period Covered:** latest week.

GASOLINE: REGULAR, 91/92 OCTANE

Source: *Commodity Trade and Price Trends.* **Price Frequency:** annually. **Effective Market(s):** Europe. **Units of Measure:** Dollars per metric ton, 1980 constant dollars per metric ton. **Time Period Covered:** latest 20 years.

GASOLINE: REGULAR, LEADED

Source: *Agricultural Prices.* **Price Frequency:** monthly. **Effective Market(s):** 10 domestic markets, United States. **Units of Measure:** Dollars per gallon. **Type of Price:** paid by farmer. **Time Period Covered:** latest month, for US quarterly for latest year.

Source: *Agricultural Prices Annual Summary.* **Price Frequency:** quarterly. **Effective Market(s):** 10 domestic markets, United States. **Units of Measure:** Dollars per gallon. **Type of Price:** average paid by farmer. **Time Period Covered:** latest year, for US monthly for latest 6 years.

Source: *Commodity Year Book.* **Price Frequency:** monthly, annually. **Units of Measure:** index. **Type of Price:** wholesale price index. **Time Period Covered:** latest 7 years.

Source: *Energy Pricing News Refined Fuel Report.* **Price Frequency:** semimonthly. **Effective Market(s):** 10 Canadian markets. **Units of Measure:** Canadian cents per liter. **Type of Price:** rack, delivered, retail. **Time Period Covered:** latest week.

Source: *National Petroleum News.* **Price Frequency:** monthly. **Effective Market(s):** Northeast, North Central, South, West, United States. **Units of Measure:** Dollars per gallon. **Type of Price:** average. **Time Period Covered:** latest month.

Source: *Oil Buyers' Guide.* **Price Frequency:** weekly. **Effective Market(s):** 6 Canadian markets. **Units of Measure:** Canadian cents per liter. **Type of Price:** rack. **Time Period Covered:** latest week.

Source: *Oil Buyers' Guide.* **Price Frequency:** weekly. **Effective Market(s):** 16 Canadian markets. **Units of Measure:** Canadian cents per liter. **Type of Price:** delivery for industrial accounts, rack. **Time Period Covered:** latest week.

Source: *Oil Buyers' Guide.* **Price Frequency:** daily. **Effective Market(s):** New York, Gulf Coast. **Units of Measure:** cents per gallon. **Type of Price:** spot. **Time Period Covered:** latest week.

Source: *OPEC Bulletin.* **Price Frequency:** monthly. **Effective Market(s):** New York. **Units of Measure:** Dollars per barrel. **Time Period Covered:** latest 2 years.

Source: *Wall Street Journal.* **Price Frequency:** daily. **Effective Market(s):** New York. **Units of Measure:** Dollars per gallon. **Time Period Covered:** latest day, day ago, year ago.

GASOLINE: REGULAR, LEADED, 89 OCTANE

Source: *Oil Buyers' Guide.* **Price Frequency:** weekly. **Effective Market(s):** East Coast. **Units of Measure:** cents per gallon. **Type of Price:** spot cargo, spot barge. **Time Period Covered:** latest week.

GASOLINE: REGULAR, LEADED, FULL SERVICE

Source: *Super Automotive Service.* **Price Frequency:** monthly. **Effective Market(s):** 19 domestic markets. **Units of Measure:** Dollars per gallon. **Type of Price:** retail. **Time Period Covered:** latest month.

GASOLINE: REGULAR, LEADED, SELF SERVICE

Source: *Super Automotive Service.* **Price Frequency:** monthly. **Effective Market(s):** 19 domestic markets. **Units of Measure:** Dollars per gallon. **Type of Price:** retail. **Time Period Covered:** latest month.

GASOLINE: REGULAR, LEADED/UNLEADED

Source: *Oil Buyers' Guide.* **Price Frequency:** daily. **Effective Market(s):** Los Angeles, San Francisco, Seattle/Portland. **Units of Measure:** cents per gallon. **Type of Price:** spot. **Time Period Covered:** latest week.

GASOLINE: REGULAR, UNLEADED

Source: *Asian Wall Street Journal.* **Price Frequency:** daily. **Effective Market(s):** New York. **Units of Measure:** Dollars per gallon. **Time Period Covered:** latest 2 days, year ago.

Source: *Energy Pricing News Refined Fuel Report.* **Price Frequency:** semimonthly. **Effective Market(s):** 10 Canadian markets. **Units of Measure:** Canadian cents per liter. **Type of Price:** contract, rack, delivered, retail. **Time Period Covered:** latest week.

Source: *National Petroleum News.* **Price Frequency:** monthly. **Effective Market(s):** Northeast, North Central, South, West, United States. **Units of Measure:** Dollars per gallon. **Type of Price:** average. **Time Period Covered:** latest month.

Source: *Oil Buyers' Guide.* **Price Frequency:** weekly. **Effective Market(s):** 6 Canadian markets. **Units of Measure:** Canadian cents per liter. **Type of Price:** rack. **Time Period Covered:** latest week.

Source: *Oil Buyers' Guide.* **Price Frequency:** weekly. **Effective Market(s):** 16 Canadian markets. **Units of Measure:** Canadian cents per liter. **Type of Price:** delivery for industrial accounts, rack. **Time Period Covered:** latest week.

Source: *Oil Buyers' Guide.* **Price Frequency:** daily. **Effective Market(s):** New York, Gulf Coast. **Units of Measure:** cents per gallon. **Type of Price:** spot. **Time Period Covered:** latest week.

Source: *OPEC Bulletin.* **Price Frequency:** monthly. **Effective Market(s):** New York, Rotterdam. **Units of Measure:** Dollars per barrel. **Time Period Covered:** latest 2 years.

Source: *Wall Street Journal.* **Price Frequency:** daily. **Effective Market(s):** New York. **Units of Measure:** Dollars per gallon. **Time Period Covered:** latest day, day ago, year ago.

GASOLINE: REGULAR, UNLEADED, 87 OCTANE

Source: *Oil Buyers' Guide International.* **Price Frequency:** weekly. **Effective Market(s):** New York. **Units of Measure:** cents per gallon. **Type of Price:** spot barge. **Time Period Covered:** latest week.

GASOLINE: REGULAR, UNLEADED, FULL SERVICE

Source: *Super Automotive Service.* **Price Frequency:** monthly. **Effective Market(s):** 21 domestic markets. **Units of Measure:** Dollars per gallon. **Type of Price:** retail. **Time Period Covered:** latest month.

GASOLINE: REGULAR, UNLEADED, FUTURES

Source: *Oil Buyers' Guide.* **Price Frequency:** weekly. **Effective Market(s):** New York. **Units of Measure:** cents per gallon. **Type of Price:** futures. **Time Period Covered:** latest week.

GASOLINE: REGULAR, UNLEADED, FUTURES, DECEMBER

Source: *Commodity Year Book.* **Price Frequency:** monthly. **Effective Market(s):** New York. **Units of Measure:** cents per gallon. **Type of Price:** futures. **Time Period Covered:** latest 3 years.

GASOLINE: REGULAR, UNLEADED, SELF SERVICE

Source: *Super Automotive Service.* **Price Frequency:** monthly. **Effective Market(s):** 21 domestic markets. **Units of Measure:** Dollars per gallon. **Type of Price:** retail. **Time Period Covered:** latest month.

GASOLINE: RIVER, NORMAL

Source: *Oil Buyers' Guide.* **Price Frequency:** daily, weekly. **Effective Market(s):** Mont Belvieu (TX). **Units of Measure:** cents per gallon. **Type of Price:** spot. **Time Period Covered:** latest week.

GASOLINE: STOVE

Source: *Oil Buyers' Guide.* **Price Frequency:** weekly. **Effective Market(s):** 6 Canadian markets. **Units of Measure:** Canadian cents per liter. **Type of Price:** rack. **Time Period Covered:** latest week.

Source: *Oil Buyers' Guide.* **Price Frequency:** weekly. **Effective Market(s):** 11 Canadian markets. **Units of Measure:** Canadian cents per liter. **Type of Price:** delivery for industrial accounts, rack. **Time Period Covered:** latest week.

GASOLINE: UNLEADED

Source: *Agricultural Prices.* **Price Frequency:** monthly. **Effective Market(s):** 10 domestic markets, United States. **Units of Measure:** Dollars per gallon. **Type of Price:** paid by farmer. **Time Period Covered:** latest month, for US quarterly for latest year.

Source: *Agricultural Prices Annual Summary.* **Price Frequency:** quarterly. **Effective Market(s):** 10 domestic markets, United States. **Units of Measure:** Dollars per gallon. **Type of Price:** average paid by farmer. **Time Period Covered:** latest year, for US monthly for latest 6 years.

Source: *Investor's Daily.* **Price Frequency:** daily. **Effective Market(s):** New York. **Units of Measure:** Dollars per gallon. **Type of Price:** barge spot. **Time Period Covered:** latest 2 days.

Source: *Oil Buyers' Guide.* **Price Frequency:** weekly. **Effective Market(s):** Venezuela. **Units of Measure:** cents per gallon. **Type of Price:** official. **Time Period Covered:** latest week.

Source: *Oil Buyers' Guide International.* **Price Frequency:** weekly. **Effective Market(s):** Venezuela. **Units of Measure:** cents per gallon. **Type of Price:** official. **Time Period Covered:** latest week.

Source: *Standard & Poor's Statistical Service Current Statistics.* **Price Frequency:** monthly, annually. **Effective Market(s):** 55-market average. **Units of Measure:** cents per gallon. **Type of Price:** retail. **Time Period Covered:** latest 3 years.

Source: *Survey of Current Business.* **Price Frequency:** monthly, annually. **Effective Market(s):** United States. **Units of Measure:** Dollars per gallon. **Type of Price:** retail. **Time Period Covered:** latest 2 years.

GASOLINE: UNLEADED, 87 OCTANE

Source: *Oil Buyers' Guide.* **Price Frequency:** weekly. **Effective Market(s):** Gulf Coast. **Units of Measure:** cents per gallon. **Type of Price:**. **Time Period Covered:** latest week.

Source: *Oil Buyers' Guide International.* **Price Frequency:** weekly. **Effective Market(s):** Gulf Coast. **Units of Measure:** cents per gallon. **Type of Price:** pipeline. **Time Period Covered:** latest week.

GASOLINE: UNLEADED, FUTURES

Source: *Asian Wall Street Journal.* **Price Frequency:** daily. **Effective Market(s):** New York. **Units of Measure:** Dollars per gallon. **Type of Price:** futures. **Time Period Covered:** latest day.

Source: *Barron's.* **Price Frequency:** weekly. **Effective Market(s):** New York. **Units of Measure:** cents per gallon. **Type of Price:** futures. **Time Period Covered:** latest week.

Source: *Los Angeles Times.* **Price Frequency:** daily. **Effective Market(s):** New York. **Units of Measure:** cents per gallon. **Type of Price:** futures. **Time Period Covered:** latest day.

Source: *New York Times.* **Price Frequency:** daily. **Effective Market(s):** New York. **Units of Measure:** cents per gallon. **Type of Price:** futures. **Time Period Covered:** latest day.

Source: *Wall Street Journal.* **Price Frequency:** daily. **Effective Market(s):** New York. **Units of Measure:** Dollars per gallon. **Type of Price:** futures. **Time Period Covered:** latest day.

GASOLINE: UNLEADED, RVP

Source: *New York Times.* **Price Frequency:** daily. **Effective Market(s):** New York. **Units of Measure:** Dollars per gallon. **Type of Price:** cash. **Time Period Covered:** latest 2 days.

GASOLINE: UNLEADED, SELF SERVICE

Source: *Oil & Gas Journal.* **Price Frequency:** weekly except last issue of month. **Effective Market(s):** 18 domestic markets. **Units of Measure:** Dollars per MMBTU. **Time Period Covered:** latest week, year ago.

GEARS: BRONZE, HIGH GRADE, SCRAP

Source: *American Metal Market.* **Price Frequency:** daily. **Effective Market(s):** 14 domestic markets, Montreal, Toronto. **Units of Measure:** cents per lb. **Type of Price:** dealer buying. **Time Period Covered:** latest day.

GEESE

Source: *HRI-Buyers Guide.* **Price Frequency:** weekly. **Effective Market(s):** Northeastern area. **Units of Measure:** Dollars per lb. **Type of Price:** price paid by dining places & institutions. **Time Period Covered:** latest week.

Source: *Lancaster Farming.* **Price Frequency:** weekly. **Effective Market(s):** Pennsylvania. **Units of Measure:** Dollars per lb. **Type of Price:** auction. **Time Period Covered:** latest week.

Source: *Weekly Insiders Turkey Letter.* **Price Frequency:** weekly. **Effective Market(s):** New York. **Units of Measure:** cents per lb. **Type of Price:** retail. **Time Period Covered:** latest week, week ago, year ago.

GEESE: FROZEN, CANADIAN

Source: *Urner Barry's Price-Current.* **Price Frequency:** daily. **Units of Measure:** Dollars per lb. **Type of Price:** sale from stores. **Time Period Covered:** latest day.

GEESE: FROZEN, MIDWESTERN

Source: *Urner Barry's Price-Current.* **Price Frequency:** daily. **Units of Measure:** Dollars per lb. **Type of Price:** sale from stores. **Time Period Covered:** latest day.

GELATIN

Source: *Journal of Commerce and Commercial.* **Price Frequency:** weekly in Friday issue. **Units of Measure:** Dollars per lb. **Type of Price:** spot. **Time Period Covered:** latest week.

GELATIN: EDIBLE

Source: *Chemical Marketing Reporter.* **Price Frequency:** weekly. **Effective Market(s):** New York. **Units of Measure:** Dollars per lb. **Type of Price:** spot. **Time Period Covered:** latest week.

GELATIN STOCKS

Source: *National Provisioner.* **Price Frequency:** weekly. **Effective Market(s):** Midwest River. **Units of Measure:** Dollars per 100 lbs. **Time Period Covered:** latest week.

GENTIAN VIOLET

see Methyl Roseaniline Chloride.

GERANIOL: NATURAL, 90-92%

Source: *Chemical Marketing Reporter.* **Price Frequency:** weekly. **Effective Market(s):** New York. **Units of Measure:** Dollars per lb. **Type of Price:** spot. **Time Period Covered:** latest week.

GERANIOL: SYNTHETIC

Source: *Journal of Commerce and Commercial.* **Price Frequency:** weekly in Tuesday issue. **Units of Measure:** Dollars per lb. **Type of Price:** spot. **Time Period Covered:** latest week.

GERANIOL: SYNTHETIC, 90-92%

Source: *Chemical Marketing Reporter.* **Price Frequency:** weekly. **Effective Market(s):** New York. **Units of Measure:** Dollars per lb. **Type of Price:** spot. **Time Period Covered:** latest week.

GERANIOL: SYNTHETIC, 96-98%

Source: *Chemical Marketing Reporter.* **Price Frequency:** weekly. **Effective Market(s):** New York. **Units of Measure:** Dollars per lb. **Type of Price:** spot. **Time Period Covered:** latest week.

GERANIUM OIL

Source: *U. S. Essential Oil Trade.* **Price Frequency:** annually. **Effective Market(s):** United States. **Units of Measure:** Dollars per kilogram. **Type of Price:** import value. **Time Period Covered:** latest 3 years.

GERANIUM OIL: BOURBON

Source: *Journal of Commerce and Commercial.* **Price Frequency:** weekly in Tuesday issue. **Units of Measure:** Dollars per lb. **Type of Price:** spot. **Time Period Covered:** latest week.

GERANIUM OIL: CHINESE

Source: *Chemical Marketing Reporter.* **Price Frequency:** weekly. **Effective Market(s):** New York. **Units of Measure:** Dollars per lb. **Type of Price:** spot. **Time Period Covered:** latest week.

Source: *Journal of Commerce and Commercial.* **Price Frequency:** weekly in Tuesday issue. **Units of Measure:** Dollars per lb. **Type of Price:** spot. **Time Period Covered:** latest week.

GERANIUM OIL: EGYPTIAN

Source: *Chemical Marketing Reporter.* **Price Frequency:** weekly. **Effective Market(s):** New York. **Units of Measure:** Dollars per lb. **Type of Price:** spot. **Time Period Covered:** latest week.

Source: *Journal of Commerce and Commercial.* **Price Frequency:** weekly in Tuesday issue. **Units of Measure:** Dollars per lb. **Type of Price:** spot. **Time Period Covered:** latest week.

GERANIUM OIL: MOROCCAN

Source: *Chemical Marketing Reporter.* **Price Frequency:** weekly. **Effective Market(s):** New York. **Units of Measure:** Dollars per lb. **Type of Price:** spot. **Time Period Covered:** latest week.

Source: *Journal of Commerce and Commercial.* **Price Frequency:** weekly in Tuesday issue. **Units of Measure:** Dollars per lb. **Type of Price:** spot. **Time Period Covered:** latest week.

GERANIUM OIL: TURKISH

see Palmarosa Oil.

GERANIUMS: BEDDING, FLATS

Source: *Floriculture Crops.* **Price Frequency:** annually. **Effective Market(s):** 26 domestic markets, United States. **Units of Measure:** Dollars per unit. **Type of Price:** commercial wholesale. **Time Period Covered:** latest 2 years.

GERANIUMS: POTTED CUTTINGS, LESS THAN 5″

Source: *Floriculture Crops.* **Price Frequency:** annually. **Effective Market(s):** 27 domestic markets, United States. **Units of Measure:** Dollars per unit. **Type of Price:** commercial wholesale. **Time Period Covered:** latest 2 years.

GERANIUMS: POTTED CUTTINGS, MORE THAN 5″

Source: *Floriculture Crops.* **Price Frequency:** annually. **Effective Market(s):** 27 domestic markets, United States. **Units of Measure:** Dollars per unit. **Type of Price:** commercial wholesale. **Time Period Covered:** latest 2 years.

GERANIUMS: POTTED FROM SEED, LESS THAN 5″

Source: *Floriculture Crops.* **Price Frequency:** annually. **Effective Market(s):** 25 domestic markets, United States. **Units of Measure:** Dollars per unit. **Type of Price:** commercial wholesale. **Time Period Covered:** latest 2 years.

GERANIUMS: POTTED FROM SEED, MORE THAN 5″

Source: *Floriculture Crops.* **Price Frequency:** annually. **Effective Market(s):** 21 domestic markets, United States. **Units of Measure:** Dollars per unit. **Type of Price:** commercial wholesale. **Time Period Covered:** latest 2 years.

GERANYL ACETATE

Source: *Chemical Marketing Reporter.* **Price Frequency:** weekly. **Effective Market(s):** New York. **Units of Measure:** Dollars per lb. **Type of Price:** spot. **Time Period Covered:** latest week.

Source: *Journal of Commerce and Commercial.* **Price Frequency:** weekly in Tuesday issue. **Units of Measure:** Dollars per lb. **Type of Price:** spot. **Time Period Covered:** latest week.

GERANYL ACETATE: NATURAL

Source: *Chemical Marketing Reporter.* **Price Frequency:** weekly. **Effective Market(s):** New York. **Units of Measure:** Dollars per lb. **Type of Price:** spot. **Time Period Covered:** latest week.

GERANYL FORMATE: NATURAL

Source: *Chemical Marketing Reporter.* **Price Frequency:** weekly. **Effective Market(s):** New York. **Units of Measure:** Dollars per lb. **Type of Price:** spot. **Time Period Covered:** latest week.

GERANYL FORMATE: SYNTHETIC

Source: *Chemical Marketing Reporter.* **Price Frequency:** weekly. **Effective Market(s):** New York. **Units of Measure:** Dollars per lb. **Type of Price:** spot. **Time Period Covered:** latest week.

GERBERAS

Source: *New Zealand Farmer.* **Price Frequency:** weekly, seasonally. **Effective Market(s):** New Zealand. **Units of Measure:** New Zealand dollars per bunch. **Time Period Covered:** latest week.

GERMANIUM

Source: *Economic and Energy Indicators.* **Price Frequency:** monthly, quarterly, annually. **Units of Measure:** Dollars per kilogram. **Time Period Covered:** latest 3 months, quarters, and years.

GERMANY, FEDERAL REPUBLIC OF

see West Germany.

GHATTI GUM: POWDER

Source: *Journal of Commerce and Commercial.* **Price Frequency:** weekly in Monday issue. **Units of Measure:** Dollars per lb. **Type of Price:** spot. **Time Period Covered:** latest week.

GILSONITE: GENERAL PURPOSE

Source: *Chemical Marketing Reporter.* **Price Frequency:** weekly. **Effective Market(s):** Bonanza (UT). **Units of Measure:** Dollars per ton. **Type of Price:** spot. **Time Period Covered:** latest week.

GILSONITE: SELECTS

Source: *Chemical Marketing Reporter.* **Price Frequency:** weekly. **Effective Market(s):** Bonanza (UT). **Units of Measure:** Dollars per ton. **Type of Price:** spot. **Time Period Covered:** latest week.

GIN

Source: *Beverage Media.* **Price Frequency:** monthly. **Effective Market(s):** New York. **Units of Measure:** Dollars per unit. **Type of Price:** wholesale by brand. **Time Period Covered:** latest month.

Source: *Colorado Beverage Analyst.* **Price Frequency:** monthly. **Effective Market(s):** Colorado. **Units of Measure:** Dollars per case. **Type of Price:** wholesale by brand. **Time Period Covered:** latest month.

Source: *Illinois Beverage Journal.* **Price Frequency:** monthly. **Effective Market(s):** Illinois. **Units of Measure:** Dollars per case. **Type of Price:** wholesale by brand. **Time Period Covered:** latest month.

Source: *Indiana Beverage Journal.* **Price Frequency:** monthly. **Effective Market(s):** Indiana. **Units of Measure:** Dollars per case, dollars per bottle. **Type of Price:** wholesale by brand. **Time Period Covered:** latest month.

Source: *Kentucky Beverage Journal.* **Price Frequency:** monthly. **Effective Market(s):** Kentucky. **Units of Measure:** Dollars per bottle, dollars per case. **Type of Price:** wholesale by brand. **Time Period Covered:** latest month.

Source: *Nevada Beverage Index.* **Price Frequency:** monthly. **Effective Market(s):** Nevada. **Units of Measure:** Dollars per unit. **Type of Price:** wholesale by brand. **Time Period Covered:** latest month.

Source: *Rhode Island Beverage Journal.* **Price Frequency:** monthly. **Effective Market(s):** Rhode Island. **Units of Measure:** Dollars per unit. **Type of Price:** wholesale by brand. **Time Period Covered:** latest month.

GINGER (FLOWER): OTHER COLORED, CUT, HAWAII

Source: *Floriculture Crops.* **Price Frequency:** annually. **Effective Market(s):** United States. **Units of Measure:** cents per unit. **Type of Price:** commercial wholesale. **Time Period Covered:** latest 2 years.

GINGER (FLOWER): PINK, CUT, HAWAII

Source: *Floriculture Crops.* **Price Frequency:** annually. **Effective Market(s):** United States. **Units of Measure:** cents per unit. **Type of Price:** commercial wholesale. **Time Period Covered:** latest 2 years.

GINGER (FLOWER): RED, CUT, HAWAII

Source: *Floriculture Crops.* **Price Frequency:** annually. **Effective Market(s):** United States. **Units of Measure:** cents per unit. **Type of Price:** commercial wholesale. **Time Period Covered:** latest 2 years.

GINGER: CHINESE

Source: *Chemical Marketing Reporter.* **Price Frequency:** weekly. **Effective Market(s):** New York. **Units of Measure:** Dollars per lb. **Type of Price:** spot. **Time Period Covered:** latest week.

Source: *Prices of Selected Asia/Pacific Products.* **Price Frequency:** monthly. **Effective Market(s):** Tokyo. **Units of Measure:** Japanese yen per kilogram. **Type of Price:** trade high, trade low. **Time Period Covered:** latest month.

GINGER: COCHIN

Source: *Chemical Marketing Reporter.* **Price Frequency:** weekly. **Effective Market(s):** New York. **Units of Measure:** Dollars per lb. **Type of Price:** spot. **Time Period Covered:** latest week.

Source: *Fruit and Tropical Products.* **Price Frequency:** monthly, seasonally. **Effective Market(s):** London. **Units of Measure:** British pounds per tonne. **Type of Price:** month end. **Time Period Covered:** latest 2 years.

Source: *Prices of Selected Asia/Pacific Products.* **Price Frequency:** monthly. **Effective Market(s):** United Kingdom/North European ports, Japan, Netherlands, United Kingdom. **Units of Measure:** Dollars per metric ton. **Type of Price:** high, low. **Time Period Covered:** latest month.

Source: *Prices of Selected Asia/Pacific Products.* **Price Frequency:** monthly. **Effective Market(s):** United States. **Units of Measure:** Dollars per metric ton. **Type of Price:** spot high, spot low. **Time Period Covered:** latest month.

GINGER: HAWAII

Source: *U. S. Spice Trade.* **Price Frequency:** monthly, annually. **Effective Market(s):** Hawaii. **Units of Measure:** cents per lb. **Type of Price:** farm. **Time Period Covered:** latest 12 years.

GINGER: INDIAN COCHIN

Source: *U. S. Spice Trade.* **Price Frequency:** monthly, annually. **Effective Market(s):** New York. **Units of Measure:** cents per lb. **Type of Price:** spot. **Time Period Covered:** latest 10 years.

GINGER: SLICED, CHINESE

Source: *Prices of Selected Asia/Pacific Products.* **Price Frequency:** monthly. **Effective Market(s):** Japan, major European ports, Netherlands. **Units of Measure:** Dollars per metric ton. **Type of Price:** high, low. **Time Period Covered:** latest month.

Source: *Prices of Selected Asia/Pacific Products.* **Price Frequency:** monthly. **Effective Market(s):** United States. **Units of Measure:** Dollars per metric ton. **Type of Price:** spot high, spot low. **Time Period Covered:** latest month.

Source: *U. S. Spice Trade.* **Price Frequency:** monthly, annually. **Effective Market(s):** New York. **Units of Measure:** cents per lb. **Type of Price:** spot. **Time Period Covered:** latest 10 years.

GINGER: SLICED, INDONESIAN

Source: *Prices of Selected Asia/Pacific Products.* **Price Frequency:** monthly. **Effective Market(s):** Netherlands, United Kingdom, United Kingdom/North European ports. **Units of Measure:** Dollars per metric ton. **Type of Price:** high, low. **Time Period Covered:** latest month.

Source: *Prices of Selected Asia/Pacific Products.* **Price Frequency:** monthly. **Effective Market(s):** United Kingdom. **Units of Measure:** British pounds per metric ton. **Type of Price:** spot high, spot low. **Time Period Covered:** latest month.

GINGER: SPLIT, NIGERIAN

Source: *Fruit and Tropical Products.* **Price Frequency:** monthly, seasonally. **Effective Market(s):** London. **Units of Measure:** British pounds per tonne. **Type of Price:** spot. **Time Period Covered:** latest 2 years.

GINGER: WHOLE PEELED, CHINESE

Source: *U. S. Spice Trade.* **Price Frequency:** monthly, annually. **Effective Market(s):** New York. **Units of Measure:** cents per lb. **Type of Price:** spot. **Time Period Covered:** latest 10 years.

GINGER: WHOLE, CHINESE

Source: *Prices of Selected Asia/Pacific Products.* **Price Frequency:** monthly. **Effective Market(s):** Japan, Hong Kong, Netherlands. **Units of Measure:** Dollars per metric ton. **Type of Price:** high, low. **Time Period Covered:** latest month.

Source: *Prices of Selected Asia/Pacific Products.* **Price Frequency:** monthly. **Effective Market(s):** United States. **Units of Measure:** Dollars per metric ton. **Type of Price:** spot high, spot low. **Time Period Covered:** latest month.

GINGER OIL

Source: *Journal of Commerce and Commercial.* **Price Frequency:** weekly in Tuesday issue. **Units of Measure:** Dollars per lb. **Type of Price:** spot. **Time Period Covered:** latest week.

GINGER OIL: CHINESE

Source: *Chemical Marketing Reporter.* **Price Frequency:** weekly. **Effective Market(s):** New York. **Units of Measure:** Dollars per kilo. **Type of Price:** spot. **Time Period Covered:** latest week.

GINGER OIL: INDIAN

Source: *Chemical Marketing Reporter.* **Price Frequency:** weekly. **Effective Market(s):** New York. **Units of Measure:** Dollars per kilo. **Type of Price:** spot. **Time Period Covered:** latest week.

GINGER OLEORESIN: NF

Source: *Chemical Marketing Reporter.* **Price Frequency:** weekly. **Effective Market(s):** New York. **Units of Measure:** Dollars per lb. **Type of Price:** spot. **Time Period Covered:** latest week.

GINGER ROOT: CHINESE

Source: *Prices of Selected Asia/Pacific Products.* **Price Frequency:** monthly, seasonally. **Effective Market(s):** New York. **Units of Measure:** Dollars per lb. **Type of Price:** spot high, spot low. **Time Period Covered:** latest month.

GINGER ROOT: CHINESE/TAIWANESE

Source: *Prices of Selected Asia/Pacific Products.* **Price Frequency:** monthly, seasonally. **Effective Market(s):** Osaka. **Units of Measure:** Japanese yen per kilogram. **Type of Price:** trade high, trade low. **Time Period Covered:** latest month.

GINGER ROOT: COCHIN

Source: *Prices of Selected Asia/Pacific Products.* **Price Frequency:** monthly, seasonally. **Effective Market(s):** New York. **Units of Measure:** Dollars per lb. **Type of Price:** spot high, spot low. **Time Period Covered:** latest month.

GINGHAM FABRIC: POLYESTER/COTTON, YARN DYED

Source: *JTN: The International Textile Magazine.* **Price Frequency:** monthly. **Effective Market(s):** Taiwan. **Units of Measure:** Dollars per yard. **Type of Price:** export. **Time Period Covered:** latest month.

GINSENG ROOT: POWDER, SIBERIAN

Source: *Journal of Commerce and Commercial.* **Price Frequency:** weekly in Monday issue. **Units of Measure:** Dollars per lb. **Type of Price:** spot. **Time Period Covered:** latest week.

GLADIOLI

Source: *Floriculture Crops.* **Price Frequency:** annually. **Effective Market(s):** 8 domestic markets, United States. **Units of Measure:** cents per unit. **Type of Price:** commercial wholesale. **Time Period Covered:** latest 2 years.

GLASS: ROSIN WINDOW

Source: *CRB Commodity Index Report.* **Price Frequency:** weekly. **Effective Market(s):** New York. **Units of Measure:** Dollars per 100 lbs. **Type of Price:** spot. **Time Period Covered:** latest week.

GLAUBER'S SALT

see Sodium Sulfate.

GLUCONIC ACID

Source: *Journal of Commerce and Commercial.* **Price Frequency:** weekly in Friday issue. **Units of Measure:** Dollars per lb. **Type of Price:** spot. **Time Period Covered:** latest week.

GLUCONIC ACID: TECHNICAL GRADE, 50%

Source: *Chemical Marketing Reporter.* **Price Frequency:** weekly. **Effective Market(s):** New York. **Units of Measure:** Dollars per lb. **Type of Price:** spot. **Time Period Covered:** latest week.

GLUE: BONE, EXTRACTED, GREEN, JELLYGRAMS

Source: *Chemical Marketing Reporter.* **Price Frequency:** weekly. **Effective Market(s):** New York. **Units of Measure:** Dollars per lb. **Type of Price:** spot. **Time Period Covered:** latest week.

GLUE: HIDE, JELLYGRAMS

Source: *Chemical Marketing Reporter.* **Price Frequency:** weekly. **Effective Market(s):** New York. **Units of Measure:** Dollars per lb. **Type of Price:** spot. **Time Period Covered:** latest week.

GLUTAMIC ACID: 99-1/2%

Source: *Chemical Marketing Reporter.* **Price Frequency:** weekly. **Effective Market(s):** New York. **Units of Measure:** Dollars per kilo. **Type of Price:** spot. **Time Period Covered:** latest week.

GLYCERINE

Source: *Purchasing.* **Price Frequency:** quarterly in January, April, July, October issues. **Units of Measure:** cents per lb. **Type of Price:** transaction. **Time Period Covered:** latest 5 quarters.

GLYCERINE: 96%, USP

Source: *Journal of Commerce and Commercial.* **Price Frequency:** weekly in Friday issue. **Units of Measure:** Dollars per lb. **Type of Price:** spot. **Time Period Covered:** latest week.

GLYCERINE: 99.5%, USP

Source: *Journal of Commerce and Commercial.* **Price Frequency:** weekly in Friday issue. **Units of Measure:** Dollars per lb. **Type of Price:** spot. **Time Period Covered:** latest week.

GLYCERINE: NATURAL, CHEMICALLY PURE, 96%, USP

Source: *Chemical Marketing Reporter.* **Price Frequency:** weekly. **Effective Market(s):** New York. **Units of Measure:** Dollars per lb. **Type of Price:** spot. **Time Period Covered:** latest week.

GLYCERINE: NATURAL, KOSHER, CHEMICALLY PURE, 99.7%

Source: *Chemical Marketing Reporter.* **Price Frequency:** weekly. **Effective Market(s):** New York. **Units of Measure:** Dollars per lb. **Type of Price:** spot. **Time Period Covered:** latest week.

GLYCERINE: NATURAL, REFINED, CHEMICALLY PURE, 99.7%, USP

Source: *Chemical Marketing Reporter.* **Price Frequency:** weekly. **Effective Market(s):** New York. **Units of Measure:** Dollars per lb. **Type of Price:** spot. **Time Period Covered:** latest week.

GLYCERINE: REFINED

Source: *Standard & Poor's Statistical Service Current Statistics.* **Price Frequency:** monthly, annually. **Effective Market(s):** New York. **Units of Measure:** cents per lb. **Time Period Covered:** latest 4 years.

GLYCERINE: SYNTHETIC, 96%

Source: *Chemical Marketing Reporter.* **Price Frequency:** weekly. **Effective Market(s):** New York. **Units of Measure:** Dollars per lb. **Type of Price:** spot. **Time Period Covered:** latest week.

GLYCERINE: SYNTHETIC, 99.7%

Source: *Chemical Marketing Reporter.* **Price Frequency:** weekly. **Effective Market(s):** New York. **Units of Measure:** Dollars per lb. **Type of Price:** spot. **Time Period Covered:** latest week.

GLYCERYL GUAIACOLATE

Source: *Chemical Marketing Reporter.* **Price Frequency:** weekly. **Effective Market(s):** New York. **Units of Measure:** Dollars per lb. **Type of Price:** spot. **Time Period Covered:** latest week.

GLYCINE

see Aminoacetic Acid.

GLYCOLIC ACID

see Hydroxyacetic Acid.

GLYOXAL: 40% SOLUTION

Source: *Chemical Marketing Reporter.* **Price Frequency:** weekly. **Effective Market(s):** New York. **Units of Measure:** Dollars per lb. **Type of Price:** spot. **Time Period Covered:** latest week.

GOATS

Source: *Farm and Dairy.* **Price Frequency:** weekly, seasonally. **Effective Market(s):** Ohio, Pennyslvania. **Units of Measure:** Dollars per head. **Type of Price:** auction high, auction low. **Time Period Covered:** latest week.

Source: *Lancaster Farming.* **Price Frequency:** weekly. **Effective Market(s):** Pennsylvania, Virginia. **Units of Measure:** Dollars per head. **Type of Price:** auction. **Time Period Covered:** latest week.

Source: *Lancaster Farming.* **Price Frequency:** weekly. **Effective Market(s):** Pennsylvania. **Units of Measure:** Dollars each. **Type of Price:** auction. **Time Period Covered:** latest week.

GOATS: KID

Source: *Lancaster Farming.* **Price Frequency:** weekly. **Effective Market(s):** Pennsylvania. **Units of Measure:** Dollars each. **Type of Price:** auction. **Time Period Covered:** latest week.

GOLD

Source: *American Metal Market.* **Price Frequency:** daily. **Effective Market(s):** London, New York, Paris, Zurich. **Units of Measure:** Dollars per troy ounce. **Time Period Covered:** latest day.

Source: *Asian Wall Street Journal.* **Price Frequency:** daily. **Effective Market(s):** Hong Kong, Paris, Zurich. **Units of Measure:** Hong Kong dollars per tael, dollars per troy ounce. **Type of Price:** cash. **Time Period Covered:** latest 2 days.

Source: *Asian Wall Street Journal.* **Price Frequency:** daily. **Effective Market(s):** New York, London. **Units of Measure:** Dollars per troy ounce. **Type of Price:** cash. **Time Period Covered:** latest 2 days.

Source: *Barron's.* **Price Frequency:** weekly. **Effective Market(s):** New York. **Units of Measure:** Dollars per troy ounce. **Time Period Covered:** latest 2 weeks.

Source: *Business Week.* **Price Frequency:** weekly. **Units of Measure:** Dollars per troy ounce. **Time Period Covered:** latest 2 weeks.

Source: *Commodity Year Book.* **Price Frequency:** annually. **Effective Market(s):** United States. **Units of Measure:** Dollars per troy ounce. **Time Period Covered:** latest 7 years.

Source: *Commodity Year Book.* **Price Frequency:** monthly, annually. **Effective Market(s):** New York. **Units of Measure:** Dollars per troy ounce. **Time Period Covered:** latest 9 years.

Source: *E&MJ.* **Price Frequency:** monthly. **Effective Market(s):** Zurich, Paris, London, New York. **Units of Measure:** Dollars per troy ounce. **Time Period Covered:** latest month.

Source: *Economic and Energy Indicators.* **Price Frequency:** monthly, quarterly, annually. **Units of Measure:** Dollars per troy ounce. **Time Period Covered:** latest 3 months, quarters, and years.

Source: *The Economist.* **Price Frequency:** weekly. **Units of Measure:** Dollars per ounce. **Time Period Covered:** latest week, week ago.

Source: *Far Eastern Economic Review.* **Price Frequency:** weekly. **Effective Market(s):** London. **Units of Measure:** Dollars per ounce. **Time Period Covered:** latest week, week ago, 3 months ago, year ago.

Source: *Financial Post.* **Price Frequency:** weekly. **Effective Market(s):** Canada, London, New York. **Units of Measure:** Canadian dollars per troy ounce, British pounds per troy ounce, dollars per troy ounce. **Time Period Covered:** latest 2 weeks.

Source: *Financial Times.* **Price Frequency:** daily. **Effective Market(s):** London. **Units of Measure:** Dollars per troy ounce. **Type of Price:** spot. **Time Period Covered:** latest day.

Source: *Financial Times.* **Price Frequency:** daily. **Effective Market(s):** London. **Units of Measure:** Dollars per fine ounce, British pounds per fine ounce. **Type of Price:** close, opening, fix. **Time Period Covered:** latest day.

Source: *Investor's Daily.* **Price Frequency:** daily. **Effective Market(s):** 6 international markets. **Units of Measure:** Dollars per troy ounce. **Type of Price:** spot. **Time Period Covered:** latest day.

Source: *Iron Age.* **Price Frequency:** monthly. **Units of Measure:** Dollars per troy ounce. **Type of Price:** consumer. **Time Period Covered:** latest month.

Source: *Los Angeles Times.* **Price Frequency:** daily. **Effective Market(s):** London, New York . **Units of Measure:** Dollars per troy ounce. **Type of Price:** cash. **Time Period Covered:** latest day.

Source: *Minerals Today.* **Price Frequency:** bimonthly. **Units of Measure:** Dollars per troy ounce. **Time Period Covered:** latest month, month ago.

Source: *New York Times.* **Price Frequency:** daily. **Effective Market(s):** 6 international markets. **Units of Measure:** Dollars per troy ounce. **Type of Price:** cash. **Time Period Covered:** latest day.

Source: *Northern Miner.* **Price Frequency:** daily. **Effective Market(s):** London, Canada. **Units of Measure:** Dollars per ounce. **Type of Price:** spot. **Time Period Covered:** week ago.

Source: *Purchasing.* **Price Frequency:** quarterly in January, April, July, October issues. **Units of Measure:** Dollars per troy ounce. **Type of Price:** transaction. **Time Period Covered:** latest 5 quarters.

Source: *Standard & Poor's Statistical Service Current Statistics.* **Price Frequency:** monthly, annually. **Effective Market(s):** New York. **Units of Measure:** Dollars per troy ounce. **Type of Price:** average. **Time Period Covered:** latest 3 years.

Source: *Wall Street Journal.* **Price Frequency:** daily. **Effective Market(s):** New York. **Units of Measure:** Dollars per troy ounce. **Time Period Covered:** latest day, day ago, year ago.

GOLD: 99.5% FINE

Source: *Monthly Commodity Price Bulletin Supplement.* **Price Frequency:** monthly, quarterly, annually. **Effective Market(s):** London. **Units of Measure:** Dollars per fine ounce. **Type of Price:** average of daily rates. **Time Period Covered:** latest 20 years.

GOLD: FABRICATED

Source: *E&MJ.* **Price Frequency:** monthly. **Units of Measure:** Dollars per troy ounce. **Time Period Covered:** latest month.

Source: *Investor's Daily.* **Price Frequency:** daily. **Effective Market(s):** New York. **Units of Measure:** Dollars per troy ounce. **Type of Price:** spot. **Time Period Covered:** latest day.

GOLD: FABRICATED FORM

Source: *American Metal Market.* **Price Frequency:** daily. **Units of Measure:** Dollars per troy ounce. **Time Period Covered:** latest day.

GOLD: FABRICATED PRODUCTS

Source: *Asian Wall Street Journal.* **Price Frequency:** daily. **Effective Market(s):** New York. **Units of Measure:** Dollars per troy ounce. **Type of Price:** cash. **Time Period Covered:** latest 2 days.

Source: *Wall Street Journal.* **Price Frequency:** daily. **Units of Measure:** Dollars per troy ounce. **Time Period Covered:** latest day, day ago, year ago.

GOLD: FUTURES

Source: *Agriculture.* **Price Frequency:** weekly. **Effective Market(s):** Chicago. **Units of Measure:** Dollars per ounce. **Type of Price:** futures. **Time Period Covered:** latest week, week ago.

Source: *Asian Wall Street Journal.* **Price Frequency:** daily. **Effective Market(s):** Hong Kong, New York. **Units of Measure:** Dollars per troy ounce. **Type of Price:** futures. **Time Period Covered:** latest day.

Source: *Asian Wall Street Journal.* **Price Frequency:** daily. **Effective Market(s):** Chicago. **Units of Measure:** Dollars per troy ounce. **Type of Price:** futures. **Time Period Covered:** latest day.

Source: *Barron's.* **Price Frequency:** weekly. **Effective Market(s):** New York. **Units of Measure:** Dollars per troy ounce. **Type of Price:** futures. **Time Period Covered:** latest week.

Source: *Financial Times.* **Price Frequency:** daily. **Effective Market(s):** New York. **Units of Measure:** Dollars per troy ounce. **Type of Price:** futures. **Time Period Covered:** latest day.

Source: *Investor's Daily.* **Price Frequency:** daily. **Effective Market(s):** New York. **Units of Measure:** Dollars per troy ounce. **Type of Price:** futures. **Time Period Covered:** latest day.

Source: *Japan Economic Journal.* **Price Frequency:** weekly. **Effective Market(s):** Tokyo. **Units of Measure:** Japanese yen per gram. **Type of Price:** futures. **Time Period Covered:** latest week.

Source: *Los Angeles Times.* **Price Frequency:** daily. **Effective Market(s):** New York. **Units of Measure:** Dollars per troy ounce. **Type of Price:** futures. **Time Period Covered:** latest day.

Source: *New York Times.* **Price Frequency:** daily. **Effective Market(s):** New York. **Units of Measure:** Dollars per troy ounce. **Type of Price:** futures. **Time Period Covered:** latest day.

Source: *Northern Miner.* **Price Frequency:** daily. **Effective Market(s):** New York. **Units of Measure:** Dollars per ounce. **Type of Price:** futures. **Time Period Covered:** selected day.

Source: *Wall Street Journal.* **Price Frequency:** daily. **Effective Market(s):** Chicago, New York. **Units of Measure:** Dollars per troy ounce. **Type of Price:** futures. **Time Period Covered:** latest day.

GOLD: FUTURES, DECEMBER

Source: *Commodity Year Book.* **Price Frequency:** monthly. **Effective Market(s):** New York. **Units of Measure:** Dollars per ounce. **Type of Price:** futures. **Time Period Covered:** latest 4 years.

GOLD: KILO, FUTURES

Source: *Investor's Daily.* **Price Frequency:** daily. **Effective Market(s):** Chicago. **Units of Measure:** Dollars per troy ounce. **Type of Price:** futures. **Time Period Covered:** latest day.

Source: *Wall Street Journal.* **Price Frequency:** daily. **Effective Market(s):** Chicago. **Units of Measure:** Dollars per troy ounce. **Type of Price:** futures. **Time Period Covered:** latest day.

GOLD: LONDON FIXING

Source: *Wall Street Journal.* **Price Frequency:** daily. **Units of Measure:** Dollars per troy ounce. **Time Period Covered:** latest day, day ago, year ago.

GOLD: MONTAGU'S

Source: *Standard & Poor's Statistical Service Current Statistics.* **Price Frequency:** monthly, annually. **Effective Market(s):** London. **Units of Measure:** Dollars per troy ounce. **Type of Price:** closing. **Time Period Covered:** latest 3 years.

GOLD: UNFABRICATED

Source: *American Metal Market.* **Price Frequency:** daily. **Units of Measure:** Dollars per troy ounce. **Type of Price:** base. **Time Period Covered:** latest day.

GOLD: UNITED KINGDOM

Source: *International Financial Statistics.* **Price Frequency:** monthly, quarterly, annually. **Effective Market(s):** London. **Units of Measure:** Dollars per fine ounce, index. **Type of Price:** market price, price index. **Time Period Covered:** latest 5 months, latest 5 quarters, latest 5 years.

Source: *International Financial Statistics Yearbook.* **Price Frequency:** annually. **Effective Market(s):** London. **Units of Measure:** Dollars per fine ounce. **Type of Price:** wholesale. **Time Period Covered:** latest 30 years.

GOLD BULLION

Source: *E&MJ.* **Price Frequency:** monthly. **Units of Measure:** Dollars per troy ounce. **Time Period Covered:** latest month.

Source: *The Times.* **Price Frequency:** daily. **Effective Market(s):** London. **Units of Measure:** Dollars per troy ounce. **Time Period Covered:** latest day.

GOLD BULLION: INDUSTRIAL

Source: *Asian Wall Street Journal.* **Price Frequency:** daily. **Effective Market(s):** New York. **Units of Measure:** Dollars per troy ounce. **Type of Price:** cash. **Time Period Covered:** latest 2 days.

Source: *Wall Street Journal.* **Price Frequency:** daily. **Units of Measure:** Dollars per troy ounce. **Time Period Covered:** latest day, day ago, year ago.

GOLD COINS

see Coins: Gold.

GOLDENSEAL ROOT: WHOLE

Source: *Journal of Commerce and Commercial.* **Price Frequency:** weekly in Monday issue. **Units of Measure:** Dollars per lb. **Type of Price:** spot. **Time Period Covered:** latest week.

GRAIN

see specific types of grain, e.g., Sorghum.

GRAIN DRILL

Source: *Agricultural Prices Annual Summary.* **Price Frequency:** semiannually. **Effective Market(s):** United States. **Units of Measure:** Dollars each. **Type of Price:** average paid by farmer. **Time Period Covered:** latest 6 years.

GRAIN DRILL: MOST COMMON SPACING

Source: *Agricultural Prices.* **Price Frequency:** semiannually. **Effective Market(s):** United States. **Units of Measure:** Dollars each. **Type of Price:** paid by farmer. **Time Period Covered:** latest year.

GRAIN SCREENINGS: GROUND

Source: *Feedstuffs.* **Price Frequency:** weekly. **Effective Market(s):** Buffalo, Ft. Worth, Kansas City. **Units of Measure:** Dollars per bulk ton. **Time Period Covered:** latest week.

Source: *Feedstuffs.* **Price Frequency:** weekly. **Effective Market(s):** Buffalo, Ft. Worth, Kansas City. **Units of Measure:** Dollars per ton. **Time Period Covered:** latest week.

GRAINS: FEED

Source: *Illinois Farm Report.* **Price Frequency:** monthly. **Effective Market(s):** Illinois. **Units of Measure:** index . **Type of Price:** index of prices received by farmers. **Time Period Covered:** latest 2 months, year ago.

GRAINS: FOOD

Source: *Illinois Farm Report.* **Price Frequency:** monthly. **Effective Market(s):** Illinois. **Units of Measure:** index . **Type of Price:** index of prices received by farmers. **Time Period Covered:** latest 2 months, year ago.

GRAPEFRUIT

Source: *Agricultural Outlook.* **Price Frequency:** monthly, annually. **Effective Market(s):** United States. **Units of Measure:** Dollars per box. **Type of Price:** price received by farmers. **Time Period Covered:** monthly latest 6 months, annually latest 3 years.

Source: *Agricultural Outlook.* **Price Frequency:** monthly. **Units of Measure:** Dollars per box. **Time Period Covered:** latest year.

Source: *Agricultural Prices.* **Price Frequency:** monthly. **Effective Market(s):** United States. **Units of Measure:** Dollars per box. **Type of Price:** received by farmer. **Time Period Covered:** latest 2 months, year ago.

Source: *Agricultural Prices Annual Summary.* **Price Frequency:** annually. **Effective Market(s):** Arizona, California, Florida, Texas, United States. **Units of Measure:** Dollars per box. **Type of Price:** average received by grower. **Time Period Covered:** latest 2 years.

Source: *Agricultural Prices Annual Summary.* **Price Frequency:** monthly. **Effective Market(s):** Arizona, California, Florida, Texas. **Units of Measure:** Dollars per box. **Type of Price:** average received by grower. **Time Period Covered:** latest 2 years.

Source: *California Farmer.* **Price Frequency:** semimonthly. **Effective Market(s):** Southern District (CA), Central District (CA), Coachella Valley(CA). **Units of Measure:** Dollars per 40 lb. carton. **Time Period Covered:** latest week, month ago, year ago.

Source: *FAO Quarterly Bulletin of Statistics.* **Price Frequency:** monthly, annually. **Effective Market(s):** United Kingdom. **Units of Measure:** British pounds per 100 kilograms, dollars per metric ton. **Type of Price:** wholesale. **Time Period Covered:** latest 3 years.

Source: *Fruit and Tree Nuts Situation and Outlook Yearbook.* **Price Frequency:** annually. **Effective Market(s):** United States. **Units of Measure:** Dollars per lb. **Type of Price:** retail. **Time Period Covered:** latest 9 years.

Source: *New Zealand Farmer.* **Price Frequency:** weekly, seasonally. **Effective Market(s):** New Zealand. **Units of Measure:** New Zealand dollars per unit. **Time Period Covered:** latest week.

Source: *The Packer.* **Price Frequency:** weekly, seasonally. **Effective Market(s):** varies. **Units of Measure:** Dollars per carton. **Type of Price:** price received by farmer. **Time Period Covered:** latest week.

GRAPEFRUIT: CALIFORNIA

Source: *Japan Economic Journal.* **Price Frequency:** weekly. **Effective Market(s):** Japan. **Units of Measure:** Japanese yen per carton. **Type of Price:** wholesale. **Time Period Covered:** latest 2 weeks.

GRAPEFRUIT: COLORED, SEEDLESS

Source: *Agricultural Prices Annual Summary.* **Price Frequency:** annually. **Effective Market(s):** Interior Florida, Indian River (FL). **Units of Measure:** Dollars per box. **Type of Price:** average received by grower. **Time Period Covered:** latest 2 years.

Source: *Agricultural Prices Annual Summary.* **Price Frequency:** monthly. **Effective Market(s):** Florida. **Units of Measure:** Dollars per box. **Type of Price:** average received by grower. **Time Period Covered:** latest 2 years.

GRAPEFRUIT: DESERT VALLEY

Source: *Agricultural Prices Annual Summary.* **Price Frequency:** annually. **Effective Market(s):** California. **Units of Measure:** Dollars per box. **Type of Price:** average received by grower. **Time Period Covered:** latest 2 years.

Source: *Agricultural Prices Annual Summary.* **Price Frequency:** monthly. **Effective Market(s):** California. **Units of Measure:** Dollars per box. **Type of Price:** average received by grower. **Time Period Covered:** latest 2 years.

GRAPEFRUIT: FRESH

Source: *Agricultural Prices.* **Price Frequency:** monthly. **Effective Market(s):** Arizona, California, Florida, Texas, United States. **Units of Measure:** Dollars per box. **Type of Price:** received by farmer. **Time Period Covered:** latest month.

GRAPEFRUIT: ISRAELI

Source: *FAO Quarterly Bulletin of Statistics.* **Price Frequency:** monthly, annually, seasonally. **Effective Market(s):** West Germany. **Units of Measure:** West German marks per 100 kilograms, dollars per metric ton. **Type of Price:** wholesale. **Time Period Covered:** latest 3 years.

GRAPEFRUIT: OTHER THAN SEEDLESS

Source: *Agricultural Prices Annual Summary.* **Price Frequency:** monthly. **Effective Market(s):** Florida. **Units of Measure:** Dollars per box. **Type of Price:** average received by grower. **Time Period Covered:** latest 2 years.

GRAPEFRUIT: RED

Source: *Fresh Fruit and Vegetable Prices.* **Price Frequency:** monthly, seasonally. **Effective Market(s):** South, Central/Coachella Valley (CA,AZ). **Units of Measure:** Dollars per carton. **Type of Price:** average price at shipping point. **Time Period Covered:** latest year.

Source: *Lancaster Farming.* **Price Frequency:** weekly, seasonally. **Effective Market(s):** Pennsylvania. **Units of Measure:** Dollars per carton. **Type of Price:** market. **Time Period Covered:** latest week.

GRAPEFRUIT: RED, CALIFORNIA

Source: *Fresh Fruit and Vegetable Prices.* **Price Frequency:** monthly, seasonally. **Effective Market(s):** Chicago, New York City. **Units of Measure:** Dollars per carton. **Type of Price:** average wholesale price. **Time Period Covered:** latest year.

GRAPEFRUIT: RED, FLORIDA INCLUDING INDIAN RIVER DISTRICT

Source: *Fresh Fruit and Vegetable Prices.* **Price Frequency:** monthly, seasonally. **Effective Market(s):** Chicago, New York City. **Units of Measure:** Dollars per carton. **Type of Price:** average wholesale price. **Time Period Covered:** latest year.

GRAPEFRUIT: RUBY RED

Source: *Fresh Fruit and Vegetable Prices.* **Price Frequency:** monthly, seasonally. **Effective Market(s):** Lower Rio Grande Valley (TX). **Units of Measure:** Dollars per carton. **Type of Price:** average price at shipping point. **Time Period Covered:** latest year.

GRAPEFRUIT: SEEDLESS

Source: *Agricultural Prices Annual Summary.* **Price Frequency:** annually. **Effective Market(s):** Florida. **Units of Measure:** Dollars per box. **Type of Price:** average received by grower. **Time Period Covered:** latest 2 years.

GRAPEFRUIT: WHITE

Source: *Lancaster Farming.* **Price Frequency:** weekly, seasonally. **Effective Market(s):** Pennsylvania. **Units of Measure:** Dollars per carton. **Type of Price:** market. **Time Period Covered:** latest week.

GRAPEFRUIT: WHITE, CALIFORNIA

Source: *Fresh Fruit and Vegetable Prices.* **Price Frequency:** monthly, seasonally. **Effective Market(s):** Chicago, New York City. **Units of Measure:** Dollars per carton. **Type of Price:** average wholesale price. **Time Period Covered:** latest year.

GRAPEFRUIT: WHITE, FLORIDA INCLUDING INDIAN RIVER DISTRICT

Source: *Fresh Fruit and Vegetable Prices.* **Price Frequency:** monthly, seasonally. **Effective Market(s):** Chicago, New York City. **Units of Measure:** Dollars per carton. **Type of Price:** average wholesale price. **Time Period Covered:** latest year.

GRAPEFRUIT: WHITE, SEEDLESS

Source: *Agricultural Prices Annual Summary.* **Price Frequency:** annually. **Effective Market(s):** Florida. **Units of Measure:** Dollars per box. **Type of Price:** average received by grower. **Time Period Covered:** latest 2 years.

Source: *Agricultural Prices Annual Summary.* **Price Frequency:** annually. **Effective Market(s):** Interior Florida, Indian River (FL). **Units of Measure:** Dollars per box. **Type of Price:** average received by grower. **Time Period Covered:** latest 2 years.

Source: *Agricultural Prices Annual Summary.* **Price Frequency:** monthly. **Effective Market(s):** Florida. **Units of Measure:** Dollars per box. **Type of Price:** average received by grower. **Time Period Covered:** latest 2 years.

GRAPEFRUIT OIL

Source: *Journal of Commerce and Commercial.* **Price Frequency:** weekly in Tuesday issue. **Units of Measure:** Dollars per lb. **Type of Price:** spot. **Time Period Covered:** latest week.

Source: *U. S. Essential Oil Trade.* **Price Frequency:** annually. **Effective Market(s):** United States. **Units of Measure:** Dollars per kilogram. **Type of Price:** import value. **Time Period Covered:** latest 3 years.

GRAPEFRUIT OIL: CALIFORNIA

Source: *Chemical Marketing Reporter.* **Price Frequency:** weekly. **Effective Market(s):** New York. **Units of Measure:** Dollars per lb. **Type of Price:** spot. **Time Period Covered:** latest week.

GRAPEFRUIT OIL: FLORIDA

Source: *Chemical Marketing Reporter.* **Price Frequency:** weekly. **Effective Market(s):** New York. **Units of Measure:** Dollars per lb. **Type of Price:** spot. **Time Period Covered:** latest week.

GRAPEFRUIT OIL: ISRAELI

Source: *Chemical Marketing Reporter.* **Price Frequency:** weekly. **Effective Market(s):** New York. **Units of Measure:** Dollars per lb. **Type of Price:** spot. **Time Period Covered:** latest week.

GRAPEFRUIT SECTIONS: FROZEN

Source: *HRI-Buyers Guide.* **Price Frequency:** weekly. **Effective Market(s):** Northeastern area. **Units of Measure:** Dollars per case. **Time Period Covered:** latest week.

GRAPES

Source: *Agricultural Prices Annual Summary.* **Price Frequency:** annually. **Effective Market(s):** 12 domestic markets. **Units of Measure:** Dollars per ton. **Type of Price:** average price received by farmer. **Time Period Covered:** latest 3 years, for US latest 6 years.

GRAPES: ALL

Source: *Fruit and Tree Nuts Situation and Outlook Yearbook.* **Price Frequency:** annually. **Effective Market(s):** United States. **Units of Measure:** Dollars per short ton. **Type of Price:** grower. **Time Period Covered:** latest 20 years.

GRAPES: ALMERIA, CHILEAN

Source: *Fresh Fruit and Vegetable Prices.* **Price Frequency:** monthly, seasonally. **Effective Market(s):** New York City/Philadelphia. **Units of Measure:** Dollars per lug. **Type of Price:** dock price. **Time Period Covered:** latest year.

GRAPES: BLACK SEEDLESS, CHILEAN

Source: *Fresh Fruit and Vegetable Prices.* **Price Frequency:** monthly, seasonally. **Effective Market(s):** New York City/Philadelphia. **Units of Measure:** Dollars per lug. **Type of Price:** dock price . **Time Period Covered:** latest year.

GRAPES: CALMERIAS, CHILEAN

Source: *Fresh Fruit and Vegetable Prices.* **Price Frequency:** monthly, seasonally. **Effective Market(s):** New York City/Philadelphia. **Units of Measure:** Dollars per lug. **Type of Price:** dock price. **Time Period Covered:** latest year.

GRAPES: CANNED

Source: *Fruit and Tree Nuts Situation and Outlook Yearbook.* **Price Frequency:** annually. **Effective Market(s):** United States. **Units of Measure:** Dollars per ton. **Type of Price:** grower. **Time Period Covered:** latest 20 years.

GRAPES: CARDINAL, CHILEAN

Source: *Fresh Fruit and Vegetable Prices.* **Price Frequency:** monthly, seasonally. **Effective Market(s):** New York City/Philadelphia. **Units of Measure:** Dollars per lug. **Type of Price:** dock price. **Time Period Covered:** latest year.

GRAPES: DRIED

Source: *Fruit and Tree Nuts Situation and Outlook Yearbook.* **Price Frequency:** annually. **Effective Market(s):** United States. **Units of Measure:** Dollars per ton. **Type of Price:** grower. **Time Period Covered:** latest 20 years.

GRAPES: EMPERORS

Source: *Fresh Fruit and Vegetable Prices.* **Price Frequency:** monthly, seasonally. **Effective Market(s):** Central San Joaquin Valley (CA), Kern District (CA). **Units of Measure:** Dollars per lug. **Type of Price:** average price at shipping point. **Time Period Covered:** latest year.

GRAPES: EMPERORS, CALIFORNIA

Source: *Fresh Fruit and Vegetable Prices.* **Price Frequency:** monthly, seasonally. **Effective Market(s):** Chicago, New York City. **Units of Measure:** Dollars per lug. **Type of Price:** average wholesale price. **Time Period Covered:** latest year.

GRAPES: EMPERORS, CHILEAN

Source: *Fresh Fruit and Vegetable Prices.* **Price Frequency:** monthly, seasonally. **Effective Market(s):** Chicago, New York City. **Units of Measure:** Dollars per lug. **Type of Price:** average wholesale price. **Time Period Covered:** latest year.

Source: *Fresh Fruit and Vegetable Prices.* **Price Frequency:** monthly, seasonally. **Effective Market(s):** New York City/Philadelphia. **Units of Measure:** Dollars per lug. **Type of Price:** dock price. **Time Period Covered:** latest year.

GRAPES: EXOTIC

Source: *Fresh Fruit and Vegetable Prices.* **Price Frequency:** monthly, seasonally. **Effective Market(s):** Central San Joaquin Valley (CA), Kern District (VA). **Units of Measure:** Dollars per lug. **Type of Price:** average price at shipping point. **Time Period Covered:** latest year.

Source: *Lancaster Farming.* **Price Frequency:** weekly, seasonally. **Effective Market(s):** Pennsylvania. **Units of Measure:** Dollars per lug. **Type of Price:** market. **Time Period Covered:** latest week.

GRAPES: EXOTIC, CALIFORNIA

Source: *Fresh Fruit and Vegetable Prices.* **Price Frequency:** monthly, seasonally. **Effective Market(s):** Chicago. **Units of Measure:** Dollars per lug. **Type of Price:** average wholesale price. **Time Period Covered:** latest year.

GRAPES: FLAME SEEDLESS

Source: *Fresh Fruit and Vegetable Prices.* **Price Frequency:** monthly, seasonally. **Effective Market(s):** Arizona, Coachella Valley (CA), Central San Joaquin Valley (CA), Kern District (CA). **Units of Measure:** Dollars per lug. **Type of Price:** average price at shipping point. **Time Period Covered:** latest year.

Source: *Lancaster Farming.* **Price Frequency:** weekly, seasonally. **Effective Market(s):** Pennsylvania. **Units of Measure:** Dollars per lug. **Type of Price:** market. **Time Period Covered:** latest week.

GRAPES: FLAME SEEDLESS, CALIFORNIA

Source: *Fresh Fruit and Vegetable Prices.* **Price Frequency:** monthly, seasonally. **Effective Market(s):** Chicago, New York City. **Units of Measure:** Dollars per lug. **Type of Price:** average wholesale price. **Time Period Covered:** latest year.

GRAPES: FLAME SEEDLESS, CHILEAN

Source: *Fresh Fruit and Vegetable Prices.* **Price Frequency:** monthly, seasonally. **Effective Market(s):** New York City/Philadelphia. **Units of Measure:** Dollars per lug. **Type of Price:** dock price. **Time Period Covered:** latest year.

Source: *Fresh Fruit and Vegetable Prices.* **Price Frequency:** monthly, seasonally. **Effective Market(s):** Chicago, New York City. **Units of Measure:** Dollars per lug. **Type of Price:** average wholesale price. **Time Period Covered:** latest year.

GRAPES: FLAME SEEDLESS, MEXICO

Source: *Fresh Fruit and Vegetable Prices.* **Price Frequency:** monthly, seasonally. **Effective Market(s):** Nogales (AZ). **Units of Measure:** Dollars per lug. **Type of Price:** price paid at point of entry. **Time Period Covered:** latest year.

GRAPES: FRESH

Source: *Fruit and Tree Nuts Situation and Outlook Yearbook.* **Price Frequency:** annually. **Effective Market(s):** United States. **Units of Measure:** Dollars per short ton. **Type of Price:** grower. **Time Period Covered:** latest 20 years.

GRAPES: JUICE

Source: *Fruit and Tree Nuts Situation and Outlook Yearbook.* **Price Frequency:** annually. **Effective Market(s):** United States. **Units of Measure:** Dollars per ton. **Type of Price:** grower. **Time Period Covered:** latest 20 years.

GRAPES: PERLETTE

Source: *Fresh Fruit and Vegetable Prices.* **Price Frequency:** monthly, seasonally. **Effective Market(s):** Arizona, Coachella Valley (CA). **Units of Measure:** Dollars per lug. **Type of Price:** average price at shipping point. **Time Period Covered:** latest year.

GRAPES: PERLETTE, CALIFORNIA

Source: *Fresh Fruit and Vegetable Prices.* **Price Frequency:** monthly, seasonally. **Effective Market(s):** Chicago. **Units of Measure:** Dollars per lug. **Type of Price:** average wholesale price. **Time Period Covered:** latest year.

GRAPES: PERLETTE, CHILEAN

Source: *Fresh Fruit and Vegetable Prices.* **Price Frequency:** monthly, seasonally. **Effective Market(s):** Chicago, New York City. **Units of Measure:** Dollars per lug. **Type of Price:** average wholesale price. **Time Period Covered:** latest year.

Source: *Fresh Fruit and Vegetable Price.* **Price Frequency:** monthly, seasonally. **Effective Market(s):** New York City/Philadelphia. **Units of Measure:** Dollars per lug. **Type of Price:** dock price. **Time Period Covered:** latest year.

GRAPES: PERLETTE, MEXICO

Source: *Fresh Fruit and Vegetable Prices.* **Price Frequency:** monthly, seasonally. **Effective Market(s):** Nogales (AZ). **Units of Measure:** Dollars per lug. **Type of Price:** price paid at point of entry. **Time Period Covered:** latest year.

GRAPES: PROCESSING

Source: *Fruit and Tree Nuts Situation and Outlook Yearbook.* **Price Frequency:** annually. **Effective Market(s):** United States. **Units of Measure:** Dollars per short ton. **Type of Price:** grower. **Time Period Covered:** latest 20 years.

GRAPES: RAISIN DRIED

Source: *Fruit and Tree Nuts Situation and Outlook Yearbook.* **Price Frequency:** annually. **Effective Market(s):** California. **Units of Measure:** Dollars per ton. **Type of Price:** grower. **Time Period Covered:** latest 20 years.

GRAPES: RAISIN NOT DRIED

Source: *Fruit and Tree Nuts Situation and Outlook Yearbook.* **Price Frequency:** annually. **Effective Market(s):** California. **Units of Measure:** Dollars per ton. **Type of Price:** grower. **Time Period Covered:** latest 20 years.

GRAPES: RAISIN TYPE

Source: *Agricultural Prices Annual Summary.* **Price Frequency:** annually. **Effective Market(s):** California, Hawaii. **Units of Measure:** Dollars per ton. **Type of Price:** average price received by farmer. **Time Period Covered:** latest 6 years.

Source: *Fruit and Tree Nuts Situation and Outlook Yearbook.* **Price Frequency:** annually. **Effective Market(s):** California. **Units of Measure:** Dollars per ton. **Type of Price:** grower. **Time Period Covered:** latest 20 years.

GRAPES: RED SEEDLESS, CHILEAN

Source: *Fresh Fruit and Vegetable Prices.* **Price Frequency:** monthly, seasonally. **Effective Market(s):** New York City/Philadelphia. **Units of Measure:** Dollars per lug. **Type of Price:** dock price. **Time Period Covered:** latest year.

GRAPES: RIBIERS

Source: *Fresh Fruit and Vegetable Prices.* **Price Frequency:** monthly, seasonally. **Effective Market(s):** Central San Joaquin Valley (CA), Kern District (CA). **Units of Measure:** Dollars per lug. **Type of Price:** average price at shipping point. **Time Period Covered:** latest year.

GRAPES: RIBIERS, CALIFORNIA

Source: *Fresh Fruit and Vegetable Prices.* **Price Frequency:** monthly, seasonally. **Effective Market(s):** Chicago, New York City. **Units of Measure:** Dollars per lug. **Type of Price:** average wholesale price. **Time Period Covered:** latest year.

GRAPES: RIBIERS, CHILEAN

Source: *Fresh Fruit and Vegetable Prices.* **Price Frequency:** monthly, seasonally. **Effective Market(s):** Chicago, New York City. **Units of Measure:** Dollars per lug. **Type of Price:** average wholesale price. **Time Period Covered:** latest year.

Source: *Fresh Fruit and Vegetable Prices.* **Price Frequency:** monthly, seasonally. **Effective Market(s):** New York City/Philadelphia. **Units of Measure:** Dollars per lug. **Type of Price:** dock price. **Time Period Covered:** latest year.

GRAPES: RUBY SEEDLESS

Source: *Fresh Fruit and Vegetable Prices.* **Price Frequency:** monthly, seasonally. **Effective Market(s):** Central San Joaquin Valley (CA). **Units of Measure:** Dollars per lug. **Type of Price:** average price at shipping point. **Time Period Covered:** latest year.

GRAPES: RUBY SEEDLESS, CHILEAN

Source: *Fresh Fruit and Vegetable Prices.* **Price Frequency:** monthly, seasonally. **Effective Market(s):** New York City/Philadelphia. **Units of Measure:** Dollars per lug. **Type of Price:** dock price. **Time Period Covered:** latest year.

GRAPES: TABLE

Source: *Agricultural Prices Annual Summary.* **Price Frequency:** annually. **Effective Market(s):** California, Hawaii. **Units of Measure:** Dollars per ton. **Type of Price:** average price received by farmer. **Time Period Covered:** latest 6 years.

GRAPES: TABLE, CALMERIA

Source: *California Farmer.* **Price Frequency:** semimonthly, seasonally. **Effective Market(s):** Kern (CA). **Units of Measure:** Dollars per 22 lb. lug. **Time Period Covered:** latest week, month ago, year ago.

GRAPES: TABLE, EMPEROR

Source: *California Farmer.* **Price Frequency:** semimonthly, seasonally. **Effective Market(s):** Kern (CA), Central San Joaquin Valley. **Units of Measure:** Dollars per 22 lb. lug. **Time Period Covered:** latest week, month ago, year ago.

GRAPES: TABLE, EXOTIC

Source: *California Farmer.* **Price Frequency:** semimonthly, seasonally. **Effective Market(s):** Kern (CA). **Units of Measure:** Dollars per 22 lb. lug. **Time Period Covered:** latest week, month ago, year ago.

Source: *The Packer.* **Price Frequency:** weekly, seasonally. **Effective Market(s):** varies. **Units of Measure:** Dollars per lug. **Type of Price:** price received by farmer. **Time Period Covered:** latest week.

GRAPES: TABLE, FLAME SEEDLESS

Source: *California Farmer.* **Price Frequency:** semimonthly, seasonally. **Effective Market(s):** Central San Joaquin Valley. **Units of Measure:** Dollars per 22 lb. lug. **Time Period Covered:** latest week, month ago, year ago.

Source: *The Packer.* **Price Frequency:** weekly, seasonally. **Effective Market(s):** varies. **Units of Measure:** Dollars per lug. **Type of Price:** price received by farmer. **Time Period Covered:** latest week.

GRAPES: TABLE, PERLETTE

Source: *California Farmer.* **Price Frequency:** semimonthly, seasonally. **Effective Market(s):** Coachella Valley (CA). **Units of Measure:** Dollars per 22 lb. lug. **Time Period Covered:** latest week, month ago, year ago.

GRAPES: TABLE, RIBIER

Source: *California Farmer.* **Price Frequency:** semimonthly, seasonally. **Effective Market(s):** Kern (CA), Central San Joaquin Valley. **Units of Measure:** Dollars per 22 lb. lug. **Time Period Covered:** latest week, month ago, year ago.

GRAPES: TABLE, THOMPSON SEEDLESS

Source: *California Farmer.* **Price Frequency:** semimonthly, seasonally. **Effective Market(s):** Central San Joaquin Valley, Kern (CA). **Units of Measure:** Dollars per 22 lb. lug. **Time Period Covered:** latest week, month ago, year ago.

Source: *The Packer.* **Price Frequency:** weekly, seasonally. **Effective Market(s):** varies. **Units of Measure:** Dollars per lug. **Type of Price:** price received by farmer. **Time Period Covered:** latest week.

GRAPES: TABLE, TOKAY

Source: *California Farmer.* **Price Frequency:** semimonthly, seasonally. **Effective Market(s):** Lodi (CA). **Units of Measure:** Dollars per 22 lb. lug. **Time Period Covered:** latest week, month ago, year ago.

GRAPES: THOMPSON SEEDLESS

Source: *Fresh Fruit and Vegetable Prices.* **Price Frequency:** monthly, seasonally. **Effective Market(s):** Arizona, Coachella Valley (CA), Central San Joaquin Valley (CA), Kern District (CA). **Units of Measure:** Dollars per lug. **Type of Price:** average price at shipping point. **Time Period Covered:** latest year.

Source: *Fruit and Tree Nuts Situation and Outlook Yearbook.* **Price Frequency:** annually. **Effective Market(s):** United States. **Units of Measure:** Dollars per lb. **Type of Price:** retail. **Time Period Covered:** latest 9 years.

Source: *Lancaster Farming.* **Price Frequency:** weekly, seasonally. **Effective Market(s):** Pennsylvania. **Units of Measure:** Dollars per lug. **Type of Price:** market. **Time Period Covered:** latest week.

GRAPES: THOMPSON SEEDLESS, CALIFORNIA

Source: *Fresh Fruit and Vegetable Prices.* **Price Frequency:** monthly, seasonally. **Effective Market(s):** Chicago, New York City. **Units of Measure:** Dollars per lug. **Type of Price:** average wholesale price. **Time Period Covered:** latest year.

GRAPES: THOMPSON SEEDLESS, CHILEAN

Source: *Fresh Fruit and Vegetable Prices.* **Price Frequency:** monthly, seasonally. **Effective Market(s):** New York City/Philadelphia. **Units of Measure:** Dollars per lug. **Type of Price:** dock price. **Time Period Covered:** latest year.

Source: *Fresh Fruit and Vegetable Prices.* **Price Frequency:** monthly, seasonally. **Effective Market(s):** Chicago, New York City. **Units of Measure:** Dollars per lug. **Type of Price:** average wholesale price. **Time Period Covered:** latest year.

GRAPES: THOMPSON SEEDLESS, MEXICO

Source: *Fresh Fruit and Vegetable Prices.* **Price Frequency:** monthly, seasonally. **Effective Market(s):** Nogales (AZ). **Units of Measure:** Dollars per lug. **Type of Price:** price paid at point of entry. **Time Period Covered:** latest year.

GRAPES: TOKAY

Source: *Fresh Fruit and Vegetable Prices.* **Price Frequency:** monthly, seasonally. **Effective Market(s):** Lodi District (CA). **Units of Measure:** Dollars per lug. **Type of Price:** average price at shipping point. **Time Period Covered:** latest year.

GRAPES: WINE

Source: *Agricultural Prices Annual Summary.* **Price Frequency:** annually. **Effective Market(s):** California, Hawaii. **Units of Measure:** Dollars per ton. **Type of Price:** average price received by farmer. **Time Period Covered:** latest 6 years.

Source: *Fruit and Tree Nuts Situation and Outlook Yearbook.* **Price Frequency:** annually. **Effective Market(s):** California, United States. **Units of Measure:** Dollars per ton. **Type of Price:** grower. **Time Period Covered:** latest 20 years.

GRAPHIDOX

Source: *American Metal Market.* **Price Frequency:** weekly. **Units of Measure:** cents per lb. **Type of Price:** producer. **Time Period Covered:** latest week.

GRAPHITE: CRYSTALLINE, 88-90%, POWDERED

Source: *Chemical Marketing Reporter.* **Price Frequency:** weekly. **Effective Market(s):** New York. **Units of Measure:** Dollars per lb. **Type of Price:** spot. **Time Period Covered:** latest week.

GRAPHITE: CRYSTALLINE, 90-92%, POWDERED

Source: *Chemical Marketing Reporter.* **Price Frequency:** weekly. **Effective Market(s):** New York. **Units of Measure:** Dollars per lb. **Type of Price:** spot. **Time Period Covered:** latest week.

GRAPHITE: CRYSTALLINE, 95-96%, POWDERED

Source: *Chemical Marketing Reporter.* **Price Frequency:** weekly. **Effective Market(s):** New York. **Units of Measure:** Dollars per lb. **Type of Price:** spot. **Time Period Covered:** latest week.

GRAPHITE: CRYSTALLINE, LARGE FLAKE

Source: *Industrial Minerals.* **Price Frequency:** monthly. **Effective Market(s):** United Kingdom port. **Units of Measure:** Dollars per metric tonne. **Type of Price:** producer & dealer. **Time Period Covered:** latest month.

GRAPHITE: CRYSTALLINE, LUMP

Source: *Industrial Minerals.* **Price Frequency:** monthly. **Effective Market(s):** United Kingdom port. **Units of Measure:** Dollars per metric tonne. **Type of Price:** producer & dealer. **Time Period Covered:** latest month.

GRAPHITE: CRYSTALLINE, MEDIUM FLAKE

Source: *Industrial Minerals.* **Price Frequency:** monthly. **Effective Market(s):** United Kingdom port. **Units of Measure:** Dollars per metric tonne. **Type of Price:** producer & dealer. **Time Period Covered:** latest month.

GRAPHITE: CRYSTALLINE, SMALL FLAKE

Source: *Industrial Minerals.* **Price Frequency:** monthly. **Effective Market(s):** United Kingdom port. **Units of Measure:** Dollars per metric tonne. **Type of Price:** producer & dealer. **Time Period Covered:** latest month.

GRAPHITE: FLAKE, NO. 1, 90-95%

Source: *Chemical Marketing Reporter.* **Price Frequency:** weekly. **Effective Market(s):** New York. **Units of Measure:** Dollars per lb. **Type of Price:** spot. **Time Period Covered:** latest week.

GRAPHITE: FLAKE, NO. 2, 90-95%

Source: *Chemical Marketing Reporter.* **Price Frequency:** weekly. **Effective Market(s):** New York. **Units of Measure:** Dollars per lb. **Type of Price:** spot. **Time Period Covered:** latest week.

GRAPHITE: FLAKE, NO. 3, 90-95%

Source: *Chemical Marketing Reporter.* **Price Frequency:** weekly. **Effective Market(s):** New York. **Units of Measure:** Dollars per lb. **Type of Price:** spot. **Time Period Covered:** latest week.

GRAPHITE POWDER

Source: *Industrial Minerals.* **Price Frequency:** monthly. **Effective Market(s):** United Kingdom port. **Units of Measure:** Dollars per metric tonne. **Type of Price:** producer & dealer. **Time Period Covered:** latest month.

GRAPHITE POWDER: AMORPHOUS

Source: *Chemical Marketing Reporter.* **Price Frequency:** weekly. **Effective Market(s):** New York. **Units of Measure:** Dollars per lb. **Type of Price:** spot. **Time Period Covered:** latest week.

Source: *Industrial Minerals.* **Price Frequency:** monthly. **Effective Market(s):** United Kingdom port. **Units of Measure:** Dollars per metric tonne. **Type of Price:** producer & dealer. **Time Period Covered:** latest month.

GRAPHITE POWDER: AMORPHOUS, CRYSTALLINE, 97% AND UP

Source: *Chemical Marketing Reporter.* **Price Frequency:** weekly. **Effective Market(s):** New York. **Units of Measure:** Dollars per lb. **Type of Price:** spot. **Time Period Covered:** latest week.

GRAPPA

Source: *Illinois Beverage Journal.* **Price Frequency:** monthly. **Effective Market(s):** Illinois. **Units of Measure:** Dollars per case. **Type of Price:** wholesale by brand. **Time Period Covered:** latest month.

GRAVEL: 3/4" DOWN TO 3/8"

Source: *ENR.* **Price Frequency:** monthly in first issue of month. **Effective Market(s):** 15 domestic markets, Montreal, Toronto. **Units of Measure:** Dollars per ton. **Type of Price:** spot. **Time Period Covered:** latest month.

GRAVEL: 1-1/2" DOWN TO 3/4"

Source: *ENR.* **Price Frequency:** monthly in first issue of month. **Effective Market(s):** 16 domestic markets, Montreal, Toronto. **Units of Measure:** Dollars per ton. **Type of Price:** spot. **Time Period Covered:** latest month.

GRAY FABRICS

see Fabric or see specific types of fabric, e.g., Pongee Fabric.

GREASE: 14-1/2 OUNCE CARTRIDGE

Source: *Agricultural Prices.* **Price Frequency:** semiannually. **Effective Market(s):** United States. **Units of Measure:** Dollars each. **Type of Price:** paid by farmer. **Time Period Covered:** latest year.

Source: *Agricultural Prices Annual Summary.* **Price Frequency:** quarterly. **Effective Market(s):** United States. **Units of Measure:** Dollars each cartridge. **Type of Price:** average paid by farmer. **Time Period Covered:** latest 6 years.

GREASE: 35 LB. PAIL

Source: *Agricultural Prices.* **Price Frequency:** semiannually. **Effective Market(s):** United States. **Units of Measure:** Dollars each. **Type of Price:** paid by farmer. **Time Period Covered:** latest year.

Source: *Agricultural Prices Annual Summary.* **Price Frequency:** quarterly. **Effective Market(s):** United States. **Units of Measure:** Dollars each. **Type of Price:** average paid by farmer. **Time Period Covered:** latest 6 years.

GREASE: ANIMAL, YELLOW

Source: *Feedstuffs.* **Price Frequency:** weekly. **Effective Market(s):** 10 domestic markets. **Units of Measure:** Dollars per lb. **Time Period Covered:** latest week.

GREASE: B-WHITE

Source: *National Provisioner.* **Price Frequency:** weekly. **Effective Market(s):** Chicago. **Units of Measure:** Dollars per 100 lbs. **Time Period Covered:** latest week.

GREASE: HOUSE

Source: *National Provisioner.* **Price Frequency:** weekly. **Effective Market(s):** Chicago. **Units of Measure:** Dollars per 100 lbs. **Time Period Covered:** latest week.

GREASE: WHITE, CHOICE

Source: *Asian Wall Street Journal.* **Price Frequency:** daily. **Effective Market(s):** Chicago. **Units of Measure:** Dollars per lb. **Type of Price:** cash. **Time Period Covered:** latest 2 days, year ago.

Source: *Chemical Marketing Reporter.* **Price Frequency:** weekly. **Effective Market(s):** New York. **Units of Measure:** cents per lb. **Type of Price:** spot. **Time Period Covered:** latest week.

Source: *National Provisioner.* **Price Frequency:** weekly. **Effective Market(s):** Chicago, Missouri River. **Units of Measure:** Dollars per 100 lbs. **Time Period Covered:** latest week.

Source: *Wall Street Journal.* **Price Frequency:** daily. **Effective Market(s):** Chicago. **Units of Measure:** Dollars per lb. **Time Period Covered:** latest day, day ago, year ago.

GREASE: WHITE, CHOICE, INEDIBLE

Source: *Livestock, Meat, Wool Market News.* **Price Frequency:** weekly, seasonally. **Effective Market(s):** Chicago, Gulf. **Units of Measure:** Dollars per 100 lbs. **Time Period Covered:** latest week.

GREASE: YELLOW

Source: *National Provisioner.* **Price Frequency:** weekly. **Effective Market(s):** Chicago, Missouri River. **Units of Measure:** Dollars per 100 lbs. **Time Period Covered:** latest week.

GREASE: YELLOW, INEDIBLE

Source: *Livestock, Meat, Wool Market News.* **Price Frequency:** weekly, seasonally. **Effective Market(s):** Gulf. **Units of Measure:** Dollars per 100 lbs. **Time Period Covered:** latest week.

GREASE: YELLOW, MAXIMUM 10%

Source: *Chemical Marketing Reporter.* **Price Frequency:** weekly. **Units of Measure:** cents per lb. **Type of Price:** spot. **Time Period Covered:** latest week.

GREASE GUN: HAND PRESSURE

Source: *Agricultural Prices.* **Price Frequency:** annually. **Effective Market(s):** United States. **Units of Measure:** Dollars each. **Type of Price:** paid by farmer. **Time Period Covered:** latest year.

Source: *Agricultural Prices Annual Summary.* **Price Frequency:** semiannually. **Effective Market(s):** United States. **Units of Measure:** Dollars each. **Type of Price:** average paid by farmer. **Time Period Covered:** latest 6 years.

GREASE OIL

see Lard Oil.

GREAT BRITAIN POUNDS STERLING

Source: *American Metal Market.* **Price Frequency:** daily. **Effective Market(s):** New York. **Units of Measure:** British pounds per United States dollar. **Type of Price:** foreign exchange. **Time Period Covered:** latest day.

Source: *Asian Wall Street Journal.* **Price Frequency:** daily. **Effective Market(s):** New York. **Units of Measure:** British pounds per ECU. **Type of Price:** foreign exchange. **Time Period Covered:** latest 2 days.

Source: *Barron's.* **Price Frequency:** weekly. **Effective Market(s):** New York. **Units of Measure:** British pounds per United States dollar. **Type of Price:** foreign exchange. **Time Period Covered:** latest 2 weeks.

Source: *Commodity Year Book.* **Price Frequency:** monthly, annually. **Units of Measure:** British pounds per United States dollar. **Type of Price:** foreign exchange. **Time Period Covered:** latest 4 years.

Source: *The Economist.* **Price Frequency:** weekly. **Effective Market(s):** London. **Units of Measure:** British pounds per ECU, per SDR, per United States dollar. **Type of Price:** foreign exchange. **Time Period Covered:** latest week.

Source: *New York Times.* **Price Frequency:** daily. **Effective Market(s):** New York. **Units of Measure:** British pounds per United States dollar. **Type of Price:** foreign exchange. **Time Period Covered:** latest 2 days.

Source: *Timber Bulletin.* **Price Frequency:** monthly, annually. **Units of Measure:** British pounds per United States dollar. **Type of Price:** foreign exchange. **Time Period Covered:** latest 2 years.

Source: *The Times.* **Price Frequency:** daily. **Effective Market(s):** 16 international markets. **Units of Measure:** British pounds per 16 national currencies. **Type of Price:** foreign exchange. **Time Period Covered:** latest day.

GREAT BRITAIN POUNDS STERLING: FUTURES

Source: *Asian Wall Street Journal.* **Price Frequency:** daily. **Effective Market(s):** Chicago. **Units of Measure:** United States dollars per British pound. **Type of Price:** foreign exchange futures. **Time Period Covered:** latest 2 days.

Source: *Barron's.* **Price Frequency:** weekly. **Effective Market(s):** New York. **Units of Measure:** United States dollars per British pound. **Type of Price:** foreign exchange futures. **Time Period Covered:** latest week.

Source: *Los Angeles Times.* **Price Frequency:** daily. **Effective Market(s):** Chicago. **Units of Measure:** United States dollars per British pound. **Type of Price:** foreign exchange futures. **Time Period Covered:** latest day.

Source: *New York Times.* **Price Frequency:** daily. **Effective Market(s):** New York. **Units of Measure:** United States dollars per British pound. **Type of Price:** foreign exchange futures. **Time Period Covered:** latest day.

Source: *Urner Barry's Price-Current.* **Price Frequency:** daily. **Units of Measure:** United States dollars per British pound. **Type of Price:** foreign exchange futures. **Time Period Covered:** latest day.

GREECE DRACHMA

Source: *Asian Wall Street Journal.* **Price Frequency:** daily. **Effective Market(s):** United States. **Units of Measure:** Greek drachma per ECU. **Type of Price:** foreign exchange. **Time Period Covered:** latest 2 days.

Source: *Barron's.* **Price Frequency:** weekly. **Effective Market(s):** New York. **Units of Measure:** Greek drachma per United States dollar. **Type of Price:** foreign exchange. **Time Period Covered:** latest 2 weeks.

Source: *New York Times.* **Price Frequency:** daily. **Effective Market(s):** New York. **Units of Measure:** Greek drachma per United States dollar. **Type of Price:** foreign exchange. **Time Period Covered:** latest 2 days.

Source: *Timber Bulletin.* **Price Frequency:** monthly, annually. **Units of Measure:** Greek drachmas per United States dollar. **Type of Price:** foreign exchange. **Time Period Covered:** latest 2 years.

Source: *The Times.* **Price Frequency:** daily. **Effective Market(s):** London. **Units of Measure:** Greek Drachma per British pound. **Type of Price:** foreign exchange. **Time Period Covered:** latest day.

GREENS: COLLARD

Source: *Lancaster Farming.* **Price Frequency:** weekly, seasonally. **Effective Market(s):** Pennsylvania. **Units of Measure:** Dollars per bushel. **Type of Price:** market. **Time Period Covered:** latest week.

GREENS: KALE

Source: *Lancaster Farming.* **Price Frequency:** weekly, seasonally. **Effective Market(s):** Pennsylvania. **Units of Measure:** Dollars per bushel. **Type of Price:** market. **Time Period Covered:** latest week.

GREENS: MUSTARD AND TURNIP TOPS

Source: *Lancaster Farming.* **Price Frequency:** weekly, seasonally. **Effective Market(s):** Pennsylvania. **Units of Measure:** Dollars per bushel. **Type of Price:** market. **Time Period Covered:** latest week.

GREIGE FABRICS

see Fabrics: Greige.

GRENADINE

Source: *Illinois Beverage Journal.* **Price Frequency:** monthly. **Effective Market(s):** Illinois. **Units of Measure:** Dollars per case. **Type of Price:** wholesale by brand. **Time Period Covered:** latest month.

GROCERY BAGS: VARIETY

Source: *Pulp & Paper Week.* **Price Frequency:** monthly, irregularly. **Units of Measure:** index. **Type of Price:** price index. **Time Period Covered:** latest 3 months.

GROUNDNUT CAKE

Source: *International Financial Statistics Yearbook.* **Price Frequency:** annually. **Effective Market(s):** Europe. **Units of Measure:** Dollars per metric ton. **Type of Price:** wholesale. **Time Period Covered:** latest 30 years.

GROUNDNUT CAKE: THAI

Source: *Prices of Selected Asia/Pacific Products.* **Price Frequency:** monthly, seasonally. **Effective Market(s):** Hong Kong. **Units of Measure:** Hong Kong dollars per picul. **Type of Price:** high, low. **Time Period Covered:** latest month.

GROUNDNUT MEAL

see also Peanut Meal.

Source: *International Financial Statistics.* **Price Frequency:** monthly, quarterly, annually. **Effective Market(s):** Europe. **Units of Measure:** Dollars per metric ton, index. **Type of Price:** market price, price index. **Time Period Covered:** latest 5 months, latest 5 quarters, latest 5 years.

GROUNDNUT MEAL: 48% INDIAN

Source: *Commodity Trade and Price Trends.* **Price Frequency:** annually. **Effective Market(s):** Hamburg. **Units of Measure:** Dollars per metric ton, 1980 constant dollars per metric ton. **Time Period Covered:** latest 37 years.

GROUNDNUT MEAL: 48-50%, ARGENTINE

Source: *Oil World.* **Price Frequency:** weekly, monthly, annually. **Effective Market(s):** Argentina. **Units of Measure:** Dollars per tonne. **Type of Price:** lowest representative asking. **Time Period Covered:** weekly latest 3 weeks, monthly latest 2 months, annually latest 2 years.

GROUNDNUT MEAL: PELLETS

Source: *Agra Europe.* **Price Frequency:** weekly, irregularly. **Effective Market(s):** Rotterdam. **Units of Measure:** Dollars per tonne . **Type of Price:** average. **Time Period Covered:** latest week.

GROUNDNUT OIL
see also Peanut Oil.

Source: *Fruit and Tropical Products.* **Price Frequency:** monthly, annually. **Effective Market(s):** Rotterdam. **Units of Measure:** Dollars per tonne. **Type of Price:** average. **Time Period Covered:** monthly latest year, annually latest 2 years.

Source: *Monthly Commodity Price Bulletin Supplement.* **Price Frequency:** monthly, quarterly, annually. **Effective Market(s):** Rotterdam. **Units of Measure:** Dollars per tonne. **Time Period Covered:** latest 20 years.

Source: *Oil World.* **Price Frequency:** weekly, monthly, annually. **Effective Market(s):** Rotterdam. **Units of Measure:** Dollars per tonne. **Type of Price:** lowest representative asking. **Time Period Covered:** weekly latest 3 weeks, monthly latest 2 months, annually latest 2 years.

Source: *UNCTAD Commodity Yearbook.* **Price Frequency:** annually. **Effective Market(s):** Rotterdam. **Units of Measure:** Dollars per metric ton. **Type of Price:** free market. **Time Period Covered:** latest 12 years.

GROUNDNUT OIL: 2-3% FREE FATTY ACID

Source: *FAO Quarterly Bulletin of Statistics.* **Price Frequency:** monthly, annually. **Effective Market(s):** Rotterdam. **Units of Measure:** Dollars per 1000 kilograms, dollars per metric ton. **Time Period Covered:** latest 3 years.

Source: *Prices of Selected Asia/Pacific Products.* **Price Frequency:** monthly. **Effective Market(s):** Rotterdam. **Units of Measure:** Dollars per metric ton. **Type of Price:** high, low. **Time Period Covered:** latest month.

GROUNDNUT OIL: ANY ORIGIN

Source: *Commodity Trade and Price Trends.* **Price Frequency:** annually. **Effective Market(s):** European ports. **Units of Measure:** Dollars per metric ton, 1980 constant dollars per metric ton. **Time Period Covered:** latest 37 years.

Source: *Monthly Commodity Price Bulletin.* **Price Frequency:** monthly, annually. **Effective Market(s):** Rotterdam. **Units of Measure:** Dollars per metric ton. **Time Period Covered:** latest 5 years.

GROUNDNUT OIL: CRUDE

Source: *Prices of Selected Asia/Pacific Products.* **Price Frequency:** monthly. **Effective Market(s):** Rotterdam. **Units of Measure:** Dollars per metric ton. **Type of Price:** high, low. **Time Period Covered:** latest month.

GROUNDNUT OIL: GRADE B, THAI

Source: *Prices of Selected Asia/Pacific Products.* **Price Frequency:** monthly, seasonally. **Effective Market(s):** Bangkok. **Units of Measure:** Thai baht per 18 kilograms. **Type of Price:** wholesale high, wholesale low. **Time Period Covered:** latest month.

GROUNDNUT OIL: NEW STOCK, TSINGTAO

Source: *Prices of Selected Asia/Pacific Products.* **Price Frequency:** monthly. **Effective Market(s):** Hong Kong. **Units of Measure:** Hong Kong dollars per picul. **Type of Price:** wholesale high, wholesale low. **Time Period Covered:** latest month.

GROUNDNUT OIL: SPECIAL, NEW STOCK, CHINESE

Source: *Prices of Selected Asia/Pacific Products.* **Price Frequency:** monthly. **Effective Market(s):** Hong Kong. **Units of Measure:** Hong Kong dollars per picul. **Type of Price:** wholesale high, wholesale low. **Time Period Covered:** latest month.

GROUNDNUT OIL: SUPREME, NEW STOCK, CHINESE

Source: *Prices of Selected Asia/Pacific Products.* **Price Frequency:** monthly. **Effective Market(s):** Hong Kong. **Units of Measure:** Hong Kong dollars per picul. **Type of Price:** wholesale high, wholesale low. **Time Period Covered:** latest month.

GROUNDNUT OIL: WEST AFRICA

Source: *International Financial Statistics.* **Price Frequency:** monthly, quarterly, annually. **Effective Market(s):** Europe. **Units of Measure:** Dollars per metric ton, index. **Type of Price:** market price, price index. **Time Period Covered:** latest 5 months, latest 5 quarters, latest 5 years.

Source: *International Financial Statistics Yearbook.* **Price Frequency:** annually. **Effective Market(s):** Europe. **Units of Measure:** Dollars per metric ton. **Type of Price:** wholesale. **Time Period Covered:** latest 30 years.

GROUNDNUTS
see also Peanuts.

GROUNDNUTS: 35/40, HPS, HSUJI

Source: *Prices of Selected Asia/Pacific Products.* **Price Frequency:** monthly, seasonally. **Effective Market(s):** United Kingdom/North European ports. **Units of Measure:** Dollars per metric ton. **Type of Price:** high, low. **Time Period Covered:** latest month.

GROUNDNUTS: 40/50, HPS, HSUJI

Source: *Prices of Selected Asia/Pacific Products.* **Price Frequency:** monthly, seasonally. **Effective Market(s):** United Kingdom/North European ports. **Units of Measure:** Dollars per metric ton. **Type of Price:** high, low. **Time Period Covered:** latest month.

GROUNDNUTS: GRADE A, THAI

Source: *Prices of Selected Asia/Pacific Products.* **Price Frequency:** monthly, seasonally. **Effective Market(s):** Bangkok. **Units of Measure:** Thai baht per kilogram. **Type of Price:** wholesale high, wholesale low. **Time Period Covered:** latest month.

GROUNDNUTS: GRADE A, UNSHELLED, THAI

Source: *Prices of Selected Asia/Pacific Products.* **Price Frequency:** monthly, seasonally. **Effective Market(s):** Bangkok. **Units of Measure:** Thai baht per 100 kilograms. **Type of Price:** wholesale high, wholesale low. **Time Period Covered:** latest month.

GROUNDNUTS: LARGE SIZE, CHINESE

Source: *Prices of Selected Asia/Pacific Products.* **Price Frequency:** monthly, seasonally. **Effective Market(s):** Osaka/Kobe. **Units of Measure:** 1000 Japanese yen per metric ton. **Type of Price:** wholesale high, wholesale low. **Time Period Covered:** latest month.

GROUNDNUTS: LARGE SIZE, UNITED STATES

Source: *Prices of Selected Asia/Pacific Products.* **Price Frequency:** monthly, seasonally. **Effective Market(s):** Osaka/Kobe. **Units of Measure:** 1000 Japanese yen per metric ton. **Type of Price:** wholesale high, wholesale low. **Time Period Covered:** latest month.

GROUNDNUTS: NIGERIA

Source: *International Financial Statistics.* **Price Frequency:** quarterly, annually. **Effective Market(s):** London. **Units of Measure:** Dollars per metric ton, index. **Type of Price:** market price, price index. **Time Period Covered:** latest 2 quarters, latest 4 years.

Source: *International Financial Statistics Yearbook.* **Price Frequency:** annually. **Effective Market(s):** London. **Units of Measure:** Dollars per metric ton. **Type of Price:** wholesale. **Time Period Covered:** latest 30 years.

GROUNDNUTS: SHELLED

Source: *Fruit and Tropical Products.* **Price Frequency:** monthly, annually. **Effective Market(s):** European ports. **Units of Measure:** Dollars per tonne. **Type of Price:** average. **Time Period Covered:** monthly latest year, annually latest 2 years.

Source: *Monthly Commodity Price Bulletin Supplement.* **Price Frequency:** monthly, quarterly, annually. **Effective Market(s):** European ports. **Units of Measure:** Dollars per tonne. **Time Period Covered:** latest 20 years.

Source: *UNCTAD Commodity Yearbook.* **Price Frequency:** annually. **Effective Market(s):** European ports. **Units of Measure:** Dollars per metric ton. **Type of Price:** free market. **Time Period Covered:** latest 12 years.

GROUNDNUTS: SHELLED, AFRICAN

Source: *Oil World.* **Price Frequency:** weekly, monthly, annually. **Effective Market(s):** Europe. **Units of Measure:** Dollars per tonne. **Type of Price:** lowest representative asking. **Time Period Covered:** weekly latest 3 weeks, monthly latest 2 months, annually latest 2 years.

GROUNDNUTS: SHELLED, ANY ORIGIN

Source: *FAO Quarterly Bulletin of Statistics.* **Price Frequency:** monthly, annually. **Effective Market(s):** Europe. **Units of Measure:** Dollars per 1000 kilograms, dollars per metric ton. **Time Period Covered:** latest 3 years.

Source: *Monthly Commodity Price Bulletin.* **Price Frequency:** monthly, annually. **Effective Market(s):** European ports. **Units of Measure:** Dollars per metric ton. **Time Period Covered:** latest 5 years.

GROUNDNUTS: SHELLED, THAI

Source: *Prices of Selected Asia/Pacific Products.* **Price Frequency:** monthly, seasonally. **Effective Market(s):** Hong Kong. **Units of Measure:** Hong Kong dollars per picul. **Type of Price:** wholesale high, wholesale low. **Time Period Covered:** latest month.

GROUPER: BLACK, FILLETS, FRESH

Source: *Seafood Price-Current.* **Price Frequency:** semiweekly. **Effective Market(s):** Gulf/Southeast. **Units of Measure:** Dollars per lb. **Type of Price:** sale by first receiver. **Time Period Covered:** latest day.

GROUPER: BLACK, FRESH

Source: *Seafood Price-Current.* **Price Frequency:** semiweekly. **Effective Market(s):** Gulf/Southeast. **Units of Measure:** Dollars per lb. **Type of Price:** sale by first receiver. **Time Period Covered:** latest day.

GROUPER: RED, FILLETS, FRESH

Source: *Seafood Price-Current.* **Price Frequency:** semiweekly. **Effective Market(s):** Gulf/Southeast. **Units of Measure:** Dollars per lb. **Type of Price:** sale by first receiver. **Time Period Covered:** latest day.

GROUPER: RED, FRESH

Source: *Seafood Price-Current.* **Price Frequency:** semiweekly. **Effective Market(s):** Gulf/Southeast. **Units of Measure:** Dollars per lb. **Type of Price:** sale by first receiver. **Time Period Covered:** latest day.

GROUPER: SNOWY, FRESH

Source: *Seafood Price-Current.* **Price Frequency:** semiweekly. **Effective Market(s):** Gulf/Southeast. **Units of Measure:** Dollars per lb. **Type of Price:** sale by first receiver. **Time Period Covered:** latest day.

GROUPER: WHOLE, FRESH

Source: *Seafood Price-Current.* **Price Frequency:** semiweekly. **Effective Market(s):** Mid-Atlantic, Boston, New Bedford (MA), Portland (ME). **Units of Measure:** Dollars per lb. **Type of Price:** sale by first receiver, auction price. **Time Period Covered:** latest day.

GROUPER: WHOLE, FRESH, MEXICAN

Source: *Seafood Price-Current.* **Price Frequency:** semiweekly. **Effective Market(s):** Miami. **Units of Measure:** Dollars per lb. **Type of Price:** sale by first receiver. **Time Period Covered:** latest day.

GROUPER: WHOLE, FRESH, PANAMA

Source: *Seafood Price-Current.* **Price Frequency:** semiweekly. **Effective Market(s):** Miami. **Units of Measure:** Dollars per lb. **Type of Price:** sale by first receiver. **Time Period Covered:** latest day.

GUAIACOL: TECHNICAL GRADE

Source: *Chemical Marketing Reporter.* **Price Frequency:** weekly. **Effective Market(s):** Wallingford (CN). **Units of Measure:** Dollars per lb. **Type of Price:** spot. **Time Period Covered:** latest week.

GUAIACWOOD OIL

Source: *Chemical Marketing Reporter.* **Price Frequency:** weekly. **Effective Market(s):** New York. **Units of Measure:** Dollars per lb. **Type of Price:** spot. **Time Period Covered:** latest week.

GUAR GUM: EDIBLE

Source: *Chemical Marketing Reporter.* **Price Frequency:** weekly. **Effective Market(s):** New York. **Units of Measure:** Dollars per lb. . **Type of Price:** spot. **Time Period Covered:** latest week.

GUAR GUM: FOOD GRADE

Source: *Journal of Commerce and Commercial.* **Price Frequency:** weekly in Monday issue. **Units of Measure:** Dollars per lb. **Type of Price:** spot. **Time Period Covered:** latest week.

GUAR GUM: INDUSTRIAL GRADE

Source: *Journal of Commerce and Commercial.* **Price Frequency:** weekly in Monday issue. **Units of Measure:** Dollars per lb. **Type of Price:** spot. **Time Period Covered:** latest week.

GUAR GUM: INDUSTRIAL GRADE, HIGH VISCOSITY

Source: *Chemical Marketing Reporter.* **Price Frequency:** weekly. **Effective Market(s):** New York. **Units of Measure:** Dollars per lb. **Type of Price:** spot. **Time Period Covered:** latest week.

GUARANA

Source: *Journal of Commerce and Commercial.* **Price Frequency:** weekly in Monday issue. **Units of Measure:** Dollars per lb. **Type of Price:** spot. **Time Period Covered:** latest week.

GUINEA FOWL

Source: *Lancaster Farming.* **Price Frequency:** weekly. **Effective Market(s):** Pennsylvania. **Units of Measure:** Dollars per lb. **Type of Price:** auction. **Time Period Covered:** latest week.

GUINEA PIGS

Source: *Lancaster Farming.* **Price Frequency:** weekly. **Effective Market(s):** Pennsylvania. **Units of Measure:** Dollars each. **Type of Price:** auction. **Time Period Covered:** latest week.

GUM ROSIN: K, DOMESTIC

Source: *Journal of Commerce and Commercial.* **Price Frequency:** weekly in Monday issue. **Effective Market(s):** South. **Units of Measure:** Dollars per 100 lbs. **Type of Price:** spot. **Time Period Covered:** latest week.

GUM ROSIN: M, DOMESTIC

Source: *Journal of Commerce and Commercial.* **Price Frequency:** weekly in Monday issue. **Effective Market(s):** South. **Units of Measure:** Dollars per 100 lbs. **Type of Price:** spot. **Time Period Covered:** latest week.

GUM ROSIN: N, DOMESTIC

Source: *Journal of Commerce and Commercial.* **Price Frequency:** weekly in Monday issue. **Effective Market(s):** South. **Units of Measure:** Dollars per 100 lbs. **Type of Price:** spot. **Time Period Covered:** latest week.

GUM ROSIN: WG, DOMESTIC

Source: *Journal of Commerce and Commercial.* **Price Frequency:** weekly in Monday issue. **Effective Market(s):** South. **Units of Measure:** Dollars per 100 lbs. **Type of Price:** spot. **Time Period Covered:** latest week.

GUM ROSIN: WW, DOMESTIC

Source: *Journal of Commerce and Commercial.* **Price Frequency:** weekly in Monday issue. **Effective Market(s):** South. **Units of Measure:** Dollars per 100 lbs. **Type of Price:** spot. **Time Period Covered:** latest week.

GUMS

Source: *Journal of Commerce and Commercial.* **Price Frequency:** weekly in Monday issue. **Units of Measure:** Dollars per lb. **Type of Price:** spot. **Time Period Covered:** latest week.

GUNNY BAG: USED, EXTRA CHOICE

Source: *Prices of Selected Asia/Pacific Products.* **Price Frequency:** monthly. **Effective Market(s):** Hong Kong. **Units of Measure:** Hong Kong dollars per piece. **Type of Price:** spot high, spot low. **Time Period Covered:** latest month.

GYPSOPHLIA

Source: *New Zealand Farmer.* **Price Frequency:** weekly, seasonally. **Effective Market(s):** New Zealand. **Units of Measure:** New Zealand dollars per bunch. **Time Period Covered:** latest week.

GYPSUM: CRUDE

Source: *Industrial Minerals.* **Price Frequency:** monthly **Effective Market(s):** United Kingdom. **Units of Measure:** British pounds per metric tonne. **Type of Price:** producer & dealer. **Time Period Covered:** latest month.

HADDOCK: BLOCKS, IMPORTED

Source: *NMFS Green Sheet Supplement.* **Price Frequency:** weekly. **Effective Market(s):** New England. **Units of Measure:** Dollars per lb. **Type of Price:** processor. **Time Period Covered:** latest week.

HADDOCK: FILLETS, BONE IN, SKIN ON, CANADIAN

Source: *NMFS Green Sheet Supplement.* **Price Frequency:** weekly. **Effective Market(s):** New England. **Units of Measure:** Dollars per lb. **Type of Price:** to primary wholesaler. **Time Period Covered:** latest week.

HADDOCK: FILLETS, BONE IN, SKIN ON, DENMARK

Source: *NMFS Green Sheet Supplement.* **Price Frequency:** weekly. **Effective Market(s):** New England. **Units of Measure:** Dollars per lb. **Type of Price:** to primary wholesaler. **Time Period Covered:** latest week.

HADDOCK: FILLETS, BONE IN, SKIN ON, ICELAND

Source: *NMFS Green Sheet Supplement.* **Price Frequency:** weekly. **Effective Market(s):** New England. **Units of Measure:** Dollars per lb. **Type of Price:** to primary wholesaler. **Time Period Covered:** latest week.

HADDOCK: FILLETS, BONE IN, SKIN ON, NORWEGIAN

Source: *NMFS Green Sheet Supplement.* **Price Frequency:** weekly. **Effective Market(s):** New England. **Units of Measure:** Dollars per lb. **Type of Price:** to primary wholesaler. **Time Period Covered:** latest week.

HADDOCK: FILLETS, BONELESS, ICELAND

Source: *NMFS Green Sheet Supplement.* **Price Frequency:** weekly. **Effective Market(s):** New England. **Units of Measure:** Dollars per lb. **Type of Price:** to primary wholesaler. **Time Period Covered:** latest week.

HADDOCK: FILLETS, BONELESS, NORWEGIAN

Source: *NMFS Green Sheet Supplement.* **Price Frequency:** weekly. **Effective Market(s):** New England. **Units of Measure:** Dollars per lb. **Type of Price:** to primary wholesaler. **Time Period Covered:** latest week.

HADDOCK: FILLETS, BONELESS, SCOTTISH

Source: *NMFS Green Sheet Supplement.* **Price Frequency:** weekly. **Effective Market(s):** New England. **Units of Measure:** Dollars per lb. **Type of Price:** to primary wholesaler. **Time Period Covered:** latest week.

HADDOCK: FILLETS, BONELESS, SKIN ON, ICELAND

Source: *NMFS Green Sheet Supplement.* **Price Frequency:** weekly. **Effective Market(s):** New England. **Units of Measure:** Dollars per lb. **Type of Price:** to primary wholesaler. **Time Period Covered:** latest week.

HADDOCK: FILLETS, BONELESS, SKIN ON, NORWEGIAN

Source: *NMFS Green Sheet Supplement.* **Price Frequency:** weekly. **Effective Market(s):** New England. **Units of Measure:** Dollars per lb. **Type of Price:** to primary wholesaler. **Time Period Covered:** latest week.

HADDOCK: FILLETS, BONELESS, SKINLESS, FROZEN, CANADIAN

Source: *Seafood Price-Current.* **Price Frequency:** semiweekly. **Effective Market(s):** Mid-Atlantic. **Units of Measure:** Dollars per lb. **Type of Price:** first receiver. **Time Period Covered:** latest day.

HADDOCK: FILLETS, BONELESS, SKINLESS, FROZEN, ICELAND

Source: *Seafood Price-Current.* **Price Frequency:** semiweekly. **Effective Market(s):** Mid-Atlantic. **Units of Measure:** Dollars per lb. **Type of Price:** first receiver. **Time Period Covered:** latest day.

HADDOCK: FILLETS, BREADED, FROZEN

Source: *HRI-Buyers Guide.* **Price Frequency:** weekly. **Effective Market(s):** New York. **Units of Measure:** Dollars per case. **Type of Price:** prices paid by dining places & institutions. **Time Period Covered:** latest week.

HADDOCK: FILLETS, FRESH

Source: *Seafood Price-Current.* **Price Frequency:** semiweekly. **Effective Market(s):** Mid-Atlantic, New England. **Units of Measure:** Dollars per lb. **Type of Price:** sale by first receiver. **Time Period Covered:** latest day.

HADDOCK: FILLETS, FROZEN

Source: *HRI-Buyers Guide.* **Price Frequency:** weekly. **Effective Market(s):** New York. **Units of Measure:** Dollars per case. **Type of Price:** prices paid by dining places & institutions. **Time Period Covered:** latest week.

HADDOCK: FILLETS, SKIN ON, FROZEN, CANADIAN

Source: *Seafood Price-Current.* **Price Frequency:** semiweekly. **Effective Market(s):** Mid-Atlantic. **Units of Measure:** Dollars per lb. **Type of Price:** first receiver. **Time Period Covered:** latest day.

HADDOCK: FILLETS, SKINLESS, FROZEN, CANADIAN

Source: *Seafood Price-Current.* **Price Frequency:** semiweekly. **Effective Market(s):** Mid-Atlantic. **Units of Measure:** Dollars per lb. **Type of Price:** first receiver. **Time Period Covered:** latest day.

HADDOCK: FISH PORTIONS, BATTERED, COOKED

Source: *NMFS Green Sheet Supplement.* **Price Frequency:** weekly. **Effective Market(s):** New England. **Units of Measure:** Dollars per lb. **Type of Price:** to primary wholesaler. **Time Period Covered:** latest week.

HADDOCK: FISH PORTIONS, BATTERED, RAW

Source: *NMFS Green Sheet Supplement.* **Price Frequency:** weekly. **Effective Market(s):** New England. **Units of Measure:** Dollars per lb. **Type of Price:** to primary wholesaler. **Time Period Covered:** latest week.

HADDOCK: FISH PORTIONS, BREADED, COOKED

Source: *NMFS Green Sheet Supplement.* **Price Frequency:** weekly. **Effective Market(s):** New England. **Units of Measure:** Dollars per lb. **Type of Price:** to primary wholesaler. **Time Period Covered:** latest week.

HADDOCK: FISH PORTIONS, BREADED, RAW

Source: *NMFS Green Sheet Supplement.* **Price Frequency:** weekly. **Effective Market(s):** New England. **Units of Measure:** Dollars per lb. **Type of Price:** to primary wholesaler. **Time Period Covered:** latest week.

HADDOCK: FISH STICKS, BATTERED, RAW

Source: *NMFS Green Sheet Supplement.* **Price Frequency:** weekly. **Effective Market(s):** New England. **Units of Measure:** Dollars per lb. **Type of Price:** to primary wholesaler. **Time Period Covered:** latest week.

HADDOCK: FISH STICKS, BATTERED, COOKED

Source: *NMFS Green Sheet Supplement.* **Price Frequency:** weekly. **Effective Market(s):** New England. **Units of Measure:** Dollars per lb. **Type of Price:** to primary wholesaler. **Time Period Covered:** latest week.

HADDOCK: FISH STICKS, BREADED, COOKED

Source: *NMFS Green Sheet Supplement.* **Price Frequency:** weekly. **Effective Market(s):** New England. **Units of Measure:** Dollars per lb. **Type of Price:** to primary wholesaler. **Time Period Covered:** latest week.

HADDOCK: FISH STICKS, BREADED, RAW

Source: *NMFS Green Sheet Supplement.* **Price Frequency:** weekly. **Effective Market(s):** New England. **Units of Measure:** Dollars per lb. **Type of Price:** to primary wholesaler. **Time Period Covered:** latest week.

HADDOCK: PROCESSOR FISH BLOCKS, CANADA/NORWAY

Source: *Seafood Price-Current.* **Price Frequency:** semiweekly. **Effective Market(s):** West Coast. **Units of Measure:** Dollars per lb. **Type of Price:** first receiver. **Time Period Covered:** latest day.

HADDOCK: SCROD, FILLETS, FRESH

Source: *Seafood Price-Current.* **Price Frequency:** semiweekly. **Effective Market(s):** Mid-Atlantic, New England. **Units of Measure:** Dollars per lb. **Type of Price:** sale by first receiver. **Time Period Covered:** latest day.

HADDOCK: SCROD, WHOLE, FRESH

Source: *Seafood Price-Current.* **Price Frequency:** semiweekly. **Effective Market(s):** Boston, Mid-Atlantic, New Bedford (MA), Portland (ME). **Units of Measure:** Dollars per lb. **Type of Price:** sale by first receiver, auction price. **Time Period Covered:** latest day.

HADDOCK: SKIN ON, FROZEN, DENMARK

Source: *Seafood Price-Current.* **Price Frequency:** semiweekly. **Effective Market(s):** Mid-Atlantic. **Units of Measure:** Dollars per lb. **Type of Price:** first receiver. **Time Period Covered:** latest day.

HADDOCK: WHOLE, FRESH

Source: *Seafood Price-Current.* **Price Frequency:** semiweekly. **Effective Market(s):** Boston, Mid-Atlantic, New Bedford (MA), Portland (ME). **Units of Measure:** Dollars per lb. **Type of Price:** sale by first receiver, auction price. **Time Period Covered:** latest day.

HAKE: WHITE, FILLETS, FRESH

Source: *Seafood Price-Current.* **Price Frequency:** semiweekly. **Effective Market(s):** Mid-Atlantic, New England. **Units of Measure:** Dollars per lb. **Type of Price:** sale by first receiver. **Time Period Covered:** latest day.

HAKE: WHITE, WHOLE, FRESH

Source: *Seafood Price-Current.* **Price Frequency:** semiweekly. **Effective Market(s):** Boston, Mid-Atlantic, New Bedford (MA), Portland (ME). **Units of Measure:** Dollars per lb. **Type of Price:** sale by first receiver, auction price. **Time Period Covered:** latest day.

HALIBUT: DRESSED, FRESH, DOMESTIC

Source: *Seafood Price-Current.* **Price Frequency:** semiweekly. **Effective Market(s):** West Coast. **Units of Measure:** Dollars per lb. **Type of Price:** sale by first receiver. **Time Period Covered:** latest day.

HALIBUT: FILLETS, FRESH, SOUTHERN CALIFORNIA

Source: *Seafood Price-Current.* **Price Frequency:** semiweekly. **Effective Market(s):** West Coast. **Units of Measure:** Dollars per lb. **Type of Price:** sale by first receiver. **Time Period Covered:** latest day.

HALIBUT: WHOLE, FRESH, EASTERN

Source: *Seafood Price-Current.* **Price Frequency:** semiweekly. **Effective Market(s):** Boston, Mid-Atlantic, New Bedford (MA), Portland (ME). **Units of Measure:** Dollars per lb. **Type of Price:** sale by first receiver, auction price. **Time Period Covered:** latest day.

HALIBUT: WHOLE, FRESH, MEXICAN

Source: *Seafood Price-Current.* **Price Frequency:** semiweekly. **Effective Market(s):** West Coast. **Units of Measure:** Dollars per lb. **Type of Price:** sale by first receiver. **Time Period Covered:** latest day.

HALIBUT: WHOLE, FRESH, NORTHERN

Source: *Seafood Price-Current.* **Price Frequency:** semiweekly. **Effective Market(s):** Seattle. **Units of Measure:** Dollars per lb. **Type of Price:** sale by first receiver. **Time Period Covered:** latest day.

HALIBUT: WHOLE, FRESH, SOUTHERN CALIFORNIA

Source: *Seafood Price-Current.* **Price Frequency:** semiweekly. **Effective Market(s):** West Coast. **Units of Measure:** Dollars per lb. **Type of Price:** sale by first receiver. **Time Period Covered:** latest day.

HALIBUT STEAKS: FROZEN

Source: *HRI-Buyers Guide.* **Price Frequency:** weekly. **Effective Market(s):** New York. **Units of Measure:** Dollars per case. **Type of Price:** prices paid by dining places & institutions. **Time Period Covered:** latest week.

HALS: MAXIMUM

Source: *Modern Plastics.* **Price Frequency:** quarterly in February, May, August, November. **Units of Measure:** Dollars per lb. **Type of Price:** list. **Time Period Covered:** latest 4 quarters.

HALS: MINIMUM

Source: *Modern Plastics.* **Price Frequency:** quarterly in February, May, August, November. **Units of Measure:** Dollars per lb. **Type of Price:** list. **Time Period Covered:** latest 4 quarters.

HAM

Source: *Livestock and Poultry Update.* **Price Frequency:** monthly. **Effective Market(s):** Central United States. **Units of Measure:** Dollars per 100 lbs. **Type of Price:** wholesale. **Time Period Covered:** latest 3 months, year ago.

HAM: 17-20 LBS

Source: *Asian Wall Street Journal.* **Price Frequency:** daily. **Effective Market(s):** Mid-United States. **Units of Measure:** Dollars per lb. **Type of Price:** cash. **Time Period Covered:** latest 2 days, year ago.

Source: *The Brock Report.* **Price Frequency:** weekly. **Units of Measure:** cents per lb. **Time Period Covered:** latest week, 2 weeks ago, year ago.

Source: *Porkpro Newsletter.* **Price Frequency:** weekly. **Units of Measure:** Dollars per lb. **Type of Price:** wholesale. **Time Period Covered:** latest day, week ago, year ago.

Source: *Wall Street Journal.* **Price Frequency:** daily. **Effective Market(s):** Mid-United States. **Units of Measure:** Dollars per lb. **Time Period Covered:** latest day, day ago, year ago.

HAM: BONED AND TIED

Source: *Meat Price Report.* **Price Frequency:** weekly. **Units of Measure:** cents per lb. **Type of Price:** price paid to wholesaler. **Time Period Covered:** latest week.

HAM: BONELESS, SKINLESS, CURED AND SMOKED, FULLY-COOKED, DRY HEAT

Source: *Meat Price Report.* **Price Frequency:** weekly. **Units of Measure:** cents per lb. **Type of Price:** price paid to wholesaler. **Time Period Covered:** latest week.

HAM: BONELESS, SKINLESS, CURED AND SMOKED, FULLY-COOKED, MOIST HEAT

Source: *Meat Price Report.* **Price Frequency:** weekly. **Units of Measure:** cents per lb. **Type of Price:** price paid to wholesaler. **Time Period Covered:** latest week.

HAM: CANADIAN

Source: *HRI-Buyers Guide.* **Price Frequency:** weekly. **Effective Market(s):** Northeastern area. **Units of Measure:** Dollars per lb. **Type of Price:** price paid by dining places & institutions. **Time Period Covered:** latest week.

HAM: CANNED

Source: *Livestock and Poultry Situation and Outlook Report.* **Price Frequency:** monthly. **Units of Measure:** Dollars per lb. **Type of Price:** retail. **Time Period Covered:** latest 3 years.

HAM: IMPORTED

Source: *HRI-Buyers Guide.* **Price Frequency:** weekly. **Effective Market(s):** Northeastern area. **Units of Measure:** Dollars per lb. **Type of Price:** price paid by dining places & institutions. **Time Period Covered:** latest week.

HAM: NO. 2, SMOKED

Source: *Journal of Commerce and Commercial.* **Price Frequency:** daily. **Effective Market(s):** New York. **Units of Measure:** Dollars per lb. **Type of Price:** spot supplier. **Time Period Covered:** latest day.

HAM: OBLONG, CANNED, IMPORTED

Source: *Meat Price Report.* **Price Frequency:** weekly. **Units of Measure:** cents per lb. **Type of Price:** price paid to wholesaler. **Time Period Covered:** latest week.

HAM: PEARSHAPED, CANNED, DOMESTIC

Source: *Meat Price Report.* **Price Frequency:** weekly. **Units of Measure:** cents per lb. **Type of Price:** price paid to wholesaler. **Time Period Covered:** latest week.

HAM: PICNIC

Source: *National Provisioner.* **Price Frequency:** daily. **Effective Market(s):** Midwest River. **Units of Measure:** cents per lb. **Time Period Covered:** latest week.

HAM: PROSCIUTTO

Source: *HRI-Buyers Guide.* **Price Frequency:** weekly. **Effective Market(s):** Northeastern area. **Units of Measure:** Dollars per lb. **Type of Price:** price paid by dining places & institutions. **Time Period Covered:** latest week.

HAM: PULLMAN STYLE, CANNED, DOMESTIC

Source: *Meat Price Report.* **Price Frequency:** weekly. **Units of Measure:** cents per lb. **Type of Price:** price paid to wholesaler. **Time Period Covered:** latest week.

HAM: PULLMAN STYLE, CANNED, IMPORTED

Source: *Meat Price Report.* **Price Frequency:** weekly. **Units of Measure:** cents per lb. **Type of Price:** price paid to wholesaler. **Time Period Covered:** latest week.

HAM: RUMP OR SHANK HALF

Source: *Livestock and Poultry Situation and Outlook Report.* **Price Frequency:** monthly. **Units of Measure:** Dollars per lb. **Type of Price:** retail. **Time Period Covered:** latest 3 years.

HAM: SHORT SHANK, PARTIALLY SKINNED, SMOKED, CURED, DRY

Source: *Meat Price Report.* **Price Frequency:** weekly. **Units of Measure:** cents per lb. **Type of Price:** price paid to wholesaler. **Time Period Covered:** latest week.

HAM: SHORT SHANK, PARTIALLY SKINNED, SMOKED, CURED, WATER ADDED

Source: *Meat Price Report.* **Price Frequency:** weekly. **Units of Measure:** cents per lb. **Type of Price:** price paid to wholesaler. **Time Period Covered:** latest week.

HAM: SHORT SHANK, SKINNED

Source: *Meat Price Report.* **Price Frequency:** weekly. **Units of Measure:** cents per lb. **Type of Price:** price paid to wholesaler. **Time Period Covered:** latest week.

HAM: SKINNED

Source: *Agricultural Outlook.* **Price Frequency:** monthly, annually. **Effective Market(s):** Midwest. **Units of Measure:** Dollars per 100 lbs. **Type of Price:** wholesale. **Time Period Covered:** monthly latest 6 months, annually latest 3 years.

Source: *Livestock and Poultry Situation and Outlook Report.* **Price Frequency:** monthly. **Effective Market(s):** Central United States. **Units of Measure:** Dollars per 100 lbs. **Type of Price:** wholesale. **Time Period Covered:** latest year.

Source: *National Provisioner.* **Price Frequency:** daily. **Effective Market(s):** Midwest River. **Units of Measure:** cents per lb. **Time Period Covered:** latest week.

HAM: SKINNED, FRESH

Source: *HRI-Buyers Guide.* **Price Frequency:** weekly. **Effective Market(s):** Northeastern area. **Units of Measure:** Dollars per lb. **Type of Price:** price paid by dining places & institutions. **Time Period Covered:** latest week.

Source: *Livestock, Meat, Wool Market News.* **Price Frequency:** weekly, seasonally. **Effective Market(s):** Central United States, California. **Units of Measure:** Dollars per 100 lbs. **Type of Price:** average. **Time Period Covered:** latest week, year ago.

HAM: SKINNED, SMOKED

Source: *Commodity Year Book.* **Price Frequency:** annually. **Effective Market(s):** Midwest. **Units of Measure:** cents per lb. **Time Period Covered:** latest 7 years.

HAM: SKINNED, SMOKED, CURED

Source: *HRI-Buyers Guide.* **Price Frequency:** weekly. **Effective Market(s):** Northeastern area. **Units of Measure:** Dollars per lb. **Type of Price:** price paid by dining places & institutions. **Time Period Covered:** latest week.

HAM: SMOKED, FULLY COOKED

Source: *HRI-Buyers Guide.* **Price Frequency:** weekly. **Effective Market(s):** Northeastern area. **Units of Measure:** Dollars per lb. **Type of Price:** price paid by dining places & institutions. **Time Period Covered:** latest week.

HAM: WHOLE, CURED

Source: *Porkpro Newsletter.* **Price Frequency:** weekly. **Effective Market(s):** Chicago. **Units of Measure:** Dollars per lb. **Type of Price:** retail. **Time Period Covered:** latest day, week ago, year ago.

HAMMER: NAIL, 16 OUNCE HEAD, WITH HANDLE

Source: *Agricultural Prices.* **Price Frequency:** semiannually. **Effective Market(s):** United States. **Units of Measure:** Dollars each. **Type of Price:** paid by farmer. **Time Period Covered:** latest year.

Source: *Agricultural Prices Annual Summary.* **Price Frequency:** semiannually. **Effective Market(s):** United States. **Units of Measure:** Dollars each. **Type of Price:** average paid by farmer. **Time Period Covered:** latest 6 years.

HANGING BASKETS: FLOWERING

Source: *Floriculture Crops.* **Price Frequency:** annually. **Effective Market(s):** 28 domestic markets, United States. **Units of Measure:** Dollars per unit. **Type of Price:** commercial wholesale. **Time Period Covered:** latest 2 years.

HANGING BASKETS: FOLIAGE

Source: *Floriculture Crops.* **Price Frequency:** annually. **Effective Market(s):** 27 domestic markets, United States. **Units of Measure:** Dollars per unit. **Type of Price:** commercial wholesale. **Time Period Covered:** latest 2 years.

HARDBOARD

Source: *Timber Bulletin.* **Price Frequency:** monthly, annually. **Effective Market(s):** United Kingdom. **Units of Measure:** British pounds per metric ton. **Type of Price:** import value. **Time Period Covered:** monthly latest 2 years, annually latest 5 years.

HARDWOOD CHIPS: CLEAN

Source: *Timber Mart-South.* **Price Frequency:** quarterly. **Effective Market(s):** 14 Southeastern domestic markets. **Units of Measure:** Dollars per ton. **Type of Price:** mill. **Time Period Covered:** latest quarter.

HARDWOOD CHIPS: WHOLE TREE

Source: *Timber Mart-South.* **Price Frequency:** quarterly. **Effective Market(s):** 14 Southeastern domestic markets. **Units of Measure:** Dollars per ton. **Type of Price:** mill. **Time Period Covered:** latest 2 quarters.

HARDWOOD PULPWOOD: CHIPS

Source: *Pulpwood Prices in the Southeast.* **Price Frequency:** annually. **Effective Market(s):** Florida, Georgia, North Carolina, South Carolina, Virginia. **Units of Measure:** Dollars per green ton. **Type of Price:** average. **Time Period Covered:** latest 2 years.

HARDWOOD PULPWOOD: ROUNDWOOD

Source: *Pulpwood Prices in the Southeast.* **Price Frequency:** annually. **Effective Market(s):** Florida, Georgia, North Carolina, South Carolina, Virginia. **Units of Measure:** Dollars per standard cord. **Type of Price:** average. **Time Period Covered:** latest 2 years.

HARDWOOD SAWTIMBER: MIXED

Source: *Timber Mart-South.* **Price Frequency:** quarterly. **Effective Market(s):** 14 Southeastern domestic markets. **Units of Measure:** Dollars per 1000 board feet. **Type of Price:** stumpage, mill, standing. **Time Period Covered:** latest 2 quarters.

Source: *Timber Mart-South.* **Price Frequency:** quarterly. **Effective Market(s):** 12 domestic markets. **Units of Measure:** Dollars per 1000 board feet. **Type of Price:** bid. **Time Period Covered:** latest quarter.

HARDWOODS: EASTERN

Source: *Volume and Value of Sawtimber Stumpage Sold From National Forests by Selected Species and Region.* **Price Frequency:** quarterly, annually. **Effective Market(s):** United States. **Units of Measure:** Dollars per 1000 board feet. **Type of Price:** average. **Time Period Covered:** latest quarter, latest year.

HARDWOODS: WESTERN

Source: *Volume and Value of Sawtimber Stumpage Sold From National Forests by Selected Species and Region.* **Price Frequency:** quarterly, annually. **Effective Market(s):** United States. **Units of Measure:** Dollars per 1000 board feet. **Type of Price:** average. **Time Period Covered:** latest quarter, latest year.

HAY

Source: *Agricultural Outlook.* **Price Frequency:** monthly, annually. **Effective Market(s):** United States. **Units of Measure:** Dollars per ton. **Type of Price:** price received by farmers. **Time Period Covered:** monthly latest 6 months, annually latest 3 years.

Source: *Agricultural Prices.* **Price Frequency:** monthly. **Effective Market(s):** United States. **Units of Measure:** Dollars per ton. **Type of Price:** received by farmer. **Time Period Covered:** latest 2 months, year ago.

Source: *Agricultural Prices.* **Price Frequency:** monthly. **Effective Market(s):** 29 domestic markets, United States. **Units of Measure:** Dollars per ton. **Type of Price:** received by farmer. **Time Period Covered:** latest month.

Source: *Agricultural Prices Annual Summary.* **Price Frequency:** annually. **Effective Market(s):** 50 domestic markets, United States. **Units of Measure:** Dollars per ton. **Type of Price:** average price received by farmer. **Time Period Covered:** latest 2 years, for US latest 6 years.

Source: *Commodity Year Book.* **Price Frequency:** annually. **Effective Market(s):** United States. **Units of Measure:** Dollars per ton. **Type of Price:** farm price. **Time Period Covered:** latest 4 years.

Source: *Commodity Year Book.* **Price Frequency:** monthly, annually. **Units of Measure:** Dollars per ton. **Type of Price:** price received by farmers. **Time Period Covered:** latest 4 years.

Source: *Dairy Market Statistics.* **Price Frequency:** monthly, annually. **Effective Market(s):** 11 domestic markets. **Units of Measure:** Dollars per ton. **Time Period Covered:** latest year.

Source: *Farm and Dairy.* **Price Frequency:** weekly, seasonally. **Effective Market(s):** Ohio, Pennsylvania. **Units of Measure:** Dollars per load. **Type of Price:** auction high, auction low. **Time Period Covered:** latest week.

Source: *Feed Situation and Outlook Report.* **Price Frequency:** monthly, annually. **Effective Market(s):** United States. **Units of Measure:** Dollars per ton. **Type of Price:** average. **Time Period Covered:** latest 5 years.

Source: *Illinois Farm Report.* **Price Frequency:** monthly. **Effective Market(s):** Illinois. **Units of Measure:** Dollars per ton. **Type of Price:** average received by farmers. **Time Period Covered:** latest 2 months, year ago.

Source: *Kansas Business Review.* **Price Frequency:** monthly. **Effective Market(s):** Kansas. **Units of Measure:** Dollars per ton. **Type of Price:** received by farmer. **Time Period Covered:** latest month, month ago, year ago.

Source: *Standard & Poor's Statistical Service Current Statistics.* **Price Frequency:** monthly, annually. **Units of Measure:** Dollars per ton. **Time Period Covered:** latest 4 years.

HAY: FAIR TO GOOD QUALITY

Source: *Utah Stockman-Farmer.* **Price Frequency:** monthly. **Effective Market(s):** Utah. **Units of Measure:** Dollars per ton. **Time Period Covered:** latest month.

HAY: GOOD QUALITY

Source: *Utah Stockman-Farmer.* **Price Frequency:** monthly. **Effective Market(s):** Utah. **Units of Measure:** Dollars per ton. **Time Period Covered:** latest month.

HAY: MEADOW, GOOD

Source: *Farmers Weekly.* **Price Frequency:** weekly, seasonally. **Effective Market(s):** 10 British markets. **Units of Measure:** British pounds per tonne. **Type of Price:** merchant's buying. **Time Period Covered:** latest week.

HAY: MEADOW, MEDIUM

Source: *Farmers Weekly.* **Price Frequency:** weekly, seasonally. **Effective Market(s):** 10 British markets. **Units of Measure:** British pounds per tonne. **Type of Price:** merchant's buying. **Time Period Covered:** latest week.

HAY: MIXED ALFALFA-GRASS

Source: *Drovers Journal.* **Price Frequency:** semiweekly, seasonally. **Effective Market(s):** 8 domestic markets. **Time Period Covered:** selected day.

HAY: NOT ALFALFA

Source: *Agricultural Prices.* **Price Frequency:** monthly. **Effective Market(s):** 29 domestic markets, United States. **Units of Measure:** Dollars per ton. **Type of Price:** received by farmer. **Time Period Covered:** latest month.

Source: *Washington Farmer-Stockman.* **Price Frequency:** monthly. **Effective Market(s):** Washington. **Units of Measure:** Dollars per ton. **Type of Price:** average received by farmer. **Time Period Covered:** latest month, month ago, year ago.

HAY: OTHER

Source: *Illinois Farm Report.* **Price Frequency:** monthly. **Effective Market(s):** Illinois. **Units of Measure:** Dollars per ton. **Type of Price:** average received by farmers. **Time Period Covered:** latest 2 months, year ago.

HAY: PRAIRIE

Source: *Drovers Journal.* **Price Frequency:** semiweekly, seasonally. **Effective Market(s):** 8 domestic markets. **Time Period Covered:** selected day.

Source: *Hay Market News.* **Price Frequency:** weekly, seasonally. **Effective Market(s):** North East Nebraska, South East Kansas. **Units of Measure:** Dollars per ton. **Time Period Covered:** latest week, month ago, year ago.

HAY: PREMIUM QUALITY

Source: *Utah Stockman-Farmer.* **Price Frequency:** monthly. **Effective Market(s):** Utah. **Units of Measure:** Dollars per ton. **Time Period Covered:** latest month.

HAY: RED CLOVER SEED

Source: *Commodity Year Book.* **Price Frequency:** annually. **Effective Market(s):** United States. **Units of Measure:** Dollars per 100 lbs. **Type of Price:** retail price paid by farmers. **Time Period Covered:** latest 2 years.

HAY: SEEDS, GOOD

Source: *Farmers Weekly.* **Price Frequency:** weekly, seasonally. **Effective Market(s):** 10 British markets. **Units of Measure:** British pounds per tonne. **Type of Price:** merchant's buying. **Time Period Covered:** latest week.

HAY: SEEDS, MEDIUM

Source: *Farmers Weekly.* **Price Frequency:** weekly, seasonally. **Effective Market(s):** 10 British markets. **Units of Measure:** British pounds per tonne. **Type of Price:** merchant's buying. **Time Period Covered:** latest week.

HAY: SUDAN GRASS

Source: *Commodity Year Book.* **Price Frequency:** annually. **Effective Market(s):** United States. **Units of Measure:** Dollars per 100 lbs. **Type of Price:** retail price paid by farmers. **Time Period Covered:** latest 2 years.

HAY: TIMOTHY SEED

Source: *Commodity Year Book.* **Price Frequency:** annually. **Effective Market(s):** United States. **Units of Measure:** Dollars per 100 lbs. **Type of Price:** retail price paid by farmers. **Time Period Covered:** latest 2 years.

HAY AND FEED GRAINS

Source: *Illinois Farm Report.* **Price Frequency:** monthly. **Effective Market(s):** Illinois. **Units of Measure:** index. **Type of Price:** index of prices received by farmers. **Time Period Covered:** latest 2 months, year ago.

HAY CUBES: OFF QUALITY

Source: *Utah Stockman-Farmer.* **Price Frequency:** monthly. **Effective Market(s):** Utah. **Units of Measure:** Dollars per ton. **Time Period Covered:** latest month.

HAY CUBES: PREMIER QUALITY

Source: *Utah Stockman-Farmer.* **Price Frequency:** monthly. **Effective Market(s):** Utah. **Units of Measure:** Dollars per ton. **Time Period Covered:** latest month.

HAYRAKE: SIDE DELIVERY, TRACTION DRIVE

Source: *Agricultural Prices.* **Price Frequency:** annually. **Effective Market(s):** United States. **Units of Measure:** Dollars each. **Type of Price:** paid by farmer. **Time Period Covered:** latest year.

Source: *Agricultural Prices Annual Summary.* **Price Frequency:** annually. **Effective Market(s):** United States. **Units of Measure:** Dollars each. **Type of Price:** average paid by farmer. **Time Period Covered:** latest 6 years.

HDPE

see Polyethylene: High Density.

HEAT STABILIZERS

Source: *Modern Plastics.* **Price Frequency:** quarterly in February, May, August, November. **Units of Measure:** Dollars per lb. **Type of Price:** list. **Time Period Covered:** latest 4 quarters.

HEATING OIL

see Oil: Heating.

HEIFERETTES AND STOCKER COWS: FEEDER, MEDIUM AND LARGE FRAME

Source: *Montana Farmer-Stockman.* **Price Frequency:** monthly. **Effective Market(s):** Billings (MT). **Units of Measure:** Dollars per 100 lbs. **Type of Price:** cash auction. **Time Period Covered:** latest month.

HEIFERETTES AND YOUNG COWS FOR FURTHER FEEDING: FEEDER

Source: *Utah Stockman-Farmer.* **Price Frequency:** monthly. **Effective Market(s):** Spanish Fork (UT). **Units of Measure:** Dollars per 100 lbs. **Type of Price:** auction. **Time Period Covered:** latest month.

HEIFERS

Source: *Farmers Weekly.* **Price Frequency:** weekly. **Effective Market(s):** England/Wales, Scotland. **Units of Measure:** British pence per kilogram. **Type of Price:** average. **Time Period Covered:** latest week.

Source: *Scottish Farmer.* **Price Frequency:** weekly. **Effective Market(s):** Scotland. **Units of Measure:** British pence per kilogram. **Type of Price:** average. **Time Period Covered:** latest week.

Source: *Scottish Farmer.* **Price Frequency:** weekly. **Effective Market(s):** 33 Scottish markets. **Units of Measure:** British pence per kilogram. **Time Period Covered:** latest week.

HEIFERS: ADULT, GOOD, STORE

Source: *New Zealand Farmer.* **Price Frequency:** weekly, seasonally. **Effective Market(s):** 7 New Zealand markets. **Units of Measure:** New Zealand dollars per head. **Time Period Covered:** latest 2 weeks.

HEIFERS: ADULT, MEDIUM, STORE

Source: *New Zealand Farmer.* **Price Frequency:** weekly, seasonally. **Effective Market(s):** 7 New Zealand markets. **Units of Measure:** New Zealand dollars per head. **Time Period Covered:** latest 2 weeks.

HEIFERS: ALL BREEDS, STORE

Source: *Scottish Farmer.* **Price Frequency:** weekly. **Effective Market(s):** Aberdeen (Scotland), Stirling (Scotland). **Units of Measure:** British pence per kilo. **Time Period Covered:** latest week.

HEIFERS: ANGUS AND ANGUS X, STORE

Source: *Farmers Weekly.* **Price Frequency:** weekly. **Effective Market(s):** England/Wales, Scotland. **Units of Measure:** British pence per kilogram. **Type of Price:** average. **Time Period Covered:** latest week.

HEIFERS: ANGUS-ANGUS AND ANGUS-ANGUS X, STORE

Source: *Scottish Farmer.* **Price Frequency:** weekly. **Effective Market(s):** Aberdeen (Scotland), Stirling (Scotland). **Units of Measure:** British pence per kilogram. **Time Period Covered:** latest week.

HEIFERS: BEEF, CHAROLAIS X, HEAVY

Source: *Farmers Weekly.* **Price Frequency:** weekly. **Effective Market(s):** England/Wales. **Units of Measure:** British pence per kilogram. **Time Period Covered:** latest week.

HEIFERS: BEEF, CHAROLAIS X, LIGHT

Source: *Farmers Weekly.* **Price Frequency:** weekly. **Effective Market(s):** England/Wales. **Units of Measure:** British pence per kilogram. **Time Period Covered:** latest week.

HEIFERS: BEEF, CHAROLAIS X, MEDIUM

Source: *Farmers Weekly.* **Price Frequency:** weekly. **Effective Market(s):** England/Wales. **Units of Measure:** British pence per kilogram. **Time Period Covered:** latest week.

HEIFERS: BEEF, CHOICE

Source: *Livestock and Poultry Situation and Outlook Report.* **Price Frequency:** monthly. **Effective Market(s):** Central United States. **Units of Measure:** Dollars per 100 lbs. **Type of Price:** wholesale. **Time Period Covered:** latest year.

Source: *Livestock and Poultry Update.* **Price Frequency:** monthly. **Effective Market(s):** Central United States. **Units of Measure:** Dollars per 100 lbs. **Type of Price:** wholesale. **Time Period Covered:** latest 3 months, year ago.

HEIFERS: BEEF, CHOICE, YIELD 3

Source: *National Provisioner.* **Price Frequency:** daily. **Effective Market(s):** Midwest Reiver area. **Units of Measure:** cents per lb. **Time Period Covered:** latest week.

HEIFERS: BEEF, CHOICE, YIELD 4

Source: *National Provisioner.* **Price Frequency:** daily. **Effective Market(s):** Midwest River area. **Units of Measure:** cents per lb. **Time Period Covered:** latest week.

HEIFERS: BEEF, DRESSED

Source: *Commodity Year Book.* **Price Frequency:** annually. **Units of Measure:** Dollars per 100 lbs. **Type of Price:** wholesale. **Time Period Covered:** latest 4 years.

HEIFERS: BEEF, FRESIAN/HOLSTEIN, HEAVY

Source: *Farmers Weekly.* **Price Frequency:** weekly. **Effective Market(s):** England/Wales. **Units of Measure:** British pence per kilogram. **Time Period Covered:** latest week.

HEIFERS: BEEF, FRESIAN/HOLSTEIN, LIGHT

Source: *Farmers Weekly.* **Price Frequency:** weekly. **Effective Market(s):** England/Wales. **Units of Measure:** British pence per kilogram. **Time Period Covered:** latest week.

HEIFERS: BEEF, FRESIAN/HOLSTEIN, MEDIUM

Source: *Farmers Weekly.* **Price Frequency:** weekly. **Effective Market(s):** England/Wales. **Units of Measure:** British pence per kilogram. **Time Period Covered:** latest week.

HEIFERS: BEEF, HEREFORD CROSS, HEAVY

Source: *Farmers Weekly.* **Price Frequency:** weekly. **Effective Market(s):** England/Wales. **Units of Measure:** British pence per kilogram. **Time Period Covered:** latest week.

HEIFERS: BEEF, HEREFORD CROSS, LIGHT

Source: *Farmers Weekly.* **Price Frequency:** weekly. **Effective Market(s):** England/Wales. **Units of Measure:** British pence per kilogram. **Time Period Covered:** latest week.

HEIFERS: BEEF, HEREFORD CROSS, MEDIUM

Source: *Farmers Weekly.* **Price Frequency:** weekly. **Effective Market(s):** England/Wales. **Units of Measure:** British pence per kilogram. **Time Period Covered:** latest week.

HEIFERS: BEEF, LIMOUSIN X, HEAVY

Source: *Farmers Weekly.* **Price Frequency:** weekly. **Effective Market(s):** England/Wales. **Units of Measure:** British pence per kilogram. **Time Period Covered:** latest week.

HEIFERS: BEEF, LIMOUSIN X, LIGHT

Source: *Farmers Weekly.* **Price Frequency:** weekly. **Effective Market(s):** England/Wales. **Units of Measure:** British pence per kilogram. **Time Period Covered:** latest week.

HEIFERS: BEEF, LIMOUSIN X, MEDIUM

Source: *Farmers Weekly.* **Price Frequency:** weekly. **Effective Market(s):** England/Wales. **Units of Measure:** British pence per kilogram. **Time Period Covered:** latest week.

HEIFERS: BEEF, SIMMENTAL X, HEAVY

Source: *Farmers Weekly.* **Price Frequency:** weekly. **Effective Market(s):** England/Wales. **Units of Measure:** British pence per kilogram. **Time Period Covered:** latest week.

HEIFERS: BEEF, SIMMENTAL X, LIGHT

Source: *Farmers Weekly.* **Price Frequency:** weekly. **Effective Market(s):** England/Wales. **Units of Measure:** British pence per kilogram. **Time Period Covered:** latest week.

HEIFERS: BEEF, SIMMENTAL X, MEDIUM

Source: *Farmers Weekly.* **Price Frequency:** weekly. **Effective Market(s):** England/Wales. **Units of Measure:** British pence per kilogram. **Time Period Covered:** latest week.

HEIFERS: BELGIAN BLUE AND BELGIAN BLUE X, STORE

Source: *Farmers Weekly.* **Price Frequency:** weekly. **Effective Market(s):** England/Wales, Scotland. **Units of Measure:** British pence per kilogram. **Type of Price:** average. **Time Period Covered:** latest week.

HEIFERS: BELGIAN BLUE X, STORE

Source: *Scottish Farmer.* **Price Frequency:** weekly. **Effective Market(s):** Aberdeen (Scotland), Stirling (Scotland). **Units of Measure:** British pence per kilogram. **Time Period Covered:** latest week.

HEIFERS: CHAROLAIS AND CHAROLAIS X, STORE

Source: *Farmers Weekly.* **Price Frequency:** weekly. **Effective Market(s):** England/Wales, Scotland. **Units of Measure:** British pence per kilogram. **Type of Price:** average. **Time Period Covered:** latest week.

HEIFERS: CHAROLAIS X, STORE

Source: *Scottish Farmer.* **Price Frequency:** weekly. **Effective Market(s):** Aberdeen (Scotland), Stirling (Scotland). **Units of Measure:** British pence per kilogram. **Time Period Covered:** latest week.

HEIFERS: CHOICE

Source: *Agriculture.* **Price Frequency:** weekly. **Effective Market(s):** Omaha (NE), Sioux City (IA), Sioux Falls (SD), St. Paul, Texas Panhandle. **Units of Measure:** Dollars per 100 lbs. **Time Period Covered:** latest week.

Source: *Farm and Dairy.* **Price Frequency:** weekly, seasonally. **Effective Market(s):** Ohio, Pennsylvania. **Units of Measure:** Dollars per head. **Type of Price:** auction high, auction low. **Time Period Covered:** latest week.

HEIFERS: CHOICE 2-4

Source: *Utah Farmer-Stockman.* **Price Frequency:** monthly, seasonally. **Effective Market(s):** Arizona/California, Central Plains, Midwest. **Units of Measure:** Dollars per 100 lbs. **Time Period Covered:** latest month.

HEIFERS: DAIRY

Source: *Scottish Farmer.* **Price Frequency:** weekly. **Effective Market(s):** Ayr (Scotland), Carlisle (Scotland), Lanark (Scotland), Paisley (Scotland), Stirling (Scotland). **Units of Measure:** British pounds per head. **Type of Price:** top, average. **Time Period Covered:** latest week.

HEIFERS: DEADWEIGHT

Source: *Farmers Weekly.* **Price Frequency:** weekly. **Effective Market(s):** Great Britain. **Units of Measure:** British pence per kilogram. **Type of Price:** average. **Time Period Covered:** latest week.

Source: *Scottish Farmer.* **Price Frequency:** weekly. **Effective Market(s):** Scotland. **Units of Measure:** British pence per kilogram. **Type of Price:** average. **Time Period Covered:** latest week.

HEIFERS: FEEDER

Source: *California Farmer.* **Price Frequency:** semimonthly. **Effective Market(s):** Stockton (CA). **Units of Measure:** Dollars per 100 lbs. **Time Period Covered:** latest week, month ago, year ago.

Source: *Farm and Dairy.* **Price Frequency:** weekly, seasonally. **Effective Market(s):** Ohio, Pennsylvania. **Units of Measure:** Dollars per head. **Type of Price:** auction high, auction low. **Time Period Covered:** latest week.

Source: *Livestock and Poultry Update.* **Price Frequency:** monthly. **Effective Market(s):** Oklahoma City. **Units of Measure:** Dollars per 100 lbs. **Time Period Covered:** latest 3 months, year ago.

Source: *Oregon Farmer-Stockman.* **Price Frequency:** monthly, seasonally. **Effective Market(s):** Portland, Klamath Falls (OR). **Units of Measure:** Dollars per 100 lbs. **Type of Price:** auction. **Time Period Covered:** latest month.

Source: *Viewpoint.* **Price Frequency:** weekly. **Effective Market(s):** 11 domestic markets. **Units of Measure:** Dollars per 100 lbs. **Time Period Covered:** latest week.

HEIFERS: FEEDER, 4-500 LBS

Source: *Doane'e Agricultural Report.* **Price Frequency:** weekly. **Effective Market(s):** Oklahoma City. **Units of Measure:** Dollars per 100 lbs. **Time Period Covered:** latest week, week ago, year ago.

HEIFERS: FEEDER, MEDIUM AND LARGE

Source: *Idaho Farmer-Stockman.* **Price Frequency:** monthly. **Effective Market(s):** Idaho. **Units of Measure:** Dollars per 100 lbs. **Time Period Covered:** latest month.

Source: *Montana Farmer-Stockman.* **Price Frequency:** monthly. **Effective Market(s):** Billings (MT), Riverton (WY), Torrington (WY). **Units of Measure:** Dollars per 100 lbs. **Type of Price:** cash auction. **Time Period Covered:** latest month.

Source: *Utah Stockman-Farmer.* **Price Frequency:** monthly. **Effective Market(s):** Spanish Fork (UT), Salinas (UT). **Units of Measure:** Dollars per 100 lbs. **Type of Price:** auction. **Time Period Covered:** latest month.

HEIFERS: FEEDER, MEDIUM AND LARGE NO. 1

Source: *Oregon Farmer-Stockman.* **Price Frequency:** monthly. **Effective Market(s):** Oregon/Washington. **Time Period Covered:** latest month.

Source: *Washington Farmer-Stockman.* **Price Frequency:** monthly. **Effective Market(s):** Washington/Oregon. **Units of Measure:** Dollars per 100 lbs. **Time Period Covered:** latest month.

HEIFERS: FEEDER, MEDIUM NO. 1

Source: *Livestock and Poultry Situation and Outlook Report.* **Price Frequency:** monthly. **Effective Market(s):** Kansas City, Oklahoma City. **Units of Measure:** Dollars per 100 lbs. **Time Period Covered:** latest year.

Source: *Livestock, Meat, Wool Market News.* **Price Frequency:** weekly, seasonally. **Effective Market(s):** 10 domestic markets. **Units of Measure:** Dollars per 100 lbs. **Type of Price:** average. **Time Period Covered:** latest week, year ago.

HEIFERS: FEEDER, MEDIUM NO. 2

Source: *Livestock, Meat, Wool Market News.* **Price Frequency:** weekly, seasonally. **Effective Market(s):** California, Colorado/Kansas, Georgia, Illinois, Kentucky. **Units of Measure:** Dollars per 100 lbs. **Type of Price:** average. **Time Period Covered:** latest week, year ago.

HEIFERS: FRIESIAN/HOLSTEIN X, STORE

Source: *Farmers Weekly.* **Price Frequency:** weekly. **Effective Market(s):** England/Wales, Scotland. **Units of Measure:** British pence per kilogram. **Type of Price:** average. **Time Period Covered:** latest week.

Source: *Scottish Farmer.* **Price Frequency:** weekly. **Effective Market(s):** Aberdeen (Scotland), Stirling (Scotland). **Units of Measure:** British pence per kilogram. **Time Period Covered:** latest week.

HEIFERS: G2

Source: *New Zealand Farmer.* **Price Frequency:** weekly, seasonally. **Effective Market(s):** 8 New Zealand markets. **Units of Measure:** New Zealand cents per kilogram. **Type of Price:** export. **Time Period Covered:** latest week.

HEIFERS: GOOD

Source: *Farm and Dairy.* **Price Frequency:** weekly, seasonally. **Effective Market(s):** Ohio, Pennsylvania. **Units of Measure:** Dollars per head. **Type of Price:** auction high, auction low. **Time Period Covered:** latest week.

HEIFERS: GOOD AND CHOICE

Source: *Commodity Year Book.* **Price Frequency:** annually. **Effective Market(s):** Omaha (NE). **Units of Measure:** Dollars per 100 lbs. **Type of Price:** wholesale. **Time Period Covered:** latest 5 years.

HEIFERS: HEAVY, PRIME

Source: *New Zealand Farmer.* **Price Frequency:** weekly, seasonally. **Effective Market(s):** 7 New Zealand markets. **Units of Measure:** New Zealand dollars per head. **Time Period Covered:** latest 2 weeks.

HEIFERS: HEREFORD AND HEREFORD X, STORE

Source: *Farmers Weekly.* **Price Frequency:** weekly. **Effective Market(s):** England/Wales, Scotland. **Units of Measure:** British pence per kilogram. **Type of Price:** average. **Time Period Covered:** latest week.

Source: *Scottish Farmer.* **Price Frequency:** weekly. **Effective Market(s):** Aberdeen (Scotland), Stirling (Scotland). **Units of Measure:** British pence per kilogram. **Time Period Covered:** latest week.

HEIFERS: HOLSTEIN

Source: *Lancaster Farming.* **Price Frequency:** weekly. **Effective Market(s):** Pennsylvania, Virginia. **Units of Measure:** Dollars per head. **Type of Price:** auction. **Time Period Covered:** latest week.

HEIFERS: HOT WEIGHT, MOSTLY CHOICE

Source: *Drovers Journal.* **Price Frequency:** semimonthly, seasonally. **Effective Market(s):** 8 domestic markets. **Units of Measure:** Dollars per 100 lbs. **Time Period Covered:** selected date.

HEIFERS: K2

Source: *New Zealand Farmer.* **Price Frequency:** weekly, seasonally. **Effective Market(s):** 8 New Zealand markets. **Units of Measure:** New Zealand cents per kilogram. **Type of Price:** export. **Time Period Covered:** latest week.

HEIFERS: LIGHT

Source: *Farmers Weekly.* **Price Frequency:** weekly. **Effective Market(s):** over 170 British markets. **Units of Measure:** British pence per kilogram. **Type of Price:** auction. **Time Period Covered:** latest week.

HEIFERS: LIGHT, PRIME

Source: *New Zealand Farmer.* **Price Frequency:** weekly, seasonally. **Effective Market(s):** 7 New Zealand markets. **Units of Measure:** New Zealand dollars per head. **Time Period Covered:** latest 2 weeks.

HEIFERS: LIMOUSIN AND LIMOUSIN X, STORE

Source: *Farmers Weekly.* **Price Frequency:** weekly. **Effective Market(s):** England/Wales, Scotland. **Units of Measure:** British pence per kilogram. **Type of Price:** average. **Time Period Covered:** latest week.

HEIFERS: LIMOUSIN X, STORE

Source: *Scottish Farmer.* **Price Frequency:** weekly. **Effective Market(s):** Aberdeen (Scotland), Stirling (Scotland). **Units of Measure:** British pence per kilogram. **Time Period Covered:** latest week.

HEIFERS: MEDIUM

Source: *Farmers Weekly.* **Price Frequency:** weekly. **Effective Market(s):** over 170 British markets. **Units of Measure:** British pence per kilogram. **Type of Price:** auction. **Time Period Covered:** latest week.

HEIFERS: MEDIUM AND LARGE NO. 1

Source: *Drovers Journal.* **Price Frequency:** semimonthly, seasonally. **Effective Market(s):** 80 domestic markets. **Units of Measure:** Dollars per 100 lbs. **Time Period Covered:** latest week.

HEIFERS: MEDIUM, PRIME

Source: *New Zealand Farmer.* **Price Frequency:** weekly, seasonally. **Effective Market(s):** 7 New Zealand markets. **Units of Measure:** New Zealand dollars per head. **Time Period Covered:** latest 2 weeks.

HEIFERS: NON-HOLSTEIN, SELECT

Source: *National Provisioner.* **Price Frequency:** daily. **Effective Market(s):** Midwest River area. **Units of Measure:** cents per lb. **Time Period Covered:** latest week.

HEIFERS: P2

Source: *New Zealand Farmer.* **Price Frequency:** weekly, seasonally. **Effective Market(s):** 8 New Zealand markets. **Units of Measure:** New Zealand cents per kilogram. **Type of Price:** export. **Time Period Covered:** latest week.

HEIFERS: RISING 1 YEAR, GOOD, STORE

Source: *New Zealand Farmer.* **Price Frequency:** weekly, seasonally. **Effective Market(s):** 7 New Zealand markets. **Units of Measure:** New Zealand dollars per head. **Time Period Covered:** latest 2 weeks.

HEIFERS: RISING 1 YEAR, MEDIUM, STORE

Source: *New Zealand Farmer.* **Price Frequency:** weekly, seasonally. **Effective Market(s):** 7 New Zealand markets. **Units of Measure:** New Zealand dollars per head. **Time Period Covered:** latest 2 weeks.

HEIFERS: RISING 2 YEAR, GOOD, STORE

Source: *New Zealand Farmer.* **Price Frequency:** weekly, seasonally. **Effective Market(s):** 7 New Zealand markets. **Units of Measure:** New Zealand dollars per head. **Time Period Covered:** latest 2 weeks.

HEIFERS: RISING 2 YEAR, MEDIUM, STORE

Source: *New Zealand Farmer.* **Price Frequency:** weekly, seasonally. **Effective Market(s):** 7 New Zealand markets. **Units of Measure:** New Zealand dollars per head. **Time Period Covered:** latest 2 weeks.

HEIFERS: SIMMENTAL AND SIMMENTAL X, STORE

Source: *Farmers Weekly.* **Price Frequency:** weekly. **Effective Market(s):** England/Wales, Scotland. **Units of Measure:** British pence per kilogram. **Type of Price:** average. **Time Period Covered:** latest week.

HEIFERS: SIMMENTAL X, STORE

Source: *Scottish Farmer.* **Price Frequency:** weekly. **Effective Market(s):** Aberdeen (Scotland), Stirling (Scotland). **Units of Measure:** British pence per kilogram. **Time Period Covered:** latest week.

HEIFERS: SLAUGHTER

Source: *Utah Farmer-Stockman.* **Price Frequency:** monthly. **Effective Market(s):** Idaho. **Units of Measure:** Dollars per 100 lbs. **Type of Price:** range. **Time Period Covered:** latest month.

HEIFERS: SLAUGHTER, CHOICE

Source: *Lancaster Farming.* **Price Frequency:** weekly. **Effective Market(s):** Pennsylvania, Virginia. **Units of Measure:** Dollars per head. **Type of Price:** auction. **Time Period Covered:** latest week.

Source: *Livestock and Poultry Situation and Outlook Report.* **Price Frequency:** monthly. **Effective Market(s):** Omaha (NE). **Units of Measure:** Dollars per 100 lbs. **Time Period Covered:** latest year.

Source: *Livestock and Poultry Update.* **Price Frequency:** monthly. **Effective Market(s):** Omaha (NE). **Units of Measure:** Dollars per 100 lbs. **Time Period Covered:** latest 3 months, year ago.

HEIFERS: SLAUGHTER, CHOICE 2-3

Source: *Utah Stockman-Farmer.* **Price Frequency:** monthly. **Effective Market(s):** Utah. **Units of Measure:** Dollars per 100 lbs. **Type of Price:** range. **Time Period Covered:** latest month.

HEIFERS: SLAUGHTER, CHOICE 2-4

Source: *Idaho Farmer-Stockman.* **Price Frequency:** monthly. **Effective Market(s):** Central Plains, Midwest. **Units of Measure:** Dollars per 100 lbs. **Time Period Covered:** latest month.

Source: *Livestock, Meat, Wool Market News.* **Price Frequency:** weekly, seasonally. **Effective Market(s):** 10 domestic markets. **Units of Measure:** Dollars per 100 lbs. **Type of Price:** average. **Time Period Covered:** latest week, year ago.

HEIFERS: SLAUGHTER, COMMON TO MEDIUM

Source: *Farm and Dairy.* **Price Frequency:** weekly, seasonally. **Effective Market(s):** Ohio, Pennsylvania. **Units of Measure:** Dollars per head. **Type of Price:** auction high, auction low. **Time Period Covered:** latest week.

HEIFERS: SLAUGHTER, DRESSED CARCASS, SELECT

Source: *Utah Stockman-Farmer.* **Price Frequency:** monthly. **Effective Market(s):** Idaho. **Units of Measure:** Dollars per 100 lbs. **Type of Price:** range. **Time Period Covered:** latest month.

HEIFERS: SLAUGHTER, DRESSED CARCASS, SELECT AND CHOICE

Source: *Washington Farmer-Stockman.* **Price Frequency:** monthly. **Effective Market(s):** Washington/Oregon. **Units of Measure:** Dollars per 100 lbs. **Time Period Covered:** latest month.

HEIFERS: SLAUGHTER, DRESSED, SELECT TO MOSTLY CHOICE 2-3

Source: *Idaho Farmer-Stockman.* **Price Frequency:** monthly. **Effective Market(s):** Idaho. **Units of Measure:** Dollars per 100 lbs. **Time Period Covered:** latest month.

HEIFERS: SLAUGHTER, DRESSED, SELECT AND CHOICE 1-3

Source: *Utah Stockman-Farmer.* **Price Frequency:** monthly. **Effective Market(s):** Idaho. **Units of Measure:** Dollars per 100 lbs. **Type of Price:** range. **Time Period Covered:** latest month.

HEIFERS: SLAUGHTER, MEDIUM TO GOOD

Source: *Farm and Dairy.* **Price Frequency:** weekly, seasonally. **Effective Market(s):** Ohio, Pennsylvania. **Units of Measure:** Dollars per head. **Type of Price:** auction high, auction low. **Time Period Covered:** latest week.

HEIFERS: SLAUGHTER, SELECT

Source: *Lancaster Farming.* **Price Frequency:** weekly. **Effective Market(s):** Pennsylvania, Virginia. **Units of Measure:** Dollars per head. **Type of Price:** auction. **Time Period Covered:** latest week.

Source: *Livestock and Poultry Situation and Outlook Report.* **Price Frequency:** monthly. **Effective Market(s):** Omaha (NE). **Units of Measure:** Dollars per 100 lbs. **Time Period Covered:** latest year.

Source: *Livestock and Poultry Update.* **Price Frequency:** monthly. **Effective Market(s):** Omaha (NE). **Units of Measure:** Dollars per 100 lbs. **Time Period Covered:** latest 3 months, year ago.

HEIFERS: SLAUGHTER, SELECT 2-3

Source: *Livestock, Meat, Wool Market News.* **Price Frequency:** weekly, seasonally. **Effective Market(s):** 10 domestic markets. **Units of Measure:** Dollars per 100 lbs. **Type of Price:** average. **Time Period Covered:** latest week, year ago.

HEIFERS: SLAUGHTER, SELECT AND CHOICE

Source: *Washington Farmer-Stockman.* **Price Frequency:** monthly. **Effective Market(s):** Washington/Oregon. **Units of Measure:** Dollars per 100 lbs. **Time Period Covered:** latest month.

HEIFERS: SLAUGHTER, SELECT AND CHOICE 1-3

Source: *Utah Stockman-Farmer.* **Price Frequency:** monthly. **Effective Market(s):** Idaho. **Units of Measure:** Dollars per 100 lbs. **Type of Price:** range. **Time Period Covered:** latest month.

HEIFERS: SLAUGHTER, SELECT AND CHOICE 2-3

Source: *Oregon Farmer-Stockman.* **Price Frequency:** monthly. **Effective Market(s):** Oregon/Washington. **Units of Measure:** Dollars per 100 lbs. **Type of Price:** range. **Time Period Covered:** latest month.

HEIFERS: SLAUGHTER, SELECT AND CHOICE 2-4

Source: *Idaho Farmer-Stockman.* **Price Frequency:** monthly. **Effective Market(s):** Arizona/California. **Units of Measure:** Dollars per 100 lbs. **Time Period Covered:** latest month.

HEIFERS: SLAUGHTER, SELECT TO MOSTLY CHOICE 1-3

Source: *Idaho Farmer-Stockman.* **Price Frequency:** monthly. **Effective Market(s):** Idaho. **Units of Measure:** Dollars per 100 lbs. **Time Period Covered:** latest month.

HEIFERS: STANDARD

Source: *Farm and Dairy.* **Price Frequency:** weekly, seasonally. **Effective Market(s):** Ohio, Pennsylvania. **Units of Measure:** Dollars per head. **Type of Price:** auction high, auction low. **Time Period Covered:** latest week.

HEIFERS: YOUNG, MOSTLY CHOICE

Source: *Drovers Journal.* **Price Frequency:** semimonthly, seasonally. **Effective Market(s):** 8 domestic markets. **Units of Measure:** Dollars per 100 lbs. **Time Period Covered:** selected date.

HEIFERS: YOUNG, MOSTLY SELECT

Source: *Drovers Journal.* **Price Frequency:** semimonthly, seasonally. **Effective Market(s):** 8 domestic markets. **Units of Measure:** Dollars per 100 lbs. **Time Period Covered:** selected date.

HELICONIA: HAWAII

Source: *Floriculture Crops.* **Price Frequency:** annually. **Effective Market(s):** United States. **Units of Measure:** cents per unit. **Type of Price:** commercial wholesale. **Time Period Covered:** latest 2 years.

HELIOTROPINE

Source: *Chemical Marketing Reporter.* **Price Frequency:** weekly. **Effective Market(s):** New York. **Units of Measure:** Dollars per lb. **Type of Price:** spot. **Time Period Covered:** latest week.

Source: *Journal of Commerce and Commercial.* **Price Frequency:** weekly in Tuesday issue. **Units of Measure:** Dollars per lb. **Type of Price:** spot. **Time Period Covered:** latest week.

HEMATITE

Source: *Journal of Commerce and Commercial.* **Price Frequency:** weekly in Wednesday issue. **Units of Measure:** Dollars per lb. **Type of Price:** spot. **Time Period Covered:** latest week.

HEMLOCK: EASTERN

Source: *Volume and Value of Sawtimber Stumpage Sold From National Forests by Selected Species and Region.* **Price Frequency:** quarterly, annually. **Effective Market(s):** Southern region. **Units of Measure:** Dollars per 1000 board feet. **Type of Price:** average. **Time Period Covered:** latest quarter, latest year.

HEMLOCK: MOUNTAIN

Source: *Volume and Value of Sawtimber Stumpage Sold From National Forests by Selected Species and Region.* **Price Frequency:** quarterly, annually. **Effective Market(s):** Northern region, Pacific Northwest. **Units of Measure:** Dollars per 1000 board feet. **Type of Price:** average. **Time Period Covered:** latest quarter, latest year.

HEMLOCK: WESTERN

Source: *Volume and Value of Sawtimber Stumpage Sold From National Forests by Selected Species and Region.* **Price Frequency:** quarterly, annually. **Effective Market(s):** Northern region, Pacific Northwest, Alaska. **Units of Measure:** Dollars per 1000 board feet. **Type of Price:** average. **Time Period Covered:** latest quarter, latest year.

HEMLOCK OIL
see Spruce Oil.

HEMLOCK SAWTIMBER
see Sawtimber: Hemlock.

HEMLOCK-FIR: INLAND

Source: *Random Lengths.* **Price Frequency:** weekly. **Effective Market(s):** 8 domestic markets. **Units of Measure:** Dollars per 1000 board feet. **Type of Price:** delivered to wholesaler. **Time Period Covered:** latest week.

HEMLOCK-FIR: KILN DRIED, NO. 2 AND BETTER

Source: *Random Lengths.* **Price Frequency:** weekly. **Effective Market(s):** Coast. **Units of Measure:** Dollars per 1000 board feet. **Type of Price:** mill price to wholesaler. **Time Period Covered:** latest week.

HEMLOCK-FIR: KILN DRIED, STANDARD AND BETTER

Source: *Random Lengths.* **Price Frequency:** weekly. **Effective Market(s):** Coast. **Units of Measure:** Dollars per 1000 board feet. **Type of Price:** mill price to wholesaler. **Time Period Covered:** latest week.

HEMP

Source: *Fibre Market News.* **Price Frequency:** weekly. **Effective Market(s):** New York. **Units of Measure:** cent per lb. **Time Period Covered:** latest week.

HEMP: TYPE G, MANILA

Source: *Prices of Selected Asia/Pacific Products.* **Price Frequency:** monthly. **Effective Market(s):** main European ports. **Units of Measure:** Dollars per metric ton. **Type of Price:** high, low. **Time Period Covered:** latest month.

HEMP: TYPE H, MANILA

Source: *Prices of Selected Asia/Pacific Products.* **Price Frequency:** monthly. **Effective Market(s):** main European ports. **Units of Measure:** Dollars per metric ton. **Type of Price:** high, low. **Time Period Covered:** latest month.

HEMP: TYPE JK, MANILA

Source: *Prices of Selected Asia/Pacific Products.* **Price Frequency:** monthly. **Effective Market(s):** main European ports. **Units of Measure:** Dollars per metric ton. **Type of Price:** high, low. **Time Period Covered:** latest month.

HENBANE LEAVES

Source: *Chemical Marketing Reporter.* **Price Frequency:** weekly. **Effective Market(s):** New York. **Units of Measure:** Dollars per lb. **Type of Price:** spot. **Time Period Covered:** latest week.

HENNA POWDER: BLACK

Source: *Journal of Commerce and Commercial.* **Price Frequency:** weekly in Monday issue. **Units of Measure:** Dollars per lb. **Type of Price:** spot. **Time Period Covered:** latest week.

HENNA POWDER: NEUTRAL

Source: *Journal of Commerce and Commercial.* **Price Frequency:** weekly in Monday issue. **Units of Measure:** Dollars per lb. **Type of Price:** spot. **Time Period Covered:** latest week.

HENNA POWDER: RED

Source: *Journal of Commerce and Commercial.* **Price Frequency:** weekly in Monday issue. **Units of Measure:** Dollars per lb. **Type of Price:** spot. **Time Period Covered:** latest week.

HENS

Source: *Commodity Year Book.* **Price Frequency:** annually. **Effective Market(s):** New York. **Units of Measure:** cents per lb. **Type of Price:** retail. **Time Period Covered:** latest 5 years.

Source: *Lancaster Farming.* **Price Frequency:** weekly. **Effective Market(s):** Pennsylvania. **Units of Measure:** Dollars per lb. **Type of Price:** auction. **Time Period Covered:** latest week.

HENS: BANTY

Source: *Lancaster Farming.* **Price Frequency:** weekly. **Effective Market(s):** Pennsylvania. **Units of Measure:** Dollars each. **Type of Price:** auction. **Time Period Covered:** latest week.

HENS: GRADE A, READY-TO-COOK

Source: *Poultry Market Statistics.* **Price Frequency:** monthly, annually. **Effective Market(s):** Chicago, Detroit, Los Angeles, North Atlantic region, San Francisco. **Units of Measure:** cents per lb. **Type of Price:** average paid to retailers. **Time Period Covered:** latest year.

HENS: LEGHORN

Source: *Lancaster Farming.* **Price Frequency:** weekly. **Effective Market(s):** Pennsylvania. **Units of Measure:** Dollars per lb. **Type of Price:** auction. **Time Period Covered:** latest week.

HENS: LIVE, HEAVY TYPE

Source: *Poultry Market Statistics.* **Price Frequency:** monthly, annually. **Effective Market(s):** North Carolina, Southeast area, Southwest area, North Central area. **Units of Measure:** cents per lb. **Type of Price:** farm. **Time Period Covered:** latest year.

HENS: LIVE, LIGHT TYPE

Source: *Poultry Market Statistics.* **Price Frequency:** monthly, annually. **Effective Market(s):** East Pennsylvania/New Jersey, Southeast area, West North Central area. **Units of Measure:** cents per lb. **Type of Price:** farm. **Time Period Covered:** latest year.

HENS: ROCK CORNISH

Source: *HRI-Buyers Guide.* **Price Frequency:** weekly. **Effective Market(s):** Northeastern area. **Units of Measure:** Dollars per lb. **Type of Price:** price paid by dining places & institutions. **Time Period Covered:** latest week.

HENS: ROCK CORNISH GAME, FRESH

Source: *Urner Barry's Price-Current.* **Price Frequency:** daily. **Units of Measure:** Dollars per hen. **Type of Price:** paid by first receiver. **Time Period Covered:** latest day.

HENS: ROCK CORNISH GAME, FROZEN

Source: *Urner Barry's Price-Current.* **Price Frequency:** daily. **Units of Measure:** Dollars per hen. **Type of Price:** paid by first receiver. **Time Period Covered:** latest day.

HEPTANE: 95%

Source: *Chemical Marketing Reporter.* **Price Frequency:** weekly. **Effective Market(s):** Houston (TX). **Units of Measure:** Dollars per gallon. **Type of Price:** spot. **Time Period Covered:** latest week.

HEPTANE: INDUSTRIAL GRADE

Source: *Chemical Marketing Reporter.* **Price Frequency:** weekly. **Effective Market(s):** Beaumont (TX). **Units of Measure:** Dollars per gallon. **Type of Price:** spot. **Time Period Covered:** latest week.

HEPTANOIC ACID: SYNTHETIC

Source: *Chemical Marketing Reporter.* **Price Frequency:** weekly. **Effective Market(s):** New York. **Units of Measure:** Dollars per lb. **Type of Price:** spot. **Time Period Covered:** latest week.

HERRING ROE: LARGE

Source: *Weekly Statistical Fishery Report.* **Price Frequency:** weekly. **Effective Market(s):** Tokyo. **Units of Measure:** Dollars per lb. **Type of Price:** wholesale. **Time Period Covered:** 2 weeks ago, month ago.

HERRING ROE: MEDIUM

Source: *Weekly Statistical Fishery Report.* **Price Frequency:** weekly. **Effective Market(s):** Tokyo. **Units of Measure:** Dollars per lb. **Type of Price:** wholesale. **Time Period Covered:** 2 weeks ago, month ago.

HERRING ROE: SMALL

Source: *Weekly Statistical Fishery Report.* **Price Frequency:** weekly. **Effective Market(s):** Tokyo. **Units of Measure:** Dollars per lb. **Type of Price:** wholesale. **Time Period Covered:** 2 weeks ago, month ago.

HESSIAN CLOTH

Source: *Prices of Selected Asia/Pacific Products.* **Price Frequency:** monthly. **Effective Market(s):** Hong Kong. **Units of Measure:** Hong Kong dollars per yard. **Type of Price:** high, low. **Time Period Covered:** latest month.

1-HEXADECANOL: SYNTHETIC

Source: *Chemical Marketing Reporter.* **Price Frequency:** weekly. **Effective Market(s):** New York. **Units of Measure:** Dollars per lb. **Type of Price:** spot. **Time Period Covered:** latest week.

HEXAHYDROPHTHALIC ANHYDRIDE: TECHNICAL GRADE

Source: *Chemical Marketing Reporter.* **Price Frequency:** weekly. **Effective Market(s):** New York. **Units of Measure:** Dollars per lb. **Type of Price:** spot. **Time Period Covered:** latest week.

HEXAMETHYLENETETRAMINE

Source: *Journal of Commerce and Commercial.* **Price Frequency:** weekly in Thursday issue. **Units of Measure:** Dollars per lb. **Type of Price:** spot. **Time Period Covered:** latest week.

HEXAMETHYLENETETRAMINE: GRANULAR

Source: *Chemical Marketing Reporter.* **Price Frequency:** weekly. **Effective Market(s):** New York. **Units of Measure:** Dollars per lb. **Type of Price:** spot. **Time Period Covered:** latest week.

HEXAMETHYLENETETRAMINE: POWDERED

Source: *Chemical Marketing Reporter.* **Price Frequency:** weekly. **Effective Market(s):** New York. **Units of Measure:** Dollars per lb. **Type of Price:** spot. **Time Period Covered:** latest week.

HEXANE: 95%

Source: *Chemical Marketing Reporter.* **Price Frequency:** weekly. **Effective Market(s):** Houston (TX). **Units of Measure:** Dollars per gallon. **Type of Price:** spot. **Time Period Covered:** latest week.

HEXANE: INDUSTRIAL GRADE

Source: *Chemical Marketing Reporter.* **Price Frequency:** weekly. **Effective Market(s):** New York. **Units of Measure:** Dollars per gallon. **Type of Price:** spot. **Time Period Covered:** latest week.

1-HEXANOL: SYNTHETIC

Source: *Chemical Marketing Reporter.* **Price Frequency:** weekly. **Effective Market(s):** New York. **Units of Measure:** Dollars per lb. **Type of Price:** spot. **Time Period Covered:** latest week.

P-HEXYL METHACRYLATE

Source: *Chemical Marketing Reporter.* **Price Frequency:** weekly. **Effective Market(s):** New York. **Units of Measure:** Dollars per lb. **Type of Price:** spot. **Time Period Covered:** latest week.

HEXYLENE GLYCOL

Source: *Chemical Marketing Reporter.* **Price Frequency:** weekly. **Effective Market(s):** New York. **Units of Measure:** Dollars per lb. **Type of Price:** spot. **Time Period Covered:** latest week.

HEXYLRESORCINOL: USP

Source: *Chemical Marketing Reporter.* **Price Frequency:** weekly. **Effective Market(s):** New York. **Units of Measure:** Dollars per lb. **Type of Price:** spot. **Time Period Covered:** latest week.

HIBISCUS: CHINESE

Source: *Journal of Commerce and Commercial.* **Price Frequency:** weekly in Monday issue. **Units of Measure:** Dollars per lb. **Type of Price:** spot. **Time Period Covered:** latest week.

HIBISCUS: TAIWANESE

Source: *Journal of Commerce and Commercial.* **Price Frequency:** weekly in Monday issue. **Units of Measure:** Dollars per lb. **Type of Price:** spot. **Time Period Covered:** latest week.

HIDES: AUSTRALIA

Source: *International Financial Statistics.* **Price Frequency:** monthly, quarterly, annually. **Effective Market(s):** Australia. **Units of Measure:** cents per lb., index. **Type of Price:** market price, price index. **Time Period Covered:** latest 2 months, latest 4 quarters, latest 5 years.

Source: *International Financial Statistics Yearbook.* **Price Frequency:** annually. **Effective Market(s):** Australia. **Units of Measure:** cents per lb. **Type of Price:** wholesale. **Time Period Covered:** latest 30 years.

HIDES: CALF

Source: *Hides and Skins.* **Price Frequency:** monthly, annually. **Effective Market(s):** Spain. **Units of Measure:** Spanish pesetas per kilogram. **Type of Price:** average. **Time Period Covered:** latest 3 years.

HIDES: CATTLE

Source: *Hides and Skins.* **Price Frequency:** monthly, annually. **Effective Market(s):** West Germany. **Units of Measure:** West German marks per kilogram. **Type of Price:** average. **Time Period Covered:** latest 3 years.

HIDES: CATTLE, EAST AFRICAN

Source: *Monthly Commodity Price Bulletin Supplement.* **Price Frequency:** monthly, quarterly, annually. **Effective Market(s):** London. **Units of Measure:** Dollars per tonne. **Type of Price:** domestic/import. **Time Period Covered:** latest 20 years.

Source: *Monthly Commodity Price Bulletin.* **Price Frequency:** monthly, annually. **Effective Market(s):** United Kingdom. **Units of Measure:** Dollars per kilogram. **Type of Price:** domestic/import. **Time Period Covered:** latest 5 years.

Source: *UNCTAD Commodity Yearbook.* **Price Frequency:** annually. **Effective Market(s):** United Kingdom. **Units of Measure:** Dollars per metric ton. **Type of Price:** domestic/import. **Time Period Covered:** latest 12 years.

HIDES: COW

Source: *Hides and Skins.* **Price Frequency:** monthly, annually. **Effective Market(s):** West Germany. **Units of Measure:** West German marks per kilogram. **Type of Price:** average. **Time Period Covered:** latest 3 years.

Source: *Hides and Skins.* **Price Frequency:** monthly, annually. **Effective Market(s):** Spain. **Units of Measure:** Spanish pesetas per kilogram. **Type of Price:** average. **Time Period Covered:** latest 3 years.

HIDES: COW, 2ND CLEAR

Source: *Hides and Skins.* **Price Frequency:** monthly, annually. **Effective Market(s):** United Kingdom. **Units of Measure:** British pence per kilogram. **Type of Price:** average. **Time Period Covered:** latest 3 years.

HIDES: COW, BRANDED

Source: *Livestock, Meat, Wool Market News.* **Price Frequency:** weekly, seasonally. **Effective Market(s):** Central United States. **Units of Measure:** Dollars per 100 lbs. **Time Period Covered:** latest week.

Source: *National Provisioner.* **Price Frequency:** weekly. **Effective Market(s):** Chicago. **Units of Measure:** Dollars per 100 lbs. **Time Period Covered:** latest week, year ago.

HIDES: GREEN BASIS, BULL

Source: *Livestock, Meat, Wool Market News.* **Price Frequency:** weekly, seasonally. **Effective Market(s):** Los Angeles, San Francisco. **Units of Measure:** Dollars per piece. **Time Period Covered:** latest week.

HIDES: GREEN BASIS, COW

Source: *Hides and Skins.* **Price Frequency:** monthly, annually. **Effective Market(s):** Italy. **Units of Measure:** Italian lire per kilogram. **Type of Price:** average. **Time Period Covered:** latest 3 years.

Source: *Livestock, Meat, Wool Market News.* **Price Frequency:** weekly, seasonally. **Effective Market(s):** Los Angeles, San Francisco. **Units of Measure:** Dollars per piece. **Time Period Covered:** latest week.

HIDES: GREEN BASIS, HEIFER

Source: *Livestock, Meat, Wool Market News.* **Price Frequency:** weekly, seasonally. **Effective Market(s):** Los Angeles, San Francisco. **Units of Measure:** Dollars per piece. **Time Period Covered:** latest week.

HIDES: GREEN BASIS, HOLSTEIN

Source: *Livestock, Meat, Wool Market News.* **Price Frequency:** weekly, seasonally. **Effective Market(s):** Los Angeles, San Francisco. **Units of Measure:** Dollars per piece. **Time Period Covered:** latest week.

HIDES: GREEN BASIS, OX HEIFER

Source: *Hides and Skins.* **Price Frequency:** monthly, annually. **Effective Market(s):** Italy. **Units of Measure:** Italian lire per kilogram. **Type of Price:** average. **Time Period Covered:** latest 3 years.

HIDES: GREEN BASIS, STEER

Source: *Livestock, Meat, Wool Market News.* **Price Frequency:** weekly, seasonally. **Effective Market(s):** Los Angeles, San Francisco. **Units of Measure:** Dollars per piece. **Time Period Covered:** latest week.

HIDES: HEAVY NATIVE COW

Source: *Commodity Year Book.* **Price Frequency:** annually. **Effective Market(s):** United States. **Units of Measure:** cents per lb. **Type of Price:** wholesale. **Time Period Covered:** latest 5 years.

Source: *National Provisioner.* **Price Frequency:** weekly. **Effective Market(s):** Chicago. **Units of Measure:** Dollars per 100 lbs. **Time Period Covered:** latest week, year ago.

HIDES: HEAVY NATIVE HEIFER

Source: *Livestock, Meat, Wool Market News.* **Price Frequency:** weekly, seasonally. **Effective Market(s):** Central United States. **Units of Measure:** Dollars per 100 lbs. **Time Period Covered:** latest week.

HIDES: HEAVY NATIVE STEER

Source: *Asian Wall Street Journal.* **Price Frequency:** daily. **Units of Measure:** Dollars per lb. **Type of Price:** cash. **Time Period Covered:** latest 2 days, year ago.

Source: *Commodity Year Book.* **Price Frequency:** annually. **Effective Market(s):** United States. **Units of Measure:** cents per lb. **Type of Price:** wholesale. **Time Period Covered:** latest 5 years.

Source: *Hides and Skins.* **Price Frequency:** monthly, annually. **Effective Market(s):** Chicago. **Units of Measure:** cents per lb. **Type of Price:** average. **Time Period Covered:** latest 3 years.

Source: *Investor's Daily.* **Price Frequency:** daily. **Units of Measure:** Dollars per lb. **Type of Price:** spot. **Time Period Covered:** latest 2 days.

Source: *Livestock, Meat, Wool Market News.* **Price Frequency:** weekly, seasonally. **Effective Market(s):** Central United States. **Units of Measure:** Dollars per 100 lbs. **Time Period Covered:** latest week.

Source: *National Provisioner.* **Price Frequency:** weekly. **Effective Market(s):** Chicago. **Units of Measure:** Dollars per 100 lbs. **Time Period Covered:** latest week, year ago.

Source: *New York Times.* **Price Frequency:** daily. **Units of Measure:** Dollars per lb. **Type of Price:** cash. **Time Period Covered:** latest 2 days.

Source: *Wall Street Journal.* **Price Frequency:** daily. **Units of Measure:** Dollars per lb. **Time Period Covered:** latest day, day ago, year ago.

HIDES: HEAVY NATIVE STEER, PACKER

Source: *Commodity Year Book.* **Price Frequency:** monthly, annually. **Units of Measure:** index. **Type of Price:** price index. **Time Period Covered:** latest 12 years.

HIDES: HEAVY NATIVE STEER, RAW

Source: *Journal of Commerce and Commercial.* **Price Frequency:** daily. **Effective Market(s):** Chicago. **Units of Measure:** Dollars per lb. **Type of Price:** spot supplier. **Time Period Covered:** latest day.

HIDES: HEAVY NATIVE STEER, RAW, UNITED STATES

Source: *Prices of Selected Asia/Pacific Products.* **Price Frequency:** monthly. **Effective Market(s):** Chicago. **Units of Measure:** Dollars per lb. **Type of Price:** spot high, spot low. **Time Period Covered:** latest month.

HIDES: HEAVY STEER, SALTED, NORTH AMERICA

Source: *Prices of Selected Asia/Pacific Products.* **Price Frequency:** monthly. **Effective Market(s):** Tokyo. **Units of Measure:** 1000 Japanese yen per piece. **Type of Price:** high, low. **Time Period Covered:** latest month.

HIDES: HEAVY STEER, TEXAS

Source: *Livestock, Meat, Wool Market News.* **Price Frequency:** weekly, seasonally. **Effective Market(s):** Central United States. **Units of Measure:** Dollars per 100 lbs. **Time Period Covered:** latest week.

HIDES: HEIFER, BRANDED

Source: *Livestock, Meat, Wool Market News.* **Price Frequency:** weekly, seasonally. **Effective Market(s):** Central United States. **Units of Measure:** Dollars per 100 lbs. **Time Period Covered:** latest week.

HIDES: LIGHT NATIVE COW

Source: *CRB Commodity Index Report.* **Price Frequency:** weekly. **Effective Market(s):** Chicago. **Units of Measure:** Dollars per lb. **Type of Price:** spot. **Time Period Covered:** latest week.

Source: *FAO Quarterly Bulletin of Statistics.* **Price Frequency:** monthly, annually, seasonally. **Effective Market(s):** Chicago. **Units of Measure:** Dollars per 100 lbs., dollars per metric ton. **Type of Price:** wholesale. **Time Period Covered:** latest 3 years.

Source: *National Provisioner.* **Price Frequency:** weekly. **Effective Market(s):** Chicago. **Units of Measure:** Dollars per 100 lbs. **Time Period Covered:** latest week, year ago.

HIDES: LIGHT NATIVE HEIFER

Source: *Livestock, Meat, Wool Market News.* **Price Frequency:** weekly, seasonally. **Effective Market(s):** Central United States. **Units of Measure:** Dollars per 100 lbs. **Time Period Covered:** latest week.

HIDES: LIGHT NATIVE STEER

Source: *Hides and Skins.* **Price Frequency:** monthly, annually. **Effective Market(s):** Chicago. **Units of Measure:** cents per lb. **Type of Price:** average. **Time Period Covered:** latest 3 years.

Source: *Livestock, Meat, Wool Market News.* **Price Frequency:** weekly, seasonally. **Effective Market(s):** Central United States. **Units of Measure:** Dollars per 100 lbs. **Time Period Covered:** latest week.

Source: *National Provisioner.* **Price Frequency:** weekly. **Effective Market(s):** Chicago. **Units of Measure:** Dollars per 100 lbs. **Time Period Covered:** latest week, year ago.

HIDES: NATIVE BULL

Source: *Livestock, Meat, Wool Market News.* **Price Frequency:** weekly, seasonally. **Effective Market(s):** Central United States. **Units of Measure:** Dollars per 100 lbs. **Time Period Covered:** latest week.

Source: *National Provisioner.* **Price Frequency:** weekly. **Effective Market(s):** Chicago. **Units of Measure:** Dollars per 100 lbs. **Time Period Covered:** latest week, year ago.

HIDES: NATIVE COW

Source: *Livestock, Meat, Wool Market News.* **Price Frequency:** weekly, seasonally. **Effective Market(s):** Central United States. **Units of Measure:** Dollars per 100 lbs. **Time Period Covered:** latest week.

HIDES: OX, 2ND CLEAR

Source: *Hides and Skins.* **Price Frequency:** monthly, annually. **Effective Market(s):** United Kingdom. **Units of Measure:** British pence per kilogram. **Type of Price:** average. **Time Period Covered:** latest 3 years.

HIDES: STEER

Source: *Hides and Skins.* **Price Frequency:** monthly, annually. **Effective Market(s):** Spain. **Units of Measure:** Spanish pesetas per kilogram. **Type of Price:** average. **Time Period Covered:** latest 3 years.

HIDES: STEER AND COW, PLUMP AND MEDIUM

Source: *National Provisioner.* **Price Frequency:** weekly. **Effective Market(s):** Chicago. **Units of Measure:** Dollars per 100 lbs. **Type of Price:** small packer. **Time Period Covered:** latest week, year ago.

HIDES: STEER, BRANDED, COLORADO

Source: *Livestock, Meat, Wool Market News.* **Price Frequency:** weekly, seasonally. **Effective Market(s):** Central United States. **Units of Measure:** Dollars per 100 lbs. **Time Period Covered:** latest week.

HIDES: STEER, BUTT BRANDED

Source: *Livestock, Meat, Wool Market News.* **Price Frequency:** weekly, seasonally. **Effective Market(s):** Central United States. **Units of Measure:** Dollars per 100 lbs. **Time Period Covered:** latest week.

Source: *National Provisioner.* **Price Frequency:** weekly. **Effective Market(s):** Chicago. **Units of Measure:** Dollars per 100 lbs. **Time Period Covered:** latest week, year ago.

HIDES: STEER, COLORADO

Source: *National Provisioner.* **Price Frequency:** weekly. **Effective Market(s):** Chicago. **Units of Measure:** Dollars per 100 lbs. **Time Period Covered:** latest week, year ago.

HIDES: SUSPENSION DRY, IMPORTED

Source: *Hides and Skins.* **Price Frequency:** monthly, annually. **Effective Market(s):** East Africa. **Units of Measure:** British pence per kilogram. **Type of Price:** average. **Time Period Covered:** latest 3 years.

HIDES: UNITED STATES

Source: *International Financial Statistics.* **Price Frequency:** monthly, quarterly, annually. **Effective Market(s):** Chicago. **Units of Measure:** cents per lb., index. **Type of Price:** market price, price index. **Time Period Covered:** latest 5 months, latest 5 quarters, latest 5 years.

Source: *International Financial Statistics Yearbook.* **Price Frequency:** annually. **Effective Market(s):** Chicago. **Units of Measure:** cents per lb. **Type of Price:** wholesale. **Time Period Covered:** latest 30 years.

HINDERED AMINE LIGHT STABILIZERS

see HALS.

HMW-HDPE

see Polyethylene: High Density, High Molecular Weight.

HOE: 6″ BLADE

Source: *Agricultural Prices.* **Price Frequency:** annually. **Effective Market(s):** United States. **Units of Measure:** Dollars each. **Type of Price:** paid by farmer. **Time Period Covered:** latest year.

Source: *Agricultural Prices Annual Summary.* **Price Frequency:** semiannually. **Effective Market(s):** United States. **Units of Measure:** Dollars each. **Type of Price:** average paid by farmer. **Time Period Covered:** latest 6 years.

HOG CONCENTRATE: 38-42% PROTEIN

Source: *Agricultural Prices Annual Summary.* **Price Frequency:** quarterly. **Effective Market(s):** 10 domestic markets, United States. **Units of Measure:** Dollars per ton. **Type of Price:** average paid by farmer. **Time Period Covered:** latest year, for US monthly for latest 6 years.

Source: *Feed Situation and Outlook Report.* **Price Frequency:** quarterly, annually. **Effective Market(s):** United States. **Units of Measure:** Dollars per ton. **Type of Price:** paid by farmer. **Time Period Covered:** latest year.

HOG FEED: 14-18% PROTEIN

Source: *Agricultural Prices.* **Price Frequency:** quarterly. **Effective Market(s):** United States. **Units of Measure:** Dollars per ton. **Type of Price:** paid by farmer. **Time Period Covered:** latest 2 quarters, year ago.

Source: *Agricultural Prices.* **Price Frequency:** monthly. **Effective Market(s):** 10 domestic markets, United States. **Units of Measure:** Dollars per ton. **Type of Price:** paid by farmer. **Time Period Covered:** latest month.

Source: *Agricultural Prices Annual Summary.* **Price Frequency:** quarterly. **Effective Market(s):** 10 domestic markets, United States. **Units of Measure:** Dollars per ton. **Type of Price:** average paid by farmer. **Time Period Covered:** latest year, for US monthly for latest 6 years.

HOG FEED: 38-42% PROTEIN

Source: *Agricultural Prices.* **Price Frequency:** quarterly. **Effective Market(s):** United States. **Units of Measure:** Dollars per ton. **Type of Price:** paid by farmer. **Time Period Covered:** latest 2 quarters, year ago.

Source: *Agricultural Prices.* **Price Frequency:** monthly. **Effective Market(s):** 10 domestic markets, United States. **Units of Measure:** Dollars per ton. **Type of Price:** paid by farmer. **Time Period Covered:** latest month.

HOGS

see also Barrows & Gilts, Pigs, Sows.

Source: *Agricultural Outlook.* **Price Frequency:** monthly, annually. **Effective Market(s):** United States. **Units of Measure:** Dollars per 100 lbs. **Type of Price:** price received by farmers. **Time Period Covered:** monthly latest 6 months, annually latest 3 years.

Source: *Agricultural Prices Annual Summary.* **Price Frequency:** monthly, seasonally. **Effective Market(s):** 20 domestic markets, United States. **Units of Measure:** Dollars per 100 lbs. **Type of Price:** average received by farmer. **Time Period Covered:** monthly latest year, for US latest 6 years.

Source: *Asian Wall Street Journal.* **Price Frequency:** daily. **Effective Market(s):** Iowa/Southern Minnesota, Omaha (NE). **Units of Measure:** Dollars per 100 lbs. **Type of Price:** cash. **Time Period Covered:** latest 2 days, year ago.

Source: *The Brock Report.* **Price Frequency:** quarterly. **Effective Market(s):** 7-market average. **Units of Measure:** Dollars per 100 lbs. **Time Period Covered:** latest 4 years.

Source: *The Brock Report.* **Price Frequency:** weekly. **Effective Market(s):** 5 domestic markets. **Units of Measure:** top price, dollars per 100 lbs. **Time Period Covered:** latest week, week ago.

Source: *Commodity Year Book.* **Price Frequency:** monthly, annually. **Effective Market(s):** United States. **Units of Measure:** cents per lb. **Type of Price:** price received by farmers. **Time Period Covered:** latest 4 years.

Source: *Commodity Year Book.* **Price Frequency:** monthly, annually. **Effective Market(s):** Sioux City (IA). **Units of Measure:** Dollars per 100 lbs. **Type of Price:** wholesale. **Time Period Covered:** latest 3 years.

Source: *Farm and Dairy.* **Price Frequency:** weekly, seasonally. **Effective Market(s):** Iowa/South Minnesota. **Units of Measure:** Dollars per average 100 lbs. **Time Period Covered:** latest week, year ago.

Source: *Farm and Dairy.* **Price Frequency:** weekly, seasonally. **Effective Market(s):** Ohio, Pennsylvania. **Units of Measure:** Dollars per head. **Type of Price:** auction high, auction low. **Time Period Covered:** latest week.

Source: *Illinois Farm Report.* **Price Frequency:** monthly. **Effective Market(s):** Illinois. **Units of Measure:** Dollars per 100 lbs. **Type of Price:** average received by farmers. **Time Period Covered:** latest 2 months, year ago.

Source: *Investor's Daily.* **Price Frequency:** daily. **Effective Market(s):** Omaha (NE). **Units of Measure:** Dollars per 100 lbs. **Type of Price:** spot. **Time Period Covered:** latest 2 days.

Source: *Kansas Business Review.* **Price Frequency:** monthly. **Effective Market(s):** Kansas. **Units of Measure:** Dollars per 100 lbs. **Type of Price:** received by farmer. **Time Period Covered:** latest month, month ago, year ago.

Source: *Lancaster Farming.* **Price Frequency:** weekly. **Effective Market(s):** Illinois, Pennsylvania, Virginia. **Units of Measure:** Dollars per head. **Type of Price:** auction. **Time Period Covered:** latest week.

Source: *Livestock and Poultry Situation and Outlook Report.* **Price Frequency:** monthly. **Units of Measure:** Dollars per 100 lbs. **Type of Price:** farm. **Time Period Covered:** latest year.

Source: *Livestock and Poultry Update.* **Price Frequency:** monthly. **Effective Market(s):** 7-market average. **Units of Measure:** Dollars per 100 lbs. **Time Period Covered:** latest 3 months, year ago.

Source: *Porkpro Newsletter.* **Price Frequency:** weekly. **Effective Market(s):** Omaha (NE). **Units of Measure:** Dollars per 100 lbs. **Type of Price:** wholesale. **Time Period Covered:** latest day, week ago, year ago.

Source: *Standard & Poor's Statistical Service Current Statistics.* **Price Frequency:** monthly. **Units of Measure:** Dollars per 100 lbs. **Time Period Covered:** latest 5 years.

Source: *Wall Street Journal.* **Price Frequency:** daily. **Effective Market(s):** Iowa/Southern Minnesota, Omaha (NE). **Units of Measure:** Dollars per 100 lbs. **Time Period Covered:** latest day, day ago, year ago.

HOGS: ALL TYPES

Source: *Agricultural Prices.* **Price Frequency:** monthly. **Effective Market(s):** United States. **Units of Measure:** Dollars per 100 lbs. **Type of Price:** received by farmer. **Time Period Covered:** latest 2 months, year ago.

Source: *Agricultural Prices.* **Price Frequency:** monthly. **Effective Market(s):** United States. **Units of Measure:** Dollars per 100 lbs. **Type of Price:** received by farmer. **Time Period Covered:** latest 2 years.

Source: *Agricultural Prices.* **Price Frequency:** monthly. **Effective Market(s):** 20 domestic markets, United States. **Units of Measure:** Dollars per 100 lbs. **Type of Price:** received by farmer. **Time Period Covered:** latest 2 months.

Source: *Agricultural Prices Annual Summary.* **Price Frequency:** annually. **Effective Market(s):** 50 domestic markets, United States. **Units of Measure:** Dollars per 100 lbs. **Type of Price:** average received by farmer. **Time Period Covered:** latest 2 years, for US latest 6 years.

HOGS: AVERAGE WEIGHT

Source: *CRB Commodity Index Report.* **Price Frequency:** weekly. **Effective Market(s):** Omaha (NE). **Units of Measure:** Dollars per 100 lbs. **Type of Price:** spot. **Time Period Covered:** latest week.

HOGS: BARROWS AND GILTS

Source: *Agricultural Prices Annual Summary.* **Price Frequency:** annually. **Effective Market(s):** 50 domestic markets, United States. **Units of Measure:** Dollars per 100 lbs. **Type of Price:** average received by farmer. **Time Period Covered:** latest 2 years, for US latest 6 years.

Source: *Agricultural Prices Annual Summary.* **Price Frequency:** monthly, seasonally. **Effective Market(s):** 20 domestic markets, United States. **Units of Measure:** Dollars per 100 lbs. **Type of Price:** average received by farmer. **Time Period Covered:** monthly latest year, for US latest 6 years.

Source: *Agriculture.* **Price Frequency:** weekly. **Effective Market(s):** 7 domestic markets, 7-market average. **Units of Measure:** Dollars per 100 lbs. **Time Period Covered:** latest week, week ago, year ago.

Source: *California Farmer.* **Price Frequency:** semimonthly. **Effective Market(s):** Dixon (CA). **Units of Measure:** Dollars per 100 lbs. **Time Period Covered:** latest week, month ago, year ago.

Source: *Fedgazette.* **Price Frequency:** monthly. **Effective Market(s):** South St. Paul (MN). **Units of Measure:** Dollars per 100 lbs. **Time Period Covered:** latest 24 months.

Source: *Lancaster Farming.* **Price Frequency:** weekly. **Effective Market(s):** Illinois, Pennsylvania, Virginia. **Units of Measure:** Dollars per head. **Type of Price:** auction. **Time Period Covered:** latest week.

HOGS: BARROWS AND GILTS, 200-240 LBS

Source: *FAO Quarterly Bulletin of Statistics.* **Price Frequency:** monthly, annually. **Effective Market(s):** Omaha (NE). **Units of Measure:** Dollars per 100 lbs., dollars per metric ton. **Type of Price:** wholesale. **Time Period Covered:** latest 3 years.

HOGS: BARROWS AND GILTS, US 1-3

Source: *Idaho Farmer-Stockman.* **Price Frequency:** monthly. **Effective Market(s):** Omaha (NE). **Units of Measure:** Dollars per 100 lbs. **Time Period Covered:** latest month.

Source: *Livestock, Meat, Wool Market News.* **Price Frequency:** weekly. **Effective Market(s):** Omaha (NE). **Units of Measure:** Dollars per 100 lbs. **Type of Price:** average. **Time Period Covered:** latest week, year ago.

Source: *Oregon Farmer-Stockman.* **Price Frequency:** monthly, seasonally. **Effective Market(s):** Omaha (NE). **Units of Measure:** Dollars per 100 lbs. **Time Period Covered:** latest month.

Source: *Utah Stockman-Farmer.* **Price Frequency:** monthly. **Effective Market(s):** Omaha (NE). **Units of Measure:** Dollars per 100 lbs. **Time Period Covered:** latest month.

HOGS: BARROWS AND GILTS, US 2-3

Source: *Oregon Farmer-Stockman.* **Price Frequency:** monthly, seasonally. **Effective Market(s):** Omaha (NE). **Units of Measure:** Dollars per 100 lbs. **Time Period Covered:** latest month.

Source: *Utah Stockman-Farmer.* **Price Frequency:** monthly. **Effective Market(s):** Omaha (NE). **Units of Measure:** Dollars per 100 lbs. **Time Period Covered:** latest month.

HOGS: FUTURES

Source: *Asian Wall Street Journal.* **Price Frequency:** daily. **Effective Market(s):** Chicago. **Units of Measure:** cents per lb. **Type of Price:** futures. **Time Period Covered:** latest day.

Source: *Barron's.* **Price Frequency:** weekly. **Effective Market(s):** Chicago. **Units of Measure:** cents per lb. **Type of Price:** futures. **Time Period Covered:** latest week.

Source: *Investor's Daily.* **Price Frequency:** daily. **Effective Market(s):** Chicago. **Units of Measure:** cents per lb. **Type of Price:** futures. **Time Period Covered:** latest day.

Source: *Lancaster Farming.* **Price Frequency:** daily. **Effective Market(s):** Chicago. **Type of Price:** futures. **Time Period Covered:** latest week.

Source: *Los Angeles Times.* **Price Frequency:** daily. **Effective Market(s):** Chicago. **Units of Measure:** cents per lb. **Type of Price:** futures. **Time Period Covered:** latest day.

Source: *Porkpro Newsletter.* **Price Frequency:** daily. **Units of Measure:** Dollars per 100 lbs. **Type of Price:** futures. **Time Period Covered:** latest week.

Source: *Wall Street Journal.* **Price Frequency:** daily. **Effective Market(s):** Chicago. **Units of Measure:** cents per lb. **Type of Price:** futures. **Time Period Covered:** next 7 contract months.

HOGS: FUTURES, JUNE

Source: *Commodity Year Book.* **Price Frequency:** monthly. **Effective Market(s):** Chicago. **Units of Measure:** cents per lb. **Type of Price:** futures. **Time Period Covered:** latest 4 years.

HOGS: LIVE, FUTURES

Source: *Agriculture.* **Price Frequency:** weekly. **Effective Market(s):** Chicago. **Units of Measure:** cents per lb. **Type of Price:** futures. **Time Period Covered:** latest week, week ago.

Source: *Drovers Journal.* **Price Frequency:** weekly. **Effective Market(s):** Chicago. **Units of Measure:** Dollars per 100 lbs. **Type of Price:** futures. **Time Period Covered:** latest 6 week.

Source: *Feedstuffs.* **Price Frequency:** weekly. **Effective Market(s):** Chicago. **Units of Measure:** cents per lb. **Type of Price:** futures. **Time Period Covered:** latest week, week ago, latest season.

Source: *Financial Times.* **Price Frequency:** daily. **Effective Market(s):** Chicago. **Units of Measure:** cents per lb. **Type of Price:** futures. **Time Period Covered:** latest day.

Source: *National Provisioner.* **Price Frequency:** daily. **Effective Market(s):** Chicago. **Type of Price:** futures. **Time Period Covered:** latest week.

Source: *New York Times.* **Price Frequency:** daily. **Effective Market(s):** Chicago. **Units of Measure:** cents per lb. **Type of Price:** futures. **Time Period Covered:** latest day.

Source: *Urner Barry's Price-Current.* **Price Frequency:** daily. **Effective Market(s):** Chicago. **Units of Measure:** cents per lb. **Type of Price:** futures. **Time Period Covered:** latest day.

Source: *Wall Street Journal.* **Price Frequency:** daily. **Effective Market(s):** Chicago. **Units of Measure:** cents per lb. **Type of Price:** futures. **Time Period Covered:** latest day.

HOGS: SLAUGHTER

Source: *Livestock and Poultry Situation and Outlook Report.* **Price Frequency:** monthly. **Effective Market(s):** Omaha (NE), Sioux City (IA), 7-market average. **Units of Measure:** Dollars per 100 lbs. **Time Period Covered:** latest year.

Source: *Survey of Current Business.* **Price Frequency:** monthly, annually. **Effective Market(s):** Sioux City (IA). **Units of Measure:** Dollars per 100 lbs. **Type of Price:** wholesale. **Time Period Covered:** latest year.

HOGS: SLAUGHTER, BARROWS AND GILTS

Source: *Agricultural Outlook.* **Price Frequency:** monthly, annually. **Effective Market(s):** 7 market average. **Units of Measure:** Dollars per 100 lbs. **Type of Price:** market. **Time Period Covered:** monthly latest 6 months, annually latest 3 years.

HOGS: SLAUGHTER, BARROWS AND GILTS, US 1-2

Source: *Livestock, Meat, Wool Market News.* **Price Frequency:** weekly, seasonally. **Effective Market(s):** 16 domestic markets. **Units of Measure:** Dollars per 100 lbs. **Type of Price:** average. **Time Period Covered:** latest week, year ago.

HOGS: SLAUGHTER, BARROWS AND GILTS, US 1-3

Source: *Livestock, Meat, Wool Market News.* **Price Frequency:** weekly, seasonally. **Effective Market(s):** 16 domestic markets. **Units of Measure:** Dollars per 100 lbs. **Type of Price:** average. **Time Period Covered:** latest week, year ago.

HOGS: SLAUGHTER, BARROWS AND GILTS, US 2-3

Source: *Livestock, Meat, Wool Market News.* **Price Frequency:** weekly, seasonally. **Effective Market(s):** 16 domestic markets. **Units of Measure:** Dollars per 100 lbs. **Type of Price:** average. **Time Period Covered:** latest week, year ago.

HOGS: SLAUGHTER, BARROWS AND GILTS, US 3-4

Source: *Livestock, Meat, Wool Market News.* **Price Frequency:** weekly, seasonally. **Effective Market(s):** 16 domestic markets. **Units of Measure:** Dollars per 100 lbs. **Type of Price:** average. **Time Period Covered:** latest week, year ago.

HOGS: SLAUGHTER, SOWS, US 1-3

Source: *Livestock, Meat, Wool Market News.* **Price Frequency:** weekly, seasonally. **Effective Market(s):** 16 domestic markets. **Units of Measure:** Dollars per 100 lbs. **Type of Price:** average. **Time Period Covered:** latest week, year ago.

HOGS: SLAUGHTER, SOWS, US 2-3

Source: *Livestock, Meat, Wool Market News.* **Price Frequency:** weekly, seasonally. **Effective Market(s):** 16 domestic markets. **Units of Measure:** Dollars per 100 lbs. **Type of Price:** average. **Time Period Covered:** latest week, year ago.

HOGS: SOWS, US 1-3

Source: *Idaho Farmer-Stockman.* **Price Frequency:** monthly. **Effective Market(s):** Omaha (NE). **Units of Measure:** Dollars per 100 lbs. **Time Period Covered:** latest month.

HOGS: US 1-2

Source: *Feedstuffs.* **Price Frequency:** weekly. **Effective Market(s):** Omaha (NE). **Units of Measure:** cents per lb. **Time Period Covered:** latest week, week ago, 6 months ago, year ago.

Source: *New York Times.* **Price Frequency:** daily. **Effective Market(s):** Omaha (NE). **Units of Measure:** Dollars per 100 lbs. **Type of Price:** cash. **Time Period Covered:** latest 2 days.

HOLLAND GUILDERS

see Netherlands Guilders.

HOMATROPINE HYDROBROMIDE: USP

Source: *Chemical Marketing Reporter.* **Price Frequency:** weekly. **Effective Market(s):** New York. **Units of Measure:** Dollars per ounce. **Type of Price:** spot. **Time Period Covered:** latest week.

HOMATROPINE METHYLBROMIDE: USP

Source: *Chemical Marketing Reporter.* **Price Frequency:** weekly. **Effective Market(s):** New York. **Units of Measure:** Dollars per lb. **Type of Price:** spot. **Time Period Covered:** latest week.

HOMEFURNISHINGS

Source: *Textile World.* **Price Frequency:** monthly. **Units of Measure:** index. **Type of Price:** producer price index. **Time Period Covered:** latest 2 months, year ago.

HOMINY FEED

Source: *Asian Wall Street Journal.* **Price Frequency:** daily. **Effective Market(s):** Central Illinois. **Units of Measure:** Dollars per ton. **Type of Price:** cash. **Time Period Covered:** latest 2 days, year ago.

Source: *Feed Situation and Outlook Report.* **Price Frequency:** monthly. **Effective Market(s):** Illinois points. **Units of Measure:** Dollars per ton. **Type of Price:** wholesale. **Time Period Covered:** latest 8 months.

Source: *Grain and Feed Market News.* **Price Frequency:** weekly, seasonally. **Effective Market(s):** Illinois points, Kansas City, Los Angeles, Northern California points, St. Louis. **Units of Measure:** Dollars per ton. **Type of Price:** wholesale. **Time Period Covered:** latest week, week ago, year ago.

Source: *Milling & Baking News.* **Price Frequency:** weekly. **Effective Market(s):** California, Chicago, Kansas City, Paris (IL). **Units of Measure:** Dollars per ton. **Time Period Covered:** latest week, week ago, year ago.

Source: *Wall Street Journal.* **Price Frequency:** daily. **Effective Market(s):** Central Illinois. **Units of Measure:** Dollars per ton. **Time Period Covered:** latest day, day ago, year ago.

HOMINY FEED: WHITE

Source: *Feedstuffs.* **Price Frequency:** weekly. **Effective Market(s):** 8 domestic markets. **Units of Measure:** Dollars per bulk ton. **Time Period Covered:** latest week.

HOMINY FEED: YELLOW

Source: *Feedstuffs.* **Price Frequency:** weekly. **Effective Market(s):** 8 domestic markets. **Units of Measure:** Dollars per bulk ton. **Time Period Covered:** latest week.

HOMINY FEED: YELLOW CORN

Source: *California Farmer.* **Price Frequency:** semimonthly. **Effective Market(s):** California. **Units of Measure:** Dollars per ton. **Time Period Covered:** latest week, month ago, year ago.

HOMINY FEED MEAL

Source: *Milling & Baking News.* **Price Frequency:** weekly. **Units of Measure:** Dollars per 100 lbs. **Time Period Covered:** latest week.

HONEY

Source: *Commodity Year Book.* **Price Frequency:** annually. **Effective Market(s):** United States. **Units of Measure:** cents per lb. **Type of Price:** support price. **Time Period Covered:** latest 11 years.

Source: *Gleanings in Bee Culture.* **Price Frequency:** monthly. **Effective Market(s):** 10 domestic markets. **Units of Measure:** Dollars per lb. **Type of Price:** retail. **Time Period Covered:** latest month.

Source: *Honey.* **Price Frequency:** annually. **Effective Market(s):** 49 domestic markets, United States. **Units of Measure:** cents per lb. **Type of Price:** average. **Time Period Covered:** latest 2 years.

Source: *World Honey Situation.* **Price Frequency:** annually. **Effective Market(s):** 10 international markets. **Units of Measure:** national currency per unit. **Time Period Covered:** latest year.

HONEY: 1 LB. JAR

Source: *Gleanings in Bee Culture.* **Price Frequency:** monthly. **Effective Market(s):** 10 domestic markets. **Units of Measure:** Dollars per case of 24 jars. **Type of Price:** wholesale. **Time Period Covered:** latest month.

HONEY: 2 LB. JARS

Source: *Gleanings in Bee Culture.* **Price Frequency:** monthly. **Effective Market(s):** 10 domestic markets. **Units of Measure:** Dollars per case of 12 jars. **Type of Price:** wholesale. **Time Period Covered:** latest month.

HONEY: 5 LB. JARS

Source: *Gleanings in Bee Culture.* **Price Frequency:** monthly. **Effective Market(s):** 10 domestic markets. **Units of Measure:** Dollars per case of 6 jars. **Type of Price:** wholesale. **Time Period Covered:** latest month.

HONEY: ALFALFA, EXTRA LIGHT AMBER

Source: *National Honey Market News.* **Price Frequency:** monthly, seasonally. **Effective Market(s):** 6 domestic markets. **Units of Measure:** cents per lb. **Type of Price:** price paid to beekeepers. **Time Period Covered:** latest month.

HONEY: ALFALFA, EXTRA WHITE

Source: *National Honey Market News.* **Price Frequency:** monthly, seasonally. **Effective Market(s):** Minnesota. **Units of Measure:** cents per lb. **Type of Price:** price paid to beekeepers. **Time Period Covered:** latest month.

HONEY: ALFALFA, LIGHT AMBER

Source: *National Honey Market News.* **Price Frequency:** monthly, seasonally. **Effective Market(s):** 3 California markets, Washington, Utah. **Units of Measure:** cents per lb. **Type of Price:** price paid to beekeepers. **Time Period Covered:** latest month.

HONEY: ALFALFA, WATER WHITE

Source: *National Honey Market News.* **Price Frequency:** monthly, seasonally. **Effective Market(s):** South Dakota, Wyoming. **Units of Measure:** cents per lb. **Type of Price:** price paid to beekeepers. **Time Period Covered:** latest month.

HONEY: ALFALFA, WHITE

Source: *National Honey Market News.* **Price Frequency:** monthly, seasonally. **Effective Market(s):** Oregon, Utah, Washington, Wyoming. **Units of Measure:** cents per lb. **Type of Price:** price paid to beekeepers. **Time Period Covered:** latest month.

HONEY: ALFALFA, WHITE, ARGENTINE

Source: *National Honey Market News.* **Price Frequency:** monthly, seasonally. **Effective Market(s):** East Coast ports. **Units of Measure:** cents per lb. **Type of Price:** price paid to importers. **Time Period Covered:** latest month.

HONEY: ALFALFA-CLOVER, CUT COMB

Source: *National Honey Market News.* **Price Frequency:** monthly, seasonally. **Effective Market(s):** Nebraska. **Units of Measure:** cents per lb. **Type of Price:** price paid to beekeepers. **Time Period Covered:** latest month.

HONEY: ALFALFA-CLOVER, EXTRA LIGHT AMBER

Source: *National Honey Market News.* **Price Frequency:** monthly, seasonally. **Effective Market(s):** North/Central California. **Units of Measure:** cents per lb. **Type of Price:** price paid to beekeepers. **Time Period Covered:** latest month.

Source: *National Honey Market News.* **Price Frequency:** monthly, seasonally. **Effective Market(s):** Minnesota. **Units of Measure:** cents per lb. **Type of Price:** price paid to beekeepers. **Time Period Covered:** latest month.

HONEY: ALFALFA-CLOVER, EXTRA WHITE

Source: *National Honey Market News.* **Price Frequency:** monthly, seasonally. **Effective Market(s):** Idaho, Utah. **Units of Measure:** cents per lb. **Type of Price:** price paid to beekeepers. **Time Period Covered:** latest month.

HONEY: ALFALFA-CLOVER, WHITE

Source: *National Honey Market News.* **Price Frequency:** monthly, seasonally. **Effective Market(s):** 5 domestic markets. **Units of Measure:** cents per lb. **Type of Price:** price paid to beekeepers. **Time Period Covered:** latest month.

HONEY: ALFALFA-CLOVER-BUCKWHEAT, EXTRA LIGHT AMBER

Source: *National Honey Market News.* **Price Frequency:** monthly, seasonally. **Effective Market(s):** Minnesota. **Units of Measure:** cents per lb. **Type of Price:** price paid to beekeepers. **Time Period Covered:** latest month.

HONEY: ALFALFA-COTTON-CLOVER

Source: *National Honey Market News.* **Price Frequency:** monthly, seasonally. **Effective Market(s):** North/ Central California. **Units of Measure:** cents per lb. **Type of Price:** price paid to beekeepers. **Time Period Covered:** latest month.

HONEY: ALFALFA-SUNFLOWERS, LIGHT AMBER

Source: *National Honey Market News.* **Price Frequency:** monthly, seasonally. **Effective Market(s):** Texas. **Units of Measure:** cents per lb. **Type of Price:** price paid to beekeepers. **Time Period Covered:** latest month.

HONEY: ALL TYPES

Source: *Honey.* **Price Frequency:** annually. **Effective Market(s):** United States. **Units of Measure:** cents per lb. **Type of Price:** coop & private, retail, average. **Time Period Covered:** latest 2 years.

HONEY: AMBER, EXTRA LIGHT

Source: *Honey.* **Price Frequency:** annually. **Effective Market(s):** United States. **Units of Measure:** cents per lb. **Type of Price:** coop & private, retail, average. **Time Period Covered:** latest 2 years.

HONEY: AMBER, EXTRACTED, UNPROCESSED

Source: *Gleanings in Bee Culture.* **Price Frequency:** monthly. **Effective Market(s):** 10 domestic markets. **Units of Measure:** Dollars per 60 lb. can, dollars per lb. **Type of Price:** price to packer. **Time Period Covered:** latest month.

HONEY: AMBER, LIGHT AMBER, DARK AMBER

Source: *Honey.* **Price Frequency:** annually. **Effective Market(s):** United States. **Units of Measure:** cents per lb. **Type of Price:** coop & private, retail, average. **Time Period Covered:** latest 2 years.

HONEY: AREA SPECIALTIES

Source: *Honey.* **Price Frequency:** annually. **Effective Market(s):** United States. **Units of Measure:** cents per lb. **Type of Price:** coop & private, retail, average. **Time Period Covered:** latest 2 years.

HONEY: BARNABY THISTLE, WHITE

Source: *National Honey Market News.* **Price Frequency:** monthly, seasonally. **Effective Market(s):** Washington. **Units of Measure:** cents per lb. **Type of Price:** price paid to beekeepers. **Time Period Covered:** latest month.

HONEY: BEESWAX

see Beeswax.

HONEY: BRAZILIAN PEPPER, AMBER

Source: *National Honey Market News.* **Price Frequency:** monthly, seasonally. **Effective Market(s):** Florida. **Units of Measure:** cents per lb. **Type of Price:** price paid to beekeepers. **Time Period Covered:** latest month.

HONEY: BRAZILIAN PEPPER, AMBER, NON-TABLE

Source: *National Honey Market News.* **Price Frequency:** monthly, seasonally. **Effective Market(s):** Florida. **Units of Measure:** cents per lb. **Type of Price:** price paid to beekeepers. **Time Period Covered:** latest month.

HONEY: BRAZILIAN PEPPER, LIGHT AMBER

Source: *National Honey Market News.* **Price Frequency:** monthly, seasonally. **Effective Market(s):** Florida. **Units of Measure:** cents per lb. **Type of Price:** price paid to beekeepers. **Time Period Covered:** latest month.

HONEY: BRAZILIAN PEPPER, NON-TABLE

Source: *National Honey Market News.* **Price Frequency:** monthly, seasonally. **Effective Market(s):** Florida. **Units of Measure:** cents per lb. **Type of Price:** price paid to beekeepers. **Time Period Covered:** latest month.

HONEY: BRAZILIAN PEPPER-GALLBERRY

Source: *National Honey Market News.* **Price Frequency:** monthly, seasonally. **Effective Market(s):** Florida. **Units of Measure:** cents per lb. **Type of Price:** price paid to beekeepers. **Time Period Covered:** latest month.

HONEY: BRAZILIAN PEPPER-GALLBERRY, AMBER

Source: *National Honey Market News.* **Price Frequency:** monthly, seasonally. **Effective Market(s):** Florida, Mississippi. **Units of Measure:** cents per lb. **Type of Price:** price paid to beekeepers. **Time Period Covered:** latest month.

HONEY: BRAZILIAN PEPPER-MANGROVE, AMBER, NON-TABLE

Source: *National Honey Market News.* **Price Frequency:** monthly, seasonally. **Effective Market(s):** Florida. **Units of Measure:** cents per lb. **Type of Price:** price paid to beekeepers. **Time Period Covered:** latest month.

HONEY: BRAZILIAN PEPPER-SAW PALMETTO-GALLBERRY, AMBER

Source: *National Honey Market News.* **Price Frequency:** monthly, seasonally. **Effective Market(s):** Florida. **Units of Measure:** cents per lb. **Type of Price:** price paid to beekeepers. **Time Period Covered:** latest month.

HONEY: BRAZILIAN PEPPER-SAW PALMETTO-GALLBERRY, LIGHT AMBER

Source: *National Honey Market News.* **Price Frequency:** monthly, seasonally. **Effective Market(s):** Florida. **Units of Measure:** cents per lb. **Type of Price:** price paid to beekeepers. **Time Period Covered:** latest month.

HONEY: BRUSH, AMBER

Source: *National Honey Market News.* **Price Frequency:** monthly, seasonally. **Effective Market(s):** Colorado, Texas. **Units of Measure:** cents per lb. **Type of Price:** price paid to beekeepers. **Time Period Covered:** latest month.

HONEY: BRUSH, LIGHT AMBER

Source: *National Honey Market News.* **Price Frequency:** monthly, seasonally. **Effective Market(s):** Louisiana, New Mexico, Texas. **Units of Measure:** cents per lb. **Type of Price:** price paid to beekeepers. **Time Period Covered:** latest month.

HONEY: BRUSH, WHITE

Source: *National Honey Market News.* **Price Frequency:** monthly, seasonally. **Effective Market(s):** Texas. **Units of Measure:** cents per lb. **Type of Price:** price paid to beekeepers. **Time Period Covered:** latest month.

HONEY: BRUSH-COTTON, LIGHT AMBER

Source: *National Honey Market News.* **Price Frequency:** monthly, seasonally. **Effective Market(s):** New Mexico. **Units of Measure:** cents per lb. **Type of Price:** price paid to beekeepers. **Time Period Covered:** latest month.

HONEY: BRUSH-COTTON-WILD FLOWERS, LIGHT AMBER

Source: *National Honey Market News.* **Price Frequency:** monthly, seasonally. **Effective Market(s):** Texas. **Units of Measure:** cents per lb. **Type of Price:** price paid to beekeepers. **Time Period Covered:** latest month.

HONEY: BRUSH-COTTON-WILD FLOWERS, WHITE

Source: *National Honey Market News.* **Price Frequency:** monthly, seasonally. **Effective Market(s):** Texas. **Units of Measure:** cents per lb. **Type of Price:** price paid to beekeepers. **Time Period Covered:** latest month.

HONEY: BUCKWHEAT, AMBER

Source: *National Honey Market News.* **Price Frequency:** monthly, seasonally. **Effective Market(s):** South Dakota. **Units of Measure:** cents per lb. **Type of Price:** price paid to beekeepers. **Time Period Covered:** latest month.

HONEY: BUCKWHEAT, EXTRA LIGHT AMBER

Source: *National Honey Market News.* **Price Frequency:** monthly, seasonally. **Effective Market(s):** North/Central California. **Units of Measure:** cents per lb. **Type of Price:** price paid to beekeepers. **Time Period Covered:** latest month.

HONEY: BUCKWHEAT, LIGHT AMBER

Source: *National Honey Market News.* **Price Frequency:** monthly, seasonally. **Effective Market(s):** North/Central California. **Units of Measure:** cents per lb. **Type of Price:** price paid to beekeepers. **Time Period Covered:** latest month.

Source: *National Honey Market News.* **Price Frequency:** monthly, seasonally. **Effective Market(s):** West Coast ports. **Units of Measure:** cents per lb. **Type of Price:** price paid to importers. **Time Period Covered:** latest month.

HONEY: CHINESE, ACACIA, EXTRA LIGHT AMBER

Source: *National Honey Market News.* **Price Frequency:** monthly, seasonally. **Effective Market(s):** West Coast ports. **Units of Measure:** cents per lb. **Type of Price:** price paid to importers. **Time Period Covered:** latest month.

HONEY: CHINESE, ACACIA, LIGHT AMBER

Source: *National Honey Market News.* **Price Frequency:** monthly, seasonally. **Effective Market(s):** West Coast ports. **Units of Measure:** cents per lb. **Type of Price:** price paid to importers. **Time Period Covered:** latest month.

HONEY: CHINESE, ACACIA, WATER WHITE

Source: *National Honey Market News.* **Price Frequency:** monthly, seasonally. **Effective Market(s):** West Coast ports. **Units of Measure:** cents per lb. **Type of Price:** price paid to importers. **Time Period Covered:** latest month.

HONEY: CHINESE, ALFALFA, LIGHT AMBER

Source: *National Honey Market News.* **Price Frequency:** monthly, seasonally. **Effective Market(s):** West Coast ports. **Units of Measure:** cents per lb. **Type of Price:** price paid to importers. **Time Period Covered:** latest month.

HONEY: CHINESE, MIXED FLOWERS, EXTRA LIGHT AMBER

Source: *National Honey Market News.* **Price Frequency:** monthly, seasonally. **Effective Market(s):** East Coast ports, West Coast ports. **Units of Measure:** cents per lb. **Type of Price:** price paid to importers. **Time Period Covered:** latest month.

HONEY: CHINESE, MIXED FLOWERS, LIGHT AMBER

Source: *National Honey Market News.* **Price Frequency:** monthly, seasonally. **Effective Market(s):** East Coast ports, West Coast ports. **Units of Measure:** cents per lb. **Type of Price:** price paid to importers. **Time Period Covered:** latest month.

HONEY: CHINESE TALLOW, AMBER

Source: *National Honey Market News.* **Price Frequency:** monthly, seasonally. **Effective Market(s):** Louisiana, Texas. **Units of Measure:** cents per lb. **Type of Price:** price paid to beekeepers. **Time Period Covered:** latest month.

Source: *National Honey Market News.* **Price Frequency:** monthly, seasonally. **Effective Market(s):** Louisiana. **Units of Measure:** cents per lb. **Type of Price:** price paid to beekeepers. **Time Period Covered:** latest month.

HONEY: CHINESE TALLOW, AMBER, NON-TABLE

Source: *National Honey Market News.* **Price Frequency:** monthly, seasonally. **Effective Market(s):** Mississippi, Texas. **Units of Measure:** cents per lb. **Type of Price:** price paid to beekeepers. **Time Period Covered:** latest month.

HONEY: CHINESE TALLOW, LIGHT AMBER, NON-TABLE

Source: *National Honey Market News.* **Price Frequency:** monthly, seasonally. **Effective Market(s):** Louisiana. **Units of Measure:** cents per lb. **Type of Price:** price paid to beekeepers. **Time Period Covered:** latest month.

HONEY: CLOVER, AMBER

Source: *National Honey Market News.* **Price Frequency:** monthly, seasonally. **Effective Market(s):** Wisconsin, North Dakota. **Units of Measure:** cents per lb. **Type of Price:** price paid to beekeepers. **Time Period Covered:** latest month.

HONEY: CLOVER, DARK AMBER

Source: *National Honey Market News.* **Price Frequency:** monthly, seasonally. **Effective Market(s):** Iowa. **Units of Measure:** cents per lb. **Type of Price:** price paid to beekeepers. **Time Period Covered:** latest month.

HONEY: CLOVER, EXTRA LIGHT AMBER

Source: *National Honey Market News.* **Price Frequency:** monthly, seasonally. **Effective Market(s):** 7 domestic markets. **Units of Measure:** cents per lb. **Type of Price:** price paid to beekeepers. **Time Period Covered:** latest month.

HONEY: CLOVER, EXTRA WHITE

Source: *National Honey Market News.* **Price Frequency:** monthly, seasonally. **Effective Market(s):** Minnesota. **Units of Measure:** cents per lb. **Type of Price:** price paid to beekeepers. **Time Period Covered:** latest month.

HONEY: CLOVER, GOLDEN

Source: *National Honey Market News.* **Price Frequency:** monthly, seasonally. **Effective Market(s):** British Columbia. **Units of Measure:** cents per lb. **Type of Price:** price paid to beekeepers. **Time Period Covered:** latest month.

HONEY: CLOVER, LIGHT AMBER

Source: *National Honey Market News.* **Price Frequency:** monthly, seasonally. **Effective Market(s):** Alabama, Idaho. **Units of Measure:** cents per lb. **Type of Price:** price paid to beekeepers. **Time Period Covered:** latest month.

HONEY: CLOVER, WATER WHITE

Source: *National Honey Market News.* **Price Frequency:** monthly, seasonally. **Effective Market(s):** South Dakota, Montana. **Units of Measure:** cents per lb. **Type of Price:** price paid to beekeepers. **Time Period Covered:** latest month.

HONEY: CLOVER, WHITE

Source: *National Honey Market News.* **Price Frequency:** monthly, seasonally. **Effective Market(s):** 14 domestic markets, Alberta, British Columbia, Manitoba. **Units of Measure:** cents per lb. **Type of Price:** price paid to beekeepers. **Time Period Covered:** latest month.

HONEY: CLOVER, WHITE, ARGENTINE

Source: *National Honey Market News.* **Price Frequency:** monthly, seasonally. **Effective Market(s):** East Coast ports, Gulf ports. **Units of Measure:** cents per lb. **Type of Price:** price paid to importers. **Time Period Covered:** latest month.

HONEY: COMB

Source: *Gleanings in Bee Culture.* **Price Frequency:** monthly. **Effective Market(s):** 10 domestic markets. **Units of Measure:** Dollars per lb. **Type of Price:** retail. **Time Period Covered:** latest month.

HONEY: COMB, ROUND PLASTIC

Source: *Gleanings in Bee Culture.* **Price Frequency:** monthly. **Effective Market(s):** 10 domestic markets. **Units of Measure:** Dollars per comb. **Type of Price:** retail. **Time Period Covered:** monthly.

HONEY: COTTON, EXTRA LIGHT AMBER

Source: *National Honey Market News.* **Price Frequency:** monthly, seasonally. **Effective Market(s):** North/Central California. **Units of Measure:** cents per lb. **Type of Price:** price paid to beekeepers. **Time Period Covered:** latest month.

HONEY: COTTON, LIGHT AMBER

Source: *National Honey Market News.* **Price Frequency:** monthly, seasonally. **Effective Market(s):** North/Central California, Texas. **Units of Measure:** cents per lb. **Type of Price:** price paid to beekeepers. **Time Period Covered:** latest month.

HONEY: COTTON, WHITE

Source: *National Honey Market News.* **Price Frequency:** monthly, seasonally. **Effective Market(s):** Texas. **Units of Measure:** cents per lb. **Type of Price:** price paid to beekeepers. **Time Period Covered:** latest month.

HONEY: CREAMED

Source: *Gleanings in Bee Culture.* **Price Frequency:** monthly. **Effective Market(s):** 10 domestic markets. **Units of Measure:** Dollars per lb. **Type of Price:** retail. **Time Period Covered:** latest month.

HONEY: CUT COMB

Source: *National Honey Market News.* **Price Frequency:** monthly, seaonally. **Effective Market(s):** Florida. **Units of Measure:** cents per lb. **Type of Price:** price paid to beekeepers. **Time Period Covered:** latest month.

HONEY: CUT COMB, LIGHT

Source: *National Honey Market News.* **Price Frequency:** monthly, seasonally. **Effective Market(s):** Florida, Iowa. **Units of Measure:** cents per lb. **Type of Price:** price paid to beekeepers. **Time Period Covered:** latest month.

HONEY: EXTRACTED, EXTRA LIGHT, FLORIDA

Source: *Commodity Year Book.* **Price Frequency:** annually. **Effective Market(s):** United States. **Units of Measure:** cents per lb. **Time Period Covered:** latest 6 years.

HONEY: FIREWEED, WHITE

Source: *National Honey Market News.* **Price Frequency:** monthly, seasonally. **Effective Market(s):** Washington. **Units of Measure:** cents per lb. **Type of Price:** price paid to beekeepers. **Time Period Covered:** latest month.

HONEY: GALLBERRY, AMBER

Source: *National Honey Market News.* **Price Frequency:** monthly, seasonally. **Effective Market(s):** Florida, Georgia. **Units of Measure:** cents per lb. **Type of Price:** price paid to beekeepers. **Time Period Covered:** latest month.

HONEY: GALLBERRY, AMBER, BAKERY-GRADE

Source: *National Honey Market News.* **Price Frequency:** monthly, seasonally. **Effective Market(s):** Florida. **Units of Measure:** cents per lb. **Type of Price:** price paid to beekeepers. **Time Period Covered:** latest month.

HONEY: GALLBERRY, EXTRA LIGHT AMBER

Source: *National Honey Market News.* **Price Frequency:** monthly, seasonally. **Effective Market(s):** Florida. **Units of Measure:** cents per lb. **Type of Price:** price paid to beekeepers. **Time Period Covered:** latest month.

HONEY: GALLBERRY, LIGHT AMBER

Source: *National Honey Market News.* **Price Frequency:** monthly, seasonally. **Effective Market(s):** Florida. **Units of Measure:** cents per lb. **Type of Price:** price paid to beekeepers. **Time Period Covered:** latest month.

HONEY: GALLBERRY, WHITE

Source: *National Honey Market News.* **Price Frequency:** monthly, seasonally. **Effective Market(s):** Florida. **Units of Measure:** cents per lb. **Type of Price:** price paid to beekeepers. **Time Period Covered:** latest month.

HONEY: GALLBERRY-SAW PALMETTO, LIGHT AMBER

Source: *National Honey Market News.* **Price Frequency:** monthly, seasonally. **Effective Market(s):** Florida. **Units of Measure:** cents per lb. **Type of Price:** price paid to beekeepers. **Time Period Covered:** latest month.

HONEY: GALLBERRY-SAW PALMETTO, EXTRA LIGHT AMBER

Source: *National Honey Market News.* **Price Frequency:** monthly, seasonally. **Effective Market(s):** Florida. **Units of Measure:** cents per lb. **Type of Price:** price paid to beekeepers. **Time Period Covered:** latest month.

HONEY: HUAJILLO, EXTRA LIGHT AMBER

Source: *National Honey Market News.* **Price Frequency:** monthly, seasonally. **Effective Market(s):** Texas. **Units of Measure:** cents per lb. **Type of Price:** price paid to beekeepers. **Time Period Covered:** latest month.

HONEY: MANGROVE, AMBER

Source: *National Honey Market News.* **Price Frequency:** monthly, seasonally. **Effective Market(s):** Florida. **Units of Measure:** cents per lb. **Type of Price:** price paid to beekeepers. **Time Period Covered:** latest month.

HONEY: MANGROVE, LIGHT AMBER

Source: *National Honey Market News.* **Price Frequency:** monthly, seasonally. **Effective Market(s):** Florida. **Units of Measure:** cents per lb. **Type of Price:** price paid to beekeepers. **Time Period Covered:** latest month.

HONEY: MESQUITE, WHITE, MEXICO

Source: *National Honey Market News.* **Price Frequency:** monthly, seasonally. **Effective Market(s):** West Coast ports. **Units of Measure:** cents per lb. **Type of Price:** price paid to importers. **Time Period Covered:** latest month.

HONEY: MINT, AMBER

Source: *National Honey Market News.* **Price Frequency:** monthly, seasonally. **Effective Market(s):** Utah. **Units of Measure:** cents per lb. **Type of Price:** price paid to beekeepers. **Time Period Covered:** latest month.

HONEY: MINT-WILDFLOWER, AMBER

Source: *National Honey Market News.* **Price Frequency:** monthly, seasonally. **Effective Market(s):** Utah. **Units of Measure:** cents per lb. **Type of Price:** price paid to beekeepers. **Time Period Covered:** latest month.

HONEY: MINT-WILDFLOWER, EXTRA LIGHT AMBER

Source: *National Honey Market News.* **Price Frequency:** monthly, seasonally. **Effective Market(s):** Utah. **Units of Measure:** cents per lb. **Type of Price:** price paid to beekeepers. **Time Period Covered:** latest month.

HONEY: MINT-WILDFLOWER, LIGHT AMBER

Source: *National Honey Market News.* **Price Frequency:** monthly, seasonally. **Effective Market(s):** Utah. **Units of Measure:** cents per lb. **Type of Price:** price paid to beekeepers. **Time Period Covered:** latest month.

HONEY: MIXED FLOWERS, AMBER

Source: *National Honey Market News.* **Price Frequency:** monthly, seasonally. **Effective Market(s):** Louisiana. **Units of Measure:** cents per lb. **Type of Price:** price paid to beekeepers. **Time Period Covered:** latest month.

HONEY: MIXED FLOWERS, EXTRA LIGHT AMBER

Source: *National Honey Market News.* **Price Frequency:** monthly, seasonally. **Effective Market(s):** North/Central California. **Units of Measure:** cents per lb. **Type of Price:** price paid to beekeepers. **Time Period Covered:** latest month.

HONEY: MIXED FLOWERS, EXTRA LIGHT AMBER, MEXICAN

Source: *National Honey Market News.* **Price Frequency:** monthly, seasonally. **Effective Market(s):** West Coast ports. **Units of Measure:** cents per lb. **Type of Price:** price paid to importers. **Time Period Covered:** latest month.

HONEY: MIXED FLOWERS, LIGHT AMBER, MEXICAN

Source: *National Honey Market News.* **Price Frequency:** monthly, seasonally. **Effective Market(s):** West Coast ports. **Units of Measure:** cents per lb. **Type of Price:** price paid to importers. **Time Period Covered:** latest month.

HONEY: MIXED FLOWERS, LIGHT AMBER

Source: *National Honey Market News.* **Price Frequency:** monthly, seasonally. **Effective Market(s):** North/Central California. **Units of Measure:** cents per lb. **Type of Price:** price paid to beekeepers. **Time Period Covered:** latest month.

HONEY: MIXED WILD FLOWERS, AMBER

Source: *National Honey Market News.* **Price Frequency:** monthly, seasonally. **Effective Market(s):** Florida. **Units of Measure:** cents per lb. **Type of Price:** price paid to beekeepers. **Time Period Covered:** latest month.

HONEY: MIXED WILD FLOWERS, LIGHT AMBER

Source: *National Honey Market News.* **Price Frequency:** monthly, seasonally. **Effective Market(s):** Florida. **Units of Measure:** cents per lb. **Type of Price:** price paid to beekeepers. **Time Period Covered:** latest month.

HONEY: NAPWEED, WHITE

Source: *National Honey Market News.* **Price Frequency:** monthly, seasonally. **Effective Market(s):** Idaho, Montana. **Units of Measure:** cents per lb. **Type of Price:** price paid to beekeepers. **Time Period Covered:** latest month.

HONEY: ORANGE BLOSSOM, AMBER

Source: *National Honey Market News.* **Price Frequency:** monthly, seasonally. **Effective Market(s):** Florida. **Units of Measure:** cents per lb. **Type of Price:** price paid to beekeepers. **Time Period Covered:** latest month.

HONEY: ORANGE BLOSSOM, EXTRA LIGHT AMBER

Source: *National Honey Market News.* **Price Frequency:** monthly, seasonally. **Effective Market(s):** Florida, Wisconsin. **Units of Measure:** cents per lb. **Type of Price:** price paid to beekeepers. **Time Period Covered:** latest month.

HONEY: ORANGE BLOSSOM, LIGHT AMBER

Source: *National Honey Market News.* **Price Frequency:** monthly, seasonally. **Effective Market(s):** Florida. **Units of Measure:** cents per lb. **Type of Price:** price paid to beekeepers. **Time Period Covered:** latest month.

HONEY: ORANGE BLOSSOM, WHITE

Source: *National Honey Market News.* **Price Frequency:** monthly, seasonally. **Effective Market(s):** Florida. **Units of Measure:** cents per lb. **Type of Price:** price paid to beekeepers. **Time Period Covered:** latest month.

HONEY: ORANGE BLOSSON-SAW PALMETTO, LIGHT AMBER

Source: *National Honey Market News.* **Price Frequency:** monthly, seasonally. **Effective Market(s):** Florida. **Units of Measure:** cents per lb. **Type of Price:** price paid to beekeepers. **Time Period Covered:** latest month.

HONEY: ORANGE, WHITE

Source: *National Honey Market News.* **Price Frequency:** monthly, seasonally. **Effective Market(s):** North/Central California. **Units of Measure:** cents per lb. **Type of Price:** price paid to beekeepers. **Time Period Covered:** latest month.

HONEY: SAGE, LIGHT AMBER

Source: *National Honey Market News.* **Price Frequency:** monthly, seasonally. **Effective Market(s):** North/Central California. **Units of Measure:** cents per lb. **Type of Price:** price paid to beekeepers. **Time Period Covered:** latest month.

HONEY: SAW PALMETTO, AMBER

Source: *National Honey Market News.* **Price Frequency:** monthly, seasonally. **Effective Market(s):** Florida. **Units of Measure:** cents per lb. **Type of Price:** price paid to beekeepers. **Time Period Covered:** latest month.

HONEY: SAW PALMETTO, EXTRA LIGHT AMBER

Source: *National Honey Market News.* **Price Frequency:** monthly, seasonally. **Effective Market(s):** Florida. **Units of Measure:** cents per lb. **Type of Price:** price paid to beekeepers. **Time Period Covered:** latest month.

HONEY: SAW PALMETTO, LIGHT AMBER

Source: *National Honey Market News.* **Price Frequency:** monthly, seasonally. **Effective Market(s):** Florida. **Units of Measure:** cents per lb. **Type of Price:** price paid to beekeepers. **Time Period Covered:** latest month.

HONEY: SOYBEAN, AMBER

Source: *National Honey Market News.* **Price Frequency:** monthly, seasonally. **Effective Market(s):** Arkansas, Louisiana. **Units of Measure:** cents per lb. **Type of Price:** price paid to beekeepers. **Time Period Covered:** latest month.

HONEY: SOYBEAN, EXTRA LIGHT AMBER

Source: *National Honey Market News.* **Price Frequency:** monthly, seasonally. **Effective Market(s):** Missouri. **Units of Measure:** cents per lb. **Type of Price:** price paid to beekeepers. **Time Period Covered:** latest month.

Source: *National Honey Market News.* **Price Frequency:** monthly, seasonally. **Effective Market(s):** Arkansas. **Units of Measure:** cents per lb. **Type of Price:** price paid to beekeepers. **Time Period Covered:** latest month.

HONEY: SOYBEAN, LIGHT AMBER

Source: *National Honey Market News.* **Price Frequency:** monthly, seasonally. **Effective Market(s):** Arkansas. **Units of Measure:** cents per lb. **Type of Price:** price paid to beekeepers. **Time Period Covered:** latest month.

HONEY: SPANISH NEEDLE, AMBER

Source: *National Honey Market News.* **Price Frequency:** monthly, seasonally. **Effective Market(s):** Arkansas, Florida. **Units of Measure:** cents per lb. **Type of Price:** price paid to beekeepers. **Time Period Covered:** latest month.

HONEY: SQUEEZE BOTTLE

Source: *Gleanings in Bee Culture.* **Price Frequency:** monthly. **Effective Market(s):** 10 domestic markets. **Units of Measure:** Dollars per 12 ounce bottle. **Type of Price:** retail. **Time Period Covered:** latest month.

HONEY: SUNFLOWER, LIGHT AMBER

Source: *National Honey Market News.* **Price Frequency:** monthly, seasonally. **Effective Market(s):** Nebraska. **Units of Measure:** cents per lb. **Type of Price:** price paid to beekeepers. **Time Period Covered:** latest month.

HONEY: TI TI, AMBER, NON-TABLE

Source: *National Honey Market News.* **Price Frequency:** monthly, seasonally. **Effective Market(s):** Florida. **Units of Measure:** cents per lb. **Type of Price:** price paid to beekeepers. **Time Period Covered:** latest month.

HONEY: TI TI, LIGHT AMBER, NON-TABLE

Source: *National Honey Market News.* **Price Frequency:** monthly, seasonally. **Effective Market(s):** Florida. **Units of Measure:** cents per lb. **Type of Price:** price paid to beekeepers. **Time Period Covered:** latest month.

HONEY: TULIP POPLAR, AMBER

Source: *National Honey Market News.* **Price Frequency:** monthly, seasonally. **Effective Market(s):** Georgia. **Units of Measure:** cents per lb. **Type of Price:** price paid to beekeepers. **Time Period Covered:** latest month.

HONEY: TULIP POPLAR, AMBER, NON-TABLE

Source: *National Honey Market News.* **Price Frequency:** monthly, seasonally. **Effective Market(s):** Alabama. **Units of Measure:** cents per lb. **Type of Price:** price paid to beekeepers. **Time Period Covered:** latest month.

HONEY: WHITE, EXTRACTED, UNPROCESSED

Source: *Gleanings in Bee Culture.* **Price Frequency:** monthly. **Effective Market(s):** 10 domestic markets. **Units of Measure:** Dollars per 60 lb. can, dollars per lb. **Type of Price:** price to packer. **Time Period Covered:** latest month.

HONEY: WHITE, WATER WHITE, EXTRA WHITE

Source: *Honey.* **Price Frequency:** annually. **Effective Market(s):** United States. **Units of Measure:** cents per lb. **Type of Price:** coop & private, retail, average. **Time Period Covered:** latest 2 years.

HONEY: WILDFLOWER, AMBER

Source: *National Honey Market News.* **Price Frequency:** monthly, seasonally. **Effective Market(s):** Arkansas. **Units of Measure:** cents per lb. **Type of Price:** price paid to beekeepers. **Time Period Covered:** latest month.

HONEYDEW MELONS

Source: *Agricultural Prices Annual Summary.* **Price Frequency:** monthly, seasonally. **Effective Market(s):** Arizona, California, Texas, United States. **Units of Measure:** Dollars per 100 lbs. **Type of Price:** average received by growers. **Time Period Covered:** monthly latest 3 years, for US latest 6 years.

Source: *California Farmer.* **Price Frequency:** semimonthly, seasonally. **Effective Market(s):** Central San Joaquin Valley, Sacramento Valley (CA), Imperial/Palo Verde Valleys. **Units of Measure:** Dollars per 2/3 carton. **Time Period Covered:** latest week, month ago, year ago.

Source: *Fresh Fruit and Vegetable Prices.* **Price Frequency:** monthly, seasonally. **Effective Market(s):** San Joaquin Valley (CA), Sacramento Valley (CA), Western Arizona/Southern California, Lower Rio Grande Valley (TX). **Units of Measure:** Dollars per carton. **Type of Price:** average price at shipping point. **Time Period Covered:** latest year.

Source: *Lancaster Farming.* **Price Frequency:** weekly, seasonally. **Effective Market(s):** Pennsylvania. **Units of Measure:** Dollars per carton. **Type of Price:** market. **Time Period Covered:** latest week.

Source: *New Zealand Farmer.* **Price Frequency:** weekly, seasonally. **Effective Market(s):** New Zealand. **Units of Measure:** New Zealand dollars per carton. **Time Period Covered:** latest week.

Source: *The Packer.* **Price Frequency:** weekly, seasonally. **Effective Market(s):** varies. **Units of Measure:** Dollars per carton. **Type of Price:** price received by farmer. **Time Period Covered:** latest week.

HONEYDEW MELONS: CALIFORNIA

Source: *Fresh Fruit and Vegetable Prices.* **Price Frequency:** monthly, seasonally. **Effective Market(s):** Chicago, New York City. **Units of Measure:** Dollars per carton. **Type of Price:** average wholesale price. **Time Period Covered:** latest year.

HONEYDEW MELONS: CARIBBEAN, IMPORTS

Source: *Fresh Fruit and Vegetable Prices.* **Price Frequency:** monthly, seasonally. **Units of Measure:** Dollars per carton. **Time Period Covered:** latest year.

HONEYDEW MELONS: FRESH

Source: *HRI-Buyers Guide.* **Price Frequency:** weekly. **Effective Market(s):** Northeastern area. **Units of Measure:** Dollars per case. **Time Period Covered:** latest week.

HONEYDEW MELONS: GUATEMALA

Source: *Fresh Fruit and Vegetable Prices.* **Price Frequency:** monthly, seasonally. **Effective Market(s):** New York City. **Units of Measure:** Dollars per carton. **Type of Price:** average wholesale price. **Time Period Covered:** latest year.

HONEYDEW MELONS: IMPORTED

Source: *New Zealand Farmer.* **Price Frequency:** weekly, seasonally. **Effective Market(s):** New Zealand. **Units of Measure:** New Zealand dollars per carton. **Time Period Covered:** latest week.

HONEYDEW MELONS: MEXICO

Source: *Fresh Fruit and Vegetable Prices.* **Price Frequency:** monthly, seasonally. **Effective Market(s):** South Texas. **Units of Measure:** Dollars per carton. **Type of Price:** price paid at point of entry. **Time Period Covered:** latest year.

Source: *Fresh Fruit and Vegetable Prices.* **Price Frequency:** monthly, seasonally. **Effective Market(s):** Chicago, New York City. **Units of Measure:** Dollars per carton. **Type of Price:** average wholesale price. **Time Period Covered:** latest year.

HONEYDEW MELONS: TEXAS

Source: *Fresh Fruit and Vegetable Prices.* **Price Frequency:** monthly, seasonally. **Effective Market(s):** Chicago, New York City. **Units of Measure:** Dollars per carton. **Type of Price:** average wholesale price. **Time Period Covered:** latest year.

HONG KONG DOLLARS

Source: *Asian Wall Street Journal.* **Price Frequency:** daily. **Effective Market(s):** Asia. **Units of Measure:** Hong Kong dollars per United States dollar. **Type of Price:** foreign exchange. **Time Period Covered:** latest 2 days.

Source: *Barron's.* **Price Frequency:** weekly. **Effective Market(s):** New York. **Units of Measure:** Hong Kong dollars per United States dollar. **Type of Price:** foreign exchange. **Time Period Covered:** latest 2 weeks.

Source: *New York Times.* **Price Frequency:** daily. **Effective Market(s):** United States. **Units of Measure:** Hong Kong dollars per United States dollar. **Type of Price:** foreign exchange. **Time Period Covered:** latest 2 days.

Source: *Prices of Selected Asia/Pacific Products.* **Price Frequency:** monthly. **Effective Market(s):** Hong Kong. **Units of Measure:** Hong Kong dollars per Australian dollar. **Type of Price:** monthly average foreign exchange. **Time Period Covered:** latest month.

Source: *Prices of Selected Asia/Pacific Products.* **Price Frequency:** monthly. **Effective Market(s):** Hong Kong. **Units of Measure:** Hong Kong dollars per Danish kroner. **Type of Price:** monthly average foreign exchange. **Time Period Covered:** latest month.

Source: *Prices of Selected Asia/Pacific Products.* **Price Frequency:** monthly. **Effective Market(s):** Hong Kong. **Units of Measure:** Hong Kong dollars per West German mark. **Type of Price:** monthly average foreign exchange. **Time Period Covered:** latest month.

Source: *Prices of Selected Asia/Pacific Products.* **Price Frequency:** monthly. **Effective Market(s):** Hong Kong. **Units of Measure:** Hong Kong dollars per French franc. **Type of Price:** monthly average foreign exchange. **Time Period Covered:** latest month.

Source: *Prices of Selected Asia/Pacific Products.* **Price Frequency:** monthly. **Effective Market(s):** Hong Kong. **Units of Measure:** Hong Kong dollars per Japanese yen. **Type of Price:** monthly average foreign exchange. **Time Period Covered:** latest month.

Source: *Prices of Selected Asia/Pacific Products.* **Price Frequency:** monthly. **Effective Market(s):** Hong Kong. **Units of Measure:** Hong Kong dollars per Dutch guilder. **Type of Price:** monthly average foreign exchange. **Time Period Covered:** latest month.

Source: *Prices of Selected Asia/Pacific Products.* **Price Frequency:** monthly. **Effective Market(s):** Hong Kong. **Units of Measure:** Hong Kong dollars per Philippines peso. **Type of Price:** monthly average foreign exchange. **Time Period Covered:** latest month.

Source: *Prices of Selected Asia/Pacific Products.* **Price Frequency:** monthly. **Effective Market(s):** Hong Kong. **Units of Measure:** Hong Kong dollars per British pound. **Type of Price:** monthly average foreign exchange. **Time Period Covered:** latest month.

Source: *Prices of Selected Asia/Pacific Products.* **Price Frequency:** monthly. **Effective Market(s):** Hong Kong. **Units of Measure:** Hong Kong dollars per Swedish kroner. **Type of Price:** monthly average foreign exchange. **Time Period Covered:** latest month.

Source: *Prices of Selected Asia/Pacific Products.* **Price Frequency:** monthly. **Effective Market(s):** Hong Kong. **Units of Measure:** Hong Kong dollars per Thai baht. **Type of Price:** monthly average foreign exchange. **Time Period Covered:** latest month.

Source: *Prices of Selected Asia/Pacific Products.* **Price Frequency:** monthly. **Effective Market(s):** Hong Kong. **Units of Measure:** Hong Kong dollars per United States dollar. **Type of Price:** monthly average foreign exchange. **Time Period Covered:** latest month.

Source: *The Times.* **Price Frequency:** daily. **Effective Market(s):** London. **Units of Measure:** Hong Kong Dollars per British pound. **Type of Price:** foreign exchange. **Time Period Covered:** latest day.

HOPS

Source: *Agricultural Prices Annual Summary.* **Price Frequency:** annually. **Effective Market(s):** Idaho, Oregon, Washington, United States. **Units of Measure:** Dollars per lb. **Type of Price:** average price received by farmer. **Time Period Covered:** latest 2 years, for US latest 6 years.

Source: *Journal of Commerce and Commercial.* **Price Frequency:** weekly in Monday issue. **Units of Measure:** Dollars per lb. **Type of Price:** spot. **Time Period Covered:** latest week.

HOREHOUND HERB

Source: *Chemical Marketing Reporter.* **Price Frequency:** weekly. **Effective Market(s):** New York. **Units of Measure:** Dollars per lb. **Type of Price:** spot. **Time Period Covered:** latest week.

HORSES

Source: *Farm and Dairy.* **Price Frequency:** weekly, seasonally. **Effective Market(s):** Ohio, Pennsylvania. **Units of Measure:** Dollars per head. **Type of Price:** auction high, auction low. **Time Period Covered:** latest week.

HORSES: COLTS

Source: *Lancaster Farming.* **Price Frequency:** weekly, seasonally. **Effective Market(s):** Pennsylvania. **Units of Measure:** Dollars per head. **Type of Price:** auction. **Time Period Covered:** latest week.

HORSES: DRIVING

Source: *Lancaster Farming.* **Price Frequency:** weekly, seasonally. **Effective Market(s):** Pennsylvania. **Units of Measure:** Dollars per head. **Type of Price:** market. **Time Period Covered:** latest week.

HORSES: GELDINGS

Source: *Lancaster Farming.* **Price Frequency:** weekly, seasonally. **Effective Market(s):** Pennsylvania. **Units of Measure:** Dollars per head. **Type of Price:** auction. **Time Period Covered:** latest week.

HORSES: HEAVYWEIGHT KILLER

Source: *Lancaster Farming.* **Price Frequency:** weekly, seasonally. **Effective Market(s):** Pennsylvania. **Units of Measure:** Dollars per head. **Type of Price:** auction. **Time Period Covered:** latest week.

HORSES: LIGHTWEIGHT KILLER

Source: *Lancaster Farming.* **Price Frequency:** weekly, seasonally. **Effective Market(s):** Pennsylvania. **Units of Measure:** Dollars per head. **Type of Price:** auction. **Time Period Covered:** latest week.

HORSES: MARES

Source: *Lancaster Farming.* **Price Frequency:** weekly, seasonally. **Effective Market(s):** Pennsylvania. **Units of Measure:** Dollars per head. **Type of Price:** auction. **Time Period Covered:** latest week.

HORSES: REGISTERED

Source: *Lancaster Farming.* **Price Frequency:** weekly, seasonally. **Effective Market(s):** Pennsylvania. **Units of Measure:** Dollars per head. **Type of Price:** auction. **Time Period Covered:** latest week.

HORSES: RIDING

Source: *Lancaster Farming.* **Price Frequency:** weekly, seasonally. **Effective Market(s):** Pennsylvania. **Units of Measure:** Dollars per head. **Type of Price:** auction. **Time Period Covered:** latest week.

HOT DOGS: TURKEY

Source: *Urner Barry's Price-Current, West Coast Edition.* **Price Frequency:** semiweekly. **Effective Market(s):** West Coast. **Units of Measure:** Dollars per lb. **Time Period Covered:** latest week.

HYDRAZINE HYDRATE: 85%

Source: *Chemical Marketing Reporter.* **Price Frequency:** weekly. **Effective Market(s):** New York. **Units of Measure:** Dollars per lb. **Type of Price:** spot. **Time Period Covered:** latest week.

HYDRIODIC ACID: PURIFIED, 47-57%

Source: *Chemical Marketing Reporter.* **Price Frequency:** weekly. **Effective Market(s):** New York. **Units of Measure:** Dollars per lb. **Type of Price:** spot. **Time Period Covered:** latest week.

HYDROABIETYL ALCOHOL: TECHNICAL GRADE, SOLID

Source: *Chemical Marketing Reporter.* **Price Frequency:** weekly. **Effective Market(s):** New York. **Units of Measure:** Dollars per lb. **Type of Price:** spot. **Time Period Covered:** latest week.

HYDROBROMIC ACID: 48%

Source: *Chemical Marketing Reporter.* **Price Frequency:** weekly. **Effective Market(s):** New York. **Units of Measure:** Dollars per lb. **Type of Price:** spot. **Time Period Covered:** latest week.

HYDROCHLORIC ACID

Source: *Chemical Marketing Reporter.* **Price Frequency:** weekly. **Effective Market(s):** East, Midwest, Gulf Coast, West Coast. **Units of Measure:** Dollars per ton. **Type of Price:** spot. **Time Period Covered:** latest week.

Source: *Journal of Commerce and Commercial.* **Price Frequency:** weekly in Friday issue. **Units of Measure:** Dollars per ton. **Type of Price:** spot. **Time Period Covered:** latest week.

Source: *Purchasing.* **Price Frequency:** quarterly in January, April, July, October issues. **Units of Measure:** Dollars per ton. **Type of Price:** transaction. **Time Period Covered:** latest 5 quarters.

HYDROCHLORIC ACID: ANHYDROUS

see Hydrogen Chloride.

HYDROCORTISONE

Source: *Journal of Commerce and Commercial.* **Price Frequency:** weekly in Friday issue. **Units of Measure:** Dollars per gram. **Type of Price:** spot. **Time Period Covered:** latest week.

HYDROCORTISONE ACETATE: MICRONIZED

Source: *Chemical Marketing Reporter.* **Price Frequency:** weekly. **Effective Market(s):** New York. **Units of Measure:** Dollars per gram. **Type of Price:** spot. **Time Period Covered:** latest week.

HYDROCORTISONE ALCOHOL: MICRONIZED

Source: *Chemical Marketing Reporter.* **Price Frequency:** weekly. **Effective Market(s):** New York. **Units of Measure:** Dollars per gram. **Type of Price:** spot. **Time Period Covered:** latest week.

HYDROFLUORIC ACID: ANHYDROUS

see Hydrogen Fluoride.

HYDROFLUORIC ACID: AQUEOUS

Source: *Journal of Commerce and Commercial.* **Price Frequency:** weekly in Thursday issue. **Units of Measure:** Dollars per lb. **Type of Price:** spot. **Time Period Covered:** latest week.

HYDROFLUORIC ACID: AQUEOUS, 70%

Source: *Chemical Marketing Reporter.* **Price Frequency:** weekly. **Effective Market(s):** New York. **Units of Measure:** Dollars per 100 lbs. **Type of Price:** spot. **Time Period Covered:** latest week.

HYDROFLUOSILICIC ACID

Source: *Chemical Marketing Reporter.* **Price Frequency:** weekly. **Effective Market(s):** New York. **Units of Measure:** Dollars per ton. **Type of Price:** spot. **Time Period Covered:** latest week.

HYDROGEN BROMIDE: ANHYDROUS

Source: *Chemical Marketing Reporter.* **Price Frequency:** weekly. **Effective Market(s):** New York. **Units of Measure:** Dollars per lb. **Type of Price:** spot. **Time Period Covered:** latest week.

HYDROGEN CHLORIDE: ANHYDROUS

Source: *Chemical Marketing Reporter.* **Price Frequency:** weekly. **Effective Market(s):** New York. **Units of Measure:** Dollars per ton. **Type of Price:** spot. **Time Period Covered:** latest week.

HYDROGEN CHLORIDE: ANHYDROUS, TUBE TRAILERS

Source: *Chemical Marketing Reporter.* **Price Frequency:** weekly. **Effective Market(s):** New York. **Units of Measure:** Dollars per lb. **Type of Price:** spot. **Time Period Covered:** latest week.

HYDROGEN CYANIDE: LIQUID, 99.5%

Source: *Chemical Marketing Reporter.* **Price Frequency:** weekly. **Effective Market(s):** New York. **Units of Measure:** Dollars per lb. **Type of Price:** spot. **Time Period Covered:** latest week.

HYDROGEN FLUORIDE: ANHYDROUS

Source: *Chemical Marketing Reporter.* **Price Frequency:** weekly. **Effective Market(s):** New York. **Units of Measure:** Dollars per lb. **Type of Price:** spot. **Time Period Covered:** latest week.

HYDROGEN PEROXIDE: 35% TECHNICAL GRADE

Source: *Chemical Marketing Reporter.* **Price Frequency:** weekly. **Effective Market(s):** New York. **Units of Measure:** Dollars per lb. **Type of Price:** spot. **Time Period Covered:** latest week.

HYDROGEN PEROXIDE: 50%

Source: *Chemical Marketing Reporter.* **Price Frequency:** weekly. **Effective Market(s):** New York. **Units of Measure:** Dollars per lb. **Type of Price:** spot. **Time Period Covered:** latest week.

HYDROGEN PEROXIDE: 70%

Source: *Chemical Marketing Reporter.* **Price Frequency:** weekly. **Effective Market(s):** New York. **Units of Measure:** Dollars per lb. **Type of Price:** spot. **Time Period Covered:** latest week.

Source: *Journal of Commerce and Commercial.* **Price Frequency:** weekly in Thursday issue. **Units of Measure:** Dollars per lb. **Type of Price:** spot. **Time Period Covered:** latest week.

HYDROGEN SULFIDE: LIQUID, 99.25% MINIMUM

Source: *Chemical Marketing Reporter.* **Price Frequency:** weekly. **Effective Market(s):** New York. **Units of Measure:** Dollars per lb. **Type of Price:** spot. **Time Period Covered:** latest week.

HYDROQUINONE: PHOTO GRADE

Source: *Journal of Commerce and Commercial.* **Price Frequency:** weekly in Friday issue. **Units of Measure:** Dollars per lb. **Type of Price:** spot. **Time Period Covered:** latest week.

HYDROQUINONE: PHOTO GRADE, CONSUMERS

Source: *Chemical Marketing Reporter.* **Price Frequency:** weekly. **Effective Market(s):** New York. **Units of Measure:** Dollars per lb. **Type of Price:** spot. **Time Period Covered:** latest week.

HYDROQUINONE: TECHNICAL GRADE

Source: *Chemical Marketing Reporter.* **Price Frequency:** weekly. **Effective Market(s):** New York. **Units of Measure:** Dollars per lb. **Type of Price:** spot. **Time Period Covered:** latest week.

HYDROSULFIDE: FLAKE, 70-72%

Source: *Journal of Commerce and Commercial.* **Price Frequency:** weekly in Thursday issue. **Units of Measure:** Dollars per lb. **Type of Price:** spot. **Time Period Covered:** latest week.

HYDROXYACETIC ACID: TECHNICAL GRADE, 70%

Source: *Chemical Marketing Reporter.* **Price Frequency:** weekly. **Effective Market(s):** Belle (WV). **Units of Measure:** Dollars per lb. **Type of Price:** spot. **Time Period Covered:** latest week.

P-HYDROXYBENZENE SULFONIC ACID

see p-Phenolsulfonic Acid.

HYDROXYCITRONELLAL

Source: *Journal of Commerce and Commercial.* **Price Frequency:** weekly in Tuesday issue. **Units of Measure:** Dollars per lb. **Type of Price:** spot. **Time Period Covered:** latest week.

HYDROXYCITRONELLAL: NATURAL

Source: *Chemical Marketing Reporter.* **Price Frequency:** weekly. **Effective Market(s):** New York. **Units of Measure:** Dollars per lb. **Type of Price:** spot. **Time Period Covered:** latest week.

HYDROXYCITRONELLAL: SYNTHETIC

Source: *Chemical Marketing Reporter.* **Price Frequency:** weekly. **Effective Market(s):** New York. **Units of Measure:** Dollars per lb. **Type of Price:** spot. **Time Period Covered:** latest week.

HYDROXYCITRONELLAL DIMETHYL ACETAL

Source: *Chemical Marketing Reporter.* **Price Frequency:** weekly. **Effective Market(s):** New York. **Units of Measure:** Dollars per lb. **Type of Price:** spot. **Time Period Covered:** latest week.

P-HYDROXYDIPHENYLAMINE

Source: *Chemical Marketing Reporter.* **Price Frequency:** weekly. **Effective Market(s):** New York. **Units of Measure:** Dollars per lb. **Type of Price:** spot. **Time Period Covered:** latest week.

HYDROXYETHYL CELLULOSE: STANDARD GRADE

Source: *Chemical Marketing Reporter.* **Price Frequency:** weekly. **Effective Market(s):** New York. **Units of Measure:** Dollars per lb. **Type of Price:** spot. **Time Period Covered:** latest week.

HYDROXYETHYL METHYLCELLULOSE

Source: *Chemical Marketing Reporter.* **Price Frequency:** weekly. **Effective Market(s):** New York. **Units of Measure:** Dollars per lb. **Type of Price:** spot. **Time Period Covered:** latest week.

HYDROXYLAMINE SULFATE

Source: *Chemical Marketing Reporter.* **Price Frequency:** weekly. **Effective Market(s):** New York. **Units of Measure:** Dollars per lb. **Type of Price:** spot. **Time Period Covered:** latest week.

HYDROXYPROPYL METHYLCELLULOSE

Source: *Chemical Marketing Reporter.* **Price Frequency:** weekly. **Effective Market(s):** New York. **Units of Measure:** Dollars per lb. **Type of Price:** spot. **Time Period Covered:** latest week.

HYDROXYPROPYL METHYLCELLULOSE: PREMIUM, USP

Source: *Chemical Marketing Reporter.* **Price Frequency:** weekly. **Effective Market(s):** New York. **Units of Measure:** Dollars per lb. **Type of Price:** spot. **Time Period Covered:** latest week.

HYDROXYPROPYL METHYLCELLULOSE: USP

Source: *Chemical Marketing Reporter.* **Price Frequency:** weekly. **Effective Market(s):** New York. **Units of Measure:** Dollars per lb. **Type of Price:** spot. **Time Period Covered:** latest week.

8-HYDROXYQUINOLINE

see Oxyquinoline.

HYPOPHOSPHITE

Source: *Journal of Commerce and Commercial.* **Price Frequency:** weekly in Thursday issue. **Units of Measure:** Dollars per lb. **Type of Price:** spot. **Time Period Covered:** latest week.

HYPOPHOSPHOROUS ACID: PURIFIED, 50%

Source: *Chemical Marketing Reporter.* **Price Frequency:** weekly. **Effective Market(s):** New York. **Units of Measure:** Dollars per lb. **Type of Price:** spot. **Time Period Covered:** latest week.

I-BEAMS: 6″ DEEP, 12.5 LB./LF

Source: *ENR.* **Price Frequency:** monthly in second issue of month. **Effective Market(s):** 17 domestic cities, Montreal, Toronto. **Units of Measure:** Dollars per 100 lbs. **Type of Price:** spot. **Time Period Covered:** latest month.

IBUPROFEN

Source: *Chemical Marketing Reporter.* **Price Frequency:** weekly. **Effective Market(s):** New York. **Units of Measure:** Dollars per kilo. **Type of Price:** spot. **Time Period Covered:** latest week.

ICE CREAM: REGULAR

Source: *Dairy Market Statistics.* **Price Frequency:** monthly, annually. **Effective Market(s):** Northeast, North Central, South, West, United States. **Units of Measure:** Dollars per half gallon. **Type of Price:** retail. **Time Period Covered:** latest year.

Source: *Federal Milk Order Market Statistics.* **Price Frequency:** monthly. **Effective Market(s):** North Central, Northeast, South, West, United States. **Units of Measure:** Dollars per 1/2 gallon. **Type of Price:** retail. **Time Period Covered:** latest year to date.

ICE CREAM AND RELATED PRODUCTS

Source: *Dairy Market Statistics.* **Price Frequency:** monthly. **Effective Market(s):** United States. **Units of Measure:** index. **Type of Price:** consumer price index. **Time Period Covered:** latest year.

ICHTHAMMOL: NF

Source: *Chemical Marketing Reporter.* **Price Frequency:** weekly. **Effective Market(s):** New York. **Units of Measure:** Dollars per lb. **Type of Price:** spot. **Time Period Covered:** latest week.

ILANG-ILANG OIL

see Ylang-Ylang Oil.

ILMENITE: 'Q' GRADE, INDIAN

Source: *Industrial Minerals.* **Price Frequency:** monthly. **Effective Market(s):** Neendakara (India). **Type of Price:** producer & dealer. **Time Period Covered:** latest month.

ILMENITE: CONCENTRATE, AUSTRALIAN

Source: *Industrial Minerals.* **Price Frequency:** monthly. **Effective Market(s):** Australia. **Units of Measure:** Australian dollars per metric tonne. **Type of Price:** producer & dealer. **Time Period Covered:** latest month.

ILMENITE: CONCENTRATE, UNITED STATES

Source: *Industrial Minerals.* **Price Frequency:** monthly. **Effective Market(s):** East Coast. **Units of Measure:** Dollars per short ton. **Type of Price:** producer & dealer. **Time Period Covered:** latest month.

IMINODIACETIC ACID: 96% MINIMUM

Source: *Chemical Marketing Reporter.* **Price Frequency:** weekly. **Effective Market(s):** New York. **Units of Measure:** Dollars per lb. **Type of Price:** spot. **Time Period Covered:** latest week.

INCONEL: SOLIDS

Source: *American Metal Market.* **Price Frequency:** daily. **Effective Market(s):** Los Angeles. **Units of Measure:** cents per lb. **Type of Price:** dealer buying. **Time Period Covered:** latest day.

INDEX CARDS

Source: *Pulp & Paper Week.* **Price Frequency:** monthly, irregularly. **Units of Measure:** index. **Type of Price:** price index. **Time Period Covered:** latest 3 months.

INDIA RUPEES

Source: *Barron's.* **Price Frequency:** weekly. **Effective Market(s):** New York. **Units of Measure:** Indian rupees per United States dollar. **Type of Price:** foreign exchange. **Time Period Covered:** latest 2 weeks.

Source: *New York Times.* **Price Frequency:** daily. **Effective Market(s):** United States. **Units of Measure:** Indian rupees per United States dollar. **Type of Price:** official foreign exchange rate. **Time Period Covered:** latest 2 days.

Source: *The Times.* **Price Frequency:** daily. **Effective Market(s):** London. **Units of Measure:** Indian rupees per British pound. **Type of Price:** foreign exchange. **Time Period Covered:** latest day.

INDIUM

Source: *Iron Age.* **Price Frequency:** monthly. **Units of Measure:** Dollars per troy ounce. **Type of Price:** consumer. **Time Period Covered:** latest month.

INDIUM INGOTS: 99.97% MINIMUM

Source: *Economic and Energy Indicators.* **Price Frequency:** monthly, quarterly, annually. **Units of Measure:** Dollars per troy ounce. **Time Period Covered:** latest 3 months, quarters, and years.

INDOLE

Source: *Chemical Marketing Reporter.* **Price Frequency:** weekly. **Effective Market(s):** New York. **Units of Measure:** Dollars per lb. **Type of Price:** spot. **Time Period Covered:** latest week.

INDONESIA RUPIAH

Source: *Asian Wall Street Journal.* **Price Frequency:** daily. **Effective Market(s):** Asia. **Units of Measure:** Indonesian rupiah per United States dollar, per SDR. **Type of Price:** foreign exchange. **Time Period Covered:** latest 2 days.

Source: *Barron's.* **Price Frequency:** weekly. **Effective Market(s):** New York. **Units of Measure:** Indonesian rupiah per United States dollar. **Type of Price:** foreign exchange. **Time Period Covered:** latest 2 weeks.

Source: *New York Times.* **Price Frequency:** daily. **Effective Market(s):** United States. **Units of Measure:** Indonesian rupiah per United States dollar. **Type of Price:** foreign exchange. **Time Period Covered:** latest 2 days.

INDUSTRIAL MATERIALS

Source: *Business Week.* **Price Frequency:** weekly. **Units of Measure:** index. **Type of Price:** price index. **Time Period Covered:** latest 2 weeks.

INOSITOL

Source: *Chemical Marketing Reporter.* **Price Frequency:** weekly. **Effective Market(s):** New York. **Units of Measure:** Dollars per kilo. **Type of Price:** spot. **Time Period Covered:** latest week.

INSECTICIDES

Source: *Journal of Commerce and Commercial.* **Price Frequency:** weekly in Thursday issue. **Units of Measure:** Dollars per lb. **Type of Price:** spot. **Time Period Covered:** latest week.

INSULATING BOARD

Source: *Timber Bulletin.* **Price Frequency:** monthly, annually. **Effective Market(s):** United Kingdom. **Units of Measure:** British pounds per metric ton. **Type of Price:** import value. **Time Period Covered:** monthly latest 2 years, annually latest 5 years.

IODINE: CRUDE

Source: *Chemical Marketing Reporter.* **Price Frequency:** weekly. **Effective Market(s):** New York. **Units of Measure:** Dollars per kilo. **Type of Price:** spot. **Time Period Covered:** latest week.

Source: *Journal of Commerce and Commercial.* **Price Frequency:** weekly in Friday issue. **Units of Measure:** Dollars per lb. **Type of Price:** spot. **Time Period Covered:** latest week.

IODINE: USP

Source: *Chemical Marketing Reporter.* **Price Frequency:** weekly. **Effective Market(s):** New York. **Units of Measure:** Dollars per lb. **Type of Price:** spot. **Time Period Covered:** latest week.

Source: *Journal of Commerce and Commercial.* **Price Frequency:** weekly in Friday issue. **Units of Measure:** Dollars per lb. **Type of Price:** spot. **Time Period Covered:** latest week.

IODINE CRYSTAL: CRUDE

Source: *Industrial Minerals.* **Price Frequency:** monthly. **Effective Market(s):** United Kingdom. **Units of Measure:** Dollars per kilogram. **Type of Price:** producer & dealer. **Time Period Covered:** latest month.

IODOCHLORHYDROXYQUIN: USP

Source: *Chemical Marketing Reporter.* **Price Frequency:** weekly. **Effective Market(s):** New York. **Units of Measure:** Dollars per kilo. **Type of Price:** spot. **Time Period Covered:** latest week.

IODOFORM: NF

Source: *Chemical Marketing Reporter.* **Price Frequency:** weekly. **Effective Market(s):** New York. **Units of Measure:** Dollars per lb. **Type of Price:** spot. **Time Period Covered:** latest week.

IONOMER

Source: *Plastics Technology.* **Price Frequency:** monthly. **Units of Measure:** cents per lb., cents per cubic inch. **Type of Price:** bulk list, market. **Time Period Covered:** latest month.

IONOMER RESIN

Source: *Journal of Commerce and Commercial.* **Price Frequency:** weekly in Tuesday issue. **Units of Measure:** Dollars per lb. **Type of Price:** spot. **Time Period Covered:** latest week.

A-IONONE

Source: *Chemical Marketing Reporter.* **Price Frequency:** weekly. **Effective Market(s):** New York. **Units of Measure:** Dollars per lb. **Type of Price:** spot. **Time Period Covered:** latest week.

B-IONONE

Source: *Chemical Marketing Reporter.* **Price Frequency:** weekly. **Effective Market(s):** New York. **Units of Measure:** Dollars per lb. **Type of Price:** spot. **Time Period Covered:** latest week.

IONONES: ALPHA

Source: *Journal of Commerce and Commercial.* **Price Frequency:** weekly in Tuesday issue. **Units of Measure:** Dollars per lb. **Type of Price:** spot. **Time Period Covered:** latest week.

IONONES: BETA

Source: *Journal of Commerce and Commercial.* **Price Frequency:** weekly in Tuesday issue. **Units of Measure:** Dollars per lb. **Type of Price:** spot. **Time Period Covered:** latest week.

IPECAC ROOT: WHOLE

Source: *Chemical Marketing Reporter.* **Price Frequency:** weekly. **Effective Market(s):** New York. **Units of Measure:** Dollars per kilo. **Type of Price:** spot. **Time Period Covered:** latest week.

Source: *Journal of Commerce and Commercial.* **Price Frequency:** weekly in Monday issue. **Units of Measure:** Dollars per lb. **Type of Price:** spot. **Time Period Covered:** latest week.

IRAN RIAL

Source: *Asian Wall Street Journal.* **Price Frequency:** daily. **Effective Market(s):** United States. **Units of Measure:** Iranian rial per SDR. **Type of Price:** foreign exchange. **Time Period Covered:** latest 2 days.

IRELAND POUNDS

Source: *Asian Wall Street Journal.* **Price Frequency:** daily. **Effective Market(s):** United States. **Units of Measure:** Irish pounds per ECU. **Type of Price:** foreign exchange. **Time Period Covered:** latest 2 days.

Source: *Barron's.* **Price Frequency:** weekly. **Effective Market(s):** New York. **Units of Measure:** Irish pounds per United States dollar. **Type of Price:** foreign exchange. **Time Period Covered:** latest 2 weeks.

Source: *New York Times.* **Price Frequency:** daily. **Effective Market(s):** United States. **Units of Measure:** Irish pounds per United States dollar. **Type of Price:** foreign exchange. **Time Period Covered:** latest 2 days.

Source: *Timber Bulletin.* **Price Frequency:** monthly, annually. **Units of Measure:** Irish pounds per United States dollar. **Type of Price:** foreign exchange. **Time Period Covered:** latest 2 years.

IRIDIUM

Source: *American Metal Market.* **Price Frequency:** daily. **Effective Market(s):** United States. **Units of Measure:** Dollars per troy ounce. **Type of Price:** producer. **Time Period Covered:** latest day.

Source: *E&MJ.* **Price Frequency:** monthly. **Units of Measure:** Dollars per troy ounce. **Type of Price:** producer. **Time Period Covered:** latest month.

Source: *Iron Age.* **Price Frequency:** monthly. **Units of Measure:** Dollars per troy ounce. **Type of Price:** consumer. **Time Period Covered:** latest month.

IRISES

Source: *New Zealand Farmer.* **Price Frequency:** weekly, seasonally. **Effective Market(s):** New Zealand. **Units of Measure:** New Zealand dollars per bunch. **Time Period Covered:** latest week.

IRISH MOSS: BLEACHED, PRIME, WHOLE

Source: *Chemical Marketing Reporter.* **Price Frequency:** weekly. **Effective Market(s):** New York. **Units of Measure:** Dollars per lb. **Type of Price:** spot. **Time Period Covered:** latest week.

IRISH WHISKEY

Source: *Colorado Beverage Analyst.* **Price Frequency:** monthly. **Effective Market(s):** Colorado. **Units of Measure:** Dollars per case. **Type of Price:** wholesale by brand. **Time Period Covered:** latest month.

Source: *Illinois Beverage Journal.* **Price Frequency:** monthly. **Effective Market(s):** Illinois. **Units of Measure:** Dollars per case. **Type of Price:** wholesale by brand. **Time Period Covered:** latest month.

Source: *Kentucky Beverage Journal.* **Price Frequency:** monthly. **Effective Market(s):** Kentucky. **Units of Measure:** Dollars per bottle, dollars per case. **Type of Price:** wholesale by brand. **Time Period Covered:** latest month.

IRON: PIG

Source: *Commodity Year Book.* **Price Frequency:** annually. **Effective Market(s):** Neville Island (PA). **Units of Measure:** Dollars per net ton. **Type of Price:** wholesale. **Time Period Covered:** latest 5 years.

Source: *Iron Age.* **Price Frequency:** weekly. **Units of Measure:** Dollars per net ton. **Type of Price:** composite. **Time Period Covered:** latest week, week ago, month ago, year ago.

IRON: PIG, BUFF

Source: *Investor's Daily.* **Price Frequency:** daily. **Units of Measure:** Dollars per gross ton. **Type of Price:** foundry spot. **Time Period Covered:** latest 2 days.

Source: *New York Times.* **Price Frequency:** daily. **Units of Measure:** Dollars per gross ton. **Type of Price:** cash. **Time Period Covered:** latest 2 days.

IRON: PIG, IRON AGE COMPOSITE

Source: *Commodity Year Book.* **Price Frequency:** annually. **Effective Market(s):** United States. **Units of Measure:** Dollars per net ton. **Type of Price:** wholesale. **Time Period Covered:** latest 5 years.

IRON: PIG, NO. 2

Source: *Commodity Year Book.* **Price Frequency:** annually. **Effective Market(s):** Birmingham. **Units of Measure:** Dollars per net ton. **Type of Price:** wholesale. **Time Period Covered:** latest 5 years.

IRON: PURIFIED, POWDERED

Source: *Chemical Marketing Reporter.* **Price Frequency:** weekly. **Effective Market(s):** New York. **Units of Measure:** Dollars per lb. **Type of Price:** spot. **Time Period Covered:** latest week.

IRON: REGULAR GRADE, BLUE

Source: *Journal of Commerce and Commercial.* **Price Frequency:** weekly in Wednesday issue. **Units of Measure:** Dollars per lb. **Type of Price:** spot. **Time Period Covered:** latest week.

IRON BLUE: ALKALI-RESISTANT

Source: *Chemical Marketing Reporter.* **Price Frequency:** weekly. **Effective Market(s):** East. **Units of Measure:** Dollars per lb. **Type of Price:** spot. **Time Period Covered:** latest week.

IRON BLUE: REGULAR

Source: *Chemical Marketing Reporter.* **Price Frequency:** weekly. **Effective Market(s):** New York. **Units of Measure:** Dollars per lb. **Type of Price:** spot. **Time Period Covered:** latest week.

IRON BORINGS: CAST

Source: *Iron Age.* **Price Frequency:** monthly. **Effective Market(s):** 9 domestic markets. **Units of Measure:** Dollars per gross ton. **Type of Price:** consumer. **Time Period Covered:** latest month.

IRON ORE: BONG RANGE CONCENTRATE C. 61% IRON, LIBERIAN

Source: *Monthly Commodity Price Bulletin.* **Price Frequency:** monthly, annually. **Effective Market(s):** North Sea ports. **Units of Measure:** Dollars per metric ton. **Time Period Covered:** latest 5 years.

Source: *UNCTAD Commodity Yearbook.* **Price Frequency:** annually. **Effective Market(s):** North Sea ports. **Units of Measure:** Dollars per metric ton. **Type of Price:** free market. **Time Period Covered:** latest 12 years.

IRON ORE: BRAZILIAN

Source: *International Financial Statistics.* **Price Frequency:** monthly, quarterly, annually. **Effective Market(s):** North Sea ports. **Units of Measure:** Dollars per metric ton, index. **Type of Price:** market price, price index. **Time Period Covered:** latest 5 months, latest 5 quarters, latest 5 years.

Source: *International Financial Statistics Yearbook.* **Price Frequency:** annually. **Effective Market(s):** North Sea ports. **Units of Measure:** Dollars per metric ton. **Type of Price:** wholesale. **Time Period Covered:** latest 30 years.

IRON ORE: C. 62% IRON, LIBERIAN

Source: *Monthly Commodity Price Bulletin Supplement.* **Price Frequency:** monthly, quarterly, annually. **Effective Market(s):** North Sea ports. **Units of Measure:** Dollars per tonne. **Time Period Covered:** latest 20 years.

IRON ORE: C. 64% IRON, AUSTRALIAN

Source: *Monthly Commodity Price Bulletin Supplement.* **Price Frequency:** monthly, quarterly, annually. **Effective Market(s):** Japan. **Units of Measure:** Dollars per tonne. **Time Period Covered:** latest 10 years.

IRON ORE: C. 64.5% IRON, BRAZILIAN

Source: *Monthly Commodity Price Bulletin Supplement.* **Price Frequency:** monthly, quarterly, annually. **Effective Market(s):** Europe. **Units of Measure:** Dollars per tonne. **Time Period Covered:** latest 10 years.

IRON ORE: FINES, C. 64% IRON, AUSTRALIAN

Source: *Monthly Commodiuty Price Bulletin.* **Price Frequency:** monthly, annually. **Effective Market(s):** Japan. **Units of Measure:** cents per unit of iron. **Time Period Covered:** latest 5 years.

IRON ORE: FINES, C.V.R.D., BRAZILIAN

Source: *UNCTAD Commodity Yearbook.* **Price Frequency:** annually. **Effective Market(s):** Europe. **Units of Measure:** cents per unit of iron. **Type of Price:** free market. **Time Period Covered:** latest 12 years.

IRON ORE: FINES, C.V.R.D., C. 64.5% IRON, BRAZILIAN TO EUROPE

Source: *Monthly Commodity Price Bulletin.* **Price Frequency:** monthly, annually. **Units of Measure:** cents per unit of iron. **Time Period Covered:** latest 5 years.

IRON ORE: MESABI

Source: *Iron Age.* **Price Frequency:** monthly. **Effective Market(s):** Lake Superior. **Units of Measure:** Dollars per gross ton. **Time Period Covered:** latest month.

IRON ORE: SINTER FINES 65%, BRAZILIAN

Source: *Commodity Trade and Price Trends.* **Price Frequency:** annually. **Effective Market(s):** North Sea ports. **Units of Measure:** Dollars per metric ton, 1980 constant dollars per metric ton. **Time Period Covered:** latest 27 years.

IRON ORE: SINTER FINES KIRUNA D, 60%, SWEDISH

Source: *Commodity Trade and Price Trends.* **Price Frequency:** annually. **Effective Market(s):** Rotterdam. **Units of Measure:** Dollars per metric ton, 1980 constant dollars per metric ton. **Type of Price:** domestic import. **Time Period Covered:** latest 33 years.

IRON ORE: TACONITE PELLETS

Source: *Northern Miner.* **Price Frequency:** daily. **Effective Market(s):** United States. **Units of Measure:** Dollars per long ton. **Type of Price:** producer. **Time Period Covered:** selected day.

IRON ORE PELLETS

Source: *Iron Age.* **Price Frequency:** monthly. **Effective Market(s):** Lake Superior. **Units of Measure:** Dollars per gross ton. **Time Period Covered:** latest month.

IRON OXIDE: BLACK

Source: *Journal of Commerce and Commercial.* **Price Frequency:** weekly in Wednesday issue. **Units of Measure:** Dollars per lb. **Type of Price:** spot. **Time Period Covered:** latest week.

IRON OXIDE: BLACK, SYNTHETIC

Source: *Chemical Marketing Reporter.* **Price Frequency:** weekly. **Effective Market(s):** New York. **Units of Measure:** Dollars per lb. **Type of Price:** spot. **Time Period Covered:** latest week.

IRON OXIDE: BROWN, SYNTHETIC

Source: *Chemical Marketing Reporter.* **Price Frequency:** weekly. **Effective Market(s):** New York. **Units of Measure:** Dollars per lb. **Type of Price:** spot. **Time Period Covered:** latest week.

Source: *Journal of Commerce and Commercial.* **Price Frequency:** weekly in Wednesday issue. **Units of Measure:** Dollars per lb. **Type of Price:** spot. **Time Period Covered:** latest week.

IRON OXIDE: BUFF, DARK

Source: *Chemical Marketing Reporter.* **Price Frequency:** weekly. **Effective Market(s):** New York. **Units of Measure:** Dollars per lb. **Type of Price:** spot. **Time Period Covered:** latest week.

IRON OXIDE: BUFF, LIGHT, NATURAL, DOMESTIC

Source: *Chemical Marketing Reporter.* **Price Frequency:** weekly. **Effective Market(s):** New York. **Units of Measure:** Dollars per lb. **Type of Price:** spot. **Time Period Covered:** latest week.

IRON OXIDE: METALLIC BROWN

Source: *Chemical Marketing Reporter.* **Price Frequency:** weekly. **Effective Market(s):** New York. **Units of Measure:** Dollars per lb. **Type of Price:** spot. **Time Period Covered:** latest week.

IRON OXIDE: OTHER SHADES

Source: *Chemical Marketing Reporter.* **Price Frequency:** weekly. **Effective Market(s):** New York. **Units of Measure:** Dollars per lb. **Type of Price:** spot. **Time Period Covered:** latest week.

IRON OXIDE: RED

Source: *Journal of Commerce and Commercial.* **Price Frequency:** weekly in Wednesday issue. **Units of Measure:** Dollars per lb. **Type of Price:** spot. **Time Period Covered:** latest week.

IRON OXIDE: RED, DOMESTIC

Source: *Journal of Commerce and Commercial.* **Price Frequency:** weekly in Wednesday issue. **Units of Measure:** Dollars per lb. **Type of Price:** spot. **Time Period Covered:** latest week.

IRON OXIDE: RED, NATURAL, DOMESTIC

Source: *Chemical Marketing Reporter.* **Price Frequency:** weekly. **Effective Market(s):** New York. **Units of Measure:** Dollars per lb. **Type of Price:** spot. **Time Period Covered:** latest week.

IRON OXIDE: YELLOW

Source: *Journal of Commerce and Commercial.* **Price Frequency:** weekly in Wednesday issue. **Units of Measure:** Dollars per lb. **Type of Price:** spot. **Time Period Covered:** latest week.

IRON OXIDE: YELLOW, SYNTHETIC

Source: *Chemical Marketing Reporter.* **Price Frequency:** weekly. **Effective Market(s):** New York. **Units of Measure:** Dollars per lb. **Type of Price:** spot. **Time Period Covered:** latest week.

IRON PIPE: DUCTILE, CL-50

Source: *ENR.* **Price Frequency:** monthly in second issue of month. **Effective Market(s):** 16 domestic cities, Montreal, Toronto. **Units of Measure:** Dollars per foot. **Type of Price:** spot. **Time Period Covered:** latest month.

IRON POWDER: ATOMIZED

Source: *American Metal Market.* **Price Frequency:** daily. **Units of Measure:** Dollars per lb. **Time Period Covered:** latest day.

IRON POWDER: CARBONYL GAF

Source: *American Metal Market.* **Price Frequency:** daily. **Units of Measure:** Dollars per lb. **Time Period Covered:** latest day.

IRON POWDER: ELECTROLYTIC

Source: *American Metal Market.* **Price Frequency:** daily. **Units of Measure:** Dollars per lb. **Time Period Covered:** latest day.

IRON POWDER: SPONGE

Source: *American Metal Market.* **Price Frequency:** daily. **Units of Measure:** Dollars per lb. **Time Period Covered:** latest day.

ISATOIC ANHYDRIDE

Source: *Chemical Marketing Reporter.* **Price Frequency:** weekly. **Effective Market(s):** New York. **Units of Measure:** Dollars per lb. **Type of Price:** spot. **Time Period Covered:** latest week.

ISO-OCTYL ALCOHOL

Source: *Chemical Marketing Reporter.* **Price Frequency:** weekly. **Effective Market(s):** New York. **Units of Measure:** Dollars per lb. **Type of Price:** spot. **Time Period Covered:** latest week.

ISOAMYL ALCOHOL: 95%

Source: *Chemical Marketing Reporter.* **Price Frequency:** weekly. **Effective Market(s):** New York. **Units of Measure:** Dollars per lb. **Type of Price:** spot. **Time Period Covered:** latest week.

ISOAMYL BUTYRATE: FCC

Source: *Chemical Marketing Reporter.* **Price Frequency:** weekly. **Effective Market(s):** New York. **Units of Measure:** Dollars per lb. **Type of Price:** spot. **Time Period Covered:** latest week.

ISOAMYL SALICYATE: FCC

Source: *Chemical Marketing Reporter.* **Price Frequency:** weekly. **Effective Market(s):** New York. **Units of Measure:** Dollars per lb. **Type of Price:** spot. **Time Period Covered:** latest week.

ISOBORNEOL

Source: *Chemical Marketing Reporter.* **Price Frequency:** weekly. **Effective Market(s):** New York. **Units of Measure:** Dollars per lb. **Type of Price:** spot. **Time Period Covered:** latest week.

ISOBORNYL ACETATE

Source: *Chemical Marketing Reporter.* **Price Frequency:** weekly. **Effective Market(s):** New York. **Units of Measure:** Dollars per kilo. **Type of Price:** spot. **Time Period Covered:** latest week.

ISOBUTANE

Source: *Energy Pricing News: Petrochemical Report.* **Price Frequency:** bimonthly. **Effective Market(s):** Sarnia (Canada). **Units of Measure:** Canadian dollars per cubic meter. **Type of Price:** contract. **Time Period Covered:** latest month.

Source: *Oil & Gas Journal.* **Price Frequency:** monthly in third issue of month. **Effective Market(s):** Conway (KS), Mont Belvieu (TX). **Units of Measure:** cents per gallon. **Type of Price:** spot. **Time Period Covered:** latest 2 months.

Source: *Oil Buyers' Guide.* **Price Frequency:** weekly. **Effective Market(s):** Venezuela. **Units of Measure:** Dollars per metric ton. **Type of Price:** official. **Time Period Covered:** latest week.

Source: *Oil Buyers' Guide.* **Price Frequency:** daily, weekly. **Effective Market(s):** Los Angeles, Mont Belvieu (TX), Conway (KS), Sarnia (Canada). **Units of Measure:** cents per gallon. **Type of Price:** spot. **Time Period Covered:** latest week.

Source: *Oil Buyers' Guide International.* **Price Frequency:** weekly. **Effective Market(s):** Venezuela. **Units of Measure:** Dollars per metric ton. **Type of Price:** official. **Time Period Covered:** latest week.

ISOBUTYL ACETATE

Source: *Journal of Commerce and Commercial.* **Price Frequency:** weekly in Wednesday issue. **Units of Measure:** Dollars per lb. **Type of Price:** spot. **Time Period Covered:** latest week.

ISOBUTYL ACETATE: SOLVENT GRADE

Source: *Chemical Marketing Reporter.* **Price Frequency:** weekly. **Effective Market(s):** New York. **Units of Measure:** Dollars per lb. **Type of Price:** spot. **Time Period Covered:** latest week.

ISOBUTYL ACRYLATE

Source: *Chemical Marketing Reporter.* **Price Frequency:** weekly. **Effective Market(s):** East. **Units of Measure:** Dollars per lb. **Type of Price:** spot. **Time Period Covered:** latest week.

ISOBUTYL ALCOHOL

Source: *Chemical Marketing Reporter.* **Price Frequency:** weekly. **Effective Market(s):** New York. **Units of Measure:** Dollars per lb. **Type of Price:** spot. **Time Period Covered:** latest week.

ISOBUTYL ISOBUTYRATE

Source: *Chemical Marketing Reporter.* **Price Frequency:** weekly. **Effective Market(s):** New York. **Units of Measure:** Dollars per lb. **Type of Price:** spot. **Time Period Covered:** latest week.

ISOBUTYL METHACRYLATE

Source: *Chemical Marketing Reporter.* **Price Frequency:** weekly. **Effective Market(s):** New York. **Units of Measure:** Dollars per lb. **Type of Price:** spot. **Time Period Covered:** latest week.

ISOBUTYL PHENYLACETATE

Source: *Chemical Marketing Reporter.* **Price Frequency:** weekly. **Effective Market(s):** New York. **Units of Measure:** Dollars per lb. **Type of Price:** spot. **Time Period Covered:** latest week.

ISOBUTYL SALICYLATE

Source: *Chemical Marketing Reporter.* **Price Frequency:** weekly. **Effective Market(s):** New York. **Units of Measure:** Dollars per lb. **Type of Price:** spot. **Time Period Covered:** latest week.

ISOBUTYLENE: 99%

Source: *Chemical Marketing Reporter.* **Price Frequency:** weekly. **Effective Market(s):** New York. **Units of Measure:** Dollars per lb. **Type of Price:** spot. **Time Period Covered:** latest week.

ISOBUTYRALDEHYDE: TECHNICAL GRADE

Source: *Chemical Marketing Reporter.* **Price Frequency:** weekly. **Effective Market(s):** New York. **Units of Measure:** Dollars per lb. **Type of Price:** spot. **Time Period Covered:** latest week.

ISOBUTYRIC ACID

Source: *Chemical Marketing Reporter.* **Price Frequency:** weekly. **Effective Market(s):** New York. **Units of Measure:** Dollars per lb. **Type of Price:** spot. **Time Period Covered:** latest week.

ISOBUTYRONITRILE

Source: *Chemical Marketing Reporter.* **Price Frequency:** weekly. **Effective Market(s):** New York. **Units of Measure:** Dollars per lb. **Type of Price:** spot. **Time Period Covered:** latest week.

ISOEUGENOL

Source: *Chemical Marketing Reporter.* **Price Frequency:** weekly. **Effective Market(s):** New York. **Units of Measure:** Dollars per lb. **Type of Price:** spot. **Time Period Covered:** latest week.

Source: *Journal of Commerce and Commercial.* **Price Frequency:** weekly in Tuesday issue. **Units of Measure:** Dollars per lb. **Type of Price:** spot. **Time Period Covered:** latest week.

ISONIAZID: POWDERED

Source: *Chemical Marketing Reporter.* **Price Frequency:** weekly. **Effective Market(s):** New York. **Units of Measure:** Dollars per kilo. **Type of Price:** spot. **Time Period Covered:** latest week.

ISONICOTINIC ACID: HYDRAZINE

see Isoniazid.

ISONONYL ALCOHOL

Source: *Chemical Marketing Reporter.* **Price Frequency:** weekly. **Effective Market(s):** New York. **Units of Measure:** Dollars per lb. **Type of Price:** spot. **Time Period Covered:** latest week.

ISOPHORONE

Source: *Chemical Marketing Reporter.* **Price Frequency:** weekly. **Effective Market(s):** New York. **Units of Measure:** Dollars per lb. **Type of Price:** spot. **Time Period Covered:** latest week.

ISOPHTHALIC ACID: 99%

Source: *Chemical Marketing Reporter.* **Price Frequency:** weekly. **Effective Market(s):** Joliet (IL). **Units of Measure:** Dollars per lb. **Type of Price:** spot. **Time Period Covered:** latest week.

ISOPHTHALONITRILE

Source: *Chemical Marketing Reporter.* **Price Frequency:** weekly. **Effective Market(s):** New York. **Units of Measure:** Dollars per lb. **Type of Price:** spot. **Time Period Covered:** latest week.

ISOPROPYL ACETATE

Source: *Chemical Marketing Reporter.* **Price Frequency:** weekly. **Effective Market(s):** New York. **Units of Measure:** Dollars per lb. **Type of Price:** spot. **Time Period Covered:** latest week.

ISOPROPYL ALCOHOL: 91%

Source: *Journal of Commerce and Commercial.* **Price Frequency:** weekly in Friday issue. **Units of Measure:** Dollars per lb. **Type of Price:** spot. **Time Period Covered:** latest week.

ISOPROPYL ALCOHOL: 99%

Source: *Journal of Commerce and Commercial.* **Price Frequency:** weekly in Friday issue. **Units of Measure:** Dollars per lb. **Type of Price:** spot. **Time Period Covered:** latest week.

ISOPROPYL ALCOHOL: ANHYDROUS, 99%

Source: *Chemical Marketing Reporter.* **Price Frequency:** weekly. **Effective Market(s):** New York. **Units of Measure:** Dollars per gallon. **Type of Price:** spot. **Time Period Covered:** latest week.

ISOPROPYL ALCOHOL: REFINED, 91%

Source: *Chemical Marketing Reporter.* **Price Frequency:** weekly. **Effective Market(s):** New York. **Units of Measure:** Dollars per gallon. **Type of Price:** spot. **Time Period Covered:** latest week.

ISOPROPYL MYRISTATE

Source: *Chemical Marketing Reporter.* **Price Frequency:** weekly. **Effective Market(s):** East. **Units of Measure:** Dollars per lb. **Type of Price:** spot. **Time Period Covered:** latest week.

ISOPROPYLAMINE

see Mono-, or Di-isopropylamine.

ISRAEL SHEKELS

Source: *Barron's.* **Price Frequency:** weekly. **Effective Market(s):** New York. **Units of Measure:** Israeli shekels per United States dollar. **Type of Price:** foreign exchange. **Time Period Covered:** latest 2 weeks.

Source: *New York Times.* **Price Frequency:** daily. **Effective Market(s):** United States. **Units of Measure:** Israeli shekels per United States dollar. **Type of Price:** foreign exchange. **Time Period Covered:** latest 2 days.

ITACONIC ACID

Source: *Chemical Marketing Reporter.* **Price Frequency:** weekly. **Effective Market(s):** New York. **Units of Measure:** Dollars per lb. **Type of Price:** spot. **Time Period Covered:** latest week.

ITALY LIRE

Source: *Asian Wall Street Journal.* **Price Frequency:** daily. **Effective Market(s):** United States. **Units of Measure:** Italian lire per ECU, per SDR. **Type of Price:** foreign exchange. **Time Period Covered:** latest 2 days.

Source: *Barron's.* **Price Frequency:** weekly. **Effective Market(s):** New York. **Units of Measure:** Italian lire per United States dollar. **Type of Price:** foreign exchange. **Time Period Covered:** latest 2 weeks.

Source: *The Economist.* **Price Frequency:** weekly. **Effective Market(s):** London. **Units of Measure:** Italina lire per United States dollar, per British pounds, per ECU, per SDR. **Type of Price:** foreign exchange. **Time Period Covered:** latest week.

Source: *New York Times.* **Price Frequency:** daily. **Effective Market(s):** United States. **Units of Measure:** Italian lire per United States dollar. **Type of Price:** foreign exchange. **Time Period Covered:** latest 2 days.

Source: *Timber Bulletin.* **Price Frequency:** monthly, annually. **Units of Measure:** Italian lire per United States dollar. **Type of Price:** foreign exchange. **Time Period Covered:** latest 2 years.

J ACID: PASTE

Source: *Chemical Marketing Reporter.* **Price Frequency:** weekly. **Effective Market(s):** New York. **Units of Measure:** Dollars per kilo. **Type of Price:** spot. **Time Period Covered:** latest week.

JABORANDI LEAVES

Source: *Journal of Commerce and Commercial.* **Price Frequency:** weekly in Monday issue. **Units of Measure:** Dollars per lb. **Type of Price:** spot. **Time Period Covered:** latest week.

JALAP ROOT: WHOLE

Source: *Journal of Commerce and Commercial.* **Price Frequency:** weekly in Monday issue. **Units of Measure:** Dollars per lb. **Type of Price:** spot. **Time Period Covered:** latest week.

JAPAN WAX

Source: *Chemical Marketing Reporter.* **Price Frequency:** weekly. **Effective Market(s):** New York. **Units of Measure:** Dollars per lb. **Type of Price:** spot. **Time Period Covered:** latest week.

JAPAN YEN

Source: *American Metal Market.* **Price Frequency:** daily. **Effective Market(s):** New York. **Units of Measure:** Japanes yen per United States dollar. **Type of Price:** foreign exchange. **Time Period Covered:** latest day.

Source: *Asian Wall Street Journal.* **Price Frequency:** daily. **Effective Market(s):** Asia. **Units of Measure:** Japanese yen per United States dollar, per ECU, per SDR. **Type of Price:** foreign exchange. **Time Period Covered:** latest 2 days.

Source: *Barron's.* **Price Frequency:** weekly. **Effective Market(s):** New York. **Units of Measure:** Japanese yen per United States dollar. **Type of Price:** foreign exchange. **Time Period Covered:** latest 2 weeks.

Source: *Commodity Year Book.* **Price Frequency:** monthly, annually. **Units of Measure:** Japanese yen per United States dollar. **Type of Price:** foreign exchange. **Time Period Covered:** latest 5 years.

Source: *The Economist.* **Price Frequency:** weekly. **Effective Market(s):** London. **Units of Measure:** Japanese yen per United States dollar, per British pounds, per ECU, per SDR. **Type of Price:** foreign exchange. **Time Period Covered:** latest week.

Source: *International Wheat Council Market Report.* **Price Frequency:** weekly. **Effective Market(s):** London. **Units of Measure:** Japanese yen per United States dollar. **Type of Price:** foreign exchange. **Time Period Covered:** latest 5 weeks.

Source: *Japan Economic Journal.* **Price Frequency:** weekly. **Effective Market(s):** Tokyo. **Units of Measure:** Japanese yen per 17 national currencies. **Type of Price:** foreign exchange. **Time Period Covered:** latest 2 weeks.

Source: *Japan Economic Journal.* **Price Frequency:** daily. **Effective Market(s):** Tokyo. **Units of Measure:** Japanese yen per United States dollar. **Type of Price:** spot foreign exchange. **Time Period Covered:** latest week.

Source: *New York Times.* **Price Frequency:** daily. **Effective Market(s):** United States. **Units of Measure:** Japanese yen per United States dollar. **Type of Price:** foreign exchange. **Time Period Covered:** latest 2 days.

Source: *Timber Bulletin.* **Price Frequency:** monthly, annually. **Units of Measure:** Japanese yen per United States dollar. **Type of Price:** foreign exchange. **Time Period Covered:** latest 2 years.

JAPAN YEN: FUTURES

Source: *Asian Wall Street Journal.* **Price Frequency:** daily. **Units of Measure:** United States dollars per Japanese yen. **Type of Price:** foreign exchange futures. **Time Period Covered:** latest day.

Source: *Barron's.* **Price Frequency:** weekly. **Effective Market(s):** Chicago. **Units of Measure:** United States per Japanese yen. **Type of Price:** foreign exchange futures. **Time Period Covered:** latest week.

Source: *Japan Economic Journal.* **Price Frequency:** daily. **Effective Market(s):** Tokyo. **Units of Measure:** Japanese yen per United States dollar. **Type of Price:** foreign exchange futures. **Time Period Covered:** latest week.

Source: *Los Angeles Times.* **Price Frequency:** daily. **Effective Market(s):** Chicago. **Units of Measure:** United States dollars per Japanese yen. **Type of Price:** foreign exchange futures. **Time Period Covered:** latest day.

Source: *New York Times.* **Price Frequency:** daily. **Effective Market(s):** Chicago. **Units of Measure:** United States dollars per Japanese yen. **Type of Price:** foreign exchange futures. **Time Period Covered:** latest day.

Source: *Urner Barry's Price-Current.* **Price Frequency:** daily. **Units of Measure:** United States cents per Japanese yen. **Type of Price:** foreign exchange futures. **Time Period Covered:** latest day.

JAPANESE WHISKEY

Source: *Colorado Beverage Analyst.* **Price Frequency:** monthly. **Effective Market(s):** Colorado. **Units of Measure:** Dollars per case. **Type of Price:** wholesale by brand. **Time Period Covered:** latest month.

Source: *Illinois Beverage Journal.* **Price Frequency:** monthly. **Effective Market(s):** Illinois. **Units of Measure:** Dollars per case. **Type of Price:** wholesale by brand. **Time Period Covered:** latest month.

JELLY FISH: CHINESE TYPE, A CLASS, MALAYSIA/INDONESIAN

Source: *Prices of Selected Asia/Pacific Products.* **Price Frequency:** monthly. **Effective Market(s):** Tokyo. **Units of Measure:** Japanese yen per kilogram. **Type of Price:** wholesale high, wholesale low. **Time Period Covered:** latest month.

JELLY FISH: DRIED, 2ND CLASS, CHINESE

Source: *Prices of Selected Asia/Pacific Products.* **Price Frequency:** monthly. **Effective Market(s):** Tokyo. **Units of Measure:** 1000 Japanese yen per 25 kgs. **Type of Price:** wholesale high, wholesale low. **Time Period Covered:** latest month.

JET KEROSENE

see Kerosene: Jet.

JOJOBA OIL

Source: *Chemical Marketing Reporter.* **Price Frequency:** weekly. **Effective Market(s):** Arizona producing point. **Units of Measure:** Dollars per kilo. **Type of Price:** spot. **Time Period Covered:** latest week.

JORDAN DINAR

Source: *Barron's.* **Price Frequency:** weekly. **Effective Market(s):** New York. **Units of Measure:** Jordanian dinar per United States dollar. **Type of Price:** foreign exchange. **Time Period Covered:** latest 2 weeks.

Source: *New York Times.* **Price Frequency:** daily. **Effective Market(s):** United States. **Units of Measure:** Jordanian dinar per United States dollar. **Type of Price:** foreign exchange. **Time Period Covered:** latest 2 days.

JUNIPER BERRY OIL

Source: *Journal of Commerce and Commercial.* **Price Frequency:** weekly in Tuesday issue. **Units of Measure:** Dollars per lb. **Type of Price:** spot. **Time Period Covered:** latest week.

JUNIPER BERRY OIL: ITALIAN

Source: *Chemical Marketing Reporter.* **Price Frequency:** weekly. **Effective Market(s):** New York. **Units of Measure:** Dollars per kilo. **Type of Price:** spot. **Time Period Covered:** latest week.

JUTE: 40-10 OUNCE/40

Source: *Fibre Market News.* **Price Frequency:** weekly. **Effective Market(s):** Chalna/Chittagong (Bangladesh). **Units of Measure:** Dollars per 100 yards. **Type of Price:** export. **Time Period Covered:** latest week.

JUTE: BANGLADESH

Source: *International Financial Statistics.* **Price Frequency:** monthly, quarterly, annually. **Effective Market(s):** Chalna/Chittagong (Bangladesh). **Units of Measure:** Dollars per metric ton, index. **Type of Price:** market price, price index. **Time Period Covered:** latest 5 months, latest 5 quarters, latest 5 years.

Source: *International Financial Statistics Yearbook.* **Price Frequency:** annually. **Effective Market(s):** Chalna/Chittagong (Bangladesh). **Units of Measure:** Dollars per metric ton. **Type of Price:** wholesale. **Time Period Covered:** latest 30 years.

JUTE: BTC, BANGLADESH

Source: *Prices of Selected Asia/Pacific Products.* **Price Frequency:** monthly. **Effective Market(s):** Chalna/Chittagong (Bangladesh). **Units of Measure:** Dollars per metric ton. **Type of Price:** high, low. **Time Period Covered:** latest month.

JUTE: BTC, RAW

Source: *Commodity Year Book.* **Price Frequency:** monthly, annually. **Effective Market(s):** New York. **Units of Measure:** index. **Type of Price:** producer price index. **Time Period Covered:** latest 7 years.

JUTE: BTD, BANGLADESH

Source: *Prices of Selected Asia/Pacific Products.* **Price Frequency:** monthly. **Effective Market(s):** Chalna/Chittagong (Bangladesh). **Units of Measure:** Dollars per metric ton. **Type of Price:** high, low. **Time Period Covered:** latest month.

JUTE: BWC, BANGLADESH

Source: *Prices of Selected Asia/Pacific Products.* **Price Frequency:** monthly. **Effective Market(s):** Chalna/Chittagong (Bangladesh). **Units of Measure:** Dollars per metric ton. **Type of Price:** high, low. **Time Period Covered:** latest month.

JUTE: BWD, BANGLADESH

Source: *FAO Quarterly Bulletin of Statistics.* **Price Frequency:** monthly, annually. **Effective Market(s):** Chalna/Chittagong (Bangladesh). **Units of Measure:** Dollars per 1000 kgs., dollars per metric ton. **Time Period Covered:** latest 3 years.

Source: *Prices of Selected Asia/Pacific Products.* **Price Frequency:** monthly. **Effective Market(s):** Chalna/Chittagong (Bangladesh). **Units of Measure:** Dollars per metric ton. **Type of Price:** high, low. **Time Period Covered:** latest month.

Source: *UNCTAD Commodity Yearbook.* **Price Frequency:** annually. **Effective Market(s):** Chalna/Chittagong (Bangladesh). **Units of Measure:** Dollars per metric ton. **Type of Price:** free market. **Time Period Covered:** latest 12 years.

JUTE: BWD, CHITTAGONG/MONGLA

Source: *Far Eastern Economic Review.* **Price Frequency:** weekly. **Effective Market(s):** Dhaka. **Units of Measure:** Dollars per tonne. **Time Period Covered:** latest week, week ago, 3 months ago, year ago.

JUTE: BWD, RAW, BANGLADESH

Source: *Monthly Commodity Price Bulletin Supplement.* **Price Frequency:** monthly, quarterly, annually. **Effective Market(s):** Chalna/Chittagong (Bangladesh). **Units of Measure:** Dollars per tonne. **Type of Price:** market. **Time Period Covered:** latest 20 years.

Source: *Monthly Commodity Price Bulletin.* **Price Frequency:** monthly, annually. **Effective Market(s):** Chalna (Chittagong, Bangladesh). **Units of Measure:** Dollars per metric ton. **Type of Price:** market. **Time Period Covered:** latest 5 years.

JUTE: CARPET BACKING CLOTH, 5.5 OUNCE/36

Source: *Fibre Market News.* **Price Frequency:** weekly. **Effective Market(s):** Chalna/Chittagong (Bangladesh). **Units of Measure:** Dollars per linear yard. **Type of Price:** export. **Time Period Covered:** latest week.

JUTE: GRADE A, SIAM

Source: *Prices of Selected Asia/Pacific Products.* **Price Frequency:** monthly. **Effective Market(s):** European ports. **Units of Measure:** Dollars per metric ton. **Type of Price:** high, low. **Time Period Covered:** latest month.

Source: *Prices of Selected Asia/Pacific Products.* **Price Frequency:** monthly. **Effective Market(s):** Bangkok. **Units of Measure:** Thai baht per kilogram. **Type of Price:** high, low. **Time Period Covered:** latest month.

JUTE: GRADE B, SIAM

Source: *Prices of Selected Asia/Pacific Products.* **Price Frequency:** monthly. **Effective Market(s):** European ports. **Units of Measure:** Dollars per metric ton. **Type of Price:** high, low. **Time Period Covered:** latest month.

Source: *Prices of Selected Asia/Pacific Products.* **Price Frequency:** monthly. **Effective Market(s):** Bangkok. **Units of Measure:** Thai baht per kilogram. **Type of Price:** high, low. **Time Period Covered:** latest month.

JUTE: SMR, MESHTA

Source: *Fibre Market News.* **Price Frequency:** weekly. **Effective Market(s):** Chalna/Chittagong (Bangladesh). **Units of Measure:** Dollars per metric ton. **Time Period Covered:** latest week.

JUTE: STANDARD B, TWILLS

Source: *Fibre Market News.* **Price Frequency:** weekly. **Effective Market(s):** Chalna/Chittagong (Bangladesh). **Units of Measure:** Dollars per 100 bags. **Type of Price:** export. **Time Period Covered:** latest week.

JUTE: WHITE C, BANGLADESH

Source: *Commodity Trade and Price Trends.* **Price Frequency:** annually. **Effective Market(s):** Dundee. **Units of Measure:** Dollars per metric ton, 1980 constant dollars per metric ton. **Time Period Covered:** latest 27 years.

Source: *Fibre Market News.* **Price Frequency:** weekly. **Effective Market(s):** Chalna/Chittagong (Bangladesh). **Units of Measure:** Dollars per metric ton. **Time Period Covered:** latest week.

JUTE: WHITE CUTTINGS A, BANGLADESH

Source: *Fibre Market News.* **Price Frequency:** weekly. **Effective Market(s):** Chalna/Chittagong (Bangladesh). **Units of Measure:** Dollars per metric ton. **Time Period Covered:** latest week.

JUTE: WHITE CUTTINGS B, BANGLADESH

Source: *Fibre Market News.* **Price Frequency:** weekly. **Effective Market(s):** Chalna/Chittagong (Bangladesh). **Units of Measure:** Dollars per metric ton. **Time Period Covered:** latest week.

JUTE: WHITE D, BANGLADESH

Source: *Commodity Trade and Price Trends.* **Price Frequency:** annually. **Effective Market(s):** Chalna/Chittagong (Bangladesh). **Units of Measure:** Dollars per metric ton, 1980 constant dollars per metric ton. **Time Period Covered:** latest 33 years.

Source: *Fibre Market News.* **Price Frequency:** weekly. **Effective Market(s):** Chalna/Chittagong (Bangladesh). **Units of Measure:** Dollars per metric ton. **Time Period Covered:** latest week.

JUTE TWINE: 3 PLY, CHINA/THAILAND

Source: *Prices of Selected Asia/Pacific Products.* **Price Frequency:** monthly. **Effective Market(s):** Hong Kong. **Units of Measure:** Hong Kong dollars per 410 lbs. **Type of Price:** spot high, spot low. **Time Period Covered:** latest month.

KAKU (FISH)

see Baracuda.

KAOLIN: AIRFLOATED SOFT, DRY GROUND

Source: *Chemical Marketing Reporter.* **Price Frequency:** weekly. **Effective Market(s):** Georgia. **Units of Measure:** Dollars per ton. **Type of Price:** spot. **Time Period Covered:** latest week.

KAOLIN: CALCINED, PAPER GRADE,

Source: *Chemical Marketing Reporter.* **Price Frequency:** weekly. **Effective Market(s):** Georgia. **Units of Measure:** Dollars per ton. **Type of Price:** spot. **Time Period Covered:** latest week.

KAOLIN: PAINT GRADE, FULLY CALCINED, WATER WASHED

Source: *Chemical Marketing Reporter.* **Price Frequency:** weekly. **Effective Market(s):** Georgia. **Units of Measure:** Dollars per ton. **Type of Price:** spot. **Time Period Covered:** latest week.

KAOLIN: POWDERED, COLLOIDAL, BACTERIA CONTROLLED, NF

Source: *Chemical Marketing Reporter.* **Price Frequency:** weekly. **Effective Market(s):** Georgia. **Units of Measure:** Dollars per ton. **Type of Price:** spot. **Time Period Covered:** latest week.

KAOLIN: PRINCIPAL GRADES, REFINED

Source: *Industrial Minerals.* **Price Frequency:** monthly. **Effective Market(s):** main European port. **Units of Measure:** British pounds per metric tonne. **Type of Price:** producer & dealer. **Time Period Covered:** latest month.

KAOLIN: UNCALCINED, DELAMINATED WATER WASHED, PAINT GRADE, 1 MICRON AVERAGE

Source: *Chemical Marketing Reporter.* **Price Frequency:** weekly. **Effective Market(s):** Georgia. **Units of Measure:** Dollars per ton. **Type of Price:** spot. **Time Period Covered:** latest week.

KAOLIN: UNCALCINED, FILLER, GENERAL PURPOSE

Source: *Chemical Marketing Reporter.* **Price Frequency:** weekly. **Effective Market(s):** Georgia. **Units of Measure:** Dollars per ton. **Type of Price:** spot. **Time Period Covered:** latest week.

KAOLIN: UNCALCINED, NO. 1 COATING

Source: *Chemical Marketing Reporter.* **Price Frequency:** weekly. **Effective Market(s):** Georgia. **Units of Measure:** Dollars per ton. **Type of Price:** spot. **Time Period Covered:** latest week.

KAOLIN: UNCALCINED, NO. 2 COATING

Source: *Chemical Marketing Reporter.* **Price Frequency:** weekly. **Effective Market(s):** Georgia. **Units of Measure:** Dollars per ton. **Type of Price:** spot. **Time Period Covered:** latest week.

KAOLIN: UNCALCINED, NO. 3 COATING

Source: *Chemical Marketing Reporter.* **Price Frequency:** weekly. **Effective Market(s):** Georgia. **Units of Measure:** Dollars per ton. **Type of Price:** spot. **Time Period Covered:** latest week.

KAOLIN: UNCALCINED, NO. 4 COATING

Source: *Chemical Marketing Reporter.* **Price Frequency:** weekly. **Effective Market(s):** Georgia. **Units of Measure:** Dollars per ton. **Type of Price:** spot. **Time Period Covered:** latest week.

KAOLIN COATING CLAYS

Source: *Industrial Minerals.* **Price Frequency:** monthly. **Effective Market(s):** main European port. **Units of Measure:** British pounds per metric tonne. **Type of Price:** producer & dealer. **Time Period Covered:** latest month.

KAOLIN FILLER CLAYS

Source: *Industrial Minerals.* **Price Frequency:** monthly. **Effective Market(s):** main European port. **Units of Measure:** British pounds per metric tonne. **Type of Price:** producer & dealer. **Time Period Covered:** latest month.

KAOLIN POTTERY CLAYS

Source: *Industrial Minerals.* **Price Frequency:** monthly. **Effective Market(s):** main European port. **Units of Measure:** British pounds per metric tonne. **Type of Price:** producer & dealer. **Time Period Covered:** latest month.

KARAYA GUM: NO. 1

Source: *Journal of Commerce and Commercial.* **Price Frequency:** weekly in Monday issue. **Units of Measure:** Dollars per lb. **Type of Price:** spot. **Time Period Covered:** latest week.

KARAYA GUM: NO. 1, POWDERED

Source: *Chemical Marketing Reporter.* **Price Frequency:** weekly. **Effective Market(s):** New York. **Units of Measure:** Dollars per lb. **Type of Price:** spot. **Time Period Covered:** latest week.

KARAYA GUM: NO. 2

Source: *Journal of Commerce and Commercial.* **Price Frequency:** weekly in Monday issue. **Units of Measure:** Dollars per lb. **Type of Price:** spot. **Time Period Covered:** latest week.

KARAYA GUM: NO. 2, POWDERED

Source: *Chemical Marketing Reporter.* **Price Frequency:** weekly. **Effective Market(s):** New York. **Units of Measure:** Dollars per lb. **Type of Price:** spot. **Time Period Covered:** latest week.

KARAYA GUM: NO. 3, POWDERED

Source: *Chemical Marketing Reporter.* **Price Frequency:** weekly. **Effective Market(s):** New York. **Units of Measure:** Dollars per lb. **Type of Price:** spot. **Time Period Covered:** latest week.

KENAF: GRADE A, THAI

Source: *FAO Quarterly Bulletin of Statistics.* **Price Frequency:** monthly, annually. **Effective Market(s):** Bangkok. **Units of Measure:** Dollars per 100 kgs., dollars per metric ton. **Time Period Covered:** latest 3 years.

Source: *Prices of Selected Asia/Pacific Products.* **Price Frequency:** monthly. **Effective Market(s):** Bangkok. **Units of Measure:** Thai baht per kilogram, Thai baht per 100 kgs. **Type of Price:** wholesale high, wholesale low. **Time Period Covered:** latest month.

KENAF: GRADE B, THAI

Source: *Prices of Selected Asia/Pacific Products.* **Price Frequency:** monthly. **Effective Market(s):** Bangkok. **Units of Measure:** Thai baht per kilogram, Thai baht per 100 kgs. **Type of Price:** wholesale high, wholesale low. **Time Period Covered:** latest month.

KENAF: GRADE C, THAI

Source: *Prices of Selected Asia/Pacific Products.* **Price Frequency:** monthly. **Effective Market(s):** Bangkok. **Units of Measure:** Thai baht per kilogram. **Type of Price:** wholesale high, wholesale low. **Time Period Covered:** latest month.

KEROSENE

Source: *Japan Economic Journal.* **Price Frequency:** weekly. **Effective Market(s):** Tokyo. **Units of Measure:** Japanese yen per kiloliter. **Type of Price:** spot. **Time Period Covered:** latest 2 weeks.

Source: *Petroleum Economist.* **Price Frequency:** monthly. **Effective Market(s):** Bahamas, Bahrain, Curacao, Pulau Buxom (Singapore), Quoin Island. **Units of Measure:** cents per gallon. **Time Period Covered:** latest month.

Source: *Statistical Bulletin of the South Pacific: Retail Price Indexes.* **Price Frequency:** annually. **Effective Market(s):** 18 South Pacific markets. **Units of Measure:** Australian dollars per. **Type of Price:** retail. **Time Period Covered:** latest year.

KEROSENE: 41-43

Source: *Oil Buyers' Guide.* **Price Frequency:** weekly. **Effective Market(s):** Gulf Coast. **Units of Measure:** cents per gallon. **Type of Price:**. **Time Period Covered:** latest week.

Source: *Oil Buyers' Guide International.* **Price Frequency:** weekly. **Effective Market(s):** Gulf Coast. **Units of Measure:** cents per gallon. **Type of Price:** pipeline. **Time Period Covered:** latest week.

KEROSENE: DUAL PURPOSE

Source: *Oil Buyers' Guide International.* **Price Frequency:** weekly. **Effective Market(s):** Japan, Singapore. **Units of Measure:** Dollars per metric ton. **Type of Price:** spot. **Time Period Covered:** latest week.

KEROSENE: GENERAL PURPOSE

Source: *Oil Buyers' Guide.* **Price Frequency:** weekly. **Effective Market(s):** Venezuela. **Units of Measure:** cents per gallon. **Type of Price:** official. **Time Period Covered:** latest week.

KEROSENE: JET

Source: *Oil Buyers' Guide.* **Price Frequency:** weekly. **Effective Market(s):** Gulf Coast. **Units of Measure:** cents per gallon. **Type of Price:**. **Time Period Covered:** latest week.

Source: *Oil Buyers' Guide.* **Price Frequency:** weekly. **Effective Market(s):** Venezuela. **Units of Measure:** cents per gallon. **Type of Price:** official. **Time Period Covered:** latest week.

Source: *Oil Buyers' Guide International.* **Price Frequency:** weekly. **Effective Market(s):** Gulf Coast. **Units of Measure:** cents per gallon. **Type of Price:** pipeline. **Time Period Covered:** latest week.

Source: *Oil Buyers' Guide International.* **Price Frequency:** weekly. **Effective Market(s):** Venezuela. **Units of Measure:** cents per gallon. **Type of Price:** official. **Time Period Covered:** latest week.

Source: *OPEC Bulletin.* **Price Frequency:** monthly. **Effective Market(s):** Caribbean, Italy, Middle East Gulf, New York, Rotterdam, Singapore. **Units of Measure:** Dollars per barrel. **Time Period Covered:** latest 2 years.

KEROSENE: JP-1

Source: *Oil Buyers' Guide.* **Price Frequency:** weekly. **Effective Market(s):** Mediterranean, Northwest Europe. **Units of Measure:** Dollars per metric ton. **Type of Price:** cargo, barge. **Time Period Covered:** latest week.

Source: *Oil Buyers' Guide International.* **Price Frequency:** weekly. **Effective Market(s):** Mediterranean, Northwest Europe. **Units of Measure:** Dollars per metric ton. **Type of Price:** cargo. **Time Period Covered:** latest week.

KEROSENE: NO. 1, LIGHT DISTILLATE

Source: *Commodity Year Book.* **Price Frequency:** monthly, annually. **Units of Measure:** index. **Type of Price:** wholesale price index. **Time Period Covered:** latest 14 years.

KIWIFRUIT

Source: *Agricultural Prices Annual Summary.* **Price Frequency:** annually. **Effective Market(s):** California, Hawaii. **Units of Measure:** Dollars per ton. **Type of Price:** average price received by farmer. **Time Period Covered:** latest 6 years.

Source: *California Farmer.* **Price Frequency:** semimonthly, seasonally. **Effective Market(s):** Central California, Northern California. **Units of Measure:** Dollars per 7 lb. flat. **Time Period Covered:** latest week, month ago, year ago.

Source: *Fruit and Tree Nuts Situation and Outlook Yearbook.* **Price Frequency:** annually. **Effective Market(s):** California. **Units of Measure:** Dollars per ton. **Type of Price:** grower. **Time Period Covered:** latest 10 years.

Source: *New Zealand Farmer.* **Price Frequency:** weekly, seasonally. **Effective Market(s):** New Zealand. **Units of Measure:** New Zealand dollars per bushel/kilogram. **Time Period Covered:** latest week.

KIWIFRUIT: NEW ZEALAND

Source: *Lancaster Farming.* **Price Frequency:** weekly, seasonally. **Effective Market(s):** Pennsylvania. **Units of Measure:** Dollars per crate. **Type of Price:** market. **Time Period Covered:** latest week.

KIWIFRUIT: NORTH ISLAND (NEW ZEALAND)

Source: *New Zealand Farmer.* **Price Frequency:** weekly, seasonally. **Effective Market(s):** New Zealand. **Units of Measure:** New Zealand dollars per kilogram. **Time Period Covered:** latest week.

KIWIFRUIT: SOUTH ISLAND (NEW ZEALAND)

Source: *New Zealand Farmer.* **Price Frequency:** weekly, seasonally. **Effective Market(s):** New Zealand. **Units of Measure:** New Zealand dollars per kilogram. **Time Period Covered:** latest week.

KNITS: POLYESTER

see Polyester Knit.

KNOCKWURST

Source: *Meat Price Report.* **Price Frequency:** weekly. **Units of Measure:** cents per lb. **Type of Price:** price paid to wholesaler. **Time Period Covered:** latest week.

KOLA NUTS

Source: *Chemical Marketing Reporter.* **Price Frequency:** weekly. **Effective Market(s):** New York. **Units of Measure:** Dollars per lb. **Type of Price:** spot. **Time Period Covered:** latest week.

KOLA NUTS: GROUND

Source: *Journal of Commerce and Commercial.* **Price Frequency:** weekly in Monday issue. **Units of Measure:** Dollars per lb. **Type of Price:** spot. **Time Period Covered:** latest week.

KUMARA SQUASH

see Squash: Kumara.

KUWAIT DINAR

Source: *Barron's.* **Price Frequency:** weekly. **Effective Market(s):** New York. **Units of Measure:** Kuwaiti dinar per United States dollar. **Type of Price:** foreign exchange. **Time Period Covered:** latest 2 weeks.

Source: *New York Times.* **Price Frequency:** daily. **Effective Market(s):** United States. **Units of Measure:** Kuwaiti dinar per United States dollar. **Type of Price:** foreign exchange. **Time Period Covered:** latest 2 days.

Source: *The Times.* **Price Frequency:** daily. **Effective Market(s):** London. **Units of Measure:** Kuwaiti Dinar per British pound. **Type of Price:** foreign exchange. **Time Period Covered:** latest day.

KYANITE: CALCINED, UNITED STATES

Source: *Industrial Minerals.* **Price Frequency:** monthly. **Effective Market(s):** United States. **Units of Measure:** Dollars per metric tonne. **Type of Price:** producer & dealer. **Time Period Covered:** latest month.

KYANITE: RAW, UNITED STATES

Source: *Industrial Minerals.* **Price Frequency:** monthly. **Effective Market(s):** United States. **Units of Measure:** Dollars per metric tonne. **Type of Price:** producer & dealer. **Time Period Covered:** latest month.

KYANITE: RAW/CALCINED

Source: *Industrial Minerals.* **Price Frequency:** monthly. **Effective Market(s):** main European port. **Units of Measure:** British pounds per metric tonne. **Type of Price:** producer & dealer. **Time Period Covered:** latest month.

LACQUER DILUENT: PETROLEUM

Source: *Chemical Marketing Reporter.* **Price Frequency:** weekly. **Effective Market(s):** New York/New Jersey, Houston (TX). **Units of Measure:** Dollars per gallon. **Type of Price:** spot. **Time Period Covered:** latest week.

LACTIC ACID: 50%

Source: *Chemical Marketing Reporter.* **Price Frequency:** weekly. **Effective Market(s):** New York. **Units of Measure:** Dollars per lb. **Type of Price:** spot. **Time Period Covered:** latest week.

LACTIC ACID: FOOD GRADE, 88%

Source: *Chemical Marketing Reporter.* **Price Frequency:** weekly. **Effective Market(s):** New York. **Units of Measure:** Dollars per lb. **Type of Price:** spot. **Time Period Covered:** latest week.

Source: *Journal of Commerce and Commercial.* **Price Frequency:** weekly in Friday issue. **Units of Measure:** Dollars per lb. **Type of Price:** spot. **Time Period Covered:** latest week.

LACTIC ACID: TECHNICAL GRADE, 88%

Source: *Chemical Marketing Reporter.* **Price Frequency:** weekly. **Effective Market(s):** New York. **Units of Measure:** Dollars per lb. **Type of Price:** spot. **Time Period Covered:** latest week.

LACTOSE

Source: *Milling & Baking News.* **Price Frequency:** weekly. **Units of Measure:** Dollars per lb. **Time Period Covered:** latest week.

LACTOSE: EDIBLE

Source: *Dairy Market Statistics.* **Price Frequency:** monthly, annually. **Effective Market(s):** Central/Western States. **Units of Measure:** Dollars per lb. **Time Period Covered:** latest year.

LACTOSE: EDIBLE, REGULAR

Source: *Chemical Marketing Reporter.* **Price Frequency:** weekly. **Effective Market(s):** New York. **Units of Measure:** Dollars per lb. **Type of Price:** spot. **Time Period Covered:** latest week.

LACTOSE: REGULAR, USP

Source: *Chemical Marketing Reporter.* **Price Frequency:** weekly. **Effective Market(s):** New York. **Units of Measure:** Dollars per lb. **Type of Price:** spot. **Time Period Covered:** latest week.

LACTOSE: SPRAY DRIED, USP

Source: *Chemical Marketing Reporter.* **Price Frequency:** weekly. **Effective Market(s):** New York. **Units of Measure:** Dollars per lb. **Type of Price:** spot. **Time Period Covered:** latest week.

LAKE C: RED TONER (RED 53)

Source: *Chemical Marketing Reporter.* **Price Frequency:** weekly. **Effective Market(s):** New York. **Units of Measure:** Dollars per lb. **Type of Price:** spot. **Time Period Covered:** latest week.

LAMB

Source: *New Zealand Farmer.* **Price Frequency:** weekly, seasonally. **Effective Market(s):** 11 New Zealand markets. **Units of Measure:** New Zealand dollars per unit weight. **Type of Price:** export value. **Time Period Covered:** latest week.

LAMB: CHUCK

Source: *HRI-Buyers Guide.* **Price Frequency:** weekly. **Effective Market(s):** Northeastern area. **Units of Measure:** Dollars per lb. **Type of Price:** price paid by dining places & institutions. **Time Period Covered:** latest week.

LAMB: GROUND

Source: *Meat Price Report.* **Price Frequency:** weekly. **Units of Measure:** cents per lb. **Type of Price:** price paid to wholesaler. **Time Period Covered:** latest week.

LAMB: NEW ZEALAND

Source: *FAO Quarterly Bulletin of Statistics.* **Price Frequency:** monthly, annually. **Effective Market(s):** London. **Units of Measure:** British pounds per 100 kgs., dollars per metric ton. **Type of Price:** wholesale. **Time Period Covered:** latest 3 years.

LAMB AND MUTTON

Source: *Agricultural Outlook.* **Price Frequency:** annually. **Effective Market(s):** United States. **Units of Measure:** Dollars per 100 lbs. **Type of Price:** past primary market. **Time Period Covered:** latest 2 years.

LAMB BREAST

Source: *HRI-Buyers Guide.* **Price Frequency:** weekly. **Effective Market(s):** Northeastern area. **Units of Measure:** Dollars per lb. **Type of Price:** price paid by dining places & institutions. **Time Period Covered:** latest week.

LAMB CARCASS: CHOICE AND PRIME

Source: *Commodity Year Book.* **Price Frequency:** annually. **Effective Market(s):** East Coast. **Units of Measure:** cents per lb. **Time Period Covered:** latest 7 years.

LAMB CARCASS: DRESSED, CHOICE AND PRIME

Source: *Livestock, Meat, Wool Market News.* **Price Frequency:** weekly, seasonally. **Effective Market(s):** East Coast, Central United States, California. **Units of Measure:** Dollars per 100 lbs. **Type of Price:** wholesale. **Time Period Covered:** latest week, year ago.

LAMB CARCASS: WHOLE, FROZEN, NEW ZEALAND

Source: *Commodity Trade and Price Trends.* **Price Frequency:** annually. **Effective Market(s):** London. **Units of Measure:** cents per kilogram, 1980 constant cents per kilogram. **Time Period Covered:** latest 37 years.

LAMB FOR STEWING

Source: *Meat Price Report.* **Price Frequency:** weekly. **Units of Measure:** cents per lb. **Type of Price:** price paid to wholesaler. **Time Period Covered:** latest week.

LAMB FOR STEWING: BONELESS

Source: *HRI-Buyers Guide.* **Price Frequency:** weekly. **Effective Market(s):** Northeastern area. **Units of Measure:** Dollars per lb. **Type of Price:** price paid by dining places & institutions. **Time Period Covered:** latest week.

LAMB FORESHANK

Source: *Meat Price Report.* **Price Frequency:** weekly. **Units of Measure:** cents per lb. **Type of Price:** price paid to wholesaler. **Time Period Covered:** latest week.

LAMB HOTEL RACK

Source: *HRI-Buyers Guide.* **Price Frequency:** weekly. **Effective Market(s):** Northeastern area. **Units of Measure:** Dollars per lb. **Type of Price:** price paid by dining places & institutions. **Time Period Covered:** latest week.

LAMB LEG

Source: *HRI-Buyers Guide.* **Price Frequency:** weekly. **Effective Market(s):** Northeastern area. **Units of Measure:** Dollars per lb. **Type of Price:** price paid by dining places & institutions. **Time Period Covered:** latest week.

Source: *Meat Price Report.* **Price Frequency:** weekly. **Units of Measure:** cents per lb. **Type of Price:** price paid to wholesaler. **Time Period Covered:** latest week.

LAMB LEG: BONELESS

Source: *HRI-Buyers Guide.* **Price Frequency:** weekly. **Effective Market(s):** Northeastern area. **Units of Measure:** Dollars per lb. **Type of Price:** price paid by dining places & institutions. **Time Period Covered:** latest week.

LAMB LEG: OVEN PREPARED, BONELESS AND TIED

Source: *Meat Price Report.* **Price Frequency:** weekly. **Units of Measure:** cents per lb. **Type of Price:** price paid to wholesaler. **Time Period Covered:** latest week.

LAMB LOIN

Source: *HRI-Buyers Guide.* **Price Frequency:** weekly. **Effective Market(s):** Northeastern area. **Units of Measure:** Dollars per lb. **Type of Price:** price paid by dining places & institutions. **Time Period Covered:** latest week.

LAMB LOIN: TRIMMED

Source: *Meat Price Report.* **Price Frequency:** weekly. **Units of Measure:** cents per lb. **Type of Price:** price paid to wholesaler. **Time Period Covered:** latest week.

LAMB LOIN CHOPS

Source: *HRI-Buyers Guide.* **Price Frequency:** weekly. **Effective Market(s):** Northeastern area. **Units of Measure:** Dollars per lb. **Type of Price:** price paid by dining places & institutions. **Time Period Covered:** latest week.

Source: *Meat Price Report.* **Price Frequency:** weekly. **Units of Measure:** cents per lb. **Type of Price:** price paid to wholesaler. **Time Period Covered:** latest week.

LAMB MEAT: HEAVY, ENGLISH

Source: *Farmers Weekly.* **Price Frequency:** weekly. **Effective Market(s):** Smithfield (England). **Units of Measure:** British pence per lb. **Type of Price:** high, low. **Time Period Covered:** latest week.

LAMB MEAT: MEDIUM, ENGLISH

Source: *Farmers Weekly.* **Price Frequency:** weekly. **Effective Market(s):** Smithfield (England). **Units of Measure:** British pence per lb. **Type of Price:** high, low. **Time Period Covered:** latest week.

LAMB MEAT: PLS, NEW SEASON, NEW ZEALAND

Source: *Farmers Weekly.* **Price Frequency:** weekly. **Effective Market(s):** Smithfield (England). **Units of Measure:** British pence per lb. **Type of Price:** high, low. **Time Period Covered:** latest week.

LAMB MEAT: PMS, NEW SEASON, NEW ZEALAND

Source: *Farmers Weekly.* **Price Frequency:** weekly. **Effective Market(s):** Smithfield (England). **Units of Measure:** British pence per lb. **Type of Price:** high, low. **Time Period Covered:** latest week.

LAMB MEAT: PXS, NEW SEASON, NEW ZEALAND

Source: *Farmers Weekly.* **Price Frequency:** weekly. **Effective Market(s):** Smithfield (England). **Units of Measure:** British pence per lb. **Type of Price:** high, low. **Time Period Covered:** latest week.

LAMB MEAT: SMALL NEW SEASON, ENGLISH

Source: *Farmers Weekly.* **Price Frequency:** weekly. **Effective Market(s):** Smithfield (England). **Units of Measure:** British pence per lb. **Type of Price:** high, low. **Time Period Covered:** latest week.

LAMB RACK: NEW ZEALAND

Source: *HRI-Buyers Guide.* **Price Frequency:** weekly. **Effective Market(s):** Northeastern area. **Units of Measure:** Dollars per lb. **Type of Price:** price paid by dining places & institutions. **Time Period Covered:** latest week.

LAMB RIB CHOPS

Source: *HRI-Buyers Guide.* **Price Frequency:** weekly. **Effective Market(s):** Northeastern area. **Units of Measure:** Dollars per lb. **Type of Price:** price paid by dining places & institutions. **Time Period Covered:** latest week.

Source: *Meat Price Report.* **Price Frequency:** weekly. **Units of Measure:** cents per lb. **Type of Price:** price paid to wholesaler. **Time Period Covered:** latest week.

LAMB RIB CHOPS: FRENCHED

Source: *Meat Price Report.* **Price Frequency:** weekly. **Units of Measure:** cents per lb. **Type of Price:** price paid to wholesaler. **Time Period Covered:** latest week.

LAMB RIB RACK

Source: *Meat Price Report.* **Price Frequency:** weekly. **Units of Measure:** cents per lb. **Type of Price:** price paid to wholesaler. **Time Period Covered:** latest week.

LAMB SHEARLINGS

Source: *National Provisioner.* **Price Frequency:** weekly. **Effective Market(s):** Chicago. **Units of Measure:** Dollars per 100 lbs. **Time Period Covered:** latest week, year ago.

LAMB SHOULDER CHOPS

Source: *Meat Price Report.* **Price Frequency:** weekly. **Units of Measure:** cents per lb. **Type of Price:** price paid to wholesaler. **Time Period Covered:** latest week.

LAMB SQUARE CUT SHOULDER

Source: *Meat Price Report.* **Price Frequency:** weekly. **Units of Measure:** cents per lb. **Type of Price:** price paid to wholesaler. **Time Period Covered:** latest week.

LAMB SQUARE CUT SHOULDER: BONELESS

Source: *Meat Price Report.* **Price Frequency:** weekly. **Units of Measure:** cents per lb. **Type of Price:** price paid to wholesaler. **Time Period Covered:** latest week.

LAMBS

Source: *Agricultural Outlook.* **Price Frequency:** monthly, annually. **Effective Market(s):** United States. **Units of Measure:** Dollars per 100 lbs. **Type of Price:** price received by farmers. **Time Period Covered:** monthly latest 6 months, annually latest 3 years.

Source: *Agricultural Prices.* **Price Frequency:** monthly. **Effective Market(s):** United States. **Units of Measure:** Dollars per 100 lbs. **Type of Price:** received by farmer. **Time Period Covered:** latest 2 months, year ago.

Source: *Agricultural Prices.* **Price Frequency:** monthly. **Effective Market(s):** 16 domestic markets, United States. **Units of Measure:** Dollars per 100 lbs. **Type of Price:** received by farmer. **Time Period Covered:** latest 2 months.

Source: *Agricultural Prices Annual Summary.* **Price Frequency:** monthly, seasonally. **Effective Market(s):** 16 domestic markets, United States. **Units of Measure:** Dollars per 100 lbs. **Type of Price:** average received by farmer. **Time Period Covered:** monthly latest year, for US latest 6 years.

Source: *Agricultural Prices Annual Summary.* **Price Frequency:** annually. **Effective Market(s):** 50 domestic markets, United States. **Units of Measure:** Dollars per 100 lbs. **Type of Price:** received by farmer. **Time Period Covered:** latest 2 years.

Source: *Commodity Year Book.* **Price Frequency:** monthly, annually. **Effective Market(s):** Omaha (NE). **Units of Measure:** Dollars per 100 lbs. **Type of Price:** wholesale. **Time Period Covered:** latest 6 years.

Source: *Commodity Year Book.* **Price Frequency:** monthly, annually. **Effective Market(s):** United States. **Units of Measure:** Dollars per 100 lbs. **Type of Price:** price received by farmers. **Time Period Covered:** latest 7 years.

Source: *Farm and Dairy.* **Price Frequency:** weekly, seasonally. **Effective Market(s):** Ohio, Pennsylvania. **Units of Measure:** Dollars per head. **Type of Price:** auction high, auction low. **Time Period Covered:** latest week.

Source: *Illinois Farm Report.* **Price Frequency:** quarterly. **Effective Market(s):** Illinois. **Units of Measure:** Dollars per 100 lbs. **Type of Price:** average received by farmers. **Time Period Covered:** latest 2 months, year ago.

Source: *Livestock and Poultry Situation and Outlook Report.* **Price Frequency:** monthly. **Units of Measure:** Dollars per 100 lbs. **Type of Price:** farm. **Time Period Covered:** latest year.

Source: *Scottish Farmer.* **Price Frequency:** weekly. **Effective Market(s):** Scotland. **Units of Measure:** British pence per kilogram. **Type of Price:** average. **Time Period Covered:** latest week.

Source: *Scottish Farmer.* **Price Frequency:** weekly. **Effective Market(s):** 33 Scottish markets. **Units of Measure:** British pence per kilogram. **Time Period Covered:** latest week.

Source: *Standard & Poor's Statistical Service Current Statistics.* **Price Frequency:** monthly. **Units of Measure:** Dollars per 100 lbs. **Time Period Covered:** latest 5 years.

LAMBS: BLACKFACE, STORE

Source: *Scottish Farmer.* **Price Frequency:** weekly. **Effective Market(s):** 9 Scottish markets average. **Units of Measure:** British pounds per head. **Type of Price:** average. **Time Period Covered:** latest 2 weeks.

LAMBS: CHEVIOT, STORE

Source: *Scottish Farmer.* **Price Frequency:** weekly. **Effective Market(s):** 9 Scottish markets average. **Units of Measure:** British pounds per head. **Type of Price:** average. **Time Period Covered:** latest 2 weeks.

LAMBS: CHOICE

Source: *Farm and Dairy.* **Price Frequency:** weekly, seasonally. **Effective Market(s):** Ohio, Pennsylvania. **Units of Measure:** Dollars per head. **Type of Price:** auction high, auction low. **Time Period Covered:** latest week.

Source: *Livestock and Poultry Update.* **Price Frequency:** monthly. **Effective Market(s):** East Coast. **Units of Measure:** Dollars per 100 lbs. **Type of Price:** wholesale. **Time Period Covered:** latest 3 months, year ago.

LAMBS: CHOICE AND PRIME

Source: *California Farmer.* **Price Frequency:** semimonthly. **Effective Market(s):** Northern California. **Units of Measure:** Dollars per 100 lbs. **Time Period Covered:** latest week, month ago, year ago.

Source: *Livestock and Poultry Situation and Outlook Report.* **Price Frequency:** monthly. **Effective Market(s):** East Coast. **Units of Measure:** Dollars per 100 lbs. **Type of Price:** wholesale. **Time Period Covered:** latest year.

Source: *Meat and Dairy Products.* **Price Frequency:** monthly. **Effective Market(s):** East Coast. **Units of Measure:** Dollars per 100 lbs. **Type of Price:** wholesale. **Time Period Covered:** latest 4 years.

LAMBS: DOWN CROSS, STORE

Source: *Scottish Farmer.* **Price Frequency:** weekly. **Effective Market(s):** 9 Scottish markets average. **Units of Measure:** British pounds per head. **Type of Price:** average. **Time Period Covered:** latest 2 weeks.

LAMBS: FAT

Source: *Meat and Dairy Products.* **Price Frequency:** monthly. **Effective Market(s):** 7 international markets. **Units of Measure:** national currency per kilogram/100 lbs. **Type of Price:** average. **Time Period Covered:** latest 3 years.

LAMBS: FEEDER

Source: *Idaho Farmer-Stockman.* **Price Frequency:** monthly. **Effective Market(s):** El Reno, Midwest, Oklahoma City. **Units of Measure:** Dollars per 100 lbs. **Time Period Covered:** latest month.

Source: *National Wool Market Review.* **Price Frequency:** weekly, seasonally. **Effective Market(s):** varies. **Units of Measure:** Dollars per 100 lbs. **Type of Price:** auction, direct trade. **Time Period Covered:** latest week.

Source: *Oregon Farmer-Stockman.* **Price Frequency:** monthly, seasonally. **Effective Market(s):** Oregon/ Washington. **Units of Measure:** Dollars per 100 lbs. **Time Period Covered:** latest month.

Source: *Oregon Farmer-Stockman.* **Price Frequency:** monthly, seasonally. **Effective Market(s):** Ft. Collins (CO), Midwest, Oklahoma City. **Units of Measure:** Dollars per 100 lbs. **Time Period Covered:** latest month.

Source: *Utah Stockman-Farmer.* **Price Frequency:** monthly. **Effective Market(s):** El Reno, Midwest, Oklahoma City. **Units of Measure:** Dollars per 100 lbs. **Time Period Covered:** latest month.

LAMBS: FEEDER, CHOICE

Source: *Agricultural Outlook.* **Price Frequency:** monthly, annually. **Effective Market(s):** San Angelo (TX). **Units of Measure:** Dollars per 100 lbs. **Type of Price:** market. **Time Period Covered:** monthly latest 6 months, annually latest 3 years.

Source: *Livestock and Poultry Situation and Outlook Report.* **Price Frequency:** monthly. **Effective Market(s):** San Angelo (TX), South St. Paul. **Units of Measure:** Dollars per 100 lbs. **Time Period Covered:** latest year.

Source: *Livestock and Poultry Update.* **Price Frequency:** monthly. **Effective Market(s):** San Angelo (TX). **Units of Measure:** Dollars per 100 lbs. **Time Period Covered:** latest 3 months, year ago.

LAMBS: FEEDER, CHOICE AND FANCY

Source: *Montana Farmer-Stockman.* **Price Frequency:** monthly. **Effective Market(s):** Billings (MT). **Units of Measure:** Dollars per 100 lbs. **Type of Price:** cash auction. **Time Period Covered:** latest month.

Source: *Washington Farmer-Stockman.* **Price Frequency:** monthly. **Effective Market(s):** Portland (OR). **Units of Measure:** Dollars per 100 lbs. **Type of Price:** auction. **Time Period Covered:** latest month.

LAMBS: FEEDER, OLD CROP

Source: *National Wool Market Review.* **Price Frequency:** weekly, seasonally. **Effective Market(s):** varies. **Units of Measure:** Dollars per 100 lbs. **Type of Price:** auction, direct trade. **Time Period Covered:** latest week.

LAMBS: FEEDER, SHORN, CHOICE AND FANCY

Source: *Livestock, Meat, Wool Market News.* **Price Frequency:** weekly, seasonally. **Effective Market(s):** Billings (MT),San Angelo (TX), West Fargo (ND), South St. Paul, Sioux Falls (SD). **Units of Measure:** Dollars per 100 lbs. **Type of Price:** average. **Time Period Covered:** latest week, year ago.

LAMBS: FEEDER, SPRING

Source: *National Wool Market Review.* **Price Frequency:** weekly, seasonally. **Effective Market(s):** varies. **Units of Measure:** Dollars per 100 lbs. **Type of Price:** auction, direct trade. **Time Period Covered:** latest week.

LAMBS: FEEDER, SPRING, CHOICE AND FANCY

Source: *Livestock, Meat, Wool Market News.* **Price Frequency:** weekly, seasonally. **Effective Market(s):** Billings (MT), San Angelo (TX), West Fargo (ND), South St. Paul, Sioux Falls (SD). **Units of Measure:** Dollars per 100 lbs. **Type of Price:** average. **Time Period Covered:** latest week, year ago.

LAMBS: FEEDER, UMATILLA

Source: *Oregon Farmer-Stockman.* **Price Frequency:** monthly, seasonally. **Effective Market(s):** Oregon/ Washington. **Units of Measure:** Dollars per 100 lbs. **Time Period Covered:** latest month.

LAMBS: FEEDER, WOOLED, CHOICE AND FANCY

Source: *Livestock, Meat, Wool Market News.* **Price Frequency:** weekly, seasonally. **Effective Market(s):** Billings (MT), San Angelo (TX), West Fargo (ND), South St. Paul, Sioux Falls (SD). **Units of Measure:** Dollars per 100 lbs. **Type of Price:** average. **Time Period Covered:** latest week, year ago.

LAMBS: FINISHED

Source: *Farmers Weekly.* **Price Frequency:** weekly. **Effective Market(s):** Great Britain. **Units of Measure:** British pence per kilogram. **Time Period Covered:** latest week, week ago, year ago.

LAMBS: GOOD

Source: *Farm and Dairy.* **Price Frequency:** weekly, seasonally. **Effective Market(s):** Ohio, Pennsylvania. **Units of Measure:** Dollars per head. **Type of Price:** auction high, auction low. **Time Period Covered:** latest week.

LAMBS: GOOD, STORE

Source: *New Zealand Farmer.* **Price Frequency:** weekly, seasonally. **Effective Market(s):** 7 New Zealand markets. **Units of Measure:** New Zealand dollars per head. **Time Period Covered:** latest 2 weeks.

LAMBS: GREYFACE, STORE

Source: *Scottish Farmer.* **Price Frequency:** weekly. **Effective Market(s):** 9 Scottish markets average. **Units of Measure:** British pounds per head. **Type of Price:** average. **Time Period Covered:** latest 2 weeks.

LAMBS: HALF-BRED, STORE

Source: *Scottish Farmer.* **Price Frequency:** weekly. **Effective Market(s):** 9 Scottish markets average. **Units of Measure:** British pounds per head. **Type of Price:** average. **Time Period Covered:** latest 2 weeks.

LAMBS: HEAVY

Source: *Farmers Weekly.* **Price Frequency:** weekly. **Effective Market(s):** over 170 British markets. **Units of Measure:** British pence per kilogram. **Type of Price:** auction. **Time Period Covered:** latest week.

LAMBS: HEAVY, PRIME

Source: *New Zealand Farmer.* **Price Frequency:** weekly, seasonally. **Effective Market(s):** 7 New Zealand markets. **Units of Measure:** New Zealand dollars per head. **Time Period Covered:** latest 2 weeks.

LAMBS: LIGHT

Source: *Farmers Weekly.* **Price Frequency:** weekly. **Effective Market(s):** over 170 British markets. **Units of Measure:** British pence per kilogram. **Type of Price:** auction. **Time Period Covered:** latest week.

LAMBS: LIGHT, PRIME

Source: *New Zealand Farmer.* **Price Frequency:** weekly, seasonally. **Effective Market(s):** 7 New Zealand markets. **Units of Measure:** New Zealand dollars per head. **Time Period Covered:** latest 2 weeks.

LAMBS: LIGHT, STORE

Source: *New Zealand Farmer.* **Price Frequency:** weekly, seasonally. **Effective Market(s):** 7 New Zealand markets. **Units of Measure:** New Zealand dollars per head. **Time Period Covered:** latest 2 weeks.

LAMBS: MEDIUM

Source: *Farmers Weekly.* **Price Frequency:** weekly. **Effective Market(s):** over 170 British markets. **Units of Measure:** British pence per kilogram. **Type of Price:** auction. **Time Period Covered:** latest week.

LAMBS: MEDIUM, ENGLISH

Source: *Meat and Dairy Products.* **Price Frequency:** monthly. **Effective Market(s):** London. **Units of Measure:** British pence per lb. **Type of Price:** average. **Time Period Covered:** latest 4 years.

LAMBS: MEDIUM, PRIME

Source: *New Zealand Farmer.* **Price Frequency:** weekly, seasonally. **Effective Market(s):** 7 New Zealand markets. **Units of Measure:** New Zealand dollars per head. **Time Period Covered:** latest 2 weeks.

LAMBS: NEW ZEALAND

Source: *International Financial Statistics.* **Price Frequency:** monthly, quarterly, annually. **Effective Market(s):** London. **Units of Measure:** cents per lb., index. **Type of Price:** market price, price index. **Time Period Covered:** latest 5 months, latest 5 quarters, latest 5 years.

Source: *International Financial Statistics.* **Price Frequency:** annually. **Effective Market(s):** New Zealand. **Units of Measure:** cents per lb., index. **Type of Price:** market price, price index. **Time Period Covered:** latest 4 years.

Source: *International Financial Statistics Yearbook.* **Price Frequency:** annually. **Effective Market(s):** London, New Zealand. **Units of Measure:** cents per lb. **Type of Price:** wholesale. **Time Period Covered:** latest 30 years.

LAMBS: PM, NEW ZEALAND

Source: *Meat and Dairy Products.* **Price Frequency:** monthly. **Effective Market(s):** London. **Units of Measure:** British pence per lb. **Type of Price:** average. **Time Period Covered:** latest 4 years.

LAMBS: SLAUGHTER

Source: *National Wool Market Review.* **Price Frequency:** weekly, seasonally. **Effective Market(s):** varies. **Units of Measure:** Dollars per 100 lbs. **Type of Price:** auction, direct trade. **Time Period Covered:** latest week.

Source: *Survey of Current Business.* **Price Frequency:** monthly, annually. **Effective Market(s):** Omaha (NE). **Units of Measure:** Dollars per 100 lbs. **Type of Price:** wholesale. **Time Period Covered:** latest year.

LAMBS: SLAUGHTER, CHOICE

Source: *Agricultural Outlook.* **Price Frequency:** monthly, annually. **Effective Market(s):** San Angelo (TX). **Units of Measure:** Dollars per 100 lbs. **Type of Price:** market. **Time Period Covered:** monthly latest 6 months, annually latest 3 years.

Source: *California Farmer.* **Price Frequency:** semimonthly. **Effective Market(s):** Dixon (CA). **Units of Measure:** Dollars per 100 lbs. **Time Period Covered:** latest week, month ago, year ago.

Source: *Doane's Agricultural Report.* **Price Frequency:** weekly. **Effective Market(s):** San Angelo (TX). **Units of Measure:** Dollars per 100 lbs. **Time Period Covered:** latest week, week ago, year ago.

Source: *Livestock and Poultry Situation and Outlook Report.* **Price Frequency:** quarterly, annually. **Effective Market(s):** San Angelo (TX). **Units of Measure:** Dollars per 100 lbs. **Time Period Covered:** latest 2 years.

Source: *Livestock and Poultry Situation and Outlook Report.* **Price Frequency:** monthly. **Effective Market(s):** San Angelo (TX), South St. Paul. **Units of Measure:** Dollars per 100 lbs. **Time Period Covered:** latest year.

Source: *Livestock and Poultry Update.* **Price Frequency:** monthly. **Effective Market(s):** San Angelo (TX). **Units of Measure:** Dollars per 100 lbs. **Time Period Covered:** latest 3 months, year ago.

LAMBS: SLAUGHTER, CHOICE AND PRIME

Source: *Idaho Farmer-Stockman.* **Price Frequency:** monthly. **Effective Market(s):** El Reno, Idaho, Midwest, Oklahoma City. **Units of Measure:** Dollars per 100 lbs. **Time Period Covered:** latest month.

Source: *Oregon Farmer-Stockman.* **Price Frequency:** monthly, seasonally. **Effective Market(s):** Midwest, Oklahoma City, Ft. Collins (CO). **Units of Measure:** Dollars per 100 lbs. **Time Period Covered:** latest month.

Source: *Utah Stockman-Farmer.* **Price Frequency:** monthly. **Effective Market(s):** Midwest, Oklahoma City, El Reno, Idaho. **Units of Measure:** Dollars per 100 lbs. **Time Period Covered:** latest month.

LAMBS: SLAUGHTER, MOSTLY CHOICE

Source: *Montana Farmer-Stockman.* **Price Frequency:** monthly. **Effective Market(s):** Billings (MT). **Units of Measure:** Dollars per 100 lbs. **Type of Price:** cash auction. **Time Period Covered:** latest month.

LAMBS: SLAUGHTER, OLD CROP

Source: *National Wool Market Review.* **Price Frequency:** weekly, seasonally. **Effective Market(s):** varies. **Units of Measure:** Dollars per 100 lbs. **Type of Price:** auction, direct trade. **Time Period Covered:** latest week.

LAMBS: SLAUGHTER, SHORN, CHOICE

Source: *Livestock, Meat, Wool Market News.* **Price Frequency:** weekly, seasonally. **Effective Market(s):** Billings (MT), San Angelo (TX), West Fargo (ND), South St. Paul, Sioux Falls (SD). **Units of Measure:** Dollars per 100 lbs. **Type of Price:** average. **Time Period Covered:** latest week, year ago.

LAMBS: SLAUGHTER, SHORN, PRIME

Source: *Livestock, Meat, Wool Market News.* **Price Frequency:** weekly, seasonally. **Effective Market(s):** Billings (MT), San Angelo (TX), West Fargo (ND), South St. Paul, Sioux Falls (SD). **Units of Measure:** Dollars per 100 lbs. **Type of Price:** average. **Time Period Covered:** latest week, year ago.

LAMBS: SLAUGHTER, SPRING

Source: *National Wool Market Review.* **Price Frequency:** weekly, seasonally. **Effective Market(s):** varies. **Units of Measure:** Dollars per 100 lbs. **Type of Price:** auction, direct trade. **Time Period Covered:** latest week.

LAMBS: SLAUGHTER, SPRING, CHOICE

Source: *Livestock, Meat, Wool Market News.* **Price Frequency:** weekly, seasonally. **Effective Market(s):** Billings (MT), San Angelo (TX), West Fargo (ND), South St. Paul, Sioux Falls (SD). **Units of Measure:** Dollars per 100 lbs. **Type of Price:** average. **Time Period Covered:** latest week, year ago.

LAMBS: SLAUGHTER, SPRING, PRIME

Source: *Livestock, Meat, Wool Market News.* **Price Frequency:** weekly, seasonally. **Effective Market(s):** Billings (MT), San Angelo (TX), West Fargo (ND), South St. Paul, Sioux Falls (SD). **Units of Measure:** Dollars per 100 lbs. **Type of Price:** average. **Time Period Covered:** latest week, year ago.

LAMBS: SLAUGHTER, UMATILLA

Source: *Oregon Farmer-Stockman.* **Price Frequency:** monthly, seasonally. **Effective Market(s):** Oregon/Washington. **Units of Measure:** Dollars per 100 lbs. **Time Period Covered:** latest month.

LAMBS: SLAUGHTER, WOOLED, CHOICE

Source: *Livestock, Meat, Wool Market News.* **Price Frequency:** weekly, seasonally. **Effective Market(s):** Billings (MT), San Angelo (TX), West Fargo (ND), South St. Paul, Sioux Falls (SD). **Units of Measure:** Dollars per 100 lbs. **Type of Price:** average. **Time Period Covered:** latest week, year ago.

LAMBS: SLAUGHTER, WOOLED, CHOICE AND PRIME

Source: *Washington Farmer-Stockman.* **Price Frequency:** monthly. **Effective Market(s):** Portland. **Units of Measure:** Dollars per 100 lbs. **Type of Price:** auction. **Time Period Covered:** latest month.

LAMBS: SLAUGHTER, WOOLED, PRIME

Source: *Livestock, Meat, Wool Market News.* **Price Frequency:** weekly, seasonally. **Effective Market(s):** Billings (MT), San Angelo (TX), West Fargo (ND), South St. Paul, Sioux Falls (SD). **Units of Measure:** Dollars per 100 lbs. **Type of Price:** average. **Time Period Covered:** latest week, year ago.

LAMBS: SPRING

Source: *Lancaster Farming.* **Price Frequency:** weekly. **Effective Market(s):** Pennsylvania, Virginia. **Units of Measure:** Dollars per head. **Type of Price:** auction. **Time Period Covered:** latest week.

LAMBS: SPRING, CHOICE

Source: *Lancaster Farming.* **Price Frequency:** weekly. **Effective Market(s):** Pennsylvania, Virginia. **Units of Measure:** Dollars per head. **Type of Price:** auction. **Time Period Covered:** latest week.

LAMBS: SPRING, CHOICE AND PRIME

Source: *Lancaster Farming.* **Price Frequency:** weekly. **Effective Market(s):** Pennsylvania, Virginia. **Units of Measure:** Dollars per head. **Type of Price:** auction. **Time Period Covered:** latest week.

LAMBS: SPRING, GOOD TO LOW CHOICE

Source: *Lancaster Farming.* **Price Frequency:** weekly. **Effective Market(s):** Pennsylvania, Virginia. **Units of Measure:** Dollars per head. **Type of Price:** auction. **Time Period Covered:** latest week.

LAMBS: STANDARD

Source: *Farmers Weekly.* **Price Frequency:** weekly. **Effective Market(s):** over 170 British markets. **Units of Measure:** British pence per kilogram. **Type of Price:** auction. **Time Period Covered:** latest week.

LANGOSTINO: CHILE

Source: *NMFS Green Sheet Supplement.* **Price Frequency:** weekly. **Effective Market(s):** New York. **Units of Measure:** Dollars per lb. **Type of Price:** warehouse. **Time Period Covered:** latest week.

LANGOSTINO: CHILE, FROZEN

Source: *Seafood Price-Current.* **Price Frequency:** semiweekly. **Effective Market(s):** Mid-Atlantic. **Units of Measure:** Dollars per lb. **Type of Price:** first receiver. **Time Period Covered:** latest day.

LANGOSTINO LOBSTERS: FROZEN

Source: *HRI-Buyers Guide.* **Price Frequency:** weekly. **Effective Market(s):** New York. **Units of Measure:** Dollars per case. **Type of Price:** prices paid by dining places & institutions. **Time Period Covered:** latest week.

LANOLIN: ANHYDROUS, COSMETIC

Source: *Chemical Marketing Reporter.* **Price Frequency:** weekly. **Effective Market(s):** New York. **Units of Measure:** Dollars per lb. **Type of Price:** spot. **Time Period Covered:** latest week.

LANOLIN: COSMETIC

Source: *Journal of Commerce and Commercial.* **Price Frequency:** weekly in Friday issue. **Units of Measure:** Dollars per lb. **Type of Price:** spot. **Time Period Covered:** latest week.

LANOLIN: PHARMACEUTICAL

Source: *Chemical Marketing Reporter.* **Price Frequency:** weekly. **Effective Market(s):** New York. **Units of Measure:** Dollars per lb. **Type of Price:** spot. **Time Period Covered:** latest week.

Source: *Journal of Commerce and Commercial.* **Price Frequency:** weekly in Friday issue. **Units of Measure:** Dollars per lb. **Type of Price:** spot. **Time Period Covered:** latest week.

LANOLIN: TECHNICAL GRADE

Source: *Chemical Marketing Reporter.* **Price Frequency:** weekly. **Effective Market(s):** New York. **Units of Measure:** Dollars per lb. **Type of Price:** spot. **Time Period Covered:** latest week.

LARCH

Source: *Volume and Value of Sawtimber Stumpage Sold From National Forests by Selected Species and Region.* **Price Frequency:** quarterly, annually. **Effective Market(s):** Northern region, Pacific Northwest. **Units of Measure:** Dollars per 1000 board feet. **Type of Price:** average. **Time Period Covered:** latest quarter, latest year.

LARD

Source: *Asian Wall Street Journal.* **Price Frequency:** daily. **Effective Market(s):** Chicago. **Units of Measure:** Dollars per lb. **Type of Price:** cash. **Time Period Covered:** latest 2 days, year ago.

Source: *Bakery Newsletter.* **Price Frequency:** weekly. **Effective Market(s):** Chicago. **Type of Price:** cash. **Time Period Covered:** latest week.

Source: *CRB Commodity Index Report.* **Price Frequency:** weekly. **Effective Market(s):** Chicago. **Units of Measure:** Dollars per lb. **Type of Price:** spot. **Time Period Covered:** latest week.

Source: *National Provisioner.* **Price Frequency:** weekly. **Effective Market(s):** Chicago. **Units of Measure:** cents per lb. **Time Period Covered:** latest week.

Source: *Wall Street Journal.* **Price Frequency:** daily. **Effective Market(s):** Chicago. **Units of Measure:** Dollars per lb. **Time Period Covered:** latest day, day ago, year ago.

LARD: EDIBLE

Source: *National Provisioner.* **Price Frequency:** weekly. **Effective Market(s):** Chicago. **Units of Measure:** Dollars per 100 lbs. **Time Period Covered:** latest week.

LARD: EDIBLE, LOOSE

Source: *Livestock, Meat, Wool Market News.* **Price Frequency:** weekly, seasonally. **Effective Market(s):** Chicago. **Units of Measure:** Dollars per 100 lbs. **Time Period Covered:** latest week.

LARD: LOOSE

Source: *Chemical Marketing Reporter.* **Price Frequency:** weekly. **Effective Market(s):** Chicago. **Units of Measure:** cents per lb. **Type of Price:** spot. **Time Period Covered:** latest week.

Source: *Commodity Year Book.* **Price Frequency:** monthly, annually. **Effective Market(s):** Chicago. **Units of Measure:** cents per lb. **Type of Price:** wholesale. **Time Period Covered:** latest 9 years.

Source: *Milling & Baking News.* **Price Frequency:** weekly. **Effective Market(s):** Chicago. **Units of Measure:** Dollars per lb. **Type of Price:** spot. **Time Period Covered:** latest week.

LARD: PRIME WEST

Source: *Journal of Commerce and Commercial.* **Price Frequency:** daily. **Effective Market(s):** Chicago. **Units of Measure:** Dollars per lb. **Type of Price:** spot supplier. **Time Period Covered:** latest day.

LARD: REFINED

Source: *National Provisioner.* **Price Frequency:** weekly. **Effective Market(s):** Chicago. **Units of Measure:** cents per lb. **Time Period Covered:** latest week.

LARD: REFINED, EUROPEAN COMMUNITY

Source: *Oil World.* **Price Frequency:** weekly, monthly, annually. **Effective Market(s):** United Kingdom. **Units of Measure:** Dollars per tonne. **Type of Price:** lowest representative asking. **Time Period Covered:** weekly latest 3 weeks, monthly latest 2 months, annually latest 2 years.

LARD OIL: EXTRA, WINTER-STRAINED

Source: *Chemical Marketing Reporter.* **Price Frequency:** weekly. **Effective Market(s):** New York. **Units of Measure:** Dollars per lb. **Type of Price:** spot. **Time Period Covered:** latest week.

LARD OIL: NO. 1

Source: *Chemical Marketing Reporter.* **Price Frequency:** weekly. **Effective Market(s):** New York. **Units of Measure:** Dollars per lb. **Type of Price:** spot. **Time Period Covered:** latest week.

LARD OIL: PRIME, BURNING

Source: *Chemical Marketing Reporter.* **Price Frequency:** weekly. **Effective Market(s):** Chicago, Texas, West Coast. **Units of Measure:** Dollars per lb. **Type of Price:** spot. **Time Period Covered:** latest week.

LAUREL LEAVES: TURKISH

Source: *Chemical Marketing Reporter.* **Price Frequency:** weekly. **Effective Market(s):** New York. **Units of Measure:** Dollars per lb. **Type of Price:** spot. **Time Period Covered:** latest week.

Source: *U. S. Spice Trade.* **Price Frequency:** annually. **Effective Market(s):** New York. **Units of Measure:** cents per lb. **Type of Price:** spot. **Time Period Covered:** latest 3 years.

LAURENT'S ACID

Source: *Chemical Marketing Reporter.* **Price Frequency:** weekly. **Effective Market(s):** New York. **Units of Measure:** Dollars per lb. **Type of Price:** spot. **Time Period Covered:** latest week.

LAURIC ACID: COMMERCIAL

Source: *Chemical Marketing Reporter.* **Price Frequency:** weekly. **Effective Market(s):** New York. **Units of Measure:** Dollars per lb. **Type of Price:** spot. **Time Period Covered:** latest week.

N-LAURYL METHACRYLATE: SYNTHETIC

Source: *Chemical Marketing Reporter.* **Price Frequency:** weekly. **Effective Market(s):** New York. **Units of Measure:** Dollars per lb. **Type of Price:** spot. **Time Period Covered:** latest week.

LAVANDIN OIL: ABRIALIS, 30-32%

Source: *Chemical Marketing Reporter.* **Price Frequency:** weekly. **Effective Market(s):** New York. **Units of Measure:** Dollars per lb. **Type of Price:** spot. **Time Period Covered:** latest week.

LAVANDIN OIL: FRENCH

Source: *Journal of Commerce and Commercial.* **Price Frequency:** weekly in Tuesday issue. **Units of Measure:** Dollars per lb. **Type of Price:** spot. **Time Period Covered:** latest week.

LAVENDER FLOWER OIL: 40-42%, ESTER, NF, FRENCH

Source: *Chemical Marketing Reporter.* **Price Frequency:** weekly. **Effective Market(s):** New York. **Units of Measure:** Dollars per lb. **Type of Price:** spot. **Time Period Covered:** latest week.

LAVENDER FLOWER OIL: SPIKE, SPANISH

Source: *Chemical Marketing Reporter.* **Price Frequency:** weekly. **Effective Market(s):** New York. **Units of Measure:** Dollars per lb. **Type of Price:** spot. **Time Period Covered:** latest week.

LAVENDER OIL

Source: *Journal of Commerce and Commercial.* **Price Frequency:** weekly in Tuesday issue. **Units of Measure:** Dollars per lb. **Type of Price:** spot. **Time Period Covered:** latest week.

Source: *U. S. Essential Oil Trade.* **Price Frequency:** annually. **Effective Market(s):** United States. **Units of Measure:** Dollars per kilogram. **Type of Price:** import value. **Time Period Covered:** latest 3 years.

LAWN FABRIC

Source: *JTN: The International Textile Magazine.* **Price Frequency:** monthly. **Effective Market(s):** Japan. **Units of Measure:** Japanese yen per yard. **Type of Price:** spot. **Time Period Covered:** latest month.

LAYING FEED

Source: *Agricultural Prices.* **Price Frequency:** quarterly. **Effective Market(s):** United States. **Units of Measure:** Dollars per ton. **Type of Price:** paid by farmer. **Time Period Covered:** latest 2 quarters, year ago.

Source: *Agricultural Prices.* **Price Frequency:** monthly. **Effective Market(s):** 10 domestic markets, United States. **Units of Measure:** Dollars per ton. **Type of Price:** paid by farmer. **Time Period Covered:** latest month.

Source: *Agricultural Prices Annual Summary.* **Price Frequency:** quarterly. **Effective Market(s):** 10 domestic markets, United States. **Units of Measure:** Dollars per ton. **Type of Price:** average paid by farmer. **Time Period Covered:** latest year, for US monthly for latest 6 years.

Source: *Feed Situation and Outlook Report.* **Price Frequency:** quarterly, annually. **Effective Market(s):** United States. **Units of Measure:** Dollars per ton. **Type of Price:** paid by farmer. **Time Period Covered:** latest year.

LCP

see Polymers: Liquid Crystal.

LDPE

see Polyethylene: Low Density.

LEAD

Source: *American Metal Market.* **Price Frequency:** daily. **Effective Market(s):** London. **Units of Measure:** British pounds per metric ton. **Type of Price:** cash. **Time Period Covered:** latest 2 days.

Source: *American Metal Market.* **Price Frequency:** daily. **Effective Market(s):** London. **Units of Measure:** Dollars per metric ton. **Type of Price:** spot fix. **Time Period Covered:** latest day.

Source: *American Metal Market.* **Price Frequency:** daily. **Units of Measure:** cents per lb. **Type of Price:** market. **Time Period Covered:** latest 3 days.

Source: *Asian Wall Street Journal.* **Price Frequency:** daily. **Effective Market(s):** London. **Units of Measure:** British pounds per metric ton. **Type of Price:** spot. **Time Period Covered:** latest day.

Source: *Asian Wall Street Journal.* **Price Frequency:** daily. **Units of Measure:** Dollars per lb. **Type of Price:** producer. **Time Period Covered:** latest 2 days, year ago.

Source: *Battery Man.* **Price Frequency:** monthly. **Effective Market(s):** United States, London. **Units of Measure:** cents per lb. **Time Period Covered:** latest year.

Source: *Chemical Marketing Reporter.* **Price Frequency:** weekly. **Effective Market(s):** New York. **Units of Measure:** Dollars per lb. **Type of Price:** spot. **Time Period Covered:** latest week.

Source: *Commodity Year Book.* **Price Frequency:** annually. **Effective Market(s):** New York, London. **Units of Measure:** cents per lb. **Time Period Covered:** latest 10 years.

Source: *E&MJ.* **Price Frequency:** monthly. **Effective Market(s):** United States, Canada. **Units of Measure:** cents per lb. **Type of Price:** producer. **Time Period Covered:** latest month.

Source: *E&MJ.* **Price Frequency:** monthly. **Effective Market(s):** London. **Units of Measure:** Dollars per metric ton. **Type of Price:** spot. **Time Period Covered:** latest month, 3 months ago.

Source: *Economic and Energy Indicators.* **Price Frequency:** monthly, quarterly, annually. **Units of Measure:** cents per lb. **Time Period Covered:** latest 3 months, quarters, and years.

Source: *Financial Times.* **Price Frequency:** daily. **Effective Market(s):** London. **Units of Measure:** cents per lb. **Type of Price:** spot. **Time Period Covered:** latest day.

Source: *Financial Times.* **Price Frequency:** daily. **Effective Market(s):** London. **Units of Measure:** British pounds per tonne. **Type of Price:** cash. **Time Period Covered:** latest day.

Source: *Investor's Daily.* **Price Frequency:** daily. **Units of Measure:** Dollars per lb. **Type of Price:** spot. **Time Period Covered:** latest 2 days.

Source: *Iron Age.* **Price Frequency:** monthly. **Effective Market(s):** London. **Units of Measure:** cents per lb. **Time Period Covered:** latest month.

Source: *Los Angeles Times.* **Price Frequency:** daily. **Units of Measure:** cents per lb. **Type of Price:** cash. **Time Period Covered:** latest day.

Source: *Minerals Today.* **Price Frequency:** bimonthly. **Units of Measure:** cents per lb. **Time Period Covered:** latest month, month ago.

Source: *Monthly Commodity Price Bulletin.* **Price Frequency:** monthly, annually. **Effective Market(s):** London. **Units of Measure:** British pounds per metric ton, cents per lb. **Type of Price:** cash settlement. **Time Period Covered:** latest 5 years.

Source: *New York Times.* **Price Frequency:** daily. **Effective Market(s):** London. **Units of Measure:** British pounds per metric ton. **Type of Price:** spot. **Time Period Covered:** latest day.

Source: *New York Times.* **Price Frequency:** daily. **Units of Measure:** Dollars per lb. **Type of Price:** cash. **Time Period Covered:** latest 2 days.

Source: *Northern Miner.* **Price Frequency:** daily. **Effective Market(s):** London. **Units of Measure:** British pounds per tonne. **Type of Price:** spot. **Time Period Covered:** week ago.

Source: *Northern Miner.* **Price Frequency:** daily. **Effective Market(s):** Canada, United States. **Units of Measure:** Canadian cents per lb., cents per lb. **Type of Price:** producer. **Time Period Covered:** selected day.

Source: *The Times.* **Price Frequency:** daily. **Effective Market(s):** London. **Units of Measure:** British pounds per metric ton. **Type of Price:** cash. **Time Period Covered:** latest day.

Source: *UNCTAD Commodity Yearbook.* **Price Frequency:** annually. **Effective Market(s):** London. **Units of Measure:** Dollars per metric ton. **Type of Price:** cash settlement. **Time Period Covered:** latest 12 years.

Source: *Wall Street Journal.* **Price Frequency:** daily. **Units of Measure:** Dollars per lb. **Time Period Covered:** latest day, day ago, year ago.

Source: *Wall Street Journal.* **Price Frequency:** daily. **Effective Market(s):** London. **Units of Measure:** British pounds per metric ton. **Type of Price:** spot. **Time Period Covered:** latest day, 3 months ago.

LEAD: 99.97% LEAD

Source: *Monthly Commodity Price Bulletin Supplement.* **Price Frequency:** monthly, quarterly, annually. **Effective Market(s):** London. **Units of Measure:** British pounds per lb., dollars per tonne. **Type of Price:** settlement & cash seller. **Time Period Covered:** latest 20 years.

LEAD: BULK BATTERY

Source: *American Metal Market.* **Price Frequency:** daily. **Units of Measure:** Dollars per 100 lbs. lead oxide. **Time Period Covered:** latest day.

LEAD: CANADIAN

Source: *American Metal Market.* **Price Frequency:** daily. **Effective Market(s):** United States. **Units of Measure:** cents per lb. **Type of Price:** primary producer. **Time Period Covered:** latest day.

LEAD: COMMON CORRODING

Source: *American Metal Market.* **Price Frequency:** daily. **Effective Market(s):** United States. **Units of Measure:** cents per lb. **Type of Price:** primary producer. **Time Period Covered:** latest day.

LEAD: COMMON GRADE

Source: *Survey of Current Business.* **Price Frequency:** monthly, annually. **Units of Measure:** Dollars per lb. **Time Period Covered:** latest year.

LEAD: ELECTROTYPE

Source: *Iron Age.* **Price Frequency:** monthly. **Units of Measure:** cents per lb. **Type of Price:** dealer. **Time Period Covered:** latest month.

LEAD: HEAVY SOFT

Source: *American Metal Market.* **Price Frequency:** daily. **Effective Market(s):** 14 domestic markets, Montreal, Toronto. **Units of Measure:** cents per lb., Canadian cents per lb. **Type of Price:** dealer buying. **Time Period Covered:** latest day.

Source: *Iron Age.* **Price Frequency:** monthly. **Units of Measure:** cents per lb. **Type of Price:** dealer. **Time Period Covered:** latest month.

LEAD: MIXED HARD

Source: *American Metal Market.* **Price Frequency:** daily. **Effective Market(s):** 14 domestic markets, Montreal, Toronto. **Units of Measure:** cents per lb., Canadian cents per lb. **Type of Price:** dealer buying. **Time Period Covered:** latest day.

LEAD: PIG, COMMON CORRODING

Source: *Commodity Year Book.* **Price Frequency:** monthly, annually. **Effective Market(s):** United States. **Units of Measure:** cents per lb. **Time Period Covered:** latest 8 years.

LEAD: PIG, COMMON GRADE

Source: *Purchasing.* **Price Frequency:** monthly. **Effective Market(s):** United States. **Units of Measure:** cents per lb. **Type of Price:** transaction. **Time Period Covered:** latest day, month ago, 6 months ago, year ago.

LEAD: PIG, DESILVERIZED

Source: *Commodity Trade and Price Trends.* **Price Frequency:** annually. **Effective Market(s):** New York. **Units of Measure:** Dollars per metric ton, 1980 constant dollars per metric ton. **Type of Price:** producer. **Time Period Covered:** latest 37 years.

LEAD: PIG, SOFT, 99.97% PURITY

Source: *Commodity Trade and Price Trends.* **Price Frequency:** annually. **Effective Market(s):** London. **Units of Measure:** Dollars per metric ton, 1980 dollars per metric ton. **Type of Price:** settlement. **Time Period Covered:** latest 37 years.

LEAD: RED

Source: *Chemical Marketing Reporter.* **Price Frequency:** weekly. **Effective Market(s):** New York. **Units of Measure:** Dollars per lb. **Type of Price:** spot. **Time Period Covered:** latest week.

LEAD: RED, 97%

Source: *Journal of Commerce and Commercial.* **Price Frequency:** weekly in Wednesday issue. **Units of Measure:** Dollars per lb. **Type of Price:** spot. **Time Period Covered:** latest week.

LEAD: RED, DRY

Source: *American Metal Market.* **Price Frequency:** daily. **Units of Measure:** Dollars per 100 lbs. lead oxide. **Time Period Covered:** latest day.

LEAD: REFINED

Source: *Lead and Zinc Statistics.* **Price Frequency:** weekly, monthly, annually. **Effective Market(s):** London, United States. **Units of Measure:** British pounds per metric ton, cents per lb. **Type of Price:** average. **Time Period Covered:** weekly latest month, monthly latest year, annually latest 4 years.

Source: *Lead and Zinc Statistics.* **Price Frequency:** daily. **Effective Market(s):** 7 international markets. **Units of Measure:** national currency per unit. **Type of Price:** varies. **Time Period Covered:** latest day.

Source: *Monthly Commodity Price Bulletin.* **Price Frequency:** monthly, annually. **Effective Market(s):** New York. **Units of Measure:** cents per lb. **Type of Price:** domestic. **Time Period Covered:** latest 5 years.

Source: *Monthly Commodity Price Bulletin Supplement.* **Price Frequency:** monthly, quarterly, annually. **Effective Market(s):** New York. **Units of Measure:** cents per lb. **Type of Price:** domestic. **Time Period Covered:** latest 20 years.

LEAD: REFINED, UNITED STATES

Source: *UNCTAD Commodity Yearbook.* **Price Frequency:** annually. **Effective Market(s):** New York. **Units of Measure:** Dollars per metric ton. **Type of Price:** domestic. **Time Period Covered:** latest 12 years.

LEAD: REMELT, HEAVY SOFT

Source: *American Metal Market.* **Price Frequency:** daily. **Units of Measure:** Dollars per 100 lbs. **Type of Price:** smelter buying. **Time Period Covered:** latest day.

LEAD: SECONDARY FOR FABRICATED PRODUCTS

Source: *American Metal Market.* **Price Frequency:** daily. **Effective Market(s):** United States. **Units of Measure:** cents per lb. **Type of Price:** primary producer. **Time Period Covered:** latest day.

Source: *E&MJ.* **Price Frequency:** monthly. **Units of Measure:** cents per lb. **Time Period Covered:** latest month.

LEAD: UNITED KINGDOM

Source: *International Financial Statistics.* **Price Frequency:** monthly, quarterly, annually. **Effective Market(s):** London. **Units of Measure:** cents per lb., index. **Type of Price:** market price, price index. **Time Period Covered:** latest 5 months, latest 5 quarters, latest 5 years.

Source: *International Financial Statistics Yearbook.* **Price Frequency:** annually. **Effective Market(s):** London. **Units of Measure:** cents per lb. **Type of Price:** wholesale. **Time Period Covered:** latest 30 years.

LEAD: UNITED STATES

Source: *International Financial Statistics.* **Price Frequency:** monthly, quarterly, annually. **Effective Market(s):** New York. **Units of Measure:** cents per lb., index. **Type of Price:** market price, price index. **Time Period Covered:** latest 4 months, latest 5 quarters, latest 5 years.

Source: *International Financial Statistics Yearbook.* **Price Frequency:** annually. **Effective Market(s):** New York. **Units of Measure:** cents per lb. **Type of Price:** wholesale. **Time Period Covered:** latest 30 years.

LEAD: VIRGIN BRANDS, CANADA

Source: *American Metal Market.* **Price Frequency:** daily. **Effective Market(s):** Canada. **Units of Measure:** Canadian cents per lb. **Time Period Covered:** latest day.

LEAD ACETATE: PURIFIED, FLAKE

Source: *Chemical Marketing Reporter.* **Price Frequency:** weekly. **Effective Market(s):** New York. **Units of Measure:** Dollars per lb. **Type of Price:** spot. **Time Period Covered:** latest week.

Source: *Journal of Commerce and Commercial.* **Price Frequency:** weekly in Thursday issue. **Units of Measure:** Dollars per lb. **Type of Price:** spot. **Time Period Covered:** latest week.

LEAD ACETATE: TECHNICAL GRADE, FLAKE

Source: *Chemical Marketing Reporter.* **Price Frequency:** weekly. **Effective Market(s):** New York. **Units of Measure:** Dollars per lb. **Type of Price:** spot. **Time Period Covered:** latest week.

LEAD CABLE: HEAVY SOFT

Source: *American Metal Market.* **Price Frequency:** daily. **Units of Measure:** Dollars per 100 lbs. **Type of Price:** smelter buying. **Time Period Covered:** latest day.

LEAD CARBONATE

see Lead White Basic Carbonate.

LEAD CHLORIDE

Source: *Chemical Marketing Reporter.* **Price Frequency:** weekly. **Effective Market(s):** New York. **Units of Measure:** Dollars per lb. **Type of Price:** spot. **Time Period Covered:** latest week.

LEAD DIOXIDE: TECHNICAL GRADE, POWDERED

Source: *Chemical Marketing Reporter.* **Price Frequency:** weekly. **Effective Market(s):** New York. **Units of Measure:** Dollars per lb. **Type of Price:** spot. **Time Period Covered:** latest week.

LEAD FLUOBORATE: LIQUID CONCENTRATED

Source: *Chemical Marketing Reporter.* **Price Frequency:** weekly. **Effective Market(s):** New York. **Units of Measure:** Dollars per lb. **Type of Price:** spot. **Time Period Covered:** latest week.

LEAD MONOSILICATE: COARSE

Source: *Chemical Marketing Reporter.* **Price Frequency:** weekly. **Effective Market(s):** New York. **Units of Measure:** Dollars per lb. **Type of Price:** spot. **Time Period Covered:** latest week.

LEAD MONOSILICATE: GRANULAR

Source: *American Metal Market.* **Price Frequency:** daily. **Units of Measure:** Dollars per 100 lbs. lead oxide. **Time Period Covered:** latest day.

LEAD MONOSILICATE: GROUND

Source: *American Metal Market.* **Price Frequency:** daily. **Units of Measure:** Dollars per 100 lbs. lead oxide. **Time Period Covered:** latest day.

LEAD MONOSILICATE: MILLED

Source: *Chemical Marketing Reporter.* **Price Frequency:** weekly. **Effective Market(s):** New York. **Units of Measure:** Dollars per lb. **Type of Price:** spot. **Time Period Covered:** latest week.

LEAD NAPHTHENATE: LIQUID, 24% LEAD

Source: *Chemical Marketing Reporter.* **Price Frequency:** weekly. **Effective Market(s):** New York. **Units of Measure:** Dollars per lb. **Type of Price:** spot. **Time Period Covered:** latest week.

LEAD NITRATE: TECHNICAL GRADE, CRYSTALLINE

Source: *Chemical Marketing Reporter.* **Price Frequency:** weekly. **Effective Market(s):** New York. **Units of Measure:** Dollars per lb. **Type of Price:** spot. **Time Period Covered:** latest week.

LEAD OXIDES

Source: *American Metal Market.* **Price Frequency:** daily. **Units of Measure:** Dollars per 100 lbs. lead oxide. **Time Period Covered:** latest day.

LEAD PEROXIDE

see Lead Dioxide.

LEAD SCRAP: HEAVY SOFT

Source: *American Metal Market.* **Price Frequency:** daily. **Units of Measure:** Dollars per 100 lbs. **Type of Price:** smelter buying. **Time Period Covered:** latest day.

LEAD SILICOCHROMATE

Source: *Chemical Marketing Reporter.* **Price Frequency:** weekly. **Effective Market(s):** New York. **Units of Measure:** Dollars per lb. **Type of Price:** spot. **Time Period Covered:** latest week.

LEAD TYPE METAL

Source: *American Metal Market.* **Price Frequency:** daily. **Effective Market(s):** 14 domestic markets, Montreal, Toronto. **Units of Measure:** cents per lb., Canadian cents per lb. **Type of Price:** dealer buying. **Time Period Covered:** latest day.

Source: *Iron Age.* **Price Frequency:** monthly. **Units of Measure:** cents per lb. **Type of Price:** dealer. **Time Period Covered:** latest month.

LEAD WHITE BASIC CARBONATE

Source: *Chemical Marketing Reporter.* **Price Frequency:** weekly. **Effective Market(s):** New York. **Units of Measure:** Dollars per lb. **Type of Price:** spot. **Time Period Covered:** latest week.

Source: *Journal of Commerce and Commercial.* **Price Frequency:** weekly in Wednesday issue. **Units of Measure:** Dollars per lb. **Type of Price:** spot. **Time Period Covered:** latest week.

LEATHER: CALF, CASE, UNITED STATES

Source: *Prices of Selected Asia/Pacific Products.* **Price Frequency:** monthly. **Effective Market(s):** Tokyo. **Units of Measure:** Japanese yen per unit. **Type of Price:** wholesale high, wholesale low. **Time Period Covered:** latest month.

LEATHER: CATTLEHIDE, SHEEP AND LAMB LEATHER

Source: *Commodity Year Book.* **Price Frequency:** annually. **Effective Market(s):** United States. **Units of Measure:** index. **Type of Price:** wholesale price index. **Time Period Covered:** latest 6 years.

LEBANON POUNDS

Source: *Barron's.* **Price Frequency:** weekly. **Effective Market(s):** New York. **Units of Measure:** Lebanese pounds per United States dollar. **Type of Price:** foreign exchange. **Time Period Covered:** latest 2 weeks.

Source: *New York Times.* **Price Frequency:** daily. **Effective Market(s):** United States. **Units of Measure:** Lebanese pounds per United States dollar. **Type of Price:** foreign exchange. **Time Period Covered:** latest 2 days.

LECITHIN: EDIBLE, TECHNICAL GRADE, BLEACHED

Source: *Chemical Marketing Reporter.* **Price Frequency:** weekly. **Effective Market(s):** New York. **Units of Measure:** Dollars per lb. **Type of Price:** spot. **Time Period Covered:** latest week.

LECITHIN: UNBLEACHED

Source: *Chemical Marketing Reporter.* **Price Frequency:** weekly. **Effective Market(s):** New York. **Units of Measure:** Dollars per lb. **Type of Price:** spot. **Time Period Covered:** latest week.

LEEKS

Source: *Lancaster Farming.* **Price Frequency:** weekly, seasonally. **Effective Market(s):** Pennsylvania. **Units of Measure:** Dollars per crate. **Type of Price:** market. **Time Period Covered:** latest week.

Source: *New Zealand Farmer.* **Price Frequency:** weekly, seasonally. **Effective Market(s):** New Zealand. **Units of Measure:** New Zealand dollars per case/crate. **Time Period Covered:** latest week.

LEEKS: FRESH

Source: *HRI-Buyers Guide.* **Price Frequency:** weekly. **Effective Market(s):** Northeastern area. **Units of Measure:** Dollars per case. **Time Period Covered:** latest week.

LEMON OIL

Source: *U. S. Essential Oil Trade.* **Price Frequency:** annually. **Effective Market(s):** United States. **Units of Measure:** Dollars per kilogram. **Type of Price:** import value. **Time Period Covered:** latest 3 years.

LEMON OIL: ARGENTINE

Source: *Chemical Marketing Reporter.* **Price Frequency:** weekly. **Effective Market(s):** New York. **Units of Measure:** Dollars per lb. **Type of Price:** spot. **Time Period Covered:** latest week.

Source: *Journal of Commerce and Commercial.* **Price Frequency:** weekly in Tuesday issue. **Units of Measure:** Dollars per lb. **Type of Price:** spot. **Time Period Covered:** latest week.

LEMON OIL: BRAZIL

Source: *Chemical Marketing Reporter.* **Price Frequency:** weekly. **Effective Market(s):** New York. **Units of Measure:** Dollars per lb. **Type of Price:** spot. **Time Period Covered:** latest week.

LEMON OIL: CALIFORNIA

Source: *Journal of Commerce and Commercial.* **Price Frequency:** weekly in Tuesday issue. **Units of Measure:** Dollars per lb. **Type of Price:** spot. **Time Period Covered:** latest week.

LEMON OIL: CALIFORNIA, USP

Source: *Chemical Marketing Reporter.* **Price Frequency:** weekly. **Effective Market(s):** New York. **Units of Measure:** Dollars per lb. **Type of Price:** spot. **Time Period Covered:** latest week.

LEMON OIL: ITALIAN

Source: *Chemical Marketing Reporter.* **Price Frequency:** weekly. **Effective Market(s):** New York. **Units of Measure:** Dollars per lb. **Type of Price:** spot. **Time Period Covered:** latest week.

Source: *Journal of Commerce and Commercial.* **Price Frequency:** weekly in Tuesday issue. **Units of Measure:** Dollars per lb. **Type of Price:** spot. **Time Period Covered:** latest week.

LEMON PEEL

Source: *Journal of Commerce and Commercial.* **Price Frequency:** weekly in Monday issue. **Units of Measure:** Dollars per lb. **Type of Price:** spot. **Time Period Covered:** latest week.

LEMONGRASS OIL

Source: *U. S. Essential Oil Trade.* **Price Frequency:** annually. **Effective Market(s):** United States. **Units of Measure:** Dollars per kilogram. **Type of Price:** import value. **Time Period Covered:** latest 3 years.

LEMONGRASS OIL: CHOCIL

Source: *Chemical Marketing Reporter.* **Price Frequency:** weekly. **Effective Market(s):** New York. **Units of Measure:** Dollars per kilo. **Type of Price:** spot. **Time Period Covered:** latest week.

LEMONGRASS OIL: GUATAMALAN

Source: *Journal of Commerce and Commercial.* **Price Frequency:** weekly in Tuesday issue. **Units of Measure:** Dollars per lb. **Type of Price:** spot. **Time Period Covered:** latest week.

LEMONGRASS OIL: GUATEMALAN

Source: *Chemical Marketing Reporter.* **Price Frequency:** weekly. **Effective Market(s):** New York. **Units of Measure:** Dollars per lb. **Type of Price:** spot. **Time Period Covered:** latest week.

LEMONGRASS OIL: INDIAN

Source: *Journal of Commerce and Commercial.* **Price Frequency:** weekly in Tuesday issue. **Units of Measure:** Dollars per lb. **Type of Price:** spot. **Time Period Covered:** latest week.

LEMONS

Source: *Agricultural Prices.* **Price Frequency:** monthly. **Effective Market(s):** United States. **Units of Measure:** Dollars per box. **Type of Price:** received by farmer. **Time Period Covered:** latest 2 months, year ago.

Source: *Agricultural Prices.* **Price Frequency:** monthly. **Effective Market(s):** Arizona, California, United States. **Units of Measure:** Dollars per box. **Type of Price:** received by farmer. **Time Period Covered:** latest month.

Source: *Agricultural Prices Annual Summary.* **Price Frequency:** annually. **Effective Market(s):** Arizona, California, United States. **Units of Measure:** Dollars per box. **Type of Price:** average received by growers. **Time Period Covered:** latest 2 years.

Source: *Agricultural Prices Annual Summary.* **Price Frequency:** monthly. **Effective Market(s):** Arizona, California, United States. **Units of Measure:** Dollars per box. **Type of Price:** average received by growers. **Time Period Covered:** latest 2 years.

Source: *California Farmer.* **Price Frequency:** semimonthly. **Effective Market(s):** Southern District (CA), Central District (CA). **Units of Measure:** Dollars per 38 lb. carton. **Time Period Covered:** latest week, month ago, year ago.

Source: *FAO Quarterly Bulletin of Statistics.* **Price Frequency:** monthly, seasonally. **Effective Market(s):** France. **Units of Measure:** French francs per kilogram, dollars per metric ton. **Type of Price:** wholesale. **Time Period Covered:** latest 3 years.

Source: *Fresh Fruit and Vegetable Prices.* **Price Frequency:** monthly, seasonally. **Effective Market(s):** South/Central California/Arizona. **Units of Measure:** Dollars per carton. **Type of Price:** average price at shipping point. **Time Period Covered:** latest year.

Source: *Fruit and Tree Nuts Situation and Outlook Yearbook.* **Price Frequency:** annually. **Effective Market(s):** United States. **Units of Measure:** Dollars per lb. **Type of Price:** retail. **Time Period Covered:** latest 9 years.

Source: *Lancaster Farming.* **Price Frequency:** weekly, seasonally. **Effective Market(s):** Pennsylvania. **Units of Measure:** Dollars per carton. **Type of Price:** market. **Time Period Covered:** latest week.

Source: *New Zealand Farmer.* **Price Frequency:** weekly, seasonally. **Effective Market(s):** New Zealand. **Units of Measure:** New Zealand dollars per bushel/carton. **Time Period Covered:** latest week.

Source: *The Packer.* **Price Frequency:** weekly, seasonally. **Effective Market(s):** varies. **Units of Measure:** Dollars per carton. **Type of Price:** price received by farmer. **Time Period Covered:** latest week.

LEMONS: ARIZONA

Source: *Fresh Fruit and Vegetable Prices.* **Price Frequency:** monthly, seasonally. **Effective Market(s):** Chicago. **Units of Measure:** Dollars per carton. **Type of Price:** average wholesale price. **Time Period Covered:** latest year.

Source: *Japan Economic Journal.* **Price Frequency:** weekly. **Effective Market(s):** Japan. **Units of Measure:** Japanese yen per carton. **Type of Price:** wholesale. **Time Period Covered:** latest 2 weeks.

LEMONS: CALIFORNIA

Source: *Fresh Fruit and Vegetable Prices.* **Price Frequency:** monthly, seasonally. **Effective Market(s):** Chicago. **Units of Measure:** Dollars per carton. **Type of Price:** average wholesale price. **Time Period Covered:** latest year.

LEMONS: CALIFORNIA AND ARIZONA

Source: *Fresh Fruit and Vegetable Prices.* **Price Frequency:** monthly, seasonally. **Effective Market(s):** New York City. **Units of Measure:** Dollars per carton. **Type of Price:** average wholesale price. **Time Period Covered:** latest year.

LEMONS: FLORIDA

Source: *Fresh Fruit and Vegetable Prices.* **Price Frequency:** monthly, seasonally. **Effective Market(s):** New York City. **Units of Measure:** Dollars per carton. **Type of Price:** average wholesale price. **Time Period Covered:** latest year.

LEMONS: FRESH

Source: *HRI-Buyers Guide.* **Price Frequency:** weekly. **Effective Market(s):** Northeastern area. **Units of Measure:** Dollars per case. **Time Period Covered:** latest week.

LEMONS: ITALIAN

Source: *FAO Quarterly Bulletin of Statistics.* **Price Frequency:** monthly, annually, seasonally. **Effective Market(s):** West Germany. **Units of Measure:** West German marks per 14 kilogram box, dollars per metric ton. **Type of Price:** wholesale. **Time Period Covered:** latest 3 years.

LEMONS: MEYER

Source: *New Zealand Farmer.* **Price Frequency:** weekly, seasonally. **Effective Market(s):** New Zealand. **Units of Measure:** New Zealand dollars per carton. **Time Period Covered:** latest week.

LEMONS: SPANISH

Source: *FAO Quarterly Bulletin of Statistics.* **Price Frequency:** monthly, annually. **Effective Market(s):** West Germany. **Units of Measure:** West German marks per 15 kilogram box, dollars per metric ton. **Type of Price:** wholesale. **Time Period Covered:** latest 3 years.

LENTILS

Source: *Bean Market News.* **Price Frequency:** weekly. **Effective Market(s):** Idaho/Washington. **Units of Measure:** Dollars per 100 lbs. **Type of Price:** dealer. **Time Period Covered:** latest week, week ago, year ago.

Source: *Bean Market News.* **Price Frequency:** weekly. **Effective Market(s):** Idaho, Washington. **Units of Measure:** Dollars per 100 lbs. **Type of Price:** grower. **Time Period Covered:** latest week, week ago.

Source: *Idaho Farmer-Stockman.* **Price Frequency:** monthly. **Effective Market(s):** Moscow (ID). **Type of Price:** bid to grower. **Time Period Covered:** latest month, month ago.

Source: *Oregon Farmer-Stockman.* **Price Frequency:** monthly, seasonally. **Effective Market(s):** Moscow (ID). **Units of Measure:** Dollars per bushel. **Type of Price:** bid to grower. **Time Period Covered:** latest month, month ago.

Source: *Vegetable Specialties Situation and Outlook Report.* **Price Frequency:** monthly, annually, seasonally. **Effective Market(s):** United States. **Units of Measure:** Dollars per 100 lbs. **Type of Price:** received by grower. **Time Period Covered:** latest 4 years.

Source: *Washington Farmer-Stockman.* **Price Frequency:** monthly. **Effective Market(s):** Moscow (ID). **Units of Measure:** Dollars per bushel. **Type of Price:** bid to grower. **Time Period Covered:** latest month, month ago.

LENTILS: DRY, TURKISH

Source: *FAO Quarterly Bulletin of Statistics.* **Price Frequency:** monthly, annually, seasonally. **Effective Market(s):** United Kingdom. **Units of Measure:** Dollars per 1000 kgs., dollars per metric ton. **Time Period Covered:** latest 3 years.

LESPEDEZA SEED: UNHULLED, KOREAN

Source: *Agricultural Prices Annual Summary.* **Price Frequency:** annually. **Effective Market(s):** United States. **Units of Measure:** Dollars per 100 lbs. **Type of Price:** average paid by farmer. **Time Period Covered:** latest 6 years.

LESPEDEZA SEED: UNHULLED, SERICEA

Source: *Agricultural Prices Annual Summary.* **Price Frequency:** annually. **Effective Market(s):** United States. **Units of Measure:** Dollars per 100 lbs. **Type of Price:** average paid by farmer. **Time Period Covered:** latest 6 years.

LESPEDEZA SEED: UNHULLED, STRIATE, KOBE

Source: *Agricultural Prices Annual Summary.* **Price Frequency:** annually. **Effective Market(s):** United States. **Units of Measure:** Dollars per 100 lbs. **Type of Price:** average paid by farmer. **Time Period Covered:** latest 6 years.

LETTUCE

Source: *Agricultural Outlook.* **Price Frequency:** monthly, annually. **Effective Market(s):** United States. **Units of Measure:** Dollars per 100 lbs. **Type of Price:** price received by farmers. **Time Period Covered:** monthly latest 6 months, annually latest 3 years.

Source: *Agricultural Prices Annual Summary.* **Price Frequency:** monthly, seasonally. **Effective Market(s):** 8 domestic markets, United States. **Units of Measure:** Dollars per 100 lbs. **Type of Price:** average received by growers. **Time Period Covered:** monthly latest 3 years, for US latest 6 years.

Source: *The Grower.* **Price Frequency:** monthly, seasonally. **Units of Measure:** Dollars per carton. **Time Period Covered:** latest year.

Source: *New Zealand Farmer.* **Price Frequency:** weekly, seasonally. **Effective Market(s):** New Zealand. **Units of Measure:** New Zealand dollars per crate. **Time Period Covered:** latest week.

LETTUCE: BIBB

Source: *Lancaster Farming.* **Price Frequency:** weekly, seasonally. **Effective Market(s):** Pennsylvania. **Units of Measure:** Dollars per carton. **Type of Price:** market. **Time Period Covered:** latest week.

LETTUCE: BIBB, FRESH

Source: *HRI-Buyers Guide.* **Price Frequency:** weekly. **Effective Market(s):** Northeastern area. **Units of Measure:** Dollars per case. **Time Period Covered:** latest week.

LETTUCE: BIG BOSTON TYPE

Source: *Lancaster Farming.* **Price Frequency:** weekly, seasonally. **Effective Market(s):** Pennsylvania. **Units of Measure:** Dollars per carton. **Type of Price:** market. **Time Period Covered:** latest week.

LETTUCE: BIG BOSTON TYPE, CALIFORNIA

Source: *Fresh Fruit and Vegetable Prices.* **Price Frequency:** monthly, seasonally. **Effective Market(s):** Chicago, New York City. **Units of Measure:** Dollars per carton. **Type of Price:** average wholesale price. **Time Period Covered:** latest year.

LETTUCE: BOSTON TYPE

Source: *Fresh Fruit and Vegetable Prices.* **Price Frequency:** monthly, seasonally. **Effective Market(s):** South Florida, Imperial/Coachella Valleys (CA), Salinas/Watsonville (CA). **Units of Measure:** Dollars per crate. **Type of Price:** average price at shipping point. **Time Period Covered:** latest year.

Source: *The Packer.* **Price Frequency:** weekly, seasonally. **Effective Market(s):** varies. **Units of Measure:** Dollars per carton. **Type of Price:** price received by farmer. **Time Period Covered:** latest week.

LETTUCE: BUTTERCRUNCH TYPE

Source: *New Zealand Farmer.* **Price Frequency:** weekly, seasonally. **Effective Market(s):** New Zealand. **Units of Measure:** New Zealand dollars per head. **Time Period Covered:** latest week.

LETTUCE: CALIFORNIA

Source: *Vegetable Specialties Situation and Outlook Report.* **Price Frequency:** weekly. **Effective Market(s):** Los Angeles. **Units of Measure:** carton of 24 count bunches. **Type of Price:** wholesale. **Time Period Covered:** latest year.

LETTUCE: FRESH

Source: *Agricultural Prices.* **Price Frequency:** monthly. **Effective Market(s):** United States. **Units of Measure:** Dollars per 100 lbs. **Type of Price:** received by farmer. **Time Period Covered:** latest 2 months, year ago.

Source: *Vegetable Specialties Situation and Outlook Report.* **Price Frequency:** monthly, annually. **Effective Market(s):** United States. **Units of Measure:** Dollars per 100 lbs. **Type of Price:** received by grower. **Time Period Covered:** latest 4 years.

LETTUCE: GREEN LEAF

Source: *The Packer.* **Price Frequency:** weekly, seasonally. **Effective Market(s):** varies. **Units of Measure:** Dollars per carton. **Type of Price:** price received by farmer. **Time Period Covered:** latest week.

LETTUCE: GREEN LEAF, CALIFORNIA

Source: *Fresh Fruit and Vegetable Prices.* **Price Frequency:** monthly, seasonally. **Effective Market(s):** Chicago. **Units of Measure:** Dollars per carton. **Type of Price:** average wholesale price. **Time Period Covered:** latest year.

LETTUCE: HOTHOUSE

Source: *New Zealand Farmer.* **Price Frequency:** weekly, seasonally. **Effective Market(s):** New Zealand. **Units of Measure:** New Zealand dollars per head. **Time Period Covered:** latest week.

LETTUCE: ICEBERG

Source: *California Farmer.* **Price Frequency:** semimonthly. **Effective Market(s):** 6 California markets. **Units of Measure:** Dollars per 50 lb. carton. **Time Period Covered:** latest week, month ago, year ago.

Source: *Fresh Fruit and Vegetable Prices.* **Price Frequency:** monthly, seasonally. **Effective Market(s):** 17 domestic markets. **Units of Measure:** Dollars per carton. **Type of Price:** average price at shipping point. **Time Period Covered:** latest year.

Source: *Lancaster Farming.* **Price Frequency:** weekly, seasonally. **Effective Market(s):** Pennsylvania. **Units of Measure:** Dollars per carton. **Type of Price:** market. **Time Period Covered:** latest week.

Source: *The Packer.* **Price Frequency:** weekly, seasonally. **Effective Market(s):** varies. **Units of Measure:** Dollars per carton. **Type of Price:** price received by farmer. **Time Period Covered:** latest week.

LETTUCE: ICEBERG, ARIZONA

Source: *Fresh Fruit and Vegetable Prices.* **Price Frequency:** monthly, seasonally. **Effective Market(s):** Chicago. **Units of Measure:** Dollars per carton. **Type of Price:** average wholesale price. **Time Period Covered:** latest year.

LETTUCE: ICEBERG, ARIZONA AND CALIFORNIA

Source: *Fresh Fruit and Vegetable Prices.* **Price Frequency:** monthly, seasonally. **Effective Market(s):** New York City. **Units of Measure:** Dollars per carton. **Type of Price:** average wholesale price. **Time Period Covered:** latest year.

LETTUCE: ICEBERG, CALIFORNIA

Source: *Fresh Fruit and Vegetable Prices.* **Price Frequency:** monthly, seasonally. **Effective Market(s):** Chicago. **Units of Measure:** Dollars per carton. **Type of Price:** average wholesale price. **Time Period Covered:** latest year.

LETTUCE: ICEBERG, FRESH

Source: *HRI-Buyers Guide.* **Price Frequency:** weekly. **Effective Market(s):** Northeastern area. **Units of Measure:** Dollars per case. **Time Period Covered:** latest week.

LETTUCE: ICEBERG, FRESH, CALIFORNIA

Source: *Vegetable Specialties Situation and Outlook Report.* **Price Frequency:** monthly. **Effective Market(s):** North Central, Northeast. **Units of Measure:** cents per lb. **Type of Price:** retail. **Time Period Covered:** latest month, year ago.

LETTUCE: INDOOR, HEAVY

Source: *Farmers Weekly.* **Price Frequency:** weekly, seasonally. **Effective Market(s):** Birmingham (England), Bristol (England), Covent Garden (England), Glasgow (Scotland), Manchester (England). **Units of Measure:** British pence per kilogram. **Type of Price:** auction. **Time Period Covered:** latest week.

LETTUCE: LEAF

Source: *Fresh Fruit and Vegetable Prices.* **Price Frequency:** monthly, seasonally. **Effective Market(s):** Imperial/Coachella Valleys (CA)/Calexico (CA), Salinas/Watsonville (CA), Florida. **Units of Measure:** Dollars per carton. **Type of Price:** average price at shipping point. **Time Period Covered:** latest year.

Source: *Lancaster Farming.* **Price Frequency:** weekly, seasonally. **Effective Market(s):** Pennsylvania. **Units of Measure:** Dollars per carton. **Type of Price:** market. **Time Period Covered:** latest week.

LETTUCE: LEAF, FRESH

Source: *HRI-Buyers Guide.* **Price Frequency:** weekly. **Effective Market(s):** Northeastern area. **Units of Measure:** Dollars per case. **Time Period Covered:** latest week.

LETTUCE: LOOSELEAF

Source: *California Farmer.* **Price Frequency:** semimonthly, seasonally. **Effective Market(s):** Imperial/Coachella Valley. **Units of Measure:** Dollars per 25 lb. carton. **Time Period Covered:** latest week, month ago, year ago.

LETTUCE: OAMARU

Source: *New Zealand Farmer.* **Price Frequency:** weekly, seasonally. **Effective Market(s):** New Zealand. **Units of Measure:** New Zealand dollars per carton. **Time Period Covered:** latest week.

LETTUCE: ORGANIC, CALIFORNIA

Source: *Vegetable Specialties Situation and Outlook Report.* **Price Frequency:** weekly. **Effective Market(s):** California. **Units of Measure:** carton of 24 count bunches. **Type of Price:** wholesale. **Time Period Covered:** latest year.

LETTUCE: RED LEAF

Source: *The Packer.* **Price Frequency:** weekly, seasonally. **Effective Market(s):** varies. **Units of Measure:** Dollars per carton. **Type of Price:** price received by farmer. **Time Period Covered:** latest week.

LETTUCE: ROMAINE

Source: *California Farmer.* **Price Frequency:** semimonthly, seasonally. **Effective Market(s):** Imperial/Coachella Valleys. **Units of Measure:** Dollars per 40 lb. carton. **Time Period Covered:** latest week, month ago, year ago.

Source: *Fresh Fruit and Vegetable Prices.* **Price Frequency:** monthly, seasonally. **Effective Market(s):** South Florida, Imperial/Coachella Valleys (CA), Salinas/Watsonville (CA). **Units of Measure:** Dollars per carton. **Type of Price:** average price at shipping point. **Time Period Covered:** latest year.

Source: *Lancaster Farming.* **Price Frequency:** weekly, seasonally. **Effective Market(s):** Pennsylvania. **Units of Measure:** Dollars per carton. **Type of Price:** market. **Time Period Covered:** latest week.

Source: *The Packer.* **Price Frequency:** weekly, seasonally. **Effective Market(s):** varies. **Units of Measure:** Dollars per carton. **Type of Price:** price received by farmer. **Time Period Covered:** latest week.

LETTUCE: ROMAINE, CALIFORNIA

Source: *Fresh Fruit and Vegetable Prices.* **Price Frequency:** monthly, seasonally. **Effective Market(s):** Chicago, New York City. **Units of Measure:** Dollars per carton. **Type of Price:** average wholesale price. **Time Period Covered:** latest year.

LETTUCE: ROMAINE, FLORIDA

Source: *Fresh Fruit and Vegetable Prices.* **Price Frequency:** monthly, seasonally. **Effective Market(s):** New York City. **Units of Measure:** Dollars per crate/carton. **Type of Price:** average wholesale price. **Time Period Covered:** latest year.

LETTUCE: ROMAINE, FRESH

Source: *HRI-Buyers Guide.* **Price Frequency:** weekly. **Effective Market(s):** Northeastern area. **Units of Measure:** Dollars per case. **Time Period Covered:** latest week.

LETTUCE: WHITLOFF

Source: *New Zealand Farmer.* **Price Frequency:** weekly, seasonally. **Effective Market(s):** New Zealand. **Units of Measure:** New Zealand dollars per 4.5 kilograms. **Time Period Covered:** latest week.

DL-LEUCINE

Source: *Chemical Marketing Reporter.* **Price Frequency:** weekly. **Effective Market(s):** New York. **Units of Measure:** Dollars per lb. **Type of Price:** spot. **Time Period Covered:** latest week.

LEUCOXENE: WESTERN AUSTRALIAN

Source: *Industrial Minerals.* **Price Frequency:** monthly. **Effective Market(s):** Australia. **Units of Measure:** Australian dollars per metric tonne. **Type of Price:** producer & dealer. **Time Period Covered:** latest month.

LICORICE ROOT: WHOLE

Source: *Chemical Marketing Reporter.* **Price Frequency:** weekly. **Effective Market(s):** New York. **Units of Measure:** Dollars per lb. **Type of Price:** spot. **Time Period Covered:** latest week.

LICORICE ROOT EXTRACT

Source: *Journal of Commerce and Commercial.* **Price Frequency:** weekly in Monday issue. **Units of Measure:** Dollars per lb. **Type of Price:** spot. **Time Period Covered:** latest week.

LICORICE ROOT POWDER

Source: *Chemical Marketing Reporter.* **Price Frequency:** weekly. **Effective Market(s):** New York. **Units of Measure:** Dollars per lb. **Type of Price:** spot. **Time Period Covered:** latest week.

Source: *Journal of Commerce and Commercial.* **Price Frequency:** weekly in Monday issue. **Units of Measure:** Dollars per lb. **Type of Price:** spot. **Time Period Covered:** latest week.

LIGHT WHISKEY

Source: *Colorado Beverage Analyst.* **Price Frequency:** monthly. **Effective Market(s):** Colorado. **Units of Measure:** Dollars per case. **Type of Price:** wholesale by brand. **Time Period Covered:** latest month.

Source: *Illinois Beverage Journal.* **Price Frequency:** monthly. **Effective Market(s):** Illinois. **Units of Measure:** Dollars per case. **Type of Price:** wholesale by brand. **Time Period Covered:** latest month.

Source: *Kentucky Beverage Journal.* **Price Frequency:** monthly. **Effective Market(s):** Kentucky. **Units of Measure:** Dollars per bottle, dollars per case. **Type of Price:** wholesale by brand. **Time Period Covered:** latest month.

LIGNALOE

Source: *U. S. Essential Oil Trade.* **Price Frequency:** annually. **Effective Market(s):** United States. **Units of Measure:** Dollars per kilogram. **Type of Price:** import value. **Time Period Covered:** latest 3 years.

LIGNOSULFONATE

see Ammonium or Sodium Lignin Sulfonate.

LILIES: POTTED, LESS THAN 5″

Source: *Floriculture Crops.* **Price Frequency:** annually. **Effective Market(s):** 7 domestic markets, United States. **Units of Measure:** Dollars per unit. **Type of Price:** commercial wholesale. **Time Period Covered:** latest 2 years.

LILIES: POTTED, MORE THAN 5″

Source: *Floriculture Crops.* **Price Frequency:** annually. **Effective Market(s):** 18 domestic markets, United States. **Units of Measure:** Dollars per unit. **Type of Price:** commercial wholesale. **Time Period Covered:** latest 2 years.

LIMA BEANS

See Beans: Lima.

LIME: CHEMICAL, HYDRATED

Source: *Chemical Marketing Reporter.* **Price Frequency:** weekly. **Effective Market(s):** New York. **Units of Measure:** Dollars per ton. **Type of Price:** spot. **Time Period Covered:** latest week.

LIME: CHEMICAL, PEBBLE (QUICKLIME)

Source: *Chemical Marketing Reporter.* **Price Frequency:** weekly. **Effective Market(s):** New York. **Units of Measure:** Dollars per ton. **Type of Price:** spot. **Time Period Covered:** latest week.

LIME: MASONS

Source: *ENR.* **Price Frequency:** monthly in first issue of month. **Effective Market(s):** 16 domestic cities, Montreal, Toronto. **Units of Measure:** Dollars per ton. **Type of Price:** spot. **Time Period Covered:** latest month.

LIME: PURIFIED, NF

Source: *Chemical Marketing Reporter.* **Price Frequency:** weekly. **Effective Market(s):** New York. **Units of Measure:** Dollars per lb. **Type of Price:** spot. **Time Period Covered:** latest week.

LIME OIL

Source: *U. S. Essential Oil Trade.* **Price Frequency:** annually. **Effective Market(s):** United States. **Units of Measure:** Dollars per kilogram. **Type of Price:** import value. **Time Period Covered:** latest 3 years.

LIME OIL: DISTILLED

Source: *Journal of Commerce and Commercial.* **Price Frequency:** weekly in Tuesday issue. **Units of Measure:** Dollars per lb. **Type of Price:** spot. **Time Period Covered:** latest week.

LIME OIL: DISTILLED, HAITIAN

Source: *Chemical Marketing Reporter.* **Price Frequency:** weekly. **Effective Market(s):** New York. **Units of Measure:** Dollars per lb. **Type of Price:** spot. **Time Period Covered:** latest week.

LIME OIL: DISTILLED, MEXICAN

Source: *Chemical Marketing.* **Price Frequency:** weekly. **Effective Market(s):** New York. **Units of Measure:** Dollars per lb. **Type of Price:** spot. **Time Period Covered:** latest week.

LIME OIL: EXPRESSED

Source: *Journal of Commerce and Commercial.* **Price Frequency:** weekly in Tuesday issue. **Units of Measure:** Dollars per lb. **Type of Price:** spot. **Time Period Covered:** latest week.

Source: *Prices of Selected Asia/Pacific Products.* **Price Frequency:** monthly, seasonally. **Effective Market(s):** New York. **Units of Measure:** Dollars per lb. **Type of Price:** spot high, spot low. **Time Period Covered:** latest month.

LIME SALTS

see Calcium.

LIMES

Source: *Agricultural Prices.* **Price Frequency:** monthly. **Effective Market(s):** United States. **Units of Measure:** Dollars per box. **Type of Price:** received by farmer. **Time Period Covered:** latest 2 months, year ago.

Source: *Agricultural Prices.* **Price Frequency:** monthly. **Effective Market(s):** Florida. **Units of Measure:** Dollars per box. **Type of Price:** received by farmer. **Time Period Covered:** latest month.

Source: *Agricultural Prices Annual Summary.* **Price Frequency:** annually. **Effective Market(s):** Florida. **Units of Measure:** Dollars per box. **Type of Price:** average received by growers. **Time Period Covered:** latest 2 years.

Source: *Agricultural Prices Annual Summary.* **Price Frequency:** monthly. **Effective Market(s):** Florida. **Units of Measure:** Dollars per box. **Type of Price:** average received by growers. **Time Period Covered:** latest 2 years.

Source: *Fruit and Tree Nuts Situation and Outlook Yearbook.* **Price Frequency:** annually. **Effective Market(s):** Florida. **Units of Measure:** Dollars per ton. **Type of Price:** grower. **Time Period Covered:** latest 20 years.

Source: *New Zealand Farmer.* **Price Frequency:** weekly, seasonally. **Effective Market(s):** New Zealand. **Units of Measure:** New Zealand dollars per quarter carton. **Time Period Covered:** latest week.

Source: *The Packer.* **Price Frequency:** weekly, seasonally. **Effective Market(s):** varies. **Units of Measure:** Dollars per carton. **Type of Price:** price received by farmer. **Time Period Covered:** latest week.

LIMES: FRESH

Source: *HRI-Buyers Guide.* **Price Frequency:** weekly. **Effective Market(s):** Northeastern area. **Units of Measure:** Dollars per case. **Time Period Covered:** latest week.

LIMES: MEXICO IMPORTS

Source: *Fresh Fruit and Vegetable Prices.* **Price Frequency:** monthly, seasonally. **Effective Market(s):** South Texas. **Units of Measure:** Dollars per carton. **Type of Price:** average price at shipping point. **Time Period Covered:** latest year.

LIMES: PERSIAN

Source: *Lancaster Farming.* **Price Frequency:** weekly, seasonally. **Effective Market(s):** Pennsylvania. **Units of Measure:** Dollars per carton. **Type of Price:** market. **Time Period Covered:** latest week.

LIMES: PERSIAN SEEDLESS

Source: *Fresh Fruit and Vegetable Prices.* **Price Frequency:** monthly, seasonally. **Effective Market(s):** South Florida. **Units of Measure:** Dollars per carton. **Type of Price:** average price at shipping point. **Time Period Covered:** latest year.

Source: *The Packer.* **Price Frequency:** weekly, seasonally. **Effective Market(s):** varies. **Units of Measure:** Dollars per carton. **Type of Price:** price received by farmer. **Time Period Covered:** latest week.

LIMES: PERSIAN SEEDLESS, FLORIDA

Source: *Fresh Fruit and Vegetable Prices.* **Price Frequency:** monthly, seasonally. **Effective Market(s):** Chicago, New York. **Units of Measure:** Dollars per carton. **Type of Price:** average wholesale price. **Time Period Covered:** latest year.

LIMES: PERSIAN SEEDLESS, MEXICO

Source: *Fresh Fruit and Vegetable Prices.* **Price Frequency:** monthly, seasonally. **Effective Market(s):** Chicago, New York City. **Units of Measure:** Dollars per carton. **Type of Price:** average wholesale price. **Time Period Covered:** latest year.

LIMES: SEEDLESS

Source: *Lancaster Farming.* **Price Frequency:** weekly, seasonally. **Effective Market(s):** Pennsylvania. **Units of Measure:** Dollars per carton. **Type of Price:** market. **Time Period Covered:** latest week.

LIMESTONE: SPREAD ON FIELD

Source: *Agricultural Prices.* **Price Frequency:** monthly. **Effective Market(s):** 9 domestic markets, United States. **Units of Measure:** Dollars per ton. **Type of Price:** paid by farmer. **Time Period Covered:** latest month.

Source: *Agricultural Prices Annual Summary.* **Price Frequency:** semiannually. **Effective Market(s):** East South Central region, North Central region, Northeast region, South Central region, Southeast region, United States. **Units of Measure:** Dollars per ton. **Type of Price:** average paid by farmer. **Time Period Covered:** latest year, for US quarterly for latest 6 years.

D-LIMONENE

Source: *Chemical Marketing Reporter.* **Price Frequency:** weekly. **Effective Market(s):** New York. **Units of Measure:** Dollars per lb. **Type of Price:** spot. **Time Period Covered:** latest week.

LINALOOL: NATURAL

Source: *Journal of Commerce and Commercial.* **Price Frequency:** weekly in Tuesday issue. **Units of Measure:** Dollars per lb. **Type of Price:** spot. **Time Period Covered:** latest week.

LINALOOL: SYNTHETIC

Source: *Journal of Commerce and Commercial.* **Price Frequency:** weekly in Tuesday issue. **Units of Measure:** Dollars per lb. **Type of Price:** spot. **Time Period Covered:** latest week.

LINALOOL EX BOIS DE ROSE OIL

Source: *Chemical Marketing Reporter.* **Price Frequency:** weekly. **Effective Market(s):** New York. **Units of Measure:** Dollars per lb. **Type of Price:** spot. **Time Period Covered:** latest week.

LINALOOL EX BOIS DE ROSE OIL: SYNTHETIC, FCC

Source: *Chemical Marketing Reporter.* **Price Frequency:** weekly. **Effective Market(s):** New York. **Units of Measure:** Dollars per lb. **Type of Price:** spot. **Time Period Covered:** latest week.

LINALOOL OXIDE: SYNTHETIC

Source: *Chemical Marketing Reporter.* **Price Frequency:** weekly. **Effective Market(s):** New York. **Units of Measure:** Dollars per lb. **Type of Price:** spot. **Time Period Covered:** latest week.

LINALYL ACETATE: 90-92%

Source: *Journal of Commerce and Commercial.* **Price Frequency:** weekly in Tuesday issue. **Units of Measure:** Dollars per lb. **Type of Price:** spot. **Time Period Covered:** latest week.

LINALYL ACETATE: 98-100%, SYNTHETIC

Source: *Chemical Marketing Reporter.* **Price Frequency:** weekly. **Effective Market(s):** New York. **Units of Measure:** Dollars per lb. **Type of Price:** spot. **Time Period Covered:** latest week.

LINALYL BENZOATE: SYNTHETIC

Source: *Chemical Marketing Reporter.* **Price Frequency:** weekly. **Effective Market(s):** New York. **Units of Measure:** Dollars per lb. **Type of Price:** spot. **Time Period Covered:** latest week.

LINALYL CINNAMATE: SYNTHETIC

Source: *Chemical Marketing Reporter.* **Price Frequency:** weekly. **Effective Market(s):** New York. **Units of Measure:** Dollars per lb. **Type of Price:** spot. **Time Period Covered:** latest week.

LINDANE: 20% FORMULATION

Source: *Chemical Marketing Reporter.* **Price Frequency:** weekly. **Effective Market(s):** New York. **Units of Measure:** Dollars per gallon. **Type of Price:** spot. **Time Period Covered:** latest week.

LINDANE: 20-25% FORMULATION

Source: *Journal of Commerce and Commercial.* **Price Frequency:** weekly in Thursday issue. **Units of Measure:** Dollars per gallon. **Type of Price:** spot. **Time Period Covered:** latest week.

LINDANE: 99.9%, TECHNICAL GRADE

Source: *Chemical Marketing Reporter.* **Price Frequency:** weekly. **Effective Market(s):** New York. **Units of Measure:** Dollars per lb. **Type of Price:** spot. **Time Period Covered:** latest week.

LINDEN FLOWERS: WITH LEAVES

Source: *Chemical Marketing Reporter.* **Price Frequency:** weekly. **Effective Market(s):** New York. **Units of Measure:** Dollars per lb. **Type of Price:** spot. **Time Period Covered:** latest week.

LINDEN FLOWERS: WITHOUT LEAVES

Source: *Chemical Marketing Reporter.* **Price Frequency:** weekly. **Effective Market(s):** New York. **Units of Measure:** Dollars per lb. **Type of Price:** spot. **Time Period Covered:** latest week.

LINERBOARD: 36 LB. OR MORE

Source: *Pulp & Paper Week.* **Price Frequency:** monthly, usually in last issue of month. **Effective Market(s):** Northern Europe. **Units of Measure:** Dollars per metric ton. **Type of Price:** estimated export transaction. **Time Period Covered:** latest 3 months, year ago.

LINERBOARD: 42 LB., DOMESTIC

Source: *Pulp & Paper Week.* **Price Frequency:** monthly, usually in last issue of month. **Effective Market(s):** Eastern United States, West Coast. **Units of Measure:** Dollars per short ton, dollars per 1000 square feet. **Type of Price:** estimated transaction. **Time Period Covered:** latest 3 months, year ago.

LINERBOARD: FOURDRINIER KRAFT

Source: *Purchasing.* **Price Frequency:** monthly. **Effective Market(s):** East/Midwest/West. **Units of Measure:** Dollars per ton. **Type of Price:** transaction. **Time Period Covered:** latest day, month ago, 6 months ago, year ago.

LING (FISH): RED HAKE, WHOLE, FRESH

Source: *Seafood Price-Current.* **Price Frequency:** semiweekly. **Effective Market(s):** Boston, Mid-Atlantic, New Bedford (MA), Portland (ME). **Units of Measure:** Dollars per lb. **Type of Price:** sale by first receiver, auction price. **Time Period Covered:** latest day.

LINSEED: 36%, ARGENTINE

Source: *Oil World.* **Price Frequency:** weekly, monthly, annually. **Effective Market(s):** Rotterdam. **Units of Measure:** Dollars per tonne. **Type of Price:** lowest representative asking export. **Time Period Covered:** weekly latest 3 weeks, monthly latest 2 months, annually latest 2 years.

LINSEED: NO. 1, CANADIAN

Source: *Commodity Trade and Price Trends.* **Price Frequency:** annually. **Effective Market(s):** European ports. **Units of Measure:** Dollars per metric ton, 1980 constant dollars per metric ton. **Time Period Covered:** latest 37 years.

Source: *Oil World.* **Price Frequency:** weekly, monthly, annually. **Effective Market(s):** Northwest Europe. **Units of Measure:** Dollars per tonne. **Type of Price:** lowest representative asking. **Time Period Covered:** weekly latest 3 weeks, monthly latest 2 months, annually latest 2 years.

Source: *World Oilseed Situation and Market Highlights.* **Price Frequency:** monthly, annually. **Effective Market(s):** Rotterdam. **Units of Measure:** Dollars per metric ton. **Time Period Covered:** monthly latest year, annually latest 9 years.

LINSEED MEAL: 34% PROTEIN

Source: *Oil Crops Situation and Outlook.* **Price Frequency:** monthly. **Effective Market(s):** Minneapolis. **Units of Measure:** Dollars per ton. **Time Period Covered:** latest 5 months.

LINSEED MEAL: 34% PROTEIN, EXTRACTED

Source: *Chemical Marketing Reporter.* **Price Frequency:** weekly. **Effective Market(s):** Fargo (ND). **Units of Measure:** Dollars per ton. **Type of Price:** spot. **Time Period Covered:** latest week.

LINSEED MEAL: 34% SOLVENT

Source: *Feed Situation and Outlook Report.* **Price Frequency:** monthly. **Effective Market(s):** Minneapolis. **Units of Measure:** Dollars per ton. **Type of Price:** wholesale. **Time Period Covered:** latest 8 months.

LINSEED MEAL: 35% PROTEIN

Source: *Milling & Baking News.* **Price Frequency:** weekly. **Effective Market(s):** Minneapolis. **Units of Measure:** Dollars per ton. **Time Period Covered:** latest week, week ago, year ago.

LINSEED MEAL: SOLVENT

Source: *Feedstuffs.* **Price Frequency:** weekly. **Effective Market(s):** 7 domestic markets. **Units of Measure:** Dollars per bulk ton. **Time Period Covered:** latest week.

Source: *Feedstuffs.* **Price Frequency:** weekly. **Effective Market(s):** Minneapolis. **Units of Measure:** Dollars per ton. **Time Period Covered:** latest week, week ago, 6 months ago, year ago.

LINSEED OIL

Source: *Commodity Year Book.* **Price Frequency:** monthly, annually. **Effective Market(s):** Minneapolis (MN). **Units of Measure:** cents per lb. **Type of Price:** wholesale. **Time Period Covered:** latest 5 years.

Source: *Commodity Year Book.* **Price Frequency:** annually. **Effective Market(s):** Rotterdam (The Netherlands). **Units of Measure:** Dollars per tonne. **Time Period Covered:** latest 6 years.

Source: *Fruit and Tropical Products.* **Price Frequency:** monthly, annually. **Effective Market(s):** Rotterdam. **Units of Measure:** Dollars per tonne. **Type of Price:** average. **Time Period Covered:** monthly latest year, annually latest 2 years.

Source: *Monthly Commodity Price Bulletin Supplement.* **Price Frequency:** monthly, quarterly, annually. **Effective Market(s):** Rotterdam. **Units of Measure:** Dollars per tonne. **Time Period Covered:** latest 20 years.

Source: *Oil World.* **Price Frequency:** weekly, monthly, annually. **Effective Market(s):** Rotterdam. **Units of Measure:** Dollars per tonne. **Type of Price:** lowest representative asking. **Time Period Covered:** weekly latest 3 weeks, monthly latest 2 months, annually latest 2 years.

Source: *UNCTAD Commodity Yearbook.* **Price Frequency:** annually. **Effective Market(s):** Rotterdam. **Units of Measure:** Dollars per metric ton. **Type of Price:** free market. **Time Period Covered:** latest 12 years.

Source: *World Oilseed Situation and Market Highlights.* **Price Frequency:** monthly, annually. **Effective Market(s):** Rotterdam. **Units of Measure:** Dollars per metric ton. **Time Period Covered:** monthly latest year, annually latest 9 years.

LINSEED OIL: 34% SOLVENT

Source: *Grain and Feed Market News.* **Price Frequency:** weekly, seasonally. **Effective Market(s):** Minneapolis. **Units of Measure:** Dollars per ton. **Type of Price:** wholesale. **Time Period Covered:** latest week, week ago, year ago.

LINSEED OIL: ANY ORIGIN

Source: *Commodity Trade and Price Trends.* **Price Frequency:** annually. **Effective Market(s):** Rotterdam. **Units of Measure:** Dollars per metric ton, 1980 constant dollars per metric ton. **Time Period Covered:** latest 37 years.

Source: *Monthly Commodity Price Bulletin.* **Price Frequency:** monthly, annually. **Effective Market(s):** Rotterdam. **Units of Measure:** Dollars per metric ton. **Time Period Covered:** latest 5 years.

LINSEED OIL: CRUDE

Source: *Chemical Marketing Reporter.* **Price Frequency:** weekly. **Effective Market(s):** Minneapolis (MN). **Units of Measure:** cents per lb. **Type of Price:** spot. **Time Period Covered:** latest week.

LINSEED OIL: RAW

Source: *Oil Crops Situation and Outlook.* **Price Frequency:** monthly. **Effective Market(s):** Minneapolis. **Units of Measure:** cents per lb. **Type of Price:** wholesale. **Time Period Covered:** latest 5 months.

Source: *Wall Street Journal.* **Price Frequency:** daily. **Effective Market(s):** Minneapolis. **Units of Measure:** Dollars per lb. **Time Period Covered:** latest day, day ago, year ago.

LINSEED OIL: UNITED STATES

Source: *International Financial Statistics.* **Price Frequency:** annually. **Effective Market(s):** Minneapolis. **Units of Measure:** cents per lb., index. **Type of Price:** market price, price index. **Time Period Covered:** latest 2 years.

Source: *International Financial Statistics Yearbook.* **Price Frequency:** annually. **Effective Market(s):** Minneapolis. **Units of Measure:** cents per lb. **Type of Price:** wholesale. **Time Period Covered:** latest 30 years.

LINSEED OIL FATTY ACID: DISTILLED

Source: *Chemical Marketing Reporter.* **Price Frequency:** weekly. **Effective Market(s):** New York. **Units of Measure:** Dollars per lb. **Type of Price:** spot. **Time Period Covered:** latest week.

LIQUEURS

Source: *Beverage Media.* **Price Frequency:** monthly. **Effective Market(s):** New York. **Units of Measure:** Dollars per unit. **Type of Price:** wholesale by brand. **Time Period Covered:** latest month.

Source: *Colorado Beverage Analyst.* **Price Frequency:** monthly. **Effective Market(s):** Colorado. **Units of Measure:** Dollars per case. **Type of Price:** wholesale by brand. **Time Period Covered:** latest month.

Source: *Illinois Beverage Journal.* **Price Frequency:** monthly. **Effective Market(s):** Illinois. **Units of Measure:** Dollars per case. **Type of Price:** wholesale by brand. **Time Period Covered:** latest month.

Source: *Indiana Beverage Journal.* **Price Frequency:** monthly. **Effective Market(s):** Indiana. **Units of Measure:** Dollars per case, dollars per bottle. **Type of Price:** wholesale by brand. **Time Period Covered:** latest month.

Source: *Kentucky Beverage Journal.* **Price Frequency:** monthly. **Effective Market(s):** Kentucky. **Units of Measure:** Dollars per bottle, dollars per case. **Type of Price:** wholesale by brand. **Time Period Covered:** latest month.

Source: *Nevada Beverage Index.* **Price Frequency:** monthly. **Effective Market(s):** Nevada. **Units of Measure:** Dollars per unit. **Type of Price:** wholesale by brand. **Time Period Covered:** latest month.

LIQUID CRYSTAL POLYMERS

see Polymers: Liquid Crystal.

LIQUORICE ROOT

Source: *Prices of Selected Asia/Pacific Products.* **Price Frequency:** monthly, seasonally. **Effective Market(s):** United Kingdom/North European ports. **Units of Measure:** British pounds per kilogram. **Time Period Covered:** latest month.

LIQUORICE ROOT POWDER

Source: *Prices of Selected Asia/Pacific Products.* **Price Frequency:** monthly, seasonally. **Effective Market(s):** New York. **Units of Measure:** Dollars per lb. **Type of Price:** spot high, spot low. **Time Period Covered:** latest month.

LITHARGE

Source: *American Metal Market.* **Price Frequency:** daily. **Units of Measure:** Dollars per 100 lbs. lead oxide. **Time Period Covered:** latest day.

LITHARGE: COMMERCIAL, POWDERED

Source: *Chemical Marketing Reporter.* **Price Frequency:** weekly. **Effective Market(s):** New York. **Units of Measure:** Dollars per lb. **Type of Price:** spot. **Time Period Covered:** latest week.

LITHARGE: YELLOW

Source: *Journal of Commerce and Commercial.* **Price Frequency:** weekly in Wednesday issue. **Units of Measure:** Dollars per lb. **Type of Price:** spot. **Time Period Covered:** latest week.

LITHIUM: 99.9%

Source: *E&MJ.* **Price Frequency:** monthly. **Units of Measure:** Dollars per lb. **Time Period Covered:** latest month.

LITHIUM: 99.9% MINIMUM

Source: *Economic and Energy Indicators.* **Price Frequency:** monthly, quarterly, annually. **Units of Measure:** Dollars per lb. **Time Period Covered:** latest 3 months, quarters, and years.

LITHIUM: CARBONATE

Source: *E&MJ.* **Price Frequency:** monthly. **Units of Measure:** Dollars per lb. **Time Period Covered:** latest month.

LITHIUM BROMIDE: ANHYDROUS

Source: *Chemical Marketing Reporter.* **Price Frequency:** weekly. **Effective Market(s):** New York. **Units of Measure:** Dollars per lb. **Type of Price:** spot. **Time Period Covered:** latest week.

LITHIUM BROMIDE: SOLUTION

Source: *Chemical Marketing Reporter.* **Price Frequency:** weekly. **Effective Market(s):** New York. **Units of Measure:** Dollars per lb. **Type of Price:** spot. **Time Period Covered:** latest week.

LITHIUM CARBONATE

Source: *Industrial Minerals.* **Price Frequency:** monthly. **Effective Market(s):** United States. **Units of Measure:** Dollars per lb. **Type of Price:** producer & dealer. **Time Period Covered:** latest month.

Source: *Journal of Commerce and Commercial.* **Price Frequency:** weekly in Friday issue. **Units of Measure:** Dollars per lb. **Type of Price:** spot. **Time Period Covered:** latest week.

LITHIUM CARBONATE: GRANULAR

Source: *Chemical Marketing Reporter.* **Price Frequency:** weekly. **Effective Market(s):** New York. **Units of Measure:** Dollars per lb. **Type of Price:** spot. **Time Period Covered:** latest week.

LITHIUM CHLORIDE: ANHYDROUS

Source: *Chemical Marketing Reporter.* **Price Frequency:** weekly. **Effective Market(s):** New York. **Units of Measure:** Dollars per lb. **Type of Price:** spot. **Time Period Covered:** latest week.

Source: *Journal of Commerce and Commercial.* **Price Frequency:** weekly in Friday issue. **Units of Measure:** Dollars per lb. **Type of Price:** spot. **Time Period Covered:** latest week.

LITHIUM CHLORIDE: SOLUTION

Source: *Chemical Marketing Reporter.* **Price Frequency:** weekly. **Effective Market(s):** New York. **Units of Measure:** Dollars per lb. **Type of Price:** spot. **Time Period Covered:** latest week.

LITHIUM FLUORIDE

Source: *Chemical Marketing Reporter.* **Price Frequency:** weekly. **Effective Market(s):** New York. **Units of Measure:** Dollars per lb. **Type of Price:** spot. **Time Period Covered:** latest week.

LITHIUM HYDRIDE

Source: *Chemical Marketing Reporter.* **Price Frequency:** weekly. **Effective Market(s):** New York. **Units of Measure:** Dollars per lb. **Type of Price:** spot. **Time Period Covered:** latest week.

LITHIUM HYDROXIDE: MONOHYDRATE

Source: *Chemical Marketing Reporter.* **Price Frequency:** weekly. **Effective Market(s):** New York. **Units of Measure:** Dollars per lb. **Type of Price:** spot. **Time Period Covered:** latest week.

LITHIUM HYPOCHLORITE

Source: *Chemical Marketing Reporter.* **Price Frequency:** weekly. **Effective Market(s):** New York. **Units of Measure:** Dollars per lb. **Type of Price:** spot. **Time Period Covered:** latest week.

LITHIUM METAL

Source: *Chemical Marketing Reporter.* **Price Frequency:** weekly. **Effective Market(s):** New York. **Units of Measure:** Dollars per lb. **Type of Price:** spot. **Time Period Covered:** latest week.

LITHIUM NITRATE: TECHNICAL GRADE

Source: *Chemical Marketing Reporter.* **Price Frequency:** weekly. **Effective Market(s):** New York. **Units of Measure:** Dollars per lb. **Type of Price:** spot. **Time Period Covered:** latest week.

LITHIUM SULFATE: ANHYDROUS

Source: *Chemical Marketing Reporter.* **Price Frequency:** weekly. **Effective Market(s):** New York. **Units of Measure:** Dollars per lb. **Type of Price:** spot. **Time Period Covered:** latest week.

LITHOL: RED TONER, BARIUM

Source: *Chemical Marketing Reporter.* **Price Frequency:** weekly. **Effective Market(s):** New York. **Units of Measure:** Dollars per lb. **Type of Price:** spot. **Time Period Covered:** latest week.

LITHOL: RED TONER, CALCIUM

Source: *Chemical Marketing Reporter.* **Price Frequency:** weekly. **Effective Market(s):** New York. **Units of Measure:** Dollars per lb. **Type of Price:** spot. **Time Period Covered:** latest week.

LITHOL: RUBINE TONER (RED 57), RESINATED

Source: *Chemical Marketing Reporter.* **Price Frequency:** weekly. **Effective Market(s):** New York. **Units of Measure:** Dollars per lb. **Type of Price:** spot. **Time Period Covered:** latest week.

LITSEA CUBEBA OIL

Source: *Chemical Marketing Reporter.* **Price Frequency:** weekly. **Effective Market(s):** New York. **Units of Measure:** Dollars per lb. **Type of Price:** spot. **Time Period Covered:** latest week.

LIVER

see Beef Liver, Calf Liver, Chicken Livers.

LIVER SAUSAGE: BRAUNSCHWEIGER, ARTIFICIAL CASING

Source: *Meat Price Report.* **Price Frequency:** weekly. **Units of Measure:** cents per lb. **Type of Price:** price paid to wholesaler. **Time Period Covered:** latest week.

LIVER SAUSAGE: BRAUNSCHWEIGER, NATURAL CASING

Source: *Meat Price Report.* **Price Frequency:** weekly. **Units of Measure:** cents per lb. **Type of Price:** price paid to wholesaler. **Time Period Covered:** latest week.

LIVESTOCK

Source: *Illinois Farm Report.* **Price Frequency:** monthly. **Effective Market(s):** Illinois. **Units of Measure:** index. **Type of Price:** index of prices received by farmers. **Time Period Covered:** latest 2 months, year ago.

LLDPE

see Polyethylene: Linear Low Density.

LOBELIA HERB

Source: *Journal of Commerce and Commercial.* **Price Frequency:** weekly in Monday issue. **Units of Measure:** Dollars per lb. **Type of Price:** spot. **Time Period Covered:** latest week.

LOBSTER: FILLETS, FRESH

Source: *Seafood Price-Current.* **Price Frequency:** semiweekly. **Effective Market(s):** Gulf/Southeast. **Units of Measure:** Dollars per lb. **Type of Price:** sale by first receiver. **Time Period Covered:** latest day.

LOBSTER: FRESH, MAINE

Source: *HRI-Buyers Guide.* **Price Frequency:** weekly. **Effective Market(s):** New York. **Units of Measure:** Dollars per case. **Type of Price:** prices paid by dining places & institutions. **Time Period Covered:** latest week.

LOBSTER: TAIL MEAT, FRESH

Source: *Seafood Price-Current.* **Price Frequency:** semiweekly. **Effective Market(s):** Mid-Atlantic, New England. **Units of Measure:** Dollars per lb. **Type of Price:** sale by first receiver. **Time Period Covered:** latest day.

LOBSTER MEAT: CANADIAN

Source: *NMFS Green Sheet Supplement.* **Price Frequency:** weekly. **Effective Market(s):** New England. **Units of Measure:** Dollars per lb. **Type of Price:** to primary wholesaler. **Time Period Covered:** latest week.

LOBSTER MEAT: COOKED, FROZEN, CANADIAN

Source: *Seafood Price-Current.* **Price Frequency:** semiweekly. **Effective Market(s):** Mid-Atlantic. **Units of Measure:** Dollars per lb. **Type of Price:** first receiver. **Time Period Covered:** latest day.

LOBSTER MEAT: FROZEN

Source: *HRI-Buyers Guide.* **Price Frequency:** weekly. **Effective Market(s):** New York. **Units of Measure:** Dollars per case. **Type of Price:** prices paid by dining places & institutions. **Time Period Covered:** latest week.

LOBSTER MEAT: PRECOOKED, CANADIAN

Source: *NMFS Green Sheet Supplement.* **Price Frequency:** weekly. **Effective Market(s):** New York. **Units of Measure:** Dollars per lb. **Type of Price:** warehouse. **Time Period Covered:** latest week.

LOBSTER TAILS: FROZEN

Source: *HRI-Buyers Guide.* **Price Frequency:** weekly. **Effective Market(s):** New York. **Units of Measure:** Dollars per case. **Type of Price:** prices paid by dining places & institutions. **Time Period Covered:** latest week.

LOBSTER TAILS: FROZEN, AUSTRALIA AND NEW ZEALAND

Source: *Seafood Price-Current.* **Price Frequency:** semiweekly. **Effective Market(s):** Mid-Atlantic. **Units of Measure:** Dollars per lb. **Type of Price:** first receiver. **Time Period Covered:** latest day.

LOBSTER TAILS: FROZEN, BRAZIL

Source: *Seafood Price-Current.* **Price Frequency:** semiweekly. **Effective Market(s):** Mid-Atlantic. **Units of Measure:** Dollars per lb. **Type of Price:** first receiver. **Time Period Covered:** latest day.

LOBSTER TAILS: FROZEN, CARIBBEAN, WARM WATER

Source: *Seafood Price-Current.* **Price Frequency:** semiweekly. **Effective Market(s):** Mid-Atlantic. **Units of Measure:** Dollars per lb. **Type of Price:** first receiver. **Time Period Covered:** latest day.

LOBSTER TAILS: SLIPPER, INDIA

Source: *NMFS Green Sheet Supplement.* **Price Frequency:** weekly. **Effective Market(s):** New York. **Units of Measure:** Dollars per lb. **Type of Price:** warehouse. **Time Period Covered:** latest week.

LOBSTER TAILS: SPINY, AUSTRALIA

Source: *NMFS Green Sheet Supplement.* **Price Frequency:** weekly. **Effective Market(s):** New York. **Units of Measure:** Dollars per lb. **Type of Price:** warehouse. **Time Period Covered:** latest week.

LOBSTER TAILS: SPINY, BRAZIL

Source: *NMFS Green Sheet Supplement.* **Price Frequency:** weekly. **Effective Market(s):** New York. **Units of Measure:** Dollars per lb. **Type of Price:** warehouse. **Time Period Covered:** latest week.

LOBSTER TAILS: SPINY, HONDURAS

Source: *NMFS Green Sheet Supplement.* **Price Frequency:** weekly. **Effective Market(s):** New York. **Units of Measure:** Dollars per lb. **Type of Price:** warehouse. **Time Period Covered:** latest week.

LOBSTER TAILS: SPINY, NEW ZEALAND

Source: *NMFS Green Sheet Supplement.* **Price Frequency:** weekly. **Effective Market(s):** New York. **Units of Measure:** Dollars per lb. **Type of Price:** warehouse. **Time Period Covered:** latest week.

LOBSTER TAILS: WHOLE, COOKED, FROZEN, CARIBBEAN

Source: *Seafood Price-Current.* **Price Frequency:** semiweekly. **Effective Market(s):** Mid-Atlantic. **Units of Measure:** Dollars per lb. **Type of Price:** first receiver. **Time Period Covered:** latest day.

LOBSTERS: FRESH, MAINE/CANADA

Source: *Seafood Price-Current.* **Price Frequency:** semiweekly. **Effective Market(s):** Mid-Atlantic, New England. **Units of Measure:** Dollars per lb. **Type of Price:** sale by first receiver. **Time Period Covered:** latest day.

LOBSTERS: SLIPPER, SHELL OFF, FROZEN

Source: *Seafood Price-Current.* **Price Frequency:** semiweekly. **Effective Market(s):** Mid-Atlantic. **Units of Measure:** Dollars per lb. **Type of Price:** first receiver. **Time Period Covered:** latest day.

LOBSTERS: SLIPPER, SHELL ON, TAIWAN/HONG KONG/THAILAND, FROZEN

Source: *Seafood Price-Current.* **Price Frequency:** semiweekly. **Effective Market(s):** West Coast. **Units of Measure:** Dollars per lb. **Type of Price:** first receiver. **Time Period Covered:** latest day.

LOBSTERS: SPINY, OCEAN RUN, FRESH

Source: *Seafood Price-Current.* **Price Frequency:** semiweekly. **Effective Market(s):** West Coast. **Units of Measure:** Dollars per lb. **Type of Price:** sale by first receiver. **Time Period Covered:** latest day.

LOCUST BEAN GUM POWDER

Source: *Chemical Marketing Reporter.* **Price Frequency:** weekly. **Effective Market(s):** New York. **Units of Measure:** Dollars per lb. **Type of Price:** spot. **Time Period Covered:** latest week.

Source: *Journal of Commerce and Commercial.* **Price Frequency:** weekly in Monday issue. **Units of Measure:** Dollars per lb. **Type of Price:** spot. **Time Period Covered:** latest week.

LOGS: BEECH

Source: *Timber Bulletin.* **Price Frequency:** monthly, annually. **Effective Market(s):** West Germany. **Units of Measure:** West German marks per cubic meter. **Time Period Covered:** monthly latest 2 years, annually latest 6 years.

Source: *Timber Bulletin.* **Price Frequency:** monthly, annually. **Effective Market(s):** Switzerland. **Units of Measure:** Swiss francs per metric ton. **Time Period Covered:** monthly latest 2 years, annually latest 6 years.

LOGS: CEDAR

Source: *FAO Quarterly Bulletin of Statistics.* **Price Frequency:** monthly, annually. **Effective Market(s):** Japan. **Units of Measure:** Japanese yen per cubic meter. **Type of Price:** wholesale. **Time Period Covered:** latest 3 years.

Source: *Timber Bulletin.* **Price Frequency:** monthly, annually. **Effective Market(s):** Japan. **Units of Measure:** Japanese yen per cubic meter. **Time Period Covered:** monthly latest 2 years, annually latest 6 years.

LOGS: CONIFEROUS

Source: *Timber Bulletin.* **Price Frequency:** monthly, annually. **Effective Market(s):** Finland. **Units of Measure:** Finnish markka per cubic meter. **Type of Price:** export value. **Time Period Covered:** monthly latest year, annually latest 5 years.

Source: *Timber Bulletin.* **Price Frequency:** monthly, annually. **Effective Market(s):** Sweden. **Units of Measure:** Swedish kronor per cubic meter. **Type of Price:** average export. **Time Period Covered:** monthly latest year, annually latest 5 years.

LOGS: LUAN FOR PLYWOOD AND VENEERS, PHILIPPINES

Source: *Commodity Trade and Price Trends.* **Price Frequency:** annually. **Effective Market(s):** Japan. **Units of Measure:** Dollars per cubic meter, 1980 constant dollars per cubic meter. **Type of Price:** wholesale. **Time Period Covered:** latest 32 years.

LOGS: MALAYSIA

Source: *International Financial Statistics.* **Price Frequency:** monthly, quarterly, annually. **Effective Market(s):** Tokyo. **Units of Measure:** Dollars per cubic meter, index. **Type of Price:** market price, price index. **Time Period Covered:** latest 5 months, latest 5 quarters, latest 5 years.

LOGS: MERANTI FOR PLYWOOD AND VENEERS, SABAH SQ BEST QUALITY, MALAYSIAN

Source: *Commodity Trade and Price Trends.* **Price Frequency:** annually. **Effective Market(s):** Japan. **Units of Measure:** Dollars per cubic meter, 1980 constant dollars per cubic meter. **Type of Price:** import. **Time Period Covered:** latest 10 years.

LOGS: OAK

Source: *Timber Bulletin.* **Price Frequency:** monthly, annually. **Effective Market(s):** Switzerland. **Units of Measure:** Swiss francs per metric ton. **Time Period Covered:** monthly latest 2 years, annually latest 6 years.

LOGS: PHILIPPINES

Source: *International Financial Statistics Yearbook.* **Price Frequency:** annually. **Effective Market(s):** Tokyo. **Units of Measure:** Dollars per cubic meter. **Type of Price:** wholesale. **Time Period Covered:** latest 30 years.

LOGS: PLY

Source: *Timber Mart-South.* **Price Frequency:** quarterly. **Effective Market(s):** 11 domestic markets. **Units of Measure:** Dollars per 1000 board feet. **Type of Price:** delivered. **Time Period Covered:** latest 2 quarters.

LOGS: ROUND, M.L.H., INDONESIAN

Source: *Prices of Selected Asia/Pacific Products.* **Price Frequency:** monthly. **Effective Market(s):** Hong Kong. **Units of Measure:** Hong Kong dollars per cubic foot. **Type of Price:** high, low. **Time Period Covered:** latest month.

LOGS: ROUND, M.L.H., SABAH

Source: *Prices of Selected Asia/Pacific Products.* **Price Frequency:** monthly. **Effective Market(s):** Hong Kong. **Units of Measure:** Hong Kong dollars per cubic foot. **Type of Price:** high, low. **Time Period Covered:** latest month.

LOGS: ROUND, M.L.H., SARAWAK

Source: *Prices of Selected Asia/Pacific Products.* **Price Frequency:** monthly. **Effective Market(s):** Hong Kong. **Units of Measure:** Hong Kong dollars per cubic foot. **Type of Price:** high, low. **Time Period Covered:** latest month.

LOGS: SAPELLI, HIGH QUALITY, LOYAL AND MARCHAND

Source: *Monthly Commodity Price Bulletin Supplement.* **Price Frequency:** monthly, quarterly, annually. **Effective Market(s):** Cameroon. **Units of Measure:** Dollars per cubic meter. **Time Period Covered:** latest 20 years.

LOGS: SAPELLI, HIGH QUALITY, WEST AFRICAN

Source: *Commodity Trade and Price Trends.* **Price Frequency:** annually. **Effective Market(s):** Cameroon. **Units of Measure:** Dollars per cubic meter, 1980 constant dollars per cubic meter. **Time Period Covered:** latest 32 years.

LOGS: SPRUCE, BARKED, WEST GERMAN

Source: *FAO Quarterly Bulletin of Statistics.* **Price Frequency:** monthly, annually. **Effective Market(s):** West Germany. **Units of Measure:** West German marks per cubic meter. **Type of Price:** producer. **Time Period Covered:** latest 3 years.

LOGS: SPRUCE/FIR

Source: *Timber Bulletin.* **Price Frequency:** monthly, annually. **Effective Market(s):** Austria. **Units of Measure:** Austrian schillings per cubic meter. **Type of Price:** ceiling, floor. **Time Period Covered:** monthly latest 2 years, annually latest 6 years.

Source: *Timber Bulletin.* **Price Frequency:** monthly, annually. **Effective Market(s):** West Germany. **Units of Measure:** West German marks cubic meter. **Time Period Covered:** monthly latest 2 years, annually latest 6 years.

LOGS: SQ FIRST CLASS, SABAH

Source: *Prices of Selected Asia/Pacific Products.* **Price Frequency:** monthly. **Effective Market(s):** Tokyo. **Units of Measure:** 1000 Japanese yen per Brerton. **Type of Price:** high, low. **Time Period Covered:** latest month.

LOGS: TROPICAL

Source: *Monthly Commodity Price Bulletin.* **Price Frequency:** monthly, annually. **Effective Market(s):** United Kingdom. **Units of Measure:** index. **Type of Price:** wholesale price index. **Time Period Covered:** latest 5 years.

Source: *Monthly Commodity Price Bulletin Supplement.* **Price Frequency:** monthly, quarterly, annually. **Effective Market(s):** United Kingdom. **Units of Measure:** Dollars per cubic meter. **Type of Price:** wholesale. **Time Period Covered:** latest 20 years.

LOGS: TROPICAL, LAUAN VENEER SHEETS

Source: *Timber Bulletin.* **Price Frequency:** monthly, annually. **Effective Market(s):** Japan. **Units of Measure:** Japanese yen per cubic meter. **Time Period Covered:** monthly latest 2 years, annually latest 6 years.

LOGS: TROPICAL, QUALTIY L AND M, SAMBA

Source: *FAO Quarterly Bulletin of Statistics.* **Price Frequency:** monthly, annually. **Effective Market(s):** Ivory Coast. **Units of Measure:** CFA francs per cubic meter, dollars per metric ton. **Time Period Covered:** latest 3 years.

LOGS: TROPICAL, SECOND GROWTH, SERAYA

Source: *FAO Quarterly Bulletin of Statistics.* **Price Frequency:** monthly, annually. **Effective Market(s):** Malaysia. **Units of Measure:** Dollars per cubic meter, dollars per metric ton. **Time Period Covered:** latest 3 years.

LOGS: TROPICAL, VENEER, LAUAN, PHILIPPINES

Source: *FAO Quarterly Bulletin of Statistics.* **Price Frequency:** monthly, annually. **Effective Market(s):** Japan. **Units of Measure:** Japanese yen per cubic meter. **Time Period Covered:** latest 3 years.

LUBRICANTS

Source: *Modern Plastics.* **Price Frequency:** quarterly in February, May, August, November. **Units of Measure:** Dollars per lb. **Type of Price:** list. **Time Period Covered:** latest 4 quarters.

LUBRICATION: AUTOMOBILE

Source: *Agricultural Prices.* **Price Frequency:** semiannually. **Effective Market(s):** United States. **Units of Measure:** Dollars each time. **Type of Price:** paid by farmer. **Time Period Covered:** latest year.

Source: *Agricultural Prices Annual Summary.* **Price Frequency:** semiannually. **Effective Market(s):** United States. **Units of Measure:** Dollars each. **Type of Price:** average paid by farmer. **Time Period Covered:** latest 6 years.

LUCERNE: HOME-GROWN

Source: *Farmers Weekly.* **Price Frequency:** weekly, seasonally. **Effective Market(s):** Great Britain. **Units of Measure:** British pounds per tonne. **Type of Price:** spot. **Time Period Covered:** latest week.

LUCERNE: IMPORTED

Source: *Farmers Weekly.* **Price Frequency:** weekly, seasonally. **Effective Market(s):** Great Britain. **Units of Measure:** British pounds per tonne. **Type of Price:** spot. **Time Period Covered:** latest week.

LUMBER

see also Logs, Pulpwood, Sawtimber, Wood, and specific types of wood, e.g., Douglas Fir.

LUMBER: BOARDS, DRESSED

Source: *Agricultural Prices.* **Price Frequency:** quarterly. **Effective Market(s):** United States. **Units of Measure:** Dollars per 1000 board feet. **Type of Price:** paid by farmer. **Time Period Covered:** latest 2 quarters, year ago.

Source: *Agricultural Prices Annual Summary.* **Price Frequency:** bimonthly. **Effective Market(s):** United States. **Units of Measure:** Dollars per 1000 board feet. **Type of Price:** average paid by farmer. **Time Period Covered:** latest 6 years.

LUMBER: BOARDS, ROUGH

Source: *Agricultural Prices.* **Price Frequency:** quarterly. **Effective Market(s):** United States. **Units of Measure:** Dollars per 1000 board feet. **Type of Price:** paid by farmer. **Time Period Covered:** latest 2 quarters, year ago.

Source: *Agricultural Prices Annual Summary.* **Price Frequency:** bimonthly. **Effective Market(s):** United States. **Units of Measure:** Dollars per 1000 board feet. **Type of Price:** average paid by farmer. **Time Period Covered:** latest 6 years.

LUMBER: BOARDS, SOUTHERN PINE, PRESSURE TREATED

Source: *Random Lengths.* **Price Frequency:** weekly. **Units of Measure:** Dollars per 1000 board feet. **Type of Price:** plant price to wholesaler. **Time Period Covered:** latest week.

LUMBER: DOUGLAS FIR

Source: *Commodity Year Book.* **Price Frequency:** annually. **Units of Measure:** Dollars per 1000 board feet. **Time Period Covered:** latest 8 years.

LUMBER: DOUGLAS FIR, GREEN

Source: *Purchasing.* **Price Frequency:** monthly. **Units of Measure:** Dollars per 1000 board feet. **Type of Price:** transaction. **Time Period Covered:** latest day, month ago, 6 months ago, year ago.

Source: *Random Lengths.* **Price Frequency:** weekly. **Effective Market(s):** varies. **Units of Measure:** Dollars per 1000 board feet. **Type of Price:** mill price to wholesaler. **Time Period Covered:** latest week.

LUMBER: DOUGLAS FIR, SOFTWOOD

Source: *Commodity Year Book.* **Price Frequency:** monthly, annually. **Units of Measure:** index. **Type of Price:** price index. **Time Period Covered:** latest 11 years.

LUMBER: FIR AND LARCH, KILN DRIED

Source: *Random Lengths.* **Price Frequency:** weekly. **Units of Measure:** Dollars per 1000 board feet. **Type of Price:** mill price to wholesaler. **Time Period Covered:** latest week.

LUMBER: FIR, STANDARD AND BETTER

Source: *Agricultural Prices.* **Price Frequency:** quarterly. **Effective Market(s):** United States. **Units of Measure:** Dollars per 1000 board feet. **Type of Price:** paid by farmer. **Time Period Covered:** latest 2 quarters, year ago.

Source: *Agricultural Prices Annual Summary.* **Price Frequency:** bimonthly. **Effective Market(s):** United States. **Units of Measure:** Dollars per 1000 board feet. **Type of Price:** average paid by farmer. **Time Period Covered:** latest 6 years.

LUMBER: FRAMING, DOUGLAS FIR, GREEN

Source: *Random Lengths.* **Price Frequency:** weekly. **Effective Market(s):** varies. **Units of Measure:** Dollars per 1000 board feet. **Type of Price:** price to wholesaler. **Time Period Covered:** latest week.

LUMBER: FRAMING, DOUGLAS FIR, KILN DRIED

Source: *Random Lengths.* **Price Frequency:** weekly. **Effective Market(s):** varies. **Units of Measure:** Dollars per 1000 board feet. **Type of Price:** price to wholesaler. **Time Period Covered:** latest week.

LUMBER: FRAMING, FIR AND LARCH, KILN DRIED

Source: *Random Lengths.* **Price Frequency:** weekly. **Effective Market(s):** varies. **Units of Measure:** Dollars per 1000 board feet. **Type of Price:** price to wholesaler. **Time Period Covered:** latest week.

LUMBER: FRAMING, FIR AND LARCH, GREEN

Source: *Random Lengths.* **Price Frequency:** weekly. **Effective Market(s):** varies. **Units of Measure:** Dollars per 1000 board feet. **Type of Price:** price to wholesaler. **Time Period Covered:** latest week.

LUMBER: FRAMING, HEMLOCK-FIR, COAST, KILN DRIED

Source: *Random Lengths.* **Price Frequency:** weekly. **Units of Measure:** Dollars per 1000 board feet. **Type of Price:** price to wholesaler. **Time Period Covered:** latest week.

LUMBER: FRAMING, HEMLOCK-FIR, GREEN

Source: *Random Lengths.* **Price Frequency:** weekly. **Effective Market(s):** varies. **Units of Measure:** Dollars per 1000 board feet. **Type of Price:** price to wholesaler. **Time Period Covered:** latest week.

LUMBER: FRAMING, HEMLOCK-FIR, INLAND, KILN DRIED

Source: *Random Lengths.* **Price Frequency:** weekly. **Effective Market(s):** varies. **Units of Measure:** Dollars per 1000 board feet. **Type of Price:** price to wholesaler. **Time Period Covered:** latest week.

LUMBER: FRAMING, PONDEROSA PINE, KILN DRIED

Source: *Random Lengths.* **Price Frequency:** weekly. **Effective Market(s):** varies. **Units of Measure:** Dollars per 1000 board feet. **Type of Price:** price to wholesaler. **Time Period Covered:** latest week.

LUMBER: FRAMING, RED CEDAR, WESTERN, GREEN

Source: *Random Lengths.* **Price Frequency:** weekly. **Effective Market(s):** varies. **Units of Measure:** Dollars per 1000 board feet. **Type of Price:** price to wholesaler. **Time Period Covered:** latest week.

LUMBER: FRAMING, SOUTHERN PINE, KILN DRIED

Source: *Random Lengths.* **Price Frequency:** weekly. **Effective Market(s):** varies. **Units of Measure:** Dollars per 1000 board feet. **Type of Price:** price to wholesaler. **Time Period Covered:** latest week.

LUMBER: FRAMING, SOUTHERN PINE, PRESSURE TREATED

Source: *Random Lengths.* **Price Frequency:** weekly. **Units of Measure:** Dollars per 1000 board feet. **Type of Price:** plant price to wholesaler. **Time Period Covered:** latest week.

LUMBER: FRAMING, SPRUCE-LODGEPOLE, KILN DRIED

Source: *Random Lengths.* **Price Frequency:** weekly. **Effective Market(s):** varies. **Units of Measure:** Dollars per 1000 board feet. **Type of Price:** price to wholesaler. **Time Period Covered:** latest week.

LUMBER: FRAMING, SPRUCE-PINE-FIR, EASTERN, GREEN

Source: *Random Lengths.* **Price Frequency:** weekly. **Effective Market(s):** varies. **Units of Measure:** Dollars per 1000 board feet. **Type of Price:** price to wholesaler. **Time Period Covered:** latest week.

LUMBER: FRAMING, SPRUCE-PINE-FIR, EASTERN, KILN DRIED

Source: *Random Lengths.* **Price Frequency:** weekly. **Effective Market(s):** varies. **Units of Measure:** Dollars per 1000 board feet. **Type of Price:** price to wholesaler. **Time Period Covered:** latest week.

LUMBER: FRAMING, SPRUCE-PINE-FIR, WESTERN, KILN DRIED

Source: *Random Lengths.* **Price Frequency:** weekly. **Effective Market(s):** varies. **Units of Measure:** Dollars per 1000 board feet. **Type of Price:** price to wholesaler. **Time Period Covered:** latest week.

LUMBER: FUTURES

Source: *Asian Wall Street Journal.* **Price Frequency:** daily. **Effective Market(s):** Chicago. **Units of Measure:** Dollars per 1000 board feet. **Type of Price:** futures. **Time Period Covered:** latest day.

Source: *Barron's.* **Price Frequency:** weekly. **Effective Market(s):** Chicago. **Units of Measure:** Dollars per 1000 board feet. **Type of Price:** futures. **Time Period Covered:** latest week.

Source: *Investor's Daily.* **Price Frequency:** daily. **Effective Market(s):** Chicago. **Units of Measure:** Dollars per 1000 board feet. **Type of Price:** futures. **Time Period Covered:** latest day.

Source: *Los Angeles Times.* **Price Frequency:** daily. **Effective Market(s):** Chicago. **Units of Measure:** Dollars per 1000 board feet. **Type of Price:** futures. **Time Period Covered:** latest day.

Source: *Wall Street Journal.* **Price Frequency:** daily. **Effective Market(s):** Chicago. **Units of Measure:** Dollars per 1000 board feet. **Type of Price:** futures. **Time Period Covered:** next 5 contract months.

LUMBER: FUTURES, MAY

Source: *Commodity Year Book.* **Price Frequency:** monthly, annually. **Effective Market(s):** Chicago. **Units of Measure:** Dollars per 1000 board feet. **Type of Price:** futures. **Time Period Covered:** latest 8 years.

LUMBER: HARDWOOD, EASTERN

Source: *Commodity Year Book.* **Price Frequency:** annually. **Units of Measure:** Dollars per 1000 board feet. **Time Period Covered:** latest 8 years.

LUMBER: HEMLOCK, SAWN, CANADIAN

Source: *Japan Economic Journal.* **Price Frequency:** weekly. **Effective Market(s):** Japan. **Units of Measure:** Japanese yen per cubic meter. **Type of Price:** wholesale. **Time Period Covered:** latest 2 weeks.

LUMBER: HEMLOCK, WESTERN

Source: *Commodity Year Book.* **Price Frequency:** annually. **Units of Measure:** Dollars per 1000 board feet. **Time Period Covered:** latest 8 years.

LUMBER: HEMLOCK-FIR, COAST, KILN DRIED

Source: *Random Lengths.* **Price Frequency:** weekly. **Units of Measure:** Dollars per 1000 board feet. **Type of Price:** mill price to wholesaler. **Time Period Covered:** latest week.

LUMBER: HEMLOCK-FIR, INLAND, KILN DRIED

Source: *Random Lengths.* **Price Frequency:** weekly. **Units of Measure:** Dollars per 1000 board feet. **Type of Price:** mill price to wholesaler. **Time Period Covered:** latest week.

LUMBER: HEMLOCK-FIR, INLAND, STANDARD AND BETTER

Source: *Purchasing.* **Price Frequency:** monthly. **Units of Measure:** Dollars per 1000 board feet. **Type of Price:** transaction. **Time Period Covered:** latest day, month ago, 6 months ago, year ago.

LUMBER: MAPLE

Source: *Commodity Year Boook.* **Price Frequency:** annually. **Units of Measure:** Dollars per 1000 board feet. **Time Period Covered:** latest 8 years.

LUMBER: PINE, STANDARD AND BETTER

Source: *Agricultural Prices.* **Price Frequency:** quarterly. **Effective Market(s):** United States. **Units of Measure:** Dollars per 1000 board feet. **Type of Price:** paid by farmer. **Time Period Covered:** latest 2 quarters, year ago.

Source: *Agricultural Prices Annual Summary.* **Price Frequency:** bimonthly. **Effective Market(s):** United States. **Units of Measure:** Dollars per 1000 board feet. **Type of Price:** average paid by farmer. **Time Period Covered:** latest 6 years.

LUMBER: PONDEROSA PINE

Source: *Commodity Year Book.* **Price Frequency:** annually. **Units of Measure:** Dollars per 1000 board feet. **Time Period Covered:** latest 8 years.

Source: *Purchasing.* **Price Frequency:** quarterly in January, April, July, October issues. **Units of Measure:** Dollars per 1000 board feet. **Type of Price:** transaction. **Time Period Covered:** latest 5 quarters.

LUMBER: ROUGH SOFTWOOD

Source: *Commodity Year Book.* **Price Frequency:** monthly, annually. **Units of Measure:** index. **Type of Price:** price index. **Time Period Covered:** latest 6 years.

LUMBER: SOUTHERN PINE

Source: *Commodity Year Book.* **Price Frequency:** annually. **Units of Measure:** Dollars per 1000 board feet. **Time Period Covered:** latest 8 years.

LUMBER: SOUTHERN PINE, KILN DRIED

Source: *Random Lengths.* **Price Frequency:** weekly. **Effective Market(s):** varies. **Units of Measure:** Dollars per 1000 board feet. **Type of Price:** mill price to wholesaler. **Time Period Covered:** latest week.

LUMBER: SPRUCE-PINE-FIR, EASTERN, GREEN

Source: *Random Lengths.* **Price Frequency:** weekly. **Effective Market(s):** varies. **Units of Measure:** Dollars per 1000 board feet. **Type of Price:** mill price to wholesaler. **Time Period Covered:** latest week.

LUMBER: SPRUCE-PINE-FIR, EASTERN, KILN DRIED

Source: *Random Lengths.* **Price Frequency:** weekly. **Effective Market(s):** Boston, Great Lakes. **Units of Measure:** Dollars per 1000 board feet. **Type of Price:** mill price to wholesaler. **Time Period Covered:** latest week.

LUMBER: SPRUCE-PINE-FIR, WESTERN, KILN DRIED

Source: *Random Lengths.* **Price Frequency:** weekly. **Effective Market(s):** varies. **Units of Measure:** Dollars per 1000 board feet. **Type of Price:** mill price to wholesaler. **Time Period Covered:** latest week.

LUMBER: SQUARES AND TIMBERS, SOUTHERN PINE, PRESSURE TREATED

Source: *Random Lengths.* **Price Frequency:** weekly. **Units of Measure:** Dollars per 1000 board feet. **Type of Price:** plant price to wholesaler. **Time Period Covered:** latest week.

2,4-LUTIDINE

Source: *Chemical Marketing Reporter.* **Price Frequency:** weekly. **Effective Market(s):** New York. **Units of Measure:** Dollars per kilo. **Type of Price:** spot. **Time Period Covered:** latest week.

LYCOPODIUM

Source: *Chemical Marketing Reporter.* **Price Frequency:** weekly. **Effective Market(s):** New York. **Units of Measure:** Dollars per lb. **Type of Price:** spot. **Time Period Covered:** latest week.

L-LYSINE MONOHYDROCHLORIDE: FEED GRADE

Source: *Chemical Marketing Reporter.* **Price Frequency:** weekly. **Effective Market(s):** New York. **Units of Measure:** Dollars per lb. **Type of Price:** spot. **Time Period Covered:** latest week.

1-LYSINE MONOHYDROCHLORIDE: FEED GRADE

Source: *Journal of Commerce and Commercial.* **Price Frequency:** weekly in Friday issue. **Units of Measure:** Dollars per lb. **Type of Price:** spot. **Time Period Covered:** latest week.

MABECHI (FISH)

see Tuna: Bigeye.

MACADAMIA NUTS

Source: *Agricultural Prices Annual Summary.* **Price Frequency:** annually. **Effective Market(s):** California, Hawaii. **Units of Measure:** Dollars per lb. **Type of Price:** average received by farmer. **Time Period Covered:** latest 6 years.

MACADAMIA NUTS: IN SHELL

Source: *Fruit and Tree Nuts Situation and Outlook Yearbook.* **Price Frequency:** annually. **Effective Market(s):** Hawaii. **Units of Measure:** cents per lb. **Type of Price:** grower. **Time Period Covered:** latest 20 years.

MACE: NO. 1, WEST INDIAN

Source: *Fruit and Tropical Products.* **Price Frequency:** monthly, seasonally. **Effective Market(s):** London. **Units of Measure:** British pounds per tonne. **Type of Price:** month end. **Time Period Covered:** latest 2 years.

MACE: NO. 2, SIAUW SIFTINGS

Source: *Chemical Marketing Reporter.* **Price Frequency:** weekly. **Effective Market(s):** New York. **Units of Measure:** Dollars per lb. **Type of Price:** spot. **Time Period Covered:** latest week.

Source: *U. S. Spice Trade.* **Price Frequency:** monthly, annually. **Effective Market(s):** New York. **Units of Measure:** Dollars per lb. **Type of Price:** spot. **Time Period Covered:** latest 10 years.

MACE: SIFTINGS, EAST INDIAN

Source: *Chemical Marketing Reporter.* **Price Frequency:** weekly. **Effective Market(s):** New York. **Units of Measure:** Dollars per lb. **Type of Price:** spot. **Time Period Covered:** latest week.

Source: *Prices of Selected Asia/Pacific Products.* **Price Frequency:** monthly. **Effective Market(s):** New York. **Units of Measure:** Dollars per lb. **Type of Price:** spot high, spot low. **Time Period Covered:** latest month.

MACKEREL: BLUE, WHOLE, FRESH

Source: *Seafood Price-Current.* **Price Frequency:** semiweekly. **Effective Market(s):** West Coast. **Units of Measure:** Dollars per lb. **Type of Price:** sale by first receiver. **Time Period Covered:** latest day.

MACKEREL: KING, FILLETS, FRESH, HAWAIIAN

Source: *Seafood Price-Current.* **Price Frequency:** semiweekly. **Effective Market(s):** Hawaii. **Units of Measure:** Dollars per lb. **Type of Price:** sale by first receiver. **Time Period Covered:** latest day.

MACKEREL: KING, WHOLE, FRESH

Source: *Seafood Price-Current.* **Price Frequency:** semiweekly. **Effective Market(s):** Boston, Mid-Atlantic, New Bedford (MA), Portland (ME). **Units of Measure:** Dollars per lb. **Type of Price:** sale by first receiver, auction price. **Time Period Covered:** latest day.

MACKEREL: KING, WHOLE, FRESH, HAWAIIAN

Source: *Seafood Price-Current.* **Price Frequency:** semiweekly. **Effective Market(s):** Hawaii. **Units of Measure:** Dollars per lb. **Type of Price:** sale by first receiver. **Time Period Covered:** latest day.

MACKEREL: WHOLE, FRESH

Source: *Seafood Price-Current.* **Price Frequency:** semiweekly. **Effective Market(s):** Boston, Mid-Atlantic, New Bedford (MA), Portland (ME). **Units of Measure:** Dollars per lb. **Type of Price:** sale by first receiver, auction price. **Time Period Covered:** latest day.

MACKEREL: WHOLE, FRESH, SPANISH

Source: *Seafood Price-Current.* **Price Frequency:** semiweekly. **Effective Market(s):** West Coast. **Units of Measure:** Dollars per lb. **Type of Price:** sale by first receiver. **Time Period Covered:** latest day.

MAGAZINE PAPER

Source: *Fibre Market News.* **Price Frequency:** weekly. **Effective Market(s):** 9 domestic markets. **Units of Measure:** Dollars per net ton. **Type of Price:** grader & packer buying price. **Time Period Covered:** latest week.

MAGNESIA: NATURAL, TECHNICAL, HEAVY, 85%, 150 MESH

Source: *Chemical Marketing Reporter.* **Price Frequency:** weekly. **Effective Market(s):** Nevada. **Units of Measure:** Dollars per ton. **Type of Price:** spot. **Time Period Covered:** latest week.

MAGNESIA: NATURAL, TECHNICAL, HEAVY, 90%, 325 MESH

Source: *Chemical Marketing Reporter.* **Price Frequency:** weekly. **Effective Market(s):** New York. **Units of Measure:** Dollars per ton. **Type of Price:** spot. **Time Period Covered:** latest week.

MAGNESIA: SYNTHETIC, TECHNICAL, CHEMICAL GRADE

Source: *Chemical Marketing Reporter.* **Price Frequency:** weekly. **Effective Market(s):** New York. **Units of Measure:** Dollars per ton. **Type of Price:** spot. **Time Period Covered:** latest week.

MAGNESIA: SYNTHETIC, TECHNICAL, CHEMICAL GRADE, DEADBURNED

Source: *Chemical Marketing Reporter.* **Price Frequency:** weekly. **Effective Market(s):** New York. **Units of Measure:** Dollars per ton. **Type of Price:** spot. **Time Period Covered:** latest week.

MAGNESIA: TECHNICAL, LIGHT, NEOPRENE GRADE

Source: *Chemical Marketing Reporter.* **Price Frequency:** weekly. **Effective Market(s):** New York. **Units of Measure:** Dollars per lb. **Type of Price:** spot. **Time Period Covered:** latest week.

MAGNESITE: CALCINED, AGRICULTURAL

Source: *Industrial Minerals.* **Price Frequency:** monthly. **Effective Market(s):** main European port. **Units of Measure:** British pounds per metric tonne. **Type of Price:** producer & dealer. **Time Period Covered:** latest month.

MAGNESITE: CALCINED, NATURAL, INDUSTRIAL GRADE

Source: *Industrial Minerals.* **Price Frequency:** monthly. **Effective Market(s):** main European port. **Units of Measure:** British pounds per metric tonne. **Type of Price:** producer & dealer. **Time Period Covered:** latest month.

MAGNESITE: CALCINED, SEA WATER, INDUSTRIAL GRADE

Source: *Industrial Minerals.* **Price Frequency:** monthly. **Effective Market(s):** main European port. **Units of Measure:** British pounds per metric tonne. **Type of Price:** producer & dealer. **Time Period Covered:** latest month.

MAGNESITE: CRUDE LUMP, GREEK

Source: *Industrial Minerals.* **Price Frequency:** monthly . **Effective Market(s):** main European port. **Units of Measure:** British pounds per metric tonne. **Type of Price:** producer & dealer. **Time Period Covered:** latest month.

MAGNESITE: DEADBURNED, BRICKMAKING

Source: *Industrial Minerals.* **Price Frequency:** monthly. **Effective Market(s):** United Kingdom. **Units of Measure:** British pounds per metric tonne. **Type of Price:** producer & dealer. **Time Period Covered:** latest month.

MAGNESITE: DEADBURNED, MAINTENANCE

Source: *Industrial Minerals.* **Price Frequency:** monthly. **Effective Market(s):** United Kingdom. **Units of Measure:** British pounds per metric tonne. **Type of Price:** producer & dealer. **Time Period Covered:** latest month.

MAGNESIUM

see also Ferromanganese.

MAGNESIUM ALLOYS

Source: *American Metal Market.* **Price Frequency:** daily. **Units of Measure:** cents per lb. **Type of Price:** contract. **Time Period Covered:** latest day.

MAGNESIUM ALLOYS: DIE CASTING, 99.8%

Source: *Chemical Marketing Reporter.* **Price Frequency:** weekly. **Effective Market(s):** New York. **Units of Measure:** Dollars per lb. **Type of Price:** spot. **Time Period Covered:** latest week.

MAGNESIUM BROMIDE: HEXAHYDRATE

Source: *Chemical Marketing Reporter.* **Price Frequency:** weekly. **Effective Market(s):** New York. **Units of Measure:** Dollars per lb. **Type of Price:** spot. **Time Period Covered:** latest week.

MAGNESIUM CARBONATE: HEAVY, USP

Source: *Chemical Marketing Reporter.* **Price Frequency:** weekly. **Effective Market(s):** New York. **Units of Measure:** Dollars per lb. **Type of Price:** spot. **Time Period Covered:** latest week.

MAGNESIUM CARBONATE: LIGHT, TECHNICAL

Source: *Chemical Marketing Reporter.* **Price Frequency:** weekly. **Effective Market(s):** New York. **Units of Measure:** Dollars per lb. **Type of Price:** spot. **Time Period Covered:** latest week.

MAGNESIUM CARBONATE: LIGHT, USP

Source: *Chemical Marketing Reporter.* **Price Frequency:** weekly. **Effective Market(s):** New York. **Units of Measure:** Dollars per lb. **Type of Price:** spot. **Time Period Covered:** latest week.

MAGNESIUM CARBONATE: TECHNICAL

Source: *Journal of Commerce and Commercial.* **Price Frequency:** weekly in Friday issue. **Units of Measure:** Dollars per lb. **Type of Price:** spot. **Time Period Covered:** latest week.

MAGNESIUM CHLORIDE: ANHYDROUS, 92%, FLAKE OR PEBBLE

Source: *Chemical Marketing Reporter.* **Price Frequency:** weekly. **Effective Market(s):** New York. **Units of Measure:** Dollars per lb. **Type of Price:** spot. **Time Period Covered:** latest week.

MAGNESIUM CHLORIDE: HYDROUS, 99%, FLAKE

Source: *Chemical Marketing Reporter.* **Price Frequency:** weekly. **Effective Market(s):** New York. **Units of Measure:** Dollars per lb. **Type of Price:** spot. **Time Period Covered:** latest week.

MAGNESIUM FERROSILICON

Source: *American Metal Market.* **Price Frequency:** weekly. **Units of Measure:** Dollars per lb. of material. **Type of Price:** producer. **Time Period Covered:** latest week.

MAGNESIUM GLUCONATE

Source: *Chemical Marketing Reporter.* **Price Frequency:** weekly. **Effective Market(s):** East. **Units of Measure:** Dollars per lb. **Type of Price:** spot. **Time Period Covered:** latest week.

MAGNESIUM GRINDING SLAB

Source: *American Metal Market.* **Price Frequency:** daily. **Units of Measure:** cents per lb. **Type of Price:** contract. **Time Period Covered:** latest day.

Source: *E&MJ.* **Price Frequency:** monthly. **Units of Measure:** cents per lb. **Time Period Covered:** latest month.

MAGNESIUM HYDROXIDE: POWDERED, NF

Source: *Chemical Marketing Reporter.* **Price Frequency:** weekly. **Effective Market(s):** New York. **Units of Measure:** Dollars per lb. **Type of Price:** spot. **Time Period Covered:** latest week.

MAGNESIUM INGOTS

Source: *Commodity Year Book.* **Price Frequency:** annually. **Effective Market(s):** Valasco (TX). **Units of Measure:** Dollars per lb. **Time Period Covered:** latest 12 years.

Source: *Purchasing.* **Price Frequency:** quarterly in January, April, July, October issues. **Units of Measure:** cents per lb. **Type of Price:** transaction. **Time Period Covered:** latest 5 quarters.

MAGNESIUM INGOTS: 99.8%

Source: *American Metal Market.* **Price Frequency:** daily. **Units of Measure:** cents per lb. **Type of Price:** contract. **Time Period Covered:** latest day.

Source: *Chemical Marketing Reporter.* **Price Frequency:** weekly. **Effective Market(s):** Freeport (TX). **Units of Measure:** Dollars per lb. **Type of Price:** spot. **Time Period Covered:** latest week.

Source: *E&MJ.* **Price Frequency:** monthly. **Units of Measure:** cents per lb. **Time Period Covered:** latest month.

Source: *Iron Age.* **Price Frequency:** monthly. **Effective Market(s):** London. **Units of Measure:** cents per lb. **Time Period Covered:** latest month.

Source: *Northern Miner.* **Price Frequency:** daily. **Effective Market(s):** United States. **Units of Measure:** Dollars per lb. **Type of Price:** producer . **Time Period Covered:** latest day.

MAGNESIUM LAURYL SULFATE

Source: *Chemical Marketing Reporter.* **Price Frequency:** weekly. **Effective Market(s):** New York. **Units of Measure:** Dollars per lb. **Type of Price:** spot. **Time Period Covered:** latest week.

MAGNESIUM NITRATE: TECHNICAL, FLAKE

Source: *Chemical Marketing Reporter.* **Price Frequency:** weekly. **Effective Market(s):** New York. **Units of Measure:** Dollars per lb. **Type of Price:** spot. **Time Period Covered:** latest week.

MAGNESIUM OXIDE: HEAVY, USP

Source: *Chemical Marketing Reporter.* **Price Frequency:** weekly. **Effective Market(s):** New York. **Units of Measure:** Dollars per lb. **Type of Price:** spot. **Time Period Covered:** latest week.

Source: *Journal of Commerce and Commercial.* **Price Frequency:** weekly in Friday issue. **Units of Measure:** Dollars per lb. **Type of Price:** spot. **Time Period Covered:** latest week.

MAGNESIUM OXIDE: LIGHT, USP

Source: *Chemical Marketing Reporter.* **Price Frequency:** weekly. **Effective Market(s):** New York. **Units of Measure:** Dollars per lb. **Type of Price:** spot. **Time Period Covered:** latest week.

Source: *Journal of Commerce and Commercial.* **Price Frequency:** weekly in Friday issue. **Units of Measure:** Dollars per lb. **Type of Price:** spot. **Time Period Covered:** latest week.

MAGNESIUM OXIDE: TECHNICAL

see Magnesia.

MAGNESIUM PHOSPHATE: TRIBASIC, TECHNICAL

Source: *Chemical Marketing Reporter.* **Price Frequency:** weekly. **Effective Market(s):** New York. **Units of Measure:** Dollars per lb. **Type of Price:** spot. **Time Period Covered:** latest week.

MAGNESIUM SILICATE

see Talc.

MAGNESIUM SILICOFLUORIDE

Source: *Chemical Marketing Reporter.* **Price Frequency:** weekly. **Effective Market(s):** New York. **Units of Measure:** Dollars per lb. **Type of Price:** spot. **Time Period Covered:** latest week.

MAGNESIUM STEARATE

Source: *Chemical Marketing Reporter.* **Price Frequency:** weekly. **Effective Market(s):** New York. **Units of Measure:** Dollars per lb. **Type of Price:** spot. **Time Period Covered:** latest week.

MAGNESIUM STICKS

Source: *American Metal Market.* **Price Frequency:** daily. **Units of Measure:** cents per lb. **Type of Price:** contract. **Time Period Covered:** latest day.

Source: *E&MJ.* **Price Frequency:** monthly. **Units of Measure:** cents per lb. **Time Period Covered:** latest month.

Source: *Iron Age.* **Price Frequency:** monthly. **Units of Measure:** Dollars per lb. **Type of Price:** consumer. **Time Period Covered:** latest month.

MAGNESIUM SULFATE

see also Epsom Salt.

MAGNESIUM SULFATE: 10% MAGNESIUM, TECHNICAL

Source: *Chemical Marketing Reporter.* **Price Frequency:** weekly. **Effective Market(s):** New York. **Units of Measure:** Dollars per lb. **Type of Price:** spot. **Time Period Covered:** latest week.

MAGNESIUM SULFATE: CRYSTALLINE, USP

Source: *Chemical Marketing Reporter.* **Price Frequency:** weekly. **Effective Market(s):** New York. **Units of Measure:** Dollars per lb. **Type of Price:** spot. **Time Period Covered:** latest week.

MAGNESIUM TRISILICATE: POWDERED, FIBER, USP

Source: *Chemical Marketing Reporter.* **Price Frequency:** weekly. **Effective Market(s):** New York. **Units of Measure:** Dollars per lb. **Type of Price:** spot. **Time Period Covered:** latest week.

MAGNESIUM TRISILICATE POWDER: MICRONIZED, USP

Source: *Chemical Marketing Reporter.* **Price Frequency:** weekly. **Effective Market(s):** New York. **Units of Measure:** Dollars per lb. **Type of Price:** spot. **Time Period Covered:** latest week.

MAGNESIUM TURNINGS

Source: *American Metal Market.* **Price Frequency:** daily. **Units of Measure:** cents per lb. **Type of Price:** contract. **Time Period Covered:** latest day.

MAHI-MAHI
see Dolphin (fish).

MAIZE
see also Corn.

Source: *Agra Europe.* **Price Frequency:** weekly. **Effective Market(s):** 9 European markets. **Units of Measure:** national currency per tonne. **Type of Price:** average. **Time Period Covered:** latest week.

Source: *Far Eastern Economic Review.* **Price Frequency:** weekly. **Effective Market(s):** Chicago. **Units of Measure:** cents per 56 lb. bushel. **Time Period Covered:** latest week, week ago, 3 months ago, year ago.

Source: *International Financial Statistics.* **Price Frequency:** monthly, quarterly, annually. **Effective Market(s):** Chicago, Gulf ports. **Units of Measure:** Dollars per bushel, index. **Type of Price:** market price, price index. **Time Period Covered:** latest 4 months, latest 5 quarters, latest 5 years.

Source: *International Financial Statistics Yearbook.* **Price Frequency:** annually. **Effective Market(s):** Chicago, Gulf ports. **Units of Measure:** Dollars per bushel. **Type of Price:** wholesale. **Time Period Covered:** latest 30 years.

MAIZE: ARGENTINE

Source: *Commodity Trade and Price Trends.* **Price Frequency:** annually. **Effective Market(s):** North Sea ports. **Units of Measure:** Dollars per metric ton, 1980 constant dollars per metric ton. **Time Period Covered:** latest 37 years.

Source: *International Wheat Council Market Report.* **Price Frequency:** weekly, seasonally. **Effective Market(s):** Rosario (Argentina). **Units of Measure:** Dollars per metric ton. **Type of Price:** export. **Time Period Covered:** latest 5 weeks.

Source: *International Wheat Council Market Report.* **Price Frequency:** weekly, seasonally. **Effective Market(s):** Rotterdam. **Units of Measure:** Dollars per metric ton. **Type of Price:** import. **Time Period Covered:** latest 5 weeks.

Source: *Monthly Commodity Price Bulletin.* **Price Frequency:** monthly, annually. **Effective Market(s):** North Sea ports. **Units of Measure:** Dollars per metric ton. **Time Period Covered:** latest 5 years.

Source: *Monthly Commodity Price Bulletin Supplement.* **Price Frequency:** monthly, quarterly, annually. **Effective Market(s):** North Sea ports. **Units of Measure:** Dollars per tonne. **Time Period Covered:** latest 20 years.

Source: *UNCTAD Commodity Yeabook.* **Price Frequency:** annually. **Effective Market(s):** North Sea ports. **Units of Measure:** Dollars per metric ton. **Type of Price:** free market. **Time Period Covered:** latest 12 years.

MAIZE: EUROPEAN COMMUNITY

Source: *International Wheat Council Market Report.* **Price Frequency:** weekly, seasonally. **Effective Market(s):** European Community. **Units of Measure:** Dollars per metric ton. **Type of Price:** export. **Time Period Covered:** latest 5 weeks.

MAIZE: FUTURES

Source: *Far Eastern Economic Review.* **Price Frequency:** weekly. **Effective Market(s):** Chicago. **Units of Measure:** cents per 56 lb. bushel. **Type of Price:** futures. **Time Period Covered:** latest week.

Source: *Financial Times.* **Price Frequency:** daily. **Effective Market(s):** Chicago. **Units of Measure:** cents per 56 lb. bushel. **Type of Price:** futures. **Time Period Covered:** latest 2 days.

Source: *International Wheat Council Market Report.* **Price Frequency:** weekly. **Effective Market(s):** Chicago. **Units of Measure:** Dollars per bushel. **Type of Price:** futures. **Time Period Covered:** latest month.

MAIZE: NO. 2, YELLOW

Source: *Commodity Trade and Price Trends.* **Price Frequency:** annually. **Effective Market(s):** Gulf ports. **Units of Measure:** Dollars per metric ton, 1980 constant dollars per metric ton. **Time Period Covered:** latest 37 years.

Source: *FAO Quarterly Bulletin of Statistics.* **Price Frequency:** monthly, annually. **Effective Market(s):** Gulf. **Units of Measure:** Dollars per 56 lbs., dollars per metric ton. **Time Period Covered:** latest 3 years.

Source: *International Wheat Council Market Report.* **Price Frequency:** monthly. **Effective Market(s):** Central Illinois. **Units of Measure:** Dollars per bushel, dollars per ton. **Type of Price:** cash. **Time Period Covered:** latest month.

MAIZE: NO. 3, YELLOW

Source: *International Wheat Council Market Report.* **Price Frequency:** weekly, seasonally. **Effective Market(s):** Gulf. **Units of Measure:** Dollars per metric ton. **Type of Price:** export. **Time Period Covered:** latest 5 weeks.

Source: *Monthly Commodity Price Bulletin.* **Price Frequency:** monthly, annually. **Effective Market(s):** Rotterdam. **Units of Measure:** Dollars per metric ton. **Time Period Covered:** latest 5 years.

Source: *UNCTAD Commodity Yearbook.* **Price Frequency:** annually. **Effective Market(s):** Rotterdam. **Units of Measure:** Dollars per metric ton. **Type of Price:** free market. **Time Period Covered:** latest 12 years.

MAIZE: NO. 3, YELLOW, UNITED STATES

Source: *Financial Times.* **Price Frequency:** daily. **Effective Market(s):** London. **Units of Measure:** British pounds per tonne. **Type of Price:** free market. **Time Period Covered:** latest day.

Source: *International Wheat Council Market Report.* **Price Frequency:** weekly, seasonally. **Effective Market(s):** Rotterdam. **Units of Measure:** Dollars per metric ton. **Type of Price:** import. **Time Period Covered:** latest 5 weeks.

Source: *Monthly Commodity Price Bulletin Supplement.* **Price Frequency:** monthly, quarterly, annually. **Effective Market(s):** Rotterdam. **Units of Measure:** Dollars per tonne. **Time Period Covered:** latest 20 years.

MAIZE: SILO, THAI

Source: *Prices of Selected Asia/Pacific Products.* **Price Frequency:** monthly. **Effective Market(s):** Bangkok. **Units of Measure:** Thai baht per 100 kilograms. **Type of Price:** wholesale high, wholesale low. **Time Period Covered:** latest month.

MAIZE: THAI

Source: *International Financial Statistics.* **Price Frequency:** monthly, quarterly, annually. **Effective Market(s):** Thailand. **Units of Measure:** Dollars per bushel, index. **Type of Price:** market price, price index. **Time Period Covered:** latest 1 month, latest 4 quarters, latest 5 years.

Source: *International Financial Statistics Yearbook.* **Price Frequency:** annually. **Effective Market(s):** Thailand. **Units of Measure:** Dollars per bushel. **Type of Price:** wholesale. **Time Period Covered:** latest 30 years.

MAIZE: UNITED STATES

Source: *Prices of Selected Asia/Pacific Products.* **Price Frequency:** monthly. **Effective Market(s):** Tokyo. **Units of Measure:** Dollars per metric ton. **Type of Price:** high, low. **Time Period Covered:** latest month.

MAIZE: YELLOW, CHINESE

Source: *Prices of Selected Asia/Pacific Products.* **Price Frequency:** monthly. **Effective Market(s):** Hong Kong. **Units of Measure:** Hong Kong dollars per picul. **Type of Price:** wholesale high, wholesale low. **Time Period Covered:** latest month.

MAIZE: YELLOW, SOUTH AFRICAN

Source: *International Wheat Council Market Report.* **Price Frequency:** weekly, seasonally. **Effective Market(s):** East London. **Units of Measure:** Dollars per metric ton. **Type of Price:** export. **Time Period Covered:** latest 5 weeks.

MAIZE: YELLOW, THAI

Source: *Prices of Selected Asia/Pacific Products.* **Price Frequency:** monthly. **Effective Market(s):** Hong Kong. **Units of Measure:** Hong Kong dollars per picul. **Type of Price:** wholesale high, wholesale low. **Time Period Covered:** latest month.

MAIZE GLUTEN: HOME PRODUCED

Source: *Farmers Weekly.* **Price Frequency:** weekly, seasonally. **Effective Market(s):** Great Britain. **Units of Measure:** British pounds per tonne. **Type of Price:** spot. **Time Period Covered:** latest week.

MAIZE GLUTEN: IMPORTED

Source: *Farmers Weekly.* **Price Frequency:** weekly, seasonally. **Effective Market(s):** Great Britain. **Units of Measure:** British pounds per tonne. **Type of Price:** spot. **Time Period Covered:** latest week.

MAKO SHARK

see Shark: Mako.

MALATHION

Source: *Journal of Commerce and Commercial.* **Price Frequency:** weekly in Thursday issue. **Units of Measure:** Dollars per lb. **Type of Price:** spot. **Time Period Covered:** latest week.

MALATHION: EMULSIFIABLE CONCENTRATE

Source: *Agricultural Prices Annual Summary.* **Price Frequency:** semiannually. **Effective Market(s):** United States. **Units of Measure:** Dollars per 5 gallons. **Type of Price:** paid by farmer. **Time Period Covered:** latest 6 years.

MALATHION: TECHNICAL

Source: *Chemical Marketing Reporter.* **Price Frequency:** weekly. **Effective Market(s):** New York. **Units of Measure:** Dollars per lb. **Type of Price:** spot. **Time Period Covered:** latest week.

MALAYSIA DOLLARS

Source: *Asian Wall Street Journal.* **Price Frequency:** daily. **Effective Market(s):** Asia. **Units of Measure:** Malaysian dollars per United States dollars, per SDR. **Type of Price:** foreign exchange. **Time Period Covered:** latest 2 days.

Source: *Monthly Commodity Price Bulletin.* **Price Frequency:** monthly, annually. **Units of Measure:** Malaysian dollars per United States dollars. **Type of Price:** foreign exchange. **Time Period Covered:** latest 5 years.

Source: *Monthly Commodity Price Bulletin Supplement.* **Price Frequency:** monthly, quarterly, annually. **Effective Market(s):** developing countries. **Units of Measure:** Malaysian dollars per United States dollars. **Type of Price:** foreign exchange. **Time Period Covered:** latest 20 years.

MALAYSIA RINGGIT

Source: *Barron's.* **Price Frequency:** weekly. **Effective Market(s):** New York. **Units of Measure:** Malaysian ringgit per United States dollar. **Type of Price:** foreign exchange. **Time Period Covered:** latest 2 weeks.

Source: *New York Times.* **Price Frequency:** daily. **Effective Market(s):** United States. **Units of Measure:** Malaysian ringgit per United States dollar. **Type of Price:** foreign exchange. **Time Period Covered:** latest 2 days.

Source: *The Times.* **Price Frequency:** daily. **Effective Market(s):** London. **Units of Measure:** Malaysian ringgits per British pound. **Type of Price:** foreign exchange. **Time Period Covered:** latest day.

MALEIC ACID: CRYSTALLINE, POWDERED

Source: *Chemical Marketing Reporter.* **Price Frequency:** weekly. **Effective Market(s):** New York. **Units of Measure:** Dollars per ton. **Type of Price:** spot. **Time Period Covered:** latest week.

MALEIC ANHYDRIDE

Source: *Chemical Marketing Reporter.* **Price Frequency:** weekly. **Effective Market(s):** New York. **Units of Measure:** Dollars per lb. **Type of Price:** spot. **Time Period Covered:** latest week.

Source: *Journal of Commerce and Commercial.* **Price Frequency:** weekly in Wednesday issue. **Units of Measure:** Dollars per lb. **Type of Price:** spot. **Time Period Covered:** latest week.

MALIC ACID

Source: *Chemical Marketing Reporter.* **Price Frequency:** weekly. **Effective Market(s):** New York. **Units of Measure:** Dollars per lb. **Type of Price:** spot. **Time Period Covered:** latest week.

Source: *Journal of Commerce and Commercial.* **Price Frequency:** weekly in Friday issue. **Units of Measure:** Dollars per lb. **Type of Price:** spot. **Time Period Covered:** latest week.

MALT BEVERAGE

Source: *Illinois Beverage Journal.* **Price Frequency:** monthly. **Effective Market(s):** Illinois. **Units of Measure:** Dollars per case. **Type of Price:** wholesale by brand. **Time Period Covered:** latest month.

Source: *Rhode Island Beverage Journal.* **Price Frequency:** monthly. **Effective Market(s):** Rhode Island. **Units of Measure:** Dollars per unit. **Type of Price:** wholesale by brand. **Time Period Covered:** latest month.

MALT SPROUTS

Source: *Grain and Feed Market News.* **Price Frequency:** weekly, seasonally. **Effective Market(s):** Chicago/Milwaukee. **Units of Measure:** Dollars per ton. **Type of Price:** wholesale. **Time Period Covered:** latest week, week ago, year ago.

MALTA LIRA

Source: *Barron's.* **Price Frequency:** weekly. **Effective Market(s):** New York. **Units of Measure:** Maltan lira per United States dollar. **Type of Price:** foreign exchange. **Time Period Covered:** latest 2 weeks.

MANDARIN OIL: BRAZILIAN

Source: *Chemical Marketing Reporter.* **Price Frequency:** weekly. **Effective Market(s):** New York. **Units of Measure:** Dollars per lb. **Type of Price:** spot. **Time Period Covered:** latest week.

MANDARIN OIL: ITALIAN

Source: *Chemical Marketing Reporter.* **Price Frequency:** weekly. **Effective Market(s):** New York. **Units of Measure:** Dollars per lb. **Type of Price:** spot. **Time Period Covered:** latest week.

MANDARINES

Source: *New Zealand Farmer.* **Price Frequency:** weekly, seasonally. **Effective Market(s):** New Zealand. **Units of Measure:** New Zealand dollars per unit. **Time Period Covered:** latest week.

MANDELIC ACID

Source: *Chemical Marketing Reporter.* **Price Frequency:** weekly. **Effective Market(s):** New York. **Units of Measure:** Dollars per kilo. **Type of Price:** spot. **Time Period Covered:** latest week.

MANEB: WETTABLE POWDER, 80%

Source: *Agricultural Prices Annual Summary.* **Price Frequency:** semiannually. **Effective Market(s):** United States. **Units of Measure:** Dollars per lb. **Type of Price:** paid by farmer. **Time Period Covered:** latest 6 years.

MANGANESE: 99.7%

Source: *Journal of Commerce and Commercial.* **Price Frequency:** daily. **Effective Market(s):** Europe. **Units of Measure:** Dollars per ton. **Type of Price:** spot. **Time Period Covered:** latest day.

MANGANESE: BATTERY GRADE, UNGROUND

Source: *Industrial Minerals.* **Price Frequency:** monthly. **Effective Market(s):** main European port. **Units of Measure:** Dollars per metric tonne. **Type of Price:** producer & dealer. **Time Period Covered:** latest month.

MANGANESE: CHEMICAL GRADE

Source: *Industrial Minerals.* **Price Frequency:** monthly. **Effective Market(s):** main European port. **Units of Measure:** British pounds per metric tonne. **Type of Price:** producer & dealer. **Time Period Covered:** latest month.

MANGANESE: ELECTROLYTIC, 99.9%

Source: *E&MJ.* **Price Frequency:** monthly. **Units of Measure:** cents per lb. **Time Period Covered:** latest month.

MANGANESE: ELECTROLYTIC, NO. 1 CHIP

Source: *Chemical Marketing Reporter.* **Price Frequency:** weekly. **Effective Market(s):** New York. **Units of Measure:** Dollars per lb. **Type of Price:** spot. **Time Period Covered:** latest week.

MANGANESE: ELECTROLYTIC, NO. 1 GRADE

Source: *American Metal Market.* **Price Frequency:** weekly. **Units of Measure:** Dollars per lb. of material. **Type of Price:** producer. **Time Period Covered:** latest week.

MANGANESE: INDIAN

Source: *International Financial Statistics.* **Price Frequency:** quarterly, annually. **Effective Market(s):** United States ports. **Units of Measure:** Dollars per long ton, index. **Type of Price:** market price, price index. **Time Period Covered:** latest 2 quarters, latest 3 years.

Source: *International Financial Statistics Yearbook.* **Price Frequency:** annually. **Effective Market(s):** United States ports. **Units of Measure:** Dollars per long ton. **Type of Price:** wholesale. **Time Period Covered:** latest 30 years.

MANGANESE ACETATE: DIHYDRATE

Source: *Chemical Marketing Reporter.* **Price Frequency:** weekly. **Effective Market(s):** New York. **Units of Measure:** Dollars per lb. **Type of Price:** spot. **Time Period Covered:** latest week.

MANGANESE ACETATE: TETRAHYDRATE

Source: *Chemical Marketing Reporter.* **Price Frequency:** weekly. **Effective Market(s):** New York. **Units of Measure:** Dollars per lb. **Type of Price:** spot. **Time Period Covered:** latest week.

MANGANESE ALUMINUM

Source: *American Metal Market.* **Price Frequency:** weekly. **Units of Measure:** Dollars per lb. of material. **Type of Price:** producer. **Time Period Covered:** latest week.

MANGANESE BORATE: TECHNICAL

Source: *Chemical Marketing Reporter.* **Price Frequency:** weekly. **Effective Market(s):** New York. **Units of Measure:** Dollars per lb. **Type of Price:** spot. **Time Period Covered:** latest week.

MANGANESE BORATE PRINTING INK DRIER

Source: *Chemical Marketing Reporter.* **Price Frequency:** weekly. **Effective Market(s):** New York. **Units of Measure:** Dollars per lb. **Type of Price:** spot. **Time Period Covered:** latest week.

MANGANESE BRONZE: SCRAP

Source: *Iron Age.* **Price Frequency:** monthly. **Units of Measure:** cents per lb. **Type of Price:** mill. **Time Period Covered:** latest month.

MANGANESE BRONZE SOLIDS

Source: *American Metal Market.* **Price Frequency:** daily. **Effective Market(s):** Montreal. **Units of Measure:** Canadian cents per lb. **Type of Price:** dealer. **Time Period Covered:** latest day.

MANGANESE BRONZE TURNINGS

Source: *American Metal Market.* **Price Frequency:** daily. **Effective Market(s):** Montreal, San Francisco. **Units of Measure:** Canadian cents per lb., cents per lb. **Type of Price:** dealer. **Time Period Covered:** latest day.

MANGANESE CARBONATE: CHEMICAL GRADE, 46% MANGANESE

Source: *Chemical Marketing Reporter.* **Price Frequency:** weeklyl. **Effective Market(s):** New York. **Units of Measure:** Dollars per lb. **Type of Price:** spot. **Time Period Covered:** latest week.

MANGANESE CHLORIDE: ANHYDROUS

Source: *Chemical Marketing Reporter.* **Price Frequency:** weekly. **Effective Market(s):** New York. **Units of Measure:** Dollars per lb. **Type of Price:** spot. **Time Period Covered:** latest week.

MANGANESE DIOXIDE: NATURAL, GROUND, AFRICAN

Source: *Chemical Marketing Reporter.* **Price Frequency:** weekly. **Effective Market(s):** New York. **Units of Measure:** Dollars per ton. **Type of Price:** spot. **Time Period Covered:** latest week.

MANGANESE DIOXIDE: SYNTHETIC, BATTERY GRADE, CRYSTALLINE

Source: *Chemical Marketing Reporter.* **Price Frequency:** weekly. **Effective Market(s):** New York. **Units of Measure:** Dollars per lb. **Type of Price:** spot. **Time Period Covered:** latest week.

MANGANESE DIOXIDE: SYNTHETIC, FERRITE GRADE, CHEMICAL

Source: *Chemical Marketing Reporter.* **Price Frequency:** weekly. **Effective Market(s):** New York. **Units of Measure:** Dollars per lb. **Type of Price:** spot. **Time Period Covered:** latest week.

MANGANESE GLUCONATE

Source: *Chemical Marketing Reporter.* **Price Frequency:** weekly. **Effective Market(s):** New York. **Units of Measure:** Dollars per lb. **Type of Price:** spot. **Time Period Covered:** latest week.

MANGANESE HYDRATE

Source: *Chemical Marketing Reporter.* **Price Frequency:** weekly. **Effective Market(s):** New York. **Units of Measure:** Dollars per lb. **Type of Price:** spot. **Time Period Covered:** latest week.

MANGANESE HYPOPHOSPHATE: NF

Source: *Chemical Marketing Reporter.* **Price Frequency:** weekly. **Effective Market(s):** New York. **Units of Measure:** Dollars per lb. **Type of Price:** spot. **Time Period Covered:** latest week.

MANGANESE NAPHTHENATE: 6% MANGANESE, LIQUID

Source: *Chemical Marketing Reporter.* **Price Frequency:** weekly. **Effective Market(s):** New York. **Units of Measure:** Dollars per lb. **Type of Price:** spot. **Time Period Covered:** latest week.

MANGANESE ORE: 46-48% MANGANESE, INDIAN

Source: *Commodity Trade and Price Trends.* **Price Frequency:** annually. **Effective Market(s):** United States ports. **Units of Measure:** cents per metric ton unit, 1980 constant cents per metric ton unit. **Time Period Covered:** latest 37 years.

MANGANESE ORE: 48% MANGANESE

Source: *Economic and Energy Indicators.* **Price Frequency:** monthly, quarterly, annually. **Units of Measure:** Dollars per long ton. **Time Period Covered:** latest 3 months, quarters, and years.

MANGANESE ORE: METALLURGICAL, 48-50% MANGANESE

Source: *Monthly Commodity Price Bulletin.* **Price Frequency:** monthly, annually. **Effective Market(s):** London. **Units of Measure:** Dollars per metric ton. **Time Period Covered:** latest 5 years.

Source: *Monthly Commodity Price Bulletin Supplement.* **Price Frequency:** monthly, quarterly, annually. **Effective Market(s):** London. **Units of Measure:** Dollars per tonne. **Time Period Covered:** latest 20 years.

Source: *UNCTAD Commodity Yeabook.* **Price Frequency:** annually. **Effective Market(s):** United Kingdom. **Units of Measure:** Dollars per metric ton. **Type of Price:** free market. **Time Period Covered:** latest 12 years.

MANGANESE SULFATE: 28.5% MANGANESE, POWDER AND MINI GRANULAR

Source: *Chemical Marketing Reporter.* **Price Frequency:** weekly. **Effective Market(s):** Mobile (AL). **Units of Measure:** Dollars per ton. **Type of Price:** spot. **Time Period Covered:** latest week.

MANGANESE SULFATE: 32% MANGANESE, GRANULAR

Source: *Chemical Marketing Reporter.* **Price Frequency:** weekly. **Effective Market(s):** New York. **Units of Measure:** Dollars per ton. **Type of Price:** spot. **Time Period Covered:** latest week.

MANGANESE TALLATE: 6% MANGANESE, LIQUID

Source: *Chemical Marketing Reporter.* **Price Frequency:** weekly. **Effective Market(s):** New York. **Units of Measure:** Dollars per lb. **Type of Price:** spot. **Time Period Covered:** latest week.

MANGOES

Source: *Fresh Fruit and Vegetable Prices.* **Price Frequency:** monthly, seasonally. **Effective Market(s):** South Florida. **Units of Measure:** Dollars per flat. **Type of Price:** average price at shipping point. **Time Period Covered:** latest year.

Source: *Fruit and Tree Nuts Situation and Outlook Yearbook.* **Price Frequency:** annually. **Effective Market(s):** United States. **Units of Measure:** Dollars per bushel. **Type of Price:** grower. **Time Period Covered:** latest 20 years.

Source: *Prices of Selected Asia/Pacific Products.* **Price Frequency:** monthly. **Effective Market(s):** Sydney (Australia). **Units of Measure:** Australian dollars per tray. **Type of Price:** wholesale high, wholesale low. **Time Period Covered:** latest month.

MANGOES: BRAZILIAN

Source: *Prices of Selected Asia/Pacific Products.* **Price Frequency:** monthly. **Effective Market(s):** Netherlands, United Kingdom. **Units of Measure:** Dutch guilders per kilogram, British pounds per kilogram. **Type of Price:** wholesale high, wholesale low. **Time Period Covered:** latest month.

MANGOES: FRANCIS, CARIBBEAN, IMPORTED

Source: *Fresh Fruit and Vegetable Prices.* **Price Frequency:** monthly. **Effective Market(s):** South Florida. **Units of Measure:** Dollars per flat. **Type of Price:** price paid at point of entry. **Time Period Covered:** latest year.

MANGOES: HADENS AND KENTS, MEXICAN

Source: *Fresh Fruit and Vegetable Prices.* **Price Frequency:** monthly, seasonally. **Effective Market(s):** South Texas. **Units of Measure:** Dollars per carton. **Type of Price:** price paid at point of entry. **Time Period Covered:** latest year.

MANGOES: KEITTS, MEXICAN

Source: *Fresh Fruit and Vegetable Prices.* **Price Frequency:** monthly, seasonally. **Effective Market(s):** South Texas. **Units of Measure:** Dollars per carton. **Type of Price:** price paid at point of entry. **Time Period Covered:** latest year.

MANGOES: KENT

Source: *Lancaster Farmer.* **Price Frequency:** weekly, seasonally. **Effective Market(s):** Pennsylvania. **Units of Measure:** Dollars per carton. **Type of Price:** market. **Time Period Covered:** latest week.

MANGOES: TOMMY ATKINS, MEXICAN

Source: *Fresh Fruit and Vegetable Prices.* **Price Frequency:** monthly, seasonally. **Effective Market(s):** South Texas. **Units of Measure:** Dollars per carton. **Type of Price:** price paid at point of entry. **Time Period Covered:** latest year.

MANGOSTEEN: THAI

Source: *Prices of Selected Asia/Pacific Products.* **Price Frequency:** monthly, seasonally. **Effective Market(s):** Denmark, Sweden. **Units of Measure:** Danish kroner per kilogram, Swedish kroner per kilogram. **Type of Price:** wholesale high, wholesale low. **Time Period Covered:** latest month.

MANMADE FIBERS
see Fibers: Manmade.

MANMADE STAPLES

Source: *JTN: The International Textile Magazine.* **Price Frequency:** monthly. **Effective Market(s):** Japan. **Units of Measure:** Japanese yen per yard. **Type of Price:** spot. **Time Period Covered:** latest month.

MANNITOL: COMMERCIAL, POWDERED

Source: *Chemical Marketing Reporter.* **Price Frequency:** weekly. **Effective Market(s):** New York. **Units of Measure:** Dollars per lb. **Type of Price:** spot. **Time Period Covered:** latest week.

MANURE LOADER

Source: *Agricultural Prices.* **Price Frequency:** annually. **Effective Market(s):** United States. **Units of Measure:** Dollars each. **Type of Price:** paid by farmer. **Time Period Covered:** latest year.

MANURE SPREADER: CONVEYOR TYPE

Source: *Agricultural Prices.* **Price Frequency:** annually. **Effective Market(s):** United States. **Units of Measure:** Dollars each. **Type of Price:** paid by farmer. **Time Period Covered:** latest year.

Source: *Agricultural Prices Annual Summary.* **Price Frequency:** annually. **Effective Market(s):** United States. **Units of Measure:** Dollars each. **Type of Price:** paid by farmer. **Time Period Covered:** latest 6 years.

MAPLE SAWTIMBER

Source: *Volume and Value of Sawtimber Stumpage Sold From National Forests by Selected Species and Region.* **Price Frequency:** quarterly, annually. **Effective Market(s):** Eastern region. **Units of Measure:** Dollars per 1000 board feet. **Type of Price:** average. **Time Period Covered:** latest quarter, latest year.

MAPLE SAWTIMBER: RED

Source: *Volume and Value of Sawtimber Stumpage Sold From National Forests by Selected Species and Region.* **Price Frequency:** quarterly, annually. **Effective Market(s):** Eastern region. **Units of Measure:** Dollars per 1000 board feet. **Type of Price:** average. **Time Period Covered:** latest quarter, latest year.

MAPLE SAWTIMBER: SUGAR

Source: *Volume and Value of Sawtimber Stumpage Sold From National Forests by Selected Species and Region.* **Price Frequency:** quarterly, annually. **Effective Market(s):** Eastern Region. **Units of Measure:** Dollars per 1000 board feet. **Type of Price:** average. **Time Period Covered:** latest quarter, latest year.

MARGARINE

Source: *HRI-Buyers Guide.* **Price Frequency:** weekly. **Effective Market(s):** Northeastern area. **Units of Measure:** cents per lb. **Type of Price:** prices paid by dining places & institutions. **Time Period Covered:** latest week.

MARGARINE: BLENDED

Source: *Urner Barry's Price-Current.* **Price Frequency:** daily. **Effective Market(s):** East. **Units of Measure:** cents per lb. **Time Period Covered:** latest day.

MARGARINE: CORN OIL

Source: *Urner Barry's Price-Current.* **Price Frequency:** daily. **Effective Market(s):** East. **Units of Measure:** cents per lb. **Time Period Covered:** latest day.

Source: *Weekly Insiders Dairy & Egg Letter.* **Price Frequency:** weekly. **Units of Measure:** Dollars per lb. **Type of Price:** retail. **Time Period Covered:** latest week, week ago, year ago.

MARGARINE: PRIVATE LABEL

Source: *Weekly Insiders Dairy & Egg Letter.* **Price Frequency:** weekly. **Units of Measure:** Dollars per lb. **Type of Price:** retail. **Time Period Covered:** latest week, week ago, year ago.

MARGARINE: REGULAR

Source: *Weekly Insiders Dairy & Egg Letter.* **Price Frequency:** weekly. **Units of Measure:** Dollars per lb. **Type of Price:** retail. **Time Period Covered:** latest week, week ago, year ago.

MARGARINE: SOFT

Source: *Weekly Insiders Dairy & Egg Letter.* **Price Frequency:** weekly. **Units of Measure:** Dollars per lb. **Type of Price:** retail. **Time Period Covered:** latest week, week ago, year ago.

MARGARINE: VEGETABLE OIL

Source: *Monthly Price Review.* **Price Frequency:** daily. **Effective Market(s):** east. **Units of Measure:** dollars per lb. **Time Period Covered:** latest month.

Source: *Urner Barry's Price-Current.* **Price Frequency:** daily. **Units of Measure:** cents per lb. **Type of Price:** sales by first receivers. **Time Period Covered:** latest day.

Source: *Urner Barry's Price-Current.* **Price Frequency:** daily. **Effective Market(s):** East. **Units of Measure:** cents per lb. **Time Period Covered:** latest day.

MARGARINE: WHITE

Source: *Agricultural Outlook.* **Price Frequency:** monthly, annually. **Effective Market(s):** Chicago. **Units of Measure:** cents per lb. **Type of Price:** wholesale. **Time Period Covered:** monthly latest 5 months, annually latest 4 years.

MARGARINE: YELLOW

Source: *Oil Crops Situation and Outlook.* **Price Frequency:** monthly. **Effective Market(s):** Chicago. **Units of Measure:** cents per lb. **Type of Price:** wholesale. **Time Period Covered:** latest 5 months.

MARJORAM: EGYPTIAN

Source: *Chemical Marketing Reporter.* **Price Frequency:** weekly. **Effective Market(s):** New York. **Units of Measure:** Dollars per lb. **Type of Price:** spot. **Time Period Covered:** latest week.

Source: *U. S. Spice Trade.* **Price Frequency:** annually. **Effective Market(s):** New York. **Units of Measure:** cents per lb. **Type of Price:** spot. **Time Period Covered:** latest 3 years.

MARJORAM: FRENCH

Source: *Chemical Marketing Reporter.* **Price Frequency:** weekly. **Effective Market(s):** New York. **Units of Measure:** Dollars per lb. **Type of Price:** spot. **Time Period Covered:** latest week.

Source: *U. S. Spice Trade.* **Price Frequency:** annually. **Effective Market(s):** New York. **Units of Measure:** cents per lb. **Type of Price:** spot. **Time Period Covered:** latest 3 years.

MARKS
see West German Marks.

MARLIN: BLUE, FILLETS, FRESH, HAWAIIAN

Source: *Seafood Price-Current.* **Price Frequency:** semiweekly. **Effective Market(s):** Hawaii. **Units of Measure:** Dollars per lb. **Type of Price:** sale by first receiver. **Time Period Covered:** latest day.

MARLIN: BLUE, WHOLE, FRESH, HAWAIIAN

Source: *Seafood Price-Current.* **Price Frequency:** semiweekly. **Effective Market(s):** Hawaii. **Units of Measure:** Dollars per lb. **Type of Price:** sale by first receiver . **Time Period Covered:** latest day.

MARLIN: STRIPED, FILLETS, FRESH, HAWAIIAN

Source: *Seafood Price-Current.* **Price Frequency:** semiweekly. **Effective Market(s):** Hawaii. **Units of Measure:** Dollars per lb. **Type of Price:** sale by first receiver. **Time Period Covered:** latest day.

MARLIN: STRIPED, WHOLE, FRESH, HAWAIIAN

Source: *Seafood Price-Current.* **Price Frequency:** semiweekly. **Effective Market(s):** Hawaii. **Units of Measure:** Dollars per lb. **Type of Price:** sale by first receiver. **Time Period Covered:** latest day.

MARLIN: WHOLE, FRESH

Source: *Seafood Price-Current.* **Price Frequency:** semiweekly. **Effective Market(s):** Boston, Mid-Atlantic, New Bedford (MA), Portland (ME). **Units of Measure:** Dollars per lb. **Type of Price:** sale by first receiver, auction price. **Time Period Covered:** latest day.

MARROWS

Source: *New Zealand Farmer.* **Price Frequency:** weekly, seasonally. **Effective Market(s):** New Zealand. **Units of Measure:** New Zealand dollars per case. **Time Period Covered:** latest week.

MASTIC GUM

Source: *Journal of Commerce and Commercial.* **Price Frequency:** weekly in Monday issue. **Units of Measure:** Dollars per lb. **Type of Price:** spot. **Time Period Covered:** latest week.

MATERIALS: CONSTRUCTION

Source: *ENR.* **Price Frequency:** weekly. **Effective Market(s):** 20-market average. **Units of Measure:** index. **Type of Price:** price index. **Time Period Covered:** latest week.

Source: *ENR.* **Price Frequency:** monthly in second issue of month. **Effective Market(s):** 20 domestic markets. **Units of Measure:** index. **Type of Price:** price index. **Time Period Covered:** latest month.

MBS
see Methacrylate Butadiene Styrene.

MBT
see 2-Mercaptobenzothiazole.

MBTS
see Mercaptobenzothiazyl Disulfide.

MCPA: EMULSIFIABLE CONCENTRATE

Source: *Agricultural Prices Annual Summary.* **Price Frequency:** semiannually. **Effective Market(s):** United States. **Units of Measure:** Dollars per 5 gallons. **Type of Price:** paid by farmer. **Time Period Covered:** latest 6 years.

MDI
see Diphenylmethane 4,4,-di-isocyanate.

MEAL
see specific types of meal, e.g., Corn Meal.

MEAT
Source: *Dairy Market Statistics.* **Price Frequency:** monthly. **Effective Market(s):** United States. **Units of Measure:** index. **Type of Price:** consumer price index. **Time Period Covered:** latest year.

MEAT AND BONE MEAL
see also Meat Meal, Bone Meal.

Source: *California Farmer.* **Price Frequency:** semimonthly. **Effective Market(s):** California. **Units of Measure:** Dollars per ton. **Time Period Covered:** latest week, month ago, year ago.

Source: *Feed Situation and Outlook Report.* **Price Frequency:** monthly. **Effective Market(s):** Kansas City. **Units of Measure:** Dollars per ton. **Type of Price:** wholesale. **Time Period Covered:** latest 8 months.

Source: *Feedstuffs.* **Price Frequency:** weekly. **Effective Market(s):** 10 domestic markets. **Units of Measure:** Dollars per bulk ton. **Time Period Covered:** latest week.

Source: *Feedstuffs.* **Price Frequency:** weekly. **Effective Market(s):** Chicago. **Units of Measure:** Dollars per ton. **Time Period Covered:** latest week, week ago, 6 months ago, year ago.

Source: *Grain and Feed Market News.* **Price Frequency:** weekly, seasonally. **Effective Market(s):** 6 domestic markets. **Units of Measure:** Dollars per ton. **Type of Price:** wholesale. **Time Period Covered:** latest week, week ago, year ago.

Source: *Livestock, Meat, Wool Market News.* **Price Frequency:** weekly, seasonally. **Effective Market(s):** Central United States. **Units of Measure:** Dollars per ton. **Time Period Covered:** latest week.

Source: *National Provisioner.* **Price Frequency:** weekly. **Effective Market(s):** Chicago. **Units of Measure:** Dollars per 100 lbs. **Time Period Covered:** latest week.

MEAT AND BONE MEAL: 50% PROTEIN
Source: *Asian Wall Street Journal.* **Price Frequency:** daily. **Effective Market(s):** Illinois. **Units of Measure:** Dollars per ton. **Type of Price:** cash. **Time Period Covered:** latest 2 days, year ago.

MEAT ANIMALS
Source: *Illinois Farm Report.* **Price Frequency:** monthly. **Effective Market(s):** Illinois. **Units of Measure:** index. **Type of Price:** index of prices received by farmers. **Time Period Covered:** latest 2 months, year ago.

MEAT BY-PRODUCTS
Source: *National Provisioner.* **Price Frequency:** weekly. **Effective Market(s):** Midwest River area. **Units of Measure:** Dollars per 100 lbs. **Time Period Covered:** latest week.

MEAT MEAL: 50% PROTEIN
Source: *Milling & Baking News.* **Price Frequency:** weekly. **Effective Market(s):** Chicago, Kansas City. **Units of Measure:** Dollars per ton. **Time Period Covered:** latest week, week ago, year ago.

MELAMINE
Source: *Chemical Marketing Reporter.* **Price Frequency:** weekly. **Effective Market(s):** New York. **Units of Measure:** Dollars per lb. **Type of Price:** spot. **Time Period Covered:** latest week.

Source: *Journal of Commerce and Commercial.* **Price Frequency:** weekly in Tuesday issue. **Units of Measure:** Dollars per lb. **Type of Price:** spot. **Time Period Covered:** latest week.

MELAMINE: CYMEL 303
Source: *Journal of Commerce and Commercial.* **Price Frequency:** weekly in Wednesday issue. **Units of Measure:** Dollars per lb. **Type of Price:** spot. **Time Period Covered:** latest week.

MELAMINE FORMALDEHYDE RESIN: GENERAL PURPOSE
Source: *Chemical Marketing Reporter.* **Price Frequency:** weekly. **Effective Market(s):** New York. **Units of Measure:** Dollars per lb. **Type of Price:** spot. **Time Period Covered:** latest week.

MELAMINE FORMALDEHYDE RESIN: MOLDING COMPOUNDS
Source: *Chemical Marketing Reporter.* **Price Frequency:** weekly. **Effective Market(s):** New York. **Units of Measure:** Dollars per lb. **Type of Price:** spot. **Time Period Covered:** latest week.

MELAMINE MOLDING COMPOUND
Source: *Plastics Technology.* **Price Frequency:** monthly. **Units of Measure:** cents per lb., cents per cubic inch. **Type of Price:** bulk list, market. **Time Period Covered:** latest month.

MELAMINE PHENOLIC COMPOUND
Source: *Plastics Technology.* **Price Frequency:** monthly. **Units of Measure:** cents per lb., cents per cubic inch. **Type of Price:** bulk list, market. **Time Period Covered:** latest month.

MELON BALLS: FROZEN
Source: *HRI-Buyers Guide.* **Price Frequency:** weekly. **Effective Market(s):** Northeastern area. **Units of Measure:** cents per lb. **Type of Price:** prices paid by dining places & institutions. **Time Period Covered:** latest week.

MELONS
see specific types of melon, e.g., Honeydew Melons.

MELONS: CRENSHAW
see Crenshaw Melons.

MELONS: HONEYDEW
see Honeydew Melons.

MELONS: ROCK
see Rock Melons.

MENHADEN
Source: *Feedstuffs.* **Price Frequency:** weekly. **Effective Market(s):** 7 domestic markets. **Units of Measure:** Dollars per bulk ton. **Time Period Covered:** latest week.

MENHADEN: DOMESTIC, 60%

Source: *Milling & Baking News.* **Price Frequency:** weekly. **Effective Market(s):** Gulf. **Units of Measure:** Dollars per ton. **Time Period Covered:** latest week, week ago, year ago.

MENHADEN OIL

Source: *Chemical Marketing Reporter.* **Price Frequency:** weekly. **Effective Market(s):** Gulf ports. **Units of Measure:** Dollars per lb. **Type of Price:** spot. **Time Period Covered:** latest week.

MENTHA ARVENSIS

Source: *U. S. Essential Oil Trade.* **Price Frequency:** annually. **Effective Market(s):** United States. **Units of Measure:** Dollars per kilogram. **Type of Price:** import value. **Time Period Covered:** latest 3 years.

MENTHA PIPERITA

Source: *U. S. Essential Oil Trade.* **Price Frequency:** annually. **Effective Market(s):** United States. **Units of Measure:** Dollars per kilogram. **Type of Price:** import value. **Time Period Covered:** latest 3 years.

MENTHOL: CHINESE

Source: *Chemical Marketing Reporter.* **Price Frequency:** weekly. **Effective Market(s):** New York. **Units of Measure:** Dollars per kilo. **Type of Price:** spot. **Time Period Covered:** latest week.

Source: *Journal of Commerce and Commercial.* **Price Frequency:** weekly in Friday issue. **Units of Measure:** Dollars per lb. **Type of Price:** spot. **Time Period Covered:** latest week.

Source: *Prices of Selected Asia/Pacific Products.* **Price Frequency:** monthly. **Effective Market(s):** United Kingdom, United Kingdom/North European ports. **Units of Measure:** British pounds per kilogram. **Type of Price:** spot high, spot low. **Time Period Covered:** latest month.

MENTHOL: CRYSTAL

Source: *Prices of Selected Asia/Pacific Products.* **Price Frequency:** monthly. **Effective Market(s):** Tokyo. **Units of Measure:** Japanese yen per kilogram. **Type of Price:** high, low. **Time Period Covered:** latest month.

MENTHOL: CRYSTAL, HONG KONG

Source: *Prices of Selected Asia/Pacific Products.* **Price Frequency:** monthly. **Effective Market(s):** Hong Kong. **Units of Measure:** Hong Kong dollars per kilogram. **Type of Price:** wholesale high, wholesale low. **Time Period Covered:** latest month.

MENTHOL: CRYSTAL, SHANGHAI

Source: *Prices of Selected Asia/Pacific Products.* **Price Frequency:** monthly. **Effective Market(s):** Hong Kong. **Units of Measure:** Hong Kong dollars per kilogram. **Type of Price:** wholesale high, wholesale low. **Time Period Covered:** latest month.

MENTHOL: INDIAN

Source: *Journal of Commerce and Commercial.* **Price Frequency:** weekly in Friday issue. **Units of Measure:** Dollars per lb. **Type of Price:** spot. **Time Period Covered:** latest week.

MENTHOL: NATURAL, LARGE AND REGULAR CRYSTALS, BRAZILIAN, USP

Source: *Chemical Marketing Reporter.* **Price Frequency:** weekly. **Effective Market(s):** New York. **Units of Measure:** Dollars per lb. **Type of Price:** spot. **Time Period Covered:** latest week.

MENTHOL: NATURAL, USP

Source: *Prices of Selected Asia/Pacific Products.* **Price Frequency:** monthly. **Effective Market(s):** New York. **Units of Measure:** Dollars per lb. **Type of Price:** spot high, spot low. **Time Period Covered:** latest month.

MENTHOL: SYNTHETIC, USP

Source: *Chemical Marketing Reporter.* **Price Frequency:** weekly. **Effective Market(s):** New York. **Units of Measure:** Dollars per lb. **Type of Price:** spot. **Time Period Covered:** latest week.

Source: *Prices of Selected Asia/Pacific Products.* **Price Frequency:** monthly. **Effective Market(s):** New York. **Units of Measure:** Dollars per lb. **Type of Price:** spot high, spot low. **Time Period Covered:** latest month.

2-MERCAPTOBENZOTHIAZOLE

Source: *Chemical Marketing Reporter.* **Price Frequency:** weekly. **Effective Market(s):** New York. **Units of Measure:** Dollars per lb. **Type of Price:** spot. **Time Period Covered:** latest week.

MERCAPTOBENZOTHIAZYL DISULFIDE

Source: *Chemical Marketing Reporter.* **Price Frequency:** weekly. **Effective Market(s):** New York. **Units of Measure:** Dollars per lb. **Type of Price:** spot. **Time Period Covered:** latest week.

MERCURIC CHLORIDE: POWDERED, GRANULAR, NF

Source: *Chemical Marketing Reporter.* **Price Frequency:** weekly. **Effective Market(s):** New York. **Units of Measure:** Dollars per lb. **Type of Price:** spot. **Time Period Covered:** latest week.

MERCURIC OXIDE: RED

Source: *Journal of Commerce and Commercial.* **Price Frequency:** weekly in Friday issue. **Units of Measure:** Dollars per lb. **Type of Price:** spot. **Time Period Covered:** latest week.

MERCURIC OXIDE: RED, PURIFIED

Source: *Chemical Marketing Reporter.* **Price Frequency:** weekly. **Effective Market(s):** New York. **Units of Measure:** Dollars per lb. **Type of Price:** spot. **Time Period Covered:** latest week.

MERCURIC OXIDE: RED, TECHNICAL

Source: *Chemical Marketing Reporter.* **Price Frequency:** weekly. **Effective Market(s):** New York. **Units of Measure:** Dollars per lb. **Type of Price:** spot. **Time Period Covered:** latest week.

MERCURIC OXIDE: YELLOW

Source: *Journal of Commerce and Commercial.* **Price Frequency:** weekly in Friday issue. **Units of Measure:** Dollars per lb. **Type of Price:** spot. **Time Period Covered:** latest week.

MERCURIC OXIDE: YELLOW, NF

Source: *Chemical Marketing Reporter.* **Price Frequency:** weekly. **Effective Market(s):** New York. **Units of Measure:** Dollars per lb. **Type of Price:** spot. **Time Period Covered:** latest week.

MERCURIC OXIDE: YELLOW, TECHNICAL

Source: *Chemical Marketing Reporter.* **Price Frequency:** weekly. **Effective Market(s):** New York. **Units of Measure:** Dollars per lb. **Type of Price:** spot. **Time Period Covered:** latest week.

MERCUROUS CHLORIDE

see Calomel.

MERCURY

Source: *Asian Wall Street Journal.* **Price Frequency:** daily. **Effective Market(s):** New York. **Units of Measure:** Dollars per 76 lb. flask. **Type of Price:** cash. **Time Period Covered:** latest 2 days, year ago.

Source: *Commodity Year Book.* **Price Frequency:** monthly, annually. **Effective Market(s):** New York. **Units of Measure:** Dollars per 76 lb. flask. **Time Period Covered:** latest 8 years.

Source: *Investor's Daily.* **Price Frequency:** daily. **Units of Measure:** Dollars per 76 lb. flask. **Type of Price:** spot. **Time Period Covered:** latest 2 days.

Source: *Iron Age.* **Price Frequency:** monthly. **Effective Market(s):** New York. **Units of Measure:** Dollars per 76 lb. flask. **Type of Price:** consumer. **Time Period Covered:** latest month.

Source: *Journal of Commerce and Commercial.* **Price Frequency:** daily. **Effective Market(s):** Europe. **Units of Measure:** Dollars per 76 lb. flask. **Type of Price:** spot. **Time Period Covered:** latest day.

Source: *Los Angeles Times.* **Price Frequency:** daily. **Effective Market(s):** New York. **Units of Measure:** Dollars per 76 lb. flask. **Type of Price:** cash. **Time Period Covered:** latest day.

Source: *New York Times.* **Price Frequency:** daily. **Units of Measure:** Dollars per 76 lb. flask. **Type of Price:** cash. **Time Period Covered:** latest 2 days.

Source: *Purchasing.* **Price Frequency:** quarterly in January, April, July, October issues. **Units of Measure:** cents per lb. **Type of Price:** transaction. **Time Period Covered:** latest 5 quarters.

Source: *Wall Street Journal.* **Price Frequency:** daily. **Effective Market(s):** New York. **Units of Measure:** Dollars per 76 lb. flask. **Time Period Covered:** latest day, day ago, year ago.

MERCURY: 99.9%

Source: *American Metal Market.* **Price Frequency:** daily. **Effective Market(s):** European port, New York. **Units of Measure:** Dollars per 76 lb. flask. **Time Period Covered:** latest day.

Source: *E&MJ.* **Price Frequency:** monthly. **Effective Market(s):** New York, European port. **Units of Measure:** Dollars per 76 lb. flask. **Time Period Covered:** latest month.

MERCURY: AMMONIATED

see White Precipitate: XV, USP.

MERCURY CHLORIDE

See also Calomel.

MERCURY CHLORIDE: NF

Source: *Journal of Commerce and Commercial.* **Price Frequency:** weekly in Friday issue. **Units of Measure:** Dollars per lb. **Type of Price:** spot. **Time Period Covered:** latest week.

METAL POWDERS

see specific types of powders, e.g., Nickel Carbonyl Powder.

METALLIC BROWN: SYNTHETIC

Source: *Journal of Commerce and Commercial.* **Price Frequency:** weekly in Wednesday issue. **Units of Measure:** Dollars per lb. **Type of Price:** spot. **Time Period Covered:** latest week.

METHACRYLATE BUTADIENE STYRENE: MAXIMUM

Source: *Modern Plastics.* **Price Frequency:** quarterly every February, May, August, November. **Units of Measure:** Dollars per lb. **Type of Price:** list. **Time Period Covered:** latest 4 quarters.

METHACRYLATE BUTADIENE STYRENE: MINIMUM

Source: *Modern Plastics.* **Price Frequency:** quarterly every February, May, August, November. **Units of Measure:** Dollars per lb. **Type of Price:** list. **Time Period Covered:** latest 4 quarters.

METHACRYLIC ACID: GLACIAL, 99%

Source: *Chemical Marketing Reporter.* **Price Frequency:** weekly. **Effective Market(s):** New York. **Units of Measure:** Dollars per lb. **Type of Price:** spot. **Time Period Covered:** latest week.

D-METHAMPHETAMINE HYDROCHLORIDE

Source: *Chemical Marketing Reporter.* **Price Frequency:** weekly. **Effective Market(s):** New York. **Units of Measure:** Dollars per lb. **Type of Price:** spot. **Time Period Covered:** latest week.

DL-METHAMPHETAMINE HYDROCHLORIDE

Source: *Chemical Marketing Reporter.* **Price Frequency:** weekly. **Effective Market(s):** New York. **Units of Measure:** Dollars per lb. **Type of Price:** spot. **Time Period Covered:** latest week.

METHANOL

Source: *Energy Pricing News: Petrochemical Report.* **Price Frequency:** bimonthly. **Units of Measure:** Canadian dollars per tonne. **Type of Price:** contract. **Time Period Covered:** latest month.

Source: *Journal of Commerce and Commercial.* **Price Frequency:** weekly in Thursday issue. **Units of Measure:** Dollars per gallon. **Type of Price:** spot. **Time Period Covered:** latest week.

METHANOL: SYNTHETIC

Source: *Chemical Marketing Reporter.* **Price Frequency:** weekly. **Effective Market(s):** Gulf Coast. **Units of Measure:** Dollars per gallon. **Type of Price:** spot. **Time Period Covered:** latest week.

Source: *Purchasing.* **Price Frequency:** monthly. **Effective Market(s):** United States. **Units of Measure:** cents per gallon. **Type of Price:** transaction. **Time Period Covered:** latest day, month ago, 6 months ago, year ago.

METHENAMINE

see Hexamethylenetetramine.

DL-METHIONINE
see Racemethionine.

METHIONINE HYDROXYANALOGUE: DRY, 86% ACTIVITY
Source: *Chemical Marketing Reporter.* **Price Frequency:** weekly. **Effective Market(s):** New York. **Units of Measure:** Dollars per lb. **Type of Price:** spot. **Time Period Covered:** latest week.

METHIONINE HYDROXYANALOGUE: LIQUID, 88% ACTIVITY
Source: *Chemical Marketing Reporter.* **Price Frequency:** weekly. **Effective Market(s):** New York. **Units of Measure:** Dollars per lb. **Type of Price:** spot. **Time Period Covered:** latest week.

METHOXYCHLOR: 50% WETTABLE POWDER
Source: *Chemical Marketing Reporter.* **Price Frequency:** weekly. **Effective Market(s):** New York. **Units of Measure:** Dollars per lb. **Type of Price:** dealer. **Time Period Covered:** latest week.

METHYL ABIETATE
Source: *Chemical Marketing Reporter.* **Price Frequency:** weekly. **Effective Market(s):** East. **Units of Measure:** Dollars per lb. **Type of Price:** spot. **Time Period Covered:** latest week.

METHYL ABIETATE: HYDROGENATED
Source: *Chemical Marketing Reporter.* **Price Frequency:** weekly. **Effective Market(s):** New York. **Units of Measure:** Dollars per lb. **Type of Price:** spot. **Time Period Covered:** latest week.

METHYL ACETOACETATE
Source: *Chemical Marketing Reporter.* **Price Frequency:** weekly. **Effective Market(s):** East. **Units of Measure:** Dollars per lb. **Type of Price:** spot. **Time Period Covered:** latest week.

METHYL ACRYLATE
Source: *Chemical Marketing Reporter.* **Price Frequency:** weekly. **Effective Market(s):** New York. **Units of Measure:** Dollars per lb. **Type of Price:** spot. **Time Period Covered:** latest week.

METHYL ALCOHOL
see Methanol.

METHYL AMYL ALCOHOL
Source: *Chemical Marketing Reporter.* **Price Frequency:** weekly. **Effective Market(s):** New York. **Units of Measure:** Dollars per lb. **Type of Price:** spot. **Time Period Covered:** latest week.

METHYL N-AMYL KETONE
Source: *Chemical Marketing Reporter.* **Price Frequency:** weekly. **Effective Market(s):** New York. **Units of Measure:** Dollars per lb. **Type of Price:** spot. **Time Period Covered:** latest week.

METHYL ANTHRANILATE
Source: *Chemical Marketing Reporter.* **Price Frequency:** weekly. **Effective Market(s):** New York. **Units of Measure:** Dollars per lb. **Type of Price:** spot. **Time Period Covered:** latest week.

Source: *Journal of Commerce and Commercial.* **Price Frequency:** weekly in Tuesday issue. **Units of Measure:** Dollars per lb. **Type of Price:** spot. **Time Period Covered:** latest week.

METHYL BENZOATE
Source: *Chemical Marketing Reporter.* **Price Frequency:** weekly. **Effective Market(s):** New York. **Units of Measure:** Dollars per lb. **Type of Price:** spot. **Time Period Covered:** latest week.

METHYL BROMIDE
Source: *Chemical Marketing Reporter.* **Price Frequency:** weekly. **Effective Market(s):** New York. **Units of Measure:** Dollars per lb. **Type of Price:** spot. **Time Period Covered:** latest week.

METHYL CHLORIDE: INDUSTRIAL
Source: *Chemical Marketing Reporter.* **Price Frequency:** weekly. **Effective Market(s):** New York. **Units of Measure:** Dollars per lb. **Type of Price:** spot. **Time Period Covered:** latest week.

METHYL CHLOROFORM
see 1,1,1-Trichloroethane.

METHYL CINNAMATE
Source: *Chemical Marketing Reporter.* **Price Frequency:** weekly. **Effective Market(s):** New York. **Units of Measure:** Dollars per lb. **Type of Price:** spot. **Time Period Covered:** latest week.

METHYL P-CRESOL
Source: *Chemical Marketing Reporter.* **Price Frequency:** weekly. **Effective Market(s):** New York. **Units of Measure:** Dollars per lb. **Type of Price:** spot. **Time Period Covered:** latest week.

METHYL ETHYL KETONE
Source: *Chemical Marketing Reporter.* **Price Frequency:** weekly. **Effective Market(s):** East. **Units of Measure:** Dollars per lb. **Type of Price:** spot. **Time Period Covered:** latest week.

METHYL EUGENOL
Source: *Chemical Marketing Reporter.* **Price Frequency:** weekly. **Effective Market(s):** New York. **Units of Measure:** Dollars per lb. **Type of Price:** spot. **Time Period Covered:** latest week.

METHYL FORMATE: PURE
Source: *Chemical Marketing Reporter.* **Price Frequency:** weekly. **Effective Market(s):** New York. **Units of Measure:** Dollars per lb. **Type of Price:** spot. **Time Period Covered:** latest week.

METHYL FORMATE: TECHNICAL
Source: *Chemical Marketing Reporter.* **Price Frequency:** weekly. **Effective Market(s):** New York. **Units of Measure:** Dollars per lb. **Type of Price:** spot. **Time Period Covered:** latest week.

METHYL HEPTENONE: TECHNICAL
Source: *Chemical Marketing Reporter.* **Price Frequency:** weekly. **Effective Market(s):** New York. **Units of Measure:** Dollars per lb. **Type of Price:** spot. **Time Period Covered:** latest week.

METHYL HEPTIN CARBONATE

Source: *Chemical Marketing Reporter.* **Price Frequency:** weekly. **Effective Market(s):** New York. **Units of Measure:** Dollars per lb. **Type of Price:** spot. **Time Period Covered:** latest week.

METHYL P-HYDROXYBENZOATE

see Methylparaben.

METHYL IONONE: STANDARD

Source: *Chemical Marketing Reporter.* **Price Frequency:** weekly. **Effective Market(s):** New York. **Units of Measure:** Dollars per lb. **Type of Price:** spot. **Time Period Covered:** latest week.

METHYL ISOAMYL KETONE

Source: *Chemical Marketing Reporter.* **Price Frequency:** weekly. **Effective Market(s):** East. **Units of Measure:** Dollars per lb. **Type of Price:** spot. **Time Period Covered:** latest week.

METHYL ISOBUTYL CARBINOL

see Methyl Amyl Alcohol.

METHYL ISOBUTYL KETONE

Source: *Chemical Marketing Reporter.* **Price Frequency:** weekly. **Effective Market(s):** California, New York, West of the Rockies. **Units of Measure:** Dollars per lb. **Type of Price:** spot. **Time Period Covered:** latest week.

Source: *Journal of Commerce and Commercial.* **Price Frequency:** weekly in Wednesday issue. **Units of Measure:** Dollars per lb. **Type of Price:** spot. **Time Period Covered:** latest week.

METHYL ISOEUGENOL

Source: *Chemical Marketing Reporter.* **Price Frequency:** weekly. **Effective Market(s):** New York. **Units of Measure:** Dollars per lb. **Type of Price:** spot. **Time Period Covered:** latest week.

METHYL METHACRYLATE

Source: *Chemical Marketing Reporter.* **Price Frequency:** weekly. **Effective Market(s):** New York. **Units of Measure:** Dollars per lb. **Type of Price:** spot. **Time Period Covered:** latest week.

METHYL NAPHTHYL KETONE: CRYSTALLINE

Source: *Chemical Marketing Reporter.* **Price Frequency:** weekly. **Effective Market(s):** New York. **Units of Measure:** Dollars per lb. **Type of Price:** spot. **Time Period Covered:** latest week.

METHYL PARATHION: 80%

Source: *Journal of Commerce and Commercial.* **Price Frequency:** weekly in Thursday issue. **Units of Measure:** Dollars per lb. **Type of Price:** spot. **Time Period Covered:** latest week.

METHYL PARATHION: EMULSIFIABLE CONCENTRATE

Source: *Agricultural Prices Annual Summary.* **Price Frequency:** semiannually. **Effective Market(s):** United States. **Units of Measure:** Dollars per 5 gallons. **Type of Price:** paid by farmer. **Time Period Covered:** latest 6 years.

METHYL PARATHION: TECHNICAL, 80%

Source: *Chemical Marketing Reporter.* **Price Frequency:** weekly. **Effective Market(s):** East. **Units of Measure:** Dollars per lb. **Type of Price:** spot. **Time Period Covered:** latest week.

METHYL PHENYLACETATE

Source: *Chemical Marketing Reporter.* **Price Frequency:** weekly. **Effective Market(s):** New York. **Units of Measure:** Dollars per lb. **Type of Price:** spot. **Time Period Covered:** latest week.

N-METHYL 2-PYRROLIDONE

Source: *Chemical Marketing Reporter.* **Price Frequency:** weekly. **Effective Market(s):** New York. **Units of Measure:** Dollars per lb. **Type of Price:** spot. **Time Period Covered:** latest week.

METHYL ROSEANILINE CHLORIDE: USP

Source: *Chemical Marketing Reporter.* **Price Frequency:** weekly. **Effective Market(s):** New York. **Units of Measure:** Dollars per lb. **Type of Price:** spot. **Time Period Covered:** latest week.

METHYL SALICYLATE: NF

Source: *Chemical Marketing Reporter.* **Price Frequency:** weekly. **Effective Market(s):** New York. **Units of Measure:** Dollars per lb. **Type of Price:** spot. **Time Period Covered:** latest week.

METHYL VIOLET

see Methyl Roseaniline Chloride.

METHYL VIOLET TONER: MOLYBDATED, PMA

Source: *Chemical Marketing Reporter.* **Price Frequency:** weekly. **Effective Market(s):** East of the Rockies. **Units of Measure:** Dollars per lb. **Type of Price:** spot. **Time Period Covered:** latest week.

METHYL VIOLET TONER: TUNGSTATED, PTA

Source: *Chemical Marketing Reporter.* **Price Frequency:** weekly. **Effective Market(s):** New York. **Units of Measure:** Dollars per lb. **Type of Price:** spot. **Time Period Covered:** latest week.

METHYLCELLULOSE

Source: *Chemical Marketing Reporter.* **Price Frequency:** weekly. **Effective Market(s):** Zone 1. **Units of Measure:** Dollars per lb. **Type of Price:** spot. **Time Period Covered:** latest week.

METHYLCELLULOSE: PREMIUM, USP

Source: *Chemical Marketing Reporter.* **Price Frequency:** weekly. **Effective Market(s):** Zone 1. **Units of Measure:** Dollars per lb. **Type of Price:** spot. **Time Period Covered:** latest week.

METHYLDIETHANOLAMINE

Source: *Chemical Marketing Reporter.* **Price Frequency:** weekly. **Effective Market(s):** New York. **Units of Measure:** Dollars per lb. **Type of Price:** spot. **Time Period Covered:** latest week.

METHYLENE CHLORIDE

Source: *Chemical Marketing Reporter.* **Price Frequency:** weekly. **Effective Market(s):** New York. **Units of Measure:** Dollars per lb. **Type of Price:** spot. **Time Period Covered:** latest week.

Source: *Journal of Commerce and Commercial.* **Price Frequency:** weekly in Wednesday issue. **Units of Measure:** Dollars per lb. **Type of Price:** spot. **Time Period Covered:** latest week.

METHYLENE DI-P-PHENYLENE DI-ISOCYANATE
see Diphenylmethane 4,4,-di-isocyanate.

4,4-METHYLENE DIANILINE: CRUDE
Source: *Chemical Marketing Reporter.* **Price Frequency:** weekly. **Effective Market(s):** New York. **Units of Measure:** Dollars per lb. **Type of Price:** spot. **Time Period Covered:** latest week.

4,4-METHYLENE DIANILINE: PURIFIED, FLAKE
Source: *Chemical Marketing Reporter.* **Price Frequency:** weekly. **Effective Market(s):** New York. **Units of Measure:** Dollars per lb. **Type of Price:** spot. **Time Period Covered:** latest week.

P-METHYLNAPHTHALENE
Source: *Chemical Marketing Reporter.* **Price Frequency:** weekly. **Effective Market(s):** New York. **Units of Measure:** Dollars per gallon. **Type of Price:** spot. **Time Period Covered:** latest week.

METHYLPARABEN: NF
Source: *Chemical Marketing Reporter.* **Price Frequency:** weekly. **Effective Market(s):** New York. **Units of Measure:** Dollars per lb. **Type of Price:** spot. **Time Period Covered:** latest week.

METHYLPARABEN: TECHNICAL
Source: *Chemical Marketing Reporter.* **Price Frequency:** weekly. **Effective Market(s):** New York. **Units of Measure:** Dollars per lb. **Type of Price:** spot. **Time Period Covered:** latest week.

METHYLPENTANEDIOL
see Hexylene Glycol.

METHYLPHENYLPYRAZOLONE
see 1-Phenyl-3-methyl-5-pyrazolone.

A-METHYLSTYRENE
Source: *Chemical Marketing Reporter.* **Price Frequency:** weekly. **Effective Market(s):** New York. **Units of Measure:** Dollars per lb. **Type of Price:** spot. **Time Period Covered:** latest week.

METOLACHLOR: EMULSIFIABLE CONCENTRATE
Source: *Agricultural Prices Annual Summary.* **Price Frequency:** semiannually. **Effective Market(s):** United States. **Units of Measure:** Dollars per gallon. **Type of Price:** paid by farmer. **Time Period Covered:** latest 6 years.

METRIBUZIN: 75%, DRY FLOWABLE
Source: *Agricultural Prices Annual Summary.* **Price Frequency:** semiannually. **Effective Market(s):** United States. **Units of Measure:** Dollars per lb. **Type of Price:** paid by farmer. **Time Period Covered:** latest 6 years.

MEXICO PESOS
Source: *Barron's.* **Price Frequency:** weekly. **Effective Market(s):** New York. **Units of Measure:** Mexican pesos per United States dollar. **Type of Price:** floating foreign exchange rate. **Time Period Covered:** latest 2 weeks.

Source: *International Wheat Council Market Report.* **Price Frequency:** weekly. **Effective Market(s):** London. **Units of Measure:** Mexican pesos per United States dollars. **Type of Price:** foreign exchange. **Time Period Covered:** latest 5 weeks.

Source: *New York Times.* **Price Frequency:** daily. **Effective Market(s):** United States. **Units of Measure:** Mexican pesos per United States dollar. **Type of Price:** floating foreign exchange rate. **Time Period Covered:** latest 2 days.

Source: *The Times.* **Price Frequency:** daily. **Effective Market(s):** London. **Units of Measure:** Mexican pesos per British pound. **Type of Price:** foreign exchange. **Time Period Covered:** latest day.

MEZCAL
Source: *Kentucky Beverage Journal.* **Price Frequency:** monthly. **Effective Market(s):** Kentucky. **Units of Measure:** Dollars per bottle, dollars per case. **Type of Price:** wholesale by brand. **Time Period Covered:** latest month.

MICA: DRY GROUND
Source: *Industrial Minerals.* **Price Frequency:** monthly. **Effective Market(s):** United Kingdom. **Units of Measure:** British pounds per metric tonne. **Type of Price:** producer & dealer. **Time Period Covered:** latest month.

MICA: DRY GROUND, INDIAN
Source: *Industrial Minerals.* **Price Frequency:** monthly. **Effective Market(s):** Antwerp (Belgium). **Units of Measure:** British pounds per metric tonne. **Type of Price:** producer & dealer. **Time Period Covered:** latest month.

MICA: DRY GROUND, JOINT CEMENT, PLASTIC
Source: *Chemical Marketing Reporter.* **Price Frequency:** weekly. **Effective Market(s):** New York. **Units of Measure:** Dollars per lb. **Type of Price:** spot. **Time Period Covered:** latest week.

MICA: DRY GROUND, ROOFING
Source: *Chemical Marketing Reporter.* **Price Frequency:** weekly. **Effective Market(s):** New York. **Units of Measure:** Dollars per lb. **Type of Price:** spot. **Time Period Covered:** latest week.

MICA: MICRONISED
Source: *Industrial Minerals.* **Price Frequency:** monthly. **Effective Market(s):** main European port. **Units of Measure:** British pounds per metric tonne. **Type of Price:** producer & dealer. **Time Period Covered:** latest month.

MICA: MICRONISED, INDIAN
Source: *Industrial Minerals.* **Price Frequency:** monthly. **Effective Market(s):** Antwerp (Belgium). **Units of Measure:** British pounds per metric tonne. **Type of Price:** producer & dealer. **Time Period Covered:** latest month.

MICA: MINE SCRAP, MUSCOVITE, NO FOREIGN MATTER
Source: *Industrial Minerals.* **Price Frequency:** monthly. **Effective Market(s):** main European port. **Units of Measure:** British pounds per metric tonne. **Type of Price:** producer & dealer. **Time Period Covered:** latest month.

MICA: RUBBER
Source: *Chemical Marketing Reporter.* **Price Frequency:** weekly. **Effective Market(s):** New York. **Units of Measure:** Dollars per lb. **Type of Price:** spot. **Time Period Covered:** latest week.

MICA: WALLPAPER

Source: *Chemical Marketing Reporter.* **Price Frequency:** weekly. **Effective Market(s):** New York. **Units of Measure:** Dollars per lb. **Type of Price:** spot. **Time Period Covered:** latest week.

MICA: WET GROUND

Source: *Industrial Minerals.* **Price Frequency:** monthly. **Effective Market(s):** United Kingdom. **Units of Measure:** British pounds per metric tonne. **Type of Price:** producer & dealer. **Time Period Covered:** latest month.

MICA: WET GROUND, PAINT OR LACQUER

Source: *Chemical Marketing Reporter.* **Price Frequency:** weekly. **Effective Market(s):** New York. **Units of Measure:** Dollars per lb. **Type of Price:** spot. **Time Period Covered:** latest week.

MICROCRYSTALLINE WAX

see Wax: Microcrystalline.

MIDDLINGS

Source: *Agricultural Prices.* **Price Frequency:** quarterly. **Effective Market(s):** United States. **Units of Measure:** Dollars per 100 lbs. **Type of Price:** paid by farmer. **Time Period Covered:** latest 2 quarters, year ago.

Source: *Agricultural Prices.* **Price Frequency:** monthly. **Effective Market(s):** 10 domestic markets, United States. **Units of Measure:** Dollars per 100 lbs. **Type of Price:** paid by farmer. **Time Period Covered:** latest month.

Source: *Agricultural Prices Annual Summary.* **Price Frequency:** quarterly. **Effective Market(s):** 10 domestic markets, United States. **Units of Measure:** Dollars per 100 lbs. **Type of Price:** paid by farmer. **Time Period Covered:** latest year, for US latest 6 years.

Source: *Milling & Baking News.* **Price Frequency:** weekly. **Effective Market(s):** Kansas City. **Units of Measure:** Dollars per ton. **Time Period Covered:** latest week, week ago, year ago.

Source: *Milling & Baking News.* **Price Frequency:** weekly. **Effective Market(s):** 6 domestic markets. **Units of Measure:** Dollars per ton. **Time Period Covered:** latest week.

MIDDLINGS MILLFEEDS

Source: *Feedstuffs.* **Price Frequency:** weekly. **Effective Market(s):** 9 domestic markets. **Units of Measure:** Dollars per ton. **Time Period Covered:** latest week.

Source: *Feedstuffs.* **Price Frequency:** weekly. **Effective Market(s):** Minneapolis. **Units of Measure:** Dollars per ton. **Time Period Covered:** latest week, week ago, 6 months ago, year ago.

MILK

Source: *Agricultural Outlook.* **Price Frequency:** quarterly, annually. **Units of Measure:** Dollars per 100 lbs. **Type of Price:** plant average. **Time Period Covered:** latest year.

Source: *Agricultural Outlook.* **Price Frequency:** annually. **Effective Market(s):** United States. **Units of Measure:** Dollars per 100 lbs. **Type of Price:** delivered to plants and dealers. **Time Period Covered:** latest 7 years.

Source: *Agricultural Prices.* **Price Frequency:** monthly. **Effective Market(s):** United States. **Units of Measure:** Dollars per 100 lbs. **Type of Price:** received by farmer. **Time Period Covered:** latest 2 months, year ago.

Source: *Agricultural Prices.* **Price Frequency:** monthly. **Effective Market(s):** 33 domestic markets, United States. **Units of Measure:** Dollars per 100 lbs. **Type of Price:** received by farmer. **Time Period Covered:** latest 2 months.

Source: *Commodity Year Book.* **Price Frequency:** monthly, annually. **Units of Measure:** Dollars per 100 lbs. **Type of Price:** price received by farmers. **Time Period Covered:** latest 5 years.

Source: *Commodity Year Book.* **Price Frequency:** annually. **Effective Market(s):** United States. **Units of Measure:** cents per quart. **Type of Price:** consumer. **Time Period Covered:** latest 5 years.

Source: *Commodity Year Book.* **Price Frequency:** annually. **Effective Market(s):** United States. **Units of Measure:** Dollars per 100 lbs. **Type of Price:** milk sold to plants and dealers. **Time Period Covered:** latest 5 years.

Source: *Commodity Year Book.* **Price Frequency:** monthly, annually. **Units of Measure:** Dollars per 100 lbs. **Type of Price:** farm price. **Time Period Covered:** latest 6 years.

Source: *Dairy Market Statistics.* **Price Frequency:** monthly, annually. **Effective Market(s):** 11 domestic markets. **Units of Measure:** Dollars per 100 lbs. **Time Period Covered:** latest year.

Source: *Fedgazette.* **Price Frequency:** monthly. **Effective Market(s):** Minnesota. **Units of Measure:** Dollars per 100 lbs. **Time Period Covered:** latest 24 months.

Source: *Illinois Farm Report.* **Price Frequency:** monthly. **Effective Market(s):** Illinois. **Units of Measure:** Dollars per 100 lbs. **Type of Price:** average received by farmers. **Time Period Covered:** latest 2 months, year ago.

Source: *Kansas Business Review.* **Price Frequency:** monthly. **Effective Market(s):** Kansas. **Units of Measure:** Dollars per 100 lbs. **Type of Price:** received by farmer. **Time Period Covered:** latest month, month ago, year ago.

Source: *Scottish Farmer.* **Price Frequency:** monthly. **Effective Market(s):** Aberdeen, Northern Scotland. **Units of Measure:** British pence per litre. **Time Period Covered:** latest 2 months.

Source: *Standard & Poor's Statistical Service Current Statistics.* **Price Frequency:** monthly, annually. **Units of Measure:** Dollars per 100 lbs. **Type of Price:** plant & dealer. **Time Period Covered:** latest 4 years.

Source: *Washington Farmer-Stockman.* **Price Frequency:** monthly. **Effective Market(s):** Washington. **Units of Measure:** Dollars per 100 lbs. **Type of Price:** average received by farmer. **Time Period Covered:** latest month, month ago, year ago.

MILK: % MILKFAT

see Milk: % Butterfat.

MILK: 3.5% BUTTERFAT

Source: *Federal Milk Order Market Statistics.* **Price Frequency:** monthly. **Effective Market(s):** United States. **Units of Measure:** Dollars per 100 lbs. **Type of Price:** wholesale. **Time Period Covered:** latest 2 years.

MILK: ALL GRADES SOLD TO PLANTS

Source: *Agricultural Outlook.* **Price Frequency:** monthly, annually. **Effective Market(s):** United States. **Units of Measure:** Dollars per 100 lbs. **Type of Price:** average received by farmer. **Time Period Covered:** monthly latest 6 months, annually latest 3 years.

Source: *Dairy Situation and Outlook.* **Price Frequency:** monthly, annually. **Units of Measure:** Dollars per 100 lbs. **Type of Price:** received by farmers. **Time Period Covered:** latest 3 years.

MILK: ALL GRADES, NONFAT, POWDER SPRAY

Source: *Dairy Foods.* **Price Frequency:** monthly. **Effective Market(s):** Central states, South, West Coast. **Units of Measure:** Dollars per lb. **Time Period Covered:** latest month.

MILK: BLEND

Source: *Federal Milk Order Market Statistics Annual Summary.* **Price Frequency:** monthly, annually. **Effective Market(s):** 49 domestic markets. **Units of Measure:** Dollars per 100 lbs. **Type of Price:** average. **Time Period Covered:** latest 2 years.

Source: *Federal Milk Order Market Statistics.* **Price Frequency:** monthly, annually. **Effective Market(s):** 36 domestic markets. **Units of Measure:** Dollars per 100 lbs. **Type of Price:** average. **Time Period Covered:** monthly latest 2 months, annually latest 2 years.

MILK: ELIGIBLE FOR FLUID MARKET

Source: *Agricultural Prices Annual Summary.* **Price Frequency:** annually. **Effective Market(s):** 50 domestic markets, United States. **Units of Measure:** Dollars per 100 lbs. **Type of Price:** average received by farmer. **Time Period Covered:** latest 2 years, for US latest 6 years.

MILK: ELIGIBLE FOR FLUID MARKET, 3.5% BUTTERFAT

Source: *Federal Milk Order Market Statistics.* **Price Frequency:** monthly. **Effective Market(s):** United States. **Units of Measure:** Dollars per 100 lbs. **Type of Price:** average. **Time Period Covered:** latest 2 years.

MILK: EVAPORATED

Source: *Dairy Market Statistics.* **Price Frequency:** monthly, annually. **Effective Market(s):** United States. **Units of Measure:** Dollars per case. **Type of Price:** wholesale. **Time Period Covered:** latest year.

Source: *Statistical Bulletin of the South Pacific: Retail Price Indexes.* **Price Frequency:** annually. **Effective Market(s):** 18 South Pacific markets. **Units of Measure:** Australian dollars per 396 grams. **Type of Price:** retail. **Time Period Covered:** latest year.

MILK: EVAPORATED, KNOWN BRANDS

Source: *Dairy Foods.* **Price Frequency:** monthly. **Effective Market(s):** New York. **Units of Measure:** Dollars per case. **Time Period Covered:** latest month.

MILK: EXTRA GRADE AND GRADE A, NONFAT, DRY

Source: *Dairy Market Statistics.* **Price Frequency:** monthly, annually. **Effective Market(s):** California manufacturing plants. **Units of Measure:** Dollars per lb. **Time Period Covered:** latest year.

MILK: EXTRA GRADE, NONFAT, DRY

Source: *Dairy Market Statistics.* **Price Frequency:** monthly, annually. **Effective Market(s):** California cities, Central states, Eastern area, Southern area. **Units of Measure:** Dollars per lb. **Type of Price:** farm, wholesale. **Time Period Covered:** latest year.

MILK: EXTRA GRADE, SKIM, DRY, SPRAY, HIGH HEAT

Source: *Urner Barry's Price-Current.* **Price Frequency:** daily. **Units of Measure:** Dollars per lb. **Time Period Covered:** latest day.

MILK: FEDERAL ORDER CLASS I

Source: *Federal Milk Order Market Statistics Annual Summary.* **Price Frequency:** monthly, annually. **Effective Market(s):** 49 domestic markets. **Units of Measure:** Dollars per 100 lbs. **Type of Price:** average. **Time Period Covered:** latest 2 years.

Source: *Federal Milk Order Market Statistics.* **Price Frequency:** monthly, annually. **Effective Market(s):** 36 domestic markets. **Units of Measure:** Dollars per 100 lbs. **Type of Price:** average. **Time Period Covered:** monthly latest 2 months, annually latest 2 years.

MILK: FEDERAL ORDER CLASS II

Source: *Federal Milk Order Market Statistics Annual Summary.* **Price Frequency:** monthly. **Effective Market(s):** 39 domestic markets. **Units of Measure:** Dollars per 100 lbs. **Type of Price:** average. **Time Period Covered:** latest 2 years.

Source: *Federal Milk Order Market Statistics.* **Price Frequency:** monthly. **Effective Market(s):** 36 domestic markets. **Units of Measure:** Dollars per 100 lbs. **Type of Price:** average. **Time Period Covered:** latest 2 months.

MILK: FEDERAL ORDER CLASS III

Source: *Federal Milk Order Market Statistics.* **Price Frequency:** monthly. **Effective Market(s):** 36 domestic markets. **Units of Measure:** Dollars per 100 lbs. **Type of Price:** average. **Time Period Covered:** latest 2 months.

Source: *Federal Milk Order Market Statistics Annual Summary.* **Price Frequency:** monthly. **Effective Market(s):** 33 domestic markets. **Units of Measure:** Dollars per 100 lbs. **Type of Price:** average. **Time Period Covered:** latest 2 years.

MILK: FLUID GRADE

Source: *Agricultural Prices.* **Price Frequency:** monthly. **Effective Market(s):** United States. **Units of Measure:** Dollars per 100 lbs. **Type of Price:** received by farmer. **Time Period Covered:** latest 2 months, year ago.

Source: *Agricultural Prices.* **Price Frequency:** monthly. **Effective Market(s):** 33 domestic markets, United States. **Units of Measure:** Dollars per 100 lbs. **Type of Price:** received by farmer. **Time Period Covered:** latest month.

Source: *Illinois Farm Report.* **Price Frequency:** monthly. **Effective Market(s):** Illinois. **Units of Measure:** Dollars per 100 lbs. **Type of Price:** average received by farmers. **Time Period Covered:** latest 2 months, year ago.

Source: *Monthly Price Review.* **Price Frequency:** daily. **Effective Market(s):** East. **Units of Measure:** dollars per 100 lbs. **Time Period Covered:** latest month.

Source: *Survey of Current Business.* **Price Frequency:** monthly, annually. **Effective Market(s):** United States. **Units of Measure:** Dollars per 100 lbs. **Type of Price:** wholesale. **Time Period Covered:** latest year.

MILK: FLUID GRADE, BOTTLING QUALITY

Source: *Urner Barry's Price-Current.* **Price Frequency:** daily. **Effective Market(s):** New York. **Units of Measure:** Dollars per 40 quart unit, dollars per 100 lbs. **Time Period Covered:** latest day.

MILK: GRADE A, NONFAT, DRY

Source: *Dairy Market Statistics.* **Price Frequency:** monthly, annually. **Effective Market(s):** California cities, Central states, Eastern area, Southern area. **Units of Measure:** Dollars per lb. **Type of Price:** farm, wholesale. **Time Period Covered:** latest year.

MILK: GRADE A, NONFAT, POWDER SPRAY

Source: *Dairy Foods.* **Price Frequency:** monthly. **Effective Market(s):** New York, Philadelphia. **Units of Measure:** Dollars per lb. **Time Period Covered:** latest month.

MILK: GRADE A, SKIM, CONCENTRATED

Source: *Monthly Price Review.* **Price Frequency:** daily. **Effective Market(s):** east. **Units of Measure:** dollars per lb. **Time Period Covered:** latest month.

MILK: GRADE A, SKIM, DRY, SPRAY, LOW HEAT

Source: *Urner Barry's Price-Current.* **Price Frequency:** daily. **Units of Measure:** Dollars per lb. **Time Period Covered:** latest day.

MILK: LACTOSE SPRAY

Source: *Dairy Foods.* **Price Frequency:** monthly. **Effective Market(s):** Midwest/West. **Units of Measure:** Dollars per lb. **Time Period Covered:** latest month.

MILK: LOWFAT

Source: *Federal Milk Order Market Statistics.* **Price Frequency:** monthly. **Effective Market(s):** Northeast, South, United States. **Units of Measure:** Dollars per 1/2 gallon. **Type of Price:** retail. **Time Period Covered:** latest year to date.

MILK: LOWFAT, FRESH

Source: *Dairy Market Statistics.* **Price Frequency:** monthly, annually. **Effective Market(s):** Northeast, South, United States. **Units of Measure:** Dollars per half gallon. **Type of Price:** retail. **Time Period Covered:** latest year.

MILK: MANUFACTURING GRADE

Source: *Agricultural Outlook.* **Price Frequency:** monthly, annually. **Effective Market(s):** United States. **Units of Measure:** Dollars per 100 lbs. **Type of Price:** average received by farmer. **Time Period Covered:** monthly latest 6 months, annually latest 3 years.

Source: *Agricultural Prices.* **Price Frequency:** monthly. **Effective Market(s):** United States. **Units of Measure:** Dollars per 100 lbs. **Type of Price:** received by farmer. **Time Period Covered:** latest 2 months, year ago.

Source: *Agricultural Prices.* **Price Frequency:** monthly. **Effective Market(s):** 33 domestic markets, United States. **Units of Measure:** Dollars per 100 lbs. **Type of Price:** received by farmer. **Time Period Covered:** latest month.

Source: *Agricultural Prices Annual Summary.* **Price Frequency:** annually. **Effective Market(s):** 27 domestic markets, United States. **Units of Measure:** Dollars per 100 lbs. **Type of Price:** average received by farmer. **Time Period Covered:** latest 2 years, for US latest 6 years.

Source: *Dairy Market Statistics.* **Price Frequency:** monthly, annually. **Effective Market(s):** 8 domestic markets. **Units of Measure:** Dollars per 100 lbs. **Time Period Covered:** latest year.

Source: *Dairy Situation and Outlook.* **Price Frequency:** monthly, annually. **Units of Measure:** Dollars per 100 lbs. **Type of Price:** received by farmers. **Time Period Covered:** latest 3 years.

Source: *Federal Milk Order Market Statistics Annual Summary.* **Price Frequency:** monthly, annually. **Effective Market(s):** Minnesota/Wisconsin. **Units of Measure:** Dollars per 100 lbs. **Type of Price:** average. **Time Period Covered:** latest 2 years.

Source: *Illinois Farm Report.* **Price Frequency:** monthly. **Effective Market(s):** Illinois. **Units of Measure:** Dollars per 100 lbs. **Type of Price:** average received by farmers. **Time Period Covered:** latest 2 months, year ago.

Source: *Minnesota-Wisconsin Manufacturing Grade Milk: Prices Received Summary.* **Price Frequency:** monthly, annually. **Effective Market(s):** Minnesota/Wisconsin. **Units of Measure:** Dollars per 100 lbs. **Type of Price:** average received. **Time Period Covered:** latest 3 years.

Source: *Minnesota-Wisconsin Manufacturing Grade Milk Price.* **Price Frequency:** monthly. **Effective Market(s):** Minnesota/Wisconsin. **Units of Measure:** Dollars per 100 lbs. **Type of Price:** average. **Time Period Covered:** latest 2 months.

MILK: MANUFACTURING GRADE, 3.5% BUTTERFAT

Source: *Agricultural Outlook.* **Price Frequency:** monthly, annually. **Effective Market(s):** Minnesota/Wisconsin. **Units of Measure:** Dollars per 100 lbs. **Time Period Covered:** monthly latest 6 months, annually latest 3 years.

Source: *Federal Milk Order Market Statistics.* **Price Frequency:** monthly. **Effective Market(s):** United States. **Units of Measure:** Dollars per 100 lbs. **Type of Price:** average. **Time Period Covered:** latest 2 years.

Source: *Federal Milk Order Market Statistics.* **Price Frequency:** monthly. **Effective Market(s):** Minnesota/Wisconsin. **Units of Measure:** Dollars per 100 lbs. **Type of Price:** average paid to producer. **Time Period Covered:** latest 2 years.

Source: *Minnesota-Wisconsin Manufacturing Grade Milk: Prices Received Summary.* **Price Frequency:** monthly, annually. **Effective Market(s):** Minnesota/Wisconsin. **Units of Measure:** Dollars per 100 lbs. **Type of Price:** average received. **Time Period Covered:** latest 3 years.

Source: *Minnesota-Wisconsin Manufacturing Grade Milk Price.* **Price Frequency:** monthly. **Effective Market(s):** Minnesota/Wisconsin. **Units of Measure:** Dollars per 100 lbs. **Type of Price:** average. **Time Period Covered:** latest 2 months.

MILK: MANUFACTURING GRADE, SOLD TO PLANTS

Source: *Agricultural Prices Annual Summary.* **Price Frequency:** monthly. **Effective Market(s):** 24 domestic markets, United States. **Units of Measure:** Dollars per 100 lbs. **Type of Price:** received by farmer. **Time Period Covered:** latest year, for US latest 6 years.

MILK: NONFAT

Source: *Agricultural Outlook.* **Price Frequency:** monthly, annually. **Effective Market(s):** Central States. **Units of Measure:** cents per lb. **Type of Price:** wholesale. **Time Period Covered:** monthly latest 6 months, annually latest 3 years.

MILK: NONFAT, DRY

Source: *Dairy Situation and Outlook.* **Price Frequency:** monthly, annually. **Effective Market(s):** Central States. **Units of Measure:** cents per lb. **Type of Price:** wholesale. **Time Period Covered:** latest year.

Source: *Survey of Current Business.* **Price Frequency:** monthly, annually. **Units of Measure:** Dollars per lb. **Type of Price:** manufacturers' average selling. **Time Period Covered:** latest year.

Source: *World Dairy Situation.* **Price Frequency:** semiannually. **Effective Market(s):** Northern Europe/World ports. **Units of Measure:** Dollars per metric ton. **Type of Price:** average. **Time Period Covered:** latest 7 years.

MILK: NONFAT, DRY, HIGH HEAT

Source: *Milling & Baking News.* **Price Frequency:** weekly. **Effective Market(s):** Chicago, Eastern States. **Units of Measure:** cents per lb. **Time Period Covered:** latest week.

MILK: NONFAT, DRY, SPRAY PROCESS

Source: *Federal Milk Order Market Statistics Annual Summary.* **Price Frequency:** monthly, annually. **Effective Market(s):** Chicago. **Units of Measure:** Dollars per lb. **Type of Price:** average. **Time Period Covered:** latest 2 years.

Source: *Federal Milk Order Market Statistics.* **Price Frequency:** monthly. **Effective Market(s):** Chicago. **Units of Measure:** Dollars per lb. **Type of Price:** wholesale. **Time Period Covered:** latest 2 years.

MILK: NONFAT, POWDER SPRAY, HIGH HEAT

Source: *Dairy Foods.* **Price Frequency:** monthly. **Effective Market(s):** Chicago, New York Philadelphia. **Units of Measure:** Dollars per lb. **Time Period Covered:** latest month.

MILK: NONFAT, POWDER SPRAY, LOW HEAT

Source: *Dairy Foods.* **Price Frequency:** monthly. **Effective Market(s):** Chicago, New York, Philadelphia. **Units of Measure:** Dollars per lb. **Time Period Covered:** latest month.

MILK: RETAILED BY FARMER

Source: *Agricultural Prices Annual Summary.* **Price Frequency:** annually. **Effective Market(s):** 25 domestic markets, United States. **Units of Measure:** Dollars per quart. **Type of Price:** average received by farmer. **Time Period Covered:** latest 2 years, for US latest 6 years.

MILK: SKIM, CONDENSED

Source: *Dairy Market Statistics.* **Price Frequency:** monthly, annually. **Effective Market(s):** Baltimore/Philadelphia/Washington, Boston, New York. **Units of Measure:** Dollars per lb. wet solids. **Type of Price:** spot. **Time Period Covered:** latest year.

Source: *Urner Barry's Price-Current.* **Price Frequency:** daily. **Effective Market(s):** New York. **Units of Measure:** Dollars per lb. solids. **Time Period Covered:** latest day.

MILK: SKIM, CONDENSED, SOLID

Source: *Monthly Price Review.* **Price Frequency:** daily. **Effective Market(s):** East. **Units of Measure:** dollars per lb. **Time Period Covered:** latest month.

MILK: SKIM, DRY

Source: *Dairy Market Statistics.* **Price Frequency:** monthly, annually. **Effective Market(s):** Central states. **Units of Measure:** Dollars per lb. **Time Period Covered:** latest year.

Source: *Feedstuffs.* **Price Frequency:** weekly. **Effective Market(s):** Ft. Worth, Minneapolis/St. Paul. **Units of Measure:** Dollars per 100 lbs. **Time Period Covered:** latest week.

MILK: SOLD TO PLANTS

Source: *Agricultural Prices Annual Summary.* **Price Frequency:** monthly. **Effective Market(s):** 33 domestic markets, United States. **Units of Measure:** Dollars per 100 lbs. **Type of Price:** received by farmer. **Time Period Covered:** latest year, for US latest 6 years.

MILK: WHOLE

Source: *Federal Milk Order Market Statistics.* **Price Frequency:** monthly. **Effective Market(s):** North Central, Northeast, South, West, United States. **Units of Measure:** Dollars per 1/2 gallon. **Type of Price:** retail. **Time Period Covered:** latest year to date.

MILK: WHOLE, DRY, SPRAY

Source: *Dairy Foods.* **Price Frequency:** monthly. **Effective Market(s):** Eastern area. **Units of Measure:** Dollars per lb. **Time Period Covered:** latest month.

MILK: WHOLE, DRY, SPRAY, 26%, KNOWN BRANDS

Source: *Urner Barry's Price-Current* . **Price Frequency:** daily. **Units of Measure:** Dollars per lb. **Time Period Covered:** latest day.

MILK: WHOLE, DRY, SPRAY, 28 TO 28-1/2%, KNOWN BRANDS

Source: *Urner Barry's Price-Current.* **Price Frequency:** daily. **Units of Measure:** Dollars per lb. **Time Period Covered:** latest day.

MILK: WHOLE, EVAPORATED, KNOWN BRANDS

Source: *Urner Barry's Price-Current.* **Price Frequency:** daily. **Units of Measure:** Dollars per case . **Time Period Covered:** latest day.

MILK: WHOLE, FRESH

Source: *Dairy Market Statistics.* **Price Frequency:** monthly. **Effective Market(s):** United States. **Units of Measure:** index. **Type of Price:** consumer price index. **Time Period Covered:** latest year.

Source: *Dairy Market Statistics.* **Price Frequency:** monthly, annually. **Effective Market(s):** North Central, Northeast, South, West, United States. **Units of Measure:** Dollars per half gallon. **Type of Price:** retail. **Time Period Covered:** latest year.

MILK COOLER

Source: *Agricultural Prices.* **Price Frequency:** semiannually. **Effective Market(s):** United States. **Units of Measure:** Dollars each. **Type of Price:** paid by farmer. **Time Period Covered:** latest year.

Source: *Agricultural Prices Annual Summary.* **Price Frequency:** annually. **Effective Market(s):** United States. **Units of Measure:** Dollars each. **Type of Price:** paid by farmer. **Time Period Covered:** latest 6 years.

MILK POWDER

Source: *Statistical Bulletin of the South Pacific: Retail Price Indexes.* **Price Frequency:** annually. **Effective Market(s):** 18 South Pacific markets. **Units of Measure:** Australian dollars per 1.250 kilograms. **Type of Price:** retail. **Time Period Covered:** latest year.

MILK POWDER: SKIM, SPRAY

Source: *FAO Quarterly Bulletin of Statistics.* **Price Frequency:** monthly, annually. **Effective Market(s):** New York. **Units of Measure:** Dollars per 100 lbs., dollars per metric ton. **Type of Price:** wholesale. **Time Period Covered:** latest 3 years.

MILK POWDER: SKIM, SPRAY, DUTCH

Source: *FAO Quarterly Bulletin of Statistics.* **Price Frequency:** monthly, annually. **Effective Market(s):** Netherlands. **Units of Measure:** Dutch guilders per kilogram, dollars per metric ton. **Type of Price:** national average. **Time Period Covered:** latest 3 years.

MILK POWDER: WHEY, SPRAY, DUTCH

Source: *FAO Quarterly Bulletin of Statistics.* **Price Frequency:** monthly, annually. **Effective Market(s):** Netherlands. **Units of Measure:** Dutch guilders per kilograms, dollars per metric ton. **Type of Price:** national average. **Time Period Covered:** latest 3 years.

MILK POWDER: WHOLE, 26% BUTTERFAT

Source: *Dairy Market Statistics.* **Price Frequency:** monthly, annually. **Effective Market(s):** Eastern area. **Units of Measure:** Dollars per lb. **Type of Price:** wholesale. **Time Period Covered:** latest year.

MILK POWDER: WHOLE, 28-1/2% BUTTERFAT

Source: *Dairy Market Statistics.* **Price Frequency:** monthly, annually. **Effective Market(s):** Eastern area. **Units of Measure:** Dollars per lb. **Type of Price:** wholesale. **Time Period Covered:** latest year.

MILK POWDER: WHOLE, SPRAY, DUTCH

Source: *FAO Quarterly Bulletin of Statistics.* **Price Frequency:** monthly, annually. **Effective Market(s):** Netherlands. **Units of Measure:** Dutch guilders per kilogram, dollars per metric ton. **Type of Price:** national average. **Time Period Covered:** latest 3 years.

MILLFEEDS: BRAN

see Bran Millfeeds.

MILLFEEDS: MIDDLINGS

see Middlings Millfeeds.

MILLFEEDS: MILLRUN

see Millrun Millfeeds.

MILLFEEDS: RICE

see Rice Millfeeds.

MILLFEEDS: SHORTS

Source: *Feedstuffs.* **Price Frequency:** weekly. **Effective Market(s):** Chicago, Ft. Worth, Los Angeles, San Francisco. **Units of Measure:** Dollars per ton. **Time Period Covered:** latest week.

MILLRUN MILLFEEDS

Source: *Feedstuffs.* **Price Frequency:** weekly. **Effective Market(s):** Chicago, Ft. Worth, Los Angeles, San Francisco. **Units of Measure:** Dollars per ton. **Time Period Covered:** latest week.

MILO

see also Sorghum.

Source: *Feedstuffs.* **Price Frequency:** weekly. **Effective Market(s):** 8 domestic markets. **Units of Measure:** Dollars per 100 lbs. **Time Period Covered:** latest week.

Source: *Feedstuffs.* **Price Frequency:** weekly. **Effective Market(s):** Kansas City. **Units of Measure:** Dollars per 100 lbs. **Time Period Covered:** latest week, week ago, 6 months ago, year ago.

MILO: NO. 2, YELLOW

Source: *Commodity Trade and Price Trends.* **Price Frequency:** annually. **Effective Market(s):** Gulf ports. **Units of Measure:** Dollars per metric ton, 1980 constant dollars per metric ton. **Time Period Covered:** latest 37 years.

Source: *FAO Quarterly Bulletin of Statistics.* **Price Frequency:** monthly, annually. **Effective Market(s):** Gulf. **Units of Measure:** Dollars per 100 lbs., dollars per metric ton. **Time Period Covered:** latest 3 years.

MINERAL OIL: 180-190 VISCOSITY, USP

Source: *Chemical Marketing Reporter.* **Price Frequency:** weekly. **Effective Market(s):** New York. **Units of Measure:** Dollars per gallon. **Type of Price:** spot. **Time Period Covered:** latest week.

MINERAL OIL: 200-210 VISCOSITY, USP

Source: *Chemical Marketing Reporter.* **Price Frequency:** weekly. **Effective Market(s):** New York. **Units of Measure:** Dollars per gallon. **Type of Price:** spot. **Time Period Covered:** latest week.

MINERAL OIL: 340-350 VISCOSITY, USP

Source: *Chemical Marketing Reporter.* **Price Frequency:** weekly. **Effective Market(s):** New York. **Units of Measure:** Dollars per lb. **Type of Price:** spot. **Time Period Covered:** latest week.

MINERAL OIL: WHITE

Source: *Journal of Commerce and Commercial.* **Price Frequency:** weekly in Friday issue. **Units of Measure:** Dollars per gallon. **Type of Price:** spot. **Time Period Covered:** latest week.

MINERAL OIL: WHITE, 50-65 VISCOSITY

Source: *Chemical Marketing Reporter.* **Price Frequency:** weekly. **Effective Market(s):** New York. **Units of Measure:** Dollars per gallon. **Type of Price:** spot. **Time Period Covered:** latest week.

MINERAL OIL: WHITE, 65-75 VISCOSITY

Source: *Chemical Marketing Reporter.* **Price Frequency:** weekly. **Effective Market(s):** New York. **Units of Measure:** Dollars per gallon. **Type of Price:** spot. **Time Period Covered:** latest week.

MINERAL OIL: WHITE, 80-90 VISCOSITY

Source: *Chemical Marketing Reporter.* **Price Frequency:** weekly. **Effective Market(s):** New York. **Units of Measure:** Dollars per gallon. **Type of Price:** spot. **Time Period Covered:** latest week.

MINERAL OIL: WHITE, 145-155 VISCOSITY

Source: *Chemical Marketing Reporter.* **Price Frequency:** weekly. **Effective Market(s):** New York. **Units of Measure:** Dollars per gallon. **Type of Price:** spot. **Time Period Covered:** latest week.

MINERAL SPIRITS: PETROLEUM, ODORLESS

Source: *Chemical Marketing Reporter.* **Price Frequency:** weekly. **Effective Market(s):** Houston (TX), New Jersey. **Units of Measure:** Dollars per gallon. **Type of Price:** spot. **Time Period Covered:** latest week.

MINERAL SPIRITS: PETROLEUM, REGULAR

Source: *Chemical Marketing Reporter.* **Price Frequency:** weekly. **Effective Market(s):** Houston (TX), New Jersey. **Units of Measure:** Dollars per lb. **Type of Price:** spot. **Time Period Covered:** latest week.

MINERAL WATER

Source: *Nevada Beverage Index.* **Price Frequency:** monthly. **Effective Market(s):** Nevada. **Units of Measure:** Dollars per unit. **Type of Price:** wholesale by brand. **Time Period Covered:** latest month.

MINERALS, ORES AND METALS

Source: *Monthly Commodity Price Bulletin.* **Price Frequency:** monthly, annually. **Effective Market(s):** developing countries. **Units of Measure:** index. **Type of Price:** free market price index. **Time Period Covered:** latest 5 years.

Source: *Monthly Commodity Price Bulletin Supplement.* **Price Frequency:** monthly, quarterly, annually. **Effective Market(s):** developing countries. **Units of Measure:** index. **Type of Price:** free market price index. **Time Period Covered:** latest 20 years.

Source: *UNCTAD Commodity Yearbook.* **Price Frequency:** annually. **Units of Measure:** index. **Type of Price:** price index. **Time Period Covered:** latest 12 years.

MINT LEAVES: PEPPERMINT

Source: *U. S. Spice Trade.* **Price Frequency:** annually. **Effective Market(s):** New York. **Units of Measure:** cents per lb. **Type of Price:** spot. **Time Period Covered:** latest 3 years.

MINT LEAVES: PEPPERMINT, CRUSHED

Source: *U. S. Spice Trade.* **Price Frequency:** annually. **Effective Market(s):** New York. **Units of Measure:** cents per lb. **Type of Price:** spot. **Time Period Covered:** latest 3 years.

MINT LEAVES: SPEARMINT

Source: *U. S. Spice Trade.* **Price Frequency:** annually. **Effective Market(s):** New York. **Units of Measure:** cents per lb. **Type of Price:** spot. **Time Period Covered:** latest 3 years.

MINT LEAVES: SPEARMINT, CRUSHED

Source: *U. S. Spice Trade.* **Price Frequency:** annually. **Effective Market(s):** New York. **Units of Measure:** cents per lb. **Type of Price:** spot. **Time Period Covered:** latest 3 years.

MINT OIL

Source: *Journal of Commerce and Commercial.* **Price Frequency:** weekly in Tuesday issue. **Units of Measure:** Dollars per lb. **Type of Price:** spot. **Time Period Covered:** latest week.

Source: *U. S. Essential Oil Trade.* **Price Frequency:** annually. **Effective Market(s):** New York. **Units of Measure:** Dollars per lb. **Type of Price:** spot. **Time Period Covered:** latest 4 years.

MIXES: COCKTAIL

Source: *Illinois Beverage Journal.* **Price Frequency:** monthly. **Effective Market(s):** Illinois. **Units of Measure:** Dollars per case. **Type of Price:** wholesale by brand. **Time Period Covered:** latest month.

Source: *Kentucky Beverage Journal.* **Price Frequency:** monthly. **Effective Market(s):** Kentucky. **Units of Measure:** Dollars per bottle, dollars per case. **Type of Price:** wholesale by brand. **Time Period Covered:** latest month.

MMA FABRIC

Source: *JTN: The International Textile Magazine.* **Price Frequency:** monthly. **Effective Market(s):** Japan. **Units of Measure:** Japanese yen per yard. **Type of Price:** spot. **Time Period Covered:** latest month.

MOGAS 98

Source: *Oil Buyers' Guide International.* **Price Frequency:** weekly. **Effective Market(s):** Mediterranean, Northwest Europe. **Units of Measure:** Dollars per metric ton. **Type of Price:** cargo. **Time Period Covered:** latest week.

MOHAIR

Source: *Wool and Mohair.* **Price Frequency:** annually. **Effective Market(s):** United States. **Units of Measure:** Dollars per lb. **Time Period Covered:** latest 3 years.

Source: *Wool and Mohair.* **Price Frequency:** annually. **Effective Market(s):** Arizona, Michigan, New Mexico, Oklahoma, Texas, United States. **Units of Measure:** Dollars per lb. **Time Period Covered:** latest 2 years.

MOHAIR: ORIGINAL BAG, ADULT GOAT, GREASE BASIS

Source: *National Wool Market Review.* **Price Frequency:** weekly, seasonally. **Effective Market(s):** Texas. **Units of Measure:** cents per lb. **Time Period Covered:** latest week.

MOHAIR: ORIGINAL BAG, KID GOAT, GREASE BASIS

Source: *National Wool Market Review.* **Price Frequency:** weekly, seasonally. **Effective Market(s):** Texas. **Units of Measure:** cents per lb. **Time Period Covered:** latest week.

MOHAIR: ORIGINAL BAG, YEARLING/ YOUNG GOAT, GREASE BASIS

Source: *National Wool Market Review.* **Price Frequency:** weekly, seasonally. **Effective Market(s):** Texas. **Units of Measure:** cents per lb. **Time Period Covered:** latest week.

MOLASSES

Source: *Agricultural Prices Annual Summary.* **Price Frequency:** quarterly. **Effective Market(s):** 10 domestic markets, United States. **Units of Measure:** Dollars per 100 lbs. **Type of Price:** paid by farmer. **Time Period Covered:** latest year, for US latest 6 years.

MOLASSES: BEET

Source: *Commodity Year Book.* **Price Frequency:** annually. **Effective Market(s):** 6 domestic markets. **Units of Measure:** Dollars per ton. **Time Period Covered:** latest 10 years.

Source: *Milling & Baking News.* **Price Frequency:** weekly. **Effective Market(s):** Colorado. **Units of Measure:** Dollars per ton. **Time Period Covered:** latest week, week ago, year ago.

MOLASSES: BEET FEED

Source: *Molasses Market News.* **Price Frequency:** weekly. **Effective Market(s):** 5 domestic markets. **Units of Measure:** Dollars per ton. **Type of Price:** wholesale. **Time Period Covered:** latest week, week ago, year ago.

MOLASSES: BEET PULP

Source: *Feed Situation and Outlook Report.* **Price Frequency:** monthly. **Effective Market(s):** Los Angeles. **Units of Measure:** Dollars per ton. **Type of Price:** wholesale. **Time Period Covered:** latest 8 months.

MOLASSES: BEET PULP, DRIED

Source: *Grain and Feed Market News.* **Price Frequency:** weekly, seasonally. **Effective Market(s):** Los Angeles, Northern California Hills. **Units of Measure:** Dollars per ton. **Type of Price:** wholesale. **Time Period Covered:** latest week, week ago, year ago.

MOLASSES: BLACKSTRAP

Source: *Commodity Year Book.* **Price Frequency:** monthly, annually. **Effective Market(s):** New Orleans. **Units of Measure:** Dollars per ton. **Type of Price:** wholesale. **Time Period Covered:** latest 5 years.

Source: *Commodity Year Book.* **Price Frequency:** Annually. **Effective Market(s):** 6 domestic markets. **Units of Measure:** Dollars per ton. **Time Period Covered:** latest 10 years.

Source: *Milling & Baking News.* **Price Frequency:** weekly. **Effective Market(s):** Kansas City. **Units of Measure:** Dollars per ton. **Time Period Covered:** latest week, week ago, year ago.

MOLASSES: CANE

Source: *Farmers Weekly.* **Price Frequency:** weekly, seasonally. **Effective Market(s):** Great Britain. **Units of Measure:** British pounds per tonne. **Type of Price:** spot. **Time Period Covered:** latest week.

Source: *Feed Situation and Outlook Report.* **Price Frequency:** monthly. **Effective Market(s):** New Orleans. **Units of Measure:** Dollars per ton. **Type of Price:** wholesale. **Time Period Covered:** latest 8 months.

Source: *Feedstuffs.* **Price Frequency:** weekly. **Effective Market(s):** 10 domestic markets. **Units of Measure:** Dollars per bulk ton. **Time Period Covered:** latest week.

Source: *Feedstuffs.* **Price Frequency:** weekly. **Effective Market(s):** New Orleans. **Units of Measure:** Dollars per ton. **Time Period Covered:** latest week, week ago, 6 months ago, year ago.

Source: *Grain and Feed Market News.* **Price Frequency:** weekly, seasonally. **Effective Market(s):** 6 domestic markets. **Units of Measure:** Dollars per ton. **Type of Price:** wholesale. **Time Period Covered:** latest week, week ago, year ago.

MOLASSES: CANE BLACKSTRAP, FEED

Source: *Molasses Market News.* **Price Frequency:** weekly. **Effective Market(s):** 11 domestic markets. **Units of Measure:** Dollars per ton. **Type of Price:** wholesale. **Time Period Covered:** latest week, week ago, year ago.

MOLASSES: CITRUS

Source: *Commodity Year Book.* **Price Frequency:** annually. **Effective Market(s):** Florida. **Units of Measure:** Dollars per ton. **Time Period Covered:** latest 10 years.

Source: *Feedstuffs.* **Price Frequency:** weekly, seasonally. **Effective Market(s):** 10 domestic markets. **Units of Measure:** Dollars per bulk ton. **Time Period Covered:** latest week.

MOLASSES: LIQUID

Source: *Agricultural Prices.* **Price Frequency:** quarterly. **Effective Market(s):** United States. **Units of Measure:** Dollars per 100 lbs. **Type of Price:** paid by farmer. **Time Period Covered:** latest 2 quarters, year ago.

Source: *Agricultural Prices.* **Price Frequency:** monthly. **Effective Market(s):** 10 domestic markest, United States. **Units of Measure:** Dollars per 100 lbs. **Type of Price:** paid by farmer. **Time Period Covered:** latest month.

MOLDING COMPOUND: CHEMICAL RESISTANT

Source: *Journal of Commerce and Commercial.* **Price Frequency:** weekly in Tuesday issue. **Units of Measure:** Dollars per lb. **Type of Price:** spot. **Time Period Covered:** latest week.

MOLDING COMPOUND: HIGH IMPACT

Source: *Journal of Commerce and Commercial.* **Price Frequency:** weekly in Tuesday issue. **Units of Measure:** Dollars per lb. **Type of Price:** spot. **Time Period Covered:** latest week.

MOLDING COMPOUND POWDER: GENERAL PURPOSE

Source: *Journal of Commerce and Commercial.* **Price Frequency:** weekly in Tuesday issue. **Units of Measure:** Dollars per lb. **Type of Price:** spot. **Time Period Covered:** latest week.

MOLYBDATED ORANGE

Source: *Journal of Commerce and Commercial.* **Price Frequency:** weekly in Wednesday issue. **Units of Measure:** Dollars per lb. **Type of Price:** spot. **Time Period Covered:** latest week.

MOLYBDENUM

Source: *American Metal Market.* **Price Frequency:** daily. **Units of Measure:** Dollars per lb. of concentrated Molybdenum. **Type of Price:** merchant, producer. **Time Period Covered:** latest day.

Source: *Iron Age.* **Price Frequency:** monthly. **Units of Measure:** Dollars per lb. **Type of Price:** consumer. **Time Period Covered:** latest month.

Source: *Purchasing.* **Price Frequency:** quarterly in January, April, July, October issues. **Units of Measure:** cents per lb. **Type of Price:** transaction. **Time Period Covered:** latest 5 quarters.

MOLYBDENUM: FERRO

see Ferromolybednum.

MOLYBDENUM OXIDE

Source: *Northern Miner.* **Price Frequency:** daily. **Effective Market(s):** Midwest. **Units of Measure:** Dollars per lb. **Type of Price:** dealer . **Time Period Covered:** latest day.

MOLYBDENUM OXIDE: 57% MINIMUM

Source: *Journal of Commerce and Commercial.* **Price Frequency:** daily. **Effective Market(s):** Europe. **Units of Measure:** Dollars per lb. **Type of Price:** spot. **Time Period Covered:** latest day.

MOLYBDENUM TRIOXIDE: CHEMICALLY PURE

Source: *Chemical Marketing Reporter.* **Price Frequency:** weekly. **Effective Market(s):** New York. **Units of Measure:** Dollars per lb. **Type of Price:** spot. **Time Period Covered:** latest week.

MOLYBDENUM TRIOXIDE: TECHNICAL, CHEMICAL

Source: *Chemical Marketing Reporter.* **Price Frequency:** weekly. **Effective Market(s):** New York. **Units of Measure:** Dollars per lb. **Type of Price:** spot. **Time Period Covered:** latest week.

MOLYBDENUM TRIOXIDE: TECHNICAL, METALLURGICAL

Source: *Chemical Marketing Reporter.* **Price Frequency:** weekly. **Effective Market(s):** New York. **Units of Measure:** Dollars per lb. **Type of Price:** spot. **Time Period Covered:** latest week.

MOLYBDIC ACID

see Ammonium Dimolybdate.

MOLYBDIC OXIDE

Source: *E&MJ.* **Price Frequency:** monthly. **Units of Measure:** Dollars per lb. **Type of Price:** producer. **Time Period Covered:** latest month.

MOLYBDIC OXIDE: CANNED

Source: *American Metal Market.* **Price Frequency:** daily. **Units of Measure:** Dollars per lb. of concentrated Molybdenum. **Type of Price:** merchant, producer. **Time Period Covered:** latest day.

MONAZITE

Source: *Industrial Minerals.* **Price Frequency:** monthly. **Effective Market(s):** Australia. **Units of Measure:** Australian dollars per metric tonne. **Type of Price:** producer & dealer. **Time Period Covered:** latest month.

MONEL CASTINGS

Source: *American Metal Market.* **Price Frequency:** daily. **Effective Market(s):** 8 domestic markets. **Units of Measure:** cents per lb. **Type of Price:** dealer. **Time Period Covered:** latest day.

MONEL CLIPPINGS AND SOLIDS: NEW

Source: *American Metal Market.* **Price Frequency:** daily. **Effective Market(s):** 8 domestic markets. **Units of Measure:** cents per lb. **Type of Price:** dealer. **Time Period Covered:** latest day.

MONEL PLATES

Source: *American Metal Market.* **Price Frequency:** daily. **Effective Market(s):** World. **Units of Measure:** Dollars per lb. of nickel. **Type of Price:** base. **Time Period Covered:** latest day.

MONEL RODS

Source: *American Metal Market.* **Price Frequency:** daily. **Effective Market(s):** World. **Units of Measure:** Dollars per lb. of nickel. **Type of Price:** base. **Time Period Covered:** latest day.

MONEL SHEETS: COLD ROLLED

Source: *American Metal Market.* **Price Frequency:** daily. **Effective Market(s):** World. **Units of Measure:** Dollars per lb. of nickel. **Type of Price:** base. **Time Period Covered:** latest day.

MONEL SHEETS AND SOLIDS: OLD

Source: *American Metal Market.* **Price Frequency:** daily. **Effective Market(s):** 8 domestic markets. **Units of Measure:** cents per lb. **Type of Price:** dealer. **Time Period Covered:** latest day.

MONEL STRIP

Source: *American Metal Market.* **Price Frequency:** daily. **Effective Market(s):** World. **Units of Measure:** Dollars per lb. of nickel. **Type of Price:** base. **Time Period Covered:** latest day.

MONEL TURNINGS AND SHAVINGS

Source: *American Metal Market.* **Price Frequency:** daily. **Effective Market(s):** 8 domestic markets. **Units of Measure:** cents per lb. **Type of Price:** dealer. **Time Period Covered:** latest day.

MONKFISH: FILLETS, FRESH

Source: *HRI-Buyers Guide.* **Price Frequency:** weekly. **Effective Market(s):** New York. **Units of Measure:** Dollars per lb. **Type of Price:** prices paid by dining places & institutions. **Time Period Covered:** latest week.

Source: *Seafood Price-Current.* **Price Frequency:** semiweekly. **Effective Market(s):** Mid-Atlantic, New England. **Units of Measure:** Dollars per lb. **Type of Price:** sale by first receiver. **Time Period Covered:** latest day.

MONKTAIL (FISH): WHOLE, FRESH

Source: *Seafood Price-Current.* **Price Frequency:** semiweekly. **Effective Market(s):** Boston, Mid-Atlantic, New Bedford (MA), Portland (ME). **Units of Measure:** Dollars per lb. **Type of Price:** sale by first receiver, auction price. **Time Period Covered:** latest day.

MONO-TERT-BUTYL-M-CRESOL

Source: *Chemical Marketing Reporter.* **Price Frequency:** weekly. **Effective Market(s):** New York. **Units of Measure:** Dollars per lb. **Type of Price:** spot. **Time Period Covered:** latest week.

MONOAMMONIUM PHOSPHATE: FERTILIZER GRADE

Source: *Chemical Marketing Reporter.* **Price Frequency:** weekly. **Effective Market(s):** Florida. **Units of Measure:** Dollars per ton. **Type of Price:** spot. **Time Period Covered:** latest week.

MONOAMMONIUM PHOSPHATE: FOOD GRADE

Source: *Chemical Marketing Reporter.* **Price Frequency:** weekly. **Effective Market(s):** New York. **Units of Measure:** Dollars per 100 lbs. **Type of Price:** spot. **Time Period Covered:** latest week.

MONOAMMONIUM PHOSPHATE: TECHNICAL GRADE

Source: *Chemical Marketing Reporter.* **Price Frequency:** weekly. **Effective Market(s):** New York. **Units of Measure:** Dollars per 100 lbs. **Type of Price:** spot. **Time Period Covered:** latest week.

MONOBUTYLAMINE

Source: *Chemical Marketing Reporter.* **Price Frequency:** weekly. **Effective Market(s):** New York. **Units of Measure:** Dollars per lb. **Type of Price:** spot. **Time Period Covered:** latest week.

MONOCHLOROACETIC ACID: PURIFIED

see Chloroacetic Acid: Mono.

MONOCHLOROBENZENE

Source: *Chemical Marketing Reporter.* **Price Frequency:** weekly. **Effective Market(s):** New York. **Units of Measure:** Dollars per lb. **Type of Price:** spot. **Time Period Covered:** latest week.

Source: *Journal of Commerce and Commercial.* **Price Frequency:** weekly in Wednesday issue. **Units of Measure:** Dollars per lb. **Type of Price:** spot. **Time Period Covered:** latest week.

MONOETHANOLAMINE

Source: *Chemical Marketing Reporter.* **Price Frequency:** weekly. **Effective Market(s):** East. **Units of Measure:** Dollars per lb. **Type of Price:** spot. **Time Period Covered:** latest week.

MONOETHYLAMINE: 70% AQUEOUS

Source: *Chemical Marketing Reporter.* **Price Frequency:** weekly. **Effective Market(s):** New York. **Units of Measure:** Dollars per lb. **Type of Price:** spot. **Time Period Covered:** latest week.

MONOETHYLAMINE: ANHYDROUS

Source: *Chemical Marketing Reporter.* **Price Frequency:** weekly. **Effective Market(s):** New York. **Units of Measure:** Dollars per lb. **Type of Price:** spot. **Time Period Covered:** latest week.

MONOISOPROPANOLAMINE

Source: *Chemical Marketing Reporter.* **Price Frequency:** weekly. **Effective Market(s):** East. **Units of Measure:** Dollars per lb. **Type of Price:** spot. **Time Period Covered:** latest week.

MONOISOPROPYLAMINE: ANHYDROUS

Source: *Chemical Marketing Reporter.* **Price Frequency:** weekly. **Effective Market(s):** New York. **Units of Measure:** Dollars per lb. **Type of Price:** spot. **Time Period Covered:** latest week.

MONOMETHYLAMINE: 25% SOLUTION

Source: *Chemical Marketing Reporter.* **Price Frequency:** weekly. **Effective Market(s):** New York. **Units of Measure:** Dollars per lb. **Type of Price:** spot. **Time Period Covered:** latest week.

MONOMETHYLAMINE: 40-60% SOLUTION

Source: *Chemical Marketing Reporter.* **Price Frequency:** weekly. **Effective Market(s):** New York. **Units of Measure:** Dollars per lb. **Type of Price:** spot. **Time Period Covered:** latest week.

MONOMETHYLAMINE: ANHYDROUS

Source: *Chemical Marketing Reporter.* **Price Frequency:** weekly. **Effective Market(s):** New York. **Units of Measure:** Dollars per lb. **Type of Price:** spot. **Time Period Covered:** latest week.

MONOPOTASSIUM GLUTAMATE

Source: *Chemical Marketing Reporter.* **Price Frequency:** weekly. **Effective Market(s):** New York. **Units of Measure:** Dollars per lb. **Type of Price:** spot. **Time Period Covered:** latest week.

MONOSODIUM GLUTAMATE

Source: *Chemical Marketing Reporter.* **Price Frequency:** weekly. **Effective Market(s):** New York. **Units of Measure:** Dollars per lb. **Type of Price:** spot. **Time Period Covered:** latest week.

Source: *Journal of Commerce and Commercial.* **Price Frequency:** weekly in Friday issue. **Units of Measure:** Dollars per lb. **Type of Price:** spot. **Time Period Covered:** latest week.

MONOSODIUM PHOSPHATE

see Sodium Phosphate: Monobasic.

MONTAN WAX

see Wax: Montan.

MOONFISH: FILLETS, FRESH, HAWAIIAN

Source: *Seafood Price-Current.* **Price Frequency:** semiweekly. **Effective Market(s):** Hawaii. **Units of Measure:** Dollars per lb. **Type of Price:** sale by first receiver. **Time Period Covered:** latest day.

MOONFISH: WHOLE, FRESH, HAWAIIAN

Source: *Seafood Price-Current.* **Price Frequency:** semiweekly. **Effective Market(s):** Hawaii. **Units of Measure:** Dollars per lb. **Type of Price:** sale by first receiver. **Time Period Covered:** latest day.

MOROCCO DIRHAM

Source: *International Wheat Council Market Report.* **Price Frequency:** weekly. **Effective Market(s):** London. **Units of Measure:** Moroccan dirham per United States dollar. **Type of Price:** foreign exchange. **Time Period Covered:** latest 5 weeks.

MORPHINE: SULFATE, USP

Source: *Journal of Commerce and Commercial.* **Price Frequency:** weekly in Friday issue. **Units of Measure:** Dollars per kilo. **Type of Price:** spot. **Time Period Covered:** latest week.

MORPHINE ALKALOID: NF

Source: *Chemical Marketing Reporter.* **Price Frequency:** weekly. **Effective Market(s):** New York. **Units of Measure:** Dollars per kilo. **Type of Price:** spot. **Time Period Covered:** latest week.

MORPHINE SULFATE: USP

Source: *Chemical Marketing Reporter.* **Price Frequency:** weekly. **Effective Market(s):** New York. **Units of Measure:** Dollars per kilo. **Type of Price:** spot. **Time Period Covered:** latest week.

MORPHOLINE

Source: *Chemical Marketing Reporter.* **Price Frequency:** weekly. **Effective Market(s):** East. **Units of Measure:** Dollars per lb. **Type of Price:** spot. **Time Period Covered:** latest week.

MOTOR: ELECTRIC

Source: *Agricultural Prices.* **Price Frequency:** annually. **Effective Market(s):** United States. **Units of Measure:** Dollars each. **Type of Price:** paid by farmer. **Time Period Covered:** latest year.

Source: *Agricultural Prices Annual Summary.* **Price Frequency:** semiannually. **Effective Market(s):** United States. **Units of Measure:** Dollars each. **Type of Price:** paid by farmer. **Time Period Covered:** latest 6 years.

MOTOR TUNE-UP: LABOR ONLY

Source: *Agricultural Prices Annual Summary.* **Price Frequency:** semiannually. **Effective Market(s):** United States. **Units of Measure:** Dollars each time. **Type of Price:** paid by farmer. **Time Period Covered:** latest 6 years.

Source: *Agricultural Prices.* **Price Frequency:** semiannually. **Effective Market(s):** United States. **Units of Measure:** Dollars each time. **Type of Price:** paid by farmer. **Time Period Covered:** latest year.

MOWER: MOUNTED OR DRAWN

Source: *Agricultural Prices.* **Price Frequency:** annually. **Effective Market(s):** United States. **Units of Measure:** Dollars each. **Type of Price:** paid by farmer. **Time Period Covered:** latest year.

Source: *Agricultural Prices Annual Summary.* **Price Frequency:** annually. **Effective Market(s):** United States. **Units of Measure:** Dollars each. **Type of Price:** paid by farmer. **Time Period Covered:** latest 6 years.

MOWER CONDITIONER

Source: *Agricultural Prices Annual Summary.* **Price Frequency:** annually. **Effective Market(s):** United States. **Units of Measure:** Dollars each. **Type of Price:** paid by farmer. **Time Period Covered:** latest 6 years.

Source: *Agricultural Prices.* **Price Frequency:** annually. **Effective Market(s):** United States. **Units of Measure:** Dollars each. **Type of Price:** paid by farmer. **Time Period Covered:** latest year.

MTBE

Source: *Journal of Commerce and Commercial.* **Price Frequency:** weekly in Wednesday issue. **Effective Market(s):** Gulf. **Units of Measure:** Dollars per gallon. **Type of Price:** spot. **Time Period Covered:** latest week.

MULCH HAY

Source: *Lancaster Farmer.* **Price Frequency:** weekly. **Effective Market(s):** Pennsylvania. **Units of Measure:** Dollars per ton. **Type of Price:** auction. **Time Period Covered:** latest week.

MULES

Source: *Farm and Dairy.* **Price Frequency:** weekly, seasonally. **Effective Market(s):** Ohio, Pennsylvania. **Units of Measure:** Dollars per head. **Type of Price:** auction high, auction low. **Time Period Covered:** latest week.

MULLET (FISH): LISA, WHOLE, FRESH

Source: *Seafood Price-Current.* **Price Frequency:** semiweekly. **Effective Market(s):** Boston, Mid-Atlantic, New Bedford (MA), Portland (ME). **Units of Measure:** Dollars per lb. **Type of Price:** sale by first receiver, auction price. **Time Period Covered:** latest day.

MURIATE OF POTASH: GRANULAR

Source: *Industrial Minerals.* **Price Frequency:** monthly. **Effective Market(s):** United Kingdom. **Units of Measure:** British pounds per metric tonne. **Type of Price:** producer & dealer. **Time Period Covered:** latest month.

MURIATE OF POTASH: STANDARD

Source: *Industrial Minerals.* **Price Frequency:** monthly. **Effective Market(s):** United Kingdom, Vancouver (Canada). **Units of Measure:** British pounds per metric tonne, dollars per metric tonne. **Type of Price:** producer & dealer. **Time Period Covered:** latest month.

MURIATE OF POTASH FERTILIZER

Source: *Agricultural Prices.* **Price Frequency:** monthly. **Effective Market(s):** 9 domestic markets, United States. **Units of Measure:** Dollars per ton. **Type of Price:** paid by farmer. **Time Period Covered:** latest month.

Source: *Agricultural Prices Annual Summary.* **Price Frequency:** semiannually. **Effective Market(s):** East South Central region, North Central region, Northern Plains region, United States. **Units of Measure:** Dollars per ton. **Type of Price:** paid by farmer. **Time Period Covered:** latest year, for US quarterly latest 6 years.

MURIATIC ACID

see also Hydrochloric Acid.

MURIATIC ACID: 20 DEGREE

Source: *Journal of Commerce and Commercial.* **Price Frequency:** weekly in Thursday issue. **Effective Market(s):** Gulf. **Units of Measure:** Dollars per lb. **Type of Price:** spot. **Time Period Covered:** latest week.

MURIATIC ACID: 22 DEGREE

Source: *Journal of Commerce and Commercial.* **Price Frequency:** weekly in Thursday issue. **Effective Market(s):** Gulf. **Units of Measure:** Dollars per lb. **Type of Price:** spot. **Time Period Covered:** latest week.

MUSCAT: DRY

Source: *California Wineletter.* **Price Frequency:** semimonthly. **Effective Market(s):** Non-California markets. **Units of Measure:** Dollars per gallon. **Type of Price:** asking. **Time Period Covered:** latest week.

MUSCAT: LIGHT SWEET

Source: *California Wineletter.* **Price Frequency:** semimonthly. **Effective Market(s):** Non-California markets. **Units of Measure:** Dollars per gallon. **Type of Price:** asking. **Time Period Covered:** latest week.

MUSCATEL: STANDARD QUALITY

Source: *California Wineletter.* **Price Frequency:** semimonthly. **Effective Market(s):** Non-California markets. **Units of Measure:** Dollars per gallon. **Type of Price:** asking. **Time Period Covered:** latest week.

MUSHROOMS

Source: *Lancaster Farmer.* **Price Frequency:** weekly, seasonally. **Effective Market(s):** Pennsylvania. **Units of Measure:** Dollars per basket. **Type of Price:** market. **Time Period Covered:** latest week.

Source: *Mushrooms.* **Price Frequency:** annually. **Effective Market(s):** United States. **Units of Measure:** Dollars per lb. **Time Period Covered:** latest 23 years.

Source: *New Zealand Farmer.* **Price Frequency:** weekly, seasonally. **Effective Market(s):** New Zealand. **Units of Measure:** New Zealand dollars per crate/tray. **Time Period Covered:** latest week.

MUSHROOMS: AGARICUS

Source: *Mushrooms.* **Price Frequency:** annually. **Effective Market(s):** 14 domestic markets, United States. **Units of Measure:** Dollars per lb. **Time Period Covered:** latest 2 years.

MUSHROOMS: AGARICUS AND EXOTIC

Source: *Mushrooms.* **Price Frequency:** annually. **Effective Market(s):** United States. **Units of Measure:** Dollars per lb. **Type of Price:** average. **Time Period Covered:** latest 3 years.

MUSHROOMS: AGARICUS, FRESH MARKET

Source: *Mushrooms.* **Price Frequency:** annually. **Effective Market(s):** Central, East, Pennsylvania, West, United States. **Units of Measure:** Dollars per lb. **Time Period Covered:** latest 2 years.

MUSHROOMS: AGARICUS, PROCESSING

Source: *Mushrooms.* **Price Frequency:** annually. **Effective Market(s):** Central, East, Pennsylvania, West, United States. **Units of Measure:** Dollars per lb. **Time Period Covered:** latest 2 years.

MUSHROOMS: EXOTIC

Source: *Mushrooms.* **Price Frequency:** annually. **Effective Market(s):** United States. **Units of Measure:** Dollars per lb. **Time Period Covered:** latest 3 years.

MUSHROOMS: FRESH

Source: *HRI-Buyers Guide.* **Price Frequency:** weekly. **Effective Market(s):** Northeastern area. **Units of Measure:** Dollars per basket. **Type of Price:** prices paid by dining places & institutions. **Time Period Covered:** latest week.

Source: *Mushrooms.* **Price Frequency:** annually. **Effective Market(s):** United States. **Units of Measure:** Dollars per lb. **Time Period Covered:** latest 23 years.

MUSHROOMS: ILLINOIS AND PENNSYLVANIA

Source: *Fresh Fruit and Vegetable Prices.* **Price Frequency:** monthly, seasonally. **Effective Market(s):** Chicago. **Units of Measure:** Dollars per carton. **Type of Price:** average wholesale price. **Time Period Covered:** latest year.

MUSHROOMS: OYSTER

Source: *Mushrooms.* **Price Frequency:** annually. **Effective Market(s):** United States. **Units of Measure:** Dollars per lb. **Time Period Covered:** latest 3 years.

MUSHROOMS: PENNSYLVANIA

Source: *Fresh Fruit and Vegetable Prices.* **Price Frequency:** monthly, seasonally. **Effective Market(s):** New York City. **Units of Measure:** Dollars per basket. **Type of Price:** average wholesale price. **Time Period Covered:** latest year.

MUSHROOMS: PROCESSING

Source: *Mushrooms.* **Price Frequency:** annually. **Effective Market(s):** United States. **Units of Measure:** Dollars per lb. **Time Period Covered:** latest 23 years.

MUSHROOMS: SHIITAKE

Source: *Lancaster Farmer.* **Price Frequency:** weekly, seasonally. **Effective Market(s):** Pennsylvania. **Units of Measure:** Dollars per unit. **Type of Price:** market. **Time Period Covered:** latest week.

Source: *Mushrooms.* **Price Frequency:** annually. **Effective Market(s):** United States. **Units of Measure:** Dollars per lb. **Time Period Covered:** latest 3 years.

MUSK: KETONE

Source: *Journal of Commerce and commercial.* **Price Frequency:** weekly in Tuesday issue. **Units of Measure:** Dollars per lb. **Type of Price:** spot. **Time Period Covered:** latest week.

MUSK: SYNTHETIC, AMBRETTE

Source: *Chemical Marketing Reporter.* **Price Frequency:** weekly. **Effective Market(s):** New York. **Units of Measure:** Dollars per lb. **Type of Price:** spot. **Time Period Covered:** latest week.

MUSK: SYNTHETIC, KETONE

Source: *Chemical Marketing Reporter.* **Price Frequency:** weekly. **Effective Market(s):** New York. **Units of Measure:** Dollars per lb. **Type of Price:** spot. **Time Period Covered:** latest week.

MUSK: SYNTHETIC, XYLOL

Source: *Chemical Marketing Reporter.* **Price Frequency:** weekly. **Effective Market(s):** New York. **Units of Measure:** Dollars per lb. **Type of Price:** spot. **Time Period Covered:** latest week.

MUSK: XYLOL

Source: *Journal of Commerce and Commercial.* **Price Frequency:** weekly in Tuesday issue. **Units of Measure:** Dollars per lb. **Type of Price:** spot. **Time Period Covered:** latest week.

MUSSELS: CULTIVATED, FRESH

Source: *Seafood Price-Current.* **Price Frequency:** semiweekly. **Effective Market(s):** Mid-Atlantic. **Units of Measure:** Dollars per bushel. **Type of Price:** sale by first receiver. **Time Period Covered:** latest day.

MUSSELS: FRESH, MAINE

Source: *Seafood Price-Current.* **Price Frequency:** semiweekly. **Effective Market(s):** Mid-Atlantic. **Units of Measure:** Dollars per bushel. **Type of Price:** sale by first receiver. **Time Period Covered:** latest day.

MUSSELS: FRESH, MASSACHUSETTS

Source: *Seafood Price-Current.* **Price Frequency:** semiweekly. **Effective Market(s):** Mid-Atlantic. **Units of Measure:** Dollars per bushel. **Type of Price:** sale by first receiver. **Time Period Covered:** latest day.

MUSSELS: FRESH, NEW JERSEY

Source: *Seafood Price-Current.* **Price Frequency:** semiweekly. **Effective Market(s):** Mid-Atlantic. **Units of Measure:** Dollars per bushel. **Type of Price:** sale by first receiver. **Time Period Covered:** latest day.

MUSSELS: FRESH, RHODE ISLAND

Source: *Seafood Price-Current.* **Price Frequency:** semiweekly. **Effective Market(s):** Mid-Atlantic. **Units of Measure:** Dollars per lb. **Type of Price:** sale by first receiver. **Time Period Covered:** latest day.

MUSTARD OIL: SYNTHETIC

see Allyl Isothiocyanate.

MUSTARD SEED: NO. 1, BROWN

Source: *Chemical Marketing Reporter.* **Price Frequency:** weekly. **Effective Market(s):** New York. **Units of Measure:** Dollars per lb. **Type of Price:** spot. **Time Period Covered:** latest week.

MUSTARD SEED: NO. 1, ORIENTAL

Source: *Chemical Marketing Reporter.* **Price Frequency:** weekly. **Effective Market(s):** New York. **Units of Measure:** Dollars per lb. **Type of Price:** spot. **Time Period Covered:** latest week.

MUSTARD SEED: NO. 1, YELLOW, CANADIAN

Source: *Chemical Marketing Reporter.* **Price Frequency:** weekly. **Effective Market(s):** New York. **Units of Measure:** Dollars per lb. **Type of Price:** spot. **Time Period Covered:** latest week.

Source: *U. S. Spice Trade.* **Price Frequency:** monthly, annually. **Effective Market(s):** New York. **Units of Measure:** cents per lb. **Type of Price:** spot. **Time Period Covered:** latest 10 years.

MUSTARD SEED: ORIENTAL/BROWN

Source: *U. S. Spice Trade.* **Price Frequency:** monthly, annually. **Effective Market(s):** New York. **Units of Measure:** Dollars per lb. **Type of Price:** spot. **Time Period Covered:** latest 10 years.

MUTTON

Source: *New Zealand Farmer.* **Price Frequency:** weekly, seasonally. **Effective Market(s):** 11 New Zealand markets. **Units of Measure:** New Zealand dollars per unit weight. **Type of Price:** export value. **Time Period Covered:** latest week.

MUTTON AND LAMB: NEW ZEALAND

Source: *FAO Quarterly Bulletin of Statistics.* **Price Frequency:** monthly, annually. **Effective Market(s):** London. **Units of Measure:** British pounds per 100 kilograms, dollars per metric ton. **Type of Price:** wholesale. **Time Period Covered:** latest 3 years.

MYRCIA OIL

see Bay Oil.

MYRISTIC ACID: COMMERCIAL, PURE

Source: *Chemical Marketing Reporter.* **Price Frequency:** weekly. **Effective Market(s):** New York. **Units of Measure:** Dollars per lb. **Type of Price:** spot. **Time Period Covered:** latest week.

MYRISTICA OIL

see Nutmeg Oil.

MYRRH GUM

Source: *Chemical Marketing Reporter.* **Price Frequency:** weekly. **Effective Market(s):** New York. **Units of Measure:** Dollars per lb. **Type of Price:** spot. **Time Period Covered:** latest week.

Source: *Journal of Commerce and Commercial.* **Price Frequency:** weekly in Monday issue. **Units of Measure:** Dollars per lb. **Type of Price:** spot. **Time Period Covered:** latest week.

NAILS: COMMON, 8D

Source: *Agricultural Prices.* **Price Frequency:** semiannually. **Effective Market(s):** United States. **Units of Measure:** Dollars per lb. **Type of Price:** paid by farmer. **Time Period Covered:** latest year.

Source: *Agricultural Prices Annual Summary.* **Price Frequency:** quarterly. **Effective Market(s):** United States. **Units of Measure:** Dollars per lb. **Type of Price:** paid by farmer. **Time Period Covered:** latest 6 years.

NAPHTHA

Source: *Financial Times.* **Price Frequency:** daily. **Effective Market(s):** London. **Units of Measure:** Dollars per tonne. **Type of Price:** spot. **Time Period Covered:** latest day.

Source: *International Butane/Propane Newsletter.* **Price Frequency:** semimonthly. **Effective Market(s):** Rotterdam. **Units of Measure:** Dollars per metric ton. **Time Period Covered:** latest week.

Source: *Japan Economic Journal.* **Price Frequency:** weekly. **Effective Market(s):** London, Singapore. **Units of Measure:** Dollars per ton, dollars per barrel. **Type of Price:** spot. **Time Period Covered:** latest 2 weeks.

Source: *OPEC Bulletin.* **Price Frequency:** monthly. **Effective Market(s):** Caribbean, Italy, Middle East Gulf, Rotterdam, Singapore. **Units of Measure:** Dollars per barrel. **Time Period Covered:** latest 2 years.

Source: *Petroleum Economist.* **Price Frequency:** monthly. **Effective Market(s):** Bahamas, Bahrain, Curacao, Pulau Bukom (Singapore), Quoin Island. **Units of Measure:** cents per gallon. **Time Period Covered:** latest month.

Source: *The Times.* **Price Frequency:** daily. **Effective Market(s):** Northwest Europe. **Units of Measure:** Dollars per metric ton. **Type of Price:** spot. **Time Period Covered:** latest day.

NAPHTHA: CATALYTIC

Source: *Oil Buyers' Guide.* **Price Frequency:** weekly. **Effective Market(s):** Venezuela. **Units of Measure:** Dollars per metric ton. **Type of Price:** official. **Time Period Covered:** latest week.

Source: *Oil Buyers' Guide International.* **Price Frequency:** weekly. **Effective Market(s):** Venezuela. **Units of Measure:** cents per gallon. **Type of Price:** official. **Time Period Covered:** latest week.

NAPHTHA: HEAVY

Source: *Oil Buyers' Guide.* **Price Frequency:** weekly. **Effective Market(s):** Venezuela. **Units of Measure:** Dollars per metric ton. **Type of Price:** official. **Time Period Covered:** latest week.

NAPHTHA: HIGH SOLVENCY

see Naphtha: Solvent, Petroleum.

NAPHTHA: LIGHT

Source: *Oil Buyers' Guide.* **Price Frequency:** weekly. **Effective Market(s):** Venezuela. **Units of Measure:** Dollars per metric ton. **Type of Price:** official. **Time Period Covered:** latest week.

Source: *Oil Buyers' Guide International.* **Price Frequency:** weekly. **Effective Market(s):** Venezuela. **Units of Measure:** cents per gallon. **Type of Price:** official. **Time Period Covered:** latest week.

NAPHTHA: PARAFFINIC

Source: *Petroleum Economist.* **Price Frequency:** monthly. **Effective Market(s):** Caribbean, Mediterranean, New York, Northwest Europe, Rotterdam. **Units of Measure:** Dollars per metric ton. **Type of Price:** spot. **Time Period Covered:** latest month.

NAPHTHA: PETROLEUM

Source: *Chemical Marketing Reporter.* **Price Frequency:** weekly. **Effective Market(s):** Houston (TX), New Jersey/New York. **Units of Measure:** Dollars per gallon. **Type of Price:** spot. **Time Period Covered:** latest week.

NAPHTHA: PETROLEUM, CLEANER'S

see Cleaner's Naphtha.

NAPHTHA: SOLVENT, PETROLEUM, STRAIGHT AROMATIC

Source: *Chemical Marketing Reporter.* **Price Frequency:** weekly. **Effective Market(s):** Illinois, Houston, New Jersey. **Units of Measure:** Dollars per gallon. **Type of Price:** spot. **Time Period Covered:** latest week.

NAPHTHA: VIRGIN

Source: *Oil Buyers' Guide.* **Price Frequency:** weekly. **Effective Market(s):** Mediterranean, Northwest Europe. **Units of Measure:** Dollars per metric ton. **Type of Price:** cargo. **Time Period Covered:** latest week.

Source: *Oil Buyers' Guide International.* **Price Frequency:** weekly. **Effective Market(s):** Mediterranean, Northwest Europe. **Units of Measure:** Dollars per metric ton. **Type of Price:** cargo. **Time Period Covered:** latest week.

Source: *Oil Buyers' Guide International.* **Price Frequency:** weekly. **Effective Market(s):** Japan, Singapore. **Units of Measure:** Dollars per metric ton. **Type of Price:** spot. **Time Period Covered:** latest week.

NAPHTHA: WHOLE

Source: *Oil Buyers' Guide.* **Price Frequency:** weekly. **Effective Market(s):** Venezuela. **Units of Measure:** Dollars per metric ton. **Type of Price:** official. **Time Period Covered:** latest week.

Source: *Oil Buyers' Guide International.* **Price Frequency:** weekly. **Effective Market(s):** Venezuela. **Units of Measure:** cents per gallon. **Type of Price:** official. **Time Period Covered:** latest week.

NAPHTHALENE: CRUDE

Source: *Journal of Commerce and Commercial.* **Price Frequency:** weekly in Wednesday issue. **Units of Measure:** Dollars per lb. **Type of Price:** spot. **Time Period Covered:** latest week.

NAPHTHALENE: CRUDE, DOMESTIC

Source: *Chemical Marketing Reporter.* **Price Frequency:** weekly. **Effective Market(s):** New York. **Units of Measure:** Dollars per lb. **Type of Price:** spot. **Time Period Covered:** latest week.

NAPHTHALENE: PETROLEUM

Source: *Chemical Marketing Reporter.* **Price Frequency:** weekly. **Effective Market(s):** New York. **Units of Measure:** Dollars per lb. **Type of Price:** spot. **Time Period Covered:** latest week.

Source: *Journal of Commerce and Commercial.* **Price Frequency:** weekly in Wednesday issue. **Units of Measure:** Dollars per lb. **Type of Price:** spot. **Time Period Covered:** latest week.

NAPHTHALENE: PHTHALIC ANHYDRIDE GRADE

Source: *Chemical Marketing Reporter.* **Price Frequency:** weekly. **Effective Market(s):** New York. **Units of Measure:** Dollars per lb. **Type of Price:** spot. **Time Period Covered:** latest week.

NAPHTHALENE: REFINED, FLAKES

Source: *Journal of Commerce and Commercial.* **Price Frequency:** weekly in Wednesday issue. **Units of Measure:** Dollars per lb. **Type of Price:** spot. **Time Period Covered:** latest week.

NAPHTHALENE: REFINED, FLAKES AND BALLS

Source: *Chemical Marketing Reporter.* **Price Frequency:** weekly. **Effective Market(s):** New York. **Units of Measure:** Dollars per lb. **Type of Price:** wholesaler & jobber. **Time Period Covered:** latest week.

NAPHTHENIC ACID: CRUDE

Source: *Chemical Marketing Reporter.* **Price Frequency:** weekly. **Effective Market(s):** New York. **Units of Measure:** Dollars per lb. **Type of Price:** spot. **Time Period Covered:** latest week.

NAPHTHENIC ACID: REFINED, 220 ACID

Source: *Chemical Marketing Reporter.* **Price Frequency:** weekly. **Effective Market(s):** New York. **Units of Measure:** Dollars per lb. **Type of Price:** spot. **Time Period Covered:** latest week.

A-NAPHTHOL

Source: *Journal of Commerce and Commercial.* **Price Frequency:** weekly in Wednesday issue. **Units of Measure:** Dollars per lb. **Type of Price:** spot. **Time Period Covered:** latest week.

A-NAPHTHOL: GROUND

Source: *Chemical Marketing Reporter.* **Price Frequency:** weekly. **Effective Market(s):** New York. **Units of Measure:** Dollars per lb. **Type of Price:** spot. **Time Period Covered:** latest week.

B-NAPHTHOL

Source: *Journal of Commerce and Commercial.* **Price Frequency:** weekly in Wednesday issue. **Units of Measure:** Dollars per lb. **Type of Price:** spot. **Time Period Covered:** latest week.

B-NAPHTHOL: TECHNICAL, FLAKE

Source: *Chemical Marketing Reporter.* **Price Frequency:** weekly. **Effective Market(s):** New York. **Units of Measure:** Dollars per lb. **Type of Price:** spot. **Time Period Covered:** latest week.

NAPHTHOL ARYLIDE RED TONER: LIGHT SHADES

Source: *Chemical Marketing Reporter.* **Price Frequency:** weekly. **Effective Market(s):** New York. **Units of Measure:** Dollars per lb. **Type of Price:** spot. **Time Period Covered:** latest week.

2-NAPHTHOL-3,6-DISULFONIC ACID, DISODIUM SALT

see R Salt.

A-NAPHTHYLAMINE

Source: *Chemical Marketing Reporter.* **Price Frequency:** weekly. **Effective Market(s):** New York. **Units of Measure:** Dollars per lb. **Type of Price:** spot. **Time Period Covered:** latest week.

Source: *Journal of Commerce and Commercial.* **Price Frequency:** weekly in Wednesday issue. **Units of Measure:** Dollars per lb. **Type of Price:** spot. **Time Period Covered:** latest week.

1-NAPHTHYLAMINE-5-SULFONIC ACID

see Laurent's Acid.

2-NAPHTHYLAMINE-4,8 DISULFONIC ACID

see Cassella Acid.

2-NAPHTHYLAMINE-1-SULFONIC ACID

see Tobias Acid.

NAPKINS AND NAPKIN STOCK

Source: *Pulp & Paper Week.* **Price Frequency:** monthly, irregulary. **Units of Measure:** index. **Type of Price:** price index. **Time Period Covered:** latest 3 months.

NASHI

Source: *New Zealand Farmer.* **Price Frequency:** weekly, seasonally. **Effective Market(s):** New Zealand. **Units of Measure:** New Zealand dollars per tray. **Time Period Covered:** latest week.

NEATSFOOT OIL

Source: *Chemical Marketing Reporter.* **Price Frequency:** weekly. **Effective Market(s):** Philadelphia, Texas, West Coast. **Units of Measure:** Dollars per lb. **Type of Price:** spot. **Time Period Covered:** latest week.

NECTARINES

Source: *Agricultural Prices Annual Summary.* **Price Frequency:** annually. **Effective Market(s):** California, Hawaii. **Units of Measure:** Dollars per ton. **Type of Price:** average received by farmer. **Time Period Covered:** latest 6 years.

Source: *California Farmer.* **Price Frequency:** semimonthly, seasonally. **Effective Market(s):** Central/Southern San Joaquin Valley. **Units of Measure:** Dollars per 25 lb. carton. **Time Period Covered:** latest week, month ago, year ago.

Source: *Fresh Fruit and Vegetable Prices.* **Price Frequency:** monthly, seasonally. **Effective Market(s):** Central San Joaquin Valley (CA), Washington. **Units of Measure:** Dollars per carton. **Type of Price:** average price at shipping point. **Time Period Covered:** latest year.

Source: *Fruit and Tree Nuts Situation and Outlook Yearbook.* **Price Frequency:** annually. **Effective Market(s):** California. **Units of Measure:** Dollars per ton. **Type of Price:** grower. **Time Period Covered:** latest 20 years.

NECTARINES: CALIFORNIA

Source: *Fresh Fruit and Vegetable Prices.* **Price Frequency:** monthly, seasonally. **Effective Market(s):** Chicago, New York City. **Units of Measure:** Dollars per lug. **Type of Price:** average wholesale price. **Time Period Covered:** latest year.

NECTARINES: CHILEAN

Source: *Fresh Fruit and Vegetable Prices.* **Price Frequency:** monthly, seasonally. **Effective Market(s):** New York City/Philadelphia. **Units of Measure:** Dollars per lug. **Type of Price:** dock price. **Time Period Covered:** latest year.

Source: *Fresh Fruit and Vegetable Prices.* **Price Frequency:** monthly, seasonally. **Effective Market(s):** Chicago, New York City. **Units of Measure:** Dollars per lug. **Type of Price:** average wholesale price. **Time Period Covered:** latest year.

NECTARINES: FANTASIA

Source: *The Packer.* **Price Frequency:** weekly, seasonally. **Effective Market(s):** varies. **Units of Measure:** Dollars per carton. **Type of Price:** price received by farmer. **Time Period Covered:** latest week.

NECTARINES: FLAMEKIST

Source: *Lancaster Farmer.* **Price Frequency:** weekly, seasonally. **Effective Market(s):** Pennsylvania. **Units of Measure:** Dollars per carton. **Type of Price:** market. **Time Period Covered:** latest week.

NECTARINES: FRESH

Source: *Fruit and Tree Nuts Situation and Outlook Yearbook.* **Price Frequency:** annually. **Effective Market(s):** California. **Units of Measure:** Dollars per ton. **Type of Price:** grower. **Time Period Covered:** latest 20 years.

NECTARINES: JULY RED

Source: *The Packer.* **Price Frequency:** weekly, seasonally. **Effective Market(s):** varies. **Units of Measure:** Dollars per carton. **Type of Price:** price received by farmer. **Time Period Covered:** latest week.

NECTARINES: LATE LEGRAND

Source: *The Packer.* **Price Frequency:** weekly, seasonally. **Effective Market(s):** varies. **Units of Measure:** Dollars per carton. **Type of Price:** price received by farmer. **Time Period Covered:** latest week.

NECTARINES: PROCESSING

Source: *Fruit and Tree Nuts Situation and Outlook Yearbook.* **Price Frequency:** annually. **Effective Market(s):** California. **Units of Measure:** Dollars per ton. **Type of Price:** grower. **Time Period Covered:** latest 20 years.

NECTARINES: ROYAL GIANT

Source: *Lancaster Farmer.* **Price Frequency:** weekly, seasonally. **Effective Market(s):** Pennsylvania. **Units of Measure:** Dollars per carton. **Type of Price:** market. **Time Period Covered:** latest week.

Source: *The Packer.* **Price Frequency:** weekly, seasonally. **Effective Market(s):** varies. **Units of Measure:** Dollars per carton. **Type of Price:** price received by farmer. **Time Period Covered:** latest week.

NECTARINES: SPARKLING RED

Source: *Lancaster Farmer.* **Price Frequency:** weekly, seasonally. **Effective Market(s):** Pennsylvania. **Units of Measure:** Dollars per carton. **Type of Price:** market. **Time Period Covered:** latest week.

Source: *The Packer.* **Price Frequency:** weekly, seasonally. **Effective Market(s):** varies. **Units of Measure:** Dollars per carton. **Type of Price:** price received by farmer. **Time Period Covered:** latest week.

NEOMYCIN SULFATE: COMMERCIAL, MICRONIZED

Source: *Journal of Commerce and Commercial.* **Price Frequency:** weekly in Friday issue. **Units of Measure:** Dollars per kilo. **Type of Price:** spot. **Time Period Covered:** latest week.

NEOMYCIN SULFATE: NON-STERILE, USP

Source: *Chemical Marketing Reporter.* **Price Frequency:** weekly. **Effective Market(s):** New York. **Units of Measure:** Dollars per kilo. **Type of Price:** spot. **Time Period Covered:** latest week.

NEOMYCIN SULFATE: USP

Source: *Journal of Commerce and Commercial.* **Price Frequency:** weekly in Friday issue. **Units of Measure:** Dollars per kilo. **Type of Price:** spot. **Time Period Covered:** latest week.

NEOPENTYL GLYCOL: POWDER, FLAKE

Source: *Chemical Marketing Reporter.* **Price Frequency:** weekly. **Effective Market(s):** New York. **Units of Measure:** Dollars per lb. **Type of Price:** spot. **Time Period Covered:** latest week.

NEOPENTYL GLYCOL: SLURRY, 90%

Source: *Chemical Marketing Reporter.* **Price Frequency:** weekly. **Effective Market(s):** New York. **Units of Measure:** Dollars per lb. **Type of Price:** spot. **Time Period Covered:** latest week.

NEPHELINE SYENITE: CERAMIC GRADE, CANADIAN

Source: *Industrial Minerals.* **Price Frequency:** monthly. **Effective Market(s):** main European port. **Units of Measure:** Dollars per short ton. **Type of Price:** producer & dealer. **Time Period Covered:** latest month.

NEPHELINE SYENITE: CERAMIC GRADE, NORWEGIAN

Source: *Industrial Minerals.* **Price Frequency:** monthly. **Effective Market(s):** United Kingdom. **Units of Measure:** British pounds per metric tonne. **Type of Price:** producer & dealer. **Time Period Covered:** latest month.

NEPHELINE SYENITE: FILLER/EXTENDER, CANADIAN

Source: *Industrial Minerals.* **Price Frequency:** monthly. **Effective Market(s):** main European port. **Units of Measure:** Dollars per short ton. **Type of Price:** producer & dealer. **Time Period Covered:** latest month.

NEPHELINE SYENITE: GLASS GRADE, HIGH IRON, CANADIAN

Source: *Industrial Minerals.* **Price Frequency:** monthly. **Effective Market(s):** main European port. **Units of Measure:** Dollars per short ton. **Type of Price:** producer & dealer. **Time Period Covered:** latest month.

NEPHELINE SYENITE: GLASS GRADE, NORWEGIAN

Source: *Industrial Minerals.* **Price Frequency:** monthly. **Effective Market(s):** United Kingdom. **Units of Measure:** British pounds per metric tonne. **Type of Price:** producer & dealer. **Time Period Covered:** latest month.

NEROL: PERFORMANCE GRADE

Source: *Chemical Marketing Reporter.* **Price Frequency:** weekly. **Effective Market(s):** New York. **Units of Measure:** Dollars per lb. **Type of Price:** spot. **Time Period Covered:** latest week.

NEROL: TECHNICAL

Source: *Chemical Marketing Reporter.* **Price Frequency:** weekly. **Effective Market(s):** New York. **Units of Measure:** Dollars per lb. **Type of Price:** spot. **Time Period Covered:** latest week.

NEROLI OIL

Source: *Journal of Commerce and Commercial.* **Price Frequency:** weekly in Tuesday issue. **Units of Measure:** Dollars per lb. **Type of Price:** spot. **Time Period Covered:** latest week.

Source: *U. S. Essential Oil Trade.* **Price Frequency:** annually. **Effective Market(s):** United States. **Units of Measure:** Dollars per kilogram. **Type of Price:** import value. **Time Period Covered:** latest 3 years.

NEROLI OIL: TUNISIAN

Source: *Chemical Marketing Reporter.* **Price Frequency:** weekly. **Effective Market(s):** New York. **Units of Measure:** Dollars per kilo. **Type of Price:** spot. **Time Period Covered:** latest week.

NEROLIDOL: SYNTHETIC

Source: *Chemical Marketing Reporter.* **Price Frequency:** weekly. **Effective Market(s):** New York. **Units of Measure:** Dollars per lb. **Type of Price:** spot. **Time Period Covered:** latest week.

NEROLIN: BROMELIN

Source: *Chemical Marketing Reporter.* **Price Frequency:** weekly. **Effective Market(s):** New York. **Units of Measure:** Dollars per kilo. **Type of Price:** spot. **Time Period Covered:** latest week.

NETHERLANDS GUILDERS

Source: *Asian Wall Street Journal.* **Price Frequency:** daily. **Effective Market(s):** United States. **Units of Measure:** Dutch guilders per ECU, per SDR. **Type of Price:** foreign exchange. **Time Period Covered:** latest 2 days.

Source: *Barron's.* **Price Frequency:** weekly. **Effective Market(s):** New York. **Units of Measure:** Dutch guilders per United States dollar. **Type of Price:** foreign exchange. **Time Period Covered:** latest 2 weeks.

Source: *The Economist.* **Price Frequency:** weekly. **Effective Market(s):** London. **Units of Measure:** Dutch guilders per British pound, per ECU, per SDR, per United States dollar. **Type of Price:** foreign exchange. **Time Period Covered:** latest week.

Source: *New York Times.* **Price Frequency:** daily. **Effective Market(s):** United States. **Units of Measure:** Dutch guilders per United States dollar. **Type of Price:** foreign exchange. **Time Period Covered:** latest 2 days.

Source: *Timber Bulletin.* **Price Frequency:** monthly, annually. **Units of Measure:** Dutch guilders per United States dollar. **Type of Price:** foreign exchange. **Time Period Covered:** latest 2 years.

NEW ZEALAND DOLLARS

Source: *Asian Wall Street Journal.* **Price Frequency:** daily. **Effective Market(s):** Asia. **Units of Measure:** United States dollars per New Zealand dollars. **Type of Price:** foreign exchange. **Time Period Covered:** latest 2 days.

Source: *Barron's.* **Price Frequency:** weekly. **Effective Market(s):** New York. **Units of Measure:** New Zealand dollars per United States dollar. **Type of Price:** foreign exchange. **Time Period Covered:** latest 2 weeks.

Source: *New York Times.* **Price Frequency:** daily. **Effective Market(s):** United States. **Units of Measure:** New Zealand dollars per United States dollar. **Type of Price:** foreign exchange. **Time Period Covered:** latest 2 days.

Source: *The Times.* **Price Frequency:** daily. **Effective Market(s):** London. **Units of Measure:** New Zealand dollars per British pound. **Type of Price:** foreign exchange. **Time Period Covered:** latest day.

NEWSPAPER: BLANK, WHITE

Source: *Fibre Market News.* **Price Frequency:** weekly. **Effective Market(s):** 9 domestic markets. **Units of Measure:** Dollars per net ton. **Type of Price:** grader & packer buying price. **Time Period Covered:** latest week.

NEWSPAPER: FOLDED

Source: *Fibre Market News.* **Price Frequency:** weekly. **Effective Market(s):** Boston, Philadelphia. **Units of Measure:** Dollars per net ton. **Type of Price:** grader & packer buying price. **Time Period Covered:** latest week.

NEWSPAPER: OVERISSUE

Source: *Fibre Market News.* **Price Frequency:** weekly. **Effective Market(s):** 9 domestic markets. **Units of Measure:** Dollars per net ton. **Type of Price:** grader & packer buying price. **Time Period Covered:** latest week.

NEWSPAPER: OVERISSUE, SPECIAL PACK

Source: *Fibre Market News.* **Price Frequency:** weekly. **Effective Market(s):** Boston, Chicago, Philadelphia. **Units of Measure:** Dollars per net ton. **Type of Price:** grader & packer buying price. **Time Period Covered:** latest week.

NEWSPAPER: REGULAR

Source: *Fibre Market News.* **Price Frequency:** weekly. **Effective Market(s):** 9 domestic markets. **Units of Measure:** Dollars per net ton. **Type of Price:** grader & packer buying price. **Time Period Covered:** latest week.

NEWSPAPER: SPECIAL

Source: *Fibre Market News.* **Price Frequency:** weekly. **Effective Market(s):** 9 domestic markets. **Units of Measure:** Dollars per net ton. **Type of Price:** grader & packer buying price. **Time Period Covered:** latest week.

NEWSPAPER: SPECIAL DE-INK

Source: *Fibre Market News.* **Price Frequency:** weekly. **Effective Market(s):** 9 domestic markets. **Units of Measure:** Dollars per net ton. **Type of Price:** grader & packer buying price. **Time Period Covered:** latest week.

NEWSPRINT

Source: *International Financial Statistics.* **Price Frequency:** monthly, quarterly, annually. **Effective Market(s):** New York. **Units of Measure:** Dollars per short ton, index. **Type of Price:** market price, price index. **Time Period Covered:** latest 4 months, latest 5 quarters, latest 5 years.

Source: *International Financial Statistics Yearbook.* **Price Frequency:** annually. **Effective Market(s):** New York. **Units of Measure:** Dollars per short ton. **Type of Price:** wholesale. **Time Period Covered:** latest 30 years.

Source: *Pulp & Paper Week.* **Price Frequency:** monthly, usually in last issue of month. **Effective Market(s):** Eastern United States, Western United States. **Units of Measure:** Dollars per metric ton. **Type of Price:** estimated transaction. **Time Period Covered:** latest 3 months, year ago.

Source: *Purchasing.* **Price Frequency:** quarterly in January, April, July, October issues. **Units of Measure:** Dollars per ton. **Type of Price:** transaction. **Time Period Covered:** latest 5 quarters.

Source: *Timber Bulletin.* **Price Frequency:** monthly, annually. **Effective Market(s):** Canada, Finland. **Units of Measure:** national currency per metric ton. **Type of Price:** export value. **Time Period Covered:** monthly latest 2 years, annually latest 6 years.

Source: *Timber Bulletin.* **Price Frequency:** monthly, annually. **Effective Market(s):** Norway. **Units of Measure:** Norwegian kroner per metric ton. **Type of Price:** export value. **Time Period Covered:** monthly latest 2 years, annually latest 2 years.

Source: *Timber Bulletin.* **Price Frequency:** monthly, annually. **Effective Market(s):** United Kingdom. **Units of Measure:** British pounds per metric ton. **Type of Price:** import value. **Time Period Covered:** monthly latest 2 years, annually latest 5 years.

NEWSPRINT: 50 GRAMS, CANADIAN

Source: *Prices of Selected Asia/Pacific Products.* **Price Frequency:** monthly. **Effective Market(s):** Hong Kong. **Units of Measure:** Hong Kong dollars per lb. **Type of Price:** wholesale high, wholesale low. **Time Period Covered:** latest month.

NEWSPRINT: 50 GRAMS, CHINESE

Source: *Prices of Selected Asia/Pacific Products.* **Price Frequency:** monthly. **Effective Market(s):** Hong Kong. **Units of Measure:** Hong Kong dollars per ream. **Type of Price:** wholesale high, wholesale low. **Time Period Covered:** latest month.

NEWSPRINT: 50 GRAMS, EUROPE

Source: *Prices of Selected Asia/Pacific Products.* **Price Frequency:** monthly. **Effective Market(s):** Hong Kong. **Units of Measure:** Hong Kong dollars per ream. **Type of Price:** wholesale high, wholesale low. **Time Period Covered:** latest month.

NEWSPRINT: 50 GRAMS, SUPERIOR, CHINESE

Source: *Prices of Selected Asia/Pacific Products.* **Price Frequency:** monthly. **Effective Market(s):** Hong Kong. **Units of Measure:** Hong Kong dollars per lb. **Type of Price:** wholesale high, wholesale low. **Time Period Covered:** latest month.

NEWSPRINT: CANADIAN

Source: *International Financial Statistics.* **Price Frequency:** annually. **Effective Market(s):** Canada. **Units of Measure:** Dollars per short ton, index. **Type of Price:** market price, price index. **Time Period Covered:** latest 4 years.

Source: *International Financial Statistics Yearbook.* **Price Frequency:** annually. **Effective Market(s):** Canada. **Units of Measure:** Dollars per short ton. **Type of Price:** wholesale. **Time Period Covered:** latest 30 years.

NEWSPRINT: FINNISH

Source: *International Financial Statistics.* **Price Frequency:** monthly, quarterly, annually. **Effective Market(s):** Finland. **Units of Measure:** Dollars per short ton, index. **Type of Price:** market price, price index. **Time Period Covered:** latest 2 months, latest 3 quarters, latest 4 years.

Source: *International Financial Statistics Yearbook.* **Price Frequency:** annually. **Effective Market(s):** Finland. **Units of Measure:** Dollars per short ton. **Type of Price:** wholesale. **Time Period Covered:** latest 30 years.

NEWSPRINT: SWEDISH

Source: *International Financial Statistics.* **Price Frequency:** quarterly, annually. **Effective Market(s):** Sweden. **Units of Measure:** Dollars per short ton, index. **Type of Price:** market price, price index. **Time Period Covered:** latest 2 quarters, latest 4 years.

Source: *International Financial Statistics Yearbook.* **Price Frequency:** annually. **Effective Market(s):** Sweden. **Units of Measure:** Dollars per short ton. **Type of Price:** wholesale. **Time Period Covered:** latest 30 years.

NEWSPRINT ROLLS

Source: *Commodity Year Book.* **Price Frequency:** monthly, annually. **Units of Measure:** index. **Type of Price:** price index. **Time Period Covered:** latest 4 years.

NEWSPRINT ROLLS: STANDARD

Source: *FAO Quarterly Bulletin of Statistics.* **Price Frequency:** monthly, annually. **Effective Market(s):** New York. **Units of Measure:** Dollars per 2000 lbs., dollars per metric ton. **Type of Price:** contract. **Time Period Covered:** latest 3 years.

NIACIN: FEED GRADE, 98-99.5%

Source: *Chemical Marketing Reporter.* **Price Frequency:** weekly. **Effective Market(s):** New York. **Units of Measure:** Dollars per kilo. **Type of Price:** spot. **Time Period Covered:** latest week.

NIACIN: NF

Source: *Chemical Marketing Reporter.* **Price Frequency:** weekly. **Effective Market(s):** New York. **Units of Measure:** Dollars per kilo. **Type of Price:** spot. **Time Period Covered:** latest week.

NIACINAMIDE: FEED GRADE

Source: *Journal of Commerce and Commercial.* **Price Frequency:** weekly in Friday issue. **Units of Measure:** Dollars per kilo. **Type of Price:** spot. **Time Period Covered:** latest week.

NIACINAMIDE: USP

Source: *Chemical Marketing Reporter.* **Price Frequency:** weekly. **Effective Market(s):** New York. **Units of Measure:** Dollars per kilo. **Type of Price:** spot. **Time Period Covered:** latest week.

Source: *Journal of Commerce and Commercial.* **Price Frequency:** weekly in Friday issue. **Units of Measure:** Dollars per lb. **Type of Price:** spot. **Time Period Covered:** latest week.

NICKEL

Source: *American Metal Market.* **Price Frequency:** daily. **Effective Market(s):** London. **Units of Measure:** Dollars per metric ton. **Type of Price:** cash. **Time Period Covered:** latest 2 days.

Source: *Asian Wall Street Journal.* **Price Frequency:** daily. **Effective Market(s):** London. **Units of Measure:** Dollars per metric ton. **Type of Price:** spot. **Time Period Covered:** latest day.

Source: *E&MJ.* **Price Frequency:** monthly. **Effective Market(s):** New York. **Units of Measure:** Dollars per lb. **Type of Price:** merchant, spot. **Time Period Covered:** latest month.

Source: *Economic and Energy Indicators.* **Price Frequency:** monthly, quarterly, annually. **Units of Measure:** Dollars per lb. **Time Period Covered:** latest 3 months, quarters, and years.

Source: *Financial Times.* **Price Frequency:** daily. **Effective Market(s):** London. **Units of Measure:** cents per lb. **Type of Price:** free market. **Time Period Covered:** latest day.

Source: *Financial Times.* **Price Frequency:** daily. **Effective Market(s):** London. **Units of Measure:** Dollars per tonne. **Type of Price:** cash. **Time Period Covered:** latest 2 days.

Source: *Iron Age.* **Price Frequency:** monthly. **Effective Market(s):** London. **Units of Measure:** cents per lb. **Type of Price:** average. **Time Period Covered:** latest month.

Source: *Monthly Commodity Price Bulletin.* **Price Frequency:** monthly, annually. **Effective Market(s):** London. **Units of Measure:** Dollars per metric ton. **Type of Price:** cash. **Time Period Covered:** latest 5 years.

Source: *New York Times.* **Price Frequency:** daily. **Effective Market(s):** London. **Units of Measure:** Dollars per metric ton. **Type of Price:** spot. **Time Period Covered:** latest day.

Source: *Northern Miner.* **Price Frequency:** daily. **Effective Market(s):** London. **Units of Measure:** Dollars per tonne. **Type of Price:** spot. **Time Period Covered:** latest week.

Source: *The Times.* **Price Frequency:** daily. **Effective Market(s):** London. **Units of Measure:** Dollars per tonne. **Type of Price:** cash. **Time Period Covered:** latest day.

Source: *UNCTAD Commodity Yearbook.* **Price Frequency:** annually. **Effective Market(s):** London. **Units of Measure:** Dollars per metric ton. **Type of Price:** cash. **Time Period Covered:** latest 12 years.

Source: *Wall Street Journal.* **Price Frequency:** daily. **Effective Market(s):** London. **Units of Measure:** Dollars per metric ton. **Type of Price:** spot. **Time Period Covered:** latest day, 3 months ago.

NICKEL: 99.5%

Source: *Journal of Commerce and Commercial.* **Price Frequency:** daily. **Effective Market(s):** Europe. **Units of Measure:** Dollars per lb. **Type of Price:** spot. **Time Period Covered:** latest day.

NICKEL: 99.5%, REFINERY

Source: *Monthly Commodity Price Bulletin Supplement.* **Price Frequency:** monthly, quarterly, annually. **Effective Market(s):** United Kingdom. **Units of Measure:** Dollars per tonne. **Type of Price:** cash. **Time Period Covered:** latest 10 years.

NICKEL: CANADIAN

Source: *International Financial Statistics Yearbook.* **Price Frequency:** annually. **Effective Market(s):** Canadian ports. **Units of Measure:** cents per lb. **Type of Price:** wholesale. **Time Period Covered:** latest 30 years.

NICKEL: UNITED KINGDOM

Source: *International Financial Statistics.* **Price Frequency:** monthly, quarterly, annually. **Effective Market(s):** Northern European ports. **Units of Measure:** cents per lb., index. **Type of Price:** market price, price index. **Time Period Covered:** latest 5 months, latest 5 quarters, latest 5 years.

NICKEL ACETATE

Source: *Chemical Marketing Reporter.* **Price Frequency:** weekly. **Effective Market(s):** East. **Units of Measure:** Dollars per lb. **Type of Price:** spot. **Time Period Covered:** latest week.

Source: *Journal of Commerce and Commercial.* **Price Frequency:** weekly in Thursday issue. **Units of Measure:** Dollars per lb. **Type of Price:** spot. **Time Period Covered:** latest week.

NICKEL ANODES: ROLLED

Source: *American Metal Market.* **Price Frequency:** daily. **Effective Market(s):** Chicago. **Units of Measure:** cents per lb. **Type of Price:** dealer. **Time Period Covered:** latest day.

NICKEL BRIQUETTES

Source: *American Metal Market.* **Price Frequency:** daily. **Effective Market(s):** New York. **Units of Measure:** Dollars per lb. of nickel. **Type of Price:** market, spot. **Time Period Covered:** latest day.

NICKEL BRIQUETTES: MELTING

Source: *E&MJ.* **Price Frequency:** monthly. **Units of Measure:** Dollars per lb. **Time Period Covered:** latest month.

NICKEL CARBONATE

Source: *Chemical Marketing Reporter.* **Price Frequency:** weekly. **Effective Market(s):** New York. **Units of Measure:** Dollars per lb. **Type of Price:** spot. **Time Period Covered:** latest week.

Source: *Journal of Commerce and Commercial.* **Price Frequency:** weekly in Thursday issue. **Units of Measure:** Dollars per lb. **Type of Price:** spot. **Time Period Covered:** latest week.

NICKEL CARBONYL POWDER

Source: *American Metal Market.* **Price Frequency:** daily. **Units of Measure:** Dollars per lb. **Type of Price:** wholesale. **Time Period Covered:** latest day.

NICKEL CATHODES

Source: *American Metal Market.* **Price Frequency:** daily. **Units of Measure:** Dollars per lb. of nickel. **Type of Price:** market. **Time Period Covered:** latest day.

Source: *American Metal Market.* **Price Frequency:** daily. **Effective Market(s):** Chicago. **Units of Measure:** cents per lb. **Type of Price:** dealer. **Time Period Covered:** latest day.

Source: *Commodity Trade and Price Trends.* **Price Frequency:** annually. **Effective Market(s):** New York. **Units of Measure:** Dollars per metric ton, 1980 constant dollars per metric ton. **Type of Price:** spot. **Time Period Covered:** latest 15 years.

Source: *Commodity Year Book.* **Price Frequency:** annually. **Effective Market(s):** New York. **Units of Measure:** Dollars per lb. **Type of Price:** free market. **Time Period Covered:** latest 7 years.

Source: *Monthly Commodity Price Bulletin.* **Price Frequency:** monthly, annually. **Effective Market(s):** New York. **Units of Measure:** cents per lb. **Type of Price:** free market. **Time Period Covered:** latest 5 years.

Source: *Monthly Commodity Price Bulletin Supplement.* **Price Frequency:** monthly, quarterly, annually. **Effective Market(s):** New York. **Units of Measure:** cents per lb. **Type of Price:** free market. **Time Period Covered:** latest 20 years.

Source: *Northern Miner.* **Price Frequency:** daily. **Effective Market(s):** New York. **Units of Measure:** Dollars per lb. **Type of Price:** dealer . **Time Period Covered:** latest day.

Source: *UNCTAD Commodity Yearbook.* **Price Frequency:** annually. **Effective Market(s):** New York. **Units of Measure:** Dollars per metric ton. **Type of Price:** dealer, free market. **Time Period Covered:** latest 12 years.

NICKEL CATHODES: ELECTROLYTIC

Source: *Chemical Marketing Reporter.* **Price Frequency:** weekly. **Effective Market(s):** New York. **Units of Measure:** Dollars per lb. **Type of Price:** spot. **Time Period Covered:** latest week.

NICKEL CATHODES: ELECTROLYTIC, CANADIAN

Source: *Commodity Trade and Price Trends.* **Price Frequency:** annually. **Effective Market(s):** London. **Units of Measure:** Dollars per metric ton, 1980 constant dollars per metric ton. **Type of Price:** contract. **Time Period Covered:** latest 37 years.

NICKEL CATHODES AND PELLETS: MELTING

Source: *Purchasing.* **Price Frequency:** monthly. **Units of Measure:** cents per lb. **Type of Price:** transaction. **Time Period Covered:** latest day, month ago, 6 months ago, year ago.

NICKEL CHLORIDE

Source: *Chemical Marketing Reporter.* **Price Frequency:** weekly. **Effective Market(s):** New York. **Units of Measure:** Dollars per lb. **Type of Price:** spot. **Time Period Covered:** latest week.

Source: *Journal of Commerce and Commercial.* **Price Frequency:** weekly in Thursday issue. **Units of Measure:** Dollars per lb. **Type of Price:** spot. **Time Period Covered:** latest week.

NICKEL CLIPPINGS AND SOLIDS: NEW

Source: *American Metal Market.* **Price Frequency:** daily. **Effective Market(s):** 8 domestic markets. **Units of Measure:** cents per lb. **Type of Price:** dealer. **Time Period Covered:** latest day.

NICKEL FLUOBORATE

Source: *Journal of Commerce and Commercial.* **Price Frequency:** weekly in Thursday issue. **Units of Measure:** Dollars per lb. **Type of Price:** spot. **Time Period Covered:** latest week.

NICKEL FLUOBORATE: LIQUID CONCENTRATE

Source: *Chemical Marketing Reporter.* **Price Frequency:** weekly. **Effective Market(s):** East. **Units of Measure:** Dollars per lb. **Type of Price:** spot. **Time Period Covered:** latest week.

NICKEL NITRATE

Source: *Chemical Marketing Reporter.* **Price Frequency:** weekly. **Effective Market(s):** East. **Units of Measure:** Dollars per lb. **Type of Price:** spot. **Time Period Covered:** latest week.

Source: *Journal of Commerce and Commercial.* **Price Frequency:** weekly in Thursday issue. **Units of Measure:** Dollars per lb. **Type of Price:** spot. **Time Period Covered:** latest week.

NICKEL OXIDE: 75-78% NICKEL

Source: *Chemical Marketing Reporter.* **Price Frequency:** weekly. **Effective Market(s):** New York. **Units of Measure:** Dollars per lb. **Type of Price:** spot. **Time Period Covered:** latest week.

NICKEL PLATES

Source: *American Metal Market.* **Price Frequency:** daily. **Effective Market(s):** World. **Units of Measure:** Dollars per lb. of nickel. **Type of Price:** base. **Time Period Covered:** latest day.

NICKEL ROD ENDS

Source: *Iron Age.* **Price Frequency:** monthly. **Effective Market(s):** New York. **Units of Measure:** cents per lb. **Type of Price:** dealer. **Time Period Covered:** latest month.

NICKEL RODS

Source: *American Metal Market.* **Price Frequency:** daily. **Effective Market(s):** World. **Units of Measure:** Dollars per lb. of nickel. **Type of Price:** base. **Time Period Covered:** latest day.

NICKEL SALTS

Source: *Journal of Commerce and Commercial.* **Price Frequency:** weekly in Thursday issue. **Units of Measure:** Dollars per lb. **Type of Price:** spot. **Time Period Covered:** latest week.

NICKEL SHEETS: CLIPPINGS

Source: *Iron Age.* **Price Frequency:** monthly. **Effective Market(s):** New York. **Units of Measure:** cents per lb. **Type of Price:** dealer. **Time Period Covered:** latest month.

NICKEL SHEETS: COLD ROLLED

Source: *American Metal Market.* **Price Frequency:** daily. **Effective Market(s):** World. **Units of Measure:** Dollars per lb. of nickel. **Type of Price:** base. **Time Period Covered:** latest day.

NICKEL SILVER POWDER

Source: *American Metal Market.* **Price Frequency:** daily. **Units of Measure:** Dollars per lb. **Type of Price:** wholesale. **Time Period Covered:** latest day.

NICKEL SILVER SOLIDS

Source: *American Metal Market.* **Price Frequency:** daily. **Effective Market(s):** San Francisco. **Units of Measure:** cents per lb. **Type of Price:** dealer. **Time Period Covered:** latest day.

NICKEL SOLIDS

Source: *Iron Age.* **Price Frequency:** monthly. **Effective Market(s):** New York. **Units of Measure:** cents per lb. **Type of Price:** dealer. **Time Period Covered:** latest month.

NICKEL STRIPS

Source: *American Metal Market.* **Price Frequency:** daily. **Effective Market(s):** World. **Units of Measure:** Dollars per lb. of nickel. **Type of Price:** base. **Time Period Covered:** latest day.

NICKEL SULFATE

Source: *Chemical Marketing Reporter.* **Price Frequency:** weekly. **Effective Market(s):** East. **Units of Measure:** Dollars per lb. **Type of Price:** spot. **Time Period Covered:** latest week.

Source: *Journal of Commerce and Commercial.* **Price Frequency:** weekly in Thursday issue. **Units of Measure:** Dollars per lb. **Type of Price:** spot. **Time Period Covered:** latest week.

NICKEL TURNINGS

Source: *American Metal Market.* **Price Frequency:** daily. **Effective Market(s):** 8 domestic markets. **Units of Measure:** cents per lb. **Type of Price:** dealer. **Time Period Covered:** latest day.

Source: *Iron Age.* **Price Frequency:** monthly. **Effective Market(s):** New York. **Units of Measure:** cents per lb. **Type of Price:** dealer. **Time Period Covered:** latest month.

NICOTINAMIDE

see Niacinamide.

NICOTINIC ACID

see Niacin.

NITRATE OF SODA

Source: *Standard & Poor's Statistical Service Current Statistics.* **Price Frequency:** monthly, annually. **Effective Market(s):** East. **Units of Measure:** cents per lb. **Time Period Covered:** latest 4 years.

NITRATE OF SODA FERTILIZER

Source: *Agricultural Prices.* **Price Frequency:** monthly. **Effective Market(s):** 9 domestic markets, United States. **Units of Measure:** Dollars per ton. **Type of Price:** paid by farmer. **Time Period Covered:** latest month.

Source: *Agricultural Prices Annual Summary.* **Price Frequency:** semiannually. **Effective Market(s):** East South Central region, Southeast region, United States. **Units of Measure:** Dollars per ton. **Type of Price:** paid by farmer. **Time Period Covered:** latest year, for US quarterly latest 6 years.

NITRIC ACID

Source: *Chemical Marketing Reporter.* **Price Frequency:** weekly. **Effective Market(s):** New York. **Units of Measure:** Dollars per ton. **Type of Price:** spot. **Time Period Covered:** latest week.

NITRIC ACID: 36 DEGREE

Source: *Journal of Commerce and Commercial.* **Price Frequency:** weekly in Thursday issue. **Units of Measure:** Dollars per ton. **Type of Price:** spot. **Time Period Covered:** latest week.

NITRIC ACID: 38 DEGREE

Source: *Journal of Commerce and Commercial.* **Price Frequency:** weekly in Thursday issue. **Units of Measure:** Dollars per ton. **Type of Price:** spot. **Time Period Covered:** latest week.

NITRIC ACID: 40 DEGREE

Source: *Journal of Commerce and Commercial.* **Price Frequency:** weekly in Thursday issue. **Units of Measure:** Dollars per ton. **Type of Price:** spot. **Time Period Covered:** latest week.

2-NITRO-P-CRESOL: TECHNICAL

Source: *Chemical Marketing Reporter.* **Price Frequency:** weekly. **Effective Market(s):** New York. **Units of Measure:** Dollars per lb. **Type of Price:** spot. **Time Period Covered:** latest week.

NITROANILINE: TNR

Source: *Journal of Commerce and Commercial.* **Price Frequency:** weekly in Wednesday issue. **Units of Measure:** Dollars per lb. **Type of Price:** spot. **Time Period Covered:** latest week.

O-NITROANILINE

Source: *Journal of Commerce and Commercial.* **Price Frequency:** weekly in Wednesday issue. **Units of Measure:** Dollars per lb. **Type of Price:** spot. **Time Period Covered:** latest week.

O-NITROANILINE: FLAKE

Source: *Chemical Marketing Reporter.* **Price Frequency:** weekly. **Effective Market(s):** New York. **Units of Measure:** Dollars per lb. **Type of Price:** spot. **Time Period Covered:** latest week.

O-NITROANILINE: MOLTEN, REFINED

Source: *Chemical Marketing Reporter.* **Price Frequency:** weekly. **Effective Market(s):** New York. **Units of Measure:** Dollars per lb. **Type of Price:** spot. **Time Period Covered:** latest week.

O-NITROANILINE: MOLTEN, TECHNICAL

Source: *Chemical Marketing Reporter.* **Price Frequency:** weekly. **Effective Market(s):** New York. **Units of Measure:** Dollars per lb. **Type of Price:** spot. **Time Period Covered:** latest week.

O-NITROANILINE ORANGE TONER

Source: *Chemical Marketing Reporter.* **Price Frequency:** weekly. **Effective Market(s):** New York. **Units of Measure:** Dollars per lb. **Type of Price:** spot. **Time Period Covered:** latest week.

P-NITROANILINE

Source: *Chemical Marketing Reporter.* **Price Frequency:** weekly. **Effective Market(s):** New York. **Units of Measure:** Dollars per lb. **Type of Price:** spot. **Time Period Covered:** latest week.

Source: *Journal of Commerce and Commercial.* **Price Frequency:** weekly in Wednesday issue. **Units of Measure:** Dollars per lb. **Type of Price:** spot. **Time Period Covered:** latest week.

O-NITROANISOLE

Source: *Chemical Marketing Reporter.* **Price Frequency:** weekly. **Effective Market(s):** New York. **Units of Measure:** Dollars per kilo. **Type of Price:** spot. **Time Period Covered:** latest week.

NITROBENZENE

Source: *Chemical Marketing Reporter.* **Price Frequency:** weekly. **Effective Market(s):** New York. **Units of Measure:** Dollars per lb. **Type of Price:** spot. **Time Period Covered:** latest week.

Source: *Journal of Commerce and Commercial.* **Price Frequency:** weekly in Wednesday issue. **Units of Measure:** Dollars per lb. **Type of Price:** spot. **Time Period Covered:** latest week.

O-NITROCHLOROBENZENE

Source: *Chemical Marketing Reporter.* **Price Frequency:** weekly. **Effective Market(s):** New York. **Units of Measure:** Dollars per lb. **Type of Price:** spot. **Time Period Covered:** latest week.

NITROETHANE

Source: *Chemical Marketing Reporter.* **Price Frequency:** weekly. **Effective Market(s):** East. **Units of Measure:** Dollars per lb. **Type of Price:** spot. **Time Period Covered:** latest week.

NITROGEN SOLUTION FERTILIZER: 28% NITROGEN

Source: *Agricultural Prices.* **Price Frequency:** monthly. **Effective Market(s):** 9 domestic markets, United States. **Units of Measure:** Dollars per ton. **Type of Price:** paid by farmer. **Time Period Covered:** latest month.

Source: *Agricultural Prices Annual Summary.* **Price Frequency:** semiannually. **Effective Market(s):** North Central region, Northern Plains region, South Central region, United States. **Units of Measure:** Dollars per ton. **Type of Price:** paid by farmer. **Time Period Covered:** latest year, for US quarterly latest 6 years.

NITROGEN SOLUTION FERTILIZER: 30% NITROGEN

Source: *Agricultural Prices.* **Price Frequency:** monthly. **Effective Market(s):** 9 domestic markets, United States. **Units of Measure:** Dollars per ton. **Type of Price:** paid by farmer. **Time Period Covered:** latest month.

Source: *Agricultural Prices Annual Summary.* **Price Frequency:** semiannually. **Effective Market(s):** Southeast region, United States. **Units of Measure:** Dollars per ton. **Type of Price:** paid by farmer. **Time Period Covered:** latest year, for US quarterly latest 6 years.

NITROGEN SOLUTION FERTILIZER: 32% NITROGEN

Source: *Agricultural Prices.* **Price Frequency:** monthly. **Effective Market(s):** 9 domestic markets, United States. **Units of Measure:** Dollars per ton. **Type of Price:** paid by farmer. **Time Period Covered:** latest month.

Source: *Agricultural Prices Annual Summary.* **Price Frequency:** semiannually. **Effective Market(s):** North Central region, Northern Plains, Southeast region, Southwest region, United States. **Units of Measure:** Dollars per ton. **Type of Price:** paid by farmer. **Time Period Covered:** latest year, for US quarterly latest 6 years.

NITROGEN SOLUTION FERTILIZER: DIRECT APPLICATION, 19-32% NITROGEN

Source: *Chemical Marketing Reporter.* **Price Frequency:** weekly. **Effective Market(s):** New York. **Units of Measure:** Dollars per unit-ton. **Type of Price:** spot. **Time Period Covered:** latest week.

NITROGEN SOLUTION FERTILIZER: DIRECT APPLICATION, OVER 32% NITROGEN

Source: *Chemical Marketing Reporter.* **Price Frequency:** weekly. **Effective Market(s):** New York. **Units of Measure:** Dollars per unit-ton. **Type of Price:** spot. **Time Period Covered:** latest week.

NITROMETHANE

Source: *Chemical Marketing Reporter.* **Price Frequency:** weekly. **Effective Market(s):** East. **Units of Measure:** Dollars per lb. **Type of Price:** spot. **Time Period Covered:** latest week.

M-NITROPARATOLUIDINE

Source: *Journal of Commerce and Commercial.* **Price Frequency:** weekly in Wednesday issue. **Units of Measure:** Dollars per lb. **Type of Price:** spot. **Time Period Covered:** latest week.

O-NITROPHENOL

Source: *Chemical Marketing Reporter.* **Price Frequency:** weekly. **Effective Market(s):** New York. **Units of Measure:** Dollars per lb. **Type of Price:** spot. **Time Period Covered:** latest week.

Source: *Journal of Commerce and Commercial.* **Price Frequency:** weekly in Wednesday issue. **Units of Measure:** Dollars per lb. **Type of Price:** spot. **Time Period Covered:** latest week.

P-NITROPHENOL

Source: *Chemical Marketing Reporter.* **Price Frequency:** weekly. **Effective Market(s):** New York. **Units of Measure:** Dollars per lb. **Type of Price:** spot. **Time Period Covered:** latest week.

Source: *Journal of Commerce and Commercial.* **Price Frequency:** weekly in Wednesday issue. **Units of Measure:** Dollars per lb. **Type of Price:** spot. **Time Period Covered:** latest week.

2-NITROPROPANE

Source: *Chemical Marketing Reporter.* **Price Frequency:** weekly. **Effective Market(s):** East. **Units of Measure:** Dollars per lb. **Type of Price:** spot. **Time Period Covered:** latest week.

M-NITROTOLUENE: TECHNICAL

Source: *Chemical Marketing Reporter.* **Price Frequency:** weekly. **Effective Market(s):** New York. **Units of Measure:** Dollars per lb. **Type of Price:** spot. **Time Period Covered:** latest week.

O-NITROTOLUENE

Source: *Chemical Marketing Reporter.* **Price Frequency:** weekly. **Effective Market(s):** New York. **Units of Measure:** Dollars per lb. **Type of Price:** spot. **Time Period Covered:** latest week.

Source: *Journal of Commerce and Commercial.* **Price Frequency:** weekly in Wednesday issue. **Units of Measure:** Dollars per lb. **Type of Price:** spot. **Time Period Covered:** latest week.

P-NITROTOLUENE: TECHNICAL

Source: *Chemical Marketing Reporter.* **Price Frequency:** weekly. **Effective Market(s):** New York. **Units of Measure:** Dollars per lb. **Type of Price:** spot. **Time Period Covered:** latest week.

NON-SPIRITUOUS ITEMS

Source: *Colorado Beverage Analyst.* **Price Frequency:** monthly. **Effective Market(s):** Colorado. **Units of Measure:** Dollars per case. **Type of Price:** wholesale by brand. **Time Period Covered:** latest month.

NONYLPHENOL

Source: *Chemical Marketing Reporter.* **Price Frequency:** weekly. **Effective Market(s):** East of the Rockies. **Units of Measure:** Dollars per lb. **Type of Price:** spot. **Time Period Covered:** latest week.

NOREPHEDRINE HYDROCHLORIDE

see Phenylpropanolamine Hydrochloride.

NORWAY KRONE

Source: *Asian Wall Street Journal.* **Price Frequency:** daily. **Effective Market(s):** United States. **Units of Measure:** Norwegian krone per ECU, per SDR. **Type of Price:** foreign exchange. **Time Period Covered:** latest 2 days.

Source: *Barron's.* **Price Frequency:** weekly. **Effective Market(s):** New York. **Units of Measure:** Norwegian krone per United States dollar. **Type of Price:** foreign exchange. **Time Period Covered:** latest 2 weeks.

Source: *New York Times.* **Price Frequency:** daily. **Effective Market(s):** United States. **Units of Measure:** Norwegian krone per United States dollar. **Type of Price:** foreign exchange. **Time Period Covered:** latest 2 days.

Source: *Timber Bulletin.* **Price Frequency:** monthly, annually. **Units of Measure:** Norwegian krone per United States dollar. **Type of Price:** foreign exchange. **Time Period Covered:** latest 2 years.

NUTMEG

Source: *Prices of Selected Asia/Pacific Products.* **Price Frequency:** monthly, seasonally. **Effective Market(s):** Tokyo. **Units of Measure:** Japanese yen per kilogram. **Type of Price:** trade high, trade low. **Time Period Covered:** latest month.

Source: *Prices of Selected Asia/Pacific Products.* **Price Frequency:** monthly, seasonally. **Effective Market(s):** Netherlands. **Units of Measure:** Dutch guilders per metric ton. **Type of Price:** spot high, spot low. **Time Period Covered:** latest month.

NUTMEG: EAST INDIAN

Source: *Prices of Selected Asia/Pacific Products.* **Price Frequency:** monthly, seasonally. **Effective Market(s):** United Kingdom/North European ports. **Units of Measure:** Dollars per metric ton. **Type of Price:** high, low. **Time Period Covered:** latest month.

Source: *U. S. Spice Trade.* **Price Frequency:** monthly, annually. **Effective Market(s):** New York. **Units of Measure:** Dollars per lb. **Type of Price:** spot. **Time Period Covered:** latest 10 years.

NUTMEG: INDONESIAN

Source: *Prices of Selected Asia/Pacific Products.* **Price Frequency:** monthly, seasonally. **Effective Market(s):** major European ports, Netherlands. **Units of Measure:** Dollars per metric ton, Dutch guilders per metric ton. **Type of Price:** high, low. **Time Period Covered:** latest month.

NUTMEG: PADANG

Source: *U. S. Spice Trade.* **Price Frequency:** monthly, annually, irregularly. **Effective Market(s):** New York. **Units of Measure:** Dollars per lb. **Type of Price:** spot. **Time Period Covered:** latest 5 years.

NUTMEG: SOUND SHRIVELS, EAST INDIAN

Source: *Prices of Selected Asia/Pacific Products.* **Price Frequency:** monthly. **Effective Market(s):** United Kingdom/North European ports. **Units of Measure:** Dollars per metric ton. **Type of Price:** high, low. **Time Period Covered:** latest month.

NUTMEG: SOUND SHRIVELS, INDONESIAN

Source: *Prices of Selected Asia/Pacific Products.* **Price Frequency:** monthly, seasonally. **Effective Market(s):** major European ports, Netherlands, United States. **Units of Measure:** Dollars per metric ton, Dutch guilders per metric ton. **Type of Price:** high, low. **Time Period Covered:** latest month.

NUTMEG: SOUND, UNASSORTED, GRENADA

Source: *Fruit and Tropical Products.* **Price Frequency:** monthly, seasonally. **Effective Market(s):** London. **Units of Measure:** British pounds per tonne. **Type of Price:** month end. **Time Period Covered:** latest 2 years.

NUTMEG: WHOLE, EAST INDIAN

Source: *Chemical Marketing Reporter.* **Price Frequency:** weekly. **Effective Market(s):** New York. **Units of Measure:** Dollars per lb. **Type of Price:** spot. **Time Period Covered:** latest week.

NUTMEG: WHOLE, WEST INDIAN

Source: *U. S. Spice Trade.* **Price Frequency:** monthly, annually. **Effective Market(s):** New York. **Units of Measure:** Dollars per lb. **Type of Price:** spot. **Time Period Covered:** latest 10 years.

NUTMEG OIL

Source: *Journal of Commerce and Commercial.* **Price Frequency:** weekly in Tuesday issue. **Units of Measure:** Dollars per lb. **Type of Price:** spot. **Time Period Covered:** latest week.

Source: *U. S. Essential Oil Trade.* **Price Frequency:** annually. **Effective Market(s):** United States. **Units of Measure:** Dollars per kilogram. **Type of Price:** import value. **Time Period Covered:** latest 3 years.

NUTMEG OIL: DISTILLED, EAST INDIAN

Source: *Chemical Marketing Reporter.* **Price Frequency:** weekly. **Effective Market(s):** New York. **Units of Measure:** Dollars per kilo. **Type of Price:** spot. **Time Period Covered:** latest week.

Source: *Prices of Selected Asia/Pacific Products.* **Price Frequency:** monthly. **Effective Market(s):** New York. **Units of Measure:** Dollars per kilogram. **Type of Price:** spot high, spot low. **Time Period Covered:** latest month.

NUTMEG OIL: INDONESIAN

Source: *Prices of Selected Asia/Pacific Products.* **Price Frequency:** monthly. **Effective Market(s):** New York. **Units of Measure:** Dollars per lb. **Type of Price:** spot high, spot low. **Time Period Covered:** latest month.

NUXVOMIC EXTRACT

Source: *Journal of Commerce and Commercial.* **Price Frequency:** weekly in Monday issue . **Units of Measure:** Dollars per lb. **Type of Price:** spot. **Time Period Covered:** latest week.

NYLON: HOSIERY FILAMENT YARN

see Yarn: Nylon Hosiery Filament.

NYLON: INDUSTRIAL FILAMENT YARN

see Yarn: Nylon Industrial Filament.

NYLON: MINERAL FILLED

Source: *Journal of Commerce and Commercial.* **Price Frequency:** weekly in Tuesday issue. **Units of Measure:** Dollars per lb. **Type of Price:** spot. **Time Period Covered:** latest week.

NYLON: TRANSPARENT, AMORPHOUS

Source: *Plastics Technology.* **Price Frequency:** monthly. **Units of Measure:** cents per lb., cents per cubic inch. **Type of Price:** bulk list, market. **Time Period Covered:** latest month.

NYLON: TYPE 6

Source: *Journal of Commerce and Commercial.* **Price Frequency:** weekly in Tuesday issue. **Units of Measure:** Dollars per lb. **Type of Price:** spot. **Time Period Covered:** latest week.

Source: *Plastics Technology.* **Price Frequency:** monthly. **Units of Measure:** cents per lb., cents per cubic inch. **Type of Price:** bulk list, market. **Time Period Covered:** latest month.

NYLON: TYPE 6, 30% GLASS

Source: *Plastics Technology.* **Price Frequency:** monthly. **Units of Measure:** cents per lb., cents per cubic inch. **Type of Price:** bulk list, market. **Time Period Covered:** latest month.

NYLON: TYPE 6, MINERAL FILLED

Source: *Plastics Technology.* **Price Frequency:** monthly. **Units of Measure:** cents per lb., cents per cubic inch. **Type of Price:** bulk list, market. **Time Period Covered:** latest month.

NYLON: TYPE 6/10

Source: *Plastics Technology.* **Price Frequency:** monthly. **Units of Measure:** cents per lb., cents per cubic inch. **Type of Price:** bulk list, market. **Time Period Covered:** latest month.

NYLON: TYPE 11

Source: *Plastics Technology.* **Price Frequency:** monthly. **Units of Measure:** cents per lb., cents per cubic inch. **Type of Price:** bulk list, market. **Time Period Covered:** latest month.

NYLON: TYPE 11, 30% GLASS

Source: *Plastics Technology.* **Price Frequency:** monthly. **Units of Measure:** cents per lb., cents per cubic inch. **Type of Price:** bulk list, market. **Time Period Covered:** latest month.

NYLON: TYPE 11, 43% GLASS

Source: *Plastics Technology.* **Price Frequency:** monthly. **Units of Measure:** cents per lb., cents per cubic inch. **Type of Price:** bulk list, market. **Time Period Covered:** latest month.

NYLON: TYPE 12

Source: *Plastics Technology.* **Price Frequency:** monthly. **Units of Measure:** cents per lb., cents per cubic inch. **Type of Price:** bulk list, market. **Time Period Covered:** latest month.

NYLON: TYPE 12, 30% GLASS

Source: *Plastics Technology.* **Price Frequency:** monthly. **Units of Measure:** cents per lb., cents per cubic inch. **Type of Price:** bulk list, market. **Time Period Covered:** latest month.

NYLON: TYPE 12, 50% BEAD

Source: *Plastics Technology.* **Price Frequency:** monthly. **Units of Measure:** cents per lb., cents per cubic inch. **Type of Price:** bulk list, market. **Time Period Covered:** latest month.

NYLON: TYPE 66

Source: *Journal of Commerce and Commercial.* **Price Frequency:** weekly in Tuesday issue. **Units of Measure:** Dollars per lb. **Type of Price:** spot. **Time Period Covered:** latest week.

Source: *Plastics Technology.* **Price Frequency:** monthly. **Units of Measure:** cents per lb., cents per cubic inch. **Type of Price:** bulk list, market. **Time Period Covered:** latest month.

NYLON: TYPE 66, 30% GLASS

Source: *Plastics Technology.* **Price Frequency:** monthly. **Units of Measure:** cents per lb., cents per cubic inch. **Type of Price:** bulk list, market. **Time Period Covered:** latest month.

NYLON: TYPE 66, MINERAL FILLED

Source: *Plastics Technology.* **Price Frequency:** monthly. **Units of Measure:** cents per lb., cents per cubic inch. **Type of Price:** bulk list, market. **Time Period Covered:** latest month.

NYLON: TYPE 69

Source: *Journal of Commerce and Commercial.* **Price Frequency:** weekly in Tuesday issue. **Units of Measure:** Dollars per lb. **Type of Price:** spot. **Time Period Covered:** latest week.

Source: *Plastics Technology.* **Price Frequency:** monthly. **Units of Measure:** cents per lb., cents per cubic inch. **Type of Price:** bulk list, market. **Time Period Covered:** latest month.

NYLON: TYPE 612

Source: *Journal of Commerce and Commercial.* **Price Frequency:** weekly in Tuesday issue. **Units of Measure:** Dollars per lb. **Type of Price:** spot. **Time Period Covered:** latest week.

Source: *Plastics Technology.* **Price Frequency:** monthly. **Units of Measure:** cents per lb., cents per cubic inch. **Type of Price:** bulk list, market. **Time Period Covered:** latest month.

NYLON: TYPE 612, 33% GLASS

Source: *Plastics Technology.* **Price Frequency:** monthly. **Units of Measure:** cents per lb., cents per cubic inch. **Type of Price:** bulk list, market. **Time Period Covered:** latest month.

NYLON: TYPE 612, 43% GLASS

Source: *Plastics Technology.* **Price Frequency:** monthly. **Units of Measure:** cents per lb., cents per cubic inch. **Type of Price:** bulk list, market. **Time Period Covered:** latest month.

NYLON CARPET STAPLE

Source: *Journal of Commerce and Commercial.* **Price Frequency:** weekly in Tuesday issue. **Units of Measure:** Dollars per lb. **Type of Price:** spot. **Time Period Covered:** latest week.

NYLON INDUSTRIAL STAPLE

Source: *Journal of Commerce and Commercial.* **Price Frequency:** weekly in Tuesday issue. **Units of Measure:** Dollars per lb. **Type of Price:** spot. **Time Period Covered:** latest week.

NYLON TAFFETA

Source: *JTN: The International Textile Magazine.* **Price Frequency:** monthly. **Effective Market(s):** Japan, Taiwan. **Units of Measure:** Japanese yen per yard, dollars per yard. **Type of Price:** spot. **Time Period Covered:** latest month.

NYLON YARN

see Yarn: Nylon.

NYSE COMPOSITE STOCK INDEX: FUTURES, DECEMBER

Source: *Commodity Year Book.* **Price Frequency:** monthly. **Effective Market(s):** New York. **Units of Measure:** stock index. **Type of Price:** futures. **Time Period Covered:** latest 4 years.

OAK BOARDS: SLAVONIAN

Source: *Timber Bulletin.* **Price Frequency:** monthly, annually. **Effective Market(s):** Italy. **Units of Measure:** 1000 Italian lire per cubic meter. **Time Period Covered:** monthly latest 2 years, annually latest 6 years.

OAK SAWLOGS

Source: *Timber Mart-South.* **Price Frequency:** quarterly. **Effective Market(s):** 13 domestic markets. **Units of Measure:** Dollars per 1000 board feet. **Type of Price:** delivered. **Time Period Covered:** latest 2 quarters.

OAK SAWTIMBER

Source: *Timber Mart-South.* **Price Frequency:** quarterly. **Effective Market(s):** 14 domestic markets. **Units of Measure:** Dollars per 1000 board feet. **Type of Price:** stumpage, mill. **Time Period Covered:** latest quarter.

Source: *Timber Mart-South.* **Price Frequency:** quarterly. **Effective Market(s):** 13 domestic markets. **Units of Measure:** Dollars per 1000 board feet. **Type of Price:** standing timber. **Time Period Covered:** latest 2 quarters.

Source: *Volume and Value of Sawtimber Stumpage Sold From National Forests by Selected Species and Region.* **Price Frequency:** quarterly, annually. **Effective Market(s):** Eastern region, Southern region. **Units of Measure:** Dollars per 1000 board feet. **Type of Price:** average. **Time Period Covered:** latest quarter, latest year.

OAK SAWTIMBER: CHESTNUT

Source: *Volume and Value of Sawtimber Stumpage Sold From National Forests by Selected Species and Region.* **Price Frequency:** quarterly, annually. **Effective Market(s):** Eastern region. **Units of Measure:** Dollars per 1000 board feet. **Type of Price:** average. **Time Period Covered:** latest quarter, latest year.

OAK SAWTIMBER: MIXED

Source: *Timber Mart-South.* **Price Frequency:** quarterly. **Effective Market(s):** 7 domestic markets. **Units of Measure:** Dollars per 1000 board feet. **Type of Price:** bid. **Time Period Covered:** latest quarter.

OAK SAWTIMBER: RED AND BLACK

Source: *Volume and Value of Sawtimber Stumpage Sold From National Forests by Selected Species and Region.* **Price Frequency:** quarterly, annually. **Effective Market(s):** Eastern region, Southern region. **Units of Measure:** Dollars per 1000 board feet. **Type of Price:** average. **Time Period Covered:** latest quarter, latest year.

OAK SAWTIMBER: WHITE

Source: *Timber Mart-South.* **Price Frequency:** quarterly. **Effective Market(s):** 7 domestic markets. **Units of Measure:** Dollars per 1000 board feet. **Type of Price:** bid. **Time Period Covered:** latest quarter.

Source: *Volume and Value of Sawtimber Stumpage Sold From National Forests by Selected Species and Region.* **Price Frequency:** quarterly, annually. **Effective Market(s):** Eastern region, Southern region. **Units of Measure:** Dollars per 1000 board feet. **Type of Price:** average. **Time Period Covered:** latest quarter, latest year.

OAT FEED: REGROUND

Source: *Feedstuffs.* **Price Frequency:** weekly. **Effective Market(s):** Chicago, Ft. Worth, Kansas City, Minneapolis/St. Paul. **Units of Measure:** Dollars per bulk ton. **Time Period Covered:** latest week.

OAT HULLS: REGROUND

Source: *Milling & Baking News.* **Price Frequency:** weekly. **Effective Market(s):** Chicago, Kansas City. **Units of Measure:** Dollars per ton. **Time Period Covered:** latest week, week ago, year ago.

OAT MEAL: FEED

Source: *Milling & Baking News.* **Price Frequency:** weekly . **Effective Market(s):** Kansas City. **Units of Measure:** Dollars per ton. **Time Period Covered:** latest week, week ago, year ago.

OAT PRODUCTS

Source: *Feedstuffs.* **Price Frequency:** weekly. **Units of Measure:** Dollars per bulk ton. **Time Period Covered:** latest week.

OAT STRAW

Source: *Scottish Farmer.* **Price Frequency:** weekly. **Effective Market(s):** Scotland. **Units of Measure:** British pounds per tonne. **Type of Price:** farmers buying-in. **Time Period Covered:** latest week.

OATS

Source: *Agricultural Outlook.* **Price Frequency:** annually. **Effective Market(s):** United States. **Units of Measure:** Dollars per bushel. **Type of Price:** farm. **Time Period Covered:** latest 6 years.

Source: *Agricultural Prices.* **Price Frequency:** monthly. **Effective Market(s):** United States. **Units of Measure:** Dollars per bushel. **Type of Price:** received by farmer. **Time Period Covered:** latest 2 months, year ago.

Source: *Agricultural Prices.* **Price Frequency:** monthly, seasonally. **Effective Market(s):** 16 domestic markest, United States. **Units of Measure:** Dollars per bushel. **Type of Price:** received by farmer. **Time Period Covered:** latest 2 months.

Source: *Agricultural Prices Annual Summary.* **Price Frequency:** annually. **Effective Market(s):** 36 domestic markets, United States. **Units of Measure:** Dollars per bushel. **Type of Price:** average received by farmer. **Time Period Covered:** latest 2 years, for US latest 6 years.

Source: *Commodity Year Book.* **Price Frequency:** monthly, annually. **Units of Measure:** cents per bushel. **Type of Price:** price received by farmers. **Time Period Covered:** latest 8 years.

Source: *Farm and Dairy.* **Price Frequency:** weekly, seasonally. **Effective Market(s):** Ohio, Pennsylvania. **Units of Measure:** Dollars per 100 lbs. **Type of Price:** auction high, auction low. **Time Period Covered:** latest week.

Source: *Feed Situation and Outlook Report.* **Price Frequency:** annually. **Units of Measure:** Dollars per bushel. **Type of Price:** received by farmer. **Time Period Covered:** latest 5 years.

Source: *Feed Situation and Outlook Report.* **Price Frequency:** monthly, annually. **Effective Market(s):** United States. **Units of Measure:** Dollars per bushel. **Type of Price:** received by farmer. **Time Period Covered:** latest 6 years.

Source: *Illinois Farm Report.* **Price Frequency:** monthly. **Effective Market(s):** Illinois. **Units of Measure:** Dollars per bushel. **Type of Price:** average received by farmers. **Time Period Covered:** latest 2 months, year ago.

Source: *Standard & Poor's Statistical Service Current Statistics.* **Price Frequency:** monthly, annually. **Effective Market(s):** Minneapolis. **Units of Measure:** cents per bushel. **Time Period Covered:** latest 4 years.

OATS: CRIMPED

Source: *Feedstuffs.* **Price Frequency:** weekly. **Effective Market(s):** 5 domestic markets. **Units of Measure:** Dollars per bulk ton. **Time Period Covered:** latest week.

OATS: FEED

Source: *Farmers Weekly.* **Price Frequency:** weekly, seasonally. **Effective Market(s):** 10 British markets. **Units of Measure:** British pounds per tonne. **Type of Price:** merchant's buying. **Time Period Covered:** latest week.

OATS: FUTURES

Source: *Asian Wall Street Journal.* **Price Frequency:** daily. **Effective Market(s):** Chicago, Winnepeg. **Units of Measure:** cents per bushel, Canadian dollars per ton. **Type of Price:** futures. **Time Period Covered:** latest day.

Source: *Barron's.* **Price Frequency:** weekly. **Effective Market(s):** Chicago. **Units of Measure:** Dollars per bushel. **Type of Price:** futures. **Time Period Covered:** latest week.

Source: *Investor's Daily.* **Price Frequency:** daily. **Effective Market(s):** Chicago, Minneapolis. **Units of Measure:** Dollars per bushel. **Type of Price:** futures. **Time Period Covered:** latest day.

Source: *Los Angeles Times.* **Price Frequency:** daily. **Effective Market(s):** Chicago. **Units of Measure:** Dollars per bushel. **Type of Price:** futures. **Time Period Covered:** latest day.

Source: *Minneapolis Grain Exchange Statistical Annual.* **Price Frequency:** daily. **Effective Market(s):** Minneapolis. **Units of Measure:** cents per bushel. **Type of Price:** futures. **Time Period Covered:** latest year.

Source: *New York Times.* **Price Frequency:** daily. **Effective Market(s):** Chicago. **Units of Measure:** Dollars per bushel. **Type of Price:** futures. **Time Period Covered:** latest day.

Source: *Urner Barry's Price-Current.* **Price Frequency:** daily. **Effective Market(s):** Chicago. **Units of Measure:** Dollars per bushel. **Type of Price:** futures. **Time Period Covered:** latest day.

Source: *Wall Street Journal.* **Price Frequency:** daily. **Effective Market(s):** Chicago. **Units of Measure:** cents per bushel. **Type of Price:** futures. **Time Period Covered:** latest day.

OATS: FUTURES, MAY

Source: *Commodity Year Book.* **Price Frequency:** monthly. **Effective Market(s):** Chicago. **Units of Measure:** cents per bushel. **Type of Price:** futures. **Time Period Covered:** latest 7 years.

OATS: MILLING

Source: *Farmers Weekly.* **Price Frequency:** daily, seasonally. **Effective Market(s):** 13 British markets. **Units of Measure:** British pounds per tonne. **Type of Price:** spot. **Time Period Covered:** latest day .

OATS: NO. 1

Source: *Utah Farmer-Stockman.* **Price Frequency:** monthly, seasonally. **Effective Market(s):** Ogden (UT). **Units of Measure:** Dollars per 100 lbs. **Type of Price:** cash. **Time Period Covered:** latest month, month ago.

OATS: NO. 1, CANADIAN

Source: *FAO Quarterly Bulletin of Statistics.* **Price Frequency:** monthly, annually. **Effective Market(s):** Thunder Bay (Canada). **Units of Measure:** Canadian dollars per 1000 kilograms, dollars per metric ton. **Time Period Covered:** latest 3 years.

OATS: NO. 1, HEAVY

Source: *Minneapolis Grain Exchange Statistical Annual.* **Price Frequency:** daily. **Effective Market(s):** Minneapolis. **Units of Measure:** cents per bushel. **Type of Price:** cash. **Time Period Covered:** latest year.

OATS: NO. 2

Source: *Feed Situation and Outlook Report.* **Price Frequency:** annually. **Effective Market(s):** Toledo (OH). **Units of Measure:** Dollars per bushel. **Type of Price:** average. **Time Period Covered:** latest 5 years.

Source: *Grain and Feed Market News.* **Price Frequency:** daily, seasonally. **Effective Market(s):** Minneapolis, Toledo (OH). **Units of Measure:** Dollars per bushel. **Type of Price:** cash bid. **Time Period Covered:** latest week, year ago.

Source: *Idaho Farmer-Stockman.* **Price Frequency:** monthly. **Effective Market(s):** Denver, Omaha (NE), Portland (OR), Stockton (CA). **Time Period Covered:** latest month.

Source: *Idaho Farmer-Stockman.* **Price Frequency:** monthly. **Effective Market(s):** Ogden (UT). **Units of Measure:** Dollars per 100 lbs. **Time Period Covered:** latest month, month ago.

Source: *Lancaster Farmer.* **Price Frequency:** weekly. **Effective Market(s):** Pennsylvania. **Units of Measure:** Dollars per bushel. **Type of Price:** auction. **Time Period Covered:** latest week.

Source: *Los Angeles Times.* **Price Frequency:** daily. **Effective Market(s):** Los Angeles. **Units of Measure:** Dollars per 100 lbs. **Type of Price:** cash. **Time Period Covered:** latest day.

Source: *Montana Farmer-Stockman.* **Price Frequency:** monthly. **Effective Market(s):** Minneapolis. **Units of Measure:** Dollars per bushel. **Type of Price:** cash. **Time Period Covered:** latest month, month ago.

Source: *Montana Farmer-Stockman.* **Price Frequency:** monthly, seasonally. **Effective Market(s):** 7 Montana markets. **Type of Price:** elevator bid. **Time Period Covered:** latest month.

Source: *Utah Farmer-Stockman.* **Price Frequency:** monthly, seasonally. **Effective Market(s):** Denver, Omaha (NE), Portland (OR), Stockton (CA). **Time Period Covered:** latest month.

OATS: NO. 2, HEAVY

Source: *Commodity Year Book.* **Price Frequency:** annually. **Effective Market(s):** Toledo (OH). **Units of Measure:** cents per bushel. **Type of Price:** cash. **Time Period Covered:** latest 10 years.

Source: *Doane's Agricultural Report.* **Price Frequency:** weekly. **Effective Market(s):** Minneapolis. **Units of Measure:** Dollars per bushel. **Time Period Covered:** latest week, week ago, year ago.

Source: *Feed Situation and Outlook Report.* **Price Frequency:** monthly, annually. **Effective Market(s):** Minneapolis. **Units of Measure:** Dollars per bushel. **Type of Price:** cash. **Time Period Covered:** latest 6 years.

Source: *Grain and Feed Market News.* **Price Frequency:** weekly, seasonally. **Effective Market(s):** 44 domestic markets. **Units of Measure:** Dollars per bushel. **Type of Price:** cash bid. **Time Period Covered:** latest week, year ago.

Source: *Grain and Feed Market News.* **Price Frequency:** weekly, seasonally. **Effective Market(s):** Minneapolis, Toledo (OH). **Units of Measure:** Dollars per ton. **Type of Price:** wholesale. **Time Period Covered:** latest week, week ago, year ago.

Source: *Minneapolis Grain Exchange Statistical Annual.* **Price Frequency:** daily, monthly, annually. **Effective Market(s):** Minneapolis. **Units of Measure:** cents per bushel. **Type of Price:** cash. **Time Period Covered:** daily latest year, monthly and annually latest 10 years.

OATS: NO. 2, HEAVY WHITE

Source: *Commodity Year Book.* **Price Frequency:** monthly, annually. **Effective Market(s):** Minneapolis. **Units of Measure:** cents per bushel. **Type of Price:** cash. **Time Period Covered:** latest 10 years.

Source: *Commodity Year Book.* **Price Frequency:** annually. **Effective Market(s):** Portland (OR). **Units of Measure:** cents per bushel. **Type of Price:** cash. **Time Period Covered:** latest 10 years.

OATS: NO. 2, MILLING

Source: *Asian Wall Street Journal.* **Price Frequency:** daily. **Effective Market(s):** Minneapolis. **Units of Measure:** Dollars per bushel. **Type of Price:** cash. **Time Period Covered:** latest 2 days, year ago.

Source: *Farm and Dairy.* **Price Frequency:** weekly, seasonally. **Effective Market(s):** Minneapolis. **Units of Measure:** Dollars per bushel. **Time Period Covered:** latest week, year ago.

Source: *Wall Street Journal.* **Price Frequency:** daily. **Effective Market(s):** Minneapolis. **Units of Measure:** Dollars per bushel. **Time Period Covered:** latest day, day ago, year ago.

OATS: NO. 2, WHITE

Source: *Journal of Commerce and Commercial.* **Price Frequency:** daily. **Effective Market(s):** Chicago. **Units of Measure:** Dollars per bushel. **Type of Price:** spot supplier. **Time Period Covered:** latest day.

OATS: NO. 2, WHITE HEAVY

Source: *Feed Situation and Outlook Report.* **Price Frequency:** annually. **Effective Market(s):** Minneapolis, Portland (OR). **Units of Measure:** Dollars per bushel. **Type of Price:** average. **Time Period Covered:** latest 5 years.

OATS: PULVERIZED

Source: *Feedstuffs.* **Price Frequency:** weekly. **Effective Market(s):** Chicago, Ft. Worth, Kansas City, Minneapolis/St. Paul. **Units of Measure:** Dollars per bulk ton. **Time Period Covered:** latest week.

OATS: ROLLED

Source: *Feedstuffs.* **Price Frequency:** weekly. **Effective Market(s):** 5 domestic markets. **Units of Measure:** Dollars per bulk ton. **Time Period Covered:** latest week.

Source: *Feedstuffs.* **Price Frequency:** weekly. **Effective Market(s):** Minneapolis. **Units of Measure:** Dollars per ton. **Time Period Covered:** latest week, week ago, 6 months ago, year ago.

Source: *Milling & Baking News.* **Price Frequency:** weekly. **Effective Market(s):** Kansas City. **Units of Measure:** Dollars per ton. **Time Period Covered:** latest week, week ago, year ago.

OATS FOR SEED
see Seed Oats.

OATS STRAW

Source: *Farm and Dairy.* **Price Frequency:** weekly, seasonally. **Effective Market(s):** Ohio, Pennsylvania. **Units of Measure:** Dollars per load. **Type of Price:** auction high, auction low. **Time Period Covered:** latest week.

OCEAN CATFISH
see Catfish: Ocean, Wolffish.

OCHRE
see also Iron Oxide: Yellow, Natural.

OCHRE: DARK

Source: *Industrial Minerals.* **Price Frequency:** monthly. **Effective Market(s):** Cartersville. **Units of Measure:** Dollars per lb. **Type of Price:** producer & dealer. **Time Period Covered:** latest month.

OCHRE: LIGHT

Source: *Industrial Minerals.* **Price Frequency:** monthly. **Effective Market(s):** Cartersville. **Units of Measure:** Dollars per lb. **Type of Price:** producer & dealer. **Time Period Covered:** latest month.

OCHRE: MEDIUM

Source: *Industrial Minerals.* **Price Frequency:** monthly . **Effective Market(s):** Cartersville. **Units of Measure:** Dollars per lb. **Type of Price:** producer & dealer. **Time Period Covered:** latest month.

OCHRE: MICRONISED, SPANISH

Source: *Industrial Minerals.* **Price Frequency:** monthly. **Effective Market(s):** Spain. **Units of Measure:** Dollars per metric tonne. **Type of Price:** producer & dealer. **Time Period Covered:** latest month.

OCHRE: STANDARD, SPANISH

Source: *Industrial Minerals.* **Price Frequency:** monthly. **Effective Market(s):** Spain. **Units of Measure:** Dollars per metric tonne. **Type of Price:** producer & dealer. **Time Period Covered:** latest month.

OCOTEA: CHINESE, 90%

Source: *Chemical Marketing Reporter.* **Price Frequency:** weekly. **Effective Market(s):** New York. **Units of Measure:** Dollars per lb. **Type of Price:** spot. **Time Period Covered:** latest week.

OCOTEA CYMBARUM OIL

Source: *Chemical Marketing Reporter.* **Price Frequency:** weekly. **Effective Market(s):** New York. **Units of Measure:** Dollars per kilo. **Type of Price:** spot. **Time Period Covered:** latest week.

OCOTEA CYMBARUN OIL

Source: *Journal of Commerce and Commercial.* **Price Frequency:** weekly in Tuesday issue. **Units of Measure:** Dollars per lb. **Type of Price:** spot. **Time Period Covered:** latest week.

1-OCTADECANOL: SYNTHETIC

Source: *Chemical Marketing Reporter.* **Price Frequency:** weekly. **Effective Market(s):** New York. **Units of Measure:** Dollars per lb. **Type of Price:** spot. **Time Period Covered:** latest week.

N-OCTANE: 97% MINIMUM

Source: *Chemical Marketing Reporter.* **Price Frequency:** weekly. **Effective Market(s):** Houston (TX). **Units of Measure:** Dollars per gallon. **Type of Price:** spot. **Time Period Covered:** latest week.

1-OCTANOL: PERFUMER'S GRADE

Source: *Chemical Marketing Reporter.* **Price Frequency:** weekly. **Effective Market(s):** New York. **Units of Measure:** Dollars per lb. **Type of Price:** spot. **Time Period Covered:** latest week.

1-OCTANOL: SYNTHETIC

Source: *Chemical Marketing Reporter.* **Price Frequency:** weekly. **Effective Market(s):** New York. **Units of Measure:** Dollars per lb. **Type of Price:** spot. **Time Period Covered:** latest week.

OCTOPUS: FULLY CLEANED, SPAIN

Source: *NMFS Green Sheet Supplement.* **Price Frequency:** weekly, seasonally. **Effective Market(s):** New York. **Units of Measure:** dollars per lb. **Type of Price:** warehouse. **Time Period Covered:** latest week.

N-OCTYL, N-DECYL PHTHALATE

Source: *Chemical Marketing Reporter.* **Price Frequency:** weekly. **Effective Market(s):** New York. **Units of Measure:** Dollars per lb. **Type of Price:** spot. **Time Period Covered:** latest week.

TERT-OCTYLAMINE

Source: *Chemical Marketing Reporter.* **Price Frequency:** weekly. **Effective Market(s):** New York. **Units of Measure:** Dollars per lb. **Type of Price:** spot. **Time Period Covered:** latest week.

OCTYLPHENOL: MOLTEN

Source: *Chemical Marketing Reporter.* **Price Frequency:** weekly. **Effective Market(s):** New York. **Units of Measure:** Dollars per lb. **Type of Price:** spot. **Time Period Covered:** latest week.

OFFICE SUPPLIES

Source: *Pulp & Paper Week.* **Price Frequency:** monthly, irregulary. **Units of Measure:** index. **Type of Price:** price index. **Time Period Covered:** latest 3 months.

OIL: 48 GRADE, UNITED STATES

Source: *Oil Buyers' Guide.* **Price Frequency:** weekly. **Effective Market(s):** Mediterranean, Northwest Europe. **Units of Measure:** Dollars per metric ton. **Type of Price:** cargo. **Time Period Covered:** latest week.

OIL: CRUDE

Source: *Economic and Energy Indicators.* **Price Frequency:** monthly, annually. **Effective Market(s):** OPEC, World. **Units of Measure:** Dollars per barrel. **Type of Price:** average. **Time Period Covered:** latest 3 months, latest 4 years.

Source: *Energy Statistics.* **Price Frequency:** monthly, annually. **Effective Market(s):** Non-OPEC, OPEC, United States, World. **Units of Measure:** Dollars per barrel. **Type of Price:** contract. **Time Period Covered:** monthly latest year, annually latest 5 years.

Source: *Energy Statistics.* **Price Frequency:** monthly, annually. **Effective Market(s):** United States. **Units of Measure:** Dollars per barrel. **Type of Price:** wellhead. **Time Period Covered:** monthly latest year, annually latest 17 years.

Source: *International Energy Statistical Review.* **Price Frequency:** monthly, quarterly, annually. **Effective Market(s):** OPEC, World. **Units of Measure:** Dollars per barrel. **Type of Price:** average. **Time Period Covered:** monthly latest 3 months, quarterly latest quarter, annually latest 5 years.

Source: *Journal of Commerce and Commercial.* **Price Frequency:** daily. **Units of Measure:** Dollars per barrel. **Type of Price:** spot supplier. **Time Period Covered:** latest day.

Source: *Modern Plastics.* **Price Frequency:** quarterly every January, April, July, October. **Effective Market(s):** Rotterdam. **Units of Measure:** cents per lb. **Type of Price:** market. **Time Period Covered:** latest 3 years.

Source: *Oil & Gas Journal.* **Price Frequency:** weekly except second issue of month. **Effective Market(s):** Non-OPEC, OPEC, World. **Units of Measure:** Dollars per barrel. **Type of Price:** official. **Time Period Covered:** latest 3 weeks, year ago.

Source: *Petroleum Economist.* **Price Frequency:** annually. **Effective Market(s):** Non-OPEC, OPEC, World. **Units of Measure:** Dollars per barrel. **Type of Price:** average. **Time Period Covered:** latest 3 years.

Source: *Purchasing.* **Price Frequency:** quarterly in January, April, July, October issues. **Effective Market(s):** Texas. **Units of Measure:** Dollars per barrel. **Type of Price:** transaction. **Time Period Covered:** latest 5 quarters.

OIL: CRUDE, AFRICAN, IMPORTED

Source: *Energy Pricing News: Crude Oil Report.* **Price Frequency:** monthly. **Effective Market(s):** Canada, Cushing (Canada), Edmonton (Canada), Sullum Voe (Canada). **Units of Measure:** Canadian dollars per barrel, Canadian dollars per cubic meter. **Time Period Covered:** latest month, month ago.

OIL: CRUDE, ALASKA NORTH SLOPE

Source: *Asian Wall Street Journal.* **Price Frequency:** daily. **Effective Market(s):** United States Gulf. **Units of Measure:** Dollars per barrel. **Type of Price:** spot. **Time Period Covered:** latest 2 days, year ago.

Source: *Investor's Daily.* **Price Frequency:** daily. **Effective Market(s):** Gulf Coast. **Units of Measure:** Dollars per barrel. **Type of Price:** spot. **Time Period Covered:** latest 2 days.

Source: *New York Times.* **Price Frequency:** daily. **Effective Market(s):** Gulf Coast. **Units of Measure:** Dollars per barrel. **Type of Price:** cash. **Time Period Covered:** latest 2 days.

Source: *Oil & Gas Journal.* **Price Frequency:** monthly in second issue of month. **Effective Market(s):** United States. **Units of Measure:** Dollars per barrel. **Type of Price:** dominant posting. **Time Period Covered:** latest date available.

Source: *Oil Buyers' Guide International.* **Price Frequency:** weekly. **Effective Market(s):** United States. **Units of Measure:** Dollars per barrel. **Type of Price:** posted, spot. **Time Period Covered:** latest week, year ago.

Source: *Oilweek.* **Price Frequency:** weekly. **Effective Market(s):** Chicago, Edmonton (Canada), Toronto. **Units of Measure:** Canadian dollars per barrel, dollars per barrel. **Type of Price:** spot. **Time Period Covered:** latest week.

Source: *Petroleum Economist.* **Price Frequency:** monthly. **Units of Measure:** Dollars per barrel. **Type of Price:** spot. **Time Period Covered:** latest month.

OIL: CRUDE, ALASKA NORTH SLOPE, COOK INLET

Source: *Oil & Gas Journal.* **Price Frequency:** monthly in second issue of month. **Effective Market(s):** United States. **Units of Measure:** Dollars per barrel. **Type of Price:** dominant posting. **Time Period Covered:** latest date available.

OIL: CRUDE, ALASKA NORTH SLOPE, KENAI PIPELINE

Source: *Oil & Gas Journal.* **Price Frequency:** monthly in second issue of month. **Effective Market(s):** United States. **Units of Measure:** Dollars per barrel. **Type of Price:** dominant posting. **Time Period Covered:** latest date available.

OIL: CRUDE, ALBERTA LIGHT

Source: *Oilweek.* **Price Frequency:** weekly. **Effective Market(s):** Chicago, Edmonton (Canada), Toronto. **Units of Measure:** Dollars per barrel, Canadian dollars per barrel. **Type of Price:** spot. **Time Period Covered:** latest week.

OIL: CRUDE, ALGERIA

Source: *Energy Prices and Taxes.* **Price Frequency:** monthly, quarterly, annually. **Effective Market(s):** International Energy Agency. **Units of Measure:** Dollars per barrel. **Type of Price:** import. **Time Period Covered:** monthly latest 2 years, quarterly latest 2 years, annually latest 9 years.

OIL: CRUDE, ARABIAN HEAVY

Source: *Asian Wall Street Journal.* **Price Frequency:** daily. **Effective Market(s):** Northwest Europe. **Units of Measure:** Dollars per barrel. **Type of Price:** spot. **Time Period Covered:** latest 2 days, year ago.

Source: *Energy Statistics.* **Price Frequency:** monthly, annually. **Effective Market(s):** Saudi Arabia. **Units of Measure:** Dollars per barrel. **Type of Price:** contract. **Time Period Covered:** monthly latest year, annually latest 5 years.

Source: *Oil Buyers' Guide International.* **Price Frequency:** weekly. **Effective Market(s):** Saudi Arabia. **Units of Measure:** Dollars per barrel. **Type of Price:** official, spot. **Time Period Covered:** latest week.

Source: *OPEC Bulletin.* **Price Frequency:** weekly, monthly. **Effective Market(s):** OPEC. **Units of Measure:** Dollars per barrel. **Type of Price:** spot. **Time Period Covered:** weekly for latest month, monthly for latest year.

Source: *Wall Street Journal.* **Price Frequency:** daily. **Effective Market(s):** Europe. **Units of Measure:** Dollars per barrel. **Type of Price:** spot. **Time Period Covered:** latest day, day ago, year ago.

OIL: CRUDE, ARABIAN LIGHT

Source: *Asian Wall Street Journal.* **Price Frequency:** daily. **Effective Market(s):** Northwest Europe. **Units of Measure:** Dollars per barrel. **Type of Price:** spot. **Time Period Covered:** latest 2 days, year ago.

Source: *Energy Statistics.* **Price Frequency:** monthly, annually. **Effective Market(s):** Saudi Arabia. **Units of Measure:** Dollars per barrel. **Type of Price:** contract. **Time Period Covered:** monthly latest year, annually latest 5 years.

Source: *Investor's Daily.* **Price Frequency:** daily. **Units of Measure:** Dollars per barrel. **Type of Price:** spot. **Time Period Covered:** latest 2 days.

Source: *New York Times.* **Price Frequency:** daily. **Units of Measure:** Dollars per barrel. **Type of Price:** cash. **Time Period Covered:** latest 2 days.

Source: *Oil & Gas Journal.* **Price Frequency:** monthly in second issue of month. **Effective Market(s):** World. **Units of Measure:** Dollars per barrel. **Type of Price:** spot. **Time Period Covered:** latest date available.

Source: *Oil Buyers' Guide International.* **Price Frequency:** weekly. **Effective Market(s):** Saudi Arabia. **Units of Measure:** Dollars per barrel. **Type of Price:** official, spot. **Time Period Covered:** latest week.

Source: *Oil Buyers' Guide International.* **Price Frequency:** weekly. **Effective Market(s):** United States. **Units of Measure:** Dollars per barrel. **Type of Price:** offshore official, offshore spot. **Time Period Covered:** latest week, year ago.

Source: *OPEC Bulletin.* **Price Frequency:** weekly, monthly. **Effective Market(s):** OPEC. **Units of Measure:** Dollars per barrel. **Type of Price:** spot. **Time Period Covered:** weekly for latest month, monthly for latest year.

Source: *Wall Street Journal.* **Price Frequency:** daily. **Effective Market(s):** Europe. **Units of Measure:** Dollars per barrel. **Type of Price:** spot. **Time Period Covered:** latest day, day ago, year ago.

OIL: CRUDE, ARABIAN MEDIUM

Source: *Energy Statistics.* **Price Frequency:** monthly, annually. **Effective Market(s):** Saudi Arabia. **Units of Measure:** Dollars per barrel. **Type of Price:** contract. **Time Period Covered:** monthly latest year, annually latest 5 years.

Source: *Oil Buyers' Guide International.* **Price Frequency:** weekly. **Effective Market(s):** Saudi Arabia. **Units of Measure:** Dollars per barrel. **Type of Price:** official, spot. **Time Period Covered:** latest week.

OIL: CRUDE, ARDJUNA

Source: *Oil Buyers' Guide International.* **Price Frequency:** weekly. **Effective Market(s):** Indonesia. **Units of Measure:** Dollars per barrel. **Type of Price:** spot. **Time Period Covered:** latest week.

OIL: CRUDE, ARUN

Source: *Oil Buyers' Guide International.* **Price Frequency:** weekly. **Effective Market(s):** Indonesia. **Units of Measure:** Dollars per barrel. **Type of Price:** spot. **Time Period Covered:** latest week.

OIL: CRUDE, BACHAQUERO

Source: *Energy Statistics.* **Price Frequency:** monthly, annually. **Effective Market(s):** Venezuela. **Units of Measure:** Dollars per barrel. **Type of Price:** contract. **Time Period Covered:** monthly latest year, annually latest 5 years.

OIL: CRUDE, BASRAH

Source: *Oil Buyers' Guide International.* **Price Frequency:** weekly. **Effective Market(s):** Iraq. **Units of Measure:** Dollars per barrel. **Type of Price:** official, spot. **Time Period Covered:** latest week.

OIL: CRUDE, BONNY LIGHT

Source: *Asian Wall Street Journal.* **Price Frequency:** daily. **Effective Market(s):** Northwest Europe. **Units of Measure:** Dollars per barrel. **Type of Price:** spot. **Time Period Covered:** latest 2 days, year ago.

Source: *Energy Statistics.* **Price Frequency:** monthly, annually. **Effective Market(s):** Nigeria. **Units of Measure:** Dollars per barrel. **Type of Price:** contract. **Time Period Covered:** monthly latest year, annually latest 5 years.

Source: *Oil Buyers' Guide International.* **Price Frequency:** weekly. **Effective Market(s):** Nigeria. **Units of Measure:** Dollars per barrel. **Type of Price:** official, spot. **Time Period Covered:** latest week.

Source: *Oil Buyers' Guide International.* **Price Frequency:** weekly. **Effective Market(s):** United States. **Units of Measure:** Dollars per barrel. **Type of Price:** offshore official, offshore spot. **Time Period Covered:** latest week, year ago.

Source: *Petroleum Economist.* **Price Frequency:** monthly. **Units of Measure:** Dollars per barrel. **Type of Price:** spot. **Time Period Covered:** latest month.

Source: *Wall Street Journal.* **Price Frequency:** daily. **Effective Market(s):** Europe. **Units of Measure:** Dollars per barrel. **Type of Price:** spot. **Time Period Covered:** latest day, day ago, year ago.

OIL: CRUDE, BONNY LIGHT, NIGERIAN

Source: *Oil & Gas Journal.* **Price Frequency:** monthly in second issue of month. **Effective Market(s):** World. **Units of Measure:** Dollars per barrel. **Type of Price:** spot. **Time Period Covered:** latest date available.

Source: *OPEC Bulletin.* **Price Frequency:** weekly, monthly. **Effective Market(s):** OPEC. **Units of Measure:** Dollars per barrel. **Type of Price:** spot. **Time Period Covered:** weekly for latest month, monthly for latest year.

OIL: CRUDE, BONNY MEDIUM

Source: *Oil Buyers' Guide International.* **Price Frequency:** weekly. **Effective Market(s):** Nigeria. **Units of Measure:** Dollars per barrel. **Type of Price:** official, spot. **Time Period Covered:** latest week.

OIL: CRUDE, BREGA

Source: *Oil Buyers' Guide International.* **Price Frequency:** weekly. **Effective Market(s):** Libya. **Units of Measure:** Dollars per barrel. **Type of Price:** official, spot. **Time Period Covered:** latest week.

OIL: CRUDE, BREGA, LIBYA

Source: *OPEC Bulletin.* **Price Frequency:** weekly, monthly. **Effective Market(s):** OPEC. **Units of Measure:** Dollars per barrel. **Type of Price:** spot. **Time Period Covered:** weekly for latest month, monthly for latest year.

OIL: CRUDE, BRENT

Source: *Asian Wall Street Journal.* **Price Frequency:** daily. **Effective Market(s):** Northwest Europe. **Units of Measure:** Dollars per barrel. **Type of Price:** spot. **Time Period Covered:** latest 2 days, year ago.

Source: *Energy Prices and Taxes.* **Price Frequency:** monthly, quarterly, annually. **Effective Market(s):** Rotterdam. **Units of Measure:** Dollars per barrel. **Type of Price:** spot. **Time Period Covered:** monthly latest 2 years, quarterly latest 2 years, annually latest 7 years.

Source: *Energy Statistics.* **Price Frequency:** monthly, annually. **Effective Market(s):** United Kingdom. **Units of Measure:** Dollars per barrel. **Type of Price:** contract. **Time Period Covered:** monthly latest year, annually latest 5 years.

Source: *Financial Times.* **Price Frequency:** daily. **Effective Market(s):** London. **Units of Measure:** Dollars per barrel. **Type of Price:** spot. **Time Period Covered:** latest day.

Source: *Japan Economic Journal.* **Price Frequency:** weekly. **Effective Market(s):** London, Tokyo. **Units of Measure:** Dollars per barrel. **Type of Price:** spot. **Time Period Covered:** latest 2 weeks.

Source: *Oil Buyers' Guide International.* **Price Frequency:** weekly. **Effective Market(s):** United Kingdom. **Units of Measure:** Dollars per barrel. **Type of Price:** spot. **Time Period Covered:** latest week.

Source: *Oil Buyers' Guide International.* **Price Frequency:** weekly. **Effective Market(s):** United States. **Units of Measure:** Dollars per barrel. **Type of Price:** offshore official, offshore spot. **Time Period Covered:** latest week, year ago.

Source: *Petroleum Economist.* **Price Frequency:** monthly. **Units of Measure:** Dollars per barrel. **Type of Price:** spot. **Time Period Covered:** latest month.

Source: *The Times.* **Price Frequency:** daily. **Effective Market(s):** United Kingdom. **Units of Measure:** Dollars per barrel. **Time Period Covered:** latest day.

Source: *Wall Street Journal.* **Price Frequency:** daily. **Effective Market(s):** Europe. **Units of Measure:** Dollars per barrel. **Type of Price:** spot. **Time Period Covered:** latest day, day ago, year ago.

OIL: CRUDE, BRENT, FUTURES

Source: *Asian Wall Street Journal.* **Price Frequency:** daily. **Effective Market(s):** London. **Units of Measure:** Dollars per barrel. **Type of Price:** futures. **Time Period Covered:** latest day.

Source: *Oilweek.* **Price Frequency:** weekly. **Effective Market(s):** World. **Units of Measure:** Dollars per barrel. **Type of Price:** futures. **Time Period Covered:** next 2 months.

Source: *The Times.* **Price Frequency:** daily. **Effective Market(s):** United Kingdom. **Units of Measure:** Dollars per barrel. **Time Period Covered:** latest day.

OIL: CRUDE, BRENT, UNITED KINGDOM

Source: *Oil & Gas Journal.* **Price Frequency:** monthly in second issue of month. **Effective Market(s):** World. **Units of Measure:** Dollars per barrel. **Type of Price:** spot. **Time Period Covered:** latest date available.

Source: *OPEC Bulletin.* **Price Frequency:** weekly, monthly. **Effective Market(s):** United Kingdom. **Units of Measure:** Dollars per barrel. **Type of Price:** spot. **Time Period Covered:** weekly for latest month, monthly for latest year.

OIL: CRUDE, CABINDA

Source: *Energy Statistics.* **Price Frequency:** monthly, annually. **Effective Market(s):** Angola. **Units of Measure:** Dollars per barrel. **Type of Price:** contract. **Time Period Covered:** monthly latest year, annually latest 5 years.

OIL: CRUDE, CALIFORNIA HEAVY

Source: *Oil & Gas Journal.* **Price Frequency:** monthly in second issue of month. **Effective Market(s):** United States. **Units of Measure:** Dollars per barrel. **Type of Price:** dominant posting. **Time Period Covered:** latest date available.

OIL: CRUDE, CALIFORNIA HEAVY, MIDWAY SUNSET

Source: *Oil & Gas Journal.* **Price Frequency:** monthly in second issue of month. **Effective Market(s):** United States. **Units of Measure:** Dollars per barrel. **Type of Price:** dominant posting. **Time Period Covered:** latest date available.

OIL: CRUDE, CANO LIMON

Source: *Energy Statistics.* **Price Frequency:** monthly, annually. **Effective Market(s):** Colombia. **Units of Measure:** Dollars per barrel. **Type of Price:** contract. **Time Period Covered:** monthly latest year, annually latest 5 years.

OIL: CRUDE, DAQING

Source: *Energy Statistics.* **Price Frequency:** monthly, annually. **Effective Market(s):** China. **Units of Measure:** Dollars per barrel. **Type of Price:** contract. **Time Period Covered:** monthly latest year, annually latest 5 years.

Source: *Oil Buyers' Guide International.* **Price Frequency:** weekly. **Effective Market(s):** China. **Units of Measure:** Dollars per barrel. **Type of Price:** spot. **Time Period Covered:** latest week.

OIL: CRUDE, DUBAI

Source: *Energy Prices and Taxes.* **Price Frequency:** monthly, quarterly, annually. **Effective Market(s):** Rotterdam. **Units of Measure:** Dollars per barrel. **Type of Price:** spot. **Time Period Covered:** monthly latest 2 years, quarterly latest 2 years, annually latest 7 years.

Source: *Financial Times.* **Price Frequency:** daily. **Effective Market(s):** London. **Units of Measure:** Dollars per barrel. **Type of Price:** spot. **Time Period Covered:** latest day.

Source: *Japan Economic Journal.* **Price Frequency:** weekly. **Effective Market(s):** London, Singapore, Tokyo. **Units of Measure:** Dollars per barrel. **Type of Price:** spot. **Time Period Covered:** latest 2 weeks.

Source: *Petroleum Economist.* **Price Frequency:** monthly. **Units of Measure:** Dollars per barrel. **Type of Price:** spot. **Time Period Covered:** latest month.

OIL: CRUDE, DUBAI, FUTURES

Source: *Oilweek.* **Price Frequency:** weekly. **Effective Market(s):** World. **Units of Measure:** Dollars per barrel. **Type of Price:** futures. **Time Period Covered:** next 2 months.

OIL: CRUDE, DUBAI, UNITED ARAB EMIRATES

Source: *OPEC Bulletin.* **Price Frequency:** weekly, monthly. **Effective Market(s):** OPEC. **Units of Measure:** Dollars per barrel. **Type of Price:** spot. **Time Period Covered:** weekly for latest month, monthly for latest year.

OIL: CRUDE, DUKHAN

Source: *Energy Statistics.* **Price Frequency:** monthly, annually. **Effective Market(s):** Qatar. **Units of Measure:** Dollars per barrel. **Type of Price:** contract. **Time Period Covered:** monthly latest year, annually latest 5 years.

OIL: CRUDE, DURI

Source: *Oil Buyers' Guide International.* **Price Frequency:** weekly. **Effective Market(s):** Indonesia. **Units of Measure:** Dollars per barrel. **Type of Price:** spot. **Time Period Covered:** latest week.

OIL: CRUDE, EAST TEXAS

Source: *Oil & Gas Journal.* **Price Frequency:** monthly in second issue of month. **Effective Market(s):** United States. **Units of Measure:** Dollars per barrel. **Type of Price:** dominant posting. **Time Period Covered:** latest date available.

OIL: CRUDE, EKOFISK

Source: *Energy Statistics.* **Price Frequency:** monthly, annually. **Effective Market(s):** Norway. **Units of Measure:** Dollars per barrel. **Type of Price:** contract. **Time Period Covered:** monthly latest year, annually latest 5 years.

Source: *Oil Buyers' Guide International.* **Price Frequency:** weekly. **Effective Market(s):** Norway. **Units of Measure:** Dollars per barrel. **Type of Price:** spot. **Time Period Covered:** latest week.

OIL: CRUDE, EKOFISK, NORWEGIAN

Source: *OPEC Bulletin.* **Price Frequency:** weekly, monthly. **Effective Market(s):** Norway. **Units of Measure:** Dollars per barrel. **Type of Price:** spot. **Time Period Covered:** weekly for latest month, monthly for latest year.

OIL: CRUDE, ES SIDER

Source: *Energy Statistics.* **Price Frequency:** monthly, annually. **Effective Market(s):** Libya. **Units of Measure:** Dollars per barrel. **Type of Price:** contract. **Time Period Covered:** monthly latest year, annually latest 5 years.

Source: *Oil Buyers' Guide International.* **Price Frequency:** weekly. **Effective Market(s):** Libya. **Units of Measure:** Dollars per barrel. **Type of Price:** official, spot. **Time Period Covered:** latest week.

OIL: CRUDE, ES SIDER, LIBYA

Source: *Oil & Gas Journal.* **Price Frequency:** monthly in second issue of month. **Effective Market(s):** World. **Units of Measure:** Dollars per barrel. **Type of Price:** spot. **Time Period Covered:** latest date available.

OIL: CRUDE, EXPORT BLEND, KUWAIT

Source: *OPEC Bulletin.* **Price Frequency:** weekly, monthly. **Effective Market(s):** OPEC. **Units of Measure:** Dollars per barrel. **Type of Price:** spot. **Time Period Covered:** weekly for latest month, monthly for latest year.

OIL: CRUDE, EXPORT BLEND, U.S.S.R

Source: *Oil & Gas Journal.* **Price Frequency:** monthly in second issue of month. **Effective Market(s):** World. **Units of Measure:** Dollars per barrel. **Type of Price:** spot. **Time Period Covered:** latest date available.

OIL: CRUDE, FATEH

Source: *Energy Statistics.* **Price Frequency:** monthly, annually. **Effective Market(s):** Dubai. **Units of Measure:** Dollars per barrel. **Type of Price:** contract. **Time Period Covered:** monthly latest year, annually latest 5 years.

Source: *Oil Buyers' Guide International.* **Price Frequency:** weekly. **Effective Market(s):** Dubai. **Units of Measure:** Dollars per barrel. **Type of Price:** official, spot. **Time Period Covered:** latest week.

OIL: CRUDE, FLOTTA

Source: *Oil Buyers' Guide International.* **Price Frequency:** weekly. **Effective Market(s):** United Kingdom. **Units of Measure:** Dollars per barrel. **Type of Price:** spot. **Time Period Covered:** latest week.

OIL: CRUDE, FORCADOS

Source: *Energy Statistics.* **Price Frequency:** monthly, annually. **Effective Market(s):** Nigeria. **Units of Measure:** Dollars per barrel. **Type of Price:** contract. **Time Period Covered:** monthly latest year, annually latest 5 years.

Source: *Oil Buyers' Guide International.* **Price Frequency:** weekly. **Effective Market(s):** Nigeria. **Units of Measure:** Dollars per barrel. **Type of Price:** official, spot. **Time Period Covered:** latest week.

OIL: CRUDE, FORTIES

Source: *Asian Wall Street Journal.* **Price Frequency:** daily. **Effective Market(s):** Northwest Europe. **Units of Measure:** Dollars per barrel. **Type of Price:** spot. **Time Period Covered:** latest 2 days, year ago.

Source: *Oil Buyers' Guide International.* **Price Frequency:** weekly. **Effective Market(s):** United Kingdom. **Units of Measure:** Dollars per barrel. **Type of Price:** spot. **Time Period Covered:** latest week.

Source: *Wall Street Journal.* **Price Frequency:** daily. **Effective Market(s):** Europe. **Units of Measure:** Dollars per barrel. **Type of Price:** spot. **Time Period Covered:** latest day, day ago, year ago.

OIL: CRUDE, FUTURES

Source: *Barron's.* **Price Frequency:** weekly. **Effective Market(s):** New York. **Units of Measure:** Dollars per barrel. **Type of Price:** futures. **Time Period Covered:** latest week.

Source: *Financial Times.* **Price Frequency:** daily. **Effective Market(s):** London, New York. **Units of Measure:** Dollars per barrel. **Type of Price:** futures. **Time Period Covered:** latest 2 days.

Source: *Investor's Daily.* **Price Frequency:** daily. **Effective Market(s):** New York. **Units of Measure:** Dollars per barrel. **Type of Price:** futures. **Time Period Covered:** latest day.

Source: *Los Angeles Times.* **Price Frequency:** daily. **Effective Market(s):** New York. **Units of Measure:** Dollars per barrel. **Type of Price:** futures. **Time Period Covered:** latest day.

Source: *New York Times.* **Price Frequency:** daily. **Effective Market(s):** New York. **Units of Measure:** Dollars per barrel. **Type of Price:** futures. **Time Period Covered:** latest day.

Source: *Oil Buyers' Guide.* **Price Frequency:** weekly. **Effective Market(s):** New York. **Units of Measure:** Dollars per barrel. **Type of Price:** futures. **Time Period Covered:** latest week.

Source: *Oil Buyers' Guide International.* **Price Frequency:** weekly. **Effective Market(s):** New York. **Units of Measure:** Dollars per barrel. **Type of Price:** futures. **Time Period Covered:** latest week, week ago.

OIL: CRUDE, FUTURES, DECEMBER

Source: *Commodity Year Book.* **Price Frequency:** monthly. **Effective Market(s):** New York. **Units of Measure:** Dollars per barrel. **Type of Price:** futures. **Time Period Covered:** latest 4 years.

OIL: CRUDE, GIPPSLAND

Source: *Energy Statistics.* **Price Frequency:** monthly, annually. **Effective Market(s):** Australia. **Units of Measure:** Dollars per barrel. **Type of Price:** contract. **Time Period Covered:** monthly latest year, annually latest 5 years.

OIL: CRUDE, GULF COAST SWEET

Source: *Oil & Gas Journal.* **Price Frequency:** monthly in second issue of month. **Effective Market(s):** United States. **Units of Measure:** Dollars per barrel. **Type of Price:** dominant posting. **Time Period Covered:** latest date available.

OIL: CRUDE, HANDIL

Source: *Oil Buyers' Guide International.* **Price Frequency:** weekly. **Effective Market(s):** Indonesia. **Units of Measure:** Dollars per barrel. **Type of Price:** spot. **Time Period Covered:** latest week.

OIL: CRUDE, HEAVY

Source: *Energy Pricing News: Crude Oil Report.* **Price Frequency:** monthly. **Effective Market(s):** Alberta (Canada). **Units of Measure:** Dollars per cubic meter. **Time Period Covered:** latest month.

OIL: CRUDE, HEAVY LOUISIANA SWEET

Source: *Oil Buyers' Guide International.* **Price Frequency:** weekly. **Effective Market(s):** Empire (LA). **Units of Measure:** Dollars per barrel. **Type of Price:** posted, spot. **Time Period Covered:** latest week, year ago.

OIL: CRUDE, HEAVY, VENEZUELA

Source: *Energy Prices and Taxes.* **Price Frequency:** monthly, quarterly, annually. **Effective Market(s):** International Energy Agency. **Units of Measure:** Dollars per barrel. **Type of Price:** import. **Time Period Covered:** monthly latest 2 years, quarterly latest 2 years, annually latest 9 years.

OIL: CRUDE, ILLINOIS BASIN SWEET

Source: *Oil & Gas Journal.* **Price Frequency:** monthly in second issue of month. **Effective Market(s):** United States. **Units of Measure:** Dollars per barrel. **Type of Price:** dominant posting. **Time Period Covered:** latest date available.

OIL: CRUDE, IMPORTED

Source: *Energy Prices and Taxes.* **Price Frequency:** monthly, quarterly, annually. **Effective Market(s):** 16 international markets. **Units of Measure:** Dollars per barrel. **Type of Price:** import. **Time Period Covered:** monthly latest 2 years, quarterly latest 2 years, annually latest 13 years.

OIL: CRUDE, INDONESIA

Source: *Energy Prices and Taxes.* **Price Frequency:** monthly, quarterly, annually. **Effective Market(s):** International Energy Agency. **Units of Measure:** Dollars per barrel. **Type of Price:** import. **Time Period Covered:** monthly latest 2 years, quarterly latest 2 years, annually latest 9 years.

OIL: CRUDE, INTERNATIONAL

Source: *Wall Street Journal.* **Price Frequency:** daily. **Effective Market(s):** West Texas. **Units of Measure:** Dollars per barrel. **Time Period Covered:** latest day, day ago, year ago.

OIL: CRUDE, IRANIAN HEAVY

Source: *Energy Statistics.* **Price Frequency:** monthly, annually. **Effective Market(s):** Iran. **Units of Measure:** Dollars per barrel. **Type of Price:** contract. **Time Period Covered:** monthly latest year, annually latest 5 years.

OIL: CRUDE, IRANIAN LIGHT

Source: *Asian Wall Street Journal.* **Price Frequency:** daily. **Effective Market(s):** Northwest Europe. **Units of Measure:** Dollars per barrel. **Type of Price:** spot. **Time Period Covered:** latest 2 days, year ago.

Source: *Energy Statistics.* **Price Frequency:** monthly, annually. **Effective Market(s):** Iran. **Units of Measure:** Dollars per barrel. **Type of Price:** contract. **Time Period Covered:** monthly latest year, annually latest 5 years.

Source: *Oil & Gas Journal.* **Price Frequency:** monthly in second issue of month. **Effective Market(s):** World. **Units of Measure:** Dollars per barrel. **Type of Price:** spot. **Time Period Covered:** latest date available.

Source: *Oil Buyers' Guide International.* **Price Frequency:** weekly. **Effective Market(s):** Iran. **Units of Measure:** Dollars per barrel. **Type of Price:** official, spot. **Time Period Covered:** latest week.

Source: *OPEC Bulletin.* **Price Frequency:** weekly, monthly. **Effective Market(s):** OPEC. **Units of Measure:** Dollars per barrel. **Type of Price:** spot. **Time Period Covered:** weekly for latest month, monthly for latest year.

Source: *Wall Street Journal.* **Price Frequency:** daily. **Effective Market(s):** Europe. **Units of Measure:** Dollars per barrel. **Type of Price:** spot. **Time Period Covered:** latest day, day ago, year ago.

OIL: CRUDE, KANSAS SWEET

Source: *Oil & Gas Journal.* **Price Frequency:** monthly in second issue of month. **Effective Market(s):** United States. **Units of Measure:** Dollars per barrel. **Type of Price:** dominant posting. **Time Period Covered:** latest date available.

OIL: CRUDE, KHAFJI

Source: *Energy Statistics.* **Price Frequency:** monthly, annually. **Effective Market(s):** Neutral Zone. **Units of Measure:** Dollars per barrel. **Type of Price:** contract. **Time Period Covered:** monthly latest year, annually latest 5 years.

OIL: CRUDE, KIRKUK

Source: *Energy Statistics.* **Price Frequency:** monthly, annually. **Effective Market(s):** Iraq. **Units of Measure:** Dollars per barrel. **Type of Price:** contract. **Time Period Covered:** monthly latest year, annually latest 5 years.

Source: *Oil Buyers' Guide International.* **Price Frequency:** weekly. **Effective Market(s):** Iraq. **Units of Measure:** Dollars per barrel. **Type of Price:** official, spot. **Time Period Covered:** latest week.

OIL: CRUDE, KIRKUK, IRAQ

Source: *Energy Prices and Taxes.* **Price Frequency:** monthly, quarterly, annually. **Effective Market(s):** International Energy Agency. **Units of Measure:** Dollars per barrel. **Type of Price:** import. **Time Period Covered:** monthly latest 2 years, quarterly latest 2 years, annually latest 9 years.

Source: *Oil & Gas Journal.* **Price Frequency:** monthly in second issue of month. **Effective Market(s):** World. **Units of Measure:** Dollars per barrel. **Type of Price:** spot. **Time Period Covered:** latest date available.

Source: *OPEC Bulletin.* **Price Frequency:** weekly, monthly. **Effective Market(s):** OPEC. **Units of Measure:** Dollars per barrel. **Type of Price:** spot. **Time Period Covered:** weekly for latest month, monthly for latest year.

OIL: CRUDE, KOLE

Source: *Energy Statistics.* **Price Frequency:** monthly, annually. **Effective Market(s):** Cameroon. **Units of Measure:** Dollars per barrel. **Type of Price:** contract. **Time Period Covered:** monthly latest year, annually latest 5 years.

OIL: CRUDE, KUWAIT BLEND

Source: *Energy Prices and Taxes.* **Price Frequency:** monthly, quarterly, annually. **Effective Market(s):** International Energy Agency. **Units of Measure:** Dollars per barrel. **Type of Price:** import. **Time Period Covered:** monthly latest 2 years, quarterly latest 2 years, annually latest 9 years.

Source: *Energy Statistics.* **Price Frequency:** monthly, annually. **Effective Market(s):** Kuwait. **Units of Measure:** Dollars per barrel. **Type of Price:** contract. **Time Period Covered:** monthly latest year, annually latest 5 years.

Source: *Oil & Gas Journal.* **Price Frequency:** monthly in second issue of month. **Effective Market(s):** World. **Units of Measure:** Dollars per barrel. **Type of Price:** spot. **Time Period Covered:** latest date available.

Source: *Oil Buyers' Guide International.* **Price Frequency:** weekly. **Effective Market(s):** Kuwait. **Units of Measure:** Dollars per barrel. **Type of Price:** official, spot. **Time Period Covered:** latest week.

OIL: CRUDE, LAND

Source: *Oil Buyers' Guide International.* **Price Frequency:** weekly. **Effective Market(s):** Qatar. **Units of Measure:** Dollars per barrel. **Type of Price:** official, spot. **Time Period Covered:** latest week.

OIL: CRUDE, LIBYAN

Source: *Energy Prices and Taxes.* **Price Frequency:** monthly, quarterly, annually. **Effective Market(s):** International Energy Agency. **Units of Measure:** Dollars per barrel. **Type of Price:** import. **Time Period Covered:** monthly latest 2 years, quarterly latest 2 years, annually latest 9 years.

OIL: CRUDE, LIGHT LOUISIANA SWEET

Source: *Oil Buyers' Guide International.* **Price Frequency:** weekly. **Effective Market(s):** St. James (LA). **Units of Measure:** Dollars per barrel. **Type of Price:** posted, spot. **Time Period Covered:** latest week, year ago.

OIL: CRUDE, LIGHT SOUR

Source: *Energy Pricing News: Crude Oil Report.* **Price Frequency:** monthly. **Effective Market(s):** Alberta (Canada). **Units of Measure:** Dollars per cubic meter. **Time Period Covered:** latest month.

OIL: CRUDE, LIGHT SWEET

Source: *Energy Pricing News: Crude Oil Report.* **Price Frequency:** daily, monthly. **Effective Market(s):** Edmonton (Canada). **Units of Measure:** Dollars per cubic meter. **Type of Price:** weighted average. **Time Period Covered:** latest month.

Source: *Energy Pricing News: Crude Oil Report.* **Price Frequency:** monthly. **Effective Market(s):** Alberta (Canada). **Units of Measure:** Dollars per cubic meter. **Time Period Covered:** latest month.

OIL: CRUDE, LIGHT SWEET, FUTURES

Source: *Asian Wall Street Journal.* **Price Frequency:** daily. **Effective Market(s):** New York. **Units of Measure:** Dollars per barrel. **Type of Price:** futures. **Time Period Covered:** latest day.

Source: *Wall Street Journal.* **Price Frequency:** daily. **Effective Market(s):** New York. **Units of Measure:** Dollars per barrel. **Type of Price:** futures. **Time Period Covered:** latest day.

OIL: CRUDE, LIGHT, VENEZUELA

Source: *Energy Prices and Taxes.* **Price Frequency:** monthly, quarterly, annually. **Effective Market(s):** International Energy Agency. **Units of Measure:** Dollars per barrel. **Type of Price:** import. **Time Period Covered:** monthly latest 2 years, quarterly latest 2 years, annually latest 9 years.

OIL: CRUDE, LLOYDMINSTER

Source: *Energy Statistics.* **Price Frequency:** monthly, annually. **Effective Market(s):** Canada. **Units of Measure:** Dollars per barrel. **Type of Price:** contract. **Time Period Covered:** monthly latest year, annually latest 5 years.

Source: *Oilweek.* **Price Frequency:** weekly. **Effective Market(s):** Chicago, Edmonton (Canada), Toronto. **Units of Measure:** Dollars per barrel, Canadian dollars per barrel. **Type of Price:** spot. **Time Period Covered:** latest week.

OIL: CRUDE, LOUISIANA SWEET

Source: *Asian Wall Street Journal.* **Price Frequency:** daily. **Effective Market(s):** St. James (LA). **Units of Measure:** Dollars per barrel. **Type of Price:** spot, refiner buying. **Time Period Covered:** latest 2 days, year ago.

OIL: CRUDE, MANDJI

Source: *Energy Statistics.* **Price Frequency:** monthly, annually. **Effective Market(s):** Gabon. **Units of Measure:** Dollars per barrel. **Type of Price:** contract. **Time Period Covered:** monthly latest year, annually latest 5 years.

OIL: CRUDE, MANDJI, GABON

Source: *Oil & Gas Journal.* **Price Frequency:** monthly in second issue of month. **Effective Market(s):** World. **Units of Measure:** Dollars per barrel. **Type of Price:** spot. **Time Period Covered:** latest date available.

OIL: CRUDE, MARINE

Source: *Oil Buyers' Guide International.* **Price Frequency:** weekly. **Effective Market(s):** Qatar. **Units of Measure:** Dollars per barrel. **Type of Price:** official, spot. **Time Period Covered:** latest week.

OIL: CRUDE, MEDIUM, VENZUELA

Source: *Energy Prices and Taxes.* **Price Frequency:** monthly, quarterly, annually. **Effective Market(s):** International Energy Agency. **Units of Measure:** Dollars per barrel. **Type of Price:** import. **Time Period Covered:** monthly latest 2 years, quarterly latest 2 years, annually latest 9 years.

OIL: CRUDE, MEXICAN ISTHMUS

Source: *Energy Prices and Taxes.* **Price Frequency:** monthly, quarterly, annually. **Effective Market(s):** International Energy Agency. **Units of Measure:** Dollars per barrel. **Type of Price:** import. **Time Period Covered:** monthly latest 2 years, quarterly latest 2 years, annually latest 9 years.

Source: *Energy Statistics.* **Price Frequency:** monthly, annually. **Effective Market(s):** Mexico. **Units of Measure:** Dollars per barrel. **Type of Price:** contract. **Time Period Covered:** monthly latest year, annually latest 5 years.

Source: *Oil & Gas Journal.* **Price Frequency:** monthly in second issue of month. **Effective Market(s):** World. **Units of Measure:** Dollars per barrel. **Type of Price:** spot. **Time Period Covered:** latest date available.

Source: *OPEC Bulletin.* **Price Frequency:** weekly, monthly. **Effective Market(s):** Mexico. **Units of Measure:** Dollars per barrel. **Type of Price:** spot. **Time Period Covered:** weekly for latest month, monthly for latest year.

OIL: CRUDE, MEXICAN ISTHMUS, IMPORTED

Source: *Energy Pricing News: Crude Oil Report.* **Price Frequency:** monthly. **Effective Market(s):** Canada, Cushing (Canada), Edmonton (Canada), Siullum Voe (Canada). **Units of Measure:** Canadian dollars per barrel, Canadian dollars per cubic meter. **Time Period Covered:** latest month, month ago.

OIL: CRUDE, MEXICAN MAYA

Source: *Energy Prices and Taxes.* **Price Frequency:** monthly, quarterly, annually. **Effective Market(s):** International Energy Agency. **Units of Measure:** Dollars per barrel. **Type of Price:** import. **Time Period Covered:** monthly latest 2 years, quarterly latest 2 years, annually latest 9 years.

Source: *Energy Statistics.* **Price Frequency:** monthly, annually. **Effective Market(s):** Mexico. **Units of Measure:** Dollars per barrel. **Type of Price:** contract. **Time Period Covered:** monthly latest year, annually latest 5 years.

Source: *Oilweek.* **Price Frequency:** weekly. **Effective Market(s):** Chicago, Edmonton (Canada), Toronto. **Units of Measure:** Canadian dollars per barrel, dollars per barrel. **Type of Price:** spot. **Time Period Covered:** latest week.

OIL: CRUDE, MEXICAN MAYA, IMPORTED

Source: *Energy Pricing News: Crude Oil Report.* **Price Frequency:** monthly. **Effective Market(s):** Canada, Cushing (Canada), Edmonton (Canada), Sullum Voe (Canada). **Units of Measure:** Canadian dollars per barrel, Canadian dollars per cubic meter. **Time Period Covered:** latest month, month ago.

OIL: CRUDE, MICHIGAN SOUR

Source: *Oil & Gas Journal.* **Price Frequency:** monthly in second issue of month. **Effective Market(s):** United States. **Units of Measure:** Dollars per barrel. **Type of Price:** dominant posting. **Time Period Covered:** latest date available.

OIL: CRUDE, MIDALE

Source: *Oilweek.* **Price Frequency:** weekly. **Effective Market(s):** Chicago, Edmonton (Canada), Toronto. **Units of Measure:** Dollars per barrel, Canadian dollars per barrel. **Type of Price:** spot. **Time Period Covered:** latest week.

OIL: CRUDE, MIDDLE EAST, IMPORTED

Source: *Energy Pricing News: Crude Oil Report.* **Price Frequency:** monthly. **Effective Market(s):** Canada, Cushing (Canada), Edmonton (Canada), Sullum Voe (Canada). **Units of Measure:** Canadian dollars per barrel, Canadian dollars per cubic meter. **Time Period Covered:** latest month, month ago.

OIL: CRUDE, MINAS

Source: *Oil Buyers' Guide International.* **Price Frequency:** weekly. **Effective Market(s):** Indonesia. **Units of Measure:** Dollars per barrel. **Type of Price:** spot. **Time Period Covered:** latest week.

OIL: CRUDE, MINAS, INDONESIA

Source: *Oil & Gas Journal.* **Price Frequency:** monthly in second issue of month. **Effective Market(s):** World. **Units of Measure:** Dollars per barrel. **Type of Price:** spot. **Time Period Covered:** latest date available.

Source: *OPEC Bulletin.* **Price Frequency:** weekly, monthly. **Effective Market(s):** OPEC. **Units of Measure:** Dollars per barrel. **Type of Price:** spot. **Time Period Covered:** weekly for latest month, monthly for latest year.

OIL: CRUDE, MIXED BLEND

Source: *Energy Statistics.* **Price Frequency:** monthly, annually. **Effective Market(s):** Canada. **Units of Measure:** Dollars per barrel. **Type of Price:** contract. **Time Period Covered:** monthly latest year, annually latest 5 years.

OIL: CRUDE, MURBAN

Source: *Energy Statistics.* **Price Frequency:** monthly, annually. **Effective Market(s):** Abu Dhabi. **Units of Measure:** Dollars per barrel. **Type of Price:** contract. **Time Period Covered:** monthly latest year, annually latest 5 years.

Source: *Oil Buyers' Guide International.* **Price Frequency:** weekly. **Effective Market(s):** Abu Dhabi. **Units of Measure:** Dollars per barrel. **Type of Price:** official, spot. **Time Period Covered:** latest week.

OIL: CRUDE, MURBAN, ABU DHABI

Source: *Oil & Gas Journal.* **Price Frequency:** monthly in second issue of month. **Effective Market(s):** World. **Units of Measure:** Dollars per barrel. **Type of Price:** spot. **Time Period Covered:** latest date available.

OIL: CRUDE, MURBAN/ZAKUM

Source: *Energy Prices and Taxes.* **Price Frequency:** monthly, quarterly, annually. **Effective Market(s):** International Energy Agency. **Units of Measure:** Dollars per barrel. **Type of Price:** import. **Time Period Covered:** monthly latest 2 years, quarterly latest 2 years, annually latest 9 years.

OIL: CRUDE, NIGERIAN

Source: *Energy Prices and Taxes.* **Price Frequency:** monthly, quarterly, annually. **Effective Market(s):** International Energy Agency. **Units of Measure:** Dollars per barrel. **Type of Price:** import. **Time Period Covered:** monthly latest 2 years, quarterly latest 2 years, annually latest 9 years.

OIL: CRUDE, NINIAN

Source: *Oil Buyers' Guide International.* **Price Frequency:** weekly. **Effective Market(s):** United Kingdom. **Units of Measure:** Dollars per barrel. **Type of Price:** spot. **Time Period Covered:** latest week.

OIL: CRUDE, NORTH SEA BRENT

Source: *The Economist.* **Price Frequency:** weekly. **Effective Market(s):** Great Britain. **Units of Measure:** Dollars per barrel. **Time Period Covered:** latest 2 weeks.

Source: *Energy Pricing News: Crude Oil Report.* **Price Frequency:** monthly. **Effective Market(s):** Canada, Cushing (Canada), Edmonton (Canada), Sullum Voe (Canada). **Units of Measure:** Canadian dollars per barrel, Canadian dollars per cubic meter. **Time Period Covered:** latest month, month ago.

Source: *Investor's Daily.* **Price Frequency:** daily. **Units of Measure:** Dollars per barrel. **Type of Price:** spot. **Time Period Covered:** latest 2 days.

Source: *New York Times.* **Price Frequency:** daily. **Units of Measure:** Dollars per barrel. **Type of Price:** cash. **Time Period Covered:** latest 2 days.

OIL: CRUDE, NORTH SEA, IMPORTED

Source: *Energy Pricing News: Crude Oil Report.* **Price Frequency:** monthly. **Effective Market(s):** Canada, Cushing (Canada), Edmonton (Canada), Sullum Voe (Canada). **Units of Measure:** Canadian dollars per barrel, Canadian dollars per cubic meter. **Time Period Covered:** latest month, month ago.

OIL: CRUDE, NORTHWEST EUROPE

Source: *Energy Prices and Taxes.* **Price Frequency:** monthly, quarterly, annually. **Effective Market(s):** International Energy Agency. **Units of Measure:** Dollars per barrel. **Type of Price:** import. **Time Period Covered:** monthly latest 2 years, quarterly latest 2 years, annually latest 9 years.

OIL: CRUDE, OKLAHOMA SWEET

Source: *Oil & Gas Journal.* **Price Frequency:** monthly in second issue of month. **Effective Market(s):** United States. **Units of Measure:** Dollars per barrel. **Type of Price:** dominant posting. **Time Period Covered:** latest date available.

OIL: CRUDE, OMAN BLEND

Source: *Energy Statistics.* **Price Frequency:** monthly, annually. **Effective Market(s):** Oman. **Units of Measure:** Dollars per barrel. **Type of Price:** contract. **Time Period Covered:** monthly latest year, annually latest 5 years.

Source: *Japan Economic Journal.* **Price Frequency:** weekly. **Effective Market(s):** London. **Units of Measure:** Dollars per barrel. **Type of Price:** spot. **Time Period Covered:** latest 2 weeks.

Source: *Oil Buyers' Guide International.* **Price Frequency:** weekly. **Effective Market(s):** Oman. **Units of Measure:** Dollars per barrel. **Type of Price:** official, spot. **Time Period Covered:** latest week.

Source: *OPEC Bulletin.* **Price Frequency:** weekly, monthly. **Effective Market(s):** Oman. **Units of Measure:** Dollars per barrel. **Type of Price:** spot. **Time Period Covered:** weekly for latest month, monthly for latest year.

Source: *Petroleum Economist.* **Price Frequency:** monthly. **Units of Measure:** Dollars per barrel. **Type of Price:** spot. **Time Period Covered:** latest month.

OIL: CRUDE, ORIENTE

Source: *Energy Statistics.* **Price Frequency:** monthly, annually. **Effective Market(s):** Ecuador. **Units of Measure:** Dollars per barrel. **Type of Price:** contract. **Time Period Covered:** monthly latest year, annually latest 5 years.

OIL: CRUDE, QATAR

Source: *Energy Prices and Taxes.* **Price Frequency:** monthly, quarterly, annually. **Effective Market(s):** International Energy Agency. **Units of Measure:** Dollars per barrel. **Type of Price:** import. **Time Period Covered:** monthly latest 2 years, quarterly latest 2 years, annually latest 9 years.

OIL: CRUDE, SAHARAN BLEND

Source: *Energy Statistics.* **Price Frequency:** monthly, annually. **Effective Market(s):** Algeria. **Units of Measure:** Dollars per barrel. **Type of Price:** contract. **Time Period Covered:** monthly latest year, annually latest 5 years.

Source: *Oil Buyers' Guide International.* **Price Frequency:** weekly. **Effective Market(s):** Algeria. **Units of Measure:** Dollars per barrel. **Type of Price:** official, spot. **Time Period Covered:** latest week.

OIL: CRUDE, SAHARAN BLEND, ALGERIA

Source: *OPEC Bulletin.* **Price Frequency:** weekly, monthly. **Effective Market(s):** OPEC. **Units of Measure:** Dollars per barrel. **Type of Price:** spot. **Time Period Covered:** weekly for latest month, monthly for latest year.

OIL: CRUDE, SERIA LIGHT

Source: *Energy Statistics.* **Price Frequency:** monthly, annually. **Effective Market(s):** Brunei. **Units of Measure:** Dollars per barrel. **Type of Price:** contract. **Time Period Covered:** monthly latest year, annually latest 5 years.

OIL: CRUDE, STATFJORD

Source: *Oil Buyers' Guide International.* **Price Frequency:** weekly. **Effective Market(s):** Norway. **Units of Measure:** Dollars per barrel. **Type of Price:** spot. **Time Period Covered:** latest week.

OIL: CRUDE, SUEZ BLEND

Source: *Energy Statistics.* **Price Frequency:** monthly, annually. **Effective Market(s):** Egypt. **Units of Measure:** Dollars per barrel. **Type of Price:** contract. **Time Period Covered:** monthly latest year, annually latest 5 years.

Source: *Oil Buyers' Guide International.* **Price Frequency:** weekly. **Effective Market(s):** Egypt. **Units of Measure:** Dollars per barrel. **Type of Price:** spot. **Time Period Covered:** latest week.

OIL: CRUDE, SUEZ BLEND, EGYPT

Source: *Oil & Gas Journal.* **Price Frequency:** monthly in second issue of month. **Effective Market(s):** World. **Units of Measure:** Dollars per barrel. **Type of Price:** spot. **Time Period Covered:** latest date available.

Source: *OPEC Bulletin.* **Price Frequency:** weekly, monthly. **Effective Market(s):** Egypt. **Units of Measure:** Dollars per barrel. **Type of Price:** spot. **Time Period Covered:** weekly for latest month, monthly for latest year.

OIL: CRUDE, SWAN HILLS SOUTH

Source: *Energy Pricing News: Crude Oil Report.* **Price Frequency:** monthly. **Effective Market(s):** Canada, Cushing (Canada), Edmonton (Canada), Sullum Voe (Canada). **Units of Measure:** Canadian dollars per barrel, Canadian dollars per cubic meter. **Time Period Covered:** latest month, month ago.

OIL: CRUDE, TAPIS BLEND

Source: *Energy Statistics.* **Price Frequency:** monthly, annually. **Effective Market(s):** Malaysia. **Units of Measure:** Dollars per barrel. **Type of Price:** contract. **Time Period Covered:** monthly latest year, annually latest 5 years.

OIL: CRUDE, TIA JUANA LIGHT

Source: *Energy Statistics.* **Price Frequency:** monthly, annually. **Effective Market(s):** Venezuela. **Units of Measure:** Dollars per barrel. **Type of Price:** contract. **Time Period Covered:** monthly latest year, annually latest 5 years.

OIL: CRUDE, TIA JUANA LIGHT, VENEZUELA

Source: *Oil & Gas Journal.* **Price Frequency:** monthly in second issue of month. **Effective Market(s):** World. **Units of Measure:** Dollars per barrel. **Type of Price:** spot. **Time Period Covered:** latest date available.

OIL: CRUDE, U.S.S.R

Source: *Energy Prices and Taxes.* **Price Frequency:** monthly, quarterly, annually. **Effective Market(s):** International Energy Agency. **Units of Measure:** Dollars per barrel. **Type of Price:** import. **Time Period Covered:** monthly latest 2 years, quarterly latest 2 years, annually latest 9 years.

OIL: CRUDE, UMM SHAIF

Source: *Oil Buyers' Guide International.* **Price Frequency:** weekly. **Effective Market(s):** Abu Dhabi. **Units of Measure:** Dollars per barrel. **Type of Price:** official, spot. **Time Period Covered:** latest week.

OIL: CRUDE, UNITED STATES, IMPORTED

Source: *Energy Pricing News: Crude Oil Report.* **Price Frequency:** monthly. **Effective Market(s):** Canada, Cushing (Canada), Edmonton (Canada), Sullum Voe (Canada). **Units of Measure:** Canadian dollars per barrel, Canadian dollars per cubic meter. **Time Period Covered:** latest month, month ago.

OIL: CRUDE, UPPER ZAKUM

Source: *Oil Buyers' Guide International.* **Price Frequency:** weekly. **Effective Market(s):** Abu Dhabi. **Units of Measure:** Dollars per barrel. **Type of Price:** official, spot. **Time Period Covered:** latest week.

OIL: CRUDE, URALS

Source: *Energy Statistics.* **Price Frequency:** monthly, annually. **Effective Market(s):** U.S.S.R. **Units of Measure:** Dollars per barrel. **Type of Price:** contract. **Time Period Covered:** monthly latest year, annually latest 5 years.

Source: *Oil Buyers' Guide International.* **Price Frequency:** weekly. **Effective Market(s):** U.S.S.R. **Units of Measure:** Dollars per barrel. **Type of Price:** spot. **Time Period Covered:** latest week.

OIL: CRUDE, URALS, U.S.S.R

Source: *OPEC Bulletin.* **Price Frequency:** weekly, monthly. **Effective Market(s):** Mediterranean. **Units of Measure:** Dollars per barrel. **Type of Price:** spot. **Time Period Covered:** weekly for latest month, monthly for latest year.

OIL: CRUDE, URALS-MEDITERRANEAN

Source: *Asian Wall Street Journal.* **Price Frequency:** daily. **Effective Market(s):** Northwest Europe. **Units of Measure:** Dollars per barrel. **Type of Price:** spot. **Time Period Covered:** latest 2 days, year ago.

Source: *Wall Street Journal.* **Price Frequency:** daily. **Effective Market(s):** Europe. **Units of Measure:** Dollars per barrel. **Type of Price:** spot. **Time Period Covered:** latest day, day ago, year ago.

OIL: CRUDE, VENEZUELAN, IMPORTED

Source: *Energy Pricing News: Crude Oil Report.* **Price Frequency:** monthly. **Effective Market(s):** Canada, Cushing (Canada), Edmonton (Canada), Sullum Voe (Canada). **Units of Measure:** Canadian dollars per barrel, Canadian dollars per cubic meter. **Time Period Covered:** latest month, month ago.

OIL: CRUDE, WEST TEXAS INTERMEDIATE

Source: *Asian Wall Street Journal.* **Price Frequency:** daily. **Units of Measure:** Dollars per barrel. **Type of Price:** spot, refiner buying. **Time Period Covered:** latest 2 days, year ago.

Source: *Energy Prices and Taxes.* **Price Frequency:** monthly, quarterly, annually. **Effective Market(s):** Rotterdam. **Units of Measure:** Dollars per barrel. **Type of Price:** spot. **Time Period Covered:** monthly latest 2 years, quarterly latest 2 years, annually latest 7 years.

Source: *Energy Pricing News: Crude Oil Report.* **Price Frequency:** monthly. **Effective Market(s):** Canada, Cushing (Canada), Edmonton (Canada), Sullum Voe (Canada). **Units of Measure:** Canadian dollars per barrel, Canadian dollars per cubic meter. **Time Period Covered:** latest month, month ago.

Source: *Financial Times.* **Price Frequency:** daily. **Effective Market(s):** London. **Units of Measure:** Dollars per barrel. **Type of Price:** spot. **Time Period Covered:** latest day.

Source: *Investor's Daily.* **Price Frequency:** daily. **Units of Measure:** Dollars per barrel. **Type of Price:** spot. **Time Period Covered:** latest 2 days.

Source: *Japan Economic Journal.* **Price Frequency:** weekly. **Effective Market(s):** New York. **Units of Measure:** Dollars per barrel. **Type of Price:** spot. **Time Period Covered:** latest 2 weeks.

Source: *New York Times.* **Price Frequency:** daily. **Units of Measure:** Dollars per barrel. **Type of Price:** cash. **Time Period Covered:** latest 2 days.

Source: *Oil & Gas Journal.* **Price Frequency:** monthly in second issue of month. **Effective Market(s):** United States. **Units of Measure:** Dollars per barrel. **Type of Price:** dominant posting. **Time Period Covered:** latest date available.

Source: *Oil Buyers' Guide International.* **Price Frequency:** weekly. **Effective Market(s):** Midland (TX). **Units of Measure:** Dollars per barrel. **Type of Price:** posted, spot. **Time Period Covered:** latest week, year ago.

Source: *Oilweek.* **Price Frequency:** weekly. **Effective Market(s):** Chicago, Edmonton (Canada), Toronto. **Units of Measure:** Dollars per barrel, Canadian dollars per barrel. **Type of Price:** spot. **Time Period Covered:** latest week.

Source: *OPEC Bulletin.* **Price Frequency:** weekly, monthly. **Effective Market(s):** United States. **Units of Measure:** Dollars per barrel. **Type of Price:** spot. **Time Period Covered:** weekly for latest month, monthly for latest year.

Source: *Petroleum Economist.* **Price Frequency:** monthly. **Units of Measure:** Dollars per barrel. **Type of Price:** spot. **Time Period Covered:** latest month.

Source: *The Times.* **Price Frequency:** daily. **Effective Market(s):** United Kingdom. **Units of Measure:** Dollars per barrel. **Time Period Covered:** latest day.

OIL: CRUDE, WEST TEXAS INTERMEDIATE, FUTURES

Source: *Oilweek.* **Price Frequency:** weekly. **Effective Market(s):** World. **Units of Measure:** Dollars per barrel. **Type of Price:** futures. **Time Period Covered:** next 2 months.

OIL: CRUDE, WEST TEXAS SOUR

Source: *Asian Wall Street Journal.* **Price Frequency:** daily. **Effective Market(s):** Midland (TX). **Units of Measure:** Dollars per barrel. **Type of Price:** spot, refiner buying. **Time Period Covered:** latest 2 days, year ago.

Source: *Oil & Gas Journal.* **Price Frequency:** monthly in second issue of month. **Effective Market(s):** United States. **Units of Measure:** Dollars per barrel. **Type of Price:** dominant posting. **Time Period Covered:** latest date available.

Source: *Oil Buyers' Guide International.* **Price Frequency:** weekly. **Effective Market(s):** Midland (TX). **Units of Measure:** Dollars per barrel. **Type of Price:** posted, spot. **Time Period Covered:** latest week, year ago.

OIL: CRUDE, WYOMING SWEET

Source: *Oil & Gas Journal.* **Price Frequency:** monthly in second issue of month. **Effective Market(s):** United States. **Units of Measure:** Dollars per barrel. **Type of Price:** dominant posting. **Time Period Covered:** latest date available.

OIL: CRUDE, ZARZAITINE

Source: *Oil Buyers' Guide International.* **Price Frequency:** weekly. **Effective Market(s):** Algeria. **Units of Measure:** Dollars per barrel. **Type of Price:** spot. **Time Period Covered:** latest week.

OIL: CRUDE, ZUEITINA

Source: *Oil Buyers' Guide International.* **Price Frequency:** weekly. **Effective Market(s):** Libya. **Units of Measure:** Dollars per barrel. **Type of Price:** official, spot. **Time Period Covered:** latest week.

OIL: GAS/DIESEL, 0.5% SULFUR

Source: *Petroleum Economist.* **Price Frequency:** monthly. **Effective Market(s):** Bahamas, Bahrain, Curacao, Pulau Bukom (Singapore), Quoin Island. **Units of Measure:** cents per gallon. **Time Period Covered:** latest month.

OIL: GAS/DIESEL, 53/57

Source: *Petroleum Economist.* **Price Frequency:** monthly. **Effective Market(s):** Bahamas, Bahrain, Curacao, Pulau Bukom (Singapore), Quoin Island. **Units of Measure:** cents per gallon. **Time Period Covered:** latest month.

OIL: GAS/DIESEL, CETANE 45 MIN

Source: *Petroleum Economist.* **Price Frequency:** monthly. **Effective Market(s):** Bahamas, Bahrain, Curacao, Pulau Bukom (Singapore), Quoin Island. **Units of Measure:** cents per gallon. **Time Period Covered:** latest month.

OIL: GAS/DIESEL, CETANE 47 MIN

Source: *Petroleum Economist.* **Price Frequency:** monthly. **Effective Market(s):** Bahamas, Bahrain, Curacao, Pulau Bukom (Singapore), Quoin Island. **Units of Measure:** cents per gallon. **Time Period Covered:** latest month.

OIL: GAS/DIESEL, INDUSTRIAL

Source: *Petroleum Economist.* **Price Frequency:** monthly. **Effective Market(s):** Bahamas, Bahrain, Curacao, Pulau Bukom (Singapore), Quoin Island. **Units of Measure:** cents per gallon. **Time Period Covered:** latest month.

OIL: HEATING

Source: *Energy Statistics.* **Price Frequency:** monthly, annually. **Effective Market(s):** United States. **Units of Measure:** cents per gallon. **Type of Price:** residential, refiner. **Time Period Covered:** monthly latest year, annually latest 15 years.

Source: *Energy Statistics.* **Price Frequency:** monthly. **Effective Market(s):** 27 domestic markets. **Units of Measure:** cents per gallon. **Type of Price:** residential. **Time Period Covered:** latest 16 months.

Source: *Energy Statistics.* **Price Frequency:** monthly, annually. **Effective Market(s):** 33 domestic markets. **Units of Measure:** cents per gallon. **Type of Price:** residential. **Time Period Covered:** monthly latest 2 years, annually latest 4 years.

OIL: HEATING, 0.2% SULFUR

Source: *Oil & Gas Journal.* **Price Frequency:** weekly except second issue of month. **Effective Market(s):** New York. **Units of Measure:** Dollars per barrel. **Type of Price:** spot. **Time Period Covered:** latest 3 weeks, year ago.

OIL: HEATING, 0.3% SULFUR

Source: *Oil & Gas Journal.* **Price Frequency:** weekly except second issue of month. **Effective Market(s):** Rotterdam. **Units of Measure:** Dollars per barrel. **Type of Price:** spot. **Time Period Covered:** latest 3 weeks, year ago.

OIL: HEATING, FUTURES

Source: *Barron's.* **Price Frequency:** weekly. **Effective Market(s):** New York. **Units of Measure:** cents per gallon. **Type of Price:** futures. **Time Period Covered:** latest week.

Source: *Financial Times.* **Price Frequency:** daily. **Effective Market(s):** New York. **Units of Measure:** Dollars per barrel. **Type of Price:** futures. **Time Period Covered:** latest 2 days.

Source: *Investor's Daily.* **Price Frequency:** daily. **Effective Market(s):** New York. **Units of Measure:** cents per gallon. **Type of Price:** futures. **Time Period Covered:** latest day.

Source: *Los Angeles Times.* **Price Frequency:** daily. **Effective Market(s):** New York. **Units of Measure:** cents per gallon. **Type of Price:** futures. **Time Period Covered:** latest day.

OIL: HEATING, NO. 2, FUTURES

Source: *Asian Wall Street Journal.* **Price Frequency:** daily. **Effective Market(s):** New York. **Units of Measure:** Dollars per gallon. **Type of Price:** futures. **Time Period Covered:** latest day.

Source: *New York Times.* **Price Frequency:** daily. **Effective Market(s):** New York. **Units of Measure:** cents per gallon. **Type of Price:** futures. **Time Period Covered:** latest day.

Source: *Wall Street Journal.* **Price Frequency:** daily. **Effective Market(s):** New York. **Units of Measure:** Dollars per gallon. **Type of Price:** futures. **Time Period Covered:** latest day.

OIL: HEATING, NO. 2, FUTURES, JANUARY

Source: *Commodity Year Book.* **Price Frequency:** monthly. **Effective Market(s):** New York. **Units of Measure:** cents per gallon. **Type of Price:** futures. **Time Period Covered:** latest 5 years.

OIL: HEAVY FUEL

Source: *Lloyd's Ship Manager.* **Price Frequency:** monthly. **Effective Market(s):** 8 international markets. **Units of Measure:** Dollars per tonne. **Type of Price:** spot. **Time Period Covered:** latest year.

OIL: INTERMEDIATE FUEL

Source: *Lloyd's Ship Manager.* **Price Frequency:** monthly. **Effective Market(s):** 10 international markets. **Units of Measure:** Dollars per tonne. **Type of Price:** spot. **Time Period Covered:** latest year.

OIL: MARINE DIESEL

Source: *Lloyd's Ship Manager.* **Price Frequency:** monthly. **Effective Market(s):** 10 international markets. **Units of Measure:** Dollars per tonne. **Type of Price:** spot. **Time Period Covered:** latest year.

Source: *Petroleum Economist.* **Price Frequency:** monthly. **Effective Market(s):** 8 international markets. **Units of Measure:** Dollars per metric ton. **Type of Price:** market. **Time Period Covered:** latest month.

OIL: MARINE FUEL

Source: *Petroleum Economist.* **Price Frequency:** monthly. **Effective Market(s):** 8 international markets. **Units of Measure:** Dollars per metric ton. **Type of Price:** market. **Time Period Covered:** latest month.

OIL: MARINE GAS/DIESEL

Source: *Petroleum Economist.* **Price Frequency:** monthly. **Effective Market(s):** Bahamas, Bahrain, Curacao, Pulau Buxom (Singapore), Quoin Island. **Units of Measure:** cents per gallon. **Time Period Covered:** latest month.

OIL: MOTOR, ALL WEATHER, HIGH DETERGENT

Source: *Agricultural Prices.* **Price Frequency:** semiannually. **Effective Market(s):** United States. **Units of Measure:** Dollars each. **Type of Price:** paid by farmer. **Time Period Covered:** latest year.

Source: *Agricultural Prices Annual Summary.* **Price Frequency:** quarterly. **Effective Market(s):** United States. **Units of Measure:** Dollars per gallon. **Type of Price:** paid by farmer. **Time Period Covered:** latest 6 years.

OIL: MOTOR, HEAVY DUTY, DETERGENT

Source: *Agricultural Prices.* **Price Frequency:** semiannually. **Effective Market(s):** United States. **Units of Measure:** Dollars each. **Type of Price:** paid by farmer. **Time Period Covered:** latest year.

Source: *Agricultural Prices Annual Summary.* **Price Frequency:** quarterly. **Effective Market(s):** United States. **Units of Measure:** Dollars per gallon. **Type of Price:** paid by farmer. **Time Period Covered:** latest 6 years.

OIL: MOTOR, REGULAR, NON-DETERGENT

Source: *Agricultural Prices.* **Price Frequency:** semiannually. **Effective Market(s):** United States. **Units of Measure:** Dollars each. **Type of Price:** paid by farmer. **Time Period Covered:** latest year.

Source: *Agricultural Prices Annual Summary.* **Price Frequency:** quarterly. **Effective Market(s):** United States. **Units of Measure:** Dollars per gallon. **Type of Price:** paid by farmer. **Time Period Covered:** latest 6 years.

OIL FILTER: CARTRIDGE REFILL

Source: *Agricultural Prices.* **Price Frequency:** semiannually. **Effective Market(s):** United States. **Units of Measure:** Dollars each. **Type of Price:** paid by farmer. **Time Period Covered:** latest year.

Source: *Agricultural Prices Annual Summary.* **Price Frequency:** semiannually. **Effective Market(s):** United States. **Units of Measure:** Dollars each. **Type of Price:** paid by farmer. **Time Period Covered:** latest 6 years.

OIL FILTER: SPIN-ON

Source: *Agricultural Prices.* **Price Frequency:** semiannually. **Effective Market(s):** United States. **Units of Measure:** Dollars each. **Type of Price:** paid by farmer. **Time Period Covered:** latest year.

Source: *Agricultural Prices Annual Summary.* **Price Frequency:** semiannually. **Effective Market(s):** United States. **Units of Measure:** Dollars each. **Type of Price:** paid by farmer. **Time Period Covered:** latest 6 years.

OILSEED AND OIL: VEGETABLE

Source: *Monthly Commodity Price Bulletin Supplement.* **Price Frequency:** monthly, quarterly, annually. **Effective Market(s):** developing countries. **Units of Measure:** index. **Type of Price:** free market price index. **Time Period Covered:** latest 20 years.

Source: *Monthly Commodity Price Bulletin.* **Price Frequency:** monthly, annually. **Effective Market(s):** developing countries. **Units of Measure:** index. **Type of Price:** free market price index. **Time Period Covered:** latest 5 years.

OITICICA OIL: LIQUID

Source: *Chemical Marketing Reporter.* **Price Frequency:** weekly. **Effective Market(s):** New York. **Units of Measure:** Dollars per lb. **Type of Price:** spot. **Time Period Covered:** latest week.

OKRA

Source: *Lancaster Farmer.* **Price Frequency:** weekly, seasonally. **Effective Market(s):** Pennsylvania. **Units of Measure:** Dollars per unit. **Type of Price:** market. **Time Period Covered:** latest week.

OLEIC ACID: DOUBLE-DISTILLED, WHITE

Source: *Chemical Marketing Reporter.* **Price Frequency:** weekly. **Effective Market(s):** New York. **Units of Measure:** Dollars per lb. **Type of Price:** spot. **Time Period Covered:** latest week.

OLEIC ACID: SINGLE-DISTILLED, RED

Source: *Chemical Marketing Reporter.* **Price Frequency:** weekly. **Effective Market(s):** New York. **Units of Measure:** Dollars per lb. **Type of Price:** spot. **Time Period Covered:** latest week.

OLEOMARGARINE: BLENDED

Source: *National Provisioner.* **Price Frequency:** weekly. **Units of Measure:** cents per lb. **Time Period Covered:** latest week.

OLEOMARGARINE: MILK CHURNED PASTRY

Source: *National Provisioner.* **Price Frequency:** weekly. **Units of Measure:** cents per lb. **Time Period Covered:** latest week.

OLEOMARGARINE: WATER CHURNED PASTRY

Source: *National Provisioner.* **Price Frequency:** weekly. **Units of Measure:** cents per lb. **Time Period Covered:** latest week.

OLEOMARGARINE: WHITE, VEGETABLE SOLIDS, DOMESTIC

Source: *National Provisioner.* **Price Frequency:** weekly. **Units of Measure:** cents per lb. **Time Period Covered:** latest week.

OLEOMARGARINE: YELLOW

Source: *National Provisioner.* **Price Frequency:** weekly. **Units of Measure:** cents per lb. **Time Period Covered:** latest week.

OLEUM

see Sulfuric Acid: Fuming.

OLIBANUM GUM: TEARS, INDIAN

Source: *Chemical Marketing Reporter.* **Price Frequency:** weekly. **Effective Market(s):** New York. **Units of Measure:** Dollars per lb. **Type of Price:** spot. **Time Period Covered:** latest week.

OLIBANUM GUM: TEARS, NO. 1

Source: *Journal of Commerce and Commercial.* **Price Frequency:** weekly in Monday issue. **Units of Measure:** Dollars per lb. **Type of Price:** spot. **Time Period Covered:** latest week.

OLIVE OIL: B-TYPE, ITALIAN

Source: *Chemical Marketing Reporter.* **Price Frequency:** weekly. **Effective Market(s):** New York. **Units of Measure:** Dollars per gallon. **Type of Price:** spot. **Time Period Covered:** latest week.

OLIVE OIL: EDIBLE, SPANISH

Source: *Chemical Marketing Reporter.* **Price Frequency:** weekly. **Effective Market(s):** New York. **Units of Measure:** Dollars per gallon. **Type of Price:** spot. **Time Period Covered:** latest week.

OLIVES

Source: *Agricultural Prices Annual Summary.* **Price Frequency:** annually. **Effective Market(s):** California, Hawaii. **Units of Measure:** Dollars per ton. **Type of Price:** average received by farmer. **Time Period Covered:** latest 6 years.

Source: *Fruit and Tree Nuts Situation and Outlook Yearbook.* **Price Frequency:** annually. **Effective Market(s):** California. **Units of Measure:** Dollars per short ton. **Type of Price:** grower. **Time Period Covered:** latest 20 years.

OLIVINE: AGGREGATE

Source: *Industrial Minerals.* **Price Frequency:** monthly. **Effective Market(s):** United States. **Units of Measure:** Dollars per metric tonne. **Type of Price:** producer & dealer. **Time Period Covered:** latest month.

OLIVINE: CRUSHED

Source: *Industrial Minerals.* **Price Frequency:** monthly. **Effective Market(s):** main European port. **Units of Measure:** British pounds per metric tonne. **Type of Price:** producer & dealer. **Time Period Covered:** latest month.

OLIVINE: DRY, GRADED REFRACTORY AGGREGATE

Source: *Industrial Minerals.* **Price Frequency:** monthly. **Effective Market(s):** main European port. **Units of Measure:** British pounds per metric tonne. **Type of Price:** producer & dealer. **Time Period Covered:** latest month.

OLIVINE: FLOUR

Source: *Industrial Minerals.* **Price Frequency:** monthly. **Effective Market(s):** United States. **Units of Measure:** Dollars per metric tonne. **Type of Price:** producer & dealer. **Time Period Covered:** latest month.

OLIVINE: FOUNDRY GRADE

Source: *Industrial Minerals.* **Price Frequency:** monthly. **Effective Market(s):** United States. **Units of Measure:** Dollars per metric tonne. **Type of Price:** producer & dealer. **Time Period Covered:** latest month.

OLIVINE: FOUNDRY SAND

Source: *Industrial Minerals.* **Price Frequency:** monthly. **Effective Market(s):** United Kingdom. **Units of Measure:** British pounds per metric tonne. **Type of Price:** producer & dealer. **Time Period Covered:** latest month.

ONAGA (FISH)

see Snapper: Red Longtail.

ONION AND GARLIC OIL

Source: *U. S. Essential Oil Trade.* **Price Frequency:** annually. **Effective Market(s):** United States. **Units of Measure:** Dollars per kilogram. **Type of Price:** import value. **Time Period Covered:** latest 3 years.

ONIONS

Source: *Agricultural Outlook.* **Price Frequency:** monthly, annually. **Effective Market(s):** United States. **Units of Measure:** Dollars per 100 lbs. **Type of Price:** average received by farmer. **Time Period Covered:** monthly latest 6 months, annually latest 3 years.

Source: *Agricultural Prices Annual Summary.* **Price Frequency:** monthly, seasonally. **Effective Market(s):** United States. **Units of Measure:** Dollars per 100 lbs. **Type of Price:** received by grower. **Time Period Covered:** latest 3 years, for US latest 6 years.

Source: *Commodity Year Book.* **Price Frequency:** annually. **Effective Market(s):** United States. **Units of Measure:** Dollars per 100 lbs. **Time Period Covered:** latest 8 years.

Source: *Commodity Year Book.* **Price Frequency:** monthly, annually. **Effective Market(s):** United States. **Units of Measure:** Dollars per 100 lbs. **Type of Price:** price received by growers. **Time Period Covered:** latest 8 years.

Source: *Statistical Bulletin of the South Pacific: Retail Price Indexes.* **Price Frequency:** annually. **Effective Market(s):** 18 South Pacific markets. **Units of Measure:** Australian dollars per kilogram. **Type of Price:** retail. **Time Period Covered:** latest year.

ONIONS: BEN SHERMAN

Source: *The Packer.* **Price Frequency:** weekly, seasonally. **Effective Market(s):** varies. **Units of Measure:** Dollars per sack. **Type of Price:** price received by farmer. **Time Period Covered:** latest week.

ONIONS: CLASS 2

Source: *Farmers Weekly.* **Price Frequency:** weekly, seasonally. **Effective Market(s):** Birmingham (England), Bristol (England), Covent Garden (England), Glasgow (Scotland), Manchester (England). **Units of Measure:** British pence per unit. **Type of Price:** wholesale. **Time Period Covered:** latest week.

ONIONS: FRESH

Source: *Agricultural Prices.* **Price Frequency:** monthly. **Effective Market(s):** United States. **Units of Measure:** Dollars per 100 lbs. **Type of Price:** received by farmer. **Time Period Covered:** latest 2 months, year ago.

Source: *Vegetable and Specialties Situation and Outlook Report.* **Price Frequency:** monthly, annually. **Effective Market(s):** United States. **Units of Measure:** Dollars per 100 lbs. **Type of Price:** received by grower. **Time Period Covered:** latest 4 years.

ONIONS: GRANO, DRY

Source: *Lancaster Farmer.* **Price Frequency:** weekly, seasonally. **Effective Market(s):** Pennsylvania. **Units of Measure:** Dollars per sack. **Type of Price:** market. **Time Period Covered:** latest week.

ONIONS: GREEN

Source: *California Farmer.* **Price Frequency:** semimonthly, seasonally. **Effective Market(s):** Imperial/Coachella Valleys. **Units of Measure:** Dollars per 13 lb. carton. **Time Period Covered:** latest week, month ago, year ago.

Source: *Fresh Fruit and Vegetable Prices.* **Price Frequency:** monthly, seasonally. **Effective Market(s):** Imperial/Coachella Valley/Calexico (CA), Lower Rio Grande Valley (TX), Vineland (NJ). **Units of Measure:** Dollars per carton or crate. **Type of Price:** average price at shipping point. **Time Period Covered:** latest year.

Source: *The Packer.* **Price Frequency:** weekly, seasonally. **Effective Market(s):** varies. **Units of Measure:** Dollars per carton. **Type of Price:** price received by farmer. **Time Period Covered:** latest week.

ONIONS: GREEN, CALIFORNIA

Source: *Fresh Fruit and Vegetable Prices.* **Price Frequency:** monthly, seasonally. **Effective Market(s):** Chicago, New York City. **Units of Measure:** Dollars per carton. **Type of Price:** average wholesale price. **Time Period Covered:** latest year.

ONIONS: GREEN, MEXICAN

Source: *Fresh Fruit and Vegetable Prices.* **Price Frequency:** monthly, seasonally. **Effective Market(s):** Chicago, New York City. **Units of Measure:** Dollars per carton. **Type of Price:** average wholesale price. **Time Period Covered:** latest year.

ONIONS: JUMBO

Source: *New Zealand Farmer.* **Price Frequency:** weekly, seasonally. **Effective Market(s):** New Zealand. **Units of Measure:** New Zealand dollars per bag. **Time Period Covered:** latest week.

ONIONS: NO. 1, DRY

Source: *Lancaster Farmer.* **Price Frequency:** weekly, seasonally. **Effective Market(s):** Pennsylvania. **Units of Measure:** Dollars per sack. **Type of Price:** market. **Time Period Covered:** latest week.

ONIONS: PICKLING

Source: *New Zealand Farmer.* **Price Frequency:** weekly, seasonally. **Effective Market(s):** New Zealand. **Units of Measure:** New Zealand dollars per bag. **Time Period Covered:** latest week.

ONIONS: RED

Source: *The Packer.* **Price Frequency:** weekly, seasonally. **Effective Market(s):** varies. **Units of Measure:** Dollars per Sack. **Type of Price:** price received by farmer. **Time Period Covered:** latest week.

ONIONS: RED, DRY

Source: *California Farmer.* **Price Frequency:** semimonthly, seasonally. **Effective Market(s):** Central San Joaquin Valley. **Units of Measure:** Dollars per 40 lb. carton. **Time Period Covered:** latest week, month ago, year ago.

Source: *California Farmer.* **Price Frequency:** semimonthly, seasonally. **Effective Market(s):** Imperial Valley. **Units of Measure:** Dollars per 50 lb. carton. **Time Period Covered:** latest week, month ago, year ago.

Source: *Lancaster Farmer.* **Price Frequency:** weekly, seasonally. **Effective Market(s):** Pennsylvania. **Units of Measure:** Dollars per sack. **Type of Price:** market. **Time Period Covered:** latest week.

ONIONS: RED, FRESH

Source: *HRI-Buyers Guide.* **Price Frequency:** weekly. **Effective Market(s):** Northeastern area. **Units of Measure:** Dollars per sack. **Type of Price:** prices paid by dining places & institutions. **Time Period Covered:** latest week.

ONIONS: RED GLOBE, DRY

Source: *Lancaster Farmer.* **Price Frequency:** weekly, seasonally. **Effective Market(s):** Pennsylvania. **Units of Measure:** Dollars per sack. **Type of Price:** market. **Time Period Covered:** latest week.

ONIONS: SPANISH HYBRID

Source: *The Packer.* **Price Frequency:** weekly, seasonally. **Effective Market(s):** varies. **Units of Measure:** Dollars per sack. **Type of Price:** price received by farmer. **Time Period Covered:** latest week.

ONIONS: SPRING

Source: *Agricultural Prices Annual Summary.* **Price Frequency:** monthly, seasonally. **Effective Market(s):** Arizona, California, Texas, United States. **Units of Measure:** Dollars per 100 lbs. **Type of Price:** received by grower. **Time Period Covered:** latest 3 years, for US latest 6 years.

ONIONS: SUMMER

Source: *Agricultural Prices Annual Summary.* **Price Frequency:** monthly, seasonally. **Effective Market(s):** United States. **Units of Measure:** Dollars per 100 lbs. **Type of Price:** received by grower. **Time Period Covered:** latest 6 years.

ONIONS: SUMMER, NON-STORAGE

Source: *Agricultural Prices Annual Summary.* **Price Frequency:** monthly, seasonally. **Effective Market(s):** 11 domestic markets, United States. **Units of Measure:** Dollars per 100 lbs. **Type of Price:** received by grower. **Time Period Covered:** latest 3 years, for US latest 6 years.

ONIONS: SUMMER, STORAGE

Source: *Agricultural Prices Annual Summary.* **Price Frequency:** monthly, seasonally. **Effective Market(s):** New Mexico, Texas, Washington, United States. **Units of Measure:** Dollars per 100 lbs. **Type of Price:** received by grower. **Time Period Covered:** latest 3 years, for US latest 6 years.

ONIONS: TABLE

Source: *New Zealand Farmer.* **Price Frequency:** weekly, seasonally. **Effective Market(s):** New Zealand. **Units of Measure:** New Zealand dollars per bag. **Time Period Covered:** latest week.

ONIONS: WHITE

Source: *The Packer.* **Price Frequency:** weekly, seasonally. **Effective Market(s):** varies. **Units of Measure:** Dollars per sack. **Type of Price:** price received by farmer. **Time Period Covered:** latest week.

ONIONS: WHITE, DRY

Source: *California Farmer.* **Price Frequency:** semimonthly, seasonally. **Effective Market(s):** Imperial Valley, Northern San Joaquin Valley. **Units of Measure:** Dollars per 50 lb. sack. **Time Period Covered:** latest week, month ago, year ago.

Source: *Fresh Fruit and Vegetable Prices.* **Price Frequency:** monthly, seasonally. **Effective Market(s):** Hereford/High Plains District (TX), Lower Rio Grande Valley (TX), Western Idaho/Malheur County (OR). **Units of Measure:** Dollars per sack. **Type of Price:** average price at shipping point. **Time Period Covered:** latest year.

Source: *Lancaster Farmer.* **Price Frequency:** weekly, seasonally. **Effective Market(s):** Pennsylvania. **Units of Measure:** Dollars per sack. **Type of Price:** market. **Time Period Covered:** latest week.

ONIONS: WHITE, DRY, MEXICAN

Source: *Fresh Fruit and Vegetable Prices.* **Price Frequency:** monthly, seasonally. **Effective Market(s):** South Texas. **Units of Measure:** Dollars per sack. **Type of Price:** price paid at point of entry. **Time Period Covered:** latest year.

ONIONS: WHITE, FRESH

Source: *HRI-Buyers Guide.* **Price Frequency:** weekly. **Effective Market(s):** Northeastern area. **Units of Measure:** Dollars per sack. **Type of Price:** prices paid by dining places & institutions. **Time Period Covered:** latest week.

ONIONS: YELLOW

Source: *California Farmer.* **Price Frequency:** semimonthly, seasonally. **Effective Market(s):** Gilroy/Hollister (CA). **Units of Measure:** Dollars per 50 lb. sack. **Time Period Covered:** latest week, month ago, year ago.

Source: *The Packer.* **Price Frequency:** weekly, seasonally. **Effective Market(s):** varies. **Units of Measure:** Dollars per sack. **Type of Price:** price received by farmer. **Time Period Covered:** latest week.

ONIONS: YELLOW COLOSSAL

Source: *The Packer.* **Price Frequency:** weekly, seasonally. **Effective Market(s):** varies. **Units of Measure:** Dollars per sack. **Type of Price:** price received by farmer. **Time Period Covered:** latest week.

ONIONS: YELLOW, DRY

Source: *California Farmer.* **Price Frequency:** semimonthly, seasonally. **Effective Market(s):** Central/Northern San Joaquin Valley. **Units of Measure:** Dollars per 50 lb. sack. **Time Period Covered:** latest week, month ago, year ago.

Source: *Fresh Fruit and Vegetable Prices.* **Price Frequency:** monthly, seasonally. **Effective Market(s):** Columbia Basin (WA)/Walla Walla District. **Units of Measure:** Dollars per sack. **Type of Price:** average price at shipping point. **Time Period Covered:** latest year.

Source: *Lancaster Farmer.* **Price Frequency:** weekly, seasonally. **Effective Market(s):** Pennsylvania. **Units of Measure:** Dollars per . **Type of Price:** market. **Time Period Covered:** latest week.

ONIONS: YELLOW, DRY, MICHIGAN

Source: *Fresh Fruit and Vegetable Prices.* **Price Frequency:** monthly, seasonally. **Effective Market(s):** Chicago. **Units of Measure:** Dollars per sack. **Type of Price:** average wholesale price. **Time Period Covered:** latest year.

Source: *Vegetable and Specialties Situation and Outlook Report.* **Price Frequency:** monthly. **Effective Market(s):** North Central. **Units of Measure:** cents per lb. **Type of Price:** retail. **Time Period Covered:** latest month, year ago.

ONIONS: YELLOW, DRY, NEW YORK

Source: *Vegetable and Specialties Situation and Outlook Report.* **Price Frequency:** monthly. **Effective Market(s):** Northeast. **Units of Measure:** cents per lb. **Type of Price:** retail. **Time Period Covered:** latest month, year ago.

ONIONS: YELLOW, DRY, ORANGE COUNTY

Source: *Fresh Fruit and Vegetable Prices.* **Price Frequency:** monthly, seasonally. **Effective Market(s):** New York City. **Units of Measure:** Dollars per sack. **Type of Price:** average wholesale price. **Time Period Covered:** latest year.

ONIONS: YELLOW GLOBE, DRY

Source: *Fresh Fruit and Vegetable Prices.* **Price Frequency:** monthly, seasonally. **Effective Market(s):** Central/Western New York, Michigan, Orange County (NY). **Units of Measure:** Dollars per sack. **Type of Price:** average price at shipping point. **Time Period Covered:** latest year.

ONIONS: YELLOW GRANEX, DRY

Source: *Fresh Fruit and Vegetable Prices.* **Price Frequency:** monthly, seasonally. **Effective Market(s):** Central Arizona, Lower Rio Grande Valley (TX), Southern New Mexico, Vidalia District (GA). **Units of Measure:** Dollars per sack. **Type of Price:** average price at shipping point. **Time Period Covered:** latest year.

ONIONS: YELLOW GRANO

Source: *The Packer.* **Price Frequency:** weekly, seasonally. **Effective Market(s):** varies. **Units of Measure:** Dollars per sack. **Type of Price:** price received by farmer. **Time Period Covered:** latest week.

ONIONS: YELLOW GRANO, DRY

Source: *California Farmer.* **Price Frequency:** semimonthly, seasonally. **Effective Market(s):** Imperial Valley, Kern District (CA). **Units of Measure:** Dollars per 50 lb. sack. **Time Period Covered:** latest week, month ago, year ago.

Source: *Fresh Fruit and Vegetable Prices.* **Price Frequency:** monthly, seasonally. **Effective Market(s):** 7 domestic markets. **Units of Measure:** Dollars per sack. **Type of Price:** average price at shipping point. **Time Period Covered:** latest year.

ONIONS: YELLOW GRANO, DRY, CALIFORNIA

Source: *Fresh Fruit and Vegetable Prices.* **Price Frequency:** monthly, seasonally. **Effective Market(s):** Chicago, New York City. **Units of Measure:** Dollars per sack. **Type of Price:** average wholesale price. **Time Period Covered:** latest year.

ONIONS: YELLOW GRANO, DRY, MEXICAN

Source: *Fresh Fruit and Vegetable Prices.* **Price Frequency:** monthly, seasonally. **Effective Market(s):** South Texas. **Units of Measure:** Dollars per sack. **Type of Price:** price paid at point of entry. **Time Period Covered:** latest year.

Source: *Fresh Fruit and Vegetable Prices.* **Price Frequency:** monthly, seasonally. **Effective Market(s):** Chicago. **Units of Measure:** Dollars per sack. **Type of Price:** average wholesale price. **Time Period Covered:** latest year.

ONIONS: YELLOW GRANO, DRY, TEXAS

Source: *Fresh Fruit and Vegetable Prices.* **Price Frequency:** monthly, seasonally. **Effective Market(s):** New York City. **Units of Measure:** Dollars per sack. **Type of Price:** average wholesale price. **Time Period Covered:** latest year.

ONIONS: YELLOW GRANO, FRESH

Source: *HRI-Buyers Guide.* **Price Frequency:** weekly. **Effective Market(s):** Northeastern area. **Units of Measure:** Dollars per sack. **Type of Price:** prices paid by dining places & institutions. **Time Period Covered:** latest week.

ONIONS: YELLOW JUMBO

Source: *Oregon Farmer-Stockman.* **Price Frequency:** monthly. **Units of Measure:** Dollars per 50 lbs. **Time Period Covered:** latest month.

ONIONS: YELLOW SPANISH

Source: *The Packer.* **Price Frequency:** weekly, seasonally. **Effective Market(s):** varies. **Units of Measure:** Dollars per sack. **Type of Price:** price received by farmer. **Time Period Covered:** latest week.

ONIONS: YELLOW SPANISH, DRY

Source: *Freshc Fruit and Vegetable Prices.* **Price Frequency:** monthly, seasonally. **Effective Market(s):** North/East Colorado, Western Idaho/Malheur County (OR), Western Slope (CO). **Units of Measure:** Dollars per sack. **Type of Price:** average price at shipping point. **Time Period Covered:** latest year.

ONIONS: YELLOW SPANISH, DRY, IDAHO/ OREGON

Source: *Fresh Fruit and Vegetable Price.* **Price Frequency:** monthly, seasonally. **Effective Market(s):** Chicago, New York City. **Units of Measure:** Dollars per sack. **Type of Price:** average wholesale price. **Time Period Covered:** latest year.

ONO (FISH)

see Mackerel: King.

OPAH (FISH)

see Moonfish.

OPAKAPAKA (FISH)

see Snapper: Pink.

OPIUM POWDER: GRANULAR, USP

Source: *Chemical Marketing Reporter.* **Price Frequency:** weekly. **Effective Market(s):** New York. **Units of Measure:** Dollars per kilo. **Type of Price:** spot. **Time Period Covered:** latest week.

OPIUM POWDER: USP

Source: *Journal of Commerce and Commercial.* **Price Frequency:** weekly in Friday issue. **Units of Measure:** Dollars per kilo. **Type of Price:** spot. **Time Period Covered:** latest week.

ORANGE CONCENTRATE

Source: *Commodity Year Book.* **Price Frequency:** monthly, annually. **Units of Measure:** index. **Type of Price:** price index. **Time Period Covered:** latest 7 years.

ORANGE CONCENTRATE: FROZEN

Source: *Dairy Foods.* **Price Frequency:** monthly. **Effective Market(s):** New York. **Units of Measure:** Dollars per lb. **Time Period Covered:** latest month.

ORANGE FLOWER OIL

Source: *U. S. Essential Oil Trade.* **Price Frequency:** annually. **Effective Market(s):** United States. **Units of Measure:** Dollars per kilogram. **Type of Price:** import value. **Time Period Covered:** latest 3 years.

ORANGE JUICE: FUTURES

Source: *Asian Wall Street Journal.* **Price Frequency:** daily. **Effective Market(s):** New York. **Units of Measure:** cents per lb. **Type of Price:** futures. **Time Period Covered:** latest day.

Source: *Barron's.* **Price Frequency:** weekly. **Effective Market(s):** New York. **Units of Measure:** cents per lb. **Type of Price:** futures. **Time Period Covered:** latest week.

Source: *Financial Times.* **Price Frequency:** daily. **Effective Market(s):** New York. **Units of Measure:** cents per lb. **Type of Price:** futures. **Time Period Covered:** latest day.

Source: *Investor's Daily.* **Price Frequency:** daily. **Effective Market(s):** New York. **Units of Measure:** cents per lb. **Type of Price:** futures. **Time Period Covered:** latest day.

Source: *Los Angeles Times.* **Price Frequency:** daily. **Effective Market(s):** New York. **Units of Measure:** cents per lb. **Type of Price:** futures. **Time Period Covered:** latest day.

Source: *New York Times.* **Price Frequency:** daily. **Effective Market(s):** New York. **Units of Measure:** cents per lb. **Type of Price:** futures. **Time Period Covered:** latest day.

Source: *Wall Street Journal.* **Price Frequency:** daily. **Effective Market(s):** New York. **Units of Measure:** cents per lb. **Type of Price:** futures. **Time Period Covered:** latest day.

ORANGE JUICE: FUTURES, MAY

Source: *Commodity Year Book.* **Price Frequency:** monthly. **Effective Market(s):** New York. **Units of Measure:** cents per lb. **Type of Price:** futures. **Time Period Covered:** latest 5 years.

ORANGE OIL

Source: *U. S. Essential Oil Trade.* **Price Frequency:** annually. **Effective Market(s):** United States. **Units of Measure:** Dollars per kilogram. **Type of Price:** import value. **Time Period Covered:** latest 3 years.

ORANGE OIL: BITTER

Source: *Journal of Commerce and Commercial.* **Price Frequency:** weekly in Tuesday issue. **Units of Measure:** Dollars per lb. **Type of Price:** spot. **Time Period Covered:** latest week.

ORANGE OIL: BITTER, X, NF, WEST INDIAN

Source: *Chemical Marketing Reporter.* **Price Frequency:** weekly. **Effective Market(s):** New York. **Units of Measure:** Dollars per lb. **Type of Price:** spot. **Time Period Covered:** latest week.

ORANGE OIL: BRAZILIAN

Source: *Chemical Marketing Reporter.* **Price Frequency:** weekly. **Effective Market(s):** New York. **Units of Measure:** Dollars per lb. **Type of Price:** spot. **Time Period Covered:** latest week.

Source: *Journal of Commerce and Commercial.* **Price Frequency:** weekly in Tuesday issue. **Units of Measure:** Dollars per lb. **Type of Price:** spot. **Time Period Covered:** latest week.

ORANGE OIL: DISTILLED, CALIFORNIAN

Source: *Chemical Marketing Reporter.* **Price Frequency:** weekly. **Effective Market(s):** New York. **Units of Measure:** Dollars per lb. **Type of Price:** spot. **Time Period Covered:** latest week.

ORANGE OIL: EXPRESSED, USP, CALIFORNIA

Source: *Chemical Marketing Reporter.* **Price Frequency:** weekly. **Effective Market(s):** New York. **Units of Measure:** Dollars per lb. **Type of Price:** spot. **Time Period Covered:** latest week.

ORANGE OIL: FLORIDA

Source: *Chemical Marketing Reporter.* **Price Frequency:** weekly. **Effective Market(s):** New York. **Units of Measure:** Dollars per lb. **Type of Price:** spot. **Time Period Covered:** latest week.

ORANGE OIL: SWEET

Source: *Journal of Commerce and Commercial.* **Price Frequency:** weekly in Tuesday issue. **Units of Measure:** Dollars per lb. **Type of Price:** spot. **Time Period Covered:** latest week.

ORANGE OIL: VALENCIA, EXPRESSED

Source: *Chemical Marketing Reporter.* **Price Frequency:** weekly. **Effective Market(s):** New York. **Units of Measure:** Dollars per lb. **Type of Price:** spot. **Time Period Covered:** latest week.

ORANGE PEEL: BITTER, HAITIAN

Source: *Chemical Marketing Reporter.* **Price Frequency:** weekly. **Effective Market(s):** New York. **Units of Measure:** Dollars per lb. **Type of Price:** spot. **Time Period Covered:** latest week.

ORANGE ROUGHY: FILLETS, SKINLESS, BONELESS, FROZEN, AUSTRALIA AND NEW Zealand

Source: *Seafood Price-Current.* **Price Frequency:** semiweekly. **Effective Market(s):** Mid-Atlantic. **Units of Measure:** Dollars per lb. **Type of Price:** first receiver. **Time Period Covered:** latest day.

ORANGES

Source: *Agricultural Outlook.* **Price Frequency:** monthly. **Units of Measure:** Dollars per box. **Type of Price:** shipping point. **Time Period Covered:** latest year.

Source: *Agricultural Prices.* **Price Frequency:** monthly. **Effective Market(s):** United States. **Units of Measure:** Dollars per box. **Type of Price:** received by farmer. **Time Period Covered:** latest 2 months, year ago.

Source: *New Zealand Farmer.* **Price Frequency:** weekly, seasonally. **Effective Market(s):** New Zealand. **Units of Measure:** New Zealand dollars per bushel/carton. **Time Period Covered:** latest week.

ORANGES: ALL USES

Source: *Agricultural Outlook.* **Price Frequency:** monthly, annually. **Effective Market(s):** United States. **Units of Measure:** Dollars per box. **Type of Price:** average received by farmer. **Time Period Covered:** monthly latest 6 months, annually latest 3 years.

ORANGES: CALIFORNIA

Source: *Commodity Year Book.* **Price Frequency:** monthly, annually. **Units of Measure:** Dollars per box. **Type of Price:** wholesale. **Time Period Covered:** latest 7 years.

Source: *Japan Economic Journal.* **Price Frequency:** weekly. **Effective Market(s):** Japan. **Units of Measure:** Japanese yen per carton. **Type of Price:** wholesale. **Time Period Covered:** latest 2 weeks.

ORANGES: EARLY AND MIDSEASONS

Source: *Agricultural Prices.* **Price Frequency:** monthly. **Effective Market(s):** Texas. **Units of Measure:** Dollars per box. **Type of Price:** received by farmer. **Time Period Covered:** latest month.

Source: *Fresh Fruit and Vegetable Prices.* **Price Frequency:** monthly, seasonally. **Effective Market(s):** Lower Rio Grande Valley (TX). **Units of Measure:** Dollars per carton. **Type of Price:** average price at shipping point. **Time Period Covered:** latest year.

ORANGES: EARLY AND MIDSEASONS, FRESH

Source: *Agricultural Prices Annual Summary.* **Price Frequency:** monthly, annually. **Effective Market(s):** Florida, Texas, United States. **Units of Measure:** Dollars per box. **Type of Price:** received by grower. **Time Period Covered:** latest 2 years.

ORANGES: EARLY AND MIDSEASONS, PROCESSING

Source: *Agricultural Prices Annual Summary.* **Price Frequency:** annually. **Effective Market(s):** Florida, Texas, United States. **Units of Measure:** Dollars per box. **Type of Price:** received by grower. **Time Period Covered:** latest 2 years.

ORANGES: FLORIDA

Source: *Fresh Fruit and Vegetable Prices.* **Price Frequency:** monthly, seasonally. **Effective Market(s):** Chicago, New York City. **Units of Measure:** Dollars per carton. **Type of Price:** average wholesale price. **Time Period Covered:** latest year.

ORANGES: FRESH

Source: *Agricultural Prices Annual Summary.* **Price Frequency:** monthly, annually. **Effective Market(s):** Arizona, California, Florida, Texas, United States. **Units of Measure:** Dollars per box. **Type of Price:** received by grower. **Time Period Covered:** latest 2 years.

ORANGES: MIKKAN

Source: *FAO Quarterly Bulletin of Statistics.* **Price Frequency:** monthly, annually. **Effective Market(s):** Japan. **Units of Measure:** Japanese yen per kilogram, dollars per metric ton. **Type of Price:** wholesale. **Time Period Covered:** latest 3 years.

ORANGES: NAVEL

Source: *California Farmer.* **Price Frequency:** semimonthly, seasonally. **Effective Market(s):** Central California. **Units of Measure:** Dollars per 40 lb. carton. **Time Period Covered:** latest week, month ago, year ago.

Source: *Fresh Fruit and Vegetable Prices.* **Price Frequency:** monthly, seasonally. **Effective Market(s):** Arizona/California. **Units of Measure:** Dollars per carton. **Type of Price:** average price at shipping point. **Time Period Covered:** latest year.

Source: *Fruit and Tree Nuts Situation and Outlook Yearbook.* **Price Frequency:** annually. **Effective Market(s):** United States. **Units of Measure:** Dollars per lb. **Type of Price:** retail. **Time Period Covered:** latest 9 years.

ORANGES: NAVEL AND MISCELLANEOUS, FRESH

Source: *Agricultural Prices Annual Summary.* **Price Frequency:** monthly, annually. **Effective Market(s):** Arizona, California. **Units of Measure:** Dollars per box. **Type of Price:** received by grower. **Time Period Covered:** latest 2 years.

ORANGES: NAVEL AND MISCELLANEOUS, PROCESSING

Source: *Agricultural Prices Annual Summary.* **Price Frequency:** annually. **Effective Market(s):** Arizona, California. **Units of Measure:** Dollars per box. **Type of Price:** received by grower. **Time Period Covered:** latest 2 years.

ORANGES: NAVEL, CALIFORNIA

Source: *Fresh Fruit and Vegetable Prices.* **Price Frequency:** monthly, seasonally. **Effective Market(s):** Chicago, New York City. **Units of Measure:** Dollars per carton. **Type of Price:** average wholesale price. **Time Period Covered:** latest year.

ORANGES: POPE SUMMER

Source: *Lancaster Farmer.* **Price Frequency:** weekly, seasonally. **Effective Market(s):** Pennsylvania. **Units of Measure:** Dollars per carton. **Type of Price:** market. **Time Period Covered:** latest week.

ORANGES: SPANISH

Source: *FAO Quarterly Bulletin of Statistics.* **Price Frequency:** monthly, annually. **Effective Market(s):** West Germany. **Units of Measure:** West German marks per 100 kilograms, dollars per metric ton. **Type of Price:** wholesale. **Time Period Covered:** latest 3 years.

ORANGES: TEMPLE

Source: *Agricultural Prices.* **Price Frequency:** monthly. **Effective Market(s):** United States. **Units of Measure:** Dollars per box. **Type of Price:** received by farmer. **Time Period Covered:** latest 2 months, year ago.

ORANGES: TEMPLE, FRESH

Source: *Agricultural Prices Annual Summary.* **Price Frequency:** monthly, annually, seasonally. **Effective Market(s):** Florida. **Units of Measure:** Dollars per lb. **Type of Price:** received by farmers. **Time Period Covered:** latest 2 years.

ORANGES: TEMPLE, PROCESSING

Source: *Agricultural Prices Annual Summary.* **Price Frequency:** monthly, annually, seasonally. **Effective Market(s):** Florida. **Units of Measure:** Dollars per lb. **Type of Price:** received by farmers. **Time Period Covered:** latest 2 years.

ORANGES: VALENCIA

Source: *Agricultural Prices.* **Price Frequency:** monthly. **Effective Market(s):** California. **Units of Measure:** Dollars per box. **Type of Price:** received by farmer. **Time Period Covered:** latest month.

Source: *California Farmer.* **Price Frequency:** semimonthly, seasonally. **Effective Market(s):** Central District (CA), Coachella Valley (CA), Southern District (CA). **Units of Measure:** Dollars per 40 lb. carton. **Time Period Covered:** latest week, month ago, year ago.

Source: *Fresh Fruit and Vegetable Prices.* **Price Frequency:** monthly, seasonally. **Effective Market(s):** Arizona/California. **Units of Measure:** Dollars per carton. **Type of Price:** average price at shipping point. **Time Period Covered:** latest year.

Source: *Fruit and Tree Nuts Situation and Outlook Yearbook.* **Price Frequency:** annually. **Effective Market(s):** United States. **Units of Measure:** Dollars per lb. **Type of Price:** retail. **Time Period Covered:** latest 9 years.

Source: *The Grower.* **Price Frequency:** monthly, seasonally. **Units of Measure:** Dollars per carton. **Time Period Covered:** latest year, year ago, 2 years ago.

Source: *Lancaster Farmer.* **Price Frequency:** weekly, seasonally. **Effective Market(s):** Pennsylvania. **Units of Measure:** Dollars per carton. **Type of Price:** market. **Time Period Covered:** latest week.

Source: *The Packer.* **Price Frequency:** weekly, seasonally. **Effective Market(s):** varies. **Units of Measure:** Dollars per carton. **Type of Price:** price received by farmer. **Time Period Covered:** latest week.

ORANGES: VALENCIA, CALIFORNIA

Source: *Fresh Fruit and Vegetable Prices.* **Price Frequency:** monthly, seasonally. **Effective Market(s):** Chicago, New York City. **Units of Measure:** Dollars per carton. **Type of Price:** average wholesale price. **Time Period Covered:** latest year.

ORANGES: VALENCIA, FRESH

Source: *Agricultural Prices Annual Summary.* **Price Frequency:** monthly, annually. **Effective Market(s):** Arizona, California, Florida, Texas, United States. **Units of Measure:** Dollars per box. **Type of Price:** received by grower. **Time Period Covered:** latest 2 years.

ORANGES: VALENCIA, PROCESSING

Source: *Agricultural Prices Annual Summary.* **Price Frequency:** annually. **Effective Market(s):** Arizona, California, Florida, Texas, United States. **Units of Measure:** Dollars per box. **Type of Price:** received by grower. **Time Period Covered:** latest 2 years.

ORCHARD GRASS

Source: *Agricultural Prices Annual Summary.* **Price Frequency:** semiannually. **Effective Market(s):** United States. **Units of Measure:** Dollars per 100 lbs. **Type of Price:** paid by farmer. **Time Period Covered:** latest 6 years.

ORCHIDS: ARANDA CHRISTINA, SINGAPORE

Source: *Prices of Selected Asia/Pacific Products.* **Price Frequency:** monthly, seasonally. **Effective Market(s):** Netherlands. **Units of Measure:** Dutch guilders per spike. **Type of Price:** wholesale high, wholesale low. **Time Period Covered:** latest month.

ORCHIDS: ARANDA CHRISTINA, THAI

Source: *Prices of Selected Asia/Pacific Products.* **Price Frequency:** monthly, seasonally. **Effective Market(s):** France. **Units of Measure:** French francs per bouquet. **Type of Price:** wholesale high, wholesale low. **Time Period Covered:** latest month.

ORCHIDS: DENDROBIUM, MEDIUM, THAI

Source: *Prices of Selected Asia/Pacific Products.* **Price Frequency:** monthly, seasonally. **Effective Market(s):** West Germany. **Units of Measure:** West German marks per spike. **Type of Price:** wholesale high, wholesale low. **Time Period Covered:** latest month.

ORCHIDS: DENDROBIUM, POTTED

Source: *Floriculture Crops.* **Price Frequency:** annually. **Effective Market(s):** United States. **Units of Measure:** Dollars per unit. **Type of Price:** commercial wholesale. **Time Period Covered:** latest 2 years.

ORCHIDS: DENDROBIUM SPRAYS, HAWAII

Source: *Floriculture Crops.* **Price Frequency:** annually. **Effective Market(s):** United States. **Units of Measure:** cents per unit. **Type of Price:** commercial wholesale. **Time Period Covered:** latest 2 years.

ORCHIDS: DENDROBIUM, SUPER LONG, THAI

Source: *Prices of Selected Asia/Pacific Products.* **Price Frequency:** monthly, seasonally. **Effective Market(s):** Netherlands. **Units of Measure:** Dutch guilders per spike. **Type of Price:** wholesale high, wholesale low. **Time Period Covered:** latest month.

ORCHIDS: HAWAII

Source: *Floriculture Crops.* **Price Frequency:** annually. **Effective Market(s):** United States. **Units of Measure:** cents per unit. **Type of Price:** commercial wholesale. **Time Period Covered:** latest 2 years.

ORCHIDS: POTTED

Source: *Floriculture Crops.* **Price Frequency:** annually. **Effective Market(s):** United States. **Units of Measure:** Dollars per unit. **Type of Price:** commercial wholesale. **Time Period Covered:** latest 2 years.

OREGANO: GREEK

Source: *Chemical Marketing Reporter.* **Price Frequency:** weekly. **Effective Market(s):** New York. **Units of Measure:** Dollars per lb. **Type of Price:** spot. **Time Period Covered:** latest week.

OREGANO: MEXICAN

Source: *Chemical Marketing Reporter.* **Price Frequency:** weekly. **Effective Market(s):** New York. **Units of Measure:** Dollars per lb. **Type of Price:** spot. **Time Period Covered:** latest week.

OREGANO: TURKISH

Source: *Chemical Marketing Reporter.* **Price Frequency:** weekly. **Effective Market(s):** New York. **Units of Measure:** Dollars per lb. **Type of Price:** spot. **Time Period Covered:** latest week.

ORIGANUM: GREEK

Source: *U. S. Spice Trade.* **Price Frequency:** annually. **Effective Market(s):** New York. **Units of Measure:** cents per lb. **Type of Price:** spot. **Time Period Covered:** latest 3 years.

ORIGANUM: MEXICAN

Source: *U. S. Spice Trade.* **Price Frequency:** annually. **Effective Market(s):** New York. **Units of Measure:** cents per lb. **Type of Price:** spot. **Time Period Covered:** latest 3 years.

ORIGANUM: TURKISH

Source: *U. S. Spice Trade.* **Price Frequency:** annually. **Effective Market(s):** New York. **Units of Measure:** cents per lb. **Type of Price:** spot. **Time Period Covered:** latest 3 years.

ORIGANUM OIL

Source: *Journal of Commerce and Commercial.* **Price Frequency:** weekly in Tuesday issue. **Units of Measure:** Dollars per lb. **Type of Price:** spot. **Time Period Covered:** latest week.

Source: *U. S. Essential Oil Trade.* **Price Frequency:** annually. **Effective Market(s):** United States. **Units of Measure:** Dollars per kilogram. **Type of Price:** import value. **Time Period Covered:** latest 3 years.

ORIGANUM OIL: SPANISH

Source: *Chemical Marketing Reporter.* **Price Frequency:** weekly. **Effective Market(s):** New York. **Units of Measure:** Dollars per kilo. **Type of Price:** spot. **Time Period Covered:** latest week.

ORRIS OIL

Source: *U. S. Essential Oil Trade.* **Price Frequency:** annually. **Effective Market(s):** United States. **Units of Measure:** Dollars per kilogram. **Type of Price:** import value. **Time Period Covered:** latest 3 years.

ORRIS ROOT: FLORENTINE

Source: *Chemical Marketing Reporter.* **Price Frequency:** weekly. **Effective Market(s):** New York. **Units of Measure:** Dollars per lb. **Type of Price:** spot. **Time Period Covered:** latest week.

ORRIS ROOT: POWDERED, FLORENTINE

Source: *Chemical Marketing Reporter.* **Price Frequency:** weekly. **Effective Market(s):** New York. **Units of Measure:** Dollars per lb. **Type of Price:** spot. **Time Period Covered:** latest week.

ORRIS ROOT: POWDERED, VERONA

Source: *Chemical Marketing Reporter.* **Price Frequency:** weekly. **Effective Market(s):** New York. **Units of Measure:** Dollars per lb. **Type of Price:** spot. **Time Period Covered:** latest week.

ORRIS ROOT: VERONA

Source: *Chemical Marketing Reporter.* **Price Frequency:** weekly. **Effective Market(s):** New York. **Units of Measure:** Dollars per lb. **Type of Price:** spot. **Time Period Covered:** latest week.

ORRIS ROOT OIL: FLORENTINE

Source: *Journal of Commerce and Commercial.* **Price Frequency:** weekly in Tuesday issue. **Units of Measure:** Dollars per lb. **Type of Price:** spot. **Time Period Covered:** latest week.

ORRIS ROOT OIL: MORROCAN

Source: *Journal of Commerce and Commercial.* **Price Frequency:** weekly in Tuesday issue. **Units of Measure:** Dollars per lb. **Type of Price:** spot. **Time Period Covered:** latest week.

ORRIS ROOT OIL: VERONA

Source: *Journal of Commerce and Commercial.* **Price Frequency:** weekly in Tuesday issue. **Units of Measure:** Dollars per lb. **Type of Price:** spot. **Time Period Covered:** latest week.

OSNABURGS

Source: *DNR: Daily News Record.* **Price Frequency:** quarterly. **Units of Measure:** Dollars per yard. **Time Period Covered:** latest 3 quarters.

OURICURY WAX: REFINED

see Wax: Ouricury, Refined.

OXALIC ACID

Source: *Chemical Marketing Reporter.* **Price Frequency:** weekly. **Effective Market(s):** New York. **Units of Measure:** Dollars per lb. **Type of Price:** spot. **Time Period Covered:** latest week.

Source: *Journal of Commerce and Commercial.* **Price Frequency:** weekly in Thursday issue. **Units of Measure:** Dollars per lb. **Type of Price:** spot. **Time Period Covered:** latest week.

OXTAILS

Source: *Market Price Report.* **Price Frequency:** weekly. **Units of Measure:** cents per lb. **Type of Price:** price paid to wholesaler. **Time Period Covered:** latest week.

OXTAILS: CUT UP, DISJOINTED

Source: *Meat Price Report.* **Price Frequency:** weekly. **Units of Measure:** cents per lb. **Type of Price:** price paid to wholesaler. **Time Period Covered:** latest week.

OXTAILS: FROZEN

Source: *National Provisioner.* **Price Frequency:** daily. **Effective Market(s):** Midwest River. **Units of Measure:** cents per lb. **Time Period Covered:** latest week.

B-OXYNAPHTHOIC ACID: TECHNICAL

Source: *Chemical Marketing Reporter.* **Price Frequency:** weekly. **Effective Market(s):** New York. **Units of Measure:** Dollars per lb. **Type of Price:** spot. **Time Period Covered:** latest week.

OXYQUINOLINE BASE: PURE

Source: *Chemical Marketing Reporter.* **Price Frequency:** weekly. **Effective Market(s):** New York. **Units of Measure:** Dollars per lb. **Type of Price:** spot. **Time Period Covered:** latest week.

OXYQUINOLINE SULFATE

Source: *Chemical Marketing Reporter.* **Price Frequency:** weekly. **Effective Market(s):** New York. **Units of Measure:** Dollars per lb. **Type of Price:** spot. **Time Period Covered:** latest week.

OYSTERS: BREADED, FROZEN

Source: *HRI-Buyers Guide.* **Price Frequency:** weekly. **Effective Market(s):** New York. **Units of Measure:** Dollars per case. **Type of Price:** prices paid by dining places & institutions. **Time Period Covered:** latest week.

OYSTERS: COUNTS, FRESH, LOUISIANA

Source: *Seafood Price-Current.* **Price Frequency:** semiweekly. **Effective Market(s):** Mid-Atlantic, Maryland/Virginia. **Units of Measure:** Dollars per gallon. **Type of Price:** sale by first receiver. **Time Period Covered:** latest day.

OYSTERS: IN SHELL, FRESH

Source: *HRI-Buyers Guide.* **Price Frequency:** weekly. **Effective Market(s):** New York. **Units of Measure:** Dollars per lb. **Type of Price:** prices paid by dining places & institutions. **Time Period Covered:** latest week.

OYSTERS: IN SHELL, FRESH, LOUISIANA

Source: *Seafood Price-Current.* **Price Frequency:** semiweekly. **Effective Market(s):** Maryland/Virginia. **Units of Measure:** Dollars per bushel. **Type of Price:** sale by first receiver. **Time Period Covered:** latest day.

OYSTERS: SELECT, FRESH

Source: *HRI-Buyers Guide.* **Price Frequency:** weekly. **Effective Market(s):** New York. **Units of Measure:** Dollars per lb. **Type of Price:** prices paid by dining places & institutions. **Time Period Covered:** latest week.

Source: *Seafood Price-Current.* **Price Frequency:** semiweekly. **Effective Market(s):** Gulf/Southeast. **Units of Measure:** Dollars per gallon. **Type of Price:** sale by first receiver. **Time Period Covered:** latest day.

OYSTERS: SELECT, FRESH, LOUISIANA

Source: *Seafood Price-Current.* **Price Frequency:** semiweekly. **Effective Market(s):** Mid-Atlantic, Maryland/Virginia. **Units of Measure:** Dollars per gallon. **Type of Price:** sale by first receiver. **Time Period Covered:** latest day.

OYSTERS: SELECT, FROZEN

Source: *Seafood Price-Current.* **Price Frequency:** semiweekly. **Effective Market(s):** Mid-Atlantic. **Units of Measure:** Dollars per 4 lb. bag. **Type of Price:** first receiver. **Time Period Covered:** latest day.

OYSTERS: STANDARD, FRESH

Source: *Seafood Price-Current.* **Price Frequency:** semiweekly. **Effective Market(s):** Gulf/Southeast. **Units of Measure:** Dollars per gallon. **Type of Price:** sale by first receiver. **Time Period Covered:** latest day.

OYSTERS: STANDARD, FRESH, LOUISIANA

Source: *Seafood Price-Current.* **Price Frequency:** semiweekly. **Effective Market(s):** Mid-Atlantic, Maryland/Virginia. **Units of Measure:** Dollars per gallon. **Type of Price:** sale by first receiver. **Time Period Covered:** latest day.

OYSTERS: STANDARD, FROZEN

Source: *Seafood Price-Current.* **Price Frequency:** semiweekly. **Effective Market(s):** Mid-Atlantic. **Units of Measure:** Dollars per 4 lb. bag. **Type of Price:** first receiver. **Time Period Covered:** latest day.

OYSTERS: X-SELECT, FRESH

Source: *HRI-Buyers Guide.* **Price Frequency:** weekly. **Effective Market(s):** New York. **Units of Measure:** Dollars per lb. **Type of Price:** prices paid by dining places & institutions. **Time Period Covered:** latest week.

Source: *Seafood Price-Current.* **Price Frequency:** semiweekly. **Effective Market(s):** Gulf/Southeast. **Units of Measure:** Dollars per gallon. **Type of Price:** sale by first receiver. **Time Period Covered:** latest day.

OYSTERS: X-SELECT, FRESH, LOUISIANA

Source: *Seafood Price-Current.* **Price Frequency:** semiweekly. **Effective Market(s):** Mid-Atlantic, Maryland/Virginia. **Units of Measure:** Dollars per gallon. **Type of Price:** sale by first receiver. **Time Period Covered:** latest day.

PACKAGING ACCESSORIES

Source: *Pulp & Paper Week.* **Price Frequency:** monthly, irregularly. **Units of Measure:** index. **Type of Price:** price index. **Time Period Covered:** latest 3 months.

PAIL: 12 QUART, METAL, HEAVY GALVANIZED

Source: *Agricultural Prices.* **Price Frequency:** semiannually. **Effective Market(s):** United States. **Units of Measure:** Dollars each. **Type of Price:** paid by farmer. **Time Period Covered:** latest year.

Source: *Agricultural Prices Annual Summary.* **Price Frequency:** quarterly. **Effective Market(s):** United States. **Units of Measure:** Dollars each. **Type of Price:** paid by farmer. **Time Period Covered:** latest 6 years.

PAINT: HOUSE, EXTERIOR

Source: *Agricultural Prices.* **Price Frequency:** quarterly. **Effective Market(s):** United States. **Units of Measure:** Dollars per gallon. **Type of Price:** paid by farmer. **Time Period Covered:** latest 2 quarters, year ago.

Source: *Agricultural Prices Annual Summary.* **Price Frequency:** bimonthly. **Effective Market(s):** United States. **Units of Measure:** Dollars per gallon. **Type of Price:** paid by farmer. **Time Period Covered:** latest 6 years.

PAINT MATERIALS

Source: *Journal of Commerce and Commercial.* **Price Frequency:** weekly in Wednesday issue. **Units of Measure:** Dollars per lb. **Type of Price:** spot. **Time Period Covered:** latest week.

PAKISTAN RUPEES

Source: *Barron's.* **Price Frequency:** weekly. **Effective Market(s):** New York. **Units of Measure:** Pakistani rupees per United States dollar. **Type of Price:** foreign exchange. **Time Period Covered:** latest 2 weeks.

Source: *New York Times.* **Price Frequency:** daily. **Effective Market(s):** United States. **Units of Measure:** Pakistani rupees per United States dollar. **Type of Price:** foreign exchange. **Time Period Covered:** latest 2 days.

PALLADIUM

Source: *American Metal Market.* **Price Frequency:** daily. **Effective Market(s):** London, United States. **Units of Measure:** Dollars per troy ounce. **Type of Price:** merchant, producer. **Time Period Covered:** latest day.

Source: *Chemical Marketing Reporter.* **Price Frequency:** weekly. **Effective Market(s):** New York. **Units of Measure:** Dollars per troy ounce. **Type of Price:** spot. **Time Period Covered:** latest week.

Source: *Commodity Year Book.* **Price Frequency:** monthly, annually. **Effective Market(s):** United States. **Units of Measure:** Dollars per troy ounce. **Type of Price:** dealer. **Time Period Covered:** latest 13 years.

Source: *E&MJ.* **Price Frequency:** monthly. **Effective Market(s):** London, New York. **Units of Measure:** Dollars per troy ounce. **Time Period Covered:** latest month.

Source: *Economic and Energy Indicators.* **Price Frequency:** monthly, quarterly, annually. **Units of Measure:** Dollars per troy ounce. **Time Period Covered:** latest 3 months, quarters, and years.

Source: *Financial Post.* **Price Frequency:** weekly. **Effective Market(s):** Canada. **Units of Measure:** Dollars per troy ounce. **Type of Price:** cash. **Time Period Covered:** latest week.

Source: *Financial Times.* **Price Frequency:** daily. **Effective Market(s):** London. **Units of Measure:** Dollars per troy ounce. **Type of Price:** spot. **Time Period Covered:** latest day.

Source: *Iron Age.* **Price Frequency:** monthly. **Units of Measure:** Dollars per troy ounce. **Type of Price:** consumer. **Time Period Covered:** latest month.

Source: *Northern Miner.* **Price Frequency:** daily. **Units of Measure:** Dollars per ounce. **Type of Price:** spot. **Time Period Covered:** latest week.

Source: *Northern Miner.* **Price Frequency:** daily. **Effective Market(s):** New York. **Units of Measure:** Dollars per ounce. **Type of Price:** dealer. **Time Period Covered:** latest day.

Source: *Purchasing.* **Price Frequency:** quarterly in January, April, July, October issues. **Units of Measure:** Dollars per troy ounce. **Type of Price:** transaction. **Time Period Covered:** latest 5 quarters.

PALLADIUM: FABRICATED PRODUCTS

Source: *American Metal Market.* **Price Frequency:** daily. **Effective Market(s):** United States. **Units of Measure:** Dollars per troy ounce. **Type of Price:** producer. **Time Period Covered:** latest day.

Source: *Asian Wall Street Journal.* **Price Frequency:** daily. **Effective Market(s):** New York. **Units of Measure:** Dollars per troy ounce. **Type of Price:** cash. **Time Period Covered:** latest 2 days.

Source: *Wall Street Journal.* **Price Frequency:** daily. **Units of Measure:** Dollars per troy ounce. **Time Period Covered:** latest day, day ago, year ago.

PALLADIUM: FUTURES

Source: *American Metal Market.* **Price Frequency:** daily. **Effective Market(s):** New York. **Units of Measure:** Dollars per troy ounce. **Type of Price:** futures. **Time Period Covered:** latest day.

Source: *Asian Wall Street Journal.* **Price Frequency:** daily. **Effective Market(s):** New York. **Units of Measure:** Dollars per troy ounce. **Type of Price:** futures. **Time Period Covered:** latest day.

Source: *Barron's.* **Price Frequency:** weekly. **Effective Market(s):** New York. **Units of Measure:** Dollars per troy ounce. **Type of Price:** futures. **Time Period Covered:** latest week.

Source: *Investor's Daily.* **Price Frequency:** daily. **Effective Market(s):** New York. **Units of Measure:** Dollars per troy ounce. **Type of Price:** futures. **Time Period Covered:** latest day.

Source: *Los Angeles Times.* **Price Frequency:** daily. **Effective Market(s):** New York. **Units of Measure:** Dollars per troy ounce. **Type of Price:** futures. **Time Period Covered:** latest day.

Source: *New York Times.* **Price Frequency:** daily. **Effective Market(s):** New York. **Units of Measure:** Dollars per troy ounce. **Type of Price:** futures. **Time Period Covered:** latest day.

Source: *Wall Street Journal.* **Price Frequency:** daily. **Effective Market(s):** New York. **Units of Measure:** Dollars per troy ounce. **Type of Price:** futures. **Time Period Covered:** latest day.

PALLADIUM: INDUSTRIAL

Source: *Asian Wall Street Journal.* **Price Frequency:** daily. **Effective Market(s):** New York. **Units of Measure:** Dollars per troy ounce. **Type of Price:** cash. **Time Period Covered:** latest 2 days.

Source: *Wall Street Journal.* **Price Frequency:** daily. **Units of Measure:** Dollars per troy ounce. **Time Period Covered:** latest day, day ago, year ago.

PALM EXPELLER PELLETS

Source: *Agra Europe.* **Price Frequency:** weekly, irregularly. **Effective Market(s):** Rotterdam. **Units of Measure:** Dollars per tonne. **Time Period Covered:** latest week.

PALM KERNEL MEAL

Source: *Farmers Weekly.* **Price Frequency:** weekly, seasonally. **Effective Market(s):** Great Britain. **Units of Measure:** British pounds per tonne. **Type of Price:** spot. **Time Period Covered:** latest week.

PALM KERNEL OIL

Source: *Chemical Marketing Reporter.* **Price Frequency:** weekly. **Effective Market(s):** United States ports. **Units of Measure:** Dollars per lb. **Type of Price:** spot. **Time Period Covered:** latest week.

Source: *Milling & Baking News.* **Price Frequency:** weekly. **Effective Market(s):** United States ports. **Units of Measure:** cents per lb. **Type of Price:** spot bulk. **Time Period Covered:** latest week.

PALM KERNEL OIL: 18%, MALAYSIAN

Source: *Oil World.* **Price Frequency:** weekly, monthly, annually. **Units of Measure:** Dollars per tonne. **Type of Price:** lowest representative asking. **Time Period Covered:** weekly latest 3 weeks, monthly latest 2 months, annually latest 2 years.

PALM KERNEL OIL: MALAYSIAN

Source: *Fruit and Tropical Products.* **Price Frequency:** monthly, annually. **Effective Market(s):** Rotterdam. **Units of Measure:** Dollars per tonne. **Type of Price:** average. **Time Period Covered:** monthly latest year, annually latest 2 years.

Source: *Monthly Commodity Price Bulletin.* **Price Frequency:** monthly, annually. **Effective Market(s):** Rotterdam. **Units of Measure:** Dollars per metric ton. **Time Period Covered:** latest 5 years.

Source: *Monthly Commodity Price Bulletin Supplement.* **Price Frequency:** monthly, quarterly, annually. **Effective Market(s):** Rotterdam. **Units of Measure:** Dollars per tonne. **Time Period Covered:** latest 20 years.

Source: *Oil World.* **Price Frequency:** weekly, monthly, annually. **Effective Market(s):** Rotterdam. **Units of Measure:** Dollars per tonne. **Type of Price:** lowest representative asking. **Time Period Covered:** weekly latest 3 weeks, monthly latest 2 months, annually latest 2 years.

Source: *UNCTAD Commodity Yearbook.* **Price Frequency:** annually. **Effective Market(s):** Rotterdam. **Units of Measure:** Dollars per metric ton. **Type of Price:** free market. **Time Period Covered:** latest 12 years.

PALM KERNELS: NIGERIAN

Source: *Commodity Trade and Price Trends.* **Price Frequency:** annually. **Effective Market(s):** European ports. **Units of Measure:** Dollars per metric ton, 1980 constant dollars per metric ton. **Time Period Covered:** latest 37 years.

Source: *Fruit and Tropical Products.* **Price Frequency:** monthly, annually. **Effective Market(s):** European ports. **Units of Measure:** Dollars per tonne. **Type of Price:** average. **Time Period Covered:** monthly latest year, annually latest 2 years.

Source: *International Financial Statistics.* **Price Frequency:** monthly, quarterly, annually. **Effective Market(s):** Europe. **Units of Measure:** Dollars per metric ton, index. **Type of Price:** market price, price index. **Time Period Covered:** latest 5 months, latest 4 quarters, latest 4 years.

Source: *International Financial Statistics Yearbook.* **Price Frequency:** annually. **Effective Market(s):** Europe. **Units of Measure:** Dollars per metric ton. **Type of Price:** wholesale. **Time Period Covered:** latest 30 years.

Source: *Monthly Commodity Price Bulletin.* **Price Frequency:** monthly, annually. **Effective Market(s):** European ports. **Units of Measure:** Dollars per metric ton. **Time Period Covered:** latest 5 years.

Source: *Monthly Commodity Price Bulletin Supplement.* **Price Frequency:** monthly, quarterly, annually. **Effective Market(s):** European ports. **Units of Measure:** Dollars per tonne. **Time Period Covered:** latest 20 years.

Source: *Oil World.* **Price Frequency:** weekly, monthly, annually. **Effective Market(s):** United Kingdom. **Units of Measure:** Dollars per tonne. **Type of Price:** lowest representative asking. **Time Period Covered:** weekly latest 3 weeks, monthly latest 2 months, annually latest 2 years.

Source: *UNCTAD Commodity Yearbook.* **Price Frequency:** annually. **Effective Market(s):** European ports. **Units of Measure:** Dollars per metric ton. **Type of Price:** free market. **Time Period Covered:** latest 12 years.

PALM OIL

Source: *Commodity Year Book.* **Price Frequency:** monthly, annually. **Effective Market(s):** United States. **Units of Measure:** cents per lb. **Type of Price:** wholesale. **Time Period Covered:** latest 5 years.

Source: *Economic and Energy Indicators.* **Price Frequency:** monthly, quarterly, annually. **Units of Measure:** Dollars per metric ton. **Time Period Covered:** latest 3 months, quarters, and years.

Source: *Far Eastern Economic Review.* **Price Frequency:** weekly. **Effective Market(s):** Kuala Lumpur. **Units of Measure:** Malaysian dollars per tonne. **Time Period Covered:** latest week, week ago, 3 months ago, year ago.

Source: *Milling & Baking News.* **Price Frequency:** weekly. **Effective Market(s):** United States ports. **Units of Measure:** cents per lb. **Type of Price:** spot bulk. **Time Period Covered:** latest week.

Source: *National Provisioner.* **Price Frequency:** weekly. **Effective Market(s):** Pacific Coast. **Units of Measure:** cents per lb. **Time Period Covered:** latest week.

Source: *Oil Crops Situation and Outlook.* **Price Frequency:** monthly. **Effective Market(s):** United States ports. **Units of Measure:** cents per lb. **Type of Price:** wholesale. **Time Period Covered:** latest 5 months.

Source: *Oil World.* **Price Frequency:** weekly, monthly, annually. **Effective Market(s):** West Coast. **Units of Measure:** Dollars per tonne. **Type of Price:** lowest representative asking. **Time Period Covered:** weekly latest 3 weeks, monthly latest 2 months, annually latest 2 years.

Source: *Prices of Selected Asia/Pacific Products.* **Price Frequency:** monthly. **Effective Market(s):** Tokyo. **Units of Measure:** Japanese yen per kilogram. **Type of Price:** high, low. **Time Period Covered:** latest month.

Source: *World Oilseed Situation and Market Highlights.* **Price Frequency:** monthly, annually. **Effective Market(s):** Malaysia, United States. **Units of Measure:** Dollars per metric ton. **Time Period Covered:** monthly latest 2 months, annually latest 2 years.

PALM OIL: 5%, MALAYSIAN

Source: *Fruit and Tropical Products.* **Price Frequency:** monthly, annually. **Effective Market(s):** European ports. **Units of Measure:** Dollars per tonne. **Type of Price:** average. **Time Period Covered:** monthly latest year, annually latest 2 years.

Source: *Monthly Commodity Price Bulletin.* **Price Frequency:** monthly, annually. **Effective Market(s):** European ports. **Units of Measure:** Dollars per metric ton. **Time Period Covered:** latest 5 years.

Source: *Monthly Commodity Price Bulletin Supplement.* **Price Frequency:** monthly, quarterly, annually. **Effective Market(s):** European ports. **Units of Measure:** Dollars per tonne. **Time Period Covered:** latest 20 years.

Source: *UNCTAD Commodity Yearbook.* **Price Frequency:** annually. **Effective Market(s):** European ports. **Units of Measure:** Dollars per metric ton. **Type of Price:** free market. **Time Period Covered:** latest 12 years.

PALM OIL: 5%, SUMATRA/MALAYSIAN

Source: *FAO Quarterly Bulletin of Statistics.* **Price Frequency:** monthly, annually. **Effective Market(s):** North Sea ports. **Units of Measure:** Dollars per 1000 kilograms, dollars per metric ton. **Time Period Covered:** latest 3 years.

PALM OIL: CRUDE

Source: *Chemical Marketing Reporter.* **Price Frequency:** weekly. **Effective Market(s):** New York. **Units of Measure:** cents per lb. **Type of Price:** spot. **Time Period Covered:** latest week.

Source: *Prices of Selected Asia/Pacific Products.* **Price Frequency:** monthly. **Effective Market(s):** Liverpool, New York. **Units of Measure:** Dollars per lb., British pounds per metric ton. **Type of Price:** spot high, spot low. **Time Period Covered:** latest month.

PALM OIL: CRUDE, 5%, SUMATRA/ MALAYSIAN

Source: *Prices of Selected Asia/Pacific Products.* **Price Frequency:** monthly. **Effective Market(s):** North European ports. **Units of Measure:** Dollars per metric ton. **Type of Price:** high, low. **Time Period Covered:** latest month.

PALM OIL: CRUDE, THAI

Source: *Prices of Selected Asia/Pacific Products.* **Price Frequency:** monthly. **Effective Market(s):** Bangkok. **Units of Measure:** Thai baht per kilogram. **Type of Price:** wholesale high, wholesale low. **Time Period Covered:** latest month.

PALM OIL: EDIBLE, MALAYSIAN

Source: *Commodity Trade and Price Trends.* **Price Frequency:** annually. **Effective Market(s):** European ports. **Units of Measure:** Dollars per metric ton, 1980 constant dollars per metric ton. **Time Period Covered:** latest 37 years.

PALM OIL: FUTURES

Source: *Asian Wall Street Journal.* **Price Frequency:** daily. **Effective Market(s):** Kuala Lumpur. **Units of Measure:** Malaysian dollars per metric ton. **Type of Price:** futures. **Time Period Covered:** latest day.

Source: *Far Eastern Economic Review.* **Price Frequency:** weekly. **Effective Market(s):** Kuala Lumpur. **Units of Measure:** Malaysian dollars per tonne. **Type of Price:** futures. **Time Period Covered:** latest week.

PALM OIL: MALAYSIAN

Source: *Financial Times.* **Price Frequency:** daily. **Effective Market(s):** Rotterdam. **Units of Measure:** Dollars per metric ton. **Type of Price:** spot. **Time Period Covered:** latest day.

Source: *International Financial Statistics.* **Price Frequency:** monthly, quarterly, annually. **Effective Market(s):** Northwest Europe. **Units of Measure:** Dollars per metric ton, index. **Type of Price:** market price, price index. **Time Period Covered:** latest 5 months, latest 5 quarters, latest 5 years.

Source: *International Financial Statistics.* **Price Frequency:** monthly, quarterly, annually. **Effective Market(s):** Malaysia. **Units of Measure:** Dollars per metric ton, index. **Type of Price:** market price, price index. **Time Period Covered:** latest 2 months, latest 4 quarters, latest 5 years.

Source: *International Financial Statistics Yearbook.* **Price Frequency:** annually. **Effective Market(s):** Europe, Malaysia. **Units of Measure:** Dollars per metric ton. **Type of Price:** wholesale. **Time Period Covered:** latest 30 years.

Source: *Oil World.* **Price Frequency:** weekly, monthly, annually. **Effective Market(s):** Malaysia. **Units of Measure:** Dollars per tonne. **Type of Price:** lowest representative asking. **Time Period Covered:** weekly latest 3 weeks, monthly latest 2 months, annually latest 2 years.

Source: *World Oilseed Situation and Market Highlights.* **Price Frequency:** monthly, annually. **Effective Market(s):** Malaysia. **Units of Measure:** Dollars per metric ton. **Time Period Covered:** monthly latest year, annually latest 9 years.

PALM OIL: REFINED

Source: *Wall Street Journal.* **Price Frequency:** daily. **Effective Market(s):** New Orleans. **Units of Measure:** Dollars per lb. **Time Period Covered:** latest day, day ago, year ago.

PALM OIL: REFINED, BLEACHED

Source: *Asian Wall Street Journal.* **Price Frequency:** daily. **Effective Market(s):** New Orleans. **Units of Measure:** Dollars per lb. **Type of Price:** cash. **Time Period Covered:** latest 2 days, year ago.

PALM OIL: REFINED, THAI

Source: *Prices of Selected Asia/Pacific Products.* **Price Frequency:** monthly. **Effective Market(s):** Bangkok. **Units of Measure:** Thai baht per kilogram. **Type of Price:** wholesale high, wholesale low. **Time Period Covered:** latest month.

PALM OIL: SUMATRA/MALAYSIAN

Source: *Oil World.* **Price Frequency:** weekly, monthly, annually. **Effective Market(s):** Northwest Europe. **Units of Measure:** Dollars per tonne. **Type of Price:** lowest representative asking. **Time Period Covered:** weekly latest 3 weeks, monthly latest 2 months, annually latest 2 years.

PALM OIL ACID: DOUBLE DISTILLED

Source: *Chemical Marketing Reporter.* **Price Frequency:** weekly. **Effective Market(s):** New York. **Units of Measure:** Dollars per lb. **Type of Price:** spot. **Time Period Covered:** latest week.

PALM OLEIN: MALAYSIAN

Source: *Oil World.* **Price Frequency:** weekly, monthly, annually. **Effective Market(s):** Malaysia, Rotterdam. **Units of Measure:** Dollars per tonne. **Type of Price:** lowest representative asking. **Time Period Covered:** weekly latest 3 weeks, monthly latest 2 months, annually latest 2 years.

PALM STEARIN: MALAYSIAN

Source: *Oil World.* **Price Frequency:** weekly, monthly, annually. **Effective Market(s):** Malaysia, Rotterdam. **Units of Measure:** Dollars per tonne. **Type of Price:** lowest representative asking. **Time Period Covered:** weekly latest 3 weeks, monthly latest 2 months, annually latest 2 years.

PALMAROSA OIL

Source: *U. S. Essential Oil Trade.* **Price Frequency:** annually. **Effective Market(s):** United States. **Units of Measure:** Dollars per kilogram. **Type of Price:** import value. **Time Period Covered:** latest 3 years.

PALMAROSA OIL: BRAZILIAN

Source: *Journal of Commerce and Commercial.* **Price Frequency:** weekly in Tuesday issue. **Units of Measure:** Dollars per lb. **Type of Price:** spot. **Time Period Covered:** latest week.

PALMAROSA OIL: INDIAN

Source: *Chemical Marketing Reporter.* **Price Frequency:** weekly. **Effective Market(s):** New York. **Units of Measure:** Dollars per kilo. **Type of Price:** spot. **Time Period Covered:** latest week.

PALMAROSA OIL: INDONESIAN

Source: *Journal of Commerce and Commercial.* **Price Frequency:** weekly in Tuesday issue. **Units of Measure:** Dollars per lb. **Type of Price:** spot. **Time Period Covered:** latest week.

PALMITATE

Source: *Journal of Commerce and Commercial.* **Price Frequency:** weekly in Friday issue. **Units of Measure:** Dollars per kilo. **Type of Price:** spot. **Time Period Covered:** latest week.

PALMITIC ACID: 85%, TECHNICAL

Source: *Chemical Marketing Reporter.* **Price Frequency:** weekly. **Effective Market(s):** New York. **Units of Measure:** Dollars per lb. **Type of Price:** spot. **Time Period Covered:** latest week.

PAN (TEXTILE)

Source: *Journal of Commerce and Commercial.* **Price Frequency:** weekly in Tuesday issue. **Units of Measure:** Dollars per lb. **Type of Price:** spot. **Time Period Covered:** latest week.

PAPAIN

Source: *Journal of Commerce and Commercial.* **Price Frequency:** weekly in Monday issue. **Units of Measure:** Dollars per kilo. **Type of Price:** spot. **Time Period Covered:** latest week.

PAPAVERINE HYDROCHLORIDE: POWDERED, NF, IMPORTED

Source: *Chemical Marketing Reporter.* **Price Frequency:** weekly. **Effective Market(s):** New York. **Units of Measure:** Dollars per kilo. **Type of Price:** spot. **Time Period Covered:** latest week.

PAPAYAS

Source: *Agricultural Prices Annual Summary.* **Price Frequency:** annually. **Effective Market(s):** California, Hawaii. **Units of Measure:** Dollars per lb. **Type of Price:** average received by farmer. **Time Period Covered:** latest 6 years.

Source: *Fruit and Tree Nuts Situation and Outlook Yearbook.* **Price Frequency:** annually. **Effective Market(s):** Hawaii. **Units of Measure:** cents per lb. **Type of Price:** grower. **Time Period Covered:** latest 20 years.

Source: *Lancaster Farmer.* **Price Frequency:** weekly, seasonally. **Effective Market(s):** Pennsylvania. **Units of Measure:** Dollars per carton. **Type of Price:** market. **Time Period Covered:** latest week.

PAPAYAS: BRAZILIAN

Source: *Prices of Selected Asia/Pacific Products.* **Price Frequency:** monthly. **Effective Market(s):** United Kingdom, France. **Units of Measure:** British pounds per kilograms, French francs per kilograms. **Type of Price:** wholesale high, wholesale low. **Time Period Covered:** latest month.

PAPAYAS: FRESH

Source: *Fruit and Tree Nuts Situation and Outlook Yearbook.* **Price Frequency:** annually. **Effective Market(s):** Hawaii. **Units of Measure:** cents per lb. **Type of Price:** grower. **Time Period Covered:** latest 20 years.

PAPAYAS: PROCESSED

Source: *Fruit and Tree Nuts Situation and Outlook Yearbook.* **Price Frequency:** annually. **Effective Market(s):** Hawaii. **Units of Measure:** cents per lb. **Type of Price:** grower. **Time Period Covered:** latest 20 years.

PAPER

see also Wastepaper.

PAPER: ALL CONVERTED PRODUCTS

Source: *Pulp & Paper Week.* **Price Frequency:** monthly, irregulary. **Units of Measure:** index. **Type of Price:** price index. **Time Period Covered:** latest 3 months.

PAPER: BLEACHED KRAFT, FOLDING CARTON STOCK

Source: *Purchasing.* **Price Frequency:** quarterly in January, April, July, October issues. **Units of Measure:** Dollars per ton. **Type of Price:** transaction. **Time Period Covered:** latest 5 quarters.

PAPER: BLEACHED KRAFT, FOR GROCERY BAG

Source: *Pulp & Paper Week.* **Price Frequency:** monthly, usually in last issue of month. **Effective Market(s):** Eastern United States. **Units of Measure:** Dollars per short ton. **Type of Price:** estimated transaction. **Time Period Covered:** latest 3 months, year ago.

PAPER: CABLE, KRAFT

Source: *Fibre Market News.* **Price Frequency:** weekly. **Effective Market(s):** Boston, Miami, New York, Philadelphia. **Units of Measure:** Dollars per net ton. **Type of Price:** grader & packer buying price. **Time Period Covered:** latest week.

PAPER: COATED BOOK, SULFITE

Source: *Fibre Market News.* **Price Frequency:** weekly. **Effective Market(s):** 9 domestic markets. **Units of Measure:** Dollars per net ton. **Type of Price:** grader & packer buying price. **Time Period Covered:** latest week.

PAPER: COATED GROUNDWOOD

Source: *Fibre Market News.* **Price Frequency:** weekly. **Effective Market(s):** 9 domestic markets. **Units of Measure:** Dollars per net ton. **Type of Price:** grader & packer buying price. **Time Period Covered:** latest week.

PAPER: COATED PRINTING, NO. 3

Source: *Commodity Year Book.* **Price Frequency:** monthly, annually. **Units of Measure:** index. **Type of Price:** price index. **Time Period Covered:** latest 3 years.

PAPER: COATED PUBLICATION, NO. 1

Source: *Pulp & Paper Week.* **Price Frequency:** monthly, usually in last issue of month. **Effective Market(s):** Eastern United States. **Units of Measure:** Dollars per short ton. **Type of Price:** estimated transaction. **Time Period Covered:** latest 3 months, year ago.

PAPER: COATED PUBLICATION, NO. 3

Source: *Pulp & Paper Week.* **Price Frequency:** monthly, usually in last issue of month. **Effective Market(s):** Eastern United States. **Units of Measure:** Dollars per short ton. **Type of Price:** estimated transaction. **Time Period Covered:** latest 3 months, year ago.

Source: *Purchasing.* **Price Frequency:** quarterly in January, April, July, October issues. **Units of Measure:** Dollars per ton. **Type of Price:** transaction. **Time Period Covered:** latest 5 quarters.

PAPER: COATED PUBLICATION, NO. 4

Source: *Pulp & Paper Week.* **Price Frequency:** monthly, usually in last issue of month. **Effective Market(s):** Eastern United States. **Units of Measure:** Dollars per short ton. **Type of Price:** estimated transaction. **Time Period Covered:** latest 3 months, year ago.

PAPER: COATED PUBLICATION, NO. 5, OFFSET

Source: *Pulp & Paper Week.* **Price Frequency:** monthly, usually in last issue of month. **Effective Market(s):** Eastern United States. **Units of Measure:** Dollars per short ton. **Type of Price:** estimated transaction. **Time Period Covered:** latest 3 months, year ago.

PAPER: COATED PUBLICATION, NO. 5, ROTO

Source: *Pulp & Paper Week.* **Price Frequency:** monthly, usually in last issue of month. **Effective Market(s):** Eastern United States. **Units of Measure:** Dollars per short ton. **Type of Price:** estimated transaction. **Time Period Covered:** latest 3 months, year ago.

PAPER: COATED, WOODFREE, CLASS A

Source: *Japan Economic Journal.* **Price Frequency:** weekly. **Effective Market(s):** Japan. **Type of Price:** wholesale. **Time Period Covered:** latest 2 weeks.

PAPER: CORRUGATED

Source: *Fibre Market News.* **Price Frequency:** weekly. **Effective Market(s):** 9 domestic markets. **Units of Measure:** Dollars per net ton. **Type of Price:** grader & packer buying price. **Time Period Covered:** latest week.

PAPER: CORRUGATED CONTAINERS

Source: *Fibre Market News.* **Price Frequency:** weekly. **Effective Market(s):** 9 domestic markets. **Units of Measure:** Dollars per net ton. **Type of Price:** grader & packer buying price. **Time Period Covered:** latest week.

Source: *Pulp & Paper Week.* **Price Frequency:** monthly, irregulary. **Units of Measure:** index. **Type of Price:** price index. **Time Period Covered:** latest 3 months.

PAPER: CORRUGATED CONTAINERS FOR FOOD AND BEVERAGES

Source: *Pulp & Paper Week.* **Price Frequency:** monthly, irregulary. **Units of Measure:** index. **Type of Price:** price index. **Time Period Covered:** latest 3 months.

PAPER: COVERED BOOK

Source: *Fibre Market News.* **Price Frequency:** weekly. **Effective Market(s):** 9 domestic markets. **Units of Measure:** Dollars per net ton. **Type of Price:** grader & packer buying price. **Time Period Covered:** latest week.

PAPER: CPO

Source: *Fibre Market News.* **Price Frequency:** weekly. **Effective Market(s):** 9 domestic markets. **Units of Measure:** Dollars per net ton. **Type of Price:** grader & packer buying price. **Time Period Covered:** latest week.

PAPER: CPO, GROUNDWOOD

Source: *Fibre Market News.* **Price Frequency:** weekly. **Effective Market(s):** 9 domestic markets. **Units of Measure:** Dollars per net ton. **Type of Price:** grader & packer buying price. **Time Period Covered:** latest week.

PAPER: CPO, LASER

Source: *Fibre Market News.* **Price Frequency:** weekly. **Effective Market(s):** 9 domestic markets. **Units of Measure:** Dollars per net ton. **Type of Price:** grader & packer buying price. **Time Period Covered:** latest week.

PAPER: CUPS AND LIQUID CONTAINERS

Source: *Pulp & Paper Week.* **Price Frequency:** monthly, irregulary. **Units of Measure:** index. **Type of Price:** price index. **Time Period Covered:** latest 3 months.

PAPER: CUTTINGS, BOX BOARD

Source: *Fibre Market News.* **Price Frequency:** weekly. **Effective Market(s):** 8 domestic markets. **Units of Measure:** Dollars per net ton. **Type of Price:** grader & packer buying price. **Time Period Covered:** latest week.

PAPER: CUTTINGS, HARD COLORED

Source: *Fibre Market News.* **Price Frequency:** weekly. **Effective Market(s):** 7 domestic markets. **Units of Measure:** Dollars per net ton. **Type of Price:** grader & packer buying price. **Time Period Covered:** latest week.

PAPER: DOUBLE-LINED, KRAFT CUTS

Source: *Fibre Market News.* **Price Frequency:** weekly. **Effective Market(s):** 9 domestic markets. **Units of Measure:** Dollars per net ton. **Type of Price:** grader & packer buying price. **Time Period Covered:** latest week.

PAPER: ENVELOPE CUTS, HARD WHITE

Source: *Fibre Market News.* **Price Frequency:** weekly. **Effective Market(s):** 9 domestic markets. **Units of Measure:** Dollars per net ton. **Type of Price:** grader & packer buying price. **Time Period Covered:** latest week.

PAPER: ENVELOPE CUTS, KRAFT

Source: *Fibre Market News.* **Price Frequency:** weekly. **Effective Market(s):** 7 domestic markets. **Units of Measure:** Dollars per net ton. **Type of Price:** grader & packer buying price. **Time Period Covered:** latest week.

PAPER: EXCEPT NEWS

Source: *Pulp & Paper Week.* **Price Frequency:** monthly, irregulary. **Units of Measure:** index. **Type of Price:** price index. **Time Period Covered:** latest 3 months.

PAPER: FIBER DRUMS

Source: *Pulp & Paper Week.* **Price Frequency:** monthly, irregulary. **Units of Measure:** index. **Type of Price:** price index. **Time Period Covered:** latest 3 months.

PAPER: FLOUR AND SUGAR SACK, KRAFT

Source: *Fibre Market News.* **Price Frequency:** weekly. **Effective Market(s):** 6 domestic markets. **Units of Measure:** Dollars per net ton. **Type of Price:** grader & packer buying price. **Time Period Covered:** latest week.

PAPER: FLYLEAF SULFITE, GROUNDWOOD FREE

Source: *Fibre Market News.* **Price Frequency:** weekly. **Effective Market(s):** 9 domestic markets. **Units of Measure:** Dollars per net ton. **Type of Price:** grader & packer buying price. **Time Period Covered:** latest week.

PAPER: FOLDING CARTONS

Source: *Pulp & Paper Week.* **Price Frequency:** monthly, irregulary. **Units of Measure:** index. **Type of Price:** price index. **Time Period Covered:** latest 3 months.

PAPER: KRAFT

Source: *Japan Economic Journal.* **Price Frequency:** weekly. **Effective Market(s):** Japan. **Type of Price:** wholesale. **Time Period Covered:** latest 2 weeks.

PAPER: KRAFTLINER, SCANDINAVIAN

Source: *FAO Quarterly Bulletin of Statistics.* **Price Frequency:** monthly, annually. **Effective Market(s):** Hamburg. **Units of Measure:** West German marks per 100 kilograms, dollars per metric ton. **Type of Price:** import. **Time Period Covered:** latest 3 years.

PAPER: LEDGER STOCK, COLOR

Source: *Fibre Market News.* **Price Frequency:** weekly. **Effective Market(s):** 9 domestic markets. **Units of Measure:** Dollars per net ton. **Type of Price:** grader & packer buying price. **Time Period Covered:** latest week.

PAPER: LEDGER STOCK, COLORED FOR REPACK

Source: *Fibre Market News.* **Price Frequency:** weekly. **Effective Market(s):** 8 domestic markets. **Units of Measure:** Dollars per net ton. **Type of Price:** grader & packer buying price. **Time Period Covered:** latest week.

PAPER: LEDGER STOCK, COMBINED

Source: *Fibre Market News.* **Price Frequency:** weekly. **Effective Market(s):** New York. **Units of Measure:** Dollars per net ton. **Type of Price:** grader & packer buying price. **Time Period Covered:** latest week.

PAPER: LEDGER STOCK, WHITE

Source: *Fibre Market News.* **Price Frequency:** weekly. **Effective Market(s):** 9 domestic markets. **Units of Measure:** Dollars per net ton. **Type of Price:** grader & packer buying price. **Time Period Covered:** latest week.

PAPER: LIGHT PRINT, BLEACH SULFATE

Source: *Fibre Market News.* **Price Frequency:** weekly. **Effective Market(s):** 8 domestic markets. **Units of Measure:** Dollars per net ton. **Type of Price:** grader & packer buying price. **Time Period Covered:** latest week.

PAPER: MAGAZINE

Source: *Fibre Market News.* **Price Frequency:** weekly. **Effective Market(s):** 9 domestic markets. **Units of Measure:** Dollars per net ton. **Type of Price:** grader & packer buying price. **Time Period Covered:** latest week.

PAPER: MILK AND MILK-TYPE CONTAINERS

Source: *Pulp & Paper Week.* **Price Frequency:** monthly, irregulary. **Units of Measure:** index. **Type of Price:** price index. **Time Period Covered:** latest 3 months.

PAPER: MILL WRAPPERS

Source: *Fibre Market News.* **Price Frequency:** weekly. **Effective Market(s):** 9 domestic markets. **Units of Measure:** Dollars per net ton. **Type of Price:** grader & packer buying price. **Time Period Covered:** latest week.

PAPER: MIXED

Source: *Fibre Market News.* **Price Frequency:** weekly. **Effective Market(s):** 9 domestic markets. **Units of Measure:** Dollars per net ton. **Type of Price:** grader & packer buying price. **Time Period Covered:** latest week.

PAPER: NEWS, BLANK, WHITE

Source: *Fibre Market News.* **Price Frequency:** weekly. **Effective Market(s):** 9 domestic markets. **Units of Measure:** Dollars per net ton. **Type of Price:** grader & packer buying price. **Time Period Covered:** latest week.

PAPER: NEWS, FOLDED

Source: *Fibre Market News.* **Price Frequency:** weekly. **Effective Market(s):** Boston, Philadelphia. **Units of Measure:** Dollars per net ton. **Type of Price:** grader & packer buying price. **Time Period Covered:** latest week.

PAPER: NEWS, OVERISSUE

Source: *Fibre Market News.* **Price Frequency:** weekly. **Effective Market(s):** 9 domestic markets. **Units of Measure:** Dollars per net ton. **Type of Price:** grader & packer buying price. **Time Period Covered:** latest week.

PAPER: NEWS, OVERISSUE, SPECIAL PACK

Source: *Fibre Market News.* **Price Frequency:** weekly. **Effective Market(s):** Boston, Chicago, Philadelphia. **Units of Measure:** Dollars per net ton. **Type of Price:** grader & packer buying price. **Time Period Covered:** latest week.

PAPER: NEWS, REGULAR

Source: *Fibre Market News.* **Price Frequency:** weekly. **Effective Market(s):** 9 domestic markets. **Units of Measure:** Dollars per net ton. **Type of Price:** grader & packer buying price. **Time Period Covered:** latest week.

PAPER: NEWS, SPECIAL

Source: *Fibre Market News.* **Price Frequency:** weekly. **Effective Market(s):** 9 domestic markets. **Units of Measure:** Dollars per net ton. **Type of Price:** grader & packer buying price. **Time Period Covered:** lates week.

PAPER: NEWS, SPECIAL DE-INK

Source: *Fibre Market News.* **Price Frequency:** weekly. **Effective Market(s):** 9 domestic markets. **Units of Measure:** Dollars per net ton. **Type of Price:** grader & packer buying price. **Time Period Covered:** latest week.

PAPER: NEWSPRINT

Source: *Pulp & Paper Week.* **Price Frequency:** monthly, usually in last issue of month. **Effective Market(s):** Eastern United States, Western United States. **Units of Measure:** Dollars per metric ton. **Type of Price:** estimated transaction. **Time Period Covered:** latest 3 months, year ago.

PAPER: OFFICE WASTE

Source: *Fibre Market News.* **Price Frequency:** weekly. **Effective Market(s):** 9 domestic markets. **Units of Measure:** Dollars per net ton. **Type of Price:** grader & packer buying price. **Time Period Covered:** latest week.

PAPER: OTHER SANITARY CONTAINERS

Source: *Pulp & Paper Week.* **Price Frequency:** monthly, irregulary. **Units of Measure:** index. **Type of Price:** price index. **Time Period Covered:** latest 3 months.

PAPER: PRINTING AND WRITING

Source: *Timber Bulletin.* **Price Frequency:** monthly, annually. **Effective Market(s):** Norway, Sweden. **Units of Measure:** national currency per metric ton. **Type of Price:** export value. **Time Period Covered:** monthly latest 2 years, annually latest 6 years.

Source: *Timber Bulletin.* **Price Frequency:** monthly, annually. **Effective Market(s):** United Kingdom. **Units of Measure:** British pounds per metric ton. **Type of Price:** import value. **Time Period Covered:** latest year.

PAPER: SHAVINGS, FLYLEAF

Source: *Fibre Market News.* **Price Frequency:** weekly. **Effective Market(s):** 7 domestic markets. **Units of Measure:** Dollars per net ton. **Type of Price:** grader & packer buying price. **Time Period Covered:** latest week.

PAPER: SHAVINGS, HARD WHITE

Source: *Fibre Market News.* **Price Frequency:** weekly. **Effective Market(s):** 9 domestic markets. **Units of Measure:** Dollars per net ton. **Type of Price:** grader & packer buying price. **Time Period Covered:** latest week.

PAPER: SHAVINGS, SOFT WHITE

Source: *Fibre Market News.* **Price Frequency:** weekly. **Effective Market(s):** 9 domestic markets. **Units of Measure:** Dollars per net ton. **Type of Price:** grader & packer buying price. **Time Period Covered:** latest week.

PAPER: SHIPPING SACK

Source: *Commodity Year Book.* **Price Frequency:** monthly, annually. **Units of Measure:** index. **Type of Price:** price index. **Time Period Covered:** latest 6 years.

Source: *Pulp & Paper Week.* **Price Frequency:** monthly, irregularly. **Units of Measure:** index. **Type of Price:** price index. **Time Period Covered:** latest 3 months.

PAPER: TAB CARDS

Source: *Fibre Market News.* **Price Frequency:** weekly. **Effective Market(s):** New York. **Units of Measure:** Dollars per net ton. **Type of Price:** grader & packer buying price. **Time Period Covered:** latest week.

PAPER: TAB CARDS, COLOR

Source: *Fibre Market News.* **Price Frequency:** weekly. **Effective Market(s):** 9 domestic markets. **Units of Measure:** Dollars per net ton. **Type of Price:** grader & packer buying price. **Time Period Covered:** latest week.

PAPER: TAB CARDS, MANILA

Source: *Fibre Market News.* **Price Frequency:** weekly. **Effective Market(s):** 9 domestic markets. **Units of Measure:** Dollars per net ton. **Type of Price:** grader & packer buying price.

PAPER: UNBLEACHED KRAFT, FOR GROCERY SACK

Source: *Pulp & Paper Week.* **Price Frequency:** monthly, usually in last issue of month. **Effective Market(s):** Eastern United States. **Units of Measure:** Dollars per short ton. **Type of Price:** estimated transaction. **Time Period Covered:** latest 3 months, year ago.

PAPER: UNBLEACHED KRAFT, FOR SHIPPING SACK

Source: *Pulp & Paper Week.* **Price Frequency:** monthly, usually in last issue of month. **Effective Market(s):** Eastern United States. **Units of Measure:** Dollars per short ton. **Type of Price:** estimated transaction. **Time Period Covered:** latest 3 months, year ago.

Source: *Purchasing.* **Price Frequency:** quarterly in January, April, July, October issues. **Units of Measure:** Dollars per ton. **Type of Price:** transaction. **Time Period Covered:** latest 5 quarters.

PAPER: UNCOATED BOND, NO. 4

Source: *Purchasing.* **Price Frequency:** quarterly in January, April, July, October issues. **Units of Measure:** Dollars per ton. **Type of Price:** transaction. **Time Period Covered:** latest 5 quarters.

PAPER: UNCOATED GROUNDWOOD, DIRECTORY, WHITE

Source: *Pulp & Paper Week.* **Price Frequency:** monthly, usually in last issue of month. **Effective Market(s):** Eastern United States. **Units of Measure:** Dollars per short ton. **Type of Price:** estimated transaction. **Time Period Covered:** latest 3 months, year ago.

PAPER: UNCOATED GROUNDWOOD, DIRECTORY, YELLOW

Source: *Pulp & Paper Week.* **Price Frequency:** monthly, usually in last issue of month. **Effective Market(s):** Eastern United States. **Units of Measure:** Dollars per short ton. **Type of Price:** estimated transaction. **Time Period Covered:** latest 3 months, year ago.

PAPER: UNCOATED GROUNDWOOD, FOR FORMS

Source: *Pulp & Paper Week.* **Price Frequency:** monthly, usually in last issue of month. **Effective Market(s):** Eastern United States. **Units of Measure:** Dollars per short ton. **Type of Price:** estimated transaction. **Time Period Covered:** latest 3 months, year ago.

PAPER: UNCOATED GROUNDWOOD, MF OFFSET, 65 BRIGHT

Source: *Pulp & Paper Week.* **Price Frequency:** monthly, usually in last issue of month. **Effective Market(s):** Eastern United States. **Units of Measure:** Dollars per short ton. **Type of Price:** estimated transaction. **Time Period Covered:** latest 3 months, year ago.

PAPER: UNCOATED GROUNDWOOD, ROTONEWS, PREMIUM

Source: *Pulp & Paper Week.* **Price Frequency:** monthly, usually in last issue of month. **Effective Market(s):** Eastern United States. **Units of Measure:** Dollars per short ton. **Type of Price:** estimated transaction. **Time Period Covered:** latest 3 months, year ago.

PAPER: UNCOATED GROUNDWOOD, ROTONEWS, STANDARD

Source: *Pulp & Paper Week.* **Price Frequency:** monthly, usually in last issue of month. **Effective Market(s):** Eastern United States. **Units of Measure:** Dollars per short ton. **Type of Price:** estimated transaction. **Time Period Covered:** latest 3 months, year ago.

PAPER: UNCOATED GROUNDWOOD, SUPERCALENDARED

Source: *Pulp & Paper Week.* **Price Frequency:** monthly, usually in last issue of month. **Effective Market(s):** Eastern United States. **Units of Measure:** Dollars per short ton. **Type of Price:** estimated transaction. **Time Period Covered:** latest 3 months, year ago.

Source: *Purchasing.* **Price Frequency:** quarterly in January, April, July, October issues. **Units of Measure:** Dollars per ton. **Type of Price:** transaction. **Time Period Covered:** latest 5 quarters.

PAPER: UNCOATED WHITE BOND, 25% COTTON

Source: *Pulp & Paper Week.* **Price Frequency:** monthly, usually in last issue of month. **Effective Market(s):** Eastern United States. **Units of Measure:** Dollars per short ton. **Type of Price:** estimated transaction. **Time Period Covered:** latest 3 months, year ago.

PAPER: UNCOATED WHITE BOND, NO. 4 REPRO, 81 BRIGHT

Source: *Pulp & Paper Week.* **Price Frequency:** monthly, usually in last issue of month. **Effective Market(s):** Eastern United States. **Units of Measure:** Dollars per short ton. **Type of Price:** estimated transaction. **Time Period Covered:** latest 3 months, year ago.

PAPER: UNCOATED WHITE BOND, NO. 4 REPRO, 83 BRIGHT

Source: *Pulp & Paper Week.* **Price Frequency:** monthly, usually in last issue of month. **Effective Market(s):** Eastern United States. **Units of Measure:** Dollars per short ton. **Type of Price:** estimated transaction. **Time Period Covered:** latest 3 months, year ago.

PAPER: UNCOATED WHITE, CARBONLESS, COATED BACK

Source: *Pulp & Paper Week.* **Price Frequency:** monthly, usually in last issue of month. **Effective Market(s):** Eastern United States. **Units of Measure:** Dollars per short ton. **Type of Price:** estimated transaction. **Time Period Covered:** latest 3 months, year ago.

PAPER: UNCOATED WHITE, FORM BOND

Source: *Pulp & Paper Week.* **Price Frequency:** monthly, usually in last issue of month. **Effective Market(s):** Eastern United States. **Units of Measure:** Dollars per short ton. **Type of Price:** estimated transaction. **Time Period Covered:** latest 3 months, year ago.

PAPER: UNCOATED WHITE, NO. 1, WATERMARKED, 20 LB. SHEETS

Source: *Pulp & Paper Week.* **Price Frequency:** monthly, usually in last issue of month. **Effective Market(s):** Eastern United States. **Units of Measure:** Dollars per short ton. **Type of Price:** estimated transaction. **Time Period Covered:** latest 3 months, year ago.

PAPER: UNCOATED WHITE, NO. 3, BOOK OFFSET, 45 LB. SHEETS

Source: *Pulp & Paper Week.* **Price Frequency:** monthly, usually in last issue of month. **Effective Market(s):** Eastern United States. **Units of Measure:** Dollars per short ton. **Type of Price:** estimated transaction. **Time Period Covered:** latest 3 months, year ago.

PAPER: UNCOATED WHITE, OFFSET

Source: *Pulp & Paper Week.* **Price Frequency:** monthly, usually in last issue of month. **Effective Market(s):** Eastern United States. **Units of Measure:** Dollars per short ton. **Type of Price:** estimated transaction. **Time Period Covered:** latest 3 months, year ago.

PAPER: UNCOATED, WOODFREE, CLASS A

Source: *Japan Economic Journal.* **Price Frequency:** weekly. **Effective Market(s):** Japan. **Type of Price:** wholesale. **Time Period Covered:** latest 2 weeks.

PAPER: UNPRINT, BLEACH SULFATE

Source: *Fibre Market News.* **Price Frequency:** weekly. **Effective Market(s):** 9 domestic markets. **Units of Measure:** Dollars per net ton. **Type of Price:** grader & packer buying price. **Time Period Covered:** latest week.

PAPER: WRAPPING

see Wrapping Paper.

PAPER AND PAPERBOARD

Source: *Timber Bulletin.* **Price Frequency:** monthly, annually. **Effective Market(s):** Norway, Sweden. **Units of Measure:** national currency per metric ton. **Type of Price:** export value. **Time Period Covered:** monthly latest year, annually latest 5 years.

Source: *Timber Bulletin.* **Price Frequency:** monthly, annually. **Effective Market(s):** United Kingdom. **Units of Measure:** British pounds per metric ton. **Type of Price:** import value. **Time Period Covered:** monthly latest 2 years, annually latest 5 years.

PAPER AND PAPERBOARD: KRAFTLINER

Source: *Timber Bulletin.* **Price Frequency:** monthly, annually. **Effective Market(s):** West Germany. **Units of Measure:** West German marks per metric ton. **Time Period Covered:** monthly latest 2 years, annually latest 6 years.

PAPER BAGS: SUGAR, 100 LB

Source: *Fibre Market News.* **Price Frequency:** weekly. **Units of Measure:** cents per bag. **Time Period Covered:** latest week.

PAPER BAGS AND SACKS

Source: *Pulp & Paper Week.* **Price Frequency:** monthly, irregulary. **Units of Measure:** index. **Type of Price:** price index. **Time Period Covered:** latest 3 months.

PAPER BOXES AND CONTAINERS

Source: *Pulp & Paper Week.* **Price Frequency:** monthly, irregulary. **Units of Measure:** index. **Type of Price:** price index. **Time Period Covered:** latest 3 months.

PAPERBOARD

Source: *Commodity Year Book.* **Price Frequency:** monthly, annually. **Units of Measure:** index. **Type of Price:** price index. **Time Period Covered:** latest 2 years.

Source: *Pulp & Paper Week.* **Price Frequency:** monthly, irregulary. **Units of Measure:** index. **Type of Price:** price index. **Time Period Covered:** latest 3 months.

PAPERBOARD: BLEACHED KRAFT, 15-PT FOLDING CARTON, C1S, 80 BRIGHT

Source: *Pulp & Paper Week.* **Price Frequency:** monthly, usually in last issue of month. **Effective Market(s):** Eastern United States. **Units of Measure:** Dollars per short ton. **Type of Price:** estimated transaction. **Time Period Covered:** latest 3 months, year ago.

PAPERBOARD: CORRUGATED MEDIUM, SEMICHEMICAL

Source: *Pulp & Paper Week.* **Price Frequency:** monthly, usually in last issue of month. **Effective Market(s):** Eastern United States. **Units of Measure:** Dollars per short ton, dollars per 1000 square feet. **Type of Price:** estimated transaction. **Time Period Covered:** latest 3 months, year ago.

Source: *Purchasing.* **Price Frequency:** monthly. **Units of Measure:** Dollars per ton. **Type of Price:** transaction. **Time Period Covered:** latest day, month ago, 6 months ago, year ago.

PAPERBOARD: UNBLEACHED KRAFT, 20-PT CLAY COATED

Source: *Pulp & Paper Week.* **Price Frequency:** monthly, usually in last issue of month. **Effective Market(s):** Eastern United States. **Units of Measure:** Dollars per short ton. **Type of Price:** estimated transaction. **Time Period Covered:** latest 3 months, year ago.

PAPRIKA: HUNGARIAN

Source: *Chemical Marketing Reporter.* **Price Frequency:** weekly. **Effective Market(s):** New York. **Units of Measure:** Dollars per lb. **Type of Price:** spot. **Time Period Covered:** latest week.

PAPRIKA: HUNGARIAN 120

Source: *U. S. Spice Trade.* **Price Frequency:** annually. **Effective Market(s):** New York. **Units of Measure:** cents per lb. **Type of Price:** spot. **Time Period Covered:** latest 3 years.

PAPRIKA: SPANISH

Source: *Chemical Marketing Reporter.* **Price Frequency:** weekly. **Effective Market(s):** New York. **Units of Measure:** Dollars per lb. **Type of Price:** spot. **Time Period Covered:** latest week.

Source: *Journal of Commerce and Commercial.* **Price Frequency:** weekly in Monday issue. **Units of Measure:** Dollars per lb. **Type of Price:** spot. **Time Period Covered:** latest week.

PAPRIKA: SPANISH 100 ASTA

Source: *U. S. Spice Trade.* **Price Frequency:** annually. **Effective Market(s):** New York. **Units of Measure:** cents per lb. **Type of Price:** spot. **Time Period Covered:** latest 3 years.

PAPRIKA: SPANISH 110 ASTA

Source: *U. S. Spice Trade.* **Price Frequency:** annually. **Effective Market(s):** New York. **Units of Measure:** cents per lb. **Type of Price:** spot. **Time Period Covered:** latest 3 years.

PAPRIKA: SPANISH 120 ASTA

Source: *U. S. Spice Trade.* **Price Frequency:** annually. **Effective Market(s):** New York. **Units of Measure:** cents per lb. **Type of Price:** spot. **Time Period Covered:** latest 3 years.

PARA TONER: RED

Source: *Chemical Marketing Reporter.* **Price Frequency:** weekly. **Effective Market(s):** New York. **Units of Measure:** Dollars per lb. **Type of Price:** spot. **Time Period Covered:** latest week.

PARA TONER: RED, CHLORINATED

Source: *Chemical Marketing Reporter.* **Price Frequency:** weekly. **Effective Market(s):** New York. **Units of Measure:** Dollars per lb. **Type of Price:** spot. **Time Period Covered:** latest week.

PARA-XYLENE

Source: *Cotton and Wool Situation and Outlook Report.* **Price Frequency:** monthly. **Units of Measure:** cents per lb. **Type of Price:** spot. **Time Period Covered:** latest year.

PARAFFIN

See Wax: Paraffin.

PARAFFIN: FULLY REFINED, ASTM

Source: *Chemical Marketing Reporter.* **Price Frequency:** weekly. **Effective Market(s):** New York. **Units of Measure:** Dollars per lb. **Type of Price:** spot. **Time Period Covered:** latest week.

PARAFFIN: SLACK WAX, 5% OIL

Source: *Chemical Marketing Reporter.* **Price Frequency:** weekly. **Effective Market(s):** New York. **Units of Measure:** Dollars per lb. **Type of Price:** spot. **Time Period Covered:** latest week.

PARAFFIN: SLACK WAX, 12% OIL

Source: *Chemical Marketing Reporter.* **Price Frequency:** weekly. **Effective Market(s):** New York. **Units of Measure:** Dollars per lb. **Type of Price:** spot. **Time Period Covered:** latest week.

PARAFFIN: SLACK WAX, 20% OIL

Source: *Chemical Marketing Reporter.* **Price Frequency:** weekly. **Effective Market(s):** New York. **Units of Measure:** Dollars per lb. **Type of Price:** spot. **Time Period Covered:** latest week.

PARAFORMALDEHYDE: 91%, FLAKE

Source: *Chemical Marketing Reporter.* **Price Frequency:** weekly. **Effective Market(s):** New York. **Units of Measure:** Dollars per lb. **Type of Price:** spot. **Time Period Covered:** latest week.

PARAFORMALDEHYDE: 95%, POWDERED

Source: *Chemical Marketing Reporter.* **Price Frequency:** weekly. **Effective Market(s):** New York. **Units of Measure:** Dollars per lb. **Type of Price:** spot. **Time Period Covered:** latest week.

PARALDEHYDE: TECHNICAL, 98%

Source: *Chemical Marketing Reporter.* **Price Frequency:** weekly. **Effective Market(s):** East. **Units of Measure:** Dollars per lb. **Type of Price:** spot. **Time Period Covered:** latest week.

PARATHION: ETHYL

Source: *Chemical Marketing Reporter.* **Price Frequency:** weekly. **Effective Market(s):** New York. **Units of Measure:** Dollars per lb. **Type of Price:** spot. **Time Period Covered:** latest week.

PARATHION METHYL

see Methyl Parathion.

PARSLEY

Source: *New Zealand Farmer.* **Price Frequency:** weekly, seasonally. **Effective Market(s):** New Zealand. **Units of Measure:** New Zealand dollars per case. **Time Period Covered:** latest week.

PARSLEY: CURLY

Source: *Lancaster Farmer.* **Price Frequency:** weekly, seasonally. **Effective Market(s):** Pennsylvania. **Units of Measure:** Dollars per unit. **Type of Price:** market. **Time Period Covered:** latest week.

PARSLEY: FRESH

Source: *HRI-Buyers Guide.* **Price Frequency:** weekly. **Effective Market(s):** Northeastern area. **Units of Measure:** Dollars per crate. **Type of Price:** prices paid by dining places & institutions. **Time Period Covered:** latest week.

PARSLEY: IMPORTED

Source: *U. S. Spice Trade.* **Price Frequency:** annually. **Effective Market(s):** New York. **Units of Measure:** cents per lb. **Type of Price:** spot. **Time Period Covered:** latest 3 years.

PARSLEY: PLAIN

Source: *Lancaster Farmer.* **Price Frequency:** weekly, seasonally. **Effective Market(s):** Pennsylvania. **Units of Measure:** Dollars per unit. **Type of Price:** market. **Time Period Covered:** latest week.

PARSNIPS

Source: *New Zealand Farmer.* **Price Frequency:** weekly, seasonally. **Effective Market(s):** New Zealand. **Units of Measure:** New Zealand dollars per bag/crate. **Time Period Covered:** latest week.

PARTICLE BOARD

Source: *Purchasing.* **Price Frequency:** quarterly in January, April, July, October issues. **Effective Market(s):** West. **Units of Measure:** Dollars per ton. **Type of Price:** transaction. **Time Period Covered:** latest 5 quarters.

Source: *Timber Bulletin.* **Price Frequency:** monthly, annually. **Effective Market(s):** United Kingdom. **Units of Measure:** British pounds per metric ton. **Type of Price:** import value. **Time Period Covered:** monthly latest 2 years, annually latest 5 years.

Source: *Timber Bulletin.* **Price Frequency:** monthly, annually. **Effective Market(s):** Norway. **Units of Measure:** Norwegian kroner per cubic meter. **Type of Price:** export value. **Time Period Covered:** monthly latest 2 years, annually latest 6 years.

PARTRIDGES: CHUKAR

Source: *HRI-Buyers Guide.* **Price Frequency:** weekly. **Effective Market(s):** Northeastern area. **Units of Measure:** Dollars per lb. **Type of Price:** wholesale. **Time Period Covered:** latest week.

Source: *Urner Barry's Price-Current.* **Price Frequency:** daily. **Units of Measure:** Dollars per bird. **Type of Price:** wholesale. **Time Period Covered:** latest day.

Source: *Urner Barry's Price-Current, West Coast Edition.* **Price Frequency:** semiweekly. **Effective Market(s):** West Coast. **Units of Measure:** Dollars each. **Type of Price:** wholesale. **Time Period Covered:** latest day.

PASSION FLOWER: HERB

Source: *Journal of Commerce and Commercial.* **Price Frequency:** weekly in Monday issue. **Units of Measure:** Dollars per lb. **Type of Price:** spot. **Time Period Covered:** latest week.

PASSION FRUIT

Source: *New Zealand Farmer.* **Price Frequency:** weekly, seasonally. **Effective Market(s):** New Zealand. **Units of Measure:** New Zealand dollars per half case/kilogram. **Time Period Covered:** latest week.

PATCHOULI OIL

Source: *Journal of Commerce and Commercial.* **Price Frequency:** weekly in Tuesday issue. **Units of Measure:** Dollars per lb. **Type of Price:** spot. **Time Period Covered:** latest week.

Source: *U. S. Essential Oil Trade.* **Price Frequency:** annually. **Effective Market(s):** United States. **Units of Measure:** Dollars per kilogram. **Type of Price:** import value. **Time Period Covered:** latest 3 years.

PATCHOULI OIL: CHINESE

Source: *Chemical Marketing Reporter.* **Price Frequency:** weekly. **Effective Market(s):** New York. **Units of Measure:** Dollars per kilo. **Type of Price:** spot. **Time Period Covered:** latest week.

Source: *Prices of Selected Asia/Pacific Products.* **Price Frequency:** monthly. **Effective Market(s):** New York. **Units of Measure:** Dollars per kilogram. **Type of Price:** spot high, spot low. **Time Period Covered:** latest month.

PATCHOULI OIL: INDONESIAN

Source: *Chemical Marketing Reporter.* **Price Frequency:** weekly. **Effective Market(s):** New York. **Units of Measure:** Dollars per kilo. **Type of Price:** spot. **Time Period Covered:** latest week.

Source: *Prices of Selected Asia/Pacific Products.* **Price Frequency:** monthly. **Effective Market(s):** New York. **Units of Measure:** Dollars per kilogram. **Type of Price:** spot high, spot low. **Time Period Covered:** latest month.

PATCHOULI OIL: STANDARD QUALITY, SINGAPORE

Source: *Prices of Selected Asia/Pacific Products.* **Price Frequency:** monthly. **Effective Market(s):** United Kingdom, United Kingdom/North European ports. **Units of Measure:** British pounds per kilogram. **Type of Price:** spot high, spot low. **Time Period Covered:** latest month.

PAWPAW: IMPORTED

Source: *New Zealand Farmer.* **Price Frequency:** weekly, seasonally. **Effective Market(s):** New Zealand. **Units of Measure:** New Zealand dollars per carton. **Time Period Covered:** latest week.

PBI STAPLE (TEXTILE): FIRE RESISTANT

Source: *Journal of Commerce and Commercial.* **Price Frequency:** weekly in Tuesday issue. **Units of Measure:** Dollars per lb. **Type of Price:** spot. **Time Period Covered:** latest week.

PBT

see Polyester: PBT Type.

PEA BEANS

Source: *Bean Market News.* **Price Frequency:** weekly. **Effective Market(s):** Michigan, N. Dakota-Minnesota. **Units of Measure:** Dollars per 100 lbs. **Type of Price:** grower. **Time Period Covered:** latest week, week ago.

Source: *Bean Market Summary.* **Price Frequency:** monthly, annually. **Effective Market(s):** Michigan. **Units of Measure:** Dollars per 100 lbs. **Type of Price:** dealer. **Time Period Covered:** latest 5 years.

PEA BEANS: NO. 1

Source: *Bean Market News.* **Price Frequency:** weekly. **Effective Market(s):** Michigan, North Dakota/Minnesota. **Units of Measure:** Dollars per 100 lbs. **Type of Price:** dealer. **Time Period Covered:** latest week, week ago, year ago.

PEACH KERNEL OIL: USP

see Apricot Kernel Oil.

PEACHES

Source: *California Farmer.* **Price Frequency:** semimonthly, seasonally. **Effective Market(s):** Central/Southern San Joaquin Valley. **Units of Measure:** Dollars per 22 lb. tray pack. **Time Period Covered:** latest week, month ago, year ago.

Source: *Fruit and Tree Nuts Situation and Outlook Yearbook.* **Price Frequency:** annually. **Effective Market(s):** United States. **Units of Measure:** cents per lb. **Type of Price:** grower. **Time Period Covered:** latest 20 years.

Source: *Marketing Florida, Georgia, South Carolina, North Carolina and Appalachian District Peaches.* **Price Frequency:** annually. **Effective Market(s):** 33 domestic markets. **Units of Measure:** Dollars per lb. **Time Period Covered:** latest 3 years.

PEACHES: BLAKE

Source: *The Packer.* **Price Frequency:** weekly, seasonally. **Effective Market(s):** varies. **Units of Measure:** Dollars per lug. **Type of Price:** received by farmer. **Time Period Covered:** latest week.

PEACHES: CAL RED

Source: *The Packer.* **Price Frequency:** weekly, seasonally. **Effective Market(s):** varies. **Units of Measure:** Dollars per lug. **Type of Price:** received by farmer. **Time Period Covered:** latest week.

PEACHES: CANNED

Source: *Fruit and Tree Nuts Situation and Outlook Yearbook.* **Price Frequency:** annually. **Effective Market(s):** United States. **Units of Measure:** Dollars per ton. **Type of Price:** grower. **Time Period Covered:** latest 20 years.

PEACHES: CREST HAVEN

Source: *The Packer.* **Price Frequency:** weekly, seasonally. **Effective Market(s):** varies. **Units of Measure:** Dollars per lug. **Type of Price:** received by farmer. **Time Period Covered:** latest week.

PEACHES: DRIED

Source: *Fruit and Tree Nuts Situation and Outlook Yearbook.* **Price Frequency:** annually. **Effective Market(s):** United States. **Units of Measure:** Dollars per ton. **Type of Price:** grower. **Time Period Covered:** latest 20 years.

PEACHES: EARLY RED HAVENS AND EARLY GLOW

Source: *Oregon Farmer-Stockman.* **Price Frequency:** monthly, seasonally. **Effective Market(s):** Yakima (WA). **Units of Measure:** Dollars per traypack carton. **Time Period Covered:** latest month.

PEACHES: EXTRA FANCY

Source: *Oregon Farmer-Stockman.* **Price Frequency:** monthly, seasonally. **Effective Market(s):** Yakima (WA). **Units of Measure:** Dollars per traypack carton. **Time Period Covered:** latest month.

PEACHES: FLAVORCREST

Source: *The Packer.* **Price Frequency:** weekly, seasonally. **Effective Market(s):** varies. **Units of Measure:** Dollars per lug. **Type of Price:** received by farmer. **Time Period Covered:** latest week.

PEACHES: FRESH

Source: *Agricultural Prices.* **Price Frequency:** monthly. **Effective Market(s):** United States. **Units of Measure:** Dollars per lb. **Type of Price:** received by farmer. **Time Period Covered:** latest 2 months, year ago.

Source: *Agricultural Prices Annual Summary.* **Price Frequency:** monthly, seasonally. **Effective Market(s):** United States. **Units of Measure:** Dollars per lb. **Type of Price:** average received by farmer. **Time Period Covered:** latest 6 years.

Source: *Agricultural Prices Annual Summary.* **Price Frequency:** annually. **Effective Market(s):** 32 domestic markets, United States. **Units of Measure:** Dollars per lb. **Type of Price:** received by farmer. **Time Period Covered:** latest 2 years, for US latest 6 years.

Source: *Fruit and Tree Nuts Situation and Outlook Yearbook.* **Price Frequency:** annually. **Effective Market(s):** United States. **Units of Measure:** cents per lb. **Type of Price:** grower. **Time Period Covered:** latest 20 years.

PEACHES: FROZEN

Source: *Fruit and Tree Nuts Situation and Outlook Yearbook.* **Price Frequency:** annually. **Effective Market(s):** United States. **Units of Measure:** Dollars per ton. **Type of Price:** grower. **Time Period Covered:** latest 20 years.

PEACHES: GLO HAVEN

Source: *The Packer.* **Price Frequency:** weekly, seasonally. **Effective Market(s):** varies. **Units of Measure:** Dollars per lug. **Type of Price:** received by farmer. **Time Period Covered:** latest week.

PEACHES: JEFFERSON

Source: *The Packer.* **Price Frequency:** weekly, seasonally. **Effective Market(s):** varies. **Units of Measure:** Dollars per lug. **Type of Price:** received by farmer. **Time Period Covered:** latest week.

PEACHES: LORING

Source: *Lancaster Farmer.* **Price Frequency:** weekly, seasonally. **Effective Market(s):** Pennsylvania. **Units of Measure:** Dollars per crate. **Type of Price:** market. **Time Period Covered:** latest week.

Source: *The Packer.* **Price Frequency:** weekly, seasonally. **Effective Market(s):** varies. **Units of Measure:** Dollars per lug. **Type of Price:** received by farmer. **Time Period Covered:** latest week.

PEACHES: MONROE

Source: *The Packer.* **Price Frequency:** weekly, seasonally. **Effective Market(s):** varies. **Units of Measure:** Dollars per lug. **Type of Price:** received by farmer. **Time Period Covered:** latest week.

PEACHES: O'HENRY

Source: *Lancaster Farmer.* **Price Frequency:** weekly, seasonally. **Effective Market(s):** Pennsylvania. **Units of Measure:** Dollars per tray pack. **Type of Price:** market. **Time Period Covered:** latest week.

Source: *The Packer.* **Price Frequency:** weekly, seasonally. **Effective Market(s):** varies. **Units of Measure:** Dollars per lug. **Type of Price:** received by farmer. **Time Period Covered:** latest week.

PEACHES: ORCHARD RUN

Source: *The Packer.* **Price Frequency:** weekly, seasonally. **Effective Market(s):** varies. **Units of Measure:** Dollars per lug. **Type of Price:** received by farmer. **Time Period Covered:** latest week.

PEACHES: PROCESSING

Source: *Fruit and Tree Nuts Situation and Outlook Yearbook.* **Price Frequency:** annually. **Effective Market(s):** United States. **Units of Measure:** Dollars per ton. **Type of Price:** grower. **Time Period Covered:** latest 20 years.

PEACHES: RED HAVEN

Source: *The Packer.* **Price Frequency:** weekly, seasonally. **Effective Market(s):** varies. **Units of Measure:** Dollars per lug. **Type of Price:** received by farmer. **Time Period Covered:** latest week.

PEACHES: REGINA

Source: *The Packer.* **Price Frequency:** weekly, seasonally. **Effective Market(s):** varies. **Units of Measure:** Dollars per lug. **Type of Price:** received by farmer. **Time Period Covered:** latest week.

PEACHES: RIO OSA GEM

Source: *The Packer.* **Price Frequency:** weekly, seasonally. **Effective Market(s):** varies. **Units of Measure:** Dollars per lug. **Type of Price:** received by farmer. **Time Period Covered:** latest week.

PEACHES: SLICED, FROZEN

Source: *HRI-Buyers Guide.* **Price Frequency:** weekly. **Effective Market(s):** Northeastern area. **Units of Measure:** cents per lb. **Type of Price:** prices paid by dining places & institutions. **Time Period Covered:** latest week.

PEACHES: SPARKLE

Source: *The Packer.* **Price Frequency:** weekly, seasonally. **Effective Market(s):** varies. **Units of Measure:** Dollars per lug. **Type of Price:** received by farmer. **Time Period Covered:** latest week.

PEACHES: SUMMER GLO

Source: *The Packer.* **Price Frequency:** weekly, seasonally. **Effective Market(s):** varies. **Units of Measure:** Dollars per lug. **Type of Price:** received by farmer. **Time Period Covered:** latest week.

PEACHES: SUN HIGH

Source: *The Packer.* **Price Frequency:** weekly, seasonally. **Effective Market(s):** varies. **Units of Measure:** Dollars per lug. **Type of Price:** received by farmer. **Time Period Covered:** latest week.

PEACHES: YELLOW FLESH

Source: *Fresh Fruit and Vegetable Prices.* **Price Frequency:** monthly, seasonally. **Effective Market(s):** 8 domestic markets. **Units of Measure:** Dollars per carton. **Type of Price:** average price at shipping point. **Time Period Covered:** latest year.

Source: *The Packer.* **Price Frequency:** weekly, seasonally. **Effective Market(s):** varies. **Units of Measure:** Dollars per lug. **Type of Price:** received by farmer. **Time Period Covered:** latest week.

PEACHES: YELLOW FLESH, APPALACHIAN DISTRICT

Source: *Marketing Florida, Georgia, South Carolina, North Carolina and Appalachian District Peaches.* **Price Frequency:** daily, seasonally. **Effective Market(s):** Appalachian District, Pittsburgh. **Units of Measure:** Dollars per bushel cartons. **Time Period Covered:** latest year.

PEACHES: YELLOW FLESH, CALIFORNIA

Source: *Fresh Fruit and Vegetable Prices.* **Price Frequency:** monthly, seasonally. **Effective Market(s):** Chicago, New York City. **Units of Measure:** Dollars per lug. **Type of Price:** average wholesale price. **Time Period Covered:** latest year.

PEACHES: YELLOW FLESH, CENTRAL GEORGIA

Source: *Marketing Florida, Georgia, South Carolina, North Carolina and Appalachian District Peaches.* **Price Frequency:** daily, seasonally. **Effective Market(s):** Central Georgia. **Units of Measure:** Dollars per bushel cartons. **Time Period Covered:** latest year.

PEACHES: YELLOW FLESH, CHILEAN

Source: *Fresh Fruit and Vegetable Prices.* **Price Frequency:** monthly, seasonally. **Effective Market(s):** New York City/Philadelphia. **Units of Measure:** Dollars per carton. **Type of Price:** dock price. **Time Period Covered:** latest year.

Source: *Fresh Fruit and Vegetable Prices.* **Price Frequency:** monthly, seasonally. **Effective Market(s):** Chicago, New York City. **Units of Measure:** Dollars per lug. **Type of Price:** average wholesale price. **Time Period Covered:** latest year.

PEACHES: YELLOW FLESH, FLORIDA

Source: *Marketing Florida, Georgia, South Carolina, North Carolina and Appalachian District Peaches.* **Price Frequency:** daily, seasonally. **Effective Market(s):** 6 domestic markets. **Units of Measure:** Dollars per bushel cartons. **Time Period Covered:** latest year.

PEACHES: YELLOW FLESH, GEORGIA

Source: *Fresh Fruit and Vegetable Prices.* **Price Frequency:** monthly, seasonally. **Effective Market(s):** Chicago, New York City. **Units of Measure:** Dollars per lug. **Type of Price:** average wholesale price. **Time Period Covered:** latest year.

Source: *Marketing Florida, Georgia, South Carolina, North Carolina and Appalachian District Peaches.* **Price Frequency:** daily, seasonally. **Effective Market(s):** 17 domestic markets. **Units of Measure:** Dollars per bushel cartons. **Time Period Covered:** latest year.

PEACHES: YELLOW FLESH, NEW JERSEY

Source: *Fresh Fruit and Vegetable Prices.* **Price Frequency:** monthly, seasonally. **Effective Market(s):** New York City. **Units of Measure:** Dollars per lug. **Type of Price:** average wholesale price. **Time Period Covered:** latest year.

PEACHES: YELLOW FLESH, NORTH FLORIDA/SOUTH GEORGIA

Source: *Marketing Florida, Georgia, South Carolina, North Carolina and Appalachian District Peaches.* **Price Frequency:** daily, seasonally. **Effective Market(s):** North Florida/South Georgia. **Units of Measure:** Dollars per bushel carton. **Time Period Covered:** latest year.

PEACHES: YELLOW FLESH, SOUTH CAROLINA

Source: *Fresh Fruit and Vegetable Prices.* **Price Frequency:** monthly, seasonally. **Effective Market(s):** Chicago, New York City. **Units of Measure:** Dollars per lug. **Type of Price:** average wholesale price. **Time Period Covered:** latest year.

Source: *Marketing Florida, Georgia, South Carolina, North Carolina and Appalachian District Peaches.* **Price Frequency:** daily, seasonally. **Effective Market(s):** South Carolina, 10 domestic markets. **Units of Measure:** Dollars per bushel cartons. **Time Period Covered:** latest year.

PEANUT MEAL

Source: *Feedstuffs.* **Price Frequency:** weekly. **Effective Market(s):** Atlanta. **Units of Measure:** Dollars per bulk ton. **Time Period Covered:** latest week.

Source: *Peanut Marketing Summary.* **Price Frequency:** monthly, seasonally. **Effective Market(s):** Southeast. **Units of Measure:** Dollars per bulk ton. **Type of Price:** average. **Time Period Covered:** latest 3 years.

Source: *Peanut Report.* **Price Frequency:** weekly, seasonally. **Effective Market(s):** Southeast. **Units of Measure:** cents per lb. **Time Period Covered:** latest week, week ago, year ago.

PEANUT MEAL: 48% PROTEIN, INDIAN

Source: *World Oilseed Situation and Market Highlights.* **Price Frequency:** monthly, annually. **Effective Market(s):** Rotterdam. **Units of Measure:** Dollars per metric ton. **Time Period Covered:** monthly latest year, annually latest 9 years.

PEANUT MEAL: 50% PROTEIN

Source: *World Oilseed Situation and Market Highlights.* **Price Frequency:** monthly, annually. **Effective Market(s):** Sotheast. **Units of Measure:** Dollars per metric ton. **Time Period Covered:** monthly latest year, annually latest 9 years.

PEANUT OIL

Source: *Milling & Baking News.* **Price Frequency:** weekly. **Effective Market(s):** Southeast. **Units of Measure:** cents per lb. **Type of Price:** spot bulk. **Time Period Covered:** latest week.

Source: *National Provisioner.* **Price Frequency:** weekly. **Units of Measure:** cents per lb. **Time Period Covered:** latest week.

Source: *Peanut Marketing Summary.* **Price Frequency:** monthly, seasonally. **Effective Market(s):** Southeast. **Units of Measure:** cents per lb. **Type of Price:** average. **Time Period Covered:** latest 3 years.

Source: *Peanut Report.* **Price Frequency:** weekly, seasonally. **Effective Market(s):** Southeast. **Units of Measure:** cents per lb. **Time Period Covered:** latest week, week ago, year ago.

Source: *World Oilseed Situation and Market Highlights.* **Price Frequency:** monthly, annually. **Effective Market(s):** Rotterdam. **Units of Measure:** Dollars per metric ton. **Time Period Covered:** monthly latest year, annually latest 9 years.

PEANUT OIL: CRUDE

Source: *Chemical Marketing Reporter.* **Price Frequency:** weekly. **Effective Market(s):** Southeast. **Units of Measure:** cents per lb. **Type of Price:** spot. **Time Period Covered:** latest week.

Source: *Journal of Commerce and Commercial.* **Price Frequency:** daily. **Effective Market(s):** Southeast. **Units of Measure:** Dollars per lb. **Type of Price:** spot supplier. **Time Period Covered:** latest day.

Source: *Oil Crops Situation and Outlook.* **Price Frequency:** monthly. **Effective Market(s):** Southeast. **Units of Measure:** cents per lb. **Type of Price:** wholesale. **Time Period Covered:** latest 5 months.

Source: *Wall Street Journal.* **Price Frequency:** daily. **Effective Market(s):** Southeast. **Units of Measure:** Dollars per lb. **Time Period Covered:** latest day, day ago, year ago.

Source: *World Oilseed Situation and Market Highlights.* **Price Frequency:** monthly, annually. **Effective Market(s):** Southeast. **Units of Measure:** Dollars per metric ton. **Time Period Covered:** monthly latest year, annually latest 9 years.

PEANUT OIL: CRUDE, DOMESTIC

Source: *Commodity Year Book.* **Price Frequency:** monthly, annually. **Effective Market(s):** Southeast mills. **Units of Measure:** cents per lb. **Time Period Covered:** latest 9 years.

PEANUT OIL: REFINED

Source: *Chemical Marketing Reporter.* **Price Frequency:** weekly. **Effective Market(s):** New York. **Units of Measure:** Dollars per lb. **Type of Price:** spot. **Time Period Covered:** latest week.

PEANUT OILMEAL: 50%

Source: *Chemical Marketing Reporter.* **Price Frequency:** weekly. **Effective Market(s):** Alabama, Southeast. **Units of Measure:** Dollars per ton. **Type of Price:** spot. **Time Period Covered:** latest week.

PEANUTS

see also Groundnuts.

Source: *Agricultural Prices Annual Summary.* **Price Frequency:** annually. **Effective Market(s):** 9 domestic markets, United States. **Units of Measure:** Dollars per lb. **Type of Price:** average received by farmer. **Time Period Covered:** latest 2 years, for US latest 6 years.

Source: *Commodity Year Book.* **Price Frequency:** annually. **Effective Market(s):** United States. **Units of Measure:** cents per lb. **Type of Price:** farm price. **Time Period Covered:** latest 14 years.

Source: *Oil Crops Situation and Outlook.* **Price Frequency:** monthly, annually. **Effective Market(s):** United States. **Units of Measure:** cents per lb. **Type of Price:** received by farmer. **Time Period Covered:** monthly latest 5 months, annually latest 10 years.

Source: *Peanut Marketing Summary.* **Price Frequency:** annually. **Effective Market(s):** United States. **Units of Measure:** cents per lb. **Type of Price:** received by farmer. **Time Period Covered:** latest 10 years.

PEANUTS: EDIBLE, SHELLED

Source: *World Oilseed Situation and Market Highlights.* **Price Frequency:** monthly, annually. **Effective Market(s):** Rotterdam. **Units of Measure:** Dollars per metric ton. **Type of Price:** farm. **Time Period Covered:** monthly latest year, annually latest 9 years.

PEANUTS: GOVERNMENT SUPPORTED

Source: *Commodity Year Book.* **Price Frequency:** annually. **Effective Market(s):** United States. **Units of Measure:** cents per lb. **Type of Price:** support. **Time Period Covered:** latest 13 years.

PEANUTS: IN SHELL

Source: *Agricultural Prices.* **Price Frequency:** monthly. **Effective Market(s):** United States. **Units of Measure:** Dollars per lb. **Type of Price:** received by farmer. **Time Period Covered:** latest 2 months, year ago.

Source: *Agricultural Prices.* **Price Frequency:** monthly, seasonally. **Effective Market(s):** 7 domestic markets, United States. **Units of Measure:** Dollars per lb. **Type of Price:** received by farmer. **Time Period Covered:** latest 2 months.

Source: *Agricultural Prices.* **Price Frequency:** monthly. **Effective Market(s):** Southeast, Southwest, United States, Virginia/Carolina. **Units of Measure:** Dollars per lb. **Type of Price:** received by farmer. **Time Period Covered:** latest 2 months, year ago.

Source: *Commodity Year Book.* **Price Frequency:** monthly, annually. **Effective Market(s):** United States. **Units of Measure:** cents per lb. **Type of Price:** price received by producers. **Time Period Covered:** latest 10 years.

Source: *World Oilseed Situation and Market Highlights.* **Price Frequency:** monthly, annually. **Effective Market(s):** United States. **Units of Measure:** Dollars per metric ton. **Type of Price:** farm. **Time Period Covered:** monthly latest year, annually latest 9 years.

PEANUTS: RUNNERS, JUMBO, SHELLED

Source: *Peanut Marketing Summary.* **Price Frequency:** monthly, seasonally. **Effective Market(s):** Southeast, Southwest. **Units of Measure:** cents per lb. **Type of Price:** average. **Time Period Covered:** latest 10 years.

Source: *Peanut Report.* **Price Frequency:** weekly. **Effective Market(s):** Southeastern Section, Southwestern Section. **Units of Measure:** cents per lb. **Type of Price:** local prices in shipping section. **Time Period Covered:** latest week, week ago, year ago.

PEANUTS: RUNNERS, MEDIUM, SHELLED

Source: *Peanut Marketing Summary.* **Price Frequency:** monthly, seasonally. **Effective Market(s):** Southeast, Southwest. **Units of Measure:** cents per lb. **Type of Price:** average. **Time Period Covered:** latest 10 years.

Source: *Peanut Report.* **Price Frequency:** weekly, seasonally. **Effective Market(s):** Southeastern Section, Southwestern Section. **Units of Measure:** cents per lb. **Type of Price:** local prices in shipping section. **Time Period Covered:** latest week, week ago, year ago.

PEANUTS: RUNNERS, NO. 1, SHELLED

Source: *Peanut Marketing Summary.* **Price Frequency:** monthly, seasonally. **Effective Market(s):** Southeast. **Units of Measure:** cents per lb. **Type of Price:** average. **Time Period Covered:** latest 10 years.

Source: *Peanut Report.* **Price Frequency:** weekly, seasonally. **Effective Market(s):** Southeastern Section, Southwestern Section. **Units of Measure:** cents per lb. **Type of Price:** local prices in shipping section. **Time Period Covered:** latest week, week ago, year ago.

PEANUTS: RUNNERS, SHELLED

Source: *Peanut Report.* **Price Frequency:** weekly, seasonally. **Effective Market(s):** Southeastern Section, Southwestern Section. **Units of Measure:** cents per lb. **Type of Price:** local prices in shipping section. **Time Period Covered:** latest week, week ago, year ago.

PEANUTS: RUNNERS, U.S. SPLITS

Source: *Peanut Marketing Summary.* **Price Frequency:** monthly, seasonally. **Effective Market(s):** Southeast, Southwest. **Units of Measure:** cents per lb. **Type of Price:** average. **Time Period Covered:** latest 10 years.

PEANUTS: RUNNERS, U.S. SPLITS, SHELLED

Source: *Peanut Report.* **Price Frequency:** weekly, seasonally. **Effective Market(s):** Southeastern Section, Southwestern Section. **Units of Measure:** cents per lb. **Type of Price:** local prices in shipping section. **Time Period Covered:** latest week, week ago, year ago.

PEANUTS: SPANISH, JUMBO, SHELLED

Source: *Peanut Marketing Summary.* **Price Frequency:** monthly, seasonally. **Effective Market(s):** Southwest. **Units of Measure:** cents per lb. **Type of Price:** average. **Time Period Covered:** latest 10 years.

Source: *Peanut Report.* **Price Frequency:** weekly, seasonally. **Effective Market(s):** Southwestern Section. **Units of Measure:** cents per lb. **Type of Price:** local prices in shipping section. **Time Period Covered:** latest week, week ago, year ago.

PEANUTS: SPANISH, NO. 1, SHELLED

Source: *Peanut Marketing Summary.* **Price Frequency:** monthly, seasonally. **Effective Market(s):** Southwest. **Units of Measure:** cents per lb. **Type of Price:** average. **Time Period Covered:** latest 10 years.

Source: *Peanut Report.* **Price Frequency:** weekly, seasonally. **Effective Market(s):** Southwestern Section. **Units of Measure:** cents per lb. **Type of Price:** local prices in shipping section. **Time Period Covered:** latest week, week ago, year ago.

PEANUTS: SPANISH, U.S. SPLITS, SHELLED

Source: *Peanut Marketing Summary.* **Price Frequency:** monthly, seasonally. **Effective Market(s):** Southwest. **Units of Measure:** cents per lb. **Type of Price:** average. **Time Period Covered:** latest 10 years.

Source: *Peanut Report.* **Price Frequency:** weekly, seasonally. **Effective Market(s):** Southwestern Section. **Units of Measure:** cents per lb. **Type of Price:** local prices in shipping section. **Time Period Covered:** latest week, week ago, year ago.

PEANUTS: VIRGINIAS, EXTRA LARGE, SHELLED

Source: *Peanut Marketing Summary.* **Price Frequency:** monthly, seasonally. **Effective Market(s):** Virginia/North Carolina. **Units of Measure:** cents per lb. **Type of Price:** average. **Time Period Covered:** latest 10 years.

Source: *Peanut Report.* **Price Frequency:** weekly, seasonally. **Effective Market(s):** Virginia/North Carolina Section. **Units of Measure:** cents per lb. **Type of Price:** local prices in shipping section. **Time Period Covered:** latest week, week ago, year ago.

PEANUTS: VIRGINIAS, FANCY, UNSHELLED

Source: *Peanut Marketing Summary.* **Price Frequency:** monthly, seasonally. **Effective Market(s):** Virginia/North Carolina. **Units of Measure:** cents per lb. **Type of Price:** average. **Time Period Covered:** latest 10 years.

Source: *Peanut Report.* **Price Frequency:** weekly, seasonally. **Effective Market(s):** Virginia/North Carolina Section. **Units of Measure:** cents per lb. **Type of Price:** local prices in shipping section. **Time Period Covered:** latest week, week ago year ago.

PEANUTS: VIRGINIAS, JUMBO, UNSHELLED

Source: *Peanut Marketing Summary.* **Price Frequency:** monthly, seasonally. **Effective Market(s):** Virginia/North Carolina. **Units of Measure:** cents per lb. **Type of Price:** average. **Time Period Covered:** latest 10 years.

Source: *Peanut Report.* **Price Frequency:** weekly, seasonally. **Effective Market(s):** Virginia/North Carolina Section. **Units of Measure:** cents per lb. **Type of Price:** local prices in shipping section. **Time Period Covered:** latest week, week ago, year ago.

PEANUTS: VIRGINIAS, MEDIUM, SHELLED

Source: *Peanut Marketing Summary.* **Price Frequency:** monthly, seasonally. **Effective Market(s):** Virginia/North Carolina. **Units of Measure:** cents per lb. **Type of Price:** average. **Time Period Covered:** latest 10 years.

Source: *Peanut Report.* **Price Frequency:** weekly, seasonally. **Effective Market(s):** Virginia/North Carolina Section. **Units of Measure:** cents per lb. **Type of Price:** local prices in shipping section. **Time Period Covered:** latest week, week ago, year ago.

PEANUTS: VIRGINIAS, NO. 1, SHELLED

Source: *Peanut Marketing Summary.* **Price Frequency:** monthly, seasonally. **Effective Market(s):** Virginia/North Carolina. **Units of Measure:** cents per lb. **Type of Price:** average. **Time Period Covered:** latest 10 years.

Source: *Peanut Report.* **Price Frequency:** weekly, seasonally. **Effective Market(s):** Virginia/North Carolina Section. **Units of Measure:** cents per lb. **Type of Price:** local prices in shipping section. **Time Period Covered:** latest week, week ago, year ago.

PEANUTS: VIRGINIAS, NO. 1 WITH SPLITS, SHELLED

Source: *Peanut Report.* **Price Frequency:** weekly, seasonally. **Effective Market(s):** Virginia/North Carolina Section. **Units of Measure:** cents per lb. **Type of Price:** local prices in shipping section. **Time Period Covered:** latest week, week ago, year ago.

PEANUTS: VIRGINIAS, NO. 2 WITH 70% SPLITS OR BETTER, SHELLED

Source: *Peanut Report.* **Price Frequency:** weekly, seasonally. **Effective Market(s):** Virginia/North Carolina Section. **Units of Measure:** cents per lb. **Type of Price:** local prices in shipping section. **Time Period Covered:** latest week, week ago, year ago.

PEANUTS: VIRGINIAS, NO. 2 WITH 70% SPLITS, SHELLED

Source: *Peanut Marketing Summary.* **Price Frequency:** monthly, seasonally. **Effective Market(s):** Virginia/North Carolina. **Units of Measure:** cents per lb. **Type of Price:** average. **Time Period Covered:** latest 10 years.

PEANUTS: VIRGINIAS, NO. 2 WITH 80% SPLITS OR BETTER, SHELLED

Source: *Peanut Report.* **Price Frequency:** weekly, seasonally. **Effective Market(s):** Virginia/North Carolina Section. **Units of Measure:** cents per lb. **Type of Price:** local prices in shipping section. **Time Period Covered:** latest week, week ago, year ago.

PEANUTS: VIRGINIAS, VIRGINIA SPLITS, SHELLED

Source: *Peanut Report.* **Price Frequency:** weekly, seasonally. **Effective Market(s):** Virginia/North Carolina Section. **Units of Measure:** cents per lb. **Type of Price:** local prices in shipping section. **Time Period Covered:** latest week, week ago, year ago.

PEANUTS FOR SEED

see Seed Peanuts.

PEARS

Source: *Agricultural Outlook.* **Price Frequency:** monthly. **Units of Measure:** Dollars per box. **Type of Price:** shipping point. **Time Period Covered:** latest year.

Source: *Agricultural Prices Annual Summary.* **Price Frequency:** annually. **Effective Market(s):** 9 domestic markets, United States. **Units of Measure:** Dollars per ton. **Type of Price:** average received by farmer. **Time Period Covered:** latest 3 years, for US latest 6 years.

PEARS: ANJOU

Source: *Fresh Fruit and Vegetable Prices.* **Price Frequency:** monthly, seasonally. **Effective Market(s):** Yakima Valley/Wenatchee (WA). **Units of Measure:** Dollars per carton. **Type of Price:** average price at shipping point. **Time Period Covered:** latest year.

Source: *Fruit and Tree Nuts Situation and Outlook Yearbook.* **Price Frequency:** annually. **Effective Market(s):** United States. **Units of Measure:** Dollars per lb. **Type of Price:** retail. **Time Period Covered:** latest 9 years.

PEARS: ANJOU, WASHINGTON

Source: *Fresh Fruit and Vegetable Prices.* **Price Frequency:** monthly, seasonally. **Effective Market(s):** Chicago, New York City. **Units of Measure:** Dollars per carton. **Type of Price:** average wholesale price. **Time Period Covered:** latest year.

PEARS: ASIAN

Source: *The Packer.* **Price Frequency:** weekly, seasonally. **Effective Market(s):** varies. **Units of Measure:** Dollars per carton. **Type of Price:** received by farmer. **Time Period Covered:** latest week.

PEARS: BARTLETT

Source: *California Farmer.* **Price Frequency:** semimonthly, seasonally. **Effective Market(s):** Sacramento District (CA), Lake County (CA). **Units of Measure:** Dollars per 36 lb. carton. **Time Period Covered:** latest week, month ago, year ago.

Source: *Fresh Fruit and Vegetable Prices.* **Price Frequency:** monthly, seasonally. **Effective Market(s):** Lake County (CA), Sacramento District (CA), Mendocino County (CA), Yakima Valley/Wenatchee (WA). **Units of Measure:** Dollars per carton. **Type of Price:** average price at shipping point. **Time Period Covered:** latest year.

Source: *Fruit and Tree Nuts Situation and Outlook Yearbook.* **Price Frequency:** annually. **Effective Market(s):** United States. **Units of Measure:** Dollars per short ton. **Type of Price:** grower. **Time Period Covered:** latest 20 years.

Source: *Lancaster Farmer.* **Price Frequency:** weekly, seasonally. **Effective Market(s):** Pennsylvania. **Units of Measure:** Dollars per carton. **Type of Price:** market. **Time Period Covered:** latest week.

Source: *The Packer.* **Price Frequency:** weekly, seasonally. **Effective Market(s):** varies. **Units of Measure:** Dollars per carton. **Type of Price:** received by farmer. **Time Period Covered:** latest week.

PEARS: BARTLETT, CALIFORNIA

Source: *Fresh Fruit and Vegetable Prices.* **Price Frequency:** monthly, seasonally. **Effective Market(s):** Chicago, New York City. **Units of Measure:** Dollars per carton. **Type of Price:** average wholesale price. **Time Period Covered:** latest year.

PEARS: BARTLETT, FRESH

Source: *Fruit and Tree Nuts Situation and Outlook Yearbook.* **Price Frequency:** annually. **Effective Market(s):** United States. **Units of Measure:** Dollars per short ton. **Type of Price:** grower. **Time Period Covered:** latest 20 years.

PEARS: BARTLETT, PROCESSING EXCLUDING DRIED

Source: *Fruit and Tree Nuts Situation and Outlook Yearbook.* **Price Frequency:** annually. **Effective Market(s):** United States. **Units of Measure:** Dollars per short ton. **Type of Price:** grower. **Time Period Covered:** latest 20 years.

PEARS: BOSC

Source: *Lancaster Farmer.* **Price Frequency:** weekly, seasonally. **Effective Market(s):** Pennsylvania. **Units of Measure:** Dollars per carton. **Type of Price:** market. **Time Period Covered:** latest week.

Source: *The Packer.* **Price Frequency:** weekly, seasonally. **Effective Market(s):** varies. **Units of Measure:** Dollars per carton. **Type of Price:** received by farmer. **Time Period Covered:** latest week.

PEARS: BOSC, CHILEAN

Source: *Fresh Fruit and Vegetable Prices.* **Price Frequency:** monthly. **Effective Market(s):** New York City/Philadelphia. **Units of Measure:** Dollars per carton. **Type of Price:** dock price. **Time Period Covered:** latest year.

PEARS: FRESH

Source: *Agricultural Outlook.* **Price Frequency:** monthly, annually. **Effective Market(s):** United States. **Units of Measure:** Dollars per 100 lbs. **Type of Price:** received by farmer. **Time Period Covered:** monthly latest 6 months, annually latest 3 years.

Source: *Agricultural Prices.* **Price Frequency:** monthly. **Effective Market(s):** United States. **Units of Measure:** Dollars per ton. **Type of Price:** received by farmer. **Time Period Covered:** latest 2 months, year ago.

Source: *Agricultural Prices Annual Summary.* **Price Frequency:** monthly, seasonally. **Effective Market(s):** United States. **Units of Measure:** Dollars per ton. **Type of Price:** average received by farmer. **Time Period Covered:** latest 6 years.

Source: *Agricultural Prices Annual Summary.* **Price Frequency:** annually. **Effective Market(s):** United States. **Units of Measure:** Dollars per ton. **Type of Price:** average received by farmer. **Time Period Covered:** latest 3 years, for US latest 6 years.

PEARS: PACKHAM TRIUMPH, CHILEAN

Source: *Fresh Fruit and Vegetable Prices.* **Price Frequency:** monthly, seasonally. **Effective Market(s):** New York City/Philadelphia. **Units of Measure:** Dollars per carton. **Type of Price:** dock price. **Time Period Covered:** latest year.

Source: *Fresh Fruit and Vegetable Prices.* **Price Frequency:** monthly, seasonally. **Effective Market(s):** Chicago, New York City. **Units of Measure:** Dollars per carton. **Type of Price:** average wholesale price. **Time Period Covered:** latest year.

PEARS: RED ANJOU

Source: *The Packer.* **Price Frequency:** weekly, seasonally. **Effective Market(s):** varies. **Units of Measure:** Dollars per carton. **Type of Price:** received by farmer. **Time Period Covered:** latest week.

PEARS: RED CRIMSON

Source: *The Packer.* **Price Frequency:** weekly, seasonally. **Effective Market(s):** varies. **Units of Measure:** Dollars per carton. **Type of Price:** received by farmer. **Time Period Covered:** latest week.

PEARS: SECKEL

Source: *The Packer.* **Price Frequency:** weekly, seasonally. **Effective Market(s):** varies. **Units of Measure:** Dollars per carton. **Type of Price:** received by farmer. **Time Period Covered:** latest week.

PEARS: SUMMER BARTLETT, CHILEAN

Source: *Fresh Fruit and Vegetable Prices.* **Price Frequency:** monthly, seasonally. **Effective Market(s):** New York City/Philadelphia. **Units of Measure:** Dollars per carton. **Type of Price:** dock price. **Time Period Covered:** latest year.

PEAS

Source: *Farmers Weekly.* **Price Frequency:** daily, seasonally. **Effective Market(s):** Essex (England), Lincolnshire (England). **Units of Measure:** British pounds per tonne. **Type of Price:** spot. **Time Period Covered:** latest day.

Source: *Fruit and Tree Nuts Situation and Outlook Yearbook.* **Price Frequency:** annually. **Effective Market(s):** United States. **Units of Measure:** Dollars per short ton. **Type of Price:** grower. **Time Period Covered:** latest 20 years.

PEAS: AUSTRIAN WINTER

Source: *Bean Market News.* **Price Frequency:** weekly. **Effective Market(s):** Idaho/Washington. **Units of Measure:** Dollars per 100 lbs. **Type of Price:** dealer. **Time Period Covered:** latest week, week ago, year ago.

Source: *Bean Market News.* **Price Frequency:** weekly. **Effective Market(s):** Idaho, Washington. **Units of Measure:** Dollars per 100 lbs. **Type of Price:** grower. **Time Period Covered:** latest week, week ago.

PEAS: BLACK

Source: *Idaho Farmer-Stockman.* **Price Frequency:** monthly. **Effective Market(s):** Moscow (ID). **Type of Price:** bid to grower. **Time Period Covered:** latest month, month ago.

Source: *Oregon Farmer-Stockman.* **Price Frequency:** monthly, seasonally. **Effective Market(s):** Moscow (ID). **Type of Price:** bid to grower. **Time Period Covered:** latest 2 months.

Source: *Washington Farmer-Stockman.* **Price Frequency:** monthly. **Effective Market(s):** Moscow (ID). **Type of Price:** bid to grower. **Time Period Covered:** latest 2 months.

PEAS: ENGLISH TYPE, FRESH

Source: *HRI-Buyers Guide.* **Price Frequency:** weekly. **Effective Market(s):** Northeastern area. **Units of Measure:** Dollars per crate. **Type of Price:** prices paid by dining places & institutions. **Time Period Covered:** latest week.

PEAS: FEED

Source: *Farmers Weekly.* **Price Frequency:** weekly. **Effective Market(s):** Great Britain. **Units of Measure:** British pounds per tonne. **Type of Price:** spot. **Time Period Covered:** latest week, week ago, year ago.

PEAS: GREEN

Source: *Bean Market News.* **Price Frequency:** weekly. **Effective Market(s):** Idaho, Washington. **Units of Measure:** Dollars per 100 lbs. **Type of Price:** grower. **Time Period Covered:** latest week, week ago.

Source: *Idaho Farmer-Stockman.* **Price Frequency:** monthly. **Effective Market(s):** Moscow (ID). **Type of Price:** bid to grower. **Time Period Covered:** latest month, month ago.

Source: *Lancaster Farmer.* **Price Frequency:** weekly, seasonally. **Effective Market(s):** Pennsylvania. **Units of Measure:** Dollars per crate. **Type of Price:** market. **Time Period Covered:** latest week.

Source: *Oregon Farmer-Stockman.* **Price Frequency:** monthly, seasonally. **Effective Market(s):** Moscow (ID). **Type of Price:** bid to grower. **Time Period Covered:** latest 2 months.

Source: *Washington Farmer-Stockman.* **Price Frequency:** monthly. **Effective Market(s):** Moscow (ID). **Type of Price:** bid to grower. **Time Period Covered:** latest 2 months.

PEAS: GREEN, CALIFORNIA

Source: *Fresh Fruit and Vegetable Prices.* **Price Frequency:** monthly, seasonally. **Effective Market(s):** Chicago, New York City. **Units of Measure:** Dollars per crate/carton. **Type of Price:** average wholesale price. **Time Period Covered:** latest year.

PEAS: GREEN, DRY

Source: *Vegetable Specialties Situation and Outlook Report.* **Price Frequency:** monthly, annually. **Effective Market(s):** United States. **Units of Measure:** Dollars per 100 lbs. **Type of Price:** received by grower. **Time Period Covered:** latest 4 years.

PEAS: GREEN, DRY, ALASKAN

Source: *FAO Quarterly Bulletin of Statistics.* **Price Frequency:** monthly, annually. **Effective Market(s):** United Kingdom. **Units of Measure:** British pounds per 1000 kilograms, per metric ton. **Time Period Covered:** latest 3 years.

PEAS: GREEN, FROZEN

Source: *HRI-Buyers Guide.* **Price Frequency:** weekly. **Effective Market(s):** Northeastern area. **Units of Measure:** cents per lb. **Type of Price:** prices paid by dining places & institutions. **Time Period Covered:** latest week.

Source: *Vegetable Specialties Situation and Outlook Report.* **Price Frequency:** monthly. **Units of Measure:** Dollars per case. **Type of Price:** food service, retail. **Time Period Covered:** latest month, year ago.

PEAS: GREEN, MEXICO

Source: *Fresh Fruit and Vegetable Prices.* **Price Frequency:** monthly, seasonally. **Effective Market(s):** Chicago, New York City. **Units of Measure:** Dollars per crate/carton. **Type of Price:** average wholesale price. **Time Period Covered:** latest year.

PEAS: GREEN, SPLIT

Source: *Bean Market News.* **Price Frequency:** weekly. **Effective Market(s):** Idaho/Washington. **Units of Measure:** Dollars per 100 lbs. **Type of Price:** dealer. **Time Period Covered:** latest week, week ago, year ago.

PEAS: GREEN, WHOLE

Source: *Bean Market News.* **Price Frequency:** weekly. **Effective Market(s):** Idaho/Washington. **Units of Measure:** Dollars per 100 lbs. **Type of Price:** dealer. **Time Period Covered:** latest week, week ago, year ago.

PEAS: SOUTHERN

Source: *Lancaster Farmer.* **Price Frequency:** weekly, seasonally. **Effective Market(s):** Pennsylvania. **Units of Measure:** Dollars per unit. **Type of Price:** market. **Time Period Covered:** latest week.

PEAS: SUGAR

Source: *Lancaster Farmer.* **Price Frequency:** weekly, seasonally. **Effective Market(s):** Pennsylvania. **Units of Measure:** Dollars per carton. **Type of Price:** market. **Time Period Covered:** latest week.

PEAS: SWEET, CANNED

Source: *Vegetable Specialties Situation and Outlook Report.* **Price Frequency:** monthly. **Units of Measure:** Dollars per case. **Type of Price:** wholesale. **Time Period Covered:** latest month, year ago.

PEAS: YELLOW

Source: *Bean Market News.* **Price Frequency:** weekly. **Effective Market(s):** Idaho, Washington. **Units of Measure:** Dollars per 100 lbs. **Type of Price:** grower. **Time Period Covered:** latest week, week ago.

Source: *Idaho Farmer-Stockman.* **Price Frequency:** monthly. **Effective Market(s):** Moscow (ID). **Type of Price:** bid to grower. **Time Period Covered:** latest month, month ago.

Source: *Oregon Farmer-Stockman.* **Price Frequency:** monthly, seasonally. **Effective Market(s):** Moscow (ID). **Type of Price:** bid to grower. **Time Period Covered:** latest 2 months.

Source: *Washington Farmer-Stockman.* **Price Frequency:** monthly. **Effective Market(s):** Moscow (ID). **Type of Price:** bid to grower. **Time Period Covered:** latest 2 months.

PEAS: YELLOW, DRY

Source: *Vegetable Specialties Situation and Outlook Report.* **Price Frequency:** monthly, annually. **Effective Market(s):** United States. **Units of Measure:** Dollars per 100 lbs. **Type of Price:** received by grower. **Time Period Covered:** latest 4 years.

PEAS: YELLOW, SPLIT

Source: *Bean Market News.* **Price Frequency:** weekly. **Effective Market(s):** Idaho/Washington. **Units of Measure:** Dollars per 100 lbs. **Type of Price:** dealer. **Time Period Covered:** latest week, week ago, year ago.

PEAS: YELLOW, WHOLE

Source: *Bean Market News.* **Price Frequency:** weekly. **Effective Market(s):** Idaho/Washington. **Units of Measure:** Dollars per 100 lbs. **Type of Price:** dealer. **Time Period Covered:** latest week, week ago, year ago.

PEAS AND CARROTS: FROZEN

Source: *HRI-Buyers Guide.* **Price Frequency:** weekly. **Effective Market(s):** Northeastern area. **Units of Measure:** cents per lb. **Type of Price:** prices paid by dining places & institutions. **Time Period Covered:** latest week.

PECANS

Source: *Agricultural Prices Annual Summary.* **Price Frequency:** annually. **Effective Market(s):** 11 domestic markets, United States. **Units of Measure:** Dollars per lb. **Type of Price:** average received by farmer. **Time Period Covered:** latest 3 years, for US latest 6 years.

PECANS: IMPROVED VARIETIES

Source: *Fresh Fruit and Vegetable Prices.* **Price Frequency:** monthly, seasonally. **Effective Market(s):** Texas. **Units of Measure:** Dollars per lb. **Type of Price:** paid to growers. **Time Period Covered:** latest year.

PECANS: IMPROVED VARIETIES, IN SHELL

Source: *Fruit and Tree Nuts Situation and Outlook Yearbook.* **Price Frequency:** annually. **Effective Market(s):** California. **Units of Measure:** cents per lb. **Type of Price:** grower. **Time Period Covered:** latest 20 years.

PECANS: IN SHELL

Source: *Fruit and Tree Nuts Situation and Outlook Yearbook.* **Price Frequency:** annually. **Effective Market(s):** California. **Units of Measure:** cents per lb. **Type of Price:** grower. **Time Period Covered:** latest 20 years.

PECANS: MONEYMAKER

Source: *Fresh Fruit and Vegetable Prices.* **Price Frequency:** monthly, seasonally. **Effective Market(s):** Florida/Georgia/Mississippi. **Units of Measure:** Dollars per lb. **Type of Price:** paid to grower. **Time Period Covered:** latest year.

PECANS: NATIVE AND SEEDLING, IN SHELL

Source: *Fruit and Tree Nuts Situation and Outlook Yearbook.* **Price Frequency:** annually. **Effective Market(s):** California. **Units of Measure:** cents per lb. **Type of Price:** grower. **Time Period Covered:** latest 20 years.

PECANS: NATIVES

Source: *Fresh Fruit and Vegetable Prices.* **Price Frequency:** monthly, seasonally. **Effective Market(s):** Texas. **Units of Measure:** Dollars per lb. **Type of Price:** paid to grower. **Time Period Covered:** latest year.

PECANS: STUARTS

Source: *Fresh Fruit and Vegetable Prices.* **Price Frequency:** monthly, seasonally. **Effective Market(s):** Florida/Georgia/Mississippi. **Units of Measure:** Dollars per lb. **Type of Price:** paid to grower. **Time Period Covered:** latest year.

PECTIN: HIGH METHOXYL

Source: *Chemical Marketing Reporter.* **Price Frequency:** weekly. **Effective Market(s):** New York. **Units of Measure:** Dollars per lb. **Type of Price:** spot. **Time Period Covered:** latest week.

PECTIN: LOW METHOXYL

Source: *Chemical Marketing Reporter.* **Price Frequency:** weekly. **Effective Market(s):** New York. **Units of Measure:** Dollars per lb. **Type of Price:** spot. **Time Period Covered:** latest week.

PEEK

Source: *Plastics Technology.* **Price Frequency:** monthly. **Units of Measure:** cents per lb., cents per cubic inch. **Type of Price:** bulk list, market. **Time Period Covered:** latest month.

PEEK: 30% GLASS

Source: *Plastics Technology.* **Price Frequency:** monthly. **Units of Measure:** cents per lb., cents per cubic inch. **Type of Price:** bulk list, market. **Time Period Covered:** latest month.

PELARGONIC ACID: SYNTHETIC

Source: *Chemical Marketing Reporter.* **Price Frequency:** weekly. **Effective Market(s):** New York. **Units of Measure:** Dollars per lb. **Type of Price:** spot. **Time Period Covered:** latest week.

PENICILLIN: POTASSIUM, NON-STERILE

Source: *Chemical Marketing Reporter.* **Price Frequency:** weekly. **Effective Market(s):** New York. **Units of Measure:** Dollars per billion units. **Type of Price:** spot. **Time Period Covered:** latest week.

PENICILLIN: POTASSIUM, STERILE

Source: *Journal of Commerce and Commercial.* **Price Frequency:** weekly in Friday issue. **Units of Measure:** Dollars per billion units. **Type of Price:** spot. **Time Period Covered:** latest week.

PENICILLIN: PROCAINE, STERILE

Source: *Chemical Marketing Reporter.* **Price Frequency:** weekly. **Effective Market(s):** New York. **Units of Measure:** Dollars per billion units. **Type of Price:** spot. **Time Period Covered:** latest week.

Source: *Journal of Commerce and Commercial.* **Price Frequency:** weekly in Friday issue. **Units of Measure:** Dollars per. **Type of Price:** spot. **Time Period Covered:** latest week.

PENTACHLOROPHENOL

Source: *Chemical Marketing Reporter.* **Price Frequency:** weekly. **Effective Market(s):** Wichita (KS). **Units of Measure:** Dollars per lb. **Type of Price:** spot. **Time Period Covered:** latest week.

PENTAERYTHRITOL

Source: *Journal of Commerce and Commercial.* **Price Frequency:** weekly in Wednesday issue. **Units of Measure:** Dollars per lb. **Type of Price:** spot. **Time Period Covered:** latest week.

PENTAERYTHRITOL: TECHNICAL

Source: *Chemical Marketing Reporter.* **Price Frequency:** weekly. **Effective Market(s):** New York. **Units of Measure:** Dollars per lb. **Type of Price:** spot. **Time Period Covered:** latest week.

PENTAERYTHRITOL, DI- AND TRI-ISOMERS

see Dipentaerythritol, Tripentaerythritol.

PENTAERYTHRITOL TRIACRYLATE

Source: *Chemical Marketing Reporter.* **Price Frequency:** weekly. **Effective Market(s):** New York. **Units of Measure:** Dollars per lb. **Type of Price:** spot. **Time Period Covered:** latest week.

PENTANES PLUS

Source: *Energy Pricing News: Petrochemical Report.* **Price Frequency:** bimonthly. **Effective Market(s):** Edmonton (Canada), Sarnia (Canada). **Units of Measure:** Canadian dollars per cubic meter. **Type of Price:** contract. **Time Period Covered:** latest month.

Source: *Oil & Gas Journal.* **Price Frequency:** monthly in third issue of month. **Effective Market(s):** Conway (KS), Mont Belvieu (TX). **Units of Measure:** cents per gallon. **Type of Price:** spot. **Time Period Covered:** latest 2 months.

PENTOBARBITAL

Source: *Chemical Marketing Reporter.* **Price Frequency:** weekly. **Effective Market(s):** New York. **Units of Measure:** Dollars per lb. **Type of Price:** spot. **Time Period Covered:** latest week.

PENTOBARBITAL-SODIUM

Source: *Chemical Marketing Reporter.* **Price Frequency:** weekly. **Effective Market(s):** New York. **Units of Measure:** Dollars per lb. **Type of Price:** spot. **Time Period Covered:** latest week.

PENTYLENE TETRAZOL: NF

Source: *Chemical Marketing Reporter.* **Price Frequency:** weekly. **Effective Market(s):** New York. **Units of Measure:** Dollars per kilo. **Type of Price:** spot. **Time Period Covered:** latest week.

PEPINOS

Source: *New Zealand Farmer.* **Price Frequency:** weekly, seasonally. **Effective Market(s):** New Zealand. **Units of Measure:** New Zealand dollars per case. **Time Period Covered:** latest week.

PEPPER: BLACK

Source: *Commodity Trade and Price Trends.* **Price Frequency:** annually. **Effective Market(s):** New York. **Units of Measure:** cents per kilogram, 1980 constant cents per kilogram. **Type of Price:** spot. **Time Period Covered:** latest 37 years.

Source: *Commodity Year Book.* **Price Frequency:** monthly, annually. **Effective Market(s):** New York. **Units of Measure:** cents per lb. **Time Period Covered:** latest 14 years.

Source: *Prices of Selected Asia/Pacific Products.* **Price Frequency:** monthly. **Effective Market(s):** Tokyo. **Units of Measure:** Japanese yen per kilogram. **Type of Price:** trade high, trade low. **Time Period Covered:** latest month.

PEPPER: BLACK, BRAZILIAN

Source: *Chemical Marketing Reporter.* **Price Frequency:** weekly. **Effective Market(s):** New York. **Units of Measure:** Dollars per lb. **Type of Price:** spot. **Time Period Covered:** latest week.

Source: *U. S. Spice Trade.* **Price Frequency:** monthly, annually. **Effective Market(s):** New York. **Units of Measure:** cents per lb. **Type of Price:** spot. **Time Period Covered:** latest 10 years.

PEPPER: BLACK, GRADE A, THAI

Source: *Prices of Selected Asia/Pacific Products.* **Price Frequency:** monthly. **Effective Market(s):** Bangkok. **Units of Measure:** Thai baht per kilogram. **Type of Price:** wholesale high, wholesale low. **Time Period Covered:** latest month.

PEPPER: BLACK, LAMPONG

Source: *Chemical Marketing Reporter.* **Price Frequency:** weekly. **Effective Market(s):** New York. **Units of Measure:** Dollars per lb. **Type of Price:** spot. **Time Period Covered:** latest week.

Source: *Prices of Selected Asia/Pacific Products.* **Price Frequency:** monthly. **Effective Market(s):** European ports, Japan, Netherlands, United Kingdom. **Units of Measure:** Dollars per metric ton. **Type of Price:** high, low. **Time Period Covered:** latest month.

Source: *Prices of Selected Asia/Pacific Products.* **Price Frequency:** monthly. **Effective Market(s):** United States. **Units of Measure:** Dollars per metric ton. **Type of Price:** spot high, spot low. **Time Period Covered:** latest month.

PEPPER: BLACK, LAMPONG, INDONESIAN

Source: *U. S. Spice Trade.* **Price Frequency:** monthly, annually. **Effective Market(s):** New York. **Units of Measure:** cents per lb. **Type of Price:** spot. **Time Period Covered:** latest 10 years.

PEPPER: BLACK, MALABAR

Source: *Chemical Marketing Reporter.* **Price Frequency:** weekly. **Effective Market(s):** New York. **Units of Measure:** Dollars per lb. **Type of Price:** spot. **Time Period Covered:** latest week.

PEPPER: BLACK, MALABAR, INDIAN

Source: *U. S. Spice Trade.* **Price Frequency:** monthly, annually. **Effective Market(s):** New York. **Units of Measure:** cents per lb. **Type of Price:** spot. **Time Period Covered:** latest 10 years.

PEPPER: BLACK, MALAYSIAN

Source: *International Financial Statistics.* **Price Frequency:** annually. **Effective Market(s):** New York. **Units of Measure:** cents per lb., index. **Type of Price:** market price, price index. **Time Period Covered:** latest 3 years.

Source: *International Financial Statistics Yearbook.* **Price Frequency:** annually. **Effective Market(s):** New York. **Units of Measure:** cent per lb. **Type of Price:** wholesale. **Time Period Covered:** latest 30 years.

Source: *UNCTAD Commodity Yearbook.* **Price Frequency:** annually. **Effective Market(s):** New York. **Units of Measure:** Dollars per metric ton. **Type of Price:** spot. **Time Period Covered:** latest 12 years.

PEPPER: BLACK, MG1, MALAYSIAN

Source: *Prices of Selected Asia/Pacific Products.* **Price Frequency:** monthly. **Effective Market(s):** Japan. **Units of Measure:** Dollars per metric ton. **Type of Price:** high, low. **Time Period Covered:** latest month.

Source: *Prices of Selected Asia/Pacific Products.* **Price Frequency:** monthly. **Effective Market(s):** United States. **Units of Measure:** Dollars per metric ton. **Type of Price:** spot high, spot low. **Time Period Covered:** latest month.

Source: *Prices of Selected Asia/Pacific Products.* **Price Frequency:** monthly. **Effective Market(s):** United Kingdom, Netherlands. **Units of Measure:** Dollars per metric ton. **Type of Price:** reseller high, reseller low. **Time Period Covered:** latest month.

PEPPER: BLACK, SARAWAK

Source: *FAO Quarterly Bulletin of Statistics.* **Price Frequency:** monthly, annually. **Effective Market(s):** London. **Units of Measure:** British pounds per 100 kilograms, dollars per metric ton. **Type of Price:** spot. **Time Period Covered:** latest 3 years.

Source: *Prices of Selected Asia/Pacific Products.* **Price Frequency:** monthly. **Effective Market(s):** major European ports. **Units of Measure:** Dollars per metric ton. **Type of Price:** high, low. **Time Period Covered:** latest month.

Source: *Prices of Selected Asia/Pacific Products.* **Price Frequency:** monthly. **Effective Market(s):** Japan. **Units of Measure:** Dollars per metric ton. **Type of Price:** spot high, spot low. **Time Period Covered:** latest month.

Source: *Prices of Selected Asia/Pacific Products.* **Price Frequency:** monthly. **Effective Market(s):** Netherlands, United Kingdom. **Units of Measure:** Dollars per metric ton. **Type of Price:** reseller high, reseller low. **Time Period Covered:** latest month.

PEPPER: BLACK, SARAWAK ASTA 100%

Source: *Far Eastern Economic Review.* **Price Frequency:** weekly. **Effective Market(s):** Singapore. **Units of Measure:** Singapore dollars per 100 kilograms. **Time Period Covered:** latest week, week ago, 3 months ago, year ago.

PEPPER: BLACK, SARAWAK, SPECIAL

Source: *Fruit and Tropical Products.* **Price Frequency:** monthly, annually, seasonally. **Effective Market(s):** London. **Units of Measure:** Dollars per tonne. **Time Period Covered:** latest 2 years.

Source: *Prices of Selected Asia/Pacific Products.* **Price Frequency:** monthly. **Effective Market(s):** United Kingdom/North European ports. **Units of Measure:** Dollars per metric ton. **Type of Price:** high, low. **Time Period Covered:** latest month.

PEPPER: BLACK, SPECIAL, BRAZILIAN

Source: *Fruit and Tropical Products.* **Price Frequency:** monthly, annually, seasonally. **Effective Market(s):** London. **Units of Measure:** Dollars per tonne. **Time Period Covered:** latest 2 years.

PEPPER: DINDICUTS, PAKISTAN

Source: *Chemical Marketing Reporter.* **Price Frequency:** weekly. **Effective Market(s):** New York. **Units of Measure:** Dollars per lb. **Type of Price:** spot. **Time Period Covered:** latest week.

PEPPER: RED, LILING, INDIAN

Source: *Chemical Marketing Reporter.* **Price Frequency:** weekly. **Effective Market(s):** New York. **Units of Measure:** Dollars per lb. **Type of Price:** spot. **Time Period Covered:** latest week.

PEPPER: TELLICHERRY EXTRA, INDIAN

Source: *U. S. Spice Trade.* **Price Frequency:** monthly, annually. **Effective Market(s):** New York. **Units of Measure:** cents per lb. **Type of Price:** spot. **Time Period Covered:** latest 10 years.

PEPPER: WHITE

Source: *Prices of Selected Asia/Pacific Products.* **Price Frequency:** monthly. **Effective Market(s):** Tokyo. **Units of Measure:** Japanese yen per kilogram. **Type of Price:** trade high, trade low. **Time Period Covered:** latest month.

PEPPER: WHITE, GRADE A, THAI

Source: *Prices of Selected Asia/Pacific Products.* **Price Frequency:** monthly. **Effective Market(s):** Bangkok. **Units of Measure:** Thai baht per kilogram. **Type of Price:** wholesale high, wholesale low. **Time Period Covered:** latest month.

PEPPER: WHITE, MUNTOK

Source: *Chemical Marketing Reporter.* **Price Frequency:** weekly. **Effective Market(s):** New York. **Units of Measure:** Dollars per lb. **Type of Price:** spot. **Time Period Covered:** latest week.

Source: *FAO Quarterly Bulletin of Statistics.* **Price Frequency:** monthly, annually. **Effective Market(s):** New York. **Units of Measure:** Dollars per 100 lbs., dollars per metric ton. **Type of Price:** spot. **Time Period Covered:** latest 3 years.

Source: *Prices of Selected Asia/Pacific Products.* **Price Frequency:** monthly. **Effective Market(s):** Japan, European ports, United Kingdom/North European ports. **Units of Measure:** Dollars per metric ton. **Type of Price:** high, low. **Time Period Covered:** latest month.

Source: *Prices of Selected Asia/Pacific Products.* **Price Frequency:** monthly. **Effective Market(s):** United States, United Kingdom. **Units of Measure:** Dollars per metric ton. **Type of Price:** spot high, spot low. **Time Period Covered:** latest month.

Source: *Prices of Selected Asia/Pacific Products.* **Price Frequency:** monthly. **Effective Market(s):** United Kingdom, Netherlands. **Units of Measure:** Dollars per metric ton. **Type of Price:** reseller high, reseller low. **Time Period Covered:** latest month.

PEPPER: WHITE, MUNTOK, INDONESIAN

Source: *U. S. Spice Trade.* **Price Frequency:** monthly, annually. **Effective Market(s):** New York. **Units of Measure:** cents per lb. **Type of Price:** spot. **Time Period Covered:** latest 10 years.

PEPPER: WHITE, SARAWAK

Source: *Prices of Selected Asia/Pacific Products.* **Price Frequency:** monthly. **Effective Market(s):** Japan, major European ports. **Units of Measure:** Dollars per metric ton. **Type of Price:** high, low. **Time Period Covered:** latest month.

Source: *Prices of Selected Asia/Pacific Products.* **Price Frequency:** monthly. **Effective Market(s):** Netherlands, United Kingdom. **Units of Measure:** Dollars per metric ton. **Type of Price:** reseller high, reseller low. **Time Period Covered:** latest month.

PEPPER: WHITE, SARAWAK 96%, SPECIAL

Source: *FAO Quarterly Bulletin of Statistics.* **Price Frequency:** monthly, annually. **Effective Market(s):** Singapore. **Units of Measure:** Singapore dollars per 100 kilograms, dollars per metric ton. **Time Period Covered:** latest 3 years.

PEPPER: WHITE, SARAWAK 100%

Source: *Fruit and Tropical Products.* **Price Frequency:** monthly, annually. **Effective Market(s):** Singapore. **Units of Measure:** cents per lb. **Type of Price:** spot. **Time Period Covered:** latest 3 years.

PEPPER: WHITE, SARAWAK 100%, SINGAPORE

Source: *Monthly Commodity Price Bulletin.* **Price Frequency:** monthly, annually. **Effective Market(s):** Singapore. **Units of Measure:** Singapore cents per kilogram, cents per lb. **Type of Price:** closing. **Time Period Covered:** latest 5 years.

Source: *Monthly Commodity Price Bulletin Supplement.* **Price Frequency:** monthly, quarterly, annually. **Effective Market(s):** Singapore. **Units of Measure:** Singapore cents per kilogram, dollars per tonne. **Time Period Covered:** latest 20 years.

PEPPER: WHITE, SARAWAK, SPECIAL

Source: *Fruit and Tropical Products.* **Price Frequency:** monthly, annually, seasonally. **Effective Market(s):** London. **Units of Measure:** Dollars per tonne. **Time Period Covered:** latest 2 years.

PEPPER: WHITE, SPECIAL, BRAZILIAN

Source: *Fruit and Tropical Products.* **Price Frequency:** monthly, annually, seasonally. **Effective Market(s):** London. **Units of Measure:** Dollars per tonne. **Time Period Covered:** latest 2 years.

PEPPER OIL: BLACK

Source: *Journal of Commerce and Commerical.* **Price Frequency:** weekly in Tuesday issue. **Units of Measure:** Dollars per lb. **Type of Price:** spot. **Time Period Covered:** latest week.

PEPPERMINT

Source: *U. S. Essential Oil Trade.* **Price Frequency:** annually. **Effective Market(s):** Idaho, Indiana, Oregon, Washington, Wisconsin, United States. **Units of Measure:** Dollars per lb. **Type of Price:** grower. **Time Period Covered:** latest 3 years.

PEPPERMINT LEAVES: IMPORTED

Source: *Chemical Marketing Reporter.* **Price Frequency:** weekly. **Effective Market(s):** New York. **Units of Measure:** Dollars per lb. **Type of Price:** spot. **Time Period Covered:** latest week.

PEPPERMINT OIL

Source: *Chemical Marketing Reporter.* **Price Frequency:** weekly. **Effective Market(s):** Midwest, Willamette (IL), Yakima (WA). **Units of Measure:** Dollars per lb. **Type of Price:** spot. **Time Period Covered:** latest week.

Source: *U. S. Essential Oil Trade.* **Price Frequency:** annually. **Effective Market(s):** United States. **Units of Measure:** Dollars per kilogram. **Type of Price:** import value. **Time Period Covered:** latest 3 years.

Source: *U. S. Essential Oil Trade.* **Price Frequency:** annually. **Effective Market(s):** New York. **Units of Measure:** Dollars per lb. **Type of Price:** spot. **Time Period Covered:** latest 4 years.

PEPPERMINT OIL: BRAZILIAN

Source: *Chemical Marketing Reporter.* **Price Frequency:** weekly. **Effective Market(s):** New York. **Units of Measure:** Dollars per kilo. **Type of Price:** spot. **Time Period Covered:** latest week.

PEPPERMINT OIL: CHINESE

Source: *Chemical Marketing Reporter.* **Price Frequency:** weekly. **Effective Market(s):** New York. **Units of Measure:** Dollars per kilo. **Type of Price:** spot. **Time Period Covered:** latest week.

PEPPERMINT OIL: MADRAS

Source: *Chemical Marketing Reporter.* **Price Frequency:** weekly. **Effective Market(s):** New York. **Units of Measure:** Dollars per lb. **Type of Price:** spot. **Time Period Covered:** latest week.

PEPPERMINT OIL: NATURAL

Source: *Journal of Commerce and Commercial.* **Price Frequency:** weekly in Tuesday issue. **Units of Measure:** Dollars per lb. **Type of Price:** spot. **Time Period Covered:** latest week.

PEPPERMINT OIL: SYNTHETIC

Source: *Chemical Marketing Reporter.* **Price Frequency:** weekly. **Effective Market(s):** New York. **Units of Measure:** Dollars per lb. **Type of Price:** spot. **Time Period Covered:** latest week.

PEPPERS

see also Capsicums.

PEPPERS: BELL, WONDER TYPE, CALIFORNIA

Source: *California Farmer.* **Price Frequency:** semimonthly, seasonally. **Effective Market(s):** Kern District (CA), Northern San Joaquin Valley, Imperial/Coachella Valleys. **Units of Measure:** Dollars per 25 lb. carton. **Time Period Covered:** latest week, month ago, year ago.

PEPPERS: CUBANELLE

Source: *Lancaster Farmer.* **Price Frequency:** weekly, seasonally. **Effective Market(s):** Pennsylvania. **Units of Measure:** Dollars per bushelbasket. **Type of Price:** market. **Time Period Covered:** latest week.

PEPPERS: GREEN, BELL, WONDER TYPE

Source: *California Farmer.* **Price Frequency:** semimonthly, seasonally. **Effective Market(s):** Gilroy/Hollister, Northern San Joaquin Valley, San Luis Obispo/Arroyo Grande/Oceano (CA). **Units of Measure:** Dollars per 1 1/2 bushel carton. **Time Period Covered:** latest week, month ago, year ago.

PEPPERS: GREEN, WONDER TYPE

Source: *Fresh Fruit and Vegetable Prices.* **Price Frequency:** monthly, seasonally. **Effective Market(s):** 8 domestic markets. **Units of Measure:** Dollars per carton or crate. **Type of Price:** average price at shipping point. **Time Period Covered:** latest year.

PEPPERS: GREEN, WONDER TYPE, CALIFORNIA

Source: *Fresh Fruit and Vegetable Prices.* **Price Frequency:** monthly, seasonally. **Effective Market(s):** Chicago, New York City. **Units of Measure:** Dollars per crate/carton. **Type of Price:** average wholesale price. **Time Period Covered:** latest year.

Source: *The Packer.* **Price Frequency:** weekly, seasonally. **Effective Market(s):** varies. **Units of Measure:** Dollars per carton. **Type of Price:** received by farmer. **Time Period Covered:** latest week.

PEPPERS: GREEN, WONDER TYPE, FLORIDA

Source: *Fresh Fruit and Vegetable Prices.* **Price Frequency:** monthly, seasonally. **Effective Market(s):** Chicago, New York City. **Units of Measure:** Dollars per crate/carton. **Type of Price:** average wholesale price. **Time Period Covered:** latest year.

PEPPERS: GREEN, WONDER TYPE, ILLINOIS

Source: *Fresh Fruit and Vegetable Prices.* **Price Frequency:** monthly, seasonally. **Effective Market(s):** Chicago. **Units of Measure:** Dollars per crate/carton. **Type of Price:** average wholesale price. **Time Period Covered:** latest year.

PEPPERS: GREEN, WONDER TYPE, MEXICO

Source: *Fresh Fruit and Vegetable Price.* **Price Frequency:** monthly, seasonally. **Effective Market(s):** Chicago, New York City. **Units of Measure:** Dollars per crate/carton. **Type of Price:** average wholesale price. **Time Period Covered:** latest year.

Source: *Fresh Fruit and Vegetable Prices.* **Price Frequency:** monthly, seasonally. **Effective Market(s):** Nogales (AZ). **Units of Measure:** Dollars per carton or crate. **Type of Price:** price paid at point of entry. **Time Period Covered:** latest year.

PEPPERS: RED

Source: *Lancaster Farmer.* **Price Frequency:** weekly, seasonally. **Effective Market(s):** Pennsylvania. **Units of Measure:** Dollars per unit. **Type of Price:** market. **Time Period Covered:** latest week.

PEPPERS: RED, MIXED

Source: *Lancaster Farmer.* **Price Frequency:** weekly, seasonally. **Effective Market(s):** Pennsylvania. **Units of Measure:** Dollars per unit. **Type of Price:** market. **Time Period Covered:** latest week.

PEPPERS: WONDER TYPE, CALIFORNIA

Source: *Lancaster Farmer.* **Price Frequency:** weekly, seasonally. **Effective Market(s):** Pennsylvania. **Units of Measure:** Dollars per unit. **Type of Price:** market. **Time Period Covered:** latest week.

PEPPERS: WONDER TYPE, FRESH

Source: *HRI-Buyers Guide.* **Price Frequency:** weekly. **Effective Market(s):** Northeastern area. **Units of Measure:** Dollars per crate. **Type of Price:** prices paid by dining places & institutions. **Time Period Covered:** latest week.

PERCH: FILLETS, SKIN ON, FRESH

Source: *Seafood Price-Current.* **Price Frequency:** semiweekly. **Effective Market(s):** West Coast. **Units of Measure:** Dollars per lb. **Type of Price:** sale by first receiver. **Time Period Covered:** latest day.

PERCH: OCEAN, FILLETS, FRESH

Source: *HRI-Buyers Guide.* **Price Frequency:** weekly. **Effective Market(s):** New York. **Units of Measure:** Dollars per lb. **Type of Price:** prices paid by dining places & institutions. **Time Period Covered:** latest week.

PERCH: OCEAN, FILLETS, FRESH, CANADIAN

Source: *Seafood Price-Current.* **Price Frequency:** semiweekly. **Effective Market(s):** Mid-Atlantic, New England. **Units of Measure:** Dollars per lb. **Type of Price:** sale by first receiver. **Time Period Covered:** latest day.

PERCH: OCEAN, FILLETS, FRESH, DOMESTIC

Source: *Seafood Price-Current.* **Price Frequency:** semiweekly. **Effective Market(s):** Mid-Atlantic, New England. **Units of Measure:** Dollars per lb. **Type of Price:** sale by first receiver. **Time Period Covered:** latest day.

PERCH: OCEAN, FILLETS, SKIN ON, BONE IN, CANADIAN

Source: *NMFS Green Sheet Supplement.* **Price Frequency:** weekly, seasonally. **Units of Measure:** dollars per lb. **Type of Price:** to primary wholesalers. **Time Period Covered:** latest week.

PERCH: OCEAN, FILLETS, SKIN ON, BONE IN, ICELANDIC

Source: *NMFS Green Sheet Supplement.* **Price Frequency:** weekly, seasonally. **Units of Measure:** dollars per lb. **Type of Price:** to primary wholesalers. **Time Period Covered:** latest week.

PERCH: OCEAN, FILLETS, SKIN ON, BONELESS, FROZEN, ICELANDIC

Source: *Seafood Price-Current.* **Price Frequency:** semiweekly. **Effective Market(s):** Mid-Atlantic. **Units of Measure:** Dollars per lb. **Type of Price:** first receiver. **Time Period Covered:** latest day.

PERCH: OCEAN, FILLETS, SKIN ON, BONELESS, ICELANDIC

Source: *NMFS Green Sheet Supplement.* **Price Frequency:** weekly, seasonally. **Units of Measure:** dollars per lb. **Type of Price:** to primary wholesalers. **Time Period Covered:** latest week.

PERCH: OCEAN, FILLETS, SKIN ON, FROZEN, CANADIAN

Source: *Seafood Price-Current.* **Price Frequency:** semiweekly. **Effective Market(s):** Mid-Atlantic. **Units of Measure:** Dollars per lb. **Type of Price:** first receiver. **Time Period Covered:** latest day.

PERCH: OCEAN, FILLETS, SKIN ON, FROZEN, ICELANDIC

Source: *Seafood Price-Current.* **Price Frequency:** semiweekly. **Effective Market(s):** Mid-Atlantic. **Units of Measure:** Dollars per lb. **Type of Price:** first receiver. **Time Period Covered:** latest day.

PERCH: OCEAN, FILLETS, SKINLESS, BONELESS, FROZEN, ICELANDIC

Source: *Seafood Price-Current.* **Price Frequency:** semiweekly. **Effective Market(s):** Mid-Atlantic. **Units of Measure:** Dollars per lb. **Type of Price:** first receiver. **Time Period Covered:** latest day.

PERCH: OCEAN, FILLETS, SKINLESS, BONELESS, ICELANDIC

Source: *NMFS Green Sheet Supplement.* **Price Frequency:** weekly, seasonally. **Units of Measure:** dollars per lb. **Type of Price:** to primary wholesalers. **Time Period Covered:** latest week.

PERCH: OCEAN, FROZEN, CANADIAN

Source: *Seafood Price-Current.* **Price Frequency:** semiweekly. **Effective Market(s):** Mid-Atlantic. **Units of Measure:** Dollars per lb. **Type of Price:** first receiver. **Time Period Covered:** latest day.

PERCH: OCEAN, PROCESSORS FISH BLOCKS, SKIN ON, CANADA/ICELAND

Source: *Seafood Price-Current.* **Price Frequency:** semiweekly. **Effective Market(s):** New England. **Units of Measure:** Dollars per lb. **Time Period Covered:** latest day.

PERCH: OCEAN, PROCESSORS FISH BLOCKS, SKINLESS, CANADA/ICELAND

Source: *Seafood Price-Current.* **Price Frequency:** semiweekly. **Effective Market(s):** New England. **Units of Measure:** Dollars per lb. **Time Period Covered:** latest day.

PERCH: OCEAN, WHOLE, FRESH

Source: *Seafood Price-Current.* **Price Frequency:** semiweekly. **Effective Market(s):** Mid-Atlantic, Boston, New Bedford (MA), Portland (ME). **Units of Measure:** Dollars per lb. **Type of Price:** sale by first receiver, auction price. **Time Period Covered:** latest day.

PERCHLOROETHYLENE: DRY CLEANING GRADE

Source: *Chemical Marketing Reporter.* **Price Frequency:** weekly. **Effective Market(s):** New York. **Units of Measure:** Dollars per lb. **Type of Price:** spot. **Time Period Covered:** latest week.

PERCHLOROETHYLENE: INDUSTRIAL GRADE, CONSUMERS

Source: *Chemical Marketing Reporter.* **Price Frequency:** weekly. **Effective Market(s):** New York. **Units of Measure:** Dollars per lb. **Type of Price:** spot. **Time Period Covered:** latest week.

PERCHLOROETHYLENE: USP

see Tetrachloroethylene.

PERI ACID

Source: *Chemical Marketing Reporter.* **Price Frequency:** weekly. **Effective Market(s):** New York. **Units of Measure:** Dollars per lb. **Type of Price:** spot. **Time Period Covered:** latest week.

PERLITE: AGGREGATE, EXPANDED

Source: *Industrial Minerals.* **Price Frequency:** monthly. **Effective Market(s):** United Kingdom. **Units of Measure:** British pounds per metric tonne. **Type of Price:** producer & dealer. **Time Period Covered:** latest month.

PERLITE: FILTER-AIDS, EXPANDED

Source: *Industrial Minerals.* **Price Frequency:** monthly. **Effective Market(s):** main European port. **Units of Measure:** British pounds per metric tonne. **Type of Price:** producer & dealer. **Time Period Covered:** latest month.

PERLITE: RAW, GRADED, CRUSHED

Source: *Industrial Minerals.* **Price Frequency:** monthly. **Effective Market(s):** main European port. **Units of Measure:** British pounds per metric tonne. **Type of Price:** producer & dealer. **Time Period Covered:** latest month.

PERMANENT RED 2B (RED 48): BARIUM SALTS

Source: *Chemical Marketing Reporter.* **Price Frequency:** weekly. **Effective Market(s):** New York. **Units of Measure:** Dollars per lb. **Type of Price:** spot. **Time Period Covered:** latest week.

PERMANENT RED 2B (RED 48): CALCIUM SALTS

Source: *Chemical Marketing Reporter.* **Price Frequency:** weekly. **Effective Market(s):** New York. **Units of Measure:** Dollars per lb. **Type of Price:** spot. **Time Period Covered:** latest week.

PERSIMMONS

Source: *New Zealand Farmer.* **Price Frequency:** weekly, seasonally. **Effective Market(s):** New Zealand. **Units of Measure:** New Zealand dollars per tray. **Time Period Covered:** latest week.

PERSIMMONS: HACHIYA

Source: *California Farmer.* **Price Frequency:** semimonthly, seasonally. **Effective Market(s):** Central San Joaquin Valley. **Units of Measure:** Dollars per 11 lb. flat. **Time Period Covered:** latest week, month ago, year ago.

PERU BALSAM

Source: *Chemical Marketing Reporter.* **Price Frequency:** weekly. **Effective Market(s):** New York. **Units of Measure:** Dollars per lb. **Type of Price:** spot. **Time Period Covered:** latest week.

PERU INTI

Source: *Barron's.* **Price Frequency:** weekly. **Effective Market(s):** New York. **Units of Measure:** Peruvian inti per United States dollar. **Type of Price:** foreign exchange. **Time Period Covered:** latest 2 weeks.

Source: *New York Times.* **Price Frequency:** daily. **Effective Market(s):** United States. **Units of Measure:** Peruvian inti per United States dollar. **Type of Price:** official foreign exchange rate. **Time Period Covered:** latest 2 days.

PET

see Polyester: PET Type.

PETALITE

Source: *Inudstrial Minerals.* **Price Frequency:** Monthly. **Effective Market(s):** Amsterdam. **Units of Measure:** British pounds per metric tonne. **Type of Price:** producer & dealer. **Time Period Covered:** latest month.

PETITGRAIN OIL

Source: *U. S. Essential Oil Trade.* **Price Frequency:** annually. **Effective Market(s):** United States. **Units of Measure:** Dollars per kilogram. **Type of Price:** import value. **Time Period Covered:** latest 3 years.

PETITGRAIN OIL: BIGRADE, FCC

Source: *Journal of Commerce and Commercial.* **Price Frequency:** weekly in Tuesday issue. **Units of Measure:** Dollars per lb. **Type of Price:** spot. **Time Period Covered:** latest week.

PETITGRAIN OIL: PARAGUAY

Source: *Chemical Marketing Reporter.* **Price Frequency:** weekly. **Effective Market(s):** New York. **Units of Measure:** Dollars per lb. **Type of Price:** spot. **Time Period Covered:** latest week.

PETROL

Source: *Statistical Bulletin of the South Pacific: Retail Price Indexes.* **Price Frequency:** annually. **Effective Market(s):** 18 South Pacific markets. **Units of Measure:** Australian dollars per litre. **Type of Price:** retail. **Time Period Covered:** latest year.

PETROLATUM: AMBER, USP

Source: *Chemical Marketing Reporter.* **Price Frequency:** weekly. **Effective Market(s):** New York. **Units of Measure:** Dollars per lb. **Type of Price:** spot. **Time Period Covered:** latest week.

PETROLATUM: CREAM, USP

Source: *Chemical Marketing Reporter.* **Price Frequency:** weekly. **Effective Market(s):** New York. **Units of Measure:** Dollars per lb. **Type of Price:** spot. **Time Period Covered:** latest week.

PETROLATUM: LILY WHITE, USP

Source: *Chemical Marketing Reporter.* **Price Frequency:** weekly. **Effective Market(s):** New York. **Units of Measure:** Dollars per lb. **Type of Price:** spot. **Time Period Covered:** latest week.

PETROLATUM: SNOW WHITE, USP

Source: *Chemical Marketing Reporter.* **Price Frequency:** weekly. **Effective Market(s):** New York. **Units of Measure:** Dollars per lb. **Type of Price:** spot. **Time Period Covered:** latest week.

PETROLATUM: SOFT WHITE, USP

Source: *Chemical Marketing Reporter.* **Price Frequency:** weekly. **Effective Market(s):** New York. **Units of Measure:** Dollars per lb. **Type of Price:** spot. **Time Period Covered:** latest week.

PETROLATUM: SOFT YELLOW, USP

Source: *Chemical Marketing Reporter.* **Price Frequency:** weekly. **Effective Market(s):** New York. **Units of Measure:** Dollars per lb. **Type of Price:** spot. **Time Period Covered:** latest week.

PETROLEUM

see also Diesel, Fuel Oil, Gasoline, Oil.

PETROLEUM: BRENT

Source: *Far Eastern Economic Review.* **Price Frequency:** weekly. **Effective Market(s):** London. **Units of Measure:** Dollars per barrel. **Time Period Covered:** latest week, week ago, 3 months ago, year ago.

PETROLEUM: CRUDE

Source: *Commodity Year Book.* **Price Frequency:** monthly, annually. **Units of Measure:** index. **Type of Price:** price index. **Time Period Covered:** latest 7 years.

Source: *Monthly Commodity Price Bulletin Supplement.* **Price Frequency:** monthly, quarterly, annually. **Effective Market(s):** worldwide. **Units of Measure:** Dollars per barrel. **Type of Price:** average spot. **Time Period Covered:** latest 20 years.

PETROLEUM: CRUDE, LIGHT, OPEC COUNTRIES

Source: *Commodity Trade and Price Trends.* **Price Frequency:** annually. **Effective Market(s):** OPEC countries. **Units of Measure:** Dollars per barrel, 1980 constant dollars per barrel. **Type of Price:** official OPEC selling. **Time Period Covered:** latest 37 years.

PETROLEUM: CRUDE, LIGHT, SAUDI ARABIAN

Source: *Commodity Trade and Price Trends.* **Price Frequency:** annually. **Effective Market(s):** Ras Tanura (Saudi Arabia). **Units of Measure:** Dollars per barrel, 1980 constant dollars per barrel. **Type of Price:** official OPEC selling. **Time Period Covered:** latest 37 years.

PETROLEUM: CRUDE, OPEC COUNTRIES

Source: *Commodity Trade and Price Trends.* **Price Frequency:** annually. **Effective Market(s):** OPEC countries. **Units of Measure:** Dollars per barrel, 1980 constant dollars per barrel. **Type of Price:** spot. **Time Period Covered:** latest 5 years.

PETROLEUM: LIBYA

Source: *International Financial Statistics.* **Price Frequency:** annually. **Effective Market(s):** Es Sidra (Libya). **Units of Measure:** Dollars per barrel, index. **Type of Price:** market price, price index. **Time Period Covered:** latest 4 years.

Source: *International Financial Statistics Yearbook.* **Price Frequency:** annually. **Effective Market(s):** Es Sidra (Libya). **Units of Measure:** Dollars per barrel. **Type of Price:** wholesale. **Time Period Covered:** latest 30 years.

PETROLEUM: SAUDI ARABIA

Source: *International Financial Statistics.* **Price Frequency:** annually. **Effective Market(s):** Ras Tanura (Saudi Arabia). **Units of Measure:** Dollars per barrel, index. **Type of Price:** market price, price index. **Time Period Covered:** latest year.

Source: *International Financial Statistics Yearbook.* **Price Frequency:** annually. **Effective Market(s):** Ras Tanura (Saudi Arabia). **Units of Measure:** Dollars per barrel. **Type of Price:** wholesale. **Time Period Covered:** latest 30 years.

PETROLEUM: SUMATRAN LIGHT

Source: *Far Eastern Economic Review.* **Price Frequency:** weekly. **Effective Market(s):** Tokyo. **Units of Measure:** Dollars per barrel. **Time Period Covered:** latest week, week ago, 3 months ago, year ago.

PETROLEUM: VENEZUELA

Source: *International Financial Statistics.* **Price Frequency:** quarterly, annually. **Effective Market(s):** Tia Juana (Venezuela). **Units of Measure:** Dollars per barrel, index. **Type of Price:** market price, price index. **Time Period Covered:** latest quarter, latest 4 years.

Source: *Interntional Financial Statistics Yearbook.* **Price Frequency:** annually. **Effective Market(s):** Tia Juana (Venezuela). **Units of Measure:** Dollars per barrel. **Type of Price:** wholesale. **Time Period Covered:** latest 30 years.

PETROLEUM PITCH

see Asphalt: Petroleum.

PETROLEUM SULFONATE: 51% SULFONIC CONTENT

Source: *Chemical Marketing Reporter.* **Price Frequency:** weekly. **Effective Market(s):** New York. **Units of Measure:** Dollars per lb. **Type of Price:** spot. **Time Period Covered:** latest week.

PETROLEUM SULFONATE: 60-62% SULFONIC CONTENT

Source: *Chemical Marketing Reporter.* **Price Frequency:** weekly. **Effective Market(s):** New York. **Units of Measure:** Dollars per lb. **Type of Price:** spot. **Time Period Covered:** latest week.

PHEASANTS: ADULT

Source: *HRI-Buyers Guide.* **Price Frequency:** weekly. **Effective Market(s):** Northeastern area. **Units of Measure:** Dollars per lb. **Type of Price:** wholesale. **Time Period Covered:** latest week.

Source: *Urner Barry's Price-Current.* **Price Frequency:** daily. **Units of Measure:** Dollars per lb. **Type of Price:** wholesale. **Time Period Covered:** latest day.

Source: *Urner Barry's Price-Current, West Coast Edition.* **Price Frequency:** semiweekly. **Effective Market(s):** west coast. **Units of Measure:** Dollars per lb. **Type of Price:** wholesale. **Time Period Covered:** latest day.

PHEASANTS: BABY

Source: *HRI-Buyers Guide.* **Price Frequency:** weekly. **Effective Market(s):** Northeastern area. **Units of Measure:** Dollars per lb. **Type of Price:** wholesale. **Time Period Covered:** latest week.

Source: *Urner Barry's Price-Current.* **Price Frequency:** daily. **Units of Measure:** Dollars per lb. **Type of Price:** wholesale. **Time Period Covered:** latest day.

Source: *Urner Barry's Price-Current, West Coast Edition.* **Price Frequency:** semiweekly. **Effective Market(s):** West Coast. **Units of Measure:** Dollars per lb. **Type of Price:** wholesale. **Time Period Covered:** latest day.

PHENACETIN: POWDERED, USP

Source: *Chemical Marketing Reporter.* **Price Frequency:** weekly. **Effective Market(s):** New York. **Units of Measure:** Dollars per lb. **Type of Price:** spot. **Time Period Covered:** latest week.

PHENOBARBITAL: USP

Source: *Chemical Marketing Reporter.* **Price Frequency:** weekly. **Effective Market(s):** New York. **Units of Measure:** Dollars per kilo. **Type of Price:** spot. **Time Period Covered:** latest week.

Source: *Journal of Commerce and Commercial.* **Price Frequency:** weekly in Friday issue. **Units of Measure:** Dollars per kilo. **Type of Price:** spot. **Time Period Covered:** latest week.

PHENOBARBITAL-SODIUM: NF

Source: *Chemical Marketing Reporter.* **Price Frequency:** weekly. **Effective Market(s):** New York. **Units of Measure:** Dollars per kilo. **Type of Price:** spot. **Time Period Covered:** latest week.

PHENOL: 99-100%

Source: *Journal of Commerce and Commercial.* **Price Frequency:** weekly in Wednesday issue. **Effective Market(s):** Gulf. **Units of Measure:** Dollars per lb. **Type of Price:** spot. **Time Period Covered:** latest week.

PHENOL: SYNTHETIC

Source: *Chemical Marketing Reporter.* **Price Frequency:** weekly. **Effective Market(s):** New York. **Units of Measure:** Dollars per lb. **Type of Price:** spot. **Time Period Covered:** latest week.

PHENOLIC MOLDING COMPOUND: MODIFIED

Source: *Plastics Technology.* **Price Frequency:** monthly. **Units of Measure:** cents per lb., cents per cubic inch. **Type of Price:** bulk list, market. **Time Period Covered:** latest month.

PHENOLIC MOLDING COMPOUND: UNMODIFIED

Source: *Plastics Technology.* **Price Frequency:** monthly. **Units of Measure:** cents per lb., cents per cubic inch. **Type of Price:** bulk list, market. **Time Period Covered:** latest month.

PHENOLIC RESIN: GENERAL PURPOSE

Source: *Journal of Commerce and Commerical.* **Price Frequency:** weekly in Tuesday issue. **Units of Measure:** Dollars per lb. **Type of Price:** spot. **Time Period Covered:** latest week.

PHENOLPHTHALEIN: WHITE

Source: *Journal of Commerce and Commercial.* **Price Frequency:** weekly in Friday issue. **Units of Measure:** Dollars per 100 kilo lot. **Type of Price:** spot. **Time Period Covered:** latest week.

PHENOLPHTHALEIN: YELLOW

Source: *Journal of Commerce and Commercial.* **Price Frequency:** weekly in Friday issue. **Units of Measure:** Dollars per 25 kilo drum. **Type of Price:** spot. **Time Period Covered:** latest week.

P-PHENOLSULFONIC ACID: 65% SOLUTION

Source: *Chemical Marketing Reporter.* **Price Frequency:** weekly. **Effective Market(s):** New York. **Units of Measure:** Dollars per lb. **Type of Price:** spot. **Time Period Covered:** latest week.

PHENOTHIAZINE: PURIFIED GRADE, GRANULAR

Source: *Chemical Marketing Reporter.* **Price Frequency:** weekly. **Effective Market(s):** New York. **Units of Measure:** Dollars per lb. **Type of Price:** spot. **Time Period Covered:** latest week.

PHENOTHIAZINE: TECHNICAL GRADE, GRANULAR

Source: *Chemical Marketing Reporter.* **Price Frequency:** weekly. **Effective Market(s):** New York. **Units of Measure:** Dollars per lb. **Type of Price:** spot. **Time Period Covered:** latest week.

PHENYL ACETATE

Source: *Chemical Marketing Reporter.* **Price Frequency:** weekly. **Effective Market(s):** New York. **Units of Measure:** Dollars per lb. **Type of Price:** spot. **Time Period Covered:** latest week.

1-PHENYL-3-CARBETHOXY PYRAZOLONE-5

Source: *Chemical Marketing Reporter.* **Price Frequency:** weekly. **Effective Market(s):** East. **Units of Measure:** Dollars per lb. **Type of Price:** spot. **Time Period Covered:** latest week.

1-PHENYL-3-METHYL-5-PYRAZOLONE

Source: *Chemical Marketing Reporter.* **Price Frequency:** weekly. **Effective Market(s):** East. **Units of Measure:** Dollars per lb. **Type of Price:** spot. **Time Period Covered:** latest week.

PHENYLACETALDEHYDE

Source: *Journal of Commerce and Commercial.* **Price Frequency:** weekly in Tuesday issue. **Units of Measure:** Dollars per lb. **Type of Price:** spot. **Time Period Covered:** latest week.

PHENYLACETIC ACID: PURE, CRYSTALLINE

Source: *Chemical Marketing Reporter.* **Price Frequency:** weekly. **Effective Market(s):** New York. **Units of Measure:** Dollars per kilo. **Type of Price:** spot. **Time Period Covered:** latest week.

DL-PHENYLALANINE

Source: *Chemical Marketing Reporter.* **Price Frequency:** weekly. **Effective Market(s):** New York. **Units of Measure:** Dollars per kilo. **Type of Price:** spot. **Time Period Covered:** latest week.

M-PHENYLENEDIAMINE

Source: *Journal of Commerce and Commercial.* **Price Frequency:** weekly in Wednesday issue. **Units of Measure:** Dollars per lb. **Type of Price:** spot. **Time Period Covered:** latest week.

M-PHENYLENEDIAMINE: CAST

Source: *Chemical Marketing Reporter.* **Price Frequency:** weekly. **Effective Market(s):** New York. **Units of Measure:** Dollars per lb. **Type of Price:** spot. **Time Period Covered:** latest week.

O-PHENYLENEDIAMINE: FLAKED

Source: *Chemical Marketing Reporter.* **Price Frequency:** weekly. **Effective Market(s):** New York. **Units of Measure:** Dollars per lb. **Type of Price:** spot. **Time Period Covered:** latest week.

P-PHENYLENEDIAMINE: FLAKED

Source: *Chemical Marketing Reporter.* **Price Frequency:** weekly. **Effective Market(s):** New York. **Units of Measure:** Dollars per lb. **Type of Price:** spot. **Time Period Covered:** latest week.

PHENYLEPHRINE HYDROCHLORIDE: USP

Source: *Chemical Marketing Reporter.* **Price Frequency:** weekly. **Effective Market(s):** New York. **Units of Measure:** Dollars per kilo. **Type of Price:** spot. **Time Period Covered:** latest week.

PHENYLETHYL ACETATE

Source: *Chemical Marketing Reporter.* **Price Frequency:** weekly. **Effective Market(s):** New York. **Units of Measure:** Dollars per lb. **Type of Price:** spot. **Time Period Covered:** latest week.

2-PHENYLETHYL ALCOHOL: NF

Source: *Chemical Marketing Reporter.* **Price Frequency:** weekly. **Effective Market(s):** New York. **Units of Measure:** Dollars per lb. **Type of Price:** spot. **Time Period Covered:** latest week.

B-PHENYLETHYLAMINE

Source: *Chemical Marketing Reporter.* **Price Frequency:** weekly. **Effective Market(s):** New York. **Units of Measure:** Dollars per lb. **Type of Price:** spot. **Time Period Covered:** latest week.

PHENYLETHYLPHENYL ACETATE

Source: *Chemical Marketing Reporter.* **Price Frequency:** weekly. **Effective Market(s):** New York. **Units of Measure:** Dollars per lb. **Type of Price:** spot. **Time Period Covered:** latest week.

PHENYLGLYCONIC ACID

see Mandelic Acid.

PHENYLHYDRAZINE

Source: *Journal of Commerce and Commercial.* **Price Frequency:** weekly in Wednesday issue. **Units of Measure:** Dollars per lb. **Type of Price:** spot. **Time Period Covered:** latest week.

PHENYLHYDRAZINE: 99% MINIMUM

Source: *Chemical Marketing Reporter.* **Price Frequency:** weekly. **Effective Market(s):** New York. **Units of Measure:** Dollars per lb. **Type of Price:** spot. **Time Period Covered:** latest week.

O-PHENYLPHENOL

Source: *Chemical Marketing Reporter.* **Price Frequency:** weekly. **Effective Market(s):** New York. **Units of Measure:** Dollars per lb. **Type of Price:** spot. **Time Period Covered:** latest week.

P-PHENYLPHENOL

Source: *Chemical Marketing Reporter.* **Price Frequency:** weekly. **Effective Market(s):** New York. **Units of Measure:** Dollars per lb. **Type of Price:** spot. **Time Period Covered:** latest week.

PHENYLPROPANOLAMINE HYDROCHLORIDE

Source: *Chemical Marketing Reporter.* **Price Frequency:** weekly. **Effective Market(s):** New York. **Units of Measure:** Dollars per kilo. **Type of Price:** spot. **Time Period Covered:** latest week.

PHENYLSALICYLATE: FLAKE

Source: *Chemical Marketing Reporter.* **Price Frequency:** weekly. **Effective Market(s):** East. **Units of Measure:** Dollars per lb. **Type of Price:** spot. **Time Period Covered:** latest week.

PHENYLSALICYLATE: PURIFIED, CRYSTALLINE

Source: *Chemical Marketing Reporter.* **Price Frequency:** weekly. **Effective Market(s):** East. **Units of Measure:** Dollars per lb. **Type of Price:** spot. **Time Period Covered:** latest week.

PHENYLSALICYLATE: TECHNICAL, CRYSTALLINE

Source: *Chemical Marketing Reporter.* **Price Frequency:** weekly. **Effective Market(s):** East. **Units of Measure:** Dollars per lb. **Type of Price:** spot. **Time Period Covered:** latest week.

PHILIPPINES PESOS

Source: *Asian Wall Street Journal.* **Price Frequency:** daily. **Effective Market(s):** Asia. **Units of Measure:** Philippines pesos per United States dollars. **Type of Price:** foreign exchange. **Time Period Covered:** latest 2 days.

Source: *Barron's.* **Price Frequency:** weekly. **Effective Market(s):** New York. **Units of Measure:** Philippines pesos per United States dollar. **Type of Price:** foreign exchange. **Time Period Covered:** latest 2 weeks.

Source: *New York Times.* **Price Frequency:** daily. **Effective Market(s):** United States. **Units of Measure:** Philippines pesos per United States dollar. **Type of Price:** floating foreign exchange rate. **Time Period Covered:** latest 2 days.

PHLOXINE TONER (RED 90)

Source: *Chemical Marketing Reporter.* **Price Frequency:** weekly. **Effective Market(s):** New York. **Units of Measure:** Dollars per lb. **Type of Price:** spot. **Time Period Covered:** latest week.

PHORATE: 20%, GRANULAR

Source: *Agricultural Prices Annual Summary.* **Price Frequency:** semiannually. **Effective Market(s):** United States. **Units of Measure:** Dollars per 50 lbs. **Type of Price:** paid by farmer. **Time Period Covered:** latest 6 years.

PHOSGENE

Source: *Chemical Marketing Reporter.* **Price Frequency:** weekly. **Effective Market(s):** New York. **Units of Measure:** Dollars per lb. **Type of Price:** spot. **Time Period Covered:** latest week.

PHOSPHATE: SODIUM

see Sodium Phosphate.

PHOSPHATE ROCK

Source: *Commodity Year Book.* **Price Frequency:** annually. **Effective Market(s):** United States. **Units of Measure:** Dollars per metric ton. **Time Period Covered:** latest 9 years.

Source: *Commodity Year Book.* **Price Frequency:** annually. **Effective Market(s):** United States. **Units of Measure:** Dollars per tonne. **Time Period Covered:** latest 8 years.

PHOSPHATE ROCK: 70% BPL, KHOURIBGA

Source: *Monthly Commodity Price Bulletin.* **Price Frequency:** monthly, annually. **Effective Market(s):** Casablanca. **Units of Measure:** Dollars per metric ton. **Time Period Covered:** latest 5 years.

Source: *Monthly Commodity Price Bulletin Supplement.* **Price Frequency:** monthly, quarterly, annually. **Effective Market(s):** Casablanca. **Units of Measure:** Dollars per tonne. **Time Period Covered:** latest 20 years.

Source: *UNCTAD Commodity Yearbook.* **Price Frequency:** annually. **Effective Market(s):** Casablanca. **Units of Measure:** Dollars per metric ton. **Type of Price:** free market. **Time Period Covered:** latest 12 years.

PHOSPHATE ROCK: 72% BPL, MOROCCAN

Source: *Commodity Trade and Price Trends.* **Price Frequency:** annually. **Effective Market(s):** Casablanca. **Units of Measure:** Dollars per metric ton, 1980 constant dollars per metric ton. **Time Period Covered:** latest 37 years.

PHOSPHATE ROCK: LAND PEBBLE, FLORIDA

Source: *Chemical Marketing Reporter.* **Price Frequency:** weekly. **Effective Market(s):** Florida. **Units of Measure:** Dollars per ton. **Type of Price:** spot. **Time Period Covered:** latest week.

PHOSPHATE ROCK: MOROCCAN

Source: *International Financial Statistics.* **Price Frequency:** monthly, quarterly, annually. **Effective Market(s):** Casablanca. **Units of Measure:** Dollars per metric ton, index. **Type of Price:** market price, price index. **Time Period Covered:** latest 5 months, latest 5 quarters, latest 5 years.

Source: *International Financial Statistics Yearbook.* **Price Frequency:** annually. **Effective Market(s):** Casablanca. **Units of Measure:** Dollars per metric ton. **Type of Price:** wholesale. **Time Period Covered:** latest 30 years.

PHOSPHATE ROCK: VESSEL, TAMPA

Source: *Chemical Marketing Reporter.* **Price Frequency:** weekly. **Effective Market(s):** Florida. **Units of Measure:** Dollars per ton. **Type of Price:** spot. **Time Period Covered:** latest week.

PHOSPHATES: LAND PEBBLE, DRY BASIS, UNGROUND

Source: *Industrial Minerals.* **Price Frequency:** monthly. **Effective Market(s):** Florida. **Units of Measure:** Dollars per metric tonne. **Type of Price:** domestic, export. **Time Period Covered:** latest month.

PHOSPHATES: MOROCCO

Source: *Industrial Minerals.* **Price Frequency:** monthly. **Effective Market(s):** Casablanca. **Units of Measure:** Dollars per metric tonne. **Type of Price:** producer & dealer. **Time Period Covered:** latest month.

PHOSPHATES: NAURU

Source: *Industrial Minerals.* **Price Frequency:** monthly. **Effective Market(s):** main European port. **Units of Measure:** Dollars per long ton. **Type of Price:** producer & dealer. **Time Period Covered:** latest month.

PHOSPHATES: TUNISIA

Source: *Industrial Minerals.* **Price Frequency:** monthly. **Effective Market(s):** main European port. **Units of Measure:** Dollars per metric tonne. **Type of Price:** producer & dealer. **Time Period Covered:** latest month.

PHOSPHORIC ACID: 52-54%

Source: *Journal of Commerce and Commercial.* **Price Frequency:** weekly in Thursday issue. **Units of Measure:** Dollars per ton. **Type of Price:** spot. **Time Period Covered:** latest week.

PHOSPHORIC ACID: AGRICULTURAL GRADE

Source: *Chemical Marketing Reporter.* **Price Frequency:** weekly. **Effective Market(s):** New York. **Units of Measure:** Dollars per unit-ton. **Type of Price:** spot. **Time Period Covered:** latest week.

PHOSPHORIC ACID: COMMERCIAL AND TECHNICAL GRADES

Source: *Chemical Marketing Reporter.* **Price Frequency:** weekly. **Effective Market(s):** New York. **Units of Measure:** Dollars per 100 lbs. **Type of Price:** spot. **Time Period Covered:** latest week.

PHOSPHORIC ACID: FOOD GRADE

Source: *Chemical Marketing Reporter.* **Price Frequency:** weekly. **Effective Market(s):** New York. **Units of Measure:** Dollars per 100 lbs. **Type of Price:** spot. **Time Period Covered:** latest week.

PHOSPHORUS: WHITE (YELLOW)

Source: *Chemical Marketing Reporter.* **Price Frequency:** weekly. **Effective Market(s):** New York. **Units of Measure:** Dollars per lb. **Type of Price:** spot. **Time Period Covered:** latest week.

PHOSPHORUS OXYCHLORIDE

Source: *Chemical Marketing Reporter.* **Price Frequency:** weekly. **Effective Market(s):** New York. **Units of Measure:** Dollars per lb. **Type of Price:** spot. **Time Period Covered:** latest week.

PHOSPHORUS PENTASULFIDE: POWDERED

Source: *Chemical Marketing Reporter.* **Price Frequency:** weekly. **Effective Market(s):** New York. **Units of Measure:** Dollars per 100 lbs. **Type of Price:** spot, seller. **Time Period Covered:** latest week.

PHOSPHORUS PENTOXIDE

Source: *Chemical Marketing Reporter.* **Price Frequency:** weekly. **Effective Market(s):** New York. **Units of Measure:** Dollars per lb. **Type of Price:** spot. **Time Period Covered:** latest week.

PHOSPHORUS TRICHLORIDE

Source: *Chemical Marketing Reporter.* **Price Frequency:** weekly. **Effective Market(s):** New York. **Units of Measure:** Dollars per lb. **Type of Price:** spot. **Time Period Covered:** latest week.

PHTHALIC ANHYDRIDE: FLAKE

Source: *Chemical Marketing Reporter.* **Price Frequency:** weekly. **Effective Market(s):** New York, West Coast. **Units of Measure:** Dollars per lb. **Type of Price:** spot. **Time Period Covered:** latest week.

Source: *Journal of Commerce and Commercial.* **Price Frequency:** weekly in Wednesday issue. **Units of Measure:** Dollars per lb. **Type of Price:** spot. **Time Period Covered:** latest week.

PHTHALIC ANHYDRIDE: MOLTEN

Source: *Chemical Marketing Reporter.* **Price Frequency:** weekly. **Effective Market(s):** New York, West Coast. **Units of Measure:** Dollars per lb. **Type of Price:** spot. **Time Period Covered:** latest week.

Source: *Journal of Commerce and Commercial.* **Price Frequency:** weekly in Wednesday issue. **Units of Measure:** Dollars per lb. **Type of Price:** spot. **Time Period Covered:** latest week.

PHTHALIC ANHYDRIDE: R SALT

Source: *Journal of Commerce and Commercial.* **Price Frequency:** weekly in Wednesday issue. **Units of Measure:** Dollars per lb. **Type of Price:** spot. **Time Period Covered:** latest week.

PHTHALIMIDE: FLAKE

Source: *Chemical Marketing Reporter.* **Price Frequency:** weekly. **Effective Market(s):** New York. **Units of Measure:** Dollars per lb. **Type of Price:** spot. **Time Period Covered:** latest week.

PHTHALOCYANINE BLUE TONER

Source: *Journal of Commerce and Commercial.* **Price Frequency:** weekly in Wednesday issue. **Units of Measure:** Dollars per lb. **Type of Price:** spot. **Time Period Covered:** latest week.

PHTHALOCYANINE BLUE TONER: GREEN SHADE

Source: *Chemical Marketing Reporter.* **Price Frequency:** weekly. **Effective Market(s):** East of the Rockies. **Units of Measure:** Dollars per lb. **Type of Price:** spot. **Time Period Covered:** latest week.

PHTHALOCYANINE BLUE TONER: RED SHADE

Source: *Chemical Marketing Reporter.* **Price Frequency:** weekly. **Effective Market(s):** East of the Rockies. **Units of Measure:** Dollars per lb. **Type of Price:** spot. **Time Period Covered:** latest week.

PHTHALOCYANINE BLUE TONER: WATER DISPERSABLE

Source: *Chemical Marketing Reporter.* **Price Frequency:** weekly. **Effective Market(s):** East of the Rockies. **Units of Measure:** Dollars per lb. **Type of Price:** spot. **Time Period Covered:** latest week.

PHTHALOCYANINE GREEN TONER

Source: *Journal of Commerce and Commercial.* **Price Frequency:** weekly in Wednesday issue. **Units of Measure:** Dollars per lb. **Type of Price:** spot. **Time Period Covered:** latest week.

PHTHALOCYANINE GREEN TONER: ALL GRADES

Source: *Chemical Marketing Reporter.* **Price Frequency:** weekly. **Effective Market(s):** East of the Rockies. **Units of Measure:** Dollars per lb. **Type of Price:** spot. **Time Period Covered:** latest week.

PHTHALYLSULFACETAMIDE

Source: *Chemical Marketing Reporter.* **Price Frequency:** weekly. **Effective Market(s):** New York. **Units of Measure:** Dollars per kilo. **Type of Price:** spot. **Time Period Covered:** latest week.

PICKLES

Source: *Lancaster Farmer.* **Price Frequency:** weekly, seasonally. **Effective Market(s):** Pennsylvania. **Units of Measure:** Dollars per bushel. **Type of Price:** market. **Time Period Covered:** latest week.

PICOLINES: REFINED, MIXED

Source: *Chemical Marketing Reporter.* **Price Frequency:** weekly. **Effective Market(s):** New York. **Units of Measure:** Dollars per kilo. **Type of Price:** spot. **Time Period Covered:** latest week.

PICRIC ACID: PURE PASTE

Source: *Chemical Marketing Reporter.* **Price Frequency:** weekly. **Effective Market(s):** Charlotte (NC). **Units of Measure:** Dollars per lb. **Type of Price:** spot. **Time Period Covered:** latest week.

PICRIC ACID: TECHNICAL GRADE, PASTE

Source: *Chemical Marketing Reporter.* **Price Frequency:** weekly. **Effective Market(s):** Charlotte (NC). **Units of Measure:** Dollars per lb. **Type of Price:** spot. **Time Period Covered:** latest week.

PIG IRON

see Iron: Pig.

PIG MEAT

Source: *Agra Europe.* **Price Frequency:** weekly. **Effective Market(s):** 9 European markets. **Units of Measure:** national currency per kilogram. **Type of Price:** average. **Time Period Covered:** latest week.

PIGEONS

Source: *Lancaster Farmer.* **Price Frequency:** weekly. **Effective Market(s):** Pennsylvania. **Units of Measure:** Dollars each. **Type of Price:** auction. **Time Period Covered:** latest week.

PIGEONS: WHITE

Source: *Lancaster Farmer.* **Price Frequency:** weekly. **Effective Market(s):** Pennsylvania. **Units of Measure:** Dollars each. **Type of Price:** auction. **Time Period Covered:** latest week.

PIGMENT GREEN B

Source: *Chemical Marketing Reporter.* **Price Frequency:** weekly. **Effective Market(s):** New York. **Units of Measure:** Dollars per lb. **Type of Price:** spot. **Time Period Covered:** latest week.

PIGMENTS

Source: *Journal of Commerce and Commercial.* **Price Frequency:** weekly in Wednesday issue. **Units of Measure:** Dollars per lb. **Type of Price:** spot. **Time Period Covered:** latest week.

PIGS

see also Barrows and Gilts, Hogs, Sows.

Source: *FAO Quarterly Bulletin of Statistics.* **Price Frequency:** monthly, annually. **Effective Market(s):** European Community. **Units of Measure:** ECU per 100 kilograms, dollars per metric ton. **Type of Price:** wholesale. **Time Period Covered:** latest 3 years.

Source: *Farm and Dairy.* **Price Frequency:** weekly, seasonally. **Effective Market(s):** Ohio, Pennsylvania. **Units of Measure:** Dollars per head. **Type of Price:** auction high, auction low. **Time Period Covered:** latest week.

Source: *Farmers Weekly.* **Price Frequency:** weekly. **Effective Market(s):** Great Britain. **Units of Measure:** British pence per kilogram. **Time Period Covered:** latest week, week ago, year ago.

Source: *The Times.* **Price Frequency:** daily. **Effective Market(s):** England/Wales, Great Britain, Scotland. **Units of Measure:** British pence per kilogram. **Type of Price:** average. **Time Period Covered:** latest day.

PIGS: BACONERS

Source: *Farmers Weekly.* **Price Frequency:** weekly, seasonally. **Effective Market(s):** over 170 British markets. **Units of Measure:** British pence per kilogram. **Type of Price:** auction. **Time Period Covered:** latest week.

Source: *Scottish Farmer.* **Price Frequency:** weekly. **Effective Market(s):** Scotland. **Units of Measure:** British pence per kilogram. **Type of Price:** average. **Time Period Covered:** latest week.

PIGS: BACONERS, HEAVY

Source: *New Zealand Farmer.* **Price Frequency:** weekly, seasonally. **Effective Market(s):** New Zealand. **Units of Measure:** New Zealand dollars per head. **Type of Price:** export. **Time Period Covered:** latest 2 weeks.

PIGS: BACONERS, LIGHT

Source: *New Zealand Farmer.* **Price Frequency:** weekly, seasonally. **Effective Market(s):** New Zealand. **Units of Measure:** New Zealand dollars per head. **Type of Price:** export. **Time Period Covered:** latest 2 weeks.

PIGS: BACONERS, LIVEWEIGHT

Source: *Scottish Farmer.* **Price Frequency:** weekly. **Effective Market(s):** 10 Scottish markets. **Units of Measure:** British pence per kilogram. **Time Period Covered:** latest week.

PIGS: CHOPPERS, HEAVY

Source: *New Zealand Farmer.* **Price Frequency:** weekly, seasonally. **Effective Market(s):** New Zealand. **Units of Measure:** New Zealand dollars per head. **Type of Price:** export. **Time Period Covered:** latest 2 weeks.

PIGS: CHOPPERS, LIGHT

Source: *New Zealand Farmer.* **Price Frequency:** weekly, seasonally. **Effective Market(s):** New Zealand. **Units of Measure:** New Zealand dollars per head. **Type of Price:** export. **Time Period Covered:** latest 2 weeks.

PIGS: CUTTERS

Source: *Farmers Weekly.* **Price Frequency:** weekly, seasonally. **Effective Market(s):** over 170 British markets. **Units of Measure:** British pence per kilogram. **Type of Price:** auction. **Time Period Covered:** latest week.

Source: *Scottish Farmer.* **Price Frequency:** weekly. **Effective Market(s):** Scotland. **Units of Measure:** British pence per kilogram. **Type of Price:** average. **Time Period Covered:** latest week.

PIGS: CUTTERS, LIVEWEIGHT

Source: *Scottish Farmer.* **Price Frequency:** weekly. **Effective Market(s):** 10 Scottish markets. **Units of Measure:** British pence per kilogram. **Time Period Covered:** latest week.

PIGS: DEADWEIGHT

Source: *Farmers Weekly.* **Price Frequency:** weekly. **Effective Market(s):** England/Wales, Great Britain, Scotland. **Units of Measure:** British pence per kilogram. **Time Period Covered:** latest week.

Source: *Scottish Farmer.* **Price Frequency:** weekly. **Effective Market(s):** Scotland. **Units of Measure:** British pence per kilogram. **Time Period Covered:** latest week.

PIGS: FAT

Source: *Agra Europe.* **Price Frequency:** weekly. **Effective Market(s):** 9 European markets. **Units of Measure:** national currency per kilogram. **Type of Price:** average. **Time Period Covered:** latest week.

Source: *Meat and Dairy Products.* **Price Frequency:** monthly. **Effective Market(s):** Canada, Irish Republic, United Kingdom, United States, West Germany. **Units of Measure:** national currency per kilogram/lb. **Type of Price:** average. **Time Period Covered:** latest 3 years.

PIGS: FEEDER

Source: *Agricultural Outlook.* **Price Frequency:** monthly, annually. **Effective Market(s):** Southern Missouri. **Units of Measure:** Dollars per head. **Type of Price:** market. **Time Period Covered:** monthly latest 6 months, annually latest 3 years.

Source: *Agricultural Prices.* **Price Frequency:** monthly. **Effective Market(s):** 10 domestic markets, United States. **Units of Measure:** Dollars per 100 lbs. **Type of Price:** paid by farmer. **Time Period Covered:** latest month.

Source: *Agricultural Prices.* **Price Frequency:** quarterly. **Effective Market(s):** United States. **Units of Measure:** Dollars per 100 lbs. **Type of Price:** paid by farmer. **Time Period Covered:** latest quarter, year ago.

Source: *Agricultural Prices Annual Summary.* **Price Frequency:** quarterly. **Effective Market(s):** 10 domestic markets, United States. **Units of Measure:** Dollars per 100 lbs. **Type of Price:** paid by farmer. **Time Period Covered:** latest 3 years, for US latest 6 years.

Source: *Farm and Dairy.* **Price Frequency:** weekly, seasonally. **Effective Market(s):** Ohio, Pennsylvania. **Units of Measure:** Dollars per head. **Type of Price:** auction high, auction low. **Time Period Covered:** latest week.

Source: *Porkpro Newsletter.* **Price Frequency:** weekly. **Effective Market(s):** 5 domestic markets. **Units of Measure:** Dollars per head. **Time Period Covered:** latest week.

Source: *Viewpoint.* **Price Frequency:** weekly. **Effective Market(s):** Alabama, Kentucky, Tennessee. **Units of Measure:** Dollars per 100 lbs. **Time Period Covered:** latest week.

Source: *Viewpoint.* **Price Frequency:** weekly. **Effective Market(s):** 9 domestic markets. **Units of Measure:** Dollars per head. **Time Period Covered:** latest week.

PIGS: FEEDER, 30-40 LBS

Source: *Agriculture.* **Price Frequency:** weekly. **Effective Market(s):** Iowa, Sioux Falls (SD), Southern Missouri, Kentucky, Tennessee. **Units of Measure:** Dollars per 100 lbs. **Time Period Covered:** latest week, week ago.

PIGS: FEEDER, 40 LBS

Source: *Feedstuffs.* **Price Frequency:** weekly. **Effective Market(s):** Sioux Falls (SD). **Units of Measure:** Dollars per head. **Time Period Covered:** latest week, week ago, 6 months ago, year ago.

PIGS: FEEDER, 40-50 LBS

Source: *Agriculture.* **Price Frequency:** weekly. **Effective Market(s):** Iowa, Sioux Falls (SD), Southern Missouri, Kentucky, Tennessee. **Units of Measure:** Dollars per 100 lbs. **Time Period Covered:** latest week, week ago.

Source: *The Brock Report.* **Price Frequency:** weekly. **Effective Market(s):** Kalona (IA), Sioux Falls (SD), Southern Missouri. **Units of Measure:** Dollars per head. **Type of Price:** top price. **Time Period Covered:** latest week, week ago, 2 weeks ago.

PIGS: FEEDER, NO. 1 AND 2

Source: *Doane's Agricultural Report.* **Price Frequency:** weekly. **Effective Market(s):** Southern Missouri. **Units of Measure:** Dollars per head. **Time Period Covered:** latest week, week ago, year ago.

Source: *Livestock and Poultry Situation and Outlook Report.* **Price Frequency:** monthly. **Effective Market(s):** Southern Missouri. **Units of Measure:** Dollars per 100 lbs. **Time Period Covered:** latest year.

Source: *Livestock and Poultry Update.* **Price Frequency:** monthly. **Effective Market(s):** Southern Missouri. **Units of Measure:** Dollars per head. **Time Period Covered:** latest 3 months, year ago.

PIGS: FEEDER, US 1-2

Source: *Livestock, Meat, Wool Market News.* **Price Frequency:** weekly, seasonally. **Effective Market(s):** Kentucky, Sioux Falls (SD), Southern Missouri, South St. Joseph (MO), Tennessee. **Units of Measure:** Dollars per 100 lbs. **Time Period Covered:** latest week, year ago.

PIGS: FEEDER, US 2-3

Source: *Livestock, Meat, Wool Market News.* **Price Frequency:** weekly, seasonally. **Effective Market(s):** Kentucky, Sioux Falls (SD), Southern Missouri, South St. Joseph (MO), Tennessee. **Units of Measure:** Dollars per 100 lbs. **Time Period Covered:** latest week, year ago.

PIGS: FINISHED

Source: *Farmers Weekly.* **Price Frequency:** weekly. **Effective Market(s):** Great Britain. **Units of Measure:** British pence per kilogram. **Time Period Covered:** latest week, week ago, year ago.

PIGS: FUTURES

Source: *Financial Times.* **Price Frequency:** daily. **Effective Market(s):** London. **Units of Measure:** British pence per kilogram. **Type of Price:** futures. **Time Period Covered:** latest day.

PIGS: HEAVY

Source: *Farmers Weekly.* **Price Frequency:** weekly, seasonally. **Effective Market(s):** over 170 British markets. **Units of Measure:** British pence per kilogram. **Type of Price:** auction. **Time Period Covered:** latest week.

PIGS: LITTLE

Source: *Farm and Dairy.* **Price Frequency:** weekly, seasonally. **Effective Market(s):** Ohio, Pennsylvania. **Units of Measure:** Dollars per head. **Type of Price:** auction high, auction low. **Time Period Covered:** latest week.

PIGS: LIVE, FUTURES

Source: *The Times.* **Price Frequency:** daily. **Effective Market(s):** London. **Units of Measure:** British pence per kilogram. **Type of Price:** futures. **Time Period Covered:** latest day.

PIGS: LIVEWEIGHT

Source: *Financial Times.* **Price Frequency:** daily. **Effective Market(s):** London. **Units of Measure:** British pence per kilogram. **Type of Price:** spot. **Time Period Covered:** latest day.

PIGS: PORKERS

Source: *Farmers Weekly.* **Price Frequency:** weekly, seasonally. **Effective Market(s):** over 170 British markets. **Units of Measure:** British pence per kilogram. **Type of Price:** auction. **Time Period Covered:** latest week.

Source: *Scottish Farmer.* **Price Frequency:** weekly. **Effective Market(s):** Scotland. **Units of Measure:** British pence per kilogram. **Type of Price:** average. **Time Period Covered:** latest week.

PIGS: PORKERS, HEAVY

Source: *New Zealand Farmer.* **Price Frequency:** weekly, seasonally. **Effective Market(s):** New Zealand. **Units of Measure:** New Zealand dollars per head. **Type of Price:** export. **Time Period Covered:** latest 2 weeks.

PIGS: PORKERS, LIGHT

Source: *New Zealand Farmer.* **Price Frequency:** weekly, seasonally. **Effective Market(s):** New Zealand. **Units of Measure:** New Zealand dollars per head. **Type of Price:** export. **Time Period Covered:** latest 2 weeks.

PIGS: PORKERS, LIVEWEIGHT

Source: *Scottish Farmer.* **Price Frequency:** weekly. **Effective Market(s):** 10 Scottish markets. **Units of Measure:** British pence per kilogram. **Time Period Covered:** latest week.

PIGS: WEANERS

Source: *Farmers Weekly.* **Price Frequency:** weekly. **Effective Market(s):** England & Wales. **Units of Measure:** British pounds per head. **Type of Price:** producer. **Time Period Covered:** latest 3 weeks.

PIGS: WEANERS, HEAVY

Source: *New Zealand Farmer.* **Price Frequency:** weekly, seasonally. **Effective Market(s):** New Zealand. **Units of Measure:** New Zealand dollars per head. **Type of Price:** export. **Time Period Covered:** latest 2 weeks.

PIGS: WEANERS, LIGHT

Source: *New Zealand Farmer.* **Price Frequency:** weekly, seasonally. **Effective Market(s):** New Zealand. **Units of Measure:** New Zealand dollars per head. **Type of Price:** export. **Time Period Covered:** latest 2 weeks.

PIGS: WEANERS, STORE

Source: *Scottish Farmer.* **Price Frequency:** weekly. **Effective Market(s):** 9 Scottish markets average. **Units of Measure:** British pounds per head. **Type of Price:** average. **Time Period Covered:** latest 2 weeks.

PIKE: NORTHERN, WHOLE, FRESH

Source: *Seafood Price-Current.* **Price Frequency:** semiweekly. **Effective Market(s):** Mid-Atlantic, New England. **Units of Measure:** Dollars per lb. **Type of Price:** sale by first receiver. **Time Period Covered:** latest day.

PIKE: YELLOW, WHOLE, FRESH

Source: *Seafood Price-Current.* **Price Frequency:** semiweekly. **Effective Market(s):** Mid-Atlantic, New England. **Units of Measure:** Dollars per lb. **Type of Price:** sale by first receiver. **Time Period Covered:** latest day.

PILOCARPINE HYDROCHLORIDE: USP

Source: *Chemical Marketing Reporter.* **Price Frequency:** weekly. **Effective Market(s):** New York. **Units of Measure:** Dollars per kilo. **Type of Price:** spot. **Time Period Covered:** latest week.

PIMENTO

see also Allspice.

Source: *Prices of Selected Asia/Pacific Products.* **Price Frequency:** monthly. **Effective Market(s):** Tokyo. **Units of Measure:** Japanese yen per kilogram. **Type of Price:** high, low. **Time Period Covered:** latest month.

PIMENTO: GUATEMALAN

Source: *U. S. Spice Trade.* **Price Frequency:** monthly, annually. **Effective Market(s):** New York. **Units of Measure:** cents per lb. **Type of Price:** spot. **Time Period Covered:** latest 10 years.

PIMENTO: HONDURAN

Source: *U. S. Spice Trade.* **Price Frequency:** monthly, annually. **Effective Market(s):** New York. **Units of Measure:** cents per lb. **Type of Price:** spot. **Time Period Covered:** latest 10 years.

PIMENTO: JAMAICAN

Source: *Fruit and Tropical Products.* **Price Frequency:** monthly, seasonally. **Effective Market(s):** London. **Units of Measure:** British pounds per tonne. **Type of Price:** month end. **Time Period Covered:** latest 2 years.

Source: *Prices of Selected Asia/Pacific Products.* **Price Frequency:** monthly. **Effective Market(s):** Netherlands, United Kingdom, United States. **Units of Measure:** Dollars per metric ton. **Type of Price:** spot high, spot low. **Time Period Covered:** latest month.

Source: *Prices of Selected Asia/Pacific Products.* **Price Frequency:** monthly. **Effective Market(s):** Japan, United Kingdom/North European ports. **Units of Measure:** Dollars per metric ton. **Type of Price:** high, low. **Time Period Covered:** latest month.

Source: *U. S. Spice Trade.* **Price Frequency:** monthly, annually. **Effective Market(s):** New York. **Units of Measure:** cents per lb. **Type of Price:** spot. **Time Period Covered:** latest 10 years.

PIMENTO: MEXICAN

Source: *U. S. Spice Trade.* **Price Frequency:** monthly, annually. **Effective Market(s):** New York. **Units of Measure:** cents per lb. **Type of Price:** spot. **Time Period Covered:** latest 10 years.

PIMENTO LEAF OIL

Source: *Chemical Marketing Reporter.* **Price Frequency:** weekly. **Effective Market(s):** New York. **Units of Measure:** Dollars per lb. **Type of Price:** spot. **Time Period Covered:** latest week.

PINE

see also Lumber, Sawtimber, Wood.

PINE: BOARDS, SOUTHERN YELLOW, KILN DRIED

Source: *Timber Mart-South.* **Price Frequency:** quarterly. **Effective Market(s):** east of Alabama/Mississippi border, west of Alabama/Mississippi border. **Units of Measure:** Dollars per 1000 board feet. **Type of Price:** wholesale. **Time Period Covered:** latest quarter.

PINE: CHIP-N-SAW

Source: *Timber Mart-South.* **Price Frequency:** quarterly. **Effective Market(s):** 12 domestic markets. **Units of Measure:** Dollars per cord, dollars per 1000 board feet. **Type of Price:** standing timber, delivered. **Time Period Covered:** latest 2 quarters.

PINE: EASTERN WHITE

Source: *Volume and Value of Sawtimber Stumpage Sold From National Forests by Selected Species and Region.* **Price Frequency:** quarterly, annually. **Effective Market(s):** Southern region, Eastern region. **Units of Measure:** Dollars per 1000 board feet. **Type of Price:** average. **Time Period Covered:** latest quarter, latest year.

PINE: IDAHO WHITE, SELECT AND COMMONS, KILN DRIED

Source: *Random Lengths.* **Price Frequency:** weekly. **Units of Measure:** Dollars per 1000 board feet. **Type of Price:** price to wholesaler. **Time Period Covered:** latest week.

PINE: JACK

Source: *Volume and Value of Sawtimber Stumpage Sold From National Forests by Selected Species and Region.* **Price Frequency:** quarterly, annually. **Effective Market(s):** Eastern region. **Units of Measure:** Dollars per 1000 board feet. **Type of Price:** average. **Time Period Covered:** latest quarter, latest year.

PINE: LODGEPOLE

Source: *Volume and Value of Sawtimber Stumpage Sold From National Forests by Selected Species and Region.* **Price Frequency:** quarterly, annually. **Effective Market(s):** Northern region, Rocky Mountain region, Intermountain region, Pacific Southwest region, Pacific Northwest region. **Units of Measure:** Dollars per 1000 board feet. **Type of Price:** average. **Time Period Covered:** latest quarter, latest year.

PINE: LUMBER, 2″ X 4″

Source: *ENR.* **Price Frequency:** monthly in first issue of month. **Effective Market(s):** 20-city average. **Units of Measure:** Dollars per 1000 board feet. **Time Period Covered:** latest month.

PINE: LUMBER, S4S

Source: *ENR.* **Price Frequency:** monthly in third issue of month. **Effective Market(s):** varied domestic markets, Montreal, Toronto. **Units of Measure:** Dollars per 1000 board feet. **Type of Price:** spot. **Time Period Covered:** latest month.

PINE: LUMBER, SOUTHERN YELLOW, KILN DRIED

Source: *Timber Mart-South.* **Price Frequency:** quarterly. **Effective Market(s):** east of Alabama/Mississippi border, west of Alabama/Mississippi border. **Units of Measure:** Dollars per 1000 board feet. **Type of Price:** wholesale. **Time Period Covered:** latest quarter.

PINE: NOT SPECIFIED

Source: *Volume and Value of Sawtimber Stumpage Sold From National Forests by Selected Species and Region.* **Price Frequency:** quarterly, annually. **Effective Market(s):** Eastern region. **Units of Measure:** Dollars per 1000 board feet. **Type of Price:** average. **Time Period Covered:** latest quarter, latest year.

PINE: PLY LOGS

Source: *Timber Mart-South.* **Price Frequency:** quarterly. **Effective Market(s):** 12 domestic markets. **Units of Measure:** Dollars per 1000 board feet. **Type of Price:** stumpage, mill. **Time Period Covered:** latest quarter.

Source: *Timber Mart-South.* **Price Frequency:** quarterly. **Effective Market(s):** 13 domestic markets. **Units of Measure:** Dollars per 1000 board feet. **Type of Price:** standing timber. **Time Period Covered:** latest 2 quarters.

PINE: PONDEROSA

Source: *Volume and Value of Sawtimber Stumpage Sold From National Forests by Selected Species and Region.* **Price Frequency:** quarterly, annually. **Effective Market(s):** 6 domestic markets. **Units of Measure:** Dollars per 1000 board feet. **Type of Price:** average. **Time Period Covered:** latest quarter, latest year.

PINE: PONDEROSA, SELECT AND COMMONS, KILN DRIED

Source: *Random Lengths.* **Price Frequency:** weekly. **Effective Market(s):** Inland mills, California mills, Rocky Mountain region. **Units of Measure:** Dollars per 1000 board feet. **Type of Price:** price to wholesaler. **Time Period Covered:** latest week.

PINE: RED

Source: *Volume and Value of Sawtimber Stumpage Sold From National Forests by Selected Species and Region.* **Price Frequency:** quarterly, annually. **Effective Market(s):** Eastern region. **Units of Measure:** Dollars per 1000 board feet. **Type of Price:** average. **Time Period Covered:** latest quarter, latest year.

PINE: RED AND EASTERN WHITE

Source: *Volume and Value of Sawtimber Stumpage Sold From National Forests by Selected Species and Region.* **Price Frequency:** quarterly, annually. **Effective Market(s):** Eastern region. **Units of Measure:** Dollars per 1000 board feet. **Type of Price:** average. **Time Period Covered:** latest quarter, latest year.

PINE: SAWLOGS

Source: *Timber Mart-South.* **Price Frequency:** quarterly. **Effective Market(s):** 13 domestic markets. **Units of Measure:** Dollars per 1000 board feet. **Type of Price:** delivered. **Time Period Covered:** latest 2 quarters.

PINE: SAWTIMBER

Source: *Timber Mart-South.* **Price Frequency:** quarterly. **Effective Market(s):** 14 domestic markets. **Units of Measure:** Dollars per 1000 board feet. **Type of Price:** stumpage, mill. **Time Period Covered:** latest quarter.

Source: *Timber Mart-South.* **Price Frequency:** quarterly. **Effective Market(s):** 13 domestic markets. **Units of Measure:** Dollars per 1000 board feet. **Type of Price:** standing timber, delivered. **Time Period Covered:** latest 2 quarters.

Source: *Timber Mart-South.* **Price Frequency:** quarterly. **Effective Market(s):** 14 domestic markets. **Units of Measure:** Dollars per 1000 board feet. **Type of Price:** bid. **Time Period Covered:** latest quarter.

PINE: SOUTHERN

Source: *Volume and Value of Sawtimber Stumpage Sold From National Forests by Selected Species and Region.* **Price Frequency:** quarterly, annually. **Effective Market(s):** Eastern region, Southern region. **Units of Measure:** Dollars per 1000 board feet. **Type of Price:** average. **Time Period Covered:** latest quarter, latest year.

PINE: SOUTHERN, FRAMING LUMBER, KILN DRIED

Source: *Random Lengths.* **Price Frequency:** weekly. **Effective Market(s):** Central region, Eastside region, Westside region. **Units of Measure:** Dollars per 1000 board feet. **Type of Price:** price to wholesaler. **Time Period Covered:** latest week.

PINE: SOUTHERN, KILN DRIED

Source: *Random Lengths.* **Price Frequency:** weekly. **Units of Measure:** Dollars per 1000 board feet. **Type of Price:** price to wholesaler. **Time Period Covered:** latest week.

PINE: SOUTHERN, RADIUS EDGE DECKING

Source: *Random Lengths.* **Price Frequency:** weekly. **Units of Measure:** Dollars per 1000 board feet. **Type of Price:** price to wholesaler. **Time Period Covered:** latest week.

PINE: SUGAR

Source: *Volume and Value of Sawtimber Stumpage Sold From National Forests by Selected Species and Region.* **Price Frequency:** quarterly, annually. **Effective Market(s):** Pacific Southwest region, Pacific Northwest region. **Units of Measure:** Dollars per 1000 board feet. **Type of Price:** average. **Time Period Covered:** latest quarter, latest year.

PINE: SUGAR, SELECT AND COMMONS, KILN DRIED

Source: *Random Lengths.* **Price Frequency:** weekly. **Units of Measure:** Dollars per 1000 board feet. **Type of Price:** price to wholesaler. **Time Period Covered:** latest week.

PINE: WESTERN WHITE

Source: *Volume and Value of Sawtimber Stumpage Sold From National Forests by Selected Species and Region.* **Price Frequency:** quarterly, annually. **Effective Market(s):** Northern region, Pacific Northwest region. **Units of Measure:** Dollars per 1000 board feet. **Type of Price:** average. **Time Period Covered:** latest quarter, latest year.

PINE: WHITE, SAWTIMBER

Source: *Timber Mart-South.* **Price Frequency:** quarterly. **Effective Market(s):** Georgia, North Carolina, Tennessee, Virginia, United States. **Units of Measure:** Dollars per 1000 board feet. **Type of Price:** bid. **Time Period Covered:** latest quarter.

PINE: WOODCHIPS, CLEAN

Source: *Timber Mart-South.* **Price Frequency:** quarterly. **Effective Market(s):** 14 domestic markets. **Units of Measure:** Dollars per ton. **Type of Price:** sawmill. **Time Period Covered:** latest quarter.

PINE: WOODCHIPS, WHOLE TREE

Source: *Timber Mart-South.* **Price Frequency:** quarterly. **Effective Market(s):** 14 domestic markets. **Units of Measure:** Dollars per ton. **Type of Price:** sawmill. **Time Period Covered:** latest quarter.

PINE OIL

Source: *U. S. Essential Oil Trade.* **Price Frequency:** annually. **Effective Market(s):** United States. **Units of Measure:** Dollars per kilogram. **Type of Price:** import value. **Time Period Covered:** latest 3 years.

PINE OIL: 80% ALCOHOL CONTENT

Source: *Journal of Commerce and Commercial.* **Price Frequency:** weekly in Monday issue. **Units of Measure:** Dollars per 100 lbs. **Type of Price:** spot. **Time Period Covered:** latest week.

PINE OIL: 80% MINIMUM ALCOHOL CONTENT

Source: *Chemical Marketing Reporter.* **Price Frequency:** weekly. **Effective Market(s):** New York. **Units of Measure:** Dollars per 100 lbs. **Type of Price:** spot. **Time Period Covered:** latest week.

PINE OIL: SIBERIAN

Source: *Journal of Commerce and Commercial.* **Price Frequency:** weekly in Tuesday issue. **Units of Measure:** Dollars per lb. **Type of Price:** spot. **Time Period Covered:** latest week.

PINEAPPLES

Source: *Agricultural Prices Annual Summary.* **Price Frequency:** annually. **Effective Market(s):** California, Hawaii. **Units of Measure:** Dollars per ton. **Type of Price:** average received by farmer. **Time Period Covered:** latest 6 years.

Source: *Lancaster Farmer.* **Price Frequency:** weekly, seasonally. **Effective Market(s):** Pennsylvania. **Units of Measure:** Dollars per carton. **Type of Price:** market. **Time Period Covered:** latest week.

PINEAPPLES: FRESH

Source: *Fruit and Tree Nuts Situation and Outlook Yearbook.* **Price Frequency:** annually. **Effective Market(s):** Hawaii. **Units of Measure:** Dollars per ton. **Type of Price:** farm. **Time Period Covered:** latest 20 years.

Source: *HRI-Buyers Guide.* **Price Frequency:** weekly. **Effective Market(s):** Northeastern area. **Units of Measure:** Dollars per carton. **Type of Price:** prices paid by dining places & institutions. **Time Period Covered:** latest week.

Source: *Prices of Selected Asia/Pacific Products.* **Price Frequency:** monthly. **Effective Market(s):** Sydney (Australia). **Units of Measure:** Australian dollars per case. **Type of Price:** wholesale high, wholesale low. **Time Period Covered:** latest month.

PINEAPPLES: FRESH, A', COTE D'IVOIRE

Source: *Prices of Selected Asia/Pacific Products.* **Price Frequency:** monthly. **Effective Market(s):** United Kingdom, France. **Units of Measure:** British pounds per piece, French francs per kilogram. **Type of Price:** wholesale high, wholesale low. **Time Period Covered:** latest month.

PINEAPPLES: FRESH, A6', COTE D'IVOIRE

Source: *Prices of Selected Asia/Pacific Products.* **Price Frequency:** monthly. **Effective Market(s):** Netherlands. **Units of Measure:** Dutch guilders per kilogram. **Type of Price:** wholesale high, wholesale low. **Time Period Covered:** latest month.

PINEAPPLES: FRESH, B', CAMEROON

Source: *Prices of Selected Asia/Pacific Products.* **Price Frequency:** monthly, seasonally. **Effective Market(s):** France. **Units of Measure:** French francs per kilogram. **Type of Price:** wholesale high, wholesale low. **Time Period Covered:** latest month.

PINEAPPLES: FRESH, B', COTE D'IVOIRE

Source: *Prices of Selected Asia/Pacific Products.* **Price Frequency:** monthly. **Effective Market(s):** France. **Units of Measure:** French francs per kilogram. **Type of Price:** wholesale high, wholesale low. **Time Period Covered:** latest month.

PINEAPPLES: FRESH, PHILIPPINES

Source: *Prices of Selected Asia/Pacific Products.* **Price Frequency:** monthly. **Effective Market(s):** Tokyo. **Units of Measure:** Japanese yen per carton. **Type of Price:** trade high, trade low. **Time Period Covered:** latest month.

PINEAPPLES: IMPORTED

Source: *The Packer.* **Price Frequency:** weekly, seasonally. **Effective Market(s):** varies. **Units of Measure:** Dollars per carton. **Type of Price:** received by farmer. **Time Period Covered:** latest week.

PINEAPPLES: JAS NO. 3 CAN, IMPORTED

Source: *Prices of Selected Asia/Pacific Products.* **Price Frequency:** monthly. **Effective Market(s):** Tokyo. **Units of Measure:** Japanese yen per can. **Type of Price:** wholesale high, wholesale low. **Time Period Covered:** latest month.

PINEAPPLES: PHILIPPINES

Source: *Japan Economic Journal.* **Price Frequency:** weekly. **Effective Market(s):** Japan. **Units of Measure:** Japanese yen per carton. **Type of Price:** wholesale. **Time Period Covered:** latest 2 weeks.

PINEAPPLES: PROCESSED

Source: *Fruit and Tree Nuts Situation and Outlook Yearbook.* **Price Frequency:** annually. **Effective Market(s):** Hawaii. **Units of Measure:** Dollars per ton. **Type of Price:** farm. **Time Period Covered:** latest 20 years.

PINEAPPLES: VARIOUS VARIETIES, CARIBBEAN IMPORTS

Source: *Fresh Fruit and Vegetable Prices.* **Price Frequency:** monthly, seasonally. **Effective Market(s):** South Florida. **Units of Measure:** Dollars per carton. **Type of Price:** price paid at point of entry. **Time Period Covered:** latest year.

PINEAPPLES: VARIOUS VARIETIES, MEXICO

Source: *Fresh Fruit and Vegetable Prices.* **Price Frequency:** monthly, seasonally. **Effective Market(s):** South Texas. **Units of Measure:** Dollars per carton. **Type of Price:** price paid at point of entry. **Time Period Covered:** latest year.

A-PINENE: PERFUME GRADE

Source: *Chemical Marketing Reporter.* **Price Frequency:** weekly. **Effective Market(s):** New York. **Units of Measure:** Dollars per kilo. **Type of Price:** spot. **Time Period Covered:** latest week.

A-PINENE: TECHNICAL GRADE

Source: *Chemical Marketing Reporter.* **Price Frequency:** weekly. **Effective Market(s):** New York. **Units of Measure:** Dollars per lb. **Type of Price:** spot. **Time Period Covered:** latest week.

B-PINENE: PERFUME GRADE

Source: *Chemical Marketing Reporter.* **Price Frequency:** weekly. **Effective Market(s):** New York. **Units of Measure:** Dollars per kilo. **Type of Price:** spot. **Time Period Covered:** latest week.

B-PINENE: TECHNICAL GRADE

Source: *Chemical Marketing Reporter.* **Price Frequency:** weekly. **Effective Market(s):** New York. **Units of Measure:** Dollars per lb. **Type of Price:** spot. **Time Period Covered:** latest week.

PINENEEDLE OIL

Source: *U. S. Essential Oil Trade.* **Price Frequency:** annually. **Effective Market(s):** United States. **Units of Measure:** Dollars per kilogram. **Type of Price:** import value. **Time Period Covered:** latest 3 years.

PIPE: IRON, GALVANIZED

Source: *Agricultural Prices.* **Price Frequency:** annually. **Effective Market(s):** United States. **Units of Measure:** Dollars per foot. **Type of Price:** paid by farmer. **Time Period Covered:** latest year.

Source: *Agricultural Prices Annual Summary.* **Price Frequency:** semiannually. **Effective Market(s):** United States. **Units of Measure:** Dollars per foot. **Type of Price:** paid by farmer. **Time Period Covered:** latest 6 years.

PIPERAZINE: 65%

Source: *Journal of Commerce and Commercial.* **Price Frequency:** weekly in Friday issue. **Units of Measure:** Dollars per lb. **Type of Price:** spot. **Time Period Covered:** latest week.

PIPERAZINE: ANHYDROUS

Source: *Chemical Marketing Reporter.* **Price Frequency:** weekly. **Effective Market(s):** East. **Units of Measure:** Dollars per lb. **Type of Price:** spot. **Time Period Covered:** latest week.

Source: *Journal of Commerce and Commercial.* **Price Frequency:** weekly in Friday issue. **Units of Measure:** Dollars per lb. **Type of Price:** spot. **Time Period Covered:** latest week.

PIPERAZINE CITRATE: 36%

Source: *Chemical Marketing Reporter.* **Price Frequency:** weekly. **Effective Market(s):** New York. **Units of Measure:** Dollars per lb. **Type of Price:** spot. **Time Period Covered:** latest week.

PIPERAZINE DIHYDROCHLORIDE: 53%

Source: *Chemical Marketing Reporter.* **Price Frequency:** weekly. **Effective Market(s):** New York. **Units of Measure:** Dollars per lb. **Type of Price:** spot. **Time Period Covered:** latest week.

PIPERAZINE HEXAHYDRATE: 44%

Source: *Chemical Marketing Reporter.* **Price Frequency:** weekly. **Effective Market(s):** New York. **Units of Measure:** Dollars per lb. **Type of Price:** spot. **Time Period Covered:** latest week.

PIPERAZINE PHOSPHATE: 42%

Source: *Chemical Marketing Reporter.* **Price Frequency:** weekly. **Effective Market(s):** New York. **Units of Measure:** Dollars per lb. **Type of Price:** spot. **Time Period Covered:** latest week.

PIPERIDINE: DISTILLED, 98% MINIMUM

Source: *Chemical Marketing Reporter.* **Price Frequency:** weekly. **Effective Market(s):** New York. **Units of Measure:** Dollars per kilo. **Type of Price:** spot. **Time Period Covered:** latest week.

PIPERONYL BUTOXIDE

Source: *Chemical Marketing Reporter.* **Price Frequency:** weekly. **Effective Market(s):** East. **Units of Measure:** Dollars per lb. **Type of Price:** spot. **Time Period Covered:** latest week.

PISTACHIOS

Source: *Agricultural Prices Annual Summary.* **Price Frequency:** annually. **Effective Market(s):** California, Hawaii. **Units of Measure:** Dollars per lb. **Type of Price:** average received by farmer. **Time Period Covered:** latest 6 years.

Source: *Fruit and Tree Nuts Situation and Outlook Yearbook.* **Price Frequency:** annually. **Effective Market(s):** California. **Units of Measure:** cents per lb. **Type of Price:** grower. **Time Period Covered:** latest 12 years.

PITCH FORK

Source: *Agricultural Prices.* **Price Frequency:** annually. **Effective Market(s):** United States. **Units of Measure:** Dollars each. **Type of Price:** paid by farmer. **Time Period Covered:** latest year.

Source: *Agricultural Prices Annual Summary.* **Price Frequency:** semiannually. **Effective Market(s):** United States. **Units of Measure:** Dollars each. **Type of Price:** paid by farmer. **Time Period Covered:** latest 6 years.

PLASTIC: PHENOLIC MOLDING COMPOUND

Source: *Commodity Year Book.* **Price Frequency:** monthly, annually. **Effective Market(s):** United States. **Units of Measure:** index. **Type of Price:** price index. **Time Period Covered:** latest 7 years.

PLASTIC RESINS

see also specific types of plastic, e.g., Polystyrene.

PLASTIC RESINS: POLYSTYRENE, RUBBER MODIFIED

Source: *Commodity Year Book.* **Price Frequency:** monthly, annually. **Effective Market(s):** United States. **Units of Measure:** index. **Type of Price:** price index. **Time Period Covered:** latest 7 years.

PLASTIC RESINS: THERMOPLASTIC

Source: *Commodity Year Book.* **Price Frequency:** monthly, annually. **Effective Market(s):** United States. **Units of Measure:** index. **Type of Price:** price index. **Time Period Covered:** latest 7 years.

PLASTIC RESINS: THERMOSETTING

Source: *Commodity Year Book.* **Price Frequency:** monthly, annually. **Effective Market(s):** United States. **Units of Measure:** index. **Type of Price:** price index. **Time Period Covered:** latest 7 years.

PLASTIC RESINS AND MATERIALS

Source: *Commodity Year Book.* **Price Frequency:** monthly, annually. **Effective Market(s):** United States. **Units of Measure:** index. **Type of Price:** price index. **Time Period Covered:** latest 7 years.

PLASTICIZERS

Source: *Modern Plastics.* **Price Frequency:** quarterly every February, May, August, November. **Units of Measure:** Dollars per lb. **Type of Price:** list. **Time Period Covered:** latest 4 quarters.

PLATINUM

Source: *American Metal Market.* **Price Frequency:** daily. **Effective Market(s):** London, United States. **Units of Measure:** Dollars per troy ounce. **Type of Price:** merchant, producer. **Time Period Covered:** latest day.

Source: *Asian Wall Street Journal.* **Price Frequency:** daily. **Effective Market(s):** New York. **Units of Measure:** Dollars per troy ounce. **Type of Price:** free market. **Time Period Covered:** latest 2 days.

Source: *Asian Wall Street Journal.* **Price Frequency:** daily. **Effective Market(s):** London. **Units of Measure:** Dollars per troy ounce. **Type of Price:** cash. **Time Period Covered:** latest 2 days, year ago.

Source: *Chemical Marketing Reporter.* **Price Frequency:** weekly. **Effective Market(s):** New York. **Units of Measure:** Dollars per troy ounce. **Type of Price:** spot. **Time Period Covered:** latest week.

Source: *Commodity Year Book.* **Price Frequency:** monthly, annually. **Effective Market(s):** New York. **Units of Measure:** Dollars per troy ounce. **Type of Price:** merchant. **Time Period Covered:** latest 15 years.

Source: *E&MJ.* **Price Frequency:** monthly. **Effective Market(s):** New York, London. **Units of Measure:** Dollars per troy ounce. **Time Period Covered:** latest month.

Source: *E&MJ.* **Price Frequency:** monthly. **Effective Market(s):** United States. **Units of Measure:** Dollars per troy ounce. **Type of Price:** merchant. **Time Period Covered:** latest month.

Source: *Economic and Energy Indicators.* **Price Frequency:** monthly, quarterly, annually. **Units of Measure:** Dollars per troy ounce. **Time Period Covered:** latest 3 months, quarters, and years.

Source: *Financial Post.* **Price Frequency:** weekly. **Effective Market(s):** Canada. **Units of Measure:** Dollars per troy ounce. **Type of Price:** cash. **Time Period Covered:** latest week.

Source: *Financial Times.* **Price Frequency:** daily. **Effective Market(s):** London. **Units of Measure:** Dollars per troy ounce. **Type of Price:** spot. **Time Period Covered:** latest day.

Source: *Investor's Daily.* **Price Frequency:** daily. **Effective Market(s):** New York. **Units of Measure:** Dollars per troy ounce. **Type of Price:** contract. **Time Period Covered:** latest day.

Source: *Iron Age.* **Price Frequency:** monthly. **Units of Measure:** Dollars per troy ounce. **Type of Price:** consumer. **Time Period Covered:** latest month.

Source: *Los Angeles Times.* **Price Frequency:** daily. **Effective Market(s):** New York. **Units of Measure:** Dollars per troy ounce. **Type of Price:** contract, spot. **Time Period Covered:** latest day.

Source: *New York Times.* **Price Frequency:** daily. **Effective Market(s):** New York. **Units of Measure:** Dollars per troy ounce. **Type of Price:** contract, spot. **Time Period Covered:** latest 2 days.

Source: *Northern Miner.* **Price Frequency:** daily. **Units of Measure:** Dollars per ounce. **Type of Price:** spot. **Time Period Covered:** latest week.

Source: *Northern Miner.* **Price Frequency:** daily. **Effective Market(s):** New York. **Units of Measure:** Dollars per ounce. **Type of Price:** dealer. **Time Period Covered:** latest day.

Source: *Purchasing.* **Price Frequency:** quarterly in January, April, July, October issues. **Units of Measure:** Dollars per troy ounce. **Type of Price:** transaction. **Time Period Covered:** latest 5 quarters.

Source: *The Times.* **Price Frequency:** daily. **Effective Market(s):** London. **Units of Measure:** Dollars per troy ounce, British pounds per troy ounce. **Type of Price:** evening fix. **Time Period Covered:** latest day.

Source: *Wall Street Journal.* **Price Frequency:** daily. **Units of Measure:** Dollars per troy ounce. **Type of Price:** free market. **Time Period Covered:** latest day, day ago, year ago.

PLATINUM: FABRICATED PRODUCTS

Source: *American Metal Market.* **Price Frequency:** daily. **Effective Market(s):** United States. **Units of Measure:** Dollars per troy ounce. **Type of Price:** producer. **Time Period Covered:** latest day.

Source: *Asian Wall Street Journal.* **Price Frequency:** daily. **Effective Market(s):** New York. **Units of Measure:** Dollars per troy ounce. **Type of Price:** cash. **Time Period Covered:** latest 2 days.

Source: *E&MJ.* **Price Frequency:** monthly. **Units of Measure:** Dollars per troy ounce. **Time Period Covered:** latest month.

Source: *Wall Street Journal.* **Price Frequency:** daily. **Units of Measure:** Dollars per troy ounce. **Time Period Covered:** latest day, day ago, year ago.

PLATINUM: FUTURES

Source: *American Metal Market.* **Price Frequency:** daily. **Effective Market(s):** New York. **Units of Measure:** Dollars per troy ounce. **Type of Price:** futures. **Time Period Covered:** latest day.

Source: *Asian Wall Street Journal.* **Price Frequency:** daily. **Effective Market(s):** New York. **Units of Measure:** Dollars per troy ounce. **Type of Price:** futures. **Time Period Covered:** latest day.

Source: *Barron's.* **Price Frequency:** weekly. **Effective Market(s):** New York. **Units of Measure:** Dollars per troy ounce. **Type of Price:** futures. **Time Period Covered:** latest week.

Source: *Financial Times.* **Price Frequency:** daily. **Effective Market(s):** New York. **Units of Measure:** Dollars per troy ounce. **Type of Price:** futures. **Time Period Covered:** latest day.

Source: *Investor's Daily.* **Price Frequency:** daily. **Effective Market(s):** New York. **Units of Measure:** Dollars per troy ounce. **Type of Price:** futures. **Time Period Covered:** latest day.

Source: *Japan Economic Journal.* **Price Frequency:** weekly. **Effective Market(s):** Tokyo. **Units of Measure:** Japanese yen per gram. **Type of Price:** futures. **Time Period Covered:** latest week.

Source: *Los Angeles Times.* **Price Frequency:** daily. **Effective Market(s):** New York. **Units of Measure:** Dollars per troy ounce. **Type of Price:** futures. **Time Period Covered:** latest day.

Source: *New York Times.* **Price Frequency:** daily. **Effective Market(s):** New York. **Units of Measure:** Dollars per troy ounce. **Type of Price:** futures. **Time Period Covered:** latest day.

Source: *Northern Miner.* **Price Frequency:** daily. **Effective Market(s):** New York. **Units of Measure:** Dollars per ounce. **Type of Price:** futures. **Time Period Covered:** latest day.

Source: *Wall Street Journal.* **Price Frequency:** daily. **Effective Market(s):** New York. **Units of Measure:** Dollars per troy ounce. **Type of Price:** futures. **Time Period Covered:** latest day.

PLATINUM: FUTURES, APRIL

Source: *Commodity Year Book.* **Price Frequency:** monthly. **Effective Market(s):** New York. **Units of Measure:** Dollars per ounce. **Type of Price:** futures. **Time Period Covered:** latest 5 years.

PLATINUM: INDUSTRIAL

Source: *Asian Wall Street Journal.* **Price Frequency:** daily. **Effective Market(s):** New York. **Units of Measure:** Dollars per troy ounce. **Type of Price:** cash. **Time Period Covered:** latest 2 days.

Source: *Wall Street Journal.* **Price Frequency:** daily. **Units of Measure:** Dollars per troy ounce. **Time Period Covered:** latest day, day ago, year ago.

PLATINUM MERCURY

Source: *Investor's Daily.* **Price Frequency:** daily. **Effective Market(s):** New York. **Units of Measure:** Dollars per troy ounce. **Type of Price:** spot. **Time Period Covered:** latest day.

PLOW: MOLDBOARD, ONE-WAY

Source: *Agricultural Prices.* **Price Frequency:** semiannually. **Effective Market(s):** United States. **Units of Measure:** Dollars each. **Type of Price:** paid by farmer. **Time Period Covered:** latest year.

Source: *Agricultural Prices Annual Summary.* **Price Frequency:** semiannually. **Effective Market(s):** United States. **Units of Measure:** Dollars each. **Type of Price:** paid by farmer. **Time Period Covered:** latest 6 years.

PLUMS

Source: *Agricultural Prices Annual Summary.* **Price Frequency:** annually. **Effective Market(s):** California, Hawaii. **Units of Measure:** Dollars per ton. **Type of Price:** average received by farmer. **Time Period Covered:** latest 6 years.

Source: *Fruit and Tree Nuts Situation and Outlook Yearbook.* **Price Frequency:** annually. **Effective Market(s):** California. **Units of Measure:** Dollars per ton. **Type of Price:** grower. **Time Period Covered:** latest 20 years.

PLUMS: ANGELINO

Source: *California Farmer.* **Price Frequency:** semimonthly, seasonally. **Effective Market(s):** Central/ Southern San Joaquin Valley. **Units of Measure:** Dollars per 28 lb. carton. **Time Period Covered:** latest week, year ago.

PLUMS: BLACK AMBER

Source: *Fresh Fruit and Vegetable Prices.* **Price Frequency:** monthly, seasonally. **Effective Market(s):** Central San Joaquin Valley (CA). **Units of Measure:** Dollars per carton. **Type of Price:** average price at shipping point. **Time Period Covered:** latest year.

PLUMS: CASSELMAN

Source: *California Farmer.* **Price Frequency:** semimonthly, seasonally. **Effective Market(s):** Central/Southern San Joaquin Valley. **Units of Measure:** Dollars per 28 lb. carton. **Time Period Covered:** latest week, year ago.

Source: *Fresh Fruit and Vegetable Prices.* **Price Frequency:** monthly, seasonally. **Effective Market(s):** Central San Joaquin Valley (CA). **Units of Measure:** Dollars per carton. **Type of Price:** average price at shipping point. **Time Period Covered:** latest year.

PLUMS: CASSELMAN, CALIFORNIA

Source: *Fresh Fruit and Vegetable Prices.* **Price Frequency:** monthly, seasonally. **Effective Market(s):** New York City. **Units of Measure:** Dollars per carton. **Type of Price:** average wholesale price. **Time Period Covered:** latest year.

PLUMS: EL DORADO

Source: *Fresh Fruit and Vegetable Prices.* **Price Frequency:** monthly, seasonally. **Effective Market(s):** Central San Joaquin Valley (CA). **Units of Measure:** Dollars per carton. **Type of Price:** average price at shipping point. **Time Period Covered:** latest year.

PLUMS: FRIAR

Source: *California Farmer.* **Price Frequency:** semimonthly, seasonally. **Effective Market(s):** Central/Southern San Joaquin Valley. **Units of Measure:** Dollars per 28 lb. carton. **Time Period Covered:** latest week, year ago.

Source: *Fresh Fruit and Vegetable Prices.* **Price Frequency:** monthly, seasonally. **Effective Market(s):** Central San Joaquin Valley (CA). **Units of Measure:** Dollars per carton. **Type of Price:** average price at shipping point. **Time Period Covered:** latest year.

Source: *Lancaster Farmer.* **Price Frequency:** weekly, seasonally. **Effective Market(s):** Pennsylvania. **Units of Measure:** Dollars per lug. **Type of Price:** market. **Time Period Covered:** latest week.

Source: *The Packer.* **Price Frequency:** weekly, seasonally. **Effective Market(s):** varies. **Units of Measure:** Dollars per carton. **Type of Price:** received by farmer. **Time Period Covered:** latest week.

PLUMS: FRIAR, CALIFORNIA

Source: *Fresh Fruit and Vegetable Prices.* **Price Frequency:** monthly, seasonally. **Effective Market(s):** Chicago, New York City. **Units of Measure:** Dollars per carton. **Type of Price:** average wholesale price. **Time Period Covered:** latest year.

PLUMS: FRONTIER

Source: *Lancaster Farmer.* **Price Frequency:** weekly, seasonally. **Effective Market(s):** Pennsylvania. **Units of Measure:** Dollars per lug. **Type of Price:** market. **Time Period Covered:** latest week.

PLUMS: IMPORTED

Source: *New Zealand Farmer.* **Price Frequency:** weekly, seasonally. **Effective Market(s):** New Zealand. **Units of Measure:** New Zealand dollars per carton. **Time Period Covered:** latest week.

PLUMS: KELSEY

Source: *Lancaster Farmer.* **Price Frequency:** weekly, seasonally. **Effective Market(s):** Pennsylvania. **Units of Measure:** Dollars per lug. **Type of Price:** market. **Time Period Covered:** latest week.

PLUMS: LARODA

Source: *Fresh Fruit and Vegetable Prices.* **Price Frequency:** monthly, seasonally. **Effective Market(s):** Central San Joaquin Valley (CA). **Units of Measure:** Dollars per carton. **Type of Price:** average price at shipping point. **Time Period Covered:** latest year.

PLUMS: LARODA, CALIFORNIA

Source: *Fresh Fruit and Vegetable Prices.* **Price Frequency:** monthly, seasonally. **Effective Market(s):** Chicago, New York City. **Units of Measure:** Dollars per carton. **Type of Price:** average wholesale price. **Time Period Covered:** latest year.

PLUMS: RED BEAUT

Source: *California Farmer.* **Price Frequency:** semimonthly, seasonally . **Effective Market(s):** Central/Southern San Joaquin Valley. **Units of Measure:** Dollars per 28 lb. carton. **Time Period Covered:** latest week, year ago.

PLUMS: RED BEAUT, CALIFORNIA

Source: *Fresh Fruit and Vegetable Prices.* **Price Frequency:** monthly, seasonally. **Effective Market(s):** Chicago, New York City. **Units of Measure:** Dollars per carton. **Type of Price:** average wholesale price. **Time Period Covered:** latest year.

PLUMS: ROYAL DIAMOND

Source: *Lancaster Farmer.* **Price Frequency:** weekly, seasonally. **Effective Market(s):** Pennsylvania. **Units of Measure:** Dollars per lug. **Type of Price:** market. **Time Period Covered:** latest week.

Source: *The Packer.* **Price Frequency:** weekly, seasonally. **Effective Market(s):** varies. **Units of Measure:** Dollars per carton. **Type of Price:** received by farmer. **Time Period Covered:** latest week.

PLUMS: ROYSUM

Source: *California Farmer.* **Price Frequency:** semimonthly, seasonally. **Effective Market(s):** Central/Southern San Joaquin Valley. **Units of Measure:** Dollars per 28 lb. carton. **Time Period Covered:** latest week, year ago.

Source: *Fresh Fruit and Vegetable Prices.* **Price Frequency:** monthly, seasonally. **Effective Market(s):** Central San Joaquin Valley (CA). **Units of Measure:** Dollars per carton. **Type of Price:** average price at shipping point. **Time Period Covered:** latest year.

PLUMS: ROYSUM, CALIFORNIA

Source: *Fresh Fruit and Vegetable Prices.* **Price Frequency:** monthly, seasonally. **Effective Market(s):** Chicago. **Units of Measure:** Dollars per carton. **Type of Price:** average wholesale price. **Time Period Covered:** latest year.

PLUMS: SANTA ROSA

Source: *California Farmer.* **Price Frequency:** semimonthly, seasonally. **Effective Market(s):** Central/Southern San Joaquin Valley. **Units of Measure:** Dollars per 28 lb. carton. **Time Period Covered:** latest week, year ago.

Source: *Fresh Fruit and Vegetable Prices.* **Price Frequency:** monthly, seasonally. **Effective Market(s):** Central San Joaquin Valley (CA). **Units of Measure:** Dollars per carton. **Type of Price:** average price at shipping point. **Time Period Covered:** latest year.

PLUMS: SANTA ROSA, CALIFORNIA

Source: *Fresh Fruit and Vegetable Prices.* **Price Frequency:** monthly, seasonally. **Effective Market(s):** Chicago, New York City. **Units of Measure:** Dollars per carton. **Type of Price:** average wholesale price. **Time Period Covered:** latest year.

PLUMS: VARIOUS VARIETIES, CHILEAN

Source: *Fresh Fruit and Vegetable Prices.* **Price Frequency:** monthly, seasonally. **Effective Market(s):** Chicago. **Units of Measure:** Dollars per carton. **Type of Price:** average wholesale price. **Time Period Covered:** latest year.

Source: *Fresh Fruit and Vegetable Prices.* **Price Frequency:** monthly, seasonally. **Effective Market(s):** New York City/Philadelphia. **Units of Measure:** Dollars per lug. **Type of Price:** dock price. **Time Period Covered:** latest year.

PLYFORM: 3/4″

Source: *ENR.* **Price Frequency:** monthly in first issue of month. **Effective Market(s):** 20-city average. **Units of Measure:** Dollars per 1000 square feet. **Time Period Covered:** latest month.

Source: *ENR.* **Price Frequency:** monthly in third issue of month. **Effective Market(s):** 20 domestic markets, Montreal, Toronto. **Units of Measure:** Dollars per 1000 square feet. **Type of Price:** spot. **Time Period Covered:** latest month.

PLYWOOD

Source: *Journal of Commerce and Commercial.* **Price Frequency:** daily. **Effective Market(s):** Chicago. **Type of Price:** spot supplier. **Time Period Covered:** latest day.

Source: *Timber Bulletin.* **Price Frequency:** monthly, annually. **Effective Market(s):** United Kingdom. **Units of Measure:** British pounds per cubic meter. **Type of Price:** import. **Time Period Covered:** monthly latest 2 years, annually latest 5 years.

Source: *Timber Bulletin.* **Price Frequency:** monthly, annually. **Effective Market(s):** Finland. **Units of Measure:** Finnish markka per cubic meter. **Type of Price:** export. **Time Period Covered:** monthly latest 2 years, annually latest 6 years.

PLYWOOD: 5/8″

Source: *ENR.* **Price Frequency:** monthly in first issue of month. **Effective Market(s):** 20-city average. **Units of Measure:** Dollars per 1000 square feet. **Time Period Covered:** latest month.

Source: *ENR.* **Price Frequency:** monthly in third issue of month. **Effective Market(s):** 20 domestic markets, Montreal, Toronto. **Units of Measure:** Dollars per 1000 square feet. **Type of Price:** spot. **Time Period Covered:** latest month.

PLYWOOD: C-D-X

Source: *Agricultural Prices.* **Price Frequency:** quarterly. **Effective Market(s):** United States. **Units of Measure:** Dollars each. **Type of Price:** paid by farmer. **Time Period Covered:** latest 2 quarters, year ago.

Source: *Agricultural Prices Annual Summary.* **Price Frequency:** bimonthly. **Effective Market(s):** United States. **Units of Measure:** Dollars per sheet. **Type of Price:** paid by farmer. **Time Period Covered:** latest 6 years.

PLYWOOD: C-D-X, 1/2″

Source: *Prices of Selected Asia/Pacific Products.* **Price Frequency:** monthly. **Effective Market(s):** Chicago. **Units of Measure:** Dollars per sheath. **Type of Price:** high, low. **Time Period Covered:** latest month.

PLYWOOD: FIR, C-D-X, 1/2″

Source: *Purchasing.* **Price Frequency:** monthly. **Units of Measure:** Dollars per 1000 square feet. **Type of Price:** transaction. **Time Period Covered:** latest day, month ago, 6 months ago, year ago.

PLYWOOD: FOR CONCRETE MOULDING BOX, IMPORTED

Source: *Prices of Selected Asia/Pacific Products.* **Price Frequency:** monthly. **Effective Market(s):** Tokyo. **Units of Measure:** Japanese yen per sheet. **Type of Price:** wholesale high, wholesale low. **Time Period Covered:** latest month.

PLYWOOD: FOR CONCRETE MOULDING BOX, JAPANESE

Source: *Prices of Selected Asia/Pacific Products.* **Price Frequency:** monthly. **Effective Market(s):** Tokyo. **Units of Measure:** Japanese yen per sheet. **Type of Price:** wholesale high, wholesale low. **Time Period Covered:** latest month.

PLYWOOD: LAUAN

Source: *Timber Bulletin.* **Price Frequency:** monthly, annually. **Effective Market(s):** Japan, South Korea. **Units of Measure:** national currency per sheet. **Time Period Covered:** monthly latest 2 years, annually latest 6 years.

PLYWOOD: LAUAN, 3 PLY, PHILIPPINES

Source: *Commodity Trade and Price Trends.* **Price Frequency:** annually. **Effective Market(s):** Tokyo. **Units of Measure:** cents per sheet. **Type of Price:** spot. **Time Period Covered:** latest 24 years.

Source: *Monthly Commodity Price Bulletin Supplement.* **Price Frequency:** monthly, quarterly, annually. **Effective Market(s):** Tokyo. **Units of Measure:** Dollars per sheet. **Type of Price:** wholesale. **Time Period Covered:** latest 20 years.

PLYWOOD: LAUAN, PHILIPPINES

Source: *FAO Quarterly Bulletin of Statistics.* **Price Frequency:** monthly, annually. **Effective Market(s):** Tokyo. **Units of Measure:** Japanese yen per sheet, dollars per metric ton. **Type of Price:** wholesale. **Time Period Covered:** latest 3 years.

PLYWOOD: LAUAN, TYPE 1

Source: *Japan Economic Journal.* **Price Frequency:** weekly. **Effective Market(s):** Japan. **Units of Measure:** Japanese yen per panel. **Type of Price:** wholesale. **Time Period Covered:** latest 2 weeks.

PLYWOOD: LAUAN, TYPE 1, PHILIPPINES

Source: *Prices of Selected Asia/Pacific Products.* **Price Frequency:** monthly. **Effective Market(s):** Hong Kong. **Units of Measure:** Hong Kong dollars per square feet. **Type of Price:** high, low. **Time Period Covered:** latest month.

PLYWOOD: PHILIPPINES

Source: *International Financial Statistics.* **Price Frequency:** monthly, quarterly, annually. **Effective Market(s):** Tokyo. **Units of Measure:** cents per sheet, index. **Type of Price:** market price, price index. **Time Period Covered:** latest 4 months, latest 5 quarters, latest 5 years.

Source: *International Financial Statistics Yearbook.* **Price Frequency:** annually. **Effective Market(s):** Tokyo. **Units of Measure:** cents per sheet. **Type of Price:** wholesale. **Time Period Covered:** latest 30 years.

PLYWOOD: SANDED, 1/4″

Source: *Purchasing.* **Price Frequency:** quarterly in January, April, July, October issues. **Units of Measure:** Dollars per ton. **Type of Price:** transaction. **Time Period Covered:** latest 5 quarters.

PLYWOOD: SOFTWOOD, SHEATHING

Source: *FAO Quarterly Bulletin of Statistics.* **Price Frequency:** monthly, annually. **Effective Market(s):** South United States. **Units of Measure:** Dollars per 1000 square feet, dollars per metric ton. **Type of Price:** wholesale. **Time Period Covered:** latest 3 years.

PLYWOOD: SOFTWOOD, WESTERN

Source: *Commodity Year Book.* **Price Frequency:** monthly, annually. **Units of Measure:** index. **Type of Price:** price index. **Time Period Covered:** latest 9 years.

PLYWOOD: TYPE 1, CHINESE

Source: *Prices of Selected Asia/Pacific Products.* **Price Frequency:** monthly. **Effective Market(s):** Hong Kong. **Units of Measure:** Hong Kong dollars per square feet. **Type of Price:** high, low. **Time Period Covered:** latest month.

PLYWOOD: TYPE 1, KAPOR-SHUTTERING FACE/BACK, KOREAN

Source: *Prices of Selected Asia/Pacific Products.* **Price Frequency:** monthly. **Effective Market(s):** Hong Kong. **Units of Measure:** Hong Kong dollars per square feet. **Type of Price:** high, low. **Time Period Covered:** latest month.

PLYWOOD: TYPE 1, KERUING-SHUTTERING FACE/BACK, MALAYSIAN

Source: *Prices of Selected Asia/Pacific Products.* **Price Frequency:** monthly. **Effective Market(s):** Hong Kong. **Units of Measure:** Hong Kong dollars per square feet. **Type of Price:** high, low. **Time Period Covered:** latest month.

PLYWOOD: TYPE 2, KOREAN

Source: *Prices of Selected Asia/Pacific Products.* **Price Frequency:** monthly. **Effective Market(s):** Hong Kong. **Units of Measure:** Hong Kong dollars per square feet. **Type of Price:** high, low. **Time Period Covered:** latest month.

PLYWOOD: TYPE 2, MALAYSIAN

Source: *Prices of Selected Asia/Pacific Products.* **Price Frequency:** monthly. **Effective Market(s):** Hong Kong. **Units of Measure:** Hong Kong dollars per square feet. **Type of Price:** high, low. **Time Period Covered:** latest month.

PLYWOOD: TYPE 2, PHILIPPINES

Source: *Prices of Selected Asia/Pacific Products.* **Price Frequency:** monthly. **Effective Market(s):** Hong Kong. **Units of Measure:** Hong Kong dollars per square feet. **Type of Price:** high, low. **Time Period Covered:** latest month.

PLYWOOD: VENEER, IMPORTED

Source: *Prices of Selected Asia/Pacific Products.* **Price Frequency:** monthly. **Effective Market(s):** Tokyo. **Units of Measure:** Japanese yen per sheet. **Type of Price:** wholesale high, wholesale low. **Time Period Covered:** latest month.

PLYWOOD: VENEER, JAPANESE

Source: *Prices of Selected Asia/Pacific Products.* **Price Frequency:** monthly. **Effective Market(s):** Tokyo. **Units of Measure:** Japanese yen per sheet. **Type of Price:** wholesale high, wholesale low. **Time Period Covered:** latest month.

PLYWOOD: WAFERBOARD

Source: *Purchasing.* **Price Frequency:** monthly. **Effective Market(s):** Northeast. **Units of Measure:** Dollars per 1000 square feet. **Type of Price:** transaction. **Time Period Covered:** latest day, month ago, 6 months ago, year ago.

PODOPHYLLIN: AMERICAN, USP

Source: *Journal of Commerce and Commercial.* **Price Frequency:** weekly in Friday issue. **Units of Measure:** Dollars per lb. **Type of Price:** spot. **Time Period Covered:** latest week.

PODOPHYLLIN: INDIAN

Source: *Journal of Commerce and Commercial.* **Price Frequency:** weekly in Friday issue. **Units of Measure:** Dollars per lb. **Type of Price:** spot. **Time Period Covered:** latest week.

POINSETTIAS: POTTED, LESS THAN 5″

Source: *Floriculture Crops.* **Price Frequency:** annually. **Effective Market(s):** 27 domestic markets, United States. **Units of Measure:** Dollars per unit. **Type of Price:** commercial wholesale. **Time Period Covered:** latest 2 years.

POINSETTIAS: POTTED, MORE THAN 5″

Source: *Floriculture Crops.* **Price Frequency:** annually. **Effective Market(s):** 27 domestic markets, United States. **Units of Measure:** Dollars per unit. **Type of Price:** commercial wholesale. **Time Period Covered:** latest 2 years.

POLLOCK: ALASKAN

Source: *Weekly Statistical Fishery Report.* **Price Frequency:** weekly. **Effective Market(s):** Tokyo. **Units of Measure:** Dollars per lb. **Type of Price:** wholesale. **Time Period Covered:** 2 weeks ago, month ago.

POLLOCK: BLOCKS, ALASKAN, DOMESTIC

Source: *NMFS Green Sheet Supplement.* **Price Frequency:** weekly, seasonally. **Units of Measure:** dollars per lb. **Type of Price:** processor. **Time Period Covered:** latest week.

POLLOCK: BLOCKS, ALASKAN, IMPORTED

Source: *NMFS Green Sheet Supplement.* **Price Frequency:** weekly, seasonally. **Units of Measure:** dollars per lb. **Type of Price:** processor. **Time Period Covered:** latest week.

POLLOCK: BLOCKS, IMPORTED

Source: *NMFS Green Sheet Supplement.* **Price Frequency:** weekly, seasonally. **Units of Measure:** dollars per lb. **Type of Price:** processor. **Time Period Covered:** latest week.

POLLOCK: FILLETS, BONELESS, CANADIAN

Source: *NMFS Green Sheet Supplement.* **Price Frequency:** weekly, seasonally. **Units of Measure:** dollars per lb. **Type of Price:** to primary wholesalers. **Time Period Covered:** latest week.

POLLOCK: FILLETS, BONELESS, ICELANDIC

Source: *NMFS Green Sheet Supplement.* **Price Frequency:** weekly, seasonally. **Units of Measure:** dollars per lb. **Type of Price:** to primary wholesalers. **Time Period Covered:** latest week.

POLLOCK: FILLETS, BONELESS, NORWEGIAN

Source: *NMFS Green Sheet Supplement.* **Price Frequency:** weekly, seasonally. **Units of Measure:** dollars per lb. **Type of Price:** to primary wholesalers. **Time Period Covered:** latest week.

POLLOCK: FILLETS, FRESH

Source: *Seafood Price-Current.* **Price Frequency:** semiweekly. **Effective Market(s):** Mid-Atlantic, New England. **Units of Measure:** Dollars per lb. **Type of Price:** sale by first receiver. **Time Period Covered:** latest day.

POLLOCK: FILLETS, FROZEN, ALASKAN

Source: *Seafood Price-Current.* **Price Frequency:** semiweekly. **Effective Market(s):** Mid-Atlantic. **Units of Measure:** Dollars per lb. **Type of Price:** first receiver. **Time Period Covered:** latest day.

POLLOCK: FILLETS, SKINLESS, BONELESS, FROZEN, CANADIAN

Source: *Seafood Price-Current.* **Price Frequency:** semiweekly. **Effective Market(s):** Mid-Atlantic. **Units of Measure:** Dollars per lb. **Type of Price:** first receiver. **Time Period Covered:** latest day.

POLLOCK: FILLETS, SKINLESS, BONELESS, FROZEN, ICELANDIC

Source: *Seafood Price-Current.* **Price Frequency:** semiweekly. **Effective Market(s):** Mid-Atlantic. **Units of Measure:** Dollars per lb. **Type of Price:** first receiver. **Time Period Covered:** latest day.

POLLOCK: FILLETS, SKINLESS, FROZEN, CANADIAN

Source: *Seafood Price-Current.* **Price Frequency:** semiweekly. **Effective Market(s):** Mid-Atlantic. **Units of Measure:** Dollars per lb. **Type of Price:** first receiver. **Time Period Covered:** latest day.

POLLOCK: FISH PORTIONS, BATTERED, COOKED

Source: *NMFS Green Sheet Supplement.* **Price Frequency:** weekly, seasonally. **Units of Measure:** dollars per lb. **Type of Price:** to primary wholesalers. **Time Period Covered:** latest week.

POLLOCK: FISH PORTIONS, BATTERED, RAW

Source: *NMFS Green Sheet Supplement.* **Price Frequency:** weekly, seasonally. **Units of Measure:** dollars per lb. **Type of Price:** to primary wholesalers. **Time Period Covered:** latest week.

POLLOCK: FISH PORTIONS, BREADED, COOKED

Source: *NMFS Green Sheet Supplement.* **Price Frequency:** weekly, seasonally. **Units of Measure:** dollars per lb. **Type of Price:** to primary wholesalers. **Time Period Covered:** latest week.

POLLOCK: FISH PORTIONS, BREADED, RAW

Source: *NMFS Green Sheet Supplement.* **Price Frequency:** weekly, seasonally. **Units of Measure:** dollars per lb. **Type of Price:** to primary wholesalers. **Time Period Covered:** latest week.

POLLOCK: FISH STICKS, BATTERED, COOKED

Source: *NMFS Green Sheet Supplement.* **Price Frequency:** weekly, seasonally. **Units of Measure:** dollars per lb. **Type of Price:** to primary wholesalers. **Time Period Covered:** latest week.

POLLOCK: FISH STICKS, BATTERED, RAW

Source: *NMFS Green Sheet Supplement.* **Price Frequency:** weekly, seasonally. **Units of Measure:** dollars per lb. **Type of Price:** to primary wholesalers. **Time Period Covered:** latest week.

POLLOCK: FISH STICKS, BREADED, COOKED

Source: *NMFS Green Sheet Supplement.* **Price Frequency:** weekly, seasonally. **Units of Measure:** dollars per lb. **Type of Price:** to primary wholesalers. **Time Period Covered:** latest week.

POLLOCK: FISH STICKS, BREADED, RAW

Source: *NMFS Green Sheet Supplement.* **Price Frequency:** weekly, seasonally. **Units of Measure:** dollars per lb. **Type of Price:** to primary wholesalers. **Time Period Covered:** latest week.

POLLOCK: PROCESSORS FISH BLOCKS, ALASKAN

Source: *Seafood Price-Current.* **Price Frequency:** semiweekly. **Effective Market(s):** New England. **Units of Measure:** Dollars per lb. **Time Period Covered:** latest day.

POLLOCK: PROCESSORS FISH BLOCKS, CANADA/ICELAND

Source: *Seafood Price-Current.* **Price Frequency:** semiweekly. **Effective Market(s):** New England. **Units of Measure:** Dollars per lb. **Time Period Covered:** latest day.

POLLOCK: PROCESSORS FISH BLOCKS, MINCED, ALASKAN

Source: *Seafood Price-Current.* **Price Frequency:** semiweekly. **Effective Market(s):** New England. **Units of Measure:** Dollars per lb. **Time Period Covered:** latest day.

POLLOCK: PROCESSORS FISH BLOCKS, TWICE FROZEN, IMPORTED

Source: *Seafood Price-Current.* **Price Frequency:** semiweekly. **Effective Market(s):** New England. **Units of Measure:** Dollars per lb. **Time Period Covered:** latest day.

POLLOCK: STEAK, HEAD OFF, FRESH

Source: *Seafood Price-Current.* **Price Frequency:** semiweekly. **Effective Market(s):** Mid-Atlantic, Boston, New Bedford (MA), Portland (ME). **Units of Measure:** Dollars per lb. **Type of Price:** sale by first receiver, auction price. **Time Period Covered:** latest day.

POLLOCK: WHOLE, FRESH

Source: *Seafood Price-Current.* **Price Frequency:** semiweekly. **Effective Market(s):** Mid-Atlantic, Boston, New Bedford (MA), Portland (ME). **Units of Measure:** Dollars per lb. **Type of Price:** sale by first receiver, auction price. **Time Period Covered:** latest day.

POLLOCK ROE: ALASKAN

Source: *Weekly Statistical Fishery Report.* **Price Frequency:** weekly. **Effective Market(s):** Tokyo. **Units of Measure:** Dollars per lb. **Type of Price:** wholesale. **Time Period Covered:** 2 weeks ago, month ago.

POLYARYLATE

Source: *Plastics Technology.* **Price Frequency:** monthly. **Units of Measure:** cents per lb., cents per cubic inch. **Type of Price:** bulk list, market. **Time Period Covered:** latest month.

POLYARYLSULFONE

Source: *Plastics Technology.* **Price Frequency:** monthly. **Units of Measure:** cents per lb., cents per cubic inch. **Type of Price:** bulk list, market. **Time Period Covered:** latest month.

POLYBUTYLENE: FILM

Source: *Journal of Commerce and Commercial.* **Price Frequency:** weekly in Tuesday issue. **Units of Measure:** Dollars per lb. **Type of Price:** spot. **Time Period Covered:** latest week.

Source: *Plastics Technology.* **Price Frequency:** monthly. **Units of Measure:** cents per lb., cents per cubic inch. **Type of Price:** bulk list, market. **Time Period Covered:** latest month.

POLYBUTYLENE: GENERAL PURPOSE

Source: *Plastics Technology.* **Price Frequency:** monthly. **Units of Measure:** cents per lb., cents per cubic inch. **Type of Price:** bulk list, market. **Time Period Covered:** latest month.

POLYBUTYLENE: PIPE, COLD WATER

Source: *Journal of Commerce and Commercial.* **Price Frequency:** weekly in Tuesday issue. **Units of Measure:** Dollars per lb. **Type of Price:** spot. **Time Period Covered:** latest week.

Source: *Plastics Technology.* **Price Frequency:** monthly. **Units of Measure:** cents per lb., cents per cubic inch. **Type of Price:** bulk list, market. **Time Period Covered:** latest month.

POLYBUTYLENE: PIPE, GENERAL PURPOSE

Source: *Journal of Commerce and Commercial.* **Price Frequency:** weekly in Tuesday issue. **Units of Measure:** Dollars per lb. **Type of Price:** spot. **Time Period Covered:** latest week.

POLYBUTYLENE: PIPE, HOT WATER

Source: *Journal of Commerce and Commercial.* **Price Frequency:** weekly in Tuesday issue. **Units of Measure:** Dollars per lb. **Type of Price:** spot. **Time Period Covered:** latest week.

Source: *Plastics Technology.* **Price Frequency:** monthly. **Units of Measure:** cents per lb., cents per cubic inch. **Type of Price:** bulk list, market. **Time Period Covered:** latest month.

POLYBUTYLENE TEREPHTHALATE

see Polyester: PBT Type.

POLYCARBONATE: BLOW MOLDING

Source: *Plastics Technology.* **Price Frequency:** monthly. **Units of Measure:** cents per lb., cents per cubic inch. **Type of Price:** bulk list, market. **Time Period Covered:** latest month.

POLYCARBONATE: COMPACT DISC GRADE

Source: *Journal of Commerce and Commercial.* **Price Frequency:** weekly in Tuesday issue. **Units of Measure:** Dollars per lb. **Type of Price:** spot. **Time Period Covered:** latest week.

Source: *Plastics Technology.* **Price Frequency:** monthly. **Units of Measure:** cents per lb., cents per cubic inch. **Type of Price:** bulk list, market. **Time Period Covered:** latest month.

POLYCARBONATE: EXTRUSION MOLDING

Source: *Plastics Technology.* **Price Frequency:** monthly. **Units of Measure:** cents per lb., cents per cubic inch. **Type of Price:** bulk list, market. **Time Period Covered:** latest month.

POLYCARBONATE: FIRE RETARDANT

Source: *Plastics Technology.* **Price Frequency:** monthly. **Units of Measure:** cents per lb., cents per cubic inch. **Type of Price:** bulk list, market. **Time Period Covered:** latest month.

POLYCARBONATE: INJECTION MOLDING

Source: *Plastics Technology.* **Price Frequency:** monthly. **Units of Measure:** cents per lb., cents per cubic inch. **Type of Price:** bulk list, market. **Time Period Covered:** latest month.

POLYCARBONATE: INJECTION, 20% GLASS

Source: *Plastics Technology.* **Price Frequency:** monthly. **Units of Measure:** cents per lb., cents per cubic inch. **Type of Price:** bulk list, market. **Time Period Covered:** latest month.

POLYCARBONATE: INJECTION, 30% GLASS

Source: *Plastics Technology.* **Price Frequency:** monthly. **Units of Measure:** cents per lb., cents per cubic inch. **Type of Price:** bulk list, market. **Time Period Covered:** latest month.

POLYCARBONATE: STANDARD GRADE

Source: *Journal of Commerce and Commercial.* **Price Frequency:** weekly in Tuesday issue. **Units of Measure:** Dollars per lb. **Type of Price:** spot. **Time Period Covered:** latest week.

POLYCARBONATE: STRUCTURAL FOAM

Source: *Plastics Technology.* **Price Frequency:** monthly. **Units of Measure:** cents per lb., cents per cubic inch. **Type of Price:** bulk list, market. **Time Period Covered:** latest month.

POLYCARBONATE: STRUCTURAL FOAM, 20% GLASS

Source: *Plastics Technology.* **Price Frequency:** monthly. **Units of Measure:** cents per lb., cents per cubic inch. **Type of Price:** bulk list, market. **Time Period Covered:** latest month.

POLYCARBONATE RESIN PELLETS: NATURAL

Source: *Chemical Marketing Reporter.* **Price Frequency:** weekly. **Effective Market(s):** New York. **Units of Measure:** Dollars per lb. **Type of Price:** spot. **Time Period Covered:** latest week.

POLYESTER 65/COTTON 35 FABRICS

Source: *JTN: The International Textile Magazine.* **Price Frequency:** monthly. **Effective Market(s):** Japan. **Units of Measure:** Japanese yen per yard. **Type of Price:** spot. **Time Period Covered:** latest month.

POLYESTER: PBT TYPE, 30% GLASS

Source: *Plastics Technology.* **Price Frequency:** monthly. **Units of Measure:** cents per lb. **Type of Price:** bulk list, market. **Time Period Covered:** latest month.

POLYESTER: PBT TYPE, FLAME RETARDANT

Source: *Plastics Technology.* **Price Frequency:** monthly. **Units of Measure:** cents per lb. **Type of Price:** bulk list, market. **Time Period Covered:** latest month.

POLYESTER: PBT TYPE, HIGH IMPACT

Source: *Plastics Technology.* **Price Frequency:** monthly. **Units of Measure:** cents per lb. **Type of Price:** bulk list, market. **Time Period Covered:** latest month.

POLYESTER: PBT TYPE, STRUCTURAL FOAM

Source: *Plastics Technology.* **Price Frequency:** monthly. **Units of Measure:** cents per lb. **Type of Price:** bulk list, market. **Time Period Covered:** latest month.

POLYESTER: PBT TYPE, TYPE IM

Source: *Journal of Commerce and Commercial.* **Price Frequency:** weekly in Tuesday issue. **Units of Measure:** Dollars per lb. **Type of Price:** spot. **Time Period Covered:** latest week.

POLYESTER: PBT TYPE, UNFILLED

Source: *Plastics Technology.* **Price Frequency:** monthly. **Units of Measure:** cents per lb. **Type of Price:** bulk list, market. **Time Period Covered:** latest month.

POLYESTER: PET TYPE, 30% GLASS, FLAME RETARDANT

Source: *Plastics Technology.* **Price Frequency:** monthly. **Units of Measure:** cents per lb. **Type of Price:** bulk list, market. **Time Period Covered:** latest month.

POLYESTER: PET TYPE, BOTTLE

Source: *Journal of Commerce and Commercial.* **Price Frequency:** weekly in Tuesday issue. **Units of Measure:** Dollars per lb. **Type of Price:** spot. **Time Period Covered:** latest week.

Source: *Modern Plastics.* **Price Frequency:** quarterly every January, April, July, October. **Units of Measure:** cents per lb. **Type of Price:** market. **Time Period Covered:** latest 3 years.

Source: *Plastics Technology.* **Price Frequency:** monthly. **Units of Measure:** cents per lb. **Type of Price:** bulk list, market. **Time Period Covered:** latest month.

POLYESTER: PET TYPE, MODIFIED, 30% GLASS

Source: *Plastics Technology.* **Price Frequency:** monthly. **Units of Measure:** cents per lb. **Type of Price:** bulk list, market. **Time Period Covered:** latest month.

POLYESTER: PET TYPE, MODIFIED, 55% GLASS

Source: *Plastics Technology.* **Price Frequency:** monthly. **Units of Measure:** cents per lb. **Type of Price:** bulk list, market. **Time Period Covered:** latest month.

POLYESTER: PET TYPE, PETG COPOLYMER

Source: *Plastics Technology.* **Price Frequency:** monthly. **Units of Measure:** cents per lb. **Type of Price:** bulk list, market. **Time Period Covered:** latest month.

POLYESTER: THERMOSET, BISPHENOL-A

Source: *Journal of Commerce and Commercial.* **Price Frequency:** weekly in Tuesday issue. **Units of Measure:** Dollars per lb. **Type of Price:** spot. **Time Period Covered:** latest week.

Source: *Plastics Technology.* **Price Frequency:** monthly. **Units of Measure:** cents per lb. **Type of Price:** bulk list, market. **Time Period Covered:** latest month.

POLYESTER: THERMOSET, ISOPHTHALIC

Source: *Journal of Commerce and Commercial.* **Price Frequency:** weekly in Tuesday issue. **Units of Measure:** Dollars per lb. **Type of Price:** spot. **Time Period Covered:** latest week.

POLYESTER: THERMOSET, ORTHOPHTHALIC, GENERAL PURPOSE

Source: *Journal of Commerce and Commercial.* **Price Frequency:** weekly in Tuesday issue. **Units of Measure:** Dollars per lb. **Type of Price:** spot. **Time Period Covered:** latest week.

Source: *Plastics Technology.* **Price Frequency:** monthly. **Units of Measure:** cents per lb. **Type of Price:** bulk list, market. **Time Period Covered:** latest month.

POLYESTER FIBER

Source: *ATI, America's Textiles International.* **Price Frequency:** monthly. **Time Period Covered:** latest month, 6 months ago, year ago.

POLYESTER FIBER: BLEND, STAPLE BRANDED

Source: *Journal of Commerce and Commercial.* **Price Frequency:** daily. **Effective Market(s):** New York. **Units of Measure:** Dollars per lb. **Type of Price:** spot supplier. **Time Period Covered:** latest day.

POLYESTER FILAMENT FABRIC

Source: *JTN: The International Textile Magazine.* **Price Frequency:** monthly. **Effective Market(s):** Japan. **Units of Measure:** Japanese yen per yard. **Type of Price:** spot. **Time Period Covered:** latest month.

POLYESTER KNIT: TEXTURED, DYEABLE

Source: *ATI, America's Textiles International.* **Price Frequency:** monthly. **Time Period Covered:** latest month, 6 months ago, year ago.

POLYESTER KNIT: TEXTURED, WHITES

Source: *ATI, America's Textiles International.* **Price Frequency:** monthly. **Time Period Covered:** latest month, 6 months ago, year ago.

POLYESTER RESIN: UNSATURATED, ISOPHTHALIC, GENERAL PURPOSE

Source: *Chemical Marketing Reporter.* **Price Frequency:** weekly. **Effective Market(s):** New York. **Units of Measure:** Dollars per lb. **Type of Price:** spot. **Time Period Covered:** latest week.

POLYESTER RESIN: UNSATURATED, ORTHOPHTHALIC, GENERAL PURPOSE

Source: *Chemical Marketing Reporter.* **Price Frequency:** weekly. **Effective Market(s):** New York. **Units of Measure:** Dollars per lb. **Type of Price:** spot. **Time Period Covered:** latest week.

POLYESTER STAPLE

Source: *JTN: The International Textile Magazine.* **Price Frequency:** monthly. **Effective Market(s):** Taiwan. **Units of Measure:** Dollars per lb. **Type of Price:** export. **Time Period Covered:** latest month.

POLYESTER STAPLE: CARPET

Source: *Journal of Commerce and Commercial.* **Price Frequency:** weekly in Tuesday issue. **Units of Measure:** Dollars per lb. **Type of Price:** spot. **Time Period Covered:** latest week.

POLYESTER STAPLE: FOR COTTON BLENDS

Source: *Cotton and Wool Situation and Outlook Report.* **Price Frequency:** monthly, annually. **Units of Measure:** cents per lb. **Type of Price:** actual. **Time Period Covered:** monthly latest 2 years, annually latest 6 years.

Source: *JTN: The International Textile Magazine.* **Price Frequency:** monthly. **Effective Market(s):** Japan. **Units of Measure:** Japanese yen per kilogram. **Type of Price:** spot. **Time Period Covered:** latest month.

POLYESTER STAPLE: FOR WOOL BLENDS

Source: *JTN: The International Textile Magazine.* **Price Frequency:** monthly. **Effective Market(s):** Japan. **Units of Measure:** Japanese yen per kilogram. **Type of Price:** spot. **Time Period Covered:** latest month.

POLYESTER STAPLE: INDUSTRIAL

Source: *Journal of Commerce and Commercial.* **Price Frequency:** weekly in Tuesday issue. **Units of Measure:** Dollars per lb. **Type of Price:** spot. **Time Period Covered:** latest week.

POLYESTER STAPLE: TEXTILE

Source: *Journal of Commerce and Commercial.* **Price Frequency:** weekly in Tuesday issue. **Units of Measure:** Dollars per lb. **Type of Price:** spot. **Time Period Covered:** latest week.

POLYESTER THERMOSET: ISOPHTHALIC

Source: *Plastics Technology.* **Price Frequency:** monthly. **Units of Measure:** cents per lb. **Type of Price:** bulk list, market. **Time Period Covered:** latest month.

POLYESTER YARN

see Yarn: Polyester.

POLYETHERIMIDE

Source: *Plastics Technology.* **Price Frequency:** monthly. **Units of Measure:** cents per lb., cents per cubic inch. **Type of Price:** bulk list, market. **Time Period Covered:** latest month.

POLYETHERIMIDE: 30% GLASS

Source: *Plastics Technology.* **Price Frequency:** monthly. **Units of Measure:** cents per lb., cents per cubic inch. **Type of Price:** bulk list, market. **Time Period Covered:** latest month.

POLYETHERKETONE

Source: *Plastics Technology.* **Price Frequency:** monthly. **Units of Measure:** cents per lb., cents per cubic inch. **Type of Price:** bulk list, market. **Time Period Covered:** latest month.

POLYETHERKETONE: 30% GLASS

Source: *Plastics Technology.* **Price Frequency:** monthly. **Units of Measure:** cents per lb., cents per cubic inch. **Type of Price:** bulk list, market. **Time Period Covered:** latest month.

POLYETHERSULFONE

Source: *Plastics Technology.* **Price Frequency:** monthly. **Units of Measure:** cents per lb., cents per cubic inch. **Type of Price:** bulk list, market. **Time Period Covered:** latest month.

POLYETHERSULFONE: 30% GLASS

Source: *Plastics Technology.* **Price Frequency:** monthly. **Units of Measure:** cents per lb., cents per cubic inch. **Type of Price:** bulk list, market. **Time Period Covered:** latest month.

POLYETHYLENE: HIGH DENSITY, BLOW MOLDING

Source: *Journal of Commerce and Commercial.* **Price Frequency:** weekly in Tuesday issue. **Units of Measure:** Dollars per lb. **Type of Price:** spot. **Time Period Covered:** latest week.

Source: *Modern Plastics.* **Price Frequency:** quarterly in January, April, July, October issues. **Units of Measure:** cent per lb. **Type of Price:** market. **Time Period Covered:** latest 3 years.

POLYETHYLENE: HIGH DENSITY, BLOW MOLDING, GENERAL PURPOSE

Source: *Chemical Marketing Reporter.* **Price Frequency:** weekly. **Effective Market(s):** New York. **Units of Measure:** Dollars per lb. **Type of Price:** spot. **Time Period Covered:** latest week.

POLYETHYLENE: HIGH DENSITY, EXTRUSION, GENERAL PURPOSE

Source: *Chemical Marketing Reporter.* **Price Frequency:** weekly. **Effective Market(s):** New York. **Units of Measure:** Dollars per lb. **Type of Price:** spot. **Time Period Covered:** latest week.

POLYETHYLENE: HIGH DENSITY, HIC GRADE, BLOW MOLDING

Source: *Puchasing.* **Price Frequency:** monthly. **Units of Measure:** cent per lb. **Type of Price:** transaction. **Time Period Covered:** latest day, month ago, 6 months ago, year ago.

POLYETHYLENE: HIGH DENSITY, HIGH MOLECULAR WEIGHT, FILM

Source: *Modern Plastics.* **Price Frequency:** quarterly in January, April, July, October issues. **Units of Measure:** cent per lb. **Type of Price:** market. **Time Period Covered:** latest 3 years.

POLYETHYLENE: HIGH DENSITY, INJECTION MOLDING

Source: *Journal of Commerce and Commercial.* **Price Frequency:** weekly in Tuesday issue. **Units of Measure:** Dollars per lb. **Type of Price:** spot. **Time Period Covered:** latest week.

POLYETHYLENE: HIGH DENSITY, INJECTION MOLDING, GENERAL PURPOSE

Source: *Chemical Marketing Reporter.* **Price Frequency:** weekly. **Effective Market(s):** New York. **Units of Measure:** Dollars per lb. **Type of Price:** spot. **Time Period Covered:** latest week.

POLYETHYLENE: HIGH DENSITY, MMW, BLOW MOLDING

Source: *Plastics Technology.* **Price Frequency:** monthly. **Units of Measure:** cents per lb. **Type of Price:** bulk list, market. **Time Period Covered:** latest month.

POLYETHYLENE: HIGH DENSITY, MMW, FILM QUALITY

Source: *Plastics Technology.* **Price Frequency:** monthly. **Units of Measure:** cents per lb. **Type of Price:** bulk list, market. **Time Period Covered:** latest month.

POLYETHYLENE: HIGH DENSITY, MMW, INJECTION MOLDING, GENERAL PURPOSE

Source: *Plastics Technology.* **Price Frequency:** monthly. **Units of Measure:** cents per lb. **Type of Price:** bulk list, market. **Time Period Covered:** latest month.

POLYETHYLENE: HMW-HDPE, BLOW MOLDING

Source: *Plastics Technology.* **Price Frequency:** monthly. **Units of Measure:** cents per lb. **Type of Price:** bulk list, market. **Time Period Covered:** latest month.

POLYETHYLENE: HMW-HDPE, FILM

Source: *Plastics Technology.* **Price Frequency:** monthly. **Units of Measure:** cents per lb. **Type of Price:** bulk list, market. **Time Period Covered:** latest month.

POLYETHYLENE: LINEAR LOW DENSITY, BLOWN FILM

Source: *Chemical Marketing Reporter.* **Price Frequency:** weekly. **Effective Market(s):** New York. **Units of Measure:** Dollars per lb. **Type of Price:** spot. **Time Period Covered:** latest week.

POLYETHYLENE: LINEAR LOW DENSITY, BUTENE-BASED, BLOW MOLDING

Source: *Plastics Technology.* **Price Frequency:** monthly. **Units of Measure:** cents per lb. **Type of Price:** bulk list, market. **Time Period Covered:** latest month.

POLYETHYLENE: LINEAR LOW DENSITY, BUTENE-BASED, FILM

Source: *Plastics Technology.* **Price Frequency:** monthly. **Units of Measure:** cents per lb. **Type of Price:** bulk list, market. **Time Period Covered:** latest month.

POLYETHYLENE: LINEAR LOW DENSITY, BUTENE-BASED, GENERAL PURPOSE MOLDING

Source: *Plastics Technology.* **Price Frequency:** monthly. **Units of Measure:** cents per lb. **Type of Price:** bulk list, market. **Time Period Covered:** latest month.

POLYETHYLENE: LINEAR LOW DENSITY, BUTENE-BASED, ROTOMOLDING

Source: *Plastics Technology.* **Price Frequency:** monthly. **Units of Measure:** cents per lb. **Type of Price:** bulk list, market. **Time Period Covered:** latest month.

POLYETHYLENE: LINEAR LOW DENSITY, CAST FILM

Source: *Chemical Marketing Reporter.* **Price Frequency:** weekly. **Effective Market(s):** New York. **Units of Measure:** Dollars per lb. **Type of Price:** spot. **Time Period Covered:** latest week.

POLYETHYLENE: LINEAR LOW DENSITY, GENERAL PURPOSE

Source: *Chemical Marketing Reporter.* **Price Frequency:** weekly. **Effective Market(s):** New York. **Units of Measure:** Dollars per lb. **Type of Price:** spot. **Time Period Covered:** latest week.

POLYETHYLENE: LINEAR LOW DENSITY, HEXANE FILM

Source: *Modern Plastics.* **Price Frequency:** quarterly in January, April, July, October issues. **Units of Measure:** cent per lb. **Type of Price:** market. **Time Period Covered:** latest 3 years.

POLYETHYLENE: LINEAR LOW DENSITY, HAO-BASED, FILM

Source: *Plastics Technology.* **Price Frequency:** monthly. **Units of Measure:** cents per lb. **Type of Price:** bulk list, market. **Time Period Covered:** latest month.

POLYETHYLENE: LINEAR LOW DENSITY, HAO-BASED, GENERAL PURPOSE MOLDING

Source: *Plastics Technology.* **Price Frequency:** monthly. **Units of Measure:** cents per lb. **Type of Price:** bulk list, market. **Time Period Covered:** latest month.

POLYETHYLENE: LINEAR LOW DENSITY, HAO-BASED, LID RESIN

Source: *Plastics Technology.* **Price Frequency:** monthly. **Units of Measure:** cents per lb. **Type of Price:** bulk list, market. **Time Period Covered:** latest month.

POLYETHYLENE: LOW DENSITY

Source: *Japan Economic Journal.* **Price Frequency:** weekly. **Effective Market(s):** Japan. **Units of Measure:** Japanese yen per kilogram. **Type of Price:** market. **Time Period Covered:** latest 2 weeks.

POLYETHYLENE: LOW DENSITY, BLOW MOLDING

Source: *Journal of Commerce and Commercial.* **Price Frequency:** weekly in Tuesday issue. **Units of Measure:** Dollars per lb. **Type of Price:** spot. **Time Period Covered:** latest week.

Source: *Plastics Technology.* **Price Frequency:** monthly. **Units of Measure:** cents per lb. **Type of Price:** bulk list, market. **Time Period Covered:** latest month.

POLYETHYLENE: LOW DENSITY, CLARITY FILM

Source: *Chemical Marketing Reporter.* **Price Frequency:** weekly. **Effective Market(s):** New York. **Units of Measure:** Dollars per lb. **Type of Price:** spot. **Time Period Covered:** latest week.

POLYETHYLENE: LOW DENSITY, EXTRUSION COATING

Source: *Chemical Marketing Reporter.* **Price Frequency:** weekly. **Effective Market(s):** New York. **Units of Measure:** Dollars per lb. **Type of Price:** spot. **Time Period Covered:** latest week.

Source: *Journal of Commerce and Commercial.* **Price Frequency:** weekly in Tuesday issue. **Units of Measure:** Dollars per lb. **Type of Price:** spot. **Time Period Covered:** latest week.

Source: *Plastics Technology.* **Price Frequency:** monthly. **Units of Measure:** cents per lb. **Type of Price:** bulk list, market. **Time Period Covered:** latest month.

POLYETHYLENE: LOW DENSITY, FILM

Source: *Journal of Commerce and Commercial.* **Price Frequency:** weekly in Tuesday issue. **Units of Measure:** Dollars per lb. **Type of Price:** spot. **Time Period Covered:** latest week.

POLYETHYLENE: LOW DENSITY, FILM LINER

Source: *Chemical Marketing Reporter.* **Price Frequency:** weekly. **Effective Market(s):** New York. **Units of Measure:** Dollars per lb. **Type of Price:** spot. **Time Period Covered:** latest week.

POLYETHYLENE: LOW DENSITY, GENERAL PURPOSE

Source: *Chemical Marketing Reporter.* **Price Frequency:** weekly. **Effective Market(s):** New York. **Units of Measure:** Dollars per lb. **Type of Price:** spot. **Time Period Covered:** latest week.

POLYETHYLENE: LOW DENSITY, INJECTION MOLDING

Source: *Journal of Commerce and Commercial.* **Price Frequency:** weekly in Tuesday issue. **Units of Measure:** Dollars per lb. **Type of Price:** spot. **Time Period Covered:** latest week.

Source: *Plastics Technology.* **Price Frequency:** monthly. **Units of Measure:** cents per lb. **Type of Price:** bulk list, market. **Time Period Covered:** latest month.

POLYETHYLENE: LOW DENSITY, INJECTION MOLDING, GENERAL PURPOSE

Source: *Chemical Marketing Reporter.* **Price Frequency:** weekly. **Effective Market(s):** New York. **Units of Measure:** Dollars per lb. **Type of Price:** spot. **Time Period Covered:** latest week.

POLYETHYLENE: LOW DENSITY, LID RESIN

Source: *Plastics Technology.* **Price Frequency:** monthly. **Units of Measure:** cents per lb. **Type of Price:** bulk list, market. **Time Period Covered:** latest month.

POLYETHYLENE: LOW DENSITY, LINER GRADE

Source: *Journal of Commerce and Commercial.* **Price Frequency:** weekly in Tuesday issue. **Units of Measure:** Dollars per lb. **Type of Price:** spot. **Time Period Covered:** latest week.

Source: *Modern Plastics.* **Price Frequency:** quarterly in January, April, July, October issues. **Units of Measure:** cent per lb. **Type of Price:** market. **Time Period Covered:** latest 3 years.

Source: *Plastics Technology.* **Price Frequency:** monthly. **Units of Measure:** cents per lb. **Type of Price:** bulk list, market. **Time Period Covered:** latest month.

Source: *Purchasing.* **Price Frequency:** monthly. **Units of Measure:** cent per lb. **Type of Price:** transaction. **Time Period Covered:** latest day, month ago, 6 months ago, year ago.

POLYETHYLENE: LOW DENSITY, MOLDING AND EXTRUSION, GENERAL PURPOSE

Source: *Plastics Technology.* **Price Frequency:** monthly. **Units of Measure:** cents per lb. **Type of Price:** bulk list, market. **Time Period Covered:** latest month.

POLYETHYLENE: LOW DENSITY, PALLET SHRINK FILM

Source: *Chemical Marketing Reporter.* **Price Frequency:** weekly. **Effective Market(s):** New York. **Units of Measure:** Dollars per lb. **Type of Price:** spot. **Time Period Covered:** latest week.

POLYETHYLENE: LOW DENSITY, ROTOMOLDING, PELLET

Source: *Plastics Technology.* **Price Frequency:** monthly. **Units of Measure:** cents per lb. **Type of Price:** bulk list, market. **Time Period Covered:** latest month.

POLYETHYLENE: LOW DENSITY, ROTOMOLDING, POWDER

Source: *Plastics Technology.* **Price Frequency:** monthly. **Units of Measure:** cents per lb. **Type of Price:** bulk list, market. **Time Period Covered:** latest month.

POLYETHYLENE: UHMW

Source: *Plastics Technology.* **Price Frequency:** monthly. **Units of Measure:** cents per lb. **Type of Price:** bulk list, market. **Time Period Covered:** latest month.

POLYETHYLENE TEREPHTHALATE

see Polyester: PET Type.

POLYMERS: LIQUID CRYSTAL, EXTRUSION, UNFILLED

Source: *Plastics Technology.* **Price Frequency:** monthly. **Units of Measure:** cents per lb., cents per cubic inch. **Type of Price:** bulk list, market. **Time Period Covered:** latest month.

POLYMERS: LIQUID CRYSTAL, INJECTION, CARBON FILLED

Source: *Plastics Technology.* **Price Frequency:** monthly. **Units of Measure:** cents per lb., cents per cubic inch. **Type of Price:** bulk list, market. **Time Period Covered:** latest month.

POLYMERS: LIQUID CRYSTAL, INJECTION, GLASS FILLED

Source: *Plastics Technology.* **Price Frequency:** monthly. **Units of Measure:** cents per lb., cents per cubic inch. **Type of Price:** bulk list, market. **Time Period Covered:** latest month.

POLYMERS: LIQUID CRYSTAL, INJECTION, MINERAL FILLED

Source: *Plastics Technology.* **Price Frequency:** monthly. **Units of Measure:** cents per lb., cents per cubic inch. **Type of Price:** bulk list, market. **Time Period Covered:** latest month.

POLYMYXIN SULFATE: USP

Source: *Chemical Marketing Reporter.* **Price Frequency:** weekly. **Effective Market(s):** New York. **Units of Measure:** Dollars per million units. **Type of Price:** spot. **Time Period Covered:** latest week.

POLYOXYETHYLENE SORBITAN MONOSTEARATE

Source: *Chemical Marketing Reporter.* **Price Frequency:** weekly. **Effective Market(s):** New York. **Units of Measure:** Dollars per lb. **Type of Price:** spot. **Time Period Covered:** latest week.

POLYOXYETHYLENE SORBITAN TRISTEARATE

Source: *Chemical Marketing Reporter.* **Price Frequency:** weekly. **Effective Market(s):** New York. **Units of Measure:** Dollars per lb. **Type of Price:** spot. **Time Period Covered:** latest week.

POLYPHENYLENE OXIDE: MODIFIED

Source: *Journal of Commerce and Commercial.* **Price Frequency:** weekly in Tuesday issue. **Units of Measure:** Dollars per lb. **Type of Price:** spot. **Time Period Covered:** latest week.

POLYPHENYLENE SULFIDE

see PPS.

POLYPROPYLENE: COLORED MATERIAL, ALL GRADES

Source: *Chemical Marketing Reporter.* **Price Frequency:** weekly. **Effective Market(s):** New York. **Units of Measure:** Dollars per lb. **Type of Price:** spot. **Time Period Covered:** latest week.

POLYPROPYLENE: COPOLYMER, HIGH IMPACT, NATURAL

Source: *Chemical Marketing Reporter.* **Price Frequency:** weekly. **Effective Market(s):** New York. **Units of Measure:** Dollars per lb. **Type of Price:** spot. **Time Period Covered:** latest week.

POLYPROPYLENE: COPOLYMER, MEDIUM IMPACT, NATURAL

Source: *Chemical Marketing Reporter.* **Price Frequency:** weekly. **Effective Market(s):** New York. **Units of Measure:** Dollars per lb. **Type of Price:** spot. **Time Period Covered:** latest week.

POLYPROPYLENE: FILLED, 30% GLASS

Source: *Plastics Technology.* **Price Frequency:** monthly. **Units of Measure:** cents per lb., cents per cubic inch. **Type of Price:** bulk list, market. **Time Period Covered:** latest month.

POLYPROPYLENE: FILLED, 40% GLASS

Source: *Plastics Technology.* **Price Frequency:** monthly. **Units of Measure:** cents per lb., cents per cubic inch. **Type of Price:** bulk list, market. **Time Period Covered:** latest month.

POLYPROPYLENE: GENERAL PURPOSE HOMOPOLYMER, EXTRUSION

Source: *Plastics Technology.* **Price Frequency:** monthly. **Units of Measure:** cents per lb., cents per cubic inch. **Type of Price:** bulk list, market. **Time Period Covered:** latest month.

POLYPROPYLENE: GENERAL PURPOSE HOMOPOLYMER, INJECTION

Source: *Plastics Technology.* **Price Frequency:** monthly. **Units of Measure:** cents per lb., cents per cubic inch. **Type of Price:** bulk list, market. **Time Period Covered:** latest month.

POLYPROPYLENE: GENERAL PURPOSE HOMOPOLYMER, NATURAL

Source: *Chemical Marketing Reporter.* **Price Frequency:** weekly. **Effective Market(s):** New York. **Units of Measure:** Dollars per lb. **Type of Price:** spot. **Time Period Covered:** latest week.

POLYPROPYLENE: HOMOPOLYMER

Source: *Purchasing.* **Price Frequency:** monthly. **Units of Measure:** cents per lb. **Type of Price:** transaction. **Time Period Covered:** latest day, month ago, 6 months ago, year ago.

POLYPROPYLENE: HOMOPOLYMER MOLDING

Source: *Modern Plastics.* **Price Frequency:** quarterly every January, April, July, October. **Units of Measure:** cents per lb. **Type of Price:** market. **Time Period Covered:** latest 3 years.

POLYPROPYLENE: IMPACT COPOLYMER, AUTOMOTIVE

Source: *Plastics Technology.* **Price Frequency:** monthly. **Units of Measure:** cents per lb., cents per cubic inch. **Type of Price:** bulk list, market. **Time Period Covered:** latest month.

POLYPROPYLENE: IMPACT COPOLYMER, HIGH IMPACT

Source: *Plastics Technology.* **Price Frequency:** monthly. **Units of Measure:** cents per lb., cents per cubic inch. **Type of Price:** bulk list, market. **Time Period Covered:** latest month.

POLYPROPYLENE: IMPACT COPOLYMER, MEDIUM IMPACT

Source: *Plastics Technology.* **Price Frequency:** monthly. **Units of Measure:** cents per lb., cents per cubic inch. **Type of Price:** bulk list, market. **Time Period Covered:** latest month.

POLYPROPYLENE: IMPACT COPOLYMER, SUPER HIGH IMPACT

Source: *Plastics Technology.* **Price Frequency:** monthly. **Units of Measure:** cents per lb., cents per cubic inch. **Type of Price:** bulk list, market. **Time Period Covered:** latest month.

POLYPROPYLENE: INJECTION MOLDING, GENERAL PURPOSE

Source: *Journal of Commerce and Commercial.* **Price Frequency:** weekly in Tuesday issue. **Units of Measure:** Dollars per lb. **Type of Price:** spot. **Time Period Covered:** latest week.

POLYPROPYLENE: RAFFIA EXTRUSION

Source: *Journal of Commerce and Commercial.* **Price Frequency:** weekly in Tuesday issue. **Units of Measure:** Dollars per lb. **Type of Price:** spot. **Time Period Covered:** latest week.

POLYPROPYLENE: RANDOM COPOLYMER, BLOW MOLDING

Source: *Plastics Technology.* **Price Frequency:** monthly. **Units of Measure:** cents per lb., cents per cubic inch. **Type of Price:** bulk list, market. **Time Period Covered:** latest month.

POLYPROPYLENE: RANDOM COPOLYMER, FILM

Source: *Plastics Technology.* **Price Frequency:** monthly. **Units of Measure:** cents per lb., cents per cubic inch. **Type of Price:** bulk list, market. **Time Period Covered:** latest month.

POLYPROPYLENE: RANDOM COPOLYMER, INJECTION

Source: *Plastics Technology.* **Price Frequency:** monthly. **Units of Measure:** cents per lb., cents per cubic inch. **Type of Price:** bulk list, market. **Time Period Covered:** latest month.

POLYSTYRENE: CRYSTAL MOLDING

Source: *Modern Plastics.* **Price Frequency:** quarterly every January, April, July, October. **Units of Measure:** cents per lb. **Type of Price:** market. **Time Period Covered:** latest 3 years.

POLYSTYRENE: CRYSTALLINE, NATURAL

Source: *Chemical Marketing Reporter.* **Price Frequency:** weekly. **Effective Market(s):** New York. **Units of Measure:** Dollars per lb. **Type of Price:** spot. **Time Period Covered:** latest week.

POLYSTYRENE: EXPANDABLE, BEAD CONSTRUCTION

Source: *Modern Plastics.* **Price Frequency:** quarterly in January, April, July, October issues. **Units of Measure:** cent per lb. **Type of Price:** market. **Time Period Covered:** latest 3 years.

POLYSTYRENE: EXPANDABLE BEADS, PACKAGING GRADE

Source: *Chemical Marketing Reporter.* **Price Frequency:** weekly. **Effective Market(s):** New York. **Units of Measure:** Dollars per lb. **Type of Price:** spot. **Time Period Covered:** latest week.

POLYSTYRENE: EXPANDABLE, MODIFIED

Source: *Plastics Technology.* **Price Frequency:** monthly. **Units of Measure:** cent per lb. **Type of Price:** bulk list, market. **Time Period Covered:** latest month.

POLYSTYRENE: EXPANDABLE, UNMODIFIED

Source: *Plastics Technology.* **Price Frequency:** monthly. **Units of Measure:** cent per lb. **Type of Price:** bulk list, market. **Time Period Covered:** latest month.

POLYSTYRENE: GENERAL PURPOSE

Source: *Purchasing.* **Price Frequency:** monthly. **Units of Measure:** cents per lb. **Type of Price:** transaction. **Time Period Covered:** latest day, month ago, 6 months ago, year ago.

POLYSTYRENE: GENERAL PURPOSE CRYSTAL

Source: *Plastics Technology.* **Price Frequency:** monthly. **Units of Measure:** cents per lb., cents per cubic inch. **Type of Price:** bulk list, market. **Time Period Covered:** latest month.

POLYSTYRENE: GENERAL PURPOSE CRYSTAL, HIGH HEAT

Source: *Plastics Technology.* **Price Frequency:** monthly. **Units of Measure:** cents per lb., cents per cubic inch. **Type of Price:** bulk list, market. **Time Period Covered:** latest month.

POLYSTYRENE: HIGH IMPACT

Source: *Journal of Commerce and Commercial.* **Price Frequency:** weekly in Tuesday issue. **Units of Measure:** Dollars per lb. **Type of Price:** spot. **Time Period Covered:** latest week.

Source: *Plastics Technology.* **Price Frequency:** monthly. **Units of Measure:** cents per lb., cents per cubic inch. **Type of Price:** bulk list, market. **Time Period Covered:** latest month.

POLYSTYRENE: HIGH IMPACT, FLAME RETARDANT

Source: *Plastics Technology.* **Price Frequency:** monthly. **Units of Measure:** cents per lb., cents per cubic inch. **Type of Price:** bulk list, market. **Time Period Covered:** latest month.

POLYSTYRENE: HIGH IMPACT, HIGH HEAT

Source: *Plastics Technology.* **Price Frequency:** monthly. **Units of Measure:** cents per lb., cents per cubic inch. **Type of Price:** bulk list, market. **Time Period Covered:** latest month.

POLYSTYRENE: HIGH IMPACT, HIGH HEAT, NATURAL

Source: *Chemical Marketing Reporter.* **Price Frequency:** weekly. **Effective Market(s):** New York. **Units of Measure:** Dollars per lb. **Type of Price:** spot. **Time Period Covered:** latest week.

POLYSTYRENE: HIGH IMPACT, STRUCTURAL FOAM

Source: *Plastics Technology.* **Price Frequency:** monthly. **Units of Measure:** cents per lb. **Type of Price:** bulk list, market. **Time Period Covered:** latest month.

POLYSTYRENE: IMPACT EXTRUSION

Source: *Modern Plastics.* **Price Frequency:** quarterly every January, April, July, October. **Units of Measure:** cents per lb. **Type of Price:** market. **Time Period Covered:** latest 3 years.

POLYSTYRENE: IMPACT, NATURAL

Source: *Chemical Marketing Reporter.* **Price Frequency:** weekly. **Effective Market(s):** New York. **Units of Measure:** Dollars per lb. **Type of Price:** spot. **Time Period Covered:** latest week.

POLYSTYRENE: MODIFIED

Source: *Chemical Marketing Reporter.* **Price Frequency:** weekly. **Effective Market(s):** New York. **Units of Measure:** Dollars per lb. **Type of Price:** spot. **Time Period Covered:** latest week.

POLYSULFONE

Source: *Journal of Commerce and Commercial.* **Price Frequency:** weekly in Tuesday issue. **Units of Measure:** Dollars per lb. **Type of Price:** spot. **Time Period Covered:** latest week.

POLYSULFONE: 10% GLASS

Source: *Plastics Technology.* **Price Frequency:** monthly. **Units of Measure:** cents per lb. **Type of Price:** bulk list, market. **Time Period Covered:** latest month.

POLYSULFONE: 30% GLASS

Source: *Plastics Technology.* **Price Frequency:** monthly. **Units of Measure:** cents per lb. **Type of Price:** bulk list, market. **Time Period Covered:** latest month.

POLYURETHANE: ESTER TYPE

Source: *Plastics Technology.* **Price Frequency:** monthly. **Units of Measure:** cents per lb. **Type of Price:** bulk list, market. **Time Period Covered:** latest month.

POLYURETHANE: ETHER TYPE

Source: *Plastics Technology.* **Price Frequency:** monthly. **Units of Measure:** cents per lb. **Type of Price:** bulk list, market. **Time Period Covered:** latest month.

POLYURETHANE ISOCYANATES: 80/20 TDI

Source: *Plastics Technology.* **Price Frequency:** monthly. **Units of Measure:** cents per lb. **Type of Price:** bulk list, market. **Time Period Covered:** latest month.

POLYURETHANE ISOCYANATES: POLYMERIC MDI

Source: *Plastics Technology.* **Price Frequency:** monthly. **Units of Measure:** cents per lb. **Type of Price:** bulk list, market. **Time Period Covered:** latest month.

POLYVINYL ACETATE ACRYLIC

Source: *Journal of Commerce and Commercial.* **Price Frequency:** weekly in Wednesday issue. **Units of Measure:** Dollars per lb. **Type of Price:** spot. **Time Period Covered:** latest week.

POLYVINYL ALCOHOL: FULLY HYDROLYZED, MEDIUM VISCOSITY

Source: *Chemical Marketing Reporter.* **Price Frequency:** weekly. **Effective Market(s):** New York. **Units of Measure:** Dollars per lb. **Type of Price:** spot. **Time Period Covered:** latest week.

POLYVINYL ALCOHOL: PARTIALLY HYDROLYZED, MEDIUM VISCOSITY

Source: *Chemical Marketing Reporter.* **Price Frequency:** weekly. **Effective Market(s):** New York. **Units of Measure:** Dollars per lb. **Type of Price:** spot. **Time Period Covered:** latest week.

POLYVINYL CHLORIDE: CHLORINATED PIPE COMPOUND

Source: *Plastics Technology.* **Price Frequency:** monthly. **Units of Measure:** cents per lb. **Type of Price:** bulk list, market. **Time Period Covered:** latest month.

POLYVINYL CHLORIDE: COPOLYMER FLOORING

Source: *Plastics Technology.* **Price Frequency:** monthly. **Units of Measure:** cents per lb. **Type of Price:** bulk list, market. **Time Period Covered:** latest month.

POLYVINYL CHLORIDE: FILM

Source: *Journal of Commerce and Commercial.* **Price Frequency:** weekly in Tuesday issue. **Units of Measure:** Dollars per lb. **Type of Price:** spot. **Time Period Covered:** latest week.

Source: *Plastics Technology.* **Price Frequency:** monthly. **Units of Measure:** cents per lb. **Type of Price:** bulk list, market. **Time Period Covered:** latest month.

POLYVINYL CHLORIDE: FILM GRADE

Source: *Chemical Marketing Reporter.* **Price Frequency:** weekly. **Effective Market(s):** New York. **Units of Measure:** Dollars per lb. **Type of Price:** spot. **Time Period Covered:** latest week.

POLYVINYL CHLORIDE: GENERAL PURPOSE

Source: *Journal of Commerce and Commercial.* **Price Frequency:** weekly in Tuesday issue. **Units of Measure:** Dollars per lb. **Type of Price:** spot. **Time Period Covered:** latest week.

Source: *Purchasing.* **Price Frequency:** monthly. **Units of Measure:** cents per lb. **Type of Price:** transaction. **Time Period Covered:** latest day, month ago, 6 months ago, year ago.

POLYVINYL CHLORIDE: GENERAL PURPOSE COPOLYMER DISPERSION

Source: *Chemical Marketing Reporter.* **Price Frequency:** weekly. **Effective Market(s):** New York. **Units of Measure:** Dollars per lb. **Type of Price:** spot. **Time Period Covered:** latest week.

POLYVINYL CHLORIDE: GENERAL PURPOSE COPOLYMER SUSPENSION

Source: *Chemical Marketing Reporter.* **Price Frequency:** weekly. **Effective Market(s):** New York. **Units of Measure:** Dollars per lb. **Type of Price:** spot. **Time Period Covered:** latest week.

POLYVINYL CHLORIDE: GENERAL PURPOSE HOMOPOLYMER

Source: *Plastics Technology.* **Price Frequency:** monthly. **Units of Measure:** cents per lb. **Type of Price:** bulk list, market. **Time Period Covered:** latest month.

POLYVINYL CHLORIDE: GENERAL PURPOSE HOMOPOLYMER DISPERSION

Source: *Chemical Marketing Reporter.* **Price Frequency:** weekly. **Effective Market(s):** New York. **Units of Measure:** Dollars per lb. **Type of Price:** spot. **Time Period Covered:** latest week.

POLYVINYL CHLORIDE: GENERAL PURPOSE SUSPENSION

Source: *Chemical Marketing Reporter.* **Price Frequency:** weekly. **Effective Market(s):** New York. **Units of Measure:** Dollars per lb. **Type of Price:** spot. **Time Period Covered:** latest week.

POLYVINYL CHLORIDE: GRANULAR, STRAIGHT

Source: *Japan Economic Journal.* **Price Frequency:** weekly. **Effective Market(s):** Japan. **Units of Measure:** Japanese yen per kilogram. **Type of Price:** market. **Time Period Covered:** latest 2 weeks.

POLYVINYL CHLORIDE: HOMOPOLYMER DISPERSION

Source: *Plastics Technology.* **Price Frequency:** monthly. **Units of Measure:** cents per lb. **Type of Price:** bulk list, market. **Time Period Covered:** latest month.

POLYVINYL CHLORIDE: PIPE GRADE

Source: *Chemical Marketing Reporter.* **Price Frequency:** weekly. **Effective Market(s):** New York. **Units of Measure:** Dollars per lb. **Type of Price:** spot. **Time Period Covered:** latest week.

Source: *Journal of Commerce and Commercial.* **Price Frequency:** weekly in Tuesday issue. **Units of Measure:** Dollars per lb. **Type of Price:** spot. **Time Period Covered:** latest week.

Source: *Modern Plastics.* **Price Frequency:** quarterly every January, April, July, October. **Units of Measure:** cents per lb. **Type of Price:** market. **Time Period Covered:** latest 3 years.

POLYVINYL CHLORIDE: SPECIALTY

Source: *Journal of Commerce and Commercial.* **Price Frequency:** weekly in Tuesday issue. **Units of Measure:** Dollars per lb. **Type of Price:** spot. **Time Period Covered:** latest week.

POLYVINYL CHLORIDE PIPE

Source: *Plastics Technology.* **Price Frequency:** monthly. **Units of Measure:** cents per lb. **Type of Price:** bulk list, market. **Time Period Covered:** latest month.

POMEGRANATES

Source: *Agricultural Prices Annual Summary.* **Price Frequency:** annually. **Effective Market(s):** California, Hawaii. **Units of Measure:** Dollars per ton. **Type of Price:** average received by farmer. **Time Period Covered:** latest 6 years.

Source: *California Farmer.* **Price Frequency:** semimonthly, seasonally. **Effective Market(s):** Central/Southern San Joaquin Valley. **Units of Measure:** Dollars per 22 lb. lug. **Time Period Covered:** latest week, month ago, year ago.

POMEGRANATES: GRANADA

Source: *Lancaster Farmer.* **Price Frequency:** weekly, seasonally. **Effective Market(s):** Pennsylvania. **Units of Measure:** Dollars per lug. **Type of Price:** market. **Time Period Covered:** latest week.

POMPANO: FRESH

Source: *Seafood Price-Current.* **Price Frequency:** semiweekly. **Effective Market(s):** Gulf/Southeast. **Units of Measure:** Dollars per lb. **Type of Price:** sale by first receiver. **Time Period Covered:** latest day.

POMPANO: WHOLE, FRESH

Source: *Seafood Price-Current.* **Price Frequency:** semiweekly. **Effective Market(s):** Boston, Mid-Atlantic, New Bedford (MA), Portland (ME). **Units of Measure:** Dollars per lb. **Type of Price:** sale by first receiver, auction price. **Time Period Covered:** latest day.

PONGEE FABRIC

Source: *JTN: The International Textile Magazine.* **Price Frequency:** monthly. **Effective Market(s):** Japan. **Units of Measure:** Japanese yen per yard. **Type of Price:** spot. **Time Period Covered:** latest month.

PONIES: LARGE

Source: *Lancaster Farmer.* **Price Frequency:** weekly, seasonally. **Effective Market(s):** Pennsylvania. **Units of Measure:** Dollars per head. **Type of Price:** auction. **Time Period Covered:** latest week.

PONIES: TOP

Source: *Farm and Dairy.* **Price Frequency:** weekly, seasonally. **Effective Market(s):** Ohio, Pennsylvania. **Units of Measure:** Dollars per head. **Type of Price:** auction high, auction low. **Time Period Covered:** latest week.

POPLAR: SAWTIMBER

Source: *Timber Mart-South.* **Price Frequency:** quarterly. **Effective Market(s):** 6 domestic markets. **Units of Measure:** Dollars per 1000 board feet. **Type of Price:** bid. **Time Period Covered:** latest quarter.

POPLAR: YELLOW

Source: *Volume and Value of Sawtimber Stumpage Sold From National Forests by Selected Species and Region.* **Price Frequency:** quarterly, annually. **Effective Market(s):** Eastern region, Southern region. **Units of Measure:** Dollars per 1000 board feet. **Type of Price:** average. **Time Period Covered:** latest quarter, latest year.

POPLAR: YELLOW, BASSWOOD AND CUCUMBER

Source: *Volume and Value of Sawtimber Stumpage Sold From National Forests by Selected Species and Region.* **Price Frequency:** quarterly, annually. **Effective Market(s):** Southern region. **Units of Measure:** Dollars per 1000 board feet. **Type of Price:** average. **Time Period Covered:** latest quarter, latest year.

POPLIN FABRIC

Source: *JTN: The International Textile Magazine.* **Price Frequency:** monthly. **Effective Market(s):** Japan. **Units of Measure:** Japanese yen per yard. **Type of Price:** spot. **Time Period Covered:** latest month.

POPPY SEED: AUSTRALIAN

Source: *U. S. Spice Trade.* **Price Frequency:** monthly, annually. **Effective Market(s):** New York. **Units of Measure:** cents per lb. **Type of Price:** spot. **Time Period Covered:** latest 10 years.

POPPY SEED: DUTCH

Source: *Chemical Marketing Reporter.* **Price Frequency:** weekly. **Effective Market(s):** New York. **Units of Measure:** Dollars per lb. **Type of Price:** spot. **Time Period Covered:** latest week.

Source: *U. S. Spice Trade.* **Price Frequency:** monthly, annually. **Effective Market(s):** New York. **Units of Measure:** cents per lb. **Type of Price:** spot. **Time Period Covered:** latest 10 years.

POPPY SEED: TURKISH

Source: *Chemical Marketing Reporter.* **Price Frequency:** weekly. **Effective Market(s):** New York. **Units of Measure:** Dollars per lb. **Type of Price:** spot. **Time Period Covered:** latest week.

Source: *U. S. Spice Trade.* **Price Frequency:** monthly, annually. **Effective Market(s):** New York. **Units of Measure:** cents per lb. **Type of Price:** spot. **Time Period Covered:** latest 10 years.

PORGIES (FISH): SCUP, WHOLE, FRESH

Source: *Seafood Price-Current.* **Price Frequency:** semi-weekly. **Effective Market(s):** Boston, Mid-Atlantic, New Bedford (MA), Portland (ME). **Units of Measure:** Dollars per lb. **Type of Price:** sale by first receiver, auction price. **Time Period Covered:** latest day.

PORK

Source: *Agricultural Outlook.* **Price Frequency:** annually. **Effective Market(s):** United States. **Units of Measure:** Dollars per 100 lbs. **Type of Price:** primary market. **Time Period Covered:** latest 2 years.

Source: *Commodity Year Book.* **Price Frequency:** annually. **Units of Measure:** cents per lb. **Type of Price:** retail. **Time Period Covered:** latest 7 years.

Source: *Livestock and Poultry Situation and Outlook Report.* **Price Frequency:** monthly, quarterly, annually. **Units of Measure:** cents per lb. **Type of Price:** retail. **Time Period Covered:** monthly latest year, quarterly latest 2 years, annually latest 5 years.

Source: *Livestock and Poultry Situation and Outlook Report.* **Price Frequency:** monthly. **Units of Measure:** cents per lb. **Type of Price:** retail. **Time Period Covered:** latest year.

PORK: CUT OUT

Source: *Livestock and Poultry Situation and Outlook Report.* **Price Frequency:** monthly. **Effective Market(s):** Central United States. **Units of Measure:** Dollars per 100 lbs. **Type of Price:** wholesale. **Time Period Covered:** latest year.

PORK: ENGLISH

Source: *Farmers Weekly.* **Price Frequency:** weekly. **Effective Market(s):** Smithfield (England). **Units of Measure:** British pence per lb. **Time Period Covered:** latest week.

Source: *Meat and Dairy Products.* **Price Frequency:** monthly. **Effective Market(s):** London. **Units of Measure:** British pence per lb. **Type of Price:** average. **Time Period Covered:** latest 4 years.

PORK: GROUND

Source: *Meat Price Report.* **Price Frequency:** weekly. **Units of Measure:** cents per lb. **Type of Price:** price paid to wholesaler. **Time Period Covered:** latest week.

PORK BACK LOIN RIBS: FROZEN

Source: *National Provisioner.* **Price Frequency:** daily. **Effective Market(s):** Midwest River. **Units of Measure:** cents per lb. **Time Period Covered:** latest week.

PORK BACK RIBS

Source: *Meat Price Report.* **Price Frequency:** weekly. **Units of Measure:** cents per lb. **Type of Price:** price paid to wholesaler. **Time Period Covered:** latest week.

PORK BELLIES

Source: *Agricultural Outlook.* **Price Frequency:** monthly, annually. **Effective Market(s):** Midwest. **Units of Measure:** Dollars per 100 lbs. **Type of Price:** wholesale. **Time Period Covered:** monthly latest 6 months, annually latest 3 years.

Source: *Asian Wall Street Journal.* **Price Frequency:** daily. **Effective Market(s):** Mid-United States. **Units of Measure:** Dollars per lb. **Type of Price:** cash. **Time Period Covered:** latest 2 days, year ago.

Source: *Commodity Year Book.* **Price Frequency:** annually. **Effective Market(s):** Midwest. **Units of Measure:** cents per lb. **Time Period Covered:** latest 7 years.

Source: *Investor's Daily.* **Price Frequency:** daily. **Effective Market(s):** Midwest. **Units of Measure:** Dollars per lb. **Type of Price:** spot. **Time Period Covered:** latest day.

Source: *Livestock and Poultry Situation and Outlook Report.* **Price Frequency:** monthly. **Effective Market(s):** Central United States. **Units of Measure:** Dollars per 100 lbs. **Type of Price:** wholesale. **Time Period Covered:** latest year.

Source: *Livestock and Poultry Update.* **Price Frequency:** monthly. **Effective Market(s):** Central United States. **Units of Measure:** Dollars per 100 lbs. **Type of Price:** wholesale. **Time Period Covered:** latest 3 months, year ago.

PORK BELLIES: 12-14 LBS

Source: *The Brock Report.* **Price Frequency:** weekly. **Units of Measure:** cents per lb. **Time Period Covered:** latest week, 2 weeks ago, year ago.

Source: *New York Times.* **Price Frequency:** daily. **Effective Market(s):** Midwest. **Units of Measure:** Dollars per 100 lbs. **Type of Price:** cash. **Time Period Covered:** latest 2 days.

Source: *Porkpro Newsletter.* **Price Frequency:** weekly. **Units of Measure:** Dollars per lb. **Type of Price:** wholesale. **Time Period Covered:** latest day, week ago, year ago.

Source: *Wall Street Journal.* **Price Frequency:** daily. **Effective Market(s):** Mid-United States. **Units of Measure:** Dollars per lb. **Time Period Covered:** latest day, day ago, year ago.

PORK BELLIES: FRESH

Source: *Livestock, Meat, Wool Market News.* **Price Frequency:** weekly, seasonally. **Effective Market(s):** Central United States, California. **Units of Measure:** Dollars per 100 lbs. **Type of Price:** average. **Time Period Covered:** latest week, year ago.

PORK BELLIES: FROZEN, FUTURES

Source: *Feedstuffs.* **Price Frequency:** weekly. **Effective Market(s):** Chicago. **Units of Measure:** cents per lb. **Type of Price:** futures. **Time Period Covered:** latest week, week ago, latest season.

PORK BELLIES: FUTURES

Source: *Asian Wall Street Journal.* **Price Frequency:** daily. **Effective Market(s):** Chicago. **Units of Measure:** cents per lb. **Type of Price:** futures. **Time Period Covered:** latest day.

Source: *Barron's.* **Price Frequency:** weekly. **Effective Market(s):** Chicago. **Units of Measure:** cents per lb. **Type of Price:** futures. **Time Period Covered:** latest week.

Source: *Financial Times.* **Price Frequency:** daily. **Effective Market(s):** Chicago. **Units of Measure:** cents per lb. **Type of Price:** futures. **Time Period Covered:** latest day.

Source: *Investor's Daily.* **Price Frequency:** daily. **Effective Market(s):** Chicago. **Units of Measure:** cents per lb. **Type of Price:** futures. **Time Period Covered:** latest day.

Source: *Los Angeles Times.* **Price Frequency:** daily. **Effective Market(s):** New York. **Units of Measure:** cents per lb. **Type of Price:** futures. **Time Period Covered:** latest day.

Source: *National Provisioner.* **Price Frequency:** daily. **Effective Market(s):** Chicago. **Type of Price:** futures. **Time Period Covered:** latest week.

Source: *New York Times.* **Price Frequency:** daily. **Effective Market(s):** Chicago. **Units of Measure:** cents per lb. **Type of Price:** futures. **Time Period Covered:** latest day.

Source: *Urner Barry's Price-Current.* **Price Frequency:** daily. **Effective Market(s):** Chicago. **Units of Measure:** cents per lb. **Type of Price:** futures. **Time Period Covered:** latest day.

Source: *Wall Street Journal.* **Price Frequency:** daily. **Effective Market(s):** Chicago. **Units of Measure:** cents per lb. **Type of Price:** futures. **Time Period Covered:** latest day.

PORK BELLIES: FUTURES, MAY

Source: *Commodity Year Book.* **Price Frequency:** monthly. **Effective Market(s):** Chicago. **Units of Measure:** cents per lb. **Type of Price:** futures. **Time Period Covered:** latest 7 years.

PORK BELLIES: GREEN, SQUARE CUT SEEDLESS

Source: *National Provisioner.* **Price Frequency:** daily. **Effective Market(s):** Midwest River. **Units of Measure:** cents per lb. **Time Period Covered:** latest week.

PORK BOSTON BUTT

Source: *Meat Price Report.* **Price Frequency:** weekly. **Units of Measure:** cents per lb. **Type of Price:** price paid to wholesaler. **Time Period Covered:** latest week.

PORK BOSTON BUTT: BONELESS, TIED

Source: *Meat Price Report.* **Price Frequency:** weekly. **Units of Measure:** cents per lb. **Type of Price:** price paid to wholesaler. **Time Period Covered:** latest week.

PORK BOSTON BUTT: CELLAR TRIM, BONELESS

Source: *Meat Price Report.* **Price Frequency:** weekly. **Units of Measure:** cents per lb. **Type of Price:** price paid to wholesaler. **Time Period Covered:** latest week.

PORK BOSTON BUTT STEAKS

Source: *Meat Price Report.* **Price Frequency:** weekly. **Units of Measure:** cents per lb. **Type of Price:** price paid to wholesaler. **Time Period Covered:** latest week.

PORK BOSTON BUTTS: FRESH

Source: *Livestock, Meat, Wool Market News.* **Price Frequency:** weekly, seasonally. **Effective Market(s):** Central United States, California. **Units of Measure:** Dollars per 100 lbs. **Type of Price:** average. **Time Period Covered:** latest week, year ago.

Source: *National Provisioner.* **Price Frequency:** daily. **Effective Market(s):** Midwest River. **Units of Measure:** cents per lb. **Time Period Covered:** latest week.

PORK BUTTS

Source: *HRI-Buyers Guide.* **Price Frequency:** weekly. **Effective Market(s):** Northeastern area. **Units of Measure:** Dollars per lb. **Type of Price:** price paid by dining places & institutions. **Time Period Covered:** latest week.

PORK BUTTS: BONELESS, FROZEN

Source: *National Provisioner.* **Price Frequency:** daily. **Effective Market(s):** Midwest River. **Units of Measure:** cents per lb. **Time Period Covered:** latest week.

PORK CANADIAN BACK

Source: *Meat Price Report.* **Price Frequency:** weekly. **Units of Measure:** cents per lb. **Type of Price:** price paid to wholesaler. **Time Period Covered:** latest week.

PORK CARCASS: US 1

Source: *Livestock, Meat, Wool Market News.* **Price Frequency:** weekly, seasonally. **Effective Market(s):** Omaha. **Units of Measure:** Dollars per 100 lbs. **Type of Price:** average. **Time Period Covered:** latest week, week ago.

PORK CARCASS: US 2

Source: *Livestock, Meat, Wool Market News.* **Price Frequency:** weekly, seasonally. **Effective Market(s):** Omaha. **Units of Measure:** Dollars per 100 lbs. **Type of Price:** average. **Time Period Covered:** latest week, week ago.

PORK CARCASS: US 3

Source: *Livestock, Meat, Wool Market News.* **Price Frequency:** weekly, seasonally. **Effective Market(s):** Omaha. **Units of Measure:** Dollars per 100 lbs. **Type of Price:** average. **Time Period Covered:** latest week, week ago.

PORK CARCASS: US 4

Source: *Livestock, Meat, Wool Market News.* **Price Frequency:** weekly, seasonally. **Effective Market(s):** Omaha. **Units of Measure:** Dollars per 100 lbs. **Type of Price:** average. **Time Period Covered:** latest week, week ago.

PORK CHEEK MEAT: FROZEN

Source: *Livestock, Meat, Wool Market News.* **Price Frequency:** weekly, seasonally. **Effective Market(s):** Central United States. **Units of Measure:** Dollars per 100 lbs. **Time Period Covered:** latest week.

Source: *National Provisioner.* **Price Frequency:** daily. **Effective Market(s):** Midwest River. **Units of Measure:** cents per lb. **Time Period Covered:** latest week.

PORK CHITTERLINGS: FROZEN

Source: *Livestock, Meat, Wool Market News.* **Price Frequency:** weekly, seasonally. **Effective Market(s):** Central United States. **Units of Measure:** Dollars per 100 lbs. **Time Period Covered:** latest week.

Source: *National Provisioner.* **Price Frequency:** daily. **Effective Market(s):** Midwest River. **Units of Measure:** cents per lb. **Time Period Covered:** latest week.

PORK CHOPS

Source: *Livestock and Poultry Update.* **Price Frequency:** monthly. **Units of Measure:** cents per lb. **Type of Price:** retail. **Time Period Covered:** latest 3 months, year ago.

PORK CHOPS: CENTER CUT

Source: *Livestock and Poultry Situation and Outlook Report.* **Price Frequency:** monthly. **Units of Measure:** Dollars per lb. **Type of Price:** retail. **Time Period Covered:** latest 3 years.

Source: *Meat Price Report.* **Price Frequency:** weekly. **Units of Measure:** cents per lb. **Type of Price:** price paid to wholesaler. **Time Period Covered:** latest week.

Source: *Porkpro Newsletter.* **Price Frequency:** weekly. **Effective Market(s):** Chicago. **Units of Measure:** Dollars per lb. **Type of Price:** retail. **Time Period Covered:** latest day, week ago, year ago.

PORK CHOPS: FROM LOIN, CUT END TO END

Source: *Meat Price Report.* **Price Frequency:** weekly. **Units of Measure:** cents per lb. **Type of Price:** price paid to wholesaler. **Time Period Covered:** latest week.

PORK EARS: FROZEN

Source: *Livestock, Meat, Wool Market News.* **Price Frequency:** weekly, seasonally. **Effective Market(s):** Central United States. **Units of Measure:** Dollars per 100 lbs. **Time Period Covered:** latest week.

Source: *National Provisioner.* **Price Frequency:** daily. **Effective Market(s):** Midwest River. **Units of Measure:** cents per lb. **Time Period Covered:** latest week.

PORK FEET: FRONT, TOES ON, FROZEN

Source: *Livestock, Meat, Wool Market News.* **Price Frequency:** weekly, seasonally. **Effective Market(s):** Central United States. **Units of Measure:** Dollars per 100 lbs. **Time Period Covered:** latest week.

Source: *National Provisioner.* **Price Frequency:** daily. **Effective Market(s):** Midwest River. **Units of Measure:** cents per lb. **Time Period Covered:** latest week.

PORK FILLETS

Source: *Meat Price Report.* **Price Frequency:** weekly. **Units of Measure:** cents per lb. **Type of Price:** price paid to wholesaler. **Time Period Covered:** latest week.

PORK FOR CHOP SUEY

Source: *Meat Price Report.* **Price Frequency:** weekly. **Units of Measure:** cents per lb. **Type of Price:** price paid to wholesaler. **Time Period Covered:** latest week.

PORK GELATIN SKINS: FROZEN

Source: *Livestock, Meat, Wool Market News.* **Price Frequency:** weekly, seasonally. **Effective Market(s):** Central United States. **Units of Measure:** Dollars per 100 lbs. **Time Period Covered:** latest week.

Source: *National Provisioner.* **Price Frequency:** daily. **Effective Market(s):** Midwest River. **Units of Measure:** cents per lb. **Time Period Covered:** latest week.

PORK HEAD MEAT: FROZEN

Source: *Livestock, Meat, Wool Market News.* **Price Frequency:** weekly, seasonally. **Effective Market(s):** Central United States. **Units of Measure:** Dollars per 100 lbs. **Time Period Covered:** latest week.

Source: *National Provisioner.* **Price Frequency:** daily. **Effective Market(s):** Midwest River. **Units of Measure:** cents per lb. **Time Period Covered:** latest week.

PORK HEARTS: FROZEN

Source: *Livestock, Meat, Wool Market News.* **Price Frequency:** weekly, seasonally. **Effective Market(s):** Central United States. **Units of Measure:** Dollars per 100 lbs. **Time Period Covered:** latest week.

Source: *National Provisioner.* **Price Frequency:** daily. **Effective Market(s):** Midwest River. **Units of Measure:** cents per lb. **Time Period Covered:** latest week.

PORK KIDNEYS: FROZEN

Source: *Livestock, Meat, Wool Market News.* **Price Frequency:** weekly, seasonally. **Effective Market(s):** Central United States. **Units of Measure:** Dollars per 100 lbs. **Time Period Covered:** latest week.

Source: *National Provisioner.* **Price Frequency:** daily. **Effective Market(s):** Midwest River. **Units of Measure:** cents per lb. **Time Period Covered:** latest week.

PORK KIDNEYS FOR PET FOOD: INEDIBLE

Source: *Livestock, Meat, Wool Market News.* **Price Frequency:** weekly, seasonally. **Effective Market(s):** Central United States. **Units of Measure:** Dollars per 100 lbs. **Time Period Covered:** latest week.

PORK LIVERS: FROZEN

Source: *Livestock, Meat, Wool Market News.* **Price Frequency:** weekly, seasonally. **Effective Market(s):** Central United States. **Units of Measure:** Dollars per 100 lbs. **Time Period Covered:** latest week.

Source: *National Provisioner.* **Price Frequency:** daily. **Effective Market(s):** Midwest River. **Units of Measure:** cents per lb. **Time Period Covered:** latest week.

PORK LIVERS FOR PET FOOD: INEDIBLE

Source: *Livestock, Meat, Wool Market News.* **Price Frequency:** weekly, seasonally. **Effective Market(s):** Central United States. **Units of Measure:** Dollars per 100 lbs. **Time Period Covered:** latest week.

PORK LOIN

Source: *Agricultural Outlook.* **Price Frequency:** monthly, annually. **Effective Market(s):** Midwest. **Units of Measure:** Dollars per 100 lbs. **Type of Price:** wholesale. **Time Period Covered:** monthly latest 6 months, annually latest 3 years.

Source: *Asian Wall Street Journal.* **Price Frequency:** daily. **Effective Market(s):** Mid-United States. **Units of Measure:** Dollars per lb. **Type of Price:** cash. **Time Period Covered:** latest 2 days, year ago.

Source: *California Farmer.* **Price Frequency:** semimonthly. **Effective Market(s):** Los Angeles. **Units of Measure:** Dollars per 100 lbs. **Time Period Covered:** latest week, month ago, year ago.

Source: *HRI-Buyers Guide.* **Price Frequency:** weekly. **Effective Market(s):** Northeastern area. **Units of Measure:** Dollars per lb. **Type of Price:** price paid by dining places & institutions. **Time Period Covered:** latest week.

Source: *Livestock and Poultry Situation and Outlook Report.* **Price Frequency:** monthly. **Effective Market(s):** Central United States. **Units of Measure:** Dollars per 100 lbs. **Type of Price:** wholesale. **Time Period Covered:** latest year.

Source: *Livestock and Poultry Update.* **Price Frequency:** monthly. **Effective Market(s):** Central United States. **Units of Measure:** Dollars per 100 lbs. **Type of Price:** wholesale. **Time Period Covered:** latest 3 months, year ago.

Source: *Meat and Dairy Products.* **Price Frequency:** monthly. **Effective Market(s):** Central United States. **Units of Measure:** Dollars per 100 lbs. **Type of Price:** wholesale. **Time Period Covered:** latest 4 years.

PORK LOIN: 14/DOWN

Source: *Meat Price Report.* **Price Frequency:** weekly. **Units of Measure:** cents per lb. **Type of Price:** price paid to wholesaler. **Time Period Covered:** latest week.

PORK LOIN: 14-17 LBS

Source: *The Brock Report.* **Price Frequency:** weekly. **Units of Measure:** cents per lb. **Time Period Covered:** latest week, 2 weeks ago, year ago.

Source: *Feedstuffs.* **Price Frequency:** weekly. **Effective Market(s):** Chicago. **Units of Measure:** cents per lb. **Time Period Covered:** latest week, week ago, 6 months ago, year ago.

Source: *Porkpro Newsletter.* **Price Frequency:** weekly. **Units of Measure:** Dollars per lb. **Type of Price:** wholesale. **Time Period Covered:** latest day, week ago, year ago.

Source: *Wall Street Journal.* **Price Frequency:** daily. **Effective Market(s):** Mid-United States. **Units of Measure:** Dollars per lb. **Time Period Covered:** latest day, day ago, year ago.

PORK LOIN: BONELESS

Source: *Meat Price Report.* **Price Frequency:** weekly. **Units of Measure:** cents per lb. **Type of Price:** price paid to wholesaler. **Time Period Covered:** latest week.

PORK LOIN: CANADIAN

Source: *Japan Economic Journal.* **Price Frequency:** weekly. **Effective Market(s):** Japan. **Units of Measure:** Japanese yen per kilogram. **Type of Price:** wholesale. **Time Period Covered:** latest 2 weeks.

PORK LOIN: CENTER CUT

Source: *Meat Price Report.* **Price Frequency:** weekly. **Units of Measure:** cents per lb. **Type of Price:** price paid to wholesaler. **Time Period Covered:** latest week.

PORK LOIN: FRESH

Source: *Commodity Year Book.* **Price Frequency:** annually. **Effective Market(s):** New York. **Units of Measure:** cents per lb. **Time Period Covered:** latest 7 years.

Source: *Economic and Energy Indicators.* **Price Frequency:** monthly, quarterly, annually. **Units of Measure:** cents per lb. **Time Period Covered:** latest 3 months, quarters, and years.

Source: *Livestock, Meat, Wool Market News.* **Price Frequency:** weekly, seasonally. **Effective Market(s):** Central United States, California. **Units of Measure:** Dollars per 100 lbs. **Type of Price:** average. **Time Period Covered:** latest week, year ago.

Source: *National Provisioner.* **Price Frequency:** daily. **Effective Market(s):** Midwest River. **Units of Measure:** cents per lb. **Time Period Covered:** latest week.

PORK LOIN: REGULAR, CURED AND SMOKED

Source: *Meat Price Report.* **Price Frequency:** weekly. **Units of Measure:** cents per lb. **Type of Price:** price paid to wholesaler. **Time Period Covered:** latest week.

PORK LOINS: FRESH

Source: *Survey of Current Business.* **Price Frequency:** monthly, annually. **Effective Market(s):** New York. **Units of Measure:** Dollars per lb. **Type of Price:** wholesale. **Time Period Covered:** latest year.

PORK LUNGS FOR PET FOOD: INEDIBLE

Source: *Livestock, Meat, Wool Market News.* **Price Frequency:** weekly, seasonally. **Effective Market(s):** Central United States. **Units of Measure:** Dollars per 100 lbs. **Time Period Covered:** latest week.

PORK MELTS: FROZEN

Source: *National Provisioner.* **Price Frequency:** daily. **Effective Market(s):** Midwest River. **Units of Measure:** cents per lb. **Time Period Covered:** latest week.

PORK MELTS FOR PET FOOD

Source: *Livestock, Meat, Wool Market News.* **Price Frequency:** weekly, seasonally. **Effective Market(s):** Central United States. **Units of Measure:** Dollars per 100 lbs. **Time Period Covered:** latest week.

PORK NECKBONES: FROZEN

Source: *Livestock, Meat, Wool Market News.* **Price Frequency:** weekly, seasonally. **Effective Market(s):** Central United States. **Units of Measure:** Dollars per 100 lbs. **Time Period Covered:** latest week.

Source: *National Provisioner.* **Price Frequency:** daily. **Effective Market(s):** Midwest River. **Units of Measure:** cents per lb. **Time Period Covered:** latest week.

PORK PICNICS

Source: *Livestock and Poultry Update.* **Price Frequency:** monthly. **Units of Measure:** cents per lb. **Type of Price:** retail. **Time Period Covered:** latest 3 months, year ago.

PORK PICNICS: FRESH

Source: *Livestock, Meat, Wool Market News.* **Price Frequency:** weekly, seasonally. **Effective Market(s):** Central United States, California. **Units of Measure:** Dollars per 100 lbs. **Type of Price:** average. **Time Period Covered:** latest week, year ago.

PORK SALIVARY GLANDS: FROZEN

Source: *Livestock, Meat, Wool Market News.* **Price Frequency:** weekly, seasonally. **Effective Market(s):** Central United States. **Units of Measure:** Dollars per 100 lbs. **Time Period Covered:** latest week.

Source: *National Provisioner.* **Price Frequency:** daily. **Effective Market(s):** Midwest River. **Units of Measure:** cents per lb. **Time Period Covered:** latest week.

PORK SAUSAGE

Source: *HRI-Buyers Guide.* **Price Frequency:** weekly. **Effective Market(s):** Northeastern area. **Units of Measure:** Dollars per lb. **Type of Price:** price paid by dining places & institutions. **Time Period Covered:** latest week.

PORK SAUSAGE: FRESH

Source: *Livestock and Poultry Situation and Outlook Report.* **Price Frequency:** monthly. **Units of Measure:** Dollars per lb. **Type of Price:** retail. **Time Period Covered:** latest 3 years.

PORK SAUSAGE: ITALIAN STYLE

Source: *HRI-Buyers Guide.* **Price Frequency:** weekly. **Effective Market(s):** Northeastern area. **Units of Measure:** Dollars per lb. **Type of Price:** price paid by dining places & institutions. **Time Period Covered:** latest week.

PORK SAUSAGE: LINKS, NATURAL CASING OR COLLAGEN

Source: *Meat Price Report.* **Price Frequency:** weekly. **Units of Measure:** cents per lb. **Type of Price:** price paid to wholeslaer. **Time Period Covered:** latest week.

PORK SAUSAGE: LINKS, SKINLESS

Source: *Meat Price Report.* **Price Frequency:** weekly. **Units of Measure:** cents per lb. **Type of Price:** price paid to wholesaler. **Time Period Covered:** latest week.

PORK SAUSAGE: PATTIES

Source: *Meat Price Report.* **Price Frequency:** weekly. **Units of Measure:** cents per lb. **Type of Price:** price paid to wholesaler. **Time Period Covered:** latest week.

PORK SAUSAGE: ROLLS

Source: *Meat Price Report.* **Price Frequency:** weekly. **Units of Measure:** cents per lb. **Type of Price:** price paid to wholesaler. **Time Period Covered:** latest week.

PORK SAUSAGE MATERIALS: FRESH

Source: *National Provisioner.* **Price Frequency:** daily. **Effective Market(s):** Midwest River. **Units of Measure:** cents per lb. **Time Period Covered:** latest week.

PORK SAUSAGE MATERIALS: FROZEN

Source: *National Provisioner.* **Price Frequency:** daily. **Effective Market(s):** Midwest River. **Units of Measure:** cents per lb. **Time Period Covered:** latest week.

PORK SHOULDER

Source: *HRI-Buyers Guide.* **Price Frequency:** weekly. **Effective Market(s):** Northeastern area. **Units of Measure:** Dollars per lb. **Type of Price:** price paid by dining places & institutions. **Time Period Covered:** latest week.

PORK SHOULDER: SKINNED

Source: *Meat Price Report.* **Price Frequency:** weekly. **Units of Measure:** cents per lb. **Type of Price:** price paid to wholesaler. **Time Period Covered:** latest week.

PORK SHOULDER: SKINNED, FRESH

Source: *National Provisioner.* **Price Frequency:** daily. **Effective Market(s):** Midwest River. **Units of Measure:** cents per lb. **Time Period Covered:** latest week.

PORK SHOULDER BUTT: BONELESS, CURED AND SMOKED

Source: *Meat Price Report.* **Price Frequency:** weekly. **Units of Measure:** cents per lb. **Type of Price:** price paid to wholesaler. **Time Period Covered:** latest week.

PORK SHOULDER HOCKS

Source: *Meat Price Report.* **Price Frequency:** weekly. **Units of Measure:** cents per lb. **Type of Price:** price paid to wholesaler. **Time Period Covered:** latest week.

PORK SHOULDER HOCKS: CURED AND SMOKED

Source: *Meat Price Report.* **Price Frequency:** weekly. **Units of Measure:** cents per lb. **Type of Price:** price paid to wholesalers. **Time Period Covered:** latest week.

PORK SHOULDER PICNIC: BONE IN

Source: *Livestock and Poultry Situation and Outlook Report.* **Price Frequency:** monthly. **Units of Measure:** Dollars per lb. **Type of Price:** retail. **Time Period Covered:** latest 3 years.

PORK SHOULDER PICNIC: CURED AND SMOKED

Source: *Meat Price Report.* **Price Frequency:** weekly. **Units of Measure:** cents per lb. **Type of Price:** price paid to wholesaler. **Time Period Covered:** latest week.

PORK SIRLOIN ROAST: BONE IN

Source: *Livestock and Poultry Situation and Outlook Report.* **Price Frequency:** monthly. **Units of Measure:** Dollars per lb. **Type of Price:** retail. **Time Period Covered:** latest 3 years.

PORK SKINS: FROZEN

Source: *National Provisioner.* **Price Frequency:** daily. **Effective Market(s):** Midwest River. **Units of Measure:** cents per lb. **Time Period Covered:** latest week.

PORK SNOUTS: LEAN-IN, FROZEN

Source: *National Provisioner.* **Price Frequency:** daily. **Effective Market(s):** Midwest River. **Units of Measure:** cents per lb. **Time Period Covered:** latest week.

PORK SNOUTS: PARTIAL LEAN-IN, FROZEN

Source: *Livestock, Meat, Wool Market News.* **Price Frequency:** weekly, seasonally. **Effective Market(s):** Central United States. **Units of Measure:** Dollars per 100 lbs. **Time Period Covered:** latest week.

PORK SPARERIBS

Source: *HRI-Buyers Guide.* **Price Frequency:** weekly. **Effective Market(s):** Northeastern area. **Units of Measure:** Dollars per lb. **Type of Price:** price paid by dining places & institutions. **Time Period Covered:** latest week.

Source: *Porkpro Newsletter.* **Price Frequency:** weekly. **Effective Market(s):** Chicago. **Units of Measure:** Dollars per lb. **Type of Price:** retail. **Time Period Covered:** latest day, week ago, year ago.

PORK SPARERIBS: 3/DOWN

Source: *Meat Price Report.* **Price Frequency:** weekly. **Units of Measure:** cents per lb. **Type of Price:** price paid to wholesaler. **Time Period Covered:** latest week.

PORK SPARERIBS: BREAST OFF

Source: *Meat Price Report.* **Price Frequency:** weekly. **Units of Measure:** cents per lb. **Type of Price:** price paid to wholesaler. **Time Period Covered:** latest week.

PORK SPARERIBS: FRESH

Source: *Livestock, Meat, Wool Market News.* **Price Frequency:** weekly, seasonally. **Effective Market(s):** Central United States, California. **Units of Measure:** Dollars per 100 lbs. **Type of Price:** average. **Time Period Covered:** latest week, year ago.

PORK SPARERIBS: FROZEN

Source: *National Provisioner.* **Price Frequency:** daily. **Effective Market(s):** Midwest River. **Units of Measure:** cents per lb. **Time Period Covered:** latest week.

PORK STOMACHS: FROZEN

Source: *Livestock, Meat, Wool Market News.* **Price Frequency:** weekly, seasonally. **Effective Market(s):** Central United States. **Units of Measure:** Dollars per 100 lbs. **Time Period Covered:** latest week.

Source: *National Provisioner.* **Price Frequency:** daily. **Effective Market(s):** Midwest River. **Units of Measure:** cents per lb. **Time Period Covered:** latest week.

PORK TAILS: FROZEN

Source: *Livestock, Meat, Wool Market News.* **Price Frequency:** weekly, seasonally. **Effective Market(s):** Central United States. **Units of Measure:** Dollars per 100 lbs. **Time Period Covered:** latest week.

Source: *National Provisioner.* **Price Frequency:** daily. **Effective Market(s):** Midwest River. **Units of Measure:** cents per lb. **Time Period Covered:** latest week.

PORK TENDERLOIN

Source: *Meat Price Report.* **Price Frequency:** weekly. **Units of Measure:** cents per lb. **Type of Price:** price paid to wholesaler. **Time Period Covered:** latest week.

PORK TENDERLOIN: TRIMMED

Source: *HRI-Buyers Guide.* **Price Frequency:** weekly. **Effective Market(s):** Northeastern area. **Units of Measure:** Dollars per lb. **Type of Price:** price paid by dining places & institutions. **Time Period Covered:** latest week.

PORK TONGUES: BONELESS, FROZEN

Source: *National Provisioner.* **Price Frequency:** daily. **Effective Market(s):** Midwest River. **Units of Measure:** cents per lb. **Time Period Covered:** latest week.

PORK TONGUES: FROZEN

Source: *Livestock, Meat, Wool Market News.* **Price Frequency:** weekly, seasonally. **Effective Market(s):** Central United States. **Units of Measure:** Dollars per 100 lbs. **Time Period Covered:** latest week.

PORK TRIMMINGS

Source: *Livestock, Meat, Wool Market News.* **Price Frequency:** weekly, seasonally. **Effective Market(s):** Central United States, California. **Units of Measure:** Dollars per 100 lbs. **Type of Price:** average. **Time Period Covered:** latest week, year ago.

PORT WINE

Source: *Beverage Media.* **Price Frequency:** monthly. **Effective Market(s):** New York. **Units of Measure:** Dollars per unit. **Type of Price:** wholesale by brand. **Time Period Covered:** latest month.

Source: *Indiana Beverage Journal.* **Price Frequency:** monthly. **Effective Market(s):** Indiana. **Units of Measure:** Dollars per case, dollars per bottle. **Type of Price:** wholesale by brand. **Time Period Covered:** latest month.

Source: *Nevada Beverage Index.* **Price Frequency:** monthly. **Effective Market(s):** Nevada. **Units of Measure:** Dollars per unit. **Type of Price:** wholesale by brand. **Time Period Covered:** latest month.

PORT WINE: DOMESTIC

Source: *Colorado Beverage Analyst.* **Price Frequency:** monthly. **Effective Market(s):** Colorado. **Units of Measure:** Dollars per case. **Type of Price:** wholesale by brand. **Time Period Covered:** latest month.

PORT WINE: IMPORTED

Source: *Colorado Beverage Analyst.* **Price Frequency:** monthly. **Effective Market(s):** Colorado. **Units of Measure:** Dollars per case. **Type of Price:** wholesale by brand. **Time Period Covered:** latest month.

PORT WINE: RED

Source: *California Wineletter.* **Price Frequency:** semiweekly. **Effective Market(s):** non-California markets. **Units of Measure:** Dollars per gallon. **Type of Price:** asking. **Time Period Covered:** latest week.

PORT WINE: WHITE

Source: *California Wineletter.* **Price Frequency:** semiweekly. **Effective Market(s):** non-California markets. **Units of Measure:** Dollars per gallon. **Type of Price:** asking. **Time Period Covered:** latest week, year ago.

PORTUGAL ESCUDOS

Source: *Asian Wall Street Journal.* **Price Frequency:** daily. **Effective Market(s):** Asia. **Units of Measure:** Portuguese escudos per ECU. **Type of Price:** foreign exchange. **Time Period Covered:** latest 2 days.

Source: *Barron's.* **Price Frequency:** weekly. **Effective Market(s):** New York. **Units of Measure:** Portuguese escudos per United States dollar. **Type of Price:** foreign exchange. **Time Period Covered:** latest 2 weeks.

Source: *New York Times.* **Price Frequency:** daily. **Effective Market(s):** United States. **Units of Measure:** Portuguese escudos per United States dollar. **Type of Price:** foreign exchange. **Time Period Covered:** latest 2 days.

Source: *Timber Bulletin.* **Price Frequency:** monthly, annually. **Units of Measure:** Portuguese escudos per United States dollar. **Type of Price:** foreign exchange. **Time Period Covered:** latest 2 years.

POTASH

Source: *Commodity Year Book.* **Price Frequency:** annually. **Effective Market(s):** United States. **Units of Measure:** Dollars per tonne. **Time Period Covered:** latest 8 years.

POTASH: AGRICULTURAL

see Potassium Muriate.

POTASH: CANADA

Source: *International Financial Statistics.* **Price Frequency:** monthly, quarterly, annually. **Effective Market(s):** Vancouver. **Units of Measure:** Dollars per metric ton, index. **Type of Price:** market price, price index. **Time Period Covered:** latest 5 months, latest 5 quarters, latest 5 years.

Source: *International Financial Statistics Yearbook.* **Price Frequency:** annually. **Effective Market(s):** Vancouver. **Units of Measure:** Dollars per metric ton. **Type of Price:** wholesale. **Time Period Covered:** latest week.

POTASH: CAUSTIC, LIQUID, 45% BASIS

Source: *Chemical Marketing Reporter.* **Price Frequency:** weekly. **Effective Market(s):** New York. **Units of Measure:** Dollars per 100 lbs. **Type of Price:** spot. **Time Period Covered:** latest week.

Source: *Journal of Commerce and Commercial.* **Price Frequency:** weekly in Thursday issue. **Units of Measure:** Dollars per 100 lbs. **Type of Price:** spot. **Time Period Covered:** latest week.

POTASH: CAUSTIC, LIQUID, 50% BASIS

Source: *Chemical Marketing Reporter.* **Price Frequency:** weekly. **Effective Market(s):** West Coast. **Units of Measure:** Dollars per 100 lbs. **Type of Price:** spot. **Time Period Covered:** latest week.

POTASH: COARSE

Source: *Industrial Minerals.* **Price Frequency:** monthly. **Effective Market(s):** Saskatchewan (Canada), Carlsbad. **Units of Measure:** Dollars per short ton, dollars per ton. **Type of Price:** producer & dealer. **Time Period Covered:** latest month.

POTASH: FLAKE, 88-92%

Source: *Chemical Marketing Reporter.* **Price Frequency:** weekly. **Effective Market(s):** New York. **Units of Measure:** Dollars per 100 lbs. **Type of Price:** spot. **Time Period Covered:** latest week.

Source: *Journal of Commerce and Commercial.* **Price Frequency:** weekly in Thursday issue. **Units of Measure:** Dollars per lb. **Type of Price:** spot. **Time Period Covered:** latest week.

POTASH: GRANULAR

Source: *Industrial Minerals.* **Price Frequency:** monthly. **Effective Market(s):** Saskatchewan (Canada), Carlsbad. **Units of Measure:** Dollars per short ton, dollars per ton. **Type of Price:** producer & dealer. **Time Period Covered:** latest month.

POTASH: STANDARD

Source: *Industrial Minerals.* **Price Frequency:** monthly. **Effective Market(s):** Saskatchewan (Canada). **Units of Measure:** Dollars per short ton. **Type of Price:** producer & dealer. **Time Period Covered:** latest month.

POTASH MURIATE: COARSE, 60-62%

Source: *Journal of Commerce and Commercial.* **Price Frequency:** weekly in Thursday issue. **Effective Market(s):** Saskatoon (Canada). **Units of Measure:** Dollars per ton. **Type of Price:** spot. **Time Period Covered:** latest week.

POTASH MURIATE: GRANULAR, 60-62%

Source: *Journal of Commerce and Commercial.* **Price Frequency:** weekly in Thursday issue. **Effective Market(s):** Saskatoon (Canada). **Units of Measure:** Dollars per ton. **Type of Price:** spot. **Time Period Covered:** latest week.

POTASH MURIATE: STANDARD, 60-62%

Source: *Journal of Commerce and Commercial.* **Price Frequency:** weekly in Thursday issue. **Effective Market(s):** Saskatoon (Canada). **Units of Measure:** Dollars per ton. **Type of Price:** spot. **Time Period Covered:** latest week.

POTASSIUM: DRY

Source: *Journal of Commerce and Commercial.* **Price Frequency:** weekly in Thursday issue. **Units of Measure:** Dollars per lb. **Type of Price:** spot. **Time Period Covered:** latest week.

POTASSIUM: LIQUID

Source: *Journal of Commerce and Commercial.* **Price Frequency:** weekly in Thursday issue. **Units of Measure:** Dollars per lb. **Type of Price:** spot. **Time Period Covered:** latest week.

POTASSIUM: USP

Source: *Journal of Commerce and Commercial.* **Price Frequency:** weekly in Thursday issue. **Units of Measure:** Dollars per lb. **Type of Price:** spot. **Time Period Covered:** latest week.

POTASSIUM ACETATE: GRANULAR, NF

Source: *Chemical Marketing Reporter.* **Price Frequency:** weekly. **Effective Market(s):** New York. **Units of Measure:** Dollars per lb. **Type of Price:** spot. **Time Period Covered:** latest week.

POTASSIUM BICARBONATE: GRANULAR, USP

Source: *Chemical Marketing Reporter.* **Price Frequency:** weekly. **Effective Market(s):** New York. **Units of Measure:** Dollars per lb. **Type of Price:** spot. **Time Period Covered:** latest week.

POTASSIUM BICARBONATE: TECHNICAL, GRANULAR

Source: *Chemical Marketing Reporter.* **Price Frequency:** weekly. **Effective Market(s):** New York. **Units of Measure:** Dollars per lb. **Type of Price:** spot. **Time Period Covered:** latest week.

POTASSIUM BICHROMATE: GRANULAR

Source: *Chemical Marketing Reporter.* **Price Frequency:** weekly. **Effective Market(s):** New York. **Units of Measure:** Dollars per lb. **Type of Price:** spot. **Time Period Covered:** latest week.

Source: *Journal of Commerce and Commercial.* **Price Frequency:** weekly in Thursday issue. **Units of Measure:** Dollars per lb. **Type of Price:** spot. **Time Period Covered:** latest week.

POTASSIUM BIFLUORIDE: TECHNICAL

Source: *Chemical Marketing Reporter.* **Price Frequency:** weekly. **Effective Market(s):** New York. **Units of Measure:** Dollars per lb. **Type of Price:** spot. **Time Period Covered:** latest week.

POTASSIUM BITARTRATE: GRANULAR, POWDERED, NF

Source: *Chemical Marketing Reporter.* **Price Frequency:** weekly. **Effective Market(s):** New York. **Units of Measure:** Dollars per lb. **Type of Price:** spot. **Time Period Covered:** latest week.

POTASSIUM BOROHYDRIDE: POWDERED

Source: *Chemical Marketing Reporter.* **Price Frequency:** weekly. **Effective Market(s):** New York. **Units of Measure:** Dollars per lb. **Type of Price:** spot. **Time Period Covered:** latest week.

POTASSIUM BROMATE: GRANULAR, POWDERED

Source: *Chemical Marketing Reporter.* **Price Frequency:** weekly. **Effective Market(s):** New York. **Units of Measure:** Dollars per lb. **Type of Price:** spot. **Time Period Covered:** latest week.

POTASSIUM BROMIDE: GRANULAR, NF

Source: *Chemical Marketing Reporter.* **Price Frequency:** weekly. **Effective Market(s):** New York. **Units of Measure:** Dollars per lb. **Type of Price:** spot. **Time Period Covered:** latest week.

POTASSIUM CARBONATE

Source: *Journal of Commerce and Commercial.* **Price Frequency:** weekly in Thursday issue. **Units of Measure:** Dollars per 100 lbs. **Type of Price:** spot. **Time Period Covered:** latest week.

POTASSIUM CARBONATE: ANHYDROUS

Source: *Chemical Marketing Reporter.* **Price Frequency:** weekly. **Effective Market(s):** New York. **Units of Measure:** Dollars per 100 lbs. **Type of Price:** spot. **Time Period Covered:** latest week.

POTASSIUM CARBONATE: GRANULAR, PURIFIED

Source: *Chemical Marketing Reporter.* **Price Frequency:** weekly. **Effective Market(s):** New York. **Units of Measure:** Dollars per lb. **Type of Price:** spot. **Time Period Covered:** latest week.

POTASSIUM CARBONATE: LIQUID

Source: *Chemical Marketing Reporter.* **Price Frequency:** weekly. **Effective Market(s):** New York. **Units of Measure:** Dollars per 100 lbs. **Type of Price:** spot. **Time Period Covered:** latest week.

POTASSIUM CHLORATE: CRYSTALLINE

Source: *Chemical Marketing Reporter.* **Price Frequency:** weekly. **Effective Market(s):** New York. **Units of Measure:** Dollars per lb. **Type of Price:** spot. **Time Period Covered:** latest week.

POTASSIUM CHLORATE: POWDERED

Source: *Chemical Marketing Reporter.* **Price Frequency:** weekly. **Effective Market(s):** New York. **Units of Measure:** Dollars per lb. **Type of Price:** spot. **Time Period Covered:** latest week.

POTASSIUM CHLORATE: PURIFIED, GRANULAR

Source: *Chemical Marketing Reporter.* **Price Frequency:** weekly. **Effective Market(s):** New York. **Units of Measure:** Dollars per lb. **Type of Price:** spot. **Time Period Covered:** latest week.

POTASSIUM CHLORIDE: AGRICULTURAL

see Potassium Muriate.

POTASSIUM CHLORIDE: CANADIAN

Source: *Commodity Trade and Price Trends.* **Price Frequency:** annually. **Effective Market(s):** Vancouver (Canada). **Units of Measure:** Dollars per metric ton, 1980 constant dollars per metric ton. **Time Period Covered:** latest 32 years.

POTASSIUM CHLORIDE: CHEMICAL GRADE

Source: *Chemical Marketing Reporter.* **Price Frequency:** weekly. **Effective Market(s):** New York. **Units of Measure:** Dollars per ton. **Type of Price:** spot. **Time Period Covered:** latest week.

POTASSIUM CHLORIDE: CRYSTALLINE, USP

Source: *Chemical Marketing Reporter.* **Price Frequency:** weekly. **Effective Market(s):** New York. **Units of Measure:** Dollars per lb. **Type of Price:** spot. **Time Period Covered:** latest week.

POTASSIUM CHLORIDE: GRANULAR, USP

Source: *Chemical Marketing Reporter.* **Price Frequency:** weekly. **Effective Market(s):** New York. **Units of Measure:** Dollars per lb. **Type of Price:** spot. **Time Period Covered:** latest week.

POTASSIUM CHLORIDE: POWDERED, USP

Source: *Chemical Marketing Reporter.* **Price Frequency:** weekly. **Effective Market(s):** New York. **Units of Measure:** Dollars per lb. **Type of Price:** spot. **Time Period Covered:** latest week.

POTASSIUM CHROMATE: PURIFIED, CRYSTALLINE

Source: *Chemical Marketing Reporter.* **Price Frequency:** weekly. **Effective Market(s):** New York. **Units of Measure:** Dollars per lb. **Type of Price:** spot. **Time Period Covered:** latest week.

POTASSIUM CITRATE: GRANULAR, USP

Source: *Chemical Marketing Reporter.* **Price Frequency:** weekly. **Effective Market(s):** East. **Units of Measure:** Dollars per lb. **Type of Price:** spot. **Time Period Covered:** latest week.

Source: *Journal of Commerce and Commercial.* **Price Frequency:** weekly in Friday issue. **Units of Measure:** Dollars per lb. **Type of Price:** spot. **Time Period Covered:** latest week.

POTASSIUM CYANIDE

Source: *Chemical Marketing Reporter.* **Price Frequency:** weekly. **Effective Market(s):** New York. **Units of Measure:** Dollars per lb. **Type of Price:** spot. **Time Period Covered:** latest week.

Source: *Journal of Commerce and Commercial.* **Price Frequency:** weekly in Thursday issue. **Units of Measure:** Dollars per lb. **Type of Price:** spot. **Time Period Covered:** latest week.

POTASSIUM DICHROMATE

see Potassium Bichromate.

POTASSIUM FLUOBORATE: TECHNICAL

Source: *Chemical Marketing Reporter.* **Price Frequency:** weekly. **Effective Market(s):** New York. **Units of Measure:** Dollars per lb. **Type of Price:** spot. **Time Period Covered:** latest week.

POTASSIUM FLUORIDE: ANHYDROUS

Source: *Chemical Marketing Reporter.* **Price Frequency:** weekly. **Effective Market(s):** New York. **Units of Measure:** Dollars per lb. **Type of Price:** spot. **Time Period Covered:** latest week.

POTASSIUM GLUCONATE

Source: *Chemical Marketing Reporter.* **Price Frequency:** weekly. **Effective Market(s):** New York, West of Denver. **Units of Measure:** Dollars per lb. **Type of Price:** spot. **Time Period Covered:** latest week.

POTASSIUM GLUCONATE: USP

Source: *Journal of Commerce and Commercial.* **Price Frequency:** weekly in Friday issue. **Units of Measure:** Dollars per lb. **Type of Price:** spot. **Time Period Covered:** latest week.

POTASSIUM GUAIACOLSULFONATE

Source: *Chemical Marketing Reporter.* **Price Frequency:** weekly. **Effective Market(s):** New York. **Units of Measure:** Dollars per kilo. **Type of Price:** spot. **Time Period Covered:** latest week.

POTASSIUM HYDROXIDE: PELLETS, USP

Source: *Chemical Marketing Reporter.* **Price Frequency:** weekly. **Effective Market(s):** New York. **Units of Measure:** Dollars per lb. **Type of Price:** spot. **Time Period Covered:** latest week.

Source: *Journal of Commerce and Commercial.* **Price Frequency:** weekly in Friday issue. **Units of Measure:** Dollars per lb. **Type of Price:** spot. **Time Period Covered:** latest week.

POTASSIUM HYDROXIDE: TECHNICAL

see Potash: Caustic.

POTASSIUM IODIDE

Source: *Journal of Commerce and Commercial.* **Price Frequency:** weekly in Friday issue. **Units of Measure:** Dollars per lb. **Type of Price:** spot. **Time Period Covered:** latest week.

POTASSIUM IODIDE: ACS GRADE

Source: *Chemical Marketing Reporter.* **Price Frequency:** weekly. **Effective Market(s):** New York. **Units of Measure:** Dollars per lb. **Type of Price:** spot. **Time Period Covered:** latest week.

POTASSIUM IODIDE: USP

Source: *Chemical Marketing Reporter.* **Price Frequency:** weekly. **Effective Market(s):** New York. **Units of Measure:** Dollars per lb. **Type of Price:** spot. **Time Period Covered:** latest week.

POTASSIUM MAGNESIUM SULFATE

Source: *Chemical Marketing Reporter.* **Price Frequency:** weekly. **Effective Market(s):** New York. **Units of Measure:** Dollars per ton. **Type of Price:** spot. **Time Period Covered:** latest week.

POTASSIUM METABISULFATE: GRANULAR

Source: *Chemical Marketing Reporter.* **Price Frequency:** weekly. **Effective Market(s):** New York. **Units of Measure:** Dollars per lb. **Type of Price:** spot. **Time Period Covered:** latest week.

POTASSIUM MURIATE

Source: *Chemical Marketing Reporter.* **Price Frequency:** weekly. **Effective Market(s):** Saskatchewan (Canada). **Units of Measure:** Dollars per ton. **Type of Price:** spot. **Time Period Covered:** latest week.

POTASSIUM MURIATE: COARSE

Source: *Chemical Marketing Reporter.* **Price Frequency:** weekly. **Effective Market(s):** Saskatchewan (Canada). **Units of Measure:** Dollars per ton. **Type of Price:** spot. **Time Period Covered:** latest week.

POTASSIUM MURIATE: GRANULAR

Source: *Chemical Marketing Reporter.* **Price Frequency:** weekly. **Effective Market(s):** Saskatchewan (Canada). **Units of Measure:** Dollars per ton. **Type of Price:** spot. **Time Period Covered:** latest week.

POTASSIUM NITRATE

Source: *Journal of Commerce and Commercial.* **Price Frequency:** weekly in Thursday issue. **Units of Measure:** Dollars per 100 lbs. **Type of Price:** spot. **Time Period Covered:** latest week.

POTASSIUM NITRATE: FERTILIZER GRADE

Source: *Chemical Marketing Reporter.* **Price Frequency:** weekly. **Effective Market(s):** Southeast. **Units of Measure:** Dollars per ton. **Type of Price:** spot. **Time Period Covered:** latest week.

POTASSIUM NITRATE: PRILLED

Source: *Chemical Marketing Reporter.* **Price Frequency:** weekly. **Effective Market(s):** Southeast. **Units of Measure:** Dollars per ton. **Type of Price:** spot. **Time Period Covered:** latest week.

POTASSIUM NITRATE: TECHNICAL GRADE, GRANULAR

Source: *Chemical Marketing Reporter.* **Price Frequency:** weekly. **Effective Market(s):** Southeast. **Units of Measure:** Dollars per ton. **Type of Price:** spot. **Time Period Covered:** latest week.

POTASSIUM OXALATE: NEUTRAL, TECHNICAL, FINE GRANULAR, POWDERED

Source: *Chemical Marketing Reporter.* **Price Frequency:** weekly. **Effective Market(s):** New York. **Units of Measure:** Dollars per lb. **Type of Price:** spot. **Time Period Covered:** latest week.

POTASSIUM PENTABORATE: GRANULAR

Source: *Chemical Marketing Reporter.* **Price Frequency:** weekly. **Effective Market(s):** New York. **Units of Measure:** Dollars per lb. **Type of Price:** spot. **Time Period Covered:** latest week.

POTASSIUM PENTABORATE: POWDER

Source: *Chemical Marketing Reporter.* **Price Frequency:** weekly. **Effective Market(s):** New York. **Units of Measure:** Dollars per lb. **Type of Price:** spot. **Time Period Covered:** latest week.

POTASSIUM PERCHLORATE

Source: *Chemical Marketing Reporter.* **Price Frequency:** weekly. **Effective Market(s):** New York. **Units of Measure:** Dollars per lb. **Type of Price:** spot. **Time Period Covered:** latest week.

POTASSIUM PERMANGANATE

Source: *Journal of Commerce and Commercial.* **Price Frequency:** weekly in Thursday issue. **Units of Measure:** Dollars per lb. **Type of Price:** spot. **Time Period Covered:** latest week.

POTASSIUM PERMANGANATE: FREE FLOWING

Source: *Chemical Marketing Reporter.* **Price Frequency:** weekly. **Effective Market(s):** New York. **Units of Measure:** Dollars per lb. **Type of Price:** spot. **Time Period Covered:** latest week.

POTASSIUM PERMANGANATE: USP

Source: *Chemical Marketing Reporter.* **Price Frequency:** weekly. **Effective Market(s):** New York. **Units of Measure:** Dollars per lb. **Type of Price:** spot. **Time Period Covered:** latest week.

POTASSIUM PERSULFATE

Source: *Chemical Marketing Reporter.* **Price Frequency:** weekly. **Effective Market(s):** New York. **Units of Measure:** Dollars per 100 lbs. **Type of Price:** spot. **Time Period Covered:** latest week.

POTASSIUM PYROPHOSPHATE TETRABASIC

Source: *Chemical Marketing Reporter.* **Price Frequency:** weekly. **Effective Market(s):** New York. **Units of Measure:** Dollars per 100 lbs. **Type of Price:** spot. **Time Period Covered:** latest week.

POTASSIUM PYROPHOSPHATE TETRABASIC: LIQUID

Source: *Chemical Marketing Reporter.* **Price Frequency:** weekly. **Effective Market(s):** New York. **Units of Measure:** Dollars per 100 lbs. **Type of Price:** spot. **Time Period Covered:** latest week.

POTASSIUM SALICYLATE: GRANULAR, USP

Source: *Chemical Marketing Reporter.* **Price Frequency:** weekly. **Effective Market(s):** New York. **Units of Measure:** Dollars per lb. **Type of Price:** spot. **Time Period Covered:** latest week.

POTASSIUM SALICYLATE: POWDERED, USP

Source: *Chemical Marketing Reporter.* **Price Frequency:** weekly. **Effective Market(s):** New York. **Units of Measure:** Dollars per lb. **Type of Price:** spot. **Time Period Covered:** latest week.

POTASSIUM SILICATE: ELECTRONICS GRADE

Source: *Chemical Marketing Reporter.* **Price Frequency:** weekly. **Effective Market(s):** New York. **Units of Measure:** Dollars per 100 lbs. **Type of Price:** spot. **Time Period Covered:** latest wee.

POTASSIUM SILICATE: SOLUTION

Source: *Chemical Marketing Reporter.* **Price Frequency:** weekly. **Effective Market(s):** New York. **Units of Measure:** Dollars per 100 lbs. **Type of Price:** spot. **Time Period Covered:** latest week.

POTASSIUM SILICOFLUORIDE

Source: *Chemical Marketing Reporter.* **Price Frequency:** weekly. **Effective Market(s):** New York. **Units of Measure:** Dollars per lb. **Type of Price:** spot. **Time Period Covered:** latest week.

POTASSIUM SODIUM TARTRATE: GRANULAR OR POWDERED, NF

Source: *Chemical Marketing Reporter.* **Price Frequency:** weekly. **Effective Market(s):** New York. **Units of Measure:** Dollars per lb. **Type of Price:** spot. **Time Period Covered:** latest week.

POTASSIUM SORBATE

Source: *Chemical Marketing Reporter.* **Price Frequency:** weekly. **Effective Market(s):** New York. **Units of Measure:** Dollars per lb. **Type of Price:** spot. **Time Period Covered:** latest week.

POTASSIUM STANNATE

Source: *Chemical Marketing Reporter.* **Price Frequency:** weekly. **Effective Market(s):** New York. **Units of Measure:** Dollars per lb. **Type of Price:** spot. **Time Period Covered:** latest week.

Source: *Journal of Commerce and Commercial.* **Price Frequency:** weekly in Thursday issue. **Units of Measure:** Dollars per lb. **Type of Price:** spot. **Time Period Covered:** latest week.

POTASSIUM SULFATE: AGRICULTURAL GRADE

Source: *Chemical Marketing Reporter.* **Price Frequency:** weekly. **Effective Market(s):** New York. **Units of Measure:** Dollars per ton. **Type of Price:** spot. **Time Period Covered:** latest week.

POTASSIUM SULFATE: GRANULAR, PURIFIED

Source: *Chemical Marketing Reporter.* **Price Frequency:** weekly. **Effective Market(s):** New York. **Units of Measure:** Dollars per lb. **Type of Price:** spot. **Time Period Covered:** latest week.

POTASSIUM TETRABORATE: GRANULAR

Source: *Chemical Marketing Reporter.* **Price Frequency:** weekly. **Effective Market(s):** New York. **Units of Measure:** Dollars per lb. **Type of Price:** spot. **Time Period Covered:** latest week.

POTASSIUM TETRABORATE: POWDER

Source: *Chemical Marketing Reporter.* **Price Frequency:** weekly. **Effective Market(s):** New York. **Units of Measure:** Dollars per lb. **Type of Price:** spot. **Time Period Covered:** latest week.

POTASSIUM THIOCYANATE: CRYSTALLINE, USP

Source: *Chemical Marketing Reporter.* **Price Frequency:** weekly. **Effective Market(s):** New York. **Units of Measure:** Dollars per lb. **Type of Price:** spot. **Time Period Covered:** latest week.

POTASSIUM THIOCYANATE: TECHNICAL GRADE, CRYSTALLINE

Source: *Chemical Marketing Reporter.* **Price Frequency:** weekly. **Effective Market(s):** New York. **Units of Measure:** Dollars per lb. **Type of Price:** spot. **Time Period Covered:** latest week.

POTASSIUM TITANATE

Source: *Chemical Marketing Reporter.* **Price Frequency:** weekly. **Effective Market(s):** New York. **Units of Measure:** Dollars per lb. **Type of Price:** spot. **Time Period Covered:** latest week.

POTASSIUM TITANIUM FLUORIDE: TECHNICAL

Source: *Chemical Marketing Reporter.* **Price Frequency:** weekly. **Effective Market(s):** New York. **Units of Measure:** Dollars per lb. **Type of Price:** spot. **Time Period Covered:** latest week.

POTASSIUM ZIRCONIUM FLUORIDE: TECHNICAL GRADE

Source: *Chemical Marketing Reporter.* **Price Frequency:** weekly. **Effective Market(s):** New York. **Units of Measure:** Dollars per lb. **Type of Price:** spot. **Time Period Covered:** latest week.

POTATOES

Source: *Agricultural Outlook.* **Price Frequency:** monthly, annually. **Effective Market(s):** United States. **Units of Measure:** Dollars per 100 lbs. **Type of Price:** received by farmer. **Time Period Covered:** monthly latest 6 months, annually latest 3 years.

Source: *Agricultural Prices.* **Price Frequency:** monthly. **Effective Market(s):** United States. **Units of Measure:** Dollars per 100 lbs. **Type of Price:** received by farmer. **Time Period Covered:** latest 2 months, year ago.

Source: *Agricultural Prices.* **Price Frequency:** monthly, seasonally. **Effective Market(s):** 20 domestic markets, United States. **Units of Measure:** Dollars per 100 lbs. **Type of Price:** received by farmer. **Time Period Covered:** latest 2 months.

Source: *Agricultural Prices Annual Summary.* **Price Frequency:** annually. **Effective Market(s):** 38 domestic markets, United States. **Units of Measure:** Dollars per 100 lbs. **Type of Price:** average received by farmer. **Time Period Covered:** latest 2 years, for US latest 6 years.

Source: *Commodity Year Book.* **Price Frequency:** monthly, annually. **Effective Market(s):** United States. **Units of Measure:** Dollars per 100 lbs. **Type of Price:** price received by farmers. **Time Period Covered:** latest 5 years.

Source: *Commodity Year Book.* **Price Frequency:** annually. **Effective Market(s):** United States. **Units of Measure:** Dollars per 100 lbs. **Type of Price:** farm price. **Time Period Covered:** latest 7 years.

Source: *FAO Quarterly Bulletin of Statistics.* **Price Frequency:** monthly, annually. **Effective Market(s):** United States. **Units of Measure:** Dollars per 100 lbs., dollars per metric ton. **Type of Price:** producer. **Time Period Covered:** latest 3 years.

Source: *Farmers Weekly.* **Price Frequency:** weekly. **Effective Market(s):** Great Britain. **Units of Measure:** British pounds per tonne. **Type of Price:** producer. **Time Period Covered:** latest week, week ago, year ago.

Source: *Farmers Weekly.* **Price Frequency:** weekly, seasonally. **Effective Market(s):** 11 British markets. **Units of Measure:** British pounds per tonne. **Type of Price:** new crop. **Time Period Covered:** latest week.

Source: *New Zealand Farmer.* **Price Frequency:** weekly, seasonally. **Effective Market(s):** New Zealand. **Units of Measure:** New Zealand dollars per unit. **Time Period Covered:** latest week.

Source: *Potatoes.* **Price Frequency:** annually. **Effective Market(s):** 37 domestic markets, United States. **Units of Measure:** Dollars per 100 lbs. **Type of Price:** received by farmer. **Time Period Covered:** latest 2 years.

Source: *Statistical Bulletin of the South Pacific: Retail Price Indexes.* **Price Frequency:** annually. **Effective Market(s):** 18 South Pacific markets. **Units of Measure:** Australian dollars per. **Type of Price:** retail. **Time Period Covered:** latest year.

Source: *Washington Farmer-Stockman.* **Price Frequency:** monthly. **Effective Market(s):** Washington. **Units of Measure:** Dollars per 100 lbs. **Type of Price:** average received by farmer. **Time Period Covered:** latest month, month ago, year ago.

POTATOES: ALASKAN

Source: *Potatoes.* **Price Frequency:** annually. **Effective Market(s):** Alaska. **Units of Measure:** Dollars per 100 lbs. **Type of Price:** received by farmer. **Time Period Covered:** latest 3 years.

POTATOES: ALL USES

Source: *Vegetable Specialties Situation and Outlook Report.* **Price Frequency:** monthly, annually. **Effective Market(s):** United States. **Units of Measure:** Dollars per 100 lbs. **Type of Price:** received by grower. **Time Period Covered:** latest 4 years.

POTATOES: ALL VARIETIES

Source: *Farmers Weekly.* **Price Frequency:** weekly, seasonally. **Effective Market(s):** Great Britain. **Units of Measure:** British pounds per tonne. **Type of Price:** producer. **Time Period Covered:** latest week, week ago, 2 weeks ago.

POTATOES: BURBANK RUSSET

Source: *California Farmer.* **Price Frequency:** semimonthly, seasonally. **Effective Market(s):** Klamath Basin (OR). **Units of Measure:** Dollars per 10 lb. bag. **Time Period Covered:** latest week, year ago.

POTATOES: BURBANK, FRESH

Source: *HRI-Buyers Guide.* **Price Frequency:** weekly. **Effective Market(s):** Northeastern area. **Units of Measure:** Dollars per crate. **Type of Price:** prices paid by dining places & institutions. **Time Period Covered:** latest week.

POTATOES: CARA

Source: *Scottish Farmer.* **Price Frequency:** weekly, seasonally. **Effective Market(s):** 7 Scottish markets. **Units of Measure:** British pounds per tonne. **Type of Price:** producer. **Time Period Covered:** latest week.

POTATOES: CENTENNIAL

Source: *California Farmer.* **Price Frequency:** semimonthly, seasonally. **Effective Market(s):** Kern (CA). **Units of Measure:** Dollars per 100 lbs. **Time Period Covered:** latest week, year ago.

Source: *Fresh Fruit and Vegetable Prices.* **Price Frequency:** monthly, seasonally. **Effective Market(s):** Kern District (CA). **Units of Measure:** Dollars per 50 lb. sack. **Type of Price:** average price at shipping point. **Time Period Covered:** latest year.

POTATOES: DANISH

Source: *FAO Quarterly Bulletin of Statistics.* **Price Frequency:** monthly, annually. **Effective Market(s):** Denmark. **Units of Measure:** Danish kroner per 100 kilograms, dollars per metric ton. **Type of Price:** producer. **Time Period Covered:** latest 3 years.

POTATOES: DESIREE

Source: *New Zealand Farmer.* **Price Frequency:** weekly, seasonally. **Effective Market(s):** New Zealand. **Units of Measure:** New Zealand dollars per unit. **Time Period Covered:** latest week.

POTATOES: DESIREE OR SIMILAR

Source: *Farmers Weekly.* **Price Frequency:** weekly, seasonally. **Effective Market(s):** Eastern Counties (Great Britain), Midland Counties (Great Britain), Northern Counties (Great Britain), Scotland. **Units of Measure:** British pounds per tonne. **Type of Price:** producer. **Time Period Covered:** latest week.

POTATOES: DUKE OF YORK

Source: *Scottish Farmer.* **Price Frequency:** weekly, seasonally. **Effective Market(s):** 7 Scottish markets. **Units of Measure:** British pounds per tonne. **Type of Price:** producer. **Time Period Covered:** latest week.

POTATOES: ESTIMA

Source: *Scottish Farmer.* **Price Frequency:** weekly, seasonally. **Effective Market(s):** 7 Scottish markets. **Units of Measure:** British pounds per tonne. **Type of Price:** producer. **Time Period Covered:** latest week.

POTATOES: FALL

Source: *Potatoes.* **Price Frequency:** annually. **Effective Market(s):** 23 domestic markets, United States. **Units of Measure:** Dollars per 100 lbs. **Type of Price:** received by farmer. **Time Period Covered:** latest 2 years.

POTATOES: FRENCH FRIED, FROZEN, IDAHO

Source: *HRI-Buyers Guide.* **Price Frequency:** weekly. **Effective Market(s):** Northeastern area. **Units of Measure:** cents per lb. **Type of Price:** prices paid by dining places & institutions. **Time Period Covered:** latest week.

POTATOES: FRESH

Source: *Agricultural Prices Annual Summary.* **Price Frequency:** annually. **Effective Market(s):** United States. **Units of Measure:** Dollars per 100 lbs. **Type of Price:** average received by farmer. **Time Period Covered:** latest 5 years.

POTATOES: FUTURES

Source: *Farmers Weekly.* **Price Frequency:** weekly. **Effective Market(s):** Baltic Exchange. **Units of Measure:** British pounds per tonne. **Type of Price:** futures. **Time Period Covered:** latest week.

Source: *Financial Times.* **Price Frequency:** daily. **Effective Market(s):** London. **Units of Measure:** British pounds per tonne. **Type of Price:** futures. **Time Period Covered:** latest day.

Source: *The Times.* **Price Frequency:** daily. **Effective Market(s):** London. **Units of Measure:** British pounds per tonne. **Type of Price:** futures. **Time Period Covered:** latest day.

POTATOES: FUTURES, MAY

Source: *Commodity Year Book.* **Price Frequency:** monthly. **Effective Market(s):** New York. **Units of Measure:** cents per lb. **Type of Price:** futures. **Time Period Covered:** latest 6 years.

POTATOES: IDAHO

Source: *Oregon Farmer-Stockman.* **Price Frequency:** monthly, seasonally. **Units of Measure:** Dollars per 100 lbs. **Time Period Covered:** latest month.

POTATOES: KERR'S PINK

Source: *Scottish Farmer.* **Price Frequency:** weekly, seasonally. **Effective Market(s):** 7 Scottish markets. **Units of Measure:** British pounds per tonne. **Type of Price:** producer. **Time Period Covered:** latest week.

POTATOES: KING EDWARD, CARA OR DESIREE

Source: *Farmers Weekly.* **Price Frequency:** weekly, seasonally. **Effective Market(s):** Birmingham (England), Cardiff (Wales), Leeds (England), London, Manchester (England). **Units of Measure:** British pence per 25 kilogram sack. **Type of Price:** wholesale. **Time Period Covered:** latest week.

POTATOES: KING EDWARD OR CARA

Source: *Farmers Weekly.* **Price Frequency:** weekly, seasonally. **Effective Market(s):** Eastern Counties (Great Britain), Midland Counties (Great Britain), Northern Counties (Great Britain), Scotland. **Units of Measure:** British pounds per tonne. **Type of Price:** producer. **Time Period Covered:** latest week.

POTATOES: LONG WHITE

Source: *California Farmer.* **Price Frequency:** semimonthly, seasonally. **Effective Market(s):** Stockton Delta (CA). **Units of Measure:** Dollars per 50 lb. carton. **Time Period Covered:** latest week, month ago, year ago.

Source: *California Farmer.* **Price Frequency:** semimonthly, seasonally. **Effective Market(s):** Kern (CA). **Units of Measure:** Dollars per 100 lbs. **Time Period Covered:** latest week, month ago, year ago.

Source: *Fresh Fruit and Vegetable Prices.* **Price Frequency:** monthly, seasonally. **Effective Market(s):** Kern District (CA). **Units of Measure:** Dollars per 100 lb. sack. **Type of Price:** average price at shipping point. **Time Period Covered:** latest year.

Source: *Lancaster Farmer.* **Price Frequency:** weekly, seasonally. **Effective Market(s):** Pennsylvania. **Units of Measure:** Dollars per sack. **Type of Price:** market. **Time Period Covered:** latest week.

Source: *The Packer.* **Price Frequency:** weekly, seasonally. **Effective Market(s):** varies. **Units of Measure:** Dollars per carton/sack. **Type of Price:** received by farmer. **Time Period Covered:** latest week.

POTATOES: LONG WHITE, CALIFORNIA

Source: *Fresh Fruit and Vegetable Prices.* **Price Frequency:** monthly, seasonally. **Effective Market(s):** Chicago, New York City. **Units of Measure:** Dollars per carton/lb. **Type of Price:** average wholesale price. **Time Period Covered:** latest year.

POTATOES: MARIS PEER

Source: *Scottish Farmer.* **Price Frequency:** weekly, seasonally. **Effective Market(s):** 7 Scottish markets. **Units of Measure:** British pounds per tonne. **Type of Price:** producer. **Time Period Covered:** latest week.

POTATOES: MARIS PIPER

Source: *Farmers Weekly.* **Price Frequency:** weekly, seasonally. **Effective Market(s):** Eastern Counties (Great Britain), Midland Counties (Great Britain), Northern Counties (Great Britain), Scotland. **Units of Measure:** British pounds per tonne. **Type of Price:** producer. **Time Period Covered:** latest week.

Source: *Scottish Farmer.* **Price Frequency:** weekly, seasonally. **Effective Market(s):** 7 Scottish markets. **Units of Measure:** British pounds per tonne. **Type of Price:** producer. **Time Period Covered:** latest week.

POTATOES: MARIS PIPER, PENTLAND SQUIRE, OR WILJA

Source: *Farmers Weekly.* **Price Frequency:** weekly, seasonally. **Effective Market(s):** Birmingham (England), Cardiff (Wales), Leeds (England), London, Manchester (England). **Units of Measure:** British pence per 25 kilogram sack. **Type of Price:** wholesale. **Time Period Covered:** latest week.

POTATOES: NEW

Source: *New Zealand Farmer.* **Price Frequency:** weekly, seasonally. **Effective Market(s):** New Zealand. **Units of Measure:** New Zealand dollars per unit. **Time Period Covered:** latest week.

POTATOES: NO. 1, RUSSET

Source: *Oregon Farmer-Stockman.* **Price Frequency:** monthly, seasonally. **Units of Measure:** Dollars per 100 lbs. **Time Period Covered:** latest month.

POTATOES: NORGOLD

Source: *Fresh Fruit and Vegetable Prices.* **Price Frequency:** monthly, seasonally. **Effective Market(s):** Northern Colorado, High Plains (TX). **Units of Measure:** Dollars per 50 lb. carton. **Type of Price:** average price at shipping price. **Time Period Covered:** latest year.

Source: *Lancaster Farmer.* **Price Frequency:** weekly, seasonally. **Effective Market(s):** Pennsylvania. **Units of Measure:** Dollars per sack. **Type of Price:** market. **Time Period Covered:** latest week.

Source: *The Packer.* **Price Frequency:** weekly, seasonally. **Effective Market(s):** varies. **Units of Measure:** Dollars per carton/sack. **Type of Price:** received by farmer. **Time Period Covered:** latest week.

POTATOES: NORGOLD AND RUSSET

Source: *Fresh Fruit and Vegetable Prices.* **Price Frequency:** monthly, seasonally. **Effective Market(s):** Klamath Basin (OR). **Units of Measure:** Dollars per 50 lb. carton. **Type of Price:** average price at shipping point. **Time Period Covered:** latest year.

POTATOES: NORGOLD, FRESH

Source: *HRI-Buyers Guide.* **Price Frequency:** weekly. **Effective Market(s):** Northeastern area. **Units of Measure:** Dollars per carton. **Type of Price:** prices paid by dining places & institutions. **Time Period Covered:** latest week.

POTATOES: NORGOLD RUSSET

Source: *California Farmer.* **Price Frequency:** semimonthly, seasonally. **Effective Market(s):** Klamath Basin (OR). **Units of Measure:** Dollars per 10 lb. bag. **Time Period Covered:** latest week, month ago, year ago.

Source: *The Packer.* **Price Frequency:** weekly, seasonally. **Effective Market(s):** varies. **Units of Measure:** Dollars per carton/sack. **Type of Price:** received by farmer. **Time Period Covered:** latest week.

POTATOES: NORKOTAH

Source: *California Farmer.* **Price Frequency:** semimonthly, seasonally. **Effective Market(s):** Klamath Basin (OR). **Units of Measure:** Dollars per 5-10 lb. sack. **Time Period Covered:** latest week, year ago.

Source: *Lancaster Farmer.* **Price Frequency:** weekly, seasonally. **Effective Market(s):** Pennsylvania. **Units of Measure:** Dollars per sack. **Type of Price:** market. **Time Period Covered:** latest week.

Source: *The Packer.* **Price Frequency:** weekly, seasonally. **Effective Market(s):** varies. **Units of Measure:** Dollars per carton/sack. **Type of Price:** received by farmer. **Time Period Covered:** latest week.

POTATOES: NORKOTAH RUSSET

Source: *The Packer.* **Price Frequency:** weekly, seasonally. **Effective Market(s):** varies. **Units of Measure:** Dollars per carton/sack. **Type of Price:** received by farmer. **Time Period Covered:** latest week.

POTATOES: PENTLAND SQUIRE

Source: *Scottish Farmer.* **Price Frequency:** weekly, seasonally. **Effective Market(s):** 7 Scottish markets. **Units of Measure:** British pounds per tonne. **Type of Price:** producer. **Time Period Covered:** latest week.

POTATOES: PENTLAND SQUIRE, WILJA OR SIMILAR VARIETIES

Source: *Farmers Weekly.* **Price Frequency:** weekly, seasonally. **Effective Market(s):** Eastern Counties (Great Britain), Midland Counties (Great Britain), Northern Counties (Great Britain), Scotland. **Units of Measure:** British pounds per tonne. **Type of Price:** producer. **Time Period Covered:** latest week.

POTATOES: PROCESSED

Source: *The Packer.* **Price Frequency:** weekly, seasonally. **Effective Market(s):** varies. **Units of Measure:** Dollars per 100 lbs. **Type of Price:** received by farmer. **Time Period Covered:** latest week.

POTATOES: PROCESSING

Source: *Agricultural Prices Annual Summary.* **Price Frequency:** annually. **Effective Market(s):** United States. **Units of Measure:** Dollars per 100 lbs. **Type of Price:** average received by farmer. **Time Period Covered:** latest 5 years.

Source: *Vegetable Specialties Situation and Outlook Report.* **Price Frequency:** monthly, annually. **Effective Market(s):** United States. **Units of Measure:** Dollars per 100 lbs. **Type of Price:** received by grower. **Time Period Covered:** latest 4 years.

POTATOES: RED KING

Source: *New Zealand Farmer.* **Price Frequency:** weekly, seasonally. **Effective Market(s):** New Zealand. **Units of Measure:** New Zealand dollars per unit. **Time Period Covered:** latest week.

POTATOES: RED MCCLURE

Source: *Fresh Fruit and Vegetable Prices.* **Price Frequency:** monthly, seasonally. **Effective Market(s):** San Luis Valley (CO). **Units of Measure:** Dollars per 100 lb. sack. **Type of Price:** average price at shipping point. **Time Period Covered:** latest year.

POTATOES: ROUND RED

Source: *California Farmer.* **Price Frequency:** semimonthly, seasonally. **Effective Market(s):** Kern (CA). **Units of Measure:** Dollars per 100 lbs. **Time Period Covered:** latest week, month ago, year ago.

Source: *California Farmer.* **Price Frequency:** semimonthly, seasonally. **Effective Market(s):** Stockton Delta (CA). **Units of Measure:** Dollars per 50 lb. carton. **Time Period Covered:** latest week, month ago, year ago.

Source: *Fresh Fruit and Vegetable Prices.* **Price Frequency:** monthly, seasonally. **Effective Market(s):** 7 domestic markets. **Units of Measure:** Dollars per 50 or 100 lb. sack. **Type of Price:** average price at shipping point. **Time Period Covered:** latest year.

Source: *Lancaster Farmer.* **Price Frequency:** weekly, seasonally. **Effective Market(s):** Pennsylvania. **Units of Measure:** Dollars per sack. **Type of Price:** market. **Time Period Covered:** latest week.

Source: *The Packer.* **Price Frequency:** weekly, seasonally. **Effective Market(s):** varies. **Units of Measure:** Dollars per carton/sack. **Type of Price:** received by farmer. **Time Period Covered:** latest week.

POTATOES: ROUND RED, CALIFORNIA

Source: *Fresh Fruit and Vegetable Prices.* **Price Frequency:** monthly, seasonally. **Effective Market(s):** New York City. **Units of Measure:** Dollars per sack. **Type of Price:** average wholesale price. **Time Period Covered:** latest year.

POTATOES: ROUND RED, FLORIDA

Source: *Fresh Fruit and Vegetable Prices.* **Price Frequency:** monthly, seasonally. **Effective Market(s):** Chicago, New York City. **Units of Measure:** Dollars per sack. **Type of Price:** average wholesale price. **Time Period Covered:** latest year.

POTATOES: ROUND RED, FRESH

Source: *HRI-Buyers Guide.* **Price Frequency:** weekly. **Effective Market(s):** Northeastern area. **Units of Measure:** Dollars per carton. **Type of Price:** prices paid by dining places & institutions. **Time Period Covered:** latest week.

POTATOES: ROUND RED, MINNESOTA/ NORTH DAKOTA

Source: *Fresh Fruit and Vegetable Prices.* **Price Frequency:** monthly, seasonally. **Effective Market(s):** Chicago, New York City. **Units of Measure:** Dollars per sack. **Type of Price:** average wholesale price. **Time Period Covered:** latest year.

POTATOES: ROUND WHITE

Source: *Fresh Fruit and Vegetable Prices.* **Price Frequency:** monthly, seasonally. **Effective Market(s):** 10 domestic markets. **Units of Measure:** Dollars per sack. **Type of Price:** average price at shipping point. **Time Period Covered:** latest year.

Source: *Lancaster Farmer.* **Price Frequency:** weekly, seasonally. **Effective Market(s):** Pennsylvania. **Units of Measure:** Dollars per sack. **Type of Price:** market. **Time Period Covered:** latest week.

Source: *The Packer.* **Price Frequency:** weekly, seasonally. **Effective Market(s):** varies. **Units of Measure:** Dollars per carton/sack. **Type of Price:** received by farmer. **Time Period Covered:** latest week.

POTATOES: ROUND WHITE, FRESH

Source: *HRI-Buyers Guide.* **Price Frequency:** weekly. **Effective Market(s):** Northeastern area. **Units of Measure:** Dollars per carton. **Type of Price:** prices paid by dining places & institutions. **Time Period Covered:** latest week.

POTATOES: ROUND WHITE, LONG ISLAND

Source: *Fresh Fruit and Vegetable Prices.* **Price Frequency:** monthly, seasonally. **Effective Market(s):** New York City. **Units of Measure:** Dollars per sack. **Type of Price:** average wholesale price. **Time Period Covered:** latest year.

POTATOES: ROUND WHITE, MAINE

Source: *Fresh Fruit and Vegetable Prices.* **Price Frequency:** monthly, seasonally. **Effective Market(s):** New York City. **Units of Measure:** Dollars per sack. **Type of Price:** average wholesale price. **Time Period Covered:** latest year.

POTATOES: ROUND WHITE, PRINCE EDWARD ISLAND

Source: *Fresh Fruit and Vegetable Prices.* **Price Frequency:** monthly, seasonally. **Effective Market(s):** New York City. **Units of Measure:** Dollars per sack. **Type of Price:** average wholesale price. **Time Period Covered:** latest year.

POTATOES: ROUND WHITE, WISCONSIN

Source: *Fresh Fruit and Vegetable Prices.* **Price Frequency:** monthly, seasonally. **Effective Market(s):** Chicago. **Units of Measure:** Dollars per 100 lbs. **Type of Price:** average wholesale price. **Time Period Covered:** latest year.

POTATOES: RUSSET

Source: *Fresh Fruit and Vegetable Prices.* **Price Frequency:** monthly, seasonally. **Effective Market(s):** Upper Valley/Twin Falls/Burley District (ID), Michigan, Yakima Valley/Columbia Basin (WA), Northwestern District (WA), Wisconsin. **Units of Measure:** Dollars per sack or carton. **Type of Price:** average price at shipping point. **Time Period Covered:** latest year.

Source: *Lancaster Farmer.* **Price Frequency:** weekly, seasonally. **Effective Market(s):** Pennsylvania. **Units of Measure:** Dollars per sack. **Type of Price:** market. **Time Period Covered:** latest week.

Source: *The Packer.* **Price Frequency:** weekly, seasonally. **Effective Market(s):** varies. **Units of Measure:** Dollars per carton/sack. **Type of Price:** received by farmer. **Time Period Covered:** latest week.

POTATOES: RUSSET AND CENTENNIAL

Source: *Fresh Fruit and Vegetable Prices.* **Price Frequency:** monthly, seasonally. **Effective Market(s):** San Luis Valley (CO). **Units of Measure:** Dollars per 50 lb. carton. **Type of Price:** average price at shipping point. **Time Period Covered:** latest year.

POTATOES: RUSSET BURBANK, IDAHO

Source: *Fresh Fruit and Vegetable Prices.* **Price Frequency:** monthly, seasonally. **Effective Market(s):** Chicago, New York City. **Units of Measure:** Dollars per carton. **Type of Price:** average wholesale price. **Time Period Covered:** latest year.

POTATOES: RUSSET BURBANK, WISCONSIN

Source: *Fresh Fruit and Vegetable Prices.* **Price Frequency:** monthly, seasonally. **Effective Market(s):** Chicago. **Units of Measure:** Dollars per carton. **Type of Price:** average wholesale price. **Time Period Covered:** latest year.

POTATOES: SPRING

Source: *Potatoes.* **Price Frequency:** annually. **Effective Market(s):** 7 domestic markets, United States. **Units of Measure:** Dollars per 100 lbs. **Type of Price:** received by farmer. **Time Period Covered:** latest 2 years.

POTATOES: SUMMER

Source: *Potatoes.* **Price Frequency:** annually. **Effective Market(s):** 16 domestic markets, United States. **Units of Measure:** Dollars per 100 lbs. **Type of Price:** received by farmer. **Time Period Covered:** latest 2 years.

POTATOES: TABLE STOCK

Source: *Vegetable Specialties Situation and Outlook Report.* **Price Frequency:** monthly, annually. **Effective Market(s):** United States. **Units of Measure:** Dollars per 100 lbs. **Type of Price:** received by grower. **Time Period Covered:** latest 4 years.

POTATOES: WASHED

Source: *New Zealand Farmer.* **Price Frequency:** weekly, seasonally. **Effective Market(s):** New Zealand. **Units of Measure:** New Zealand dollars per unit. **Time Period Covered:** latest week.

POTATOES: WILJA

Source: *Scottish Farmer.* **Price Frequency:** weekly, seasonally. **Effective Market(s):** 7 Scottish markets. **Units of Measure:** British pounds per tonne. **Type of Price:** producer. **Time Period Covered:** latest week.

POTATOES: WINTER

Source: *Potatoes.* **Price Frequency:** annually. **Effective Market(s):** California, Florida, United States. **Units of Measure:** Dollars per 100 lbs. **Type of Price:** received by farmer. **Time Period Covered:** latest 2 years.

POTATOES FOR SEED

see Seed Potatoes.

POULTRY

see also specific types of poultry, eg. Chickens.

Source: *Dairy Market Statistics.* **Price Frequency:** monthly. **Effective Market(s):** United States. **Units of Measure:** index. **Type of Price:** consumer price index. **Time Period Covered:** latest year.

POULTRY AND EGGS

Source: *Fedgazette.* **Price Frequency:** monthly. **Effective Market(s):** Minnesota. **Units of Measure:** index. **Type of Price:** price index. **Time Period Covered:** latest 24 months.

Source: *Illinois Farm Report.* **Price Frequency:** monthly. **Effective Market(s):** Illinois. **Units of Measure:** index. **Type of Price:** index of prices received by farmers. **Time Period Covered:** latest 2 months, year ago.

POULTRY BYPRODUCT MEAL

Source: *Feedstuffs.* **Price Frequency:** weekly. **Effective Market(s):** 7 domestic markets. **Units of Measure:** Dollars per bulk ton. **Time Period Covered:** latest week.

POULTRY FEED

Source: *Agricultural Prices.* **Price Frequency:** quarterly. **Effective Market(s):** United States. **Units of Measure:** Dollars per ton. **Type of Price:** paid by farmer. **Time Period Covered:** latest 2 quarters, year ago.

Source: *Agricultural Prices.* **Price Frequency:** monthly. **Effective Market(s):** 10 domestic markets, United States. **Units of Measure:** Dollars per ton. **Type of Price:** paid by farmer. **Time Period Covered:** latest month.

POUNDS

see Great Britain Pounds Sterling.

POUNDS STERLING

see Great Britain Pounds Sterling.

POUSSIN

Source: *Urner Barry's Price Current.* **Price Frequency:** daily. **Units of Measure:** Dollars per bird. **Type of Price:** wholesale. **Time Period Covered:** latest day.

Source: *Urner Barry's Price-Current, West Coast Edition.* **Price Frequency:** semiweekly. **Effective Market(s):** west coast. **Units of Measure:** Dollars each. **Type of Price:** wholesale. **Time Period Covered:** latest day.

PPE/PPO-BASED RESIN

Source: *Plastics Technology.* **Price Frequency:** monthly. **Units of Measure:** cents per lb., cents per cubic inch. **Type of Price:** bulk list, market. **Time Period Covered:** latest month.

PPE/PPO-BASED RESIN: 20% GLASS

Source: *Plastics Technology.* **Price Frequency:** monthly. **Units of Measure:** cents per lb., cents per cubic inch. **Type of Price:** bulk list, market. **Time Period Covered:** latest month.

PPE/PPO-BASED RESIN: 30% GLASS

Source: *Plastics Technology.* **Price Frequency:** monthly. **Units of Measure:** cents per lb., cents per cubic inch. **Type of Price:** bulk list, market. **Time Period Covered:** latest month.

PPE/PPO-BASED RESIN: EXTRUSION

Source: *Plastics Technology.* **Price Frequency:** monthly. **Units of Measure:** cents per lb., cents per cubic inch. **Type of Price:** bulk list, market. **Time Period Covered:** latest month.

PPE/PPO-BASED RESIN: INJECTION

Source: *Plastics Technology.* **Price Frequency:** monthly. **Units of Measure:** cents per lb., cents per cubic inch. **Type of Price:** bulk list, market. **Time Period Covered:** latest month.

PPE/PPO-BASED RESIN: STRUCTURAL FOAM

Source: *Plastics Technology.* **Price Frequency:** monthly. **Units of Measure:** cents per lb., cents per cubic inch. **Type of Price:** bulk list, market. **Time Period Covered:** latest month.

PPS: 20% GLASS

Source: *Plastics Technology.* **Price Frequency:** monthly. **Units of Measure:** cents per lb., cents per cubic inch. **Type of Price:** bulk list, market. **Time Period Covered:** latest month.

PPS: 35% FILLER

Source: *Plastics Technology.* **Price Frequency:** monthly. **Units of Measure:** cents per lb., cents per cubic inch. **Type of Price:** bulk list, market. **Time Period Covered:** latest month.

PPS: 35% GLASS

Source: *Plastics Technology.* **Price Frequency:** monthly. **Units of Measure:** cents per lb., cents per cubic inch. **Type of Price:** bulk list, market. **Time Period Covered:** latest month.

PPS: 40% GLASS

Source: *Plastics Technology.* **Price Frequency:** monthly. **Units of Measure:** cents per lb., cents per cubic inch. **Type of Price:** bulk list, market. **Time Period Covered:** latest month.

PRAWNS: SPOT, FRESH

Source: *Seafood Price-Current.* **Price Frequency:** semiweekly. **Effective Market(s):** West Coast. **Units of Measure:** Dollars per lb. **Type of Price:** sale by first receiver. **Time Period Covered:** latest day.

PREDNISOLONE: ANHYDROUS, USP

Source: *Chemical Marketing Reporter.* **Price Frequency:** weekly. **Effective Market(s):** New York. **Units of Measure:** Dollars per gram. **Type of Price:** spot. **Time Period Covered:** latest week.

PREDNISOLONE ACETATE: USP

Source: *Chemical Marketing Reporter.* **Price Frequency:** weekly. **Effective Market(s):** New York. **Units of Measure:** Dollars per gram. **Type of Price:** spot. **Time Period Covered:** latest week.

PREDNISONE: USP

Source: *Chemical Marketing Reporter.* **Price Frequency:** weekly. **Effective Market(s):** New York. **Units of Measure:** Dollars per gram. **Type of Price:** spot. **Time Period Covered:** latest week.

PRINT CLOTH

see Cloth: Print.

PROCAINE HYDROCHLORIDE: AMPULE GRADE, USP

Source: *Chemical Marketing Reporter.* **Price Frequency:** weekly. **Effective Market(s):** New York. **Units of Measure:** Dollars per lb. **Type of Price:** spot. **Time Period Covered:** latest week.

PROCAINE HYDROCHLORIDE: ANTIBIOTIC GRADE, USP

Source: *Chemical Marketing Reporter.* **Price Frequency:** weekly. **Effective Market(s):** New York. **Units of Measure:** Dollars per lb. **Type of Price:** spot. **Time Period Covered:** latest week.

PROCESSED YARNS AND THREADS

see Yarns and Threads: Processed.

PROPANE

Source: *Asian Wall Street Journal.* **Price Frequency:** daily. **Effective Market(s):** Mont Belvieu (TX). **Units of Measure:** Dollars per gallon. **Time Period Covered:** latest 2 days, year ago.

Source: *Energy Pricing News: Petrochemical Report.* **Price Frequency:** bimonthly. **Effective Market(s):** Edmonton (Canada), Sarnia (Canada). **Units of Measure:** Canadian dollars per cubic meter. **Type of Price:** contract. **Time Period Covered:** latest month.

Source: *International Butane/Propane Newsletter.* **Price Frequency:** semimonthly. **Effective Market(s):** East Coast, Japan, Mediterranean, Rotterdam, South Korea. **Units of Measure:** Dollars per metric ton. **Time Period Covered:** latest week.

Source: *Oil & Gas Journal.* **Price Frequency:** monthly in third issue of month. **Effective Market(s):** Conway (KS), Mont Belvieu (TX). **Units of Measure:** cents per gallon. **Type of Price:** spot. **Time Period Covered:** latest 2 months.

Source: *Oil Buyers' Guide.* **Price Frequency:** weekly. **Effective Market(s):** Venezuela. **Units of Measure:** Dollars per metric ton. **Type of Price:** official. **Time Period Covered:** latest week.

Source: *Oil Buyers' Guide.* **Price Frequency:** daily, weekly. **Effective Market(s):** Los Angeles, Mont Belvieu (TX), Conway (KS), Sarnia (Canada). **Units of Measure:** cents per gallon. **Type of Price:** spot. **Time Period Covered:** latest week.

Source: *Oil Buyers' Guide.* **Price Frequency:** weekly. **Effective Market(s):** 14 international markets. **Units of Measure:** Dollars per metric ton. **Type of Price:** spot. **Time Period Covered:** latest week.

Source: *Oil Buyers' Guide International.* **Price Frequency:** weekly. **Effective Market(s):** Venezuela. **Units of Measure:** Dollars per metric ton. **Type of Price:** official. **Time Period Covered:** latest week.

Source: *Oil Buyers' Guide International.* **Price Frequency:** weekly. **Effective Market(s):** 7 international markets. **Units of Measure:** Dollars per metric ton. **Type of Price:** posted, spot. **Time Period Covered:** latest week.

Source: *Petroleum Economist.* **Price Frequency:** monthly. **Effective Market(s):** Mediterranean, North Europe, United States. **Units of Measure:** Dollars per metric tonne, cents per gallon. **Type of Price:** spot. **Time Period Covered:** latest month.

Source: *Petroleum Economist.* **Price Frequency:** monthly. **Effective Market(s):** Middle East, Northwest Europe, United States. **Units of Measure:** Dollars per metric tonne, cents per gallon. **Time Period Covered:** latest month.

Source: *Wall Street Journal.* **Price Frequency:** daily. **Effective Market(s):** Mont Belvieu (TX). **Units of Measure:** Dollars per gallon. **Time Period Covered:** latest day, day ago, year ago.

PROPANE: ABU DHABI

Source: *International Butane/Propane Newsletter.* **Price Frequency:** semimonthly. **Effective Market(s):** Abu Dhabi. **Units of Measure:** Dollars per metric ton. **Type of Price:** producer. **Time Period Covered:** latest week.

PROPANE: ALGERIA

Source: *International Butane/Propane Newsletter.* **Price Frequency:** semimonthly. **Effective Market(s):** Algeria. **Units of Measure:** Dollars per metric ton. **Type of Price:** producer. **Time Period Covered:** latest week.

PROPANE: FUTURES

Source: *Asian Wall Street Journal.* **Price Frequency:** daily. **Effective Market(s):** New York. **Units of Measure:** cents per gallon. **Type of Price:** futures. **Time Period Covered:** latest day.

Source: *Wall Street Journal.* **Price Frequency:** daily. **Effective Market(s):** New York. **Units of Measure:** cents per gallon. **Type of Price:** futures. **Time Period Covered:** latest day.

PROPANE: ISO-BUTANE, VENEZUELA

Source: *International Butane/Propane Newsletter.* **Price Frequency:** semimonthly. **Effective Market(s):** Venezuela. **Units of Measure:** Dollars per metric ton. **Type of Price:** producer. **Time Period Covered:** latest week.

PROPANE: KUWAIT

Source: *International Butane/Propane Newsletter.* **Price Frequency:** semimonthly. **Effective Market(s):** Kuwait. **Units of Measure:** Dollars per metric ton. **Type of Price:** producer. **Time Period Covered:** latest week.

PROPANE: MONT BELVIEU

Source: *International Butane/Propane Newsletter.* **Price Frequency:** semimonthly. **Effective Market(s):** Mont Belvieu (TX). **Units of Measure:** cents per gallon. **Type of Price:** producer. **Time Period Covered:** latest week.

PROPANE: NORMAL, VENEZUELA

Source: *International Butane/Propane Newsletter.* **Price Frequency:** semimonthly. **Effective Market(s):** Venezuela. **Units of Measure:** Dollars per metric ton. **Type of Price:** producer. **Time Period Covered:** latest week.

PROPANE: NORTH SEA

Source: *International Butane/Propane Newsletter.* **Price Frequency:** semimonthly. **Effective Market(s):** North Sea. **Units of Measure:** Dollars per metric ton. **Type of Price:** producer. **Time Period Covered:** latest week.

PROPANE: QATAR

Source: *International Butane/Propane Newsletter.* **Price Frequency:** semimonthly. **Effective Market(s):** Qatar. **Units of Measure:** Dollars per metric ton. **Type of Price:** producer. **Time Period Covered:** latest week.

PROPANE: SAUDI ARABIA

Source: *International Butane/Propane Newsletter.* **Price Frequency:** semimonthly. **Effective Market(s):** Saudi Arabia. **Units of Measure:** Dollars per metric ton. **Type of Price:** producer. **Time Period Covered:** latest week.

PROPIONALDEHYDE

Source: *Chemical Marketing Reporter.* **Price Frequency:** weekly. **Effective Market(s):** New York. **Units of Measure:** Dollars per lb. **Type of Price:** spot. **Time Period Covered:** latest week.

PROPIONIC ACID: SYNTHETIC, PURE

Source: *Chemical Marketing Reporter.* **Price Frequency:** weekly. **Effective Market(s):** East. **Units of Measure:** Dollars per lb. **Type of Price:** spot. **Time Period Covered:** latest week.

N-PROPYL ACETATE

Source: *Chemical Marketing Reporter.* **Price Frequency:** weekly. **Effective Market(s):** New York. **Units of Measure:** Dollars per lb. **Type of Price:** spot. **Time Period Covered:** latest week.

N-PROPYL ALCOHOL

Source: *Chemical Marketing Reporter.* **Price Frequency:** weekly. **Effective Market(s):** New York. **Units of Measure:** Dollars per lb. **Type of Price:** spot. **Time Period Covered:** latest week.

N-PROPYL GALLATE

Source: *Chemical Marketing Reporter.* **Price Frequency:** weekly. **Effective Market(s):** New York. **Units of Measure:** Dollars per lb. **Type of Price:** spot. **Time Period Covered:** latest week.

N-PROPYL-P-HYDROXYBENZOATE: NF

Source: *Chemical Marketing Reporter.* **Price Frequency:** weekly. **Effective Market(s):** New York. **Units of Measure:** Dollars per lb. **Type of Price:** spot. **Time Period Covered:** latest week.

N-PROPYL-P-HYDROXYBENZOATE: TECHNICAL GRADE

Source: *Chemical Marketing Reporter.* **Price Frequency:** weekly. **Effective Market(s):** New York. **Units of Measure:** Dollars per lb. **Type of Price:** spot. **Time Period Covered:** latest week.

PROPYL PARABEN

see n-Propyl-p-hydroxybenzoate.

PROPYL THIOURACIL

Source: *Chemical Marketing Reporter.* **Price Frequency:** weekly. **Effective Market(s):** New York. **Units of Measure:** Dollars per kilo. **Type of Price:** spot. **Time Period Covered:** latest week.

N-PROPYLAMINE

Source: *Chemical Marketing Reporter.* **Price Frequency:** weekly. **Effective Market(s):** New York. **Units of Measure:** Dollars per lb. **Type of Price:** spot. **Time Period Covered:** latest week.

PROPYLENE

Source: *Cotton and Wool Situation and Outlook Report.* **Price Frequency:** monthly. **Units of Measure:** cents per lb. **Type of Price:** spot. **Time Period Covered:** latest year.

Source: *Energy Pricing News: Petrochemical Report.* **Price Frequency:** bimonthly. **Effective Market(s):** Eastern Canada. **Units of Measure:** Canadian dollars per tonne. **Type of Price:** contract. **Time Period Covered:** latest month.

Source: *Japan Economic Journal.* **Price Frequency:** weekly. **Effective Market(s):** Japan. **Units of Measure:** Japanese yen per kilogram. **Type of Price:** market. **Time Period Covered:** latest 2 weeks.

Source: *Purchasing.* **Price Frequency:** quarterly in January, April, July, October issues. **Effective Market(s):** West. **Units of Measure:** Dollars per ton. **Type of Price:** transaction. **Time Period Covered:** latest 5 quarters.

PROPYLENE: CHEMICAL GRADE

Source: *Chemical Marketing Reporter.* **Price Frequency:** weekly. **Effective Market(s):** Texas/Louisiana Gulf Coast points. **Units of Measure:** Dollars per lb. **Type of Price:** spot. **Time Period Covered:** latest week.

Source: *Journal of Commerce and Commercial.* **Price Frequency:** weekly in Thursday issue. **Units of Measure:** Dollars per lb. **Type of Price:** spot. **Time Period Covered:** latest week.

Source: *Oil & Gas Journal.* **Price Frequency:** monthly in first issue of month. **Units of Measure:** cents per lb. **Time Period Covered:** latest month.

PROPYLENE: POLYMER GRADE

Source: *Chemical Marketing Reporter.* **Price Frequency:** weekly. **Effective Market(s):** $ per lb. **Units of Measure:** TX & LA Gulf Coast points. **Type of Price:** spot. **Time Period Covered:** latest week.

Source: *Journal of Commerce and Commercial.* **Price Frequency:** weekly in Thursday issue. **Units of Measure:** Dollars per lb. **Type of Price:** spot. **Time Period Covered:** latest week.

Source: *Modern Plastics.* **Price Frequency:** quarterly every January, April, July, October. **Units of Measure:** cents per lb. **Type of Price:** market. **Time Period Covered:** latest 3 years.

PROPYLENE GLYCOL: INDUSTRIAL GRADE

Source: *Chemical Marketing Reporter.* **Price Frequency:** weekly. **Effective Market(s):** New York. **Units of Measure:** Dollars per lb. **Type of Price:** spot. **Time Period Covered:** latest week.

Source: *Journal of Commerce and Commercial.* **Price Frequency:** weekly in Thursday issue. **Units of Measure:** Dollars per lb. **Type of Price:** spot. **Time Period Covered:** latest week.

PROPYLENE GLYCOL: USP

Source: *Chemical Marketing Reporter.* **Price Frequency:** weekly. **Effective Market(s):** East. **Units of Measure:** Dollars per lb. **Type of Price:** spot. **Time Period Covered:** latest week.

Source: *Journal of Commerce and Commercial.* **Price Frequency:** weekly in Friday issue. **Units of Measure:** Dollars per lb. **Type of Price:** spot. **Time Period Covered:** latest week.

PROPYLENE GLYCOL MONOMETHYL ETHER

Source: *Chemical Marketing Reporter.* **Price Frequency:** weekly. **Effective Market(s):** East. **Units of Measure:** Dollars per lb. **Type of Price:** spot. **Time Period Covered:** latest week.

PROPYLENE OXIDE

Source: *Chemical Marketing Reporter.* **Price Frequency:** weekly. **Effective Market(s):** New York. **Units of Measure:** Dollars per lb. **Type of Price:** spot. **Time Period Covered:** latest week.

Source: *Journal of Commerce and Commercial.* **Price Frequency:** weekly in Thursday issue. **Units of Measure:** Dollars per lb. **Type of Price:** spot. **Time Period Covered:** latest week.

PROTEA: HAWAII

Source: *Floriculture Crops.* **Price Frequency:** annually. **Effective Market(s):** United States. **Units of Measure:** cents per unit. **Type of Price:** commercial wholesale. **Time Period Covered:** latest 2 years.

PRUNES

Source: *Fruit and Tree Nuts Situation and Outlook Yearbook.* **Price Frequency:** annually. **Effective Market(s):** California. **Units of Measure:** Dollars per ton. **Type of Price:** grower. **Time Period Covered:** latest 20 years.

PRUNES: DRIED

Source: *Agricultural Prices Annual Summary.* **Price Frequency:** annually. **Effective Market(s):** California, Hawaii. **Units of Measure:** Dollars per ton. **Type of Price:** average received by farmer. **Time Period Covered:** latest 6 years.

PRUNES: EARLY ITALIAN TYPE

Source: *Lancaster Farmer.* **Price Frequency:** weekly, seasonally. **Effective Market(s):** Pennsylvania. **Units of Measure:** Dollars per carton. **Type of Price:** market. **Time Period Covered:** latest week.

PRUNES: ITALIAN TYPE, FRESH

Source: *Fresh Fruit and Vegetable Prices.* **Price Frequency:** monthly, seasonally. **Effective Market(s):** Yakima Valley/Wenatchee (WA). **Units of Measure:** Dollars per carton. **Type of Price:** average price at shipping point. **Time Period Covered:** latest year.

PRUNES: ITALIAN TYPE, FRESH, NORTHWEST

Source: *Fresh Fruit and Vegetable Prices.* **Price Frequency:** monthly, seasonally. **Effective Market(s):** Chicago, New York City. **Units of Measure:** Dollars per carton. **Type of Price:** average wholesale price. **Time Period Covered:** latest year.

PRUNES: STANLEY, FRESH, MICHIGAN

Source: *Fresh Fruit and Vegetable Prices.* **Price Frequency:** monthly, seasonally. **Effective Market(s):** Chicago, New York City. **Units of Measure:** Dollars per carton. **Type of Price:** average wholesale price. **Time Period Covered:** latest year.

PRUNES AND PLUMS

Source: *Agricultural Prices Annual Summary.* **Price Frequency:** annually. **Effective Market(s):** Idaho, Michigan, Oregon, Washington, United States. **Units of Measure:** Dollars per ton. **Type of Price:** average received by farmer. **Time Period Covered:** latest 3 years, for US latest 6 years.

Source: *Fruit and Tree Nuts Situation and Outlook Yearbook.* **Price Frequency:** annually. **Effective Market(s):** Idaho/Michigan/Oregon/Washington. **Units of Measure:** Dollars per short ton. **Type of Price:** grower. **Time Period Covered:** latest 20 years.

PSYLLIUM: 85% HUSKS

Source: *Journal of Commerce and Commercial.* **Price Frequency:** weekly in Monday issue. **Units of Measure:** Dollars per lb. **Type of Price:** spot. **Time Period Covered:** latest week.

PSYLLIUM SEED: POWDERED, USP

Source: *Chemical Marketing Reporter.* **Price Frequency:** weekly. **Effective Market(s):** New York. **Units of Measure:** Dollars per lb. **Type of Price:** spot. **Time Period Covered:** latest week.

PSYLLIUM SEED HUSKS

Source: *Chemical Marketing Reporter.* **Price Frequency:** weekly. **Effective Market(s):** New York. **Units of Measure:** Dollars per kilo. **Type of Price:** spot. **Time Period Covered:** latest week.

PULLETS

Source: *Lancaster Farmer.* **Price Frequency:** weekly. **Effective Market(s):** Pennsylvania. **Units of Measure:** Dollars per lb. **Type of Price:** auction. **Time Period Covered:** latest week.

PULP: BLEACHED CHEMI-THERMOMECHANICAL, CANADIAN

Source: *Pulp & Paper Week.* **Price Frequency:** quarterly, irregularly. **Effective Market(s):** United States. **Units of Measure:** Dollars per metric ton. **Type of Price:** actual transaction. **Time Period Covered:** latest 2 quarters, year ago.

PULP: BLEACHED HARDWOOD KRAFT

Source: *Purchasing.* **Price Frequency:** monthly. **Effective Market(s):** North. **Units of Measure:** Dollars per metric ton. **Type of Price:** transaction. **Time Period Covered:** latest day, month ago, 6 months ago, year ago.

PULP: BLEACHED HARDWOOD KRAFT, BIRCH, NORDIC

Source: *Pulp & Paper Week.* **Price Frequency:** quarterly, irregularly. **Effective Market(s):** Northern Europe. **Units of Measure:** Dollars per metric ton. **Type of Price:** actual transaction. **Time Period Covered:** latest 2 quarters, year ago.

PULP: BLEACHED HARDWOOD KRAFT, CANADIAN

Source: *Pulp & Paper Week.* **Price Frequency:** quarterly, irregularly. **Effective Market(s):** United States, Northern Europe. **Units of Measure:** Dollars per metric ton. **Type of Price:** actual transaction. **Time Period Covered:** latest 2 quarters, year ago.

PULP: BLEACHED HARDWOOD KRAFT, EUCALYPTUS

Source: *Pulp & Paper Week.* **Price Frequency:** quarterly, irregularly. **Effective Market(s):** Northern Europe. **Units of Measure:** Dollars per metric ton. **Type of Price:** actual transaction. **Time Period Covered:** latest 2 quarters, year ago.

PULP: BLEACHED HARDWOOD KRAFT, EUCALYPTUS, BRAZILIAN

Source: *Pulp & Paper Week.* **Price Frequency:** quarterly, irregularly. **Effective Market(s):** United States. **Units of Measure:** Dollars per metric ton. **Type of Price:** actual transaction. **Time Period Covered:** latest 2 quarters, year ago.

PULP: BLEACHED HARDWOOD KRAFT, NORTHERN UNITED STATES

Source: *Pulp & Paper Week.* **Price Frequency:** quarterly, irregularly. **Effective Market(s):** United States. **Units of Measure:** Dollars per metric ton. **Type of Price:** actual transaction. **Time Period Covered:** latest 2 quarters, year ago.

PULP: BLEACHED HARDWOOD KRAFT, SOUTHERN UNITED STATES

Source: *Pulp & Paper Week.* **Price Frequency:** quarterly, irregularly. **Effective Market(s):** United States, Northern Europe, Japan. **Units of Measure:** Dollars per metric ton. **Type of Price:** actual transaction. **Time Period Covered:** latest 2 quarters, year ago.

PULP: BLEACHED SOFTWOOD KRAFT

Source: *Purchasing.* **Price Frequency:** monthly. **Effective Market(s):** North/South. **Units of Measure:** Dollars per metric ton. **Type of Price:** transaction. **Time Period Covered:** latest day, month ago, 6 months ago, year ago.

PULP: BLEACHED SOFTWOOD KRAFT, CANADIAN

Source: *Pulp & Paper Week.* **Price Frequency:** quarterly, irregularly. **Effective Market(s):** Northern Europe, Japan. **Units of Measure:** Dollars per metric ton. **Type of Price:** actual transaction. **Time Period Covered:** latest 2 quarters, year ago.

PULP: BLEACHED SOFTWOOD KRAFT, CANADIAN/UNITED STATES

Source: *Pulp & Paper Week.* **Price Frequency:** quarterly, irregularly. **Effective Market(s):** United States. **Units of Measure:** Dollars per metric ton. **Type of Price:** actual transaction. **Time Period Covered:** latest 2 quarters, year ago.

PULP: BLEACHED SOFTWOOD KRAFT, NORDIC

Source: *Pulp & Paper Week.* **Price Frequency:** quarterly, irregularly. **Effective Market(s):** Northern Europe. **Units of Measure:** Dollars per metric ton. **Type of Price:** actual transaction. **Time Period Covered:** latest 2 quarters, year ago.

PULP: BLEACHED SOFTWOOD KRAFT, SOUTHERN UNITED STATES

Source: *Pulp & Paper Week.* **Price Frequency:** quarterly, irregularly. **Effective Market(s):** United States, Northern Europe, Japan. **Units of Measure:** Dollars per metric ton. **Type of Price:** actual transaction. **Time Period Covered:** latest 2 quarters, year ago.

PULP: BLEACHED SOFTWOOD, SULPHATE, IMPORTED

Source: *Japan Economic Journal.* **Price Frequency:** weekly. **Effective Market(s):** Japan. **Type of Price:** wholesale. **Time Period Covered:** latest 2 weeks.

PULP: BLEACHED SULFITE, CANADIAN/ UNITED STATES

Source: *Pulp & Paper Week.* **Price Frequency:** quarterly, irregularly. **Effective Market(s):** United States. **Units of Measure:** Dollars per metric ton. **Type of Price:** actual transaction. **Time Period Covered:** latest 2 quarters, year ago.

PULP: CANADA

Source: *International Financial Statistics.* **Price Frequency:** annually. **Effective Market(s):** Canada. **Units of Measure:** Dollars per metric ton, index. **Type of Price:** market price, price index. **Time Period Covered:** latest 2 years.

Source: *International Financial Statistics Yearbook.* **Price Frequency:** annually. **Effective Market(s):** Canada. **Units of Measure:** Dollars per metric ton. **Type of Price:** wholesale. **Time Period Covered:** latest 30 years.

PULP: DISSOLVING

Source: *Purchasing.* **Price Frequency:** monthly. **Effective Market(s):** North. **Units of Measure:** Dollars per metric ton. **Type of Price:** transaction. **Time Period Covered:** latest day, month ago, 6 months ago, year ago.

PULP: DISSOLVING, UNITED STATES/ CANADIAN

Source: *Pulp & Paper Week.* **Price Frequency:** quarterly, irregularly. **Effective Market(s):** United States. **Units of Measure:** Dollars per metric ton. **Type of Price:** actual transaction. **Time Period Covered:** latest 2 quarters, year ago.

PULP: FLUFF, SOUTHERN UNITED STATES

Source: *Pulp & Paper Week.* **Price Frequency:** quarterly, irregularly. **Effective Market(s):** United States, Northern Europe. **Units of Measure:** Dollars per metric ton. **Type of Price:** actual transaction. **Time Period Covered:** latest 2 quarters, year ago.

PULP: PRESSED, MOLDED PRODUCTS

Source: *Pulp & Paper Week.* **Price Frequency:** monthly, irregulary. **Units of Measure:** index. **Type of Price:** price index. **Time Period Covered:** latest 3 months.

PULP: SWEDEN

Source: *International Financial Statistics.* **Price Frequency:** monthly, quarterly, annually. **Effective Market(s):** Swedish ports. **Units of Measure:** Dollars per metric ton, index. **Type of Price:** market price, price index. **Time Period Covered:** latest month, latest 4 quarters, latest 5 years.

Source: *International Financial Statistics.* **Price Frequency:** annually. **Effective Market(s):** Sweden. **Units of Measure:** Dollars per metric ton, index. **Type of Price:** market price, price index. **Time Period Covered:** latest 4 years.

Source: *International Financial Statistics Yearbook.* **Price Frequency:** annually. **Effective Market(s):** Swedish ports, Sweden. **Units of Measure:** Dollars per metric ton. **Type of Price:** wholesale. **Time Period Covered:** latest 30 years.

PULP: UNBLEACHED SOFTWOOD KRAFT, CANADIAN/UNITED STATES

Source: *Pulp & Paper Week.* **Price Frequency:** quarterly, irregularly. **Effective Market(s):** United States. **Units of Measure:** Dollars per metric ton. **Type of Price:** actual transaction. **Time Period Covered:** latest 2 quarters, year ago.

PULPO (FISH): WHOLE, FROZEN, SPAIN

Source: *Seafood Price-Current.* **Price Frequency:** semiweekly. **Effective Market(s):** Mid-Atlantic. **Units of Measure:** Dollars per lb. **Type of Price:** sale by first receiver. **Time Period Covered:** latest day.

PULPWOOD

Source: *FAO Quarterly Bulletin of Statistics.* **Price Frequency:** monthly, annually. **Effective Market(s):** Sweden. **Units of Measure:** Swedish kronor per cubic meter, dollars per metric ton. **Type of Price:** export. **Time Period Covered:** latest 3 years.

PULPWOOD: BIRCH

Source: *Timber Bulletin.* **Price Frequency:** monthly, annually. **Effective Market(s):** Finland. **Units of Measure:** Finnish markka per cubic meter. **Time Period Covered:** latest year.

PULPWOOD: CHIPS

Source: *Timber Bulletin.* **Price Frequency:** monthly, annually. **Effective Market(s):** Sweden. **Units of Measure:** Swedish kronor per cubic meter. **Time Period Covered:** latest year.

PULPWOOD: CHIPS, HARDWOOD

Source: *Pulpwood Prices in the Southeast.* **Price Frequency:** annually. **Effective Market(s):** Florida, Georgia, North Carolina, South Carolina, Virginia. **Units of Measure:** Dollars per green ton. **Type of Price:** average. **Time Period Covered:** latest 2 years.

PULPWOOD: CHIPS, SOFTWOOD

Source: *Pulpwood Prices in the Southeast.* **Price Frequency:** annually. **Effective Market(s):** Florida, Georgia, North Carolina, South Carolina, Virginia. **Units of Measure:** Dollars per green ton. **Type of Price:** average. **Time Period Covered:** latest 2 years.

PULPWOOD: CHIPS/PARTICLES

Source: *Timber Bulletin.* **Price Frequency:** monthly, annually. **Effective Market(s):** Japan. **Units of Measure:** Japanese yen per cubic meter. **Time Period Covered:** monthly latest 2 years, annually latest 6 years.

PULPWOOD: HARDWOOD

Source: *Timber Mart-South.* **Price Frequency:** quarterly. **Effective Market(s):** 13 domestic markets. **Units of Measure:** Dollars per standard cord. **Type of Price:** standing timber, delivered. **Time Period Covered:** latest 2 quarters.

Source: *Timber Mart-South.* **Price Frequency:** quarterly. **Effective Market(s):** 11 domestic markets. **Units of Measure:** Dollars per 100 cubic feet. **Type of Price:** bid. **Time Period Covered:** latest quarter.

Source: *Timber Mart-South.* **Price Frequency:** quarterly. **Effective Market(s):** 14 domestic markets. **Units of Measure:** Dollars per cord. **Type of Price:** stumpage, gate. **Time Period Covered:** latest quarter.

PULPWOOD: PINE

Source: *Timber Bulletin.* **Price Frequency:** monthly, annually. **Effective Market(s):** Finland, Sweden. **Units of Measure:** national currency per cubic meter. **Type of Price:** import value. **Time Period Covered:** latest year.

Source: *Timber Mart-South.* **Price Frequency:** quarterly. **Effective Market(s):** 13 domestic markets. **Units of Measure:** Dollars per standard cord. **Type of Price:** standing timber, delivered. **Time Period Covered:** latest 2 quarters.

Source: *Timber Mart-South.* **Price Frequency:** quarterly. **Effective Market(s):** 13 domestic markets. **Units of Measure:** Dollars per 100 cubic feet. **Type of Price:** bid. **Time Period Covered:** latest quarter.

Source: *Timber Mart-South.* **Price Frequency:** quarterly. **Effective Market(s):** 14 domestic markets. **Units of Measure:** Dollars per cord. **Type of Price:** stumpage, gate. **Time Period Covered:** latest quarter.

PULPWOOD: ROUNDWOOD, HARDWOOD

Source: *Pulpwood Prices in the Southeast.* **Price Frequency:** annually. **Effective Market(s):** Florida, Georgia, North Carolina, South Carolina, Virginia. **Units of Measure:** Dollars per standard cord. **Type of Price:** average. **Time Period Covered:** latest 2 years.

PULPWOOD: ROUNDWOOD, SOFTWOOD

Source: *Pulpwood Prices in the Southeast.* **Price Frequency:** annually. **Effective Market(s):** Florida, Georgia, North Carolina, South Carolina, Virginia. **Units of Measure:** Dollars per standard cord. **Type of Price:** average. **Time Period Covered:** latest 2 years.

PULPWOOD: SPRUCE/FIR

Source: *Timber Bulletin.* **Price Frequency:** monthly, annually. **Effective Market(s):** Austria. **Units of Measure:** Austrian schillings per cubic meter. **Time Period Covered:** monthly latest 2 years, annually latest 6 years.

PULPWOOD: SPRUCE/FIR, FREE ROADSIDE STYRIA

Source: *FAO Quarterly Bulletin of Statistics.* **Price Frequency:** monthly, annually. **Effective Market(s):** Austria. **Units of Measure:** Austrian shillings per cubic meter, dollars per metric ton. **Time Period Covered:** latest 3 years.

PUMICE: COARSE, DOMESTIC

Source: *Chemical Marketing Reporter.* **Price Frequency:** weekly. **Effective Market(s):** New York. **Units of Measure:** Dollars per ton. **Type of Price:** spot. **Time Period Covered:** latest week.

PUMICE: COARSE, ITALIAN, IMPORTED

Source: *Chemical Marketing Reporter.* **Price Frequency:** weekly. **Effective Market(s):** East Coast. **Units of Measure:** Dollars per ton. **Type of Price:** spot. **Time Period Covered:** latest week.

PUMICE: FINE, DOMESTIC

Source: *Chemical Marketing Reporter.* **Price Frequency:** weekly. **Effective Market(s):** New York. **Units of Measure:** Dollars per ton. **Type of Price:** spot. **Time Period Covered:** latest week.

PUMICE: FINE, ITALIAN, IMPORTED

Source: *Chemical Marketing Reporter.* **Price Frequency:** weekly. **Effective Market(s):** East Coast. **Units of Measure:** Dollars per ton. **Type of Price:** spot. **Time Period Covered:** latest week.

PUMICE: MEDIUM, DOMESTIC

Source: *Chemical Marketing Reporter.* **Price Frequency:** weekly. **Effective Market(s):** New York. **Units of Measure:** Dollars per ton. **Type of Price:** spot. **Time Period Covered:** latest week.

PUMICE: MEDIUM, ITALIAN, IMPORTED

Source: *Chemical Marketing Reporter.* **Price Frequency:** weekly. **Effective Market(s):** East Coast. **Units of Measure:** Dollars per ton. **Type of Price:** spot. **Time Period Covered:** latest week.

PUMPKIN

Source: *Lancaster Farmer.* **Price Frequency:** weekly, seasonally. **Effective Market(s):** Pennsylvania. **Units of Measure:** Dollars each. **Type of Price:** market. **Time Period Covered:** latest week.

PUMPKIN: BUTTERCUP

Source: *New Zealand Farmer.* **Price Frequency:** weekly, seasonally. **Effective Market(s):** New Zealand. **Units of Measure:** New Zealand dollars per case. **Time Period Covered:** latest week.

PUMPKIN: BUTTERNUT

Source: *New Zealand Farmer.* **Price Frequency:** weekly, seasonally. **Effective Market(s):** New Zealand. **Units of Measure:** New Zealand dollars per case/crate. **Time Period Covered:** latest week.

PUMPKIN: CROWN

Source: *New Zealand Farmer.* **Price Frequency:** weekly, seasonally. **Effective Market(s):** New Zealand. **Units of Measure:** New Zealand dollars per case. **Time Period Covered:** latest week.

PVDC: EXTRUDABLE

Source: *Plastics Technology.* **Price Frequency:** monthly. **Units of Measure:** cents per lb., cents per cubic inch. **Type of Price:** bulk list, market. **Time Period Covered:** latest month.

PYRAZOLONE: RED

Source: *Chemical Marketing Reporter.* **Price Frequency:** weekly. **Effective Market(s):** New York. **Units of Measure:** Dollars per lb. **Type of Price:** spot. **Time Period Covered:** latest week.

PYRETHROIDS: SYNTHETIC

Source: *Agricultural Prices Annual Summary.* **Price Frequency:** semiannually. **Effective Market(s):** United States. **Units of Measure:** Dollars per gallon. **Type of Price:** paid by farmer. **Time Period Covered:** latest 6 years.

PYRETHRUM: FINE GROUND, 0.9%

Source: *Journal of Commerce and Commercial.* **Price Frequency:** weekly in Thursday issue. **Units of Measure:** Dollars per lb. **Type of Price:** spot. **Time Period Covered:** latest week.

PYRETHRUM: PURIFIED, 20% PYRETHRINS

Source: *Chemical Marketing Reporter.* **Price Frequency:** weekly. **Effective Market(s):** New York. **Units of Measure:** Dollars per lb. **Type of Price:** spot. **Time Period Covered:** latest week.

PYRIDINE

Source: *Journal of Commerce and Commercial.* **Price Frequency:** weekly in Wednesday issue. **Units of Measure:** Dollars per kilo. **Type of Price:** spot. **Time Period Covered:** latest week.

PYRIDINE: REFINED

Source: *Chemical Marketing Reporter.* **Price Frequency:** weekly. **Effective Market(s):** New York. **Units of Measure:** Dollars per kilo. **Type of Price:** spot. **Time Period Covered:** latest week.

PYRIDOXINE HYDROCHLORIDE

Source: *Journal of Commerce and Commercial.* **Price Frequency:** weekly in Friday issue. **Units of Measure:** Dollars per kilo. **Type of Price:** spot. **Time Period Covered:** latest week.

PYRIDOXINE HYDROCHLORIDE: USP

Source: *Chemical Marketing Reporter.* **Price Frequency:** weekly. **Effective Market(s):** New York. **Units of Measure:** Dollars per kilo. **Type of Price:** spot. **Time Period Covered:** latest week.

PYROGALLIC ACID

see Pyrogallol.

PYROGALLIC ACID: TECHNICAL GRADE

Source: *Journal of Commerce and Commercial.* **Price Frequency:** weekly in Thursday issue. **Units of Measure:** Dollars per lb. **Type of Price:** spot. **Time Period Covered:** latest week.

PYROGALLOL

Source: *Chemical Marketing Reporter.* **Price Frequency:** weekly. **Effective Market(s):** New York. **Units of Measure:** Dollars per lb. **Type of Price:** spot. **Time Period Covered:** latest week.

PYROPHYLLITE: CERAMIC AND FILLER GRADES

Source: *Industrial Minerals.* **Price Frequency:** monthly. **Effective Market(s):** main European port. **Units of Measure:** Dollars per metric tonne. **Type of Price:** producer & dealer. **Time Period Covered:** latest month.

PYROPHYLLITE: REFRACTORY GRADE, AUSTRALIAN

Source: *Industrial Minerals.* **Price Frequency:** monthly. **Effective Market(s):** main European port. **Units of Measure:** Dollars per metric tonne. **Type of Price:** producer & dealer. **Time Period Covered:** latest month.

PYROPHYLLITE: UNITED STATES

Source: *Industrial Minerals.* **Price Frequency:** monthly. **Effective Market(s):** United States. **Units of Measure:** Dollars per ton. **Type of Price:** export. **Time Period Covered:** latest month.

QUAIL: PHAROAH

Source: *HRI-Buyers Guide.* **Price Frequency:** weekly. **Effective Market(s):** Northeastern area. **Units of Measure:** Dollars per lb. **Type of Price:** wholesale. **Time Period Covered:** latest week.

Source: *Urner Barry's Price-Current, West Coast Edition.* **Price Frequency:** semiweekly. **Effective Market(s):** West Coast. **Units of Measure:** Dollars each. **Type of Price:** wholesale. **Time Period Covered:** latest day.

QUAIL: PHAROAH, BONED

Source: *Urner Barry's Price-Current.* **Price Frequency:** daily. **Units of Measure:** Dollars per lb. **Type of Price:** wholesale. **Time Period Covered:** latest day.

QUAIL: PHAROAH, WHOLE

Source: *Urner Barry's Price-Current.* **Price Frequency:** daily. **Units of Measure:** Dollars per bird. **Type of Price:** wholesale. **Time Period Covered:** latest day.

QUASSIA

Source: *Journal of Commerce and Commercial.* **Price Frequency:** weekly in Monday issue. **Units of Measure:** Dollars per lb. **Type of Price:** spot. **Time Period Covered:** latest week.

QUASSIA CHIPS

Source: *Chemical Marketing Reporter.* **Price Frequency:** weekly. **Effective Market(s):** New York. **Units of Measure:** Dollars per lb. **Type of Price:** spot. **Time Period Covered:** latest week.

QUINACRIDONE: MAROON

Source: *Chemical Marketing Reporter.* **Price Frequency:** weekly. **Effective Market(s):** New York. **Units of Measure:** Dollars per lb. **Type of Price:** spot. **Time Period Covered:** latest week.

QUINACRIDONE: RED

Source: *Chemical Marketing Reporter.* **Price Frequency:** weekly. **Effective Market(s):** New York. **Units of Measure:** Dollars per lb. **Type of Price:** spot. **Time Period Covered:** latest week.

QUINACRIDONE: VIOLET

Source: *Chemical Marketing Reporter.* **Price Frequency:** weekly. **Effective Market(s):** New York. **Units of Measure:** Dollars per lb. **Type of Price:** spot. **Time Period Covered:** latest week.

QUINCE SEED

Source: *Chemical Marketing Reporter.* **Price Frequency:** weekly. **Effective Market(s):** New York. **Units of Measure:** Dollars per lb. **Type of Price:** spot. **Time Period Covered:** latest week.

QUINIDINE SULFATE

Source: *Journal of Commerce and Commercial.* **Price Frequency:** weekly in Friday issue. **Units of Measure:** Dollars per ounce. **Type of Price:** spot. **Time Period Covered:** latest week.

QUINIDINE SULFATE: USP

Source: *Chemical Marketing Reporter.* **Price Frequency:** weekly. **Effective Market(s):** New York. **Units of Measure:** Dollars per ounce. **Type of Price:** spot. **Time Period Covered:** latest week.

QUININE HYDROCHLORIDE

Source: *Journal of Commerce and Commercial.* **Price Frequency:** weekly in Friday issue. **Units of Measure:** Dollars per ounce. **Type of Price:** spot. **Time Period Covered:** latest week.

QUININE HYDROCHLORIDE: NF

Source: *Chemical Marketing Reporter.* **Price Frequency:** weekly. **Effective Market(s):** New York. **Units of Measure:** Dollars per ounce. **Type of Price:** spot. **Time Period Covered:** latest week.

QUININE SULFATE

Source: *Journal of Commerce and Commercial.* **Price Frequency:** weekly in Friday issue. **Units of Measure:** Dollars per ounce. **Type of Price:** spot. **Time Period Covered:** latest week.

QUININE SULFATE: USP XVIII

Source: *Chemical Marketing Reporter.* **Price Frequency:** weekly. **Effective Market(s):** New York. **Units of Measure:** Dollars per ounce. **Type of Price:** spot. **Time Period Covered:** latest week.

QUINOLINE

Source: *Chemical Marketing Reporter.* **Price Frequency:** weekly. **Effective Market(s):** New York. **Units of Measure:** Dollars per lb. **Type of Price:** spot. **Time Period Covered:** latest week.

R SALT : TECHNICAL

Source: *Chemical Marketing Reporter.* **Price Frequency:** weekly. **Effective Market(s):** New York. **Units of Measure:** Dollars per lb. **Type of Price:** spot. **Time Period Covered:** latest week.

RABBITS

Source: *Lancaster Farmer.* **Price Frequency:** weekly. **Effective Market(s):** Pennsylvania. **Units of Measure:** Dollars per lb. **Type of Price:** auction. **Time Period Covered:** latest week.

RABBITS: CUT UP, READY-TO-COOK, FROZEN

Source: *Poultry Market Statistics.* **Price Frequency:** monthly, annually. **Effective Market(s):** Los Angeles. **Units of Measure:** Dollars per lb. **Type of Price:** average delivered to retailer. **Time Period Covered:** latest year.

RABBITS: FRYERS

Source: *HRI-Buyers Guide.* **Price Frequency:** weekly. **Effective Market(s):** Northeastern area. **Units of Measure:** Dollars per lb. **Type of Price:** price paid by dining places & institutions. **Time Period Covered:** latest week.

RABBITS: ROASTERS

Source: *HRI-Buyers Guide.* **Price Frequency:** weekly. **Effective Market(s):** Northeastern area. **Units of Measure:** Dollars per lb. **Type of Price:** price paid by dining places & institutions. **Time Period Covered:** latest week.

RABBITS: WHOLE, READY-TO-COOK, FROZEN

Source: *Poultry Market Statistics.* **Price Frequency:** monthly, annually. **Effective Market(s):** Los Angeles, San Francisco. **Units of Measure:** Dollars per lb. **Type of Price:** average delivered to retailer. **Time Period Covered:** latest year.

RACEMETHIONINE: USP

Source: *Chemical Marketing Reporter.* **Price Frequency:** weekly. **Effective Market(s):** New York. **Units of Measure:** Dollars per kilo. **Type of Price:** spot. **Time Period Covered:** latest week.

RADIATORS: AUTOMOBILE, UNSWEATED

Source: *American Metal Market.* **Price Frequency:** daily. **Effective Market(s):** 14 domestic markets, Montreal, Toronto. **Units of Measure:** cents per lb. **Type of Price:** dealer buying. **Time Period Covered:** latest day.

RADIATORS: SCRAP

Source: *Iron Age.* **Price Frequency:** monthly. **Units of Measure:** cents per lb. **Type of Price:** mill, dealer. **Time Period Covered:** latest month.

RADIATORS: SCRAP, BRASS

Source: *American Metal Market.* **Price Frequency:** daily. **Effective Market(s):** East, Midwest. **Units of Measure:** Dollars per troy ounce. **Time Period Covered:** latest day.

RADISHES

Source: *California Farmer.* **Price Frequency:** semimonthly, seasonally. **Effective Market(s):** Imperial/Coachella Valleys. **Units of Measure:** Dollars per 35 lb. carton. **Time Period Covered:** latest week, month ago, year ago.

Source: *New Zealand Farmer.* **Price Frequency:** weekly, seasonally. **Effective Market(s):** New Zealand. **Units of Measure:** New Zealand dollars per case. **Time Period Covered:** latest week.

Source: *The Packer.* **Price Frequency:** weekly, seasonally. **Effective Market(s):** varies. **Units of Measure:** Dollars per carton. **Type of Price:** received by farmer. **Time Period Covered:** latest week.

RADISHES: RED

Source: *Fresh Fruit and Vegetable Prices.* **Price Frequency:** monthly, seasonally. **Effective Market(s):** Florida, Michigan. **Units of Measure:** Dollars per carton. **Type of Price:** average price at shipping point. **Time Period Covered:** latest year.

Source: *Lancaster Farmer.* **Price Frequency:** weekly, seasonally. **Effective Market(s):** Pennsylvania. **Units of Measure:** Dollars per unit. **Type of Price:** market. **Time Period Covered:** latest week.

RADISHES: RED, FLORIDA

Source: *Fresh Fruit and Vegetable Prices.* **Price Frequency:** monthly, seasonally. **Effective Market(s):** Chicago, New York City. **Units of Measure:** Dollars per carton. **Type of Price:** average wholesale price. **Time Period Covered:** latest year.

RADISHES: RED, FRESH

Source: *HRI-Buyers Guide.* **Price Frequency:** weekly. **Effective Market(s):** Northeastern area. **Units of Measure:** Dollars per bag. **Type of Price:** prices paid by dining places & institutions. **Time Period Covered:** latest week.

RADISHES: RED, MEXICO

Source: *Fresh Fruit and Vegetable Prices.* **Price Frequency:** monthly, seasonally. **Effective Market(s):** Calexico (CA). **Units of Measure:** Dollars per carton. **Type of Price:** price paid at point of entry. **Time Period Covered:** latest year.

RADISHES: RED, OHIO

Source: *Fresh Fruit and Vegetable Prices.* **Price Frequency:** monthly, seasonally. **Effective Market(s):** Chicago, New York City. **Units of Measure:** Dollars per carton. **Type of Price:** average wholesale price. **Time Period Covered:** latest year.

RADISHES: WHITE, FRESH

Source: *HRI-Buyers Guide.* **Price Frequency:** weekly. **Effective Market(s):** Northeastern area. **Units of Measure:** Dollars per bag. **Type of Price:** prices paid by dining places & institutions. **Time Period Covered:** latest week.

RAISINS: AUSTRALIAN

Source: *Prices of Selected Asia/Pacific Products.* **Price Frequency:** monthly. **Effective Market(s):** Tokyo. **Units of Measure:** Japanese yen per 453 grams. **Type of Price:** wholesale high, wholesale low. **Time Period Covered:** latest month.

RAISINS: FIRST CLASS, UNITED STATES

Source: *Prices of Selected Asia/Pacific Products.* **Price Frequency:** monthly. **Effective Market(s):** Tokyo. **Units of Measure:** Japanese yen per 453 grams. **Type of Price:** wholesale high, wholesale low. **Time Period Covered:** latest month.

RAPE OILSEED

Source: *Farmers Weekly.* **Price Frequency:** weekly. **Effective Market(s):** Great Britain. **Units of Measure:** British pounds per tonne. **Type of Price:** spot. **Time Period Covered:** latest week, week ago, year ago.

RAPESEED: 40% OIL, CANADA

Source: *World Oilseed Situation and Market Highlights.* **Price Frequency:** monthly, annually. **Effective Market(s):** Rotterdam. **Units of Measure:** Dollars per metric ton. **Time Period Covered:** monthly latest year, annually latest 9 years.

RAPESEED: 40%, CANADIAN

Source: *FAO Quarterly Bulletin of Statistics.* **Price Frequency:** monthly, annually. **Effective Market(s):** Northwest Europe. **Units of Measure:** Dollars per 1000 kilograms, dollars per metric ton. **Time Period Covered:** latest 3 years.

Source: *Fruit and Tropical Products.* **Price Frequency:** monthly, annually. **Effective Market(s):** Northwest Europe. **Units of Measure:** Dollars per tonne. **Type of Price:** average. **Time Period Covered:** monthly latest year, annually latest 2 years.

Source: *Oil World.* **Price Frequency:** weekly, monthly, annually. **Effective Market(s):** Northwest Europe. **Units of Measure:** Dollars per tonne. **Type of Price:** lowest representative asking. **Time Period Covered:** weekly latest 3 weeks, monthly latest 2 months, annually latest 2 years.

RAPESEED: FUTURES

Source: *Wall Street Journal.* **Price Frequency:** daily. **Effective Market(s):** Winnipeg. **Units of Measure:** Canadian dollars per ton. **Type of Price:** futures. **Time Period Covered:** latest day.

RAPESEED: FUTURES, JUNE

Source: *Commodity Year Book.* **Price Frequency:** monthly. **Effective Market(s):** Winnipeg. **Units of Measure:** Dollars per tonne. **Type of Price:** futures. **Time Period Covered:** latest 7 years.

RAPESEED: HOME PRODUCED

Source: *Farmers Weekly.* **Price Frequency:** weekly, seasonally. **Effective Market(s):** Great Britain. **Units of Measure:** British pounds per tonne. **Type of Price:** spot. **Time Period Covered:** latest week.

RAPESEED: IMPORTED

Source: *Farmers Weekly.* **Price Frequency:** weekly, seasonally. **Effective Market(s):** Great Britain. **Units of Measure:** British pounds per tonne. **Type of Price:** spot. **Time Period Covered:** latest week.

RAPESEED: STANDARD

Source: *Farmers Weekly.* **Price Frequency:** daily, seasonally. **Effective Market(s):** 13 British markets. **Units of Measure:** British pounds per tonne. **Type of Price:** spot. **Time Period Covered:** latest day.

RAPESEED MEAL: 34% PROTEIN

Source: *Oil World.* **Price Frequency:** weekly, monthly, annually. **Effective Market(s):** Hamburg. **Units of Measure:** Dollars per tonne. **Type of Price:** lowest representative asking. **Time Period Covered:** weekly latest 3 weeks, monthly latest 2 months, annually latest 2 years.

Source: *World Oilseed Situation and Market Highlights.* **Price Frequency:** monthly, annually. **Effective Market(s):** Hamburg. **Units of Measure:** Dollars per metric ton. **Time Period Covered:** monthly latest year, annually latest 9 years.

RAPESEED OIL

Source: *World Oilseed Situation and Market Highlights.* **Price Frequency:** monthly, annually. **Effective Market(s):** Rotterdam. **Units of Measure:** Dollars per metric ton. **Time Period Covered:** monthly latest year, annually latest 9 years.

RAPESEED OIL: DUTCH

Source: *Oil World.* **Price Frequency:** weekly, monthly, annually. **Effective Market(s):** Netherlands. **Units of Measure:** Dollars per tonne. **Type of Price:** lowest representative asking. **Time Period Covered:** weekly latest 3 weeks, monthly latest 2 months, annually latest 2 years.

RAPESEED OIL: OVER 45% ERUCIC ACID

Source: *Chemical Marketing Reporter.* **Price Frequency:** weekly. **Effective Market(s):** New York. **Units of Measure:** Dollars per lb. **Type of Price:** spot. **Time Period Covered:** latest week.

RAPESEED OIL: REFINED, DENATURED

Source: *Commodity Year Book.* **Price Frequency:** monthly, annually. **Effective Market(s):** New York. **Units of Measure:** cents per lb. **Type of Price:** wholesale. **Time Period Covered:** latest 12 years.

Source: *Oil Crops Situation and Outlook.* **Price Frequency:** monthly. **Effective Market(s):** New York. **Units of Measure:** cents per lb. **Type of Price:** wholesale. **Time Period Covered:** latest 5 months.

RAPESEED OIL: WEST GERMAN

Source: *Oil World.* **Price Frequency:** weekly, monthly, annually. **Effective Market(s):** Hamburg. **Units of Measure:** Dollars per tonne. **Type of Price:** lowest representative asking. **Time Period Covered:** weekly latest 3 weeks, monthly latest 2 months, annually latest 2 years.

RASPBERRIES

Source: *Fresh Fruit and Vegetable Prices.* **Price Frequency:** monthly, seasonally. **Effective Market(s):** California. **Units of Measure:** Dollars per flat. **Type of Price:** average price at shipping point. **Time Period Covered:** latest year.

Source: *The Packer.* **Price Frequency:** weekly, seasonally. **Effective Market(s):** varies. **Units of Measure:** Dollars per flat. **Type of Price:** received by farmer. **Time Period Covered:** latest week.

RASPBERRIES: CHILEAN

Source: *Fresh Fruit and Vegetable Prices.* **Price Frequency:** monthly, seasonally. **Effective Market(s):** Washington D.C./Miami. **Units of Measure:** Dollars per flat. **Type of Price:** price paid at point of entry. **Time Period Covered:** latest year.

RASPBERRIES: RED

Source: *California Farmer.* **Price Frequency:** semimonthly, seasonally. **Effective Market(s):** Central Coast (CA). **Units of Measure:** Dollars per 12-1/2 tray. **Time Period Covered:** latest week, month ago, year ago.

Source: *Lancaster Farmer.* **Price Frequency:** weekly, seasonally. **Effective Market(s):** Pennsylvania. **Units of Measure:** Dollars per flat. **Type of Price:** market. **Time Period Covered:** latest week.

RASPBERRIES: RED, CALIFORNIA

Source: *Fresh Fruit and Vegetable Prices.* **Price Frequency:** monthly, seasonally. **Effective Market(s):** Chicago, New York City. **Units of Measure:** Dollars per 1/2 pint. **Type of Price:** average wholesale price. **Time Period Covered:** latest year.

RASPBERRIES: RED, CHILEAN

Source: *Fresh Fruit and Vegetable Prices.* **Price Frequency:** monthly, seasonally. **Effective Market(s):** Chicago, New York City. **Units of Measure:** Dollars per 1/2 pint. **Type of Price:** average wholesale price. **Time Period Covered:** latest year.

RASPBERRIES: RED, OREGON

Source: *Fresh Fruit and Vegetable Prices.* **Price Frequency:** monthly, seasonally. **Effective Market(s):** Chciago. **Units of Measure:** Dollars per 1/2 pint. **Type of Price:** average wholesale price. **Time Period Covered:** latest year.

RASPBERRIES: RED, WASHINGTON

Source: *Fresh Fruit and Vegetable Prices.* **Price Frequency:** monthly, seasonally. **Effective Market(s):** Chicago. **Units of Measure:** Dollars per 1/2 pint. **Type of Price:** average wholesale price. **Time Period Covered:** latest year.

RAUWOLFIA SERPENTINA

Source: *Journal of Commerce and Commercial.* **Price Frequency:** weekly in Monday issue. **Units of Measure:** Dollars per lb. **Type of Price:** spot. **Time Period Covered:** latest week.

RAUWOLFIA SERPENTINA ROOT: POWDERED

Source: *Chemical Marketing Reporter.* **Price Frequency:** weekly. **Effective Market(s):** New York. **Units of Measure:** Dollars per kilo. **Type of Price:** spot. **Time Period Covered:** latest week.

RAYON CHALLIS FABRIC

Source: *DNR: Daily News Record.* **Price Frequency:** quarterly. **Units of Measure:** dollars per yard. **Time Period Covered:** latest 3 quarters.

RAYON FIBER: HIGH-WET MODULUS

Source: *ATI, America's Textiles International.* **Price Frequency:** monthly. **Time Period Covered:** latest month, 6 months ago, year ago.

RAYON FIBER: REGULAR TENACITY

Source: *ATI, America's Textiles International.* **Price Frequency:** monthly. **Time Period Covered:** latest month, 6 months ago, year ago.

RAYON FILAMENT FABRIC

Source: *JTN: The International Textile Magazine.* **Price Frequency:** monthly. **Effective Market(s):** Japan. **Units of Measure:** Japanese yen per yard. **Type of Price:** spot. **Time Period Covered:** latest month.

RAYON STAPLE

Source: *Cotton and Wool Situation and Outlook Report.* **Price Frequency:** monthly, annually. **Units of Measure:** cents per lb. **Type of Price:** actual. **Time Period Covered:** monthly latest 2 years, annually latest 6 years.

Source: *JTN: The International Textile Magazine.* **Price Frequency:** monthly. **Effective Market(s):** Japan. **Units of Measure:** Japanese yen per kilogram. **Type of Price:** spot. **Time Period Covered:** latest month.

RAYON TEXTILE STAPLE

Source: *Journal of Commerce and Commercial.* **Price Frequency:** weekly in Tuesday issue. **Units of Measure:** Dollars per lb. **Type of Price:** spot. **Time Period Covered:** latest week.

RED CARMINE: NO. 40

see Carmine: No. 40.

RED PRECIPITATE

see Mercuric Oxide: Red.

REDFIN (FISH): WHOLE, FRESH

Source: *Seafood Price-Current.* **Price Frequency:** semiweekly. **Effective Market(s):** Mid-Atlantic, New England. **Units of Measure:** Dollars per lb. **Type of Price:** sale by first receiver. **Time Period Covered:** latest day.

REINFORCING BARS

Source: *ENR.* **Price Frequency:** monthly in first issue of month. **Effective Market(s):** 20-city average. **Units of Measure:** Dollars per cwt. **Time Period Covered:** latest month.

REINFORCING BARS: NEW BILLET, GRADE 40

Source: *ENR.* **Price Frequency:** monthly in second issue of month. **Effective Market(s):** 16 domestic markets, Montreal. **Units of Measure:** Dollars per 100 lbs. **Type of Price:** spot. **Time Period Covered:** latest month.

RELINING OF BRAKES: MATERIALS AND LABOR

Source: *Agricultural Prices.* **Price Frequency:** semiannually. **Effective Market(s):** United States. **Units of Measure:** Dollars each time. **Type of Price:** paid by farmer. **Time Period Covered:** latest year.

RESERPINE: CRYSTALLINE, USP

Source: *Chemical Marketing Reporter.* **Price Frequency:** weekly. **Effective Market(s):** New York. **Units of Measure:** Dollars per gram. **Type of Price:** spot. **Time Period Covered:** latest week.

RESERPINE: MICRONIZED

Source: *Journal of Commerce and Commercial.* **Price Frequency:** weekly in Friday issue. **Units of Measure:** Dollars per kilo. **Type of Price:** spot. **Time Period Covered:** latest week.

RESERPINE: USP

Source: *Journal of Commerce and Commercial.* **Price Frequency:** weekly in Friday issue. **Units of Measure:** Dollars per kilo. **Type of Price:** spot. **Time Period Covered:** latest week.

RESINS: COATING

Source: *Journal of Commerce and Commercial.* **Price Frequency:** weekly in Wednesday issue. **Units of Measure:** Dollars per lb. **Type of Price:** spot. **Time Period Covered:** latest week.

RESISTORS: 8-PIN SIP NETWORK, COATED

Source: *Purchasing.* **Price Frequency:** monthly. **Units of Measure:** cents each. **Type of Price:** transaction. **Time Period Covered:** latest day, month ago, 6 months ago, year ago.

RESORCINOL: CRYSTALLINE, USP

Source: *Chemical Marketing Reporter.* **Price Frequency:** weekly. **Effective Market(s):** New York. **Units of Measure:** Dollars per kilo. **Type of Price:** spot. **Time Period Covered:** latest week.

RESORCINOL: POWDERED, USP

Source: *Chemical Marketing Reporter.* **Price Frequency:** weekly. **Effective Market(s):** New York. **Units of Measure:** Dollars per kilo. **Type of Price:** spot. **Time Period Covered:** latest week.

RESORCINOL: TECHNICAL

Source: *Chemical Marketing Reporter.* **Price Frequency:** weekly. **Effective Market(s):** New York. **Units of Measure:** Dollars per kilo. **Type of Price:** spot. **Time Period Covered:** latest week.

RESORCINOL: TECHNICAL GRADE

Source: *Journal of Commerce and Commercial.* **Price Frequency:** weekly in Wednesday issue. **Units of Measure:** Dollars per kilo. **Type of Price:** spot. **Time Period Covered:** latest week.

RESORCINOL: USP

Source: *Journal of Commerce and Commercial.* **Price Frequency:** weekly in Friday issue. **Units of Measure:** Dollars per kilo. **Type of Price:** spot. **Time Period Covered:** latest week.

RHODAMINE RED TONER: MOLYBDATED, PMA

Source: *Chemical Marketing Reporter.* **Price Frequency:** weekly. **Effective Market(s):** New York. **Units of Measure:** Dollars per lb. **Type of Price:** spot. **Time Period Covered:** latest week.

RHODAMINE RED TONER: TUNGSTATED, PTMA

Source: *Chemical Marketing Reporter.* **Price Frequency:** weekly. **Effective Market(s):** New York. **Units of Measure:** Dollars per lb. **Type of Price:** spot. **Time Period Covered:** latest week.

RHODINOL

Source: *Chemical Marketing Reporter.* **Price Frequency:** weekly. **Effective Market(s):** New York. **Units of Measure:** Dollars per lb. **Type of Price:** spot. **Time Period Covered:** latest week.

RHODINOL: SYNTHETIC

Source: *Chemical Marketing Reporter.* **Price Frequency:** weekly. **Effective Market(s):** New York. **Units of Measure:** Dollars per lb. **Type of Price:** spot. **Time Period Covered:** latest week.

RHODIUM

Source: *American Metal Market.* **Price Frequency:** daily. **Effective Market(s):** United States. **Units of Measure:** Dollars per troy ounce. **Type of Price:** merchant, producer. **Time Period Covered:** latest day.

Source: *E&MJ.* **Price Frequency:** monthly. **Units of Measure:** Dollars per troy ounce. **Type of Price:** producer, merchant. **Time Period Covered:** latest month.

Source: *Economic and Energy Indicators.* **Price Frequency:** monthly, quarterly, annually. **Units of Measure:** Dollars per troy ounce. **Time Period Covered:** latest 3 months, quarters, and years.

Source: *Iron Age.* **Price Frequency:** monthly. **Units of Measure:** Dollars per troy ounce. **Type of Price:** consumer. **Time Period Covered:** latest month.

Source: *Northern Miner.* **Price Frequency:** daily. **Effective Market(s):** New York. **Units of Measure:** Dollars per ounce. **Type of Price:** dealer. **Time Period Covered:** latest day.

RHUBARB

Source: *New Zealand Farmer.* **Price Frequency:** weekly, seasonally. **Effective Market(s):** New Zealand. **Units of Measure:** New Zealand dollars per bushel. **Time Period Covered:** latest week.

RHUBARB ROOT: WHOLE, INDIA

Source: *Chemical Marketing Reporter.* **Price Frequency:** weekly. **Effective Market(s):** New York. **Units of Measure:** Dollars per lb. **Type of Price:** spot. **Time Period Covered:** latest week.

RHUBARB ROOT POWDER

Source: *Chemical Marketing Reporter.* **Price Frequency:** weekly. **Effective Market(s):** New York. **Units of Measure:** Dollars per lb. **Type of Price:** spot. **Time Period Covered:** latest week.

Source: *Journal of Commerce and Commercial.* **Price Frequency:** weekly in Monday issue. **Units of Measure:** Dollars per lb. **Type of Price:** spot. **Time Period Covered:** latest week.

RIBOFLAVIN 5-PHOSPHATE-SODIUM

Source: *Chemical Marketing Reporter.* **Price Frequency:** weekly. **Effective Market(s):** New York. **Units of Measure:** Dollars per kilo. **Type of Price:** spot. **Time Period Covered:** latest week.

RIBOFLAVIN: FEED GRADE

Source: *Chemical Marketing Reporter.* **Price Frequency:** weekly. **Effective Market(s):** New York. **Units of Measure:** Dollars per kilo. **Type of Price:** spot. **Time Period Covered:** latest week.

RIBOFLAVIN: USP

Source: *Chemical Marketing Reporter.* **Price Frequency:** weekly. **Effective Market(s):** New York. **Units of Measure:** Dollars per kilo. **Type of Price:** spot. **Time Period Covered:** latest week.

Source: *Journal of Commerce and Commercial.* **Price Frequency:** weekly in Friday issue. **Units of Measure:** Dollars per kilo. **Type of Price:** spot. **Time Period Covered:** latest week.

RICE

Source: *Agricultural Outlook.* **Price Frequency:** annually. **Units of Measure:** Dollars per 100 lbs. **Type of Price:** farm. **Time Period Covered:** latest 6 years.

Source: *Agricultural Outlook.* **Price Frequency:** monthly, annually. **Effective Market(s):** Houston. **Units of Measure:** Dollars per 100 lbs. **Type of Price:** export. **Time Period Covered:** monthly latest 6 months, annually latest 3 years.

Source: *Agricultural Prices.* **Price Frequency:** monthly. **Effective Market(s):** United States. **Units of Measure:** Dollars per 100 lbs. **Type of Price:** received by farmer. **Time Period Covered:** latest 3 months.

Source: *Agricultural Prices Annual Summary.* **Price Frequency:** annually. **Effective Market(s):** United States. **Units of Measure:** Dollars per 100 lbs. **Type of Price:** average received by farmer. **Time Period Covered:** latest 2 years, for US latest 6 years.

Source: *Agricultural Prices Annual Summary.* **Price Frequency:** monthly. **Effective Market(s):** United States. **Units of Measure:** Dollars per 100 lbs. **Type of Price:** average received by farmer. **Time Period Covered:** latest 6 years.

Source: *Rice Situation and Outlook Report.* **Price Frequency:** annually in July issue. **Units of Measure:** Dollars per 100 lbs. **Type of Price:** farm. **Time Period Covered:** latest 36 years.

Source: *Rice Situation and Outlook Report.* **Price Frequency:** annually. **Effective Market(s):** United States. **Units of Measure:** Dollars per 100 lbs. **Type of Price:** average market. **Time Period Covered:** latest 4 years.

RICE: BREWERS'

Source: *Rice Market News.* **Price Frequency:** weekly, seasonally. **Effective Market(s):** Arkansas, Texas, Louisiana, California. **Units of Measure:** Dollars per 100 lbs. **Type of Price:** bulk. **Time Period Covered:** latest week, year ago.

Source: *Rice Situation and Outlook Report.* **Price Frequency:** monthly, annually. **Effective Market(s):** Arkansas. **Units of Measure:** Dollars per 100 lbs. **Type of Price:** average. **Time Period Covered:** latest 9 years.

RICE: BURMA

Source: *International Financial Statistics.* **Price Frequency:** monthly, quarterly, annually. **Effective Market(s):** Burma. **Units of Measure:** Dollars per metric ton, index. **Type of Price:** market price, price index. **Time Period Covered:** latest month, latest 4 quarters, latest 5 years.

Source: *International Financial Statistics Yearbook.* **Price Frequency:** annually. **Effective Market(s):** Burma. **Units of Measure:** Dollars per metric ton. **Type of Price:** wholesale. **Time Period Covered:** latest 30 years.

RICE: FUTURES

Source: *Rice Market News.* **Price Frequency:** weekly, seasonally. **Units of Measure:** Dollars per 100 lbs. **Type of Price:** futures. **Time Period Covered:** latest week.

RICE: HUSKED, 2ND GRADE, THAI

Source: *FAO Quarterly Bulletin of Statistics.* **Price Frequency:** monthly, annually. **Effective Market(s):** Bangkok. **Units of Measure:** Dollars per 1000 kilograms, dollars per metric ton. **Time Period Covered:** latest 3 years.

RICE: LONG GRAIN

Source: *Agricultural Prices Annual Summary.* **Price Frequency:** annually. **Effective Market(s):** United States. **Units of Measure:** Dollars per 100 lbs. **Type of Price:** average received by farmer. **Time Period Covered:** latest 5 years.

Source: *Commodity Year Book.* **Price Frequency:** annually. **Effective Market(s):** Houston. **Units of Measure:** Dollars per 100 lbs. **Type of Price:** wholesale. **Time Period Covered:** latest 5 years.

Source: *Rice Situation and Outlook Report.* **Price Frequency:** annually. **Effective Market(s):** United States. **Units of Measure:** Dollars per 100 lbs. **Type of Price:** average market. **Time Period Covered:** latest 4 years.

RICE: MEDIUM AND SHORT GRAIN

Source: *Agricultural Prices Annual Summary.* **Price Frequency:** annually. **Effective Market(s):** United States. **Units of Measure:** Dollars per 100 lbs. **Type of Price:** average received by farmer. **Time Period Covered:** latest 5 years.

Source: *Rice Situation and Outlook Report.* **Price Frequency:** annually. **Effective Market(s):** United States. **Units of Measure:** Dollars per 100 lbs. **Type of Price:** average market. **Time Period Covered:** latest 4 years.

RICE: MEDIUM GRAIN

Source: *Commodity Year Book.* **Price Frequency:** annually. **Effective Market(s):** Arkansas. **Units of Measure:** Dollars per 100 lbs. **Type of Price:** wholesale. **Time Period Covered:** latest 5 years.

RICE: MILLED, "A", THAI

Source: *Commodity Year Book.* **Price Frequency:** annually. **Effective Market(s):** Rotterdam. **Units of Measure:** Dollars per tonne. **Time Period Covered:** latest 5 years.

RICE: MILLED, "B", THAI

Source: *Commodity Year Book.* **Price Frequency:** annually. **Effective Market(s):** Rotterdam. **Units of Measure:** Dollars per tonne. **Time Period Covered:** latest 5 years.

RICE: MILLED, 100% 1ST GRADE, THAI

Source: *Rice Situation and Outlook Report.* **Price Frequency:** monthly, annually. **Effective Market(s):** Bangkok. **Units of Measure:** Dollars per metric ton. **Time Period Covered:** latest 5 years.

RICE: MILLED, 100% 2ND GRADE, THAI

Source: *Rice Situation and Outlook Report.* **Price Frequency:** monthly, annually. **Effective Market(s):** Bangkok. **Units of Measure:** Dollars per metric ton. **Time Period Covered:** latest 5 years.

RICE: MILLED, 5% BROKEN, THAI

Source: *Commodity Trade and Price Trends.* **Price Frequency:** annually. **Effective Market(s):** Bangkok. **Units of Measure:** Dollars per metric ton, 1980 constant dollars per metric ton. **Time Period Covered:** latest 37 years.

Source: *Rice Situation and Outlook Report.* **Price Frequency:** monthly, annually. **Effective Market(s):** Bangkok. **Units of Measure:** Dollars per metric ton. **Time Period Covered:** latest 5 years.

RICE: MILLED, A1 SUPER, BROKEN, THAI

Source: *FAO Quarterly Bulletin of Statistics.* **Price Frequency:** monthly, annually. **Effective Market(s):** Bangkok. **Units of Measure:** Dollars per 1000 kilograms, dollars per metric ton. **Time Period Covered:** latest 3 years.

RICE: MILLED, LONG GRAIN

Source: *Agricultural Outlook.* **Price Frequency:** monthly, annually. **Effective Market(s):** Southwest Louisiana. **Units of Measure:** Dollars per 100 lbs. **Type of Price:** wholesale. **Time Period Covered:** monthly latest 5 months, annually latest 4 years.

Source: *Rice Market News.* **Price Frequency:** weekly, seasonally. **Effective Market(s):** Arkansas, Texas, Louisiana, California. **Units of Measure:** Dollars per 100 lbs. **Time Period Covered:** latest week, year ago.

RICE: MILLED, LONG GRAIN, PARBOILED 5%, THAI

Source: *FAO Quarterly Bulletin of Statistics.* **Price Frequency:** monthly, annually. **Effective Market(s):** Bangkok. **Units of Measure:** Dollars per 1000 kilograms, dollars per metric ton. **Time Period Covered:** latest 3 years.

RICE: MILLED, MEDIUM GRAIN

Source: *Rice Market News.* **Price Frequency:** weekly, seasonally. **Effective Market(s):** Arkansas, Texas, Louisiana, California. **Units of Measure:** Dollars per 100 lbs. **Time Period Covered:** latest week, year ago.

RICE: MILLED, NO. 1, MEDIUM GRAIN

Source: *California Farmer.* **Price Frequency:** semimonthly. **Effective Market(s):** Northern California. **Units of Measure:** Dollars per 100 lbs. **Time Period Covered:** latest week, month ago, year ago.

RICE: MILLED, NO. 1, SHORT GRAIN, CALIFORNIA

Source: *FAO Quarterly Bulletin of Statistics.* **Price Frequency:** monthly, annually. **Effective Market(s):** United States. **Units of Measure:** Dollars per 1000 kilograms, dollars per metric ton. **Time Period Covered:** latest 3 years.

RICE: MILLED, NO. 2

Source: *Economic and Energy Indicators.* **Price Frequency:** monthly, quarterly, annually. **Effective Market(s):** United States. **Units of Measure:** Dollars per metric ton. **Time Period Covered:** latest 3 months, quarters, and years.

RICE: MILLED, NO. 2, LONG GRAIN, TEXAS

Source: *FAO Quarterly Bulletin of Statistics.* **Price Frequency:** monthly, annually. **Effective Market(s):** United States. **Units of Measure:** Dollars per 1000 kilograms, dollars per metric ton. **Time Period Covered:** latest 3 years.

RICE: MILLED, NO. 2, UNITED STATES

Source: *Commodity Year Book.* **Price Frequency:** annually. **Effective Market(s):** Rotterdam. **Units of Measure:** Dollars per tonne. **Time Period Covered:** latest 5 years.

Source: *Rice Situation and Outlook Report.* **Price Frequency:** monthly, annually. **Effective Market(s):** Rotterdam. **Units of Measure:** Dollars per metric ton. **Type of Price:** average. **Time Period Covered:** latest 6 years.

RICE: MILLED, NO. 4 OR BETTER

Source: *Rice Situation and Outlook Report.* **Price Frequency:** monthly, annually. **Effective Market(s):** Southwest Louisiana. **Units of Measure:** Dollars per 100 lbs. **Type of Price:** average. **Time Period Covered:** latest 9 years.

RICE: MILLED, SECOND HEAD

Source: *Rice Market News.* **Price Frequency:** weekly, seasonally. **Effective Market(s):** Arkansas, California, Louisiana, Texas. **Units of Measure:** Dollars per 100 lbs. **Time Period Covered:** latest week, year ago.

RICE: MILLED, SHORT GRAIN

Source: *Rice Market News.* **Price Frequency:** weekly, seasonally. **Effective Market(s):** Arkansas, Texas, Louisiana, California. **Units of Measure:** Dollars per 100 lbs. **Time Period Covered:** latest week, year ago.

RICE: MILLED, WHITE, 5% BROKEN, THAI

Source: *FAO Quarterly Bulletin of Statistics.* **Price Frequency:** monthly, annually. **Effective Market(s):** Bangkok. **Units of Measure:** Dollars per 1000 kilograms, dollars per metric ton. **Time Period Covered:** latest 3 years.

RICE: NO. 1, MEDIUM GRAIN

Source: *Rice Situation and Outlook Report.* **Price Frequency:** monthly, annually. **Effective Market(s):** California. **Units of Measure:** Dollars per 100 lbs. **Type of Price:** average. **Time Period Covered:** latest 9 years.

RICE: NO. 1, SHORT GRAIN

Source: *Rice Situation and Outlook Report.* **Price Frequency:** monthly, annually. **Effective Market(s):** California. **Units of Measure:** Dollars per 100 lbs. **Type of Price:** average. **Time Period Covered:** latest 9 years.

RICE: NO. 2, LONG GRAIN

Source: *Rice Situation and Outlook Report.* **Price Frequency:** monthly, annually. **Effective Market(s):** Arkansas, Houston, Southwest Louisiana. **Units of Measure:** Dollars per 100 lbs. **Type of Price:** average. **Time Period Covered:** latest 9 years.

RICE: NO. 2, MEDIUM GRAIN

Source: *Commodity Year Book.* **Price Frequency:** monthly, annually. **Effective Market(s):** Southwest Louisiana. **Units of Measure:** Dollars per 100 lbs. **Type of Price:** wholesale. **Time Period Covered:** latest 8 years.

Source: *Rice Situation and Outlook Report.* **Price Frequency:** monthly, annually. **Effective Market(s):** Arkansas, Southwest Louisiana. **Units of Measure:** Dollars per 100 lbs. **Type of Price:** average. **Time Period Covered:** latest 9 years.

RICE: NO. 2, MEDIUM GRAIN, LOUISIANA

Source: *Commodity Trade and Price Trends.* **Price Frequency:** annually. **Effective Market(s):** Lousiana. **Units of Measure:** Dollars per metric ton, 1980 constant dollars per metric ton. **Time Period Covered:** latest 28 years.

RICE: ROUGH

Source: *Agricultural Outlook.* **Price Frequency:** monthly, annually. **Effective Market(s):** United States. **Units of Measure:** Dollars per 100 lbs. **Type of Price:** received by farmer. **Time Period Covered:** monthly latest 6 months, annually latest 3 years.

Source: *Agricultural Prices.* **Price Frequency:** monthly. **Effective Market(s):** United States. **Units of Measure:** Dollars per 100 lbs. **Type of Price:** received by farmer. **Time Period Covered:** latest 2 months, year ago.

Source: *Commodity Year Book.* **Price Frequency:** monthly, Annually. **Effective Market(s):** United States. **Units of Measure:** Dollars per 100 lbs. **Type of Price:** price received by farmers. **Time Period Covered:** latest 5 years.

Source: *Rice Situation and Outlook Report.* **Price Frequency:** annually. **Effective Market(s):** 6 domestic markets. **Units of Measure:** Dollars per 100 lbs. **Type of Price:** received by farmer. **Time Period Covered:** latest 10 years.

Source: *Rice Situation and Outlook Report.* **Price Frequency:** monthly, annually. **Effective Market(s):** United States. **Units of Measure:** Dollars per 100 lbs. **Type of Price:** received by farmer. **Time Period Covered:** latest 10 years.

RICE: ROUGH, BROKENS

Source: *Rice Market News.* **Price Frequency:** weekly, seasonally. **Effective Market(s):** world. **Units of Measure:** Dollars per 100 lbs. **Time Period Covered:** latest week, year ago.

RICE: ROUGH, FUTURES

Source: *Asian Wall Street Journal.* **Price Frequency:** daily. **Units of Measure:** Dollars per 100 lbs. **Type of Price:** futures. **Time Period Covered:** latest day.

Source: *Wall Street Journal.* **Price Frequency:** daily. **Effective Market(s):** Chicago. **Units of Measure:** Dollars per 100 lbs. **Type of Price:** futures. **Time Period Covered:** latest day.

RICE: ROUGH, LONG GRAIN

Source: *Rice Market News.* **Price Frequency:** weekly, seasonally. **Effective Market(s):** world. **Units of Measure:** Dollars per 100 lbs. **Time Period Covered:** latest week, year ago.

Source: *Rice Situation and Outlook Report.* **Price Frequency:** annually. **Effective Market(s):** United States. **Units of Measure:** Dollars per 100 lbs. **Type of Price:** received by farmer. **Time Period Covered:** latest 10 years.

RICE: ROUGH, MEDIUM GRAIN

Source: *Rice Market News.* **Price Frequency:** weekly, seasonally. **Effective Market(s):** world. **Units of Measure:** Dollars per 100 lbs. **Time Period Covered:** latest week, year ago.

Source: *Rice Situation and Outlook Report.* **Price Frequency:** annually. **Effective Market(s):** United States. **Units of Measure:** Dollars per 100 lbs. **Type of Price:** received by farmer. **Time Period Covered:** latest 10 years.

RICE: ROUGH, SHORT GRAIN

Source: *Rice Market News.* **Price Frequency:** weekly, seasonally. **Effective Market(s):** world. **Units of Measure:** Dollars per 100 lbs. **Time Period Covered:** latest week, year ago.

RICE: SWR, 100% GRADE A, THAI

Source: *Rice Situation and Outlook Report.* **Price Frequency:** monthly, annually. **Effective Market(s):** Rotterdam. **Units of Measure:** Dollars per metric ton. **Type of Price:** average. **Time Period Covered:** latest 6 years.

RICE: SWR, 100% GRADE B, THAI

Source: *Economic and Energy Indicators.* **Price Frequency:** monthly, quarterly, annually. **Units of Measure:** cents per lb. **Time Period Covered:** latest 3 months, quarters, and years.

Source: *Rice Situation and Outlook Report.* **Price Frequency:** monthly, annually. **Effective Market(s):** Rotterdam. **Units of Measure:** Dollars per metric ton. **Type of Price:** average. **Time Period Covered:** latest 6 years.

RICE: THAI

Source: *International Financial Statistics.* **Price Frequency:** monthly, quarterly, annually. **Effective Market(s):** Bangkok. **Units of Measure:** Dollars per metric ton, index. **Type of Price:** market price, price index. **Time Period Covered:** latest 5 months, latest 5 quarters, latest 5 years.

Source: *International Financial Statistics.* **Price Frequency:** monthly, quarterly, annually. **Effective Market(s):** Thailand. **Units of Measure:** Dollars per metric ton, index. **Type of Price:** market price, price index. **Time Period Covered:** latest month, latest 4 quarters, latest 5 years.

Source: *International Financial Statistics Yearbook.* **Price Frequency:** annually. **Effective Market(s):** Bangkok, Thailand. **Units of Measure:** Dollars per metric ton. **Type of Price:** wholesale. **Time Period Covered:** latest 30 years.

RICE: UNITED STATES

Source: *International Financial Statistics.* **Price Frequency:** monthly, quarterly, annually. **Effective Market(s):** New Orleans. **Units of Measure:** Dollars per metric ton, index. **Type of Price:** market price, price index. **Time Period Covered:** latest 4 months, latest 5 quarters, latest 5 years.

Source: *International Financial Statistics Yearbook.* **Price Frequency:** annually. **Effective Market(s):** New Orleans. **Units of Measure:** Dollars per metric ton. **Type of Price:** wholesale. **Time Period Covered:** latest 30 years.

RICE: WHITE

Source: *Statistical Bulletin of the South Pacific: Retail Price Indexes.* **Price Frequency:** annually. **Effective Market(s):** 18 South Pacific markets. **Units of Measure:** Australian dollars per. **Type of Price:** retail. **Time Period Covered:** latest year.

RICE: WHITE, 5% BROKEN

Source: *Far Eastern Economic Review.* **Price Frequency:** weekly. **Effective Market(s):** Bangkok. **Units of Measure:** Dollars per tonne. **Time Period Covered:** latest week, week ago, 3 months ago, year ago.

RICE: WHITE, 5% BROKEN, THAI

Source: *Monthly Commodity Price Bulletin.* **Price Frequency:** monthly, annually. **Effective Market(s):** Bangkok. **Units of Measure:** Dollars per metric ton. **Time Period Covered:** latest 5 years.

Source: *Monthly Commodity Price Bulletin Supplement.* **Price Frequency:** monthly, quarterly, annually. **Effective Market(s):** Bangkok. **Units of Measure:** Dollars per tonne. **Type of Price:** end of month. **Time Period Covered:** latest 20 years.

Source: *UNCTAD Commodity Yearbook.* **Price Frequency:** annually. **Effective Market(s):** Bangkok. **Units of Measure:** Dollars per metric ton. **Type of Price:** free market. **Time Period Covered:** latest 12 years.

RICE: WHOLE KERNEL, MILLED, BROKEN

Source: *Rice Situation and Outlook Report.* **Price Frequency:** weekly, seasonally. **Effective Market(s):** World. **Units of Measure:** cents per lb. **Type of Price:** market. **Time Period Covered:** latest 3 years.

RICE: WHOLE KERNEL, MILLED, LONG GRAIN

Source: *Rice Situation and Outlook Report.* **Price Frequency:** weekly, seasonally. **Effective Market(s):** World. **Units of Measure:** cents per lb. **Type of Price:** market. **Time Period Covered:** latest 3 years.

RICE: WHOLE KERNEL, MILLED, MEDIUM GRAIN

Source: *Rice Situation and Outlook Report.* **Price Frequency:** weekly, seasonally. **Effective Market(s):** World. **Units of Measure:** cents per lb. **Type of Price:** market. **Time Period Covered:** latest 3 years.

RICE: WHOLE KERNEL, MILLED, SHORT GRAIN

Source: *Rice Situation and Outlook Report.* **Price Frequency:** weekly, seasonally. **Effective Market(s):** World. **Units of Measure:** cents per lb. **Type of Price:** market. **Time Period Covered:** latest 3 years.

RICE: WHOLE KERNEL, ROUGH, LONG GRAIN

Source: *Rice Situation and Outlook Report.* **Price Frequency:** weekly, seasonally. **Effective Market(s):** World. **Units of Measure:** Dollars per 100 lbs. **Type of Price:** market. **Time Period Covered:** latest 3 years.

RICE: WHOLE KERNEL, ROUGH, MEDIUM GRAIN

Source: *Rice Situation and Outlook Report.* **Price Frequency:** weekly, seasonally. **Effective Market(s):** World. **Units of Measure:** Dollars per 100 lbs. **Type of Price:** market. **Time Period Covered:** latest 3 years.

RICE: WHOLE KERNEL, ROUGH, SHORT GRAIN

Source: *Rice Situation and Outlook Report.* **Price Frequency:** weekly, seasonally. **Effective Market(s):** World. **Units of Measure:** Dollars per 100 lbs. **Type of Price:** market. **Time Period Covered:** latest 3 years.

RICE BRAN

Source: *California Farmer.* **Price Frequency:** semimonthly. **Effective Market(s):** Northern California. **Units of Measure:** Dollars per ton. **Time Period Covered:** latest week, month ago, year ago.

Source: *Feed Situation and Outlook Report.* **Price Frequency:** monthly. **Effective Market(s):** Arkansas. **Units of Measure:** Dollars per ton. **Type of Price:** wholesale. **Time Period Covered:** latest 8 months.

Source: *Feedstuffs.* **Price Frequency:** weekly. **Effective Market(s):** 8 domestic markets. **Units of Measure:** Dollars per bulk ton. **Time Period Covered:** latest week.

Source: *Grain and Feed Market News.* **Price Frequency:** weekly, seasonally. **Effective Market(s):** Arkansas, California, Southwest Louisiana, Texas. **Units of Measure:** Dollars per ton. **Type of Price:** wholesale. **Time Period Covered:** latest week, week ago, year ago.

Source: *Rice Market News.* **Price Frequency:** weekly, seasonally. **Effective Market(s):** Arkansas, California, Louisiana, Texas. **Units of Measure:** Dollars per ton. **Type of Price:** bulk. **Time Period Covered:** latest week, year ago.

Source: *Rice Situation and Outlook Report.* **Price Frequency:** monthly, annually. **Effective Market(s):** Southwest Louisiana. **Units of Measure:** Dollars per ton. **Type of Price:** average. **Time Period Covered:** latest 9 years.

RICE BRAN: 16%, FOR OIL EXTRACTION, INDIAN

Source: *Prices of Selected Asia/Pacific Products.* **Price Frequency:** monthly. **Effective Market(s):** Rotterdam. **Units of Measure:** Dollars per metric ton. **Type of Price:** high, low. **Time Period Covered:** latest month.

RICE BRAN: EXTRA, 16%, INDIA

Source: *Oil World.* **Price Frequency:** weekly, monthly, annually. **Effective Market(s):** Rotterdam. **Units of Measure:** Dollars per tonne. **Type of Price:** lowest representative asking. **Time Period Covered:** weekly latest 3 weeks, monthly latest 2 months, annually latest 2 years.

RICE BRAN: FOR OIL EXTRACTION, JAPANESE

Source: *Prices of Selected Asia/Pacific Products.* **Price Frequency:** monthly. **Effective Market(s):** Tokyo. **Units of Measure:** Japanese yen per 30 kilograms. **Type of Price:** wholesale high, wholesale low. **Time Period Covered:** latest month.

RICE BRAN OIL: REFINED

Source: *Chemical Marketing Reporter.* **Price Frequency:** weekly. **Effective Market(s):** New York. **Units of Measure:** Dollars per lb. **Type of Price:** spot. **Time Period Covered:** latest week.

RICE MILL BY-PRODUCT

Source: *Rice Market News.* **Price Frequency:** weekly, seasonally. **Effective Market(s):** Arkansas, Texas, Louisiana, California. **Units of Measure:** Dollars per ton. **Time Period Covered:** latest week, year ago.

RICE MILLFEED

Source: *Feedstuffs.* **Price Frequency:** weekly. **Effective Market(s):** 7 domestic markets. **Units of Measure:** Dollars per bulk ton. **Time Period Covered:** latest week.

Source: *Feedstuffs.* **Price Frequency:** weekly. **Effective Market(s):** 7 domestic markets. **Units of Measure:** Dollars per ton. **Time Period Covered:** latest week.

Source: *Rice Situation and Outlook Report.* **Price Frequency:** monthly, annually. **Effective Market(s):** Southwest Louisiana. **Units of Measure:** Dollars per ton. **Type of Price:** average. **Time Period Covered:** latest 9 years.

RICINOLEIC ACID

see Castor Oil Acids.

ROASTER BREASTS

Source: *Urner Barry's Price-Current.* **Price Frequency:** daily. **Units of Measure:** cents per lb. **Type of Price:** paid by first receiver. **Time Period Covered:** latest day.

ROASTER LEGS

Source: *Urner Barry's Price-Current.* **Price Frequency:** daily. **Units of Measure:** cents per lb. **Type of Price:** paid by first receiver. **Time Period Covered:** latest day.

ROASTER WINGS

Source: *Urner Barry's Price Current.* **Price Frequency:** daily. **Units of Measure:** cents per lb. **Type of Price:** paid by first receiver. **Time Period Covered:** latest day.

ROASTERS

Source: *HRI-Buyers Guide.* **Price Frequency:** weekly. **Effective Market(s):** Northeastern area. **Units of Measure:** Dollars per lb. **Type of Price:** price paid by dining places & institutions. **Time Period Covered:** latest week.

ROASTERS: 5 LBS. AND UP

Source: *Urner Barry's Price-Current.* **Price Frequency:** daily. **Effective Market(s):** New York. **Units of Measure:** cents per lb. **Type of Price:** price delivered warehouse. **Time Period Covered:** latest day.

ROASTERS: GRADE A, CRYOVAC

Source: *Urner Barry's Price-Current.* **Price Frequency:** daily. **Units of Measure:** cents per lb. **Type of Price:** paid by first receiver. **Time Period Covered:** latest day.

ROASTERS: GRADE A, ICED

Source: *Urner Barry's Price-Current.* **Price Frequency:** daily. **Units of Measure:** cents per lb. **Type of Price:** paid by first receiver. **Time Period Covered:** latest day.

ROASTERS: GRADE A, READY-TO-COOK

Source: *Poultry Market Statistics.* **Price Frequency:** monthly, annually. **Effective Market(s):** Los Angeles, North Atlantic area, San Francisco. **Units of Measure:** cents per lb. **Type of Price:** average paid to retailer. **Time Period Covered:** latest year.

ROASTERS: ICED

Source: *Weekly Insiders Poultry Report.* **Price Frequency:** annually. **Units of Measure:** cents per lb. **Type of Price:** wholesale. **Time Period Covered:** latest 3 years.

ROCHELLE SALT

see Potassium-sodium Tartrate.

ROCK CORNISH HENS

Source: *HRI-Buyers Guide.* **Price Frequency:** weekly. **Effective Market(s):** Northeastern area. **Units of Measure:** Dollars per lb. **Type of Price:** price paid by dining places & institutions. **Time Period Covered:** latest week.

ROCK MELONS

Source: *New Zealand Farmer.* **Price Frequency:** weekly, seasonally. **Effective Market(s):** New Zealand. **Units of Measure:** New Zealand dollars per carton. **Time Period Covered:** latest week.

ROCKSALT: GROUND

Source: *Industrial Minerals.* **Price Frequency:** monthly. **Effective Market(s):** United Kingdom. **Units of Measure:** British pounds per metric tonne. **Type of Price:** producer & dealer. **Time Period Covered:** latest month.

ROE

see specific types, eg. Salmon Roe.

ROOFING: GALVANIZED STEEL

Source: *Agricultural Prices.* **Price Frequency:** quarterly. **Effective Market(s):** United States. **Units of Measure:** Dollars per 100 square feet. **Type of Price:** paid by farmer. **Time Period Covered:** latest 2 quarters, year ago.

Source: *Agricultural Prices Annual Summary.* **Price Frequency:** bimonthly. **Effective Market(s):** United States. **Units of Measure:** Dollars per 100 square foot. **Type of Price:** paid by farmer. **Time Period Covered:** latest 6 years.

ROOFING PITCH
see Coaltar Pitch: Roofing.

ROOSTERS: BANTY
Source: *Lancaster Farmer.* **Price Frequency:** weekly. **Effective Market(s):** Pennsylvania. **Units of Measure:** Dollars each. **Type of Price:** auction. **Time Period Covered:** latest week.

ROOSTERS: LEGHORN
Source: *Lancaster Farmer.* **Price Frequency:** weekly. **Effective Market(s):** Pennsylvania. **Units of Measure:** Dollars per lb. **Type of Price:** auction. **Time Period Covered:** latest week.

ROPE: POLYPROPYLENE, 1/2″
Source: *Agricultural Prices.* **Price Frequency:** semiannually. **Effective Market(s):** United States. **Units of Measure:** Dollars each. **Type of Price:** paid by farmer. **Time Period Covered:** latest year.

Source: *Agricultural Prices Annual Summary.* **Price Frequency:** quarterly. **Effective Market(s):** United States. **Units of Measure:** Dollars per 100 feet. **Type of Price:** paid by farmer. **Time Period Covered:** latest 6 years.

ROSE OIL
Source: *U. S. Essential Oil Trade.* **Price Frequency:** annually. **Effective Market(s):** United States. **Units of Measure:** Dollars per kilogram. **Type of Price:** import value. **Time Period Covered:** latest 3 years.

ROSE OIL: BULGARIAN
Source: *Journal of Commerce and Commercial.* **Price Frequency:** weekly in Tuesday issue. **Units of Measure:** Dollars per kilo. **Type of Price:** spot. **Time Period Covered:** latest week.

ROSE OIL: NATURAL, NF, BULGARIAN
Source: *Chemical Marketing Reporter.* **Price Frequency:** weekly. **Effective Market(s):** New York. **Units of Measure:** Dollars per kilo. **Type of Price:** spot. **Time Period Covered:** latest week.

ROSE OIL: NATURAL, NF, TURKISH
Source: *Chemical Marketing Reporter.* **Price Frequency:** weekly. **Effective Market(s):** New York. **Units of Measure:** Dollars per kilo. **Type of Price:** spot. **Time Period Covered:** latest week.

ROSE OIL: TURKISH
Source: *Journal of Commerce and Commercial.* **Price Frequency:** weekly in Tuesday issue. **Units of Measure:** Dollars per kilo. **Type of Price:** spot. **Time Period Covered:** latest week.

ROSEBUDS: PINK, MOROCCAN
Source: *Journal of Commerce and Commercial.* **Price Frequency:** weekly in Monday issue. **Units of Measure:** Dollars per lb. **Type of Price:** spot. **Time Period Covered:** latest week.

ROSEMARY: FRENCH/YUGOSLAVIAN/ALBANIAN
Source: *U. S. Spice Trade.* **Price Frequency:** annually. **Effective Market(s):** New York. **Units of Measure:** cents per lb. **Type of Price:** spot. **Time Period Covered:** latest 3 years.

ROSEMARY: PORTUGUESE/SPANISH/MOROCCAN
Source: *U. S. Spice Trade.* **Price Frequency:** annually. **Effective Market(s):** New York. **Units of Measure:** cents per lb. **Type of Price:** spot. **Time Period Covered:** latest 3 years.

ROSEMARY OIL
Source: *U. S. Essential Oil Trade.* **Price Frequency:** annually. **Effective Market(s):** United States. **Units of Measure:** Dollars per kilogram. **Type of Price:** import value. **Time Period Covered:** latest 3 years.

ROSEMARY OIL: NF, SPANISH
Source: *Chemical Marketing Reporter.* **Price Frequency:** weekly. **Effective Market(s):** New York. **Units of Measure:** Dollars per kilo. **Type of Price:** spot. **Time Period Covered:** latest week.

ROSEMARY OIL: NF, TUNISIAN
Source: *Chemical Marketing Reporter.* **Price Frequency:** weekly. **Effective Market(s):** New York. **Units of Measure:** Dollars per kilo. **Type of Price:** spot. **Time Period Covered:** latest week.

ROSEMARY OIL: SPANISH
Source: *Journal of Commerce and Commercial.* **Price Frequency:** weekly in Tuesday issue. **Units of Measure:** Dollars per lb. **Type of Price:** spot. **Time Period Covered:** latest week.

ROSES
Source: *New Zealand Farmer.* **Price Frequency:** weekly, seasonally. **Effective Market(s):** New Zealand. **Units of Measure:** New Zealand dollars per bunch. **Time Period Covered:** latest week.

ROSES: STOCK
Source: *New Zealand Farmer.* **Price Frequency:** weekly, seasonally. **Effective Market(s):** New Zealand. **Units of Measure:** New Zealand dollars per bunch. **Time Period Covered:** latest week.

ROSES: SWEETHEART
Source: *Floriculture Crops.* **Price Frequency:** annually. **Effective Market(s):** 10 domestic markets, United States. **Units of Measure:** cents per unit. **Type of Price:** commercial wholesale. **Time Period Covered:** latest 2 years.

ROSES: TEA, HYBRID
Source: *Floriculture Crops.* **Price Frequency:** annually. **Effective Market(s):** 11 domestic markets, United States. **Units of Measure:** cents per unit. **Type of Price:** commercial wholesale. **Time Period Covered:** latest 2 years.

ROSINS
see also specific kinds of Rosin.

Source: *Journal of Commerce and Commercial.* **Price Frequency:** weekly in Monday issue. **Units of Measure:** Dollars per lb., dollars per 100 lbs. **Type of Price:** spot. **Time Period Covered:** latest week.

ROTARY HOE

Source: *Agricultural Prices.* **Price Frequency:** annually. **Effective Market(s):** United States. **Units of Measure:** Dollars each. **Type of Price:** paid by farmer. **Time Period Covered:** latest year.

Source: *Agricultural Prices Annual Summary.* **Price Frequency:** annually. **Effective Market(s):** United States. **Units of Measure:** Dollars each. **Type of Price:** paid by farmer. **Time Period Covered:** latest 6 years.

ROTENONE RESIN: 30-45%

Source: *Chemical Marketing Reporter.* **Price Frequency:** weekly. **Effective Market(s):** New York. **Units of Measure:** Dollars per unit-lb. **Type of Price:** spot. **Time Period Covered:** latest week.

RUBBER

Source: *Agricultural Outlook.* **Price Frequency:** monthly, annually. **Effective Market(s):** New York. **Units of Measure:** cents per lb. **Type of Price:** import. **Time Period Covered:** monthly latest 6 months, annually latest 3 years.

Source: *Financial Times.* **Price Frequency:** daily. **Effective Market(s):** London. **Units of Measure:** British pence per kilogram. **Type of Price:** spot. **Time Period Covered:** latest day.

Source: *International Financial Statistics.* **Price Frequency:** monthly, quarterly, annually. **Effective Market(s):** New York. **Units of Measure:** cents per lb., index. **Type of Price:** market price, price index. **Time Period Covered:** latest 4 months, latest 5 quarters, latest 5 years.

Source: *International Financial Statistics Yearbook.* **Price Frequency:** annually. **Effective Market(s):** New York. **Units of Measure:** cents per lb. **Type of Price:** wholesale. **Time Period Covered:** latest 30 years.

Source: *Monthly Commodity Price Bulletin.* **Price Frequency:** monthly, annually. **Units of Measure:** Malaysian/Singapore cents per kilogram. **Type of Price:** average of daily market indicator price. **Time Period Covered:** latest 5 years.

Source: *Monthly Commodity Price Bulletin Supplement.* **Price Frequency:** monthly, quarterly, annually. **Effective Market(s):** Kuala Lumpur (Malaysia). **Units of Measure:** Malaysian/Singapore cents per kilogram. **Type of Price:** average daily market indicator price. **Time Period Covered:** latest 20 years.

Source: *Rubber Statistical Bulletin.* **Price Frequency:** monthly, annually. **Effective Market(s):** Malaysia. **Units of Measure:** Malaysian cents per kilo. **Time Period Covered:** latest 12 months, latest 6 years.

RUBBER: CRUDE

Source: *Standard & Poor's Statistical Service Current Statistics.* **Price Frequency:** monthly, annually. **Units of Measure:** cents per lb. **Time Period Covered:** latest 4 years.

RUBBER: CRUDE, SMOKED SHEETS

Source: *Commodity Year Book.* **Price Frequency:** monthly, annually. **Effective Market(s):** New York. **Units of Measure:** cents per lb. **Type of Price:** spot. **Time Period Covered:** latest 7 years.

RUBBER: FUTURES

Source: *Japan Economic Journal.* **Price Frequency:** weekly. **Effective Market(s):** Tokyo. **Units of Measure:** Japanese yen per kilogram. **Type of Price:** futures. **Time Period Covered:** latest week.

RUBBER: MALAYSIAN

Source: *International Financial Statistics.* **Price Frequency:** monthly, quarterly, annually. **Effective Market(s):** Singapore, Malaysia. **Units of Measure:** cents per lb., index. **Type of Price:** market price, price index. **Time Period Covered:** latest 5 months, latest 5 quarters, latest 5 years.

Source: *International Financial Statistics.* **Price Frequency:** monthly, quarterly, annually. **Effective Market(s):** Malaysia. **Units of Measure:** cents per lb., index. **Type of Price:** market price, price index. **Time Period Covered:** latest 2 months, latest 4 quarters, latest 5 years.

Source: *International Financial Statistics Yearbook.* **Price Frequency:** annually. **Effective Market(s):** Singapore, Malaysia. **Units of Measure:** cents per lb. **Type of Price:** wholesale. **Time Period Covered:** latest 30 years.

RUBBER: NATURAL

Source: *Economic and Energy Indicators.* **Price Frequency:** monthly, quarterly, annually. **Units of Measure:** cents per lb. **Time Period Covered:** latest 3 months, quarters, and years.

RUBBER: NATURAL, LATEX

Source: *Rubber Statistical Bulletin.* **Price Frequency:** monthly, annually. **Effective Market(s):** London. **Units of Measure:** British pounds per metric tonne. **Type of Price:** average of daily market indicator price. **Time Period Covered:** latest 12 months, latest 6 years.

RUBBER: NATURAL, NO. 1, RSS

Source: *Commodity Trade and Price Trends.* **Price Frequency:** annually. **Effective Market(s):** London, New York. **Units of Measure:** cents per kilogram, 1980 constant cents per kilogram. **Type of Price:** spot. **Time Period Covered:** latest 37 years.

Source: *FAO Quarterly Bulletin of Statistics.* **Price Frequency:** monthly, annually. **Effective Market(s):** London. **Units of Measure:** British pounds per 1000 kilograms, dollars per metric ton. **Time Period Covered:** latest 3 years.

Source: *Rubber Statistical Bulletin.* **Price Frequency:** monthly, annually. **Effective Market(s):** Kuala Lumpur, London, New York, Singapore. **Units of Measure:** national currency per metric tonne. **Type of Price:** average of daily market indicator price. **Time Period Covered:** latest 12 months, latest 6 years.

RUBBER: NATURAL, NO. 1, RSS, KUALA LUMPUR

Source: *FAO Quarterly Bulletin of Statistics.* **Price Frequency:** monthly, annually. **Effective Market(s):** Malaysia. **Units of Measure:** ringgits per 1000 kilograms, dollars per metric ton. **Time Period Covered:** latest 3 years.

RUBBER: NATURAL, NO. 3, RSS

Source: *Rubber Statistical Bulletin.* **Price Frequency:** monthly, annually. **Effective Market(s):** Kuala Lumpur, London, New York, Tokyo. **Units of Measure:** national currency per metric tonne. **Type of Price:** average of daily market indicator price. **Time Period Covered:** latest 12 months, latest 6 years.

RUBBER: NATURAL, NO. 10, SMR

Source: *Rubber Statistical Bulletin.* **Price Frequency:** monthly, annually. **Effective Market(s):** Kuala Lumpur. **Units of Measure:** Ringgit per metric tonne. **Type of Price:** average of daily market indicator price. **Time Period Covered:** latest 12 months, latest 6 years.

RUBBER: NATURAL, NO. 20, SMR

Source: *Rubber Statistical Bulletin.* **Price Frequency:** monthly, annually. **Effective Market(s):** Kuala Lumpur, London. **Units of Measure:** national currency per metric tonne. **Type of Price:** average of daily market indicator price. **Time Period Covered:** latest 12 months, latest 6 years.

RUBBER: NATURAL, SMRL

Source: *Rubber Statistical Bulletin.* **Price Frequency:** monthly, annually. **Effective Market(s):** Kuala Lumpur. **Units of Measure:** Ringgit per metric tonne. **Type of Price:** average of daily market indicator price. **Time Period Covered:** latest 12 months, latest 6 years.

RUBBER: NO. 1, CRUDE

Source: *Journal of Commerce and Commercial.* **Price Frequency:** daily. **Effective Market(s):** New York. **Units of Measure:** Dollars per lb. **Type of Price:** spot supplier. **Time Period Covered:** latest day.

RUBBER: NO. 1, PSS

Source: *Far Eastern Economic Review.* **Price Frequency:** weekly. **Effective Market(s):** Kuala Lumpur. **Units of Measure:** Malaysian cents per kilogram. **Time Period Covered:** latest week, week ago, 3 months ago, year ago.

RUBBER: NO. 1, PSS, FUTURES

Source: *Far Eastern Economic Review.* **Price Frequency:** weekly. **Units of Measure:** Malaysian cents per kilograms. **Type of Price:** futures. **Time Period Covered:** latest week.

RUBBER: NO. 1, RSS

Source: *CRB Commodity Index Report.* **Price Frequency:** weekly. **Effective Market(s):** New York. **Units of Measure:** Dollars per lb. **Type of Price:** spot. **Time Period Covered:** latest week.

Source: *Financial Times.* **Price Frequency:** daily. **Effective Market(s):** Kuala Lumpur. **Units of Measure:** Malaysian cents per kilogram. **Type of Price:** spot. **Time Period Covered:** latest day.

RUBBER: NO. 1, RSS, FUTURES

Source: *Asian Wall Street Journal.* **Price Frequency:** daily. **Effective Market(s):** Kuala Lumpur, Singapore. **Units of Measure:** Malaysian cents per kilogram, Singapore cents per kilogram. **Type of Price:** futures. **Time Period Covered:** latest day.

RUBBER: NO. 1, RSS, SINGAPORE

Source: *Monthly Commodity Price Bulletin.* **Price Frequency:** monthly, annually. **Effective Market(s):** Singapore. **Units of Measure:** Singapore cents per kilogram, cents per lb. **Type of Price:** closing. **Time Period Covered:** latest 5 years.

Source: *Monthly Commodity Price Bulletin Supplement.* **Price Frequency:** monthly, quarterly, annually. **Effective Market(s):** Singapore. **Units of Measure:** Singapore cents per kilogram, dollars per tonne. **Type of Price:** closing. **Time Period Covered:** latest 20 years.

Source: *UNCTAD Commodity Yearbook.* **Price Frequency:** annually. **Units of Measure:** Dollars per metric ton. **Type of Price:** free market. **Time Period Covered:** latest 12 years.

RUBBER: NO. 1, SMOKED SHEETS

Source: *Investor's Daily.* **Price Frequency:** daily. **Effective Market(s):** New York. **Units of Measure:** Dollars per lb. **Type of Price:** spot. **Time Period Covered:** latest day.

Source: *New York Times.* **Price Frequency:** daily. **Effective Market(s):** New York. **Units of Measure:** Dollars per lb. **Type of Price:** cash. **Time Period Covered:** latest 2 days.

RUBBER: NO. 2, RSS, FUTURES

Source: *Asian Wall Street Journal.* **Price Frequency:** daily. **Effective Market(s):** Singapore. **Units of Measure:** Singapore cents per kilogram. **Type of Price:** futures. **Time Period Covered:** latest day.

RUBBER: NO. 3, RSS, FUTURES

Source: *Asian Wall Street Journal.* **Price Frequency:** daily. **Effective Market(s):** Singapore. **Units of Measure:** Singapore cents per kilogram. **Type of Price:** futures. **Time Period Covered:** latest day.

RUBBER: NO. 4, RSS, FUTURES

Source: *Asian Wall Street Journal.* **Price Frequency:** daily. **Effective Market(s):** Singapore. **Units of Measure:** Singapore cents per kilogram. **Type of Price:** futures. **Time Period Covered:** latest day.

RUBBER: NO. 5, RSS, FUTURES

Source: *Asian Wall Street Journal.* **Price Frequency:** daily. **Effective Market(s):** Singapore. **Units of Measure:** Singapore cents per kilogram. **Type of Price:** futures. **Time Period Covered:** latest day.

RUBBER: NO. 20, SMR, FUTURES

Source: *Asian Wall Street Journal.* **Price Frequency:** daily. **Effective Market(s):** Kuala Lumpur. **Units of Measure:** Malaysian cents per kilogram. **Type of Price:** futures. **Time Period Covered:** latest day.

RUBBER: SMOKED SHEETS

Source: *Asian Wall Street Journal.* **Price Frequency:** daily. **Effective Market(s):** New York. **Units of Measure:** Dollars per lb. **Type of Price:** cash. **Time Period Covered:** latest 2 days, year ago.

Source: *Wall Street Journal.* **Price Frequency:** daily. **Effective Market(s):** New York. **Units of Measure:** Dollars per lb. **Time Period Covered:** latest day, day ago, year ago.

RUBBER: SYNTHETIC, BR

Source: *Rubber Statistical Bulletin.* **Price Frequency:** quarterly, annually. **Effective Market(s):** Canada, Italy, United Kingdom, West Germany. **Units of Measure:** national currency per metric ton. **Time Period Covered:** latest 12 quarters, latest 8 years.

RUBBER: SYNTHETIC, SBR

Source: *Rubber Statistical Bulletin.* **Price Frequency:** quarterly, annually. **Effective Market(s):** Canada, Italy, United Kingdom, West Germany. **Units of Measure:** national currency per metric ton. **Time Period Covered:** latest 12 quarters, latest 8 years.

RUBBER: THAI

Source: *International Financial Statistics.* **Price Frequency:** monthly, quarterly, annually. **Effective Market(s):** Thailand. **Units of Measure:** cents per lb., index. **Type of Price:** market price, price index. **Time Period Covered:** latest month, latest 4 quarters, latest 5 years.

Source: *International Financial Statistics Yearbook.* **Price Frequency:** annually. **Effective Market(s):** Thailand. **Units of Measure:** cents per lb. **Type of Price:** wholesale. **Time Period Covered:** latest 30 years.

RUM

Source: *Beverage Media.* **Price Frequency:** monthly. **Effective Market(s):** New York. **Units of Measure:** Dollars per unit. **Type of Price:** wholesale by brand. **Time Period Covered:** latest month.

Source: *Colorado Beverage Analyst.* **Price Frequency:** monthly. **Effective Market(s):** Colorado. **Units of Measure:** Dollars per case. **Type of Price:** wholesale by brand. **Time Period Covered:** latest month.

Source: *Illinois Beverage Journal.* **Price Frequency:** monthly. **Effective Market(s):** Illinois. **Units of Measure:** Dollars per case. **Type of Price:** wholesale by brand. **Time Period Covered:** latest month.

Source: *Indiana Beverage Journal.* **Price Frequency:** monthly. **Effective Market(s):** Indiana. **Units of Measure:** Dollars per case, dollars per bottle. **Type of Price:** wholesale by brand. **Time Period Covered:** latest month.

Source: *Kentucky Beverage Journal.* **Price Frequency:** monthly. **Effective Market(s):** Kentucky. **Units of Measure:** Dollars per bottle, dollars per case. **Type of Price:** wholesale by brand. **Time Period Covered:** latest month.

Source: *Nevada Beverage Index.* **Price Frequency:** monthly. **Effective Market(s):** Nevada. **Units of Measure:** Dollars per unit. **Type of Price:** wholesale by brand. **Time Period Covered:** latest month.

Source: *Rhode Island Beverage Journal.* **Price Frequency:** monthly. **Effective Market(s):** Rhode Island. **Units of Measure:** Dollars per unit. **Type of Price:** wholesale by brand. **Time Period Covered:** latest month.

RUSSIAN SPIRITS

Source: *Colorado Beverage Analyst.* **Price Frequency:** monthly. **Effective Market(s):** Colorado. **Units of Measure:** Dollars per case. **Type of Price:** wholesale by brand. **Time Period Covered:** latest month.

RUTABAGAS

Source: *Lancaster Farmer.* **Price Frequency:** weekly, seasonally. **Effective Market(s):** Pennsylvania. **Units of Measure:** Dollars per carton. **Type of Price:** market. **Time Period Covered:** latest week.

RUTHENIUM

Source: *American Metal Market.* **Price Frequency:** daily. **Effective Market(s):** United States. **Units of Measure:** Dollars per troy ounce. **Type of Price:** merchant, producer. **Time Period Covered:** latest day.

Source: *E&MJ.* **Price Frequency:** monthly. **Units of Measure:** Dollars per troy ounce. **Type of Price:** producer, merchant. **Time Period Covered:** latest month.

RUTILE: AUSTRALIAN CONCENTRATE

Source: *Industrial Minerals.* **Price Frequency:** monthly. **Effective Market(s):** Australia. **Units of Measure:** Australian dollars per metric tonne. **Type of Price:** producer & dealer. **Time Period Covered:** latest month.

RUTILE: UNITED STATES CONCENTRATE

Source: *Industrial Minerals.* **Price Frequency:** monthly. **Effective Market(s):** East Coast. **Units of Measure:** Dollars per short ton. **Type of Price:** producer & dealer. **Time Period Covered:** latest month.

RUTIN

Source: *Journal of Commerce and Commercial.* **Price Frequency:** weekly in Monday issue. **Units of Measure:** Dollars per kilo. **Type of Price:** spot. **Time Period Covered:** latest week.

RYE

Source: *Agricultural Prices Annual Summary.* **Price Frequency:** annually. **Effective Market(s):** 27 domestic markets, United States. **Units of Measure:** Dollars per bushel. **Type of Price:** average received by farmer. **Time Period Covered:** latest 2 years, for US latest 6 years.

Source: *Lancaster Farmer.* **Price Frequency:** weekly. **Effective Market(s):** Pennsylvania. **Units of Measure:** Dollars per bushel. **Type of Price:** auction. **Time Period Covered:** latest week.

Source: *Wheat Situation and Outlook Report.* **Price Frequency:** annually. **Units of Measure:** Dollars per bushel. **Type of Price:** season average. **Time Period Covered:** latest 8 years.

RYE: FUTURES

Source: *Asian Wall Street Journal.* **Price Frequency:** daily. **Effective Market(s):** Winnepeg. **Units of Measure:** Canadian dollars per ton. **Type of Price:** futures. **Time Period Covered:** latest day.

Source: *Investor's Daily.* **Price Frequency:** daily. **Effective Market(s):** Winnepeg. **Units of Measure:** Canadian dollars per ton. **Type of Price:** futures. **Time Period Covered:** latest day.

Source: *Wall Street Journal.* **Price Frequency:** daily. **Effective Market(s):** Winnipeg. **Units of Measure:** Canadian dollars per ton. **Type of Price:** futures. **Time Period Covered:** latest day.

RYE: FUTURES, MAY

Source: *Commodity Year Book.* **Price Frequency:** monthly. **Effective Market(s):** Winnipeg. **Units of Measure:** Canadian Dollars per tonne. **Type of Price:** futures. **Time Period Covered:** latest 8 years.

RYE: NO. 1, PLUMP

Source: *Minneapolis Grain Exchange Statistical Annual.* **Price Frequency:** daily. **Effective Market(s):** Minneapolis. **Units of Measure:** cents per bushel. **Type of Price:** cash. **Time Period Covered:** latest year.

RYE: NO. 2

Source: *Commodity Year Book.* **Price Frequency:** monthly, annually. **Effective Market(s):** Minneapolis. **Units of Measure:** cents per bushel. **Type of Price:** cash. **Time Period Covered:** latest 8 years.

Source: *Grain and Feed Market News.* **Price Frequency:** daily, seasonally. **Effective Market(s):** Minneapolis. **Units of Measure:** Dollars per bushel. **Type of Price:** cash bid. **Time Period Covered:** latest week, year ago.

Source: *Journal of Commerce and Commercial.* **Price Frequency:** daily. **Effective Market(s):** Minneapolis. **Units of Measure:** Dollars per bushel. **Type of Price:** spot supplier. **Time Period Covered:** latest day.

Source: *Minneapolis Grain Exchange Statistical Annual.* **Price Frequency:** daily. **Effective Market(s):** Minneapolis. **Units of Measure:** cents per bushel. **Type of Price:** cash. **Time Period Covered:** latest year.

Source: *Minneapolis Grain Exchange Statistical Annual.* **Price Frequency:** monthly, annually. **Effective Market(s):** Minneapolis. **Units of Measure:** cents per bushel. **Type of Price:** cash. **Time Period Covered:** latest 10 years.

Source: *Montana Farmer-Stockman.* **Price Frequency:** monthly, seasonally. **Effective Market(s):** Minneapolis. **Type of Price:** cash. **Time Period Covered:** latest 2 months.

Source: *Standard & Poor's Statistical Service Current Statistics.* **Price Frequency:** monthly, annually. **Effective Market(s):** Minneapolis. **Units of Measure:** cents per bushel. **Time Period Covered:** latest 4 years.

RYE WHISKEY

see also Whiskey.

Source: *Colorado Beverage Analyst.* **Price Frequency:** monthly. **Effective Market(s):** Colorado. **Units of Measure:** Dollars per case. **Type of Price:** wholesale by brand. **Time Period Covered:** latest month.

Source: *Kentucky Beverage Journal.* **Price Frequency:** monthly. **Effective Market(s):** Kentucky. **Units of Measure:** Dollars per bottle, dollars per case. **Type of Price:** wholesale by brand. **Time Period Covered:** latest month.

RYEGRASS: ANNUAL

Source: *Agricultural Prices Annual Summary.* **Price Frequency:** semiannually. **Effective Market(s):** United States. **Units of Measure:** Dollars per 100 lbs. **Type of Price:** paid by farmer. **Time Period Covered:** latest 6 years.

SABADILLA POWDER

Source: *Journal of Commerce and Commercial.* **Price Frequency:** weekly in Monday issue. **Units of Measure:** Dollars per lb. **Type of Price:** spot. **Time Period Covered:** latest week.

SABLEFISH: DRESSED, FROZEN, ALASKAN/CANADIAN

Source: *Weekly Statistical Fishery Report.* **Price Frequency:** weekly. **Effective Market(s):** Tokyo. **Units of Measure:** Dollars per lb. **Type of Price:** wholesale. **Time Period Covered:** 2 weeks ago, month ago.

SACCHARIN: GRANULAR, SOLUBLE

Source: *Chemical Marketing Reporter.* **Price Frequency:** weekly. **Effective Market(s):** New York. **Units of Measure:** Dollars per lb. **Type of Price:** spot. **Time Period Covered:** latest week.

Source: *Journal of Commerce and Commercial.* **Price Frequency:** weekly in Friday issue. **Units of Measure:** Dollars per lb. **Type of Price:** spot. **Time Period Covered:** latest week.

SACCHARIN: INSOLUBLE

Source: *Journal of Commerce and Commercial.* **Price Frequency:** weekly in Friday issue. **Units of Measure:** Dollars per lb. **Type of Price:** spot. **Time Period Covered:** latest week.

SACCHARIN POWDER

Source: *Journal of Commerce and Commercial.* **Price Frequency:** weekly in Friday issue. **Units of Measure:** Dollars per lb. **Type of Price:** spot. **Time Period Covered:** latest week.

SACCHARIN POWDER: SOLUBLE, FCC

Source: *Chemical Marketing Reporter.* **Price Frequency:** weekly. **Effective Market(s):** New York. **Units of Measure:** Dollars per lb. **Type of Price:** spot. **Time Period Covered:** latest week.

SACKS: SHIPPING

see Paper: Shipping Sack.

SAFFLOWER MEAL

Source: *California Farmer.* **Price Frequency:** semimonthly. **Effective Market(s):** Northern California. **Units of Measure:** Dollars per ton. **Time Period Covered:** latest week, month ago, year ago.

SAFFLOWER MEAL: 25% PROTEIN

Source: *Feedstuffs.* **Price Frequency:** weekly. **Effective Market(s):** Los Angeles, San Francisco. **Units of Measure:** Dollars per bulk ton. **Time Period Covered:** latest week.

SAFFLOWER OIL

Source: *Chemical Marketing Reporter.* **Price Frequency:** weekly. **Effective Market(s):** New York. **Units of Measure:** Dollars per lb. **Type of Price:** spot. **Time Period Covered:** latest week.

Source: *Oil Crops Situation and Outlook.* **Price Frequency:** monthly. **Effective Market(s):** New York. **Units of Measure:** cents per lb. **Type of Price:** wholesale. **Time Period Covered:** latest 5 months.

SAFFRON

Source: *Journal of Commerce and Commercial.* **Price Frequency:** weekly in Monday issue. **Units of Measure:** Dollars per ounce. **Type of Price:** spot. **Time Period Covered:** latest week.

Source: *Prices of Selected Asia/Pacific Products.* **Price Frequency:** monthly. **Effective Market(s):** New York. **Units of Measure:** Dollars per ounce. **Type of Price:** spot high, spot low. **Time Period Covered:** latest month.

SAFFRON: JAPANESE

Source: *Prices of Selected Asia/Pacific Products.* **Price Frequency:** monthly. **Effective Market(s):** Osaka (Japan). **Units of Measure:** Japanese yen per gram. **Type of Price:** trade high, trade low. **Time Period Covered:** latest month.

SAFFRON: SPANISH

Source: *U. S. Spice Trade.* **Price Frequency:** monthly, annually. **Effective Market(s):** New York. **Units of Measure:** Dollars per lb. **Type of Price:** spot. **Time Period Covered:** latest 10 years.

SAGE: ALBANIAN

Source: *Chemical Marketing Reporter.* **Price Frequency:** weekly. **Effective Market(s):** New York. **Units of Measure:** Dollars per lb. **Type of Price:** spot. **Time Period Covered:** latest week.

Source: *U. S. Spice Trade.* **Price Frequency:** annually. **Effective Market(s):** New York. **Units of Measure:** cents per lb. **Type of Price:** spot. **Time Period Covered:** latest 3 years.

SAGE: NO. 1, DALMATIAN

Source: *Chemical Marketing Reporter.* **Price Frequency:** weekly. **Effective Market(s):** New York. **Units of Measure:** Dollars per lb. **Type of Price:** spot. **Time Period Covered:** latest week.

Source: *U. S. Spice Trade.* **Price Frequency:** annually. **Effective Market(s):** New York. **Units of Measure:** cents per lb. **Type of Price:** spot. **Time Period Covered:** latest 3 years.

SAGE: TURKISH

Source: *Chemical Marketing Reporter.* **Price Frequency:** weekly. **Effective Market(s):** New York. **Units of Measure:** Dollars per lb. **Type of Price:** spot. **Time Period Covered:** latest week.

Source: *U. S. Spice Trade.* **Price Frequency:** annually. **Effective Market(s):** New York. **Units of Measure:** cents per lb. **Type of Price:** spot. **Time Period Covered:** latest 3 years.

SAGE: YUGOSLAVIAN

Source: *U. S. Spice Trade.* **Price Frequency:** annually. **Effective Market(s):** New York. **Units of Measure:** cents per lb. **Type of Price:** spot. **Time Period Covered:** latest 3 years.

SAGE OIL: CLARY

Source: *Journal of Commerce and Commercial.* **Price Frequency:** weekly in Tuesday issue. **Units of Measure:** Dollars per lb. **Type of Price:** spot. **Time Period Covered:** latest week.

SAGE OIL: CLARY, FRENCH

Source: *Chemical Marketing Reporter.* **Price Frequency:** weekly. **Effective Market(s):** New York. **Units of Measure:** Dollars per kilo. **Type of Price:** spot. **Time Period Covered:** latest week.

SAGE OIL: DALMATIAN

Source: *Chemical Marketing Reporter.* **Price Frequency:** weekly. **Effective Market(s):** New York. **Units of Measure:** Dollars per lb. **Type of Price:** spot. **Time Period Covered:** latest week.

Source: *Journal of Commerce and Commercial.* **Price Frequency:** weekly in Tuesday issue. **Units of Measure:** Dollars per lb. **Type of Price:** spot. **Time Period Covered:** latest week.

SAGE OIL: SPANISH

Source: *Chemical Marketing Reporter.* **Price Frequency:** weekly. **Effective Market(s):** New York. **Units of Measure:** Dollars per kilo. **Type of Price:** spot. **Time Period Covered:** latest week.

Source: *Journal of Commerce and Commercial.* **Price Frequency:** weekly in Tuesday issue. **Units of Measure:** Dollars per lb. **Type of Price:** spot. **Time Period Covered:** latest week.

SAILCLOTH

Source: *DNR: Daily News Record.* **Price Frequency:** quarterly. **Units of Measure:** Dollars per yard. **Type of Price:** spot. **Time Period Covered:** latest 3 quarters.

SAKE

Source: *Beverage Media.* **Price Frequency:** monthly. **Effective Market(s):** New York. **Units of Measure:** Dollars per unit. **Type of Price:** wholesale by brand. **Time Period Covered:** latest month.

Source: *Illinois Beverage Journal.* **Price Frequency:** monthly. **Effective Market(s):** Illinois. **Units of Measure:** Dollars per case. **Type of Price:** wholesale by brand. **Time Period Covered:** latest month.

SAL SODA

Source: *Journal of Commerce and Commercial.* **Price Frequency:** weekly in Thursday issue. **Units of Measure:** Dollars per 100 lbs. **Type of Price:** spot. **Time Period Covered:** latest week.

SALAMI: COOKED

Source: *Meat Price Report.* **Price Frequency:** weekly. **Units of Measure:** cents per lb. **Type of Price:** price paid to wholesaler. **Time Period Covered:** latest week.

SALICYLALDEHYDE

Source: *Chemical Marketing Reporter.* **Price Frequency:** weekly. **Effective Market(s):** New York. **Units of Measure:** Dollars per lb. **Type of Price:** spot. **Time Period Covered:** latest week.

SALICYLAMIDE: GRANULAR, POWDERED, NF

Source: *Chemical Marketing Reporter.* **Price Frequency:** weekly. **Effective Market(s):** New York. **Units of Measure:** Dollars per lb. **Type of Price:** spot. **Time Period Covered:** latest week.

SALICYLIC ACID: CRYSTALLINE, USP

Source: *Chemical Marketing Reporter.* **Price Frequency:** weekly. **Effective Market(s):** New York. **Units of Measure:** Dollars per lb. **Type of Price:** spot. **Time Period Covered:** latest week.

SALICYLIC ACID: POWDERED, USP

Source: *Chemical Marketing Reporter.* **Price Frequency:** weekly. **Effective Market(s):** New York. **Units of Measure:** Dollars per lb. **Type of Price:** spot. **Time Period Covered:** latest week.

SALICYLIC ACID: TECHNICAL

Source: *Chemical Marketing Reporter.* **Price Frequency:** weekly. **Effective Market(s):** New York. **Units of Measure:** Dollars per lb. **Type of Price:** spot. **Time Period Covered:** latest week.

SALMON: BRITE CHUM, GILLNET, FRESH

Source: *Seafood Price-Current.* **Price Frequency:** semiweekly. **Effective Market(s):** Seattle. **Units of Measure:** Dollars per lb. **Type of Price:** sale by first receiver. **Time Period Covered:** latest day.

SALMON: BRITE CHUM, GILLNET, FROZEN

Source: *Seafood Price-Current.* **Price Frequency:** semiweekly. **Effective Market(s):** Seattle. **Units of Measure:** Dollars per lb. **Type of Price:** sale by first receiver. **Time Period Covered:** latest day.

SALMON: BRITE CHUM, TROLL, FRESH

Source: *Seafood Price-Current.* **Price Frequency:** semiweekly. **Effective Market(s):** Seattle. **Units of Measure:** Dollars per lb. **Type of Price:** sale by first receiver. **Time Period Covered:** latest day.

SALMON: BRITE CHUM, TROLL, FROZEN

Source: *Seafood Price-Current.* **Price Frequency:** semiweekly. **Effective Market(s):** Seattle. **Units of Measure:** Dollars per lb. **Type of Price:** sale by first receiver. **Time Period Covered:** latest day.

SALMON: CHUM, GRADE A, DRESSED, FROZEN, ALASKAN

Source: *Weekly Statistical Fishery Report.* **Price Frequency:** weekly. **Effective Market(s):** Tokyo. **Units of Measure:** Dollars per lb. **Type of Price:** wholesale. **Time Period Covered:** 2 weeks ago, month ago.

SALMON: COHO, FARM RAISED, FRESH, CANADIAN

Source: *Seafood Price-Current.* **Price Frequency:** semiweekly. **Effective Market(s):** Seattle. **Units of Measure:** Dollars per lb. **Type of Price:** sale by first receiver. **Time Period Covered:** latest day.

SALMON: COHO, FRESH, CHILEAN

Source: *Seafood Price-Current.* **Price Frequency:** semi-weekly. **Effective Market(s):** Miami. **Units of Measure:** Dollars per lb. **Type of Price:** sale by first receiver. **Time Period Covered:** latest day.

SALMON: DARK CHUM, GILLNET, FROZEN

Source: *Seafood Price-Current.* **Price Frequency:** semi-weekly. **Effective Market(s):** Seattle. **Units of Measure:** Dollars per lb. **Type of Price:** sale by first receiver. **Time Period Covered:** latest day.

SALMON: DARK CHUM, PALE MEAT, GILLNET, FROZEN

Source: *Seafood Price-Current.* **Price Frequency:** semi-weekly. **Effective Market(s):** Seattle. **Units of Measure:** Dollars per lb. **Type of Price:** sale by first receiver. **Time Period Covered:** latest day.

SALMON: DARK CHUM, PALE MEAT, TROLL, FRESH

Source: *Seafood Price-Current.* **Price Frequency:** semi-weekly. **Effective Market(s):** Seattle. **Units of Measure:** Dollars per lb. **Type of Price:** sale by first receiver. **Time Period Covered:** latest day.

SALMON: DARK CHUM, RED MEAT, GILLNET, FRESH

Source: *Seafood Price-Current.* **Price Frequency:** semi-weekly. **Effective Market(s):** Seattle. **Units of Measure:** Dollars per lb. **Type of Price:** sale by first receiver. **Time Period Covered:** latest day.

SALMON: FARM RAISED, FRESH, DOMESTIC/CANADIAN ATLANTIC

Source: *Seafood Price-Current.* **Price Frequency:** semi-weekly. **Effective Market(s):** Mid-Atlantic/New England. **Units of Measure:** Dollars per lb. **Type of Price:** sale by first receiver. **Time Period Covered:** latest day.

SALMON: FARM RAISED, FRESH, NORWEGIAN

Source: *Seafood Price-Current.* **Price Frequency:** semi-weekly. **Effective Market(s):** Mid-Atlantic/New England. **Units of Measure:** Dollars per lb. **Type of Price:** sale by first receiver. **Time Period Covered:** latest day.

SALMON: KING CHINOOK, GILLNET, FRESH

Source: *Seafood Price-Current.* **Price Frequency:** semi-weekly. **Effective Market(s):** Seattle. **Units of Measure:** Dollars per lb. **Type of Price:** sale by first receiver. **Time Period Covered:** latest day.

SALMON: KING CHINOOK, GILLNET, FROZEN

Source: *Seafood Price-Current.* **Price Frequency:** semi-weekly. **Effective Market(s):** Seattle. **Units of Measure:** Dollars per lb. **Type of Price:** sale by first receiver. **Time Period Covered:** latest day.

SALMON: KING CHINOOK, TROLL, FRESH

Source: *Seafood Price-Current.* **Price Frequency:** semi-weekly. **Effective Market(s):** Seattle. **Units of Measure:** Dollars per lb. **Type of Price:** sale by first receiver. **Time Period Covered:** latest day.

SALMON: KING, FARM RAISED, FRESH, CANADIAN

Source: *Seafood Price-Current.* **Price Frequency:** semi-weekly. **Effective Market(s):** Seattle. **Units of Measure:** Dollars per lb. **Type of Price:** sale by first receiver. **Time Period Covered:** latest day.

SALMON: KING, FARM RAISED, FRESH, NEW ZEALAND

Source: *Seafood Price-Current.* **Price Frequency:** semi-weekly. **Effective Market(s):** Seattle. **Units of Measure:** Dollars per lb. **Type of Price:** sale by first receiver. **Time Period Covered:** latest day.

SALMON: KING, FILLETS, FRESH

Source: *Seafood Price-Current.* **Price Frequency:** semi-weekly. **Effective Market(s):** West Coast. **Units of Measure:** Dollars per lb. **Type of Price:** sale by first receiver. **Time Period Covered:** latest day.

SALMON: PINK, GRADE A, DRESSED, FROZEN, ALASKAN

Source: *Weekly Statistical Fishery Report.* **Price Frequency:** weekly. **Effective Market(s):** Tokyo. **Units of Measure:** Dollars per lb. **Type of Price:** wholesale. **Time Period Covered:** 2 weeks ago, month ago.

SALMON: PINK SOCKEYE, GILLNET, FRESH

Source: *Seafood Price-Current.* **Price Frequency:** semi-weekly. **Effective Market(s):** Seattle. **Units of Measure:** Dollars per lb. **Type of Price:** sale by first receiver. **Time Period Covered:** latest day.

SALMON: PINK SOCKEYE, GILLNET, FROZEN

Source: *Seafood Price-Current.* **Price Frequency:** semi-weekly. **Effective Market(s):** Seattle. **Units of Measure:** Dollars per lb. **Type of Price:** sale by first receiver. **Time Period Covered:** latest day.

SALMON: PINK SOCKEYE, TROLL, FRESH

Source: *Seafood Price-Current.* **Price Frequency:** semi-weekly. **Effective Market(s):** Seattle. **Units of Measure:** Dollars per lb. **Type of Price:** sale by first receiver. **Time Period Covered:** latest day.

SALMON: PINK SOCKEYE, TROLL, FROZEN

Source: *Seafood Price-Current.* **Price Frequency:** semi-weekly. **Effective Market(s):** Seattle. **Units of Measure:** Dollars per lb. **Type of Price:** sale by first receiver. **Time Period Covered:** latest day.

SALMON: RED, GRADE A, DRESSED, FROZEN, ALASKAN

Source: *Weekly Statistical Fishery Report.* **Price Frequency:** weekly. **Effective Market(s):** Tokyo. **Units of Measure:** Dollars per lb. **Type of Price:** wholesale. **Time Period Covered:** 2 weeks ago, month ago.

SALMON: RED SOCKEYE, GILLNET, FRESH

Source: *Seafood Price-Current.* **Price Frequency:** semi-weekly. **Effective Market(s):** Seattle. **Units of Measure:** Dollars per lb. **Type of Price:** sale by first receiver. **Time Period Covered:** latest day.

SALMON: RED SOCKEYE, GILLNET, FROZEN

Source: *Seafood Price-Current.* **Price Frequency:** semi-weekly. **Effective Market(s):** Seattle. **Units of Measure:** Dollars per lb. **Type of Price:** sale by first receiver. **Time Period Covered:** latest day.

SALMON: RED SOCKEYE, PRINCESS DRESSED, GILLNET, FROZEN

Source: *Seafood Price-Current.* **Price Frequency:** semi-weekly. **Effective Market(s):** Seattle. **Units of Measure:** Dollars per lb. **Type of Price:** sale by first receiver. **Time Period Covered:** latest day.

SALMON: RED SOCKEYE, PRINCESS DRESSED, TROLL, FROZEN

Source: *Seafood Price-Current.* **Price Frequency:** semi-weekly. **Effective Market(s):** Seattle. **Units of Measure:** Dollars per lb. **Type of Price:** sale by first receiver. **Time Period Covered:** latest day.

SALMON: RED SOCKEYE, TROLL, FRESH

Source: *Seafood Price-Current.* **Price Frequency:** semi-weekly. **Effective Market(s):** Seattle. **Units of Measure:** Dollars per lb. **Type of Price:** sale by first receiver. **Time Period Covered:** latest day.

SALMON: RED SOCKEYE, TROLL, FROZEN

Source: *Seafood Price-Current.* **Price Frequency:** semi-weekly. **Effective Market(s):** Seattle. **Units of Measure:** Dollars per lb. **Type of Price:** sale by first receiver. **Time Period Covered:** latest day.

SALMON: SEMI-BRITE CHUM, GILLNET, FROZEN

Source: *Seafood Price-Current.* **Price Frequency:** semi-weekly. **Effective Market(s):** Seattle. **Units of Measure:** Dollars per lb. **Type of Price:** sale by first receiver. **Time Period Covered:** latest day.

SALMON: SEMI-BRITE CHUM, TROLL, FROZEN

Source: *Seafood Price-Current.* **Price Frequency:** semi-weekly. **Effective Market(s):** Seattle. **Units of Measure:** Dollars per lb. **Type of Price:** sale by first receiver. **Time Period Covered:** latest day.

SALMON: SILVER, GRADE A, DRESSED, FROZEN, ALASKAN

Source: *Weekly Statistical Fishery Report.* **Price Frequency:** weekly. **Effective Market(s):** Tokyo. **Units of Measure:** Dollars per lb. **Type of Price:** wholesale. **Time Period Covered:** 2 weeks ago, month ago.

SALMON: SILVER/COHO, GILLNET, FRESH

Source: *Seafood Price-Current.* **Price Frequency:** semi-weekly. **Effective Market(s):** Seattle. **Units of Measure:** Dollars per lb. **Type of Price:** sale by first receiver. **Time Period Covered:** latest day.

SALMON: SILVER/COHO, GILLNET, FROZEN

Source: *Seafood Price-Current.* **Price Frequency:** semi-weekly. **Effective Market(s):** Seattle. **Units of Measure:** Dollars per lb. **Type of Price:** sale by first receiver. **Time Period Covered:** latest day.

SALMON: SILVER/COHO, TROLL, FRESH

Source: *Seafood Price-Current.* **Price Frequency:** semi-weekly. **Effective Market(s):** Seattle. **Units of Measure:** Dollars per lb. **Type of Price:** sale by first receiver. **Time Period Covered:** latest day.

SALMON: SILVER/COHO, TROLL, FROZEN

Source: *Seafood Price-Current.* **Price Frequency:** semi-weekly. **Effective Market(s):** Seattle. **Units of Measure:** Dollars per lb. **Type of Price:** sale by first receiver. **Time Period Covered:** latest day.

SALMON: STEELHEAD, GILLNET, FRESH

Source: *Seafood Price-Current.* **Price Frequency:** semi-weekly. **Effective Market(s):** Seattle. **Units of Measure:** Dollars per lb. **Type of Price:** sale by first receiver. **Time Period Covered:** latest day.

SALMON: TROLL KING, FRESH, ALASKAN

Source: *Seafood Price-Current.* **Price Frequency:** semi-weekly. **Effective Market(s):** Seattle. **Units of Measure:** Dollars per lb. **Type of Price:** sale by first receiver. **Time Period Covered:** latest day.

SALMON: TROLL KING, FROZEN, ALASKAN

Source: *Seafood Price-Current.* **Price Frequency:** semi-weekly. **Effective Market(s):** Seattle. **Units of Measure:** Dollars per lb. **Type of Price:** sale by first receiver. **Time Period Covered:** latest day.

SALMON: WHOLE, FRESH, NORWEGIAN

Source: *HRI-Buyer's Guide.* **Price Frequency:** weekly. **Effective Market(s):** New York. **Units of Measure:** Dollars per lb. **Type of Price:** dealer. **Time Period Covered:** latest week.

SALMON ROE: CHUM, GRADE A, SALTED, PROCESSED

Source: *Weekly Statistical Fishery Report.* **Price Frequency:** weekly, seasonally. **Effective Market(s):** Tokyo. **Units of Measure:** Dollars per lb. **Type of Price:** wholesale. **Time Period Covered:** 2 weeks ago, month ago.

SALMON ROE: CHUM, GRADE B, SALTED, PROCESSED

Source: *Weekly Statistical Fishery Report.* **Price Frequency:** weekly, seasonally. **Effective Market(s):** Tokyo. **Units of Measure:** Dollars per lb. **Type of Price:** wholesale. **Time Period Covered:** 2 weeks ago, month ago.

SALMON ROE: CHUM, GRADE C, SALTED, PROCESSED

Source: *Weekly Statistical Fishery Report.* **Price Frequency:** weekly, seasonally. **Effective Market(s):** Tokyo. **Units of Measure:** Dollars per lb. **Type of Price:** wholesale. **Time Period Covered:** 2 weeks ago, month ago.

SALMON ROE: PINK, GRADE A, SALTED, PROCESSED

Source: *Weekly Statistical Fishery Report.* **Price Frequency:** weekly, seasonally. **Effective Market(s):** Tokyo. **Units of Measure:** Dollars per lb. **Type of Price:** wholesale. **Time Period Covered:** 2 weeks ago, month ago.

SALMON ROE: PINK, GRADE B, SALTED, PROCESSED

Source: *Weekly Statistical Fishery Report.* **Price Frequency:** weekly, seasonally. **Effective Market(s):** Tokyo. **Units of Measure:** Dollars per lb. **Type of Price:** wholesale. **Time Period Covered:** 2 weeks ago, month ago.

SALMON ROE: PINK, GRADE C, SALTED, PROCESSED

Source: *Weekly Statistical Fishery Report.* **Price Frequency:** weekly, seasonally. **Effective Market(s):** Tokyo. **Units of Measure:** Dollars per lb. **Type of Price:** wholesale. **Time Period Covered:** 2 weeks ago, month ago.

SALMON ROE: RED, GRADE A, SALTED, PROCESSED

Source: *Weekly Statistical Fishery Report.* **Price Frequency:** weekly, seasonally. **Effective Market(s):** Tokyo. **Units of Measure:** Dollars per lb. **Type of Price:** wholesale. **Time Period Covered:** 2 weeks ago, month ago.

SALMON ROE: RED, GRADE B, SALTED, PROCESSED

Source: *Weekly Statistical Fishery Report.* **Price Frequency:** weekly, seasonally. **Effective Market(s):** Tokyo. **Units of Measure:** Dollars per lb. **Type of Price:** wholesale. **Time Period Covered:** 2 weeks ago, month ago.

SALMON ROE: RED, GRADE C, SALTED, PROCESSED

Source: *Weekly Statistical Fishery Report.* **Price Frequency:** weekly, seasonally. **Effective Market(s):** Tokyo. **Units of Measure:** Dollars per lb. **Type of Price:** wholesale. **Time Period Covered:** 2 weeks ago, month ago.

SALMON TROUT: FARM RAISED, FRESH, CANADIAN

Source: *Seafood Price-Current.* **Price Frequency:** semiweekly. **Effective Market(s):** Seattle. **Units of Measure:** Dollars per lb. **Type of Price:** sale by first receiver. **Time Period Covered:** latest day.

SALMON TROUT: FRESH, CHILEAN

Source: *Seafood Price-Current.* **Price Frequency:** semiweekly. **Effective Market(s):** Miami. **Units of Measure:** Dollars per lb. **Type of Price:** sale by first receiver. **Time Period Covered:** latest day.

SALMON TROUT: FRESHWATER, WHOLE, FRESH

Source: *Seafood Price-Current.* **Price Frequency:** semiweekly. **Effective Market(s):** Mid-Atlantic, New England. **Units of Measure:** Dollars per lb. **Type of Price:** sale by first receiver. **Time Period Covered:** latest day.

SALOL

see Phenylsalicylate.

SALT

Source: *Feedstuffs.* **Price Frequency:** weekly. **Effective Market(s):** 6 domestic markets. **Units of Measure:** Dollars per bulk ton. **Time Period Covered:** latest week.

SALT: CHEMICAL GRADE

Source: *Chemical Marketing Reporter.* **Price Frequency:** weekly. **Effective Market(s):** New York. **Units of Measure:** Dollars per 80 lbs. **Type of Price:** spot. **Time Period Covered:** latest week.

SALT: EVAPORATED, COMMON

Source: *Chemical Marketing Reporter.* **Price Frequency:** weekly. **Effective Market(s):** New York. **Units of Measure:** Dollars per 80 lbs., dollars per ton. **Type of Price:** spot. **Time Period Covered:** latest week.

SALT: GROUND

Source: *Industrial Minerals.* **Price Frequency:** monthly. **Effective Market(s):** United Kingdom. **Units of Measure:** British pounds per metric tonne. **Type of Price:** producer & dealer. **Time Period Covered:** latest month.

SALT: ROCK, MEDIUM COARSE

Source: *Chemical Marketing Reporter.* **Price Frequency:** weekly. **Effective Market(s):** New York. **Units of Measure:** Dollars per 80 lbs., dollars per ton. **Type of Price:** spot. **Time Period Covered:** latest week.

SALT: STOCK

Source: *Agricultural Prices.* **Price Frequency:** quarterly. **Effective Market(s):** United States. **Units of Measure:** Dollars per 50 lbs. **Type of Price:** paid by farmer. **Time Period Covered:** latest 2 quarters, year ago.

Source: *Agricultural Prices.* **Price Frequency:** monthly. **Effective Market(s):** 10 domestic markets, United States. **Units of Measure:** Dollars per 50 lbs. **Type of Price:** paid by farmer. **Time Period Covered:** latest month.

Source: *Agricultural Prices Annual Summary.* **Price Frequency:** quarterly. **Effective Market(s):** 10 domestic markets, United States. **Units of Measure:** Dollars per ton. **Type of Price:** average paid by farmer. **Time Period Covered:** latest year, for US latest 6 years.

Source: *Feed Situation and Outlook Report.* **Price Frequency:** quarterly, annually. **Effective Market(s):** United States. **Units of Measure:** Dollars per 100 lbs. **Type of Price:** paid by farmer. **Time Period Covered:** latest year.

SALT: TABLE

Source: *Statistical Bulletin of the South Pacific: Retail Price Indexes.* **Price Frequency:** annually. **Effective Market(s):** 18 South Pacific markets. **Units of Measure:** Australian dollars per 500 grams. **Type of Price:** retail. **Time Period Covered:** latest year.

SALTCAKE

Source: *Chemical Marketing Reporter.* **Price Frequency:** weekly. **Effective Market(s):** East, West. **Units of Measure:** Dollars per ton. **Type of Price:** spot. **Time Period Covered:** latest week.

Source: *Journal of Commerce and Commercial.* **Price Frequency:** weekly in Thursday issue. **Effective Market(s):** East. **Units of Measure:** Dollars per ton. **Type of Price:** spot. **Time Period Covered:** latest week.

SALTPETER

Source: *Journal of Commerce and Commercial.* **Price Frequency:** weekly in Thursday issue. **Units of Measure:** Dollars per 100 lbs. **Type of Price:** spot. **Time Period Covered:** latest week.

SAN

see Styrene Acrylonitrile.

SAND

Source: *ENR.* **Price Frequency:** monthly in first issue of month. **Effective Market(s):** 20-city average. **Units of Measure:** Dollars per ton. **Time Period Covered:** latest month.

SAND: CONCRETE

Source: *ENR.* **Price Frequency:** monthly in first issue of month. **Effective Market(s):** 16 domestic market, Montreal, Toronto. **Units of Measure:** Dollars per ton. **Type of Price:** spot. **Time Period Covered:** latest month.

SAND: MASONRY

Source: *ENR.* **Price Frequency:** monthly in first issue of month. **Effective Market(s):** 16 domestic markets, Montreal. **Units of Measure:** Dollars per ton. **Type of Price:** spot. **Time Period Covered:** latest month.

SANDABS

see Dabs.

SANDALWOOD OIL

Source: *U. S. Essential Oil Trade.* **Price Frequency:** annually. **Effective Market(s):** United States. **Units of Measure:** Dollars per kilogram. **Type of Price:** import value. **Time Period Covered:** latest 3 years.

SANDALWOOD OIL: EAST INDIAN

Source: *Chemical Marketing Reporter.* **Price Frequency:** weekly. **Effective Market(s):** New York. **Units of Measure:** Dollars per kilo. **Type of Price:** spot. **Time Period Covered:** latest week.

Source: *Journal of Commerce and Commercial.* **Price Frequency:** weekly in Tuesday issue. **Units of Measure:** Dollars per lb. **Type of Price:** spot. **Time Period Covered:** latest week.

SANDALWOOD OIL: INDONESIAN

Source: *Chemical Marketing Reporter.* **Price Frequency:** weekly. **Effective Market(s):** New York. **Units of Measure:** Dollars per kilo. **Type of Price:** spot. **Time Period Covered:** latest week.

SANDARAC GUM

Source: *Journal of Commerce and Commercial.* **Price Frequency:** weekly in Monday issue. **Units of Measure:** Dollars per lb. **Type of Price:** spot. **Time Period Covered:** latest week.

SANITARY PAPERS AND STOCK

Source: *Pulp & Paper Week.* **Price Frequency:** monthly, irregularly. **Units of Measure:** index. **Type of Price:** price index. **Time Period Covered:** latest 3 month.

SARCOSINE: TECHNICAL

Source: *Chemical Marketing Reporter.* **Price Frequency:** weekly. **Effective Market(s):** New York. **Units of Measure:** Dollars per lb. **Type of Price:** spot. **Time Period Covered:** latest week.

SARSPARILLA: INDIAN

Source: *Journal of Commerce and Commercial.* **Price Frequency:** weekly in Monday issue. **Units of Measure:** Dollars per lb. **Type of Price:** spot. **Time Period Covered:** latest week.

SARSPARILLA: MEXICAN

Source: *Journal of Commerce and Commercial.* **Price Frequency:** weekly in Monday issue. **Units of Measure:** Dollars per lb. **Type of Price:** spot. **Time Period Covered:** latest week.

SASSAFRAS BARK: ORDINARY

Source: *Journal of Commerce and Commercial.* **Price Frequency:** weekly in Monday issue. **Units of Measure:** Dollars per lb. **Type of Price:** spot. **Time Period Covered:** latest week.

SASSAFRAS BARK: SPECIAL

Source: *Journal of Commerce and Commercial.* **Price Frequency:** weekly in Monday issue. **Units of Measure:** Dollars per lb. **Type of Price:** spot. **Time Period Covered:** latest week.

SASSAFRAS OIL

Source: *U. S. Essential Oil Trade.* **Price Frequency:** annually. **Effective Market(s):** United States. **Units of Measure:** Dollars per kilogram. **Type of Price:** import value. **Time Period Covered:** latest 3 years.

SATSUMAS: MIKKAN

Source: *FAO Quarterly Bulletin of Statistics.* **Price Frequency:** monthly, annually. **Effective Market(s):** Japan. **Units of Measure:** Japanese yen per kilogram, dollars per metric ton. **Type of Price:** wholesale. **Time Period Covered:** latest 3 years.

SATSUMAS: SPANISH

Source: *FAO Quarterly Bulletin of Statistics.* **Price Frequency:** monthly, annually. **Effective Market(s):** West Germany. **Units of Measure:** West German marks per 100 kilograms, dollars per metric ton. **Type of Price:** wholesale. **Time Period Covered:** latest 3 years.

SAUDI ARABIA RIYAL

Source: *Asian Wall Street Journal.* **Price Frequency:** daily. **Effective Market(s):** United States. **Units of Measure:** Saudi Arabian riyal per SDR. **Type of Price:** foreign exchange. **Time Period Covered:** latest 2 days.

Source: *Barron's.* **Price Frequency:** weekly. **Effective Market(s):** New York. **Units of Measure:** Saudi Arabian riyal per United States dollar. **Type of Price:** foreign exchange. **Time Period Covered:** latest 2 weeks.

Source: *New York Times.* **Price Frequency:** daily. **Effective Market(s):** United States. **Units of Measure:** Saudi Arabian riyal per United States dollar. **Type of Price:** foreign exchange. **Time Period Covered:** latest 2 days.

Source: *The Times.* **Price Frequency:** daily. **Effective Market(s):** London. **Units of Measure:** Saudi Arabian riyal per British pound. **Type of Price:** foreign exchange. **Time Period Covered:** latest day.

SAUSAGE: ITALIAN

Source: *Meat Price Report.* **Price Frequency:** weekly. **Units of Measure:** cents per lb. **Type of Price:** price paid to wholesaler. **Time Period Covered:** latest week.

SAUSAGE: POLISH

Source: *Meat Price Report.* **Price Frequency:** weekly. **Units of Measure:** cents per lb. **Type of Price:** price paid to wholesaler. **Time Period Covered:** latest week.

SAVORY: FRENCH

Source: *U. S. Spice Trade.* **Price Frequency:** annually. **Effective Market(s):** New York. **Units of Measure:** cents per lb. **Type of Price:** spot. **Time Period Covered:** latest 3 years.

SAVORY: YUGOSLAVIAN

Source: *U. S. Spice Trade.* **Price Frequency:** annually. **Effective Market(s):** New York. **Units of Measure:** cents per lb. **Type of Price:** spot. **Time Period Covered:** latest 3 years.

SAWLOGS: HARDWOOD, MIXED

Source: *Timber Mart-South.* **Price Frequency:** quarterly. **Effective Market(s):** 13 domestic markets. **Units of Measure:** Dollars per 1000 board feet. **Type of Price:** delivered. **Time Period Covered:** latest 2 quarters.

SAWLOGS: OAK

Source: *Timber Mart-South.* **Price Frequency:** quarterly. **Effective Market(s):** 13 domestic markets. **Units of Measure:** Dollars per 1000 board feet. **Type of Price:** delivered. **Time Period Covered:** latest 2 quarters.

SAWLOGS: PINE

Source: *Timber Mart-South.* **Price Frequency:** quarterly. **Effective Market(s):** 13 domestic markets. **Units of Measure:** Dollars per 1000 board feet. **Type of Price:** delivered. **Time Period Covered:** latest 2 quarters.

SAWNWOOD: BEECH,

Source: *FAO Quarterly Bulletin of Statistics.* **Price Frequency:** monthly, annually. **Effective Market(s):** West Germany. **Units of Measure:** West German marks per cubic meter, dollars per metric ton. **Type of Price:** producer. **Time Period Covered:** latest 3 years.

SAWNWOOD: BROADLEAVED

Source: *Timber Bulletin.* **Price Frequency:** monthly, annually. **Effective Market(s):** Italy. **Units of Measure:** 1000 Italian lire per cubic meter. **Time Period Covered:** monthly latest 2 months, annually latest 6 years.

SAWNWOOD: CONIFEROUS, CANADA

Source: *Timber Bulletin.* **Price Frequency:** monthly, annually. **Effective Market(s):** United Kingdom. **Units of Measure:** British pounds per cubic meter. **Type of Price:** import. **Time Period Covered:** monthly latest 2 months, annually latest 5 years.

SAWNWOOD: CONIFEROUS, LUMBER

Source: *Timber Bulletin.* **Price Frequency:** monthly, annually. **Effective Market(s):** Finland. **Units of Measure:** Finnish markka per cubic meter. **Type of Price:** export value. **Time Period Covered:** monthly latest 2 months, annually latest 2 years.

SAWNWOOD: CONIFEROUS, SWEDEN

Source: *Timber Bulletin.* **Price Frequency:** monthly, annually. **Effective Market(s):** United Kingdom. **Units of Measure:** British pounds per cubic meter. **Type of Price:** import. **Time Period Covered:** monthly latest 2 months, annually latest 5 years.

SAWNWOOD: CONIFEROUS, U.S.S.R

Source: *Timber Bulletin.* **Price Frequency:** monthly, annually. **Effective Market(s):** United Kingdom. **Units of Measure:** British pounds per cubic meter. **Type of Price:** import. **Time Period Covered:** monthly latest 2 months, annually latest 5 years.

SAWNWOOD: DARK RED MERANTI, MALAYSIAN

Source: *Commodity Trade and Price Trends.* **Price Frequency:** annually. **Effective Market(s):** French ports. **Units of Measure:** Dollars per cubic meter, 1980 constant dollars per cubic meter. **Time Period Covered:** latest 29 years.

Source: *Monthly Commodity Price Bulletin Supplement.* **Price Frequency:** monthly, quarterly, annually. **Effective Market(s):** French ports. **Units of Measure:** Dollars per cubic meter. **Time Period Covered:** latest 20 years.

SAWNWOOD: LAUAN, WHITE, PLANK

Source: *Prices of Selected Asia/Pacific Products.* **Price Frequency:** monthly. **Effective Market(s):** Tokyo. **Units of Measure:** 1000 Japanese yen per cubic meter. **Type of Price:** wholesale high, wholesale low. **Time Period Covered:** latest month.

SAWNWOOD: MALAYSIAN

Source: *International Financial Statistics.* **Price Frequency:** monthly, quarterly, annually. **Effective Market(s):** French ports. **Units of Measure:** Dollars per cubic meter, index. **Type of Price:** market price, price index. **Time Period Covered:** latest 3 months, latest 4 quarters, latest 5 years.

Source: *International Financial Statistics Yearbook.* **Price Frequency:** annually. **Effective Market(s):** French ports. **Units of Measure:** Dollars per cubic meter. **Type of Price:** wholesale. **Time Period Covered:** latest 30 years.

SAWNWOOD: MERANTI, MALAYSIAN

Source: *FAO Quarterly Bulletin of Statistics.* **Price Frequency:** monthly, annually. **Effective Market(s):** Malaysia. **Units of Measure:** Malaysian ringgits per ton 50 cubic feet, dollars per metric ton. **Type of Price:** export. **Time Period Covered:** latest 3 years.

SAWNWOOD: REDWOOD

Source: *Timber Bulletin.* **Price Frequency:** monthly, annually. **Effective Market(s):** Sweden. **Units of Measure:** Swedish kronor per cubic meter. **Type of Price:** export. **Time Period Covered:** monthly latest 2 months, annually latest 6 years.

SAWNWOOD: REDWOOD, UNITED STATES

Source: *FAO Quarterly Bulletin of Statistics.* **Price Frequency:** monthly, annually. **Effective Market(s):** Sweden. **Units of Measure:** Swedish kronor per cubic meter, dollars per metric ton. **Type of Price:** export. **Time Period Covered:** latest 3 years.

SAWNWOOD: SPRUCE/FIR

Source: *Timber Bulletin.* **Price Frequency:** monthly, annually. **Effective Market(s):** Austria. **Units of Measure:** Austrian schillings per cubic meter. **Type of Price:** wholesale. **Time Period Covered:** monthly latest 2 months, annually latest 6 years.

SAWNWOOD: SPRUCE/FIR BATTENS

Source: *Timber Bulletin.* **Price Frequency:** monthly, annually. **Effective Market(s):** West Germany. **Units of Measure:** West German marks per cubic meter. **Time Period Covered:** monthly latest 2 months, annually latest 6 years.

SAWNWOOD: SPRUCE/PINE/FIR

Source: *FAO Quarterly Bulletin of Statistics.* **Price Frequency:** monthly, annually. **Effective Market(s):** United States. **Units of Measure:** Dollars per 1000 board feet, dollars per metric ton. **Time Period Covered:** latest 3 years.

SAWNWOOD: WHITEWOOD

Source: *Timber Bulletin.* **Price Frequency:** monthly, annually. **Effective Market(s):** Sweden. **Units of Measure:** Swedish kronor per cubic meter. **Type of Price:** export. **Time Period Covered:** monthly latest 2 months, annually latest 6 years.

SAWTIMBER: HEMLOCK

Source: *Timber Mart-South.* **Price Frequency:** quarterly. **Effective Market(s):** Kentucky. **Units of Measure:** Dollars per 1000 board feet. **Type of Price:** bid. **Time Period Covered:** latest quarter.

SCALLOPS: BAY, FRESH, MEXICAN

Source: *Seafood Price-Current.* **Price Frequency:** semiweekly. **Effective Market(s):** West Coast. **Units of Measure:** Dollars per lb. **Type of Price:** sale by first receiver. **Time Period Covered:** latest day.

SCALLOPS: BAY, FRESH, NORTHERN

Source: *Seafood Price-Current.* **Price Frequency:** semiweekly. **Effective Market(s):** Mid-Atlantic, New England. **Units of Measure:** Dollars per lb. **Type of Price:** sale by first receiver. **Time Period Covered:** latest day.

SCALLOPS: BAY, FRESH, SOUTHERN

Source: *HRI-Buyer's Guide.* **Price Frequency:** weekly. **Effective Market(s):** New York. **Units of Measure:** Dollars per lb. **Type of Price:** dealer. **Time Period Covered:** latest week.

SCALLOPS: CALICO BAY, FRESH

Source: *Seafood Price-Current.* **Price Frequency:** semiweekly. **Effective Market(s):** Gulf/Southeast. **Units of Measure:** Dollars per gallon. **Type of Price:** sale by first receiver. **Time Period Covered:** latest day.

SCALLOPS: CALICO BAY, SHUCKED, FRESH, SOUTHERN

Source: *Seafood Price-Current.* **Price Frequency:** semiweekly. **Effective Market(s):** Mid-Atlantic, New England. **Units of Measure:** Dollars per gallon. **Type of Price:** sale by first receiver. **Time Period Covered:** latest day.

SCALLOPS: SEA, BAY, FROZEN, UNITED KINGDOM

Source: *Seafood Price-Current.* **Price Frequency:** semiweekly. **Effective Market(s):** Mid-Atlantic. **Units of Measure:** Dollars per lb. **Type of Price:** first receiver. **Time Period Covered:** latest day.

SCALLOPS: SEA, CANADIAN

Source: *NMFS Green Sheet Supplement.* **Price Frequency:** weekly, seasonally. **Effective Market(s):** New England. **Units of Measure:** Dollars per lb. **Type of Price:** to primary wholesalers. **Time Period Covered:** latest week.

SCALLOPS: SEA, DOMESTIC

Source: *NMFS Green Sheet Supplement.* **Price Frequency:** weekly, seasonally. **Effective Market(s):** New York. **Units of Measure:** Dollars per lb. **Type of Price:** warehouse. **Time Period Covered:** latest week.

SCALLOPS: SEA, FROZEN

Source: *HRI-Buyer's Guide.* **Price Frequency:** weekly. **Effective Market(s):** Northeastern area. **Units of Measure:** Dollars per 5 lb. case. **Type of Price:** price paid by dining places & institutions. **Time Period Covered:** latest week.

SCALLOPS: SEA, FROZEN, CANADIAN

Source: *Seafood Price-Current.* **Price Frequency:** semiweekly. **Effective Market(s):** Mid-Atlantic. **Units of Measure:** Dollars per lb. **Type of Price:** first receiver. **Time Period Covered:** latest day.

SCALLOPS: SEA, FROZEN, DOMESTIC

Source: *Seafood Price-Current.* **Price Frequency:** semiweekly. **Effective Market(s):** Mid-Atlantic. **Units of Measure:** Dollars per lb. **Type of Price:** first receiver. **Time Period Covered:** latest day.

SCALLOPS: SEA, FROZEN, ICELANDIC

Source: *Seafood Price-Current.* **Price Frequency:** semiweekly. **Effective Market(s):** Mid-Atlantic. **Units of Measure:** Dollars per lb. **Type of Price:** first receiver. **Time Period Covered:** latest day.

SCALLOPS: SEA, FROZEN, JAPANESE

Source: *Seafood Price-Current.* **Price Frequency:** semiweekly. **Effective Market(s):** Mid-Atlantic. **Units of Measure:** Dollars per lb. **Type of Price:** first receiver. **Time Period Covered:** latest day.

SCALLOPS: SEA, FROZEN, PERUVIAN

Source: *Seafood Price-Current.* **Price Frequency:** semiweekly. **Effective Market(s):** Mid-Atlantic. **Units of Measure:** Dollars per lb. **Type of Price:** first receiver. **Time Period Covered:** latest day.

SCALLOPS: SEA, ICELANDIC

Source: *NMFS Green Sheet Supplement.* **Price Frequency:** weekly, seasonally. **Effective Market(s):** New England. **Units of Measure:** Dollars per lb. **Type of Price:** to primary wholesalers. **Time Period Covered:** latest week.

SCALLOPS: SEA, JAPANESE

Source: *NMFS Green Sheet Supplement.* **Price Frequency:** weekly, seasonally. **Effective Market(s):** New England. **Units of Measure:** Dollars per lb. **Type of Price:** to primary wholesalers. **Time Period Covered:** latest week.

SCALLOPS: SEA, NORWEGIAN

Source: *NMFS Green Sheet Supplement.* **Price Frequency:** weekly, seasonally. **Effective Market(s):** New England. **Units of Measure:** Dollars per lb. **Type of Price:** to primary wholesalers. **Time Period Covered:** latest week.

SCALLOPS: SEA, RAW, DOMESTIC

Source: *NMFS Green Sheet Supplement.* **Price Frequency:** weekly, seasonally. **Effective Market(s):** New England. **Units of Measure:** Dollars per lb. **Type of Price:** to primary wholesalers. **Time Period Covered:** latest week.

SCALLOPS: SEA, SHUCKED, FRESH

Source: *HRI-Buyer's Guide.* **Price Frequency:** weekly. **Effective Market(s):** New York. **Units of Measure:** Dollars per lb. **Type of Price:** dealer. **Time Period Covered:** latest week.

Source: *Seafood Price-Current.* **Price Frequency:** semiweekly. **Effective Market(s):** Mid-Atlantic, New Engalnd. **Units of Measure:** Dollars per lb. **Type of Price:** sale by first receiver. **Time Period Covered:** latest day.

SCHAEFFER'S SALT

Source: *Journal of Commerce and Commercial.* **Price Frequency:** weekly in Wednesday issue. **Units of Measure:** Dollars per lb. **Type of Price:** spot. **Time Period Covered:** latest week.

SCHAEFFER'S SALT: PASTE

Source: *Chemical Marketing Reporter.* **Price Frequency:** weekly. **Effective Market(s):** New York. **Units of Measure:** Dollars per lb. **Type of Price:** spot. **Time Period Covered:** latest week.

SCOPOLAMINE HYDROBROMIDE: USP

Source: *Chemical Marketing Reporter.* **Price Frequency:** weekly. **Effective Market(s):** New York. **Units of Measure:** Dollars per ounce. **Type of Price:** spot. **Time Period Covered:** latest week.

SCOTCH

Source: *Beverage Media.* **Price Frequency:** monthly. **Effective Market(s):** New York. **Units of Measure:** Dollars per unit. **Type of Price:** wholesale by brand. **Time Period Covered:** latest month.

Source: *Colorado Beverage Analyst.* **Price Frequency:** monthly. **Effective Market(s):** Colorado. **Units of Measure:** Dollars per case. **Type of Price:** wholesale by brand. **Time Period Covered:** latest month.

Source: *Illinois Beverage Journal.* **Price Frequency:** monthly. **Effective Market(s):** Illinois. **Units of Measure:** Dollars per case. **Type of Price:** wholesale by brand. **Time Period Covered:** latest month.

Source: *Kentucky Beverage Journal.* **Price Frequency:** monthly. **Effective Market(s):** Kentucky. **Units of Measure:** Dollars per bottle, dollars per case. **Type of Price:** wholesale by brand. **Time Period Covered:** latest month.

SCREENINGS: GROUND GRAIN
see Grain Screenings: Ground.

SEA BASS
see Bass: Sea.

SEA DABS
see Dabs: Sea.

SEA URCHIN ROE: FRESH, CANADIAN

Source: *Weekly Statistical Fishery Report.* **Price Frequency:** weekly. **Effective Market(s):** Tokyo. **Units of Measure:** Dollars per lb. **Type of Price:** wholesale. **Time Period Covered:** 2 weeks ago, month ago.

SEA URCHIN ROE: FRESH, LOS ANGELES

Source: *Weekly Statistical Fishery Report.* **Price Frequency:** weekly. **Effective Market(s):** Tokyo. **Units of Measure:** Dollars per lb. **Type of Price:** wholesale. **Time Period Covered:** 2 weeks ago, month ago.

SEA URCHIN ROE: FRESH, SOUTH KOREAN

Source: *Weekly Statistical Fishery Report.* **Price Frequency:** weekly. **Effective Market(s):** Tokyo. **Units of Measure:** Dollars per lb. **Type of Price:** wholesale. **Time Period Covered:** 2 weeks ago, month ago.

SEBACIC ACID: CHEMICALLY PURE

Source: *Chemical Marketing Reporter.* **Price Frequency:** weekly. **Effective Market(s):** New York. **Units of Measure:** Dollars per lb. **Type of Price:** spot. **Time Period Covered:** latest week.

SEBACIC ACID: PURIFIED

Source: *Chemical Marketing Reporter.* **Price Frequency:** weekly. **Effective Market(s):** New York. **Units of Measure:** Dollars per lb. **Type of Price:** spot. **Time Period Covered:** latest week.

SEED BARLEY

Source: *Agricultural Prices Annual Summary.* **Price Frequency:** semiannually. **Effective Market(s):** United States. **Units of Measure:** Dollars per bushel. **Type of Price:** average paid by farmer. **Time Period Covered:** latest 6 years.

SEED CORN: HYBRID

Source: *Agricultural Prices Annual Summary.* **Price Frequency:** annually. **Effective Market(s):** United States. **Units of Measure:** Dollars per bushel. **Type of Price:** average paid by farmer. **Time Period Covered:** latest 6 years.

SEED FLAX

Source: *Agricultural Prices Annual Summary.* **Price Frequency:** annually. **Effective Market(s):** United States. **Units of Measure:** Dollars per bushel. **Type of Price:** average paid by farmer. **Time Period Covered:** latest 6 years.

SEED HAY

Source: *Scottish Farmer.* **Price Frequency:** weekly, seasonally. **Effective Market(s):** Scotland. **Units of Measure:** British pounds per tonne. **Type of Price:** average farmers buying-in. **Time Period Covered:** latest week.

SEED OATS

Source: *Agricultural Prices Annual Summary.* **Price Frequency:** semiannually. **Effective Market(s):** United States. **Units of Measure:** Dollars per bushel. **Type of Price:** average paid by farmer. **Time Period Covered:** latest 6 years.

SEED PEANUTS

Source: *Agricultural Prices Annual Summary.* **Price Frequency:** semiannually. **Effective Market(s):** United States. **Units of Measure:** Dollars per 100 lbs. **Type of Price:** average paid by farmer. **Time Period Covered:** latest 6 years.

SEED POTATOES

Source: *Agricultural Prices Annual Summary.* **Price Frequency:** annually. **Effective Market(s):** United States. **Units of Measure:** Dollars per 100 lbs. **Type of Price:** average paid by farmer. **Time Period Covered:** latest 6 years.

SEED SOYBEANS
see Soybeans for Seed.

SEED SUNFLOWER

Source: *Agricultural Prices Annual Summary.* **Price Frequency:** annually. **Effective Market(s):** United States. **Units of Measure:** Dollars per 100 lbs. **Type of Price:** average paid by farmer. **Time Period Covered:** latest 6 years.

SEED WHEAT

Source: *Agricultural Prices Annual Summary.* **Price Frequency:** annually. **Effective Market(s):** United States. **Units of Measure:** Dollars per bushel. **Type of Price:** average paid by farmer. **Time Period Covered:** latest 6 years.

SELENIUM: 99.5% MINIMUM

Source: *Economic and Energy Indicators.* **Price Frequency:** biweekly. **Units of Measure:** Dollars per lb. **Time Period Covered:** latest 3 months, quarters, and years.

Source: *Journal of Commerce and Commercial.* **Price Frequency:** daily. **Effective Market(s):** Europe. **Units of Measure:** Dollars per lb.. **Type of Price:** spot. **Time Period Covered:** latest day.

SELENIUM POWDER: COMMERCIAL

Source: *American Metal Market.* **Price Frequency:** daily. **Units of Measure:** Dollars per lb. **Time Period Covered:** latest day.

SELENIUM POWDER: HIGH PURITY

Source: *American Metal Market.* **Price Frequency:** daily. **Units of Measure:** Dollars per lb. **Time Period Covered:** latest day.

SEMICONDUCTORS: 1M DRAM

Source: *Japan Economic Journal.* **Price Frequency:** weekly. **Effective Market(s):** Japan. **Units of Measure:** Japanese yen each. **Type of Price:** wholesale. **Time Period Covered:** latest 2 weeks.

SEMICONDUCTORS: 256K DRAM

Source: *Japan Economic Journal.* **Price Frequency:** weekly. **Effective Market(s):** Japan. **Units of Measure:** Japanese yen each. **Type of Price:** wholesale. **Time Period Covered:** latest 2 weeks.

SEMICONDUCTORS: 256K EPROM, 150 NANOSECOND

Source: *Purchasing.* **Price Frequency:** monthly. **Units of Measure:** Dollars each. **Type of Price:** transaction. **Time Period Covered:** latest day, month ago, 6 months ago, year ago.

SEMICONDUCTORS: 256K RAM, 150 NANOSECOND

Source: *Purchasing.* **Price Frequency:** monthly. **Units of Measure:** Dollars each. **Type of Price:** transaction. **Time Period Covered:** latest day, month ago, 6 months ago, year ago.

SEMICONDUCTORS: 256K SRAM

Source: *Japan Economic Journal.* **Price Frequency:** weekly. **Effective Market(s):** Japan. **Units of Measure:** Japanese yen each. **Type of Price:** wholesale. **Time Period Covered:** latest 2 weeks.

SEMICONDUCTORS: 512K EPROM

Source: *Japan Economic Journal.* **Price Frequency:** weekly. **Effective Market(s):** Japan. **Units of Measure:** Japanese yen each. **Type of Price:** wholesale. **Time Period Covered:** latest 2 weeks.

SEMOLINA

Source: *Milling & Baking News.* **Price Frequency:** weekly. **Effective Market(s):** Minneapolis. **Units of Measure:** Dollars per 100 lbs. **Time Period Covered:** latest week.

SENNA LEAVES: TINNEVELLY

Source: *Journal of Commerce and Commercial.* **Price Frequency:** weekly in Monday issue. **Units of Measure:** Dollars per lb. **Type of Price:** spot. **Time Period Covered:** latest week.

Source: *Prices of Selected Asia/Pacific Products.* **Price Frequency:** monthly. **Effective Market(s):** New York. **Units of Measure:** Dollars per lb. **Type of Price:** spot high, spot low. **Time Period Covered:** latest month.

SENNA LEAVES: TINNEVELLY, NO. 1

Source: *Chemical Marketing Reporter.* **Price Frequency:** weekly. **Effective Market(s):** New York. **Units of Measure:** Dollars per lb. **Type of Price:** spot. **Time Period Covered:** latest week.

SENNA LEAVES: WHOLE

Source: *Journal of Commerce and Commercial.* **Price Frequency:** weekly in Monday issue. **Units of Measure:** Dollars per lb. **Type of Price:** spot. **Time Period Covered:** latest week.

SENNA LEAVES: WHOLE AND HALF, ALEXANDRIA

Source: *Chemical Marketing Reporter.* **Price Frequency:** weekly. **Effective Market(s):** New York. **Units of Measure:** Dollars per lb. **Type of Price:** spot. **Time Period Covered:** latest week.

Source: *Prices of Selected Asia/Pacific Products.* **Price Frequency:** monthly. **Effective Market(s):** New York. **Units of Measure:** Dollars per lb. **Type of Price:** spot high, spot low. **Time Period Covered:** latest month.

SENNA LEAVES POWDER

Source: *Journal of Commerce and Commercial.* **Price Frequency:** weekly in Monday issue. **Units of Measure:** Dollars per lb. **Type of Price:** spot. **Time Period Covered:** latest week.

Source: *Prices of Selected Asia/Pacific Products.* **Price Frequency:** monthly. **Effective Market(s):** New York. **Units of Measure:** Dollars per lb. **Type of Price:** spot high, spot low. **Time Period Covered:** latest month.

SENNA LEAVES POWDER: TINNEVELLY, NO. 1

Source: *Chemical Marketing Reporter.* **Price Frequency:** weekly. **Effective Market(s):** New York. **Units of Measure:** Dollars per lb. **Type of Price:** spot. **Time Period Covered:** latest week.

SESAME OIL: USP

Source: *Chemical Marketing Reporter.* **Price Frequency:** weekly. **Effective Market(s):** New York. **Units of Measure:** Dollars per lb. **Type of Price:** spot. **Time Period Covered:** latest week.

SESAME SEED: BLACK, FOR COOKING USE, CHINESE

Source: *Selected Prices of Asia/Pacific Products.* **Price Frequency:** monthly. **Effective Market(s):** Tokyo. **Units of Measure:** 1000 Japanese yen per metric ton. **Type of Price:** high, low. **Time Period Covered:** latest month.

SESAME SEED: BLACK, FOR COOKING USE, THAI

Source: *Selected Prices of Asia/Pacific Products.* **Price Frequency:** monthly. **Effective Market(s):** Tokyo. **Units of Measure:** 1000 Japanese yen per metric ton. **Type of Price:** high, low. **Time Period Covered:** latest month.

SESAME SEED: BLACK, LARGE, GRADE A, THAI

Source: *Selected Prices of Asia/Pacific Products.* **Price Frequency:** monthly. **Effective Market(s):** Bangkok. **Units of Measure:** Thai baht per 100 kilograms. **Type of Price:** wholesale high, wholesale low. **Time Period Covered:** latest month.

SESAME SEED: BLACK, UNHULLED, INDONESIAN

Source: *Selected Prices of Asia/Pacific Products.* **Price Frequency:** monthly. **Effective Market(s):** Hong Kong. **Units of Measure:** Hong Kong dollars per picul. **Type of Price:** wholesale high, wholesale low. **Time Period Covered:** latest month.

SESAME SEED: HULLED, CENTRAL AMERICAN

Source: *Chemical Marketing Reporter.* **Price Frequency:** weekly. **Effective Market(s):** New York. **Units of Measure:** Dollars per lb. **Type of Price:** spot. **Time Period Covered:** latest week.

Source: *U. S. Spice Trade.* **Price Frequency:** monthly, annually. **Effective Market(s):** New York. **Units of Measure:** Dollars per lb. **Type of Price:** spot. **Time Period Covered:** latest 10 years.

SESAME SEED: MIXED, FOR OIL EXTRACTION, CHINESE

Source: *Selected Prices of Asia/Pacific Products.* **Price Frequency:** monthly. **Effective Market(s):** Tokyo. **Units of Measure:** 1000 Japanese yen per metric ton. **Type of Price:** high, low. **Time Period Covered:** latest month.

SESAME SEED: NATURAL, CENTRAL AMERICAN

Source: *U. S. Spice Trade.* **Price Frequency:** monthly, annually. **Effective Market(s):** New York. **Units of Measure:** Dollars per lb. **Type of Price:** spot. **Time Period Covered:** latest 10 years.

SESAME SEED: RED, UNHULLED, HO CHI MINH CITY

Source: *Selected Prices of Asia/Pacific Products.* **Price Frequency:** monthly. **Effective Market(s):** Hong Kong. **Units of Measure:** Hong Kong dollars per picul. **Type of Price:** wholesale high, wholesale low. **Time Period Covered:** latest month.

SEWER PIPE: CONCRETE, PREMIUM JOINT

Source: *ENR.* **Price Frequency:** monthly in first issue of month. **Effective Market(s):** 20-city average. **Units of Measure:** Dollars per foot. **Time Period Covered:** latest month.

SEWER PIPE: POLYVINYL CHLORIDE, SDR 35

Source: *ENR.* **Price Frequency:** monthly in second issue of month. **Effective Market(s):** 10 domestic markets, Montreal, Toronto. **Units of Measure:** Dollars per foot. **Type of Price:** spot. **Time Period Covered:** latest month.

SEWER PIPE: VITREOUS CLAY, PREMIUM JOINT

Source: *ENR.* **Price Frequency:** monthly in first issue of month. **Effective Market(s):** 20-city average. **Units of Measure:** Dollars per foot. **Time Period Covered:** latest month.

SHAD ROE: PAIRS, WHOLE, FRESH

Source: *Seafood Price-Current.* **Price Frequency:** semiweekly. **Effective Market(s):** Boston, Mid-Atlantic, New Bedford (MA), Portland (ME). **Units of Measure:** Dollars per lb. **Type of Price:** sale by first receiver, auction price. **Time Period Covered:** latest day.

SHAKES: WESTERN RED CEDAR

Source: *Random Lengths.* **Price Frequency:** weekly. **Units of Measure:** Dollars per 1000 board feet. **Type of Price:** price to wholesaler. **Time Period Covered:** latest week.

SHALLOTS: NEW JERSEY

Source: *HRI-Buyer's Guide.* **Price Frequency:** weekly. **Effective Market(s):** Northeastern area. **Units of Measure:** Dollars per lb. **Type of Price:** price paid to dining places & institutions. **Time Period Covered:** latest week.

SHARK: ANGEL, FILLETS, FRESH

Source: *Seafood Price-Current.* **Price Frequency:** semiweekly. **Effective Market(s):** West Coast. **Units of Measure:** Dollars per lb. **Type of Price:** sale by first receiver. **Time Period Covered:** latest day.

SHARK: MAKO, FILLETS, DRESSED, FRESH, HAWAIIAN

Source: *Seafood Price-Current.* **Price Frequency:** semiweekly. **Effective Market(s):** Hawaii. **Units of Measure:** Dollars per lb. **Type of Price:** sale by first receiver. **Time Period Covered:** latest day.

SHARK: MAKO, WHOLE, DRESSED, FRESH

Source: *Seafood Price-Current.* **Price Frequency:** semiweekly. **Effective Market(s):** West Coast. **Units of Measure:** Dollars per lb. **Type of Price:** sale by first receiver. **Time Period Covered:** latest day.

SHARK: MAKO, WHOLE, DRESSED, FRESH, HAWAIIAN

Source: *Seafood Price-Current.* **Price Frequency:** semiweekly. **Effective Market(s):** Hawaii. **Units of Measure:** Dollars per lb. **Type of Price:** sale by first receiver. **Time Period Covered:** latest day.

SHARK: MAKO, WHOLE, FRESH

Source: *Seafood Price-Current.* **Price Frequency:** semiweekly. **Effective Market(s):** Boston, Mid-Atlantic, New Bedford (MA), Portland (ME). **Units of Measure:** Dollars per lb. **Type of Price:** sale by first receiver, auction price. **Time Period Covered:** latest day.

SHARK: MAKO, WHOLE, FRESH, CENTRAL/SOUTH AMERICA, IMPORTED

Source: *Seafood Price-Current.* **Price Frequency:** semiweekly. **Effective Market(s):** Miami. **Units of Measure:** Dollars per lb. **Type of Price:** sale by first receiver. **Time Period Covered:** latest day.

SHARK: SANDBAR, FRESH

Source: *Seafood Price-Current.* **Price Frequency:** semiweekly. **Effective Market(s):** Gulf/Southeast. **Units of Measure:** Dollars per lb. **Type of Price:** sale by first receiver. **Time Period Covered:** latest day.

SHARK: SOUPFIN, FILLETS, FRESH

Source: *Seafood Price-Current.* **Price Frequency:** semiweekly. **Effective Market(s):** West Coast. **Units of Measure:** Dollars per lb. **Type of Price:** sale by first receiver. **Time Period Covered:** latest day.

SHARK: THRESHER, FILLETS, FRESH

Source: *Seafood Price-Current.* **Price Frequency:** semiweekly. **Effective Market(s):** West Coast. **Units of Measure:** Dollars per lb. **Type of Price:** sale by first receiver. **Time Period Covered:** latest day.

SHARK: THRESHER, WHOLE, DRESSED, FRESH

Source: *Seafood Price-Current.* **Price Frequency:** semiweekly. **Effective Market(s):** West Coast. **Units of Measure:** Dollars per lb. **Type of Price:** sale by first receiver. **Time Period Covered:** latest day.

SHARK: THRESHER, WHOLE, FRESH, CENTRAL/SOUTH AMERICA, IMPORTED

Source: *Seafood Price-Current.* **Price Frequency:** semiweekly. **Effective Market(s):** Miami. **Units of Measure:** Dollars per lb. **Type of Price:** sale by first receiver. **Time Period Covered:** latest day.

SHARK'S FIN: CAKEFORMED, FIRST QUALITY, JAPANESE

Source: *Prices of Selected Asia/Pacific Products.* **Price Frequency:** monthly, seasonally. **Effective Market(s):** Hong Kong. **Units of Measure:** Hong Kong dollars per picul. **Type of Price:** wholesale high, wholesale low. **Time Period Covered:** latest month.

SHARK'S FIN: CAKEFORMED, HONG KONG

Source: *Prices of Selected Asia/Pacific Products.* **Price Frequency:** monthly, seasonally. **Effective Market(s):** Hong Kong. **Units of Measure:** Hong Kong dollars per picul. **Type of Price:** wholesale high, wholesale low. **Time Period Covered:** latest month.

SHARK'S FIN: CAKEFORMED, SINGAPORE

Source: *Prices of Selected Asia/Pacific Products.* **Price Frequency:** monthly, seasonally. **Effective Market(s):** Hong Kong. **Units of Measure:** Hong Kong dollars per picul. **Type of Price:** wholesale high, wholesale low. **Time Period Covered:** latest month.

SHARK'S FIN: LARGEST, JAPANESE

Source: *Prices of Selected Asia/Pacific Products.* **Price Frequency:** monthly, seasonally. **Effective Market(s):** Hong Kong. **Units of Measure:** Hong Kong dollars per picul. **Type of Price:** wholesale high, wholesale low. **Time Period Covered:** latest month.

SHEARLINGS

Source: *National Provisioner.* **Price Frequency:** weekly. **Effective Market(s):** Chicago. **Units of Measure:** Dollars per 100 lbs. **Time Period Covered:** latest week, year ago.

SHEARLINGS: PACKER, FULL CLIPS

Source: *National Provisioner.* **Price Frequency:** weekly. **Effective Market(s):** Chicago. **Units of Measure:** Dollars per 100 lbs. **Time Period Covered:** latest week, year ago.

SHEARLINGS: PACKER, NO. 1

Source: *National Provisioner.* **Price Frequency:** weekly. **Effective Market(s):** Chicago. **Units of Measure:** Dollars per 100 lbs. **Time Period Covered:** latest week, year ago.

SHEARLINGS: PACKER, NO. 2

Source: *National Provisioner.* **Price Frequency:** weekly. **Effective Market(s):** Chicago. **Units of Measure:** Dollars per 100 lbs. **Time Period Covered:** latest week, year ago.

SHEARLINGS: PACKER, NO. 3

Source: *National Provisioner.* **Price Frequency:** weekly. **Effective Market(s):** Chicago. **Units of Measure:** Dollars per 100 lbs. **Time Period Covered:** latest week, year ago.

SHEATHING: INSULATING, ASPHALT TREATED

Source: *Agricultural Prices.* **Price Frequency:** quarterly. **Effective Market(s):** United States. **Units of Measure:** Dollars per sheet. **Type of Price:** paid by farmer. **Time Period Covered:** latest 2 quarters, year ago.

Source: *Agricultural Prices Annual Summary.* **Price Frequency:** bimonthly. **Effective Market(s):** United States. **Units of Measure:** Dollars per sheet. **Type of Price:** average paid by farmer. **Time Period Covered:** latest 6 years.

SHEEP

see also Ewes, Lambs, Shearlings.

Source: *Agricultural Prices.* **Price Frequency:** monthly. **Effective Market(s):** United States. **Units of Measure:** Dollars per 100 lbs. **Type of Price:** received by farmer. **Time Period Covered:** latest 2 months, year ago.

Source: *Agricultural Prices.* **Price Frequency:** monthly. **Effective Market(s):** 16 domestic markets, United States. **Units of Measure:** Dollars per 100 lbs. **Type of Price:** received by farmer. **Time Period Covered:** latest 2 months.

Source: *Agricultural Prices Annual Summary.* **Price Frequency:** annually. **Effective Market(s):** 50 domestic markets, United States. **Units of Measure:** Dollars per 100 lbs. **Type of Price:** average received by farmer. **Time Period Covered:** latest 2 years, for US latest 6 years.

Source: *Agricultural Prices Annual Summary.* **Price Frequency:** monthly. **Effective Market(s):** 16 domestic markets, United States. **Units of Measure:** Dollars per 100 lbs. **Type of Price:** average received by farmer. **Time Period Covered:** latest year, for US latest 6 years.

Source: *Commodity Year Book.* **Price Frequency:** monthly, annually. **Effective Market(s):** United States. **Units of Measure:** Dollars per 100 lbs. **Type of Price:** price received by farmers. **Time Period Covered:** latest 7 years.

Source: *FAO Quarterly Bulletin of Statistics.* **Price Frequency:** monthly, annually. **Effective Market(s):** European Community. **Units of Measure:** ECU per 100 kilograms, dollars per metric ton. **Type of Price:** wholesale. **Time Period Covered:** latest 3 years.

Source: *Farm and Dairy.* **Price Frequency:** weekly, seasonally. **Effective Market(s):** Ohio, Pennsylvania. **Units of Measure:** Dollars per head. **Type of Price:** auction high, auction low. **Time Period Covered:** latest week.

Source: *Financial Times.* **Price Frequency:** daily. **Effective Market(s):** London. **Units of Measure:** British pence per kilogram. **Type of Price:** spot. **Time Period Covered:** latest day.

Source: *Illinois Farm Report.* **Price Frequency:** quarterly. **Effective Market(s):** Illinois. **Units of Measure:** Dollars per 100 lbs. **Type of Price:** average received by farmers. **Time Period Covered:** latest 2 months, year ago.

Source: *Lancaster Farming.* **Price Frequency:** weekly. **Effective Market(s):** Pennsylvania, Virginia. **Units of Measure:** Dollars per head. **Type of Price:** auction. **Time Period Covered:** latest week.

Source: *Livestock and Poultry Situation and Outlook Report.* **Price Frequency:** monthly. **Units of Measure:** Dollars per 100 lbs. **Type of Price:** farm. **Time Period Covered:** latest year.

Source: *Standard & Poor's Statistical Service Current Statistics.* **Price Frequency:** monthly, annually. **Units of Measure:** Dollars per 100 lbs. **Time Period Covered:** latest 5 years.

Source: *The Times.* **Price Frequency:** daily. **Effective Market(s):** England/Wales, Great Britain, Scotland. **Units of Measure:** British pence per kilogram liveweight. **Time Period Covered:** latest day.

SHEEP: AUSTRALIAN

Source: *FAO Quarterly Bulletin of Statistics.* **Price Frequency:** monthly, annually. **Effective Market(s):** Melbourne. **Units of Measure:** Australian dollars per 100 kilograms, dollars per metric ton. **Type of Price:** wholesale. **Time Period Covered:** latest 3 years.

SHEEP: HOGGET, DOWN CROSS, STORE

Source: *Scottish Farmer.* **Price Frequency:** weekly, seasonally. **Effective Market(s):** 9 Scottish markets average. **Units of Measure:** British pounds per head. **Type of Price:** average. **Time Period Covered:** latest 2 weeks.

SHEEP: HOGGET, FINISHED

Source: *Farmers Weekly.* **Price Frequency:** weekly. **Effective Market(s):** Great Britain. **Units of Measure:** British pence per kilogram. **Type of Price:** spot. **Time Period Covered:** latest week, week ago, year ago.

SHEEP: HOGGET, GREYFACE, STORE

Source: *Scottish Farmer.* **Price Frequency:** weekly, seasonally. **Effective Market(s):** 9 Scottish markets average. **Units of Measure:** British pounds per head. **Type of Price:** average. **Time Period Covered:** latest 2 weeks.

SHEEP: HOGGET, HALF-BRED, STORE

Source: *Scottish Farmer.* **Price Frequency:** weekly, seasonally. **Effective Market(s):** 9 Scottish markets average. **Units of Measure:** British pounds per head. **Type of Price:** average. **Time Period Covered:** latest 2 weeks.

SHEEP: HOGGET, HEAVY, PRIME

Source: *New Zealand Farmer.* **Price Frequency:** weekly, seasonally. **Effective Market(s):** 7 New Zealand markets. **Units of Measure:** New Zealand dollars per head. **Time Period Covered:** latest 2 weeks.

SHEEP: HOGGET, LIGHT, PRIME

Source: *New Zealand Farmer.* **Price Frequency:** weekly, seasonally. **Effective Market(s):** 7 New Zealand markets. **Units of Measure:** New Zealand dollars per head. **Time Period Covered:** latest 2 weeks.

SHEEP: HOGGET, MEDIUM, PRIME

Source: *New Zealand Farmer.* **Price Frequency:** weekly, seasonally. **Effective Market(s):** 7 New Zealand markets. **Units of Measure:** New Zealand dollars per head. **Time Period Covered:** latest 2 weeks.

SHEEP: PRIME

Source: *New Zealand Farmer.* **Price Frequency:** weekly, seasonally. **Effective Market(s):** 7 New Zealand markets. **Units of Measure:** New Zealand dollars per head. **Time Period Covered:** latest 2 weeks.

SHEEP: STORE

Source: *New Zealand Farmer.* **Price Frequency:** weekly, seasonally. **Effective Market(s):** 7 New Zealand markets. **Units of Measure:** New Zealand dollars per head. **Time Period Covered:** latest 2 weeks.

SHEEP: TWO-TOOTHS, GOOD, STORE

Source: *New Zealand Farmer.* **Price Frequency:** weekly, seasonally. **Effective Market(s):** 7 New Zealand markets. **Units of Measure:** New Zealand dollars per head. **Time Period Covered:** latest 2 weeks.

SHEEP: TWO-TOOTHS, LIGHT, STORE

Source: *New Zealand Farmer.* **Price Frequency:** weekly, seasonally. **Effective Market(s):** 7 New Zealand markets. **Units of Measure:** New Zealand dollars per head. **Time Period Covered:** latest 2 weeks.

SHEEP: WETHER, PRIME

Source: *New Zealand Farmer.* **Price Frequency:** weekly, seasonally. **Effective Market(s):** 7 New Zealand markets. **Units of Measure:** New Zealand dollars per head. **Time Period Covered:** latest 2 weeks.

SHEEPSHEAD (FISH): WHOLE, FRESH

Source: *Seafood Price-Current.* **Price Frequency:** semiweekly. **Effective Market(s):** Mid-Atlantic, New England. **Units of Measure:** Dollars per lb. **Type of Price:** sale by first receiver. **Time Period Covered:** latest day.

SHEETINGS CLOTH

Source: *DNR: Daily News Record.* **Price Frequency:** quarterly. **Units of Measure:** Dollars per yard. **Time Period Covered:** latest 3 quarters.

SHERRY

Source: *Beverage Media.* **Price Frequency:** monthly. **Effective Market(s):** New York. **Units of Measure:** Dollars per unit. **Type of Price:** wholesale by brand. **Time Period Covered:** latest month.

Source: *California Wineletter.* **Price Frequency:** semimonthly. **Effective Market(s):** Non-California markets. **Units of Measure:** Dollars per gallon. **Type of Price:** asking. **Time Period Covered:** latest week.

Source: *Indiana Beverage Journal.* **Price Frequency:** monthly. **Effective Market(s):** Indiana. **Units of Measure:** Dollars per case, dollars per bottle. **Type of Price:** wholesale by brand. **Time Period Covered:** latest month.

Source: *Nevada Beverage Index.* **Price Frequency:** monthly. **Effective Market(s):** Nevada. **Units of Measure:** Dollars per unit. **Type of Price:** wholesale by brand. **Time Period Covered:** latest month.

SHERRY: CREAM

Source: *California Wineletter.* **Price Frequency:** semimonthly. **Effective Market(s):** Non-California markets. **Units of Measure:** Dollars per gallon. **Type of Price:** asking. **Time Period Covered:** latest week.

SHERRY: DOMESTIC

Source: *Colorado Beverage Analyst.* **Price Frequency:** monthly. **Effective Market(s):** Colorado. **Units of Measure:** Dollars per case. **Type of Price:** wholesale by brand. **Time Period Covered:** latest month.

SHERRY: IMPORTED

Source: *Colorado Beverage Analyst.* **Price Frequency:** monthly. **Effective Market(s):** Colorado. **Units of Measure:** Dollars per case. **Type of Price:** wholesale by brand. **Time Period Covered:** latest month.

SHERRY: PALE DRY

Source: *California Wineletter.* **Price Frequency:** semimonthly. **Effective Market(s):** Non-California markets. **Units of Measure:** Dollars per gallon. **Type of Price:** asking. **Time Period Covered:** latest week.

SHINGLES: FIBERGLASS

Source: *Agricultural Prices.* **Price Frequency:** quarterly. **Effective Market(s):** United States. **Units of Measure:** Dollars per square. **Type of Price:** paid by farmer. **Time Period Covered:** latest 2 quarters, year ago.

Source: *Agricultural Prices Annual Summary.* **Price Frequency:** bimonthly. **Effective Market(s):** United States. **Units of Measure:** Dollars per square. **Type of Price:** average paid by farmer. **Time Period Covered:** latest 6 years.

SHINGLES: WESTERN RED CEDAR

Source: *Random Lengths.* **Price Frequency:** weekly. **Units of Measure:** Dollars per 1000 board feet. **Type of Price:** price to wholesaler. **Time Period Covered:** latest week.

SHOES: UPPER, WOMEN'S LEATHER

Source: *Commodity Year Book.* **Price Frequency:** annually. **Effective Market(s):** United States. **Units of Measure:** index. **Type of Price:** wholesale price index. **Time Period Covered:** latest 6 years.

SHORTENING

Source: *National Provisioner.* **Price Frequency:** daily. **Effective Market(s):** Chicago. **Units of Measure:** cents per lb. **Time Period Covered:** latest week.

SHORTENING: HYDROGENATED

Source: *National Provisioner.* **Price Frequency:** daily. **Effective Market(s):** North/South. **Units of Measure:** cents per lb. **Time Period Covered:** latest week.

SHORTENING: VEGETABLE, ALL PURPOSE

Source: *National Provisioner.* **Price Frequency:** daily. **Effective Market(s):** North/South. **Units of Measure:** cents per lb. **Time Period Covered:** latest week.

SHOVEL: ALUMINUM SCOOP

Source: *Agricultural Prices.* **Price Frequency:** annually. **Effective Market(s):** United States. **Units of Measure:** Dollars each. **Type of Price:** paid by farmer. **Time Period Covered:** latest year.

Source: *Agricultural Prices Annual Summary.* **Price Frequency:** semiannually. **Effective Market(s):** United States. **Units of Measure:** Dollars each. **Type of Price:** average paid by farmer. **Time Period Covered:** latest 6 years.

SHRIMP

Source: *International Financial Statistics.* **Price Frequency:** monthly, quarterly, annually. **Effective Market(s):** Gulf ports. **Units of Measure:** Dollars per lb., index. **Type of Price:** market price, price index. **Time Period Covered:** latest 5 months, latest 5 quarters, latest 5 years.

Source: *International Financial Statistics Yearbook.* **Price Frequency:** annually. **Effective Market(s):** Gulf ports. **Units of Measure:** Dollars per lb. **Type of Price:** wholesale. **Time Period Covered:** latest 30 years.

SHRIMP: BANGLADESH

Source: *NMFS Green Sheet Supplement.* **Price Frequency:** weekly, seasonally. **Effective Market(s):** New York. **Units of Measure:** Dollars per lb. **Type of Price:** warehouse. **Time Period Covered:** latest week.

SHRIMP: BLACK TIGER, BANGLADESH

Source: *NMFS Green Sheet Supplement.* **Price Frequency:** weekly, seasonally. **Effective Market(s):** New York. **Units of Measure:** Dollars per lb. **Type of Price:** warehouse. **Time Period Covered:** latest week.

SHRIMP: BLACK TIGER, INDONESIAN

Source: *NMFS Green Sheet Supplement.* **Price Frequency:** weekly, seasonally. **Effective Market(s):** New York. **Units of Measure:** Dollars per lb. **Type of Price:** warehouse. **Time Period Covered:** latest week.

SHRIMP: BLACK TIGER, SALTWATER, FROZEN, BANGLADESH

Source: *Seafood Price-Current.* **Price Frequency:** semiweekly. **Effective Market(s):** Mid-Atlantic. **Units of Measure:** Dollars per lb. **Type of Price:** first receiver. **Time Period Covered:** latest day.

SHRIMP: BLACK TIGER, SALTWATER, SOUTHEAST ASIAN, FROZEN

Source: *Seafood Price-Current.* **Price Frequency:** semiweekly. **Effective Market(s):** Mid-Atlantic. **Units of Measure:** Dollars per lb. **Type of Price:** first receiver. **Time Period Covered:** latest day.

SHRIMP: BLACK TIGER, TAIWANESE

Source: *Prices of Selected Asia/Pacific Products.* **Price Frequency:** monthly. **Effective Market(s):** Tokyo. **Units of Measure:** 100 Japanese yen per 1.8 kilograms. **Type of Price:** wholesale high, wholesale low. **Time Period Covered:** latest month.

SHRIMP: BLACK TIGER, THAI

Source: *NMFS Green Sheet Supplement.* **Price Frequency:** weekly, seasonally. **Effective Market(s):** New York. **Units of Measure:** Dollars per lb. **Type of Price:** warehouse. **Time Period Covered:** latest week.

SHRIMP: BREADED, "ORIENTAL STYLE"

Source: *NMFS Green Sheet Supplement.* **Price Frequency:** weekly, seasonally. **Effective Market(s):** New York. **Units of Measure:** Dollars per lb. **Type of Price:** warehouse. **Time Period Covered:** latest week.

SHRIMP: BROWN, GULF

Source: *NMFS Green Sheet Supplement.* **Price Frequency:** weekly, seasonally. **Effective Market(s):** New York. **Units of Measure:** Dollars per lb. **Type of Price:** warehouse. **Time Period Covered:** latest week.

SHRIMP: BROWN, NO. 1, MEXICAN

Source: *NMFS Green Sheet Supplement.* **Price Frequency:** weekly, seasonally. **Effective Market(s):** New York. **Units of Measure:** Dollars per lb. **Type of Price:** warehouse. **Time Period Covered:** latest week.

SHRIMP: BROWN, NO. 2, MEXICAN

Source: *NMFS Green Sheet Supplement.* **Price Frequency:** weekly, seasonally. **Effective Market(s):** New York. **Units of Measure:** Dollars per lb. **Type of Price:** warehouse. **Time Period Covered:** latest week.

SHRIMP: BROWN, SALTWATER, DOMESTIC/GULF OF MEXICO, FROZEN

Source: *Seafood Price-Current.* **Price Frequency:** semiweekly. **Effective Market(s):** Mid-Atlantic. **Units of Measure:** Dollars per lb. **Type of Price:** first receiver. **Time Period Covered:** latest day.

SHRIMP: BROWN, SALTWATER, PEELED, DRESSED, DOMESTIC/MEXICAN, FROZEN

Source: *Seafood Price-Current.* **Price Frequency:** semiweekly. **Effective Market(s):** Mid-Atlantic. **Units of Measure:** Dollars per lb. **Type of Price:** first receiver. **Time Period Covered:** latest day.

SHRIMP: COLUMBIA PINK, CARIBBEAN AREA

Source: *NMFS Green Sheet Supplement.* **Price Frequency:** weekly, seasonally. **Effective Market(s):** New York. **Units of Measure:** Dollars per lb. **Type of Price:** warehouse. **Time Period Covered:** latest week.

SHRIMP: COOKED FOR SALAD, FROZEN

Source: *HRI-Buyer's Guide.* **Price Frequency:** weekly. **Effective Market(s):** Northeastern area. **Units of Measure:** Dollars per case. **Type of Price:** price paid by dining places & institutions. **Time Period Covered:** latest week.

SHRIMP: COOKED, PEELED, FROZEN, CANADIAN

Source: *Seafood Price-Current.* **Price Frequency:** semiweekly. **Effective Market(s):** Mid-Atlantic. **Units of Measure:** Dollars per lb. **Type of Price:** first receiver. **Time Period Covered:** latest day.

SHRIMP: COOKED, PEELED, FROZEN, ICELANDIC

Source: *Seafood Price-Current.* **Price Frequency:** semiweekly. **Effective Market(s):** Mid-Atlantic. **Units of Measure:** Dollars per lb. **Type of Price:** first receiver. **Time Period Covered:** latest day.

SHRIMP: COOKED, PEELED, FROZEN, NORWEGIAN

Source: *Seafood Price-Current.* **Price Frequency:** semiweekly. **Effective Market(s):** Mid-Atlantic. **Units of Measure:** Dollars per lb. **Type of Price:** first receiver. **Time Period Covered:** latest day.

SHRIMP: COOKED, PEELED, FROZEN, OREGON

Source: *Seafood Price-Current.* **Price Frequency:** semiweekly. **Effective Market(s):** West Coast. **Units of Measure:** Dollars per lb. **Type of Price:** first receiver. **Time Period Covered:** latest day.

SHRIMP: COOKED, PEELED, TIN, OREGON

Source: *Seafood Price-Current.* **Price Frequency:** semiweekly. **Effective Market(s):** West Coast. **Units of Measure:** Dollars per lb. **Type of Price:** first receiver. **Time Period Covered:** latest day.

SHRIMP: ECUADOR

Source: *NMFS Green Sheet Supplement.* **Price Frequency:** weekly, seasonally. **Effective Market(s):** New York. **Units of Measure:** Dollars per lb. **Type of Price:** warehouse. **Time Period Covered:** latest week.

SHRIMP: FIRST BRAND, FROZEN, CHINESE

Source: *Prices of Selected Asia/Pacific Products.* **Price Frequency:** monthly. **Effective Market(s):** Tokyo. **Units of Measure:** 100 Japanese yen per 2 kilograms. **Type of Price:** wholesale high, wholesale low. **Time Period Covered:** latest month.

SHRIMP: FRESH WATER, THAI

Source: *NMFS Green Sheet Supplement.* **Price Frequency:** weekly, seasonally. **Effective Market(s):** New York. **Units of Measure:** Dollars per lb. **Type of Price:** warehouse. **Time Period Covered:** latest week.

SHRIMP: FRESHWATER, FROZEN, ASIAN

Source: *Seafood Price-Current.* **Price Frequency:** semiweekly. **Effective Market(s):** Mid-Atlantic. **Units of Measure:** Dollars per lb. **Type of Price:** first receiver. **Time Period Covered:** latest day.

SHRIMP: GULF/MEXICO

Source: *NMFS Green Sheet Supplement.* **Price Frequency:** weekly, seasonally. **Effective Market(s):** New York. **Units of Measure:** Dollars per lb. **Type of Price:** warehouse. **Time Period Covered:** latest week.

SHRIMP: HEAD-OFF, SHELL-ON, FROZEN, CHINESE

Source: *Weekly Statistical Fishery Report.* **Price Frequency:** weekly. **Effective Market(s):** Tokyo. **Units of Measure:** Dollars per lb. **Type of Price:** wholesale. **Time Period Covered:** 2 weeks ago, month ago.

SHRIMP: INDIAN

Source: *NMFS Green Sheet Supplement.* **Price Frequency:** weekly, seasonally. **Effective Market(s):** New York. **Units of Measure:** Dollars per lb. **Type of Price:** warehouse. **Time Period Covered:** latest week.

SHRIMP: NIGERIAN

Source: *NMFS Green Sheet Supplement.* **Price Frequency:** weekly, seasonally. **Effective Market(s):** New York. **Units of Measure:** Dollars per lb. **Type of Price:** warehouse. **Time Period Covered:** latest week.

SHRIMP: NORTHERN PINK, BRAZILIAN

Source: *NMFS Green Sheet Supplement.* **Price Frequency:** weekly, seasonally. **Effective Market(s):** New York. **Units of Measure:** Dollars per lb. **Type of Price:** warehouse. **Time Period Covered:** latest week.

SHRIMP: NORWEGIAN

Source: *NMFS Green Sheet Supplement.* **Price Frequency:** weekly, seasonally. **Effective Market(s):** New York. **Units of Measure:** Dollars per lb. **Type of Price:** warehouse. **Time Period Covered:** latest week.

SHRIMP: OREGON

Source: *NMFS Green Sheet Supplement.* **Price Frequency:** weekly, seasonally. **Effective Market(s):** New York. **Units of Measure:** Dollars per lb. **Type of Price:** warehouse. **Time Period Covered:** latest week.

SHRIMP: PEELED, DEVEINED, FROZEN

Source: *HRI-Buyer's Guide.* **Price Frequency:** weekly. **Effective Market(s):** Northeastern area. **Units of Measure:** Dollars per case. **Type of Price:** price paid by dining places & institutions. **Time Period Covered:** latest week.

SHRIMP: PEELED, INDIAN

Source: *Prices of Selected Asia/Pacific Products.* **Price Frequency:** monthly. **Effective Market(s):** Tokyo. **Units of Measure:** 100 Japanese yen per 2 kilograms. **Type of Price:** wholesale high, wholesale low. **Time Period Covered:** latest month.

SHRIMP: PERUVIAN

Source: *NMFS Green Sheet Supplement.* **Price Frequency:** weekly, seasonally. **Effective Market(s):** New York. **Units of Measure:** Dollars per lb. **Type of Price:** warehouse. **Time Period Covered:** latest week.

SHRIMP: PINK AND WHITE, SALTWATER, PEELED, DRESSED, FROZEN, DOMESTIC/MEXICAN

Source: *Seafood Price-Current.* **Price Frequency:** semiweekly. **Effective Market(s):** Mid-Atlantic. **Units of Measure:** Dollars per lb. **Type of Price:** first receiver. **Time Period Covered:** latest day.

SHRIMP: PINK, PANAMANIAN

Source: *NMFS Green Sheet Supplement.* **Price Frequency:** weekly, seasonally. **Effective Market(s):** New York. **Units of Measure:** Dollars per lb. **Type of Price:** warehouse. **Time Period Covered:** latest week.

SHRIMP: PINK, SALTWATER, FROZEN, SOUTH AMERICAN

Source: *Seafood Price-Current.* **Price Frequency:** semiweekly. **Effective Market(s):** Mid-Atlantic. **Units of Measure:** Dollars per lb. **Type of Price:** first receiver. **Time Period Covered:** latest day.

SHRIMP: PRAWN AND SHRIMP, SECOND QUALITY, HO CHI MINH CITY

Source: *Prices of Selected Asia/Pacific Products.* **Price Frequency:** monthly. **Effective Market(s):** Hong Kong. **Units of Measure:** Hong Kong dollars per picul. **Type of Price:** wholesale high, wholesale low. **Time Period Covered:** latest month.

SHRIMP: PRAWN AND SHRIMP, THAI

Source: *Prices of Selected Asia/Pacific Products.* **Price Frequency:** monthly. **Effective Market(s):** Hong Kong. **Units of Measure:** Hong Kong dollars per picul. **Type of Price:** wholesale high, wholesale low. **Time Period Covered:** latest month.

SHRIMP: RAW, SHELL-ON, FROZEN

Source: *HRI-Buyer's Guide.* **Price Frequency:** weekly. **Effective Market(s):** Northeastern area. **Units of Measure:** Dollars per case. **Type of Price:** price paid by dining places & institutions. **Time Period Covered:** latest week.

SHRIMP: SALTWATER, PUD, FROZEN, DOMESTIC/GULF OF MEXICO

Source: *Seafood Price-Current.* **Price Frequency:** semiweekly. **Effective Market(s):** Mid-Atlantic. **Units of Measure:** Dollars per lb. **Type of Price:** first receiver. **Time Period Covered:** latest day.

SHRIMP: TIGER, HEAD-OFF, SHELL-ON, FROZEN, TAIWANESE

Source: *Weekly Statistical Fishery Report.* **Price Frequency:** weekly. **Effective Market(s):** Tokyo. **Units of Measure:** Dollars per lb. **Type of Price:** wholesale. **Time Period Covered:** 2 weeks ago, month ago.

SHRIMP: UNCOOKED FOR SALAD, FROZEN

Source: *HRI-Buyer's Guide.* **Price Frequency:** weekly. **Effective Market(s):** Northeastern area. **Units of Measure:** Dollars per case. **Type of Price:** price paid by dining places & institutions. **Time Period Covered:** latest week.

SHRIMP: VENEZUELAN

Source: *NMFS Green Sheet Supplement.* **Price Frequency:** weekly, seasonally. **Effective Market(s):** New York. **Units of Measure:** Dollars per lb. **Type of Price:** warehouse. **Time Period Covered:** latest week.

SHRIMP: WHITE, CHINESE

Source: *NMFS Green Sheet Supplement.* **Price Frequency:** weekly, seasonally. **Effective Market(s):** New York. **Units of Measure:** Dollars per lb. **Type of Price:** warehouse. **Time Period Covered:** latest week.

SHRIMP: WHITE, COLUMBIAN

Source: *NMFS Green Sheet Supplement.* **Price Frequency:** weekly, seasonally. **Effective Market(s):** New York. **Units of Measure:** Dollars per lb. **Type of Price:** warehouse. **Time Period Covered:** latest week.

SHRIMP: WHITE, ECUADOR

Source: *NMFS Green Sheet Supplement.* **Price Frequency:** weekly, seasonally. **Effective Market(s):** New York. **Units of Measure:** Dollars per lb. **Type of Price:** warehouse. **Time Period Covered:** latest week.

SHRIMP: WHITE, FROZEN, INDIAN

Source: *Japan Economic Journal.* **Price Frequency:** weekly. **Effective Market(s):** Japan. **Units of Measure:** Japanese yen per 2 kilograms. **Type of Price:** wholesale. **Time Period Covered:** latest 2 weeks.

Source: *Prices of Selected Asia/Pacific Products.* **Price Frequency:** monthly. **Effective Market(s):** Tokyo. **Units of Measure:** 100 Japanese yen per 2 kilograms. **Type of Price:** wholesale high, wholesale low. **Time Period Covered:** latest month.

SHRIMP: WHITE, FROZEN, INDONESIAN

Source: *Prices of Selected Asia/Pacific Products.* **Price Frequency:** monthly. **Effective Market(s):** Tokyo. **Units of Measure:** 100 Japanese yen per 4 lbs. **Type of Price:** wholesale high, wholesale low. **Time Period Covered:** latest month.

SHRIMP: WHITE, GULF

Source: *NMFS Green Sheet Supplement.* **Price Frequency:** weekly, seasonally. **Effective Market(s):** New York. **Units of Measure:** Dollars per lb. **Type of Price:** warehouse. **Time Period Covered:** latest week.

SHRIMP: WHITE, HEAD-OFF, SHELL-ON, FROZEN, INDIAN

Source: *Weekly Statistical Fishery Report.* **Price Frequency:** weekly. **Effective Market(s):** Tokyo. **Units of Measure:** Dollars per lb. **Type of Price:** wholesale. **Time Period Covered:** 2 weeks ago, month ago.

SHRIMP: WHITE, NO. 1, MEXICAN

Source: *NMFS Green Sheet Supplement.* **Price Frequency:** weekly, seasonally. **Effective Market(s):** New York. **Units of Measure:** Dollars per lb. **Type of Price:** warehouse. **Time Period Covered:** latest week.

SHRIMP: WHITE, NO. 1, SALTWATER, FROZEN, MEXICAN

Source: *Seafood Price-Current.* **Price Frequency:** semiweekly. **Effective Market(s):** West Coast. **Units of Measure:** Dollars per lb. **Type of Price:** frist receiver. **Time Period Covered:** latest day.

SHRIMP: WHITE, NO. 2, MEXICAN

Source: *NMFS Green Sheet Supplement.* **Price Frequency:** weekly, seasonally. **Effective Market(s):** New York. **Units of Measure:** Dollars per lb. **Type of Price:** warehouse. **Time Period Covered:** latest week.

SHRIMP: WHITE, PANAMANIAN

Source: *NMFS Green Sheet Supplement.* **Price Frequency:** weekly, seasonally. **Effective Market(s):** New York. **Units of Measure:** Dollars per lb. **Type of Price:** warehouse. **Time Period Covered:** latest week.

SHRIMP: WHITE, SALTWATER, FROZEN, DOMESTIC/GULF OF MEXICO

Source: *Seafood Price-Current.* **Price Frequency:** semiweekly. **Effective Market(s):** Mid-Atlantic. **Units of Measure:** Dollars per lb. **Type of Price:** first receiver. **Time Period Covered:** latest day.

SHRIMP: WHITE, SALTWATER, POND RAISED, FROZEN, ECUADOR

Source: *Seafood Price-Current.* **Price Frequency:** semiweekly. **Effective Market(s):** Mid-Atlantic. **Units of Measure:** Dollars per lb. **Type of Price:** first receiver. **Time Period Covered:** latest day.

SHRIMP: WHITE, SALTWATER, POND RAISED, FROZEN, CHINESE

Source: *Seafood Price-Current.* **Price Frequency:** semiweekly. **Effective Market(s):** Mid-Atlantic. **Units of Measure:** Dollars per lb. **Type of Price:** first receiver. **Time Period Covered:** latest day.

SIDING: WESTERN RED CEDAR

Source: *Random Lengths.* **Price Frequency:** weekly. **Units of Measure:** Dollars per 1000 board feet. **Type of Price:** price to wholesaler. **Time Period Covered:** latest week.

SIENNA PIGMENT: BURNT

Source: *Chemical Marketing Reporter.* **Price Frequency:** weekly. **Effective Market(s):** New York. **Units of Measure:** Dollars per lb. **Type of Price:** spot. **Time Period Covered:** latest week.

SIENNA PIGMENT: BURNT, NATURAL, BROWN

Source: *Journal of Commerce and Commercial.* **Price Frequency:** weekly in Wednesday issue. **Units of Measure:** Dollars per lb. **Type of Price:** spot. **Time Period Covered:** latest week.

SIENNA PIGMENT: RAW

Source: *Chemical Marketing Reporter.* **Price Frequency:** weekly. **Effective Market(s):** New York. **Units of Measure:** Dollars per Lb. **Type of Price:** spot. **Time Period Covered:** latest week.

SIENNA PIGMENT: RAW, NATURAL, BROWN

Source: *Journal of Commerce and Commercial.* **Price Frequency:** weekly in Wednesday issue. **Units of Measure:** Dollars per lb. **Type of Price:** spot. **Time Period Covered:** latest week.

SILANE: AMINO FUNCTIONAL, MAXIMUM

Source: *Modern Plastics.* **Price Frequency:** quarterly in February, May, August, November issues. **Units of Measure:** Dollars per lb. **Type of Price:** list. **Time Period Covered:** latest year.

SILANE: AMINO FUNCTIONAL, MINIMUM

Source: *Modern Plastics.* **Price Frequency:** quarterly in February, May, August, November issues. **Units of Measure:** Dollars per lb. **Type of Price:** list. **Time Period Covered:** latest year.

SILANE: EPOXY FUNCTIONAL, MAXIMUM

Source: *Modern Plastics.* **Price Frequency:** quarterly in February, May, August, November issues. **Units of Measure:** Dollars per lb. **Type of Price:** list. **Time Period Covered:** latest year.

SILANE: EPOXY FUNCTIONAL, MINIMUM

Source: *Modern Plastics.* **Price Frequency:** quarterly in February, May, August, November issues. **Units of Measure:** Dollars per lb. **Type of Price:** list. **Time Period Covered:** latest year.

SILICA: AMORPHOUS, DRY GROUND, 93%, 200 MESH

Source: *Chemical Marketing Reporter.* **Price Frequency:** weekly. **Effective Market(s):** New York. **Units of Measure:** Dollars per ton. **Type of Price:** spot. **Time Period Covered:** latest week.

SILICA: AMORPHOUS, DRY GROUND, 98%, 200 MESH

Source: *Chemical Marketing Reporter.* **Price Frequency:** weekly. **Effective Market(s):** New York. **Units of Measure:** Dollars per ton. **Type of Price:** spot. **Time Period Covered:** latest week.

SILICA: AMORPHOUS, DRY GROUND, 97%, 325 MESH

Source: *Chemical Marketing Reporter.* **Price Frequency:** weekly. **Effective Market(s):** New York. **Units of Measure:** Dollars per ton. **Type of Price:** spot. **Time Period Covered:** latest week.

SILICA: AMORPHOUS, DRY GROUND, 98.5%, 325 MESH

Source: *Chemical Marketing Reporter.* **Price Frequency:** weekly. **Effective Market(s):** New York. **Units of Measure:** Dollars per ton. **Type of Price:** spot. **Time Period Covered:** latest week.

SILICA: AMORPHOUS, DRY GROUND, 99.5%, 325 MESH

Source: *Chemical Marketing Reporter.* **Price Frequency:** weekly. **Effective Market(s):** New York. **Units of Measure:** Dollars per ton. **Type of Price:** spot. **Time Period Covered:** latest week.

SILICA: DRY GROUND, 99% UNDER 10 MICRONS, MICRONIZED

Source: *Chemical Marketing Reporter.* **Price Frequency:** weekly. **Effective Market(s):** New York. **Units of Measure:** Dollars per ton. **Type of Price:** spot. **Time Period Covered:** latest week.

SILICA: DRY GROUND, 99% UNDER 15 MICRONS, MICRONIZED

Source: *Chemical Marketing Reporter.* **Price Frequency:** weekly. **Effective Market(s):** New York. **Units of Measure:** Dollars per ton. **Type of Price:** spot. **Time Period Covered:** latest week.

SILICA: DRY GROUND, 99.9%, 400 MESH, MICRONIZED

Source: *Chemical Marketing Reporter.* **Price Frequency:** weekly. **Effective Market(s):** New York. **Units of Measure:** Dollars per ton. **Type of Price:** spot. **Time Period Covered:** latest week.

SILICA: HARD QUARTZ, 140 MESH

Source: *Chemical Marketing Reporter.* **Price Frequency:** weekly. **Effective Market(s):** New York. **Units of Measure:** Dollars per ton. **Type of Price:** spot. **Time Period Covered:** latest week.

SILICA: HARD QUARTZ, 325 MESH

Source: *Chemical Marketing Reporter.* **Price Frequency:** weekly. **Effective Market(s):** New York. **Units of Measure:** Dollars per ton. **Type of Price:** spot. **Time Period Covered:** latest week.

SILICA SAND: FOUNDRY GRADE

Source: *Industrial Minerals.* **Price Frequency:** monthly. **Effective Market(s):** main European port. **Units of Measure:** British pounds per metric tonne. **Type of Price:** producer & dealer. **Time Period Covered:** latest month.

SILICA SAND: GLASS GRADE

Source: *Industrial Minerals.* **Price Frequency:** monthly. **Effective Market(s):** main European port. **Units of Measure:** British pounds per metric tonne. **Type of Price:** producer & dealer. **Time Period Covered:** latest month.

SILICOMANGANESE

Source: *American Metal Market.* **Price Frequency:** weekly. **Units of Measure:** cents per lb. **Type of Price:** producer. **Time Period Covered:** latest week.

SILICON

Source: *American Metal Market.* **Price Frequency:** weekly. **Units of Measure:** cents per lb. **Type of Price:** producer. **Time Period Covered:** latest week.

SILICON CARBIDE: BLACK, GRADE 1

Source: *Industrial Minerals.* **Price Frequency:** monthly. **Effective Market(s):** main European port. **Units of Measure:** British pounds per metric tonne. **Type of Price:** producer & dealer. **Time Period Covered:** latest month.

SILICON CARBIDE: BLACK, GRADE 2

Source: *Industrial Minerals.* **Price Frequency:** monthly. **Effective Market(s):** main European port. **Units of Measure:** British pounds per metric tonne. **Type of Price:** producer & dealer. **Time Period Covered:** latest month.

SILICON CARBIDE: GREEN

Source: *Industrial Minerals.* **Price Frequency:** monthly. **Effective Market(s):** main European port. **Units of Measure:** British pounds per metric tonne. **Type of Price:** producer & dealer. **Time Period Covered:** latest month.

SILICON LUMPS: 99.8% MINIMUM

Source: *Journal of Commerce and Commercial.* **Price Frequency:** daily. **Effective Market(s):** Europe. **Units of Measure:** Dollars per ton. **Type of Price:** spot. **Time Period Covered:** latest day.

SILICON TETRACHLORIDE: TECHNICAL

Source: *Chemical Marketing Reporter.* **Price Frequency:** weekly. **Effective Market(s):** New York. **Units of Measure:** Dollars per lb. **Type of Price:** spot. **Time Period Covered:** latest week.

SILICONES: MOLDING COMPOUND

Source: *Plastics Technology.* **Price Frequency:** monthly. **Units of Measure:** cents per lb., cents per cubic inch. **Type of Price:** bulk list, market. **Time Period Covered:** latest month.

SILICONES: SILICONE/EPOXY

Source: *Plastics Technology.* **Price Frequency:** monthly. **Units of Measure:** cents per lb., cents per cubic inch. **Type of Price:** bulk list, market. **Time Period Covered:** latest month.

SILICONES: SPECIALTY GRADE

Source: *Plastics Technology.* **Price Frequency:** monthly. **Units of Measure:** cents per lb., cents per cubic inch. **Type of Price:** bulk list, market. **Time Period Covered:** latest month.

SILK: RAW

Source: *Japan Economic Journal.* **Price Frequency:** weekly. **Effective Market(s):** Yokohama. **Units of Measure:** Japanese yen per kilogram. **Type of Price:** market. **Time Period Covered:** latest 2 weeks.

Source: *Prices of Selected Asia/Pacific Products.* **Price Frequency:** monthly. **Effective Market(s):** Yokohama (Japan). **Units of Measure:** 1000 Japanese yen per kilogram. **Type of Price:** wholesale high, wholesale low. **Time Period Covered:** latest month.

SILK: YOKOHAMA

Source: *Asian Wall Street Journal.* **Price Frequency:** daily. **Effective Market(s):** Yokohama. **Units of Measure:** Japanese yen per kilogram. **Type of Price:** spot. **Time Period Covered:** latest day.

SILK: YOKOHAMA, FUTURES

Source: *Asian Wall Street Journal.* **Price Frequency:** daily. **Effective Market(s):** Tokyo. **Units of Measure:** Japanese yen per kilogram. **Type of Price:** futures. **Time Period Covered:** latest day.

SILK FABRIC: 10 MONMME, HABUTAE

Source: *Prices of Selected Asia/Pacific Products.* **Price Frequency:** monthly. **Effective Market(s):** Fukui (Japan). **Units of Measure:** Japanese yen per yard. **Type of Price:** export supplier's high, export supplier's low. **Time Period Covered:** latest month.

SILK FABRIC: 14 MONMME, HABUTAE

Source: *Prices of Selected Asia/Pacific Products.* **Price Frequency:** monthly. **Effective Market(s):** Fukui (Japan). **Units of Measure:** Japanese yen per yard. **Type of Price:** domestic supplier's high, domestic supplier's low. **Time Period Covered:** latest month.

SILLIMANITE: SOUTH AFRICAN

Source: *Industrial Minerals.* **Price Frequency:** monthly. **Effective Market(s):** main European port. **Units of Measure:** British pounds per metric tonne. **Type of Price:** producer & dealer. **Time Period Covered:** latest month.

SILVER

Source: *American Metal Market.* **Price Frequency:** daily. **Effective Market(s):** London, New York, Zurich. **Units of Measure:** cents per troy ounce. **Type of Price:** selling. **Time Period Covered:** latest day.

Source: *American Metal Market.* **Price Frequency:** daily. **Effective Market(s):** New York. **Units of Measure:** cents per troy ounce. **Type of Price:** market. **Time Period Covered:** latest 3 days.

Source: *Asian Wall Street Journal.* **Price Frequency:** daily. **Effective Market(s):** London, New York. **Units of Measure:** British pounds per troy ounce, dollars per troy ounce. **Type of Price:** cash. **Time Period Covered:** latest 2 days.

Source: *Barron's.* **Price Frequency:** weekly. **Effective Market(s):** New York. **Units of Measure:** Dollars per troy ounce. **Time Period Covered:** latest 2 weeks.

Source: *Commodity Year Book.* **Price Frequency:** monthly, annually. **Effective Market(s):** New York. **Units of Measure:** cents per troy ounce. **Time Period Covered:** latest 15 years.

Source: *E&MJ.* **Price Frequency:** monthly. **Effective Market(s):** New York, Zurich. **Units of Measure:** cents per troy ounce. **Time Period Covered:** latest month.

Source: *E&MJ.* **Price Frequency:** monthly. **Effective Market(s):** London. **Units of Measure:** cents per troy ounce. **Type of Price:** spot. **Time Period Covered:** latest month, 6 months ago, 12 months ago.

Source: *Economic and Energy Indicators.* **Price Frequency:** biweekly. **Units of Measure:** Dollars per troy ounce. **Time Period Covered:** latest 3 months, quarters, and years.

Source: *Financial Post.* **Price Frequency:** weekly. **Effective Market(s):** Canada, London, New York. **Units of Measure:** Dollars per troy ounce. **Type of Price:** cash. **Time Period Covered:** latest week.

Source: *Financial Times.* **Price Frequency:** daily. **Effective Market(s):** London. **Units of Measure:** British pence per fine ounce, cents per fine/troy ounce. **Type of Price:** spot. **Time Period Covered:** latest day.

Source: *International Financial Statistics.* **Price Frequency:** monthly, quarterly, annually. **Effective Market(s):** New York. **Units of Measure:** cents per troy ounce, index. **Type of Price:** market price, price index. **Time Period Covered:** latest 5 months, latest 5 quarters, latest 5 years.

Source: *International Financial Statistics Yearbook.* **Price Frequency:** annually. **Effective Market(s):** New York. **Units of Measure:** cents per troy ounce. **Type of Price:** wholesale. **Time Period Covered:** latest 30 years.

Source: *Investor's Daily.* **Price Frequency:** daily. **Units of Measure:** Dollars per troy ounce. **Type of Price:** spot. **Time Period Covered:** latest day.

Source: *Journal of Commerce and Commercial.* **Price Frequency:** daily. **Units of Measure:** Dollars per troy ounce. **Type of Price:** spot supplier. **Time Period Covered:** latest day.

Source: *Los Angeles Times.* **Price Frequency:** daily. **Effective Market(s):** London, New York. **Units of Measure:** Dollars per troy ounce. **Type of Price:** cash. **Time Period Covered:** latest day.

Source: *New York Times.* **Price Frequency:** daily. **Effective Market(s):** New York. **Units of Measure:** Dollars per troy ounce. **Type of Price:** cash. **Time Period Covered:** latest 2 days.

Source: *Northern Miner.* **Price Frequency:** daily. **Effective Market(s):** London, New York, Toronto. **Units of Measure:** national currency per ounce. **Type of Price:** spot. **Time Period Covered:** latest week.

Source: *Purchasing.* **Price Frequency:** quarterly in January, April, July, October issues. **Units of Measure:** Dollars per troy ounce. **Type of Price:** transaction. **Time Period Covered:** latest 5 quarters.

Source: *The Times.* **Price Frequency:** daily. **Effective Market(s):** London. **Units of Measure:** Dollars per troy ounce, British pence per troy ounce. **Time Period Covered:** latest day.

Source: *Wall Street Journal.* **Price Frequency:** daily. **Units of Measure:** Dollars per troy ounce. **Type of Price:** base. **Time Period Covered:** latest day, day ago, year ago.

Source: *Wall Street Journal.* **Price Frequency:** daily. **Effective Market(s):** London. **Units of Measure:** British pounds per troy ounce. **Type of Price:** spot fixing. **Time Period Covered:** latest day, day ago, year ago.

SILVER: FABRICATED FORMS

Source: *American Metal Market.* **Price Frequency:** daily. **Effective Market(s):** New York. **Units of Measure:** cents per troy ounce. **Type of Price:** selling. **Time Period Covered:** latest day.

SILVER: FABRICATED PRODUCTS

Source: *Asian Wall Street Journal.* **Price Frequency:** daily. **Effective Market(s):** New York. **Units of Measure:** Dollars per troy ounce. **Type of Price:** cash. **Time Period Covered:** latest 2 days.

Source: *E&MJ.* **Price Frequency:** monthly. **Units of Measure:** cents per troy ounce. **Time Period Covered:** latest month.

Source: *Wall Street Journal.* **Price Frequency:** daily. **Units of Measure:** Dollars per troy ounce. **Time Period Covered:** latest day, day ago, year ago.

SILVER: FUTURES

Source: *Asian Wall Street Journal.* **Price Frequency:** daily. **Effective Market(s):** Chicago, New York. **Units of Measure:** cents per troy ounce. **Type of Price:** futures. **Time Period Covered:** latest day.

Source: *Barron's.* **Price Frequency:** weekly. **Effective Market(s):** Chicago, New York. **Units of Measure:** cents per troy ounce. **Type of Price:** futures. **Time Period Covered:** latest week.

Source: *Financial Times.* **Price Frequency:** daily. **Effective Market(s):** New York. **Units of Measure:** cents per troy ounce. **Type of Price:** futures. **Time Period Covered:** latest day.

Source: *Investor's Daily.* **Price Frequency:** daily. **Effective Market(s):** Chicago, New York. **Units of Measure:** cents per troy ounce, cents per ounce. **Type of Price:** futures. **Time Period Covered:** latest day.

Source: *Japan Economic Journal.* **Price Frequency:** weekly. **Effective Market(s):** Tokyo. **Units of Measure:** Japanese yen per 10 grams. **Type of Price:** futures. **Time Period Covered:** latest week.

Source: *Los Angeles Times.* **Price Frequency:** daily. **Effective Market(s):** Chicago, New York. **Units of Measure:** Dollars per troy ounce. **Type of Price:** futures. **Time Period Covered:** latest day.

Source: *New York Times.* **Price Frequency:** daily. **Effective Market(s):** Chicago, New York. **Units of Measure:** cents per troy ounce. **Type of Price:** futures. **Time Period Covered:** latest day.

Source: *Northern Miner.* **Price Frequency:** daily. **Effective Market(s):** New York. **Units of Measure:** cents per ounce. **Type of Price:** futures. **Time Period Covered:** daily.

Source: *Wall Street Journal.* **Price Frequency:** daily. **Effective Market(s):** Chicago, New York. **Units of Measure:** cents per troy ounce. **Type of Price:** futures. **Time Period Covered:** latest day.

SILVER: FUTURES, DECEMBER

Source: *Commodity Year Book.* **Price Frequency:** monthly. **Effective Market(s):** New York. **Units of Measure:** Dollars per ounce. **Type of Price:** futures. **Time Period Covered:** latest 8 years.

SILVER: REFINED, 99.9% GRADE

Source: *Monthly Commodity Price Bulletin Supplement.* **Price Frequency:** monthly, quarterly, annually. **Effective Market(s):** New York. **Units of Measure:** Dollars per fine ounce. **Type of Price:** average. **Time Period Covered:** latest 20 years.

SILVER BUILLON

Source: *American Metal Market.* **Price Frequency:** daily. **Effective Market(s):** New York. **Units of Measure:** cents per troy ounce. **Type of Price:** base. **Time Period Covered:** latest day.

SILVER BULLION

Source: *E&MJ.* **Price Frequency:** monthly. **Units of Measure:** cents per troy ounce. **Time Period Covered:** latest month.

SILVER BULLION: INDUSTRIAL

Source: *Asian Wall Street Journal.* **Price Frequency:** daily. **Effective Market(s):** New York. **Units of Measure:** Dollars per troy ounce. **Type of Price:** cash. **Time Period Covered:** latest 2 days.

Source: *Wall Street Journal.* **Price Frequency:** daily. **Units of Measure:** Dollars per troy ounce. **Time Period Covered:** latest day, day ago, year ago.

SILVER BULLION INGOTS

Source: *Chemical Marketing Reporter.* **Price Frequency:** weekly. **Effective Market(s):** New York. **Units of Measure:** Dollars per troy ounce. **Type of Price:** spot. **Time Period Covered:** latest week.

SILVER COINS

see Coins: Silver.

SILVER CYANIDE: 80% SILVER

Source: *Chemical Marketing Reporter.* **Price Frequency:** weekly. **Effective Market(s):** New York. **Units of Measure:** Dollars per ounce. **Type of Price:** spot. **Time Period Covered:** latest week.

SILVER INGOTS

Source: *Iron Age.* **Price Frequency:** monthly. **Units of Measure:** Dollars per gross ton. **Type of Price:** consumer. **Time Period Covered:** latest month.

SILVER NITRATE

Source: *Chemical Marketing Reporter.* **Price Frequency:** weekly. **Effective Market(s):** New York. **Units of Measure:** Dollars per ounce. **Type of Price:** spot. **Time Period Covered:** latest week.

SILVERBEET

Source: *New Zealand Farmer.* **Price Frequency:** weekly, seasonally. **Effective Market(s):** New Zealand. **Units of Measure:** New Zealand dollars per case/crate. **Time Period Covered:** latest week.

SINGAPORE DOLLARS

Source: *Asian Wall Street Journal.* **Price Frequency:** daily. **Effective Market(s):** Asia. **Units of Measure:** Singapore dollars per United States dollar, per SDR. **Type of Price:** foreign exchange. **Time Period Covered:** latest 2 days.

Source: *Barron's.* **Price Frequency:** weekly. **Effective Market(s):** New York. **Units of Measure:** Singapore dollars per United States dollar. **Type of Price:** foreign exchange. **Time Period Covered:** latest 2 weeks.

Source: *Monthly Commodity Price Bulletin.* **Price Frequency:** monthly, annually. **Units of Measure:** Singapore dollars to United States dollar. **Type of Price:** foreign exchange. **Time Period Covered:** latest 5 years.

Source: *New York Times.* **Price Frequency:** daily. **Effective Market(s):** United States. **Units of Measure:** Singapore dollars per United States dollar. **Type of Price:** foreign exchange. **Time Period Covered:** latest 2 days.

Source: *The Times.* **Price Frequency:** daily. **Effective Market(s):** London. **Units of Measure:** Singapore dollars per British pound. **Type of Price:** foreign exchange. **Time Period Covered:** latest day.

SISAL: EAST AFRICAN

Source: *Commodity Trade and Price Trends.* **Price Frequency:** annually. **Effective Market(s):** European ports. **Units of Measure:** Dollars per metric ton, 1980 constant dollars per metric ton. **Time Period Covered:** latest 32 years.

Source: *FAO Quarterly Bulletin of Statistics.* **Price Frequency:** monthly, annually. **Effective Market(s):** European ports. **Units of Measure:** Dollars per 1000 kilograms, dollars per metric ton. **Time Period Covered:** latest 3 years.

Source: *Fibre Market News.* **Price Frequency:** weekly. **Effective Market(s):** Gulf. **Units of Measure:** cents per lb. **Time Period Covered:** latest week.

Source: *International Financial Statistics.* **Price Frequency:** monthly, quarterly, annually. **Effective Market(s):** Europe. **Units of Measure:** Dollars per metric ton, index. **Type of Price:** market price, price index. **Time Period Covered:** latest 5 months, latest 5 quarters, latest 5 years.

Source: *International Financial Statistics Yearbook.* **Price Frequency:** annually. **Effective Market(s):** London. **Units of Measure:** Dollars per metric ton. **Type of Price:** wholesale. **Time Period Covered:** latest 30 years.

Source: *Monthly Commodity Price Bulletin.* **Price Frequency:** monthly, annually. **Effective Market(s):** London. **Units of Measure:** Dollars per metric ton. **Time Period Covered:** latest 5 years.

Source: *Monthly Commodity Price Bulletin Supplement.* **Price Frequency:** monthly, quarterly, annually. **Effective Market(s):** London. **Units of Measure:** Dollars per tonne. **Time Period Covered:** latest 20 years.

Source: *UNCTAD Commodity Yearbook.* **Price Frequency:** annually. **Effective Market(s):** London. **Units of Measure:** Dollars per metric ton. **Type of Price:** free market. **Time Period Covered:** latest 12 years.

SISAL: GRADE A, EAST AFRICAN

Source: *Fibre Market News.* **Price Frequency:** weekly. **Effective Market(s):** Gulf. **Units of Measure:** cents per lb. **Time Period Covered:** latest week.

SISAL: NO. 1, EAST AFRICAN

Source: *Fibre Market News.* **Price Frequency:** weekly. **Effective Market(s):** Gulf. **Units of Measure:** cents per lb. **Time Period Covered:** latest week.

SISAL: NO. 2, BRAZILIAN

Source: *Fibre Market News.* **Price Frequency:** weekly. **Effective Market(s):** Gulf. **Units of Measure:** cents per lb. **Time Period Covered:** latest week.

SISAL: NO. 2, EAST AFRICAN

Source: *Fibre Market News.* **Price Frequency:** weekly. **Effective Market(s):** Gulf. **Units of Measure:** cents per lb. **Time Period Covered:** latest week.

SISAL: NO. 3, BRAZILIAN

Source: *FAO Quarterly Bulletin of Statistics.* **Price Frequency:** monthly, annually. **Effective Market(s):** European ports. **Units of Measure:** Dollars per 1000 kilograms, dollars per metric ton. **Time Period Covered:** latest 3 years.

Source: *Fibre Market News.* **Price Frequency:** weekly. **Effective Market(s):** Gulf. **Units of Measure:** cents per lb. **Time Period Covered:** latest week.

SISAL: NO. 3, EAST AFRICAN

Source: *Fibre Market News.* **Price Frequency:** weekly. **Effective Market(s):** Gulf. **Units of Measure:** cents per lb. **Time Period Covered:** latest week.

SISAL: NO. 3, KENYAN/TANZANIAN

Source: *Commodity Trade and Price Trends.* **Price Frequency:** annually. **Effective Market(s):** London. **Units of Measure:** Dollars per metric ton, 1980 constant dollars per metric ton. **Time Period Covered:** latest 37 years.

SISAL: NO. 3, LONG, EAST AFRICAN

Source: *FAO Quarterly Bulletin of Statistics.* **Price Frequency:** monthly, annually. **Effective Market(s):** European ports. **Units of Measure:** Dollars per 1000 kilograms, dollars per metric ton. **Time Period Covered:** latest 3 years.

Source: *Fibre Market News.* **Price Frequency:** weekly. **Effective Market(s):** Gulf. **Units of Measure:** cents per lb. **Time Period Covered:** latest week.

SISAL: NO. 3, LONG, KENYAN/TANZANIAN

Source: *Monthly Commodity Price Bulletin Supplement.* **Price Frequency:** monthly, quarterly, annually. **Effective Market(s):** London. **Units of Measure:** Dollars per tonne. **Time Period Covered:** latest 20 years.

Source: *Monthly Commodity Price Bulletin.* **Price Frequency:** monthly, annually. **Effective Market(s):** London. **Units of Measure:** Dollars per metric ton. **Time Period Covered:** latest 5 years.

Source: *UNCTAD Commodity Yearbook.* **Price Frequency:** annually. **Effective Market(s):** London. **Units of Measure:** Dollars per metric ton. **Type of Price:** free market. **Time Period Covered:** latest 12 years.

SISAL: TANZANIAN

Source: *International Financial Statistics Yearbook.* **Price Frequency:** annually. **Effective Market(s):** Tanzania. **Units of Measure:** Dollars per metric ton. **Type of Price:** wholesale. **Time Period Covered:** latest 30 years.

SKATE WING (FISH): WHOLE, FRESH

Source: *Seafood Price-Current.* **Price Frequency:** semiweekly. **Effective Market(s):** Boston, Mid-Atlantic, New Bedford (MA), Portland (ME). **Units of Measure:** Dollars per lb. **Type of Price:** sale by first receiver, auction price. **Time Period Covered:** latest day.

SKINS: CALF, SQUARE TRIMMED

Source: *Hides and Skins.* **Price Frequency:** monthly, annually. **Effective Market(s):** Italy. **Units of Measure:** Italian lire per kilogram. **Type of Price:** average. **Time Period Covered:** latest 3 years.

SLATE: DELABOLE

Source: *Industrial Minerals.* **Price Frequency:** monthly. **Effective Market(s):** main European port. **Units of Measure:** British pounds per metric tonne. **Type of Price:** producer & dealer. **Time Period Covered:** latest month.

SLATE: POWDER

Source: *Industrial Minerals.* **Price Frequency:** monthly. **Effective Market(s):** main European port. **Units of Measure:** British pounds per metric tonne. **Type of Price:** producer & dealer. **Time Period Covered:** latest month.

SMELTS: WHOLE, FRESH

Source: *Seafood Price-Current.* **Price Frequency:** semiweekly. **Effective Market(s):** Mid-Atlantic, New England. **Units of Measure:** Dollars per lb. **Type of Price:** sale by first receiver. **Time Period Covered:** latest day.

SNAPPER: B-LINE, FRESH

Source: *Seafood Price-Current.* **Price Frequency:** semiweekly. **Effective Market(s):** Gulf/Southeast. **Units of Measure:** Dollars per lb. **Type of Price:** sale by first receiver. **Time Period Covered:** latest day.

SNAPPER: B-LINE, WHOLE, FRESH

Source: *Seafood Price-Current.* **Price Frequency:** semiweekly. **Effective Market(s):** Boston, Mid-Atlantic, New Bedford (MA), Portland (ME). **Units of Measure:** Dollars per lb. **Type of Price:** sale by first receiver, auction price. **Time Period Covered:** latest day.

SNAPPER: GREY, FILLETS, FRESH, HAWAIIAN

Source: *Seafood Price-Current.* **Price Frequency:** semiweekly. **Effective Market(s):** Hawaii. **Units of Measure:** Dollars per lb. **Type of Price:** sale by first receiver. **Time Period Covered:** latest day.

SNAPPER: GREY, WHOLE, FRESH, HAWAIIAN

Source: *Seafood Price-Current.* **Price Frequency:** semiweekly. **Effective Market(s):** Hawaii. **Units of Measure:** Dollars per lb. **Type of Price:** sale by first receiver. **Time Period Covered:** latest day.

SNAPPER: MANGROVE, FRESH

Source: *Seafood Price-Current.* **Price Frequency:** semi-weekly. **Effective Market(s):** Gulf/Southeast. **Units of Measure:** Dollars per lb. **Type of Price:** sale by first receiver. **Time Period Covered:** latest day.

SNAPPER: MUTTON, FILLETS, FRESH

Source: *Seafood Price-Current.* **Price Frequency:** semi-weekly. **Effective Market(s):** Gulf/Southeast. **Units of Measure:** Dollars per lb. **Type of Price:** sale by first receiver. **Time Period Covered:** latest day.

SNAPPER: MUTTON, FRESH

Source: *Seafood Price-Current.* **Price Frequency:** semi-weekly. **Effective Market(s):** Gulf/Southeast. **Units of Measure:** Dollars per lb. **Type of Price:** sale by first receiver. **Time Period Covered:** latest day.

SNAPPER: PINK, FILLETS, FRESH, HAWAIIAN

Source: *Seafood Price-Current.* **Price Frequency:** semi-weekly. **Effective Market(s):** Hawaii. **Units of Measure:** Dollars per lb. **Type of Price:** sale by first receiver. **Time Period Covered:** latest day.

SNAPPER: PINK, WHOLE, FRESH, HAWAIIAN

Source: *Seafood Price-Current.* **Price Frequency:** semi-weekly. **Effective Market(s):** Hawaii. **Units of Measure:** Dollars per lb. **Type of Price:** sale by first receiver. **Time Period Covered:** latest day.

SNAPPER: RED ATLANTIC, WHOLE, FRESH, CENTRAL/SOUTH AMERICA, IMPORTED

Source: *Seafood Price-Current.* **Price Frequency:** semi-weekly. **Effective Market(s):** Miami. **Units of Measure:** Dollars per lb. **Type of Price:** sale by first receiver. **Time Period Covered:** latest day.

SNAPPER: RED, FILLETS, FRESH

Source: *Seafood Price-Current.* **Price Frequency:** semi-weekly. **Effective Market(s):** Gulf/Southeast. **Units of Measure:** Dollars per lb. **Type of Price:** sale by first receiver. **Time Period Covered:** latest day.

SNAPPER: RED, FILLETS, NATURAL, FROZEN, BRAZIL

Source: *Seafood Price-Current.* **Price Frequency:** semi-weekly. **Effective Market(s):** Mid-Atlantic. **Units of Measure:** Dollars per lb. **Type of Price:** first receiver. **Time Period Covered:** latest day.

SNAPPER: RED, FILLETS, NATURAL, FROZEN, THAI

Source: *Seafood Price-Current.* **Price Frequency:** semi-weekly. **Effective Market(s):** Mid-Atlantic. **Units of Measure:** Dollars per lb. **Type of Price:** first receiver. **Time Period Covered:** latest day.

SNAPPER: RED, FILLETS, ONE CUTS, FROZEN

Source: *Seafood Price-Current.* **Price Frequency:** semi-weekly. **Effective Market(s):** Mid-Atlantic. **Units of Measure:** Dollars per lb. **Type of Price:** first receiver. **Time Period Covered:** latest day.

SNAPPER: RED, FRESH, DOMESTIC

Source: *Seafood Price-Current.* **Price Frequency:** semi-weekly. **Effective Market(s):** Gulf/Southeast. **Units of Measure:** Dollars per lb. **Type of Price:** sale by first receiver. **Time Period Covered:** latest day.

SNAPPER: RED LONGTAIL, FILLETS, FRESH, HAWAIIAN

Source: *Seafood Price-Current.* **Price Frequency:** semi-weekly. **Effective Market(s):** Hawaii. **Units of Measure:** Dollars per lb. **Type of Price:** sale by first receiver. **Time Period Covered:** latest day.

SNAPPER: RED LONGTAIL, WHOLE, FRESH, HAWAIIAN

Source: *Seafood Price-Current.* **Price Frequency:** semi-weekly. **Effective Market(s):** Hawaii. **Units of Measure:** Dollars per lb. **Type of Price:** sale by first receiver. **Time Period Covered:** latest day.

SNAPPER: RED PACIFIC, WHOLE, FRESH, CENTRAL/SOUTH AMERICA, IMPORTED

Source: *Seafood Price-Current.* **Price Frequency:** semi-weekly. **Effective Market(s):** Miami. **Units of Measure:** Dollars per lb. **Type of Price:** sale by first receiver. **Time Period Covered:** latest day.

SNAPPER: RED, WHOLE, GUTTED, FRESH, DOMESTIC

Source: *Seafood Price-Current.* **Price Frequency:** semi-weekly. **Effective Market(s):** Boston, Mid-Atlantic, New Bedford (MA), Portland (ME). **Units of Measure:** Dollars per lb. **Type of Price:** sale by first receiver, auction price. **Time Period Covered:** latest day.

SNAPPER: YELLOWTAIL, FILLETS, FRESH

Source: *Seafood Price-Current.* **Price Frequency:** semi-weekly. **Effective Market(s):** Gulf/Southeast. **Units of Measure:** Dollars per lb. **Type of Price:** sale by first receiver. **Time Period Covered:** latest day.

SNAPPER: YELLOWTAIL, FRESH

Source: *Seafood Price-Current.* **Price Frequency:** semi-weekly. **Effective Market(s):** Gulf/Southeast. **Units of Measure:** Dollars per lb. **Type of Price:** sale by first receiver. **Time Period Covered:** latest day.

SOAP BARK: CRUSHED

Source: *Chemical Marketing Reporter.* **Price Frequency:** weekly. **Effective Market(s):** New York. **Units of Measure:** Dollars per lb. **Type of Price:** spot. **Time Period Covered:** latest week.

Source: *Journal of Commerce and Commercial.* **Price Frequency:** weekly in Monday issue. **Units of Measure:** Dollars per lb. **Type of Price:** spot. **Time Period Covered:** latest week.

SOAP BARK: POWDERED

Source: *Chemical Marketing Reporter.* **Price Frequency:** weekly. **Effective Market(s):** New York. **Units of Measure:** Dollars per lb. **Type of Price:** spot. **Time Period Covered:** latest week.

SOAP BARK: WHOLE

Source: *Journal of Commerce and Commercial.* **Price Frequency:** weekly in Monday issue. **Units of Measure:** Dollars per lb. **Type of Price:** spot. **Time Period Covered:** latest week.

SODA: CAUSTIC, BEAD

Source: *Chemical Marketing Reporter.* **Price Frequency:** weekly. **Effective Market(s):** New York. **Units of Measure:** Dollars per 100 lbs. **Type of Price:** spot. **Time Period Covered:** latest week.

Source: *Journal of Commerce and Commercial.* **Price Frequency:** weekly in Thursday issue. **Effective Market(s):** East Coast, West Coast. **Units of Measure:** Dollars per lb. **Type of Price:** spot. **Time Period Covered:** latest week.

SODA: CAUSTIC, DIAPHRAGM LIQUID, 50% BASIS

Source: *Journal of Commerce and Commercial.* **Price Frequency:** weekly in Thursday issue. **Effective Market(s):** East Coast, West Coast. **Units of Measure:** Dollars per lb. **Type of Price:** spot. **Time Period Covered:** latest week.

SODA: CAUSTIC, DIAPHRAGM LIQUID, 73% BASIS

Source: *Journal of Commerce and Commercial.* **Price Frequency:** weekly in Thursday issue. **Effective Market(s):** East Coast, West Coast. **Units of Measure:** Dollars per lb. **Type of Price:** spot. **Time Period Covered:** latest week.

SODA: CAUSTIC, FLAKE

Source: *Chemical Marketing Reporter.* **Price Frequency:** weekly. **Effective Market(s):** New York. **Units of Measure:** Dollars per 100 lbs. **Type of Price:** spot. **Time Period Covered:** latest week.

SODA: CAUSTIC, GRANULAR

Source: *Chemical Marketing Reporter.* **Price Frequency:** weekly. **Effective Market(s):** New York. **Units of Measure:** Dollars per ton. **Type of Price:** spot. **Time Period Covered:** latest week.

SODA: CAUSTIC, LIQUID

Source: *Chemical Marketing Reporter.* **Price Frequency:** weekly. **Effective Market(s):** Gulf Coast. **Units of Measure:** Dollars per ton. **Type of Price:** seller. **Time Period Covered:** latest week.

SODA: CAUSTIC, LIQUID, 50% BASIS

Source: *Purchasing.* **Price Frequency:** monthly. **Effective Market(s):** United States. **Units of Measure:** Dollars per ton. **Type of Price:** transaction. **Time Period Covered:** latest day, month ago, 6 months ago, year ago.

SODA: CAUSTIC, RAYON TYPE, LIQUID

Source: *Chemical Marketing Reporter.* **Price Frequency:** weekly. **Effective Market(s):** New York. **Units of Measure:** Dollars per ton. **Type of Price:** spot. **Time Period Covered:** latest week.

SODA: CAUSTIC, SOLID

Source: *Chemical Marketing Reporter.* **Price Frequency:** weekly. **Effective Market(s):** New York. **Units of Measure:** Dollars per ton. **Type of Price:** spot. **Time Period Covered:** latest week.

SODA ASH

Source: *Purchasing.* **Price Frequency:** quarterly in January, April, July, October issues. **Units of Measure:** Dollars per ton. **Type of Price:** transaction. **Time Period Covered:** latest 5 quarters.

SODA ASH: DENSE

Source: *Chemical Marketing Reporter.* **Price Frequency:** weekly. **Effective Market(s):** New York. **Units of Measure:** Dollars per ton. **Type of Price:** spot. **Time Period Covered:** latest week.

Source: *Industrial Minerals.* **Price Frequency:** monthly. **Effective Market(s):** Wyoming. **Units of Measure:** Dollars per metric tonne. **Type of Price:** producer & dealer. **Time Period Covered:** latest month.

Source: *Journal of Commerce and Commercial.* **Price Frequency:** weekly in Thursday issue. **Units of Measure:** Dollars per lb. **Type of Price:** spot. **Time Period Covered:** latest week.

SODA ASH: LIGHT

Source: *Chemical Marketing Reporter.* **Price Frequency:** weekly. **Effective Market(s):** New York. **Units of Measure:** Dollars per lb. **Type of Price:** spot. **Time Period Covered:** latest week.

Source: *Journal of Commerce and Commercial.* **Price Frequency:** weekly in Thursday issue. **Units of Measure:** Dollars per ton. **Type of Price:** spot. **Time Period Covered:** latest week.

SODIUM: FUSED

Source: *Chemical Marketing Reporter.* **Price Frequency:** weekly. **Effective Market(s):** New York. **Units of Measure:** Dollars per lb. **Type of Price:** spot. **Time Period Covered:** latest week.

SODIUM: METALLIC

Source: *Chemical Marketing Reporter.* **Price Frequency:** weekly. **Effective Market(s):** New York. **Units of Measure:** Dollars per lb. **Type of Price:** spot. **Time Period Covered:** latest week.

SODIUM ACETATE: 60%, GRANULAR, USP

Source: *Chemical Marketing Reporter.* **Price Frequency:** weekly. **Effective Market(s):** New York. **Units of Measure:** Dollars per lb. **Type of Price:** spot. **Time Period Covered:** latest week.

SODIUM ACETATE: ANHYDROUS

Source: *Chemical Marketing Reporter.* **Price Frequency:** weekly. **Effective Market(s):** New York. **Units of Measure:** Dollars per lb. **Type of Price:** spot. **Time Period Covered:** latest week.

Source: *Journal of Commerce and Commercial.* **Price Frequency:** weekly in Thursday issue. **Units of Measure:** Dollars per lb.. **Type of Price:** spot. **Time Period Covered:** latest week.

SODIUM ALGINATE: WHITE, POWDERED, NF, DOMESTIC

Source: *Chemical Marketing Reporter.* **Price Frequency:** weekly. **Effective Market(s):** New York. **Units of Measure:** Dollars per lb. **Type of Price:** spot. **Time Period Covered:** latest week.

SODIUM P-AMINOSALICYLATE

Source: *Chemical Marketing Reporter.* **Price Frequency:** weekly. **Effective Market(s):** New York. **Units of Measure:** Dollars per lb. **Type of Price:** spot. **Time Period Covered:** latest week.

SODIUM-AMMONIUM PHOSPHATE: PURIFIED, CRYSTALLINE

Source: *Chemical Marketing Reporter.* **Price Frequency:** weekly. **Effective Market(s):** New York. **Units of Measure:** Dollars per lb. **Type of Price:** spot. **Time Period Covered:** latest week.

SODIUM ANTIMONATE

Source: *Chemical Marketing Reporter.* **Price Frequency:** weekly. **Effective Market(s):** East. **Units of Measure:** Dollars per lb. **Type of Price:** spot. **Time Period Covered:** latest week.

SODIUM ASCORBATE: USP

Source: *Chemical Marketing Reporter.* **Price Frequency:** weekly. **Effective Market(s):** New York. **Units of Measure:** Dollars per kilo. **Type of Price:** spot. **Time Period Covered:** latest week.

Source: *Journal of Commerce and Commercial.* **Price Frequency:** weekly in Friday issue. **Units of Measure:** Dollars per kilo. **Type of Price:** spot. **Time Period Covered:** latest week.

SODIUM BENZOATE

Source: *Journal of Commerce and Commercial.* **Price Frequency:** weekly in Friday issue. **Units of Measure:** Dollars per lb. **Type of Price:** spot. **Time Period Covered:** latest week.

SODIUM BENZOATE: TECHNICAL

Source: *Chemical Marketing Reporter.* **Price Frequency:** weekly. **Effective Market(s):** New York. **Units of Measure:** Dollars per lb. **Type of Price:** spot. **Time Period Covered:** latest week.

SODIUM BENZOATE: USP

Source: *Chemical Marketing Reporter.* **Price Frequency:** weekly. **Effective Market(s):** New York. **Units of Measure:** Dollars per lb. **Type of Price:** spot. **Time Period Covered:** latest week.

SODIUM BICARBONATE: GRANULAR, FINE, USP

Source: *Chemical Marketing Reporter.* **Price Frequency:** weekly. **Effective Market(s):** New York. **Units of Measure:** Dollars per 100 lbs. **Type of Price:** spot. **Time Period Covered:** latest week.

SODIUM BICARBONATE: GRANULAR, USP

Source: *Chemical Marketing Reporter.* **Price Frequency:** weekly. **Effective Market(s):** New York. **Units of Measure:** Dollars per 100 lbs. **Type of Price:** spot. **Time Period Covered:** latest week.

SODIUM BICARBONATE POWDER

Source: *Journal of Commerce and Commercial.* **Price Frequency:** weekly in Thursday issue. **Units of Measure:** Dollars per 100 lbs. **Type of Price:** spot. **Time Period Covered:** latest week.

SODIUM BICARBONATE POWDER: COARSE, USP

Source: *Chemical Marketing Reporter.* **Price Frequency:** weekly. **Effective Market(s):** New York. **Units of Measure:** Dollars per 100 lbs. **Type of Price:** spot. **Time Period Covered:** latest week.

SODIUM BICARBONATE POWDER: FINE, USP

Source: *Chemical Marketing Reporter.* **Price Frequency:** weekly. **Effective Market(s):** New York. **Units of Measure:** Dollars per 100 lbs. **Type of Price:** spot. **Time Period Covered:** latest week.

SODIUM BICARBONATE POWDER: REGULAR GRADE, USP

Source: *Chemical Marketing Reporter.* **Price Frequency:** weekly. **Effective Market(s):** New York. **Units of Measure:** Dollars per 100 lbs. **Type of Price:** spot. **Time Period Covered:** latest week.

SODIUM BICHROMATE: CRYSTAL

Source: *Chemical Marketing Reporter.* **Price Frequency:** weekly. **Effective Market(s):** New York. **Units of Measure:** Dollars per lb. **Type of Price:** spot. **Time Period Covered:** latest week.

SODIUM BICHROMATE: GRANULAR

Source: *Journal of Commerce and Commercial.* **Price Frequency:** weekly in Thursday issue. **Units of Measure:** Dollars per lb. **Type of Price:** spot. **Time Period Covered:** latest week.

SODIUM BICHROMATE: LIQUID

Source: *Chemical Marketing Reporter.* **Price Frequency:** weekly. **Effective Market(s):** New York. **Units of Measure:** Dollars per lb. **Type of Price:** spot. **Time Period Covered:** latest week.

SODIUM BIFLUORIDE

Source: *Chemical Marketing Reporter.* **Price Frequency:** weekly. **Effective Market(s):** New York. **Units of Measure:** Dollars per lb. **Type of Price:** spot. **Time Period Covered:** latest week.

SODIUM BISULFATE

Source: *Chemical Marketing Reporter.* **Price Frequency:** weekly. **Effective Market(s):** East, West. **Units of Measure:** Dollars per ton, dollars per 100 lbs. **Type of Price:** spot. **Time Period Covered:** latest week.

SODIUM BISULFITE: ANHYDROUS

Source: *Chemical Marketing Reporter.* **Price Frequency:** weekly. **Effective Market(s):** East, West. **Units of Measure:** Dollars per 100 lbs. **Type of Price:** spot. **Time Period Covered:** latest week.

Source: *Journal of Commerce and Commercial.* **Price Frequency:** weekly in Thursday issue. **Effective Market(s):** East. **Units of Measure:** Dollars per 100 lbs. **Type of Price:** spot. **Time Period Covered:** latest week.

SODIUM BISULFITE: SOLUTION, 38%

Source: *Chemical Marketing Reporter.* **Price Frequency:** weekly. **Effective Market(s):** East. **Units of Measure:** Dollars per 100 lbs. **Type of Price:** spot. **Time Period Covered:** latest week.

SODIUM BISULFITE: SOLUTION, 43%, PHOTOGRAPHIC GRADE

Source: *Chemical Marketing Reporter.* **Price Frequency:** weekly. **Effective Market(s):** New York. **Units of Measure:** Dollars per 100 lbs. **Type of Price:** spot. **Time Period Covered:** latest week.

SODIUM BISULFITE: SOLUTION, 100%

Source: *Chemical Marketing Reporter.* **Price Frequency:** weekly. **Effective Market(s):** West. **Units of Measure:** Dollars per 100 lbs. **Type of Price:** spot. **Time Period Covered:** latest week.

SODIUM BORATE: GRANULAR, NF

Source: *Chemical Marketing Reporter.* **Price Frequency:** weekly. **Effective Market(s):** New York. **Units of Measure:** Dollars per lb. **Type of Price:** spot. **Time Period Covered:** latest week.

SODIUM BORATE: POWDERED, NF

Source: *Chemical Marketing Reporter.* **Price Frequency:** weekly. **Effective Market(s):** New York. **Units of Measure:** Dollars per lb. **Type of Price:** spot. **Time Period Covered:** latest week.

SODIUM BOROHYDRIDE: POWDERED

Source: *Chemical Marketing Reporter.* **Price Frequency:** weekly. **Effective Market(s):** New York. **Units of Measure:** Dollars per lb. **Type of Price:** spot. **Time Period Covered:** latest week.

SODIUM BOROHYDRIDE: STABILIZED WATER SOLUTION

Source: *Chemical Marketing Reporter.* **Price Frequency:** weekly. **Effective Market(s):** New York. **Units of Measure:** Dollars per lb. **Type of Price:** spot. **Time Period Covered:** latest week.

SODIUM BROMIDE: TECHNICAL

Source: *Chemical Marketing Reporter.* **Price Frequency:** weekly. **Effective Market(s):** New York. **Units of Measure:** Dollars per lb. **Type of Price:** spot. **Time Period Covered:** latest week.

SODIUM CARBONATE: CRYSTALLINE, MONOHYDRATE

see Soda Ash.

SODIUM CARBONATE: DECAHYDRATE

Source: *Chemical Marketing Reporter.* **Price Frequency:** weekly. **Effective Market(s):** New York. **Units of Measure:** Dollars per ton. **Type of Price:** spot. **Time Period Covered:** latest week.

SODIUM CARBONATE: MONOHYDRATED

Source: *Chemical Marketing Reporter.* **Price Frequency:** weekly. **Effective Market(s):** New York. **Units of Measure:** Dollars per ton. **Type of Price:** spot. **Time Period Covered:** latest week.

SODIUM CARBOXYMETHYL CELLULOSE

see CMC.

SODIUM CHLORATE: CRYSTAL

Source: *Chemical Marketing Reporter.* **Price Frequency:** weekly. **Effective Market(s):** Northeast, Southeast. **Units of Measure:** Dollars per ton. **Type of Price:** spot. **Time Period Covered:** latest week.

SODIUM CHLORIDE: GRANULAR, USP

Source: *Chemical Marketing Reporter.* **Price Frequency:** weekly. **Effective Market(s):** New York. **Units of Measure:** Dollars per lb. **Type of Price:** spot. **Time Period Covered:** latest week.

SODIUM CHLORIDE: TECHNICAL

see Salt.

SODIUM CHLORITE: TECHNICAL

Source: *Chemical Marketing Reporter.* **Price Frequency:** weekly. **Effective Market(s):** New York. **Units of Measure:** Dollars per lb. **Type of Price:** spot. **Time Period Covered:** latest week.

SODIUM CHROMATE: ANHYDROUS

Source: *Chemical Marketing Reporter.* **Price Frequency:** weekly. **Effective Market(s):** New York. **Units of Measure:** Dollars per lb. **Type of Price:** spot. **Time Period Covered:** latest week.

SODIUM CHROMATE: TETRAHYDRATE

Source: *Chemical Marketing Reporter.* **Price Frequency:** weekly. **Effective Market(s):** New York. **Units of Measure:** Dollars per lb. **Type of Price:** spot. **Time Period Covered:** latest week.

SODIUM CITRATE: GRANULAR, DIHYDRATE, USP

Source: *Chemical Marketing Reporter.* **Price Frequency:** weekly. **Effective Market(s):** East. **Units of Measure:** Dollars per lb. **Type of Price:** spot. **Time Period Covered:** latest week.

SODIUM CITRATE: GRANULAR, USP

Source: *Journal of Commerce and Commercial.* **Price Frequency:** weekly in Friday issue. **Units of Measure:** Dollars per lb. **Type of Price:** spot. **Time Period Covered:** latest week.

SODIUM CYANATE

Source: *Chemical Marketing Reporter.* **Price Frequency:** weekly. **Effective Market(s):** New York. **Units of Measure:** Dollars per lb. **Type of Price:** spot. **Time Period Covered:** latest week.

SODIUM CYANIDE: BRIQUETTES OR GRANULAR, 99% MINIMUM

Source: *Chemical Marketing Reporter.* **Price Frequency:** weekly. **Effective Market(s):** New York. **Units of Measure:** Dollars per lb. **Type of Price:** spot. **Time Period Covered:** latest week.

SODIUM DIACETATE: ANHYDROUS

Source: *Chemical Marketing Reporter.* **Price Frequency:** weekly. **Effective Market(s):** New York. **Units of Measure:** Dollars per lb. **Type of Price:** spot. **Time Period Covered:** latest week.

SODIUM DIACETATE: FCC

Source: *Chemical Marketing Reporter.* **Price Frequency:** weekly. **Effective Market(s):** East of the Rockies. **Units of Measure:** Dollars per lb. **Type of Price:** spot. **Time Period Covered:** latest week.

SODIUM ERYTHORBATE: POWDERED, GRANULAR

Source: *Chemical Marketing Reporter.* **Price Frequency:** weekly. **Effective Market(s):** New York, West of Denver. **Units of Measure:** Dollars per lb. **Type of Price:** spot. **Time Period Covered:** latest week.

SODIUM FERROCYANIDE

Source: *Chemical Marketing Reporter.* **Price Frequency:** weekly. **Effective Market(s):** New York. **Units of Measure:** Dollars per lb. **Type of Price:** spot. **Time Period Covered:** latest week.

SODIUM FLUOBORATE: TECHNICAL, GRANULAR

Source: *Chemical Marketing Reporter.* **Price Frequency:** weekly. **Effective Market(s):** New York. **Units of Measure:** Dollars per lb. **Type of Price:** spot. **Time Period Covered:** latest week.

SODIUM FLUORIDE: POWDERED, USP

Source: *Chemical Marketing Reporter.* **Price Frequency:** weekly. **Effective Market(s):** New York. **Units of Measure:** Dollars per lb. **Type of Price:** spot. **Time Period Covered:** latest week.

SODIUM FLUORIDE: WHITE, 97%

Source: *Chemical Marketing Reporter.* **Price Frequency:** weekly. **Effective Market(s):** New York. **Units of Measure:** Dollars per lb. **Type of Price:** spot. **Time Period Covered:** latest week.

SODIUM FORMALDEHYDE SULFOXYLATE

Source: *Chemical Marketing Reporter.* **Price Frequency:** weekly. **Effective Market(s):** New York. **Units of Measure:** Dollars per lb. **Type of Price:** spot. **Time Period Covered:** latest week.

SODIUM FORMATE

Source: *Chemical Marketing Reporter.* **Price Frequency:** weekly. **Effective Market(s):** New York. **Units of Measure:** Dollars per lb. **Type of Price:** spot. **Time Period Covered:** latest week.

SODIUM GLUCONATE

Source: *Journal of Commerce and Commercial.* **Price Frequency:** weekly in Friday issue. **Units of Measure:** Dollars per lb. **Type of Price:** spot. **Time Period Covered:** latest week.

SODIUM GLUCONATE: TECHNICAL

Source: *Chemical Marketing Reporter.* **Price Frequency:** weekly. **Effective Market(s):** New York. **Units of Measure:** Dollars per lb. **Type of Price:** spot. **Time Period Covered:** latest week.

SODIUM GLYCEROPHOSPHATE

Source: *Journal of Commerce and Commercial.* **Price Frequency:** weekly in Friday issue. **Units of Measure:** Dollars per lb. **Type of Price:** spot. **Time Period Covered:** latest week.

SODIUM HYDRIDE: OIL DISPERSION, 60% SODIUM HYDRIDE

Source: *Chemical Marketing Reporter.* **Price Frequency:** weekly. **Effective Market(s):** New York. **Units of Measure:** Dollars per lb. **Type of Price:** spot. **Time Period Covered:** latest week.

SODIUM HYDROSULFIDE
see Sodium Sulfhydrate.

SODIUM HYDROSULFITE

Source: *Chemical Marketing Reporter.* **Price Frequency:** weekly. **Effective Market(s):** East. **Units of Measure:** Dollars per lb. **Type of Price:** spot. **Time Period Covered:** latest week.

SODIUM HYDROXIDE: TECHNICAL
see Soda: Caustic.

SODIUM HYDROXIDE PELLETS: USP

Source: *Chemical Marketing Reporter.* **Price Frequency:** weekly. **Effective Market(s):** New York. **Units of Measure:** Dollars per lb. **Type of Price:** spot. **Time Period Covered:** latest week.

SODIUM HYPOPHOSPHITE

Source: *Chemical Marketing Reporter.* **Price Frequency:** weekly. **Effective Market(s):** New York. **Units of Measure:** Dollars per lb. **Type of Price:** spot. **Time Period Covered:** latest week.

SODIUM HYPOSULFITE
see Sodium Thiosulfate.

SODIUM IODIDE

Source: *Journal of Commerce and Commercial.* **Price Frequency:** weekly in Friday issue. **Units of Measure:** Dollars per lb. **Type of Price:** spot. **Time Period Covered:** latest week.

SODIUM IODIDE: USP

Source: *Chemical Marketing Reporter.* **Price Frequency:** weekly. **Effective Market(s):** New York. **Units of Measure:** Dollars per lb. **Type of Price:** spot. **Time Period Covered:** latest week.

SODIUM LAURYL SULFATE: 30%

Source: *Chemical Marketing Reporter.* **Price Frequency:** Weekly. **Effective Market(s):** New York. **Units of Measure:** Dollars per lb. **Type of Price:** spot. **Time Period Covered:** latest week.

SODIUM LIGNIN SULFONATE

Source: *Chemical Marketing Reporter.* **Price Frequency:** weekly. **Effective Market(s):** New York. **Units of Measure:** Dollars per ton. **Type of Price:** spot. **Time Period Covered:** latest week.

SODIUM METABISULFITE
see Sodium Bisulfite.

SODIUM METABORATE: OCTAHYDRATE, GRANULAR

Source: *Chemical Marketing Reporter.* **Price Frequency:** weekly. **Effective Market(s):** New York. **Units of Measure:** Dollars per lb. **Type of Price:** spot. **Time Period Covered:** latest week.

SODIUM METABORATE: TETRAHYDRATE

Source: *Chemical Marketing Reporter.* **Price Frequency:** weekly. **Effective Market(s):** New York. **Units of Measure:** Dollars per lb. **Type of Price:** spot. **Time Period Covered:** latest week.

SODIUM METAPHOSPHATE: FOOD GRADE

Source: *Chemical Marketing Reporter.* **Price Frequency:** weekly. **Effective Market(s):** New York. **Units of Measure:** Dollars per 100 lbs. **Type of Price:** spot. **Time Period Covered:** latest week.

SODIUM METAPHOSPHATE: TECHNICAL

Source: *Chemical Marketing Reporter.* **Price Frequency:** weekly. **Effective Market(s):** New York. **Units of Measure:** Dollars per 100 lbs. **Type of Price:** spot. **Time Period Covered:** latest week.

SODIUM METASILICATE: ANHYDROUS

Source: *Chemical Marketing Reporter.* **Price Frequency:** weekly. **Effective Market(s):** New York. **Units of Measure:** Dollars per 100 lbs. **Type of Price:** spot. **Time Period Covered:** latest week.

Source: *Journal of Commerce and Commercial.* **Price Frequency:** weekly in Thursday issue. **Units of Measure:** Dollars per 100 lbs. **Type of Price:** spot. **Time Period Covered:** latest week.

SODIUM METASILICATE: PENTAHYDRATE

Source: *Chemical Marketing Reporter.* **Price Frequency:** weekly. **Effective Market(s):** New York. **Units of Measure:** Dollars per 100 lbs. **Type of Price:** spot. **Time Period Covered:** latest week.

Source: *Journal of Commerce and Commercial.* **Price Frequency:** weekly in Thursday issue. **Units of Measure:** Dollars per 100 lbs. **Type of Price:** spot. **Time Period Covered:** latest week.

SODIUM MOLYBDATE: ANHYDROUS

Source: *Chemical Marketing Reporter.* **Price Frequency:** weekly. **Effective Market(s):** New York. **Units of Measure:** Dollars per lb. **Type of Price:** spot. **Time Period Covered:** latest week.

SODIUM MOLYBDATE: CRYSTALLINE

Source: *Chemical Marketing Reporter.* **Price Frequency:** weekly. **Effective Market(s):** New York. **Units of Measure:** Dollars per lb. **Type of Price:** spot. **Time Period Covered:** latest week.

SODIUM MOLYBDATE: LIQUID, 35% SOLUTION

Source: *Chemical Marketing Reporter.* **Price Frequency:** weekly. **Effective Market(s):** New York. **Units of Measure:** Dollars per lb. **Type of Price:** spot. **Time Period Covered:** latest week.

SODIUM NAPHTHIONATE

Source: *Chemical Marketing Reporter.* **Price Frequency:** weekly. **Effective Market(s):** New York. **Units of Measure:** Dollars per lb. **Type of Price:** spot. **Time Period Covered:** latest week.

Source: *Journal of Commerce and Commercial.* **Price Frequency:** weekly in Wednesday issue. **Units of Measure:** Dollars per lb. **Type of Price:** spot. **Time Period Covered:** latest week.

SODIUM NITRATE: AGRICULTURAL, IMPORTED

Source: *Chemical Marketing Reporter.* **Price Frequency:** weekly. **Effective Market(s):** New York. **Units of Measure:** Dollars per ton. **Type of Price:** spot. **Time Period Covered:** latest week.

SODIUM NITRATE: CHILEAN

Source: *Industrial Minerals.* **Price Frequency:** monthly. **Effective Market(s):** main European port. **Units of Measure:** British pounds per metric tonne. **Type of Price:** producer & dealer. **Time Period Covered:** latest month.

SODIUM NITRATE: COMMERCIAL, IMPORTED

Source: *Chemical Marketing Reporter.* **Price Frequency:** weekly. **Effective Market(s):** Atlantic/Gulf. **Units of Measure:** Dollars per ton. **Type of Price:** wholesale. **Time Period Covered:** latest week.

SODIUM NITRATE: INDUSTRIAL GRADE

Source: *Journal of Commerce and Commercial.* **Price Frequency:** weekly in Thursday issue. **Units of Measure:** Dollars per ton. **Type of Price:** spot. **Time Period Covered:** latest week.

SODIUM NITRATE: USP

Source: *Chemical Marketing Reporter.* **Price Frequency:** weekly. **Effective Market(s):** New York. **Units of Measure:** Dollars per 100 lbs. **Type of Price:** spot. **Time Period Covered:** latest week.

SODIUM ORTHOSILICATE: TECHNICAL, ANHYDROUS

Source: *Chemical Marketing Reporter.* **Price Frequency:** weekly. **Effective Market(s):** New York. **Units of Measure:** Dollars per 100 lbs. **Type of Price:** spot. **Time Period Covered:** latest week.

SODIUM ORTHOSILICATE: TECHNICAL, HYDRATED, FLAKE

Source: *Chemical Marketing Reporter.* **Price Frequency:** weekly. **Effective Market(s):** New York. **Units of Measure:** Dollars per 100 lbs. **Type of Price:** spot. **Time Period Covered:** latest week.

SODIUM PENTACHLOROPHENATE: BEADS

Source: *Chemical Marketing Reporter.* **Price Frequency:** weekly. **Effective Market(s):** New York. **Units of Measure:** Dollars per lb. **Type of Price:** spot. **Time Period Covered:** latest week.

SODIUM PENTOBARBITAL

see Pentobarbital-sodium.

SODIUM PERBORATE: TETRAHYDRATE, TECHNICAL

Source: *Chemical Marketing Reporter.* **Price Frequency:** weekly. **Effective Market(s):** New York. **Units of Measure:** Dollars per lb. **Type of Price:** spot. **Time Period Covered:** latest week.

SODIUM PERSULFATE

Source: *Chemical Marketing Reporter.* **Price Frequency:** weekly. **Effective Market(s):** New York. **Units of Measure:** Dollars per lb. **Type of Price:** spot. **Time Period Covered:** latest week.

SODIUM PHENOBARBITAL

see Phenobarbital-sodium.

SODIUM PHENOSULFONATE: POWDERED

Source: *Chemical Marketing Reporter.* **Price Frequency:** weekly. **Effective Market(s):** New York. **Units of Measure:** Dollars per lb. **Type of Price:** spot. **Time Period Covered:** latest week.

SODIUM PHOSPHATE: ANHYDROUS, DIBASIC, FOOD GRADE

Source: *Chemical Marketing Reporter.* **Price Frequency:** weekly. **Effective Market(s):** New York. **Units of Measure:** Dollars per 100 lbs. **Type of Price:** spot. **Time Period Covered:** latest week.

SODIUM PHOSPHATE: ANHYDROUS, DIBASIC, TECHNICAL GRADE

Source: *Chemical Marketing Reporter.* **Price Frequency:** weekly. **Effective Market(s):** New York. **Units of Measure:** Dollars per 100 lbs. **Type of Price:** spot. **Time Period Covered:** latest week.

SODIUM PHOSPHATE: DRIED, POWDERED, USP

Source: *Chemical Marketing Reporter.* **Price Frequency:** weekly. **Effective Market(s):** New York. **Units of Measure:** Dollars per lb. **Type of Price:** spot. **Time Period Covered:** latest week.

SODIUM PHOSPHATE: MONOBASIC, FOOD GRADE

Source: *Chemical Marketing Reporter.* **Price Frequency:** weekly. **Effective Market(s):** New York. **Units of Measure:** Dollars per 100 lbs. **Type of Price:** spot. **Time Period Covered:** latest week.

SODIUM PHOSPHATE: MONOBASIC, TECHNICAL GRADE

Source: *Chemical Marketing Reporter.* **Price Frequency:** weekly. **Effective Market(s):** New York. **Units of Measure:** Dollars per 100 lbs. **Type of Price:** spot. **Time Period Covered:** latest week.

Source: *Journal of Commerce and Commercial.* **Price Frequency:** weekly in Thursday issue. **Units of Measure:** Dollars per 100 lbs. **Type of Price:** spot. **Time Period Covered:** latest week.

SODIUM PHOSPHATE: TRIBASIC, CHLORINATED

Source: *Chemical Marketing Reporter.* **Price Frequency:** weekly. **Effective Market(s):** New York. **Units of Measure:** Dollars per 100 lbs. **Type of Price:** spot. **Time Period Covered:** latest week.

SODIUM PHOSPHATE: TRIBASIC, FOOD GRADE

Source: *Chemical Marketing Reporter.* **Price Frequency:** weekly. **Effective Market(s):** New York. **Units of Measure:** Dollars per 100 lbs. **Type of Price:** spot. **Time Period Covered:** latest week.

SODIUM PHOSPHATE: TRIBASIC, FOOD GRADE, CRYSTALLINE

Source: *Chemical Marketing Reporter.* **Price Frequency:** weekly. **Effective Market(s):** New York. **Units of Measure:** Dollars per 100 lbs. **Type of Price:** spot. **Time Period Covered:** latest week.

SODIUM PHOSPHATE: TRIBASIC, TECHNICAL GRADE

Source: *Chemical Marketing Reporter.* **Price Frequency:** weekly. **Effective Market(s):** New York. **Units of Measure:** Dollars per 100 lbs. **Type of Price:** spot. **Time Period Covered:** latest week.

Source: *Journal of Commerce and Commercial.* **Price Frequency:** weekly in Thursday issue. **Units of Measure:** Dollars per lb. **Type of Price:** spot. **Time Period Covered:** latest week.

SODIUM PHOSPHATE: TRIBASIC, TECHNICAL GRADE, CRYSTALLINE

Source: *Chemical Marketing Reporter.* **Price Frequency:** weekly. **Effective Market(s):** New York. **Units of Measure:** Dollars per 100 lbs. **Type of Price:** spot. **Time Period Covered:** latest week.

SODIUM PICRAMATE: TECHNICAL, PASTE

Source: *Chemical Marketing Reporter.* **Price Frequency:** weekly. **Effective Market(s):** New York. **Units of Measure:** Dollars per lb. **Type of Price:** spot. **Time Period Covered:** latest week.

SODIUM PROPIONATE

Source: *Chemical Marketing Reporter.* **Price Frequency:** weekly. **Effective Market(s):** New York. **Units of Measure:** Dollars per lb. **Type of Price:** spot. **Time Period Covered:** latest week.

SODIUM PYROPHOSPHATE: ACID, FOOD GRADE, NON-LEAVENING

Source: *Chemical Marketing Reporter.* **Price Frequency:** weekly. **Effective Market(s):** New York. **Units of Measure:** Dollars per 100 lbs. **Type of Price:** spot. **Time Period Covered:** latest week.

SODIUM PYROPHOSPHATE: ACID, TECHNICAL GRADE

Source: *Chemical Marketing Reporter.* **Price Frequency:** weekly. **Effective Market(s):** New York. **Units of Measure:** Dollars per 100 lbs. **Type of Price:** spot. **Time Period Covered:** latest week.

SODIUM PYROPHOSPHATE: ANHYDROUS, TETRABASIC, FOOD GRADE

Source: *Chemical Marketing Reporter.* **Price Frequency:** weekly. **Effective Market(s):** New York. **Units of Measure:** Dollars per 100 lbs. **Type of Price:** spot. **Time Period Covered:** latest week.

SODIUM PYROPHOSPHATE: ANHYDROUS, TETRABASIC, TECHNICAL GRADE

Source: *Chemical Marketing Reporter.* **Price Frequency:** weekly. **Effective Market(s):** New York. **Units of Measure:** Dollars per 100 lbs. **Type of Price:** spot. **Time Period Covered:** latest week.

SODIUM PYROPHOSPHATE: FERRIC

Source: *Chemical Marketing Reporter.* **Price Frequency:** weekly. **Effective Market(s):** New York. **Units of Measure:** Dollars per lb. **Type of Price:** spot. **Time Period Covered:** latest week.

SODIUM SALICYLATE: CRYSTALLINE, USP

Source: *Chemical Marketing Reporter.* **Price Frequency:** weekly. **Effective Market(s):** New York. **Units of Measure:** Dollars per lb. **Type of Price:** spot. **Time Period Covered:** latest week.

SODIUM SALICYLATE: POWDERED, USP

Source: *Chemical Marketing Reporter.* **Price Frequency:** weekly. **Effective Market(s):** New York. **Units of Measure:** Dollars per lb. **Type of Price:** spot. **Time Period Covered:** latest week.

SODIUM SESQUICARBONATE

Source: *Chemical Marketing Reporter.* **Price Frequency:** weekly. **Effective Market(s):** New York. **Units of Measure:** Dollars per ton, dollars per 100 lbs. **Type of Price:** spot. **Time Period Covered:** latest week.

SODIUM SILICATE: SOLID OR GLASS

Source: *Chemical Marketing Reporter.* **Price Frequency:** weekly. **Effective Market(s):** New York. **Units of Measure:** Dollars per 100 lbs. **Type of Price:** spot. **Time Period Covered:** latest week.

SODIUM SILICATE: SOLUTION

Source: *Chemical Marketing Reporter.* **Price Frequency:** weekly. **Effective Market(s):** New York. **Units of Measure:** Dollars per 100 lbs. **Type of Price:** spot. **Time Period Covered:** latest week.

Source: *Journal of Commerce and Commercial.* **Price Frequency:** weekly in Thursday issue. **Units of Measure:** Dollars per 100 lbs. **Type of Price:** spot. **Time Period Covered:** latest week.

SODIUM SILICOFLUORIDE

Source: *Chemical Marketing Reporter.* **Price Frequency:** weekly. **Effective Market(s):** New York. **Units of Measure:** Dollars per 100 lbs. **Type of Price:** spot. **Time Period Covered:** latest week.

SODIUM STANNATE

Source: *Chemical Marketing Reporter.* **Price Frequency:** weekly. **Effective Market(s):** New York. **Units of Measure:** Dollars per lb. **Type of Price:** spot. **Time Period Covered:** latest week.

Source: *Journal of Commerce and Commercial.* **Price Frequency:** weekly in Thursday issue. **Units of Measure:** Dollars per lb. **Type of Price:** spot. **Time Period Covered:** latest week.

SODIUM SULFANILATE POWDER: DRY

Source: *Chemical Marketing Reporter.* **Price Frequency:** weekly. **Effective Market(s):** New York. **Units of Measure:** Dollars per lb. **Type of Price:** spot. **Time Period Covered:** latest week.

SODIUM SULFATE

Source: *Chemical Marketing Reporter.* **Price Frequency:** weekly. **Effective Market(s):** East, West. **Units of Measure:** Dollars per ton. **Type of Price:** spot. **Time Period Covered:** latest week.

SODIUM SULFATE: PHOTO GRADE

Source: *Chemical Marketing Reporter.* **Price Frequency:** weekly. **Effective Market(s):** New York. **Units of Measure:** Dollars per 100 lbs. **Type of Price:** spot. **Time Period Covered:** latest week.

SODIUM SULFATE: RAYON GRADE, TECHNICAL, DETERGENT

Source: *Chemical Marketing Reporter.* **Price Frequency:** weekly. **Effective Market(s):** Gulf. **Units of Measure:** Dollars per ton. **Type of Price:** spot. **Time Period Covered:** latest week.

SODIUM SULFATE: TECHNICAL GRADE, GRANULAR

Source: *Journal of Commerce and Commercial.* **Price Frequency:** weekly in Thursday issue. **Effective Market(s):** East. **Units of Measure:** Dollars per lb. **Type of Price:** spot. **Time Period Covered:** latest week.

SODIUM SULFATE POWDER: XII, NF

Source: *Chemical Marketing Reporter.* **Price Frequency:** weekly. **Effective Market(s):** New York. **Units of Measure:** Dollars per lb. **Type of Price:** spot. **Time Period Covered:** latest week.

SODIUM SULFHYDRATE: FLAKE, 70-72%

Source: *Chemical Marketing Reporter.* **Price Frequency:** weekly. **Effective Market(s):** New York. **Units of Measure:** Dollars per ton. **Type of Price:** spot. **Time Period Covered:** latest week.

SODIUM SULFHYDRATE: LIQUID, 44-46%

Source: *Chemical Marketing Reporter.* **Price Frequency:** weekly. **Effective Market(s):** New York. **Units of Measure:** Dollars per ton. **Type of Price:** spot. **Time Period Covered:** latest week.

SODIUM SULFIDE: FLAKE

Source: *Chemical Marketing Reporter.* **Price Frequency:** weekly. **Effective Market(s):** East. **Units of Measure:** Dollars per ton. **Type of Price:** spot. **Time Period Covered:** latest week.

Source: *Journal of Commerce and Commercial.* **Price Frequency:** weekly in Thursday issue. **Units of Measure:** Dollars per ton. **Type of Price:** spot. **Time Period Covered:** latest week.

SODIUM SULFITE

Source: *Journal of Commerce and Commercial.* **Price Frequency:** weekly in Thursday issue. **Units of Measure:** Dollars per 100 lbs. **Type of Price:** spot. **Time Period Covered:** latest week.

SODIUM SULFITE: ANHYDROUS, TECHNICAL, 95-100%

Source: *Chemical Marketing Reporter.* **Price Frequency:** weekly. **Effective Market(s):** New York. **Units of Measure:** Dollars per 100 lbs. **Type of Price:** spot. **Time Period Covered:** latest week.

SODIUM SULFOCYANIDE: CHEMICALLY PURE

see Sodium Thiocyanate.

SODIUM TETRABORATE

see Borax.

SODIUM TETRASULFIDE: LIQUID, 34%

Source: *Chemical Marketing Reporter.* **Price Frequency:** weekly. **Effective Market(s):** New York. **Units of Measure:** Dollars per ton. **Type of Price:** spot. **Time Period Covered:** latest week.

SODIUM THIOCYANATE: ANHYDROUS, TECHNICAL

Source: *Chemical Marketing Reporter.* **Price Frequency:** weekly. **Effective Market(s):** New York. **Units of Measure:** Dollars per lb. **Type of Price:** spot. **Time Period Covered:** latest week.

SODIUM THIOCYANATE: PHOTO GRADE

Source: *Chemical Marketing Reporter.* **Price Frequency:** weekly. **Effective Market(s):** New York. **Units of Measure:** Dollars per lb. **Type of Price:** spot. **Time Period Covered:** latest week.

SODIUM THIOSULFATE: ANHYDROUS, TECHNICAL, PHOTO GRADE

Source: *Chemical Marketing Reporter.* **Price Frequency:** weekly. **Effective Market(s):** New York. **Units of Measure:** Dollars per 100 lbs. **Type of Price:** spot. **Time Period Covered:** latest week.

SODIUM THIOSULFATE: PENTAHYDRATE, CRYSTALLINE

Source: *Chemical Marketing Reporter.* **Price Frequency:** weekly. **Effective Market(s):** New York. **Units of Measure:** Dollars per 100 lbs. **Type of Price:** spot. **Time Period Covered:** latest week.

SODIUM TITANATE

Source: *Chemical Marketing Reporter.* **Price Frequency:** weekly. **Effective Market(s):** New York. **Units of Measure:** Dollars per lb. **Type of Price:** spot. **Time Period Covered:** latest week.

SODIUM TRICHLOROACETATE: 95%

Source: *Chemical Marketing Reporter.* **Price Frequency:** weekly. **Effective Market(s):** East. **Units of Measure:** Dollars per lb. **Type of Price:** spot. **Time Period Covered:** latest week.

SODIUM TRIPOLYPHOSPHATE: ANHYDROUS, TECHNICAL GRADE

Source: *Journal of Commerce and Commercial.* **Price Frequency:** weekly in Thursday issue. **Units of Measure:** Dollars per lb. **Type of Price:** spot. **Time Period Covered:** latest week.

SODIUM TRIPOLYPHOSPHATE: FOOD GRADE

Source: *Chemical Marketing Reporter.* **Price Frequency:** weekly. **Effective Market(s):** New York. **Units of Measure:** Dollars per 100 lbs. **Type of Price:** spot. **Time Period Covered:** latest week.

SODIUM TRIPOLYPHOSPHATE: TECHNICAL GRADE

Source: *Chemical Marketing Reporter.* **Price Frequency:** weekly. **Effective Market(s):** New York. **Units of Measure:** Dollars per 100 lbs. **Type of Price:** spot. **Time Period Covered:** latest week.

SODIUM TUNGSTATE: FOLIN GRADE

Source: *Chemical Marketing Reporter.* **Price Frequency:** weekly. **Effective Market(s):** New York. **Units of Measure:** Dollars per lb. **Type of Price:** spot. **Time Period Covered:** latest week.

SODIUM TUNGSTATE: TECHNICAL

Source: *Chemical Marketing Reporter.* **Price Frequency:** weekly. **Effective Market(s):** New York. **Units of Measure:** Dollars per lb. **Type of Price:** spot. **Time Period Covered:** latest week.

SOFTWOOD PULPWOOD: CHIPS

Source: *Pulpwood Prices in the Southeast.* **Price Frequency:** annually. **Effective Market(s):** Florida, Georgia, North Carolina, South Carolina, Virginia. **Units of Measure:** Dollars per green ton. **Type of Price:** average. **Time Period Covered:** latest 2 years.

SOFTWOOD PULPWOOD: ROUNDWOOD

Source: *Pulpwood Prices in the Southeast.* **Price Frequency:** annually. **Effective Market(s):** Florida, Georgia, North Carolina, South Carolina, Virginia. **Units of Measure:** Dollars per standard cord. **Type of Price:** average. **Time Period Covered:** latest 2 years.

SOFTWOODS: EASTERN

Source: *Volume and Value of Sawtimber Stumpage Sold From National Forests by Selected Species and Region.* **Price Frequency:** quarterly, annually. **Effective Market(s):** Eastern region, Southern region. **Units of Measure:** Dollars per 1000 board feet. **Type of Price:** average. **Time Period Covered:** latest quarter, latest year.

SOFTWOODS: WESTERN

Source: *Volume and Value of Sawtimber Stumpage Sold From National Forests by Selected Species and Region.* **Price Frequency:** quarterly, annually. **Effective Market(s):** 8 domestic markets. **Units of Measure:** Dollars per 1000 board feet. **Type of Price:** average. **Time Period Covered:** latest quarter, latest year.

SOLDER POWDER

Source: *American Metal Market.* **Price Frequency:** daily. **Units of Measure:** Dollars per lb. **Time Period Covered:** latest day.

SOLE: DOVER, FILLETS, FRESH

Source: *Seafood Price-Current.* **Price Frequency:** semiweekly. **Effective Market(s):** West Coast. **Units of Measure:** Dollars per lb. **Type of Price:** sale by first receiver. **Time Period Covered:** latest day.

SOLE: DOVER, WHOLE, HOLLAND DRESSED, FROZEN

Source: *Seafood Price-Current.* **Price Frequency:** semiweekly. **Effective Market(s):** Mid-Atlantic. **Units of Measure:** Dollars per lb. **Type of Price:** sale by first receiver. **Time Period Covered:** latest day.

SOLE: ENGLISH, FILLETS, FRESH

Source: *Seafood Price-Current.* **Price Frequency:** semiweekly. **Effective Market(s):** West Coast. **Units of Measure:** Dollars per lb. **Type of Price:** sale by first receiver. **Time Period Covered:** latest day.

SOLE: GRAY, FILLETS, FRESH

Source: *Seafood Price-Current.* **Price Frequency:** semiweekly. **Effective Market(s):** Mid-Atlantic, New England. **Units of Measure:** Dollars per lb. **Type of Price:** sale by first receiver. **Time Period Covered:** latest day.

SOLE: GRAY, WHOLE, FRESH

Source: *Seafood Price-Current.* **Price Frequency:** semiweekly. **Effective Market(s):** Boston, Mid-Atlantic, New Bedford (MA), Portland (ME). **Units of Measure:** Dollars per lb. **Type of Price:** sale by first receiver, auction price. **Time Period Covered:** latest day.

SOLE: GREY, FILLETS, FRESH

Source: *HRI-Buyer's Guide.* **Price Frequency:** weekly. **Effective Market(s):** New York. **Units of Measure:** Dollars per lb. **Type of Price:** dealer. **Time Period Covered:** latest week.

SOLE: LEMON, WHOLE, FRESH

Source: *Seafood Price-Current.* **Price Frequency:** semiweekly. **Effective Market(s):** Boston, Mid-Atlantic, New Bedford (MA), Portland (ME). **Units of Measure:** Dollars per lb. **Type of Price:** sale by first receiver, auction price. **Time Period Covered:** latest day.

SOLE: PETRALE, FILLETS, FRESH

Source: *Seafood Price-Current.* **Price Frequency:** semiweekly. **Effective Market(s):** West Coast. **Units of Measure:** Dollars per lb. **Type of Price:** sale by first receiver. **Time Period Covered:** latest day.

SOLE: PROCESSORS FISH BLOCKS, CANADIAN

Source: *Seafood Price-Current.* **Price Frequency:** semiweekly. **Effective Market(s):** New England. **Units of Measure:** Dollars per lb. **Time Period Covered:** latest day.

SOLE: REX, WHOLE, SKINNED, TRIMMED, FRESH

Source: *Seafood Price-Current.* **Price Frequency:** semiweekly. **Effective Market(s):** West Coast. **Units of Measure:** Dollars per lb. **Type of Price:** sale by first receiver. **Time Period Covered:** latest day.

SOLE: YELLOWFIN, FILLETS, FROZEN, KOREAN

Source: *Seafood Price-Current.* **Price Frequency:** semi-weekly. **Effective Market(s):** Mid-Atlantic. **Units of Measure:** Dollars per lb. **Type of Price:** first receiver. **Time Period Covered:** latest day.

SOLE: YELLOWFIN, PROCESSORS FISH BLOCKS, KOREAN

Source: *Seafood Price-Current.* **Price Frequency:** semi-weekly. **Effective Market(s):** New England. **Units of Measure:** Dollars per lb. **Time Period Covered:** latest day.

SOLVENT NAPHTHA

see Naphtha: Solvent.

SOLVENTS: AROMATIC

Source: *Journal of Commerce and Commercial.* **Price Frequency:** weekly in Wednesday issue. **Units of Measure:** Dollars per lb. **Type of Price:** spot. **Time Period Covered:** latest week.

SORBIC ACID

Source: *Chemical Marketing Reporter.* **Price Frequency:** weekly. **Effective Market(s):** New York. **Units of Measure:** Dollars per lb. **Type of Price:** spot. **Time Period Covered:** latest week.

Source: *Journal of Commerce and Commercial.* **Price Frequency:** weekly in Friday issue. **Units of Measure:** Dollars per lb. **Type of Price:** spot. **Time Period Covered:** latest week.

SORBITAN MONOSTEARATE

Source: *Chemical Marketing Reporter.* **Price Frequency:** weekly. **Effective Market(s):** New York. **Units of Measure:** Dollars per lb. **Type of Price:** spot. **Time Period Covered:** latest week.

SORBITAN TRISTEARATE

Source: *Chemical Marketing Reporter.* **Price Frequency:** weekly. **Effective Market(s):** New York. **Units of Measure:** Dollars per lb. **Type of Price:** spot. **Time Period Covered:** latest week.

SORBITOL: 70% AQUEOUS, REGULAR, USP

Source: *Chemical Marketing Reporter.* **Price Frequency:** weekly. **Effective Market(s):** New York. **Units of Measure:** Dollars per lb. **Type of Price:** spot. **Time Period Covered:** latest week.

SORBITOL: 70% SOLUTION

Source: *Journal of Commerce and Commercial.* **Price Frequency:** weekly in Friday issue. **Units of Measure:** Dollars per lb. **Type of Price:** spot. **Time Period Covered:** latest week.

SORBITOL: GRANULAR

Source: *Chemical Marketing Reporter.* **Price Frequency:** weekly. **Effective Market(s):** New York. **Units of Measure:** Dollars per lb. **Type of Price:** spot. **Time Period Covered:** latest week.

SORBITOL: POWDERED

Source: *Chemical Marketing Reporter.* **Price Frequency:** weekly. **Effective Market(s):** New York. **Units of Measure:** Dollars per lb. **Type of Price:** spot. **Time Period Covered:** latest week.

SORGHUM

see also Milo.

Source: *Agricultural Outlook.* **Price Frequency:** monthly, annually. **Effective Market(s):** United States. **Units of Measure:** Dollars per 100 lbs. **Type of Price:** received by farmer. **Time Period Covered:** monthly latest 6 months, annually latest 3 years.

Source: *Agricultural Outlook.* **Price Frequency:** annually. **Units of Measure:** Dollars per bushel. **Type of Price:** farm. **Time Period Covered:** latest 6 years.

Source: *Agricultural Outlook.* **Price Frequency:** monthly, annually. **Effective Market(s):** Gulf ports. **Units of Measure:** Dollars per bushel. **Type of Price:** export. **Time Period Covered:** monthly latest 6 months, annually latest 3 years.

Source: *Agricultural Prices.* **Price Frequency:** monthly. **Effective Market(s):** United States. **Units of Measure:** Dollars per 100 lbs. **Type of Price:** received by farmer. **Time Period Covered:** latest 2 months, year ago.

Source: *Agricultural Prices.* **Price Frequency:** monthly, seasonally. **Effective Market(s):** 9 domestic markets, United States. **Units of Measure:** Dollars per 100 lbs. **Type of Price:** received by farmer. **Time Period Covered:** latest 2 months.

Source: *Agricultural Prices Annual Summary.* **Price Frequency:** annually. **Effective Market(s):** 20 domestic markets, United States. **Units of Measure:** Dollars per 100 lbs. **Type of Price:** average received by farmer. **Time Period Covered:** latest 2 years, for US latest 6 years.

Source: *Agricultural Trade Highlights.* **Price Frequency:** weekly. **Effective Market(s):** United States. **Units of Measure:** Dollars per metric ton. **Type of Price:** farm. **Time Period Covered:** latest week, week ago, year ago.

Source: *Feed Situation and Outlook Report.* **Price Frequency:** monthly, annually. **Effective Market(s):** United States. **Units of Measure:** Dollars per 100 lbs. **Type of Price:** received by farmer. **Time Period Covered:** latest 5 years.

Source: *Idaho Farmer-Stockman.* **Price Frequency:** monthly. **Effective Market(s):** Denver, Omaha (NE), Portland (OR), Stockton (CA). **Time Period Covered:** latest month.

Source: *International Financial Statistics.* **Price Frequency:** monthly, quarterly, annually. **Effective Market(s):** Gulf ports. **Units of Measure:** Dollars per metric ton, index. **Type of Price:** market price, price index. **Time Period Covered:** latest 5 months, latest 5 quarters, latest 5 years.

Source: *International Financial Statistics Yearbook.* **Price Frequency:** annually. **Effective Market(s):** Gulf ports. **Units of Measure:** Dollars per metric ton. **Type of Price:** wholesale. **Time Period Covered:** latest 30 years.

Source: *International Wheat Council Market Report.* **Price Frequency:** weekly, seasonally. **Effective Market(s):** Gulf. **Units of Measure:** Dollars per metric ton. **Type of Price:** export. **Time Period Covered:** latest 5 weeks.

Source: *Kansas Business Review.* **Price Frequency:** monthly. **Effective Market(s):** Kansas. **Units of Measure:** Dollars per 100 lbs. **Type of Price:** received by farmer. **Time Period Covered:** latest month, month ago, year ago.

Source: *Utah Farmer-Stockman.* **Price Frequency:** monthly, seasonally. **Effective Market(s):** Denver, Omaha, Portland (OR), Stockton (CA). **Time Period Covered:** latest month.

SORGHUM: ARGENTINE

Source: *International Wheat Council Market Report.* **Price Frequency:** weekly, seasonally. **Effective Market(s):** Rosario (Argentina). **Units of Measure:** Dollars per metric ton. **Type of Price:** export. **Time Period Covered:** latest 5 weeks.

SORGHUM: NO. 2

Source: *Asian Wall Street Journal.* **Price Frequency:** daily. **Effective Market(s):** Gulf. **Units of Measure:** Dollars per 100 lbs. **Type of Price:** cash. **Time Period Covered:** latest 2 days, year ago.

Source: *Doane's Agricultural Report.* **Price Frequency:** weekly. **Effective Market(s):** Kansas City. **Units of Measure:** Dollars per 100 lbs. **Time Period Covered:** latest week, week ago, year ago.

Source: *Farm and Dairy.* **Price Frequency:** weekly. **Effective Market(s):** Gulf. **Units of Measure:** Dollars per 100 lbs. **Time Period Covered:** latest week, year ago.

Source: *Grain and Feed Market News.* **Price Frequency:** daily, seasonally. **Effective Market(s):** Texas High Plains. **Units of Measure:** Dollars per 100 lbs. **Type of Price:** cash bid. **Time Period Covered:** latest week, year ago.

Source: *Grain and Feed Market News.* **Price Frequency:** weekly, seasonally. **Effective Market(s):** Ft. Worth, Kansas City, Texas High Plains. **Units of Measure:** Dollars per ton. **Type of Price:** wholesale. **Time Period Covered:** latest week, week ago, year ago.

Source: *Lancaster Farming.* **Price Frequency:** weekly. **Effective Market(s):** Pennsylvania. **Units of Measure:** Dollars per bushel. **Time Period Covered:** latest week.

Source: *Wall Street Journal.* **Price Frequency:** daily. **Effective Market(s):** Gulf. **Units of Measure:** Dollars per 100 lbs. **Time Period Covered:** latest day, day ago, year ago.

SORGHUM: NO. 2, MAXIMUM 14% MOISTURE

Source: *Los Angeles Times.* **Price Frequency:** daily. **Effective Market(s):** Los Angeles. **Units of Measure:** Dollars per 100 lbs. **Type of Price:** cash. **Time Period Covered:** latest day.

SORGHUM: NO. 2, YELLOW

Source: *Agricultural Outlook.* **Price Frequency:** monthly, annually. **Effective Market(s):** Kansas City. **Units of Measure:** Dollars per 100 lbs. **Type of Price:** wholesale. **Time Period Covered:** monthly latest 5 months, annually latest 4 years.

Source: *California Farmer.* **Price Frequency:** semimonthly. **Effective Market(s):** Los Angeles, Stockton (CA). **Units of Measure:** Dollars per 100 lbs. **Time Period Covered:** latest week, month ago, year ago.

Source: *Commodity Year Book.* **Price Frequency:** monthly, annually. **Effective Market(s):** Kansas City. **Units of Measure:** Dollars per 100 lbs. **Time Period Covered:** latest 9 years.

Source: *Commodity Year Book.* **Price Frequency:** annually. **Effective Market(s):** Gulf ports, Kansas City, Louisiana, Texas High Plains. **Units of Measure:** Dollars per 100 lbs. **Time Period Covered:** latest 7 years.

Source: *FAO Quarterly Bulletin of Statistics.* **Price Frequency:** monthly, annually. **Effective Market(s):** Gulf. **Units of Measure:** Dollars per 100 lbs., dollars per metric ton. **Time Period Covered:** latest 3 years.

Source: *Feed Situation and Outlook Report.* **Price Frequency:** annually. **Effective Market(s):** Gulf ports, Kansas City, Texas. **Units of Measure:** Dollars per 100 lbs. **Type of Price:** average. **Time Period Covered:** latest 5 years.

Source: *Feed Situation and Outlook Report.* **Price Frequency:** monthly, annually. **Effective Market(s):** Kansas City, Texas High Plains. **Units of Measure:** Dollars per 100 lbs. **Type of Price:** cash. **Time Period Covered:** latest 5 years.

Source: *Grain and Feed Market News.* **Price Frequency:** daily, seasonally. **Effective Market(s):** Kansas City, Los Angeles. **Units of Measure:** Dollars per 100 lbs. **Type of Price:** cash bid. **Time Period Covered:** latest week, year ago.

Source: *Grain and Feed Market News.* **Price Frequency:** weekly, seasonally. **Effective Market(s):** 44 domestic markets. **Units of Measure:** Dollars per 100 lbs. **Type of Price:** cash bid. **Time Period Covered:** latest week.

Source: *Grain and Feed Market News.* **Price Frequency:** daily, seasonally. **Effective Market(s):** Gulf. **Units of Measure:** Dollars per 100 lbs. **Type of Price:** export bid. **Time Period Covered:** latest week, year ago.

SORGHUM GRAIN

see Sorghum.

SORGHUM SEED: HYBIRD

Source: *Agricultural Prices Annual Summary.* **Price Frequency:** semiannually. **Effective Market(s):** United States. **Units of Measure:** Dollars per 100 lbs. **Type of Price:** average paid by farmer. **Time Period Covered:** latest 6 years.

SOUTH AFRICA RAND

Source: *Barron's.* **Price Frequency:** weekly. **Effective Market(s):** New York. **Units of Measure:** South African rand per United States dollar. **Type of Price:** commercial foreign exchange rate, financial foreign exchange rate. **Time Period Covered:** latest 2 weeks.

Source: *New York Times.* **Price Frequency:** daily. **Effective Market(s):** United States. **Units of Measure:** South African rand per United States dollar. **Type of Price:** foreign exchange. **Time Period Covered:** latest 2 days.

Source: *The Times.* **Price Frequency:** daily. **Effective Market(s):** London. **Units of Measure:** South African rand per British pound. **Type of Price:** foreign exchange. **Time Period Covered:** latest day.

SOUTH KOREA WON

Source: *Asian Wall Street Journal.* **Price Frequency:** daily. **Effective Market(s):** Asia. **Units of Measure:** South Korean won per United States dollar. **Type of Price:** foreign exchange. **Time Period Covered:** latest 2 days.

Source: *Barron's.* **Price Frequency:** weekly. **Effective Market(s):** New York. **Units of Measure:** South Korean won per United States dollar. **Type of Price:** foreign exchange. **Time Period Covered:** latest 2 weeks.

Source: *New York Times.* **Price Frequency:** daily. **Effective Market(s):** United States. **Units of Measure:** South Korean won per United States dollar. **Type of Price:** foreign exchange. **Time Period Covered:** latest 2 days.

SOUTHERN PINE

see Pine: Southern.

SOWS

Source: *Agricultural Prices.* **Price Frequency:** monthly. **Effective Market(s):** United States. **Units of Measure:** Dollars per 100 lbs. **Type of Price:** received by farmer. **Time Period Covered:** latest 2 months, year ago.

Source: *Agricultural Prices.* **Price Frequency:** monthly. **Effective Market(s):** 20 domestic markets, United States. **Units of Measure:** Dollars per 100 lbs. **Type of Price:** received by farmer. **Time Period Covered:** latest 2 months.

Source: *Agricultural Prices Annual Summary.* **Price Frequency:** annually. **Effective Market(s):** 50 domestic markets, United States. **Units of Measure:** Dollars per 100 lbs. **Type of Price:** average received by farmer. **Time Period Covered:** latest 2 years, for US latest 6 years.

Source: *Agricultural Prices Annual Summary.* **Price Frequency:** monthly. **Effective Market(s):** 20 domestic markets, United States. **Units of Measure:** Dollars per 100 lbs. **Type of Price:** average received by farmer. **Time Period Covered:** latest year, for US latest 6 years.

Source: *Lancaster Farming.* **Price Frequency:** weekly. **Effective Market(s):** Pennsylvania, Virginia. **Units of Measure:** Dollars per head. **Type of Price:** auction. **Time Period Covered:** latest week.

Source: *Livestock and Poultry Update.* **Price Frequency:** monthly. **Effective Market(s):** 7-market average. **Units of Measure:** Dollars per 100 lbs. **Time Period Covered:** latest 3 month, year ago.

Source: *Scottish Farmer.* **Price Frequency:** weekly. **Effective Market(s):** Scotland. **Units of Measure:** British pence per kilogram. **Type of Price:** average. **Time Period Covered:** latest week.

SOWS: CULL

Source: *Farmers Weekly.* **Price Frequency:** weekly. **Effective Market(s):** 7 British markets. **Units of Measure:** British pence per kilogram. **Time Period Covered:** latest week.

Source: *Farmers Weekly.* **Price Frequency:** weekly. **Effective Market(s):** 9 British markets. **Units of Measure:** British pounds per head. **Time Period Covered:** latest week.

SOWS: HEAVY

Source: *Farm and Dairy.* **Price Frequency:** weekly, seasonally. **Effective Market(s):** Ohio, Pennsylvania. **Units of Measure:** Dollars per head. **Type of Price:** auction high, auction low. **Time Period Covered:** latest week.

SOWS: LIGHT

Source: *Farm and Dairy.* **Price Frequency:** weekly, seasonally. **Effective Market(s):** Ohio, Pennsylvania. **Units of Measure:** Dollars per head. **Type of Price:** auction high, auction low. **Time Period Covered:** latest week.

SOWS: SLAUGHTER

Source: *Livestock and Poultry Situation and Outlook Report.* **Price Frequency:** monthly. **Effective Market(s):** 7-market average. **Units of Measure:** Dollars per 100 lbs. **Time Period Covered:** latest year.

SOWS: US 1-3

Source: *Oregon Farmer-Stockman.* **Price Frequency:** monthly. **Effective Market(s):** Omaha. **Units of Measure:** Dollars per 100 lbs. **Time Period Covered:** latest month.

Source: *Utah Farmer-Stockman.* **Price Frequency:** monthly. **Effective Market(s):** Omaha. **Units of Measure:** Dollars per 100 lbs. **Time Period Covered:** latest month.

SOY FLOUR

see Flour: Soy.

SOYABEANS

see Soybeans.

SOYBEAN MEAL

Source: *Agra Europe.* **Price Frequency:** weekly, irregularly. **Effective Market(s):** Rotterdam. **Units of Measure:** Dollars per tonne. **Time Period Covered:** latest week.

Source: *Agricultural Outlook.* **Price Frequency:** monthly, annually. **Effective Market(s):** Decatur (IL). **Units of Measure:** Dollars per ton. **Type of Price:** export. **Time Period Covered:** monthly latest 6 months, annually latest 3 years.

Source: *Asian Wall Street Journal.* **Price Frequency:** daily. **Effective Market(s):** Decatur (IL). **Units of Measure:** Dollars per ton. **Type of Price:** cash. **Time Period Covered:** latest 2 days, year ago.

Source: *California Farmer.* **Price Frequency:** semimonthly. **Effective Market(s):** California. **Units of Measure:** Dollars per ton. **Time Period Covered:** latest week, month ago, year ago.

Source: *Economic and Energy Indicators.* **Price Frequency:** biweekly. **Units of Measure:** Dollars per metric ton. **Time Period Covered:** latest 3 months, quarters, and years.

Source: *Farm and Dairy.* **Price Frequency:** weekly. **Effective Market(s):** Illinois. **Units of Measure:** Dollars per ton. **Time Period Covered:** latest week, year ago.

Source: *Investor's Daily.* **Price Frequency:** daily. **Effective Market(s):** Decatur (IL). **Units of Measure:** Dollars per ton. **Type of Price:** spot. **Time Period Covered:** latest day.

Source: *Japan Economic Journal.* **Price Frequency:** weekly. **Effective Market(s):** Japan. **Units of Measure:** Japanese yen per ton. **Type of Price:** wholesale. **Time Period Covered:** latest 2 weeks.

Source: *New York Times.* **Price Frequency:** daily. **Effective Market(s):** Decatur (IL). **Units of Measure:** Dollars per ton. **Type of Price:** cash. **Time Period Covered:** latest 2 days.

Source: *Wall Street Journal.* **Price Frequency:** daily. **Effective Market(s):** Decatur (IL). **Units of Measure:** Dollars per ton. **Time Period Covered:** latest day, day ago, year ago.

Source: *World Oilseed Situation and Market Highlights.* **Price Frequency:** monthly, annually. **Effective Market(s):** Brazil, Decatur (IL), Rotterdam. **Units of Measure:** Dollars per metric ton. **Time Period Covered:** monthly latest 2 months, annually latest 2 years.

SOYBEAN MEAL: 44% PROTEIN

Source: *Agricultural Outlook.* **Price Frequency:** annually. **Effective Market(s):** Decatur (IL). **Units of Measure:** Dollars per ton. **Type of Price:** farm. **Time Period Covered:** latest 6 years.

Source: *Agricultural Outlook.* **Price Frequency:** monthly, annually. **Effective Market(s):** Decatur (IL). **Units of Measure:** Dollars per ton. **Type of Price:** wholesale. **Time Period Covered:** monthly latest 5 months, annually latest 4 years.

Source: *Agricultural Prices.* **Price Frequency:** quarterly. **Effective Market(s):** United States. **Units of Measure:** Dollars per 100 lbs. **Type of Price:** paid by farmer. **Time Period Covered:** latest 2 quarters, year ago.

Source: *Agricultural Prices.* **Price Frequency:** monthly. **Effective Market(s):** 10 domestic markets, United States. **Units of Measure:** Dollars per 50 lbs. **Type of Price:** paid by farmer. **Time Period Covered:** latest month.

Source: *Agricultural Prices Annual Summary.* **Price Frequency:** quarterly. **Effective Market(s):** 10 domestic markets, United States. **Units of Measure:** Dollars per ton. **Type of Price:** average paid by farmer. **Time Period Covered:** latest year, for US latest 6 years.

Source: *Agricultural Trade Highlights.* **Price Frequency:** weekly. **Effective Market(s):** Rotterdam. **Units of Measure:** Dollars per metric ton. **Type of Price:** asking. **Time Period Covered:** latest week, week ago, year ago.

Source: *Commodity Trade and Price Trends.* **Price Frequency:** annually. **Effective Market(s):** Rotterdam. **Units of Measure:** Dollars per metric ton, 1980 constant dollars per metric ton. **Time Period Covered:** latest 37 years.

Source: *Farmers Weekly.* **Price Frequency:** weekly, seasonally. **Effective Market(s):** Great Britain. **Units of Measure:** British pounds per tonne. **Type of Price:** spot. **Time Period Covered:** latest week.

Source: *Feed Situation and Outlook Report.* **Price Frequency:** quarterly, annually. **Effective Market(s):** United States. **Units of Measure:** Dollars per 100 lbs. **Type of Price:** paid by farmer. **Time Period Covered:** latest year.

Source: *Feedstuffs.* **Price Frequency:** weekly. **Effective Market(s):** 11 domestic markets. **Units of Measure:** Dollars per bulk ton. **Time Period Covered:** latest week.

Source: *Feedstuffs.* **Price Frequency:** weekly. **Effective Market(s):** Decatur (IL). **Units of Measure:** Dollars per ton. **Time Period Covered:** latest week, week ago, 6 months ago, year ago.

Source: *Milling & Baking News.* **Price Frequency:** weekly. **Effective Market(s):** Kansas City. **Units of Measure:** Dollars per ton. **Time Period Covered:** latest week, week ago, year ago.

Source: *Monthly Commodity Price Bulletin.* **Price Frequency:** monthly, annually. **Effective Market(s):** Rotterdam. **Units of Measure:** Dollars per metric ton. **Time Period Covered:** latest 5 years.

Source: *Oil Crops Situation and Outlook.* **Price Frequency:** monthly, annually. **Effective Market(s):** Decatur (IL). **Units of Measure:** Dollars per ton. **Time Period Covered:** monthly latest year, annually 10 years.

Source: *Standard & Poor's Statistical Service Current Statistics.* **Price Frequency:** monthly, annually. **Effective Market(s):** Decatur (IL). **Units of Measure:** Dollars per ton. **Time Period Covered:** latest 4 years.

Source: *World Agriculture Situation and Outlook.* **Price Frequency:** monthly, annually. **Effective Market(s):** Decatur (IL), Hamburg. **Units of Measure:** Dollars per metric ton. **Time Period Covered:** monthly latest year, annually latest 9 years.

Source: *World Oilseed Situation and Market Highlights.* **Price Frequency:** monthly, annually. **Effective Market(s):** Decatur (IL). **Units of Measure:** Dollars per metric ton. **Type of Price:** wholesale. **Time Period Covered:** monthly latest year, annually latest 9 years.

SOYBEAN MEAL: 44% SOLVENT

Source: *Commodity Year Book.* **Price Frequency:** annually. **Effective Market(s):** Decatur (IL). **Units of Measure:** Dollars per ton, dollars per tonne. **Time Period Covered:** latest 6 years.

Source: *Commodity Year Book.* **Price Frequency:** monthly, annually. **Effective Market(s):** Decatur (IL). **Units of Measure:** Dollars per short ton. **Time Period Covered:** latest 6 years.

Source: *Doane's Agriculutral Report.* **Price Frequency:** weekly. **Effective Market(s):** Decatur (IL). **Units of Measure:** Dollars per ton. **Time Period Covered:** latest week, week ago, year ago.

Source: *Feed Situation and Outlook Report.* **Price Frequency:** monthly. **Effective Market(s):** Decatur (IL). **Units of Measure:** Dollars per ton. **Type of Price:** wholesale. **Time Period Covered:** latest 8 months.

Source: *Grain and Feed Market News.* **Price Frequency:** weekly, seasonally. **Effective Market(s):** Decatur (IL), Kansas City, Memphis (TN), Minneapolis, St. Louis. **Units of Measure:** Dollars per ton. **Type of Price:** wholesale. **Time Period Covered:** latest week, week ago, year ago.

Source: *Livestock and Poultry Update.* **Price Frequency:** monthly. **Effective Market(s):** Decatur (IL). **Units of Measure:** Dollars per bushel. **Time Period Covered:** latest 3 month, year ago.

SOYBEAN MEAL: 44%, UNITED STATES

Source: *FAO Quarterly Bulletin of Statistics.* **Price Frequency:** monthly, annually. **Effective Market(s):** Rotterdam. **Units of Measure:** Dollars per 1000 kilograms, dollars per metric ton. **Time Period Covered:** latest 3 years.

Source: *Monthly Commodity Price Bulletin Supplement.* **Price Frequency:** monthly, quarterly, annually. **Effective Market(s):** Rotterdam. **Units of Measure:** Dollars per tonne. **Time Period Covered:** latest 20 years.

Source: *Oil World.* **Price Frequency:** weekly, monthly, annually. **Effective Market(s):** Rotterdam. **Units of Measure:** Dollars per tonne. **Type of Price:** lowest representative asking. **Time Period Covered:** weekly latest 3 weeks, monthly latest 2 months, annually latest 2 years.

SOYBEAN MEAL: 44-45% PROTEIN, HAMBURG

Source: *Oil World.* **Price Frequency:** weekly, monthly, annually. **Units of Measure:** Dollars per tonne. **Type of Price:** lowest representative asking. **Time Period Covered:** weekly latest 3 weeks, monthly latest 2 months, annually latest 2 years.

SOYBEAN MEAL: 44-47% PROTEIN

Source: *Farmers Weekly.* **Price Frequency:** weekly, seasonally. **Effective Market(s):** Great Britain. **Units of Measure:** British pounds per tonne. **Type of Price:** spot. **Time Period Covered:** latest week.

SOYBEAN MEAL: 45-46% PROTEIN

Source: *Commodity Year Book.* **Price Frequency:** annually. **Effective Market(s):** Brazil. **Units of Measure:** Dollars per tonne. **Time Period Covered:** latest 6 years.

Source: *World Oilseed Situation and Market Highlights.* **Price Frequency:** monthly, annually. **Effective Market(s):** Rio Grande (Brazil). **Units of Measure:** Dollars per metric ton. **Time Period Covered:** monthly latest year, annually latest 9 years.

SOYBEAN MEAL: 45-46% PROTEIN, ARGENTINE

Source: *World Oilseed Situation and Market Highlights.* **Price Frequency:** monthly, annually. **Effective Market(s):** Rotterdam. **Units of Measure:** Dollars per metric ton. **Time Period Covered:** monthly latest year, annually latest 9 years.

SOYBEAN MEAL: 47% PROTEIN

Source: *Los Angeles Times.* **Price Frequency:** daily. **Effective Market(s):** Los Angeles. **Units of Measure:** Dollars per ton. **Type of Price:** cash. **Time Period Covered:** latest day.

SOYBEAN MEAL: 47-1/2% PROTEIN

Source: *Milling & Baking News.* **Price Frequency:** weekly. **Effective Market(s):** Kansas City. **Units of Measure:** Dollars per ton. **Time Period Covered:** latest week, week ago, year ago.

SOYBEAN MEAL: 48% PROTEIN

Source: *Feedstuffs.* **Price Frequency:** weekly. **Effective Market(s):** Decatur (IL). **Units of Measure:** Dollars per ton. **Time Period Covered:** latest week, week ago, 6 months ago, year ago.

SOYBEAN MEAL: 49% PROTEIN

Source: *Feedstuffs.* **Price Frequency:** weekly. **Effective Market(s):** 11 domestic markets. **Units of Measure:** Dollars per bulk ton. **Time Period Covered:** latest week.

SOYBEAN MEAL: 49-50% PROTEIN

Source: *Oil Crops Situation and Outlook.* **Price Frequency:** monthly. **Effective Market(s):** Decatur (IL). **Units of Measure:** Dollars per ton. **Time Period Covered:** latest 5 months.

SOYBEAN MEAL: FUTURES

Source: *Agriculture.* **Price Frequency:** weekly. **Effective Market(s):** Chicago. **Units of Measure:** Dollars per ton. **Type of Price:** futures. **Time Period Covered:** latest week, week ago.

Source: *Asian Wall Street Journal.* **Price Frequency:** daily. **Effective Market(s):** Chicago. **Units of Measure:** Dollars per ton. **Type of Price:** futures. **Time Period Covered:** latest day.

Source: *Barron's.* **Price Frequency:** weekly. **Effective Market(s):** Chicago. **Units of Measure:** Dollars per ton. **Type of Price:** futures. **Time Period Covered:** latest week.

Source: *Feedstuffs.* **Price Frequency:** weekly. **Effective Market(s):** Chicago. **Units of Measure:** Dollars per ton. **Type of Price:** futures. **Time Period Covered:** latest week, week ago, latest season.

Source: *Financial Times.* **Price Frequency:** daily. **Effective Market(s):** Chicago, London. **Units of Measure:** Dollars per ton, British pounds per tonne. **Type of Price:** futures. **Time Period Covered:** latest day.

Source: *Grain and Feed Market News.* **Price Frequency:** weekly. **Effective Market(s):** Chicago. **Units of Measure:** Dollars per ton. **Type of Price:** futures. **Time Period Covered:** latest week.

Source: *Investor's Daily.* **Price Frequency:** daily. **Effective Market(s):** Chicago. **Units of Measure:** Dollars per ton. **Type of Price:** futures. **Time Period Covered:** latest day.

Source: *Lancaster Farming.* **Price Frequency:** daily. **Type of Price:** futures. **Time Period Covered:** latest week.

Source: *Los Angeles Times.* **Price Frequency:** daily. **Effective Market(s):** Chicago. **Units of Measure:** Dollars per ton. **Type of Price:** futures. **Time Period Covered:** latest day.

Source: *Milling & Baking News.* **Price Frequency:** weekly. **Units of Measure:** Dollars per ton. **Type of Price:** futures. **Time Period Covered:** latest week, year ago.

Source: *New York Times.* **Price Frequency:** daily. **Effective Market(s):** Chicago. **Units of Measure:** Dollars per ton. **Type of Price:** futures. **Time Period Covered:** latest day.

Source: *Urner Barry's Price-Current.* **Price Frequency:** daily. **Effective Market(s):** Chicago. **Units of Measure:** Dollars per ton. **Type of Price:** futures. **Time Period Covered:** latest day.

Source: *Wall Street Journal.* **Price Frequency:** daily. **Effective Market(s):** Chicago. **Units of Measure:** Dollars per ton. **Type of Price:** futures. **Time Period Covered:** latest day.

SOYBEAN MEAL: FUTURES, MAY

Source: *Commodity Year Book.* **Price Frequency:** monthly. **Effective Market(s):** Chicago. **Units of Measure:** Dollars per ton. **Type of Price:** futures. **Time Period Covered:** latest 7 years.

SOYBEAN MEAL: HIGH PROTEIN

Source: *Farmers Weekly.* **Price Frequency:** weekly, seasonally. **Effective Market(s):** Great Britain. **Units of Measure:** British pounds per tonne. **Type of Price:** spot. **Time Period Covered:** latest week.

Source: *Feed Situation and Outlook Report.* **Price Frequency:** monthly. **Effective Market(s):** Decatur (IL). **Units of Measure:** Dollars per ton. **Type of Price:** wholesale. **Time Period Covered:** latest 8 months.

Source: *Grain and Feed Market News.* **Price Frequency:** weekly, seasonally. **Effective Market(s):** 8 domestic markets. **Units of Measure:** Dollars per ton. **Type of Price:** wholesale. **Time Period Covered:** latest week, week ago, year ago.

SOYBEAN MEAL: UNITED STATES

Source: *International Financial Statistics.* **Price Frequency:** monthly, quarterly, annually. **Effective Market(s):** Rotterdam. **Units of Measure:** Dollars per metric ton, index. **Type of Price:** market price, price index. **Time Period Covered:** latest 5 months, latest 5 quarters, latest 5 years.

Source: *International Financial Statistics Yearbook.* **Price Frequency:** annually. **Effective Market(s):** Rotterdam. **Units of Measure:** Dollars per metric ton. **Type of Price:** wholesale. **Time Period Covered:** latest 30 years.

SOYBEAN OIL

Source: *Agricultural Outlook.* **Price Frequency:** annually. **Effective Market(s):** Decatur (IL). **Units of Measure:** cents per lb. **Type of Price:** farm. **Time Period Covered:** latest 6 years.

Source: *Agricultural Outlook.* **Price Frequency:** monthly, annually. **Effective Market(s):** Decatur (IL). **Units of Measure:** cents per lb. **Type of Price:** export. **Time Period Covered:** monthly latest 6 months, annually latest 3 years.

Source: *Bakery Newsletter.* **Price Frequency:** weekly. **Effective Market(s):** Decatur (IL). **Units of Measure:** cents per lb. **Type of Price:** cash. **Time Period Covered:** latest week, week ago.

Source: *Dairy Foods.* **Price Frequency:** weekly. **Effective Market(s):** Decatur (IL). **Units of Measure:** Dollars per lb. **Time Period Covered:** latest 2 weeks.

Source: *Economic and Energy Indicators.* **Price Frequency:** biweekly. **Units of Measure:** Dollars per metric ton. **Time Period Covered:** latest 3 months, quarters, and years.

Source: *Grain and Feed Market News.* **Price Frequency:** weekly, seasonally. **Effective Market(s):** Decatur (IL). **Units of Measure:** cents per lb. **Type of Price:** wholesale. **Time Period Covered:** latest week, week ago, year ago.

Source: *International Financial Statistics.* **Price Frequency:** monthly, quarterly, annually. **Effective Market(s):** Dutch ports. **Units of Measure:** Dollars per metric ton, index. **Type of Price:** market price, price index. **Time Period Covered:** latest 5 months, latest 5 quarters, latest 5 years.

Source: *International Financial Statistics Yearbook.* **Price Frequency:** annually. **Effective Market(s):** Dutch ports. **Units of Measure:** Dollars per metric ton. **Type of Price:** wholesale. **Time Period Covered:** latest 30 years.

Source: *Milling & Baking News.* **Price Frequency:** weekly. **Effective Market(s):** Decatur (IL). **Units of Measure:** cents per lb. **Type of Price:** spot bulk. **Time Period Covered:** latest week.

Source: *National Provisioner.* **Price Frequency:** daily. **Units of Measure:** cents per lb. **Time Period Covered:** latest week.

Source: *World Agriculture Situation and Outlook.* **Price Frequency:** monthly, annually. **Effective Market(s):** Decatur (IL). **Units of Measure:** Dollars per metric ton. **Time Period Covered:** monthly latest year, annually latest 9 years.

Source: *World Oilseed Situation and Market Highlights.* **Price Frequency:** monthly, annually. **Effective Market(s):** Brazil, Decatur (IL), Rotterdam. **Units of Measure:** Dollars per metric ton. **Time Period Covered:** monthly latest 2 months, annually latest 2 years.

SOYBEAN OIL: 44% PROTEIN

Source: *UNCTAD Commodity Yearbook.* **Price Frequency:** annually. **Effective Market(s):** Rotterdam. **Units of Measure:** Dollars per metric ton. **Type of Price:** free market. **Time Period Covered:** latest 12 years.

SOYBEAN OIL: ACID, DOUBLE DISTILLED

Source: *Chemical Marketing Reporter.* **Price Frequency:** weekly. **Effective Market(s):** New York. **Units of Measure:** Dollars per lb. **Type of Price:** spot. **Time Period Covered:** latest week.

SOYBEAN OIL: ACID, SINGLE DISTILLED

Source: *Chemical Marketing Reporter.* **Price Frequency:** weekly. **Effective Market(s):** New York. **Units of Measure:** Dollars per lb. **Type of Price:** spot. **Time Period Covered:** latest week.

SOYBEAN OIL: ACIDULATED, SOAPSTOCK, 95% ACID

Source: *Chemical Marketing Reporter.* **Price Frequency:** weekly. **Effective Market(s):** New York. **Units of Measure:** Dollars per lb. **Type of Price:** spot. **Time Period Covered:** latest week.

SOYBEAN OIL: BRAZILIAN

Source: *Oil World.* **Price Frequency:** weekly, monthly, annually. **Units of Measure:** Dollars per tonne. **Type of Price:** lowest representative asking. **Time Period Covered:** weekly latest 3 weeks, monthly latest 2 months, annually latest 2 years.

Source: *World Oilseed Situation and Market Highlights.* **Price Frequency:** monthly, annually. **Effective Market(s):** Rio Grande (Brazil). **Units of Measure:** Dollars per metric ton. **Time Period Covered:** monthly latest year, annually latest 9 years.

SOYBEAN OIL: CRUDE

Source: *Agricultural Outlook.* **Price Frequency:** monthly, annually. **Effective Market(s):** Decatur (IL). **Units of Measure:** cents per lb. **Type of Price:** wholesale. **Time Period Covered:** monthly latest 5 months, annually latest 4 years.

Source: *Asian Wall Street Journal.* **Price Frequency:** daily. **Effective Market(s):** Decatur (IL). **Units of Measure:** Dollars per lb. **Type of Price:** cash. **Time Period Covered:** latest 2 days, year ago.

Source: *Chemical Marketing Reporter.* **Price Frequency:** weekly. **Effective Market(s):** Decatur (IL). **Units of Measure:** Dollars per lb. **Type of Price:** spot. **Time Period Covered:** latest week.

Source: *Commodity Trade and Price Trends.* **Price Frequency:** annually. **Units of Measure:** Dollars per metric ton, 1980 constant dollars per metric ton. **Time Period Covered:** latest 37 years.

Source: *CRB Commodity Index Report.* **Price Frequency:** weekly. **Effective Market(s):** Decatur (IL). **Units of Measure:** Dollars per lb. **Type of Price:** spot. **Time Period Covered:** latest week.

Source: *Investor's Daily.* **Price Frequency:** daily. **Effective Market(s):** Decatur (IL). **Units of Measure:** Dollars per lb. **Type of Price:** spot. **Time Period Covered:** latest day.

Source: *Journal of Commerce and Commercial.* **Price Frequency:** daily. **Effective Market(s):** Decatur (IL). **Units of Measure:** Dollars per lb. **Type of Price:** spot supplier. **Time Period Covered:** latest day.

Source: *Milling & Baking News.* **Price Frequency:** weekly. **Effective Market(s):** Decatur (IL), West. **Units of Measure:** Dollars per lb. **Type of Price:** bulk. **Time Period Covered:** latest week.

Source: *New York Times.* **Price Frequency:** daily. **Effective Market(s):** Decatur (IL). **Units of Measure:** Dollars per lb. **Type of Price:** cash. **Time Period Covered:** latest 2 days.

Source: *Oil Crops Situation and Outlook.* **Price Frequency:** monthly, annually. **Effective Market(s):** Decatur (IL). **Units of Measure:** cents per lb. **Time Period Covered:** monthly latest year, annually latest 10 years.

Source: *Oil Crops Situation and Outlook.* **Price Frequency:** monthly. **Effective Market(s):** Decatur (IL). **Units of Measure:** cents per lb. **Type of Price:** wholesale. **Time Period Covered:** latest 5 months.

Source: *Standard & Poor's Statistical Service Current Statistics.* **Price Frequency:** monthly, annually. **Effective Market(s):** Decatur (IL). **Units of Measure:** cents per lb. **Time Period Covered:** latest 4 years.

Source: *Wall Street Journal.* **Price Frequency:** daily. **Effective Market(s):** Decatur (IL). **Units of Measure:** Dollars per lb. **Time Period Covered:** latest day, day ago, year ago.

Source: *World Oilseed Situation and Market Highlights.* **Price Frequency:** monthly, annually. **Effective Market(s):** Decatur (IL). **Units of Measure:** Dollars per metric ton. **Type of Price:** average wholesale. **Time Period Covered:** monthly latest year, annually latest 9 years.

SOYBEAN OIL: CRUDE, DOMESTIC

Source: *Commodity Year Book.* **Price Frequency:** monthly, annually. **Effective Market(s):** Decatur (IL). **Units of Measure:** cents per lb. **Time Period Covered:** latest 9 years.

SOYBEAN OIL: CRUDE, DUTCH

Source: *FAO Quarterly Bulletin of Statistics.* **Price Frequency:** monthly, annually. **Effective Market(s):** Rotterdam. **Units of Measure:** Dollars per 1000 kilograms, dollars per metric ton. **Type of Price:** import. **Time Period Covered:** latest 3 years.

Source: *Fruit and Tropical Products.* **Price Frequency:** monthly, annually. **Effective Market(s):** Netherlands. **Units of Measure:** Dollars per tonne. **Type of Price:** average. **Time Period Covered:** monthly latest year, annually latest 2 years.

Source: *Monthly Commodity Price Bulletin.* **Price Frequency:** monthly, annually. **Units of Measure:** Dollars per metric ton. **Time Period Covered:** latest 5 years.

Source: *Monthly Commodity Price Bulletin Supplement.* **Price Frequency:** monthly, quarterly, annually. **Effective Market(s):** Netherlands. **Units of Measure:** Dollars per tonne. **Time Period Covered:** latest 20 years.

Source: *Selected Prices of Asia/Pacific Products.* **Price Frequency:** monthly. **Effective Market(s):** Dutch ports. **Units of Measure:** Dollars per metric ton. **Type of Price:** high, low. **Time Period Covered:** latest month.

Source: *UNCTAD Commodity Yearbook.* **Price Frequency:** annually. **Units of Measure:** Dollars per metric ton. **Type of Price:** free market. **Time Period Covered:** latest 12 years.

SOYBEAN OIL: CRUDE, UNITED STATES

Source: *Selected Prices of Asia/Pacific Products.* **Price Frequency:** monthly. **Effective Market(s):** Decatur (IL). **Units of Measure:** Dollars per metric ton. **Type of Price:** high, low. **Time Period Covered:** latest month.

SOYBEAN OIL: DUTCH

Source: *Oil World.* **Price Frequency:** weekly, monthly, annually. **Effective Market(s):** Netherlands. **Units of Measure:** Dollars per tonne. **Type of Price:** lowest representative asking. **Time Period Covered:** weekly latest 3 weeks, monthly latest 2 months, annually latest 2 years.

Source: *Selected Prices of Asia/Pacific Products.* **Price Frequency:** monthly. **Effective Market(s):** Netherlands. **Units of Measure:** Dutch guilders per 100 kilograms. **Type of Price:** high, low. **Time Period Covered:** latest month.

Source: *World Oilseed Situation and Market Highlights.* **Price Frequency:** monthly, annually. **Effective Market(s):** Rotterdam. **Units of Measure:** Dollars per metric ton. **Time Period Covered:** monthly latest year, annually latest 9 years.

SOYBEAN OIL: FUTURES

Source: *Agriculture.* **Price Frequency:** weekly. **Effective Market(s):** Chicago. **Units of Measure:** cents per lb. **Type of Price:** futures. **Time Period Covered:** latest week, week ago.

Source: *Asian Wall Street Journal.* **Price Frequency:** daily. **Effective Market(s):** Chicago. **Units of Measure:** cents per lb. **Type of Price:** futures. **Time Period Covered:** latest day.

Source: *Barron's.* **Price Frequency:** weekly. **Effective Market(s):** Chicago. **Units of Measure:** Dollars per 100 lbs. **Type of Price:** futures. **Time Period Covered:** latest week.

Source: *Financial Times.* **Price Frequency:** daily. **Effective Market(s):** Chicago. **Units of Measure:** cents per lb. **Type of Price:** futures. **Time Period Covered:** latest day.

Source: *Grain and Feed Market News.* **Price Frequency:** weekly. **Effective Market(s):** Chicago. **Units of Measure:** cents per lb. **Type of Price:** futures. **Time Period Covered:** latest week.

Source: *Investor's Daily.* **Price Frequency:** daily. **Effective Market(s):** Chicago. **Units of Measure:** Dollars per 100 lbs. **Type of Price:** futures. **Time Period Covered:** latest day.

Source: *Los Angeles Times.* **Price Frequency:** daily. **Effective Market(s):** Chicago. **Units of Measure:** Dollars per 100 lbs. **Type of Price:** futures. **Time Period Covered:** latest day.

Source: *Milling & Baking News.* **Price Frequency:** weekly. **Effective Market(s):** Chicago. **Units of Measure:** Dollars per lb. **Type of Price:** futures. **Time Period Covered:** latest week, year ago.

Source: *National Provisioner.* **Price Frequency:** daily. **Effective Market(s):** Chicago. **Units of Measure:** cents per lb. **Type of Price:** futures. **Time Period Covered:** latest week.

Source: *New York Times.* **Price Frequency:** daily. **Effective Market(s):** Chicago. **Units of Measure:** cents per lb. **Type of Price:** futures. **Time Period Covered:** latest day.

Source: *Urner Barry's Price-Current.* **Price Frequency:** daily. **Effective Market(s):** Chicago. **Units of Measure:** cents per lb. **Type of Price:** futures. **Time Period Covered:** latest day.

Source: *Wall Street Journal.* **Price Frequency:** daily. **Effective Market(s):** Chicago. **Units of Measure:** cents per lb. **Type of Price:** futures. **Time Period Covered:** latest day.

SOYBEAN OIL: FUTURES, MAY

Source: *Commodity Year Book.* **Price Frequency:** monthly. **Effective Market(s):** Chicago. **Units of Measure:** cents per lb. **Type of Price:** futures. **Time Period Covered:** latest 6 years.

SOYBEAN OIL: JAPAN/EUROPE

Source: *Selected Prices of Asia/Pacific Products.* **Price Frequency:** monthly. **Effective Market(s):** Hong Kong. **Units of Measure:** Hong Kong dollars per picul. **Type of Price:** high, low. **Time Period Covered:** latest month.

SOYBEAN OIL: REFINED

Source: *Selected Prices of Asia/Pacific Products.* **Price Frequency:** monthly. **Effective Market(s):** Tokyo. **Units of Measure:** Japanese yen per kilogram. **Type of Price:** high, low. **Time Period Covered:** latest month.

SOYBEAN OIL: REFINED, BLEACHED, DEODORIZED, UNITED KINGDOM

Source: *Selected Prices of Asia/Pacific Products.* **Price Frequency:** monthly. **Effective Market(s):** United Kingdom. **Units of Measure:** British pounds per metric ton. **Type of Price:** high, low. **Time Period Covered:** latest month.

SOYBEAN OIL: UNITED STATES

Source: *Oil World.* **Price Frequency:** weekly, monthly, annually. **Effective Market(s):** Decatur (IL). **Units of Measure:** Dollars per tonne. **Type of Price:** lowest representative asking. **Time Period Covered:** weekly latest 3 weeks, monthly latest 2 months, annually latest 2 years.

SOYBEAN OILMEAL: 44% PROTEIN

Source: *Chemical Marketing Reporter.* **Price Frequency:** weekly. **Effective Market(s):** Decatur (IL). **Units of Measure:** Dollars per ton. **Type of Price:** spot. **Time Period Covered:** latest week.

SOYBEAN PELLETS: 45/46%, ARGENTINE

Source: *Oil World.* **Price Frequency:** weekly, monthly, annually. **Effective Market(s):** Rotterdam. **Units of Measure:** Dollars per tonne. **Type of Price:** lowest representative asking. **Time Period Covered:** weekly latest 3 weeks, monthly latest 2 months, annually latest 2 years.

SOYBEAN PELLETS: 48%, BRAZILIAN

Source: *Agricultural Trade Highlights.* **Price Frequency:** weekly. **Effective Market(s):** Rotterdam. **Units of Measure:** Dollars per metric ton. **Type of Price:** asking. **Time Period Covered:** latest week, week ago, year ago.

Source: *Oil World.* **Price Frequency:** weekly, monthly, annually. **Effective Market(s):** Rotterdam. **Units of Measure:** Dollars per tonne. **Type of Price:** lowest representative asking. **Time Period Covered:** weekly latest 3 weeks, monthly latest 2 months, annually latest 2 years.

SOYBEAN SALAD OIL: FIRST CLASS

Source: *Selected Prices of Asia/Pacific Products.* **Price Frequency:** monthly. **Effective Market(s):** Tokyo. **Units of Measure:** Japanese yen per can. **Type of Price:** wholesale high, wholesale low. **Time Period Covered:** latest month.

SOYBEAN SALAD OIL: REFINED

Source: *Chemical Marketing Reporter.* **Price Frequency:** weekly. **Effective Market(s):** New York. **Units of Measure:** Dollars per lb. **Type of Price:** spot. **Time Period Covered:** latest week.

SOYBEANS

Source: *Agricultural Outlook.* **Price Frequency:** quarterly, annually. **Effective Market(s):** Chicago. **Units of Measure:** Dollars per bushel. **Type of Price:** average. **Time Period Covered:** latest year.

Source: *Agricultural Outlook.* **Price Frequency:** monthly, annually. **Effective Market(s):** United States. **Units of Measure:** Dollars per bushel. **Type of Price:** received by farmer. **Time Period Covered:** monthly latest 6 months, annually latest 3 years.

Source: *Agricultural Outlook.* **Price Frequency:** annually. **Units of Measure:** Dollars per bushel. **Type of Price:** farm. **Time Period Covered:** latest 6 years.

Source: *Agricultural Outlook.* **Price Frequency:** monthly, annually. **Effective Market(s):** Gulf ports. **Units of Measure:** Dollars per bushel. **Type of Price:** export. **Time Period Covered:** monthly latest 6 months, annually latest 3 years.

Source: *Agricultural Prices.* **Price Frequency:** monthly. **Effective Market(s):** United States. **Units of Measure:** Dollars per bushel. **Type of Price:** received by farmer. **Time Period Covered:** latest 2 months, year ago.

Source: *Agricultural Prices.* **Price Frequency:** monthly. **Effective Market(s):** United States. **Units of Measure:** Dollars per bushel. **Type of Price:** received by farmer. **Time Period Covered:** latest 2 years.

Source: *Agricultural Prices.* **Price Frequency:** monthly, seasonally. **Effective Market(s):** 20 domestic markets, United States. **Units of Measure:** Dollars per bushel. **Type of Price:** received by farmer. **Time Period Covered:** latest 2 months.

Source: *Agricultural Prices.* **Price Frequency:** annually. **Effective Market(s):** 20 domestic markets, United States. **Units of Measure:** Dollars per bushel. **Type of Price:** marketing year average received by farmer. **Time Period Covered:** latest year.

Source: *Agricultural Prices Annual Summary.* **Price Frequency:** annually. **Effective Market(s):** 29 domestic markets, United States. **Units of Measure:** Dollars per bushel. **Type of Price:** average received by farmer. **Time Period Covered:** latest 2 years, for US latest 6 years.

Source: *Agricultural Trade Highlights.* **Price Frequency:** weekly. **Effective Market(s):** Central Illinois. **Units of Measure:** Dollars per metric ton. **Type of Price:** processors bid. **Time Period Covered:** latest week, week ago, year ago.

Source: *Agriculture.* **Price Frequency:** weekly. **Effective Market(s):** 7 domestic markets. **Units of Measure:** Dollars per bushel. **Time Period Covered:** latest week, week ago.

Source: *The Brock Report.* **Price Frequency:** weekly. **Effective Market(s):** 10 domestic markets, Chatham (Canada). **Units of Measure:** Dollars per bushel. **Time Period Covered:** latest week, week ago.

Source: *Commodity Year Book.* **Price Frequency:** annually. **Effective Market(s):** United States. **Units of Measure:** Dollars per bushel. **Type of Price:** farm price. **Time Period Covered:** latest 14 years.

Source: *Commodity Year Book.* **Price Frequency:** monthly, annually. **Effective Market(s):** United States. **Units of Measure:** cents per bushel. **Type of Price:** price received by farmers. **Time Period Covered:** latest 9 years.

Source: *Far Eastern Economic Review.* **Price Frequency:** weekly. **Effective Market(s):** Chicago. **Units of Measure:** cents per 60 lb. bushel. **Time Period Covered:** latest week, week ago, 3 months ago, year ago.

Source: *Feedstuffs.* **Price Frequency:** weekly. **Effective Market(s):** Chicago. **Units of Measure:** Dollars per bushel. **Type of Price:** processor bid. **Time Period Covered:** latest week, week ago, 6 months ago, year ago.

Source: *Illinois Farm Report.* **Price Frequency:** monthly. **Effective Market(s):** Illinois. **Units of Measure:** Dollars per bushel. **Type of Price:** average received by farmers. **Time Period Covered:** latest 2 months, year ago.

Source: *Illinois Farm Report.* **Price Frequency:** monthly. **Effective Market(s):** Illinois. **Units of Measure:** index. **Type of Price:** index of prices received by farmers. **Time Period Covered:** latest 2 months, year ago.

Source: *Kansas Business Review.* **Price Frequency:** monthly. **Effective Market(s):** Kansas. **Units of Measure:** Dollars per bushel. **Type of Price:** received by farmer. **Time Period Covered:** latest month, month ago, year ago.

Source: *Oil Crops Situation and Outlook.* **Price Frequency:** monthly, annually. **Effective Market(s):** United States. **Units of Measure:** Dollars per bushel. **Type of Price:** received by farmer. **Time Period Covered:** monthly latest year, annually latest 10 years.

Source: *Oil Crops Situation and Outlook.* **Price Frequency:** monthly. **Effective Market(s):** United States. **Units of Measure:** Dollars per bushel. **Type of Price:** received by farmer. **Time Period Covered:** latest 5 months.

Source: *World Oilseed Situation and Market Highlights.* **Price Frequency:** monthly, annually. **Effective Market(s):** United States. **Units of Measure:** Dollars per metric ton. **Type of Price:** farm. **Time Period Covered:** monthly latest year, annually latest 9 years.

Source: *World Oilseed Situation and Market Highlights.* **Price Frequency:** monthly, annually. **Effective Market(s):** Brazil, Illinois, Rotterdam. **Units of Measure:** Dollars per metric ton. **Time Period Covered:** monthly latest 2 months, annually latest 2 years.

SOYBEANS: ARGENTINE

Source: *Oil World.* **Price Frequency:** weekly, monthly, annually. **Effective Market(s):** Rotterdam. **Units of Measure:** Dollars per tonne. **Type of Price:** lowest representative asking. **Time Period Covered:** weekly latest 3 weeks, monthly latest 2 months, annually latest 2 years.

SOYBEANS: BRAZILIAN

Source: *World Oilseed Situation and Market Highlights.* **Price Frequency:** monthly, annually. **Effective Market(s):** Rio Grande (Brazil). **Units of Measure:** Dollars per metric ton. **Time Period Covered:** monthly latest year, annually latest 9 years.

SOYBEANS: CANADIAN, FUTURES

Source: *Japan Economic Journal.* **Price Frequency:** weekly. **Effective Market(s):** Tokyo. **Units of Measure:** Japanese yen per 60 kilograms. **Type of Price:** futures. **Time Period Covered:** latest week.

SOYBEANS: CHINESE

Source: *Selected Prices of Asia/Pacific Products.* **Price Frequency:** monthly. **Effective Market(s):** Tokyo. **Units of Measure:** 1000 Japanese yen per metric ton. **Type of Price:** high, low. **Time Period Covered:** latest month.

SOYBEANS: DARIEN

Source: *Selected Prices of Asia/Pacific Products.* **Price Frequency:** monthly. **Effective Market(s):** Hong Kong. **Units of Measure:** Hong Kong dollars per picul. **Type of Price:** wholesale high, wholesale low. **Time Period Covered:** latest month.

SOYBEANS: FUTURES

Source: *Agriculture.* **Price Frequency:** weekly. **Effective Market(s):** Chicago. **Units of Measure:** cents per bushel. **Type of Price:** futures. **Time Period Covered:** latest week, week ago.

Source: *Asian Wall Street Journal.* **Price Frequency:** daily. **Effective Market(s):** Chicago. **Units of Measure:** cents per bushel. **Type of Price:** futures. **Time Period Covered:** latest day.

Source: *Asian Wall Street Journal.* **Price Frequency:** daily. **Effective Market(s):** Hong Kong, Manila. **Units of Measure:** Hong Kong dollars per bag, Philippine pesos per 60 kilos. **Type of Price:** futures. **Time Period Covered:** latest day.

Source: *Barron's.* **Price Frequency:** weekly. **Effective Market(s):** Chicago. **Units of Measure:** Dollars per bushel. **Type of Price:** futures. **Time Period Covered:** latest week.

Source: *Far Eastern Economic Review.* **Price Frequency:** weekly. **Effective Market(s):** Chicago. **Units of Measure:** cents per 60 lb. bushel. **Time Period Covered:** next contract month.

Source: *Feedstuffs.* **Price Frequency:** weekly. **Effective Market(s):** Chicago. **Units of Measure:** cents per bushel. **Type of Price:** futures. **Time Period Covered:** latest week, week ago, latest season.

Source: *Financial Times.* **Price Frequency:** daily. **Effective Market(s):** Chicago. **Units of Measure:** cents per bushel. **Type of Price:** futures. **Time Period Covered:** latest day.

Source: *Grain and Feed Market News.* **Price Frequency:** weekly. **Effective Market(s):** Chicago. **Units of Measure:** Dollars per bushel. **Type of Price:** futures. **Time Period Covered:** latest week.

Source: *International Wheat Council Market Report.* **Price Frequency:** weekly. **Effective Market(s):** Chicago. **Units of Measure:** Dollars per bushel, dollars per metric ton. **Type of Price:** futures. **Time Period Covered:** latest month.

Source: *Investor's Daily.* **Price Frequency:** daily. **Effective Market(s):** Chicago. **Units of Measure:** Dollars per bushel. **Type of Price:** futures. **Time Period Covered:** latest day.

Source: *Lancaster Farming.* **Price Frequency:** daily. **Type of Price:** futures. **Time Period Covered:** latest week.

Source: *Los Angeles Times.* **Price Frequency:** daily. **Effective Market(s):** Chicago. **Units of Measure:** Dollars per bushel. **Type of Price:** futures. **Time Period Covered:** latest day.

Source: *Milling & Baking News.* **Price Frequency:** weekly. **Units of Measure:** Dollars per bushel. **Type of Price:** futures. **Time Period Covered:** latest week, year ago.

Source: *New York Times.* **Price Frequency:** daily. **Effective Market(s):** Chicago. **Units of Measure:** Dollars per bushel. **Type of Price:** futures. **Time Period Covered:** latest day.

Source: *The Times.* **Price Frequency:** daily. **Effective Market(s):** London. **Units of Measure:** British pounds per metric ton. **Type of Price:** futures. **Time Period Covered:** latest day.

Source: *Urner Barry's Price-Current.* **Price Frequency:** daily. **Effective Market(s):** Chicago. **Units of Measure:** Dollars per bushel. **Type of Price:** futures. **Time Period Covered:** latest day.

Source: *Wall Street Journal.* **Price Frequency:** daily. **Effective Market(s):** Chicago. **Units of Measure:** cents per bushel. **Type of Price:** futures. **Time Period Covered:** latest day.

SOYBEANS: FUTURES, MAY

Source: *Commodity Year Book.* **Price Frequency:** monthly. **Effective Market(s):** Chicago. **Units of Measure:** cents per bushel. **Type of Price:** futures. **Time Period Covered:** latest 7 years.

SOYBEANS: GRADE A, CHIANGMAI, THAI

Source: *Selected Prices of Asia/Pacific Products.* **Price Frequency:** monthly. **Effective Market(s):** Bangkok. **Units of Measure:** Thai baht per 100 kilograms, Thai baht per kilogram. **Type of Price:** wholesale high, wholesale low. **Time Period Covered:** latest month.

SOYBEANS: GRADE B, CHIANGMAI, THAI

Source: *Selected Prices of Asia/Pacific Products.* **Price Frequency:** monthly. **Effective Market(s):** Bangkok. **Units of Measure:** Thai baht per kilogram. **Type of Price:** wholesale high, wholesale low. **Time Period Covered:** latest month.

SOYBEANS: NO. 1

Source: *Lancaster Farming.* **Price Frequency:** weekly. **Effective Market(s):** Pennsylvania. **Units of Measure:** Dollars per bushel. **Time Period Covered:** latest week.

SOYBEANS: NO. 1, YELLOW

Source: *Agricultural Outlook.* **Price Frequency:** monthly, annually. **Effective Market(s):** Chicago. **Units of Measure:** Dollars per bushel. **Type of Price:** wholesale. **Time Period Covered:** monthly latest 5 months, annually latest 4 years.

Source: *Asian Wall Street Journal.* **Price Frequency:** daily. **Effective Market(s):** Central Illinois. **Units of Measure:** Dollars per bushel. **Type of Price:** cash. **Time Period Covered:** latest 2 days, year ago.

Source: *Commodity Year Book.* **Price Frequency:** monthly, annually. **Effective Market(s):** Illinois. **Units of Measure:** cents per bushel. **Type of Price:** cash. **Time Period Covered:** latest 11 years.

Source: *Doane's Agricultural Report.* **Price Frequency:** weekly. **Effective Market(s):** Central Illinois. **Units of Measure:** Dollars per bushel. **Time Period Covered:** latest week, week ago, year ago.

Source: *Farm and Dairy.* **Price Frequency:** weekly. **Effective Market(s):** Central Illinois. **Units of Measure:** Dollars per bushel. **Time Period Covered:** latest week, year ago.

Source: *Fedgazette.* **Price Frequency:** monthly. **Effective Market(s):** Minneapolis (MN). **Units of Measure:** Dollars per bushel. **Time Period Covered:** latest 24 months.

Source: *Grain and Feed Market News.* **Price Frequency:** daily, seasonally. **Effective Market(s):** 6 domestic markets. **Units of Measure:** Dollars per 100 lbs. **Type of Price:** cash bid. **Time Period Covered:** latest week, year ago.

Source: *Grain and Feed Market News.* **Price Frequency:** weekly, seasonally. **Effective Market(s):** 44 domestic markets. **Units of Measure:** Dollars per bushel. **Type of Price:** cash bid. **Time Period Covered:** latest week.

Source: *International Wheat Council Market Report.* **Price Frequency:** monthly. **Effective Market(s):** Central Illinois. **Units of Measure:** Dollars per bushel, dollars per ton. **Type of Price:** cash. **Time Period Covered:** latest month.

Source: *Investor's Daily.* **Price Frequency:** daily. **Units of Measure:** Dollars per bushel. **Type of Price:** spot. **Time Period Covered:** latest day.

Source: *Journal of Commerce and Commercial.* **Price Frequency:** daily. **Effective Market(s):** Chicago. **Units of Measure:** Dollars per bushel. **Type of Price:** spot supplier. **Time Period Covered:** latest day.

Source: *Minneapolis Grain Exchange Statistical Annual.* **Price Frequency:** daily. **Effective Market(s):** Minneapolis. **Units of Measure:** cents per bushel. **Type of Price:** cash. **Time Period Covered:** latest year.

Source: *Minneapolis Grain Exchange Statistical Annual.* **Price Frequency:** monthly, annually. **Effective Market(s):** Minneapolis. **Units of Measure:** cents per bushel. **Type of Price:** cash. **Time Period Covered:** latest 10 years.

Source: *New York Times.* **Price Frequency:** daily. **Units of Measure:** Dollars per bushel. **Type of Price:** cash. **Time Period Covered:** latest 2 days.

Source: *Oil Crops Situation and Outlook.* **Price Frequency:** monthly, annually. **Effective Market(s):** Illinois. **Units of Measure:** Dollars per bushel. **Type of Price:** spot. **Time Period Covered:** monthly latest year, annually latest 6 years.

Source: *Wall Streeet Journal.* **Price Frequency:** daily. **Effective Market(s):** Central Illinois. **Units of Measure:** Dollars per bushel. **Time Period Covered:** latest day, day ago, year ago.

Source: *World Oilseed Situation and Market Highlights.* **Price Frequency:** monthly, annually. **Effective Market(s):** Central Illinois. **Units of Measure:** Dollars per metric ton. **Type of Price:** cash. **Time Period Covered:** monthly latest year, annually latest 9 years.

SOYBEANS: NO. 2

Source: *Commodity Trade and Price Trends.* **Price Frequency:** annually. **Effective Market(s):** Rotterdam. **Units of Measure:** Dollars per metric ton, 1980 constant dollars per metric ton. **Time Period Covered:** latst 37 years.

SOYBEANS: NO. 2, YELLOW

Source: *Agricultural Trade Highlights.* **Price Frequency:** weekly. **Effective Market(s):** Rotterdam. **Units of Measure:** Dollars per metric ton. **Type of Price:** asking. **Time Period Covered:** latest week, week ago, year ago.

Source: *Economic and Energy Indicators.* **Price Frequency:** biweekly. **Units of Measure:** Dollars per metric ton. **Time Period Covered:** latest 3 months, quarters, and years.

Source: *Grain and Feed Market News.* **Price Frequency:** daily, seasonally. **Effective Market(s):** East Coast, Gulf. **Units of Measure:** Dollars per bushel. **Type of Price:** export bid. **Time Period Covered:** latest week, year ago.

Source: *Monthly Commodity Price Bulletin.* **Price Frequency:** monthly, annually. **Effective Market(s):** Rotterdam. **Units of Measure:** Dollars per metric ton. **Time Period Covered:** latest 5 years.

Source: *UNCTAD Commodity Yearbook.* **Price Frequency:** annually. **Effective Market(s):** Rotterdam. **Units of Measure:** Dollars per metric ton. **Type of Price:** free market. **Time Period Covered:** latest 12 years.

SOYBEANS: NO. 2, YELLOW, UNITED STATES

Source: *Fruit and Tropical Products.* **Price Frequency:** monthly, annually. **Effective Market(s):** Rotterdam. **Units of Measure:** Dollars per tonne. **Type of Price:** average. **Time Period Covered:** monthly latest year, annually latest 2 years.

Source: *Monthly Commodity Price Bulletin Supplement.* **Price Frequency:** monthly, quarterly, annually. **Effective Market(s):** Rotterdam. **Units of Measure:** Dollars per tonne. **Time Period Covered:** latest 20 years.

Source: *World Oilseed Situation and Market Highlights.* **Price Frequency:** monthly, annually. **Effective Market(s):** Rotterdam. **Units of Measure:** Dollars per metric ton. **Time Period Covered:** monthly latest year, annually latest 9 years.

SOYBEANS: NO. 3, YELLOW

Source: *World Agriculture Situation and Outlook.* **Price Frequency:** monthly, annually. **Effective Market(s):** Gulf ports. **Units of Measure:** Dollars per metric ton. **Time Period Covered:** monthly latest year, annually latest 9 years.

SOYBEANS: ORDINARY SIZE, SELECTED, UNITED STATES

Source: *Selected Prices of Asia/Pacific Products.* **Price Frequency:** monthly. **Effective Market(s):** Tokyo. **Units of Measure:** 1000 Japanese yen per metric ton. **Type of Price:** high, low. **Time Period Covered:** latest month.

SOYBEANS: UNITED STATES

Source: *FAO Quarterly Bulletin of Statistics.* **Price Frequency:** monthly, annually. **Effective Market(s):** Rotterdam. **Units of Measure:** Dollars per 1000 kilograms, dollars per metric ton. **Time Period Covered:** latest 3 years.

Source: *Financial Times.* **Price Frequency:** daily. **Effective Market(s):** London. **Units of Measure:** British pounds per tonne. **Type of Price:** spot. **Time Period Covered:** latest day.

Source: *International Financial Statistics.* **Price Frequency:** monthly, quarterly, annually. **Effective Market(s):** Rotterdam. **Units of Measure:** Dollars per metric ton, index. **Type of Price:** market price, price index. **Time Period Covered:** latest 5 months, latest 5 quarters, latest 5 years.

Source: *International Financial Statistics.* **Price Frequency:** annually. **Effective Market(s):** Rotterdam. **Units of Measure:** Dollars per metric ton. **Type of Price:** wholesale. **Time Period Covered:** latest 30 years.

Source: *Oil World.* **Price Frequency:** weekly, monthly, annually. **Effective Market(s):** Rotterdam. **Units of Measure:** Dollars per tonne. **Type of Price:** lowest representative asking. **Time Period Covered:** weekly latest 3 weeks, monthly latest 2 months, annually latest 2 years.

Source: *Selected Prices of Asia/Pacific Products.* **Price Frequency:** monthly. **Effective Market(s):** Rotterdam. **Units of Measure:** Dollars per metric ton. **Type of Price:** high, low. **Time Period Covered:** latest month.

SOYBEANS: UNITED STATES, FUTURES

Source: *Japan Economic Journal.* **Price Frequency:** weekly. **Effective Market(s):** Tokyo. **Units of Measure:** Japanese yen per 60 kilograms. **Type of Price:** futures. **Time Period Covered:** latest week.

SOYBEANS FOR SEED

Source: *Agricultural Prices Annual Summary.* **Price Frequency:** annually. **Effective Market(s):** United States. **Units of Measure:** Dollars per bushel. **Type of Price:** average paid by farmer. **Time Period Covered:** latest 6 years.

SPAIN PESETAS

Source: *Asian Wall Street Journal.* **Price Frequency:** daily. **Effective Market(s):** United States. **Units of Measure:** Spanish pesetas per ECU, per SDR. **Type of Price:** foreign exchange. **Time Period Covered:** latest 2 days.

Source: *Barron's.* **Price Frequency:** weekly. **Effective Market(s):** New York. **Units of Measure:** Spanish pesetas per United States dollar. **Type of Price:** foreign exchange. **Time Period Covered:** latest 2 weeks.

Source: *The Economist.* **Price Frequency:** weekly. **Effective Market(s):** London. **Units of Measure:** Spanish pesetas per British pounds. **Type of Price:** foreign exchange. **Time Period Covered:** latest week, year ago.

Source: *New York Times.* **Price Frequency:** daily. **Effective Market(s):** United States. **Units of Measure:** Spanish pesetas per United States dollar. **Type of Price:** foreign exchange. **Time Period Covered:** latest 2 days.

Source: *Timber Bulletin.* **Price Frequency:** monthly, annually. **Units of Measure:** Spanish pesetas per United States dollar. **Type of Price:** foreign exchange. **Time Period Covered:** latest 2 years.

SPARK PLUGS

Source: *Agricultural Prices.* **Price Frequency:** semiannually. **Effective Market(s):** United States. **Units of Measure:** Dollars each. **Type of Price:** paid by farmer. **Time Period Covered:** latest year.

Source: *Agricultural Prices Annual Summary.* **Price Frequency:** semiannually. **Effective Market(s):** United States. **Units of Measure:** Dollars each. **Type of Price:** average paid by farmer. **Time Period Covered:** latest 6 years.

SPEARFISH: FILLETS, FRESH, HAWAIIAN

Source: *Seafood Price-Current.* **Price Frequency:** semiweekly. **Effective Market(s):** Hawaii. **Units of Measure:** Dollars per lb. **Type of Price:** sale by first receiver. **Time Period Covered:** latest day.

SPEARFISH: WHOLE, FRESH, HAWAIIAN

Source: *Seafood Price-Current.* **Price Frequency:** semiweekly. **Effective Market(s):** Hawaii. **Units of Measure:** Dollars per lb. **Type of Price:** sale by first receiver. **Time Period Covered:** latest day.

SPEARMINT

Source: *U. S. Essential Oil Trade.* **Price Frequency:** annually. **Effective Market(s):** 6 domestic markets, United States. **Units of Measure:** Dollars per lb. **Type of Price:** grower. **Time Period Covered:** latest 3 years.

SPEARMINT LEAVES: IMPORTED

Source: *Chemical Marketing Reporter.* **Price Frequency:** weekly. **Effective Market(s):** New York. **Units of Measure:** Dollars per lb. **Type of Price:** spot. **Time Period Covered:** latest week.

SPEARMINT OIL

Source: *Journal of Commerce and Commercial.* **Price Frequency:** weekly in Tuesday issue. **Units of Measure:** Dollars per lb. **Type of Price:** spot. **Time Period Covered:** latest week.

Source: *U. S. Essential Oil Trade.* **Price Frequency:** annually. **Effective Market(s):** United States. **Units of Measure:** Dollars per kilogram. **Type of Price:** import value. **Time Period Covered:** latest 3 years.

SPEARMINT OIL: 60%, CHINESE

Source: *Chemical Marketing Reporter.* **Price Frequency:** weekly. **Effective Market(s):** New York. **Units of Measure:** Dollars per lb. **Type of Price:** spot. **Time Period Covered:** latest week.

SPEARMINT OIL: 80%, CHINESE

Source: *Chemical Marketing Reporter.* **Price Frequency:** weekly. **Effective Market(s):** New York. **Units of Measure:** Dollars per lb. **Type of Price:** spot. **Time Period Covered:** latest week.

SPEARMINT OIL: NATIVE

Source: *Chemical Marketing Reporter.* **Price Frequency:** weekly. **Effective Market(s):** Far West. **Units of Measure:** Dollars per lb. **Type of Price:** spot. **Time Period Covered:** latest week.

Source: *U. S. Essential Oil Trade.* **Price Frequency:** annually. **Effective Market(s):** New York. **Units of Measure:** Dollars per lb. **Type of Price:** spot. **Time Period Covered:** latest 4 years.

SPEARMINT OIL: SCOTCH

Source: *Chemical Marketing Reporter.* **Price Frequency:** weekly. **Effective Market(s):** Far West. **Units of Measure:** Dollars per lb. **Type of Price:** spot. **Time Period Covered:** latest week.

Source: *U. S. Essential Oil Trade.* **Price Frequency:** annually. **Effective Market(s):** New York. **Units of Measure:** Dollars per lb. **Type of Price:** spot. **Time Period Covered:** latest 4 years.

SPERMACETI SUBSTITUTE

Source: *Journal of Commerce and Commercial.* **Price Frequency:** weekly in Monday issue. **Units of Measure:** Dollars per lb. **Type of Price:** spot. **Time Period Covered:** latest week.

SPINACH

Source: *Lancaster Farming.* **Price Frequency:** weekly, seasonally. **Effective Market(s):** Pennsylvania. **Units of Measure:** Dollars per carton. **Type of Price:** market. **Time Period Covered:** latest week.

Source: *New Zealand Farmer.* **Price Frequency:** weekly, seasonally. **Effective Market(s):** New Zealand. **Units of Measure:** New Zealand dollars per case/crate. **Time Period Covered:** latest week.

SPINACH: GRADE A, CHOPPED

Source: *HRI-Buyer's Guide.* **Price Frequency:** weekly. **Effective Market(s):** Northeastern area. **Units of Measure:** Dollars per case. **Type of Price:** price paid by dining places & institutions. **Time Period Covered:** latest week.

SPINACH: LEAF, GRADE A

Source: *HRI-Buyer's Guide.* **Price Frequency:** weekly. **Effective Market(s):** Northeastern area. **Units of Measure:** Dollars per case. **Type of Price:** price paid by dining places & institutions. **Time Period Covered:** latest week.

SPINACH: LONG ISLAND

Source: *HRI-Byuer's Guide.* **Price Frequency:** weekly. **Effective Market(s):** Northeastern area. **Units of Measure:** Dollars per bushel basket. **Type of Price:** price paid by dining places & institutions. **Time Period Covered:** latest week.

SPINACH: SAVOY TYPE

Source: *Fresh Fruit and Vegetable Prices.* **Price Frequency:** monthly, seasonally. **Effective Market(s):** San Antonio/Winter Garden (TX), Vineland (NJ). **Units of Measure:** Dollars per unit. **Type of Price:** average price at shipping point. **Time Period Covered:** latest year.

SPINACH: SAVOY TYPE, CALIFORNIA

Source: *Fresh Fruit and Vegetable Prices.* **Price Frequency:** monthly, seasonally. **Effective Market(s):** Chicago, New York City. **Units of Measure:** Dollars per bushel basket/crate. **Type of Price:** average wholesale price. **Time Period Covered:** latest year.

SPINACH: SAVOY TYPE, COLORADO

Source: *Fresh Fruit and Vegetable Prices.* **Price Frequency:** monthly, seasonally. **Effective Market(s):** New York City. **Units of Measure:** Dollars per bushel basket/crate. **Type of Price:** average wholesale price. **Time Period Covered:** latest year.

SPINACH: SAVOY TYPE, ILLINOIS

Source: *Fresh Fruit and Vegetable Prices.* **Price Frequency:** monthly, seasonally. **Effective Market(s):** Chicago. **Units of Measure:** Dollars per bushel basket/crate. **Type of Price:** average wholesale price. **Time Period Covered:** latest year.

SPINACH: SAVOY TYPE, NEW JERSEY

Source: *Fresh Fruit and Vegetable Prices.* **Price Frequency:** monthly, seasonally. **Effective Market(s):** New York City. **Units of Measure:** Dollars per bushel basket/crate. **Type of Price:** average wholesale price. **Time Period Covered:** latest year.

SPINACH: SAVOY TYPE, TEXAS

Source: *Fresh Fruit and Vegetable Prices.* **Price Frequency:** monthly, seasonally. **Effective Market(s):** New York City. **Units of Measure:** Dollars per bushel basket/crate. **Type of Price:** average wholesale price. **Time Period Covered:** latest year.

SPODUMENE: GLASS GRADE

Source: *Industrial Minerals.* **Price Frequency:** monthly. **Effective Market(s):** Amsterdam. **Units of Measure:** Dollars per metric tonne. **Type of Price:** producer & dealer. **Time Period Covered:** latest month.

SPODUMENE CONCENTRATE

Source: *Industrial Minerals.* **Price Frequency:** monthly. **Effective Market(s):** Amsterdam. **Units of Measure:** Dollars per metric tonne. **Type of Price:** producer & dealer. **Time Period Covered:** latest month.

SPOT (FISH): WHOLE, FRESH

Source: *Seafood Price-Current.* **Price Frequency:** semiweekly. **Effective Market(s):** Boston, Mid-Atlantic, New Bedford (MA), Portland (ME). **Units of Measure:** Dollars per lb. **Type of Price:** sale by first receiver, auction price. **Time Period Covered:** latest day.

SPRAYER: FIELD CROP, POWER

Source: *Agricultural Prices.* **Price Frequency:** annually. **Effective Market(s):** United States. **Units of Measure:** Dollars each. **Type of Price:** paid by farmer. **Time Period Covered:** latest year.

Source: *Agricultural Prices Annual Summary.* **Price Frequency:** annually. **Effective Market(s):** United States. **Units of Measure:** Dollars each. **Type of Price:** average paid by farmer. **Time Period Covered:** latest 6 years.

SPRAYER: HAND

Source: *Agricultural Prices.* **Price Frequency:** annually. **Effective Market(s):** United States. **Units of Measure:** Dollars each. **Type of Price:** paid by farmer. **Time Period Covered:** latest year.

Source: *Agricultural Prices Annual Summary.* **Price Frequency:** semiannually. **Effective Market(s):** United States. **Units of Measure:** Dollars each. **Type of Price:** average paid by farmer. **Time Period Covered:** latest 6 years.

SPRING ONIONS

Source: *New Zealand Farmer.* **Price Frequency:** weekly, seasonally. **Effective Market(s):** New Zealand. **Units of Measure:** New Zealand dollars per case/dozen. **Time Period Covered:** latest week.

SPRUCE: BLACK, RED, AND WHITE

Source: *Volume and Value of Sawtimber Stumpage Sold From National Forests by Selected Species and Region.* **Price Frequency:** quarterly, annually. **Effective Market(s):** Alaska, Eastern region, Intermountain region. **Units of Measure:** Dollars per 1000 board feet. **Type of Price:** average. **Time Period Covered:** latest quarter, latest year.

SPRUCE: ENGELMANN

Source: *Volume and Value of Sawtimber Stumpage Sold From National Forests by Selected Species and Region.* **Price Frequency:** quarterly, annually. **Effective Market(s):** Intermountain region, Northern region, Pacific Northwest region, Rocky Mountain region, Southwestern region. **Units of Measure:** Dollars per 1000 board feet. **Type of Price:** average. **Time Period Covered:** latest quarter, latest year.

SPRUCE: ENGELMANN, KILN DRIED

Source: *Random Lengths.* **Price Frequency:** weekly. **Units of Measure:** Dollars per 1000 board feet. **Type of Price:** price to wholesaler. **Time Period Covered:** latest week.

SPRUCE: SITKA

Source: *Volume and Value of Sawtimber Stumpage Sold From National Forests by Selected Species and Region.* **Price Frequency:** quarterly, annually. **Effective Market(s):** Alaska, Pacific Northwest region. **Units of Measure:** Dollars per 1000 board feet. **Type of Price:** average. **Time Period Covered:** latest quarter, latest year.

SPRUCE OIL

Source: *Chemical Marketing Reporter.* **Price Frequency:** weekly. **Effective Market(s):** New York. **Units of Measure:** Dollars per lb. **Type of Price:** spot. **Time Period Covered:** latest week.

SPRUCE-PINE-FIR: EASTERN, DRY

Source: *Random Lengths.* **Price Frequency:** weekly. **Effective Market(s):** Boston, Great Lakes. **Units of Measure:** Dollars per 1000 board feet. **Type of Price:** price to wholesaler. **Time Period Covered:** latest week.

SPRUCE-PINE-FIR: EASTERN, GREEN

Source: *Random Lengths.* **Price Frequency:** weekly. **Effective Market(s):** 7 domestic markets, Toronto. **Units of Measure:** Dollars per 1000 board feet. **Type of Price:** price to wholesaler. **Time Period Covered:** latest week.

SPRUCE-PINE-FIR: EASTERN, KILN DRIED

Source: *Random Lengths.* **Price Frequency:** weekly. **Effective Market(s):** 13 domestic markets. **Units of Measure:** Dollars per 1000 board feet. **Type of Price:** price to wholesaler. **Time Period Covered:** latest week.

SPRUCE-PINE-FIR: WESTERN, DRY

Source: *Random Lengths.* **Price Frequency:** weekly. **Units of Measure:** Dollars per 1000 board feet. **Type of Price:** price to wholesaler. **Time Period Covered:** latest week.

SPRUCE-PINE-FIR: WESTERN, FRAMING LUMBER, KILN DRIED

Source: *Random Lengths.* **Price Frequency:** weekly. **Units of Measure:** Dollars per 1000 board feet. **Type of Price:** price to wholesaler. **Time Period Covered:** latest week.

SPRUCE-PINE-FIR: WESTERN, KILN DRIED

Source: *Random Lengths.* **Price Frequency:** weekly. **Effective Market(s):** 9 domestic markets. **Units of Measure:** Dollars per 1000 board feet. **Type of Price:** price to wholesaler. **Time Period Covered:** latest week.

SQUAB

Source: *HRI-Buyer's Guide.* **Price Frequency:** weekly. **Effective Market(s):** Northeastern area. **Units of Measure:** Dollars per dozen. **Type of Price:** wholesale. **Time Period Covered:** latest week.

Source: *Urner Barry's Price-Current.* **Price Frequency:** daily. **Units of Measure:** Dollars per dozen. **Type of Price:** wholesale. **Time Period Covered:** latest day.

Source: *Urner Barry's Price-Current, West Coast Edition.* **Price Frequency:** semiweekly. **Effective Market(s):** West Coast. **Units of Measure:** Dollars per dozen. **Type of Price:** wholesale. **Time Period Covered:** latest day.

SQUAB: NEW YORK DRESSED

Source: *HRI-Buyer's Guide.* **Price Frequency:** weekly. **Effective Market(s):** Northeastern area. **Units of Measure:** Dollars per lb. **Type of Price:** wholesale. **Time Period Covered:** latest week.

Source: *Urner Barry's Price-Current.* **Price Frequency:** daily. **Units of Measure:** Dollars per lb. **Type of Price:** wholesale. **Time Period Covered:** latest day.

Source: *Urner Barry's Price-Current, West Coast Edition.* **Price Frequency:** semiweekly. **Effective Market(s):** West Coast. **Units of Measure:** Dollars per lb. **Type of Price:** wholesale. **Time Period Covered:** latest day.

SQUAB: PROCESSED, FROZEN

Source: *Poultry Market Statistics.* **Price Frequency:** monthly, annually. **Effective Market(s):** New York. **Units of Measure:** cents per dozen. **Type of Price:** wholesale. **Time Period Covered:** latest year.

SQUASH: ACORN

Source: *Fresh Fruit and Vegetable Prices.* **Price Frequency:** monthly, seasonally. **Effective Market(s):** Florida. **Units of Measure:** Dollars per carton or crate. **Type of Price:** average price at shipping point. **Time Period Covered:** latest year.

SQUASH: ACORN, FLORIDA

Source: *Fresh Fruit and Vegetable Prices.* **Price Frequency:** monthly, seasonally. **Effective Market(s):** Chicago. **Units of Measure:** Dollars per crate/carton. **Type of Price:** average wholesale price. **Time Period Covered:** latest year.

Source: *HRI-Buyer's Guide.* **Price Frequency:** weekly. **Effective Market(s):** Northeastern area. **Units of Measure:** Dollars per bushel. **Type of Price:** price paid by dining places & institutions. **Time Period Covered:** latest week.

SQUASH: ACORN, ILLINOIS

Source: *Fresh Fruit and Vegetable Prices.* **Price Frequency:** monthly, seasonally. **Effective Market(s):** Chicago. **Units of Measure:** Dollars per crate/carton. **Type of Price:** average wholesale price. **Time Period Covered:** latest year.

SQUASH: ACORN, MEXICO

Source: *Fresh Fruit and Vegetable Prices.* **Price Frequency:** monthly, seasonally. **Effective Market(s):** Chicago. **Units of Measure:** Dollars per crate/carton. **Type of Price:** average wholesale price. **Time Period Covered:** latest year.

SQUASH: ACORN, NEW JERSEY

Source: *Fresh Fruit and Vegetable Prices.* **Price Frequency:** monthly, seasonally. **Effective Market(s):** New York City. **Units of Measure:** Dollars per crate/carton. **Type of Price:** average wholesale price. **Time Period Covered:** latest year.

SQUASH: BUTTER, NEW JERSEY

Source: *HRI-Buyer's Guide.* **Price Frequency:** weekly. **Effective Market(s):** Northeastern area. **Units of Measure:** Dollars per bushel. **Type of Price:** price paid by dining places & institutions. **Time Period Covered:** latest week.

SQUASH: BUTTERNUT

Source: *Fresh Fruit and Vegetable Prices.* **Price Frequency:** monthly, seasonally. **Effective Market(s):** North Carolina. **Units of Measure:** Dollars per carton or crate. **Type of Price:** average price at shipping point. **Time Period Covered:** latest year.

SQUASH: BUTTERNUT, ILLINOIS

Source: *Fresh Fruit and Vegetable Prices.* **Price Frequency:** monthly, seasonally. **Effective Market(s):** Chicago. **Units of Measure:** Dollars per crate/carton. **Type of Price:** average wholesale price. **Time Period Covered:** latest year.

SQUASH: BUTTERNUT, NEW JERSEY

Source: *Fresh Fruit and Vegetable Prices.* **Price Frequency:** monthly, seasonally. **Effective Market(s):** New York City. **Units of Measure:** Dollars per crate/carton. **Type of Price:** average wholesale price. **Time Period Covered:** latest year.

SQUASH: CROWN

Source: *New Zealand Farmer.* **Price Frequency:** weekly, seasonally. **Effective Market(s):** New Zealand. **Units of Measure:** New Zealand dollars per crate. **Time Period Covered:** latest week.

SQUASH: ITALIAN, NEW JERSEY

Source: *HRI-Buyer's Guide.* **Price Frequency:** weekly. **Effective Market(s):** Northeastern area. **Units of Measure:** Dollars per carton, dollars per bushel. **Type of Price:** price paid by dining places & institutions. **Time Period Covered:** latest week.

SQUASH: KUMARA

Source: *New Zealand Farmer.* **Price Frequency:** weekly, seasonally. **Effective Market(s):** New Zealand. **Units of Measure:** New Zealand dollars per case. **Time Period Covered:** latest week.

SQUASH: KUMARA, GOLD

Source: *New Zealand Farmer.* **Price Frequency:** weekly, seasonally. **Effective Market(s):** New Zealand. **Units of Measure:** New Zealand dollars per crate. **Time Period Covered:** latest week.

SQUASH: KUMARA, RED

Source: *New Zealand Farmer.* **Price Frequency:** weekly, seasonally. **Effective Market(s):** New Zealand. **Units of Measure:** New Zealand dollars per crate. **Time Period Covered:** latest week.

SQUASH: PATTYPAN

Source: *Lancaster Farming.* **Price Frequency:** weekly, seasonally. **Effective Market(s):** Pennsylvania. **Units of Measure:** Dollars per bushel. **Type of Price:** market. **Time Period Covered:** latest week.

SQUASH: YELLOW CROOKNECK

Source: *Fresh Fruit and Vegetable Prices.* **Price Frequency:** monthly, seasonally. **Effective Market(s):** Florida, South Georgia, Vineland (NJ), Western North Carolina. **Units of Measure:** Dollars per carton or crate. **Type of Price:** average price at shipping point. **Time Period Covered:** latest year.

Source: *The Packer.* **Price Frequency:** weekly, seasonally. **Effective Market(s):** varies. **Units of Measure:** Dollars per bushel crate. **Type of Price:** average received by farmer. **Time Period Covered:** latest week.

SQUASH: YELLOW STRAIGHTNECK

Source: *Fresh Fruit and Vegetable Prices.* **Price Frequency:** monthly, seasonally. **Effective Market(s):** North Carolina, Pompano Beach (FL), Vineland (NJ). **Units of Measure:** Dollars per carton or crate. **Type of Price:** average price at shipping point. **Time Period Covered:** latest year.

Source: *Lancaster Farming.* **Price Frequency:** weekly, seasonally. **Effective Market(s):** Pennsylvania. **Units of Measure:** Dollars per carton. **Type of Price:** market. **Time Period Covered:** latest week.

Source: *The Packer.* **Price Frequency:** weekly, seasonally. **Effective Market(s):** varies. **Units of Measure:** Dollars per bushel crate. **Type of Price:** average received by farmer. **Time Period Covered:** latest week.

SQUASH: YELLOW STRAIGHTNECK, FLORIDA

Source: *Fresh Fruit and Vegetable Prices.* **Price Frequency:** monthly, seasonally. **Effective Market(s):** Chicago, New York City. **Units of Measure:** Dollars per crate/carton. **Type of Price:** average wholesale price. **Time Period Covered:** latest year.

SQUASH: YELLOW STRAIGHTNECK, ILLINOIS

Source: *Fresh Fruit and Vegetable Prices.* **Price Frequency:** monthly, seasonally. **Effective Market(s):** Chicago. **Units of Measure:** Dollars per crate/carton. **Type of Price:** average wholesale price. **Time Period Covered:** latest year.

SQUASH: YELLOW STRAIGHTNECK, MEXICO

Source: *Fresh Fruit and Vegetable Prices.* **Price Frequency:** monthly, seasonally. **Effective Market(s):** Chicago. **Units of Measure:** Dollars per lug. **Type of Price:** average wholesale price. **Time Period Covered:** latest year.

SQUASH: YELLOW STRAIGHTNECK, NEW JERSEY

Source: *Fresh Fruit and Vegetable Prices.* **Price Frequency:** monthly, seasonally. **Effective Market(s):** New York City. **Units of Measure:** Dollars per crate/carton. **Type of Price:** average wholesale price. **Time Period Covered:** latest year.

SQUASH: YELLOW STRAIGHTNECK, NORTH CAROLINA

Source: *Fresh Fruit and Vegetable Prices.* **Price Frequency:** monthly, seasonally. **Effective Market(s):** New York City. **Units of Measure:** Dollars per crate/carton. **Type of Price:** average wholesale price. **Time Period Covered:** latest year.

SQUASH: ZUCCHINI

Source: *Fresh Fruit and Vegetable Prices.* **Price Frequency:** monthly, seasonally. **Effective Market(s):** 6 domestic markets. **Units of Measure:** Dollars per carton or crate. **Type of Price:** average price at shipping point. **Time Period Covered:** latest year.

Source: *Lancaster Farming.* **Price Frequency:** weekly, seasonally. **Effective Market(s):** Pennsylvania. **Units of Measure:** Dollars per carton. **Type of Price:** market. **Time Period Covered:** latest week.

Source: *The Packer.* **Price Frequency:** weekly, seasonally. **Effective Market(s):** varies. **Units of Measure:** Dollars per bushel crate. **Type of Price:** average received by farmer. **Time Period Covered:** latest week.

SQUASH: ZUCCHINI, FLORIDA

Source: *Fresh Fruit and Vegetable Prices.* **Price Frequency:** monthly, seasonally. **Effective Market(s):** Chicago, New York City. **Units of Measure:** Dollars per crate/carton. **Type of Price:** average wholesale price. **Time Period Covered:** latest year.

SQUASH: ZUCCHINI, ILLINOIS

Source: *Fresh Fruit and Vegetable Prices.* **Price Frequency:** monthly, seasonally. **Effective Market(s):** Chicago. **Units of Measure:** Dollars per crate/carton. **Type of Price:** average wholesale price. **Time Period Covered:** latest year.

SQUASH: ZUCCHINI, MEXICAN

Source: *Fresh Fruit and Vegetable Prices.* **Price Frequency:** monthly, seasonally. **Effective Market(s):** Nogales (AZ). **Units of Measure:** Dollars per carton or crate. **Type of Price:** price paid at point of entry. **Time Period Covered:** latest year.

Source: *Fresh Fruit and Vegetable Prices.* **Price Frequency:** monthly, seasonally. **Effective Market(s):** Chicago, New York City. **Units of Measure:** Dollars per lug. **Type of Price:** average wholesale price. **Time Period Covered:** latest year.

SQUASH: ZUCCHINI, NEW JERSEY

Source: *Fresh Fruit and Vegetable Prices.* **Price Frequency:** monthly, seasonally. **Effective Market(s):** New York City. **Units of Measure:** Dollars per crate/carton. **Type of Price:** average wholesale price. **Time Period Covered:** latest year.

SQUASH: ZUCCHINI, NORTH CAROLINA

Source: *Fresh Fruit and Vegetable Prices.* **Price Frequency:** monthly, seasonally. **Effective Market(s):** New York City. **Units of Measure:** Dollars per crate/carton. **Type of Price:** average wholesale price. **Time Period Covered:** latest year.

SQUID: WHOLE, CLEANED, PEELED, FROZEN, TAIWANESE

Source: *Seafood Price-Current.* **Price Frequency:** semiweekly. **Effective Market(s):** Mid-Atlantic. **Units of Measure:** Dollars per lb. **Type of Price:** sale by first receiver. **Time Period Covered:** latest day.

SQUID: WHOLE, FRESH

Source: *Seafood Price-Current.* **Price Frequency:** semiweekly. **Effective Market(s):** Boston, Mid-Atlantic, New Bedford (MA), Portland (ME), West Coast. **Units of Measure:** Dollars per lb. **Type of Price:** sale by first receiver, auction price. **Time Period Covered:** latest day.

ST. JOHN'S BREAD: EDIBLE

Source: *Chemical Marketing Reporter.* **Price Frequency:** weekly. **Effective Market(s):** New York. **Units of Measure:** Dollars per lb. **Type of Price:** spot. **Time Period Covered:** latest week.

STANNIC CHLORIDE: ANHYDROUS

Source: *Chemical Marketing Reporter.* **Price Frequency:** weekly. **Effective Market(s):** New York. **Units of Measure:** Dollars per lb. **Type of Price:** spot. **Time Period Covered:** latest week.

STANNOUS CHLORIDE: ANHYDROUS

Source: *Chemical Marketing Reporter.* **Price Frequency:** weekly. **Effective Market(s):** New York. **Units of Measure:** Dollars per lb. **Type of Price:** spot. **Time Period Covered:** latest week.

Source: *Journal of Commerce and Commercial.* **Price Frequency:** weekly in Thursday issue. **Units of Measure:** Dollars per lb. **Type of Price:** spot. **Time Period Covered:** latest week.

STANNOUS FLUOBORATE

Source: *Journal of Commerce and Commercial.* **Price Frequency:** weekly in Thursday issue. **Units of Measure:** Dollars per lb. **Type of Price:** spot. **Time Period Covered:** latest week.

STANNOUS FLUOBORATE: LIQUID CONCENTRATE

Source: *Chemical Marketing Reporter.* **Price Frequency:** weekly. **Effective Market(s):** New York. **Units of Measure:** Dollars per lb. **Type of Price:** spot. **Time Period Covered:** latest week.

STANNOUS OXIDE

Source: *Chemical Marketing Reporter.* **Price Frequency:** weekly. **Effective Market(s):** New York. **Units of Measure:** Dollars per lb. **Type of Price:** spot. **Time Period Covered:** latest week.

STANNOUS SULFATE

Source: *Chemical Marketing Reporter.* **Price Frequency:** weekly. **Effective Market(s):** New York. **Units of Measure:** Dollars per lb. **Type of Price:** spot. **Time Period Covered:** latest week.

Source: *Journal of Commerce and Commercial.* **Price Frequency:** weekly in Thursday issue. **Units of Measure:** Dollars per lb. **Type of Price:** spot. **Time Period Covered:** latest week.

STAPLES (TEXTILE)

see specific types of staples, e.g., Polyester Staple.

STAPLES: FENCE

Source: *Agricultural Prices.* **Price Frequency:** annually. **Effective Market(s):** United States. **Units of Measure:** Dollars per lb. **Type of Price:** paid by farmer. **Time Period Covered:** latest year.

Source: *Agricultural Prices Annual Summary.* **Price Frequency:** semiannually. **Effective Market(s):** United States. **Units of Measure:** Dollars each. **Type of Price:** average paid by farmer. **Time Period Covered:** latest 6 years.

STATIONERY

Source: *Pulp & Paper Week.* **Price Frequency:** monthly, irregularly. **Units of Measure:** index. **Type of Price:** price index. **Time Period Covered:** latest 3 month.

STEAK

see also Beef.

STEAK: RUMP

Source: *Statistical Bulletin of the South Pacific: Retail Price Indexes.* **Price Frequency:** annually. **Effective Market(s):** 18 South Pacific markets. **Units of Measure:** Australian dollars per kilogram. **Type of Price:** retail. **Time Period Covered:** latest year.

STEARIC ACID: 90%

Source: *Journal of Commerce and Commercial.* **Price Frequency:** weekly in Friday issue. **Units of Measure:** Dollars per lb. **Type of Price:** spot. **Time Period Covered:** latest week.

STEARIC ACID: DOUBLE PRESSED

Source: *Chemical Marketing Reporter.* **Price Frequency:** weekly. **Effective Market(s):** New York. **Units of Measure:** Dollars per lb. **Type of Price:** spot. **Time Period Covered:** latest week.

STEARIC ACID: SINGLE PRESSED

Source: *Chemical Marketing Reporter.* **Price Frequency:** weekly. **Effective Market(s):** New York. **Units of Measure:** Dollars per lb. **Type of Price:** spot. **Time Period Covered:** latest week.

STEARIC ACID: TRIPLE PRESSED

Source: *Chemical Marketing Reporter.* **Price Frequency:** weekly. **Effective Market(s):** New York. **Units of Measure:** Dollars per lb. **Type of Price:** spot. **Time Period Covered:** latest week.

Source: *Journal of Commerce and Commercial.* **Price Frequency:** weekly in Friday issue. **Units of Measure:** Dollars per lb. **Type of Price:** spot. **Time Period Covered:** latest week.

STEEL

Source: *Minerals Today.* **Price Frequency:** bimonthly. **Units of Measure:** Dollars per short ton. **Time Period Covered:** latest month, month ago.

STEEL: AUTOMOBILE CAST SCRAP

Source: *Iron Age.* **Price Frequency:** monthly. **Effective Market(s):** Detroit. **Units of Measure:** Dollars per gross ton. **Type of Price:** dealer. **Time Period Covered:** latest month.

STEEL: AUTOMOBILE CAST SCRAP, CLEAN

Source: *American Metal Market.* **Price Frequency:** daily. **Effective Market(s):** varies. **Units of Measure:** Dollars per gross ton. **Type of Price:** broker buying, consumer buying, export yard buying. **Time Period Covered:** latest day.

STEEL: BREAKABLE FOUNDRY SCRAP

Source: *American Metal Market.* **Price Frequency:** daily. **Effective Market(s):** Houston. **Units of Measure:** Dollars per gross ton. **Type of Price:** consumer buying. **Time Period Covered:** latest day.

STEEL: CAST BORINGS SCRAP, CLEAN

Source: *Iron Age.* **Price Frequency:** monthly. **Effective Market(s):** New York. **Units of Measure:** Dollars per gross ton. **Type of Price:** dealer. **Time Period Covered:** latest month.

STEEL: CAST BORINGS SCRAP, IRON

Source: *American Metal Market.* **Price Frequency:** daily. **Effective Market(s):** varies. **Units of Measure:** Dollars per gross ton. **Type of Price:** broker buying, consumer buying, export yard buying. **Time Period Covered:** latest day.

STEEL: CAST SCRAP

Source: *Iron Age.* **Price Frequency:** monthly. **Effective Market(s):** Hamilton (Ontario). **Units of Measure:** Dollars per gross ton. **Type of Price:** broker buying. **Time Period Covered:** latest month.

STEEL: COLD ROLLED

Source: *Standard & Poor's Statistical Service Current Statistics.* **Price Frequency:** monthly, annually. **Units of Measure:** cents per lb. **Time Period Covered:** latest 4 years.

STEEL: CRUSHED TURNINGS SCRAP

Source: *American Metal Market.* **Price Frequency:** daily. **Effective Market(s):** Houston. **Units of Measure:** Dollars per gross ton. **Type of Price:** consumer buying. **Time Period Covered:** latest day.

Source: *Iron Age.* **Price Frequency:** monthly. **Effective Market(s):** Houston. **Units of Measure:** Dollars per gross ton. **Type of Price:** dealer. **Time Period Covered:** latest month.

STEEL: CUPOLA CAST SCRAP

Source: *American Metal Market.* **Price Frequency:** daily. **Effective Market(s):** varies. **Units of Measure:** Dollars per gross ton. **Type of Price:** broker buying, consumer buying, export yard buying. **Time Period Covered:** latest day.

Source: *Iron Age.* **Price Frequency:** monthly. **Effective Market(s):** Chicago, Houston, Philadelphia, Pittsburgh, St. Louis. **Units of Measure:** Dollars per gross ton. **Type of Price:** dealer. **Time Period Covered:** latest month.

STEEL: CUT AUTOMOBILE FOUNDRY SCRAP

Source: *American Metal Market.* **Price Frequency:** daily. **Effective Market(s):** Cleveland. **Units of Measure:** Dollars per gross ton. **Type of Price:** consumer buying. **Time Period Covered:** latest day.

STEEL: CUT PLATE AND STRUCTURAL SCRAP

Source: *Iron Age.* **Price Frequency:** monthly. **Effective Market(s):** Birmingham, Buffalo, Cleveland, Houston. **Units of Measure:** Dollars per gross ton. **Type of Price:** dealer. **Time Period Covered:** latest month.

STEEL: CUT STRUCTURAL PLATE SCRAP

Source: *American Metal Market.* **Price Frequency:** daily. **Effective Market(s):** varies. **Units of Measure:** Dollars per gross ton. **Type of Price:** broker buying, consumer buying. **Time Period Covered:** latest day.

STEEL: DROP BROKEN CAST SCRAP

Source: *American Metal Market.* **Price Frequency:** daily. **Effective Market(s):** varies. **Units of Measure:** Dollars per gross ton. **Type of Price:** broker buying, consumer buying, export yard buying. **Time Period Covered:** latest day.

Source: *Iron Age.* **Price Frequency:** monthly. **Effective Market(s):** Cincinnati. **Units of Measure:** Dollars per gross ton. **Type of Price:** dealer. **Time Period Covered:** latest month.

STEEL: DROP FORGE FLASHINGS SCRAP

Source: *Iron Age.* **Price Frequency:** monthly. **Effective Market(s):** Detroit. **Units of Measure:** Dollars per gross ton. **Type of Price:** dealer. **Time Period Covered:** latest month.

STEEL: ELECTRIC FURNACE SCRAP

Source: *American Metal Market.* **Price Frequency:** daily. **Effective Market(s):** Birmingham. **Units of Measure:** Dollars per gross ton. **Type of Price:** consumer buying. **Time Period Covered:** latest day.

Source: *Iron Age.* **Price Frequency:** monthly. **Effective Market(s):** Birmingham, Los Angeles. **Units of Measure:** Dollars per gross ton. **Type of Price:** dealer. **Time Period Covered:** latest month.

STEEL: FINISHED

Source: *Standard & Poor's Statistical Service Current Statistics.* **Price Frequency:** monthly, annually. **Units of Measure:** cents per lb. **Type of Price:** composite. **Time Period Covered:** latest 4 years.

STEEL: FINISHED, SCRAP

Source: *Iron Age.* **Price Frequency:** weekly. **Units of Measure:** Dollars per gross ton. **Type of Price:** composite. **Time Period Covered:** latest week, week ago, month ago, year ago.

STEEL: FOUNDRY SCRAP

Source: *American Metal Market.* **Price Frequency:** daily. **Effective Market(s):** varies. **Units of Measure:** Dollars per gross ton. **Type of Price:** consumer buying. **Time Period Covered:** latest day.

Source: *Iron Age.* **Price Frequency:** monthly. **Effective Market(s):** Cleveland. **Units of Measure:** Dollars per gross ton. **Type of Price:** dealer. **Time Period Covered:** latest month.

STEEL: H-SHAPES

Source: *Japan Economic Journal.* **Price Frequency:** weekly. **Effective Market(s):** Tokyo. **Units of Measure:** Japanese yen per ton. **Type of Price:** market. **Time Period Covered:** latest 2 weeks.

STEEL: HEAVY BREAKABLE CAST SCRAP

Source: *American Metal Market.* **Price Frequency:** daily. **Effective Market(s):** varies. **Units of Measure:** Dollars per gross ton. **Type of Price:** broker buying, consumer buying, export yard buying. **Time Period Covered:** latest day.

Source: *Iron Age.* **Price Frequency:** monthly. **Effective Market(s):** 7 domestic markets. **Units of Measure:** Dollars per gross ton. **Type of Price:** dealer. **Time Period Covered:** latest month.

STEEL: HEAVY FORGE BAR CROPS, SCRAP

Source: *American Metal Market.* **Price Frequency:** daily. **Effective Market(s):** Chicago. **Units of Measure:** Dollars per gross ton. **Type of Price:** consumer buying. **Time Period Covered:** latest day.

STEEL: HEAVY TURNINGS SCRAP

Source: *Iron Age.* **Price Frequency:** monthly. **Effective Market(s):** Pittsburgh. **Units of Measure:** Dollars per gross ton. **Type of Price:** dealer. **Time Period Covered:** latest month.

STEEL: HOT ROLLED

Source: *Standard & Poor's Statistical Service Current Statistics.* **Price Frequency:** monthly, annually. **Units of Measure:** cents per lb. **Time Period Covered:** latest 4 years.

STEEL: LOW PHOSPHATE SCRAP

Source: *Iron Age.* **Price Frequency:** monthly. **Effective Market(s):** Cincinnati, Philadelphia, Youngstown (OH). **Units of Measure:** Dollars per gross ton. **Type of Price:** dealer. **Time Period Covered:** latest month.

STEEL: MACHINE SHOP TURNINGS SCRAP

Source: *American Metal Market.* **Price Frequency:** daily. **Effective Market(s):** varies. **Units of Measure:** Dollars per gross ton. **Type of Price:** broker buying, consumer buying, export yard buying. **Time Period Covered:** latest day.

Source: *Iron Age.* **Price Frequency:** monthly. **Effective Market(s):** 14 domestic markets. **Units of Measure:** Dollars per gross ton. **Type of Price:** dealer. **Time Period Covered:** latest month.

STEEL: MIXED BORINGS AND TURNINGS SCRAP

Source: *American Metal Market.* **Price Frequency:** daily. **Effective Market(s):** varies. **Units of Measure:** Dollars per gross ton. **Type of Price:** broker buying, consumer buying. **Time Period Covered:** latest day.

Source: *Iron Age.* **Price Frequency:** monthly. **Effective Market(s):** Buffalo, Chicago, Detroit, Hamilton (Ontario), New York, Philadelphia. **Units of Measure:** Dollars per gross ton. **Type of Price:** dealer. **Time Period Covered:** latest month.

STEEL: MIXED CAST SCRAP

Source: *American Metal Market.* **Price Frequency:** daily. **Effective Market(s):** Boston. **Units of Measure:** Dollars per gross ton. **Type of Price:** consumer buying, export yard buying. **Time Period Covered:** latest day.

Source: *Iron Age.* **Price Frequency:** monthly. **Effective Market(s):** Cleveland. **Units of Measure:** Dollars per gross ton. **Type of Price:** dealer. **Time Period Covered:** latest month.

STEEL: MIXED CUPOLA CAST SCRAP

Source: *Iron Age.* **Price Frequency:** monthly. **Effective Market(s):** Boston, Detroit. **Units of Measure:** Dollars per gross ton. **Type of Price:** dealer. **Time Period Covered:** latest month.

STEEL: MIXED SCRAP

Source: *Iron Age.* **Price Frequency:** monthly. **Effective Market(s):** Hamilton (Ontario). **Units of Measure:** Dollars per gross ton. **Type of Price:** broker buying. **Time Period Covered:** latest month.

STEEL: MIXED YARD CAST SCRAP

Source: *Iron Age.* **Price Frequency:** monthly. **Effective Market(s):** New York, Seattle. **Units of Measure:** Dollars per gross ton. **Type of Price:** dealer. **Time Period Covered:** latest month.

STEEL: NO. 1, CUPOLA CAST SCRAP

Source: *Iron Age.* **Price Frequency:** monthly. **Effective Market(s):** 6 domestic markets. **Units of Measure:** Dollars per gross ton. **Type of Price:** dealer. **Time Period Covered:** latest month.

STEEL: NO. 1, HEAVY MELTING, INDUSTRIAL, SCRAP

Source: *American Metal Market.* **Price Frequency:** daily. **Effective Market(s):** Chicago. **Units of Measure:** Dollars per gross ton. **Type of Price:** consumer buying. **Time Period Covered:** latest day.

STEEL: NO. 1, HEAVY MELTING, RAILROAD, EXTRA DENSE, SCRAP

Source: *American Metal Market.* **Price Frequency:** daily. **Effective Market(s):** Pittsburgh. **Units of Measure:** Dollars per gross ton. **Type of Price:** consumer buying. **Time Period Covered:** latest day.

STEEL: NO. 1, HEAVY MELTING, RAILROAD, SCRAP

Source: *American Metal Market.* **Price Frequency:** daily. **Effective Market(s):** varies. **Units of Measure:** Dollars per gross ton. **Type of Price:** consumer buying. **Time Period Covered:** latest day.

Source: *Iron Age.* **Price Frequency:** monthly. **Effective Market(s):** Birmingham, Chicago, Cleveland, Pittsburgh, St. Louis. **Units of Measure:** Dollars per gross ton. **Type of Price:** dealer. **Time Period Covered:** latest month.

STEEL: NO. 1, HEAVY MELTING, SCRAP

Source: *American Metal Market.* **Price Frequency:** daily. **Effective Market(s):** varies. **Units of Measure:** Dollars per gross ton. **Type of Price:** broker buying, consumer buying, export yard buying. **Time Period Covered:** latest day.

Source: *American Metal Market.* **Price Frequency:** weekly. **Effective Market(s):** Chicago, Philadelphia, Pittsburgh, 3-market average. **Units of Measure:** Dollars per gross ton. **Time Period Covered:** latest 2 weeks, year ago.

Source: *Asian Wall Street Journal.* **Price Frequency:** daily. **Effective Market(s):** Chicago. **Units of Measure:** Dollars per ton. **Type of Price:** cash. **Time Period Covered:** latest 2 days, year ago.

Source: *Business Week.* **Price Frequency:** weekly. **Units of Measure:** Dollars per ton. **Time Period Covered:** latest 2 weeks.

Source: *Commodity Year Book.* **Price Frequency:** annually. **Effective Market(s):** Pittsburgh, Chicago. **Units of Measure:** Dollars per net ton. **Type of Price:** wholesale. **Time Period Covered:** latest 8 years.

Source: *Commodity Year Book.* **Price Frequency:** monthly, annually. **Effective Market(s):** Chicago. **Units of Measure:** Dollars per gross ton. **Type of Price:** wholesale. **Time Period Covered:** latest 10 years.

Source: *CRB Commodity Index Report.* **Price Frequency:** weekly. **Effective Market(s):** Chicago. **Units of Measure:** Dollars per ton. **Type of Price:** spot. **Time Period Covered:** latest week.

Source: *Investor's Daily.* **Price Frequency:** daily. **Units of Measure:** Dollars per gross ton. **Type of Price:** spot. **Time Period Covered:** latest day.

Source: *Iron Age.* **Price Frequency:** monthly. **Effective Market(s):** 17 domestic markets. **Units of Measure:** Dollars per gross ton. **Type of Price:** dealer. **Time Period Covered:** latest month.

Source: *Iron Age.* **Price Frequency:** weekly. **Units of Measure:** Dollars per gross ton. **Type of Price:** composite. **Time Period Covered:** latest week, week ago, month ago, year ago.

Source: *Journal of Commerce and Commercial.* **Price Frequency:** daily. **Effective Market(s):** Pittsburgh, Chicago, Philadelphia. **Units of Measure:** Dollars per ton. **Type of Price:** spot supplier. **Time Period Covered:** latest day.

Source: *New York Times.* **Price Frequency:** daily. **Units of Measure:** Dollars per gross ton. **Type of Price:** cash. **Time Period Covered:** latest 2 days.

Source: *Purchasing.* **Price Frequency:** monthly. **Effective Market(s):** Chicago, Pittsburgh. **Units of Measure:** Dollars per gross ton. **Type of Price:** transaction. **Time Period Covered:** latest day, month ago, 6 months ago, year ago.

Source: *Standard & Poor's Statistical Service Current Statistics.* **Price Frequency:** monthly, annually. **Effective Market(s):** Chicago, Philadelphia, Pittsburgh, Chicago/Philadelphia/Pittsburgh. **Units of Measure:** Dollars per gross ton. **Time Period Covered:** latest 4 years.

Source: *Survey of Current Business.* **Price Frequency:** monthly, annually. **Units of Measure:** Dollars per long ton. **Type of Price:** composite. **Time Period Covered:** latest year.

Source: *Wall Street Journal.* **Price Frequency:** daily. **Effective Market(s):** Chicago. **Units of Measure:** Dollars per ton. **Time Period Covered:** latest day, day ago, year ago.

STEEL: NO. 1, MACHINERY CAST, SCRAP

Source: *Iron Age.* **Price Frequency:** monthly. **Effective Market(s):** 6 domestic markets. **Units of Measure:** Dollars per gross ton. **Type of Price:** dealer. **Time Period Covered:** latest month.

Source: *Iron Age.* **Price Frequency:** monthly. **Effective Market(s):** Philadelphia. **Units of Measure:** Dollars per gross ton. **Type of Price:** dealer. **Time Period Covered:** latest month.

Source: *Iron Age.* **Price Frequency:** monthly. **Effective Market(s):** Chicago, Philadelphia, Pittsburgh. **Units of Measure:** Dollars per gross ton. **Time Period Covered:** latest month.

STEEL: NO. 1, RAIL, STANDARD

Source: *American Metal Market.* **Price Frequency:** weekly in Friday issue. **Units of Measure:** Dollars per 100 lbs. **Type of Price:** producer list. **Time Period Covered:** latest week.

STEEL: NO. 1, RAILROAD CAST, SCRAP

Source: *American Metal Market.* **Price Frequency:** daily. **Effective Market(s):** Cleveland. **Units of Measure:** Dollars per gross ton. **Type of Price:** consumer buying. **Time Period Covered:** latest day.

STEEL: NO. 1, SCRAP

Source: *American Metal Market.* **Price Frequency:** daily. **Effective Market(s):** Pittsburgh. **Units of Measure:** Dollars per gross ton. **Type of Price:** market. **Time Period Covered:** latest 3 days.

Source: *Iron Age.* **Price Frequency:** monthly. **Effective Market(s):** Chicago, Philadelphia, Pittsburgh. **Units of Measure:** Dollars per gross ton. **Time Period Covered:** latest month.

STEEL: NO. 1, SHEARING, SCRAP

Source: *American Metal Market.* **Price Frequency:** daily. **Effective Market(s):** varies. **Units of Measure:** Dollars per gross ton. **Type of Price:** export yard buying. **Time Period Covered:** latest day.

STEEL: NO. 2, HEAVY MELTING, SCRAP

Source: *American Metal Market.* **Price Frequency:** daily. **Effective Market(s):** varies. **Units of Measure:** Dollars per gross ton. **Type of Price:** broker buying, consumer buying, export yard buying. **Time Period Covered:** latest day.

Source: *Iron Age.* **Price Frequency:** monthly. **Effective Market(s):** 17 domestic markets. **Units of Measure:** Dollars per gross ton. **Type of Price:** dealer. **Time Period Covered:** latest month.

STEEL: PLATE

Source: *Japan Economic Journal.* **Price Frequency:** weekly. **Effective Market(s):** Tokyo. **Units of Measure:** Japanese yen per ton. **Type of Price:** market. **Time Period Covered:** latest 2 weeks.

Source: *Standard & Poor's Statistical Service Current Statistics.* **Price Frequency:** monthly, annually. **Effective Market(s):** Pittsburgh. **Units of Measure:** cents per lb. **Time Period Covered:** latest 4 years.

STEEL: PLATE ALLOY

Source: *American Metal Market.* **Price Frequency:** daily. **Effective Market(s):** Midwest. **Units of Measure:** Dollars per 100 lbs. **Type of Price:** mill. **Time Period Covered:** latest day.

Source: *American Metal Market.* **Price Frequency:** weekly in Friday issue. **Effective Market(s):** United States. **Units of Measure:** Dollars per 100 lbs. **Type of Price:** mill. **Time Period Covered:** latest week.

STEEL: PLATE AND PUNCHING, SCRAP

Source: *American Metal Market.* **Price Frequency:** daily. **Effective Market(s):** Chicago. **Units of Measure:** Dollars per gross ton. **Type of Price:** consumer buying. **Time Period Covered:** latest day.

STEEL: PLATE AND STRUCTURAL, LOW ALLOY, SCRAP

Source: *Iron Age.* **Price Frequency:** monthly. **Effective Market(s):** Chicago. **Units of Measure:** Dollars per gross ton. **Type of Price:** dealer. **Time Period Covered:** latest month.

STEEL: PLATE AND STRUCTURAL, SCRAP

Source: *Iron Age.* **Price Frequency:** monthly. **Effective Market(s):** St. Louis. **Units of Measure:** Dollars per gross ton. **Type of Price:** dealer. **Time Period Covered:** latest month.

STEEL: PLATE CARBON

Source: *American Metal Market.* **Price Frequency:** weekly in Friday issue. **Effective Market(s):** Canada, United States. **Units of Measure:** Canadian dollars per 100 lbs., dollars per 100 lbs. **Type of Price:** mill. **Time Period Covered:** latest week.

Source: *American Metal Market.* **Price Frequency:** daily. **Effective Market(s):** Midwest. **Units of Measure:** Dollars per 100 lbs. **Type of Price:** mill. **Time Period Covered:** latest day.

Source: *Commodity Trade and Price Trends.* **Price Frequency:** annually. **Effective Market(s):** Midwestern points. **Units of Measure:** Dollars per metric ton, 1980 constant dollars per metric ton. **Time Period Covered:** latest 37 years.

Source: *Commodity Year Book.* **Price Frequency:** annually. **Effective Market(s):** Pittsburgh. **Units of Measure:** cents per lb. **Type of Price:** wholesale. **Time Period Covered:** latest 7 years.

Source: *Purchasing.* **Price Frequency:** monthly. **Units of Measure:** Dollars per ton. **Type of Price:** transaction. **Time Period Covered:** latest day, month ago, 6 months ago, year ago.

STEEL: PLATE, LOW PHOSPHATE, SCRAP

Source: *American Metal Market.* **Price Frequency:** daily. **Units of Measure:** Dollars per gross ton. **Type of Price:** consumer buying. **Time Period Covered:** latest day.

Source: *Iron Age.* **Price Frequency:** monthly. **Effective Market(s):** Buffalo, Youngstown. **Units of Measure:** Dollars per gross ton. **Type of Price:** dealer. **Time Period Covered:** latest month.

STEEL: PLATE, SAFETY

Source: *American Metal Market.* **Price Frequency:** weekly in Friday issue. **Effective Market(s):** Canada, United States. **Units of Measure:** Canadian dollars per 100 lbs., dollars per 100 lbs. **Type of Price:** mill. **Time Period Covered:** latest week.

STEEL: PLATE, STRIP MILL

Source: *American Metal Market.* **Price Frequency:** weekly in Friday issue. **Effective Market(s):** United States. **Units of Measure:** Dollars per 100 lbs. **Type of Price:** mill. **Time Period Covered:** latest week.

Source: *American Metal Market.* **Price Frequency:** daily. **Effective Market(s):** Midwest. **Units of Measure:** Dollars per 100 lbs. **Type of Price:** mill. **Time Period Covered:** latest day.

STEEL: PUNCHINGS PLATE, LOW ALLOY, SCRAP

Source: *Iron Age.* **Price Frequency:** monthly. **Effective Market(s):** Chicago. **Units of Measure:** Dollars per gross ton. **Type of Price:** dealer. **Time Period Covered:** latest month.

STEEL: PUNCHINGS PLATE, LOW PHOSPHATE, SCRAP

Source: *Iron Age.* **Price Frequency:** monthly. **Effective Market(s):** Cleveland, Pittsburgh. **Units of Measure:** Dollars per gross ton. **Type of Price:** dealer. **Time Period Covered:** latest month.

STEEL: RAIL, CRANE

Source: *American Metal Market.* **Price Frequency:** weekly in Friday issue. **Units of Measure:** Dollars per 100 lbs. **Type of Price:** producer list. **Time Period Covered:** latest week.

STEEL: RAIL CROPS, SCRAP

Source: *American Metal Market.* **Price Frequency:** daily. **Effective Market(s):** varies. **Units of Measure:** Dollars per gross ton. **Type of Price:** broker buying, consumer buying. **Time Period Covered:** latest day.

STEEL: RAIL, LIGHT MINE

Source: *American Metal Market.* **Price Frequency:** weekly in Friday issue. **Units of Measure:** Dollars per 100 lbs. **Type of Price:** producer list. **Time Period Covered:** latest week.

STEEL: RAIL, PREMIUM

Source: *American Metal Market.* **Price Frequency:** weekly in Friday issue. **Units of Measure:** Dollars per 100 lbs. **Type of Price:** producer list. **Time Period Covered:** latest week.

STEEL: SHORT TURNINGS SCRAP

Source: *Iron Age.* **Price Frequency:** monthly. **Effective Market(s):** Hamilton (Ontario). **Units of Measure:** Dollars per gross ton. **Type of Price:** broker buying. **Time Period Covered:** latest month.

STEEL: SHOVELING TURNINGS SCRAP

Source: *American Metal Market.* **Price Frequency:** daily. **Effective Market(s):** varies. **Units of Measure:** Dollars per gross ton. **Type of Price:** broker buying, consumer buying, export yard buying. **Time Period Covered:** latest day.

Source: *Iron Age.* **Price Frequency:** monthly. **Effective Market(s):** 13 domestic markets. **Units of Measure:** Dollars per gross ton. **Type of Price:** dealer. **Time Period Covered:** latest month.

STEEL: SHREDDED AUTO SCRAP

Source: *American Metal Market.* **Price Frequency:** daily. **Effective Market(s):** varies. **Units of Measure:** Dollars per gross ton. **Type of Price:** broker buying, consumer buying. **Time Period Covered:** latest day.

STEEL: SHREDDED SCRAP

Source: *American Metal Market.* **Price Frequency:** daily. **Effective Market(s):** 6 domestic markets, 6-market average. **Units of Measure:** Dollars per gross ton. **Time Period Covered:** latest 2 weeks, year ago.

Source: *American Metal Market.* **Price Frequency:** daily. **Effective Market(s):** Buffalo. **Units of Measure:** Dollars per gross ton. **Type of Price:** consumer buying. **Time Period Covered:** latest day.

Source: *Iron Age.* **Price Frequency:** monthly. **Effective Market(s):** Birmingham, Boston, Chicago, Houston, Philadelphia. **Units of Measure:** Dollars per gross ton. **Type of Price:** dealer. **Time Period Covered:** latest month.

STEEL: STAINLESS, COLD ROLLED

Source: *Purchasing.* **Price Frequency:** monthly. **Units of Measure:** Dollars per ton. **Type of Price:** transaction. **Time Period Covered:** latest day, month ago, 6 months ago, year ago.

STEEL: STAINLESS, MIXED SOLIDS SCRAP

Source: *American Metal Market.* **Price Frequency:** daily. **Effective Market(s):** varies. **Units of Measure:** cents per lb. **Type of Price:** dealers' buying. **Time Period Covered:** latest day.

STEEL: STAINLESS, MIXED TURNINGS SCRAP

Source: *American Metal Market.* **Price Frequency:** daily. **Effective Market(s):** varies. **Units of Measure:** cents per lb. **Type of Price:** dealers' buying. **Time Period Covered:** latest day.

STEEL: STAINLESS PLATE

Source: *ENR.* **Price Frequency:** monthly in second issue of month. **Effective Market(s):** 15 domestic markets, Montreal. **Units of Measure:** Dollars per 100 lbs. **Type of Price:** spot. **Time Period Covered:** latest month.

Source: *Purchasing.* **Price Frequency:** quarterly in January, April, July, October issues. **Units of Measure:** cents per lb. **Type of Price:** transaction. **Time Period Covered:** latest 5 quarters.

STEEL: STAINLESS PLATE, COILED

Source: *American Metal Market.* **Price Frequency:** weekly in Friday issue. **Units of Measure:** cents per lb. **Type of Price:** base, distributor. **Time Period Covered:** latest week.

STEEL: STAINLESS PLATE, UNCOILED

Source: *American Metal Market.* **Price Frequency:** weekly in Friday issue. **Units of Measure:** cents per lb. **Type of Price:** base, distributor. **Time Period Covered:** latest week.

STEEL: STAINLESS, REDRAWN GRADE

Source: *American Metal Market.* **Price Frequency:** weekly in Friday issue. **Units of Measure:** cents per lb. **Type of Price:** base, distributor. **Time Period Covered:** latest week.

STEEL: STAINLESS, SCRAP

Source: *Iron Age.* **Price Frequency:** monthly. **Effective Market(s):** Chicago, Cleveland, Detroit, New York, Pittsburgh. **Units of Measure:** Dollars per gross ton. **Type of Price:** dealer. **Time Period Covered:** latest month.

STEEL: STAINLESS, SLABS AND BILLETS

Source: *American Metal Market.* **Price Frequency:** weekly in Friday issue. **Units of Measure:** cents per lb. **Type of Price:** base, distributor. **Time Period Covered:** latest week.

STEEL: STAINLESS, TURNINGS SCRAP

Source: *American Metal Market.* **Price Frequency:** daily. **Effective Market(s):** varies. **Units of Measure:** cents per lb., dollars per gross ton. **Type of Price:** dealers' buying, consumer buying, export yard buying. **Time Period Covered:** latest day.

STEEL: STOVE PLATE

Source: *American Metal Market.* **Price Frequency:** daily. **Effective Market(s):** Birmingham, Chicago. **Units of Measure:** Dollars per gross ton. **Type of Price:** consumer buying. **Time Period Covered:** latest day.

Source: *Iron Age.* **Price Frequency:** monthly. **Effective Market(s):** Chicago, St. Louis. **Units of Measure:** Dollars per gross ton. **Type of Price:** dealer. **Time Period Covered:** latest month.

STEEL: STRUCTURAL

Source: *ENR.* **Price Frequency:** monthly in first issue of month. **Effective Market(s):** 20-city average. **Units of Measure:** Dollars per 100 lbs. **Time Period Covered:** latest month.

STEEL: STRUCTURAL SHAPES

Source: *Commodity Year Book.* **Price Frequency:** annually. **Effective Market(s):** Pittsburgh. **Units of Measure:** cents per lb. **Type of Price:** wholesale. **Time Period Covered:** latest 6 years.

Source: *Standard & Poor's Statistical Service Current Statistics.* **Price Frequency:** monthly, annually. **Units of Measure:** cents per lb. **Time Period Covered:** latest 4 years.

STEEL: STRUCTURAL SHAPES, STANDARD CARBON

Source: *American Metal Market.* **Price Frequency:** daily. **Effective Market(s):** Midwest. **Units of Measure:** Dollars per 100 lbs. **Type of Price:** mill. **Time Period Covered:** latest day.

STEEL: STRUCTURAL SHAPES, WIDE-FLANGED CARBON

Source: *American Metal Market.* **Price Frequency:** daily. **Effective Market(s):** Midwest. **Units of Measure:** Dollars per 100 lbs. **Type of Price:** mill. **Time Period Covered:** latest day.

STEEL: TIN-FREE, FOR CANMAKING

Source: *American Metal Market.* **Price Frequency:** weekly in Friday issue. **Effective Market(s):** National mills, West Coast. **Units of Measure:** Dollars per base box. **Type of Price:** list. **Time Period Covered:** latest week.

STEEL: TOOL, COLD WORK

Source: *American Metal Market.* **Price Frequency:** weekly in Friday issue. **Units of Measure:** Dollars per lb. **Type of Price:** market. **Time Period Covered:** latest week.

STEEL: TOOL, HIGH SPEED

Source: *American Metal Market.* **Price Frequency:** weekly in Friday issue. **Units of Measure:** Dollars per lb. **Type of Price:** market. **Time Period Covered:** latest week.

STEEL: TOOL, HOT WORK

Source: *American Metal Market.* **Price Frequency:** weekly in Friday issue. **Units of Measure:** Dollars per lb. **Type of Price:** market. **Time Period Covered:** latest week.

STEEL: TOOL, MOLD, IN BLOCK FORM

Source: *American Metal Market.* **Price Frequency:** weekly in Friday issue. **Units of Measure:** Dollars per lb. **Type of Price:** market. **Time Period Covered:** latest week.

STEEL: TOOL, THICK PLATE FORM

Source: *American Metal Market.* **Price Frequency:** weekly in Friday issue. **Units of Measure:** Dollars per lb. **Type of Price:** market. **Time Period Covered:** latest week.

STEEL AUTO SLABS: SCRAP

Source: *American Metal Market.* **Price Frequency:** daily. **Effective Market(s):** Philadelphia. **Units of Measure:** Dollars per gross ton. **Type of Price:** consumer buying. **Time Period Covered:** latest day.

STEEL AXLES: SCRAP

Source: *American Metal Market.* **Price Frequency:** daily. **Effective Market(s):** Chicago. **Units of Measure:** Dollars per gross ton. **Type of Price:** consumer buying. **Time Period Covered:** latest day.

STEEL AXLES: UNTREATED

Source: *American Metal Market.* **Price Frequency:** weekly in Friday issue. **Units of Measure:** Dollars per 100 lbs. **Type of Price:** producer list. **Time Period Covered:** latest week.

STEEL BAR: ALLOY, CARBON, HOT ROLLED

Source: *American Metal Market.* **Price Frequency:** daily. **Effective Market(s):** Midwest. **Units of Measure:** Dollars per 100 lbs. **Type of Price:** mill. **Time Period Covered:** latest day.

STEEL BAR: ALLOY, HOT ROLLED

Source: *American Metal Market.* **Price Frequency:** daily. **Effective Market(s):** Midwest. **Units of Measure:** Dollars per lb., dollars per 100 lbs. **Type of Price:** mill. **Time Period Covered:** latest day.

STEEL BAR: ANGLE

Source: *American Metal Market.* **Price Frequency:** weekly in Friday issue. **Units of Measure:** Dollars per 100 lbs. **Type of Price:** base. **Time Period Covered:** latest week.

STEEL BAR: ANGLE AND SPLICE SCRAP

Source: *American Metal Market.* **Price Frequency:** daily. **Effective Market(s):** Chicago. **Units of Measure:** Dollars per gross ton. **Type of Price:** consumer buying. **Time Period Covered:** latest day.

Source: *Iron Age.* **Price Frequency:** monthly. **Effective Market(s):** Birmingham. **Units of Measure:** Dollars per gross ton. **Type of Price:** dealer. **Time Period Covered:** latest month.

STEEL BAR: BESSEMER, WEST GERMANY

Source: *Commodity Trade and Price Trends.* **Price Frequency:** annually. **Effective Market(s):** Oberhausen (West Germany). **Units of Measure:** Dollars per metric ton, 1980 constant dollars per metric ton. **Type of Price:** domestic/export. **Time Period Covered:** latest 37 years.

STEEL BAR: CARBON, HOT ROLLED

Source: *American Metal Market.* **Price Frequency:** daily. **Effective Market(s):** Midwest. **Units of Measure:** Dollars per 100 lbs. **Type of Price:** mill. **Time Period Covered:** latest day.

STEEL BAR: COLD FINISHED

Source: *American Metal Market.* **Price Frequency:** weekly in Friday issue. **Units of Measure:** Dollars per 100 lbs. **Type of Price:** composite mill. **Time Period Covered:** latest week.

Source: *American Metal Market.* **Price Frequency:** daily. **Effective Market(s):** Midwest. **Units of Measure:** Dollars per lb. **Type of Price:** mill. **Time Period Covered:** latest day.

Source: *Commodity Year Book.* **Price Frequency:** annually. **Effective Market(s):** Pittsburgh. **Units of Measure:** cents per lb. **Type of Price:** wholesale. **Time Period Covered:** latest 7 years.

STEEL BAR: COLD FINISHED, SPECIAL QUALITY

Source: *Purchasing.* **Price Frequency:** monthly. **Units of Measure:** Dollars per ton. **Type of Price:** transaction. **Time Period Covered:** latest day, month ago, 6 months ago, year ago.

STEEL BAR: DEFORMED

Source: *Japan Economic Journal.* **Price Frequency:** weekly. **Effective Market(s):** Tokyo. **Units of Measure:** Japanese yen per ton. **Type of Price:** market. **Time Period Covered:** latest 2 weeks.

STEEL BAR: FLAT

Source: *American Metal Market.* **Price Frequency:** weekly in Friday issue. **Units of Measure:** Dollars per 100 lbs. **Type of Price:** base. **Time Period Covered:** latest week.

STEEL BAR: HOT ROLLED

Source: *American Metal Market.* **Price Frequency:** weekly in Friday issue. **Units of Measure:** Dollars per 100 lbs. **Type of Price:** composite mill. **Time Period Covered:** latest week.

Source: *Commodity Year Book.* **Price Frequency:** annually. **Effective Market(s):** Pittsburgh. **Units of Measure:** cents per lb. **Type of Price:** wholesale. **Time Period Covered:** latest 7 years.

STEEL BAR: REINFORCING

Source: *American Metal Market.* **Price Frequency:** daily. **Effective Market(s):** Midwest. **Units of Measure:** Dollars per lb. **Type of Price:** mill. **Time Period Covered:** latest day.

Source: *American Metal Market.* **Price Frequency:** weekly in Friday issue. **Units of Measure:** Dollars per 100 lbs. **Type of Price:** base. **Time Period Covered:** latest week.

Source: *Purchasing.* **Price Frequency:** quarterly in January, April, July, October issues. **Units of Measure:** Dollars per ton. **Type of Price:** transaction. **Time Period Covered:** latest 5 quarters.

STEEL BAR: ROUND

Source: *American Metal Market.* **Price Frequency:** weekly in Friday issue. **Units of Measure:** Dollars per 100 lbs. **Type of Price:** base. **Time Period Covered:** latest week.

STEEL BAR: STAINLESS

Source: *American Metal Market.* **Price Frequency:** daily. **Effective Market(s):** Midwest. **Units of Measure:** Dollars per lb. **Type of Price:** mill. **Time Period Covered:** latest day.

Source: *American Metal Market.* **Price Frequency:** weekly in Friday issue. **Units of Measure:** cents per lb. **Type of Price:** base, distributor. **Time Period Covered:** latest week.

STEEL BEAM: WIDE FLANGE

Source: *Purchasing.* **Price Frequency:** monthly. **Units of Measure:** Dollars per ton. **Type of Price:** transaction. **Time Period Covered:** latest day, month ago, 6 months ago, year ago.

STEEL BLACKPLATE

Source: *American Metal Market.* **Price Frequency:** daily. **Effective Market(s):** Midwest. **Units of Measure:** Dollars per base box. **Type of Price:** mill. **Time Period Covered:** latest day.

STEEL BLACKPLATE: DOUBLE REDUCED

Source: *American Metal Market.* **Price Frequency:** weekly in Friday issue. **Effective Market(s):** National mills, West Coast. **Units of Measure:** Dollars per base box. **Type of Price:** list. **Time Period Covered:** latest week.

STEEL BLACKPLATE: ELECTROLYTIC, CHROMIUM-COATED, DOUBLE REDUCED

Source: *American Metal Market.* **Price Frequency:** weekly in Friday issue. **Effective Market(s):** National mills, West Coast. **Units of Measure:** Dollars per base box. **Type of Price:** list. **Time Period Covered:** latest week.

STEEL BLACKPLATE: ELECTROLYTIC, CHROMIUM-COATED, SINGLE REDUCED

Source: *American Metal Market.* **Price Frequency:** weekly in Friday issue. **Effective Market(s):** National mills, West Coast. **Units of Measure:** Dollars per base box. **Type of Price:** list. **Time Period Covered:** latest week.

STEEL BLACKPLATE: SINGLE REDUCED

Source: *American Metal Market.* **Price Frequency:** weekly in Friday issue. **Effective Market(s):** National mills, West Coast. **Units of Measure:** Dollars per base box. **Type of Price:** list. **Time Period Covered:** latest week.

STEEL BLACKPLATE: TIN-FREE

Source: *American Metal Market.* **Price Frequency:** daily. **Effective Market(s):** Midwest. **Units of Measure:** Dollars per base box. **Type of Price:** mill. **Time Period Covered:** latest day.

STEEL BRIQUETTABLE BORINGS: SCRAP

Source: *American Metal Market.* **Price Frequency:** daily. **Effective Market(s):** Cincinnati. **Units of Measure:** Dollars per gross ton. **Type of Price:** consumer buying. **Time Period Covered:** latest day.

STEEL BUNDLES: ELECTRIC FURNACE SCRAP

Source: *American Metal Market.* **Price Frequency:** daily. **Effective Market(s):** varies. **Units of Measure:** Dollars per gross ton. **Type of Price:** consumer buying. **Time Period Covered:** latest day.

Source: *Iron Age.* **Price Frequency:** monthly. **Effective Market(s):** Birmingham, Philadelphia, Youngstown. **Units of Measure:** Dollars per gross ton. **Type of Price:** dealer. **Time Period Covered:** latest month.

STEEL BUNDLES: GALVANIZED, SCRAP

Source: *Iron Age.* **Price Frequency:** monthly. **Effective Market(s):** Youngstown. **Units of Measure:** Dollars per gross ton. **Type of Price:** dealer. **Time Period Covered:** latest month.

STEEL BUNDLES: NO. 1, DEALER, SCRAP

Source: *Iron Age.* **Price Frequency:** monthly. **Effective Market(s):** 13 Domestic markets. **Units of Measure:** Dollars per gross ton. **Type of Price:** dealer. **Time Period Covered:** latest month.

STEEL BUNDLES: NO. 1, FACTORY, SCRAP

Source: *American Metal Market.* **Price Frequency:** daily. **Effective Market(s):** varies. **Units of Measure:** Dollars per gross ton. **Type of Price:** consumer buying. **Time Period Covered:** latest day.

Source: *Iron Age.* **Price Frequency:** monthly. **Effective Market(s):** Cleveland, Pittsburgh. **Units of Measure:** Dollars per gross ton. **Type of Price:** dealer. **Time Period Covered:** latest month.

STEEL BUNDLES: NO. 1, SCRAP

Source: *American Metal Market.* **Price Frequency:** daily. **Effective Market(s):** varies. **Units of Measure:** Dollars per gross ton. **Type of Price:** broker buying, consumer buying, export buying. **Time Period Covered:** latest day.

Source: *Iron Age.* **Price Frequency:** monthly. **Effective Market(s):** Detroit. **Units of Measure:** Dollars per gross ton. **Time Period Covered:** latest month.

STEEL BUNDLES: NO. 2, DEALER, SCRAP

Source: *Iron Age.* **Price Frequency:** monthly. **Effective Market(s):** 6 domestic markets. **Units of Measure:** Dollars per gross ton. **Type of Price:** dealer. **Time Period Covered:** latest month.

STEEL BUNDLES: NO. 2, SCRAP

Source: *American Metal Market.* **Price Frequency:** daily. **Effective Market(s):** varies. **Units of Measure:** Dollars per gross ton. **Type of Price:** broker buying, consumer buying, export yard buying. **Time Period Covered:** latest day.

Source: *Iron Age.* **Price Frequency:** monthly. **Effective Market(s):** 11 domestic markets. **Units of Measure:** Dollars per gross ton. **Type of Price:** dealer. **Time Period Covered:** latest month.

Source: *Iron Age.* **Price Frequency:** weekly. **Units of Measure:** Dollars per gross ton. **Type of Price:** composite. **Time Period Covered:** latest week, week ago, month ago, year ago.

STEEL BUNDLES: STAINLESS, SOLIDS AND CLIPPINGS, SCRAP

Source: *American Metal Market.* **Price Frequency:** daily. **Effective Market(s):** varies. **Units of Measure:** cents per lb., dollars per gross ton. **Type of Price:** dealers' buying, consumer buying, export yard buying. **Time Period Covered:** latest day.

STEEL BUNDLES AND SOLIDS: STAINLESS, SCRAP

Source: *American Metal Market.* **Price Frequency:** daily. **Effective Market(s):** varies. **Units of Measure:** Dollars per gross ton. **Type of Price:** consumer buying, export yard buying. **Time Period Covered:** latest day.

STEEL BUSHELING: NO. 1, SCRAP

Source: *American Metal Market.* **Price Frequency:** daily. **Effective Market(s):** varies. **Units of Measure:** Dollars per gross ton. **Type of Price:** broker buying, consumer buying, export yard buying. **Time Period Covered:** latest day.

Source: *Iron Age.* **Price Frequency:** monthly. **Effective Market(s):** 10 domestic markets. **Units of Measure:** Dollars per gross ton. **Type of Price:** dealer. **Time Period Covered:** latest month.

STEEL BUSHELING: PREPARED, NEW FACTORY, SCRAP

Source: *Iron Age.* **Price Frequency:** monthly. **Effective Market(s):** Hamilton (Ontario). **Units of Measure:** Dollars per gross ton. **Type of Price:** broker buying. **Time Period Covered:** latest month.

STEEL BUSHELING: UNPREPARED, NEW FACTORY, SCRAP

Source: *Iron Age.* **Price Frequency:** monthly. **Effective Market(s):** Hamilton (Ontario). **Units of Measure:** Dollars per gross ton. **Type of Price:** broker buying. **Time Period Covered:** latest month.

STEEL BUSHELING: UNPREPARED, SCRAP

Source: *American Metal Market.* **Price Frequency:** daily. **Effective Market(s):** varies. **Units of Measure:** Dollars per gross ton. **Type of Price:** broker buying. **Time Period Covered:** latest day.

STEEL CANS: SCRAP, CLEAN, USED, DENSIFIED

Source: *American Metal Market.* **Price Frequency:** daily. **Effective Market(s):** varies. **Units of Measure:** Dollars per gross ton. **Type of Price:** consumer buying. **Time Period Covered:** latest day.

STEEL CAR AXLES: RAILROAD, SCRAP

Source: *Iron Age.* **Price Frequency:** monthly. **Effective Market(s):** Chicago. **Units of Measure:** Dollars per gross ton. **Type of Price:** dealer. **Time Period Covered:** latest month.

STEEL CAR WHEELS: SCRAP

Source: *American Metal Market.* **Price Frequency:** daily. **Effective Market(s):** Chicago. **Units of Measure:** Dollars per gross ton. **Type of Price:** consumer buying. **Time Period Covered:** latest day.

Source: *Iron Age.* **Price Frequency:** monthly. **Effective Market(s):** Chicago, St. Louis. **Units of Measure:** Dollars per gross ton. **Type of Price:** dealer. **Time Period Covered:** latest month.

STEEL CASING

Source: *American Metal Market.* **Price Frequency:** monthly in Friday issue. **Effective Market(s):** Houston. **Units of Measure:** Dollars per ton. **Type of Price:** market. **Time Period Covered:** latest 2 months.

STEEL CLIPPINGS: STAINLESS, NEW, SCRAP

Source: *American Metal Market.* **Price Frequency:** daily. **Effective Market(s):** varies. **Units of Measure:** cents per lb. **Type of Price:** dealers' buying. **Time Period Covered:** latest day.

STEEL COUPLERS AND KNUCKLERS: RAILROAD, SCRAP

Source: *Iron Age.* **Price Frequency:** monthly. **Effective Market(s):** Chicago. **Units of Measure:** Dollars per gross ton. **Type of Price:** dealer. **Time Period Covered:** latest month.

STEEL COUPLERS AND KNUCKLERS: SCRAP

Source: *American Metal Market.* **Price Frequency:** daily. **Effective Market(s):** Chicago. **Units of Measure:** Dollars per gross ton. **Type of Price:** consumer buying. **Time Period Covered:** latest day.

STEEL GIRDER: RAIL, NO. 1

Source: *American Metal Market.* **Price Frequency:** weekly in Friday issue. **Units of Measure:** Dollars per 100 lbs. **Type of Price:** producer list. **Time Period Covered:** latest week.

STEEL JOINT BAR

Source: *American Metal Market.* **Price Frequency:** weekly in Friday issue. **Units of Measure:** Dollars per 100 lbs. **Type of Price:** producer list. **Time Period Covered:** latest week.

STEEL MOTOR BLOCKS: UNSTRIPPED, SCRAP

Source: *American Metal Market.* **Price Frequency:** daily. **Effective Market(s):** varies. **Units of Measure:** Dollars per gross ton. **Type of Price:** broker buying, consumer buying, export yard buying. **Time Period Covered:** latest day.

Source: *Iron Age.* **Price Frequency:** monthly. **Effective Market(s):** Birmingham, Houston, St. Louis. **Units of Measure:** Dollars per gross ton. **Type of Price:** dealer. **Time Period Covered:** latest month.

STEEL POWDER: STAINLESS

Source: *American Metal Market.* **Price Frequency:** daily. **Units of Measure:** Dollars per lb. **Time Period Covered:** latest day.

STEEL RAILROAD SPECIALTIES: SCRAP

Source: *American Metal Market.* **Price Frequency:** daily. **Effective Market(s):** Pittsburgh. **Units of Measure:** Dollars per gross ton. **Type of Price:** consumer buying. **Time Period Covered:** latest day.

Source: *Iron Age.* **Price Frequency:** monthly. **Effective Market(s):** Philadelphia, Pittsburgh. **Units of Measure:** Dollars per gross ton. **Type of Price:** dealer. **Time Period Covered:** latest month.

STEEL RAILS: SCRAP

Source: *American Metal Market.* **Price Frequency:** daily. **Effective Market(s):** varies. **Units of Measure:** Dollars per gross ton. **Type of Price:** broker buying, consumer buying. **Time Period Covered:** latest day.

Source: *Iron Age.* **Price Frequency:** monthly. **Effective Market(s):** 10 domestic markets. **Units of Measure:** Dollars per gross ton. **Type of Price:** dealer. **Time Period Covered:** latest month.

STEEL REROLLING RAILS: SCRAP

Source: *American Metal Market.* **Price Frequency:** daily. **Effective Market(s):** varies. **Units of Measure:** Dollars per gross ton. **Type of Price:** broker buying, consumer buying. **Time Period Covered:** latest day.

Source: *Iron Age.* **Price Frequency:** monthly. **Effective Market(s):** Chicago, St. Louis. **Units of Measure:** Dollars per gross ton. **Type of Price:** dealer. **Time Period Covered:** latest month.

STEEL SCREW SPIKES

Source: *American Metal Market.* **Price Frequency:** weekly in Friday issue. **Units of Measure:** Dollars per 100 lbs. **Type of Price:** producer list. **Time Period Covered:** latest week.

STEEL SEMI-FINISHED BILLETS: ALLOY FORGING QUALITY

Source: *American Metal Market.* **Price Frequency:** daily. **Effective Market(s):** Midwest. **Units of Measure:** Dollars per net ton. **Type of Price:** mill. **Time Period Covered:** latest day.

STEEL SEMI-FINISHED BILLETS: CARBON FORGING QUALITY

Source: *American Metal Market.* **Price Frequency:** daily. **Effective Market(s):** Midwest. **Units of Measure:** Dollars per net ton. **Type of Price:** mill. **Time Period Covered:** latest day.

STEEL SEMI-FINISHED BILLETS: CARBON REROLLING

Source: *American Metal Market.* **Price Frequency:** daily. **Effective Market(s):** Midwest. **Units of Measure:** Dollars per net ton. **Type of Price:** mill. **Time Period Covered:** latest day.

STEEL SHEET: ALUMINIZED

Source: *American Metal Market.* **Price Frequency:** weekly in Friday issue. **Effective Market(s):** Midwest. **Units of Measure:** Dollars per 100 lbs. **Type of Price:** list. **Time Period Covered:** latest week.

STEEL SHEET: COLD ROLLED

Source: *American Metal Market.* **Price Frequency:** weekly in Friday issue. **Effective Market(s):** Canada, Midwest, West Coast. **Units of Measure:** Canadian dollars per 100 lbs., dollars per 100 lbs. **Type of Price:** list. **Time Period Covered:** latest week.

Source: *American Metal Market.* **Price Frequency:** daily. **Effective Market(s):** Midwest. **Units of Measure:** Dollars per lb. **Type of Price:** mill. **Time Period Covered:** latest day.

STEEL SHEET: COLD ROLLED, CLASS 1

Source: *Purchasing.* **Price Frequency:** monthly. **Units of Measure:** Dollars per ton. **Type of Price:** transaction. **Time Period Covered:** latest day, month ago, 6 months ago, year ago.

STEEL SHEET: ELECTROGALVANIZED

Source: *American Metal Market.* **Price Frequency:** weekly in Friday issue. **Effective Market(s):** Midwest. **Units of Measure:** Dollars per 100 lbs. **Type of Price:** list. **Time Period Covered:** latest week.

Source: *American Metal Market.* **Price Frequency:** daily. **Effective Market(s):** Midwest. **Units of Measure:** Dollars per lb. **Type of Price:** mill. **Time Period Covered:** latest day.

STEEL SHEET: ENAMELING

Source: *American Metal Market.* **Price Frequency:** weekly in Friday issue. **Effective Market(s):** Midwest. **Units of Measure:** Dollars per 100 lbs. **Type of Price:** list. **Time Period Covered:** latest week.

STEEL SHEET: GALVALUME

Source: *American Metal Market.* **Price Frequency:** weekly in Friday issue. **Effective Market(s):** Midwest. **Units of Measure:** Dollars per 100 lbs. **Type of Price:** list. **Time Period Covered:** latest week.

STEEL SHEET: GALVANIZED

Source: *American Metal Market.* **Price Frequency:** daily. **Effective Market(s):** Midwest. **Units of Measure:** Dollars per lb. **Type of Price:** mill. **Time Period Covered:** latest day.

Source: *Commodity Year Book.* **Price Frequency:** annually. **Effective Market(s):** Pittsburgh. **Units of Measure:** cents per lb. **Type of Price:** wholesale. **Time Period Covered:** latest 7 years.

Source: *Purchasing.* **Price Frequency:** monthly. **Units of Measure:** Dollars per ton. **Type of Price:** transaction. **Time Period Covered:** latest day, month ago, 6 months ago, year ago.

Source: *Standard & Poor's Statistical Service Current Statistics.* **Price Frequency:** monthly, annually. **Effective Market(s):** Pittsburgh. **Units of Measure:** cents per lb. **Time Period Covered:** latest 4 years.

STEEL SHEET: GALVANIZED CULVERT

Source: *American Metal Market.* **Price Frequency:** weekly in Friday issue. **Effective Market(s):** Midwest, West Coast. **Units of Measure:** Dollars per 100 lbs. **Type of Price:** list. **Time Period Covered:** latest week.

STEEL SHEET: GALVANNEALED

Source: *American Metal Market.* **Price Frequency:** weekly in Friday issue. **Effective Market(s):** Midwest, West Coast. **Units of Measure:** Dollars per 100 lbs. **Type of Price:** list. **Time Period Covered:** latest week.

STEEL SHEET: HOT DIPPED, GALVANIZED

Source: *American Metal Market.* **Price Frequency:** weekly in Friday issue. **Effective Market(s):** Midwest, West Coast. **Units of Measure:** Dollars per 100 lbs. **Type of Price:** list. **Time Period Covered:** latest week.

STEEL SHEET: HOT ROLLED

Source: *American Metal Market.* **Price Frequency:** weekly in Friday issue. **Effective Market(s):** Canada, Midwest, West Coast. **Units of Measure:** Canadian dollars per 100 lbs., dollars per 100 lbs. **Type of Price:** list. **Time Period Covered:** latest week.

Source: *American Metal Market.* **Price Frequency:** daily. **Effective Market(s):** Midwest. **Units of Measure:** Dollars per lb. **Type of Price:** mill. **Time Period Covered:** latest day.

Source: *Commodity Year Book.* **Price Frequency:** annually. **Effective Market(s):** Pittsburgh. **Units of Measure:** cents per lb. **Type of Price:** wholesale. **Time Period Covered:** latest 7 years.

STEEL SHEET: HOT ROLLED BAND

Source: *American Metal Market.* **Price Frequency:** weekly in Friday issue. **Units of Measure:** Dollars per 100 lbs. **Type of Price:** list. **Time Period Covered:** latest week.

Source: *American Metal Market.* **Price Frequency:** daily. **Effective Market(s):** Midwest. **Units of Measure:** Dollars per lb. **Type of Price:** mill. **Time Period Covered:** latest day.

STEEL SHEET: HOT ROLLED, CLASS 1

Source: *Purchasing.* **Price Frequency:** monthly. **Units of Measure:** Dollars per ton. **Type of Price:** transaction. **Time Period Covered:** latest day, month ago, 6 months ago, year ago.

STEEL SHEET: LONG TERNE

Source: *American Metal Market.* **Price Frequency:** weekly in Friday issue. **Effective Market(s):** Midwest. **Units of Measure:** Dollars per 100 lbs. **Type of Price:** list. **Time Period Covered:** latest week.

STEEL SHEET: LOW ALLOY, HIGH STRENGTH

Source: *American Metal Market.* **Price Frequency:** weekly in Friday issue. **Units of Measure:** Dollars per 100 lbs. **Type of Price:** list. **Time Period Covered:** latest week.

Source: *American Metal Market.* **Price Frequency:** daily. **Effective Market(s):** Midwest. **Units of Measure:** Dollars per lb. **Type of Price:** mill. **Time Period Covered:** latest day.

STEEL SHEET: MOTOR LAMINATION

Source: *American Metal Market.* **Price Frequency:** weekly in Friday issue. **Effective Market(s):** Midwest, West Coast. **Units of Measure:** Dollars per 100 lbs. **Type of Price:** list. **Time Period Covered:** latest week.

STEEL SHEET: STAINLESS

Source: *American Metal Market.* **Price Frequency:** daily. **Effective Market(s):** Midwest. **Units of Measure:** Dollars per lb. **Type of Price:** mill. **Time Period Covered:** latest day.

Source: *ENR.* **Price Frequency:** monthly in second issue of month. **Effective Market(s):** 15 domestic markets, Montreal. **Units of Measure:** Dollars per 100 lbs. **Type of Price:** spot. **Time Period Covered:** latest month.

STEEL SHEET: STAINLESS, COLD ROLLED

Source: *American Metal Market.* **Price Frequency:** weekly in Friday issue. **Units of Measure:** cents per lb. **Type of Price:** base, distributor. **Time Period Covered:** latest week.

STEEL SLAB

Source: *Economic and Energy Indicators.* **Price Frequency:** biweekly. **Units of Measure:** Dollars per long ton. **Time Period Covered:** latest 3 months, quarters, and years.

STEEL STRIP: ALLOY, COLD ROLLED

Source: *American Metal Market.* **Price Frequency:** daily. **Effective Market(s):** Midwest. **Units of Measure:** Dollars per 100 lbs. **Type of Price:** mill. **Time Period Covered:** latest day.

Source: *American Metal Market.* **Price Frequency:** weekly in Friday issue. **Units of Measure:** Dollars per 100 lbs. **Type of Price:** base, composite. **Time Period Covered:** latest week.

STEEL STRIP: ALLOY, HOT ROLLED

Source: *American Metal Market.* **Price Frequency:** daily. **Effective Market(s):** Midwest. **Units of Measure:** Dollars per 100 lbs. **Type of Price:** mill. **Time Period Covered:** latest day.

Source: *American Metal Market.* **Price Frequency:** weekly in Friday issue. **Units of Measure:** Dollars per 100 lbs. **Type of Price:** base, composite. **Time Period Covered:** latest week.

STEEL STRIP: CARBON, COLD ROLLED

Source: *American Metal Market.* **Price Frequency:** daily. **Effective Market(s):** Midwest. **Units of Measure:** Dollars per 100 lbs. **Type of Price:** mill. **Time Period Covered:** latest day.

Source: *American Metal Market.* **Price Frequency:** weekly in Friday issue. **Units of Measure:** Dollars per 100 lbs. **Type of Price:** base, composite. **Time Period Covered:** latest week.

STEEL STRIP: CARBON, HOT ROLLED

Source: *American Metal Market.* **Price Frequency:** daily. **Effective Market(s):** Midwest. **Units of Measure:** Dollars per 100 lbs. **Type of Price:** mill. **Time Period Covered:** latest day.

Source: *American Metal Market.* **Price Frequency:** weekly in Friday issue. **Units of Measure:** Dollars per 100 lbs. **Type of Price:** base, composite. **Time Period Covered:** latest week.

STEEL STRIP: COLD ROLLED

Source: *Commodity Year Book.* **Price Frequency:** annually. **Effective Market(s):** Pittsburgh. **Units of Measure:** cents per lb. **Type of Price:** wholesale. **Time Period Covered:** latest 7 years.

STEEL STRIP: SPRING

Source: *American Metal Market.* **Price Frequency:** daily. **Effective Market(s):** Midwest. **Units of Measure:** Dollars per 100 lbs. **Type of Price:** mill. **Time Period Covered:** latest day.

STEEL STRIP: SPRING, HIGH CARBON, COLD ROLLED

Source: *American Metal Market.* **Price Frequency:** weekly in Friday issue. **Units of Measure:** Dollars per 100 lbs. **Type of Price:** base, composite. **Time Period Covered:** latest week.

STEEL STRIP: STAINLESS

Source: *American Metal Market.* **Price Frequency:** daily. **Effective Market(s):** Midwest. **Units of Measure:** Dollars per 100 lbs. **Type of Price:** mill. **Time Period Covered:** latest day.

STEEL STRIP: STAINLESS, COLD ROLLED

Source: *American Metal Market.* **Price Frequency:** weekly in Friday issue. **Units of Measure:** cents per lb. **Type of Price:** base, distributor. **Time Period Covered:** latest week.

STEEL TINPLATE

Source: *American Metal Market.* **Price Frequency:** weekly in Friday issue. **Units of Measure:** Dollars per 100 lbs. **Type of Price:** producer list. **Time Period Covered:** latest week.

Source: *Commodity Year Book.* **Price Frequency:** annually. **Effective Market(s):** Pittsburgh. **Units of Measure:** cents per lb. **Type of Price:** wholesale. **Time Period Covered:** latest 6 years.

Source: *Standard & Poor's Statistical Service Current Statistics.* **Price Frequency:** monthly, annually. **Units of Measure:** Dollars per base box. **Time Period Covered:** latest 4 years.

STEEL TINPLATE: BLACK

Source: *American Metal Market.* **Price Frequency:** daily. **Effective Market(s):** Midwest. **Units of Measure:** Dollars per base box. **Type of Price:** mill. **Time Period Covered:** latest day.

STEEL TINPLATE: ELECTROLYTIC

Source: *American Metal Market.* **Price Frequency:** daily. **Effective Market(s):** Midwest. **Units of Measure:** Dollars per base box. **Type of Price:** mill. **Time Period Covered:** latest day.

STEEL TINPLATE: ELECTROLYTIC, DOUBLE REDUCED

Source: *American Metal Market.* **Price Frequency:** weekly in Friday issue. **Effective Market(s):** National mills, West Coast. **Units of Measure:** Dollars per base box. **Type of Price:** list. **Time Period Covered:** latest week.

STEEL TINPLATE: ELECTROLYTIC, SINGLE REDUCED

Source: *American Metal Market.* **Price Frequency:** weekly in Friday issue. **Effective Market(s):** National mills, West Coast. **Units of Measure:** Dollars per base box. **Type of Price:** list. **Time Period Covered:** latest week.

STEEL TRACK BOLTS: UNTREATED

Source: *American Metal Market.* **Price Frequency:** weekly in Friday issue. **Units of Measure:** Dollars per 100 lbs. **Type of Price:** producer list. **Time Period Covered:** latest week.

STEEL TRACK SPIKES: STANDARD

Source: *American Metal Market.* **Price Frequency:** weekly in Friday issue. **Units of Measure:** Dollars per 100 lbs. **Type of Price:** producer list. **Time Period Covered:** latest week.

STEEL TUBING

Source: *American Metal Market.* **Price Frequency:** monthly in Friday issue. **Effective Market(s):** Houston. **Units of Measure:** Dollars per ton. **Type of Price:** market. **Time Period Covered:** latest 2 months.

STEEL WIRE: MANUFACTURERS' BRIGHT COARSE

Source: *American Metal Market.* **Price Frequency:** daily. **Effective Market(s):** Midwest. **Units of Measure:** Dollars per lb. **Type of Price:** mill. **Time Period Covered:** latest day.

STEEL WIRE: MERCHANT QUALITY, GALVANIZED

Source: *American Metal Market.* **Price Frequency:** daily. **Effective Market(s):** Midwest. **Units of Measure:** Dollars per lb. **Type of Price:** mill. **Time Period Covered:** latest day.

STEEL WIRE: SPRING, HIGH CARBON

Source: *American Metal Market.* **Price Frequency:** daily. **Effective Market(s):** Midwest. **Units of Measure:** Dollars per lb. **Type of Price:** mill. **Time Period Covered:** latest day.

STEEL WIRE: STAINLESS

Source: *American Metal Market.* **Price Frequency:** weekly in Friday issue. **Units of Measure:** cents per lb. **Type of Price:** base, distributor. **Time Period Covered:** latest week.

Source: *American Metal Market.* **Price Frequency:** daily. **Effective Market(s):** Midwest. **Units of Measure:** Dollars per lb. **Type of Price:** mill. **Time Period Covered:** latest day.

STEEL WIRE ROD

Source: *American Metal Market.* **Price Frequency:** daily. **Effective Market(s):** Midwest. **Units of Measure:** Dollars per lb. **Type of Price:** mill. **Time Period Covered:** latest day.

Source: *Commodity Year Book.* **Price Frequency:** annually. **Effective Market(s):** Chicago. **Units of Measure:** Dollars per ton. **Type of Price:** wholesale. **Time Period Covered:** latest 7 years.

STEEL WIRE ROD: CARBON

Source: *Purchasing.* **Price Frequency:** monthly. **Units of Measure:** Dollars per ton. **Type of Price:** transaction. **Time Period Covered:** latest day, month ago, 6 months ago, year ago.

STEER BEEF

see Beef: Steer.

STEER CARCASS: CHOICE, 700-900 LBS

Source: *Feedstuffs.* **Price Frequency:** weekly. **Effective Market(s):** Chicago. **Units of Measure:** cents per lb. **Time Period Covered:** latest week, week ago, 6 months ago, year ago.

STEERS

see also Bulls, Cattle, Cows, Heifers.

Source: *FAO Quarterly Bulletin of Statistics.* **Price Frequency:** monthly, annually. **Effective Market(s):** Omaha (NE). **Units of Measure:** Dollars per 100 lbs., dollars per metric ton. **Type of Price:** wholesale. **Time Period Covered:** latest 3 years.

Source: *Farm and Dairy.* **Price Frequency:** weekly. **Effective Market(s):** Oklahoma/Texas. **Units of Measure:** Dollars per 100 lbs. **Time Period Covered:** latest week, year ago.

Source: *Scottish Farmer.* **Price Frequency:** weekly. **Effective Market(s):** Scotland. **Units of Measure:** British pence per kilogram. **Type of Price:** average. **Time Period Covered:** latest week.

Source: *Scottish Farmer.* **Price Frequency:** weekly. **Effective Market(s):** 33 Scottish markets. **Units of Measure:** British pence per kilogram. **Time Period Covered:** latest week.

Source: *Wall Street Journal.* **Price Frequency:** daily. **Effective Market(s):** Oklahoma/Texas. **Units of Measure:** Dollars per 100 lbs. **Time Period Covered:** latest day, day ago, year ago.

STEERS: ADULT, STORE, GOOD

Source: *New Zealand Farmer.* **Price Frequency:** weekly, seasonally. **Effective Market(s):** 7 New Zealand markets. **Units of Measure:** New Zealand dollars per head. **Time Period Covered:** latest 2 weeks.

STEERS: ADULT, STORE, MEDIUM

Source: *New Zealand Farmer.* **Price Frequency:** weekly, seasonally. **Effective Market(s):** 7 New Zealand markets. **Units of Measure:** New Zealand dollars per head. **Time Period Covered:** latest 2 weeks.

STEERS: ALL BREEDS, STORE

Source: *Farmers Weekly.* **Price Frequency:** weekly. **Effective Market(s):** Great Britain. **Units of Measure:** British pence per kilogram. **Type of Price:** spot. **Time Period Covered:** latest week, week ago, year ago.

Source: *Scottish Farmer.* **Price Frequency:** weekly. **Effective Market(s):** Aberdeen (Scotland), Stirling (Scotland). **Units of Measure:** British pence per kilogram. **Time Period Covered:** latest week.

STEERS: ANGUS AND ANGUS X, STORE

Source: *Farmers Weekly.* **Price Frequency:** weekly. **Effective Market(s):** 15 British market average. **Units of Measure:** British pence per kilogram. **Type of Price:** average. **Time Period Covered:** latest week.

STEERS: ANGUS-ANGUS AND ANGUS-ANGUS X, STORE

Source: *Scottish Farmer.* **Price Frequency:** weekly. **Effective Market(s):** Aberdeen (Scotland), Stirling (Scotland). **Units of Measure:** British pence per kilogram. **Time Period Covered:** latest week.

STEERS: BEEF

Source: *Commodity Year Book.* **Price Frequency:** monthly, annually. **Effective Market(s):** Omaha (NE). **Units of Measure:** Dollars per 100 lbs. **Type of Price:** wholesale. **Time Period Covered:** latest 4 years.

Source: *Survey of Current Business.* **Price Frequency:** monthly, annually. **Effective Market(s):** Omaha (NE). **Units of Measure:** Dollars per 100 lbs. **Type of Price:** wholesale. **Time Period Covered:** latest year.

STEERS: BEEF, CHAROLAIS X, HEAVY

Source: *Farmers Weekly.* **Price Frequency:** weekly. **Effective Market(s):** England/Wales. **Units of Measure:** British pence per kilogram. **Time Period Covered:** latest week.

STEERS: BEEF, CHAROLAIS X, LIGHT

Source: *Farmers Weekly.* **Price Frequency:** weekly. **Effective Market(s):** England/Wales. **Units of Measure:** British pence per kilogram. **Time Period Covered:** latest week.

STEERS: BEEF, CHAROLAIS X, MEDIUM

Source: *Farmers Weekly.* **Price Frequency:** weekly. **Effective Market(s):** England/Wales. **Units of Measure:** British pence per kilogram. **Time Period Covered:** latest week.

STEERS: BEEF, CHOICE

Source: *Agricultural Outlook.* **Price Frequency:** monthly, annually. **Effective Market(s):** Chicago. **Units of Measure:** Dollars per 100 lbs. **Type of Price:** wholesale. **Time Period Covered:** monthly latest 6 months, annually latest 3 years.

Source: *Economic and Energy Indicators.* **Price Frequency:** monthly, quarterly, annually. **Units of Measure:** cents per lb. **Time Period Covered:** latest 3 months, quarters and years.

Source: *Livestock and Poultry Situation and Outlook Report.* **Price Frequency:** monthly. **Effective Market(s):** Central United States, West Coast. **Units of Measure:** Dollars per 100 lbs. **Type of Price:** wholesale. **Time Period Covered:** latest year.

Source: *Livestock and Poultry Update.* **Price Frequency:** monthly. **Effective Market(s):** Central United States. **Units of Measure:** Dollars per 100 lbs. **Type of Price:** wholesale. **Time Period Covered:** latest 3 months, year ago.

Source: *Meat and Dairy Products.* **Price Frequency:** monthly. **Effective Market(s):** Central United States. **Units of Measure:** Dollars per 100 lbs. **Type of Price:** wholesale. **Time Period Covered:** latest 4 years.

STEERS: BEEF, CHOICE, 900-1,300 LBS

Source: *Feedstuffs.* **Price Frequency:** weekly. **Effective Market(s):** Omaha (NE). **Units of Measure:** cents per lb. **Time Period Covered:** latest week, week ago, 6 months ago, year ago.

STEERS: BEEF, CHOICE AND GOOD

Source: *Commodity Year Book.* **Price Frequency:** annually. **Effective Market(s):** Omaha (NE). **Units of Measure:** Dollars per 100 lbs. **Type of Price:** wholesale. **Time Period Covered:** latest 5 years.

STEERS: BEEF, CHOICE, DRESSED

Source: *Commodity Year Book.* **Price Frequency:** annually. **Units of Measure:** Dollars per 100 lbs. **Type of Price:** wholesale. **Time Period Covered:** latest 4 years.

STEERS: BEEF, CHOICE, YIELD 3

Source: *National Provisioner.* **Price Frequency:** daily. **Effective Market(s):** Midwest River area. **Units of Measure:** cents per lb. **Time Period Covered:** latest week.

STEERS: BEEF, CHOICE, YIELD 4

Source: *National Provisioner.* **Price Frequency:** daily. **Effective Market(s):** Midwest River area. **Units of Measure:** cents per lb. **Time Period Covered:** latest week.

STEERS: BEEF, DRESSED, 700-900 LBS

Source: *Journal of Commerce and Commercial.* **Price Frequency:** daily. **Effective Market(s):** Midwest. **Units of Measure:** Dollars per 100 lbs. **Type of Price:** spot supplier. **Time Period Covered:** latest day.

STEERS: BEEF, FRESIAN/HOLSTEIN, HEAVY

Source: *Farmers Weekly.* **Price Frequency:** weekly. **Effective Market(s):** England/Wales. **Units of Measure:** British pence per kilogram. **Time Period Covered:** latest week.

STEERS: BEEF, FRESIAN/HOLSTEIN, LIGHT

Source: *Farmers Weekly.* **Price Frequency:** weekly. **Effective Market(s):** England/Wales. **Units of Measure:** British pence per kilogram. **Time Period Covered:** latest week.

STEERS: BEEF, FRESIAN/HOLSTEIN, MEDIUM

Source: *Farmers Weekly.* **Price Frequency:** weekly. **Effective Market(s):** England/Wales. **Units of Measure:** British pence per kilogram. **Time Period Covered:** latest week.

STEERS: BEEF, HEREFORD CROSS, HEAVY

Source: *Farmers Weekly.* **Price Frequency:** weekly. **Effective Market(s):** England/Wales. **Units of Measure:** British pence per kilogram. **Time Period Covered:** latest week.

STEERS: BEEF, HEREFORD CROSS, LIGHT

Source: *Farmers Weekly.* **Price Frequency:** weekly. **Effective Market(s):** England/Wales. **Units of Measure:** British pence per kilogram. **Time Period Covered:** latest week.

STEERS: BEEF, HEREFORD CROSS, MEDIUM

Source: *Farmers Weekly.* **Price Frequency:** weekly. **Effective Market(s):** England/Wales. **Units of Measure:** British pence per kilogram. **Time Period Covered:** latest week.

STEERS: BEEF, LIMOUSIN X, HEAVY

Source: *Farmers Weekly.* **Price Frequency:** weekly. **Effective Market(s):** England/Wales. **Units of Measure:** British pence per kilogram. **Time Period Covered:** latest week.

STEERS: BEEF, LIMOUSIN X, LIGHT

Source: *Farmers Weekly.* **Price Frequency:** weekly. **Effective Market(s):** England/Wales. **Units of Measure:** British pence per kilogram. **Time Period Covered:** latest week.

STEERS: BEEF, LIMOUSIN X, MEDIUM

Source: *Farmers Weekly.* **Price Frequency:** weekly. **Effective Market(s):** England/Wales. **Units of Measure:** British pence per kilogram. **Time Period Covered:** latest week.

STEERS: BEEF, SIMMENTAL X, HEAVY

Source: *Farmers Weekly.* **Price Frequency:** weekly. **Effective Market(s):** England/Wales. **Units of Measure:** British pence per kilogram. **Time Period Covered:** latest week.

STEERS: BEEF, SIMMENTAL X, LIGHT

Source: *Farmers Weekly.* **Price Frequency:** weekly. **Effective Market(s):** England/Wales. **Units of Measure:** British pence per kilogram. **Time Period Covered:** latest week.

STEERS: BEEF, SIMMENTAL X, MEDIUM

Source: *Farmers Weekly.* **Price Frequency:** weekly. **Effective Market(s):** England/Wales. **Units of Measure:** British pence per kilogram. **Time Period Covered:** latest week.

STEERS: BELGIAN BLUE AND BELGIAN BLUE X, STORE

Source: *Farmers Weekly.* **Price Frequency:** weekly. **Effective Market(s):** 15 British market average. **Units of Measure:** British pence per kilogram. **Type of Price:** average. **Time Period Covered:** latest week.

STEERS: BELGIAN BLUE X, STORE

Source: *Scottish Farmer.* **Price Frequency:** weekly. **Effective Market(s):** Aberdeen (Scotland), Stirling (Scotland). **Units of Measure:** British pence per kilogram. **Time Period Covered:** latest week.

STEERS: BULLS

Source: *Farm and Dairy.* **Price Frequency:** weekly, seasonally. **Effective Market(s):** Ohio, Pennsylvania. **Units of Measure:** Dollars per head. **Type of Price:** auction high, auction low. **Time Period Covered:** latest week.

STEERS: CHAROLAIS AND CHAROLAIS X, STORE

Source: *Farmers Weekly.* **Price Frequency:** weekly. **Effective Market(s):** 15 British market average. **Units of Measure:** British pence per kilogram. **Type of Price:** average. **Time Period Covered:** latest week.

STEERS: CHAROLAIS X, STORE

Source: *Scottish Farmer.* **Price Frequency:** weekly. **Effective Market(s):** Aberdeen (Scotland), Stirling (Scotland). **Units of Measure:** British pence per kilogram. **Time Period Covered:** latest week.

STEERS: CHOICE

Source: *Agricultural Outlook.* **Price Frequency:** quarterly, annually. **Effective Market(s):** Omaha (NE). **Units of Measure:** Dollars per 100 lbs. **Type of Price:** average. **Time Period Covered:** latest year.

Source: *Agricultural Outlook.* **Price Frequency:** monthly, annually. **Effective Market(s):** Omaha (NE). **Units of Measure:** Dollars per 100 lbs. **Type of Price:** market. **Time Period Covered:** monthly latest 6 months, annually latest 3 years.

Source: *Agriculture.* **Price Frequency:** weekly. **Effective Market(s):** Omaha (NE), Sioux City (IA), Sioux Falls (SD), St. Paul, Texas Panhandle. **Units of Measure:** Dollars per 100 lbs. **Time Period Covered:** latest week.

Source: *Asian Wall Street Journal.* **Price Frequency:** daily. **Effective Market(s):** Oklahoma/Texas. **Units of Measure:** Dollars per 100 lbs. **Type of Price:** cash. **Time Period Covered:** latest 2 days, year ago.

Source: *Doane's Agricultural Report.* **Price Frequency:** weekly. **Effective Market(s):** Omaha (NE). **Units of Measure:** Dollars per 100 lbs. **Time Period Covered:** latest week, week ago, year ago.

Source: *Farm and Dairy.* **Price Frequency:** weekly, seasonally. **Effective Market(s):** Ohio, Pennsylvania. **Units of Measure:** Dollars per head. **Type of Price:** auction high, auction low. **Time Period Covered:** latest week.

Source: *Livestock and Poultry Situation and Outlook Report.* **Price Frequency:** quarterly, annually. **Effective Market(s):** Omaha (NE). **Units of Measure:** Dollars per 100 lbs. **Time Period Covered:** latest 2 years.

Source: *Livestock and Poultry Situation and Outlook Report.* **Price Frequency:** monthly. **Effective Market(s):** California, Colorado, Omaha (NE), Texas. **Units of Measure:** Dollars per 100 lbs. **Time Period Covered:** latest year.

Source: *Wall Street Journal.* **Price Frequency:** daily. **Effective Market(s):** Oklahoma/Texas. **Units of Measure:** Dollars per 100 lbs. **Time Period Covered:** latest day, day ago, year ago.

STEERS: CHOICE 2-4

Source: *Livestock, Meat, Wool Market News.* **Price Frequency:** weekly, seasonally. **Units of Measure:** Dollars per 100 lbs. **Type of Price:** average. **Time Period Covered:** latest week, year ago.

Source: *Utah Farmer-Stockman.* **Price Frequency:** monthly, seasonally. **Effective Market(s):** Arizona/California, Central Plains, Midwest. **Units of Measure:** Dollars per 100 lbs. **Time Period Covered:** latest month.

STEERS: DEADWEIGHT

Source: *Farmers Weekly.* **Price Frequency:** weekly. **Effective Market(s):** Great Britain. **Units of Measure:** British pence per kilogram. **Time Period Covered:** latest week.

Source: *Scottish Farmer.* **Price Frequency:** weekly. **Effective Market(s):** Scotland. **Units of Measure:** British pence per kilogram. **Time Period Covered:** latest week.

STEERS: FAT

Source: *Lancaster Farming.* **Price Frequency:** weekly. **Effective Market(s):** Pennsylvania, Virginia. **Units of Measure:** Dollars per head. **Type of Price:** auction. **Time Period Covered:** latest week.

STEERS: FEEDER

Source: *Agriculture.* **Price Frequency:** weekly. **Effective Market(s):** 8 domestic markets. **Units of Measure:** Dollars per 100 lbs. **Time Period Covered:** latest week, week ago, year ago.

Source: *Asian Wall Street Journal.* **Price Frequency:** daily. **Effective Market(s):** Oklahoma City. **Units of Measure:** Dollars per 100 lbs. **Type of Price:** cash. **Time Period Covered:** latest 2 days, year ago.

Source: *California Farmer.* **Price Frequency:** semimonthly. **Effective Market(s):** Stockton (CA). **Units of Measure:** Dollars per 100 lbs. **Time Period Covered:** latest week, month ago, year ago.

Source: *Commodity Year Book.* **Price Frequency:** annually. **Effective Market(s):** Kansas City. **Units of Measure:** Dollars per 100 lbs. **Type of Price:** wholesale. **Time Period Covered:** latest 5 years.

Source: *Farm and Dairy.* **Price Frequency:** weekly. **Effective Market(s):** Oklahoma City. **Units of Measure:** Dollars per 100 lbs. **Time Period Covered:** latest week, year ago.

Source: *Farm and Dairy.* **Price Frequency:** weekly, seasonally. **Effective Market(s):** Ohio, Pennsylvania. **Units of Measure:** Dollars per head. **Type of Price:** auction high, auction low. **Time Period Covered:** latest week.

Source: *Fedgazette.* **Price Frequency:** monthly. **Effective Market(s):** South St. Paul. **Units of Measure:** Dollars per 100 lbs. **Time Period Covered:** latest 24 months.

Source: *Oregon Farmer-Stockman.* **Price Frequency:** monthly. **Effective Market(s):** Klamath Falls (OR), Portland (OR). **Units of Measure:** Dollars per 100 lbs. **Type of Price:** auction. **Time Period Covered:** latest month.

Source: *Utah Farmer-Stockman.* **Price Frequency:** monthly. **Effective Market(s):** Salina (UT), Spanish Fork (UT). **Units of Measure:** Dollars per 100 lbs. **Type of Price:** auction. **Time Period Covered:** latest month.

Source: *Viewpoint.* **Price Frequency:** weekly. **Effective Market(s):** 11 domestic markets. **Units of Measure:** Dollars per 100 lbs. **Time Period Covered:** latest week.

Source: *Wall Street Journal.* **Price Frequency:** daily. **Effective Market(s):** Oklahoma City. **Units of Measure:** Dollars per 100 lbs. **Time Period Covered:** latest day, day ago, year ago.

STEERS: FEEDER, 4-500 LBS

Source: *Doane's Agricultural Report.* **Price Frequency:** weekly. **Effective Market(s):** Oklahoma City. **Units of Measure:** Dollars per 100 lbs. **Time Period Covered:** latest week, week ago, year ago.

STEERS: FEEDER, 6-700 LBS

Source: *Doane's Agricultural Report.* **Price Frequency:** weekly. **Effective Market(s):** Oklahoma City. **Units of Measure:** Dollars per 100 lbs. **Time Period Covered:** latest week, week ago, year ago.

Source: *Feedstuffs.* **Price Frequency:** weekly. **Effective Market(s):** Oklahoma City. **Units of Measure:** cents per lb. **Time Period Covered:** latest week, week ago, 6 months ago, year ago.

STEERS: FEEDER, MEDIUM NO.1

Source: *Livestock, Meat, Wool Market News.* **Price Frequency:** weekly, seasonally. **Units of Measure:** Dollars per 100 lbs. **Type of Price:** average. **Time Period Covered:** latest week, year ago.

STEERS: FEEDER, MEDIUM AND LARGE NO. 1

Source: *Idaho Farmer-Stockman.* **Price Frequency:** monthly. **Effective Market(s):** Idaho. **Units of Measure:** Dollars per 100 lbs. **Time Period Covered:** latest month.

Source: *Montana Farmer-Stockman.* **Price Frequency:** monthly. **Effective Market(s):** Billings (MT), Riverton (WY), Torrington (WY). **Units of Measure:** Dollars per 100 lbs. **Type of Price:** auction. **Time Period Covered:** latest month.

Source: *Oregon Farmer-Stockman.* **Price Frequency:** monthly. **Effective Market(s):** Oregon/Washington. **Time Period Covered:** latest month.

Source: *Washington Farmer-Stockman.* **Price Frequency:** monthly. **Effective Market(s):** Oregon/Washington. **Units of Measure:** Dollars per 100 lbs. **Time Period Covered:** latest month.

STEERS: FEEDER, MEDIUM NO. 1

Source: *Livestock and Poultry Situation and Outlook Report.* **Price Frequency:** monthly. **Effective Market(s):** Amarillo (TX), Georgia, Kansas City, Oklahoma City. **Units of Measure:** Dollars per 100 lbs. **Time Period Covered:** latest year.

Source: *Livestock and Poultry Update.* **Price Frequency:** monthly. **Effective Market(s):** Oklahoma City. **Units of Measure:** Dollars per 100 lbs. **Time Period Covered:** latest 3 month, year ago.

Source: *Livestock, Meat, Wool Market News.* **Price Frequency:** weekly, seasonally. **Effective Market(s):** 10 domestic markets. **Units of Measure:** Dollars per 100 lbs. **Type of Price:** average. **Time Period Covered:** latest week, year ago.

STEERS: FEEDER, MEDIUM NO. 2

Source: *Livestock and Poultry Situation and Outlook Report.* **Price Frequency:** monthly. **Effective Market(s):** Georgia. **Units of Measure:** Dollars per 100 lbs. **Time Period Covered:** latest year.

Source: *Livestock, Meat, Wool Market News.* **Price Frequency:** weekly, seasonally. **Effective Market(s):** California, Colorado/Kansas, Georgia, Illinois, Kentucky. **Units of Measure:** Dollars per 100 lbs. **Type of Price:** average. **Time Period Covered:** latest week, year ago.

STEERS: FINISHED

Source: *Farmers Weekly.* **Price Frequency:** weekly. **Effective Market(s):** Great Britain. **Units of Measure:** British pence per kilogram. **Type of Price:** spot. **Time Period Covered:** latest week, week ago, year ago.

STEERS: FRIESIAN/HOLSTEIN, STORE

Source: *Farmers Weekly.* **Price Frequency:** weekly. **Effective Market(s):** 15 British market average. **Units of Measure:** British pence per kilogram. **Type of Price:** average. **Time Period Covered:** latest week.

Source: *Scottish Farmer.* **Price Frequency:** weekly. **Effective Market(s):** Aberdeen (Scotland), Stirling (Scotland). **Units of Measure:** British pence per kilogram. **Time Period Covered:** latest week.

STEERS: G2

Source: *New Zealand Farmer.* **Price Frequency:** weekly, seasonally. **Effective Market(s):** 8 New Zealand markets. **Units of Measure:** New Zealand cents per kilogram. **Type of Price:** export price. **Time Period Covered:** latest week.

STEERS: GOOD

Source: *Farm and Dairy.* **Price Frequency:** weekly, seasonally. **Effective Market(s):** Ohio, Pennsylvania. **Units of Measure:** Dollars per head. **Type of Price:** auction high, auction low. **Time Period Covered:** latest week.

STEERS: HEAVY

Source: *Farmers Weekly.* **Price Frequency:** weekly, seasonally. **Effective Market(s):** over 170 British markets. **Units of Measure:** British pence per kilogram. **Type of Price:** auction. **Time Period Covered:** latest week.

STEERS: HEAVY, PRIME

Source: *New Zealand Farmer.* **Price Frequency:** weekly, seasonally. **Effective Market(s):** 7 New Zealand markets. **Units of Measure:** New Zealand dollars per head. **Time Period Covered:** latest 2 weeks.

STEERS: HEREFORD AND HEREFORD X, STORE

Source: *Farmers Weekly.* **Price Frequency:** weekly. **Effective Market(s):** 15 British market average. **Units of Measure:** British pence per kilogram. **Type of Price:** average. **Time Period Covered:** latest week.

Source: *Scottish Farmer.* **Price Frequency:** weekly. **Effective Market(s):** Aberdeen (Scotland), Stirling (Scotland). **Units of Measure:** British pence per kilogram. **Time Period Covered:** latest week.

STEERS: HOLSTEIN

Source: *Farm and Dairy.* **Price Frequency:** weekly, seasonally. **Effective Market(s):** Ohio, Pennsylvania. **Units of Measure:** Dollars per head. **Type of Price:** auction high, auction low. **Time Period Covered:** latest week.

STEERS: HOLSTEIN, CHOICE

Source: *National Provisioner.* **Price Frequency:** daily. **Effective Market(s):** Midwest River area. **Units of Measure:** cents per lb. **Time Period Covered:** latest week.

STEERS: HOLSTEIN, LARGE NO. 2

Source: *Montana Farmer-Stockman.* **Price Frequency:** monthly. **Effective Market(s):** Billings (MT). **Units of Measure:** Dollars per 100 lbs. **Type of Price:** auction. **Time Period Covered:** latest month.

STEERS: HOLSTEIN, SELECT

Source: *National Provisioner.* **Price Frequency:** daily. **Effective Market(s):** Midwest River area. **Units of Measure:** cents per lb. **Time Period Covered:** latest week.

STEERS: HOT WEIGHT, MOSTLY CHOICE

Source: *Drovers Journal.* **Price Frequency:** semimonthly. **Effective Market(s):** 8 domestic markets. **Units of Measure:** Dollars per 100 lbs. **Time Period Covered:** selected date.

STEERS: K2

Source: *New Zealand Farmer.* **Price Frequency:** weekly, seasonally. **Effective Market(s):** 8 New Zealand markets. **Units of Measure:** New Zealand cents per kilogram. **Type of Price:** export price. **Time Period Covered:** latest week.

STEERS: LIGHT

Source: *Farmers Weekly.* **Price Frequency:** weekly, seasonally. **Effective Market(s):** over 170 British markets. **Units of Measure:** British pence per kilogram. **Type of Price:** auction. **Time Period Covered:** latest week.

STEERS: LIGHT, PRIME

Source: *New Zealand Farmer.* **Price Frequency:** weekly, seasonally. **Effective Market(s):** 7 New Zealand markets. **Units of Measure:** New Zealand dollars per head. **Time Period Covered:** latest 2 weeks.

STEERS: LIMOUSIN AND LIMOUSIN X, STORE

Source: *Farmers Weekly.* **Price Frequency:** weekly. **Effective Market(s):** 15 British market average. **Units of Measure:** British pence per kilogram. **Type of Price:** average. **Time Period Covered:** latest week.

STEERS: LIMOUSIN X, STORE

Source: *Scottish Farmer.* **Price Frequency:** weekly. **Effective Market(s):** Aberdeen (Scotland), Stirling (Scotland). **Units of Measure:** British pence per kilogram. **Time Period Covered:** latest week.

STEERS: MEDIUM

Source: *Farmers Weekly.* **Price Frequency:** weekly, seasonally. **Effective Market(s):** over 170 British markets. **Units of Measure:** British pence per kilogram. **Type of Price:** auction. **Time Period Covered:** latest week.

STEERS: MEDIUM AND LARGE 1

Source: *Drovers Journal.* **Price Frequency:** semimonthly. **Effective Market(s):** 80 domestic markets. **Units of Measure:** Dollars per 100 lbs. **Time Period Covered:** latest week.

STEERS: MEDIUM, PRIME

Source: *New Zealand Farmer.* **Price Frequency:** weekly, seasonally. **Effective Market(s):** 7 New Zealand markets. **Units of Measure:** New Zealand dollars per head. **Time Period Covered:** latest 2 weeks.

STEERS: NON-HOLSTEIN, SELECT

Source: *National Provisioner.* **Price Frequency:** daily. **Effective Market(s):** Midwest River area. **Units of Measure:** cents per lb. **Time Period Covered:** latest week.

STEERS: P2

Source: *New Zealand Farmer.* **Price Frequency:** weekly, seasonally. **Effective Market(s):** 8 New Zealand markets. **Units of Measure:** New Zealand cents per kilogram. **Type of Price:** export price. **Time Period Covered:** latest week.

STEERS: RISING 1 YEAR, STORE, GOOD

Source: *New Zealand Farmer.* **Price Frequency:** weekly, seasonally. **Effective Market(s):** 7 New Zealand markets. **Units of Measure:** New Zealand dollars per head. **Time Period Covered:** latest 2 weeks.

STEERS: RISING 1 YEAR, STORE, MEDIUM

Source: *New Zealand Farmer.* **Price Frequency:** weekly, seasonally. **Effective Market(s):** 7 New Zealand markets. **Units of Measure:** New Zealand dollars per head. **Time Period Covered:** latest 2 weeks.

STEERS: RISING 2 YEAR, STORE, GOOD

Source: *New Zealand Farmer.* **Price Frequency:** weekly, seasonally. **Effective Market(s):** 7 New Zealand markets. **Units of Measure:** New Zealand dollars per head. **Time Period Covered:** latest 2 weeks.

STEERS: RISING 2 YEAR, STORE, MEDIUM

Source: *New Zealand Farmer.* **Price Frequency:** weekly, seasonally. **Effective Market(s):** 7 New Zealand markets. **Units of Measure:** New Zealand dollars per head. **Time Period Covered:** latest 2 weeks.

STEERS: SELECT

Source: *Livestock and Poultry Situation and Outlook Report.* **Price Frequency:** monthly. **Effective Market(s):** Omaha (NE). **Units of Measure:** Dollars per 100 lbs. **Time Period Covered:** latest year.

STEERS: SIMMENTAL AND SIMMENTAL X, STORE

Source: *Farmers Weekly.* **Price Frequency:** weekly. **Effective Market(s):** 15 British market average. **Units of Measure:** British pence per kilogram. **Type of Price:** average. **Time Period Covered:** latest week.

STEERS: SIMMENTAL X, STORE

Source: *Scottish Farmer.* **Price Frequency:** weekly. **Effective Market(s):** Aberdeen (Scotland), Stirling (Scotland). **Units of Measure:** British pence per kilogram. **Time Period Covered:** latest week.

STEERS: SLAUGHTER

Source: *Utah Farmer-Stockman.* **Price Frequency:** monthly. **Effective Market(s):** Idaho, Utah. **Units of Measure:** Dollars per 100 lbs. **Type of Price:** range. **Time Period Covered:** latest month.

Source: *Utah Farmer-Stockman.* **Price Frequency:** monthly, seasonally. **Effective Market(s):** Idaho. **Units of Measure:** Dollars per 100 lbs. **Type of Price:** range. **Time Period Covered:** latest month.

STEERS: SLAUGHTER, CHOICE

Source: *Fedgazette.* **Price Frequency:** monthly. **Effective Market(s):** Omaha (NE). **Units of Measure:** Dollars per 100 lbs. **Time Period Covered:** latest 24 months.

Source: *Lancaster Farming.* **Price Frequency:** weekly. **Effective Market(s):** Pennsylvania, Virginia. **Units of Measure:** Dollars per head. **Type of Price:** auction. **Time Period Covered:** latest week.

Source: *Livestock and Poultry Update.* **Price Frequency:** monthly. **Effective Market(s):** Omaha (NE), Texas Panhandle. **Units of Measure:** Dollars per 100 lbs. **Time Period Covered:** latest 3 month, year ago.

STEERS: SLAUGHTER, CHOICE 2-4

Source: *Idaho Farmer-Stockman.* **Price Frequency:** monthly. **Effective Market(s):** Arizona/California, Central Plains, Midwest. **Units of Measure:** Dollars per 100 lbs. **Time Period Covered:** latest month.

Source: *Livestock, Meat, Wool Market News.* **Price Frequency:** weekly, seasonally. **Effective Market(s):** 10 domestic markets. **Units of Measure:** Dollars per 100 lbs. **Type of Price:** average. **Time Period Covered:** latest week, year ago.

STEERS: SLAUGHTER, COMMON TO MEDIUM

Source: *Farm and Dairy.* **Price Frequency:** weekly, seasonally. **Effective Market(s):** Ohio, Pennsylvania. **Units of Measure:** Dollars per head. **Type of Price:** auction high, auction low. **Time Period Covered:** latest week.

STEERS: SLAUGHTER, DRESSED CARCASSES, SELECT AND CHOICE

Source: *Oregon Farmer-Stockman.* **Price Frequency:** monthly. **Effective Market(s):** Oregon/Washington. **Units of Measure:** Dollars per 100 lbs. **Time Period Covered:** latest month.

STEERS: SLAUGHTER, DRESSED CARCASSES, SELECT TO MOSTLY CHOICE

Source: *Washington Farmer-Stockman.* **Price Frequency:** monthly. **Effective Market(s):** Oregon/Washington. **Units of Measure:** Dollars per 100 lbs. **Time Period Covered:** latest month.

STEERS: SLAUGHTER, DRESSED, SELECT AND CHOICE

Source: *Idaho Farmer-Stockman.* **Price Frequency:** monthly. **Effective Market(s):** Idaho. **Units of Measure:** Dollars per 100 lbs. **Time Period Covered:** latest month.

STEERS: SLAUGHTER, HIGH CHOICE AND PRIME

Source: *Lancaster Farming.* **Price Frequency:** weekly. **Effective Market(s):** Pennsylvania, Virginia. **Units of Measure:** Dollars per head. **Type of Price:** auction. **Time Period Covered:** latest week.

STEERS: SLAUGHTER, HOLSTEIN

Source: *Farm and Dairy.* **Price Frequency:** weekly, seasonally. **Effective Market(s):** Ohio, Pennsylvania. **Units of Measure:** Dollars per head. **Type of Price:** auction high, auction low. **Time Period Covered:** latest week.

STEERS: SLAUGHTER, MEDIUM TO GOOD

Source: *Farm and Dairy.* **Price Frequency:** weekly, seasonally. **Effective Market(s):** Ohio, Pennsylvania. **Units of Measure:** Dollars per head. **Type of Price:** auction high, auction low. **Time Period Covered:** latest week.

STEERS: SLAUGHTER, PRIME 3-4

Source: *Livestock, Meat, Wool Market News.* **Price Frequency:** weekly, seasonally. **Effective Market(s):** 10 domestic markets. **Units of Measure:** Dollars per 100 lbs. **Type of Price:** average. **Time Period Covered:** latest week, year ago.

STEERS: SLAUGHTER, SELECT

Source: *Lancaster Farming.* **Price Frequency:** weekly. **Effective Market(s):** Pennsylvania, Virginia. **Units of Measure:** Dollars per head. **Type of Price:** auction. **Time Period Covered:** latest week.

Source: *Livestock and Poultry Update.* **Price Frequency:** monthly. **Effective Market(s):** Omaha (NE). **Units of Measure:** Dollars per 100 lbs. **Time Period Covered:** latest 3 month, year ago.

STEERS: SLAUGHTER, SELECT 2-3

Source: *Livestock, Meat, Wool Market News.* **Price Frequency:** weekly, seasonally. **Effective Market(s):** 10 domestic markets. **Units of Measure:** Dollars per 100 lbs. **Type of Price:** average. **Time Period Covered:** latest week, year ago.

STEERS: SLAUGHTER, SELECT AND CHOICE

Source: *California Farmer.* **Price Frequency:** semimonthly. **Effective Market(s):** California. **Units of Measure:** Dollars per 100 lbs. **Time Period Covered:** latest week, month ago, year ago.

Source: *Oregon Farmer-Stockman.* **Price Frequency:** monthly. **Effective Market(s):** Oregon/Washington. **Units of Measure:** Dollars per 100 lbs. **Time Period Covered:** latest month.

Source: *Washington Farmer-Stockman.* **Price Frequency:** monthly. **Effective Market(s):** Oregon/Washington. **Units of Measure:** Dollars per 100 lbs. **Time Period Covered:** latest month.

STEERS: SLAUGHTER, SELECT AND CHOICE 2-3

Source: *Oregon Farmer-Stockman.* **Price Frequency:** monthly. **Effective Market(s):** Oregon/Washington. **Time Period Covered:** latest month.

STEERS: SLAUGHTER, SELECT AND CHOICE 2-3, DRESSED BASIS

Source: *Oregon Farmer-Stockman.* **Price Frequency:** monthly. **Effective Market(s):** Oregon/Washington. **Time Period Covered:** latest month.

STEERS: SLAUGHTER, SELECT AND LOW CHOICE

Source: *Lancaster Farming.* **Price Frequency:** weekly. **Effective Market(s):** Pennsylvania, Virginia. **Units of Measure:** Dollars per head. **Type of Price:** auction. **Time Period Covered:** latest week.

STEERS: SLAUGHTER, SELECT TO MOSTLY CHOICE

Source: *Idaho Farmer-Stockman.* **Price Frequency:** monthly. **Effective Market(s):** Idaho. **Units of Measure:** Dollars per 100 lbs. **Time Period Covered:** latest month.

STEERS: STANDARD

Source: *Farm and Dairy.* **Price Frequency:** weekly, seasonally. **Effective Market(s):** Ohio, Pennsylvania. **Units of Measure:** Dollars per head. **Type of Price:** auction high, auction low. **Time Period Covered:** latest week.

STEERS: STOCKER AND FEEDER

Source: *Commodity Year Book.* **Price Frequency:** monthly, annually. **Effective Market(s):** Kansas City. **Units of Measure:** Dollars per 100 lbs. **Time Period Covered:** latest 4 years.

Source: *Survey of Current Business.* **Price Frequency:** monthly, annually. **Effective Market(s):** Kansas City. **Units of Measure:** Dollars per 100 lbs. **Type of Price:** wholesale. **Time Period Covered:** latest year.

STEERS: YOUNG, HOT WEIGHT

Source: *Drovers Journal.* **Price Frequency:** semimonthly. **Effective Market(s):** 8 domestic markets. **Units of Measure:** Dollars per 100 lbs. **Time Period Covered:** selected date.

STEERS: YOUNG, LIVE, HOLSTEINS

Source: *Drovers Journal.* **Price Frequency:** semimonthly. **Effective Market(s):** 8 domestic markets. **Units of Measure:** Dollars per 100 lbs. **Time Period Covered:** selected date.

STEERS: YOUNG, LIVE, MOSTLY CHOICE

Source: *Drovers Journal.* **Price Frequency:** semimonthly. **Effective Market(s):** 8 domestic markets. **Units of Measure:** Dollars per 100 lbs. **Time Period Covered:** selected date.

STEERS: YOUNG, LIVE, MOSTLY SELECT

Source: *Drovers Journal.* **Price Frequency:** semimonthly. **Effective Market(s):** 8 domestic markets. **Units of Measure:** Dollars per 100 lbs. **Time Period Covered:** selected date.

STEERS AND HEIFERS

Source: *Agricultural Prices.* **Price Frequency:** monthly. **Effective Market(s):** United States. **Units of Measure:** Dollars per 100 lbs. **Type of Price:** received by farmer. **Time Period Covered:** latest 2 months, year ago.

Source: *Agricultural Prices.* **Price Frequency:** monthly. **Effective Market(s):** 35 domestic markets, United States. **Units of Measure:** Dollars per 100 lbs. **Type of Price:** received by farmer. **Time Period Covered:** latest 2 months.

Source: *Agricultural Prices Annual Summary.* **Price Frequency:** annually. **Effective Market(s):** 50 domestic markets, United States. **Units of Measure:** Dollars per 100 lbs. **Type of Price:** average received by farmer. **Time Period Covered:** latest 2 years, for US latest 6 years.

Source: *Agricultural Prices Annual Summary.* **Price Frequency:** monthly. **Effective Market(s):** 35 domestic markets, United States. **Units of Measure:** Dollars per 100 lbs. **Type of Price:** average received by farmer. **Time Period Covered:** latest year, for US latest 6 years.

Source: *Kansas Business Review.* **Price Frequency:** monthly. **Effective Market(s):** Kansas. **Units of Measure:** Dollars per 100 lbs. **Type of Price:** received by farmer. **Time Period Covered:** latest month, month ago, year ago.

Source: *Washington Farmer-Stockman.* **Price Frequency:** monthly. **Effective Market(s):** Washington. **Units of Measure:** Dollars per 100 lbs. **Type of Price:** average received by farmer. **Time Period Covered:** latest month, month ago, year ago.

STEERS AND HEIFERS: BEEF

Source: *Agricultural Prices.* **Price Frequency:** monthly. **Effective Market(s):** United States. **Units of Measure:** Dollars per 100 lbs. **Type of Price:** received by farmer. **Time Period Covered:** latest 2 months, year ago.

STEERS: CHOICE

Source: *CRB Commodity Index Report.* **Price Frequency:** weekly. **Effective Market(s):** Oklahoma/Texas. **Units of Measure:** Dollars per 100 lbs. **Type of Price:** spot. **Time Period Covered:** latest week.

STONE: CRUSHED, 1-1/2″

Source: *ENR.* **Price Frequency:** monthly in first issue of month. **Effective Market(s):** 20-city average. **Units of Measure:** Dollars per ton. **Time Period Covered:** latest month.

STONE: CRUSHED, ASPHALT COURSE

Source: *ENR.* **Price Frequency:** monthly in first issue of month. **Effective Market(s):** 8 domestic markets, Montreal, Toronto. **Units of Measure:** Dollars per ton. **Type of Price:** spot. **Time Period Covered:** latest month.

STONE: CRUSHED, BASE COURSE

Source: *ENR.* **Price Frequency:** monthly in first issue of month. **Effective Market(s):** 17 domestic markets, Montreal, Toronto. **Units of Measure:** Dollars per ton. **Type of Price:** spot. **Time Period Covered:** latest month.

STONE: CRUSHED, CONCRETE COURSE

Source: *ENR.* **Price Frequency:** monthly in first issue of month. **Effective Market(s):** 7 domestic markets, Montreal, Toronto. **Units of Measure:** Dollars per ton. **Type of Price:** spot. **Time Period Covered:** latest month.

STRAMONIUM

Source: *Journal of Commerce and Commercial.* **Price Frequency:** weekly in Monday issue. **Units of Measure:** Dollars per lb. **Type of Price:** spot. **Time Period Covered:** latest week.

STRAW

Source: *Lancaster Farming.* **Price Frequency:** weekly. **Effective Market(s):** Pennsylvania. **Units of Measure:** Dollars per ton. **Type of Price:** dealer. **Time Period Covered:** latest week.

STRAWBERRIES

Source: *California Farmer.* **Price Frequency:** semimonthly, seasonally. **Effective Market(s):** 5 California markets. **Units of Measure:** Dollars per 12 lb. tray. **Time Period Covered:** latest week, month ago, year ago.

Source: *Fresh Fruit and Vegetable Prices.* **Price Frequency:** monthly, seasonally. **Effective Market(s):** Central Coast California, Southern California, Central Florida, Louisiana. **Units of Measure:** Dollars per flat. **Type of Price:** average price at shipping point. **Time Period Covered:** latest year.

Source: *Lancaster Farming.* **Price Frequency:** weekly, seasonally. **Effective Market(s):** Pennsylvania. **Units of Measure:** Dollars per flat. **Type of Price:** market. **Time Period Covered:** latest week.

Source: *New Zealand Farmer.* **Price Frequency:** weekly, seasonally. **Effective Market(s):** New Zealand. **Units of Measure:** New Zealand dollars per carton. **Time Period Covered:** latest week.

Source: *The Packer.* **Price Frequency:** weekly, seasonally. **Effective Market(s):** varies. **Units of Measure:** Dollars per flat. **Type of Price:** average received by farmer. **Time Period Covered:** latest week.

STRAWBERRIES: ALL VARIETIES

Source: *Agricultural Prices Annual Summary.* **Price Frequency:** monthly, annually. **Effective Market(s):** United States. **Units of Measure:** Dollars per 100 lbs. **Type of Price:** average received by farmer. **Time Period Covered:** latest 6 years.

STRAWBERRIES: CALIFORNIA

Source: *Fresh Fruit and Vegetable Prices.* **Price Frequency:** monthly, seasonally. **Effective Market(s):** Chicago, New York City. **Units of Measure:** Dollars per pint. **Type of Price:** average wholesale price. **Time Period Covered:** latest year.

STRAWBERRIES: CARIBBEAN IMPORTS

Source: *Fresh Fruit and Vegetable Prices.* **Price Frequency:** monthly, seasonally. **Units of Measure:** Dollars per flat. **Time Period Covered:** latest year.

STRAWBERRIES: FLORIDA

Source: *Fresh Fruit and Vegetable Prices.* **Price Frequency:** monthly, seasonally. **Effective Market(s):** Chicago, New York City. **Units of Measure:** Dollars per pint. **Type of Price:** average wholesale price. **Time Period Covered:** latest year.

STRAWBERRIES: FRESH

Source: *Agricultural Prices.* **Price Frequency:** monthly. **Effective Market(s):** United States. **Units of Measure:** Dollars per lb. **Type of Price:** received by farmer. **Time Period Covered:** latest 2 months, year ago.

Source: *Fruit and Tree Nuts Situation and Outlook Yearbook.* **Price Frequency:** annually. **Effective Market(s):** United States. **Units of Measure:** Dollars per 100 lbs. **Type of Price:** grower. **Time Period Covered:** latest 20 years.

STRAWBERRIES: GRADE A, SLICED, FROZEN

Source: *HRI-Buyer's Guide.* **Price Frequency:** weekly. **Effective Market(s):** Northeastern area. **Units of Measure:** Dollars per case. **Type of Price:** price paid by dining places & institutions. **Time Period Covered:** latest week.

STRAWBERRIES: GRADE A, WHOLE, FROZEN, MEXICAN

Source: *HRI-Buyer's Guide.* **Price Frequency:** weekly. **Effective Market(s):** Northeastern area. **Units of Measure:** Dollars per case. **Type of Price:** price paid by dining places & institutions. **Time Period Covered:** latest week.

STRAWBERRIES: MEDIUM/LARGE, CALIFORNIA

Source: *HRI-Buyer's Guide.* **Price Frequency:** weekly. **Effective Market(s):** Northeastern area. **Units of Measure:** Dollars per 12 pint flat. **Type of Price:** price paid by dining places & institutions. **Time Period Covered:** latest week.

STRAWBERRIES: MEXICAN

Source: *Fresh Fruit and Vegetable Prices.* **Price Frequency:** monthly, seasonally. **Effective Market(s):** Chicago, New York City. **Units of Measure:** Dollars per pint. **Type of Price:** average wholesale price. **Time Period Covered:** latest year.

STRAWBERRIES: PROCESSING

Source: *Fruit and Tree Nuts Situation and Outlook Yearbook.* **Price Frequency:** annually. **Effective Market(s):** United States. **Units of Measure:** Dollars per 100 lbs. **Type of Price:** grower. **Time Period Covered:** latest 20 years.

STRAWBERRIES: SPRING

Source: *Agricultural Prices Annual Summary.* **Price Frequency:** monthly, annually. **Effective Market(s):** California, Michigan, Oregon, Washington, United States. **Units of Measure:** Dollars per 100 lbs. **Type of Price:** average received by farmer. **Time Period Covered:** latest 6 years.

STRAWBERRIES: WINTER

Source: *Agricultural Prices Annual Summary.* **Price Frequency:** monthly, annually. **Effective Market(s):** Florida, United States. **Units of Measure:** Dollars per 100 lbs. **Type of Price:** average received by farmer. **Time Period Covered:** latest 6 years.

STREPTOMYCIN SULFATE: USP

Source: *Chemical Marketing Reporter.* **Price Frequency:** weekly. **Effective Market(s):** New York. **Units of Measure:** Dollars per kilo. **Type of Price:** spot. **Time Period Covered:** latest week.

STRONTIUM CARBONATE: GLASS GROUND

Source: *Chemical Marketing Reporter.* **Price Frequency:** weekly. **Effective Market(s):** New York. **Units of Measure:** Dollars per lb. **Type of Price:** spot. **Time Period Covered:** latest week.

STRONTIUM NITRATE

Source: *Chemical Marketing Reporter.* **Price Frequency:** weekly. **Effective Market(s):** New York. **Units of Measure:** Dollars per 100 lbs. **Type of Price:** spot. **Time Period Covered:** latest week.

Source: *Journal of Commerce and Commercial.* **Price Frequency:** weekly in Friday issue. **Effective Market(s):** Georgia. **Units of Measure:** Dollars per lb. **Type of Price:** spot. **Time Period Covered:** latest week.

STRYCHNINE: ALKALOID POWDER

Source: *Journal of Commerce and Commercial.* **Price Frequency:** weekly in Friday issue. **Units of Measure:** Dollars per ounce. **Type of Price:** spot. **Time Period Covered:** latest week.

STRYCHNINE: SULFATE POWDER

Source: *Journal of Commerce and Commercial.* **Price Frequency:** weekly in Friday issue. **Units of Measure:** Dollars per ounce. **Type of Price:** spot. **Time Period Covered:** latest week.

STYRENE

Source: *Modern Plastics.* **Price Frequency:** quarterly every January, April, July, October. **Units of Measure:** cents per lb. **Type of Price:** market. **Time Period Covered:** latest 3 years.

Source: *Purchasing.* **Price Frequency:** quarterly in January, April, July, October issues. **Units of Measure:** cents per lb. **Type of Price:** transaction. **Time Period Covered:** latest 5 quarters.

STYRENE ACRYLIC

Source: *Plastics Technology.* **Price Frequency:** monthly. **Units of Measure:** cents per lb., cents per cubic inch. **Type of Price:** bulk list, market. **Time Period Covered:** latest month.

STYRENE ACRYLONITRILE

Source: *Journal of Commerce and Commercial.* **Price Frequency:** weekly in Tuesday issue. **Units of Measure:** Dollars per lb. **Type of Price:** spot. **Time Period Covered:** latest week.

STYRENE ACRYLONITRILE: GENERAL PURPOSE

Source: *Plastics Technology.* **Price Frequency:** monthly. **Units of Measure:** cents per lb., cents per cubic inch. **Type of Price:** bulk list, market. **Time Period Covered:** latest month.

STYRENE ACRYLONITRILE RESIN: CLEAR

Source: *Chemical Marketing Reporter.* **Price Frequency:** weekly. **Effective Market(s):** New York. **Units of Measure:** Dollars per lb. **Type of Price:** spot. **Time Period Covered:** latest week.

STYRENE ACRYLONITRILE RESIN: CRYSTALLINE

Source: *Chemical Marketing Reporter.* **Price Frequency:** weekly. **Effective Market(s):** New York. **Units of Measure:** Dollars per lb. **Type of Price:** spot. **Time Period Covered:** latest week.

STYRENE ACRYLONITRILE RESIN: NATURAL

Source: *Chemical Marketing Reporter.* **Price Frequency:** weekly. **Effective Market(s):** New York. **Units of Measure:** Dollars per lb. **Type of Price:** spot. **Time Period Covered:** latest week.

STYRENE AMLEIC ANHYDRIDE: HIGH IMPACT

Source: *Plastics Technology.* **Price Frequency:** monthly. **Units of Measure:** cents per lb., cents per cubic inch. **Type of Price:** bulk list, market. **Time Period Covered:** latest month.

STYRENE BUTADIENE LATEX

Source: *Journal of Commerce and Commercial.* **Price Frequency:** weekly in Wednesday issue. **Units of Measure:** Dollars per lb. **Type of Price:** spot. **Time Period Covered:** latest week.

STYRENE MALEIC ANHYDRIDE: FIRE RETARDANT

Source: *Plastics Technology.* **Price Frequency:** monthly. **Units of Measure:** cents per lb., cents per cubic inch. **Type of Price:** bulk list, market. **Time Period Covered:** latest month.

STYRENE MALEIC ANHYDRIDE: GENERAL PURPOSE

Source: *Plastics Technology.* **Price Frequency:** monthly. **Units of Measure:** cents per lb., cents per cubic inch. **Type of Price:** bulk list, market. **Time Period Covered:** latest month.

STYRENE MONOMER

Source: *Japan Economic Journal.* **Price Frequency:** weekly. **Effective Market(s):** Tokyo. **Units of Measure:** Japanese yen per kilogram. **Type of Price:** market. **Time Period Covered:** latest 2 weeks.

Source: *Journal of Commerce and Commercial.* **Price Frequency:** weekly in Tuesday issue. **Units of Measure:** Dollars per lb. **Type of Price:** spot. **Time Period Covered:** latest week.

STYRENE MONOMER: 99.6% MINIMUM

Source: *Chemical Marketing Reporter.* **Price Frequency:** weekly. **Effective Market(s):** New York. **Units of Measure:** Dollars per lb. **Type of Price:** spot. **Time Period Covered:** latest week.

SUCCINIC ACID: PURIFIED, CRYSTALLINE

Source: *Chemical Marketing Reporter.* **Price Frequency:** weekly. **Effective Market(s):** New York. **Units of Measure:** Dollars per lb. **Type of Price:** spot. **Time Period Covered:** latest week.

SUCCINIC ANHYDRIDE

Source: *Chemical Marketing Reporter.* **Price Frequency:** weekly. **Effective Market(s):** New York. **Units of Measure:** Dollars per lb. **Type of Price:** spot. **Time Period Covered:** latest week.

SUCROSE: REFINED, WHITE

Source: *Chemical Marketing Reporter.* **Price Frequency:** weekly. **Effective Market(s):** New York. **Units of Measure:** Dollars per 100 lbs. **Type of Price:** spot. **Time Period Covered:** latest week.

SUCROSE ACETATE: ISOBUTYRATE, 90%

Source: *Chemical Marketing Reporter.* **Price Frequency:** weekly. **Effective Market(s):** New York. **Units of Measure:** Dollars per lb. **Type of Price:** spot. **Time Period Covered:** latest week.

SUCROSE ACETATE: ISOBUTYRATE, 100%

Source: *Chemical Marketing Reporter.* **Price Frequency:** weekly. **Effective Market(s):** New York. **Units of Measure:** Dollars per lb. **Type of Price:** spot. **Time Period Covered:** latest week.

SUCROSE OCTA-ACETATE: DENATURING GRADE

Source: *Chemical Marketing Reporter.* **Price Frequency:** weekly. **Effective Market(s):** New York. **Units of Measure:** Dollars per kilo. **Type of Price:** spot. **Time Period Covered:** latest week.

SUDANGRASS

Source: *Agricultural Prices Annual Summary.* **Price Frequency:** annually. **Effective Market(s):** United States. **Units of Measure:** Dollars per 100 lbs. **Type of Price:** average paid by farmer. **Time Period Covered:** latest 6 years.

SUEDE FABRIC

Source: *JTN: The International Textile Magazine.* **Price Frequency:** monthly. **Effective Market(s):** Japan. **Units of Measure:** Japanese yen per yard. **Type of Price:** spot. **Time Period Covered:** latest month.

SUGAR

Source: *Dairy Foods.* **Price Frequency:** weekly. **Effective Market(s):** New York. **Units of Measure:** Dollars per 100 lbs. **Time Period Covered:** latest 2 weeks.

Source: *Far Eastern Economic Review.* **Price Frequency:** weekly. **Effective Market(s):** New York. **Units of Measure:** cents per lb. **Time Period Covered:** latest week, week ago, 3 months ago, year ago.

Source: *Financial Times.* **Price Frequency:** daily. **Effective Market(s):** London. **Units of Measure:** British pounds per tonne. **Type of Price:** export. **Time Period Covered:** latest day.

Source: *International Financial Statistics.* **Price Frequency:** monthly, quarterly, annually. **Effective Market(s):** United States. **Units of Measure:** cents per lb., index. **Type of Price:** import price, price index. **Time Period Covered:** latest 5 months, latest 5 quarters, latest 5 years.

Source: *International Financial Statistics Yearbook.* **Price Frequency:** annually. **Effective Market(s):** United States. **Units of Measure:** cents per lb. **Type of Price:** import. **Time Period Covered:** latest 30 years.

Source: *Monthly Commodity Price Bulletin.* **Price Frequency:** monthly, annually. **Effective Market(s):** Caribbean ports. **Units of Measure:** cents per lb. **Time Period Covered:** latest 5 years.

Source: *Monthly Commodity Price Bulletin Supplement.* **Price Frequency:** monthly, quarterly, annually. **Effective Market(s):** Caribbean ports. **Units of Measure:** cents per lb. **Time Period Covered:** latest 20 years.

Source: *Sugar Year Book.* **Price Frequency:** monthly, annually. **Effective Market(s):** Caribbean ports. **Units of Measure:** cents per lb. **Type of Price:** spot, International Sugar Agreement. **Time Period Covered:** monthly latest 3 years, annually latest 8 years.

Source: *UNCTAD Commodity Yearbook.* **Price Frequency:** annually. **Effective Market(s):** Caribbean ports. **Units of Measure:** Dollars per metric ton. **Type of Price:** free market. **Time Period Covered:** latest 12 years.

SUGAR: AUSTRALIAN

Source: *International Financial Statistics.* **Price Frequency:** monthly, quarterly, annually. **Effective Market(s):** Australia. **Units of Measure:** cents per lb., index. **Type of Price:** market price, price index. **Time Period Covered:** latest 2 months, latest 4 quarters, latest 5 years.

Source: *International Financial Statistics Yearbook.* **Price Frequency:** annually. **Effective Market(s):** Australia. **Units of Measure:** cents per lb. **Type of Price:** wholesale. **Time Period Covered:** latest 30 years.

SUGAR: BEET

Source: *Milling & Baking News.* **Price Frequency:** weekly. **Effective Market(s):** Midwest, Pacific. **Units of Measure:** cents per lb. **Time Period Covered:** latest week, year ago.

SUGAR: BEET, HOME PRODUCED

Source: *Farmers Weekly.* **Price Frequency:** weekly, seasonally. **Effective Market(s):** Great Britain. **Units of Measure:** British pounds per tonne. **Type of Price:** spot. **Time Period Covered:** latest week.

SUGAR: BEET, MOLASSED, IMPORTED

Source: *Farmers Weekly.* **Price Frequency:** weekly, seasonally. **Effective Market(s):** Great Britain. **Units of Measure:** British pounds per tonne. **Type of Price:** spot. **Time Period Covered:** latest week.

SUGAR: BEET, RAW

Source: *Bakery Newsletter.* **Price Frequency:** weekly. **Effective Market(s):** Midwest, West. **Units of Measure:** cents per lb. **Type of Price:** cash. **Time Period Covered:** latest week, week ago.

SUGAR: BEET, REFINED

Source: *Sugar and Sweetner Situation and Outlook Report.* **Price Frequency:** monthly, quarterly, annually. **Effective Market(s):** Midwest. **Units of Measure:** cents per lb. **Type of Price:** wholesale. **Time Period Covered:** latest 10 years.

SUGAR: BEET, UNMOLASSED, IMPORTED

Source: *Farmers Weekly.* **Price Frequency:** weekly, seasonally. **Effective Market(s):** Great Britain. **Units of Measure:** British pounds per tonne. **Type of Price:** spot. **Time Period Covered:** latest week.

SUGAR: BRAZILIAN

Source: *International Financial Statistics.* **Price Frequency:** quarterly, annually. **Effective Market(s):** Brazil. **Units of Measure:** cents per lb., index. **Type of Price:** market price, price index. **Time Period Covered:** latest 3 quarters, latest 4 years.

Source: *International Financial Statistics Yearbook.* **Price Frequency:** annually. **Effective Market(s):** Brazil. **Units of Measure:** cents per lb. **Type of Price:** wholesale. **Time Period Covered:** latest 30 years.

SUGAR: BROWN, FIJI

Source: *Statistical Bulletin of the South Pacific: Retail Price Indexes.* **Price Frequency:** annually. **Effective Market(s):** 18 South Pacific markets. **Units of Measure:** Australian dollars per kilogram. **Type of Price:** retail. **Time Period Covered:** latest year.

SUGAR: CANE, RAW

Source: *Asian Wall Street Journal.* **Price Frequency:** daily. **Effective Market(s):** World. **Units of Measure:** Dollars per lb. **Type of Price:** cash. **Time Period Covered:** latest 2 days, year ago.

Source: *Bakery Newsletter.* **Price Frequency:** weekly. **Effective Market(s):** Caribbean. **Units of Measure:** cents per lb. **Type of Price:** cash. **Time Period Covered:** latest week, week ago.

Source: *Economic and Energy Indicators.* **Price Frequency:** biweekly. **Units of Measure:** cents per lb. **Type of Price:** spot. **Time Period Covered:** latest 3 months, quarters, and years.

Source: *Wall Street Journal.* **Price Frequency:** daily. **Effective Market(s):** World. **Units of Measure:** Dollars per lb. **Time Period Covered:** latest day, day ago, year ago.

SUGAR: CANE, RAW, DOMESTIC

Source: *Bakery Newsletter.* **Price Frequency:** weekly. **Effective Market(s):** New York. **Units of Measure:** cents per lb. **Type of Price:** cash. **Time Period Covered:** latest week, week ago.

SUGAR: CANE, REFINED

Source: *Commodity Year Book.* **Price Frequency:** monthly, annually. **Effective Market(s):** Chicago, West. **Units of Measure:** cents per lb. **Type of Price:** wholesale. **Time Period Covered:** latest 8 years.

SUGAR: CARIBBEAN

Source: *International Financial Statistics.* **Price Frequency:** monthly, quarterly, annually. **Effective Market(s):** New York. **Units of Measure:** cents per lb., index. **Type of Price:** market price, price index. **Time Period Covered:** latest 5 months, latest 5 quarters, latest 5 years.

Source: *International Financial Statistics Yearbook.* **Price Frequency:** annually. **Effective Market(s):** New York. **Units of Measure:** cents per lb. **Type of Price:** wholesale. **Time Period Covered:** latest 30 years.

SUGAR: CONTRACT NO. 11

Source: *Investor's Daily.* **Price Frequency:** daily. **Units of Measure:** cents per lb. **Type of Price:** spot. **Time Period Covered:** latest day.

Source: *New York Times.* **Price Frequency:** daily. **Units of Measure:** cents per lb. **Type of Price:** cash. **Time Period Covered:** latest 2 days.

SUGAR: CONTRACT NO. 11, FUTURES

Source: *Barron's.* **Price Frequency:** weekly. **Effective Market(s):** New York. **Units of Measure:** cents per lb. **Type of Price:** futures. **Time Period Covered:** latest week.

Source: *Financial Times.* **Price Frequency:** daily. **Effective Market(s):** New York. **Units of Measure:** cents per lb. **Type of Price:** futures. **Time Period Covered:** latest day.

Source: *Investor's Daily.* **Price Frequency:** daily. **Effective Market(s):** New York. **Units of Measure:** cents per lb. **Type of Price:** futures. **Time Period Covered:** latest day.

Source: *Journal of Commerce and Commercial.* **Price Frequency:** daily. **Effective Market(s):** World/NY. **Units of Measure:** cents per lb. **Type of Price:** futures. **Time Period Covered:** latest day.

Source: *Los Angeles Times.* **Price Frequency:** daily. **Effective Market(s):** New York. **Units of Measure:** cents per lb. **Type of Price:** futures. **Time Period Covered:** latest day.

SUGAR: CONTRACT NO. 11, FUTURES, MARCH

Source: *Commodity Year Book.* **Price Frequency:** monthly. **Effective Market(s):** New York. **Units of Measure:** cents per lb. **Type of Price:** futures. **Time Period Covered:** latest 6 years.

SUGAR: CONTRACT NO. 14, FUTURES

Source: *Barron's.* **Price Frequency:** weekly. **Effective Market(s):** New York. **Units of Measure:** cents per lb. **Type of Price:** futures. **Time Period Covered:** latest week.

Source: *Investor's Daily.* **Price Frequency:** daily. **Effective Market(s):** New York. **Units of Measure:** cents per lb. **Type of Price:** futures. **Time Period Covered:** latest day.

SUGAR: CONVERTED

Source: *Journal of Commerce and Commercial.* **Price Frequency:** daily. **Effective Market(s):** London. **Units of Measure:** cents per lb. **Type of Price:** spot supplier. **Time Period Covered:** latest day.

SUGAR: DOMESTIC, FUTURES

Source: *Asian Wall Street Journal.* **Price Frequency:** daily. **Effective Market(s):** New York. **Units of Measure:** cents per lb. **Type of Price:** futures. **Time Period Covered:** latest day.

Source: *Los Angeles Times.* **Price Frequency:** daily. **Effective Market(s):** New York. **Units of Measure:** cents per lb. **Type of Price:** futures. **Time Period Covered:** latest day.

Source: *New York Times.* **Price Frequency:** daily. **Effective Market(s):** New York. **Units of Measure:** cents per lb. **Type of Price:** futures. **Time Period Covered:** latest day.

Source: *Wall Street Journal.* **Price Frequency:** daily. **Effective Market(s):** New York. **Units of Measure:** cents per lb. **Type of Price:** futures. **Time Period Covered:** latest day.

SUGAR: EUROPEAN COMMUNITY

Source: *International Financial Statistics Yearbook.* **Price Frequency:** annually. **Effective Market(s):** European Community. **Units of Measure:** cents per lb. **Type of Price:** import. **Time Period Covered:** latest 30 years.

Source: *International Financial Statistics.* **Price Frequency:** monthly, quarterly, annually. **Effective Market(s):** European Community. **Units of Measure:** cents per lb., index. **Type of Price:** import price, price index. **Time Period Covered:** latest 5 months, latest 5 quarters, latest 5 years.

SUGAR: FUTURES

Source: *Asian Wall Street Journal.* **Price Frequency:** daily. **Effective Market(s):** Hong Kong, Manila. **Units of Measure:** cents per lb., Philippine centavos per lb. **Type of Price:** futures. **Time Period Covered:** latest day.

Source: *Far Eastern Economic Review.* **Price Frequency:** weekly. **Effective Market(s):** New York. **Units of Measure:** cents per lb. **Time Period Covered:** next contract month.

Source: *Milling & Baking News.* **Price Frequency:** weekly. **Effective Market(s):** New York. **Units of Measure:** cents per lb. **Type of Price:** futures. **Time Period Covered:** latest week, year ago.

Source: *The Times.* **Price Frequency:** daily. **Effective Market(s):** London. **Units of Measure:** British pounds per metric ton. **Type of Price:** futures. **Time Period Covered:** latest day.

SUGAR: HFCS, 42%

Source: *Commodity Year Book.* **Price Frequency:** annually. **Effective Market(s):** North East. **Units of Measure:** cents per lb. **Type of Price:** wholesale. **Time Period Covered:** latest 11 years.

SUGAR: PHILIPPINES

Source: *International Financial Statistics.* **Price Frequency:** quarterly, annually. **Effective Market(s):** Philippines. **Units of Measure:** cents per lb., index. **Type of Price:** market price, price index. **Time Period Covered:** latest 3 quarters, latest 4 years.

Source: *International Financial Statistics Yearbook.* **Price Frequency:** annually. **Effective Market(s):** Philippines. **Units of Measure:** cents per lb. **Type of Price:** wholesale. **Time Period Covered:** latest 30 years.

SUGAR: RAW

Source: *Commodity Trade and Price Trends.* **Price Frequency:** annually. **Effective Market(s):** World, London. **Units of Measure:** cents per kilogram, 1980 constant cents per kilogram. **Time Period Covered:** latest 32 years.

Source: *Commodity Year Book.* **Price Frequency:** annually. **Effective Market(s):** World, New York. **Units of Measure:** cents per lb. **Time Period Covered:** latest 11 years.

Source: *Commodity Year Book.* **Price Frequency:** monthly, annually. **Effective Market(s):** New York. **Units of Measure:** cents per lb. **Type of Price:** spot. **Time Period Covered:** latest 7 years.

Source: *Commodity Year Book.* **Price Frequency:** monthly, annually. **Effective Market(s):** World. **Units of Measure:** cents per lb. **Type of Price:** spot, International Sugar Agreement. **Time Period Covered:** latest 7 years.

Source: *CRB Commodity Index Report.* **Price Frequency:** weekly. **Effective Market(s):** New York. **Units of Measure:** Dollars per lb. **Type of Price:** spot. **Time Period Covered:** latest week.

Source: *FAO Quarterly Bulletin of Statistics.* **Price Frequency:** monthly, annually. **Effective Market(s):** Caribbean ports. **Units of Measure:** Dollars per 1000 kilograms, dollars per metric ton. **Time Period Covered:** latest 3 years.

Source: *Financial Times.* **Price Frequency:** daily. **Effective Market(s):** London. **Units of Measure:** Dollars per tonne. **Type of Price:** spot. **Time Period Covered:** latest day.

Source: *International Sugar Organization Statistical Bulletin.* **Price Frequency:** monthly. **Effective Market(s):** London. **Units of Measure:** Dollars per tonne. **Type of Price:** spot. **Time Period Covered:** latest 4 months.

Source: *International Sugar Organization Statistical Bulletin.* **Price Frequency:** monthly. **Effective Market(s):** London, New York, International Sugar Agreement. **Units of Measure:** cents per lb. **Type of Price:** spot. **Time Period Covered:** latest 4 months.

Source: *Sugar and Sweetner Situation and Outlook Report.* **Price Frequency:** monthly, quarterly, annually. **Effective Market(s):** New York. **Units of Measure:** cents per lb. **Time Period Covered:** latest 10 years.

Source: *Sugar Year Book.* **Price Frequency:** monthly, annually. **Effective Market(s):** Caribbean/United Kingdom, London. **Units of Measure:** British pounds per tonne. **Type of Price:** average daily. **Time Period Covered:** monthly latest 3 years, annually latest 8 years.

SUGAR: RAW, CONTRACT NO. 11

Source: *Sugar and Sweetner Situation and Outlook Report.* **Price Frequency:** monthly, quarterly, annually. **Effective Market(s):** World. **Units of Measure:** cents per lb. **Type of Price:** spot. **Time Period Covered:** latest 10 years.

Source: *World Sugar Situation and Outlook.* **Price Frequency:** monthly, annually. **Effective Market(s):** New York. **Units of Measure:** cents per lb. **Type of Price:** spot. **Time Period Covered:** latest 2 years.

SUGAR: RAW, CONTRACT NO. 14

Source: *World Sugar Situation and Outlook.* **Price Frequency:** monthly, annually. **Effective Market(s):** New York. **Units of Measure:** cents per lb. **Type of Price:** nearby contract. **Time Period Covered:** latest 2 years.

SUGAR: RAW, FUTURES

Source: *Financial Times.* **Price Frequency:** daily. **Effective Market(s):** London. **Units of Measure:** Dollars per tonne. **Type of Price:** futures. **Time Period Covered:** latest day.

Source: *Japan Economic Journal.* **Price Frequency:** weekly. **Effective Market(s):** Tokyo. **Units of Measure:** Japanese yen per kilogram. **Type of Price:** futures. **Time Period Covered:** latest week.

SUGAR: REFINED

Source: *Sugar and Sweetner Situation and Outlook Report.* **Price Frequency:** monthly, quarterly, annually. **Effective Market(s):** United States. **Units of Measure:** cents per lb. **Type of Price:** retail. **Time Period Covered:** latest 10 years.

SUGAR: REFINED, CONTRACT NO. 5

Source: *Sugar and Sweetner Situation and Outlook Report.* **Price Frequency:** monthly, quarterly, annually. **Effective Market(s):** Europe. **Units of Measure:** cents per lb. **Type of Price:** spot. **Time Period Covered:** latest 10 years.

SUGAR: WHITE

Source: *Financial Times.* **Price Frequency:** daily. **Effective Market(s):** London. **Units of Measure:** Dollars per tonne. **Type of Price:** spot. **Time Period Covered:** latest day.

Source: *Statistical Bulletin of the South Pacific: Retail Price Indexes.* **Price Frequency:** annually. **Effective Market(s):** 18 South Pacific markets. **Units of Measure:** Australian dollars per kilogram. **Type of Price:** retail. **Time Period Covered:** latest year.

SUGAR: WHITE, FUTURES

Source: *Financial Times.* **Price Frequency:** daily. **Effective Market(s):** London. **Units of Measure:** Dollars per tonne. **Type of Price:** futures. **Time Period Covered:** latest day.

SUGAR: WHITE, REFINED

Source: *Sugar Year Book.* **Price Frequency:** annually. **Effective Market(s):** 38 international markets. **Units of Measure:** cents per lb. **Type of Price:** wholesale, retail. **Time Period Covered:** latest 2 years.

SUGAR: WORLD, FUTURES

Source: *Asian Wall Street Journal.* **Price Frequency:** daily. **Effective Market(s):** New York. **Units of Measure:** cents per lb. **Type of Price:** futures. **Time Period Covered:** latest day.

Source: *New York Times.* **Price Frequency:** daily. **Effective Market(s):** New York. **Units of Measure:** cents per lb. **Type of Price:** futures. **Time Period Covered:** latest day.

Source: *Wall Street Journal.* **Price Frequency:** daily. **Effective Market(s):** New York. **Units of Measure:** cents per lb. **Type of Price:** futures. **Time Period Covered:** latest day.

SUGARBEETS

Source: *Agricultural Prices Annual Summary.* **Price Frequency:** annually. **Effective Market(s):** 12 domestic markets, United States. **Units of Measure:** Dollars per ton. **Type of Price:** average received by farmer. **Time Period Covered:** latest 2 years, for US latest 6 years.

SUGARCANE

Source: *Agricultural Prices Annual Summary.* **Price Frequency:** annually. **Effective Market(s):** Florida, Hawaii, Louisiana, Texas, United States. **Units of Measure:** Dollars per ton. **Type of Price:** average received by farmer. **Time Period Covered:** latest 2 years, for US latest 6 years.

SUJIKO

see Salmon Roe.

SULFACETAMIDE: USP

Source: *Chemical Marketing Reporter.* **Price Frequency:** weekly. **Effective Market(s):** New York. **Units of Measure:** Dollars per kilo. **Type of Price:** spot. **Time Period Covered:** latest week.

SULFADIAZINE: POWDERED, USP

Source: *Chemical Marketing Reporter.* **Price Frequency:** weekly. **Effective Market(s):** New York. **Units of Measure:** Dollars per kilo. **Type of Price:** spot. **Time Period Covered:** latest week.

SULFADIAZINE-SODIUM: USP

Source: *Chemical Marketing Reporter.* **Price Frequency:** weekly. **Effective Market(s):** New York. **Units of Measure:** Dollars per kilo. **Type of Price:** spot. **Time Period Covered:** latest week.

SULFAMERAZINE: USP

Source: *Chemical Marketing Reporter.* **Price Frequency:** weekly. **Effective Market(s):** New York. **Units of Measure:** Dollars per kilo. **Type of Price:** spot. **Time Period Covered:** latest week.

SULFAMETHAZINE POWDER

Source: *Chemical Marketing Reporter.* **Price Frequency:** weekly. **Effective Market(s):** New York. **Units of Measure:** Dollars per kilo. **Type of Price:** spot. **Time Period Covered:** latest week.

SULFAMETHAZINE-SODIUM: POWDERED, USP

Source: *Chemical Marketing Reporter.* **Price Frequency:** weekly. **Effective Market(s):** New York. **Units of Measure:** Dollars per kilo. **Type of Price:** spot. **Time Period Covered:** latest week.

SULFAMIC ACID

Source: *Chemical Marketing Reporter.* **Price Frequency:** weekly. **Effective Market(s):** New York. **Units of Measure:** Dollars per lb. **Type of Price:** spot. **Time Period Covered:** latest week.

SULFANILAMIDE: NF

Source: *Journal of Commerce and Commercial.* **Price Frequency:** weekly in Friday issue. **Units of Measure:** Dollars per kilo. **Type of Price:** spot. **Time Period Covered:** latest week.

SULFANILAMIDE: REGULAR, NF

Source: *Chemical Marketing Reporter.* **Price Frequency:** weekly. **Effective Market(s):** New York. **Units of Measure:** Dollars per kilo. **Type of Price:** spot. **Time Period Covered:** latest week.

SULFANILIC ACID: TECHNICAL

Source: *Chemical Marketing Reporter.* **Price Frequency:** weekly. **Effective Market(s):** New York. **Units of Measure:** Dollars per lb. **Type of Price:** spot. **Time Period Covered:** latest week.

SULFAPYRIDINE: USP

Source: *Journal of Commerce and Commercial.* **Price Frequency:** weekly in Friday issue. **Units of Measure:** Dollars per kilo. **Type of Price:** spot. **Time Period Covered:** latest week.

SULFAQUINOXALINE

Source: *Chemical Marketing Reporter.* **Price Frequency:** weekly. **Effective Market(s):** New York. **Units of Measure:** Dollars per kilo. **Type of Price:** spot. **Time Period Covered:** latest week.

SULFATE OF AMMONIA FERTILIZER

Source: *Agricultural Prices.* **Price Frequency:** monthly. **Effective Market(s):** 9 domestic markets, United States. **Units of Measure:** Dollars per ton. **Type of Price:** paid by farmer. **Time Period Covered:** latest month.

Source: *Agricultural Prices Annual Summary.* **Price Frequency:** semiannually. **Effective Market(s):** Mountain region, North Central region, Northwest region, South Central region, Southwest region, United States. **Units of Measure:** Dollars per ton. **Type of Price:** average paid by farmer. **Time Period Covered:** latest year, for US latest 6 years.

SULFATHIAZOLE

Source: *Chemical Marketing Reporter.* **Price Frequency:** weekly. **Effective Market(s):** New York. **Units of Measure:** Dollars per kilo. **Type of Price:** spot. **Time Period Covered:** latest week.

SULFATHIAZOLE: USP

Source: *Journal of Commerce and Commercial.* **Price Frequency:** weekly in Friday issue. **Units of Measure:** Dollars per kilo. **Type of Price:** spot. **Time Period Covered:** latest week.

SULFUR

Source: *Energy Pricing News: Petrochemical Report.* **Price Frequency:** bimonthly. **Effective Market(s):** Vancouver (Canada). **Units of Measure:** Dollars per tonne. **Type of Price:** offshore market. **Time Period Covered:** latest month.

Source: *Minerals Today.* **Price Frequency:** bimonthly. **Units of Measure:** Dollars per long ton. **Time Period Covered:** latest month, month ago.

SULFUR: CRUDE, 99.5% MINIMUM PURITY, FLOUR, COMMERCIAL

Source: *Chemical Marketing Reporter.* **Price Frequency:** weekly. **Effective Market(s):** New York. **Units of Measure:** Dollars per 100 lbs. **Type of Price:** spot. **Time Period Covered:** latest week.

SULFUR: CRUDE, 99.5% MINIMUM PURITY, LUMP

Source: *Chemical Marketing Reporter.* **Price Frequency:** weekly. **Effective Market(s):** New York. **Units of Measure:** Dollars per 100 lbs. **Type of Price:** spot. **Time Period Covered:** latest week.

SULFUR: CRUDE, BRIGHT, MOLTEN

Source: *Chemical Marketing Reporter.* **Price Frequency:** weekly. **Effective Market(s):** Rotterdam, Vancouver (Canada). **Units of Measure:** Dollars per metric ton. **Type of Price:** spot. **Time Period Covered:** latest week.

SULFUR: CRUDE, BRIGHT, MOLTEN, DOMESTIC

Source: *Chemical Marketing Reporter.* **Price Frequency:** weekly. **Effective Market(s):** Port Sulfur, Alberta (Canada). **Units of Measure:** Dollars per long ton. **Type of Price:** spot. **Time Period Covered:** latest week.

SULFUR: CRUDE, BRIGHT, MOLTEN, RECOVERED, DOMESTIC

Source: *Chemical Marketing Reporter.* **Price Frequency:** weekly. **Effective Market(s):** Houston, New Orleans. **Units of Measure:** Dollars per long ton. **Type of Price:** spot. **Time Period Covered:** latest week.

SULFUR: CRUDE, DARK, MOLTEN, DOMESTIC

Source: *Chemical Marketing Reporter.* **Price Frequency:** weekly. **Effective Market(s):** Tampa (FL). **Units of Measure:** Dollars per long-ton. **Type of Price:** spot. **Time Period Covered:** latest week.

SULFUR: LIQUID, POLISH, FRENCH

Source: *Industrial Minerals.* **Price Frequency:** monthly. **Effective Market(s):** Northwest Europe. **Units of Measure:** Dollars per long ton. **Type of Price:** producer & dealer. **Time Period Covered:** latest month.

SULFUR: REFINED, 99.5% MINIMUM PURITY, LIGHT, FLOUR

Source: *Chemical Marketing Reporter.* **Price Frequency:** weekly. **Effective Market(s):** New York. **Units of Measure:** Dollars per 100 lbs. **Type of Price:** spot. **Time Period Covered:** latest week.

SULFUR: REFINED, 99.5% MINIMUM PURITY, ROLLS

Source: *Chemical Marketing Reporter.* **Price Frequency:** weekly. **Effective Market(s):** New York. **Units of Measure:** Dollars per 100 lbs. **Type of Price:** spot. **Time Period Covered:** latest week.

SULFUR: REFINED, 99.85% MINIMUM PURITY, SUBLIMED, NF

Source: *Chemical Marketing Reporter.* **Price Frequency:** weekly. **Effective Market(s):** New York. **Units of Measure:** Dollars per 100 lbs. **Type of Price:** spot. **Time Period Covered:** latest week.

SULFUR: RUBBERMAKERS, 98% MINIMUM PURITY, FINE

Source: *Chemical Marketing Reporter.* **Price Frequency:** weekly. **Effective Market(s):** New York. **Units of Measure:** Dollars per 100 lbs. **Type of Price:** spot. **Time Period Covered:** latest week.

SULFUR: RUBBERMAKERS, 99.5% MINIMUM PURITY, REGULAR, COMMERCIAL

Source: *Chemical Marketing Reporter.* **Price Frequency:** weekly. **Effective Market(s):** New York. **Units of Measure:** Dollars per 100 lbs. **Type of Price:** spot. **Time Period Covered:** latest week.

SULFUR DICHLORIDE

Source: *Chemical Marketing Reporter.* **Price Frequency:** weekly. **Effective Market(s):** New York. **Units of Measure:** Dollars per lb. **Type of Price:** spot. **Time Period Covered:** latest week.

Source: *Journal of Commerce and Commercial.* **Price Frequency:** weekly in Thursday issue. **Units of Measure:** Dollars per 100 lbs., dollars per lb. **Type of Price:** spot. **Time Period Covered:** latest week.

SULFUR DIOXIDE: LIQUID

Source: *Chemical Marketing Reporter.* **Price Frequency:** weekly. **Effective Market(s):** New York. **Units of Measure:** Dollars per ton. **Type of Price:** spot. **Time Period Covered:** latest week.

Source: *Journal of Commerce and Commercial.* **Price Frequency:** weekly in Thursday issue. **Units of Measure:** Dollars per ton. **Type of Price:** spot. **Time Period Covered:** latest week.

SULFUR MONOCHLORIDE

Source: *Chemical Marketing Reporter.* **Price Frequency:** weekly. **Effective Market(s):** New York. **Units of Measure:** Dollars per lb. **Type of Price:** spot. **Time Period Covered:** latest week.

Source: *Journal of Commerce and Commercial.* **Price Frequency:** weekly in Thursday issue. **Units of Measure:** Dollars per 100 lbs. **Type of Price:** spot. **Time Period Covered:** latest week.

SULFUR-FRASCH: CRUDE

Source: *Journal of Commerce and Commercial.* **Price Frequency:** weekly in Thursday issue. **Effective Market(s):** Tampa (FL). **Units of Measure:** Dollars per ton. **Type of Price:** spot. **Time Period Covered:** latest week.

Source: *Journal of Commerce and Commercial.* **Price Frequency:** weekly in Thursday issue. **Units of Measure:** Dollars per 100 lbs. **Type of Price:** spot. **Time Period Covered:** latest week.

SULFUR-FRASCH: CRUDE, LIGHT, FLOUR

Source: *Journal of Commerce and Commercial.* **Price Frequency:** weekly in Thursday issue. **Units of Measure:** Dollars per 100 lbs. **Type of Price:** spot. **Time Period Covered:** latest week.

SULFUR-FRASCH: CRUDE, RUBBERMAKERS

Source: *Journal of Commerce and Commercial.* **Price Frequency:** weekly in Thursday issue. **Units of Measure:** Dollars per 100 lbs. **Type of Price:** spot. **Time Period Covered:** latest week.

SULFUR-FRASCH: LIQUID, BRIGHT, UNITED STATES

Source: *Industrial Minerals.* **Price Frequency:** monthly. **Effective Market(s):** Tampa (FL), Rotterdam. **Units of Measure:** Dollars per long ton. **Type of Price:** producer & dealer. **Time Period Covered:** latest month.

SULFUR-FRASCH: REFINED, 99.5%, MEXICAN

Source: *Journal of Commerce and Commercial.* **Price Frequency:** weekly in Thursday issue. **Units of Measure:** Dollars per 100 lbs. **Type of Price:** spot. **Time Period Covered:** latest week.

SULFURIC ACID: 100%

Source: *Journal of Commerce and Commercial.* **Price Frequency:** weekly in Thursday issue. **Units of Measure:** Dollars per ton. **Type of Price:** spot. **Time Period Covered:** latest week.

SULFURIC ACID: FUMING, 20%

Source: *Chemical Marketing Reporter.* **Price Frequency:** weekly. **Effective Market(s):** Gulf Coast, New Mexico, Southeast, Northwest. **Units of Measure:** Dollars per ton. **Type of Price:** spot. **Time Period Covered:** latest week.

SULFURIC ACID: SMELTER, 93%

Source: *Chemical Marketing Reporter.* **Price Frequency:** weekly. **Effective Market(s):** Northwest. **Units of Measure:** Dollars per ton. **Type of Price:** spot. **Time Period Covered:** latest week.

SULFURIC ACID: SMELTER, 100%

Source: *Chemical Marketing Reporter.* **Price Frequency:** weekly. **Effective Market(s):** Gulf Coast, New Mexico, Southeast. **Units of Measure:** Dollars per ton. **Type of Price:** spot. **Time Period Covered:** latest week.

SULFURIC ACID: VIRGIN, 100%

Source: *Chemical Marketing Reporter.* **Price Frequency:** weekly. **Effective Market(s):** East Coast, Gulf Coast, Midwest, Southeast, West Coast. **Units of Measure:** Dollars per ton. **Type of Price:** spot. **Time Period Covered:** latest week.

Source: *Purchasing.* **Price Frequency:** monthly. **Effective Market(s):** United States. **Units of Measure:** Dollars per ton. **Type of Price:** transaction. **Time Period Covered:** latest day, month ago, 6 months ago, year ago.

SULPHATE OF AMMONIA

Source: *Standard & Poor's Statistical Service Current Statistics.* **Price Frequency:** monthly, annually. **Units of Measure:** Dollars per 100 lbs. **Time Period Covered:** latest 4 years.

SULPHIDE ORE: LUMP

Source: *Industrial Minerals.* **Price Frequency:** monthly. **Effective Market(s):** main European port. **Units of Measure:** Dollars per metric tonne. **Type of Price:** producer & dealer. **Time Period Covered:** latest month.

SULPHUR

see Sulfur.

SULPHUR: SOLID/SLATE, CANADIAN

Source: *Industrial Minerals.* **Price Frequency:** monthly. **Effective Market(s):** Vancouver (Canada). **Units of Measure:** Dollars per metric tonne. **Type of Price:** spot, contract. **Time Period Covered:** latest month.

SUNFLOWER FOR SEED

see Seed Sunflower.

SUNFLOWER MEAL: 28% PROTEIN

Source: *Grain and Feed Market News.* **Price Frequency:** weekly, seasonally. **Effective Market(s):** Minneapolis. **Units of Measure:** Dollars per ton. **Type of Price:** wholesale. **Time Period Covered:** latest week, week ago, year ago.

Source: *Oil Crops Situation and Outlook.* **Price Frequency:** monthly. **Units of Measure:** Dollars per ton. **Time Period Covered:** latest 5 months.

SUNFLOWER MEAL PELLETS

Source: *Agra Europe.* **Price Frequency:** weekly, irregularly. **Effective Market(s):** Rotterdam. **Units of Measure:** Dollars per tonne. **Time Period Covered:** latest week.

SUNFLOWER OIL

Source: *Fruit and Tropical Products.* **Price Frequency:** monthly, annually. **Effective Market(s):** Rotterdam. **Units of Measure:** Dollars per tonne. **Type of Price:** average. **Time Period Covered:** monthly latest year, annually latest 2 years.

Source: *Grain and Feed Market News.* **Price Frequency:** weekly, seasonally. **Effective Market(s):** Minneapolis. **Units of Measure:** cents per lb. **Type of Price:** wholesale. **Time Period Covered:** latest week, week ago, year ago.

Source: *Monthly Commodity Price Bulletin.* **Price Frequency:** monthly, annually. **Effective Market(s):** Rotterdam. **Units of Measure:** Dollars per metric ton. **Time Period Covered:** latest 5 years.

Source: *Monthly Commodity Price Bulletin Supplement.* **Price Frequency:** monthly, quarterly, annually. **Effective Market(s):** Rotterdam. **Units of Measure:** Dollars per tonne. **Time Period Covered:** latest 20 years.

Source: *UNCTAD Commodity Yearbook.* **Price Frequency:** annually. **Effective Market(s):** Rotterdam. **Units of Measure:** Dollars per metric ton. **Type of Price:** free market. **Time Period Covered:** latest 12 years.

SUNFLOWER OIL: CRUDE

Source: *Oil Crops Situation and Outlook.* **Price Frequency:** monthly. **Effective Market(s):** Minneapolis. **Units of Measure:** cents per lb. **Type of Price:** wholesale. **Time Period Covered:** latest 5 months.

SUNFLOWER OIL SEED

Source: *Minneapolis Grain Exchange Statistical Annual.* **Price Frequency:** monthly, annually. **Effective Market(s):** Duluth (MN), Minneapolis. **Units of Measure:** cents per bushel. **Type of Price:** cash. **Time Period Covered:** latest 10 years.

Source: *Minneapolis Grain Exchange Statistical Annual.* **Price Frequency:** monthly, annually. **Effective Market(s):** Duluth (MN), Minneapolis. **Units of Measure:** Dollars per bushel. **Type of Price:** cash. **Time Period Covered:** latest 10 years.

SUNFLOWERS

Source: *Agricultural Prices.* **Price Frequency:** monthly. **Effective Market(s):** United States. **Units of Measure:** Dollars per lb. **Type of Price:** received by farmer. **Time Period Covered:** latest 2 months, year ago.

Source: *Agricultural Prices Annual Summary.* **Price Frequency:** annually. **Effective Market(s):** Minnesota, North Dakota, South Dakota, Texas, United States. **Units of Measure:** Dollars per 100 lbs. **Type of Price:** average received by farmer. **Time Period Covered:** latest 2 years, for US latest 6 years.

Source: *Minneapolis Grain Exchange Statistical Annual.* **Price Frequency:** daily. **Effective Market(s):** Duluth (MN), Minneapolis. **Units of Measure:** cents per bushel. **Type of Price:** cash. **Time Period Covered:** latest year.

SUNFLOWERS: CRUSHING PLANTS

Source: *Doane's Agricultural Report.* **Price Frequency:** weekly. **Effective Market(s):** Eastern North Dakota. **Units of Measure:** Dollars per 100 lbs. **Time Period Covered:** latest week, week ago, year ago.

SUNFLOWERSEED

Source: *Commodity Year Book.* **Price Frequency:** annually. **Effective Market(s):** United States. **Units of Measure:** Dollars per metric ton. **Type of Price:** farm price. **Time Period Covered:** latest 4 years.

Source: *Oil Crops Situation and Outlook.* **Price Frequency:** annually. **Effective Market(s):** United States. **Units of Measure:** Dollars per metric ton. **Type of Price:** average received by farmer. **Time Period Covered:** latest 10 years.

Source: *Oil Crops Situation and Outlook.* **Price Frequency:** monthly. **Effective Market(s):** United States. **Units of Measure:** Dollars per 100 lbs. **Type of Price:** received by farmer. **Time Period Covered:** latest 5 months.

Source: *World Oilseed Situation and Market Highlights.* **Price Frequency:** monthly, annually. **Effective Market(s):** United States. **Units of Measure:** Dollars per metric ton. **Type of Price:** farm. **Time Period Covered:** monthly latest year, annually latest 9 years.

SUNFLOWERSEED: NO. 1

Source: *Grain and Feed Market News.* **Price Frequency:** daily, seasonally. **Effective Market(s):** Duluth (MN). **Units of Measure:** Dollars per 100 lbs. **Type of Price:** cash bid. **Time Period Covered:** latest week, year ago.

Source: *Wall Street Journal.* **Price Frequency:** daily. **Effective Market(s):** Duluth (MN). **Units of Measure:** Dollars per 100 lbs. **Time Period Covered:** latest day, day ago, year ago.

SUNFLOWERSEED: UNITED STATES/ CANADIAN

Source: *FAO Quarterly Bulletin of Statistics.* **Price Frequency:** monthly, annually. **Effective Market(s):** Rotterdam. **Units of Measure:** Dollars per 1000 kilograms, dollars per metric ton. **Time Period Covered:** latest 3 years.

Source: *Oil World.* **Price Frequency:** weekly, monthly, annually. **Effective Market(s):** Rotterdam. **Units of Measure:** Dollars per tonne. **Type of Price:** lowest representative asking. **Time Period Covered:** weekly latest 3 weeks, monthly latest 2 months, annually latest 2 years.

Source: *World Oilseed Situation and Market Highlights.* **Price Frequency:** monthly, annually. **Effective Market(s):** Rotterdam. **Units of Measure:** Dollars per metric ton. **Time Period Covered:** monthly latest year, annually latest 9 years.

SUNFLOWERSEED MEAL: 20% PROTEIN

Source: *Oil Crops Situation and Outlook.* **Price Frequency:** annually. **Effective Market(s):** United States. **Units of Measure:** Dollars per metric ton. **Type of Price:** average. **Time Period Covered:** latest 10 years.

SUNFLOWERSEED MEAL: 28% PROTEIN

Source: *Commodity Year Book.* **Price Frequency:** annually. **Effective Market(s):** United States. **Units of Measure:** Dollars per metric ton. **Time Period Covered:** latest 4 years.

Source: *Feedstuffs.* **Price Frequency:** weekly. **Effective Market(s):** Fargo (ND), Minneapolis. **Units of Measure:** Dollars per bulk ton. **Time Period Covered:** latest week.

Source: *Milling & Baking News.* **Price Frequency:** weekly. **Effective Market(s):** Minneapolis. **Units of Measure:** Dollars per ton. **Time Period Covered:** latest week, week ago, year ago.

SUNFLOWERSEED MEAL: 32% PROTEIN

Source: *Feedstuffs.* **Price Frequency:** weekly. **Effective Market(s):** Fargo (ND), Minneapolis. **Units of Measure:** Dollars per bulk ton. **Time Period Covered:** latest week.

Source: *World Oilseed Situation and Market Highlights.* **Price Frequency:** monthly, annually. **Effective Market(s):** Minneapolis. **Units of Measure:** Dollars per metric ton. **Time Period Covered:** monthly latest year, annually latest 9 years.

SUNFLOWERSEED MEAL PELLETS: 37-38% PROTEIN, ARGENTINA/URUGUAY

Source: *World Oilseed Situation and Market Highlights.* **Price Frequency:** monthly, annually. **Effective Market(s):** Rotterdam. **Units of Measure:** Dollars per metric ton. **Time Period Covered:** monthly latest year, annually latest 9 years.

SUNFLOWERSEED OIL

Source: *FAO Quarterly Bulletin of Statistics.* **Price Frequency:** monthly, annually. **Effective Market(s):** Rotterdam. **Units of Measure:** Dollars per 1000 kilograms, dollars per metric ton. **Time Period Covered:** latest 3 years.

Source: *Milling & Baking News.* **Price Frequency:** weekly. **Effective Market(s):** Midwest. **Units of Measure:** cents per lb. **Type of Price:** spot bulk. **Time Period Covered:** latest week.

Source: *Oil World.* **Price Frequency:** weekly, monthly, annually. **Effective Market(s):** Rotterdam. **Units of Measure:** Dollars per tonne. **Type of Price:** lowest representative asking. **Time Period Covered:** weekly latest 3 weeks, monthly latest 2 months, annually latest 2 years.

Source: *World Oilseed Situation and Market Highlights.* **Price Frequency:** monthly, annually. **Effective Market(s):** Rotterdam. **Units of Measure:** Dollars per metric ton. **Time Period Covered:** monthly latest year, annually latest 9 years.

Source: *World Oilseed Situation and Market Highlights.* **Price Frequency:** monthly, annually. **Effective Market(s):** Minneapolis. **Units of Measure:** Dollars per metric ton. **Time Period Covered:** monthly latest year, annually latest 9 years.

SUNFLOWERSEED OIL: CRUDE

Source: *Chemical Marketing Reporter.* **Price Frequency:** weekly. **Effective Market(s):** Gulf Coast. **Units of Measure:** Dollars per lb. **Type of Price:** spot. **Time Period Covered:** latest week.

Source: *Commodity Year Book.* **Price Frequency:** annually. **Effective Market(s):** Minneapolis. **Units of Measure:** Dollars per metric ton. **Time Period Covered:** latest 4 years.

Source: *Oil Crops Situation and Outlook.* **Price Frequency:** annually. **Effective Market(s):** Minneapolis. **Units of Measure:** Dollars per metric ton. **Type of Price:** average. **Time Period Covered:** latest 10 years.

SUNFLOWERSEED PELLETS: 37/38% PROTEIN, ARGENTINA/URUGUAY

Source: *Oil World.* **Price Frequency:** weekly, monthly, annually. **Effective Market(s):** Rotterdam. **Units of Measure:** Dollars per tonne. **Type of Price:** lowest representative asking. **Time Period Covered:** weekly latest 3 weeks, monthly latest 2 months, annually latest 2 years.

SUPERPHOSPHATE

Source: *International Financial Statistics.* **Price Frequency:** monthly, quarterly, annually. **Effective Market(s):** Gulf ports. **Units of Measure:** Dollars per metric ton, index. **Type of Price:** market price, price index. **Time Period Covered:** latest 5 months, latest 5 quarters, latest 5 years.

Source: *International Financial Statistics Yearbook.* **Price Frequency:** annually. **Effective Market(s):** Gulf ports. **Units of Measure:** Dollars per metric ton. **Type of Price:** wholesale. **Time Period Covered:** latest 30 years.

SUPERPHOSPHATE: TRIPLE, 46%

Source: *Journal of Commerce and Commercial.* **Price Frequency:** weekly in Thursday issue. **Units of Measure:** Dollars per ton. **Type of Price:** spot. **Time Period Covered:** latest week.

SUPERPHOSPHATE: TRIPLE, 46% OR MORE, GRANULAR

Source: *Chemical Marketing Reporter.* **Price Frequency:** weekly. **Effective Market(s):** Florida. **Units of Measure:** Dollars per ton. **Type of Price:** spot. **Time Period Covered:** latest week.

SUPERPHOSPHATE: TRIPLE, 46% OR MORE, RUN-OF-PILE

Source: *Chemical Marketing Reporter.* **Price Frequency:** weekly. **Effective Market(s):** Florida. **Units of Measure:** Dollars per unit-ton. **Type of Price:** spot. **Time Period Covered:** latest week.

SUPERPHOSPHATE FERTILIZER: 44-46% PHOSPHATE

Source: *Agricultural Prices.* **Price Frequency:** monthly. **Effective Market(s):** 9 domestic markets, United States. **Units of Measure:** Dollars per ton. **Type of Price:** paid by farmer. **Time Period Covered:** latest month.

Source: *Agricultural Prices Annual Summary.* **Price Frequency:** semiannually. **Effective Market(s):** 6 domestic markets, United States. **Units of Measure:** Dollars per ton. **Type of Price:** average paid by farmer. **Time Period Covered:** latest year, for US latest 6 years.

SURIMI (FISH): PROCESSORS FISH BLOCKS

Source: *Seafood Price-Current.* **Price Frequency:** semiweekly. **Effective Market(s):** Seattle. **Units of Measure:** Dollars per lb. **Time Period Covered:** latest day.

SWEDEN KRONA

Source: *Asian Wall Street Journal.* **Price Frequency:** daily. **Effective Market(s):** United States. **Units of Measure:** Swedish krona per ECU, per SDR. **Type of Price:** foreign exchange. **Time Period Covered:** latest 2 days.

Source: *Barron's.* **Price Frequency:** weekly. **Effective Market(s):** New York. **Units of Measure:** Swedish krona per United States dollar. **Type of Price:** foreign exchange. **Time Period Covered:** latest 2 weeks.

Source: *The Economist.* **Price Frequency:** weekly. **Effective Market(s):** London. **Units of Measure:** Swedish krona per British pounds. **Type of Price:** foreign exchange. **Time Period Covered:** latest week, year ago.

Source: *New York Times.* **Price Frequency:** daily. **Effective Market(s):** United States. **Units of Measure:** Swedish krona per United States dollar. **Type of Price:** foreign exchange. **Time Period Covered:** latest 2 days.

Source: *Timber Bulletin.* **Price Frequency:** monthly, annually. **Units of Measure:** Swedish krona per United States dollar. **Type of Price:** foreign exchange. **Time Period Covered:** latest 2 years.

SWEDES (VEGETABLE)

Source: *New Zealand Farmer.* **Price Frequency:** weekly, seasonally. **Effective Market(s):** New Zealand. **Units of Measure:** New Zealand dollars per bag. **Time Period Covered:** latest week.

SWEDES: CLEAN

Source: *Farmers Weekly.* **Price Frequency:** weekly, seasonally. **Effective Market(s):** Birmingham (England), Bristol (England), Covent Garden (England), Glasgow (Scotland), Manchester (England). **Units of Measure:** British pounds per unit. **Type of Price:** wholesale. **Time Period Covered:** latest week.

SWEET POTATOES

Source: *Agricultural Prices Annual Summary.* **Price Frequency:** annually. **Effective Market(s):** 12 domestic markets, United States. **Units of Measure:** Dollars per 100 lbs. **Type of Price:** average received by farmer. **Time Period Covered:** latest 2 years, for US latest 6 years.

Source: *Statistical Bulletin of the South Pacific: Retail Price Indexes.* **Price Frequency:** annually. **Effective Market(s):** 18 South Pacific markets. **Units of Measure:** Australian dollars per kilogram. **Type of Price:** retail. **Time Period Covered:** latest year.

SWEET POTATOES: BEAUREGARD

Source: *The Packer.* **Price Frequency:** weekly, seasonally. **Effective Market(s):** varies. **Units of Measure:** Dollars per carton. **Type of Price:** average received by farmer. **Time Period Covered:** latest week.

SWEET POTATOES: GARNET

Source: *California Farmer.* **Price Frequency:** semimonthly, seasonally. **Effective Market(s):** Atwater/Livingston (CA). **Units of Measure:** Dollars per 40 lb. carton. **Time Period Covered:** latest week, month ago, year ago.

Source: *Fresh Fruit and Vegetable Prices.* **Price Frequency:** monthly, seasonally. **Effective Market(s):** Atwater Livingston (CA). **Units of Measure:** Dollars per carton. **Type of Price:** average price at shipping point. **Time Period Covered:** latest year.

SWEET POTATOES: JEWEL

Source: *Fresh Fruit and Vegetable Prices.* **Price Frequency:** monthly, seasonally. **Effective Market(s):** Atwater/Livingston (CA), Eastern North Carolina, Georgia. **Units of Measure:** Dollars per carton. **Type of Price:** average price at shipping point. **Time Period Covered:** latest year.

Source: *Lancaster Farming.* **Price Frequency:** weekly, seasonally. **Effective Market(s):** Pennsylvania. **Units of Measure:** Dollars per carton. **Type of Price:** market. **Time Period Covered:** latest week.

Source: *The Packer.* **Price Frequency:** weekly, seasonally. **Effective Market(s):** varies. **Units of Measure:** Dollars per carton. **Type of Price:** average received by farmer. **Time Period Covered:** latest week.

SWEET POTATOES: JEWEL, NORTH CAROLINA

Source: *Fresh Fruit and Vegetable Prices.* **Price Frequency:** monthly, seasonally. **Effective Market(s):** Chicago, New York City. **Units of Measure:** Dollars per carton/crate. **Type of Price:** average wholesale price. **Time Period Covered:** latest year.

SWEET POTATOES: LOUISIANA

Source: *Fresh Fruit and Vegetable Prices.* **Price Frequency:** monthly, seasonally. **Effective Market(s):** Chicago. **Units of Measure:** Dollars per carton/crate. **Type of Price:** average wholesale price. **Time Period Covered:** latest year.

SWEET POTATOES: PORTO RICO

Source: *Fresh Fruit and Vegetable Prices.* **Price Frequency:** monthly, seasonally. **Effective Market(s):** Eastern North Carolina, Louisiana. **Units of Measure:** Dollars per carton. **Type of Price:** average price at shipping point. **Time Period Covered:** latest year.

Source: *Fresh Fruit and Vegetable Prices.* **Price Frequency:** monthly, seasonally. **Effective Market(s):** Chicago, New York City. **Units of Measure:** Dollars per carton/crate. **Type of Price:** average wholesale price. **Time Period Covered:** latest year.

Source: *The Packer.* **Price Frequency:** weekly, seasonally. **Effective Market(s):** varies. **Units of Measure:** Dollars per carton. **Type of Price:** average received by farmer. **Time Period Covered:** latest week.

SWEET POTATOES: TRAVIS

Source: *The Packer.* **Price Frequency:** weekly, seasonally. **Effective Market(s):** varies. **Units of Measure:** Dollars per carton. **Type of Price:** average received by farmer. **Time Period Covered:** latest week.

SWEET POTATOES: YELLOW JERSEY

Source: *California Farmer.* **Price Frequency:** semimonthly, seasonally. **Effective Market(s):** Atwater/Livingston (CA). **Units of Measure:** Dollars per 40 lb. carton. **Time Period Covered:** latest week, month ago, year ago.

Source: *Fresh Fruit and Vegetable Prices.* **Price Frequency:** monthly, seasonally. **Effective Market(s):** Atwater/Livingston (CA). **Units of Measure:** Dollars per carton. **Type of Price:** average price at shipping point. **Time Period Covered:** latest year.

SWITCHES: ELECTRICAL

Source: *Purchasing.* **Price Frequency:** monthly. **Units of Measure:** cents each. **Type of Price:** transaction. **Time Period Covered:** latest day, month ago, 6 months ago, year ago.

SWITZERLAND FRANCS

Source: *Asian Wall Street Journal.* **Price Frequency:** daily. **Effective Market(s):** United States. **Units of Measure:** Swiss francs per ECU. **Type of Price:** foreign exchange. **Time Period Covered:** latest 2 days.

Source: *Barron's.* **Price Frequency:** weekly. **Effective Market(s):** New York. **Units of Measure:** Swiss francs per United States dollar. **Type of Price:** foreign exchange. **Time Period Covered:** latest 2 weeks.

Source: *The Economist.* **Price Frequency:** weekly. **Effective Market(s):** London. **Units of Measure:** Swiss francs per British pounds. **Type of Price:** foreign exchange. **Time Period Covered:** latest week, year ago.

Source: *New York Times.* **Price Frequency:** daily. **Effective Market(s):** United States. **Units of Measure:** Swiss francs per United States dollar. **Type of Price:** foreign exchange. **Time Period Covered:** latest 2 days.

Source: *Timber Bulletin.* **Price Frequency:** monthly, annually. **Units of Measure:** Swiss francs per United States dollar. **Type of Price:** foreign exchange. **Time Period Covered:** latest 2 years.

SWITZERLAND FRANCS: FUTURES

Source: *Asian Wall Street Journal.* **Price Frequency:** daily. **Effective Market(s):** Chicago. **Units of Measure:** United States dollars per Swiss francs. **Type of Price:** foreign exchange futures. **Time Period Covered:** latest day.

Source: *Barron's.* **Price Frequency:** weekly. **Effective Market(s):** Chicago. **Units of Measure:** United States dollars per Swiss franc. **Type of Price:** foreign exchange futures. **Time Period Covered:** latest week.

Source: *Los Angeles Times.* **Price Frequency:** daily. **Effective Market(s):** Chicago. **Units of Measure:** United States dollars per Swiss franc. **Type of Price:** foreign exchange futures. **Time Period Covered:** latest day.

Source: *New York Times.* **Price Frequency:** daily. **Effective Market(s):** Chicago. **Units of Measure:** United States dollars per Swiss francs. **Type of Price:** foreign exchange futures. **Time Period Covered:** latest day.

Source: *Urner Barry's Price-Current.* **Price Frequency:** daily. **Units of Measure:** United States dollars per Swiss francs. **Type of Price:** foreign exchange futures. **Time Period Covered:** latest day.

SWORDFISH: CLIPPER, WHOLE, FROZEN, JAPANESE

Source: *Seafood Price-Current.* **Price Frequency:** semiweekly. **Effective Market(s):** Mid-Atlantic. **Units of Measure:** Dollars per lb. **Type of Price:** sale by first receiver. **Time Period Covered:** latest day.

SWORDFISH: FILLETS, FRESH, HAWAIIAN

Source: *Seafood Price-Current.* **Price Frequency:** semiweekly. **Effective Market(s):** Hawaii. **Units of Measure:** Dollars per lb. **Type of Price:** sale by first receiver. **Time Period Covered:** latest day.

SWORDFISH: FRESH, DOMESTIC

Source: *Seafood Price-Current.* **Price Frequency:** semiweekly. **Effective Market(s):** Gulf/Southeast. **Units of Measure:** Dollars per lb. **Type of Price:** sale by first receiver. **Time Period Covered:** latest day.

SWORDFISH: WHOLE, FRESH

Source: *HRI-Buyer's Guide.* **Price Frequency:** weekly. **Effective Market(s):** New York. **Units of Measure:** Dollars per lb. **Type of Price:** dealer. **Time Period Covered:** latest week.

Source: *Seafood Price-Current.* **Price Frequency:** semiweekly. **Effective Market(s):** Boston, Mid-Atlantic, New Bedford (MA), Portland (ME), West Coast. **Units of Measure:** Dollars per lb. **Type of Price:** sale by first receiver, auction price. **Time Period Covered:** latest day.

SWORDFISH: WHOLE, FRESH, CENTRAL/ SOUTH AMERICA, IMPORTED

Source: *Seafood Price-Current.* **Price Frequency:** semi-weekly. **Effective Market(s):** Miami. **Units of Measure:** Dollars per lb. **Type of Price:** sale by first receiver. **Time Period Covered:** latest day.

SWORDFISH: WHOLE, FRESH, CHILEAN, IMPORTED

Source: *Seafood Price-Current.* **Price Frequency:** semi-weekly. **Effective Market(s):** Miami. **Units of Measure:** Dollars per lb. **Type of Price:** sale by first receiver. **Time Period Covered:** latest day.

SWORDFISH: WHOLE, FRESH, HAWAIIAN

Source: *Seafood Price-Current.* **Price Frequency:** semi-weekly. **Effective Market(s):** Hawaii. **Units of Measure:** Dollars per lb. **Type of Price:** sale by first receiver. **Time Period Covered:** latest day.

SWORDFISH LOIN: WHOLE, FRESH

Source: *Seafood Price-Current.* **Price Frequency:** semi-weekly. **Effective Market(s):** West Coast. **Units of Measure:** Dollars per lb. **Type of Price:** sale by first receiver. **Time Period Covered:** latest day.

SWORDFISH LOIN: WHOLE, FRESH, CHILEAN, IMPORTED

Source: *Seafood Price-Current.* **Price Frequency:** semi-weekly. **Effective Market(s):** Miami. **Units of Measure:** Dollars per lb. **Type of Price:** sale by first receiver. **Time Period Covered:** latest day

TABLETS: PAPER

Source: *Pulp & Paper Week.* **Price Frequency:** monthly, irregularly. **Units of Measure:** index. **Type of Price:** price index. **Time Period Covered:** latest 3 month.

TAFFETA

Source: *DNR: Daily News Record.* **Price Frequency:** quarterly. **Units of Measure:** Dollars per yard. **Type of Price:** spot. **Time Period Covered:** latest 3 quarters.

TAFFETA: ACETATE

Source: *DNR: Daily News Record.* **Price Frequency:** quarterly. **Units of Measure:** Dollars per yard. **Type of Price:** spot. **Time Period Covered:** latest 3 quarters.

TAFFETA: NYLON

Source: *JTN: The International Textile Magazine.* **Price Frequency:** monthly. **Effective Market(s):** Japan. **Units of Measure:** Japanese yen per meter. **Type of Price:** spot. **Time Period Covered:** latest month.

TAFFETA: NYLON, PLAIN DYED

Source: *JTN: The International Textile Magazine.* **Price Frequency:** monthly. **Effective Market(s):** Taiwan. **Units of Measure:** Dollars per yard. **Type of Price:** export. **Time Period Covered:** latest month.

TAFFETA: NYLON, WATERPROOF

Source: *JTN: The International Textile Magazine.* **Price Frequency:** monthly. **Effective Market(s):** Taiwan. **Units of Measure:** Dollars per yard. **Type of Price:** export. **Time Period Covered:** latest month.

TAIWAN DOLLARS

Source: *Asian Wall Stree Journal.* **Price Frequency:** daily. **Effective Market(s):** Asia. **Units of Measure:** Taiwan dollars per United States dollar. **Type of Price:** foreign exchange. **Time Period Covered:** latest 2 days.

Source: *Barron's.* **Price Frequency:** weekly. **Effective Market(s):** New York. **Units of Measure:** Taiwan dollars per United States dollar. **Type of Price:** foreign exchange. **Time Period Covered:** latest 2 weeks.

Source: *New York Times.* **Price Frequency:** daily. **Effective Market(s):** New York. **Units of Measure:** Taiwan dollars per United States dollar. **Type of Price:** foreign exchange. **Time Period Covered:** latest 2 days.

TALC: 99.5%, MICRONIZED, DOMESTIC

Source: *Chemical Marketing Reporter.* **Price Frequency:** weekly. **Effective Market(s):** New York. **Units of Measure:** Dollars per ton. **Type of Price:** spot. **Time Period Covered:** latest week.

TALC: COSMETIC, ITALIAN

Source: *Industrial Minerals.* **Price Frequency:** monthly. **Effective Market(s):** main European port. **Units of Measure:** British pounds per metric tonne. **Type of Price:** producer & dealer. **Time Period Covered:** latest month.

TALC: FINE GROUND, FRENCH

Source: *Industrial Minerals.* **Price Frequency:** monthly. **Effective Market(s):** main European port. **Units of Measure:** British pounds per metric tonne. **Type of Price:** producer & dealer. **Time Period Covered:** latest month.

TALC: GROUND, CANADIAN, IMPORTED

Source: *Chemical Marketing Reporter.* **Price Frequency:** weekly. **Effective Market(s):** New York. **Units of Measure:** Dollars per ton. **Type of Price:** spot. **Time Period Covered:** latest week.

TALC: GROUND, DOMESTIC

Source: *Chemical Marketing Reporter.* **Price Frequency:** weekly. **Effective Market(s):** New York. **Units of Measure:** Dollars per ton. **Type of Price:** spot. **Time Period Covered:** latest week.

TALC: GROUND, NORWEGIAN

Source: *Industrial Minerals.* **Price Frequency:** monthly. **Effective Market(s):** United Kingdom. **Units of Measure:** British pounds per metric tonne. **Type of Price:** producer & dealer. **Time Period Covered:** latest month.

TALC: MICRONIZED, NORWEGIAN

Source: *Industrial Minerals.* **Price Frequency:** monthly. **Effective Market(s):** United Kingdom. **Units of Measure:** British pounds per metric tonne. **Type of Price:** producer & dealer. **Time Period Covered:** latest month.

TALC: NORMAL, CHINESE

Source: *Industrial Minerals.* **Price Frequency:** monthly. **Effective Market(s):** United Kingdom. **Units of Measure:** British pounds per metric tonne. **Type of Price:** producer & dealer. **Time Period Covered:** latest month.

TALC: ORDINARY, GROUND, CALIFORNIAN

Source: *Chemical Marketing Reporter.* **Price Frequency:** weekly. **Effective Market(s):** New York. **Units of Measure:** Dollars per ton. **Type of Price:** spot. **Time Period Covered:** latest week.

TALC: ORDINARY, GROUND, OFF-COLOR, VERMONT

Source: *Chemical Marketing Reporter.* **Price Frequency:** weekly. **Effective Market(s):** New York. **Units of Measure:** Dollars per ton. **Type of Price:** spot. **Time Period Covered:** latest week.

TALC: PAINT, NEW YORK

Source: *Industrial Minerals.* **Price Frequency:** monthly. **Effective Market(s):** main European port. **Units of Measure:** Dollars per ton. **Type of Price:** producer & dealer. **Time Period Covered:** latest month.

TALL OIL: CRUDE

Source: *Chemical Marketing Reporter.* **Price Frequency:** weekly. **Effective Market(s):** Southeast. **Units of Measure:** Dollars per ton. **Type of Price:** spot. **Time Period Covered:** latest week.

TALL OIL: DISTILLED

Source: *Chemical Marketing Reporter.* **Price Frequency:** weekly. **Effective Market(s):** New York. **Units of Measure:** Dollars per lb. **Type of Price:** spot. **Time Period Covered:** latest week.

TALL OIL: REFINED, ACID

Source: *Chemical Marketing Reporter.* **Price Frequency:** weekly. **Effective Market(s):** New York. **Units of Measure:** Dollars per lb. **Type of Price:** spot. **Time Period Covered:** latest week.

TALL OIL ACID: 2% ROSIN ACID

Source: *Chemical Marketing Reporter.* **Price Frequency:** weekly. **Effective Market(s):** New York. **Units of Measure:** Dollars per lb. **Type of Price:** spot. **Time Period Covered:** latest week.

TALL OIL ROSIN

Source: *Journal of Commerce and Commercial.* **Price Frequency:** weekly in Monday issue. **Effective Market(s):** South. **Units of Measure:** Dollars per 100 lbs. **Type of Price:** spot. **Time Period Covered:** latest week.

TALL OIL ROSIN: CRUDE

Source: *Journal of Commerce and Commercial.* **Price Frequency:** weekly in Monday issue. **Effective Market(s):** South. **Units of Measure:** Dollars per ton. **Type of Price:** spot. **Time Period Covered:** latest week.

TALLOW

Source: *CRB Commodity Index Report.* **Price Frequency:** weekly. **Effective Market(s):** Chicago. **Units of Measure:** Dollars per lb. **Type of Price:** spot. **Time Period Covered:** latest week.

TALLOW: BLEACHABLE

Source: *Asian Wall Street Journal.* **Price Frequency:** daily. **Effective Market(s):** Chicago. **Units of Measure:** Dollars per lb. **Type of Price:** cash. **Time Period Covered:** latest 2 days, year ago.

Source: *Wall Street Journal.* **Price Frequency:** daily. **Effective Market(s):** Chicago. **Units of Measure:** Dollars per lb. **Time Period Covered:** latest day, day ago, year ago.

TALLOW: EDIBLE

Source: *Asian Wall Street Journal.* **Price Frequency:** daily. **Effective Market(s):** Chicago. **Units of Measure:** Dollars per lb. **Type of Price:** cash. **Time Period Covered:** latest 2 days, year ago.

Source: *Livestock, Meat, Wool Market News.* **Price Frequency:** weekly. **Effective Market(s):** Chicago, Gulf/Texas. **Units of Measure:** Dollars per 100 lbs. **Time Period Covered:** latest week, year ago.

Source: *Milling & Baking News.* **Price Frequency:** weekly. **Effective Market(s):** Chicago. **Units of Measure:** cents per lb. **Type of Price:** spot bulk. **Time Period Covered:** latest week.

Source: *National Provisioner.* **Price Frequency:** weekly. **Effective Market(s):** Chicago. **Units of Measure:** Dollars per 100 lbs. **Time Period Covered:** latest week.

Source: *Wall Street Journal.* **Price Frequency:** daily. **Effective Market(s):** Chicago. **Units of Measure:** Dollars per lb. **Time Period Covered:** latest day, day ago, year ago.

TALLOW: EDIBLE, LOOSE

Source: *Commodity Year Book.* **Price Frequency:** annually. **Effective Market(s):** Chicago. **Units of Measure:** cents per lb. **Type of Price:** wholesale. **Time Period Covered:** latest 8 years.

TALLOW: FANCY, BLEACHABLE

Source: *Feedstuffs.* **Price Frequency:** weekly. **Effective Market(s):** 7 domestic markets. **Units of Measure:** Dollars per lb. **Time Period Covered:** latest week.

TALLOW: FANCY, BLEACHABLE, UNITED STATES

Source: *Oil World.* **Price Frequency:** weekly, monthly, annually. **Effective Market(s):** Rotterdam. **Units of Measure:** Dollars per tonne. **Type of Price:** lowest representative asking. **Time Period Covered:** weekly latest 3 weeks, monthly latest 2 months, annually latest 2 years.

TALLOW: FANCY, INEDIBLE

Source: *Chemical Marketing Reporter.* **Price Frequency:** weekly. **Effective Market(s):** New York. **Units of Measure:** cents per lb. **Type of Price:** spot. **Time Period Covered:** latest week.

Source: *National Provisioner.* **Price Frequency:** weekly. **Effective Market(s):** Chicago, Missouri River. **Units of Measure:** Dollars per 100 lbs. **Time Period Covered:** latest week.

TALLOW: FATTY ACIDS, TECHNICAL

Source: *Chemical Marketing Reporter.* **Price Frequency:** weekly. **Effective Market(s):** New York. **Units of Measure:** Dollars per lb. **Type of Price:** spot. **Time Period Covered:** latest week.

TALLOW: HYDROGENATED, TECHNICAL, FLAKE

Source: *Chemical Marketing Reporter.* **Price Frequency:** weekly. **Effective Market(s):** New York. **Units of Measure:** Dollars per lb. **Type of Price:** spot. **Time Period Covered:** latest week.

TALLOW: INEDIBLE

Source: *Agricultural Outlook.* **Price Frequency:** monthly, annually. **Effective Market(s):** Chicago. **Units of Measure:** cents per lb. **Type of Price:** export. **Time Period Covered:** monthly latest 6 months, annually latest 3 years.

TALLOW: NO. 1, INEDIBLE

Source: *Commodity Year Book.* **Price Frequency:** annually. **Effective Market(s):** Chicago. **Units of Measure:** cents per lb. **Type of Price:** wholesale. **Time Period Covered:** latest 8 years.

Source: *National Provisioner.* **Price Frequency:** weekly. **Effective Market(s):** Chicago. **Units of Measure:** Dollars per 100 lbs. **Time Period Covered:** latest week.

Source: *Oil Crops Situation and Outlook.* **Price Frequency:** monthly. **Effective Market(s):** Chicago. **Units of Measure:** cents per lb. **Type of Price:** wholesale. **Time Period Covered:** latest 5 months.

TALLOW: NO. 1, PRIME, INEDIBLE

Source: *Commodity Year Book.* **Price Frequency:** monthly, annually. **Effective Market(s):** Chicago. **Units of Measure:** cents per lb. **Type of Price:** wholesale. **Time Period Covered:** latest 8 years.

TALLOW: NO. 2, INEDIBLE

Source: *National Provisioner.* **Price Frequency:** weekly. **Effective Market(s):** Chicago. **Units of Measure:** Dollars per 100 lbs. **Time Period Covered:** latest week.

TALLOW: PACKER BLEACHABLE, INEDIBLE

Source: *Livestock, Meat, Wool Market News.* **Price Frequency:** weekly. **Effective Market(s):** Chicago, Gulf. **Units of Measure:** Dollars per 100 lbs. **Time Period Covered:** latest week, year ago.

TALLOW: PRIME

Source: *Feedstuffs.* **Price Frequency:** weekly. **Effective Market(s):** 10 domestic markets. **Units of Measure:** Dollars per lb. **Time Period Covered:** latest week.

TALLOW: PRIME, INEDIBLE

Source: *Journal of Commerce and Commercial.* **Price Frequency:** daily. **Effective Market(s):** Chicago. **Units of Measure:** Dollars per lb. **Type of Price:** spot supplier. **Time Period Covered:** latest day.

Source: *National Provisioner.* **Price Frequency:** weekly. **Effective Market(s):** Chicago. **Units of Measure:** Dollars per 100 lbs. **Time Period Covered:** latest week.

TALLOW: RENDERER BLEACHABLE, INEDIBLE

Source: *Livestock, Meat, Wool Market News.* **Price Frequency:** weekly. **Effective Market(s):** Chicago, Gulf. **Units of Measure:** Dollars per 100 lbs. **Time Period Covered:** latest week, year ago.

TALLOW: SPECIAL, INEDIBLE

Source: *National Provisioner.* **Price Frequency:** weekly. **Effective Market(s):** Chicago. **Units of Measure:** Dollars per 100 lbs. **Time Period Covered:** latest week.

TAMARILLOS

Source: *New Zealand Farmer.* **Price Frequency:** weekly, seasonally. **Effective Market(s):** New Zealand. **Units of Measure:** New Zealand dollars per unit. **Time Period Covered:** latest week.

TAMARIND SEED POWDER

Source: *Journal of Commerce and Commercial.* **Price Frequency:** weekly in Monday issue. **Units of Measure:** Dollars per lb. **Type of Price:** spot. **Time Period Covered:** latest week.

TANGELOS

Source: *Agricultural Prices.* **Price Frequency:** monthly. **Effective Market(s):** United States. **Units of Measure:** Dollars per box. **Type of Price:** received by farmer. **Time Period Covered:** latest 2 months, year ago.

Source: *Fresh Fruit and Vegetable Prices.* **Price Frequency:** monthly, seasonally. **Effective Market(s):** Central/South California. **Units of Measure:** Dollars per carton. **Type of Price:** average price at shipping point. **Time Period Covered:** latest year.

Source: *New Zealand Farmer.* **Price Frequency:** weekly, seasonally. **Effective Market(s):** New Zealand. **Units of Measure:** New Zealand dollars per bushel. **Time Period Covered:** latest week.

TANGELOS: CALIFORNIA

Source: *Fresh Fruit and Vegetable Prices.* **Price Frequency:** monthly, seasonally. **Effective Market(s):** Chicago, New York City. **Units of Measure:** Dollars per crate/carton. **Type of Price:** average wholesale price. **Time Period Covered:** latest year.

TANGELOS: FLORIDA

Source: *Fresh Fruit and Vegetable Prices.* **Price Frequency:** monthly, seasonally. **Effective Market(s):** Chicago. **Units of Measure:** Dollars per crate/carton. **Type of Price:** average wholesale price. **Time Period Covered:** latest year.

TANGELOS: FRESH

Source: *Agricultural Prices Annual Summary.* **Price Frequency:** monthly, annually, seasonally. **Effective Market(s):** Florida. **Units of Measure:** Dollars per lb. **Type of Price:** average received by grower. **Time Period Covered:** latest 2 years.

TANGELOS: MINEOLA

Source: *California Farmer.* **Price Frequency:** semimonthly, seasonally. **Effective Market(s):** Coachella Valley (CA). **Units of Measure:** Dollars per 40 lb. cartons. **Time Period Covered:** latest week, month ago, year ago.

TANGELOS: MINEOLA, FLORIDA

Source: *Fresh Fruit and Vegetable Prices.* **Price Frequency:** monthly, seasonally. **Effective Market(s):** New York City. **Units of Measure:** Dollars per crate/carton. **Type of Price:** average wholesale price. **Time Period Covered:** latest year.

TANGELOS: ORLANDO

Source: *California Farmer.* **Price Frequency:** semimonthly, seasonally. **Effective Market(s):** Coachella Valley (CA). **Units of Measure:** Dollars per 30 lb. carton. **Time Period Covered:** latest week, month ago, year ago.

TANGELOS: PROCESSING

Source: *Agricultural Prices Annual Summary.* **Price Frequency:** monthly, annually, seasonally. **Effective Market(s):** Florida. **Units of Measure:** Dollars per lb. **Type of Price:** average received by grower. **Time Period Covered:** latest 2 years.

TANGERINE OIL: BRAZILIAN

Source: *Chemical Marketing Reporter.* **Price Frequency:** weekly. **Effective Market(s):** New York. **Units of Measure:** Dollars per lb. **Type of Price:** spot. **Time Period Covered:** latest week.

TANGERINE OIL: FLORIDA

Source: *Chemical Marketing Reporter.* **Price Frequency:** weekly. **Effective Market(s):** New York. **Units of Measure:** Dollars per lb. **Type of Price:** spot. **Time Period Covered:** latest week.

TANGERINES

Source: *Agricultural Prices.* **Price Frequency:** monthly. **Effective Market(s):** United States. **Units of Measure:** Dollars per box. **Type of Price:** received by farmer. **Time Period Covered:** latest 2 months, year ago.

Source: *California Farmer.* **Price Frequency:** semimonthly, seasonally. **Effective Market(s):** Coachella Valley (CA). **Time Period Covered:** Latest week, month ago, year ago.

Source: *Fresh Fruit and Vegetable Prices.* **Price Frequency:** monthly, seasonally. **Effective Market(s):** Coachella Valley (CA). **Units of Measure:** Dollars per carton. **Type of Price:** average price at shipping point. **Time Period Covered:** latest year.

TANGERINES: DANCY, FLORIDA

Source: *Fresh Fruit and Vegetable Prices.* **Price Frequency:** monthly, seasonally. **Effective Market(s):** Chicago, New York City. **Units of Measure:** Dollars per crate/carton. **Type of Price:** average wholesale price. **Time Period Covered:** latest year.

TANGERINES: DANCY, MEXICAN

Source: *Fresh Fruit and Vegetable Prices.* **Price Frequency:** monthly, seasonally. **Effective Market(s):** Chicago. **Units of Measure:** Dollars per crate/carton. **Type of Price:** average wholesale price. **Time Period Covered:** latest year.

TANGERINES: FRESH

Source: *Agricultural Prices Annual Summary.* **Price Frequency:** monthly, annually, seasonally. **Effective Market(s):** Arizona, California, Florida, United States. **Units of Measure:** Dollars per lb. **Type of Price:** average received by grower. **Time Period Covered:** latest 2 years.

TANGERINES: HONEY, FLORIDA

Source: *Fresh Fruit and Vegetable Prices.* **Price Frequency:** monthly, seasonally. **Effective Market(s):** Chicago, New York City. **Units of Measure:** Dollars per crate/carton. **Type of Price:** average wholesale price. **Time Period Covered:** latest year.

TANGERINES: MEXICAN

Source: *Fresh Fruit and Vegetable Prices.* **Price Frequency:** monthly, seasonally. **Effective Market(s):** South Texas. **Units of Measure:** Dollars per crate or carton. **Type of Price:** price paid at point of entry. **Time Period Covered:** latest year.

TANGERINES: PROCESSING

Source: *Agricultural Prices Annual Summary.* **Price Frequency:** monthly, annually, seasonally. **Effective Market(s):** Arizona, California, Florida, United States. **Units of Measure:** Dollars per lb. **Type of Price:** average received by grower. **Time Period Covered:** latest 2 years.

TANKAGE

Source: *Feedstuffs.* **Price Frequency:** weekly. **Effective Market(s):** 10 domestic markets. **Units of Measure:** Dollars per bulk ton. **Time Period Covered:** latest week.

Source: *Feedstuffs.* **Price Frequency:** weekly. **Effective Market(s):** Chicago. **Units of Measure:** Dollars per ton. **Time Period Covered:** latest week, week ago, 6 months ago, year ago.

TANNIC ACID

Source: *Journal of Commerce and Commercial.* **Price Frequency:** weekly in Friday issue. **Units of Measure:** Dollars per lb. **Type of Price:** spot. **Time Period Covered:** latest week.

TANNIC ACID: FLUFFY, NF

Source: *Chemical Marketing Reporter.* **Price Frequency:** weekly. **Effective Market(s):** New York. **Units of Measure:** Dollars per lb. **Type of Price:** spot. **Time Period Covered:** latest week.

TANNIC ACID: FOOD GRADE

Source: *Journal of Commerce and Commercial.* **Price Frequency:** weekly in Friday issue. **Units of Measure:** Dollars per lb. **Type of Price:** spot. **Time Period Covered:** latest week.

TANNIC ACID: TECHNICAL GRADE

Source: *Journal of Commerce and Commerical.* **Price Frequency:** weekly in Thursday issue. **Units of Measure:** Dollars per lb. **Type of Price:** spot. **Time Period Covered:** latest week.

TANNIC ACID POWDER: TECHNICAL GRADE

Source: *Chemical Marketing Reporter.* **Price Frequency:** weekly. **Effective Market(s):** New York. **Units of Measure:** Dollars per lb. **Type of Price:** spot. **Time Period Covered:** latest week.

Source: *Journal of Commerce and Commercial.* **Price Frequency:** weekly in Friday issue. **Units of Measure:** Dollars per lb. **Type of Price:** spot. **Time Period Covered:** latest week.

TAPE: GUMMED SEALING

Source: *Pulp & Paper Week.* **Price Frequency:** monthly, irregularly. **Units of Measure:** index. **Type of Price:** price index. **Time Period Covered:** latest 3 month.

TAPIOCA FLOUR: SUPER, THAI

Source: *Selected Prices of Asia/Pacific Products.* **Price Frequency:** monthly. **Effective Market(s):** Rotterdam. **Units of Measure:** Dollars per metric ton. **Type of Price:** high, low. **Time Period Covered:** latest month.

TAPIOCA PELLETS

Source: *Agra Europe.* **Price Frequency:** weekly, irregularly. **Effective Market(s):** Rotterdam. **Units of Measure:** Dollars per tonne. **Time Period Covered:** latest week.

TAPIOCA PELLETS: HARD

Source: *Oil World.* **Price Frequency:** weekly, monthly, annually. **Effective Market(s):** Rotterdam. **Units of Measure:** Dollars per tonne. **Type of Price:** lowest representative asking. **Time Period Covered:** weekly latest 3 weeks, monthly latest 2 months, annually latest 2 years.

Source: *Selected Prices of Asia/Pacific Products.* **Price Frequency:** monthly. **Effective Market(s):** Rotterdam. **Units of Measure:** Dollars per metric ton. **Type of Price:** high, low. **Time Period Covered:** latest month.

TAR ACID OIL: 15-18%

Source: *Chemical Marketing Reporter.* **Price Frequency:** weekly. **Effective Market(s):** New York. **Units of Measure:** Dollars per gallon. **Type of Price:** spot. **Time Period Covered:** latest week.

TAR ACID OIL: 25-28%

Source: *Chemical Marketing Reporter.* **Price Frequency:** weekly. **Effective Market(s):** New York. **Units of Measure:** Dollars per gallon. **Type of Price:** spot. **Time Period Covered:** latest week.

TAR ACID OIL: 50-53%

Source: *Chemical Marketing Reporter.* **Price Frequency:** weekly. **Effective Market(s):** New York. **Units of Measure:** Dollars per gallon. **Type of Price:** spot. **Time Period Covered:** latest week.

TARO

Source: *Agricultural Prices Annual Summary.* **Price Frequency:** annually. **Effective Market(s):** California, Hawaii. **Units of Measure:** Dollars per lb. **Type of Price:** average received by farmer. **Time Period Covered:** latest 6 years.

Source: *Statistical Bulletin of the South Pacific: Retail Price Indexes.* **Price Frequency:** annually. **Effective Market(s):** 18 South Pacific markets. **Units of Measure:** Australian dollars per kilogram. **Type of Price:** retail. **Time Period Covered:** latest year.

TARRAGON: DOMESTIC

Source: *U. S. Spice Trade.* **Price Frequency:** annually. **Effective Market(s):** New York. **Units of Measure:** cents per lb. **Type of Price:** spot. **Time Period Covered:** latest 3 years.

TARRAGON: FRENCH

Source: *U. S. Spice Trade.* **Price Frequency:** annually. **Effective Market(s):** New York. **Units of Measure:** cents per lb. **Type of Price:** spot. **Time Period Covered:** latest 3 years.

TARTAR EMETIC: TECHNICAL GRADE

Source: *Journal of Commerce and Commercial.* **Price Frequency:** weekly in Friday issue. **Units of Measure:** Dollars per lb. **Type of Price:** spot. **Time Period Covered:** latest week.

TARTARIC ACID

Source: *Journal of Commerce and Commercial.* **Price Frequency:** weekly in Friday issue. **Units of Measure:** Dollars per lb. **Type of Price:** spot. **Time Period Covered:** latest week.

TARTARIC ACID: NF

Source: *Chemical Marketing Reporter.* **Price Frequency:** weekly. **Effective Market(s):** New York. **Units of Measure:** Dollars per lb. **Type of Price:** spot. **Time Period Covered:** latest week.

TDI

see Toluene Di-isocyanate.

TEA

Source: *Commodity Trade and Price Trends.* **Price Frequency:** annually. **Effective Market(s):** London. **Units of Measure:** cents per kilogram, 1980 constant cents per kilogram. **Type of Price:** auction. **Time Period Covered:** latest 36 years.

Source: *Commodity Year Book.* **Price Frequency:** monthly, annually. **Effective Market(s):** London. **Units of Measure:** United States cents per lb. **Type of Price:** auction. **Time Period Covered:** latest 7 years.

Source: *Economic and Energy Indicators.* **Price Frequency:** biweekly. **Effective Market(s):** London. **Units of Measure:** cents per lb. **Type of Price:** average auction. **Time Period Covered:** latest 3 months, quarters, and years.

Source: *FAO Quarterly Bulletin of Statistics.* **Price Frequency:** monthly, annually. **Effective Market(s):** London. **Units of Measure:** British pounds per 100 kilograms, dollars per metric ton. **Type of Price:** auction. **Time Period Covered:** latest 3 years.

Source: *International Financial Statistics.* **Price Frequency:** monthly, quarterly, annually. **Effective Market(s):** London. **Units of Measure:** cents per lb., index. **Type of Price:** auction price, price index. **Time Period Covered:** latest 5 months, latest 5 quarters, latest 5 years.

Source: *International Financial Statistics Yearbook.* **Price Frequency:** annually. **Effective Market(s):** London. **Units of Measure:** cents per lb. **Type of Price:** auction. **Time Period Covered:** latest 30 years.

Source: *International Tea Committee Annual Bulletin of Statistics.* **Price Frequency:** monthly, annually. **Effective Market(s):** London. **Units of Measure:** British pence per kilogram. **Type of Price:** auction. **Time Period Covered:** latest 40 years.

Source: *International Tea Committee Limited Monthly Statistical Summary.* **Price Frequency:** weekly, year-to-date, seasonally. **Effective Market(s):** London. **Units of Measure:** British new pence per kilogram. **Type of Price:** auction. **Time Period Covered:** latest 4 weeks and year-to-date, same time last year.

Source: *Monthly Commodity Price Bulletin.* **Price Frequency:** monthly, annually. **Effective Market(s):** London. **Units of Measure:** new pence per kilogram, cents per lb. **Type of Price:** auction. **Time Period Covered:** latest 5 years.

Source: *Monthly Commodity Price Bulletin Supplement.* **Price Frequency:** monthly, quarterly, annually. **Effective Market(s):** London. **Units of Measure:** British new pence per kilogram, dollars per tonne. **Type of Price:** auction. **Time Period Covered:** latest 20 years.

Source: *Statistical Bulletin of the South Pacific: Retail Price Indexes.* **Price Frequency:** annually. **Effective Market(s):** 18 South Pacific markets. **Units of Measure:** Australian dollars per 250 grams. **Type of Price:** retail. **Time Period Covered:** latest year.

Source: *UNCTAD Commodity Yearbook.* **Price Frequency:** annually. **Effective Market(s):** London. **Units of Measure:** Dollars per metric ton. **Type of Price:** auction. **Time Period Covered:** latest 12 years.

Source: *World Tea Situation.* **Price Frequency:** monthly, annually. **Effective Market(s):** London. **Units of Measure:** cents per lb. **Type of Price:** auction. **Time Period Covered:** latest 15 years.

TEA: AFRICAN

Source: *International Tea Committee Annual Bulletin of Statistics.* **Price Frequency:** annually. **Effective Market(s):** London, Mombasa (Kenya). **Units of Measure:** British pence per kilogram, Kenyan shillings per kilogram. **Type of Price:** auction. **Time Period Covered:** latest 12 years.

TEA: ARGENTINE

Source: *International Tea Committee Annual Bulletin of Statistics.* **Price Frequency:** annually. **Effective Market(s):** London. **Units of Measure:** British pence per kilogram. **Type of Price:** auction. **Time Period Covered:** latest 12 years.

TEA: BANGLADESH

Source: *International Tea Committee Annual Bulletin of Statistics.* **Price Frequency:** annually. **Effective Market(s):** London. **Units of Measure:** British pence per kilogram. **Type of Price:** auction. **Time Period Covered:** latest 12 years.

Source: *International Tea Committee Limited Monthly Statistical Summary.* **Price Frequency:** weekly, year-to-date, seasonally. **Effective Market(s):** London. **Units of Measure:** British new pence per kilogram. **Type of Price:** offshore auction, auction. **Time Period Covered:** latest 4 weeks and year-to-date, same time last year.

TEA: BRAZILIAN

Source: *International Tea Committee Annual Bulletin of Statistics.* **Price Frequency:** annually. **Effective Market(s):** London. **Units of Measure:** British pence per kilogram. **Type of Price:** auction. **Time Period Covered:** latest 12 years.

TEA: BURUNDI

Source: *International Tea Committee Annual Bulletin of Statistics.* **Price Frequency:** annually. **Effective Market(s):** London, Mombasa (Kenya). **Units of Measure:** British pence per kilogram, Kenyan shillings per kilogram. **Type of Price:** auction. **Time Period Covered:** latest 12 years.

Source: *International Tea Committee Limited Monthly Statistical Summary.* **Price Frequency:** weekly, year-to-date, seasonally. **Effective Market(s):** London. **Units of Measure:** British new pence per kilogram. **Type of Price:** auction. **Time Period Covered:** latest 4 weeks and year-to-date, same time last year.

TEA: CAMEROON

Source: *International Tea Committee Annual Bulletin of Statistics.* **Price Frequency:** annually. **Effective Market(s):** London. **Units of Measure:** British pence per kilogram. **Type of Price:** auction. **Time Period Covered:** latest 12 years.

TEA: CHINESE

Source: *International Tea Committee Annual Bulletin of Statistics.* **Price Frequency:** annually. **Effective Market(s):** London. **Units of Measure:** British pence per kilogram. **Type of Price:** auction. **Time Period Covered:** latest 12 years.

TEA: DUST, ASSAM

Source: *International Tea Committee Annual Bulletin of Statistics.* **Price Frequency:** annually. **Effective Market(s):** Calcutta, Guwahati (India). **Units of Measure:** Indian rupees per kilogram. **Type of Price:** auction. **Time Period Covered:** latest 12 years.

TEA: DUST, BANGLADESH

Source: *International Tea Committee Annual Bulletin of Statistics.* **Price Frequency:** annually. **Effective Market(s):** Chittagong (Bangladesh). **Units of Measure:** Bangladesh taka per kilogram. **Type of Price:** auction. **Time Period Covered:** latest 12 years.

Source: *International Tea Committee Limited Monthly Statistical Summary.* **Price Frequency:** weekly, year-to-date, seasonally. **Effective Market(s):** Chittagong (Bangladesh). **Units of Measure:** Bangladesh ban taka per kilogram. **Type of Price:** auction. **Time Period Covered:** latest 4 weeks and year-to-date, same time last year.

TEA: DUST, CACHAR

Source: *International Tea Committee Annual Bulletin of Statistics.* **Price Frequency:** annually. **Effective Market(s):** Calcutta, Guwahati (India). **Units of Measure:** Indian rupees per kilogram. **Type of Price:** auction. **Time Period Covered:** latest 12 years.

TEA: DUST, DARJEELING

Source: *International Tea Committee Annual Bulletin of Statistics.* **Price Frequency:** annually. **Effective Market(s):** Calcutta. **Units of Measure:** Indian rupees per kilogram. **Type of Price:** auction. **Time Period Covered:** latest 12 years.

TEA: DUST, DOOARS

Source: *International Tea Committee Annual Bulletin of Statistics.* **Price Frequency:** annually. **Effective Market(s):** Calcutta, Guwahati (India). **Units of Measure:** Indian rupees per kilogram. **Type of Price:** auction. **Time Period Covered:** latest 12 years.

TEA: DUST, INDIAN

Source: *International Tea Committee Annual Bulletin of Statistics.* **Price Frequency:** annually. **Effective Market(s):** 6 Indian markets. **Units of Measure:** Indian rupees per kilogram. **Type of Price:** auction. **Time Period Covered:** latest 12 years.

Source: *International Tea Committee Limited Monthly Statistical Summary.* **Price Frequency:** weekly, year-to-date, seasonally. **Effective Market(s):** Calcutta, Cochin. **Units of Measure:** Indian rupees per kilogram. **Type of Price:** auction. **Time Period Covered:** latest 4 weeks and year-to-date, same time last year.

TEA: DUST, TERAI

Source: *International Tea Committee Annual Bulletin of Statistics.* **Price Frequency:** annually. **Effective Market(s):** Calcutta. **Units of Measure:** Indian rupees per kilogram. **Type of Price:** auction. **Time Period Covered:** latest 12 years.

TEA: ECUADOR

Source: *International Tea Committee Annual Bulletin of Statistics.* **Price Frequency:** annually. **Effective Market(s):** London. **Units of Measure:** British pence per kilogram. **Type of Price:** auction. **Time Period Covered:** latest 12 years.

Source: *International Tea Committee Limited Monthly Statistical Summary.* **Price Frequency:** weekly, year-to-date, seasonally. **Effective Market(s):** London. **Units of Measure:** British new pence per kilogram. **Type of Price:** auction. **Time Period Covered:** latest 4 weeks and year-to-date, same time last year.

TEA: GUATEMALAN

Source: *International Tea Committee Annual Bulletin of Statistics.* **Price Frequency:** annually. **Effective Market(s):** London. **Units of Measure:** British pence per kilogram. **Type of Price:** auction. **Time Period Covered:** latest 12 years.

Source: *International Tea Committee Limited Monthly Statistical Summary.* **Price Frequency:** weekly, year-to-date, seasonally. **Effective Market(s):** London. **Units of Measure:** British new pence per kilogram. **Type of Price:** auction. **Time Period Covered:** latest 4 weeks and year-to-date, same time last year.

TEA: HIGH GROWN, SRI LANKAN

Source: *International Tea Committee Annual Bulletin of Statistics.* **Price Frequency:** annually. **Effective Market(s):** Colombo (Sri Lanka), London. **Units of Measure:** Sri Lankan rupees per kilogram, British pence per kilogram. **Type of Price:** auction. **Time Period Covered:** latest 12 years.

Source: *International Tea Committee Limited Monthly Statistical Summary.* **Price Frequency:** weekly, year-to-date, seasonally. **Effective Market(s):** Colombo (Sri Lanka). **Units of Measure:** Sri Lankan rupees per kilogram. **Type of Price:** auction. **Time Period Covered:** latest 4 weeks and year-to-date, same time last year.

Source: *International Tea Committee Limited Monthly Statistical Summary.* **Price Frequency:** weekly, year-to-date, seasonally. **Effective Market(s):** London. **Units of Measure:** British new pence per kilogram. **Type of Price:** auction. **Time Period Covered:** latest 4 weeks and year-to-date, same time last year.

TEA: HIGH, MEDIUM, AND LOW GROWN, COLOMBO

Source: *FAO Quarterly Bulletin of Statistics.* **Price Frequency:** monthly, annually. **Effective Market(s):** Sri Lanka. **Units of Measure:** Sri Lankan rupees per kilogram, dollars per metric ton. **Type of Price:** auction. **Time Period Covered:** latest 3 years.

TEA: INDIAN

Source: *International Tea Committee Annual Bulletin of Statistics.* **Price Frequency:** annually. **Effective Market(s):** London. **Units of Measure:** British pence per kilogram. **Type of Price:** auction. **Time Period Covered:** latest 12 years.

Source: *International Tea Committee Annual Bulletin of Statistics.* **Price Frequency:** annually. **Effective Market(s):** 6 Indian markets. **Units of Measure:** Indian rupees per kilogram. **Type of Price:** auction. **Time Period Covered:** latest 12 years.

TEA: INDONESIAN

Source: *International Tea Committee Annual Bulletin of Statistics.* **Price Frequency:** annually. **Effective Market(s):** Jakarta, London. **Units of Measure:** United States cents per kilogram, British pence per kilogram. **Type of Price:** auction. **Time Period Covered:** latest 12 years.

Source: *International Tea Committee Limited Monthly Statistical Summary.* **Price Frequency:** weekly, year-to-date, seasonally. **Effective Market(s):** Jakarta. **Units of Measure:** cents per kilogram. **Type of Price:** auction. **Time Period Covered:** latest 4 weeks and year-to-date, same time last year.

Source: *International Tea Committee Limited Monthly Statistical Summary.* **Price Frequency:** weekly, year-to-date, seasonally. **Effective Market(s):** London. **Units of Measure:** British new pence per kilogram. **Type of Price:** auction. **Time Period Covered:** latest 4 weeks and year-to-date, same time last year.

TEA: KENYAN

Source: *Commodity Trade and Price Trends.* **Price Frequency:** annually. **Effective Market(s):** London. **Units of Measure:** cents per kilogram, 1980 constant cents per kilogram. **Type of Price:** auction. **Time Period Covered:** latest 36 years.

Source: *FAO Quarterly Bulletin of Statistics.* **Price Frequency:** monthly, annually. **Effective Market(s):** Kenya. **Units of Measure:** Kenyan shillings per kilogram, dollars per metric ton. **Type of Price:** auction. **Time Period Covered:** latest 3 years.

Source: *International Tea Committee Annual Bulletin of Statistics.* **Price Frequency:** annually. **Effective Market(s):** London, Mombasa (Kenya). **Units of Measure:** British pence per kilogram, Kenyan shillings per kilogram. **Type of Price:** auction, offshore auction. **Time Period Covered:** latest 12 years, offshore latest 7 years.

Source: *International Tea Committee Limited Monthly Statistical Summary.* **Price Frequency:** weekly, year-to-date, seasonally. **Effective Market(s):** London. **Units of Measure:** British new pence per kilogram. **Type of Price:** offshore auction, auction. **Time Period Covered:** latest 4 weeks and year-to-date, same time last year.

Source: *International Tea Committee Limited Monthly Statistical Summary.* **Price Frequency:** weekly, year-to-date, seasonally. **Effective Market(s):** Mombasa (Kenya). **Units of Measure:** Kenyan shillings per kilogram. **Type of Price:** auction. **Time Period Covered:** latest 4 weeks and year-to-date, same time last year.

TEA: LEAF AND DUST, CALCUTTA

Source: *FAO Quarterly Bulletin of Statistics.* **Price Frequency:** monthly, annually. **Effective Market(s):** India. **Units of Measure:** Indian rupees per kilogram, dollars per metric ton. **Type of Price:** auction. **Time Period Covered:** latest 3 years.

TEA: LEAF AND DUST, COCHIN

Source: *FAO Quarterly Bulletin of Statistics.* **Price Frequency:** monthly, annually. **Effective Market(s):** India. **Units of Measure:** Indian rupees per kilogram, dollars per metric ton. **Type of Price:** auction. **Time Period Covered:** latest 3 years.

TEA: LEAF, ASSAM

Source: *International Tea Committee Annual Bulletin of Statistics.* **Price Frequency:** annually. **Effective Market(s):** Calcutta, Guwahati (India). **Units of Measure:** Indian rupees per kilogram. **Type of Price:** auction. **Time Period Covered:** latest 12 years.

TEA: LEAF, BANGLADESH

Source: *International Tea Committee Annual Bulletin of Statistics.* **Price Frequency:** annually. **Effective Market(s):** Chittagong (Bangladesh). **Units of Measure:** Bangladesh taka per kilogram. **Type of Price:** auction. **Time Period Covered:** latest 12 years.

Source: *International Tea Committee Limited Monthly Statistical Summary.* **Price Frequency:** weekly, year-to-date, seasonally. **Effective Market(s):** Chittagong (Bangladesh). **Units of Measure:** Bangladesh ban taka per kilogram. **Type of Price:** auction. **Time Period Covered:** latest 4 weeks and year-to-date, same time last year.

TEA: LEAF, CACHAR

Source: *International Tea Committee Annual Bulletin of Statistics.* **Price Frequency:** annually. **Effective Market(s):** Calcutta, Guwahati (India). **Units of Measure:** Indian rupees per kilogram. **Type of Price:** auction. **Time Period Covered:** latest 12 years.

TEA: LEAF, DARJEELING

Source: *International Tea Committee Annual Bulletin of Statistics.* **Price Frequency:** annually. **Effective Market(s):** Calcutta. **Units of Measure:** Indian rupees per kilogram. **Type of Price:** auction. **Time Period Covered:** latest 12 years.

TEA: LEAF, DOOARS

Source: *International Tea Committee Annual Bulletin of Statistics.* **Price Frequency:** annually. **Effective Market(s):** Calcutta, Guwahati (India). **Units of Measure:** Indian rupees per kilogram. **Type of Price:** auction. **Time Period Covered:** latest 12 years.

TEA: LEAF, INDIAN

Source: *International Tea Committee Annual Bulletin of Statistics.* **Price Frequency:** annually. **Effective Market(s):** 6 Indian markets. **Units of Measure:** Indian rupees per kilogram. **Type of Price:** auction. **Time Period Covered:** latest 12 years.

Source: *International Tea Committee Limited Monthly Statistical Summary.* **Price Frequency:** weekly, year-to-date, seasonally. **Effective Market(s):** Calcutta, Cochin. **Units of Measure:** Indian rupees per kilogram. **Type of Price:** auction. **Time Period Covered:** latest 4 weeks and year-to-date, same time last year.

TEA: LEAF, TERAI

Source: *International Tea Committee Annual Bulletin of Statistics.* **Price Frequency:** annually. **Effective Market(s):** Calcutta. **Units of Measure:** Indian rupees per kilogram. **Type of Price:** auction. **Time Period Covered:** latest 12 years.

TEA: LOW GROWN, SRI LANKAN

Source: *International Tea Committee Annual Bulletin of Statistics.* **Price Frequency:** annually. **Effective Market(s):** Colombo (Sri Lanka), London. **Units of Measure:** Sri Lankan rupees per kilogram, British pence per kilogram. **Type of Price:** auction. **Time Period Covered:** latest 12 years.

Source: *International Tea Committee Limited Monthly Statistical Summary.* **Price Frequency:** weekly, year-to-date, seasonally. **Effective Market(s):** Colombo (Sri Lanka). **Units of Measure:** Sri Lankan rupees per kilogram. **Type of Price:** auction. **Time Period Covered:** latest 4 weeks and year-to-date, same time last year.

Source: *International Tea Committee Limited Monthly Statistical Summary.* **Price Frequency:** weekly, year-to-date, seasonally. **Effective Market(s):** London. **Units of Measure:** British new pence per kilogram. **Type of Price:** auction. **Time Period Covered:** latest 4 weeks and year-to-date, same time last year.

TEA: MADAGASCAR

Source: *International Tea Committee Annual Bulletin of Statistics.* **Price Frequency:** annually. **Effective Market(s):** London. **Units of Measure:** British pence per kilogram. **Type of Price:** auction. **Time Period Covered:** latest 12 years.

TEA: MALAWI

Source: *International Tea Committee Annual Bulletin of Statistics.* **Price Frequency:** annually. **Effective Market(s):** London. **Units of Measure:** British pence per kilogram. **Type of Price:** auction, offshore auction. **Time Period Covered:** latest 12 years, offshore latest 7 years.

Source: *International Tea Committee Limited Monthly Statistical Summary.* **Price Frequency:** weekly, year-to-date, seasonally. **Effective Market(s):** London. **Units of Measure:** British new pence per kilogram. **Type of Price:** offshore auction, auction. **Time Period Covered:** latest 4 weeks and year-to-date, same time last year.

Source: *International Tea Committee Limited Monthly Statistical Summary.* **Price Frequency:** weekly, year-to-date, seasonally. **Effective Market(s):** Limbe (Malawi). **Units of Measure:** Malawi tamb per kilogram. **Type of Price:** auction. **Time Period Covered:** latest 4 weeks and year-to-date, same time last year.

TEA: MAURITIUS

Source: *International Tea Committee Annual Bulletin of Statistics.* **Price Frequency:** annually. **Effective Market(s):** London, Mombasa (Kenya). **Units of Measure:** British pence per kilogram, Kenyan shillings per kilogram. **Type of Price:** auction, offshore auction. **Time Period Covered:** latest 12 years, offshore latest 7 years.

Source: *International Tea Committee Limited Monthly Statistical Summary.* **Price Frequency:** weekly, year-to-date, seasonally. **Effective Market(s):** London. **Units of Measure:** British new pence per kilogram. **Type of Price:** offshore auction, auction. **Time Period Covered:** latest 4 weeks and year-to-date, same time last year.

TEA: MEDIUM GROWN, ASSAM AND KENYAN

Source: *International Tea Committee Annual Bulletin of Statistics.* **Price Frequency:** monthly. **Effective Market(s):** London. **Units of Measure:** British pence per kilogram. **Type of Price:** auction. **Time Period Covered:** latest 13 years.

TEA: MEDIUM GROWN, MALAWI

Source: *International Tea Committee Annual Bulletin of Statistics.* **Price Frequency:** monthly. **Effective Market(s):** London. **Units of Measure:** British pence per kilogram. **Type of Price:** auction. **Time Period Covered:** latest 7 years.

TEA: MEDIUM GROWN, SRI LANKAN

Source: *International Tea Committee Annual Bulletin of Statistics.* **Price Frequency:** annually. **Effective Market(s):** Colombo (Sri Lanka), London. **Units of Measure:** Sri Lankan rupees per kilogram, British pence per kilogram. **Type of Price:** auction. **Time Period Covered:** latest 12 years.

Source: *International Tea Committee Limited Monthly Statistical Summary.* **Price Frequency:** weekly, year-to-date, seasonally. **Effective Market(s):** Colombo (Sri Lanka). **Units of Measure:** Sri Lankan rupees per kilogram. **Type of Price:** auction. **Time Period Covered:** latest 4 weeks and year-to-date, same time last year.

Source: *International Tea Committee Limited Monthly Statistical Summary.* **Price Frequency:** weekly, year-to-date, seasonally. **Effective Market(s):** London. **Units of Measure:** British new pence per kilogram. **Type of Price:** auction. **Time Period Covered:** latest 4 weeks and year-to-date, same time last year.

TEA: MOZAMBIQUE

Source: *International Tea Committee Annual Bulletin of Statistics.* **Price Frequency:** annually. **Effective Market(s):** London. **Units of Measure:** British pence per kilogram. **Type of Price:** auction. **Time Period Covered:** latest 12 years.

TEA: NORTH INDIAN

Source: *Commodity Trade and Price Trends.* **Price Frequency:** annually. **Effective Market(s):** London. **Units of Measure:** cents per kilogram, 1980 constant cents per kilogram. **Type of Price:** auction. **Time Period Covered:** latest 36 years.

Source: *International Tea Committee Annual Bulletin of Statistics.* **Price Frequency:** annually. **Effective Market(s):** London. **Units of Measure:** British pence per kilogram. **Type of Price:** auction. **Time Period Covered:** latest 12 years.

Source: *International Tea Committee Annual Bulletin of Statistics.* **Price Frequency:** annually. **Effective Market(s):** Singapore. **Units of Measure:** United States cents per kilogram. **Type of Price:** auction. **Time Period Covered:** latest 6 years.

Source: *International Tea Committee Limited Monthly Statistical Summary.* **Price Frequency:** weekly, year-to-date, seasonally. **Effective Market(s):** London. **Units of Measure:** British new pence per kilogram. **Type of Price:** auction. **Time Period Covered:** latest 4 weeks and year-to-date, same time last year.

TEA: PAPUA NEW GUINEA

Source: *International Tea Committee Annual Bulletin of Statistics.* **Price Frequency:** annually. **Effective Market(s):** London. **Units of Measure:** British pence per kilogram. **Type of Price:** auction, offshore auction. **Time Period Covered:** latest 12 years, offshore latest 7 years.

Source: *International Tea Committee Limited Monthly Statistical Summary.* **Price Frequency:** weekly, year-to-date, seasonally. **Effective Market(s):** London. **Units of Measure:** British new pence per kilogram. **Type of Price:** auction. **Time Period Covered:** latest 4 weeks and year-to-date, same time last year.

TEA: QUALITY

Source: *International Tea Committee Annual Bulletin of Statistics.* **Price Frequency:** monthly. **Effective Market(s):** London. **Units of Measure:** British pence per kilogram. **Type of Price:** auction. **Time Period Covered:** latest 13 years.

TEA: RWANDAN

Source: *International Tea Committee Annual Bulletin of Statistics.* **Price Frequency:** annually. **Effective Market(s):** London, Mombasa (Kenya). **Units of Measure:** British pence per kilogram, Kenyan shillings per kilogram. **Type of Price:** auction, offshore. **Time Period Covered:** latest 12 years, offshore latest 7 years.

Source: *International Tea Committee Limited Monthly Statistical Summary.* **Price Frequency:** weekly, year-to-date, seasonally. **Effective Market(s):** London. **Units of Measure:** British new pence per kilogram. **Type of Price:** offshore auction, auction. **Time Period Covered:** latest 4 weeks and year-to-date, same time last year.

Source: *International Tea Committee Limited Monthly Statistical Summary.* **Price Frequency:** weekly, year-to-date, seasonally. **Effective Market(s):** Mombasa (Kenya). **Units of Measure:** Kenyan shillings per kilogram. **Type of Price:** auction. **Time Period Covered:** latest 4 weeks and year-to-date, same time last year.

TEA: SOUTH INDIAN

Source: *International Tea Committee Annual Bulletin of Statistics.* **Price Frequency:** annually. **Effective Market(s):** London. **Units of Measure:** British pence per kilogram. **Type of Price:** auction. **Time Period Covered:** latest 12 years.

Source: *International Tea Committee Limited Monthly Statistical Summary.* **Price Frequency:** weekly, year-to-date, seasonally. **Effective Market(s):** London. **Units of Measure:** British new pence per kilogram. **Type of Price:** auction. **Time Period Covered:** latest 4 weeks and year-to-date, same time last year.

TEA: SRI LANKAN

Source: *Commodity Trade and Price Trends.* **Price Frequency:** annually. **Effective Market(s):** London. **Units of Measure:** cents per kilogram, 1980 constant cents per kilogram. **Type of Price:** auction. **Time Period Covered:** latest 36 years.

Source: *International Financial Statistics.* **Price Frequency:** monthly, quarterly, annually. **Effective Market(s):** Sri Lanka. **Units of Measure:** cents per lb., index. **Type of Price:** market price, price index. **Time Period Covered:** latest month, latest 4 quarters, latest 5 years.

Source: *International Financial Statistics Yearbook.* **Price Frequency:** annually. **Effective Market(s):** Sri Lanka. **Units of Measure:** cents per lb. **Type of Price:** wholesale. **Time Period Covered:** latest 30 years.

Source: *International Tea Committee Annual Bulletin of Statistics.* **Price Frequency:** annually. **Effective Market(s):** Colombo (Sri Lanka), London. **Units of Measure:** Sri Lankan rupees per kilogram, British pence per kilogram. **Type of Price:** auction. **Time Period Covered:** latest 12 years.

Source: *International Tea Committee Limited Monthly Statistical Summary.* **Price Frequency:** weekly, year-to-date, seasonally. **Effective Market(s):** Colombo (Sri Lanka). **Units of Measure:** Sri Lankan rupees per kilogram. **Type of Price:** auction. **Time Period Covered:** latest 4 weeks and year-to-date, same time last year.

Source: *International Tea Committee Limited Monthly Statistical Summary.* **Price Frequency:** weekly, year-to-date, seasonally. **Effective Market(s):** London. **Units of Measure:** British new pence per kilogram. **Type of Price:** offshore auction, auction. **Time Period Covered:** latest 4 weeks and year-to-date, same time last year.

TEA: SRI LANKAN/INDIAN

Source: *International Financial Statistics Yearbook.* **Price Frequency:** annually. **Effective Market(s):** New York. **Units of Measure:** cents per lb. **Type of Price:** wholesale. **Time Period Covered:** latest 30 years.

TEA: TANZANIAN

Source: *International Tea Committee Annual Bulletin of Statistics.* **Price Frequency:** annually. **Effective Market(s):** London, Mombasa (Kenya). **Units of Measure:** British pence per kilogram, Kenyan shillings per kilogram. **Type of Price:** auction. **Time Period Covered:** latest 12 years.

Source: *International Tea Committee Limited Monthly Statistical Summary.* **Price Frequency:** weekly, year-to-date, seasonally. **Effective Market(s):** London. **Units of Measure:** British new pence per kilogram. **Type of Price:** auction. **Time Period Covered:** latest 4 weeks and year-to-date, same time last year.

TEA: TRANSKEI

Source: *International Tea Committee Annual Bulletin of Statistics.* **Price Frequency:** annually. **Effective Market(s):** London. **Units of Measure:** British pence per kilogram. **Type of Price:** auction. **Time Period Covered:** latest 12 years.

TEA: UGANDAN

Source: *International Tea Committee Annual Bulletin of Statistics.* **Price Frequency:** annually. **Effective Market(s):** London, Mombasa (Kenya). **Units of Measure:** British pence per kilogram, Kenyan shillings per kilogram. **Type of Price:** auction, offshore. **Time Period Covered:** latest 12 years, offshore latest 7 years.

Source: *International Tea Committee Limited Monthly Statistical Summary.* **Price Frequency:** weekly, year-to-date, seasonally. **Effective Market(s):** London. **Units of Measure:** British new pence per kilogram. **Type of Price:** offshore auction, auction. **Time Period Covered:** latest 4 weeks and year-to-date, same time last year.

TEA: ZAIRE

Source: *International Tea Committee Annual Bulletin of Statistics.* **Price Frequency:** annually. **Effective Market(s):** London, Mombasa (Kenya). **Units of Measure:** British pence per kilogram, Kenyan shillings per kilogram. **Type of Price:** auction. **Time Period Covered:** latest 12 years.

Source: *International Tea Committee Limited Monthly Statistical Summary.* **Price Frequency:** weekly, year-to-date, seasonally. **Effective Market(s):** Mombasa (Kenya). **Units of Measure:** Kenyan shillings per kilogram. **Type of Price:** auction. **Time Period Covered:** latest 4 weeks and year-to-date, same time last year.

Source: *International Tea Committee Limited Monthly Statistical Summary.* **Price Frequency:** weekly, year-to-date, seasonally. **Effective Market(s):** London. **Units of Measure:** British new pence per kilogram. **Type of Price:** auction. **Time Period Covered:** latest 4 weeks and year-to-date, same time last year.

TEA: ZIMBABWE

Source: *International Tea Committee Annual Bulletin of Statistics.* **Price Frequency:** annually. **Effective Market(s):** London. **Units of Measure:** British pence per kilogram. **Type of Price:** auction, offshore auction. **Time Period Covered:** latest 12 years, offshore latest 7 years.

Source: *International Tea Committee Limited Monthly Statistical Summary.* **Price Frequency:** weekly, year-to-date, seasonally. **Effective Market(s):** London. **Units of Measure:** British new pence per kilogram. **Type of Price:** offshore auction, auction. **Time Period Covered:** latest 4 weeks and year-to-date, same time last year.

TELLURIUM: METALLURGICAL

Source: *Chemical Marketing Reporter.* **Price Frequency:** weekly. **Effective Market(s):** New York. **Units of Measure:** Dollars per lb. **Type of Price:** spot. **Time Period Covered:** latest week.

TEMPLE ORANGES

see Oranges: Temple.

TEQUILA

Source: *Beverage Media.* **Price Frequency:** monthly. **Effective Market(s):** New York. **Units of Measure:** Dollars per unit. **Type of Price:** wholesale by brand. **Time Period Covered:** latest month.

Source: *Colorado Beverage Analyst.* **Price Frequency:** monthly. **Effective Market(s):** Colorado. **Units of Measure:** Dollars per case. **Type of Price:** wholesale by brand. **Time Period Covered:** latest month.

Source: *Illinois Beverage Journal.* **Price Frequency:** monthly. **Effective Market(s):** Illinois. **Units of Measure:** Dollars per case. **Type of Price:** wholesale by brand. **Time Period Covered:** latest month.

Source: *Indiana Beverage Journal.* **Price Frequency:** monthly. **Effective Market(s):** Indiana. **Units of Measure:** Dollars per case, dollars per bottle. **Type of Price:** wholesale by brand. **Time Period Covered:** latest month.

Source: *Kentucky Beverage Journal.* **Price Frequency:** monthly. **Effective Market(s):** Kentucky. **Units of Measure:** Dollars per bottle, dollars per case. **Type of Price:** wholesale by brand. **Time Period Covered:** latest month.

Source: *Nevada Beverage Index.* **Price Frequency:** monthly. **Effective Market(s):** Nevada. **Units of Measure:** Dollars per unit. **Type of Price:** wholesale by brand. **Time Period Covered:** latest month.

Source: *Rhode Island Beverage Journal.* **Price Frequency:** monthly. **Effective Market(s):** Rhode Island. **Units of Measure:** Dollars per unit. **Type of Price:** wholesale by brand. **Time Period Covered:** latest month.

TERBUFOS: 15% GRANULAR

Source: *Agricultural Prices Annual Summary.* **Price Frequency:** semiannually. **Effective Market(s):** United States. **Units of Measure:** Dollars per 50 lbs. **Type of Price:** average paid by farmer. **Time Period Covered:** latest 6 years.

TEREPHTHALIC ACID

Source: *Journal of Commerce and Commercial.* **Price Frequency:** weekly in Thursday issue. **Units of Measure:** Dollars per lb. **Type of Price:** spot. **Time Period Covered:** latest week.

TERPIN HYDRATE: CRYSTALLINE, NF

Source: *Journal of Commerce and Commercial.* **Price Frequency:** weekly in Friday issue. **Units of Measure:** Dollars per lb. **Type of Price:** spot. **Time Period Covered:** latest week.

TERPIN HYDRATE: CRYSTALLINE, POWDERED, NF, IMPORTED

Source: *Chemical Marketing Reporter.* **Price Frequency:** weekly. **Effective Market(s):** New York. **Units of Measure:** Dollars per lb. **Type of Price:** spot. **Time Period Covered:** latest week.

TERPINEOL

Source: *Journal of Commerce and Commercial.* **Price Frequency:** weekly in Tuesday issue. **Units of Measure:** Dollars per lb. **Type of Price:** spot. **Time Period Covered:** latest week.

TERPINEOL: TECHNICAL GRADE

Source: *Chemical Marketing Reporter.* **Price Frequency:** weekly. **Effective Market(s):** New York. **Units of Measure:** Dollars per lb. **Type of Price:** spot. **Time Period Covered:** latest week.

TERPINYL ACETATE: EXTRA

Source: *Chemical Marketing Reporter.* **Price Frequency:** weekly. **Effective Market(s):** New York. **Units of Measure:** Dollars per lb. **Type of Price:** spot. **Time Period Covered:** latest week.

TERPINYL ACETATE: PRIME

Source: *Chemical Marketing Reporter.* **Price Frequency:** weekly. **Effective Market(s):** New York. **Units of Measure:** Dollars per lb. **Type of Price:** spot. **Time Period Covered:** latest week.

TERPINYL PROPIONATE

Source: *Chemical Marketing Reporter.* **Price Frequency:** weekly. **Effective Market(s):** New York. **Units of Measure:** Dollars per lb. **Type of Price:** spot. **Time Period Covered:** latest week.

TETRACHLOROETHYLENE: TECHNICAL

see Perchloroethylene.

TETRACHLOROETHYLENE: USP

Source: *Chemical Marketing Reporter.* **Price Frequency:** weekly. **Effective Market(s):** New York. **Units of Measure:** Dollars per lb. **Type of Price:** spot. **Time Period Covered:** latest week.

TETRAETHYL ORTHOSILICATE

Source: *Chemical Marketing Reporter.* **Price Frequency:** weekly. **Effective Market(s):** New York. **Units of Measure:** Dollars per lb. **Type of Price:** spot. **Time Period Covered:** latest week.

TETRAETHYLENE GLYCOL

Source: *Chemical Marketing Reporter.* **Price Frequency:** weekly. **Effective Market(s):** New York. **Units of Measure:** Dollars per lb. **Type of Price:** spot. **Time Period Covered:** latest week.

TETRAETHYLENE GLYCOL DIACRYLATE

Source: *Chemical Marketing Reporter.* **Price Frequency:** weekly. **Effective Market(s):** New York. **Units of Measure:** Dollars per lb. **Type of Price:** spot. **Time Period Covered:** latest week.

TETRAETHYLENEPENTAMINE

Source: *Chemical Marketing Reporter.* **Price Frequency:** weekly. **Effective Market(s):** New York. **Units of Measure:** Dollars per lb. **Type of Price:** spot. **Time Period Covered:** latest week.

TETRAETHYLTHIURAM DISULFIDE: TECHNICAL, FLAKE

Source: *Chemical Marketing Reporter.* **Price Frequency:** weekly. **Effective Market(s):** New York. **Units of Measure:** Dollars per lb. **Type of Price:** spot. **Time Period Covered:** latest week.

TETRAHYDROFURAN

Source: *Chemical Marketing Reporter.* **Price Frequency:** weekly. **Effective Market(s):** New York. **Units of Measure:** Dollars per lb. **Type of Price:** spot. **Time Period Covered:** latest week.

TETRAHYDROFURFURYL ALCOHOL

Source: *Chemical Marketing Reporter.* **Price Frequency:** weekly. **Effective Market(s):** Memphis (TN). **Units of Measure:** Dollars per lb. **Type of Price:** spot. **Time Period Covered:** latest week.

TETRAHYDROPHTHALIC ANHYDRIDE

Source: *Chemical Marketing Reporter.* **Price Frequency:** weekly. **Effective Market(s):** New York. **Units of Measure:** Dollars per lb. **Type of Price:** spot. **Time Period Covered:** latest week.

TETRAPOTASSIUM PHOSPHATE

see Potassium Phosphate: Tetrabasic.

TETRASODIUM PYROPHOSPHATE

see Sodium Pyrophosphate: Tetrabasic.

TEXTILES: SYNTHETIC, CELLULOSIC

Source: *Journal of Commerce and Commercial.* **Price Frequency:** weekly in Tuesday issue. **Units of Measure:** Dollars per lb. **Type of Price:** spot. **Time Period Covered:** latest week.

TEXTILES: SYNTHETIC, NON-CELLULOSIC

Source: *Journal of Commerce and Commercial.* **Price Frequency:** weekly in Tuesday issue. **Units of Measure:** Dollars per lb. **Type of Price:** spot. **Time Period Covered:** latest week.

THAILAND BAHT

Source: *Asian Wall Street Journal.* **Price Frequency:** daily. **Effective Market(s):** Asia. **Units of Measure:** Thai baht per United States dollar. **Type of Price:** foreign exchange. **Time Period Covered:** latest 2 days.

Source: *Barron's.* **Price Frequency:** weekly. **Effective Market(s):** New York. **Units of Measure:** Thai baht per United States dollar. **Type of Price:** foreign exchange. **Time Period Covered:** latest 2 weeks.

Source: *New York Times.* **Price Frequency:** daily. **Effective Market(s):** New York. **Units of Measure:** Thai baht per United States dollar. **Type of Price:** foreign exchange. **Time Period Covered:** latest 2 days.

THALLIUM METAL

Source: *Chemical Marketing Reporter.* **Price Frequency:** weekly. **Effective Market(s):** New York. **Units of Measure:** Dollars per lb. **Type of Price:** spot. **Time Period Covered:** latest week.

THALLIUM SULFATE: 99%

Source: *Chemical Marketing Reporter.* **Price Frequency:** weekly. **Effective Market(s):** New York. **Units of Measure:** Dollars per kilo. **Type of Price:** spot. **Time Period Covered:** latest week.

THEOBROMINE

Source: *Chemical Marketing Reporter.* **Price Frequency:** weekly. **Effective Market(s):** New York. **Units of Measure:** Dollars per kilo. **Type of Price:** spot. **Time Period Covered:** latest week.

Source: *Journal of Commerce and Commercial.* **Price Frequency:** weekly in Friday issue. **Units of Measure:** Dollars per lb. **Type of Price:** spot. **Time Period Covered:** latest week.

THEOPHYLLINE: ANHYDROUS, USP

Source: *Chemical Marketing Reporter.* **Price Frequency:** weekly. **Effective Market(s):** New York. **Units of Measure:** Dollars per kilo. **Type of Price:** spot. **Time Period Covered:** latest week.

THERMOPLASTIC ELASTOMERS: COPOLYESTER

Source: *Plastics Technology.* **Price Frequency:** monthly. **Units of Measure:** cents per lb., cents per cubic inch. **Type of Price:** bulk list, market. **Time Period Covered:** latest month.

THERMOPLASTIC ELASTOMERS: OLEFINIC

Source: *Plastics Technology.* **Price Frequency:** monthly. **Units of Measure:** cents per lb., cents per cubic inch. **Type of Price:** bulk list, market. **Time Period Covered:** latest month.

THERMOPLASTIC ELASTOMERS: PEBA

Source: *Plastics Technology.* **Price Frequency:** monthly. **Units of Measure:** cents per lb., cents per cubic inch. **Type of Price:** bulk list, market. **Time Period Covered:** latest month.

THERMOPLASTIC ELASTOMERS: STYRENIC

Source: *Plastics Technology.* **Price Frequency:** monthly. **Units of Measure:** cents per lb., cents per cubic inch. **Type of Price:** bulk list, market. **Time Period Covered:** latest month.

THIAMINE HYDROCHLORIDE

Source: *Journal of Commerce and Commercial.* **Price Frequency:** weekly in Friday issue. **Units of Measure:** Dollars per kilo. **Type of Price:** spot. **Time Period Covered:** latest week.

THIAMINE HYDROCHLORIDE: USP

Source: *Chemical Marketing Reporter.* **Price Frequency:** weekly. **Effective Market(s):** New York. **Units of Measure:** Dollars per kilo. **Type of Price:** spot. **Time Period Covered:** latest week.

THIAMINE MONONITRATE: USP

Source: *Chemical Marketing Reporter.* **Price Frequency:** weekly. **Effective Market(s):** New York. **Units of Measure:** Dollars per kilo. **Type of Price:** spot. **Time Period Covered:** latest week.

THIODIPHENOL: 98%

Source: *Chemical Marketing Reporter.* **Price Frequency:** weekly. **Effective Market(s):** New York. **Units of Measure:** Dollars per lb. **Type of Price:** spot. **Time Period Covered:** latest week.

THIOFLAVIN GREEN TONERS: MOLYBDATED

Source: *Chemical Marketing Reporter.* **Price Frequency:** weekly. **Effective Market(s):** New York. **Units of Measure:** Dollars per lb. **Type of Price:** spot. **Time Period Covered:** latest week.

THIOFLAVIN GREEN TONERS: TUNGSTATED

Source: *Chemical Marketing Reporter.* **Price Frequency:** weekly. **Effective Market(s):** New York. **Units of Measure:** Dollars per lb. **Type of Price:** spot. **Time Period Covered:** latest week.

THIOGLYCOLIC ACID: REFINED

Source: *Chemical Marketing Reporter.* **Price Frequency:** weekly. **Effective Market(s):** New York. **Units of Measure:** Dollars per lb. **Type of Price:** spot. **Time Period Covered:** latest week.

THIOINDIGOLD: MAROON

Source: *Chemical Marketing Reporter.* **Price Frequency:** weekly. **Effective Market(s):** New York. **Units of Measure:** Dollars per lb. **Type of Price:** spot. **Time Period Covered:** latest week.

THIOINDIGOLD: RED

Source: *Chemical Marketing Reporter.* **Price Frequency:** weekly. **Effective Market(s):** New York. **Units of Measure:** Dollars per lb. **Type of Price:** spot. **Time Period Covered:** latest week.

THIONYL CHLORIDE: HIGH PURITY, 99.6%

Source: *Chemical Marketing Reporter.* **Price Frequency:** weekly. **Effective Market(s):** New York. **Units of Measure:** Dollars per lb. **Type of Price:** spot. **Time Period Covered:** latest week.

THORIUM NITRATE: PURIFIED

Source: *Chemical Marketing Reporter.* **Price Frequency:** weekly. **Effective Market(s):** New York. **Units of Measure:** Dollars per lb. **Type of Price:** spot. **Time Period Covered:** latest week.

L-THREONINE: FEED GRADE

Source: *Chemical Marketing Reporter.* **Price Frequency:** weekly. **Effective Market(s):** New York. **Units of Measure:** Dollars per kilo. **Type of Price:** spot. **Time Period Covered:** latest week.

L-THREONINE: USP

Source: *Chemical Marketing Reporter.* **Price Frequency:** weekly. **Effective Market(s):** New York. **Units of Measure:** Dollars per kilo. **Type of Price:** spot. **Time Period Covered:** latest week.

THYME LEAVES: FRENCH

Source: *Chemical Marketing Reporter.* **Price Frequency:** weekly. **Effective Market(s):** New York. **Units of Measure:** Dollars per lb. **Type of Price:** spot. **Time Period Covered:** latest week.

Source: *U. S. Spice Trade.* **Price Frequency:** annually. **Effective Market(s):** New York. **Units of Measure:** cents per lb. **Type of Price:** spot. **Time Period Covered:** latest 3 years.

THYME LEAVES: MOROCCAN

Source: *U. S. Spice Trade.* **Price Frequency:** annually. **Effective Market(s):** New York. **Units of Measure:** cents per lb. **Type of Price:** spot. **Time Period Covered:** latest 3 years.

THYME LEAVES: SPANISH

Source: *Chemical Marketing Reporter.* **Price Frequency:** weekly. **Effective Market(s):** New York. **Units of Measure:** Dollars per lb. **Type of Price:** spot. **Time Period Covered:** latest week.

Source: *U. S. Spice Trade.* **Price Frequency:** annually. **Effective Market(s):** New York. **Units of Measure:** cents per lb. **Type of Price:** spot. **Time Period Covered:** latest 3 years.

THYME OIL

Source: *U. S. Essential Oil Trade.* **Price Frequency:** annually. **Effective Market(s):** United States. **Units of Measure:** Dollars per kilogram. **Type of Price:** import value. **Time Period Covered:** latest 3 years.

THYME OIL: RED, FCC

Source: *Journal of Commerce and Commercial.* **Price Frequency:** weekly in Tuesday issue. **Units of Measure:** Dollars per lb. **Type of Price:** spot. **Time Period Covered:** latest week.

THYME OIL: RED, NF

Source: *Chemical Marketing Reporter.* **Price Frequency:** weekly. **Effective Market(s):** New York. **Units of Measure:** Dollarsper kilo. **Type of Price:** spot. **Time Period Covered:** latest week.

THYME OIL: WHITE

Source: *Journal of Commerce and Commercial.* **Price Frequency:** weekly in Tuesday issue. **Units of Measure:** Dollars per lb. **Type of Price:** spot. **Time Period Covered:** latest week.

THYME OIL: WHITE, NF

Source: *Chemical Marketing Reporter.* **Price Frequency:** weekly. **Effective Market(s):** New York. **Units of Measure:** Dollars per kilo. **Type of Price:** spot. **Time Period Covered:** latest week.

THYMIDINE: 97% PURE

Source: *Chemical Marketing Reporter.* **Price Frequency:** weekly. **Effective Market(s):** New York. **Units of Measure:** Dollars per gram, dollars per 100 grams. **Type of Price:** spot. **Time Period Covered:** latest week.

THYMOL: NF

Source: *Chemical Marketing Reporter.* **Price Frequency:** weekly. **Effective Market(s):** New York. **Units of Measure:** Dollars per lb. **Type of Price:** spot. **Time Period Covered:** latest week.

Source: *Journal of Commerce and Commercial.* **Price Frequency:** weekly in Friday issue. **Units of Measure:** Dollars per lb. **Type of Price:** spot. **Time Period Covered:** latest week.

THYMOL IODIDE

Source: *Chemical Marketing Reporter.* **Price Frequency:** weekly. **Effective Market(s):** New York. **Units of Measure:** Dollars per lb. **Type of Price:** spot. **Time Period Covered:** latest week.

TILEFISH: GOLD, FRESH

Source: *Seafood Price-Current.* **Price Frequency:** semiweekly. **Effective Market(s):** Gulf/Southeast. **Units of Measure:** Dollars per lb. **Type of Price:** sale by first receiver. **Time Period Covered:** latest day.

TILEFISH: GOLD, WHOLE, FRESH

Source: *Seafood Price-Current.* **Price Frequency:** semiweekly. **Effective Market(s):** Boston, Mid-Atlantic, New Bedford (MA), Portland (ME). **Units of Measure:** Dollars per lb. **Type of Price:** sale by first receiver, auction price. **Time Period Covered:** latest day.

TILEFISH: GREY, FILLETS, FRESH

Source: *Seafood Price-Current.* **Price Frequency:** semiweekly. **Effective Market(s):** Gulf/Southeast. **Units of Measure:** Dollars per lb. **Type of Price:** sale by first receiver. **Time Period Covered:** latest day.

TILEFISH: GREY, FRESH

Source: *Seafood Price-Current.* **Price Frequency:** semiweekly. **Effective Market(s):** Gulf/Southeast. **Units of Measure:** Dollars per lb. **Type of Price:** sale by first receiver. **Time Period Covered:** latest day.

TIMBER

see Logs, Lumber, Sawtimber, Wood, specific types of timber, e.g., Oak Sawtimber.

TIMBER: TROPICAL

Source: *UNCTAD Commodity Yearbook.* **Price Frequency:** annually. **Effective Market(s):** United Kingdom. **Units of Measure:** index. **Type of Price:** wholesale price index. **Time Period Covered:** latest 12 years.

TIMOTHY

Source: *Lancaster Farming.* **Price Frequency:** weekly. **Effective Market(s):** Pennsylvania. **Units of Measure:** Dollars per ton. **Type of Price:** dealer. **Time Period Covered:** latest week.

TIMOTHY SEED

Source: *Agricultural Prices Annual Summary.* **Price Frequency:** semiannually. **Effective Market(s):** United States. **Units of Measure:** Dollars 100 lbs. **Type of Price:** average paid by farmer. **Time Period Covered:** latest 6 years.

TIN

Source: *American Metal Market.* **Price Frequency:** daily. **Effective Market(s):** London. **Units of Measure:** Dollars per metric ton. **Type of Price:** cash. **Time Period Covered:** latest 2 days.

Source: *American Metal Market.* **Price Frequency:** daily. **Effective Market(s):** Kuala Lumpur (Malaysia), New York. **Units of Measure:** Malaysian ringgit per kilo, cents per lb. **Type of Price:** spot, settlement. **Time Period Covered:** latest day.

Source: *Asian Wall Street Journal.* **Price Frequency:** daily. **Units of Measure:** Dollars per lb. **Type of Price:** composite. **Time Period Covered:** latest 2 days, year ago.

Source: *Chemical Marketing Reporter.* **Price Frequency:** weekly. **Effective Market(s):** New York. **Units of Measure:** Dollars per lb. **Type of Price:** spot. **Time Period Covered:** latest week.

Source: *Commodity Year Book.* **Price Frequency:** monthly, annually. **Effective Market(s):** New York. **Units of Measure:** cents per lb. **Type of Price:** export. **Time Period Covered:** latest 12 years.

Source: *E&MJ.* **Price Frequency:** monthly. **Effective Market(s):** Kuala Lumpur (Malaysia). **Units of Measure:** Malaysian ringgit per kilo. **Type of Price:** spot. **Time Period Covered:** latest month.

Source: *E&MJ.* **Price Frequency:** monthly. **Effective Market(s):** New York. **Units of Measure:** Dollars per lb. **Time Period Covered:** latest month.

Source: *Economic and Energy Indicators.* **Price Frequency:** biweekly. **Units of Measure:** cents per lb. **Time Period Covered:** latest 3 months, quarters, and years.

Source: *Far Eastern Economic Review.* **Price Frequency:** weekly. **Effective Market(s):** Kuala Lumpur (Malaysia). **Units of Measure:** Malysian dollars per kilogram. **Time Period Covered:** latest week, week ago, 3 months ago, year ago.

Source: *Financial Times.* **Price Frequency:** daily. **Effective Market(s):** Kuala Lumpur (Malaysia), New York. **Units of Measure:** Malaysian ringgit per kilogram, cents per lb. **Type of Price:** spot. **Time Period Covered:** latest day.

Source: *Financial Times.* **Price Frequency:** daily. **Effective Market(s):** London. **Units of Measure:** British pounds per tonne. **Type of Price:** cash. **Time Period Covered:** latest 2 days.

Source: *International Financial Statistics.* **Price Frequency:** monthly, quarterly, annually. **Effective Market(s):** London. **Units of Measure:** cents per lb. **Time Period Covered:** latest 5 months, latest 5 quarters, latest 5 years.

Source: *International Financial Statistics Yearbook.* **Price Frequency:** annually. **Effective Market(s):** London, New York. **Units of Measure:** cents per lb. **Type of Price:** wholesale. **Time Period Covered:** latest 30 years.

Source: *International Tin Statistics.* **Price Frequency:** quarterly, annually. **Effective Market(s):** Kuala Lumpur (Malaysia), New York, Rotterdam. **Units of Measure:** Malaysian dollars per kilogram, dollars per lb., British pounds per tonne. **Time Period Covered:** latest 4 years.

Source: *International Tin Statistics.* **Price Frequency:** daily. **Effective Market(s):** Kuala Lumpur (Malaysia), New York. **Units of Measure:** Malaysian dollars per kilogram, dollars per lb. **Time Period Covered:** latest 4 months.

Source: *Investor's Daily.* **Price Frequency:** daily. **Units of Measure:** Dollars per lb. **Type of Price:** spot composite. **Time Period Covered:** latest 2 days.

Source: *Los Angeles Times.* **Price Frequency:** daily. **Units of Measure:** dollars per lb. **Type of Price:** composite. **Time Period Covered:** latest day.

Source: *Monthly Commodity Price Bulletin.* **Price Frequency:** monthly, annually. **Effective Market(s):** Kuala Lumpur (Malaysia). **Units of Measure:** Malaysian dollars per kilogram, cents per lb. **Time Period Covered:** latest 5 years.

Source: *New York Times.* **Price Frequency:** daily. **Units of Measure:** Dollars per lb. **Type of Price:** composite. **Time Period Covered:** latest 2 days.

Source: *New York Times.* **Price Frequency:** daily. **Effective Market(s):** London. **Units of Measure:** Dollars per metric ton. **Type of Price:** spot. **Time Period Covered:** latest day.

Source: *Northern Miner.* **Price Frequency:** weekly. **Effective Market(s):** New York. **Units of Measure:** Dollars per lb. **Type of Price:** producer. **Time Period Covered:** latest week.

Source: *The Times.* **Price Frequency:** daily. **Effective Market(s):** London. **Units of Measure:** Dollars per tonne. **Type of Price:** cash. **Time Period Covered:** latest day.

Source: *UNCTAD Commodity Yearbook.* **Price Frequency:** annually. **Effective Market(s):** London. **Units of Measure:** Dollars per metric ton. **Type of Price:** free market. **Time Period Covered:** latest 12 years.

Source: *UNCTAD Commodity Yearbook.* **Price Frequency:** annually. **Effective Market(s):** Kuala Lumpur (Malaysia), London. **Units of Measure:** Dollars per metric ton. **Type of Price:** free market. **Time Period Covered:** latest 12 years.

TIN: ALLOYERS' GRADE

Source: *Purchasing.* **Price Frequency:** monthly. **Units of Measure:** cents per lb. **Type of Price:** transaction. **Time Period Covered:** latest day, month ago, 6 months ago, year ago.

TIN: BOLIVIAN

Source: *International Financial Statistics.* **Price Frequency:** monthly, quarterly, annually. **Effective Market(s):** Bolivia. **Units of Measure:** cents per lb., index. **Type of Price:** market price, price index. **Time Period Covered:** latest month, latest 4 quarters, latest 5 years.

Source: *International Financial Statistics Yearbook.* **Price Frequency:** annually. **Effective Market(s):** Bolivia. **Units of Measure:** cents per lb. **Type of Price:** wholesale. **Time Period Covered:** latest 30 years.

TIN: COMPOSITE

Source: *Wall Street Journal.* **Price Frequency:** daily. **Units of Measure:** Dollars per lb. **Time Period Covered:** latest day, day ago, year ago.

TIN: GRADE A

Source: *CRB Commodity Index Report.* **Price Frequency:** weekly. **Effective Market(s):** New York. **Units of Measure:** Dollars per lb. **Type of Price:** spot. **Time Period Covered:** latest week.

Source: *Journal of Commerce and Commercial.* **Price Frequency:** daily. **Effective Market(s):** New York. **Units of Measure:** Dollars per lb. **Type of Price:** spot merchant. **Time Period Covered:** latest day.

TIN: HIGH GRADE

Source: *International Tin Statistics.* **Price Frequency:** daily. **Effective Market(s):** Euro Free Market. **Units of Measure:** British pounds per tonne. **Time Period Covered:** latest 4 months.

TIN: HIGH GRADE, FUTURES

Source: *International Tin Statistics.* **Price Frequency:** daily. **Effective Market(s):** London. **Units of Measure:** Dollars per tonne. **Type of Price:** futures. **Time Period Covered:** latest 4 months.

TIN: KUALA LUMPUR

Source: *Asian Wall Street Journal.* **Price Frequency:** daily. **Effective Market(s):** Kuala Lumpur (Malaysia). **Units of Measure:** Malaysian dollars per kilo. **Type of Price:** cash. **Time Period Covered:** latest 2 days.

Source: *Monthly Commodity Price Bulletin Supplement.* **Price Frequency:** monthly, quarterly, annually. **Effective Market(s):** Kuala Lumpur (Malaysia). **Units of Measure:** Malaysian dollars per kilogram, dollars per tonne. **Time Period Covered:** latest 20 years.

TIN: MALAYSIAN

Source: *International Financial Statistics.* **Price Frequency:** monthly, quarterly, annually. **Effective Market(s):** Penang (Malaysia). **Units of Measure:** cents per lb., index. **Type of Price:** market price, price index. **Time Period Covered:** latest 4 months, latest 5 quarters, latest 5 years.

Source: *International Financial Statistics.* **Price Frequency:** monthly, quarterly, annually. **Effective Market(s):** Malaysia. **Units of Measure:** cents per lb., index. **Type of Price:** market price, price index. **Time Period Covered:** latest 2 months, latest 4 quarters, latest 5 years.

Source: *International Financial Statistics Yearbook.* **Price Frequency:** annually. **Effective Market(s):** Malaysia, Penang (Malaysia). **Units of Measure:** cents per lb. **Type of Price:** wholesale. **Time Period Covered:** latest 30 years.

Source: *Iron Age.* **Price Frequency:** monthly. **Effective Market(s):** Kuala Lumpur (Malaysia). **Units of Measure:** cents per lb. **Type of Price:** smelter. **Time Period Covered:** latest month.

TIN: MINIMUM 99.85% TIN

Source: *Monthly Commodity Price Bulletin Supplement.* **Price Frequency:** monthly, quarterly, annually. **Effective Market(s):** United Kingdom. **Units of Measure:** British pounds per tonne, dollars per tonne. **Type of Price:** free market spot. **Time Period Covered:** latest 20 years.

TIN: PIG GRADE, STRAITS QUALITY

Source: *Commodity Trade and Price Trends.* **Price Frequency:** annually. **Effective Market(s):** New York. **Units of Measure:** Dollars per metric ton, 1980 constant dollars per metric ton. **Time Period Covered:** latest 37 years.

TIN: STANDARD, MINIMUM 99.75% TIN

Source: *Commodity Trade and Price Trends.* **Price Frequency:** annually. **Effective Market(s):** London. **Units of Measure:** Dollars per metric ton, 1980 constant dollars per metric ton. **Type of Price:** settlement. **Time Period Covered:** latest 37 years.

TIN: STANDARD, MINIMUM 99.85% TIN

Source: *Monthly Commodity Price Bulletin.* **Price Frequency:** monthly, annually. **Effective Market(s):** London. **Units of Measure:** British pounds per metric ton, cents per lb. **Type of Price:** free market spot. **Time Period Covered:** latest 5 years.

TIN: STRAITS QUALITY

Source: *Survey of Current Business.* **Price Frequency:** monthly, annually. **Units of Measure:** Dollars per lb. **Time Period Covered:** latest year.

TIN: STRAITS QUALITY, MINIMUM 99.85% TIN, MALAYSIAN

Source: *Commodity Trade and Price Trends.* **Price Frequency:** annually. **Effective Market(s):** Penang (Malaysia). **Units of Measure:** Dollars per metric ton, 1980 constant dollars per metric ton. **Type of Price:** settlement. **Time Period Covered:** latest 28 years.

TIN: THAI

Source: *International Financial Statistics.* **Price Frequency:** monthly, quarterly, annually. **Effective Market(s):** Thailand. **Units of Measure:** cents per lb., index. **Type of Price:** market price, price index. **Time Period Covered:** latest month, latest 4 quarters, latest 5 years.

Source: *International Financial Statistics Yearbook.* **Price Frequency:** annually. **Effective Market(s):** Thailand. **Units of Measure:** cents per lb. **Type of Price:** wholesale. **Time Period Covered:** latest 30 years.

TIN BABBITT

see also Babbitt.

TIN BABBITT AND PEWTER : HIGH GRADE

Source: *American Metal Market.* **Price Frequency:** daily. **Effective Market(s):** 6 domestic markets, Montreal, Toronto. **Units of Measure:** cents per lb. **Type of Price:** market. **Time Period Covered:** latest day.

TIN BLOCK PIPE

Source: *American Metal Market.* **Price Frequency:** daily. **Effective Market(s):** 6 domestic markets, Montreal, Toronto. **Units of Measure:** cents per lb. **Type of Price:** market. **Time Period Covered:** latest day.

TIN CHLORIDE: ANHYDROUS

Source: *Journal of Commerce and Commercial.* **Price Frequency:** weekly in Thursday issue. **Units of Measure:** Dollars per lb. **Type of Price:** spot. **Time Period Covered:** latest week.

TIN FLUOBORATE

Source: *Journal of Commerce and Commercial.* **Price Frequency:** weekly in Thursday issue. **Units of Measure:** Dollars per lb. **Type of Price:** spot. **Time Period Covered:** latest week.

TIN PLATE: SCRAP

Source: *Commodity Year Book.* **Price Frequency:** annually. **Effective Market(s):** United States. **Units of Measure:** Dollars per metric ton. **Time Period Covered:** latest 9 years.

TIN POWDER

Source: *American Metal Market.* **Price Frequency:** daily. **Units of Measure:** Dollars per lb. **Time Period Covered:** latest day.

TIN SALTS: ANHYDROUS

Source: *Journal of Commerce and Commercial.* **Price Frequency:** weekly in Thursday issue. **Units of Measure:** Dollars per lb. **Type of Price:** spot. **Time Period Covered:** latest week.

TIN SULFATE

Source: *Journal of Commerce and Commercial.* **Price Frequency:** weekly in Thursday issue. **Units of Measure:** Dollars per lb. **Type of Price:** spot. **Time Period Covered:** latest week.

TIRES: AUTO, TUBELESS, BIAS BELTED

Source: *Agricultural Prices.* **Price Frequency:** semiannually. **Effective Market(s):** United States. **Units of Measure:** Dollars each. **Type of Price:** paid by farmer. **Time Period Covered:** latest year.

Source: *Agricultural Prices Annual Summary.* **Price Frequency:** quarterly. **Effective Market(s):** United States. **Units of Measure:** Dollars each. **Type of Price:** average paid by farmer. **Time Period Covered:** latest 6 years.

TIRES: AUTO, TUBELESS, RADIAL, STEEL BELTED

Source: *Agricultural Prices.* **Price Frequency:** semiannually. **Effective Market(s):** United States. **Units of Measure:** Dollars each. **Type of Price:** paid by farmer. **Time Period Covered:** latest year.

Source: *Agricultural Prices Annual Summary.* **Price Frequency:** quarterly. **Effective Market(s):** United States. **Units of Measure:** Dollars each. **Type of Price:** average paid by farmer. **Time Period Covered:** latest 6 years.

TIRES: TRACTOR

Source: *Agricultural Prices.* **Price Frequency:** semiannually. **Effective Market(s):** United States. **Units of Measure:** Dollars each. **Type of Price:** paid by farmer. **Time Period Covered:** latest year.

Source: *Agricultural Prices Annual Summary.* **Price Frequency:** quarterly. **Effective Market(s):** United States. **Units of Measure:** Dollars each. **Type of Price:** average paid by farmer. **Time Period Covered:** latest 6 years.

TIRES: TRUCK

Source: *Agricultural Prices.* **Price Frequency:** semiannually. **Effective Market(s):** United States. **Units of Measure:** Dollars each. **Type of Price:** paid by farmer. **Time Period Covered:** latest year.

Source: *Agricultural Prices Annual Summary.* **Price Frequency:** quarterly. **Effective Market(s):** United States. **Units of Measure:** Dollars each. **Type of Price:** average paid by farmer. **Time Period Covered:** latest 6 years.

TITANIUM: RUTILE GRADE

Source: *Commodity Year Book.* **Price Frequency:** annually. **Effective Market(s):** Australia. **Units of Measure:** Dollars per short ton. **Time Period Covered:** latest 4 years.

Source: *Commodity Year Book.* **Price Frequency:** annually. **Effective Market(s):** East Coast. **Units of Measure:** Dollars per short ton. **Time Period Covered:** latest 12 years.

TITANIUM: SYNTHETIC

Source: *Commodity Year Book.* **Price Frequency:** annually. **Effective Market(s):** Mobile (AL). **Units of Measure:** Dollars per short ton. **Time Period Covered:** latest 8 years.

TITANIUM DIOXIDE

Source: *Modern Plastics.* **Price Frequency:** quarterly every February, May, August, November. **Units of Measure:** Dollars per lb. **Type of Price:** list. **Time Period Covered:** latest 4 quarters.

Source: *Purchasing.* **Price Frequency:** quarterly in January, April, July, October issues. **Units of Measure:** cents per lb. **Type of Price:** transaction. **Time Period Covered:** latest 5 quarters.

TITANIUM DIOXIDE: ANATASE GRADE

Source: *Chemical Marketing Reporter.* **Price Frequency:** weekly. **Effective Market(s):** New York. **Units of Measure:** Dollars per lb. **Type of Price:** spot. **Time Period Covered:** latest week.

Source: *Commodity Year Book.* **Price Frequency:** annually. **Effective Market(s):** United States. **Units of Measure:** Dollars per lb. **Time Period Covered:** latest 12 years.

TITANIUM DIOXIDE: ANATASE GRADE, DRY

Source: *Journal of Commerce and Commercial.* **Price Frequency:** weekly in Wednesday issue. **Units of Measure:** Dollars per lb. **Type of Price:** spot. **Time Period Covered:** latest week.

TITANIUM DIOXIDE: RUTILE GRADE

Source: *Chemical Marketing Reporter.* **Price Frequency:** weekly. **Effective Market(s):** New York. **Units of Measure:** Dollars per lb. **Type of Price:** spot. **Time Period Covered:** latest week.

Source: *Commodity Year Book.* **Price Frequency:** annually. **Effective Market(s):** United States. **Units of Measure:** Dollars per lb. **Time Period Covered:** latest 12 years.

TITANIUM DIOXIDE: RUTILE GRADE, DRY

Source: *Journal of Commerce and Commercial.* **Price Frequency:** weekly in Wednesday issue. **Units of Measure:** Dollars per lb. **Type of Price:** spot. **Time Period Covered:** latest week.

TITANIUM DIOXIDE: RUTILE GRADE, NON-CHALKING

Source: *Chemical Marketing Reporter.* **Price Frequency:** weekly. **Effective Market(s):** New York. **Units of Measure:** Dollars per lb. **Type of Price:** spot. **Time Period Covered:** latest week.

TITANIUM HYDRIDE: ELECTRONICS GRADE, POWDERED

Source: *Chemical Marketing Reporter.* **Price Frequency:** weekly. **Effective Market(s):** New York. **Units of Measure:** Dollars per lb. **Type of Price:** spot. **Time Period Covered:** latest week.

TITANIUM ILMENITE

Source: *Commodity Year Book.* **Price Frequency:** annually. **Effective Market(s):** East Coast. **Units of Measure:** Dollars per tonne. **Time Period Covered:** latest 7 years.

Source: *Commodity Year Book.* **Price Frequency:** annually. **Effective Market(s):** Australia. **Units of Measure:** Dollars per tonne. **Time Period Covered:** latest 12 years.

TITANIUM SHEET: GRADE 2

Source: *E&MJ.* **Price Frequency:** monthly. **Units of Measure:** Dollars per lb. **Time Period Covered:** latest month.

TITANIUM SLAG: 85% TITANIUM OXIDE

Source: *Commodity Year Book.* **Price Frequency:** annually. **Effective Market(s):** Richard's Bay (South Africa). **Units of Measure:** Dollars per tonne. **Time Period Covered:** latest 6 years.

TITANIUM SPONGE

Source: *Commodity Year Book.* **Price Frequency:** annually. **Effective Market(s):** United States. **Units of Measure:** Dollars per lb. **Time Period Covered:** latest 11 years.

Source: *E&MJ.* **Price Frequency:** monthly. **Units of Measure:** Dollars per lb. **Time Period Covered:** latest month.

Source: *Economic and Energy Indicators.* **Price Frequency:** biweekly. **Units of Measure:** Dollars per lb. **Time Period Covered:** latest 3 months, quarters, and years.

TITANIUM SPONGE: 99.3% MINIMUM

Source: *Chemical Marketing Reporter.* **Price Frequency:** weekly. **Effective Market(s):** New York. **Units of Measure:** Dollars per lb. **Type of Price:** spot. **Time Period Covered:** latest week.

TITANIUM SPONGE: 99.7% MINIMUN

Source: *Journal of Commerce and Commercial.* **Price Frequency:** daily. **Effective Market(s):** Europe. **Units of Measure:** Dollars per kilogram. **Type of Price:** spot. **Time Period Covered:** latest day.

TITANIUM SPONGE: MELTING GRADE

Source: *Iron Age.* **Price Frequency:** monthly. **Units of Measure:** Dollars per lb. **Type of Price:** consumer. **Time Period Covered:** latest month.

TITANIUM TETRACHLORIDE: TECHNICAL

Source: *Chemical Marketing Reporter.* **Price Frequency:** weekly. **Effective Market(s):** New York. **Units of Measure:** Dollars per lb. **Type of Price:** spot. **Time Period Covered:** latest week.

TOBACCO

Source: *Agricultural Outlook.* **Price Frequency:** monthly, annually. **Units of Measure:** cents per lb. **Type of Price:** auction for export. **Time Period Covered:** monthly latest 6 months, annually latest 3 years.

Source: *Agricultural Prices.* **Price Frequency:** monthly. **Effective Market(s):** United States. **Units of Measure:** Dollars per lb. **Type of Price:** received by farmer. **Time Period Covered:** latest 2 months, year ago.

Source: *Agricultural Prices.* **Price Frequency:** monthly, seasonally. **Effective Market(s):** 6 domestic markets, United States. **Units of Measure:** Dollars per lb. **Type of Price:** received by farmer. **Time Period Covered:** latest month.

Source: *Agricultural Prices Annual Summary.* **Price Frequency:** monthly, seasonally. **Effective Market(s):** 12 domestic markets. **Units of Measure:** Dollars per lb. **Type of Price:** average received by farmer. **Time Period Covered:** latest 3 years.

Source: *Agricultural Prices Annual Summary.* **Price Frequency:** annually. **Effective Market(s):** 16 domestic markets, United States. **Units of Measure:** Dollars per lb. **Type of Price:** average received by farmer. **Time Period Covered:** latest 3 years.

Source: *Annual Report on Tobacco Statistics.* **Price Frequency:** annually. **Effective Market(s):** 16 domestic markets, United States. **Units of Measure:** cents per lb. **Time Period Covered:** latest 6 years.

Source: *Commodity Year Book.* **Price Frequency:** annually. **Effective Market(s):** United States. **Units of Measure:** cents per lb. **Type of Price:** farm. **Time Period Covered:** latest 8 years.

TOBACCO: BURLEY

Source: *Agricultural Outlook.* **Price Frequency:** quarterly, annually, seasonally. **Units of Measure:** Dollars per lb. **Type of Price:** auction. **Time Period Covered:** quarterly latest 5 quarters, annually latest 5 years.

Source: *Tobacco Market Review: Burley.* **Price Frequency:** annually. **Effective Market(s):** 8 domestic markets, United States. **Units of Measure:** Dollars per 100 lbs. **Type of Price:** gross sale, producer, resale. **Time Period Covered:** latest 3 years.

Source: *Tobacco Market Review: Burley.* **Price Frequency:** annually. **Effective Market(s):** 62 domestic markets. **Units of Measure:** Dollars per 100 lbs. **Type of Price:** average. **Time Period Covered:** latest 2 years.

Source: *Tobacco Situation and Outlook Report.* **Price Frequency:** monthly. **Units of Measure:** cents per lb. **Type of Price:** grower. **Time Period Covered:** latest 3 months, year ago.

TOBACCO: BURLEY, FLYINGS

Source: *Tobacco Market Review: Burley.* **Price Frequency:** annually. **Effective Market(s):** United States. **Units of Measure:** Dollars per 100 lbs. **Type of Price:** average. **Time Period Covered:** latest year.

TOBACCO: BURLEY, LEAF

Source: *Tobacco Market Review: Burley.* **Price Frequency:** annually. **Effective Market(s):** United States. **Units of Measure:** Dollars per 100 lbs. **Type of Price:** average. **Time Period Covered:** latest year.

TOBACCO: BURLEY, LUGS

Source: *Tobacco Market Review: Burley.* **Price Frequency:** annually. **Effective Market(s):** United States. **Units of Measure:** Dollars per 100 lbs. **Type of Price:** average. **Time Period Covered:** latest year.

TOBACCO: BURLEY, MALAWI, LEAF

Source: *Tobacco Quarterly.* **Price Frequency:** weekly, annually, seasonally. **Effective Market(s):** Malawi. **Units of Measure:** Malawi tambala per kilogram. **Type of Price:** average. **Time Period Covered:** latest 2 years.

TOBACCO: BURLEY, MIXED GROUP

Source: *Tobacco Market Review: Burley.* **Price Frequency:** annually. **Effective Market(s):** United States. **Units of Measure:** Dollars per 100 lbs. **Type of Price:** average. **Time Period Covered:** latest year.

TOBACCO: BURLEY, NONDESCRIPT

Source: *Tobacco Market Review: Burley.* **Price Frequency:** annually. **Effective Market(s):** United States. **Units of Measure:** Dollars per 100 lbs. **Type of Price:** average. **Time Period Covered:** latest year.

TOBACCO: BURLEY, TIPS

Source: *Tobacco Market Review: Burley.* **Price Frequency:** annually. **Effective Market(s):** United States. **Units of Measure:** Dollars per 100 lbs. **Type of Price:** average. **Time Period Covered:** latest year.

TOBACCO: BURLEY, TYPE 31

Source: *Annual Report on Tobacco Statistics.* **Price Frequency:** annually. **Effective Market(s):** United States/Puerto Rico. **Units of Measure:** cents per lb. **Type of Price:** price paid to growers. **Time Period Covered:** latest 6 years.

Source: *Commodity Year Book.* **Price Frequency:** annually. **Effective Market(s):** United States. **Units of Measure:** cents per lb. **Type of Price:** farm. **Time Period Covered:** latest 9 years.

TOBACCO: DARK AIR-CURED, KENTUCKY/ TENNESSEE

Source: *Tobacco Situation and Outlook Report.* **Price Frequency:** monthly. **Units of Measure:** cents per lb. **Type of Price:** grower. **Time Period Covered:** latest 3 months, year ago.

TOBACCO: DARK AIR-CURED, TYPE 35

Source: *Agricultural Prices Annual Summary.* **Price Frequency:** monthly, annually, seasonally. **Effective Market(s):** Kentucky, Tennessee, United States. **Units of Measure:** Dollars per lb. **Type of Price:** average received by farmer. **Time Period Covered:** latest 2 years, for US latest 6 years.

TOBACCO: DARK AIR-CURED, TYPE 36

Source: *Agricultural Prices Annual Summary.* **Price Frequency:** monthly, annually, seasonally. **Effective Market(s):** Kentucky, United States. **Units of Measure:** Dollars per lb. **Type of Price:** average received by farmer. **Time Period Covered:** latest 2 years, for US latest 6 years.

TOBACCO: DARK AIR-CURED, TYPE 37

Source: *Agricultural Prices Annual Summary.* **Price Frequency:** monthly, annually, seasonally. **Effective Market(s):** Virginia, United States. **Units of Measure:** Dollars per lb. **Type of Price:** average received by farmer. **Time Period Covered:** latest 2 years, for US latest 6 years.

TOBACCO: DARK AIR-CURED, TYPES 35-36

Source: *Agricultural Prices Annual Summary.* **Price Frequency:** monthly, annually, seasonally. **Effective Market(s):** United States. **Units of Measure:** Dollars per lb. **Type of Price:** average received by farmer. **Time Period Covered:** latest 6 years.

TOBACCO: DARK AIR-CURED, TYPES 35-37

Source: *Agricultural Prices Annual Summary.* **Price Frequency:** monthly, annually, seasonally. **Effective Market(s):** United States. **Units of Measure:** Dollars per lb. **Type of Price:** average received by farmer. **Time Period Covered:** latest 2 years, for US latest 6 years.

Source: *Tobacco Market Review: Fire-Cured and Dark Air-Cured.* **Price Frequency:** annually. **Effective Market(s):** United States. **Units of Measure:** Dollars per 100 lbs. **Type of Price:** average, gross sale, resale. **Time Period Covered:** latest 6 years.

TOBACCO: FIRE-CURED, KENTUCKY/ TENNESSEE

Source: *Tobacco Situation and Outlook Report.* **Price Frequency:** monthly. **Units of Measure:** cents per lb. **Type of Price:** grower. **Time Period Covered:** latest 3 months, year ago.

TOBACCO: FIRE-CURED, MALAWI, LEAF

Source: *Tobacco Quarterly.* **Price Frequency:** weekly, annually, seasonally. **Effective Market(s):** Malawi. **Units of Measure:** Malawi tambala per kilogram. **Type of Price:** average. **Time Period Covered:** latest 2 years.

TOBACCO: FIRE-CURED, TYPE 21

Source: *Agricultural Prices Annual Summary.* **Price Frequency:** monthly, annually, seasonally. **Effective Market(s):** Virginia, United States. **Units of Measure:** Dollars per lb. **Type of Price:** average received by farmer. **Time Period Covered:** latest 2 years, for US latest 6 years.

TOBACCO: FIRE-CURED, TYPE 21, VIRGINIA

Source: *Annual Report on Tobacco Statistics.* **Price Frequency:** annually. **Effective Market(s):** United States/Puerto Rico. **Units of Measure:** cents per lb. **Type of Price:** price paid to growers. **Time Period Covered:** latest 6 years.

Source: *Tobacco Market Review: Fire-Cured and Dark Air-Cured.* **Price Frequency:** annually. **Effective Market(s):** United States. **Units of Measure:** Dollars per 100 lbs. **Type of Price:** auction, gross sale, resale. **Time Period Covered:** latest 6 years.

Source: *Tobacco Market Review: Fire-Cured and Dark Air-Cured.* **Price Frequency:** annually. **Effective Market(s):** Blackstone (VA), Farmville (VA), Lynchburg (VA), other Virginia markets. **Units of Measure:** Dollars per 100 lbs. **Type of Price:** gross sale, producer, resale. **Time Period Covered:** latest 2 years.

TOBACCO: FIRE-CURED, TYPE 21, VIRGINIA, HEAVY LEAF

Source: *Tobacco Market Review: Fire-Cured and Dark Air-Cured.* **Price Frequency:** annually. **Effective Market(s):** United States. **Units of Measure:** Dollars per 100 lbs. **Type of Price:** auction. **Time Period Covered:** latest year.

TOBACCO: FIRE-CURED, TYPE 21, VIRGINIA, LUGS

Source: *Tobacco Market Review: Fire-Cured and Dark Air-Cured.* **Price Frequency:** annually. **Effective Market(s):** United States. **Units of Measure:** Dollars per 100 lbs. **Type of Price:** auction. **Time Period Covered:** latest year.

TOBACCO: FIRE-CURED, TYPE 21, VIRGINIA, NONDESCRIPT

Source: *Tobacco Market Review: Fire-Cured and Dark Air-Cured.* **Price Frequency:** annually. **Effective Market(s):** United States. **Units of Measure:** Dollars per 100 lbs. **Type of Price:** auction. **Time Period Covered:** latest year.

TOBACCO: FIRE-CURED, TYPE 21, VIRGINIA, THIN LEAF

Source: *Tobacco Market Review: Fire-Cured and Dark Air-Cured.* **Price Frequency:** annually. **Effective Market(s):** United States. **Units of Measure:** Dollars per 100 lbs. **Type of Price:** auction. **Time Period Covered:** latest year.

TOBACCO: FIRE-CURED, TYPE 21, VIRGINIA, WRAPPERS

Source: *Tobacco Market Review: Fire-Cured and Dark Air-Cured.* **Price Frequency:** annually. **Effective Market(s):** United States. **Units of Measure:** Dollars per 100 lbs. **Type of Price:** auction. **Time Period Covered:** latest year.

TOBACCO: FIRE-CURED, TYPE 22

Source: *Agricultural Prices Annual Summary.* **Price Frequency:** monthly, annually, seasonally. **Effective Market(s):** Kentucky, Tennessee, United States. **Units of Measure:** Dollars per lb. **Type of Price:** average received by farmer. **Time Period Covered:** latest 2 years, for US latest 6 years.

TOBACCO: FIRE-CURED, TYPE 23

Source: *Agricultural Prices Annual Summary.* **Price Frequency:** monthly, annually, seasonally. **Effective Market(s):** Kentucky, Tennessee, United States. **Units of Measure:** Dollars per lb. **Type of Price:** average received by farmer. **Time Period Covered:** latest 2 years, for US latest 6 years.

TOBACCO: FIRE-CURED, TYPES 21-23

Source: *Agricultural Prices Annual Summary.* **Price Frequency:** monthly, annually, seasonally. **Effective Market(s):** United States. **Units of Measure:** Dollars per lb. **Type of Price:** average received by farmer. **Time Period Covered:** latest 6 years.

Source: *Tobacco Market Review: Fire-Cured and Dark Air-Cured.* **Price Frequency:** annually. **Effective Market(s):** United States. **Units of Measure:** Dollars per 100 lbs. **Type of Price:** average, gross sale, resale. **Time Period Covered:** latest 6 years.

TOBACCO: FIRE-CURED, TYPES 22-23

Source: *Agricultural Prices Annual Summary.* **Price Frequency:** monthly, annually, seasonally. **Effective Market(s):** United States. **Units of Measure:** Dollars per lb. **Type of Price:** average received by farmer. **Time Period Covered:** latest 6 years.

TOBACCO: FIRE-CURED, TYPES 22-23, KENTUCKY AND TENNESSEE

Source: *Annual Report on Tobacco Statistics.* **Price Frequency:** annually. **Effective Market(s):** United States/Puerto Rico. **Units of Measure:** cents per lb. **Type of Price:** price paid to growers. **Time Period Covered:** latest 6 years.

Source: *Tobacco Market Review: Fire-Cured and Dark Air-Cured.* **Price Frequency:** annually. **Effective Market(s):** United States. **Units of Measure:** Dollars per 100 lbs. **Type of Price:** average, auction, country, gross sale, resale. **Time Period Covered:** latest 6 years.

Source: *Tobacco Market Review: Fire-Cured and Dark Air-Cured.* **Price Frequency:** annually. **Effective Market(s):** 7 Kentucky/Tennessee markets. **Units of Measure:** Dollars per 100 lbs. **Type of Price:** gross sale, producer, resale. **Time Period Covered:** latest 2 years.

TOBACCO: FIRE-CURED, TYPES 22-23, KENTUCKY AND TENNESSEE, HEAVY LEAF

Source: *Tobacco Market Review: Fire-Cured and Dark Air-Cured.* **Price Frequency:** annually. **Effective Market(s):** United States. **Units of Measure:** Dollars per 100 lbs. **Type of Price:** auction. **Time Period Covered:** latest year.

TOBACCO: FIRE-CURED, TYPES 22-23, KENTUCKY AND TENNESSEE, LUGS

Source: *Tobacco Market Review: Fire-Cured and Dark Air-Cured.* **Price Frequency:** annually. **Effective Market(s):** United States. **Units of Measure:** Dollars per 100 lbs. **Type of Price:** auction. **Time Period Covered:** latest year.

TOBACCO: FIRE-CURED, TYPES 22-23, KENTUCKY AND TENNESSEE, NONDESCRIPT

Source: *Tobacco Market Review: Fire-Cured and Dark Air-Cured.* **Price Frequency:** annually. **Effective Market(s):** United States. **Units of Measure:** Dollars per 100 lbs. **Type of Price:** auction. **Time Period Covered:** latest year.

TOBACCO: FIRE-CURED, TYPES 22-23, KENTUCKY AND TENNESSEE, THIN LEAF

Source: *Tobacco Market Review: Fire-Cured and Dark Air-Cured.* **Price Frequency:** annually. **Effective Market(s):** United States. **Units of Measure:** Dollars per 100 lbs. **Type of Price:** auction. **Time Period Covered:** latest year.

TOBACCO: FIRE-CURED, TYPES 22-23, KENTUCKY AND TENNESSEE, WRAPPERS

Source: *Tobacco Market Review: Fire-Cured and Dark Air-Cured.* **Price Frequency:** annually. **Effective Market(s):** United States. **Units of Measure:** Dollars per 100 lbs. **Type of Price:** auction. **Time Period Covered:** latest year.

TOBACCO: FIRE-CURED, VIRGINIA

Source: *Tobacco Situation and Outlook Report.* **Price Frequency:** monthly. **Units of Measure:** cents per lb. **Type of Price:** grower. **Time Period Covered:** latest 3 months, year ago.

TOBACCO: FLUE-CURED

Source: *Agricultural Outlook.* **Price Frequency:** quarterly, annually, seasonally. **Units of Measure:** Dollars per lb. **Type of Price:** auction. **Time Period Covered:** quarterly latest 5 quarters, annually latest 5 years.

Source: *Tobacco Situation and Outlook Report.* **Price Frequency:** monthly. **Units of Measure:** cents per lb. **Type of Price:** grower. **Time Period Covered:** latest 3 months, year ago.

TOBACCO: FLUE-CURED, INDIAN

Source: *Commodity Trade and Price Trends.* **Price Frequency:** annually. **Effective Market(s):** India. **Units of Measure:** Dollars per metric ton, 1980 constant dollars per metric ton. **Type of Price:** export. **Time Period Covered:** latest 37 years.

TOBACCO: FLUE-CURED, MALAWI, LEAF

Source: *Tobacco Quarterly.* **Price Frequency:** weekly, annually, seasonally. **Effective Market(s):** Malawi. **Units of Measure:** Malawi tambala per kilogram. **Type of Price:** average. **Time Period Covered:** latest 2 years.

TOBACCO: FLUE-CURED, TYPE 11

Source: *Agricultural Prices Annual Summary.* **Price Frequency:** monthly, annually, seasonally. **Effective Market(s):** North Carolina, Virginia, United States. **Units of Measure:** Dollars per lb. **Type of Price:** average received by farmer. **Time Period Covered:** latest 2 years, for US latest 6 years.

TOBACCO: FLUE-CURED, TYPE 11, OLD AND MIDDLE BELT

Source: *Agricultural Prices.* **Price Frequency:** monthly. **Effective Market(s):** United States. **Units of Measure:** Dollars per lb. **Type of Price:** received by farmer. **Time Period Covered:** latest month, year ago.

Source: *Tobacco Market Review: Flue-Cured.* **Price Frequency:** annually. **Effective Market(s):** United States. **Units of Measure:** Dollars per 100 lbs. **Type of Price:** gross resale, producer, resale. **Time Period Covered:** latest 2 years.

Source: *Tobacco Market Review: Flue-Cured.* **Price Frequency:** annually. **Effective Market(s):** 24 North Carolina/Virginia markets. **Units of Measure:** Dollars per 100 lbs. **Type of Price:** gross resale, producer, resale. **Time Period Covered:** latest 2 years.

Source: *Tobacco Market Review: Flue-Cured.* **Price Frequency:** weekly, annually, seasonally. **Units of Measure:** Dollars per 100 lbs. **Type of Price:** average. **Time Period Covered:** latest year.

Source: *Tobacco Quarterly.* **Price Frequency:** weekly, seasonally. **Effective Market(s):** United States. **Units of Measure:** cents per kilogram. **Type of Price:** average. **Time Period Covered:** latest 2 years.

TOBACCO: FLUE-CURED, TYPE 11, OLD AND MIDDLE BELT, CUTTERS

Source: *Tobacco Market Review: Flue-Cured.* **Price Frequency:** annually. **Effective Market(s):** United States. **Units of Measure:** Dollars per 100 lbs. **Type of Price:** average. **Time Period Covered:** latest year.

TOBACCO: FLUE-CURED, TYPE 11, OLD AND MIDDLE BELT, LEAF

Source: *Tobacco Market Review: Flue-Cured.* **Price Frequency:** annually. **Effective Market(s):** United States. **Units of Measure:** Dollars per 100 lbs. **Type of Price:** average. **Time Period Covered:** latest year.

TOBACCO: FLUE-CURED, TYPE 11, OLD AND MIDDLE BELT, LUGS

Source: *Tobacco Market Review: Flue-Cured.* **Price Frequency:** annually. **Effective Market(s):** United States. **Units of Measure:** Dollars per 100 lbs. **Type of Price:** average. **Time Period Covered:** latest year.

TOBACCO: FLUE-CURED, TYPE 11, OLD AND MIDDLE BELT, NONDESCRIPT

Source: *Tobacco Market Review: Flue-Cured.* **Price Frequency:** annually. **Effective Market(s):** United States. **Units of Measure:** Dollars per 100 lbs. **Type of Price:** average. **Time Period Covered:** latest year.

TOBACCO: FLUE-CURED, TYPE 11, OLD AND MIDDLE BELT, PRIMINGS

Source: *Tobacco Market Review: Flue-Cured.* **Price Frequency:** annually. **Effective Market(s):** United States. **Units of Measure:** Dollars per 100 lbs. **Type of Price:** average. **Time Period Covered:** latest year.

TOBACCO: FLUE-CURED, TYPE 11, OLD AND MIDDLE BELT, SMOKING LEAF

Source: *Tobacco Market Review: Flue-Cured.* **Price Frequency:** annually. **Effective Market(s):** United States. **Units of Measure:** Dollars per 100 lbs. **Type of Price:** average. **Time Period Covered:** latest year.

TOBACCO: FLUE-CURED, TYPE 12, EASTERN NORTH CAROLINA

Source: *Agricultural Prices.* **Price Frequency:** monthly. **Effective Market(s):** United States. **Units of Measure:** Dollars per lb. **Type of Price:** received by farmer. **Time Period Covered:** latest month, year ago.

Source: *Agricultural Prices Annual Summary.* **Price Frequency:** monthly, annually, seasonally. **Effective Market(s):** North Carolina, United States. **Units of Measure:** Dollars per lb. **Type of Price:** average received by farmer. **Time Period Covered:** latest 2 years, for US latest 6 years.

Source: *Tobacco Market Review: Flue-Cured.* **Price Frequency:** annually. **Effective Market(s):** United States. **Units of Measure:** Dollars per 100 lbs. **Type of Price:** gross resale, producer, resale. **Time Period Covered:** latest 6 years.

Source: *Tobacco Market Review: Flue-Cured.* **Price Frequency:** annually. **Effective Market(s):** 16 North Carolina markets. **Units of Measure:** Dollars per 100 lbs. **Type of Price:** gross resale, producer, resale. **Time Period Covered:** latest 6 years.

Source: *Tobacco Market Review: Flue-Cured.* **Price Frequency:** weekly, annually, seasonally. **Units of Measure:** Dollars per 100 lbs. **Type of Price:** average. **Time Period Covered:** latest year.

Source: *Tobacco Quarterly.* **Price Frequency:** weekly, seasonally. **Effective Market(s):** United States. **Units of Measure:** cents per kilogram. **Type of Price:** average. **Time Period Covered:** latest 2 years.

TOBACCO: FLUE-CURED, TYPE 12, EASTERN NORTH CAROLINA, CUTTERS

Source: *Tobacco Market Review: Flue-Cured.* **Price Frequency:** annually. **Effective Market(s):** United States. **Units of Measure:** Dollars per 100 lbs. **Type of Price:** average. **Time Period Covered:** latest year.

TOBACCO: FLUE-CURED, TYPE 12, EASTERN NORTH CAROLINA, LEAF

Source: *Tobacco Market Review: Flue-Cured.* **Price Frequency:** annually. **Effective Market(s):** United States. **Units of Measure:** Dollars per 100 lbs. **Type of Price:** average. **Time Period Covered:** latest year.

TOBACCO: FLUE-CURED, TYPE 12, EASTERN NORTH CAROLINA, LUGS

Source: *Tobacco Market Review: Flue-Cured.* **Price Frequency:** annually. **Effective Market(s):** United States. **Units of Measure:** Dollars per 100 lbs. **Type of Price:** average. **Time Period Covered:** latest year.

TOBACCO: FLUE-CURED, TYPE 12, EASTERN NORTH CAROLINA, NONDESCRIPT

Source: *Tobacco Market Review: Flue-Cured.* **Price Frequency:** annually. **Effective Market(s):** United States. **Units of Measure:** Dollars per 100 lbs. **Type of Price:** average. **Time Period Covered:** latest year.

TOBACCO: FLUE-CURED, TYPE 12, EASTERN NORTH CAROLINA, PRIMINGS

Source: *Tobacco Market Review: Flue-Cured.* **Price Frequency:** annually. **Effective Market(s):** United States. **Units of Measure:** Dollars per 100 lbs. **Type of Price:** average. **Time Period Covered:** latest year.

TOBACCO: FLUE-CURED, TYPE 12, EASTERN NORTH CAROLINA, SMOKING LEAF

Source: *Tobacco Market Review: Flue-Cured.* **Price Frequency:** annually. **Effective Market(s):** United States. **Units of Measure:** Dollars per 100 lbs. **Type of Price:** average. **Time Period Covered:** latest year.

TOBACCO: FLUE-CURED, TYPE 13

Source: *Agricultural Prices Annual Summary.* **Price Frequency:** monthly, annually, seasonally. **Effective Market(s):** North Carolina, South Carolina, United States. **Units of Measure:** Dollars per lb. **Type of Price:** average received by farmer. **Time Period Covered:** latest 2 years, for US latest 6 years.

TOBACCO: FLUE-CURED, TYPE 13, SOUTH CAROLINA AND BORDER NORTH CAROLINA

Source: *Agricultural Prices.* **Price Frequency:** monthly. **Effective Market(s):** United States. **Units of Measure:** Dollars per lb. **Type of Price:** received by farmer. **Time Period Covered:** latest month, year ago.

Source: *Tobacco Market Review: Flue-Cured.* **Price Frequency:** annually. **Effective Market(s):** United States. **Units of Measure:** Dollars per 100 lbs. **Type of Price:** gross resale, producer, resale. **Time Period Covered:** latest 6 years.

Source: *Tobacco Market Review: Flue-Cured.* **Price Frequency:** annually. **Effective Market(s):** 17 North Carolina/South Carolina markets. **Units of Measure:** Dollars per 100 lbs. **Type of Price:** gross resale, producer, resale. **Time Period Covered:** latest 6 years.

Source: *Tobacco Market Review: Flue-Cured.* **Price Frequency:** weekly, annually, seasonally. **Units of Measure:** Dollars per 100 lbs. **Type of Price:** average. **Time Period Covered:** latest year.

Source: *Tobacco Quarterly.* **Price Frequency:** weekly, seasonally. **Effective Market(s):** United States. **Units of Measure:** cents per kilogram. **Type of Price:** average. **Time Period Covered:** latest 2 years.

TOBACCO: FLUE-CURED, TYPE 13, SOUTH CAROLINA AND BORDER NORTH CAROLINA, CUTTERS

Source: *Tobacco Market Review: Flue-Cured.* **Price Frequency:** annually. **Effective Market(s):** United States. **Units of Measure:** Dollars per 100 lbs. **Type of Price:** average. **Time Period Covered:** latest year.

TOBACCO: FLUE-CURED, TYPE 13, SOUTH CAROLINA AND BORDER NORTH CAROLINA, LEAF

Source: *Tobacco Market Review: Flue-Cured.* **Price Frequency:** annually. **Effective Market(s):** United States. **Units of Measure:** Dollars per 100 lbs. **Type of Price:** average. **Time Period Covered:** latest year.

TOBACCO: FLUE-CURED, TYPE 13, SOUTH CAROLINA AND BORDER NORTH CAROLINA, LUGS

Source: *Tobacco Market Review: Flue-Cured.* **Price Frequency:** annually. **Effective Market(s):** United States. **Units of Measure:** Dollars per 100 lbs. **Type of Price:** average. **Time Period Covered:** latest year.

TOBACCO: FLUE-CURED, TYPE 13, SOUTH CAROLINA AND BORDER NORTH CAROLINA, NONDESCRIPT

Source: *Tobacco Market Review: Flue-Cured.* **Price Frequency:** annually. **Effective Market(s):** United States. **Units of Measure:** Dollars per 100 lbs. **Type of Price:** average. **Time Period Covered:** latest year.

TOBACCO: FLUE-CURED, TYPE 13, SOUTH CAROLINA AND BORDER NORTH CAROLINA, PRIMINGS

Source: *Tobacco Market Review: Flue-Cured.* **Price Frequency:** annually. **Effective Market(s):** United States. **Units of Measure:** Dollars per 100 lbs. **Type of Price:** average. **Time Period Covered:** latest year.

TOBACCO: FLUE-CURED, TYPE 13, SOUTH CAROLINA AND BORDER NORTH CAROLINA, SMOKING LEAF

Source: *Tobacco Market Review: Flue-Cured.* **Price Frequency:** annually. **Effective Market(s):** United States. **Units of Measure:** Dollars per 100 lbs. **Type of Price:** average. **Time Period Covered:** latest year.

TOBACCO: FLUE-CURED, TYPE 14

Source: *Agricultural Prices Annual Summary.* **Price Frequency:** monthly, annually, seasonally. **Effective Market(s):** FL, GA, United States. **Units of Measure:** Dollars per lb. **Type of Price:** average received by farmer. **Time Period Covered:** latest 2 years, for US latest 6 years.

TOBACCO: FLUE-CURED, TYPE 14, GEORGIA AND FLORIDA

Source: *Agricultural Prices.* **Price Frequency:** monthly. **Effective Market(s):** United States. **Units of Measure:** Dollars per lb. **Type of Price:** received by farmer. **Time Period Covered:** latest month, year ago.

Source: *Tobacco Market Review: Flue-Cured.* **Price Frequency:** annually. **Effective Market(s):** United States. **Units of Measure:** Dollars per 100 lbs. **Type of Price:** gross resale, producer, resale. **Time Period Covered:** latest 6 years.

Source: *Tobacco Market Review: Flue-Cured.* **Price Frequency:** annually. **Effective Market(s):** United States. **Units of Measure:** Dollars per 100 lbs. **Type of Price:** average. **Time Period Covered:** latest year.

Source: *Tobacco Market Review: Flue-Cured.* **Price Frequency:** annually. **Effective Market(s):** 20 Georgia/Florida markets. **Units of Measure:** Dollars per 100 lbs. **Type of Price:** gross resale, producer, resale. **Time Period Covered:** latest 6 years.

Source: *Tobacco Market Review: Flue-Cured.* **Price Frequency:** weekly, annually, seasonally. **Units of Measure:** Dollars per 100 lbs. **Type of Price:** average. **Time Period Covered:** latest year.

Source: *Tobacco Quarterly.* **Price Frequency:** weekly, seasonally. **Effective Market(s):** United States. **Units of Measure:** cents per kilogram. **Type of Price:** average. **Time Period Covered:** latest 2 years.

TOBACCO: FLUE-CURED, TYPE 14, GEORGIA AND FLORIDA, CUTTERS

Source: *Tobacco Market Review: Flue-Cured.* **Price Frequency:** annually. **Effective Market(s):** United States. **Units of Measure:** Dollars per 100 lbs. **Type of Price:** average. **Time Period Covered:** latest year.

TOBACCO: FLUE-CURED, TYPE 14, GEORGIA AND FLORIDA, LEAF

Source: *Tobacco Market Review: Flue-Cured.* **Price Frequency:** annually. **Effective Market(s):** United States. **Units of Measure:** Dollars per 100 lbs. **Type of Price:** average. **Time Period Covered:** latest year.

TOBACCO: FLUE-CURED, TYPE 14, GEORGIA AND FLORIDA, LUGS

Source: *Tobacco Market Review: Flue-Cured.* **Price Frequency:** annually. **Effective Market(s):** United States. **Units of Measure:** Dollars per 100 lbs. **Type of Price:** average. **Time Period Covered:** latest year.

TOBACCO: FLUE-CURED, TYPE 14, GEORGIA AND FLORIDA, NONDESCRIPT

Source: *Tobacco Market Review: Flue-Cured.* **Price Frequency:** annually. **Effective Market(s):** United States. **Units of Measure:** Dollars per 100 lbs. **Type of Price:** average. **Time Period Covered:** latest year.

TOBACCO: FLUE-CURED, TYPE 14, GEORGIA AND FLORIDA, PRIMINGS

Source: *Tobacco Market Review: Flue-Cured.* **Price Frequency:** annually. **Effective Market(s):** United States. **Units of Measure:** Dollars per 100 lbs. **Type of Price:** average. **Time Period Covered:** latest year.

TOBACCO: FLUE-CURED, TYPE 14, GEORGIA AND FLORIDA, SMOKING LEAF

Source: *Tobacco Market Review: Flue-Cured.* **Price Frequency:** annually. **Effective Market(s):** United States. **Units of Measure:** Dollars per 100 lbs. **Type of Price:** average. **Time Period Covered:** latest year.

TOBACCO: FLUE-CURED, TYPES 11-14

Source: *Agricultural Prices.* **Price Frequency:** monthly. **Effective Market(s):** United States. **Units of Measure:** Dollars per lb. **Type of Price:** received by farmer. **Time Period Covered:** latest month, year ago.

Source: *Agricultural Prices Annual Summary.* **Price Frequency:** monthly, annually, seasonally. **Effective Market(s):** United States. **Units of Measure:** Dollars per lb. **Type of Price:** average received by farmer. **Time Period Covered:** latest 6 years.

Source: *Annual Report on Tobacco Statistics.* **Price Frequency:** annually. **Effective Market(s):** United States/Puerto Rico. **Units of Measure:** cents per lb. **Type of Price:** price paid to growers. **Time Period Covered:** latest 6 years.

Source: *Commodity Year Book.* **Price Frequency:** annually. **Effective Market(s):** United States. **Units of Measure:** cents per lb. **Type of Price:** farm. **Time Period Covered:** latest 9 years.

Source: *Commodity Year Book.* **Price Frequency:** annually. **Effective Market(s):** United States. **Units of Measure:** cents per lb. **Type of Price:** parity price. **Time Period Covered:** latest 7 years.

Source: *Commodity Year Book.* **Price Frequency:** annually. **Effective Market(s):** United States. **Units of Measure:** cents per lb. **Type of Price:** support price. **Time Period Covered:** latest 9 years.

Source: *Tobacco Market Review: Flue-Cured.* **Price Frequency:** annually. **Effective Market(s):** United States. **Units of Measure:** Dollars per 100 lbs. **Type of Price:** gross resale, producer, resale. **Time Period Covered:** latest 6 years.

TOBACCO: FLUE-CURED, TYPES 11-14, CUTTERS

Source: *Tobacco Market Review: Flue-Cured.* **Price Frequency:** annually. **Effective Market(s):** United States. **Units of Measure:** Dollars per 100 lbs. **Type of Price:** average. **Time Period Covered:** latest year.

TOBACCO: FLUE-CURED, TYPES 11-14, LEAF

Source: *Tobacco Market Review: Flue-Cured.* **Price Frequency:** annually. **Effective Market(s):** United States. **Units of Measure:** Dollars per 100 lbs. **Type of Price:** average. **Time Period Covered:** latest year.

TOBACCO: FLUE-CURED, TYPES 11-14, LUGS

Source: *Tobacco Market Review: Flue-Cured.* **Price Frequency:** annually. **Effective Market(s):** United States. **Units of Measure:** Dollars per 100 lbs. **Type of Price:** average. **Time Period Covered:** latest year.

TOBACCO: FLUE-CURED, TYPES 11-14, NONDESCRIPT

Source: *Tobacco Market Review: Flue-Cured.* **Price Frequency:** annually. **Effective Market(s):** United States. **Units of Measure:** Dollars per 100 lbs. **Type of Price:** average. **Time Period Covered:** latest year.

TOBACCO: FLUE-CURED, TYPES 11-14, PRIMINGS

Source: *Tobacco Market Review: Flue-Cured.* **Price Frequency:** annually. **Effective Market(s):** United States. **Units of Measure:** Dollars per 100 lbs. **Type of Price:** average. **Time Period Covered:** latest year.

TOBACCO: FLUE-CURED, TYPES 11-14, SMOKING LEAF

Source: *Tobacco Market Review: Flue-Cured.* **Price Frequency:** annually. **Effective Market(s):** United States. **Units of Measure:** Dollars per 100 lbs. **Type of Price:** average. **Time Period Covered:** latest year.

TOBACCO: FLUE-CURED, TYPES 11-37

Source: *Agricultural Prices.* **Price Frequency:** monthly. **Effective Market(s):** United States. **Units of Measure:** Dollars per lb. **Type of Price:** received by farmer. **Time Period Covered:** latest month, year ago.

TOBACCO: FLUE-CURED, ZIMBABWE, LEAF

Source: *Tobacco Quarterly.* **Price Frequency:** weekly, seasonally. **Effective Market(s):** Zimbabwe. **Units of Measure:** Zimbabwe cents per kilogram. **Type of Price:** average. **Time Period Covered:** latest 3 years.

TOBACCO: FLUE-CURED, ZIMBABWE, LUGS

Source: *Tobacco Quarterly.* **Price Frequency:** weekly, seasonally. **Effective Market(s):** Zimbabwe. **Units of Measure:** Zimbabwe cents per kilogram. **Type of Price:** average. **Time Period Covered:** latest 3 years.

TOBACCO: FLUE-CURED, ZIMBABWE, PRIMINGS

Source: *Tobacco Quarterly.* **Price Frequency:** weekly, seasonally. **Effective Market(s):** Zimbabwe. **Units of Measure:** Zimbabwe cents per kilogram. **Type of Price:** average. **Time Period Covered:** latest 3 years.

TOBACCO: FLUE-CURED, ZIMBABWE, STRIP

Source: *Tobacco Quarterly.* **Price Frequency:** weekly, seasonally. **Effective Market(s):** Zimbabwe. **Units of Measure:** Zimbabwe cents per kilogram. **Type of Price:** average. **Time Period Covered:** latest 3 years.

TOBACCO: GREEN RIVER, TYPE 36

Source: *Annual Report on Tobacco Statistics.* **Price Frequency:** annually. **Effective Market(s):** United States/Puerto Rico. **Units of Measure:** cents per lb. **Type of Price:** price paid to growers. **Time Period Covered:** latest 6 years.

Source: *Tobacco Market Review: Fire-Cured and Dark Air-Cured.* **Price Frequency:** annually. **Effective Market(s):** United States. **Units of Measure:** Dollars per 100 lbs. **Type of Price:** auction, gross sale, resale. **Time Period Covered:** latest 6 years.

Source: *Tobacco Market Review: Fire-Cured and Dark Air-Cured.* **Price Frequency:** annually. **Effective Market(s):** Owensboro (KY). **Units of Measure:** Dollars per 100 lbs. **Type of Price:** gross sale, producer, resale. **Time Period Covered:** latest 2 years.

TOBACCO: GREEN RIVER, TYPE 36, HEAVY LEAF

Source: *Tobacco Market Review: Fire-Cured and Dark Air-Cured.* **Price Frequency:** annually. **Effective Market(s):** United States. **Units of Measure:** Dollars per 100 lbs. **Type of Price:** auction. **Time Period Covered:** latest year.

TOBACCO: GREEN RIVER, TYPE 36, LUGS

Source: *Tobacco Market Review: Fire-Cured and Dark Air-Cured.* **Price Frequency:** annually. **Effective Market(s):** United States. **Units of Measure:** Dollars per 100 lbs. **Type of Price:** auction. **Time Period Covered:** latest year.

TOBACCO: GREEN RIVER, TYPE 36, NONDESCRIPT

Source: *Tobacco Market Review: Fire-Cured and Dark Air-Cured.* **Price Frequency:** annually. **Effective Market(s):** United States. **Units of Measure:** Dollars per 100 lbs. **Type of Price:** auction. **Time Period Covered:** latest year.

TOBACCO: GREEN RIVER, TYPE 36, THIN LEAF

Source: *Tobacco Market Review: Fire-Cured and Dark Air-Cured.* **Price Frequency:** annually. **Effective Market(s):** United States. **Units of Measure:** Dollars per 100 lbs. **Type of Price:** auction. **Time Period Covered:** latest year.

TOBACCO: GREEN RIVER, TYPE 36, WRAPPERS

Source: *Tobacco Market Review: Fire-Cured and Dark Air-Cured.* **Price Frequency:** annually. **Effective Market(s):** United States. **Units of Measure:** Dollars per 100 lbs. **Type of Price:** auction. **Time Period Covered:** latest year.

TOBACCO: LEAF

Source: *Monthly Commodity Price Bulletin Supplement.* **Price Frequency:** monthly, quarterly, annually. **Units of Measure:** cents per lb. **Type of Price:** price paid to producers. **Time Period Covered:** latest 20 years.

TOBACCO: LIGHT AIR-CURED, TYPE 31

Source: *Agricultural Prices Annual Summary.* **Price Frequency:** monthly, annually, seasonally. **Effective Market(s):** 8 domestic markets, United States. **Units of Measure:** Dollars per lb. **Type of Price:** average received by farmer. **Time Period Covered:** latest 2 years, for US latest 6 years.

TOBACCO: LIGHT AIR-CURED, TYPE 32

Source: *Agricultural Prices Annual Summary.* **Price Frequency:** monthly, annually, seasonally. **Effective Market(s):** Maryland, United States. **Units of Measure:** Dollars per lb. **Type of Price:** average received by farmer. **Time Period Covered:** latest 2 years, for US latest 6 years.

TOBACCO: MARYLAND

Source: *Tobacco Situation and Outlook Report.* **Price Frequency:** monthly. **Units of Measure:** cents per lb. **Type of Price:** grower. **Time Period Covered:** latest 3 months, year ago.

TOBACCO: ONE SUCKER, TYPE 35

Source: *Annual Report on Tobacco Statistics.* **Price Frequency:** annually. **Effective Market(s):** United States/Puerto Rico. **Units of Measure:** cents per lb. **Type of Price:** price paid to growers. **Time Period Covered:** latest 6 years.

TOBACCO: ONE-SUCKER, TYPE 35

Source: *Tobacco Market Review: Fire-Cured and Dark Air-Cured.* **Price Frequency:** annually. **Effective Market(s):** United States. **Units of Measure:** Dollars per 100 lbs. **Type of Price:** average, auction, country, gross sale, resale. **Time Period Covered:** latest 6 years.

Source: *Tobacco Market Review: Fire-Cured and Dark Air-Cured.* **Price Frequency:** annually. **Effective Market(s):** 6 Kentucky/Tennessee markets. **Units of Measure:** Dollars per 100 lbs. **Type of Price:** gross sale, producer, resale. **Time Period Covered:** latest 2 years.

TOBACCO: ONE-SUCKER, TYPE 35, HEAVY LEAF

Source: *Tobacco Market Review: Fire-Cured and Dark Air-Cured.* **Price Frequency:** annually. **Effective Market(s):** United States. **Units of Measure:** Dollars per 100 lbs. **Type of Price:** auction. **Time Period Covered:** latest year.

TOBACCO: ONE-SUCKER, TYPE 35, LUGS

Source: *Tobacco Market Review: Fire-Cured and Dark Air-Cured.* **Price Frequency:** annually. **Effective Market(s):** United States. **Units of Measure:** Dollars per 100 lbs. **Type of Price:** auction. **Time Period Covered:** latest year.

TOBACCO: ONE-SUCKER, TYPE 35, NONDESCRIPT

Source: *Tobacco Market Review: Fire-Cured and Dark Air-Cured.* **Price Frequency:** annually. **Effective Market(s):** United States. **Units of Measure:** Dollars per 100 lbs. **Type of Price:** auction. **Time Period Covered:** latest year.

TOBACCO: ONE-SUCKER, TYPE 35, THIN LEAF

Source: *Tobacco Market Review: Fire-Cured and Dark Air-Cured.* **Price Frequency:** annually. **Effective Market(s):** United States. **Units of Measure:** Dollars per 100 lbs. **Type of Price:** auction. **Time Period Covered:** latest year.

TOBACCO: ONE-SUCKER, TYPE 35, WRAPPERS

Source: *Tobacco Market Review: Fire-Cured and Dark Air-Cured.* **Price Frequency:** annually. **Effective Market(s):** United States. **Units of Measure:** Dollars per 100 lbs. **Type of Price:** auction. **Time Period Covered:** latest year.

TOBACCO: SUN-CURED, TYPE 37, VIRGINIA

Source: *Annual Report on Tobacco Statistics.* **Price Frequency:** annually. **Effective Market(s):** United States/Puerto Rico. **Units of Measure:** cents per lb. **Type of Price:** price paid to growers. **Time Period Covered:** latest 6 years.

Source: *Tobacco Market Review: Fire-Cured and Dark Air-Cured.* **Price Frequency:** annually. **Effective Market(s):** United States. **Units of Measure:** Dollars per 100 lbs. **Type of Price:** auction, gross sale, resale. **Time Period Covered:** latest 6 years.

Source: *Tobacco Market Review: Fire-Cured and Dark Air-Cured.* **Price Frequency:** annually. **Effective Market(s):** Farmville (VA). **Units of Measure:** Dollars per 100 lbs. **Type of Price:** gross sale, producer, resale. **Time Period Covered:** latest 2 years.

TOBACCO: SUN-CURED, TYPE 37, VIRGINIA, HEAVY LEAF

Source: *Tobacco Market Review: Fire-Cured and Dark Air-Cured.* **Price Frequency:** annually. **Effective Market(s):** United States. **Units of Measure:** Dollars per 100 lbs. **Type of Price:** auction. **Time Period Covered:** latest year.

TOBACCO: SUN-CURED, TYPE 37, VIRGINIA, LUGS

Source: *Tobacco Market Review: Fire-Cured and Dark Air-Cured.* **Price Frequency:** annually. **Effective Market(s):** United States. **Units of Measure:** Dollars per 100 lbs. **Type of Price:** auction. **Time Period Covered:** latest year.

TOBACCO: SUN-CURED, TYPE 37, VIRGINIA, NONDESCRIPT

Source: *Tobacco Market Review: Fire-Cured and Dark Air-Cured.* **Price Frequency:** annually. **Effective Market(s):** United States. **Units of Measure:** Dollars per 100 lbs. **Type of Price:** auction. **Time Period Covered:** latest year.

TOBACCO: SUN-CURED, TYPE 37, VIRGINIA, THIN LEAF

Source: *Tobacco Market Review: Fire-Cured and Dark Air-Cured.* **Price Frequency:** annually. **Effective Market(s):** United States. **Units of Measure:** Dollars per 100 lbs. **Type of Price:** auction. **Time Period Covered:** latest year.

TOBACCO: SUN-CURED, TYPE 37, VIRGINIA, WRAPPERS

Source: *Tobacco Market Review: Fire-Cured and Dark Air-Cured.* **Price Frequency:** annually. **Effective Market(s):** United States. **Units of Measure:** Dollars per 100 lbs. **Type of Price:** auction. **Time Period Covered:** latest year.

TOBACCO: SUN-CURED, VIRGINIA

Source: *Tobacco Situation and Outlook Report.* **Price Frequency:** monthly. **Units of Measure:** cents per lb. **Type of Price:** grower. **Time Period Covered:** latest 3 months, year ago.

TOBACCO: SUN/AIR-CURED, MALAWI, LEAF

Source: *Tobacco Quarterly.* **Price Frequency:** weekly, annually, seasonally. **Effective Market(s):** Malawi. **Units of Measure:** Malawi tambala per kilogram. **Type of Price:** average. **Time Period Covered:** latest 2 years.

TOBACCO: TYPE 21

Source: *Annual Report on Tobacco Statistics.* **Price Frequency:** annually. **Effective Market(s):** United States. **Units of Measure:** Dollars per 1000 lbs. **Type of Price:** auction. **Time Period Covered:** latest 6 years.

TOBACCO: TYPE 31

Source: *Annual Report on Tobacco Statistics.* **Price Frequency:** annually. **Effective Market(s):** United States. **Units of Measure:** Dollars per 1000 lbs. **Type of Price:** auction. **Time Period Covered:** latest 6 years.

TOBACCO: TYPE 32, MARYLAND

Source: *Annual Report on Tobacco Statistics.* **Price Frequency:** annually. **Effective Market(s):** United States/Puerto Rico. **Units of Measure:** cents per lb. **Type of Price:** price paid to growers. **Time Period Covered:** latest 6 years.

TOBACCO: TYPE 41, CIGAR FILLER

Source: *Agricultural Prices Annual Summary.* **Price Frequency:** annually. **Effective Market(s):** Pennsylvania, United States. **Units of Measure:** Dollars per lb. **Type of Price:** average received by farmer. **Time Period Covered:** latest 2 years, for US latest 6 years.

TOBACCO: TYPE 41, PENNSYLVANIA, SEED-LEAF FILLER

Source: *Annual Report on Tobacco Statistics.* **Price Frequency:** annually. **Effective Market(s):** United States/Puerto Rico. **Units of Measure:** cents per lb. **Type of Price:** price paid to growers. **Time Period Covered:** latest 6 years.

TOBACCO: TYPE 46, PUERTO RICO, FILLER

Source: *Annual Report on Tobacco Statistics.* **Price Frequency:** annually. **Effective Market(s):** United States/Puerto Rico. **Units of Measure:** cents per lb. **Type of Price:** price paid to growers. **Time Period Covered:** latest 6 years.

TOBACCO: TYPE 51, CIGAR BINDER

Source: *Agricultural Prices Annual Summary.* **Price Frequency:** annually. **Effective Market(s):** Connecticut, Massachusetts, United States. **Units of Measure:** Dollars per lb. **Type of Price:** average received by farmer. **Time Period Covered:** latest 2 years, for US latest 6 years.

TOBACCO: TYPE 52, CIGAR BINDER

Source: *Agricultural Prices Annual Summary.* **Price Frequency:** annually. **Effective Market(s):** United States. **Units of Measure:** Dollars per lb. **Type of Price:** average received by farmer. **Time Period Covered:** latest 6 years.

TOBACCO: TYPE 54, CIGAR BINDER

Source: *Agricultural Prices Annual Summary.* **Price Frequency:** annually. **Effective Market(s):** Wisconsin, United States. **Units of Measure:** Dollars per lb. **Type of Price:** average received by farmer. **Time Period Covered:** latest 2 years, for US latest 6 years.

TOBACCO: TYPE 55, CIGAR BINDER

Source: *Agricultural Prices Annual Summary.* **Price Frequency:** annually. **Effective Market(s):** Wisconsin, United States. **Units of Measure:** Dollars per lb. **Type of Price:** average received by farmer. **Time Period Covered:** latest 2 years, for US latest 6 years.

TOBACCO: TYPE 61, CIGAR WRAPPER

Source: *Agricultural Prices Annual Summary.* **Price Frequency:** annually. **Effective Market(s):** Connecticut, Massachusetts, United States. **Units of Measure:** Dollars per lb. **Type of Price:** average received by farmer. **Time Period Covered:** latest 2 years, for US latest 6 years.

TOBACCO: TYPES 11-14

Source: *Annual Report on Tobacco Statistics.* **Price Frequency:** annually. **Effective Market(s):** United States. **Units of Measure:** Dollars per 1000 lbs. **Type of Price:** auction. **Time Period Covered:** latest 6 years.

TOBACCO: TYPES 11-37

Source: *Agricultural Prices Annual Summary.* **Price Frequency:** monthly, annually, seasonally. **Effective Market(s):** United States. **Units of Measure:** Dollars per lb. **Type of Price:** average received by farmer. **Time Period Covered:** latest 6 years.

TOBACCO: TYPES 11-62

Source: *Annual Report on Tobacco Statistics.* **Price Frequency:** annually. **Effective Market(s):** United States/Puerto Rico. **Units of Measure:** cents per lb. **Type of Price:** price paid to growers. **Time Period Covered:** latest 6 years.

TOBACCO: TYPES 11-72

Source: *Agricultural Prices Annual Summary.* **Price Frequency:** annually. **Effective Market(s):** United States. **Units of Measure:** Dollars per lb. **Type of Price:** average received by farmer. **Time Period Covered:** latest 6 years.

TOBACCO: TYPES 41-44, CIGAR FILLER

Source: *Agricultural Prices Annual Summary.* **Price Frequency:** annually. **Effective Market(s):** United States. **Units of Measure:** Dollars per lb. **Type of Price:** average received by farmer. **Time Period Covered:** latest 6 years.

TOBACCO: TYPES 41-61, CIGAR

Source: *Agricultural Prices Annual Summary.* **Price Frequency:** annually. **Effective Market(s):** United States. **Units of Measure:** Dollars per lb. **Type of Price:** average received by farmer. **Time Period Covered:** latest 6 years.

TOBACCO: TYPES 42-44 AND 54-55, CIGAR FILLER AND BINDER

Source: *Agricultural Prices Annual Summary.* **Price Frequency:** annually. **Effective Market(s):** United States. **Units of Measure:** Dollars per lb. **Type of Price:** average received by farmer. **Time Period Covered:** latest 6 years.

TOBACCO: TYPES 42-44, CIGAR FILLER

Source: *Agricultural Prices Annual Summary.* **Price Frequency:** annually. **Effective Market(s):** Ohio, United States. **Units of Measure:** Dollars per lb. **Type of Price:** average received by farmer. **Time Period Covered:** latest 2 years, for US latest 6 years.

TOBACCO: TYPES 42-44, MIAMI VALLEY

Source: *Annual Report on Tobacco Statistics.* **Price Frequency:** annually. **Effective Market(s):** United States/Puerto Rico. **Units of Measure:** cents per lb. **Type of Price:** price paid to growers. **Time Period Covered:** latest 6 years.

TOBACCO: TYPES 51-52, CIGAR BINDER

Source: *Agricultural Prices Annual Summary.* **Price Frequency:** annually. **Effective Market(s):** United States. **Units of Measure:** Dollars per lb. **Type of Price:** average received by farmer. **Time Period Covered:** latest 6 years.

TOBACCO: TYPES 51-52, CONNECTICUT VALLEY, BINDER

Source: *Annual Report on Tobacco Statistics.* **Price Frequency:** annually. **Effective Market(s):** United States/Puerto Rico. **Units of Measure:** cents per lb. **Type of Price:** price paid to growers. **Time Period Covered:** latest 6 years.

TOBACCO: TYPES 51-55, CIGAR BINDER

Source: *Agricultural Prices Annual Summary.* **Price Frequency:** annually. **Effective Market(s):** United States. **Units of Measure:** Dollars per lb. **Type of Price:** average received by farmer. **Time Period Covered:** latest 6 years.

TOBACCO: TYPES 54-55, CIGAR BINDER

Source: *Agricultural Prices Annual Summary.* **Price Frequency:** annually. **Effective Market(s):** United States. **Units of Measure:** Dollars per lb. **Type of Price:** average received by farmer. **Time Period Covered:** latest 6 years.

TOBACCO: TYPES 54-55, WISCONSIN, BINDER

Source: *Annual Report on Tobacco Statistics.* **Price Frequency:** annually. **Effective Market(s):** United States/Puerto Rico. **Units of Measure:** cents per lb. **Type of Price:** price paid to growers. **Time Period Covered:** latest 6 years.

TOBACCO: UNITED STATES

Source: *International Financial Statistics.* **Price Frequency:** monthly, quarterly, annually. **Effective Market(s):** World. **Units of Measure:** cents per lb., index. **Type of Price:** market price, price index. **Time Period Covered:** latest 4 months, latest 5 quarters, latest 5 years.

Source: *International Financial Statistics Yearbook.* **Price Frequency:** annually. **Effective Market(s):** World. **Units of Measure:** cents per lb. **Type of Price:** wholesale. **Time Period Covered:** latest 30 years.

TOBIAS ACID

Source: *Chemical Marketing Reporter.* **Price Frequency:** weekly. **Effective Market(s):** New York. **Units of Measure:** Dollars per lb. **Type of Price:** spot. **Time Period Covered:** latest week.

A-TOCOPHEROL

Source: *Journal of Commerce and Commercial.* **Price Frequency:** weekly in Friday issue. **Units of Measure:** Dollars per kilo. **Type of Price:** spot. **Time Period Covered:** latest week.

DI-A-TOCOPHEROL ACETATE

Source: *Journal of Commerce and Commercial.* **Price Frequency:** weekly in Friday issue. **Units of Measure:** Dollars per kilo. **Type of Price:** spot. **Time Period Covered:** latest week.

D-A-TOCOPHEROLS: 67%

Source: *Chemical Marketing Reporter.* **Price Frequency:** weekly. **Effective Market(s):** New York. **Units of Measure:** Dollars per kilo. **Type of Price:** spot. **Time Period Covered:** latest week.

D-A-TOCOPHERYL ACETATE: 81% CONCENTRATE

Source: *Chemical Marketing Reporter.* **Price Frequency:** weekly. **Effective Market(s):** New York. **Units of Measure:** Dollars per kilo. **Type of Price:** spot. **Time Period Covered:** latest week.

DL-A-TOCOPHERYL ACETATE: 50% DRY POWDERED

Source: *Chemical Marketing Reporter.* **Price Frequency:** weekly. **Effective Market(s):** New York. **Units of Measure:** Dollars per lb. **Type of Price:** spot. **Time Period Covered:** latest week.

DL-A-TOCOPHERYL ACETATE: USP

Source: *Chemical Marketing Reporter.* **Price Frequency:** weekly. **Effective Market(s):** New York. **Units of Measure:** Dollars per kilo. **Type of Price:** spot. **Time Period Covered:** latest week.

D-A-TOCOPHERYL ACID SUCCINATE: CRYSTALLINE

Source: *Chemical Marketing Reporter.* **Price Frequency:** weekly. **Effective Market(s):** New York. **Units of Measure:** Dollars per kilo. **Type of Price:** spot. **Time Period Covered:** latest week.

TOILET TISSUE: STOCK

Source: *Pulp & Paper Week.* **Price Frequency:** monthly, irregularly. **Units of Measure:** index. **Type of Price:** price index. **Time Period Covered:** latest 3 month.

TOKAY

Source: *California Wineletter.* **Price Frequency:** semiweekly. **Effective Market(s):** Non-California markets. **Units of Measure:** Dollars per gallon. **Type of Price:** asking. **Time Period Covered:** latest week.

TOLUENE

Source: *Energy Pricing News: Petrochemical Report.* **Price Frequency:** bimonthly. **Units of Measure:** Canadian dollars per tonne. **Type of Price:** contract. **Time Period Covered:** latest month.

Source: *Journal of Commerce and Commercial.* **Price Frequency:** weekly in Wednesday issue. **Effective Market(s):** Gulf. **Units of Measure:** Dollars per gallon. **Type of Price:** spot. **Time Period Covered:** latest week.

TOLUENE: PETROLEUM, INDUSTRIAL OR NITRATION

Source: *Chemical Marketing Reporter.* **Price Frequency:** weekly. **Effective Market(s):** 11 domestic markets. **Units of Measure:** Dollars per gallon. **Type of Price:** spot. **Time Period Covered:** latest week.

TOLUENE DI-ISOCYANATE

Source: *Chemical Marketing Reporter.* **Price Frequency:** weekly. **Effective Market(s):** New York. **Units of Measure:** Dollars per lb. **Type of Price:** spot. **Time Period Covered:** latest week.

Source: *Journal of Commerce and Commercial.* **Price Frequency:** weekly in Thursday issue. **Units of Measure:** Dollars per lb. **Type of Price:** spot. **Time Period Covered:** latest week.

2,4-TOLUENEDIAMINE

Source: *Journal of Commerce and Commercial.* **Price Frequency:** weekly in Wednesday issue. **Units of Measure:** Dollars per lb. **Type of Price:** spot. **Time Period Covered:** latest week.

P-TOLUENESULFONAMIDE: POWDERED

Source: *Chemical Marketing Reporter.* **Price Frequency:** weekly. **Effective Market(s):** New York. **Units of Measure:** Dollars per lb. **Type of Price:** spot. **Time Period Covered:** latest week.

O-TOLUIDINE

Source: *Journal of Commerce and Commercial.* **Price Frequency:** weekly in Wednesday issue. **Units of Measure:** Dollars per lb. **Type of Price:** spot. **Time Period Covered:** latest week.

P-TOLUIDINE: FLAKE

Source: *Chemical Marketing Reporter.* **Price Frequency:** weekly. **Effective Market(s):** New York. **Units of Measure:** Dollars per lb. **Type of Price:** spot. **Time Period Covered:** latest week.

Source: *Journal of Commerce and Commercial.* **Price Frequency:** weekly in Wednesday issue. **Units of Measure:** Dollars per lb. **Type of Price:** spot. **Time Period Covered:** latest week.

M-TOLUIDINE: TECHNICAL

Source: *Chemical Marketing Reporter.* **Price Frequency:** weekly. **Effective Market(s):** New York. **Units of Measure:** Dollars per lb. **Type of Price:** spot. **Time Period Covered:** latest week.

TOLUIDINE: TECHNICAL GRADE

Source: *Journal of Commerce and Commercial.* **Price Frequency:** weekly in Wednesday issue. **Units of Measure:** Dollars per lb. **Type of Price:** spot. **Time Period Covered:** latest week.

P-TOLUIDINE: TECHNICAL, CAST SOLID

Source: *Chemical Marketing Reporter.* **Price Frequency:** weekly. **Effective Market(s):** New York. **Units of Measure:** Dollars per lb. **Type of Price:** spot. **Time Period Covered:** latest week.

O-TOLUIDINE: TECHNICAL, LIQUID

Source: *Chemical Marketing Reporter.* **Price Frequency:** weekly. **Effective Market(s):** New York. **Units of Measure:** Dollars per lb. **Type of Price:** spot. **Time Period Covered:** latest week.

P-TOLUIDINE: TECHNICAL, LIQUID

Source: *Chemical Marketing Reporter.* **Price Frequency:** weekly. **Effective Market(s):** New York. **Units of Measure:** Dollars per lb. **Type of Price:** spot. **Time Period Covered:** latest week.

TOLUIDINES: MIXED, O-M-P, TECHNICAL, LIQUID

Source: *Chemical Marketing Reporter.* **Price Frequency:** weekly. **Effective Market(s):** New York. **Units of Measure:** Dollars per lb. **Type of Price:** spot. **Time Period Covered:** latest week.

TOLYTRIAZOLE

Source: *Chemical Marketing Reporter.* **Price Frequency:** weekly. **Effective Market(s):** Cincinnati (OH). **Units of Measure:** Dollars per lb. **Type of Price:** spot. **Time Period Covered:** latest week.

TOMATO PASTE: CANNED

Source: *Vegetable and Specialties Situation and Outlook Report.* **Price Frequency:** monthly. **Units of Measure:** cents per lb. **Type of Price:** wholesale. **Time Period Covered:** latest month, year ago.

TOMATOES

Source: *Agricultural Outlook.* **Price Frequency:** monthly, annually. **Effective Market(s):** United States. **Units of Measure:** Dollars per 100 lbs. **Type of Price:** received by farmer. **Time Period Covered:** monthly latest 6 months, annually latest 3 years.

Source: *Agricultural Prices.* **Price Frequency:** monthly. **Effective Market(s):** United States. **Units of Measure:** Dollars per 100 lbs. **Type of Price:** received by farmer. **Time Period Covered:** latest 2 months, year ago.

Source: *Agricultural Prices Annual Summary.* **Price Frequency:** monthly, seasonally. **Effective Market(s):** 9 domestic markets, United States. **Units of Measure:** Dollars per 100 lbs. **Type of Price:** average received by farmer. **Time Period Covered:** latest 3 years, for US latest 6 years.

Source: *Statistical Bulletin of the South Pacific: Retail Price Indexes.* **Price Frequency:** annually. **Effective Market(s):** 18 South Pacific markets. **Units of Measure:** Australian dollars per kilogram. **Type of Price:** retail. **Time Period Covered:** latest year.

TOMATOES: AUCKLAND

Source: *New Zealand Farmer.* **Price Frequency:** weekly, seasonally. **Effective Market(s):** New Zealand. **Units of Measure:** New Zealand dollars per 7 kilograms. **Time Period Covered:** latest week.

TOMATOES: BLENHEIM

Source: *New Zealand Farmer.* **Price Frequency:** weekly, seasonally. **Effective Market(s):** New Zealand. **Units of Measure:** New Zealand dollars per 4.5 kilograms. **Time Period Covered:** latest week.

TOMATOES: BREAKERS TO LIGHT RED

Source: *California Farmer.* **Price Frequency:** semimonthly, seasonally. **Effective Market(s):** Baja Crossings, San Joaquin Valley (CA), Southern California/Baja. **Units of Measure:** Dollars per 2 layer flat. **Time Period Covered:** latest week, month ago, year ago.

TOMATOES: CHERRY TYPE

Source: *California Farmer.* **Price Frequency:** semimonthly, seasonally. **Effective Market(s):** Central San Joaquin Valley. **Units of Measure:** Dollars per 15 lb. tray. **Time Period Covered:** latest week, month ago, year ago.

Source: *Fresh Fruit and Vegetable Prices.* **Price Frequency:** monthly, seasonally. **Effective Market(s):** Central San Joaquin Valley (CA), Florida. **Units of Measure:** Dollars per flat. **Type of Price:** average price at shipping point. **Time Period Covered:** latest year.

Source: *Lancaster Farming.* **Price Frequency:** weekly, seasonally. **Effective Market(s):** Pennsylvania. **Units of Measure:** Dollars per flat. **Type of Price:** market. **Time Period Covered:** latest week.

Source: *The Packer.* **Price Frequency:** weekly, seasonally. **Effective Market(s):** varies. **Units of Measure:** Dollar per pint tray. **Type of Price:** received by farmer. **Time Period Covered:** latest week.

TOMATOES: CHERRY TYPE, CALIFORNIA

Source: *Fresh Fruit and Vegetable Prices.* **Price Frequency:** monthly, seasonally. **Effective Market(s):** Chicago, New York City. **Units of Measure:** Dollars per flat. **Type of Price:** average wholesale price. **Time Period Covered:** latest year.

Source: *HRI-Buyer's Guide.* **Price Frequency:** weekly. **Effective Market(s):** Northeastern area. **Units of Measure:** Dollars per 12 pint tray. **Type of Price:** price paid by dining places & institutions. **Time Period Covered:** latest week.

TOMATOES: CHERRY TYPE, FLORIDA

Source: *Fresh Fruit and Vegetable Prices.* **Price Frequency:** monthly, seasonally. **Effective Market(s):** Chicago, New York City. **Units of Measure:** Dollars per flat. **Type of Price:** average wholesale price. **Time Period Covered:** latest year.

TOMATOES: CHERRY TYPE, MEXICAN

Source: *Fresh Fruit and Vegetable Prices.* **Price Frequency:** monthly. **Effective Market(s):** Nogales (AZ), South Texas. **Units of Measure:** Dollars per flat. **Type of Price:** price paid at point of entry. **Time Period Covered:** latest year.

Source: *Fresh Fruit and Vegetable Prices.* **Price Frequency:** monthly, seasonally. **Effective Market(s):** Chicago, New York City. **Units of Measure:** Dollars per flat. **Type of Price:** average wholesale price. **Time Period Covered:** latest year.

TOMATOES: CHERRY TYPE, MICHIGAN

Source: *Fresh Fruit and Vegetable Prices.* **Price Frequency:** monthly, seasonally. **Effective Market(s):** Chicago. **Units of Measure:** Dollars per flat. **Type of Price:** average wholesale price. **Time Period Covered:** latest year.

TOMATOES: CHERRY TYPE, RED, CALIFORNIA

Source: *Vegetable and Specialties Situation and Outlook Report.* **Price Frequency:** weekly. **Effective Market(s):** Los Angeles. **Units of Measure:** Dollars per carton. **Type of Price:** wholesale. **Time Period Covered:** latest year.

TOMATOES: CHERRY TYPE, RED, ORGANIC, CALIFORNIA

Source: *Vegetable and Specialties Situation and Outlook Report.* **Price Frequency:** weekly. **Effective Market(s):** California. **Units of Measure:** Dollars per carton. **Type of Price:** grower, wholesale. **Time Period Covered:** latest year.

TOMATOES: CLASS 1

Source: *Farmers Weekly.* **Price Frequency:** weekly, seasonally. **Effective Market(s):** Birmingham (England), Bristol (England), Covent Garden (England), Glasgow (Scotland), Manchester (England). **Units of Measure:** British pounds per unit. **Type of Price:** wholesale. **Time Period Covered:** latest week.

TOMATOES: COCKTAIL

Source: *New Zealand Farmer.* **Price Frequency:** weekly, seasonally. **Effective Market(s):** New Zealand. **Units of Measure:** New Zealand dollars per tray. **Time Period Covered:** latest week.

TOMATOES: FRESH

Source: *Vegetable and Specialties Situation and Outlook Report.* **Price Frequency:** monthly, annually. **Effective Market(s):** United States. **Units of Measure:** Dollars per 100 lbs. **Type of Price:** received by grower. **Time Period Covered:** latest 4 years.

TOMATOES: GLASSHOUSE

Source: *New Zealand Farmer.* **Price Frequency:** weekly, seasonally. **Effective Market(s):** New Zealand. **Units of Measure:** New Zealand dollars per bag. **Time Period Covered:** latest week.

TOMATOES: GREEN

Source: *Fresh Fruit and Vegetable Prices.* **Price Frequency:** monthly, seasonally. **Effective Market(s):** Charleston/Beauford District (SC), Eastern Shore Virginia/Maryland, Florida, Gonzales/King City District (CA), Northern San Joa**Units of Measure:** Dollars per 25 lb. carton. **Type of Price:** average price at shipping point. **Time Period Covered:** latest year.

TOMATOES: GREEN, CALIFORNIA

Source: *Fresh Fruit and Vegetable Prices.* **Price Frequency:** monthly, seasonally. **Effective Market(s):** Chicago, New York City. **Units of Measure:** Dollars per carton. **Type of Price:** average wholesale price. **Time Period Covered:** latest year.

TOMATOES: GREEN, FLORIDA

Source: *Fresh Fruit and Vegetable Prices.* **Price Frequency:** monthly, seasonally. **Effective Market(s):** Chicago, New York City. **Units of Measure:** Dollars per carton. **Type of Price:** average wholesale price. **Time Period Covered:** latest year.

TOMATOES: GREEN, MEXICAN

Source: *Fresh Fruit and Vegetable Prices.* **Price Frequency:** monthly, seasonally. **Effective Market(s):** Nogales (AZ). **Units of Measure:** Dollars oer 25 lb. carton. **Type of Price:** price paid at point of entry. **Time Period Covered:** latest year.

TOMATOES: GREEN TO RED

Source: *Lancaster Farming.* **Price Frequency:** weekly, seasonally. **Effective Market(s):** Pennsylvania. **Units of Measure:** Dollars per carton. **Type of Price:** market. **Time Period Covered:** latest week.

TOMATOES: LARGE, CALIFORNIA

Source: *HRI-Buyer's Guide.* **Price Frequency:** weekly. **Effective Market(s):** Northeastern area. **Units of Measure:** Dollars per 25 lb. carton. **Type of Price:** price paid by dining places & institutions. **Time Period Covered:** latest week.

TOMATOES: MATURE GREEN

Source: *California Farmer.* **Price Frequency:** semimonthly, seasonally. **Effective Market(s):** Salinas Valley, San Joaquin Valley. **Units of Measure:** Dollars per 25 lb. carton. **Time Period Covered:** latest week, month ago, year ago.

Source: *The Packer.* **Price Frequency:** weekly, seasonally. **Effective Market(s):** varies. **Units of Measure:** Dollar per carton. **Type of Price:** received by farmer. **Time Period Covered:** latest week.

TOMATOES: MEXICAN

Source: *Fresh Fruit and Vegetable Prices.* **Price Frequency:** monthly, seasonally. **Effective Market(s):** Chicago, New York City. **Units of Measure:** Dollars per flat. **Type of Price:** average wholesale price. **Time Period Covered:** latest year.

TOMATOES: MOUNTAIN PRIDE

Source: *The Packer.* **Price Frequency:** weekly, seasonally. **Effective Market(s):** varies. **Units of Measure:** Dollar per carton. **Type of Price:** received by farmer. **Time Period Covered:** latest week.

TOMATOES: NELSON

Source: *New Zealand Farmer.* **Price Frequency:** weekly, seasonally. **Effective Market(s):** New Zealand. **Units of Measure:** New Zealand dollars per 4.5 kilograms. **Time Period Covered:** latest week.

TOMATOES: PINK

Source: *Fresh Fruit and Vegetable Prices.* **Price Frequency:** monthly, seasonally. **Effective Market(s):** Southern California/Otay Mesa (CA), Western North Carolina. **Units of Measure:** Dollars per unit. **Type of Price:** average price at shipping point. **Time Period Covered:** latest year.

TOMATOES: PINK, MEXICAN

Source: *Fresh Fruit and Vegetable Prices.* **Price Frequency:** monthly, seasonally. **Effective Market(s):** Nogales (AZ). **Units of Measure:** Dollars per unit. **Type of Price:** price paid at point of entry. **Time Period Covered:** latest year.

TOMATOES: PINK TO LIGHT RED

Source: *Lancaster Farming.* **Price Frequency:** weekly, seasonally. **Effective Market(s):** Pennsylvania. **Units of Measure:** Dollars per carton. **Type of Price:** market. **Time Period Covered:** latest week.

TOMATOES: PLUM, CALIFORNIA

Source: *HRI-Buyer's Guide.* **Price Frequency:** weekly. **Effective Market(s):** Northeastern area. **Units of Measure:** Dollars per 25 lb. carton. **Type of Price:** price paid by dining places & institutions. **Time Period Covered:** latest week.

TOMATOES: ROMA

Source: *The Packer.* **Price Frequency:** weekly, seasonally. **Effective Market(s):** varies. **Units of Measure:** Dollar per carton. **Type of Price:** received by farmer. **Time Period Covered:** latest week.

TOMATOES: TURNING-LIGHT RED

Source: *Fresh Fruit and Vegetable Prices.* **Price Frequency:** monthly, seasonlly. **Effective Market(s):** Michigan, Swedesboro (NJ), Vineland (NJ). **Units of Measure:** Dollars per 25 lb. carton. **Type of Price:** average price at shipping point. **Time Period Covered:** latest year.

TOMATOES: WHOLE, CANNED

Source: *Vegetable and Specialties Situation and Outlook Report.* **Price Frequency:** monthly. **Units of Measure:** Dollars per case. **Type of Price:** wholesale. **Time Period Covered:** latest month, year ago.

TOMBU AHI (FISH)

see Tuna: Albacore.

TONKA BEANS: PRIME, ANGOSTURA

Source: *Chemical Marketing Reporter.* **Price Frequency:** weekly. **Effective Market(s):** New York. **Units of Measure:** Dollars per lb. **Type of Price:** spot. **Time Period Covered:** latest week.

TOWELS: PAPER

Source: *Pulp & Paper Week.* **Price Frequency:** monthly, irregularly. **Units of Measure:** index. **Type of Price:** price index. **Time Period Covered:** latest 3 month.

TOXAPHENE

Source: *Journal of Commerce and Commercial.* **Price Frequency:** weekly in Thursday issue. **Units of Measure:** Dollars per lb. **Type of Price:** spot. **Time Period Covered:** latest week.

TRACTOR: 2-WHEEL DRIVE

Source: *Agricultural Prices.* **Price Frequency:** semiannually. **Effective Market(s):** United States. **Units of Measure:** Dollars each. **Type of Price:** paid by farmer. **Time Period Covered:** latest year.

Source: *Agricultural Prices Annual Summary.* **Price Frequency:** trimonthly. **Effective Market(s):** United States. **Units of Measure:** Dollars each. **Type of Price:** average paid by farmer. **Time Period Covered:** latest 6 years.

TRACTOR: 4-WHEEL DRIVE

Source: *Agricultural Prices.* **Price Frequency:** semiannually. **Effective Market(s):** United States. **Units of Measure:** Dollars each. **Type of Price:** paid by farmer. **Time Period Covered:** latest year.

Source: *Agricultural Prices Annual Summary.* **Price Frequency:** trimonthly. **Effective Market(s):** United States. **Units of Measure:** Dollars each. **Type of Price:** average paid by farmer. **Time Period Covered:** latest 6 years.

TRAGACANTH GUM: FLAKE

Source: *Journal of Commerce and Commercial.* **Price Frequency:** weekly in Monday issue. **Units of Measure:** Dollars per lb. **Type of Price:** spot. **Time Period Covered:** latest week.

TRAGACANTH GUM POWDER

Source: *Journal of Commerce and Commercial.* **Price Frequency:** weekly in Monday issue. **Units of Measure:** Dollars per lb. **Type of Price:** spot. **Time Period Covered:** latest week.

TRAGACANTH GUM POWDER: FLAKED

Source: *Chemical Marketing Reporter.* **Price Frequency:** weekly. **Effective Market(s):** New York. **Units of Measure:** Dollars per lb. **Type of Price:** spot. **Time Period Covered:** latest week.

TRAGACANTH GUM RIBBON: NO. 1

Source: *Chemical Marketing Reporter.* **Price Frequency:** weekly. **Effective Market(s):** New York. **Units of Measure:** Dollars per lb. **Type of Price:** spot. **Time Period Covered:** latest week.

Source: *Journal of Commerce and Commercial.* **Price Frequency:** weekly in Monday issue. **Units of Measure:** Dollars per lb. **Type of Price:** spot. **Time Period Covered:** latest week.

TREE PEONY CORTAX: CHINA/KOREA

Source: *Prices of Selected Asia/Pacific Products.* **Price Frequency:** monthly. **Effective Market(s):** Osaka (Japan). **Units of Measure:** Japanese yen per kilogram. **Type of Price:** trade high, trade low. **Time Period Covered:** latest month.

TRI-ISOBUTYLENE

Source: *Chemical Marketing Reporter.* **Price Frequency:** weekly. **Effective Market(s):** New York. **Units of Measure:** Dollars per lb. **Type of Price:** spot. **Time Period Covered:** latest week.

TRI-ISOPROPANOLAMINE

Source: *Chemical Marketing Reporter.* **Price Frequency:** weekly. **Effective Market(s):** East. **Units of Measure:** Dollars per lb. **Type of Price:** spot. **Time Period Covered:** latest week.

TRIACETIN

Source: *Chemical Marketing Reporter.* **Price Frequency:** weekly. **Effective Market(s):** East. **Units of Measure:** Dollars per lb. **Type of Price:** spot. **Time Period Covered:** latest week.

TRIBUTYL CITRATE

Source: *Chemical Marketing Reporter.* **Price Frequency:** weekly. **Effective Market(s):** New York. **Units of Measure:** Dollars per lb. **Type of Price:** spot. **Time Period Covered:** latest week.

TRIBUTYL PHOSPHATE

Source: *Chemical Marketing Reporter.* **Price Frequency:** weekly. **Effective Market(s):** New York. **Units of Measure:** Dollars per lb. **Type of Price:** spot. **Time Period Covered:** latest week.

TRIBUTYLAMINE

Source: *Chemical Marketing Reporter.* **Price Frequency:** weekly. **Effective Market(s):** New York. **Units of Measure:** Dollars per lb. **Type of Price:** spot. **Time Period Covered:** latest week.

TRICHLOROACETIC ACID: TECHNICAL

Source: *Chemical Marketing Reporter.* **Price Frequency:** weekly. **Effective Market(s):** New York. **Units of Measure:** Dollars per lb. **Type of Price:** spot. **Time Period Covered:** latest week.

TRICHLOROACETIC ACID: USP

Source: *Chemical Marketing Reporter.* **Price Frequency:** weekly. **Effective Market(s):** New York. **Units of Measure:** Dollars per lb. **Type of Price:** spot. **Time Period Covered:** latest week.

1,2,4-TRICHLOROBENZENE: PURE

Source: *Chemical Marketing Reporter.* **Price Frequency:** weekly. **Effective Market(s):** New York. **Units of Measure:** Dollars per lb. **Type of Price:** spot. **Time Period Covered:** latest week.

1,1,1-TRICHLOROETHANE

Source: *Chemical Marketing Reporter.* **Price Frequency:** weekly. **Effective Market(s):** New York. **Units of Measure:** Dollars per lb. **Type of Price:** spot. **Time Period Covered:** latest week.

1,1,2-TRICHLOROETHANE

Source: *Chemical Marketing Reporter.* **Price Frequency:** weekly. **Effective Market(s):** New York. **Units of Measure:** Dollars per lb. **Type of Price:** spot. **Time Period Covered:** latest week.

TRICHLOROETHYLENE

Source: *Chemical Marketing Reporter.* **Price Frequency:** weekly. **Effective Market(s):** New York. **Units of Measure:** Dollars per lb. **Type of Price:** spot. **Time Period Covered:** latest week.

Source: *Journal of Commerce and Commercial.* **Price Frequency:** weekly in Thursday issue. **Units of Measure:** Dollars per lb. **Type of Price:** spot. **Time Period Covered:** latest week.

TRICHLOROISOCYANURIC ACID

Source: *Chemical Marketing Reporter.* **Price Frequency:** weekly. **Effective Market(s):** New York. **Units of Measure:** Dollars per lb. **Type of Price:** spot. **Time Period Covered:** latest week.

TRICRESYL PHOSPHATE

Source: *Chemical Marketing Reporter.* **Price Frequency:** weekly. **Effective Market(s):** New York. **Units of Measure:** Dollars per lb. **Type of Price:** spot. **Time Period Covered:** latest week.

TRIDECYL ALCOHOL: MIXED ISOMERS

Source: *Chemical Marketing Reporter.* **Price Frequency:** weekly. **Effective Market(s):** New York. **Units of Measure:** Dollars per lb. **Type of Price:** spot. **Time Period Covered:** latest week.

TRIETHANOLAMINE: 85%

Source: *Chemical Marketing Reporter.* **Price Frequency:** weekly. **Effective Market(s):** East. **Units of Measure:** Dollars per lb. **Type of Price:** spot. **Time Period Covered:** latest week.

TRIETHANOLAMINE: 99%

Source: *Chemical Marketing Reporter.* **Price Frequency:** weekly. **Effective Market(s):** East. **Units of Measure:** Dollars per lb. **Type of Price:** spot. **Time Period Covered:** latest week.

TRIETHANOLAMINE LAURYL SULFATE

Source: *Chemical Marketing Reporter.* **Price Frequency:** weekly. **Effective Market(s):** New York. **Units of Measure:** Dollars per lb. **Type of Price:** spot. **Time Period Covered:** latest week.

TRIETHYL CITRATE

Source: *Chemical Marketing Reporter.* **Price Frequency:** weekly. **Effective Market(s):** New York. **Units of Measure:** Dollars per lb. **Type of Price:** spot. **Time Period Covered:** latest week.

TRIETHYL PHOSPHATE

Source: *Chemical Marketing Reporter.* **Price Frequency:** weekly. **Effective Market(s):** New York. **Units of Measure:** Dollars per lb. **Type of Price:** spot. **Time Period Covered:** latest week.

TRIETHYLAMINE

Source: *Chemical Marketing Reporter.* **Price Frequency:** weekly. **Effective Market(s):** New York. **Units of Measure:** Dollars per lb. **Type of Price:** spot. **Time Period Covered:** latest week.

TRIETHYLENE GLYCOL

Source: *Chemical Marketing Reporter.* **Price Frequency:** weekly. **Effective Market(s):** East. **Units of Measure:** Dollars per lb. **Type of Price:** spot. **Time Period Covered:** latest week.

TRIETHYLENE GLYCOL DIPELARGONATE

Source: *Chemical Marketing Reporter.* **Price Frequency:** weekly. **Effective Market(s):** New York. **Units of Measure:** Dollars per lb. **Type of Price:** spot. **Time Period Covered:** latest week.

TRIETHYLENETETRAMINE

Source: *Chemical Marketing Reporter.* **Price Frequency:** weekly. **Effective Market(s):** New York. **Units of Measure:** Dollars per lb. **Type of Price:** spot. **Time Period Covered:** latest week.

TRIFLURALIN: EMULSIFIABLE CONCENTRATE

Source: *Agricultural Prices Annual Summary.* **Price Frequency:** seminannually. **Effective Market(s):** United States. **Units of Measure:** Dollars per 5 gallons. **Type of Price:** average paid by farmer. **Time Period Covered:** latest 6 years.

TRIMETHYLAMINE: 25% SOLUTION

Source: *Chemical Marketing Reporter.* **Price Frequency:** weekly. **Effective Market(s):** New York. **Units of Measure:** Dollars per lb. **Type of Price:** spot. **Time Period Covered:** latest week.

TRIMETHYLAMINE: 40% SOLUTION

Source: *Chemical Marketing Reporter.* **Price Frequency:** weekly. **Effective Market(s):** New York. **Units of Measure:** Dollars per lb. **Type of Price:** spot. **Time Period Covered:** latest week.

TRIMETHYLAMINE: ANHYDROUS

Source: *Chemical Marketing Reporter.* **Price Frequency:** weekly. **Effective Market(s):** New York. **Units of Measure:** Dollars per lb. **Type of Price:** spot. **Time Period Covered:** latest week.

TRIMETHYLOLPROPANE

Source: *Chemical Marketing Reporter.* **Price Frequency:** weekly. **Effective Market(s):** New York. **Units of Measure:** Dollars per lb. **Type of Price:** spot. **Time Period Covered:** latest week.

TRIMETHYLOLPROPANE TRIACRYLATE

Source: *Chemical Marketing Reporter.* **Price Frequency:** weekly. **Effective Market(s):** New York. **Units of Measure:** Dollars per lb. **Type of Price:** spot. **Time Period Covered:** latest week.

TRIPE: HONEY COMB

Source: *HRI-Buyer's Guide.* **Price Frequency:** weekly. **Effective Market(s):** Northeastern area. **Units of Measure:** Dollars per lb. **Type of Price:** price paid by dining places & institutions. **Time Period Covered:** latest week.

TRIPENTAERYTHRITOL

Source: *Chemical Marketing Reporter.* **Price Frequency:** weekly. **Effective Market(s):** New York. **Units of Measure:** Dollars per lb. **Type of Price:** spot. **Time Period Covered:** latest week.

TRIPHENYL PHOSPHATE

Source: *Chemical Marketing Reporter.* **Price Frequency:** weekly. **Effective Market(s):** New York. **Units of Measure:** Dollars per lb. **Type of Price:** spot. **Time Period Covered:** latest week.

TRIPLE SUPERPHOSPHATE

Source: *Commodity Trade and Price Trends.* **Price Frequency:** annually. **Effective Market(s):** Gulf ports. **Units of Measure:** Dollars per metric ton, 1980 constant dollars per metric ton. **Time Period Covered:** latest 20 years.

TRIPROPYLENE GLYCOL

Source: *Chemical Marketing Reporter.* **Price Frequency:** weekly. **Effective Market(s):** New York. **Units of Measure:** Dollars per lb. **Type of Price:** spot. **Time Period Covered:** latest week.

TRIS- (HYDROMETHYL) NITROMETHANE: SOLID

Source: *Chemical Marketing Reporter.* **Price Frequency:** weekly. **Effective Market(s):** New York. **Units of Measure:** Dollars per lb. **Type of Price:** spot. **Time Period Covered:** latest week.

TRISODIUM PHOSPHATE

see Sodium Phosphate: Tribasic.

TROUT: FRESHWATER, WHOLE, DRESSED, FRESH

Source: *Seafood Price-Current.* **Price Frequency:** semiweekly. **Effective Market(s):** Mid-Atlantic, New England. **Units of Measure:** Dollars per lb. **Type of Price:** sale by first receiver. **Time Period Covered:** latest day.

TROUT: SEA, FILLETS, FROZEN, ARGENTINA/URUGUAY

Source: *Seafood Price-Current.* **Price Frequency:** semiweekly. **Effective Market(s):** Mid-Atlantic. **Units of Measure:** Dollars per lb. **Type of Price:** first receiver. **Time Period Covered:** latest day.

TROUT: SEA, FRESH

Source: *Seafood Price-Current.* **Price Frequency:** semiweekly. **Effective Market(s):** Gulf/Southeast. **Units of Measure:** Dollars per lb. **Type of Price:** sale by first receiver. **Time Period Covered:** latest day.

TROUT: SEA, WEAKFISH, WHOLE, FRESH

Source: *Seafood Price-Current.* **Price Frequency:** semiweekly. **Effective Market(s):** Boston, Mid-Atlantic, New Bedford (MA), Portland (ME). **Units of Measure:** Dollars per lb. **Type of Price:** sale by first receiver, auction price. **Time Period Covered:** latest day.

TRUCKS: 3/4 TON PICKUP

Source: *Agricultural Prices Annual Summary.* **Price Frequency:** semiannually. **Effective Market(s):** United States. **Units of Measure:** Dollars each. **Type of Price:** average paid by farmer. **Time Period Covered:** latest 6 years.

TRUCKS: 1-1/2 TO 2 TONS, CAB AND CHASIS

Source: *Agricultural Prices Annual Summary.* **Price Frequency:** semiannually. **Effective Market(s):** United States. **Units of Measure:** Dollars each. **Type of Price:** average paid by farmer. **Time Period Covered:** latest 6 years.

L-TRYPTOPHAN

Source: *Chemical Marketing Reporter.* **Price Frequency:** weekly. **Effective Market(s):** New York. **Units of Measure:** Dollars per kilo. **Type of Price:** spot. **Time Period Covered:** latest week.

TUBING: PLASTIC

Source: *Agricultural Prices.* **Price Frequency:** annually. **Effective Market(s):** United States. **Units of Measure:** Dollars each. **Type of Price:** paid by farmer. **Time Period Covered:** latest year.

Source: *Agricultural Prices Annual Summary.* **Price Frequency:** semiannually. **Effective Market(s):** United States. **Units of Measure:** Dollars per foot. **Type of Price:** average paid by farmer. **Time Period Covered:** latest 6 years.

TULIPS

Source: *New Zealand Farmer.* **Price Frequency:** weekly, seasonally. **Effective Market(s):** New Zealand. **Units of Measure:** New Zealand dollars per bunch. **Time Period Covered:** latest week.

TUNA: ALBACORE, FILLETS, FRESH, HAWAIIAN

Source: *Seafood Price-Current.* **Price Frequency:** semiweekly. **Effective Market(s):** Hawaii. **Units of Measure:** Dollars per lb. **Type of Price:** sale by first receiver. **Time Period Covered:** latest day.

TUNA: ALBACORE, WHOLE, FRESH

Source: *Seafood Price-Current.* **Price Frequency:** semiweekly. **Effective Market(s):** West Coast. **Units of Measure:** Dollars per lb. **Type of Price:** sale by first receiver. **Time Period Covered:** latest day.

TUNA: ALBACORE, WHOLE, FRESH, HAWAIIAN

Source: *Seafood Price-Current.* **Price Frequency:** semiweekly. **Effective Market(s):** Hawaii. **Units of Measure:** Dollars per lb. **Type of Price:** sale by first receiver. **Time Period Covered:** latest day.

TUNA: BIGEYE, FILLETS, FRESH, HAWAIIAN

Source: *Seafood Price-Current.* **Price Frequency:** semiweekly. **Effective Market(s):** Hawaii. **Units of Measure:** Dollars per lb. **Type of Price:** sale by first receiver. **Time Period Covered:** latest day.

TUNA: BIGEYE, FRESH, AUSTRALIAN

Source: *Weekly Statistical Fishery Report.* **Price Frequency:** weekly, seasonally. **Effective Market(s):** Tokyo. **Units of Measure:** Dollars per lb. **Type of Price:** wholesale. **Time Period Covered:** 2 weeks ago, month ago.

TUNA: BIGEYE, FRESH, INDONESIAN

Source: *Weekly Statistical Fishery Report.* **Price Frequency:** weekly, seasonally. **Effective Market(s):** Tokyo. **Units of Measure:** Dollars per lb. **Type of Price:** wholesale. **Time Period Covered:** 2 weeks ago, month ago.

TUNA: BIGEYE, FRESH, NEW YORK

Source: *Weekly Statistical Fishery Report.* **Price Frequency:** weekly, seasonally. **Effective Market(s):** Tokyo. **Units of Measure:** Dollars per lb. **Type of Price:** wholesale. **Time Period Covered:** 2 weeks ago, month ago.

TUNA: BIGEYE, WHOLE, FRESH, HAWAIIAN

Source: *Seafood Price-Current.* **Price Frequency:** semiweekly. **Effective Market(s):** Hawaii. **Units of Measure:** Dollars per lb. **Type of Price:** sale by first receiver. **Time Period Covered:** latest day.

TUNA: BLUEFIN, FRESH, AUSTRALIAN

Source: *Weekly Statistical Fishery Report.* **Price Frequency:** weekly, seasonally. **Effective Market(s):** Tokyo. **Units of Measure:** Dollars per lb. **Type of Price:** wholesale. **Time Period Covered:** 2 weeks ago, month ago.

TUNA: BLUEFIN, FRESH, BOSTON

Source: *Weekly Statistical Fishery Report.* **Price Frequency:** weekly, seasonally. **Effective Market(s):** Tokyo. **Units of Measure:** Dollars per lb. **Type of Price:** wholesale. **Time Period Covered:** 2 weeks ago, month ago.

TUNA: BLUEFIN, WHOLE, FRESH

Source: *Seafood Price-Current.* **Price Frequency:** semiweekly. **Effective Market(s):** West Coast. **Units of Measure:** Dollars per lb. **Type of Price:** sale by first receiver. **Time Period Covered:** latest day.

TUNA: YELLOWFIN, FRESH, AUSTRALIAN

Source: *Weekly Statistical Fishery Report.* **Price Frequency:** weekly. **Effective Market(s):** Tokyo. **Units of Measure:** Dollars per lb. **Type of Price:** wholessale. **Time Period Covered:** 2 weeks ago, month ago.

TUNA: YELLOWFIN, FRESH, INDONESIAN

Source: *Weekly Statistical Fishery Report.* **Price Frequency:** weekly, seaonally. **Effective Market(s):** Tokyo. **Units of Measure:** Dollars per lb. **Type of Price:** wholesale. **Time Period Covered:** 2 weeks ago, month ago.

TUNA: YELLOWFIN, FRESH, NEW YORK

Source: *Weekly Statistical Fishery Report.* **Price Frequency:** weekly, seasonally. **Effective Market(s):** Tokyo. **Units of Measure:** Dollars per lb. **Type of Price:** wholesale. **Time Period Covered:** 2 weeks ago, month ago.

TUNA: YELLOWFIN, NO. 1, FILLETS, FRESH, HAWAIIAN

Source: *Seafood Price-Current.* **Price Frequency:** semiweekly. **Effective Market(s):** Hawaii. **Units of Measure:** Dollars per lb. **Type of Price:** sale by first receiver. **Time Period Covered:** latest day.

TUNA: YELLOWFIN, NO. 1, FRESH

Source: *Seafood Price-Current.* **Price Frequency:** semiweekly. **Effective Market(s):** Gulf/Southeast. **Units of Measure:** Dollars per lb. **Type of Price:** sale by first receiver. **Time Period Covered:** latest day.

TUNA: YELLOWFIN, NO. 1, WHOLE, FRESH, HAWAIIAN

Source: *Seafood Price-Current.* **Price Frequency:** semiweekly. **Effective Market(s):** Hawaii. **Units of Measure:** Dollars per lb. **Type of Price:** sale by first receiver. **Time Period Covered:** latest day.

TUNA: YELLOWFIN, NO. 2, WHOLE, FRESH

Source: *Seafood Price-Current.* **Price Frequency:** semiweekly. **Effective Market(s):** Boston, Mid-Atlantic, New Bedford (MA), Portland (ME), West Coast. **Units of Measure:** Dollars per lb. **Type of Price:** sale by first receiver, auction price. **Time Period Covered:** latest day.

TUNA: YELLOWFIN, NO. 2, WHOLE, FRESH, CENTRAL/SOUTH AMERICA, IMPORTED

Source: *Seafood Price-Current.* **Price Frequency:** semiweekly. **Effective Market(s):** Miami. **Units of Measure:** Dollars per lb. **Type of Price:** sale by first receiver. **Time Period Covered:** latest day.

TUNA MEAL: BLENDED, WEST COAST

Source: *Feedstuffs.* **Price Frequency:** weekly. **Effective Market(s):** Los Angeles, San Francisco. **Units of Measure:** Dollars per bulk ton. **Time Period Covered:** latest week.

TUNG OIL

Source: *Fruit and Tropical Products.* **Price Frequency:** monthly, annually. **Effective Market(s):** Rotterdam. **Units of Measure:** Dollars per tonne. **Type of Price:** average. **Time Period Covered:** monthly latest year, annually latest 2 years.

Source: *Oil World.* **Price Frequency:** weekly, monthly, annually. **Effective Market(s):** Rotterdam. **Units of Measure:** Dollars per tonne. **Type of Price:** lowest representative asking. **Time Period Covered:** weekly latest 3 weeks, monthly latest 2 months, annually latest 2 years.

Source: *Standard & Poor's Statistical Service Current Statistics.* **Price Frequency:** monthly, annually. **Units of Measure:** cents per lb. **Time Period Covered:** latest 5 years.

TUNG OIL: IMPORTED

Source: *Chemical Marketing Reporter.* **Price Frequency:** weekly. **Effective Market(s):** New York. **Units of Measure:** Dollars per lb. **Type of Price:** spot. **Time Period Covered:** latest week.

Source: *Commodity Year Book.* **Price Frequency:** monthly, annually. **Effective Market(s):** New York. **Units of Measure:** cents per lb. **Time Period Covered:** latest 7 years.

Source: *Oil Crops Situation and Outlook.* **Price Frequency:** monthly. **Effective Market(s):** Chicago. **Units of Measure:** cents per lb. **Type of Price:** wholesale. **Time Period Covered:** latest 5 months.

TUNGSTEN

Source: *Commodity Year Book.* **Price Frequency:** annually. **Effective Market(s):** United States, Europe. **Units of Measure:** Dollars per short ton unit. **Time Period Covered:** latest 6 years.

TUNGSTEN ORE

Source: *American Metal Market.* **Price Frequency:** daily. **Effective Market(s):** London, World. **Units of Measure:** Dollars per metric ton. **Type of Price:** buying, indicator. **Time Period Covered:** latest day.

Source: *Economic and Energy Indicators.* **Price Frequency:** biweekly. **Units of Measure:** Dollars per metric ton. **Time Period Covered:** latest 3 months, quarters, and years.

Source: *Northern Miner.* **Price Frequency:** weekly. **Units of Measure:** Dollars per tonne. **Type of Price:** producer. **Time Period Covered:** latest week.

TUNGSTEN ORE: SCHEELITE

Source: *Monthly Commodity Price Bulletin Supplement.* **Price Frequency:** monthly, quarterly, annually. **Effective Market(s):** European ports. **Units of Measure:** Dollars per metric ton unit of WO3. **Time Period Covered:** latest 6 years.

Source: *Monthly Commodity Price Bulletin.* **Price Frequency:** monthly, annually. **Effective Market(s):** United Kingdom. **Units of Measure:** Dollars per metric ton unit of WO3. **Time Period Covered:** latest 5 years.

Source: *UNCTAD Commodity Yearbook.* **Price Frequency:** annually. **Effective Market(s):** United Kingdom. **Units of Measure:** Dollars per metric ton unit of WO3. **Type of Price:** free market. **Time Period Covered:** latest 12 years.

TUNGSTEN ORE: WOLFRAMITE

Source: *Monthly Commodity Price Bulletin.* **Price Frequency:** monthly, annually. **Effective Market(s):** United Kingdom. **Units of Measure:** Dollars per metric ton unit of WO3. **Time Period Covered:** latest 5 years.

Source: *Monthly Commodity Price Bulletin Supplement.* **Price Frequency:** monthly, quarterly, annually. **Effective Market(s):** United Kingdom. **Units of Measure:** Dollars per metric ton unit of WO3. **Time Period Covered:** latest 6 years.

Source: *UNCTAD Commodity Yearbook.* **Price Frequency:** annually. **Effective Market(s):** United Kingdom. **Units of Measure:** Dollars per metric ton unit of WO3. **Type of Price:** free market. **Time Period Covered:** latest 12 years.

TUNGSTEN POWDER

Source: *Iron Age.* **Price Frequency:** monthly. **Units of Measure:** Dollars per lb. **Type of Price:** consumer. **Time Period Covered:** latest month.

TUNISIA DINAR

Source: *International Wheat Council Market Report.* **Price Frequency:** weekly. **Effective Market(s):** London. **Units of Measure:** Tunisian dinar per United States dollar. **Type of Price:** foreign exchange. **Time Period Covered:** latest 5 weeks.

TURBOT: FILLETS, FROZEN, CANADIAN

Source: *Seafood Price-Current.* **Price Frequency:** semiweekly. **Effective Market(s):** Mid-Atlantic. **Units of Measure:** Dollars per lb. **Type of Price:** first receiver. **Time Period Covered:** latest day.

TURBOT: FILLETS, FROZEN, ICELANDIC

Source: *Seafood Price-Current.* **Price Frequency:** semiweekly. **Effective Market(s):** Mid-Atlantic. **Units of Measure:** Dollars per lb. **Type of Price:** first receiver. **Time Period Covered:** latest day.

TURBOT: FILLETS, GREENLAND/CANADA

Source: *NMFS Green Sheet Supplement.* **Price Frequency:** weekly. **Units of Measure:** Dollars per lb. **Time Period Covered:** latest week.

TURBOT: FILLETS, GREENLAND/ICELAND

Source: *NMFS Green Sheet Supplement.* **Price Frequency:** weekly. **Units of Measure:** Dollars per lb. **Time Period Covered:** latest week.

TURBOT: FILLETS, SKINLESS, BONELESS, FROZEN, CANADIAN

Source: *Seafood Price-Current.* **Price Frequency:** semiweekly. **Effective Market(s):** Mid-Atlantic. **Units of Measure:** Dollars per lb. **Type of Price:** first receiver. **Time Period Covered:** latest day.

TURBOT: PROCESSORS FISH BLOCKS

Source: *Seafood Price-Current.* **Price Frequency:** semiweekly. **Effective Market(s):** New England. **Units of Measure:** Dollars per lb. **Time Period Covered:** latest day.

TURKEY BODY SKIN

Source: *Urner Barry's Price-Current.* **Price Frequency:** daily. **Units of Measure:** cents per lb. **Time Period Covered:** latest day.

TURKEY BOLOGNA

Source: *Urner Barry's Price-Current.* **Price Frequency:** daily. **Units of Measure:** Dollars per lb. **Type of Price:** deli, retail chub. **Time Period Covered:** latest day.

Source: *Urner Barry's Price-Current, West Coast Edition.* **Price Frequency:** semiweekly. **Units of Measure:** Dollars per lb. **Type of Price:** deli, retail chub. **Time Period Covered:** latest day.

TURKEY BREAST

Source: *Livestock and Poultry Update.* **Price Frequency:** monthly. **Effective Market(s):** Eastern region. **Units of Measure:** cents per lb. **Type of Price:** wholesale. **Time Period Covered:** latest 3 months, year ago.

Source: *Urner Barry's Price-Current, West Coast Edition.* **Price Frequency:** semiweekly. **Effective Market(s):** West Coast. **Units of Measure:** Dollars per lb. **Time Period Covered:** latest day.

Source: *Weekly Insiders Turkey Letter.* **Price Frequency:** weekly. **Effective Market(s):** New York. **Units of Measure:** cents per lb. **Type of Price:** retail. **Time Period Covered:** latest week, week ago, year ago.

Source: *Weekly Insiders Turkey Letter.* **Price Frequency:** monthly. **Effective Market(s):** east. **Units of Measure:** cents per lb. **Time Period Covered:** latest 5 years.

TURKEY BREAST: BASTED, NETTED

Source: *Urner Barry's Price-Current, West Coast Edition.* **Price Frequency:** semiweekly. **Effective Market(s):** West Coast. **Units of Measure:** Dollars per lb. **Time Period Covered:** latest day.

TURKEY BREAST: BONE IN, RAW

Source: *Meat Price Report.* **Price Frequency:** weekly. **Units of Measure:** cents per lb. **Type of Price:** price paid to wholesaler. **Time Period Covered:** latest week.

TURKEY BREAST: BONELESS, RAW

Source: *Meat Price Report.* **Price Frequency:** weekly. **Units of Measure:** cents per lb. **Type of Price:** price paid to wholesaler. **Time Period Covered:** latest week.

TURKEY BREAST: FRESH

Source: *Weekly Insiders Turkey Letter.* **Price Frequency:** annually. **Units of Measure:** cents per lb. **Type of Price:** wholesale. **Time Period Covered:** latest 3 years.

TURKEY BREAST: FRESH TRAY PACK

Source: *Urner Barry's Price-Current.* **Price Frequency:** daily. **Units of Measure:** cents per lb. **Type of Price:** delivered warehouse. **Time Period Covered:** latest day.

TURKEY BREAST: GRADE A, BASTED, NETTED, CONSUMER PACKAGED

Source: *Urner Barry's Price-Current.* **Price Frequency:** daily. **Units of Measure:** cents per lb. **Type of Price:** trucklot. **Time Period Covered:** latest day.

TURKEY BREAST: GRADE A, FROZEN, READY-TO-COOK

Source: *Poultry Market Statistics.* **Price Frequency:** monthly, annually. **Effective Market(s):** Los Angeles. **Units of Measure:** Dollars per lb. **Type of Price:** average paid by restaurants and institutions. **Time Period Covered:** latest year.

TURKEY BREAST: GRADE A, INSTITUTIONAL PACKAGED

Source: *Urner Barry's Price-Current.* **Price Frequency:** daily. **Units of Measure:** cents per lb. **Type of Price:** trucklot. **Time Period Covered:** latest day.

TURKEY BREAST: HEN, YOUNG, SKINLESS, BONELESS, FROZEN

Source: *Urner Barry's Price-Current.* **Price Frequency:** daily. **Units of Measure:** cents per lb. **Time Period Covered:** latest day.

TURKEY BREAST: OVEN PREPARED, SKIN ON

Source: *Urner Barry's Price-Current, West Coast Edition.* **Price Frequency:** semiweekly. **Units of Measure:** Dollars per lb. **Time Period Covered:** latest day.

TURKEY BREAST: OVEN PREPARED, SKINLESS

Source: *Urner Barry's Price-Current, West Coast Edition.* **Price Frequency:** semiweekly. **Units of Measure:** Dollars per lb. **Time Period Covered:** latest day.

TURKEY BREAST: OVEN ROASTED, BONELESS, COOKED

Source: *HRI-Buyer's Guide.* **Price Frequency:** weekly. **Effective Market(s):** Northeastern area. **Units of Measure:** Dollars per lb. **Type of Price:** price paid by dining places & institutions. **Time Period Covered:** latest week.

TURKEY BREAST: OVEN ROASTED, SKIN ON

Source: *Urner Barry's Price-Current.* **Price Frequency:** daily. **Units of Measure:** Dollars per lb. **Time Period Covered:** latest day.

Source: *Urner Barry's Price-Current, West Coast Edition.* **Price Frequency:** semiweekly. **Units of Measure:** Dollars per lb. **Time Period Covered:** latest day.

TURKEY BREAST: OVEN ROASTED, SKIN ON, BROWN TOP, NATURAL

Source: *Urner Barry's Price-Current, West Coast Edition.* **Price Frequency:** semiweekly. **Units of Measure:** Dollars per lb. **Time Period Covered:** latest day.

TURKEY BREAST: OVEN ROASTED, SKIN ON, NATURAL

Source: *Urner Barry's Price-Current.* **Price Frequency:** daily. **Units of Measure:** Dollars per lb. **Time Period Covered:** latest day.

Source: *Urner Barry's Price-Current, West Coast Edition.* **Price Frequency:** semiweekly. **Units of Measure:** Dollars per lb. **Time Period Covered:** latest day.

TURKEY BREAST: OVEN ROASTED, SKINLESS

Source: *Urner Barry's Price-Current.* **Price Frequency:** daily. **Units of Measure:** Dollars per lb. **Time Period Covered:** latest day.

Source: *Urner Barry's Price-Current, West Coast Edition.* **Price Frequency:** semiweekly. **Units of Measure:** Dollars per lb. **Time Period Covered:** latest day.

TURKEY BREAST: OVEN ROASTED, SKINLESS, BROWN TOP, NATURAL

Source: *Urner Barry's Price-Current, West Coast Edition.* **Price Frequency:** semiweekly. **Units of Measure:** Dollars per lb. **Time Period Covered:** latest day.

TURKEY BREAST: OVEN ROASTED, SKINLESS, NATURAL

Source: *Urner Barry's Price-Current.* **Price Frequency:** daily. **Units of Measure:** Dollars per lb. **Time Period Covered:** latest day.

Source: *Urner Barry's Price-Current, West Coast Edition.* **Price Frequency:** semiweekly. **Units of Measure:** Dollars per lb. **Time Period Covered:** latest day.

TURKEY BREAST: RAW

Source: *HRI-Buyer's Guide.* **Price Frequency:** weekly. **Effective Market(s):** Northeastern area. **Units of Measure:** Dollars per lb. **Type of Price:** price paid by dining places & institutions. **Time Period Covered:** latest week.

TURKEY BREAST: SKINLESS, BONELESS, COOKED

Source: *Meat Price Report.* **Price Frequency:** weekly. **Units of Measure:** cents per lb. **Type of Price:** price paid to wholesaler. **Time Period Covered:** latest week.

TURKEY BREAST: SKINLESS, BONELESS, FRESH

Source: *Poultry Market Statistics.* **Price Frequency:** monthly, annually. **Effective Market(s):** Central region, Eastern region, Western region. **Units of Measure:** Dollars per lb. **Type of Price:** average to first receiver. **Time Period Covered:** latest year.

TURKEY BREAST: SKINLESS, BONELESS, FROZEN

Source: *Poultry Market Statistics.* **Price Frequency:** monthly, annually. **Effective Market(s):** Central region, Eastern region, Western region. **Units of Measure:** Dollars per lb. **Type of Price:** average to first receiver. **Time Period Covered:** latest year.

TURKEY BREAST: SMOKED, SKIN ON

Source: *Urner Barry's Price-Current, West Coast Edition.* **Price Frequency:** semiweekly. **Units of Measure:** Dollars per lb. **Time Period Covered:** latest day.

TURKEY BREAST: SMOKED, SKIN ON, READY-TO-EAT

Source: *Urner Barry's Price-Current.* **Price Frequency:** daily. **Units of Measure:** Dollars per lb. **Time Period Covered:** latest day.

TURKEY BREAST: SMOKED, SKINLESS

Source: *Urner Barry's Price-Current, West Coast Edition.* **Price Frequency:** semiweekly. **Units of Measure:** Dollars per lb. **Time Period Covered:** latest day.

TURKEY BREAST: SMOKED, SKINLESS, READY-TO-EAT

Source: *Urner Barry's Price-Current.* **Price Frequency:** daily. **Units of Measure:** Dollars per lb. **Time Period Covered:** latest day.

TURKEY BREAST: TOM, YOUNG, SKINLESS, BONELESS, FRESH

Source: *Urner Barry's Price-Current.* **Price Frequency:** daily. **Units of Measure:** cents per lb. **Time Period Covered:** latest day.

TURKEY BREAST: TOM, YOUNG, SKINLESS, BONELESS, FROZEN

Source: *Urner Barry's Price-Current.* **Price Frequency:** daily. **Units of Measure:** cents per lb. **Time Period Covered:** latest day.

TURKEY BREAST MEAT: BREEDER, FROZEN

Source: *Urner Barry's Price-Current, West Coast Edition.* **Price Frequency:** semiweekly. **Effective Market(s):** West Coast. **Units of Measure:** Dollars per lb. **Time Period Covered:** latest day.

TURKEY BREAST MEAT: FROZEN

Source: *Monthly Price Review.* **Price Frequency:** daily. **Units of Measure:** Dollars per lb. **Time Period Covered:** latest month.

TURKEY BREAST MEAT: SKINLESS, BONELESS, FRESH

Source: *Monthly Price Review.* **Price Frequency:** daily. **Units of Measure:** Dollars per lb. **Time Period Covered:** latest month.

TURKEY BREAST MEAT: SKINLESS, BONELESS, FROZEN

Source: *Monthly Price Review.* **Price Frequency:** daily. **Units of Measure:** Dollars per lb. **Time Period Covered:** latest month.

Source: *Urner Barry's Price-Current, West Coast Edition.* **Price Frequency:** semiweekly. **Effective Market(s):** West Coast. **Units of Measure:** Dollars per lb. **Time Period Covered:** latest day.

TURKEY BREAST SKIN

Source: *Urner Barry's Price-Current.* **Price Frequency:** daily. **Units of Measure:** cents per lb. **Time Period Covered:** latest day.

TURKEY BREAST TENDERLOINS: YOUNG, FROZEN

Source: *Urner Barry's Price-Current.* **Price Frequency:** daily. **Units of Measure:** cents per lb. **Time Period Covered:** latest day.

TURKEY BREAST TRIM

Source: *Urner Barry's Price-Current.* **Price Frequency:** daily. **Units of Measure:** cents per lb. **Time Period Covered:** latest day.

TURKEY BREAST WITH RIB, BACK AND WING MEAT: READY-TO-COOK, FROZEN

Source: *Poultry Market Statistics.* **Price Frequency:** monthly, annually. **Effective Market(s):** Central region, Eastern region, Western region. **Units of Measure:** Dollars per lb. **Type of Price:** average to first receiver. **Time Period Covered:** latest year.

TURKEY BREEDER BREAST MEAT

Source: *Urner Barry's Price-Current.* **Price Frequency:** daily. **Units of Measure:** cents per lb. **Time Period Covered:** latest day.

TURKEY CUTLETS: FRESH TRAY PACK

Source: *Urner Barry's Price-Current.* **Price Frequency:** daily. **Units of Measure:** cents per lb. **Type of Price:** delivered warehouse. **Time Period Covered:** latest day.

TURKEY DRUMSTICK MEAT: BONELESS, FROZEN

Source: *Urner Barry's Price-Current, West Coast Edition.* **Price Frequency:** semiweekly. **Effective Market(s):** West Coast. **Units of Measure:** Dollars per lb. **Time Period Covered:** latest day.

TURKEY DRUMSTICKS

Source: *Livestock and Poultry Update.* **Price Frequency:** monthly. **Effective Market(s):** Eastern region. **Units of Measure:** cents per lb. **Type of Price:** wholesale. **Time Period Covered:** latest 3 months, year ago.

Source: *Meat Price Report.* **Price Frequency:** weekly. **Units of Measure:** cents per lb. **Type of Price:** price paid to wholesaler. **Time Period Covered:** latest week.

Source: *Monthly Price Review.* **Price Frequency:** daily. **Units of Measure:** Dollars per lb. **Time Period Covered:** latest month.

Source: *Weekly Insiders Turkey Letter.* **Price Frequency:** weekly. **Effective Market(s):** New York. **Units of Measure:** cents per lb. **Type of Price:** retail. **Time Period Covered:** latest week, week ago, year ago.

TURKEY DRUMSTICKS: FRESH

Source: *Urner Barry's Price-Current, West Coast Edition.* **Price Frequency:** semiweekly. **Effective Market(s):** West Coast. **Units of Measure:** Dollars per lb. **Time Period Covered:** latest day.

TURKEY DRUMSTICKS: FROZEN

Source: *Urner Barry's Price-Current, West Coast Edition.* **Price Frequency:** semiweekly. **Effective Market(s):** West Coast. **Units of Measure:** Dollars per lb. **Time Period Covered:** latest day.

TURKEY DRUMSTICKS: HEN, FRESH

Source: *Urner Barry's Price-Current.* **Price Frequency:** daily. **Units of Measure:** cents per lb. **Time Period Covered:** latest day.

TURKEY DRUMSTICKS: HEN, FRESH TRAY PACK

Source: *Urner Barry's Price-Current.* **Price Frequency:** daily. **Units of Measure:** cents per lb. **Type of Price:** delivered warehouse. **Time Period Covered:** latest day.

TURKEY DRUMSTICKS: READY-TO-COOK, FROZEN

Source: *Poultry Market Statistics.* **Price Frequency:** monthly, annually. **Effective Market(s):** Central region, Eastern region, Western region. **Units of Measure:** Dollars per lb. **Type of Price:** average to first receiver. **Time Period Covered:** latest year.

TURKEY DRUMSTICKS: TOM

Source: *Weekly Insiders Turkey Letter.* **Price Frequency:** monthly. **Effective Market(s):** east. **Units of Measure:** cents per lb. **Time Period Covered:** latest 5 years.

TURKEY DRUMSTICKS: TOM, FRESH

Source: *Urner Barry's Price-Current.* **Price Frequency:** daily. **Units of Measure:** cents per lb. **Time Period Covered:** latest day.

TURKEY DRUMSTICKS: TOM, FRESH TRAY PACK

Source: *Urner Barry's Price-Current.* **Price Frequency:** daily. **Units of Measure:** cents per lb. **Type of Price:** delivered warehouse. **Time Period Covered:** latest day.

TURKEY GIZZARDS: FRESH

Source: *Urner Barry's Price-Current, West Coast Edition.* **Price Frequency:** semiweekly. **Effective Market(s):** West Coast. **Units of Measure:** Dollars per lb. **Time Period Covered:** latest day.

TURKEY GIZZARDS: FROZEN

Source: *Urner Barry's Price-Current, West Coast Edition.* **Price Frequency:** semiweekly. **Effective Market(s):** West Coast. **Units of Measure:** Dollars per lb. **Time Period Covered:** latest day.

TURKEY GIZZARDS: FROZEN, READY-TO-COOK

Source: *Urner Barry's Price-Current.* **Price Frequency:** daily. **Units of Measure:** cents per lb. **Type of Price:** price for bulk carlots & trucklots. **Time Period Covered:** daily.

TURKEY GROWER FEED

Source: *Agricultural Outlook.* **Price Frequency:** monthly, annually. **Units of Measure:** Dollars per ton. **Time Period Covered:** monthly latest 6 months, annually latest 3 years.

Source: *Agricultural Prices.* **Price Frequency:** quarterly. **Effective Market(s):** United States. **Units of Measure:** Dollars per ton. **Type of Price:** paid by farmer. **Time Period Covered:** latest 2 quarters, year ago.

Source: *Agricultural Prices.* **Price Frequency:** monthly. **Effective Market(s):** 10 domestic markets, United States. **Units of Measure:** Dollars per ton. **Type of Price:** paid by farmer. **Time Period Covered:** latest month.

Source: *Agricultural Prices Annual Summary.* **Price Frequency:** quarterly. **Effective Market(s):** 10 domestic markets, United States. **Units of Measure:** Dollars per ton. **Type of Price:** average paid by farmer. **Time Period Covered:** latest year, for US latest 6 years.

Source: *Feed Situation and Outlook Report.* **Price Frequency:** quarterly, annually. **Effective Market(s):** United States. **Units of Measure:** Dollars per ton. **Type of Price:** paid by farmer. **Time Period Covered:** latest year.

TURKEY HALF BREASTS: FRESH TRAY PACK

Source: *Urner Barry's Price-Current.* **Price Frequency:** daily. **Units of Measure:** cents per lb. **Type of Price:** delivered warehouse. **Time Period Covered:** latest day.

TURKEY HALF BREASTS: HEN, FRESH

Source: *Urner Barry's Price-Current, West Coast Edition.* **Price Frequency:** semiweekly. **Effective Market(s):** West Coast. **Units of Measure:** Dollars per lb. **Time Period Covered:** latest day.

TURKEY HALF BREASTS: HEN, FROZEN

Source: *Urner Barry's Price-Current, West Coast Edition.* **Price Frequency:** semiweekly. **Effective Market(s):** West Coast. **Units of Measure:** Dollars per lb. **Time Period Covered:** latest day.

TURKEY HAM

Source: *Urner Barry's Price-Current.* **Price Frequency:** daily. **Units of Measure:** Dollars per lb. **Type of Price:** deli, retail chub. **Time Period Covered:** latest day.

Source: *Urner Barry's Price-Current, West Coast Edition.* **Price Frequency:** semiweekly. **Units of Measure:** Dollars per lb. **Type of Price:** deli, retail chub. **Time Period Covered:** latest day.

TURKEY HEARTS: FRESH

Source: *Urner Barry's Price-Current, West Coast Edition.* **Price Frequency:** semiweekly. **Effective Market(s):** West Coast. **Units of Measure:** Dollars per lb. **Time Period Covered:** latest day.

TURKEY HEARTS: FROZEN

Source: *Urner Barry's Price-Current, West Coast Edition.* **Price Frequency:** semiweekly. **Effective Market(s):** West Coast. **Units of Measure:** Dollars per lb. **Time Period Covered:** latest day.

TURKEY HEARTS: FROZEN, READY-TO-COOK

Source: *Urner Barry's Price-Current.* **Price Frequency:** daily. **Units of Measure:** cents per lb. **Type of Price:** price for bulk carlots & trucklots, price for bulk pack, price for consumer pack. **Time Period Covered:** latest day.

TURKEY HOT DOGS

Source: *Urner Barry's Price-Current.* **Price Frequency:** daily. **Units of Measure:** Dollars per lb. **Type of Price:** retail, bulk. **Time Period Covered:** latest day.

Source: *Urner Barry's Price-Current, West Coast Edition.* **Price Frequency:** semiweekly. **Units of Measure:** Dollars per lb. **Type of Price:** bulk, retail. **Time Period Covered:** latest day.

TURKEY LIRA

Source: *Barron's.* **Price Frequency:** weekly. **Effective Market(s):** New York. **Units of Measure:** Turkish lira per United States dollar. **Type of Price:** foreign exchange. **Time Period Covered:** latest 2 weeks.

Source: *New York Times.* **Price Frequency:** daily. **Effective Market(s):** New York. **Units of Measure:** Turkish lira per United States dollar. **Type of Price:** foreign exchange. **Time Period Covered:** latest 2 days.

Source: *Timber Bulletin.* **Price Frequency:** monthly, annually. **Units of Measure:** Turkish lira per United States dollar. **Type of Price:** foreign exchange. **Time Period Covered:** latest 2 years.

TURKEY LIVERS: FRESH

Source: *Urner Barry's Price-Current, West Coast Edition.* **Price Frequency:** semiweekly. **Effective Market(s):** West Coast. **Units of Measure:** Dollars per lb. **Time Period Covered:** latest day.

TURKEY LIVERS: FROZEN

Source: *Urner Barry's Price-Current, West Coast Edition.* **Price Frequency:** semiweekly. **Effective Market(s):** West Coast. **Units of Measure:** Dollars per lb. **Time Period Covered:** latest day.

TURKEY LIVERS: FROZEN, READY-TO-COOK

Source: *Urner Barry's Price-Current.* **Price Frequency:** daily. **Units of Measure:** cents per lb. **Type of Price:** price for bulk carlots & trucklots. **Time Period Covered:** latest day.

TURKEY MEAT: BODY SKIN, FROZEN

Source: *Urner Barry's Price-Current, West Coast Edition.* **Price Frequency:** semiweekly. **Effective Market(s):** West Coast. **Units of Measure:** Dollars per lb. **Time Period Covered:** latest day.

TURKEY MEAT: BREAST SKIN, FROZEN

Source: *Urner Barry's Price-Current, West Coast Edition.* **Price Frequency:** semiweekly. **Effective Market(s):** West Coast. **Units of Measure:** Dollars per lb. **Time Period Covered:** latest day.

TURKEY MEAT: COMMINUTED, FRESH

Source: *Urner Barry's Price-Current.* **Price Frequency:** daily. **Effective Market(s):** Eastern area. **Units of Measure:** cents per lb. **Time Period Covered:** latest day.

TURKEY MEAT: COMMINUTED, FROZEN

Source: *Urner Barry's Price-Current.* **Price Frequency:** daily. **Effective Market(s):** Eastern area. **Units of Measure:** cents per lb. **Time Period Covered:** latest day.

TURKEY MEAT: COMMINUTED, NO SKIN, FRESH

Source: *Urner Barry's Price-Current.* **Price Frequency:** daily. **Effective Market(s):** Eastern area. **Units of Measure:** cents per lb. **Time Period Covered:** latest day.

Source: *Urner Barry's Price-Current, West Coast Edition.* **Price Frequency:** semiweekly. **Effective Market(s):** West Coast. **Units of Measure:** Dollars per lb. **Time Period Covered:** latest day.

TURKEY MEAT: COMMINUTED, NO SKIN, FROZEN

Source: *Monthly Price Review.* **Price Frequency:** daily. **Units of Measure:** Dollars per lb. **Time Period Covered:** latest month.

Source: *Urner Barry's Price-Current.* **Price Frequency:** daily. **Effective Market(s):** Eastern area. **Units of Measure:** cents per lb. **Time Period Covered:** latest day.

Source: *Urner Barry's Price-Current, West Coast Edition.* **Price Frequency:** semiweekly. **Effective Market(s):** West Coast. **Units of Measure:** Dollars per lb. **Time Period Covered:** latest day.

TURKEY MEAT: COMMINUTED, SOME SKIN, FRESH

Source: *Urner Barry's Price-Current.* **Price Frequency:** daily. **Effective Market(s):** Eastern area. **Units of Measure:** cents per lb. **Time Period Covered:** latest day.

Source: *Urner Barry's Price-Current, West Coast Edition.* **Price Frequency:** semiweekly. **Effective Market(s):** West Coast. **Units of Measure:** Dollars per lb. **Time Period Covered:** latest day.

TURKEY MEAT: COMMINUTED, SOME SKIN, FROZEN

Source: *Urner Barry's Price-Current.* **Price Frequency:** daily. **Effective Market(s):** Eastern area. **Units of Measure:** cents per lb. **Time Period Covered:** latest day.

Source: *Urner Barry's Price-Current, West Coast Edition.* **Price Frequency:** semiweekly. **Effective Market(s):** West Coast. **Units of Measure:** Dollars per lb. **Time Period Covered:** latest day.

TURKEY MEAT: COMMINUTED, WITH SKIN, FROZEN

Source: *Monthly Price Review.* **Price Frequency:** daily. **Units of Measure:** Dollars per lb. **Time Period Covered:** latest month.

TURKEY MEAT: COOKED, DICED

Source: *Meat Price Report.* **Price Frequency:** weekly. **Units of Measure:** cents per lb. **Type of Price:** price paid to wholesaler. **Time Period Covered:** latest week.

TURKEY MEAT: DARK, GROUND COARSE

Source: *Urner Barry's Price-Current.* **Price Frequency:** daily. **Units of Measure:** cents per lb. **Time Period Covered:** latest day.

TURKEY MEAT: DARK, GROUND COARSE, FROZEN

Source: *Urner Barry's Price-Current, West Coast Edition.* **Price Frequency:** semiweekly. **Effective Market(s):** West Coast. **Units of Measure:** Dollars per lb. **Time Period Covered:** latest day.

TURKEY MEAT: DARK, GROUND FINE

Source: *Urner Barry's Price-Current.* **Price Frequency:** daily. **Units of Measure:** cents per lb. **Time Period Covered:** latest day.

TURKEY MEAT: DARK, GROUND FINE, FROZEN

Source: *Urner Barry's Price-Current, West Coast Edition.* **Price Frequency:** semiweekly. **Effective Market(s):** West Coast. **Units of Measure:** Dollars per lb. **Time Period Covered:** latest day.

TURKEY MEAT: DRUMSTICK, BONELESS

Source: *Urner Barry's Price-Current.* **Price Frequency:** daily. **Units of Measure:** cents per lb. **Time Period Covered:** latest day.

TURKEY MEAT: FRIED IN OIL, SKIN ON

Source: *Urner Barry's Price-Current, West Coast Edition.* **Price Frequency:** semiweekly. **Units of Measure:** Dollars per lb. **Time Period Covered:** latest day.

TURKEY MEAT: FRIED IN OIL, SKIN ON, READY-TO-EAT

Source: *Urner Barry's Price-Current.* **Price Frequency:** daily. **Units of Measure:** Dollars per lb. **Time Period Covered:** latest day.

TURKEY MEAT: FRIED IN OIL, SKINLESS

Source: *Urner Barry's Price-Current, West Coast Edition.* **Price Frequency:** semiweekly. **Units of Measure:** Dollars per lb. **Time Period Covered:** latest day.

TURKEY MEAT: FRIED IN OIL, SKINLESS, READY-TO-EAT

Source: *Urner Barry's Price-Current.* **Price Frequency:** daily. **Units of Measure:** Dollars per lb. **Time Period Covered:** latest day.

TURKEY MEAT: SKIN ON, FULLY COOKED

Source: *Urner Barry's Price-Current, West Coast Edition.* **Price Frequency:** semiweekly. **Units of Measure:** Dollars per lb. **Time Period Covered:** latest day.

TURKEY MEAT: SKIN ON, FULLY COOKED, READY-TO-EAT

Source: *Urner Barry's Price-Current.* **Price Frequency:** daily. **Units of Measure:** Dollars per lb. **Time Period Covered:** latest day.

TURKEY MEAT: SKINLESS, FULLY COOKED

Source: *Urner Barry's Price-Current, West Coast Edition.* **Price Frequency:** semiweekly. **Units of Measure:** Dollars per lb. **Time Period Covered:** latest day.

TURKEY MEAT: SKINLESS, FULLY COOKED, READY-TO-EAT

Source: *Urner Barry's Price-Current.* **Price Frequency:** daily. **Units of Measure:** Dollars per lb. **Time Period Covered:** latest day.

TURKEY MEAT: WHITE, COOKED, PULLED

Source: *Meat Price Report.* **Price Frequency:** weekly. **Units of Measure:** cents per lb. **Type of Price:** price paid to wholesaler. **Time Period Covered:** latest week.

TURKEY MEAT: WHITE TRIM, FROZEN

Source: *Urner Barry's Price-Current, West Coast Edition.* **Price Frequency:** semiweekly. **Effective Market(s):** West Coast. **Units of Measure:** Dollars per lb. **Time Period Covered:** latest day.

TURKEY MINI: SKINLESS, FULLY COOKED, READY-TO-EAT

Source: *Urner Barry's Price-Current.* **Price Frequency:** daily. **Units of Measure:** Dollars per lb. **Time Period Covered:** latest day.

TURKEY NECKS

Source: *Monthly Price Review.* **Price Frequency:** daily. **Units of Measure:** Dollars per lb. **Time Period Covered:** latest month.

Source: *Poultry Market Statistics.* **Price Frequency:** monthly, annually. **Effective Market(s):** Central region, Eastern region, Western region. **Units of Measure:** Dollars per lb. **Type of Price:** average to first receiver. **Time Period Covered:** latest year.

TURKEY NECKS: HEN, FRESH

Source: *Urner Barry's Price-Current, West Coast Edition.* **Price Frequency:** semiweekly. **Effective Market(s):** West Coast. **Units of Measure:** Dollars per lb. **Time Period Covered:** latest day.

TURKEY NECKS: HEN, FROZEN, READY-TO-COOK

Source: *Urner Barry's Price-Current.* **Price Frequency:** daily. **Units of Measure:** cents per lb. **Type of Price:** price for bulk carlots & trucklost, price for bulk pack, price for consumer pack. **Time Period Covered:** latest day.

TURKEY NECKS: TOM

Source: *Weekly Insiders Turkey Letter.* **Price Frequency:** monthly. **Effective Market(s):** east. **Units of Measure:** cents per lb. **Time Period Covered:** latest 5 years.

TURKEY NECKS: TOM, FRESH

Source: *Urner Barry's Price-Current, West Coast Edition.* **Price Frequency:** semiweekly. **Effective Market(s):** West Coast. **Units of Measure:** Dollars per lb. **Time Period Covered:** latest day.

TURKEY NECKS: TOM, FRESH TRAY PACK

Source: *Urner Barry's Price-Current.* **Price Frequency:** daily. **Units of Measure:** cents per lb. **Type of Price:** delivered warehouse. **Time Period Covered:** latest day.

TURKEY NECKS: TOM, FROZEN

Source: *Urner Barry's Price-Current, West Coast Edition.* **Price Frequency:** semiweekly. **Effective Market(s):** West Coast. **Units of Measure:** Dollars per lb. **Time Period Covered:** latest day.

TURKEY PASTRAMI

Source: *Urner Barry's Price-Current.* **Price Frequency:** daily. **Units of Measure:** Dollars per lb. **Type of Price:** deli, retail chub. **Time Period Covered:** latest day.

Source: *Urner Barry's Price-Current, West Coast Edition.* **Price Frequency:** semiweekly. **Units of Measure:** Dollars per lb. **Type of Price:** deli, retail chub. **Time Period Covered:** latest day.

TURKEY POULTS

Source: *Agricultural Prices.* **Price Frequency:** quarterly. **Effective Market(s):** United States. **Units of Measure:** Dollars each. **Type of Price:** paid by farmer. **Time Period Covered:** latest 2 quarters, year ago.

Source: *Agricultural Prices Annual Summary.* **Price Frequency:** quarterly, annually. **Effective Market(s):** United States. **Units of Measure:** Dollars each. **Type of Price:** average paid by farmer. **Time Period Covered:** latest 6 years.

TURKEY POULTS: HEAVY BREEDS

Source: *Agricultural Prices Annual Summary.* **Price Frequency:** annually. **Effective Market(s):** United States. **Units of Measure:** Dollars each. **Type of Price:** average paid by farmer. **Time Period Covered:** latest 6 years.

TURKEY POULTS: LIGHT BREEDS

Source: *Agricultural Prices Annual Summary.* **Price Frequency:** annually. **Effective Market(s):** United States. **Units of Measure:** Dollars each. **Type of Price:** average paid by farmer. **Time Period Covered:** latest 6 years.

TURKEY ROAST: ALL WHITE, RAW

Source: *Weekly Insiders Turkey Letter.* **Price Frequency:** weekly. **Effective Market(s):** New York. **Units of Measure:** cents per lb. **Type of Price:** retail. **Time Period Covered:** latest week, week ago, year ago.

TURKEY ROAST: BONED, TIED, SEASONED, READY-TO-COOK

Source: *Urner Barry's Price-Current.* **Price Frequency:** daily. **Units of Measure:** Dollars per lb. **Time Period Covered:** latest day.

Source: *Urner Barry's Price-Current, West Coast Edition.* **Price Frequency:** semiweekly. **Units of Measure:** Dollars per lb. **Time Period Covered:** latest day.

TURKEY ROAST: BONED, TIED, UNSEASONED, READY-TO-COOK

Source: *Urner Barry's Price-Current.* **Price Frequency:** daily. **Units of Measure:** Dollars per lb. **Time Period Covered:** latest day.

Source: *Urner Barry's Price-Current, West Coast Edition.* **Price Frequency:** semiweekly. **Units of Measure:** Dollars per lb. **Time Period Covered:** latest day.

TURKEY ROAST: RAW

Source: *Weekly Insiders Turkey Letter.* **Price Frequency:** weekly. **Effective Market(s):** New York. **Units of Measure:** cents per lb. **Type of Price:** retail. **Time Period Covered:** latest week, week ago, year ago.

TURKEY ROAST: SKIN ON, FOIL WRAPPED, READY-TO-COOK

Source: *Urner Barry's Price-Current.* **Price Frequency:** daily. **Units of Measure:** Dollars per lb. **Time Period Covered:** latest day.

Source: *Urner Barry's Price-Current, West Coast Edition.* **Price Frequency:** semiweekly. **Units of Measure:** Dollars per lb. **Time Period Covered:** latest day.

TURKEY ROLL: ALL WHITE

Source: *HRI-Buyer's Guide.* **Price Frequency:** weekly. **Effective Market(s):** Northeastern area. **Units of Measure:** Dollars per lb. **Type of Price:** price paid by dining places & institutions. **Time Period Covered:** latest week.

TURKEY ROLL: ALL WHITE, FULLY COOKED

Source: *Urner Barry's Price-Current, West Coast Edition.* **Price Frequency:** semiweekly. **Units of Measure:** Dollars per lb. **Time Period Covered:** latest day.

TURKEY ROLL: ALL WHITE, FULLY COOKED, READY-TO-EAT

Source: *Urner Barry's Price-Current.* **Price Frequency:** daily. **Units of Measure:** Dollars per lb. **Time Period Covered:** latest day.

TURKEY ROLL: ECONOMY ALL WHITE

Source: *HRI-Buyer's Guide.* **Price Frequency:** weekly. **Effective Market(s):** Northeastern area. **Units of Measure:** Dollars per lb. **Type of Price:** price paid by dining places & institutions. **Time Period Covered:** latest week.

TURKEY ROLL: ECONOMY WHITE AND DARK

Source: *HRI-Buyer's Guide.* **Price Frequency:** weekly. **Effective Market(s):** Northeastern area. **Units of Measure:** Dollars per lb. **Type of Price:** price paid by dining places & institutions. **Time Period Covered:** latest week.

TURKEY ROLL: ECONOMY WHITE AND DARK, FULLY COOKED

Source: *Urner Barry's Price-Current, West Coast Edition.* **Price Frequency:** semiweekly. **Units of Measure:** Dollars per lb. **Time Period Covered:** latest day.

TURKEY ROLL: ECONOMY WHITE AND DARK, FULLY COOKED, READY-TO-EAT

Source: *Urner Barry's Price-Current.* **Price Frequency:** daily. **Units of Measure:** Dollars per lb. **Time Period Covered:** latest day.

TURKEY ROLL: ECONOMY WHITE, FULLY COOKED

Source: *Urner Barry's Price-Current, West Coast Edition.* **Price Frequency:** semiweekly. **Units of Measure:** Dollars per lb. **Time Period Covered:** latest day.

TURKEY ROLL: ECONOMY WHITE, FULLY COOKED, READY-TO-EAT

Source: *Urner Barry's Price-Current.* **Price Frequency:** daily. **Units of Measure:** Dollars per lb. **Time Period Covered:** latest day.

TURKEY ROLL: WHITE AND DARK, FULLY COOKED

Source: *Urner Barry's Price-Current, West Coast Edition.* **Price Frequency:** semiweekly. **Units of Measure:** Dollars per lb. **Time Period Covered:** latest day.

TURKEY ROLL: WHITE AND DARK, FULLY COOKED, READY-TO-EAT

Source: *Urner Barry's Price-Current.* **Price Frequency:** daily. **Units of Measure:** Dollars per lb. **Time Period Covered:** latest day.

TURKEY SALAMI

Source: *Urner Barry' Price-Current.* **Price Frequency:** daily. **Units of Measure:** Dollars per lb. **Type of Price:** deli, retail chub. **Time Period Covered:** latest day.

Source: *Urner Barry's Price-Current, West Coast Edition.* **Price Frequency:** semiweekly. **Units of Measure:** Dollars per lb. **Type of Price:** deli, retail chub. **Time Period Covered:** latest day.

TURKEY SAUSAGE PRODUCTS: DARK, GROUND

Source: *Urner Barry's Price-Current, West Coast Edition.* **Price Frequency:** semiweekly. **Units of Measure:** Dollars per lb. **Type of Price:** bulk, retail. **Time Period Covered:** latest day.

TURKEY SAUSAGE PRODUCTS: DARK MEAT, GROUND, READY-TO-COOK

Source: *Urner Barry's Price-Current.* **Price Frequency:** daily. **Units of Measure:** Dollars per lb. **Type of Price:** retail, bulk. **Time Period Covered:** latest day.

TURKEY SCAPULA

Source: *Urner Barry's Price-Current.* **Price Frequency:** daily. **Units of Measure:** cents per lb. **Time Period Covered:** latest day.

TURKEY SCAPULA MEAT: FROZEN

Source: *Urner Barry's Price-Current, West Coast Edition.* **Price Frequency:** semiweekly. **Effective Market(s):** West Coast. **Units of Measure:** Dollars per lb. **Time Period Covered:** latest day.

TURKEY TAILS: FRESH

Source: *Urner Barry's Price-Current, West Coast Edition.* **Price Frequency:** semiweekly. **Effective Market(s):** West Coast. **Units of Measure:** Dollars per lb. **Time Period Covered:** latest day.

TURKEY TAILS: FROZEN

Source: *Urner Barry's Price-Current, West Coast Edition.* **Price Frequency:** semiweekly. **Effective Market(s):** West Coast. **Units of Measure:** Dollars per lb. **Time Period Covered:** latest day.

TURKEY TAILS: FROZEN, READY-TO-COOK

Source: *Urner Barry's Price-Current.* **Price Frequency:** daily. **Units of Measure:** cents per lb. **Type of Price:** price for bulk carlots & trucklots. **Time Period Covered:** latest day.

TURKEY THIGH MEAT: FRESH

Source: *Weekly Insiders Turkey Letter.* **Price Frequency:** monthly. **Effective Market(s):** east. **Units of Measure:** cents per lb. **Time Period Covered:** latest 5 years.

TURKEY THIGH MEAT: SKINLESS, BONELESS, FRESH

Source: *Monthly Price Review.* **Price Frequency:** daily. **Units of Measure:** Dollars per lb. **Time Period Covered:** latest month.

TURKEY THIGH MEAT: SKINLESS, BONELESS, FROZEN

Source: *Monthly Price Review.* **Price Frequency:** daily. **Units of Measure:** Dollars per lb. **Time Period Covered:** latest month.

Source: *Urner Barry's Price-Current, West Coast Edition.* **Price Frequency:** semiweekly. **Effective Market(s):** West Coast. **Units of Measure:** Dollars per lb. **Time Period Covered:** latest day.

TURKEY THIGHS

Source: *Weekly Insiders Turkey Letter.* **Price Frequency:** weekly. **Effective Market(s):** New York. **Units of Measure:** cents per lb. **Type of Price:** retail. **Time Period Covered:** latest week, week ago, year ago.

TURKEY THIGHS: BONE IN, FRESH TRAY PACK

Source: *Urner Barry's Price-Current.* **Price Frequency:** daily. **Units of Measure:** cents per lb. **Type of Price:** delivered warehouse. **Time Period Covered:** latest day.

TURKEY THIGHS: DARK MEAT, BONELESS, COOKED

Source: *Meat Price Report.* **Price Frequency:** weekly. **Units of Measure:** cents per lb. **Type of Price:** price paid to wholesaler. **Time Period Covered:** latest week.

TURKEY THIGHS: FRESH

Source: *Urner Barry's Price-Current, West Coast Edition.* **Price Frequency:** semiweekly. **Effective Market(s):** West Coast. **Units of Measure:** Dollars per lb. **Time Period Covered:** latest day.

Source: *Weekly Insiders Turkey Letter.* **Price Frequency:** annually. **Units of Measure:** cents per lb. **Type of Price:** wholesale. **Time Period Covered:** latest 3 years.

TURKEY THIGHS: FROZEN

Source: *Urner Barry's Price-Current, West Coast Edition.* **Price Frequency:** semiweekly. **Effective Market(s):** West Coast. **Units of Measure:** Dollars per lb. **Time Period Covered:** latest day.

TURKEY THIGHS: SKINLESS, BONELESS, FRESH

Source: *Poultry Market Statistics.* **Price Frequency:** monthly, annually. **Effective Market(s):** Central region, Eastern region, Western region. **Units of Measure:** Dollars per lb. **Type of Price:** average to first receiver. **Time Period Covered:** latest year.

Source: *Urner Barry's Price-Current.* **Price Frequency:** daily. **Units of Measure:** cents per lb. **Time Period Covered:** latest day.

TURKEY THIGHS: SKINLESS, BONELESS, FROZEN

Source: *Poultry Market Statistics.* **Price Frequency:** monthly, annually. **Effective Market(s):** Central region, Eastern region, Western region. **Units of Measure:** Dollars per lb. **Type of Price:** average to first receiver. **Time Period Covered:** latest year.

Source: *Urner Barry's Price-Current.* **Price Frequency:** daily. **Units of Measure:** cents per lb. **Time Period Covered:** latest day.

TURKEY TRIM: WHITE

Source: *Urner Barry's Price-Current.* **Price Frequency:** daily. **Units of Measure:** cents per lb. **Time Period Covered:** latest day.

TURKEY V-WINGS

Source: *Poultry Market Statistics.* **Price Frequency:** monthly, annually. **Effective Market(s):** Central region, Eastern region, Western region. **Units of Measure:** Dollars per lb. **Type of Price:** average to first receiver. **Time Period Covered:** latest year.

TURKEY V-WINGS: HEN, FRESH TRAY PACK

Source: *Urner Barry's Price-Current.* **Price Frequency:** daily. **Units of Measure:** cents per lb. **Type of Price:** delivered warehouse. **Time Period Covered:** latest day.

TURKEY V-WINGS: TOM

Source: *Weekly Insiders Turkey Letter.* **Price Frequency:** monthly. **Effective Market(s):** east. **Units of Measure:** cents per lb. **Time Period Covered:** latest 5 years.

TURKEY V-WINGS: TOM, FRESH TRAY PACK

Source: *Urner Barry's Price-Current.* **Price Frequency:** daily. **Units of Measure:** cents per lb. **Type of Price:** delivered warehouse. **Time Period Covered:** latest day.

TURKEY WING DRUMETTES: FRESH TRAY PACK

Source: *Urner Barry's Price-Current.* **Price Frequency:** daily. **Units of Measure:** cents per lb. **Type of Price:** delivered warehouse. **Time Period Covered:** latest day.

TURKEY WING MEAT: WITH SKIN

Source: *Urner Barry's Price-Current.* **Price Frequency:** daily. **Units of Measure:** cents per lb. **Time Period Covered:** latest day.

TURKEY WING MEAT: WITH SKIN, FROZEN

Source: *Urner Barry' Price-Current, West Coast Edition.* **Price Frequency:** semiweekly. **Effective Market(s):** West Coast. **Units of Measure:** Dollars per lb. **Time Period Covered:** latest day.

TURKEY WINGS

Source: *Meat Price Report.* **Price Frequency:** weekly. **Units of Measure:** cents per lb. **Type of Price:** price paid to wholesaler. **Time Period Covered:** latest week.

Source: *Monthly Price Review.* **Price Frequency:** daily. **Units of Measure:** Dollars per lb. **Time Period Covered:** latest month.

Source: *Weekly Insiders Turkey Letter.* **Price Frequency:** weekly. **Effective Market(s):** New York. **Units of Measure:** cents per lb. **Type of Price:** retail. **Time Period Covered:** latest week, week ago, year ago.

TURKEY WINGS: FULL CUT

Source: *Livestock and Poultry Update.* **Price Frequency:** monthly. **Effective Market(s):** Eastern region. **Units of Measure:** cents per lb. **Type of Price:** wholesale. **Time Period Covered:** latest 3 months, year ago.

Source: *Poultry Market Statistics.* **Price Frequency:** monthly, annually. **Effective Market(s):** Central region, Eastern region, Western region. **Units of Measure:** Dollars per lb. **Type of Price:** average to first receiver. **Time Period Covered:** latest year.

TURKEY WINGS: WHOLE

Source: *Weekly Insiders Turkey Letter.* **Price Frequency:** monthly. **Effective Market(s):** east. **Units of Measure:** cents per lb. **Time Period Covered:** latest 5 years.

TURKEY WINGS: WHOLE, FRESH

Source: *Urner Barry's Price-Current, West Coast Edition.* **Price Frequency:** semiweekly. **Effective Market(s):** West Coast. **Units of Measure:** Dollars per lb. **Time Period Covered:** latest day.

TURKEY WINGS: WHOLE, FRESH TRAY PACK

Source: *Urner Barry's Price-Current.* **Price Frequency:** daily. **Units of Measure:** cents per lb. **Type of Price:** delivered warehouse. **Time Period Covered:** latest day.

TURKEY WINGS: WHOLE, FROZEN

Source: *Urner Barry's Price-Current, West Coast Edition.* **Price Frequency:** semiweekly. **Effective Market(s):** West Coast. **Units of Measure:** Dollars per lb. **Time Period Covered:** latest day.

TURKEYS

Source: *Agricultural Outlook.* **Price Frequency:** monthly, annually. **Effective Market(s):** United States. **Units of Measure:** cents per lb. **Type of Price:** received by farmer. **Time Period Covered:** monthly latest 6 months, annaually latest 3 years.

Source: *Agricultural Outlook.* **Price Frequency:** annually. **Effective Market(s):** United States. **Units of Measure:** cents per lb. **Type of Price:** primary market. **Time Period Covered:** latest 2 years.

Source: *Agricultural Prices.* **Price Frequency:** monthly. **Effective Market(s):** 9 domestic markets, United States. **Units of Measure:** Dollars per lb. **Type of Price:** received by farmer. **Time Period Covered:** latest month.

Source: *Agricultural Prices Annual Summary.* **Price Frequency:** annually. **Effective Market(s):** 50 domestic markets, United States. **Units of Measure:** Dollars per lb. **Type of Price:** average received by farmer. **Time Period Covered:** latest 2 years, for US latest 6 years.

Source: *Agricultural Prices Annual Summary.* **Price Frequency:** monthly. **Effective Market(s):** 10 domestic markets, United States. **Units of Measure:** Dollars per lb. **Type of Price:** average received by farmer. **Time Period Covered:** latest year, for US latest 6 years.

Source: *Illinois Farm Report.* **Price Frequency:** quarterly. **Effective Market(s):** Illinois. **Units of Measure:** Dollars per lb. **Type of Price:** average received by farmers. **Time Period Covered:** latest 2 months, year ago.

Source: *Livestock and Poultry Situation and Outlook Report.* **Price Frequency:** monthly, annually. **Units of Measure:** cents per lb. **Type of Price:** farm. **Time Period Covered:** latest 3 years.

TURKEYS: BELTVILLES, DRESSED, FRESH, DEEP CHILLED

Source: *Urner Barry's Price-Current.* **Price Frequency:** daily. **Units of Measure:** cents per lb. **Time Period Covered:** latest day.

TURKEYS: BELTVILLES, GRADE A, FROZEN, READY-TO-COOK

Source: *Urner Barry's Price-Current, West Coast Edition.* **Price Frequency:** semiweekly. **Effective Market(s):** West Coast. **Units of Measure:** Dollars per lb. **Time Period Covered:** latest day.

TURKEYS: BELTVILLES, GRADE A OR COMPARABLE, DRESSED, FROZEN, Ready-to-Cook

Source: *Urner Barry's Price-Current.* **Price Frequency:** daily. **Units of Measure:** cents per lb. **Type of Price:** truck load, sale from stores and warehouses. **Time Period Covered:** latest day.

TURKEYS: BREEDER HENS, FRESH, REGULAR PACK

Source: *Urner Barry's Price-Current, West Coast Edition.* **Price Frequency:** semiweekly. **Effective Market(s):** Midwest. **Units of Measure:** Dollars per lb. **Time Period Covered:** latest day.

TURKEYS: BREEDER HENS, FROZEN, REGULAR PACK

Source: *Urner Barry's Price-Current, West Coast Edition.* **Price Frequency:** semiweekly. **Effective Market(s):** Midwest. **Units of Measure:** Dollars per lb. **Time Period Covered:** latest day.

TURKEYS: COCKS, GRADE A, UNEVISERATED, FRESH

Source: *Farmers Weekly.* **Price Frequency:** weekly. **Effective Market(s):** Smithfield (England). **Units of Measure:** British pence per lb. **Type of Price:** wholesale bottom, wholesale top. **Time Period Covered:** latest week.

TURKEYS: HENS

Source: *Commodity Year Book.* **Price Frequency:** monthly, annually. **Effective Market(s):** New York. **Units of Measure:** cents per lb. **Type of Price:** wholesale. **Time Period Covered:** latest 14 years.

Source: *Commodity Year Book.* **Price Frequency:** annually. **Effective Market(s):** 4-market average. **Units of Measure:** cents per lb. **Type of Price:** retail. **Time Period Covered:** latest 6 years.

Source: *Commodity Year Book.* **Price Frequency:** annually. **Effective Market(s):** New York, United States. **Units of Measure:** cents per lb. **Type of Price:** farm. **Time Period Covered:** latest 14 years.

Source: *Livestock and Poultry Update.* **Price Frequency:** monthly. **Effective Market(s):** Eastern region. **Units of Measure:** cents per lb. **Type of Price:** wholesale. **Time Period Covered:** latest 3 months, year ago.

Source: *Monthly Price Review.* **Price Frequency:** daily. **Units of Measure:** Dollars per lb. **Time Period Covered:** latest month.

Source: *Weekly Insiders Turkey Letter.* **Price Frequency:** weekly. **Effective Market(s):** New York. **Units of Measure:** cents per lb. **Type of Price:** retail. **Time Period Covered:** latest week, week ago, year ago.

TURKEYS: HENS, BASTED

Source: *Weekly Insiders Turkey Letter.* **Price Frequency:** weekly. **Effective Market(s):** New York. **Units of Measure:** cents per lb. **Type of Price:** retail. **Time Period Covered:** latest week, week ago, year ago.

TURKEYS: HENS, DRESSED, FRESH, DEEP CHILLED

Source: *Urner Barry's Price-Current.* **Price Frequency:** daily. **Units of Measure:** cents per lb. **Time Period Covered:** latest day.

TURKEYS: HENS, FRESH, DEEP CHILLED

Source: *Urner Barry's Price-Current.* **Price Frequency:** daily. **Effective Market(s):** Midwest. **Units of Measure:** cents per lb. **Type of Price:** truck load, sale from stores and warehouses. **Time Period Covered:** latest day.

TURKEYS: HENS, GRADE A

Source: *Weekly Statistical Fishery Report.* **Price Frequency:** weekly. **Effective Market(s):** New York. **Units of Measure:** Dollars per lb. **Type of Price:** market. **Time Period Covered:** latest week.

TURKEYS: HENS, GRADE A, FROZEN

Source: *Poultry Times.* **Price Frequency:** biweekly. **Effective Market(s):** Central, East, West. **Units of Measure:** cents per lb. **Type of Price:** delivered price. **Time Period Covered:** week ago, 3 weeks ago.

TURKEYS: HENS, GRADE A, UNEVISERATED, FRESH

Source: *Farmers Weekly.* **Price Frequency:** weekly. **Effective Market(s):** Smithfield (England). **Units of Measure:** British pence per lb. **Type of Price:** wholesale bottom, wholesale top. **Time Period Covered:** latest week.

TURKEYS: HENS, READY-TO-COOK

Source: *Livestock and Poultry Situation and Outlook Report.* **Price Frequency:** monthly, annually. **Effective Market(s):** New York. **Units of Measure:** cents per lb. **Type of Price:** wholesale. **Time Period Covered:** latest 3 years.

TURKEYS: HENS, YOUNG

Source: *Agricultural Outlook.* **Price Frequency:** monthly, annually. **Effective Market(s):** Eastern United States. **Units of Measure:** cents per lb. **Type of Price:** wholesale. **Time Period Covered:** monthly latest 6 months, annually latest 3 years.

Source: *Livestock and Poultry Situation and Outlook Report.* **Price Frequency:** quarterly, annually. **Effective Market(s):** Eastern region. **Units of Measure:** cents per lb. **Type of Price:** wholesale. **Time Period Covered:** latest 2 years.

TURKEYS: HENS, YOUNG, FRESH

Source: *Urner Barry's Price-Current, West Coast Edition.* **Price Frequency:** semiweekly. **Effective Market(s):** West Coast. **Units of Measure:** Dollars per lb. **Time Period Covered:** latest day.

TURKEYS: HENS, YOUNG, FRESH, REGULAR PACK

Source: *Urner Barry's Price-Current, West Coast Edition.* **Price Frequency:** semiweekly. **Effective Market(s):** Midwest. **Units of Measure:** Dollars per lb. **Time Period Covered:** latest day.

TURKEYS: HENS, YOUNG, FROZEN

Source: *Weekly Insiders Turkey Letter.* **Price Frequency:** annually. **Units of Measure:** cents per lb. **Type of Price:** wholesale. **Time Period Covered:** latest 3 years.

TURKEYS: HENS, YOUNG, FROZEN, CANNER PACK

Source: *Poultry Market Statistics.* **Price Frequency:** weekly, seasonally. **Effective Market(s):** Central region. **Units of Measure:** cents per lb. **Time Period Covered:** latest year.

TURKEYS: HENS, YOUNG, FROZEN, REGULAR PACK

Source: *Urner Barry's Price-Current, West Coast Edition.* **Price Frequency:** semiweekly. **Effective Market(s):** Midwest. **Units of Measure:** Dollars per lb. **Time Period Covered:** latest day.

TURKEYS: HENS, YOUNG, GRADE A, FROZEN, READY-TO-COOK

Source: *Feedstuffs.* **Price Frequency:** weekly. **Effective Market(s):** New York. **Units of Measure:** cents per lb. **Time Period Covered:** latest week, week ago, 6 months ago, year ago.

Source: *Poultry Market Statistics.* **Price Frequency:** monthly, annually. **Effective Market(s):** Central region, Eastern region, Los Angeles, San Francisco, Western region. **Units of Measure:** cents per lb. **Time Period Covered:** latest year.

TURKEYS: HENS, YOUNG, GRADE A OR COMPARABLE, DRESSED, FROZEN, Ready-to-Cook

Source: *Urner Barry's Price-Current.* **Price Frequency:** daily. **Units of Measure:** cents per lb. **Type of Price:** truck load, sale from stores and warehouses. **Time Period Covered:** latest day.

TURKEYS: HENS, YOUNG, GRADE A OR COMPARABLE, FROZEN, READY-TO-COOK

Source: *Urner Barry's Price-Current.* **Price Frequency:** daily. **Effective Market(s):** Midwest. **Units of Measure:** cents per lb. **Type of Price:** truck load, sale from stores and warehouses. **Time Period Covered:** latest day.

TURKEYS: HENS, YOUNG, HEAVY BREEDS, GRADE A, FROZEN, READY-TO-COOK

Source: *Urner Barry's Price-Current, West Coast Edition.* **Price Frequency:** semiweekly. **Effective Market(s):** West Coast. **Units of Measure:** Dollars per lb. **Time Period Covered:** latest day.

TURKEYS: HENS, YOUNG, LINE RUN, FRESH

Source: *Urner Barry's Price-Current, West Coast Edition.* **Price Frequency:** semiweekly. **Effective Market(s):** Midwest. **Units of Measure:** Dollars per lb. **Time Period Covered:** latest day.

TURKEYS: HENS, YOUNG, LINE RUN, FROZEN

Source: *Urner Barry's Price-Current, West Coast Edition.* **Price Frequency:** semiweekly. **Effective Market(s):** Midwest. **Units of Measure:** Dollars per lb. **Time Period Covered:** latest day.

TURKEYS: LIGHT

Source: *Weekly Insiders Turkey Letter.* **Price Frequency:** weekly. **Effective Market(s):** New York. **Units of Measure:** cents per lb. **Type of Price:** retail. **Time Period Covered:** latest week, week ago, year ago.

TURKEYS: LIGHT, BASTED

Source: *Weekly Insiders Turkey Letter.* **Price Frequency:** weekly. **Effective Market(s):** New York. **Units of Measure:** cents per lb. **Type of Price:** retail. **Time Period Covered:** latest week, week ago, year ago.

TURKEYS: LIVE

Source: *Agricultural Prices.* **Price Frequency:** monthly. **Effective Market(s):** United States. **Units of Measure:** Dollars per lb. **Type of Price:** received by farmer. **Time Period Covered:** latest 2 months, year ago.

TURKEYS: READY-TO-COOK

Source: *Commodity Year Book.* **Price Frequency:** annually. **Effective Market(s):** 3-market composite. **Units of Measure:** cents per lb. **Type of Price:** wholesale. **Time Period Covered:** latest 10 years.

TURKEYS: READY-TO-COOK, FROZEN

Source: *HRI-Buyer's Guide.* **Price Frequency:** weekly. **Effective Market(s):** Northeastern area. **Units of Measure:** Dollars per lb. **Type of Price:** price paid by dining places & institutions. **Time Period Covered:** latest week.

TURKEYS: TOMS

Source: *Livestock and Poultry Update.* **Price Frequency:** monthly. **Effective Market(s):** Eastern region. **Units of Measure:** cents per lb. **Type of Price:** wholesale. **Time Period Covered:** latest 3 months, year ago.

Source: *Weekly Insiders Turkey Letter.* **Price Frequency:** weekly. **Effective Market(s):** New York. **Units of Measure:** cents per lb. **Type of Price:** retail. **Time Period Covered:** latest week, week ago, year ago.

TURKEYS: TOMS, BASTED

Source: *Weekly Insiders Turkey Letter.* **Price Frequency:** weekly. **Effective Market(s):** New York. **Units of Measure:** cents per lb. **Type of Price:** retail. **Time Period Covered:** latest week, week ago, year ago.

TURKEYS: TOMS, DRESSED, FRESH, DEEP CHILLED

Source: *Urner Barry's Price Current.* **Price Frequency:** daily. **Units of Measure:** cents per lb. **Time Period Covered:** latest day.

TURKEYS: TOMS, FRESH, DEEP CHILLED

Source: *Urner Barry's Price-Current.* **Price Frequency:** daily. **Effective Market(s):** Midwest. **Units of Measure:** cent per lb. **Type of Price:** truck load, sales from stores and warehouses. **Time Period Covered:** latest day.

TURKEYS: TOMS, FROZEN

Source: *Monthly Price Review.* **Price Frequency:** daily. **Units of Measure:** Dollars per lb. **Time Period Covered:** latest month.

Source: *Weekly Insiders Turkey Letter.* **Price Frequency:** monthly. **Effective Market(s):** east. **Units of Measure:** cents per lb. **Time Period Covered:** latest 5 years.

TURKEYS: TOMS, GRADE A

Source: *Weekly Statistical Fishery Report.* **Price Frequency:** weekly. **Effective Market(s):** New York. **Units of Measure:** Dollars per lb. **Type of Price:** market. **Time Period Covered:** latest week.

TURKEYS: TOMS, GRADE A, FROZEN

Source: *Poultry Times.* **Price Frequency:** biweekly. **Effective Market(s):** Central, East, West. **Units of Measure:** cents per lb. **Type of Price:** delivered price. **Time Period Covered:** week ago, 3 weeks ago.

TURKEYS: TOMS, YOUNG

Source: *Poultry Market Statistics.* **Price Frequency:** weekly, seasonally. **Effective Market(s):** Central region. **Units of Measure:** cents per lb. **Time Period Covered:** latest year.

TURKEYS: TOMS, YOUNG, FRESH

Source: *Urner Barry's Price-Current, West Coast Edition.* **Price Frequency:** semiweekly. **Effective Market(s):** West Coast. **Units of Measure:** Dollars per lb. **Time Period Covered:** latest day.

TURKEYS: TOMS, YOUNG, FRESH, CANNER PACKED/REGULAR PACK

Source: *Urner Barry's Price-Current.* **Price Frequency:** daily. **Effective Market(s):** Eastern area, Midwestern area. **Units of Measure:** cents per lb. **Type of Price:** carlot or trucklot. **Time Period Covered:** latest day.

TURKEYS: TOMS, YOUNG, FRESH, REGULAR PACK

Source: *Urner Barry's Price-Current, West Coast Edition.* **Price Frequency:** semiweekly. **Effective Market(s):** Midwest, West Coast. **Units of Measure:** Dollars per lb. **Time Period Covered:** latest day.

TURKEYS: TOMS, YOUNG, FROZEN

Source: *Weekly Insiders Turkey Letter.* **Price Frequency:** annually. **Units of Measure:** cents per lb. **Type of Price:** wholesale. **Time Period Covered:** latest 3 years.

TURKEYS: TOMS, YOUNG, FROZEN, CANNER PACKED/REGULAR PACK

Source: *Urner Barry's Price-Current.* **Price Frequency:** daily. **Effective Market(s):** Eastern area, Midwestern area. **Units of Measure:** cents per lb. **Type of Price:** carlot or trucklot. **Time Period Covered:** latest day.

TURKEYS: TOMS, YOUNG, FROZEN, REGULAR PACK

Source: *Urner Barry's Price-Current, West Coast Edition.* **Price Frequency:** semiweekly. **Effective Market(s):** Midwest, West Coast. **Units of Measure:** Dollars per lb. **Time Period Covered:** latest day.

TURKEYS: TOMS, YOUNG, GRADE A, FROZEN, READY-TO-COOK

Source: *Feedstuffs.* **Price Frequency:** weekly. **Effective Market(s):** New York. **Units of Measure:** cents per lb. **Time Period Covered:** latest week, week ago, 6 months ago, year ago.

Source: *Poultry Market Statistics.* **Price Frequency:** monthly, annually. **Effective Market(s):** Central region, Eastern region, Los Angeles, San Francisco, Western region. **Units of Measure:** cents per lb. **Time Period Covered:** latest year.

Source: *Poultry Market Statistics.* **Price Frequency:** monthly, annually. **Effective Market(s):** Los Angeles. **Units of Measure:** Dollars per lb. **Type of Price:** average paid by restaurants and institutions. **Time Period Covered:** latest year.

TURKEYS: TOMS, YOUNG, GRADE A OR COMPARABLE, DRESSED, FROZEN, Ready-to-Cook

Source: *Urner Barry's Price-Current.* **Price Frequency:** daily. **Units of Measure:** cents per lb. **Type of Price:** truck load, sale from stores and warehouses. **Time Period Covered:** latest day.

TURKEYS: TOMS, YOUNG, GRADE A OR COMPARABLE, FROZEN, READY-TO-COOK

Source: *Urner Barry's Price-Current.* **Price Frequency:** daily. **Effective Market(s):** Midwest. **Units of Measure:** cents per lb. **Type of Price:** truck load, sale from stores and warehouses. **Time Period Covered:** latest day.

TURKEYS: TOMS, YOUNG, HEAVY BREEDS, GRADE A, FROZEN, READY-TO-COOK

Source: *Urner Barry's Price-Current, West Coast Edition.* **Price Frequency:** semiweekly. **Effective Market(s):** West Coast. **Units of Measure:** Dollars per lb. **Time Period Covered:** latest day.

TURKEYS: TOMS, YOUNG, LINE RUN, FRESH

Source: *Urner Barry's Price-Current, West Coast Edition.* **Price Frequency:** semiweekly. **Effective Market(s):** Midwest, West Coast. **Units of Measure:** Dollars per lb. **Time Period Covered:** latest day.

TURKEYS: TOMS, YOUNG, LINE RUN, FRESH, CANNER PACKED

Source: *Urner Barry's Price-Current.* **Price Frequency:** daily. **Effective Market(s):** Eastern area, Midwestern area. **Units of Measure:** cents per lb. **Type of Price:** carlot or trucklot. **Time Period Covered:** latest day.

TURKEYS: TOMS, YOUNG, LINE RUN, FROZEN

Source: *Urner Barry's Price-Current, West Coast Edition.* **Price Frequency:** semiweekly. **Effective Market(s):** Midwest, West Coast. **Units of Measure:** Dollars per lb. **Time Period Covered:** latest day.

TURKEYS: TOMS, YOUNG, LINE RUN, FROZEN, CANNER PACKED

Source: *Urner Barry's Price-Current.* **Price Frequency:** daily. **Effective Market(s):** Midwestern area. **Units of Measure:** cents per lb. **Type of Price:** carlot or trucklot. **Time Period Covered:** latest day.

TURKEYS: WHOLE

Source: *Livestock and Poultry Situation and Outlook Report.* **Price Frequency:** monthly, annually. **Effective Market(s):** 4-market average. **Units of Measure:** cents per lb. **Type of Price:** retail. **Time Period Covered:** latest 3 years.

TURKEYS: WHOLE, FROZEN

Source: *Livestock and Poultry Update.* **Price Frequency:** monthly. **Units of Measure:** cents per lb. **Type of Price:** retail. **Time Period Covered:** latest 3 months, year ago.

TURKEYS: WHOLE, RAW, FRESH/FROZEN

Source: *Meat Price Report.* **Price Frequency:** weekly. **Units of Measure:** cents per lb. **Type of Price:** price paid to wholesaler. **Time Period Covered:** latest week.

TURMERIC: ALLEPPEY 5%

Source: *Chemical Marketing Reporter.* **Price Frequency:** weekly. **Effective Market(s):** New York. **Units of Measure:** Dollars per lb. **Type of Price:** spot. **Time Period Covered:** latest week.

TURMERIC: ALLEPPEY OVER 6%

Source: *Chemical Marketing Reporter.* **Price Frequency:** weekly. **Effective Market(s):** New York. **Units of Measure:** Dollars per lb. **Type of Price:** spot. **Time Period Covered:** latest week.

TURMERIC: ALLEPPEY, INDIAN

Source: *U. S. Spice Trade.* **Price Frequency:** monthly, annually. **Effective Market(s):** New York. **Units of Measure:** cents per lb. **Type of Price:** spot. **Time Period Covered:** latest 10 years.

TURMERIC: CHINESE

Source: *Prices of Selected Asia/Pacific Products.* **Price Frequency:** monthly. **Effective Market(s):** Tokyo. **Units of Measure:** Japanese yen per kilogram. **Type of Price:** trade high, trade low. **Time Period Covered:** latest month.

Source: *U. S. Spice Trade.* **Price Frequency:** monthly, annually. **Effective Market(s):** New York. **Units of Measure:** cents per lb. **Type of Price:** spot. **Time Period Covered:** latest 5 years.

TURMERIC: INDIAN

Source: *Prices of Selected Asia/Pacific Products.* **Price Frequency:** monthly. **Effective Market(s):** Tokyo. **Units of Measure:** Japanese yen per kilogram. **Type of Price:** trade high, trade low. **Time Period Covered:** latest month.

TURMERIC FINGERS: MADRAS

Source: *Fruit and Tropical Products.* **Price Frequency:** monthly, seasonally. **Effective Market(s):** London. **Units of Measure:** British pounds per tonne. **Type of Price:** month end. **Time Period Covered:** latest 2 years.

Source: *Prices of Selected Asia/Pacific Products.* **Price Frequency:** monthly. **Effective Market(s):** United Kingdom, United Kingdom/North European ports. **Units of Measure:** British pounds per metric ton, dollars per metric ton. **Type of Price:** spot high, spot low. **Time Period Covered:** latest month.

TURNIPS

Source: *Lancaster Farming.* **Price Frequency:** weekly, seasonally. **Effective Market(s):** Pennsylvania. **Units of Measure:** Dollars per bag. **Type of Price:** market. **Time Period Covered:** latest week.

TURNIPS: WHITE

Source: *New Zealand Farmer.* **Price Frequency:** weekly, seasonally. **Effective Market(s):** New Zealand. **Units of Measure:** New Zealand dollars per bag/case. **Time Period Covered:** latest week.

TURPENTINE: GUM

Source: *Journal of Commerce and Commercial.* **Price Frequency:** weekly in Monday issue. **Effective Market(s):** South. **Units of Measure:** Dollars per gallon. **Type of Price:** spot. **Time Period Covered:** latest week.

TURPENTINE: STEAMED, DISTILLED

Source: *Journal of Commerce and Commercial.* **Price Frequency:** weekly in Monday issue. **Effective Market(s):** South. **Units of Measure:** Dollars per gallon. **Type of Price:** spot. **Time Period Covered:** latest week.

TURPENTINE SULFATE: CRUDE

Source: *Chemical Marketing Reporter.* **Price Frequency:** weekly. **Effective Market(s):** Southeast. **Units of Measure:** Dollars per gallon. **Type of Price:** spot. **Time Period Covered:** latest week.

Source: *Journal of Commerce and Commercial.* **Price Frequency:** weekly in Monday issue. **Effective Market(s):** South. **Units of Measure:** Dollars per gallon. **Type of Price:** spot. **Time Period Covered:** latest week.

TWILL FABRIC

Source: *JTN: The International Textile Magazine.* **Price Frequency:** monthly. **Effective Market(s):** Japan. **Units of Measure:** Japanese yen per meter. **Type of Price:** spot. **Time Period Covered:** latest month.

TWILLS: POLYESTER/RAYON

Source: *DNR: Daily News Record.* **Price Frequency:** quarterly. **Units of Measure:** Dollars per yard. **Type of Price:** spot. **Time Period Covered:** latest 3 quarters.

UGLIFRUIT

Source: *New Zealand Farmer.* **Price Frequency:** weekly, seasonally. **Effective Market(s):** New Zealand. **Units of Measure:** New Zealand dollars per case. **Time Period Covered:** latest week.

UKU (FISH)

see Snapper: Grey.

ULTRAMARINE BLUE PIGMENTS

Source: *Chemical Marketing Reporter.* **Price Frequency:** weekly. **Effective Market(s):** New York. **Units of Measure:** Dollars per lb. **Type of Price:** spot. **Time Period Covered:** latest week.

Source: *Journal of Commerce and Commercial.* **Price Frequency:** weekly in Wednesday issue. **Units of Measure:** Dollars per lb. **Type of Price:** spot. **Time Period Covered:** latest week.

ULTRAMARINE VIOLET PIGMENTS

Source: *Chemical Marketing Reporter.* **Price Frequency:** weekly. **Effective Market(s):** New York. **Units of Measure:** Dollars per lb. **Type of Price:** spot. **Time Period Covered:** latest week.

UMBER PIGMENT: BURNT, AMERICAN

Source: *Chemical Marketing Reporter.* **Price Frequency:** weekly. **Effective Market(s):** New York. **Units of Measure:** Dollars per lb. **Type of Price:** spot. **Time Period Covered:** latest week.

UMBER PIGMENT: BURNT, NATURAL, BROWN

Source: *Journal of Commerce and Commercial.* **Price Frequency:** weekly in Wednesday issue. **Units of Measure:** Dollars per lb. **Type of Price:** spot. **Time Period Covered:** latest week.

UMBER PIGMENT: RAW, AMERICAN

Source: *Chemical Marketing Reporter.* **Price Frequency:** weekly. **Effective Market(s):** New York. **Units of Measure:** Dollars per lb. **Type of Price:** spot. **Time Period Covered:** latest week.

UMBER PIGMENT: RAW, NATURAL, BROWN

Source: *Journal of Commerce and Commercial.* **Price Frequency:** weekly in Wednesday issue. **Units of Measure:** Dollars per lb. **Type of Price:** spot. **Time Period Covered:** latest week.

UNDECYLENIC ACID

Source: *Chemical Marketing Reporter.* **Price Frequency:** weekly. **Effective Market(s):** New York. **Units of Measure:** Dollars per lb. **Type of Price:** spot. **Time Period Covered:** latest week.

UNITED ARAB EMIRATES DIRHAM

Source: *Barron's.* **Price Frequency:** weekly. **Effective Market(s):** New York. **Units of Measure:** United Arab Emirates dirham per United States dollar. **Type of Price:** foreign exchange. **Time Period Covered:** latest 2 weeks.

Source: *New York Times.* **Price Frequency:** daily. **Effective Market(s):** New York. **Units of Measure:** United Arab Emirates dirham per United States dollar. **Type of Price:** foreign exchange. **Time Period Covered:** latest 2 days.

Source: *The Times.* **Price Frequency:** daily. **Effective Market(s):** London. **Units of Measure:** United Arab Emirates dirham per British pound. **Type of Price:** foreign exchange. **Time Period Covered:** latest day.

UNITED KINGDOM POUNDS

see Great Britain Pounds Sterling.

UNITED STATES DOLLARS

Source: *American Metal Market.* **Price Frequency:** daily. **Effective Market(s):** New York. **Units of Measure:** United States dollars per 8 national currencies. **Type of Price:** foreign exchange. **Time Period Covered:** latest day.

Source: *Asian Wall Street Journal.* **Price Frequency:** daily. **Effective Market(s):** United States. **Units of Measure:** United States dollars per ECU, per SDR. **Type of Price:** foreign exchange. **Time Period Covered:** latest 2 days.

Source: *Barron's.* **Price Frequency:** weekly. **Effective Market(s):** New York. **Units of Measure:** United States dollars per 49 national currencies, per ECU, per SDR. **Type of Price:** foreign exchange. **Time Period Covered:** latest 2 weeks.

Source: *The Economist.* **Price Frequency:** weekly. **Effective Market(s):** London. **Units of Measure:** United States dollars per British pound, per ECU, per SDR. **Type of Price:** foreign exchange. **Time Period Covered:** latest week, year ago.

Source: *Energy Prices and Taxes.* **Price Frequency:** annually. **Units of Measure:** United States dollars per 22 national currencies. **Type of Price:** foreign exchange. **Time Period Covered:** latest 8 years.

Source: *Far Eastern Economic Review.* **Price Frequency:** weekly. **Units of Measure:** United States dollars per 7 national currencies. **Type of Price:** spot foreign exchange. **Time Period Covered:** latest week.

Source: *Monthly Commodity Price Bulletin.* **Price Frequency:** monthly. **Units of Measure:** Dollars per SDR. **Type of Price:** foreign exchange. **Time Period Covered:** latest 5 years.

Source: *Monthly Commodity Price Bulletin.* **Price Frequency:** monthly, annually. **Units of Measure:** Dollars per British pounds. **Type of Price:** foreign exchange. **Time Period Covered:** latest 5 years.

Source: *Monthly Commodity Price Bulletin Supplement.* **Price Frequency:** monthly, quarterly, annually. **Units of Measure:** Dollars per SDR. **Type of Price:** foreign exchange. **Time Period Covered:** latest 20 years.

Source: *Monthly Commodity Price Bulletin Supplement.* **Price Frequency:** monthly, quarterly, annually. **Units of Measure:** Dollars per British pound. **Type of Price:** foreign exchange. **Time Period Covered:** latest 20 years.

Source: *New York Times.* **Price Frequency:** daily. **Effective Market(s):** New York. **Units of Measure:** United States dollars per 50 national currencies. **Type of Price:** foreign exchange. **Time Period Covered:** latest 2 days.

Source: *Standard & Poor's Statistical Service Current Statistics.* **Price Frequency:** monthly, annually. **Effective Market(s):** New York. **Units of Measure:** United States cents/dollars per British pounds, per Canadian dollars, per French francs, per Japanese yen, per Swiss francs, per West German marks. **Type of Price:** foreign exchange. **Time Period Covered:** latest 3 years.

Source: *The Times.* **Price Frequency:** daily. **Effective Market(s):** London. **Units of Measure:** United States dollars per 18 national currencies. **Type of Price:** spot foreign exchange. **Time Period Covered:** latest day.

URANIUM

Source: *American Metal Market.* **Price Frequency:** daily. **Units of Measure:** Dollars per lb. of U3O8. **Time Period Covered:** latest day.

Source: *E&MJ.* **Price Frequency:** monthly. **Units of Measure:** Dollars per lb. **Time Period Covered:** latest month.

Source: *Energy Statistics.* **Price Frequency:** annually. **Effective Market(s):** United States. **Units of Measure:** Dollars per lb. U3O8. **Type of Price:** delivered, import. **Time Period Covered:** latest 9 years.

Source: *Northern Miner.* **Price Frequency:** weekly. **Units of Measure:** Dollars per lb. U3O8. **Type of Price:** producer. **Time Period Covered:** latest week.

UREA

Source: *Commodity Trade and Price Trends.* **Price Frequency:** annually. **Effective Market(s):** Europe. **Units of Measure:** Dollars per metric ton, 1980 constant dollars per metric ton. **Time Period Covered:** latest 24 years.

Source: *Feedstuffs.* **Price Frequency:** weekly. **Effective Market(s):** 6 domestic markets. **Units of Measure:** Dollars per bulk ton. **Time Period Covered:** latest week.

Source: *International Financial Statistics.* **Price Frequency:** monthly, quarterly, annually. **Effective Market(s):** Europe. **Units of Measure:** Dollars per metric ton, index. **Type of Price:** market price, price index. **Time Period Covered:** latest 5 months, latest 5 quarters, latest 5 years.

Source: *International Financial Statistics Yearbook.* **Price Frequency:** annually. **Effective Market(s):** Europe. **Units of Measure:** Dollars per metric ton. **Type of Price:** wholesale. **Time Period Covered:** latest 30 years.

UREA: 42% NITROGEN

Source: *Feed Situation and Outlook Report.* **Price Frequency:** monthly. **Effective Market(s):** Fort Worth (TX). **Units of Measure:** Dollars per ton. **Type of Price:** wholesale. **Time Period Covered:** latest 8 months.

UREA: 44-46% NITROGEN

Source: *Agricultural Prices.* **Price Frequency:** monthly. **Effective Market(s):** 9 domestic markets, United States. **Units of Measure:** Dollars per ton. **Type of Price:** paid by farmer. **Time Period Covered:** latest month.

Source: *Agricultural Prices Annual Summary.* **Price Frequency:** semiannually. **Effective Market(s):** 8 domestic markets, United States. **Units of Measure:** Dollars per ton. **Type of Price:** average paid by farmer. **Time Period Covered:** latest year, for US latest 6 years.

UREA: 46% NITROGEN, AGRICULTURAL GRADE, GRANULAR

Source: *Chemical Marketing Reporter.* **Price Frequency:** weekly. **Effective Market(s):** Gulf Coast, Midwest. **Units of Measure:** Dollars per ton. **Type of Price:** spot. **Time Period Covered:** latest week.

UREA: 46% NITROGEN, AGRICULTURAL GRADE, PRILLED

Source: *Journal of Commerce and Commercial.* **Price Frequency:** weekly in Thursday issue. **Effective Market(s):** Louisiana. **Units of Measure:** Dollars per ton. **Type of Price:** spot. **Time Period Covered:** latest week.

UREA: 46% NITROGEN, INDUSTRIAL GRADE

Source: *Chemical Marketing Reporter.* **Price Frequency:** weekly. **Effective Market(s):** Gulf Coast. **Units of Measure:** Dollars per ton. **Type of Price:** spot. **Time Period Covered:** latest week.

Source: *Journal of Commerce and Commercial.* **Price Frequency:** weekly in Thursday issue. **Units of Measure:** Dollars per ton. **Type of Price:** spot. **Time Period Covered:** latest week.

UREA FORMALDELHYDE

Source: *Journal of Commerce and Commercial.* **Price Frequency:** weekly in Tuesday issue. **Units of Measure:** Dollars per lb. **Type of Price:** spot. **Time Period Covered:** latest week.

UREA MOLDING COMPOUND: BLACK AND BROWN

Source: *Plastics Technology.* **Price Frequency:** monthly. **Units of Measure:** cents per lb., cents per cubic inch. **Type of Price:** bulk list, market. **Time Period Covered:** latest month.

UREA MOLDING COMPOUND: WHITE AND IVORY

Source: *Plastics Technology.* **Price Frequency:** monthly. **Units of Measure:** cents per lb., cents per cubic inch. **Type of Price:** bulk list, market. **Time Period Covered:** latest month.

URUGUAY PESOS

Source: *Barron's.* **Price Frequency:** weekly. **Effective Market(s):** New York. **Units of Measure:** Uruguay pesos per United States dollar. **Type of Price:** financial foreign exchange rate. **Time Period Covered:** latest 2 weeks.

Source: *New York Times.* **Price Frequency:** daily. **Effective Market(s):** New York. **Units of Measure:** Uruguay pesos per United States dollar. **Type of Price:** financial foreign exchange rate. **Time Period Covered:** latest 2 days.

UVA URSI LEAVES

Source: *Chemical Marketing Reporter.* **Price Frequency:** weekly. **Effective Market(s):** New York. **Units of Measure:** Dollars per lb. **Type of Price:** spot. **Time Period Covered:** latest week.

Source: *Journal of Commerce and Commercial.* **Price Frequency:** weekly in Monday issue. **Units of Measure:** Dollars per lb. **Type of Price:** spot. **Time Period Covered:** latest week.

VALERIAN ROOT

Source: *Journal of Commerce and Commercial.* **Price Frequency:** weekly in Monday issue. **Units of Measure:** Dollars per lb. **Type of Price:** spot. **Time Period Covered:** latest week.

VALERIAN ROOT: BELGIAN

Source: *Chemical Marketing Reporter.* **Price Frequency:** weekly. **Effective Market(s):** New York. **Units of Measure:** Dollars per lb. **Type of Price:** spot. **Time Period Covered:** latest week.

VALERIAN ROOT: INDIAN

Source: *Chemical Marketing Reporter.* **Price Frequency:** weekly. **Effective Market(s):** New York. **Units of Measure:** Dollars per lb. **Type of Price:** spot. **Time Period Covered:** latest week.

VANADIUM

Source: *Iron Age.* **Price Frequency:** monthly. **Units of Measure:** Dollars per lb. **Type of Price:** consumer. **Time Period Covered:** latest month.

VANADIUM OXYTRICHLORIDE

Source: *Chemical Marketing Reporter.* **Price Frequency:** weekly. **Effective Market(s):** New York. **Units of Measure:** Dollars per lb. **Type of Price:** spot. **Time Period Covered:** latest week.

VANADIUM PENTOXIDE

Source: *Commodity Year Book.* **Price Frequency:** annually. **Effective Market(s):** United States. **Units of Measure:** Dollars per lb. **Time Period Covered:** latest 7 years.

VANADIUM PENTOXIDE: FUSED OR FLAKE

Source: *Chemical Marketing Reporter.* **Price Frequency:** weekly. **Effective Market(s):** New York. **Units of Measure:** Dollars per lb. **Type of Price:** spot. **Time Period Covered:** latest week.

VANADIUM PENTOXIDE: HIGH PURITY

Source: *American Metal Market.* **Price Frequency:** weekly. **Units of Measure:** Dollars per lb. **Type of Price:** producer. **Time Period Covered:** latest week.

VANADIUM PENTOXIDE: TECHNICAL, FUSED OR FLAKE

Source: *American Metal Market.* **Price Frequency:** weekly. **Units of Measure:** Dollars per lb. **Type of Price:** producer. **Time Period Covered:** latest week.

VANADIUM PENTOXIDE: TECHNICAL, GRANULAR

Source: *American Metal Market.* **Price Frequency:** weekly. **Units of Measure:** Dollars per lb. **Type of Price:** producer. **Time Period Covered:** latest week.

Source: *Chemical Marketing Reporter.* **Price Frequency:** weekly. **Effective Market(s):** New York. **Units of Measure:** Dollars per lb. **Type of Price:** spot. **Time Period Covered:** latest week.

VANDYKE BROWN

Source: *Chemical Marketing Reporter.* **Price Frequency:** weekly. **Effective Market(s):** New York. **Units of Measure:** Dollars per lb. **Type of Price:** spot. **Time Period Covered:** latest week.

Source: *Journal of Commerce and Commercial.* **Price Frequency:** weekly in Wednesday issue. **Units of Measure:** Dollars per lb. **Type of Price:** spot. **Time Period Covered:** latest week.

VANILLA BEANS: JAVANESE

Source: *Chemical Marketing Reporter.* **Price Frequency:** weekly. **Effective Market(s):** New York. **Units of Measure:** Dollars per lb. **Type of Price:** spot. **Time Period Covered:** latest week.

Source: *Journal of Commerce and Commercial.* **Price Frequency:** weekly in Monday issue. **Units of Measure:** Dollars per lb. **Type of Price:** spot. **Time Period Covered:** latest week.

Source: *U. S. Spice Trade.* **Price Frequency:** annually. **Effective Market(s):** New York. **Units of Measure:** cents per lb. **Type of Price:** spot. **Time Period Covered:** latest 3 years.

VANILLA BEANS: MADAGASCAR

Source: *Chemical Marketing Reporter.* **Price Frequency:** weekly. **Effective Market(s):** New York. **Units of Measure:** Dollars per lb. **Type of Price:** spot. **Time Period Covered:** latest week.

Source: *Journal of Commerce and Commercial.* **Price Frequency:** weekly in Monday issue. **Units of Measure:** Dollars per lb. **Type of Price:** spot. **Time Period Covered:** latest week.

Source: *U. S. Spice Trade.* **Price Frequency:** annually. **Effective Market(s):** New York. **Units of Measure:** cents per lb. **Type of Price:** spot. **Time Period Covered:** latest 3 years.

VANILLIN: IMPORTED

Source: *Chemical Marketing Reporter.* **Price Frequency:** weekly. **Effective Market(s):** New York. **Units of Measure:** Dollars per lb. **Type of Price:** spot. **Time Period Covered:** latest week.

VANILLIN: USP

Source: *Chemical Marketing Reporter.* **Price Frequency:** weekly. **Effective Market(s):** New York. **Units of Measure:** Dollars per lb. **Type of Price:** spot. **Time Period Covered:** latest week.

Source: *Journal of Commerce and Commercial.* **Price Frequency:** weekly in Monday issue. **Units of Measure:** Dollars per ounce. **Type of Price:** spot. **Time Period Covered:** latest week.

VARNISH GUM: BATU, EAST INDIAN

Source: *Journal of Commerce and Commercial.* **Price Frequency:** weekly in Wednesday issue. **Units of Measure:** Dollars per lb. **Type of Price:** spot. **Time Period Covered:** latest week.

VARNISH GUM: DAMMAR, NO. 1, SINGAPORE

Source: *Journal of Commerce and Commercial.* **Price Frequency:** weekly in Wednesday issue. **Units of Measure:** Dollars per lb. **Type of Price:** spot. **Time Period Covered:** latest week.

VARNISH GUM: DDB, MANILA

Source: *Journal of Commerce and Commercial.* **Price Frequency:** weekly in Wednesday issue. **Units of Measure:** Dollars per lb. **Type of Price:** spot. **Time Period Covered:** latest week.

VARNISH GUM: LOBA C, MANILA

Source: *Journal of Commerce and Commercial.* **Price Frequency:** weekly in Wednesday issue. **Units of Measure:** Dollars per lb. **Type of Price:** spot. **Time Period Covered:** latest week.

VEAL

Source: *Agricultural Outlook.* **Price Frequency:** annually. **Effective Market(s):** United States. **Units of Measure:** Dollars per 100 lbs. **Type of Price:** primary market. **Time Period Covered:** latest 2 years.

VEAL: GROUND

Source: *Meat Price Report.* **Price Frequency:** weekly. **Units of Measure:** cents per lb. **Type of Price:** price paid to wholesaler. **Time Period Covered:** latest week.

VEAL BREAST

Source: *HRI-Buyer's Guide.* **Price Frequency:** weekly. **Effective Market(s):** Northeastern area. **Units of Measure:** Dollars per lb. **Type of Price:** price paid by dining places & institutions. **Time Period Covered:** latest week.

VEAL CALVES

Source: *Lancaster Farming.* **Price Frequency:** weekly. **Effective Market(s):** Pennsylvania, Virginia. **Units of Measure:** Dollars per head. **Type of Price:** auction. **Time Period Covered:** latest week.

Source: *Livestock and Poultry Update.* **Price Frequency:** monthly. **Effective Market(s):** South St. Paul. **Units of Measure:** Dollars per head. **Time Period Covered:** latest 3 months, year ago.

Source: *Survey of Current Business.* **Price Frequency:** monthly, annually. **Effective Market(s):** South St. Paul. **Units of Measure:** Dollars per head. **Time Period Covered:** latest year.

VEAL CALVES: CHOICE

Source: *Livestock and Poultry Situation and Outlook Report.* **Price Frequency:** monthly. **Effective Market(s):** South St. Paul. **Units of Measure:** Dollars per 100 lbs. **Time Period Covered:** latest year.

VEAL CALVES: COMMON TO MEDIUM

Source: *Farm and Dairy.* **Price Frequency:** weekly, seasonally. **Effective Market(s):** Ohio, Pennsylvania. **Units of Measure:** Dollars per head. **Type of Price:** auction high, auction low. **Time Period Covered:** latest week.

VEAL CALVES: CULL

Source: *Farm and Dairy.* **Price Frequency:** weekly, seasonally. **Effective Market(s):** Ohio, Pennsylvania. **Units of Measure:** Dollars per head. **Type of Price:** auction high, auction low. **Time Period Covered:** latest week.

VEAL CALVES: GOOD TO CHOICE

Source: *Farm and Dairy.* **Price Frequency:** weekly, seasonally. **Effective Market(s):** Ohio, Pennsylvania. **Units of Measure:** Dollars per head. **Type of Price:** auction high, auction low. **Time Period Covered:** latest week.

VEAL CALVES: HIGH GOOD TO LOW CHOICE

Source: *Lancaster Farming.* **Price Frequency:** weekly. **Effective Market(s):** Pennsylvania, Virginia. **Units of Measure:** Dollars per head. **Type of Price:** auction. **Time Period Covered:** latest week.

VEAL CALVES: MEDIUM TO GOOD

Source: *Farm and Dairy.* **Price Frequency:** weekly, seasonally. **Effective Market(s):** Ohio, Pennsylvania. **Units of Measure:** Dollars per head. **Type of Price:** auction high, auction low. **Time Period Covered:** latest week.

VEAL CALVES: STANDARD TO LOW GOOD

Source: *Lancaster Farming.* **Price Frequency:** weekly. **Effective Market(s):** Pennsylvania, Virginia. **Units of Measure:** Dollars per head. **Type of Price:** auction. **Time Period Covered:** latest week.

VEAL CARCASS: GOOD AND CHOICE, DRESSED

Source: *Livestock, Meat, Wool Market News.* **Price Frequency:** weekly, seasonally. **Effective Market(s):** California, Central United States, East Coast. **Units of Measure:** Dollars per 100 lbs. **Type of Price:** wholesale. **Time Period Covered:** latest week, year ago.

VEAL CARCASS: PRIME, SPECIAL FED, DRESSED

Source: *Livestock, Meat, Wool Market News.* **Price Frequency:** weekly, seasonally. **Effective Market(s):** California, Central United States, East Coast. **Units of Measure:** Dollars per 100 lbs. **Type of Price:** wholesale. **Time Period Covered:** latest week, year ago.

VEAL CUBED STEAKS

Source: *Meat Price Report.* **Price Frequency:** weekly. **Units of Measure:** cents per lb. **Type of Price:** price paid to wholesaler. **Time Period Covered:** latest week.

VEAL CUBED STEAKS: SPECIAL

Source: *Meat Price Report.* **Price Frequency:** weekly. **Units of Measure:** cents per lb. **Type of Price:** price paid to wholesalers. **Time Period Covered:** latest week.

VEAL FOR STEWING

Source: *HRI-Buyer's Guide.* **Price Frequency:** weekly. **Effective Market(s):** Northeastern area. **Units of Measure:** Dollars per lb. **Type of Price:** price paid by dining places & institutions. **Time Period Covered:** latest week.

Source: *Meat Price Report.* **Price Frequency:** weekly. **Units of Measure:** cents per lb. **Type of Price:** price paid to wholesaler. **Time Period Covered:** latest week.

VEAL FORESHANK

Source: *Meat Price Report.* **Price Frequency:** weekly. **Units of Measure:** cents per lb. **Type of Price:** price paid to wholesaler. **Time Period Covered:** latest week.

VEAL HOTEL RACK

Source: *HRI-Buyer's Guide.* **Price Frequency:** weekly. **Effective Market(s):** Northeastern area. **Units of Measure:** Dollars per lb. **Type of Price:** price paid by dining places & institutions. **Time Period Covered:** latest week.

VEAL HOTEL RACK: 7 RIBS

Source: *Meat Price Report.* **Price Frequency:** weekly. **Units of Measure:** cents per lb. **Type of Price:** price paid to wholesaler. **Time Period Covered:** latest week.

VEAL LEG

Source: *Meat Price Report.* **Price Frequency:** weekly. **Units of Measure:** cents per lb. **Type of Price:** price paid to wholesaler. **Time Period Covered:** latest week.

VEAL LEG: ROAST READY, BONELESS

Source: *Meat Price Report.* **Price Frequency:** weekly. **Units of Measure:** cents per lb. **Type of Price:** price paid to wholesaler. **Time Period Covered:** latest week.

VEAL LEG: SPECIAL FED

Source: *Meat Price Report.* **Price Frequency:** weekly. **Units of Measure:** cents per lb. **Type of Price:** price paid to wholesaler. **Time Period Covered:** latest week.

VEAL LEG CUTLETS

Source: *HRI-Buyer's Guide.* **Price Frequency:** weekly. **Effective Market(s):** Northeastern area. **Units of Measure:** Dollars per lb. **Type of Price:** price paid by dining places & institutions. **Time Period Covered:** latest week.

VEAL LEG CUTLETS: MATURES

Source: *HRI-Buyer's Guide.* **Price Frequency:** weekly. **Effective Market(s):** Northeastern area. **Units of Measure:** Dollars per lb. **Type of Price:** price paid by dining places & institutions. **Time Period Covered:** latest week.

VEAL LEG CUTLETS: SPECIAL, REGULAR OR CUBED

Source: *Meat Price Report.* **Price Frequency:** weekly. **Units of Measure:** cents per lb. **Type of Price:** price paid to wholesalers. **Time Period Covered:** latest week.

VEAL LEGS: MATURES

Source: *HRI-Buyer's Guide.* **Price Frequency:** weekly. **Effective Market(s):** Northeastern area. **Units of Measure:** Dollars per lb. **Type of Price:** price paid by dining places & institutions. **Time Period Covered:** latest week.

VEAL LOIN

Source: *HRI-Buyer's Guide.* **Price Frequency:** weekly. **Effective Market(s):** Northeastern area. **Units of Measure:** Dollars per lb. **Type of Price:** price paid by dining places & institutions. **Time Period Covered:** latest week.

VEAL LOIN: 2 RIBS, TRIMMED

Source: *Meat Price Report.* **Price Frequency:** weekly. **Units of Measure:** cents per lb. **Type of Price:** price paid to wholesaler. **Time Period Covered:** latest week.

VEAL LOIN CHOPS

Source: *Meat Price Report.* **Price Frequency:** weekly. **Units of Measure:** cents per lb. **Type of Price:** price paid to wholesaler. **Time Period Covered:** latest week.

VEAL RIB CHOPS

Source: *Meat Price Report.* **Price Frequency:** weekly. **Units of Measure:** cents per lb. **Type of Price:** price paid to wholesalers. **Time Period Covered:** latest week.

VEAL SHOULDER CLOD

Source: *Meat Price Report.* **Price Frequency:** weekly. **Units of Measure:** cents per lb. **Type of Price:** price paid to wholesaler. **Time Period Covered:** latest week.

VEAL SHOULDER CUTLETS

Source: *HRI-Buyer's Guide.* **Price Frequency:** weekly. **Effective Market(s):** Northeastern area. **Units of Measure:** Dollars per lb. **Type of Price:** price paid by dining places & institutions. **Time Period Covered:** latest week.

VEAL SQUARE CUT CHUCKS: 4 RIBS

Source: *Meat Price Report.* **Price Frequency:** weekly. **Units of Measure:** cents per lb. **Type of Price:** price paid to wholesaler. **Time Period Covered:** latest week.

VEAL SQUARE CUT CHUCKS: 4 RIBS, BONELESS

Source: *Meat Price Report.* **Price Frequency:** weekly. **Units of Measure:** cents per lb. **Type of Price:** price paid to wholesalers. **Time Period Covered:** latest week.

VEAL SWEETBREADS: JUMBO

Source: *HRI-Buyer's Guide.* **Price Frequency:** weekly. **Effective Market(s):** Northeastern area. **Units of Measure:** Dollars per lb. **Type of Price:** price paid by dining places & institutions. **Time Period Covered:** latest week.

VEALERS: CHOICE

Source: *Agricultural Outlook.* **Price Frequency:** monthly, annually. **Effective Market(s):** South St. Paul (MN). **Units of Measure:** Dollars per head. **Type of Price:** market. **Time Period Covered:** monthly latest 6 months, annually latest 3 years.

Source: *Commodity Year Book.* **Price Frequency:** annually. **Effective Market(s):** South St. Paul (MN). **Units of Measure:** Dollars per 100 lbs. **Type of Price:** wholesale. **Time Period Covered:** latest 5 years.

VEGETABLE AND ANIMAL FAT

Source: *Feedstuffs.* **Price Frequency:** weekly. **Effective Market(s):** 7 domestic markets. **Units of Measure:** Dollars per lb. **Time Period Covered:** latest week.

VEGETABLE OILS

Source: *National Provisioner.* **Price Frequency:** daily. **Units of Measure:** cents per lb. **Time Period Covered:** latest week.

VEGETABLE OILSEEDS AND OILS

Source: *Monthly Commodity Price Bulletin Supplement.* **Price Frequency:** monthly, quarterly, annually. **Units of Measure:** index. **Type of Price:** free market price index. **Time Period Covered:** latest 20 years.

Source: *Monthly Commodity Price Bulletin.* **Price Frequency:** monthly, annually. **Effective Market(s):** developing countries. **Units of Measure:** index. **Type of Price:** free market price index. **Time Period Covered:** latest 5 years.

Source: *UNCTAD Commodity Yearbook.* **Price Frequency:** annually. **Units of Measure:** index. **Type of Price:** price index. **Time Period Covered:** latest 12 years.

VELVETEEN FABRIC

Source: *JTN: The International Textile Magazine.* **Price Frequency:** monthly. **Effective Market(s):** Japan. **Units of Measure:** Japanese yen per yard. **Type of Price:** spot. **Time Period Covered:** latest month.

VENEER SHEETS: FIR

Source: *Purchasing.* **Price Frequency:** quarterly in January, April, July, October issues. **Units of Measure:** Dollars per 1000 square feet. **Type of Price:** transaction. **Time Period Covered:** latest 5 quarters.

VENEER SHEETS: HARDWOOD

Source: *Timber Mart-South.* **Price Frequency:** quarterly. **Effective Market(s):** United States. **Units of Measure:** Dollars per 1000 board feet. **Type of Price:** stumpage, delivered. **Time Period Covered:** latest quarter.

VENEER SHEETS: LAUAN

Source: *Timber Bulletin.* **Price Frequency:** monthly, annually. **Effective Market(s):** Japan. **Units of Measure:** Japanese yen per cubic meter. **Time Period Covered:** monthly latest 2 years, annually latest 6 years.

VENEER SHEETS: SOFTWOOD

Source: *Timber Mart-South.* **Price Frequency:** quarterly. **Effective Market(s):** United States. **Units of Measure:** Dollars per 1000 board feet. **Type of Price:** stumpage, delivered. **Time Period Covered:** latest quarter.

VENEZUELA BOLIVAR

Source: *Barron's.* **Price Frequency:** weekly. **Effective Market(s):** New York. **Units of Measure:** Venezuelan bolivars per United States dollar. **Type of Price:** floating foreign exchange rate. **Time Period Covered:** latest 2 weeks.

Source: *New York Times.* **Price Frequency:** daily. **Effective Market(s):** New York. **Units of Measure:** Venezuelan bolivars per United States dollar. **Type of Price:** floating foreign exchange rate. **Time Period Covered:** latest 2 days.

VENISON: AF1/AT

Source: *New Zealand Farmer.* **Price Frequency:** weekly, seasonally. **Effective Market(s):** New Zealand. **Units of Measure:** New Zealand cents per kilogram carcase weight. **Type of Price:** export price. **Time Period Covered:** latest week.

VENISON: AF2

Source: *New Zealand Farmer.* **Price Frequency:** weekly, seasonally. **Effective Market(s):** New Zealand. **Units of Measure:** New Zealand cents per kilogram carcase weight. **Type of Price:** export price. **Time Period Covered:** latest week.

VENISON: AP

Source: *New Zealand Farmer.* **Price Frequency:** weekly, seasonally. **Effective Market(s):** New Zealand. **Units of Measure:** New Zealand cents per kilogram carcase weight. **Type of Price:** export price. **Time Period Covered:** latest week.

VENISON HIND LEG: BONELESS, DESINEWED

Source: *HRI-Buyer's Guide.* **Price Frequency:** weekly. **Effective Market(s):** Northeastern area. **Units of Measure:** Dollars per lb. **Type of Price:** price paid by dining places & institutions. **Time Period Covered:** latest week.

Source: *Urner Barry's Price-Current, West Coast Edition.* **Price Frequency:** semiweekly. **Effective Market(s):** West Coast. **Units of Measure:** Dollars per lb. **Time Period Covered:** latest day.

VENISON HIND LEG: BONELESS, DESINEWED, IMPORTED

Source: *Urner Barry's Price-Current.* **Price Frequency:** daily. **Units of Measure:** cents per lb. **Type of Price:** wholesale. **Time Period Covered:** latest day.

VENISON HINDS: IMPORTED

Source: *HRI-Buyer's Guide.* **Price Frequency:** weekly. **Effective Market(s):** Northeastern area. **Units of Measure:** Dollars per lb. **Type of Price:** price paid by dining places & institutions. **Time Period Covered:** latest week.

Source: *Urner Barry's Price-Current.* **Price Frequency:** daily. **Units of Measure:** cents per lb. **Type of Price:** wholesale. **Time Period Covered:** latest day.

Source: *Urner Barry's Price-Current, West Coast Edition.* **Price Frequency:** semiweekly. **Effective Market(s):** West Coast. **Units of Measure:** Dollars per lb. **Type of Price:** watest day.

VENISON SADDLES: IMPORTED

Source: *HRI-Buyer's Guide.* **Price Frequency:** weekly. **Effective Market(s):** Northeastern area. **Units of Measure:** Dollars per lb. **Type of Price:** price paid by dining places & institutions. **Time Period Covered:** latest week.

Source: *Urner Barry's Price-Current.* **Price Frequency:** daily. **Units of Measure:** cents per lb. **Type of Price:** wholesale. **Time Period Covered:** latest day.

Source: *Urner Barry's Price-Current, West Coast Edition.* **Price Frequency:** semiweekly. **Effective Market(s):** West Coast. **Units of Measure:** Dollars per lb. **Time Period Covered:** latest day.

VERMICULITE: CRUDE, SOUTH AFRICAN

Source: *Industrial Minerals.* **Price Frequency:** monthly. **Effective Market(s):** Gulf Coast. **Units of Measure:** Dollars per short ton. **Type of Price:** producer & dealer. **Time Period Covered:** latest month.

VERMICULITE: RAW, UNITED STATES

Source: *Industrial Minerals.* **Price Frequency:** monthly. **Effective Market(s):** United States. **Units of Measure:** Dollars per short ton. **Type of Price:** producer & dealer. **Time Period Covered:** latest month.

VERMICULITE: SOUTH AFRICAN

Source: *Industrial Minerals.* **Price Frequency:** monthly. **Effective Market(s):** Rotterdam. **Units of Measure:** Dollars per short ton. **Type of Price:** producer & dealer. **Time Period Covered:** latest month.

VERMOUTH

Source: *Beverage Media.* **Price Frequency:** monthly. **Effective Market(s):** New York. **Units of Measure:** Dollars per unit. **Type of Price:** wholesale by brand. **Time Period Covered:** latest month.

Source: *Colorado Beverage Analyst.* **Price Frequency:** monthly. **Effective Market(s):** Colorado. **Units of Measure:** Dollars per case. **Type of Price:** wholesale by brand. **Time Period Covered:** latest month.

Source: *Illinois Beverage Journal.* **Price Frequency:** monthly. **Effective Market(s):** Illinois. **Units of Measure:** Dollars per case. **Type of Price:** wholesale by brand. **Time Period Covered:** latest month.

Source: *Indiana Beverage Journal.* **Price Frequency:** monthly. **Effective Market(s):** Indiana. **Units of Measure:** Dollars per case, dollars per bottle. **Type of Price:** wholesale by brand. **Time Period Covered:** latest month.

Source: *Nevada Beverage Index.* **Price Frequency:** monthly. **Effective Market(s):** Nevada. **Units of Measure:** Dollars per unit. **Type of Price:** wholesale by brand. **Time Period Covered:** latest month.

Source: *Rhode Island Beverage Journal.* **Price Frequency:** monthly. **Effective Market(s):** Rhode Island. **Units of Measure:** Dollars per unit. **Type of Price:** wholesale by brand. **Time Period Covered:** latest month.

VETIVER OIL

Source: *U. S. Essential Oil Trade.* **Price Frequency:** annually. **Effective Market(s):** United States. **Units of Measure:** Dollars per kilogram. **Type of Price:** import value. **Time Period Covered:** latest 3 years.

VETIVER OIL: BOURBON

Source: *Chemical Marketing Reporter.* **Price Frequency:** weekly. **Effective Market(s):** New York. **Units of Measure:** Dollars per lb. **Type of Price:** spot. **Time Period Covered:** latest week.

VETIVER OIL: CHINESE

Source: *Chemical Marketing Reporter.* **Price Frequency:** weekly. **Effective Market(s):** New York. **Units of Measure:** Dollars per lb. **Type of Price:** spot. **Time Period Covered:** latest week.

VETIVER OIL: HAITIAN

Source: *Chemical Marketing Reporter.* **Price Frequency:** weekly. **Effective Market(s):** New York. **Units of Measure:** Dollars per lb. **Type of Price:** spot. **Time Period Covered:** latest week.

VETIVER OIL: JAVANESE

Source: *Chemical Marketing Reporter.* **Price Frequency:** weekly. **Effective Market(s):** New York. **Units of Measure:** Dollars per lb. **Type of Price:** spot. **Time Period Covered:** latest week.

Source: *Journal of Commerce and Commercial.* **Price Frequency:** weekly in Tuesday issue. **Units of Measure:** Dollars per lb. **Type of Price:** spot. **Time Period Covered:** latest week.

VETIVERYL ACETATE

Source: *Chemical Marketing Reporter.* **Price Frequency:** weekly. **Effective Market(s):** New York. **Units of Measure:** Dollars per kilo. **Type of Price:** spot. **Time Period Covered:** latest week.

VICTORIA BLUE TONERS: MOLYBDATED

Source: *Chemical Marketing Reporter.* **Price Frequency:** weekly. **Effective Market(s):** New York. **Units of Measure:** Dollars per lb. **Type of Price:** spot. **Time Period Covered:** latest week.

VICTORIA BLUE TONERS: TUNGSTATED

Source: *Chemical Marketing Reporter.* **Price Frequency:** weekly. **Effective Market(s):** New York. **Units of Measure:** Dollars per lb. **Type of Price:** spot. **Time Period Covered:** latest week.

VINYL ACETATE MONOMER

Source: *Chemical Marketing Reporter.* **Price Frequency:** weekly. **Effective Market(s):** New York. **Units of Measure:** Dollars per lb. **Type of Price:** spot. **Time Period Covered:** latest week.

Source: *Japan Economic Journal.* **Price Frequency:** weekly. **Effective Market(s):** Tokyo. **Units of Measure:** Japanese yen per kilogram. **Type of Price:** market. **Time Period Covered:** latest 2 weeks.

Source: *Journal of Commerce and Commercial.* **Price Frequency:** weekly in Tuesday issue. **Units of Measure:** Dollars per lb. **Type of Price:** spot. **Time Period Covered:** latest week.

VINYL CHLORIDE MONOMER

Source: *Chemical Marketing Reporter.* **Price Frequency:** weekly. **Effective Market(s):** New York. **Units of Measure:** Dollars per lb. **Type of Price:** spot. **Time Period Covered:** latest week.

Source: *Journal of Commerce and Commercial.* **Price Frequency:** weekly in Thursday issue. **Units of Measure:** Dollars per lb. **Type of Price:** spot. **Time Period Covered:** latest week.

Source: *Modern Plastics.* **Price Frequency:** quarterly every January, April, July, October. **Units of Measure:** cents per lb. **Type of Price:** market. **Time Period Covered:** latest 3 years.

Source: *Purchasing.* **Price Frequency:** quarterly in January, April, July, October issues. **Units of Measure:** cents per lb. **Type of Price:** transaction. **Time Period Covered:** latest 5 quarters.

VINYL ESTER: CORROSION RESISTANT

Source: *Plastics Technology.* **Price Frequency:** monthly. **Units of Measure:** cents per lb. **Type of Price:** bulk list, market. **Time Period Covered:** latest month.

VINYL ESTER: HEAT AND CORROSION RESISTANT

Source: *Plastics Technology.* **Price Frequency:** monthly. **Units of Measure:** cents per lb. **Type of Price:** bulk list, market. **Time Period Covered:** latest month.

2-VINYLPYRIDINE

Source: *Chemical Marketing Reporter.* **Price Frequency:** weekly. **Effective Market(s):** New York. **Units of Measure:** Dollars per kilo. **Type of Price:** spot. **Time Period Covered:** latest week.

VINYLTOLUENE

Source: *Chemical Marketing Reporter.* **Price Frequency:** weekly. **Effective Market(s):** New York. **Units of Measure:** Dollars per lb. **Type of Price:** spot. **Time Period Covered:** latest week.

VINYON STAPLE

Source: *Journal of Commerce and Commercial.* **Price Frequency:** weekly in Tuesday issue. **Units of Measure:** Dollars per lb. **Type of Price:** spot. **Time Period Covered:** latest week.

VIOLET METHYL TONER
see Methyl Violet Toner.

VIOLET TONER: BLUE

Source: *Journal of Commerce and Commercial.* **Price Frequency:** weekly in Wednesday issue. **Units of Measure:** Dollars per lb. **Type of Price:** spot. **Time Period Covered:** latest week.

VITAMIN A

Source: *Journal of Commerce and Commercial.* **Price Frequency:** weekly in Friday issue. **Units of Measure:** Dollars per kilo. **Type of Price:** spot. **Time Period Covered:** latest week.

VITAMIN A: FEED GRADE

Source: *Chemical Marketing Reporter.* **Price Frequency:** weekly. **Effective Market(s):** New York. **Units of Measure:** Dollars per kilo. **Type of Price:** spot. **Time Period Covered:** latest week.

VITAMIN A: LIQUID IN OIL

Source: *Chemical Marketing Reporter.* **Price Frequency:** weekly. **Effective Market(s):** New York. **Units of Measure:** Dollars per kilo. **Type of Price:** spot. **Time Period Covered:** latest week.

VITAMIN A: SYNTHETIC, DRY, PHARMACEUTICAL

Source: *Chemical Marketing Reporter.* **Price Frequency:** weekly. **Effective Market(s):** New York. **Units of Measure:** Dollars per kilo. **Type of Price:** spot. **Time Period Covered:** latest week.

VITAMIN B1
see Thiamine Hydrochloride.

VITAMIN B2: USP

Source: *Journal of Commerce and Commercial.* **Price Frequency:** weekly in Friday issue. **Units of Measure:** Dollars per kilo. **Type of Price:** spot. **Time Period Covered:** latest week.

VITAMIN B5: USP

Source: *Journal of Commerce and Commercial.* **Price Frequency:** weekly in Friday issue. **Units of Measure:** Dollars per kilo. **Type of Price:** spot. **Time Period Covered:** latest week.

VITAMIN B6

Source: *Journal of Commerce and Commercial.* **Price Frequency:** weekly in Friday issue. **Units of Measure:** Dollars per kilo. **Type of Price:** spot. **Time Period Covered:** latest week.

VITAMIN B12
see also Riboflavin, Yeast.

Source: *Chemical Marketing Reporter.* **Price Frequency:** weekly. **Effective Market(s):** New York. **Units of Measure:** Dollars per gram, dollars per kilo. **Type of Price:** spot. **Time Period Covered:** latest week.

Source: *Journal of Commerce and Commercial.* **Price Frequency:** weekly in Friday issue. **Units of Measure:** Dollars per kilo. **Type of Price:** spot. **Time Period Covered:** latest week.

VITAMIN C
see Ascorbic Acid.

VITAMIN D
see Cholecalciferol.

VITAMIN D2
see Codliver Oil.

VITAMIN D3

Source: *Journal of Commerce and Commercial.* **Price Frequency:** weekly in Friday issue. **Units of Measure:** Dollars per kilo. **Type of Price:** spot. **Time Period Covered:** latest week.

VITAMIN E
see a-Tocopherol, Wheat Germ Oil.

VITAMIN H
see Biotin.

VODKA

Source: *Beverage Media.* **Price Frequency:** monthly. **Effective Market(s):** New York. **Units of Measure:** Dollars per unit. **Type of Price:** wholesale by brand. **Time Period Covered:** latest month.

Source: *Colorado Beverage Analyst.* **Price Frequency:** monthly. **Effective Market(s):** Colorado. **Units of Measure:** Dollars per case. **Type of Price:** wholesale by brand. **Time Period Covered:** latest month.

Source: *Illinois Beverage Journal.* **Price Frequency:** monthly. **Effective Market(s):** Illinois. **Units of Measure:** Dollars per case. **Type of Price:** wholesale by brand. **Time Period Covered:** latest month.

Source: *Indiana Beverage Journal.* **Price Frequency:** monthly. **Effective Market(s):** Indiana. **Units of Measure:** Dollars per case, dollars per bottle. **Type of Price:** wholesale by brand. **Time Period Covered:** latest month.

Source: *Kentucky Beverage Journal.* **Price Frequency:** monthly. **Effective Market(s):** Kentucky. **Units of Measure:** Dollars per bottle, dollars per case. **Type of Price:** wholesale by brand. **Time Period Covered:** latest month.

Source: *Nevada Beverage Index.* **Price Frequency:** monthly. **Effective Market(s):** Nevada. **Units of Measure:** Dollars per unit. **Type of Price:** wholesale by brand. **Time Period Covered:** latest month.

Source: *Rhode Island Beverage Journal.* **Price Frequency:** monthly. **Effective Market(s):** Rhode Island. **Units of Measure:** Dollars per unit. **Type of Price:** wholesale by brand. **Time Period Covered:** latest month.

VODKA: FLAVORED

Source: *Colorado Beverage Analyst.* **Price Frequency:** monthly. **Effective Market(s):** Colorado. **Units of Measure:** Dollars per case. **Type of Price:** wholesale by brand. **Time Period Covered:** latest month.

VOILE CLOTH

Source: *DNR: Daily News Record.* **Price Frequency:** quarterly. **Units of Measure:** Dollars per yard. **Type of Price:** spot. **Time Period Covered:** latest 3 quarters.

WAGON: GRAVITY UNLOAD, BOX AND RUNNING GEAR

Source: *Agricultural Prices.* **Price Frequency:** annually. **Effective Market(s):** United States. **Units of Measure:** Dollars each. **Type of Price:** paid by farmer. **Time Period Covered:** latest year.

Source: *Agricultural Prices Annual Summary.* **Price Frequency:** annually. **Effective Market(s):** United States. **Units of Measure:** Dollars each. **Type of Price:** average paid by farmer. **Time Period Covered:** latest 6 years.

WAGON: RUNNING GEAR, WITHOUT BOX OR TIRES

Source: *Agricultural Prices Annual Summary.* **Price Frequency:** annually. **Effective Market(s):** United States. **Units of Measure:** Dollars each. **Type of Price:** average paid by farmer. **Time Period Covered:** latest 6 years.

WALNUT SAWTIMBER: BLACK

Source: *Timber Mart-South.* **Price Frequency:** quarterly. **Effective Market(s):** Arkansas, Kentucky, United States. **Units of Measure:** Dollars per 1000 board feet. **Type of Price:** bid. **Time Period Covered:** latest quarter.

WALNUTS

Source: *Agricultural Prices Annual Summary.* **Price Frequency:** annually. **Effective Market(s):** California, Hawaii. **Units of Measure:** Dollars per lb. **Type of Price:** average received by farmer. **Time Period Covered:** latest 6 years.

WALNUTS: ENGLISH TYPE, IN SHELL

Source: *Fruit and Tree Nuts Situation and Outlook Yearbook.* **Price Frequency:** annually. **Effective Market(s):** California. **Units of Measure:** Dollars per ton. **Type of Price:** grower. **Time Period Covered:** latest 20 years.

WALNUTS: LIGHT AMBER, BROKEN, INDIAN

Source: *Prices of Selected Asia/Pacific Products.* **Price Frequency:** monthly, seasonally. **Effective Market(s):** United Kingdom/North European ports. **Units of Measure:** British pounds per metric ton. **Type of Price:** high, low. **Time Period Covered:** latest month.

WALNUTS: LIGHT, BROKEN, INDIAN

Source: *Prices of Selected Asia/Pacific Products.* **Price Frequency:** monthly, seasonally. **Effective Market(s):** United Kingdom/North European ports. **Units of Measure:** British pounds per metric ton. **Type of Price:** high, low. **Time Period Covered:** latest month.

WALNUTS: LIGHT, HALVES, INDIAN

Source: *Prices of Selected Asia/Pacific Products.* **Price Frequency:** monthly, seasonally. **Effective Market(s):** United Kingdom/North European ports. **Units of Measure:** British pounds per metric ton. **Type of Price:** high, low. **Time Period Covered:** latest month.

WARFARIN: 0.5%

Source: *Chemical Marketing Reporter.* **Price Frequency:** weekly. **Effective Market(s):** New York, Chicago. **Units of Measure:** Dollars per lb. **Type of Price:** spot. **Time Period Covered:** latest week.

WASTEPAPER: BOXBOARD CUTTINGS

Source: *Pulp & Paper Week.* **Price Frequency:** monthly, usually in last issue of month. **Effective Market(s):** Atlanta, Chicago, New York, San Francisco/Los Angeles. **Units of Measure:** Dollars per short ton. **Type of Price:** purchase. **Time Period Covered:** latest month.

WASTEPAPER: COATED BOOK STOCK

Source: *Pulp & Paper Week.* **Price Frequency:** monthly, usually in last issue of month. **Effective Market(s):** Atlanta, Chicago, New York, San Francisco/Los Angeles. **Units of Measure:** Dollars per short ton. **Type of Price:** purchase. **Time Period Covered:** latest month.

WASTEPAPER: COMPUTER PRINTOUT

Source: *Pulp & Paper Week.* **Price Frequency:** monthly, usually in last issue of month. **Effective Market(s):** Atlanta, Chicago, New York, San Francisco/Los Angeles. **Units of Measure:** Dollars per short ton. **Type of Price:** purchase. **Time Period Covered:** latest month.

WASTEPAPER: CORRUGATED CONTAINERS

Source: *Pulp & Paper Week.* **Price Frequency:** monthly, usually in last issue of month. **Effective Market(s):** Atlanta, Chicago, New York, San Francisco/Los Angeles. **Units of Measure:** Dollars per short ton. **Type of Price:** purchase. **Time Period Covered:** latest month.

WASTEPAPER: DOUBLE-LINED KRAFT CORRUGATED CLIPPINGS, NEW

Source: *Pulp & Paper Week.* **Price Frequency:** monthly, usually in last issue of month. **Effective Market(s):** Atlanta, Chicago, New York, San Francisco/Los Angeles. **Units of Measure:** Dollars per short ton. **Type of Price:** purchase. **Time Period Covered:** latest month.

WASTEPAPER: HARD WHITE ENVELOPE CUTTINGS

Source: *Pulp & Paper Week.* **Price Frequency:** monthly, usually in last issue of month. **Effective Market(s):** Atlanta, Chicago, New York, San Francisco/Los Angeles. **Units of Measure:** Dollars per short ton. **Type of Price:** purchase. **Time Period Covered:** latest month.

WASTEPAPER: HARD WHITE SHAVINGS

Source: *Pulp & Paper Week.* **Price Frequency:** monthly, usually in last issue of month. **Effective Market(s):** Atlanta, Chicago, New York, San Francisco/Los Angeles. **Units of Measure:** Dollars per short ton. **Type of Price:** purchase. **Time Period Covered:** latest month.

WASTEPAPER: MANIFOLD, COLORED LEDGER

Source: *Pulp & Paper Week.* **Price Frequency:** monthly, usually in last issue of month. **Effective Market(s):** Atlanta, Chicago, New York, San Francisco/Los Angeles. **Units of Measure:** Dollars per short ton. **Type of Price:** purchase. **Time Period Covered:** latest month.

WASTEPAPER: MANIFOLD, WHITE LEDGER

Source: *Pulp & Paper Week.* **Price Frequency:** monthly, usually in last issue of month. **Effective Market(s):** Atlanta, Chicago, New York, San Francisco/Los Angeles. **Units of Measure:** Dollars per short ton. **Type of Price:** purchase. **Time Period Covered:** latest month.

WASTEPAPER: MIXED

Source: *Pulp & Paper Week.* **Price Frequency:** monthly, usually in last issue of month. **Effective Market(s):** Atlanta, Chicago, New York, San Francisco/Los Angeles. **Units of Measure:** Dollars per short ton. **Type of Price:** purchase. **Time Period Covered:** latest month.

WASTEPAPER: NEWS

Source: *Pulp & Paper Week.* **Price Frequency:** monthly, usually in last issue of month. **Effective Market(s):** Atlanta, Chicago, New York, San Francisco/Los Angeles. **Units of Measure:** Dollars per short ton. **Type of Price:** purchase. **Time Period Covered:** latest month.

WASTEPAPER: WHITE NEWS BLANKS

Source: *Pulp & Paper Week.* **Price Frequency:** monthly, usually in last issue of month. **Effective Market(s):** Atlanta, Chicago, New York, San Francisco/Los Angeles. **Units of Measure:** Dollars per short ton. **Type of Price:** purchase. **Time Period Covered:** latest month.

WATER HEATER: ELECTRIC

Source: *Agricultural Prices Annual Summary.* **Price Frequency:** semiannually. **Effective Market(s):** United States. **Units of Measure:** Dollars each. **Type of Price:** average paid by farmer. **Time Period Covered:** latest 6 years.

WATER HEATER: GAS

Source: *Agricultural Prices Annual Summary.* **Price Frequency:** semiannually. **Effective Market(s):** United States. **Units of Measure:** Dollars each. **Type of Price:** average paid by farmer. **Time Period Covered:** latest 6 years.

WATER HEATERS: ELECTRIC

Source: *Agricultural Prices.* **Price Frequency:** annually. **Effective Market(s):** United States. **Units of Measure:** Dollars each. **Type of Price:** paid by farmer. **Time Period Covered:** latest year.

WATER HEATERS: GAS

Source: *Agricultural Prices.* **Price Frequency:** annually. **Effective Market(s):** United States. **Units of Measure:** Dollars each. **Type of Price:** paid by farmer. **Time Period Covered:** latest year.

WATER TUBING: COPPER, TYPE L

Source: *ENR.* **Price Frequency:** monthly in second issue of month. **Effective Market(s):** 17 domestic markets, Montreal, Toronto. **Units of Measure:** Dollars per foot. **Type of Price:** spot. **Time Period Covered:** latest month.

WATERCRESS

Source: *Lancaster Farming.* **Price Frequency:** weekly, seasonally. **Effective Market(s):** Pennsylvania. **Units of Measure:** Dollars per carton. **Type of Price:** market. **Time Period Covered:** latest week.

Source: *New Zealand Farmer.* **Price Frequency:** weekly, seasonally. **Effective Market(s):** New Zealand. **Units of Measure:** New Zealand dollars per case. **Time Period Covered:** latest week.

WATERCRESS: FLORIDA

Source: *HRI-Buyer's Guide.* **Price Frequency:** weekly. **Effective Market(s):** Northeastern area. **Units of Measure:** Dollars per 24s bunch. **Type of Price:** price paid by dining places & institutions. **Time Period Covered:** latest week.

WATERMELON: DELAWARE

Source: *Fresh Fruit and Vegetable Prices.* **Price Frequency:** monthly, seasonally. **Effective Market(s):** New York City. **Units of Measure:** Dollars per lb. **Type of Price:** average wholesale price. **Time Period Covered:** latest year.

WATERMELON: FLORIDA

Source: *Fresh Fruit and Vegetable Prices.* **Price Frequency:** monthly, seasonally. **Effective Market(s):** Chicago, New York City. **Units of Measure:** Dollars per lb. **Type of Price:** average wholesale price. **Time Period Covered:** latest year.

WATERMELON: GEORGIA

Source: *Fresh Fruit and Vegetable Prices.* **Price Frequency:** monthly, seasonally. **Effective Market(s):** Chicago. **Units of Measure:** Dollars per lb. **Type of Price:** average wholesale price. **Time Period Covered:** latest year.

WATERMELON: INDIANA

Source: *Fresh Fruit and Vegetable Prices.* **Price Frequency:** monthly, seasonally. **Effective Market(s):** Chicago. **Units of Measure:** Dollars per lb. **Type of Price:** average wholesale price. **Time Period Covered:** latest year.

WATERMELON: MEXICAN

Source: *Fresh Fruit and Vegetable Prices.* **Price Frequency:** monthly, seasonally. **Effective Market(s):** Chicago, New York City. **Units of Measure:** Dollars per carton. **Type of Price:** average wholesale price. **Time Period Covered:** latest year.

WATERMELON: MISSOURI

Source: *Fresh Fruit and Vegetable Prices.* **Price Frequency:** monthly, seasonally. **Effective Market(s):** Chicago. **Units of Measure:** Dollars per lb. **Type of Price:** average wholesale price. **Time Period Covered:** latest year.

WATERMELON: NORTH CAROLINA

Source: *Fresh Fruit and Vegetable Prices.* **Price Frequency:** monthly, seasonally. **Effective Market(s):** New York City. **Units of Measure:** Dollars per lb. **Type of Price:** average wholesale price. **Time Period Covered:** latest year.

WATERMELON: TEXAS

Source: *Fresh Fruit and Vegetable Prices.* **Price Frequency:** monthly, seasonally. **Effective Market(s):** Chicago, New York City. **Units of Measure:** Dollars per carton. **Type of Price:** average wholesale price. **Time Period Covered:** latest year.

Source: *Fresh Fruit and Vegetable Prices.* **Price Frequency:** monthly, seasonally. **Effective Market(s):** Chicago. **Units of Measure:** Dollars per lb. **Type of Price:** average wholesale price. **Time Period Covered:** latest year.

WATERMELONS

Source: *Fresh Fruit and Vegetable Prices.* **Price Frequency:** monthly, seasonally. **Effective Market(s):** Central/Western Arizona, Imperial/Coachella/Palo Verde Valleys (CA). **Units of Measure:** Dollars per lb. **Type of Price:** average price at shipping points. **Time Period Covered:** latest year.

Source: *Fresh Fruit and Vegetable Prices.* **Price Frequency:** monthly, seasonally. **Effective Market(s):** 9 domestic markets. **Units of Measure:** Dollars per 100 lbs. **Type of Price:** average price at shipping point. **Time Period Covered:** latest year.

WATERMELONS: ALLSWEET

Source: *The Packer.* **Price Frequency:** weekly, seasonally. **Effective Market(s):** varies. **Units of Measure:** Dollar per 100 lbs. **Type of Price:** received by farmer. **Time Period Covered:** latest week.

WATERMELONS: CAL SWEET

Source: *California Farmer.* **Price Frequency:** semimonthly, seasonally. **Effective Market(s):** Kern (CA), San Joaquin Valley (CA). **Units of Measure:** cents per lb. **Time Period Covered:** latest week, month ago, year ago.

WATERMELONS: CARIBBEAN, IMPORTED

Source: *Fresh Fruit and Vegetable Prices.* **Price Frequency:** monthly, seasonally. **Effective Market(s):** South Florida. **Units of Measure:** Dollars per lb. **Type of Price:** price paid at point of entry. **Time Period Covered:** latest year.

WATERMELONS: CRIMSON SWEET

Source: *Lancaster Farming.* **Price Frequency:** weekly, seasonally. **Effective Market(s):** Pennsylvania. **Units of Measure:** Dollars per unit. **Type of Price:** market. **Time Period Covered:** latest week.

Source: *The Packer.* **Price Frequency:** weekly, seasonally. **Effective Market(s):** varies. **Units of Measure:** Dollar per 100 lbs. **Type of Price:** received by farmer. **Time Period Covered:** latest week.

WATERMELONS: FLORIDA

Source: *HRI-Buyer's Guide.* **Price Frequency:** weekly. **Effective Market(s):** Northeastern area. **Type of Price:** price paid by dining places & institutions. **Time Period Covered:** latest week.

WATERMELONS: IMPORTED

Source: *New Zealand Farmer.* **Price Frequency:** weekly, seasonally. **Effective Market(s):** New Zealand. **Units of Measure:** New Zealand dollars per kilogram. **Time Period Covered:** latest week.

WATERMELONS: JUBILEE

Source: *Lancaster Farming.* **Price Frequency:** weekly, seasonally. **Effective Market(s):** Pennsylvania. **Units of Measure:** Dollars per unit. **Type of Price:** market. **Time Period Covered:** latest week.

WATERMELONS: LONG GRAY

Source: *The Packer.* **Price Frequency:** weekly, seasonally. **Effective Market(s):** varies. **Units of Measure:** Dollar per 100 lbs. **Type of Price:** received by farmer. **Time Period Covered:** latest week.

WATERMELONS: MEXICAN

Source: *Fresh Fruit and Vegetable Prices.* **Price Frequency:** monthly, seasonally. **Effective Market(s):** Nogales (AZ), South Texas. **Units of Measure:** Dollars per lb. **Type of Price:** price paid at point of entry. **Time Period Covered:** latest year.

WATERMELONS: MIRAGE

Source: *The Packer.* **Price Frequency:** weekly, seasonally. **Effective Market(s):** varies. **Units of Measure:** Dollar per 100 lbs. **Type of Price:** received by farmer. **Time Period Covered:** latest week.

WATERMELONS: PARADISE

Source: *The Packer.* **Price Frequency:** weekly, seasonally. **Effective Market(s):** varies. **Units of Measure:** Dollar per 100 lbs. **Type of Price:** received by farmer. **Time Period Covered:** latest week.

WATERMELONS: PEACOCK

Source: *California Farmer.* **Price Frequency:** semimonthly, seasonally. **Effective Market(s):** Coachella/Imperial District (CA). **Units of Measure:** cents per lb. **Time Period Covered:** latest week, year ago.

WATERMELONS: PICNIC

Source: *The Packer.* **Price Frequency:** weekly, seasonally. **Effective Market(s):** varies. **Units of Measure:** Dollar per 100 lbs. **Type of Price:** received by farmer. **Time Period Covered:** latest week.

WATERMELONS: ROYAL SWEET

Source: *California Farmer.* **Price Frequency:** semimonthly, seasonally. **Effective Market(s):** Kern (CA), San Joaquin Valley (CA). **Units of Measure:** cents per lb. **Time Period Covered:** latest week, month ago, year ago.

Source: *The Packer.* **Price Frequency:** weekly, seasonally. **Effective Market(s):** varies. **Units of Measure:** Dollar per 100 lbs. **Type of Price:** received by farmer. **Time Period Covered:** latest week.

WATERMELONS: ROYAL WINDSOR

Source: *California Farmer.* **Price Frequency:** semimonthly, seasonally. **Effective Market(s):** Imperial/Coachella Valleys. **Units of Measure:** cents per lb. **Time Period Covered:** latest week, year ago.

WATERMELONS: SUGAR BABIES

Source: *Lancaster Farming.* **Price Frequency:** weekly, seasonally. **Effective Market(s):** Pennsylvania. **Units of Measure:** Dollars per lb. **Type of Price:** market. **Time Period Covered:** latest week.

WATERMELONS: YELLOW DOLLS

Source: *Lancaster Farming.* **Price Frequency:** weekly, seasonally. **Effective Market(s):** Pennsylvania. **Units of Measure:** Dollars each. **Type of Price:** market. **Time Period Covered:** latest week.

WAX: BEES

see Beeswax.

WAX: CANDELILLA, CRUDE

Source: *Journal of Commerce and Commercial.* **Price Frequency:** weekly in Monday issue. **Units of Measure:** Dollars per lb. **Type of Price:** spot. **Time Period Covered:** latest week.

WAX: CANDELILLA, REFINED

Source: *Journal of Commerce and Commercial.* **Price Frequency:** weekly in Monday issue. **Units of Measure:** Dollars per lb. **Type of Price:** spot. **Time Period Covered:** latest week.

WAX: CARNAUBA, JAPANESE

Source: *Journal of Commerce and Commercial.* **Price Frequency:** weekly in Monday issue. **Units of Measure:** Dollars per lb. **Type of Price:** spot. **Time Period Covered:** latest week.

WAX: CARNAUBA, NO. 1, YELLOW, PARNAHYBA

Source: *Chemical Marketing Reporter.* **Price Frequency:** weekly. **Effective Market(s):** New York. **Units of Measure:** Dollars per lb. **Type of Price:** spot. **Time Period Covered:** latest week.

WAX: CARNAUBA, NO. 1, YELLOW, REFINED

Source: *Journal of Commerce and Commercial.* **Price Frequency:** weekly in Monday issue. **Units of Measure:** Dollars per lb. **Type of Price:** spot. **Time Period Covered:** latest week.

WAX: CARNAUBA, NO. 2, REFINED

Source: *Chemical Marketing Reporter.* **Price Frequency:** weekly. **Effective Market(s):** New York. **Units of Measure:** Dollars per lb. **Type of Price:** spot. **Time Period Covered:** latest week.

WAX: CARNAUBA, NO. 3, CENTRIFUGED

Source: *Chemical Marketing Reporter.* **Price Frequency:** weekly. **Effective Market(s):** New York. **Units of Measure:** Dollars per lb. **Type of Price:** spot. **Time Period Covered:** latest week.

WAX: CARNAUBA, NO. 3, CRUDE

Source: *Journal of Commerce and Commercial.* **Price Frequency:** weekly in Monday issue. **Units of Measure:** Dollars per lb. **Type of Price:** spot. **Time Period Covered:** latest week.

WAX: CARNAUBA, NO. 3, REFINED

Source: *Chemical Marketing Reporter.* **Price Frequency:** weekly. **Effective Market(s):** New York. **Units of Measure:** Dollars per lb. **Type of Price:** spot. **Time Period Covered:** latest week.

Source: *Journal of Commerce and Commercial.* **Price Frequency:** weekly in Monday issue. **Units of Measure:** Dollars per lb. **Type of Price:** spot. **Time Period Covered:** latest week.

WAX: CARNAUBA, POWDERED, 20 TO 100 MESH

Source: *Chemical Marketing Reporter.* **Price Frequency:** weekly. **Effective Market(s):** New York. **Units of Measure:** Dollars per lb. **Type of Price:** spot. **Time Period Covered:** latest week.

WAX: PARAFFIN, 123-127 DEGREE AMP, CRUDE SCALE

Source: *Journal of Commerce and Commercial.* **Price Frequency:** weekly in Friday issue. **Units of Measure:** Dollars per lb. **Type of Price:** spot. **Time Period Covered:** latest week.

WAX: PARAFFIN, 128/130 DEGREE AMP, LIQUID

Source: *Journal of Commerce and Commercial.* **Price Frequency:** weekly in Friday issue. **Effective Market(s):** Gulf. **Units of Measure:** Dollars per lb. **Type of Price:** spot. **Time Period Covered:** latest week.

WAX: PARAFFIN, 128/130 DEGREE AMP, SLAB

Source: *Journal of Commerce and Commercial.* **Price Frequency:** weekly in Friday issue. **Units of Measure:** Dollars per lb. **Type of Price:** spot. **Time Period Covered:** latest week.

WAX: PARAFFIN, 150 DEGREE AMP, LIQUID

Source: *Journal of Commerce and Commercial.* **Price Frequency:** weekly in Friday issue. **Units of Measure:** Dollars per lb. **Type of Price:** spot. **Time Period Covered:** latest week.

WAX: PARAFFIN, 150 DEGREE AMP, SLAB

Source: *Journal of Commerce and Commercial.* **Price Frequency:** weekly in Friday issue. **Units of Measure:** Dollars per lb. **Type of Price:** spot. **Time Period Covered:** latest week.

WELDER: ACETYLENE

Source: *Agricultural Prices.* **Price Frequency:** annually. **Effective Market(s):** United States. **Units of Measure:** Dollars each. **Type of Price:** paid by farmer. **Time Period Covered:** latest year.

Source: *Agricultural Prices Annual Summary.* **Price Frequency:** semiannually. **Effective Market(s):** United States. **Units of Measure:** Dollars each. **Type of Price:** average paid by farmer. **Time Period Covered:** latest 6 years.

WELL PUMP: SUBMERSIBLE

Source: *Agricultural Prices.* **Price Frequency:** annually. **Effective Market(s):** United States. **Units of Measure:** Dollars each. **Type of Price:** paid by farmer. **Time Period Covered:** latest year.

Source: *Agricultural Prices Annual Summary.* **Price Frequency:** semiannually. **Effective Market(s):** United States. **Units of Measure:** Dollars each. **Type of Price:** average paid by farmer. **Time Period Covered:** latest 6 years.

WEST GERMAN MARKS

Source: *American Metal Market.* **Price Frequency:** daily. **Effective Market(s):** New York. **Units of Measure:** West German marks per United States dollar. **Type of Price:** foreign exchange. **Time Period Covered:** latest day.

Source: *Asian Wall Street Journal.* **Price Frequency:** daily. **Effective Market(s):** United States. **Units of Measure:** West German marks per ECU, per SDR. **Type of Price:** foreign exchange. **Time Period Covered:** latest 2 days.

Source: *Barron's.* **Price Frequency:** weekly. **Effective Market(s):** New York. **Units of Measure:** West German marks per United States dollar. **Type of Price:** foreign exchange. **Time Period Covered:** latest 2 weeks.

Source: *Commodity Year Book.* **Price Frequency:** monthly, annually. **Units of Measure:** West German marks per United States dollar. **Type of Price:** foreign exchange. **Time Period Covered:** latest 5 years.

Source: *The Economist.* **Price Frequency:** weekly. **Effective Market(s):** London. **Units of Measure:** West German marks per British pound, per ECU, per SDR, per United States dollar. **Type of Price:** foreign exchange. **Time Period Covered:** latest week, year ago.

Source: *Monthly Commodity Price Bulletin.* **Price Frequency:** monthly, annually. **Units of Measure:** West German marks per United States dollar. **Type of Price:** foreign exchange. **Time Period Covered:** latest 5 years.

Source: *New York Times.* **Price Frequency:** daily. **Effective Market(s):** New York. **Units of Measure:** West German marks per United States dollar. **Type of Price:** foreign exchange. **Time Period Covered:** latest 2 days.

Source: *Timber Bulletin.* **Price Frequency:** monthly, annually. **Units of Measure:** West German marks per United States dollar. **Type of Price:** foreign exchange. **Time Period Covered:** latest 2 years.

WEST GERMAN MARKS: FUTURES

Source: *Asian Wall Street Journal.* **Price Frequency:** daily. **Effective Market(s):** Chicago. **Units of Measure:** United States dollars per West German mark. **Type of Price:** foreign exchange futures. **Time Period Covered:** latest day.

Source: *Barron's.* **Price Frequency:** weekly. **Effective Market(s):** Chicago. **Units of Measure:** United States dollars per West German mark. **Type of Price:** foreign exchange futures. **Time Period Covered:** latest week.

Source: *Los Angeles Times.* **Price Frequency:** daily. **Effective Market(s):** Chicago. **Units of Measure:** United States dollars per West German mark. **Type of Price:** foreign exchange futures. **Time Period Covered:** latest day.

Source: *New York Times.* **Price Frequency:** daily. **Effective Market(s):** Chicago. **Units of Measure:** United States dollars per West German mark. **Type of Price:** foreign exchange futures. **Time Period Covered:** latest day.

Source: *Urner Barry's Price-Current.* **Price Frequency:** daily. **Units of Measure:** United States dollars per West German mark. **Type of Price:** foreign exchange futures. **Time Period Covered:** latest day.

WESTERN RED CEDAR SAWTIMBER

Source: *Random Lengths.* **Price Frequency:** weekly. **Units of Measure:** Dollars per 1000 board feet. **Type of Price:** price to wholesaler. **Time Period Covered:** latest week.

WHEAT

see also Flour.

Source: *Agra Europe.* **Price Frequency:** weekly. **Effective Market(s):** 9 European markets. **Units of Measure:** national currency per tonne. **Type of Price:** average. **Time Period Covered:** latest week.

Source: *Agricultural Outlook.* **Price Frequency:** annually. **Units of Measure:** Dollars per bushel. **Type of Price:** farm. **Time Period Covered:** latest 6 years.

Source: *Agricultural Outlook.* **Price Frequency:** monthly, annually. **Effective Market(s):** Gulf ports. **Units of Measure:** Dollars per bushel. **Type of Price:** export. **Time Period Covered:** monthly latest 6 months, annually latest 3 years.

Source: *Agricultural Outlook.* **Price Frequency:** monthly, annually. **Effective Market(s):** United States. **Units of Measure:** Dollars per bushel. **Type of Price:** received by farmer. **Time Period Covered:** monthly latest 6 months, annually latest 3 years.

Source: *Agricultural Prices.* **Price Frequency:** monthly, seasonally. **Effective Market(s):** 21 domestic markets, United States. **Units of Measure:** Dollars per bushel. **Type of Price:** received by farmer. **Time Period Covered:** latest 2 months, for US latest 2 years.

Source: *Agricultural Prices Annual Summary.* **Price Frequency:** annually. **Effective Market(s):** 42 domestic markets, United States. **Units of Measure:** Dollars per bushel. **Type of Price:** average received by farmer. **Time Period Covered:** latest 2 years, for US latest 6 years.

Source: *Agricultural Trade Highlights.* **Price Frequency:** weekly. **Effective Market(s):** United States. **Units of Measure:** Dollars per metric ton. **Type of Price:** farm. **Time Period Covered:** latest week, month ago, year ago.

Source: *Agriculture.* **Price Frequency:** weekly. **Effective Market(s):** 8 domestic markets. **Units of Measure:** Dollars per bushel. **Time Period Covered:** latest week, week ago.

Source: *The Brock Report.* **Price Frequency:** weekly. **Effective Market(s):** 5 domestic markets. **Units of Measure:** Dollars per bushel. **Time Period Covered:** latest week, week ago.

Source: *Commodity Year Book.* **Price Frequency:** monthly, annually. **Effective Market(s):** United States. **Units of Measure:** cents per bushel. **Type of Price:** price received by farmers. **Time Period Covered:** latest 6 years.

Source: *Commodity Year Book.* **Price Frequency:** annually. **Effective Market(s):** United States. **Units of Measure:** Dollars per bushel. **Type of Price:** cash price received by farmers. **Time Period Covered:** latest 5 years.

Source: *Far Eastern Economic Review.* **Price Frequency:** weekly. **Effective Market(s):** Chicago. **Units of Measure:** cents per 60 lb. bushel. **Time Period Covered:** latest week, week ago, 3 months ago, year ago.

Source: *Farmers Weekly.* **Price Frequency:** weekly, seasonally. **Effective Market(s):** 10 British markets. **Units of Measure:** British pounds per tonne. **Type of Price:** merchant's buying. **Time Period Covered:** latest week.

Source: *Illinois Farm Report.* **Price Frequency:** monthly. **Effective Market(s):** Illinois. **Units of Measure:** Dollars per bushel. **Type of Price:** average received by farmers. **Time Period Covered:** latest 2 months, year ago.

Source: *International Financial Statistics.* **Price Frequency:** monthly, quarterly, annually. **Effective Market(s):** Gulf ports. **Units of Measure:** Dollars per bushel, index. **Type of Price:** market price, price index. **Time Period Covered:** latest 5 months, latest 5 quarters, latest 5 years.

Source: *International Financial Statistics Yearbook.* **Price Frequency:** annually. **Effective Market(s):** Gulf ports. **Units of Measure:** Dollars per bushel. **Type of Price:** wholesale. **Time Period Covered:** latest 30 years.

Source: *International Wheat Council Market Report.* **Price Frequency:** weekly. **Units of Measure:** index. **Type of Price:** price index. **Time Period Covered:** latest 5 weeks and same time last year.

Source: *Kansas Business Review.* **Price Frequency:** monthly. **Effective Market(s):** Kansas. **Units of Measure:** Dollars per bushel. **Type of Price:** received by farmer. **Time Period Covered:** latest month, month ago, year ago.

Source: *Washington Farmer-Stockman.* **Price Frequency:** monthly. **Effective Market(s):** Washington. **Units of Measure:** Dollars per bushel. **Type of Price:** average received by farmer. **Time Period Covered:** latest month, month ago, year ago.

Source: *Wheat Situation and Outlook Report.* **Price Frequency:** annually. **Effective Market(s):** United States. **Units of Measure:** Dollars per bushel. **Type of Price:** received by farmer. **Time Period Covered:** latest 35 years.

Source: *Wheat Situation and Outlook Report.* **Price Frequency:** monthly, annually. **Effective Market(s):** United States. **Units of Measure:** Dollars per bushel. **Type of Price:** farm. **Time Period Covered:** latest 10 years.

WHEAT: ARGENTINE

Source: *International Financial Statistics.* **Price Frequency:** quarterly, annually. **Effective Market(s):** Argentina. **Units of Measure:** Dollars per bushel, index. **Type of Price:** market price, price index. **Time Period Covered:** latest quarter, latest 4 years.

Source: *International Financial Statistics Yearbook.* **Price Frequency:** annually. **Effective Market(s):** Argentina. **Units of Measure:** Dollars per bushel. **Type of Price:** wholesale. **Time Period Covered:** latest 30 years.

Source: *Wheat Situation and Outlook Report.* **Price Frequency:** monthly, annually. **Effective Market(s):** Buenos Aires. **Units of Measure:** Dollars per bushel. **Time Period Covered:** monthly latest 2 years, annuall latest 8 years.

Source: *World Agriculture Situation and Outlook.* **Price Frequency:** monthly, annually. **Effective Market(s):** Buenos Aires. **Units of Measure:** Dollars per metric ton. **Time Period Covered:** monthly latest year, annually latest 9 years.

Source: *World Grain Situation and Outlook.* **Price Frequency:** weekly, monthly, annually. **Effective Market(s):** Argentina. **Units of Measure:** Dollars per metric ton. **Type of Price:** export. **Time Period Covered:** weekly latest 3 months, monthly latest 3 years, annually latest 7 years.

WHEAT: AUSTRALIAN

Source: *International Financial Statistics.* **Price Frequency:** monthly, quarterly, annually. **Effective Market(s):** Sydney (Australia), Australia. **Units of Measure:** Dollars per bushel, index. **Type of Price:** market price, price index. **Time Period Covered:** latest 3 months, latest 4 quarters, latest 5 years.

Source: *International Financial Statistics Yearbook.* **Price Frequency:** annually. **Effective Market(s):** Sydney (Australia), Australia. **Units of Measure:** Dollars per bushel. **Type of Price:** wholesale. **Time Period Covered:** latest 30 years.

WHEAT: BREAD MILLING

Source: *Scottish Farmer.* **Price Frequency:** monthly, seasonally. **Effective Market(s):** United Kingdom. **Units of Measure:** British pounds per tonne. **Type of Price:** spot. **Time Period Covered:** latest 2 months.

WHEAT: CANADIAN

Source: *International Financial Statistics.* **Price Frequency:** annually. **Effective Market(s):** Canada. **Units of Measure:** Dollars per bushel, index. **Type of Price:** market price, price index. **Time Period Covered:** latest 4 years.

Source: *International Financial Statistics Yearbook.* **Price Frequency:** annually. **Effective Market(s):** Canada. **Units of Measure:** Dollars per bushel. **Type of Price:** wholesale. **Time Period Covered:** latest 30 years.

WHEAT: DARK NORTHERN SPRING, 13% PROTEIN

Source: *Montana Farmer-Stockman.* **Price Frequency:** monthly, seasonally. **Effective Market(s):** 9 Montana markets. **Units of Measure:** Dollars per bushel. **Type of Price:** cash. **Time Period Covered:** latest month.

WHEAT: DARK NORTHERN SPRING, 14% PROTEIN

Source: *Doane's Agricultural Report.* **Price Frequency:** weekly. **Effective Market(s):** Minneapolis. **Units of Measure:** Dollars per bushel. **Time Period Covered:** latest week, week ago, year ago.

Source: *International Wheat Council Report for the Crop Year.* **Price Frequency:** monthly, quarterly, annually. **Effective Market(s):** Lakehead. **Units of Measure:** Dollars per metric ton. **Time Period Covered:** latest year.

Source: *Montana Farmer-Stockman.* **Price Frequency:** monthly, seasonally. **Effective Market(s):** 9 Montana markets. **Units of Measure:** Dollars per bushel. **Type of Price:** cash. **Time Period Covered:** latest month.

WHEAT: DARK NORTHERN SPRING, 15% PROTEIN

Source: *Montana Farmer-Stockman.* **Price Frequency:** monthly, seasonally. **Effective Market(s):** 9 Montana markets. **Units of Measure:** Dollars per bushel. **Type of Price:** cash. **Time Period Covered:** latest month.

WHEAT: DARK NORTHERN SPRING, ORDINARY PROTEIN

Source: *Agricultural Outlook.* **Price Frequency:** monthly, annually. **Effective Market(s):** Minneapolis. **Units of Measure:** Dollars per bushel. **Type of Price:** wholesale. **Time Period Covered:** monthly latest 5 months, annually latest 4 years.

WHEAT: DARK NORTHERN SPRING, UNITED STATES

Source: *Financial Times.* **Price Frequency:** daily. **Effective Market(s):** London. **Units of Measure:** British pounds per tonne. **Type of Price:** spot. **Time Period Covered:** latest day.

WHEAT: DURUM

Source: *Agricultural Prices.* **Price Frequency:** monthly, seasonally. **Effective Market(s):** 6 domestic markets, United States. **Units of Measure:** Dollars per bushel. **Type of Price:** received by farmer. **Time Period Covered:** latest 2 months.

Source: *Agricultural Prices Annual Summary.* **Price Frequency:** annually. **Effective Market(s):** 6 domestic markets, United States. **Units of Measure:** Dollars per bushel. **Type of Price:** average received by farmer. **Time Period Covered:** latest 2 years, for US latest 6 years.

Source: *Montana Farmer-Stockman.* **Price Frequency:** monthly, seasonally. **Effective Market(s):** 9 Montana markets. **Units of Measure:** Dollars per bushel. **Type of Price:** cash. **Time Period Covered:** latest month.

Source: *Montana Farmer-Stockman.* **Price Frequency:** monthly, seasonally. **Effective Market(s):** Minneapolis. **Units of Measure:** Dollars per bushel. **Type of Price:** cash. **Time Period Covered:** latest 2 months.

WHEAT: DURUM, MILLING

Source: *Minneapolis Grain Exchange Statistical Annual.* **Price Frequency:** daily. **Effective Market(s):** Duluth (MN), Minneapolis. **Units of Measure:** cents per bushel. **Type of Price:** cash. **Time Period Covered:** latest year.

WHEAT: FEED

Source: *Farmers Weekly.* **Price Frequency:** weekly. **Effective Market(s):** Great Britain. **Units of Measure:** British pounds per tonne. **Type of Price:** spot. **Time Period Covered:** latest week, week ago, year ago.

Source: *Farmers Weekly.* **Price Frequency:** weekly, seasonally. **Effective Market(s):** 50 British markets. **Units of Measure:** British pounds per tonne. **Type of Price:** farm. **Time Period Covered:** latest week.

Source: *Farmers Weekly.* **Price Frequency:** weekly, seasonally. **Effective Market(s):** 13 British markets. **Units of Measure:** British pounds per tonne. **Type of Price:** spot. **Time Period Covered:** latest week.

Source: *Feedstuffs.* **Price Frequency:** weekly. **Effective Market(s):** Atlanta, Kansas City, Los Angeles, San Francisco. **Units of Measure:** Dollars per bushel, dollars per 100 lbs. **Time Period Covered:** latest week.

Source: *Feedstuffs.* **Price Frequency:** weekly. **Effective Market(s):** Kansas City. **Units of Measure:** Dollars per bushel. **Time Period Covered:** latest week, week ago, 6 months ago, year ago.

Source: *Los Angeles Times.* **Price Frequency:** daily. **Effective Market(s):** Los Angeles. **Units of Measure:** Dollars per 100 lbs. **Type of Price:** spot. **Time Period Covered:** latest day.

Source: *Scottish Farmer.* **Price Frequency:** monthly, seasonally. **Effective Market(s):** 7 Scottish markets, United Kingdom. **Units of Measure:** British pounds per tonne. **Type of Price:** spot. **Time Period Covered:** latest 2 months.

WHEAT: FEED, CANADIAN

Source: *International Wheat Council Market Report.* **Price Frequency:** weekly, seasonally. **Effective Market(s):** St. Lawrence (Canada). **Units of Measure:** Dollars per metric ton. **Type of Price:** export. **Time Period Covered:** latest 5 weeks.

WHEAT: FEED, EUROPEAN COMMUNITY

Source: *World Oilseed Situation and Market Highlights.* **Price Frequency:** monthly, annually. **Effective Market(s):** Rotterdam. **Units of Measure:** Dollars per metric ton, ECU per metric ton. **Type of Price:** reference. **Time Period Covered:** monthly latest 2 months, annually latest 2 years.

WHEAT: FUTURES

Source: *Agriculture.* **Price Frequency:** weekly. **Effective Market(s):** Chicago, Kansas City. **Units of Measure:** cents per bushel. **Type of Price:** futures. **Time Period Covered:** latest week, week ago.

Source: *Asian Wall Street Journal.* **Price Frequency:** daily. **Effective Market(s):** Chicago, Kansas City, Minneapolis, Winnepeg. **Units of Measure:** cents per bushel, Canadian dollars per ton. **Type of Price:** futures. **Time Period Covered:** latest day.

Source: *Bakery Newsletter.* **Price Frequency:** weekly. **Effective Market(s):** Chicago, Kansas City, Minneapolis. **Units of Measure:** Dollars per bushel. **Type of Price:** futures. **Time Period Covered:** latest week, week ago.

Source: *Barron's.* **Price Frequency:** weekly. **Effective Market(s):** Chicago, Kansas City. **Units of Measure:** Dollars per bushel. **Type of Price:** futures. **Time Period Covered:** latest week.

Source: *Far Eastern Economic Review.* **Price Frequency:** weekly. **Effective Market(s):** Chicago. **Units of Measure:** cents per 60 lb. bushel. **Type of Price:** futures. **Time Period Covered:** latest week.

Source: *Farmers Weekly.* **Price Frequency:** weekly. **Effective Market(s):** Baltic Exchange. **Units of Measure:** British pounds per tonne. **Type of Price:** futures. **Time Period Covered:** latest week.

Source: *Feedstuffs.* **Price Frequency:** weekly. **Effective Market(s):** Chicago. **Units of Measure:** cents per bushel. **Type of Price:** futures. **Time Period Covered:** latest week, week ago, latest season.

Source: *Financial Times.* **Price Frequency:** daily. **Effective Market(s):** London. **Units of Measure:** British pounds per tonne. **Type of Price:** futures. **Time Period Covered:** latest day.

Source: *Financial Times.* **Price Frequency:** daily. **Effective Market(s):** Chicago. **Units of Measure:** cents per bushel. **Type of Price:** futures. **Time Period Covered:** latest day.

Source: *Grain and Feed Market News.* **Price Frequency:** weekly. **Effective Market(s):** Chicago, Kansas City, Minneapolis. **Units of Measure:** Dollars per bushel. **Type of Price:** futures. **Time Period Covered:** latest week.

Source: *Investor's Daily.* **Price Frequency:** daily. **Effective Market(s):** Chicago, Kansas City, Minneapolis, Winnepeg. **Units of Measure:** Dollars per bushel. **Type of Price:** futures. **Time Period Covered:** latest day.

Source: *Los Angeles Times.* **Price Frequency:** daily. **Effective Market(s):** Chicago, Kansas City. **Units of Measure:** Dollars per bushel. **Type of Price:** futures. **Time Period Covered:** latest day.

Source: *Milling & Baking News.* **Price Frequency:** weekly. **Effective Market(s):** Chicago, Kansas City, Minneapolis. **Units of Measure:** Dollars per bushel. **Type of Price:** futures. **Time Period Covered:** latest week, year ago, latest season.

Source: *New York Times.* **Price Frequency:** daily. **Effective Market(s):** Chicago, Kansas City, Minneapolis. **Units of Measure:** Dollars per bushel. **Type of Price:** futures. **Time Period Covered:** latest day.

Source: *The Times.* **Price Frequency:** daily. **Effective Market(s):** London. **Units of Measure:** British pounds per tonne. **Type of Price:** futures. **Time Period Covered:** latest day.

Source: *Urner Barry's Price-Current.* **Price Frequency:** daily. **Effective Market(s):** Chicago, Kansas City, Minneapolis. **Units of Measure:** Dollars per bushel. **Type of Price:** futures. **Time Period Covered:** latest day.

Source: *Wall Street Journal.* **Price Frequency:** daily. **Effective Market(s):** Chicago, Kansas City, Minneapolis, Winnepeg. **Units of Measure:** cents per bushel, Canadian dollars per ton. **Type of Price:** futures. **Time Period Covered:** latest day.

WHEAT: FUTURES, MAY

Source: *Commodity Year Book.* **Price Frequency:** monthly. **Effective Market(s):** Chicago. **Units of Measure:** cents per bushel. **Type of Price:** futures. **Time Period Covered:** latest 6 years.

WHEAT: HARD

Source: *Bakery Newsletter.* **Price Frequency:** weekly. **Effective Market(s):** Gulf. **Units of Measure:** Dollars per bushel. **Type of Price:** cash. **Time Period Covered:** latest week, week ago.

WHEAT: HARD RED

Source: *Agricultural Prices.* **Price Frequency:** monthly. **Effective Market(s):** United States. **Units of Measure:** Dollars per bushel. **Type of Price:** received by farmer. **Time Period Covered:** latest 2 months, year ago.

Source: *Agricultural Prices Annual Summary.* **Price Frequency:** monthly. **Effective Market(s):** United States. **Units of Measure:** Dollars per bushel. **Type of Price:** average received by farmer. **Time Period Covered:** latest 6 years.

WHEAT: HARD RED SPRING, FUTURES

Source: *Washington Farmer-Stockman.* **Price Frequency:** monthly. **Effective Market(s):** Minneapolis. **Units of Measure:** Dollars per bushel. **Type of Price:** futures. **Time Period Covered:** latest month.

WHEAT: HARD RED WINTER

Source: *Agricultural Outlook.* **Price Frequency:** quarterly, annually. **Effective Market(s):** Kansas City. **Units of Measure:** Dollars per bushel. **Type of Price:** average. **Time Period Covered:** latest year.

Source: *Wheat Situation and Outlook Report.* **Price Frequency:** monthly, annually. **Effective Market(s):** United States. **Units of Measure:** Dollars per metric ton. **Type of Price:** farm. **Time Period Covered:** monthly latest 2 years, annually latest 8 years.

WHEAT: HARD RED WINTER, 11% PROTEIN

Source: *Montana Farmer-Stockman.* **Price Frequency:** monthly, seasonally. **Effective Market(s):** 9 Montana markets. **Units of Measure:** Dollars per bushel. **Type of Price:** cash. **Time Period Covered:** latest month.

WHEAT: HARD RED WINTER, 12% PROTEIN

Source: *Montana Farmer-Stockman.* **Price Frequency:** monthly, seasonally. **Effective Market(s):** 9 Montana markets. **Units of Measure:** Dollars per bushel. **Type of Price:** cash. **Time Period Covered:** latest month.

WHEAT: HARD RED WINTER, 13% PROTEIN

Source: *Montana Farmer-Stockman.* **Price Frequency:** monthly, seasonally. **Effective Market(s):** 9 Montana markets. **Units of Measure:** Dollars per bushel. **Type of Price:** cash. **Time Period Covered:** latest month.

WHEAT: HARD RED WINTER, FUTURES

Source: *Washington Farmer-Stockman.* **Price Frequency:** monthly. **Effective Market(s):** Kansas City. **Units of Measure:** Dollars per bushel. **Type of Price:** futures. **Time Period Covered:** latest month.

WHEAT: HARD RED WINTER, ORDINARY PROTEIN

Source: *International Wheat Council Report for the Crop Year.* **Price Frequency:** monthly, quarterly, annually. **Effective Market(s):** Gulf. **Units of Measure:** Dollars per metric ton. **Time Period Covered:** latest year.

Source: *Livestock and Poultry Update.* **Price Frequency:** monthly. **Effective Market(s):** Kansas City. **Units of Measure:** Dollars per bushel. **Time Period Covered:** latest 3 months, year ago.

Source: *Montana Farmer-Stockman.* **Price Frequency:** monthly, seasonally. **Effective Market(s):** 9 Montana markets. **Units of Measure:** Dollars per bushel. **Type of Price:** cash. **Time Period Covered:** latest month.

WHEAT: HARD WINTER

Source: *Wheat Situation and Outlook Report.* **Price Frequency:** monthly, annually. **Effective Market(s):** Central/Southern Plains. **Units of Measure:** Dollars per bushel. **Type of Price:** farm. **Time Period Covered:** latest 10 years.

WHEAT: MILLING

Source: *Farmers Weekly.* **Price Frequency:** weekly. **Effective Market(s):** Great Britain. **Units of Measure:** British pounds per tonne. **Type of Price:** spot. **Time Period Covered:** latest week, week ago, year ago.

Source: *Farmers Weekly.* **Price Frequency:** weekly, seasonally. **Effective Market(s):** 50 British markets. **Units of Measure:** British pounds per tonne. **Type of Price:** farm. **Time Period Covered:** latest week.

Source: *Scottish Farmer.* **Price Frequency:** monthly, seasonally. **Effective Market(s):** United Kingdom. **Units of Measure:** British pounds per tonne. **Type of Price:** spot. **Time Period Covered:** latest 2 months.

WHEAT: MILLING, 11% PROTEIN

Source: *Farmers Weekly.* **Price Frequency:** weekly, seasonally. **Effective Market(s):** 13 British markets. **Units of Measure:** British pounds per tonne. **Type of Price:** spot. **Time Period Covered:** latest week.

WHEAT: NO. 1

Source: *Idaho Farmer-Stockman.* **Price Frequency:** monthly. **Effective Market(s):** Denver, Omaha (NE), Portland (OR), Stockton (CA). **Time Period Covered:** latest month.

Source: *Utah Farmer-Stockman.* **Price Frequency:** monthly, seasonally. **Effective Market(s):** Denver, Omaha, Portland (OR), Stockton (CA). **Units of Measure:** Dollars per bushel. **Time Period Covered:** latest month.

WHEAT: NO. 1, DARK NORTHERN, 14% PROTEIN

Source: *Investor's Daily.* **Price Frequency:** daily. **Effective Market(s):** Minneapolis. **Units of Measure:** Dollars per bushel. **Type of Price:** spot. **Time Period Covered:** latest 2 days.

Source: *New York Times.* **Price Frequency:** daily. **Effective Market(s):** Minneapolis. **Units of Measure:** Dollars per bushel. **Type of Price:** cash. **Time Period Covered:** latest 2 days.

WHEAT: NO. 1, DARK NORTHERN SPRING

Source: *Journal of Commercial and Commercial.* **Price Frequency:** daily. **Effective Market(s):** Minneapolis. **Units of Measure:** Dollars per bushel. **Type of Price:** spot supplier. **Time Period Covered:** latest day.

WHEAT: NO. 1, DARK NORTHERN SPRING, 13% PROTEIN

Source: *Grain and Feed Market News.* **Price Frequency:** daily, seasonally. **Effective Market(s):** Minneapolis. **Units of Measure:** Dollars per bushel. **Type of Price:** cash bid. **Time Period Covered:** latest week, year ago.

Source: *Idaho Farmer-Stockman.* **Price Frequency:** monthly. **Effective Market(s):** Portland (OR). **Units of Measure:** Dollars per bushel. **Time Period Covered:** latest month, month ago.

Source: *Montana Farmer-Stockman.* **Price Frequency:** monthly, seasonally. **Effective Market(s):** Minneapolis, Portland (OR). **Units of Measure:** Dollars per bushel. **Type of Price:** cash. **Time Period Covered:** latest 2 months.

Source: *Oregon Farmer-Stockman.* **Price Frequency:** monthly. **Effective Market(s):** Portland (OR). **Units of Measure:** Dollars per bushel. **Type of Price:** cash. **Time Period Covered:** latest 2 months.

Source: *Washington Farmer-Stockman.* **Price Frequency:** monthly. **Effective Market(s):** Portland (OR). **Units of Measure:** Dollars per bushel. **Type of Price:** cash. **Time Period Covered:** latest 2 months.

WHEAT: NO. 1, DARK NORTHERN SPRING, 14% PROTEIN

Source: *Commodity Year Book.* **Price Frequency:** monthly, annually. **Effective Market(s):** Minneapolis. **Units of Measure:** cents per bushel. **Time Period Covered:** latest 6 years.

Source: *Commodity Year Book.* **Price Frequency:** annually. **Effective Market(s):** Minneapolis. **Units of Measure:** Dollars per bushel. **Type of Price:** cash. **Time Period Covered:** latest 5 years.

Source: *Fedgazette.* **Price Frequency:** monthly. **Effective Market(s):** Minneapolis. **Units of Measure:** Dollars per bushel. **Time Period Covered:** latest 24 months.

Source: *Grain and Feed Market News.* **Price Frequency:** daily, seasonally. **Effective Market(s):** Minneapolis, Portland. **Units of Measure:** Dollars per bushel. **Type of Price:** cash bid. **Time Period Covered:** latest week, year ago.

Source: *Minneapolis Grain Exchange Statistical Annual.* **Price Frequency:** monthly, annually. **Effective Market(s):** Minneapolis. **Units of Measure:** cents per bushel. **Type of Price:** cash. **Time Period Covered:** latest 10 years.

Source: *Montana Farmer-Stockman.* **Price Frequency:** monthly, seasonally. **Effective Market(s):** Minneapolis, Portland (OR). **Units of Measure:** Dollars per bushel. **Type of Price:** cash. **Time Period Covered:** latest 2 months.

Source: *Washington Farmer-Stockman.* **Price Frequency:** monthly. **Effective Market(s):** Portland (OR). **Units of Measure:** Dollars per bushel. **Type of Price:** cash. **Time Period Covered:** latest 2 months.

Source: *Wheat Situation and Outlook Report.* **Price Frequency:** monthly, annually. **Effective Market(s):** Minneapolis. **Units of Measure:** Dollars per bushel. **Time Period Covered:** latest 16 years.

WHEAT: NO. 1, DARK NORTHERN SPRING, 15% PROTEIN

Source: *Grain and Feed Market News.* **Price Frequency:** daily, seasonally. **Effective Market(s):** Minneapolis. **Units of Measure:** Dollars per bushel. **Type of Price:** cash bid. **Time Period Covered:** latest week, year ago.

Source: *Montana Farmer-Stockman.* **Price Frequency:** monthly, seasonally. **Effective Market(s):** Minneapolis, Portland (OR). **Units of Measure:** Dollars per bushel. **Type of Price:** cash. **Time Period Covered:** latest 2 months.

Source: *Washington Farmer-Stockman.* **Price Frequency:** monthly. **Effective Market(s):** Portland (OR). **Units of Measure:** Dollars per bushel. **Type of Price:** cash. **Time Period Covered:** latest 2 months.

WHEAT: NO. 1, DARK NORTHERN SPRING, ORDINARY PROTEIN

Source: *Grain and Feed Market News.* **Price Frequency:** daily, seasonally. **Effective Market(s):** Minneapolis. **Units of Measure:** Dollars per bushel. **Type of Price:** cash bid. **Time Period Covered:** latest week, year ago.

WHEAT: NO. 1, DARK NORTHERN SPRING/ NO.1 NORTHERN SPRING, ORDINARY PROTEIN

Source: *Minneapolis Grain Exchange Statistical Annual.* **Price Frequency:** daily. **Effective Market(s):** Minneapolis. **Units of Measure:** cents per bushel. **Type of Price:** cash. **Time Period Covered:** latest year.

WHEAT: NO. 1, DURUM, CANADIAN

Source: *Agricultural Trade Highlights.* **Price Frequency:** weekly. **Effective Market(s):** Rotterdam. **Units of Measure:** Dollars per metric ton. **Type of Price:** asking. **Time Period Covered:** latest week, month ago, year ago.

WHEAT: NO. 1, HARD AMBER DURUM

Source: *Commodity Year Book.* **Price Frequency:** annually. **Effective Market(s):** Minneapolis. **Units of Measure:** Dollars per bushel. **Type of Price:** cash. **Time Period Covered:** latest 5 years.

Source: *Quarterly Durum Report.* **Price Frequency:** monthly, annually. **Effective Market(s):** Minneapolis, North Dakota. **Units of Measure:** cents per bushel. **Type of Price:** spot, average price received by farmer. **Time Period Covered:** latest four years.

Source: *Wheat Situation and Outlook Report.* **Price Frequency:** monthly, annually. **Effective Market(s):** Minneapolis. **Units of Measure:** Dollars per bushel. **Time Period Covered:** latest 16 years.

WHEAT: NO. 1, HARD AMBER DURUM, MILLING

Source: *Grain and Feed Market News.* **Price Frequency:** daily, seasonally. **Effective Market(s):** Minneapolis. **Units of Measure:** Dollars per bushel. **Type of Price:** cash bid. **Time Period Covered:** latest week, year ago.

WHEAT: NO. 1, HARD AMBER DURUM, TERMINAL

Source: *Milling & Baking News.* **Price Frequency:** weekly. **Effective Market(s):** Duluth (MN), Minneapolis. **Units of Measure:** Dollars per bushel. **Time Period Covered:** latest week.

WHEAT: NO. 1, HARD AMBER DURUM, TRACK MILLING

Source: *Milling & Baking News.* **Price Frequency:** weekly. **Effective Market(s):** Minneapolis. **Units of Measure:** Dollars per bushel. **Time Period Covered:** latest week.

WHEAT: NO. 1, HARD AMBER DURUM, TRACK BALANCE MILLING

Source: *Milling & Baking News.* **Price Frequency:** weekly. **Effective Market(s):** Minneapolis. **Units of Measure:** Dollars per bushel. **Time Period Covered:** latest week.

WHEAT: NO. 1, HARD RED WINTER

Source: *Doane's Agricultural Report.* **Price Frequency:** weekly. **Effective Market(s):** Kansas City. **Units of Measure:** Dollars per bushel. **Time Period Covered:** latest week, week ago, year ago.

Source: *Grain and Feed Market News.* **Price Frequency:** weekly, seasonally. **Effective Market(s):** 44 domestic markets. **Units of Measure:** Dollars per bushel. **Type of Price:** cash bid. **Time Period Covered:** latest week.

WHEAT: NO. 1, HARD RED WINTER, 10% PROTEIN

Source: *Washington Farmer-Stockman.* **Price Frequency:** monthly. **Effective Market(s):** Portland (OR). **Units of Measure:** Dollars per bushel. **Type of Price:** cash. **Time Period Covered:** latest 2 months.

WHEAT: NO. 1, HARD RED WINTER, 11% PROTEIN

Source: *Montana Farmer-Stockman.* **Price Frequency:** monthly, seasonally. **Effective Market(s):** Portland (OR). **Units of Measure:** Dollars per bushel. **Type of Price:** cash. **Time Period Covered:** latest 2 months.

Source: *Washington Farmer-Stockman.* **Price Frequency:** monthly. **Effective Market(s):** Portland (OR). **Units of Measure:** Dollars per bushel. **Type of Price:** cash. **Time Period Covered:** latest 2 months.

WHEAT: NO. 1, HARD RED WINTER, 11% PROTEIN, TRACK

Source: *Milling & Baking News.* **Price Frequency:** weekly. **Effective Market(s):** Portland (OR). **Units of Measure:** Dollars per bushel. **Type of Price:** exporter. **Time Period Covered:** latest week.

WHEAT: NO. 1, HARD RED WINTER, 12% PROTEIN

Source: *Idaho Farmer-Stockman.* **Price Frequency:** monthly. **Effective Market(s):** Portland (OR). **Units of Measure:** Dollars per bushel. **Time Period Covered:** latest month, month ago.

Source: *Montana Farmer-Stockman.* **Price Frequency:** monthly, seasonally. **Effective Market(s):** Minneapolis, Portland (OR). **Units of Measure:** Dollars per bushel. **Type of Price:** cash. **Time Period Covered:** latest 2 months.

Source: *Oregon Farmer-Stockman.* **Price Frequency:** monthly. **Effective Market(s):** Portland (OR). **Units of Measure:** Dollars per bushel. **Type of Price:** cash. **Time Period Covered:** latest 2 months.

Source: *Washington Farmer-Stockman.* **Price Frequency:** monthly. **Effective Market(s):** Portland (OR). **Units of Measure:** Dollars per bushel. **Type of Price:** cash. **Time Period Covered:** latest 2 months.

WHEAT: NO. 1, HARD RED WINTER, 13% PROTEIN

Source: *Grain and Feed Market News.* **Price Frequency:** daily, seasonally. **Effective Market(s):** Kansas City. **Units of Measure:** Dollars per bushel. **Type of Price:** cash bid. **Time Period Covered:** latest week, year ago.

Source: *Los Angeles Times.* **Price Frequency:** daily. **Effective Market(s):** Los Angeles. **Units of Measure:** Dollars per bushel. **Type of Price:** cash. **Time Period Covered:** latest day.

Source: *Montana Farmer-Stockman.* **Price Frequency:** monthly, seasonally. **Effective Market(s):** Portland (OR). **Units of Measure:** Dollars per bushel. **Type of Price:** cash. **Time Period Covered:** latest 2 months.

Source: *Washington Farmer-Stockman.* **Price Frequency:** monthly. **Effective Market(s):** Portland (OR). **Units of Measure:** Dollars per bushel. **Type of Price:** cash. **Time Period Covered:** latest 2 months.

Source: *Wheat Situation and Outlook Report.* **Price Frequency:** monthly, annually. **Effective Market(s):** Kansas City. **Units of Measure:** Dollars per bushel. **Time Period Covered:** latest 16 years.

WHEAT: NO. 1, HARD RED WINTER, ORDINARY PROTEIN

Source: *Agricultural Outlook.* **Price Frequency:** monthly, annually. **Effective Market(s):** Kansas City. **Units of Measure:** Dollars per bushel. **Type of Price:** wholesale. **Time Period Covered:** monthly latest 5 months, annually latest 4 years.

Source: *Commodity Year Book.* **Price Frequency:** annually. **Effective Market(s):** Kansas City. **Units of Measure:** Dollars per bushel. **Type of Price:** cash. **Time Period Covered:** latest 5 years.

Source: *Commodity Year Book.* **Price Frequency:** monthly, annually. **Effective Market(s):** Kansas City. **Units of Measure:** cents per bushel. **Time Period Covered:** latest 6 years.

Source: *Grain and Feed Market News.* **Price Frequency:** daily, seasonally. **Effective Market(s):** Kansas City, Houston, Omaha (NE), Portland (OR). **Units of Measure:** Dollars per bushel. **Type of Price:** cash bid. **Time Period Covered:** latest week, year ago.

Source: *Grain and Feed Market News.* **Price Frequency:** daily, seasonally. **Effective Market(s):** Gulf. **Units of Measure:** Dollars per bushel. **Type of Price:** export bid. **Time Period Covered:** latest week, year ago.

Source: *Idaho Farmer-Stockman.* **Price Frequency:** monthly. **Effective Market(s):** Portland (OR). **Units of Measure:** Dollars per bushel. **Time Period Covered:** latest month, month ago.

Source: *Montana Farmer-Stockman.* **Price Frequency:** monthly, seasonally. **Effective Market(s):** Portland (OR). **Units of Measure:** Dollars per bushel. **Type of Price:** cash. **Time Period Covered:** latest 2 months.

Source: *Oregon Farmer-Stockman.* **Price Frequency:** monthly. **Effective Market(s):** Portland (OR). **Units of Measure:** Dollars per bushel. **Type of Price:** cash. **Time Period Covered:** latest 2 months.

Source: *Washington Farmer-Stockman.* **Price Frequency:** monthly. **Effective Market(s):** Portland (OR). **Units of Measure:** Dollars per bushel. **Type of Price:** cash. **Time Period Covered:** latest 2 months.

Source: *Wheat Situation and Outlook Report.* **Price Frequency:** monthly, annually. **Effective Market(s):** Kansas City. **Units of Measure:** Dollars per bushel. **Time Period Covered:** latest 16 years.

WHEAT: NO. 1, HARD WINTER

Source: *CRB Commodity Index Report.* **Price Frequency:** weekly. **Effective Market(s):** Kansas City. **Units of Measure:** Dollars per bushel. **Type of Price:** spot. **Time Period Covered:** latest week.

WHEAT: NO. 1, HARD WINTER, 11% PROTEIN

Source: *Utah Farmer-Stockman.* **Price Frequency:** monthly, seasonally. **Effective Market(s):** Ogden (UT). **Units of Measure:** Dollars per bushel. **Type of Price:** cash. **Time Period Covered:** latest 2 months.

WHEAT: NO. 1, HARD WINTER, 12% PROTEIN

Source: *Utah Farmer-Stockman.* **Price Frequency:** monthly, seasonally. **Effective Market(s):** Ogden (UT). **Units of Measure:** Dollars per bushel. **Type of Price:** cash. **Time Period Covered:** latest 2 months.

WHEAT: NO. 1, HARD WINTER, 13% PROTEIN

Source: *Utah Farmer-Stockman.* **Price Frequency:** monthly, seasonally. **Effective Market(s):** Ogden (UT). **Units of Measure:** Dollars per bushel. **Type of Price:** cash. **Time Period Covered:** latest 2 months.

WHEAT: NO. 1, HARD WINTER, ORDINARY PROTEIN

Source: *Wheat Situation and Outlook Report.* **Price Frequency:** monthly, annually. **Effective Market(s):** Kansas City. **Units of Measure:** Dollars per bushel. **Time Period Covered:** monthly latest 2 years, annuall latest 8 years.

WHEAT: NO. 1, HARD, 11% PROTEIN

Source: *Idaho Farmer-Stockman.* **Price Frequency:** monthly. **Effective Market(s):** Ogden (UT). **Units of Measure:** Dollars per bushel. **Time Period Covered:** latest month, month ago.

WHEAT: NO. 1, HARD, 12% PROTEIN

Source: *Idaho Farmer-Stockman.* **Price Frequency:** monthly. **Effective Market(s):** Ogden (UT). **Units of Measure:** Dollars per bushel. **Time Period Covered:** latest month, month ago.

WHEAT: NO. 1, HARD, 13% PROTEIN

Source: *Idaho Farmer-Stockman.* **Price Frequency:** monthly. **Effective Market(s):** Ogden (UT). **Units of Measure:** Dollars per bushel. **Time Period Covered:** latest month, month ago.

WHEAT: NO. 1, HARD, ORDINARY PROTEIN, TRACK

Source: *Milling & Baking News.* **Price Frequency:** weekly. **Effective Market(s):** Gulf. **Units of Measure:** Dollars per bushel. **Type of Price:** exporter. **Time Period Covered:** latest week.

WHEAT: NO. 1, HARD, ORDINARY PROTEIN

Source: *Idaho Farmer-Stockman.* **Price Frequency:** monthly. **Effective Market(s):** Ogden (UT). **Units of Measure:** Dollars per bushel. **Time Period Covered:** latest month, month ago.

Source: *Utah Farmer-Stockman.* **Price Frequency:** monthly, seasonally. **Effective Market(s):** Ogden (UT). **Units of Measure:** Dollars per bushel. **Type of Price:** cash. **Time Period Covered:** latest 2 months.

WHEAT: NO. 1, NORTHERN SPRING

Source: *Minneapolis Grain Exchange Statistical Annual.* **Price Frequency:** monthly. **Effective Market(s):** Minneapolis. **Units of Measure:** cents per bushel. **Type of Price:** cash high, cash low. **Time Period Covered:** latest 70 years.

WHEAT: NO. 1, SOFT RED WINTER

Source: *Commodity Trade and Price Trends.* **Price Frequency:** annually. **Effective Market(s):** Atlantic ports. **Units of Measure:** Dollars per metric ton, 1980 constant dollars per metric ton. **Time Period Covered:** latest 37 years.

Source: *Grain and Feed Market News.* **Price Frequency:** daily, seasonally. **Effective Market(s):** Kansas City, Portland (OR). **Units of Measure:** Dollars per bushel. **Type of Price:** cash bid. **Time Period Covered:** latest week, year ago.

Source: *Grain and Feed Market News.* **Price Frequency:** weekly, seasonally. **Effective Market(s):** 44 domestic markets. **Units of Measure:** Dollars per bushel. **Type of Price:** cash bid. **Time Period Covered:** latest week.

WHEAT: NO. 1, SOFT WHITE

Source: *California Farmer.* **Price Frequency:** semimonthly. **Effective Market(s):** Portland (OR). **Units of Measure:** Dollars per 100 lbs. **Time Period Covered:** latest week, month ago, year ago.

Source: *Idaho Farmer-Stockman.* **Price Frequency:** monthly. **Effective Market(s):** Ogden (UT), Portland (OR). **Units of Measure:** Dollars per bushel. **Time Period Covered:** latest month, month ago.

Source: *Montana Farmer-Stockman.* **Price Frequency:** monthly, seasonally. **Effective Market(s):** Portland (OR). **Units of Measure:** Dollars per bushel. **Type of Price:** cash. **Time Period Covered:** latest 2 months.

Source: *Oregon Farmer-Stockman.* **Price Frequency:** monthly. **Effective Market(s):** Portland (OR). **Units of Measure:** Dollars per bushel. **Type of Price:** cash. **Time Period Covered:** latest 2 months.

Source: *Utah Farmer-Stockman.* **Price Frequency:** monthly, seasonally. **Effective Market(s):** Ogden (UT). **Units of Measure:** Dollars per bushel. **Type of Price:** cash. **Time Period Covered:** latest 2 months.

Source: *Washington Farmer-Stockman.* **Price Frequency:** monthly. **Effective Market(s):** Portland (OR). **Units of Measure:** Dollars per bushel. **Type of Price:** cash. **Time Period Covered:** latest 2 months.

Source: *Wheat Situation and Outlook Report.* **Price Frequency:** monthly, annually. **Effective Market(s):** Portland (OR). **Units of Measure:** Dollars per bushel. **Time Period Covered:** latest 16 years.

WHEAT: NO. 1, SOFT WHITE, TRACK

Source: *Milling & Baking News.* **Price Frequency:** weekly. **Effective Market(s):** Portland (OR). **Units of Measure:** Dollars per bushel. **Type of Price:** exporter. **Time Period Covered:** latest week.

WHEAT: NO. 1, SPRING

Source: *CRB Commodity Index Report.* **Price Frequency:** weekly. **Effective Market(s):** Minneapolis. **Units of Measure:** Dollars per bushel. **Type of Price:** spot. **Time Period Covered:** latest week.

WHEAT: NO. 1, SPRING, 14% PROTEIN, TRACK

Source: *Milling & Baking News.* **Price Frequency:** weekly. **Effective Market(s):** Portland (OR). **Units of Measure:** Dollars per bushel. **Type of Price:** exporter. **Time Period Covered:** latest week.

WHEAT: NO. 1, WESTERN AMBER DURUM, CANADIAN

Source: *International Wheat Council Market Report.* **Price Frequency:** weekly, seasonally. **Effective Market(s):** Rotterdam, St. Lawrence (Canada). **Units of Measure:** Dollars per metric ton. **Type of Price:** cash. **Time Period Covered:** latest 5 weeks.

Source: *International Wheat Council Report for the Crop Year.* **Price Frequency:** monthly, quarterly, annually. **Effective Market(s):** Thunder Bay (Canada). **Units of Measure:** Dollars per metric ton. **Time Period Covered:** latest year.

WHEAT: NO. 1, WESTERN RED SPRING, 13.5% PROTEIN, CANADIAN

Source: *Agricultural Trade Highlights.* **Price Frequency:** weekly. **Effective Market(s):** Rotterdam. **Units of Measure:** Dollars per metric ton. **Type of Price:** asking. **Time Period Covered:** latest week, month ago, year ago.

Source: *FAO Quarterly Bulletin of Statistics.* **Price Frequency:** monthly, annually. **Effective Market(s):** Thunder Bay (Canada). **Units of Measure:** Canadian dollars per 100 kilograms,, dollars per metric ton. **Time Period Covered:** latest 3 years.

Source: *International Wheat Council Market Report.* **Price Frequency:** weekly, seasonally. **Effective Market(s):** Rotterdam, United Kingdom. **Units of Measure:** Dollars per metric ton, British pounds per metric ton. **Type of Price:** cash. **Time Period Covered:** latest 5 weeks.

Source: *International Wheat Council Market Report.* **Price Frequency:** weekly, seasonally. **Effective Market(s):** St. Lawrence (Canada), Vancouver (Canada). **Units of Measure:** Dollars per metric ton. **Type of Price:** export. **Time Period Covered:** latest 5 weeks.

Source: *International Wheat Council Report for the Crop Year.* **Price Frequency:** monthly, quarterly, annually. **Effective Market(s):** St. Lawrence (Canada), Thunder Bay (Canada). **Units of Measure:** Dollars per metric ton. **Time Period Covered:** latest year.

Source: *Wheat Situation and Outlook Report.* **Price Frequency:** monthly, annually. **Effective Market(s):** St. Lawrence (Canada). **Units of Measure:** Dollars per bushel. **Time Period Covered:** monthly latest 2 years, annuall latest 8 years.

Source: *World Agriculture Situation and Outlook.* **Price Frequency:** monthly, annually. **Effective Market(s):** Thunder Bay (Canada). **Units of Measure:** Dollars per metric ton. **Time Period Covered:** monthly latest year, annually latest 9 years.

WHEAT: NO. 1, WESTERN RED SPRING, CANADIAN

Source: *Commodity Trade and Price Trends.* **Price Frequency:** annually. **Effective Market(s):** St. Lawrence (Canada). **Units of Measure:** Dollars per metric ton, 1980 constant dollars per metric ton. **Type of Price:** export. **Time Period Covered:** latest 37 years.

Source: *International Wheat Council Report for the Crop Year.* **Price Frequency:** monthly, quarterly, annually. **Effective Market(s):** Pacific (Canada). **Units of Measure:** Dollars per metric ton. **Time Period Covered:** latest year.

Source: *World Grain Situation and Outlook.* **Price Frequency:** weekly, monthly, annually. **Effective Market(s):** Canada. **Units of Measure:** Dollars per metric ton. **Type of Price:** export. **Time Period Covered:** weekly latest 3 months, monthly latest 3 years, annually latest 7 years.

WHEAT: NO. 1, WHITE

Source: *Doane's Agricultural Report.* **Price Frequency:** weekly. **Effective Market(s):** Portland (OR). **Units of Measure:** Dollars per bushel. **Time Period Covered:** latest week, week ago, year ago.

WHEAT: NO. 1, WHITE CLUB

Source: *Idaho Farmer-Stockman.* **Price Frequency:** monthly. **Effective Market(s):** Portland (OR). **Units of Measure:** Dollars per bushel. **Time Period Covered:** latest month, month ago.

Source: *Montana Farmer-Stockman.* **Price Frequency:** monthly, seasonally. **Effective Market(s):** Portland (OR). **Units of Measure:** Dollars per bushel. **Type of Price:** cash. **Time Period Covered:** latest 2 months.

Source: *Oregon Farmer-Stockman.* **Price Frequency:** monthly. **Effective Market(s):** Portland (OR). **Units of Measure:** Dollars per bushel. **Type of Price:** cash. **Time Period Covered:** latest 2 months.

Source: *Washington Farmer-Stockman.* **Price Frequency:** monthly. **Effective Market(s):** Portland (OR). **Units of Measure:** Dollars per bushel. **Type of Price:** cash. **Time Period Covered:** latest 2 months.

WHEAT: NO. 2

Source: *Economic and Energy Indicators.* **Price Frequency:** biweekly. **Units of Measure:** Dollars per metric ton. **Time Period Covered:** latest 3 months, quarters, and years.

Source: *Lancaster Farming.* **Price Frequency:** weekly. **Effective Market(s):** Pennsylvania. **Units of Measure:** Dollars per bushel. **Time Period Covered:** latest week.

WHEAT: NO. 2 OR BETTER, 13% PROTEIN, CALIFORNIA

Source: *Los Angeles Times.* **Price Frequency:** daily. **Effective Market(s):** Los Angeles. **Units of Measure:** Dollars per bushel. **Type of Price:** cash. **Time Period Covered:** latest day.

WHEAT: NO. 2 OR BETTER, HARD RED WINTER

Source: *California Farmer.* **Price Frequency:** semimonthly. **Effective Market(s):** Los Angeles. **Units of Measure:** Dollars per 100 lbs. **Time Period Covered:** latest week, month ago, year ago.

WHEAT: NO. 2 OR BETTER, SOFT WINTER

Source: *Grain and Feed Market News.* **Price Frequency:** daily, seasonally. **Effective Market(s):** Pacific Northwest. **Units of Measure:** Dollars per bushel. **Type of Price:** export bid. **Time Period Covered:** latest week, year ago.

WHEAT: NO. 2, 14% PROTEIN, UNITED STATES

Source: *Oil World.* **Price Frequency:** weekly, monthly, annually. **Effective Market(s):** Rotterdam. **Units of Measure:** Dollars per tonne. **Type of Price:** lowest representative asking. **Time Period Covered:** weekly latest 3 weeks, monthly latest 2 months, annually latest 2 years.

WHEAT: NO. 2, DARK NORTHERN SPRING, 14% PROTEIN

Source: *Grain and Feed Market News.* **Price Frequency:** daily, seasonally. **Effective Market(s):** Duluth (MN), Gulf, Pacific Northwest. **Units of Measure:** Dollars per bushel. **Type of Price:** export bid. **Time Period Covered:** latest week, year ago.

Source: *International Wheat Council Market Report.* **Price Frequency:** weekly, seasonally. **Effective Market(s):** Lakehead. **Units of Measure:** Dollars per metric ton. **Type of Price:** export. **Time Period Covered:** latest 5 weeks.

WHEAT: NO. 2, DARK NORTHERN SPRING, 14% PROTEIN, UNITED STATES

Source: *Agricultural Trade Highlights.* **Price Frequency:** weekly. **Effective Market(s):** Rotterdam. **Units of Measure:** Dollars per metric ton. **Type of Price:** asking. **Time Period Covered:** latest week, month ago, year ago.

Source: *International Wheat Council Market Report.* **Price Frequency:** weekly, seasonally. **Effective Market(s):** Rotterdam. **Units of Measure:** Dollars per metric ton. **Type of Price:** cash. **Time Period Covered:** latest 5 weeks.

Source: *International Wheat Council Market Report.* **Price Frequency:** weekly, seasonally. **Effective Market(s):** United Kingdom. **Units of Measure:** British pounds per metric ton. **Type of Price:** cash. **Time Period Covered:** latest 5 weeks.

Source: *Wheat Situation and Outlook Report.* **Price Frequency:** monthly, annually. **Effective Market(s):** Rotterdam. **Units of Measure:** Dollars per bushel. **Time Period Covered:** monthly latest 2 years, annuall latest 8 years.

Source: *World Grain Situation and Outlook.* **Price Frequency:** weekly, monthly, annually, seasonally. **Effective Market(s):** Rotterdam. **Units of Measure:** Dollars per metric ton. **Time Period Covered:** weekly latest 7 months, monthly latest 2 years, annually latest 17 years.

WHEAT: NO. 2, HARD

Source: *Asian Wall Street Journal.* **Price Frequency:** daily. **Effective Market(s):** Kansas City. **Units of Measure:** Dollars per bushel. **Type of Price:** cash. **Time Period Covered:** latest 2 days, year ago.

Source: *Business Week.* **Price Frequency:** weekly. **Units of Measure:** Dollars per bushel. **Time Period Covered:** latest 2 weeks.

Source: *Farm and Dairy.* **Price Frequency:** weekly. **Effective Market(s):** Kansas City. **Units of Measure:** Dollars per bushel. **Time Period Covered:** latest week, year ago.

Source: *Investor's Daily.* **Price Frequency:** daily. **Effective Market(s):** Kansas City. **Units of Measure:** Dollars per bushel. **Type of Price:** spot. **Time Period Covered:** latest 2 days.

Source: *Journal of Commerce and Commercial.* **Price Frequency:** daily. **Effective Market(s):** Kansas City. **Units of Measure:** Dollars per bushel. **Type of Price:** spot supplier. **Time Period Covered:** latest day.

Source: *New York Times.* **Price Frequency:** daily. **Effective Market(s):** Kansas City. **Units of Measure:** Dollars per bushel. **Type of Price:** cash. **Time Period Covered:** latest 2 days.

Source: *Wall Street Journal.* **Price Frequency:** daily. **Effective Market(s):** Kansas City. **Units of Measure:** Dollars per bushel. **Time Period Covered:** latest day, day ago, year ago.

WHEAT: NO. 2, HARD AMBER DURUM, UNITED STATES

Source: *Agricultural Trade Highlights.* **Price Frequency:** weekly. **Effective Market(s):** Rotterdam. **Units of Measure:** Dollars per metric ton. **Type of Price:** asking. **Time Period Covered:** latest week, month ago, year ago.

WHEAT: NO. 2, HARD RED WINTER

Source: *Commodity Year Book.* **Price Frequency:** annually. **Effective Market(s):** Rotterdam. **Units of Measure:** Dollars per metric ton. **Type of Price:** export. **Time Period Covered:** latest 5 years.

Source: *UNCTAD Commodity Yearbook.* **Price Frequency:** annually. **Effective Market(s):** Gulf. **Units of Measure:** Dollars per metric ton. **Type of Price:** free market. **Time Period Covered:** latest 12 years.

WHEAT: NO. 2, HARD RED WINTER, 13.5% PROTEIN, UNITED STATES

Source: *International Wheat Council Market Report.* **Price Frequency:** weekly, seasonally. **Effective Market(s):** Rotterdam. **Units of Measure:** Dollars per metric ton. **Type of Price:** cash. **Time Period Covered:** latest 5 weeks.

WHEAT: NO. 2, HARD RED WINTER, FEED

Source: *California Farmer.* **Price Frequency:** semimonthly. **Effective Market(s):** Stockton (CA). **Units of Measure:** Dollars per 100 lbs. **Time Period Covered:** latest week, month ago, year ago.

WHEAT: NO. 2, HARD RED WINTER, ORDINARY PROTEIN

Source: *Grain and Feed Market News.* **Price Frequency:** daily, seasonally. **Effective Market(s):** Pacific Northwest. **Units of Measure:** Dollars per bushel. **Type of Price:** export bid. **Time Period Covered:** latest week, year ago.

Source: *International Wheat Council Market Report.* **Price Frequency:** weekly, seasonally. **Effective Market(s):** Gulf. **Units of Measure:** Dollars per metric ton. **Type of Price:** export. **Time Period Covered:** latest 5 weeks.

Source: *Monthly Commodity Price Bulletin.* **Price Frequency:** monthly, annually. **Effective Market(s):** Gulf. **Units of Measure:** Dollars per metric ton. **Time Period Covered:** latest 5 years.

Source: *Monthly Commodity Price Bulletin Supplement.* **Price Frequency:** monthly, quarterly, annually. **Effective Market(s):** Gulf. **Units of Measure:** Dollars per tonne. **Time Period Covered:** latest 20 years.

WHEAT: NO. 2, HARD RED WINTER, ORDINARY PROTEIN, UNITED STATES

Source: *International Wheat Council Market Report.* **Price Frequency:** weekly, seasonally. **Effective Market(s):** Rotterdam. **Units of Measure:** Dollars per metric ton. **Type of Price:** cash. **Time Period Covered:** latest 5 weeks.

WHEAT: NO. 2, HARD WINTER

Source: *International Wheat Council Market Report.* **Price Frequency:** monthly. **Effective Market(s):** Kansas City. **Units of Measure:** Dollars per bushel, dollars per ton. **Type of Price:** target, cash. **Time Period Covered:** latest month.

Source: *World Grain Situation and Outlook.* **Price Frequency:** weekly, monthly, annually. **Effective Market(s):** Gulf. **Units of Measure:** Dollars per metric ton. **Type of Price:** export. **Time Period Covered:** weekly latest 3 months, monthly latest 3 years, annually latest 7 years.

WHEAT: NO. 2, HARD WINTER, FUTURES

Source: *International Wheat Council Market Report.* **Price Frequency:** weekly. **Effective Market(s):** Kansas City. **Units of Measure:** Dollars per bushel, dollars per metric ton. **Type of Price:** futures. **Time Period Covered:** latest month.

WHEAT: NO. 2, HARD WINTER, ORDINARY PROTEIN

Source: *FAO Quarterly Bulletin of Statistics.* **Price Frequency:** monthly, annually. **Effective Market(s):** Gulf. **Units of Measure:** Dollars per 1000 kilograms, dollars per metric ton. **Time Period Covered:** latest 3 years.

Source: *Wheat Situation and Outlook Report.* **Price Frequency:** monthly, annually. **Effective Market(s):** Gulf ports. **Units of Measure:** Dollars per bushel. **Time Period Covered:** monthly latest 2 years, annuall latest 8 years.

Source: *World Agriculture Situation and Outlook.* **Price Frequency:** monthly, annually. **Effective Market(s):** Gulf ports. **Units of Measure:** Dollars per metric ton. **Time Period Covered:** monthly latest year, annually latest 9 years.

WHEAT: NO. 2, NORTHERN SPRING, FUTURES

Source: *International Wheat Council Market Report.* **Price Frequency:** weekly. **Effective Market(s):** Minneapolis. **Units of Measure:** Dollars per bushel, dollars per metric ton. **Type of Price:** futures. **Time Period Covered:** latest month.

WHEAT: NO. 2, RED WINTER

Source: *Standard & Poor's Statistical Service Current Statistics.* **Price Frequency:** monthly, annually. **Effective Market(s):** St. Louis. **Units of Measure:** Dollars per bushel. **Time Period Covered:** latest 5 years.

WHEAT: NO. 2, SOFT

Source: *Commodity Year Book.* **Price Frequency:** annually. **Effective Market(s):** Portland (OR). **Units of Measure:** Dollars per bushel. **Type of Price:** cash. **Time Period Covered:** latest 5 years.

Source: *Investor's Daily.* **Price Frequency:** daily. **Units of Measure:** Dollars per bushel. **Type of Price:** spot. **Time Period Covered:** latest 2 days.

Source: *New York Times.* **Price Frequency:** daily. **Units of Measure:** Dollars per bushel. **Type of Price:** cash. **Time Period Covered:** latest 2 days.

WHEAT: NO. 2, SOFT RED

Source: *Asian Wall Street Journal.* **Price Frequency:** daily. **Effective Market(s):** St. Louis. **Units of Measure:** Dollars per bushel. **Type of Price:** cash. **Time Period Covered:** latest 2 days, year ago.

Source: *Farm and Dairy.* **Price Frequency:** weekly. **Effective Market(s):** St. Louis. **Units of Measure:** Dollars per bushel. **Time Period Covered:** latest week, year ago.

Source: *Journal of Commerce and Commercial.* **Price Frequency:** daily. **Effective Market(s):** Chicago. **Units of Measure:** Dollars per bushel. **Type of Price:** spot supplier. **Time Period Covered:** latest day.

Source: *Milling & Baking News.* **Price Frequency:** weekly. **Effective Market(s):** New Orleans. **Units of Measure:** Dollars per bushel. **Type of Price:** exporter. **Time Period Covered:** latest week.

Source: *Wall Street Journal.* **Price Frequency:** daily. **Effective Market(s):** St. Louis. **Units of Measure:** Dollars per bushel. **Time Period Covered:** latest day, day ago, year ago.

WHEAT: NO. 2, SOFT RED WINTER

Source: *Commodity Year Book.* **Price Frequency:** annually. **Effective Market(s):** Chicago, St. Louis. **Units of Measure:** Dollars per bushel. **Type of Price:** cash. **Time Period Covered:** latest 5 years.

Source: *Commodity Year Book.* **Price Frequency:** monthly, annually. **Effective Market(s):** Chicago. **Units of Measure:** Dollars per bushel. **Time Period Covered:** latest 10 years.

Source: *Grain and Feed Market News.* **Price Frequency:** daily, seasonally. **Effective Market(s):** Chicago, St. Louis, Toledo (OH). **Units of Measure:** Dollars per bushel. **Type of Price:** cash bid. **Time Period Covered:** latest week, year ago.

Source: *Grain and Feed Market News.* **Price Frequency:** daily, seasonally. **Effective Market(s):** East Coast, Gulf. **Units of Measure:** Dollars per bushel. **Type of Price:** export bid. **Time Period Covered:** latest week, year ago.

Source: *International Wheat Council Market Report.* **Price Frequency:** weekly, seasonally. **Effective Market(s):** Gulf. **Units of Measure:** Dollars per metric ton. **Type of Price:** export. **Time Period Covered:** latest 5 weeks.

Source: *Wheat Situation and Outlook Report.* **Price Frequency:** monthly, annually. **Effective Market(s):** Chicago, St. Louis, Toledo (OH). **Units of Measure:** Dollars per bushel. **Time Period Covered:** latest 16 years.

WHEAT: NO. 2, SOFT RED WINTER, FUTURES

Source: *International Wheat Council Market Report.* **Price Frequency:** weekly. **Effective Market(s):** Chicago. **Units of Measure:** Dollars per bushel, dollars per metric ton. **Type of Price:** futures. **Time Period Covered:** latest month.

WHEAT: NO. 2, SOFT RED WINTER, UNITED STATES

Source: *Agricultural Trade Highlights.* **Price Frequency:** weekly. **Effective Market(s):** Rotterdam. **Units of Measure:** Dollars per metric ton. **Type of Price:** asking. **Time Period Covered:** latest week, month ago, year ago.

Source: *International Wheat Council Market Report.* **Price Frequency:** weekly, seasonally. **Effective Market(s):** Rotterdam. **Units of Measure:** Dollars per metric ton. **Type of Price:** cash. **Time Period Covered:** latest 5 weeks.

WHEAT: NO. 2, SOFT WHITE

Source: *Commodity Year Book.* **Price Frequency:** annually. **Effective Market(s):** Toledo (OH). **Units of Measure:** Dollars per bushel. **Type of Price:** cash. **Time Period Covered:** latest 5 years.

Source: *Grain and Feed Market News.* **Price Frequency:** daily, seasonally. **Effective Market(s):** Toledo (OH). **Units of Measure:** Dollars per bushel. **Type of Price:** cash bid. **Time Period Covered:** latest week, year ago.

Source: *Wheat Situation and Outlook Report.* **Price Frequency:** monthly, annually. **Effective Market(s):** Toledo (OH). **Units of Measure:** Dollars per bushel. **Time Period Covered:** latest 16 years.

WHEAT: NO. 2, WESTERN WHITE

Source: *Commodity Year Book.* **Price Frequency:** annually. **Effective Market(s):** Pacific Northwest. **Units of Measure:** Dollars per bushel. **Type of Price:** cash. **Time Period Covered:** latest 5 years.

Source: *International Wheat Council Market Report.* **Price Frequency:** weekly, seasonally. **Effective Market(s):** Pacific. **Units of Measure:** Dollars per metric ton. **Type of Price:** export. **Time Period Covered:** latest 5 weeks.

WHEAT: NO. 3, HARD AMBER DURUM

Source: *International Wheat Council Market Report.* **Price Frequency:** weekly, seasonally. **Effective Market(s):** Lakehead. **Units of Measure:** Dollars per metric ton. **Type of Price:** export. **Time Period Covered:** latest 5 weeks.

Source: *International Wheat Council Report for the Crop Year.* **Price Frequency:** monthly, quarterly, annually. **Effective Market(s):** Lakehead. **Units of Measure:** Dollars per metric ton. **Time Period Covered:** latest year.

WHEAT: NO. 3, HARD AMBER DURUM, UNITED STATES

Source: *International Wheat Council Market Report.* **Price Frequency:** weekly, seasonally. **Effective Market(s):** Rotterdam. **Units of Measure:** Dollars per metric ton. **Type of Price:** cash. **Time Period Covered:** latest 5 weeks.

WHEAT: PRIME HARD, 14% PROTEIN, AUSTRALIAN

Source: *International Wheat Council Market Report.* **Price Frequency:** weekly, seasonally. **Effective Market(s):** United Kingdom. **Units of Measure:** British pounds per metric ton. **Type of Price:** cash. **Time Period Covered:** latest 5 weeks.

WHEAT: SOFT RED

Source: *Agricultural Prices.* **Price Frequency:** monthly. **Effective Market(s):** United States. **Units of Measure:** Dollars per bushel. **Type of Price:** received by farmer. **Time Period Covered:** latest 2 months, year ago.

Source: *Agricultural Prices Annual Summary.* **Price Frequency:** monthly. **Effective Market(s):** United States. **Units of Measure:** Dollars per bushel. **Type of Price:** average received by farmer. **Time Period Covered:** latest 6 years.

WHEAT: SOFT RED WINTER

Source: *Doane's Agricultural Report.* **Price Frequency:** weekly. **Effective Market(s):** St. Louis. **Units of Measure:** Dollars per bushel. **Time Period Covered:** latest week, week ago, year ago.

Source: *International Wheat Council Report for the Crop Year.* **Price Frequency:** monthly, quarterly, annually. **Effective Market(s):** Gulf. **Units of Measure:** Dollars per metric ton. **Time Period Covered:** latest year.

Source: *Wheat Situation and Outlook Report.* **Price Frequency:** monthly, annually. **Effective Market(s):** Corn Belt. **Units of Measure:** Dollars per bushel. **Type of Price:** farm. **Time Period Covered:** latest 10 years.

WHEAT: SOFT WHITE

Source: *Asian Wall Street Journal.* **Price Frequency:** daily. **Effective Market(s):** Portland (OR). **Units of Measure:** Dollars per bushel. **Type of Price:** cash. **Time Period Covered:** latest 2 days, year ago.

Source: *Montana Farmer-Stockman.* **Price Frequency:** monthly, seasonally. **Effective Market(s):** 9 Montana markets. **Units of Measure:** Dollars per bushel. **Type of Price:** cash. **Time Period Covered:** latest month.

WHEAT: SOFT WHITE, FUTURES

Source: *Washington Farmer-Stockman.* **Price Frequency:** monthly. **Effective Market(s):** Minneapolis. **Units of Measure:** Dollars per bushel. **Type of Price:** futures. **Time Period Covered:** latest month.

WHEAT: SPRING

Source: *Wheat Situation and Outlook Report.* **Price Frequency:** monthly, annually. **Effective Market(s):** Northern Plains. **Units of Measure:** Dollars per bushel. **Type of Price:** farm. **Time Period Covered:** latest 10 years.

WHEAT: SPRING, 11% PROTEIN

Source: *Minneapolis Grain Exchange Statistical Annual.* **Price Frequency:** daily. **Effective Market(s):** Minneapolis. **Units of Measure:** cents per bushel. **Type of Price:** cash. **Time Period Covered:** latest year.

WHEAT: SPRING, 12% PROTEIN

Source: *Minneapolis Grain Exchange Statistical Annual.* **Price Frequency:** daily. **Effective Market(s):** Minneapolis. **Units of Measure:** cents per bushel. **Type of Price:** cash. **Time Period Covered:** latest year.

WHEAT: SPRING, 13% PROTEIN

Source: *Minneapolis Grain Exchange Statistical Annual.* **Price Frequency:** daily. **Effective Market(s):** Minneapolis. **Units of Measure:** cents per bushel. **Type of Price:** cash. **Time Period Covered:** latest year.

WHEAT: SPRING, 14% PROTEIN

Source: *Asian Wall Street Journal.* **Price Frequency:** daily. **Effective Market(s):** Minneapolis. **Units of Measure:** Dollars per bushel. **Type of Price:** cash. **Time Period Covered:** latest 2 days, year ago.

Source: *Minneapolis Grain Exchange Statistical Annual.* **Price Frequency:** daily. **Effective Market(s):** Minneapolis. **Units of Measure:** cents per bushel. **Type of Price:** cash. **Time Period Covered:** latest year.

Source: *Wall Street Journal.* **Price Frequency:** daily. **Effective Market(s):** Minneapolis. **Units of Measure:** Dollars per bushel. **Time Period Covered:** latest day, day ago, year ago.

WHEAT: SPRING, 15% PROTEIN

Source: *Minneapolis Grain Exchange Statistical Annual.* **Price Frequency:** daily. **Effective Market(s):** Minneapolis. **Units of Measure:** cents per bushel. **Type of Price:** cash. **Time Period Covered:** latest year.

WHEAT: SPRING, 16% PROTEIN

Source: *Minneapolis Grain Exchange Statistical Annual.* **Price Frequency:** daily. **Effective Market(s):** Minneapolis. **Units of Measure:** cents per bushel. **Type of Price:** cash. **Time Period Covered:** latest year.

WHEAT: SPRING, 17% PROTEIN

Source: *Minneapolis Grain Exchange Statistical Annual.* **Price Frequency:** daily. **Effective Market(s):** Minneapolis. **Units of Measure:** cents per bushel. **Type of Price:** cash. **Time Period Covered:** latest year.

WHEAT: SPRING, FUTURES

Source: *Minneapolis Grain Exchange Statistical Annual.* **Price Frequency:** daily. **Effective Market(s):** Minneapolis. **Units of Measure:** cents per bushel. **Type of Price:** futures. **Time Period Covered:** latest year.

WHEAT: SPRING, OTHER TYPES

Source: *Agricultural Prices.* **Price Frequency:** monthly. **Effective Market(s):** United States. **Units of Measure:** Dollars per bushel. **Type of Price:** received by farmer. **Time Period Covered:** latest 2 months, year ago.

Source: *Agricultural Prices.* **Price Frequency:** monthly, seasonally. **Effective Market(s):** 7 domestic markets, United States. **Units of Measure:** Dollars per bushel. **Type of Price:** received by farmer. **Time Period Covered:** latest 2 months.

Source: *Agricultural Prices Annual Summary.* **Price Frequency:** annually. **Effective Market(s):** 12 domestic markets, United States. **Units of Measure:** Dollars per bushel. **Type of Price:** average received by farmer. **Time Period Covered:** latest 2 years, for US latest 6 years.

WHEAT: STANDARD

Source: *International Wheat Council Report for the Crop Year.* **Price Frequency:** monthly, quarterly, annually. **Effective Market(s):** European Economic Community. **Units of Measure:** Dollars per metric ton. **Time Period Covered:** latest year.

WHEAT: STANDARD, EUROPEAN COMMUNITY

Source: *International Wheat Council Market Report.* **Price Frequency:** weekly, seasonally. **Effective Market(s):** 12 international markets. **Units of Measure:** Dollars per metric ton. **Type of Price:** export. **Time Period Covered:** latest 5 weeks.

WHEAT: STANDARD WHITE, AUSTRALIAN

Source: *Commodity Year Book.* **Price Frequency:** annually. **Effective Market(s):** Australia. **Units of Measure:** Dollars per metric ton. **Type of Price:** export. **Time Period Covered:** latest 5 years.

Source: *International Wheat Council Market Report.* **Price Frequency:** weekly, seasonally. **Effective Market(s):** Australia. **Units of Measure:** Dollars per metric ton. **Type of Price:** export. **Time Period Covered:** latest 5 weeks.

Source: *International Wheat Council Report for the Crop Year.* **Price Frequency:** monthly, quarterly, annually. **Effective Market(s):** Australia. **Units of Measure:** Dollars per metric ton. **Time Period Covered:** latest year.

Source: *Wheat Situation and Outlook Report.* **Price Frequency:** monthly, annually. **Effective Market(s):** Australia. **Units of Measure:** Dollars per bushel. **Time Period Covered:** monthly latest 2 years, annuall latest 8 years.

Source: *World Agriculture Situation and Outlook.* **Price Frequency:** monthly, annually. **Effective Market(s):** Australia. **Units of Measure:** Dollars per metric ton. **Type of Price:** selling. **Time Period Covered:** monthly latest year, annually latest 9 years.

Source: *World Grain Situation and Outlook.* **Price Frequency:** weekly, monthly, annually. **Effective Market(s):** Australia. **Units of Measure:** Dollars per metric ton. **Type of Price:** export. **Time Period Covered:** weekly latest 3 months, monthly latest 3 years, annually latest 7 years.

WHEAT: TRIGO PAN

Source: *International Wheat Council Report for the Crop Year.* **Price Frequency:** monthly, quarterly, annually. **Effective Market(s):** Argentina. **Units of Measure:** Dollars per metric ton. **Time Period Covered:** latest year.

WHEAT: TRIGO PAN, ARGENTINE

Source: *International Wheat Council Market Report.* **Price Frequency:** weekly, seasonally. **Effective Market(s):** Argentina. **Units of Measure:** Dollars per metric ton. **Type of Price:** export. **Time Period Covered:** latest 5 weeks.

Source: *International Wheat Council Market Report.* **Price Frequency:** weekly, seasonally. **Effective Market(s):** Rotterdam. **Units of Measure:** Dollars per metric ton. **Type of Price:** cash. **Time Period Covered:** latest 5 weeks.

Source: *Monthly Commodity Price Bulletin.* **Price Frequency:** monthly, annually. **Units of Measure:** Dollars per metric ton. **Time Period Covered:** latest 5 years.

Source: *Monthly Commodity Price Bulletin Supplement.* **Price Frequency:** monthly, quarterly, annually. **Effective Market(s):** Argentina. **Units of Measure:** Dollars per tonne. **Time Period Covered:** latest 20 years.

Source: *UNCTAD Commodity Yearbook.* **Price Frequency:** annually. **Units of Measure:** Dollars per metric ton. **Type of Price:** free market. **Time Period Covered:** latest 12 years.

WHEAT: WESTERN RED SPRING, 13-1/2% PROTEIN, CANADIAN

Source: *World Grain Situation and Outlook.* **Price Frequency:** weekly, monthly, annually, seasonally. **Effective Market(s):** Rotterdam. **Units of Measure:** Dollars per metric ton. **Time Period Covered:** weekly latest 7 months, monthly latest 2 years, annually latest 17 years.

WHEAT: WESTERN WHITE

Source: *International Wheat Council Report for the Crop Year.* **Price Frequency:** monthly, quarterly, annually. **Effective Market(s):** Pacific. **Units of Measure:** Dollars per metric ton. **Time Period Covered:** latest year.

WHEAT: WHITE

Source: *Agricultural Prices.* **Price Frequency:** monthly. **Effective Market(s):** United States. **Units of Measure:** Dollars per bushel. **Type of Price:** received by farmer. **Time Period Covered:** latest 2 months, year ago.

Source: *Agricultural Prices Annual Summary.* **Price Frequency:** monthly. **Effective Market(s):** United States. **Units of Measure:** Dollars per bushel. **Type of Price:** average received by farmer. **Time Period Covered:** latest 6 years.

Source: *Wheat Situation and Outlook Report.* **Price Frequency:** monthly, annually. **Effective Market(s):** Pacific Northwest. **Units of Measure:** Dollars per bushel. **Type of Price:** farm. **Time Period Covered:** latest 10 years.

WHEAT: WHITE, FUTURES

Source: *Minneapolis Grain Exchange Statistical Annual.* **Price Frequency:** daily. **Effective Market(s):** Minneapolis. **Units of Measure:** cents per bushel. **Type of Price:** futures. **Time Period Covered:** latest year.

WHEAT: WINTER

Source: *Agricultural Prices.* **Price Frequency:** monthly. **Effective Market(s):** United States. **Units of Measure:** Dollars per bushel. **Type of Price:** received by farmer. **Time Period Covered:** latest 2 months, year ago.

Source: *Agricultural Prices.* **Price Frequency:** monthly, seasonally. **Effective Market(s):** 20 domestic markets, United States. **Units of Measure:** Dollars per bushel. **Type of Price:** received by farmer. **Time Period Covered:** latest 2 months.

Source: *Agricultural Prices Annual Summary.* **Price Frequency:** annually. **Effective Market(s):** 42 domestic markets, United States. **Units of Measure:** Dollars per bushel. **Type of Price:** average received by farmer. **Time Period Covered:** latest 2 years, for US latest 6 years.

WHEAT: WINTER, MINNESOTA/SOUTH DAKOTA

Source: *Minneapolis Grain Exchange Statistical Annual.* **Price Frequency:** daily. **Effective Market(s):** Minneapolis. **Units of Measure:** cents per bushel. **Type of Price:** cash. **Time Period Covered:** latest year.

WHEAT: WINTER, MONTANA/NORTH DAKOTA

Source: *Minneapolis Grain Exchange Statistical Annual.* **Price Frequency:** daily. **Effective Market(s):** Minneapolis. **Units of Measure:** cents per bushel. **Type of Price:** cash. **Time Period Covered:** latest year.

WHEAT BRAN

Source: *Feed Situation and Outlook Report.* **Price Frequency:** monthly. **Effective Market(s):** Kansas City. **Units of Measure:** Dollars per ton. **Type of Price:** wholesale. **Time Period Covered:** latest 8 months.

Source: *Feed Situation and Outlook Report.* **Price Frequency:** quarterly, annually. **Effective Market(s):** United States. **Units of Measure:** Dollars per 100 lbs. **Type of Price:** paid by farmer. **Time Period Covered:** latest year.

Source: *Grain and Feed Market News.* **Price Frequency:** weekly, seasonally. **Effective Market(s):** Kansas City, Minneapolis. **Units of Measure:** Dollars per ton. **Type of Price:** wholesale. **Time Period Covered:** latest week, week ago, year ago.

WHEAT BRAN MIDDLINGS

Source: *Asian Wall Street Journal.* **Price Frequency:** daily. **Effective Market(s):** Kansas City. **Units of Measure:** Dollars per ton. **Type of Price:** cash. **Time Period Covered:** latest 2 days, year ago.

Source: *Wall Street Journal.* **Price Frequency:** daily. **Effective Market(s):** Kansas City. **Units of Measure:** Dollars per ton. **Time Period Covered:** latest day, day ago, year ago.

WHEAT FOR SEED

see Seed Wheat.

WHEAT GERM OIL: COLD PRESSED

Source: *Chemical Marketing Reporter.* **Price Frequency:** weekly. **Effective Market(s):** New York. **Units of Measure:** Dollars per gallon. **Type of Price:** spot. **Time Period Covered:** latest week.

WHEAT GERM OIL: COLD PROCESSED

Source: *Chemical Marketing Reporter.* **Price Frequency:** weekly. **Effective Market(s):** New York. **Units of Measure:** Dollars per gallon. **Type of Price:** spot. **Time Period Covered:** latest week.

WHEAT MIDDLINGS

Source: *Feed Situation and Outlook Report.* **Price Frequency:** monthly. **Effective Market(s):** Kansas City. **Units of Measure:** Dollars per ton. **Type of Price:** wholesale. **Time Period Covered:** latest 8 months.

Source: *Feed Situation and Outlook Report.* **Price Frequency:** quarterly, annually. **Effective Market(s):** United States. **Units of Measure:** Dollars per 100 lbs. **Type of Price:** paid by farmer. **Time Period Covered:** latest year.

Source: *Grain and Feed Market News.* **Price Frequency:** weekly, seasonally. **Effective Market(s):** Buffalo, Kansas City, Memphis (TN), Minneapolis, St. Louis. **Units of Measure:** Dollars per ton. **Type of Price:** wholesale. **Time Period Covered:** latest week, week ago, year ago.

WHEAT MILLRUN

Source: *California Farmer.* **Price Frequency:** semi-monthly. **Effective Market(s):** Los Angeles, Northern California. **Units of Measure:** Dollars per ton. **Time Period Covered:** latest week, month ago, year ago.

Source: *Grain and Feed Market News.* **Price Frequency:** weekly, seasonally. **Effective Market(s):** Los Angeles, Northern California points, Portland (OR). **Units of Measure:** Dollars per ton. **Type of Price:** wholesale. **Time Period Covered:** latest week, week ago, year ago.

Source: *Los Angeles Times.* **Price Frequency:** daily. **Effective Market(s):** Los Angeles. **Units of Measure:** Dollars per ton. **Type of Price:** cash. **Time Period Covered:** latest day.

WHEAT STRAW

Source: *Farm and Dairy.* **Price Frequency:** weekly, seasonally. **Effective Market(s):** Ohio, Pennsylvania. **Units of Measure:** Dollars per load. **Type of Price:** auction high, auction low. **Time Period Covered:** latest week.

Source: *Scottish Farmer.* **Price Frequency:** weekly. **Effective Market(s):** Scotland. **Units of Measure:** British pounds per tonne. **Type of Price:** average farmers buying-in. **Time Period Covered:** latest week.

WHEY

Source: *Milling & Baking News.* **Price Frequency:** weekly. **Effective Market(s):** Kansas City. **Units of Measure:** Dollars per 100 lbs. **Time Period Covered:** latest week, week ago, year ago.

WHEY: DARK COLOR, DRY, SPRAY, BAGS

Source: *Urner Barry's Price-Current.* **Price Frequency:** daily. **Units of Measure:** cents per lb. **Time Period Covered:** latest day.

WHEY: DELACTOSE, EDIBLE, REGULAR

Source: *Milling & Baking News.* **Price Frequency:** weekly. **Units of Measure:** cents per lb. **Time Period Covered:** latest week.

WHEY: DELACTOSE, SACKED

Source: *Feedstuffs.* **Price Frequency:** weekly. **Effective Market(s):** Chicago, Ft. Worth, Kansas City, Minneapolis/St. Paul. **Units of Measure:** Dollars per 100 lbs. **Time Period Covered:** latest week.

WHEY: HYGROSCOPIC

Source: *Milling & Baking News.* **Price Frequency:** weekly. **Units of Measure:** cents per lb. **Time Period Covered:** latest week.

WHEY: LIGHT COLOR, DRY, SPRAY, BAGS

Source: *Urner Barry's Price-Current.* **Price Frequency:** daily. **Units of Measure:** cents per lb. **Time Period Covered:** latest day.

WHEY: NONHYGROSCOPIC

Source: *Milling & Baking News.* **Price Frequency:** weekly. **Units of Measure:** cents per lb. **Time Period Covered:** latest week.

WHEY: NONHYGROSCOPIC, EDIBLE, DRIED

Source: *Federal Milk Order Market Statistics.* **Price Frequency:** monthly, annually. **Effective Market(s):** Central States. **Units of Measure:** Dollars per lb. **Type of Price:** wholesale. **Time Period Covered:** latest year.

WHEY: WHOLE, SACKED

Source: *Feedstuffs.* **Price Frequency:** weekly. **Effective Market(s):** Chicago, Ft. Worth, Kansas City, Minneapolis/St. Paul. **Units of Measure:** Dollars per 100 lbs. **Time Period Covered:** latest week.

Source: *Feedstuffs.* **Price Frequency:** weekly. **Effective Market(s):** Chicago. **Units of Measure:** Dollars per 100 lbs. **Time Period Covered:** latest week, week ago, 6 months ago, year ago.

WHEY POWDER: DELACTOSE, USED FOR ANIMAL FEED

Source: *Dairy Market Statistics.* **Price Frequency:** monthly, annually. **Effective Market(s):** Central States. **Units of Measure:** Dollars per lb. **Type of Price:** farm. **Time Period Covered:** latest year.

WHEY POWDER: EDIBLE

Source: *Dairy Market Statistics.* **Price Frequency:** monthly, annually. **Effective Market(s):** Central States, Western area. **Units of Measure:** Dollars per lb. **Type of Price:** wholesale. **Time Period Covered:** latest year.

WHEY POWDER: EXTRA GRADE, EDIBLE

Source: *Dairy Market Statistics.* **Price Frequency:** monthly, annually. **Effective Market(s):** Eastern area, Southern area. **Units of Measure:** Dollars per lb. **Type of Price:** wholesale. **Time Period Covered:** latest year.

WHEY POWDER: GRADE A, EDIBLE

Source: *Dairy Market Statistics.* **Price Frequency:** monthly, annually. **Effective Market(s):** Eastern area, Southern area. **Units of Measure:** Dollars per lb. **Type of Price:** wholesale. **Time Period Covered:** latest year.

WHEY POWDER: USED FOR ANIMAL FEED, ROLLER PROCESS, GROUND

Source: *Dairy Market Statistics.* **Price Frequency:** monthly, annually. **Effective Market(s):** Central States. **Units of Measure:** Dollars per lb. **Type of Price:** farm. **Time Period Covered:** latest year.

WHEY POWDER: USED FOR ANIMAL FEED, SPRAY PROCESS, MILK REPLACER

Source: *Dairy Market Statistics.* **Price Frequency:** monthly, annually. **Effective Market(s):** Central States, Eastern area. **Units of Measure:** Dollars per lb. **Type of Price:** farm. **Time Period Covered:** latest year.

WHEY POWDER: USED FOR ANIMAL FEED, SPRAY PROCESS, STANDARD

Source: *Dairy Market Statistics.* **Price Frequency:** monthly, annually. **Effective Market(s):** Central States. **Units of Measure:** Dollars per lb. **Type of Price:** farm. **Time Period Covered:** latest year.

WHEY PROTEIN CONCENTRATE

Source: *Dairy Foods.* **Price Frequency:** monthly. **Effective Market(s):** Central States. **Units of Measure:** Dollars per lb. **Time Period Covered:** latest month.

WHEY PROTEIN CONCENTRATE: CALF-MILK REPLACER

Source: *Milling & Baking News.* **Price Frequency:** weekly. **Units of Measure:** cents per lb. **Time Period Covered:** latest week.

WHEY PROTEIN CONCENTRATE: EDIBLE

Source: *Dairy Market Statistics.* **Price Frequency:** monthly, annually. **Effective Market(s):** Central/Western areas. **Units of Measure:** Dollars per lb. **Type of Price:** farm. **Time Period Covered:** latest year.

WHEY PROTEIN CONCENTRATE: EDIBLE, REGULAR

Source: *Milling & Baking News.* **Price Frequency:** weekly. **Units of Measure:** cents per lb. **Time Period Covered:** latest week.

WHEY SPRAY

Source: *Dairy Foods.* **Price Frequency:** monthly. **Effective Market(s):** Eastern area, South. **Units of Measure:** Dollars per lb. **Time Period Covered:** latest month.

WHISKEY

Source: *Beverage Media.* **Price Frequency:** monthly. **Effective Market(s):** New York. **Units of Measure:** Dollars per unit. **Type of Price:** wholesale by brand. **Time Period Covered:** latest month.

Source: *Illinois Beverage Journal.* **Price Frequency:** monthly. **Effective Market(s):** Illinois. **Units of Measure:** Dollars per case. **Type of Price:** wholesale by brand. **Time Period Covered:** latest month.

Source: *Indiana Beverage Journal.* **Price Frequency:** monthly. **Effective Market(s):** Indiana. **Units of Measure:** Dollars per case, dollars per bottle. **Type of Price:** wholesale by brand. **Time Period Covered:** latest month.

Source: *Nevada Beverage Index.* **Price Frequency:** monthly. **Effective Market(s):** Nevada. **Units of Measure:** Dollars per unit. **Type of Price:** wholesale by brand. **Time Period Covered:** latest month.

Source: *Rhode Island Beverage Journal.* **Price Frequency:** monthly. **Effective Market(s):** Rhode Island. **Units of Measure:** Dollars per unit. **Type of Price:** wholesale by brand. **Time Period Covered:** latest month.

WHISKEY: BLENDED

Source: *Colorado Beverage Analyst.* **Price Frequency:** monthly. **Effective Market(s):** Colorado. **Units of Measure:** Dollars per case. **Type of Price:** wholesale by brand. **Time Period Covered:** latest month.

Source: *Kentucky Beverage Journal.* **Price Frequency:** monthly. **Effective Market(s):** Kentucky. **Units of Measure:** Dollars per bottle, dollars per case. **Type of Price:** wholesale by brand. **Time Period Covered:** latest month.

WHISKEY: BONDED

Source: *Colorado Beverage Analyst.* **Price Frequency:** monthly. **Effective Market(s):** Colorado. **Units of Measure:** Dollars per case. **Type of Price:** wholesale by brand. **Time Period Covered:** latest month.

Source: *Kentucky Beverage Journal.* **Price Frequency:** monthly. **Effective Market(s):** Kentucky. **Units of Measure:** Dollars per bottle, dollars per case. **Type of Price:** wholesale by brand. **Time Period Covered:** latest month.

WHISKEY: CANADIAN

Source: *Colorado Beverage Analyst.* **Price Frequency:** monthly. **Effective Market(s):** Colorado. **Units of Measure:** Dollars per case. **Type of Price:** wholesale by brand. **Time Period Covered:** latest month.

Source: *Illinois Beverage Journal.* **Price Frequency:** monthly. **Effective Market(s):** Illinois. **Units of Measure:** Dollars per case. **Type of Price:** wholesale by brand. **Time Period Covered:** latest month.

Source: *Kentucky Beverage Journal.* **Price Frequency:** monthly. **Effective Market(s):** Kentucky. **Units of Measure:** Dollars per bottle, dollars per case. **Type of Price:** wholesale by brand. **Time Period Covered:** latest month.

WHISKEY: CHINESE

Source: *Colorado Beverage Analyst.* **Price Frequency:** monthly. **Effective Market(s):** Colorado. **Units of Measure:** Dollars per case. **Type of Price:** wholesale by brand. **Time Period Covered:** latest month.

WHISKEY: CORN

Source: *Colorado Beverage Analyst.* **Price Frequency:** monthly. **Effective Market(s):** Colorado. **Units of Measure:** Dollars per case. **Type of Price:** wholesale by brand. **Time Period Covered:** latest month.

Source: *Kentucky Beverage Journal.* **Price Frequency:** monthly. **Effective Market(s):** Kentucky. **Units of Measure:** Dollars per bottle, dollars per case. **Type of Price:** wholesale by brand. **Time Period Covered:** latest month.

WHISKEY: IRISH

Source: *Colorado Beverage Analyst.* **Price Frequency:** monthly. **Effective Market(s):** Colorado. **Units of Measure:** Dollars per case. **Type of Price:** wholesale by brand. **Time Period Covered:** latest month.

Source: *Illinois Beverage Journal.* **Price Frequency:** monthly. **Effective Market(s):** Illinois. **Units of Measure:** Dollars per case. **Type of Price:** wholesale by brand. **Time Period Covered:** latest month.

Source: *Kentucky Beverage Journal.* **Price Frequency:** monthly. **Effective Market(s):** Kentucky. **Units of Measure:** Dollars per bottle, dollars per case. **Type of Price:** wholesale by brand. **Time Period Covered:** latest month.

WHISKEY: JAPANESE

Source: *Colorado Beverage Analyst.* **Price Frequency:** monthly. **Effective Market(s):** Colorado. **Units of Measure:** Dollars per case. **Type of Price:** wholesale by brand. **Time Period Covered:** latest month.

Source: *Illinois Beverage Journal.* **Price Frequency:** monthly. **Effective Market(s):** Illinois. **Units of Measure:** Dollars per case. **Type of Price:** wholesale by brand. **Time Period Covered:** latest month.

WHISKEY: LIGHT

Source: *Colorado Beverage Analyst.* **Price Frequency:** monthly. **Effective Market(s):** Colorado. **Units of Measure:** Dollars per case. **Type of Price:** wholesale by brand. **Time Period Covered:** latest month.

Source: *Illinois Beverage Journal.* **Price Frequency:** monthly. **Effective Market(s):** Illinois. **Units of Measure:** Dollars per case. **Type of Price:** wholesale by brand. **Time Period Covered:** latest month.

Source: *Kentucky Beverage Journal.* **Price Frequency:** monthly. **Effective Market(s):** Kentucky. **Units of Measure:** Dollars per bottle, dollars per case. **Type of Price:** wholesale by brand. **Time Period Covered:** latest month.

WHISKEY: RYE

Source: *Colorado Beverage Analyst.* **Price Frequency:** monthly. **Effective Market(s):** Colorado. **Units of Measure:** Dollars per case. **Type of Price:** wholesale by brand. **Time Period Covered:** latest month.

Source: *Kentucky Beverage Journal.* **Price Frequency:** monthly. **Effective Market(s):** Kentucky. **Units of Measure:** Dollars per bottle, dollars per case. **Type of Price:** wholesale by brand. **Time Period Covered:** latest month.

WHISKEY: STRAIGHT

Source: *Colorado Beverage Analyst.* **Price Frequency:** monthly. **Effective Market(s):** Colorado. **Units of Measure:** Dollars per case. **Type of Price:** wholesale by brand. **Time Period Covered:** latest month.

Source: *Kentucky Beverage Journal.* **Price Frequency:** monthly. **Effective Market(s):** Kentucky. **Units of Measure:** Dollars per bottle, dollars per case. **Type of Price:** wholesale by brand. **Time Period Covered:** latest month.

WHITE ARSENIC

See Arsenic Trioxide.

WHITE PRECIPITATE: POWDERED, USP

Source: *Chemical Marketing Reporter.* **Price Frequency:** weekly. **Effective Market(s):** New York. **Units of Measure:** Dollars per lb. **Type of Price:** spot. **Time Period Covered:** latest week.

WHITEFISH: WHOLE, DRESSED, FRESH, CANADIAN

Source: *Seafood Price-Current.* **Price Frequency:** semiweekly. **Effective Market(s):** Mid-Atlantic, New England. **Units of Measure:** Dollars per lb. **Type of Price:** sale by first receiver. **Time Period Covered:** latest day.

WHITEFISH: WHOLE, FRESH

Source: *Seafood Price-Current.* **Price Frequency:** semiweekly. **Effective Market(s):** Mid-Atlantic, New England. **Units of Measure:** Dollars per lb. **Type of Price:** sale by first receiver. **Time Period Covered:** latest day.

WHITING (CHEMICAL)

see Calcium Carbonate.

WHITING: BLOCKS, DEFATTED

Source: *NMFS Green Sheet Supplement.* **Price Frequency:** weekly. **Units of Measure:** Dollars per lb. **Time Period Covered:** latest week.

WHITING: BLOCKS, IMPORTED

Source: *NMFS Green Sheet Supplement.* **Price Frequency:** weekly. **Units of Measure:** Dollars per lb. **Time Period Covered:** latest week.

WHITING: FILLETS, DOMESTIC

Source: *NMFS Green Sheet Supplement.* **Price Frequency:** weekly. **Units of Measure:** Dollars per lb. **Time Period Covered:** latest week.

WHITING: FILLETS, SKIN ON

Source: *NMFS Green Sheet Supplement.* **Price Frequency:** weekly. **Units of Measure:** Dollars per lb. **Time Period Covered:** latest week.

WHITING: FILLETS, SKINLESS, FROZEN, ARGENTINA/URUGUAY

Source: *Seafood Price-Current.* **Price Frequency:** semiweekly. **Effective Market(s):** Mid-Atlantic. **Units of Measure:** Dollars per lb. **Type of Price:** first receiver. **Time Period Covered:** latest day.

WHITING: FILLETS, SOUTH AMERICAN

Source: *NMFS Green Sheet Supplement.* **Price Frequency:** weekly. **Units of Measure:** Dollars per lb. **Time Period Covered:** latest week.

WHITING: FISH PORTIONS, BATTERED, COOKED

Source: *NMFS Green Sheet Supplement.* **Price Frequency:** weekly, seasonally. **Effective Market(s):** New England. **Units of Measure:** Dollars per lb. **Type of Price:** to primary wholesalers. **Time Period Covered:** latest week.

WHITING: FISH PORTIONS, BATTERED, RAW

Source: *NMFS Green Sheet Supplement.* **Price Frequency:** weekly, seasonally. **Effective Market(s):** New England. **Units of Measure:** Dollars per lb. **Type of Price:** to primary wholesalers. **Time Period Covered:** latest week.

WHITING: FISH PORTIONS, BREADED, COOKED

Source: *NMFS Green Sheet Supplement.* **Price Frequency:** weekly, seasonally. **Effective Market(s):** New England. **Units of Measure:** Dollars per lb. **Type of Price:** to primary wholesalers. **Time Period Covered:** latest week.

WHITING: FISH PORTIONS, BREADED, RAW

Source: *NMFS Green Sheet Supplement.* **Price Frequency:** weekly, seasonally. **Effective Market(s):** New England. **Units of Measure:** Dollars per lb. **Type of Price:** to primary wholesalers. **Time Period Covered:** latest week.

WHITING: FISH STICKS, BATTERED, COOKED

Source: *NMFS Green Sheet Supplement.* **Price Frequency:** weekly, seasonally. **Effective Market(s):** New England. **Units of Measure:** Dollars per lb. **Type of Price:** to primary wholesalers. **Time Period Covered:** latest week.

WHITING: FISH STICKS, BATTERED, RAW

Source: *NMFS Green Sheet Supplement.* **Price Frequency:** weekly, seasonally. **Effective Market(s):** New England. **Units of Measure:** Dollars per lb. **Type of Price:** to primary wholesalers. **Time Period Covered:** latest week.

WHITING: FISH STICKS, BREADED, COOKED

Source: *NMFS Green Sheet Supplement.* **Price Frequency:** weekly, seasonally. **Effective Market(s):** New England. **Units of Measure:** Dollars per lb. **Type of Price:** to primary wholesalers. **Time Period Covered:** latest week.

WHITING: FISH STICKS, BREADED, RAW

Source: *NMFS Green Sheet Supplement.* **Price Frequency:** weekly, seasonally. **Effective Market(s):** New England. **Units of Measure:** Dollars per lb. **Type of Price:** to primary wholesalers. **Time Period Covered:** latest week.

WHITING: KING, WHOLE, FRESH

Source: *Seafood Price-Current.* **Price Frequency:** semiweekly. **Effective Market(s):** Boston, Mid-Atlantic, New Bedford (MA), Portland (ME). **Units of Measure:** Dollars per lb. **Type of Price:** sale by first receiver, auction price. **Time Period Covered:** latest day.

WHITING: PROCESSORS FISH BLOCKS, DEFATTED, SOUTH AMERICAN

Source: *Seafood Price-Current.* **Price Frequency:** semiweekly. **Effective Market(s):** New England. **Units of Measure:** Dollars per lb. **Time Period Covered:** latest day.

WHITING: PROCESSORS FISH BLOCKS, MINCED, SOUTH AMERICAN

Source: *Seafood Price-Current.* **Price Frequency:** semiweekly. **Effective Market(s):** New England. **Units of Measure:** Dollars per lb. **Time Period Covered:** latest day.

WHITING: PROCESSORS FISH BLOCKS, SOUTH AMERICAN

Source: *Seafood Price-Current.* **Price Frequency:** semiweekly. **Effective Market(s):** New England. **Units of Measure:** Dollars per lb. **Time Period Covered:** latest day.

WHITING: WHOLE, DRESSED, FRESH

Source: *Seafood Price-Current.* **Price Frequency:** semiweekly. **Effective Market(s):** West Coast. **Units of Measure:** Dollars per lb. **Type of Price:** sale by first receiver. **Time Period Covered:** latest day.

WHITING: WHOLE, FRESH

Source: *Seafood Price-Current.* **Price Frequency:** semiweekly. **Effective Market(s):** Boston, Mid-Atlantic, New Bedford (MA), Portland (ME). **Units of Measure:** Dollars per lb. **Type of Price:** sale by first receiver, auction price. **Time Period Covered:** latest day.

WHITING: WHOLE, SKIN ON, FROZEN, DOMESTIC

Source: *Seafood Price-Current.* **Price Frequency:** semiweekly. **Effective Market(s):** Mid-Atlantic. **Units of Measure:** Dollars per lb. **Type of Price:** sale by first receiver. **Time Period Covered:** latest day.

WHITING: WHOLE, SKIN ON, FROZEN, SOUTH AMERICAN

Source: *Seafood Price-Current.* **Price Frequency:** semiweekly. **Effective Market(s):** Mid-Atlantic. **Units of Measure:** Dollars per lb. **Type of Price:** sale by first receiver. **Time Period Covered:** latest day.

WIDE-FLANGE

Source: *ENR.* **Price Frequency:** monthly in second issue of month. **Effective Market(s):** 17 domestic markets, Montreal, Toronto. **Units of Measure:** Dollars per 100 lbs. **Type of Price:** spot. **Time Period Covered:** latest month.

WILD CHERRY BARK: THIN, NATURAL

Source: *Journal of Commerce and Commercial.* **Price Frequency:** weekly in Monday issue. **Units of Measure:** Dollars per lb. **Type of Price:** spot. **Time Period Covered:** latest week.

WINDROWER: SELF-PROPELLED

Source: *Agricultural Prices.* **Price Frequency:** semiannually. **Effective Market(s):** United States. **Units of Measure:** Dollars each. **Type of Price:** paid by farmer. **Time Period Covered:** latest year.

Source: *Agricultural Prices Annual Summary.* **Price Frequency:** annually. **Effective Market(s):** United States. **Units of Measure:** Dollars each. **Type of Price:** average paid by farmer. **Time Period Covered:** latest 6 years.

WINE

see also Port, Sherry, Tokay.

WINE: AMERICAN

Source: *Rhode Island Beverage Journal.* **Price Frequency:** monthly. **Effective Market(s):** Rhode Island. **Units of Measure:** Dollars per unit. **Type of Price:** wholesale by brand. **Time Period Covered:** latest month.

WINE: CARBONATED, AMERICAN

Source: *Nevada Beverage Index.* **Price Frequency:** monthly. **Effective Market(s):** Nevada. **Units of Measure:** Dollars per unit. **Type of Price:** wholesale by brand. **Time Period Covered:** latest month.

WINE: CARBONATED, IMPORTED

Source: *Nevada Beverage Index.* **Price Frequency:** monthly. **Effective Market(s):** Nevada. **Units of Measure:** Dollars per unit. **Type of Price:** wholesale by brand. **Time Period Covered:** latest month.

WINE: CHABLIS

Source: *California Wineletter.* **Price Frequency:** semiweekly. **Effective Market(s):** Non-California markets. **Units of Measure:** Dollars per gallon. **Type of Price:** asking. **Time Period Covered:** latest week.

WINE: CHENIN BLANC

Source: *California Wineletter.* **Price Frequency:** semiweekly. **Effective Market(s):** Non-California markets. **Units of Measure:** Dollars per gallon. **Type of Price:** asking. **Time Period Covered:** latest week.

WINE: CHINESE

Source: *Colorado Beverage Analyst.* **Price Frequency:** monthly. **Effective Market(s):** Colorado. **Units of Measure:** Dollars per case. **Type of Price:** wholesale by brand. **Time Period Covered:** latest month.

WINE: COLOMBARD

Source: *California Wineletter.* **Price Frequency:** semi-weekly. **Effective Market(s):** Non-California markets. **Units of Measure:** Dollars per gallon. **Type of Price:** asking. **Time Period Covered:** latest week.

WINE: DESSERT

Source: *California Wineletter.* **Price Frequency:** semi-weekly. **Effective Market(s):** Non-California markets. **Units of Measure:** Dollars per gallon. **Type of Price:** asking. **Time Period Covered:** latest week.

WINE: DOMESTIC

Source: *Colorado Beverage Analyst.* **Price Frequency:** monthly. **Effective Market(s):** Colorado. **Units of Measure:** Dollars per case. **Type of Price:** wholesale by brand. **Time Period Covered:** latest month.

Source: *Kentucky Beverage Journal.* **Price Frequency:** monthly. **Effective Market(s):** Kentucky. **Units of Measure:** Dollars per bottle, dollars per case. **Type of Price:** wholesale by brand. **Time Period Covered:** latest month.

WINE: GRENACHE ROSE

Source: *California Wineletter.* **Price Frequency:** semi-weekly. **Effective Market(s):** Non-California markets. **Units of Measure:** Dollars per gallon. **Type of Price:** asking. **Time Period Covered:** latest week.

WINE: IMPORTED

Source: *Colorado Beverage Analyst.* **Price Frequency:** monthly. **Effective Market(s):** Colorado. **Units of Measure:** Dollars per case. **Type of Price:** wholesale by brand. **Time Period Covered:** latest month.

Source: *Kentucky Beverage Journal.* **Price Frequency:** monthly. **Effective Market(s):** Kentucky. **Units of Measure:** Dollars per bottle, dollars per case. **Type of Price:** wholesale by brand. **Time Period Covered:** latest month.

Source: *Rhode Island Beverage Journal.* **Price Frequency:** monthly. **Effective Market(s):** Rhode Island. **Units of Measure:** Dollars per unit. **Type of Price:** wholesale by brand. **Time Period Covered:** latest month.

WINE: JAPANESE

Source: *Colorado Beverage Analyst.* **Price Frequency:** monthly. **Effective Market(s):** Colorado. **Units of Measure:** Dollars per case. **Type of Price:** wholesale by brand. **Time Period Covered:** latest month.

WINE: RED, DRY

Source: *California Wineletter.* **Price Frequency:** semi-weekly. **Effective Market(s):** Non-California markets. **Units of Measure:** Dollars per gallon. **Type of Price:** asking. **Time Period Covered:** latest week.

WINE: RED, DRY, CABERNET

Source: *California Wineletter.* **Price Frequency:** semi-weekly. **Effective Market(s):** Non-California markets. **Units of Measure:** Dollars per gallon. **Type of Price:** asking. **Time Period Covered:** latest week.

WINE: RED, SWEET

Source: *California Wineletter.* **Price Frequency:** semi-weekly. **Effective Market(s):** Non-California markets. **Units of Measure:** Dollars per gallon. **Type of Price:** asking. **Time Period Covered:** latest week.

WINE: RED, TABLE

Source: *FAO Quarterly Bulletin of Statistics.* **Price Frequency:** monthly, annually. **Effective Market(s):** European Economic Community. **Units of Measure:** ECU per degree per hectoliter, dollars per metric ton. **Time Period Covered:** latest 3 years.

WINE: ROSE

Source: *California Wineletter.* **Price Frequency:** semi-weekly. **Effective Market(s):** Non-California markets. **Units of Measure:** Dollars per gallon. **Type of Price:** asking. **Time Period Covered:** latest week.

WINE: SPARKLING

see also Champagne.

WINE: SPARKLING, AMERICAN

Source: *Beverage Media.* **Price Frequency:** monthly. **Effective Market(s):** New York. **Units of Measure:** Dollars per unit. **Type of Price:** wholesale by brand. **Time Period Covered:** latest month.

Source: *Indiana Beverage Journal.* **Price Frequency:** monthly. **Effective Market(s):** Indiana. **Units of Measure:** Dollars per case, dollars per bottle. **Type of Price:** wholesale by brand. **Time Period Covered:** latest month.

Source: *Nevada Beverage Index.* **Price Frequency:** monthly. **Effective Market(s):** Nevada. **Units of Measure:** Dollars per unit. **Type of Price:** wholesale by brand. **Time Period Covered:** latest month.

Source: *Rhode Island Beverage Journal.* **Price Frequency:** monthly. **Effective Market(s):** Rhode Island. **Units of Measure:** Dollars per unit. **Type of Price:** wholesale by brand. **Time Period Covered:** latest month.

WINE: SPARKLING, DOMESTIC

Source: *Colorado Beverage Analyst.* **Price Frequency:** monthly. **Effective Market(s):** Colorado. **Units of Measure:** Dollars per case. **Type of Price:** wholesale by brand. **Time Period Covered:** latest month.

Source: *Illinois Beverage Journal.* **Price Frequency:** monthly. **Effective Market(s):** Illinois. **Units of Measure:** Dollars per case. **Type of Price:** wholesale by brand. **Time Period Covered:** latest month.

WINE: SPARKLING, IMPORTED

Source: *Beverage Media.* **Price Frequency:** monthly. **Effective Market(s):** New York. **Units of Measure:** Dollars per unit. **Type of Price:** wholesale by brand. **Time Period Covered:** latest month.

Source: *Colorado Beverage Analyst.* **Price Frequency:** monthly. **Effective Market(s):** Colorado. **Units of Measure:** Dollars per case. **Type of Price:** wholesale by brand. **Time Period Covered:** latest month.

Source: *Illinois Beverage Journal.* **Price Frequency:** monthly. **Effective Market(s):** Illinois. **Units of Measure:** Dollars per case. **Type of Price:** wholesale by brand. **Time Period Covered:** latest month.

Source: *Indiana Beverage Journal.* **Price Frequency:** monthly. **Effective Market(s):** Indiana. **Units of Measure:** Dollars per case, dollars per bottle. **Type of Price:** wholesale by brand. **Time Period Covered:** latest month.

Source: *Nevada Beverage Index.* **Price Frequency:** monthly. **Effective Market(s):** Nevada. **Units of Measure:** Dollars per unit. **Type of Price:** wholesale by brand. **Time Period Covered:** latest month.

Source: *Rhode Island Beverage Journal.* **Price Frequency:** monthly. **Effective Market(s):** Rhode Island. **Units of Measure:** Dollars per unit. **Type of Price:** wholesale by brand. **Time Period Covered:** latest month.

WINE: STILL, AMERICAN

Source: *Beverage Media.* **Price Frequency:** monthly. **Effective Market(s):** New York. **Units of Measure:** Dollars per unit. **Type of Price:** wholesale by brand. **Time Period Covered:** latest month.

Source: *Indiana Beverage Journal.* **Price Frequency:** monthly. **Effective Market(s):** Indiana. **Units of Measure:** Dollars per case, dollars per bottle. **Type of Price:** wholesale by brand. **Time Period Covered:** latest month.

Source: *Nevada Beverage Index.* **Price Frequency:** monthly. **Effective Market(s):** Nevada. **Units of Measure:** Dollars per unit. **Type of Price:** wholesale by brand. **Time Period Covered:** latest month.

WINE: STILL, DOMESTIC

Source: *Illinois Beverage Journal.* **Price Frequency:** monthly. **Effective Market(s):** Illinois. **Units of Measure:** Dollars per case. **Type of Price:** wholesale by brand. **Time Period Covered:** latest month.

WINE: STILL, IMPORTED

Source: *Beverage Media.* **Price Frequency:** monthly. **Effective Market(s):** New York. **Units of Measure:** Dollars per unit. **Type of Price:** wholesale by brand. **Time Period Covered:** latest month.

Source: *Illinois Beverage Journal.* **Price Frequency:** monthly. **Effective Market(s):** Illinois. **Units of Measure:** Dollars per case. **Type of Price:** wholesale by brand. **Time Period Covered:** latest month.

Source: *Indiana Beverage Journal.* **Price Frequency:** monthly. **Effective Market(s):** Indiana. **Units of Measure:** Dollars per case, dollars per bottle. **Type of Price:** wholesale by brand. **Time Period Covered:** latest month.

Source: *Nevada Beverage Index.* **Price Frequency:** monthly. **Effective Market(s):** Nevada. **Units of Measure:** Dollars per unit. **Type of Price:** wholesale by brand. **Time Period Covered:** latest month.

WINE: TABLE

Source: *California Wineletter.* **Price Frequency:** semiweekly. **Effective Market(s):** Non-California markets. **Units of Measure:** Dollars per gallon. **Type of Price:** asking. **Time Period Covered:** latest week.

WINE: WHITE, STANDARD DRY

Source: *California Wineletter.* **Price Frequency:** semiweekly. **Effective Market(s):** Non-California markets. **Units of Measure:** Dollars per gallon. **Type of Price:** asking. **Time Period Covered:** latest week.

WINE: WHITE, TABLE

Source: *FAO Quarterly Bulletin of Statistics.* **Price Frequency:** monthly, annually. **Effective Market(s):** European Economic Community. **Units of Measure:** ECU per degree per hectoliter, dollars per metric ton. **Time Period Covered:** latest 3 years.

WINE: ZINFANDEL

Source: *California Wineletter.* **Price Frequency:** semiweekly. **Effective Market(s):** Non-California markets. **Units of Measure:** Dollars per gallon. **Type of Price:** asking. **Time Period Covered:** latest week.

WINE COOLERS

Source: *Beverage Media.* **Price Frequency:** monthly. **Effective Market(s):** New York. **Units of Measure:** Dollars per unit. **Type of Price:** wholesale by brand. **Time Period Covered:** latest month.

Source: *Colorado Beverage Analyst.* **Price Frequency:** monthly. **Effective Market(s):** Colorado. **Units of Measure:** Dollars per case. **Type of Price:** wholesale by brand. **Time Period Covered:** latest month.

Source: *Illinois Beverage Journal.* **Price Frequency:** monthly. **Effective Market(s):** Illinois. **Units of Measure:** Dollars per case. **Type of Price:** wholesale by brand. **Time Period Covered:** latest month.

Source: *Indiana Beverage Journal.* **Price Frequency:** monthly. **Effective Market(s):** Indiana. **Units of Measure:** Dollars per case, dollars per bottle. **Type of Price:** wholesale by brand. **Time Period Covered:** latest month.

Source: *Kentucky Beverage Journal.* **Price Frequency:** monthly. **Effective Market(s):** Kentucky. **Units of Measure:** Dollars per bottle, dollars per case. **Type of Price:** wholesale by brand. **Time Period Covered:** latest month.

Source: *Nevada Beverage Index.* **Price Frequency:** monthly. **Effective Market(s):** Nevada. **Units of Measure:** Dollars per unit. **Type of Price:** wholesale by brand. **Time Period Covered:** latest month.

Source: *Rhode Island Beverage Journal.* **Price Frequency:** monthly. **Effective Market(s):** Rhode Island. **Units of Measure:** Dollars per unit. **Type of Price:** wholesale by brand. **Time Period Covered:** latest month.

WINTERGREEN OIL: SOUTHERN

Source: *Journal of Commerce and Commercial.* **Price Frequency:** weekly in Tuesday issue. **Units of Measure:** Dollars per lb. **Type of Price:** spot. **Time Period Covered:** latest week.

WINTERGREEN OIL: SYNTHETIC

see Methyl Salicylate.

WIRE: BARBED, GALVANIZED

Source: *Agricultural Prices Annual Summary.* **Price Frequency:** quarterly. **Effective Market(s):** United States. **Units of Measure:** Dollars per 20 rod spool. **Type of Price:** average paid by farmer. **Time Period Covered:** latest 6 years.

WITCH HAZEL BARK

Source: *Chemical Marketing Reporter.* **Price Frequency:** weekly. **Effective Market(s):** New York. **Units of Measure:** Dollars per lb. **Type of Price:** spot. **Time Period Covered:** latest week.

Source: *Journal of Commerce and Commercial.* **Price Frequency:** weekly in Monday issue. **Units of Measure:** Dollars per lb. **Type of Price:** spot. **Time Period Covered:** latest week.

WITCH HAZEL LEAVES

Source: *Chemical Marketing Reporter.* **Price Frequency:** weekly. **Effective Market(s):** New York. **Units of Measure:** Dollars per lb. **Type of Price:** spot. **Time Period Covered:** latest week.

Source: *Journal of Commerce and Commercial.* **Price Frequency:** weekly in Monday issue. **Units of Measure:** Dollars per lb. **Type of Price:** spot. **Time Period Covered:** latest week.

WITCH HAZEL LEAVES: 325 MESH

Source: *Chemical Marketing Reporter.* **Price Frequency:** weekly. **Effective Market(s):** New York. **Units of Measure:** Dollars per ton. **Type of Price:** spot. **Time Period Covered:** latest week.

WITCH HAZEL LEAVES: 400 MESH

Source: *Chemical Marketing Reporter.* **Price Frequency:** weekly. **Effective Market(s):** New York. **Units of Measure:** Dollars per ton. **Type of Price:** spot. **Time Period Covered:** latest week.

WITCH HAZEL LEAVES: HIGH ASPECT RATIO

Source: *Chemical Marketing Reporter.* **Price Frequency:** weekly. **Effective Market(s):** New York. **Units of Measure:** Dollars per ton. **Type of Price:** spot. **Time Period Covered:** latest week.

WOLFFISH: FILLETS, BONELESS, CANADIAN

Source: *NMFS Green Sheet Supplement.* **Price Frequency:** weekly. **Units of Measure:** Dollars per lb. **Time Period Covered:** latest week.

WOLFFISH: FILLETS, BONELESS, ICELANDIC

Source: *NMFS Green Sheet Supplement.* **Price Frequency:** weekly. **Units of Measure:** Dollars per lb. **Time Period Covered:** latest week.

WOLFFISH: FILLETS, BONELESS, NORWEGIAN

Source: *NMFS Green Sheet Supplement.* **Price Frequency:** weekly. **Units of Measure:** Dollars per lb. **Time Period Covered:** latest week.

WOLFFISH: PROCESSORS FISH BLOCKS, CANADA/GREENLAND

Source: *Seafood Price-Current.* **Price Frequency:** semiweekly. **Effective Market(s):** New England. **Units of Measure:** Dollars per lb. **Time Period Covered:** latest day.

WOLFFISH: WHOLE, FRESH

Source: *Seafood Price-Current.* **Price Frequency:** semiweekly. **Effective Market(s):** Boston, Mid-Atlantic, New Bedford (MA), Portland (ME). **Units of Measure:** Dollars per lb. **Type of Price:** sale by first receiver, auction price. **Time Period Covered:** latest day.

WOLLASTONITE: 325 MESH

Source: *Chemical Marketing Reporter.* **Price Frequency:** weekly. **Effective Market(s):** New York. **Units of Measure:** Dollars per ton. **Type of Price:** spot. **Time Period Covered:** latest week.

WOLLASTONITE: 400 MESH

Source: *Chemical Marketing Reporter.* **Price Frequency:** weekly. **Effective Market(s):** New York. **Units of Measure:** Dollars per ton. **Type of Price:** spot. **Time Period Covered:** latest week.

WOLLASTONITE: 1250 MESH

Source: *Chemical Marketing Reporter.* **Price Frequency:** weekly. **Effective Market(s):** New York. **Units of Measure:** Dollars per ton. **Type of Price:** spot. **Time Period Covered:** latest week.

WOLLASTONITE: ACICULAR, UNITED STATES

Source: *Industrial Minerals.* **Price Frequency:** monthly. **Effective Market(s):** United States. **Units of Measure:** Dollars per short ton. **Type of Price:** producer & dealer. **Time Period Covered:** latest month.

WOLLASTONITE: FINNISH

Source: *Industrial Minerals.* **Price Frequency:** monthly. **Effective Market(s):** United Kingdom. **Units of Measure:** British pounds per metric tonne. **Type of Price:** producer & dealer. **Time Period Covered:** latest month.

WOLLASTONITE: GENERAL GRADE

Source: *Chemical Marketing Reporter.* **Price Frequency:** weekly. **Effective Market(s):** New York. **Units of Measure:** Dollars per ton. **Type of Price:** spot. **Time Period Covered:** latest week.

WOLLASTONITE: UNITED STATES

Source: *Industrial Minerals.* **Price Frequency:** monthly. **Effective Market(s):** United States. **Units of Measure:** Dollars per short ton. **Type of Price:** producer & dealer. **Time Period Covered:** latest month.

WOOD CHIP-N-SAW

Source: *Timber Mart-South.* **Price Frequency:** quarterly. **Effective Market(s):** 14 domestic markets. **Units of Measure:** Dollars per cord. **Type of Price:** stumpage, mill. **Time Period Covered:** latest quarter.

WOOD CHIP-N-SAW: PINE

Source: *Timber Mart-South.* **Price Frequency:** quarterly. **Effective Market(s):** 12 domestic markets. **Units of Measure:** Dollars per cord, dollars per 1000 board feet. **Type of Price:** standing timber, delivered. **Time Period Covered:** latest 2 quarters.

WOOD CHIPS: HARDWOOD, CLEAN

Source: *Timber Mart-South.* **Price Frequency:** quarterly. **Effective Market(s):** 13 domestic markets. **Units of Measure:** Dollars per ton. **Type of Price:** delivered. **Time Period Covered:** latest 2 quarters.

WOOD CHIPS: HARDWOOD, WHOLE TREE

Source: *Timber Mart-South.* **Price Frequency:** quarterly. **Effective Market(s):** 13 domestic markets. **Units of Measure:** Dollars per ton. **Type of Price:** delivered. **Time Period Covered:** latest 2 quarters.

WOOD CHIPS: PINE, CLEAN

Source: *Timber Mart-South.* **Price Frequency:** quarterly. **Effective Market(s):** 13 domestic markets. **Units of Measure:** Dollars per ton. **Type of Price:** delivered. **Time Period Covered:** latest 2 quarters.

WOOD POLES

Source: *Timber Mart-South.* **Price Frequency:** quarterly. **Effective Market(s):** 14 domestic markets. **Units of Measure:** Dollars per 1000 board feet. **Type of Price:** stumpage, mill. **Time Period Covered:** latest quarter.

Source: *Timber Mart-South.* **Price Frequency:** quarterly. **Effective Market(s):** 11 domestic markets. **Units of Measure:** Dollars per 1000 board feet. **Type of Price:** standing timber, delivered. **Time Period Covered:** latest 2 quarters.

WOOD ROSIN: 4 B

Source: *Journal of Commerce and Commercial.* **Price Frequency:** weekly in Monday issue. **Effective Market(s):** New York. **Units of Measure:** Dollars per lb. **Type of Price:** spot. **Time Period Covered:** latest week.

WOOD ROSIN: B

Source: *Journal of Commerce and Commercial.* **Price Frequency:** weekly in Monday issue. **Effective Market(s):** South. **Units of Measure:** Dollars per lb. **Type of Price:** spot. **Time Period Covered:** latest week.

WOOD ROSIN: FF

Source: *Journal of Commerce and Commercial.* **Price Frequency:** weekly in Monday issue. **Effective Market(s):** South, New York. **Units of Measure:** Dollars per lb. **Type of Price:** spot. **Time Period Covered:** latest week.

WOOD ROSIN: N

Source: *Journal of Commerce and Commercial.* **Price Frequency:** weekly in Monday issue. **Effective Market(s):** South. **Units of Measure:** Dollars per lb. **Type of Price:** spot. **Time Period Covered:** latest week.

WOOD ROSIN: WG

Source: *Journal of Commerce and Commercial.* **Price Frequency:** weekly in Monday issue. **Effective Market(s):** South. **Units of Measure:** Dollars per lb. **Type of Price:** spot. **Time Period Covered:** latest week.

WOODEN MOLDING: PONDEROSA PINE

Source: *Random Lengths.* **Price Frequency:** weekly. **Units of Measure:** Dollars per 1000 board feet. **Type of Price:** price to wholesaler. **Time Period Covered:** latest week.

WOODEN MOLDING: WHITE FIR

Source: *Random Lengths.* **Price Frequency:** weekly. **Units of Measure:** Dollars per 1000 board feet. **Type of Price:** price to wholesaler. **Time Period Covered:** latest week.

WOODEN POSTS, BEAMS AND TIMBERS: DOUGLAS FIR

Source: *Random Lengths.* **Price Frequency:** weekly. **Effective Market(s):** Eureka (CA), Portland (OR). **Units of Measure:** Dollars per 1000 board feet. **Type of Price:** price to wholesaler. **Time Period Covered:** latest week.

WOODEN POSTS, BEAMS AND TIMBERS: SOUTHERN PINE

Source: *Random Lengths.* **Price Frequency:** weekly. **Units of Measure:** Dollars per 1000 board feet. **Type of Price:** price to wholesaler. **Time Period Covered:** latest week.

WOODEN SHOP: PONDEROSA PINE

Source: *Random Lengths.* **Price Frequency:** weekly. **Units of Measure:** Dollars per 1000 board feet. **Type of Price:** price to wholesaler. **Time Period Covered:** latest week.

WOODEN SHOP: WHITE FIR

Source: *Random Lengths.* **Price Frequency:** weekly. **Units of Measure:** Dollars per 1000 board feet. **Type of Price:** price to wholesaler. **Time Period Covered:** latest week.

WOODPULP: MECHANICAL

Source: *Timber Bulletin.* **Price Frequency:** monthly, annually. **Effective Market(s):** Canada, Finland, Sweden. **Units of Measure:** national currency per metric ton. **Type of Price:** export value. **Time Period Covered:** monthly latest 2 years, annually latest 6 years.

Source: *Timber Bulletin.* **Price Frequency:** monthly, annually. **Effective Market(s):** United Kingdom. **Units of Measure:** British pounds per metric ton. **Type of Price:** import value. **Time Period Covered:** monthly latest 2 years, annually latest 5 years.

WOODPULP: SULPHATE, BLEACHED, SOFTWOOD

Source: *Commodity Year Book.* **Price Frequency:** monthly, annually. **Units of Measure:** index. **Type of Price:** price index. **Time Period Covered:** latest 4 years.

WOODPULP: SULPHATE, CHEMICAL

Source: *Timber Bulletin.* **Price Frequency:** monthly, annually. **Effective Market(s):** United Kingom. **Units of Measure:** British pounds per metric ton. **Type of Price:** import value. **Time Period Covered:** monthly latest 2 years, annually latest 5 years.

Source: *Timber Bulletin.* **Price Frequency:** monthly, annually. **Effective Market(s):** Canada, Finland, Sweden. **Units of Measure:** national currency per metric ton. **Type of Price:** export value. **Time Period Covered:** monthly latest 2 years, annually latest 6 years.

WOODPULP: SULPHATE, CHEMICAL, SWEDISH

Source: *Timber Bulletin.* **Price Frequency:** monthly, annually. **Effective Market(s):** West Germany. **Units of Measure:** West German marks per metric ton. **Time Period Covered:** monthly latest 2 years, annually latest 6 years.

WOODPULP: SULPHATE, UNBLEACHED, AIR DRY

Source: *FAO Quarterly Bulletin of Statistics.* **Price Frequency:** monthly, annually. **Effective Market(s):** Sweden. **Units of Measure:** Dollars per 1000 kilograms, dollars per metric ton. **Type of Price:** export. **Time Period Covered:** latest 3 years.

WOODPULP: SULPHITE, CHEMICAL

Source: *Timber Bulletin.* **Price Frequency:** monthly, annually. **Effective Market(s):** Canada. **Units of Measure:** Canadian dollars per metric ton. **Type of Price:** export value. **Time Period Covered:** monthly latest 2 years, annually latest 6 years.

WOOL

Source: *Agricultural Outlook.* **Price Frequency:** monthly, annually. **Effective Market(s):** United States. **Units of Measure:** cents per lb. **Type of Price:** received by farmer. **Time Period Covered:** monthly latest 6 months, annaually latest 3 years.

Source: *Agricultural Prices.* **Price Frequency:** monthly. **Effective Market(s):** United States. **Units of Measure:** Dollars per lb. **Type of Price:** local average received by farmer. **Time Period Covered:** latest 2 months, year ago.

Source: *Agricultural Prices.* **Price Frequency:** monthly. **Effective Market(s):** 13 domestic markets, United States. **Units of Measure:** Dollars per lb. **Type of Price:** received by farmer. **Time Period Covered:** latest month.

Source: *Agricultural Prices Annual Summary.* **Price Frequency:** annually. **Effective Market(s):** 50 domestic markets, United States. **Units of Measure:** Dollars per lb. **Type of Price:** average received by farmer. **Time Period Covered:** latest 2 years, for US latest 6 years.

Source: *Agricultural Prices Annual Summary.* **Price Frequency:** monthly. **Effective Market(s):** 16 domestic markets, United States. **Units of Measure:** Dollars per lb. **Type of Price:** average received by farmer. **Time Period Covered:** latest year, for US latest 6 years.

Source: *Commodity Year Book.* **Price Frequency:** annually. **Effective Market(s):** United States. **Units of Measure:** cents per lb. **Time Period Covered:** latest 8 years.

Source: *Illinois Farm Report.* **Price Frequency:** quarterly. **Effective Market(s):** Illinois. **Units of Measure:** Dollars per lb. **Type of Price:** average. **Time Period Covered:** latest 2 months, year ago.

Source: *Wool and Mohair.* **Price Frequency:** annually. **Effective Market(s):** United States. **Units of Measure:** Dollars per lb. **Time Period Covered:** latest 3 years.

Source: *Wool and Mohair.* **Price Frequency:** annually. **Effective Market(s):** 42 domestic markets, United States. **Units of Measure:** Dollars per lb. **Time Period Covered:** latest 2 years.

WOOL: 48'S, AUSTRALIAN/NEW ZEALAND

Source: *International Financial Statistics.* **Price Frequency:** monthly, quarterly, annually. **Effective Market(s):** United Kingdom. **Units of Measure:** cents per kilogram, index. **Type of Price:** market price, price index. **Time Period Covered:** latest 5 months, latest 5 quarters, latest 5 years.

WOOL: 48'S, CLEAN BASIS, DRY COMBED BASIS

Source: *Monthly Commodity Price Bulletin.* **Price Frequency:** monthly, annually. **Effective Market(s):** United Kingdom. **Units of Measure:** new pence per kilogram, cents per lb. **Time Period Covered:** latest 5 years.

Source: *UNCTAD Commodity Yearbook.* **Price Frequency:** annually. **Effective Market(s):** United Kingdom. **Units of Measure:** Dollars per metric ton. **Type of Price:** free market. **Time Period Covered:** latest 12 years.

WOOL: 48'S, DRY COMBED BASIS, NEW ZEALAND

Source: *Monthly Commodity Price Bulletin Supplement.* **Price Frequency:** monthly, quarterly, annually. **Effective Market(s):** United Kingdom. **Units of Measure:** British new pence per kilogram, dollars per tonne. **Time Period Covered:** latest 20 years.

WOOL: 50'S, AUSTRALIAN/NEW ZEALAND

Source: *International Financial Statistics Yearbook.* **Price Frequency:** annually. **Effective Market(s):** United Kingdom. **Units of Measure:** cents per kilogram. **Type of Price:** wholesale. **Time Period Covered:** latest 30 years.

WOOL: 54'S, CLEAN BASIS, TERRITORY

Source: *National Wool Market Review.* **Price Frequency:** weekly. **Effective Market(s):** United States. **Units of Measure:** Dollars per lb. **Type of Price:** market. **Time Period Covered:** latest week.

WOOL: 54'S, GRADED FLEECE

Source: *National Wool Market Review.* **Price Frequency:** weekly. **Effective Market(s):** United States. **Units of Measure:** Dollars per lb. **Type of Price:** market. **Time Period Covered:** latest week.

WOOL: 54'S, GREASE BASIS, TERRITORY

Source: *National Wool Market Review.* **Price Frequency:** weekly. **Effective Market(s):** United States. **Units of Measure:** Dollars per lb. **Type of Price:** market. **Time Period Covered:** latest week.

WOOL: 56'S, CLEAN BASIS, TERRITORY

Source: *National Wool Market Review.* **Price Frequency:** weekly. **Effective Market(s):** United States. **Units of Measure:** Dollars per lb. **Type of Price:** market. **Time Period Covered:** latest week.

WOOL: 56'S, CROSSBRED, CLEAN BASIS, NEW ZEALAND

Source: *Commodity Trade and Price Trends.* **Price Frequency:** annually. **Effective Market(s):** United Kingdom. **Units of Measure:** cents per kilogram, 1980 constant cents per kilogram. **Type of Price:** auction. **Time Period Covered:** latest 37 years.

WOOL: 56'S, GREASE BASIS, TERRITORY

Source: *National Wool Market Review.* **Price Frequency:** weekly. **Effective Market(s):** United States. **Units of Measure:** Dollars per lb. **Type of Price:** market. **Time Period Covered:** latest week.

WOOL: 58'S, CLEAN BASIS, TERRITORY

Source: *National Wool Market Review.* **Price Frequency:** weekly. **Effective Market(s):** United States. **Units of Measure:** Dollars per lb. **Type of Price:** market. **Time Period Covered:** latest week.

WOOL: 58'S, GREASE BASIS, TERRITORY

Source: *National Wool Market Review.* **Price Frequency:** weekly. **Effective Market(s):** United States. **Units of Measure:** Dollars per lb. **Type of Price:** market. **Time Period Covered:** latest week.

WOOL: 60'S, CLEAN BASIS, TERRITORY

Source: *National Wool Market Review.* **Price Frequency:** weekly. **Effective Market(s):** United States. **Units of Measure:** Dollars per lb. **Type of Price:** market. **Time Period Covered:** latest week.

WOOL: 60'S, GREASE BASIS, TERRITORY

Source: *National Wool Market Review.* **Price Frequency:** weekly. **Effective Market(s):** United States. **Units of Measure:** Dollars per lb. **Type of Price:** market. **Time Period Covered:** latest week.

WOOL: 60/62'S, TYPE 64A, AUSTRALIAN

Source: *Agricultural Outlook.* **Price Frequency:** monthly, annually. **Effective Market(s):** Boston. **Units of Measure:** cents per lb. **Type of Price:** import. **Time Period Covered:** monthly latest 6 months, annually latest 3 years.

WOOL: 62'S, CLEAN BASIS, TERRITORY

Source: *National Wool Market Review.* **Price Frequency:** weekly. **Effective Market(s):** United States. **Units of Measure:** Dollars per lb. **Type of Price:** market. **Time Period Covered:** latest week.

WOOL: 62'S, GREASE BASIS, TERRITORY

Source: *National Wool Market Review.* **Price Frequency:** weekly. **Effective Market(s):** United States. **Units of Measure:** Dollars per lb. **Type of Price:** market. **Time Period Covered:** latest week.

WOOL: 64'S, AUSTRALIAN/NEW ZEALAND

Source: *International Financial Statistics.* **Price Frequency:** monthly, quarterly, annually. **Effective Market(s):** United Kingdom. **Units of Measure:** cents per kilogram, index. **Type of Price:** market price, price index. **Time Period Covered:** latest 5 months, latest 5 quarters, latest 5 years.

Source: *International Financial Statistics Yearbook.* **Price Frequency:** annually. **Effective Market(s):** United Kingdom. **Units of Measure:** cents per kilogram. **Type of Price:** wholesale. **Time Period Covered:** latest 30 years.

WOOL: 64'S, CLEAN BASIS, DRY COMBED BASIS

Source: *Monthly Commodity Price Bulletin.* **Price Frequency:** monthly, annually. **Effective Market(s):** United Kingdom. **Units of Measure:** new pence per kilogram, cents per lb. **Time Period Covered:** latest 5 years.

Source: *UNCTAD Commodity Yearbook.* **Price Frequency:** annually. **Effective Market(s):** United Kingdom. **Units of Measure:** Dollars per metric ton. **Type of Price:** free market. **Time Period Covered:** latest 12 years.

WOOL: 64'S, CLEAN BASIS, TERRITORY

Source: *National Wool Market Review.* **Price Frequency:** weekly. **Effective Market(s):** United States. **Units of Measure:** Dollars per lb. **Type of Price:** market. **Time Period Covered:** latest week.

WOOL: 64'S, DRY COMBED BASIS, NEW ZEALAND

Source: *Monthly Commodity Price Bulletin Supplement.* **Price Frequency:** monthly, quarterly, annually. **Effective Market(s):** United Kingdom. **Units of Measure:** British new pence per kilogram, dollars per tonne. **Time Period Covered:** latest 20 years.

WOOL: 64'S, GRADED TERRITORY

Source: *Agricultural Outlook.* **Price Frequency:** monthly, annually. **Effective Market(s):** Boston. **Units of Measure:** cents per lb. **Time Period Covered:** monthly latest 6 months, annually latest 3 years.

WOOL: 64'S, GREASE BASIS, TERRITORY

Source: *National Wool Market Review.* **Price Frequency:** weekly. **Effective Market(s):** United States. **Units of Measure:** Dollars per lb. **Type of Price:** market. **Time Period Covered:** latest week.

WOOL: 64'S, ORIGINAL BAG, TEXAS

Source: *National Wool Market Review.* **Price Frequency:** weekly. **Effective Market(s):** United States. **Units of Measure:** Dollars per lb. **Type of Price:** market. **Time Period Covered:** latest week.

WOOL: 64'S, STAPLE

Source: *Asian Wall Street Journal.* **Price Frequency:** daily. **Units of Measure:** Dollars per lb. **Type of Price:** cash. **Time Period Covered:** latest 2 days, year ago.

WOOL: 64'S, STAPLE 2-3/4″ AND UP, CLEAN BASIS, GRADED TERRITORY, RAW, Domestic

Source: *Survey of Current Business.* **Price Frequency:** monthly, annually. **Effective Market(s):** United States. **Units of Measure:** Dollars per lb. **Time Period Covered:** latest year.

WOOL: 64'S, STAPLE 2-3/4″ AND UP, GRADED TERRITORY, DOMESTIC

Source: *Commodity Year Book.* **Price Frequency:** monthly, annually. **Effective Market(s):** United States. **Units of Measure:** cents per lb. **Time Period Covered:** latest 11 years.

WOOL: 64'S, STAPLE, TERRITORY

Source: *Wall Street Journal.* **Price Frequency:** daily. **Units of Measure:** Dollars per lb. **Time Period Covered:** latest day, day ago, year ago.

WOOL: 64'S, TYPE 62, AUSTRALIAN

Source: *Commodity Year Book.* **Price Frequency:** monthly, annually. **Effective Market(s):** United States. **Units of Measure:** cents per lb. **Time Period Covered:** latest 7 years.

WOOL: 64'S, TYPE 62, RAW, AUSTRALIAN

Source: *Survey of Current Business.* **Price Frequency:** monthly, annually. **Effective Market(s):** United States. **Units of Measure:** Dollars per lb. **Time Period Covered:** latest year.

WOOL: AUSTRALIAN

Source: *National Wool Market Review.* **Price Frequency:** weekly. **Effective Market(s):** Charleston (SC). **Units of Measure:** cents per lb. **Type of Price:** auction. **Time Period Covered:** latest week.

WOOL: CROSSBRED, BELLIES

Source: *New Zealand Farmer.* **Price Frequency:** weekly, seasonally. **Effective Market(s):** New Zealand. **Units of Measure:** New Zealand cents per kilogram. **Type of Price:** growers, clean market. **Time Period Covered:** latest week.

WOOL: CROSSBRED, COTT

Source: *New Zealand Farmer.* **Price Frequency:** weekly, seasonally. **Effective Market(s):** New Zealand. **Units of Measure:** New Zealand cents per kilogram. **Type of Price:** growers, clean market. **Time Period Covered:** latest week.

WOOL: CROSSBRED, CRUTCHINGS

Source: *New Zealand Farmer.* **Price Frequency:** weekly, seasonally. **Effective Market(s):** New Zealand. **Units of Measure:** New Zealand cents per kilogram. **Type of Price:** growers, clean market. **Time Period Covered:** latest week.

WOOL: CROSSBRED, FLEECE

Source: *New Zealand Farmer.* **Price Frequency:** weekly, seasonally. **Effective Market(s):** New Zealand. **Units of Measure:** New Zealand cents per kilogram. **Type of Price:** growers, clean market. **Time Period Covered:** latest week.

WOOL: CROSSBRED, LOX

Source: *New Zealand Farmer.* **Price Frequency:** weekly, seasonally. **Effective Market(s):** New Zealand. **Units of Measure:** New Zealand cents per kilogram. **Type of Price:** growers, clean market. **Time Period Covered:** latest week.

WOOL: CROSSBRED, PIECES

Source: *New Zealand Farmer.* **Price Frequency:** weekly, seasonally. **Effective Market(s):** New Zealand. **Units of Measure:** New Zealand cents per kilogram. **Type of Price:** growers, clean market. **Time Period Covered:** latest week.

WOOL: FINE STAPLE

Source: *New York Times.* **Price Frequency:** daily. **Effective Market(s):** Boston. **Units of Measure:** Dollars per lb. **Type of Price:** cash. **Time Period Covered:** latest 2 days.

WOOL: FINE STAPLE, SCOURED BASIS, TERRITORY

Source: *Standard & Poor's Statistical Service Current Statistics.* **Price Frequency:** monthly, annually. **Effective Market(s):** Boston. **Units of Measure:** cents per lb. **Time Period Covered:** latest 5 years.

WOOL: FINE STAPLE, TERRITORY

Source: *Investor's Daily.* **Price Frequency:** daily. **Effective Market(s):** Boston. **Units of Measure:** Dollars per lb. **Type of Price:** spot. **Time Period Covered:** latest 2 days.

WOOL: GREASY, AUSTRALIAN

Source: *International Financial Statistics.* **Price Frequency:** monthly, quarterly, annually. **Effective Market(s):** Australia. **Units of Measure:** cents per kilogram, index. **Type of Price:** market price, price index. **Time Period Covered:** latest 2 months, latest 4 quarters, latest 5 years.

Source: *International Financial Statistics Yearbook.* **Price Frequency:** annually. **Effective Market(s):** Australia. **Units of Measure:** cents per kilogram. **Type of Price:** wholesale. **Time Period Covered:** latest 30 years.

WOOL: GREASY BASIS, SHORN

Source: *Cotton and Wool Situation and Outlook Report.* **Price Frequency:** monthly, annually. **Effective Market(s):** United States. **Units of Measure:** cents per lb. **Type of Price:** farm. **Time Period Covered:** latest 6 years.

Source: *FAO Quarterly Bulletin of Statistics.* **Price Frequency:** monthly, annually. **Effective Market(s):** United States. **Units of Measure:** Dollars per 100 lbs., dollars per metric ton. **Type of Price:** producer. **Time Period Covered:** latest 3 years.

WOOL: GREASY, NEW ZEALAND

Source: *International Financial Statistics.* **Price Frequency:** annually. **Effective Market(s):** New Zealand. **Units of Measure:** cents per kilogram, index. **Type of Price:** market price, price index. **Time Period Covered:** latest 4 years.

Source: *International Financial Statistics Yearbook.* **Price Frequency:** annually. **Effective Market(s):** New Zealand. **Units of Measure:** cents per kilogram. **Type of Price:** wholesale. **Time Period Covered:** latest 30 years.

WOOL: HALFBRED AND CORRIEDALE, BELLIES

Source: *New Zealand Farmer.* **Price Frequency:** weekly, seasonally. **Effective Market(s):** New Zealand. **Units of Measure:** New Zealand cents per kilogram. **Type of Price:** growers, clean market. **Time Period Covered:** latest week.

WOOL: HALFBRED AND CORRIEDALE, CRUTCHINGS

Source: *New Zealand Farmer.* **Price Frequency:** weekly, seasonally. **Effective Market(s):** New Zealand. **Units of Measure:** New Zealand cents per kilogram. **Type of Price:** growers, clean market. **Time Period Covered:** latest week.

WOOL: HALFBRED AND CORRIEDALE, FLEECE

Source: *New Zealand Farmer.* **Price Frequency:** weekly, seasonally. **Effective Market(s):** New Zealand. **Units of Measure:** New Zealand cents per kilogram. **Type of Price:** growers, clean market. **Time Period Covered:** latest week.

WOOL: HALFBRED AND CORRIEDALE, LAMBS

Source: *New Zealand Farmer.* **Price Frequency:** weekly, seasonally. **Effective Market(s):** New Zealand. **Units of Measure:** New Zealand cents per kilogram. **Type of Price:** growers, clean market. **Time Period Covered:** latest week.

WOOL: HALFBRED AND CORRIEDALE, LOX

Source: *New Zealand Farmer.* **Price Frequency:** weekly, seasonally. **Effective Market(s):** New Zealand. **Units of Measure:** New Zealand cents per kilogram. **Type of Price:** growers, clean market. **Time Period Covered:** latest week.

WOOL: HALFBRED AND CORRIEDALE, PIECES

Source: *New Zealand Farmer.* **Price Frequency:** weekly, seasonally. **Effective Market(s):** New Zealand. **Units of Measure:** New Zealand cents per kilogram. **Type of Price:** growers, clean market. **Time Period Covered:** latest week.

WOOL: MERINO, BELLIES

Source: *New Zealand Farmer.* **Price Frequency:** weekly, seasonally. **Effective Market(s):** New Zealand. **Units of Measure:** New Zealand cents per kilogram. **Type of Price:** growers, clean market. **Time Period Covered:** latest week.

WOOL: MERINO, FLEECE

Source: *New Zealand Farmer.* **Price Frequency:** weekly, seasonally. **Effective Market(s):** New Zealand. **Units of Measure:** New Zealand cents per kilogram. **Type of Price:** growers, clean market. **Time Period Covered:** latest week.

WOOL: MERINO, PIECES

Source: *New Zealand Farmer.* **Price Frequency:** weekly, seasonally. **Effective Market(s):** New Zealand. **Units of Measure:** New Zealand cents per kilogram. **Type of Price:** growers, clean market. **Time Period Covered:** latest week.

WOOL: RAW, AUSTRALIAN

Source: *Wool Quarterly.* **Price Frequency:** weekly, monthly, annually. **Effective Market(s):** Australia. **Units of Measure:** Australian cents per kilogram clean. **Type of Price:** auction. **Time Period Covered:** weekly latest year, monthly latest 5 years, annually latest 14 years.

WOOL: RAW, NEW ZEALAND

Source: *Wool Quarterly.* **Price Frequency:** weekly, monthly, annually. **Effective Market(s):** New Zealand. **Units of Measure:** New Zealand cents per kilogram clean. **Type of Price:** auction. **Time Period Covered:** weekly latest year, monthly latest 5 years, annually latest 14 years.

WOOL: RAW, SOUTH AFRICAN

Source: *Wool Quarterly.* **Price Frequency:** weekly, monthly, annually. **Units of Measure:** South African cents per kilogram clean. **Type of Price:** auction. **Time Period Covered:** weekly latest year, monthly latest 5 years, annually latest 14 years.

WOOL: SECOND SHEAR, BELLIES AND PIECES

Source: *New Zealand Farmer.* **Price Frequency:** weekly, seasonally. **Effective Market(s):** New Zealand. **Units of Measure:** New Zealand cents per kilogram. **Type of Price:** growers, clean market. **Time Period Covered:** latest week.

WOOL: SECOND SHEAR, FLEECE

Source: *New Zealand Farmer.* **Price Frequency:** weekly, seasonally. **Effective Market(s):** New Zealand. **Units of Measure:** New Zealand cents per kilogram. **Type of Price:** growers, clean market. **Time Period Covered:** latest week.

WOOL: SECOND SHEAR, LAMBS

Source: *New Zealand Farmer.* **Price Frequency:** weekly, seasonally. **Effective Market(s):** New Zealand. **Units of Measure:** New Zealand cents per kilogram. **Type of Price:** growers, clean market. **Time Period Covered:** latest week.

WOOL: SHORN

Source: *Commodity Year Book.* **Price Frequency:** monthly, annually. **Effective Market(s):** United States. **Units of Measure:** cents per lb. **Type of Price:** price received by farmers. **Time Period Covered:** latest 4 years.

WOOL GREASE: USP

see Lanolin.

WOOL POOLS: 60/62'S

Source: *Oregon Farmer-Stockman.* **Price Frequency:** monthly. **Effective Market(s):** Montana. **Units of Measure:** Dollars per lb. **Time Period Covered:** latest month.

WOOL TOPS

Source: *CRB Commodity Index Report.* **Price Frequency:** weekly. **Effective Market(s):** Boston. **Units of Measure:** Dollars per lb. **Type of Price:** spot. **Time Period Covered:** latest week.

WOOLTOPS: 64'S, SUPER

Source: *Financial Times.* **Price Frequency:** daily. **Effective Market(s):** London. **Units of Measure:** British pence per kilogram. **Type of Price:** spot. **Time Period Covered:** latest day.

WORMSEED: AMERICAN

Source: *Journal of Commerce and Commercial.* **Price Frequency:** weekly in Monday issue. **Units of Measure:** Dollars per lb. **Type of Price:** spot. **Time Period Covered:** latest week.

WORMSEED OIL

see Chenopodium Oil: NF.

WORMWOOD OIL

Source: *Chemical Marketing Reporter.* **Price Frequency:** weekly. **Effective Market(s):** New York. **Units of Measure:** Dollars per lb. **Type of Price:** spot. **Time Period Covered:** latest week.

WRAPPING PAPER: KRAFT, HEAVY WRAPPING, JAPANESE

Source: *Selected Prices of Asia/Pacific Products.* **Price Frequency:** monthly. **Effective Market(s):** Tokyo. **Units of Measure:** Japanese yen per kilogram. **Type of Price:** wholesale high to paper bag manufacturers, wholesale low to paper bag manufacturers. **Time Period Covered:** latest month.

WRAPPING PAPER: KRAFT, LIGHT WRAPPING, JAPANESE

Source: *Selected Prices of Asia/Pacific Products.* **Price Frequency:** monthly. **Effective Market(s):** Tokyo. **Units of Measure:** Japanese yen per kilogram. **Type of Price:** wholesale high, wholesale low. **Time Period Covered:** latest month.

WRAPPING PAPER: MACHINE GLAZED, WHITE SULPHITE, CZECHOSLOVAKIA/FINLAND

Source: *Selected Prices of Asia/Pacific Products.* **Price Frequency:** monthly. **Effective Market(s):** Hong Kong. **Units of Measure:** Hong Kong dollars per ream. **Type of Price:** wholesale high, wholesale low. **Time Period Covered:** latest month.

WRAPPING PAPER: MACHINE GLAZED KRAFT, WHITE, JAPANESE

Source: *Selected Prices of Asia/Pacific Products.* **Price Frequency:** monthly. **Effective Market(s):** Tokyo. **Units of Measure:** Japanese yen per kilogram. **Type of Price:** wholesale high, wholesale low. **Time Period Covered:** latest month.

WRAPPING PAPER: UNGLAZED KRAFT, CANADIAN

Source: *Selected Prices of Asia/Pacific Products.* **Price Frequency:** monthly. **Effective Market(s):** Hong Kong. **Units of Measure:** Hong Kong dollars per lb. **Type of Price:** wholesale high, wholesale low. **Time Period Covered:** latest month.

WRAPPING PAPER: UNGLAZED KRAFT, CHINESE

Source: *Selected Prices of Asia/Pacific Products.* **Price Frequency:** monthly. **Effective Market(s):** Hong Kong. **Units of Measure:** Hong Kong dollars per ream, Hong Kong dollars per lb. **Type of Price:** wholesale high, wholesale low. **Time Period Covered:** latest month.

WRAPPING PAPER: UNGLAZED KRAFT, JAPANESE

Source: *Selected Prices of Asia/Pacific Products.* **Price Frequency:** monthly. **Effective Market(s):** Hong Kong. **Units of Measure:** Hong Kong dollars per ream. **Type of Price:** wholesale high, wholesale low. **Time Period Covered:** latest month.

WRAPPING PAPER: UNGLAZED KRAFT, UNITED STATES

Source: *Selected Prices of Asia/Pacific Products.* **Price Frequency:** monthly. **Effective Market(s):** Hong Kong. **Units of Measure:** Hong Kong dollars per lb. **Type of Price:** wholesale high, wholesale low. **Time Period Covered:** latest month.

WRENCH: ADJUSTABLE END

Source: *Agricultural Prices.* **Price Frequency:** semiannually. **Effective Market(s):** United States. **Units of Measure:** Dollars each. **Type of Price:** paid by farmer. **Time Period Covered:** latest year.

Source: *Agricultural Prices Annual Summary.* **Price Frequency:** quarterly. **Effective Market(s):** United States. **Units of Measure:** Dollars each. **Type of Price:** average paid by farmer. **Time Period Covered:** latest 6 years.

XANTHAN GUM: FOOD GRADE

Source: *Chemical Marketing Reporter.* **Price Frequency:** weekly. **Effective Market(s):** New York. **Units of Measure:** Dollars per lb. **Type of Price:** spot. **Time Period Covered:** latest week.

Source: *Journal of Commerce and Commercial.* **Price Frequency:** weekly in Monday issue. **Units of Measure:** Dollars per lb. **Type of Price:** spot. **Time Period Covered:** latest week.

XANTHAN GUM: INDUSTRIAL GRADE

Source: *Chemical Marketing Reporter.* **Price Frequency:** weekly. **Effective Market(s):** New York. **Units of Measure:** Dollars per lb. **Type of Price:** spot. **Time Period Covered:** latest week.

Source: *Journal of Commerce and Commercial.* **Price Frequency:** weekly in Monday issue. **Units of Measure:** Dollars per lb. **Type of Price:** spot. **Time Period Covered:** latest week.

XYLENE

Source: *Energy Pricing News: Petrochemical Report.* **Price Frequency:** bimonthly. **Units of Measure:** Canadian dollars per tonne. **Type of Price:** contract. **Time Period Covered:** latest month.

O-XYLENE

Source: *Chemical Marketing Reporter.* **Price Frequency:** weekly. **Effective Market(s):** New York. **Units of Measure:** Dollars per lb. **Type of Price:** spot. **Time Period Covered:** latest week.

P-XYLENE

Source: *Chemical Marketing Reporter.* **Price Frequency:** weekly. **Effective Market(s):** New York. **Units of Measure:** Dollars per lb. **Type of Price:** spot. **Time Period Covered:** latest week.

M-XYLENE: HIGH PURITY

Source: *Chemical Marketing Reporter.* **Price Frequency:** weekly. **Effective Market(s):** Texas City (TX). **Units of Measure:** Dollars per lb. **Type of Price:** spot. **Time Period Covered:** latest week.

XYLENE: MIXED

Source: *Journal of Commerce and Commercial.* **Price Frequency:** weekly in Wednesday issue. **Effective Market(s):** Gulf. **Units of Measure:** Dollars per gallon. **Type of Price:** spot. **Time Period Covered:** latest week.

XYLENE: PARA

Source: *Journal of Commerce and Commercial.* **Price Frequency:** weekly in Wednesday issue. **Effective Market(s):** Gulf. **Units of Measure:** Dollars per lb. **Type of Price:** spot. **Time Period Covered:** latest week.

XYLENE: PETROLEUM, INDUSTRIAL OR NITRATION

Source: *Chemical Marketing Reporter.* **Price Frequency:** weekly. **Effective Market(s):** 13 domestic markets. **Units of Measure:** Dollars per gallon. **Type of Price:** spot. **Time Period Covered:** latest week.

M-XYLENEDIAMINE

Source: *Chemical Marketing Reporter.* **Price Frequency:** weekly. **Effective Market(s):** New York. **Units of Measure:** Dollars per lb. **Type of Price:** spot. **Time Period Covered:** latest week.

2,4-XYLIDINE: TECHNICAL, LIQUID

Source: *Chemical Marketing Reporter.* **Price Frequency:** weekly. **Effective Market(s):** New York. **Units of Measure:** Dollars per lb. **Type of Price:** spot. **Time Period Covered:** latest week.

XYLIDINES: MIXED, O-M-P

Source: *Chemical Marketing Reporter.* **Price Frequency:** weekly. **Effective Market(s):** New York. **Units of Measure:** Dollars per lb. **Type of Price:** spot. **Time Period Covered:** latest week.

YAMS

Source: *New Zealand Farmer.* **Price Frequency:** weekly, seasonally. **Effective Market(s):** New Zealand. **Units of Measure:** New Zealand dollars per bag/crate. **Time Period Covered:** latest week.

YAMS: COLUMBIA

Source: *HRI-Buyer's Guide.* **Price Frequency:** weekly. **Effective Market(s):** Northeastern area. **Units of Measure:** Dollars per 45 lb. carton. **Type of Price:** price paid by dining places & institutions. **Time Period Covered:** latest week.

YARA YARA

Source: *Chemical Marketing Reporter.* **Price Frequency:** weekly. **Effective Market(s):** New York. **Units of Measure:** Dollars per lb. **Type of Price:** spot. **Time Period Covered:** latest week.

Time Period Covered: latest week.

YARN: ACETATE FILAMENT, 75 DENIER

Source: *Journal of Commerce and Commercial.* **Price Frequency:** weekly in Tuesday issue. **Units of Measure:** Dollars per lb. **Type of Price:** spot. **Time Period Covered:** latest week.

YARN: ACETATE FILAMENT, 150 DENIER

Source: *Journal of Commerce and Commercial.* **Price Frequency:** weekly in Tuesday issue. **Units of Measure:** Dollars per lb. **Type of Price:** spot. **Time Period Covered:** latest week.

YARN: ACRYLIC

Source: *JTN: The International Textile Magazine.* **Price Frequency:** monthly. **Effective Market(s):** Taiwan. **Units of Measure:** Dollars per lb. **Type of Price:** export. **Time Period Covered:** latest month.

YARN: ACRYLIC, BRANDED, OPEN-END SPUN

Source: *ATI, America's Textiles International.* **Price Frequency:** monthly. **Time Period Covered:** latest month, 6 months ago, year ago.

YARN: ACRYLIC, UNBRANDED, OPEN-END SPUN

Source: *ATI, America's Textiles International.* **Price Frequency:** monthly. **Time Period Covered:** latest month, 6 months ago, year ago.

YARN: ACRYLIC/COTTON (CARDED), OPEN-END SPUN

Source: *ATI, America's Textiles International.* **Price Frequency:** monthly. **Time Period Covered:** latest month, 6 months ago, year ago.

YARN: COIR, ANJENGO A3, INDIAN

Source: *Prices of Selected Asia/Pacific Products.* **Price Frequency:** monthly. **Effective Market(s):** Cochin (India). **Units of Measure:** British pounds per metric ton. **Type of Price:** high, low. **Time Period Covered:** latest month.

YARN: COIR, ANJENGO A7, INDIAN

Source: *Prices of Selected Asia/Pacific Products.* **Price Frequency:** monthly. **Effective Market(s):** Cochin (India). **Units of Measure:** British pounds per metric ton. **Type of Price:** high, low. **Time Period Covered:** latest month.

YARN: COTTON, 16S, PAKISTAN

Source: *Prices of Selected Asia/Pacific Products.* **Price Frequency:** monthly, seasonally. **Effective Market(s):** Osaka. **Units of Measure:** 1000 Japanese yen per bag. **Type of Price:** trade high, trade low. **Time Period Covered:** latest month.

YARN: COTTON, 20S, PAKISTAN

Source: *Prices of Selected Asia/Pacific Products.* **Price Frequency:** monthly, seasonally. **Effective Market(s):** Osaka. **Units of Measure:** 1000 Japanese yen per bag. **Type of Price:** trade high, trade low. **Time Period Covered:** latest month.

YARN: COTTON, 21S, PAKISTAN

Source: *Prices of Selected Asia/Pacific Products.* **Price Frequency:** monthly, seasonally. **Effective Market(s):** Hong Kong. **Units of Measure:** Hong Kong dollars per bale. **Type of Price:** wholesale spot high, wholesale spot low. **Time Period Covered:** latest month.

YARN: COTTON, 30S, CHINESE

Source: *Prices of Selected Asia/Pacific Products.* **Price Frequency:** monthly, seasonally. **Effective Market(s):** Osaka. **Units of Measure:** 1000 Japanese yen per bag. **Type of Price:** trade high, trade low. **Time Period Covered:** latest month.

YARN: COTTON, 30S, KOREAN

Source: *Prices of Selected Asia/Pacific Products.* **Price Frequency:** monthly, seasonally. **Effective Market(s):** Osaka. **Units of Measure:** 1000 Japanese yen per bag. **Type of Price:** trade high, trade low. **Time Period Covered:** latest month.

YARN: COTTON, 40S, CHINESE

Source: *Prices of Selected Asia/Pacific Products.* **Price Frequency:** monthly, seasonally. **Effective Market(s):** Osaka. **Units of Measure:** 1000 Japanese yen per bag. **Type of Price:** trade high, trade low. **Time Period Covered:** latest month.

YARN: COTTON, 40S, KOREAN

Source: *Prices of Selected Asia/Pacific Products.* **Price Frequency:** monthly, seasonally. **Effective Market(s):** Osaka. **Units of Measure:** 1000 Japanese yen per bag. **Type of Price:** trade high, trade low. **Time Period Covered:** latest month.

YARN: COTTON, CARDED

Source: *JTN: The International Textile Magazine.* **Price Frequency:** monthly. **Effective Market(s):** Taiwan. **Units of Measure:** Dollars per bale. **Type of Price:** export. **Time Period Covered:** latest month.

YARN: COTTON, CARDED, 10S

Source: *JTN: The International Textile Magazine.* **Price Frequency:** monthly. **Effective Market(s):** Japan. **Units of Measure:** 1000 Japanese yen per bale. **Type of Price:** spot. **Time Period Covered:** latest month.

YARN: COTTON, CARDED, 16S

Source: *JTN: The International Textile Magazine.* **Price Frequency:** monthly. **Effective Market(s):** Japan. **Units of Measure:** 1000 Japanese yen per bale. **Type of Price:** spot. **Time Period Covered:** latest month.

YARN: COTTON, CARDED, 20S

Source: *JTN: The International Textile Magazine.* **Price Frequency:** monthly. **Effective Market(s):** Japan. **Units of Measure:** 1000 Japanese yen per bale. **Type of Price:** spot. **Time Period Covered:** latest month.

YARN: COTTON, CARDED, 30S

Source: *JTN: The International Textile Magazine.* **Price Frequency:** monthly. **Effective Market(s):** Japan. **Units of Measure:** 1000 Japanese yen per bale. **Type of Price:** spot. **Time Period Covered:** latest month.

YARN: COTTON, CARDED, 40S

Source: *JTN: The International Textile Magazine.* **Price Frequency:** monthly. **Effective Market(s):** Japan. **Units of Measure:** 1000 Japanese yen per bale. **Type of Price:** spot. **Time Period Covered:** latest month.

YARN: COTTON, CARDED, 40S, SINGLES

Source: *Japan Economic Journal.* **Price Frequency:** weekly. **Effective Market(s):** Osaka. **Units of Measure:** Japanese yen per 400 lbs. **Type of Price:** market. **Time Period Covered:** latest 2 weeks.

YARN: COTTON, CARDED, OPEN-END SPUN

Source: *ATI, America's Textiles International.* **Price Frequency:** monthly. **Time Period Covered:** latest month, 6 months ago, year ago.

YARN: COTTON, CARDED, RING-SPUN

Source: *ATI, America's Textiles International.* **Price Frequency:** monthly. **Time Period Covered:** latest month, 6 months ago, year ago.

YARN: COTTON, COMBED, 30S

Source: *JTN: The International Textile Magazine.* **Price Frequency:** monthly. **Effective Market(s):** Japan. **Units of Measure:** 1000 Japanese yen per bale. **Type of Price:** spot. **Time Period Covered:** latest month.

YARN: COTTON, COMBED, 40S

Source: *JTN: The International Textile Magazine.* **Price Frequency:** monthly. **Effective Market(s):** Japan. **Units of Measure:** 1000 Japanese yen per bale. **Type of Price:** spot. **Time Period Covered:** latest month.

YARN: COTTON, COMBED, 60S, EGYPTIAN

Source: *Prices of Selected Asia/Pacific Products.* **Price Frequency:** monthly, seasonally. **Effective Market(s):** Osaka. **Units of Measure:** 1000 Japanese yen per bag. **Type of Price:** trade high, trade low. **Time Period Covered:** latest month.

YARN: COTTON, COMBED FOR STRAND, 30S, UNITED STATES

Source: *Prices of Selected Asia/Pacific Products.* **Price Frequency:** monthly, seasonally. **Effective Market(s):** Osaka. **Units of Measure:** 1000 Japanese yen per bag. **Type of Price:** trade high, trade low. **Time Period Covered:** latest month.

YARN: COTTON, COMBED, RING-SPUN

Source: *ATI, America's Textiles International.* **Price Frequency:** monthly. **Time Period Covered:** latest month, 6 months ago, year ago.

YARN: COTTON, FULL COMBED, 32S, CHINESE

Source: *Prices of Selected Asia/Pacific Products.* **Price Frequency:** monthly, seasonally. **Effective Market(s):** Hong Kong. **Units of Measure:** Hong Kong dollars per bale. **Type of Price:** wholesale spot high, wholesale spot low. **Time Period Covered:** latest month.

YARN: COTTON, FULL COMBED, 40S, CHINESE

Source: *Prices of Selected Asia/Pacific Products.* **Price Frequency:** monthly, seasonally. **Effective Market(s):** Hong Kong. **Units of Measure:** Hong Kong dollars per bale. **Type of Price:** wholesale spot high, wholesale spot low. **Time Period Covered:** latest month.

YARN: COTTON, NATURAL STOCK, COMBED, KNITTING

Source: *Commodity Year Book.* **Price Frequency:** monthly, annually. **Units of Measure:** index. **Type of Price:** wholesale price index. **Time Period Covered:** latest 5 years.

YARN: COTTON, SEMI-COMBED, 32S, HONG KONG

Source: *Prices of Selected Asia/Pacific Products.* **Price Frequency:** monthly, seasonally. **Effective Market(s):** Hong Kong. **Units of Measure:** Hong Kong dollars per bale. **Type of Price:** wholesale spot high, wholesale spot low. **Time Period Covered:** latest month.

YARN: COTTON, SEMI-COMBED, 40S, HONG KONG

Source: *Prices of Selected Asia/Pacific Products.* **Price Frequency:** monthly, seasonally. **Effective Market(s):** Hong Kong. **Units of Measure:** Hong Kong dollars per bale. **Type of Price:** wholesale spot high, wholesale spot low. **Time Period Covered:** latest month.

YARN: FIBERGLASS FILAMENT

Source: *Journal of Commerce and Commercial.* **Price Frequency:** weekly in Tuesday issue. **Units of Measure:** Dollars per lb. **Type of Price:** spot. **Time Period Covered:** latest week.

YARN: NYLON FILAMENT

Source: *JTN: The International Textile Magazine.* **Price Frequency:** monthly. **Effective Market(s):** Japan. **Units of Measure:** Japanese yen per kilogram. **Type of Price:** spot. **Time Period Covered:** latest month.

Source: *JTN: The International Textile Magazine.* **Price Frequency:** monthly. **Effective Market(s):** Taiwan. **Units of Measure:** Dollars per kilogram. **Type of Price:** export. **Time Period Covered:** latest month.

YARN: NYLON FILAMENT, TEXTURED

Source: *ATI, America's Textiles International.* **Price Frequency:** monthly. **Time Period Covered:** latest month, 6 months ago, year ago.

Source: *JTN: The International Textile Magazine.* **Price Frequency:** monthly. **Effective Market(s):** Japan. **Units of Measure:** Japanese yen per kilogram. **Type of Price:** spot. **Time Period Covered:** latest month.

Source: *JTN: The International Textile Magazine.* **Price Frequency:** monthly. **Effective Market(s):** Taiwan. **Units of Measure:** Dollars per kilogram. **Type of Price:** export. **Time Period Covered:** latest month.

YARN: NYLON HOSIERY FILAMENT

Source: *Journal of Commerce and Commercial.* **Price Frequency:** weekly in Tuesday issue. **Units of Measure:** Dollars per lb. **Type of Price:** spot. **Time Period Covered:** latest week.

YARN: NYLON INDUSTRIAL FILAMENT

Source: *Journal of Commerce and Commercial.* **Price Frequency:** weekly in Tuesday issue. **Units of Measure:** Dollars per lb. **Type of Price:** spot. **Time Period Covered:** latest week.

YARN: POLYESTER, BRANDED, RING-SPUN

Source: *ATI, America's Textiles International.* **Price Frequency:** monthly. **Time Period Covered:** latest month, 6 months ago, year ago.

YARN: POLYESTER FILAMENT

Source: *JTN: The International Textile Magazine.* **Price Frequency:** monthly. **Effective Market(s):** Japan. **Units of Measure:** Japanese yen per lb. **Type of Price:** spot. **Time Period Covered:** latest month.

Source: *JTN: The International Textile Magazine.* **Price Frequency:** monthly. **Effective Market(s):** Taiwan. **Units of Measure:** Dollars per kilogram. **Type of Price:** export. **Time Period Covered:** latest month.

YARN: POLYESTER FILAMENT, PARTIALLY ORIENTED, 70 DENIER

Source: *ATI, America's Textiles International.* **Price Frequency:** monthly. **Time Period Covered:** latest month, 6 months ago, year ago.

YARN: POLYESTER FILAMENT, PARTIALLY ORIENTED, 100 DENIER

Source: *ATI, America's Textiles International.* **Price Frequency:** monthly. **Time Period Covered:** latest month, 6 months ago, year ago.

YARN: POLYESTER FILAMENT, PARTIALLY ORIENTED, 150 DENIER

Source: *ATI, America's Textiles International.* **Price Frequency:** monthly. **Time Period Covered:** latest month, 6 months ago, year ago.

YARN: POLYESTER FILAMENT, TEXTURED

Source: *JTN: The International Textile Magazine.* **Price Frequency:** monthly. **Effective Market(s):** Taiwan. **Units of Measure:** Dollars per kilogram. **Type of Price:** export. **Time Period Covered:** latest month.

YARN: POLYESTER FILAMENT, TEXTURED, ONE HEATER

Source: *JTN: The International Textile Magazine.* **Price Frequency:** monthly. **Effective Market(s):** Japan. **Units of Measure:** Japanese yen per lb. **Type of Price:** spot. **Time Period Covered:** latest month.

YARN: POLYESTER FILAMENT, TEXTURED, TWO HEATER

Source: *JTN: The International Textile Magazine.* **Price Frequency:** monthly. **Effective Market(s):** Japan. **Units of Measure:** Japanese yen per lb. **Type of Price:** spot. **Time Period Covered:** latest month.

YARN: POLYESTER TEXTILE FILAMENT

Source: *Journal of Commerce and Commercial.* **Price Frequency:** weekly in Tuesday issue. **Units of Measure:** Dollars per lb. **Type of Price:** spot. **Time Period Covered:** latest week.

YARN: POLYESTER TEXTILE FILAMENT, 150 DENIER

Source: *Journal of Commerce and Commercial.* **Price Frequency:** weekly in Tuesday issue. **Units of Measure:** Dollars per lb. **Type of Price:** spot. **Time Period Covered:** latest week.

YARN: POLYESTER, UNBRANDED, WHITES ONLY, RING-SPUN

Source: *ATI, America's Textiles International.* **Price Frequency:** monthly. **Time Period Covered:** latest month, 6 months ago, year ago.

YARN: POLYESTER/COTTON BLEND, 34S

Source: *JTN: The International Textile Magazine.* **Price Frequency:** monthly. **Effective Market(s):** Japan. **Units of Measure:** Japanese yen per lb. **Type of Price:** spot. **Time Period Covered:** latest month.

YARN: POLYESTER/COTTON BLEND, 45S

Source: *JTN: The International Textile Magazine.* **Price Frequency:** monthly. **Effective Market(s):** Japan. **Units of Measure:** Japanese yen per lb. **Type of Price:** spot. **Time Period Covered:** latest month.

Source: *JTN: The International Textile Magazine.* **Price Frequency:** monthly. **Effective Market(s):** Taiwan. **Units of Measure:** Dollars per lb. **Type of Price:** export. **Time Period Covered:** latest month.

YARN: POLYESTER/COTTON (CARDED), OPEN-END SPUN

Source: *ATI, America's Textiles International.* **Price Frequency:** monthly. **Time Period Covered:** latest month, 6 months ago, year ago.

YARN: POLYESTER/COTTON (CARDED), RING-SPUN

Source: *ATI, America's Textiles International.* **Price Frequency:** monthly. **Time Period Covered:** latest month. 6 months ago, year ago.

YARN: RAYON FILAMENT, VISCOSE, BRIGHT

Source: *JTN: The International Textile Magazine.* **Price Frequency:** monthly. **Effective Market(s):** Japan. **Units of Measure:** Japanese yen per kilogram. **Type of Price:** spot. **Time Period Covered:** latest month.

YARN: RAYON FILAMENT, VISCOSE, DULL

Source: *JTN: The International Textile Magazine.* **Price Frequency:** monthly. **Effective Market(s):** Japan. **Units of Measure:** Japanese yen per kilogram. **Type of Price:** spot. **Time Period Covered:** latest month.

YARN: RAYON, SPUN, BRIGHT

Source: *JTN: The International Textile Magazine.* **Price Frequency:** monthly. **Effective Market(s):** Japan. **Units of Measure:** Japanese yen per lb. **Type of Price:** spot. **Time Period Covered:** latest month.

YARN: RAYON, SPUN, DULL

Source: *JTN: The International Textile Magazine.* **Price Frequency:** monthly. **Effective Market(s):** Japan. **Units of Measure:** Japanese yen per lb. **Type of Price:** spot. **Time Period Covered:** latest month.

YARN: WOOLEN, WORSTED, WEAVING, 48S, DOUBLES

Source: *Japan Economic Journal.* **Price Frequency:** weekly. **Effective Market(s):** Nagoya. **Units of Measure:** Japanese yen per kilogram. **Type of Price:** market. **Time Period Covered:** latest 2 weeks.

YARN: WORSTED

Source: *JTN: The International Textile Magazine.* **Price Frequency:** monthly. **Effective Market(s):** Japan. **Units of Measure:** Japanese yen per kilogram. **Type of Price:** spot. **Time Period Covered:** latest month.

YARNS: COTTON, CARDED

Source: *DNR: Daily News Record.* **Price Frequency:** daily. **Units of Measure:** Dollars per yard. **Time Period Covered:** latest day.

YARNS: COTTON, COMBED

Source: *DNR: Daily News Record.* **Price Frequency:** daily. **Units of Measure:** Dollars per yard. **Time Period Covered:** latest day.

YARNS: COTTON, OPEN-END SPUN

Source: *DNR: Daily News Record.* **Price Frequency:** daily. **Units of Measure:** Dollars per yard. **Time Period Covered:** latest day.

YARNS: POLYESTER/BLEND, CARDED

Source: *DNR: Daily News Record.* **Price Frequency:** daily. **Units of Measure:** Dollars per yard. **Time Period Covered:** latest day.

YARNS: POLYESTER/COTTON (COMBED), 50S

Source: *DNR: Daily News Record.* **Price Frequency:** daily. **Units of Measure:** Dollars per yard. **Time Period Covered:** latest day.

YARNS: POLYESTER/COTTON, OPEN-END SPUN

Source: *DNR: Daily News Record.* **Price Frequency:** daily. **Units of Measure:** Dollars per yard. **Time Period Covered:** latest day.

YARNS AND THREADS: PROCESSED

Source: *Textile World.* **Price Frequency:** monthly. **Units of Measure:** index. **Type of Price:** producer price index. **Time Period Covered:** latest 2 months, year ago.

YEARLINGS: BULLS

Source: *Farm and Dairy.* **Price Frequency:** weekly, seasonally. **Effective Market(s):** Ohio, Pennsylvania. **Units of Measure:** Dollars per head. **Type of Price:** auction high, auction low. **Time Period Covered:** latest week.

YEARLINGS: HEIFERS

Source: *Farm and Dairy.* **Price Frequency:** weekly, seasonally. **Effective Market(s):** Ohio, Pennsylvania. **Units of Measure:** Dollars per head. **Type of Price:** auction high, auction low. **Time Period Covered:** latest week.

YEARLINGS: STEER

Source: *Farm and Dairy.* **Price Frequency:** weekly, seasonally. **Effective Market(s):** Ohio, Pennsylvania. **Units of Measure:** Dollars per head. **Type of Price:** auction high, auction low. **Time Period Covered:** latest week.

YEAST: DRIED

Source: *Feedstuffs.* **Price Frequency:** weekly. **Effective Market(s):** 8 domestic markets. **Units of Measure:** Dollars per lb. **Time Period Covered:** latest week.

YEAST: PURE BREWER'S, DEBITTERED

Source: *Chemical Marketing Reporter.* **Price Frequency:** weekly. **Effective Market(s):** New York. **Units of Measure:** Dollars per lb. **Type of Price:** spot. **Time Period Covered:** latest week.

YELLOWTAIL: FILLETS, FRESH

Source: *Seafood Price-Current.* **Price Frequency:** semiweekly. **Effective Market(s):** Mid-Atlantic, New England. **Units of Measure:** Dollars per lb. **Type of Price:** sale by first receiver. **Time Period Covered:** latest day.

YELLOWTAIL: FILLETS, LARGE, MIXED, FRESH

Source: *HRI-Buyer's Guide.* **Price Frequency:** weekly. **Effective Market(s):** New York. **Units of Measure:** Dollars per lb. **Type of Price:** dealer. **Time Period Covered:** latest week.

YELLOWTAIL: FILLETS, REGULAR, FRESH

Source: *HRI-Buyer's Guide.* **Price Frequency:** weekly. **Effective Market(s):** New York. **Units of Measure:** Dollars per lb. **Type of Price:** dealer. **Time Period Covered:** latest week.

YELLOWTAIL: WHOLE, FRESH

Source: *Seafood Price-Current.* **Price Frequency:** semiweekly. **Effective Market(s):** West Coast. **Units of Measure:** Dollars per lb. **Type of Price:** sale by first receiver. **Time Period Covered:** latest day.

YEN

See Japan Yen.

YERBA, SANTA LEAVES

Source: *Chemical Marketing Reporter.* **Price Frequency:** weekly. **Effective Market(s):** New York. **Units of Measure:** Dollars per lb. **Type of Price:** spot. **Time Period Covered:** latest week.

YERBA, SANTA LEAVES: EXTRA

Source: *Chemical Marketing Reporter.* **Price Frequency:** weekly. **Effective Market(s):** New York. **Units of Measure:** Dollars per lb. **Type of Price:** spot. **Time Period Covered:** latest week.

YLANG-YLANG OIL

Source: *U. S. Essential Oil Trade.* **Price Frequency:** annually. **Effective Market(s):** United States. **Units of Measure:** Dollars per kilogram. **Type of Price:** import value. **Time Period Covered:** latest 3 years.

YLANG-YLANG OIL: EXTRA GRADE

Source: *Chemical Marketing Reporter.* **Price Frequency:** weekly. **Effective Market(s):** New York. **Units of Measure:** Dollars per lb. **Type of Price:** spot. **Time Period Covered:** latest week.

Source: *Journal of Commerce and Commercial.* **Price Frequency:** weekly in Tuesday issue. **Units of Measure:** Dollars per lb. **Type of Price:** spot. **Time Period Covered:** latest week.

YLANG-YLANG OIL: GRADE 1

Source: *Chemical Marketing Reporter.* **Price Frequency:** weekly. **Effective Market(s):** New York. **Units of Measure:** Dollars per lb. **Type of Price:** spot. **Time Period Covered:** latest week.

YLANG-YLANG OIL: GRADE 2

Source: *Chemical Marketing Reporter.* **Price Frequency:** weekly. **Effective Market(s):** New York. **Units of Measure:** Dollars per lb. **Type of Price:** spot. **Time Period Covered:** latest week.

YLANG-YLANG OIL: GRADE 3

Source: *Chemical Marketing Reporter.* **Price Frequency:** weekly. **Effective Market(s):** New York. **Units of Measure:** Dollars per lb. **Type of Price:** spot. **Time Period Covered:** latest week.

YOGURT: NATURAL, FLAVORED

Source: *Dairy Market Statistics.* **Price Frequency:** monthly, annually. **Effective Market(s):** South, United States. **Units of Measure:** Dollars per lb. **Type of Price:** retail. **Time Period Covered:** latest year.

Source: *Federal Milk Order Market Statistics.* **Price Frequency:** monthly. **Effective Market(s):** South, West, United States. **Units of Measure:** Dollars per 1/2 pint. **Type of Price:** retail. **Time Period Covered:** latest year to date.

YTTRIUM CONCENTRATE

Source: *Industrial Minerals.* **Price Frequency:** monthly. **Effective Market(s):** Malaysia. **Units of Measure:** Dollars per kilogram. **Type of Price:** producer & dealer. **Time Period Covered:** latest month.

YUGOSLAVIA DINAR

Source: *New York Times.* **Price Frequency:** daily. **Effective Market(s):** New York. **Units of Measure:** Yugoslav dinar per United States dollar. **Type of Price:** foreign exchange. **Time Period Covered:** latest 2 days.

Source: *Timber Bulletin.* **Price Frequency:** monthly, annually. **Units of Measure:** Yugoslav dinars per United States dollar. **Type of Price:** foreign exchange. **Time Period Covered:** latest 2 years.

ZEIN

Source: *Chemical Marketing Reporter.* **Price Frequency:** weekly. **Effective Market(s):** New York. **Units of Measure:** Dollars per lb. **Type of Price:** spot. **Time Period Covered:** latest week.

ZINC

Source: *E&MJ.* **Price Frequency:** monthly. **Effective Market(s):** Europe. **Units of Measure:** Dollars per metric ton. **Type of Price:** producer. **Time Period Covered:** latest month.

Source: *Economic and Energy Indicators.* **Price Frequency:** biweekly. **Units of Measure:** cents per lb. **Time Period Covered:** latest 3 months, quarters, and years.

Source: *International Financial Statistics.* **Price Frequency:** monthly, quarterly, annually. **Effective Market(s):** New York. **Units of Measure:** cents per lb., index. **Type of Price:** market price, price index. **Time Period Covered:** latest 4 months, latest 5 quarters, latest 5 years.

Source: *International Financial Statistics Yearbook.* **Price Frequency:** annually. **Effective Market(s):** New York. **Units of Measure:** cents per lb. **Type of Price:** wholesale. **Time Period Covered:** latest 30 years.

Source: *Lead and Zinc Statistics.* **Price Frequency:** weekly, monthly, annually. **Effective Market(s):** London, United States. **Units of Measure:** British pounds per metric ton, cents per lb. **Type of Price:** average. **Time Period Covered:** weekly latest month, monthly latest year, annually latest 4 years.

Source: *Lead and Zinc Statistics.* **Price Frequency:** daily. **Effective Market(s):** 8 international markets. **Units of Measure:** national currency per unit. **Time Period Covered:** latest day available.

Source: *Los Angeles Times.* **Price Frequency:** daily. **Units of Measure:** cents per lb. **Type of Price:** cash. **Time Period Covered:** latest day.

Source: *Minerals Today.* **Price Frequency:** bimonthly. **Units of Measure:** cents per lb. **Time Period Covered:** latest month, month ago.

Source: *Monthly Commodity Price Bulletin.* **Price Frequency:** monthly, annually. **Effective Market(s):** outside North America. **Units of Measure:** Dollars per metric ton. **Type of Price:** producer. **Time Period Covered:** latest 5 years.

Source: *Northern Miner.* **Price Frequency:** daily. **Effective Market(s):** London. **Units of Measure:** Dollars per tonne. **Type of Price:** spot. **Time Period Covered:** latest week.

Source: *UNCTAD Commodity Yearbook.* **Price Frequency:** annually. **Effective Market(s):** London. **Units of Measure:** Dollars per metric ton. **Type of Price:** cash. **Time Period Covered:** latest 12 years.

Source: *UNCTAD Commodity Yearbook.* **Price Frequency:** annually. **Effective Market(s):** outside North America. **Units of Measure:** Dollars per metric ton. **Type of Price:** producer. **Time Period Covered:** latest 12 years.

ZINC: 50% SOLUTION, TECHNICAL GRADE

Source: *Journal of Commerce and Commercial.* **Price Frequency:** weekly in Thursday issue. **Units of Measure:** Dollars per 100 lbs. **Type of Price:** spot. **Time Period Covered:** latest week.

ZINC: BOLIVIAN

Source: *International Financial Statistics.* **Price Frequency:** monthly, quarterly, annually. **Effective Market(s):** Bolivia. **Units of Measure:** cents per lb., index. **Type of Price:** market price, price index. **Time Period Covered:** latest month, latest 4 quarters, latest 5 years.

ZINC: CANADIAN

Source: *International Financial Statistics.* **Price Frequency:** annually. **Effective Market(s):** Canada. **Units of Measure:** cents per lb., index. **Type of Price:** market price, price index. **Time Period Covered:** latest 3 years.

Source: *International Financial Statistics Yearbook.* **Price Frequency:** annually. **Effective Market(s):** Canada. **Units of Measure:** cents per lb. **Type of Price:** wholesale. **Time Period Covered:** latest 30 years.

ZINC: CONTINUOUS GALVINIZING

Source: *E&MJ.* **Price Frequency:** monthly. **Units of Measure:** cents per lb. **Time Period Covered:** latest month.

ZINC: CONTINUOUS GALVANIZING GRADE, CANADIAN

Source: *American Metal Market.* **Price Frequency:** daily. **Effective Market(s):** Canada. **Units of Measure:** Canadian cents per lb. **Time Period Covered:** latest day.

ZINC: CONTINUOUS GALVANIZING GRADE, DOMESTIC

Source: *American Metal Market.* **Price Frequency:** daily. **Effective Market(s):** United States. **Units of Measure:** cents per lb. **Type of Price:** producer. **Time Period Covered:** latest day.

ZINC: CONTINUOUS GALVANIZING GRADE, IMPORTED

Source: *American Metal Market.* **Price Frequency:** daily. **Effective Market(s):** United States. **Units of Measure:** cents per lb. **Type of Price:** producer. **Time Period Covered:** latest day.

ZINC: DIE CAST, NEW

Source: *American Metal Market.* **Price Frequency:** daily. **Effective Market(s):** 13 domestic markets, Montreal, Toronto. **Units of Measure:** cents per lb., Canadian cents per lb. **Type of Price:** dealer buying. **Time Period Covered:** latest day.

Source: *American Metal Market.* **Price Frequency:** weekly in Wednesday issue. **Effective Market(s):** Los Angeles, San Francisco. **Units of Measure:** cents per lb. **Type of Price:** dealer buying. **Time Period Covered:** latest week.

ZINC: DIE CAST, NO. 3

Source: *Purchasing.* **Price Frequency:** quarterly in January, April, July, October issues. **Units of Measure:** cents per lb. **Type of Price:** transaction. **Time Period Covered:** latest 5 quarters.

ZINC: DIE CAST, OLD

Source: *American Metal Market.* **Price Frequency:** daily. **Effective Market(s):** 13 domestic markets, Montreal, Toronto. **Units of Measure:** cents per lb., Canadian cents per lb. **Type of Price:** dealer buying. **Time Period Covered:** latest day.

Source: *American Metal Market.* **Price Frequency:** weekly in Wednesday issue. **Effective Market(s):** Los Angeles, San Francisco. **Units of Measure:** cents per lb. **Type of Price:** dealer buying. **Time Period Covered:** latest week.

Source: *Iron Age.* **Price Frequency:** monthly. **Effective Market(s):** New York. **Units of Measure:** cents per lb. **Type of Price:** dealer. **Time Period Covered:** latest month.

ZINC: DIE CAST, SCRAP

Source: *American Metal Market.* **Price Frequency:** daily. **Units of Measure:** cents per lb. **Type of Price:** smelters. **Time Period Covered:** latest day.

ZINC: EXTRA HIGH GRADE

Source: *Iron Age.* **Price Frequency:** monthly. **Effective Market(s):** London. **Units of Measure:** cents per lb. **Time Period Covered:** latest month.

ZINC: HIGH GRADE

Source: *American Metal Market.* **Price Frequency:** daily. **Effective Market(s):** New York. **Units of Measure:** cents per lb. **Type of Price:** market. **Time Period Covered:** latest 3 days.

Source: *Chemical Marketing Reporter.* **Price Frequency:** weekly. **Effective Market(s):** New York. **Units of Measure:** Dollars per lb. **Type of Price:** spot. **Time Period Covered:** latest week.

Source: *Commodity Trade and Price Trends.* **Price Frequency:** annually. **Effective Market(s):** London. **Units of Measure:** Dollars per metric ton, 1980 constant dollars per metric ton. **Type of Price:** settlement. **Time Period Covered:** latest 37 years.

Source: *E&MJ.* **Price Frequency:** monthly. **Units of Measure:** cents per lb. **Time Period Covered:** latest month.

Source: *Investor's Daily.* **Price Frequency:** daily. **Units of Measure:** Dollars per lb. **Type of Price:** spot. **Time Period Covered:** latest 2 days.

Source: *Monthly Commodity Price Bulletin.* **Price Frequency:** monthly, annually. **Effective Market(s):** London. **Units of Measure:** Dollars per metric ton. **Type of Price:** cash settlement. **Time Period Covered:** latest 5 years.

Source: *Monthly Commodity Price Bulletin Supplement.* **Price Frequency:** monthly, quarterly, annually. **Effective Market(s):** United Kingdom ports. **Units of Measure:** Dollars per tonne. **Type of Price:** cash. **Time Period Covered:** latest 20 years.

Source: *Monthly Commodity Price Bulletin Supplement.* **Price Frequency:** monthly, quarterly, annually. **Effective Market(s):** United States. **Units of Measure:** cents per lb. **Type of Price:** daily weighted average. **Time Period Covered:** latest 20 years.

Source: *New York Times.* **Price Frequency:** daily. **Units of Measure:** Dollars per lb. **Type of Price:** cash. **Time Period Covered:** latest 2 days.

Source: *Purchasing.* **Price Frequency:** monthly. **Effective Market(s):** United States. **Units of Measure:** cents per lb. **Type of Price:** transaction. **Time Period Covered:** latest day, month ago, 6 months ago, year ago.

Source: *Survey of Current Business.* **Price Frequency:** monthly, annually. **Units of Measure:** Dollars per lb. **Time Period Covered:** latest year.

Source: *Wall Street Journal.* **Price Frequency:** daily. **Effective Market(s):** London. **Units of Measure:** Dollars per troy ounce. **Type of Price:** spot. **Time Period Covered:** latest day, 3 months ago.

ZINC: HIGH GRADE, 99.98%, CANADIAN

Source: *American Metal Market.* **Price Frequency:** daily. **Effective Market(s):** Canada. **Units of Measure:** Canadian cents per lb. **Time Period Covered:** latest day.

ZINC: HIGH GRADE, DOMESTIC

Source: *American Metal Market.* **Price Frequency:** daily. **Effective Market(s):** United States. **Units of Measure:** cents per lb. **Type of Price:** producer. **Time Period Covered:** latest day.

ZINC: HIGH GRADE, IMPORTED

Source: *American Metal Market.* **Price Frequency:** daily. **Effective Market(s):** United States. **Units of Measure:** cents per lb. **Type of Price:** producer. **Time Period Covered:** latest day.

ZINC: OLD, CLEAN, SCRAP

Source: *American Metal Market.* **Price Frequency:** daily. **Units of Measure:** cents per lb. **Type of Price:** smelters. **Time Period Covered:** latest day.

ZINC: OLD, SCRAP

Source: *American Metal Market.* **Price Frequency:** daily. **Effective Market(s):** 13 domestic markets, Montreal, Toronto. **Units of Measure:** cents per lb., Canadian cents per lb. **Type of Price:** dealer buying. **Time Period Covered:** latest day.

Source: *American Metal Market.* **Price Frequency:** weekly in Wednesday issue. **Effective Market(s):** Los Angeles, San Francisco. **Units of Measure:** cents per lb. **Type of Price:** dealer buying. **Time Period Covered:** latest week.

ZINC: PERUVIAN

Source: *International Financial Statistics Yearbook.* **Price Frequency:** annually. **Effective Market(s):** Peru. **Units of Measure:** cents per lb. **Type of Price:** wholesale. **Time Period Covered:** latest 30 years.

ZINC: PRIME WESTERN GRADE

Source: *Commodity Trade and Price Trends.* **Price Frequency:** annually. **Effective Market(s):** New York. **Units of Measure:** Dollars per metric ton, 1980 constant dollars per metric ton. **Type of Price:** domestic producer. **Time Period Covered:** latest 37 years.

Source: *CRB Commodity Index Report.* **Price Frequency:** weekly. **Effective Market(s):** New York. **Units of Measure:** Dollars per lb. **Type of Price:** spot. **Time Period Covered:** latest week.

Source: *E&MJ.* **Price Frequency:** monthly. **Units of Measure:** cents per lb. **Time Period Covered:** latest month.

Source: *Monthly Commodity Price Bulletin.* **Price Frequency:** monthly, annually. **Units of Measure:** cents per lb. **Time Period Covered:** latest 5 years.

Source: *UNCTAD Commodity Yearbook.* **Price Frequency:** annually. **Effective Market(s):** West. **Units of Measure:** Dollars per metric ton. **Type of Price:** free market. **Time Period Covered:** latest 12 years.

ZINC: PRIME WESTERN GRADE, CANADIAN

Source: *American Metal Market.* **Price Frequency:** daily. **Effective Market(s):** Canada. **Units of Measure:** Canadian cents per lb. **Time Period Covered:** latest day.

ZINC: PRIME WESTERN GRADE, DOMESTIC

Source: *American Metal Market.* **Price Frequency:** daily. **Effective Market(s):** United States. **Units of Measure:** cents per lb. **Type of Price:** producer. **Time Period Covered:** latest day.

ZINC: PRIME WESTERN GRADE, IMPORTED

Source: *American Metal Market.* **Price Frequency:** daily. **Effective Market(s):** United States. **Units of Measure:** cents per lb. **Type of Price:** producer. **Time Period Covered:** latest day.

ZINC: PRIME WESTERN GRADE, UNITED STATES

Source: *Financial Times.* **Price Frequency:** daily. **Effective Market(s):** London. **Units of Measure:** cents per lb. **Type of Price:** spot. **Time Period Covered:** latest day.

ZINC: PRIME WESTERN SLAB

Source: *Commodity Year Book.* **Price Frequency:** monthly, annually. **Effective Market(s):** United States. **Units of Measure:** cents per lb. **Time Period Covered:** latest 13 years.

ZINC: SPECIAL HIGH GRADE

Source: *American Metal Market.* **Price Frequency:** daily. **Effective Market(s):** London. **Units of Measure:** Dollars per metric ton. **Type of Price:** cash. **Time Period Covered:** latest 2 days.

Source: *Asian Wall Street Journal.* **Price Frequency:** daily. **Effective Market(s):** London. **Units of Measure:** Dollars per metric ton. **Type of Price:** spot. **Time Period Covered:** latest day.

Source: *Asian Wall Street Journal.* **Price Frequency:** daily. **Units of Measure:** Dollars per lb. **Type of Price:** producer. **Time Period Covered:** latest 2 days, year ago.

Source: *E&MJ.* **Price Frequency:** monthly. **Units of Measure:** cents per lb. **Time Period Covered:** latest month.

Source: *Financial Times.* **Price Frequency:** daily. **Effective Market(s):** London. **Units of Measure:** Dollars per tonne. **Type of Price:** cash. **Time Period Covered:** latest 2 days.

Source: *Journal of Commerce and Commercial.* **Price Frequency:** daily. **Units of Measure:** Dollars per lb. **Type of Price:** spot supplier. **Time Period Covered:** latest day.

Source: *New York Times.* **Price Frequency:** daily. **Effective Market(s):** London. **Units of Measure:** Dollars per metric ton. **Type of Price:** spot. **Time Period Covered:** latest day.

Source: *Northern Miner.* **Price Frequency:** weekly. **Effective Market(s):** Canada, United States. **Units of Measure:** Canadian dollars per lb., dollars per lb. **Type of Price:** producer. **Time Period Covered:** latest week.

Source: *The Times.* **Price Frequency:** daily. **Effective Market(s):** London. **Units of Measure:** Dollars per per tonne. **Type of Price:** cash. **Time Period Covered:** latest day.

Source: *Wall Street Journal.* **Price Frequency:** daily. **Units of Measure:** Dollars per lb. **Type of Price:** producer. **Time Period Covered:** latest day, day ago, year ago.

ZINC: SPECIAL HIGH GRADE, 99.99%, CANADIAN

Source: *American Metal Market.* **Price Frequency:** daily. **Effective Market(s):** Canada. **Units of Measure:** Canadian cents per lb. **Time Period Covered:** latest day.

ZINC: SPECIAL HIGH GRADE, DOMESTIC

Source: *American Metal Market.* **Price Frequency:** daily. **Effective Market(s):** United States. **Units of Measure:** cents per lb. **Type of Price:** producer. **Time Period Covered:** latest day.

ZINC: SPECIAL HIGH GRADE, IMPORTED

Source: *American Metal Market.* **Price Frequency:** daily. **Effective Market(s):** United States. **Units of Measure:** cents per lb. **Type of Price:** producer. **Time Period Covered:** latest day.

ZINC: UNITED KINGDOM

Source: *International Financial Statistics.* **Price Frequency:** monthly, quarterly, annually. **Effective Market(s):** London. **Units of Measure:** cents per lb., index. **Type of Price:** market price, price index. **Time Period Covered:** latest 5 months, latest 5 quarters, latest 5 years.

Source: *International Financial Statistics Yearbook.* **Price Frequency:** annually. **Effective Market(s):** London. **Units of Measure:** cents per lb. **Type of Price:** wholesale. **Time Period Covered:** latest 30 years.

ZINC ACETATE: NF

Source: *Chemical Marketing Reporter.* **Price Frequency:** weekly. **Effective Market(s):** New York. **Units of Measure:** Dollars per lb. **Type of Price:** spot. **Time Period Covered:** latest week.

ZINC ACETATE: TECHNICAL, DIHYDRATE

Source: *Chemical Marketing Reporter.* **Price Frequency:** weekly. **Effective Market(s):** New York. **Units of Measure:** Dollars per lb. **Type of Price:** spot. **Time Period Covered:** latest week.

ZINC ALLOY: DIE CASTING

Source: *American Metal Market.* **Price Frequency:** daily. **Units of Measure:** cents per lb. **Type of Price:** wholesale. **Time Period Covered:** latest day.

ZINC AMMONIUM CHLORIDE

Source: *Chemical Marketing Reporter.* **Price Frequency:** weekly. **Effective Market(s):** New York. **Units of Measure:** Dollars per lb. **Type of Price:** spot. **Time Period Covered:** latest week.

ZINC AUTOMOTIVE GRILLES: DIE CAST

Source: *American Metal Market.* **Price Frequency:** daily. **Effective Market(s):** 13 domestic markets, Montreal, Toronto. **Units of Measure:** cents per lb., Canadian cents per lb. **Type of Price:** dealer buying. **Time Period Covered:** latest day.

ZINC BORATE: TECHNICAL

Source: *Chemical Marketing Reporter.* **Price Frequency:** weekly. **Effective Market(s):** New York. **Units of Measure:** Dollars per lb. **Type of Price:** spot. **Time Period Covered:** latest week.

ZINC CHLORIDE: GRANULAR

Source: *Journal of Commerce and Commercial.* **Price Frequency:** weekly in Thursday issue. **Units of Measure:** Dollars per 100 lbs. **Type of Price:** spot. **Time Period Covered:** latest week.

ZINC CHLORIDE: GRANULAR, USP

Source: *Chemical Marketing Reporter.* **Price Frequency:** weekly. **Effective Market(s):** New York. **Units of Measure:** Dollars per kilo. **Type of Price:** spot. **Time Period Covered:** latest week.

ZINC CHLORIDE: TECHNICAL, 50% SOLUTION

Source: *Chemical Marketing Reporter.* **Price Frequency:** weekly. **Effective Market(s):** New York. **Units of Measure:** Dollars per 100 lbs. **Type of Price:** spot. **Time Period Covered:** latest week.

ZINC CHLORIDE: TECHNICAL, 65% SOLUTION

Source: *Chemical Marketing Reporter.* **Price Frequency:** weekly. **Effective Market(s):** New York. **Units of Measure:** Dollars per 100 lbs. **Type of Price:** spot. **Time Period Covered:** latest week.

ZINC CHLORIDE: TECHNICAL, 70% SOLUTION

Source: *Chemical Marketing Reporter.* **Price Frequency:** weekly. **Effective Market(s):** New York. **Units of Measure:** Dollars per 100 lbs. **Type of Price:** spot. **Time Period Covered:** latest week.

ZINC CHLORIDE: TECHNICAL, 72% SOLUTION

Source: *Chemical Marketing Reporter.* **Price Frequency:** weekly. **Effective Market(s):** New York. **Units of Measure:** Dollars per 100 lbs. **Type of Price:** spot. **Time Period Covered:** latest week.

ZINC CHROMATE

Source: *Chemical Marketing Reporter.* **Price Frequency:** weekly. **Effective Market(s):** New York. **Units of Measure:** Dollars per lb. **Type of Price:** spot. **Time Period Covered:** latest week.

ZINC CHROMATE: YELLOW

Source: *Journal of Commerce and Commercial.* **Price Frequency:** weekly in Wednesday issue. **Units of Measure:** Dollars per lb. **Type of Price:** spot. **Time Period Covered:** latest week.

ZINC CLIPPINGS: MIXED HIGH, SCRAP

Source: *American Metal Market.* **Price Frequency:** daily. **Units of Measure:** cents per lb. **Type of Price:** secondary smelter buying. **Time Period Covered:** latest day.

ZINC CLIPPINGS: NEW

Source: *American Metal Market.* **Price Frequency:** daily. **Effective Market(s):** 13 domestic markets, Montreal, Toronto. **Units of Measure:** cents per lb., Canadian cents per lb. **Type of Price:** dealer buying. **Time Period Covered:** latest day.

Source: *American Metal Market.* **Price Frequency:** weekly in Wednesday issue. **Effective Market(s):** Los Angeles, San Francisco. **Units of Measure:** cents per lb. **Type of Price:** dealer buying. **Time Period Covered:** latest week.

Source: *Iron Age.* **Price Frequency:** monthly. **Effective Market(s):** New York. **Units of Measure:** cents per lb. **Type of Price:** dealer. **Time Period Covered:** latest month.

ZINC CLIPPINGS: NEW, SCRAP

Source: *American Metal Market.* **Price Frequency:** daily. **Units of Measure:** cents per lb. **Type of Price:** smelters. **Time Period Covered:** latest day.

ZINC CYANIDE

Source: *Chemical Marketing Reporter.* **Price Frequency:** weekly. **Effective Market(s):** New York. **Units of Measure:** Dollars per lb. **Type of Price:** spot. **Time Period Covered:** latest week.

Source: *Journal of Commerce and Commercial.* **Price Frequency:** weekly in Thursday issue. **Units of Measure:** Dollars per lb. **Type of Price:** spot. **Time Period Covered:** latest week.

ZINC DIE CASTING ALLOY: NO. 3

Source: *E&MJ.* **Price Frequency:** monthly. **Effective Market(s):** United States. **Units of Measure:** cents per lb. **Type of Price:** producer. **Time Period Covered:** latest month.

ZINC DIE CASTING ALLOY: NO. 5

Source: *E&MJ.* **Price Frequency:** monthly. **Effective Market(s):** United States. **Units of Measure:** cents per lb. **Type of Price:** producer. **Time Period Covered:** latest month.

ZINC DROSS: GALVANIZERS', SCRAP

Source: *American Metal Market.* **Price Frequency:** daily. **Units of Measure:** cents per lb. **Type of Price:** smelters. **Time Period Covered:** latest day.

ZINC DROSS: HOT DIP GALVANIZERS' UNSWEATED

Source: *American Metal Market.* **Price Frequency:** daily. **Effective Market(s):** 13 domestic markets, Montreal, Toronto. **Units of Measure:** cents per lb., Canadian cents per lb. **Type of Price:** dealer buying. **Time Period Covered:** latest day.

ZINC DUST

Source: *American Metal Market.* **Price Frequency:** daily. **Units of Measure:** cents per lb. **Type of Price:** wholesale. **Time Period Covered:** latest day.

Source: *Journal of Commerce and Commercial.* **Price Frequency:** weekly in Wednesday issue. **Units of Measure:** Dollars per lb. **Type of Price:** spot. **Time Period Covered:** latest week.

ZINC DUST PIGMENT: TYPE 1 AND 2

Source: *Chemical Marketing Reporter.* **Price Frequency:** weekly. **Effective Market(s):** New York. **Units of Measure:** Dollars per lb. **Type of Price:** spot. **Time Period Covered:** latest week.

ZINC ETHYLENEDIAMINE TETRACETIC ACID: 8.4% ZINC

Source: *Chemical Marketing Reporter.* **Price Frequency:** weekly. **Effective Market(s):** New York. **Units of Measure:** Dollars per lb. **Type of Price:** spot. **Time Period Covered:** latest week.

ZINC ETHYLENEDIAMINE TETRACETIC ACID: 9% ZINC

Source: *Chemical Marketing Reporter.* **Price Frequency:** weekly. **Effective Market(s):** New York. **Units of Measure:** Dollars per lb. **Type of Price:** spot. **Time Period Covered:** latest week.

ZINC FLUOBORATE: LIQUID CONCENTRATE

Source: *Chemical Marketing Reporter.* **Price Frequency:** weekly. **Effective Market(s):** New York. **Units of Measure:** Dollars per lb. **Type of Price:** spot. **Time Period Covered:** latest week.

ZINC FORMALDEHYDE SULFOXYLATE: BASIC

Source: *Chemical Marketing Reporter.* **Price Frequency:** weekly. **Effective Market(s):** New York. **Units of Measure:** Dollars per lb. **Type of Price:** spot. **Time Period Covered:** latest week.

ZINC NAPHTHENATE: LIQUID, 8% ZINC

Source: *Chemical Marketing Reporter.* **Price Frequency:** weekly. **Effective Market(s):** New York. **Units of Measure:** Dollars per lb. **Type of Price:** spot. **Time Period Covered:** latest week.

ZINC NITRATE: TECHNICAL, FLAKE

Source: *Chemical Marketing Reporter.* **Price Frequency:** weekly. **Effective Market(s):** New York. **Units of Measure:** Dollars per lb. **Type of Price:** spot. **Time Period Covered:** latest week.

ZINC OXIDE: AMERICAN PROCESS, LEAD FREE

Source: *Chemical Marketing Reporter.* **Price Frequency:** weekly. **Effective Market(s):** New York. **Units of Measure:** Dollars per lb. **Type of Price:** spot. **Time Period Covered:** latest week.

Source: *Journal of Commerce and Commercial.* **Price Frequency:** weekly in Wednesday issue. **Units of Measure:** Dollars per lb. **Type of Price:** spot. **Time Period Covered:** latest week.

ZINC OXIDE: FRENCH PROCESS

Source: *Chemical Marketing Reporter.* **Price Frequency:** weekly. **Effective Market(s):** New York. **Units of Measure:** Dollars per lb. **Type of Price:** spot. **Time Period Covered:** latest week.

Source: *Journal of Commerce and Commercial.* **Price Frequency:** weekly in Wednesday issue. **Units of Measure:** Dollars per lb. **Type of Price:** spot. **Time Period Covered:** latest week.

ZINC OXIDE: PHOTO CONDUCTIVE

Source: *Chemical Marketing Reporter.* **Price Frequency:** weekly. **Effective Market(s):** New York. **Units of Measure:** Dollars per lb. **Type of Price:** spot. **Time Period Covered:** latest week.

ZINC OXIDE: USP

Source: *Chemical Marketing Reporter.* **Price Frequency:** weekly. **Effective Market(s):** New York. **Units of Measure:** Dollars per lb. **Type of Price:** spot. **Time Period Covered:** latest week.

ZINC PHENOLSULFONATE: PURIFIED, GRANULAR

Source: *Chemical Marketing Reporter.* **Price Frequency:** weekly. **Effective Market(s):** New York. **Units of Measure:** Dollars per lb. **Type of Price:** spot. **Time Period Covered:** latest week.

ZINC POWDER

Source: *American Metal Market.* **Price Frequency:** daily. **Units of Measure:** Dollars per lb. **Time Period Covered:** latest day.

ZINC PYRIDINETHIONE: 48% DISPERSION

Source: *Chemical Marketing Reporter.* **Price Frequency:** weekly. **Effective Market(s):** New York. **Units of Measure:** Dollars per lb. **Type of Price:** spot. **Time Period Covered:** latest week.

ZINC PYRIDINETHIONE: INDUSTRIAL GRADE

Source: *Chemical Marketing Reporter.* **Price Frequency:** weekly. **Effective Market(s):** New York. **Units of Measure:** Dollars per lb. **Type of Price:** spot. **Time Period Covered:** latest week.

ZINC RESINATE: PRECIPITATED, 7.2-7.6% ZINC

Source: *Chemical Marketing Reporter.* **Price Frequency:** weekly. **Effective Market(s):** New York. **Units of Measure:** Dollars per lb. **Type of Price:** spot. **Time Period Covered:** latest week.

ZINC SILICOFLUORIDE

Source: *Chemical Marketing Reporter.* **Price Frequency:** weekly. **Effective Market(s):** New York. **Units of Measure:** Dollars per lb. **Type of Price:** spot. **Time Period Covered:** latest week.

ZINC STEARATE: USP

Source: *Chemical Marketing Reporter.* **Price Frequency:** weekly. **Effective Market(s):** New York. **Units of Measure:** Dollars per lb. **Type of Price:** spot. **Time Period Covered:** latest week.

ZINC SULFATE: AGRICULTURAL GRADE, POWDERED

Source: *Chemical Marketing Reporter.* **Price Frequency:** weekly. **Effective Market(s):** New York. **Units of Measure:** Dollars per ton. **Type of Price:** spot. **Time Period Covered:** latest week.

ZINC SULFATE: MONOHYDRATE, INDUSTRIAL GRADE, GRANULAR

Source: *Chemical Marketing Reporter.* **Price Frequency:** weekly. **Effective Market(s):** New York. **Units of Measure:** Dollars per 100 lbs. **Type of Price:** spot. **Time Period Covered:** latest week.

ZINC UNDECYLENATE

Source: *Chemical Marketing Reporter.* **Price Frequency:** weekly. **Effective Market(s):** New York. **Units of Measure:** Dollars per lb. **Type of Price:** spot. **Time Period Covered:** latest week.

ZINC YELLOW

see Zinc Chromate.

ZIRCON: CONCENTRATE

Source: *Industrial Minerals.* **Price Frequency:** monthly. **Effective Market(s):** East Coast. **Units of Measure:** Dollars per short ton. **Type of Price:** producer & dealer. **Time Period Covered:** latest month.

ZIRCON: GRANULAR

Source: *Chemical Marketing Reporter.* **Price Frequency:** weekly. **Effective Market(s):** New York. **Units of Measure:** Dollars per ton. **Type of Price:** spot. **Time Period Covered:** latest week.

ZIRCON: INTERMEDIATE

Source: *Industrial Minerals.* **Price Frequency:** monthly. **Effective Market(s):** Australia. **Units of Measure:** Australian dollars per metric tonne. **Type of Price:** producer & dealer. **Time Period Covered:** latest month.

ZIRCON: MILLED, 200 AND 325 MESH

Source: *Chemical Marketing Reporter.* **Price Frequency:** weekly. **Effective Market(s):** New York. **Units of Measure:** Dollars per ton. **Type of Price:** spot. **Time Period Covered:** latest week.

ZIRCON: PREMIUM

Source: *Industrial Minerals.* **Price Frequency:** monthly. **Effective Market(s):** Australia. **Units of Measure:** Australian dollars per metric tonne. **Type of Price:** producer & dealer. **Time Period Covered:** latest month.

ZIRCON: STANDARD

Source: *Industrial Minerals.* **Price Frequency:** monthly. **Effective Market(s):** Australia. **Units of Measure:** Australina dollars per metric tonne. **Type of Price:** producer & dealer. **Time Period Covered:** latest month.

ZIRCONIUM ACETATE: SOLUTION

Source: *Chemical Marketing Reporter.* **Price Frequency:** weekly. **Effective Market(s):** New York. **Units of Measure:** Dollars per lb. **Type of Price:** spot. **Time Period Covered:** latest week.

ZIRCONIUM HYDRIDE: POWDERED, ELECTRONIC GRADE

Source: *Chemical Marketing Reporter.* **Price Frequency:** weekly. **Effective Market(s):** New York. **Units of Measure:** Dollars per lb. **Type of Price:** spot. **Time Period Covered:** latest week.

ZIRCONIUM OXIDE: DENSE, STABILIZED

Source: *Chemical Marketing Reporter.* **Price Frequency:** weekly. **Effective Market(s):** New York. **Units of Measure:** Dollars per lb. **Type of Price:** spot. **Time Period Covered:** latest week.

ZIRCONIUM OXIDE: ELECTRONIC

Source: *Chemical Marketing Reporter.* **Price Frequency:** weekly. **Effective Market(s):** New York. **Units of Measure:** Dollars per lb. **Type of Price:** spot. **Time Period Covered:** latest week.

ZIRCONIUM OXIDE: INSULATING, STABILIZED

Source: *Chemical Marketing Reporter.* **Price Frequency:** weekly. **Effective Market(s):** New York. **Units of Measure:** Dollars per lb. **Type of Price:** spot. **Time Period Covered:** latest week.

ZIRCONIUM OXIDE: INSULATING, UNSTABILIZED

Source: *Chemical Marketing Reporter.* **Price Frequency:** weekly. **Effective Market(s):** New York. **Units of Measure:** Dollars per lb. **Type of Price:** spot. **Time Period Covered:** latest week.

ZIRCONIUM OXIDE: POWDERED, COMMERCIAL

Source: *Chemical Marketing Reporter.* **Price Frequency:** weekly. **Effective Market(s):** New York. **Units of Measure:** Dollars per lb. **Type of Price:** spot. **Time Period Covered:** latest week.

ZIRCONIUM OXYCHLORIDE: LIQUID

Source: *Chemical Marketing Reporter.* **Price Frequency:** weekly. **Effective Market(s):** New York. **Units of Measure:** Dollars per lb. **Type of Price:** spot. **Time Period Covered:** latest week.

ZIRCONIUM POWDER

Source: *American Metal Market.* **Price Frequency:** daily. **Units of Measure:** Dollars per lb. **Time Period Covered:** latest day.

Source: *E&MJ.* **Price Frequency:** monthly. **Units of Measure:** Dollars per lb. **Time Period Covered:** latest month.

ZIRCONIUM SPONGE

Source: *E&MJ.* **Price Frequency:** monthly. **Units of Measure:** Dollars per lb. **Time Period Covered:** latest month.

Source: *Iron Age.* **Price Frequency:** monthly. **Units of Measure:** Dollars per lb. **Type of Price:** consumer. **Time Period Covered:** latest month.

ZUCCHINI

see also Squash: Zucchini, Courgettes.

ZUCCHINI: GREEN

Source: *Lancaster Farming.* **Price Frequency:** weekly, seasonally. **Effective Market(s):** Pennsylvania. **Units of Measure:** Dollars per bushel. **Type of Price:** market. **Time Period Covered:** latest week.

ZUCCHINI: YELLOW

Source: *Lancaster Farming.* **Price Frequency:** weekly, seasonally. **Effective Market(s):** Pennsylvania. **Units of Measure:** Dollars per bushel. **Type of Price:** market. **Time Period Covered:** latest week.

Publishers Index

Publishers Index

A

AGRA EUROPE
Agra Europe (London)
25 Frant Road
Tunbridge Wells
Kent TN2 5JT
England
08.923.3813
weekly
Annual Price: 512.00 British pounds
Prices of major agricultural products in several European countries.

AGRICULTURAL OUTLOOK
Superintendent of Documents
U.S. Government Printing Office
Washington, D.C. 20402
(202) 783-3238
monthly
Annual Price: $36.00
Single Issue Price: not sold
Several pages of agricultural commodity prices.

AGRICULTURAL PRICES
Superintendent of Documents
U.S. Government Printing Office
Washington, D.C. 20402
(202) 783-3238
monthly
Annual Price: $28.00
Single Issue Price: $5.50
Exceptional source of price statistics for agricultural commodities, farming equipment, and farm chemicals.

AGRICULTURAL PRICES ANNUAL SUMMARY
Agricultural Statistics Board Publications
U.S.D.A.
Room 5829
South Building
Washington, D.C. 20250
(202) 783-3238
annual
Annual Price: $8.00
Annual cumulation of prices of agricultural commodities, farming equipment, and farm chemicals.

AGRICULTURAL TRADE HIGHLIGHTS
U.S.D.A., Foreign Agricultural Service
Information Division
Washington, D.C. 20250
(202) 783-3238
monthly
Annual Price: contact publisher
Quotations of selected international farm prices.

AGRICULTURE
AgriData Resources, Inc.
330 E. Kilbourn Avenue
Milwaukee, WI 53202
(414) 278-7676
weekly
Annual Price: $40.00
Single Issue Price: $1.00
Futures and cash market prices for major agricultural commodities.

AMERICAN METAL MARKET
Fairchild Publications
7 E. 12th Street
New York, NY 10003
(212) 741-4160
daily
Annual Price: $435.00
Single Issue Price: $1.25
Extensive listing of metal and metal product prices.

ANNUAL REPORT ON TOBACCO STATISTICS
Agricultural Marketing Service
Information Staff
Room 3068-S
Washington, D.C. 20250
(202) 783-3238
annual
Annual Price: contact publisher
Prices of tobacco prices by type.

AQUACULTURE SITUATION AND OUTLOOK REPORT
Economic Research Service
ERS-NASS Publications
P.O. Box 1608
Rockville, MD 20850
annual
Annual Price: $10.00
Catfish prices.

ASIAN WALL STREET JOURNAL
Asian Wall Street Journal
(Dow Jones Publishing Co., Asia, Inc.)
Circulation Department
P.O. Box 9825
Hong Kong
5.737121
daily
Annual Price: $370.00
Cash and futures prices of selected agricultural and metal commodities, also has foreign exchange rates.

ATI: AMERICA'S TEXTILE INTERNATIONAL
Billian Publishing Co.
2100 Powers Ferry Road
Suite 125
Atlanta, GA 30339
(404) 955-5656
monthly
Annual Price: $43.00
Single Issue Price: $5.00
Prices for spun cotton, spun blend, and man-made fibers and filaments.

B

BAKERY NEWSLETTER
Gorman Publishing Co.
Presidents Plaza III
8750 W. Bryn Mawr Avenue
Chicago, IL 60631
(312) 693-3200
weekly
Annual Price: $165.00
Selected prices of commodities important to the baking industry.

BARRON'S
(Barron's National Business and Financial Weekly)
Barron's
200 Burnett Road
Chicopee, MA 01021
(212) 416-2000
weekly
Annual Price: $96.00
Commodity price futures and foreign currency exchange rates.

BATTERY MAN
Independent Battery Manufacturers Association, Inc.
100 Larchwood Dr.
Largo, FL 34640
(813) 586-1400
monthly
Annual Price: $12.00
Single Issue Price: $3.00
Lead prices.

BEAN MARKET NEWS
Agricultural Marketing Service
U.S.D.A.
Information Staff
Room 3068-S
Washington, D.C. 20250
(202) 783-3238
weekly
Annual Price: $30.00, includes *Bean Market Summary*
Current prices of different varieties of beans.

BEAN MARKET SUMMARY
Agricultural Marketing Service
U.S.D.A.
Information Staff
Room 3068-S
Washington, D.C. 20250
(202) 783-3238
annual
Annual Price: $30.00, includes *Bean Market News*
Annual summary of prices for several varieties of beans.

BEVERAGE MEDIA
Beverage Media Ltd.
161 Avenue of the Americas
New York, NY 10013
(212) 620-0100
monthly
Annual Price: $27.50
Prices of alcoholic beverages in the New York area.

THE BROCK REPORT
Brock & Associates
2050 W. Good Hope Road
Milwaukee, WI 53209
(414) 351-5500
weekly
Annual Price: $355.00
Provides prices for major agricultural commodities.

BUSINESS WEEK
McGraw-Hill
1221 Avenue of the Americas
New York, NY 10020
(212) 512-2000
weekly
Annual Price: $40.00
Single Issue Price: $2.00
Small number of important commodity prices.

C

CALIFORNIA FARMER
HBJ Farm Publications
731 Market Street
San Francisco, CA 94103
(415) 495-3340
semimonthly
Annual Price: $10.00
Prices of California produce.

CALIFORNIA WINELETTER
California Wineletter
P.O. Box 70
Mill Valley, CA 94942
(415) 388-2578
semimonthly
Annual Price: $55.00
Selected prices of bulk California wines sold out-of-state.

CATFISH
Superintendent of Documents
U.S. Government Printing Office
Washington, D.C. 20402
(202) 783-3238
monthly
Annual Price: $14.00
Single Issue Price: not sold
Processed catfish prices.

CATFISH PRODUCTION
Economic Research Service
ERS-NASS Publications
P.O. Box 1608
Rockville, MD 20850
semiannual
Annual Price: $15.00 including *Catfish*
Single Issue Price: $5.50
Basic catfish prices.

CHEMICAL MARKETING REPORTER
Schnell Publishing Co., Inc.
80 Broad Street
New York, NY 10004-2203
(212) 248-4177
weekly
Annual Price: $70.00
Single Issue Price: $2.25
Comprehensive reporting of current chemical and related material prices.

COLORADO BEVERAGE ANALYST
BevAn Inc.
2403 Champa Street
Denver, CO 80205
(303) 296-1600
monthly
Annual Price: $12.00
Single Issue Price: $3.00
Prices of alcoholic beverages in Colorado.

COMMODITY TRADE AND PRICE TRENDS
International Bank for Reconstruction and Development/The World Bank
Distributed for the World Bank by the Johns Hopkins University Press
Journals Division
701 W. 40th Street, Suite 275
Baltimore, MD 21211
annual
Annual Price: $25.00
Prices for food, non-food, fuel, metal, and mineral commodities in several international markets.

COMMODITY YEAR BOOK
Commodity Research Bureau
100 Church Street
Suite 1850
New York, NY 10007
(212) 406-4545
annual
Annual Price: $49.95
Prices for over 100 major commodities.

COTTON AND WOOL SITUATION AND OUTLOOK REPORT
Superintendent of Documents
U.S. Government Printing Office
Washington, D.C. 20402
(202) 783-3238
quarterly
Annual Price: $9.50
Single Issue Price: $2.50
Basic cotton and fiber prices.

COTTON PRICE STATISTICS
Agricultural Marketing Service
U.S.D.A., Cotton Division
Information Staff
Room 3068-S
Washington, D.C. 20250
(202) 783-3238
monthly
Annual Price: $30.00, includes *Cotton Price Statistics Annual*
Cotton prices by type and market.

COTTON PRICE STATISTICS ANNUAL
Agricultural Marketing Service
U.S.D.A., Cotton Division
Information Staff
Room 3068-S
Washington, D.C. 20250
(202) 783-3238
annual
Annual Price: $5.00
Annual summary of cotton prices by type.

COTTON: REVIEW OF THE WORLD SITUATION
International Cotton Advisory Committee
1901 Pennsylvania Avenue N.W.
Washington, D.C. 20006
(202) 463-6660
bimonthly
Annual Price: $45.00, includes *Cotton: World Statistics*
Price indexes for cotton.

COTTON: WORLD STATISTICS
International Cotton Advisory Committee
1901 Pennsylvania Avenue N.W.
Washington, D.C. 20006
(202) 463-6660
monthly
Annual Price: $45.00, includes *Cotton: Review of the World Situation*
Cash, index, and futures prices of different types of cotton.

COTTONSEED REVIEW
Agricultural Marketing Service
U.S.D.A., Cotton Division
Information Staff
Room 3068-S
Washington, D.C. 20250
(202) 783-3238
weekly during season
Annual Price: $15.00
Seasonal cottonseed prices from selected domestic markets.

CRB COMMODITY INDEX REPORT
Commodity Research Bureau
100 Church Street
Suite 1850
New York, NY 10007
(212) 406-4545
weekly
Annual Price: $175.00
Spot market prices for primary foodstuffs and raw industrial materials.

D

DAIRY FOODS
Gorman Publishing Co.
8750 W. Bryn Mawr Avenue
Chicago, IL 60631
(312) 693-3200
monthly
Annual Price: $64.00
Single Issue Price: $8.00
Prices for dairy and dairy industry products.

DAIRY MARKET STATISTICS
Agricultural Marketing Service
U.S.D.A., Dairy Division
Information Staff
Room 3068-S
Washington, D.C. 20250
(202) 447-7461
annual
Annual Price: $4.00
Extensive coverage of dairy product prices.

DAIRY SITUATION AND OUTLOOK REPORT
Superintendent of Documents
U.S. Government Printing Office
Washington, D.C. 20402
(202) 783-3238
5 issues per year
Annual Price: $8.00
Single Issue Price: $1.75
Prices of cows and dairy products.

DNR: DAILY NEWS RECORD
Fairchild Publications
7 E. 12th Street
New York, NY 10003
(212) 741-4000
daily
Annual Price: $62.00
Single Issue Price: $.50
Market prices for gray goods and fibers.

DOANE'S AGRICULTURAL REPORT
Doane Information Services
11701 Borman Dr.
St. Louis, MO 63146
(314) 569-2700
weekly
Annual Price: $75.00
Prices for primary livestock and grains.

DROVERS JOURNAL
Vance Livestock Publications
Box 2939
Shawnee Mission, KS 66201
(913) 451-2200
weekly
Annual Price: $20.00
Cash prices for hay and cattle by market, and futures prices for hogs, corn, and cattle.

E

E&MJ
(E&MJ--Engineering and Mining Journal)
Maclean Hunter Publishing Co.
Fulfillment Manager
Engineering & Mining Journal
29 N. Wacker
Chicago, IL 60606
monthly
Annual Price: $40.00
Single Issue Price: $6.00

ECONOMIC AND ENERGY INDICATORS
Photoduplication Service
Library of Congress
Publications Officer
Washington, D.C. 20515
biweekly
Annual Price: contact publisher
Basic energy prices.

THE ECONOMIST
Economist Newspaper
10 Rockefeller Plaza, 10th Fl.
New York, NY 10020
(212) 541-5730
weekly
Annual Price: $98.00
Commodity price indexes and foreign exchange rates.

ENERGY PRICES AND TAXES
International Energy Agency
OECD Publications and Information Center
2001 "L" Street N.W.
Washington, D.C. 20036
(202) 785-6323
quarterly
Annual Price: $140.00
Single Issue Price: $42.00
Prices of different types of energy in several international markets.

ENERGY PRICING NEWS
(Crude Oil Report, Natural Gas Report, Petrochemical Report, Refined Fuel Report)
Southam Business Information & Communications Group, Inc.
1450 Don Mills Road
Don Mills, ON M3B 2X7
Canada
(403) 265-4750
monthly
Annual Price: $467.00
Prices for gasoline, natural gas, petrochemicals and crude oil in a variety of Canadian markets.

ENERGY STATISTICS
Institute of Gas Technology
Technical Information Center
3424 S. State Street
Chicago, IL 60616
(312) 567-3848
quarterly
Annual Price: $100.00
Single Issue Price: $25.00
Natural gas and crude oil prices.

ENR
(ENR--Engineering News Record)
McGraw-Hill
Fulfillment Manager
ENR
P.O. Box 518
Hightstown, NJ 08520
(609) 426-7070
weekly
Annual Price: $49.00
Single Issue Price: $5.00
Market prices for materials, including steel, metals, and lumber.

F

FAO QUARTERLY BULLETIN OF STATISTICS
Food and Agriculture Organization United Nations
Unipub
4611-F Assembly Drive
Lanham, MD 20706-4391
1-800-274-4888
quarterly
Annual Price: $14.00
Excellent coverage of commodity prices in several international markets.

FAR EASTERN ECONOMIC REVIEW
Review Publishing Co. Ltd.
G.P.O. Box 160
Hong Kong, Hong Kong
(212) 564-5040
weekly
Annual Price: $98.00
Prices of selected grain, metal, and food commodities.

FARM AND DAIRY
Lyle Printing and Publishing Company
Box 38
Salem, OH 44460
(216) 337-3419
weekly
Annual Price: $17.00
Prices for Ohio and Pennyslvania cattle, sheep, hogs, and hay.

FARMERS WEEKLY
Reed Business Publishing Ltd.
Oakfield House
Perrymount Road
Haywards Heath
Sussex RH16 3DH
England
04.44.441212
weekly
Annual Price: $156.00
Livestock, vegetable, and grain prices in several United Kingdom markets.

FEDERAL MILK ORDER MARKET STATISTICS
Agricultural Marketing Service, U.S.D.A.
Information Staff
Room 3068-S
Washington, D.C. 20250
(202) 783-3238
monthly
Annual Price: free
Federal milk order prices in several domestic markets.

FEDERAL MILK ORDER MARKET STATISTICS ANNUAL SUMMARY
Agricultural Marketing Service U.S.D.A.
Information Staff
Room 3068-S
Washington, D.C. 20250
(202) 783-3238
annual
Annual Price: free
Federal milk order and selected dairy product prices in several domestic markets.

FEDGAZETTE
Public Affairs
Federal Reserve Bank of Minneapolis
250 Marquette Avenue
Minneapolis, MN 55480
monthly
Annual Price: free
Price charts of major farm commodities.

FEED SITUATION AND OUTLOOK REPORT
Superintendent of Documents
U.S. Government Printing Office
Washington, D.C. 20402
(202) 783-3238
quarterly
Annual Price: $11.00
Single Issue Price: $3.00
Prices for several different types of grain.

FEEDSTUFFS
Miller Publishing Co.
191 S. Gary Avenue
Carol Stream, IL 60188-2089
(612) 931-0211
weekly
Annual Price: $45.00
Single Issue Price: $1.00
Commodity cash and ingredient market prices for several domestic markets.

FIBRE MARKET NEWS
G.I.E. Inc.
4012 Bridge Avenue
Cleveland, OH 44113
(216) 961-4130
weekly
Annual Price: $110.00
Single Issue Price: $2.50
Burlap, jute and fibre, including paper stock, prices in selected domestic and international markets.

FINANCIAL POST
Financial Post
777 Bay Street
Toronto, ON M5G 2E4
Canada
(416) 596-5147
weekly
Annual Price: contact publisher
Basic prices of metals.

FINANCIAL TIMES
Financial Times Ltd.
Bracken House
10 Cannon Street
London EC4P 4BY
England
01.248.8000
daily
Annual Price: $365.00
Spot and futures prices for selected commodities in mostly British markets.

FLORICULTURE CROPS
Economic Research Service
ERS-NASS Publications
P.O. Box 1608
Rockville, MD 20850
annual
Annual Price: $6.50
Plant and flower prices in the United States.

FRESH FRUIT AND VEGETABLE PRICES
Agricultural Marketing Service
U.S.D.A.
Information Staff
Rm. 3068-S
Washington, D.C. 20250
(202) 783-3238
annual
Annual Price: $8.00
Good coverage of fruit and vegetable prices by type.

FRUIT AND TREE NUTS SITUATION AND OUTLOOK
Superintendent of Documents
U.S. Government Printing Office
Washington, D.C. 20402
(202) 783-3238
quarterly
Annual Price: $11.00
Single Issue Price: $3.00
Fruit and nut prices for the United States.

FRUIT AND TROPICAL PRODUCTS
Commonwealth Secretariat
Publications Division
Marlborough House
Pall Mall
London SW1Y 5HX
England
semiannual
Annual Price: 45.00 British pounds
Prices of fruits, coffee, oilseeds, oils, and spices.

GAS STATS: MONTHLY GAS UTILITY STATISTICAL REPORT
American Gas Association
Department of Statistics
1515 Wilson Boulevard
Arlington, VA 22209
(703) 841-8507
monthly
Annual Price: contact publisher
Prices of natural gas by use.

GAS STATS: QUARTERLY REPORT OF GAS INDUSTRY OPERATIONS
American Gas Association
Department of Statistics
1515 Wilson Boulevard
Arlington, VA 22209
(703) 841-8507
quarterly
Annual Price: contact publisher
Prices of natural gas by use.

GLEANINGS IN BEE CULTURE
A.I. Root Co.
Box 706
Medina, OH 44258
(216) 725-6677
monthly
Annual Price: $13.00
Honey prices for several different domestic regions.

GRAIN AND FEED MARKET NEWS
Agricultural Marketing Service
U.S.D.A., Livestock & Seed Division
Information Staff
Room 3068-S
Washington, D.C. 20250
(202) 783-3238
weekly
Annual Price: $45.00
Daily prices for grains, grain products and feed.

GRAIN MARKET NEWS: QUARTERLY DURUM REPORT
Agricultural Marketing Service
U.S.D.A.
Livestock, Grain & Seed Division
Information Staff
Room 3068-S
Washington, D.C. 20250
(202) 783-3238
quarterly
Annual Price: $5.00
Gives durum wheat prices.

THE GROWER
Vance Publishing Co.
7950 College Boulevard
Overland Park, KS 66210
(913) 451-2200
monthly
Annual Price: $15.00
Fruit and vegetable prices in selected domestic markets.

H

HAY MARKET NEWS
Agricultural Marketing Service
U.S.D.A.
Livestock Division
Information Staff
Room 3068-S
Washington, D.C. 20250
(202) 783-3238
weekly
Annual Price: $30.00
Hay prices for selected domestic markets.

HIDES AND SKINS
Commonwealth Secretariat
Publications Division
Marlborough House
Pall Mall
London SW1Y 5HX
England
semiannual
Annual Price: 25.00 British pounds
Prices of hides and skins in several international markets.

HONEY
Economic Research Service
ERS-NASS Publications
P.O. Box 1608
Rockville, MD 20850
annual
Annual Price: $4.00
Honey prices by type and market.

HRI-BUYER'S GUIDE
Urner Barry's Publications, Inc.
Box 389
Toms River, NJ 08754-0389
(201) 240-5330
weekly
Annual Price: $67.00
Prices paid by dining places and institutions for perishable food items.

I

IDAHO FARMER-STOCKMAN
Western Farmer-Stockman Magazines
Box 2160
999 W. Riverside
Spokane, WA 99210-1615
(509) 459-5361
monthly
Annual Price: $15.00
Single Issue Price: $.75
Prices for livestock and farm products in selected Idaho and Northwestern markets.

ILLINOIS BEVERAGE JOURNAL
Illinois Beverage Media, Inc.
1 LaSalle Street, Suite 3030
Chicago, IL 60602
(312) 263-5680
monthly
Annual Price: $30.00
Single Issue Price: $5.00
Prices of alcoholic beverages in Illinois.

ILLINOIS FARM REPORT
Illinois Agricultural Statistics Service
Illinois Department of Agriculture
P.O. Box 19283
Springfield, IL 62794-9283
(217) 492-4295
monthly
Annual Price: contact publisher
Prices of Illinois farm products.

INDIANA BEVERAGE JOURNAL
Indiana Beverage Life, Inc.
2511 E. 46th Street, Suite A-7
Indianapolis, IN 46205
(317) 545-5262
monthly
Annual Price: $20.00
Single Issue Price: $3.00
Prices of alcoholic beverages in Indiana.

INTERNATIONAL MINERALS
Metal Bulletin PLC
220 Fifth Avenue
New York, NY 10001
(212) 213-6202
monthly
Annual Price: $272.00
Prices of industrial minerals, primarily in the European market.

INTERNATIONAL BUTANE-PROPANE NEWSLETTER
Butane-Propane News, Inc.
Box 419
338 E. Foothill Boulevard
Arcadia, CA 91006
(818) 357-2168
biweekly
Annual Price: $195.00
World prices of butane and propane.

INTERNATIONAL ENERGY STATISTICAL REVIEW
Library of Congress
Photoduplication Service
Publications Officer
Washington, D.C. 20515
biweekly
Annual Price: contact publisher
Crude oil prices for OPEC and world.

INTERNATIONAL FINANCIAL STATISTICS
International Monetary Fund
700 19th Street N.W., Suite C-100
Washington, D.C. 20431
(202) 473-7430
monthly
Annual Price: $148.00, includes *International Financial Statistics Yearbook*
Single Issue Price: $15.00
Prices for several primary commodities.

INTERNATIONAL FINANCIAL STATISTICS YEARBOOK
International Monetary Fund
700 19th Street N.W., Suite C-100
Washington, D.C. 20431
(202) 473-7430
annual
Annual Price: Comes with *International Financial Statistics.*
Prices for several primary commodities.

INTERNATIONAL SUGAR ORGANIZATION STATISTICAL BULLETIN
International Sugar Organization
Haymarket House
28 Haymarket
London SW1Y 4SP
England
01.930.3666
monthly
Annual Price: 35.00 British pounds
Single Issue Price: 5.00 British pounds
Daily spot prices for raw sugar.

INTERNATIONAL TEA COMMITTEE ANNUAL BULLETIN OF STATISTICS
International Tea Committee Ltd.
Sir John Lyon House
5 Timber Street
London EC4V 3NH
England
01.248.4672
annual
Annual Price: 110.00 British pounds
Annual summary of tea prices by type and market.

INTERNATIONAL TEA COMMITTEE LIMITED MONTHLY STATISTICAL SUMMARY
International Tea Committee Ltd.
Sir John Lyon House
5 Timber Street
London EC4V 3NH
England
01.248.4672
monthly
Annual Price: 85.00 British pounds
Extensive coverage of tea prices by type and market.

INTERNATIONAL TIN STATISTICS
International Tin Statistics
Haymarket House
4th Floor
28 Haymarket
London SW1Y 4EQ
England
01.930.0451
quarterly
Annual Price: contact publisher
Single Issue Price: 25.00 British pounds
Tin prices.

INTERNATIONAL WHEAT COUNCIL MARKET REPORT
International Wheat Council
Haymarket House
28 Haymarket
London SW1Y 4SS
England
01.930.4128
9 issues per year
Annual Price: $100.00
Current cash and futures prices for selected wheats, coarse grains, and soybeans.

INTERNATIONAL WHEAT COUNCIL REPORT FOR THE CROP YEAR
International Wheat Council
Haymarket House
28 Haymarket
London SW1Y 4SS
England
01.930.4128
annual
Annual Price: $30.00
Prices for different varieties of wheat in different international markets.

INVESTOR'S DAILY
Investor's Daily
Box 25970
Los Angeles, CA 90025
daily
Annual Price: $94.00
Spot and futures prices of agricultural, metal and other commodities.

IRON AGE
Fairchild Publications, Inc.
7 E. 12th Street
New York, NY 10003
(212) 741-4140
monthly
Annual Price: $50.00
Single Issue Price: $5.00
Prices of steel, steel products, and metals in several domestic markets.

J

JAPAN ECONOMIC JOURNAL
Nihon Keizai Shimbun, Inc.
9-5 Otemachi 1-chome
Chiyoda-ku
Tokyo 100-66
Japan
or OCS America, Inc.
5 E. 44 Street
New York, NY 10017
weekly
Annual Price: $108.00
Asian market prices for selected commodities, including oil, steel, and foodstuffs.

JOURNAL OF COMMERCE AND COMMERCIAL
Journal of Commerce, Inc.
110 Wall Street
New York, NY 10005
(212) 425-1616
daily
Annual Price: $225.00
Extensive coverage of commodity prices.

JTN: THE INTERNATIONAL TEXTILE MAGAZINE
Toshio Hikiba
16-8, Nihonbashi-Kodenmacho
Chuo-ku
Tokyo 103, Japan
03.663.8751
monthly
Annual Price: $132.00
Yarn, staple, and gray fabric prices in Japan and Taiwan.

K

KANSAS BUSINESS REVIEW
Institute for Public Policy and Business Research
University of Kansas
607 Blake Hall
The University of Kansas
Lawrence, KS 66045-2960
quarterly
Annual Price: free
Selective coverage of Kansas farm commodities.

KENTUCKY BEVERAGE JOURNAL
Feature Publications, Inc.
Box 3309
Frankfort, KY 40603
(502) 223-1621
monthly
Annual Price: $18.00
Single Issue Price: $1.50
Alcoholic beverage prices in Kentucky.

L

LANCASTER FARMING
Lancaster Farming
P.O. Box 609
1 East Main Street
Ephrata, PA 17522
(717) 394-3047
weekly
Annual Price: $12.50
Single Issue Price: $.50
Prices for livestock, grain, feed, and produce in eastern domestic markets.

LEAD AND ZINC STATISTICS
International Lead and Zinc Study Group
58 St. James's Street
London SW1A 1LD
England
01.499.9373
monthly
Annual Price: $140.00
Several prices for lead and zinc, including several international market quotations.

LIVESTOCK AND POULTRY SITUATION AND OUTLOOK REPORT
Superintendent of Documents
U.S. Government Printing Office
Washington, D.C. 20402
(202) 783-3238
bimonthly
Annual Price: $12.00
Single Issue Price: $2.25
Prices of livestock, meat products, and poultry in selected domestic markets.

LIVESTOCK AND POULTRY UPDATE
Economic Research Service
ERS-NASS Publications
P.O. Box 1608
Rockville, MD 20850
monthly
Annual Price: $15.00
Livestock and poultry prices for selected domestic markets.

LIVESTOCK, MEAT, WOOL MARKET NEWS
Agricultural Marketing Service
U.S.D.A., Livestock Division
Information Staff
Room 3068-S
Washington, D.C. 20250
(202) 783-3238
weekly
Annual Price: $30.00
Livestock, meat and wool prices for mostly domestic markets.

LLOYD'S SHIP MANAGER
Lloyd's of London Press Inc.
611 Broadway
Suite 523
New York, NY 10012
(212) 529-9500
monthly
Annual Price: $250.00
Spot prices of fuel oil in several international markets.

LONG STAPLE COTTON REVIEW
Agricultural Marketing Service
U.S.D.A., Cotton Division
Information Staff
Room 3068-S
Washington, D.C. 20250
(202) 783-3238
monthly
Annual Price: $12.00
Prices of long staple cotton.

LOS ANGELES TIMES
Los Angeles Times
Times Mirror Square
Los Angeles, CA 90053
(213) 237-5000
daily
Annual Price: $150.00
Futures and cash prices of selected commodities, including grains, livestock, and metals.

M

MARKETING APPALACHIAN DISTRICT APPLES
Agricultural Marketing Service
U.S.D.A., Fruit and Vegetable Division
Federal-State Market News
P.O. Box 66
Inwood, WV 25428
annual
Annual Price: $8.00
Apple prices by type for selected Appalachian markets.

MARKETING FLORIDA, GEORGIA, SOUTH CAROLINA, NORTH CAROLINA AND APPLACHIAN DISTRICT PEACHES
Agricultural Marketing Service
U.S.D.A., Fruit and Vegetable Division
Federal-State Market News
P.O.Box 66
Inwood, WV 25428
annual
Annual Price: $8.00
Contains seasonal peach prices for selected Southeastern markets.

MEAT AND DAIRY PRODUCTS
Commonwealth Secretariat
Publications Division
Marlborough House
Pall Mall
London SW1Y 5HX
England
semiannual
Annual Price: 25.00 British pounds
Prices of meat and dairy products in several international markets.

MEAT PRICE REPORT
National Provisioner, Inc.
15 W. Huron Street
Chicago, IL 60610
(312) 944-3380
weekly
Annual Price: $125.00
Prices of meat by cut and type.

MILLING & BAKING NEWS
Sosland Publishing Co.
9000 W. 67th Street
Merriam, KS 66202
(913) 236-7300
weekly
Annual Price: $64.00
Single Issue Price: $2.00
Prices of commodities important to the baking and milling industries.

MINERALS TODAY
Superintendent of Documents
U.S. Government Printing Office
Washington, D.C. 20402
(202) 783-3238
bimonthly
Annual Price: $13.00
Single Issue Price: $3.00
Prices for primary metals and building materials.

MINNEAPOLIS GRAIN EXCHANGE STATISTICAL ANNUAL
Minneaplois Grain Exchange
Statistical Information
130 Grain Exchange Building
Minneapolis, MN 55415
(612) 338-6212
annual
Annual Price: $30.00
Prices of grains at the Grain Exchange.

MINNESOTA-WISCONSIN MANUFACTURING GRADE MILK PRICE
Economic Research Service
ERS-NASS Publications
P.O. Box 1608
Rockville, MD 20850
monthly
Annual Price: $5.00
Prices of manufacturing grade milk in selected market.

MINNESOTA-WISCONSIN MANUFACTURING GRADE MILK: PRICES RECEIVED SUMMARY
Economic Research Service
ERS-NASS Publications
P.O. Box 1608
Rockville, MD 20850
annual
Annual Price: $4.00
Prices of manufacturing grade milk in selected market.

MODERN PLASTICS
McGraw-Hill
1221 Avenue of the Americas
New York, NY 10020
(212) 512-2000
monthly
Annual Price: $34.00
Single Issue Price: $5.00
Good source of plastics prices.

MOLASSES MARKET NEWS
Agricultural Marketing Service
U.S.D.A., Livestock Division
Information Staff
Room 3068-S
Washington, D.C. 20250
(202) 783-3238
weekly
Annual Price: $45.00, includes *Molasses Market News, News Summary*
Current prices of molasses in several domestic markets.

MONTANA FARMER-STOCKMAN
Western Farmer-Stockman Magazines
Box 2160
999 W. Riverside
Spokane, WA 99210-1615
(509) 459-5361
monthly
Annual Price: $15.00
Single Issue Price: $.75
Cash prices of livestock and grain in Montana and Northwestern markets.

MONTHLY COMMODITY PRICE BULLETIN
United Nations Conference on Trade and Development
Editorial and Documents Division
Palais des Nations
CH-1211 Geneva 10
Switzerland
22.34.60.11
monthly
Annual Price: $36.00, includes *Monthly Commodity Price Supplement*
Single Issue Price: $4.00
Prices for several important food, non-food, mineral, and metal commodities.

MONTHLY COMMODITY PRICE BULLETIN SUPPLEMENT
United Nations Conference on Trade and Development
Editorial and Documents Division
Palais des Nations
CH-1211 Geneva 10
Switzerland
22.34.60.11
annual
Annual Price: Comes with *Monthly Commodity Price Bulletin*
Supplement to provide price series for important commodities, including food, non-food, and minerals.

MONTHLY COTTON LINTERS REPORT
Agricultural Marketing Service
U.S.D.A., Cotton Division
Information Staff
Room 3068-S
Washington, D.C. 20250
(202) 783-3238
monthly
Annual Price: $12.00
Cotton linters prices by market.

MONTHLY PRICE REVIEW
Urner Barry's Publications, Inc.
Box 389
Toms River, NJ 08754-0389
(201) 240-5330
monthly
Annual Price: $93.00
Single Issue Price: $7.00
Spot prices for selected poultry and dairy products.

MUSHROOMS
Economic Research Service
ERS-NASS Publications
P.O. Box 1608
Rockville, MD 20850
annual
Annual Price: $4.00
Prices of domestic and agaricus mushrooms.

N

NATIONAL HONEY MARKET NEWS
Agricultural Marketing Service
U.S.D.A., Fruit and Vegetable Division
Information Staff
Room 3068-S
Washington, D.C. 20250
(202) 783-3238
monthly
Annual Price: $18.00
Honey prices by variety and market.

NATIONAL PETROLEUM NEWS
Hunter Publishing Ltd. Partnership
950 Lee Street
Des Plaines, IL 60016
(708) 296-0770
monthly
Annual Price: $71.00
Single Issue Price: $8.00
Average gasoline prices in the United States.

NATIONAL PROVISIONER
National Provisioner, Inc.
15 W. Huron Street
Chicago, IL 60610
(312) 944-3380
weekly
Annual Price: $14.00
Single Issue Price: $.75
Prices of cattle, beef cuts, and pork products.

NATIONAL WOOL MARKET REVIEW
Agricultural Marketing Service
U.S.D.A.
Information Staff
Room 3068-S
Washington, D.C. 20250
(202) 783-3238
weekly February to June, biweekly July to January
Annual Price: $30.00
Prices of livestock, wool and mohair.

NEVADA BEVERAGE INDEX
Nevada Publishing Company
300 East 1st Street
P.O. Box 99
Reno, NV 89501
(202) 786-5553
monthly
Annual Price: $12.00
Alcoholic beverage prices for the state of Nevada.

NEW YORK TIMES
New York Times Co.
229 W. 43rd Street
New York, NY 10036
(212) 556-1234
daily
Annual Price: $185.00
Commodity futures and cash prices, foreign exchange rates.

NEW ZEALAND FARMER
New Zealand Rural Press Ltd.
540 Great South Road
Box 4233
Auckland, New Zealand
09.591.124
weekly
Annual Price: 70.50 New Zealand dollars
Prices for vegetables, fruit, flowers, sheep, and cattle in the New Zealand market.

NMFS GREEN SHEET SUPPLEMENT
Urner Barry Publications, Inc.
P.O. Box 389
Toms River, NJ 08754-0389
(201) 240-5330
weekly
Annual Price: contact publisher
Fish, processed fish, shellfish, and shrimp prices.

NORTHERN MINER
Northern Miner Press Ltd.
7 Labatt Avenue
Toronto, ON M5A 3P2
Canada
(416) 368-3483
weekly
Annual Price: $50.00
Single Issue Price: $1.25
Free market, producer, and futures prices for metals.

O

OIL AND GAS JOURNAL
PennWell Publishing Co.
Box 1260
1421 S. Sheridan
Tulsa, OK 74101
(918) 835-3161
weekly
Annual Price: $95.00
Single Issue Price: $3.00
Prices of oil, oil products, gasoline, and natural gases.

OIL BUYERS' GUIDE
Petroleum Publications
Box 998
Lakewood, NJ 08701
(201) 367-1600
weekly
Annual Price: $675.00
Oil, oil product, and natural gas prices for selected domestic markets.

OIL BUYERS' GUIDE INTERNATIONAL
Petroleum Publications
Box 998
Lakewood, NJ 08701
(201) 367-1600
weekly
Annual Price: $775.00
Oil, oil product, and natural gas prices for selected international markets.

OIL CROPS SITUATION AND OUTLOOK
Superintendent of Documents
U.S. Government Printing Office
Washington, D.C. 20402
(202) 783-3238
quarterly
Annual Price: $7.00
Single Issue Price: $2.50
Prices for all types of domestic oilseeds.

OIL WORLD
ISTA Mielke GmbH
Langenberg 25
D-2100 Hamburg 90
West Germany
040.7602081
weekly
Annual Price: 759.00 West German marks
Prices for edible oilseeds, crude oils, fats, meals and grains.

OILWEEK
Maclean-Hunter Ltd.
200-1015 Cantre Street N.
Calgary, AB T2E 2P8
Canada
(403) 276-7881
weekly
Annual Price: 33.00 Canadian dollars
Spot crude oil prices in North American markets.

OPEC BULLETIN
Organization of the Petroleum Exporting Countries
Obere Donaustrasse 93
1020 Vienna
Austria
10 issues per year
Annual Price: free
Single Issue Price: free
Crude oil and gasoline prices in several international markets.

OREGON FARMER-STOCKMAN
Western Farmer-Stockman Magazines
Box 2160
999 W. Riverside
Spokane, WA 99210
(509) 459-5234
monthly
Annual Price: $9.00
Single Issue Price: $.75
Prices for livestock and grain in selected Northwestern markets.

THE PACKER
Vance Publishing Corp.
7950 College Boulevard
Overland Park, KS 66210
(913) 451-2200
weekly
Annual Price: $40.00
Single Issue Price: $1.00
Prices of produce for selected domestic markets.

P

PEANUT MARKETING SUMMARY
Agricultural Marketing Service
U.S.D.A., Fruit and Vegetable Division
Federal-State Marketing News
P.O. Box 1447
Thomasville, GA 31799
(912) 228-1208
annual
Annual Price: $10.00
Annual cumulation of peanut and peanut product prices.

PEANUT REPORT
Agricultural Marketing Service
U.S.D.A., Fruit and Vegetable Division
Federal-State Marketing News
P.O. Box 1447
Thomasville, GA 31799
(912) 228-1208
weekly
Annual Price: $80.00
Current prices of peanuts and peanut products.

PETROLEUM ECONOMIST
Petroleum Economist
P.O. Box 105
25/31 Ironmonger Row
London EC1V 3PN
England
01.251.3501
monthly
Annual Price: $210.00
Crude oil and oil products.

PLASTICS TECHNOLOGY
Bill Communications, Inc.
633 Third Avenue
New York, NY 10017
(212) 986-4800
monthly
Annual Price: $45.00
Single Issue Price: $5.00
Good source of plastics prices.

PORKPRO NEWSLETTER
Professional Farmers of America, Inc.
219 Parkade
Cedar Falls, IA 50613-9985
weekly
Annual Price: contact publisher
Contains cash prices for various cuts of meat and futures prices for hogs.

POTATOES
Agricultural Statistics Board
U.S.D.A.
ERS/NASS
P.O. Box 1608
Rockville, MD 20850
1-800-999-6779
annual
Annual Price: $9.00, includes *Potato Stock*
Prices of different varieties of potatoes in selected domestic markets.

POULTRY MARKET STATISTICS
Agricultural Marketing Service
U.S.D.A.
Poultry Marketing News
Statistical Reports Office
811 Grand Avenue, Rm. 119
Kansas City, MO 64106
annual
Annual Price: $4.00
Good coverage of poultry and egg prices.

POULTRY TIMES
Poultry Times
345 Green Street N.W.
Box 1338
Gainesville, GA 30503
(404) 536-2476
biweekly
Annual Price: $7.00
Single Issue Price: $.50
Prices of chickens, turkeys and eggs.

PRICES OF SELECTED ASIA/PACIFIC PRODUCTS
Economic and Social Commission for Asia and the Pacific
United Nations Building
Rajadamnern Avenue
Bangkok 2
Thailand
2.2829161.200
monthly
Annual Price: free
Price information for selected exportable products.

PULP & PAPER WEEK
Miller Freeman Publications
500 Howard Street
San Francisco, CA 94105
(415) 995-2424
weekly
Annual Price: $547.00
Single Issue Price: $25.00
Pulp, paper, and paper product prices for the United States.

PULPWOOD PRICES IN THE SOUTHEAST
Southeastern Experiment Station
U.S.D.A., Forest Service
200 Weaver Boulevard
Asheville, NC 28804
(202) 783-3238
annual
Annual Price: contact publisher
Prices for different types of pulpwood in the Southeast market.

PURCHASING
Cahners Publishing Co.
275 Washington Street
Newton, MA 02158-1630
(617) 964-3030
biweekly
Annual Price: $65.00
Single Issue Price: $5.00
Prices for a number of commodities, including paper products, chemicals, and electronic components.

R

RANDOM LENGTHS
Random Lengths Publications, Inc.
Box 867
Eugene, OR 97440-0867
(503) 686-9925
weekly
Annual Price: $155.00
Single Issue Price: $2.50
Lumber prices by type.

RHODE ISLAND BEVERAGE JOURNAL
Rhode Island Beverage Journal, Inc.
2529 Whitney Avenue
Hamden, CT 06518
(410) 751-2397
monthly
Annual Price: $10.00
Single Issue Price: $3.00
Alcoholic beverage prices in Rhode Island.

RICE MARKET NEWS
Agricultural Marketing Service
U.S.D.A., Livestock and Seed Division
Information Staff
Room 3068-S
Washington, D.C. 20250
(202) 783-3238
weekly
Annual Price: $45.00
Contains rice and rice by-product prices for rice-producing markets in the United States.

RICE SITUATION AND OUTLOOK
Superintendent of Documents
U.S. Government Printing Office
Washington, D.C. 20402
(202) 783-3238
3 issues per year
Annual Price: $7.50
Single Issue Price: $2.75
Rice and rice product prices.

RUBBER STATISTICAL BULLETIN
International Rubber Study Group
8th Fl., York House
Empire Way
Wembley HA9 0PA
England
01.493.6711
monthly
Annual Price: $140.00
Average natural and synthetic rubber prices.

S

SCOTTISH FARMER
Holmes MacDougall Ltd.
Ravenseft House
302-304 St. Vincent Street
Glasgow G2 5NL
Scotland
weekly
Annual Price: 36.50 British pounds
Prices for livestock, grains, and potatoes in Scotland.

SEAFOOD PRICE-CURRENT
Urner Barry Publications, Inc.
Box 389
Toms River, NJ 08754-0389
(210) 240-5330
semiweekly
Annual Price: $150.00
Single Issue Price: $3.00
Current prices for fresh, frozen, and processed fish.

STANDARD & POOR'S STATISTICAL SERVICE CURRENT STATISTICS
Standard & Poor's Corporation
25 Broadway
New York, NY 10004
monthly
Annual Price: $420.00
Wide variety of commodity prices.

STATISTICAL BULLETIN OF THE SOUTH PACIFIC: RETAIL PRICE INDEXES
South Pacific Commission
Publications Bureau
P.O. Box A245
Sydney N.S.W. 2000
Australia
annual
Annual Price: $50.00, included in subscription to Statistical Bulletin of the South Pacific.
Average retail prices of selected commodities in the South Pacific market.

SUGAR AND SWEETNER SITUATION AND OUTLOOK REPORT
Superintendent of Documents
U.S. Government Printing Office
Washington, D.C. 20402
(202) 783-3238
quarterly
Annual Price: $12.00
Single Issue Price: $3.75
Prices of sugar and other sweetners in the United States.

SUGAR YEAR BOOK
International Sugar Organization
28 Haymarket
London SW1Y 4SP
England
01.930.3666
annual
Annual Price: 15.00 British pounds
Prices of sugar in selected world markets.

SUPER AUTOMOTIVE NEWS
Irving-Cloud Publications
7300 N. Cicero
Lincolnwood, IL 60646-1696
(312) 588-7300
monthly
Annual Price: $30.00
Single Issue Price: $3.00
Retail gasoline prices by market.

SURVEY OF CURRENT BUSINESS
Superintendent of Documents
U.S. Government Printing Office
Washington, D.C. 20402
(202) 783-3238
monthly
Annual Price: $52.00
Single Issue Price: $6.50
Small selection of domestic commodity prices.

T

TIMBER BULLETIN
United Nations
United Nations Publications
Palais des Nations
CH 1211 Geneva 10
Switzerland
22.34.28.06
monthly
Annual Price: $80.00
Prices for forest products in several international markets.

TIMBER MART-SOUTH
Timber Mart-South, Inc.
P.O. Box 1278
Highlands, NC 28741
(704) 526-3653
quarterly
Annual Price: $175.00
Raw forest product prices for several Southeast markets.

THE TIMES
Times Newspapers of Great Britain
10 E. 53rd Street
New York, NY 10022
(212) 527-2469
daily
Annual Price: 433.68 British pounds, airmail
Selective list of primary commodity prices.

TOBACCO MARKET REVIEW: BURLEY
Agricultural Marketing Service
U.S.D.A.
Information Staff
Room 3068-S
Washington, D.C. 20250
(202) 783-3238
annual
Annual Price: $2.00
Prices for burley tobacco by type and domestic market.

TOBACCO MARKET REVIEW: FIRE-CURED AND DARK AIR-CURED
Agricultural Marketing Service
U.S.D.A.
Information Staff
Room 3068-S
Washington, D.C. 20250
(202) 783-3238
annual
Annual Price: $2.00
Prices for fire-cured and dark air-cured tobacco by type and domestic market.

TOBACCO MARKET REVIEW: FLUE-CURED
Agricultural Marketing Service
U.S.D.A.
Information Staff
Room 3068-S
Washington, D.C. 20250
(202) 783-3238
annual
Annual Price: $2.00
Prices for flue-cured tobacco by type and domestic market.

TOBACCO QUARTERLY
Commonwealth Secretariat
Publications Division
Marlborough House
Pall Mall
London SW1Y 5HX
England
quarterly
Annual Price: 70.00 British pounds
Tobacco prices in selected international markets.

TOBACCO SITUATION AND OUTLOOK REPORT
Superintendent of Documents
U.S. Government Printing Office
Washington, D.C. 20402
(202) 783-3238
quarterly
Annual Price: $9.50
Single Issue Price: $2.50
Prices of cigarettes.

U

U. S. ESSENTIAL OIL TRADE
U.S.D.A., Foreign Agricultural Service
Information Division
Washington, D.C. 20250
(202) 783-3238
annual
Annual Price: $7.00, includes *U. S. Spice Trade and World Tea Situation*
Prices for several essential oils.

U. S. SPICE TRADE
U.S.D.A., Foreign Agricultural Service
Information Division
Washington, D.C. 20250
(202) 783-3238
annual
Annual Price: $7.00, includes *U. S. Essential Oil Trade and World Tea Situation*
Spot spice prices.

UNCTAD COMMODITY YEARBOOK
United Nations
United Nations Publications
Room DC-2-0853
New York, NY 10017
(212) 963-8301
annual
Annual Price: $60.00
Free market prices and price indexes of selected primary commodities.

URNER BARRY'S PRICE-CURRENT
Urner Barry Publications, Inc.
Box 389
Toms River, NJ 08754-0389
(201) 240-5330
daily
Annual Price: $306.00
Single Issue Price: $3.00
Wide range of fowl prices.
West Coast Edition

Urner Barry's Publications, Inc.
Box 389
Toms River, NJ 08754-0389
(201) 240-5330
semiweekly
Annual Price: $103.00
Single Issue Price: $3.00
Gives West Coast prices for fowl and egg products.

UTAH FARMER-STOCKMAN
Western Farmer-Stockman Magazines
Box 2160
999 W. Riverside
Spokane, WA 99210
(509) 459-5361
monthly
Annual Price: $9.00
Single Issue Price: $.75
Prices of livestock and grain in selected Northwestern markets.

V

VEGETABLE AND SPECIALTIES SITUATION AND OUTLOOK REPORT
Superintendent of Documents
U.S. Government Printing Office
Washington, D.C. 20402
(202) 783-3238
3 issues per year
Annual Price: $8.00
Single Issue Price: $3.00
Very selective list of prices for vegetables.

VIEWPOINT
Farmers Grain and Livestock Corp.
P.O. Box 65537
1400 50th Street
West Des Moines, IA 50265-0914
(515) 223-2200
weekly
Annual Price: $125.00
Selected livestock prices for different domestic markets.

VOLUME AND VALUE OF SAWTIMBER STUMPAGE SOLD FROM NATIONAL FORESTS BY SELECTED SPECIES AND REGIONS
Forest Service, U.S.D.A.
Information Division
Washington, D.C. 20250
(202) 783-3238
quarterly
Annual Price: contact publisher
Average price value of types of sawtimber stumpage sold in different markets in the United States.

W

WALL STREET JOURNAL
Dow Jones & Company, Inc.
Box 300
Princeton, NJ 08540
(212) 285-5000
daily
Annual Price: $114.00
Cash and futures prices for several commodities, including grains, oils, and textiles.

WASHINGTON FARMER-STOCKMAN
Western Farmer-Stockman Magazines
Box 2160
999 W. Riverside
Spokane, WA 99210
(509) 459-5361
monthly
Annual Price: $9.00
Single Issue Price: $.75
Prices for livestock and farm products in selected Northwestern markets.

WEEKLY INSIDERS DAIRY & EGG LETTER
Urner Barry Publications, Inc.
Box 389
Toms River, NJ 08754-0389
(201) 240-5330
weekly
Annual Price: $131.00
Single Issue Price: $3.00
Has cash prices for egg and dairy products.

WEEKLY INSIDERS POULTRY REPORT
Urner Barry Publications, Inc.
Box 389
Toms River, NJ 08754-0389
(201) 240-5330
weekly
Annual Price: $131.00
Single Issue Price: $3.00
Contains prices for poultry and poultry products.

WEEKLY INSIDERS TURKEY LETTER
Urner Barry Publications, Inc.
Box 389
Toms River, NJ 08754-0389
(201) 240-5330
weekly
Annual Price: $131.00
Single Issue Price: $3.00
Contains prices for turkeys and turkey products.

WEEKLY STATISTICAL FISHERY REPORT
Urner Barry Publications, Inc.
Box 389
Toms River, NJ 08754-0389
(201) 240-5330
weekly
Annual Price: $150.00
Provides prices for fresh, frozen, and processed fish.

WHEAT SITUATION AND OUTLOOK REPORT
Superintendent of Documents
U.S. Government Printing Office
Washington, D.C. 20402
(202) 783-3238
quarterly
Annual Price: $10.00
Single Issue Price: $3.00
Wheat prices by type and market.

WOOL AND MOHAIR
Economic Research Service
ERS-NASS Publications
P.O. Box 1608
Rockville, MD 20850
annual
Annual Price: $4.00
Wool and mohair prices in the United States.

WOOL QUARTERLY
Commonwealth Secretariat
Publications Division
Marlborough House
Pall Mall
London SW1Y 5HX
England
quarterly
Annual Price: 80.00 British pounds
Prices of wool in selected Commonwealth markets.

WORLD AGRICULTURE SITUATION AND OUTLOOK
Superintendent of Documents
U.S. Government Printing Office
Washington, D.C. 20402
(202) 783-3238
3 issues per year
Annual Price: $9.00
Basic grain prices for a small number of international markets.

WORLD COCOA SITUATION
U.S.D.A., Foreign Agricultural Service
Information Division
Washington, D.C. 20250
(202) 783-3238
semiannual
Annual Price: $5.00
Prices of cocoa beans and cocoa products by market.

WORLD DAIRY SITUATION
U.S.D.A., Foreign Agricultural Service
Information Division
Washington, D.C. 20250
(202) 783-3238
semiannual
Annual Price: $4.00
Basic dairy product prices.

WORLD GRAIN SITUATION AND OUTLOOK
U.S.D.A., Foreign Agricultural Service
Information Division
Washington, D.C. 20250
(202) 783-3238
monthly
Annual Price: $24.00
Prices for different types of grain, including wheat and coarse grains.

WORLD HONEY SITUATION
U.S.D.A., Foreign Agricultural Service
Information Division
Washington, D.C. 20250
(202) 783-3238
annual
Annual Price: $7.00, includes several other publications
Average annual honey prices in 10 international markets.

WORLD OIL
Gulf Publishing Co.
3301 Allen Parkway
Houston, TX 77019
(713) 529-4301
monthly
Annual Price: $24.00
Single Issue Price: $8.00
Gasoline prices for selected South Central markets.

WORLD OILSEED SITUATION AND MARKET HIGHLIGHTS
U.S.D.A., Foreign Agricultural Service
Information Division
Washington, D.C. 20250
(202) 783-3238
monthly
Annual Price: $28.00
Oilseed prices for domestic and international markets.

WORLD SUGAR SITUATION AND OUTLOOK
U.S.D.A., Foreign Agricultural Service
Information Division
Washington, D.C. 20250
(202) 783-3238
annual
Annual Price: $7.00
Raw sugar spot and contract prices.

WORLD TEA SITUATION
U.S.D.A., Foreign Agricultural Service
Information Division
Washington, D.C. 20250
(202) 783-3238
annual
Annual Price: $7.00, includes *U. S. Spice Trade and U. S. Essential Oil Trade*
Average auction tea prices.